CASSELL'S COMPACT
French–English
English–French
Dictionary

Compiled by
J. H. DOUGLAS

DENIS GIRARD

W. THOMPSON

D0044302

Published by
Dell Publishing Co., Inc.
1 Dag Hammarskjold Plaza
New York, New York 10017

Copyright © Cassell & Company Ltd., 1968

Laurel ® TM 674623, Dell Publishing Co., Inc.

ISBN: 0-440-31128-4

Reprinted by arrangement with
Macmillan Publishing Co., Inc.

Printed in the United States of America
One Previous Laurel Edition
New Laurel Edition
First printing—September 1981
Fourth printing—July 1983

Contents

Cassell has published outstanding dictionaries for virtually every major foreign language. Now, for the first time, many of them are being made available in compact paperback editions. Besides the present French–English, English–French dictionary, the Dell series includes the Cassell's Compact Spanish–English, German–English, and Latin–English dictionaries. These handy reference books are invaluable aids for students in foreign-language courses or for those who want to polish up their language skills on their own. Additionally, they are designed for the traveler and the reader of contemporary literature, newspapers, and magazines.

J. H. Douglas is Headmaster of the Caldew School, Cumberland, England, and Chevalier dans l'Ordre des Palmes Académiques.

Denis Girard is affiliated with the Academy of Paris and is the editor of *The New Cassell's French Dictionary*, on which this volume is based.

W. Thompson is Deputy Headmaster, The White House Grammar School, Cumberland, England.

Preface

This new edition of a work which appeared for the first time in 1904 represents a departure from tradition in that it is not a revised version of its immediate predecessor, but an entirely new work based on 'Cassell's New French Dictionary' compiled by Denis Girard and first published in 1962.

The availability of such a recent publication, and one moreover which has been widely accepted as a reliable work, has made the editors' task much easier than it could ever have been otherwise. The dead wood had already been cut away and many new words had been introduced, but it will come as no surprise that there are entries in the 'Compact' which do not appear in the 'New', e.g. 'escalate', and that others which were included in the 'New' for the first time in 1962 have already been discarded as obsolete, e.g. 'teddy boy'.

It is, of course, the question of selection which poses the greatest problem for anyone concerned with the compilation of a dictionary of limited size. Many uncommon words inevitably fail to find a place, as do the less frequent uses of some which have been included. We have tried wherever possible to illustrate by examples, but we have not attempted to incorporate information which properly belongs to a grammar book rather than a dictionary. It is assumed that the user will have a knowledge not only of parts of speech but also of the essential basic grammar of both languages. Although personal preference may have played a part, we have always tried to regard suitability for this type of dictionary as the primary consideration for or against the inclusion of a word, and we hope that we have, if anything, erred on the safe side.

Several features in the general layout of the 'New French Dictionary' have been incorporated for the first time in the 'Compact'. These include the use of the symbols of the International Phonetic Association throughout, the detailed information given in the 'Advice to the User' and the tables of English and French verbs. Completely new features are the notes at the head of the verb tables and the increased use of French in the explanatory parentheses in the English–French section.

J. H. D.

Advice to the User

Grouping of Words
In both sections of the dictionary alphabetical order has been strictly observed for all entries, including proper nouns.

Numbering of Identical Words
Words which are spelt alike but which differ in origin or pronunciation are numbered separately.

Punctuation
When several translations are given for one word it can generally be assumed that those which are separated by commas have much the same meaning; semi-colons are used where there is a clear difference in meaning or usage.

Words or meanings marked with an asterisk (*) are obsolete.

Pronunciation
The phonetic transcription is given in square brackets immediately after the key-word and alternative pronunciations have been given where necessary. The mark (ˈ) precedes the syllable which carries the stress.

The symbols of the International Phonetic Association have been used throughout the dictionary, and the user who is unfamiliar with these should refer to the Key to Pronunciation.

Daniel Jones' *English Pronouncing Dictionary* has usually been followed in the English–French section.

Grammatical Information
It is assumed that the user will have a reasonable knowledge of the basic grammar of the two languages. For example, when a noun merely adds -s for the plural or an adjective -e for the feminine, it has not been considered necessary to show this. Parts of speech are indicated by an abbreviation in italics (*a., n.m., v.t., adv.* etc.) except in the case of proper nouns where in English no indication has been given and in French only the gender. For the meanings of the abbreviations the user is referred to the list on page xiv.

Nouns and Adjectives
In the French–English section French nouns are classed as *n.m.* for the masculine, *n.f.* for the feminine or *n.* for a noun which may be masculine or feminine according to context. In the English–French section the gender of French nouns is shown by the abbreviations *m.* or *f.*; where a noun, without change of form, may be masculine or feminine both genders are given. In a list of nouns the gender is not given after each one and the user should therefore read on to the next gender mentioned, e.g. under **damage** he will find 'dommage; tort,

Groupement des Mots

Dans les deux parties du dictionnaire l'ordre alphabétique a été strictement suivi pour tous les articles, y compris les noms propres.

Numérotage de Mots Identiques

Les mots qui ont la même orthographe sont numérotés séparément lorsqu'ils ont une racine ou une prononciation différente.

Ponctuation

Quand plusieurs traductions sont données pour un même mot, celles qui ne sont séparées que par des virgules ont en règle générale des sens à peu près identiques; le point virgule est utilisé pour indiquer des différences très nettes de sens ou d'emploi.

Les mots précédés d'un astérisque (*) sont désuets.

Prononciation

La transcription phonétique est donnée entre crochets immédiatement après le mot principal. Lorsqu'il y a d'autres prononciations possibles, elles sont également indiquées. L'accent (') précède la syllabe qui porte l'accent tonique.

Les signes de l'Association Internationale de Phonétique sont utilisés dans les deux parties du dictionnaire et le lecteur qui n'est pas familiarisé avec ces signes devra consulter la Table de Prononciation.

Pour la section Anglais–Français, on a généralement suivi le dictionnaire de M. Daniel Jones, *An English Pronouncing Dictionary*.

Indications Grammaticales

Le lecteur est considéré comme ayant une connaissance suffisante de la grammaire de base des deux langues. Par exemple, quand un nom français forme son pluriel en **-s** et quand un adjectif forme son féminin en **-e**, il n'a pas paru nécessaire de l'indiquer. La nature des mots est indiquée par une abréviation en italique (*a.*, *n.m.*, *v.t.*, *adv.* etc.) excepté dans le cas des noms propres pour lesquels aucune indication n'a été donnée dans la partie Anglais–Français et seulement le genre dans la partie Français–Anglais. On trouvera la signification des abréviations à la page xiv.

Noms et adjectifs

Dans la partie Français–Anglais, les noms français sont classés en *n.m.* pour les noms masculins, en *n.f.* pour les noms féminins et *n.* pour ceux qui se modifient selon le contexte. Dans la partie Anglais–Français, le genre des noms français est indiqué par les abréviations *m.* ou *f.*; lorsqu'un nom peut, sans changer de forme, être soit du masculin soit du féminin, les deux genres sont donnés. Dans une dégât; (*fig.*) préjudice, détriment, *m.*' and he will know from this that all these five nouns are masculine. In the English–French section the feminine forms of French adjectives and nouns (where applicable) are not normally given. The user should consult the relevant French word in the French–English section.

Where plurals or feminines of nouns or adjectives are given, abbreviated forms are used. For example the entry **cheval** (pl. **-aux**) means that the full plural word is **chevaux**. Similarly, **acteur** (*fem.* **-trice**) indicates that the feminine form is **actrice**.

Verbs

All Verbs, other than reflexive verbs, form their compound tenses with **avoir** unless there is an indication with the entry that they take **être**. For all further information on verb entries please consult notes on Verb Tables below.

Verb Tables

1. French verbs have been listed in the tables as follows:

    a. A pattern verb for each of the three regular conjugations.
    b. Pattern verbs which may best be described as 'anomalous', i.e. verbs which are basically regular but which, for one reason or another, show slight variations from the normal forms.
    c. An alphabetical list of irregular verbs, some of which are used as a reference for other verbs which show similar irregularities.

Full conjugations have been given for the regular verbs but elsewhere only where it is considered necessary or desirable.

2. An alphabetical list of all irregular English verbs included in this dictionary is given. The user is referred to the Verb Tables for a note on the following:

    a. Verbs ending in **-y** preceded by one or more consonants.
    b. Certain verbs ending in a consonant preceded by a vowel.

3. The following explanation of verb entries in the dictionary may be helpful:

    a. *irr.* See the verb in question in the list of irregular verbs.
    b. *irr.* (*conjug. like* . . . . . .) See the pattern verb in the list of irregular verbs.
    c. (*see Verb Tables*) See the verb in question in the list of anomalous verbs.
    d. (*conjug. like* . . . . . .) See the pattern verb in the list of anomalous verbs.

liste de noms, le genre n'est pas donné après chacun d'eux et le lecteur doit alors se référer au premier genre indiqué, e.g. pour **damage** il trouvera 'dommage; tort, dégât; (*fig.*) préjudice, détriment, *m.*' et il en déduira que ces cinq noms sont du masculin. Dans la partie Anglais–Français, le féminin des mots français, lorsqu'il existe, n'est en principe pas indiqué; on le trouvera dans la partie Français–Anglais.

Lorsque le pluriel ou le féminin des noms ou des adjectifs est indiqué, il est donné en abrégé. Par exemple, **cheval** (*pl.* **-aux**) signifie que la forme de ce mot au pluriel est **chevaux**. De même, **acteur** (*fem.* **-trice**) signifie que la forme du féminin est **actrice**.

Verbes
Tous les verbes, autres que les .erbes réfléchis, forment leurs temps composés avec l'auxiliaire **avoir**, à moins qu'il soit indiqué qu'ils se conjuguent avec **être**. On trouvera ci-dessous des renseignements complémentaires sur les verbes.

Tables des Verbes
1. Les verbes français sont présentés de la façon suivante:

    a. un verbe-type pour chacune des trois conjugaisons régulières.

    b. des verbes-types 'anomaux', c'est-à-dire, des verbes qui sont fondamentalement réguliers mais qui comportent de légères variations par rapport aux formes normales.

    c. une liste alphabétique des verbes irréguliers dont certains servent de références à d'autres verbes présentant des irrégularités analogues.

La conjugaison des verbes réguliers a été donnée en entier, mais pour les autres verbes elle ne figure que lorsque cela paraît nécessaire.

2. On trouvera une liste alphabétique de tous les verbes irréguliers anglais qui sont donnés dans ce dictionnaire, précédée par des renseignements sur les groupes suivants:

    a. Verbes qui se terminent en **-y** précédé d'une ou plus d'une consonne.

    b. Certains verbes qui se terminent en une consonne précédée d'une voyelle.

3. Les renseignements suivants concernant la présentation des verbes dans le dictionnaire pourront s'avérer utiles:

    a. *irr.* Se reporter à la liste des verbes irréguliers .

    b. *irr.* (*conjug. like* . . . . . .) Voir le verbe-type dans la liste des verbes irréguliers.

    c. (*see Verb Tables*) Voir ce verbe dans la liste des verbes anomaux.

    d. (*conjug. like* . . . . . .) Voir le verbe-type dans la liste des verbes anomaux.

Key to Pronunciation

VOWELS

French (1)

i   as in cri [kri], difficile [difi'sil]
i: ,, ,, écrire [e'kri:r], finir [fi'ni:r]
e   ,, ,, thé [te], mélodie [melo'di]
ε   ,, ,, réel [re'ɛl], aile [ɛl]
ε: ,, ,, bête [bɛ:t], dentaire [dɑ̃'tɛ:r]
a   ,, ,, patte [pat], apparat [apa'ra]
a: ,, ,, tard [ta:r], barbare [bar'ba:r]
ɑ   ,, ,, pas [pɑ], tailler [tɑ'je]
ɑ: ,, ,, gaz [gɑ:z], pâte [pɑ:t]
ɔ   ,, ,, coter [kɔ'te], voler [vɔ'le]
ɔ: ,, ,, confort [kɔ'fɔ:r], porc [pɔ:r]
o   ,, ,, côté [ko'te], gros [gro], tôt [to]
o: ,, ,, dôme [do:m], rôle [ro:l]
u   ,, ,, coup [ku], tourner [tur'ne]
u: ,, ,, bourre [bu:r], cour [ku:r]
y   ,, ,, cru [kry], salut [sa'ly]
y: ,, ,, littérature [litera'ty:r]
ø   ,, ,, neveu [nə'vø], rocheux [rɔ'ʃø]
ø: ,, ,, mitrailleuse [mitra'jø:z]
œ   ,, ,, feuillet [fœ'je]
œ: ,, ,, faveur [fa'vœ:r]
ə   ,, ,, le [lə], refaire [rə'fɛ:r]

English (1)

i: as in seat [si:t]
i   ,, ,, finish ['finiʃ], physics ['fiziks]
e   ,, ,, neck [nek], bread [bred]
æ   ,, ,, man [mæn], malefactor ['mælifæktə]
ɑ: ,, ,, father ['fɑ:ðə], task [tɑ:sk]
ə   ,, ,, block [blɔk], waddle [wɔdl]
ɔ: ,, ,, shawl [ʃɔ:l], tortoise ['tɔ:təs]
o   ,, ,, domain [do'mein]
u   ,, ,, good [gud], July [dʒu'lai]
u: ,, ,, moon [mu:n], tooth [tu:θ]
ʌ   ,, ,, cut [kʌt], somewhere ['sʌmwɛə]
ə: ,, ,, search [sə:tʃ], surgeon ['sə:dʒən]
ə   ,, ,, cathedral [kə'θi:drəl], never ['nevə]

Nasal Vowels

ɛ̃   as in faim [fɛ̃], vingt [vɛ̃]
ɛ̃:   ,, ,, feindre [fɛ̃:dr], poindre [pwɛ̃:dr]
ɑ̃   ,, ,, ensemencement [ɑ̃smɑ̃s'mɑ̃]
ɑ̃:   ,, ,, défendre [de'fɑ̃:dr]
ɔ̃   ,, ,, son [sɔ̃], fonder [fɔ̃'de]
ɔ̃:   ,, ,, contre [kɔ̃:tr], trompe [trɔ̃:p]
œ̃   ,, ,, défunt [de'fœ̃], un [œ̃]
œ̃:   ,, . humble [œ̃:bl]

Diphthongs

ei   as in great [greit]
ou   ,, ,, show [ʃou]
ai   ,, ,, high [hai]
au   ,, ,, crowd [kraud]
ɔi   ,, ,, boy [bɔi]
iə   ,, ,, steer [stiə]
ɛə   ,, ,, hair [hɛə]
uə   ,, ,, moor [muə]

Key to Pronunciation

CONSONANTS

FRENCH (1)

p as in peine [pɛn], papier [pa'pje]
b ,, ,, bon [bɔ̃]
t ,, ,, tâter [tɑ'te], thé [te]
d ,, ,, dinde [dɛ̃:d]
k ,, ,, coquelicot [kɔkli'ko]
g ,, ,, gare [gɑ:r]
m ,, ,, maman [ma'mɑ̃], même [mɛ:m]
n ,, ,, nonne [nɔn]

ɲ ,, ,, agneau [a'ɲo], soigner [swa'ɲe]
f ,, ,, fier [fjɛ:r]
v ,, ,, vivre [vi:vr]

s ,, ,, sucre [sykr]
z ,, ,, raser [rɑ'ze]
l ,, ,, lettre [lɛtr], valise [va'li:z]
ʃ ,, ,, charme [ʃarm]
ʒ ,, ,, ronger [rɔ̃'ʒe], joue [ʒu]
r ,, ,, arrière [a'rjɛ:r]

ENGLISH (1)

p as in paper ['peipə]
b ,, ,, ball [bɔ:l]
t ,, ,, tea [ti:], till [til]
d ,, ,, deed [di:d]
k ,, ,, cake [keik]
g ,, ,, game [geim]
m ,, ,, mammoth ['mæməθ]
n ,, ,, nose [nouz], nun [nʌn]
ŋ ,, ,, bring [briŋ], finger ['fiŋgə]

f ,, ,, fair [fɛə], far [fɑ:]
v ,, ,, vine [vain]
θ ,, . thin [θin], bath [bɑ:θ]
ð ,, ,, this [ðis], bathe [beið]
s ,, ,, since [sins]
z ,, ,, busy ['bizi]
l ,, ,, land [lænd], hill [hil]
ʃ ,, ,, shield [ʃi:ld], sugar ['ʃugə]
ʒ ,, ,, visionary ['viʒənəri]
r ,, ,, rut [rʌt], brain [brein]
h ,, ,, here [hiə], horse [hɔ:s]
x ,, ,, loch [lɔx]

SEMI-CONSONANTS

j as in rien [rjɛ̃]
w ,, ,, ouate [wat], oui [wi]
ɥ ,, ,, huile [ɥil]

j as in yellow ['jelou], yes [jes]
w ,, ,, wall [wɔ:l]

When the same symbol is used in both English and French it often represents a different sound in each language.

′ denotes that the stress is on the following syllable.
: denotes that the preceding vowel is long.
~ placed over a vowel-symbol shows that the vowel has a nasal sound.

List of Abbreviations

a.	adjective	*foll.*	the following	*pers.*	person, personal
abbr.	abbreviation	*Fort.*	Fortification	*Pharm.*	Pharmacy
Adm.	Administration	*Fr.*	French	*Phil.*	Philosophy
adv.	adverb	*Ftb.*	Assoc. Football	*Philol.*	Philology
adv. phr.	adverbial phrase	*fut.*	future	*Phon.*	Phonetics
affirm.	affirmative	*Gard.*	Gardening	*Phot.*	Photography
Agric.	Agriculture	*Geog.*	Geography	*phr.*	phrase
Alg.	Algebra	*Geol.*	Geology	*Phys.*	Physics
Am.	American	*Geom.*	Geometry	*Physiol.*	Physiology
Anat.	Anatomy	*Gr.*	Greek	*pl.*	plural
Ant.	Antiquities	*Gram.*	Grammar	*poet.*	poetical
Arch.	Architecture	*Gym.*	Gymnastics	*Polit.*	Politics
Archaeol.	Archaeology	*Her.*	Heraldry	*pop.*	popular
Arith.	Arithmetic	*Hist.*	History	*poss.*	possessive
art.	article	*Horol.*	Horology	*p.p.*	past participle
Artill.	Artillery	*Hort.*	Horticulture	*prec.*	the preceding
Astron.	Astronomy	*Hunt.*	Hunting	*pref.*	prefix
aux.	auxiliary	*Hydr.*	Hydrostatics	*prep.*	preposition
Av.	Aviation	*i.*	intransitive	*pres.*	present
Bibl.	Bible, Biblical	*Ichth.*	Ichthyology	*pres. p.*	present participle
Biol.	Biology	*imp.*	imperfect	*Print.*	Printing
Bookb.	Bookbinding	*impers.*	impersonal	*pron.*	pronoun
Bot.	Botany	*Ind.*	Industry	*prop.*	proper, properly
Box.	Boxing	*indec.*	indecent	*Pros.*	Prosody
Build.	Building	*indef.*	indefinite	*Psych.*	Psychology
(C)	Canadian usage	*indic.*	indicative	*Pyro.*	Pyrotechnics
Carp.	Carpentry	*inf.*	infinitive	*r.*	reflexive; recipro-
Ch.	Church	*int.*	interjection		cal
Chem.	Chemistry	*inter.*	interrogative	*Rad.*	Radio
Cine.	Cinema	*inv.*	invariable	*Rail.*	Railway
Civ. Eng.	Civil Engineering	*iron.*	ironical	*R.C.*	Roman Catholic
Coin.	Coinage	*irr.*	irregular (see	*reg.*	registered
collect.	collective		table of Irregular	*rel.*	relative
colloq.	colloquially		Verbs, pp. 636–	*Relig.*	Religion
comb.	combination		58)	*rhet.*	rhetoric
comb. form	combining form	*It.*	Italian	*Rom.*	Roman
Comm.	Commerce	*Jew.*	Jewish	*Row.*	Rowing
comp.	comparative	*Journ.*	Journalism	*Sc.*	Scottish
Conch.	Conchology	*L.*	Latin	*Sch.*	Schools
cond.	conditional	*Lit.*	Literature	*Sci.*	Science
conj.	conjunction	*Log.*	Logic	*Sculp.*	Sculpture
conjug.	conjugated	*m.*	masculine	*sing.*	singular
contr.	contraction	*Mach.*	Machinery	*s.o.'s*	someone's
Cook.	Cookery	*Manuf.*	Manufacturing	*Spt.*	Sport
Cost.	Costume	*masc.*	masculine	*St. Exch.*	Stock Exchange
Cycl.	Cycling	*Math.*	Mathematics	*subj.*	subjunctive
dat.	dative	*Mech.*	Mechanics	*superl.*	superlative
def.	definite	*Med.*	Medicine	*Surg.*	Surgery
dem.	demonstrative	*Metal.*	Metallurgy	*Surv.*	Surveying
Dent.	Dentistry	*Meteor.*	Meteorology	*Swim.*	Swimming
dial.	dialect	*Mil.*	Military	*t.*	transitive
dim.	diminutive	*Min.*	Mineralogy	*Tech.*	Technical
Dress.	Dressmaking	*Motor.*	Motoring	*Tel.*	Television
Eccles.	Ecclesiastical	*Mount.*	Mountaineering	*Teleg.*	Telegraphy
Econ.	Economics	*Mus.*	Music	*Teleph.*	Telephone
Elec.	Electricity	*Myth.*	Mythology	*Ten.*	Tennis
ellipt.	elliptic	*n.*	noun	*Tex.*	Textiles
emphat.	emphatic	*Nat.*	Natural	*Theat.*	Theatrical
Eng.	Engineering	*Naut.*	Nautical	*Theol.*	Theological
Engl.	English	*neg.*	negative	*Trig.*	Trigonometry
Engr.	Engraving	*obj.*	object	*Univ.*	University
Ent.	Entomology	*obs.*	obsolete	*U.S.*	United States
esp.	especially	*Opt.*	Optics	*usu.*	usually
Exam.	Examination	*Orn.*	Ornithology	*v.*	verb
f.	feminine	*Paint.*	Painting	*Vet.*	Veterinary
fam.	familiarly	*Parl.*	Parliamentary	*v.i.*	intransitive verb
facet.	facetiously	*part.*	participle, par-	*v.r.*	reflexive *or* reci-
fem.	feminine		ticipial		procal verb
Fenc.	Fencing	*Path.*	Pathology	*v.t.*	transitive verb
Feud.	Feudal	*pej.*	pejorative	*vulg.*	vulgar
fig.	figuratively	*perf.*	perfect	*Zool.*	Zoology
Fin.	Financial				

A

A, a [a], *n.m.* in French *a* has two sounds: (1) as in *part*, shown in this dictionary by 'a'; (2) as in *pas*, shown by 'ɑ'.

à [a], *prep.* [*see also* AU, AUX] to, at, in, into, on, by, for, from, with.

abaisse [a'bɛ:s], *n.f.* undercrust of pastry.

abaissement [abɛs'mã], *n.m.* lowering, falling, abatement, depression; humiliation, abasement.

abaisser [abɛ'se], *v.t.* to let down, to let fall, to lower; to diminish, to reduce; (*fig.*) to bring low, to humble, to depress; to roll out (*paste*). **s'abaisser,** *v.r.* to sink, to subside, to decrease, to abate, to decline; to humble oneself, to stoop, to cringe.

abajoue [aba'ʒu], *n.f.* (*Zool.*) cheek pouch.

abalourdir [abalur'di:r], *v.t.* to make dull *or* stupid.

abalourdissement [abalurdis'mã], *n.m.* dullness, stupidity.

abandon [abã'dõ], *n.m.* relinquishment, surrender, cession; abandonment, forlornness, destitution; lack of restraint; *à l'abandon,* at random, in confusion, at sixes and sevens; (*Naut.*) adrift.

abandonné [abãdɔ'ne], *a.* abandoned, forsaken; lost to decency, shameless, profligate.

abandonnement [abãdɔn'mã], *n.m.* abandonment; desertion; (*fig.*) dissoluteness, profligacy.

abandonnément [abãdɔne'mã], *adv.* freely, unreservedly.

abandonner [abãdɔ'ne], *v.t.* to give up, to hand over, to surrender; to renounce; to forsake, to desert, to abandon; to leave, to quit; to neglect. **s'abandonner,** *v.r.* to give oneself up, to give way (*à*); to indulge (*à*); to neglect oneself.

abaque [a'bak], *n.m.* (*Arch.*) abacus; (*Arith.*) abacus.

abasourdir [abazur'di:r], *v.t.* to stun, to dumbfound; (*fig.*) to astound.

abasourdissant [abazurdi'sã], *a.* astounding, overwhelming.

abasourdissement [abazurdis'mã], *n.m.* stupefaction, bewilderment.

*abat [a'ba], *n.m.* killing, knocking down; heavy shower.

abâtardi [abatar'di], *a.* degenerate, corrupt, debased.

abâtardir [abatar'di:r], *v.t.* to render degenerate; to debase, to corrupt. **s'abâtardir,** *v.r.* to degenerate.

abâtardissement [abatardis'mã], *n.m.* degeneracy.

abatée *or* **abattée** [aba'te], *n.f.* swoop (*of plane*).

abat-jour [aba'ʒu:r], *n.m. inv.* sky-light; lamp shade; shade for the eyes.

abat-son [aba'sõ], *n.m.* (*pl. unchanged or* abat-sons) a series of sloping louvres in the window of a bell tower for directing the sound downwards.

abattage [aba'ta:ʒ], *n.m.* cutting down, felling (*of trees*); slaughtering (*of animals*).

abattant [aba'tã], *n.m.* flap (*of a counter etc.*).

abattée [ABATÉE].

abattement [abat'mã], *n.m.* weakening; prostration; dejection, despondency, low spirits.

abatteur [aba'tœ:r], *n.m.* one who fells (*trees etc.*); slaughterer.

abattis [aba'ti], *n.m.* things *or* materials brought down (*such as houses, walls, trees*); slaughtered animals, game etc.; killing of game; giblets (*of poultry*).

abattoir [aba'twa:r], *n.m.* slaughter-house.

abattre [a'batr], *v.t.* (*conjug. like* BATTRE) to throw *or* hurl down; to knock, beat *or* batter down; to pull down; to fell; to kill, to slaughter; to overthrow, to demolish; to dishearten, to discourage, to depress. **s'abattre,** *v.r.* to throw oneself down, to fall, to tumble down; to crash (down); to abate; to be cast down *or* dejected; to pounce upon; *le vent s'abat,* the wind is dropping.

abattu [aba'ty], *a.* cast down, depressed, dejected; humbled, crestfallen.

abat-vent [aba'vã], *n.m. inv.* louvre-boards (*of a window*); wind-cowl (*of a chimney*).

abat-voix [aba'vwa], *n.m. inv.* sounding board (*of a pulpit*).

abbaye [abɛ'i], *n.f.* monastery, abbey.

abbé [a'be], *n.m.* abbot, abbé; *l'abbé Martin,* Father Martin.

abbesse [a'bɛs], *n.f.* abbess.

A.B.C. [abe'se], *n.m.* alphabet; primer, spelling-book.

abcéder [apse'de], *v.i.* (*conjug. like* CÉDER) to turn into an abscess, to gather.

abcès [ap'sɛ], *n.m.* abscess, gathering; *abcès aux gencives,* gumboil.

abdication [abdika'sjõ], *n.f.* abdication; renunciation (*of property etc.*); surrender (*of authority*).

abdiquer [abdi'ke], *v.t.* to abdicate, to resign, to renounce.

abdomen [abdɔ'mɛn], *n.m.* abdomen.

abdominal [abdɔmi'nal], *a.* abdominal.

abducteur [abdyk'tœ:r], *a.* (*Anat.*) abducent. —*n.m.* (*Anat.*) abductor.

abduction [abdyk'sjõ], *n.f.* abduction.

abécédaire [abese'dɛ:r], *a.* alphabetical; *ordre abécédaire,* alphabetical order.—*n.m.* spelling book; elementary reading book; primer.

abecquer [abɛ'ke], *v.t.* to feed (*a bird*).

abeille [a'bɛ:j], *n.f.* bee; *abeille mère,* queen bee.

aberration [abɛra'sjõ], *n.f.* deviation from the normal *or* the correct course; (*Astron., Opt. etc.*) aberration.

abêtir [abɛ'ti:r], *v.t.* to render stupid; to dull, to blunt.—*v.i.* to become dull *or* stupid. **s'abêtir,** *v.r.* to grow stupid.

abêtissement [abetis'mã], *n.m.* stultification.

1

abhorrer [abɔ're], *v.t.* to abhor, to hate, to loathe.

abîme [a'biːm], *n.m.* abyss, the deep, chasm; hell.

abîmé [abi'me], *a.* swallowed up, engulfed; ruined; damaged.

abîmer [abi'me], *v.t.* *to engulf, to swallow up; to ruin; to damage. **s'abîmer**, *v.r.* to fall into ruin; to be spoiled.

abject [ab'ʒɛkt], *a.* abject, base.

abjectement [abʒɛktə'mã], *adv.* abjectly.

abjection [abʒɛk'sjɔ̃], *n.f.* abasement, humiliation; vileness.

abjuration [abʒyra'sjɔ̃], *n.f.* solemn renunciation, abjuration.

abjurer [abʒy're], *v.t.* to abjure, to renounce; to foreswear.

ablatif [abla'tif], *a.* (*fem.* -**tive**) ablative. —*n.m.* (*Gram.*) ablative (case).

ablation [abla'sjɔ̃], *n.f.* (*Surg.*) removal (*of a part*).

able [abl], *n.m.* any small freshwater fish of the bleak family [ABLETTE].

ablette [a'blɛt], *n.f.* bleak [ABLE].

ablution [ably'sjɔ̃], *n.f.* ablution, washing, purification.

abnégation [abnega'sjɔ̃], *n.f.* abnegation, renunciation, sacrifice, self-denial.

aboi [a'bwa], *n.m.* (*dog's*) bark, barking, baying; (*fig.*) desperate condition; *aux abois*, at bay.

aboiement [abwa'mã], *n.m.* barking, baying.

abolir [abɔ'liːr], *v.t.* to abolish, to repeal, to annul, to suppress.

abolissement [abolis'mã], *n.m.* abolition.

abolition [aboli'sjɔ̃], *n.f.* abolition, repeal.

abominable [abomi'nabl], *a.* abominable, execrable; heinous.

abominablement [abominablə'mã], *adv.* abominably.

abomination [abomina'sjɔ̃], *n.f.* abomination, detestation, horror.

abominer [abomi'ne], *v.t.* to abominate, to detest.

abondamment [abɔ̃da'mã], *adv.* abundantly.

abondance [abɔ̃'dãːs], *n.f.* a great quantity, abundance, plenty; affluence.

abondant [abɔ̃'dã], *a.* abundant, plentiful, copious; exuberant, effusive.

abonder [abɔ̃'de], *v.i.* to abound, to be plentiful, to be in great quantity; *abonder dans le sens de quelqu'un*, to support somebody's views strongly.

abonné [abɔ'ne], *n.m.* (*fem.* -**ée**) subscriber (*to periodicals etc.*); season ticket holder.

abonnement [abɔn'mã], *n.m.* subscription (*to periodicals, theatres etc.*); agreement; season ticket; *carte d'abonnement*, season ticket.

abonner (s') [sabɔ'ne], *v.r.* to become a subscriber.

abonnir [abɔ'niːr], *v.t.* to mend, to improve (*wine*).—*v.i.* to become good. **s'abonnir**, *v.r.* to mend, to grow better.

abonnissement [abonis'mã], *n.m.* improvement.

abord [a'bɔːr], *n.m.* landing; arrival; access, approach, meeting; onset, attack; (*pl.*) approaches, surroundings; *d'abord*, at first.

abordable [abɔr'dabl], *a.* accessible, easily approached, affable.

abordage [abɔr'daːʒ], *n.m.* (*Naut.*) boarding; fouling, colliding.

abordée [abɔr'de], *n.f.* the act of meeting, accosting *or* beginning.

aborder [abɔr'de], *v.t.* to arrive at; to approach, to accost; to enter upon (*a subject etc.*); to grapple (*a vessel*); to run foul of (*a ship*).—*v.i.* to arrive; to land. **s'aborder**, *v.r.* to accost each other; to run foul of each other.

aborigène [abɔri'ʒɛːn], *a.* native, original.— *n.m.* aboriginal, aborigine.

aborner [abɔr'ne], *v.t.* to mark out, to delimit.

abortif [abɔr'tif], *a.* (*fem.* -**tive**) abortive.

abouchement [abuʃ'mã], *n.m.* interview, conference.

aboucher [abu'ʃe], *v.t.* to bring (*things or persons*) together. **s'aboucher**, *v.r.* to have an interview, to confer (*with*); to get in touch (*with*).

aboutement [abut'mã], *n.m.* abutment; placing *or* fitting end to end.

abouter [abu'te], *v.t.* to join end to end.

aboutir [abu'tiːr], *v.i.* to end at *or* in, to result (*à*); (*Surg.*) to come to a head (*with aux.* ÊTRE *or* AVOIR).

aboutissant [abuti'sã], *a.* bordering upon, abutting on, ending in.

aboutissement [abutis'mã], *n.m.* result, issue.

aboyer [abwa'je], *v.i.* (*conjug. like* EMPLOYER) to bark, to bay, to yelp.

abracadabra [abrakada'bra], *n.m.* abracadabra (*magic word*).

abracadabrant [abrakada'brã], *a.* stupendous, amazing, stunning.

abrasif [abra'zif], *n.m.* abrasive.

abrégé [abre'ʒe], *a.* short, summary.—*n.m.* abridgment, résumé, précis, abstract, summary.

abrégement [abreʒ'mã], *n.m.* abridging, abridgment.

abréger [abre'ʒe], *v.t.* (*conjug. like* ASSIÉGER) to abridge, to shorten; to abbreviate.

abreuvage [abrœ'vaːʒ], **abreuvement** [a brœv'mã], *n.m.* watering, soaking, steaming.

abreuver [abrœ've], *v.t.* to water (*animals*); to water (*the ground etc.*). **s'abreuver**, *v.r.* to drink, to be watered (*of animals*).

abreuvoir [abrœ'vwaːr], *n.m.* watering place, horse pond; drinking trough.

abréviation [abrevja'sjɔ̃], *n.f.* abbreviation, shortening.

abri [a'bri], *n.m.* shelter, cover, refuge, dugout.

abricot [abri'ko], *n.m.* apricot.

abricotier [abriko'tje], *n.m.* apricot tree.

abriter [abri'te], *v.t.* to shelter, to shade, to protect. **s'abriter**, *v.r.* to take refuge.

abrogation [abrɔga'sjɔ̃], *n.f.* abrogation, repeal, annulment.

abroger [abrɔ'ʒe], *v.t.* (*conjug. like* MANGER) to abrogate, to repeal, to annul. **s'abroger**, *v.r.* to fall into disuse.

abrupt [a'brypt], *a.* abrupt, steep, sheer; (*fig.*) blunt, rugged, rough (*of style etc.*).

abruptement [abryptə'mã], *adv.* abruptly.

abruti [abry'ti], *a.* and *n.m.* (*fem.* -**e**) brutalized, stupid (person).

abrutir [abry'tiːr], *v.t.* to stupefy, to brutalize. **s'abrutir**, *v.r.* to become brutalized *or* stupid.

abrutissant [abryti'sɑ̃], *a.* brutalizing, stupefying.

abrutissement [abrytis'mɑ̃], *n.m.* the act of brutalizing; brutishness, degradation.

absence [ap'sɑ̃:s], *n.f.* absence; want, lack; *absence d'esprit,* absence of mind.

absent [ap'sɑ̃], *a.* absent, away from home; wandering, woolgathering.—*n.m.* (*fem.* **-e**) absentee.

absentéisme [apsɑ̃te'ism], *n.m.* absenteeism.

absenter (s') [apsɑ̃'te], *v.r.* to absent oneself, to play truant.

abside [ap'si:d], *n.f.* apse.

absinthe [ap'sɛ̃:t], *n.f.* absinth; wormwood.

absolu [apsɔ'ly], *a.* absolute; despotic, arbitrary; unrestricted; peremptory; positive.

absolument [apsɔly'mɑ̃], *adv.* absolutely; arbitrarily.

absolution [apsɔly'sjɔ̃], *n.f.* absolution, acquittal.

absolutisme [apsɔly'tism], *n.m.* absolutism.

absorbant [apsɔr'bɑ̃], *a.* absorptive, absorbent; engrossing.—*n.m.* absorbent.

absorber [apsɔr'be], *v.t.* to absorb, to imbibe; to eat *or* drink; (*fig.*) to engross. **s'absorber,** *v.r.* to be absorbed; (*fig.*) to be entirely taken up with (*dans*).

absorption [apsɔrp'sjɔ̃], *n.f.* absorption.

absoudre [ap'sudr], *v.t. irr.* to absolve, to acquit; to exonerate, to forgive.

abstenir (s') [apsta'ni:r], *v.r. irr.* (*conjug. like* TENIR) to abstain (*from voting*); to refrain, to forbear, to forgo.

abstention [apstɑ̃'sjɔ̃], *n.f.* abstention.

abstinence [apsti'nɑ̃:s], *n.f.* abstinence; temperance, sobriety; (*pl.*) fasts, fasting.

abstinent [apsti'nɑ̃], *a.* abstemious, sober.

abstraction [apstrak'sjɔ̃], *n.f.* abstraction, abstract question *or* idea.

abstraire [aps'trɛ:r], *v.t. irr.* (*conjug. like* TRAIRE) to abstract; to separate, to isolate.

abstrait [aps'trɛ], *a.* abstract, abstruse; absent-minded.

abstraitement [apstrɛt'mɑ̃], *adv.* abstractedly; separately; in the abstract.

abstrus [aps'try], *a.* abstruse, obscure.

absurde [ap'syrd], *a.* absurd, nonsensical, stupid, silly, preposterous.

absurdement [apsyrdə'mɑ̃], *adv.* absurdly, nonsensically.

absurdité [apsyrdi'te], *n.f.* absurdity, nonsense.

abus [a'by], *n.m.* abuse; grievance; misuse.

abuser [aby'ze], *v.t.* to deceive, to lead astray, to delude.—*v.i.* to misuse, to make ill use (*de*); to take advantage (*de*). **s'abuser,** *v.r.* to be mistaken, to deceive oneself.

abusif [aby'zif], *a.* (*fem.* **-sive**) irregular, improper.

abusivement [abyziv'mɑ̃], *adv.* irregularly, improperly.

abyssal [abi'sal], *a.* unfathomable.

abysse [a'bis], *n.m.* abyss, unfathomable gulf *or* depth.

Abyssinie [abisi'ni], *l',* *f.* Abyssinia.

abyssinien [abisi'njɛ̃] (*fem.* **-enne**), **abyssin** [abi'sɛ̃], *a.* Abyssinian.—*n.m.* (**Abyssinien,** *fem.* **-enne**) Abyssinian (*person*).

acabit [aka'bi], *n.m.* quality (*of fruits, vegetables*); character, nature, stamp (*of persons*).

acacia [aka'sja], *n.m.* (*Bot.*) acacia.

académicien [akademi'sjɛ̃], *n.m.* academician.

académie [akade'mi], *n.f.* academy, society of learned men, *esp.* the Académie Française; school (*of dancing, fencing, riding etc.*).

académique [akade'mik], *a.* proper, appropriate *or* belonging to an academy, academic(al).

acagnarder [akaɲar'de], *v.t.* to make lazy. **s'acagnarder,** *v.r.* to drift into an idle, slothful life.

acajou [aka'ʒu], *n.m.* mahogany.

acanthe [a'kɑ̃:t], *n.f.* acanthus.

acariâtre [aka'rjo:tr], *a.* contrary, crabbed, cross-grained, quarrelsome, shrewish.

acariâtreté [akarjotrə'te], *n.f.* crabbedness, peevishness, shrewishness.

accablant [aka'blɑ̃], *a.* oppressive, overwhelming, crushing.

accablement [akablə'mɑ̃], *n.m.* prostration, oppression, extreme discouragement *or* dejection.

accabler [aka'ble], *v.t.* to crush, to overpower, to overcome; (*fig.*) to weigh down, to overload, to overwhelm.

accalmie [akal'mi], *n.f.* (*Naut.*) lull.

accaparant [akapa'rɑ̃], *a.* engrossing.

accaparement [akapar'mɑ̃], *n.m.* monopoly, monopolizing.

accaparer [akapa're], *v.t.* to monopolize, to hoard, to engross.

accapareur [akapa'rœr], *n.m.* (*fem.* **-euse**) monopolist, monopolizer, hoarder.

accéder [akse'de], *v.i.* (*conjug. like* CÉDER) to arrive, to reach, to have access, to accede, to comply with.

accélérateur [akselera'tœ:r], *a.* (*fem.* **-trice**) accelerative, with increasing speed.—*n.m.* (*Elec., Mech., Phot. etc.*) accelerator; (*fam.*) *appuyer sur l'accélérateur,* to step on the gas.

accélération [akselera'sjɔ̃], *n.f.* acceleration.

accéléré [aksele're], *a.* accelerated.

accélérer [aksele're], *v.t.* (*conjug. like* CÉDER) to accelerate, to quicken, to hasten, to press, to dispatch.

accent [ak'sɑ̃], *n.m.* pitch, accent, stress, tone; pronunciation; expression (*of the voice*).

accentuation [aksɑ̃tɥa'sjɔ̃], *n.f.* accentuation, stressing.

accentuer [aksɑ̃'tɥe], *v.t.* to accent, to accentuate, to stress.

acceptable [aksɛp'tabl], *a.* acceptable, worth accepting.

acceptation [aksɛpta'sjɔ̃], *n.f.* acceptance; acceptation.

accepter [aksɛp'te], *v.t.* to accept, to agree to, to welcome (*what is offered* or *proposed*).

acception [aksɛp'sjɔ̃], *n.f.* respect, regard, sense, meaning, acceptation.

accès [ak'sɛ], *n.m.* access, opportunity of approach, admittance; attack, fit, paroxysm.

accessibilité [aksɛsibili'te], *n.f.* accessibility.

accessible [aksɛ'sibl], *a.* accessible, approachable; within reach.

accession [aksɛ'sjɔ̃], *n.f.* accession; adhesion, union (*of a country, province etc. to another*).

accessit [aksɛ'sit], *n.m.* award of merit, honorable mention; 'proxime accessit'.

accessoire [aksɛ'swa:r], *a.* accessory, additional, subordinate.—*n.m.* an accessory; (*pl.*) (*Theat.*) properties.

accessoiriste [aksɛswa'rist], *n.m.* props man.

3

accident [aksi'dā], *n.m.* accident, fortuitous incident; casualty, mishap, mischance; unevenness, irregularity (*in the ground*).

accidenté [aksidā'te], *a.* varied, unequal (*of style etc.*); rough, uneven, broken, hilly (*of ground*); chequered (*of life, career etc.*).— *n.m.* (*fem.* **-ée**) one injured by an accident.

accidentel [aksidā'tel], *a.* (*fem.* **-elle**) accidental, adventitious, fortuitous, unexpected; *signe accidentel*, (*Mus.*) accidental.

accidentellement [aksidātel'mā], *adv.* accidentally, casually, by chance.

accidenter [aksidā'te], *v.t.* to make irregular *or* uneven; to diversify, to chequer, to make picturesque.

accise [ak'siːz], *n.f.* (*Law*) inland duty, excise; *préposé à l'accise*, exciseman.

acclamation [aklama'sjɔ̃], *n.f.* acclamation, cheering.

acclamer [akla'me], *v.t.* to acclaim, to applaud, to cheer.

acclimatable [aklima'tabl], *a.* that may be acclimatized.

acclimatation [aklimata'sjɔ̃], *n.f.* acclimatization.

acclimater [aklima'te], *v.t.* to acclimatize. **s'acclimater**, *v.r.* to become acclimatized.

accointance [akwɛ̃'tãːs], *n.f.* (*used generally in pl. and in a bad sense*) intimacy, familiarity; *avoir des accointances* (*avec*), to have dealings (*with*).

accointer [akwɛ̃'te], *v.t.* to make acquainted.

accolade [akɔ'lad], *n.f.* embrace; kiss; accolade (*in knighting*).

accolader (**s'**) [sakɔla'de], *v.r.* to embrace mutually.

accolage [akɔ'laːʒ], *n.m.* tying up, training (*branches etc.*).

accolement [akɔl'mã], *n.m.* joining, uniting.

accoler [akɔ'le], *v.t.* to embrace; to tie up, to fasten, to place against; (*fig.*) to couple, to join together, to bracket.

accommodable [akɔmɔ'dabl], *a.* that may be arranged; adjustable.

accommodage [akɔmɔ'daːʒ], *n.m.* preparation *or* dressing (*of meat*).

accommodant [akɔmɔ'dã], *a.* accommodating, easy-going, courteous.

accommodation [akɔmɔda'sjɔ̃], *n.f.* accommodation.

accommodement [akɔmɔd'mã], *n.m.* accommodation, arrangement, composition; settlement, reconciliation, compromise.

accommoder [akɔmɔ'de], *v.t.* to adapt, to accommodate, to fit, to adjust; to reconcile; to conciliate; to dress, to trim; to cook, to do up; to suit, to be convenient. **s'accommoder**, *v.r.* to agree, to come to terms; to accommodate oneself, to adapt oneself (*à*); to put up with (*de*).

accompagnateur [akɔ̃paɲa'tœːr], *n.m.* (*fem.* **-trice**) accompanist (*with instrument or voice*); conductor (*of a tour*).

accompagnement [akɔ̃paɲ'mã], *n.m.* accompanying; attendance, retinue; an accompaniment, an accessory; (*Mus.*) accompaniment.

accompagner [akɔ̃pa'ɲe], *v.t.* to accompany, to attend on; to go with, to escort; (*Mus.*) to accompany.

accompli [akɔ̃'pli], *a.* accomplished, performed, fulfilled; complete, faultless, perfect, out and out.

accomplir [akɔ̃'pliːr], *v.t.* to fulfil, to effect, to perform; to realize, to carry out.

accomplissement [akɔ̃plis'mã], *n.m.* accomplishment, fulfilment, realization.

accon, acconier [ACON etc.].

accord [a'kɔːr], *n.m.* accord, concurrence, unanimity, harmony; agreement, bargain; convention, settlement; (*Mus.*) chord; *être d'accord*, to agree; *d'accord*, granted, agreed.

accordable [akɔr'dabl], *a.* that may be accorded; reconcilable; (*Mus.*) tunable.

accordage [akɔr'daːʒ], **accordement** [akɔrdə'mã], *n.m.* tuning (*of a musical instrument*).

accordailles [akɔr'daːj], *n.f.* (*used only in pl.*) betrothal.

accordant [akɔr'dã], *a.* accordant, harmonious.

accordé [akɔr'de], *n.m.* (*fem.* **-ée**) fiancé, fiancée; *les accordés*, the bride and bridegroom.

accordéon [akɔrde'ɔ̃], *n.m.* accordion.

accordéoniste [akɔrdeɔ'nist], *n.* accordionist.

accorder [akɔr'de], *v.t.* to bring into harmony *or* accord, to make agree, to reconcile; to concede, to grant; to admit, to avow; (*Mus.*) to tune, to harmonize; to bestow (*hand in marriage*). **s'accorder**, *v.r.* to agree, to concur; to correspond; to suit, to be suited.

accordeur [akɔr'dœːr], *n.m.* tuner (*of musical instruments*).

accordoir [akɔr'dwaːr], *n.m.* tuning hammer, key *or* cone.

accore [a'kɔːr], *a.* abrupt, sheer, vertical (*of a coast*).

accort [a'kɔːr], *a.* gracious, courteous.

accostable [akɔs'tabl], *a.* easy of access, approachable.

accostage [akɔs'taːʒ], *n.m.* the act of accosting, approaching *or* drawing alongside.

accoster [akɔs'te], *v.t.* to accost, to go up to; (*Naut.*) to come alongside.

accotement [akɔt'mã], *n.m.* (*Civ. Eng.*) roadside; footpath.

accoter [akɔ'te], *v.t.* to prop up, to support, to stay. **s'accoter**, *v.r.* to lean (*contre*).

accotoir [akɔ'twaːr], *n.m.* prop, support, leaning post.

accouardir [akwar'diːr], *v.t.* to make a coward. **s'accouardir**, *v.r.* to turn coward.

accouchée [aku'ʃe], *n.f.* woman in childbirth, woman who has just had a child.

accouchement [akuʃ'mã], *n.m.* childbirth, delivery, confinement; *centre d'accouchement*, maternity home.

accoucher [aku'ʃe], *v.t.* to deliver (*a woman*). —*v.i.* to lie in, to be brought to bed, to be delivered.

accoucheur [aku'ʃœːr], *n.m.* male midwife, accoucheur.

accoucheuse [aku'ʃøːz], *n.f.* midwife.

accoudement [akud'mã], *n.m.* the act of leaning (*on*).

accouder (**s'**) [saku'de], *v.r.* to lean on one's elbow.

accoudoir [aku'dwaːr], *n.m.* elbow rest; (*Arch.*) rail, balustrade.

accouple [a'kupl], *n.f.* leash (*for tying dogs in couples*).

accouplement [akuplə'mɑ̃], *n.m.* coupling; pairing.

accoupler [aku'ple], *v.t.* to couple; to join together in pairs; (*Elec.*) to connect, to group (*batteries etc.*).

accourci [akur'si], *n.m.* abridgement (*of a book*).

accourcir [akur'si:r], *v.t.* to shorten, to abridge, to curtail. **s'accourcir**, *v.r.* to become shorter, to decrease.

accourcissement [akursis'mɑ̃], *n.m.* shortening, diminution.

accourir [aku'ri:r], *v.i.* irr. (*conjug. like* COURIR) to run up to, to hasten, to flock.

accoutrement [akutrə'mɑ̃], *n.m.* garb, dress, *esp.* as an object of ridicule.

accoutrer [aku'tre], *v.t.* to rig out, to dress. **s'accoutrer**, *v.r.* to dress absurdly, to rig oneself out.

accoutumance [akuty'mɑ̃:s], *n.f.* habit, custom, wont, usage.

accoutumé [akuty'me], *a.* ordinary, accustomed, habitual.

accoutumer [akuty'me], *v.t.* to accustom, to habituate, to inure.—*v.i.* (*only in compound tenses*) to use, to be wont. **s'accoutumer**, *v.r.* to be accustomed, to be used (*à*).

accouvage [aku'va:ʒ], *n.m.* hatching (*esp. by artificial means*), incubation.

accouver [aku've], *v.t.* to set (*a hen etc.*).— *v.i.* to sit, to hatch.

accréditation [akredita'sjɔ̃], *n.f.* accreditation, accrediting (*of an ambassador*).

accréditer [akredi'te], *v.t.* to give credit, standing *or* sanction to; to authorize; to accredit (*an ambassador etc.*); to confirm, to spread (*rumors etc.*). **s'accréditer**, *v.r.* to gain credit *or* reputation; to ingratiate oneself; to spread (*of rumors etc.*).

accréditeur [akredi'tœ:r], *n.m.* guarantor, surety.

accroc [a'kro], *n.m.* impediment, hitch; hindrance; rent, tear.

accrochage [akro'ʃa:ʒ], *n.m.* hanging, hooking, hitching; catching, retarding, stopping; grazing (*vehicles*).

accroche-cœur [akroʃ'kœ:r], *n.m. inv.* spit curl.

accrochement [akroʃ'mɑ̃], *n.m.* hooking, catching (*in something*).

accrocher [akro'ʃe], *v.t.* to hang upon a hook; to hook, to catch, to hitch, to catch and tear; to get hold of; to pick up (*a radio station*). **s'accrocher**, *v.r.* to catch in, to be caught *or* hooked (*par*); to lay hold of, to cling (*à*).

accroire [a'krwa:r], *v.t. irr.* (*used only in the infinitive after faire*) to believe.

accroissement [akrwas'mɑ̃], *n.m.* increase, growth, enlargement, extension.

accroître [a'krwa:tr], *v.t. irr.* (*conjug. like* CROÎTRE except for p.p. **accru**) to increase, to augment, to enlarge, to amplify. **s'accroître**, *v.r.* to increase, to grow.

accroupi [akru'pi], *a.* crouched, crouching, cowering, squatting.

accroupir (**s'**) [sakru'pi:r], *v.r.* to sit down on the hams *or* heels, to squat, to crouch.

accroupissement [akrupis'mɑ̃], *n.m.* cowering, squatting, crouching.

accru [a'kry], *n.m.* (*Gard.*) sucker, scion.

accrue [a'kry], *n.f.* increase of land through the retreat of waters; encroachment of a forest on adjoining land.

accu [a'ky], *n.m. abbr.* [ACCUMULATEUR].

accueil [a'kœ:j], *n.m.* reception, welcome, greeting.

accueillir [akœ'ji:r], *v.t. irr.* (*conjug. like* CUEILLIR) to receive (*well* or *ill*); to receive graciously, to welcome.

acculer [aky'le], *v.t.* to drive into a corner; to bring to a standstill. **s'acculer**, *v.r.* to set one's back against something.

accumulateur [akymyla'tœ:r], *a.* (*fem.* **-trice**) storing, heaping up, hoarding up.—*n.m.* accumulator (*person* or *thing*); (*Elec.*) storage cell *or* battery.

accumulation [akymyla'sjɔ̃], *n.f.* accumulation; mass, pile.

accumuler [akymy'le], *v.t.* to accumulate, to pile up, to amass. **s'accumuler**, *v.r.* to accumulate, to increase.

accusable [aky'zabl], *a.* accusable, chargeable.

accusateur [akyza'tœ:r], *a.* (*fem.* **-trice**) accusing, accusatory.—*n.m.* (*fem.* **-trice**) accuser, denouncer.

accusatif [akyza'tif], *a.* (*fem.* **-tive**) and *n.m.* (*Gram.*) accusative (*case*); **à l'accusatif**, in the accusative.

accusation [akyza'sjɔ̃], *n.f.* accusation, indictment, charge; (*fig.*) prosecution; **mise ₂n accusation**, arraignment.

accusatoire [akyza'twa:r], *a.* accusatory.

accusé [aky'ze], *n.m.* (*fem.* **-ée**) the accused, prisoner, defendant; **accusé de réception**, acknowledgment of a letter, receipt.

accuser [aky'ze], *v.t.* to impute, to charge with; to reproach, to blame; to indict, to impeach, to prosecute. **s'accuser**, *v.r.* to admit, to avow, to confess.

acéphale [ase'fal], *a.* acephalous, headless.

acérain [ase'rɛ̃], *a.* like *or* pertaining to steel, steely.

acerbe [a'sɛrb], *a.* sour, harsh, sharp, astringent; (*fig.*) bitter, acrimonious.

acerbité [asɛrbi'te], *n.f.* acerbity, harshness; (*fig.*) bitterness, severity.

acéré [ase're], *a.* steely, steeled; sharp, keen; (*fig.*) mordant, trenchant, acute.

acérer [ase're], *v.t.* (*conjug. like* CÉDER) to steel; to sharpen, to render biting, incisive *or* mordant.

acétate [ase'tat], *n.m.* (*Chem.*) acetate.

acéteux [ase'tø], *a.* (*fem.* **-euse**) acetous, sour, tasting like vinegar.

acétique [ase'tik], *a.* acetic.

acétone [ase'tɔn], *n.m.* acetone.

acétoselle [aseto'sɛl], *n.f.* wood-sorrel.

acétylène [aseti'lɛːn], *n.m.* acetylene.

achalandage [aʃalɑ̃'da:ʒ], *n.m.* custom, customers; goodwill (*of a shop*).

achalandé [aʃalɑ̃'de], *a.* having plenty of custom; **boutique bien achalandée**, a well-frequented shop.

achalander [aʃalɑ̃'de], *v.t.* to get custom, to attract customers, to draw trade.

acharné [aʃar'ne], *a.* fleshed, fierce, tenacious, implacable; stubborn, obstinate, intense.

acharnement [aʃarnə'mɑ̃], *n.m.* tenacity; rancor, animosity, fury; stubbornness, obstinacy, desperation.

acharner

acharner [aʃar'ne], *v.t.* to flesh; to set on; to excite, to madden; to embitter, to envenom. **s'acharner**, *v.r.* to be intent, bent *or* obstinately set upon; to set one's heart upon, to persist in; to be infuriated *or* implacable.

achat [a'ʃa], *n.m.* purchasing, buying; purchase; *faire des achats*, to go shopping; *pouvoir d'achat*, purchasing power.

acheminement [aʃmin'mã], *n.m.* progress, advance, conveying.

acheminer [aʃmi'ne], *v.t.* to send on (*towards a place* or *object*); to train (*a horse*). **s'acheminer**, *v.r.* to set out (*pour*), to make one's way towards.

achetable [aʃ'tabl], *a.* purchasable.

acheter [aʃ'te], *v.t.* (*conjug. like* AMENER) to buy, to purchase; (*fig.*) to bribe. **s'acheter**, *v.r.* to be bought; to be for sale, to be venal.

acheteur [aʃ'tœːr], *n.m.* (*fem.* -**euse**) buyer, purchaser.

achevage [aʃ'vaːʒ], *n.m.* completion, finishing; finish (*of a work of art*).

achevé [aʃ've], *a.* finished, accomplished, perfect, exquisite; absolute, downright, consummate, arrant.

achèvement [aʃɛv'mã], *n.m.* completion, conclusion.

achever [aʃ've], *v.t.* (*conjug. like* AMENER) to finish, to terminate; to put the finishing touch to; to complete, to achieve; to consummate, to perfect; (*fig.*) to do for completely, to ruin, to kill.

Achille [a'ʃil], *m.* Achilles.

achoppement [aʃɔp'mã], *n.m.* obstacle, impediment; unforeseen difficulty, embarrassment; *pierre d'achoppement*, stumbling block.

achopper [aʃɔ'pe], *v.i.* and **s'achopper**, *v.r.* to stumble, to knock against something; (*fig.*) to come to grief; to fail.

achromatopsie [akromatɔp'si], *n.f.* achromatopsy, color blindness.

acide [a'sid], *a.* acid, sour, tart, sharp.—*n.m.* acid.

acidifier [asidi'fje], *v.t.* to acidify. **s'acidifier**, *v.r.* to become acidified.

acidité [asidi'te], *n.f.* acidity, sourness, sharpness, tartness.

acidule [asi'dyl], *a.* subacid, acidulous.

acidulé [asidy'le], *a.* acidulated; *bonbons acidulés*, acid drops, sour balls.

aciduler [asidy'le], *v.t.* to acidulate.

acier [a'sje], *n.m.* steel; *acier chromé*, chrome steel; *acier coulé* or *fondu*, cast steel; *acier doux*, mild steel; *acier inoxydable*, stainless steel.

aciération [asjera'sjɔ̃], *n.f.* steeling, plating with steel.

aciérer [asje're], *v.t.* (*conjug. like* CÉDER) to convert into steel, to cover with steel; to acierate. **s'aciérer**, *v.r.* to steel oneself.

aciéreux [asje're], *a.* (*fem.* -**euse**) steely, like steel.

aciérie [asje'ri], *n.f.* steel factory, steelworks.

acné [ak'ne], *n.f.* (*Med.*) acne.

acolyte [akɔ'lit], *n.m.* (*Eccles.*) acolyte; (*fig.*) assistant, confederate, associate, accomplice.

acompte [a'kɔ̃ːt], *n.m.* instalment, partial payment.

acon or **accon** [a'kɔ̃], *n.m.* small lighter, punt.

aconier or **acconier** [akɔ'nje], *n.m.* lighterman.

aconit [akɔ'nit], *n.m.* aconite.

acoquinant [akɔki'nã], *a.* alluring, engaging, captivating.

acoquiner [akɔki'ne], *v.t.* to make fond, to allure, to bewitch, to captivate. **s'acoquiner**, *v.r.* (*fam.*) to be bewitched, to be greatly attached to.

Açores [a'sɔːr], **les**, *f.pl.* the Azores.

à-côté [ako'te], *n.m.* aside; (*pl.*) little extras.

à-coup [a'ku], *n.m.* jerk, jolt; sudden stop.

acousticien [akusti'sjɛ̃], *n.m.* (*fem.* -**enne**) acoustician.

acoustique [akus'tik], *a.* acoustic.—*n.f.* acoustics.

acquéreur [ake'rœːr], *n.m.* (*fem.* -**euse**) buyer, purchaser.

acquérir [ake'riːr], *v.t. irr.* to purchase, to buy, to get; to earn, to win, to gain; to acquire, to obtain. **s'acquérir**, *v.r.* to get or win for oneself; to be acquired, obtained or purchased.

acquiescement [akjɛs'mã], *n.m.* acquiescence, compliance, consent, willingness.

acquiescer [akjɛ'se], *v.i.* (*conjug. like* COMMENCER) to acquiesce, to agree, to assent, to yield, to comply.

acquis [a'ki], *a.* acquired, secured.—*n.m.* acquirements, attainments, experience.

acquisitif [akizi'tif], *a.* (*fem.* -**tive**) acquisitive.

acquisition [akizi'sjɔ̃], *n.f.* acquisition, acquiring, attaining, acquirement, attainment; purchase, conquest.

acquisivité [akizivi'te], *n.f.* acquisitiveness.

acquit [a'ki], *n.m.* receipt, discharge, release, acquittance; (*Billiards*) break (*i.e. start*).

acquittement [akit'mã], *n.m.* payment, quittance; (*Law*) acquittal.

acquitter [aki'te], *v.t.* to pay; to discharge, to pay off (*a dependant*); to acquit. **s'acquitter**, *v.r.* to fulfil, to perform; to pay off one's debts, to be quits (*in gambling*); to acquit oneself (*well* or *ill*).

acre [akr], *n.f.* acre.

âcre [ɑːkr], *a.* sour, sharp, tart, acrid; (*fig.*) bitter, pungent, caustic.

âcrement [ɑːkrə'mã], *adv.* tartly, sourly.

âcreté [ɑːkrə'te], *n.f.* sourness, acridity, sharpness, tartness, acrimony.

acrimonie [akrimɔ'ni], *n.f.* bitterness, sharpness, keenness, acrimony.

acrimonieux [akrimɔ'njø], *a.* (*fem.* -**euse**) pungent, acrimonious, ill-natured, sharp.

acrobate [akrɔ'bat], *n.* acrobat, rope-dancer.

acrobatie [akrɔba'si], *n.f.* acrobatics; (*Av.*) stunt.

acrobatique [akrɔba'tik], *a.* acrobatic.

acrobatisme [akrɔba'tism], *n.m.* acrobatics.

acrocéphale [akrɔse'fal], *a.* having a pointed head, acrocephalic, acrocephalous.—*n.* a person with such a head.

acropole [akrɔ'pɔl], *n.f.* acropolis.

acrostiche [akrɔs'tiʃ], *a.* and *n.m.* acrostic.

acrotère [akrɔ'tɛːr], *n.m.* (*Arch.*) acroterium, ornamental summit (*of a pediment*).

acte [akt], *n.m.* action, deed; (*Law*) deed, indenture; instrument; document, charter; (*Theat.*) act; (*pl.*) records, public registers, rolls, transactions, proceedings; *acte de naissance*, birth certificate.

acteur [ak'tœːr], *n.m.* (*fem.* -**trice**) actor; actress; player.

6

actif [ak'tif], *a.* (*fem.* **-tive**) active, busy, energetic, assiduous; nimble, brisk, agile; (*Gram. etc.*) active.—*n.m.* (*Gram.*) active voice; assets, credit balance.

action [ak'sjɔ̃], *n.f.* action, operation, work; activity, motion, deed, feat, performance; fight, engagement, battle; (*Law*) action, law-suit; (*Theat.*) gesture; (*Lit.*) subject, action, plot; (*Comm.*) share, stock.

actionnaire [aksjɔ'nɛːr], *n.* shareholder.

actionnariat [aksjɔna'rja], *n.m.* shareholding; **actionnariat ouvrier**, industrial co-partnership.

actionner [aksjɔ'ne], *v.t.* to bring an action against, to sue at law; to bestir, to rouse up, to set going; to operate; to run, to drive. **s'actionner**, *v.r.* to bestir oneself.

activement [aktiv'mã], *adv.* actively, vigorously.

activer [akti've], *v.t.* to press, to accelerate, to forward, to expedite, to stir up (*a fire, people*).

activisme [akti'vism], *n.m.* (*Polit.*) militancy, activism.

activiste [akti'vist], *n.m.* activist.

activité [aktivi'te], *n.f.* activity, full swing; nimbleness, alacrity, promptitude, dispatch.

actrice [ak'tris], [ACTEUR].

actuaire [ak'tɥɛːr], *n.m.* actuary.

actualisation [aktɥaliza'sjɔ̃], *n.f.* actualization; realization.

actualiser [aktɥali'ze], *v.t.* to bring up to date. **s'actualiser**, *v.r.* to become real.

actualité [aktɥali'te], *n.f.* actuality; event of the moment, present interest; (*Cine.*) **les actualités**, the newsreel.

actuel [ak'tɥɛl], *a.* (*fem.* **-elle**) present, of the present time.

actuellement [aktɥɛl'mã], *adv.* now, at the present time.

acuité [akɥi'te], *n.f.* sharpness, acuteness, keenness.

acutangle [aky'tã:gl], **acutangulaire** [a kytãgy'lɛːr], *a.* acute-angled (*of triangles etc.*).

acutesse [aky'tɛs], *n.f.* acuteness, sharpness.

adage [a'da:ʒ], *n.m.* adage, proverb, saying.

Adam [a'dã], *m.* Adam.

adamantin [adamã'tɛ̃], *a.* adamantine.

adaptable [adap'tabl], *a.* adaptable.

adaptateur [adapta'tœːr], *n.m.* adapter, converter.

adaptation [adapta'sjɔ̃], *n.f.* adaptation.

adapter [adap'te], *v.t.* to adapt, to adjust, to apply (à); to fit, to make suitable. **s'adapter**, *v.r.* to fit, to suit, to adapt oneself (*to*).

addition [adi'sjɔ̃], *n.f.* adding up, addition; an addition; bill, reckoning; check.

additionnel [adisjɔ'nɛl], *a.* (*fem.* **-elle**) additional.

additionner [adisjɔ'ne], *v.t.* to add up.

Adélaïde [adela'id], *f.* Adelaide.

Adèle [a'dɛl], *f.* Adela.

adénite [ade'nit], *n.f.* adenitis, inflammation of the glands.

adénoïde [adenɔ'id], *a.* adenoid; **végétations adénoïdes**, adenoids.

adent [a'dã], *n.m.* dovetail, tenon.

adenter [adã'te], *v.t.* to dovetail, to join with mortise and tenon.

adepte [a'dɛpt], *n.m.* adept, initiate, follower.

adéquat [ade'kwa], *a.* adequate; (*Phil.*) equal in content; appropriate.

adhérence [ade'rãːs], *n.f.* adhesion, adherence; (*fig.*) attachment.

adhérent [ade'rã], *a.* adherent.—*n.m.* (*fem.* **-e**) adherent, follower, partisan.

adhérer [ade're], *v.i.* (*conjug. like* CÉDER) to adhere, to cling; (*fig.*) to hold (à), to cleave (*to a sect etc.*).

adhésif [ade'zif], *a.* (*fem.* **-sive**) adhesive.—*n.m.* (*Phot.*) dry-mounting tissue.

adhésion [ade'zjɔ̃], *n.f.* adhesion, adherence, union; compliance; joining (*a party*).

adhésivité [adezivi'te], *n.f.* adhesiveness.

adieu [a'djø], *int.* adieu, good-bye, farewell. —*n.m.* (*pl.* **-eux**) farewell, parting, leave; **faire ses adieux à**, to take leave of, to say good-bye to.

adipeux [adi'pø], *a.* (*fem.* **-euse**) adipose, fat.

adiposité [adipozi'te], *n.f.* adipose *or* fatty condition.

adjacence [adʒa'sã:s], *n.f.* adjacency.

adjacent [adʒa'sã], *a.* adjacent, bordering upon, contiguous.

adjectif [adʒɛk'tif], *a.* (*fem.* **-tive**) (*Gram.*) adjectival.—*n.m.* adjective.

adjectivement [adʒɛktiv'mã], *adv.* adjectivally.

adjoindre [ad'ʒwɛ̃:dr], *v.t. irr.* (*conjug. like* CRAINDRE) to adjoin, to associate, to add as an assistant. **s'adjoindre**, *v.r.* to join as a partner *or* associate; to take on.

adjoint [ad'ʒwɛ̃], *a.* adjunct, associate.—*n.m.* (*fem.* **-e**) associate, assistant, deputy; **adjoint au maire**, deputy mayor.

adjonction [adʒɔ̃k'sjɔ̃], *n.f.* adjunction.

adjudant [adʒy'dã], *n.m.* company sergeant-major; warrant officer; **adjudant-major**, adjutant.

adjudicataire [adʒydika'tɛːr], *a.* and *n.* contracting party; successful tenderer, highest bidder.

adjudicateur [adʒydika'tœːr], *n.m.* (*fem.* **-trice**) adjudicator, awarder; auctioneer.

adjudication [adʒydika'sjɔ̃], *n.f.* auction; knocking down; adjudication.

adjuger [adʒy'ʒe], *v.t.* (*conjug. like* MANGER) to adjudge, to adjudicate, to knock down (*to the highest bidder*); to award; **adjugé!** (*at auctions*) gone!

adjuration [adʒyra'sjɔ̃], *n.f.* adjuration, imprecation.

adjurer [adʒy're], *v.t.* to adjure, to conjure; to call upon, to beseech.

admettre [ad'mɛtr], *v.t. irr.* (*conjug. like* METTRE) to admit, to let in; to concede, to allow, to acknowledge.

administrateur [administra'tœːr], *n.m.* (*fem.* **-trice**) manager, director; administrator, administratrix, trustee (*of an estate*).

administratif [administra'tif], *a.* (*fem.* **-tive**) administrative.

administration [administra'sjɔ̃], *n.f.* administration, management, direction, government; (*collect.*) the management, the administration.

administré [adminis'tre], *n.m.* (*fem.* **-ée**) person under one's administration *or* jurisdiction.

administrer [adminis'tre], *v.t.* to manage, to govern, to direct; to administer, to dispense.

7

admirable [admi'rabl], *a.* admirable; wonderful.

admirablement [admirablə'mã], *adv.* admirably; wonderfully.

admirateur [admira'tœ:r], *n.m. (fem.* -trice) admirer, praiser.

admiratif [admira'tif], *a. (fem.* -tive) admiring, wondering.

admiration [admira'sjɔ̃], *n.f.* admiration.

admirer [admi're], *v.t.* to admire.

admissibilité [admisibili'te], *n.f.* admissibility.

admissible [admi'sibl], *a.* admittable, admissible.

admission [admi'sjɔ̃], *n.f.* admission, admittance; *soupape d'admission,* inlet valve.

admonestation [admɔnɛsta'sjɔ̃], *n.f.* admonishment, admonition.

admonester [admɔnɛs'te], *v.t.* to reprimand, to admonish.

admoniteur [admɔni'tœ:r], *n.m. (fem.* -trice) admonisher.

admonitif [admɔni'tif], *a. (fem.* -tive) admonitory.

admonition [admɔni'sjɔ̃], *n.f. (chiefly R.-C. Ch.)* admonition, advice, reprimand.

adolescence [adɔlɛ'sã:s], *n.f.* adolescence.

adolescent [adɔlɛ'sã], *a.* adolescent.—*n.m. (fem.* -e) adolescent, youth, teenager.

Adonis [adɔ'ni:s], *n.m.* Adonis, beau.

adonné [adɔ'ne], *a.* given to, addicted, devoted. **s'adonner,** *v.r.* to give, devote *or* addict oneself (*à*).

adopté [adɔp'te], *a.* adopted *or* adoptive (*child*).

adopter [adɔp'te], *v.t.* to adopt; to embrace, to espouse; to pass, to carry (*a bill*).

adoptif [adɔp'tif], *a. (fem.* -tive) adoptive, by adoption.

adoption [adɔp'sjɔ̃], *n.f.* adoption.

adorable [adɔ'rabl], *a.* adorable, charming, delightful, exquisite.

adorablement [adɔrablə'mã], *adv.* adorably, delightfully.

adorateur [adɔra'tœ:r], *n.m. (fem.* -trice) adorer, worshipper.

adoration [adɔra'sjɔ̃], *n.f.* adoration, worship; admiration, respect, reverence.

adorer [adɔ're], *v.t.* to adore, to worship.

adossé [adɔ'se], *a.* with one's back against.

adosser [adɔ'se], *v.t.* to set *or* lean with the back r iinst; to put back to back. **s'adosser,** *v.r.* to 1ean one's back (*à, contre*).

adoucir [adu'si:r], *v.t.* to soften; to sweeten; to mitigate, to alleviate, to smooth. **s'adoucir,** *v.r.* to grow mild *or* soft; to get milder (*of weather*).

adoucissement [adusis'mã], *n.m.* softening, sweetening; assuaging, appeasing; ease, mitigation, alleviation; consolation.

adrénaline [adrena'lin], *n.f.* adrenalin.

adresse [a'drɛs], *n.f.* address; memorial, a document addressed to an assembly *or* person in authority; skill, dexterity, cleverness.

adresser [adrɛ'se], *v.t.* to direct, to address; to turn, to direct (*one's steps etc.*). **s'adresser,** *v.r.* to be directed; to speak, to address oneself, to make application, to appeal (*à*); *s'adresser ici,* apply within.

Adriatique [adria'tik], **l',** *f.* the Adriatic.

adroit [a'drwa], *a.* ingenious, clever, skilful; artful.

adroitement [adrwat'mã], *adv.* skilfully, artfully, cleverly.

adulateur [adyla'tœ:r], *a. (fem.* -trice) flattering, adulatory.—*n.m. (fem.* -trice) adulator, flatterer, sycophant.

adulatif [adyla'tif], *a. (fem.* -tive) flattering, adulatory.

adulation [adyla'sjɔ̃], *n.,* adulation, flattery, sycophancy.

aduler [ady'le], *v.t.* to flatter, to fawn upon.

adulte [a'dylt], *a.* adult, grown-up.—*n.* adult.

adultère [adyl'tɛ:r], *a.* adulterous; *femme adultère,* adulteress.—*n.m.* adultery.—*n.* adulterer, adulteress.

adultérer [adylte're], *v.t. (conjug. like* CÉDER) (*Pharm.*) to adulterate; (*Law*) to falsify (*money*); (*fig.*) to corrupt, to pervert, to falsify.

adultérin [adylte'rɛ̃], *a.* adulterine.

advenir [adva'ni:r], *v.i. irr.* (*used only in inf. and 3rd pers.*) to occur, to happen, to befall.

adventice [advã'tis], *a.* adventitious.

adventif [advã'tif], *a. (fem.* -tive) (*Bot.*) adventitious, casual.

adverbe [ad'vɛrb], *n.m.* adverb.

adverbial [advɛr'bjal], *a.* adverbial.

adverbialement [advɛrbjal'mã], *adv.* adverbially.

adversaire [advɛr'sɛ:r], *n.* adversary, opponent.

adverse [ad'vɛrs], *a.* adverse, opposite, contrary; calamitous.

adversité [advɛrsi'te], *n.f.* adversity, misfortune.

aérage [ae'ra:ʒ], *n.m.* ventilation, airing.

aérateur [aera'tœ:r], *n.m.* ventilator.

aération [aera'sjɔ̃], *n.f.* ventilation, airing.

aéré [ae're], *p.p.* ventilated.—*a.* airy.

aérer [ae're], *v.t. (conjug. like* CÉDER) to ventilate, to air, to renew the air of; (*Chem.*) to aerate.

aérien [ae'rjɛ̃], *a. (fem.* -enne) aerial; living *or* occurring in the air, celestial; (*fig.*) light, airy; *base aérienne,* air base; *fil aérien,* overhead wire; *ligne aérienne,* airline; *pont aérien,* airlift; *raid aérien,* air raid.

aérifère [aeri'fɛ:r], *a.* air-conducting.

aérification [aerifika'sjɔ̃], *n.f.* gasification.

aérifier [aeri'fje], *v.t.* to gasify.

aéro-club [aero'klœb], *n.m.* (*pl.* **aéro-clubs**) flying club.

aérodrome [aero'dro:m], *n.m.* aerodrome, airfield.

aérodynamique [aerodina'mik], *a.* aerodynamic, streamlined.—*n.f.* aerodynamics.

aérogare [aero'ga:r], *n.f.* air terminal.

aérographe [aero'graf], *n.m.* aerograph.

aérographie [aerogra'fi], *n.f.* aerography.

aérolithe [aero'lit], *n.m.* aerolite.

aérolithique [aeroli'tik], *a.* aerolitic.

aérologie [aerolɔ'ʒi], *n.f.* aerology.

aéromètre [aero'mɛtr], *n.m.* aerometer, air-poise.

aéronaute [aero'no:t], *n.* aeronaut.

aéronautique [aerono'tik], *a.* aeronautic.—*n.f.* aeronautics, aerial navigation.

aéronef [aero'nɛf], *n.m.* airship.

aéroplane [aero'plan], *n.m.* airplane.

aéroport [aero'pɔ:r], *n.m.* airport.

aéroporté [aeropɔr'te], *a.* airborne (*troops*).

aérosphère [aerɔ'sfɛːr], *n.f.* the mass of air surrounding the globe, atmosphere.

aérostat [aerɔs'ta], *n.m.* aerostat, air-balloon.

aérostation [aerɔsta'sjɔ̃], *n.f.* aerostation, air navigation.

aérostatique [aerɔsta'tik], *a.* aerostatic.— *n.f.* aerostatics.

aérostier [aerɔs'tje], *n.m.* aeronaut, one directing an aerostat.

aérothérapie [aerɔtera'pi], *n.f.* aerotherapy.

affabilité [afabili'te], *n.f.* affability, kindness, courtesy.

affable [a'fabl], *a.* affable, courteous.

affadir [afa'diːr], *v.t.* to make unsavory *or* insipid; (*fig.*) to make flat *or* dull. **s'affadir**, *v.r.* to become insipid.

affadissement [afadis'mã], *n.m.* insipidity, nausea, sickliness.

affaiblir [afɛ'bliːr], *v.t.* to enfeeble, to weaken; to lessen. **s'affaiblir**, *v.r.* to grow weak; to abate.

affaiblissement [afɛblis'mã], *n.m.* weakening; allaying, abatement.

affaire [a'fɛːr], *n.f.* affair, business, concern, matter; trouble, scrape; lawsuit; transaction, bargain; *c'est mon affaire*, it is my own concern; *mêlez-vous de vos affaires!*, mind your own business!; *être dans les affaires*, to be in business; *homme d'affaires*, business man, legal adviser.

affairé [afɛ're], *a.* busy.

affairement [afɛr'mã], *n.m.* hurry, bustle, ado.

affaissement [afɛs'mã], *n.m.* depression, subsidence, giving way, collapse.

affaisser [afɛ'se], *v.t.* to cause to sink, to weigh down, to press down; to bear down, to overwhelm. **s'affaisser**, *v.r.* to sink, to subside; to give way; to be bent down (*by age*); to collapse.

affamé [afa'me], *a.* famished, hungry, starving; greedy, craving; *être affamé de*, to be greedy *or* eager for.

affamer [afa'me], *v.t.* to starve, to famish, to deprive of food.

affectation [afɛkta'sjɔ̃], *n.f.* appropriation, destination *or* attribution (*to a certain object*); simulation, show, pretence, affectation; preference; distinction; (*Mil.*) *recevoir une affectation*, to be posted.

affecté [afɛk'te], *a.* affected, assumed, simulated, put on; attributed, destined (*to a certain object*); (*Path.*) affected (*by a disease etc.*); (*Mil.*) posted to.

affecter [afɛk'te], *v.t.* to affect, to make frequent *or* habitual use of, to have a predilection for; to assume (*a certain shape etc.*); to feign, to pretend; to set apart, to earmark, to destine; to appropriate (*to a certain object*); to move, to touch, to impress emotionally. **s'affecter**, *v.r.* to be affected.

affection [afɛk'sjɔ̃], *n.f.* affection, love, attachment; (*Med.*) affection, ailment.

affectionné [afɛksjɔ'ne], *a.* affectionate, loving, attached, loved, liked.

affectionner [afɛksjɔ'ne], *v.t.* to love, to be fond of, to like.

affectueusement [afɛktɥøz'mã], *adv.* affectionately, fondly.

affectueux [afɛk'tɥø], *a.* (*fem.* **-euse**) affectionate, tender, warm-hearted.

afférent [afe'rã], *a.* reverting; relating to; assignable to; accruing to.

affermage [afɛr'maːʒ], *n.m.* farming, renting.

affermataire [afɛrma'tɛːr], *n.m.* tenant farmer.

affermateur [afɛrma'tœːr], *n.m.* (*fem.* **-trice**) lessor.

affermer [afɛr'me], *v.t.* to farm *or* let out by lease; to take a lease of, to rent.

affermir [afɛr'miːr], *v.t.* to strengthen, to make firm; to confirm, to establish, to consolidate. **s'affermir**, *v.r.* to become strong, firm, *or* fast; to become established.

affermissement [afɛrmis'mã], *n.m.* strengthening, consolidation, establishment; support, prop, stay.

affété [afe'te], *a.* affected, prim, finical; canting, mincing, pretty-pretty.

afféterie [afe'tri], *n.f.* affectation, mannerisms, primness.

affichage [afi'ʃaːʒ], *n.m.* bill-posting; placarding.

affiche [a'fiʃ], *n.f.* placard, bill, poster; *homme affiche*, sandwichman; *affiche électorale*, election poster.

afficher [afi'ʃe], *v.t.* to post up; to publish, to divulge, to proclaim; to make a show of, to parade; *défense d'afficher*, post no bills; billposting prohibited. **s'afficher**, *v.r.* to set up (*for*); to attract public notice.

afficheur [afi'ʃœːr], *n.m.* bill-poster.

affidavit [afida'vit], *n.m.* affidavit.

affidé [afi'de], *a.* trusty, trustworthy; in the know.—*n.m.* (*fem.* **-ée**) confederate, confidential agent; spy.

affilage [afi'laːʒ], **affilement** [afil'mã], *n.m.* whetting, sharpening, setting.

affilé [afi'le], *a.* sharp; nimble, glib (*of the tongue*).

affilée (d') [dafi'le], *adv. phr.* at a stretch; *trois heures d'affilée*, three hours at a stretch.

affiler [afi'le], *v.t.* to sharpen, to set, to put an edge on.

affiliation [afilja'sjɔ̃], *n.f.* affiliation (*to a society, company, plot etc.*).

affilié [afi'lje], *a.* affiliated, admitted a member *or* associate.—*n.m.* (*fem.* **-ée**) affiliated member, associate, confederate.

affilier [afi'lje], *v.t.* to admit, to affiliate, to receive. **s'affilier**, *v.r.* to become admitted *or* affiliated, to join.

affiloir [afi'lwaːr], *n.m.* hone, oilstone, steel, strop.

affinage [afi'naːʒ], **affinement** [afin'mã], *n.m.* refining, fining (*of metals, sugar etc.*); heckling (*of hemp*), maturing (*of a wine*), ripening (*of a cheese*).

affiner [afi'ne], *v.t.* to fine, to refine. **s'affiner**, *v.r.* to be refined, to be fined; to become finer, wittier etc. (*of the mind*).

affinerie [afin'ri], *n.f.* metal refinery.

affineur [afi'nœːr], *n.m.* metal refiner.

affinité [afini'te], *n.f.* affinity, relationship.

affinoir [afi'nwaːr], *n.m.* carding brush.

affiquet [afi'kɛ], *n.m.* knitting sheath; (*pl.*) gewgaws, trinkets.

affirmatif [afirma'tif], *a.* (*fem.* **-tive**) affirmative, asserting.—*n.f.* (**-tive**) affirmative statement, answer etc.; asseveration; *répondre par l'affirmative*, to answer in the affirmative.

affirmation [afirma'sjɔ̃], *n.f.* affirmation, assertion.

9

affirmativement [afirmativ'mã], *adv.* affirmatively.

affirmer [afir'me], *v.t.* to affirm, to assert, to vouch, to declare; to confirm by *or* on oath **s'affirmer**, *v.r.* to grow stronger, to assert oneself.

affixe [a'fiks], *n.m.* affix.

affleurement [aflœr'mã], *n.m.* levelling, making flush; (*Mining*) outcrop.

affleurer [aflœ're], *v.t.* to make even, to level; (*Arch.*) to make flush.—*v.i.* to be level, to be flush (*with*); (*Mining*) to crop out.

affliction [aflik'sjõ], *n.f.* affliction, trouble, distress; trial, vexation.

affligé [afli'ʒe], *a.* afflicted, grieved, distressed.

affliger [afli'ʒe], *v.t.* (*conjug. like* MANGER) to afflict, to trouble, to distress, to grieve, to vex, to torment; to mortify, to chasten. **s'affliger**, *v.r.* to grieve, to be afflicted, troubled *or* cast down; to take something to heart.

afflouage [aflu'a:ʒ], *n.m.* (*Naut.*) refloating (*of a ship*).

afflouer [aflu'e], *v.t.* to refloat.

affluence [afly'ã:s], *n.f.* affluence, abundance; concourse, crowd; **heures d'affluence**, rush hour.

affluent [afly'ã], *a.* falling into, running into (*of rivers*).—*n.m.* tributary.

affluer [afly'e], *v.i.* to fall, run *or* flow into (*as a tributary*) (**dans**); to abound; to come in great quantity (**à, vers**).

affolant [afɔ'lã], *a.* distracting.

affolé [afɔ'le], *a.* distracted, panic-stricken; (*Mech.*) disconnected, defective.

affolement [afɔl'mã], *n.m.* distraction, panic.

affoler [afɔ'le], *v.t.* to distract; to infatuate; to bewitch; to madden, to drive crazy. **s'affoler**, *v.r.* to fall into a panic, to stampede.

afforestage [afɔrɛs'ta:ʒ], *n.m.* right of cutting firewood, estovers.

afforestation [afɔrɛstɑ'sjõ], *n.f.* afforestation.

affouillable [afu'jabl], *a.* subject *or* liable to undermining.

affouillement [afuj'mã], *n.m.* undermining, washing away.

affouiller [afu'je], *v.t.* to undermine, to wash away.

affouragement or **affourragement** [afuraʒ'mã], *n.m.* foraging, foddering.

affourager or **affourrager** [afura'ʒe], *v.t.* (*conjug. like* MANGER) to fodder, to give fodder to.

affourcher [afur'ʃe], *v.t.* to seat astride; (*Carp.*) to join a tongue and groove.

affranchi [afrã'ʃi], *a.* set free, freed.—*n.m.* (*fem.* **-e**) freedman; freedwoman.

affranchir [afrã'ʃi:r], *v.t.* to free, to set free, to enfranchise; to absolve, to exempt; to frank (*a letter*), to stamp. **s'affranchir**, *v.r.* to free oneself; to rid oneself of (**de**), to shake off, to break away from.

affranchissement [afrãʃis'mã], *n.m.* enfranchisement; exemption; discharge; deliverance; payment of postage (*of a letter*).

affranchisseur [afrãʃi'sœ:r], *n.m.* emancipator, liberator.

affres [a:fr], *n.f.* (*used only in pl.*) dread, horror, agony; **les affres de la mort**, the pangs of death, death throes.

affrètement [afrɛt'mã], *n.m.* chartering, freighting.

affréter [afre'te], *v.t.* (*conjug. like* CÉDER) (*Naut.*) to charter, to freight (*a vessel*).

affréteur [afre'tœ:r], *n.m.* charterer, freighter.

affreusement [afrœz'mã], *adv.* frightfully, horribly, dreadfully.

affreux [a'frø], *a.* (*fem.* **-euse**) frightful, hideous, shocking, horrible, ghastly.

affriander [afriã'de], *v.t.* to allure, to entice to tempt.

affricher [afri'ʃe], *v.t.* to leave fallow.

affrioler [afriɔ'le], *v.t.* to allure, to entice.

affront [a'frõ], *n.m.* affront, insult; disgrace.

affronter [afrõ'te], *v.t.* to face, to confront, to brave; to attack boldly.

affruiter [afrɥi'te], *v.t.* to plant with fruit-trees.—*v.i.* to bear *or* supply fruit. **s'affruiter**, *v.r.* to come into fruit.

affublement [afyblə'mã], *n.m.* grotesque make-up *or* rig-out (*of dress*).

affubler [afy'ble], *v.t.* to dress up, to rig out (*grotesquely*). **s'affubler**, *v.r.* to dress up ridiculously.

affût [a'fy], *n.m.* stand *or* place for lying in wait, watch; gun carriage; **être à l'affût**, to lie in wait.

affûtage [afy'ta:ʒ], *n.m.* setting *or* sharpening (*of tools*).

affûter [afy'te], *v.t.* to grind, to sharpen.

affûteur [afy'tœ:r], *n.m.* sharpener, setter, grinder; stalker.—*n.f.* (**-euse**) sharpening machine.

afghan [af'gã], *a.* Afghan.—*n.m.* (**Afghan**, *fem.* **-ane**) Afghan (*person*).

Afghanistan [afganis'tã], l', *m.* Afghanistan.

afin [a'fɛ̃], *conj.* **afin de** (*with inf.*) to, in order to, so as to; **afin que** (*with subj.*) to, in order that, so that.

africain [afri'kɛ̃], *a.* African.—*n.m.* (**Africain** *fem.* **-aine**) African (*person*).

Afrique [a'frik], l', *f.* Africa.

agaçant [aga'sã], *a.* irritating, worrying; provoking, provocative; alluring, enticing.

agace or **agasse** [a'gas], *n.f.* magpie.

agacement [agas'mã], *n.m.* irritation, setting on edge.

agacer [aga'se], *v.t.* (*conjug. like* COMMENCER) to worry, to irritate, to set on edge; to excite, to provoke; to entice, to allure.

agacerie [aga'sri], *n.f.* allurement, coquetry, enticement.

agaillardir [agajar'di:r], *v.t.* to cheer up.

agate [a'gat], *n.f.* agate.

Agathe [a'gat], *f.* Agatha.

âge [ɑ:ʒ], *n.m.* age, years; period, epoch, era, (*pl.*) the ages, time; **Moyen Âge**, Middle Ages; **d'un certain âge**, elderly; **entre deux âges**, of uncertain age.

âgé [ɑ'ʒe], *a.* aged (*so many years*); old, elderly; **âgé de vingt ans**, twenty years old.

agence [a'ʒã:s], *n.f.* agency, bureau, branch office.

agencement [aʒãs'mã], *n.m.* arrangement, grouping, ordering; (*Arch.*) composition, layout.

agencer [aʒã'se], *v.t.* (*conjug. like* COMMENCER) to arrange, to dispose.

agenda [aʒɛ̃'da], *n.m.* notebook; diary; engagement book.

agenouiller (s') [saʒnu'je], *v.r.* to kneel down, to fall on one's knees; (*fig.*) to bow down (*devant*).

agenouilloir [aʒnuj'wa:r], *n.m.* hassock.

agent [a'ʒɑ̃], *n.m.* agent; deputy; middleman; broker; **agent de change**, stockbroker; **agent électoral**, canvasser; **agent de liaison**, liaison officer; **agent de police**, policeman.

agglomération [aglɔmera'sjɔ̃], *n.f.* agglomeration, build-up area.

aggloméré [aglɔme're], *n.m.* compressed fuel, briquette.

agglomérer [aglɔme're], *v.t.* (*conjug. like* CÉDER) to agglomerate, to mass together, to pile up, to assemble.

agglutinant [aglyti'nɑ̃], *a.* adhesive.

agglutiner [aglyti'ne], *v.t.* to bind, to cake. **s'agglutiner**, *v.r.* to unite, to cohere; to heal over (*wound*).

aggravant [agra'vɑ̃], *a.* (*Law*) aggravating, making more heinous.

aggravation [agrava'sjɔ̃], *n.f.* aggravation, additional penalty; **aggravation de peine**, increase of punishment.

aggraver [agra've], *v.t.* to aggravate, to make worse. **s'aggraver**, *v.r.* to worsen (*illness, situation*).

agile [a'ʒil], *a.* agile, nimble.

agilement [aʒil'mɑ̃], *adv.* nimbly, with agility.

agilité [aʒili'te], *n.f.* agility, nimbleness, lightness.

agio [a'ʒjo], *n.m.* stock-jobbing, speculation.

agiotage [aʒjo'ta:ʒ], *n.m.* stockjobbing; **faire l'agiotage**, to deal in stocks.

agioter [aʒjo'te], *v.i.* to speculate, to job.

agioteur [aʒjo'tœ:r], *n.m.* speculator, jobber.

agir [a'ʒi:r], *v.i.* to act, to do; to operate; to have an effect (*sur*); to negotiate, to manage a business; to sue, to prosecute, to proceed (*contre*); to behave. **s'agir**, *v.r.* (*impers.*) to be in question, to be the matter; **de quoi s'agit-il?** what is it about? **il s'agit de votre vie**, your life is at stake.

agissant [aʒi'sɑ̃], *a.* active, busy; efficacious, effective.

agitateur [aʒita'tœ:r], *n.m.* (*fem* -trice) agitator.—*n.m.* stirring rod.

agitation [aʒita'sjɔ̃], *n.f.* agitation; disturbance, tossing, shaking, tumult; trouble, emotion, uneasiness, restlessness.

agité [aʒi'te], *a.* restless (*sleep*); rough (*sea*); fretful (*child*).

agiter [aʒi'te], *v.t.* to agitate, to put in motion, to shake, to stir; to disturb, to trouble; to excite, to perturb; to debate, to discuss. **s'agiter**, *v.r.* to be agitated *or* in movement; to get rough; to be restless, disturbed *or* uneasy; to toss, to wave, to flutter; to be debated.

agneau [a'ɲo], *n.m.* (*fem.* **-elle**, *pl.* **-eaux**) lamb.

agnelage [aɲə'la:ʒ], **agnèlement** [aɲɛl'mɑ̃], *n.m.* lambing; lambing time.

agneler [aɲə'le], *v.i.* (*conjug. like* AMENER) to lamb, to yean.

Agnès [a'ɲɛ:s], *f.* Agnes.

agnès [a'ɲɛ:s], *n.f.* raw young girl.

agnosticisme [agnɔsti'sism], *n.m.* agnosticism.

agnosticiste [agnɔsti'sist], **agnostique** [agnɔs'tik], *a.* and *n.* agnostic.

agonie [agɔ'ni], *n.f.* agony, death pangs;

(*fig.*) trouble, anguish, torture; **être à l'agonie**, to be at the point of death.

agonir [agɔ'ni:r], *v.t.* to insult grossly.

agonisant [agɔni'zɑ̃], *a.* dying, in a dying condition.—*n.m.* (*fem.* -e) dying person.

agoniser [agɔni'ze], *v.i.* to be at the point of death.

agoraphobie [agɔrafɔ'bi], *n.f.* agoraphobia.

agrafe [a'graf], *n.f.* fastener, clasp, clip, staple (*for papers*); **agrafe et porte**, hook and eye.

agrafer [agra'fe], *v.t.* to hook, to clasp, to fasten with a clasp; to staple.

agrafeuse [agra'fø:z], *n.f.* stapler.

agraire [a'grɛ:r], *a.* agrarian.

agrandir [agrɑ̃'di:r], *v.t.* to make greater, to enlarge, to augment; to widen; to exaggerate; to promote, to advance; (*fig.*) to elevate. **s'agrandir**, *v.r.* to become greater *or* larger.

agrandissement [agrɑ̃dis'mɑ̃], *n.m.* enlargement, increase; aggrandizement, elevation.

agran-'isseur [agrɑ̃di'sœ:r], *n.m.* (*Phot.*) enlarger.

agréable [agre'abl], *a.* agreeable, pleasing, pleasant, acceptable.

agréablement [agreablə'mɑ̃], *adv.* agreeably, pleasantly.

agréé [agre'e], *n.m.* solicitor; attorney.

agréer [agre'e], *v.t.* to accept, to approve, to allow, to receive kindly.—*v.i.* to please, to be agreeable; **veuillez agréer mes salutations**, yours truly.

agrégat [agre'ga], *n.m.* aggregate, composite mass.

agrégation [agrega'sjɔ̃], *n.f.* (*Phys.*) aggregation, aggregate; (= **concours d'agrégation**) competitive examination for admission on the teaching staff of State secondary schools *or* on faculties of law, medicine, pharmacy.

agrégé [agre'ʒe], *a.* and *n.m.* **professeur agrégé**, one who has passed the **agrégation**.

agréger [agre'ʒe], *v.t.* (*conjug. like* ASSIÉGER) to admit into a society, to incorporate; (*Phys.*) to aggregate.

agrément [agre'mɑ̃], *n.m.* consent, approbation; pleasure, charm, gracefulness; amenity; (*pl.*) ornaments, embellishments, amenities (*of life*); **arts d'agrément**, accomplishments.

agrémenter [agremɑ̃'te], *v.t.* to set off, to ornament, to adorn.

agrès [a'grɛ], *n.m.* (*used only in pl.*) rigging (*of a ship etc.*); apparatus, gear (*of a gymnasium etc.*).

agresseur [agre'sœ:r], *n.m.* aggressor.

agressif [agre'sif], *a.* (*fem.* -ive) aggressive.

agression [agre'sjɔ̃], *n.f.* aggression.

agressivité [agresivi'te], *n.f.* aggressiveness.

agreste [a'grɛst], *a.* rustic; countrified (*manners*).

agrestement [agrestə'mɑ̃], *adv.* rustically.

agricole [agri'kɔl], *a.* agricultural.

agriculteur [agrikyl'tœ:r], *n.m.* agriculturist, husbandman, farmer.

agriculture [agrikyl'ty:r], *n.f.* agriculture, husbandry, tillage.

agriffer [agri'fe], *v.t.* to claw; to clutch, to grip. **s'agriffer**, *v.r.* to claw (*at*).

agrion [agri'ɔ̃], *n.m.* dragonfly.

agripper [agri'pe], *v.t.* to grip, to snatch. **s'agripper**, *v.r.* to cling (*to*).

agronome [agrɔ'nɔm], *n.m.* agriculturist.

aguerri [agɛ'ri], *a.* inured to war; disciplined.

aguerrir [agɛ'ri:r], *v.t.* to train *or* inure to the hardships of war; to accustom, to inure (*to hardships etc.*). **s'aguerrir**, *v.r.* to inure *or* accustom oneself (*to hardships, abstinence etc.*), to be inured.

aguerrissement [agɛris'mã], *n.m.* inuring to war, hardening.

aguets [a'gɛ], *n.m.* (*used only in pl.*) watch, lookout; **être aux aguets**, to be on the watch.

aheurter (s') [saœr'te], *v.r.* to persist (*in*).

ahuri [ay'ri], *a.* bewildered, perplexed, flurried.

ahurir [ay'ri:r], *v.t.* to bewilder, to flurry, to stupefy.

ahurissant [ayri'sã], *a.* bewildering.

ahurissement [ayris'mã], *n.m.* bewilderment, confusion, perplexity.

aï [a'i], *n.m.* (*Zool.*) sloth.

aide [ɛ:d], *n.f.* help, relief, assistance; succor, support, protection, rescue; relief (*of the poor etc.*); helper, female assistant, help; à l'aide de, with the help of.—*n.m.* a male assistant; **aide de camp** (*pl.* **aides de camp**), aide-de-camp.

aide-mémoire [ɛdme'mwa:r], *n.m.* *inv.* précis; memorandum.

aider [ɛ'de], *v.t.* to aid, to help, to relieve, to assist, to succor; to abet; to conduce to, to further.—*v.i.* to be helpful, to be of assistance (à). **s'aider**, *v.r.* to make use (*de*); to avail oneself.

aïe! [aj], *int.* oh! oh dear!

aïeul [a'jœl], *n.m.* (*fem.* **aïeule**, *pl.* **aïeuls**, **aïeules**) grandfather, grandsire; grandmother, grandam; (*pl.* **aïeux**) forebears, ancestors.

aigle [ɛ:gl], *n.* eagle; (*fig.*) clever *or* brilliant person, genius.—*n.m.* reading desk, lectern (*with effigy of an eagle*).

aiglefin [ɛglə'fɛ], **aigrefin** (1) [ɛgrə'fɛ], *n.m.* haddock.

aiglon [ɛ'glɔ̃], *n.m.* (*fem.* -**onne**) eaglet.

aigre [ɛgr], *a.* sour, tart; (*fig.*) harsh, bitter, shrill.—*n.m.* sourness, mustiness.

aigre-doux [ɛgrə'du], *a.* (*fem.* -**douce**) sourish, bitter-sweet.

aigrefin (2) [ɛgrə'fɛ̃], *n.m.* sharper, swindler; adventurer; [AIGLEFIN].

aigrelet [ɛgrə'lɛ], *a.* (*fem.* -**ette**) sourish.

aigrement [ɛgrə'mã], *adv.* acrimoniously, sourly, bitterly; roughly, harshly.

aigret [ɛ'grɛ], *a.* (*fem.* -**ette** (1)) sourish.

aigrette (2) [ɛ'grɛt], *n.f.* aigrette, tuft, cluster *or* plume (*of feathers, diamonds etc.*); horn (*of an owl*); crest (*of a peacock*); egret, tufted heron.

aigreur [ɛ'grœ:r], *n.f.* sourness, sharpness, tartness; (*fig.*) harshness, bitterness, surliness, animosity, spite.

aigrir [ɛ'gri:r], *v.t.* to make sour *or* sharp, to sour; (*fig.*) to irritate, to embitter, to make worse, to incense; to make ill-humoured. **s'aigrir**, *v.r.* to turn sour; (*fig.*) to grow worse, to be exasperated, to be irritated.

aigrissement [ɛgris'mã], *n.m.* souring, embittering.

aigu [ɛ'gy], *a.* (*fem.* **aiguë**) pointed, sharp, keen, acute; (*fig.*) shrill, piercing; **accent aigu**, acute accent.

aiguë [AIGU].

aigue-marine [ɛgma'rin], *n.f.* (*pl.* **aigues-marines**) aquamarine.

aiguière [ɛ'gjɛ:r], *n.f.* ewer.

aiguillage [ɛgɥi'ja:ʒ], *n.m.* (*Rail.*) shunting, switch.

aiguillat [ɛgɥi'ja], *n.m.* dogfish.

aiguille [ɛ'gɥi:j], *n.f.* needle; index, pointer, hand (*of a dial, watch etc.*); spire (*steeple*); point (*of an obelisk, peak etc.*); rock pinnacle *or* needle-shaped peak; **trou d'une aiguille**, eye of a needle; (*pl.*, *Rail.*) switch.

aiguiller [ɛgɥi'je], *v.t.* (*Rail.*) to shunt.

aiguillette [ɛgɥi'jɛt], *n.f.* aglet, point; (*Mil.*) ornamental shoulder-knot.

aiguilleur [ɛgɥi'jœ:r], *n.m.* (*Rail.*) switchman, shunter.

aiguillier [ɛgɥi'je], *n.m.* (*fem.* -**ière**) needlemaker.

aiguillon [ɛgɥi'jɔ̃], *n.m.* goad, sting; (*fig.*) spur, incentive; (*Bot.*) prickle.

aiguillonner [ɛgɥijɔ'ne], *v.t.* to goad, to prick; (*fig.*) to incite, to spur on; to stimulate.

aiguisage [ɛgi'za:ʒ], **aiguisement** [ɛgiz'mã], *n.m.* whetting, sharpening.

aiguisé [ɛgi'ze], *a.* whetted, sharpened.

aiguiser [ɛgi'ze], *v.t.* to whet, to sharpen, to set an edge on; to point; (*fig.*) to make keen, acid, piquant etc.; to excite, to stimulate.

aiguiseur [ɛgi'zœ:r], *n.m.* knife-grinder, sharpener.

aiguisoir [ɛgi'zwa:r], *n.m.* sharpening-tool, whetstone.

ail [a:j], *n.m.* (*pl.* (*Cook.*) **aulx** [o:], (*Bot.*) **ails**) garlic.

aile [ɛl], *n.f.* wing; brim (*of a hat*); flipper (*of a penguin*); blade (*of a propeller*); vane, sail (*of a windmill*); flank *or* wing (*of an army, building etc.*); fender, mudguard (*of a car*).

ailé [ɛ'le], *a.* winged.

aileron [ɛl'rɔ̃], *n.m.* pinion (*of a bird*); aileron, balancing flap (*of an aircraft*); fin (*of some fish*).

ailette [ɛ'lɛt], *n.f.* small wing; vane (*of a torpedo etc.*); (*Motor.*) rib, fin, flange.

ailier [ɛ'lje], *n.m.* (*Ftb.*) wing forward, wing three-quarter.

ailleurs [a'jœ:r], *adv.* elsewhere, somewhere else; **d'ailleurs**, besides, moreover, in other respects.

aimable [ɛ'mabl], *a.* kind, amiable, obliging.

aimablement [ɛmablə'mã], *adv.* amiably, kindly.

aimant [ɛ'mã], *a.* loving, affectionate.—*n.m.* magnet; (*fig.*) attractiveness.

aimantation [ɛmãta'sjɔ̃], *n.f.* magnetization.

aimanter [ɛmã'te], *v.t.* to magnetize.

Aimée [ɛ'me], *f.* Amy.

aimer [ɛ'me], *v.t.* to love, to be fond of, to be in love with; to like; **aimer mieux**, to prefer. **s'aimer**, *v.r.* to love oneself, to be vain; to love each other.

aine (1) [ɛ:n], *n.f.* groin.

aine (2) [ɛ:n], *n.f.* herring-stick; leather band on organ bellows.

aîné [ɛ'ne], *a.* (*fem.* -**ée**) eldest, elder, senior.—*n.m.* (*fem.* -**ée**) eldest son *or* daughter.

aînesse [ɛ'nɛs], *n.f.* seniority, priority by age, primogeniture; **droit d'aînesse**, birthright.

ainsi [ɛ̃'si], *adv.* thus, so, in this *or* that manner; **ainsi de suite,** and so on and so forth; **ainsi soit-il,** so be it, amen; *pour ainsi dire,* so to speak, as it were; *uinsi que,* in the same way (*as*).

air (1) [ɛːr], *n.m.* air; wind; (*Chem. etc.*) gas; (*pl.*) atmosphere; *chambre à air,* inner tube; *courant d'air,* draught; *en plein air,* in the open air.

air (2) [ɛːr], *n.m.* mien, look, expression, air, manner, appearance.

air (3) [ɛːr], *n.m.* (*Mus.*) tune.

airain [ɛ'rɛ̃], *n.m.* bronze; (*Poet.*) cannon, bell.

aire [ɛːr], *n.f.* area, space; threshing floor; eyrie; *aire d'atterrissage,* (*Av.*) landing area, apron.

airelle [ɛ'rɛl], *n.f.* whortleberry, bilberry.

ais [ɛ], *n.m.* board, plank; stave (*of a barrel*).

aisance [ɛ'zãːs], *n.f.* ease, facility; easiness, affluence; competency; (*Mach.*) play; freedom; the comforts *or* conveniences of life; *cabinet* (*or lieu*) *d'aisances,* public convenience.

aisceau [AISSETTE].

aise [ɛːz], *a.* glad, well pleased; *je suis bien aise de vous voir,* I am very glad to see you.—*n.f.* ease, comfort, convenience; (*pl.*) comforts, comfortable circumstances; *à l'aise,* at ease, comfortable; *être à son aise,* to be well off.

aisé [ɛ'ze], *a.* easy; convenient, comfortable; in easy circumstances.

aisément [ɛze'mã], *adv.* easily, readily, freely; comfortably.

aisseau [ɛ'so], *n.m.* furze, gorse.

aisseau [ɛ'so], *n.m.* (*pl.* -eaux), **aissante** [ɛ'sãːt], *n.f.* (*Carp.*) shingle, wooden tile.

aisselier [csɔ'lje], *n.m.* (*Carp.*) tie beam, brace, strut.

aisselle [ɛ'sɛl], *n.f.* armpit; (*Bot.*) axil.

aissette [ɛ'sɛt], *n.f.*, **aisceau** [ɛ'so] (*pl.* -eaux), *n.m.* adze (*of a cooper*); hooked hammer (*of a tiler*).

Aix-la-Chapelle [ɛkslafa'pɛl], *f.* Aachen.

ajointer [aʒwɛ̃'te], *v.t.* to join on to, to fit.

ajonc [a'ʒɔ̃], *n.m.* furze, gorse.

ajournement [aʒurnə'mã], *n.m.* adjournment, postponement; (*Law*) summons.

ajourner [aʒur'ne], *v.t.* to adjourn; to defer; (*Law*) to summon (*for a specified day*).

ajouter [aʒu'te], *v.t.* to add, to join, to subjoin, to interpolate. **s'ajouter,** *v.r.* to be joined, to attach oneself.

ajusté [aʒys'te], *a.* close-fitting (*clothes*).

ajustement [aʒysta'mã], *n.m.* adjustment, arranging, fitting, settlement; laying out; attire, apparel.

ajuster [aʒys'te], *v.t.* to adjust, to regulate, to square; to fit, to adapt (*one thing to another*); to take aim at; to set in order; (*Mus.*) to tune; to bedeck; to settle *or* arrange (*a dispute*). **s'ajuster,** *v.r.* to accommodate oneself, to be adapted; to dress, to deck oneself out.

ajusteur [aʒys'tœːr], *n.m.* fitter; weigher (*at the mint*).

alacrité [alakri'te], *n.f.* alacrity, cheerful briskness.

Aladin [ala'dɛ̃], *m.* Aladdin.

Alain [a'lɛ̃], *m.* Alan.

alaise [a'lɛːz], *n.f.* rubber sheet for pram *or* cot.

alambic [alã'bik], *n.m.* alembic, still.

alambiquer [alãbi'ke], *v.t.* to distil, to refine.

alangui [alã'gi:], *a.* languid, downcast.

alanguir [alã'giːr], *v.t.* to enfeeble, to make languid. **s'alanguir,** *v.r.* to languish, to flag, to become languid.

alanguissement [alãgis'mã], *n.m.* languor.

alarmant [alar'mã], *a.* alarming, startling.

alarme [a'larm], *n.f.* alarm, affright, sudden fear, uneasiness.

alarmer [alar'me], *v.t.* to alarm; to startle, to render anxious *or* frightened. **s'alarmer,** *v.r.* to take alarm, to be alarmed.

alarmiste [alar'mist], *a.* and *n.* alarmist.

albanais [alba'nɛ], *a.* Albanian.—*n.m.* Albanian (*language*); (**Albanais,** *fem.* -**aise**) Albanian (*person*).

Albanie [alba'ni:], **l',** *f.* Albania.

albâtre [al'bɑːtr], *n.m.* alabaster; (*fig.*) whiteness.

albatros [alba'tros], *n.m.* albatross.

albinisme [albi'nism], *n.m.* albinism.

albinⅰ [albi'nɔs], *a.* and *n.* albino.

album [al'bɔm], *n.m.* album, scrapbook, sketch book.

albumine [alby'min], *n.f.* albumen.

alcaïque [alka'ik], *a.* alcaic (*verse*).

alcali [alka'li], *n.m.* alkali.

alcalin [alka'lɛ̃], *a.* alkaline.

alcalinité [alkalini'te], *n.f.* alkalinity.

alcaliser [alkali'ze], **alcaliniser** [alkalini 'ze], *v.t.* to alkalify.

alchimie [alʃi'mi], *n.f.* alchemy.

alchimique [alʃi'mik], *a.* alchemical.

alchimiste [alʃi'mist], *n.m.* alchemist.

alcool [al'kɔl], *n.m.* alcohol; spirit(s); *alcool à brûler, alcool dénaturé,* methylated spirit.

alcoolique [alkɔ'lik], *a.* alcoholic.

alcoolisme [alkɔ'lism], *n.m.* alcoholism.

Alcoran [alkɔ'rã], [CORAN].

alcôve [al'koːv], *n.f.* alcove, recess.

alcyon [al'sjɔ̃], *n.m.* halcyon; (*Orn.*) kingfisher.

alcyonien [alsjɔ'njɛ̃], *a.* (*fem.* -**enne**) halcyon, peaceful.

aléa [ale'a], *n.m.* chance, hazard.

aléatoire [alea'twaːr], *a.* hazardous, uncertain.

alène [a'lɛn], *n.f.* awl.

alentour *or* **à l'entour** [alã'tuːr], *adv.* about, around, round about.

alentours, [alã'tuːr], *n.m.* (*used only in pl.*) environs, neighborhood.

Aléoutiennes [aleu'sjɛn], **les,** *f.pl.* the Aleutian Islands.

alerte [a'lɛrt], *a.* alert, vigilant; active, lively, agile.—*n.f.* alarm, warning; *alerte aérienne,* air-raid warning.

alerter [alɛr'te], *v.t.* to give the alarm to, to warn.

alésage [ale'zaːʒ], *n.m.* boring, drilling; bore (*of cylinder*).

aléser [ale'ze], *v.t.* (*conjug. like* CÉDER) to smooth *or* enlarge the bore of (*a tube, gun etc*); *aléser un canon,* to bore a cannon.

aléseuse [ale'zøːz], *n.f.* boring machine.

alésoir [ale'zwaːr], *n.m.* borer, boring tool.

alester [alɛs'te], **alestir** [alɛs'tiːr], *v.t.* (*Naut.*) to lighten *or* disencumber (*a vessel*).

alésure [ale'zyːr], *n.f.* metal turnings *or* filings.

alevin [al'vɛ̃], *n.m.* fry, young fish.

aleviner [alvi'ne], *v.t.* to stock with fry.

13

alevinier [alvi′nje], *n.m.* breeding pond.
Alexandre [alɛk′sɑ̃:dr], *m.* Alexander.
Alexandrie [alɛksɑ̃′dri], *f.* Alexandria.
alexandrin [alɛksɑ̃′drɛ̃], *a.* and *n.m.* (*Pros.*) Alexandrine.
alezan [al′zɑ̃], *a.* and *n.m.* chestnut (horse).
alèze or **alèse** [a′lɛ:z], [ALAISE].
alfa [al′fa], *n.m.* esparto grass.
algarade [alga′rad], *n.f.* insult, affront; rating.
algèbre [al′ʒɛbr], *n.f.* algebra.
algébrique [alʒe′brik], *a.* algebraical.
algébriquement [alʒebrik′mɑ̃], *adv.* algebraically.
Alger [al′ʒe], *m.* Algiers.
Algérie [alʒe′ri], *f.* Algeria.
algérien [alʒe′rjɛ̃], *a.* (*fem.* **-enne**) Algerian.—*n.m.* (**Algérien**, *fem.* **-enne**) Algerian (*person*).
algie [al′ʒi:], *n.f.* ache.
algue [alg], *n.f.* seaweed, alga.
alibi [ali′bi], *n.m.* (*Law*) alibi.
aliboron [alibɔ′rɔ̃], *n.m.* jackass, stupid *or* self-conceited fellow.
aliénable [alje′nabl], *a.* alienable, transferable.
aliénation [aljenɑ′sjɔ̃], *n.f.* (*Law*) conveyance of property to another; (*fig.*) alienation, mental derangement; estrangement, aversion.
aliéné [alje′ne], *a.* lunatic, mad.—*n.m.* (*fem.* **-ée**) lunatic.
aliéner [alje′ne], *v.t.* (*conjug. like* CÉDER) to alienate, to give away (*property*), to transfer, to make over; to estrange, to make hostile; to derange (*the mind*). **s'aliéner**, *v.r.* to become estranged (*from*).
aliéniste [alje′nist], *n.m.* alienist.
alignée [ali′ɲe], *n.f.* line, row.
alignement [aliɲə′mɑ̃], *n.m.* alignment; laying out in line; (*Mil.*) dressing; (*Print.*) ranging.
aligner [ali′ɲe], *v.t.* to align, to lay out in line; to put in a straight line; (*Mil.*) to dress; (*Print.*) to range. **s'aligner**, *v.r.* (*Mil.*) to dress.
aliment [ali′mɑ̃], *n.m.* aliment, food, nourishment, nutriment; (*Law*, *pl.*) alimony, maintenance.
alimentaire [alimɑ̃′tɛ:r], *a.* alimental, alimentary; (*Mech.*) **pompe alimentaire**, feed pump, donkey engine.
alimentateur [alimɑ̃ta′tœ:r], *a.* (*fem.* **-trice**) alimentary.
alimentation [alimɑ̃tɑ′sjɔ̃], *n.f.* alimentation; nourishment, feeding; **rayon d'alimentation**, food department.
alimenter [alimɑ̃′te], *v.t.* to feed, to nourish; to maintain; to supply, to provision; to fuel, to keep up.
alimenteux [alimɑ̃′tø], *a.* (*fem.* **-euse**) nutritive.
alinéa [aline′a], *n.m.* indented line; new paragraph.
alisé [ALIZÉ].
aliter [ali′te], *v.t.* to confine to bed; **être alité**, to be bedridden. **s'aliter**, *v.r.* to take to one's bed.
alizé or **alisé** [ali′ze], *a.* soft (*said of the trade winds*); **vents alizés**, trade winds.—*n.m.* trade wind.
alkali etc. [ALCALI].
Alkoran [alkɔ′rɑ̃], [CORAN].

Allah [a′la], *m.* Allah.
allaitement [alɛt′mɑ̃], *n.m.* lactation, nursing, suckling; **allaitement artificiel**, bottle feeding.
allaiter [ale′te], *v.t.* to suckle, to nurse.
alléchant [ale′ʃɑ̃], *a.* alluring, seductive.
allèchement [alɛʃ′mɑ̃], *n.m.* allurement, enticement, seduction, attraction.
allécher [ale′ʃe], *v.t.* (*conjug. like* CÉDER) to allure, to entice, to attract.
allée [a′le], *n.f.* passage, drive, alley, avenue, walk; (*pl.*) goings.
allégation [alega′sjɔ̃], *n.f.* allegation, assertion.
allège [a′lɛ:ʒ], *n.f.* lighter, hopper; (*Arch.*) window basement, sill of window.
allégeance [ale′ʒɑ̃:s], *n.f.* alleviation, relief; allegiance.
allégement [aleʒ′mɑ̃], *n.m.* alleviation, relief; reduction.
alléger [ale′ʒe], *v.t.* (*conjug. like* ASSIÉGER) to ease, to unburden, to lighten; to unload (*a boat*); to alleviate, to relieve, to assuage (*pain or grief*).
allégorie [alegɔ′ri], *n.f.* allegory.
allégorique [alegɔ′rik], *a.* allegorical.
allégoriquement [alegɔrik′mɑ̃], *adv.* allegorically.
allégoriser [alegɔri′ze], *v.t.* to allegorize.
allégoriste [alegɔ′rist], *n.m.* allegorist.
allègre [al′lɛgr], *a.* lively, nimble, sprightly; jolly, cheerful.
allègrement [allɛgrə′mɑ̃], *adv.* briskly; joyfully, merrily, joyously.
allégresse [alle′grɛs], *n.f.* gaiety, joy, mirth, cheerfulness; sprightliness.
alléguer [alle′ge], *v.t.* (*conjug. like* CÉDER) to allege, to advance, to urge; (*Law*) to quote, to adduce, to cite, to plead.
alléluia [allely′ja], *n.m.* and *int.* hallelujah.
Allemagne [al′maɲ], *f.* Germany.
allemand [al′mɑ̃], *a.* German.—*n.m.* German (*language*); (**Allemand**, *fem.* **-ande**) German (*person*).
aller [a′le], *v.i. irr.* (*with aux.* ÊTRE) to go, to go on, to proceed, to progress (*well, ill etc.*); to be (*in good or ill health*); to act (*in a certain way*); to suit, to fit (*well or ill*); to be going to; **aller au pas**, to go at a walking pace; **aller et venir**, to go up and down; **je ne ferai qu'aller et venir**, I won't be a minute; **cela va tout seul**, it is plain sailing; **cet enfant ira loin**, this child will go far; **comment allez-vous?** how are you? **je vais bien**, I am well; (*fam.*) **ça va!** all right! **cet habit vous va mal**, this coat does not fit you; **allons!** come on! **allons donc!** surely not! **cela va sans dire**, it stands to reason; **il y va de sa vie**, his life is at stake; **se laisser aller**, to yield, to give way, to abandon oneself to a thing. **s'en aller**, *v.r.* to go away, to run away; to vanish, to disappear; to die, to wear out; **va-t'en! allez-vous-en!** go away! be off with you!—*n.m.* going, course, run; outward voyage, trip, journey; **billet d'aller et retour**, return ticket.
allergie [alɛr′ʒi], *n.f.* allergy.
allergique [alɛr′ʒik], *a.* allergic.
alliage [a′lja:ʒ], *n.m.* alloy, mixture; (*fig.*) impure mixture *or* combination.

alumine

alliance [a'ljɑ̃:s], *n.f.* alliance; marriage; union, league, coalition, confederacy; compact, covenant; mixture, blending; wedding ring.

allié [a'lje], *a.* allied; related (*by marriage*); akin, kindred.—*n.m.* (*fem.* **-ée**) ally; connection (*by marriage*).

allier [a'lje], *v.t.* to mix; to combine; to join, to unite, to ally, to marry; to reconcile; to match. **s'allier**, *v.r.* to be incorporated *or* mixed; to become allied, to join forces (*avec*); to combine (*of metals*).

alligator [aliga'to:r], *n.m.* alligator.

allitération [alitera'sjɔ̃], *n.f.* alliteration.

allo! [a'lo], *int.* (*Teleph.*) hello!

allocataire [aloka'tɛ:r], *n.* recipient of an allowance.

allocation [aloka'sjɔ̃], *n.f.* allocation, allowance; *allocation de chômage*, unemployment benefit; *allocations familiales*, family allowances.

allocution [aloky'sjɔ̃], *n.f.* allocution, short address, speech.

allonge [a'lɔ̃:ʒ], *n.f.* leaf (*of a table*); flyleaf, addendum; rider (*of a document*); reach (*in boxing*); *allonge de boucher*, meat hook.

allongé [alɔ̃'ʒe], *a.* lengthened, elongated, out-stretched; downcast, long (*of face*).

allongement [alɔ̃ʒ'mɑ̃], *n.m.* lengthening, elongation, protraction.

allonger [alɔ̃'ʒe], *v.t.* (*conjug. like* MANGER) to lengthen, to elongate, to eke out; to stretch; to drag out, to protract. **s'allonger**, *v.r.* to stretch out, to grow longer; to stretch, to lie down at full length.

allouer [a'lwe], *v.t.* to allow, to grant, to accord; to allocate.

alluchon [aly'ʃɔ̃], *n.m.* cog, tooth (*of a wheel*).

allumage [aly'ma:ʒ], *n.m.* lighting, kindling; ignition; *un raté d'allumage*, misfire; *mettre l'allumage*, to switch on; *couper l'allumage*, to switch off.

allumé [aly'me], *a.* lighted, ignited; (*colloq.*) excited; drunk, lit-up.

allume-feu [alym'fø], *n.m. inv.* firewood, firelighter, kindling.

allume-gaz [alym'ga:z], *n.m. inv.* gas lighter.

allumer [aly'me], *v.t.* to light; to kindle, to set on fire; (*fig.*) to inflame, to incite, to stir up. **s'allumer**, *v.r.* to light, to take *or* catch fire; to blaze, to sparkle, to glare; to flare up, to break out.

allumette [aly'mɛt], *n.f.* match.

allumeur [aly'mœ:r], *n.m.* (*fem.* **-euse**) lighter.

allure [aly're], *n.f.* carriage, gait, pace, way of walking; demeanor; aspect, look; speed; (*pl.*) ways (*of a person*); *à toute allure*, at full speed.

allusion [aly'zjɔ̃], *n.f.* allusion, hint, innuendo.

alluvial [aly'vjal], *a.* (*m. pl.* **-aux**) alluvial.

alluvion [aly'vjɔ̃], *n.f.* alluvium.

almanach [alma'na], *n.m.* almanac, calendar.

aloès [alɔ'ɛ:s], *n.m.* aloe; aloes.

aloi [a'lwa], *n.m.* the statutory degree of purity of gold and silver; (*fig.*) standard (*good or bad*), quality, kind (*of persons etc.*).

alors [a'lɔ:r], *adv.* then, that time; in that case; *d'alors*, of that time; *alors que*, while, whereas; *jusqu'alors*, up to then,

till that moment; *alors même que*, even though.

alose [a'lo:z], *n.f.* shad.

alouette [a'lwɛt], *n.f.* (*Orn.*) lark.

alourdir [alur'di:r], *v.t.* to make heavy, dull *or* stupid. **s'alourdir**, *v.r.* to grow heavy *or* dull.

alourdissant [alurdi'sɑ̃], *a.* oppressive, burdensome.

alourdissement [alurdis'mɑ̃], *n.m.* heaviness, dullness.

aloyau [alwa'jo], *n.m.* (*pl.* **-aux**) sirloin.

alpaca [alpa'ka], **alpaga** [alpa'ga], *n.m.* alpaca.

alpenstock [alpɛn'stɔk], *n.m.* alpenstock.

Alpes [alp], **les**, *f.pl.* the Alps.

alpestre [al'pɛstr], *a.* Alpine (*scenery, flora*).

alpha [al'fa], *n.m.* alpha; (*fig.*) beginning.

alphabet [alfa'bɛ], *n.m.* alphabet.

alphabétique [alfabe'tik], *a.* alphabetical.

alphabétiquement [alfabetik'mɑ̃], *adv.* alphabetically.

alpin [al'pɛ̃], *a.* Alpine (*club etc.*).

alpinisme [alpi'nism], *n.m.* mountaineering.

alpiniste [alpi'nist], *n.m.* Alpinist, mountaineer.

Alsace [al'zas], **l'**, *f.* Alsace.

alsacien [alza'sjɛ̃], *a.* (*fem.* **-enne**) Alsatian. —*n.m.* (**Alsacien**, *fem.* **-enne**) inhabitant of Alsace.

altérable [alte'rabl], *a.* alterable, corruptible, adulterable.

altérant [alte'rɑ̃], *a.* causing thirst.

altération [altera'sjɔ̃], *n.f.* deterioration; falsification, adulteration, debasing (*of money etc.*); weakening, impairing.

altercation [altɛrka'sjɔ̃], *n.f.* altercation, wrangle, dispute, quarrel.

altérer [alte're], *v.t.* (*conjug. like* CÉDER) to alter for the worse; to impair, to adulterate, to corrupt, to pervert, to debase, to falsify; to disturb, to trouble, to upset; to make thirsty. **s'altérer**, *v.r.* to be impaired, to degenerate.

alternance [altɛr'nɑ̃:s], *n.f.* alternation, rotation.

alternant [altɛr'nɑ̃], *a.* alternating, rotating (*as crops*).

alternat [altɛr'na], *n.m.* rotation (*of crops etc*).

alternatif [altɛrna'tif], *a.* (*fem.* **-tive**) alternate, alternating, alternative.—*n.f.* (**-tive**) alternation; alternative, choice, option (*between two possible actions*).

alternativement [altɛrnativ'mɑ̃], *adv.* alternately, by turns.

alterne [al'tɛrn], *a.* (*Geom.*) alternate (*of angles*); (*Bot.*) alternate.

alterner [altɛr'ne], *v.t.* to grow (*crops*) in rotation.—*v.i.* to alternate, to succeed each other alternately.

Altesse [al'tɛs], *n.f.* Highness.

altier [al'tje], *a.* (*fem.* **-ière**) haughty, proud, arrogant, lordly, lofty.

altimètre [alti'mɛtr], *n.m.* altimeter.

altitude [alti'tyd], *n.f.* altitude.

alto [al'to], *n.m.* alto; tenor violin; tenor saxhorn.

altruisme [altry'ism], *n.m.* altruism.

altruiste [altry'ist], *a.* altruistic.—*n.* altruist.

alumine [aly'min], *n.f.* alumina, oxide of aluminum.

aluminer [alymi'ne], *v.t.* to aluminate, to aluminize.

aluminium [alymi'njɔm], *n.m.* aluminum.

alun [a'lœ̃], *n.m.* alum.

alunage [aly'na:ʒ], *n.m.* (*Dyeing*) steeping in alum; (*Phot.*) hardening (*negatives etc.*) in an alum bath.

aluner [aly'ne], *v.t.* (*Dyeing*) to steep in alum water; (*Phot.*) to harden in an alum bath.

alunière [aly'njɛ:r], *n.f.* alum pit *or* mine, alum-works.

alunir [aly'ni:r], *v.i.* to land on the moon.

alvéole [alve'ɔl], *n.m.* alveolus, cell (*in a honey-comb*); socket (*of a tooth*).

amabilité [amabili'te], *n.f.* amiability, affability, kindness.

amadou [ama'du], *n.m.* amadou, (German) tinder; touchwood.

amadouer [ama'dwe], *v.t.* to coax, to wheedle, to cajole.

amaigrir [amɛ'gri:r], *v.t.* to make lean, meager *or* thin, to emaciate; to reduce, to lessen (*in bulk etc.*); to impoverish; to exhaust (*soil etc.*).—*v.i.* to fall away; to grow lean or thin. **s'amaigrir**, *v.r.* to grow thin, to fall away.

amaigrissant [amɛgri'sɑ̃], *a.* causing emaciation; *régime amaigrissant*, slimming diet.

amaigrissement [amɛgris'mɑ̃], *n.m.* emaciation, wasting away.

amalgamation [amalgama'sjɔ̃], *n.f.* amalgamation.

amalgame [amal'gam], *n.m.* amalgam; (*fig.*) medley, heterogeneous mixture.

amalgamer [amalga'me], *v.t.* to amalgamate, to blend, to combine. **s'amalgamer**, *v.r.* to amalgamate, to blend, to combine.

amande [a'mɑ̃:d], *n.f.* almond; kernel; *amandes lissées*, sugar-plums.

amandier [amɑ̃'dje], *n.m.* almond tree.

amant [a'mɑ̃], *n.m.* (*fem.* -e) lover, suitor; sweetheart, mistress; gallant, paramour; passionate admirer.

amarante [ama'rɑ̃:t], *n.f.* amaranth.

amareilleur *or* **amareyeur** [amarɛ'jœ:r], *n.m.* worker on an oyster bed.

amarinage [amari'na:ʒ], *n.m.* (*Naut.*) manning (*a prize*).

amariner [amari'ne], *v.t.* to man (*a p. ize*); to inure (*a crew etc.*) to sea. **s'amariner**, *v.r.* to become used to the sea.

amarrage [ama'ra:ʒ], *n.m.* (*Naut.*) mooring; anchorage; lashing.

amarre [a'ma:r], *n.f.* (*Naut.*) cable, rope, hawser.

amarrer [ama're], *v.t.* to moor, to belay, to make fast.

amaryllis [amari'lis], *n.f.* amaryllis.

amas [a'ma], *n.m.* mass, heap, pile, accumulation.

amasser [ama'se], *v.t.* to accumulate, to heap up, to amass; to hoard; to collect, to get together. **s'amasser**, *v.r.* to gather, to get together, to accumulate, to be collected, to crowd, to assemble.

amassette [ama'sɛt], *n.f.* small palette knife.

amasseur [ama'sœ:r], *n.m.* (*fem.* -euse) hoarder.

amateur [ama'tœ:r], *n.m.* amateur; devotee; connoisseur.

amazone [ama'zo:n], *n.f.* Amazon, female warrior; horse-woman; riding habit; *habit d'amazone*, riding habit; *monter en amazone*, to ride side-saddle.

ambages [ɑ̃'ba:ʒ], *n.f.* (*pl.*) circumlocution; *sans ambages*, straight out.

ambassade [ɑ̃ba'sad], *n.f.* embassy, ambassador's staff.

ambassadeur [ɑ̃basa'dœ:r], *n.m.* ambassador; (*fig.*) envoy, messenger.

ambassadrice [ɑ̃basa'dris], *n.f.* ambassadress.

ambiance [ɑ̃'bjɑ̃:s], *n.f.* surroundings, environment; atmosphere.

ambiant [ɑ̃'bjɑ̃], *a.* ambient, surrounding.

ambidextre [ɑ̃bi'dɛkstr], *a.* ambidextrous.—*n.* ambidexter.

ambigu [ɑ̃bi'gy], *a.* (*fem.* -guë) ambiguous, equivocal.—*n.m.* heterogeneous mixture, medley.

ambiguïté [ɑ̃bigui'te], *n.f.* ambiguity.

ambigument [ɑ̃bigy'mɑ̃], *adv.* ambiguously.

ambitieusement [ɑ̃bisjøz'mɑ̃], *adv.* ambitiously.

ambitieux [ɑ̃bi'sjø], *a.* (*fem.* -euse) ambitious.—*n.m.* (*fem.* -euse) ambitious person.

ambition [ɑ̃bi'sjɔ̃], *n.f.* ambition.

ambitionner [ɑ̃bisjo'ne], *v.t.* to desire earnestly; to be ambitious of, to aspire to.

ambivalence [ɑ̃biva'lɑ̃:s], *n.f.* ambivalence.

ambivalent [ɑ̃biva'lɑ̃], *a.* ambivalent.

amble [ɑ̃:bl], *n.m.* amble.

ambler [ɑ̃'ble], *v.i.* to amble.

ambleur [ɑ̃'blœ:r], *a.* (*fem.* -euse) ambling.

amblyope [ɑ̃'bljɔp], *a.* amblyopic, weak-sighted.—*n.* weak-sighted person.

ambre [ɑ̃:br], *n.m.* amber; *ambre gris*, ambergris.

ambré [ɑ̃'bre], *a.* amber-colored.

ambrer [ɑ̃'bre], *v.t.* to perfume with amber.

ambrette [ɑ̃'brɛt], *n.f.* amber seed; musk seed.

ambroisie [ɑ̃brwa'zi], *n.f.* ambrosia.

ambulance [ɑ̃by'lɑ̃:s], *n.f.* ambulance; field hospital; peripatetic clerkship; *chirurgien d'ambulance*, field surgeon.

ambulancier [ɑ̃bylɑ̃'sje], *n.m.* (*fem.* -ière) ambulance man, stretcher-bearer, nurse.

ambulant [ɑ̃by'lɑ̃], *a.* ambulant, ambulatory, itinerant, peripatetic; travelling (*of a railway post office*); strolling (*players*).

ambulatoire [ɑ̃byla'twa:r], *a.* ambulatory; (*Law*) movable.

âme (1) [ɑ:m], *n.f.* soul, spirit; sentiment, sensibility; (*fig.*) inhabitant, person (*on a lost ship etc.*); core, pith, heart (*of a thing etc.*); **rendre l'âme**, to give up the ghost.

âme (2) [ɑ:m], *n.f.* sounding board (*of a violin etc.*); bore (*of gun*).

amélioration [ameljɔra'sjɔ̃], *n.f.* amelioration, improvement; (*pl.*) repairs, decorations (*of a house etc.*).

améliorer [ameljo're], *v.t.* to ameliorate, to improve, to better. **s'améliorer**, *v.r.* to get better, to mend, to improve.

amen [a'mɛn], *int.* and *n.m.* amen.

aménagement [amena3'mɑ̃], *n.m.* arrangement; disposition (*of a house etc.*); management (*of a forest*).

16

aménager [amena'ʒe], *v.t.* (*conjug. like* MANGER) to dispose, to arrange, to lay out; to regulate the felling of (*a wood* or *forest*).

amendable [amɑ̃'dabl], *a.* improvable, mendable.

amende [a'mɑ̃:d], *n.f.* fine, penalty, forfeit, compensation, reparation; *faire amende honorable*, to make a full apology; *mettre* or *condamner à l'amende*, to fine.

amendement [amɑ̃d'mɑ̃], *n.m.* amendment; improvement; manuring (*of land*).

amender [amɑ̃'de], *v.t.* to amend, to better; to manure (*land*). **s'amender**, *v.r.* to mend, to grow better.

amène [a'mɛ:n], *a.* agreeable, pleasant (*site*).

amener [am'ne], *v.t.* (*see Verb Tables*) to lead (*hither*), to bring; to induce, prevail upon; to introduce; to bring about; to occasion, to lead to; (*Naut.*) to lower, to strike (*colors, sails etc.*); *mandat d'amener*, warrant.

aménité [ameni'te], *n.f.* amenity, pleasantness, affability; grace, urbanity.

amenuiser [amənɥi'ze], *v.t.* to make thinner or smaller. **s'amenuiser**, *v.r.* to grow thinner or smaller.

amer (1) [a'mɛ:r], *a.* (*fem.* **amère**) bitter, harsh; painful, grievous; biting, galling.—*n.m.* something bitter; gall; bitterness; (*pl.*) bitters.

amer (2) [a'mɛ:r], *n.m.* (*Naut.*) any landmark or leading mark.

amèrement [amɛr'mɑ̃], *adv.* bitterly, grievously.

américain [ameri'kɛ̃], *a.* American.—*n.m.* (**Américain**, *fem.* **-aine**) American (*person*).

américanisme [amerika'nism], *n.m.* Americanism.

Amérique [ame'rik], **l'**, *f.* America.

amérir or **amerrir** [ame'ri:r], *v.i.* (*Av.*) to alight on the water.

amerrissage [ameri'sa:ʒ], *n.m.* alighting (*on the water*).

amertume [amɛr'tym], *n.f.* bitterness, grief; gall, venom.

améthyste [ame'tist], *n.f.* amethyst.

ameublement [amœblə'mɑ̃], *n.m.* furniture, suite of furniture.

ameublir [amœ'bli:r], *v.t.* (*Agric.*) to make (*soil*) more broken up or lighter.

ameublissement [amœblis'mɑ̃], *n.m.* (*Agric.*) loosening, mellowing.

ameulonner [amœlɔ'ne], *v.t.* to stack (*hay, corn etc.*).

ameuter [amø'te], *v.t.* to train dogs as a pack; (*fig.*) to stir up, to rouse, to excite.

ami [a'mi], *n.m.* (*fem.* **amie**) friend; well-wisher, partisan; lover; *chambre d'ami*, spare room.—*a.* friendly; sympathetic, favorable, kindly-disposed; kind, propitious.

amiable [a'mjabl], *a.* friendly, courteous; amicable, conciliatory; *vente à l'amiable*, sale by private contract.

amiablement [amjablə'mɑ̃], *adv.* amicably.

amiante [a'mjɑ̃:t], *n.m.* asbestos.

amibe [a'mib], *n.f.* amoeba.

amical [ami'kal], *a.* (*m. pl.* **-aux**) amicable, friendly

amicalement [amikal'mɑ̃], *adv.* amicably, in a friendly manner.

amidon [ami'dɔ̃], *n.m.* starch.

amidonner [amidɔ'ne], *v.t.* to starch.

amincir [amɛ̃'si:r], *v.t.* to make thinner. **s'amincir**, *v.r.* to become thinner.

amincissement [amɛ̃sis'mɑ̃], *n.m.* thinning.

amiral [ami'ral], *n.m.* (*pl.* **-aux**) admiral; *contre-amiral*, rear admiral; *grand amiral*, high admiral; *vice-amiral*, vice admiral; *vaisseau amiral*, flagship.

Amirauté [amiro'te], **Îles de l'**, *f.* Admiralty Islands.

amirauté [amiro'te], *n.f.* admiralship; admiralty.

amitié [ami'tje], *n.f.* friendship, affection; favor, kindness; (*pl.*) kind regards, compliments; *mes amitiés à tout le monde*, love to all; *par amitié*, out of friendship.

ammoniac [amɔ'njak], *a.* (*fem.* **-iaque**) ammoniac; *sel ammoniac*, sal ammoniac. —*n.f.* (**-iaque**) ammonia.

ammonite [amɔ'nit], *n.f.* ammonite.

amnésie [amne'zi], *n.f.* amnesia.

amnistie [amnis'ti], *n.f.* amnesty, pardon.

amnistier [amnis'tje], *v.t.* to pardon by amnesty.

amoindrir [amwɛ̃'dri:r], *v.t.* to lessen, to decrease, to diminish. **s'amoindrir**, *v.r.* to grow less.

amoindrissement [amwɛ̃dris'mɑ̃], *n.m.* lessening, decrease.

amollir [amɔ'li:r], *v.t.* to soften; (*fig.*) to mollify. **s'amollir**, *v.r.* to soften, to grow soft; to grow effeminate or weak.

amollissant [amɔli'sɑ̃], *a.* softening; enervating.

amollissement [amɔlis'mɑ̃], *n.m.* softening, enervation, effeminacy.

amonceler [amɔ̃s'le], *v.t.* (*conjug. like* APPELER) to heap up, to lay in a heap; (*fig.*) to accumulate. **s'amonceler**, *v.r.* to gather; to accumulate, to drift together.

amoncellement [amɔ̃sɛl'mɑ̃], *n.m.* accumulation; heap.

amont [a'mɔ̃], *n.m.* upstream water (*used chiefly in en amont*, up-stream, up-river).

amoral [amɔ'ral], *a.* (*m. pl.* **-aux**) amoral.

amorçage [amɔr'sa:ʒ], *n.m.* priming (*of pumps, motors, guns etc.*); baiting (*of hook*).

amorce [a'mɔrs], *n.f.* bait; (*fig.*) allurement, charm; priming, percussion cap (*of guns etc.*); priming (*for a pump*).

amorcer [amɔr'se], *v.t.* (*conjug. like* COMMENCER) to bait; (*fig.*) to allure, to entice, to decoy; (*Hydraulics*) to prime; (*Artill.*) to cap (*a shell*).

amorphe [a'mɔrf], *a.* amorphous.

amortir [amɔr'ti:r], *v.t.* to deaden, to allay, to moderate; to weaken, to break (*a fall, shock etc.*); to redeem, to pay off; to cool (*passions*).

amortissable [amɔrti'sabl], *a.* redeemable.

amortissement [amɔrtis'mɑ̃], *n.m.* redemption, buying up; liquidation; deadening (*of a blow etc.*); *fonds d'amortissement*, sinking fund.

amortisseur [amɔrti'sœ:r], *n.m.* shock absorber.

amour [a'mu:r], *n.m.* (*usu. fem. in pl.*) love, affection, passion; the object of love, flame, fancy; *l'Amour*, (*Myth.*) Eros, Cupid.

amouracher(s') [samura'ʃe], *v.r.* to be smitten with, to become enamored (*de*).

amourette [amu'rɛt], *n.f.* passing amour, love affair.

amoureusement [amurøz'mā], *adv.* amorously, lovingly; tenderly.

amoureux [amu'rø], *a.* (*fem.* **-euse**) loving, in love, smitten, enamored (*de*); amorous. —*n.m.* (*fem.* **-euse**) lover, sweetheart; fiancé or fiancée.

amour-propre [amur'prɔpr], *n.m.* self-respect; vanity, conceit.

amovibilité [amɔvibili'te], *n.f.* removability, liability to removal; precariousness of tenure.

amovible [amɔ'vibl], *a.* removable, revocable.

ampère [ɑ̃'pɛ:r], *n.m.* (*Elec.*) ampere.

amphibie [ɑ̃fi'bi], *a.* amphibious.—*n.m.* amphibian.

amphibiens [ɑ̃fi'bjɛ̃], *n.m. pl.* (*Zool.*) Amphibia.

amphigouri [ɑ̃figu'ri], *n.m.* rigmarole, gibberish.

amphithéâtre [ɑ̃fite'a:tr], *n.m.* amphitheatre; the whole body of occupants of this; the gallery in a theatre rising above the boxes and facing the stage; lecture room; *en amphithéâtre*, in semi-circular tiers.

Amphitryon [ɑ̃fitri'ɔ̃], *n.m.* Amphitryon; host, entertainer.

amphore [ɑ̃'fo:r], *n.f.* amphora.

ample [ɑ̃:pl], *a.* ample, full; large, vast, spacious; copious.

amplement [ɑ̃plə'mā], *adv.* amply, fully; largely, plentifully.

ampleur [ɑ̃'plœ:r], *n.f.* width, fullness (*of clothes*); abundance; profusion; dignity (*of style etc.*); volume (*of voice*).

amplifiant [ɑ̃pli'fjā], *a.* magnifying (*of a lens etc.*); amplifying.

amplificateur [ɑ̃plifika'tœ:r], *a.* (*fem.* **-trice**) magnifying; amplifying.—*n.m.* (*Phot.*) enlarger.

amplification [ɑ̃plifika's͜ɔ̃], *n.f.* amplification; magnification, enlargement; (*fig.*) exaggeration.

amplifier [ɑ̃pli'tyd], *v.t.* to amplify, to develop, to enlarge.

amplitude [ɑ̃pli'tyd], *n.f.* extent, amplitude.

ampoule [ɑ̃'pul], *n.f.* blister, swelling; (*Elec.*) bulb; (*Med.*) ampoule.

ampoulé [ɑ̃pu'le], *a.* bombastic, turgid.

amputation [ɑ̃pyta'sjɔ̃], *n.f.* amputation; (*fig.*) curtailment.

amputer [ɑ̃py'te], *v.t.* to amputate, to cut off.

amulette [amy'lɛt], *n.f.* amulet, charm.

amusant [amy'zā], *a.* amusing, diverting, entertaining.

amusement [amyz'mā], *n.m.* amusement, entertainment, diversion; fooling, trifling.

amuser [amy'ze], *v.t.* to amuse, to divert, to entertain; to fool, to beguile; to dupe; to detain, to delay. **s'amuser**, *v.r.* to amuse oneself, to divert oneself; to trifle; to have a good time; *s'amuser de quelqu'un*, to make fun of someone; *amusez-vous bien !* enjoy yourselves, have a good time.

amusette [amy'zɛt], *n.f.* petty amusement.

amuseur [amy'zœ:r], *n.m.* (*fem.* **-euse**) amuser, entertainer.

amygdale [ami'dal], *n.f.* (*Anat.*) tonsil.

an [ɑ̃], *n.m.* year; (*pl.*) years, time, age; *elle a quinze ans*, she is fifteen; *le jour de l'an*, New Year's day.

anacarde [ana'kard], *n.m.* cashew nut.

anachorète [anakɔ'rɛt], *n.* anchorite, hermit.

anachronisme [anakrɔ'nism], *n.m.* anachronism.

anaéroïde [ANÉROÏDE].

anagramme [ana'gram], *n.f.* anagram.

analgésie [analʒe'zi], **analgie** [anal'ʒi], *n.f.* (*Med.*) analgesia.

analgésique [analʒe'zik], **analgique** [anal'ʒik], *a.* and *n.m.* analgesic.

analogie [analɔ'ʒi], *n.f.* analogy.

analogique [analɔ'ʒik], *a.* analogous, analogical.

analogue [ana'lɔg], *a.* analogous, similar.

analyse [ana'li:ʒ], *n.f.* analysis; outline, précis, abstract (*of a book etc.*); (*Gram.*) parsing, analysis.

analyser [anali'ze], *v.t.* to analyze.

analyste [ana'list], *n.m.* analyst.

analytique [anali'tik], *a.* analytic, analytical.

analytiquement [analitik'mā], *adv.* analytically.

ananas [ana'nɑ], *n.m.* pineapple.

anarchie [anar'ʃi], *n.f.* anarchy; (*fig.*) disorder, confusion.

anarchique [anar'ʃik], *a.* anarchical.

anarchiste [anar'ʃist], *n.* anarchist.

anathème [ana'tɛ:m], *n.m.* anathema; sentence of reprobation *or* excommunication, ban, curse.

anatomie [anatɔ'mi], *n.f.* anatomy; dissection; (*fam.*) body, figure.

anatomique [anatɔ'mik], *a.* anatomical.

anatomiquement [anatɔmik'mā], *adv.* anatomically.

anatomiser [anatɔmi'ze], *v.t.* to anatomize, to dissect.

anatomiste [anatɔ'mist], *n.* anatomist.

ancêtre [ɑ̃'sɛ:tr], *n.* ancestor, ancestress.—*n.m. pl.* ancestors, forefathers.

anchois [ɑ̃'ʃwa], *n.m.* anchovy.

ancien [ɑ̃'sjɛ̃], *a.* (*fem.* **-ienne**) ancient, old; former, late, ex-; antique; *un ancien élève*, an old boy.—*n.m.* (*fem.* **-ienne**) senior; ancient; (*Eccles.*) elder; (*Mil.*) veteran; (*pl.*) the ancients; our forefathers.

anciennement [ɑ̃sjɛn'mā], *adv.* formerly; *of* yore; in former times.

ancienneté [ɑ̃sjɛn'te], *n.f.* antiquity; seniority.

ancillaire [ɑ̃sil'lɛ:r], *a.* ancillary.

ancrage [ɑ̃'kra:ʒ], *n.m.* anchorage.

ancre [ɑ̃:kr], *n.f.* anchor; *ancre de miséricorde* (or *de salut*), sheet anchor; (*fig.*) last resource; cramp iron, tie plate (*of a wall*).

ancrer [ɑ̃'kre], *v.t.* to anchor; (*fig.*) to fix *or* establish firmly.—*v.i.* to anchor. **s'ancrer**, *v.r.* to establish oneself, to get a footing (*in a place*), to take deep root (*in*).

Andalousie [ɑ̃dalu'zi], **l'**, *f.* Andalusia.

Andes [ɑ̃:d], **les**, *f. pl.* the Andes.

Andorre [ɑ̃'dɔ:r], **l'**, *m.* Andorra.

andouille [ɑ̃'du:j], *n.f.* pork sausage (*made of chitterlings*); (*pop.*) imbecile, duffer.

andouiller [ɑ̃du'je], *n.m.* tine (*of antler*).

André [ɑ̃'dre], *m.* Andrew.

Andromède [ɑ̃drɔ'mɛd], *f.* Andromeda.

âne [ɑ:n], *n.m.* ass, donkey; blockhead, stupid, ignorant *or* foolish person, idiot.

anéantir [aneɑ̃'ti:r], *v.t.* to annihilate, to destroy utterly, to abolish; (*fig.*) to overwhelm.

anéantissement [aneɑ̃tis'mɑ̃], n.m. annihilation; destruction, ruin, overthrow; humiliation, prostration.

anecdote [anɛg'dɔt], n.f. anecdote.

anecdotique [anɛgdɔ'tik], a. anecdotic.

anémie [ane'mi], n.f. anaemia.

anémique [ane'mik], a. anaemic.

anémone [ane'mɔn], n.f. anemone, windflower.

ânerie [ɑn'ri], n.f. stupidity; gross ignorance; gross blunder.

anéroïde [anerɔ'id], **anaéroïde** [anaerɔ'id], a. aneroid.—n.m. aneroid barometer.

ânesse [ɑ'nɛs], n.f. she-ass.

anesthésie [anɛste'zi], n.f. (Med.) anaesthesia.

anesthésier [anɛste'zje], v.t. to anaesthetize.

anesthésique [anɛste'zik], a. and n.m. anaesthetic.

anesthésiste [anɛste'zist], n.m. anaesthetist.

anévrisme [ane'vrism], n.m. aneurism.

anfractueux [ɑ̃frak'tɥø], a. (fem. -euse) anfractuous, winding, sinuous, craggy.

anfractuosité [ɑ̃fraktɥozi'te], n.f. anfractuosity, cragginess, twist, jagged or rugged outlines.

ange [ɑ̃ʒ], n.m. angel; (fig.) an adorable or beloved person.

Angèle [ɑ̃'ʒɛl], f. Angela.

angélique [ɑ̃ʒe'lik], a. angelic, angelical.

angélus [ɑ̃ʒe'ly:s], n.m. angelus.

angevin [ɑ̃ʒə'vɛ̃], a. of Anjou.—n.m. (Angevin, fem. -ine) native of Anjou.

angine [ɑ̃'ʒin], n.f. angina, quinsy, sore throat.

anglais [ɑ̃'glɛ], a. English; British.—n.m. English (language); (Anglais, fem. -aise) Englishman, English girl or woman; (pl.) the English.

angle [ɑ̃:gl], n.m. angle, corner; (Arch.) quoin; **angle aigu**, acute angle; **angle droit**, right angle.

Angleterre [ɑ̃glə'tɛ:r], l', f. England.

anglican [ɑ̃gli'kɑ̃], a. and n.m. (fem. -e) Anglican.

angliciser [ɑ̃glisi'ze], v.t. to Anglicize. **s'angliciser**, v.r. to become Anglicized or English.

anglicisme [ɑ̃gli'sism], n.m. Anglicism.

anglomanie [ɑ̃glɔma'ni], n.f. Anglomania.

anglo-normand [ɑ̃glonɔr'mɑ̃], a. and n.m. (fem. -e) Anglo-Norman; **les Iles anglo-normandes**, the Channel Islands.

anglophile [ɑ̃glɔ'fil], a. and n. Anglophil.

anglo-saxon [ɑ̃glɔsak'sɔ̃], a. and n.m. (fem. -saxonne) Anglo-Saxon.

angoisse [ɑ̃'gwas], n.f. anguish, agony, great distress; (Med.) angor, anguish.

angora [ɑ̃gɔ'ra], a. Angora.—n.m. Angora cat.

anguille [ɑ̃'gi:j], n.f. eel; (pl., Naut.) launching ways, slips; **il y a anguille sous roche**, I smell a rat.

angulaire [ɑ̃gy'lɛ:r], a. angular.

angusture [ɑ̃gys'ty:r], n.f. (Pharm.) angostura.

anhélation [anela'sjɔ̃], n.f. panting.

anhéler [ane'le], v.i. (conjug. like CÉDER) to pant.

anhydre [a'nidr], a. (Chem.) anhydrous.

anhydride [ani'drid], n.m. anhydride; **anhydride carbonique**, carbon dioxide.

anicroche [ani'krɔʃ], n.f. slight obstacle.

animadversion [animadver'sjɔ̃], n.f. animadversion, reproof, reprimand, censure.

animal [ani'mal], n.m. (pl. -aux) animal; beast, brute; **société protectrice des animaux**, Society for the Prevention of Cruelty to Animals.—a. (m.pl. -aux) animal; sensual, carnal.

animateur [anima'tœ:r], a. (fem. -trice) animating.

animation [anima'sjɔ̃], n.f. animation, vitality, life; liveliness; excitement; irritation.

animé [ani'me], a. animated; spirited, gay, sprightly; **rue animée**, busy street.

animer [ani'me], v.t. to animate, to give life to; to arouse, to excite, to urge on; to enliven, to give force to (style etc.). **s'animer**, v.r. to become animated or lively; to cheer up; to become angry.

animosité [animozi'te], n.f. animosity, ill will, spite, rancor.

anis [a'ni], n.m. anise, aniseed.

aniser [ani'ze], v.t. to flavor with aniseed.

anisette [ani'zɛt], n.f. aniseed cordial.

ankylose [ɑ̃ki'lo:z], n.f. (Path.) anchylosis, stiffness in the joints.

annales [a'nal], n.f. (used only in pl.) annals, public records.

annaliste [ana'list], n.m. annalist.

anneau [a'no], n.m. (pl. anneaux) ring; link (of a chain); ringlet (of hair).

année [a'ne], n.f. year, period of twelve months; **année bissextile**, leap year; **souhaiter la bonne année**, to wish a happy New Year.

année-lumière [anely'mjɛ:r], n.f. (pl. années-lumière) light-year.

annelé [an'le], a. having or arranged in rings, ringed; (Zool.) annulated.

annelet [an'lɛ], n.m. ringlet, small ring.

annexe [a'nɛks], n.f. annex; appendage; appendix, schedule, rider; chapel of ease.

annexer [anɛk'se], v.t. to annex, to attach.

annexion [anɛk'sjɔ̃], n.f. annexation.

annihilation [aniila'sjɔ̃], n.f. annihilation; (Law) annulment.

annihiler [anii'le], v.t. to annihilate, to destroy; (Law) to annul.

anniversaire [aniver'sɛ:r], a. and n.m. anniversary, birthday.

annonce [a'nɔ̃:s], n.f. announcement, notification; indication, sign, mark; advertisement; **annonce de mariage**, banns of marriage.

annoncer [anɔ̃'se], v.t. (conjug. like COMMENCER) to announce, to give notice of; to advertise; to announce (a visitor), to usher or show in; to proclaim; to foretell, **s'annoncer**, v.r. to present oneself; to manifest itself.

Annonciation [anɔ̃sja'sjɔ̃], n.f. Annunciation; Lady Day (March 25).

annoncier [anɔ̃'sje], n.m. publicity manager.

annotateur [anɔta'tœ:r], n.m. (fem. -trice) annotator (of a book etc.).

annotation [anɔta'sjɔ̃], n.f. annotation.

annoter [anɔ'te], v.t. to annotate, to make notes on (a text etc.).

annuaire [a'nɥɛ:r], n.m. annual, year-book; **l'Annuaire des Téléphones**, the telephone directory.

annuel [a'nɥɛl], a. (fem. -elle) annual, yearly.

annuellement [anɥɛl'mɑ̃], adv. annually, yearly.

19

annuité [anɥi'te], *n.f.* annuity.

annulable [any'labl], *a.* revocable.

annulaire [any'lɛ:r], *a.* annular, ring-shaped. —*n m.* ring finger, third finger.

annulation [anylɑ'sjɔ̃], *n.f.* annulment, cancellation, repeal, abolition.

annuler [any'le], *v.t.* to annul, to rescind, to cancel, to abolish, to set aside, to make void.

anobli [anɔ'bli], *a.* ennobled.—*n.m.* newly created nobleman.

anoblir [anɔ'bli:r], *v.t.* to ennoble, to raise to the rank of the nobility.

anoblissement [anɔblis'mɑ̃], *n.m.* ennoblement.

anode [a'nɔd], *n.f.* (*Elec.*) anode, positive pole.

anodin [anɔ'dɛ̃], *a.* (*Med.*) anodyne, soothing; (*fig.*) harmless, mild, inoffensive, insignificant.

anomal [anɔ'mal], *a.* (*m. pl.* **-aux**) (*Gram.*) anomalous, irregular.

anomalie [anɔma'li], *n.f.* anomaly, irregularity.

ânon [ɑ'nɔ̃], *n.m.* ass's foal, young ass; (*fig.*) a little fool.

ânonnement [anɔn'mɑ̃], *n.m.* faltering, mumbling way of reading a text.

ânonner [anɔ'ne], *v.t.* to mumble and blunder through (*a lesson etc.*).—*v.i.* to read in a faltering way.

anonymat [anɔni'ma], *n.m.* anonymity.

anonyme [anɔ'nim], *a.* anonymous, nameless; *société anonyme*, joint-stock company. —*n.* anonymous person.

anonymement [anɔnim'mɑ̃], *adv.* anonymously.

anorak [anɔ'rak], *n.m.* (*reg. trade mark*) anorak.

anormal [anɔr'mal], *a.* (*m. pl.* **-aux**) abnormal, irregular, mentally deficient.

anormalement [anɔrmal'mɑ̃], *adv.* abnormally.

anse [ɑ̃:s], *n.f.* handle (*of a pot, basket etc.*); bay, cove.

antagonique [ɑ̃tagɔ'nik], *a.* antagonistic.

antagonisme [ɑ̃tagɔ'nism], *n.m.* antagonism.

antagoniste [ɑ̃tagɔ'nist], *a.* antagonistic.— *n.m.* antagonist, adversary, opponent; competitor, rival.

*****antan** [ɑ̃'tɑ̃], *n.m.* yesteryear; *les neiges d'antan*, the snows of yesteryear.

antarctique [ɑ̃tark'tik], *a.* Antarctic.

antécédent [ɑ̃tese'dɑ̃], *a.* antecedent, preceding, foregoing, previous.—*n.m.* precedent; (*Gram.*) antecedent.

antéchrist [ɑ̃te'krist], *n.m.* Antichrist.

antédiluvien [ɑ̃tedily'vjɛ̃], *a.* (*fem.* **-ienne**) antediluvian.

antenne [ɑ̃'tɛn], *n.f.* (*Rad., Tel.*) aerial; (*Ent.*) antenna, (*pl.*) antennae.

antépénultième [ɑ̃tepenyl'tjɛm], *a.* antepenultimate.

antérieur [ɑ̃te'rjœːr], *a.* anterior, earlier, antecedent, previous, former.

antérieurement [ɑ̃terjœr'mɑ̃], *adv.* previously, before.

antériorité [ɑ̃terjɔri'te], *n.f.* anteriority, priority, precedence.

anthologie [ɑ̃tɔlɔ'ʒi], *n.f.* anthology.

anthracite [ɑ̃tra'sit], *n.m.* anthracite.

anthrax [ɑ̃'traks], *n.m.* (*Med.*) anthrax.

anthropoïde [ɑ̃trɔpɔ'id], *a.* and *n.m.* (*Zool.*) anthropoid.

anthropologie [ɑ̃trɔpɔlɔ'ʒi], *n.f.* anthropology.

anthropologiste [ɑ̃trɔpɔlɔ'ʒist], **anthropologue** [ɑ̃trɔpɔ'lɔg], *n.* anthropologist.

anthropophage [ɑ̃trɔpɔ'fa:ʒ], *n.* cannibal.

anti-aérien [ɑ̃tiae'rjɛ̃], *a.* (*fem.* **-enne**) anti-aircraft.

antibiotique [ɑ̃tibiɔ'tik], *a.* and *n.m.* antibiotic.

anti-brouillard [ɑ̃tibru'ja:r], *n.m.* (*Motor.*) fog light.

anti-buée [ɑ̃ti'bye], *a.* (*Motor.*) demisting.— *n.m.* demister.

antichambre [ɑ̃ti'ʃɑ̃:br], *n.f.* (*formerly m.*) antechamber, anteroom.

anti-char [ɑ̃ti'fa:r], *a.* anti-tank.

antichrétien [ɑ̃tikre'tjɛ̃], *a.* and *n.m.* (*fem.* **-ienne**) antichristian.

anticipation [ɑ̃tisipa'sjɔ̃], *n.f.* anticipation; encroachment, trespass; *par anticipation*, in advance, beforehand.

anticipé [ɑ̃tisi'pe], *a.* done *or* occurring in advance.

anticiper [ɑ̃tisi'pe], *v.t.* to anticipate, to forestall.—*v.i.* to encroach *or* trespass (*sur*).

anticlimax [ɑ̃tikli'maks], *n.m.* anticlimax.

anticommunisme [ɑ̃tikɔmy'nism], *n.m.* anti-communism.

anticonstitutionnellement [ɑ̃tikɔ̃stitysjɔnɛl'mɑ̃], *adv.* (*the longest French word*) anticonstitutionally.

anticorps [ɑ̃ti'kɔ:r], *n.m.* (*Med.*) antibody.

anticyclone [ɑ̃tisi'klo:n], *n.m.* (*Meteor.*) anticyclone.

antidate [ɑ̃ti'dat], *n.f.* antedate.

antidater [ɑ̃tida'te], *v.t.* to antedate.

antidérapant [ɑ̃tidera'pɑ̃], *a.* non-skidding; *pneu antidérapant*, non-skid tire.

antidote [ɑ̃ti'dɔt], *n.m.* antidote, antitoxin; (*fig.*) cure.

anti-éblouissant [ɑ̃tieblui'sɑ̃], *a.* (*Motor.*) antidazzle.

antienne [ɑ̃'tjɛn], *n.f.* antiphon; anthem.

antigel [ɑ̃ti'ʒɛl], *n.m. inv.* anti-freeze.

antillais [ɑ̃ti'jɛ], *a.* West Indian. *n.m.* (**Antillais**, *fem.* **-aise**) West Indian (*person*).

Antilles [ɑ̃'ti:j], **les**, *s.f.pl.* the West Indies; *la mer des Antilles*, the Caribbean Sea.

antilope [ɑ̃ti'lɔp], *n.f.* antelope.

anti-mite [ɑ̃ti'mit], *a.* moth-proof.

antimoine [ɑ̃ti'mwan], *n.m.* antimony.

Antioche [ɑ̃'tjɔʃ], *f.* Antioch.

antiparasite [ɑ̃tipara'zit], *n.m.* suppressor.

antiparlementaire [ɑ̃tiparləmɑ̃'tɛːr], *a.* unparliamentary.

antipathie [ɑ̃tipa'ti], *n.f.* antipathy, aversion.

antipathique [ɑ̃tipa'tik], *a.* antipathetic, repugnant.

antiphonaire [ɑ̃tifɔ'nɛːr], *n.m.* antiphonal.

antipode [ɑ̃ti'pɔd], *n.m.* the region of the globe diametrically opposite; (*pl.*) antipodes.

antiputride [ɑ̃ti'grid], *a.* and *n.m.* antiseptic.

antiquaire [ɑ̃ti'kɛːr], *n.m.* antiquary, antiquarian, antique dealer.

antique [ɑ̃'tik], *a.* antique, ancient; old-fashioned.—*n.f.* antique, ancient work of art.

antiquité [ɑ̃tiki'te], *n.f.* antiquity; old times; (*pl.*) antiquities; *magasin d'antiquités*, old curiosity shop.

antirouille [ɑ̃ti'ru:j], *n.m.* rust preventive.

antirrhine [ãti′rin], *n.f.* (*Bot.*) antirrhinum, snapdragon.

antisémite [ãtise′mit], *n.* anti-Semite.

antisémitique [ãtisemi′tik], *a.* anti-Semitic.

antisemitisme [ãtisemi′tism], *n.m.* anti-Semitism.

antiseptique [ãtisɛp′tik], *a.* and *n.m.* (*Med.*) antiseptic.

antisocial [ãtiso′sjal], *a.* (*m. pl.* **-aux**) antisocial.

antisportif [ãtispor′tif], *a.* (*fem.* **-ive**) unsportsmanlike; opposed to sports.

antithèse [ãti′tɛ:z], *n.f.* antithesis.

antitoxine [ãtitok′sin], *n.f.* (*Med.*) antitoxin.

anti-vol [ãti′vol], *a. inv.* anti-theft.—*n.m.* burglar-proof device.

antivivisection [ãtivivisɛk′sjõ], *n.f.* antivivisection.

Antoine [ã′twan], *m.* Anthony.

antre [ã:tr], *n.m.* den, lair; cavern.

anuiter (**s′**) [sãɥi′te], *v.r.* to be benighted.

anus [a′ny:s], *n.m.* anus.

Anvers [ã′vɛr], *m.* Antwerp.

anxiété [ãksje′te], *n.f.* anxiety; uneasiness; (*Med.*) pain in the heart.

anxieusement [ãksjøz′mã], *adv.* anxiously.

anxieux [ãk′sjø], *a.* (*fem.* **-euse**) anxious, uneasy, restless.

aorte [a′ort], *n.f.* (*Anat.*) aorta.

août [u(t)], *n.m.* August; (*fig.*) harvest; **la mi-août**, the middle of August.

noûté [u′te], *a.* ripened by the heat of August.

noûter (**s′**) [su′te], *v.r.* to ripen (*in August*).

apache [a′paʃ], *n.m.* ruffian of the Paris streets, hooligan.

apaisement [apɛz′mã], *n.m.* appeasement; abatement, lull.

apaiser [apɛ′ze], *v.t.* to pacify, to calm, to appease; to quiet; to mitigate, to alleviate (*pain, sorrow etc.*); to stay (*hunger*); to quench (*thirst*). **s′apaiser**, *v.r.* to be appeased; to sober down; to grow quiet; to abate, to subside.

Apalaches [apa′laʃ], *m.pl.* Appalachians. (**C**) **apalachien** [apala′ʃjɛ̃], *a.* (*fem.* **-chienne**) Appalachian.

apanage [apa′na:ʒ], *n.m.* apanage; (*fig.*) lot.

apanager [apana′ʒe], *v.t.* (*conjug. like* MANGER) to endow.

aparté [apar′te], *n.m.* aside.

apathie [apa′ti], *n.f.* apathy, indolence, listlessness.

apathique [apa′tik], *a.* apathetic, listless.

apatride [apa′trid], *a.* and *n.* stateless (person).

Apennins [apɛ′nɛ̃], **les**, *m.pl.* the Apennines.

apepsie [apɛp′si], *n.f.* (*Path.*) apepsy, indigestion.

apeptique [apɛp′tik], *a.* dyspeptic.

apercevable [apɛrsə′vabl], *a.* perceivable, perceptible.

apercevoir [apɛrsə′vwa:r], *v.t.* (*conjug. like* RECEVOIR) to catch sight of, to notice; to perceive, to understand, to comprehend. **s′apercevoir**, *v.r.* (**de quelque chose**) to remark, to notice, to be aware of; to find out, to discover; to be visible.

aperçu [apɛr′sy], *n.m.* rapid view, glance or survey; rough estimate or summary; judgment, idea.

apéritif [aperi′tif], *a.* (*fem.* **-ive**) aperient, appetizing.—*n.m.* (*Med.*) aperient, laxative; appetizer, aperitif (*e.g. vermouth, bitters*).

à peu près [apø′prɛ], *n.m.* approximation, approach; a word roughly standing for another.—*adv.* nearly, about.

apeuré [apø′re], *a.* frightened, scared.

apex [a′pɛks], *n.m.* apex.

aphélie [afe′li], *n.m.* (*Astron.*) aphelion.

aphidé [afi′de], **aphidien** [afi′d̃ɛ̃], *n.m.* (*Ent.*) aphis, greenfly.

aphone [a′fon], *a.* voiceless.

aphonie [afo′ni], *n.f.* aphony, loss of voice.

aphorisme [afo′rism], *n.m.* aphorism.

à-pic [a′pik], *n.m.* steep hill, cliff.

apiculteur [apikyl′tœ:r], *n.m.* bee-keeper.

apiculture [apikyl′ty:r], *n.f.* apiculture, bee-keeping.

apitoiement [apitwa′mã], *n.m.* pity, compassion.

apitoyant [apitwa′jã], *a.* piteous.

apitoyer [apitwa′je], *v.t.* (*conjug. like* EMPLOYER) to move to pity, to soften. **s′apitoyer**, *v.r.* to pity.

aplanir [apla′ni:r], *v.t.* to smooth, to level, to make even; (*fig.*) to level down *or* remove (*obstacles, difficulties etc.*). **s′aplanir**, *v.r.* to grow easy, smooth etc.

aplanissement [aplanis′mã], *n.m.* smoothing, levelling, making even; smoothness, evenness.

aplat [a′pla], *n.m.* flat tint.

aplatir [apla′ti:r], *v.t.* to flatten, to beat flat; (*fig.*) to vanquish, to silence, to floor. **s′aplatir**, *v.r.* to become flat, to be flattened; (*fig.*) to crouch, to cringe.

aplatissement [aplatis′mã], **aplatissage** [aplati′sa:ʒ], *n.m.* flattening, flatness; (*fig.*) humiliation.

aplomb [a′plõ], *n.m.* perpendicularity; equilibrium; (*fig.*) assurance, self-possession, steadiness, coolness; impudence, cheek; **d′aplomb**, perpendicularly, upright.

apocalypse [apoka′lips], *n.f.* Apocalypse, the Book of Revelation.

apocalyptique [apokalip′tik], *a.* apocalyptic, obscure.

apocryphe [apo′krif], *a.* apocryphal, spurious.

apode [a′pod], *a.* (*Zool.*) apodal, footless.

apogée [apo′ʒe], *n.m.* apogee; (*fig.*) acme, height, zenith.

apologétique [apoloʒe′tik], *a.* by way of apology, apologetic.

apologie [apolo′ʒi], *n.f.* apology, vindication, justification.

apologue [apo′log], *n.m.* apologue, fable.

apoplectique [apoplɛk′tik], *a.* and *n.* apoplectic.

apoplexie [apoplɛk′si], *n.f.* apoplexy.

apostasie [aposta′zi], *n.f.* apostasy.

apostat [apos′ta], *a.* and *n.m.* (*fem.* **-e**) apostate.

aposter [apos′te], *v.t.* to place in ambush, to station.

apostille [apos′ti:j], *n.f.* marginal note, postscript, footnote.

apostiller [aposti′je], *v.t.* to add a postscript *or* marginal recommendation.

apostolat [aposto′la], *n.m.* apostleship.

apostolique [aposto′lik], *a.* apostolic; papal.

apostrophe [apos′trof], *n.f.* (*Rhet. and Gram.*) apostrophe; address; (*fig.*) reprimand, attack.

apostropher [apɔstrɔ'fe], *v.t.* to apostrophize, to address; (*fig.*) to reprimand.
apothéose [apɔte'o:z], *n.f.* apotheosis.
apothicaire [apɔti'kɛ:r], *n.m.* apothecary.
apôtre [a'po:tr], *n.m.* apostle; (*fig.*) leader of a cause.
apparaître [apa'rɛ:tr], *v.i. irr.* (*conjug. like* CONNAÎTRF) to appear, to become visible; to be evident.
apparat [apa'ra], *n.m.* pomp, show, ostentation, parade.
apparaux [apa'ro], *n.m.* (*used only in pl.*) (*Naut.*) gear, tackle, outfit etc.
appareil [apa'rɛ:j], *n.m.* formal preparation; pomp, display; appearance, show; apparatus, appliances, machinery, paraphernalia; (*Surg.*) dressing; **appareil (photographique)**, camera; **qui est à l'appareil?** who is speaking?
appareillage [aparɛ'ja:ʒ], *n.m.* installation; (*Naut.*) act of getting under sail, weighing.
appareillement [aparɛj'mɑ̃], *n.m.* coupling, yoking; pairing (*for breeding*).
appareiller [aparɛ'je], *v.t.* to install equipment; to match; to pair (*animals*).—*v.i.* to get under way, to weigh anchor. **s'appareiller**, *v.r.* to pair (*of birds*).
appareilleur [aparɛ'jœ:r], *n.m.* (*Building*) stone dresser; **appareilleur à gaz**, gas fitter.
apparemment [apara'mɑ̃], *adv.* apparently.
apparence [apa'rɑ̃:s], *n.f.* appearance, look, semblance, likelihood, probability; **en apparence**, seemingly, apparently.
apparent [apa'rɑ̃], *a.* visible, prominent.
apparenté [aparɑ̃'te], *a.* related; **bien apparenté**, well connected.
apparentement [aparɑ̃t'mɑ̃], *n.m.* political alliance.
apparenter [aparɑ̃'te], *v.t.* to ally, to connect by marriage. **s'apparenter**, *v.r.* to ally oneself (*by marriage*).
appariement or **apparîment** [apari'mɑ̃], *n.m.* pairing, matching, coupling, mating; **appariement d'écoles**, school consolidation.
apparier [apa'rje], *v.t.* to assort by pairs, to pair (*birds etc.*), to match (*horses, gloves etc.*).
apparition [apari'sjɔ̃], *n.f.* apparition, sudden appearance; phantom, ghost; **apparition d'anges**, vision of angels.
appartement [apartə'mɑ̃], *n.m.* apartment.
appartenances [apartə'nɑ̃:s], *n.f.* (*used in pl.*) appurtenances.
appartenant [apartə'nɑ̃], *a.* belonging, appertaining.
appartenir [apartə'ni:r], *v.i. irr.* (*conjug. like* TENIR) to belong, to appertain; to relate, to pertain, to concern; to behoove, to be the right, privilege, duty etc. of (**à**); **il appartient,** (*v. impers.*) it is meet or fit; it behooves, concerns. **s'appartenir,** *v.r.* to be master of one's own actions, to be free.
appas [a'pɑ], *n.m. pl.* feminine charms, attractions.
appât [a'pɑ], *n.m.* bait; lure, allurement, enticement.
appâter [apɑ'te], *v.t.* to attract with a bait, to allure; to fatten (*fowls etc.*).
appauvrir [apo'vri:r], *v.t.* to impoverish. **s'appauvrir,** *v.r.* to grow poor, to become impoverished.
appauvrissement [apovris'mɑ̃], *n.m.* impoverishment.
appel [a'pɛl], *n.m.* appeal, call, summons; (*Mil.*) roll call, muster; summoning of conscripts to the colors; (*Law*) appeal to a higher court; **battre** or **sonner l'appel**, (*Mil.*) to sound the fall-in.
appelé [ap'le], *a.* called up.—*n.m.* soldier called up for service.
appeler [ap'le], *v.t.* (*see Verb Tables*) to call, to send for; to call over; to call up, to call together; to summon, to cite, to invoke, to call upon, to invite; to name, to term; to challenge.—*v.i.* to appeal (*to a higher court*). **s'appeler,** *v.r.* to be called, to call oneself.
appellation [apɛlɑ'sjɔ̃], *n.f.* calling; appelation; trade name; **appellation contrôlée**, registered trade name.
appendice [apɑ̃'dis], *n.m.* appendix, appendage, addition.
appendicite [apɑ̃di'sit], *n.f.* (*Path.*) appendicitis.
appendre [a'pɑ̃:dr], *v.t.* to hang up, to suspend; to attach.
appentis [apɑ̃'ti], *n.m.* shed, lean-to.
appesantir [apəzɑ̃'ti:r], *v.t.* to make heavy, to weigh down; (*fig.*) to make dull. **s'appesantir,** *v.r.* to grow heavy and dull, to be weighed down; to dwell on, to expatiate (*sur*).
appesantissement [apəzɑ̃tis'mɑ̃], *n.m.* heaviness, dullness.
appétissant [apeti'sɑ̃], *a.* desirable, appetizing, tempting; dainty, delicious.
appétit [ape'ti], *n.m.* appetite, relish; desire, sensuous craving (*usu. in pl.*); appetite (*for food*); (*fig.*) inclination, taste, stomach.
applaudir [aplo'di:r], *v.t., v.i.* to clap the hands, to applaud; to praise, to commend, to approve. **s'applaudir,** *v.r.* to boast, to glory (*in a thing*); to congratulate oneself (*de*); to rejoice (*de*).
applaudissement [aplodis'mɑ̃], *n.m.* (*usually pl.*) applause, public praise; cheering.
applicabilité [aplikabili'te], *n.f.* applicability, appositeness.
applicable [apli'kabl], *a.* applicable, apposite, relevant, suitable.
application [aplikɑ'sjɔ̃], *n.f.* application, applying; employment (*of a sum of money*); infliction (*of a penalty*); attention, care, diligence; appliqué lace.
applique [a'plik], *n.f.* ornamental accessories, candelabrum or bracket fixed to a wall.
appliqué [apli'ke], *a.* studious; **sciences appliquées**, applied sciences.
appliquer [apli'ke], *v.t.* to apply (**à**); to stick; to apply (*one's mind*); to adapt, to employ; to inflict, to impose (*a penalty etc.*). **s'appliquer,** *v.r.* to apply oneself, to work hard.
appoint [a'pwɛ̃], *n.m.* money paying off an account, balance; change; contribution; **faire l'appoint**, to pay the exact sum.
appointé [apwɛ̃'te], *a.* receiving a salary.
appointement [apwɛ̃t'mɑ̃], *n.m.* (*pl.*) salary (*of employee*); emoluments; (*Eccles.*) stipend.
appointer (1) [apwɛ̃'te], *v.t.* to give a salary to.
appointer (2) [apwɛ̃'te], *v.t.* to sharpen to a point, to point.
appontement [apɔ̃t'mɑ̃], *n.m.* (*Naut.*) bridge-

like structure for loading vessels; (*wooden*) wharf *or* pier.

apport [a'pɔːr], *n.m.* property brought by a husband or wife into the common stock; a shareholder's contribution to the assets of a company.

apporter [apor'te], *v.t.* to bring; to furnish, to supply; to bring to bear, to employ (*trouble, pains etc.*); to cause, to produce, to bring about.

apposer [apo'ze], *v.t.* to set, to put, to affix; to insert (*a clause etc.*).

apposition [apozi'sjɔ̃], *n.f.* setting, putting, affixing; (*Gram.*) apposition.

appréciable [apre'sjabl], *a.* appreciable, perceptible.

appréciateur [apresja'tœːr], *n.m.* (*fem.* **-trice**) valuer.

appréciatif [apresja'tif], *a.* (*fem.* **-ive**) denoting the value of; *état* or *devis appréciatif,* estimate.

appréciation [apresja'sjɔ̃], *n.f.* appreciation, valuation, estimation; rise in value.

apprécier [apre'sje], *v.t.* to value, to estimate, to appraise, to judge; to appreciate, to esteem.

appréhender [apreɑ̃'de], *v.t.* to arrest, to apprehend, to be apprehensive of, to fear, to dread.

appréhensible [apreɑ̃'sibl], *a.* apprehensible, comprehensible.

appréhensif [apreɑ̃'sif], *a.* (*fem.* **-ive**) apprehensive, timid.

appréhension [apreɑ̃'sjɔ̃], *n.f.* apprehension, fear, dread.

apprendre [a'prɑ̃ːdr], *v.t. irr.* (*conjug. like* PRENDRE) to learn; to hear of, to be informed of; to acquire (*a habit etc.*); to tell, to inform; to teach, to impart knowledge of (*a subject*).

apprenti [aprɑ̃'ti], *a.* apprenticed, articled.— *n.m.* (*fem.* **-e**) apprentice; (*fig.*) novice.

apprentissage [aprɑ̃ti'saːʒ], *n.m.* apprenticeship; trial, experiment.

apprêt [a'prɛ], *n.m.* preparation; cooking, dressing (*of food*); manner of preparing cloth, silk, lace etc.; the substance used in this process; (*pl.*) preparations.

apprêtage [aprɛ'taːʒ], *n.m.* dressing, application of the preliminary preparation to cloth, silk etc.

apprêté [aprɛ'te], *a.* studied, affected, stiff.

apprêter [aprɛ'te], *v.t.* to prepare, to get ready; to dress, to cook; to apply the *apprêts* [*q.v.*] to. **s'apprêter,** *v.r.* to prepare oneself, to get ready (*à*).

apprêteur [aprɛ'tœːr], *a. and n.m.* (*fem.* **-euse**) dresser, finisher.—*n.f.* (**-euse**) hat trimmer.

apprivoisé [aprivwa'ze], *a.* tame.

apprivoisement [aprivwaz'mɑ̃], *n.m.* taming.

apprivoiser [aprivwa'ze], *v.t.* to tame (*animals*); to win (*people*) over, to make sociable or tractable.

apprivoiseur [aprivwa'zœːr], *n.m.* (*fem.* **-euse**) tamer.

approbateur [aproba'tœːr], *a.* (*fem.* **-trice**) approving.

approbatif [aproba'tif], *a.* (*fem.* **-tive**) approbatory; *geste approbatif,* nod of approbation *or* approval.

approbation [aproba'sjɔ̃], *n.f.* approbation, consent, approval.

approbativement [aprobativ'mɑ̃], *adv.* approvingly.

approchable [apro'ʃabl], *a.* approachable, easy of access.

approchant [apro'ʃɑ̃], *a.* like, much the same, something like, approximate, bordering on.

approche [a'prɔʃ], *n.f.* approach, coming, advance, nearness; (*pl.*) approaches, access.

approcher [apro'ʃe], *v.t.* to bring, put *or* draw near *or* nearer; to come near *or* nearer; to approach.—*v.i.* to approach, to draw near, to come near; to be something like, to be nearly. **s'approcher,** *v.r.* to approach, to advance.

approfondir [aprofɔ̃'diːr], *v.t.* to deepen, to make deeper; to examine thoroughly, to investigate. **s'approfondir,** *v.r.* to become deeper.

approfondissement [aprofɔ̃dis'mɑ̃], *n.m.* deepening; fathoming; thorough investigation.

appropriation [aproprja'sjɔ̃], *n.f.* adaptation, assimilation; appropriation.

approprier [aroprj'e], *v.t.* to make appropriate, to accommodate, to adapt; to clean, to tidy etc.; to suit, to fit, (*style to subject etc.*). **s'approprier,** *v.r.* to appropriate a thing to oneself; to conform, to adapt oneself.

approuver [apru've], *v.t.* to sanction, to consent to, to ratify, to authorize; to approve, to approve of; to pass (*accounts*).

approvisionnement [aprovizjon'mɑ̃], *n.m.* victualling, supply, stock.

approvisionner [aprovizjo'ne], *v.t.* to supply with necessaries, to victual, to stock. **s'approvisionner,** *v.r.* to supply oneself; to lay in supplies.

approvisionneur [aprovizjo'nœːr], *n.m.* (*fem.* **-euse**) caterer, purveyor.

approximatif [aproksima'tif], *a.* (*fem.* **-tive**) approximate.

approximation [aproksima'sjɔ̃], *n.f.* approximation, rough estimate.

approximativement [aproksimativ'mɑ̃], *adv.* approximately.

appui [a'pɥi], *n.m.* support, prop, stay; any kind of mechanical support, *as* buttress, rail, handrail, sill (*of windows*); (*Mech.*) fulcrum; (*fig.*) corroboration; (*Gram.*) stress.

appui-main [apɥi'mɛ̃], *n.m.* (*pl.* **appuis-main**) painter's maulstick *or* hand rest.

appuyer [apɥi'je], *v.t.* (*conjug. like* EMPLOYER) to prop up, to support; to lean (*something against a wall etc.*); (*fig.*) to second, to back up, to uphold, to stand by, to reinforce.— *v.i.* to weigh upon, to lay stress on (*sur*); (*fig.*) to insist; *appuyer à droite,* to bear to the right. **s'appuyer,** *v.r.* to lean, to rest (*sur*); to rely upon, to depend (*sur*); to lay stress *or* a stress on, to dwell (*sur*).

âpre [ɑːpr], *a.* hard, rough, harsh, rugged; sharp, tart, sour; bitter, biting, bleak raw; grating (*of sound*); (*fig.*) austere; crabbed; violent, eager (*in pursuit of something*); *âpre à la curée,* out for the kill (*of animals*); (*fig.*) on the make (*of persons*).

âprement [ɑːprə'mɑ̃], *adv.* harshly, roughly; peevishly, crabbedly; violently, eagerly.

23

après [a'prɛ], *prep.* after, behind (*in time, order etc.*); next to; in pursuit of; **d'après,** after, according to.—*adv.* afterwards, later; **et après?** (*ellipt.*) what next? what then? so what?—*conj.* **après que,** after, when.

après-demain [aprɛd'mɛ̃], *adv.* the day after tomorrow.

après-midi [aprɛmi'di], *n.m.* or *f. inv.* afternoon.

âpreté [ɑprə'te], *n.f.* harshness, tartness, sharpness; roughness, ruggedness; (*fig.*) acrimony, asperity; eagerness; keenness; greediness.

à-propos [apro'po], *n.m.* aptness, suitability.

apside [ap'sid], *n.f.* (*Astron.*) apsis.

apte [apt], *a.* apt, fit, proper, suitable.

aptitude [apti'tyd], *n.f.* aptitude, natural disposition *or* capacity (*for*).

apurement [apyr'mɑ̃], *n.m.* verification *or* audit (*of accounts*).

apurer [apy're], *v.t.* to verify, to audit.

aquaplane [akwa'plan], *n.f.* surf-board; **faire de l'aquaplane,** to go surf-riding.

aquarelle [akwa'rɛl], *n.f.* painting in water-colors, aquarelle.

aquarelliste [akwarɛ'list], *n.m.* painter in water-colors.

aquarium [akwa'rjɔm], *n.m.* aquarium.

aquatique [akwa'tik], *a.* aquatic.

aqueduc [akə'dyk], *n.m.* aqueduct, conduit; (*Anat.*) duct.

aqueux [a'kø], *a.* (*fem.* **-euse**) aqueous, watery.

aquilin [aki'lɛ̃], *a.* aquiline, curved, hooked, Roman (*of noses etc.*).

aquilon [aki'lɔ̃], *n.m.* north wind, cold blast.

ara [a'ra], *n.m.* (*Orn.*) ara, macaw.

arabe [a'rab], *a.* Arabic, Arabian.—*n.m.* Arabic (*language*).—*n.* (**Arabe**) Arab, Arabian.

arabesque [ara'bɛsk], *n.f.* arabesque.

Arabie [ara'bi], **l'**, *f.* Arabia; **Arabie Séoudite,** Saudi Arabia.

arabique [ara'bik], *a.* Arabic, Arabian; **gomme arabique,** gum arabic.

arable [a'rabl], *a.* arable, tillable.

arachide [ara'ʃid], *n.f.* pea-nut, ground-nut.

araignée [arɛ'ne], *n.f.* spider; a spider-like implement etc.; (*Mil.*) a series of branching galleries in a mine; (*Naut.*) crowfoot; **toile d'araignée,** cobweb.

arasement [araz'mɑ̃], *n.m.* levelling, making even.

araser [ara'ze], *v.t.* to level (*a wall, a building etc.*).

aratoire [ara'twa:r], *a.* pertaining to farming.

arbalète [arba'lɛt], *n.f.* arbalest, cross-bow.

arbalétrier [arbale'trje], *n.m.* cross-bowman; (*Carp.*) principal rafters of a roof; strut (*of plane*); (*Orn.*) (black) swift.

arbitrage [arbi'tra:ʒ], *n.m.* arbitration; (*Banking*) arbitrage.

arbitraire [arbi'trɛ:r], *a.* arbitrary; absolute, despotic.

arbitrairement [arbitrɛr'mɑ̃], *adv.* arbitrarily; despotically.

arbitral [arbi'tral], *a.* (*m. pl.* **-aux**) by arbitration; composed of arbitrators (*of a tribunal etc.*).

arbitralement [arbitral'mɑ̃], *adv.* by arbitration.

arbitre [ar'bitr], *n.m.* arbitrator, umpire, referee; arbiter, disposer; will.

arbitrer [arbi'tre], *v.t.* to arbitrate, to judge, to settle (*a dispute etc.*), to referee *or* umpire (*a match*).

arborer [arbɔ're], *v.t.* to put up, to hoist, to unfurl (*a flag or as a flag*); (*fig.*) to put on.

arbre [arbr], *n.m.* tree; (*fig.*) anything resembling this (*e.g. a genealogical tree*); (*Mach.*) arbor, shaft, spindle, axle-tree; (*Naut.*) mast; (*Motor.*) **arbre moteur,** mainshaft; **arbre coudé,** crankshaft.

arbrisseau [arbri'so], *n.m.* (*pl.* **-eaux**) shrubby tree.

arbuste [ar'byst], *n.m.* bush, shrub.

arc [ark], *n.m.* bow, long-bow; (*Arch.*) arch; (*Geom., Phys. etc.*) arc.

arcade [ar'kad], *n.f.* arch-shaped opening; (*pl.*) arcade.

arcanes [ar'kan], *n.m. pl.* secrets, mysteries.

arc-boutant [arkbu'tɑ̃], *n.m.* (*pl.* **arcs-boutants**) (*fig.*) buttress, arched flying buttress; supporter, pillar.

arc-bouter [arkbu'te], *v.t.* to strengthen by a flying buttress; (*fig.*) to support, to buttress.

arceau [ar'so], *n.m.* (*pl.* **-eaux**) curved part of a vault *or* arch; anything shaped like an arch; (*croquet*) hoop.

arc-en-ciel [arkɑ̃'sjɛl], *n.m.* (*pl.* **arcs-en-ciel**) rainbow.

archaïque [arka'ik], *a.* archaic.

archaïsme [arka'ism], *n.m.* archaism, obsolete word etc.

archange [ar'kɑ̃:ʒ], *n.m.* archangel.

arche (1) [arʃ], *n.f.* arch (*of a bridge*).

arche (2) [arʃ], *n.f.* ark; **l'arche de Noé,** Noah's ark.

archéologie [arkeolo'ʒi], *n.f.* archaeology.

archéologique [arkeolo'ʒik], *a.* archaeological.

archéologue [arkeo'log], *n.m.* archaeologist.

archer [ar'ʃe], *n.m.* archer, bowman.

archet [ar'ʃɛ], *n.m.* (*Mus.*) bow, fiddle-stick.

archevêché [arʃəve'ʃe], *n.m.* archbishopric; archiepiscopal diocese; archbishop's residence.

archevêque [arʃə'vɛk], *n.m.* archbishop.

archi- [ar'ʃi or ar'ki], *pref.* arch-, archi-, chief; extremely *as in* **archiriche** etc.

archidiacre [arʃi'djakr], *n.m.* archdeacon.

archiduc [arʃi'dyk], *n.m.* archduke.

archiduché [arʃidy'ʃe], *n.m.* archdukedom, archduchy.

archiduchesse [arʃidy'ʃɛs], *n.f.* archduchess.

archiépiscopal [arʃiepisko'pal], *a.* (*m. pl.* **-aux**) archiepiscopal.

archière [ar'ʃjɛ:r], *n.f.* loophole.

Archimède [arʃi'mɛd], *m.* Archimedes.

archipel [arʃi'pɛl], *n.m.* archipelago.

archiprêtre [arʃi'prɛ:tr], *n.m.* arch-priest, high priest.

architecte [arʃi'tɛkt], *n.m.* architect; **architecte paysagiste,** landscape gardener.

architectural [arʃitɛkty'ral], *a.* (*m.pl.* **-aux**) architectural.

architecture [arʃitɛk'ty:r], *n.f.* architecture.

architrave [arʃi'tra:v], *n.f.* (*Arch.*) architrave.

archives [ar'ʃi:v], *n.f.* (*used only in pl.*) archives; state, civic *or* family records; record office, muniment room.

archiviste [arʃi'vist], *n.m.* archivist, keeper of records, registrar; filing clerk.

arçon [ar'sɔ̃], *n.m.* saddle-bow; bow-shaped tool used by hat makers etc.

arcot [ar'ko], *n.m.* dross, slag.

arctique [ark'tik], *a.* Arctic.

ardemment [arda'mɑ̃], *adv.* ardently.

ardent [ar'dɑ̃], *a.* burning, hot, fiery, scorching; (*fig.*) violent, intense; ardent, vehement, fervent, earnest, energetic, active; red, reddish (*of hair*); **charbons ardents**, live coals; **buisson ardent**, the burning bush.

ardeur [ar'dœːr], *n.f.* intense heat; ardor, intense activity, fervor, earnestness; fire, spirit, mettle.

ardoise [ar'dwaːz], *n.f.* slate; (*colloq.*) score, account.

ardoisé [ardwa'ze], *a.* slate-colored.

ardoiser [ardwa'ze], *v.t.* to cover (*a roof*) with slates.

ardoisier [ardwa'zje], *n.m.* owner of *or* workman in a slate quarry.

ardoisière [ardwa'zjeːr], *n.f.* slate quarry.

ardu [ar'dy], *a.* steep, abrupt; (*fig.*) arduous, difficult.

are [aːr], *n.m.* 100 sq. metres (*approx. 120 sq. yds.*).

arène [a'rɛːn], *n.f.* (*poet.*) sand; arena; (*fig.*) cock-pit, battle ground, theatre, scene; (*pl.*) the ancient Roman amphitheatres.

arénière [are'njɛːr], *n.f.* sand pit.

aréomètre [areɔ'mɛtr], *n.m.* areometer, hydrometer.

aréopage [areɔ'paːʒ], *n.m.* areopagus.

arête [a'rɛːt], *n.f.* fish-bone; awn *or* beard of wheat etc.; (*Geog. etc.*) ridge; **arête du nez**, bridge of the nose.

argent [ar'ʒɑ̃], *n.m.* silver; silver money; money, cash; (*fig.*) wealth, riches; (*Her.*) argent; **argent doré**, silver-gilt; **vif-argent**, quicksilver; **argent comptant**, ready money.

argentage [ARGENTURE].

argenté [arʒɑ̃'te], *a.* plated, silvered over; silvery.

argenter [arʒɑ̃'te], *v.t.* to silver over, to plate; to give the appearance of silver to.

argenterie [arʒɑ̃'tri], *n.f.* plate, silver plate.

argentin [arʒɑ̃'tɛ̃], *a.* silvery, argentine (*tint*); silver-toned (*ringing*); Argentinian, Argentine.—*n.m.* (**Argentin**, *fem.* **-ine** (1)) Argentinian (*person*).

Argentine (2) [arʒɑ̃'tin], l', *f.* Argentina, the Argentine.

argenture [arʒɑ̃'tyːr], *n.f.*, **argentage** [arʒɑ̃'taːʒ], *n.m.* silvering, silver-plating.

argile [ar'ʒil], *n.f.* clay, potter's clay, argil; **argile à porcelaine**, china clay; **argile réfractaire**, fire clay.

argileux [arʒi'lø], *a.* (*fem.* **-euse**) clayey, clayish.

argilière [arʒi'ljɛːr], *n.f.* clay pit.

argon [ar'gɔ̃], *n.m.* (*Chem.*) argon.

argonaute [argɔ'noːt], *n.m.* argonaut, nautilus.

argot [ar'go], *n.m.* slang, cant.

arguer [ar'gɥe], *v.t.* to infer, to deduce, to argue. (j'argue, nous arguions)

argument [argy'mɑ̃], *n.m.* argument, reasoning; proof, evidence; summary; theme, subject.

argumentateur [argymɑ̃ta'tœːr], *n.m.* (*fem.* **-trice**) habitual arguer *or* disputer.

argumentation, [argymɑ̃ta'sjɔ̃], *n.f.* argumentation, reasoning.

argumenter [argymɑ̃'te], *v.i.* to argue; to quibble.

argutie [argy'si], *n.f.* quibble, hair-splitting, cavil.

aria [a'rja], *n.m.* (*Mus.*) aria; (*pop.*) nuisance; fuss, bother.

arianisme [arja'nism], *n.m.* Arianism.

aride [a'rid], *a.* arid, dry; sterile.

aridité [aridi'te], *n.f.* aridity, dryness, barrenness, sterility.

arien [a'rjɛ̃] *a.* (*fem.* **a-ienne**) Arian.—*n.m.* (**Arien**, *fem.* **Arienne**) Arian (*person*).

aristocrate [aristɔ'krat], *a.* aristocratic.—*n.* aristocrat.

aristocratie [aristɔkra'si], *n.f.* aristocracy.

aristocratique [aristɔkra'tik], *a.* aristocratic.

aristocratiquement [aristɔkratik'mɑ̃], *adv.* aristocratically.

Aristote [aris'tɔt], *m.* Aristotle.

arithmétique [aritme'tik], *n.f.* arithmetic.—*a.* arithmetical.

arithmétiquement [aritmetik'mɑ̃], *adv.* arithmetically.

arlequin [arlə'kɛ̃], *n.m.* harlequin; (*fig.*) turn-coat; weathercock; **habit d'arlequin**, patchwork, motley.

arlequinade [arlɔki'nad], *n.f.* harlequinade.

armagnac [armɔ'nak], *n.m.* brandy (*made in Armagnac, S. of France*).

armateur [arma'tœːr], *n.m.* shipowner; captain of a privateer; privateer.

armature [arma'tyːr], *n.f.* armature, iron braces, stays, casing, gear etc.

arme [arm], *n.f.* arm, weapon; branch *or* arm (*of the service*); (*Her.*) armorial bearings; **arme blanche**, cold steel; **aux armes!** to arms! **un maître d'armes**, a fencing master.

armé [ar'me], *a.* armed, equipped; (*Her.*) armed (*with claws, horns, teeth etc.*); **béton armé**, reinforced concrete.

armée [ar'me], *n.f.* army; forces, troops, host; (*fig.*) body (*of officials etc.*); **l'Armée du Salut**, the Salvation Army.

armement [armə'mɑ̃], *n.m.* arming, raising of forces, warlike preparations; armament, equipment; (*Am.*) ordnance.

Arménie [arme'ni], l', *f.* Armenia.

arménien [arme'njɛ̃], *a.* (*fem.* **-enne**) Armenian.—*n.m.* Armenian (*language*); (**Arménien**, *fem.* **-enne**) Armenian (*person*).

armer [ar'me], *v.t.* to equip, to arm; (*Artill.*) to load, to mount (*guns etc.*); to cock (*a gun etc.*); (*fig.*) to fortify; to strengthen; (*Naut.*) to fit out. **s'armer**, *v.r.* to arm oneself, to take up arms; to protect oneself (*against something*).

armistice [armis'tis], *n.m.* armistice.

armoire [ar'mwaːr], *n.f.* closet, cupboard; clothes-press, wardrobe.

armoiries [armwa'ri], *n.f.* (*used only in pl.*) arms, armorial bearings.

armorial [armɔ'rjal], *a.* (*m. pl.* **-aux**) armorial, pertaining to heraldry.—*n.m.* armorial, book of heraldry.

armoricain [armɔri'kɛ̃], *a.* Armorican (*of Brittany*).

armorier [armɔ'rje], *v.t.* to put *or* paint a coat of arms upon, to blazon.

Armorique [armɔ'rik], l', *f.* Armorica.

armoriste [armɔ'rist], *n.m.* armorist, heraldic engraver.

armure [ar'my:r], *n.f.* armor, arms and armor; casing, wrapper; armature (*of a magnet, dynamo etc.*); (*Agric.*) tree-guard; (*Naut.*) fish (*of a mast, yard etc.*); (*fig.*) defence, protection.

armurerie [armyrə'ri], *n.f.* armory; manufacture of arms; arms factory.

armurier [army'rje], *n.m.* armorer, gunsmith.

arnica [arni'ka], *n.m.* (*Bot.*) arnica.

aromatique [arɔma'tik], *a.* aromatic, fragrant, spicy.

aromatiser [arɔmati'ze], *v.t.* to aromatize, to perfume, to flavor.

arome [a'ro:m], *n.m.* aroma, perfume, scent.

aronde [a'rɔ:d], *n.f.* (*Carp.*) dovetail, tenon.

arpège [ar'pɛ:ʒ], *n.m.* arpeggio.

arpéger [arpe'ʒe], *v.i.* (*conjug. like* ASSIÉGER) to play arpeggios.

arpent [ar'pɑ̃], *n.m.* acre (*French; about one and a half English or American acres*).

arpentage [arpɑ̃'ta:ʒ], *n.m.* land measurement; survey, measurement.

arpenter [arpɑ̃'te], *v.t.* to survey, to measure (*land*); (*fig.*) to stride up and down.

arpenteur [arpɑ̃'tœ:r], *n.m.* land surveyor.

arpon [ar'pɔ̃], *n.m.* ripsaw, crosscut saw.

arqué [ar'ke], *a.* bent, curved, arched (*of horses*).

arquebuse [arkə'by:z], *n.f.* arquebus.

arquebusier [arkəby'zje], *n.m.* arquebusier; gunsmith, armorer.

arquer [ar'ke], *v.t., v.i.* to bend, to curve, to arch.

arraché [ara'ʃe], *a.* uprooted.

arrachement [araʃ'mɑ̃], *n.m.* tearing up or away, pulling or rooting up or out; drawing, extraction.

arrache-pied (d') [daraʃ'pje], *adv. phr.* without interruption; *travailler d'arrache-pied*, to work with a will.

arracher [ara'ʃe], *v.t.* to pull or tear away, up or out; to extract, to uproot, to grub up; (*fig.*) to extort. **s'arracher**, *v.r.* to tear oneself away, to get away; to break away or off.

arraisonner [arɛzɔ'ne], *v.t.* (*Naut.*) to hail (*a ship*); to stop and examine (*a ship*).

arrangeant [arɑ̃'ʒɑ̃], *a.* accommodating, easy to deal with or get on with.

arrangement [arɑ̃ʒ'mɑ̃], *n.m.* arrangement, disposition, adjustment, setting in order; order, plan, method; agreement, settlement; (*pl.*) terms; measures; (*Math.*) permutations.

arranger [arɑ̃'ʒe], *v.t.* (*conjug. like* MANGER) to arrange, to put in order; to settle, to compromise, to compose (*a difference etc.*); to manage, to regulate; to make suitable; to fit up (*a house*); to trim up; *cela m'arrange*, that suits me; *comme vous voilà arrangé!* what a sight you look! **s'arranger**, *v.r.* to prepare oneself, to make arrangements (*pour*); to come to an agreement; to be satisfied (*de*); *arrangez-vous*, that is your lookout.

arrérages [are'ra:ʒ], *n.m.* (*used only in pl.*) arrears.

arrestation [arɛstɑ'sjɔ̃], *n.f.* arrest, apprehension; custody.

arrêt [a'rɛ], *n.m.* stoppage, stop, check, pause, halt; suspension, cessation; (*Law*) award, judgment; arrest, apprehension; (*fig.*) decree; (*pl.*) imprisonment; *arrêt fixe*, regular (bus) stop; *arrêt facultatif*, request stop; *arrêt de mort*, sentence of death; *chien d'arrêt*, setter, pointer; *robinet d'arrêt*, stopcock.

arrêté (1) [arɛ'te], *a.* stopped; decreed, agreed upon, resolved; arrested; fastened.

arrêté (2) [arɛ'te], *n.m.* departmental minute, order, decree, decision; *arrêté ministériel*, order in council.

arrêter [arɛ'te], *v.t.* to check, to stop the movement of, to throw out of gear; to delay, to detain, to hinder, to impede, to hold up; to arrest; to decide, to resolve; to settle (*an account*). **s'arrêter**, *v.r.* to stop, to pause, to hesitate; to remain, to loiter; to lag; to leave off; to be concluded, determined or resolved (*of bargains etc.*); to resolve upon; to dwell (*upon*), to insist (*sur*).

arrhes [ar], *n.f. pl.* earnest (*money*), deposit.

arrière [a'rjɛ:r], *adv.* behind (*of time and place*); backward; (*Naut.*) aft, abaft; *en arrière*, backward; behindhand, in arrears; at the back, at the rear (*of a train*); *en arrière de*, behind.—*int.* away!—*n.m.* back part, rear; (*Naut.*) stern (*of a vessel*); (*Ftb.*) back.

arriéré [arje're], *a.* in arrears; behindhand, backward, poorly developed.—*n.m.* arrears.

[In *pl.* of all the following compounds *arrière* is *inv.* The *n.* has its normal *pl.*]

arrière-boutique [arjɛrbu'tik], *n.f.* room at the back of a shop.

arrière-cour [arjɛr'ku:r], *n.f.* back yard.

arrière-cousin [arjɛrku'zɛ̃], *n.m.* (*fem.* **cousine**) distant cousin, cousin several times removed.

arrière-cuisine [arjɛrkɥi'zin], *n.f.* back kitchen, scullery.

arrière-garde [arjɛr'gard], *n.f.* rear guard.

arrière-goût [arjɛr'gu], *n.m.* after-taste.

arrière-grand-mère [arjɛrgrɑ̃'mɛ:r], *n.f.* (*pl.* **-grand-mères**) great-grandmother.

arrière-grand-père [arjɛrgrɑ̃'pɛ:r], *n.m.* (*pl.* **-grands-pères**) great-grandfather.

arrière-main [arjɛr'mɛ̃], *n.f.* back of the hand; (*Ten.*) backhand (stroke).—*n.m.* hindquarters (*of a horse*).

arrière-neveu [arjɛrnə've], *n.m.* (*pl.* **-eux**) grand-nephew.

arrière-nièce [arjɛr'njɛs], *n.f.* grand-niece.

arrière-pays [arjɛr'pei], *n.m. inv.* hinterland.

arrière-pensée [arjɛrpɑ̃'se], *n.f.* mental reservation, hidden motive, underlying design.

arrière-petite-fille [arjɛrpətit'fi:j], *n.f.* (*pl.* **-petites-filles**) great-granddaughter.

arrière-petit-fils [arjɛrpəti'fis], *n.m.* (*pl.* **-petits-fils**) great-grandson.

arrière-petits-enfants [arjɛrpətizɑ̃'fɑ̃], *n.m. pl.* great-grandchildren.

arrière-plan [arjɛr'plɑ̃], *n.m.* (*Paint., Cine.*) background.

arrière-point [arjɛr'pwɛ̃], *n.m.* back-stitch.

arrière-port [arjɛr'pɔ:r], *n.m.* inner harbor.

arriérer [arje're], v.t. (conjug. like CÉDER) to defer, to put off; to leave in arrears.
s'arriérer, v.r. to stay behind; to be in arrears.

arrière-saison [arjɛrsɛ'zɔ̃], n.f. end of autumn.

arrière-train [arjɛr'trɛ̃], n.m. hindquarters (of an animal).

arrimage [ari'ma:ʒ], n.m. (Naut.) stowage.

arrimer [ari'me], v.t. (Naut.) to stow (cargo etc.).

arrimeur [ari'mœ:r], n.m. stower, stevedore.

arrivée [ari've], n.f. arrival, moment of landing, coming etc., advent.

arriver [ari've], v.i. (conjug. with ÊTRE) to arrive, to come; to arrive at, to attain, to get to, to reach (à); to make one's way, to succeed; to happen, to occur, to take place; to veer; quoi qu'il arrive, come what may.

arrivisme [ari'vism], n.m. push, unscrupulous ambition.

arriviste [ari'vist], n.m. an unscrupulously ambitious person.

arrogamment [arɔga'mã], adv. arrogantly, haughtily; insolently.

arrogance [arɔ'gɑ̃:s], n.f. arrogance, haughtiness, superciliousness.

arrogant [arɔ'gɑ̃], a. arrogant, haughty, supercilious, overbearing.

arroger (s') [sarɔ'ʒe], v.r. (conjug. like MANGER) to assume or claim presumptuously.

arrondi [arɔ̃'di], a. rounded.—n.m. curve (of shoulder, face etc.).

arrondir [arɔ̃'di:r], v.t. to make round; to give a curved shape to, to round off; (fig.) to enlarge, to extend. s'arrondir, v.r. to grow or become round; to increase one's estate.

arrondissement [arɔ̃dis'mã], n.m. rounding, making round; roundness; division of a (French) department; (in Paris) one of the 20 wards.

arrosage [arɔ'za:ʒ], n.m. watering, sprinkling; irrigation.

arrosement [arɔz'mã], n.m. watering, sprinkling; irrigation.

arroser [arɔ'ze], v.t. to water, to wet, to sprinkle; to irrigate (land); to soak, to moisten; to flow through (of a river); to bathe (with tears).

arrosoir [arɔ'zwa:r], n.m. watering can.

arsenal [arsa'nal], n.m. arsenal; arsenal maritime, naval dockyard.

arsenic [arsə'nik], n.m. arsenic.

arsenical [arsəni'kal], a. (m.pl. -aux) arsenical.—n.m. pl. (-aux) arsenical compounds.

art [a:r], n.m. art; skill, dexterity, artifice; arts d'agrément, accomplishments; les beaux-arts, the fine arts.

artère [ar'tɛ:r], n.f. artery; (fig.) thoroughfare (in a town).

artériel [arte'rjɛl], a. (fem. -elle) arterial; tension artérielle, blood pressure.

artériole [arte'rjɔl], n.f. small artery.

artésien [arte'zjɛ̃], a. (fem. -enne) artesian; puits artésien, artesian well.—n.m. (Artésien, fem. -enne) inhabitant or native of Artois.

arthrite [ar'trit], n.f. arthritis.

arthritique [artri'tik], a. arthritic.

artichaut [arti'ʃo], n.m. globe artichoke.

article [ar'tikl], n.m. article (in all English senses); clause, provision (of a treaty etc.); item; commodity; (pl.) goods; article de fond, leading article, éditorial.

articulaire [artiky'lɛ:r], a. articular.

articulation [artikyla'sjɔ̃], n.f. articulation, pronunciation; (Bot., Anat.) joint, articulation; (Law) enumeration of facts.

articulé [artiky'le], a. articulate, clear, distinct; jointed, articulated.

articuler [artiky'le], v.t. to articulate, to put together by the joints; to pronounce distinctly; (Law) to enumerate. s'articuler, v.r. to be connected by joints.

artifice [arti'fis], n.m. artifice, contrivance, expedient; dodge, trick, stratagem; craft, ruse; un feu d'artifice, fireworks.

artificiel [artifi'sjɛl], a. (fem. -elle) artificial; fictitious, spurious.

artificiellement [artifisjɛl'mã], adv. artificially.

artificieusement [artifisjøz'mã], adv. cunningly, craftily, artfully, slyly.

artificieux [artifi'sjø], a. (fem. -euse) artful, cunning.

artillerie [artij'ri], n.f. artillery, ordnance.

artilleur [arti'jœ:r], n.m. artilleryman, gunner.

artimon [arti'mɔ̃], n.m. mizen-mast or -sail.

artisan [arti'zɑ̃], n.m. artisan, operative, mechanic; (fig.) author, architect, contriver, maker.

artiste [ar'tist], a. artistic (of persons).—n. artist; player, performer.

artistement [artista'mã], adv. in an artistic manner; skilfully, artistically.

artistique [artis'tik], a. artistic, pertaining to art.

as [ɑ:s], n.m. ace (at cards, dice); as (Roman coin and weight).

asbeste [az'bɛst], n.m. asbestos.

ascendance [asɑ̃'dɑ̃:s], n.f. ascent; ancestry.

ascendant [asɑ̃'dɑ̃], n.m. ascendant; ascendency, influence; (pl.) ancestors.—a. ascending, ascendant; going upward, rising.

ascenseur [asɑ̃'sœ:r], n.m. lift, (Am.) elevator.

ascension [asɑ̃'sjɔ̃], n.f. ascent, climbing, rising; upstroke (of machinery); (Jour de) l'Ascension, Ascension Day.

ascète [a'sɛt], n. ascetic.

ascétique [ase'tik], a. ascetic, rigid, severe.

ascétisme [ase'tism], n.m. asceticism.

asepsie [asɛp'si], n.f. (Med.) asepsis.

aseptique [asɛp'tik], a. and n.m. aseptic.

aseptiser [asɛpti'ze], v.t. to render aseptic.

asexué [asɛk'sɥe], **asexuel** [asɛk'sɥel] (fem. -elle), a. asexual.

asiatique [azja'tik], a. Asiatic; grippe asiatique, Asian flu.—n. (Asiatique) native of Asia.

Asie [a'zi], f. Asia; Asie Mineure, Asia Minor.

asile [a'zil], n.m. asylum, place of refuge, sanctuary, retreat, home (for the aged etc.); (fig.) protection, refuge; asile d'aliénés, mental hospital.

asine [a'zin], a. asinine.

aspect [as'pɛ], n.m. aspect, view, look; countenance; phase, bearing; point of view.

asperge [as'pɛrʒ], n.f. asparagus (head of).

aspergement [aspɛrʒə'mã], n.m. sprinkling.

asperger [aspɛr'ʒe], v.t. (conjug. like MANGER) to sprinkle.

aspergerie [aspɛrʒə'ri], **aspergière** [aspɛr'ʒjɛ:r], n.f. asparagus bed.

aspérité

aspérité [asperi'te], *n.f.* roughness, harshness; unevenness, ruggedness; (*fig.*) asperity.

aspersion [asper'sjɔ̃], *n.f.* aspersion, sprinkling.

aspersoir [asper'swa:r], *n.m.* holy water sprinkler; rose (*of a watering can*).

asphaltage [asfal'ta:ʒ], *n.m.* asphalting.

asphalte [as'falt], *n.m.* bitumen, asphalt.

asphalter [asfal'te], *v.t.* to asphalt.

asphodèle [asfo'dɛl], *n.m.* asphodel.

asphyxiant [asfik'sjɑ̃], *a.* asphyxiating, suffocating; **gaz asphyxiant**, poison gas.

asphyxie [asfik'si], *n.f.* (*Med.*) asphyxia, suffocation.

asphyxié [asfik'sje], *a.* asphyxiated.—*n.m.* (*fem.* -ée) person in a state of asphyxia.

asphyxier [asfik'sje], *v.t.* to asphyxiate, to suffocate. **s'asphyxier**, *v.r.* to commit suicide by suffocation.

aspic [as'pik], *n.m.* asp, viper; (*Bot.*) spike lavender; (*Cook.*) cold meat *or* fish, in jelly.

aspidistra [aspidis'tra], *n.m.* aspidistra.

aspirail [aspi'ra:j], *n.m.* (*pl.* -aux) airhole (*in a stove, oven etc.*).

aspirant (1) [aspi'rɑ̃], *a.* suction, sucking (*of pumps*).

aspirant (2) [aspi'rɑ̃], *n.m.* aspirant, candidate; suitor; officer-cadet; midshipman.

aspirateur [aspira'tœ:r], *n.m.* ventilator; suction pump; vacuum cleaner.

aspiration [aspira'sjɔ̃], *n.f.* aspiration (*of the letter* h *etc.*); inhaling, inspiration; (*of pumps*) exhaustion, suction; (*fig.*) yearning, aspiration; (*Motor.*) suction, intake.

aspirer [aspi're], *v.t.* to inspire, to inhale; to draw in, to suck in; (*Gram.*) to aspirate. —*v.i.* to aspire, to aim at.

aspirine [aspi'rin], *n.f.* aspirin.

assagir [asa'ʒi:r], *v.t.* to make wiser, to impart wisdom to. **s'assagir**, *v.r.* to become wiser; to settle down.

assaillant [asa'jɑ̃], *a.* attacking, aggressive.— *n.m.* (*fem.* -e) aggressor, assailant, besieger.

assaillir [asa'ji:r], *v.t. irr.* to assault, to assail; to worry, to molest, to beset.

assainir [ase'ni:r], *v.t.* to render healthy; (*fig.*) to cleanse, to purify morally etc. **s'assainir**, *v.r.* to become healthy.

assainissement [asenis'mɑ̃], *n.m.* purification, sanitation salubrity; drainage.

assaisonnement [asezɔn'mɑ̃], *n.m.* condiment, seasoning, dressing.

assaisonner [asezɔ'ne], *v.t.* to season, to dress, to give a relish to.

assassin [asa'sɛ̃], *a.* killing, murderous.— *n.m.* (*fem.* -e) assassin, murderer; ruffian.

assassinat [asasi'na], *n.m.* assassination, wilful murder, homicide.

assassiner [asasi'ne], *v.t.* to assassinate, to murder; (*fig.*) to bore; to tease, to importune.

assaut [a'so], *n.m.* assault, onset, attack.

assèchement [asɛʃ'mɑ̃], *n.m.* drying up, drainage.

assécher [ase'ʃe], *v.t.* (*conjug. like* CÉDER) to drain (*a mine, pond etc.*).—*v.i.* to become dry, to be drained.

assemblage [asɑ̃'bla:ʒ], *n.m.* assemblage, collection, union, combination; (*Print.*) gathering; (*Carp.*) joint, scarf; **chaine d'assemblage**, assembly line.

assemblée [asɑ̃'ble], *n.f.* assembly, meeting, company, party; convocation, congregation (*of churches*); meet (*of hunters*).

assembler [asɑ̃'ble], *v.t.* to assemble, to call together; to collect, to gather; to bring together; (*Print.*) to gather; (*Carp.*) to trim, to scarf. **s'assembler**, *v.r.* to assemble, to meet, to congregate.

asséner [ase'ne], *v.t.* (*conjug. like* CÉDER) to strike *or* deal (*a blow*).

assentiment [asɑ̃ti'mɑ̃], *n.m.* assent, agreement.

asseoir [a'swa:r], *v.t. irr.* to seat, to put on a seat, to set, to place, to fix, to establish; to pitch (*a camp etc.*). **s'asseoir**, *v.r.* to sit, to sit down, to take a seat, to settle, to perch.

assermenté [asɛrmɑ̃'te], *a.* sworn in, attested.

assermenter [asɛrmɑ̃'te], *v.t.* to swear in.

assertif [asɛr'tif], *a.* (*fem.* -tive) assertive.

assertion [asɛr'sjɔ̃], *n.f.* assertion, affirmation.

asservir [asɛr'vi:r], *v.t.* to enslave, to reduce to servitude; to subdue, to conquer. **s'asservir**, *v.r.* to obey, to submit (*à*).

asservissant [asɛrvi'sɑ̃], *a.* enslaving, subjecting, coercive.

asservissement [asɛrvis'mɑ̃], *n.m.* bondage, servitude, slavery, subjection.

assez [a'se], *adv.* enough, sufficiently; tolerably, passably, rather.

assidu [asi'dy], *a.* assiduous, diligent, attentive; punctual; regular, constant.

assiduité [asidɥi'te], *n.f.* assiduity, application, diligence, attention.

assidûment [asidy'mɑ̃], *adv.* assiduously, diligently, constantly; punctually.

assiéger [asje'ʒe], *v.t.* (*see Verb Tables*) to besiege; to lay siege to; to surround; to importune.

assiette [a'sjɛt], *n.f.* plate; plateful; attitude *or* posture (*in sitting etc.*), pose, situation, bearing, basis; seat (*in the saddle*); position, site; tone, state, disposition (*of the mind etc.*).

assiettée [asjɛ'te], *n.f.* plateful.

assignation [asiɲa'sjɔ̃], *n.f.* order to pay, transfer; (*Law*) summons, subpoena, writ; appointment, rendezvous, assignation.

assigner [asi'ɲe], *v.t.* to assign (*property in payment of a debt etc.*); to cite, to summon, to subpoena; to appoint, to make (*a rendezvous etc.*).

assimilation [asimila'sjɔ̃], *n.f.* assimilation.

assimiler [asimi'le], *v.t.* to make like; to liken, to compare, to assimilate.

assis [a'si], *a.* seated, sitting; situated; established.

assise [a'si:z], *n.f.* course (*of stones etc.*), foundation, basis; (*Geol.*) stratum; (*Mining*) measure (*of coal*); (*pl.*) assizes; **cour d'assises**, assize court.

assistance [asis'tɑ̃:s], *n.f.* audience, company, bystanders; congregation (*in a church*); assistance, help, aid; relief.

assistant [asis'tɑ̃], *n.m.* (*fem.* -ante) assistant (*priest, teacher etc.*); person present, bystander, witness etc.; **assistant(e) social(e)**, social welfare worker.

assisté [asis'te], *a.* receiving public assistance. —*n.m.* (*fem.* -ée) person in receipt of relief.

28

assister [asis'te], *v.t.* to assist, to help, to succor.— *v.i.* to be at, to be present (*à*), to look on, to be a witness (*à*).

association [asɔsja'sjɔ̃], *n.f.* association; union; partnership, fellowship, society, order.

associé [asɔ'sje], *a.* associated, admitted (*as a member*).—*n.m.* (*fem.* **-ée**) associate, fellow, member, partner.

associer [asɔ'sje], *v.t.* to associate, to take into partnership etc.; to divide *or* share something with someone; to link together, to connect (*ideas etc.*). **s'associer**, *v.r.* to enter into partnership, to associate oneself, to combine (*with*).

assoiffé [aswa'fe], *a.* thirsty; eager (*for*).

assolement [asɔl'mɑ̃], *n.m.* (*Agric.*) rotation (*of crops*).

assoler [asɔ'le], *v.t.* to vary *or* rotate (*crops*).

assombrir [asɔ̃'briːr], *v.t.* to darken, to throw a gloom over, to cloud. **s'assombrir**, *v.r.* to become dark *or* gloomy; to darken (*of the brow*).

assombrissement [asɔ̃bris'mɑ̃], *n.m.* darkening, gloom.

assommant [asɔ'mɑ̃], *a.* wearisome, tiresome, boring.

assommer [asɔ'me], *v.t.* to beat to death, to knock on the head; to overpower; to overwhelm, to stun; (*fig.*) to bore, to importune, to oppress.

assommeur [asɔ'mœːr], *n.m.* (*fem.* **-euse**) slaughterer (*of oxen etc.*).

assommoir [asɔ'mwaːr], *n.m.* poleaxe; bludgeon.

Assomption [asɔ̃p'sjɔ̃], *n.f.* (*Eccles.*) Assumption of the Blessed Virgin (August 15).

assomption [asɔ̃p'sjɔ̃], *n.f.* assumption.

assonance [asɔ'nɑ̃ːs], *n.f.* assonance.

assonant [asɔ'nɑ̃], *a.* assonant.

assorti [asɔr'ti], *a.* assorted, matched, paired.

assortiment [asɔrti'mɑ̃], *n.m.* suitability, match; assortment, set.

assortir [asɔr'tiːr], *v.t.* to assort, to match, to pair; to stock, to furnish (*with things that go together or match*).—*v.i.* to match, to suit, to go well together. **s'assortir**, *v.r.* to match, to agree, to go well together.

assortissant [asɔrti'sɑ̃], *a.* suitable, matching, going well (*with something else*).

assoupi [asu'pi], *a.* dozing; dormant (*volcano*).

assoupir [asu'piːr], *v.t.* to make drowsy, sleepy, heavy *or* dull; (*fig.*) to assuage, to allay, to deaden. **s'assoupir**, *v.r.* to grow drowsy, sleepy, dull *or* heavy; to doze; (*fig.*) to be assuaged, to be appeased, to be stilled.

assoupissant [asupi'sɑ̃], *a.* making drowsy *or* sleepy, soporific.

assoupissement [asupis'mɑ̃], *n.m.* drowsiness, sleepiness, heaviness; (*fig.*) carelessness, sloth; (*Med.*) coma.

assouplir [asu'pliːr], *v.t.* to make supple, flexible *or* tractable; to break in (*a horse*). **s'assouplir**, *v.r.* to become supple, tractable *or* manageable.

assouplissement [asupis'mɑ̃], *n.m.* suppleness, tractability, docility.

assourdir [asur'diːr], *v.t.* to deafen, to stun; to muffle.

assourdissant [asurdi'sɑ̃], *a.* deafening.

assourdissement [asurdis'mɑ̃], *n.m.* deafening, muffling, deadening; deafening noise; temporary deafness.

assouvir [asu'viːr], *v.t.* to glut, to satiate, to surfeit; to gratify; to cloy. **s'assouvir**. *v.r,* to be satiated, gratified *or* cloyed.

assouvissement [asuvis'mɑ̃], *n.m.* glutting, satiating.

assujettir [asyʒe'tiːr], *v.t.* to subdue, to subjugate; to compel; to fix, to fasten. **s'assujettir**, *v.r.* to subject oneself, to submit.

assujettissant [asyʒeti'sɑ̃], *a.* binding, constraining, fettering, restrictive.

assujettissement [asyʒetis'mɑ̃], *n.m.* subjection, subjugation; obligation, fixing.

assumer [asy'me], *v.t.* to take upon oneself, to assume.

assurance [asy'rɑ̃ːs], *n.f.* confidence, security, assurance; certainty, conviction; warrant, pledge; insurance, underwriting; (*fig.*) boldness, **(les) assurances sociales**, the French equivalent of social security.

assuré [asy're], *a.* assured, confident; sure, secure, positive, certain; trusty; insured.— *n.m.* (*fem.* **-ée**) insured person.

assurément [asyre'mɑ̃], *adv.* assuredly, confidently; surely, undoubtedly; certainly.

assurer [asy're], *v.t.* to fix securely, to fasten, to steady; (*Naut.* and *Mount.*) to belay; to assure, to guarantee; to insure; to underwrite; to assert, to affirm. **s'assurer**, *v.r.* to make sure of, to ascertain.

assureur [asy'rœːr], *n.m.* underwriter, insurer, assurer.

Assyrie [asi'ri], *f.* Assyria.

assyrien [asi'rjɛ̃], *a.* (*fem.* **-enne**) Assyrian.— *n.m.* (**Assyrien**, *fem.* **-enne**) Assyrian (*person*).

aster [as'tɛːr], *n.m.* (*Bot.*) aster.

astérie [aste'ri], *n.f.* starfish.

astérisque [aste'risk], *n.m.* asterisk.

astéroïde [asterɔ'id], *n.m.* asteroid.

asthmatique [asma'tik], *a.* asthmatic.

asthme [asm], *n.m.* asthma.

asticot [asti'ko], *n.m.* gentle (*bait for fishing*); maggot.

asticoter [astikɔ'te], *v.t.* (*colloq.*) to tease, to worry.

astigmate [astig'mat], *a.* astigmatic.

astigmatisme [astigma'tism], *n.m.* astigmatism.

astiquer [asti'ke], *v.t.* to polish, to furbish, to glaze.

astracan *or* **astrakan** [astra'kɑ̃], *n.m.* astrakhan, Persian lamb (*fur*).

astral [as'tral], *a.* (*m. pl.* **-aux**) astral.

astre [astr], *n.m.* star; (*fig.*) celebrity.

astreindre [as'trɛ̃ːdr], *v.t. irr.* (*conjug. like* CRAINDRE) to oblige, to compel, to subject. **s'astreindre**, *v.r.* to confine oneself, to tie oneself down (*à*).

astreinte [as'trɛ̃ːt], *n.f.* (*Law*) compulsion: fine for delay in the performance of a contract.

astringence [astrɛ̃'ʒɑ̃ːs], *n.f.* astringency.

astringent [astrɛ̃'ʒɑ̃], *a.* and *n.m.* astringent.

astroïde [astrɔ'id], *a.* star-shaped.

astrologie [astrɔlɔ'ʒi], *n.f.* astrology.

astrologique [astrɔlɔ'ʒik], *a.* astrological.

astrologue [astrɔ'lɔg], *n.m.* astrologer.

astronaute [astrɔ'noːt], *n.m.* astronaut.

astronautique [astrɔnɔ'tik], *n.f.* astronautics.

astronome [astrɔ'nɔm], *n.m.* astronomer.

astronomie [astronɔ'mi], *n.f.* astronomy.
astronomique [astronɔ'mik], *a.* astronomical, astronomic.
astrophysique [astrofi'zik], *a.* astrophysical. —*n.f.* astrophysics.
astuce [as'tys], *n.f.* craft, guile; cunning.
astucieusement [astysjøz'mã], *adv.* craftily, cunningly.
astucieux [asty'sjø], *a.* (*fem.* **-euse**) crafty, wily.
Asturies [asty'ri], **les,** *f. pl.* the Asturias.
asymétrie [asime'tri], *n.f.* asymmetry.
asymétrique [asime'trik], *a.* asymmetrical.
atelier [atə'lje], *n.m.* workshop, studio, atelier; (*collect.*) gang of workmen etc.; (*Freemasonry*) lodge, lodge meeting.
atermoyer [atɛrmwa'je], *v.t.* (*conjug. like* EMPLOYER) to put off, to delay (*a payment*). —*v.i.* (*fig.*) to put off, to make shifts. **s'atermoyer,** *v.r.* to compound with one's creditors.
athée [a'te], *a.* atheistic.—*n.* atheist.
athéisme [ate'ism], *n.m.* atheism.
Athènes [a'tɛːn], *f.* Athens.
athénien [ate'njɛ̃], *a.* (*fem.* **-enne**) Athenian. —*n.m.* (**Athénien,** *fem.* **-enne**) Athenian (*person*).
athlète [at'lɛt], *n.m.* athlete.
athlétique [atle'tik], *a.* athletic.
athlétisme [atle'tism], *n.m.* athleticism; athletics.
Atlantide [atlɑ̃'tid], *f.* Atlantis.
atlantique [atlɑ̃'tik], *a.* Atlantic.—*n.m.* (**L'Atlantique**) the Atlantic (Ocean).
atlas [a'tlɑːs], *n.m.* atlas.
atmosphère [atmos'fɛːr], *n.f.* atmosphere.
atmosphérique [atmosfe'rik], *a.* atmospheric; *pression atmosphérique,* atmospheric pressure.
atoll [a'tɔl], *n.m.* atoll.
atome [a'toːm], *n.m.* atom; corpuscle.
atomicité [atomisi'te], *n.f.* (*Chem.*) atomicity, valency.
atomique [atɔ'mik], *a.* atomic(al); *commissariat à l'énergie atomique,* atomic energy authority.
atomiser [atomi'ze], *v.t.* to pulverize.
atomiste [atɔ'mist], *n.m.* atomist.
atomistique [atomis'tik], *a.* atomic(al).
atone [a'tɔn], *a.* atonic, debilitated, dull; lacklustre, expressionless (*of eyes*); (*Gram.*) atonic, unaccentuated.
atonie [atɔ'ni], *n.f.* atony, debility.
atonique [atɔ'nik], *a.* atonic.
atours [a'tuːr], *n.m.* (*used only in pl.*) woman's attire, dress, ornament.
atout [a'tu], *n.m.* trump; trump card.
atoxique [atɔk'sik], *a.* non-poisonous.
atrabilaire [atrabi'lɛːr], *a.* morose, peevish.
âtre [ɑːtr], *n.m.* hearth; fireplace.
atroce [a'trɔs], *a.* atrocious, cruel, excruciating; heinous, odious, dreadful.
atrocement [atrɔs'mã], *adv.* atrociously, cruelly, outrageously.
atrocité [atrɔsi'te], *n.f.* atrociousness, heinousness; atrocity, cruelty.
atrophie [atrɔ'fi], *n.f.* (*Path.*) atrophy.
atrophié [atrɔ'fje], *a.* atrophied, wasted, withered, stunted.
atrophier [atrɔ'fje], *v.t.* to cause to waste *or* wither. **s'atrophier,** *v.r.* to waste away, to atrophy.

atrophique [atrɔ'fik], *a.* atrophic.
attablé [ata'ble], *a.* seated at table.
attabler (s') [sata'ble], *v.r.* to sit down to *or* take one's place at table.
attachant [ata'ʃã], *a.* engaging, winning, attractive.
attache [a'taʃ], *n.f.* bond, cord, leash, strap; (*fig.*) attachment, affection for.
attaché [ata'ʃe], *n.m.* attaché (*of an embassy*).
attachement [ataʃ'mã], *n.m.* attachment; affection, liaison; eagerness, zeal.
attacher [ata'ʃe], *v.t.* to fasten, to tie, to attach, to fix; (*fig.*) to apply, to affix; to connect, to associate; to engage, to endear.— **s'attacher,** *v.r.* to take hold, to attach *or* fasten oneself; to cling, to adhere; to have an affection for; to apply oneself to.
attaquable [ata'kabl], *a.* assailable; of doubtful validity.
attaquant [ata'kã], *n.m.* assailant.
attaque [a'tak], *n.f.* attack, assault, aggression; fit, stroke.
attaquer [ata'ke], *v.t.* to attack, to assail, to assault; to seize suddenly (*of illness etc.*); to criticize; *attaquer en justice,* to sue for. **s'attaquer,** *v.r.* to make *or* conduct an attack (*à*), to set upon.
attaqueur [ata'kœːr], *n.m.* attacker.
attardé [atar'de], *a.* late, behindhand; mentally retarded (*child*).
attarder [atar'de], *v.t.* to make late, to delay. **s'attarder,** *v.r.* to be belated; to loiter, to linger.
atteindre [a'tɛ̃ːdr], *v.t. irr.* (*conjug. like* CRAINDRE) to reach, to hit, to attain; to arrive at; to overtake, to come up to.—*v.i.* to reach with difficulty, to attain (*à*); *atteindre à la perfection,* to attain to perfection.
atteint [a'tɛ̃], *a.* hit, struck; attacked, seized, affected; reached.
atteinte [a'tɛ̃ːt], *n.f.* reach, blow, stroke, touch; attack, fit, seizure (*of disease*); injury, damage, harm, wrong.
attelage [at'laːʒ], *n.m.* harnessing, yoking; team, yoke; set, pair; carriage, horses; (*Rail.*) coupling.
atteler [at'le], *v.t.* (*conjug. like* APPELER) to put horses etc. (*to*); to harness, to yoke; (*fig.*) to subjugate. **s'atteler,** *v.r.* to settle down to (*à*); (*fig.*) to apply oneself to, to hitch one's wagon to.
attelle [a'tɛl], *n.f.* hame; (*Surg.*) splint.
attenant [at'nã], *a.* contiguous, adjoining, next door to, close by (*à*).
attendre [a'tɑ̃ːdr], *v.t.* to await, to wait for, to stay for; to look forward to, to expect; to look for, to count upon. **s'attendre,** *v.r.* to rely upon, to count upon, to trust (*à*); to expect, to look forward (*à*).
attendrir [atɑ̃'driːr], *v.t.* to make tender, to soften; to touch, to move. **s'attendrir,** *v.r.* to grow tender; to be moved, to melt, to pity, to relent.
attendrissant [atɑ̃dri'sã], *a.* moving, touching.
attendrissement [atɑ̃dris'mã], *n.m.* compassion, pity; tears, sensibility; tenderness.
attendu [atɑ̃'dy], *prep.* considering, on account of, in consideration of.—*conj. attendu que,* seeing that, as, whereas, since.
attenir [at'niːr], *v.i. irr.* (*conjug. like* TENIR) to adjoin, to be contiguous (*à*); to be related.

attentat [atɑ̃'ta], *n.m.* attempt at crime; crime, attempt; outrage, violation.
attente [a'tɑ̃:t], *n.f.* waiting, expectation; hope; *salle d'attente*, waiting-room.
attenter [atɑ̃'te], *v.i.* to make a criminal attempt.
attentif [atɑ̃'tif], *a.* (*fem.* **-tive**) attentive, heedful; considerate.
attention [atɑ̃'sjɔ̃], *n.f.* attention, notice; heed, care, vigilance; regard, respect, consideration; *attention!* look out! stand by!
attentionné [atɑ̃sjɔ'ne], *a.* attentive, considerate.
attentivement [atɑ̃tiv'mɑ̃], *adv.* attentively, carefully.
atténuant [ate'nɥɑ̃], *a.* mitigating; (*Law*) extenuating.
atténuation [atenɥa'sjɔ̃], *n.f.* attenuation, extenuation, mitigation.
atténué [ate'nɥe], *a.* attenuated, wasted, emaciated.
atténuer [ate'nɥe], *v.t.* to make smaller, thinner, feebler etc.; to attenuate; to extenuate, to mitigate.
atterrant [ate'rɑ̃], *a.* astounding, startling, overwhelming.
atterrement [ater'mɑ̃], *n.m.* overthrow; prostration, amazement.
atterré [ate're], *a.* horror-stricken, dumbfounded.
atterrer [ate're], *v.t.* to overwhelm; to astound.
atterrir [ate'ri:r], *v.i.* to land, to make land.
atterrissage [ateri'sa:ʒ], *n.m.* landing; *terrain d'atterrissage*, landing-ground.
atterrissement [ateris'mɑ̃], *n.m.* alluvion, accretion, alluvium.
attestation [atɛsta'sjɔ̃], *n.f.* attestation, evidence; certificate, voucher, testimonial; *attestation sous serment*, affidavit.
attester [atɛs'te], *v.t.* to attest, to certify, to avouch, to witness, to testify.
attiédir [atje'di:r], *v.t.* to cool, to make lukewarm; to take the chill off. **s'attiédir**, *v.r.* to grow cool or lukewarm; to cool off.
attiédissement [atjedis'mɑ̃], *n.m.* lukewarmness, coolness; abatement.
attifage [ati'fa:ʒ], **attifement** [atif'mɑ̃], *n.m.* get-up, rig-out.
attifer [ati'fe] (*always in a bad sense*), *v.t.* to dress up. **s'attifer**, *v.r.* to dress up, to rig oneself out.
attique [a'tik], *a.* Attic; (*fig.*) witty, urbane.—*n.m.* (*Arch.*) attic.
attirail [ati'ra:j], *n.m.* (*collect.*) apparatus, implements, utensils, gear, tackle; baggage, paraphernalia; show, pomp.
attirance [ati'rɑ̃:s], *n.f.* attraction (*vers*).
attirant [ati'rɑ̃], *a.* attractive, alluring, enticing, engaging.
attirer [ati're], *v.t.* to attract, to draw; to win or gain over, to lure, to wheedle, to entice; to occasion. **s'attirer**, *v.r.* to draw to or down upon one, to bring upon one; to incur, to win.
attisage [ati'za:ʒ], **attisement** [atiz'mɑ̃], *n.m.* the act of stirring up, poking (*a fire*), fanning (*flame*).
(C) **attisée** [ati'ze], *n.f.* a good fire; armful (*of stove wood*).
attiser [ati'ze], *v.t.* to make or stir up (*a fire*); to poke; (*fig.*) to incense, to stir up.

attisoir [ati'zwa:r], **attisonnoir** [atizɔ'nwa:r], *n.m.* poker (*especially in foundries*), fire rake.
attitré [ati'tre], *a.* recognized, appointed, regular, ordinary; hired.
attitude [ati'tyd], *n.f.* attitude; (*Paint.*) posture; (*fig.*) attitude of mind etc.
attouchement [atuʃ'mɑ̃], *n.m.* touch, contact.
attracteur [atrak'tœ:r], *a.* (*fem.* **-trice**) attractile.
attractif [atrak'tif], *a.* (*fem.* **-tive**) attractive.
attraction [atrak'sjɔ̃], *n.f.* attraction; (*pl.*) cabaret show.
attractivement [atraktiv'mɑ̃], *adv.* attractively.
attrait [a'trɛ], *n.m.* allurement, attraction, charm; inclination, bent; (*pl.*) attractions, charms; bait.
attrape [a'trap], *n.f.* trap, gin; (*fig.*) trick, take- in, sell, hoax; (*Naut.*) hawser.
attrape-mouche or **attrape-mouches** [atrap'muʃ], *n.m. inv.* flycatcher.
attrape-nigaud [atrapni'go], *n.m.* (*pl.* **attrape-nigauds**) booby trap.
attraper [atra'pe], *v.t.* to catch; to entrap, to ensnare; to take in, to trick, to bamboozle; to imitate; (*fam.*) to scold; to hit; to overtake, to catch up; to get accidentally (*a cold etc.*); *attrape!* take that! **s'attraper**, *v.r.* to hit (*against*); to be caught (*in*); to get hold of; to seize, to stick (*à*).
attrapeur [atra'pœ:r], *n.m.* (*fem.* **-euse**) deceiver, cheat, trickster.
attrayant [atrɛ'jɑ̃], *a.* attractive, winning, engaging, charming.
attribuable [atri'bɥabl], *a.* attributable, due to.
attribuer [atri'bɥe], *v.t.* to assign, to confer; to attribute, to ascribe, to impute (*a thing to someone*). **s'attribuer**, *v.r.* to assume, to take upon oneself, to claim.
attribut [atri'by], *n.m.* attribute, prerogative; special symbol or emblem; (*Gram.*) predicate.
attributif [atriby'tif], *a.* (*fem.* **-tive**) (*Gram.*) attributive; predicative; (*Law*) conferring a right.
attribution [atriby'sjɔ̃], *n.f.* attribution, conferment, awarding (*of a grant*); (*usu. in pl.*) privilege, prerogative (*of a person*); province, department, jurisdiction.
attristant [atris'tɑ̃], *a.* saddening, sorrowful, melancholy, grievous.
attrister [atris'te], *v.t.* to grieve, to sadden, to trouble. **s'attrister**, *v.r.* to be sad, to become sorrowful.
attrition [atri'sjɔ̃], *n.f.* attrition, friction.
attroupement [atrup'mɑ̃], *n.m.* riotous assemblage, mob, crowd, gathering of people.
attrouper [atru'pe], *v.t.* to assemble, to gather together in troops or a mob. **s'attrouper**, *v.r.* to flock together, to gather in crowds.
au [o], (*contraction of* à LE) to the.
aubade [o'bad], *n.f.* aubade, dawn song; (*iron.*) hot reception.
aubaine [o'bɛn], *n.f.* (*Law*) escheat; windfall, piece of good luck.
aube [o:b], *n.f.* the dawn; alb (*priest's vestment*).

aubépine [obe′pin], *n.f.* hawthorn, white-thorn, may.

aubère [o′bɛːr], *a.* red roan (*horse*).

auberge [o′bɛrʒ], *n.f.* inn, public-house, tavern; *auberge de (la) jeunesse*, youth hostel.

aubergine [ober′ʒin], *n.f.* aubergine, egg-plant.

aubergiste [ober′ʒist], *n.* innkeeper, publican, landlord, host.

aubour [o′buːr], *n.m.* laburnum; guelder-rose.

aucun [o′kœ̃], *a.* and *pron.* none, no one, not one; not any; anyone; any.

aucunement [okyn′mɑ̃], *adv.* in no wise, not at all, not in the least; at all.

audace [o′das], *n.f.* audacity, daring, bold-ness; impudence, insolence; *payer d′audace*, to brazen it out.

audacieusement [odasjøz′mɑ̃], *adv.* audaci-ously, daringly, boldly; rashly; impudently.

audacieux [oda′sjø], *a.* (*fem.* -**euse**) audaci-ous, bold, daring; impudent, presumptuous.

au deçà, au dedans, au dehors, au delà [DEÇÀ, DEDANS, DEHORS, DELÀ].

au-dessous [od′su], *prep.* below.

au-dessus [od′sy], *prep.* above.

au-devant [od′vɑ̃], *prep.* towards; *aller au-devant d′un danger*, to anticipate danger.

audibilité [odibili′te], *n.f.* audibility.

audible [o′dibl], *a.* audible.

audience [o′djɑ̃ːs], *n.f.* audience, hearing; reception; sitting, session, court, tribunal.

audiomètre [odjo′mɛtr], **audimètre** [odi′metr], *n.m.* audiometer.

audiophone [odjo′fɔn], **audiphone** [odi′fɔn], *n.m.* audiphone.

audio-visuel [odjovi′zɥɛl], *a.* (*fem.* -**elle**) audio-visual; *moyens audio-visuels*, audio-visual aids.

auditeur [odi′tœːr], *n.m.* (*fem.* -**trice**) hearer, listener.

auditif [odi′tif], *a.* (*fem.* -**tive**) auditory.

audition [odi′sjɔ̃], *n.f.* hearing; (*Law*) hearing (*of a case etc.*); audition (*of a singer etc.*).

auditionner [odisjɔ′ne], *v.t.* to audition.

auditoire [odi′twaːr], *n.m.* auditory; congre-gation (*in church*), audience (*theatre etc.*).

auditrice [odi′tris], [AUDITEUR].

auge [o:ʒ], *n.f.* trough (*for drinking etc.*); (*plasterer′s*) hod; (*Elec.*) cell.

auget [o′ʒɛ], *n.m.* small trough; seed box.

augmentation [ɔgmɑ̃ta′sjɔ̃], *n.f.* augmenta-tion, increase, addition, rise (*in salary*).

augmenter [ɔgmɑ̃′te], *v.t.* to augment, to increase; to enlarge; to raise the salary of.—*v.i.* to augment, to increase, to grow, to rise (*in price*), to multiply. **s′augmenter**, *v.r.* to increase, to enlarge, to improve.

augural [ogy′ral], *a.* (*m. pl.* -**aux**) augural.

augure [o′gyːr], *n.m.* augur, soothsayer; augury, omen, sign; *de mauvais augure*, ominous, portentous.

augurer [ogy′re], *v.t.* to augur; (*fig.*) to con-jecture, to surmise.

Auguste [o′gyst], *m.* Augustus.

auguste [o′gyst], *a.* august, majestic.

augustin [ogys′tɛ̃], *n.m.* (*fem.* -**ine**) Augustin-ian or Austin friar or (*f.*) nun.

aujourd′hui [oʒur′dɥi], *adv.* today, during this day; nowadays, now, at present.

aulnaie [AUNAIE].

aulne [AUNE].

aulx [o:], [AIL].

aumône [o′mɔn], *n.f.* alms, alms-giving; (*fig.*) charity, favor.

aumônerie [omon′ri], *n.f.* chaplaincy.

aumônier [omo′nje], *n.m.* (*Eccles.*) almoner, chaplain; *aumônier militaire*, army chap-lain, padre.

aunaie or **aulnaie** [o′nɛ], *n.f.* grove of alders.

aune (1) or **aulne** [o:n], *n.m.* alder tree.

aune (2) [o:n], *n.f.* ell; (*fig.*) measure, standard.

aunée [o′ne], *n.f.* length of an ell.

auparavant [opara′vɑ̃], *adv.* before, formerly previously.

auprès [o′prɛ], *adv.* near, by, close by.—*prep. auprès de*, near to, close to; in com-parison with; in the service of; in the opinion of.

auquel [o′kɛl], *contraction* of À LEQUEL (*fem.* **à laquelle**, *pl.* **auxquels, auxquelles**) to whom, to which.

auréole [ore′ɔl], *n.f.* aureole, halo, nimbus; (*fig.*) glory, prestige.

auréoler [oreo′le], *v.t.* to crown with a halo.

auriculaire [oriky′lɛːr], *a.* auricular.—*n.m.* the little finger.

auricule [ori′kyl], *n.f.* lower lobe of the ear, auricle; (*Bot.*) auricula.

auriculiste [oriky′list], *n.m.* ear specialist.

aurifère [ori′fɛːr], *a.* auriferous.

auriste [o′rist], *n.m.* ear specialist.

aurore [o′rɔːr], *n.f.* dawn, morn, daybreak; (*fig.*) promise, beginning, the East; (*Astron.*) aurora.

auscultation [oskylta′sjɔ̃], *n.f.* (*Med.*) auscul-tation.

ausculter [oskyl′te], *v.t.* to sound a patient.

auspice [os′pis], *n.m.* auspice, omen, presage; (*pl.*) protection, patronage.

aussi [o′si], *adv.* also, likewise, too, besides; as; so.—*conj.* and so, accordingly, therefore, consequently; but then.

aussière [o′sjɛːr], *n.f.* (*Naut.*) hawser.

aussitôt [osi′to], *adv.* immediately, forthwith. —*conj. aussitôt que*, as soon as.

austère [os′tɛːr], *a.* austere, severe, stern.

austèrement [ostɛr′mɑ̃], *adv.* austerely.

austérité [osteri′te], *n.f.* austerity; severity; strictness.

austral [os′tral], *a.* (*m. pl.* -**als** or -**aux**) austral, southern.

Australasie [ostrala′zi], **l′**, *f.* Australasia.

australasien [ostrala′zjɛ̃], *a.* (*fem.* -**enne**) Australasian.

Australie [ostra′li], **l′**, *f.* Australia.

australien [ostra′ljɛ̃], *a.* (*fem.* -**enne**) Austra-lian.—*n.m.* (**Australien**, *fem.* -**enne**) Aus-tralian (*person*).

autant [o′tɑ̃], *adv.* as much, so much, as many, so many; *autant de têtes, autant d′avis*, there are as many opinions as there are men; *autant que*, as much as, as many as, as far as, in the same way as; *d′autant*, in the same proportion; *d′autant mieux* or *d′autant plus*, the more, so much the more.—*conj. d′autant que*, seeing that, since, more especially as.

autel [o′tɛl], *n.m.* altar; (*fig.*) ministry, Church, religious life.

auteur [o'tœːr], *n.m.* author, creator, maker; writer (*of a book etc.*); perpetrator; achiever; contriver, framer; composer, sculptor; informant, authority; *droit d'auteur*, royalty.

authenticité [otütisi'te], *n.f.* authenticity, genuineness.

authentique [otɑ̃'tik], *a.* authenticated, genuine, incontestable, positive.

authentiquement [otɑ̃tik'mɑ̃], *adv.* authentically.

authentiquer [otɑ̃ti'ke], *v.t.* to authenticate; (*Law*) to make legal and binding.

auto [o'to], *n.f. abbr.* [AUTOMOBILE].

auto-allumage [otoaly'maːʒ], *n.m.* knocking (*of a car*).

autobiographe [otobjɔ'graf], *n.m.* autobiographer.

autobiographie [otobjɔgra'fi], *n.f.* autobiography.

autobiographique [otobjɔgra'fik], *a.* autobiographical.

autobus [oto'bys], *n.m.* bus.

autocar [oto'kaːr], *n.m.* motor coach.

autochenille [oto'ʃniːj], *n.f.* caterpillar tractor; half-track vehicle.

autoclave [oto'klaːv], *a.* and *n.m.* vacuum pan, sterilizer; *marmite autoclave*, autoclave, digester; pressure cooker.

autocopie [otokɔ'pi], *n.f.* cyclostyling.

autocopier [otokɔ'pje], *v.t.* to cyclostyle.

autocopiste [otokɔ'pist], *n.m.* duplicator, cyclostyle.

autocrate [oto'krat], *n.m.* autocrat.

autocratie [otokra'si], *n.f.* autocracy.

autocratique [otokra'tik], *a.* autocratic.

autocratiquement [otokratik'mɑ̃], *adv.* autocratically.

autocritique [otokri'tik], *n.f.* self-criticism.

auto-cuiseur [otokɥi'zœːr], *n.m.* pressure cooker.

autodidacte [otodi'dakt], *n.* self-taught person.

autodrome [oto'droːm], *n.m.* race-track for motor cars.

auto-école [otoe'kɔl], *n.f.* school of motoring.

autogare [oto'gaːr], *n.f.* bus or coach station.

autographe [oto'graf], *a.* autographic.—*n.m.* autograph.

autographie [otogra'fi], *n.f.* autography.

autographier [otogra'fje], *v.t.* to autograph.

autogyre [oto'ʒiːr], *n.m.* autogyro.

automate [oto'mat], *n.m.* automaton, robot.

automation [otoma'sjɔ̃], *n.f.* automation.

automatique [otoma'tik], *a.* automatic; *distributeur automatique*, (penny-in-the-) slot machine; *machine à vente automatique*, vending machine.—*n.m.* *l'Automatique*, automatic telephone.

automatiquement [otomatik'mɑ̃], *adv.* automatically.

automatisme [otoma'tism], *n.m.* automatism, purely mechanical movement.

automitrailleuse [otomitra'jøːz], *n.f.* light armored car.

automnal [oto'nal], *a.* (*m. pl.* **-aux**) autumnal.

automne [o'tɔn], *n.m.* or *f.* autumn.

automobile [otomɔ'bil], *a.* self-moving, self-propelling; *canot automobile*, motor-boat.—*n.f.* motor car; *salon de l'automobile*, motor show.

automobilisme [otomɔbi'lism], *n.m.* automobilism, motoring.

automobiliste [otomɔbi'list], *n.* motorist.

automoteur [otomɔ'tœːr], *a.* (*fem.* **-trice**) self-acting, self-moving, self-propelling. (*C*) **auto-neige** [oto'nɛːʒ], *n.f.* snowmobile.

autonome [oto'nɔm], *a.* autonomous.

autonomie [otonɔ'mi], *n.f.* autonomy, self-government; cruising range.

autonomiste [otono'mist], *n.m.* autonomist.

autoplastie [otoplas'ti], *n.f.* (*Surg.*) plastic surgery.

auto-portrait [otopɔr'trɛ], *n.m.* self-portrait.

auto-propulsé [otoprɔpyl'se], *a.* self-propelled.

auto-propulsion [otoprɔpyl'sjɔ̃], *n.f.* self-propulsion.

autopsie [otop'si], *n.f.* autopsy; post-mortem examination.

autorail [oto'raːj], *n.m.* rail car.

autorisation [otoriza'sjɔ̃], *n.f.* authorization; authority, warrant; written consent or permission, license (*of a preacher*).

autoriser [otori'ze], *v.t.* to authorize, to empower, to commission; to license, to warrant, to permit, to sanction. **s'autoriser**, *v.r.* to have, get or assume authority; to act on the authority (*of*), to be warranted by (*de*).

autoritaire [otori'tɛːr], *a.* and *n.* authoritative, commanding, arbitrary (person).

autoritairement [otoritɛr'mɑ̃], *adv.* authoritatively.

autorité [otori'te], *n.f.* authority, legal or legitimate power; an authority; (*fig.*) control.

autoroute [oto'rut], *n.f.* motorway; (*Am.*) speedway.

auto-stop [oto'stɔp], *n.m.* hitch-hiking; *faire de l'auto-stop*, to hitch-hike.

autostrade [oto'strad], *n.f.* special road for motor cars, motorway.

autosuggestion [otosygʒɛs'tjɔ̃], *n.f.* autosuggestion.

autour (1) [o'tuːr], *adv.* about, round about.—*prep. phr. autour de*, about, round, around.

autour (2) [o'tuːr], *n.m.* (*Orn.*) goshawk.

autre [oːtr], *a.* other; second; another different, distinct (*but of the same kind*).—*pron. indef.* another person, someone else; (*pl.*) the others, the rest.

autrefois [otrə'fwa], *adv.* formerly, in former times; of old; *d'autrefois*, former, bygone; *des mœurs d'autrefois*, bygone customs.

autrement [otrə'mɑ̃], *adv.* otherwise, after another manner; else; or else; *autrement dit*, in other words.

Autriche [o'triʃ], **l'**, *f.* Austria.

autrichien [otri'ʃjɛ̃], *a.* (*fem.* **-enne**) Austrian. —*n.m.* (**Autrichien**, *fem.* **-enne**) Austrian (*person*).

autruche [o'tryʃ], *n.f.* ostrich.

autrucherie [otryʃ'ri], *n.f.* ostrich farm.

autrui [o'trɥi], *pron. indef. inv.* others, other people, one's or our neighbors.

auvent [o'vɑ̃], *n.m.* weather-board, porch roof; *auvent de capot*, hood louver.

aux [o], *pl.* [AU].

auxiliaire [oksi'ljɛːr], *a.* auxiliary, aiding, subsidiary.—*n.* auxiliary; helper, assistant.

auxquels [o'kɛl], *pl.* (*fem.* **-elles**) [AUQUEL].

avachi [ava'ʃi], *a.* out of shape, worn out; (*fam.*) flabby, floppy, downcast (*of a person*).

avachir (s') [sava'ʃiːr], v.r. to flag; to grow fat and flabby; to get out of shape or down at heel.
avachissement [avaʃis'mɑ̃], n.m. flabbiness; lack of energy.
aval (1) [a'val], n.m. (pl. **avals**) guarantee, endorsement.
aval (2) [a'val], n.m. down stream; **en aval de**, below.
avalaison [avalɛ'zɔ̃], **avalasse** [ava'las], n.f. sudden flood, spate; (Naut.) a long-continued wind from the sea.
avalanche [ava'lɑ̃ːʃ], n.f. avalanche.
avalasse [AVALAISON].
avalement [aval'mɑ̃], n.m. descent, lowering, letting down; swallowing.
avaler [ava'le], v.t. to swallow, to swallow down; to drink, to gulp down; to let down, to lower (things into a cellar); (fig.) to endure, to pocket (an affront); to believe.—v.i. to go down (a river etc. with the stream).
avaliser [avali'ze], v.t. to guarantee, to endorse [AVAL (1)].
avance [a'vɑ̃ːs], n.f. part of a building etc. projecting forwards; advance; start, distance in advance; payment of money in advance; (fig., pl.) attentions, first steps in an acquaintanceship.
avancé [avɑ̃'se], a. advanced, forward, early; late (of the hour); over-ripe, tainted, high; liberal, progressive (of opinions etc.); paid in advance; put forward, enunciated.
avancement [avɑ̃s'mɑ̃], n.m. projection; progress, advancement; preferment, promotion, rise.
avancer [avɑ̃'se], v.t. (conjug. like COMMENCER) to move, bring, put or hold forward, to advance; to pay beforehand or in advance; to assert, to bring forward, to urge; to promote, to give promotion to; to advantage, to profit; (fig.) to bring nearer, to hasten, to forward; to put on (a clock),—v.i. to advance, to proceed, to keep on; to project, to jut out; to make progress, to thrive, to get on, to gain ground; to go too fast; **l'horloge avance**, the clock is fast. **s'avancer**, v.r. to advance, to go on, to move forward; to get on, to improve; to get promoted, to be successful; to grow old; to project.
avanie [ava'ni], n.f. insult, affront; snub.
avant [a'vɑ̃], prep. before, in advance of (of time and order); **avant J.-C.**, B.C.—adv. before, previously; forward, in front; farther in advance.—conj. **avant que**, before; **en avant!** forward!—n.m. front; prow, head, bow (of a ship); (Ftb.) forward.
avantage [avɑ̃'taːʒ], n.m. advantage, benefit, profit, superiority, whip-hand; (Ten.) advantage, vantage.
avantager [avɑ̃ta'ʒe], v.t. (conjug. like MANGER) to advantage, to give an advantage to; to favor. **s'avantager**, v.r. to take advantage.
avantageusement [avɑ̃taʒøz'mɑ̃], adv. advantageously, to advantage; usefully, favorably.
avantageux [avɑ̃ta'ʒø], a. (fem. **-euse**) advantageous, profitable, favorable; conceited, presumptuous; (of dress) becoming.

[In pl. of the following compounds **avant** is inv. The n. has its normal pl.]

avant-bassin [avɑ̃ba'sɛ̃], n.m. outer dock.
avant-bras [avɑ̃'brɑ], n.m. inv. forearm.
avant-centre [avɑ̃'sɑ̃ːtr], n.m. (Ftb.) centre-forward.
avant-corps [avɑ̃'kɔːr], n.m. inv. (Arch.) forepart (of a building).
avant-cour [avɑ̃'kuːr], n.f. fore-court.
avant-coureur [avɑ̃ku'rœːr], a. going in front, preceding, presaging.—n.m. forerunner, precursor, harbinger.
avant-courrier [avɑ̃ku'rje], n.m. (fem. **-ière**) (fig.) herald, forerunner, harbinger.
avant-dernier [avɑ̃dɛr'nje], a. and n.m. (fem. **-ière**) the last but one.
avant-garde [avɑ̃'gard], n.f. vanguard, van.
avant-goût [avɑ̃'gu], n.m. foretaste; earnest; anticipation.
avant-guerre [avɑ̃'gɛːr], n.m. the pre-war period.
avant-hier [avɑ̃'tjɛːr], adv. and n.m. the day before yesterday.
avant-main [avɑ̃'mɛ̃], n.m. flat of the hand; forehand (of a horse); (Ten.) forehand (stroke); (Cards) lead.
avant-port [avɑ̃'pɔːr], n.m. outer harbor, tide dock.
avant-poste [avɑ̃'pɔst], n.m. (Mil.) advanced post, outpost; (fig.) outer defence.
avant-première [avɑ̃prə'mjɛːr], n.f. dress rehearsal; (Cine.) preview.
avant-projet [avɑ̃prɔ'ʒɛ], n.m. rough draft.
avant-propos [avɑ̃prɔ'po], n.m. inv. preface, preamble, introduction, foreword.
avant-scène [avɑ̃'sɛːn], n.f. front of the stage (between curtain and orchestra), proscenium.
avant-toit [avɑ̃'twa], n.m. eaves.
avant-train [avɑ̃'trɛ̃], n.m. fore-carriage, limber.
avant-veille [avɑ̃'vɛːj], n.f. two days before.
avare [a'vaːr], a. avaricious, miserly, covetous, stingy, close-fisted.—n.m. miser, niggard.
avarement [avar'mɑ̃], adv. stingily.
avariable [ava'rjɑbl], a. perishable, damageable.
avarice [ava'ris], n.f. avarice, greed, covetousness; niggardliness, stinginess.
avaricieusement [avarisjøz'mɑ̃], adv. avariciously.
avaricieux [avari'sjø], a. (fem. **-euse**) avaricious, covetous, stingy.
avarie [ava'ri], n.f. damage (to a ship or cargo); deterioration.
avarié [ava'rje], a. damaged, spoiled, deteriorated.
avarier [ava'rje], v.t. to damage, to spoil. **s'avarier**, v.r. to become damaged.
avec [a'vɛk], prep. with, at the same time as, along or together with; by means of, by; regarding; against, in spite of; **avec ça!** (colloq.) nonsense!
aveline [a'vlin], n.f. filbert, Kentish cob.
avelinier [avli'nje], n.m. filbert tree, hazel tree.
aven [a'vɛ̃], n.m. pothole, swallow, chasm (in mountain limestone).
avenant [av'nɑ̃], a. personable, prepossessing, comely, pleasing, taking.—adv. phr. **à l'avenant**, in keeping, in the same proportions, of a piece.—n.m. additional clause (to an insurance policy); rider (to a verdict); codicil (to a treaty).

avènement [avɛn'mɑ̃], *n.m.* coming, advent; accession, succession (*to a throne etc.*).

avenir [av'ni:r], *n.m.* future, future ages; posterity; (*fig.*) prospects; *à l'avenir*, in future, henceforth.

Avent [a'vɑ̃], *n.m.* (*Ch.*) Advent.

aventure [avɑ̃'ty:r], *n.f.* surprising *or* unexpected event *or* experience, chance, accident, luck; adventure, daring enterprise, hazardous exploit; love affair *or* intrigue; *à l'aventure*, at random; *d'aventure* or *par aventure*, by chance, perchance.

aventurer [avɑ̃ty're], *v.t.* to venture, to hazard, to risk. **s'aventurer**, *v.r.* to venture, to take one's chance, to take risks.

aventureux [avɑ̃ty'rø], *a.* (*fem.* **-euse**) venturesome, adventurous; left to chance.

aventurier [avɑ̃ty'rje], *n.m.* (*fem.* **-ière**) adventurer, adventuress.

avenue [av'ny], *n.f.* approach; avenue.

avéré [ave're], *a.* authenticated, established by evidence.

avérer [ave're], *v.t.* (*conjug. like* CÉDER) to verify, to confirm, to establish. **s'avérer**, *v.r.* (*used only in inf. and p.p.*) to appear, to be distinctly, to turn out to be, to prove.

avers [a'vɛ:r], *n.m.* obverse (*of coins etc.*).

averse [a'vɛrs], *n.f.* sudden and heavy shower of rain, downpour; (*fig.*) flood (*of talk etc.*).

aversion [avɛr'sjɔ̃], *n.f.* aversion, dislike, detestation.

averti [avɛr'ti], *a.* warned, informed; wide awake; well-informed, experienced.

avertir [avɛr'ti:r], *v.t.* to inform, to acquaint with, to give notice, to warn, to admonish (*de*).

avertissement [avɛrtis'mɑ̃], *n.m.* information, notification, advice, warning, caution; *avertissement au lecteur*, foreword (*of a book*).

avertisseur [avɛrti'sœ:r], *n.m.* look-out man; (*Theat.*) callboy; call bell, hooter; *avertisseur d'incendie*, fire-alarm.

aveu [a'vø], *n.m.* (*pl.* **-eux**) admission, avowal, confession; approbation, consent; *homme sans aveu*, vagrant, vagabond.

aveuglant [avœ'glɑ̃], *a.* blinding, dazzling; (*fig.*) distracting, misleading.

aveugle [a'vœgl], *a.* blind, sightless; blinded by passion etc., deluded.—*n.* blind person.

aveuglement [avœglə'mɑ̃], *n.m.* blindness; (*fig.*) infatuation, delusion.

aveuglément [avœgle'mɑ̃], *adv.* blindly, rashly; implicitly.

aveugle-né [avœglə'ne], *a.* and *n.m.* (*fem.* **-née**, *pl.* **aveugles-nés**) blind from birth.

aveugler [avœ'gle], *v.t.* to blind, to make blind; (*fig.*) to dazzle; to delude. **s'aveugler**, *v.r.* to shut one's eyes (*to*); (*fig.*) to be blinded, to be infatuated.

aveuglette [avœ'glɛt], *n.f.* (*only used in*) *à l'aveuglette*, blindly; *aller à l'aveuglette*, to go groping along, to go blindly *or* rashly; (*Av.*) *voler à l'aveuglette*, to fly blind.

aveulir [avø'li:r], *v.t.* to render weak, to enfeeble, to enervate. **s'aveulir**, *v.r.* to sink into sloth.

aveulissant [avøli'sɑ̃], *a.* enfeebling, enervating.

aveulissement [avølis'mɑ̃], *n.m.* enfeeblement, enervation.

aviateur [avja'tœ:r], *n.m.* (*fem.* **-trice**) aviator; air-man, air-woman; flyer.

aviation [avja'sjɔ̃], *n.f.* aviation; *terrain d'aviation*, flying ground, airfield.

aviculteur [avikyl'tœ:r], *n.m.* one who raises birds *or* poultry; bird fancier.

aviculture [avikyl'ty:r], *n.f.* bird raising; poultry farming.

avide [a'vid], *a.* greedy, voracious, rapacious; eager for, grasping.

avidement [avid'mɑ̃], *adv.* greedily, voraciously; eagerly.

avidité [avidi'te], *n.f.* avidity, greediness; eagerness.

avilir [avi'li:r], *v.t.* to debase, to depreciate, to disparage; to lower; to degrade, to disgrace. **s'avilir**, *v.r.* to degrade oneself, to stoop to (*doing something*).

avilissant [avili'sɑ̃], *a.* debasing, degrading, humiliating.

avilissement [avilis'mɑ̃], *n.m.* debasement, degradation; depreciation, disparagement.

avilisseur [avili'sœ:r], *a.* (*fem.* **-euse**) debasing, degrading.—*n.m.* (*fem.* **-euse**) one who debases, disparages *or* degrades.

aviné [avi'ne], *a.* drunk, unsteady (*from drink*); wine-soaked (*of a cask*).

aviner [avi'ne], *v.t.* to soak *or* fill with wine. **s'aviner**, *v.r.* to get drunk.

avion [a'vjɔ̃], *n.m.* airplane, aircraft; *avion de bombardement*, bomber; *avion de chasse*, fighter; *avion de ligne*, airliner; *avion à réaction*, jet-plane; *avion-fusée*, rocket-plane; *avion-taxi*, charter-plane; *par avion*, by air, by air mail.

aviron [avi'rɔ̃], *n.m.* oar; (*Spt.*) rowing.

avis [a'vi], *n.m.* opinion, way of thinking, judgment; vote, motion; advice, counsel; information, notice, warning, caution, intelligence; *à mon avis*, in my opinion; *j'ai changé d'avis*, I have changed my mind; *avis au public*, notice.

avisé [avi'ze], *a.* shrewd, clear-sighted, wary, circumspect, prudent.

aviser [avi'ze], *v.t.* to perceive, to espy; to inform, to apprise; (*Comm.*) to advise by letter.—*v.i.* to consider, to think (*about*), to look (*to*). **s'aviser**, *v.r.* to think (*of*), to be minded (*to*); to venture to do.

avivage [avi'va:ʒ], *n.m.* brightening, reviving (*of colors*).

aviver [avi've], *v.t.* to revive, to brighten; to sharpen the edges of, to polish, to burnish; to irritate, to exacerbate (*a wound, resentment etc.*). **s'aviver**, *v.r.* to revive.

avocat (1) [avɔ'ka], *n.m.* (*fem.* **-e**) barrister, advocate, counsel; (*fig.*) pleader, intercessor, champion.

avocat (2) [avɔ'ka], *n.m.* avocado, alligator pear.

avoine [a'vwan], *n.f.* oats.

avoir [a'vwa:r], *v.t.* *irr.* to have, to possess; to experience, to feel (*pain, hunger etc.*); to obtain, to get, to buy etc.; to be aged (*so many years*); to have on, to wear; to ail; *avoir à*, to have to, to be under obligation to (*do etc.*); *y avoir* (*impers.*), to be; *avoir faim*, to be hungry; *combien y a-t-il de Paris à Londres?* how far is it from Paris to London? *il a quarante ans*, he is forty; *il n'y a pas de quoi*, don't mention it, no offence taken; *il y a deux mois que je* *suis ici,* I have been here two months; *il est arrivé il y a trois semaines,* he arrived three weeks ago; *j'ai à vous parler,* I have something to tell you; *qu'avez-vous donc?* what's the matter? *quel âge avez-vous?* how old are you? *qu'est-ce que vous avez?* what is the matter with you? *la pièce a cinq mètres de large,* the room is fifteen feet wide.—*n.m.* possessions, property, what one is worth.

avoisinant [avwazi'nɑ̃], *a.* neighboring, adjoining, close by.

avoisiner [avwazi'ne], *v.t.* to border upon, to be contiguous to.

avortement [avɔrtə'mɑ̃], *n.m.* abortion, miscarriage; failure.

avorter [avɔr'te], *v.i.* to miscarry, to have a miscarriage; to fail to develop, ripen etc. (*of plants, fruit etc.*); to prove abortive, to fail.

avorton [avɔr'tɔ̃], *n.m.* abortion; abortive child; (*fig.*) a paltry *or* miserable person *or* thing, a miserable specimen.

avoué [a'vwe], *n.m.* attorney, solicitor; *une étude d'avoué,* a solicitor's office.

avouer [a'vwe], *v.t.* to own, to acknowledge, to confess; to approve; to recognize as one's own, to avow.

avril [a'vril], *n.m.* April.

avunculaire [avɔ̃ky'lɛːr], *a.* avuncular.

axe [aks], *n.m.* axis; axle, axle-tree, spindle, trunnion; (*Bot., Geol., Anat. etc.*) axis; (*fig.*) central support *or* main axis of a system of ideas etc.; (*Polit.*) the Nazi-Fascist Axis.

axiomatique [aksjɔma'tik], *a.* axiomatic.

axiome [ak'sjoːm], *n.m.* axiom; (*fig.*) an accepted proposition, truism.

ayant [ɛ'jɑ̃], *pres. p.* [AVOIR].

ayant cause [ɛjɑ̃'koːz], *n.m.* (*pl.* **ayants cause**) (*Law*) trustee, executor, assign.

ayant droit [ɛjɑ̃'drwa], *n.m.* (*pl.* **ayants droit**) beneficiary, rightful claimant.

azalée [aza'le], *n.f.* azalea.

azotate [azɔ'tat], *n.m.* nitrate.

azote [a'zɔt], *a.* nitric.—*n.m.* nitrogen.

azoté [azɔ'te], *a.* nitrogenized.

azoter [azɔ'te], *v.t.* to charge with nitrogen; to azotize.

azoteux [azɔ'tø], *a.* (*fem.* **-euse**) nitrous.

azotique [azɔ'tik], *a.* nitric.

azur [a'zyːr], *n.m.* azure, blue, sky-color; washing blue; *la Côte d'Azur,* the French Riviera.

azuré [azy're], *a.* azure, sky-colored; *la voûte azurée,* the azure skies.

azyme [a'zim], *a.* azymous, unleavened (*bread*).—*n.m.* azyme, unleavened bread; *fête des azymes,* feast of unleavened bread.

B

B, b [be], *n.m.* the second letter of the alphabet.

baba [ba'ba], *n.m.* a sponge cake, with sultanas, steeped in rum and syrup.

Babel [ba'bɛl], *n.f.* Babel; (*fig.*) uproar, disorder.

babeurre [ba'bœːr], *n.m.* buttermilk.

babil [ba'bi], *n.m.* babble, prattle; chit-chat, tattle; chattering, babbling.

babillage [babi'jaːʒ], **babillement** [babij'mɑ̃], *n.m.* prattle, babbling, twaddle; tittle-tattle.

babillard [babi'jaːr], *a.* babbling, prattling, talkative, garrulous; gossiping, tell-tale.— *n.m.* (*fem.* **-e**) chatterer, babbler; tattler, blabber, gossip, tell-tale.

babillement [BABILLAGE].

babiller [babi'je], *v.i.* to babble, to prattle, to chat; to gossip, to chatter; (*fig.*) to blab, to backbite.

babine [ba'bin], **babouine** [ba'bwin], *n.f.* the pendulous lip (*of certain animals*); (*colloq.*) chops.

babiole [ba'bjɔl], *n.f.* bauble, trinket, toy; (*fig.*) trifle, trumpery affair.

bâbord [bɑ'bɔːr], *n.m.* (*Naut.*) port (*side*).

babouche [ba'buʃ], *n.f.* Turkish heelless slipper, babouche.

babouin [ba'bwɛ̃], *n.m.* baboon, monkey.

Babylone [babi'lɔn], *f.* Babylon.

babylonien [babilɔ'njɛ̃], *a.* (*fem.* **-enne**) Babylonian.—*n.m.* (**Babylonien,** *fem.* **-enne**) Babylonian (*person*).

bac [bak], *n.m.* ferry, ferry-boat; vat; (*Elec.*) *bac d'accumulateurs,* accumulator-jar.

baccalauréat [bakalɔre'a], *n.m.* baccalaureate, bachelorship (*of arts, science etc.*), school-leaving certificate.

bacchanal [baka'nal], *n.m.* (*colloq.*) racket, uproar.

bacchante [ba'kɑ̃ːt], *n.f.* bacchante, lewd woman.

bâche [bɑːʃ], *n.f.* cart tilt; awning; tank, cistern; *bâche (goudronnée),* tarpaulin.

bachelier [baʃə'lje], *n.m.* (*fem.* **-ière**) Bachelor (*ès Lettres, ès Sciences, of Arts, Science*).

bachique [ba'ʃik], *a.* bacchic, jovial, convivial; *chant bachique,* drinking song.

bachot [ba'ʃo], *n.m.* wherry, small ferry-boat; (*Univ. slang*) baccalaureate.

bachoteur [baʃɔ'tœːr], *n.m.* ferryman.

bacille [ba'sil], *n.m.* (*Biol.*) bacillus; *porteur de bacilles,* germ carrier.

bacillose [basi'loːz], [TUBERCULOSE].

bâclage [bɑ'klaːʒ], *n.m.* closing of a port by means of chains, booms etc.; line of boats (*in a port*) for the discharge *or* loading of cargo; (*fig.*) hasty, scamped work.

bâcle [bɑːkl], *n.f.* bar (*for door or gate*).

bâcler [bɑ'kle], *v.t.* to bar, fasten *or* secure (*a door, window etc.*); to stop, obstruct *or* interrupt (*traffic, navigation etc.*); (*fig.*) to do hastily, to polish off, to scamp (*work*); to bungle.

bactérie [bakte'ri], *n.f.* bacterium, microbe.

bactérien [bakte'rjɛ̃], *a.* (*fem.* **-enne**) bacterial.

bactériologie [bakterjɔlɔ'ʒi], *n.f.* bacteriology.

bactériologique [bakterjɔlɔ'ʒik], *a.* bacteriological; *guerre bactériologique,* germ warfare.

bactériologiste [bakterjɔlɔ'ʒist], *n.m.* bacteriologist.

bactériothérapie [bakterjɔtera'pi], *n.f.* medical treatment by means of bacteria.

badaud [ba'do], *n.m.* (*fem.* **-e**) ninny, booby, star-gazer; lounger, idler, rubber-neck.

badaudage [bado'da:ʒ], *n.m.* star-gazing, lounging, loitering, idling.

badauder [bado'de], *v.i.* to go gaping about; to lounge, to saunter, to loiter.

badauderie [bado'dri], *n.f.* star-gazing, silliness; lounging, idling, sauntering.

Bade [bad], *f.* Baden.

badigeon [badi'ʒɔ̃], *n.m.* badigeon, filling paste; whitewash; calcimine.

badigeonnage [badiʒɔ'naːʒ], *n.m.* filling up with badigeon, making up; daubing; whitewashing.

badigeonner [badiʒɔ'ne], *v.t.* to fill up (*stonework, sculpture etc.*) with badigeon; to whitewash; (*fig.*) to disguise defects with varnish, rouge etc.; (*Med.*) to anoint.

badigeonneur [badiʒɔ'nœːr], *n.m.* whitewasher; (*pej.*) dauber.

badin [ba'dɛ̃], *a.* waggish, jocular, roguish, droll.—*n.m.* (*fem.* **-e** (1)) wag, joker; buffoon.

badinage [badi'naːʒ], *n.m.* badinage, raillery, banter; playfulness, jocularity (*of style*); mere child's-play.

badine (2) [ba'din], *n.f.* switch, light cane, wand; (*pl.*) small tongs.

badiner [badi'ne], *v.i.* to trifle, to dally, to toy; to speak *or* write banteringly *or* playfully.

badinerie [badin'ri], *n.f.* jesting, foolery, trifling; silliness, childishness.

(C) **bâdrant** [ba'drɑ̃], *a.* bothersome.

(C) **bâdrer** [ba'dre], *v.t.* to annoy, to bother.

bafouer [ba'fwe], *v.t.* to scoff at, to make game of.

bafouillage [bafu'jaːʒ], *n.f.* gibberish, rigmarole; spluttering; bad running (*of engine*).

bafouiller [bafu'je], *v.i.* (*colloq.*) to stammer; to splutter; to miss, to chatter (*of engine*).

bafouilleur [bafu'jœːr], *n.m.* (*fem.* **-euse**) stammerer.

bagages [ba'gaːʒ], *n.m. pl.* luggage; *bagages enregistrés,* checked luggage.

bagarre [ba'gaːr], *n.f.* riot; uproar; crush, squabble, scuffle.

bagatelle [baga'tɛl], *n.f.* bauble, trinket, trifle, anything frivolous; trifling sum, mere nothing.

bagne [baɲ], *n.m.* penitentiary; penal servitude.

bagnole [ba'ɲɔl], *n.f.* (*fam.*) (old) motor car.

bague [bag], *n.f.* ring; ring band (*for birds*).

bague-agrafe [bag'graf], *n.f.* (*d'un stylo*) (fountain-pen) clip.

baguer [ba'ge], *v.t.* to baste, to tack, to stitch; to decorate *or* hang with rings; (*Hort.*) to ring (*trees*); to ring (*a bird*).

baguette [ba'gɛt], *n.f.* switch, rod, wand; pointer; clock (*of stockings*); glove-stretcher; long roll (*French bread*).

baguier [ba'gje], *n.m.* casket for rings, jewels etc., jewel box, ring stand.

bah! [ba], *int.* pooh! pshaw! nonsense! fudge!

bahut [ba'y], *n.m.* cabinet, trunk, chest; press, cupboard; (*Sch. slang*) grammar school.

bahutier [bay'tje], *n.m.* maker of trunks, chests, cabinets, etc.

bai [bɛ], *a.* bay, *une jument baie,* a bay mare.

baie (1) [bɛ], *n.f.* bay, gulf; (*Arch.*) bay, opening.

baie (2) [bɛ], *n.f.* berry.

baignade [bɛ'ɲad], *n.f.* bathing; bathing place.

baigner [bɛ'ɲe], *v.t.* to bathe, to give a bath to, to dip; (*fig.*) to wash, to water (*a coast etc.*); to wet, to suffuse.—*v.i.* to be plunged into; to welter (*in blood etc.*). **se baigner,** *v.r.* to bathe, to wash.

baigneur [bɛ'ɲœːr], *n.m.* (*fem.* **-euse**) bather; bathkeeper *or* attendant, bathing attendant.

baignoire [bɛ'ɲwaːr], *n.f.* bathtub, bath; (*Theat.*) ground-floor box.

bail [baːj], *n.m.* (*pl.* **baux** [bo]) lease.

bâillement [baj'mɑ̃], *n.m.* yawning, yawn.

bâiller [ba'je], *v.i.* to yawn, to gape; to open (*of fissures etc.*); to be ajar (*of doors*).

bailleur [ba'jœːr], *n.m.* (*fem.* **-eresse**) one who leases, lessor.

bâilleur [ba'jœːr], *n.m.* (*fem.* **-euse**) yawner; gaper.

bailli [ba'ji], *n.m.* (*Fr. Hist.*) bailiff.

bâillon [ba'jɔ̃], *n.m.* gag, muzzle.

bâillonnement [bajɔn'mɑ̃], *n.m.* gagging.

bâillonner [bajɔ'ne], *v.t.* to stop the mouth of, to gag, to muzzle; (*fig.*) to silence.

bain [bɛ̃], *n.m.* bath; bathing tub; (*pl.*) baths, bathing establishment, watering place, spa; *la salle de bain(s),* the bathroom.

bain-douche [bɛ̃'duʃ], *n.m.* shower bath.

bain-marie [bɛ̃ma'ri], *n.m.* (*pl.* **bains-marie**) (*Cook.*) double saucepan for foods that burn easily; boiler (*in a kitchen range etc.*).

baïonnette [bajɔ'nɛt], *n.f.* bayonet.

baiser [bɛ'ze], *v.t.* (*of strictly literary use, no longer decent in conversation, practically replaced by* **embrasser**) to kiss.—*n.m.* kiss, kissing; salute.

baisse [bɛːs], *n.f.* fall, abatement, decline; reduction *or* fall (*of prices etc.*); falling off (*of credit etc.*).

baisser [bɛ'se], *v.t.* to let down, to lower; to reduce the height of; to strike (*a flag etc.*); to bow (*the head etc.*).—*v.i.* (*with aux.* ÊTRE *or* AVOIR) to go down; to ebb; to be on the decline *or* the wane; to flag, to droop; to fail, to diminish. **se baisser,** *v.r.* to stoop; to bow down; to be lowered.

bajoue [ba'ʒu], *n.f.* jowl, chap (*of pigs etc.*); full and pendulous cheek.

bakélite [bake'lit], *n.f.* bakelite (*trade mark*).

bal [bal], *n.m.* ball, dance; *bal costumé,* fancy-dress ball.

baladeuse [bala'døːz], *n.f.* street vendor's barrow; portable lamp; trailer (*for cycle or tram*).

baladin [bala'dɛ̃], *n.m.* (*fem.* **-e**) mountebank; buffoon.

balafre [ba'laːfr], *n.f.* gash, slash, cut; scar.

balafrer [bala'fre], *v.t.* to gash, to slash.

balai (1) [ba'lɛ], *n.m.* broom, besom; (*Elec.*) brush.

(C) **balai** (2) [ba'lɛ], *n.m.* cedar.

balalaïka [balalai'ka], *n.f.* balalaika.

balance [ba'lɑ̃ːs], *n.f.* balance, scales, pair of scales; (*Comm.*) balance (*of an account*), balance sheet.

balancement [balɑ̃s'mɑ̃], *n.m.* balancing, poising; rocking, see-saw; (*fig.*) fluctuation, wavering, hesitation.

balancer [balɑ̃'se], *v.t.* (*conjug. like* COM-
MENCER) to balance, to poise, to hold in
equilibrium; to swing to and fro, to rock;
(*fig.*) to weigh, to consider; to square (*accounts*); to counterbalance.—*v.i.* to hesitate,
to be in suspense, to waver; to fluctuate, to
oscillate, to remain undecided. **se balancer**
v.r. to swing, to rock.

balancier [balɑ̃'sje], *n.m.* maker of weights
and scales; pendulum, balance; balancing-
pole.

balançoire [balɑ̃'swaːr], *n.f.* see-saw; swing.

balandre [ba'lɑ̃ːdr], *n.f.* flat canal boat.

balayage [balɛ'jaːʒ], **balayement** [balɛ
'mɑ̃], *n.m.* sweeping; (*Tel.*) scanning.

balayer [balɛ'je], *v.t.* (*conjug. like* PAYER) to
sweep, to clean with a broom; (*Tel.*) to scan.

balayette [balɛ'jɛt], *n.f.* small broom, whisk.

balayeur [balɛ'jœːr], *n.m.* (*fem.* **-euse**)
sweeper, scavenger.—*n.f.* (**-euse**) sweeping-
machine.

balayures [balɛ'jyːr], *n.f.* (*used only in pl.*)
sweepings.

balbutier [balby'sje], *v.t.* to pronounce
indistinctly.—*v.i.* to stammer, to stutter;
to mumble.

balbutieur [balby'sjœːr], *n.m.* (*fem.* **-euse**)
stutterer, stammerer.

balcon [bal'kɔ̃], *n.m.* balcony; (*Theat.*) dress
circle.

baldaquin [balda'kɛ̃], *n.m.* baldachin,
canopy; tester (*of bed*).

Bâle [bɑːl], *f.* Basel, Basle.

Baléares [bale'aːr], **les**, *f. pl.* the Balearic
Isles.

baleine [ba'lɛːn], *n.f.* whale; whalebone; rib
of an umbrella.

baleiné [balɛ'ne], *a.* stiffened with whalebone.

baleineau [balɛ'no], *n.m.* (*pl.* **-eaux**) young
whale.

baleinier [balɛ'nje], *n.m.* (*fem.* **-ière**) whaler.
—*n.f.* (**-ière**) whaleboat.

balisage [bali'zaːʒ], *n.m.* (*Naut.*) buoying,
signalling; (*Av.*) ground lights.

balise [ba'liːz], *n.f.* sea mark, buoy, beacon;
(*Av.*) ground light.

baliser [bali'ze], *v.t.* to buoy; to mark with
beacons *or* ground lights.

balistique [balis'tik], *a.* ballistic.—*n.f.* bal-
listics.

balivage [bali'vaːʒ], *n.m.* *staddling.

baliveau [bali'vo], *n.m.* (*pl.* **-eaux**) *staddle;
sapling.

baliverne [bali'vɛrn], *n.f.* nonsense, humbug.

baliverner [balivɛr'ne], *v.i.* to talk idly, to
talk twaddle.

balkanique [balka'nik], *a.* Balkan.

ballade [ba'lad], *n.f.* ballade; ballad.

ballant [ba'lɑ̃], *a.* waving, swinging, dangling.

ballast [ba'last], *n.m.* (*Rail.*) ballast.

balle [bal], *n.f.* ball; bullet, shot; bale, pack.

ballerine [bal'rin], *n.f.* ballerina.

ballet [ba'lɛ], *n.m.* ballet.

ballon [ba'lɔ̃], *n.m.* hand-ball; football; balloon; air balloon (*child's*).

ballonné [balɔ'ne], *a.* distended, swollen.

ballonnier [balɔ'nje], *n.m.* maker *or* vendor of
toy balloons.

ballon-sonde [balɔ̃'sɔ̃ːd], *n.m.* sounding
balloon.

ballot [ba'lo], *n.m.* small pack (*of wares for
sale*).

ballottement [balɔt'mɑ̃], *n.m.* tossing,
shaking.

ballotter [balɔ'te], *v.t.* to toss, to toss about;
to bandy; to keep in suspense.—*v.i.* to
shake, to rattle.

balnéaire [balne'ɛːr], *a.* pertaining to baths
etc.; *station balnéaire,* watering place;
seaside resort.

balourd [ba'luːr], *a.* dull, heavy, thick-
headed.—*n.m.* (*fem.* **-e**) stupid *or* dull person,
numskull, dunce.

balourdise [balur'diːz], *n.f.* gross blunder;
stupidity.

balsamier [balza'mje], **baumier** [bo'mje],
n.m. balsam tree.

balsamine [balza'min], *n.f.* balsamine.

Baltique [bal'tik], **la**, *f.* the Baltic (Sea).

balustrade [balys'trad], *n.f.* balustrade; low
railing etc.

balustre [ba'lystr], *n.m.* baluster, hand rail.

balustrer [balys'tre], *v.t.* to rail in, to surround.

balzane [bal'zan], *n.f.* white stocking (*of a
horse*).

bambin [bɑ̃'bɛ̃], *n.m.* (*fem.* **-e**) (*colloq.*) urchin,
brat, tiny tot.

bambou [bɑ̃'bu], *n.m.* bamboo (cane).

ban [bɑ̃], *n.m.* ban, announcement, public
order, edict *or* proclamation; banishment,
proscription; (*pl.*) banns (*of matrimony*).

banal [ba'nal], *a.* (*m. pl.* **-aux**) common,
commonplace, trite.

banalité [banali'te], *n.f.* vulgarity; banality,
commonplace, trite expression.

banane [ba'nan], *n.f.* banana.

bananier [bana'nje], *n.m.* banana tree;
banana boat.

banc [bɑ̃], *n.m.* bench, settle, form; reef,
sand bank; shoal (*of fish*); (*Geol.*) layer, bed;
dock, bar; *banc d'essai,* (*Motor.*) test
bench; (C) *banc de neige,* heap of snow;
banc d'huîtres, oyster bed.

bancal [bɑ̃'kal], *a.* (*m. pl.* **-als**) bandy-
legged.—*n.m.* (*fem.* **-e**) bandy-legged person.

bandage [bɑ̃'daːʒ], *n.m.* application of
bandages; bandage; belt; truss; tire (*of
wheels*).

bande (1) [bɑ̃ːd], *n.f.* band, belt, strip; ribbon;
bandage; *bande de papier,* slip of paper,
wrapper.

bande (2) [bɑ̃ːd], *n.f.* band, troop, company;
gang, crew, set (*of brigands etc.*); flock,
pack.

bandé [bɑ̃'de], *a.* bandaged, taut, stretched.

bandeau [bɑ̃'do], *n.m.* (*pl.* **-eaux**) headband,
bandage (*for the eyes*).

bandelette [bɑ̃'dlɛt], *n.f.* little band, string
fillet.

bander [bɑ̃'de], *v.t.* to bind *or* tie up; to
bandage; to tighten, to bend (*a bow etc.*).—
v.i. to be stretched, to be taut *or* too tight.

banderole [bɑ̃'drɔl], *n.f.* banderole, streamer.

bandit [bɑ̃'di], *n.m.* brigand, bandit; ruffian,
blackguard; scamp.

bandoulière [bɑ̃du'ljɛːr], *n.f.* shoulder strap,
bandolier; *en bandoulière,* slung across
the back.

banjo [bɑ̃'ʒo], *n.m.* banjo.

banlieue [bɑ̃'ljø], *n.f.* suburbs, outskirts (*of
a town*).

banne [ban], *n.f.* hamper; awning; tilt,
tarpaulin.

banni [ba'ni], *a.* banished, outlawed; (*fig.*) banned, forbidden.—*n.m.* (*fem.* **-e**) exile, outlaw.
bannière [ba'njɛːr], *n.f.* banner, standard, flag.
bannir [ba'niːr], *v.t.* to banish; (*fig.*) to expel, to dismiss.
bannissement [banis'mã], *n.m.* banishment.
banque [bãːk], *n.f.* bank, banking.
banqueroute [bã'krut], *n.f.* bankruptcy; (*fig.*) failure, collapse.
banqueroutier [bãkru'tje], *n.m.* (*fem.* **-ière**) bankrupt.
banquet [bã'kɛ], *n.m.* banquet, feast.
banquette [bã'kɛt], *n.f.* bench; towing path; (*Fort.*) banquette.
banquier [bã'kje], *n.m.* banker.
banquise [bã'kiːz], *n.f.* ice floe, ice pack.
bantam [bã'tam], *n.m.* bantam.
baptême [ba'tɛːm], *n.m.* baptism, christening; *nom de baptême*, Christian name.
baptiser [bati'ze], *v.t.* to baptize; (*fig.*) to christen, to give a name *or* nickname to.
baptismal [batiz'mal], *a.* (*m. pl.* **-aux**) baptismal.
baptistaire [batis'tɛːr], *a.* of baptism; *registre baptistaire*, parish register.
Baptiste [ba'tist], *n.m.* Baptist.
baquet [ba'kɛ], *n.m.* tub; (*Av.*) cockpit.
bar (1) [baːr], *n.m.* bass.
bar (2) [baːr], *n.m.* bar (*of a public-house etc.*).
baragouin [bara'gwɛ̃], *n.m.* gibberish, jargon, lingo.
baragouinage [baragwi'naːʒ], *n.m.* talking, gibberish, jargon etc.
baragouiner [baragwi'ne], *v.t.* to sputter out (*words*).—*v.i.* to talk gibberish; to gabble.
baraque [ba'rak], *n.f.* hut, shed, shanty; (*fam.*) hovel; booth (*at a fair*).
baraquement [barak'mã], *n.m.* (*Mil.*) hutting.
barattage [bara'taːʒ], *n.m.* churning.
baratte [ba'rat], *n.f.* churn.
baratter [bara'te], *v.t.* to churn.
barbacane [barba'kan], *n.f.* (*Fort.*) barbican.
Barbade [bar'bad], *f.* Barbados.
barbare [bar'baːr], *a.* barbarous, barbarian; cruel, inhuman; (*fig.*) uncouth, rude; incorrect, ungrammatical.—*n.m.* (*usu. in pl.*) barbarians.
barbarement [barbar'mã], *adv.* barbarously.
barbaresque [barba'rɛsk], *a.* of *or* pertaining to Barbary.
Barbarie [barba'ri], **la**, *f.* Barbary.
barbarie [barba'ri], *n.f.* barbarity, rudeness; (*fig.*) cruelty.
barbarisme [barba'rism], *n.m.* (*Gram.*) barbarism.
barbe (1) [barb], *n.f.* beard; whiskers (*of cats, dogs etc.*); beard (*of grain*); wattles (*of fowls*).
barbe (2) [barb], *n.m.* barb, barbary horse.
barbeau [bar'bo], *n.m.* (*pl.* **-eaux**) barbel; (*Bot.*) bluebottle, cornflower.
barbelé [barbə'le], *a.* barbed, spiked; *fil de fer*) *barbelé*, barbed wire.
barbiche [bar'biʃ], **barbichette** [barbi'ʃɛt], *n.f.* beard growing only on the chin, goatee.
barbier [bar'bje], *n.m.* barber.
barbiturate [barbity'rat], **barbiturique** [barbity'rik], *n.m.* (*Chem.*) barbiturate.

barboter [barbɔ'te], *v.i.* to dabble about in mud *or* water (*with the beak, like a duck*); to paddle, to flounder about in the mud; (*fig.*) to mumble.
barboteuse [barbɔ'tøːz], *n.f.* rompers.
barbotière [barbɔ'tjɛːr], *n.f.* duck pond; trough.
barbouillage [barbu'jaːʒ], *n.m.* daubing; daub; scrawl; (*fig.*) twaddle.
barbouiller [barbu'je], *v.t.* to soil, to dirty, to blot; to daub, to besmear; to scrawl, to scribble; to splutter out, to mumble; to bungle.
barbouilleur [barbu'jœːr], *n.m.* (*fem.* **-euse**) dauber, scribbler; mumbler.
barbu [bar'by], *a.* bearded.
barbue [bar'by], *n.f.* brill.
barcarolle [barka'rɔl], *n.f.* (*Mus.*) barcarolle.
Barcelone [barsa'lɔn], *f.* Barcelona.
bardane [bar'dan], *n.f.* burr, burdock.
barde (1) [bard], *n.m.* bard.
barde (2) [bard], *n.f.* bard (*iron armor for horses*); thin rasher of bacon used for larding poultry etc.
bardé [bar'de], *a.* barded; larded.
barder [bar'de], *v.t.* to bard a horse; to cover with thin slices of bacon, to lard; (*slang*) *ça barde* or *ça va barder*, things are beginning to hum.
bardot or **bardeau** (*pl.* **-eaux**) [bar'do], *n.m.* hinny; pack mule.
barème [ba'rɛːm], *n.m.* ready-reckoner.
barguignage [bargi'naːʒ], *n.m.* (*colloq.*) hesitation, wavering, dilly-dallying.
barguigner [bargi'ne], *v.i.* to be irresolute, to waver, to shilly-shally.
barguigneur [bargi'nœːr], *n.m.* (*fem.* **-euse**) waverer, haggler.
baril [ba'ri], *n.m.* small barrel, cask, keg.
bariolage [barjɔ'laːʒ], *n.m.* variegation, odd medley of colors, motley.
bariolé [barjɔ'le], *a.* gaudy, motley, many-colored.
barioler [barjɔ'le], *v.t.* to streak with several colors, to variegate.
barnache [BERNACLE].
baromètre [barɔ'mɛtr], *n.m.* barometer.
barométrique [barɔme'trik], *a.* barometrical.
baron [ba'rõ], *n.m.* (*fem.* **-onne**) baron, baroness.
baronnet [barɔ'nɛ], *n.m.* baronet.
baronnial [barɔ'njal], *a.* (*m. pl.* **-aux**) baronial.
baronnie [barɔ'ni], *n.f.* barony.
baroque [ba'rɔk], *a.* irregular, grotesque, odd; baroque.
barque [bark], *n.f.* bark, boat, small craft.
barquerolle [barkə'rɔl], *n.f.* small mastless barge.
barquette [bar'kɛt], *n.f.* small craft; light puff-biscuit.
barrage [ba'raːʒ], *n.m.* barrier; toll bar; dam, weir, barrage.
barre [baːr], *n.f.* bar (*of metal, wood etc.*); dash, cross, stroke (*of the pen etc.*); bar (*in courts*) of justice; (*Naut.*) helm, tiller, bar; (*Mus.*) bar; bore (*of river*).
barreau [ba'ro], *n.m.* (*pl.* **-eaux**) small bar (*of wood, metal etc.*); bench reserved for barristers; (*fig.*) lawyers, barristers; rung (*of a ladder*): *être reçu* or *admis au barreau*, to be admitted to the bar.

barrer [ba're], *v.t.* to bar up, to fence off; to obstruct, to thwart; to cross off, to erase.

barrette (1) or **barette** [ba'rɛt], *n.f.* square flat cap, biretta; cardinal's hat.

barrette (2) [ba'rɛt], *n.m.* axle, pin, bolt, etc. (*in watches, jewelry etc.*); bar (*of medal*).

barreur [ba'rœ:r], *n.m.* helmsman, coxswain.

barricade [bari'kad], *n.f.* barricade.

barricader [barika'de], *v.t.* to barricade, to obstruct.

barrière [ba'rjɛ:r], *n.f.* railing, barrier; gateway; farm gate.

barrique [ba'rik], *n.f.* large barrel *or* cask, hogshead.

baryton [bari'tɔ̃], *n.m.* baritone.

baryum [ba'rjɔm], *n.m.* barium.

bas (1) [bɑ], *a.* (*fem.* **basse** (1)) low; in a low situation; inferior; (*fig.*) vile, base, sordid; mean; subdued (*of sounds*); decadent; **la marée est basse**, it is low tide; **les Pays-Bas**, the Netherlands.—*adv.* low, down; in a subdued voice, tone, etc.; **ici bas**, here below; **là-bas**, over there, yonder.—*n.m.* the lower part, bottom *or* foot (*of something*); **en bas**, below, downstairs; **le bas de l'escalier**, the foot of the stairs.

bas (2) [bɑ], *n.m. inv.* stocking.

basalte [ba'zalt], *n.m.* basalt.

basane [ba'zan], *n.f.* sheepskin.

basané [baza'ne], *a.* sunburnt, bronzed, swarthy, tawny.

bascule [bas'kyl], *n.f.* see-saw; weighing machine.

basculer [basky'le], *v.i.* to see-saw; to rock, to swing.

base [ba:z], *n.f.* base, foundation; lower part, bottom; basis.

base-ball [bes'bol], *n.m.* baseball.

baser [ba'ze], *v.t.* to found, to base, to ground. **se baser**, *v.r.* to be grounded; to depend, to rely.

bas-fond [bɑ'fɔ̃], *n.m.* (*pl.* **bas-fonds**) low-lying ground, hollow, bottom; shallow, shallow water; (*fig., pl.*) underworld.

basilic [bazi'lik], *n.m.* (*Bot.*) basil, sweet basil; (*Myth.*) basilisk, cockatrice.

basilique [bazi'lik], *n.f.* basilica.

basket-ball [basket'bol], *n.m.* basketball.

basketteur [baske'tœ:r], *n.m.* (*fem.* **-euse**) basketball player.

basque (1) [bask], *n.f.* flap, skirt, tail (*of a garment*).

basque (2) [bask], *a.* Basque.—*n.m.* Basque (*language*).—*n.* (**Basque**) Basque (*person*).

bas-relief [barə'ljɛf], *n.m.* (*pl.* **bas-reliefs**) bas-relief.

basse (1) [bɑ:s], [BAS (1)].

basse (2) [bɑ:s], *n.f.* bass; violoncello; saxhorn.

basse (3) [bɑ:s], *n.f.* shallow, reef.

basse-contre [bɑs'kɔ̃:tr], *n.f.* (*pl.* **basses-contre**) (*Mus.*) contra-bass, lower tenor.

basse-cour [bɑs'ku:r], *n.f.* (*pl.* **basses-cours**) farmyard, poultry yard.

bassement [bɑs'mã], *adv.* basely, meanly, vilely.

bassesse [bɑ'sɛs], *n.f.* baseness; lowness (*of station etc.*); meanness, vileness; mean *or* sordid action.

basset [ba'sɛ], *n.m.* basset hound; **basset allemand**, dachshund.

basse-taille [bɑs'ta:j], *n.f.* (*pl.* **basses-tailles**) (*Mus.*) baritone; (*Sculp.*) bas-relief.

bassin [ba'sɛ̃], *n.m.* basin; pond; dock; (*Anat.*) pelvis.

bassine [ba'sin], *n.f.* deep, wide pan.

bassiner [basi'ne], *v.t.* to warm (*a bed etc.*); to bathe (*with warm lotions*), to foment, to steep; to water, to sprinkle (*crops etc.*).

bassinet [basi'nɛ], *n.m.* small basin, pan, bowl.

bassinoire [basi'nwa:r], *n.f.* warming pan; (*pop.*) bore.

bassiste [ba'sist], *n.m.* saxhorn player; 'cellist.

basson [bɑ'sɔ̃], *n.m.* bassoon; bassoonist.

bastide [bas'tid], *n.f.* (*Provence*) country cottage, villa.

bastille [bas'ti:j], *n.f.* bastille, fort.

bastion [bas'tjɔ̃], *n.m.* bastion.

bastionner [bastjɔ'ne], *v.t.* to bastion, to fortify with bastions.

bastonnade [bastɔ'nad], *n.f.* bastinado; caning.

bastringue [bas'trɛ̃:g], *n.m.* (*pop.*) dance hall; (*slang*) noise.

bas-ventre [ba'vã:tr], *n.m.* (*pl.* **bas-ventres**) lower part of the belly.

bât [bɑ], *n.m.* pack-saddle.

bataclan [bata'klã], *n.m.* (*fam.*) paraphernalia.

bataille [ba'ta:j], *n.f.* battle, fight, engagement.

batailler [bata'je], *v.i.* to give battle; to be at war, to fight; to struggle hard, to strive.

batailleur [bata'jœ:r], *a.* (*fem.* **-euse**) combative, pugnacious, quarrelsome; disputatious.

bataillon [bata'jɔ̃], *n.m.* battalion; (*fig.*) host; (*pl.*) troops.

bâtard [ba'ta:r], *a.* and *n.m.* (*fem.* **-e**) bastard, illegitimate *or* natural (child).

bâté [ba'te], *a.* saddled with a pack; **c'est un âne bâté**, he is an ignorant lout.

bateau [ba'to], *n.m.* (*pl.* **-eaux**) boat; **bateau mouche**, pleasure steamer (*Paris and Lyons*).

batelage [ba'tla:ʒ], *n.m.* juggling, legerdemain; lighterage charges.

bateleur [ba'tlœ:r], *n.m.* (*fem.* **-euse**) juggler, buffoon, mountebank.

batelier [batə'lje], *n.m.* (*fem.* **-ière**) boatman, boatwoman, ferryman, ferrywoman.

bâter [ba'te], *v.t.* to load with a pack-saddle.

bathyscaphe [batis'kaf], *n.m.* bathyscape.

bâti [ba'ti], *n.m.* framing, structure; basting, tacking (*of a garment*).

batifolage [batifɔ'la:ʒ], *n.m.* romping; fondling.

batifoler [batifɔ'le], *v.i.* to play, to romp; to fondle.

bâtiment [bati'mã], *n.m.* building, structure, edifice; building trade; ship, vessel.

bâtir [ba'ti:r], *v.t.* to build, to erect, to construct; **faire bâtir**, to have built, to build; **terrain à bâtir**, building site.

bâtisse [ba'tis], *n.f.* masonry, ramshackle building.

batiste [ba'tist], *n.f.* cambric.

bâton [ba'tɔ̃], *n.m.* stick, staff, cudgel, cane.

bâtonner [batɔ'ne], *v.t.* to cudgel, to cane.

batracien [batra'sjɛ̃], *n.m.* (*Zool.*) batrachian.

battant (1) [ba'tã], *n.m.* clapper (*of a bell*); leaf (*of a table or door*); fly (*of a flag*); **porte à deux battants**, double door.

battant (2) [baˈtɑ̃], a. beating, pelting, falling heavily (of rain etc.); *mener tambour battant*, to hurry on (a business).

batte [bat], n.f. long wooden staff or beater; *batte de blanchisseuse*, washing board; *batte (de cricket)*, (cricket) bat.

battée [baˈte], n.f. jamb of door or window.

battement [batˈmɑ̃], n.m. beating; clapping (of hands), stamping (of feet), flapping (of wings); beating (of the heart); shuffling (of cards).

batterie [baˈtri], n.f. (Artill., Elec., Cook. etc.) battery; *batterie de cuisine*, complete set of kitchen utensils.

batteur [baˈtœːr], n.m. (fem. **-euse**) beater; (cricket etc.) batsman; (jazz) drummer.—n.f. (**-euse**) threshing machine.

battre [batr], v.t. (see Verb Tables) to strike upon, against etc.; to beat, to thrash, to whip (a horse etc.); to beat up, to mix; to defeat; to shuffle (cards); *battre des mains*, to clap; *la fête battait son plein*, the party was in full swing.—v.i. to beat, to knock; to pant, to throb. **se battre**, v.r. to fight, to combat; to hit oneself (contre etc.).

battu [baˈty], a. beaten (of a path, road etc.); frequented; (fig.) trite, commonplace.

battue [baˈty], n.f. (Shooting) wholesale slaughter, battue.

baudet [boˈdɛ], n.m. ass; (fig.) dolt, donkey; sawyer's trestle.

bauge [boːʒ], n.f. lair of a wild boar; squirrel's nest; (fig.) a dirty hovel.

baume [boːm], n.m. balm; balsam; (fig.) consolation.

baumier [BALSAMIER].

baux [BAIL].

bauxite [boˈsit], n.f. bauxite.

bavard [baˈvaːr], a. prating, talkative, loquacious.—n.m. (fem. **-e**) prater, babbler, chatterer.

bavardage [bavarˈdaːʒ], n.m. babbling, prattling; (fig.) twaddle, nonsense.

bavarder [bavarˈde], v.i. to babble, to prattle.

bavarois [bavaˈrwa], a. Bavarian.—n.m. (**Bavarois**, fem. **-oise**) Bavarian (person).

bave [baːv], n.f. slaver, dribble; foam; (fig.) slime.

baver [baˈve], v.i. to slobber, to dribble.

bavette [baˈvɛt], n.f. bib.

baveux [baˈvø], a. (fem. **-euse**) dribbling, slobbering.

Bavière [baˈvjɛːr], **la**, f. Bavaria.

bavure [baˈvyːr], n.f. seam (left by a mold); smudge (of a pen).

bazar [baˈzaːr], n.m. bazaar; ill-kept, untidy house; (fam.) *mettre tout son bazar dans une malle*, to put all one's belongings in a trunk.

bazooka [bazuˈka], n.m. (Artill.) bazooka.

béant [beˈɑ̃], a. gaping, yawning, wide open.

béat [beˈa], a. blessed; devout; sanctimonious.

béatement [beatˈmɑ̃], adv. sanctimoniously.

béatification [beatifikaˈsjɔ̃], n.f. beatification.

béatifier [beatiˈfje], v.t. to beatify.

béatifique [beatiˈfik], a. beatific, blissful.

béatitude [beatiˈtyd], n.f. beatitude, blessedness.

beau [bo], **bel** [bɛl] (before nouns singular beginning with a vowel or h mute), a. (fem. **belle**, pl. **beaux**, **belles**) beautiful, fine, handsome, fair; smart, spruce; glorious; lofty, noble;

seemly, becoming; (iron.) nice, precious; *au beau milieu*, in the very middle; *il fait beau*, it is a fine day; *il l'a échappé belle*, he has had a narrow escape.—adv. finely, promisingly; in vain; *avoir beau dire*, to speak in vain; *de plus belle*, with renewed ardor, worse than ever; *tout beau*, gently, not so fast.—n.m. that which is beautiful, fine, excellent etc.; beauty; beau.—n.f. (**belle**) belle; *la Belle et la Bête*, Beauty and the Beast.

beaucoup [boˈku], adv. many, much; a great many, a great deal; *avoir beaucoup d'argent*, to have plenty of money.

beau-fils [boˈfis], n.m. (pl. **beaux-fils**) stepson.

beau-frère [boˈfrɛːr], n.m. (pl. **beaux-frères**) brother-in-law.

beau-père [boˈpɛːr], n.m. (pl. **beaux-pères**) father-in-law; step-father.

beaupré [boˈpre], n.m. (Naut.) bowsprit.

beauté [boˈte], n.f. beauty, fineness, loveliness, comeliness, elegance, agreeableness.

beaux-arts [boˈzaːr], n.m. pl. fine arts.

beaux-parents [bopaˈrɑ̃], n.m. pl. father-in-law and mother-in-law.

bébé [beˈbe], n.m. baby; baby doll.

bec [bɛk], n.m. beak, bill; (fig.) mouth; snout (of some fishes); lip (of a jug), spout (of a kettle etc.); gas jet, burner; mouthpiece (of musical instrument); nib (pen); *avoir bon bec*, to have the gift of the gab.

bécane [beˈkan], n.f. (pop.) bike.

bécarre [beˈkaːr], a. and n.m. (Mus.) natural.

bécasse [beˈkas], n.f. woodcock; (fam.) stupid woman.

bécassine [bekaˈsin], n.f. snipe.

bec-de-lièvre [bɛkdəˈljɛːvr], n.m. (pl. **becs-de-lièvre**) harelip; harelipped person.

bec-fin [bɛkˈfɛ̃], n.m. (pl. **becs-fins**) warbler; pipit.

béchamel [beʃaˈmɛl], n.f. cream sauce, béchamel sauce.

bêche [bɛːʃ], n.f. spade.

bêcher [bɛˈʃe], v.t. to dig.

becquée [bɛˈke], **béquée** [beˈke], n.f. billful; *donner la becquée*, to feed.

becqueter [bɛkˈte], **béqueter** [bekˈte], v.t. (conjug. like AMENER) to peck; (colloq.) to eat. **se becqueter**, **se béqueter**, v.r. to peck one another.

bedaine [bəˈdɛn], n.f. (colloq.) paunch.

bedeau [bəˈdo], n.m. (pl. **-eaux**) beadle, verger.

bedonnant [bədɔˈnɑ̃], a. stout, pot-bellied.

bedonner [bədɔˈne], v.i. to get or grow stout.

bédouin [beˈdwɛ̃], a. Bedouin.—n.m. (**Bédouin**, fem. **-e**) Bedouin.

bée [be], a. only used in *bouche bée*, gaping, open-mouthed.

beffroi [bɛˈfrwa], n.m. belfry.

bégaiement [begɛˈmɑ̃], n.m., **bégayant** [begɛˈjɑ̃], a. stammering, faltering.

bégayer [begɛˈje], v.t. (conjug. like PAYER) to stammer out, to stutter, to lisp.—v.i. to stammer.

bégayeur [begɛˈjœːr], n.m. (fem. **-euse**) stammerer, stutterer.

bégonia [begɔˈnja], n.m. begonia.

bègue [bɛg], a. stammering, stuttering.—n. stammerer, stutterer.

bégueule [beˈgœl], a. prudish, squeamish; straitlaced.—n.f. (fam.) prude.

bégueulerie [begœl'ri], *n.f.* prudery, prudish airs, squeamishness.

béguin [be'gɛ̃], *n.m.* hood, child's cap; *avoir un béguin pour*, to be sweet on; *c'est mon béguin*, he or she is my darling.

béguine [be'gin], *n.f.* beguine (*Flemish nun*); nun; bigoted person.

bégum [be'gɔm], *n.f.* begum.

beige [bɛːʒ], *a.* natural, undyed (*of wool*); beige.—*n.f.* unbleached serge.

beignet [be'nɛ], *n.m.* fritter.

béjaune [be'ʒoːn], *n.m.* (*Falconry*) eyas, unfledged hawk; (*fig.*) ninny, novice; blunder, silliness, mistake.

bel [BEAU].

bêlant [be'lɑ̃], *a.* bleating.

bêlement [bɛl'mɑ̃], *n.m.* bleating (*of sheep*).

bêler [be'le], *v.i.* to bleat.

belette [bə'lɛt], *n.f.* weasel.

belge [bɛlʒ], *a.* Belgian.—*n.* (**Belge**) Belgian (*person*).

Belgique [bɛl'ʒik], **la**, *f.* Belgium.

bélier [be'lje], *n.m.* ram; battering-ram; Aries.

bélière [be'ljɛːr], *n.f.* sheep bell; clapper ring (*of a bell*); watch ring; sword sling.

bélitre [be'litr], *n.m.* rascal, cad.

belladone [bɛla'dɔn], *n.f.* belladonna, deadly nightshade.

bellâtre [bɛ'laːtr], *a.* having insipid beauty; foppish.—*n.m.* insipid beauty; fop, coxcomb.

belle-fille [bɛl'fiːj], *n.f.* (*pl.* **belles-filles**) daughter-in-law: stepdaughter.

belle-maman [bɛlma'mɑ̃], (*colloq.*) [BELLE-MÈRE].

bellement [bɛl'mɑ̃], *adv.* prettily, charmingly, softly, gently.

belle-mère [bɛl'mɛːr], *n.f.* (*pl.* **belles-mères**) mother-in-law; stepmother.

belles-lettres [bɛl'lɛtr], *n.f. pl.* polite literature, belles-lettres.

belle-sœur [bɛl'sœːr], *n.f.* (*pl.* **belles-sœurs**) sister-in-law; stepsister.

belligérance [bɛliʒe'rɑ̃ːs], *n.f.* belligerence, belligerency.

belligérant [bɛliʒe'rɑ̃], *a.* and *n.m.* (*fem.* **-e**) belligerent.

belliqueux [bɛli'kø], *a.* (*fem.* **-euse**) warlike, martial; bellicose, quarrelsome.

belvédère [bɛlve'dɛːr], *n.m.* turret, terrace, belvedere, gazebo.

bémol [be'mɔl], *a.* and *n.m.* (*Mus.*) flat.

bémoliser [bemɔli'ze], *v.t.* (*Mus.*) to mark flat or with a flat.

bénédicité [benedisi'te], *n.m.* grace (*before meals*).

bénédictin [benedik'tɛ̃], *a.* and *n.m.* (*fem.* **-e**) Benedictine.

bénédiction [benedik'sjɔ̃], *n.f.* benediction, blessing, consecration; (*fig.*) expression of thanks.

bénéfice [bene'fis], *n.m.* benefit, gain, profit; privilege, advantage; (*Eccles.*) benefice, living.

bénéficiaire [benefi'sjɛːr], *a.* receiving a benefit or benefice.—*n.* beneficiary, recipient.

bénéficial [benefi'sjal], *n.m.* beneficiary (*of ecclesiastical livings*).

bénéficier [benefi'sje], *v.i.* to gain, to profit.—*n.m.* beneficed clergyman, incumbent.

benêt [bə'nɛ], *a.* silly, foolish, simple.—*n.m* booby, fool, simpleton.

bénévole [bene'vɔl], *a.* well-disposed, kindly; unpaid.

bénévolement [benevɔl'mɑ̃], *adv.* out of good will; voluntarily, spontaneously.

Bengale [bɛ̃'gal], **le**, *m.* Bengal.

bengali [bɛ̃ga'li], *a.* Bengali.—*n.m.* Bengali (*language*).—*n.* (**Bengali**) Bengali (*person*).

Béni-oui-oui [beniwi'wi], *n.m. inv.* (*fam.*) yes-man.

bénignement [beniɲ'mɑ̃], *adv.* benignly, kindly; graciously.

bénignité [beniɲi'te], *n.f.* benignity, kindness; mildness (*of a disease*).

bénin [be'nɛ̃], *a.* (*fem.* **bénigne**) benign, good-natured, indulgent; mild (*of attacks of disease, remedies etc.*).

bénir [be'niːr], *v.t.* to bless, to hallow, to consecrate; to call down blessings on; to thank; to praise.

bénit [be'ni], *a.* hallowed, consecrated.

bénitier [beni'tje], *n.m.* holy-water basin; font.

benjamin [bɛ̃ʒa'mɛ̃], *n.m.* favorite (*especially the youngest child*).

benjoin [bɛ̃'ʒwɛ̃], *n.m.* benjamin, benzoin.

benne [bɛn], *n.f.* hamper, basket; (*Mining*) hopper, bucket.

benzine [bɛ̃'zin], *n.f.* benzine.

benzol [bɛ̃'zɔl], *n.m.* benzol.

béquillard [beki'jaːr], *a.* (*pop.*) crippled, going on crutches.—*n.m.* (*fem.* **-e**) cripple.

béquille [be'kiːj], *n.f.* crutch; (*Av.*) tail-skid.

béquiller [beki'je], *v.i.* to walk on crutches.

berbère [bɛr'bɛːr], *a.* Berber.—*n.* (**Berbère**) Berber (*person*).

berbéris [bɛrbe'ris], *n.m.* (*Bot.*) barberry, berberis.

bercail [bɛr'kaːj], *n.m.* (*used only in sing.*) sheepfold, fold.

berce [bɛrs], *n.f.* cow-parsnip.

berceau [bɛr'so], *n.m.* (*pl.* **-eaux**) cradle: (*fig.* infancy; origin, source; (*Hort.*) arbor, bower.

bercement [bɛrsə'mɑ̃], *n.m.* rocking; lulling.

bercer [bɛr'se], *v.t.* (*conjug. like* COMMENCER) to rock, to lull asleep; to lull, to soothe; (*fig.*) to delude or flatter with vain hopes. **se bercer**, *v.r.* to rock; (*fig.*) to delude oneself (*de*).

berceuse [bɛr'søːz], *n.f.* woman who rocks an infant; rocking chair; cradle that rocks; (*Mus.*) lullaby.

béret [be'rɛ], *n.m.* beret, tam-o'-shanter (*worn by the French Alpine regiments*).

berge [bɛrʒ], *n.f.* steep bank (*of a river*); side (*of a canal, ditch, roadway etc.*).

berger [bɛr'ʒe], *n.m.* (*fem.* **-ère** (1)) shepherd, shepherdess; (*poet.*) swain; (*fig.*) pastor, guardian (*of the people etc.*); (*Chess*) *le coup du berger*, fool's mate.

bergère (2) [bɛr'ʒɛːr], *n.f.* large and deep armchair.

bergerie [bɛrʒə'ri], *n.f.* sheepfold, pen; (*Lit.*) (*chiefly used in the plural*) pastoral.

bergeronnette [bɛrʒərɔ'nɛt], *n.f.* (*Orn.*) wagtail.

berlue [bɛr'ly], *n.f.* dimness of sight.

Bermudes [bɛr'myd], **les**, *f. pl.* the Bermudas.

bernacle [bɛr'nakl], **bernache** [bɛr'naʃ], **barnache** [bar'naʃ], *n.f.* barnacle goose; barnacle (*shell-fish*).

bernard-l'ermite [bɛrnarlɛr'mit], *n.m.* hermit crab.

berne (1) [bɛrn], *n.f.* tossing in a blanket.

berne (2) [bɛrn], *n.f.* (*Naut.*) *mettre le pavillon en berne*, to fly the flag at half-mast.

berner [bɛr'ne], *v.t.* to toss in a blanket; (*fig.*) to ridicule, to make a fool of, to deride; to deceive, to hoax.

bernique [bɛr'nik], *int.* (*pop.*) no use; not a bit of it, no go.

berthon [bɛr'tɔ̃], *n.m.* a small collapsible boat.

béryl or **béril** [be'ril], *n.m.* beryl.

besace [bə'zas], *n.f.* beggar's wallet, scrip.

bésigue [be'zig], *n.m.* bezique (*card game*).

besogne [bə'zɔɲ], *n.f.* work, business, labor; job, piece of work.

besogner [bəzɔ'ɲe], *v.i.* to work, to labor.

besogneux [bəzɔ'ɲø], *a.* and *n.m.* (*fem.* **-euse**) necessitous, needy (person).

besoin [bə'zwɛ̃], *n.m.* need, want; necessity; poverty, distress, emergency; *au besoin*, at a pinch, if need be.

Bessarabie [bɛsara'bi], la, *f.* Bessarabia.

bestial [bɛs'tjal], *a.* (*m. pl.* **-aux** (1)) bestial, brutish.

bestialement [bɛstjal'mɑ̃], *adv.* bestially, brutally, like a beast.

bestialité [bɛstjali'te], *n.f.* bestiality.

bestiaux [BESTIAL, BÉTAIL].

bestiole [bɛs'tjɔl], *n.f.* little animal.

bêta [be'ta], *n.m.* (*fem.* **-asse**) a bit of a blockhead, rather a simpleton.

bétail [be'taj], *n.m.* (*pl.* **bestiaux** (2) [bɛs'tjo]) cattle, livestock; *gros bétail*, oxen etc.; *menu bétail*, sheep, goats etc.

bêtasse [be'taːs], [BÊTA].

bête [bɛːt], *a.* silly, stupid, nonsensical.—*n.f.* animal, beast, brute; fool, blockhead, stupid creature; *bête noire*, pet aversion; *bête sauvage*, wild animal.

bêtement [bɛt'mɑ̃], *adv.* like a fool, foolishly, stupidly.

Bethléem [bɛtle'ɛm], *f.* Bethlehem.

bêtise [be'tiːz], *n.f.* silliness, stupidity; tomfoolery, foolish act, suggestion etc., silly thing, absurdity.

béton [be'tɔ̃], *n.m.* (*Masonry*) beton (*a kind of concrete*); *béton armé*, reinforced concrete.

bétonnière [betɔ'njɛːr], **bétonneuse** [betɔ'nøːz], *n.f.* concrete mixer.

bette [bɛt], **blette** (2) [blɛt], *n.f.* beet.

betterave [bɛ'traːv], *n.f.* beets; *betterave à sucre*, sugar beet; *betterave fourragère*, mangel-wurzel.

beuglement [bøglə'mɑ̃], *n.m.* bellowing, lowing (*of cattle*).

beugler [bø'gle], *v.i.* to bellow, to low.

beurre [bœːr], *n.m.* butter.

beurrée [bœ're], *n.f.* slice of bread and butter.

beurrer [bœ're], *v.t.* to butter (*bread etc.*).

beurrerie [bœr'ri], *n.f.* butter factory.

beurrier [bœ'rje], *n.m.* butter dish.

bévue [be'vy], *n.f.* blunder, oversight, mistake; (*colloq.*) howler.

bey [be], *n.m.* bey.

biais [bjɛ], *a.* slanting, sloping, askew; oblique.—*n.m.* bias, obliquity, slope; (*fig.*) shift, subterfuge.

biaisement [bjɛz'mɑ̃], *n.m.* sloping, slanting, shift, evasion.

biaiser [bjɛ'ze], *v.i.* to be oblique, to go obliquely, to slope, to slant, to lean on one side; to use shifts or evasions.

bibelot [bi'blo], *n.m.* trinket, knick-knack.

biberon (1) [bi'brɔ̃], *n.m.* (*Med.*) feeding cup; feeding bottle (*for infants*).

biberon (2) [bi'brɔ̃], *n.m.* (*fem.* **-onne**) tippler, toper.

Bible [bibl], *n.f.* Bible.

bibliographe [bibliɔ'graf], *n.m.* bibliographer.

bibliographie [bibliɔgra'fi], *n.f.* bibliography.

bibliographique [bibliɔgra'fik], *a.* bibliographical.

bibliomane [bibliɔ'man], *n.m.* book collector.

bibliomanie [bibliɔma'ni], *n.f.* bibliomania.

bibliophile [bibliɔ'fil], *n.m.* book lover.

biblio-hécaire [bibliɔte'kɛːr], *n.m.* librarian.

bibliothèque [bibliɔ'tɛk], *n.f.* library; bookcase.

biblique [bi'blik], *a.* Biblical.

bicarbonate [bikarbɔ'nat], *n.m.* (*Chem.*) bicarbonate.

biceps [bi'sɛps], *n.m.* biceps.

biche [biʃ], *n.f.* hind, doe.

bichon [bi'ʃɔ̃], *n.m.* (*fem.* **-onne**) lap dog with long, silky hair.

bichonner [biʃɔ'ne], *v.t.* to curl; (*fig.*) to caress. **se bichonner**, *v.r.* to curl one's hair; to make oneself smart.

biconcave [bikɔ'kaːv], *a.* bi-concave.

biconvexe [bikɔ'vɛks], *a.* bi-convex.

bicoque [bi'kɔk], *n.f.* (*colloq.*) ramshackle house, shanty.

bicorne [bi'kɔrn], *a.* and *n.m.* cocked (hat).

bicyclette [bisi'klɛt], *n.f.* bicycle.

bidet [bi'de], *n.m.* pony, small nag; bidet (*bath*).

bidon [bi'dɔ̃], *n.m.* tin, can (*esp. gas can*); camp kettle; soldier's water bottle.

bidonville [bidɔ̃'vil], *n.m.* shanty town.

bielle [bjɛl], *n.f.* (*Mach.*) connecting rod.

Blélorussie [bjelory'si], la, *f.* Byelorussia, White Russia.

bien [bjɛ̃], *n.m.* good; that which is pleasant, useful or advantageous; benefit, welfare, well-being, blessing; wealth, estate, property; gift, boon, mercy; (*pl.*) goods, chattels; fruits (*of the soil etc.*); *biens de consommation*, consumer goods; *biens immobiliers*, real estate.—*adv.* well; rightly, finely; much, very, far, entirely, completely; about, well-nigh; favorably, successfully; well off; on good terms, in favor; certainly, truly, indeed; formally, clearly, expressly; *aussi bien*, anyhow, in any case; *bien de*, plenty of, many; *bien mieux*, far better; *bien plus*, besides, moreover; *bien que*, although; *c'est bien*, that's right; *cette femme est bien*, that woman is good-looking; *eh bien!* well! or well? *je vous l'avais bien dit*, I told you so; *ou bien*, or else; *si bien que*, so that; *tant bien que mal*, so-so.—*int.* (*sometimes pronounced colloq.* [bɛ̃]) well!

bien-aimé [bjɛ̃nɛ'me], *a.* beloved, well-beloved.—*n.m.* (*fem.* **-ée**) darling, dear.

bien-dire [bjɛ̃'diːr], *n.m.* (*no pl.*) fine speaking.

43

bien-être [bjɛ̃'nɛːtr], *n.m.* (*no pl.*) well-being, welfare, comfort.
bienfaisance [bjɛ̃fə'zɑ̃ːs], *n.f.* beneficence, charity, munificence.
bienfaisant [bjɛ̃fə'zɑ̃], *a.* charitable, beneficent, kind, gracious; beneficial, salutary.
bienfait [bjɛ̃'fɛ], *n.m.* good turn, kindness, benefit, favor, courtesy.
bienfaiteur [bjɛ̃fɛ'tœːr], *n.m.* (*fem.* **-trice**) benefactor, benefactress, patron.
bien-fonds [bjɛ̃'fɔ̃], *n.m.* (*pl.* **biens-fonds**) real estate.
bienheureux [bjɛ̃nœ'rø], *a.* (*fem.* **-euse**) happy, fortunate; (*Eccles.*) blessed.
biennal [biɛ'nal], *a.* (*m. pl.* **-aux**) biennial.
bienséance [bjɛ̃se'ɑ̃ːs], *n.f.* propriety decency, decorum, seemliness.
bienséant [bjɛ̃se'ɑ̃], *a.* decent, becoming, seemly, decorous, fit.
bientôt [bjɛ̃'to], *adv.* soon, before long, shortly; *à bientôt!* see you soon!
bienveillance [bjɛ̃vɛ'jɑ̃ːs], *n.f.* benevolence, goodwill, favor, kindness.
bienveillant [bjɛ̃vɛ'jɑ̃], *a.* benevolent, kind, friendly, favorable.
bienvenu [bjɛ̃v'ny], *a.* welcome; *soyez le bienvenu,* it's nice to have you with us.
bienvenue [bjɛ̃v'ny], *n.f.* welcome; *souhaiter la bienvenue à quelqu'un,* to greet *or* welcome someone.
bière (1) [bjɛːr], *n.f.* beer.
bière (2) [bjɛːr], *n.f.* coffin.
biffer [bi'fe], *v.t.* to cancel, to blot out, to erase.
biflore [bi'flɔːr], *a.* (*Bot.*) biflorate.
bifocal [bifɔ'kal], *a.* (*m. pl.* **-aux**) bifocal.
bifolié [bifɔ'lje], *a.* (*Bot.*) bifoliate.
bifteck [bif'tɛk], *n.m.* beefsteak.
bifurcation [bifyrka'sjɔ̃], *n.f.* bifurcation; fork (*of a road*).
bigame [bi'gam], *a.* bigamous.—*n.* bigamist.
bigamie [biga'mi], *n.f.* bigamy.
bigarré [biga're], *a.* parti-colored, streaked.
bigarrer [biga're], *v.t.* to chequer, to streak, to variegate.
bigarrure [biga'ryːr], *n.f.* medley, mixture, motley, variegation.
bigot [bi'go], *a.* bigoted.—*n.m.* (*fem.* **-e**) bigot.
bigoterie [bigɔ'tri], *n.f.*, **bigotisme** [bigɔ'tism], *n.m.* bigotry.
bigoudi [bigu'di], *n.m.* curling pin *or* curler (*for the hair*).
bijou [bi'ʒu], *n.m.* (*pl.* **-oux**) jewel, gem; (*fig.*) darling.
bijouterie [biʒu'tri], *n.f.* jewelry.
bijoutier [biʒu'tje], *n.m.* (*fem.* **-ière**) jeweler.
bilan [bi'lɑ̃], *n.m.* balance sheet.
bilatéral [bilate'ral], *a.* (*m. pl.* **-aux**) bilateral.
bilboquet [bilbɔ'kɛ], *n.m.* cup-and-ball (*toy*); small weighted figure that balances itself.
bile [bil], *n.f.* bile, spleen, gall; (*fig.*) anger.
bilieux [bi'ljø], *a.* (*fem.* **-euse**) bilious; (*fig.*) choleric, passionate.
bilingue [bi'lɛ̃ːg], *a.* bilingual.
billard [bi'jaːr], *n.m.* billiards; billiard table; billiard room.
bille [biːj], *n.f.* billiard ball; marble, taw; log, unworked piece of timber; *roulement à billes,* ball bearings.
billet [bi'jɛ], *n.m.* note, missive; bill, handbill; ticket, lottery ticket; promissory note;

billet (*for quartering soldiers*); *billet de banque,* bank note; *billet d'aller et retour,* return ticket; *billet doux,* love letter.
billevesée [bilvə'ze], *n.f.* idle story, stuff, nonsense, bunkum.
billion [bi'ljɔ̃], *n.m.* (*since* 1948 = 1 *followed by* 12 *ciphers*), billion, one million million(s); (*Am.*) trillion.
billot [bi'jo], *n.m.* block; executioner's block.
bimbelot [bɛ̃'blo], *n.m.* plaything, toy, bauble.
bimensuel [bimɑ̃'sɥɛl], *a.* (*fem.* **-elle**) twice monthly, fortnightly.
bimoteur [bimɔ'tœːr], *a.* and *n.m.* twin-engined (plane).
binaire [bi'nɛːr], *a.* binary.
biner [bi'ne], *v.t.* (*Agric.*) to dig again; to hoe.
binette [bi'nɛt], *n.f.* hoe; (*colloq.*) face.
biniou [bi'nju], *n.m.* Breton bagpipe.
binôme [bi'noːm], *n.m.* (*Alg.*) binomial.
biochimie [biɔʃi'mi], *n.f.* biochemistry.
biographe [biɔ'graf], *n.m.* biographer.
biographie [biɔgra'fi], *n.f.* biography.
biographique [biɔgra'fik], *a.* biographical.
biologie [biɔlɔ'ʒi], *n.f.* biology.
biologique [biɔlɔ'ʒik], *a.* biological.
biologiste [biɔlɔ'ʒist], **biologue** [biɔ'lɔg], *n.m.* biologist.
bion [bjɔ̃], *n.m.* sucker, shoot.
bioxyde [biɔk'sid], *n.m.* dioxide.
biparti [bipar'ti], **bipartite** [bipar'tit], *a.* bipartite.
bipède [bi'pɛd], *a.* and *n.* (*Zool.*) biped.
biplan [bi'plɑ̃], *n.m.* biplane.
bipolaire [bipɔ'lɛːr], *a.* bipolar.
bique [bik], *n.f.* nanny goat.
biréacteur [bireak'tœːr], *n.m.* twin-engined jet plane.
birloir [bir'lwaːr], *n.m.* window catch.
birman [bir'mɑ̃], *a.* Burmese.—*n.m.* (**Birman,** *fem.* **-ane**) Burmese (*person*).
Birmanie [birma'ni], **la,** *f.* Burma.
bis (1) [bi], *a.* brown; tawny, swarthy; *du pain bis,* brown bread.
bis (2) [bis], *adv.* twice.—*int.* encore!
bisaïeul [biza'jœl], *n.m.* great-grandfather.
bisaïeule [biza'jœl], *n.f.* great-grandmother.
bisannuel [biza'nɥɛl], *a.* (*fem.* **-elle**) (*Bot.*) biennial.
bisbille [biz'biːj], *n.f.* (*fam.*) petty quarrel, tiff, bickering.
biscornu [biskɔr'ny], *a.* irregular, misshapen; (*fig.*) outlandish, odd, queer.
biscotte [bis'kɔt], *n.f.* rusk.
biscuit [bis'kɥi], *n.m.* biscuit; pastry made with flour, eggs, and sugar; (*Am.*) cracker; unglazed porcelain.
bise [biːz], *n.f.* dry and cold north wind; (*colloq.*) kiss.
biseau [bi'zo], *n.m.* (*pl.* **-eaux**) bevel, chamfer; bevelling tool.
biseauter [bizo'te], *v.t.* to bevel.
bismuth [biz'myt], *n.m.* bismuth.
bison [bi'zɔ̃], *n.m.* bison, buffalo.
bisque [bisk], *n.f.* soup made of crayfish, chicken *or* game, fish etc.; (*colloq.*) ill-humor, spite.
bisquer [bis'ke], *v.i.* (*colloq.*) to be vexed *or* riled.
bissac [bi'sak], *n.m.* double wallet, sack *or* bag, haversack.
bissecter [bisɛk'te], *v.t.* to bisect.

bisser [bi'se], *v.t.* to encore.

bissextile [bisɛks'til], *a.* **année bissextile**, leap year.

bissexué [bisɛk'sɥe], **bissexuel** [-sɥɛl] (*fem.* **-elle**), *a.* (*Bot.*) bisexual.

bistouri [bistu'ri], *n.m.* bistoury, lancet.

bistourner [bistur'ne], *v.t.* to twist, to distort; to castrate.

bistre [bistr], *n.m.* bistre, sepia.

bistro or **bistrot** [bis'tro], *n.m.* (*slang*) pub.

bitume [bi'tym], *n.m.* bitumen.

bituminer [bitymi'ne], *v.t.* to asphalt.

bitumineux [bitymi'nø], **bitumeux** [bity'mø], *a.* (*fem.* **-euse**) bituminous.

bivalent [biva'lã], *a.* divalent, bivalent.

bivalve [bi'valv], *a.* bivalvular.—*n.m.* bivalve.

bivouac [bi'vwak], *n.m.* bivouac.

bivouaquer [bivwa'ke], *v.i.* to bivouac.

bizarre [bi'za:r], *a.* queer, strange, whimsical, bizarre.

bizarrement [bizar'mã], *adv.* oddly, queerly, whimsically.

bizarrerie [bizar'ri], *n.f.* singularity, oddness; caprice, whim.

black-out [blak'aut], *n.m.* black-out.

blafard [bla'fa:r], *a.* pale, wan; livid.

blague [blag], *n.f.* tobacco pouch; (*slang*) chaff, humbug, hoax, fib; trick, practical joke; *sans blague!* you don't say!

blaguer [bla'ge], *v.i.* to chaff, to hoax, to humbug.

blagueur [bla'gœ:r], *n.m.* (*fem.* **-euse**) wag, hoaxer, humbug.

blaireau [blɛ'ro], *n.m.* (*pl.* **-eaux**) badger; shaving brush; badger-hair brush.

blâmable [blɑ'mabl], *a.* blameworthy.

blâme [blɑ:m], *n.m.* blame; reproach, reprimand.

blâmer [blɑ'me], *v.t.* to blame, to criticize; to censure, to reprimand.

blanc [blɑ̃], *a.* (*fem.* **blanche** (1) [blɑ̃:ʃ]) white; hoar, hoary; clean; blank; *gelée blanche*, hoar frost; *passer une nuit blanche*, to have a sleepless night; *vers blancs*, blank verse.—*n.m.* white; blank; target, mark; *blanc de chaux*, whitewash; *de but en blanc*, point-blank; *en blanc*, left blank.

blanc-bec [blɑ̃'bɛk], *n.m.* (*pl.* **blancs-becs**) beardless youth, youngster; greenhorn; sucker.

blanchaille [blɑ̃'ʃa:j], *n.f.* whitebait.

blanchâtre [blɑ̃'ʃɑ:tr], *a.* whitish.

blanche (1) [BLANC].

blanche (2) [blɑ̃:ʃ], *n.f.* (*Mus.*) minim.

blancheur [blɑ̃'ʃœ:r], *n.f.* whiteness; cleanliness; light; (*fig.*) purity, innocence.

blanchiment [blɑ̃ʃi'mã], *n.m.* whitening, bleaching; blanching.

blanchir [blɑ̃'ʃi:r], *v.t.* to whiten; to whitewash; to wash, to bleach, to clean; to blanch.—*v.i.* to whiten.

blanchissage [blɑ̃ʃi'sa:ʒ], *n.m.* washing; refining (*of sugar etc.*).

blanchissant [blɑ̃ʃi'sã], *a.* that whitens or grows white; foaming.

blanchisserie [blɑ̃ʃis'ri], *n.f.* laundry, washhouse.

blanchisseuse [blɑ̃ʃi'sø:z], *n.f.* washerwoman; laundress.

blanc-manger [blɑ̃mɑ̃'ʒe], *n.m.* (*pl.* **blancs-mangers**) blancmange.

blaser [blɑ'ze], *v.t.* to blunt, to cloy, to sicken, to surfeit.

blason [blɑ'zõ], *n.m.* coat of arms; blazon; heraldry, blazonry.

blasonner [blɑzo'ne], *v.t.* to blazon; to interpret (*coats of arms*).

blasphémateur [blasfema'tœ:r], *n.m.* (*fem.* **-trice**) blasphemer.

blasphématoire [blasfema'twa:r], *a.* blasphemous.

blasphème [blas'fɛ:m], *n.m.* blasphemy.

blasphémer [blasfe'me], *v.t., v.i.* (*conjug. like* CÉDER) to blaspheme, to curse.

blatte [blat], *n.f.* cockroach, black beetle.

blé [ble], *n.m.* corn, wheat; *halle au blé*, corn exchange; *manger son blé en herbe*, to spend one's money before one has it.

blême [blɛ:m], *a.* sallow, pale, wan; ghastly.

blêmir [blɛ'mi:r], *v.i.* to turn or grow pale.

blèsement [blɛz'mã], *n.m.* lisping.

bléser [ble'ze], *v.i.* (*conjug. like* CÉDER) to lisp.

blessant [blɛ'sã], *a.* wounding; (*fig.*) offensive, mortifying.

blessé [blɛ'se], *a.* wounded; (*fig.*) offended.—*n.m.* (*fem.* **-ée**) (*Mil.*) casualty.

blesser [blɛ'se], *v.t.* to wound; to hurt; to offend, to injure; to shock. **se blesser**, *v.r.* to hurt oneself; (*fig.*) to take offence.

blessure [blɛ'sy:r], *n.f.* wound, hurt, injury; offence; *coups et blessures*, assault and battery.

blet [blɛ], *a.* (*fem.* **-ette** (1)) over-ripe, sleepy (*of fruit*).

blette (2) [BETTE].

bleu [blø], *a.* blue, black and blue (*as a bruise*); (*fig.*) amazed; *cordon bleu*, first-rate cook. —*n.m.* blue, blueness; blueprint; greenhorn, novice; (*C*) Conservative, Tory.

bleuâtre [blø'ɑ:tr], *a.* bluish.

bleuet [BLUET].

bleuir [blø'i:r], *v.t.* to make blue, to blue (*in washing*).—*v.i.* to become blue.

blindage [blɛ̃'da:ʒ], *n.m.* iron-plating, armor-plating.

blindé [blɛ̃'de], *a.* armored, armor-plated; screened; (*slang*) drunk.

blinder [blɛ̃'de], *v.t.* to armor-plate (*a ship, fort etc.*).

bloc [blok], *n.m.* block, lump, the whole lot.

blocage (1) [blo'ka:ʒ], *n.m.* blockading; blocking; block (*of traffic*); obstruction; (*Fin.*) freezing.

blocage (2) [blo'ka:ʒ], *n.m.* rubble.

blockhaus [blo'ko:s], *n.m. inv.* blockhouse.

bloc-note(s) [blok'not], *n.m.* writing pad.

blocus [blo'ky:s], *n.m. inv.* blockade.

blond [blõ], *a.* blond, fair; light (*ale*); *blond ardent*, auburn; *blond cendré*, ash-blond. —*n.f.* (**-e**) (*C*) sweetheart.

blondin [blõ'dɛ̃], *a.* fair-haired.—*n.m.* (*fem.* **-e**) fair-haired child.—*n.m.* spark, beau.

blondir [blõ'di:r], *v.i.* to grow blond or fair.

blondissant [blõdi'sã], *a.* growing yellow or golden (*of corn etc.*).

bloquer [blo'ke], *v.t.* to block up, to fill up (*cavities in walls*) with mortar; (*Mil.*) to blockade; (*Fin.*) to freeze; to jam on (*brakes*).

blottir (**se**) [sablo'ti:r], *v.r.* to curl up, to snuggle, to huddle; to cower, to crouch.

blouse [blu:z], *n.f.* smock; tunic; blouse; pinafore; overall.

blouser [blu'ze], *v.t.* to mislead, to cheat. **se blouser**, *v.r.* (*Billiards*) to pocket one's own ball; (*fig.*) to blunder; to bark up the wrong tree.

blouson [blu'zõ], *n.m.* lumber-jacket, wind-cheater.

bluet [bly'ɛ], **bleuet** [blœ'ɛ], *n.m.* blue-bottle, corn-flower; (C) blueberry.

bluette [bly'ɛt], *n.f.* spark; (*fig.*) literary trifle, novelette.

bluff [blœf], *n.m.* bluff.

bluffer [blœ'fe], *v.t.* to bluff.

blutage [bly'ta:ʒ], *n.m.* bolting, sifting (*of flour*).

bluter [bly'te], *v.t.* to bolt, to sift (*flour etc.*).

boa [bo'a], *n.m.* boa (*snake*); boa (*of feathers*).

bobèche [bɔ'bɛʃ], *n.f.* socket (*of a candlestick*); sconce.

bobine [bɔ'bin], *n.f.* bobbin, spool, reel; (*Cine.*) reel; **bobine d'induction**, induction coil.

bobiner [bɔbi'ne], *v.t.* to wind on a bobbin, to spool.

bobineuse [bɔbi'nø:z], *n.f.* winder, winding machine.

bobo [bo'bo], *n.m.* (*Childish*) hurt, sore, bump; **avoir bobo** or **du bobo**, to have a slight pain, sore etc.; **faire bobo**, to hurt.

bocage [bɔ'ka:ʒ], *n.m.* copse, grove.

bocager [bɔka'ʒe], *a.* (*fem.* **-ère**) of groves *or* woodlands; shady.

bocal [bɔ'kal], *n.m.* (*pl.* **-aux**) druggist's short-necked bottle; carboy; glass jar, fish-bowl.

boche [bɔʃ] (*aphæresis of* **Alboche**), *n.* (*pej.*) German, Jerry.

bock [bɔk], *n.m.* bock *or* glass (*beer*).

bœuf [bœf], *n.m.* (*pl.* **bœufs** [bø]) ox; beef.

Bohême [bɔ'ɛːm], **la,** *f.* Bohemia.

bohème [bɔ'ɛːm], *a.* Bohemian.—*n.* Bohemian, person of careless, unconventional habits.

bohémien [bɔe'mjɛ̃], *a.* and *n.m.* (*fem.* **-enne**) Bohemian; gipsy.

boire [bwa:r], *v.t. irr.* to drink; to consume *or* waste on drink; to absorb; to swallow (*an insult etc.*).—*v.i.* to drink (*to someone's health*); to tipple; to blot (*of paper*).—*n.m.* drink; drinking.

bois [bwa], *n.m.* wood, forest; wood, ʹtimber; wooden part *or* object; horns (*of a deer etc.*).

boisage [bwa'za:ʒ], *n.m.* wood-work; timber-ing (*of mines etc.*); wainscotting.

(C) **bois-brûlé** [bwabry'le], *n.m.* half-breed.

(C) **bois-debout** [bwad'bu], *n.m.* standing timber.

boisé [bwa'ze], *a.* wooded, well-timbered.

boisement [bwaz'mã], *n.m.* planting land with trees.

boiser [bwa'ze], *v.t.* to put woodwork to; to timber (*a mine etc.*); to wainscot; to pant with woods.

boiserie [bwaz'ri], *n.f.* wainscot, wainscotting.

boisseau [bwa'so], *n.m.* (*pl.* **-eaux**) bushel.

boisson [bwa'sõ], *n.f.* drink; beverage; (*fig.*) drinking, drunkenness; (C) hard liquor; **boisson forte**, strong drink, (*Am.*) liquor.

boîte [bwat], *n.f.* box; casket, caddy, chest; case (*of a watch, rudder etc.*); (*pop.*) mouth; **boîte à feu**, stoke-hole; (*Motor.*) **boîte de vitesses**, gear box; **boîte de nuit**, night club; (*pop.*) **ta boîte!** shut your big mouth!

boitement [bwat'mã], *n.m.* halting, limping.

boiter [bwa'te], *v.i.* to limp; to be lame.

boiteux [bwa'tø], *a.* (*fem.* **-euse**) lame, halt, limping; rickety (*furniture*).—*n.m.* (*fem.* **-euse**) lame man *or* woman.

boîtier [bwa'tje], *n.m.* surgeon's case of in-struments; case (*of a watch, an electric torch*).

bol [bɔl], *n.m.* bowl, basin.

bolchevik [bɔlʃə'vik], *n.m.* Bolshevik.

bolchevisme [bɔlʃə'vism], *n.m.* Bolshevism.

bolée [bɔ'le], *n.f.* bowlful.

boléro [bole'ro], *n.m.* bolero (*dance and gar-ment*).

Bolivie [bɔli'vi], **la,** *f.* Bolivia.

bolivien [bɔli'vjɛ̃], *a.* (*fem.* **-enne**) Bolivian.—*n.m.* (**Bolivien,** *fem.* **-enne**) Bolivian (*person*).

bombance [bõ'bã:s], *n.f.* feasting, junketing.

bombardement [bõbardə'mã], *n.m.* bom-bardment, shelling; **bombardement en piqué**, dive-bombing.

bombarder [bõbar'de], *v.t.* to bombard, to bomb; **quartier bombardé**, bombed site.

bombardier [bõbar'dje], *n.m.* bombardier.

bombe [bõ:b], *n.f.* bomb; spray flask; **bombe atomique**, atom bomb; **bombe à hydro-gène**, H-bomb; **bombe incendiaire**, incendiary bomb; (*colloq.*) **faire la bombe**, to be on a binge.

bombé [bõ'be], *a.* convex, arched.

bombement [bõbə'mã], *n.m.* convexity, swell-ing, bulge.

bomber [bõ'be], *v.t.* to cause (*something*) to bulge, jut, swell out, arch, curve *or* barrel.—*v.i.* to bulge, to jut out.

bombyx [bõ'biks], *n.m.* (*Ent.*) bombyx; silk-worm.

bon (1) [bõ], *a.* (*fem.* **bonne** (1)) good; kind, favorable; fine, convenient, advantageous, profitable, proper; well-executed, cleverly done etc.; easy, good-natured; (*iron.*) simple, credulous; **à quoi bon tant de peine?** what is the good of so much trouble? **il fait bon dans cette pièce**, this room is nice and warm; **pour de bon**, for good and all.—*n.m.* that which is good; the best.—*adv.* well, right, properly; **tout de bon**, seriously, truly.

bon (2) [bõ], *n.m.* bond, coupon, voucher; **bon du trésor**, treasury bond; **bon d'essence**, gasoline coupon.

bonasse [bo'nas], *a.* simple-minded, credul-ous; soft.

bon-bec [bõ'bɛk], *n.m.* (*pl.* **bons-becs**) chatterbox, gossip.

bonbon [bõ'bõ], *n.m.* sweet, (*Am.*) candy.

bond [bõ], *n.m.* bound, leap, jump, caper; **faire faux bond**, to give (*someone*) the slip.

bonde [bõ:d], *n.f.* bung-hole, bung; sluice, flood-gate.

bondé [bõ'de], *a.* chock-full, packed, crammed.

bondir [bõ'di:r], *v.i.* to bound, to leap, to bounce, to caper, to frisk.

bondissant [bõdi'sã], *a.* bounding, skipping.

bondissement [bõdis'mã], *n.m.* bounding, skipping, frisking.

bonheur [bɔ'nœːr], *n.m.* happiness, prosper-ity, welfare; good fortune, good luck, success.

bouclé

bonhomie [bɔnɔ'mi], *n.f.* good nature; simplicity, credulity.

bonhomme [bɔ'nɔm], *n.m.* (*pl.* **bonshommes** [bɔ'zɔm]) simple, good-natured man; foolish *or* credulous person; (*fig.*) rough drawing *or* effigy of a man; *bonhomme de neige*, snowman.

boni [bɔ'ni], *n.m.* bonus.

boniface [bɔni'fas], *a.* and *n.* (*pop.*) simple, artless (person).

bonification [bɔnifika'sjɔ̃], *n.f.* amelioration, improvement (*of land*); (*Fin.*) bonus, discount.

bonifier [bɔni'fje], *v.t.* to better, to improve; (*Fin.*) to pay, to transfer.

boniment [bɔni'mã], *n.m.* quack's show; (*fig.*) humbug.

bonjour [bɔ̃'ʒuːr], *n.m.* and *int.* good morning, good afternoon, good day.

bonne (1) [BON (1)].

bonne (2) [bɔn], *n.f.* servant-maid; housemaid; *bonne d'enfants*, nursery-maid; *bonne à tout faire*, general maid.

bonnement [bɔn'mã], *adv.* plainly, simply, honestly; *tout bonnement*, quite frankly.

bonnet [bɔ'nɛ], *n.m.* cap; *c'est bonnet blanc et blanc bonnet*, it is six of one and half a dozen of the other.

bonneterie [bɔn'tri], *n.f.* hosiery business; hosiery.

bonnetier [bɔn'tje], *n.m.* (*fem.* **-ière**) hosier.

bon-prime [bɔ̃'prim], *n.m.* (*Comm.*) free-gift coupon.

bonsoir [bɔ̃'swaːr], *n.m.* and *int.* good evening, good night.

bonté [bɔ̃'te], *n.f.* goodness, kindness.

boom [bum], *n.m.* (*Fin.*) boom.

borax [bɔ'raks], *n.m.* borax.

bord [bɔːr], *n.m.* edge, margin, brink, brim, border, rim; shore, bank, side; *au bord de la mer*, at the seaside; *à bord*, on board; *par-dessus bord*, overboard.

bordage [bɔr'daːʒ], *n.m.* bordering, hemming etc.; (*Naut.*) planking, bulwarks.

bordé [bɔr'de], *n.m.* hem, edging, bordering (*of a garment*); (*Naut.*) planking.

bordeaux [bɔr'do], *n.m.* Bordeaux wine; *bordeaux rouge*, claret.

bordée [bɔr'de], *n.f.* (*Naut.*) broadside; volley, salvo; (*C*) *une bordée de neige*, a snow-fall.

bordelais [bɔrdə'lɛ:], *a.* of Bordeaux.—*n.m.* (**Bordelais**, *fem.* **-aise**) native of Bordeaux.

border [bɔr'de], *v.t.* to border, to edge, to hem, to skirt, to bind; to tuck in (*bedclothes*); (*Naut.*) to haul (*the sheets*).

bordereau [bɔrdə'ro], *n.m.* (*pl.* **-eaux**) memorandum, note, schedule, account.

bordure [bɔr'dyːr], *n.f.* frame, edging, edging; margin, border, curb; rim.

boréal [bɔre'al], *a.* (*m. pl.* **-aux**) boreal, northern.

borée [bɔ're], *n.m.* Boreas, north wind (*poet.*).

borgne [bɔrn], *a.* one-eyed; *rue borgne*, blind alley.—*n.* one-eyed person.

borique [bɔ'rik], *a.* boric.

borne [bɔrn], *n.f.* landmark; boundary, limit, confine; milestone; (*Elec.*) terminal; *borne kilométrique*, milestone.

borné [bɔr'ne], *a.* bounded, limited, confined; narrow, mean, hide-bound.

borne-fontaine [bɔrnfɔ̃'tɛ:n], *n.f.* (*pl.* **bornes-fontaines**) street fountain (*like a boundary post*).

borner [bɔr'ne], *v.t.* to set landmarks to; to bound, to limit, to confine.

Bosphore [bɔs'fɔːr], **le**, *m.* the Bosphorus.

bosquet [bɔs'kɛ], *n.m.* grove, thicket, arbor.

bosse [bɔs], *n.f.* hump, hunch; bump, bruise; knob, protuberance, lump, boss; (*Arch.*) embossment; (*Sculp.*) relief.

bosselage [bɔs'laːʒ], *n.m.* embossing.

bosseler [bɔs'le], *v.t.* (*conjug. like* APPELER) to dent; to emboss.

bossu [bɔ'sy], *a.* hunch-backed; deformed, crooked; pigeon-breasted.—*n.m.* (*fem.* **-e**) hunch-back; *rire comme un bossu*, to split one's sides with laughter.

bossuer [bɔ'sɥe], *v.t.* to dent, to batter.

boston [bɔs'tɔ̃], *n.m.* boston (*card game, dance*).

bot [bo], *a.* *pied bot*, club foot; club-footed.

botanique [bɔta'nik], *a.* botanical.—*n.f.* botany.

botaniser [bɔtani'ze], *v.i.* to botanize.

botaniste [bɔta'nist], *n.* botanist.

botte (1) [bɔt], *n.f.* wellington boot, jack-boot.

botte (2) [bɔt], *n.f.* bunch, truss, bale.

botte (3) [bɔt], *n.f.* (*Fenc.*) pass, thrust

bottelage [bɔt'laːʒ], *n.m.* tying up in bundles.

botteler [bɔt'le], *v.t.* (*conjug. like* APPELER) to put up in bundles, to truss.

botteloir [bɔt'lwaːr], *n.m.*, **botteleuse** [bɔt'løːz], *n.f.* sheaf-binding machine, binder.

botter [bɔ'te], *v.t.* to put boots on (*a person*).

bottier [bɔ'tje], *n.m.* bootmaker.

bottin [bɔ'tɛ̃], *n.m.* a directory published by the firm of Didot Bottin.

bottine [bɔ'tin], *n.f.* (ankle) boot.

bouc [buk], *n.m.* billy goat; *bouc émissaire* scapegoat.

boucanage [buka'naːʒ], *n.m.* smoke-drying.

boucaner [buka'ne], *v.t.* to smoke (*meat, hides etc.*).

boucanier [buka'nje], *n.m.* buccaneer; freebooter.

(*C*) **boucanière** [buka'nɛːr], *n.f.* smokehouse (*for fish*).

bouchage [bu'ʃaːʒ], *n.m.* stopping, corking.

bouche [buʃ], *n.f.* mouth; lips; tongue; voice; victuals; muzzle (*of a cannon*); *bouche d'eau*, hydrant.

bouchée [bu'ʃe], *n.f.* mouthful.

boucher (1) [bu'ʃe], *v.t.* to stop, to choke.

boucher (2) [bu'ʃe], *n.m.* butcher.

bouchère [bu'ʃɛːr], *n.f.* butcher's wife; woman keeping a butcher's shop.

boucherie [buʃ'ri], *n.f.* butcher's shop; butchery, slaughter.

bouche-trou [buʃ'tru], *n.m.* (*pl.* **bouchetrous**) stopgap.

bouchon [bu'ʃɔ̃], *n.m.* stopper, cork; wisp (*of straw etc.*).

bouchonner [buʃɔ'ne], *v.t.* to rub down (*a horse*).

bouchonnier [buʃɔ'nje], *n.m.* one who cuts *or* sells corks.

boucle [bukl], *n.f.* buckle; curl, lock (*of hair*); loop (*of a river etc.*).

bouclé [bu'kle], *a.* buckled, curled.

47

boucler [bu'kle], *v.t.* to buckle; to put a ring to; to curl (*hair*); **boucler la boucle**, to loop the loop. **se boucler**, *v.r.* to curl one's hair.

bouclier [bu'klje], *n.m.* buckler, shield; (*fig.*) defense.

Bouddha [bu'da], *m.* Buddha.

bouddhisme [bu'dism], *n.m.* Buddhism.

bouddhiste [bu'dist], *n.* Buddhist.

bouder [bu'de], *v.i.* to sulk, to be sullen, to pout. **se bouder**, *v.r.* to be cool towards each other.

bouderie [bu'dri], *n.f.* pouting, sulkiness.

boudeur [bu'dœ:r], *a.* (*fem.* **-euse**) sulky, sullen.

boudin [bu'dɛ̃], *n.m.* blood sausage; spring (*of a coach*).

boudoir [bu'dwa:r], *n.m.* boudoir, lady's private room.

boue [bu], *n.f.* mud, mire, dirt, filth.

bouée [bu'e], *n.f.* buoy.

boueux [bu'ø], *a.* (*fem.* **-euse**) muddy, dirty, miry; foul.—*n.m.* scavenger; garbage man.

bouffant [bu'fɑ̃], *a.* puffed (*sleeve*), baggy (*trousers*).

bouffe [buf], *a.* comic.—*n.m. pl. Les Bouffes*, the Italian opera (*in Paris*).

bouffée [bu'fe], *n.f.* puff, gust, blast, whiff.

bouffette [bu'fɛt], *n.f.* bow of ribbon; tassel.

bouffi [bu'fi], *a.* puffed up, swollen, inflated.

bouffir [bu'fi:r], *v.t.* to puff up, to swell, to bloat.—*v.i.* to swell.

bouffissure [bufi'sy:r], *n.f.* swelling, puffing up.

bouffon [bu'fɔ̃], *a.* (*fem.* **-onne**) jocose, facetious, comical.—*n.m.* buffoon, clown, jester.

bouffonner [bufɔ'ne], *v.i.* to play the buffoon; to be jocose or full of jests.

bouffonnerie [bufɔn'ri], *n.f.* buffoonery, drollery, jesting.

bougainvillée [bugɛ̃vi'le], *n.f.*, **bougain-villier** [bugɛ̃vi'lje], *n.m.* bougainvillea.

bouge [bu:ʒ], *n.m.* den, dirty hole, hovel.

bougeoir [bu'ʒwa:], *n.m.* flat candlestick.

bouger [bu'ʒe], *v.i.* (*conjug. like* MANGER) to stir, to budge, to fidget.

bougie [bu'ʒi], *n.f.* wax candle; (*Elec.*) candlepower; **bougie d'allumage**, (*Motor.*) spark plug.

bougran [bu'grɑ̃], *n.m.* buckram.

bouillabaisse [buja'bɛs], *n.f.* Provençal fish soup with saffron etc.

bouillant [bu'jɑ̃], *a.* boiling, hot, scalding.

bouilleur [bu'jœ:r], *n.m.* brandy distiller; boiler tube (*of an engine*).

bouilli [bu'ji], *n.m.* boiled beef.

bouillie [bu'ji], *n.f.* pap (*for infants*), porridge; pulp.

bouillir [bu'ji:r], *v.t. irr.* to boil (*milk etc.*). —*v.i.* to boil.

bouilloire [bu'jwa:r], *n.f.* kettle.

bouillon [bu'jɔ̃], *n.m.* broth, beef tea; bubble; ebullition.

bouillonnement [bujɔn'mɑ̃], *n.m.* bubbling up, spouting, gushing.

bouillonner [bujɔ'ne], *v.i.* to bubble, to boil; (*fig.*) to be in a state of excitement.

bouillotte [bu'jɔt]. *n.f.* foot warmer; hot-water bottle; small kettle.

boulanger [bulɑ̃'ʒe], *n.m.* (*fem.* **-ère**) baker, baker's wife.—*v.t.* (*conjug. like* MANGER) to make, knead or bake (*bread*).

boulangerie [bulɑ̃'ʒri], *n.f.* baking, baker's business; baker's shop.

boule [bul], *n.f.* ball; bowl; (*pop.*) face, pate, head.

bouleau [bu'lo], *n.m.* (*pl.* **-eaux**) birch, birch tree.

bouledogue [bul'dɔg], *n.m.* bulldog.

boulet [bu'lɛ], *n.m.* cannon or musket ball.

boulette [bu'lɛt], *n.f.* pellet; forcemeat ball.

boulevard [bul'va:r], *n.m.* rampart; boulevard.

bouleversement [bulvɛrsə'mɑ̃], *n.m.* overthrow; commotion, confusion; destruction, ruin.

bouleverser [bulvɛr'se], *v.t.* to overthrow, to throw down; to subvert; (*fig.*) to agitate, to upset.

boulier [bu'lje], *n.m.* (*Fishing*) bag net; scoring board (*at billiards*).

bouline [bu'lin], *n.f.* (*Naut.*) bowline.

boulon [bu'lɔ̃], *n.m.* bolt, large iron pin.

boulonner [bulɔ'ne], *v.t.* to fasten with iron pins, to bolt.

boulot [bu'lo], *a.* (*fem.* **-otte**) fat, dumpy, squat.

bouquet [bu'kɛ], *n.m.* bunch (*of flowers*), nosegay, bouquet; aroma (*of wine*), perfume.

bouquetier [buk'tje], *n.f.* flower vase.

bouquetière [buk'tjɛ:r], *n.f.* flower girl.

bouquetin [buk'tɛ̃], *n.m.* ibex.

bouquin (1) [bu'kɛ̃], *n.m.* (*Zool.*) old billy goat; old hare.

bouquin (2) [bu'kɛ̃], *n.m.* old book; second-hand book; (*colloq.*) book.

bouquiner [buki'ne], *v.i.* to hunt after old books; (*colloq.*) to read.

bouquineur [buki'nœ:r], *n.m.* (*colloq.*) lover of old books, book fancier.

bouquiniste [buki'nist], *n.m.* dealer in second-hand books.

bourbe [burb], *n.f.* mud, mire, slush.

bourbeux [bur'bø], *a.* (*fem.* **-euse**) miry, muddy, sloshy.

bourbier [bur'bje], *n.m.* slough, puddle, mire.

bourdaine [bur'dɛn], **bourgène** [bur'ʒɛn], *n.f.* black alder.

bourdon (1) [bur'dɔ̃], *n.m.* pilgrim's staff.

bourdon (2) [bur'dɔ̃], *n.m.* bumblebee; great bell; (*Organ*) drone.

bourdonnant [burdɔ'nɑ̃], *a.* humming, buzzing.

bourdonnement [burdɔn'mɑ̃], *n.m.* buzz, buzzing; humming.

bourdonner [burdɔ'ne], *v.t.* to hum.—*v.i.* to buzz, to hum; to murmur.

bourdonneur [burdɔ'nœ:r], *a.* humming.— *n.m.* hummingbird, colibri.

bourg [bu:r], *n.m.* borough, market-town.

bourgade [bur'gad], *n.f.* small market-town.

bourgène [BOURDAINE].

bourgeois [bur'ʒwa], *a.* middle-class; plain, common, ordinary.—*n.m.* (*fem.* **-e**) citizen, townsman, townswoman; commoner; middle-class person, bourgeois.

bourgeoisie [burʒwa'zi], *n.f.* bourgeoisie, middle class.

bourgeon [bur'ʒɔ̃], *n.m.* (*Bot.*) bud, shoot; pimple.

bourgeonnement [burʒɔn'mɑ̃], *n.m.* budding.

bourgeonner [burʒɔ'ne], *v.i.* to bud; to break out in pimples.

bourgeron [burʒə'rɔ̃], *n.m.* workman's blouse, smock frock.

bourgmestre [burg'mɛstr], *n.m.* burgomaster.

Bourgogne [bur'gɔɲ], **la**, *f.* Burgundy.

bourguignon [burgi'ɲɔ̃], *a.* (*fem.* **-onne**) Burgundian, of Burgundy.—*n.m.* (**Bourguignon**, *fem.* **-onne**) native *or* inhabitant of Burgundy.

bourrade [bu'rad], *n.f.* blow, thrust, buffet.

bourrasque [bu'rask], *n.f.* squall, gust; fit of anger.

bourre [bu:r], *n.f.* hair, fluff (*of animals*); flock (*of wool*); floss (*of silk*); (*fig.*) stuff, trash.

bourreau [bu'ro], *n.m.* (*pl.* **-eaux**) hangman, executioner; tyrant.

bourrée [bu're], *n.f.* brushwood, faggot; an Auvergne dance.

bourreler [bur'le], *v.t.* (*conjug. like* APPELER) to torment, to rack.

bourrelet [bur'le], *n.m.* pad, cushion.

bourrelier [burə'lje], *n.m.* harness maker.

bourrellerie [burɛl'ri], *n.f.* harness maker's shop.

bourrer [bu're], *v.t.* to tamp; to stuff, to cram; (*fig.*) to ill-treat, to thrash. **se bourrer**, *v.r.* to cram oneself; to thrash each other.

bourriche [bu'riʃ], *n.f.* game basket, basket of game.

bourrique [bu'rik], *n.f.* she-ass; (*fig.*) stupid person, dolt.

bourriquet [buri'kɛ], *n.m.* ass's colt *or* small ass; hand barrow.

bourru [bu'ry], *a.* cross, peevish, moody, surly.

Bourse [burs], *n.f.* Stock Exchange; *Bourse du travail*, labor exchange.

bourse [burs], *n.f.* purse, bag; scholarship, grant, bursary; rabbit net.

boursier [bur'sje], *a.* (*fem.* **-ière**) pertaining to the Stock Exchange.—*n.m.* (*fem.* **-ière**) speculator on the Stock Exchange, exchange broker; purse maker; scholarship holder.

boursouflage [bursu'flaːʒ], *n.m.* bombast.

boursouflé [bursu'fle], *a.* bloated; bombastic, swollen.

boursouflement [bursuflə'mã], *n.m.* bloatedness, puffiness; blister (*of paint*).

boursoufler [bursu'fle], *v.t.* to bloat, to puff up.

boursouflure [bursu'flyːr], *n.f.* bloatedness (*of face etc.*); (*fig.*) turgidity (*of style*).

bousculade [busky'lad], *n.m.* jostling, hustling; scrimmage.

bousculer [busky'le], *v.t.* to throw into disorder; to jostle, to hustle. **se bousculer**, *v.r.* to jostle each other.

boussole [bu'sɔl], *n.f.* compass.

bout [bu], *n.m.* end, tip, top, point; fragment, bit; *venir à bout de*, to succeed, to get through (*something*).

boutade [bu'tad], *n.f.* whim, fit, start, caprice; witticism.

boute-en-train [butã'trɛ̃], *n.m. inv.* one who promotes gaiety in others, merry-maker; *être le boute-en-train*, to be the life and soul of the party.

boutefeu [but'fø], *n.m.* (*pl.* **-eux**) (*fig.*) incendiary, fire-brand.

bouteille [bu'tɛːj], *n.f.* bottle; bottleful.

bouteillerie [butɛj'ri], *n.f.* bottle-works.

boutique [bu'tik], *n.f.* shop; work-shop; (*collect.*) tools, implements.

boutiquier [buti'kje], *n.m.* (*fem.* **-ière**) shopkeeper.—*a.* (*fem.* **-ière**) shopkeeping.

bouton [bu'tɔ̃], *n.m.* bud; pimple; button, stud, knob; (*Elec. etc.*) switch.

bouton d'or [butɔ̃'dɔːr], *n.m.* (*pl.* **boutons d'or**) (*Bot.*) buttercup.

boutonné [butɔ'ne], *a.* buttoned; pimpled.

boutonner [butɔ'ne], *v.t.* to button; (*Fenc.*) to touch.—*v.i.* to bud; to button up. **se boutonner**, *v.r.* to button one's coat.

boutonnière [butɔ'njɛːr], *n.f.* buttonhole.

bouture [bu'tyːr], *n.f.* slip, cutting.

bouveau [bu'vo] (*pl.* **-eaux**), **bouvelet** [buv'le], *n.m.* young ox.

bouverie [bu'vri], *n.f.* cattle shed, byre.

bouvet [bu'vɛ], *n.m.* joiner's grooving-plane.

bouvetage [buv'taːʒ], *n.m.* grooving and tonguing.

bouveter [buv'te], *v.t.* (*conjug. like* APPELER) to groove and tongue.

bouvier [bu'vje], *n.m.* (*fem.* **-ière**) cow-herd, ox-drover.

bouvillon [buvi'jɔ̃], *n.m.* young bullock, steer.

bouvreuil [bu'vrœj], *n.m.* bullfinch.

bovin [bɔ'vɛ̃], *a.* bovine.

box [bɔks], *n.m.* (*pl.* **boxes**) horse box, loose box; lock-up garage; *le box des accusés*, the dock.

boxe [bɔks], *n.f.* boxing.

boxer [bɔk'se], *v.i.* to box, to spar.

boxeur [bɔk'sœːr], *n.m.* boxer, prize-fighter.

boy [bɔj], *n.m.* groom; native servant.

boyau [bwa'jo], *n.m.* (*pl* **-aux**) bowel, gut; catgut; hose-pipe; (*Cycl.*) racing tire.

brabançon [brabã'sɔ̃], *a.* (*fem.* **-onne**) Brabantine, Belgian.—*n.m.* (**Brabançon**, *fem.* **-onne**) Brabantine, Belgian (*person*).

bracelet [bras'lɛ], *n.m.* bracelet, armlet, bangle.

bracelet-montre [braslɛ'mɔ̃:tr], *n.m.* (*pl.* **bracelets-montres**) wrist watch.

braconnage [brakɔ'naːʒ], *n.m.* poaching.

braconner [brakɔ'ne], *v.i.* to poach, to steal game.

braconnier [brakɔ'nje], *n.m.* (*fem.* **-ière**) poacher.—*a.* (*fem.* **-ière**) poaching; pertaining to poaching.

braguette [bra'gɛt], *n.f.* fly (*of trousers*).

brahmane [bra'man], **brahme** [bram], *n.m.* Brahmin.

brahmanisme [brama'nism], *n.m.* Brahminism.

brahme [BRAHMANE].

brai [brɛ], *n.m.* resin, rosin, pitch.

braillard [bra'jaːr], *a.* brawling, squalling; obstreperous.—*n.m.* (*fem.* **-e**) brawler, squaller.—*n.m.* small speaking-trumpet.

braille [braj], *n.m.* braille.

braillement [braj'mã], *n.m.* squalling.

brailler [bra'je], *v.i.* to bawl, to shout, to be noisy.

brailleur [bra'jœːr], *a.* and *n.m.* (*fem.* **-euse**) [BRAILLARD].

braiment [brɛ'mã], *n.m.* braying (*of an ass*).

braire [brɛːr], *v.i. irr.* to bray; (*fig.*) to cry, to whine.

braise [brɛːz], *n.f.* wood embers, live coals.

49

braiser [brɛ'ze], v.t. to braise.
braisier [brɛ'zje], n.m. brazier.
braisière [brɛ'zjɛːr], n.f. braising pan.
bramer [bra'me], v.i. to bell (of deer).
brancard [brɑ̃'kaːr], n.m. stretcher, litter; hand barrow; shaft (of a cart).
brancardier [brɑ̃kar'dje], n.m. stretcher bearer, ambulance man.
branchage [brɑ̃'ʃaːʒ], n.m. (collect.) branches, boughs.
branche [brɑ̃ːʃ], n.f. branch, bough; part, division.
brancher [brɑ̃'ʃe], v.t. to divide into branches; (Elec.) to connect, to plug in; to tap (a gas or water pipe).—v.i. to branch off.
branchu [brɑ̃'ʃy], a. forked, bifurcated, ramifying.
brande [brɑ̃ːd], n.f. heather; heath.
Brandebourg [brɑ̃d'buːr], m. Brandenburg.
brandebourgs [brɑ̃d'buːr], n.m. pl. braid, frogs and loops (on a uniform).
brandillement [brɑ̃dij'mɑ̃], n.m. tossing; swinging.
brandiller [brɑ̃di'je], v.t. to swing, to shake to and fro.—v.i. to move, to move to and fro. **se brandiller**, v.r. to swing.
brandir [brɑ̃'diːr], v.t. to brandish, to flourish.
brandissement [brɑ̃dis'mɑ̃], n.m. brandishing, flourishing.
brandon [brɑ̃'dɔ̃], n.m. torch, fire-brand.
branlant [brɑ̃'lɑ̃], a. shaking, loose, tottering.
branle [brɑ̃ːl], n.m. oscillation, shaking or tossing motion; jog; an old-fashioned dance.
branle-bas [brɑ̃l'bɑ] n.m. inv. (Naut.) clearing for action; (fig.) commotion, disturbance.
branlement [brɑ̃l'mɑ̃], n.m. oscillation, shaking, swing.
branler [brɑ̃'le], v.t. to shake, to wag.—v.i. to shake, to stagger, to rock; to move; to waver.
braquage [bra'kaːʒ], n.m. aiming, steering, lock (of a car).
braque (1) [brak], n.m. French pointer.
braque (2) [brak], a. madcap, hare-brained.
braquer [bra'ke], v.t. to aim, to level, to point.
bras [bra], n.m. arm; bracket; branch (of a stream etc.); (fig.) power, action, assistance.
braser [bra'ze], v.t. to braze.
brasier [bra'zje], n.m. quick clear fire; brazier, furnace.
brasiller [brazi'je], v.t. to grill, to broil.—v.i. to glitter, to shine (of the sea).
brassage [bra'saːʒ], n.m. mashing, brewing.
brassard [bra'saːr], n.m. brace (armor); armlet.
brasse [bras], n.f. fathom, six feet; armful; stroke (in swimming).
brassée [bra'se], n.f. armful; stroke (in swimming).
brassement [bras'mɑ̃], n.m. brewing; mixing.
brasser [bra'se], v.t. to mix; to brew, to mash; to stir up.
brasserie [bras'ri], n.f. brewery; brewing; drinking-saloon, 'pub'.
brasseur [bra'sœːr], n.m. brewer.
brassière [bra'sjɛːr], n.f. shoulder strap (of a knapsack etc.); infant's undershirt.
brassin [bra'sɛ̃], n.m. brewing tub; mash tub; a boiling (quantity boiled or brewed).

50

bravache [bra'vaʃ], n.m. bully, swaggerer, blusterer.—a. blustering, bullying.
bravade [bra'vad], n.f. bravado, boast, bluster.
brave [braːv], a. brave, courageous, gallant; worthy, honest, good.—n.m. brave or courageous man; good fellow.
bravement [brav'mɑ̃], adv. bravely, stoutly, valiantly; skilfully, finely.
braver [bra've], v.t. to defy, to dare; to brave, to beard.
bravo [bra'vo], n.m. (pl. bravos) and int. bravo; hear, hear!
bravoure [bra'vuːr], n.f. bravery, courage, gallantry; (pl.) exploits.
break [brɛk], n.m. break (carriage).
brebis [brə'bi], n.f. ewe; (fig.) sheep; (pl.) flock.
brèche [brɛʃ], n.f. breach, flaw; notch, gap.
bréchet [bre'ʃe], n.m. (Orn.) breast-bone.
bredouillage [brəduja:ʒ], n.m. bredouillement
bredouillement [brəduj'mɑ̃], n.m. stammering, stuttering, sputtering.
bredouille [brə'duːj], n.f.(backgammon)lurch. a. inv. empty-handed; revenir bredouille, to return with an empty bag (of sportsmen).
bredouillement [BREDOUILLAGE].
bredouiller [brədu'je], v.t., v.i. to stammer, to stutter.
bredouilleur [brədu'jœːr], a. (fem. -euse) stammering, stuttering.—n.m. (fem. -euse) stammerer, stutterer.
bref [brɛf], a. (fem. brève (1)) short, brief, concise; brusque.—adv. in short, in fine, in a word.
brelan [brə'lɑ̃], n.m. brelan (card game); gaming house.
brêler or **breller** [brɛ'le], v.t. to lash.
breller [BRÊLER].
breloque [brə'lɔk], n.f. trinket, gewgaw, charm.
Brême [brɛːm], m. Bremen.
brème [brɛːm], n.f. bream.
Brésil [bre'zil], le, m. Brazil.
brésil [bre'zil], n.m. Brazil-wood (for dyeing).
brésilien [brezi'ljɛ̃], a. (fem. -enne) Brazilian.—n.m. (Brésilien, fem. -enne) Brazilian (person).
Bretagne [brə'taɲ], la, f. Brittany; la Grande-Bretagne, Great Britain; la Nouvelle-Bretagne, New Britain.
bretelle [brə'tɛl], n.f. strap; brace; (pl.) pair of braces; (Rail.) switch; (rifle) sling.
breton [brə'tɔ̃], a. (fem. -onne) Breton.—n.m. Breton (language); (Breton, fem. -onne) Breton (person).
bretteur [brɛ'tœːr], n.m. swashbuckler, duellist.
bretzel [brɛt'sɛl], n.m. pretzel.
breuil [brœːj], n.m. enclosed coppice, covert.
breuvage [brœ'vaːʒ], n.m. beverage, drink, liquor.
brève (1) [brɛːv], [BREF].
brève (2) [brɛːv], n.f. short syllable; (Mus.) breve.
brevet [bra'vɛ], n.m. warrant, brevet, certificate (school etc.); diploma, license (of printers); patent; badge (of boy scouts); (Mil.) commission.
breveté [brəv'te], a. patented; (Mil.) certificated—n.m. (fem. -ée) patentee.

breveter [brəv'te], *v.t.* (*conjug. like* APPELER) to patent; to license; to certificate.

bréviaire [bre'vjɛːr], *n.m.* breviary.

brévité [brevi'te], *n.f.* shortness (*of syllables*).

bribes [brib], *n.f. pl.* scraps, bits; odds and ends.

bric-à-brac [brika'brak], *n.m. inv.* curios, bric-a-brac; curiosity shop.

brick [brik], *n.m.* brig.

bricolage [briko'la:ʒ], *n.m.* puttering.

bricoler [briko'le], *v.i.* to putter, to do odds and ends.

bricoleur [briko'lœːr], *n.m.* (*fem.* **-euse**) odd job man, handyman *or* woman.

bride [brid], *n.f.* bridle, bridle rein; check. curb; string (*of a woman's cap, bonnet etc.*).

brider [bri'de], *v.t.* to bridle; to restrain, to curb; to truss (*a fowl*); to tie; to check.

bridge [brid3], *n.m.* bridge (*card game*); bridge (*in dentistry*).

bridger [bri'd3e], *v.i.* to play bridge.

bridgeur [bri'd3œːr], *n.m.* (*fem.* **-euse**) bridge player.

bridon [bri'dɔ̃], *n.m.* snaffle bridle.

brie [bri], *n.m.* Brie cheese.

brièvement [briɛv'mã], *adv.* briefly, succinctly, in short.

brièveté [briɛv'te], *n.f.* brevity, briefness, conciseness.

brigade [bri'gad], *n.f.* brigade; (*fig.*) troop, gang, body.

brigadier [briga'dje], *n.m.* corporal (*in cavalry, artillery*); sergeant (*of police*).

brigand [bri'gã], *n.m.* brigand; (*fig.*) robber, thief.

brigandage [brigã'da:ʒ], *n.m.* brigandage, plunder.

brigander [brigã'de], *v.i.* to rob, to plunder.

brigantin [brigã'tɛ̃], *n.m.* brigantine.

brigantine [brigã'tin], *n.f.* (*Naut.*) spanker; small vessel.

brigue [brig], *n.f.* intrigue, cabal, faction.

briguer [bri'ge], *v.t.* to canvass for, to solicit, to court.

brigueur [bri'gœːr], *n.m.* (*fem.* **-euse**) intriguer, canvasser.

brillamment [brija'mã], *adv.* brilliantly, in a brilliant manner.

brillance [bri'jã:s], *n.f.* (*Opt.*) brilliancy.

brillant [bri'jã], *a.* brilliant, sparkling, glittering; radiant.—*n.m.* brilliance, splendor; brilliant (*diamond*).

brillanter [brijã'te], *v.t.* to cut into a brilliant.

brillantine [brijã'tin], *n.f.* brilliantine (*hair-oil*); glossy cotton cloth.

briller [bri'je], *v.i.* to shine, to glitter, to sparkle; (*fig.*) to distinguish oneself, to stand out.

brimade [bri'mad], *n.f.* ragging; vexation, persecution.

brimborion [brɛ̃bo'rjɔ̃], *n.m.* knick-knack, bauble.

brimer [bri'me], *v.t.* to rag, to bully.

brin [brɛ̃], *n.m.* blade, slender stalk, shoot (*of corn etc.*); (*fig.*) bit, jot.

brindille [brɛ̃'di:j], *n.f.* sprig, twig.

brio [bri'o] [It.], *n.m.* (*Mus. etc.*) dash, spirit, go.

brioche [bri'ɔʃ], *n.f.* brioche, bun; (*fig.*) blunder.

brique [brik], *n.f.* brick; *brique anglaise,* Bath brick.

briquet [bri'kɛ], *n.m.* tinder box; (cigarette) lighter.

briquetage [brik'ta:ʒ], *n.m.* brick work; imitation brick work.

briqueter [brik'te], *v.t.* (*conjug. like* APPELER) to brick, to pave with bricks.

briqueterie [brik'tri], *n.f.* brick field, brick making; brickworks.

briqueteur [brik'tœːr], *n.m.* bricklayer.

briquetier [brik'tje], *n.m.* brick maker.

briquette [bri'kɛt], *n.f.* briquette; compressed slack.

brisant [bri'zã], *n.m.* sand bank, reef, shoal; (*pl.*) breakers.

brise [bri:z], *n.f.* breeze; strong wind.

brisé [bri'ze], *a.* broken to pieces; (*fig.*) harassed.

brise-bise [briz'bi:z], *n.m. inv.* draft excluder; sash curtain.

brisées [bri'ze], *n.f.* (*used only in pl.*) footsteps, wake; *aller* or *marcher sur les brisées de quelqu'un,* to poach on someone's preserves.

brise-glace [briz'glas], *n.m.* (*pl.* **brise-glace** or **-glaces**) ice-breaker (*ship*).

brise-jet [briz'3e], *n.m. inv.* anti-splash tap nozzle.

brise-lames [briz'lam], *n.m. inv.* breakwater.

brisement [briz'mã], *n.m.* breaking, dashing (*of waves*); (*fig.*) trouble, contrition.

briser [bri'ze], *v.t.* to break to pieces, to smash, to break, to shatter; to burst; to crack; to destroy.—*v.i.* to break; to dash (*of waves*).

brise-tout [briz'tu], *n.m. inv.* person who breaks everything; rough, clumsy fellow.

briseur [bri'zœːr], *n.m.* (*fem.* **-euse**) one who breaks or likes to break anything; iconoclast.

brise-vent [briz'vã], *n.m.* (*pl.* **brise-vent** or **brise-vents**) wind-screen (*for protecting plants*).

brisque [brisk], *n.f.* a card game; (*Mil.*) stripe; war service chevron.

brisure [bri'zyːr], *n.f.* break; folding-point in a piece of joiner's work; small fragment.

britannique [brita'nik], *a.* British, Britannic; *Les Îles Britanniques,* the British Isles.

broc [bro], *n.m.* large jug *or* quart pot.

brocantage [brokã'ta:ʒ], *n.m.* dealing in second-hand goods, broker's business; bartering.

brocante [bro'kã:t], *n.f.* second-hand trade; article of trifling value.

brocanter [brokã'te], *v.i.* to deal in second-hand goods; to exchange, to barter.

brocanteur [brokã'tœːr], *n.m.* (*fem.* **-euse**) dealer in second-hand goods, junk-shop owner.

brocard [bro'ka:r], *n.m.* taunt, jeer; lampoon.

brocarder [brokar'de], *v.t.* to taunt, to ridicule.

brocardeur [brokar'dœːr], *n.m.* (*fem.* **-euse**) scoffer, jeerer.

brocart *or* **broquart** [bro'ka:r], *n.m.* brocade.

brochage [bro'ʃa:ʒ], *n.m.* stitching (*of books*).

broche [brɔʃ], *n.f.* spit; spindle; skewer; spigot; knitting needle; brooch; (*pl.*) tusks (*of wild boars*); (*Elec.*) *fiche à deux broches,* two-pin plug.

broché [brɔ'ʃe], a. embossed (of linen); brocaded, figured (of other materials); *livre broché*, paper-bound book.

brocher [brɔ'ʃe], v.t. to stitch (a book etc.); to figure (materials); to emboss (linen).

brochet [brɔ'ʃe], n.m. pike (fish).

brocheter [brɔʃ'te], v.t. (conjug. like APPELER) to skewer.

brochette [brɔ'ʃet], n.f. (Cook.) small spit.

brocheur [brɔ'ʃœːr], n.m. (fem. **-euse**) stitcher, esp. book-stitcher.

brochure [brɔ'ʃyːr], n.f. stitching; booklet, brochure, pamphlet, tract; embroidery.

brocoli [brɔkɔ'li], n.m. broccoli.

brodequin [brɔd'kɛ̃], n.m. buskin, half-boot.

broder [brɔ'de], v.t. to embroider; to adorn, to embellish (a story etc.).—v.i. to romance.

broderie [brɔd'ri], n.f. embroidery; (fig.) embellishment.

brodeur [brɔ'dœːr], n.m. (fem. **-euse**) embroiderer.

broiement or **broîment** [brwa'mã], **broyage** [brwa'jaːʒ], n.m. grinding, powdering.

bromure [brɔ'myːr], n.m. bromide.

bronche [brɔ̃ːʃ], n.f. (pl.) (Anat.) bronchial tubes.

bronchement [brɔ̃ʃ'mã], n.m. stumbling; flinching.

broncher [brɔ̃'ʃe], v.i. to stumble, to trip, to reel; to falter.

bronchial [brɔ̃'ʃjal], a. (m. pl. **-aux**) (Anat.) bronchial.

bronchique [brɔ̃'ʃik], a. bronchial.

bronchite [brɔ̃'ʃit], n.f. (Path.) bronchitis.

broncho-pneumonie [brɔ̃kɔpnømɔ'ni], n.f. broncho-pneumonia.

bronze [brɔ̃ːz], n.m. bronze; bronze statue or medal.

bronzer [brɔ̃'ze], v.t. to bronze; to tan (the face etc.).

broquart [BROCART].

broquette [brɔ'ket], n.f. tack; carpet nail.

brosse [brɔs], n.f. brush; painter's brush or pencil; *cheveux en brosse*, crew-cut hair.

brosser [brɔ'se], v.t. to brush. **se brosser**, v.r. to brush oneself.

brosserie [brɔs'ri], n.f. brushmaking business; brush factory.

brou [bru], n.m. husk or peel (of nuts, esp. walnuts); *brou de noix*, walnut stain, walnut liquor.

brouet [bru'ɛ], n.m. thin broth.

brouette [bru'ɛt], n.f. wheelbarrow.

brouettée [bruɛ'te], n.f. barrow load.

brouetter [bruɛ'te], v.t. to wheel in a barrow.

brouetteur [bruɛ'tœːr], **brouettier** [bruɛ'tje], n.m. barrowman.

brouhaha [brua'a], n.m. hubbub, uproar, hurly-burly.

brouillage [bru'jaːʒ], n.m. (Rad.) atmospherics, jamming.

brouillard [bru'jaːr], n.m. fog, mist, haze; (Comm.) daybook.

brouillasse [bru'jas], n.f. drizzle, Scotch mist.

brouillasser [bruja'se], v.impers. to drizzle.

brouille [bru:j], n.f. quarrel, falling-out.

brouillé [bru'je], a. scrambled (eggs); blurred; on bad terms.

brouillement [bruj'mã], n.m. mixing together, jumbling.

brouiller [bru'je], v.t. to mix together, to jumble up, to shuffle; to embroil, to confuse; (Rad.) to jam. **se brouiller**, v.r. to fall out (with someone).

brouillerie [BROUILLE].

brouillon [bru'jɔ̃], a. (fem. **-onne**) mischief-making; blundering.—n.m. rough draft, rough copy; blunderer, bungler.

brouillonner [brujɔ'ne], v.t. to write in a blundering or confused way, to botch.

brouir [bru'iːr], v.t. to blight, to nip, to parch.

brouissure [brui'syːr], n.f. blight, scorching.

broussailles [bru'saːj], n.f. (usu. in pl.) bushes, brushwood, undergrowth.

broussailleux [brusa'jø], a. (fem. **-euse**) bushy, covered with bushes.

brousse [brus], n.f. brushwood, bush (Australia etc.).

brouter [bru'te], v.t., v.i. to browse, to graze.

broutilles [bru'tiːj], n.f. pl. sprigs; (fig.) trifles.

brownien [brɔ'nɛ̃], a. *mouvements browniens*, molecular motion.

browning [brɔ'niŋ], n.m. automatic pistol.

broyage [brwa'jaːʒ], n.m. crushing (of ore), grinding (of colors).

broyer [brwa'je], v.t. (conjug. like EMPLOYER) to grind, to pound, to pulverize.

broyeur [brwa'jœːr], a. (fem. **-euse**) grinding.—n.m. (fem. **-euse**) grinding; grinder, pounder.

bru [bry], n.f. daughter-in-law.

brucelles [bry'sɛl], n.f. pl. tweezers.

brugnon [bry'ɲɔ̃], n.m. nectarine.

bruine [brɥin], n.f. light drizzling rain.

bruiner [brɥi'ne], v.impers. to drizzle.

bruineux [brɥi'nø], a. (fem. **-euse**) drizzly, drizzling.

bruire [brɥiːr], v.t. irr. to make a noise; to rustle, to rattle; to roar, to sough (of the wind).

bruissant [brɥi'sã], a. rustling, rattling; roaring.

bruissement [brɥis'mã], n.m. rustling noise, rattling, roaring.

bruit [brɥi], n.m. noise, din, uproar, clamor; fame, renown; report, talk, rumor.

bruitage [brɥi'taːʒ], n.m. sound effects.

bruiter [brɥi'te], v.i. to make sound effects.

bruiteur [brɥi'tœːr], n.m. sound-effects specialist.

brûlage [bry'laːʒ], n.m. burning (of rubbish); singeing (of hair); roasting (of coffee).

brûlant [bry'lã], a. burning, scorching, hot, torrid; (fig.) eager, ardent.

brûlé [bry'le], n.m. smell of burning; (C) burnt-out area or field.

brûle-gueule [bryl gœl], n.m. inv. (colloq.) short pipe, cutty.

brûle-pourpoint, à [abrylpur'pwɛ̃], adv. point-blank (of shooting).

brûler [bry'le], v.t. to burn; to cauterize; to scorch, to parch; to singe (hair).—v.i. to burn, to be on fire; (fig.) to be eager. **se brûler**, v.r. to burn oneself, to be burnt.

brûleur [bry'lœːr], n.m. (fem. **-euse**) burner; incendiary; *brûleur à gaz*, gas-ring, gas jet.

brûlis [bry'li], n.m. burnt part of a wood or field.

brûloir [bry'lwaːr], n.m. coffee burner or roaster.

brûlot [bry'lo], *n.m.* fire ship; (*fig.*) firebrand, incendiary; (C) kind of gnat *or* midge.

brûlure [bry'ly:r], *n.f.* burn, frost nip, scald.

brumaire [bry'mɛ:r], *n.m.* Brumaire (*second month of the calendar of the first French Republic, from Oct. 22nd to Nov. 20th*).

brume [brym], *n.f.* haze, mist.

brumeux [bry'mø], *a.* (*fem.* -euse) hazy, misty; (*fig.*) sombre.

brun [brœ̃], *a.* brown, dark, dusky.—*n.m.* brown (*color*); (*fem.* -e (1)) dark-complexioned person.

brunâtre [bry'nɑ:tr], *a.* brownish.

brune (2) [bryn], *n.f.* dusk (*of the evening*); dark woman, dark girl, brunette.

brunet [bry'nɛ], *a.* (*fem.* -ette) brownish.—*n.f.* (-ette) dark woman, dark girl.

brunir [bry'ni:r], *v.t.* to make brown; to burnish.—*v.i.* to turn brown. **se brunir**, *v.r.* to turn dark *or* brown.

brunissage [bryni'sa:ʒ], *n.m.* burnishing.

brunisseur [bryni'sœ:r], *n.m.* (*fem.* -euse) burnisher.

brunissoir [bryni'swa:r], *n.m.* burnisher (*tool*).

brunissure [bryni'sy:r], *n.f.* burnishing; polish.

brusque [brysk], *a.* blunt, abrupt, rough; unexpected.

brusquement [bryskə'mɑ̃], *adv.* bluntly, abruptly; uncivilly.

brusquer [brys'ke], *v.t.* to be sharp with (*someone*); to offend; (*fig.*) to precipitate.

brusquerie [bryskə'ri], *n.f.* abruptness, bluntness; hastiness.

brut [bryt], *a.* rough, raw, unhewn; uncultured.—*adv.* (*Comm.*) gross (*as opposed to* net).

brutal [bry'tal], *a.* (*m.pl.* -aux) brutal; surly, churlish.—*n.m.* (*fem.* -e) brute, brutal person.

brutalement [brytal'mɑ̃], *adv.* brutally.

brutaliser [brytali'ze], *v.t.* to bully; to brutalize.

brutalité [brytali'te], *n.f.* brutality, brutishness.

brute [bryt], *n.f.* brute, brutal person; boor.

Bruxelles [bry'sɛl], *f.* Brussels.

bruyamment [bryja'mɑ̃], *adv.* noisily.

bruyère [bry'jɛ:r], *n.f.* heath, heather.

buanderie [buɑ̃'dri], *n.f.* wash house, laundry.

buandier [buɑ̃'dje], *n.m.* (*fem.* -ière) bleacher; washerman, washerwoman.

bube [byb], *n.f.* pimple.

bubonique [bybo'nik], *a.* bubonic.

Bucarest [byka'rest], *m.* Bucharest.

buccin [byk'sɛ̃], *n.m.* (*Mus. Ant.*) long trumpet; (*Conch.*) whelk.

bûche [byʃ], *n.f.* log; (*fig.*) blockhead, dolt.

bûcher (1) [by'ʃe], *n.m.* wood house; funeral pile, pyre; stake.

bûcher (2) [by'ʃe], *v.t.* to roughhew.—*v.i.* to cram, to bone.

bûcheron [byʃ'rõ], *n.m.* (*fem.* -onne) wood cutter.

bûchette [by'ʃɛt], *n.f.* stick of dry wood.

bucolique [byko'lik], *a.* bucolic.

budget [byd'ʒɛ], *n.m.* budget.

budgétaire [bydʒe'tɛ:r], *a.* a budgetary.

buée [bue], *n.f.* steam (*on window panes*).

buffet [by'fɛ], *n.m.* sideboard; buffet; refreshment room.

buffetier [byf'tje], *n.m.* (*fem.* -ière) refreshment room manager.

buffle [byfl], *n.m.* buffalo; buffalo hide; buff leather.

buffleterie [byflə'tri], *n.f.* buff belts, straps etc. (*of a soldier*).

bugle [bygl], *n.m.* key bugle.

buis [bui], *n.m.* box; box tree, boxwood.

buissaie [bui'sɛ], **buissière** [bui'sjɛ:r], *n.f.* box grove.

buisson [bui'sõ], *n.m.* bush; thicket.

buissonner [buisɔ'ne], *v.i.* to grow into a bush.

buissonnet [buisɔ'nɛ], *n.m.* little bush.

buissonneux [buisɔ'nø], *a.* (*fem.* -euse) bushy.

buissonnier [buisɔ'nje], *a.* (*fem.* -ière) retiring into the bushes; *faire l'école buissonnière*, to play truant; *lapins buissonniers*, thicket-rabbits.—*n.m.* shrubbery.

bulbe [bylb], *n.m.* bulb.

bulbeux [byl'bø], *a.* (*fem.* -euse) bulbous.

bulgare [byl'ga:r], *a.* Bulgarian.—*n.m.* Bulgarian (*language*).—*n.* (**Bulgare**) Bulgarian (*person*).

Bulgarie [bylga'ri], **la**, *f.* Bulgaria.

bulle [byl], *n.f.* bubble; blister; a papal bull.

bullé [by'le], *a.* authenticated with a seal; by papal bull.

bulletin [byl'tɛ̃], *n.m.* bulletin, official report (*school etc.*); certificate, receipt; ballot; ticket; *bulletin d'information* news bulletin; *bulletin météorologique*, weather forecast.

bulleux [by'lø], *a.* (*fem.* -euse) bubbly, blistery.

buraliste [byra'list], *n.* receiver of taxes; tobacco dealer.

bure [by:r], *n.f.* drugget; fustian, baize.

bureau [by'ro], *n.m.* (*pl.* -eaux) writing table, desk; office; board; committee; *Deuxième Bureau*, Intelligence Service, M.I.5.

bureaucrate [byro'krat], *n.m.* (*pej.*) bureaucrat.

bureaucratie [byrokra'si], *n.f.* bureaucracy; (*fig.*) red tape.

bureaucratique [byrokra'tik], *a.* bureaucratic; formal.

burette [by'rɛt], *n.f.* cruet; oil-can; (*Chem.*) burette.

burin [by'rɛ̃], *n.m.* graver, graving tool; (*fig.*) pen.

buriner [byri'ne], *v.t.* to engrave; to drill (*a tooth*).

burineur [byri'nœ:r], *n.m.* engraver.

burlesque [byr'lesk], *a.* burlesque, ludicrous.—*n.m.* burlesque.

burnous [byr'nus], *n.m.* burnous, hooded Arab cloak.

busard [by'za:r], *n.m.* buzzard.

buse (1) [by:z], *n.f.* buzzard; (*fig.*) blockhead.

buse (2) [by:z], *n.f.* channel, pipe; nozzle; (*Mining*) air shaft.

busqué [bys'ke], *a.* aquiline (*nose*).

buste [byst], *n.m.* bust, head and shoulders.

but [by(t)], *n.m.* mark; object, end; purpose, design, goal, objective; *de but en blanc* bluntly; (*Ftb.*) *marquer un but*, to score.

buté [by'te], *a.* stubborn, (*fam.*) dead set on.

buter *or* **butter** (1) [by'te], *v.t.* to support, to prop.—*v.i.* to rest *or* abut (*contre*); to stumble *or* hit (*contre*). **se buter**, *v.r.* to be bent on, to stick (*à*).

butin [by'tɛ̃], *n.m.* booty, spoils, prize, plunder.
butiner [byti'ne], *v.t., v.i.* to pillage, to plunder.
butoir [by'twaːr], *n.m.* buffer, buffer-stop (*on railway*); tappet.
butor [by'tɔːr], *n.m.* bittern; (*fig.*) churl, lout, booby.
butte [byt], *n.f.* rising ground; knoll, mound.
butter (1) [BUTER].
butter (2) [by'te], *v.t.* to earth up.
butteur [BUTTOIR].
buttoir [by'twaːr], **butteur** [by'tœːr], *n.m.* ridging plough.
buvable [by'vabl], *a.* drinkable, fit to drink.
buvard [by'vaːr], *a.* *papier buvard*, blotting paper.—*n.m.* blotting pad, blotter.
buvetier [byv'tje], *n.m.* (*fem.* -**ière**) innkeeper, publican.
buvette [by'vɛt], *n.f.* refreshment room (*railway station*); pump room (*at spa*).
buveur [by'vœːr], *n.m.* (*fem.* -**euse**) drinker; toper; *buveur d'eau*, teetotaller.
buvoter [byvɔ'te], *v.i.* to sip, to tipple.
Byzance [bi'zãːs], *f.* Byzantium.
byzantin [bizã'tɛ̃], *a.* Byzantine.—*n.m.* (**Byzantin,** *fem.* -**ine**) Byzantine (*person*).

C

C, c [se], *n.m.* the third letter of the alphabet.
ça [sa], *pron.* [*contraction of* cela] that; *comme ci comme ça*, only so-so; *donnez-moi ça*, give me that.
çà [sa], *adv.* here; *çà et là*, here and there. —*int* now; *çà alors!* well, I never!
cabale [ka'bal], *n.f.* cabal, faction.
cabaler [kaba'le], *v.i.* to cabal, to plot.
cabaleur [kaba'lœːr], *n.m.* (*fem.* -**euse**) caballer, intriguer.
caban [ka'bã], *n.m.* hooded cloak, oilskins.
cabane [ka'ban], *n.f.* hut, shed, cabin, shanty; central part (*of an airplane*).
cabanon [kaba'nɔ̃], *n.m.* small hut; prison cell; padded room.
cabaret [kaba'rɛ], *n.m.* inferior kind of wine shop, tavern; night club.
cabaretier [kabar'tje], *n.m.* (*fem.* -**ière**) publican, tavern keeper.
cabas [ka'ba], *n.m.* flat two-handled basket.
cabeliau [CABILLAUD].
cabestan [kabɛs'tã], *n.m.* capstan, windlass.
cabillaud [kabi'jo], **cabeliau** [kab'ljo] (*pl.* -**aux**), *n.m.* fresh cod.
cabine [ka'bin], *n.f.* cabin; (*Av.*) *cabine de pilotage*, cockpit; *cabine téléphonique*, telephone booth.
cabinet [kabi'nɛ], *n.m.* closet, study; practice (*of a professional man*); office (*of a lawyer, barrister etc.*); (*Polit.*) Cabinet; *cabinet d'aisances* or *les cabinets*, lavatory.
câblage [kɑ'blaːʒ], *n.m.* (*Elec.*) wiring.
câble [kɑːbl], *n.m.* cable.
câbler [kɑ'ble], *v.t.* to twist into a cord; to telegraph by cable.

câblogramme [kɑblɔ'gram], *n.m.* cablegram.
cabochon [kabɔ'ʃɔ̃], *n.m.* fancy brass nail; (*Cycl.*) *cabochon rouge*, red reflector.
cabosse [ka'bɔs], *n.f.* (*pop.*) bruise, bump.
cabosser [kabɔ'se], *v.t.* to bump, to bruise; to dent.
cabotage [kabɔ'taːʒ], *n.m.* coasting, coasting trade.
caboter [kabɔ'te], *v.i.* to coast.
caboteur [kabɔ'tœːr], **cabotier** [kabɔ'tje], *n.m.* coasting vessel; coaster.
cabotin [kabɔ'tɛ̃], *n.m.* strolling player; bad actor, mummer.
cabotiner [kabɔti'ne], *v.i.* to act badly; (*fig.*) to strut.
cabré [ka'bre], *a.* rearing (*of a horse*); bucking (*of a plane*).
cabrer [ka'bre], *v.t.* to make (*a horse, a plane*) rear. **se cabrer**, *v.r.* to prance, to rear; (*fig.*) to revolt, to fly into a passion.
cabri [ka'bri], *n.m.* kid.
cabriole [kabri'ɔl], *n.f.* caper, leap.
cabrioler [kabriɔ'le], *v.i.* to caper, to cut capers.
cabriolet [kabriɔ'lɛ], *n.m.* cabriolet, cab.
cacahouète [kaka'wɛt], **cacahuète** [kaka'ɥɛt], *n.f.* peanut, monkey nut.
cacao [kaka'o], *n.m.* cacao, chocolate nut.
cacaoyer [kakaɔ'je], **cacaotier** [kakaɔ'tje], *n.m.* cacao tree.
cacaoyère [kakaɔ'jɛːr], **cacaotière** [kakaɔ'tjɛːr], *n.f.* cacao plantation.
cacatois [kaka'twa], **cacatoès** [kakatɔ'ɛːs], *n.m.* cockatoo.
cachalot [kaʃa'lo], *n.m.* sperm whale.
cachalotier [kaʃalɔ'tje], *n.m.* whaler.
cache [kaʃ], *n.f.* hiding place.
cache-cache [kaʃ'kaʃ], *n.m.* hide-and-seek.
cachemire [kaʃ'miːr], *n.m.* cashmere.
cache-nez [kaʃ'ne], *n.m.* muffler, comforter.
cacher [ka'ʃe], *v.t.* to hide, to conceal; to mask. **se cacher**, *v.r.* to hide, to lurk.
cache-sexe [kaʃ'sɛks], *n.m.* trunks; panties; (*colloq.*) G-string.
cachet [ka'ʃɛ], *n.m.* seal, stamp; signet ring; ticket; tablet (*of aspirin*); (*fig.*) character, stamp, mark.
cacheter [kaʃ'te], *v.t.* (*conjug. like* APPELER) to seal.
cachette [ka'ʃɛt], *n.f.* hiding place.
cachot [ka'ʃo], *n.m.* dungeon, prison.
cachotter [kaʃɔ'te], *v.t.* to make a mystery of, to conceal.
cachotterie [kaʃɔ'tri], *n.f.* mysterious ways; underhand work.
cachottier [kaʃɔ'tje], *a.* (*fem.* -**ière**) mysterious, sly.—*n.m.* (*fem.* -**ière**) one who makes a mystery of things.
cachou [ka'ʃu], *n.m.* cachou.
cacophonie [kakɔfɔ'ni], *n.f.* cacophony.
cacophonique [kakɔfɔ'nik], *a.* cacophonous.
cactier [kak'tje], **cactus** [kak'tyːs], *n.m.* cactus.
cadastral [kadas'tral], *a.* (*m. pl.* -**aux**) cadastral, referring to the register of lands.
cadastre [ka'dastr], *n.m.* cadastre, register of the survey of lands.
cadastrer [kadas'tre], *v.t.* to survey.
cadavéreux [kadave'rø], *a.* (*fem.* -**euse**) cadaverous, corpse-like, ghastly.
cadavérique [kadave'rik], *a.* of *or* pertaining to a corpse.

cadavre [ka'dɑ:vr], *n.m.* corpse, dead body.

cadeau [ka'do], *n.m.* (*pl.* **-eaux**) present, gift.

cadenas [kad'nɑ], *n.m.* padlock; clasp.

cadenasser [kadna'se], *v.t.* to padlock; to snap, clasp.

cadence [ka'dɑ̃:s], *n.f.* cadence, rhythm, time (*in dancing*).

cadencer [kadɑ̃'se], *v.t.* (*conjug. like* COMMENCER) to cadence, to harmonize.

cadène [ka'dɛ:n], *n.f.* chain (*for convicts*); chain gang.

cadenette [kad'nɛt], *n.f.* tress (*of hair*).

cadet [ka'dɛ], *a.* and *n.m.* (*fem.* **-ette**) younger, junior (*of two*).

Cadix [ka'diks], *f.* Cadiz.

cadmium [kad'mjɔm], *n.m.* cadmium.

cadrage [ka'drɑ:ʒ], *n.m.* (*Phot., Cine.*) centering.

cadran [ka'drɑ̃], *n.m.* dial plate, dial; **cadran solaire**, sundial.

cadre [kɑ:dr], *n.m.* frame, framework; (*Mil.*) the staff; (*pl.*) the higher staff (*of an administration* or *a firm*).

cadrer [ka'dre], *v.t.* (*Phot., Cine.*) to center.— *v.i.* to agree, to tally, to square (*à* or *avec*).

caduc [ka'dyk], *a.* (*fem.* **-uque**) decrepit, decayed; frail, tumble-down; lapsed, null, void (*of legacies*); (*Bot.*) deciduous.

caducité [kadysi'te], *n.f.* caducity, decrepitude.

cafard [ka'fa:r], *a.* hypocritical, sanctimonious.—*n.m.* (*fem.* **-e**) hypocrite, sanctimonious person; humbug; (*Sch.*) sneak.—*n.m.* cockroach.

cafarder [kafar'de], *v.i.* (*fam.*) to sneak, to tell tales (*at school*).

cafarderie [kafar'dri], *n.f.* cant, hypocrisy, sanctimoniousness.

café [ka'fe], *n.m.* coffee; café, coffee house; coffee berry.

caféière [kafe'jɛ:r], *n.f.* coffee plantation.

caféine [kafe'in], *n.f.* caffeine.

cafetan or **caftan** [kaf'tɑ̃], *n.m.* caftan.

cafetier [kaf'tje], *n.m.* (*fem.* **cafetière** (1)) coffee-house keeper.

cafetière (2) [kaf'tjɛ:r], *n.f.* coffee pot, percolator.

cafouillage [kafu'ja:ʒ], *n.m.* floundering.

cafre [ka:fr], *a.* and *n.* (**Cafre**) Kaffir, Bantu.

caftan [CAFETAN].

cage [ka:ʒ], *n.f.* cage; coop.

cageot [ka'ʒo], *n.m.* little cage, hamper, crate.

cagibi [kaʒi'bi], *n.m.* small hut or room.

cagneux [ka'nø], *a.* (*fem.* **-euse**) knock-kneed, pigeon-toed.

cagnotte [ka'nɔt], *n.f.* kitty, pool, jackpot.

cagot [ka'go], *a.* (*fem.* **-otte**) bigoted, hypocritical.—*n.m.* (*fem.* **-otte**) bigot, hypocrite.

cagoterie [kago'tri], *n.f.* an act or word of hypocrisy or bigotry.

cagotisme [kago'tism], *n.m.* hypocrisy, bigotry.

cagoule [ka'gul], *n.f.* monk's cloak; penitent's cowl; hood.

cahier [ka'je], *n.m.* stitched paper-book; exercise book; quarter of a quire of paper.

cahot [ka'o], *n.m.* jerk, jolt.

cahotage [kao'ta:ʒ], **cahotement** [kaot'mɑ̃], *n.m.* jolting, jerking.

cahotant [kao'tɑ̃], *a.* rough, jolting.

cahoter [kao'te], *v.i.* to jolt, to be jerked about.

cahute [ka'yt], *n.f.* hut, hovel.

cïad [ka'id], *n.m.* Arab chief or judge.

caïeu or **cayeu** [ka'jø], *n.m.* (*pl.* **-eux**) (*Hort.*) offshoot of a bulb, clove.

caillage [ka'ja:ʒ], *n.m.* curdling, congealing.

caille [kɑ:j], *n.f.* quail.—(*C*) *a.* piebald.

caillé [ka'je], *n.m.* curdled milk, curds.—*a.* curdled.

caillebottage [kajbo'ta:ʒ], *n.m.* curdling.

caillebotte [kaj'bɔt], *n.f.* curds.

caillebotter (se) [sakajbɔ'te], *v.r.* to curdle.

caille-lait [kaj'lɛ], *n.m. inv.* rennet.

caillement [kaj'mɑ̃], *n.m.* curdling, coagulating.

cailler [ka'je], *v.t.* to curdle, to clot. **se cailler**, *v.r.* to coagulate, to turn to curds.

cailleteau [kaj'to], *n.m.* (*pl.* **-eaux**) young quail.

caillette (1) [ka'jɛt], *n.f.* rennet.

caillette (2) [ka'jɛt], *n.f.* (*Orn.*) petrel; flirt.

caillot [ka'jo], *n.m.* clot of blood, coagulum.

caillou [ka'ju], *n.m.* (*pl.* **-oux**) pebble, small stone, flint, flint stone.

cailloutage [kaju'ta:ʒ], *n.m.* gravelling; ballasting; rough-cast, pebble-work.

caillouter [kaju'te], *v.t.* to gravel, to ballast.

caillouteux [kaju'tø], *a.* (*fem.* **-euse**) pebbly, flinty.

cailloutis [kaju'ti], *n.m.* broken stones, gravel; road metal.

caïman [kai'mɑ̃], *n.m.* American crocodile, cayman.

Caïn [ka'ɛ̃], *m.* Cain.

caïque or **caïc** [ka'ik], *n.m.* (*Naut.*) caique.

Caire [kɛ:r], **Le**, *m.* Cairo.

caisse [kɛ:s], *n.f.* chest, case, box, trunk; till; cash; cashier's office, pay desk; **la grosse caisse**, the (big) drum; **caisse d'épargne**, savings bank.

caissette [kɛ'sɛt], *n.f.* small box.

caissier [kɛ'sje], *n.m.* (*fem.* **-ière**) treasurer, cashier.

caisson [kɛ'sɔ̃], *n.m.* ammunition wagon; (*Naut.*) locker.

cajoler [kaʒo'le], *v.t.* to cajole, to coax.

cajolerie [kaʒol'ri], *n.f.* cajolery, coaxing.

cajoleur [kaʒo'lœ:r], *n.m.* (*fem.* **-euse**) cajoler, coaxer.—*a.* cajoling, coaxing.

cal [kal], *n.m.* callosity, callus.

Calabre [ka'la:br], **la**, *f.* Calabria.

calage [ka'la:ʒ], *n.m.* lowering (*of sails etc.*) propping, wedging (*of furniture*).

calaison [kalɛ'zɔ̃], *n.f.* load line, sea gauge.

calaminage [kalami'na:ʒ], *n.m.* (*Motor.*) carbonizing.

calamine [kala'min], *n.f.* carbon (*on plugs of a car etc.*).

calamité [kalami'te], *n.f.* calamity, misfortune.

calamiteusement [kalamitøz'mɑ̃], *adv.* calamitously.

calamiteux [kalami'tø], *a.* (*fem.* **-euse**) calamitous.

calandrage [kalɑ̃'dra:ʒ], *n.m.* calendering, hot-pressing.

calandre [ka'lɑ̃:dr], *n.f.* mangle, calender; (*Motor.*) radiator grill.

calandrer [kalɑ̃'dre], *v.t.* to calender, to press, to smooth.

calandrette [kalɑ̃'drɛt], *n.f.* song-thrush.

calcaire [kal'kɛ:r], *a.* calcareous.—*n.m.* limestone.

calcéolaire [kalseo'lɛ:r], *n.f.* calceolaria.

calcination [kalsinɑ'sjɔ̃], *n.f.* calcination.
calciner [kalsi'ne], *v.t.* to calcine, to burn. **se calciner**, *v.r.* to calcine.
calcium [kal'sjɔm], *n.m.* calcium.
calcul [kal'kyl], *n.m.* calculation; arithmetic; reckoning, counting; (*Math.*) calculus; (*fig.*) design, selfish motive; (*Med.*) calculus (*stone*).
calculable [kalky'labl], *a.* computable, calculable.
calculateur [kalkyla'tœ:r], *a.* (*fem.* **-trice**) calculating, scheming.—*n.m.* (*fem.* **-trice**) calculator, reckoner; schemer.—*n.f.* (**-trice**) computer.
calculer [kalky'le], *v.t.* to calculate, to compute, to estimate; **machine à calculer**, computer.
cale (1) [kal], *n.f.* hold (*of a ship*); stocks, slip; ducking, keel-hauling (*punishment*); **cale sèche**, dry dock.
cale (2) [kal], *n.f.* wedge, block; prop, strut.
calebasse [kal'bas], *n.f.* calabash, gourd.
calèche [ka'lɛʃ], *n.f.* calash; barouche, open carriage.
caleçon [kal'sɔ̃], *n.m.* (*men's*) drawers, pants; **caleçon de bain**, bathing trunks.
Calédonie [kaledɔ'ni], **la**, *f.* Caledonia.
calédonien [kaledɔ'njɛ̃], *a.* (*fem.* **-enne**) Caledonian.—*n.m.* (**Calédonien**, *fem.* **-enne**) Caledonian (*person*).
caléfaction [kalefak'sjɔ̃], *n.f.* heating, calefaction.
calembour [kalɑ̃'bu:r], *n.m.* pun.
calembourdiste [kalɑ̃bur'dist], *n.m.* punster.
calembredaine [kalɑ̃brə'dɛn], *n.f.* quibble, subterfuge, nonsense.
calendes [ka'lɑ̃:d], *n.f. pl.* (*Ant.*) calends; convocation of the clergy of a diocese.
calendrier [kalɑ̃dri'e], *n.m.* calendar, almanac.
calendule [kalɑ̃'dyl], *n.f.* calendula.
cale-pied [kal'pje], *n.m.* toe clip.
calepin [kal'pɛ̃], *n.m.* notebook, memorandum book.
caler (1) [ka'le], *v.t.* (*Naut.*) to lower, to strike; to draw, to have a draft of.
caler (2) [ka'le], *v.t.* to prop up, to wedge; to steady; to jam; (*Motor.*) to stall.—*v.i.* (*Motor.*) to stall.
calfeutrage [kalfø'tra:ʒ], **calfeutrement** [kalføtr'mɑ̃], *n.m.* stopping of chinks.
calfeutrer [kalfø'tre], *v.t.* to stop up the chinks of, to make air-tight. **se calfeutrer**, *v.r.* to shut oneself up.
calibre [ka'libr], *n.m.* calibre, bore (*of a gun*); size (*of a bullet*); (*fig.*) kind, sort.
calibrer [kali'bre], *v.t.* to calibrate; to give the proper calibre to (*bullets etc.*).
calice (1) [ka'lis], *n.m.* chalice, communion cup; (*fig.*) grief, sacrifice.
calice (2) [ka'lis], *n.m.* (*Bot.*) calyx, flower, cup.
calicot [kali'ko], *n.m.* unbleached muslin; (*slang*) dry-goods store clerk.
calicule [kali'kyl], *n.m.* calicle, caliculus.
califat [kali'fa], *n.m.* caliphate.
calife [ka'lif] *n.m.* caliph.
Californie [kalifɔr'ni], **la**, *f.* California.
californfourchon [kalifur'ʃɔ̃], *n.m.* **à califourchon**, astride.
câlin [ka'lɛ̃], *a.* wheedling, winning, coaxing.—*n.m.* (*fem.* **-e**) wheedler, cajoler.

câliner [kɑ:li'ne], *v.t.* to cajole, to wheedle. **se câliner**, *v.r.* to coddle oneself, to take one's ease.
câlinerie [kɑ:lin'ri], *n.f.* wheedling, cajolery, caressing.
calleux [ka'lø], *a.* (*fem.* **-euse**) callous, horny.
calligraphe [kali'graf], *n.m.* calligrapher, good penman.
calligraphie [kaligra'fi], *n.f.* calligraphy, penmanship.
callisthénie [kaliste'ni], *n.f.* callisthenics.
callosité [kalozi'te], *n.f.* callosity.
calmant [kal'mɑ̃], *a.* calming, soothing, sedative.—*n.m.* (*Med.*) anodyne, sedative.
calme [kalm], *a.* tranquil, quiet, serene, calm; composed, dispassionate.—*n.m.* calm, stillness, quiet; composure.
calmer [kal'me], *v.t.* to calm, to still, to quiet, to allay, to soothe.—*v.i.* (*Naut.*) to lull, to become calm. **se calmer**, *v.r.* to become calm to compose oneself; to blow over.
calomel [kalɔ'mɛl], *n.m.* calomel.
calomniateur [kalɔmnja'tœ:r], *a.* (*fem.* **-trice**) slanderous.—*n.m.* (*fem.* **-trice**) calumniator, slanderer.
calomnie [kalɔm'ni], *n.f.* calumny, slander.
calomnier [kalɔm'nje], *v.t.* to calumniate, to slander.
calomnieusement [kalɔmnjøz'mɑ̃], *adv.* calumniously, slanderously.
calomnieux [kalɔm'njø], *a.* (*fem.* **-euse**) calumnious, slanderous.
calorie [kalɔ'ri], *n.f.* calorie, unit of heat.
calorifère [kalɔri'fɛ:r], *n.m.* hot-air stove *or* pipe; central heating.—*a.* heat-conveying.
calorifique [kalɔri'fik], *a.* calorific.
calorifuger [kalɔrify'ʒe], *v.t.* (*conjug. like* MANGER) to insulate, to lag (*pipes*).
calorique [kalɔ'rik], *a.* and *n.m.* caloric, heat.
calotte [ka'lɔt], *n.f.* skullcap (*esp. that worn by priests*); small dome; box on the ears.
calotter [kalɔ'te], *v.t.* to box the ears of.
calque [kalk], *n.m.* tracing; close copy.—*a. papier calque*, tracing paper.
calquer [kal'ke], *v.t.* to trace; to copy, to imitate closely. **se calquer**, *v.r.* (*sur*) to model oneself (*on*).
calumet [kaly'me], *n.m.* pipe, calumet.
calvados [kalva'dos], *n.m.* apple brandy, calvados.
calvaire [kal've:r], *n.m.* calvary; (*fig.*) torture, suffering, tribulation.
calvinisme [kalvi'nism], *n.m.* Calvinism.
calviniste [kalvi'nist], *a.* Calvinistic.—*n.* (**Calviniste**) Calvinist.
calvitie [kalvi'si], *n.f.* baldness.
camaïeu [kama'jø], *n.m.* (*pl.* **-eux**) cameo (*brooch etc.*).
camail [ka'ma:j], *n.m.* (*pl.* **-ails**) hood, capuchin; hackles (*of poultry*).
camarade [kama'rad], *n.* comrade, fellow, mate, chum, playmate.
camaraderie [kamara'dri], *n.f.* comradeship, intimacy.
camard [ka'ma:r], *a.* snub-nosed, flat.—*n.m.* (*fem.* **-e**) snub-nosed person.
Cambodge [kɑ̃'bɔdʒ], **le**, *m.* Cambodia.
cambodgien [kɑ̃bɔ'djɛ̃], *a.* (*fem.* **-enne**) Cambodian.—*n.m.* (**Cambodgien**, *fem.* **-enne**) Cambodian (*person*).
cambouis [kɑ̃'bwi], *n.m.* dirty cart-grease, dirty lubricating oil.

cambrage [kɑ̃'braː3], *n.m.* cambering, bending.

cambrai [kɑ̃'brɛ], *n.m.* machine-made lace; cambric.

cambré [kɑ̃'bre], *a.* bent, cambered.

cambrement [kɑ̃brə'mɑ̃], *n.m.* arching, curving.

cambrer [kɑ̃'bre], *v.t.* to arch, to bend, to curve. **se cambrer**, *v.r.* to be cambered; to warp; to draw oneself up.

cambriolage [kɑ̃briɔ'laː3], *n.m.* housebreaking, burglary.

cambrioler [kɑ̃briɔ'le], *v.t.* to break into (*a house*), to burgle.

cambrioleur [kɑ̃briɔ'lœːr], *n.m.* housebreaker, burglar.

cambrure [kɑ̃'bryːr], *n.f.* bend, curvature, arch; the arched part in a shoe.

cambuse [kɑ̃'byːz], *n.f.* (*Naut.*) storeroom, canteen.

came [kam], *n.f.* cam, wiper; *arbre à cames* camshaft.

camée [ka'me], *n.m.* cameo.

caméléon [kamele'ɔ̃], *n.m.* chameleon.

camélia [kame'lja], *n.m.* camellia.

camelot [kam'lo], *n.m.* camlet; cheap-jack, pedlar, hawker.

camelote [kam'lɔt], *n.f.* inferior merchandise, shoddy; (*fig.*) trash.

caméra [kame'ra], *n.f.* ciné camera.

camérier [kame'rje], *n.m.* chamberlain (*of the Pope etc.*).

Cameroun [kamə'run], **le**, *m.* Cameroon.

camion [ka'mjɔ̃], *n.m.* dray, low wagon,truck.

camionnage [kamjɔ'naː3], *n.m.* carting, carriage.

camionner [kamjɔ'ne], *v.t.* to convey on a dray, lorry, truck etc.

camionnette [kamjɔ'nɛt], *n.f.* light motor lorry; van.

camionneur [kamjɔ'nœːr], *n.m.* drayman; vanman; haulage contractor, trucker.

camisole [kami'zɔl], *n.f.* woman's morning jacket; *camisole de force*, strait jacket.

camomille [kamɔ'miːj], *n.f.* camomile.

camouflage [kamu'flaː3], **camouflement** [kamuflə'mɑ̃], *n.m.* disguise; camouflage.

camoufler [kamu'fle], *v.t.* to disguise; to camouflage. **se camoufler**, *v.r.* to disguise or camouflage oneself.

camouflet [kamu'flɛ], *n.m.* whiff of smoke (*in the face*); (*fig.*) affront, snub.

camp [kɑ̃], *n.m.* camp; (*fig.*) army; party; (C) country cottage.

campagnard [kɑ̃pa'naːr], *a.* rustic, countrified, rural.—*n.m.* (*fem.* **-e**) countryman *or* countrywoman, peasant; clodhopper.

campagne [kɑ̃'paɲ], *n.f.* the country, the fields, plain; seat, estate, country house; campaign; (*Naut.*) cruise.

campagnol [kɑ̃pa'nɔl], *n.m.* vole, field mouse.

campanile [kɑ̃pa'nil], *n.m.* campanile, bell tower.

campanule [kɑ̃pa'nyl], *n.f.* campanula, bellflower, bluebell.

campé [kɑ̃'pe], *a.* established, firmly planted, well set up.

campement [kɑ̃p'mɑ̃], *n.m.* encamping; encampment; camp party, billeting party.

camper [kɑ̃'pe], *v.t.* to encamp (*troops etc.*); to place, to seat, to clap down.—*v.i.* to live in camp, to encamp. **se camper**, *v.r.* to encamp; to plant oneself.

campeur [kɑ̃'pœːr], *n.m.* (*fem.* **-euse**) camper.

camphre [kɑ̃:fr], *n.m.* camphor.

camphré [kɑ̃'fre], *a.* camphorated.

camphrier [kɑ̃fri'e], *n.f.* camphor tree.

camus [ka'my], *a.* flat-nosed, snub-nosed.

Canada [kana'da], **le**, *m.* Canada.

canadien [kana'djɛ̃], *a.* (*fem.* **-enne**) Canadian.—*n.m.* (**Canadien**, *fem.* **-enne**) Canadian (*person*).

canaille [ka'naːj], *n.f.* rabble, riffraff, mob.

canaillerie [kanaːj'ri], *n.f.* blackguardism; vulgarity.

canal [ka'nal], *n.m.* (*pl.* **-aux**) canal; conduit, drain; pipe, tube, spout; water-course.

canalisation [kanaliza'sjɔ̃], *n.f.* canalization; mains; *canalisation de gaz*, gas mains.

canaliser [kanali'ze], *v.t.* to canalize;to install pipes (*for gas etc.*).

canamelle [kana'mɛl], *n.f.* sugar cane.

canapé [kana'pe], *n.m.* sofa, couch.

canapé-lit [kanape'li], *n.m.* divan-bed.

canard [ka'naːr], *n.m.* duck; drake; (*fig.*) hoax.

canardeau [kanar'do], *n.m.* (*pl.* **-eaux**) young duck.

canarder [kanar'de], *v.t.* to shoot from behind a shelter; to snipe.—*v.i.* (*Naut.*) to pitch heavily.

canardière [kanar'djɛːr], *n.f.* duck pond; duck gun.

canari [kana'ri], *n.m.* canary (*bird*).

Canaries [kana'ri], **les Îles**, *f. pl.* the Canary Islands.

canasta [kanas'ta], *n.f.* canasta.

cancan [kɑ̃'kɑ̃], *n.m.* tittle-tattle, scandal; French cancan.

cancaner [kɑ̃ka'ne], *v.i.* to tattle, to invent stories.

cancanier [kɑ̃ka'nje], *a.* (*fem.* **-ière**) addicted to gossip.—*n.m.* (*fem.* **-ière**)scandal-monger.

cancer [kɑ̃'sɛːr], *n.m.* (*Astron., Geol., Med.*) cancer.

cancéreux [kɑ̃se'rø], *a.* (*fem.* **-euse**) cancerous.

cancre [kɑ̃:kr], *n.m.* crab; (*fig.*) dunce (*at school*).

cancrelat *or* **cancrelas** [kɑ̃krə'la], *n.m.* cockroach.

candélabre [kɑ̃de'laːbr], *n.m.* candelabrum, sconce.

candeur [kɑ̃'dœːr], *n.f.* artlessness, guilelessness, ingenuousness.

candi [kɑ̃'di], *a.m.* candied; *fruits candis*, crystallized fruits.—*n.m.* sugar candy.

candidat [kɑ̃di'da], *n.m.* candidate.

candidature [kɑ̃dida'tyːr], *n.f.* candidature.

candide [kɑ̃'did], *a.* ingenuous, artless.

candidement [kɑ̃did'mɑ̃], *adv.* ingenuously.

candir [kɑ̃'diːr], *v.i. or* **se candir**, *v.r.* to candy, to crystallize.

cane [kan], *n.f.* (*female*) duck.

canebière [CANNEBIÈRE].

canepetière [kanpə'tjɛːr], *n.f.* lesser bustard.

caneton [kan'tɔ̃], *n.m.* duckling.

canette (1) *or* **cannette** (1) [ka'nɛt], *n.f.* small duck, duckling; teal.

canette (2) *or* **cannette** (2) [ka'nɛt], *n.f.* measure for beer; spool (*inside shuttle*).

canevas [kan'va], *n.m.* canvas; sailcloth; outline sketch, rough draft.

caniche [ka'niʃ], *n.m.* poodle.

canichon [kani'ʃɔ], *n.m.* small poodle; duckling.

caniculaire [kaniky'lɛːr], *a.* canicular.

canicule [kani'kyl], *n.f.* dog-days; (*Astron.*) Dog Star.

canif [ka'nif], *n.m.* penknife.

canin [ka'nɛ̃], *a.* canine.—*n.f.* (*dent*) *canine*, canine (tooth).

canitie [kani'si], *n.f.* whiteness of the hair.

caniveau [kani'vo], *n.m.* (*pl.* **-eaux**) (*Arch.*) channel stone, gutter.

cannage [ka'naːʒ], *n.m.* cane work (*in chairs etc.*).

cannaie [ka'nɛ], *n.f.* cane plantation, cane field.

canne [kan], *n.f.* cane, reed; walking stick; glass-blower's pipe.

canneberge [kan'bɛrʒ], *n.f.* cranberry.

cannebière *or* **canebière** [kan'bjɛːr], *n.f.* (*S.-E. France*) [CHENEVIÈRE]

cannelé [kan'le], *a.* fluted (*column*); grooved (*tire*).—*n.m.* ribbed silk.

canneler [kan'le], *v.t.* (*conjug. like* APPELER) to flute, to channel, to groove.

cannelier [kanə'lje], *n.m.* cinnamon tree.

cannelle (1) [ka'nɛl], *n.f.* cinnamon bark, cinnamon.

cannelle (2) [ka'nɛl], **cannette** (3) [ka'nɛt], *n.f.* spigot, tap.

cannelure [kan'lyːr], *n.f.* fluting, channelling.

cannette (1) [CANETTE (1).]

cannette (2) [CANETTE (2).]

cannette (3) [CANNELLE (2].

cannibale [kani'bal], *n.m.* cannibal.

cannibalisme [kaniba'lism], *n.m.* cannibalism; (*fig.*) ferocity.

canon (1) [ka'nɔ̃], *n.m.* cannon, gun; barrel (*of a gun*); cylinder, pipe, tube (*of lock*).

canon (2) [ka'nɔ̃], *n.m.* (*Eccles.*) canon; (*Mus.*) round, canon.

cañon [ka'nɔ̃], *n.m.* canyon.

canonial [kanɔ'njal], *a.* (*m.pl.* **-aux**) canonical.

canonicat [kanɔni'ka], *n.m.* canonry; (*fig.*) sinecure.

canonicité [kanɔnisi'te], *n.f.* canonicity.

canonique [kanɔ'nik], *a.* canonical.

canonisation [kanɔniza'sjɔ̃], *n.f.* canonization.

canoniser [kanɔni'ze], *v.t.* to canonize.

canonnade [kanɔ'nad], *n.f.* cannonading, cannonade.

canonner [kanɔ'ne], *v.t.* to attack with heavy artillery, to cannonade.

canonnier [kanɔ'nje], *n.m.* gunner.

canonnière [kanɔ'njɛːr], *n.f.* pop-gun; gunboat.

canot [ka'no], *n.m.* small open boat, dinghy; (*C*) Canadian canoe; *canot automobile*, motor-boat; *canot de sauvetage*, lifeboat.

canotage [kanɔ'taːʒ], *n.m.* boating, rowing.

cantate [kɑ̃'tat], *n.f.* (*Mus.*) cantata.

cantatrice [kɑ̃ta'tris], *n.f.* cantatrice, (*classical*) singer.

cantharide [kɑ̃ta'rid], *n.f.* (*Ent.*) cantharis, Spanish fly.

cantilène [kɑ̃ti'lɛːn], *n.f.* cantilena, ballad, popular song.

cantine [kɑ̃'tin], *n.f.* canteen; kit-case.

cantique [kɑ̃'tik], *n.m.* canticle, hymn.

canton [kɑ̃'tɔ̃], *n.m.* canton (*district*); (*C*) township.

cantonade [kɑ̃tɔ'nad], *n.f.* (*Theat.*) either of the wings; *parler à la cantonade*, to speak to an actor off the stage.

cantonnement [kɑ̃tɔn'mɑ̃], *n.m.* (*Mil.*) cantonment, billet, quarters.

cantonner [kɑ̃tɔ'ne], *v.t.* (*Mil.*) to billet (*troops*). **se cantonner**, *v.r.* to take up a position, quarters *or* abode; to fortify oneself.

cantonnier [kɑ̃tɔ'nje], *n.m.* roadman; (*Rail.*) platelayer.

cantonnière [kɑ̃tɔ'njɛːr], *n.f.* valance.

canule [ka'nyl], *n.f.* clyster pipe, injection tube, douche tube.

caoutchouc [kau'tʃu], *n.m.* (India-)rubber mackintosh; (*pl.*) galoshes.

cap [kap], *n.m.* head; bow (*of a ship*); cape, headland, promontory.

capable [ka'pabl], *a.* able, fit, capable; apt; competent.

capacité [kapasi'te], *n.f.* extent, size; ability.

caparaçon [kapara'sɔ̃], *n.m.* caparison, trappings.

caparaçonner [kaparasɔ'ne], *v.t.* to caparison (*a horse*).

cape [kap], *n.f.* cape, mantle *or* cloak with a hood.

capharnaüm [kafarna'ɔm], *n.m.* lumberroom, storeroom for odds and ends.

capillaire [kapi'lɛːr], *a.* capillary.—*n.m.* capillary; maidenhair fern.

capilotade [kapilɔ'tad], *n.f.* hash, ragoût; (*fig.*) thrashing.

capitaine [kapi'tɛn], *n.m.* captain; (*fig.*) eminent commander.

capital [kapi'tal], *a.* (*m.pl.* **-aux**) capital, main, chief, principal.—*n.m.* capital, principal; property stock.

capitale [kapi'tal], *n.f.* capital, chief city; capital letter.

capitaliser [kapitali'ze], *v.t.* to put at compound interest; to add to the capital; to realize, to capitalize.—*v.i.* to save, to lay by.

capitaliste [kapita'list], *n.* capitalist, moneyed man *or* woman.

capitan [kapi'tɑ̃], *n.m.* braggadocio, swaggerer.

capitation [kapita'sjɔ̃], *n.f.* capitation, poll tax.

capiteux [kapi'tø], *a.* (*fem.* **-euse**) heady, strong.

Capitole [kapi'tɔl], *n.m.* Capitol (*of Rome etc.*).

capitonner [kapitɔ'ne], *v.t.* to stuff, to pad.

capitulaire [kapity'lɛːr], *a.* and *n.m.* capitulary.

capitulation [kapityla'sjɔ̃], *n.f.* capitulation; compromise.

capituler [kapity'le], *v.i.* to capitulate; to compound, to compromise.

capoc [ka'pɔk], *n.m.* kapok.

capon [ka'pɔ̃], *a.* (*fem.* **-onne**) cowardly.—*n.m.* (*fem.* **-onne**) mean fellow, sneak; coward.

caponner [kapɔ'ne], *v.i.* to cheat; to be cowardly; to rat.

caporal [kapɔ'ral], *n.m.* (*pl.* **-aux**) corporal; sort of 'shag' (*tobacco*).

capot (1) [ka'po], *n.m.* (*Motor.*) bonnet, (*Am.*) hood.

capot (2) [ka'po], *a. inv.* capot (*at piquet etc.*); flabbergasted.

capote [ka'pɔt], *n.f.* capote, large cloak with a hood; (*soldier's*) overcoat; baby's bonnet.

capoter [kapɔˈte], v.i. (Naut. etc.) to capsize; to turn turtle.

câpre [kɑːpr], n.f. (Bot.) caper.

caprice [kaˈpris], n.m. caprice, whim, humor; flight, sally.

capricieusement [kaprisjøzˈmã], adv. capriciously, whimsically.

capricieux [kapriˈsjø], a. (fem. -euse) capricious, whimsical, fickle.

capricorne [kapriˈkɔrn], n.m. (Astron.) Capricorn.

capsule [kapˈsyl], n.f. capsule; pod; percussion cap (of firearms).

captation [kaptaˈsjã], n.f. captation, inveigling; intercepting.

captatoire [kaptaˈtwaːr], a. inveigling.

capter [kapˈte], v.t. to obtain by underhand methods; to win by bribery etc.

captieusement [kapsjøzˈmã], adv. insidiously, cunningly, deceitfully.

captieux [kapˈsjø], a. (fem. -euse) insidious, cunning, specious.

captif [kapˈtif], a. and n.m.(fem. -tive) captive.

captivant [kaptiˈvã], a. captivating; enthralling.

captiver [kaptiˈve], v.t. to captivate, to charm.

captivité [kaptiviˈte], n.f. captivity, bondage.

capture [kapˈtyːr], n.f. capture, prize, booty.

capturer [kaptyˈre], v.t. to capture; to arrest.

capuchon [kapyˈʃã], n.m. hood, cowl.

capuchonné [kapyʃɔˈne], a. cowled; hooded.

capucin [kapyˈsɛ̃], n.m. (fem. **capucine** (1) [kapyˈsin]) Capuchin friar or nun.

capucine (1) [CAPUCIN].

capucine (2) [kapyˈsin], n.f. nasturtium.

caque [kak], n.f. keg, barrel.

caquet [kaˈkɛ], n.m. cackle (of geese etc.); tittle-tattle, gossip, scandal.

caquetage [kakˈtaːʒ], n.m., **caqueterie** [kak(ə)ˈtri], n.f. babbling, prattling; tattling, gossiping.

caqueter [kakˈte], v.i. (conjug. like APPELER) to cackle, to chatter; to gossip.

car (1) [kaːr], conj. for, because.

car (2) [kaːr], n.m. (fam.) coach, long-distance bus.

carabin [karaˈbɛ̃], n.m. (colloq.) saw-bones, medical student.

carabine [karaˈbin], n.f. carbine, rifle.

carabiné [karabiˈne], a. rifled; (colloq.) strong, violent.

carabiner [karabiˈne], v.t. to rifle (a gun barrel).

carabinier [karabiˈnje], n.m. carabinier, rifleman.

caractère [karakˈtɛːr], n.m. character, letter; handwriting; nature, disposition; temper, spirit; stamp; quality.

caractériser [karakteriˈze], v.t. to characterize, to describe.

caractéristique [karakterisˈtik], a. and n.f. characteristic.

carafe [kaˈraf], n.f. carafe, decanter, water-bottle.

carafon [karaˈfã], n.m. small carafe or decanter.

Caraïbes [karaˈib], les, f.pl. the Caribbean Isles.

carambolage [karãbɔˈlaːʒ], n.m. (Billiards) carom; (pop.) affray, shindy; (fig.) rebound (against).

caramboler [karãbɔˈle], v.i. (Billiards) to carom.

caramel [karaˈmɛl], n.m. caramel.

carapace [karaˈpas], n.f. (Zool.) carapace, shell.

carat [kaˈra], n.m. (Gold) carat.

caravane [karaˈvan], n.f. caravan, convoy; trailer (car).

carbonate [karbɔˈnat], n.m. (Chem.) carbonate.

carbone [karˈbɔn], n.m. carbon.

carboné [karbɔˈne], a. carbonated, carbonized.

carbonique [karbɔˈnik], a. carbonic.

carboniser [karbɔniˈze], v.t. to carbonize.

carburant [karbyˈrã], a. and n.m. motor fuel.

carburateur [karbyraˈtœːr], n.m. carburetor.

carbure [karˈbyːr], n.m. (Chem.) carbide.

carburé [karbyˈre], a. carburetted.

carcasse [karˈkas], n.f. carcass, skeleton.

cardage [karˈdaːʒ], n.m. carding.

carda.. [karˈdã], n.m. (Mech.) universal joint.

carde [kard], n.f. (Bot.) cardoon.

carder [karˈde], v.t. to card, to comb.

cardialgie [kardjalˈʒi], n.f. cardialgy, heartburn.

cardiaque [karˈdjak], a. and n. cardiac (case).

cardinal [kardiˈnal], a. (m. pl. -aux) cardinal, chief, principal.—n.m. (pl. -aux) (Eccles.) cardinal.

cardinalat [kardinaˈla], n.m. cardinalate, cardinalship.

cardiogramme [kardjɔˈgram], n.m. cardiogram.

cardiographe [kardjɔˈgraf], n.m. cardiograph.

cardon [karˈdã], n.m. (Bot.) cardoon.

carême [kaˈrɛːm], n.m. Lent; Lent sermons.

carénage [kareˈnaːʒ], n.m. careening.

carence [kaˈrãs], n.f. (Law) insolvency.

carène [kaˈrɛːn], n.f. (Naut.) bottom (keel and sides up to water-mark).

caréné [kareˈne], a. (Bot.) carinate; keeled; (Motor.) streamlined.

caréner [kareˈne], v.t. (conjug. like CÉDER) to careen; to streamline.

caressant [kareˈsã], a. caressing, endearing; tender.

caresse [kaˈrɛs], n.f. caress, endearment.

caresser [kareˈse], v.t. to caress, to fondle, to stroke.

caret (1) [kaˈrɛ], n.m. rope-maker's reel.

caret (2) [kaˈrɛ], n.m. turtle.

cargaison [kargɛˈzã], n.f. cargo, freight.

cargo [karˈgo], n.m. (Naut.) tramp, cargo boat.

carguer [karˈge], v.t. to reef (sails).

cargueur [karˈgœːr], n.m. (Naut.) reefer.

cari [kaˈri], n.m. curry powder.

cariatide [karjaˈtid], n.f. caryatid.

caribou [kariˈbu], n.m. cariboo.

caricature [karikaˈtyːr], n.f. caricature; (fam.) fright (person).

caricaturer [karikatyˈre], v.t. to caricature.

caricaturiste [karikatyˈrist], n. caricaturist.

carie [kaˈri], n.f. (Path.) caries, decay; (Bot.) brown rust; rot (of timber).

carier [kaˈrje], v.t. to make carious, to rot.

carillon [kariˈjã], n.m. carillon; chime, peal.

carillonnement [karijɔnˈmã], n.m. chiming, jingling.

carillonner [karijɔ'ne], *v.i.* to chime; to ring the changes; to jingle.
carillonneur [karijɔ'nœːr], *n.m.* bell ringer.
carlin [kar'lɛ̃], *a.* pug; turned-up (*nose*).
carlingue [kar'lɛ̃ːg], *n.f.* (*Av.*) cockpit.
carmagnole [karma'ɲɔl], *n.f.* Piedmontese jacket; carmagnole.
carme [karm], *n.m.* Carmelite friar, White friar.
carmélite [karme'lit], *n.f.* Carmelite nun.— *a.* light brown.
carmin [kar'mɛ̃], *a.* and *n.m.* carraine.
carnage [kar'naːʒ], *n.m.* carnage, slaughter.
carnassier [karna'sje], *a.* (*fem.* **-ière**) carnivorous, flesh-eating.—*n.m.* feline animal; flesh-eater.—*n.f.* (**-ière**) game bag.
carnation [karna'sjɔ̃], *n.f.* complexion; flesh color.
carnaval [karna'val], *n.m.* carnival; masquerade, festival; good fellow.
carné [kar'ne], *a.* flesh-colored; composed of meat.
carnet [kar'nɛ], *n.m.* notebook, log book.
carnier [kar'nje], *n.m.* game bag.
carnivore [karni'vɔːr], *a.* carnivorous.—*n.* carnivore.
carogne [ka'rɔɲ], *n.f.* hag, jade, impudent slut.
carotide [karɔ'tid], *a.* and *n.f.* carotid.
carotte [ka'rɔt], *n.f.* carrot; (*slang*) fake, ruse, hoax; sign outside a tobacconist's shop.—*a.* (*inv.*) ginger (*hair*).
carotter [karɔ'te], *v.t.* to cheat.
carotteur [karɔ'tœːr], **carottier** [karɔ'tje], *n.m.* (*fem.* **-euse, -ière**) cheat, trickster; wangler.
carpe (1) [karp], *n.f.* (*Ichth.*) carp.
carpe (2) [karp], *n.m.* (*Anat.*) wrist.
carquois [kar'kwa], *n.m.* quiver.
carrare [ka'raːr], *n.m.* Carrara marble.
carré [ka're], *a.* square; well-set; plain, straightforward.—*n.m.* square; landing, floor; (*Hort.*) plot.
carreau [ka'ro], *n.m.* (*pl.* **-eaux**) small square; square tile *or* brick, small flagstone; pane (*of glass*); diamond (*at cards*).
carrefour [kar'fuːr], *n.m.* crossroads.
carrelage [kar'laːʒ], *n.m.* tile flooring, paving squares.
carreler [kar'le], *v.t.* (*conjug. like* APPELER) to pave (*a floor*) with square tiles, bricks, stones etc.; to cobble (*shoes etc.*).
carrelet [kar'lɛ], *n.m.* plaice.
carrelette [kar'lɛt], *n.f.* flat file.
carreleur [kar'lœːr], *n.m.* floor tiler.
carrément [kare'mā], *adv.* squarely; (*fig.*) bluntly, plainly.
carrer [ka're], *v.t.* to square. **se carrer**, *v.r.* to strut, to pose.
carrier [ka'rje], *n.m.* quarryman.
carrière (1) [ka'rjɛːr], *n.f.* career; course; scope, play, vent; profession, vocation; *la Carrière*, the diplomatic service.
carrière (2) [ka'rjɛːr], *n.f.* quarry.
carriole [ka'rjɔl], *n.f.* light covered cart.
carrossable [karɔ'sabl], *a.* practicable for vehicles (*of roads*).
carrosse [ka'rɔs], *n.m.* state-coach, four-wheeled carriage.
carrosserie [karɔ'sri], *n.f.* coach-building; body (*of motors*).

carrossier [karɔ'sje], *n.m.* coach maker, carriage builder.
carrousel [karu'zɛl], *n.m.* merry-go-round; tournament.
carrure [ka'ryːr], *n.f.* breadth of shoulders.
cartable [kar'tabl], *n.m.* school satchel.
carte [kart], *n.f.* pasteboard; card, playing card, postcard; ticket; bill of fare; map, chart; *avoir carte blanche*, to have full power; *carte d'abonnement*, season ticket; *carte d'alimentation*, ration card, ration book; *un jeu de cartes*, a pack of cards.
cartel [kar'tɛl], *n.m.* challenge; cartel; dial case; wall clock; frieze panel.
carte-lettre [kartə'lɛtr], *n.f.* (*pl.* **cartes-lettres**) letter-card.
carter [kar'tɛr], *n.m.* gearcase (*of bicycle*); crankcase (*of car*).
cartésianisme [kartezja'nism], *n.m.* Cartesian philosophy.
cartésien [karte'zjɛ̃], *a.* and *n.m.* (*fem.* **-ienne**) Cartesian.
cartilage [karti'laːʒ], *n.m.* cartilage, gristle.
cartilagineux [kartilaʒi'nø], *a.* (*fem.* **-euse**) cartilaginous, gristly.
cartographe [kartɔ'graf], *n.m.* cartographer.
cartographie [kartɔgra'fi], *n.f.* cartography.
carton [kar'tɔ̃], *n.m.* cardboard, pasteboard; cardboard box, hatbox; (*Paint.*) cartoon; (*Phot.*) mount.
cartonnage [kartɔ'naːʒ], *n.m.* (*Bookb.*) boarding.
cartonneur [kartɔ'nœːr], *n.m.* (*fem.* **-euse**) binder (*of books*).
carton-pâte [kartɔ̃'paːt], *n.m.* millboard; papier mâché.
carton-pierre [kartɔ̃'pjɛːr], *n.m.* pasteboard for making ornaments.
cartothèque [kartɔ'tɛk], *n.f.* card index.
cartouche (1) [kar'tuʃ], *n.m.* escutcheon, scroll.
cartouche (2) [kar'tuʃ], *n.f.* cartridge.
cartouchier [kartu'ʃje], *n.m.*, **cartouchière** [kartu'ʃjɛːr], *n.f.* cartridge pouch *or* box.
cas [kɑ], *n.m.* case; instance, circumstance, state of things, conjuncture; (*Law*) cause; *c'est le cas ou jamais*, it is now or never; *en tout cas*, at all events.
casanier [kaza'nje], *a.* (*fem.* **-ière**) domestic, stay-at-home, home-loving.
cascade [kas'kad], *n.f.* cascade, waterfall.
case [kɑːz], *n.f.* cabin, hut, small house; division, compartment; box (*for animals*); pigeonhole; square (*of chess-* or *draught-board*); (*Naut.*) berth.
casemate [kaz'mat], *n.f.* (*Fort.*) casemate.
caser [kɑ'ze], *v.t.* to put in order, to file (*documents*), (*fam.*) to provide for; to marry off.—*v.i.* (*backgammon*) to make a point. **se caser**, *v.r.* to take up one's abode, to settle.
caserne [ka'zɛrn], *n.f.* barracks.
caserner [kazɛr'ne], *v.t.* to quarter in barracks.—*v.i.* to be in barracks.
casier [kɑ'zje], *n.m.* rack, card *or* music stand, set of pigeonholes; *casier judiciaire*, police record.
casilleux [kazi'jø], *a.* (*fem.* **-euse**) brittle.
casino [kazi'no], *n.m.* casino, club.
casque [kask], *n.m.* helmet, headpiece; (*Nat. Hist.*) crest; headphone (*radio*).

casquette [kas′kɛt], *n.f.* cap.
cassable [kɑ′sabl], *a.* breakable.
cassage [kɑ′saːʒ], *n.m.* breakage.
cassant [kɑ′sã], *a.* brittle; crisp; breakable; (*fig.*) abrupt, gruff.
cassation [kasɑ′sjɔ̃], *n.f.* (*Law*) cassation, annulment, repeal; *cour de cassation*, the highest court of appeal in France.
casse (1) [kɑːs], *n.f.* breakage(s); damage, losses.
casse (2) [kɑːs], *n.f.* (*Print.*) case; *bas de casse*, lower case.
casse-cou [kɑs′ku], *n.m. inv.* death trap; roughrider; daredevil.
casse-croûte [kɑs′krut], *n.m. inv.* quick meal, snack.
casse-noisette [kɑsnwa′zɛt], *n.m.* (*pl.* **casse-noisettes**) nutcracker; (*Orn.*) nuthatch.
casse-noix [kɑs′nwɑ], *n.m. inv.* nutcrackers.
casse-pipes [kɑs′pip], *n.m. inv.* shooting gallery; (*pop.*) war.
casser [kɑ′se], *v.t.* to break, to smash; to cashier (*an officer*), to reduce to the ranks, to dissolve (*Parliament etc.*); to annul, to rescind. **se casser**, *v.r.* to break, to snap; to break down.
casserole [kas′rɔl], *n.f.* saucepan, stewpan.
casse-tête [kɑs′tɛːt], *n.m. inv.* cudgel, club; (*fig.*) din; conundrum.
cassette [kɑ′sɛt], *n.f.* casket; cash box.
casseur [kɑ′sœːr], *n.m.* (*fem.* **-euse**) breaker, smasher.
cassis [kɑ′sis], *n.m.* black currant.
casson [kɑ′sɔ̃], *n.m.* piece of broken glass *or* pottery; rough lump (*of sugar*).
cassonade [kasɔ′nad], *n.f.* moist brown sugar.
cassoulet [kasu′lɛ], *n.m.* stew of beans with mutton and pork.
cassure [kɑ′syːr], *n.f.* break, crack, fracture; broken piece.
castagnette [kasta′ɲɛt], *n.f.* castanet.
caste [kast], *n.f.* caste.
castillan [kasti′jã], *a.* Castilian.—*n.m.* Castilian (*speech*); (**Castillan**, *fem.* **-ane**) Castilian (*person*).
castine [kas′tin], *n.f.* (*Metal.*) flux.
castor [kas′tɔːr], *n.m.* beaver.
casuel [ka′zɥɛl], *a.* (*fem.* **-uelle**) casual, fortuitous, accidental.—*n.m.* perquisites, fees.
casuiste [ka′zɥist], *n.m.* casuist.
cataclysme [kata′klism], *n.m.* cataclysm; (*fig.*) disaster.
catacombes [kata′kɔ̃:b], *n.f. pl.* catacombs.
catafalque [kata′falk], *n.m.* catafalque.
cataire [ka′tɛːr], *n.f.* (*Bot.*) catmint.
catalan [kata′lã], *a.* Catalan.—*n.m.* Catalan (*language*); (**Catalan**, *fem.* **-ane**) Catalan (*person*).
catalepsie [katalɛp′si], *n.f.* catalepsy.
catalogue [kata′lɔg], *n.m.* list, catalogue.
cataloguer [katalɔ′ge], *v.t.* to catalogue.
catalyse [kata′liːz], *n.f.* (*Chem.*) catalysis.
catalyseur [katali′zœːr], *n.m.* catalyst.
catalytique [katali′tik], *a.* catalytic.
cataphote [kata′fɔt], *n.m.* cat's eye (*reflector*).
cataplasme [kata′plasm], *n.m.* cataplasm, poultice.
cataracte [kata′rakt], *n.f.* cataract, waterfall; (*Path.*) cataract.
catarrhal [kata′ral], *a.* (*m.pl.* **-aux**) catarrhal.
catarrhe [ka′taːr], *n.m.* catarrh.

catastrophe [katas′trɔf], *n.f.* catastrophe, calamity.
catastrophique [katastrɔ′fik], *a.* catastrophic.
catéchiser [kate′ʃize], *v.t.* to catechize; (*fig.*) to reason with; to lecture.
catéchisme [kate′ʃism], *n.m.* catechism.
catégorie [katego′ri], *n.f.* category.
catégorique [katego′rik], *a.* categorical, explicit.
catégoriquement [kategorik′mã], *adv.* categorically.
catharsis [katar′sis], *n.f.* (*Med.*) catharsis.
cathédral [kate′dral], *a.* (*m.pl.* **-aux**) cathedral.
cathédrale [kate′dral], *n.f.* cathedral.
cathode [ka′tɔd], *n.f.* cathode.
cathodique [katɔ′dik], *a.* cathode.
catholicisme [katɔli′sism], *n.m.* Catholicism.
catholique [katɔ′lik], *a.* catholic; moral, orthodox.—*n.* Catholic (*person*).
cati [ka′ti], *n.m.* gloss, luster.
catir [′a′tiːr], *v.t.* to give a gloss to.
catissage [kati′saːʒ], *n.m.* glossing, pressing.
catisseur [kati′sœːr], *a.* and *n.m.* (*fem.* **-euse**) presser.
Caucase [ko′kɑːz], **le**, *m.* the Caucasus.
caucasien [koka′zjɛ̃], *a.* (*fem.* **-enne**) Caucasian.—*n.m.* (**Caucasien**, *fem.* **-enne**) Caucasian (*person*).
cauchemar [koʃ′maːr], *n.m.* nightmare.
caudataire [kodɑ′tɛːr], *n.m.* train-bearer.
cauri, cauris *or* **coris** [ko′ri], *n.m.* cowrie.
causal [ko′zal], *a.* causal.
causant [ko′zã], *a.* chatty, talkative.
causatif [koza′tif], *a.* (*fem.* **-tive**) (*Gram.*) causative, causal.
cause [koːz], *n.f.* cause; grounds, motive; interest; case, trial, suit, action; *à cause de*, because of; *mettre en cause*, to sue.
causer (1) [ko′ze], *v.t.* to cause, to be the cause of.
causer (2) [ko′ze], *v.i.* to chat, to talk; to prate.
causerie [ko′zri], *n.f.* talk, chat, gossip; chatty essay, review etc.
causette [ko′zɛt], *n.f.* chit-chat, small talk.
causeur [ko′zœːr], *a.* (*fem.* **-euse**) talkative, chatty.—*n.m.* (*fem.* **-euse**) talker.—*n.f.* (**-euse**) small sofa, settee for two.
causticité [kostisi′te], *n.f.* causticity.
caustique [kos′tik], *a.* caustic, biting, cutting.—*n.m.* caustic.
caustiquement [kostik′mã], *adv.* caustically.
cauteleusement [kotløz′mã], *adv.* craftily, slyly.
cauteleux [kot′lø], *a.* (*fem.* **-euse**) cunning, crafty.
cautère [ko′tɛːr], *n.m.* (*Med.*) cautery; issue.
cautérisation [koteriza′sjɔ̃], *n.f.* cauterization.
cautériser [koteri′ze], *v.t.* to cauterize.
caution [ko′sjɔ̃], *n.f.* security, bail, surety; (*fig.*) pledge, guarantee; *verser une caution*, to pay a deposit.
cautionnement [kosjɔn′mã], *n.m.* bail; security.
cautionner [kosjɔ′ne], *v.t.* to stand bail for someone.
cavage [ka′vaːʒ], *n.m.* cellarage.
cavalcade [kaval′kad], *n.f.* procession; cavalcade.
cavale [ka′val], *n.f.* mare.
cavalerie [kaval′ri], *n.f.* cavalry.

cavalier

cavalier [kava'lje], *n.m.* horseman, rider, trooper; (*Dancing*) partner; (*C*) lover, sweetheart; (*Chess*) knight.—*a.* (*fem.* **-ière**) cavalier, unceremonious (*of manners etc.*); off-hand, flippant.

cavalièrement [kavaljɛr'mɑ̃], *adv.* cavalierly, bluntly.

cave (1) [ka:v], *a.* hollow.

cave (2) [ka:v], *n.f.* (*wine*) cellar, vault; cellarage.

caveau [ka'vo], *n.m.* (*pl.* **-eaux**) small cellar; burial vault.

caver [ka've], *v.t.* to hollow, to scoop out, to dig under; (*fig.*) to undermine; (*Fenc.*) to lunge. **se caver**, *v.r.* to become hollow or sunken.

caverne [ka'vɛrn], *n.f.* cavern, cave, hollow; (*fig.*) retreat, lair.

caverneux [kavɛr'nø], *a.* (*fem.* **-euse**) cavernous, hollow.

caviar [ka'vja:r], *n.m.* caviare.

cavillation [kavilo'sjɔ̃], *n.f.* sophistry, cavil.

cavité [kavi'te], *n.f.* cavity, hollow.

ce (1) [sə], *dem. a.* (*before vowels* **cet**, *fem.* **cette**, *pl.* **ces**) this, that, (*pl.*) these, those.

ce (2) [sə], *dem. pron. inv.* it, that (*sometimes* = he, she, or, *with plural verb*, they); *c'en est fait*, it is all over, it is done; *c'est-à-dire*, that is to say; *c'est que*, the fact is that; *pour ce qui est de* . . . , as for . . . .

*céans [se'ɑ̃], *adv.* within, here within, in this house, at home.

ceci [sə'si], *dem. pron.* this, this thing.

cécité [sesi'te], *n.f.* blindness.

cédant [se'dɑ̃], *a.* that grants; (*Law*) that assigns, transfers.—*n.m.* (*fem.* **-e**) (*Law*) grantor, assignor, transferrer.

céder [se'de], *v.t.* (*see Verb Tables*) to give up, to yield, to surrender, to cede; to transfer, to make over.—*v.i.* to give way; to submit.

cédille [se'di:j], *n.f.* cedilla.

cédrat [se'dra], *n.m.* citron tree; citron.

cèdre [sɛ:dr], *n.m.* cedar.

cédule [se'dyl], *n.f.* schedule, memorandum; notice; (*Law*) notification.

cégétiste [seʒe'tist], *n.m.* a member of the C.G.T. (Confédération Générale du Travail.)

ceindre [sɛ̃:dr], *v.t. irr.* (*conjug. like* CRAINDRE) to gird, to encircle, to encompass, to surround; to bind or gird on. **se ceindre**, *v.r.* to bind round one, to put on (*a scarf etc.*).

ceinture [sɛ̃'ty:r], *n.f.* sash, girdle, belt, waistband; waist; enclosure, circle; *ceinture de sauvetage*, life belt.

ceinturer [sɛ̃ty're], *v.t.* to girdle, to surround.

ceinturon [sɛ̃ty'rɔ̃], *n.m.* belt, sword belt.

cela [sə'la, sla], *dem. pron.* that, that thing (*in opposition to this, of which we are speaking*); *c'est cela*, that's it. *In popular speech* **cela** becomes **ça**; *pas de ça*, none of that; *comme ci comme ça*, middling.

céladon [sela'dɔ̃], *a.* and *n.m.* sea-green (*color*).

célébrant [sele'brɑ̃], *n.m.* celebrant.

célébration [selebra'sjɔ̃], *n.f.* solemn performance, celebration.

célèbre [se'lɛbr], *a.* celebrated, famous, renowned.

célébrer [sele'bre], *v.t.* (*conjug. like* CÉDER) to celebrate, to praise, to extol; to solemnize.

célébrité [selebri'te], *n.f.* celebrity.

*celer [sə'le], *v.t.* (*conjug. like* AMENER) to conceal, to keep secret. ***se celer**, *v.r.* to conceal oneself, to hide.

céleri [sel'ri], *n.m.* celery; *un pied de céleri*, a stick of celery.

célerin [sel'rɛ̃], *n.m.* (*Ichth.*) pilchard.

célérité [seleri'te], *n.f.* celerity, rapidity.

céleste [se'lɛst], *a.* celestial, heavenly, divine.

célibat [seli'ba], *n.m.* celibacy, single life.

célibataire [seliba'tɛ:r], *a.* single.—*n.m.* bachelor.—*n.f.* spinster.

celle [sɛl], [CELUI].

cellérier [sele'rje], *n.m.* (*fem.* **-ière**) cellarer.

cellier [se'lje], *n.m.* cellar, storeroom.

cellophane [selo'fan], *n.f.* cellophane.

cellulaire [sely'lɛ:r], *a.* cellular.

cellule [se'lyl], *n.f.* cell; *cellule photo-électrique*, electric eye.

celluleux [sely'lø], *a.* (*fem.* **-euse**) cellular.

celluloïd or **celluloïde** [selylo'id], *n.m.* celluloid.

cellulose [sely'lo:z], *n.f.* cellulose.

Celte [sɛlt], *n.* Celt.

celtique [sɛl'tik], *a.* Celtic.—*n.m.* Celtic (*language*).

celui [sə'lɥi], *dem. pron. m.* (*fem.* **celle**, *pl.* **ceux**, **celles**) the one, that, those (*sometimes* = he or she). Followed by **-ci** or **-là** = this one, that one etc. or the latter *and* the former.

cément [se'mɑ̃], *n.m.* (*Metal.*) cement.

cémentation [semɑ̃ta'sjɔ̃], *n.f.* (*Metal.*) cementation.

cémenter [semɑ̃'te], *v.t.* (*Metal.*) to cement.

cénacle [se'nakl], *n.m.* (*Ant.*) guest chamber; (*fig.*) literary society or coterie.

cendre [sɑ̃:dr], *n.f.* ashes, embers, cinders; dust, ashes (*of the dead*).

cendré [sɑ̃'dre], *a.* ashy, ashen.

cendrée [sɑ̃'dre], *n.f.* small shot; cinders (*for track*); *piste en cendrée*, dirt track, cinder track.

cendrer [sɑ̃'dre], *v.t.* to paint ash-grey; to mix or cover with ashes.

cendreux [sɑ̃'drø], *a.* (*fem.* **-euse**) ashy.

cendrier [sɑ̃dri'e], *n.m.* ash pan, ash pit; ash tray.

cendrière [sɑ̃dri'ɛ:r], *n.f.* peat.

Cendrillon [sɑ̃dri'jɔ̃], *n.f.* Cinderella, drudge.

Cène [sɛ:n], *n.f.* The Lord's Supper, Holy Communion.

cenelle [sə'nɛl], *n.f.* haw.

cénobite [seno'bit], *n.m.* coenobite.

cénotaphe [seno'taf], *n.m.* cenotaph.

cens [sɑ̃:s], *n.m.* census; rating.

censé [sɑ̃'se], *a.* accounted, reputed, supposed.

censeur [sɑ̃'sœ:r], *n.m.* censor; critic; proctor (*of Engl. Univ.*); assistant headmaster (*in French Lycée*).

censure [sɑ̃'sy:r], *n.f.* censorship; criticism, censure; audit (*of accounts*).

censurer [sɑ̃sy're], *v.t.* to find fault with, to criticize; to censure.

cent [sɑ̃], *a.* one hundred; *faire les cent pas*, to walk up and down.—*n.m.* a hundred; *cinq pour cent*, five per cent.

centaine [sɑ̃'tɛn], *n.f.* a hundred; a hundred or so.

centaure [sɑ̃'to:r], *n.m.* centaur.

centenaire [sɑ̃t'nɛ:r], *a.* a hundred years old. —*n.* centenarian.—*n.m.* centenary.

centième [sã'tjɛm], *a.* hundredth.—*n.m.* hundredth part.

centigrade [sãti'grad], *a.* centigrade.

centigramme [sãti'gram], *n.m.* centigram, the hundredth part of a gram (.1543 grain).

centilitre [sãti'litr], *n.m.* centiliter, hundredth part of a liter (.61028 cubic in.).

centime [sã'tim], *n.m.* centime, hundredth part of a franc.

centimètre [sãti'metr], *n.m.* centimeter, hundredth part of a meter (.39371 in.).

centipède [sãti'pɛd], *n.m.* centipede.

central [sã'tral], *a.* (*m. pl.* **-aux**) central; chief, principal, head.—*n.m.* **central téléphonique**, telephone exchange.—*n.f.* **centrale électrique**, electric power station.

centralement [sãtral'mã], *adv.* centrally.

centralisateur [sãtraliza'tœːr], *a.* (*fem.* **-trice**) centralizing.

centralisation [sãtraliza'sjã], *n.f.* centralization.

centraliser [sãtrali'ze], *v.t.* to centralize.

centre [sãːtr], *n.m.* center, middle.

centrer [sã'tre], *v.t.* to center.

centrifuge [sãtri'fyːʒ], *a.* centrifugal.

centripète [sãtri'pɛt], *a.* centripetal.

centuple [sã'typl], *a.* and *n.m.* centuple, hundredfold.

centupler [sãty'ple], *v.t.* to multiply a hundredfold.

centurion [sãty'rjã], *n.m.* centurion.

cep [sep], *n.m.* vine stock.

cépage [se'paːʒ], *n.m.* vine plant.

cépée [se'pe], *n.f.* (*Agric.*) tuft of shoots from a pollarded stump; copse of one or two years' growth.

cependant [spã'dã], *adv.* in the meantime, meanwhile.—*conj.* yet, still, however, nevertheless.

céramique [sera'mik], *a.* ceramic.—*n.f.* ceramics.

Cerbère [sɛr'bɛːr], *m.* (*Myth.*) Cerberus.

cerceau [sɛr'so], *n.m.* (*pl.* **-eaux**) hoop, ring; hoop net.

cerclage [sɛr'klaːʒ], *n.m.* hooping (*of casks*).

cercle [sɛrkl], *n.m.* circle, ring; circumference; club, club-house.

cercler [sɛr'kle], *v.t.* to bind with hoops, to hoop.

cercueil [sɛr'kœːj], *n.m.* coffin; (*fig.*) the tomb.

céréale [sere'al], *n.f.* cereal, corn, grain.

cérébral [sere'bral], *a.* (*m.pl.* **-aux**) cerebral.

cérémonial [seremo'njal], *a.* (*m.pl.* **-aux**) ceremonial.—*n.m.* (*no pl.*) ceremonial, pomp.

cérémonie [seremo'ni], *n.f.* ceremony; pomp; fuss, ado.

cérémonieux [seremo'njø], *a.* (*fem.* **-euse**) ceremonious, formal.

cerf [sɛːr], *n.m.* stag, hart, deer.

cerfeuil [sɛr'fœːj], *n.m.* chervil.

cerf-volant [sɛrvo'lã], *n.m.* (*pl.* **cerfs-volants**) stag beetle; kite, paper kite.

cerisaie [sri'zɛ], *n.f.* cherry orchard.

cerise [sə'riːz], *n.f.* cherry.—*n.m.* cherry-color, cerise.—*a.* cherry-colored, cerise.

cerisier [səri'zje], *n.m.* cherry tree, cherry wood.

cerner [sɛr'ne], *v.t.* to cut *or* dig round (*a tree*), to ring (*a tree*); to surround, to encompass, to hem in.

certain [sɛr'tɛ], *a.* certain, sure, positive; fixed, determined; **d'un certain âge**, not so young.—*n.m.* certainty; a sure thing.

certainement [sɛrtɛn'mã], *adv.* certainly.

certes [sɛrt], *adv.* indeed, most certainly.

certificat [sɛrtifi'ka], *n.m.* certificate; testimonial; diploma.

certification [sɛrtifika'sjã], *n.f.* certification.

certifier [sɛrti'fje], *v.t.* to certify, to testify, to vouch for.

certitude [sɛrti'tyd], *n.f.* certitude, certainty.

cerveau [sɛr'vo], *n.m.* (*pl.* **-eaux**) brain; mind, intellect, intelligence.

cervelas [sɛrvə'la], *n.m.* saveloy.

cervelle [sɛr'vɛl], *n.f.* brains; mind, intelligence.

cervin [sɛr'vɛ], *a.* cervine; *le* (*Mont*) *Cervin*, the Matterhorn.

César [se'zaːr], *m.* Caesar.—*n.m.* Caesar, emperor.

césari·n [seza'rjɛ], *a.* (*fem.* **-ienne**) Caesarean.—*n.f.* (**-ienne**) Caesarean operation.

cessant [se'sã], *a.* ceasing, suspended.

cessation [sɛsa'sjã], *n.f.* cessation, suspension, stoppage.

cesse [sɛs], *n.f.* ceasing, intermission, respite.

cesser [se'se], *v.t.* to leave off, to break off, to stop.—*v.i.* to cease, to leave off, to stop.

cession [se'sjã], *n.f.* transfer, assignment (*of property*).

cessionnaire [sesjo'nɛːr], *n.m.* grantee, assignee.

césure [se'zyːr], *n.f.* caesura.

cet, cette [sɛt], [CE].

cétacé [seta'se], *a.* cetaceous.—*n.m.* cetacean.

ceux [sø·], [CELUI].

Ceylan [se'lã], *le*, m. Ceylon.

chablis (1) [ʃa'bli], *n.m.* deadwood.

chablis (2) [ʃa'bli], *n.m.* Chablis (*white wine*).

chacal [ʃa'kal], *n.m.* jackal.

chacun [ʃa'kœ], *pron. indef. sing.* each, each one, every one.

chafouin [ʃa'fwɛ], *a.* weasel-faced, mean-looking.

chagrin (1), [ʃa'grɛ], *n.m.* grief, chagrin; sorrow.—*a.* gloomy, melancholy, sad.

chagrin (2) [ʃa'grɛ], *n.m.* shagreen.

chagrinant [ʃagri'nã], *a.* distressing, sad.

chagriner [ʃagri'ne], *v.t.* to grieve, to afflict; to cross, to vex. **se chagriner**, *v.r.* to fret, to grieve.

chahut [ʃa'y], *n.m.* row, shindy.

chahuter [ʃay'te], *v.i.* to make a row, to kick up a shindy.

chaîne [ʃɛːn], *n.f.* chain; shackle, fetters; bonds, bondage; (*Naut.*) cable; (*fig.*) series, range; (*Ind.*) **chaîne de montage**, assembly line.

chaîner [ʃɛ'ne], *v.t.* (*Surveying*) to measure (*land*) with the chain.

chaînette [ʃɛ'nɛt], *n.f.* little chain; (*Arch.*) catenary arch.

chaînon [ʃɛ'nã], *n.m.* link.

chaintre [ʃɛːtr], *n.m.* (*Agric.*) balk, headland.

chair [ʃɛːr], *n.f.* flesh; meat; (*fig.*) the human body, the flesh; (*Paint., pl.*) naked flesh.

chaire [ʃɛːr], *n.f.* pulpit; professorship; bishop's throne.

chaise [ʃɛːz], *n.f.* chair, seat; post chaise.

chaland (1) [ʃa'lã], *n.m.* lighter, barge.

chaland (2) [ʃa'lã], *n.m.* (*fem.* **-e**) customer, client.

chalandeau [ʃalɑ̃'do], *n.m.* (*pl.* **-eaux**) lighterman, bargeman.

chalcographe [kalkɔ'graf], *n.m.* chalcographer, engraver on metal.

chalcographie [kalkɔgra'fi], *n.f.* chalcography; engraving establishment.

chaldaïque [kalda'ik], *a.* Chaldaic.

Chaldée [kal'de], *f.* Chaldea.

chaldéen [kalde'ɛ̃], *a.* (*fem.* **-éenne**) Chaldean. —*n.m.* (**Chaldéen,** *fem.* **-éenne**) Chaldean (*person*).

châle [ʃɑ:l], *n.m.* shawl.

chalet [ʃa'lɛ], *n.m.* chalet, Swiss cottage.

chaleur [ʃa'lœ:r], *n.f.* heat; warmth, warm weather; (*fig.*) glow; zeal, ardor; '*craint la chaleur*', 'store in a cool place'.

chaleureusement [ʃalœrøz'mɑ̃], *adv.* cordially, warmly.

chaleureux [ʃalœ'rø], *a.* (*fem.* **-euse**) warm, cordial.

chalicose [ʃali'ko:z], *n.f.* silicosis.

châlit [ʃa'li], *n.m.* bedstead.

chaloupe [ʃa'lup], *n.f.* ship's boat, launch.

chalumeau [ʃaly'mo], *n.m.* (*pl.* **-eaux**) stalk of wheat; drinking-straw; flute, pipe.

chalut [ʃa'ly], *n.m.* dragnet, trawl.

chalutier [ʃaly'tje], *n.m.* trawler.

chamaillard [ʃama'ja:r], *a.* squabbling, quarrelsome.

chamailler [ʃama'je], *v.i.* to bicker, to squabble. **se chamailler**, *v.r.* to squabble, to wrangle.

chamaillis [ʃama'ji], *n.m.* fray; squabble; uproar.

chamarrer [ʃama're], *v.t.* to bedizen, to bedeck.

chambellan [ʃɑ̃be'lɑ̃], *n.m.* chamberlain.

chambranle [ʃɑ̃'brɑ̃:l], *n.m.* door frame, window frame.

chambre [ʃɑ̃:br], *n.f.* chamber, room; apartment; House (*of Parliament*); court (*of justice*); *chambre à air*, inner tube (*bicycle etc.*); *chambre à un* (*deux*) *lit*(*s*), single (double) room; *chambre d'unis*, spare bedroom; *chambre d'écluse*, lock; *chambre noire*, camera obscura.

chambrée [ʃɑ̃'bre], *n.f.* barrack room; roomful (*of*) (*Theat. etc.*) house.

chambrer [ʃɑ̃'bre], *v.t.* to keep (*someone*) confined; to bring wine to room temperature.—*v.i.* to lodge (*together*). **se chambrer**, *v.r.* to become pitted.

chambrette [ʃɑ̃'brɛt], *n.f.* little room.

chameau [ʃa'mo], *n.m.* (*pl.* **-eaux**) camel; (*pop.*) nasty, evil-minded person.

chamelier [ʃamə'lje], *n.m.* camel driver.

chamelle [ʃa'mɛl], *n.f.* female camel.

chamelon [ʃam'lɔ̃], *n.m.* young camel.

chamois [ʃa'mwa], *n.m.* chamois; chamois leather.—*a.* chamois-colored; buff.

chamoiseur [ʃamwa'zœ:r], *n.m.* chamois or leather dresser.

champ [ʃɑ̃], *n.m.* field, piece of ground; scope, range; (*poet.*) land; (*fig.*) space; *sur-le-champ*, at once, immediately.

champagne [ʃɑ̃'paɲ], *n.m.* champagne; *champagne frappé*, iced champagne; *champagne mousseux*, sparkling champagne; *fine champagne*, liqueur brandy.

champenois [ʃɑ̃pə'nwa], *a.* of Champagne. —*n.m.* (**Champenois,** *fem.* **-oise**) inhabitant of Champagne.

champêtre [ʃɑ̃'pɛ:tr], *a.* rural, rustic; *garde champêtre*, village policeman.

champignon [ʃɑ̃pi'ɲɔ̃], *n.m.* mushroom, fungus.

champion [ʃɑ̃'pjɔ̃], *n.m.* (*fem.* **-onne**) champion.

championnat [ʃɑ̃pjo'na], *n.m.* championship.

chançard [ʃɑ̃'sa:r], *a.* and *n.m.* (*fem.* **-e**) (*fam.*) lucky (*person*).

chance [ʃɑ̃:s], *n.f.* chance; luck, good luck, good fortune; (*pl.*) chances, (*fam.*) odds.

chancelant [ʃɑ̃s'lɑ̃], *a.* staggering, tottering.

chanceler [ʃɑ̃s'le], *v.i.* (*conjug. like* APPELER) to stagger, to totter; to reel.

chancelier [ʃɑ̃sə'lje], *n.m.* chancellor.

chancellement [ʃɑ̃sɛl'mɑ̃], *n.m.* tottering, staggering.

chancellerie [ʃɑ̃sɛl'ri], *n.f.* chancellery.

chanceux [ʃɑ̃'sø], *a.* (*fem.* **-euse**) lucky, fortunate; risky, doubtful (*of things*).

chanci [ʃɑ̃'si], *a.* moldy.

chancir [ʃɑ̃'si:r], *v.i.* to grow musty or moldy.

chancissure [ʃɑ̃si'sy:r], *n.f.* mustiness, moldiness.

chancre [ʃɑ̃:kr], *n.m.* ulcer, tumor; canker.

chancreux [ʃɑ̃'krø], *a.* (*fem.* **-euse**) ulcerous; cankered.

chandail [ʃɑ̃'da:j], *n.m.* jersey, sweater.

Chandeleur [ʃɑ̃'dlœ:r], *n.f.* Candlemas.

chandelier [ʃɑ̃də'lje], *n.m.* candlestick.

chandelle [ʃɑ̃'dɛl], *n.f.* (*tallow*) candle; (*fig.*) light; (*Tennis*) lob.

change [ʃɑ̃:ʒ], *n.m.* exchange; exchange of money; exchange office; agio; (*Hunt.*) wrong scent; *agent de change*, stockbroker; *cours du change*, rate of exchange.

changeant [ʃɑ̃'ʒɑ̃], *a.* changeable, fickle; unstable; unsettled (*of the weather*).

changement [ʃɑ̃ʒ'mɑ̃], *n.m.* change, alteration; (*Law*) amendment.

changer [ʃɑ̃'ʒe], *v.t., v.i.* (*conjug. like* MANGER) to change, to exchange; to alter.

changeur [ʃɑ̃'ʒœ:r], *n.m.* (*fem.* **-euse**) money-changer.

chanoine [ʃa'nwan], *n.m.* canon.

chanson [ʃɑ̃'sɔ̃], *n.f.* song, ballad; (*fig.*) idle story, stuff, trash; *chansons que tout cela!* humbug!

chansonner [ʃɑ̃so'ne], *v.t.* to lampoon.

chansonnette [ʃɑ̃so'nɛt], *n.f.* little song, ditty.

chansonneur [ʃɑ̃so'nœ:r], *n.m.* lampooner.

chansonnier [ʃɑ̃so'nje], *n.m.* (*fem.* **-ière**) song-writer, ballad writer; singer of satirical songs.

chant [ʃɑ̃], *n.m.* singing; song; air, tune; poem; canto; chant, hymn.

chantable [ʃɑ̃'tabl], *a.* fit to be sung, worth singing.

chantage [ʃɑ̃'ta:ʒ], *n.m.* extortion of hush money, blackmail.

chantant [ʃɑ̃'tɑ̃], *a.* easily sung; tuneful, harmonious.

chanteau [ʃɑ̃'to], *n.m.* (*pl.* **-eaux**) hunk (*of bread*), bit (*of material etc.*), remnant; (*Dress.*) gore.

chantepleure [ʃɑ̃t'plœ:r], *n.f.* funnel pierced with holes; strainer.

charpentier [ʃarpɑ̃'tje], *n.m.* carpenter.

charpie [ʃar'pi], *n.f.* lint.

charretée [ʃar'te], *n.f.* cartload.

charretier [ʃar'tje], *n.m.* (*fem.* **-ière**) carter, wagoner. —*a.* passable for carts etc.

charrette [ʃa'rɛt], *n.f.* cart; *charrette à bras*, hand cart.

charriage [ʃa'ria:ʒ], *n.m.* cartage; haulage.

charrier [ʃa'rje], *v.t.* to cart.—*v.i.* to drift (*of ice*).

charroi [ʃa'rwa], *n.m.* cartage.

charron [ʃa'rɔ̃], *n.m.* wheelwright.

charroyer [ʃarwa'je], *v.t.* (*conjug. like* EMPLOYER) to cart (*heavy things*).

charrue [ʃa'ry], *n.f.* plow.

charte [ʃart], *n.f.* charter.

chartreuse [ʃar'trø:z], *n.f.* Carthusian monastery *or* convent; Carthusian nun; isolated country house; chartreuse (*liqueur*).

chartreux [ʃar'trø], *n.m.* Carthusian friar; cat of a bluish-grey color.

chartrier [ʃartri'e], *n.m.* keeper of charters; archives; muniment room.

Charybde [ka'ribd], *n.m.* Charybdis.

chas [ʃɑ], *n.m.* eye (*of a needle*).

chasme [kasm], *n.m.* chasm.

châsse [ʃɑ:s], *n.f.* reliquary, shrine; frame.

chasse [ʃas], *n.f.* hunting, shooting, fowling; the hunt, the chase; game preserve; play (*of machinery etc.*); flush (*of lavatory*).

chassé [ʃa'se], *n.m.* chassé (*a step in dancing*).

chassé-croisé [ʃasekrwa'ze], *n.m.* (*pl. chassés-croisés*) (*Dancing*) a dance step; (*fig.*) *faire un chassé-croisé*, to exchange places.

chasselas [ʃas'la], *n.m.* table grapes.

[In the following compounds **chasse** is *inv.*]

chasse-marée [ʃasma're], *n.m.* fish cart.

chasse-mouches [ʃas'muʃ], *n.m.* a form of fan; fly swatter.

chasse-neige [ʃas'nɛ:ʒ], *n.m.* snow plow.

chasse-pierre(s) [ʃas'pjɛ:r], *n.m.* (*Rail.*) guard-iron, cow-catcher.

chasser [ʃa'se], *v.t.* to hunt; to chase, to pursue; to drive in (*a nail etc.*); to expel, to turn out, to discharge; to propel.—*v.i.* to go shooting *or* hunting; to glide along; (*Motor.*) to skid.

chasseresse [ʃas'rɛs], *n.f.* huntress.

chasseur [ʃa'sœ:r], *n.m.* (*fem.* **-euse**) hunter *or* huntress, sportsman *or* sportswoman.— *n.m.* page boy; light infantry soldier; (*Av.*) fighter.

chassie [ʃa'si], *n.f.* gum on the edge of the eyelids.

chassieux [ʃa'sjø], *a.* (*fem.* **-euse**) blear-eyed.

châssis [ʃa'si], *n.m.* case, frame; window sash; garden frame; printer's chase; (*Motor.*) chassis; (*Theat.*) flat for scenery.

chaste [ʃast], *a.* chaste; pure, virtuous.

chastement [ʃastə'mã], *adv.* chastely, purely, virtuously.

chasteté [ʃastə'te], *n.f.* chastity, purity.

chasuble [ʃa'zybl], *n.f.* chasuble.

chat [ʃa], *n.m.* (*fem.* **chatte**) cat; darling, dear little thing; *à bon chat bon rat*, set a thief to catch a thief; (*C*) *chat sauvage*, raccoon; *Le Chat Botté*, Puss in Boots.

châtaigne [ʃa'tɛɲ], *n.f.* chestnut.

châtaignier [ʃatɛ'ɲje], *n.m.* chestnut tree.

châtain [ʃa'tɛ̃], *a. inv.* chestnut, nut-brown, auburn.

chat-cervier [ʃasɛr'vje], *n.m.* (*pl.* **chats-cerviers**) lynx.

château [ʃa'to], *n.m.* (*pl.* **-eaux**) castle, fortress; country seat, mansion, hall, palace.

châteaubriant [ʃatobri'ã], *n.m.* large grilled rump steak.

châtelain [ʃa'tlɛ̃], *n.m.* (*fem.* **-aine**) lord *or* lady of a manor, squire *or* squire's wife.

chat-huant [ʃa'ɥã], *n.m.* (*pl.* **chats-huants**) tawny owl.

châtiable [ʃa'tjabl], *a.* chastisable, punishable.

châtier [ʃa'tje], *v.t.* to chastise, to punish; (*fig.*) to correct.

chatière [ʃa'tjɛ:r], *n.f.* cat's hole (*in door etc.*).

châtiment [ʃati'mã], *n.m.* chastisement, punishment.

chatoiement *or* **chatoîment** [ʃatwa'mã], *n.m.* play of colors, changing luster (*as of shot silk, opals etc.*).

chaton (1) [ʃa'tɔ̃], *n.m.* kitten; catkin.

chaton (2) [ʃa'tɔ̃], *n.m.* setting of a gem; stone in a setting.

chatouillant [ʃatu'jã], *a.* tickling.

chatouillement [ʃatuj'mã], *n.m.* tickling, titillation.

chatouiller [ʃatu'je], *v.t.* to tickle, to titillate; (*fig.*) to please, to gratify, to flatter.

chatouilleux [ʃatu'jø], *a.* (*fem.* **-euse**) ticklish; (*fig.*) delicate, touchy.

chatoyant [ʃatwa'jã], *a.* shot, glistening (*of colors etc.*).

chatoyer [ʃatwa'je], *v.i.* (*conjug. like* EMPLOYER) to shimmer, to glisten.

châtrer [ʃa'tre], *v.t.* to castrate, to geld; (*Hort.*) to lop, to prune; (*fig.*) to expurgate.

chattée [ʃa'te], *n.f.* litter of kittens.

chatte [ʃat], [CHAT].

chatterie [ʃat'ri], *n.f.* playfulness, pretty *or* coaxing way; wheedling caress; (*pl.*) tidbits.

chatterton [ʃatɛr'tɔ̃], *n.m.* insulating tape.

chaud [ʃo], *a.* hot, warm, burning, glowing.— *n.m.* heat, warmth; *il fait chaud*, it is hot. —*adv.* hot, warm.

chaudeau [ʃo'do], *n.m.* (*pl.* **-eaux**) egg flip.

chaudement [ʃod'mã], *adv.* warmly; (*fig.*) quickly, eagerly, fiercely, hotly.

chaud-froid [ʃo'frwa], *n.m.* cold jellied chicken *or* game with mayonnaise.

chaudière [ʃo'djɛ:r], *n.f.* copper; boiler (*of a steam engine etc.*); (*C*) pail.

chaudron [ʃo'drɔ̃], *n.m.* cauldron.

chaudronnerie [ʃodrɔn'ri], *n.f.* boiler works.

chaudronnier [ʃodrɔ'nje], *n.m.* brazier, coppersmith, tinker.

chauffage [ʃo'fa:ʒ], *n.m.* heating, warming; stoking; fuel, firewood; *chauffage central*, central heating.

chauffard [ʃo'fa:r], *n.m.* (*pop.*) road hog.

chauffe [ʃo:f], *n.f.* furnace.

chauffe-bain [ʃof'bɛ̃], *n.m.* (*pl.* **chauffe-bains**) geyser.

chauffe-eau [ʃof'o], *n.m. inv.* water heater.

chauffelinge [ʃof'lɛ:ʒ], *n.m. inv.* clothes-horse, airing cupboard.

chauffer [ʃo'fe], *v.t.* to heat, to warm; (*fig.*) to excite.—*v.i.* to grow hot; to be brewing; (*fig.*) to be urgent *or* pressing. **se chauffer**, *v.r.* to warm oneself.

chaufferette [ʃo'frɛt], *n.f.* foot warmer.

chauffeur [ʃoˈfœːr], *n.m.* fireman; (*fem.* **-euse**)(*Motor.*) driver, chauffeur, chauffeuse.
chaufour [ʃoˈfuːr], *n.m.* lime kiln.
chaulage [ʃoˈlaːʒ], *n.m.* (*Agric.*) liming.
chauler [ʃoˈle], *v.t.* to lime (*soil*).
chaume [ʃoːm], *n.m.* stubble; stubble field; thatch.
chaumer [ʃoˈme], *v.t., v.i.* (*Agric.*) to cut stubble.
chaumière [ʃoˈmjɛːr], *n.f.* thatched house, cottage.
chausse [ʃoːs], *n.f.* shoulder band (*worn in universities etc.*); *(pl.)* hose (*covering the body from waist to foot*).
chaussée [ʃoˈse], *n.f.* embankment, dike; causeway; roadway, (*Am.*) pavement; *le rez-de-chaussée*, the ground floor.
chausse-pied [ʃosˈpje], *n.m.* (*pl.* **chaussepieds**) shoe-horn.
chausser [ʃoˈse], *v.t.* to put on (*footwear*); to shoe, to make (*the shoes etc.*) for; (*colloq.*) to fit, to suit.—*v.i. chausser du* 40, to take a 7 (*in shoes*). **se chausser**, *v.r.* to put on one's shoes etc.
chausse-trape [ʃosˈtrap], *n.f.* (*pl.* **chaussetrapes**) snare, trap.
chaussette [ʃoˈsɛt], *n.f.* sock.
chausseur [ʃoˈsœːr], *n.m.* footwear dealer.
chausson [ʃoˈsɔ̃], *n.m.* slipper; gym shoe; bootee (*for infants*).
chaussure [ʃoˈsyːr], *n.f.* footwear.
chauve [ʃoːv], *a.* bald.
chauve-souris [ʃovsuˈri], *n.f.* (*pl.* **chauvessouris**) bat, flittermouse.
chauvin [ʃoˈvɛ̃], *n.m.* fanatical patriot.—*a.* chauvinistic, jingoistic.
chaux [ʃo], *n.f.* lime; limestone.
chavirage [ʃaviˈraːʒ], **chavirement** [ʃavirˈmã], *n.m.* capsizing, upsetting.
chavirer [ʃaviˈre], *v.t., v.i.* to capsize, to upset.
chef [ʃɛf], *n.m.* chief, commander, conductor, master, principal, ringleader; chef.
chef-d'œuvre [ʃeˈdœːvr], *n.m.* (*pl.* **chefs-d'œuvre**) chef-d'œuvre, masterpiece.
chef-lieu [ʃeˈljø], *n.m.* (*pl.* **chefs-lieux**) chief town, county seat.
cheik [SCHEIK].
chelem or **schelem** [ʃlɛm], *n.m. inv.* slam (*at cards*).
chemin [ʃəˈmɛ̃], *n.m.* way, road, path, track; (*fig.*) means; course; *chemin de fer*, railway, (*Am.*) railroad.
chemineau [ʃəmiˈno], *n.m.* (*pl.* **-eaux**) tramp.
cheminée [ʃəmiˈne], *n.f.* chimney; funnel; fire-place; mantelpiece; nipple (*of a percussion gun*).
cheminer [ʃəmiˈne], *v.i.* to walk, to tramp; to proceed.
cheminot [ʃəmiˈno], *n.m.* railwayman; rail layer.
chemise [ʃəˈmiːz], *n.f.* shirt; wrapper, cover.
chemiserie [ʃəmiˈzri], *n.f.* shirt factory; shirt making.
chemisette [ʃəmiˈzɛt], *n.f.* short-sleeved shirt (*men*).
chemisier [ʃəmiˈzje], *n.m.* (*fem.* **-ière**) shirt maker *or* seller.
chênaie [ʃeˈnɛ], *n.f.* oak plantation.
chenal [ʃəˈnal], *n.m.* channel, fairway.
chenapan [ʃənaˈpã], *n.m.* vagabond, good-for-nothing, scamp.

chêne [ʃɛːn], *n.m.* oak.
chêneau [ʃeˈno], *n.m.* (*pl.* **-eaux**) young oak.
chéneau [ʃeˈno], *n.m.*(*pl.* **-eaux**)(eaves) gutter.
chenet [ʃəˈnɛ], *n.m.* fire-dog.
chènevière [ʃɛnvjɛːr], *n.f.* hemp-field.
chènevis [ʃɛnˈvi], *n.m.* hemp-seed.
chènevotte [ʃɛnˈvɔt], *n.f.* stalk (*of hemp*).
chenil [ʃəˈni], *n.m.* dog-kennel; kennels; dirty hovel.
chenille [ʃəˈniːj], *n.f.* caterpillar; kind of silk cord, chenille; *tracteur à chenille*, caterpillar tractor.
chenillère [ʃəniˈjɛːr], *n.f.* nest of caterpillars.
chenillette [ʃəniˈjɛt], *n.f.* (*Mil.*) caterpillar.
chenu [ʃəˈny], *a.* hoary, grey-headed; snow-capped.
cheptel [ʃəˈtɛl, ʃɛpˈtɛl], *n.m.* live-stock (*of a country*).
chèque [ʃɛk], *n.m.* cheque, (*Am.*) check.
chéquier [ʃeˈkje], *n.m.* cheque-book.
cher [ʃɛːr], *a.* (*fem.* **chère** (1)) dear, beloved; precious; expensive.—*adv.* dear, dearly, expensively.
chercher [ʃɛrˈʃe], *v.t.* to seek, to look for, to search for; to endeavour, to try, to attempt; *aller chercher*, to go for; to fetch.
chercheur [ʃɛrˈʃœːr], *n.m.* (*fem.* **-euse**) seeker, searcher; research worker.
chère (1) [ʃɛːr], [CHER].
chère (2) [ʃɛːr], *n.f.* entertainment, fare; *bonne chère*, good cheer, good living.
chèrement [ʃɛrˈmã], *adv.* dearly, tenderly; dear, at a high price.
chéri [ʃeˈri], *a.* beloved; cherished.—*n.m.* (*fem.* **-e**) darling, dearest.
chérif [ʃeˈrif], *n.m.* shereef (*Arabian prince*).
chérir [ʃeˈriːr], *v.t.* to love dearly, to cherish.
cherté [ʃɛrˈte], *n.f.* dearness, high price.
chérubin [ʃeryˈbɛ̃], *n.m.* cherub.
chérubique [ʃeryˈbik], *a.* cherubic.
chester [ʃɛsˈtɛr], *n.m.* Cheshire cheese.
chétif [ʃeˈtif], *a.* (*fem.* **-tive**) puny, pitiful; worthless.
chétivement [ʃetivˈmã], *adv.* meanly, pitifully, poorly, feebly.
chétiveté [ʃetivˈte], *n.f.* puniness, paltriness.
cheval [ʃəˈval], *n.m.* (*pl.* **-aux**) horse; nag, steed; *aller à cheval*, to ride; *cheval d'arçons, cheval de bois*, (*Gym.*) vaulting horse; *cheval à bascule*, rocking-horse; *chevaux de bois*, merry-go-round; *cheval marin*, sea horse; walrus.
chevaleresque [ʃəvalˈrɛsk], *a.* chivalrous, knightly.
chevaleresquement [ʃəvalrɛskˈmã], *adv.* chivalrously.
chevalerie [ʃəvalˈri], *n.f.* knighthood, chivalry.
chevalet [ʃəvaˈlɛ], *n.m.* easel; bridge (*of a stringed instrument*); sawing-trestle; buttress, prop; clothes-horse.
chevalier (1) [ʃəvaˈlje], *n.m.* knight.
chevalier (2) [ʃəvaˈlje], *n.m.* (*Orn.*) sandpiper; redshank.
chevalière [ʃəvaˈljɛːr], *n.f.* knight's lady; signet-ring.
chevalin [ʃəvaˈlɛ̃], *a.* equine; *boucherie chevaline*, horse butcher's shop.
cheval-vapeur [ʃəvalvaˈpœːr], *n.m.* (*pl.* **chevaux-vapeur**) horsepower.
chevauchant [ʃəvoˈʃã], *a.* overlapping.
chevauchée [ʃəvoˈʃe], *n.f.* ride, excursion on horseback; cavalcade.

chevauchement [ʃəvoʃ'mɑ̃], *n.m.* overlap *or* crossing (*tiles, wires*).

chevaucher [ʃəvo'ʃe], *v.i.* to ride on horseback; to be astride; to overlap.

chevaucheur [ʃəvo'ʃœːr], *n.m.* rider, horseman.

chevauchure [ʃəvo'ʃyːr], *n.f.* overlapping.

chevelu [ʃə'vly], *a.* hairy, long-haired; (*Bot.*) fibrous.

chevelure [ʃə'vlyːr], *n.f.* hair, head of hair.

chevesne [ʃə'vɛn], *n.m.* (*Ichth.*) chub.

chevet [ʃə've], *n.m.* head (*of a bed*); bolster; pillow; bedside.

cheveu [ʃə'vø], *n.m.* (*pl.* **-eux**) a single hair; *pl.* the hair (*of the head*).

chevillage [ʃəvi'jaːʒ], *n.m.* fastening, bolting, dowelling.

cheville [ʃə'viːj], *n.f.* ankle; peg, pin, dowel, bolt; plug.

cheviller [ʃəvi'je], *v.t.* to dowel, to peg, to bolt.

cheviotte [ʃə'vjɔt], *n.f.* cheviot (*tweed*).

chèvre [ʃɛːvr], *n.f.* goat, nanny goat.

chevreau [ʃə'vro], *n.m.* (*pl.* **-eaux**) kid (*animal or skin*).

chèvrefeuille [ʃɛvrə'fœːj], *n.m.* honeysuckle.

chèvrerie [ʃɛvrə'ri], *n.f.* goat pen.

chevrette [ʃə'vrɛt], *n.f.* small goat; young roe.

chevreuil [ʃə'vrœːj], *n.m.* roe, roe deer.

chevrier [ʃəvri'e], *n.m.* (*fem.* **-ière**) goatherd.

chevron [ʃə'vrɔ̃], *n.m.* rafter; chevron, stripe.

chevronnage [ʃəvrɔ'naːʒ], *n.m.* rafters, raftering.

chevronné [ʃəvrɔ'ne], *a.* (*fam.*) experienced

chevrotain or **chevrotin** [ʃəvrɔ'tɛ̃], *n.m.* chevrotain, musk deer.

chevrotant [ʃəvrɔ'tɑ̃], *a.* quavering, tremulous.

chevrotement [ʃəvrɔt'mɑ̃], *n.m.* tremulous motion, trembling (*of the voice etc.*).

chevroter [ʃəvrɔ'te], *v.i.* to sing *or* speak in a tremulous voice.

chevrotin (1) [CHEVROTAIN].

chevrotin (2) [ʃəvrɔ'tɛ̃], *n.m.* fawn of roe deer; kid (*leather*).

chevrotine [ʃəvrɔ'tin], *n.f.* buckshot.

chez [ʃe], *prep.* at, to, in (*the house, family or country of*); in, with, among; in the works of, (*on letters*) care of.

chiasse [ʃjas], *n.f.* dross, scum.

chibouque or **chibouk** [ʃi'buk], *n.f.* chibouk (*Turkish pipe*).

chic [ʃik], *n.m.* style, chic; aplomb, ease and elegance.—*a. inv.* stylish, smart.

chicane [ʃi'kan], *n.f.* cavil, evasion, quibble; chicanery.

chicaner [ʃika'ne], *v.t.* to quarrel *or* wrangle with.—*v.i.* to cavil, to quibble.

chicanerie [ʃikan'ri], *n.f.* chicanery, quibbling, cavilling.

chicaneur [ʃika'nœːr], *n.m.* (*fem.* **-euse**) or **chicanier** [ʃika'nje], *n.m.* (*fem.* **-ière**) caviller, pettifogger.—*a.* litigious, cavilling, wrangling.

chiche (1) [ʃiʃ], *a.* niggardly, stingy.

chiche (2) [ʃiʃ], *a.* **pois chiches**, chickpeas.

chichement [ʃiʃ'mɑ̃], *adv.* stingily.

chicorée [ʃikɔ're], *n.f.* endive, chicory.

chicot [ʃi'ko], *n.m.* stub *or* stump (*of tree or tooth*).

chicotin [ʃiko'tɛ̃], *n.m.* bitter juice of aloes.

chien [ʃjɛ̃], *n.m.* (*fem.* **chienne**) dog; hammer, cock (*of a gun or pistol*); **chien de mer**, dogfish.

chiendent [ʃjɛ̃'dɑ̃], *n.m.* couch grass.

chiennée [ʃje'ne], *n.f.* litter of pups.

chiffe [ʃif], *n.f.* poor stuff, rag; (*fig.*) weakling; spineless person.

chiffon [ʃi'fɔ̃], *n.m.* rag, scrap, bit; frippery.

chiffonnage [ʃifɔ'naːʒ], *n.m.* rumpled drapery, rumpling, crumpling.

chiffonner [ʃifɔ'ne], *v.t.* to rumple, to crumple; (*colloq.*) to ruffle, to tease, to vex. —*v.i.* to be a rag collector.

chiffonnier [ʃifɔ'nje], *n.m.* (*fem.* **-ière**) ragpicker; chiffonnier.

chiffrage [ʃi'fraːʒ], **chiffrement** [ʃifr'mɑ̃], *n.m.* figuring, figures; calculation; writing in cipher, coding.

chiffre [ʃifr], *n.m.* figure, number; total amount; cipher; monogram.

chiffrer [ʃi'fre], *v.t.* to calculate, to tot up; to code.—*v.i.* to cipher.

chiffreur [ʃi'frœːr], *n.m.* (*fem.* **-euse**) reckoner, cipherer.

chignole [ʃi'nɔl], *n.f.* ratchet drill.

chignon [ʃi'nɔ̃], *n.m.* chignon, coil of hair.

Chili [ʃi'li], **le**, *m.* Chile.

chilien [ʃi'ljɛ̃], *a.* (*fem.* **-enne**) Chilean.—*n.m.* (**Chilien,** *fem.* **-enne**) Chilean (*person*).

chimère [ʃi'mɛːr], *n.f.* chimera; myth, idle fancy.

chimérique [ʃime'rik], *a.* chimerical, visionary.

chimériquement [ʃimerik'mɑ̃], *adv.* chimerically.

chimie [ʃi'mi], *n.f.* chemistry.

chimique [ʃi'mik], *a.* chemical.

chimiquement [ʃimik'mɑ̃], *adv.* chemically.

chimiste [ʃi'mist], *n.m.* chemist (*not pharmaceutical chemist*).

chimpanzé [ʃɛ̃pɑ̃'ze], *n.m.* chimpanzee.

chinchilla [ʃɛ̃fil'ta], *n.m.* chinchilla.

Chine [ʃin], **la**, *f.* China.

chiner [ʃi'ne], *v.t.* to color differently; to figure (*stuffs*).

chinois [ʃi'nwa], *a.* Chinese.—*n.m.* Chinese (*language*); **un chinois,** a small green orange preserved in brandy; (**Chinois,** *fem.* **-oise**) Chinese (*person*).

chinoiserie [ʃinwa'zri], *n.f.* Chinese thing, curio; (*fig.*) trick; red tape.

chiot [ʃjo], *n.m.* puppy.

chiourme [ʃjurm], *n.f.* convict gang.

chipolata [ʃipɔla'ta], *n.f.* onion stew; small sausage.

chipotage [ʃipɔ'taːʒ], *n.m.* dawdling; haggling.

chipoter [ʃipɔ'te], *v.i.* to dally, to dawdle (*s*); to haggle; to peck at a dish.

chipotier [ʃipɔ'tje], *n.m.* (*fem.* **-ière**) trifler, dallier, shuffler.

chique [ʃik], *n.f.* quid of tobacco.

chiquement [ʃik'mɑ̃], *adv.* smartly.

chiquenaude [ʃik'noːd], *n.f.* flick.

chiquenauder [ʃikno'de], *v.t.* to flick.

chiquer [ʃi'ke], *v.i.* to chew tobacco.

chiquet [ʃi'ke], *n.m.*, **chiquette** [ʃi'kɛt], *n.f.* driblet, bit, shred.

chiqueur [ʃi'kœːr], *n.m.* chewer of tobacco; pretender.

chiromancie [kirɔmɑ̃'si], *n.f.* chiromancy, palmistry.
chiromancien [kirɔmɑ̃'sjɛ̃], *n.m.* (*fem.* **-ienne**) chiromancer, palmist.
chirurgical [ʃiryrʒi'kal], *a.* (*m. pl.* **-aux**) surgical.
chirurgicalement [ʃiryrʒikal'mɑ̃], *adv.* surgically.
chirurgie [ʃiryr'ʒi], *n.f.* surgery.
chirurgien [[ʃiryr'ʒjɛ̃], *n.m.* surgeon.
chirurgique [ʃiryr'ʒik], *a.* surgical.
chiure [ʃjy:r], *n.f.* flyspeck.
chlorate [klɔ'rat], *n.m.* chlorate.
chlore [klɔ:r], *n.m.* (*Chem.*) chlorine.
chloré [klɔ're], *a.* containing chlorine.
chlorhydrate [klɔri'drat], *n.m.* (*Chem.*) hydrochlorate.
chlorhydrique [klɔri'drik], *a.* hydrochloric.
chloroforme [klɔrɔ'fɔrm], *n.m.* chloroform.
chloroformer [klɔrɔfɔr'me], *v.t.* to chloroform.
chlorure [klɔ'ry:r], *n.m.* (*Chem.*) chloride.
choc [ʃɔk], *n.m.* shock; impact; clash, encounter.
chocolat [ʃɔkɔ'la], *n.m.* chocolate.—*a.* chocolate-colored.
chocolaterie [ʃɔkɔla'tri], *n.f.* chocolate-making; chocolate factory.
chocolatier [ʃɔkɔla'tje], *n.m.* (*fem.* **-ière**) chocolate maker *or* seller.—*n.f.* (**-ière**) chocolate pot.
chœur [kœ:r], *n.m.* choir; chancel; (*Ant. and fig.*) chorus.
choir [ʃwa:r], *v.i. irr.* to fall, to drop.
choisir [ʃwa'zi:r], *v.t.* to choose, to single out, to select.
choix [ʃwa], *n.m.* choice, alternative; selection; distinction.
choléra [kɔle'ra], *n.m.* cholera.
cholérique [kɔle'rik], *a.* choleraic.—*n.* person affected with cholera.
chômable [ʃo'mabl], *a.* (*of days, fêtes etc.*) to be kept as a holiday.
chômage [ʃo'ma:ʒ], *n.m.* unemployment, enforced idleness; stoppage; *allocation de chômage,* unemployment benefit, 'dole'.
chômer [ʃo'me], *v.i.* to be doing nothing; to be unemployed.
chômeur [ʃo'mœ:r], *n.m.* (*fem.* **-euse**) idle *or* unemployed person.
chope [ʃɔp], *n.f.* large beer glass; mug of beer.
chopper [ʃɔ'pe], *v.i.* to stumble, to trip (*contre*).
choquant [ʃɔ'kɑ̃], *a.* offensive, unpleasant, improper.
choquer [ʃɔ'ke], *v.t.* to shock, to strike *or* dash against; to displease, to offend.—*v.i.* to clink glasses; to be offensive, to be shocking. **se choquer,** *v.r.* to take offence; to come into collision with each other.
choral [kɔ'ral], *a.* choral.—*n.m.* (*pl.* **-als**) choral(e).—*n.f.* (**chorale**) choir, choral society.
chorée [kɔ're], *n.f.* chorea, St. Vitus's dance.
chorégraphe [kɔre'graf], *n.m.* choreographer.
chorégraphie [kɔregra'fi], *n.f.* choreography.
choriste [kɔ'rist], *n.m.* chorister; (*Theat.*) member of the chorus.
chorus [kɔ'ry:s], *n.m.* chorus.

chose [ʃo:z], *n.f.* thing; matter, business, affair; (*Law*) chattel, property.
chou [ʃu], *n.m.* (*pl.* **choux**) cabbage, kale; (*colloq.*) puff paste; darling, dear; bow, rosette; *choux de Bruxelles,* Brussels sprouts.
chouan [ʃwɑ̃], *n.m.* Chouan, Breton royalist insurgent (*during the French Revolution*).
choucas [ʃu'ka], *n.m.,* **chouchette** [ʃu'ʃɛt] *n.f.* jackdaw.
choucroute [ʃu'krut], *n.f.* sauerkraut.
chouette (1) [ʃwɛt], *n.f.* owl.
chouette (2) [ʃwɛt], *int.* (*pop.*) fine, marvellous.—*a.* nice, fine, good of its kind.
chou-fleur [ʃu'flœ:r], *n.m.* (*pl.* **choux-fleurs**) cauliflower.
chou-rave [ʃu'ra:v], *n.m.* (*pl.* **choux-raves**) kohl rabi, turnip-cabbage.
choyer [ʃwa'je], *v.t.* (*conjug. like* EMPLOYER) to take great care of, to be fond of, to pamper, to pet. **se choyer,** *v.r.* to pamper oneself.
chrème [krɛ:m], *n.m.* chrism, holy oil.
chrémeau [kre'mo], *n.m.* (*pl.* **-eaux**) chrism cloth.
chrétien [kre'tjɛ̃], *a.* and *n.m.* (*fem.* **-enne**) Christian.
chrétiennement [kretjɛn'mɑ̃], *adv.* like a Christian.
chrétienté [kretjɛ̃'te], *n.f.* Christendom.
christ [krist], *n.m.* crucifix; representation of Christ crucified; *le Christ,* Jesus Christ.
christianisme [kristja'nism], *n.m.* Christianity.
Christophe [kris'tɔf], *m.* Christopher.
chromage [kro'ma:ʒ], *n.m.* chromium plating.
chromate [kro'mat] *n.m.* (*Chem.*) chromate.
chromatique [krɔma'tik], *a.* (*Chem., Mus.*) chromatic.—*n.f.* (*Mus., Paint.*) chromatics.
chrome [kro:m], *n.m.* chromium, chrome.
chromé [kro'me], *a.* chromium-plated.
chromer [kro'me], *v.t.* to chrome.
chromique [kro'mik], *a.* chromic.
chromosome [kromo'zo:m], *n.m.* chromosome.
chronique (1) [krɔ'nik], *n.f.* chronicle, history; news summary.
chronique (2) [krɔ'nik], *a.* (*Med.*) chronic.
chroniqueur [krɔni'kœ:r], *n.m.* (*fem.* **-euse**) chronicler; newswriter, columnist.
chronologie [krɔnɔlɔ'ʒi], *n.f.* chronology.
chronologique [krɔnɔlɔ'ʒik], *a.* chronological.
chronomètre [krɔnɔ'mɛ:tr], *n.m.* chronometer.
chronométrer [krɔnɔme'tre], *v.t.* (*conjug. like* CÉDER) to time.
chronométreur [krɔnɔme'trœ:r], *n.m.* timekeeper.
chrysalide [kriza'lid], *n.f.* chrysalis.
chrysanthème [krizɑ̃'tɛ:m], *n.m.* chrysanthemum.
chuchotement [ʃyʃɔt'mɑ̃], *n.m.* whispering, whisper, rustling.
chuchoter [ʃyʃɔ'te], *v.t., v.i.* to whisper.
chuchoterie [ʃyʃɔ'tri], *n.f.* whispering.
chuchoteur [ʃyʃɔ'tœ:r], *n.m.* (*fem.* **-euse**) whisperer.
chuinter [ʃyɛ̃'te], *v.i.* to hoot (*of owls*); to hiss (*of gas*).
chut [ʃ:t], *int.* and *n.m.* hush!

69

chute [ʃyt], *n.f.* fall, tumble; collapse, ruin, downfall; disaster.
chuter [ʃy'te], *v.i.* (*fam.*) to fall, to fail.
Chypre [ʃipr], *f.* Cyprus.
ci [si], *adv.* here.
cible [sibl], *n.f.* target, mark; (*fig.*) purpose.
ciboire [si'bwa:r], *n.m.* sacred vase, pyx.
ciboule [si'bul], *n.f.* Welsh onion, scallion.
ciboulette [sibu'lɛt], *n.f.* chive.
cicatrice [sika'tris], *n.f.* scar, seam, mark.
cicatrisant [sikatri'zɑ̃], *a.* cicatrizing.
cicatrisation [sikatriza'sjɔ̃], *n.f.* cicatrization.
cicatriser [sikatri'ze], *v.t.* to cicatrize; to close, to heal up. **se cicatriser**, *v.r.* to skin over, to heal up.
Cicéron [sise'rɔ̃], *m.* Cicero.
cicérone [sise'rɔn], *n.m.* cicerone, guide.
cicéronien [sisero'njɛ̃], *a.* (*fem.* **-enne**) Ciceronian.
cidre [sidr], *n.m.* cider.
cidrerie [sidrə'ri], *n.f.* cider making; cider factory.
ciel [sjɛl], *n.m.* (*pl.* **cieux**) the heavens, the firmament, the sky; heaven.
cierge [sjɛrʒ], *n.m.* taper, church candle.
cigale [si'gal], *n.f.* cicada.
cigare [si'ga:r], *n.m.* cigar.
cigarette [siga'rɛt], *n.f.* cigarette.
cigogne [si'gɔɲ], *n.f.* stork.
cigogneau [sigɔ'no], *n.m.* (*pl.* **-eaux**) young stork.
ciguë [si'gy], *n.f.* hemlock (*plant or poison*).
cil [sil], *n.m.* eyelash.
cilice [si'lis], *n.m.* cilice, hair shirt.
cillement [sij'mɑ̃], *n.m.* blink, winking.
ciller [si'je], *v.t.*, *v.i.* to wink, to blink (*the eyes*).
cimaise *or* **cymaise** [si'mɛ:z], *n.f.* cyma, ogee; dado rail, picture rail.
cime [sim], *n.f.* top, summit, peak.
ciment [si'mɑ̃], *n.m.* cement.
cimenter [simɑ̃'te], *v.t.* to cement; to strengthen, to consolidate.
cimentier [simɑ̃'tje], *n.m.* cement maker.
cimeterre [sim'tɛ:r], *n.m.* scimitar.
cimetière [sim'tjɛ:r], *n.m.* cemetery, church-yard.
cimier [si'mje], *n.m.* crest (*of a helmet*); rump (*of beef*).
cinéaste [sine'ast], *n.m.* film producer.
cinéma [sine'ma], *n.m.* cinema.
cinémascope [sinemas'kɔp], *n.m.* cinema-scope.
cinémathèque [sinema'tɛk], *n.f.* film library.
cinématographier [sinematogra'fje], *v.t.* to film.
cinérama [sinera'ma], *n.m.* cinerama.
cinétique [sine'tik], *n.f.* kinetics.—*a.* kinetic, motive (*energy*).
cinétiquement [sinetik'mɑ̃], *adv.* kinetically.
cingalais [sɛ̃ga'lɛ], *a.* Sin(g)halese *or* Cingalese.—*n.m.* Sin(g)halese *or* Cingalese (*language*); (**Cingalais**, *fem.* **-aise**) Sin(g)halese *or* Cingalese (*person*).
cinglage [sɛ̃'gla:ʒ], *n.m.* sailing, ship's course, run of a ship in twenty-four hours.
cinglement [sɛ̃gl'mɑ̃], *n.m.* lashing, slashing.
cingler (1) [sɛ̃'gle], *v.i.* to sail before the wind.
cingler (2) [sɛ̃'gle], *v.t.* to lash; (*fig.*) to chastize.
cinname [si'nam], **cinnamome** [sina'mɔm], *n.m.* cinnamon.

cinq [sɛ̃:k], *a.* five.—*n.m.* five.
cinquantaine [sɛ̃kɑ̃'tɛn], *n.f.* about fifty.
cinquante [sɛ̃'kɑ̃:t], *a.* fifty.
cinquantenaire [sɛ̃kɑ̃t'nɛ:r], *a.* and *n.* quinquagenarian.—*n.m.* fiftieth anniversary, jubilee.
cinquantième [sɛ̃kɑ̃'tjɛm], *a.* fiftieth.—*n.m.* fiftieth part.
cinquième [sɛ̃'kjɛm], *a.* fifth.—*n.m.* fifth part; fifth floor.
cintrage [sɛ̃'tra:ʒ], *n.m.* arching, curving (*of arches etc.*).
cintre [sɛ̃:tr], *n.m.* curve of an arch; coat-hanger.
cintrer [sɛ̃'tre], *v.t.* to arch, to curve.
cipaye [si'pa:j], **cipahi** [si'pai], *n.m.* sepoy.
cipolin [sipɔ'lɛ̃], *n.m.* cipollino, cipolin marble.
cippe [sip], *n.m.* cippus (*half-column*).
cirage [si'ra:ʒ], *n.m.* waxing; blacking (*composit.on or process*); shoe polish.
circoncire [sirkɔ̃'si:r], *v.t.* *irr.* (*conjug. like* CONFIRE *except for p.p.* **circoncis**) to circumcise.
circoncis [sirkɔ̃'si], *a.* circumcised.—*n.m.* one who is circumcised.
circoncision [sirkɔ̃si'zjɔ̃], *n.f.* circumcision.
circonférence [sirkɔ̃fe'rɑ̃:s], *n.f.* circumference.
circonflexe [sirkɔ̃'flɛks], *a.* and *n.m.* circumflex.
circonlocution [sirkɔ̃lɔky'sjɔ̃], *n.f.* circumlocution.
circonscription [sirkɔ̃skrip'sjɔ̃], *n.f.* circumscription; district; constituency.
circonscrire [sirkɔ̃s'kri:r], *v.t.* *irr.* (*conjug. like* ÉCRIRE) to circumscribe, to encircle; to limit.
circonspect [sirkɔ̃s'pɛkt, -spɛ], *a.* circumspect, wary, discreet, reserved.
circonspection [sirkɔ̃spɛk'sjɔ̃], *n.f.* circumspection, wariness, caution.
circonstance [sirkɔ̃s'tɑ̃:s], *n.f.* circumstance; occurrence, event.
circonstanciel [sirkɔ̃stɑ̃'sjɛl], *a.* (*fem.* **-elle**) circumstantial.
circonstancier [sirkɔ̃stɑ̃'sje], *v.t.* to state circumstantially, to particularize.
circonvenir [sirkɔ̃v'ni:r], *v.t.* *irr.* (*conjug. like* TENIR) to circumvent, to outwit.
circonvention [sirkɔ̃vɑ̃'sjɔ̃], *n.f.* circumvention, fraud.
circonvoisin [sirkɔ̃vwa'zɛ̃], *a.* circumjacent, neighboring, adjoining.
circonvolution [sirkɔ̃vɔly'sjɔ̃] *n.f.* circumvolution.
circuit [sir'kɥi], *n.m.* circuit, circumference; detour; lap; (*Elec.*) **court circuit**, short circuit; **en circuit**, switched on.
circulaire [sirky'lɛ:r], *a.* circular, round.—*n.f.* circular.
circulation [sirkyla'sjɔ̃], *n.f.* circulation; currency; traffic.
circulatoire [sirkyla'twa:r], *a.* circulatory, circulating.
circuler [sirky'le], *v.i.* to circulate, to revolve, to move round; to be current.
cire [si:r], *n.f.* beeswax; wax; taper.
ciré [si're], *n.m.* (*Naut.*) (suit of) oilskins.
cirer [si're], *v.t.* to wax; to black *or* to polish (*boots*).

claquette

cireur [si'rœ:r], *n.m.* (*fem.* **cireuse** (1)) polisher; *cireuse électrique*, electric polisher.

cireux [si'rø], *a.* (*fem.* **cireuse** (2)) waxy.

ciron [si'rɔ̃], *n.m.* mite.

cirque [sirk], *n.m.* circus.

cirrus [sir'ry:s], *n.m.* cirrus (*cloud*).

cirure [si'ry:r], *n.f.* prepared wax.

cisaille [si'zɑ:j], *n.f.* clipping *or* shearing of metals; (*pl.*) shears; (*Bookb.*) guillotine.

cisailler [siza'je], *v.t.* to pare, to clip (*coins etc.*); to cut with shears.

cisalpin [sizal'pɛ̃], *a.* cisalpine.

ciseau [si'zo], *n.m.* (*pl.* **-eaux**) chisel; (*pl.*) scissors.

ciseler [siz'le], *v.t.* (*conjug. like* AMENER) to chisel; to chase.

ciselet [siz'lɛ], *n.m.* small chisel, graver.

ciseleur [siz'lœ:r], *n.m.* chaser; carver, sculptor.

ciselure [siz'ly:r], *n.f.* chasing, sculpture, carving.

cisoires [si'zwa:r], *n.f.* (*used only in pl.*) big bench-shears (*to cut sheet iron*).

ciste [sist], *n.m.* cistus, rockrose.

citadelle [sita'dɛl], *n.f.* citadel; (*fig.*) stronghold.

citadin [sita'dɛ̃], *n.m.* (*fem.* **-e**) citizen, townsman *or* -woman.

citation [sita'sjɔ̃], *n.f.* citation, quotation; summons.

cité [si'te], *n.f.* city; town.

citer [si'te], *v.t.* to cite, to quote; to summon.

citérieur [site'rjœ:r], *a.* (*Geog.*) nearer, hithermost.

citerne [si'tɛrn], *n.f.* cistern, reservoir; (*Naut.*) tanker.

cithare [si'ta:r], *n.f.* zither.

citoyen [sitwa'jɛ̃], *n.m.* (*fem.* **-enne**) citizen, burgess; (*fig.*) patriot.

citrate [si'trat], *n.m.* citrate.

citrin [si'trɛ̃], *a.* citrine, lemon-colored.

citrique [si'trik], *a.* citric.

citron [si'trɔ̃], *a.* lemon-colored. —*n.m.* lemon, citron.

citronnade [sitrɔ'nad], *n.f.* lemon squash.

citronnat [sitrɔ'na], *n.m.* candied lemon peel.

citronné [sitrɔ'ne], *a.* lemon-flavored.

citronnier [sitrɔ'nje], *n.m.* citron tree.

citrouille [si'tru:j], *n.f.* pumpkin, gourd.

cive [si:v], **civette** (1) [si'vɛt], [CIBOULETTE].

civet [si'vɛ], *n.m.* wine stew (*of venison*); *civet de lièvre*, jugged hare.

civette (1) [CIVE].

civette (2) [si'vɛt], *n.f.* civet cat; civet.

civière [si'vjɛ:r], *n.f.* hand barrow; stretcher; bier.

civil [si'vil], *a.* civil; private; plain; polite.—*n.m.* civilian.

civilement [sivil'mɑ̃], *adv.* civilly; courteously.

civilisable [sivili'zabl], *a.* civilizable.

civilisateur [siviliza'tœ:r], *a.* (*fem.* **-trice**) civilizing.

civilisation [siviliza'sjɔ̃], *n.f.* civilization.

civiliser [sivili'ze], *v.t.* to civilize. **se civiliser,** *v.r.* to become civilized.

civilité [sivili'te], *n.f.* civility, good manners; (*pl.*) compliments.

civique [si'vik], *a.* civic.

civisme [si'vism], *n.m.* good citizenship.

clabaudage [klabo'da:ʒ], *n.m.* barking, bawling.

clabauder [klabo'de], *v.i.* to clamor, to bawl out.

clabaudeur [klabo'dœ:r], *n.m.* (*fem.* **-euse**) brawler, scandalmonger.

claie [klɛ], *n.f.* wattle, hurdle; screen (*of a sieve*).

clair [klɛ:r], *a.* clear, bright, luminous; light-colored, pure, cloudless; thin (*of liquids etc.*); plain, intelligible, obvious.—*adv.* clearly, distinctly, plainly.—*n.m.* light, clearness; (*Paint.*) highlight.

Claire [klɛ:r], *f.* Clara, Cla(i)re.

clairement [klɛr'mɑ̃], *adv.* clearly, plainly, distinctly.

clairet [klɛ'rɛ], *a.* (*fem.* **clairette** (1)) palish, lightish (*of wines*).—*n.m.* light-red wine.

clairette (2) [klɛ'rɛt], *n.f.* white grape.

claire-voie [klɛr'vwa], *n.f.* (*pl.* **claires-voies**) wooden fencing; opening (*in garden wall*), wicket; skylight.

clairière [klɛ'rjɛ:r], *n.f.* clearing, glade.

clair-obscur [klɛrɔps'ky:r], *n.m.* (*pl.* **clairs-obscurs**) chiaroscuro; light and shade.

clairon [klɛ'rɔ̃], *n.m.* clarion, bugle; bugler.

clairsemé [klɛrsə'me], *a.* thin, thinly sown, scattered.

clairvoyance [klɛrvwa'jɑ̃:s], *n.f.* sharpness, perspicacity; clairvoyance.

clairvoyant [klɛrvwa'jɑ̃], *a.* clear-sighted, discerning; clairvoyant.

clamer [kla'me], *v.t.* to cry out, to shout.

clameur [kla'mœ:r], *n.f.* clamor, outcry.

clan [klɑ̃], *n.m.* clan.

clandestin [klɑ̃dɛs'tɛ̃], *a.* clandestine, secret.

clandestinement [klɑ̃dɛstin'mɑ̃], *adv.* clandestinely, secretly.

clapement [CLAPPEMENT].

clapet [kla'pɛ], *n.m.* valve, clapper.

clapier [kla'pje], *n.m.* hutch (*for rabbits*).

clapir [kla'pi:r], *v.i.* to squeak (*of rabbits*). **se clapir,** *v.r.* to hide in a hole, to squat, to cower.

clapotage [klapɔ'ta:ʒ], *n.m.* rippling, plashing; lapping.

clapotement [klapɔt'mɑ̃], *n.m.* [CLAPOTAGE].

clapoter [klapɔ'te], *v.i.* to plash, to chop.

clapoteux [klapɔ'tø], *a.* (*fem.* **-euse**) plashing, choppy, rough.

clapotis [klapɔ'ti], *n.m.* [CLAPOTAGE].

clappement *or* **clapement** [klap'mɑ̃], *n.m.* clacking, smacking.

clapper [kla'pe], *v.i.* to clack, to smack (*of the tongue*).

claque (1) [klak], *n.f.* slap, smack; claque (*paid applauders at theatres*); (*pl.*) (*C*) clogs, galoshes.

claque (2) [klak], *n.m.* opera hat, crush hat.

claquebois [klak'bwa], *n.m.* xylophone.

claquement [klak'mɑ̃], *n.m.* clapping, clap; snapping; cracking; chattering; slamming.

claquemurer [klakmy're], *v.t.* to coop up, to imprison. **se claquemurer,** *v.r.* to shut oneself up.

claquer [kla'ke], *v.t.* to slap, to crack, to slam.—*v.i.* to snap, to crack, to clap, to clack; to slam, to bang.

claqueter [klak'te], *v.i.* (*conjug. like* APPELER) to cackle (*of a hen*); to cry (*of the stork*).

claquette [kla'kɛt], *n.f.* clapper, rattle; *danseur à claquettes*, tap dancer.

71

claquoir [kla'kwa:r], *n.m.* [CLAQUETTE].
clarification [klarifika'sjɔ̃], *n.f.* clarification.
clarifier [klari'fje], *v.t.* to clarify; to purify, to fine. **se clarifier**, *v.r.* to clarify, to settle.
clarine [kla'rin], *n.f.* bell (*attached to cattle*).
clarinette [klari'nɛt], *n.f.* clarinet.
clarinettiste [klarinɛ'tist], *n.* clarinetist.
clarté [klar'te], *n.f.* light, splendor; clearness.
classe [klɑ:s], *n.f.* class, order, rank; kind, tribe; class *or* grade (*in a school*); classroom; lesson; (*pl.*) school hours; school time.
classement [klɑs'mɑ̃], *n.m.* classing, classification, filing.
classer [klɑ'se], *v.t.* to class, to classify, to sort; to file.
classeur [klɑ'sœ:r], *n.m.* card index; file.
classification [klasifika'sjɔ̃], *n.f.* classification.
classifier [klasi'fje], *v.t.* to classify.
classique [kla'sik], *a.* classic, classical; standard (*of authors, books etc.*); conventional.—*n.m.* classic (*author, book etc.*).
claudicant [klodi'kɑ̃], *a.* lame, limping.
claudication [klodika'sjɔ̃], *n.f.* lameness, limping, halting.
clause [klo:z], *n.f.* clause.
claustral [klos'tral], *a.* (*m. pl.* **-aux**) claustral; monastic.
claustration [klostra'sjɔ̃], *n.f.* claustration, confinement.
claustrer [klos'tre], *v.t.* to cloister, to confine.
claustrophobie [klostrɔfɔ'bi], *n.f.* claustrophobia.
clavecin [klav'sɛ̃], *n.m.* harpsichord, clavecin.
clavette [kla'vɛt], *n.f.* (*Tech.*) peg, pin; key, cotter.
claviculaire [klaviky'lɛ:r], *a.* clavicular.
clavicule [klavi'kyl], *n.f.* clavicle, collarbone.
clavier [kla'vje], *n.m.* clavier, keyboard (*piano, typewriter*), key frame.
clayère [klɛ'jɛ:r], *n.f.* oyster bed *or* breeding ground.
clayon [klɛ'jɔ̃], *n.m.* wattle; stand (*for draining cheese*).
clef *or* **clé** [kle], *n.f.* key; plug (*of a cock*); spanner; keystone (*of arch*); (*Mus.*) clef, tuning key.
clématite [klema'tit], *n.f.* (*Bot.*) clematis.
clémence [kle'mɑ̃:s], *n.f.* clemency, mercy.
clément [kle'mɑ̃], *a.* clement, merciful, lenient; mild (*of the weather*).
Clémentine [klemɑ̃'tin], *f.* Clementine.
clenche [klɑ̃:ʃ], **clenchette** [klɑ̃'ʃɛt], *n.f.* catch *or* latch (*of a lock*).
cleptomane [klɛptɔ'man], *n.* kleptomaniac.
cleptomanie [klɛptɔma'ni], *n.f.* kleptomania.
clerc [klɛːr], *n.m.* clergyman; (*fig.*) scholar.
clergé [klɛr'ʒe], *n.m.* clergy.
clérical [kleri'kal], *a.* (*m. pl.* **-aux**) clerical.
cléricalisme [klerika'lism], *n.m.* clericalism.
cléricaliste [klerika'list], *n.* clericalist.
clic-clac [klik'klak], *n.m.* cracking (*of a whip*).
clichage [kli'ʃa:ʒ], *n.m.* stereotyping, stereotype.
cliché [kli'ʃe], *n.m.* stereotype plate, cliché; (*fig.*) stereotyped phrase; (*Phot.*) negative; (*Sculp.*) cast.
clicher [kli'ʃe], *v.t.* to stereotype.
client [kli'ɑ̃], *n.m.* (*fem.* **-e**) client (*of law-*

yers etc.); patient (*of physicians*); customer (*of tradesmen*).
clientèle [kliɑ̃'tɛl], *n.f.* clientele; practice; connection; custom; goodwill (*of a business*).
clignement [kliɲ'mɑ̃], *n.m.* winking, blinking, wink.
cligner [kli'ɲe], *v.t., v.i.* to wink, to blink.
clignotant [kliɲɔ'tɑ̃], *a.* winking, blinking.—*n.m.* (*Motor.*) winker, flashing indicator.
clignotement [kliɲɔt'mɑ̃], *n.m.* winking, blinking.
clignoter [kliɲɔ'te], *v.i.* to wink, to blink.
climat [kli'ma], *n.m.* climate; region, country.
climatérique [klimate'rik], **climatique** [klima'tik], *a.* climatic.
climatisation [klimatiza'sjɔ̃], *n.f.* air conditioning.
climatisé [klimati'ze], *a.* air-conditioned.
climatiser [klimati'ze], *v.t.* to air-condition.
clin [klɛ̃], *n.m.* wink (*of an eye*).
clinicien [klini'sjɛ̃], *a.m.* clinical.—*n.m.* clinical physician.
clinique [kli'nik], *a.* clinical.—*n.f.* clinical surgery; clinic, nursing home.
clinquant [klɛ̃'kɑ̃], *a.* showy, gaudy, trumpery.—*n.m.* tinsel; (*fig.*) glitter, affectation.
clip [klip], *n.m.* clip-fastened jewel.
clipper [kli'pɛr], *n.m.* (*Naut.* and *Av.*) clipper.
clique [klik], *n.f.* set, coterie, party, clique.
cliquet [kli'kɛ], *n.m.* catch, pawl.
cliqueter [klik'te], *v.i.* (*conjug. like* APPELER) to click or jingle; (*Motor.*) to knock.
cliquetis [klik'ti], *n.m.* clanking, clash.
cliquette [kli'kɛt], *n.f.* sinker (*of net*); (*usu. pl.*) bones (*a kind of castanets*).
clissage [kli'sa:ʒ], *n.m.* wickering.
clisse [klis], *n.f.* wicker mat for draining cheese; basket-work cover for a bottle; (*Surg.*) splint.
clisser [kli'se], *v.t.* to wicker, to cover with wicker-work etc.
clivage [kli'va:ʒ], *n.m.* (*Min.*) cleavage; cleaving.
cliver [kli've], *v.t.* to cleave (*diamonds etc.*). **se cliver**, *v.r.* to split, to be cleft.
cloaque [klɔ'ak], *n.m.* drain, sewer, sink, cesspool; (*fig.*) filthy hole.
clochage [klɔ'ʃa:ʒ], *n.m.* cultivation under cloches.
clochard [klɔ'ʃa:r], *n.m.* (*fam.*) tramp, vagrant; (*Am.*) hobo.
cloche [klɔʃ], *n.f.* bell; dish cover; blister; stewpan; (*Gard.*) cloche.
clochement [klɔʃ'mɑ̃], *n.m.* hobbling, halting.
cloche-pied [klɔʃ'pje], *n.m.* hopping on one leg.
clocher (1) [klɔ'ʃe], *n.m.* steeple, belfry; (*fig.*) parish, native place.
clocher (2) [klɔ'ʃe], *v.t.* (*Gard.*) to cover with a cloche.
clocher (3) [klɔ'ʃe], *v.i.* to limp, to hobble; (*fig., fam.*) to go wrong somewhere, to be defective.
clocheton [klɔʃ'tɔ̃], *n.m.* bell turret.
clochette [klɔ'ʃɛt], *n.f.* small bell, hand bell; bellflower.
cloison [klwa'zɔ̃], *n.f.* partition, division; compartment; (*Naut.*) bulkhead.
cloisonnage [klwazɔ'na:ʒ], **cloisonnement** [klwazɔn'mɑ̃], *n.m.* partition work, wainscotting.

cloisonner [klwazɔ'ne], *v.t.* to partition.
cloître [klwɑ:tr], *n.m.* cloister.
cloîtrer [klwɑ'tre], *v.t.* to shut up in a cloister, to immure. **se cloîtrer**, *v.r.* to enter a monastery *or* convent.
cloîtrier [klwɑ'trie], *n.m.* (*fem.* **-ière**) cloistered monk *or* nun.
clopin-clopant [klɔpɛ̃klɔ'pɑ̃], *adv.* limpingly, hobbling along.
clopiner [klɔpi'ne], *v.i.* to limp, to halt, to hobble.
cloporte [klɔ'pɔrt], *n.m.* woodlouse.
cloque [klɔk], *n.f.* blister (*on skin, paint etc.*); blight, rust (*of plants*).
cloquer [klɔ'ke], *v.i.* to blister (*of paint*).
clore [klɔ:r], *v.t. irr.* (*chiefly used in p.p.*) to close, to shut; to enclose; to end.—*v.i.* to close, to shut. **se clore**, *v.r.* to close, to be closed; to end.
clos [klo], *a.* closed, sealed; completed; *à huis clos*, in camera.—*n.m.* close; enclosure, field.
closeau [klo'zo], *n.m.* (*pl.* **-eaux**) small garden.
closerie [kloz'ri], *n.f.* small enclosed farm *or* garden.
clôture [klo'ty:r], *n.f.* enclosure, fence; closing, close; closure; (*Relig.*) enclosure (*of nuns etc.*).
clôturer [kloty're], *v.t.* to close.
clou [klu], *n.m.* nail, spike, stud; (*Path.*) carbuncle, boil; *clou de girofle*, clove.
clouage [klu'a:ʒ], **clouement** [klu'mɑ̃], *n.m.* nailing.
clouer [klu'e], *v.t.* to nail; to fix; (*fig.*) to detain.
clouter [klu'te], *v.t.* to adorn with nails, to stud; *passage clouté*, pedestrian crossing.
clouterie [klu'tri], *n.f.* nail factory; nail trade.
cloutier [klu'tje], *n.m.* nail maker, nail dealer.
cloutière [klu'tjɛ:r], *n.f.* nail box.
clovisse [klɔ'vis], *n.f.* winkle; cockle.
clown [klun], *n.m.* clown.
cloyère [klwa'jɛ:r], *n.f.* oyster basket.
club [klʌb, klyb], *n.m.* club (*sporting or political*).
clystère [klis'tɛ:r] *n.m.* clyster, injection, enema.
coaccusé [koaky'ze], *n.m.* (*fem.* **-ée**) fellow prisoner; co-defendant.
coacquéreur [koakɛ'rœ:r], *n.m.* (*fem.* **-euse**) co-purchaser, joint buyer.
coacquisition [koakizi'sjɔ̃], *n.f.* joint purchase.
coactif [koak'tif], *a.* (*fem.* **-tive**) coactive.
coaction [koak'sjɔ̃], *n.f.* coercion, compulsion.
coadjuteur [koadʒy'tœ:r], *n.m.* coadjutor.
coadjutrice [koadʒy'tris], *n.f.* coadjutrix.
coagulant [koagy'lɑ̃], *a.* coagulant.
coagulation [koagyla'sjɔ̃], *n.f.* coagulation.
coaguler [koagy'le], *v.t.* to coagulate. **se coaguler**, *v.r.* to coagulate.
coaliser [koali'ze], *v.t.* to unite in a coalition. **se coaliser**, *v.r.* to coalesce, to league, to unite, to combine.
coalition [koali'sjɔ̃], *n.f.* coalition, union, league.
coassement [koas'mɑ̃], *n.m.* croaking (*of frogs*).
coasser [koa'se], *v.i.* to croak (*of frogs*).

coassocié [koasɔ'sje], *n.m.* (*fem.* **-ée**) co-partner.
coauteur [koo'tœ:r], *n.m.* co-author.
cobalt [kɔ'balt], *n.m.* cobalt.
cobaye [kɔ'ba:j], *n.m.* guinea pig.
cobra [kɔ'bra], *n.m.* cobra, hooded snake.
cocagne [kɔ'kaɲ], *n.f. mât de cocagne*, greasy pole; *pays de cocagne*, land of plenty.
cocaïne [kɔka'in], *n.f.* cocaine.
cocarde [kɔ'kard], *n.f.* cockade; rosette.
cocasse [kɔ'kas], *a.* (*fam.*) odd, laughable, comical.
cocasserie [kɔkas'ri], *n.f.* drollery, foolery, farce.
coccinelle [kɔksi'nɛl], *n.f.* ladybug.
coche (1) [kɔʃ], *n.m.* coach; *c'est la mouche du coche*, he is a busybody.
coche (2) [kɔʃ], *n.f.* notch, score.
coche (3) [kɔʃ], *n.f.* sow.
cochenille [kɔʃ'ni:j], *n.f.* cochineal.
cocher (1) [kɔ'ʃe], *n.m.* coachman, driver.
cocher (2) [kɔ'ʃe], *v.t.* to notch.
cochère [kɔ'ʃɛ:r], *a.f.* for carriages; *porte cochère*, carriage entrance, gateway.
cochet [kɔ'ʃɛ], *n.m.* young cock, cockerel.
cochon [kɔ'ʃɔ̃], *n.m.* hog, pig; pork; *cochon d'Inde*, guinea pig.
cochonnée [kɔʃɔ'ne], *n.f.* litter (*of pigs*).
cochonner [kɔʃɔ'ne], *v.i.* to farrow, to pig.
cochonnerie [kɔʃɔn'ri], *n.f.* nastiness, filth.
cochonnet [kɔʃɔ'nɛ], *n.m.* young pig; jack (*at bowls*).
cocktail [kɔk'tɛl], *n.m.* cocktail; cocktail party.
coco [kɔ'ko], *n.m.* coconut.
cocon [kɔ'kɔ̃], *n.m.* cocoon.
cocotier [kɔkɔ'tje], *n.m.* coconut palm.
coction [kɔk'sjɔ̃], *n.f.* coction, boiling; digestion (*of food*).
code [kɔd], *n.m.* code (*digest or collection of laws*), law, rule.
codemandeur [kɔdəmɑ̃'dœ:r], *n.m.* (*fem.* **-eresse**) co-plaintiff.
coder [kɔ'de], *v.t.* to code (*telegram*).
codétenteur [kɔdetɑ̃'tœ:r], *n.m.* (*fem.* **-trice**) joint holder.
codétenu [kɔdet'ny], *n.m.* (*fem.* **-e**) fellow prisoner.
codicillaire [kɔdisi'lɛ:r], *a.* contained in a codicil.
codicille [kɔdi'sil], *n.m.* codicil, rider.
codifier [kɔdi'fje], *v.t.* to codify.
codirecteur [kɔdirɛk'tœ:r], *n.m.* (*fem.* **-trice**) joint manager.
codonataire [kɔdɔna'tɛ:r], *n.* joint donee.
codonateur [kɔdɔna'tœ:r], *n.m.* (*fem.* **-trice**) joint donor.
coéquipier [kɔeki'pje], *n.m.* fellow member (*of a crew, team etc.*).
coercer [kɔɛr'se], *v.t.* to coerce.
coercition [kɔɛrsi'sjɔ̃], *n.f.* coercion.
cœur [kœ:r], *n.m.* heart; (*fig.*) bosom, mind, soul; courage; core, middle; love, affection; hearts (*cards*).
coexistant [kɔɛgzis'tɑ̃], *a.* coexistent.
coexistence [kɔɛgzis'tɑ̃:s], *n.f.* coexistence.
coexister [kɔɛgzis'te], *v.i.* to coexist.
coffre [kɔfr], *n.m.* chest, trunk; coffer; (*Naut.*) mooring buoy; boot (*of a car*).
coffre-fort [kɔfrə'fɔ:r], *n.m.* (*pl.* **coffres-forts**) strongbox, safe.

coffret [kɔ'frɛ], *n.m.* little chest, casket.

cogitation [kɔʒita'sjɔ̃], *n.f.* cogitation, reflection.

cognac [kɔ'ɲak], *n.m.* cognac, brandy.

cognasse [kɔ'ɲas], *n.f.* wild quince.

cognassier [kɔɲa'sje], *n.m.* quince tree.

cognée [kɔ'ɲe], *n.f.* axe, hatchet.

cogner [kɔ'ɲe], *v.t.* to knock in, to drive in; to thump.—*v.i.* to hit, to bump (*contre*); to knock (*engine*). **se cogner**, *v.r.* to knock (*against*).

cohabitant [koabi'tɑ̃], *a.* cohabiting (*with*).

cohabitation [koabita'sjɔ̃], *n.f.* cohabitation.

cohabiter [koabi'te], *v.i.* to cohabit.

cohérence [kɔe'rɑ̃:s], *n.f.* coherence.

cohérent [kɔe'rɑ̃], *a.* coherent.

cohériter [koeri'te], *v.i.* to inherit conjointly.

cohéritier [koeri'tje], *n.m.* (*fem.* **-ière**) co-heir, co-heiress.

cohésif [kɔe'zif], *a.* (*fem.* **-sive**) cohesive.

cohésion [kɔe'zjɔ̃], *n.f.* cohesion.

cohorte [kɔ'ɔrt], *n.f.* cohort; (*poet.*) troop, host; (*colloq.*) crew, gang.

cohue [kɔ'y], *n.f.* throng, mob, crush.

coi [kwa], *a.* (*fem.* **coite** (1)) quiet, calm, still.

coiffe [kwaf], *n.f.* hood, headdress.

coiffer [kwa'fe], *v.t.* to put on the head of; to dress the hair of; (*fig.*) to infatuate.—*v.i.* to dress hair; to become; to suit. **se coiffer**, *v.r.* to put one's hat on; to do one's hair.

coiffeur [kwa'fœ:r], *n.m.* (*fem.* **-euse**) hairdresser.—*n.f.* lady's dressing-table.

coiffure [kwa'fy:r], *n.f.* headdress, hairstyle.

coin [kwɛ̃], *n.m.* corner, angle, nook; (*Coin. etc.*) stamp.

coincer [kwɛ̃'se], *v.t.* (*conjug. like* COMMENCER) to wedge. **se coincer**, *v.r.* to jam (*of machines*).

coïncidence [kɔɛ̃si'dɑ̃:s], *n.f.* coincidence.

coïncident [kɔɛ̃si'dɑ̃], *a.* coincident.

coïncider [kɔɛ̃si'de], *v.i.* to coincide, to be coincident.

coing [kwɛ̃], *n.m.* quince

cointéressé [kɔɛ̃terɛ'se], *a.* jointly interested. —*n.m.* (*fem.* **-ée**) associate, partner.

coite (1) [kwat], [COI].

coite (2), **coitte** [COUETTE].

cojouissance [kɔʒwi'sɑ̃:s], *n.f.* (*Law*) joint use.

coke [kɔk], *n.m.* coke.

cokéfier [koke'fje], *v.t.* to coke.

col [kɔl], *n.m.* neck (*of a bottle, dress etc.*); collar; pass, col (*of mountain*).

colback [kɔl'bak], *n.m.* busby.

colchique [kɔl'ʃik], *n.m.* (*Bot.*) meadow saffron, colchicum.

colégataire [kolega'tɛ:r], *n.* co-legatee.

coléoptère [koleɔp'tɛ:r], *a.* coleopterous.— *n.m.* beetle.

colère [kɔ'lɛ:r], *n.f.* anger, wrath, rage, fury.

colérique [kɔle'rik], *a.* choleric, irascible.

colibri [kɔli'bri], *n.m.* hummingbird.

colifichet [kɔlifi'ʃɛ], *n.m.* trinket, knick-knack.

colimaçon [kɔlima'sɔ̃], *n.m.* snail; *escalier en colimaçon*, spiral staircase.

colin-maillard [kɔlɛ̃ma'ja:r], *n.m. inv.* blind-man's-buff.

colique [kɔ'lik], *n.f.* colic, stomach ache.

colis [kɔ'li], *n.m.* package, parcel, case.

collaborateur [kɔlabɔra'tœ:r], *n.m.* (*fem.* **-trice**) collaborator.

collaboration [kɔlabɔra'sjɔ̃], *n.f.* collaboration.

collaborer [kɔlabɔ're], *v.i.* to collaborate.

collage [kɔ'la:ʒ], *n.m.* pasting, gluing; paper-hanging; (*Art*) collage.

collant [kɔ'lɑ̃], *a.* sticky; tight, close-fitting.

collatéral [kɔllate'ral], *a.* (*m. pl.* **-aux**) collateral.

collatéralement [kɔllateral'mɑ̃], *adv.* collaterally.

collation [kɔlla'sjɔ̃], *n.f.* light meal; comparison (*of documents etc.*).

collationnement [kɔllasjɔn'mɑ̃], *n.m.* collating, comparing.

collationner [kɔllasjɔ'ne], *v.t.* to collate, to compare.—*v.i.* to have a snack.

colle [kɔl], *n.f.* paste, gum; poser; sham, fib.

collecte [kɔ'lɛkt], *n.f.* collection (*of money etc.*); collect (*prayer*).

collecteur [kɔlɛk'tœ:r], *n.m.* (*fem.* **-trice**) collector.

collectif [kɔlɛk'tif], *a.* (*fem.* **-tive**) collective.

collection [kɔlɛk'sjɔ̃], *n.f.* collection; set.

collectionner [kɔlɛksjɔ'ne], *v.t.* to collect, to make collections of things.

collectionneur [kɔlɛksjɔ'nœ:r], *n.m.* (*fem.* **-euse**) collector.

collectivement [kɔlɛktiv'mɑ̃], *adv.* collectively.

collectivisme [kɔlɛkti'vism], *n.m.* collectivism.

collectiviste [kɔlɛkti'vist], *n.* collectivist.

collectivité [kɔlɛktivi'te], *n.f.* collectivity; common ownership.

collège [kɔ'lɛ:ʒ], *n.m.* college; grammar school.

collégien [kɔle'ʒjɛ̃], *n.m.* (*fem.* **-enne**) high-school boy or girl.

collègue [kɔl'lɛg], *n.* colleague.

coller [kɔ'le], *v.t.* to paste, to glue; to stick together.—*v.i.* to stick, to adhere. **se coller**, *v.r.* to stick to.

collerette [kɔl'rɛt], *n.f.* collar (*for ladies*).

collet [kɔ'lɛ], *n.m.* collar (*of gown etc.*); cape; flange; snare.

colleter [kɔl'te], *v.t.* (*conjug. like* APPELER) to collar, to seize by the neck.—*v.i.* to set snares. **se colleter**, *v.r.* to come to grips (*with someone*).

colleur [kɔ'lœ:r], *n.m.* (*fem.* **-euse**) gluer; paster, paperhanger; billposter.

collier [kɔ'lje], *n.m.* necklace; gold chain (*of knightly orders etc.*); collar (*for animals*).

colline [kɔ'lin], *n.f.* hill, hillock.

collision [kɔli'zjɔ̃], *n.f.* collision.

collocation [kɔllɔka'sjɔ̃], *n.f.* classification.

colloque [kɔl'lɔk], *n.m.* colloquy, conference.

collusion [kɔlly'zjɔ̃], *n.f.* collusion.

collusoire [kɔlly'zwa:r], *a.* collusory, collusive.

Colomb [kɔ'lɔ̃], *m.* Columbus.

colombe [kɔ'lɔ̃:b], *n.f.* (*poet.*) pigeon, dove.

Colombie [kɔlɔ̃'bi], **la**, *f.* Colombia.

colombien [kɔlɔ̃'bjɛ̃], *a.* (*fem.* **-enne**) Colombian.—*n.m.* (**Colombien**, *fem.* **-enne**) Colombian (*person*).

colombier [kɔlɔ̃'bje], *n.m.* dovecot, pigeon house.

colombin [kɔlɔ̃'bɛ̃], *a.* columbine; dove-color.

colombophile [kɔlɔ̃bɔ'fil], *a.* and *n.* pigeon fancier.

colon [kɔ'lɔ̃], *n.m.* colonist, planter; settler.
côlon [ko'lɔ̃], *n.m.* (*Anat.*) colon.
colonel [kɔlɔ'nɛl], *n.m.* colonel; (*Av.*) group captain.
colonial [kɔlɔ'njal], *a.* (*m. pl.* **-aux**) colonial. —*n.m.* (*fem.* **-e**) colonial.
colonie [kɔlɔ'ni], *n.f.* colony, settlement; *colonie de vacances*, holiday camp.
colonisation [kɔlɔniza'sjɔ̃], *n.f.* colonization.
coloniser [kɔlɔni'ze], *v.t.* to colonize.
colonnade [kɔlɔ'nad], *n.f.* (*Arch.*) colonnade.
colonne [kɔ'lɔn], *n.f.* column, pillar; column (*of units, tens etc.*).
colonnette [kɔlɔ'nɛt], *n.f.* little column.
colorant [kɔlɔ'rɑ̃], *a.* coloring.—*n.m.* dye.
coloration [kɔlɔra'sjɔ̃], *n.f.* coloration, staining.
colorer [kɔlɔ're], *v.t.* to color, to dye; to varnish. **se colorer**, *v.r.* to color (*of a thing*).
coloriage [kɔlɔ'rja:ʒ], *n.m.* (*Paint.*) coloring.
colorier [kɔlɔ'rje], *v.t.* to color, to stain (*a drawing etc.*).
coloris [kɔlɔ'ri], *n.m.* coloring, art of coloring.
coloriste [kɔlɔ'rist], *n.* colorer; colorist.
colossal [kɔlɔ'sal], *a.* (*m. pl.* **-aux**) colossal.
colosse [kɔ'los], *n.m.* colossus, giant.
colportage [kɔlpɔr'ta:ʒ], *n.m.* hawking, peddling.
colporter [kɔlpɔr'te], *v.t.* to hawk about; to spread.
colporteur [kɔlpɔr'tœːr], *n.m.* hawker, pedlar.
coltiner [kɔlti'ne], *v.t.* to carry heavy loads (*on head and back*).
coltineur [kɔlti'nœːr], *n.m.* coal heaver, loadporter.
colza [kɔl'za], *n.m.* colza, rape, rape seed.
coma [kɔ'ma], *n.m.* coma.
comateux [kɔma'tø], *a.* (*fem.* **-euse**) comatose.
combat [kɔ̃'ba], *n.m.* combat, fight, battle, contest; struggle; *hors de combat*, disabled.
combattant [kɔ̃ba'tɑ̃], *n.m.* combatant; champion; *anciens combattants*, ex-service men.
combattre [kɔ̃'batr], *v.t.* (*conjug. like* BATTRE) to fight, to combat, to wage war against, to strive against.—*v.i.* to fight, to vie, to struggle. **se combattre**, *v.r.* to combat; to contend with each other.
combien [kɔ̃'bjɛ̃], *adv.* how much, how many; how; how far; how long.
combinaison [kɔ̃binɛ'zɔ̃], *n.f.* combination; contrivance, scheme; overalls; slip (*woman's undergarment*).
combiné [kɔ̃bi'ne], *n.m.* (*Chem.*) compound; (*Rad.*) radiogram.
combiner [kɔ̃bi'ne], *v.t.* to combine; (*fig.*) to contrive.
comble [kɔ̃bl], *n.m.* heaping up above a full measure; summit; (*fig.*) zenith; (*pl.*) roof timbers.—*a.* full, heaped up, full to the top; *salle comble*, house full.
comblement [kɔ̃blə'mɑ̃], *n.m.* filling up, heaping up.
combler [kɔ̃'ble], *v.t.* to heap up, to fill up; to complete; to overwhelm.
comburant [kɔ̃by'rɑ̃], *a.* (*Chem.*) causing burning (*of oxygen etc.*).—*n.m.* fuel.
combustibilité [kɔ̃bystibili'te], *n.f.* combustibility.

combustible [kɔ̃bys'tibl], *a.* combustible.— *n.m.* combustible; fuel, firing.
combustion [kɔ̃bys'tjɔ̃], *n.f.* combustion, flame.
comédie [kɔme'di], *n.f.* comedy; theatre; players.
comédien [kɔme'djɛ̃], *n.m.* (*fem.* **-enne**) comedian, actor, actress, player; (*fig.*) hypocrite.
comestible [kɔmɛs'tibl], *a.* edible, eatable.— *n.m.* eatable; (*pl.*) eatables.
comète [kɔ'mɛt], *n.f.* comet.
comice [kɔ'mis], *n.m.* meeting; electoral meeting; *comice agricole*, agricultural show.
comique [kɔ'mik], *a.* comic; comical, ludicrous.—*n.m.* comic art, comedy.
comiquement [kɔmik'mɑ̃], *adv.* comically.
comité [kɔmi'te], *n.m.* committee, board.
commandant [kɔmɑ̃'dɑ̃], *a.* commanding.— *n.m.* (*fem.* **-e**) commander, commanding officer, commandant; major.
commande [kɔ'mɑ̃:d], *n.f.* order; (*Mach.*) driving wheel.
commandement [kɔmɑ̃d'mɑ̃], *n.m.* command; authority, control; order; commandment, law.
commander [kɔmɑ̃'de], *v.t.* to command, to order; to govern; to overlook.—*v.i.* to command, to have authority. **se commander**, *v.r.* to command oneself.
commandeur [kɔmɑ̃'dœːr], *n.m.* commander (*in orders of knighthood*).
commanditaire [kɔmɑ̃di'tɛːr], *n.* silent partner.
commandite [kɔmɑ̃'dit], *n.f.* limited partnership.
commanditer [kɔmɑ̃di'te], *v.t.* to finance (*a commercial undertaking*).
commando [kɔmɑ̃'do], *n.m.* commando.
comme [kɔm], *adv.* as; like, such as; almost, nearly, as if; how, in what way, to what extent.—*conj.* as, since, because.
commémoraison [kɔmemɔre'zɔ̃], *n.f.* (*R.-C. Ch.*) commemoration, remembrance.
commémoratif [kɔmemɔra'tif], *a.* (*fem.* **-tive**) commemorative.
commémoration [kɔmemɔra'sjɔ̃], *n.f.* commemoration.
commémorer [kɔmemɔ're], *v.t.* to commemorate, to remember.
commençant [kɔmɑ̃'sɑ̃], *n.m.* (*fem.* **-e**) beginner, novice.
commencement [kɔmɑ̃s'mɑ̃], *n.m.* beginning, commencement.
commencer [kɔmɑ̃'se], *v.t., v.i.* (*see Verb Tables*) to begin, to commence; to initiate.
commensal [kɔmɑ̃'sal], *n.m.* (*m. pl.* **-aux**) habitual guest; fellow boarder, messmate.
commensurable [kɔmɑ̃sy'rabl], *a.* commensurable.
comment [kɔ'mɑ̃], *adv.* how, in what manner; why, wherefore.—*int.* what! indeed!— *n.m.* the why and wherefore.
commentaire [kɔmɑ̃'tɛːr], *n.m.* commentary, exposition; (*fig.*) unfavorable comment.
commentateur [kɔmɑ̃ta'tœːr], *n.m.* (*fem.* **-trice**) commentator, annotator.
commenter [kɔmɑ̃'te], *v.t.* to comment on, to explain, to annotate.—*v.i.* to criticize adversely.

commérage

commérage [kɔme'ra:ʒ], *n.m.* gossip, tittle-tattle.
commerçant [kɔmɛr'sā], · *a.* commercial, mercantile, trading.—*n.m.* (*fem.* **-e**) merchant, tradesman, shopkeeper.
commerce [kɔ'mɛrs], *n.m.* commerce, trade, trading, traffic; intercourse, dealings.
commercer [kɔmɛr'se], *v.i.* (*conjug. like* COMMENCER) to trade, to deal.
commercial [kɔmɛr'sjal], *a.* (*m. pl.* **-aux**) commercial.
commercialement [kɔmɛrsjal'mā], *adv.* commercially.
commercialisation [kɔmɛrsjaliza'sjō], *n.f.* commercialization.
commercialiser [kɔmɛrsjali'ze], *v.t.* to commercialize.
commère [kɔ'mɛr], *n.f.* godmother; gossip.
commettre [kɔ'mɛtr], *v.t. irr.* (*conjug. like* METTRE) to commit, to perpetrate; to appoint, to empower; to entrust. **se commettre**, *v.r.* to commit oneself.
commis (1) [kɔ'mi], *n.m.* (*fem.* **commise**) clerk; **commis voyageur**, commercial traveller.
commis (2) [kɔ'mi], *a.* committed, appointed.
commisération [kɔmizera'sjō], *n.f.* commiseration, compassion, pity.
commissaire [kɔmi'sɛːr], *n.m.* commissioner; manager, steward, trustee; purser (*of a vessel*).
commissaire-priseur [kɔmisɛrpri'zœːr], *n.m.* auctioneer; valuer, appraiser.
commissariat [kɔmisa'rja], *n.m.* commissaryship, trusteeship; (*Mil., Navy*) commissariat; police station.
commission [kɔmi'sjō], *n.f.* commission, charge; errand; power; (*Comm.*) percentage; warrant.
commissionnaire [kɔmisjɔ'nɛːr], *n.m.* commission agent, commissionnaire; messenger, porter.
commissionner [kɔmisjɔ'ne], *v.t.* to empower, to commission; to order (*goods*).
commode [kɔ'mɔd], *a.* convenient, commodious, handy; comfortable, suitable; easy.—*n.f.* chest of drawers, commode.
commodément [kɔmɔde'mā], *adv.* commodiously, conveniently; comfortably, suitably.
commodité [kɔmɔdi'te], *n.f.* convenience, accommodation.
commotion [kɔmo'sjō], *n.f.* commotion; shock; concussion.
commotionné [kɔmosjɔ'ne], *a.* suffering from concussion.
commuable [kɔ'mɥabl], *a.* commutable.
commun [kɔ'mœ̃], *a.* common; usual, ordinary; mean, vulgar; **le bien commun**, the common weal; **lieux communs**, commonplaces.—*n.m.* common people.
communal [kɔmy'nal], *a.* (*m. pl.* **-aux**) communal, parochial; common.—*n.m. pl.* (**biens**) **communaux**, communal property.
communauté [kɔmyno'te], *n.f.* community, society, corporation.
commune [kɔ'myn], *n.f.* commune (*parish, township, in France*).
communément [kɔmyne'mā], *adv.* commonly, usually.
communiant [kɔmy'njā], *n.m.* (*fem.* **-e**) communicant.

communicatif [kɔmynika'tif], *a.* (*fem.* **-tive**) communicative, open.
communication [kɔmynika'sjō], *n.f.* intercourse, communication; (*Teleph.*) call.
communicativement [kɔmynikativ'mā], *adv.* communicatively.
communier [kɔmy'nje], *v.i.* to communicate, to receive the sacrament.
communion [kɔmy'njō], *n.f.* communion, fellowship; persuasion; sacrament.
communiqué [kɔmyni'ke], *n.m.* statement, communiqué.
communiquer [kɔmyni'ke], *v.t.* to communicate, to impart; to tell, to acquaint.—*v.i.* to be in contact *or* correspondence (*with*).
communisant [kɔmyni'zā], *a.* communistic.—*n.m.* (*fem.* **-e**) fellow traveller.
communisme [kɔmy'nism], *n.m.* communism.
communiste [kɔmy'nist], *n.* communist.
commutable [kɔmy'tabl], [COMMUABLE].
commutateur [kɔmyta'tœːr], *n.m.* (*Elec.*) switch.
compact [kɔ̃'pakt], *a.* compact, dense.
compagne [kɔ̃'paɲ], *n.f.* female companion, consort; playmate.
compagnie [kɔ̃pa'ɲi], *n.f.* society, companionship; company; (*Comm.*) company.
compagnon [kɔ̃pa'ɲō], *n.m.* companion, comrade; playmate; mate; (*Bot.*) campion.
comparable [kɔ̃pa'rabl], *a.* comparable.
comparablement [kɔ̃parablə'mā], *adv.* in comparison (*with*).
comparaison [kɔ̃parɛ'zō], *n.f.* comparison; similitude.
comparaître [kɔ̃pa'rɛːtr], *v.i. irr.* (*conjug. like* CONNAÎTRE) to appear (*before a tribunal*).
comparant [kɔ̃pa'rā], *n.m.* (*fem.* **-e**) person appearing in court on a summons.
comparatif [kɔ̃para'tif], *a.* (*fem.* **-tive**) comparative.—*n.m.* comparative degree.
comparativement [kɔ̃parativ'mā], *adv.* comparatively.
comparer [kɔ̃pa're], *v.t.* to compare. **se comparer**, *v.r.* to be compared.
compartiment [kɔ̃parti'mā], *n.m.* compartment, division.
compas [kɔ̃'pa], *n.m.* pair of compasses; mariner's compass.
compassé [kɔ̃pa'se], *a.* formal, stiff, starchy.
compasser [kɔ̃pa'se], *v.t.* to measure, set out; to proportion, to regulate; (*fig.*) to weigh, to consider.
compassion [kɔ̃pa'sjō], *n.f.* compassion, pity, mercy.
compatibilité [kɔ̃patibili'te], *n.f.* compatibility.
compatible [kɔ̃pa'tibl], *a.* compatible, consistent.
compatir [kɔ̃pa'tiːr], *v.i.* to sympathize; to agree, to be compatible (*with*).
compatissant [kɔ̃pati'sā], *a.* compassionate, tender.
compatriote [kɔ̃patri'ɔt], *n.* compatriot, fellow countryman.
compendium [kɔ̃pɑ̃'djɔm], *n.m.* summary, compendium.
compensable [kɔ̃pɑ̃'sabl], *a.* that may be compensated.
compensation [kɔ̃pɑ̃sa'sjō], *n.f.* compensation, amends, reparation.

compensatoire [kɔ̃pɑ̃sa'twa:r], *a.* compensatory.

compenser [kɔ̃pɑ̃'se], *v.t.* to counterbalance, to compensate, to make up for. **se compenser**, *v.r.* to compensate each other; to be set off against.

compère [kɔ̃'pɛ:r], *n.m.* godfather; (*fig.*) gossip, crony; confederate.

compétence [kɔ̃pe'tɑ̃:s], *n.f.* competence, cognizance; (*fig.*) department, province; proficiency.

compétent [kɔ̃pe'tɑ̃], *a.* competent, qualified; (*fig.*) suitable, requisite.

compétiteur [kɔ̃peti'tœ:r], *n.m.* (*fem.* **-trice**) competitor, candidate.

compétitif [kɔ̃peti'tif], *a.* (*fem.* **-tive**) competitive.

compétition [kɔ̃peti'sjɔ̃], *n.f.* competition, rivalry.

compilateur [kɔ̃pila'tœ:r], *n.m.* compiler.

compilation [kɔ̃pila'sjɔ̃], *n.f.* compilation.

compiler [kɔ̃pi'le], *v.t.* to compile.

complainte [kɔ̃'plɛ̃:t], *n.f.* tragic *or* plaintive ballad, lament; (*fig.*) lamentation.

complaire [kɔ̃'plɛ:r], *v.i. irr.* (*conjug. like* PLAIRE) to be pleasing (*à*). **se complaire**, *v.r.* to delight (*dans* or *à*).

complaisamment [kɔ̃plɛza'mɑ̃], *adv.* complaisantly, obligingly.

complaisance [kɔ̃plɛ'zɑ̃:s], *n.f.* complaisance, good nature; complacency.

complaisant [kɔ̃plɛ'zɑ̃], *a.* affable, civil, obliging, kind.—*n.m.* (*fem.* **-e**) flatterer; go-between.

complément [kɔ̃ple'mɑ̃], *n.m.* complement; (*Gram.*) object; extension (*of subject*).

complémentaire [kɔ̃plemɑ̃'tɛ:r], *a.* complementary, completing.

complet [kɔ̃'plɛ], *a.* (*fem.* **-plète**) complete, whole; full, filled.—*n.m.* complement, full number; suit (*of clothes*).

complètement [kɔ̃plɛt'mɑ̃], *adv.* completely, entirely, thoroughly.

complétement [kɔ̃plet'mɑ̃], *n.m.* finishing, completion.

compléter [kɔ̃ple'te], *v.t.* (*conjug. like* CÉDER) to complete, to perfect; to fill up.

complexe [kɔ̃'plɛks], *a.* complex, complicated.—*n.m.* **complexe d'infériorité**, inferiority complex.

complexion [kɔ̃plɛk'sjɔ̃], *n.f.* constitution; disposition, humor, temper.

complexité [kɔ̃plɛksi'te], *n.f.* complexity.

complication [kɔ̃plika'sjɔ̃], *n.f.* complication, intricacy.

complice [kɔ̃'plis], *a.* accessory, privy to.—*n.* accomplice, accessory.

complicité [kɔ̃plisi'te], *n.f.* complicity, participation.

compliment [kɔ̃pli'mɑ̃], *n.m.* compliment; (*pl.*) regards, congratulations.

complimenter [kɔ̃plimɑ̃'te], *v.t.* to compliment, to congratulate.

complimenteur [kɔ̃plimɑ̃'tœ:r], *a.* and *n.m.* (*fem.* **-euse**) over-complimentary; obsequious (person).

compliqué [kɔ̃pli'ke], *a.* complicated, intricate.

compliquer [kɔ̃pli'ke], *v.t.* to complicate, to entangle. **se compliquer**, *v.r.* to become complicated.

complot [kɔ̃'plo], *n.m.* plot, conspiracy; *chef du complot*, ringleader.

comploter [kɔ̃plɔ'te], *v.t.* to plot.

comploteur [kɔ̃plɔ'tœ:r], *n.m.* plotter, schemer.

componction [kɔ̃pɔ̃k'sjɔ̃], *n.f.* compunction; solemn manners *or* expression.

comportement [kɔ̃pɔrtə'mɑ̃], *n.m.* demeanor, deportment, behavior.

comporter [kɔ̃pɔr'te], *v.t.* to permit, to allow; to require; to comprise. **se comporter**, *v.r.* to behave; to act, to manage.

composant [kɔ̃po'zɑ̃], *n.m.* (*Chem.*) component, constituent.

composé [kɔ̃po'ze], *a.* composed, compound. —*n.m.* compound.

composer [kɔ̃po'ze], *v.t.* to compose, to compound, to make up; to form, to create; to adjust, to regulate; *composer un numéro*, to dial a number.—*v.i.* to compound, to compromise, to make up.

composeuse [kɔ̃po'zø:z], *n.f.* type-setting machine.

composite [kɔ̃po'zit], *a.* composite.

compositeur [kɔ̃pozi'tœ:r], *n.m.* (*fem.* **-trice**) composer (*of music*); (*Print.*) compositor.

composition [kɔ̃pozi'sjɔ̃], *n.f.* composition; chemical composition; settlement; (*fig.*) disposition; (*Print.*) composing.

compost [kɔ̃'pɔst], *n.m.* (*Agric.*) compost.

composter [kɔ̃pɔs'te], *v.t.* to compost; to date *or* obliterate (*ticket etc.*).

compote [kɔ̃'pɔt], *n.f.* stewed fruit, compote.

compotier [kɔ̃po'tje], *n.m.* fruit dish.

compréhensibilité [kɔ̃preɑ̃sibili'te], *n.f.* comprehensibility.

compréhensible [kɔ̃preɑ̃'sibl], *a.* understandable, intelligible.

compréhensif [kɔ̃preɑ̃'sif], *a.* (*fem.* **-sive**) comprehensive; broadminded.

compréhension [kɔ̃preɑ̃'sjɔ̃], *n.f.* comprehension; (*fig.*) understanding, intelligence.

compréhensivité [kɔ̃preɑ̃sivi'te], *n.f.* comprehensiveness, faculty of comprehending.

comprendre [kɔ̃'prɑ̃:dr], *v.t. irr.* (*conjug. like* PRENDRE) to include, to comprise; to understand, to conceive, to realize.

compresse [kɔ̃'prɛ:s], *n.f.* (*Surg.*) compress, pledget.

compresseur [kɔ̃prɛ'sœ:r], *a.* compressive.— *n.m.* compressor, roller.

compressif [kɔ̃prɛ'sif], *a.* (*fem.* **-ssive**) compressive, repressive.

compression [kɔ̃prɛ'sjɔ̃], *n.f.* compression; (*fig.*) constraint.

comprimable [kɔ̃pri'mabl], *a.* compressible.

comprimé [kɔ̃pri'me], *a.* compressed, condensed; kept under.—*n.m.* (*Pharm.*) tabloid, tablet.

comprimer [kɔ̃pri'me], *v.t.* to compress, to condense; to repress, to restrain.

compris [kɔ̃'pri], *a.* understood; included.

compromettant [kɔ̃promɛ'tɑ̃], *a.* compromising; damaging.

compromettre [kɔ̃pro'mɛtr], *v.t. irr.* (*conjug. like* METTRE) to expose, to commit, to compromise; to jeopardize.—*v.i.* to compromise; to submit to arbitration. **se compromettre**, *v.r.* to compromise oneself.

compromis [kɔ̃prɔ'mi], *n.m.* mutual agreement, compromise.

comptabilité [kɔ̃tabili'te], *n.f.* accountancy, bookkeeping; accountant's department.

comptable [kɔ̃'tabl], *a.* responsible for accounts; accountable, responsible.—*n.m.* accountant, bookkeeper; (*Naut.*) purser.

comptant [kɔ̃'tɑ̃], *a.m.* (*of money*) ready; (*of payment*) in cash.—*n.m.* ready money, cash.

compte [kɔ̃:t], *n.m.* reckoning; account, score, statement, report; (*fig.*) profit; esteem, value; **se rendre compte de**, to realize.

compte-gouttes [kɔ̃t'gut], *n.m. inv.* (*Med.*) drop-tube, dropper; filler; (*fig.*) **au compte-gouttes**, sparingly.

compte-pas [kɔ̃tə'pa], *n.m.* pedometer.

compter [kɔ̃'te], *v.t.* to count, to calculate, to compute; to pay down; to comprise.—*v.i.* to reckon, to count; to be reckoned; to expect; to intend; to rely (*sur*). **se compter**, *v.r.* to be reckoned *or* included.

compteur [kɔ̃'tœ:r], *a.* and *n.m.* (*fem.* **-euse**) that counts; computer.—*n.m.* meter; (C) **compteur de stationnement**, parking meter.

comptoir [kɔ̃'twa:r], *n.m.* counter; cashier's desk; counting-house; branch bank; factory.

compulser [kɔ̃pyl'se], *v.t.* to inspect (*documents etc.*).

computation [kɔ̃pyta'sjɔ̃], *n.f.* computation.

computer [kɔ̃py'te], *v.t.* to compute.

comtal [kɔ̃'tal], *a.* (*m. pl.* **-aux**) pertaining to an earl *or* a countess.

comte [kɔ̃:t], *n.m.* count; earl.

comté [kɔ̃'te], *n.m.* county, shire; earldom.

comtesse [kɔ̃'tɛs], *n.f.* countess.

concassage [kɔ̃ka'sa:ʒ], *n.m.* pounding, crushing.

concasser [kɔ̃ka'se], *v.t.* to pound, to crush.

concasseur [kɔ̃ka'sœ:r], *n.m.* crushing-mill; steam roller.

concave [kɔ̃'ka:v], *a.* concave.

concavité [kɔ̃kavi'te], *n.f.* concave; concavity.

concéder [kɔ̃se'de], *v.t.* (*conjug. like* CÉDER) to grant, to concede, to allow.

concentration [kɔ̃sɑ̃tra'sjɔ̃], *n.f.* concentration; condensation; **camp de concentration**, concentration camp.

concentré [kɔ̃sɑ̃'tre], *a.* concentrated; (*fig.*) silent, reserved.—*n.m.* extract.

concentrer [kɔ̃sɑ̃'tre], *v.t.* to concentrate, to focus; (*fig.*) to repress, to smother (*anger etc.*). **se concentrer**, *v.r.* to concentrate; to withdraw within oneself.

concentrique [kɔ̃sɑ̃'trik], *a.* concentric.

concentriquement [kɔ̃sɑ̃trik'mɑ̃], *adv.* concentrically.

concept [kɔ̃'sɛpt], *n.m.* concept.

conceptibilité [kɔ̃sɛptibili'te], *n.f.* conceivability.

conceptible [kɔ̃sɛp'tibl], *a.* conceivable.

conceptif [kɔ̃sɛp'tif], *a.* (*fem.* **-tive**) conceptive.

conception [kɔ̃sɛp'sjɔ̃], *n.f.* conception; thought, notion; understanding.

concernant [kɔ̃sɛr'nɑ̃], *prep.* concerning, relating to.

concerner [kɔ̃sɛr'ne], *v.t.* to relate (*to*), to concern, to regard.

concert [kɔ̃'sɛ:r], *n.m.* harmony; concert; (*fig.*) concord.

concertant [kɔ̃sɛr'tɑ̃], *a.* in concert (*of a piece of music*).—*n.m.* (*fem.* **-e**) performer in a concert.

concerté [kɔ̃sɛr'te], *a.* concerted, united; studied, stiff.

concerter [kɔ̃sɛr'te], *v.t.* to contrive, to concert; to plan, to devise; to compose (*one's demeanor etc.*). **se concerter**, *v.r.* to plan together, to concert.

concertiste [kɔ̃sɛr'tist], *n.* performer (*at a concert*).

concerto [kɔ̃sɛr'to], *n.m.* concerto.

concession [kɔ̃se'sjɔ̃], *n.f.* concession, privilege.

concessionnaire [kɔ̃sesjɔ'nɛ:r], *a.* concessionary.—*n.* grantee.

concevable [kɔ̃s'vabl], *a.* conceivable, imaginable.

concevoir [kɔ̃sə'vwa:r], *v.t. irr.* (*conjug. like* RECEVOIR) to become pregnant, to conceive; to imagine, to understand; to comprehend.

concierge [kɔ̃'sjɛr:ʒ], *n.* concierge, hall-porter, caretaker.

conciergerie [kɔ̃sjɛrʒə'ri], *n.f.* caretaker's lodge; **La Conciergerie**, a prison in Paris (*during French Revolution*).

concile [kɔ̃'sil], *n.m.* an assembly of prelates and doctors, council, synod.

conciliable [kɔ̃si'ljabl], *a.* reconcilable.

conciliabule [kɔ̃silja'byl], *n.m.* conventicle, secret meeting.

conciliaire [kɔ̃si'lje:r], *a.* of *or* belonging to a council.

conciliant [kɔ̃si'ljɑ̃], *a.* conciliating, reconciling.

conciliateur [kɔ̃silja'tœ:r], *a.* (*fem.* **-trice**) conciliatory.—*n.m.* (*fem.* **-trice**) conciliator.

conciliation [kɔ̃silja'sjɔ̃], *n.f.* reconciliation.

conciliatoire [kɔ̃silja'twa:r], *a.* conciliatory.

concilier [kɔ̃si'lje], *v.t.* to conciliate, to reconcile; to gain, to win, to procure. **se concilier**, *v.r.* to gain, to win.

concis [kɔ̃'si], *a.* concise, brief, short.

concision [kɔ̃si'zjɔ̃], *n.f.* brevity, conciseness.

concitoyen [kɔ̃sitwa'jɛ̃], *n.m.* (*fem.* **-enne**) fellow citizen.

conclave [kɔ̃'kla:v], *n.m.* conclave, assembly of all the cardinals.

concluant [kɔ̃kly'ɑ̃], *a.* conclusive, decisive.

conclure [kɔ̃'kly:r], *v.t. irr.* to conclude; to infer; to judge.

conclusif [kɔ̃kly'zif], *a.* (*fem.* **-sive**) conclusive.

conclusion [kɔ̃kly'zjɔ̃], *n.f.* conclusion, upshot.

concombre [kɔ̃'kɔ̃:br], *n.m.* cucumber.

concomitance [kɔ̃kɔmi'tɑ̃:s], *n.f.* concomitance.

concomitant [kɔ̃kɔmi'tɑ̃], *a.* concomitant.

concordance [kɔ̃kɔr'dɑ̃:s], *n.f.* agreement; (*Bibl. etc.*) concordance.

concordant [kɔ̃kɔr'dɑ̃], *a.* concordant.

concordat [kɔ̃kɔr'da], *n.m.* concordat, agreement; bankrupt's certificate.

concordataire [kɔ̃kɔrda'tɛ:r], *n.m.* certificated bankrupt.

concorde [kɔ̃'kɔrd], *n.f.* concord, agreement, harmony; good understanding.

concorder [kɔ̃kɔr'de], *v.i.* to be in accord, to agree, to concur.

concourir [kɔ̃ku'ri:r], *v.i. irr.* (*conjug. like* COURIR) to concur; to contribute to; to co-operate; to compete; to converge.

concours [kɔ̃'kuːr], *n.m.* concourse, meeting; coincidence; competition; co-operation; competitive examination; assistance.

concret [kɔ̃'krɛ], *a.* (*fem.* **-crète**) concrete, solid.

concubine [kɔ̃ky'bin], *n.f.* concubine.

concupiscence [kɔ̃kypi'sɑ̃ːs], *n.f.* concupiscence, lust.

concurremment [kɔ̃kyra'mɑ̃], *adv.* concurrently; jointly, together.

concurrence [kɔ̃ky'rɑ̃ːs], *n.f.* competition; rivalry, opposition.

concurrent [kɔ̃ky'rɑ̃], *n.m.* (*fem.* **-e**) competitor, rival.

concussion [kɔ̃ky'sjɔ̃], *n.f.* extortion, embezzlement.

concussionnaire [kɔ̃kysjɔ'nɛːr], *a.* guilty of peculation, of bribery *or* of extortion.—*n.m.* extortioner, peculator, embezzler.

condamnable [kɔ̃dɑ'nabl], *a.* condemnable, blamable.

condamnation [kɔ̃dɑnɑ'sjɔ̃], *n.f.* condemnation, judgment, sentence; penalty.

condamné [kɔ̃dɑ'ne], *a.* condemned, convicted.—*n.m.* (*fem.* **-ée**) convict.

condamner [kɔ̃dɑ'ne], *v.t.* to condemn, to sentence, to convict; (*fig.*) to blame, to censure.

condensateur [kɔ̃dɑsɑ'tœːr], *n.m.* (*Phys.*) condenser.

condensation [kɔ̃dɑsɑ'sjɔ̃], *n.f.* condensation.

condensé [kɔ̃dɑ'se], *a.* condensed.—*n.m.* digest.

condenser [kɔ̃dɑ'se], *v.t.* to condense.

condenseur [kɔ̃dɑ'sœːr], *n.m.* condenser.

condescendance [kɔ̃desɑ'dɑ̃ːs], *n.f.* condescension.

condescendant [kɔ̃desɑ'dɑ̃], *a.* condescending, complying.

condescendre [kɔ̃de'sɑ̃ːdr], *v.i.* to condescend, to comply.

condiment [..ɔ̃di'mɑ̃], *n.m.* condiment, seasoning.

condisciple [kɔ̃di'sipl], *n.m.* schoolfellow.

condit [kɔ̃'di], *n.m.* candied fruit.

condition [kɔ̃di'sjɔ̃], *n.f.* condition; rank, station; domestic service; situation, circumstances; terms; *à condition or sous condition*, on condition, on approval.

conditionné [kɔ̃disjɔ'ne], *a.* conditioned (*bien* or *mal*); well-conditioned, sound.

conditionnel [kɔ̃disjɔ'nɛl], *a.* conditional.—*n.m.* (*Gram.*) conditional.

conditionnellement [kɔ̃disjɔnɛl'mɑ̃], *adv.* conditionally, on condition.

conditionner [kɔ̃disjɔ'ne], *v.t.* to condition; to dry (*silk*); to season (*wood*).

condoléance [kɔ̃dɔle'ɑ̃ːs], *n.f.* condolence.

condominium [kɔ̃dɔmi'njɔm], *n.m.* condominium.

condor [kɔ̃'dɔːr], *n.m.* condor.

conductance [kɔ̃dyk'tɑ̃ːs], *n.f.* (*Elec.*) conductance.

conducteur [kɔ̃dyk'tœːr], *n.m.* (*fem.* **-trice**) conductor, conductress, leader, guide; driver, drover.—*a.* (*Phys.*) conducting.

conductibilité [kɔ̃dyktibili'te], *n.f.* conductibility.

conductible [kɔ̃dyk'tibl], *a.* conductible.

conduction [kɔ̃dyk'sjɔ̃], *n.f.* (*Phys.*) conduction; (*Civic Law*) hiring.

conduire [kɔ̃'dɥiːr], *v.t. irr.* to conduct, to lead, to guide; to drive; to accompany; to bring, to take; to be at the head of.—*v.i.* to lead (*à*); to drive. **se conduire**, *v.r.* to conduct *or* behave oneself.

conduit [kɔ̃'dɥi], *n.m.* conduit, duct, pipe, passage, tube, canal.

conduite [kɔ̃'dɥit], *n.f.* conducting, leading, driving, steering; management, direction, administration; conveyance, distribution; scheme, plan; water-pipe, conduit; behavior, demeanor; prudence, discretion.

cône [koːn], *n.m.* cone; *en cône*, conical.

confection [kɔ̃fɛk'sjɔ̃], *n.f.* preparation, making; making of ready-made clothes; (*Pharm.*) confection; *vêtements de confection*, ready-made clothes.

confectionner [kɔ̃fɛksjɔ'ne], *v.t.* to make, to manufacture, to finish.

confectionneur [kɔ̃fɛksjɔ'nœːr], *n.m.* (*fem.* **-euse :**) maker, finisher (*of wearing apparel*), clothier, outfitter.

confédération [kɔ̃federɑ'sjɔ̃], *n.f.* confederation, confederacy; *la Confédération Générale du Travail* (*abbr.* **C.G.T.**), the French equivalent of the C.I.O.

confédéré [kɔ̃fede're], *a.* and *n.m.* (*fem.* **-ée**) confederate, associate.

confédérer (se) [səkɔ̃fede're], *v.r.* (*conjug. like* **CÉDER**) to combine, to enter into confederation.

conférence [kɔ̃fe'rɑ̃ːs], *n.f.* conference; lecture.

conférencier [kɔ̃ferɑ̃'sje], *n.m.* (*fem.* **-ière**) lecturer.

conférer [kɔ̃fe're], *v.t.* (*conjug. like* **CÉDER**) to confer, to bestow, to grant; to compare.—*v.i.* to consult together, to confer.

confesse [kɔ̃'fɛs], *n.f.* (*always used with* **à** *or* **de**) *aller à confesse*, to go to confession; *venir de confesse*, to come from confession.

confesser [kɔ̃fɛ'se], *v.t.* to confess; to acknowledge, to admit; to shrive. **se confesser**, *v.r.* to confess one's sins, to confess (*to a priest*).

confesseur [kɔ̃fɛ'sœːr], *n.m.* (father) confessor.

confession [kɔ̃fɛ'sjɔ̃], *n.f.* confession, acknowledgment, avowal.

confessionnal [kɔ̃fɛsjɔ'nal], *n.m.* confessional.

confetti [kɔ̃fɛt'ti], *n.m. pl.* confetti.

confiance [kɔ̃'fjɑ̃ːs], *n.f.* confidence, reliance, trust.

confiant [kɔ̃'fjɑ̃], *a.* confident, unsuspecting, sanguine; self-conceited.

confidemment [kɔ̃fida'mɑ̃], *adv.* confidentially.

confidence [kɔ̃fi'dɑ̃ːs], *n.f.* confidence; secret.

confident [kɔ̃fi'dɑ̃], *n.m.* (*fem.* **-ente**) confidant, confidante.

confidentiel [kɔ̃fidɑ̃'sjɛl], *a.* confidential.

confidentiellement [kɔ̃fidɑ̃sjɛl'mɑ̃], *adv.* confidentially.

confier [kɔ̃'fje], *v.t.* to confide, to entrust, to commit (*à*). **se confier**, *v.r.* to trust in; to unbosom oneself (*à*).

configuration [kɔ̃figyrɑ'sjɔ̃], *n.f.* configuration, form, shape, lay (*of the land*).

confinement [kɔ̃fin'mɑ̃], *n.m.* confinement; overcrowding.

confiner [kɔ̃fi'ne], *v.t.* to confine, to imprison; *air confiné*, stuffy atmosphere.—*v.i.* to border upon, to be adjoining. **se confiner**, *v.r.* to confine *or* to limit oneself.

confins [kɔ̃'fɛ̃], *n.m. (used only in pl.)* confines, borders, limits.

confire [kɔ̃'fi:r], *v.t. irr.* to preserve; to candy, to pickle.

confirmatif [kɔ̃firma'tif], *a. (fem. -tive)* confirmative.

confirmation [kɔ̃firma'sjɔ̃], *n.f.* confirmation, ratification.

confirmer [kɔ̃fir'me], *v.t.* to strengthen, to corroborate; to confirm; to ratify. **se confirmer**, *v.r.* to be confirmed.

confiscable [kɔ̃fis'kabl], *a.* confiscable, forfeitable.

confiscation [kɔ̃fiska'sjɔ̃], *n.f.* confiscation, forfeiture.

confiserie [kɔ̃fiz'ri], *n.f.* confectionery; confectioner's shop.

confiseur [kɔ̃fi'zœ:r] *n.m. (fem. -euse)* confectioner.

confisquer [kɔ̃fis'ke], *v.t.* to confiscate, to forfeit, to impound; to seize.

confit (1) [kɔ̃'fi], *p.p.* [CONFIRE].

confit (2) [kɔ̃'fi], *n.m.* meat, poultry etc. preserved in fat; bran mash *(for pigs etc.).*

confiture [kɔ̃fi'ty:r], *n.f.* preserve, jam.

conflagration [kɔ̃flagra'sjɔ̃], *n.f.* conflagration.

conflit [kɔ̃'fli], *n.m.* conflict, collision, encounter; contention, strife, contest, rivalry; jar, clash.

confluent [kɔ̃fly'ɑ̃], *n.m.* confluence, junction *(of rivers).*

confluer [kɔ̃fly'e], *v.i.* to meet, to unite *(of streams etc.).*

confondre [kɔ̃'fɔ̃:dr], *v.t.* to confound, to confuse; to mix, to mingle; *(fig.)* to amaze, to astound. **se confondre**, *v.r.* to mingle, to be lost in; to be confounded, to be abashed.

conformation [kɔ̃fɔrma'sjɔ̃], *n.f.* conformation, structure.

conforme [kɔ̃'fɔrm], *a.* conformable; congenial, consistent; *pour copie conforme*, certified true copy.

conformé [kɔ̃fɔr'me], *a.* formed, shaped *(bien or mal).*

conformément [kɔ̃fɔrme'mɑ̃], *adv.* suitably; according to.

conformer [kɔ̃fɔr'me], *v.t.* to give form to. **se conformer**, *v.r.* to conform, to comply *(with).*

conformisme [kɔ̃fɔr'mism], *n.m.* conformity, orthodoxy.

conformité [kɔ̃fɔrmi'te], *n.f.* likeness, conformity, compliance.

confort [kɔ̃'fɔ:r], *n.m.* comfort, ease.

confortable [kɔ̃fɔr'tabl], *a.* cosy, comfortable.

confortablement [kɔ̃fɔrtablə'mɑ̃], *adv.* comfortably.

confraternité [kɔ̃fraterni'te], *n.f.* fraternity, brotherhood.

confrère [kɔ̃'frɛ:r], *n.m.* colleague; fellow member.

confrérie [kɔ̃fre'ri], *n.f.* brotherhood, fraternity.

confrontation [kɔ̃frɔ̃ta'sjɔ̃], *n.f.* confrontation; comparing.

confronter [kɔ̃frɔ̃'te], *v.t.* to confront; to compare.

confus [kɔ̃'fy], *a.* confused, muddled, vague, indistinct, obscure; abashed, crestfallen.

confusément [kɔ̃fyze'mɑ̃], *adv.* confusedly, vaguely, dimly.

confusion [kɔ̃fy'zjɔ̃], *n.f.* confusion, disorder; bewilderment; embarrassment, shame, blush; misunderstanding.

congé [kɔ̃'ʒe], *n.m.* leave, permission; leave of absence, holiday; discharge, dismissal; notice (to quit); permit.

congédier [kɔ̃ʒe'dje], *v.t.* to discharge, to dismiss, to pay off; to disband.

congélateur [kɔ̃ʒela'tœ:r], *n.m.* refrigerator.

congeler [kɔ̃ʒ'le], *v.t.*, **se congeler**, *v.r.* *(conjug. like* AMENER*)* to congeal, to freeze; to coagulate.

congénère [kɔ̃ʒe'nɛ:r], *a.* congeneric; of same species; *(Philol.)* cognate.

congénial [kɔ̃ʒe'njal], *a. (m. pl. -aux)* congenial, of the same nature.

congénital [kɔ̃ʒeni'tal], *a. (m. pl. -aux)* congenital, hereditary.

congère [kɔ̃'ʒɛ:r], *n.f.* snowdrift.

congestion [kɔ̃ʒes'tjɔ̃], *n.f.* congestion.

conglomération [kɔ̃glɔmera'sjɔ̃], *n.f.* conglomeration.

conglomérer [kɔ̃glɔme're], *v.t. (conjug. like* CÉDER*)* to conglomerate.

congolais [kɔ̃gɔ'lɛ], *a.* Congolese.— **(Congolais**, *fem. -aise)* Congolese *(person).*

congratulation [kɔ̃gratyla'sjɔ̃], *n.f.* congratulation.

congratulatoire [kɔ̃gratyla'twa:r], *a.* congratulatory.

congratuler [kɔ̃graty'le], *v.t.* to congratulate.

congre [kɔ̃:gr], *n.m.* conger, conger eel.

congrégation [kɔ̃grega'sjɔ̃], *n.f.* fraternity, brotherhood, general body *(of an order etc.).*

congrès [kɔ̃'grɛ], *n.m.* congress.

congressiste [kɔ̃grɛ'sist], *n.m. (Am.)* congressman.

congru [kɔ̃'gry], *a.* suitable, consistent, congruous, proper.

congruité [kɔ̃gryi'te], *n.f.* congruity, consistency, propriety.

congrûment [kɔ̃gry'mɑ̃], *adv.* congruously, properly.

conifère [kɔni'fɛ:r], *a.* coniferous.—*n.m.* conifer.

conique [kɔ'nik], *a.* conical.

conjecture [kɔ̃ʒek'ty:r], *n.f.* conjecture, surmise, guess.

conjecturer [kɔ̃ʒɛkty're], *v.t.* to conjecture, to guess, to surmise.

conjoindre [kɔ̃'ʒwɛ̃:dr], *v.t. irr. (conjug. like* CRAINDRE*)* to conjoin, to unite together; to marry.

conjoint [kɔ̃'ʒwɛ̃], *a.* conjoined, united, joint. —*n.m. (fem. -e)* spouse.

conjointement [kɔ̃ʒwɛ̃'mɑ̃], *adv.* conjointly, unitedly.

conjoncteur [kɔ̃ʒɔ̃k'tœ:r], *n.m. (Elec.)* circuit breaker, switch key.

conjonctif [kɔ̃ʒɔ̃k'tif], *a. (fem. -tive)* conjunctive.

conjonction [kɔ̃ʒɔ̃k'sjɔ̃], *n.f.* conjunction; union, connection; coition.

conjoncture [kɔ̃ʒɔ̃k'ty:r], *n.f.* conjuncture, juncture.

conjugaison [kɔ̃ʒygɛ'zɔ̃], *n.f.* conjugation.

conjugal [kɔ̃ʒy'gal], *a.* (*m. pl.* **-aux**) conjugal.
conjugalement [kɔ̃ʒygal'mã], *adv.* conjugally.
conjugué [kɔ̃ʒy'ge], *a.* (*Mech.*) twin.
conjuguer [kɔ̃ʒy'ge], *v.t.* (*Gram.*) to conjugate.
conjuration [kɔ̃ʒyra'sjɔ̃], *n.f.* conspiracy, plot.
conjuré [kɔ̃ʒy're], *a.* confederate, sworn.—*n.m.* (*fem.* **-ée**) conspirator, plotter.
conjurer [kɔ̃ʒy're], *v.t.* to implore; to conspire; to swear; to conjure up; to exorcize, to ward off.
connaissable [kɔnɛ'sabl], *a.* recognizable.
connaissance [kɔnɛ'sã:s], *n.f.* knowledge, learning; consciousness (*de*); acquaintance; intercourse; (*Law*) cognizance; (*pl.*) attainments.
connaisseur [kɔnɛ'sœːr], *a.* (*fem.* **-euse**) expert, skilled.—*n.m.* connoisseur, expert.
connaître [kɔ'nɛːtr], *v.t. irr.* to know, to perceive; to understand; to be acquainted with.—*v.i.* to have or take cognizance of; to deal with (*a matter*). **se connaître**, *v.r.* to know oneself; to know each other; to be a connoisseur.
connecter [kɔnɛk'te], *v.t.* to connect; (*Elec.*) to couple (up), to group.
connétable [kɔne'tabl], *n.m.* high constable.
connexion [kɔnɛk'sjɔ̃], *n.f.* connection, affinity.
connexité [kɔnɛksi'te], *n.f.* connection.
connivence [kɔni'vã:s], *n.f.* connivance.
connotation [kɔnɔta'sjɔ̃], *n.f.* connotation.
connu [kɔ'ny], *a.* known, understood.—*n.m.* that which is known.
conque [kɔ̃:k], *n.f.* conch, sea-shell.
conquérant [kɔ̃ke'rã], *a.* conquering.—*n.m.* (*fem.* **-e**) conqueror.
conquérir [kɔ̃ke'ri:r], *v.t. irr.* (*conjug. like* ACQUÉRIR) to conquer, to subdue (*a country*); (*fig.*) to gain, to win over.
conquête [kɔ̃'kɛːt], *n.f.* conquest, acquisition.
conquis [kɔ̃'ki], *a.* conquered.
consacrant [kɔ̃sa'krã], *a.* consecrating, officiating.—*n.m.* consecrator, officiant.
consacrer [kɔ̃sa'kre], *v.t.* to consecrate, to dedicate, to sanctify; to sanction; to authorize. **se consacrer**, *v.r.* to devote oneself.
consciemment [kɔ̃sja'mã], *adv.* consciously, knowingly.
conscience [kɔ̃'sjã:s], *n.f.* consciousness, perception; conscience, conscientiousness.
consciencieusement [kɔ̃sjãsjøz'mã], *adv.* conscientiously.
consciencieux [kɔ̃sjã'sjø], *a.* (*fem.* **-euse**) conscientious.
conscient [kɔ̃'sjã], *a.* conscious (*de*); self-conscious.
conscription [kɔ̃skrip'sjɔ̃], *n.f.* enlistment; conscription.
conscrit [kɔ̃'skri], *a.* conscript.—*n.m.* conscript; (raw) recruit.
consécrateur [kɔ̃sekra'tœːr], [CONSACRANT].
consécration [kɔ̃sekra'sjɔ̃], *n.f.* consecration; ordination.
consécutif [kɔ̃seky'tif], *a.* (*fem.* **-tive**) consecutive, following.
consécutivement [kɔ̃sekytiv'mã], *adv.* consecutively.
conseil [kɔ̃'sɛːj], *n.m.* counsel, advice; resolution; council, board; (*Law*) counsel;

conseil d'administration, board of directors; **Conseil d'État**, Council of State; **Conseil de Sécurité (de l'O.N.U.)**, (U.N.) Security Council; **conseil judiciaire**, guardian; **conseil de guerre**, court-martial; council of war; **conseil municipal**, town council, corporation.
conseiller [kɔ̃sɛ'je], *v.t.* to advise, to counsel; to recommend.—*n.m.* (*fem.* **-ère**) counsellor, adviser, councillor.
consensus [kɔ̃sã'sy:s], *n.m.* consent, consensus.
consentant [kɔ̃sã'tã], *a.* consenting, willing.
consentement [kɔ̃sãt'mã], *n.m.* consent, assent.
consentir [kɔ̃sã'tiːr], *v.i. irr.* (*conjug. like* SENTIR) to consent, to agree, to acquiesce (*à*).
conséquemment [kɔ̃seka'mã], *adv.* consequently, accordingly.
conséquence [kɔ̃se'kã:s], *n.f.* consequence, sequel; issue, result; inference, conclusion.
conséquent [kɔ̃se'kã], *a.* rational, consistent.—*n.m.* (*Log., Math.*) consequent; **par conséquent**, consequently.
conservateur [kɔ̃sɛrva'tœːr], *a.* (*fem.* **-trice**) preserving, conservative.—*n.m.* (*fem.* **-trice**) Conservative, Tory.—*n.m.* guardian, keeper, curator.
conservatif [kɔ̃sɛrva'tif], *a.* (*fem.* **-tive**) conservative, preservative.—*n.m.* preservative.
conservation [kɔ̃sɛrva'sjɔ̃], *n.f.* conservation, preservation; registration (*of mortgages etc.*).
conservatisme [kɔ̃sɛrva'tism], *n.m.* conservatism.
Conservatoire [kɔ̃sɛrva'twa:r], *n.m.* academy of music and school of elocution in Paris.
conserve [kɔ̃'sɛrv], *n.f.* preserve; tinned (*Am.* canned) food.
conserver [kɔ̃sɛr've], *v.t.* to preserve; to keep. **se conserver**, *v.r.* to be preserved; to bear one's age well; to keep (*of meat, fruit etc.*).
considérable [kɔ̃side'rabl], *a.* considerable, notable, eminent; **peu considérable**, of little importance.
considérablement [kɔ̃siderablə'mã], *adv.* considerably.
considérant [kɔ̃side'rã], *conj. phr.* **considérant que**, whereas.
considération [kɔ̃sidera'sjɔ̃], *n.f.* consideration, attention; motive, grounds; regard, respect.
considérément [kɔ̃sidere'mã], *adv.* considerately, prudently.
considérer [kɔ̃side're], *v.t.* (*conjug. like* CÉDER) to consider, to look at, to view; to ponder; to value, to esteem; to pay attention to. **se considérer**, *v.r.* to esteem oneself.
consignataire [kɔ̃sina'tɛ:r], *n.* trustee, depositary.
consignateur [kɔ̃sina'tœ:r], *n.m.* (*fem.* **-trice**) (*Comm.*) consignor, shipper.
consignation [kɔ̃sina'sjɔ̃], *n.f.* (*Comm.*) deposit, consignment.
consigne [kɔ̃'siɲ], *n.f.* (*Mil.*) order, password; (*fig.*) strict command, prohibition; (*Rail.*) baggage check room, cloak-room; (*sch.*) gating, detention.

consigner [kɔ̃si'ɲe], v.t. to deposit; to consign; to record, to register; to keep in; to refuse admittance to.

consistance [kɔ̃sis'tãːs], n.f. consistency; firmness, stability; (fig.) credit, consideration.

consistant [kɔ̃sis'tã], a. consisting of; consistent, firm, solid.

consister [kɔ̃sis'te], v.i. to consist; to be composed of.

consistoire [kɔ̃sis'twaːr], n.m. consistory.

consolable [kɔ̃sɔ'labl], a. consolable.

consolant [kɔ̃sɔ'lã], a. consoling, comforting.

consolateur [kɔ̃sɔla'tœːr], a. (fem. -trice) consoling.—n.m. (fem. -trice) comforter, consoler.

consolation [kɔ̃sɔla'sjɔ̃], n.f. consolation, comfort, solace.

console [kɔ̃'sɔl], n.f. console, bracket.

consoler [kɔ̃sɔ'le], v.t. to console, to comfort. **se consoler**, v.r. to console oneself.

consolidation [kɔ̃sɔlida'sjɔ̃], n.f. consolidation; strengthening; funding (of interest).

consolidé [kɔ̃sɔli'de], a. funded.—n.m. (Fin., used only in pl.) consols.

consolider [kɔ̃sɔli'de], v.t. to consolidate; to strengthen. **se consolider**, v.r. to consolidate, to grow firm.

consommable [kɔ̃sɔ'mabl], a. consumable, edible.

consommateur [kɔ̃sɔma'tœːr], n.m. (fem. -trice) consumer (as opposed to producer), eater, drinker.

consommation [kɔ̃sɔma'sjɔ̃], n.f. consumption; consummation; food, drinks, refreshments.

consommé [kɔ̃sɔ'me], a. consumed; consummated; consummate; accomplished.—n.m. clear soup.

consommer [kɔ̃sɔ'me], v.t. to consume, to use; (fig.) to consummate, to accomplish.—v.i. (pop.) to have a drink.

consomption [kɔ̃sɔ̃p'sjɔ̃], n.f. consumption, using up; (Path.) phthisis, decline.

consonance [kɔ̃sɔ'nãːs], n.f. consonance; (fig.) concord.

consonant [kɔ̃sɔ'nã], a. consonant.

consonne [kɔ̃'sɔn], n.f. consonant.

consort [kɔ̃'sɔːr], a. consort (of the husband or wife of a sovereign).—n.m. (used only in pl.) consorts, confederates; (Law) associates.

consortium [kɔ̃sɔr'sjɔm], n.m. consortium.

conspirateur [kɔ̃spira'tœːr], n.m. (fem. -trice) conspirator.—a. conspiring.

conspiration [kɔ̃spira'sjɔ̃], n.f. conspiracy, plot.

conspirer [kɔ̃spi're], v.t. to plot.—v.i. to conspire, to concur; to plot.

conspuer [kɔ̃s'pɥe], v.t. to despise, to spurn; to boo, to barrack.

constamment [kɔ̃sta'mã] adv. steadily; continually, constantly.

constance [kɔ̃s'tãːs], n.f. constancy; perseverance.

constant [kɔ̃s'tã], a. constant, faithful, unshaken; persevering.

constatation [kɔ̃stata'sjɔ̃], n.f. authentication; statement; findings.

constater [kɔ̃sta'te], v.t. to prove, to verify; to ascertain; to state, to declare.

constellation [kɔ̃stɛla'sjɔ̃], n.f. constellation.

constellé [kɔ̃stɛ'le], a. constellated; studded.

consteller [kɔ̃stɛ'le], v.t. to constellate, to stud.

consternation [kɔ̃stɛrna'sjɔ̃], n.f. consternation, dismay.

consterné [kɔ̃stɛr'ne], a. dismayed, overwhelmed.

consterner [kɔ̃stɛr'ne], v.t. to dismay, to dishearten; to astound, to amaze.

constipation [kɔ̃stipa'sjɔ̃], n.f. constipation, costiveness.

constipé [kɔ̃sti'pe], a. costive, constipated.

constiper [kɔ̃sti'pe], v.t. to constipate, to bind.

constituant [kɔ̃sti'tɥã], a. constituent.

constituer [kɔ̃sti'tɥe], v.t. to constitute; to establish; to appoint; to settle, to assign. **se constituer**, v.r. to constitute oneself.

constitution [kɔ̃stity'sjɔ̃], n.f. constitution; establishment; settlement (of an annuity etc.); temperament.

constitutionnel [kɔ̃stitysjɔ'nɛl], a. (fem. -elle) constitutional.

constitutionnellement [kɔ̃stitysjɔnɛl'mã], adv. constitutionally.

constriction [kɔ̃strik'sjɔ̃], n.f. constriction.

constringent [kɔ̃strɛ̃'ʒã], a. constringent.

constructeur [kɔ̃stryk'tœːr], n.m. constructor, builder; shipbuilder, shipwright.

construction [kɔ̃stryk'sjɔ̃], n.f. building, construction; erection, structure.

constructivité [kɔ̃stryktivi'te], n.f. constructiveness.

construire [kɔ̃s'trɥiːr], v.t. irr. (conjug. like CONDUIRE) to construct, to build, to erect.

consul [kɔ̃'syl], n.m. consul.

consulaire [kɔ̃sy'lɛːr], a. consular.

consulat [kɔ̃sy'la], n.m. consulate, consulship.

consultant [kɔ̃syl'tã], a. consulting.—n.m. (fem. -e) consultant, consulting physician.

consultatif [kɔ̃sylta'tif], a. (fem. -tive) consultative, deliberative.

consultation [kɔ̃sylta'sjɔ̃], n.f. consultation; opinion, advice; cabinet de consultation, surgery.

consulter [kɔ̃syl'te], v.t. to consult; to refer to.—v.i. to deliberate, to take counsel (together). **se consulter**, v.r. to consider, to reflect, to deliberate.

consumable [kɔ̃sy'mabl], a. consumable.

consumant [kɔ̃sy'mã], a. consuming, devouring, burning.

consumer [kɔ̃sy'me], v.t. to consume; to destroy, to wear out, to wear away, to squander, to waste. **se consumer**, v.r. to decay, to waste away, to wear out; to undermine one's health.

contact [kɔ̃'takt], n.m. contact; touch; connection; (Motor.) clé de contact, ignition key; (Opt.) verres de contact, contact lenses.

contagieux [kɔ̃ta'ʒjø], a. (fem. -euse) contagious, infectious.

contagion [kɔ̃ta'ʒjɔ̃], n.f. contagion, infection.

contamination [kɔ̃tamina'sjɔ̃], n.f. contamination, pollution.

contaminé [kɔ̃tami'ne], a. polluted, contaminated.

contaminer [kɔ̃tami'ne], v.t. to contaminate.

conte [kɔ̃ːt], n.m. story, tale; (fig.) fib, fairytale.

contemplateur [kɔ̃tɑ̃plaˈtœːr], *n.m.* (*fem.* -trice) contemplator.

contemplatif [kɔ̃tɑ̃plaˈtif], *a.* (*fem.* -tive) contemplative.

contemplation [kɔ̃tɑ̃plɑˈsjɔ̃], *n.f.* contemplation, meditation.

contempler [kɔ̃tɑ̃ˈple], *v.t.* to contemplate, to survey, to gaze on.—*v.i.* to contemplate, to meditate, to reflect.

contemporain [kɔ̃tɑ̃pɔˈrɛ̃], *a.* and *n.m.* (*fem.* -e) contemporary.

contempteur [kɔ̃tɑ̃pˈtœːr], *a.* (*jem.* -trice) contemptuous, scornful, insolent, disdainful.—*n.m.* contemner, despiser, scorner.

contenance [kɔ̃tˈnɑ̃ːs], *n.f.* capacity; volume; (*fig.*) countenance, air, bearing.

contenant [kɔ̃tˈnɑ̃], *a.* holding, containing.—*n.m.* holder, container.

contenir [kɔ̃tˈniːr], *v.t. irr.* (*conjug. like* TENIR) to contain, to comprise, to hold, to include; to restrain. **se contenir**, *v.r.* to keep within bounds, to be moderate; to control oneself.

content [kɔ̃ˈtɑ̃], *a.* content, satisfied; pleased, glad, gratified.

contentement [kɔ̃tɑ̃tˈmɑ̃], *n.m.* contentment, satisfaction; comfort, pleasure.

contenter [kɔ̃tɑ̃ˈte], *v.t.* to content, to satisfy; to please, to gratify. **se contenter**, *v.r.* to be satisfied, to be content.

contentieusement [kɔ̃tɑ̃sjøzˈmɑ̃], *adv.* contentiously, litigiously.

contentieux [kɔ̃tɑ̃ˈsjø], *a.* (*fem.* -euse) contentious, disputable; litigious; in dispute; quarrelsome.—*n.m.* debatable matter; *bureau du contentieux*, legal department.

contention [kɔ̃tɑ̃ˈsjɔ̃], *n.f.* application, vehemence; contention, contest, debate, strife.

contenu [kɔ̃tˈny], *a.* contained; (*fig.*) kept in control.—*n.m.* contents; enclosure; terms (*of a letter etc.*).

conter [kɔ̃ˈte], *v.t.* to tell, to relate; *en conter*, to tell fibs.

contestable [kɔ̃tɛsˈtabl], *a.* disputable, debatable.

contestant [kɔ̃tɛsˈtɑ̃], *a.* contending (*at law*).—*n.m.* (*fem.* -e) contesting party, litigant.

contestation [kɔ̃tɛstɑˈsjɔ̃], *n.f.* contestation, contest; dispute, debate; litigation.

contester [kɔ̃tɛsˈte], *v.t.* to dispute, 'o contest; to contend, to debate.—*v.i.* to quarrel; to be contentious.

conteur [kɔ̃ˈtœːr], *a.* (*fem.* -euse) who tells stories.—*n.m.* (*fem.* -euse) story teller; (*fig.*) fibber.

contexte [kɔ̃ˈtɛkst], *n.m.* context; text (*of a deed*).

contexture [kɔ̃tɛksˈtyːr], *n.f.* contexture (*of the muscles etc.*); texture (*of materials*).

contigu [kɔ̃tiˈgy], *a.* (*fem.* -ë) contiguous, adjoining.

contiguïté [kɔ̃tiguiˈte], *n.f.* contiguity.

continence [kɔ̃tiˈnɑ̃ːs], *n.f.* continency, chastity.

continent (1) [kɔ̃tiˈnɑ̃], *a.* chaste, continent.

continent (2) [kɔ̃tiˈnɑ̃], *n.m.* continent, mainland.

continental [kɔ̃tinɑ̃ˈtal], *a.* (*m. pl.* -aux) continental.

contingence [kɔ̃tɛ̃ˈʒɑ̃ːs], *n.f.* contingency, casualty.

contingent [kɔ̃tɛ̃ˈʒɑ̃], *a.* contingent, accidental, casual.—*n.m.* quota; contingent.

continu [kɔ̃tiˈny], *a.* continuous, continual, uninterrupted; incessant.

continuation [kɔ̃tinɥɑˈsjɔ̃], *n.f.* continuation.

continuel [kɔ̃tiˈnɥɛl], *a.* (*fem.* -elle) continual, perpetual.

continuellement [kɔ̃tinɥɛlˈmɑ̃], *adv.* continually, perpetually.

continuer [kɔ̃tiˈnɥe], *v.t.* to continue, to proceed with; to lengthen.—*v.i.* to continue, to keep on. **se continuer**, *v.r.* to be continued, to last.

continuité [kɔ̃tinɥiˈte], *n.f.* continuity; continuance.

continûment [kɔ̃tinyˈmɑ̃], *adv.* unremittingly, continuously, without cessation.

contorsion [kɔ̃tɔrˈsjɔ̃], *n.f.* contortion; grimace.

contorsionniste [kɔ̃tɔrsjɔˈnist], *n.* contortionist.

contour [kɔ̃ˈtuːr], *n.m.* circuit, circumference; contour, outline.

contourné [kɔ̃turˈne], *a.* distorted, bizarre.

contournement [kɔ̃turnəˈmɑ̃], *n.m.* outlining, tracing; winding, convolution; *route de contournement*, by-pass (*road*).

contourner [kɔ̃turˈne], *v.t.* to outline; to distort, to twist; to twist, turn, go *or* wind round. **se contourner**, *v.r.* to grow crooked, to become bent.

contractant [kɔ̃trakˈtɑ̃], *a. partie contractante*, contracting party.—*n.m.* (*fem.* -e) stipulator.

contracté [kɔ̃trakˈte], *a.* contracted, shortened.

contracter [kɔ̃trakˈte], *v.t.* to contract; to covenant, to stipulate, to bargain; to make a contract; to acquire. **se contracter**, *v.r.* to contract, to shrink; to shorten; to be settled by contract.

contraction [kɔ̃trakˈsjɔ̃], *n.f.* contraction.

contractuel [kɔ̃trakˈtɥɛl], *a.* (*fem.* -elle) stipulated, done by contract.

contractuellement [kɔ̃traktɥɛlˈmɑ̃], *adv.* by contract.

contradicteur [kɔ̃tradikˈtœːr], *n.m.* contradictor; (*Law*) adversary.

contradiction [kɔ̃tradikˈsjɔ̃], *n.f.* contradiction, denial; opposition; discrepancy.

contradictoire [kɔ̃tradikˈtwaːr], *a.* contradictory, inconsistent, conflicting; *examen contradictoire*, cross-examination.

contraindre [kɔ̃ˈtrɛ̃ːdr], *v.t. irr.* (*conjug. like* CRAINDRE) to constrain, to compel, to coerce; to restrain; to squeeze. **se contraindre**, *v.r.* to restrain oneself, to refrain.

contraint [kɔ̃ˈtrɛ̃], *a.* constrained, forced.

contrainte [kɔ̃ˈtrɛ̃ːt], *n.f.* constraint, compulsion, coercion; restraint; uneasiness.

contraire [kɔ̃ˈtreːr], *a.* contrary, opposite, inconsistent; adverse; prejudicial.—*n.m.* contrary, opposite, reverse.

contrairement [kɔ̃trɛrˈmɑ̃], *adv.* contrarily, in opposition.

contralte [kɔ̃ˈtralt], **contralto** [kɔ̃tralˈto], *n.m.* contralto, counter-tenor.

contrariant [kɔ̃traˈrjɑ̃], *a.* thwarting, annoying.

contrarier [kɔ̃traˈrje], *v.t.* to thwart, to counteract, to baffle; to annoy; to disappoint.

83

contrariété [kɔ̃trarje'te], *n.f.* contrariety, contradiction; annoyance; hindrance, disappointment; *quelle contrariété!* how annoying!

contrastant [kɔ̃tras'tɑ̃], *a.* contrasting.

contraste [kɔ̃'trast], *n.m.* contrast, opposition.

contraster [kɔ̃tras'te], *v.t., v.i.* to contrast.

contrat [kɔ̃'tra], *n.m.* contract, deed; agreement, bargain.

contravention [kɔ̃travɑ̃'sjɔ̃], *n.f.* contravention.

contre [kɔ̃:tr], *prep.* against, versus, contrary to; close up against, near; in exchange for; *ci-contre,* opposite, in the margin; *par contre,* on the other hand; *pour et contre,* pro and con.—*adv.* against.—*n.m.* the opposite side of the question; *le pour et le contre,* the pros and cons.

contre-allée [kɔ̃tra'le], *n.f.* side lane, side alley.

contre-amiral [kɔ̃trami'ral], *n.m.* (*pl.* **contre-amiraux**) rear-admiral.

contre-attaque [kɔ̃tra'tak], *n.f.* (*Mil.*) counter-attack.

contre-avions [kɔ̃tra'vjɔ̃], *a.* anti-aircraft.

contrebalancer [kɔ̃trəbalɑ̃'se], *v.t.* (*conjug. like* COMMENCER) to counterbalance, to counterpoise.

contrebande [kɔ̃trə'bɑ̃:d], *n.f.* contraband, smuggling; smuggled goods.

contrebandier [kɔ̃trəbɑ̃'dje], *n.m.* smuggler, gunrunner; smuggling vessel.

contre-bas (en) [ɑ̃kɔ̃trə'ba], *adv.* downwards.

contrebasse [kɔ̃trə'ba:s], *n.f.* double bass.

contre-bord (à) [akɔ̃trə'bɔ:r], *adv.* (*Naut.*) on the opposite tack.

contre-boutant [kɔ̃trəbu'tɑ̃], **contre-boutement** [kɔ̃trəbut'mɑ̃], *n.m.* abutment, buttress.

contre-bouter [kɔ̃trəbu'te], *v.t.* to buttress; to shore up.

contrecarrer [kɔ̃trəka're], *v.t.* to thwart, to oppose.

contre-cœur [kɔ̃trə'kœ:r], *n.m.* chimney-back; *à contre-cœur,* reluctantly.

contre-coup [kɔ̃trə'ku], *n.m.* rebound, repercussion; (*fig.*) consequence, result; *par contre-coup,* as a consequence.

contredanse [kɔ̃trə'dɑ̃:s], *n.f.* quadrille.

contredire [kɔ̃trə'di:r], *v.t. irr.* (*conjug. like* MÉDIRE) to contradict, to gainsay; (*Law*) to disprove. **se contredire,** *v.r.* to contradict oneself; to be contradictory.

contredisant [kɔ̃trədi'zɑ̃], *a.* contradicting.

contredit [kɔ̃trə'di], *n.m.* contradiction; answer, reply; *sans contredit,* incontestably.

contrée [kɔ̃'tre], *n.f.* country, region, district.

contre-échange [kɔ̃tre'ʃɑ̃:ʒ], *n.m.* mutual exchange.

contre-écrou [kɔ̃tre'kru], *n.m.* lock nut.

contre-épreuve [kɔ̃tre'prœ:v], *n.f.* (*Engraving*) counter-proof; (*fig.*) feeble imitation.

contre-espionnage [kɔ̃trespjɔ'na:ʒ], *n.m.* counter-espionage.

contrefaçon [kɔ̃trəfa'sɔ̃], *n.f.* counterfeiting, forgery.

contrefacteur [kɔ̃trəfak'tœ:r], *n.m.* counterfeiter (*of coins etc.*); forger (*of bills etc.*); infringer (*of patents etc.*).

contrefaire [kɔ̃trə'fɛ:r], *v.t. irr.* (*conjug. like* FAIRE) to counterfeit, to imitate; to copy; to forge; to mimic; to disguise. **se contrefaire,** *v.r.* to dissemble, to sham.

contrefaiseur [kɔ̃trəfə'zœ:r], *n.m.* (*fem.* -euse) counterfeiter, mimic, imitator.

contrefait [kɔ̃trə'fɛ], *a.* counterfeit; deformed.

contre-fiche [kɔ̃trə'fiʃ], *n.f.* (*Carp.*) prop, strut.

contre-haut (en) [ɑ̃kɔ̃trə'o], *adv.* upwards.

contre-jour [kɔ̃trə'ʒu:r], *n.m.* (*Phot.*) low light; *à contre-jour,* against the light.

contremaître [kɔ̃trə'mɛ:tr], *n.m.* overseer, foreman.

contremander [kɔ̃trəmɑ̃'de], *v.t.* to countermand.

contremarche [kɔ̃trə'marʃ], *n.f.* countermarch.

contremarcher [kɔ̃trəmar'ʃe], *v.i.* to countermarch.

contremarque [kɔ̃trə'mark], *n.f.* countermark; (*Theat.*) pass-out check.

contre-mesure [kɔ̃trəmə'zy:r], *n.f.* countermeasure.

contre-offensive [kɔ̃trɔfɑ̃'si:v], *n.f.* counterattack.

contre-partie [kɔ̃trəpar'ti], *n.f.* counterpart; (*fig.*) opposite, contrary; return match.

contre-pédaler [kɔ̃trəpeda'le], *v.i.* to back-pedal.

contre-pied [kɔ̃trə'pje], *n.m.* (*Hunt.*) backscent; (*fig.*) reverse way, contrary.

contre-plaqué [kɔ̃trəpla'ke], *a.* laminated. —*n.m.* two- (*or* three-) ply wood.

contrepoids [kɔ̃trə'pwa], *n.m. inv.* counterpoise, counter-balance; (*fig.*) equilibrium.

contre-poil [kɔ̃trə'pwal], *n.m.* wrong way of the hair *or* of the nap; *à contre-poil,* against the grain.

contrepoint [kɔ̃trə'pwɛ̃], *n.m.* counterpoint.

contrepoison [kɔ̃trəpwa'zɔ̃], *n.m.* antidote, counter-poison.

contre-poser [kɔ̃trəpo'ze], *v.t.* to misplace; (*Comm.*) to set down wrong.

contrer [kɔ̃'tre], *v.t.* (*Bridge*) to double.

contre-ressort [kɔ̃trərə'sɔ:r], *n.m.* shock absorber.

contre-révolution [kɔ̃trərevɔly'sjɔ̃], *n.f.* counter-revolution.

contre-saison (à) [akɔ̃trəsɛ'zɔ̃], *adv. phr.* (*flower*) produced out of season; ill-timed.

contresens [kɔ̃trə'sɑ̃:s], *n.m.* contrary sense; wrong construction *or* meaning; mistranslation; wrong side (*of material*).

contresigner [kɔ̃trəsi'ne], *v.t.* to countersign.

contretemps [kɔ̃trə'tɑ̃], *n.m. inv.* untoward accident, disappointment, mishap; (*Mus.*) syncopation; *à contretemps,* at the wrong time.

contre-torpilleur [kɔ̃trətɔrpi'jœ:r], *n.m.* torpedo-boat destroyer.

contrevenant [kɔ̃trəv'nɑ̃], *n.m.* (*fem.* -e) contravener, infringer, offender, transgressor.

contrevenir [kɔ̃trəv'ni:r], *v.i. irr.* (*conjug. like* TENIR) to contravene, infringe.

contrevent [kɔ̃trə'vɑ̃], *n.m.* outside window-shutter.

contribuable [kɔ̃tri'bɥabl], *a.* taxable. —*n.* tax-payer.

contribuer [kɔ̃tri'bɥe], *v.i.* to contribute, to pay; (*fig.*) to conduce, to be an accessory (*à*).

contributaire [kɔ̃triby'tɛːr], *a.* contributory.

contribution [kɔ̃triby'sjɔ̃], *n.f.* contribution; tax; share, portion; *contribution foncière*, land tax.

contrister [kɔ̃tris'te], *v.t.* to grieve, to vex, to sadden.

contrit [kɔ̃'tri], *a.* contrite, penitent; afflicted.

contrition [kɔ̃tri'sjɔ̃], *n.f.* contrition.

contrôlable [kɔ̃tro'labl], *a.* that may be checked, verified.

contrôle [kɔ̃'troːl], *n.m.* muster roll; roll, list; controller's office; stamp, hall-mark; *(Theat.)* ticket-checking counter; *(fig.)* control, censure.

contrôler [kɔ̃tro'le], *v.t.* to register; to stamp; to check, to verify; to audit; to censure.

contrôleur [kɔ̃tro'lœːr], *n.m.* *(fem. -euse)* controller; *(Taxes, Theat., Rail.)* inspector; time-keeper; ticket collector; *(fig.)* critic.

controuver [kɔ̃tru've], *v.t.* to forge, to fabricate.

controversable [kɔ̃trovɛr'sabl], *a.* controvertible, controversial.

controverse [kɔ̃trɔ'vɛrs], *n.f.* controversy, discussion, dispute.

controverser [kɔ̃trɔvɛr'se], *v.t.* to dispute, to discuss.

contumace [kɔ̃ty'mas], *n.f.* contumacy, non-appearance *or* default, contempt of court; obstinacy.—*a.* contumacious.—*n.* defaulter.

contus [kɔ̃'ty], *a.* bruised, contused.

contusion [kɔ̃ty'zjɔ̃], *n.f.* contusion, bruise.

contusionner [kɔ̃tyzjɔ'ne], *v.t.* to contuse, to bruise.

convaincant [kɔ̃vɛ̃'kã], *a.* convincing.

convaincre [kɔ̃'vɛ̃:kr], *v.t. irr. (conjug. like* VAINCRE) to convince; to persuade. **se convaincre,** *v.r.* to convince oneself.

convaincu [kɔ̃vɛ̃'ky], *a.* convinced; sincere; convicted.

convalescence [kɔ̃valɛ'sãːs], *n.f.* convalescence.

convalescent [kɔ̃valɛ'sã], *a.* and *n.m. (fem. -e)* convalescent (person).

convection [kɔ̃vɛk'sjɔ̃], *n.f.* convection.

convenable [kɔ̃v'nabl], *a.* suitable, fit, proper; convenient; becoming.

convenablement [kɔ̃vənablə'mã], *adv.* suitably, becomingly, decently.

convenance [kɔ̃v'nãːs], *n.f.* fitness, propriety; seasonableness *(of time)*; decency, seemliness; *(pl.)* propriety, decorum; *mariage de convenance,* marriage of convenience.

convenir [kɔ̃v'niːr], *v.i. irr. (conjug. like* TENIR, *but with aux.* ÊTRE) to agree; to admit, to own, to acknowledge *(de)*; *(with aux.* AVOIR) to suit, to fit, to match; *(impers.)* to be fitting. **se convenir,** *v.r.* to suit each other, to agree.

convention [kɔ̃vã'sjɔ̃], *n.f.* agreement, treaty; *(social and other)* convention; *(pl.)* conditions *(of an agreement).*

conventionnel [kɔ̃vãsjɔ'nɛl], *a. (fem. -elle)* conventional.

conventionnellement [kɔ̃vãsjɔnɛl'mã], *adv.* by agreement.

convenu [kɔ̃v'ny], *a.* agreed; conventional; banal.

convergent [kɔ̃vɛr'ʒã], *a.* convergent.

converger [kɔ̃vɛr'ʒe], *v.i. (conjug. like* MANGER) to converge.

conversation [kɔ̃vɛrsa'sjɔ̃], *n.f.* conversation, converse, talk.

converse [kɔ̃'vɛrs], *a.* and *n.f. (Log.)* converse; *(Math.)* inverted.

converser [kɔ̃vɛr'se], *v.i.* to converse, to discourse.

conversible [kɔ̃vɛr'sibl], [CONVERTIBLE].

conversion [kɔ̃vɛr'sjɔ̃], *n.f.* conversion; transformation; change.

converti [kɔ̃vɛr'ti], *n.m. (fem. -e)* convert.

convertible [kɔ̃vɛr'tibl], *a.* convertible.

convertir [kɔ̃vɛr'tiːr], *v.t.* to convert, to transform, to change, to turn. **se convertir,** *v.r.* to be converted, to turn.

convertissement [kɔ̃vɛrtis'mã], *n.m.* conversion.

convexe [kɔ̃'vɛks], *a.* convex.

convexité [kɔ̃vɛksi'te], *n.f.* convexity.

conviction [kɔ̃vik'sjɔ̃], *n.f.* conviction, convincing proof.

convié [kɔ̃'vje], *a.* invited.—*n.m. (fem. -ée)* guest.

convier [kɔ̃'vje], *v.t.* to invite, to bid; *(fig.)* to urge.

convive [kɔ̃'viv], *n.* guest; fellow diner.

convocation [kɔ̃vɔka'sjɔ̃], *n.f.* convocation; summons.

convoi [kɔ̃'vwa], *n.m. (Mil., Navy)* convoy; *(Rail. etc.)* train; *convoi funèbre,* funeral procession.

convoiter [kɔ̃vwa'te], *v.t.* to covet, to hanker after.

convoitise [kɔ̃vwa'tiːz], *n.f.* covetousness; lust.

convolution [kɔ̃vɔly'sjɔ̃], *n.f.* convolution.

convolvulus [kɔ̃vɔlvy'lyːs], *n.m. (Bot.)* convolvulus.

convoquer [kɔ̃vɔ'ke], *v.t.* to convoke, to convene; to summon.

convoyer [kɔ̃vwa'je], *v.t. (conjug. like* EMPLOYER) to convoy, to escort.

convoyeur [kɔ̃vwa'jœːr], *n.m.* convoy *(ship)*; *(Mech.)* conveyor.

convulser [kɔ̃vyl'se], *v.t.* to convulse. **se convulser,** *v.r.* to be *or* become convulsed.

convulsif [kɔ̃vyl'sif], *a. (fem. -sive)* convulsive.

convulsion [kɔ̃vyl'sjɔ̃], *n.f.* convulsion.

convulsionner [kɔ̃vylsjɔ'ne], *v.t. (Med.)* to convulse.

convulsivement [kɔ̃vylsiv'mã], *adv.* convulsively.

coolie or **coulis** [ku'li], *n.m.* coolie.

coopérateur [koɔpera'tœːr], *n.m. (fem. -trice)* co-operator, fellow workman.—*a. (fem. -trice)* co-operating.

coopératif [koɔpera'tif], *a. (fem. -tive)* co-operative.

coopération [koɔpera'sjɔ̃], *n.f.* co-operation.

coopérer [koɔpe're], *v.i. (conjug. like* CÉDER) to co-operate.

coopter [koɔp'te], *v.t.* to co-opt.

coordination [koɔrdina'sjɔ̃], *n.f.* co-ordination.

coordonné [koɔrdɔ'ne], *a.* co-ordinate.—*n.f. pl. (-ées) (Gram., Geom.)* co-ordinates.

coordonner [koɔrdɔ'ne], *v.t.* to co-ordinate.

copain [kɔ'pɛ̃], *n.m. (colloq.)* pal, mate.

copal [kɔ'pal], *n.m.* copal.

copeau [kɔ'po], *n.m. (pl. -eaux)* shaving, chip *(of wood).*

Copenhague [kɔpə'nag], *f.* Copenhagen.

cophte [COPTE].
copie [kɔ'pi], n.f. copy, transcript; reproduction; (Print.) 'copy'; candidate's paper.
copier [kɔ'pje], v.t. to copy; to imitate; to
mimic.
copieusement [kɔpjøz'mã], adv. copiously,
heartily (of drinking, eating).
copieux [kɔ'pjø], a. (fem. -euse) copious,
plentiful.
co-pilote [kopi'lɔt], n.m. second pilot.
copiste [kɔ'pist], n. copier, transcriber,
copyist.
copte or cophte [kɔpt], a. Coptic.—n. (Copte,
Cophte) Copt.
coq [kɔk], n.m. cock, rooster; cock- (as opposed
to hen); weathercock; au chant du coq, at
cock-crow; coq de bruyère, grouse; coq
d'Inde, turkey cock; poids coq, (Box.)
bantam weight.
coq-à-l'âne [kɔka'laːn], n.m. inv. nonsense,
cock-and-bull story.
coque [kɔk], n.f. shell (of eggs, walnuts, fruits,
snails etc.); cocoon; cockle-shell (small
boat); (Naut.) hull.
coquelicot [kɔkli'ko], n.m. corn-poppy.
coqueluche [kɔ'klyʃ], n.f. the rage, favorite;
(Med.) whooping-cough.
coquerico [kɔkri'ko], n.m. cock-a-doodle-doo.
coqueriquer [kɔkri'ke], v.i. to crow.
coquet [kɔ'kɛ], a. (fem. -ette) coquettish;
stylish, smart.—n.m. (fem. -ette) coquette,
flirt; dandy.
coqueter [kɔk'te], v.i. (conjug. like APPELER)
to coquet, to flirt.
coquetier [kɔk'tje], n.m. egg merchant,
poulterer; egg cup.
coquetterie [kɔkɛ'tri], n.f. coquettishness,
flirtation; affectation (in dress etc.).
coquillage [kɔki'jaː3], n.m. shell-fish; shell.
coquille [kɔ'kiːj], n.f. shell (of shell-fish, egg,
fruits etc.); (Cook.) Dutch oven; pat (of
butter); (Print.) wrong letter; thumb (of a
latch); (Ornament) conch.
coquin [kɔ'kɛ̃], a. roguish; rascally.—n.m.
knave, rascal, rogue, scamp.—n.f. (-e)
slut, hussy, jade.
coquinerie [kɔkin'ri], n.f. knavery, rascality,
roguery.
coquinet [kɔki'nɛ], n.m. little rascal.
cor (1) [kɔːr], n.m. horn, hunting horn.
cor (2) [kɔːr], n.m. corn (on the foot).
cor (3) [kɔːr], n.m. tine (of antler).
corail [kɔ'raːj], n.m. (pl. -aux) coral.
corailleur [kɔra'jœːr], n.m. coral fisher;
coral-fishing boat.
Coran [kɔ'rã], n.m. Koran.
corbeau [kɔr'bo], n.m. (pl. -eaux) crow;
raven.
corbeille [kɔr'bɛːj], n.f. flat, wide basket.
corbillard [kɔrbi'jaːr], n.m. hearse.
corbillon [kɔrbi'jɔ̃], n.m. small basket;
crambo (game).
corbin [kɔr'bɛ̃], n.m. crow.
corbine [kɔr'bin], n.f. carrion crow.
corbleu! [kɔr'blø], int. by Jove!
cordage [kɔr'daː3], n.m. cord, rope, cordage,
rigging.
corde [kɔrd], n.f. cord, rope; twine, twist;
string (musical instrument, racquet); line;
(Mus., Geom. etc.) chord; tone, note; corde
à boyau, catgut.
cordé (1) [kɔr'de], a. twisted, corded.

cordé (2) [kɔr'de], a. cordate, heart-shaped.
cordeau [kɔr'do], n.m. (pl. -eaux) cord; line;
fuse; tape.
cordée [kɔr'de], n.f. fishing line; line of
roped mountaineers.
cordeler [kɔrdə'le], v.t. (conjug. like APPELER)
to twist, to twine.
cordelette [kɔrdə'lɛt], n.f. small cord; string.
cordelier [kɔrdə'lje], n.m. Franciscan friar.
cordelière [kɔrdə'ljɛːr], n.f. girdle (of
dressing-gown etc.).
cordelle [kɔr'dɛl], n.f. towline, tow-rope.
corder [kɔr'de], v.t. to twist (into cord); to
cord; to bind with a cord; to string (racquet).
se corder, v.r. to be corded; to become
stringy (of plants etc.).
corderie [kɔrdə'ri], n.f. rope walk.
cordial [kɔr'djal], a. (m. pl. -aux) cordial,
hearty, sincere.—n.m. cordial.
cordialement [kɔrdjal'mã], adv. cordially,
heartily, sincerely.
cordialité [kɔrdjali'te], n.f. cordiality, heartiness.
cordier [kɔr'dje], n.m. rope maker.
Cordillères [kɔrdi'jɛːr], les, f.pl. the Cor-
dilleras.
cordite [kɔr'dit], n.f. cordite.
cordon [kɔr'dɔ̃], n.m. strand (of a rope); twist,
string; cord; ribbon (of an order); border,
edging; cordon bleu, blue ribbon, first-
rate cook.
cordonner [kɔrdɔ'ne], v.t. to twist, to twine,
to braid; to mill (coins).
cordonnerie [kɔrdɔn'ri], n.f. shoe-making;
cobbler's shop.
cordonnet [kɔrdɔ'nɛ], n.m. twist; milled edge
(of coins).
cordonnier [kɔrdɔ'nje], n.m. shoe-maker.
Corée [kɔ're], la, f. Korea.
coréen [kɔre'ɛ̃], a. (fem. -enne) Korean.—
n.m. Korean (language); (Coréen, fem.
-enne) Korean (person).
coriace [kɔ'rjas], a. tough, leathery; (fig.)
close, niggardly; dogged.
coricide [kɔri'sid], n.m. corn cure.
corinthien [kɔrɛ̃'tjɛ̃], a. (fem. -enne)
Corinthian.—n.m. (Corinthien, fem. -enne)
Corinthian.
coris [CAURI].
corli [kɔr'li], courlis [kur'li], corlieu
[kɔr'ljø], n.m. curlew.
cormoran [kɔrmɔ'rã], n.m. cormorant.
cornac [kɔr'nak], n.m. elephant driver,
mahout; mentor.
corne [kɔrn], n.f. horn, hoof; shoe horn;
dog's-ear (on books, leaves); chapeau à
trois cornes, three-cornered hat.
corné [kɔr'ne], a. corneous, horny.
cornée [kɔr'ne], n.f. cornea.
corneille [kɔr'nɛːj], n.f. crow, rook, jackdaw.
cornement [kɔrnə'mã], n.m. buzzing in the
ears.
cornemuse [kɔrnə'myːz], n.f. bagpipes.
corner (1) [kɔr'ne], v.t. to blurt out, to
trumpet; to dog's-ear (a leaf).—v.i. to blow,
wind or sound a horn; to tingle (of the ears).
corner (2) [kɔr'nɛr], n.m. (Ftb.) corner (-kick).
cornet [kɔr'nɛ], n.m. horn, hooter; ink horn;
cone.
cornette [kɔr'nɛt], n.f. mob-cap; pennant
of cavalry.
corniche [kɔr'niʃ], n.f. cornice; ledge.

cornichon [kɔrni'ʃɔ̃], *n.m.* gherkin; (*fig.*) greenhorn.

corniste [kɔr'nist], *n.* horn player.

Cornouaille [kɔr'nwaːj], **la**, *f.* Cornwall.

cornu [kɔr'ny], *a.* horned; angular, cornered; (*fig.*) absurd.

cornue [kɔr'ny], *n.f.* (*Chem.*) retort.

corollaire [kɔrɔ'leːr], *n.m.* corollary.

corolle [kɔ'rɔl], *n.f.* corolla.

coronaire [kɔrɔ'nɛːr], *a.* (*Anat.*) coronary.

coronal [kɔrɔ'nal], *a.* (*m. pl.* **-aux**) (*Anat.*) coronal.

corporation [kɔrpɔra'sjɔ̃], *n.f.* corporation, corporate body.

corporel [kɔrpɔ'rɛl], *a.* (*fem.* **-elle**) corporal, bodily.

corps [kɔːr], *n.m.* body; matter, substance; thickness, consistence; chief part; corporation, company; society, college; corps; fellow creature; *à corps perdu*, desperately; *à son corps défendant*, (*fig.*) reluctantly; *corps à corps*, hand to hand, (*Box.*) in-fight(ing); *corps morts*, (*Naut.*) fixed moorings; *garde du corps*, lifeguard; *sombrer corps et biens*, to founder with all hands.

corpulence [kɔrpy'lɑ̃ːs], *n.f.* corpulence, stoutness.

corpulent [kɔrpy'lɑ̃], *a.* corpulent, stout.

corpuscule [kɔrpys'kyl], *n.m.* corpuscule, corpuscle.

correct [kɔ'rɛkt], *a.* correct, accurate.

correctement [kɔrɛkt'mɑ̃], *adv.* correctly, accurately.

correctif [kɔrɛk'tif], *a.* (*fem.* **-tive**) corrective. —*n.m.* corrective.

correction [kɔrɛk'sjɔ̃], *n.f.* correction; correctness, accuracy; (*Print.*) reading, alteration (*of a proof etc.*); (*fig.*) reprimand, reproof; punishment; thrashing.

correctionnel [kɔrɛksjɔ'nɛl], *a.* (*fem.* **-elle**) within the jurisdiction of the *tribunal de police correctionnelle*, court of petty sessions.

corrélation [kɔrela'sjɔ̃], *n.f.* correlation.

correspondance [kɔrɛspɔ̃'dɑ̃ːs], *n.f.* correspondence; connection; intercourse; conformity; (*Rail.*) connection.

correspondant [kɔrɛspɔ̃'dɑ̃], *a.* correspondent, corresponding. —*n.m.* (*fem.* **-ᵉ**) correspondent, corresponding member.

correspondre [kɔrɛs'pɔ̃ːdr], *v.i.* to correspond, to communicate, to be in correspondence; to agree.

corridor [kɔri'dɔːr], *n.m.* corridor, gallery, passage.

corrigé [kɔri'ʒe], *n.m.* corrected (*schoolboy's*) exercise; key (*book*), crib.

corriger [kɔri'ʒe], *v.t.* (*conjug. like* MANGER) to correct, to rectify; to repair, to amend; to reprove, to chide, to chastise. **se corriger**, *v.r.* to correct oneself, to amend, to reform.

corroboration [kɔrɔbɔra'sjɔ̃], *n.f.* corroboration, strengthening.

corroborer [kɔrɔbɔ're], *v.t.* to strengthen; to corroborate.

corrodant [kɔrɔ'dɑ̃], *a.* corroding, corrosive.

corroder [kɔrɔ'de], *v.t.* to corrode.

corrompre [kɔ'rɔ̃ːpr], *v.t.* (*conjug. like* ROMPRE) to corrupt, to infect; to spoil; to taint (*meat*); (*fig.*) to pervert; to bribe. **se**

corrompre, *v.r.* to grow corrupt; to become tainted.

corrompu [kɔrɔ̃'py], *a.* corrupted, unsound; bribed.

corrosif [kɔrɔ'zif], *a.* (*fem.* **-sive**) and *n.m.* corrosive.

corrosion [kɔrɔ'zjɔ̃], *n.f.* corrosion.

corroyer [kɔrwa'je], *v.t.* (*conjug. like* EMPLOYER) to curry (*leather*); to plane (*wood*).

corroyeur [kɔrwa'jœːr], *n.m.* currier.

corrupteur [kɔryp'tœːr], *a.* (*fem.* **-trice**) corrupting, perverting, infectious. —*n.m.* (*fem.* **-trice**) corrupter, seducer; briber.

corruptibilité [kɔryptibili'te], *n.f.* corruptibility.

corruptible [kɔryp'tibl], *a.* corruptible.

corruptif [kɔryp'tif], *a.* (*fem.* **-tive**) corruptive.

corruption [kɔryp'sjɔ̃], *n.f.* corruption; rottenness; (*fig.*) depravity; (*Polit.*) bribery.

corsage [kɔr'saːʒ], *n.m.* chest (*of the body*); corsage, bodice.

corsaire [kɔr'sɛːr], *n.m.* privateer, corsair; (*fig.*) shark.

Corse [kɔrs], **la**, *f.* Corsica.—*n.* Corsican (*person*).

corse [kɔrs], *a.* Corsican.

corsé [kɔr'se], *a.* rich, full-bodied; (*colloq.*) strong, thick; (*of stories etc.*) spicy.

corser [kɔr'se], *v.t.* to stiffen, to thicken; to complicate.

corset [kɔr'sɛ], *n.m.* corset, stays.

corsetier [kɔrsə'tje], *n.m.* (*fem.* **-ière**) corset maker.

cortège [kɔr'tɛːʒ], *n.m.* train, retinue, suite, procession.

corvée [kɔr've], *n.f.* (*Feud.*) forced *or* statute labor; fatigue party; (*fig.*) drudgery.

corvette [kɔr'vɛt], *n.f.* corvette, sloop of war.

Cosaque [kɔ'zak], *n.m.* Cossack.

cosinus [kɔsi'nyːs], *n.m.* cosine.

cosmétique [kɔsme'tik], *a.* and *n.m.* cosmetic.

cosmique [kɔs'mik], *a.* cosmic.

cosmographie [kɔsmɔgra'fi], *n.f.* cosmography.

cosmopolite [kɔsmɔpɔ'lit], *n.* cosmopolite. —*a.* cosmopolitan.

cosmos [kɔs'mos], *n.m.* cosmos.

cosse [kɔs], *n.f.* pod, shell, husk, rind.

cossu [kɔ'sy], *a.* substantial, wealthy.

costume [kɔs'tym], *n.m.* costume, dress; uniform.

costumer [kɔsty'me], *v.t.* to dress (*in a certain style etc.*). **se costumer**, *v.r.* to dress (*oneself*) up.

costumier [kɔsty'mje], *n.m.* (*fem.* **-ière**) costumier.

cote [kɔt], *n.f.* quota, share; letter, number, figure (*to indicate order etc.*); (*St. Exch.*) quotation; (*Comm.*) price list; odds.

côte [koːt], *n.f.* rib (*of the body, cloth, fruit etc.*); slope, hill; shore, sea coast; *à mi-côte*, half-way up.

côté [ko'te], *n.m.* side; part, quarter, hand, way, direction; face, aspect; *à côté de*, by, near; *d'à côté*, adjoining, next.

coté [kɔ'te], *a.* marked; classed; backed; *point coté*, (*on a map*) trig-point; *cheval bien coté*, well-backed horse.

coteau [kɔ'to], *n.m.* (*pl.* **-eaux**) slope; little hill.

côtelette [koˈtlɛt], *n.f.* cutlet, chop.

coter [koˈte], *v.t.* to number; to price; (*St. Exch.*) to quote.

coterie [koˈtri], *n.f.* coterie, set, circle, clique.

cothurne [koˈtyrn], *n.m.* buskin.

côtier [koˈtje], *a.* (*fem.* -**ière**) coasting.—*n.m.* coaster (*ship*).

cotillon [kotiˈjɔ̃], *n.m.* under-petticoat; cotillion.

cotisation [kotizaˈsjɔ̃], *n.f.* assessment, quota, share; subscription.

cotiser [kotiˈze], *v.t.* to assess, to rate. **se cotiser**, *v.r.* to club together; to get up a subscription, to subscribe.

coton [koˈtɔ̃], *n.m.* cotton; fluff, down (*of fruit, and hair on the face*);absorbent cotton.

cotonnade [kotoˈnad], *n.f.* cotton cloth.

cotonné [kotoˈne], *a.* covered with *or* full of cotton; downy; woolly (*of hair*); padded.

cotonner [kotoˈne], *v.t.* to fill *or* to stuff with cotton; to pad. **se cotonner**, *v.r.* to be covered with down.

cotonneux [kotoˈnø], *a.* (*fem.* -**euse**) cottony, downy; spongy, mealy.

cotonnier [kotoˈnje], *n.m.* cotton bush.

côtoyer [kotwaˈje], *v.t.* (*conjug. like* EMPLOYER) to go by the side of, to skirt; to coast; (*fig.*) to keep close to.

cotre [koˈtr], *n.m.* cutter (*vessel*).

cotret [koˈtrɛ], *n.m.* faggot; stick.

cottage [koˈtaːʒ], *n.m.* cottage.

cotte [kot], *n.f.* short petticoat; (*engineer's*) overalls.

cotuteur [kotyˈtœːr], *n.m.* (*fem.* -**trice**) joint guardian.

cou [ku], *n.m.* neck.

couac [kwak], *n.m.* false note; squawk.

couard [kwaːr], *a.* coward, cowardly.—*n.m.* (*fem.* -**e**) coward.

couardise [kwarˈdiːz], *n.f.* cowardice.

couchage [kuˈʃaːʒ], *n.m.* act of lying in bed; bed, night's lodging; bedding.

couchant [kuˈʃɑ̃], *a.* setting; lying; (*fig.*) fawning; **un chien couchant**, a setter.—*n.m.* west; (*fig.*) decline.

couche [kuʃ], *n.f.* bed, couch; confinement; diaper; layer, row; (*Min.*) seam; (*Gard.*) hotbed, bed; coat (*of varnish or color*); (*fig.*) social stratum.

couché [kuˈʃe], *a.* in bed, gone to bed, lying down, recumbent; (*Her.*) couchant.

couchée [kuˈʃe], *n.f.* act of lying down; sleeping place; night's lodging.

coucher [kuˈʃe], *v.t.* to put to bed; to lay down; to knock down; to lay on; to stake.—*v.i.* to sleep, to lie (down), to rest; **coucher à la belle étoile**, to sleep in the open air. **se coucher**, *v.r.* to go to bed; to lie down; to set, to go down (*of the sun etc.*).—*n.m.* going to bed; bed time; setting (*of the sun etc.*).

couchette [kuˈʃɛt], *n.f.* small bed, crib; berth; bunk (*on a ship*); **wagon à couchettes**, second-class sleeper.

coucou [kuˈku], *n.m.* cuckoo; cuckoo clock; (*Bot.*) cowslip.

coude [kud], *n.m.* elbow; bend, angle; turning.

coudé [kuˈde], *a.* bent, elbowed, cranked.

coudée [kuˈde], *n.f.* length of arm from elbow to tip of middle finger, cubit.

cou-de-pied [kudˈpje], *n.m.* (*pl.* **cous-de-pied**) instep.

couder [kuˈde], *v.t.* to bend, to make an elbow in. **se couder**, *v.r.* to elbow, to form an elbow.

coudoyer [kudwaˈje], *v.t.* (*conjug. like* EMPLOYER) to elbow, to jostle. **se coudoyer**, *v.r.* to elbow *or* jostle each other.

coudraie [kuˈdrɛ], *n.f.* hazel copse; filbert orchard.

coudre [kudr], *v.t. irr.* to sew, to stitch; (*fig.*) to attach, to connect.

coudrier [kuˈdrje], *n.m.* hazel tree.

couenne [kwan], *n.f.* scraped pig-skin; crackling (*of pork*); rind; (*Med.*) birth-mark.

couette [kwɛt], **coit(t)e** (2) [kwat], *n.f.* feather-bed; sea-gull; (*hare's*) scut.

couguar [kuˈgaːr], *n.m.* cougar, puma.

coulage [kuˈlaːʒ], *n.m.* flow (*of metal in fusion*); melting, casting; leakage, waste; pilferage.

coulant [kuˈlɑ̃], *a.* flowing, smooth, natural (*of s.yle etc.*); (*fig.*) easy; **nœud coulant**, slip knot.—*n.m.* sliding ring (*for a necktie, umbrella etc.*).

coulé [kuˈle], *n.m.* (*Mus.*) slur; (*Billiards*) follow through; (*Swim.*) plunge.

coulée [kuˈle], *n.f.* running hand (*of writing*); (*Metal.*) tapping; flow, rush (*of a torrent etc.*); (*Hunt.*) track, path.

couler [kuˈle], *v.t.* to cast; to strain; to slip (*dans*); to sink, to run down; (*Mus.*) to slur.—*v.i.* to flow; to glide; to trickle; to leak; to slip away (*of time etc.*); to founder (*of a ship etc.*). **se couler**, *v.r.* to slip, to creep, to steal, to glide; to be cast (*of metals*).

couleur [kuˈlœːr], *n.f.* color; coloring-matter, paint; coloring; (*fig.*) appearance; pretence; suit (*at cards*).

couleuvre [kuˈlœːvr], *n.f.* (grass) snake.

coulis [kuˈli], *n.m.* strained juice from meat etc. slowly stewed.

coulisse [kuˈlis], *n.f.* groove, channel; running string; (*Theat.*) wing; (*fig.*) behind the scenes; **porte à coulisse**, sliding door; **faire les yeux en coulisse**, to make sheep's eyes.

coulissé [kuliˈse], *a.* grooved.

coulissier [kuliˈsje], *n.m.* stock jobber, outside broker.

couloir [kuˈlwaːr], *n.m.* passage, corridor, lobby, gangway.

couloire [kuˈlwaːr], *n.f.* colander, strainer.

coup [ku], *n.m.* blow, stroke, hit, thump, knock, stab, thrust; beat (*of a drum*); draft (*of liquids*); clap (*of thunder*); (*Artill.*) charge; gust (*of wind*); throw; shot; moment; bout; attempt; deed; event; **à coup sûr**, unquestionably; (*Ftb.*) **coup d'envoi**, kick-off; **coup d'œil**, glance; **coup de télé-phone**, telephone call; **le coup de grâce**, the finishing stroke; **tout à coup**, all of a sudden; **tout d'un coup**, all at once.

coupable [kuˈpabl], *a.* culpable, guilty.—*n.* guilty person, culprit.

coupage [kuˈpaːʒ], *n.m.* cutting; diluting (*of wine*); blending (*of spirits*).

coupant [kuˈpɑ̃], *a.* cutting, sharp.—*n.m.* edge (*of a sword etc.*).

coupe (1) [kup], *n.f.* cutting, felling (*of wood*); wood felled; the cut end; cut (*clothes etc.*); shape; (*Pros.*) cadence; (*Swim.*) overarm stroke.

coupe (2) [kup], *n.f.* cup, goblet, chalice; basin (*of a fountain etc.*).

coupé (1) [ku'pe], *a.* intersected; diluted; (*fig.*) laconic.

coupé (2) [ku'pe], *n.m.* coupé (*kind of brougham*); a dance step.

[In the following compounds *coupe* is *inv.*]

coupe-circuit [kupsir'kɥi], *n.m. inv.* cut-out, circuit breaker; fuse.

coupée [ku'pe], *n.f.* (*Naut.*) gangway; *échelle de coupée*, accommodation ladder.

coupe-file [kup'fil], *n.m. inv.* police pass.

coupe-gorge [kup'gɔrʒ], *n.m. inv.* cut-throat place, den.

coupe-jarret [kupʒa'rɛ], *n.m.* cut-throat, assassin, ruffian.

coupe-papier [kuppa'pje], *n.m. inv.* paper knife.

couper [ku'pe], *v.t.* to cut; to dock. to strike off; to clip, to pare; to geld; (*Mil.*) to intercept; to dilute (*milk, wine, with water*); to intersect; to interrupt.—*v.i.* to make an incision; to cut, to trump (*at cards*). **se couper**, *v.r.* to cut oneself; to intersect.

couperet [ku'prɛ], *n.m.* (*butcher's*) chopper; knife (*of guillotine*).

couperose [ku'pro:z], *n.f.* copperas.

couperosé [kupro'ze], *a.* blotched.

coupeur [ku'pœ:r], *n.m.* (*fem.* **-euse**) cutter. —*n.f.* (**-euse**) cutting machine.

(C) **coupe-vent** [kup'vɑ̃], *n.m.* wind breaker.

couplage [ku'plaʒ], *n.m.* coupling.

couple [kupl], *n.f.* brace, couple.—*n.m.* married couple; pair (*of animals, male and female*); (*Naut.*) frame.

coupler [ku'ple], *v.t.* to couple, to link.

couplet [ku'plɛ], *n.m.* couplet; verse of song; (*fig.*) tirade; (*Tech.*) hinge.

coupleur [ku'plœ:r], *n.m.* (*Elec.*) make-and-break, cut-out.

coupoir [ku'pwa:r], *n.m.* cutter (*instrument*).

coupole [ku'pɔl], *n.f.* cupola; (*Naut.*) revolving gun turret.

coupon [ku'pɔ̃], *n.m.* remnant; coupon; dividend check, check; (*Theat.*) ticket.

coupure [ku'py:r], *n.f.* cut, incision, slit; cutting; suppression; drain; (*Banking*) small note.

cour [ku:r], *n.f.* court (*of a prince, of justice etc.*); yard, courtyard; (*fig.*) courtsh.p, suit.

courage [ku'ra:ʒ], *n.m.* courage, daring; spirit, mettle; fortitude, greatness of soul.

courageusement [kuraʒøz'mɑ̃], *adv.* courageously, bravely, resolutely.

courageux [kura'ʒø], *a.* (*fem.* **-euse**) courageous, daring, fearless, plucky.

couramment [kura'mɑ̃], *adv.* fluently, readily.

courant [ku'rɑ̃], *a.* running; current, present; usual; fair, middling (*of goods*); lineal (*of measures*).—*n.m.* stream, current, tide; course (*of time etc.*); routine; present price; present (*time*).

courbage [kur'ba:ʒ], *n.m.* bending, curving.

courbatu [kurba'ty], *a.* foundered (*of horses*); stiff in the joints; (*Med.*) affected with lumbago.

courbature [kurba'ty:r], *n.f.* foundering, lameness; (*Path.*) stiffness in the limbs, lumbago.

courbaturer [kurbaty're], *v.t.* to make (*someone*) feel stiff all over.

courbe [kurb], *a.* curved, bent, crooked.—*n.f.* curve; (*Naut., Carp.*) knee; (*Vet.*) curb; (*Math.*) graph.

courber [kur'be], *v.t.* to curve, to bend, to warp, to make crooked.—*v.i.* to bend, to sag. **se courber**, *v.r.* to bend, to stoop; to bow down.

courbette [kur'bɛt], *n.f.* curvet; (*pl.*) bowing and scraping, cringing.

courbetter [kurbe'te], *v.i.* to curvet.

courbure [kur'by:r], *n.f.* curvature, curve; bend; sagging.

coureur [ku'rœ:r], *a.* (*fem.* **-euse**) swift.—*n.m.* runner, racer; hunter (*horse*); light porter; rover; rake, libertine; (*Mil.*) scout.

courge [kurʒ], *n.f.* gourd; *courge à la moelle*, vegetable marrow, squash.

courir [ku'ri:r], *v.t. irr.* to pursue; to travel over; to hunt; to frequent; to expose oneself to.—*v.i.* to run; to hasten; to ramble, to rove; to flow; to stretch; to circulate.

courlis [kur'li], **courlieu** [kur'ljø], *n.m.* curlew.

couronne [ku'ron], *n.f.* crown; coronet; wreath; crown (*a coin*).

couronnement [kuron'mɑ̃], *n.m.* crowning, coronation; completion.

couronner [kuro'ne], *v.t.* to crown; to award a prize, to honor (*avec*); to consummate; to wreathe.

courre [ku:r], *v.t.* only used in *chasse à courre*, hunting.

courrier [ku'rje], *n.m.* messenger, courier; mail, post; letters, correspondence.

courriériste [kurje'rist], *n.m.* columnist.

courroie [ku'rwa], *n.f.* strap, thong; driving belt or band.

courroucer [kuru'se], *v.t.* (*conjug. like* COMMENCER) to provoke, to anger, to incense, to irritate. **se courroucer**, *v.r.* to become angry, to rage.

courroux [ku'ru], *n.m.* wrath, anger, rage.

cours [ku:r], *n.m.* course, stream, current, flow; lapse; path, orbit; vent, scope; public drive or walk; vogue; currency; series of lectures; (*pl.*) classes; (*St. Exch.*) market price, rate.

course [kurs], *n.f.* running, run; course; drive, walk, excursion; career; race; errand; privateering; cruise; length of the stroke (*of a piece of machinery*).

coursier [kur'sje], *n.m.* charger; (*poet.*) steed; (*Naut.*) bow gun.

coursive [kur'si:v], *n.f.* (*Naut.*) gangway.

court (1) [ku:r], *a.* short; brief; concise, curt; limited; scanty; fleeting.—*adv.* short, abruptly; *demeurer court*, to stop short; *être à court d'argent*, to be short of money.

court (2) [kort, ku:r], *n.m.* tennis court.

courtage [kur'ta:ʒ], *n.m.* brokerage, commission.

courtaud [kur'to], *a.* thick-set, dumpy, docked, crop-eared.—*n.m.* (*fem.* **-e**) short, thick-set person; docked or crop-eared horse.

courtauder [kurto'de], *v.t.* to dock, to crop (*horses etc.*).

court-circuit [kursir'kɥi], *n.m.* (*pl.* **courts-circuits**) short circuit.

89

court-circuiter [kursirkɥi'te], *v.t.* to short-circuit.

courtement [kurtə'mã], *adv.* shortly, briefly.

courtepointe [kurtə'pwɛ̃:t], *n.f.* counterpane, quilt.

courtier [kur'tje], *n.m.* (*fem.* **-ière**) broker, agent.

courtil [kur'til], *n.m.* *small garden; garth.

courtisan [kurti'zã], *n.m.* courtier; fawner.

courtisane [kurti'zan], *n.f.* courtesan.

courtisanerie [kurtizan'ri], *n.f.* court flattery, toadyism.

courtisanesque [kurtiza'nɛsk], *a.* courtier-like.

courtiser [kurti'ze], *v.t.* to court; to woo; to flatter.

courtois [kur'twa] *a.* courteous, polite.

courtoisement [kurtwaz'mã], *adv.* courteously.

courtoisie [kurtwa'zi], *n.f.* courtesy; kindness, good turn.

couseur [ku'zœ:r], *n.m.* (*fem.* **-euse**) sewer, stitcher (*of books*).

cousin [ku'zɛ̃], *n.m.* (*fem.* **-e**) cousin; (*fig.*) friend, crony.

cousinage [kuzi'na:ʒ], *n.m.* cousinhood; cousins; relationship.

cousiner [kuzi'ne], *v.t.* to call cousin; to hob-nob with.—*v.i.* to live on others; to be friends *or* cronies.

coussin [ku'sɛ̃], *n.m.* cushion, hassock; pad.

coussiner [kusi'ne], *v.t.* to pad, to cushion.

coussinet [kusi'nɛ], *n.m.* small cushion, pad; iron wedge; pillion.

cousu [ku'zy], *a.* sewn, stitched.

coût [ku], *n.m.* costs, charge; *le coût de la vie*, the cost of living.

coûtant [ku'tã], *a.* costing; *à prix coûtant*, at cost price.

couteau [ku'to], *n.m.* (*pl.* **-eaux**) knife.

coutelas [kut'lɑ], *n.m.* cutlass.

coutelier [kutə'lje], *n.m.* cutler.

coutelière [kutə'ljɛ:r], *n.f.* knife case; cutler's wife.

coutellerie [kutel'ri], *n.f.* cutler's shop *or* business; cutlery.

coûter [ku'te], *v.i.* to cost, to cause, to occasion.—*v.i.* to cost (*cher etc.*); to be expensive; (*fig.*) to be painful, troublesome.

coûteusement [kutøz'mã], *adv.* expensively.

coûteux [ku'tø], *a.* (*fem.* **-euse**) expensive, costly.

coutil [ku'ti], *n.m.* tick, ticking; (*Tex.*) drill.

coutre [kutr], *n.m.* plough-share, coulter, axe.

coutume [ku'tym], *n.f.* custom, habit, practice.

coutumier [kuty'mje], *a.* (*fem.* **-ière**) customary, common, ordinary; habitual.

couture [ku'ty:r], *n.f.* sewing, needlework; seam, suture; scar.

couturer [kuty're], *v.t.* to seam.

couturier [kuty'rje], *n.m.* ladies' tailor.—*a.* sartorial.

couturière [kuty'rjɛ:r], *n.f.* dressmaker, seamstress.

couvage [ku'va:ʒ], **couvaison** [kuvɛ'zõ], *n.f.* brooding-time, sitting, incubation.

couvée [ku've], *n.f.* sitting (*of eggs*); brood, covey.

couvent [ku'vã], *n.m.* convent, monastery, nunnery; convent school.

couver [ku've], *v.t.* to sit on, to incubate, to hatch; to brood, to prepare in secret (*a plot etc.*); to brood over.—*v.i.* to lie hidden, to lurk; to smoulder.

couvercle [ku'vɛrkl], *n.m.* cover, lid, cap, shutter.

couvert [ku'vɛ:r], *a.* covered; clad, clothed; cloudy, overcast; obscure, ambiguous (*of words*).—*n.m.* cover (*plate, spoon, knife, fork*); shelter; cover, wrapper; covert, thicket; *le vivre et le couvert*, board and lodging.

couverte [ku'vɛrt], *n.f.* glaze, glazing.

couverture [kuvɛr'ty:r], *n.f.* covering, wrapper; blanket, rug, counterpane, quilt; cover (*of a book*); (*Comm.*) guaranty, security; *couverture chauffante*, electric blanket.

couveuse [ku'vø:z], *n.f.* broody hen; *couveuse artificielle*, incubator.

couvi [ku'vi], *a.* addled, rotten (*egg*).

couvoir [ku'vwa:r], *n.m.* incubator.

[In the following compounds *couvre* is *inv.*]

couvre-chef [kuvrə'ʃɛf], *n.m.* headgear.

couvre-feu [kuvrə'fø], *n.m. inv.* curfew; curfew-bell; fire cover, fire plate; black-out.

couvre-plat [kuvrə'pla], *n.m.* dish cover.

couvre-théière [kuvrəte'jɛ:r], *n.m.* tea cosy.

couvreur [ku'vrœ:r], *n.m.* roofer.

couvrir [ku'vri:r], *v.t. irr.* (*conjug. like* OUVRIR) to cover; to wrap up; to roof; to overwhelm; to clothe; to defend, to protect; to overrun, to overflow; to excuse; to disguise; to defray (*expenses etc.*). **se couvrir**, *v.r.* to cover oneself, to put on (*one's hat*); to get under cover; to be overcast (*of the weather*); (*Comm.*) to reimburse oneself.

coyote [ko'jɔt], *n.m.* prairie wolf.

crabe [kra:b], *n.m.* crab.

crac! [krak], *int.* crack! pop!

crachat [kra'ʃa], *n.m.* spittle, expectoration.

crachement [kraʃ'mã], *n.m.* spitting.

cracher [kra'ʃe], *v.t.* to spit; (*fig.*) to spit out, to come out with.—*v.i.* to spit, to splutter; (*Mach. etc.*) to spark, to backfire.

crachoir [kra'ʃwa:r], *n.m.* spittoon.

crachoter [kraʃɔ'te], *v.i.* to spit often.

Cracovie [krakɔ'vi], *f.* Cracow.

craie [krɛ], *n.f.* chalk.

craillement [kraj'mã], *n.m.* cawing (*of crows*).

crailler [kra'je], *v.i.* to caw.

craindre [krɛ̃:dr], *v.t. irr.* to fear; to dread; to dislike.

crainte [krɛ̃:t], *n.f.* fear, apprehension; dread, awe.

craintif [krɛ̃'tif], *a.* (*fem.* **-tive**) fearful, apprehensive, timid.

craintivement [krɛ̃tiv'mã], *adv.* fearfully, timorously.

cramoisi [kramwa'zi], *a.* and *n.m.* crimson.

crampe [krɑ̃:p], *n.f.* cramp; crampon.

crampon [krɑ̃'põ], *n.m.* crampon, cramp-iron, grappling iron.

cramponner [krɑ̃pɔ'ne], *v.t.* to cramp, to fasten with a cramp-iron. **se cramponner**, *v.r.* to hold fast, to cling like grim death.

cramponnet [krɑ̃pɔ'nɛ], *n.m.* small cramp, tack; staple (*of a lock*).

cran (1) [krɑ̃], *n.m.* notch; cog; (*Print.*) nick; (*fam.*) pluck.

cran (2) [krɑ̃], *n.m.* horse-radish.

crâne [krɑːn], *a.* bold, plucky.—*n.m.* skull, cranium.

crânement [krɑn'mɑ̃], *adv.* pluckily; in style, famously.

craner [krɑ'ne], *v.t.* to notch, to indent (*a clock wheel*).

crâner [krɑ'ne], *v.i.* to swagger.

cranologie [krɑnɔlɔ'ʒi], **craniologie** [krɑnjɔlɔ'ʒi], *n.f.* craniology.

crapaud [krɑ'po], *n.m.* toad; jumping cracker; (*fig.*) urchin, brat.

crapaudière [krɑpo'djɛːr], *n.f.* nest of toads; (*fig.*) low, swampy place.

crapaudine [krɑpo'din], *n.f.* toadstone; grating (*of an escape-pipe*); *à la crapaudine*, cut open and broiled.

crapouillot [krɑpu'jo], *n.m.* trench-mortar.

crapule [krɑ'pyl], *n.f.* low vulgar debauchery, gluttony, drunkenness; blackguards.

crapuleusement [krɑpyløz'mɑ̃], *adv.* dissolutely.

crapuleux [krɑpy'lø], *a.* (*fem.* **-euse**) low, debauched, vicious, dissolute.

craque [krak], *n.f.* fib, humbug.

craqueler [krɑ'kle], *v.t.* (*conjug. like* APPELER) to crackle (*china*).

craquelot [krɑ'klo], *n.m.* bloater.

craquelure [krɑ'klyːr], *n.f.* crack (*in china*).

craquement [krak'mɑ̃], *n.m.* cracking noise, creaking, snapping (*boughs*).

craquer [krɑ'ke], *v.i.* to crack, to crackle, to snap, to creak, to crunch.

craquètement [krakɛt'mɑ̃], *n.m.* crackling; chattering (*of the teeth*); gabbling (*of a stork and other birds*).

craqueter [krak'te], *v.i.* (*conjug. like* APPELER) to crackle, to crepitate; to gabble (*birds*).

crasse (1) [kras], *a.* gross, thick, coarse, crass.

crasse (2) [krɑs], *n.f.* dirt, filth, squalor; stinginess; dross.

crasser [krɑ'se], *v.t.* to foul, to dirty (*fire-arms etc.*). **se crasser**, *v.r.* to become foul (*of fire-arms etc.*).

crasseux [krɑ'sø], *a.* (*fem.* **-euse**) dirty, filthy, nasty, squalid, sordid; stingy, mean.—*n.m.* (*fem.* **-euse**) sloven, slut; skinflint.

crassier [krɑ'sje], *n.m.* slag heap; rubbish dump.

cratère [krɑ'tɛːr], *n.m.* crater (*mouth of volcano*); (*Gr. or Rom.*) bowl *or* cup.

cravache [krɑ'vaʃ], *n.f.* riding whip.

cravacher [krava'ʃe], *v.t.* to horse whip.

cravate [krɑ'vat], *n.f.* cravat, (neck-)tie.

cravater (**se**) [səkrava'te], *v.r.* to put on one's (neck-)tie.

cravatier [krava'tje], *n.m.* maker *or* vendor of neckties.

crawl [krol], *n.m.* (*Swim.*) crawl.

crawleur [kro'lœːr], *n.m.* crawl swimmer.

crayer [krɛ'je], *v.t.* (*conjug. like* PAYER) to chalk, to mark up etc. with chalk.

crayère [krɛ'jɛːr], *n.f.* chalk pit.

crayeux [krɛ'jø], *a.* (*fem.* **-euse**) chalky.

crayon [krɛ'jɔ̃], *n.m.* pencil; drawing *or* portrait in crayon; (*fig.*) style; sketch; *crayon à bille*, ball-point pen.

crayonnage [krɛjɔ'naːʒ], *n.m.* pencil drawing.

crayonner [krɛjɔ'ne], *v.t.* to draw with a pencil; to mark with a pencil; (*fig.*) to sketch.

crayonneux [krɛjɔ'nø], *a.* (*fem.* **-euse**) chalky.

créance [kre'ɑ̃s], *n.f.* credence, trust, belief; credit; money owing; (*Hunt.*) command.

créancier [kreɑ̃'sje], *n.m.* (*fem.* **-ière**) creditor.

créateur [krea'tœːr], *a.* (*fem.* **-trice**) creative, inventive.—*n.m.* (*fem.* **-trice**) creator, maker, author.

création [krea'sjɔ̃], *n.f.* creation; universe; establishment; (*Dress.*) design.

créature [krea'tyːr], *n.f.* creature; man, as opposed to God.

crécelle [kre'sɛl], *n.f.* child's *or* hand rattle.

crécerelle [kres'rɛl], *n.f.* (*Orn.*) kestrel.

crèche [krɛːʃ], *n.f.* manger; crib; crèche.

crédence [kre'dɑ̃ːs], *n.f.* credence table; side-board.

crédibilité [kredibili'te], *n.f.* credibility.

crédit [kre'di], *n.m.* credit; trust; authority, influence; esteem; vogue; parliamentary grant.

créditer [kredi'te], *v.t.* to credit.

créditeur [kredi'tœːr], *a.* credit.—*n.m.* (*fem.* **-trice**) creditor.

credo [kre'do], *n.m.* (*no pl.*) creed, belief.

crédule [kre'dyl], *a.* credulous.

crédulement [kredyl'mɑ̃], *adv.* credulously.

crédulité [kredyli'te], *n.f.* credulity.

créer [kre'e], *v.t.* to create; to produce; to invent, to imagine; to establish.

crémaillère [krema'jɛːr], *n.f.* pot-hook.

crémation [krema'sjɔ̃], *n.f.* cremation.

crématorium [krematɔ'rjɔm], *n.m.* (*pl.* **-ia**) crematorium.

crème [krɛːm], *n.f.* cream; custard; sweet liqueur; the best part of a thing.

crémer (1) [kre'me], *v.i.* (*conjug. like* CÉDER) to dye cream color.—*v.i.* to cream.

crémer (2) [kre'me], *v.t.* (*conjug. like* CÉDER) to cremate.

crémerie [krem'ri], *n.f.* creamery, dairy.

crémeux [kre'mø], *a.* (*fem.* **-euse**) creamy.

crémier [kre'mje], *n.m.* (*fem.* **-ière**) milkman, dairyman *or* -woman.—*n.f.* (**-ière**) cream pitcher.

créneau [kre'no], *n.m.* (*pl.* **-eaux**) battlement.

crénelage [kren'laːʒ], *n.m.* milling, milled edge (*on coins*), crenellation.

créneler [kren'le], *v.t.* (*conjug. like* APPELER) to embattle; to indent, to notch.

crénelure [kren'lyːr], *n.f.* crenellation; notching.

créole [kre'ɔl], *a.* Creole.—*n.* (**Créole**) Creole.

créosote [kreɔ'zɔt], *n.f.* creosote.

créosoter [kreɔzɔ'te], *v.t.* to creosote.

crêpe (1) [krɛːp], *n.m.* crape; (*fig.*) veil; crêpe rubber.

crêpe (2) [krɛːp], *n.f.* pancake.

crêpelu [krɛ'ply], *a.* frizzy (*hair*).

crêper [krɛ'pe], *v.t.* to crisp, to frizz.

crépi [kre'pi], *n.m.* rough-cast, parget.

crépir [kre'piːr], *v.t.* to rough-cast, to plaster.

crépissage [krepi'saːʒ], **crépissement** [krepis'mɑ̃], *n.m.* plastering, pargeting, rough-casting.

crépissure [krepi'syːr], *n.m.* parget; rough-casting.

crépitant [krepi'tɑ̃], a. crepitating; crackling.
crépitation [krepitɑ'sjɔ̃], n.f., **crépite-ment** [krepit'mɑ̃], n.m. crepitation; crackling.
crépiter [krepi'te], v.i. to crackle; to crepitate.
crépu [kre'py], a. crisped, frizzy; woolly.
crépure [kre'py:r], n.f. crisping; craping.
crépusculaire [krepysky'lɛ:r], a. crepuscular, twilight.
crépuscule [krepys'kyl], n.m. twilight; dawn.
créquier [kre'kje], n.m. sloe tree.
cresson [kre'sɔ̃], n.m. cress.
cressonnière [krɛsɔ'njɛ:r], n.f. water-cress bed.
Crésus [kre'zy:s], m. Croesus.
crésus [kre'zy:s], n.m. inv. very rich man.
crétacé [kreta'se], a. cretaceous, chalky.
Crète [krɛ:t], **la**, f. Crete.
crète [krɛ:t], n.f. crest, comb (of a cock or hen); tuft; ridge; coping.
crèté [krɛ'te], a. crested, tufted.
crèteler [krɛ'tle], v.i. (conjug. like APPELER) to cackle (of hens).
crétin [kre'tɛ̃], a. cretinous; idiotic.—n.m. (fem. -e) cretin; idiot, dunce.
crétinerie [kretin'ri], n.f. idiotic behavior; foolishness.
crétiniser [kretini'ze], v.t. to make cretinous, to brutalize, to make an idiot of.
crétinisme [kreti'nism], n.m. cretinism.
crétois [kre'twa], a. Cretan.—n.m. (**Crétois**, fem. -oise) Cretan (person).
cretonne [krə'tɔn], n.f. cretonne.
creusage [krə'za:ʒ], **creusement** [krøz'mɑ̃], n.m. deepening, hollowing; excavation.
creuser [krø'ze], v.t. to dig, to hollow, to excavate, to scoop out; to sink, to drive (a well, shaft etc.); to make hollow or empty. **se creuser**, v.r. to become hollow.
creuset [krø'ze], n.m. crucible, melting pot; (fig.) test, trial.
creux [krø], a. (fem. **creuse**) hollow; cavernous; deep; empty; (fig.) airy, extravagant. —n.m. hollow, cavity; pit, hole, chasm; mold, mortar, trough.—adv. hollow; **sonner creux**, to sound hollow.
crevaison [krə'vɛzɔ̃], n.f. puncture (of a tire).
crevant [krə'vɑ̃], a. (vulg.) tiresome; killing (toil etc.); killing (funny).
crevasse [krə'vas], n.f. crevice, rift, crack, chink, crevasse; gap, cranny; chap (in the hands etc.).
crevasser [krəva'se], v.t. to split; to crack; to chap. **se crevasser**, v.r. to crack, to become chapped.
crevé [krə've], n.m. (Dress.) opening, slash (in sleeves).
crève-cœur [krɛv'kœ:r], n.m. inv. heart-break; heart-breaking thing.
crever [krə've], v.t. (conjug. like AMENER) to burst, to split, to break open, to rend; to stave in; to puncture.—v.i. to burst; to die (animals); (vulg.) to die (human beings). **se crever**, v.r. to burst; to kill oneself.
crevette [krə'vɛt], n.f. shrimp, prawn.
cri [kri], n.m. cry; scream, roar, yell, shriek, screech, wail, outcry, clamor.
criaillement [kriɑj'mɑ̃], n.m. shouting, wrangling, brawling; scolding.

criailler [kriɑ'je], v.i. to bawl, to cry, to clamor; to scold; to brawl; to gabble (of geese).
criaillerie [kriɑj'ri], n.f. brawling, clamoring, wrangling.
criailleur [kriɑ'jœ:r], n.m. (fem. -euse) brawler, wrangler; shrew, scold.
criant [kri'ɑ̃], a. crying; (fig.) glaring, shocking.
criard [kri'a:r], a. crying, noisy, clamorous; scolding; (fig.) shrill, discordant, crude.— n.m. (fem. -e) bawler, clamorer; scold, shrew.
criblage [kri'bla:ʒ], n.m. sifting, screening (of coals etc.).
crible [kribl], n.m. sieve, riddle.
cribler [kri'ble], v.t. to sift, to riddle; to pierce all over, to riddle (with wounds etc.); (fig.) to overwhelm.
cric [kri], n.m. jack, screw-jack, hand-screw.
cri-cri [kri'kri], n.m. inv. (fam.) cricket (insect); chirping.
criée [kri'e], n.f. (public) auction.
crier [kri'e], v.t. to cry, to proclaim, to put up for sale; to publish, to announce.—v.i. to cry out; to shout, to scream, to shriek; to call out; to whine; to complain loudly, to exclaim; to chirp; to creak.
crieur [kri'jœ:r], n.m. (fem. -euse) bawler; crier; (Theat.) call-boy; auctioneer; hawker; **crieur public**, town crier; **crieur de journaux**, newsboy.
crime [krim], n.m. crime, offence.
Crimée [kri'me], **la**, f. the Crimea.
criminel [krimi'nɛl], a. (fem. -elle) criminal, felonious, guilty.—n.m. (fem. -elle) criminal, felon, culprit, offender.
criminellement [kriminɛl'mɑ̃], adv. criminally, culpably, guiltily.
crin [krɛ̃], n.m. horse-hair, bristles, fibres, mane.
crinière [kri'njɛ:r], n.f. mane (of animal).
crinoline [krino'lin], n.f. crinoline.
crique [krik], n.f. creek, cove; flaw, crack.
criquet [kri'kɛ], n.m. locust; (fig.) bad horse.
criqueter [krik'te], v.i. (conjug. like APPELER) to rasp, to grate.
crise [kri:z], n.f. crisis; fit, convulsion; slump.
crispation [krispɑ'sjɔ̃], n.f. shrivelling, crispation; fidgets.
crisper [kris'pe], v.t. to shrivel; to irritate (the nerves), to give (someone) the fidgets. **se crisper**, v.r. to shrivel, to contract.
crissement [kris'mɑ̃], n.m. grating (of teeth, of brakes etc.).
crisser [kri'se], v.i. to grate, to grind; to squeak.
cristal [kris'tal], n.m. (pl. -aux) crystal, cut glass; (fig.) limpidity; **cristal de mine**, quartz; **cristal de roche**, rock crystal.
cristallerie [kristal'ri], n.f. glass-cutting; crystal manufactory, glass works.
cristallier [krista'lje], n.m. glass-cutter; glass cupboard.
cristallière [krista'ljɛ:r], n.f. rock-crystal mine; machine for glass-cutting.
cristallin [krista'lɛ̃], a. crystalline; pellucid. —n.m. (Anat.) crystalline lens (of the eye); (Astron.) crystalline heaven.
cristallisant [kristali'zɑ̃], a. crystallizing.
cristallisation [kristaliza'sjɔ̃], n.f. crystallization.

cristalliser [kristali'ze], v.t., v.i. to crystallize. **se cristalliser**, v.r. to crystallize; to candy.

critère [kri'tɛːr], **critérium** [krite'rjɔm], n.m. criterion, standard, test.

critiquable [kriti'kabl], a. open to criticism, censurable, exceptionable.

critique [kri'tik], a. critical; censorious, carping; ticklish, momentous; critical (in the literary sense).—n.m. critic; censor, carper.—n.f. criticism, science of criticism; review.

critiquer [kriti'ke], v.t. to criticize unfavorably; to censure, to find fault with.

critiqueur [kriti'kœːr], n.m. (fem. -euse) criticizer, fault-finder, carper.

croassement [krɔas'mã], n.m. croak, croaking, cawing (of rooks).

croasser [krɔa'se], v.i. to croak, to caw (of crows, rooks etc.).

croate [krɔ'at], a. Croatian.—n.m. Croatian (language).—n. (Croate) Croat.

Croatie [krɔa'si], la, f. Croatia.

croc [kro], n.m. hook; fang (of dog), tusk (of walrus).

croc-en-jambe [krɔkã'ʒãːb], n.m. (pl. **crocs-en-jambe**) trip up; dirty trick.

croche [krɔʃ], a. crooked, bent.—n.f. (Mus.) quaver; (pl.) smith's tongs; **double croche**, semi-quaver; **triple croche**, demi-semi-quaver.

crocher [krɔ'ʃe], v.t. to hook; to bend like a hook.

crochet [krɔ'ʃe], n.m. small hook; knitting needle, crochet hook; (Print.) square bracket; teeth of certain animals.

crochetable [krɔʃ'tabl], a. pickable (of locks).

crochetage [krɔʃ'taːʒ], n.m. lock picking.

crocheter [krɔʃ'te], v.t. (conjug. like AMENER) to pick (a lock); to crochet.

crochetier [krɔʃ'tje], n.m. hook maker, clasp maker.

crochu [krɔ'ʃy], a. crooked, hooked.

crocodile [krɔkɔ'dil], n.m. crocodile; (Rail.) automatic stop.

crocus [krɔ'kyːs], n.m. (Bot.) crocus.

croire [krwaːr], v.t. irr. to believe; to have faith in; to think, to deem.—v.i. to believe, to have faith (à), to be a believer. **se croire**, v.r. to believe or think oneself, to consider oneself; to be believed, to be credible.

croisade [krwa'zad], n.f. crusade.

croisé [krwa'ze], a. crossed; twilled, double-milled (of cloth); cross (of breeds of animals); **mots croisés**, a crossword.—n.m. crusader; twill; crossing (a step in dancing).

croisée [krwa'ze], n.f. crossing point; casement window (opening inside).

croisement [krwaz'mã], n.m. crossing (of two roads etc.); meeting; cross-breeding (of animals).

croiser [krwa'ze], v.t. to cross; to lay across; to cross (breeds of animals); to pass (a person); to thwart.—v.i. to overlap; to cruise. **se croiser**, v.r. to cross or pass each other; to be crossed; to thwart one another.

croiseur [krwa'zœːr], n.m. cruiser.

croisière [krwa'zjɛːr], n.f. cruise, cruising; (Rail.) crossing.

croissance [krwa'sãːs], n.f. growth, increase.

croissant [krwa'sã], a. growing, increasing.—n.m. the moon in her increase; crescent; pruning hook, hedging bill; crescent roll.

croît [krwa], n.m. increase (from breeding).

croître [krwaːtr], v.i. irr. to grow; to increase; to wax (moon); to spring up, to sprout; to lengthen; to swell.

croix [krwa], n.f. cross; the Holy Rood; (fig.) affliction; (Coin.) obverse.

cromlech [krɔm'lɛk], n.m. (Archaeol.) stone circle.

crône [kroːn], n.m. crane (on a wharf).

croquade [krɔ'kad], n.f. rough sketch.

croquant [krɔ'kã], a. crisp, crackling, short.—n.m. poor wretch; clodhopper.—n.f. crisp almond cake.

croque-au-sel (à la) [krɔko'sɛl], adv. phr. with salt only.

croque-mitaine [krɔkmi'tɛn], n.m. (pl. **croque-mitaines**) bogy man.

croquer [krɔ'ke], v.t. irr. to crunch; to devour; to draft, to sketch.—v.i. to crackle between the teeth, to make a scrunching noise.

croquet [krɔ'kɛ], n.m. crisp biscuit; croquet (game).

croquette [krɔ'kɛt], n.f. croquette.

croquignole [krɔki'ɲɔl], n.f. cracknel; fillip; (C) doughnut.

croquis [krɔ'ki], n.m. first sketch, rough draft, outline.

cross [krɔs], n.m. (Box.) cross-counter; cross-country running.

crosse [krɔs], n.f. crooked stick, crosier (of bishops); butt (of rifle); stock; hockey stick, golf club etc.; (C) **jeu de crosse**, lacrosse.

crossé [krɔ'se], a. crosiered, mitred.

crosser [krɔ'se], v.t. to strike (a ball etc.).

crosseur [krɔ'sœːr], n.m. hockey player, lacrosse player.

crotale [krɔ'tal], n.m. rattlesnake.

crotte [krɔt], n.f. dung; dirt, mud, mire.

crotté [krɔ'te], a. dirty, muddy; (fig.) squalid.

crotter [krɔ'te], v.t. to dirty; to draggle, to bespatter. **se crotter**, v.r. to get dirty.

crottin [krɔ'tɛ̃], n.m. dung.

croulant [kru'lã], a. sinking, crumbling; tottering, tumbledown.

croulement [krul'mã], n.m. sinking, falling in, collapse.

crouler [kru'le], v.i. to give way, to fall in, to collapse.

croup [krup], n.m. (Path.) croup, diphtheria.

croupal [kru'pal], a. (m. pl. -aux) pertaining to the croup; laryngitic.

croupe [krup], n.f. croup, crupper, buttocks (of a horse), rump; top or brow (of a hill); **monter en croupe**, to ride pillion.

croupé [kru'pe], a. with a rump or crupper.

croupi [kru'pi], a. stagnant, putrid; **de l'eau croupie**, ditch water.

croupier [kru'pje], n.m. croupier (at a gaming table); partner (of a financier etc.).

croupière [kru'pjɛːr], n.f. saddle tie, crupper.

croupion [kru'pjɔ̃], n.m. rump; **le croupion (d'une volaille)**, the parson's nose.

croupir [kru'piːr], v.i. to stagnate; to wallow.

croupissant [krupi'sã], a. stagnant, putrescent.

croupon [kru'pɔ̃], n.m. butt (leather).

croustillant [krusti'jã], a. crisp, crusty.

croustille [krus'tiːj], n.f. little crust; (fig.) snack.

croustiller [krusti′je], *v.i.* to bite, eat, crunch a crust, to munch.

croûte [krut], *n.f.* crust; pie crust; scab; *casser la croûte*, to have a snack; (*C*) crust (*of the snow*); (*fig.*) bad painting, daub.

croûton [kru′tɔ̃], *n.m.* bit of crust, crusty end; sippet.

croyable [krwɑ′jabl], *a.* credible, likely.

croyance [krwɑ′jɑ̃:s], *n.f.* belief; creed, faith.

croyant [krwɑ′jɑ̃], *a.* believing.—*n.m.* (*fem.* -**e**) believer.

cru (1) [kry], *n.m.* growth; production (*esp. of wine*).

cru (2) [kry], *a.* raw, uncooked; unwrought; (*fig.*) crude, coarse, indecent; *à cru*, on the bare skin.

cruauté [kryo′te], *n.f.* cruelty, inhumanity.

cruche [kryʃ], *n.f.* pitcher, jar, jug; (*colloq.*) blockhead.

cruchée [kry′ʃe], *n.f.* pitcherful, jugful, jarful.

cruchon [kry′ʃɔ̃], *n.m.* little pitcher; (*stone*) hot-water bottle.

crucial [kry′sjal], *a.* (*m. pl.* -**aux**) cross-shaped, crucial; (*fig.*) decisive.

cruciement [krysifi′mɑ̃], *n.m.* crucifixion.

crucifier [krysi′fje], *v.t.* to crucify.

crucifix [krysi′fi], *n.m.* crucifix.

crucifixion [krysifik′sjɔ̃], *n.f.* crucifixion.

cruciforme [krysi′fɔrm], *a.* cruciform, cross-shaped.

crudité [krydi′te], *n.f.* crudity, rawness; coarse expression; (*pl.*) raw vegetables *or* fruit.

crue [kry], *n.f.* growth, increase; rise, swelling (*of river etc.*); flood.

cruel [kry′ɛl], *a.* (*fem.* -**elle**) cruel, merciless; bloodthirsty; hard; grievous, sad.

cruellement [kryɛl′mɑ̃], *adv.* cruelly; unmercifully; severely.

crûment [kry′mɑ̃], *adv.* roughly, coarsely; crudely.

crustacé [krysta′se], *a.* crustaceous.—*n.m.* crustacean; shell-fish.

crypte [kript], *n.f.* crypt.

cryptogramme [kripto′gram], *n.m.* cryptogram, cipher.

cryptographe [kripto′graf], *n.* cryptographer.

cryptographie [kriptɔgra′fi], *n.f.* cryptography.

cryptographique [kriptɔgra′fik], *a.* cryptographic.

cubage [ky′ba:ʒ], *n.m.* cubage, cubature; cubic content.

cubain [ky′bɛ̃], *a.* Cuban.—*n.m.* (**Cubain,** *fem.* -**aine**) Cuban (*person*).

cubature [kyba′ty:r], *n.f.* cubature.

cube [kyb], *a.* cubic.—*n.m.* cube (*shape and measure*).

cuber [ky′be], *v.t.* to cube.

cubique [ky′bik], *a.* cubic; cubical.

cubisme [ky′bism], *n.m.* (*Art*) cubism.

cubiste [ky′bist], *a.* and *n.* cubist.

cueillage [kœ′ja:ʒ], *n.m.,* **cueillaison** [kœjɛ′zɔ̃], **cueille** [kœ:j], *n.f.* gathering time, gathering.

cueillette [kœ′jɛt], *n.f.* gathering of a crop; harvesting time.

cueilleur [kœ′jœ:r], *n.m.* (*fem.* -**euse**) gatherer, picker.

cueillir [kœ′ji:r], *v.t. irr.* to gather, to cull, to pick, to pluck; to acquire.

cueilloir [kœj′wa:r], *n.m.* fruit basket; implement for picking fruit.

cuiller [kɥi′je], **cuillère** [kɥi′jɛ:r], *n.f.* spoon; scoop.

cuillerée [kɥij′re], *n.f.* spoonful.

cuilleron [kɥij′rɔ̃], *n.m.* bowl of a spoon.

cuir [kɥi:r], *n.m.* hide; leather; strop.

cuirasse [kɥi′ras], *n.f.* cuirass, breast-plate.

cuirassé [kɥira′se], *a.* armed with a cuirass; armour-plated; hardened; secret.—*n.m.* (*Naut.*) battleship.

cuirassement [kɥiras′mɑ̃], *n.m.* armor-plating.

cuirasser [kɥira′se], *v.t.* to arm with a cuirass; to armor-plate; (*fig.*) to steel, to harden. **se cuirasser,** *v.r.* to put on a cuirass; to harden *or* fortify oneself.

cuirassier [kɥira′sje], *n.m.* cuirassier.

cuire [kɥi:r], *v.t. irr.* (*conjug. like* CONDUIRE) to cook; to burn (*of the sun*); to ripen.—*v.i.* to cook, to be cooked, to be done; to bake, boil etc.; to smart.

cuisage [kɥi′za:ʒ], *n.m.* burning (*of charcoal*), charring.

cuisant [kɥi′zɑ̃], *a.* sharp, smarting; piercing.

cuiseur [kɥi′zœ:r], *n.m.* pressure cooker.

cuisine [kɥi′zin], *n.f.* kitchen; cookery; cooks; fare, living; (*Naut.*) galley.

cuisiner [kɥizi′ne], *v.t., v.i.* to cook.

cuisinier [kɥizi′nje], *n.m.* (*fem.* -**ière**) cook.— *n.f.* (-**ière**) Dutch oven.

cuisse [kɥis], *n.f.* thigh; quarter (*of venison*); leg (*of poultry*).

cuisseau [kɥi′so], *n.m.* (*pl.* -**eaux**) leg (*of veal*).

cuisson [kɥi′sɔ̃], *n.f.* cooking (*baking, boiling, roasting etc.*); smart (*pain*).

cuissot [kɥi′so], *n.m.* haunch (*of venison*).

cuit [kɥi], *a.* cooked, done (*roasted, boiled, baked etc.*); (*fig.*) done for, dished.

cuite [kɥit], *n.f.* baking; burning (*of bricks etc.*); ovenful, kilnful; (*slang*) intoxication.

cuivrage [kɥi′vra:ʒ], *n.m.* coppering; copper-plating.

cuivre [kɥi:vr], *n.m.* copper; copper money; copper-plate; *cuivre battu*, wrought copper; *cuivre jaune*, brass; *cuivre rouge*, copper.

cuivré [kɥi′vre], *a.* copper-colored; (*fig.*) bronzed (*complexion*); ringing, clear.

cuivrer [kɥi′vre], *v.t.* to cover with copper.

cuivrerie [kɥivrə′ri], *n.f.* copper-works; copper wares.

cuivreux [kɥi′vrø], *a.* (*fem.* -**euse**) coppery.

cul [ky], *n.m.* (*indec.*) backside, posterior; bottom (*of bottle or bag*); stern (*of ship*).

culasse [ky′las], *n.f.* breech (*of a cannon etc.*); cylinder head (*of car engine*).

culbute [kyl′byt], *n.f.* somersault; fall, tumble; (*fig.*) ruin, bankruptcy.

culbuter [kylby′te], *v.t.* to throw over, to upset violently; to overthrow.—*v.i.* to fall head over heels.

culbutis [kylby′ti], *n.m.* confused heap, jumble.

cul de bouteille [kydbu′tɛ:j], *a.* bottle-green. —*n.m.* bottom of bottle.

cul-de-jatte [kyd′ʒat], *n.m.* (*pl.* **culs-de-jatte**) legless cripple.

cul-de-lampe [kyd′lɑ̃p], *n.m.* (*Print.*) tail-piece.

cul-de-sac [kyd′sak], *n.m.* (*pl.* **culs-de-sac**) blind alley, cul-de-sac; (*fig.*) deadlock.

cylindre

culée [ky'le], *n.f.* abutment (*of bridges*); (*Naut.*) stern-way.

culer [ky'le], *v.i.* to go backwards; to fall astern.

culière [ky'ljɛːr], *n.f.* hind girth, crupper (*of harness*); gutter stone.

culinaire [kyli'nɛːr], *a.* culinary.

culminance [kylmi'nɑ̃ːs], *n.f.* culmination, highest point.

culminant [kylmi'nɑ̃], *a.* culminating; prominent.

culmination [kylmina'sjɔ̃], *n.f.* culmination.

culminer [kylmi'ne], *v.i.* to culminate.

culot [ky'lo], *n.m.* bottom (*of lamps, crucibles etc.*); residuum, (*fam.*) dottle (*in a pipe*).

culottage [kylɔ'taːʒ], *n.m.* coloring, seasoning (*of pipes*).

culotte [ky'lɔt], *n.f.* breeches; (*pl.*) shorts; tights; (*Cook.*) rump (*of an ox*).

culotter [kylɔ'te], *v.t.* to breech; to put in breeches; to color (*pipes*). **se culotter**, *v.r.* to put on one's breeches; to become colored (*of pipes*).

culottier [kylɔ'tje], *n.m.* (*fem.* **-ière**) breeches maker.

culpabilité [kylpabili'te], *n.f.* culpability; guilt.

culte [kylt], *n.m.* worship, adoration; (*fig.*) cult, religion, creed; veneration, love.

cultivable [kylti'vabl], *a.* cultivable, arable.

cultivateur [kyltiva'tœːr], *a.* agricultural.— *n.m.* (*fem.* **-trice**) cultivator, farmer, agriculturist; cultivator (*implement*).

cultivé [kylti've], *a.* cultivated; (*of the mind*) cultured.

cultiver [kylti've], *v.t.* to cultivate; to till; to improve (*the mind*); to study, to practise; to cultivate the acquaintance of.

cultural [kylty'ral], *a.* (*m. pl.* **-aux**) cultural (*in relation to agriculture*).

culture [kyl'tyːr], *n.f.* culture, cultivation, tillage, husbandry; education, improvement.

culturel [kylty'rɛl], *a.* (*fem.* **-elle**) cultural (*in relation to intellectual culture*).

cumulatif [kymyla'tif], *a.* (*fem.* **-tive**) cumulative.

cumulativement [kymylativ'mɑ̃], *adv.* by accumulation.

cumuler [kymy'le], *v.t.* to accumulate; to hold several (*offices, salaries etc.*).

cumulus [kymy'lyːs], *n.m.* cumulus.

cupide [ky'pid], *a.* covetous, greedy, grasping.

cupidement [kypid'mɑ̃], *adv.* greedily, covetously.

cupidité [kypidi'te], *n.f.* cupidity, covetousness, greed.

Cupidon [kypi'dɔ̃], *n.m.* (*Myth.*) Cupid, Love.

curable [ky'rabl], *a.* curable.

curaçao [kyra'so], *n.m.* curaçao (*liqueur*).

curage [ky'raːʒ], *n.m.* **curement** [kyr'mɑ̃], *n.m.* cleansing.

curatelle [kyra'tɛl], *n.f.* guardianship, trusteeship.

curateur [kyra'tœːr], *n.m.* (*fem.* **-trice**) guardian, trustee.

curatif [kyra'tif], *a.* (*fem.* **-tive**) curative.— *n.m.* curative agent.

cure [kyːr], *n.f.* medical treatment, cure, healing; living, rectorship; vicarage, rectory.

curé [ky're], *n.m.* parish priest; parson, rector, vicar.

cure-dent [kyr'dɑ̃], *n.m.* (*pl.* **cure-dents**) tooth-pick.

curée [ky're], *n.f.* (*Hunt.*) quarry, chase; (*fig.*) prey, booty.

curement [CURAGE].

cure-môle [kyr'moːl], *n.m.* (*pl.* **cure-môles**) dredging machine.

cure-ongles [kyr'ɔ̃gl], *n.m. inv.* nail file.

curer [ky're], *v.t.* to cleanse, to clean out (*harbors, sewers etc.*); to pick (*teeth, ears etc.*).

curial (1) [ky'rjal], *a.* (*m. pl.* **-aux**) vicarial, rectorial.

curial (2) or **curiale** [ky'rjal], *a.* (*Rom. Ant.*) curial.

curie [ky'ri], *n.f.* (*Rom. Ant.*) curia.

curieusement [kyrjøz'mɑ̃], *adv.* curiously; inquisitively; carefully; quaintly.

curieux [ky'rjø], *a.* (*fem.* **-euse**) curious; inquisitive, prying; inquiring; careful; dainty; particular; strange.—*n.m.* (*fem.* **-euse**) interested person; inquisitive person; sightseer, looker-on.—*n.m.* curious fact.

curiosité [kyrjozi'te], *n.f.* curiosity; inquisitiveness; curio, rarity; quaintness.

cursif [kyr'sif], *a.* (*fem.* **-sive**) cursive, running; cursory.

cursivement [kyrsiv'mɑ̃], *adv.* cursively; cursorily.

curure [ky'ryːr], *n.f.* dirt, sewage.

cussonné [kyso'ne], *a.* worm-eaten (*of wood*).

custode [kys'tod], *n.m.* warden (*among monks*); custodian, inspector.

cutané [kyta'ne], *a.* cutaneous.

cuticule [kyti'kyl], *n.f.* cuticle.

cuvage [ky'va:ʒ], *n.m.*, **cuvaison** [kyvɛ'zɔ̃], *n.f.* fermenting (*of wine*).

cuve [kyːv], *n.f.* tub, vat.

cuvée [ky've], *n.f.* tubful; vatful.

cuvelage [ky'vlaːʒ], *n.m.*, **cuvellement** [kyvɛl'mɑ̃], *n.m.* lining, casing (*of mine shafts*).

cuveler [ky'vle], *v.t.* (*conjug. like* APPELER) to line, to case (*mine shafts etc.*).

cuver [ky've], *v.t.* to ferment; (*fam.*) to sleep off the effects of (*wine*).—*v.i.* to work, to ferment, to settle.

cuvette [ky'vɛt], *n.f.* shallow basin; wash basin; lavatory bowl.

cuvier [ky'vje], *n.m.* wash tub.

cyanure [sja'nyːr], *n.m.* (*Chem.*) cyanide.

cybernétique [sibɛrne'tik], *n.f.* cybernetics.

cyclamen [sikla'mɛn], *n.m.* cyclamen, sowbread.

cycle [sikl], *n.m.* cycle (*of events*); **cycle à 4 temps** (*d'un moteur*), 4-stroke cycle (*of an engine*).

cyclique [si'klik], *a.* cyclical.

cyclisme [si'klism], *n.m.* cycling.

cycliste [si'klist], *n.* cyclist.

cyclomoteur [siklomo'tœːr], *n.m.* motorbike.

cyclonal [siklo'nal], *a.* (*m. pl.* **-aux**) cyclonic.

cyclone [si'kloːn], *n.m.* cyclone.

cyclonique [siklo'nik], *a.* cyclonic.

Cyclope [si'klɔp], *n.m.* Cyclops.

cygne [sin], *n.m.* swan.

cylindrage [silɛ̃'draːʒ], *n.m.* mangling (*of linen etc.*); rolling (*of roads*).

cylindre [si'lɛ̃dr], *n.m.* cylinder; roller; garden roller; mangle, calender.

95

cylindrée [silɛ̃'dre], *n.f.* cubic capacity of an engine.
cylindrer [silɛ̃'dre], *v.t.* to calender; to roll.
cylindrique [silɛ̃'drik], *a.* cylindrical.
cymaise [CIMAISE].
cymbale [sɛ̃'bal], *n.f.* (*Mus.*) cymbal.
cymbalier [sɛ̃ba'lje], *n.m.* cymbal player.
cynancie [sinɑ̃'si], [ESQUINANCIE].
cynégétique [sineʒe'tik], *a.* relating to hunting and dogs.—*n.f.* the art of hunting with dogs, cynegetics.
cynique [si'nik], *a.* cynical; snarling, snappish; impudent.—*n.* cynic.
cyniquement [sinik'mɑ̃], *adv.* cynically.
cynisme [si'nism], *n.m.* cynicism; impudence.
cynodrome [sinɔ'droːm], *n.m.* greyhound racing track.
cynosure [sinɔ'syːr], *n.f.* (*Astron.*) Cynosure, Little Bear.
cyprès [si'prɛ], *n.m.* cypress, cypress tree.
cyprière [si'prjɛːr], *n.f.* cypress grove.
cypriote [si'prjɔt], *a.* Cypriot.—*n.* (**Cypriote**) Cypriot (*person*).
cytise [si'tiːz], *n.m.* cytisus, laburnum.
czar [tsaːr], [TZAR].

D

D, d [de], *n.m.* the fourth letter of the alphabet.
d', *abbr.* [DE].
da [da], *particle* (*used after* oui, non) truly, indeed; *oui-da*, yes indeed.
d'abord [da'bɔːr], [ABORD].
dactylo [dakti'lo], *n.f. abbr. of* [DACTYLO-GRAPHE].
dactylographe [daktilɔ'graf], *n.f.* typist.
dactylographie [daktilɔgra'fi], *n.f.* typewriting.
dactylographier [daktilɔgra'fje], *v.t.* to type(write).
dactylographique [daktilɔgra'fik], *a.* typewritten (*report*); typewriting (*material*).
dactyloptère [daktilɔp'tɛːr], *n.m.* flying fish.
dada [da'da], *n.m.* (*childish*) horse. cockhorse; gee-gee.
dadais [da'dɛ], *n.m.* booby, clown, ninny.
dague [dag], *n.f.* dagger, dirk.
daguerréotype [dagereɔ'tip], *n.m.* daguerreotype.
dahlia [da'lja], *n.m.* dahlia.
daigner [dɛ'ne], *v.i.* to deign, to condescend.
d'ailleurs [da'jœːr], [AILLEURS].
daim [dɛ̃], *n.m.* deer, fallow deer; buck.
daine [dɛn], *n.f.* doe.
dais [dɛ], *n.m.* canopy.
dallage [da'laːʒ], *n.m.* paving with flagstones.
dalle [dal], *n.f.* flag, flagstone; slab.
daller [da'le], *v.t.* to pave with flagstones, to flag.
dalleur [da'lœːr], *n.m.* pavior.
dalmate [dal'mat], *a.* Dalmatian.—*n.* (**Dalmate**) Dalmatian (*person*).
dalmatique [dalma'tik], *n.f.* dalmatic.
daltonisme [daltɔ'nism], *n.m.* color blindness.

damas [da'mɑ], *n.m.* damask; damson; Damascus blade.
damasquiner [damaski'ne], *v.t.* to damascene.
damassé [dama'se], *n.m.* damask linen, damask cloth.
damasser [dama'se], *v.t.* to damask.
damassin [dama'sɛ̃], *n.m.* figured linen cloth.
damassure [dama'syːr], *n.f.* damasking (*of linen*); damask work.
dame (1) [dam], *n.f.* (*married*) lady, dame; rowlock; beetle, rammer; (*Cards*, and *Chess*) queen.
dame (2) [dam], *int.* **dame oui**! why, yes!
dame-jeanne [dam'ʒaːn], *n.f.* (*pl.* **dames-jeannes**) demijohn, carboy.
damer [da'me], *v.t.* (*Draughts*) to crown (*a man*); (*Chess*) to queen; to ram (*earth etc.*).
damier [da'mje], *n.m.* draught board.
damnable [dɑ'nabl], *a.* damnable.
damnablement [dɑnablə'mɑ̃],*adv.*damnably.
damnation [dɑna'sjɔ̃], *n.f.* damnation.
damné [dɑ'ne], *a.* and *n.m.* (*fem.* **-ée**) damned (person).
damner [dɑ'ne], *v.t.* to damn. **se damner**, *v.r.* to damn oneself.
dancing [dɑ̃'siŋ], *n.m.* dance hall, palais de danse.
dandin [dɑ̃'dɛ̃], *n.m.* ninny.
dandinement [dɑ̃din'mɑ̃], *n.m.* swinging (*of the body*); rolling gait.
dandiner [dɑ̃di'ne], *v.i.* to swing (*of the body*) to dandle (*of a baby*). **se dandiner**, *v.r.* to waddle.
dandy [dɑ̃'di], *n.m.* dandy.
dandysme [dɑ̃'dism], *n.m.* dandyism.
Danemark [dan'mark], le, *m.* Denmark.
danger [dɑ̃'ʒe], *n.m.* danger, peril, risk, hazard.
dangereusement [dɑ̃ʒrøz'mɑ̃], *adv.* dangerously.
dangereux [dɑ̃'ʒrø], *a.* (*fem.* **-euse**) dangerous.
danois [da'nwa], *a.* Danish.—*n.m.* Danish (*language*); Great Dane (*dog*); (**Danois**, *fem.* **-oise**) Dane (*person*).
dans [dɑ̃], *prep.* in, within; into; with, according to; during; out of.
danse [dɑ̃ːs], *n.f.* dance; dancing; (*fig.*) beating, hiding; **danse de Saint-Guy**, St. Vitus's dance.
danser [dɑ̃'se], *v.t., v.i.* to dance.
danseur [dɑ̃'sœːr], *n.m.* (*fem.* **-euse**) dancer, ballet girl.
dard [daːr], *n.m.* dart; sting; forked tongue (*of a snake*); pistil.
darder [dar'de], *v.t.* to hurl; to spear; to shoot forth, to beam, to dart.
dardillon [dardi'jɔ̃], *n.m.* small dart; barb (*of a fish-hook*).
dare-dare [dar'daːr], *adv.* (*fam.*) in great haste, in double-quick time.
darne [darn], *n.f.* slice (*of fish*).
dartre [dartr], *n.f.* slight and dry eruption (*of the skin*), scurf.
dartreux [dar'trø], *a.* (*fem.* **-euse**) herpetic, scurfy.
date [dat], *n.f.* date.
dater [da'te], *v.t.* to date (*a letter etc.*).—*v.i.* to date (*de*); to reckon.
datif [da'tif], *n.m.* (*Gram.*) dative, dative case.

datte [dat], *n.f.* date.

dattier [da'tje], *n.m.* date palm.

datura [daty'ra], *n.m.* datura, thorn apple.

daube [do:b], *n.f.* stew.

dauber [do'be], *v.t.* to cuff, to drub; (*fig.*) to banter, to jeer at; (*Cook.*) to stew.

daubeur [do'bœ:r], *n.m.* (*fem.* -euse) jeerer, banterer, sneerer.

daubière [do'bjɛ:r], *n.f.* stew pan.

dauphin [do'fɛ̃], *n.m.* dolphin; dauphin (*eldest son of the king of France*).

dauphine [do'fin], *n.f.* wife of the dauphin.

dauphinelle [dofi'nɛl], *n.f.* (*Bot.*) larkspur, delphinium.

daurade [do'rad], *n.f.* gilt-head (*fish*).

davantage [davã'ta:ʒ], *adv.* more, any more; any longer, any further.

davier [da'vje], *n.m.* dentist's forceps; cramp; (*Naut.*) davit.

de [də], *prep.* of; out of, made of, composed of, from; by, with; at, for; concerning, about.

dé (1) [de], *n.m.* die (*for playing*); (*fig.*) throw, hazard.

dé (2) [de], *n.m.* thimble.

débâcher [deba'ʃe], *v.t.* to uncover, to untilt.

débâcle [de'ba:kl], *n.f.* breaking up (*of ice*); (*fig.*) downfall, collapse.

débâcler [deba'kle], *v.t.* to break up (*of ice*).

débâcleur [deba'klœ:r], *n.m.* water or port bailiff.

déballage [deba'la:ʒ], *n.m.* unpacking.

déballer [deba'le], *v.t.* to unpack.

débandade [debã'dad], *n.f.* rout, stampede; **à la débandade**, in confusion.

débander [debã'de], *v.t.* to unbind; to loosen; to remove a bandage from. **se débander**, *v.r.* to slacken; to relax; to disband.

débaptiser [debati'ze], *v.t.* to change the name of.

débarbouillage [debarbu'ja:ʒ], *n.m.* washing, cleansing.

débarbouiller [debarbu'je], *v.t.* to wash, to cleanse. **se débarbouiller**, *v.r.* to wash one's face etc.; (*fig.*) to extricate oneself.

débarcadère [debarka'dɛ:r], *n.m.* landing place, wharf; (*Rail.*) station; arrival platform.

débardage [debar'da:ʒ], *n.m.* unloading (*of wood etc.*).

débarder [debar'de], *v.t.* to unload (*wood etc.*); to clear (*a wood etc.*) of felled trees.

débardeur [debar'dœ:r], *n.m.* stevedore, lighterman, docker.

débarquement [debarkə'mã], *n.m.* landing, disembarkation (*of persons*); unloading (*of goods*).

débarquer [debar'ke], *v.t., v.i.* to disembark, to land.

débarras [deba'ra], *n.m.* riddance, disencumbrance; **chambre de débarras**, lumber-room, box room.

débarrasser [debara'se], *v.t.* to disencumber, to rid; to disentangle, to extricate; to clear (*the table*). **se débarrasser**, *v.r.* to extricate oneself, to rid oneself of, to shake off; to get clear.

débarrer [deba're], *v.t.* to unbar.

débat [de'ba], *n.m.* dispute, contest; debate, discussion; (*pl.*) parliamentary debates.

débateler [debata'le], *v.t.* (*conjug. like* APPELER) to unlade (*boats etc.*).

débâter [debɑ'te], *v.t.* to unsaddle; to take a packsaddle off.

débâtir [debɑ'ti:r], *v.t.* to pull down, to demolish; to unbaste, to untack (*garments*).

débattre [de'batr], *v.t. irr.* (*conjug. like* BATTRE) to debate, to discuss, to argue. **se débattre**, *v.r.* to struggle, to strive; to flounder, to flutter.

débauche [de'bo:ʃ], *n.f.* debauchery; dissoluteness.

débauché [debo'ʃe], *n.m.* debauchee, rake.

débaucher [debo'ʃe], *v.t.* to debauch; to corrupt; to lead astray. **se débaucher**, *v.r.* to become debauched.

débet [de'bɛ], *n.m.* debit.

débile [de'bil], *a.* weak, feeble.

débilement [debil'mã], *adv.* feebly, weakly.

débilité [debili'te], *n.f.* debility, weakness.

débiliter [debili'te], *v.t.* to debilitate, to enfeeble.

débit [de'bi], *n.m.* sale; market; retail; retail shop; (*fig.*) delivery, utterance; (*Book-keeping*) debit.

débitage [debi'ta:ʒ], *n.m.* cutting up (*of stones, timber etc.*).

débitant [debi'tã], *n.m.* (*fem.* -e) retailer, dealer.

débiter [debi'te], *v.t.* to sell; to retail; to supply; to debit; to cut up (*wood, stone etc.*); (*fig.*) to spread, to report, to utter.

débiteur (1) [debi'tœ:r], *n.m.* (*fem.* -trice) debtor.

débiteur (2) [debi'tœ:r], *n.m.* (*fem.* -euse) prattler, gossipmonger.

déblai [de'blɛ], *n.m.* clearing; excavation; (*pl.*) earth, stones etc. cleared away.

déblaiement or **déblayement** [deblɛ'mã], *n.m.* clearance; cutting, excavation, digging.

déblatérer [deblate're], *v.i.* (*conjug. like* CÉDER) to utter violent abuse, to rail (*contre*).

déblayement [DÉBLAIEMENT].

déblayer [deblɛ'je], *v.t.* (*conjug. like* PAYER) to clear away; to clear; (*fig.*) to sweep away (*obstacles etc.*).

déblocage [deblɔ'ka:ʒ], *n.m.* (*Print.*) turning letters.

débloquer [deblɔ'ke], *v.t.* to raise the blockade from; (*Print.*) to turn letters; to unlock; to release.

débobiner [debobi'ne], *v.t.* to unwind.

déboire [de'bwa:r], *n.m.* after-taste; (*fig.*) disappointment, vexation.

déboisement [debwaz'mã], *n.m.* clearing of trees, deforestation.

déboiser [debwa'ze], *v.t.* to clear of trees.

déboîtement [debwat'mã], *n.m.* dislocation.

déboîter [debwa'te], *v.t.* to put out of joint, to dislocate; (*Elec.*) to disconnect. **se déboîter**, *v.r.* to be dislocated.

débonder [debɔ̃'de], *v.t.* to unplug, to unstopper; to loosen, to unbind.—*v.i.* or **se débonder**, *v.r.* to gush, to break out, to burst forth; to be relaxed (*of a person*).

débonnaire [debɔ'nɛ:r], *a.* good-natured, easy-tempered.

débonnairement [debɔnɛr'mã], *adv.* compliantly, easily.

débonnaireté [debɔnɛr'te], *n.f.* compliance, good nature.

débordé [debɔr'de], *a.* overflowing (*river*); overwhelmed (*man*); outflanked (*troops*).

97

débordement [debɔrdə'mã], *n.m.* overflowing, flood; outburst; (*fig.*) dissoluteness.
déborder [debɔr'de], *v.t.* to take off the border from; to go beyond; to outrun.—*v.i.* to overflow, to run over; to project, to jut out. **se déborder**, *v.r.* to overflow; to run over, to burst forth.
débordoir [debɔr'dwa:r], *n.m.* edging tool; spoke shave.
débosseler [debɔs'le], *v.t.* (*conjug. like* APPELER) to take the dents out of.
débotté or **débotter** (1) [debɔ'te], *n.m.* the moment of taking boots off; (*fig.*) *au débotté*, at once.
débotter (2) [debɔ'te], *v.t.* to pull off (*someone's*) boots. **se débotter**, *v.r.* to take off one's boots.
débouché [debu'ʃe], *n.m.* outlet, issue; waterway; (*Comm.*) market, sale.
débouchage [debu'ʃa:3], **débouchement** [debuʃ'mã], *n.m.* uncorking; outlet; market, sale.
déboucher [debu'ʃe], *v.t.* to open, to clear; to uncork; to unplug.—*v.i.* to emerge; to empty itself (*of rivers*); (*Mil.*) to debouch.
déboucler [debu'kle], *v.t.* to unbuckle; to uncurl.
débouler [debu'le], *v.i.* to roll down (*like a ball*); to start off suddenly (*like a hare*).
déboulonner [debulɔ'ne], *v.t.* to unrivet, to unbolt.
débourrer [debu're], *v.t.* to draw the wad or wadding out of (*fire arms*); to empty the tobacco out of (*a pipe*); (*fig.*) to polish (*a person's manners*).
débours [de'bu:r], **déboursé** [debur'se], *n.m.* disbursement, outlay.
déboursement [deburs'mã], *n.m.* outlay, expenditure.
débourser [debur'se], *v.t.* to disburse, to expend, to lay out.
debout [də'bu], *adv.* upright, on end, standing up; out of bed, up; in existence; (*Naut.*) ahead (*of the wind*).
déboutonner [debutɔ'ne], *v.t.* to unbutton. **se déboutonner**, *v.r.* to unbutton oneself; (*colloq.*) to unbosom oneself.
débraillé [debra'je], *a.* loosely dressed, in disorder.—*n.m.* disorder, untidiness; (*fig.*) license.
débrailler (se) [sadebra'je], *v.r.* to uncover one's breast, to be untidy or disordered.
débrancher [debrã'ʃe], *v.t.* (*Elec.*) to disconnect.
débrayage [debrɛ'ja:3], **désembrayage** [dezãbrɛ'ja:3], *n.m.* disengaging gear (*of motors etc.*); declutching.
débrayer [debrɛ'je], *v.t.* (*conjug. like* PAYER) to throw out of gear, to disengage, to declutch.
débridement [debrid'mã], *n.m.* unbridling; (*fig.*) dispatch, hurry.
débrider [debri'de], *v.t. v.i.* to unbridle (*horse*); to halt.
débris [de'bri], *n.m.* (*usu. in pl.*) remains, debris; rubbish.
débrouillard [debru'ja:r], *a.* and *n.m.* (*fem.* -e) (*colloq.*) resourceful (person).
débrouiller [debru'je], *v.t.* to disentangle, to unravel; (*fig.*) to explain. **se débrouiller**, *v.r.* to be cleared up; to get out of difficulties, to manage.

débusquement [debyska'mã], *n.m.* driving out, dislodging.
débusquer [debys'ke], *v.t.* to turn out, to oust, to expel; (*Hunt.*) to start.
début [de'by], *n.m.* lead; outset; début.
débutant [deby'tã], *n.m.* (*fem.* -e) actor or actress appearing for the first time; beginner.
débuter [deby'te], *v.i.* to lead, to play first; to open; to start; to make one's début.
deçà [də'sa], *prep.* on this side of; short of, well within.—*adv.* here, on this side; *deçà* (*et*) *delà*, here and there.
décachetage [dekaʃ'ta:3], *n.m.* unsealing, opening.
décacheter [dekaʃ'te], *v.t.* (*conjug. like* APPELER) to unseal, to open.
décadaire [deka'dɛ:r], *a.* decadal.
décade [de'kad], *n.f.* decade, group of ten.
décadenasser [dekadna'se], *v.t.* to unpadlock.
décadence [deka'dã:s], *n.f.* decadence, decline, wane.
décadent [deka'dã], *a.* and *n.m.* (*fem.* -e) decadent (person).
décaèdre [deka'edr], *a.* decahedral.—*n.m.* decahedron.
décagonal [dekagɔ'nal], *a.* (*pl.* -aux) decagonal (*ten-sided*).
décagone [deka'gɔn], *n.m.* decagon.
décagramme [deka'gram], *n.m.* decagramme, ten grammes.
décaissement [dekɛs'mã], **décaissage** [dekɛ'sa:3], *n.m.* uncasing, unpacking.
décaisser [dekɛ'se], *v.t.* to unpack; to pay out.
décaler [deka'le], *v.t.* to unwedge.
décalaminage [dekalami'na:3], *n.m.* (*Motor.*) decarbonizing.
décalaminer [dekalami'ne], *v.t.* to decarbonize.
décalitre [deka'litr], *n.m.* decalitre (2·2 gallons).
décalquer [dekal'ke], *v.t.* to transfer (*a tracing*), to countertrace.
décamètre [deka'mɛtr], *n.m.* decametre.
décamper [dekã'pe], *v.i.* to decamp; (*fig.*) to bolt.
décanter [dekã'te], *v.t.* to decant, to pour off gently.
décapitation [dekapita'sjõ], *n.f.* decapitation, beheading.
décapiter [dekapi'te], *v.t.* to behead, to decapitate.
décapotable [dekapɔ'tabl], *a.* (*Motor.*) convertible.
décarboniser [dekarbɔni'ze], *v.t.* to decarbonize.
décarburation [dekarbyra'sjõ], *n.f.* decarbonization.
décarburer [dekarby're], *v.t.* to decarburize, to decarbonize.
décastère [deka'stɛ:r], *n.m.* measure of 10 steres or cubic metres (13.1 cubic yards).
décathlon [dekat'lõ], *n.m.* (*spt.*) decathlon.
décauville [dəko'vil], *n.m.* narrow gauge railway.
décaver [deka've], *v.t.* to win the whole of the stakes from, (*fam.*) to clean out; (*fig.*) to ruin, to beggar.
décédé [dese'de], *n.m.* (*fem.* -ée) deceased (*person*).
décéder [dese'de], *v.i.* (*conjug. like* CÉDER) to die, to decease.

décèlement [desɛl'mã], *n.m.* disclosure, exposure, discovery.

déceler [des'le], *v.t.* (*conjug. like* AMENER) to disclose, to reveal, to betray. **se déceler,** *v.r.* to betray oneself.

déceleur [des'lœːr], *n.m.* (*fem.* **-euse**) betrayer, revealer.

décembre [de'sãːbr], *n.m.* December.

décemment [desa'mã], *adv.* decently.

décence [de'sãːs], *n.f.* decency, propriety.

décent [de'sã], *a.* decent, becoming; modest.

décentralisation [desãtraliza'sjõ], *n.f.* decentralization.

décentraliser [desãtrali'ze], *v.t.* to decentralize.

déception [desɛp'sjõ], *n.f.* disappointment; deception, deceit.

décernement [desɛrnə'mã], *n.m.* awarding.

décerner [desɛr'ne], *v.t.* to decree, to enact; to award, to confer (*an honor*); to issue (*a summons etc.*).

décès [de'sɛ], *n.m.* decease, demise, death.

décevant [des'vã], *a.* deceptive; disappointing.

décevoir [desə'vwaːr], *v.t. irr.* (*conjug. like* RECEVOIR) to deceive; to disappoint.

déchaînement [deʃɛn'mã], *n.m.* unbridling, bursting (*of storm*); outburst (*of passion*); fury, rage; invective.

déchaîner [deʃɛ'ne], *v.t.* to unchain, to let loose; to give vent to (*passion*). **se déchaîner,** *v.r.* to break loose; to burst out; to run wild (*of passions etc.*).

déchaler [deʃa'le], *v.i.* to ebb; to lie dry.

déchanter [deʃã'te], *v.i.* to lower one's key (*in singing*); (*fig.*) to lower one's pretensions, to sing another tune.

déchaperonner [deʃaprɔ'ne], *v.t.* to unhood (*a hawk etc.*); to uncope (*a wall*).

décharge [de'ʃarʒ], *n.f.* unloading; rebate (*on a tax*); outlet, discharge (*of water etc.*); (*Law*) discharge, acquittal; (*Mil.*) volley.

déchargement [deʃarʒə'mã], *n.m.* unloading, unlading.

décharger [deʃar'ʒe], *v.t.* (*conjug. like* MANGER) to unload; to empty; to disburden; to discharge; to fire (*fire-arms*); to acquit (*de*). **se décharger,** *v.r.* to be unloaded, to discharge; to give vent (*to*); to unburden oneself.

déchargeur [deʃar'ʒœːr], *n.m.* unloader, wharf porter, heaver, lumper.

décharné [deʃar'ne], *a.* fleshless; lean, emaciated.

décharnement [deʃarnə'mã], *n.m.* emaciation.

décharner [deʃar'ne], *v.t.* to strip the flesh off; to emaciate.

déchaumage [deʃo'maːʒ], *n.m.* (*Agric.*) ploughing up fallow ground.

déchaumer [deʃo'me], *v.t.* to plough up the stubble on; to break up (*fallow land*).

déchaussé [deʃo'se], *a.* barefooted.

déchausser [deʃo'se], *v.t.* to pull off (*some-one's*) shoes and stockings; to lay bare the root or base (*of trees, buildings, teeth etc.*). **se déchausser,** *v.r.* to take off one's shoes and stockings.

déchéance [deʃe'ãːs], *n.f.* forfeiture; disgrace; deposition.

déchet [de'ʃɛ], *n.m.* loss, waste, offal.

décheveler [deʃə'vle], *v.t.* (*conjug. like* APPELER) to dishevel [ÉCHEVELER].

déchevêtrer [deʃəvɛ'tre], *v.t.* to unhalter (*a beast of burden*).

décheviller [deʃəvi'je], *v.t.* to unpeg, to unpin.

déchiffrable [deʃi'frabl], *a.* legible.

déchiffrement [deʃifrə'mã], *n.m.* deciphering; reading or playing at sight.

déchiffrer [deʃi'fre], *v.t.* to decipher, to unravel; to read or play at sight. **se déchiffrer,** *v.r.* to be deciphered.

déchiffreur [deʃi'frœːr], *n.m.* (*fem.* **-euse**) decipherer; sight reader; *déchiffreur de radar,* radar scanner.

déchiqueté [deʃik'te], *a.* jagged, indented.

déchiqueter [deʃik'te], *v.t.* (*conjug. like* APPELER) to cut, to slash, to hack; to cut into long pieces.

déchiqueture [deʃik'tyːr], *n.f.* tear, slash.

déchirage [deʃi'raːʒ], *n.m.* ripping up, breaking up (*of a ship etc.*).

déchirant [deʃi'rã], *a.* heart-rending, piercing; excruciating.

déchirement [deʃir'mã], *n.m.* rending, tearing, laceration; (*fig.*) heart-break.

déchirer [deʃi're], *v.t.* to tear to pieces, to rend; (*fig.*) to torture; to revile. **se déchirer,** *v.r.* to tear, to be torn; to defame each other.

déchirure [deʃi'ryːr], *n.f.* rent, tear; fissure.

déchoir [de'ʃwaːr], *v.i. irr.* to decay, to fall off, to decline; to sink.

déchouer [deʃu'e], *v.t.* to get off, to set afloat.

déchu [de'ʃy], *a.* fallen, decayed; sunken; *ange déchu,* fallen angel.

décidé [desi'de], *a.* decided, determined, resolved.

décidément [deside'mã], *adv.* decidedly, positively; firmly; definitely.

décider [desi'de], *v.t.* to decide, to determine, to settle; to induce, to persuade.—*v.i.* to decide. **se décider,** *v.r.* to decide, to determine, to make up one's mind.

décigramme [desi'gram], *n.m.* decigram (*one-tenth of a gramme,* 1.54 *grains*).

décilitre [desi'litr], *n.m.* decilitre (*one-tenth of a·litre*).

décimal [desi'mal], *a.* (*m.pl.* **-aux**) decimal.— *n.f.* (**-e**) a decimal.

décimalisation [desimaliza'sjõ], *n.f.* decimalization.

décimaliser [desimali'ze], *v.t.* to decimalize.

décimateur [desima'tœːr], *n.m.* tithe owner.

décime [de'sim], *n.f.* tithe.

décimer [desi'me], *v.t.* to decimate, to destroy, to annihilate.

décimètre [desi'mɛtr], *n.m.* decimetre (3.937 *inches*).

décimo [desi'mo], *adv.* tenthly.

décintrer [desɛ̃'tre], *v.t.* to remove the centerings from (*arches*).

décisif [desi'zif], *a.* (*fem.* **-sive**) decisive, conclusive.

décision [desi'zjõ], *n.f.* decision, determination; resolution.

décisivement [desiziv'mã], *adv.* decisively; peremptorily, positively.

décistère [desi'stɛːr], *n.m.* tenth of a stere (3·53 *cubic feet*).

déciviliser [desivili'ze], *v.t.* to decivilize.

déclamateur [deklama'tœːr], *n.m.* (*fem.* **-trice**) declaimer; (*fig.*) tub-thumper.—*a.* (*fem.* **-trice**) declamatory, bombastic.

déclamation [deklama'sjɔ̃], *n.f.* declamation, elocution.

déclamatoire [deklama'twaːr], *a.* declamatory.

déclamer [dekla'me], *v.t., v.i.* to declaim; to spout, to mouth.

déclarant [dekla'rɑ̃], *n.m.* (*Law*) informant.

déclaration [deklara'sjɔ̃], *n.f.* declaration, proclamation; disclosure; notification; *déclaration sous serment*, affidavit.

déclaratoire [deklara'twaːr], *a.* declaratory.

déclarer [dekla're], *v.t.* to declare, to make known; to proclaim; to certify. **se déclarer,** *v.r.* to speak one's mind; to declare oneself *or* itself; to show oneself *or* itself.

déclassé [dekla'se], *a.* come down in the world.—*n.m.* (*fem.* **-ée**) one who has come down in the world; one rejected by his own class *or* sphere.

déclassement [deklas'mɑ̃], *n.m.* loss of social position.

déclasser [dekla'se], *v.t.* to alter the classing of; to transfer from one class to another (*on trains, boats etc.*); to strike off the rolls, to dismiss from the service.

déclencher [deklɑ̃'ʃe], *v.t.* to unlatch (*a door*); to unhook, to detach; to release; (*Mil.*) to launch (*an attack*).

déclic [de'klik], *n.m.* pawl, catch.

déclin [de'klɛ̃], *n.m.* decline; decay; wane (*of the moon*); ebb; close (*of day etc.*).

déclinaison [deklinɛ'zɔ̃], *n.f.* (*Gram.*) declension.

déclinant [dekli'nɑ̃], *a.* declining.

décliner [dekli'ne], *v.t.* to refuse; (*Gram.*) to decline; to state.—*v.i.* to decline, to be on the wane, to fall off.

déclive [de'kliːv], *a.* declivous, sloping.

déclivité [deklivi'te], *n.f.* declivity, slope.

décloîtrer (**se**) [sədeklwa'tre], *v.r.* to leave the cloister, to return to the world.

déclore [de'klɔːr], *v.t. irr.* (*conjug. like* CLORE) to unclose, to throw open.

décochement [dekɔʃ'mɑ̃], *n.m.* discharge, shooting (*of arrows, shafts etc.*).

décocher [dekɔ'ʃe], *v.t.* to discharge, to dart (*arrows etc.*); to let fly (*insults etc.*).

décoiffer [dekwa'fe], *v.t.* to remove *or* undo the coiffure of, to undress the hair of. **se décoiffer,** *v.r.* to undo one's head-dress; to take off one's hat.

décoincer (**se**) [sədekwɛ̃'se], *v.r.* (*conjug. like* COMMENCER) to work loose.

décollage [dekɔ'laːʒ], *n.m.* (*Av.*) taking off.

décollement [dekɔl'mɑ̃], *n.m.* ungluing, unpasting; coming off; detachment (*of retina*).

décoller [dekɔ'le], *v.t.* to unglue.—*v.i.* (*Av.*) to take off. **se décoller,** *v.r.* to become unglued, to come off.

décolletage [dekɔl'taːʒ], *n.m.* lowness in the neck (*of dresses*); baring the neck and shoulders.

décolleté [dekɔl'te], *a.* (*Dress.*) low-necked.

décolleter [dekɔl'te], *v.t.* (*conjug. like* APPELER) to uncover the neck, shoulders etc., of; to cut (*a dress*) low. **se décolleter,** *v.r.* to bare one's shoulders; to wear a low dress.

décoloration [dekɔlɔra'sjɔ̃], *n.f.* discoloration.

décoloré [dekɔlɔ're], *a.* discolored, faded.

décolorer [dekɔlɔ're], *v.t.* to discolor. **se décolorer,** *v.r.* to become discolored, to fade.

décombres [de'kɔ̃ːbr], *n.m.* (*used only in pl.*) rubbish, debris, ruins.

décommander [dekɔmɑ̃'de], *v.t.* to countermand; to cancel.

décomposé [dekɔpo'ze], *a.* decomposed.

décomposer [dekɔpo'ze], *v.t.* to decompose; to break up; to distort. **se décomposer,** *v.r.* to decompose, to rot; (*fig.*) to be distorted (*of the face etc.*).

décomposition [dekɔpozi'sjɔ̃], *n.f.* decomposition, analysis.

décompresseur [dekɔprɛ'sœːr], *n.m.* (*Motor.*) exhaust valve.

décompte [de'kɔ̃ːt], *n.m.* deduction, discount, allowance; deficit; balance due; (*fig.*) drawback; disappointment.

décompter [dekɔ̃'te], *v.t.* to deduct.—*v.i.* (*fig.*) to be disappointed.

déconcertant [dekɔ̃sɛr'tɑ̃], *a.* disconcerting.

déconcerter [dekɔ̃sɛr'te], *v.t.* to disconcert; to baffle. **se déconcerter,** *v.r.* to be disconcerted *or* put out.

déconfiture [dekɔ̃fi'tyːr], *n.f.* discomfiture; break-down; insolvency.

décongeler [dekɔ̃'ʒle], *v.t.* (*conjug. like* AMENER) to thaw (*chilled meat*).

déconseiller [dekɔ̃sɛ'je], *v.t.* to dissuade.

déconsidération [dekɔ̃sidera'sjɔ̃], *n.f.* disrepute, discredit.

déconsidérer [dekɔ̃side're], *v.t.* (*conjug. like* CÉDER) to bring into disrepute, to discredit. **se déconsidérer,** *v.r.* to fall into disrepute.

décontenancement [dekɔ̃tnɑ̃s'mɑ̃], *n.m.* mortification, embarrassment.

décontenancer [dekɔ̃tnɑ̃'se], *v.t.* (*conjug. like* COMMENCER) to abash, to put out of countenance. **se décontenancer,** *v.r.* to be put out of countenance, to be abashed.

déconvenue [dekɔ̃v'ny], *n.f.* discomfiture; disappointment, set-back.

décor [de'kɔːr], *n.m.* decoration; (*Theat., pl.*) scenery.

décorateur [dekɔra'tœːr], *n.m.* (*fem.* **-trice**) ornamental painter, decorator; scene painter.

décoratif [dekɔra'tif], *a.* (*fem.* **-tive**) decorative, ornamental.

décoration [dekɔra'sjɔ̃], *n.f.* decoration, embellishment; medal, insignia (*of an order*).

décorder [dekɔr'de], *v.t.* to untwist, to untwine (*a cord etc.*); to untie the rope (*of a box*).

décoré [dekɔ're], *a.* decorated; wearing the insignia of some order *or* its ribbon in one's buttonhole.

décorer [dekɔ're], *v.t.* to decorate; to set off; to confer the Legion of Honor etc. upon.

décorner [dekɔr'ne], *v.t.* to dishorn.

décortiquer [dekɔrti'ke], *v.t.* to decorticate, to bark, to husk, to shell, to peel.

décorum [dekɔ'rɔm], *n.m.* decorum, propriety.

découcher [deku'ʃe], *v.i.* to sleep away from home; to stay out all night.

découdre [de'kudr] *v.t. irr. (conjug. like* COUDRE) to unsew, to unstitch; to rip up. **se découdre**, *v.r.* to come unstitched.

découler [deku'le], *v.i.* to trickle, to flow; to spring, to proceed *(from)*.

découpage [deku'pa:ʒ], *n.m.* cutting out, carving out.

découpé [deku'pe], *a. (Bot.)* cut, denticulated.

découper [deku'pe], *v.t.* to cut up; to pink, to cut out; to punch. **se découper**, *v.r.* to stand out, to show up *(against)*.

découpeur [deku'pœ:r], *n.m. (fem.* **-euse**) carver; pinker, cutter.

découplé [deku'ple], *a.* strapping.

découpler [deku'ple], *v.t.* to uncouple, to unleash, to let loose *(in pursuit)*.

découpoir [deku'pwa:r], *n.m.* punch, stamping machine, stamping press.

découpure [deku'py:r], *n.f.* cutting out, pinking, work cut out; cut paper-work; indentation.

décourageant [dekuraʒ'ɑ̃], *a.* discouraging, disheartening.

découragement [dekuraʒ'mɑ̃], *n.m.* discouragement.

décourager [dekura'ʒe], *v.t. (conjug. like* MANGER) to discourage, to dishearten. **se décourager**, *v.r.* to be disheartened.

décours [de'ku:r], *n.m.* decrease; wane *(of the moon)*.

décousu [deku'zy], *a.* unsewn, unstitched; *(fig.)* desultory *(of style etc.)*.

décousure [deku'zy:r], *n.f.* unpicked stitching.

découvert [deku'vɛ:r], *a.* uncovered; discovered; open, unguarded; bare, bareheaded.—*n.m. (Comm.)* overdraft, deficit.

découverte [deku'vɛrt], *n.f.* discovery, detection; *(Mil.)* reconnoitring; *(Naut.)* look out.

découvreur [deku'vrœ:r], *n.m. (fem.* **-euse**) discoverer.

découvrir [deku'vri:r], *v.t. (conjug. like* OUVRIR) to uncover, to expose; to discover, to disclose, to detect. **se découvrir**, *v.r.* to uncover oneself, to take off one's hat; to unbosom oneself; to expose oneself; to lie open or bare; to clear up *(of the sky)*.

décramponner (se) [sədekrɑ̃pɔ'ne], *v.r.* to let go one's hold.

décrasser [dekra'se], *v.t.* to take the dirt off, to scour; *(fig.)* to make presentable. **se décrasser**, *v.r.* to wash, to clean oneself; to become polished.

décrassoir [dekra'swa:r], *n.m.* fine-tooth comb.

décréditement [dekredit'mɑ̃], *n.m.* discrediting.

décrépi [dekre'pi], *a.* unplastered.

décrépir (se) [sədekre'pi:r], *v.r.* to lose its plaster *(of a wall etc.)*.

décrépit [dekre'pi], *a.* decrepit, broken-down.

décrépitude [dekrepi'tyd], *n.f.* decrepitude.

décret [de'krɛ], *n.m.* decree, order, enactment; *(Law)* writ, warrant.

décret-loi [dekrɛ'lwa], *n.m.* Order in Council.

décréter [dekre'te], *v.t. (conjug. like* CÉDER) to decree, to order, to enact.

décri [de'kri], *n.m.* official crying down *or* depreciation *(of coinage)*; *(fig.)* discredit.

décrier [dekri'e], *v.t.* to decry, to run down;

(fig.) to discredit. **se décrier**, *v.r.* to bring oneself into disrepute; to decry one another.

décrire [de'kri:r], *v.t. irr. (conjug. like* ÉCRIRE) to describe, to depict. **se décrire**, *v.r.* to be described.

décrocher [dekrɔ'ʃe], *v.t.* to unhook, to take down, to disconnect.

décroiser [dekrwa'ze], *v.t.* to uncross *(the legs etc.)*.

décroissant [dekrwa'sɑ̃], *a.* decreasing, diminishing; subsiding.

décroissement [dekrwas'mɑ̃], *n.m.*, **décroissance** [dekrwa'sɑ̃:s], *n.f.* decrease, diminution, wane.

décroît [de'krwa], *n.m.* wane *(of the moon)*.

décroître [de'krwa:tr], *v.i. irr. (conjug. like* CROÎTRE) to decrease, to diminish, to wane.

décrottage [dekrɔ'ta:ʒ], *n.m.* cleaning *(of boots, trousers etc.)*.

décrotter [dekrɔ'te], *v.t.* to rub the dirt off; *(fig.)* to improve the manners of. **se décrotter**, *v.r.* to clean oneself; to clean one's shoes etc.

décrotteur [dekrɔ'tœ:r], *n.m. (fem.* **-euse**) bootblack.

décrottoir [dekrɔ'twa:r], *n.m.* scraper *(for shoes)*.

décrottoire [dekrɔ'twa:r], *n.f.* shoe brush.

décrue [de'kry], *n.f.* decrease; fall *(of water)*.

décrypter [dekrip'te], *v.t.* to decipher.

déculotter [dekylɔ'te], *v.t.* to take off *(s.o.'s)* breeches, *(a child's)* pants.

décuple [de'kypl], *a.* and *n.m.* tenfold.

décupler [deky'ple], *v.t.* to increase tenfold.

décuvage [deky'va:ʒ], *n.m.*, **décuvaison** [dekyvɛ'zɔ̃], *n.f.* tunning *(of wine)*.

décuver [deky've], *v.t.* to tun.

dédaigner [dedɛ'ɲe], *v.t.* to disdain, to scorn, to despise.

dédaigneusement [dedɛɲøz'mɑ̃], *adv.* disdainfully, scornfully.

dédaigneux [dedɛ'ɲø], *a. (fem.* **-euse**) disdainful, scornful.

dédain [de'dɛ̃], *n.m.* disdain, scorn, disregard.

dédale [de'dal], *n.m.* labyrinth, maze.

dedans [dǝ'dɑ̃], *adv.* within, in, inside; at home.—*n.m.* inside, interior.

dédicace [dedi'kas], *n.f.* dedication, consecration *(of a church etc.)*.

dédication [dedika'sjɔ̃], *n.f. (Law)* dedication *(of a temple etc.)*.

dédier [de'dje], *v.t.* to dedicate, to consecrate; to devote; to inscribe *(a book etc.)*.

dédire [de'di:r], *v.t. irr. (conjug. like* MÉDIRE) to disown; gainsay, to contradict. **se dédire**, *v.r.* to recant, to retract, to go back on one's word.

dédit [de'di], *n.m.* retraction; forfeit.

dédommagement [dedɔmaʒ'mɑ̃], *n.m.* indemnification; compensation, damages.

dédommager [dedɔma'ʒe], *v.t. (conjug. like* MANGER) to make amends for; to compensate, to make up for. **se dédommager**, *v.r.* to indemnify oneself.

dédorer [dedɔ're], *v.t.* to ungild. **se dédorer**, *v.r.* to lose its gilt *(of metal etc.)*.

dédouanement [dedwan'mɑ̃], *n.m. (customs)* clearance.

dédouaner [dedwa'ne], *v.t.* to clear *(goods)* from the custom house.

dédoublement

dédoublement [dedubləˈmɑ̃], **dédoublage** [deduˈblaː3], *n.m.* dividing into two; un-lining (*of a garment*); diluting.

dédoubler [deduˈble], *v.t.* to take out the lining of; to divide into two; *dédoubler un autocar (un train),* to run a relief coach (train). **se dédoubler,** *v.r.* to be divided into two.

déductif [dedykˈtif], *a.* (*fem.* **-tive**) deductive.

déduction [dedykˈsjɔ̃], *n.f.* deduction, allowance; inference.

déduire [deˈdɥiːr], *v.t. irr.* (*conjug. like* CONDUIRE) to deduct, to subtract; to deduce, to infer.

déesse [deˈɛs], *n.f.* goddess, female deity.

défâcher [defaˈʃe], *v.t.* to pacify. **se dé-fâcher,** *v.r.* to be pacified, to cool down.

défaillance [defaˈjɑ̃ːs], *n.f.* fainting fit, swoon, faintness; exhaustion; extinction (*of a family etc.*).

défaillant [defaˈjɑ̃], *a.* failing, falling off; decaying; without heirs; weak, feeble.—*n.m.* (*fem.* **-e**) (*Law*) defaulter.

défaillir [defaˈjiːr], *v.i. irr.* (*conjug. like* ASSAILLIR) to fail, to default; to decay; to swoon, to faint away.

défaire [deˈfɛːr], *v.t. irr.* (*conjug. like* FAIRE) to undo, to unmake; to defeat; to emaciate; to embarrass; to foil. **se défaire,** *v.r.* to come undone; *se défaire de,* to get rid of, to give up.

défait [deˈfɛ], *a.* undone, defeated; meager, wasted; worn out.

défaite [deˈfɛt], *n.f.* defeat, overthrow; evasion, pretence, excuse.

défaitisme [defeˈtism], *n.m.* defeatism.

défaitiste [defeˈtist], *a.* and *n.* defeatist.

défalcation [defalkaˈsjɔ̃], *n.f.* deduction.

défalquer [defalˈke], *v.t.* to take off, to deduct.

défausser [defoˈse], *v.t.* to straighten.

défaut [deˈfo], *n.m.* absence, lack, default; defect, fault, flaw; (*Law*) non-appearance; *à défaut de,* instead of, for want of; *faire défaut,* to be wanting, to be missing.

défaveur [defaˈvœːr], *n.f.* disfavor, discredit.

défavorable [defavoˈrabl], *a.* unfavorable.

défavorablement [defavorabləˈmɑ̃], *adv.* unfavorably.

défectif [defɛkˈtif], *a.* (*fem.* **-tive**) (*Gram.*) defective.

défection [defɛkˈsjɔ̃], *n.f.* defection, falling off, disloyalty.

défectueux [defɛkˈtɥø], *a.* (*fem.* **-euse**) defective, imperfect.

défectuosité [defɛktɥoziˈte], *n.f.* defect, imperfection, flaw.

défendable [defɑ̃ˈdabl], *a.* defensible, tenable.

défendeur [defɑ̃ˈdœːr], *n.m.* (*fem.* **-eresse**) defendant; respondent.

défendre [deˈfɑ̃ːdr], *v.t.* to defend, to protect; to shield; to support; to forbid. **se défendre,** *v.r.* to defend oneself; to clear oneself; to deny.

défense [deˈfɑ̃ːs], *n.f.* defense, protection; prohibition; apology, plea; (*Law*) the defense; (*Fort., pl.*) outworks; tusk, fang (*of animals*); (*Naut.*) fender; *défense de fumer,* no smoking.

défenseur [defɑ̃ˈsœːr], *n.m.* defender, supporter; advocate, counsel.

défensif [defɑ̃ˈsif], *a.* (*fem.* **-sive**) defensive. —*n.f.* (**-sive**) defensive.

déféquer [defeˈke], *v.t.* (*conjug. like* CÉDER) to purify.—*v.i.* to defecate.

déférence [defeˈrɑ̃ːs], *n.f.* deference, regard, respect.

déférent [defeˈrɑ̃], *a.* deferential, compliant.

déférer [defeˈre], *v.t.* (*conjug. like* CÉDER) * to confer, to bestow; to tender; to accuse, to inform against.—*v.i.* to defer, to yield, to comply.

déferler [defɛrˈle], *v.t.* (*Naut.*) to unfurl.—*v.i.* to break into foam (*of the sea*).

déferrer [defɛˈre], *v.t.* to unshoe (*a horse*). **se déferrer,** *v.r.* to come unshod, to lose a shoe.

défeuiller [defœˈje], *v.t.* to take the leaves off. **se défeuiller,** *v.r.* to shed its leaves.

défi [deˈfi], *n.m.* defiance, challenge.

défiance [deˈfjɑ̃ːs], *n.f.* distrust, mistrust; caution.

défiant [deˈfjɑ̃], *a.* distrustful, suspicious.

déficeler [defisˈle], *v.t.* (*conjug. like* APPELER) to untie; to undo.

déficient [defiˈsjɑ̃], *a.* deficient.

déficit [defiˈsit], *n.m.* deficit, deficiency.

défier [deˈfje], *v.t.* to defy, to challenge; to brave, to face; to set at defiance. **se défier,** *v.r.* to defy *or* to challenge each other; to distrust, to beware (*de*).

défiger [defiˈ3e], *v.t.* (*conjug. like* MANGER) to liquefy.

défiguration [defigyraˈsjɔ̃], *n.f.,* **défigurement** [defigyrˈmɑ̃], *n.m.* disfigurement, defacement.

défigurer [defigyˈre], *v.t.* to disfigure, to mar; to distort. **se défigurer,** *v.r.* to disfigure oneself; to become deformed.

défilade [defiˈlad], *n.f.* filing off *or* past, marching past; succession.

défilé [defiˈle], *n.m.* defile, narrow pass, gorge; (*fig.*) strait, difficulty; (*Mil.*) filing past; *un défilé de mannequins,* a mannequin parade.

défiler [defiˈle], *v.t.* to unstring, to unthread; to untwist.—*v.i.* to file off, to march past. **se défiler,** *v.r.* to come unthreaded *or* unstrung; (*Mil.*) to take cover; to slip away.

défini [defiˈni], *a.* definite, determined, defined.

définir [defiˈniːr], *v.t.* to define; to determine; to describe.

définissable [definiˈsabl], *a.* definable.

définitif [definiˈtif], *a.* (*fem.* **-tive**) definitive, final; ultimate, eventual.

définition [definiˈsjɔ̃], *n.f.* definition.

définitivement [definitivˈmɑ̃], *adv.* definitively, positively, decidedly; eventually.

déflation [defloˈsjɔ̃], *n.f.* deflation.

défléchir [defleˈʃiːr], *v.t., v.i.* to turn from *or* aside, to deflect.

déflecteur [deflɛkˈtœːr], *n.m.* (*Motor.*) ventilating window; deflector.

défleuraison [deflœrɛˈzɔ̃] (DÉFLORAISON).

défleurir [deflœˈriːr], *v.t.* to nip *or* strip off blossoms.—*v.i.* to lose its flowers.

déflexion [deflɛkˈsjɔ̃], *n.f.* deviation; (*Gram.*) deflection.

défloraison [deflorɛˈzɔ̃], **défleuraison** [deflœrɛˈzɔ̃], *n.f.* fall *or* withering of the blossom.

déflorer [defloˈre], *v.t.* to deflower, to seduce.

défonçage [defɔ̃'saːʒ], **défoncement** [defɔ̃s'mã], *n.m.* staving in (*of the head of casks*), breaking *or* smashing in; (*Agric.*) deep trenching.

défoncer [defɔ̃'se], *v.t.* (*conjug. like* COMMENCER) to stave in, to bilge (*a cask*); to dig deeply, to trench (*ground*). **se défoncer**, *v.r.* to give way; to break up (*of roads*); to get battered.

défonceuse [defɔ̃'søːz], *n.f.* trenching plough.

déforestation [defɔrɛsta'sjɔ̃], *n.f.* deforestation.

déformant [defɔr'mã], *a.* distorting (*mirror etc.*).

déformation [defɔrma'sjɔ̃], *n.f.* distortion, buckling.

déformer [defɔr'me], *v.t.* to deform, to distort. **se déformer**, *v.r.* to lose its shape.

défortifier [defɔrti'fje], *v.t.* to dismantle the fortifications of.

défourner [defur'ne], *v.t.* to draw out of an oven *or* kiln.

défourrer [defu're], *v.t.* to unwrap, to take out of its cover; to thresh (*grain*).

défraîchir [defrɛ'ʃiːr], *v.t.* to tarnish, to take away the brilliancy, gloss *or* freshness of. **se défraîchir**, *v.r.* to lose its brilliancy, freshness etc., to tarnish.

défrayer [defrɛ'je], *v.t.* (*conjug. like* PAYER) to defray, to bear the cost of; to amuse.

défriche [de'friʃ], *n.f.*, **défriché** [defri'ʃe], *n.m.* piece of cleared land.

défrichement [defriʃ'mã], **défrichage** [defri'ʃaːʒ], *n.m.* clearing, breaking up (*of land for tillage*).

défricher [defri'ʃe], *v.t.* to clear, to break up (*ground*) for tillage; to reclaim.

défricheur [defri'ʃœːr], *n.m.* clearer; settler.

défriper [defri'pe], *v.t.* to smooth out.

défrisement [defriz'mã], *n.m.* uncurling.

défriser [defri'ze], *v.t.* to uncurl; (*fam.*) to disappoint, to ruffle.

défroque [de'frɔk], *n.f.* the effects left by a dying monk; *hence,* old things, effects, cast-off clothes, etc.

défrooué [defrɔ'ke], *a.* and *n.m.* unfrocked (*priest*).

défroquer [defrɔ'ke], *v.t.* to unfrock. **se défroquer**, *v.r.* to renounce one's order (*of monks*).

défunt [de'fœ̃], *a.* defunct, deceased late.— *n.m.* (*fem.* **-e**) the deceased.

dégagé [dega'ʒe], *a.* free, easy, unconstrained; flippant; bold; slender, graceful.

dégagement [degaʒ'mã], *n.m.* disengagement, redemption; clearance; discharge (*of gas etc.*); (*fig.*) unconcern.

dégager [dega'ʒe], *v.t.* (*conjug. like* MANGER) to disengage, to extricate; to clear; to deliver, to rescue; to release, to emit (*fumes etc.*); to redeem, to take out of pawn. **se dégager**, *v.r.* to be liberated (*de*); to extricate, disengage *or* disentangle oneself; to get away; (*Chem.*) to be emitted.

dégaine [de'gɛːn], *n.f.* (*colloq.*) awkward gait.

dégainer [degɛ'ne], *v.t.* to unsheathe (*one's sword etc.*).

déganter [degã'te], *v.t.* to unglove. **se déganter**, *v.r.* to take off one's gloves.

dégarnir [degar'niːr], *v.t.* to strip; to dismantle; to thin (*trees, woods etc.*). **se dégarnir**, *v.r.* to strip oneself (*de*); to

become empty; to grow thin; to lose branches etc.

dégât [de'gɑ], *n.m.* havoc, damage, ravage.

dégauchir [dego'ʃiːr], *v.t.* to smooth, to plane, to level, to straighten; (*fig.*) to polish.

dégauchissement [degoʃis'mã], **dégauchissage** [degoʃi'saːʒ], *n.m.* planing, straightening, levelling, smoothing.

dégazonner [degazɔ'ne], *v.t.* to remove the turf.

dégel [de'ʒɛl], *n.m.* thaw.

dégeler [de'ʒle], *v.t., v.i.* (*conjug. like* AMENER) to thaw. **se dégeler**, *v.r.* to thaw (*of persons*).

dégénération [deʒenera'sjɔ̃], *n.f.* degeneration, degeneracy.

dégénéré [deʒene're], *a.* and *n.m.* (*fem.* **-ée**) degenerate (person).

dégénérer [deʒene're], *v.i. irr.* (*conjug. like* CÉDER) to decline, to degenerate.

dégénérescence [deʒeneres'sãːs], *n.f.* degeneracy, degeneration.

dégénérescent [deʒeneres'sã], *a.* degenerating.

dégingandé [deʒɛ̃gã'de], *a.* ungainly, gawky, awkward in one's gait; clumsy, disjointed, irregular.

dégivrer [deʒi'vre], *v.t.* to de-ice.

dégivreur [deʒi'vrœːr], *n.m.* (*Motor., Av.*) de-icer.

déglutir [degly'tiːr], *v.t.* to swallow.

déglutition [deglyti'sjɔ̃], *n.f.* deglutition, swallowing.

dégommer [degɔ'me], *v.t.* to wash the gum out of; (*slang*) to sack.

dégonflement [degɔ̃flə'mã], *n.m.* deflating (*of tire, balloon*); collapse; reduction.

dégonfler [degɔ̃'fle], *v.t.* to cause to collapse; to deflate; to reduce (*a swelling*). **se dégonfler**, *v.r.* to go down, to be reduced; to subside; (*pop.*) to sing small.

dégorgement [degɔrʒ'mã], *n.m.* breaking out, overflow; unstopping.

dégorger [degɔr'ʒe], *v.t.* (*conjug. like* MANGER) to disgorge; to unstop, to clear; to cleanse.—*v.i.* to discharge, to overflow. **se dégorger**, *v.r.* to discharge *or* empty itself *or* oneself, to be unstopped, to be cleared.

dégourdi [degur'di], *a.* quick, sharp, acute, smart; tepid (*of water*).—*n.m.* (*fem.* **-e**) a shrewd *or* forward person.

dégourdir [degur'diːr], *v.t.* to revive, to quicken; to take the chill off; (*fig.*) to sharpen, to render shrewd; to polish. **se dégourdir**, *v.r.* to lose numbness, to feel warmer; to brighten up.

dégourdissement [degurdis'mã], *n.m.* return of circulation; quickening, reviving.

dégoût [de'gu], *n.m.* dislike, distaste; disgust, aversion; mortification.

dégoûtant [degu'tã], *a.* disgusting, distasteful, nauseous; loathsome; unpleasant.

dégoûté [degu'te], *a.* disgusted; fastidious.— *n.m.* (*fem.* **-ée**) fastidious person.

dégoûter [degu'te], *v.t.* to disgust. **se dégoûter**, *v.r.* to take a dislike to.

dégouttant [degu'tã], *a.* dripping.

dégouttement [degut'mã], *n.m.* dripping, falling in drops.

dégoutter [degu'te], *v.i.* to drip, to fall in drops, to trickle.

dégradant [degra'dã], *a.* degrading, debasing.

dégradation [degradɑ'sjɔ̃], *n.f.* degradation; debasement; (*Paint.*) gradation of light and shade; (*Law*) *dégradation nationale* or *civile*, loss of civil rights; *dégradation militaire*, cashiering.

dégrader [degra'de], *v.t.* to degrade, to debase; to deface; (*Mil.*) to reduce to the ranks; to cashier; (*Paint.*) to graduate the light and shade. **se dégrader**, *v.r.* to degrade, debase *or* disgrace oneself; to become damaged *or* defaced.

dégrafer [degra'fe], *v.t.* to unclasp, to unhook. **se dégrafer**, *v.r.* to come unfastened (*of garments etc.*); to unfasten one's clothes.

dégraissage [degrɛ'sa:ʒ], **dégraissement** [degrɛs'mɑ̃], *n.m.* dry-cleaning (*garments*); scouring (*wool*).

dégraisser [degrɛ'se], *v.t.* to remove greasy stains from.

dégraisseur [degrɛ'sœːr], *n.m.* (*fem.* -**euse**) scourer (*of wool*); dry-cleaner (*of clothes etc.*).

dégraissoir [degrɛ'swa:r], *n.m.* scraper.

degré [də'gre], *n.m.* step, stair; stage, grade, degree; point, extent, height, pitch.

dégréer [degre'e], *v.t.* to unrig; to strip a mast.

dégrèvement [degrɛv'mɑ̃], *n.m.* reduction; tax allowance, relief.

dégrever [degra've], *v.t.* (*conjug. like* AMENER) to diminish, to reduce (*a tax etc.*); to relieve (*someone of a tax*); to disencumber (*an estate etc.*); to pay off (*a mortgage*).

dégringolade [degrɛ̃gɔ'lad], *n.f.* (*fam.*) fall, tumble.

dégringoler [degrɛ̃gɔ'le], *v.i.* to tumble down, to topple over.

dégrisement [degriz'mɑ̃], *n.m.* (*colloq.*) sobering, getting sober; (*fig.*) cooling down.

dégriser [degri'ze], *v.t.* to sober; (*fig.*) to cool down, to bring to one's senses. **se dégriser**, *v.r.* to sober up; (*fig.*) to come to one's senses; to lose one's illusions.

dégrossir [degro'si:r], *v.t.* to rough-hew; (*fig.*) to make a rough sketch of.

dégrossissage [degrosi'sa:ʒ], **dégrossissement** [degrosis'mɑ̃], *n.m.* rough-hewing; (*Carp.*) dressing, trimming.

déguenillé [degani'je], *a.* tattered, ragged.— *n.m.* (*fem.* -ée) ragamuffin.

déguerpir [degɛr'piːr], *v.i.* to move off; to be gone.

déguerpissement [degɛrpis'mɑ̃], *n.m.* quitting, giving up, abandonment.

dégueuler [degœ'le], *v.t.* (*vulg.*) to spew.

déguignonner [degiɲɔ'ne], *v.t.* to lift a curse from, to bring better luck to.

déguisable [degi'zabl], *a.* disguisable.

déguisement [degiz'mɑ̃], *n.m.* disguise, concealment; *parlez sans déguisement*, speak openly.

déguiser [degi'ze], *v.t.* to disguise, to cloak; to misrepresent. **se déguiser**, *v.r.* to disguise oneself; to put on fancy dress.

dégustateur [degysta'tœːr], *n.m.* (*fem.* -**trice**) taster (*of wines etc.*).

dégustation [degysta'sjɔ̃], *n.f.* tasting (*of wines etc.*).

déguster [degys'te], *v.t.* to taste; to sip, to savor.

déhaler [dea'le], *v.t.* (*Naut.*) to tow out; to haul off.

déhâler [dea'le], *v.t.* to take away sun-burn, freckles, tan etc. from. **se déhâler**, *v.r.* to clear one's complexion.

déhanché [deɑ̃'fe], *a.* having the hip dislocated; (*fig.*) ungainly.

déhanchement [deɑ̃f'mɑ̃], *n.m.* waddling gait, waddle.

déhancher (se) [sədeɑ̃'fe], *v.r.* to sway one's hips; to have a waddling, loose gait.

déharnachement [dearnaf'mɑ̃], *n.m.* unharnessing.

déharnacher [dearna'fe], *v.t.* to unharness.

dehors [də'ɔːr], *adv.* out, *without*, outside; out of doors; abroad; externally; (*Naut.*) at sea; *au dedans et au dehors*, at home and abroad; *au dehors*, outwardly; *de dehors*, from without; *en dehors*, outside, *without*; *mettre quelqu'un dehors*, to turn someone out.— *n.m. inv.* outside, exterior; (*pl.*) appearances; (*Fort.*) outworks; dependencies, approaches, grounds (*of a house*); *sauver les dehors*, to save appearances.

déification [deifikɑ'sjɔ̃], *n.f.* deification.

déifier [dei'fje], *v.t.* to deify.

déisme [de'ism], *n.m.* deism.

déiste [de'ist], *a.* deistic.—*n.* deist.

déité [dei'te], *n.f.* deity (*god, goddess*), divinity.

déjà [de'ʒa], *adv.* already, before, previously.

déjection [deʒɛk'sjɔ̃], *n.f.* (*Med.*) dejection, ejection, evacuation.

déjeté [deʒ'te], *a.* awry, lopsided, off the straight.

déjeter [deʒ'te], *v.t.* (*conjug. like* APPELER) to warp. **se déjeter**, *v.r.* to warp (*of wood etc.*); (*Path.*) to deviate.

déjettement [deʒɛt'mɑ̃], *n.m.* warping; deviation.

déjeuner [deʒœ'ne], *n.m.* lunch; *petit déjeuner*, breakfast; *un déjeuner de porcelaine*, a china breakfast-set.—*v.i.* to breakfast, to lunch.

déjouer [de'ʒwe], *v.t.* to baffle, to frustrate, to foil; (*Mil.*) to outmaneuver.

déjucher [deʒy'fe], *v.t.* to dislodge.—*v.i.* to come down from the roost *or* from one's perch.

déjuger (se) [sədeʒy'ʒe], *v.r.* (*conjug. like* MANGER) to reverse one's opinion *or* decision.

delà [də'la], *prep.* on the other side of; beyond; *au delà, de delà, par delà,* or *en delà,* beyond; *deçà et delà*, both here and there, both this and that; *l'au-delà*, the hereafter.

délabré [dela'bre], *a.* tattered, shabby (*garments*); tumbledown, ramshackle (*building*).

délabrement [delabrə'mɑ̃], *n.m.* decay, dilapidation; shabbiness.

délabrer [dela'bre], *v.t.* to shatter, to ruin, to tear to tatters. **se délabrer**, *v.r.* to fall to pieces, to go to ruin.

délacer [dela'se], *v.t.* (*conjug. like* COMMENCER) to unlace (*shoes etc.*). **se délacer**, *v.r.* to unlace oneself; to come undone (*of shoes, strings etc.*).

délai [de'le], *n.m.* delay; respite.

délaissé [delɛ'se], *a.* abandoned, friendless.

délaissement [delɛs'mã], *n.m.* desertion; destitution, helplessness.
délaisser [delɛ'se], *v.t.* to forsake, to abandon; to neglect.
délassant [dela'sã], *a.* refreshing, diverting.
délassement [delas'mã], *n.m.* relaxation; repose.
délasser [dela'se], *v.t.* to refresh, to relax, to divert. **se délasser**, *v.r.* to refresh oneself, to rest.
délateur [dela'tœːr], *n.m.* (*fem.* **-trice**) informer, accuser.
délation [dela'sjɔ̃], *n.f.* informing.
délavage [dela'va:ʒ], *n.m.* diluting of color; soaking.
délaver [dela've], *v.t.* to dilute *or* wash (*color*); to soak into. **se délaver**, *v.r.* to become soaked; to lose color.
délayable [delɛ'jabl], *a.* dilutable.
délayage [delɛ'ja:ʒ], *n.m.* diluting, dilution.
délayé [delɛ'je], *a.* watery.
délayer [delɛ'je], *v.t.* (*conjug. like* PAYER) to dilute; (*fig.*) to spin out.
délectable [delɛk'tabl], *a.* delectable, delightful.
délecter (se) [sədelɛk'te], *v.r.* to take delight.
délégation [delega'sjɔ̃], *n.f.* delegation, assignment.
délégatoire [delega'twaːr], *a.* delegatory.
délégué [dele'ge], *n.m.* (*fem.* **-ée**) delegate, deputy; proxy.
déléguer [dele'ge], *v.t.* (*conjug. like* CÉDER) to delegate; to assign. **se déléguer**, *v.r.* to be delegated.
délester [delɛs'te], *v.t.* to unballast.
délétère [dele'tɛːr], *a.* deleterious.
délibérant [delibe'rã], *a.* deliberative.
délibératif [delibera'tif], *a.* (*fem.* **-tive**) deliberative.
délibération [delibera'sjɔ̃], *n.f.* deliberation; resolution.
délibéré [delibe're], *a.* deliberate, determined, resolute.
délibérément [delibere'mã], *adv.* deliberately, resolutely.
délibérer [delibe're], *v.i.* (*conjug. like* CÉDER) to deliberate; to resolve.
délicat [deli'ka], *a.* delicate, dainty; nice, fastidious; frail.—*n.m.* (*fem.* **-e**) fastidious person.
délicatement [delikat'mã], *adv.* delicately, daintily, tenderly.
délicatesse [delika'tɛs], *n.f.* delicacy, fragility; tenderness; daintiness; fastidiousness; refinement, squeamishness; nicety (*of language etc.*); considerateness; (*pl.*) dainties.
délice [de'lis], *n.m. in sing.* (*used chiefly in f.pl.*) delight, pleasure.
délicieusement [delisjøz'mã], *adv.* deliciously, delightfully.
délicieux [deli'sjø], *a.* (*fem.* **-euse**) delicious, delightful.
délié [de'lje], *a.* slender, fine; sharp, shrewd; glib, flowing (*of style etc.*); untied, loose.
délier [de'lje], *v.t.* to unbind, to untie; to liberate, to release; to absolve. **se délier**, *v.r.* to come untied, to get loose.
délimitation [delimita'sjɔ̃], *n.f.* delimitation, fixing of boundaries.
délimiter [delimi'te], *v.t.* to delimit, to settle the boundaries of.

délinéation [delinea'sjɔ̃], *n.f.* delineation.
délinéer [deline'e], *v.t.* to delineate.
délinquance [delɛ̃'kã:s], *n.f.* delinquency.
délinquant [delɛ̃'kã], *n;a.* (*fem.* **-e**) delinquent, offender.— *enfance délinquante*, juvenile delinquents.
délirant [deli'rã], *a.* delirious, frenzied, frantic; rapturous, ecstatic.—*n.m.* (*fem.* **-e**) a delirious *or* ecstatic person.
délire [de'li:r], *n.m.* delirium, frenzy, folly.
délirer [deli're], *v.i.* to be delirious, to rave, to wander.
délit [de'li], *n.m.* misdemeanor, offence; *en flagrant délit*, in the very act, redhanded.
délivrance [deli'vrã:s], *n.f.* rescue, deliverance; issue (*of tickets*); delivery (*of certificates etc.*); accouchement.
délivre [de'livr], *n.m.* (*Anat.*) after-birth, placenta.
délivrer [deli'vre], *v.t.* to deliver, to release, to set free; to hand over; to issue; to deliver (*a woman of a baby*).
délogement [delɔʒ'mã], *n.m.* removal, change of quarters, decamping.
déloger [delɔ'ʒe], *v.t.* (*conjug. like* MANGER) to turn out (*of house etc.*), to oust; to drive away; (*Mil.*) to dislodge.—*v.i.* to remove, to go (*from one's house etc.*), to go away, to march off.
déloyal [delwa'jal], *a.* (*m.pl.* **-aux**) disloyal, false, treacherous, unfair; foul.
déloyalement [delwajal'mã], *adv.* disloyally, unfairly.
déloyauté [delwajo'te], *n.f.* disloyalty, treachery.
delta [dɛl'ta], *n.m.* delta.
déluge [de'ly:ʒ], *n.m.* deluge, flood.
déluré [dely're], *a.* wide-awake, sharp.
délustrer [delys'tre], *v.t.* to take the luster *or* gloss from.
démagnétiser [demaɲeti'ze], *v.t.* to demagnetize.
démagogue [dema'gɔg], *n.* demagogue.
démailler [dema'je], *v.t.* to undo the meshes of (*a net etc.*).
demain [də'mɛ̃] *adv.* and *n.m.* tomorrow; *à demain!* see you tomorrow!
démancher [demã'ʃe], *v.t.* to take off the handle of; (*fig.*) to dislocate. **se démancher**, *v.r.* to lose its handle; to go wrong.
demande [də'mã:d], *n.f.* question; request, application, petition; claim; (*Comm.*) demand; order.
demander [dəmã'de], *v.t.* to ask, to beg, to request; to desire, to wish; to require, to call for; to need, to want; to inquire about; to ask to see; to seek in marriage; (*Comm.*) to order. **se demander**, *v.r.* to ask oneself, to wonder.
demandeur [dəmã'dœːr], *a.* (*fem.* **-euse**) always asking.—*n.m.* (*fem.* **-eresse**) asker, applicant; (*Law*) plaintiff.
démangeaison [demãʒɛ'zɔ̃], *n.f.* itching; longing.
démanger [demã'ʒe], *v.i.* (*conjug. like* MANGER) to itch; to long.
démantibuler [demãtiby'le], *v.t.* to break, to dislocate.
démaquiller [demaki'je], *v.t.* to take off someone's make-up. **se démaquiller**, *v.r.* to take off one's make-up.

105

démarcation [demarkaˈsjɔ̃], *n.f.* demarcation; *ligne de démarcation*, line of demarcation.

démarche [deˈmarʃ], *n.f.* gait, walk, bearing; proceeding, measure, step, course.

démarcheur [demarˈʃœːr], *n.m.* canvasser.

démarier [demaˈrje], *v.t.* (*fam.*) to annul the marriage of; (*Hort.*) to thin out. **se démarier**, *v.r.* to be divorced.

démarrer [demaˈre], *v.t.* to cast off; to unfasten.—*v.i.* to leave, to slip her moorings (*of a ship*); to move, to get away, to start.

démarreur [demaˈrœːr], *n.m.* (*Motor.*) self-starter.

démasquer [demasˈke], *v.t.* to unmask; to show up.

démâter [demaˈte], *v.t.* to dismast.—*v.i.* to lose her masts (*of a ship*).

démêlage [demeˈlaːʒ], *n.m.* combing (*of wool*).

démêlé [demeˈle], *n.m.* strife, contest, quarrel.

démêler [demeˈle], *v.t.* to unravel, to disentangle, to separate; to clear up; to distinguish, to discern; to comb out (*hair*), to tease (*wool*). **se démêler**, *v.r.* to be disentangled; to extricate oneself; to stand out (*clearly*); to comb out one's hair.

démembrement [demɑ̃brəˈmɑ̃], *n.m.* dismemberment; breaking up.

démembrer [demɑ̃ˈbre], *v.t.* to tear limb from limb, to dismember; to break up.

déménagement [demenaʒˈmɑ̃], *n.m.* (*household*) removal.

déménager [demenaˈʒe], *v.t.* (*conjug. like* MANGER) to remove (*one's furniture*).—*v.i.* to (re)move.

déménageur [demenaˈʒœːr], *n.m.* furniture mover.

démence [deˈmɑ̃ːs], *n.f.* insanity, madness.

démener (*se*) [sademəˈne], *v.r.* (*conjug. like* AMENER) to stir, to struggle, to make a great fuss, to strive hard.

démenti [demɑ̃ˈti], *n.m.* denial, flat contradiction; lie.

démentir [demɑ̃ˈtiːr], *v.t.* (*conjug. like* SENTIR) to give the lie to, to contradict; to deny; to belie, to refute. **se démentir**, *v.r.* to contradict oneself; to fall off, to flag.

démériter [demeˈrite], *n.m.* demerit.

démériter [demeriˈte], *v.i.* to lose esteem or favor.

démesuré [deməzyˈre], *a.* inordinate, excessive, enormous.

démesurément [deməzyreˈmɑ̃], *adv.* inordinately, excessively.

démettre [deˈmɛtr], *v.t. irr.* (*conjug. like* METTRE) to put out of joint, to dislocate; to dismiss; (*Law*) to overrule. **se démettre**, *v.r.* to be put out of joint; to resign.

démeubler [demœˈble], *v.t.* to strip of furniture.

demeurant [dəmœˈrɑ̃], *a.* dwelling, living.—*n.m.* remainder; **au demeurant**, after all, nevertheless.

demeure [dəˈmœːr], *n.f.* abode, home, dwelling; stay; (*Law*) delay.

demeurer [dəmœˈre], *v.i.* to live, to lodge, to reside; to stop, to stand; to continue, to stay.

demi [dəˈmi], *a.* and *adv.* half.—*n.m.* (*Arith.*) half; (*Ftb. etc.*) half-back; glass of beer.—*n.f.* (-e) (the) half-hour.

[In the following compounds *demi* is *inv.* The noun has its regular plural, unless otherwise indicated.]

demi-bain [dəmiˈbɛ̃], *n.m.* hip bath.

demi-bas [dəmiˈbɑ], *n.m. inv.* knee-length stocking.

demi-botte [dəmiˈbɔt], *n.f.* Wellington boot.

demi-cercle [dəmiˈsɛrkl], *n.m.* semicircle.

demi-finale [dəmifiˈnal], *n.f.* (*Spt.*) semifinal.

demi-fond [dəmiˈfɔ̃], *n.m. inv.* middle distance (*race*).

demi-heure [dəmiˈœːr], *n.f.* half-hour; *une demi-heure*, half an hour.

demi-jour [dəmiˈʒuːr], *n.m.* twilight.

demi-mot [dəmiˈmo], *adv. phr.* *comprendre à demi-mot*, to take the hint.

déminage [demiˈnaːʒ], *n.m.* mine clearing.

déminer [demiˈne], *v.t.* to clear of mines.

demi-pension [dəmipɑ̃ˈsjɔ̃], *n.f.* half-board.

demi-pensionnaire [dəmipɑ̃sjɔˈnɛːr], *n.* day-boarder.

demi-place [dəmiˈplas], *n.f.* half-fare.

demi-saison [dəmisɛˈzɔ̃], *n.f.* autumn or spring.

demi-sang [dəmiˈsɑ̃], *n.m. inv.* half-bred horse.

demi-sel [dəmiˈsɛl], *n.m.* slightly salted cream cheese.

demi-solde [dəmiˈsɔld], *n.f.* half-pay.

démission [demiˈsjɔ̃], *n.f.* resignation.

démissionnaire [demisjɔˈnɛːr], *a.* who has resigned or vacated his seat, outgoing.

démissionner [demisjɔˈne], *v.i.* to resign.

demi-tour [dəmiˈtuːr], *n.m.* half-turn; (*Mil.*) about turn; *faire demi-tour*, to turn back.

démobilisation [demobilizaˈsjɔ̃], *n.f.* demobilization.

démobiliser [demobiliˈze], *v.t.* to demobilize.

démocrate [demoˈkrat], *a.* democratic.—*n.* democrat.

démocratie [demokraˈsi], *n.f.* democracy.

démocratique [demokraˈtik], *a.* democratic.

démocratiquement [demokratikˈmɑ̃], *adv.* democratically.

démocratiser [demokratiˈze], *v.t.* to democratize.

démodé [demoˈde], *a.* old-fashioned, antiquated.

demoiselle [dəmwaˈzɛl], *n.f.* young lady; unmarried woman, spinster; young girl; dragon-fly; *demoiselle d'honneur*, bridesmaid.

démolir [demoˈliːr], *v.t.* to demolish, to pull down.

démolisseur [demoliˈsœːr], *n.m.* (*fem.* -**euse**) demolisher.

démolition [demoliˈsjɔ̃], *n.f.* demolition; (*pl.*) old building materials.

démon [deˈmɔ̃], *n.m.* demon; (*good or evil*) genius; devil, fiend.

démonétisation [demonetizaˈsjɔ̃], *n.f.* withdrawal from circulation (*of money*).

démonétiser [demonetiˈze], *v.t.* to withdraw from circulation, to call in (*money*).

démoniaque [demoˈnjak], *a.* demoniac(al).—*n.* demoniac, demon, devil.

démonstrateur [demɔ̃straˈtœːr], *n.m.* (*fem.* -**euse**) demonstrator, lecturer.

démonstratif [demɔ̃straˈtif], *a.* (*fem.* -**tive**) demonstrative.

dépaqueter

démonstration [demɔ̃stra'sjɔ̃], *n.f.* demonstration, proof; exhibition.

démontable [demɔ̃'tabl], *a.* that can be taken to pieces; collapsible (*canoe*).

démontage [demɔ̃'ta:ʒ], *n.m.* taking to pieces, dismantling.

démonte-pneu [demɔ̃t'pnø], *n.m.* tire lever.

démonter [demɔ̃'te], *v.t.* to unhorse, to dismount; to take to pieces, to dismantle; (*fig.*) to nonplus, to baffle; **mer démontée,** very rough sea. **se démonter,** *v.r.* to take *or* come to pieces (*of machinery*); to lose countenance, to be nonplussed; to be getting out of order (*of machinery etc.*).

démontrer [demɔ̃'tre], *v.t.* to demonstrate, to prove.

démoralisant [demɔrali'zɑ̃], *a.* demoralizing.

démoralisateur [demɔraliza'tœːr], *a.* (*fem.* **-trice**) corrupting, demoralizing.

démoralisation [demɔraliza'sjɔ̃], *n.f.* demoralization.

démoraliser [demɔrali'ze], *v.t.* to demoralize; to corrupt.

démordre [de'mɔrdr], *v.i.* to let go one's hold; to desist, to yield, to give in.

démoucheter [demuʃ'te], *v.t.* (*conjug. like* APPELER) to take off the button from (*a foil*), to uncap.

démoulage [demu'la:ʒ], *n.m.* taking from the mold.

démouler [demu'le], *v.t.* to take from the mold.

démunir [demy'ni:r], *v.t.* to strip (*of ammunition*), to leave unprovided. **se démunir,** *v.r.* to deprive oneself, to leave oneself unprovided for.

démuseler [demyz'le], *v.t.* (*conjug. like* APPELER) to unmuzzle; (*fig.*) to let loose.

dénatalité [denatali'te], *n.f.* fall in the birthrate.

dénationalisation [denasjɔnaliza'sjɔ̃], *n.f.* denationalization.

dénationaliser [denasjɔnali'ze], *v.t.* to denationalize.

dénatter [dena'te], *v.t.* to unplait (*hair etc.*).

dénaturé [denaty're], *a.* unnatural, barbarous, cruel.

dénaturer [denaty're], *v.t.* to alter the nature of; to misrepresent, to distort; to disfigure; to methylate (*alcohol*).

dénégation [denega'sjɔ̃], *n.f.* denial, denegation.

déni [de'ni], *n.m.* denial, refusal.

déniaiser [denjɛ'ze], *v.t.* to sharpen the wits of; to initiate; to seduce. **se déniaiser,** *v.r.* to learn to be sharp, to grow cunning; (*fam.*) to lose one's innocence.

dénicher [deni'ʃe], *v.t.* to take out of the nest; to hunt out, to find out.—*v.i.* to forsake its nest (*of a bird*); to make off, to run away.

dénicheur [deni'ʃœːr], *n.m.* nest robber.

denier [də'nje], *n.m.* (*Rom. Ant.*) denarius; (*Fr. Ant.*) denier; penny; farthing, mite; (*pl.*) state revenues.

dénier [de'nje], *v.t.* to deny, to refuse.

dénigrant [deni'grɑ̃], *a.* disparaging.

dénigrement [denigrə'mɑ̃], *n.m.* disparagement.

dénigrer [deni'gre], *v.t.* to disparage; to vilify.

dénivellation [denivɛlla'sjɔ̃], *n.f.,* **dénivellement** [denivɛl'mɑ̃], *n.m.* difference of level; unevenness.

dénombrement [denɔ̃brə'mɑ̃], *n.m.* enumeration; census.

dénombrer [denɔ̃'bre], *v.t.* to number, to enumerate.

dénominateur [denɔmina'tœːr], *n.m.* (*Arith.*) denominator.

dénomination [denɔmina'sjɔ̃], *n.f.* denomination, name.

dénommer [denɔ'me], *v.t.* to designate.

dénoncer [denɔ̃'se], *v.t.* (*conjug. like* COMMENCER) to denounce, to inform against; to give notice of, to declare (*war etc.*). **se dénoncer,** *v.r.* to own up; to give oneself up.

dénonciateur [denɔ̃sja'tœːr], *n.m.* (*fem.* **-trice**) informer, accuser.

dénonciation [denɔ̃sja'sjɔ̃], *n.f.* denunciation, declaration.

dénoter [denɔ'te], *v.t.* to denote, to betoken.

dénouement *or* **dénoûment** [denu'mɑ̃], *n.m.* dénouement, unravelling (*esp. of a play etc.*).

dénouer [denu'e], *v.t.* to untie, to loosen; to solve (*difficulties etc.*); to unravel (*plots*). **se dénouer,** *v.r.* to come untied, to be unravelled; to be solved.

denrée [dɑ̃'re], *n.f.* commodity, produce provisions.

dense [dɑ̃:s], *a.* dense, close, thick.

densité [dɑ̃si'te], *n.f.* density, thickness.

dent [dɑ̃], *n.f.* tooth; fang; notch; cog; prong; **faire ses dents,** to cut one's teeth.

dentaire [dɑ̃'tɛːr], *a.* dental.

dental [dɑ̃'tal], *a.* (*m.pl.* **-aux**) (*Phon.*) dental.

dent-de-lion [dɑ̃də'ljɔ̃], *n.m.* (*pl.* **dents-de-lion**) dandelion.

denté [dɑ̃'te], *a.* toothed; (*Bot.*) dentate; **roue dentée,** cogged wheel.

dentelé [dɑ̃'tle], *a.* notched, denticulated, indented, jagged.

denteler [dɑ̃'tle], *v.t.* (*conjug. like* APPELER) to indent, to notch.

dentelle [dɑ̃'tɛl], *n.f.* lace, lace work.

dentellier [dɑ̃tɛ'lje], *n.m.* (*fem.* **-ière**) lace maker.

dentelure [dɑ̃'tlyːr], *n.f.* denticulation, indenting; scallop.

denticule [dɑ̃ti'kyl], *n.m.* denticle.

dentier [dɑ̃'tje], *n.m.* set of teeth (*esp. artificial*), denture.

dentifrice [dɑ̃ti'fris], *n.m.* toothpaste.

dentiste [dɑ̃'tist], *n.m.* dentist.

denture [dɑ̃'tyːr], *n.f.* set of teeth; (*Horol.*) teeth of a wheel.

dénudation [denyda'sjɔ̃], *n.f.* denudation.

dénuder [deny'de], *v.t.* to denude; to lay bare.

dénuement *or* **dénûment** [deny'mɑ̃], *n.m.* destitution, penury, want.

dénuer [de'nɥe], *v.t.* to strip, to leave destitute. **se dénuer,** *v.r.* to strip oneself; to leave oneself destitute.

dépannage [depa'na:ʒ], *n.m.* (*Mach., Elec.*) repairing; **service de dépannage,** breakdown *or* repair service.

dépanner [depa'ne], *v.t.* (*Mach., Elec.*) to repair (*a breakdown*).

dépanneuse [depa'nøːz], *n.f.* breakdown vehicle, repair car, wrecker.

dépaqueter [depak'te], *v.t.* (*conjug. like* APPELER) to unpack.

dépareillé

dépareillé [depare'je], a. unmatched, odd.
déparer [depa're], v.t. to strip (of ornaments); (fig.) to mar, to disfigure.
déparier [depa'rje], v.t. to take away one (of a pair); to separate (a pair of animals).
départ [de'pa:r], n.m. departure, start, setting out.
départager [departa'ʒe], v.t. (conjug. like MANGER) to settle by a vote.
département [departə'mã], n.m. department; line, business.
départemental [departəmã'tal], a. (m. pl. -aux) departmental.
départir [depar'ti:r], v.t. irr. (conjug. like SENTIR) to separate; to distribute, to divide, to endow, to bestow. **se départir**, v.r. to desist; to deviate (from).
dépassement [depas'mã], n.m. overstepping (of credit etc.); (Motor.) passing.
dépasser [depa'se], v.t. to go beyond, to pass, to overtake; to exceed, to surpass; to be taller etc. than; to show; **son jupon dépasse**, her slip is showing.
dépaver [depa've], v.t. to unpave, to take up the pavement etc.
dépaysé [depei'ze], a. away from home, out of one's element.
dépayser [depei'ze], v.t. to send away from home; to remove from his natural sphere etc.; (fig.) to bewilder. **se dépayser**, v.r. to leave one's home; to go abroad; to get out of one's element.
dépècement [depɛs'mã], **dépeçage** [depə'sa:ʒ], n.m. cutting up, carving, dismemberment.
dépecer [dep'se], v.t. (see Verb Tables) to cut up (a carcass), to carve.
dépêche [de'pɛ:ʃ], n.f. dispatch (letter on affairs of State); communication (esp. a telegram).
dépêcher [depe'ʃe], v.t. to dispatch, to do quickly; to send quickly, to send by messenger; to kill. **se dépêcher**, v.r. to hurry, to make haste; **dépêchez-vous**, hurry up.
dépeigner [depe'ɲe], v.t. to ruffle (hair).
dépeindre [de'pɛ:dr], v.t. irr. (conjug. like CRAINDRE) to depict, to describe; to portray, to paint.
dépelotonner [deplɔtɔ'ne], v.t. to unwind. **se dépelotonner**, v.r. to come unwound; to uncurl (of cat).
dépenaillé [depna'je], a. tattered, ragged.
dépendance [depã'dã:s], n.f. subordination; dependence; appendage, annex, outhouse, (pl.) out-buildings.
dépendant [depã'dã], a. dependent.
dépendre (1) [de'pã:dr], v.t. to take down; to unhang.
dépendre (2) [de'pã:dr], v.i. to depend, to be dependent (de).
dépens [de'pã], n.m. (used only in pl.) expense, cost.
dépense [de'pã:s], n.f. expense; expenditure, outlay; waste, flow.
dépenser [depã'se], v.t. to spend, to consume; to waste.
dépensier [depã'sje], a. (fem. -ière) extravagant.—n.m. (fem. -ière) extravagant person, spend-thrift; bursar.
déperdition [deperdi'sjɔ̃], n.f. loss, waste.
dépérir [depe'ri:r], v.i. to decline, to pine away, to wither, to dwindle, to waste away.

dépérissement [deperis'mã], n.m. decay, withering, wasting away.
dépêtrer [depe'tre], v.t. to disentangle, to extricate. **se dépêtrer**, v.r. to get clear of.
dépeuplement [depœplə'mã], n.m. depopulation; thinning (of forests etc.).
dépeupler [depœ'ple], v.t. to depopulate; to thin. **se dépeupler**, v.r. to become depopulated, to be unstocked (of river).
dépilage [depi'la:ʒ], n.m. removal of hairs, bristles, etc. (from hides etc.).
dépilation [depilo'sjɔ̃], n.f. depilation.
dépiquage [depi'ka:ʒ], n.m. threshing or treading out (grain).
dépiquer (1) [depi'ke], v.t. to unquilt, to unstitch.
dépiquer (2) [depi'ke], v.t. to tread out (grain).
dépister [depis'te], v.t. to track down; to hunt out; (fig.) to throw off the scent.
dépit [de'pi], n.m. spite; vexation.
dépiter [depi'te], v.t. to vex, to spite. **se dépiter**, v.r. to be vexed, to fret.
déplacé [depla'se], a. displaced, misplaced, ill-timed, unbecoming.
déplacement [deplas'mã], n.m. removal; displacement; **frais de déplacement**, travelling expenses.
déplacer [depla'se], v.t. (conjug. like COMMENCER) to displace; to remove, to change; to misplace. **se déplacer**, v.r. to move, to change one's place, to leave one's residence; to be displaced (of things).
déplaire [de'plɛ:r], v.i. irr. (conjug. like PLAIRE) to displease, to offend; to be disagreeable, to give offence. **se déplaire**, v.r. to be displeased or dissatisfied (with).
déplaisant [deplɛ'zã], a. unpleasant, disagreeable.
déplaisir [deplɛ'zi:r], n.m. displeasure, annoyance; grief.
déplanter [deplã'te], v.t. to dig or take up (a plant).
déplantoir [deplã'twa:r], n.m. garden trowel.
dépliant [depli'ã], n.m. folding page; folder, prospectus, leaflet.
déplier [depli'e], v.t. to unfold, to open out; to lay out.
déplisser [depli'se], v.t. to unpleat. **se déplisser**, v.r. to come unpleated; to lose its pleats (of a skirt etc.).
déploiement or **déploîment** [deplwa'mã], n.m. unfolding; display, show; (Mil.) deployment.
déplombage [deplɔ̃'ba:ʒ], n.m. unsealing; unstopping.
déplomber [deplɔ̃'be], v.t. to take the custom-house seal off (goods); to unstop (a tooth).
déplorable [deplɔ'rabl], a. deplorable, lamentable.
déplorablement [deplɔrablə'mã], adv. deplorably, wretchedly.
déplorer [deplɔ're], v.t. to deplore, to bewail, to lament, to mourn.
déployer [deplwa'je], v.t. (conjug. like EMPLOYER) to unfold, to unroll, to unfurl, to spread out; to display, to show; (Mil.) to deploy; **à gorge déployée**, at the top of one's voice. **se déployer**, v.r. to unroll; to display oneself; (Mil.) to deploy.
déplumer [deply'me], v.t. to pluck; (fig.) to despoil; to tear the hair from. **se déplumer**, v.r. to molt, to shed feathers.

dépolariser [depɔlari'ze], *v.t.* to depolarize.
dépolir [depɔ'li:r], *v.t.* to make the surface (*of metal etc.*) dull, to frost (*glass*).
dépopulation [depɔpyla'sjɔ̃], *n.m.* depopulation.
déportation [depɔrta'sjɔ̃], *n.f.* deportation.
déporté [depɔr'te], *n.m.* (*fem.* -ée) deported person.
déportements [depɔrtə'mɑ̃], *n.m. pl.* misconduct, evil-doings.
déporter [depɔr'te], *v.t.* to deport, to transport for life; to swerve; to carry away, to drift. **se déporter**, *v.r.* (*Law*) to desist (*from*).
déposant [depo'zɑ̃], *a.* giving evidence; depositing.—*n.m.* (*fem.* -e) witness; depositor.
déposer [depo'ze], *v.t.* to lay down or aside; to divest oneself of; to depose; to deposit; to lodge (*a complaint etc.*); *marque déposée*, registered trademark.—*v.i.* to give evidence; to settle, to leave a sediment.
dépositaire [depozi'tɛ:r], *n.m.* depositary, trustee; agent.
déposition [depozi'sjɔ̃], *n.f.* deposition, evidence.
dépositoire [depozi'twa:r], *n.m.* depository, mortuary.
déposséder [depose'de], *v.t.* (*conjug. like* CÉDER) to dispossess, to oust.
dépossession [depose'sjɔ̃], *n.f.* dispossession, deprivation.
dépôt [de'po], *n.m.* depositing; deposit; sediment; depository, warehouse; (*Mil.*) depot; (*Med.*) tumor, abscess; *dépôt d'essence*, gas station; *en dépôt*, as a deposit in trust, (*Comm.*) on sale; *mandat de dépôt*, writ of imprisonment.
dépotage [depo'ta:ʒ], **dépotement** [depɔt'mɑ̃], *n.m.* unpotting; decanting.
dépoter [depo'te], *v.t.* to take out of a pot; to decant.
dépouille [de'pu:j], *n.f.* slough, cast-off skin or hide; spoil; remains, wardrobe (*of persons deceased*); (*pl.*) spoils, booty; *dépouille mortelle*, mortal remains.
dépouillement [depuj'mɑ̃], *n.m.* spoliation, despoiling; scrutiny (*of a ballot box*); abstract (*of an account*).
dépouiller [depu'je], *v.t.* to strip, to skin; to unclothe; to despoil; to throw off; to cast (*of insects*); to reap (*crops*); to inspect, to count up (*a ballot-box*); to present an abstract (*of accounts*). **se dépouiller**, *v.r.* to shed its skin (*of insects and animals*), to molt; *se dépouiller de*, to divest oneself of, to strip oneself of, to renounce (*possessions etc.*).
dépourvoir [depur'vwa:r], *v.t. irr.* (*conjug. like* POURVOIR) to leave unprovided (*with*) or destitute (*of*). **se dépourvoir**, *v.r.* to leave oneself unequipped.
dépourvu [depur'vy], *a.* destitute, unprovided; *au dépourvu*, unawares, unexpectedly.
dépravation [depravɑ'sjɔ̃], *n.f.* vitiation, depravity.
dépravé [depra've], *a.* vitiated, depraved, corrupt.
dépraver [depra've], *v.t.* to deprave, to corrupt, to pervert. **se dépraver**, *v.r.* to become depraved or corrupted.

dépréciation [depresja'sjɔ̃], *n.f.* depreciation.
déprécier [depre'sje], *v.t.* to depreciate, to undervalue, to underrate; to disparage. **se déprécier**, *v.r.* to underrate oneself; to fall in value (*of things*).
déprédateur [depreda'tœ:r], *n.m.* (*fem.* -trice) depredator, plunderer.
déprédation [depredɑ'sjɔ̃], *n.f.* plundering, depredation.
déprendre [de'prɑ̃:dr], *v.t. irr.* (*conjug. like* PRENDRE) to loosen, to detach. **se déprendre**, *v.r.* to get loose; to detach oneself (*de*).
dépression [deprɛ'sjɔ̃], *n.f.* depression, hollow; (*fig.*) recession, slump (*of business*); *dépression nerveuse*, nervous breakdown.
déprimer [depri'me], *v.t.* to press down, to depress; (*fig.*) to discourage.
depuis [də'pɥi], *prep.* since, for; from; after; *depuis longtemps*, for a long time; *depuis peu*, lately; *depuis quand?* since when?—*adv.* since (then), afterwards, since that time.—*conj. phr. depuis que*, since.
députation [depytɑ'sjɔ̃], *n.f.* deputation; deputyship.
député [depy'te], *n.m.* deputy, delegate; Member of Parliament.
députer [depy'te], *v.t.* to send as representative, to depute.
déracinement [derasin'mɑ̃], *n.m.* uprooting, eradication.
déraciner [derasi'ne], *v.t.* to uproot; to eradicate, to extirpate.
déraidir [derɛ'di:r], *v.t.* to unstiffen; to make pliant. **se déraidir**, *v.r.* to grow soft or supple; to unbend.
déraillement [deraj'mɑ̃], *n.m.* derailment.
dérailler [derɑ'je], *v.i.* to run off the rails.
déraison [derɛ'zɔ̃], *n.f.* unreasonableness, folly.
déraisonnable [derɛzɔ'nabl], *a.* unreasonable, senseless.
déraisonnablement [derɛzɔnablə'mɑ̃], *adv.* unreasonably, irrationally.
déraisonner [derɛzɔ'ne], *v.i.* to reason falsely, to talk nonsense; to rave.
dérangement [derɑ̃ʒ'mɑ̃], *n.m.* derangement; trouble; disorder, disturbance.
déranger [derɑ̃'ʒe], *v.t.* (*conjug. like* MANGER) to derange, to put out of place or order; to discompose, to disconcert; to disturb, to upset; to unsettle. **se déranger**, *v.r.* to move; to be deranged, to get out of order; to trouble or disturb oneself, to put oneself out.
déraper [dera'pe], *v.i.* to skid, to side-slip (*bicycle, car etc.*).
dératé [dera'te], *n.m. only used in courir comme un dératé*, to run like a greyhound.
derechef [dər'ʃɛf], *adv.* over again, afresh, anew.
déréglé [dere'gle], *a.* out of order; irregular; intemperate, (*fig.*) unruly, dissolute.
dérèglement [derɛglə'mɑ̃], *n.m.* irregularity, disorder; dissoluteness, licentiousness.
dérégler [dere'gle], *v.t.* (*conjug. like* CÉDER) to put out of order. **se dérégler**, *v.r.* to get out of order; to be deranged; to lead a disorderly life.

dérider

dérider [deri'de], *v.t.* to unwrinkle, to smooth; to brighten, to cheer up. **se dérider**, *v.r.* to smooth one's brow; to cheer up.

dérision [deri'zjɔ̃], *n.f.* derision, mockery, ridicule.

dérisoire [deri'zwa:r], *a.* derisive, mocking.

dérivatif [deriva'tif], *a.* (*fem.* **-tive**) derivative.—*n.m.* (*Med.*) derivative, counter-irritant.

dérivation [deriva'sjɔ̃], *n.f.* derivation; diversion (*of water etc.*); (*Elec.*) branching, shunting; (*Naut.*) drift, leeway; (*Av.*) windage; (*Elec.*) **circuit en dérivation**, branch circuit.

dérive [de'ri:v], *n.f.* (*Naut.*) drift, leeway; (*Av.*) fin.

dérivé [deri've], *a.* drifted.—*n.m.* (*Gram.*) derivative.

dériver [deri've], *v.t.* to divert; to derive.—*v.i.* to be turned from its proper course; (*Naut.*) to drift (*from the shore*), to go adrift.

dermatite [dɛrma'tit], *n.f.* dermatitis.

dernier [dɛr'nje], *a.* (*fem.* **-ière**) last, latest; vilest, meanest; extreme (*highest, greatest etc.*); the one just past; youngest (*of a family of children*).—*n.m.* (*fem.* **-ière**) the last; the highest, lowest etc.

dernièrement [dɛrnjɛr'mɑ̃], *adv.* lately, recently.

dérobé [derɔ'be], *a.* stolen, hidden, secret; **à la dérobée**, stealthily.

dérober [derɔ'be], *v.t.* to steal; to remove; to conceal; to protect, to screen. **se dérober**, *v.r.* to steal away, to escape, to disappear.

dérogation [derɔga'sjɔ̃], *n.f.* derogation.

dérogatoire [derɔga'twa:r], *a.* derogatory.

déroger [derɔ'ʒe], *v.i.* (*conjug. like* MANGER) to derogate; to detract; to condescend, to stoop.

dérouillement [deruj'mɑ̃], *n.m.* removal of rust.

dérouiller [deru'je], *v.t.* to remove the rust from; (*fig.*) to polish. **se dérouiller**, *v.r.* to lose its *or* one's rust; to brighten up; to read a subject up again.

déroulement [derul'mɑ̃], *n.m.* unrolling, unfolding.

dérouler [deru'le], *v.t.* to unroll; to spread out, to display. **se dérouler**, *v.r.* to unroll; to open to the view; to roll in (*of the waves*); to take place (*of events*).

déroutant [deru'tɑ̃], *a.* baffling, confusing.

déroute [de'rut], *n.f.* rout, overthrow; ruin; disorder, confusion.

dérouter [deru'te], *v.t.* to lead astray; to embarrass, to disconcert; to baffle; to divert (*ship, train etc.*).

derrière [dɛ'rjɛ:r], *prep.* behind, on the other side of.—*adv.* behind, after.—*n.m.* back, hinder part; posterior; behind; **pattes de derrière**, hind legs; **porte de derrière**, back door.

derviche [dɛr'viʃ], **dervis** [dɛr'vi], *n.m.* dervish.

des [de], (*contr. of* DE LES).

dès [dɛ], *prep.* from, since, as early as.—*conj. phr.* **dès que**, when, as soon as, since.

désabonnement [dezabɔn'mɑ̃], *n.m.* withdrawal of subscription.

désabonner (se) [sədezabɔ'ne], *v.r.* to withdraw one's subscription (*to a magazine etc.*).

désabuser [dezaby'ze], *v.t.* to disabuse, to undeceive. **se désabuser**, *v.r.* to be undeceived, to face the facts.

désaccord [deza'kɔːr], *n.m.* disagreement, discord.

désaccorder [dezakɔr'de], *v.t.* to untune; (*fig.*) to set at variance. **se désaccorder**, *v.r.* to get out of tune.

désaccouplement [dezakupla'mɑ̃], *n.m.* uncoupling.

désaccoupler [dezaku'ple], *v.t.* to uncouple. **se désaccoupler**, *v.r.* to become uncoupled; to come asunder.

désaccoutumer [dezakuty'me], *v.t.* to disaccustom. **se désaccoutumer**, *v.r.* to break oneself of, to lose the habit of.

désaffecter [dezafɛk'te], *v.t.* to secularize (*a church*); (*Mil.*) to transfer; to put a building to another use.

désaffection [dezafɛk'sjɔ̃], *n.f.* loss of affection.

désaffectionner [dezafɛksjɔ'ne], *v.t.* to cause (*someone*) to lose his *or* her affection, to disaffect. **se désaffectionner**, *v.r.* to lose affection.

désagencement [dezaʒɑ̃s'mɑ̃], *n.m.* throwing out of gear.

désagencer [dezaʒɑ̃'se], *v.t.* (*conjug. like* COMMENCER) to throw out of gear, to disarrange.

désagréable [dezagre'abl], *a.* disagreeable, unpleasant.

désagréablement [dezagreabla'mɑ̃], *adv.* disagreeably, unpleasantly.

désagréger [dezagre'ʒe], *v.t.* (*conjug. like* ASSIÉGER) to disaggregate, to break up, to separate.

désagrément [dezagre'mɑ̃], *n.m.* disagreeableness, unpleasantness; annoyance, discomfort.

désaimanter [dezɛmɑ̃'te], *v.t.* to demagnetize.

désajustement [dezaʒysta'mɑ̃], *n.m.* disarrangement, disorder.

désajuster [dezaʒys'te], *v.t.* to disarrange, to disturb, to put out of order. **se désajuster**, *v.r.* to become disarranged, to get out of order.

désaltérant [dezalte'rɑ̃], *a.* thirst-quenching.

désaltérer [dezalte're], *v.t.* (*conjug. like* CÉDER) to quench the thirst of, to refresh. **se désaltérer**, *v.r.* to quench one's thirst.

désamorcer [dezamɔr'se], *v.t.* (*conjug. like* COMMENCER) to unprime, to uncap (*fire-arms etc.*). **se désamorcer**, *v.r.* to run down (*dynamo*); to run dry (*pump*).

désappointement [dezapwɛ̃'mɑ̃], *n.m.* disappointment.

désappointer [dezapwɛ̃'te], *v.t.* to disappoint.

désapprendre [deza'prɑ̃:dr], *v.t. irr.* (*conjug. like* PRENDRE) to unlearn, to forget.

désapprobateur [dezaprɔba'tœːr], *a.* (*fem.* **-trice**) disapproving, censuring, carping.—*n.m.* (*fem.* **-trice**) censurer, fault-finder.

désapprobation [dezaprɔba'sjɔ̃], *n.f.* disapprobation, disapproval.

désappropriation [dezaprɔpria'sjɔ̃], *n.f.* renunciation (*of property*).

désapprouver [dezapru've], *v.t.* to disapprove of, to blame.

110

désarçonner [dezarsɔ'ne], v.t. to unhorse; (fig.) to baffle, to floor.
désarmement [dezarmə'mɑ̃], n.m. disarming, disarmament; (Naut.) laying up.
désarmer [dezar'me], v.t. to disarm, to unarm; (fig.) to appease, to calm; to uncock (a gun); (Naut.) to lay up (a vessel).—v.i. to disarm; to give up maintaining troops.
désarroi [deza'rwa], n.m. disorder, disarray, confusion.
désarticulation [dezartikylɑ'sjɔ̃], n.f. disarticulation.
désarticuler [dezartiky'le], v.t. to disarticulate, to disjoint.
désassemblage [dezasɑ̃'bla:ʒ], **désassemblement** [dezasɑ̃blə'mɑ̃], n.m. dismantling.
désassembler [dezasɑ̃'ble], v.t. to take to pieces, to separate, to dismantle.
désassocier [dezasɔ'sje], v.t. to disassociate, to dissociate.
désassortiment [dezasɔrti'mɑ̃], n.m. unmatching, ill-assortment; unstocking.
désastre [de'zastr], n.m. disaster.
désastreusement [dezastrøz'mɑ̃], adv. disastrously.
désastreux [dezas'trø], a. (fem. -euse) disastrous, unfortunate, very sad.
désavantage [dezavɑ̃'ta:ʒ], n.m. disadvantage; detriment, prejudice; drawback, handicap.
désavantager [dezavɑ̃ta'ʒe], v.t. (conjug. like MANGER) to disadvantage, to handicap.
désavantageusement [dezavɑ̃taʒøz'mɑ̃], adv. disadvantageously; disparagingly.
désavantageux [dezavɑ̃ta'ʒø], a. (fem. -euse) disadvantageous; detrimental, prejudicial, unfavorable.
désaveu [deza'vø], n.m. (pl. -eux) disavowal; denial; retractation.
désavouer [deza'vwe], v.t. to disown, to disclaim, to disavow; to retract.
désaxé [deza'kse], a. offset, out of true (of a wheel, etc.); (fig.) out of joint.
descellement [desɛl'mɑ̃], n.m. loosening, unsealing.
desceller [desɛ'le], v.t. to unseal; to loosen (masonry etc.). **se desceller**, v.r. to become loose or unsealed.
descendance [desɑ̃'dɑ̃:s], n.f. descent, lineage.
descendant [desɑ̃'dɑ̃], a. descending, going down; (Mil.) coming off duty.—n.m. (fem. -e) descendant, offspring, issue.
descendre [de'sɑ̃:dr], v.t. (with aux. AVOIR) to take down, to bring or let down; to go or come down (a staircase etc.); to drop off (of a cab etc.); to land.—v.i. (with aux. ÊTRE) to descend, to go down; to go downstairs; to alight, to land; to slope, to incline; to fall, to subside.
descente [de'sɑ̃:t], n.f. descent; taking down; subsidence (of waters etc.); dismounting; disembarkation; declivity; raid; (pop.) rupture; **descente de lit**, bedside rug; **descente de bain**, bath mat.
descriptif [deskrip'tif], a. (fem. -tive) descriptive.
description [deskrip'sjɔ̃], n.f. description; inventory.
désemballage [dezɑ̃ba'la:ʒ], n.m. unpacking.
désemballer [dezɑ̃ba'le], v.t. to unpack.

désembarquement [dezɑ̃barka'mɑ̃], n.m. disembarkation, landing.
désembarquer [dezɑ̃bar'ke], v.t. to disembark, to land; to unship, to unload.
désemboîter [dezɑ̃bwa'te], v.t. to dislocate. **se désemboîter**, v.r. to become disjointed.
désembourber [dezɑ̃bur'be], v.t. to draw out of the mire.
désemparé [dezɑ̃pa're], a. in distress, helpless.
désemparer [dezɑ̃pa're], v.t. (Naut.) to disable.—v.i. to quit, to go away; **sans désemparer**, on the spot, at once.
désempeser [dezɑ̃pə'ze], v.t. (conjug. like AMENER) to unstarch. **se désempeser**, v.r. to become limp.
désemplir [dezɑ̃'pli:r], v.t. to make less full, to empty in part.—v.i. to become less full (used only in negative). **se désemplir**, v.r. to become less full.
désen̄haîner [dezɑ̃ʃɛ'ne], v.t. to unchain.
désenchantement [dezɑ̃ʃɑ̃t'mɑ̃], n.m. disenchantment, disillusion.
désenchanter [dezɑ̃ʃɑ̃'te], v.t. to disenchant, to disillusion.
désenchanteur [dezɑ̃ʃɑ̃'tœ:r], a. (fem. -eresse) disenchanting.
désencombrement [dezɑ̃kɔ̃brə'mɑ̃], n.m. disencumbrance; dispersal.
désencombrer [dezɑ̃kɔ̃'bre], v.t. to disencumber, to clear (a road etc.).
désenfiler [dezɑ̃fi'le], v.t. to unthread, to unstring. **se désenfiler**, v.r. to come unthreaded or unstrung.
désenfler [dezɑ̃'fle], v.t. to reduce the swelling of.—v.i. and **se désenfler**, v.r. to become less swollen.
désenflure [dezɑ̃'fly:r], n.f., **désenflement** [dezɑ̃flə'mɑ̃], n.m. diminution or disappearance of a swelling.
désengager [dezɑ̃ga'ʒe], v.t. (conjug. like MANGER) to disengage, to release from an engagement.
désengrener [dezɑ̃grə'ne], v.t. (conjug. like AMENER) to throw out of gear.
désenivrer [dezɑ̃ni'vre], v.t., to make sober again.—v.i. to sober. **se désenivrer**, v.r. to become sober (again), to sober up.
désenlaidir [dezɑ̃lɛ'di:r], v.t. to render less ugly.—v.i. to become less ugly.
désennuyer [dezɑ̃nɥi'je], v.t. (conjug. like EMPLOYER) to enliven, to cheer. **se désennuyer**, v.r. to find amusement, to kill time.
désenrayer [dezɑ̃rɛ'je], v.t. (conjug. like PAYER) to unlock or unskid (a wheel etc.).
désenrhumer [dezɑ̃ry'me], v.t. to cure (someone) of a cold. **se désenrhumer**, v.r. to get rid of a cold.
désenrôlement [dezɑ̃rol'mɑ̃], n.m. (Mil.) discharge.
désenrôler [dezɑ̃ro'le], v.t. to discharge.
désensevelir [dezɑ̃sə'vli:r], v.t. to unshroud, to exhume.
désensevelissement [dezɑ̃səvlis'mɑ̃], n.m. unshrouding, exhumation, disinterment.
désentortiller [dezɑ̃tɔrti'je], v.t. to untwist, to unravel.
désentraver [dezɑ̃tra've], v.t. to untrammel, to unhobble (a horse etc.).
déséquilibre [dezeki'libr], n.m. lack of balance, unbalance; imbalance.

111

déséquilibré

déséquilibré [dezekili'bre], *a.* and *n.m.* (*fem.* **-ée**) unbalanced (person).

déséquilibrer [dezekili'bre], *v.t.* to unbalance.

désert [de'zɛːr], *a.* uninhabited, solitary; wild, waste, deserted.—*n.m.* desert, wilderness; solitary place; (*C*) clearing in a forest.

déserter [dezɛrte], *v.t.* to desert, to abandon, to forsake; to quit, to leave; (*C*) to clear land, to break up (*ground*) for tillage.—*v.i.* to desert, to go over to the enemy.

déserteur [dezɛr'tœːr], *n.m.* deserter.

désertion [dezɛr'sjɔ̃], *n.f.* desertion.

désespérance [dezɛspe'rɑ̃ːs], *n.f.* despair.

désespérant [dezɛspe'rɑ̃], *a.* desperate, hopeless; disheartening, distressing.

désespéré [dezɛspe're], *a.* hopeless, desperate; disconsolate.—*n.m.* (*fem.* **-ée**) person in despair; madman, madwoman.

désespérément [dezɛspere'mɑ̃], *adv.* desperately, despairingly.

désespérer [dezɛspe're], *v.t.* (*conjug. like* CÉDER) to drive to despair; to dishearten; to distress.—*v.i.* to despair. **se désespérer**, *v.r.* to be in despair.

désespoir [dezɛs'pwaːr], *n.m.* despair, hopelessness, despondency, grief; **en désespoir de cause**, as a last resource.

déshabiliter [dezabili'te], *v.t.* to disqualify.

déshabillé [dezabi'je], *n.m.* deshabille, undress; **en déshabillé**, partly or scantily dressed.

déshabiller [dezabi'je], *v.t.* to undress, to strip. **se déshabiller**, *v.r.* to undress oneself.

déshabituer [dezabi'tɥe], *v.t.* to disaccustom, to break off. **se déshabituer**, *v.r.* to lose the habit of; to break oneself of.

déshérence [deze'rɑ̃ːs], *n.f.* (*Law*) escheat.

déshériter [dezeri'te], *v.t.* to disinherit.

déshonnête [dezɔ'nɛːt], *a.* immodest, indecent, unseemly.

déshonnêtement [dezɔnɛt'mɑ̃], *adv.* indecently, immodestly.

déshonnêteté [dezɔnɛt'te], *n.f.* indecency, unseemliness.

déshonneur [dezɔ'nœːr], *n.m.* dishonor, disgrace, shame.

déshonorable [dezɔnɔ'rabl], *a.* dishonorable.

déshonorablement [dezɔnɔrablə'mɑ̃], *adv.* dishonorably.

déshonorant [dezɔnɔ'rɑ̃], *a.* dishonorable, disgraceful.

déshonorer [dezɔnɔ're], *v.t.* to dishonor, to disgrace. **se déshonorer**, *v.r.* to dishonor or disgrace oneself.

déshydrater [dezidra'te], *v.t.* to dehydrate.

désignatif [deziɲa'tif], *a.* (*fem.* **-tive**) indicative.

désignation [deziɲa'sjɔ̃], *n.f.* designation, indication.

désigner [dezi'ɲe], *v.t.* to designate, to denote; to appoint, to nominate; to point out; (*Mil.*) to detail.

désillusion [dezily'zjɔ̃], *n.f.*, **désillusionnement** [dezilyzjɔn'mɑ̃], *n.m.* disillusion.

désillusionner [dezilyzjɔ'ne], *v.t.* to disillusion, to disappoint.

désinfectant [dezɛ̃fɛk'tɑ̃], *a.* disinfecting.—*n.m.* disinfectant.

désinfecter [dezɛ̃fɛk'te], *v.t.* to disinfect, to decontaminate.

désinfection [dezɛ̃fɛk'sjɔ̃], *n.f.* disinfection.

désintégration [dezɛ̃tegrɑ'sjɔ̃], *n.f.* disintegration; fission.

désintégrer [dezɛ̃te'gre], *v.t.* (*conjug. like* CÉDER) to disintegrate; to split (*atom*).

désintéressé [dezɛ̃tere'se], *a.* disinterested, unselfish, unbiased.

désintéressement [dezɛ̃teres'mɑ̃], *n.m.* disinterestedness.

désintéresser [dezɛ̃tere'se], *v.t.* to indemnify.

désinvestir [dezɛ̃vɛs'tiːr], *v.t.* (*Mil.*) to raise the siege of.

désinvolte [dezɛ̃'vɔlt], *a.* free, easy; offhand.

désinvolture [dezɛ̃vɔl'tyːr], *n.f.* casual, easy bearing or gait; offhandedness.

désir [de'ziːr], *n.m.* desire, wish, longing.

désirable [dezi'rabl], *a.* desirable.

désirer [dezi're], *v.t.* to desire, to wish for, to long for; to want.

désireux [dezi'rø], *a.* (*fem.* **-euse**) desirous, anxious, eager (*to*).

désistement [dezista'mɑ̃], *n.m.* desistance, withdrawal.

désister (se) [sədezis'te], *v.r.* to desist from, to renounce, to withdraw.

désobéir [dezɔbe'iːr], *v.i.* to disobey.

désobéissance [dezɔbei'sɑ̃ːs], *n.f.* disobedience.

désobéissant [dezɔbei'sɑ̃], *a.* disobedient.

désobligeamment [dezɔbliʒa'mɑ̃], *adv.* disobligingly; unkindly.

désobligeance [dezɔbli'ʒɑ̃ːs], *n.f.* lack of complaisance; unkindness.

désobligeant [dezɔbli'ʒɑ̃], *a.* disobliging; uncivil.

désobliger [dezɔbli'ʒe], *v.t.* (*conjug. like* MANGER) to disoblige, to displease.

désodorisant [dezɔdɔri'zɑ̃], *a.* and *n.m.* deodorant.

désœuvré [dezœ'vre], *a.* unoccupied, idle.

désœuvrement [dezœvrə'mɑ̃], *n.m.* want of occupation, idleness.

désolant [dezɔ'lɑ̃], *a.* grievous, distressing.

désolation [dezɔlɑ'sjɔ̃], *n.f.* desolation, ruin; deep affliction, grief.

désolé [dezɔ'le], *a.* afflicted, broken-hearted; very sorry, grieved; dreary, desolate (*place*).

désoler [dezɔ'le], *v.t.* to devastate, to desolate, to lay waste; to afflict, to grieve; to annoy, to torment. **se désoler**, *v.r.* to grieve, to be disconsolate.

désolidariser [desɔlidari'ze], *v.t.* to break the ties which keep together (*a party, friends etc.*).

désopilant [dezɔpi'lɑ̃], *a.* very funny, side-splitting.

désopiler [dezɔpi'le], *v.t.* (*Med.*) to clear of obstruction; (*fig.*) to cheer up, to enliven.

désordonné [dezɔrdɔ'ne], *a.* disorderly; (*fig.*) dissolute, unruly; inordinate.

désordonner [dezɔrdɔ'ne], *v.t.* to disturb; to throw into confusion.

désordre [de'zɔrdr], *n.m.* disorder, confusion; disorderly life; perturbation; (*pl.*) disturbances, riots.

désorganisation [dezɔrganizɑ'sjɔ̃], *n.f.* disorganization.

désorganiser [dezɔrgani'ze], *v.t.* to disorganize. **se désorganiser**, *v.r.* to become disorganized.

désorienter [dezɔrjɑ̃'te], *v.t.* to lead astray, to mislead, to bewilder; to put out, to disconcert.

désormais [dezɔr'mɛ], *adv.* henceforth, hereafter.

désossé [dezɔ'se], *a.* boneless, flabby.

désosser [dezɔ'se], *v.t.* to bone. **se désosser,** *v.r.* to become disjointed, limp, flabby etc.

despote [dɛs'pɔt], *n.m.* despot.

despotique [dɛspɔ'tik], *a.* despotic.

despotiquement [dɛspɔtik'mɑ̃], *adv.* despotically.

despotisme [dɛspɔ'tism], *n.m.* despotism.

desquels [de'kɛl], *m.pl. (fem.* **-elles**) [DUQUEL].

dessaisir [desɛ'ziːr], *v.t.* to let go; to dispossess. **se dessaisir,** *v.r.* to give up, to part with.

dessaisissement [desɛzis'mɑ̃], *n.m.* parting with, abandonment.

dessalé [desa'le], *a.* unsalted, free from salt; *(fam.)* sharp.—*n.m. (fem.* **-ée**) sharp person.

dessaler [desa'le], *v.t.* to remove salt from *(meat etc.); (fig.)* to make sharp, cunning etc.

dessangler [desɑ̃'gle], *v.t.* to loosen the girth of *(a horse etc.)*.

desséchant [dese'ʃɑ̃], *a.* drying, parching.

dessèchement [deseʃ'mɑ̃], *n.m.* drying up; dryness.

dessécher [dese'ʃe], *v.t.* to dry up; to parch; *(fig.)* to wither *(the heart etc.);* to emaciate. **se dessécher,** *v.r.* to become dry, to dry up; *(fig.)* to waste away.

dessein [de'sɛ̃], *n.m.* design, plan, scheme; intention, resolution.

desseller [dese'le], *v.t.* to unsaddle.

desserrer [dese're], *v.t.* to loosen, to relax; to ease. **se desserrer,** *v.r.* to become loose, to relax.

dessert [de'sɛːr], *n.m.* dessert.

desserte [de'sɛrt], *n.f.* leavings, remains *(of a meal);* small sideboard; parochial duty; railway service.

desservant [desɛr'vɑ̃], *n.m.* officiating minister *(of a parish etc.)*.

desservir [desɛr'viːr], *v.t. irr. (conjug. like* SENTIR) to clear *(a table);* to officiate *(of clergymen);* to ply between *(of boats etc.); (fig.)* to do someone a disservice.

dessiller or **déciller** [desi'je], *v.t.* to open *(someone's eyes);* to undeceive.

dessin [de'sɛ̃], *n.m.* drawing; sketch; pattern, design; *dessin animé, (Cine.)* cartoon.

dessinateur [desina'tœːr], *n.m. (fem.* **-trice**) draftsman; designer.

dessiner [desi'ne], *v.t.* to draw, to sketch; to set off, to indicate; to lay out. **se dessiner,** *v.r.* to be delineated, to be visible, to stand out.

dessous [dɔ'su], *adv.* under, underneath, below.—*n.m.* lower part; under, hidden or wrong side; worst; lee *(of the wind); (pl.)* underclothing *(of women)*.—*prep. phr.* **au-dessous de,** beneath.

dessus [dɔ'sy], *adv.* on, upon, over, above; *là-dessus,* thereupon; *par-dessus,* over, besides; *sens dessus dessous,* upside down.—*n.m.* top, upper part; right side; upper hand, advantage.—*prep. phr.* **au-dessus de,** above.

destin [dɛs'tɛ̃], *n.m.* destiny, fate; career.

destinataire [dɛstina'tɛːr], *n.* addressee; recipient; *(Comm.)* consignee; payee.

destination [dɛstina'sjɔ̃], *n.f.* destination; object, end.

destinée [dɛsti'ne], *n.f.* fate, destiny, doom.

destiner [dɛsti'ne], *v.t.* to destine, to purpose; to reserve *(for a particular fate etc.).* **se destiner,** *v.r.* to be destined.

destituer [dɛsti'tɥe], *v.t.* to dismiss, to discharge.

destitution [dɛstity'sjɔ̃], *n.f.* dismissal, removal *(from office)*.

destroyer [dɛstrwa'jœːr], *n.m. (Navy)* destroyer.

destructeur [dɛstryk'tœːr], *a. (fem.* **-trice**) destructive, deadly, ruinous.—*n.m. (fem.* **-trice**) ravager, spoiler.

destructif [dɛstryk'tif], *a. (fem.* **-tive**) destructive, destroying.

destruction [dɛstryk'sjɔ̃], *n.f.* destruction.

désuet [desɥ'ɛ], *a. (fem.* **-ète**) obsolete, out-of-date.

désuétude [desɥe'tyd], *n.f.* disuse, desuetude.

désunion [dezy'njɔ̃], *n.f.* disunion; disjunction.

désunir [dezy'niːr], *v.t.* to disunite, to disjoin, to part. **se désunir,** *v.r.* to disunite, to come asunder.

détachage [deta'ʃaːʒ], *n.m.* cleaning, scouring.

détachant [deta'ʃɑ̃], *n.m.* cleaner, stain-remover.

détachement [detaʃ'mɑ̃], *n.m.* indifference, unconcern; *(Mil.)* detachment, draft.

détacher (1) [deta'ʃe], *v.t.* to remove stains, spots etc.

détacher (2) [deta'ʃe], *v.t.* to detach, to untie, to unfasten, to undo; to cut off; *(Mil.)* to detail. **se détacher,** *v.r.* to come unfastened, to come undone; to disengage oneself; to break away; to stand out clearly.

détail [de'taːj], *n.m.* detail, small matter, trifle; retail.

détaillant [deta'jɑ̃], *n.m. (fem.* **-e**) retailer, small dealer.

détailler [deta'je], *v.t.* to cut in pieces; to retail; to relate minutely.

détaxation [detaksa'sjɔ̃], *n.f.* decontrol *(of prices)*.

détaxer [detak'se], *v.t.* to reduce or take off a tax; to decontrol.

détecter [detɛk'te], *v.t.* to detect.

détecteur [detɛk'tœːr], *n.m.* detector.

détection [detɛk'sjɔ̃], *n.f.* detection.

détective [detɛk'tiːv], *n.m.* detective.

déteindre [de'tɛ̃ːdr], *v.t. irr. (conjug. like* CRAINDRE) to take the dye or color out of.—*v.i.* to lose color, to run, to fade.

dételage [de'tlaːʒ], *n.m.* unharnessing.

dételer [de'tle], *v.t. (conjug. like* APPELER) to unharness, to unyoke.

détendre [de'tɑ̃ːdr], *v.t.* to slacken, to relax; to reduce the pressure of; to take down. **se détendre,** *v.r.* to slacken, to unbend, to become easier, to relax.

détenir [det'niːr], *v.t. irr. (conjug. like* TENIR) to detain, to withhold; to confine.

détente [de'tɑ̃ːt], *n.f.* trigger *(of a gun etc.);* cut-off *(of an engine);* relaxation, easing.

détenteur [detɑ̃'tœːr], *n.m. (fem.* **-trice**) holder, detainer.

113

détention [detɑ̃'sjɔ̃], *n.f.* detention; imprisonment.

détenu [det'ny], *a.* detained, imprisoned.—*n.m.* (*fem.* **-e**) prisoner.

détergent [deter'ʒɑ̃], *a.* (*Med.*) detergent.—*n.m.* detergent.

déterger [deter'ʒe], *v.t.* (*conjug. like* MANGER) to cleanse, to purify.

détérioration [deterjɔrɑ'sjɔ̃], *n.f.* deterioration; wear and tear.

détériorer [deterjɔ're], *v.t.* to impair, to make worse. **se détériorer**, *v.r.* to deteriorate.

déterminable [determi'nabl], *a.* determinable.

déterminant [determi'nɑ̃], *a.* determinative, decisive.—*n.m.* (*Math.*) determinant.

détermination [determinɑ'sjɔ̃], *n.f.* determination, resolution.

déterminé [determi'ne], *a.* determined, decided, fixed; resolute, firm.

déterminer [determi'ne], *v.t.* to determine, to settle; to ascertain; to decide; to cause to take a resolution. **se déterminer**, *v.r.* to resolve, to determine.

déterré [dete're], *n.m.* exhumed body.

déterrer [dete're], *v.t.* to dig up, to disinter; to unearth, to bring to light.

détestable [detes'tabl], *a.* detestable, hateful, odious; wretched.

détestablement [detestablə'mɑ̃], *adv.* detestably, abominably.

détestation [detestɑ'sjɔ̃], *n.f.* detestation, abhorrence.

détester [detes'te], *v.t.* to detest, to hate.

détirer [deti're], *v.t.* to draw out, to stretch.

détisser [deti'se], *v.t.* to unweave.

détonateur [detɔna'tœ:r], *n.m.* detonator.

détonation [detɔna'sjɔ̃], *n.f.* detonation, report.

détoner [detɔ'ne], *v.t., v.i.* to detonate.

détonneler [detɔn'le], *v.t.* (*conjug. like* APPELER) to draw from a cask.

détonner [detɔ'ne], *v.i.* to be out of tune; to jar.

détordre [de'tɔrdr], *v.t.* to untwist; to unravel. **se détordre**, *v.r.* to come untwisted.

détors [de'tɔ:r], *a.* untwisted.

détortiller [detɔrti'je], *v.t.* to untwist; to unravel. **se détortiller**, *v.r.* to become untwisted; to be unravelled.

détour [de'tu:r], *n.m.* turning, change of direction; roundabout way; (*fig.*) shift, evasion, trick.

détourné [detur'ne], *a.* out of the way, unfrequented; indirect.

détournement [deturnə'mɑ̃], *n.m.* turning aside; embezzlement; *détournement de mineur*, (*Law*) abduction of a minor.

détourner [detur'ne], *v.t.* to turn away; to lead astray; to divert; to ward off; to embezzle; to deter.—*v.i.* to turn, to turn off. **se détourner**, *v.r.* to turn aside; to abandon (*de*).

détracteur [detrak'tœ:r], *a.* (*fem.* **-trice**) detractive, detracting.—*n.m.* (*fem.* **-trice**) detractor, disparager.

détraqué [detra'ke], *a.* out of order; deranged, (*colloq.*) crazy.—*n.m.* (*fem.* **-ée**) person shattered in mind or body.

détraquement [detrak'mɑ̃], *n.m.* breakdown (*of mechanism, mind, health*).

détraquer [detra'ke], *v.t.* to spoil (*a horse's*) paces; (*fig.*) to put out of order. **se détraquer**, *v.r.* to lose its paces (*of a horse*); (*fig.*) to be disordered.

détrempe [de'trɑ̃:p], *n.f.* calcimine (*paint*).

détremper [detrɑ̃'pe], *v.t.* to dilute, to dissolve.

détresse [de'trɛs], *n.f.* distress, grief, trouble.

détresser [detrɛ'se], *v.t.* to unravel; to unplait.

détriment [detri'mɑ̃], *n.m.* detriment, injury, prejudice.

détritus [detri'tys], *n.m.* residue, refuse; offal.

détroit [de'trwa], *n.m.* strait, channel, sound, narrow firth.

détromper [detrɔ̃'pe], *v.t.* to undeceive. **se détromper**, *v.r.* to be undeceived.

détrônement [detron'mɑ̃], *n.m.* dethronement.

détrôner [detro'ne], *v.t.* to dethrone.

détrousser [detru'se], *v.t.* to untruss, to let down; (*fig.*) to rob.

détrousseur [detru'sœ:r], *n.m.* (*fem.* **-euse**) highwayman, robber.

détruire [de'trɥi:r], *v.t. irr.* (*conjug. like* CONDUIRE) to destroy, to demolish, to ruin; to exterminate, to do away with; to efface, to suppress. **se détruire**, *v.r.* to fall into ruin *or* decay; to destroy each other.

dette [dɛt], *n.f.* debt; obligation.

deuil [dœ:j], *n.m.* mourning; grief, sorrow; gloom; period of mourning; bereavement; mourning clothes; funeral cortège.

Deutéronome [døterɔ'nɔm], *n.m.* Deuteronomy.

deux [dø], *a.* two, both; second.—*n.m.* two; second (*of the month*); (*Cards, Dice etc.*) deuce.

deuxième [dø'zjɛm], *a.* second.—*n.m.* second; second floor.

deuxièmement [døzjɛm'mɑ̃], *adv.* secondly.

deux-pièces [dø'pjɛs], *n.m. inv.* (*women's*) two-piece (*suit*).

deux-points [dø'pwɛ̃], *n.m. inv.* (*Print.*) colon.

dévaler [deva'le], *v.t.* to descend; to lower.—*v.i.* to descend, to slope; to go *or* rush down (*of streams etc.*).

dévaliser [devali'ze], *v.t.* to rifle, to strip, to rob.

dévaliseur [devali'zœ:r], *n.m.* (*fem.* **-euse**) thief, burglar.

dévaluation [devalɥa'sjɔ̃], *n.f.* devaluation.

dévaluer [deva'lɥe], *v.t.* to devalue.

devancer [dəvɑ̃'se], *v.t.* (*conjug. like* COMMENCER) to precede; to outstrip; to forestall, to anticipate; to surpass.

devancier [dəvɑ̃'sje], *n.m.* (*fem.* **-ière**) predecessor; (*pl.*) ancestors, forefathers.

devant [də'vɑ̃], *prep.* before; in front of, over against.—*adv.* in front, ahead.—*n.m.* front, foreport.

devanture [dəvɑ̃'ty:r], *n.f.* front(age) (*of a building*); shop front.

dévaser [deva'ze], *v.t.* to dredge.

dévastateur [devasta'tœ:r], *a.* (*fem.* **-trice**) devastating, destructive.—*n.m.* (*fem.* **-trice**) devastator.

dévastation [devastɑ'sjɔ̃], *n.f.* devastation, ravage, havoc.

dévaster [devas'te], *v.t.* to devastate, to lay waste.

développement [devlɔp'mɑ̃], *n.m.* unfolding, opening; development, progress; (*Mil.*) deployment.

développer [devlɔ'pe], *v.t.* to open, to unwrap; to expand, to explain; to develop. **se développer**, *v.r.* to expand, to unfold; to be unravelled; to extend; to develop.

devenir [dǝv'ni:r], *v.i. irr.* (*conjug. like* TENIR) to become, to grow, to get, to turn into.— *n.m.* gradual development (*of beings or of things*).

dévergondage [devergɔ̃'da:ʒ], *n.m.* shamelessness; profligacy, dissoluteness.

dévergonder (se) [sǝdevergɔ̃'de], *v.r.* to become dissolute.

déverrouillement [deveruj'mɑ̃], *n.m.* unbolting.

déverrouiller [deveru'je], *v.t.* to unbolt; (*fig.*) to set free.

devers [dǝ'vɛ:r], *prep.* towards; **par devers**, in the presence of.

dévers [de'vɛ:r], *a.* inclined; out of alignment. —*n.m.* inclination; warping.

déverser [dever'se], *v.t.* to bend; to dump; to pour out (*water etc.*).—*v.i.* to lean, to jut out; to warp. **se déverser**, *v.r.* to empty (*of rivers, canals etc.*).

déversoir [dever'swa:r], *n.m.* overflow (*of a canal etc.*); outfall.

dévêtir [deve'ti:r], *v.t. irr.* (*conjug. like* VÊTIR) to undress, to strip of clothes; (*Law*) to divest. **se dévêtir**, *v.r.* to take off one's clothes, to undress.

déviation [devja'sjɔ̃], *n.f.* deviation, curvature; detour (*of a road*).

déviationnisme [devjasjɔ'nism], *n.m.* (*Polit.*) deviationism.

déviationniste [devjasjɔ'nist], *n.* deviationist.

dévidage [devi'da:ʒ], *n.m.* winding *or* reeling off.

dévider [devi'de], *v.t.* to wind off (*into skeins etc.*); (*fig.*) to explain.

dévideur [devi'dœ:r], *n.m.* (*fem.* **-euse**) winder, reeler.

dévidoir [devi'dwa:r], *n.m.* reel, skein winder, spool.

dévier [de'vje], *v.i.* and **se dévier**, *v.r.* to deviate; to swerve.

devin [dǝ'vɛ̃], *n.m.* (*fem.* **devineresse**) diviner, augur; fortune-teller.

deviner [dǝvi'ne], *v.t.* to divine, to predict; to guess. **se deviner**, *v.r.* to understand each other.

devinette [dǝvi'nɛt], *n.f.* poser, riddle, conundrum.

devineur [dǝvi'nœ:r], *n.m.* (*fem.* **-euse**) guesser.

devis [dǝ'vi], *n.m.* estimate; specification.

dévisager [deviza'ʒe], *v.t.* (*conjug. like* MANGER) to disfigure; to stare at.

devise [dǝ'vi:z], *n.f.* device, emblem; motto, slogan; (*Fin.*) currency; **des devises étrangères**, foreign currency.

deviser [dǝvi'ze], *v.i.* to talk casually, to chat.

dévissage [devi'sa:ʒ], **dévissement** [devis 'mɑ̃], *n.m.* unscrewing.

dévisser [devi'se], *v.t.* to unscrew. **se dévisser**, *v.r.* to come unscrewed.

dévitaliser [devitali'ze], *v.t.* to kill the nerve (*of a tooth etc.*).

dévoiement [devwa'mɑ̃], *n.m.* looseness (*of the bowels*); (*Arch.*) inclination, slope; (*fig.*) departure from the normal path.

dévoilement [devwal'mɑ̃], *n.m.* unveiling, disclosure.

dévoiler [devwa'le], *v.t.* to unveil, to reveal, to disclose. **se dévoiler**, *v.r.* to be revealed.

dévoîment [DÉVOIEMENT].

devoir [dǝ'vwa:r], *v.t. irr.* to owe (*money, gratitude*); to be obliged to, to be bound to, to have to, must. **se devoir**, *v.r.* to owe oneself; to owe it to oneself.—*n.m.* duty; (*Sch.*) work set, homework; (*pl.*) respects, compliments.

dévoltage [devɔl'ta:ʒ], *n.m.* (*Elec.*) reduction of voltage.

dévolter [devɔl'te], *v.t.* to reduce the voltage, to step down (*current*).

dévolteur [devɔl'tœ:r], *n.m.* reducing transformer.

dévolu [devɔ'ly], *a.* (*Law*) devolved, vested.— *n.m.* choice, preference.

dévolution [devɔly'sjɔ̃], *n.f.* devolution; escheat.

dévorant [devɔ'rɑ̃], *a.* devouring, ravenous; (*fig.*) wasting.

dévorateur [devɔra'tœ:r], *a.* (*fem.* **-trice**) devouring.—*n.m.* (*fem.* **-trice**) devourer, destroyer.

dévorer [devɔ're], *v.t.* to devour; to destroy; to squander; to gaze at eagerly.

dévot [de'vo], *a.* devout, pious; sanctimonious; holy (*of books etc.*).—*n.m.* (*fem.* **-e**) devout person, devotee; bigot.

dévotement [devɔt'mɑ̃], *adv.* devoutly, piously.

dévotion [devɔ'sjɔ̃], *n.f.* devotion, piety; disposal; devoutness.

dévouement *or* **dévoûment** [devu'mɑ̃], *n.m.* self-sacrifice; devotion, devotedness; zeal.

dévouer [de'vwe], *v.t.* to devote, to dedicate. **se dévouer**, *v.r.* to devote oneself; to dedicate oneself.

dévoyé [devwa'je], *a.* stray, gone astray.—*n.m.* (*fem.* **-ée**) (*fig.*) black sheep.

dévoyer [devwa'je], *v.t.* (*conjug. like* EMPLOYER) to corrupt; to lead astray. **se dévoyer**, *v.r.* to become corrupted.

dextérité [deksteri'te], *n.f.* dexterity, skill.

dextrine [dɛks'trin], *n.f.* dextrin.

dextrose [dɛks'tro:z], *n.f.* dextrose, glucose.

diabète [dja'bɛt], *n.m.* diabetes.

diabétique [djabe'tik], *a.* and *n.* diabetic.

diable [dja:bl], *n.m.* devil; wayward child; jack-in-the-box; luggage-truck; drag; **un bon diable**, a good-natured fellow; **un pauvre diable**, a poor wretch.—*int.* the devil! the deuce! confound it! hang it!

diablement [djablǝ'mɑ̃], *adv.* devilishly.

diablerie [djablǝ'ri], *n.f.* devilry, witchcraft; mischief.

diablesse [dja'blɛs], *n.f.* she-devil; shrew, vixen.

diablotin [djablɔ'tɛ̃], *n.m.* imp; (Christmas) cracker.

diabolique [djabɔ'lik], *a.* diabolical, devilish.

diaboliquement [djabɔlik'mɑ̃], *adv.* diabolically, devilishly.

diaconal [djakɔ'nal], *a.* (*m. pl.* **-aux**) diaconal.

diaconat [djakɔ'na], *n.m.* diaconate, deaconry.

diaconesse [djakɔ'nɛs], *n.f.* deaconess.
diacre [djakr], *n.m.* deacon.
diadème [dja'dɛ:m], *n.m.* diadem; coronet.
diagnose [djag'no:z], *n.f.* (*art of*) diagnosis.
diagnostic [djagnɔs'tik], *n.m.* diagnosis.
diagnostique [djagnɔs'tik], *a.* diagnostic.
diagnostiquer [djagnɔsti'ke], *v.t.* to diagnose.
diagonal [djagɔ'nal], *a.* (*m. pl.* **-aux**) diagonal.—*n.f.* (**-e**) diagonal.
diagonalement [djagɔnal'mã], *adv.* diagonally.
diagramme [dja'gram], *n.m.* diagram.
dialecte [dja'lɛkt], *n.m.* dialect.
dialecticien [djalɛkti'sjɛ̃], *n.m.* dialectician.
dialectique [djalɛk'tik], *a.* dialectical.—*n.f.* dialectics, logic.
dialogue [dja'lɔg], *n.m.* dialogue, colloquy.
dialoguer [djalɔ'ge], *v.t.* to write in dialogue form.—*v.i.* to converse, to chat.
dialoguiste [djalɔ'gist], *n.m.* (*Cine.*) script writer.
diamant [dja'mã], *n.m.* diamond.
diamantaire [djamã'tɛ:r], *a.* of diamond brilliancy.—*n.m.* diamond cutter *or* seller.
diamanter [djamã'te], *v.t.* to set with diamonds; to tinsel, to frost.
diamétral [djame'tral], *a.* (*m. pl.* **-aux**) diametrical.
diamétralement [djametral'mã], *adv.* diametrically.
diamètre [dja'metr], *n.m.* diameter.
diane [djan], *n.f.* reveille.
diantre [djã:tr], *int.* the deuce! dash! blast!
diapason [djapa'zɔ̃], *n.m.* diapason, pitch; tuning fork.
diaphane [dja'fan], *a.* diaphanous, transparent.
diaphragme [dja'fragm], *n.m.* diaphragm, midriff.
diapositive [djapozi'ti:v], *n.f.* transparency, slide.
diapré [dja'pre], *a.* dappled, variegated.
diaprer [dja'pre], *v.t.* to dapple, to variegate, to mottle.
diarrhée [dja're], *n.f.* diarrhoea.
diatribe [dja'trib], *n.f.* diatribe, bitter criticism *or* dissertation.
dictamen [dikta'mɛn], *n.m.* dictate (*of one's conscience*).
dictateur [dikta'tœ:r], *n.m.* dictator.
dictatorial [diktatɔ'rjal], *a.* (*m. pl.* **-aux**) dictatorial.
dictature [dikta'ty:r], *n.f.* dictatorship.
dictée [dik'te], *n.f.* act of dictating, dictation.
dicter [dik'te], *v.t.* to dictate; (*fig.*) to suggest, to inspire.
diction [dik'sjɔ̃], *n.f.* diction; delivery.
dictionnaire [diksjɔ'nɛ:r], *n.m.* dictionary.
dicton [dik'tɔ̃], *n.m.* common saying, saw, proverb.
didactique [didak'tik], *a.* didactic.—*n.f.* didactic art.
didactiquement [didaktik'mã], *adv.* didactically.
dièse [dje:z], *n.m.* (*Mus.*) sharp.
diesel [dje'zɛl], *n.m.* diesel (*engine*).
diète (1) [djɛt], *n.f.* diet (*regimen*).
diète (2) [djɛt], *n.f.* (*Hist.*) diet.
diététicien [djeteti'sjɛ̃], *n.m.* (*fem.* **-enne**) dietician, dietist.

diététique [djete'tik], *a.* dietetical.—*n.f.* dietetics.
Dieu [djø], *n.m.* God.
dieu [djø], *n.m.* (*pl.* **dieux**) god.
diffamant [difa'mã], *a.* defamatory, libellous, slanderous.
diffamateur [difama'tœ:r], *n.m.* (*fem.* **-trice**) defamer, slanderer.
diffamation [difama'sjɔ̃], *n.f.* defamation, aspersion, calumny.
diffamatoire [difama'twa:r], *a.* defamatory, libelous, slanderous.
diffamer [difa'me], *v.t.* to defame, to slander, to libel.
différemment [difera'mã], *adv.* differently.
différence [dife'rã:s], *n.f.* difference, diversity, contrast.
différenciation [diferãsja'sjɔ̃], *n.f.* differentiation.
différencier [diferã'sje], *v.t.* to make a difference, to distinguish; (*Math.*) to differentiate.
différend [dife'rã], *n.m.* difference, quarrel, dispute.
différent [dife'rã], *a.* different, dissimilar, unlike.
différentiel [diferã'sjɛl], *a.* (*fem.* **-elle**) differential.—*n.m.* (*Motor.*) differential.
différer [dife're], *v.t.* (*conjug. like* CÉDER) to defer, to postpone, to adjourn.—*v.i.* to defer, to put off; to differ, to disagree.
difficile [difi'sil], *a.* difficult; hard, trying; hard to please, particular.
difficilement [difisil'mã], *adv.* with difficulty.
difficulté [difikyl'te], *n.f.* difficulty; obstacle; rub; objection.
difficultueux [difikyl'tɥø], *a.* (*fem.* **-euse**) prone to raise difficulties; hard to please.
difforme [di'fɔrm], *a.* deformed, misshapen.
difformité [difɔrmi'te], *n.f.* deformity; hideousness.
diffus [di'fy], *a.* diffuse, prolix, verbose.
diffusément [difyze'mã], *adv.* diffusely, wordily.
diffuser [dify'ze], *v.t.* to diffuse; (*Rad. Tel.*) to broadcast.
diffuseur [dify'zœ:r], *n.m.* diffuser, spray cone; loudspeaker.
diffusion [dify'zjɔ̃], *n.f.* diffusion; diffusiveness, wordiness; propagation; broadcasting.
digérer [diʒe're], *v.t.* (*conjug. like* CÉDER) to digest; to ponder, to discuss; to put up with.
digestible [diʒɛs'tibl], *a.* digestible.
digestif [diʒɛs'tif], *a.* (*fem.* **-tive**) and *n.m.* digestive.
digestion [diʒɛs'tjɔ̃], *n.f.* digestion.
digital [diʒi'tal], *a.* (*m. pl.* **-aux**) digital; *empreinte digitale*, finger-print.
digitale [diʒi'tal], *n.f.* foxglove.
digitaline [diʒita'lin], *n.f.* (*Pharm.*) digitalis.
digne [diɲ], *a.* deserving, worthy; dignified.
dignement [diɲ'mã], *adv.* worthily, deservedly; with dignity.
dignitaire [diɲi'tɛ:r], *n.m.* dignitary.
dignité [diɲi'te], *n.f.* dignity, nobility, seriousness; self-respect.
digresser [digrɛ'se], *v.i.* to digress, to depart from the main subject.
digressif [digrɛ'sif], *a.* (*fem.* **-ive**) digressive.
digression [digrɛ'sjɔ̃], *n.f.* digression.

digressivement [digrɛsiv'mã], *adv.* digressively.
digue [dig], *n.f.* dike, dam, embankment; (*fig.*) limit; security.
diguer [di'ge], *v.t.* to dam, to embank.
dilacération [dilasera'sjɔ̃], *n.f.* tearing, rending.
dilacérer [dilase're], *v.t.* (*conjug. like* CÉDER) to tear to pieces.
dilapidateur [dilapida'tœ:r], *a.* (*fem.* -trice) wasteful, extravagant.—*n.m.* (*fem.* -trice) squanderer.
dilapidation [dilapida'sjɔ̃], *n.f.* waste; embezzlement.
dilapider [dilapi'de], *v.t.* to waste, to squander (*a fortune*); to embezzle.
dilatation [dilata'sjɔ̃] *n.f.* dilatation, expansion, distension.
dilater [dila'te], *v.t.* to dilate, to distend, to expand. **se dilater,** *v.r.* to dilate, to be dilated.
dilatoire [dila'twa:r], *a.* (*Law*) dilatory.
dilemme [di'lɛm], *n.m.* dilemma.
dilettante [dilɛ'tã:t], *n.* dilettante.
dilettantisme [dilɛtã'tism], *n.m.* dilettantism, amateurism.
diligemment [diliʒa'mã], *adv.* diligently, promptly.
diligence [dili'ʒã:s], *n.f.* diligence; dispatch, application; stage-coach.
diligent [dili'ʒã], *a.* diligent, assiduous, active.
diluer [di'lɥe], *v.t.* to dilute.
dilution [dily'sjɔ̃], *n.f.* dilution.
diluvien [dily'vjɛ̃], *a.* (*fem.* -enne) diluvian.
dimanche [di'mã:ʃ], *n.m.* Sunday, Sabbath.
dîme [dim], *n.f.* tithe; (U.S.) dime.
dimension [dimã'sjɔ̃], *n.f.* dimension, size.
dîmer [di'me], *v.t.* to tithe.—*v.i.* to levy a tithe.
diminuer [dimi'nɥe], *v.t.* to diminish, to lessen; to impair.—*v.i.* to diminish, to abate, to fall (*in price etc.*); to grow shorter(*of days*).
diminutif [diminy'tif], *a.* (*fem.* ive) and *n.m.* diminutive.
diminution [diminy'sjɔ̃], *n.f.* diminution, reduction, abatement.
dinde [dɛ̃:d], *n.f.* turkey hen; turkey.
dindon [dɛ̃'dɔ̃], *n.m.* turkey cock.
dindonneau [dɛ̃dɔ'no], *n.m.* (*pl.* -eaux) young turkey.
dindonner [dɛ̃dɔ'ne], *v.t.* to dupe, to take in.
dindonnier [dɛ̃dɔ'nje], *n.m.* (*fem.* -ière) turkey keeper.
dîné [DÎNER].
dîner [di'ne], *v.i.* to dine, to have dinner.—*n.m.* or **dîné** [di'ne], dinner; dinner party.
dînette [di'nɛt], *n.f.* child's or doll's dinner.
dîneur [di'nœ:r], *n.m.* (*fem.* -euse) diner; diner-out.
diocésain [djɔse'zɛ̃], *a.* diocesan.
diocèse [djɔ'sɛ:z], *n.m.* diocese.
diphasé [difa'ze], *a.* (*Elec.*) two-phase, diphasic.
diphtérie [difte'ri], *n.f.* diphtheria.
diphtongue [dif'tɔ̃:g], *n.f.* diphthong.
diplomate [diplɔ'mat], *a.* diplomatic.—*n.* diplomatist, diplomat.
diplomatie [diplɔma'si], *n.f.* diplomacy; diplomatic service.
diplomatique [diplɔma'tik], *a.* diplomatic; tactful.

diplomatiquement [diplɔmatik'mã], *adv.* diplomatically.
diplôme [di'plo:m], *n.m.* diploma.
diplômé [diplo'me], *a.* (*fem.* -ée) qualified.—*n.m.* (*fem.* -ée) qualified person.
dipsomane [dipsɔ'man], *n.m.* dipsomaniac.
dipsomanie [dipsɔma'ni], *n.f.* dipsomania.
dire [di:r], *v.t. irr.* to say, to speak; to tell; to recite; to order; to express. **se dire,** *v.r.* to call oneself, to be called; to say to oneself; to be said.—*n.m.* what one says, statement; (*Law*) allegation.
direct [di'rɛkt], *a.* direct, straight, immediate.—*n.m.* (*Box.*) straight blow; *un direct du gauche,* a straight left.
directement [dirɛktə'mã], *adv.* directly, point-blank.
directeur [dirɛk'tœ:r], *n.m.* (*fem.* -trice) director, manager, superintendent, head; principal, head master, head mistress; conductor (*of orchestra*).
direction [dirɛk'sjɔ̃], *n.f.* directing, direction; management; directorship; (*Motor.*) steering.
directives [dirɛk'ti:v], *n.f. pl.* general rules, directives.
directoire [dirɛk'twa:r], *n.m.* (*Eccles.*) directory.
directorat [dirɛktɔ'ra], *n.m.* directorship, directorate.
dirigeable [diri'ʒabl], *n.m.* dirigible balloon *or* airship.
dirigeant [diri'ʒã], *a.* directing, leading.—*n.* ruler, leader.
diriger [diri'ʒe], *v.t.* (*conjug. like* MANGER) to direct; to control; to steer, to manage, to govern; to send, to aim. **se diriger,** *v.r.* to make for, to go (*towards*); to govern oneself.
dirigisme [diri'ʒism], *n.m.* (*Polit.*) state planning *or* controls.
discernement [disɛrnə'mã], *n.m.* discernment; discrimination; judgment.
discerner [disɛr'ne], *v.t.* to discern; to distinguish, to discriminate.
disciple [di'sipl], *n.m.* disciple, follower.
disciplinaire [disipli'nɛ:r], *a.* disciplinary.
discipline [disi'plin], *n.f.* discipline; education, training; (*sch.*) subject.
discipliner [disipli'ne], *v.t.* to discipline. **se discipliner,** *v.r.* to be disciplined.
discontinu [diskɔ̃ti'ny], *a.* discontinuous.
discontinuation [diskɔ̃tinɥa'sjɔ̃], *n.f.* discontinuance, discontinuation.
discontinuer [diskɔ̃ti'nɥe], *v.t.* to discontinue, to interrupt, to suspend.—*v.i.* to cease, to leave off.
discontinuité [diskɔ̃tinɥi'te], *n.f.* discontinuity, discontinuance, interruption.
disconvenance [diskɔ̃v'nã:s], *n.f.* incongruity, unsuitability; dissimilarity.
disconvenir [diskɔ̃v'ni:r], *v.i. irr.* (*conjug. like* TENIR) to deny, to disown; to disagree.
discord [dis'kɔ:r], *a.* (*Mus.*) out of tune, discordant.
discordance [diskɔr'dã:s], *n.f.* discordancy, dissonance.
discordant [diskɔr'dã], *a.* discordant, dissonant, out of tune; inharmonious, incongruous.
discorde [dis'kɔrd], *n.f.* discord, disagreement, strife.

117

discorder

discorder [diskɔr'de], *v.i.* (*Mus.*) to be out of tune; to be in a state of dissension.
discothèque [diskɔ'tɛk], *n.f.* record library; discothèque.
discoureur [disku'rœːr], *n.m.* (*fem.* -**euse**) talker, chatterer.
discourir [disku'riːr], *v.i. irr.* (*conjug. like* COURIR) to discourse; to descant (*sur*); to babble.
discours [dis'kuːr], *n.m.* discourse; speech, address; diction; treatise.
discourtois [diskur'twa], *a.* discourteous.
discourtoisement [diskurtwaz'mã], *adv.* discourteously.
discourtoisie [diskurtwa'zi], *n.f.* discourtesy, incivility.
discrédit [diskre'di], *n.m.* discredit, disrepute.
discréditer [diskredi'te], *v.t.* to discredit.
discret [dis'krɛ], *a.* (*fem.* -**ète**) discreet; cautious, shy; secret, close.
discrètement [diskrɛt'mã], *adv.* discreetly; warily.
discrétion [diskre'sjɔ̃], *n.f.* circumspection, prudence; discretion; reserve; *pain à discrétion*, bread ad lib.
discrétionnaire [diskresjɔ'nɛːr], *a.* discretionary.
discrimination [diskriminɑ'sjɔ̃], *n.f.* discrimination.
discriminer [diskrimi'ne], *v.t.* to discriminate.
disculper [diskyl'pe], *v.t.* to exculpate, to vindicate, to exonerate.
discursif [diskyr'sif], *a.* (*fem.* -**sive**) discursive.
discussion [disky'sjɔ̃], *n.f.* discussion, debate; altercation, dispute.
discutable [disky'tabl], *a.* debatable, disputable, contestable.
discuter [disky'te], *v.t.* to discuss, to debate, to argue; to examine, to inquire into, to sift.
discuteur, [disky'tœːr] *n.m.* (*fem.* -**euse**) disputant.
disert [di'zɛːr], *a.* copious, fluent, eloquent.
disertement [dizɛrtə'mã], *adv.* copiously, fluently.
disette [di'zɛt], *n.f.* scarcity, dearth, famine; poverty, penury.
diseur [di'zœːr], *n.m.* (*fem.* -**euse**) sayer, teller; diseuse.
disgrâce [diz'grɑːs], *n.f.* disfavor; disgrace, misfortune; plainness (*of features*).
disgracié [dizgra'sje], *a.* out of favor; (*fig.*) ill-favored, deformed.
disgracier [dizgra'sje], *v.t.* to disgrace, to put out of favor.
disgracieusement [dizgrasjœz'mã], *adv.* awkwardly, ungracefully.
disgracieux [dizgra'sjø], *a.* (*fem.* -**euse**) awkward, uncouth, disagreeable.
disjoindre [diz'ʒwɛ̃ːdr], *v.t. irr.* (*conjug. like* CRAINDRE) to disjoin, to disunite. **se disjoindre**, *v.r.* to come apart, to disunite.
disjoncteur [diʒɔ̃k'tœːr], *n.m.* (*Elec.*) circuit breaker.
disjonction [diʒɔ̃k'sjɔ̃], *n.f.* disjunction, separation.
dislocation [dislɔka'sjɔ̃], *n.f.* dislocation, dismemberment.
disloquement [dislɔk'mã], *n.m.* dislocation.

disloquer [dislɔ'ke], *v.t.* to dislocate, to dismember; to take to pieces (*machines etc.*); (*Mil.*) to break up (*an army*). **se disloquer**, *v.r.* to dislocate one's arm etc.; to be taken to pieces; to come apart.
dispache [dis'paʃ], *n.f.* (*Maritime Insurance*) assessment; average adjustment.
dispacheur [dispa'ʃœːr], **dispatcheur** [dispa'tʃœːr], *n.m.* assessor, average adjuster.
disparaître [dispa'rɛːtr], *v.i. irr.* (*conjug. like* CONNAÎTRE) to vanish, to disappear; to abscond; to die.
disparate [dispa'rat], *a.* dissimilar, incongruous, unlike, ill-matched.—*n.f.* incongruity, dissimilarity.
disparité [dispari'te], *n.f.* disparity, dissimilarity.
disparition [dispari'sjɔ̃], *n.f.* disappearance.
dispendieusement [dispãdjœz'mã], *adv.* expensively.
dispendieux [dispã'djø], *a.* (*fem.* -**euse**) expensively, costly.
dispensaire [dispã'sɛːr], *n.m.* dispensary; out-patients' department.
dispensateur [dispãsa'tœːr], *n.m.* (*fem.* -**trice**) dispenser; bestower, giver.
dispensation [dispãsa'sjɔ̃], *n.f.* dispensation; distribution; dispensing.
dispense [dis'pãːs], *n.f.* dispensation (*from fasting*); exemption (*from military service*).
dispenser [dispã'se], *v.t.* to dispense, to bestow; to exempt; to dispense (*with*). **se dispenser**, *v.r.* to dispense with; to exempt or excuse oneself (*from*); to spare oneself.
disperser [disper'se], *v.t.* to disperse, to scatter. **se disperser**, *v.r.* to be dispersed, to break up, to be scattered.
dispersion [disper'sjɔ̃], *n.f.* dispersion, breaking up.
disponibilité [disponibili'te], *n.f.* (*Law*) state of being disposable, disposal (*of property*); (*Mil.*) state of being unattached.
disponible [dispɔ'nibl], *a.* disposable, available; disengaged.—*n.m.* realizable assets.
dispos [dis'po], *a.* fit and well, in good fettle, nimble; cheerful.
disposer [dispo'ze], *v.t.* to dispose, to arrange, to prepare; to incline, to prevail upon.—*v.i.* to dispose (*de*); to prescribe, to ordain. **se disposer**, *v.r.* to dispose oneself, to be disposed; to get ready.
disposition [dispozi'sjɔ̃], *n.f.* disposition, arrangement; inclination, frame of mind; mind, intention.
disproportion [dispropor'sjɔ̃], *n.f.* disproportion.
disproportionné [disproporsjɔ'ne], *a.* disproportionate, inadequate.
disproportionnel [disproporsjɔ'nɛl], *a.* (*fem.* -**elle**) disproportional.
disputable [dispy'tabl], *a.* disputable, debatable, doubtful.
dispute [dis'pyt], *n.f.* dispute, debate, controversy, wrangle; quarrel.
disputer [dispy'te], *v.t.* to contend for; to dispute, to call in question.—*v.i.* to discuss, to argue, to dispute; to contend, to wrangle. **se disputer**, *v.r.* to dispute; to contend, to quarrel.
disputeur [dispy'tœːr], *a.* (*fem.* -**euse**) contentious, quarrelsome.—*n.m.* (*fem.* -**euse**) wrangler.

118

disqualification [diskalifika'sjɔ̃], *n.f.* disqualification.

disqualifier [diskali'fje], *v.t.* to disqualify.

disquaire [dis'kɛːr], *n.* phonograph record seller.

disque [disk], *n.m.* discus, quoit; disk; (*Rail.*) signal disk; phonograph record; *disque longue durée* or *microsillon*, long-playing record.

disruptif [disryp'tif], *a.* (*fem.* -**tive**) disruptive.

disrupteur [disryp'tœːr], *n.m.* (*Elec.*) interrupter.

dissecteur [disɛk'tœːr], *n.m.* dissector.

dissection [disɛk'sjɔ̃], *n.f.* dissection.

dissemblable [disɑ̃'blabl], *a.* dissimilar, unlike.

dissemblablement [disɑ̃blabblə'mɑ̃], *adv.* dissimilarly.

dissemblance [disɑ̃'blɑ̃ːs], *n.f.* dissimilarity, difference.

dissemblant [disɑ̃'blɑ̃], *a.* dissimilar, different.

dissémination [disemina'sjɔ̃], *n.f.* dissemination, scattering (*of seeds etc.*).

disséminer [disemi'ne], *v.t.* to disseminate, to scatter.

dissension [disɑ̃'sjɔ̃], *n.f.* dissension, discord, strife.

dissentiment [disɑ̃ti'mɑ̃], *n.m.* dissent, disagreement.

disséquer [dise'ke], *v.t.* (*conjug. like* CÉDER) to dissect; to analyse.

disséqueur [dise'kœːr], [DISSECTEUR].

dissertation [disɛrta'sjɔ̃], *n.f.* dissertation, treatise; essay (*in schools*).

disserter [disɛr'te], *v.i.* to dissert.

dissidence [disi'dɑ̃ːs], *n.f.* dissidence, difference of opinion, dissent.

dissident [disi'dɑ̃], *a.* dissident.—*n.m.* (*fem.* -**e**) dissenter, rebel.

dissimilaire [disimi'lɛːr], *a.* dissimilar, different, unlike.

dissimilarité [disimilari'te], *n.f.* dissimilarity.

dissimilitude [disimili'tyd], *n.f.* dissimilitude, difference.

dissimulateur [disimyla'tœːr], *n.m.* (*fem.* -**trice**) dissembler; hypocrite.

dissimulation [disimyla'sjɔ̃], *n.f.* dissimulation; double-dealing.

dissimulé [disimy'le], *a.* two-faced, artful.—*n.m.* (*fem.* -**ée**) dissembler; hypocrite.

dissimuler [disimy'le], *v.t.* to dissemble, to conceal. **se dissimuler**, *v.r.* to hide oneself, to pass unnoticed.

dissipateur [disipa'tœːr], *a.* (*fem.* -**trice**) lavish, extravagant.—*n.m.* (*fem.* -**trice**) squanderer, spendthrift.

dissipation [disipa'sjɔ̃], *n.f.* dissipation, waste; idleness.

dissipé [disi'pe], *a.* dissipated, profligate; inattentive.

dissiper [disi'pe], *v.t.* to dissipate, to dispel; to scatter, to squander. **se dissiper**, *v.r.* to be dispersed; to vanish; to be squandered; to be inattentive (*in class-room*).

dissolu [disɔ'ly], *a.* dissolute, profligate, licentious.

dissolubilité [disɔlybili'te], *n.f.* dissolubility.

dissoluble [disɔ'lybl], *a.* dissoluble, dissolvable.

dissolution [disɔly'sjɔ̃], *n.f.* dissolution; solution; dissoluteness.

dissolvant [disɔl'vɑ̃], *a.* and *n.m.* dissolvent, solutive, solvent.

dissonance [disɔ'nɑ̃ːs], *n.f.* dissonance, discord.

dissonant [disɔ'nɑ̃], *a.* dissonant, discordant.

dissoudre [di'sudr], *v.t. irr.* (*conjug. like* ABSOUDRE) to dissolve; to break up; to annul. **se dissoudre**, *v.r.* to dissolve, to be dissolved; to break up.

dissous [di'su], *a.* (*fem.* -**oute**) dissolved; broken up.

dissuader [disɥa'de], *v.t.* to dissuade.

dissuasif [disɥa'zif], *a.* (*fem.* -**sive**) dissuasive.

dissymétrique [disime'trik], *a.* assymetric(al).

distance [dis'tɑ̃ːs], *n.f.* distance; interval (*of place or time*).

distancer [distɑ̃'se], *v.t.* (*conjug. like* COMMENCER) to out-distance, to outrun; (*fig.*) to surpass, to outdo.

distant [dis'tɑ̃], *a.* distant, remote; aloof, stand-offish.

distendre [dis'tɑ̃ːdr], *v.t.* to distend.

distension [distɑ̃'sjɔ̃], *n.f.* distension, strain.

distillable [disti'labl], *a.* distillable.

distillateur [distila'tœːr], *n.m.* distiller.

distillation [distila'sjɔ̃], *n.f.* distillation.

distiller [disti'le], *v.t.* to distil; to discharge; to vent.—*v.i.* to drop, to distil, to trickle.

distillerie [distil'ri], *n.f.* distillery; distilling.

distinct [dis'tɛ̃], *a.* distinct, different, separate.

distinctement [distɛ̃ktə'mɑ̃], *adv.* distinctly, clearly, plainly.

distinctif [distɛ̃k'tif], *a.* (*fem.* -**tive**) distinctive, characteristic.

distinction [distɛ̃k'sjɔ̃], *n.f.* distinction; division, difference; eminence; refinement.

distinctivement [distɛ̃ktiv'mɑ̃], *adv.* distinctively.

distingué [distɛ̃'ge], *a.* distinguished, eminent, noted; elegant, well-bred.

distinguer [distɛ̃'ge], *v.t.* to distinguish, to discern; to discriminate; to honor. **se distinguer**, *v.r.* to be conspicuous; to gain distinction.

distique [dis'tik], *n.m.* distich; couplet.

distordre [dis'tɔrdr], *v.t.* to distort; to sprain. **se distordre**, *v.r.* to become distorted.

distorsion [distɔr'sjɔ̃], *n.f.* distortion; sprain.

distraction [distrak'sjɔ̃], *n.f.* separation; absence of mind, inattention; diversion, hobby.

distraire [dis'trɛːr], *v.t. irr.* (*conjug. like* TRAIRE) to separate; to distract, to disturb; to entertain. **se distraire**, *v.r.* to be disturbed; to be diverted (*de*); to amuse oneself.

distrait [dis'trɛ], *a.* absent-minded, heedless; vacant (*person*).—*n.m.* (*fem.* -**e**) absent-minded person.

distraitement [distrɛt'mɑ̃], *adv.* absent-mindedly.

distrayant [distrɛ'jɑ̃], *a.* diverting, pleasing.

distribuable [distri'bɥabl], *a.* distributable.

distribuer [distri'bɥe], *v.t.* to distribute, to divide; to dispose; to arrange.

distributaire [distriby'tɛːr], *n.* recipient, receiver; sharer.

distributeur [distriby'tœ:r], *a.* (*fem.* **-trice**) distributing.—*n.m.* (*fem.* **-trice**) distributer, bestower, dispenser; **distributeur automatique**, vending machine.

distributif [distriby'tif], *a.* (*fem.* **-tive**) distributive.

distribution [distriby'sjɔ̃], *n.f.* distribution; division; disposition; delivery (*of mail*).

district [dis'trikt], *n.m.* (administrative) district; region.

dit [di], *a.* said, spoken; surnamed, called; **aussitôt dit, aussitôt fait**, no sooner said than done; **autrement dit**, in other words.—*n.m.* maxim; saying.

dito [di'to], *adv.* (*Comm.*) ditto. (*abbr.*) do.

diurnal [djyr'nal], *a.* (*m. pl.* **-aux**) diurnal.—*n.m.* diurnal, daily-prayer book.

diurne [djyrn], *a.* diurnal, daily.—*n.m.* diurnal insect.

divagant [diva'gɑ̃], *a.* wandering, rambling.

divagateur [divaga'tœ:r], *a.* (*fem.* **-trice**) desultory, rambling.—*n.m.* (*fem.* **-trice**) rambling speaker.

divagation [divaga'sjɔ̃], *n.f.* divagation, wandering.

divaguer [diva'ge], *v.i.* to ramble, to wander from the question; to be incoherent (*in writing* or *speaking*).

divan [di'vɑ̃], *n.m.* divan; couch.

divergence [diver'ʒɑ̃:s], *n.f.* divergence.

divergent [diver'ʒɑ̃], *a.* divergent; different.

diverger [diver'ʒe], *v.i.* (*conjug. like* MANGER) to diverge, to branch off.

divers [di've:r], *a.* diverse, miscellaneous; changing; (*pl.*) various, divers, sundry.

diversement [diversə'mɑ̃], *adv.* diversely, variously.

diversifier [diversi'fje], *v.t.* to diversify; to variegate. **se diversifier**, *v.r.* to be varied *or* diversified.

diversion [diver'sjɔ̃], *n.f.* diversion; change.

diversité [diversi'te], *n.f.* diversity, variety, difference.

divertir [diver'ti:r], *v.t.* to amuse, to delight; to divert; to embezzle. **se divertir**, *v.r.* to amuse oneself.

divertissant [diverti'sɑ̃], *a.* diverting, entertaining.

divertissement [divertis'mɑ̃], *n.m.* diversion, amusement, entertainment; (*Law*) embezzlement.

divette [di'vɛt], *n.f.* musical comedy actress.

dividende [divi'dɑ̃:d], *n.m.* dividend.

divin [di'vɛ̃], *a.* divine, heavenly; (*fig.*) admirable, exquisite.

divinateur [divina'tœ:r], *a.* (*fem.* **-trice**) prophetic.—*n.m.* (*fem.* **-trice**) diviner, seer.

divination [divina'sjɔ̃], *n.f.* divination.

divinatoire [divina'twa:r], *a.* divinatory, divining.

divinement [divin'mɑ̃], *adv.* divinely; (*fig.*) admirably, exquisitely.

diviniser [divini'ze], *v.t.* to deify; to laud to the skies.

divinité [divini'te], *n.f.* divinity, godhead, deity.

diviser [divi'ze], *v.t.* to divide, to portion out; to disunite. **se diviser**, *v.r.* to be divided; to fall (*into*), to break up (*into*).

diviseur [divi'zœ:r], *a.* divisive, dividing.—*n.m.* (*Arith.*) divisor; divider.

divisibilité [divizibili'te], *n.f.* divisibility.

divisible [divi'zibl], *a.* divisible.

division [divi'zjɔ̃], *n.f.* division, partition, dividing; (*Mil.*) division.

divisionnaire [divizjɔ'nɛ:r], *a.* divisional, divisionary.

divorce [di'vors], *n.m.* divorce; (*fig.*) variance.

divorcer [divor'se], *v.i.* (*conjug. like* COMMENCER) to divorce oneself (*de*); to break with; to divorce *or* get a divorce from someone (*d'avec quelqu'un*).

divulgation [divylga'sjɔ̃], *n.f.* divulgence; revelation.

divulguer [divyl'ge], *v.t.* to divulge, to reveal, to make public. **se divulguer**, *v.r.* to leak out (*secret*).

dix [dis], *when other words follow* [di] *or* [diz], *a.* ten; tenth.—*n.m.* ten.

dix-huit [di'zɥit], *a.* and *n.m.* eighteen.

dix-huitième [dizɥi'tjɛm], *a.* and *n.* eighteenth.

dixième [di'zjɛm], *a.* and *n.* tenth.

dixièmement [dizjɛm'mɑ̃], *adv.* tenthly.

dix-neuf [diz'nœf], *a.* and *n.m.* nineteen; nineteenth.

dix-neuvième [diznœ'vjɛm], *a.* and *n.* nineteenth.

dix-sept [dis'sɛt], *a.* and *n.m.* seventeen; seventeenth.

dix-septième [dissɛ'tjɛm], *a.* and *n.* seventeenth.

dizaine [di'zɛn], *n.f.* half a score; about ten.

djinn [dʒin], *n.m.* jinn(ee).

do [do], *n.m.* (*Mus.*) do *or* ut; (the note) C.

docile [dɔ'sil], *a.* docile, tractable, submissive.

docilement [dɔsil'mɑ̃], *adv.* with docility.

docilité [dɔsili'te], *n.f.* docility, tractability.

dock [dɔk], *n.m.* dock; warehouse.

docker [dɔ'kɛ:r], *n.m.* docker.

docte [dɔkt], *a.* erudite, learned.

doctement [dɔktə'mɑ̃], *adv.* learnedly, pedantically.

docteur [dɔk'tœ:r], *n.* doctor.

doctoral [dɔktɔ'ral], *a.* (*m. pl.* **-aux**) doctoral.

doctorat [dɔktɔ'ra], *n.m.* doctorate, doctor's degree.

doctrinaire [dɔktri'nɛ:r], *a.* stiff, formal, pedantic.—*n.m.* doctrinaire.

doctrinairement [dɔktrinɛr'mɑ̃], *adv.* stiffly, formally, pedantically.

doctrine [dɔk'trin], *n.f.* doctrine.

document [dɔky'mɑ̃], *n.m.* document; (*pl.*) records.

documentaire [dɔkymɑ̃'tɛ:r], *a.* documentary.—*n.m.* (*Cine.*) documentary film.

documentation [dɔkymɑ̃tɑ'sjɔ̃], *n.f.* documentation.

documenter [dɔkymɑ̃'te], *v.t.* to give information. **se documenter**, *v.r.* to gather evidence.

dodelinement [dɔdlin'mɑ̃], *n.m.* wagging, nodding (*of head*); dandling.

dodeliner [dɔdli'ne], *v.t.* to dandle, to rock (*a child*).—*v.i.* to wag, nod (*head*).

dodiner [dɔdi'ne], *v.t.* to rock, to dandle.—*v.i.* to oscillate. **se dodiner**, *v.r.* to rock one's body; to nurse or coddle oneself.

dodo [do'do], *n.m.* (*Infantile*) bye-bye; (*fig.*) sleep, bed.

dodu [do'dy], *a.* plump.

dogaresse [dɔga'rɛs], *n.f.* dogaressa, wife of a doge.

doge [dɔ:ʒ], *n.m.* doge.

dogmatique [dɔgma'tik], *a.* dogmatic.
dogmatiquement [dɔgmatik'mã], *adv.* dogmatically.
dogmatiser [dɔgmɑti'ze], *v.t.* to state dogmatically.—*v.i.* to dogmatize.
dogmatisme [dɔgma'tism], *n.m.* dogmatism.
dogmatiste [dɔgma'tist], *n.* dogmatist.
dogme [dɔgm], *n.m.* dogma, tenet.
dogue [dɔg], *n.m.* mastiff; (*fig.*) bull-dog (*of a man*).
doguin [dɔ'gɛ̃], *n.m.* pug.
doigt [dwa], *n.m.* finger, digit; toe.
doigté [dwa'te], *n.m.* (*Mus.*) fingering, touch; (*fig.*) tact, adroitness.
doigtier [dwa'tje], *n.m.* finger-stall.
dol [dɔl], *n.m.* deceit, fraud.
dolage [dɔ'la:ʒ], *n.m.* planing.
doléances [dɔle'ã:s], *n.f. pl.* complaints; grievances.
dolemment [dɔla'mã], *adv.* dolefully.
dolent [dɔ'lã], *a.* doleful, piteous, plaintive.
doler [dɔ'le], *v.t.* to smooth with the adze; to plane.
dolmen [dɔl'mɛn], *n.m.* dolmen.
doloir [dɔ'lwa:r], *n.m.* paring knife, parer.
doloire [dɔ'lwa:r], *n.f.* cooper's adze; mason's axe.
dolosif [dɔlɔ'zif], *a.* (*fem.* **-sive**) fraudulent.
domaine [dɔ'mɛ:n], *n.m.* domain, estate, property; province, sphere.
dôme [do:m], *n.m.* dome; canopy, vault.
domestication [dɔmestika'sjɔ̃], *n.f.* domestication.
domesticité [dɔmɛstisi'te], *n.f.* domesticity; (*collect.*) domestic servants.
domestique [dɔmɛs'tik], *a.* domestic; tame, domesticated.—*n.* servant, domestic.—*n.m.* household.
domestiquer [dɔmɛsti'ke], *v.t.* to domesticate, to tame.
domicile [dɔmi'sil], *n.m.* domicile, residence.
domiciliaire [dɔmisi'ljɛ:r], *a.* domiciliary.
domicilié [dɔmisi'lje], *a.* resident, domiciled.
domicilier (se) [sədɔmisi'lje], *v.r.* to settle down in a place.
dominance [dɔmi'nã:s], *n.f.* dominance.
dominant [dɔmi'nã], *a.* dominant, predominant, prevalent.
dominateur [dɔminɑ'tœ:r], *a.* (*fem.* **-trice**) ruling, domineering, arrogant.—*n.m.* (*fem.* **-trice**) dominator, ruler, tyrant.
domination [dɔminɑ'sjɔ̃], *n.f.* domination; dominion, rule, sway.
dominer [dɔmi'ne], *v.t.* to dominate; to rule; to prevail over; to overlook, to tower over.—*v.i.* to rule, to control; to dominate, to prevail; to lord it; to tower. **se dominer** *v.r.* to control oneself.
dominicain [dɔmini'kɛ̃], *a.* (*Relig.*, *Polit.*) Dominican.—*n.m.* (**Dominicain**, *fem.* **-aine**) (*Polit.*) Dominican (*person*), Dominican friar *or* nun; **la République Dominicaine**, the Dominican Republic.
dominical [dɔmini'kal], *a.* (*m. pl.* **-aux**) dominical.
dominicale [dɔmini'kal], *n.f.* Sunday sermon.
dominion [dɔmi'njɔ̃], *n.m.* dominion.
domino [dɔmi'no], *n.m.* domino.
dommage [dɔ'ma:ʒ], *n.m.* damage, injury, loss; **c'est dommage**, it is a pity.

dommageable [dɔma'ʒabl], *a.* hurtful, prejudicial, injurious; damageable (*goods*).
domptable [dɔ̃'tabl], *a.* tamable, manageable.
dompter [dɔ̃'te], *v.t.* to subdue, to subjugate, to tame. **se dompter**, *v.r.* to quell *or* overcome one's passions.
dompteur [dɔ̃'tœ:r], *n.m.* (*fem.* **-euse**) subduer; tamer; breaker-in.
don [dɔ̃], *n.m.* gift, donation; (*fig.*) aptitude, talent.
donataire [dɔna'tɛ:r], *n.* donee, recipient.
donateur [dɔna'tœ:r], *n.m.* (*fem.* **-trice**) donor, giver.
donation [dɔna'sjɔ̃], *n.f.* donation, free gift.
donc [dɔ̃:k, dɔ̃], *conj.* then, therefore, accordingly, hence; consequently; of course, to be sure.
donjon [dɔ̃'ʒɔ̃], *n.m.* keep, castle keep; turret.
donnant [dɔ'nã], *a.* open-handed, generous; **donnant donnant**, give and take.
donne [dɔn], *n.f.* deal (*at cards*).
donnée [dɔ'ne], *n.f.* given fact, datum; notion; (*Math.*) known quantity; (*pl.*) data.
donner [dɔ'ne], *v.t.* to give, to bestow; to grant; to present (*a play etc.*); to deal (*at cards*).—*v.i.* to give way; to hit, to stumble (*dans*); to be addicted to (*dans*); to attack (*of troops etc.*); to yield; to overlook. **se donner**, *v.r.* to procure; to take place (*of battles etc.*); to give oneself out (*pour*).
donneur [dɔ'nœ:r], *n.m.* (*fem.* **-euse**) giver, donor; dealer (*of cards*); **donneur de sang**, blood donor.
don Quichotte [dɔ̃ki'ʃɔt], *n.m.* Don Quixote, quixotic person.
dont [dɔ̃], *pron.* whose, of which, of whom, from whom etc.
doper [dɔ'pe], *v.t.* (*Spt.*) to dope (*a horse etc.*).
doping [dɔ'piŋ], *n.m.* dope; doping.
dorade [dɔ'rad], *n.f.* (*Ichth.*) sea bream.
doré [dɔ're], *a.* gilt, gilded, golden.
dorénavant [dɔrena'vã], *adv.* henceforth, hereafter.
dorer [dɔ're], *v.t.* to gild; to glaze (*pastry*). **se dorer**, *v.r.* to gild; to become yellow.
doreur [dɔ'rœ:r], *n.m.* (*fem.* **-euse**) gilder.
dorien [dɔ'rjɛ̃], *a.* and *n.m.* (*fem.* **-enne**) Dorian; Doric.
dorique [dɔ'rik], *a.* and *n.m.* Doric.
dorloter [dɔrlɔ'te], *v.t.* to fondle, to pamper, to coddle, to pet. **se dorloter**, *v.r.* to coddle oneself; to indulge oneself.
dormant [dɔr'mã], *a.* sleeping, asleep; dormant, stagnant.—*n.m.* fixed frame (*of window etc.*).
dormeur [dɔr'mœ:r], *a.* (*fem.* **-euse**) sleepy, drowsy, sluggish.—*n.m.* (*fem.* **-euse**) sleeper; sluggard.—*n.f.* (**-euse** (1)) sort of chaise longue.
dormeuse (2) [dɔr'mø:z], *n.f.* stud ear-ring.
dormir [dɔr'mi:r], *v.i. irr.* (*conjug. like* SENTIR) to sleep, to be asleep; to lie still; to lie dormant (*of money*); to be stagnant (*of water*).
dormitif [dɔrmi'tif], *a.* (*fem.* **-tive**) soporific, dormitive.
Dorothée [dɔrɔ'te], *f.* Dorothy.
dorsal [dɔr'sal], *a.* dorsal.
dortoir [dɔr'twa:r], *n.m.* dormitory.
dorure [dɔ'ry:r], *n.f.* gilding; glazing (*of pastry*).

121

doryphore [dɔri'fɔːr], *n.m.* Colorado beetle.
dos [do], *n.m. inv.* back; rear; top, ridge.
dosable [do'zabl], *a.* measurable.
dosage [do'zaːʒ], *n.m.* dosage; titration.
dose [doːz], *n.f.* dose; quantity; portion.
doser [do'ze], *v.t.* to dose; to proportion.
dossier [do'sje], *n.m.* back (*of chair etc.*); brief (*of a lawyer*); record, file, dossier.
dossière [do'sjɛːr], *n.f.* back band, ridge band (*of harness*); back plate (*of a cuirass*).
dot [dɔt], *n.f.* marriage portion, dowry.
dotal [dɔ'tal], *a.* (*m. pl.* **-aux**) of or concerning dowry.
dotation [dɔta'sjɔ̃], *n.f.* endowment.
doter [dɔ'te], *v.t.* to endow; to make a grant.
douaire [dwɛːr], *n.m.* (*widow's*) dower; jointure, marriage settlement.
douairière [dwɛ'rjɛːr], *n.f.* dowager.
douane [dwan], *n.f.* customs; custom house; custom duty.
douanier [dwa'nje], *a.* relating to the custom house, of customs.—*n.m.* customs officer.
doublage [du'blaːʒ], *n.m.* lining, plating; (*Cine.*) dubbing.
double [dubl], *a.* twofold, double, duplicate; (*fig.*) deceitful, downright.—*n.m.* double; carbon copy, duplicate, replica; (*Ten.*) doubles.—*adv.* double; **voir double,** to see double.
doublé [du'ble], *n.m.* gold- or silver-plated ware; (*Billiards*) carom off the cushion.
doubleau [du'blo], *n.m.* (*pl.* **-eaux**) ceiling beam.
doublement [dublə'mã], *n.m.* doubling.—*adv.* doubly.
doubler [du'ble], *v.t.* to double; to line (*clothes etc.*); to overtake, to pass; (*Theat.*) to understudy; (*Cine.*) to dub.
doublet [du'blɛ], *n.m.* doublet.
doubleur [du'blœːr], *n.m.* (*fem.* **-euse**) doubler, twister.
doublure [du'blyːr], *n.f.* lining; (*Theat.*) understudy.
douce-amère [dusa'mɛːr], *n.f.* (*pl.* **douces-amères**) woody nightshade, bitter-sweet.
douceâtre [du'saːtr], *a.* sweetish, sickly.
doucement [dus'mã], *adv.* gently, tenderly; slowly, quietly; mildly, calmly; so-so.
doucereux [dus'rø], *a.* (*fem.* **-euse**) sweetish; mawkish, mealy-mouthed.
doucet [du'sɛ], *a.* and *n.m.* (*fem.* **-ette** (1)) demure, mild, affected (person).
doucette (2) [du'sɛt], *n.f.* corn salad.
doucette (3) [du'sɛt], *n.f.* Venus's-looking-glass.
douceur [du'sœːr], *n.f.* sweetness, softness; fragrance; kindness; peacefulness; gentleness; (*pl.*) sweets; gallantries.
douche [duʃ], *n.f.* shower-bath.
doucher [du'ʃe], *v.t.* to give someone a shower-bath; to cool down (*excitement etc.*). **se doucher,** *v.r.* to take a shower.
doucir [du'siːr], *v.t.* to polish (*looking-glasses etc.*).
doucissage [dusi'saːʒ], *n.m.* polishing.
doucisseur [dusi'sœːr], *n.m.* polisher.
doué [dwe], *a.* gifted.
douer [dwe], *v.t.* to endow, to bestow upon.
douille [du:j], *n.f.* socket; case or shell (*of cartridges*); **douille d'embrayage,** clutch casing: **douille de lampe,** lamp socket, lamp holder.

douillet [du'jɛ], *a.* effeminate, delicate; sensitive; soft.
douillettement [dujɛt'mã], *adv.* softly; delicately; cosily.
douleur [du'lœːr], *n.f.* pain, suffering, ache; anguish, grief, sorrow.
douloureusement [dulurøz'mã], *adv.* painfully; grievously.
douloureux [dulu'rø], *a.* (*fem.* **-euse**) painful, smarting, sore; grievous, afflicting, sad.
doute [dut], *n.m.* doubt, irresolution; suspicion; scepticism; fear; **sans doute,** no doubt.
douter [du'te], *v.i.* (**de**) to doubt, to question; to hesitate; to distrust, to fear. **se douter,** *v.r.* (**de, que**) to suspect, to conjecture.
douteur [du'tœːr], *a.* (*fem.* **-euse** (1)) doubting.—*n.m.* (*fem.* **-euse**) doubter.
douteusement [dutøz'mã], *adv.* doubtfully.
douteux [du'tø], *a.* (*fem.* **-euse** (2)) doubtful, questionable.
douve [du:v], *n.f.* stave (*for casks*); trench, moat.
Douvres [du:vr], *m.* Dover.
doux [du], *a.* (*fem.* **douce**) sweet; fragrant; kindly, charming; easy; gentle; calm; fresh (*of water*).—*adv.* gently; submissively.
douzaine [du'zɛn], *n.f.* dozen.
douze [du:z], *a.* twelve, twelfth.—*n.m.* twelve.
douzième [du'zjɛm], *a.* and *n.* twelfth.
douzièmement [duzjɛm'mã], *adv.* twelfthly.
doyen [dwa'jɛ̃], *n.m.* (*fem.* **-enne**) senior, oldest member; dean.
doyenné [dwajɛ'ne], *n.m.* deanship, deanery.
drachme [drakm], *n.f.* drachma; (*Pharm.*) dram.
draconien [drakɔ'njɛ̃], *a.* (*fem.* **-enne**) draconian, harsh, severe.
dragage [dra'gaːʒ], *n.m.* dredging, dragging (*of a river etc.*).
dragée [dra'ʒe], *n.f.* sugar-almond, sugar-plum; small shot.
drageoir [dra'ʒwaːr], *n.m.* comfit dish.
drageon [dra'ʒɔ̃], *n.m.* sucker.
drageonner [draʒɔ'ne], *v.i.* to put forth suckers.
dragon [dra'gɔ̃], *a.* dragonish—*n.m.* dragon; (*fig.*) vixen; dragoon.
dragonne [dra'gɔn], *n.f.* sword-knot.
drague [drag], *n.f.* dredger; dredge net; grappling iron.
draguer [dra'ge], *v.t.* to drag, to dredge.
dragueur [dra'gœːr], *n.m.* dredger; **dragueur de mines,** minesweeper.
drain [drɛ̃], *n.m.* drain, drain-pipe.
drainage [drɛ'naːʒ], *n.m.* drainage.
drainer [drɛ'ne], *v.t.* to drain.
dramatique [drama'tik], *a.* dramatic.
dramatiser [dramati'ze], *v.t.* to dramatize.
dramaturge [drama'tyrʒ], *n.m.* dramatist, playwright.
drame [dram], *n.m.* drama.
drap [dra], *n.m.* cloth; (*bed*) sheet; pall.
drapeau [dra'po], *n.m.* (*pl.* **-eaux**) flag, standard, ensign, streamer, colors.
draper [dra'pe], *v.t.* to cover with cloth; to drape. **se draper,** *v.r.* to wrap oneself up; to make a show, to parade.
draperie [dra'pri], *n.f.* drapery; cloth trade, cloth making.
drapier [dra'pje], *n.m.* draper, clothier.

drastique [dras'tik], *a.* and *n.m.* (*Med.*) drastic.
(*C*) **drave** [drav], *n.f.* drive, log-running.
(*C*) **draver** [dra've], *v.t.* to drive, to drift.
(*C*) **draveur** [dra'vœːr], *n.m.* wood-floater, rafter.
drayage [drɛ'jaːʒ], *n.m.* fleshing (*of hides*).
drayer [drɛ'je], *v.t.* (*conjug. like* PAYER) to flesh (*hides*).
dressage [drɛ'saːʒ], *n.m.* erection; training (*of animals*); pitching (*of a tent*).
dresser [drɛ'se], *v.t.* to erect, to set up, to raise; to straighten; to lay out; to lay (*a snare*); to pitch (*a tent*); to draw up (*a report*); to prick up (*the ears*); to train (*animals*). **se dresser**, *v.r.* to stand on end (*of hair*); to stand erect; to rear.
dresseur [drɛ'sœːr], *n.m.* (*fem.* **-euse**) trainer (*of dogs etc.*).
dressoir [drɛ'swaːr], *n.m.* dresser, sideboard.
drille [driːj], *n.f.* hand-drill, borer.
driller [dri'je], *v.t.* to drill, to bore.
drive [driv], *n.m.* (*Ten.*) drive.
drogue [drɔg], *n.f.* drug; rubbish; dope.
droguer [drɔ'ge], *v.t.* to drug, to physic. **se droguer**, *v.r.* to physic *or* doctor oneself, to dope oneself.
droguerie [drɔ'gri], *n.f.* drug-store; drug-trade, drysaltery.
droguiste [drɔ'gist], *n.* retailer in drugs and chemicals.
droguet [drɔ'gɛ], *n.m.* (*Tex.*) drugget.
droit [drwa], *a.* straight, right, direct; vertical, upright; just, sincere; right (*opposed to left*).—*adv.* straight, straight on.—*n.m.* right, equity; law; right (*to*), claim, title; fee; due (*tax*), duty, customs duty.
droite [drwat], *n.f.* right hand, right.
droitement [drwat'mã], *adv.* rightly; sincerely, straightforwardly.
droitier [drwa'tje], *a.* and *n.m.* (*fem.* **-ière**) right-handed (person).
droiture [drwa'tyːr], *n.f.* equity, justice; uprightness, integrity.
drolatique [drola'tik], *a.* amusing, laughable, facetious.
drôle [droːl], *a.* funny, droll, ludicrous; strange, curious.—*n.* rogue, rascal, scoundrel.
drôlement [drol'mã], *adv.* comically, facetiously, jocosely.
drôlerie [drol'ri], *n.f.* drollery; buffoonery.
drôlesse [dro'lɛs], *n.f.* jade, hussy.
dromadaire [droma'dɛːr], *n.m.* dromedary.
dru [dry], *a.* sturdy; dense (*of rain*); brisk, lively; close-planted; fledged (*of birds*).—*adv.* thick, fast, hard.
druide [drɥid], *n.m.* druid.
druidesse [drɥi'dɛs], *n.f.* druidess.
druidique [drɥi'dik], *a.* druidical.
druidisme [drɥi'dism], *n.m.* druidism.
dryade [dri'ad], *n.f.* dryad; (*Bot.*) dryas.
du [dy], (*contraction of* DE LE) of the, from the, by the; some, any.
dû [dy], *n.m.* due, what is owed, what is owing.
dualisme [dɥa'lism], *n.m.* dualism.
dualiste [dɥa'list], *a.* and *n.* dualist.
dualité [dɥali'te], *n.f.* duality.
duc [dyk], *n.m.* duke; horned owl.
ducal [dy'kal], *a.* (*m. pl.* **-aux**) ducal.
ducat [dy'ka], *n.m.* ducat.

duché [dy'ʃe], *n.m.* dukedom, duchy.
duchesse [dy'ʃɛs], *n.f.* duchess.
ductile [dyk'til], *a.* ductile, malleable.
ductilité [dyktili'te], *n.f.* ductility.
duègne [dɥɛɲ], *n.f.* duenna, chaperon.
duel [dɥɛl], *n.m.* duel; struggle.
duelliste [dɥɛ'list], *n.* duellist.
dulcifier [dylsi'fje], *v.t.* to dulcify.
dulcinée [dylsi'ne], *n.f.* sweetheart.
dûment [dy'mã], *adv.* duly, properly.
dumping [dam'piŋ], *n.m.* dumping, unfair competition.
dune [dyn], *n.f.* dune, sand-hill.
dunette [dy'nɛt], *n.f.* poop-deck.
duo [dɥo], *n.m.* duet.
duodécimal [dɥodesi'mal], *a.* (*m. pl.* **-aux**) duodecimal.
duodénal [dɥode'nal], *a.* (*m. pl.* **-aux**) duodenal.
duodénum [dɥode'nɔm], *n.m.* duodenum.
dupe [dyp], *n.f.* dupe.
duper [dy'pe], *v.t.* to dupe, to gull, to take in.
duperie [dy'pri], *n.f.* dupery, trickery.
dupeur [dy'pœːr], *n.m.* (*fem.* **-euse**) cheat, trickster.
duplicata [dyplika'ta], *n.m.* duplicate.
duplicateur [dyplika'tœːr], *n.m.* (*Elec.*) duplicator; duplicating machine.
duplicité [dyplisi'te], *n.f.* duplicity, double-dealing, deceit.
duquel [dy'kɛl], (*contraction of* DE LEQUEL) of whom, of which.
dur [dyːr], *a.* hard; tough; (*fig.*) unyielding, harsh, unkind; difficult.—*adv.* hard; firmly; **travailler dur**, to work hard.
durabilité [dyrabili'te], *n.f.* durability.
durable [dy'rabl], *a.* durable, lasting, solid.
durablement [dyrabla'mã], *adv.* durably, lastingly.
duralumin [dyraly'mɛ̃], *n.m.* duralumin.
durant [dy'rã], *prep.* during.
durcir [dyr'siːr], *v.t.* to harden.—*v.i.* to harden, to stiffen. **se durcir**, *v.r.* to harden, to harden.
durcissement [dyrsis'mã], *n.m.* hardening, stiffening, induration.
dure [dyːr], *n.f.* hard ground *or* floor *in* **coucher sur la dure**.
durée [dy're], *n.f.* duration; continuance.
durement [dyr'mã], *adv.* hard; harshly, roughly.
durer [dy're], *v.i.* to last, to remain; to endure.
dureté [dyr'te], *n.f.* hardness; harshness, austerity, unkindness; (*pl.*) harsh *or* offensive words.
durillon [dyri'jɔ̃], *n.m.* callosity, corn.
duvet [dy've], *n.m.* down; wool, nap; fluff.
duveté [dyv'te], *a.* downy (*of birds etc.*); like down.
duveteux [dyv'tø], *a.* (*fem.* **-euse**) downy, fluffy.
dynamique [dina'mik], *a.* dynamic.—*n.f.* dynamics.
dynamisme [dina'mism], *n.m.* dynamism.
dynamiste [dina'mist], *n.* dynamist.
dynamitage [dinami'taːʒ], *n.m.* blasting, blowing up.
dynamite [dina'mit], *n.f.* dynamite.
dynamiter [dinami'te], *v.t.* to dynamite, to blow up.
dynamo [dina'mo], *n.f.* dynamo.
dynastie [dinas'ti], *n.f.* dynasty.

dynastique [dinas'tik], *a.* dynastic.
dysenterie [disɑ̃'tri], *n.f.* dysentery.
dyspepsie [dispɛp'si], *n.f.* dyspepsia.
dyspepsique [dispɛp'sik], **dyspeptique** [dispɛp'tik], *a.* dyspeptic.

E

E, e [ə], *n.m.* the fifth letter of the alphabet.
eau [o], *n.f.* water; rain, flood; (*pl.*) mineral *or* thermal waters; watering place; stream; track; gloss; *à fleur d'eau*, on a level with the water; (*Chem.*) *eau lourde*, heavy water.
eau-de-vie [o'dvi], *n.f.* (*pl.* **eaux-de-vie**) brandy.
ébahi [eba'i], *a.* astonished, dumbfounded.
ébahir (s') [seba'i:r], *v.r.* to wonder (at), to be amazed.
ébahissement [ebais'mɑ̃], *n.m.* amazement, astonishment.
ébats [e'ba], *n.m. pl.* pastime, sport, gambol, frolic.
ébattre (s') [se'batr], *v.r.* (*conjug. like* BATTRE) to sport, to gambol, to frolic.
ébauchage [ebo'ʃa:ʒ], *n.m.* sketching.
ébauche [e'boːʃ], *n.f.* rough draft, outline.
ébaucher [ebo'ʃe], *v.t.* to make the first draft of, to draw an outline of, to sketch.
ébauchoir [ebo'ʃwaːr], *n.m.* (*Sculp.*) roughing chisel; (*Carp.*) mortise chisel.
ébène [e'bɛːn], *n.f.* ebony, ebony work.
ébéner [ebe'ne], *v.t.* (*conjug. like* CÉDER) to ebonize.
ébénier [ebe'nje], *n.m.* ebony tree.
ébéniste [ebe'nist], *n.* cabinet-maker.
ébénisterie [ebenis'tri], *n.f.* cabinet-work.
ébiseler [ebi'zle], *v.t.* (*conjug. like* APPELER) to chamfer, to bevel.
éblouir [eblu'iːr], *v.t.* to dazzle; (*fig.*) to fascinate, to amaze. **s'éblouir**, *v.r.* to be dazzled *or* fascinated.
éblouissant [eblui'sɑ̃], *a.* dazzling, resplendent.
éblouissement [ebluis'mɑ̃], *n.m.* dazzle, daze; (*fig.*) bewilderment.
ébonite [ebɔ'nit], *n.f.* ebonite; vulcanite.
ébouage [ebu'aːʒ], *n.m.* scavenging.
ébouer [ebu'e], *v.t.* to scavenge.
éboueur [ebu'œːr], *n.m.* (*fem.* -**euse**) road-sweeper, scavenger.—*n.f.* (-**euse**) road-sweeping machine.
ébouillanter [ebujɑ̃'te], *v.t.* to dip in hot water, to scald.
éboulement [ebul'mɑ̃], *n.m.* falling in, fall; caving in, collapse; landslide, landslip.
ébouler [ebu'le], *v.i.* to fall in, to fall down, to sink. **s'ébouler**, *v.r.* to fall in, to cave in.
éboulis [ebu'li], *n.m. inv.* debris, fallen rocks.
ébourgeonner [eburʒɔ'ne], *v.t.* to disbud.
ébouriffé [eburi'fe], *a.* disordered, ruffled, in disorder; (*fig.*) in a flutter.
ébouriffer [eburi'fe], *v.t.* to ruffle, to disorder; (*fig.*) to startle, to amaze.
ébouter [ebu'te], *v.t.* to cut off (*the end*).

ébranchage [ebrɑ̃'ʃa:ʒ], **ébranchement** [ebrɑ̃ʃ'mɑ̃], *n.m.* (*Hort.*) pruning, lopping, trimming.
ébrancher [ebrɑ̃'ʃe], *v.t.* to prune, to lop, to trim.
ébranlement [ebrɑ̃l'mɑ̃], *n.m.* shock, shaking; (*fig.*) perturbation, disturbance.
ébranler [ebrɑ̃'le], *v.t.* to shake; to disturb, to unsettle. **s'ébranler**, *v.r.* to get under way, to move off.
ébrécher [ebre'ʃe], *v.t.* (*conjug. like* CÉDER) to notch, to indent; to crack, to chip; (*fig.*) to impair.
ébriété [ebrie'te], *n.f.* drunkenness, inebriety.
ébrouement [ebru'mɑ̃], *n.m.* snorting.
ébrouer (s') [sebru'e], *v.r.* to snort from fear (*of horses*).
ébruiter [ebrɥi'te], *v.t.* to make known, to spread about. **s'ébruiter**, *v.r.* to spread, to be noised abroad.
ébullition [ebyli'sjɔ̃], *n.f.* boiling, ebullition.
écaille [ekɑ:j], *n.f.* scale; shell.
écaillé [ekɑ'je], *a.* scaly.
écailler (1) [ekɑ'je], *v.t.* to scale. **s'écailler** *v.r.* to peel off, to scale.
écailler (2) [ekɑ'je], *n.m.* (*fem.* -**ère**) oyster-man, oyster-woman.
écailleux [ekɑ'jø], *a.* (*fem.* -**euse**) scaly, squamous.
écale [e'kal], *n.f.* shell, pod (*of peas etc.*); hull, husk (*of walnut*).
écaler [ekɑ'le], *v.t.* to shell (*beans, peas etc.*); to hull, to husk (*almonds, nuts etc.*). **s'écaler**, *v.r.* to come out of the shell.
écarlate [ekar'lat], *a.* and *n.f.* scarlet; hectic red.
écarquillement [ekarkij'mɑ̃], *n.m.* spreading out, opening wide (*of one's eyes, legs etc.*).
écarquiller [ekarki'je], *v.t.* to spread out, to open wide.
écart [e'kaːr], *n.m.* stepping aside, swerving; fault; deviation; *à l'écart*, aside; *faire un écart*, to step aside.
écarté (1) [ekar'te], n.m. écarté (*game of cards*).
écarté (2) [ekar'te], *a.* remote, lonely, secluded.
écartelé [ekartə'le], *a.* (*of mind, heart, etc.*) divided, torn asunder; (*Her.*) quartered.
écartèlement [ekartɛl'mɑ̃], *n.m.* tearing to pieces, quartering.
écarteler [ekartə'le], *v.t.* (*conjug. like* AMENER) to tear to pieces; (*Her.*) to quarter.
écartement [ekartə'mɑ̃], *n.m.* putting aside; removal; spacing; spread.
écarter [ekar'te], *v.t.* to open, to throw wide apart; to set aside; to avert; to dispel, to deviate; to spread. **s'écarter**, *v.r.* to turn aside, to swerve; to stray; to make way.
ecchymose [ɛki'moːz], *n.f.* (*Med.*) ecchymosis.
ecclésiastique [ɛklezjas'tik], *a.* ecclesiastic; clerical.—*n.m.* clergyman, ecclesiastic.
écervelé [esɛrvə'le], *a.* hare-brained, rash, giddy.—*n.m.* (*fem.* -**ée**) madcap; scatter-brain.
échafaud [eʃa'fo], *n.m.* scaffold.
échafaudage [eʃafo'da:ʒ], *n.m.* scaffolding; (*fig.*) structure.
échafauder [eʃafo'de], *v.t.* to pile up; (*fig.*) to lay out (*a plan*).—*v.i.* to erect scaffolding.

échalas [eʃɑ'lɑ], *n.m.* vine prop; hop pole.
échalassage [eʃɑlɑ'sa:ʒ], **échalassement** [eʃɑlɑs'mɑ̃], *n.m.* propping.
échalasser [eʃɑlɑ'se], *v.t.* to prop (*vines etc.*).
échalier [eʃɑ'lje], **échalis** [eʃɑ'li], *n.m.* stile; wooden fence.
échalote [eʃɑ'lɔt], *n.f.* (*Bot.*) shallot.
échancrer [eʃɑ̃'kre], *v.t.* to make a crescent-shaped cut; to indent.
échancrure [eʃɑ̃'kry:r], *n.f.* notch, cut, indentation; opening.
échandole [eʃɑ̃'dɔl], *n.f.* shingle (*for roofing*).
échange [e'ʃɑ̃:ʒ], *n.m.* exchange, barter; *libre échange*, free trade.
échangeable [eʃɑ̃'ʒabl], *a.* exchangeable.
échanger [eʃɑ̃'ʒe], *v.t.* (*conjug. like* MANGER) to exchange, to barter; to interchange.
échanson [eʃɑ̃'sɔ̃], *n.m.* cup-bearer; butler.
échantillon [eʃɑ̃ti'jɔ̃], *n.m.* sample, pattern, specimen; (*fig.*) model.
échantillonner [eʃɑ̃tijɔ'ne], *v.t.* to sample.
échappatoire [eʃapa'twa:r], *n.f.* shift, subterfuge, loop-hole, evasion.
échappée [eʃa'pe], *a.* runaway.—*n.m.* (*fem.* -ée (1)) one who has escaped, runaway.
échappée (2) [eʃa'pe], *n.f.* escapade, prank; short space of time.
échappement [eʃap'mɑ̃], *n.m.* escape; leakage; (*Horol.*) escapement; exhaust.
échapper [eʃa'pe], *v.t.* to escape, to avoid; *l'échapper belle*, to have a narrow escape. —*v.i.* to escape, to make good one's escape; to be overlooked. **s'échapper**, *v.r.* to escape; to vanish.
écharde [e'ʃard], *n.f.* prickle (*of a thistle etc.*); splinter.
écharner [eʃar'ne], *v.t.* to flesh *or* scrape (*hides*).
écharnoir [eʃar'nwa:r], *n.m.* fleshing-knife.
écharpe [e'ʃarp], *n.f.* scarf, sash; arm-sling.
écharper [eʃar'pe], *v.t.* to slash, to cut.
échasse [e'ʃɑ:s], *n.f.* stilt; long-legged plover.
échassier [eʃɑ'sje], *n.m.* (*fem.* -ière) stilt-walker; (*colloq.*) long-legged person.—*n.m.* (*Orn.*) wader.
échauboulure [eʃobu'ly:r], *n.f.* pimple, blotch.
échaudage [eʃo'da:ʒ], *n.m.* whitewash; white-washing; scalding.
échaudé (1) [eʃo'de], *n.m.* simnel, cracknel.
échaudé (2) [eʃo'de], *a.* scalded.
échauder [eʃo'de], *v.t.* to scald. **s'échauder**, *v.r.* to burn oneself.
échaudoir [eʃo'dwa:r], *n.m.* scalding-house; scalding-tub.
échaudure [eʃo'dy:r], *n.f.* scald.
échauffant [eʃo'fɑ̃], *a.* heating; binding (*food*).
échauffement [eʃof'mɑ̃], *n.m.* heating; over-excitement.
échauffer [eʃo'fe], *v.t.* to warm, to heat, to over-heat; to excite, to irritate. **s'échauffer**, *v.r.* to grow warm, to overheat oneself; to grow angry, to chafe.
échauffourée [eʃofu're], *n.f.* rash *or* blundering enterprise; brush, scuffle.
échauffure [eʃo'fy:r], *n.f.* red rash.
échauguette [eʃo'gɛt], *n.f.* (*Mil.*) watch-tower.
échéable [eʃe'abl], *a.* due, payable.
échéance [eʃe'ɑ̃:s], *n.f.* falling due (*of bill*); date (*of payment, of maturity*); expiration (*of tenancy*).

échéant [eʃe'ɑ̃], *a.* falling due; *le cas échéant*, in that case, if need be.
échec [e'ʃɛk], *n.m.* check, defeat, blow, loss.
échecs [e'ʃɛk], *n.m. pl.* chess; chess-men.
échelle [e'ʃɛl], *n.f.* ladder; scale; gradation.
échelon [eʃ'lɔ̃], *n.m.* round, rung, step (*of a ladder*); degree; (*Mil.*) echelon.
échelonner [eʃlɔ'ne], *v.t.* to draw up in echelon; to arrange according to gradation; to spread (*over a period of time*); to place (*at regular intervals*); *vacances échelonnées*, staggered holidays. **s'échelonner**, *v.r.* to be graduated; to slope gradually; to be arranged in echelon.
écheniller [eʃni'je], *v.t.* to rid (*plants, trees etc.*) of caterpillars.
écheveau [eʃ'vo], *n.m.* (*pl.* -eaux) hank, skein.
échevelé [eʃə'vle], *a.* dishevelled; (*fig.*) wild, extravagant.
écheveler [eʃə'vle], *v.t.* (*conjug. like* APPELER) to dishevel.
*****échevin** [eʃ'vɛ̃], *n.m.* sheriff; alderman; (*C*) municipal magistrate.
échine [e'ʃin], *n.f.* spine, backbone, chine.
échiner [eʃi'ne], *v.t.* to beat unmercifully; to tire out. **s'échiner**, *v.r.* (*pop.*) to work oneself to death.
échiqueté [eʃik'te], *a.* chequered.
échiquier [eʃi'kje], *n.m.* chess-board; exchequer; square net.
écho [e'ko], *n.m.* echo.
échoir [e'ʃwa:r], *v.i. irr.* (*aux.* ÊTRE) to expire, to fall due, to lapse; to happen, to befall.
échoppe [e'ʃɔp], *n.f.* booth, covered stall.
échopper [eʃɔ'pe], *v.t.* to gouge.
échotier [eko'tje], *n.m.* (*fem.* -ière) gossip writer, columnist.
échouage [e'ʃwa:ʒ], **échouement** [eʃu'mɑ̃], *n.m.* (*Naut.*) beaching, running aground.
échouer [e'ʃwe], *v.t.* to run (*a vessel*) aground. —*v.i.* to run aground, to be stranded; (*fig.*) to miscarry, to fail.
écimer [esi'me], *v.t.* to top (*plants etc.*), to pollard (*trees*).
éclaboussement [eklabus'mɑ̃], *n.m.* splashing, bespattering.
éclabousser [eklabu'se], *v.t.* to splash, to bespatter.
éclaboussure [eklabu'sy:r], *n.f.* splash.
éclair [e'klɛ:r], *n.m.* lightning, flash of lightning; variety of chocolate cake.
éclairage [eklɛ'ra:ʒ], *n.m.* lighting, illumination, light.
éclaircie [eklɛr'si], *n.f.* opening, rift (*in clouds etc.*); glade, clearing; (*fig.*) favorable change of affairs.
éclaircir [eklɛr'si:r], *v.t.* to make clear *or* clearer, to brighten; to clarify; to make thin *or* thinner; to elucidate, to explain. **s'éclaircir**, *v.r.* to become clear, bright *or* fine; to grow light; to be explained.
éclaircissement [eklɛrsis'mɑ̃], *n.m.* clearing up, explanation, solution; hint, light.
éclaire [e'klɛ:r], *n.f.* celandine.
éclairé [ekle're], *a.* lighted; well-lighted; (*fig.*) well-informed; enlightened; enlightened.
éclairer [ekle're], *v.t.* to light, to give light to, to illuminate; to enlighten; to observe; (*Mil.*) to reconnoitre.—*v.i.* to sparkle, to shine, to glitter. **s'éclairer**, *v.r.* to become enlightened; to instruct *or* enlighten one another; to light up.

125

éclaireur [eklɛ'rœ:r], *n.m.* (*Mil.*) scout; boy scout.

éclanche [e'klɑ̃:ʃ], *n.f.* shoulder of mutton.

éclat [e'kla], *n.m.* burst; crash, peal; splinter (*of wood, stone, brick etc.*); brightness, glare, glitter; luster, pomp; renown; gaudiness (*of colors*); rumor, scandal; *un éclat de rire*, a burst of laughter; *un grand éclat de voix*, a loud shout; *voler en éclats*, to fly into a thousand pieces.

éclatant [ekla'tɑ̃], *a.* bright, sparkling, brilliant; striking; piercing, shrill.

éclatement [eklat'mɑ̃], *n.m.* bursting, explosion.

éclater [ekla'te], *v.i.* to split, to burst, to explode; to cry out; to shine, to sparkle, to flash; to break out (*war etc.*); *éclater de rire*, to burst out laughing.

éclectique [eklɛk'tik], *a.* and *n.f.* eclectic; dilettante.

éclectisme [eklɛk'tism], *n.m.* eclecticism.

éclipse [e'klips], *n.f.* eclipse; (*fig.*) disappearance.

éclipser [eklip'se], *v.t.* to eclipse, (*fig.*) to surpass. **s'éclipser**, *v.r.* (*fig.*) to disappear, to vanish.

écliptique [eklip'tik], *a.* and *n.f.* ecliptic.

éclisse [e'klis], *n.f.* (*Surg.*) splint.

éclisser [ekli'se], *v.t.* (*Surg.*) to splint.

éclopé [eklɔ'pe], *a.* crippled, footsore, lame.— *n.m.* (*fem.* **-ée**) cripple.

écloper [eklɔ'pe], *v.t.* to lame, to disable.

éclore [e'klɔ:r], *v.i. irr.* (*conjug. like* CLORE, *but with aux.* ÊTRE) to hatch; to open, to bloom (*of flowers*); (*fig.*) to show itself.

éclosion [eklo'zjɔ̃], *n.f.* hatching; (*fig.*) opening, blooming; appearance.

écluse [e'kly:z], *n.f.* lock (*on canals etc.*); dam, weir; *porte d'écluse*, sluice, floodgate.

écluser [ekly'ze], *v.t.* to furnish with locks; to take (*a boat etc.*) through a lock.

éclusier [ekly'zje], *n.m.* (*fem.* **-ière**) lock keeper.

écœurant [ekœ'rɑ̃], *a.* disgusting, nauseating.

écœurement [ekœr'mɑ̃], *n.m.* disgust; nausea.

écœurer [ekœ're], *v.t.* to disgust, to sicken; (*fig.*) to shock, to dishearten.

école [e'kɔl], *n.f.* school, college; scholastic philosophy; sect; (*Mil.*) training; (*fig.*) manner, practice.

écolier [ekɔ'lje], *n.m.* (*fem.* **-ière**) schoolboy, schoolgirl, pupil, student.

éconduire [ekɔ̃'dɥi:r], *v.t. irr.* (*conjug. like* CONDUIRE) to show out, to dismiss; to refuse.

économat [ekɔnɔ'ma], *n.m.* stewardship, bursarship.

économe [ekɔ'nɔm], *a.* economical, saving, thrifty.—*n.* steward, housekeeper, bursar, treasurer (*of colleges, hospitals etc.*).

économie [ekɔnɔ'mi], *n.f.* economy; thrift, saving.

économique [ekɔnɔ'mik], *a.* (*applied to things only*) economic, economical, cheap.—*n.f.* economics.

économiquement [ekɔnɔmik'mɑ̃], *adv.* economically.

économiser [ekɔnɔmi'ze], *v.t.*, *v.i.* to economize, to save (up).

économiste [ekɔnɔ'mist], *n.* economist.

écope [e'kɔp], *n.f.* scoop, ladle; (*Naut.*) bailer.

écorce [e'kɔrs], *n.f.* bark, rind, peel; shell; (*Geol.*) crust (*of the earth*).

écorcement [ekɔrs'mɑ̃], **écorçage** [ekɔr'sa:ʒ], *n.m.* barking *or* stripping (*of trees etc.*); peeling.

écorcer [ekɔr'se], *v.t.* (*conjug. like* COMMENCER) to bark, to strip (*trees etc.*), to peel.

écorchement [ekɔrʃə'mɑ̃], *n.m.* excoriation, flaying, skinning.

écorcher [ekɔr'ʃe], *v.t.* to flay, to skin; to graze (*skin*); to peel, to bark; (*fig.*) to strip, to fleece. **s'écorcher**, *v.r.* to graze oneself.

écorcheur [ekɔr'ʃœ:r], *n.m.* (*fem.* **-euse**) knacker, flayer; (*fig.*) fleecer.

écorchure [ekɔr'ʃy:r], *n.f.* scratch, graze.

écorner [ekɔr'ne], *v.t.* to break the horns of; to break the corners of, to dog-ear; to curtail, to impair.

écornifler [ekɔrni'fle], *v.t.* to sponge upon.

écornure [ekɔr'ny:r], *n.f.* broken-off corner, chip.

écossais [ekɔ'sɛ], *a.* Scottish.—*n.m.* Scots (*language*); plaid, tartan cloth; (**Écossais**, *fem.* **-aise**) Scot, Scotsman, Scotswoman.

Écosse [e'kɔs], **l'**, *f.* Scotland; *La Nouvelle Écosse*, *f.* Nova Scotia.

écosser [ekɔ'se], *v.t.* to shell, to husk (*peas or beans*).

écosseur [ekɔ'sœ:r], *n.m.* (*fem.* **-euse**) sheller.

écot (1) [e'ko], *n.m.* share (*of a reckoning*); bill, reckoning, score (*usually in the expression payer son écot, to pay one's share*).

écot (2) [e'ko], *n.m.* stump of a tree.

écoulement [ekul'mɑ̃], *n.m.* flowing, flow, running; outlet, (*Comm.*) sale, disposal; export.

écouler [eku'le], *v.t.* to dispose of, to sell. **s'écouler**, *v.r.* to run *or* flow away, to pass, to slip away; (*Comm.*) to be disposed of.

écourter [ekur'te], *v.t.* to shorten, to dock, to crop.

écoutant [eku'tɑ̃], *a.* listening; *avocat écoutant*, briefless attorney.

écoute (1) [e'kut], *n.f.* hiding place for listening; *être aux écoutes*, to be on the watch.

écoute (2) [e'kut], *n.f.* (*Naut.*) sheet (*of sail*).

écouter [eku'te], *v.t.* to listen to, to hearken to; to pay attention to. **s'écouter**, *v.r.* to like the sound of one's own voice; to indulge oneself.

écouteur [eku'tœ:r], *n.m.* (*fem.* **-euse**) listener, listener-in; (*Teleph.*) receiver; (*Teleg.*) ear-phone.

écoutille [eku'ti:j], *n.f.* (*Naut.*) hatchway.

écran [e'krɑ̃], *n.m.* screen; *vedette de l'écran*, film star.

écrasant [ekra'zɑ̃], *a.* crushing; (*fig.*) humiliating, excessive; overwhelming.

écrasé [ekra'ze], *a.* crushed, ruined.

écrasement [ekraz'mɑ̃], *n.m.* crushing, bruising; (*fig.*) overwhelming.

écraser [ekra'ze], *v.t.* to crush; to bruise; to overwhelm, to ruin; to run over.

écraseur [ekra'zœ:r], *n.m.* crusher; (*Motor.*) road hog; steam-roller.

écrémer [ekre'me], *v.t.* (*conjug. like* CÉDER) to take the cream off, to skim.

écrémeuse [ekre'mø:z] *n.f.* separator.

écrevisse [ekra'vis], *n.f.* crayfish; (*Am.*) crawfish; (*Astron.*) Cancer.

écrier (s') [sekri'je], *v.r.* to cry out, to exclaim.

écrin [e'krɛ̃], n.m. casket, jewel box or case.
écrire [e'kri:r], v.t. irr. to write; to spell. s'écrire, v.r. to be written; to be spelled; to write to each other.
écrit [e'kri], n.m. writing; pamphlet.
écriteau [ekri'to], n.m. (pl. -eaux) bill (poster); board.
écritoire [ekri'twa:r], n.f. writing desk; inkstand.
écriture [ekri'ty:r], n.f. writing, handwriting; scripture; (pl.) accounts, documents.
écrivain [ekri'vɛ̃], n.m. writer, author; femme écrivain, authoress, woman writer.
écrivassier [ekriva'sje], n.m. (fem. -ière) (colloq.) scribbler.
écrou [e'kru], n.m. screw nut; écrou à oreilles, wing nut.
écrouelles [ekru'ɛl], n.f. pl. king's evil, scrofula.
écrouelleux [ekru'lø], a. (fem. -euse) scrofulous.
écrouer [ekru'e], v.t. to imprison, to lock up.
écroulement [ekrul'mɑ̃], n.m. falling in, collapse; wreck, ruin.
écrouler (s') [sekru'le], v.r. to fall in, to fall to pieces, to collapse.
écru [e'kry], a. raw, unbleached; toile écrue, (brown) holland.
ectoplasme [ɛkto'plasm], n.m. ectoplasm.
écu [e'ky], n.m. shield; crown (coin); (fig.) money, cash.
écueil [e'kœ:j], n.m. reef, rock; (fig.) danger, stumbling-block.
écuelle [e'kɥɛl], n.f. porringer, bowl, basin.
écuellée [ekɥe'le], n.f. bowlful.
éculer [eky'le], v.t. to tread down at heel; des souliers éculés, down-at-heel shoes.
écumage [eky'ma:ʒ], n.m. skimming.
écumant [eky'mɑ̃], a. foaming, frothing, seething.
écume [e'kym], n.f. foam, froth; lather; (fig.) scum, dregs.
écumer [eky'me], v.t. to skim; to scour; écumer la marmite, to be a sponger.—v.i. to foam, to froth.
écumeur [eky'mœ:r], n.m. (fem. écumeuse (1)) skimmer; hanger-on, parasite.
écumeux [eky'mø], a. (fem. écumeuse (2)) frothy, foaming.
écumoire [eky'mwa:r], n.f. skimmer.
écurage [eky'ra:ʒ], n.m. scouring, cleaning.
écurer [eky're], v.t. to scour, to cleanse.
écureuil [eky'rœ:j], n.m. squirrel.
écurie [eky'ri], n.f. stable, mews; stud.
écusson [eky'sɔ̃], n.m. escutcheon; shield.
écuyer [ekɥi'je], n.m. squire; equerry; riding-master; rider; wall hand-rail (of a staircase).
écuyère [ekɥi'jɛ:r], n.f. horsewoman; female equestrian performer; bottes à l'écuyère, top boots, riding boots.
eczéma [ɛgze'ma], n.m. eczema.
édenté [edɑ̃'te], a. toothless.
édenter [edɑ̃'te], v.t. to break the teeth of (combs, saws etc.).
édicter [edik'te], v.t. to enact, to decree.
édicule [edi'kyl], n.m. small building (pavilion, kiosk etc.).
édifiant [edi'fjɑ̃], a. edifying.
édification [edifika'sjɔ̃], n.f. building, erection; (fig.) edification.
édifice [edi'fis], n.m. edifice, building, pile.

édifier [edi'fje], v.t. to build, to erect, to construct; (fig.) to edify, to improve; to instruct, to enlighten; to satisfy.
édile [e'dil], n.m. ædile; town councillor.
Édimbourg [edɛ̃'bu:r], m. or f. Edinburgh.
édit [e'di], n.m. edict.
éditer [edi'te], v.t. to publish; to edit.
éditeur [edi'tœ:r], n.m. (fem. -trice) publisher.
édition [edi'sjɔ̃], n.f. edition.
éditorial [edito'rjal], n.m. (pl. -aux) leading article, leader, editorial.
éditorialiste [editɔrja'list], n. leader writer.
Édouard [e'dwa:r], m. Edward.
édredon [edrə'dɔ̃], n.m. eider-down; eider-down quilt.
éducateur [edyka'tœ:r], a. (fem. -trice) educative, instructing.—n.m. (fem. -trice) educator; breeder.
éducatif [edyka'tif], a. (fem. -tive) educational.
éducation [edyka'sjɔ̃], n.f. education; training; rearing (of animals); breeding, manners.
éduquer [edy'ke], v.t. to bring up, to educate (children).
effacement [efas'mɑ̃], n.m. effacement, obliteration; disappearance; humility, self-effacement.
effacer [efa'se], v.t. (conjug. like COMMENCER) to efface, to erase, to rub out, to blot out, to obliterate. s'effacer, v.r. to become obliterated; to wear away; to draw aside, to give way.
effaçure [efa'sy:r], n.f. erasure, blotting out, obliteration.
effaré [efa're], a. wild, scared, bewildered; astounded.
effarement [efar'mɑ̃], n.m. bewilderment, terror, affright.
effarer [efa're], v.t. to frighten, to scare. s'effarer, v.r. to be scared, to take fright.
effarouchant [efaru'ʃɑ̃], a. startling, disquieting; shocking; annoying.
effaroucher [efaru'ʃe], v.t. to startle, to frighten away. s'effaroucher, v.r. to be scared, to be startled.
effectif [efɛk'tif], a. (fem. -tive) actual, real, positive.—n.m. effective force (of troops etc.); size (of a class).
effectivement [efɛktiv'mɑ̃], adv. in effect, actually, indeed, in fact; (in answer) that is so.
effectuer [efɛk'tɥe], v.t. to effect, to accomplish, to carry out. s'effectuer, v.r. to be accomplished, to take place.
effémination [efemina'sjɔ̃], n.f. effeminacy.
efféminé [efemi'ne], a. effeminate, womanish.
effervescence [efɛrvɛ'sɑ̃:s], n.f. effervescence; (fig.) agitation, ferment.
effervescent [efɛrvɛ'sɑ̃], a. effervescent; (fig.) excitable, irascible.
effet [e'fɛ], n.m. effect, result; performance; impression; power (transmitted by machinery etc.); (Comm.) bill of exchange; (pl.) belongings; en effet, indeed, in fact.
effeuillaison [efœjɛ'zɔ̃], n.f., effeuillement [efœj'mɑ̃], n.m. fall of the leaves.
effeuiller [efœ'je], v.t. to strip off leaves, to pick (a flower) to pieces. s'effeuiller, v.r. to lose or shed its leaves.
efficace [efi'kas], a. efficacious, effective.

127

efficacité [efikasi'te], *n.f.* efficacy, effectiveness; efficiency.

effigie [efi'ʒi], *n.f.* effigy.

effilé [efi'le], *a.* slender, slim; sharp, keen, trenchant.—*n.m.* fringe.

effiler [efi'le], *v.t.* to unweave, to unravel; to taper. **s'effiler**, *v.r.* to unravel; to taper, to become sharp; to fray.

effiloche [efi'lɔʃ], **effiloque** [efi'lɔk], *n.f.* floss silk, light refuse silk.

effilocher [efilɔ'ʃe], **effiloquer** [efilɔ'ke], *v.t.* to unravel, to undo.

efflanqué [eflɑ̃'ke], *a.* lean, thin, lank.

efflanquer [eflɑ̃'ke], *v.t.* to make lean, to emaciate.

effleurer [eflœ're], *v.t.* to graze, to skim the surface of, to touch lightly; (*fig.*) to touch upon.

efflorescence [eflɔrɛ'sɑ̃:s], *n.f.* efflorescence.

efflorescent [eflɔrɛ'sɑ̃], *a.* efflorescent.

effluent [efly'ɑ̃], *a.* effluent.

effluve [e'fly:v], *n.m.* effluvium.

effondrement [efɔ̃drə'mɑ̃], *n.m.* (*Agric.*) trenching; falling in, sinking; collapse.

effondrer [efɔ̃'dre], *v.t.* to dig deeply; to break in; to overwhelm. **s'effondrer**, *v.r.* to fall in, to collapse.

efforcer (s') [efɔr'se], *v.r.* (*conjug. like* COMMENCER) to exert oneself, to strain, to strive.

effort [e'fɔ:r], *n.m.* effort, exertion, endeavor; stress; (*Med.*) strain, rupture.

effraction [efrak'sjɔ̃], *n.f.* breaking into, house-breaking; **vol avec effraction**, burglary.

effraie [e'frɛ], *n.f.* barn owl, screech owl.

effrayant [efrɛ'jɑ̃], *a.* frightful, dreadful.

effrayer [efrɛ'je], *v.t.* (*conjug. like* PAYER) to frighten, to alarm, to terrify. **s'effrayer**, *v.r.* to be frightened, to be startled.

effréné [efre'ne], *a.* unrestrained; lawless; wild.

effritement [efrit'mɑ̃], *n.m.* crumbling into dust.

effriter [efri'te], *v.r.* to crumble.

effroi [e'frwa], *n.m.* fright, terror, dread.

effronté [efrɔ̃'te], *a.* and *n.m.* (*fem.* -ée) shameless, brazen, impudent (person).

effrontément [efrɔ̃te'mɑ̃], *adv.* impudently, shamelessly.

effronterie [efrɔ̃'tri], *n.f.* effrontery, impudence.

effroyable [efrwa'jabl], *a.* frightful, dreadful, hideous.

effroyablement [efrwajablə'mɑ̃], *adv.* frightfully, horribly, dreadfully.

effusion [efy'zjɔ̃], *n.f.* effusion; overflowing.

égal [e'gal], *a.* (*m. -i. -aux*) equal, alike; even, level, smooth; all the same.—*n.m.* (*fem.* -e) equal.

également [egal'mɑ̃], *adv.* equally, alike.

égaler [ega'le], *v.t.* to equal; to make equal; to compare. **s'égaler**, *v.r.* to equal; to compare oneself (*à*).

égalisation [egaliza'sjɔ̃], *n.f.* equalization.

égaliser [egali'ze], *v.t.* to equalize; to level.

égalitaire [egali'tɛ:r], *a.* and *n.* egalitarian.

égalité [egali'te], *n.f.* equality, parity; uniformity.

égard [e'ga:r], *n.m.* regard, consideration, respect.

égaré [ega're], *a.* wandering, strayed; misled; mislaid; distracted.

égarement [egar'mɑ̃], *n.m.* straying, losing one's way; mistake; ill-conduct.

égarer [ega're], *v.t.* to mislead; to lose; to lead astray; to bewilder; to impair (*intellect*). **s'égarer**, *v.r.* to lose one's way, to stray; to err.

égayer [egɛ'je], *v.t.* (*conjug. like* PAYER) to enliven, to cheer up; (*Hort.*) to prune (*trees*). **s'égayer**, *v.r.* to brighten up; to make merry.

églantier [eglɑ̃'tje], *n.m.* eglantine, briar, dog-rose (*bush*).

églantine [eglɑ̃'tin], *n.f.* eglantine, dog-rose (*flower*).

église [e'gli:z], *n.f.* church.

églogue [e'glɔg], *n.f.* eclogue.

égocentrique [egosɑ̃'trik], *a.* egocentric, self-centered.

égoïsme [egɔ'ism], *n.m.* egoism, selfishness.

égoïste [egɔ'ist], *a.* egoistic, selfish.—*n.* egoist, selfish person.

égorger [egɔr'ʒe], *v.t.* (*conjug. like* MANGER) to cut the throat of, to slaughter.

égorgeur [egɔr'ʒœ:r], *n.m.* (*fem.* -euse) slaughterer, murderer.

égosiller (s') [segozi'je], *v.r.* to make oneself hoarse; to bawl.

égotisme [egɔ'tism], *n.m.* egotism.

égotiste [egɔ'tist], *a.* egotistic(al).—*n.* egotist.

égout [e'gu], *n.m.* running or falling of water; sink, drain, sewer.

égouttage [egu'ta:ʒ], **égouttement** [egut'mɑ̃], *n.m.* drainage, draining; dripping.

égoutter [egu'te], *v.t., v.i.* to drain, to drip. **s'égoutter**, *v.r.* to drip, to drain.

égouttoir [egu'twa:r], *n.m.* drainer (*plate-rack etc.*).

égrapper [egra'pe], *v.t.* to pick (*grapes, currants etc.*) from the bunch.

égratigner [egrati'ne], *v.t.* to scratch.

égratignure [egrati'ny:r], *n.f.* scratch; slight wound.

égrenage [egrə'na:ʒ], *n.m.* picking off (*of grapes etc.*).

égrener [egrə'ne], *v.t.* (*conjug. like* AMENER) to tell (*beads*); to unstring (*beads etc.*); to pick off (*grapes etc.*) from the bunch. **s'égrener**, *v.r.* to fall from the stalk, to drop one by one.

égrillard [egri'ja:r], *a.* lewd, broad, naughty; **propos égrillards**, spicy talk.

égrilloir [egri'jwa:r], *n.m.* weir; grate (*to confine fish in a pond*).

égrisé, *n.m.* or **égrisée** [egri'ze], *n.f.* diamond dust.

égriser [egri'ze], *v.t.* to grind, to polish (*diamonds etc.*).

égrugeoir [egry'ʒwa:r], *n.m.* mortar.

égruger [egry'ʒe], *v.t.* (*conjug. like* MANGER) to pound, to grind in a mortar.

égueuler [egœ'le], *v.t.* to break off the mouth or neck (*of glass and other vessels*).

Égypte [e'ʒipt], **l'**, *f.* Egypt.

égyptien [eʒip'sjɛ̃], *a.* (*fem.* -enne) Egyptian.—*n.m.* (**Égyptien**, *fem.* -enne) Egyptian (*person*).

eh! [e], *int.* ah! well! hey! **eh bien !** well!

éhonté [eɔ̃'te], *a.* shameless.

émacié

éjaculation [eʒakylɑ'sjɔ̃], *n.f.* throwing out with force, discharge; ejaculation.
éjaculer [eʒaky'le], *v.t.* to discharge, to ejaculate.
éjecter [eʒɛk'te], *v.t.* to eject.
éjecteur [eʒɛk'tœːr], *a.* (*fem.* **-trice**) ejecting; (*Av.*) **siège éjecteur**, ejector seat.—*n.m.* ejector (*of firearm*).
élaboration [elabɔrɑ'sjɔ̃], *n.f.* elaboration.
élaboré [elabɔ're], *a.* wrought; elaborate.
élaborer [elabɔ're], *v.t.* to elaborate, to work out.
élaguer [ela'ge], *v.t.* to lop, to prune; (*fig.*) to curtail, to cut down.
élagueur [ela'gœːr], *n.m.* (*Hort.*) pruner.
élan (1) [e'lɑ̃], *n.m.* start, spring, bound; flight; burst; dash.
élan (2) [e'lɑ̃], *n.m.* elk; moose, wapiti (*Canada*), eland (*S. Africa*).
élancé [elɑ̃'se], *a.* slender, slim.
élancement [elɑ̃s'mɑ̃], *n.m.* darting forward; shooting pain, twinge; (*pl.*) transports.
élancer [elɑ̃'se], *v.i.* (*conjug. like* COMMENCER) to dart, to hurl.—*v.i.* to shoot, to twitch (*of pain*). **s'élancer**, *v.r.* to bound, to shoot *or* dart forth, to rush, to dash; to soar up.
élargir [elar'ʒiːr], *v.t.* to widen, to enlarge; to release. **s'élargir**, *v.r.* to widen; to stretch; to enlarge one's estate.
élargissement [elarʒis'mɑ̃], *n.m.* widening, enlarging; discharge (*from prison etc.*).
élasticité [elastisi'te], *n.f.* elasticity, springiness.
élastique [elas'tik], *a.* elastic, springy.—*n.m.* India rubber; elastic band.
électeur [elɛk'tœːr], *n.m.* (*fem.* **-trice**) (*Hist.*) elector, electress; (*Polit.*) voter.
élection [elɛk'sjɔ̃], *n.f.* election, polling; choice; appointment.
électoral [elɛktɔ'ral], *a.* (*m. pl.* **-aux**) electoral.
électorat [elɛktɔ'ra], *n.m.* electorate.
électricien [elɛktri'sjɛ̃], *n.m.* electrician.
électricité [elɛktrisi'te], *n.f.* electricity.
électrification [elɛktrifikɑ'sjɔ̃], *n.f.* electrification.
électrifier [elɛktri'fje], *v.t.* to provide with current, to electrify.
électrique [elɛk'trik], *a.* electric; **secousse électrique**, electric shock.
électriquement [elɛktrik'mɑ̃], *adv.* electrically.
électriser [elɛktri'ze], *v.t.* to electrify.
électro-aimant [elɛktrɔɛ'mɑ̃], *n.m.* (*pl.* **électro-aimants**) electro-magnet.
électrocuter [elɛktrɔky'te], *v.t.* to electrocute.
électrocution [elɛktrɔky'sjɔ̃], *n.f.* electrocution.
électron [elɛk'trɔ̃], *n.m.* electron.
électronique [elɛktrɔ'nik], *a.* electronic.
élégamment [elega'mɑ̃], *adv.* elegantly, stylishly.
élégance [ele'gɑ̃ːs], *n.f.* elegance, style.
élégant [ele'gɑ̃], *a.* elegant, smart, fashionable, stylish.—*n.m.* (*fem.* **-ée**) gentleman *or* lady of fashion.
élégiaque [ele'ʒjak], *a.* elegiac.—*n.* elegist.
élégie [ele'ʒi], *n.f.* elegy.
élément [ele'mɑ̃], *n.m.* element, component part.

élémentaire [elemɑ̃'tɛːr], *a.* elementary, elemental.
éléphant [ele'fɑ̃], *n.m.* elephant.
éléphantin [elefɑ̃'tɛ̃], *a.* elephantine.
élevage [el'vaːʒ], *n.m.* breeding, rearing (*of cattle*); stud.
élévateur [eleva'tœːr], *a.* (*fem.* **-trice**) raising, lifting.—*n.m.* elevator, lift, hoist.
élévation [eleva'sjɔ̃], *n.f.* elevation, raising; eminence, height; promotion; greatness (*of soul*); rise (*in prices etc.*).
élève [e'lɛːv], *n.* pupil; student, disciple; apprentice.
élevé [el've], *a.* raised, grand; reared; heroic, eminent; high (*of prices etc.*); exalted; **bien élevé**, well-bred; **mal élevé**, ill-bred.
élever [el've], *v.t.* (*conjug. like* AMENER) to raise, to lift up; to erect; to exalt; to run up (*accounts etc.*); to bring up, to rear; to educate; to foster. **s'élever**, *v.r.* to rise, to ascend, to go up; to be constructed; to increase; to break out.
éleveur [el'vœːr], *n.m.* (*fem.* **-euse**) raiser; cattle breeder.—*n.f.* (**-euse**) incubator.
elfe [ɛlf], *n.m.* elf, brownie.
élider [eli'de], *v.t.* (*Gram.*) to cut off, to elide. **s'élider**, *v.r.* to be elided.
éligibilité [eliʒibili'te], *n.f.* eligibility.
éligible [eli'ʒibl], *a.* eligible.
élimer [eli'me], *v.t.* to wear out. **s'élimer**, *v.r.* to wear threadbare (*of clothes etc.*).
élimination [eliminɑ'sjɔ̃], *n.f.* elimination.
éliminatoire [eliminɑ'twaːr], *a.* and *n.f.* (*Spt.*) eliminating (heat); disqualifying.
éliminer [elimi'ne], *v.t.* to eliminate; to expel; to remove.
élire [e'liːr], *v.t. irr.* (*conjug. like* LIRE) to elect, to choose; to return, to appoint.
élision [eli'zjɔ̃], *n.f.* elision.
élite [e'lit], *n.f.* choice, pick, select few, élite.
élixir [elik'siːr], *n.m.* elixir.
elle [ɛl], *pron.* (*pl.* **elles**) she, her, it; (*pl.*) they.
ellébore [ele'bɔːr], *n.m.* hellebore.
ellipse [e'lips], *n.f.* ellipse; (*Gram.*) ellipsis.
elliptique [elip'tik], *a.* elliptical.
élocution [elɔky'sjɔ̃], *n.f.* elocution.
éloge [e'lɔːʒ], *n.m.* eulogy, praise; panegyric.
élogieux [elɔ'ʒjø], *a.* (*fem.* **-euse**) laudatory, eulogistic, flattering.
éloigné [elwa'ɲe], *a.* removed, distant, remote; absent.
éloignement [elwaɲ'mɑ̃], *n.m.* removal; remoteness; dislike; unwillingness.
éloigner [elwa'ɲe], *v.t.* to remove; to dismiss; to set aside, to repudiate; to waive; to banish; to put off; to alienate. **s'éloigner**, *v.r.* to go away, to withdraw; to digress; to deviate; to be alienated.
éloquemment [elɔka'mɑ̃], *adv.* eloquently.
éloquence [elɔ'kɑ̃ːs], *n.f.* eloquence, oratory.
éloquent [elɔ'kɑ̃], *a.* eloquent.
élu [e'ly], *a.* elected, chosen, elect; appointed.—*n.m.* (*fem.* **-e**) elected *or* chosen person.
élucidation [elysidɑ'sjɔ̃], *n.f.* elucidation.
élucider [elysi'de], *v.t.* to elucidate, to clear up.
éluder [ely'de], *v.t.* to elude, to evade.
Élysée [eli'ze], *n.m.* Elysium; **l'Élysée**, the residence (*in Paris*) of the President of the Republic.
émaciation [emasjɑ'sjɔ̃], *n.f.* emaciation.
émacié [ema'sje], *a.* emaciated.

129

émail

émail [e′ma:j], *n.m.* (*pl.* **émaux**) enamel.
émaillage [ema′ja:ʒ], *n.m.* enamelling.
émailler [ema′je], *v.t.* to enamel; (*fig.*) to adorn.
émailleur [ema′jœr], *n.m.* enameller.
émaillure [ema′jy:r], *n.f.* enamelling.
émanation [emana′sjɔ̃], *n.f.* emanation.
émancipation [emãsipa′sjɔ̃], *n.f.* emancipation.
émanciper [emãsi′pe], *v.t.* to emancipate. **s'émanciper**, *v.r.* to gain one's liberty; to overstep the mark, to forget oneself.
émaner [ema′ne], *v.i.* to emanate.
émargement [emarʒə′mã], *n.m.* writing in the margin, marginal note; signature in the margin.
émarger [emar′ʒe], *v.t.* (*conjug. like* MANGER) to write *or* sign in the margin, *esp. on receipt*; *hence*, to draw one's salary.
embâcle [ã′ba:kl], *n.m.* ice-pack (*in a river etc.*).
emballage [ãba′la:ʒ], *n.m.* packing up, packing; package; (*Spt.*) spurt.
emballement [ãbal′mã], *n.m.* excitement; flying into a temper; burst of enthusiasm.
emballer [ãba′le], *v.t.* to pack up, to wrap up; (*colloq.*) to pack off; to arrest; to tell (*someone*) off. **s'emballer**, *v.r.* to bolt (*of a horse etc.*); to wrap oneself up; to be carried away (*by rage, enthusiasm etc.*), to race (*of an engine*).
emballeur [ãba′lœr], *n.m.* packer.
embarbouiller [ãbarbu′je], *v.t.* to besmear. **s'embarbouiller**, *v.r.* to get muddled.
embarcadère [ãbarka′dɛ:r], *n.m.* wharf, pier, landing-stage.
embarcation [ãbarka′sjɔ̃], *n.f.* small boat, craft.
embardée [ãbar′de], *n.f.* lurch (*of a boat, a car etc.*); **faire une embardée**, to lurch (*of boat*); to swerve, to skid (*of car*).
embargo [ãbar′go], *n.m.* embargo.
embarquement [ãbarkə′mã], *n.m.* embarkation, embarking; shipment.
embarquer [ãbar′ke], *v.t.* to embark, to take on board; to ship (*water etc.*). **s'embarquer**, *v.r.* to embark, to go on board; **s'embarquer dans**, (*fig.*) to embark upon.
embarras [ãba′ra], *n.m.* encumbrance, hindrance; difficulty, fuss; (*pl.*) embarrassing circumstances; trouble, nervousness.
embarrassant [ãbara′sã], *a.* embarrassing, puzzling, awkward; troublesome.
embarrassé [ãbara′se], *a.* embarrassed, perplexed.
embarrasser [ãbara′se], *v.t.* to embarrass, to obstruct; to trouble, to confound; to puzzle. **s'embarrasser**, *v.r.* to entangle oneself; to be embarrassed; to concern oneself (*with*).
embâter [ãba′te], *v.t.* to put a pack-saddle on, to saddle.
embauchage [ãbo′ʃa:ʒ], *n.m.*, **embauche** [ã′boʃ], *n.f.* hiring, engaging (*of workmen*); enlisting, recruiting (*soldiers*).
embaucher [ãbo′ʃe], *v.t.* to hire, to engage, to sign on (*workmen*); to enlist (*soldiers*).
embaucheur [ãbo′ʃœ:r], *n.m.* (*fem.* **-euse**) hirer, recruiting officer.
embauchoir [ãbo′ʃwa:r], *n.m.* boot tree, boot last.

embaumement [ãbom′mã], *n.m.* embalming.
embaumer [ãbo′me], *v.t.* to embalm; to perfume.—*v.i.* to smell sweet.
embaumeur [ãbo′mœ:r], *n.m.* embalmer.
embecquer [ãbɛ′ke], *v.t.* to feed (*a bird*); to bait (*a hook*).
embéguiner [ãbegi′ne], *v.t.* to muffle up. **s'embéguiner**, *v.r.* to wrap oneself up; (*fig.*) to be infatuated with.
embellir [ãbɛ′li:r], *v.t.* to embellish, to beautify.—*v.i.* to grow more beautiful. **s'embellir**, *v.r.* to grow more beautiful; to enhance one's looks.
embellissement [ãbɛlis′mã], *n.m.* embellishment; improvement.
embêtant [ãbɛ′tã], *a.* (*colloq.*) boring, annoying.
embêtement [ãbɛt′mã], *n.m.* (*colloq.*) annoyance; nuisance, bore.
embêter [ãbɛ′te], *v.t.* to bore; to annoy, to rile; to worry. **s'embêter**, *v.r.* to feel dull *or* bored.
emblée (d') [dã′ble], *adv.* at the first, at the first attempt, immediately.
emblématique [ãblema′tik], *a.* emblematical.
emblème [ã′blɛ:m], *n.m.* emblem.
emboîtage [ãbwa′ta:ʒ], *n.m.* boards, cover (*book*).
emboîtement [ãbwat′mã], *n.m.* fitting in, jointing, clamping.
emboîter [ãbwa′te], *v.t.* to fit in, to put (*a book*) into its boards; to clamp. **s'emboîter**, *v.r.* to fit, to fit in; (*fig.*) to model oneself upon.
emboîture [ãbwa′ty:r], *n.f.* socket, clamp.
embolie [ãbɔ′li], *n.f.* (*Path.*) embolism.
embonpoint [ãbɔ̃′pwɛ̃], *n.m.* plumpness, stoutness, obesity.
emboucher [ãbu′ʃe], *v.t.* to put to one's mouth, to sound (*wind instruments*); to bit (*a horse*).
embouchure [ãbu′ʃy:r], *n.f.* mouth (*of a river, harbor etc.*); mouth-piece (*of wind instruments*); opening (*of a receptacle*).
embourber [ãbur′be], *v.t.* to put in the mire; (*fig.*) to implicate in a dirty affair. **s'embourber**, *v.r.* to stick in the mire, to get bogged down; (*fig.*) to be involved (*in some trouble*); to put one's foot in it.
embourser [ãbur′se], *v.t.* to receive, to swallow (*affronts etc.*).
embout [ã′bu], *n.m.* ferrule.
embouteillage [ãbutɛ′ja:ʒ], *n.m.* bottling; traffic jam.
embouteiller [ãbutɛ′je], *v.t.* to bottle; to bottle up; to block up.
emboutir [ãbu′ti:r], *v.t.* to beat out (*coppersmith's work etc.*); to scoop out, to stamp; (*fam.*) to bump into. **s'emboutir**, *v.r.* to crash into, to collide with.
embranchement [ãbrãʃ′mã], *n.m.* branching off; branch road, branch line etc.; junction.
embrancher [ãbrã′ʃe], *v.t.* to put together, to join up (*roads, railways, pipes etc.*). **s'embrancher**, *v.r.* to join (*of a minor road or line joining a major one*).
embrasement [ãbraz′mã], *n.m.* conflagration; illumination.

embraser [ãbrɑ'ze], v.t. to fire, to set on fire; (fig.) to inflame; to illuminate. **s'embraser**, v.r. to kindle, to catch fire; to glow.
embrassade [ãbra'sad], n.f. embrace, hug; kissing, kiss.
embrasse [ã'bras], n.f. curtain loop.
embrassement [ãbras'mã], n.m. embrace, embracing.
embrasser [ãbra'se], v.t. to embrace, to clasp; to kiss; (fig.) to encircle; to comprise. **s'embrasser**, v.r. to embrace or kiss one another; to be included.
embrassure [ãbras'sy:r], n.f. band of iron.
embrasure [ãbra'zy:r], n.f. embrasure, recess.
embrayage [ãbrɛ'ja:ʒ], n.m. (Motor.) coupling gear, clutch.
embrayer [ãbrɛ'je], v.t. (conjug. like PAYER) to connect up, to throw into gear.—v.i. to let in the clutch.
embrèvement [ãbrɛv'mã], n.m. (Carp.) mortise.
embrocation [ãbrɔka'sjɔ̃], n.f. embrocation.
embrocher [ãbrɔ'ʃe], v.t. to put on the spit.
embrouillement [ãbruj'mã], n.m. embroilment, entanglement, perplexity.
embrouiller [ãbru'je], v.t. to embroil, to confuse; to perplex; to obscure. **s'embrouiller**, v.r. to become intricate or entangled; to get confused or muddled.
embrouilleur [ãbru'jœ:r], n.m. (fem. -euse) muddler, blunderer.
embrumer (s') [sãbry'me], v.r. to be covered with fog etc; to become misty or hazy; (fig.) to grow somber or gloomy.
embrun [ã'brœ̃], n.m. (usu. pl.) spray, spindrift.
embrunir [ãbry'ni:r], v.t. to brown.
embryon [ãbri'jɔ̃], n.m. embryo; germ; (fig.) dwarf, shrimp.
embryonnaire [ãbrijɔ'nɛ:r], a. embryonic, in embryo.
embûche [ã'byʃ], n.f. ambush, snare.
embuscade [ãbys'kad], n.f. ambuscade, ambush.
embusqué [ãbys'ke], n.m. (Mil. slang) shirker.
embusquer [ãbys'ke], v.t. to place in ambuscade, to post. **s'embusquer**, v.r. to lie in wait.
émender [emã'de], v.t. (Law) to amend, to correct.
émeraude [em'ro:d], n.f. emerald.
émergence [emɛr'ʒã:s], n.f. emergence; emersion.
émergent [emɛr'ʒã], a. emergent.
émerger [emɛr'ʒe], v.i. (conjug. like MANGER) to emerge, to rise out.
émeri [em'ri], n.m. emery.
émerillon [emri'jɔ̃], n.m. (Orn.) merlin.
émeriser [emri'ze], v.t. to cover with emery; **papier émerisé**, emery paper.
émérite [eme'rit], a. emeritus; practised, perfect; eminent.
émersion [emɛr'sjɔ̃], n.f. emersion.
émerveillement [emɛrvɛj'mã], n.m. wonder, astonishment.
émerveiller [emɛrvɛ'je], v.t. to astonish, to amaze. **s'émerveiller**, v.r. to marvel, to be astonished.
émétique [eme'tik], a. and n.m. emetic.
émetteur [eme'tœ:r] a. (fem. -trice)

(Rad., Tel.) **poste émetteur** or **station émettrice**, broadcasting station.—n.m. transmitter; **émetteur-récepteur**, transmitter-receiver, (fam.) walkie-talkie.
émettre [e'mɛtr], v.t. irr. (conjug. like METTRE) to emit, to give out; to utter, to express; (Rad., Tel.) to broadcast.
émeu [e'mø], n.m. (Orn.) emu.
émeute [e'mø:t], n.f. riot, disturbance, tumult, rising; **chef d'émeute**, ringleader.
émeuter [emø'te], v.t. to rouse, to stir up, to excite.
émeutier [emø'tje], n.m. (fem. -ière) rioter.
émiettement [emjɛt'mã], n.m. crumbling.
émietter [emjɛ'te], v.t. to crumble. **s'émietter**, v.r. to crumble.
émigrant [emi'grã], a. emigrating.—n.m. (fem. -e) emigrant.
émigration [emigra'sjɔ̃], n.f. emigration, migration.
émigré [emi'gre], n.m. (fem. -ée) emigrant; refugee.
émigrer [emi'gre], v.i. to emigrate; to migrate.
émincé [emɛ̃'se], n.m. (Cook.) thin slices (of meat).
émincer [emɛ̃'se], v.t. (conjug. like COMMENCER) to slice (meat).
éminemment [emina'mã], adv. eminently.
éminence [emi'nã:s], n.f. eminence, elevation, rising ground, height.
éminent [emi'nã], a. eminent, high, lofty.
émissaire [emi'sɛ:r], n.m. emissary, messenger; **bouc émissaire**, scapegoat.
émission [emi'sjɔ̃], n.f. emission; issue, uttering; broadcasting.
emmagasinage [ãmagazi'na:ʒ], n.m. storage, warehousing.
emmagasiner [ãmagazi'ne], v.t. to warehouse, to store.
emmaillotement [ãmajɔt'mã], n.m. swaddling, swathing.
emmailloter [ãmajɔ'te], v.t. to swaddle, to swathe.
emmanchement [ãmãʃ'mã], n.m. hafting, helving (putting a handle on); (fig.) joining.
emmancher [ãmã'ʃe], v.t. to put a handle to, to haft, to helve. **s'emmancher**, v.r. to fit on a handle; (fig.) to start (of an affair).
emmanchure [ãmã'ʃy:r], n.f. armhole.
emmarchement [ãmarʃə'mã], n.m. tread (of stair).
emmêlement [ãmɛl'mã], n.m. tangle, muddle.
emmêler [ãmɛ'le], v.t. to entangle. **s'emmêler**, v.r. to get entangled.
emménagement [ãmena'ʒmã], n.m. moving into (a new house), installation.
emménager [ãmena'ʒe], v.t. (conjug. like MANGER) to move in; to fit out (a ship etc.).—v.i. and **s'emménager**, v.r. to move in.
emmener [ãm'ne], v.t. (conjug. like AMENER) to take away, to lead away, to fetch away, to convey away.
emmenotter [ãmnɔ'te], v.t. to handcuff.
emmeuler [ãmø'le], v.t. to stack (hay etc.).
emmiellé [ãmjɛ'le], a. honeyed, sweet.
emmieller [ãmjɛ'le], v.t. to honey, to sweeten with or as with honey.
emmitoufler [ãmitu'fle], v.t. to wrap up warmly.

émoi [e'mwa], *n.m.* emotion, anxiety, flutter.

émollient [emɔ'ljã], *a.* emollient, softening. —*n.m.* emollient.

émolument [emɔly'mã], *n.m.* emolument, fee; (*pl.*) salary.

émondage [emɔ̃'da:ʒ], *n.m.* pruning, lopping, trimming.

émonder [emɔ̃'de], *v.t.* to prune, to lop.

émondeur [emɔ̃'dœ:r], *n.m.* (*fem.* **-euse**) pruner, trimmer.

émotion [emo'sjɔ̃], *n.f.* emotion; stir, commotion.

émotter [emɔ'te], *v.t.* to break up (*soil, a field etc.*).

émoucher [emu'ʃe], *v.t.* to drive flies away from. **s'émoucher**, *v.r.* to whisk away the flies.

émouchet [emu'ʃɛ], *n.m.* sparrow hawk.

émouchette [emu'ʃɛt], *n.f.* fly net (*for horses etc.*).

émouchoir [emu'ʃwa:r], *n.m.* fly whisk.

émoudre [e'mudr], *v.t. irr.* (*conjug. like* MOUDRE) to grind, to sharpen.

émouleur [emu'lœ:r], *n.m.* knifegrinder.

émoulu [emu'ly], *a.* sharpened, sharp.

émousser [emu'se], *v.t.* to blunt, to take the edge off; (*fig.*) to dull; to deaden. **s'émousser**, *v.r.* to get blunt; to become dull.

émoustiller [emusti'je], *v.t.* (*colloq.*) to exhilarate, to put into good spirits; (*fam.*) to ginger up. **s'émoustiller**, *v.r.* to bestir oneself.

émouvant [emu'vã], *a.* touching, moving, stirring.

émouvoir [emu'vwa:r], *v.t. irr.* (*conjug. like* MOUVOIR) to move, to affect; to excite, to rouse. **s'émouvoir**, *v.r.* to be roused *or* moved; to be agitated.

empaillage [ãpa'ja:ʒ], **empaillement** [ãpaj'mã], *n.m.* bottoming (*with straw*); stuffing (*of animals*).

empaillé [ãpa'je], *a.* stuffed; (*fam.*) **avoir l'air empaillé**, to be slow *or* dull-witted.

empailler [ãpa'je], *v.t.* to pack in straw; to straw-bottom; to stuff (*birds etc.*).

empailleur [ãpa'jœ:r], *n.m.* (*fem.* **-euse**) chair mender; bird *or* animal stuffer, taxidermist.

empaler [ãpa'le], *v.t.* to impale.

empanacher [ãpana'ʃe], *v.t.* to adorn with a plume; (*colloq.*) to touch up.

empaquetage [ãpak'ta:ʒ], *n.m.* packing.

empaqueter [ãpak'te], *v.t.* (*conjug. like* APPELER) to pack up, to make up into a bundle, to do up. **s'empaqueter**, *v.r.* to wrap oneself up.

emparer (s') [sãpa're], *v.r.* to possess oneself (*of*), to get hold (*of*); to seize, to secure.

empâtement [ãpat'mã], *n.m.* stickiness, clamminess.

empâter [ãpa'te], *v.t.* to make clammy *or* sticky; to cram (*fowls*).

empattement [ãpat'mã], *n.m.* footing, foundation, base; (*Motor. etc.*) wheel-base.

empaumer [ãpo'me], *v.t.* to catch *or* strike (*a ball etc.*) in *or* with the palm of the hand; (*fig.*)to get hold of, to grasp, to take possession of.

empêchement [ãpɛʃ'mã], *n.m.* hindrance, obstacle, impediment, objection

empêcher [ãpe'ʃe], *v.t.* to oppose, to prevent; to hinder. **s'empêcher**, *v.r.* (*always in the negative*) to forbear, to refrain from; **je ne peux m'empêcher de rire**, I cannot help laughing.

empeigne [ã'pɛɲ], *n.f.* upper (leather) (*of shoe*).

empenner [ãpɛ'ne], *v.t.* to feather (*arrows*); to fit on (*fins*).

empereur [ã'prœ:r], *n.m.* emperor.

empesage [ãpə'za:ʒ], *n.m.* starching.

empesé [ãpə'ze], *a.* starched; stiff (*of style etc.*), formal.

empeser [ãpə'ze], *v.t.* (*conjug. like* AMENER) to starch.

empester [ãpɛs'te], *v.t.* to infect, to taint; to cause to stink horribly; (*fig.*) to corrupt.

empêtrer [ãpɛ'tre], *v.t.* to entangle; to embarrass. **s'empêtrer**, *v.r.* to become entangled.

emphase [ã'fa:z], *n.f.* grandiloquence; emphasis, stress.

emphatique [ãfa'tik], *a.* bombastic, affected; emphatic.

emplècement [ãpjɛs'mã], *n.m.* yoke (*of blouse*).

empierrement [ãpjɛr'mã], *n.m.* stoning, metalling, surfacing (*a road etc.*).

empierrer [ãpjɛ're], *v.t.* to stone, to metal, to surface (*roads etc.*).

empiétement [ãpjet'mã], *n.m.* encroaching, infringement.

empiéter [ãpje'te], *v.t.* (*conjug. like* CÉDER) to encroach upon, to invade, to trespass upon.—*v.i.* to encroach (*sur*).

empilement [ãpil'mã], *n.m.* piling, stacking.

empiler [ãpi'le], *v.t.* to pile up, to stack.

empire [ã'pi:r], *n.m.* empire, sovereignty, control, authority, dominion; (*fig.*) prestige, sway, mastery.

empirer [ãpi're], *v.t.* to make worse.—*v.i.* to grow worse.

empirique [ãpi'rik], *a.* empiric(al).

empirisme [ãpi'rism], *n.m.* empiricism.

emplacement [ãplas'mã], *n.m.* site, place, piece of ground.

emplâtre [ã'pla:tr], *n.m.* plaster, ointment; (*fig.*) palliative; (*colloq.*) helpless creature.

emplette [ã'plɛt], *n.f.* purchase; **faire des emplettes**, to go shopping.

emplir [ã'pli:r], *v.t.* to fill. **s'emplir**, *v.r.* to fill; to be filled.

emploi [ã'plwa], *n.m.* employ, employment; use, function; situation, post.

employé [ãplwa'je], *a.* employed.—*n.m.* (*fem.* **-ée**) employee, assistant, clerk.

employer [ãplwa'je], *v.t.* (*see Verb Tables*) to employ, to use; to give employment to; to spend, to invest. **s'employer**, *v.r.* to employ oneself, to exert *or* busy oneself; to use one's interest; to be used.

employeur [ãplwa'jœ:r], *n.m.* (*fem.* **-euse**) employer.

emplumer (s') [sãply'me], *v.r.* to become fledged.

empocher [ãpɔ'ʃe], *v.t.* to pocket.

empoignade [ãpɔ'ɲad, ãpwa'ɲad], *n.f.* (*colloq.*) dispute, row, set-to.

empoignant [ãpɔ'ɲã, ãpwa'ɲã], *a.* thrilling, poignant.

empoigner [ãpɔ'ɲe, ãpwa'ɲe], *v.t.* to grasp, to seize. **s'empoigner**, *v.r.* to lay hold of each other, to grapple.

empois [ã'pwa], *n.m.* starch.

empoisonné [ăpwazo′ne], *a.* poisoned; (*fig.*) poisonous.

empoisonner [ăpwazo′ne], *v.t.* to poison; (*fig.*) to infect; to corrupt; to embitter; (*slang*) to bore to death. **s'empoisonner**, *v.r.* to poison oneself.

empoisonneur [ăpwazo′nœːr], *a.* (*fem.* **-euse**) poisonous; (*fig.*) corrupting.—*n.m.* (*fem.* **-euse**) poisoner; (*fig.*) corrupter.

empoissonner [ăpwaso′ne], *v.t.* to stock with fish.

emporté [ăpor′te], *a.* fiery, passionate, hotheaded; runaway, unmanageable.

emportement [ăport′mă], *n.m.* transport, fit of passion, outburst (*of anger, rage etc.*).

emporte-pièce [ăportə′pjɛs], *n.m.* punch (*instrument*), cutting-out machine; *c'est une réponse à l'emporte-pièce*, it is a very cutting answer.

emporter [ăpor′te], *v.t.* to carry away, to take away; to remove (*stains etc.*); to transport (*of emotion etc.*); to entail, to involve; to gain, to obtain. **s'emporter**, *v.r.* to fly into a passion, to flare up; to declaim (*contre*); to bolt (*of horses*).

empotage [ăpo′taːʒ], *n.m.* potting (*of plants*).

empoter [ăpo′te], *v.t.* to pot (*plants*).

empourpré [ăpur′pre], *a.* crimson.

empourprer [ăpur′pre], *v.t.* to color red or purple. **s'empourprer**, *v.r.* to turn red or purple; to flush, to blush.

empreindre [ă′prɛ̃ːdr], *v.t. irr.* (*conjug. like* CRAINDRE) to imprint, to stamp, to impress. **s'empreindre**, *v.r.* to become tinged.

empreinte [ă′prɛ̃ːt], *n.f.* stamp, print, impression; mark; *empreintes digitales*, fingerprints.

empressé [ăprɛ′se], *a.* eager, earnest; assiduous.

empressement [ăprɛs′mă], *n.m.* alacrity, eagerness; haste, hurry.

empresser (s') [săprɛ′se], *v.r.* to be eager (*to*); to crowd, to press.

emprisonnement [ăprizɔn′mă], *n.m.* imprisonment.

emprisonner [ăprizɔ′ne], *v.t.* to imprison, to confine.

emprunt [ă′prœ̃], *n.m.* borrowing; loan.

emprunter [ăprœ̃′te], *v.t.* to borrow; to assume.

emprunteur [ăprœ̃′tœːr], *a.* (*fem.* **-euse**) borrowing.—*n.m.* (*fem.* **-euse**) borrower.

empuantir [ăpɥă′tiːr], *v.t.* to give an ill smell to, to infect.

ému [e′my], *a.* moved, affected.

émulation [emyla′sjɔ̃], *n.f.* emulation, rivalry.

émule [e′myl], *n.* rival, competitor.

émulgent [emyl′ʒă], *a.* (*Physiol.*) emulgent.

émulsif [emyl′sif], *a.* (*fem.* **-sive**) emulsive.

émulsion [emyl′sjɔ̃], *n.f.* emulsion.

en (1) [ă], *prep.* in; to; within; into; at; like, in the form of, as; out of, by, through; from; for, on.

en (2) [ă], *pron. inv.* of him, of her, of it, its, of them, their; from him, by him, about him etc.; thence, from thence; some of it, any.

enamourer (s') [sănamu′re], *v.r.* to fall in love; to be enamored (*de*).

encadrement [ăkadrə′mă], *n.m.* framing, frame; border; (*fig.*) environment.

encadrer [ăka′dre], *v.t.* to frame; to surround; to insert; (*Mil.*) to bracket (*target*);

to officer (*troops*). **s'encadrer**, *v.r.* to be inserted *or* enclosed.

encadreur [ăka′drœːr], *n.m.* (*fem.* **-euse**) picture-frame maker.

encager [ăka′ʒe], *v.t.* (*conjug. like* MANGER) to cage, to put in a cage.

encaissage [ăkɛ′saːʒ], *n.m.* encasing.

encaisse [ă′kɛs], *n.f.* cash in hand; cash balance.

encaissé [ăkɛ′se], *a.* encased; sunk, hollow; steeply *or* deeply embanked.

encaissement [ăkɛs′mă], *n.m.* packing, putting in boxes etc.; embankment; paying in (*of money*).

encaisser [ăkɛ′se], *v.t.* to encase, to pack; to bank, pay in; to collect, to receive (*money*).

encaisseur [ăkɛ′sœːr], *n.m.* (*fem.* **-euse**) cashier.

encan [ă′kă], *n.m.* public auction.

encapuchonner (s') [săkapyʃɔ′ne], *v.r.* to put on a cowl; to wrap one's head up; to arch the neck (*of horses*).

encarter [ăkar′te], *v.t.* to card-index.

en-cas [ă′ka], *n.m. inv.* anything kept for use in emergency; small umbrella; light meal prepared in case of need.

encastrement [ăkastr′mă], *n.m.* fitting, fitting in.

encastrer [ăkas′tre], *v.t.* to fit in, to imbed.

encaustiquage [ăkosti′kaːʒ], *n.m.* waxpolishing.

encavement [ăkav′mă], *n.m.* storing (*in cellar*), cellaring.

encaver [ăka′ve], *v.t.* to put *or* store in a cellar.

enceindre [ă′sɛ̃ːdr], *v.t. irr.* (*conjug. like* CRAINDRE) to surround, to enclose.

enceinte [ă′sɛ̃ːt], *n.f.* circuit, enclosure; (*Fort.*) enceinte. *a.* pregnant

encens [ă′să], *n.m.* incense; (*fig.*) fragrance; flattery.

encensement [ăsăs′mă], *n.m.* incensing; (*fig.*) flattery.

encenser [ăsă′se], *v.t.* to incense; (*fig.*) to flatter.

encenseur [ăsă′sœːr], *n.m.* (*fem.* **-euse**) burner of incense; (*fig.*) flatterer.

encensoir [ăsă′swaːr], *n.m.* censer; (*fig.*) flattery.

encerclement [ăsɛrklə′mă], *n.m.* encircling; (*Polit.*) encirclement.

encercler [ăsɛr′kle], *v.t.* to encircle.

enchaînement [ăʃɛn′mă], *n.m.* chaining, linking; series, connection.

enchaîner [ăʃɛ′ne], *v.t.* to chain up, to bind in chains; (*Cine.*) to fade in; (*fig.*) to restrain; to captivate; to link. **s'enchaîner**, *v.r.* to be connected *or* linked together.

enchanté [ăʃă′te], *a.* enchanted; (*fig.*) charmed, delighted.

enchantement [ăʃăt′mă], *n.m.* enchantment, magic; (*fig.*) charm, delight.

enchanter [ăʃă′te], *v.t.* to enchant; (*fig.*) to fascinate, to charm.

enchanteur [ăʃă′tœːr], *a.* (*fem.* **-eresse**) enchanting, entrancing, captivating.—*n.m.* (*fem.* **-eresse**) enchanter, enchantress, charmer.

enchâsser [ăʃa′se], *v.t.* to enchase; to enshrine; to insert.

enchâssure [ăʃa′syːr], *n.f.* setting, mount; insertion.

enchère

enchère [ɑ̃'ʃɛːr], *n.f.* bid (*at an auction*); auction.

enchérir [ɑ̃ʃe'riːr], *v.t.* to bid for, to outbid; to raise (*prices etc.*).—*v.i.* to rise (*in price*); (*fig.*) to surpass, to outdo; to bid, to outbid (*sur*).

enchérissement [ɑ̃ʃeris'mɑ̃], *n.m.* rise, increase.

enchérisseur [ɑ̃ʃeri'sœːr], *n.m.* bidder (*at an auction*).

enchevêtrement [ɑ̃ʃvɛtrə'mɑ̃], *n.m.* entanglement.

enchevêtrer [ɑ̃ʃve'tre], *v.t.* to halter (*a horse etc.*); to entangle. **s'enchevêtrer**, *v.r.* to get entangled, confused *or* embarrassed.

enclave [ɑ̃'klaːv], *n.f.* enclave, piece of enclosed land.

enclaver [ɑ̃kla've], *v.t.* to enclose, to hem in.

enclenchement [ɑ̃klɑ̃ʃ'mɑ̃], *n.m.* throwing into gear; automatic clutch.

enclin [ɑ̃'klɛ̃], *a.* inclined; prone, addicted, apt, given to.

enclore [ɑ̃'kloːr], *v.t. irr.* (*conjug. like* CLORE) to enclose, to fence in, to take in, to shut in.

enclos [ɑ̃'klo], *n.m.* enclosure, yard; paddock; fencing, wall.

enclume [ɑ̃'klym], *n.f.* anvil.

encoche [ɑ̃'kɔʃ], *n.f.* notch.

encoffrer [ɑ̃kɔ'fre], *v.t.* to shut in a coffer; (*fig.*) to cage.

encoignure [ɑ̃kɔ'ɲyːr], *n.f.* corner, angle (*of a street*); corner piece; corner cupboard.

encollage [ɑ̃kɔ'laːʒ], *n.m.* sizing, gluing; glue, size.

encoller [ɑ̃kɔ'le], *v.t.* to size, to glue.

encolure [ɑ̃kɔ'lyːr], *n.f.* neck and shoulders (*of a horse*); neck-line (*of a garment*); size (*of collars*); (*fig.*) appearance (*of a person*).

encombrant [ɑ̃kɔ̃'brɑ̃], *a.* cumbersome.

encombre [ɑ̃'kɔ̃ːbr], *n.m.* (*now only used after* sans) impediment, hindrance.

encombrement [ɑ̃kɔ̃brə'mɑ̃], *n.m.* obstruction; crowding, congestion (*of traffic*).

encombrer [ɑ̃kɔ̃'bre], *v.t.* to obstruct; to crowd, to throng.

encontre (à l' . . . de) [alɑ̃'kɔ̃ːtrdə], *prep. phr.* against, counter to.

encore [ɑ̃'kɔːr], *adv.* yet, still, as yet; anew, again, once more; further, moreover, besides; even, but, only.

encorner [ɑ̃kɔr'ne], *v.t.* to gore, to toss.

encourageant [ɑ̃kura'ʒɑ̃], *a.* encouraging, cheering.

encouragement [ɑ̃kuraʒ'mɑ̃], *n.m.* encouragement.

encourager [ɑ̃kura'ʒe], *v.t.* (*conjug. like* MANGER) to encourage, to stimulate. **s'encourager**, *v.r.* to encourage each other, to take courage.

encourir [ɑ̃ku'riːr], *v.t. irr.* (*conjug. like* COURIR) to incur (*disgrace, reproach, obligation etc.*).

encrasser [ɑ̃kra'se], *v.t.* to make dirty, to foul. **s'encrasser**, *v.r.* to become dirty.

encre [ɑ̃ːkr], *n.f.* ink.

encrier [ɑ̃kri'e], *n.m.* ink-stand, ink-pot.

encroûté [ɑ̃kru'te], *a.* covered with a crust; (*fig.*) full of prejudices.—*n.m.* (*fem.* -ée) old fogy.

encroûter (s') [sɑ̃kru'te], *v.r.* to crust, to get hard; to become dull, stupid *or* hide-bound.

encuvage [ɑ̃ky'vaːʒ], **encuvement** [ɑ̃kyv'mɑ̃], *n.m.* tubbing.

encuver [ɑ̃ky've], *v.t.* to put into a vat, to tub.

encyclopédie [ɑ̃siklɔpe'di], *n.f.* encyclopaedia.

endémique [ɑ̃de'mik], *a.* endemic.

endenté [ɑ̃dɑ̃'te], *a.* indented.

endenter [ɑ̃dɑ̃'te], *v.t.* to cog, to tooth.

endetter [ɑ̃dɛ'te], *v.t.* to get (*a person*) into debt. **s'endetter**, *v.r.* to run into debt.

endeuiller [ɑ̃dœ'je], *v.t.* to put into mourning; to sadden.

endiablé [ɑ̃dja'ble], *a.* possessed; (*fig.*) devilish.

endiabler [ɑ̃dja'ble], *v.i.* to be furious; **faire endiabler**, to torment.

endiguement [ɑ̃dig'mɑ̃], *n.m.* damming up.

endiguer [ɑ̃di'ge], *v.t.* to dam up, to embank.

endimancher (s') [sɑ̃dimɑ̃'ʃe], *v.r.* to put on one's Sunday best.

endive [ɑ̃'diːv], *n.f.* (*broad-leaved*) chicory.

endoctrinement [ɑ̃dɔktrin'mɑ̃], *n.m.* indoctrination.

endoctriner [ɑ̃dɔktri'ne], *v.t.* to indoctrinate.

endolorir [ɑ̃dɔlɔ'riːr], *v.t.* to make sore; to make (*the heart etc.*) ache. **s'endolorir**, *v.r.* to become sore.

endolorissement [ɑ̃dɔlɔris'mɑ̃], *n.m.* pain, soreness.

endommagement [ɑ̃dɔmaʒ'mɑ̃], *n.m.* loss, injury, damage.

endommager [ɑ̃dɔma'ʒe], *v.t.* (*conjug. like* MANGER) to damage, to injure.

endormeur [ɑ̃dɔr'mœːr], *n.m.* (*fem.* -euse) cajoler, flatterer; bore.

endormi [ɑ̃dɔr'mi], *a.* asleep; sleepy; benumbed.—*n.m.* (*fem.* -e) sleepy-head.

endormir [ɑ̃dɔr'miːr], *v.t. irr.* (*conjug. like* SENTIR) to send to sleep, to rock to sleep; to anesthetize; to wheedle, to deceive; to benumb; to bore. **s'endormir**, *v.r.* to fall asleep.

endos [ɑ̃'do], **endossement** [ɑ̃dɔs'mɑ̃], *n.m.* endorsement.

endosser [ɑ̃dɔ'se], *v.t.* to put on one's back, to put on; to saddle oneself with (*an obligation etc.*); to endorse.

endroit [ɑ̃'drwa], *n.m.* place, spot; point; right side (*of a material*); part, passage (*of a book etc.*).

enduire [ɑ̃'dɥiːr], *v.t. irr.* (*conjug. like* CONDUIRE) to do over, to coat, to smear.

enduit [ɑ̃'dɥi], *n.m.* coating, layer, plaster, glaze, varnish, polish.

endurance [ɑ̃dy'rɑ̃ːs], *n.f.* endurance, fortitude; **épreuve d'endurance**, endurance *or* reliability test.

endurant [ɑ̃dy'rɑ̃], *a.* patient, tolerant.

endurci [ɑ̃dyr'si], *a.* hardened; inured, callous.

endurcir [ɑ̃dyr'siːr], *v.t.* to harden, to toughen, to inure; to render callous. **s'endurcir**, *v.r.* to harden, to grow hard; to become callous.

endurcissement [ɑ̃dyrsis'mɑ̃], *n.m.* hardening, obduracy; callousness.

endurer [ɑ̃dy're], *v.t.* to endure, to bear; to put up with.

énergie [ener'ʒi], *n.f.* energy, strength, vigor, power.

énergique [ener'ʒik], *a.* energetic, vigorous.

134

énergiquement [enɛrʒik'mã], *adv.* energetically, vigorously.

énervant [enɛr'vã], *a.* enervating; debilitating, nerve-racking.

énervé [enɛr've],*a.*nerveless;on edge, fidgety.

énervement [enɛrv'mã], *n.m.* nervous tension.

énerver [enɛr've], *v.t.* to enervate, to debilitate; to weaken; to unnerve; (*fam.*) to get on the nerves. **s'énerver**, *v.r.* to become enervated, unnerved, irritable *or* fidgety.

enfance [ã'fã:s], *n.f.* infancy, childhood; childishness.

enfant [ã'fã], *n.* child; infant, baby; descendant; citizen, native.

enfantement [ãfãt'mã], *n.m.* childbirth.

enfanter [ãfã'te], *v.t.* to bring forth, to bear; (*fig.*) to beget, to give birth to.

enfantillage [ãfãti'ja:ʒ], *n.m.* child's-play, childishness.

enfantin [ãfã'tɛ̃], *a.* infantile, childish.

enfariner [ãfari'ne], *v.t.* to flour, to sprinkle with flour.

enfer [ã'fɛ:r], *n.m.* hell; (*fig.*) torment, misery.

enfermer [ãfɛr'me], *v.t.* to shut in *or* up; to lock up; to enclose; to conceal; to comprise. **s'enfermer**, *v.r.* to lock oneself in.

enficeler [ãfis'le], *v.t.* (*conjug. like* APPELER) to tie with string etc.

enfièvrement [ãfjɛvrɑ'mã], *n.m.* feverishness.

enfilade [ãfi'lad], *n.f.* suite (*of chambers etc.*); string (*of phrases etc.*); (*Mil.*) enfilade.

enfiler [ãfi'le], *v.t.* to thread (*a needle*); to string (*beads*); to pierce; to pass through; (*Mil.*) to enfilade; to slip on (*clothes*). **s'enfiler**, *v.r.* to be threaded; to be pierced; to get involved in.

enfin [ã'fɛ̃], *adv.* at last, finally, at length, after all, lastly; in short, in a word.

enflammé [ãfla'me], *a.* on fire, in flames, ignited.

enflammer [ãfla'me], *v.t.* to set on fire, to kindle; (*fig.*) to incense, to provoke. **s'enflammer**, *v.r.* to catch fire, to blaze; (*fig.*) to be incensed.

enflé [ã'fle], *a.* swollen, puffed up; (*fig.*) bombastic, high-flown (*style etc.*).

enfler [ã'fle], *v.t.* to swell out, to puff up, to distend; (*fig.*) to excite; to exaggerate. **s'enfler**, *v.r.* to swell; to be puffed up.

enflure [ã'fly:r], *n.f.* bloatedness, swelling; bombast.

enfoncé [ãfõ'se], *a.* broken open; sunken; (*pop.*) done for.

enfoncement [ãfõs'mã], *n.m.* breaking in; sinking; recess; (*Paint.*) background.

enfoncer [ãfõ'se], *v.t.* (*conjug. like* COMMENCER) to push *or* drive in, down etc.; to sink; to break in; to get the better of.— *v.i.* to sink, to founder. **s'enfoncer**, *v.r.* to sink; to bury oneself; to plunge; (*fig.*) to fail.

enfoncure [ãfõ'sy:r], *n.f.* cavity, hole, hollow.

enforcir [ãfɔr'si:r], *v.t.* to strengthen.—*v.i.* and **s'enforcir**, *v.r.* to gather strength; to grow stronger.

enfouir [ã'fwi:r], *v.t.* to put *or* bury in the ground; (*fig.*) to hide. **s'enfouir**, *v.r.* to bury oneself (*in an out-of-the-way place etc.*).

enfourcher [ãfur'ʃe], *v.t.* to bestride, to straddle; to pierce with a pitch-fork etc.

enfourchure [ãfur'ʃy:r], *n.f.* fork; crotch.

enfourner [ãfur'ne], *v.t.* to put in the oven. **s'enfourner**, *v.r.* to get into a blind alley, a scrape etc.

enfreindre [ã'frɛ̃:dr], *v.t. irr.* (*conjug. like* CRAINDRE) to infringe, to break, to violate.

enfuir (s') [sã'fɥi:r], *v.r. irr.* (*conjug. like* FUIR) to run away, to escape.

enfumer [ãfy'me], *v.t.* to smoke, to fill with smoke, to smoke (*vermin etc.*) out.

enfûtage [ãfy'ta:ʒ], *n.m.* casking.

enfutailler [ãfyta'je], **enfuter** [ãfy'te], *v.t.* to cask, to barrel, to tun (*wine etc.*).

engagé [ãga'ʒe], *a.* pledged; engaged, enlisted; in action; (*Naut.*) water-logged.

engageant [ãga'ʒã], *a.* engaging, winning.

engagement [ãgaʒ'mã], *n.m.* engagement, commitment; pledging; mortgage; appointment; (*Mil.*) enlisting; action; entry (*for a sporting event*); (*pl.*) liabilities.

engager [ãga'ʒe], *v.t.* (*conjug. like* MANGER) to pledge, to pawn; to engage; to begin; to invite, to induce, to urge; to involve. **s'engager**, *v.r.* to engage oneself, to undertake, to promise; to stand security; to begin; to enter; to enlist; to get involved.

engeance [ã'ʒã:s], *n.f.* breed; brood (*esp. of poultry*).

engelure [ãʒ'ly:r], *n.f.* chilblain.

engendrer [ãʒã'dre], *v.t.* to beget, to engender; (*fig.*) to produce.

engin [ã'ʒɛ̃], *n.m.* machine, engine; snare; tool; *engin téléguidé*, guided missile.

englober [ãglɔ'be], *v.t.* to unite, to put together; (*fig.*) to include, to embrace.

engloutir [ãglu'ti:r], *v.t.* to swallow, to devour. **s'engloutir**, *v.r.* to be swallowed up.

engloutissement [ãglutis'mã], *n.m.* engulfing, swallowing up.

engoncé [ãgõ'se], *a. avoir l'air engoncé*, to look awkward and stiff.

engorgement [ãgɔrʒə'mã], *n.m.* obstruction, stopping up (*of a pipe etc.*); (*Med.*) congestion; (*Econ.*) glut.

engorger [ãgɔr'ʒe], *v.t.* (*conjug. like* MANGER) to obstruct, to block. **s'engorger**, *v.r.* to be obstructed *or* choked up.

engouement *or* **engoûment** [ãgu'mã], *n.m.* (*Med.*) choking, obstruction; (*fig.*) infatuation.

engouer [ã'gwe], *v.t.* to obstruct (*the throat etc.*); (*fig.*) to infatuate. **s'engouer**, *v.r.* to half choke oneself; (*fig.*) to be infatuated.

engouffrer [ãgu'fre], *v.t.* to engulf; (*fig.*) to swallow up. **s'engouffrer**, *v.r.* to be engulfed; to be swallowed up; to blow hard (*of the wind*).

engourdi [ãgur'di], *a.* torpid; benumbed.

engourdir [ãgur'di:r], *v.t.* to benumb; to dull, to enervate. **s'engourdir**, *v.r.* to get benumbed; to become sluggish.

engourdissement [ãgurdis'mã], *n.m.* numbness; torpor, enervation.

engrais [ã'grɛ], *n.m.* manure, fertilizer; fattening (*cattle*).

engraissant [ãgrɛ'sã], *a.* fattening.

engraissement [ãgrɛs'mã], *n.m.* fattening.

engraisser [ãgrɛ'se], *v.t.* to fatten; to manure; (*fig.*) to enrich.—*v.i.* to grow fat; (*fig.*) to thrive. **s'engraisser**, *v.r.* to grow fat *or* stout.

engrenage [ãgrə'na:ʒ], *n.m.* gear, gearing etc.; action of these; (*fig.*) correlation (*of circumstances etc.*).

engrener (1) [ãgrə'ne], *v.t.* (*conjug. like* AMENER) to put corn into (*the mill-hopper*); to feed with corn.

engrener (2) [ãgrə'ne], *v.t.* (*conjug. like* AMENER) (*Mach.*) to throw into gear. **s'engrener**, *v.r.* to work into each other (*of toothed wheels*); to be put in gear.

engrenure [ãgrə'ny:r], *n.f.* engagement of teeth, cogs etc.

engrumeler (s') [sãgrym'le], *v.r.* (*conjug. like* APPELER) to clot, to coagulate.

enhardir [ãar'di:r], *v.t.* to embolden, to encourage. **s'enhardir**, *v.r.* to grow bold.

enherber [ãnɛr'be], *v.t.* to put land under grass.

énigmatique [enigma'tik], *a.* enigmatical.

énigmatiquement [enigmatik'mã], *adv.* enigmatically.

énigme [e'nigm], *n.f.* enigma, riddle.

enivrant [ãni'vrã], *a.* intoxicating.

enivrement [ãnivrə'mã], *n.m.* intoxication; (*fig.*) elation.

enivrer [ãni'vre], *v.t.* to intoxicate, to inebriate; (*fig.*) to elate. **s'enivrer**, *v.r.* to get intoxicated; (*fig.*) to be elated.

enjambée [ãʒã'be], *n.f.* stride.

enjambement [ãʒãb'mã], *n.m.* (*Pros.*) run-on line, enjambment.

enjamber [ãʒã'be], *v.t.* to skip *or* leap over; to stride; (*fig.*) to encroach upon; (*Pros.*) to make enjambment.

enjeu [ã'ʒø], *n.m.* (*pl.* **-eux**) stake (*gaming and fig.*).

enjoindre [ã'ʒwɛ̃:dr], *v.t. irr.* (*conjug. like* CRAINDRE) to enjoin, to charge, to direct, to prescribe.

enjôlement [ãʒɔl'mã], *n.m.* wheedling, coaxing, cajoling.

enjôler [ãʒɔ'le], *v.t.* to coax, to wheedle.

enjôleur [ãʒɔ'lœ:r], *n.m.* (*fem.* **-euse**) wheedler, coaxer.

enjolivement [ãʒɔliv'mã], *n.m.* embellishment, decoration, ornament.

enjoliver [ãʒɔli've], *v.t.* to embellish, to set off.

enjoliveur [ãʒɔli'vœ:r], *n.m.* (*fem.* **-euse**) embellisher.

enjolivure [ãʒɔli'vy:r], *n.f.* (*small*) embellishment.

enjoué [ã'ʒwe], *a.* playful, sprightly, lively, jovial, sportive.

enjouement or **enjoûment** [ãʒu'mã], *n.m.* playfulness, sportiveness, sprightliness.

enlacement [ãlas'mã], *n.m.* lacing, interlacing, entwining.

enlacer [ãla'se], *v.t.* (*conjug. like* COMMENCER) to lace; to entwine; to clasp. **s'enlacer**, *v.r.* to entwine, to be interlaced.

enlaidir [ãlɛ'di:r], *v.t.* to make ugly; to disfigure.—*v.i.* to grow ugly, to be disfigured.

enlaidissement [ãlɛdis'mã], *n.m.* disfigurement.

enlèvement [ãlɛv'mã], *n.m.* carrying off; removal; wiping off; kidnapping.

enlever [ãla've], *v.t.* (*conjug. like* AMENER) to remove, to take off; to carry off; to kidnap; to wipe off; to charm. **s'enlever**, *v.r.* to rise, to be lifted; to come off, to peel off; to come out; to be snapped up (*of goods on sale*); to get into a passion.

enlève-taches [ãlɛv'taʃ], *n.m. inv.* stain remover.

enliasser [ãlja'se], *v.t.* to tie up in a bundle.

enlignement [ãliɲ'mã], *n.m.* alignment.

enligner [ãli'ɲe], *v.t.* to put in line.

enlisement [ãliz'mã], *n.m.* sinking, swallowing up (*in quicksand*).

enliser [ãli'ze], *v.t.* to engulf. **s'enliser**, *v.r.* to be engulfed *or* swallowed up.

enluminer [ãlymi'ne], *v.t.* to color; to illuminate. **s'enluminer**, *v.r.* to rouge, to paint; to flush.

enlumineur [ãlymi'nœ:r], *n.m.* (*fem.* **-euse**) colorer of maps, prints etc.

enluminure [ãlymi'ny:r], *n.f.* coloring; colored print; tinsel (*of style*).

enneigé [ãnɛ'ʒe], *a.* snow-covered.

ennemi [ɛn'mi], *a.* hostile; injurious.—*n.m.* (*fem.* **-e**) enemy, foe.

ennoblir [ãnɔ'bli:r], *v.t.* to dignify, to exalt. **s'ennoblir**, *v.r.* to be ennobled *or* exalted.

ennoblissement [ãnɔblis'mã], *n.m.* ennoblement, exaltation.

ennui [ã'nɥi], *n.m.* trouble, worry; nuisance; boredom.

ennuyer [ãnɥi'je], *v.t.* (*conjug. like* EMPLOYER) to bore, to weary; to pester; (*fig.*) to annoy. **s'ennuyer**, *v.r.* to be bored, to feel dull; to miss.

ennuyeusement [ãnɥijøz'mã], *adv.* tediously, irksomely.

ennuyeux [ãnɥi'jø], *a.* (*fem.* **-euse**) boring, tedious, dull, tiresome; annoying.—*n.m.* (*fem.* **-euse**) tiresome person, bore.

énoncé [enɔ̃'se], *n.m.* statement.

énoncer [enɔ̃'se], *v.t.* (*conjug. like* COMMENCER) to state, to express, to enunciate. **s'énoncer**, *v.r.* to be worded *or* expressed.

énonciatif [enɔ̃sja'tif], *a.* (*fem.* **-tive**) enunciative.

énonciation [enɔ̃sja'sjɔ̃], *n.f.* enunciation, delivery; statement; wording.

enorgueillir [ãnɔrgœ'ji:r], *v.t.* to make proud, to elate. **s'enorgueillir**, *v.r.* to be *or* grow proud of, to be elated, to glory in (*de*).

énorme [e'nɔrm], *a.* enormous, huge.

énormément [enɔrme'mã], *adv.* enormously, beyond measure.

énormité [enɔrmi'te], *n.f.* hugeness, vastness; enormity.

enquérir (s') [sãke'ri:r], *v.r. irr.* (*conjug. like* ACQUÉRIR) to inquire, to make inquiries.

enquête [ã'kɛ:t], *n.f.* inquiry, investigation; inquest.

enquêter [ãkɛ'te], *v.i.* to inquire into a matter (*sur*), to conduct an inquiry.

enquêteur [ãkɛ'tœ:r], *n.m.* (*fem.* **-euse**) investigator.

enraciner [ãrasi'ne], *v.t.* to root; (*fig.*) to implant. **s'enraciner**, *v.r.* to take root.

enragé [ãra'ʒe], *a.* mad, rabid; (*fig.*) enthusiastic.—*n.m.* (*fem.* **-ée**) madman, mad woman; desperate person.

enrageant [ãra'ʒã], *a.* maddening, vexing.

enrager [ãra'ʒe], *v.i.* (*conjug. like* MANGER) to be mad, to go mad; to be enraged, to fume.

enrayage [ãrɛ'ja:ʒ], *n.m.* (*Mil.*) jam (*in rifle*).

enrayement or **enraiement** [ārɛj'mā], *n.m.* skidding, locking.

enrayer (1) [ārɛ'je], *v.t. (conjug. like* PAYER) to put spokes to (*a wheel*); to skid (*a wheel*), to apply brakes to; (*fig.*) to check, to slow up (*an attack*); to stem (*an epidemic*); to jam (*a machine-gun*).

enrayer (2) [ārɛ'je], *v.t. (conjug. like* PAYER) (*Agric.*) to plough the first furrow in.

enrayure (1) [ārɛ'jy:r], *n.f.* drag, skid, lock-chain.

enrayure (2) [ārɛ'jy:r], *n.m.* (*Agric.*) first furrow.

enrégimenter [āreʒimā'te], *v.t.* to form into regiments; (*fig.*) to enroll.

enregistrement [ārəʒistrə'mā], *n.m.* registration, recording; checking(*of luggage*).

enregistrer [ārəʒis'tre], *v.t.* to register, to record; to check(*luggage*).

enregistreur [ārəʒis'trœ:r], *n.m.* registrar; recording machine.

enrêner [ārɛ'ne], *v.t.* to rein in; to tie up by the reins.

enrhumer [āry'me], *v.t.* to give a cold to (*someone*). **s'enrhumer**, *v.r.* to catch a cold.

enrichi [āri'ʃi], *n.m.* (*fem.* **-e**) upstart, parvenu, new rich.

enrichir [āri'ʃi:r], *v.t.* to enrich; (*fig.*) to embellish. **s'enrichir**, *v.r.* to enrich oneself, to thrive.

enrichissement [āriʃis'mā], *n.m.* enrichment; (*fig.*) embellishment.

enrôlement [ārol'mā], *n.m.* enrolment; (*Mil.*) enlistment.

enrôler [āro'le], *v.t.* to enlist; to enroll. **s'enrôler**, *v.r.*to enroll oneself, to enlist.

enroué [ā'rwe], *a.* hoarse, husky.

enrouement [āru'mā], *n.m.* hoarseness, huskiness.

enrouer [ā'rwe], *v.t.* to make hoarse. **s'enrouer**, *v.r.* to become hoarse or husky.

enroulement [ārul'mā], *n.m.* rolling up; (*Arch.*) scroll.

enrouler [āru'le], *v.t.* to roll up, to coil. **s'enrouler**, *v.r.* to roll oneself up; to twine (*of plants etc.*).

enrubanner [āryba'ne], *v.t.* to deck out with ribbons. **s'enrubanner**, *v.r.* to beribbon oneself.

ensablement [āsablə'mā], *n.m.* sand-bank; ballasting; stranding (*of a ship*).

ensabler [āsa'ble], *v.t.* to ballast; to run aground, to strand. **s'ensabler**, *v.r.* to run aground; to sink in sand; to silt up.

ensacher [āsa'ʃe], *v.t.* to put in bags or sacks.

ensanglanter [āsāglā'te], *v.t.* to make bloody, to stain with blood.

enseignant [āsɛ'ɲā], *a.* teaching.—*n.m.* (*pl.*) teachers.

enseigne [ā'sɛɲ], *n.f.* sign, signboard; mark, token; ensign, flag.—*n.m.* (*Navy*) sublieutenant; (*U.S.*) ensign.

enseignement [āsɛɲ'mā], *n.m.* teaching, education; teaching profession.

enseigner [āsɛ'ɲe], *v.t.* to teach, to instruct; to inform, to direct.

ensemble [āsā'bl], *adv.* together, at the same time.—*n.m.* whole, general effect, mass; two- or three-piece (*clothing*); suite (*furniture*); (*Math.*) set.

ensemencement [āsmās'mā], *n.m.* sowing.

ensemencer [āsmā'se], *v.t.* (*conjug. like* COMMENCER) to sow.

enserrer [āsɛ're], *v.t.* to enclose; to lock up; to hem in.

ensevelir [āsə'vli:r], *v.t.* to shroud; (*fig.*) to bury; to swallow up, to entomb; to absorb. **s'ensevelir**, *v.r.* to bury oneself.

ensevelissement [āsəvlis'mā], *n.m.* putting in a shroud; burial.

ensoleillé [āsɔlɛ'je], *a.* sunny.

ensoleiller [āsɔlɛ'je], *v.t.* to light up with sunshine; (*fig.*) to brighten.

ensommeillé [āsɔmɛ'je], *a.* heavy with sleep; (*fig.*) torpid.

ensorceler [āsɔrsə'le], *v.t.* (*conjug. like* APPELER) to bewitch.

ensorceleur [āsɔrsə'lœ:r], *a.* (*fem.* **-euse**) bewitching.—*n.m.* (*fem.* **-euse**) enchanter, enchantress.

ensorcellement [āsɔrsɛl'mā], *n.m.* bewitchment.

ensuite [ā'sɥit], *adv.* after, afterwards, then, in the next place; what then? what next? well!

ensuivre (s') [sā'sɥi:vr], *v.r. irr.* (*conjug. like* SUIVRE) to follow, to result, to ensue.

entacher [āta'ʃe], *v.t.* to sully; to taint; to cast a slur on.

entaille [ā'ta:j], *n.f.* notch; cut; gash; groove.

entailler [āta'je], *v.t.* to notch, to cut.

entamer [āta'me], *v.t.* to make the first cut in; to make an incision in; to broach; to break into.

entartrer (s') [sātar'tre], *v.r.* to scale, to become furred.

entassement [ātas'mā], *n.m.* accumulation; heap, pile; crowding together.

entasser [āta'se], *v.t.* to heap or pile up, to accumulate; to hoard up; to pack together. **s'entasser**, *v.r.* to heap up; to crowd together.

entendement [ātād'mā], *n.m.* understanding; judgment, sense.

entendre [ā'tā:dr], *v.t.* to hear; to understand; to know; to intend; to mean. **s'entendre**, *v.r.* to hear each other; to hear one's own voice; to be heard; to be understood; to understand one another; to act in concert; to come to terms (*avec*); to agree with; to be skilful.

entendu [ātā'dy], *a.* heard; understood; agreed; skilful.

enténébrer [ātene'bre], *v.t.* (*conjug. like* CÉDER) to plunge or wrap in darkness.

entente [ā'tā:t], *n.f.* meaning; skill, judgment; understanding, agreement.

enter [ā'te], *v.t.* to graft upon, to engraft; to join.

entériner [āteri'ne], *v.t.* to ratify, to confirm.

entérique [āte'rik], *a.* enteric.

entérite [āte'rit], *n.f.* enteritis.

enterrement [ātɛr'mā], *n.m.* burial, interment, funeral.

enterrer [ātɛ're], *v.t.* to bury, to inter; (*fig.*) to survive, to outlive; to end. **s'enterrer**, *v.r.* to bury oneself.

en-tête [ā'tɛ:t], *n.m.* (*pl.* **-têtes**) heading, headline.

entêté [ātɛ'te], *a.* stubborn, obstinate.— *n.m.* (*fem.* **-ée**) stubborn person.

137

entêtement [ătet'mã], *n.m.* stubbornness, obstinacy; infatuation.

entêter [ăte'te], *v.t.* to give a headache to; to make giddy, to intoxicate. **s'entêter,** *v.r.* to be stubborn, to persist (*in*); to be infatuated (*de*).

enthousiasme [ătu'zjasm], *n.m.* enthusiasm, rapture, ecstasy.

enthousiasmer [ătuzjas'me], *v.t.* to render enthusiastic, to enrapture. **s'enthousiasmer,** *v.r.* to be enthusiastic, to be in raptures (*de*).

enthousiaste [ătu'zjast], *a.* enthusiastic.—*n.* enthusiast.

entiché [ăti'ʃe], *a.* infatuated, keen on.

entichement [ătiʃ'mã], *n.m.* infatuation, addiction.

enticher [ăti'ʃe], *v.t.* to infatuate. **s'enticher,** *v.r.* to be infatuated with (*de*).

entier [ă'tje], *a.* (*fem.* **-ière**) entire, whole; total; positive.—*n.m.* entirety, totality; (*Arith.*) integral.

entièrement [ătjɛr'mã], *adv.* entirely, wholly.

entité [ăti'te], *n.f.* entity.

entonner [ăto'ne], *v.t.* to tun, to put into casks.

entonner (2) [ăto'ne], *v.t.* to begin to sing, to strike up.

entonnoir [ăto'nwa:r], *n.m.* funnel; shell hole.

entorse [ă'tɔrs], *n.f.* sprain; strain, twist.

entortillage [ătɔrti'ja:ʒ], **entortillement** [ătɔrtij'mã], *n.m.* entanglement; winding, coiling; abstruseness; subterfuge; equivocation.

entortiller [ătɔrti'je], *v.t.* to wrap, to roll round; to distort; to entangle. **s'entortiller,** *v.r.* to wind oneself round; to twine; to be obscure.

entour [ă'tu:r], *n.m.* (*used only in pl. except in the adverbial expression* **à l'entour,** around) environs, adjacent parts.

entourage [ătu'ra:ʒ], *n.m.* frame; entourage; friends, relations, circle, attendants.

entourer [ătu're], *v.t.* to surround; to gather round.

entournure [ătur'ny:r], *n.f.* arm-hole.

entracte [ă'trakt], *n.m.* intermission (*Theat.*); interlude.

entraide [ă'trɛd], *n.f.* (*no pl.*) mutual aid.

entraider (s') or **entr'aider** (s') [sătre'de], *v.r.* to help one another.

entrailles [ă'tra:j], *n.f. pl.* intestines, entrails, bowels; (*fig.*) feelings, tenderness, pity.

entrain [ă'trɛ̃], *n.m.* warmth, heartiness; spirit, animation, life, go.

entraînant [ătre'nã], *a.* captivating, seductive.

entraînement [ătren'mã], *n.m.* enthusiasm, rapture; impulse, temptation; (*Spt.*) coaching, training.

entraîner [ătre'ne], *v.t.* to drag along; to carry away; to win over; to involve; to train.

entraîneur [ătre'nœ:r], *n.m.* (*fem.* **-euse**) trainer (*esp. of horses*); pace-maker; coach (*of teams*).

entrant [ă'trã], *a.* ingoing, incoming.—*n.m.* (*fem.* **-e**) person going or coming in.

entr'apercevoir [ătrapersa'vwa:r], *v.t. irr.* (*conjug. like* RECEVOIR) to catch a quick glimpse of.

entr'appeler (s') [sătra'ple], *v.r.* (*conjug. like* APPELER) to call one another.

entrave [ă'tra:v], *n.f.* clog, fetter, hobble; (*fig.*) hindrance, impediment.

entraver [ătra've], *v.t.* to shackle; to hinder, to thwart.

entre [ă:tr], *prep.* between, betwixt; among, amongst; into.

entrebâillé [ătrəbα'je], *a.* ajar, half-open.

entrebâillement [ătrəbαj'mã], *n.m.* small opening, gap, chink.

entrebâiller [ătrəbα'je], *v.t.* to half-open.

entrechat [ătrə'ʃa], *n.m.* caper in dancing, entrechat.

entrechoquement [ătrəʃɔk'mã], *n.m.* clash, collision, conflict.

entrechoquer (s') [sătrəʃo'ke], *v.r.* to knock, to run or dash against each other.

entre-clos [ătrə'klo], *a.* half-closed; half-drawn.

entr'éclos [ătre'klo], *a.* half-opened (*flower*).

entrecôte [ătrə'ko:t], *n.f.* steak cut from between the ribs.

entrecoupé [ătrəku'pe], *a.* broken (*of words, speech etc.*).

entrecouper [ătrəku'pe], *v.t.* to intersect; to interrupt; to intersperse.

entrecroisement [ătrəkrwaz'mã], *n.m.* intersection, crossing.

entrecroiser [ătrəkrwa'ze], *v.t.* to intersect. **s'entrecroiser,** *v.r.* to cross one other, to intersect.

entre-deux [ătrə'dø], *n.m. inv.* partition; insertion (*of lace etc.*).

entrée [ă'tre], *n.f.* entry, entrance; mouth; reception; beginning; first course.

entrefaites [ătrə'fɛt], *n.f. pl.* interval, meantime; **sur ces entrefaites,** meanwhile.

entrefilet [ătrəfi'lɛ], *n.m.* (short) paragraph, note (*in a newspaper*).

entregent [ătrə'ʒã], *n.m.* tact, cleverness (*in dealing with people*).

entrelacement [ătrəlas'mã], *n.m.* interlacing, interweaving, intertwining.

entrelacer [ătrəla'se], *v.t.* to interlace, to intertwine. **s'entrelacer,** *v.r.* to entwine, to twist round each other.

entrelardé [ătrəlar'de], *a.* interlarded; streaky.

entrelarder [ătrəlar'de], *v.t.* to lard.

entremêlement [ătrəmɛl'mã], *n.m.* intermixing, intermingling.

entremêler [ătrəmɛ'le], *v.t.* to intermingle, to intermix. **s'entremêler,** *v.r.* to intermingle, to meddle.

entremets [ătrə'mɛ], *n.m. inv.* side dish, sweet.

entremetteur [ătrəme'tœ:r], *n.m.* (*fem.* **-euse**) go-between, mediator.

entremettre (s') [sătrə'mɛtr], *v.r. irr.* (*conjug. like* METTRE) to interpose; to interfere, to meddle.

entremise [ătrə'mi:z], *n.f.* intervention, mediation.

entrepont [ătrə'põ], *n.m.* (*Naut.*) between decks; **passagers d'entrepont,** steerage passengers.

entreposer [ătrəpo'ze], *v.t.* to store, to warehouse; to put in bond.

entrepositaire [ătrəpozi'tɛ:r], *n.* bonder; depositor (*of goods*).

entrepôt [ătrə'po], *n.m.* bonded warehouse, store; mart, emporium, depot.

entreprenant [ātrəprə'nā], *a.* enterprising, adventurous; daring, bold.

entreprendre [ātrə'prā:dr], *v.t. irr. (conjug. like* PRENDRE) to undertake, to attempt; to contract for *or* to; to venture.—*v.i.* to encroach, to infringe (*sur*).

entrepreneur [ātrəprə'nœ:r], *n.m.* (*fem.* **-euse**) contractor; master builder; *entrepreneur de pompes funèbres,* undertaker.

entreprise [ātrə'pri:z], *n.f.* enterprise, undertaking; concern, company.

entrer [ā'tre], *v.i.* (*with aux.* ÊTRE) to enter, to come *or* go in; to run into.

entre-rail [ātrə'ra:j], *n.m.* (*pl.* **-rails**) (*Rail.*) gauge.

entresol [ātrə'sɔl], *n.m.* mezzanine, entresol (*rooms between the ground floor and the first floor*).

entre-temps [ātrə'tā], *n.m. inv.* interval; *dans l'entre-temps,* meanwhile.—*adv.* meanwhile.

entretenir [ātrət'ni:r], *v.t. irr. (conjug. like* TENIR) to hold together, to keep up, to keep in good order; to maintain; to support; to entertain. **s'entretenir,** *v.r.* to be kept up, to be maintained; to subsist; to converse.

entretien [ātrə'tjɛ̃], *n.m.* maintenance, servicing (*of car etc.*); preservation; living, livelihood; conversation, interview, conference.

entrevoir [ātrə'vwa:r], *v.t. irr. (conjug. like* VOIR) to catch a glimpse of; to foresee confusedly.

entrevue [ātrə'vy], *n.f.* interview.

entr'ouvert [ātru'vɛ:r], *a.* partly open, ajar; gaping.

entr'ouvrir [ātru'vri:r], *v.t. irr. (conjug. like* OUVRIR) to open a little, to half-open. **s'entr'ouvrir,** *v.r.* to be ajar; to open up.

énumérateur [enymera'tœ:r], *n.m.* (*fem.* **-trice**) enumerator.

énumératif [enymera'tif], *a.* (*fem.* **-tive**) enumerative.

énumération [enymera'sjɔ̃], *n.f.* enumeration.

énumérer [enyme're], *v.t. (conjug. like* CÉDER) to enumerate, to count, to reckon.

envahir [āva'i:r], *v.t.* to invade, to overrun; to encroach upon.

envahissant [āvai'sā], *a.* invading, encroaching.

envahissement [āvais'mā], *n.m.* invasion, overrunning; encroachment.

envahisseur [āvai'sœ:r], *a.* (*fem.* **-euse**) invading, encroaching.—*n.m.* (*fem.* **-euse**) invader.

envaser [āva'ze], *v.t.* to fill up *or* choke with silt. **s'envaser,** *v.r.* to stick fast in the mud; to silt up.

enveloppe [ā'vlɔp], *n.f.* wrapper, cover; envelope; exterior; tire casing.

enveloppement [āvlɔp'mā], *n.m.* enveloping, wrapping up.

envelopper [āvlɔ'pe], *v.t.* to envelop, to wrap up, to cover; to surround; to disguise. **s'envelopper,** *v.r.* to cover *or* wrap oneself up.

envenimement [āvnima'mā], *n.m.* poisoning; aggravation (*of a quarrel*).

envenimer [āvni'me], *v.t.* to poison; to inflame, to exasperate. **s'envenimer,** *v.r.* to be envenomed; to fester, to rankle.

envergure [āvɛr'gy:r], *n.f.* spread (*of sail*); spread, span (*of a bird's wings, of an airplane*).

envers [ā'vɛ:r], *prep.* towards, to (*in respect of*).—*n.m.* wrong side, reverse side, back; *à l'envers,* on the wrong side, inside out.

envi (à l') [alā'vi], *adv. phr.* emulously, vying with each other.

enviable [ā'vjabl], *a.* enviable, to be envied.

envie [ā'vi], *n.f.* envy; desire, longing; birthmark; *avoir envie de,* to have a mind to, to long for, to feel like.

envier [ā'vje], *v.t.* to envy; to long for; to grudge.

envieux [ā'vjø], *a.* and *n.m.* (*fem.* **-euse**) envious, jealous (person).

environ [āvi'rɔ̃], *adv.* about, nearly, thereabouts.—*n.m.* (*pl.*) environs, vicinity, neighborhood.

environnant [āvirɔ'nā], *a.* surrounding.

environner [āvirɔ'ne], *v.t.* to surround, to stand round, to encircle, to enclose.

envisager [āviza'ʒe], *v.t. (conjug. like* MANGER) to look, to stare in the face; to face; to consider, to envisage.

envoi [ā'vwa], *n.m.* sending (*of thing sent*); packet, parcel, consignment, shipment; (*Pros.*) envoy.

envol [ā'vɔl], *n.m.* taking wing (*of birds*), taking off (*of airplanes*), start; *piste d'envol,* runway.

envolée [āvɔ'le], *n.f.* flight; (*fig.*) élan.

envoler (s') [sāvɔ'le], *v.r.* to fly away; to take off; (*fig.*) to be carried off (*by the wind etc.*); (*fig.*) to disappear.

envoûtement [āvut'mā], *n.m.* spell, magical charm.

envoûter [āvu'te], *v.t.* to cast a spell on (*someone*).

envoyé [āvwa'je], *n.m.* (*fem.* **-ée**) envoy, delegate, messenger; *envoyé spécial* (*of a paper*), special correspondent.

envoyer [āvwa'je], *v.t. irr.* to send, to forward, to dispatch.

envoyeur [āvwa'jœ:r], *n.m.* (*fem.* **-euse**) sender.

enzyme [ā'ʒim], *n.f.* enzyme.

éon [e'ɔ̃], *n.m.* eon.

épagneul [epa'nœl], *n.m.* spaniel.

épais [e'pɛ], *a.* thick, dense; thickset; (*fig.*) dull, gross.—*adv.* thick, thickly.

épaisseur [epɛ'sœ:r], *n.f.* thickness, density; stoutness; dullness.

épaissir [epɛ'si:r], *v.t.* to thicken.—*v.i.* and **s'épaissir,** *v.r.* to become thick, to grow big; to become heavy.

épaississement [epɛsis'mā], *n.m.* thickening.

épanchement [epā'ʃmā], *n.m.* pouring out, discharge; (*fig.*) outpouring (*emotion etc.*).

épancher [epā'ʃe], *v.t.* to pour out, to shed; to discharge. **s'épancher,** *v.r.* to be discharged, to overflow; to open one's heart.

épanchoir [epā'ʃwa:r], *n.m.* outlet, overflow.

épandre [e'pā:dr], *v.t.* to scatter, to strew; to shed (*light etc.*). **s'épandre,** *v.r.* to spread; (*fig.*) to stretch (*of a sheet of water etc.*).

épanoui [epa'nwi], *a.* in full bloom; (*fig.*) beaming.

épanouir [epa'nwi:r], *v.t.* to cause to open *or* expand; (*fig.*) to gladden. **s'épanouir,** *v.r.* to blossom, to open (*of flowers*); to brighten up (*of the face etc.*).

chanter [ʃɑ̃'te], *v.t.* to extol, to praise, to celebrate; to sing.—*v.i.* to sing; to chirp, to warble, to crow; *cela vous chante-t-il?* how do you like the idea ? **se chanter,** *v.r.* to be sung.

chanterelle [ʃɑ̃'trɛl], *n.f.* first string of a violin etc.; decoy bird.

chanteur [ʃɑ̃'tœːr], *a.* (*fem.* **-euse**) singing.— *n.m.* (*fem.* **-euse**) singer, vocalist.

chantier [ʃɑ̃'tje], *n.m.* timber-yard, wood-yard; stone-yard; dockyard; site; (*C*) shanty, lumber camp.

chantonner [ʃɑ̃tɔ'ne], *v.t.*, *v.i.* to hum.

chantourner [ʃɑ̃tur'ne], *v.t.* to cut in profile; *scie à chantourner,* bow saw.

chantre [ʃɑ̃ːtr], *n.m.* singer, *esp.* a chorister; precentor, lay clerk; (*fig.*) songster (*of birds*).

chanvre [ʃɑ̃ːvr], *n.m.* hemp.

chanvreux [ʃɑ̃'vrø], *a.* (*fem.* **-euse**) hempen.

chaos [ka'o], *n.m.* chaos; (*fig.*) confusion, disorder.

chaotique [kao'tik], *a.* chaotic.

chaparder [ʃapar'de], *v.t.* (*slang*) to steal, to scrounge.

chape [ʃap], *n.f.* cope (*ecclesiastical vestment*); tread (*of a tire*).

chapeau [ʃa'po], *n.m.* (*pl.* **-eaux**) hat; (*Mech. etc.*) cap; *un coup de chapeau,* a bow.

chapelain [ʃa'plɛ̃], *n.m.* chaplain.

chapelet [ʃa'plɛ], *n.m.* rosary, beads; (*Arch. etc.*) chaplet; *chapelet de bombes,* stick of bombs; *chapelet d'oignons,* string of onions.

chapelier [ʃapə'lje], *n.m.* (*fem.* **-ière**) hatter.

chapelle [ʃa'pɛl], *n.f.* chapel, coterie, school (*of literature etc.*); church plate; living.

chapellenie [ʃapɛl'ni], *n.f.* chaplaincy.

chapellerie [ʃapɛl'ri], *n.f.* hat-making; hat trade, shop *or* business.

chapelure [ʃa'plyːr], *n.f.* grated bread-crumbs.

chaperon [ʃa'prɔ̃], *n.m.* hood; (*fig.*) chaperon; *Le Petit Chaperon Rouge,* Little Red Riding Hood.

chaperonner [ʃapro'ne], *v.t.* to cope (*a wall*); (*fig.*) to chaperon.

chapiteau [ʃapi'to], *n.m.* (*pl.* **-eaux**) capital (*of column etc.*); cornice (*of a wardrobe etc.*); big top (*circus*).

chapitre [ʃa'pitr], *n.m.* chapter (*of a book, of knights, of a cathedral*); subject matter of discourse.

chapitrer [ʃapi'tre], *v.t.* to reprimand, to rebuke.

chapon [ʃa'pɔ̃], *n.m.* capon; sop in broth.

chaponner [ʃapo'ne], *v.t.* to caponize.

chaque [ʃak], *a.* each, every.

char [ʃaːr], *n.m.* chariot, carriage, vehicle; *char d'assaut* (*Mil.*) tank.

charabia [ʃara'bja], *n.m.* gibberish.

charade [ʃa'rad], *n.f.* charade.

charançon [ʃarɑ̃'sɔ̃], *n.m.* weevil.

charbon [ʃar'bɔ̃], *n.m.* coal, charcoal; (*pl.*) embers; (*Path.*) anthrax; (*Chem.*) carbon.

charbonnée [ʃarbo'ne], *n.f.* piece of grilled meat; charcoal drawing.

charbonner [ʃarbo'ne], *v.t.* to char; to black with coal. **se charbonner,** *v.r.* to be charred, to burn black.

charbonnerie [ʃarbon'ri], *n.f.* coal depot.

charbonneux [ʃarbo'nø], *a.* (*fem.* **-euse**) coaly; affected *or* infected with anthrax.

charbonnier [ʃarbo'nje], *n.m.* (*fem.* **-ière**) charcoal burner; coal man.—*n.m.* coal heaver; coal hole; (*Naut.*) collier.—*n.f.* (**-ière**) charcoal kiln; coal scuttle; (*Orn.*) great tit.

charcuter [ʃarky'te], *v.t.* to hack and hew (*meat*); to hack, to butcher (*of a surgeon*).

charcuterie [ʃarky'tri], *n.f.* pork-butcher's meat; pork-butcher's business *or* shop.

charcutier [ʃarky'tje], *n.m.* (*fem.* **-ière**) pork-butcher; (*colloq.*) sawbones.

chardon [ʃar'dɔ̃], *n.m.* thistle; spikes (*on a wall or railing*).

chardonneret [ʃardɔn're], *n.m.* goldfinch.

charge [ʃarʒ], *n.f.* pack; load; expense, cost; accusation; post, employment; care, custody; charge, onset; *à charge de revanche,* provided that I may return the favor.

chargé [ʃar'ʒe], *a.* loaded, burdened.

chargement [ʃarʒə'mɑ̃], *n.m.* cargo, freight; bill of lading; load; charging (*of a battery*).

charger [ʃar'ʒe], *v.t.* (*conjug. like* MANGER) to load, to charge; to burden; to charge with; to register (*a letter*). **se charger,** *v.r.* to take upon oneself, to saddle oneself with (*de*).

chargeur [ʃar'ʒœːr], *n.m.* loader, shipper; stoker; (*Phot., Cine.*) cassette.

chariot [ʃa'rjo], *n.m.* wagon, go-cart; (*Mach.*) truck, trolley.

charitable [ʃari'tabl], *a.* charitable.

charitablement [ʃaritablə'mɑ̃], *adv.* charitably.

charité [ʃari'te], *n.f.* charity; benevolence, alms.

charivari [ʃariva'ri], *n.m.* rough music; hubbub, clatter.

charlatan [ʃarla'tɑ̃], *n.m.* charlatan, mountebank, quack.

charlatanisme [ʃarlata'nism], *n.m.* quackery, charlatanism.

charlot [ʃar'lo], *n.m.* (*Orn.*) curlew.

charmant [ʃar'mɑ̃], *a.* charming, delightful.

charme (1) [ʃarm], *n.m.* charm; spell, enchantment.

charme (2) [ʃarm], *n.m.* (*Bot.*) hornbeam.

charmer [ʃar'me], *v.t.* to charm, to enchant, to bewitch, to fascinate, to captivate, to delight.

charmeur [ʃar'mœːr], *n.m.* (*fem.* **-euse**) charmer, enchanter; bewitching woman, enchantress.

charmille [ʃar'miːj], *n.f.* hedge of young hornbeam; bower, arbor.

charnel [ʃar'nɛl], *a.* (*fem.* **-elle**) carnal; sensual (*person*).

charnellement [ʃarnɛl'mɑ̃], *adv.* carnally.

charnier [ʃar'nje], *n.m.* charnel house.

charnière [ʃar'njɛːr], *n.f.* hinge; joint, articulation.

charnu [ʃar'ny], *a.* fleshy, plump; pulpy (*of fruits*).

charogne [ʃa'rɔɲ], *n.f.* carrion; (*pop.*) blackguard; slut.

charpente [ʃar'pɑ̃ːt], *n.f.* frame, framework.

charpenter [ʃarpɑ̃'te], *v.t.* to square (*timber*); (*fig.*) to frame, to construct.

charpenterie [ʃarpɑ̃'tri], *n.f.* carpentry, carpenter's work *or* trade.

épanouissement [epanwis'mā], *n.m.* blossoming, opening (*of flowers*); (*fig.*) brightness, glow.

épargnant [epar'nā], *a.* sparing, saving; parsimonious.—*n.m.* (*fem.* **-e**) small investor.

épargne [e'parɲ], *n.f.* saving, thrift; parsimony; **caisse d'épargne**, savings bank.

épargner [epar'ne], *v.t.* to save; to spare; to economize.

éparpillement [eparpij'mā], *n.m.* scattering, dispersion.

éparpiller [eparpi'je], *v.t.* to scatter; to spread, to disperse; to squander.

épars [e'pa:r], *a.* scattered, dispersed, sparse; dishevelled (*of hair*).

épaté [epa'te], *a.* flat (*of noses*); (*fam.*) amazed.

épaule [e'po:l], *n.f.* shoulder.

épaulement [epol'mā], *n.m.* shoulder; (*Naut.*) bows; (*Fort.*) breast-work.

épauler [epo'le], *v.t.* to splay the shoulder (*a horse etc.*); to bring (*a rifle*) to the shoulder.

épaulette [epo'lɛt], *n.f.* shoulder strap; epaulet.

épave [e'pa:v], *n.f.* wreck; flotsam, jetsam; waif.

épée [e'pe], *n.f.* sword; (*fig.*) brand, steel.

épeler [e'ple], *v.t.* (*conjug. like* APPELER) to spell.

épellation [epɛla'sjɔ̃], *n.f.* spelling.

éperdu [epɛr'dy], *a.* distracted, bewildered.

éperdument [epɛrdy'mā], *adv.* madly, distractedly.

éperon [e'prɔ̃], *n.m.* spur; (*Arch.*) buttress, starling (*of a bridge etc.*); (*Naut.*) prow.

éperonné [epro'ne], *a.* spurred.

éperonner [epro'ne], *v.t.* to spur; to urge forward.

éperonnière [epro'nje:r], *n.f.* (*Bot.*) larkspur.

épervier [epɛr'vje], *n.m.* sparrow hawk; casting net.

épeuré [epø're], *a.* scared.

éphélide [efe'lid], *n.f.* sunburn; freckle.

éphémère [efe'mɛ:r], *a.* ephemeral, short-lived.—*n.m.* ephemera, May fly.

épi [e'pi], *n.m.* ear of corn; (*Rail.*) system of marshalling tracks, spur tracks.

épice [e'pis], *n.f.* spice.

épicé [epi'se], *a.* spiced; seasoned.

épicer [epi'se], *v.t.* (*conjug. like* COMMENCER) to spice.

épicerie [epi'sri], *n.f.* spices; grocery.

épicier [epi'sje], *n.m.* (*fem.* **-ière**) grocer.

épicurien [epiky'rjɛ̃], *a.* (*fem.* **-enne**) epicurean, voluptuous.—*n.m.* (*fem.* **-enne**) epicure.

épicurisme [epiky'rism], *n.m.* epicureanism, epicurism.

épidémie [epide'mi], *n.f.* epidemic.

épidémique [epide'mik], *a.* epidemic.

épiderme [epi'dɛrm], *n.m.* epidermis, cuticle.

épidermique [epidɛr'mik], *a.* epidermic, epidermal.

épier (1) [e'pje], *v.i.* to ear (*of grain*).

épier (2) [e'pje], *v.t.* to watch; to spy upon; to lie in wait for.

épieu [e'pjø], *n.m.* (*pl.* **-eux**) boar spear, hunting pole.

épigrammatique [epigrama'tik], *a.* epigrammatical.

épigrammatiste [epigrama'tist], *n.* epigrammatist.

épigramme [epi'gram], *n.f.* epigram.

épigraphe [epi'graf], *n.f.* epigraph.

épilation [epila'sjɔ̃], *n.f.* depilation.

épilatoire [epila'twa:r], *a.* depilatory.

épilepsie [epilɛp'si], *n.f.* epilepsy.

épileptique [epilɛp'tik], *a.* and *n.* epileptic.

épiler [epi'le], *v.t.* to depilate. **s'épiler**, *v.r.* to pluck out one's hairs.

épileur [epi'lœ:r], *n.m.* (*fem.* **-euse**) depilator (*person*).

épilogue [epi'lɔg], *n.m.* epilogue.

épiloguer [epilɔ'ge], *v.t.* to censure, to criticize.—*v.i.* to carp, to find fault.

épilogueur [epilɔ'gœ:r], *a.* (*fem.* **-euse**) fault-finding.—*n.m.* (*fem.* **-euse**) critic, fault-finder, carper.

épiloir [epi'lwa:r], *n.m.* tweezers.

épinaie [epi'nɛ], *n.f.* brake, thorny thicket.

épinard [epi'na:r], *n.m.* spinach.

épine [e'pin], *n.f.* thorn, prickle; (*fig.*) obstacle, difficulty; (*Anat.*) spine.

épinette [epi'nɛt], *n.f.* *spinet; (*Bot.*) spruce.

épineux [epi'nø], *a.* (*fem.* **-euse**) thorny, prickly; (*fig.*) irritable; ticklish, intricate.

épingle [e'pɛ̃gl], *n.f.* pin; scarf pin, breast pin.

épinglé [epɛ̃'gle], *a.* pinned; corded, terry.—*n.m.* terry velvet.

épingler [epɛ̃'gle], *v.t.* to pin.

épinglier [epɛ̃'glje], *n.m.* pin tray; (*fem.* **-ière**) pin maker.

épinière [epi'nje:r], *a.* (*Anat.*) spinal.

Épiphanie [epifa'ni], *n.f.* Epiphany.

épique [e'pik], *a.* epic(al).

épiscopal [episkɔ'pal], *a.* (*m.pl.* **-aux**) episcopal.

épiscopalien [episkɔpa'ljɛ̃], *a.* and *n.m.* (*fem.* **-enne**) episcopalian.

épiscopat [episkɔ'pa], *n.m.* episcopate, episcopacy.

épisode [epi'zɔd], *n.m.* episode.

épistolaire [episto'lɛ:r], *a.* epistolary.

épitaphe [epi'taf], *n.f.* epitaph.

épithète [epi'tɛt], *n.f.* epithet.

épitomé [epito'me], *n.m.* epitome, abridgment.

épître [e'pi:tr], *n.f.* epistle, letter, missive.

éploré [eplɔ're], *a.* in tears, distressed.

épluchage [eply'ʃa:3], **épluchement** [eplyʃ'mā], *n.m.* cleaning; picking; peeling.

éplucher [eply'ʃe], *v.t.* to pick; to clean; to peel; (*fig.*) to sift.

éplucheur [eply'ʃœ:r], *n.m.* (*fem.* **-euse**) picker; fault-finder, hair-splitter.

épluchures [eply'ʃy:r], *n.f. pl.* parings, peelings.

épointé [epwɛ̃'te], *a.* blunt (*pencil, needle*).

épointement [epwɛ̃t'mā], *n.m.* bluntness.

épointer [epwɛ̃'te], *v.t.* to break the point off, to blunt. **s'épointer**, *v.r.* to have its point broken off.

éponge [e'pɔ̃:3], *n.f.* sponge.

épongeage [epɔ̃'3a:3], *n.m.* sponging.

éponger [epɔ̃'3e], *v.t.* (*conjug. like* MANGER) to sponge.

épopée [epɔ'pe], *n.f.* epic.

époque [e'pɔk], *n.f.* epoch, period, era; time.

époumoner [epumɔ'ne], *v.t.* to tire the lungs of, to exhaust. **s'époumoner**, *v.r.* to tire one's lungs; (*fig.*) to shout oneself hoarse.

épouse [e'pu:z], *n.f.* spouse, bride, wife.

épouser [epu'ze], *v.t.* to marry; to wed; (*fig.*) to take up. **s'épouser**, *v.r.* to marry (*each other*).

époussetage [epus'ta:ʒ], *n.m.* dusting.
épousseter [epus'te], *v.t.* (*conjug. like* AP-PELER) to dust.
époussette [epu'set], *n.f.* dusting brush, duster.
épouvantable [epuvɑ̃'tabl], *a.* frightful, dreadful, horrible, appalling.
épouvantablement [epuvɑ̃tablə'mɑ̃], *adv.* frightfully; dreadfully.
épouvantail [epuvɑ̃'ta:j], *n.m.* scarecrow; (*fig.*) bugbear.
épouvante [epu'vɑ̃:t], *n.f.* terror, fright; dismay.
épouvanter [epuvɑ̃'te], *v.t.* to terrify, to frighten. **s'épouvanter**, *v.r.* to be frightened *or* terrified.
époux [e'pu], *n.m.* husband, bridegroom; (*pl.*) married couple.
épreindre [e'prɛ̃:dr], *v.t. irr.* (*conjug. like* CRAINDRE) to squeeze out, to press.
éprendre (s') [se'prɑ̃:dr], *v.r. irr.* (*conjug. like* PRENDRE) to fall in love (*de*).
épreuve [e'prœ:v], *n.f.* proof, test; ordeal; examination; (*Print.*) proof sheet; (*Phot.*) print.
épris [e'pri], *a.* in love, taken with.
éprouvé [epru've], *a.* tried, tested; stricken with misfortune.
éprouver [epru've], *v.t.* to try, to test; to put to the proof; (*fig.*) to feel, to experience.
éprouvette [epru'vet], *n.f.* gauge; test tube; eprouvette (*for testing gunpowder*); (*Surg.*) probe.
épuisable [epɥi'zabl], *a.* exhaustible.
épuisement [epɥiz'mɑ̃], *n.m.* exhaustion, draining; enervation.
épuiser [epɥi'ze], *v.t.* to exhaust, to drain; to use up; to tire out, to wear out. **s'épuiser**, *v.r.* to be exhausted; to use up one's strength.
épuisette [epɥi'zet], *n.f.* landing-net; scoop.
épurateur [epyra'tœ:r], *a.* (*fem.* **-trice**) purifying.—*n.m.* purifier.
épuratif [epyra'tif], *a.* (*fem.* **-tive**) purifying, refining.
épuration [epyra'sjɔ̃], *n.f.* purification; refining; (*Polit.*) purge.
épuratoire [epyra'twa:r], *a.* purifying.
épurement [epyr'mɑ̃], *n.m.* purifying.
épurer [epy're], *v.t.* to purify; to clarify; to refine; to purge. **s'épurer**, *v.r.* to be purified, to become pure.
équanime [ekwa'nim], *a.* even-tempered.
équanimité [ekwanimi'te], *n.f.* equanimity.
équarrir [eka'ri:r], *v.t.* to square; to cut up (*a carcass*).
équarrissage [ekari'sa:ʒ], **équarrissement** [ekaris'mɑ̃], *n.m.* squaring; squareness; flaying and cutting up (*of horses etc.*).
équarrisseur [ekari'sœ:r], *n.m.* knacker.
Équateur [ekwa'tœ:r], **l'**, *m.* Ecuador.
équateur [ekwa'tœ:r], *n.m.* equator.
équation [ekwa'sjɔ̃], *n.f.* equation.
équatorial [ekwatɔ'rjal], *a.* (*m. pl.* **-aux**) equatorial.
équatorien [ekwatɔ'rjɛ̃], *a.* (*fem.* **-enne**) Ecuadorean.—*n.m.* (**Équatorien**, *fem.* **-enne**) Ecuadorean (*person*).
équerre [e'ke:r], *n.f.* square, set-square.
équerrer [eke're], *v.t.* to square, to bevel.
équestre [e'kestr], *a.* equestrian.

équilibre [eki'libr], *n.m.* equilibrium, poise, balance; (*Hist.*) balance of power.
équilibrer [ekili'bre], *v.t.* to equilibrate, to balance.
équilibriste [ekili'brist], *n.* tight-rope walker, acrobat.
équin [e'kɛ̃], *a.* equine; *pied équin*, club foot.
équinoxe [eki'nɔks], *n.m.* equinox.
équinoxial [ekinɔk'sjal], *a.* (*m. pl.* **-aux**) equinoctial.
équipage [eki'pa:ʒ], *n.m.* equipage; carriage; dress; gear, tackle; personnel, crew.
équipe [e'kip], *n.f.* train of boats; gang (*of workmen etc.*); team (*of sportsmen*).
équipement [ekip'mɑ̃], *n.m.* outfit, fitting out; equipment.
équiper [eki'pe], *v.t.* to equip, to fit out; to furnish; to man. **s'équiper**, *v.r.* to fit oneself out; to rig oneself out.
équitable [eki'tabl], *a.* equitable, just, fair.
équitablement [ekitablə'mɑ̃], *adv.* equitably, justly, fairly.
équitation [ekita'sjɔ̃], *n.f.* horsemanship, riding.
équité [eki'te], *n.f.* equity, fairness.
équivalence [ekiva'lɑ̃:s], *n.f.* equivalence.
équivalent [ekiva'lɑ̃], *a.* equivalent; tantamount (to).—*n.m.* equivalent.
équivaloir [ekiva'lwa:r], *v.i. irr.* (*conjug. like* VALOIR) to be equivalent, to be tantamount (*à*).
équivoque [eki'vɔk], *a.* equivocal, ambiguous; doubtful.—*n.f.* equivocation, ambiguity; evasion.
équivoquer [ekivɔ'ke], *v.t.* to equivocate, to speak ambiguously, to quibble.
érable [e'rabl], *n.m.* maple, maple tree.
éradication [eradika'sjɔ̃], *n.f.* eradication.
érafler [era'fle], *v.t.* to scratch slightly, to graze.
éraflure [era'fly:r], *n.f.* slight scratch, graze.
éraillé [erɑ'je], *a.* frayed; wrinkled; bloodshot (*of the eyes*); raucous, hoarse (*of the voice*).
éraillement [erɑj'mɑ̃], *n.m.* eversion of the eyelids; fraying; huskiness.
érailler [erɑ'je], *v.t.* to unravel; to fray. **s'érailler**, *v.r.* to fray; to become bloodshot (*of the eyes*); to become husky (*of the voice*).
éraillure [erɑ'jy:r], *n.f.* fret, fraying; scratch.
ère [e:r], *n.f.* era, epoch.
érection [erek'sjɔ̃], *n.f.* erection, erecting.
éreinter [erɛ̃'te], *v.t.* to break the back (*of*); to tire out; to beat unmercifully; (*fig.*) to slate, to lash (*satire etc.*). **s'éreinter**, *v.r.* to break one's back, to tire oneself out, to drudge.
érésipèle [ERYSIPÈLE].
ergot [ɛr'go], *n.m.* spur (*of certain birds etc.*); catch, stop (*of machine*).
ergotage [ɛrgɔ'ta:ʒ], **ergotement** [ɛrgɔt'mɑ̃] *n.m.*, **ergoterie** [ɛrgɔ'tri], *n.f.* cavilling, quibbling.
ergoter [ɛrgɔ'te], *v.i.* (*colloq.*) to cavil; to wrangle.
ergoteur [ɛrgɔ'tœ:r], *a.* (*fem.* **-euse**) cavilling.—*n.m.* (*fem.* **-euse**) caviller, quibbler.
ériger [eri'ʒe], *v.t.* (*conjug. like* MANGER) to erect, to raise, to rear; to set up; to exalt. **s'ériger**, *v.r.* to set up for, to pose (*en*); to be erected.
ermitage [ɛrmi'ta:ʒ], *n.m.* hermitage.

ermite [ɛrˈmit], *n.* hermit, recluse.

éroder [eroˈde], *v.t.* to erode.

érosif [eroˈzif], *a.* (*fem.* **-sive**) erosive.

érosion [eroˈzjɔ̃], *n.f.* erosion.

érotique [erɔˈtik], *a.* erotic.

errant [ɛˈrɑ̃], *a.* wandering, roving, errant; erring; *chevalier errant*, knight errant.

erratique [ɛraˈtik], *a.* erratic.

erre [ɛːr], *n.f.* course, way; (*pl.*) track (*of a stag etc.*).

errements [ɛrˈmɑ̃], *n.m.* (*used only in pl.*) manner, way; vagaries, follies.

errer [ɛˈre], *v.i.* to wander, to stray; to range to rove; to err, to go astray.

erreur [ɛˈrœːr], *n.f.* error, mistake.

erroné [erɔˈne], *a.* erroneous, mistaken, false.

erronément [erɔneˈmɑ̃], *adv.* erroneously.

érudit [eryˈdi], *a.* erudite, learned.—*n.m.* (*fem.* **-e**) scholar, learned person.

érudition [erydiˈsjɔ̃], *n.f.* erudition, scholarship.

éruptif [erypˈtif], *a.* (*fem.* **-tive**) eruptive.

éruption [erypˈsjɔ̃], *n.f.* eruption; cutting (*of teeth*); breaking out (*of a rash*).

érysipèle [eriziˈpɛl], **érésipèle** [ereziˈpɛl], *n.m.* erysipelas.

ès [ɛs], contraction of EN (I) LES (*survives only in a few set expressions*) in, of; *licencié ès lettres*, bachelor of arts.

escabeau [ɛskaˈbo], *n.m.* (*pl.* **-eaux**) stool; step ladder.

escabelle [ɛskaˈbɛl], *n.f.* three-legged stool.

escadre [ɛsˈkaːdr], *n.f.* (*Naut.*) squadron; (*Av.*) wing.

escadrille [ɛskaˈdriːj], *n.f.* small squadron, flotilla.

escadron [ɛskaˈdrɔ̃], *n.m.* squadron (*of horse*).

escalade [ɛskaˈlad], *n.f.* scaling (*a wall*); rock-climbing; escalation (*of a war etc.*).

escalader [ɛskalaˈde], *v.t.* to scale, to climb over.

escale [ɛsˈkal], *n.f.* port of call, stopping place.

escalier [ɛskaˈlje], *n.m.* staircase, stairs, steps; *escalier roulant*, escalator.

escalope [ɛskaˈlɔp], *n.f.* escalope, collop (*of veal*); steak (*of fish*).

escamotable [ɛskamɔˈtabl], *a.* which can be tucked away; (*Av.*) *train escamotable*, retractable landing-gear.

escamotage [ɛskamɔˈtaːʒ], *n.m.* juggling, sleight of hand; (*fig.*) filching.

escamoter [ɛskamɔˈte], *v.t.* to conjure away; to pilfer, to make away with; (*Av.*) to retract (*the undercarriage*).

escamoteur [ɛskamɔˈtœːr], *n.m.* (*fem.* **-euse**) juggler, conjurer; pilferer, pickpocket.

escapade [ɛskaˈpad], *n.f.* escapade, prank.

escarbille [ɛskarˈbiːj], *n.f.* cinder (*of coal*).

escarboucle [ɛskarˈbukl], *n.f.* carbuncle (*precious stone*).

escargot [ɛskarˈgo], *n.m.* snail (*edible*).

escarmouche [ɛskarˈmuʃ], *n.f.* skirmish; brush; (*fig.*) bickering.

escarmoucher [ɛskarmuˈʃe], *v.i.* to skirmish; (*fig.*) to bicker.

escarpé [ɛskarˈpe], *a.* scarped, steep, precipitous; (*fig.*) difficult.

escarpement [ɛskarpəˈmɑ̃], *n.m.* escarpment; steep face *or* slope.

escarpin [ɛskarˈpɛ̃], *n.m.* pump, dancing shoe.

escarpolette [ɛskarpɔˈlɛt], *n.f.* (*child's*) swing.

escarre *or* **eschare** [ɛsˈkaːr], *n.f.* scab.

escient [ɛˈsjɑ̃], *n.m.* used only in *à bon escient*, wittingly, knowingly.

esclaffer (s') [sɛsklaˈfe], *v.r.* to laugh noisily, to guffaw.

esclandre [ɛsˈklɑ̃ːdr], *n.m.* scandal, exposure, scene.

esclavage [ɛsklaˈvaːʒ], *n.m.* slavery; bondage.

esclave [ɛsˈklaːv], *a.* slavish.—*n.* slave, bondsman; drudge.

escogriffe [ɛskɔˈgrif], *n.m.* (*colloq.*) tall, lanky, ungainly fellow.

escompte [ɛsˈkɔ̃ːt], *n.m.* discount, rebate.

escompter [ɛskɔ̃ˈte], *v.t.* to discount; (*fig.*) to anticipate; *escompter un billet*, to cash a bill.

escorte [ɛsˈkɔrt], *n.f.* escort; (*Navy*) convoy; (*fig.*) retinue, attendants.

escorter [ɛskɔrˈte], *v.t.* to escort, to accompany, to attend.

escorteur [ɛskɔrˈtœːr], *n.m.* escort vessel.

escouade [ɛsˈkwad], *n.f.* squad, small party (*of soldiers*); gang (*of workmen*).

escrime [ɛsˈkrim], *n.f.* fencing.

escrimer [ɛskriˈme], *v.i.* to fence; (*fig.*) to have a trial of skill etc. **s'escrimer**, *v.r.* (*colloq.*) to strive; to try hard.

escrimeur [ɛskriˈmœːr], *n.m.* (*fem.* **-euse**) fencer.

escroc [ɛsˈkro], *n.m.* sharper, swindler.

escroquer [ɛskrɔˈke], *v.t.* to swindle out of; to cheat.

escroquerie [ɛskrɔˈkri], *n.f.* swindling.

espace [ɛsˈpuːs], *n.m.* space, room; duration.—*n.f.* (*Print.*) space.

espacement [ɛspasˈmɑ̃], *n.m.* interval; (*Print.*) spacing.

espacer [ɛspaˈse], *v.t.* (*conjug. like* COM-MENCER) to leave a space between; to separate. **s'espacer**, *v.r.* to become less frequent *or* numerous.

espadrille [ɛspaˈdriːj], *n.f.* canvas shoe with cord soles.

Espagne [ɛsˈpaɲ], **l'**. *f.* Spain.

espagnol [ɛspaˈɲɔl], *a.* Spanish.—*n.m.* Spanish (*language*); (**Espagnol**, *fem.* **-ole**) Spaniard.

espagnolette [ɛspaɲɔˈlɛt], *n.f.* bolt of French window.

espalier [ɛspaˈlje], *n.m.* espalier (*tree or wall*).

espèce [ɛsˈpɛs], *n.f.* species; sort, nature; (*pl.*) ready money, hard cash.

espérance [ɛspeˈrɑ̃ːs], *n.f.* hope, trust, expectation.

espéranto [ɛsperɑ̃ˈto], *n.m.* Esperanto.

espérer [ɛspeˈre], *v.t.* (*conjug. like* CÉDER) to hope for; to expect; to trust.—*v.i.* to hope; to put one's trust in.

espiègle [ɛsˈpjɛgl], *a.* and *n.* mischievous, roguish (person).

espièglerie [ɛspjɛgləˈri], *n.f.* frolic, roguish trick, prank.

espion [ɛsˈpjɔ̃], *n.m.* (*fem.* **-onne**) spy.

espionnage [ɛspjɔˈnaːʒ], *n.m.* espionage.

espionner [ɛspjɔˈne], *v.t.* to spy, to pry into.

esplanade [ɛsplaˈnad], *n.f.* esplanade, parade.

espoir [ɛsˈpwaːr], *n.m.* hope.

esprit [ɛsˈpri], *n.m.* spirit, ghost; soul; mind, sense, intellect; wit; humor, character.

esquif [ɛsˈkif], *n.m.* small boat.

esquille [ɛsˈkiːj], *n.f.* splinter (*of a bone*).

étalage

esquimau [ɛski'mo], a. (pl. -aux) and n. (Esquimau or Eskimo) Eskimo.
esquinancie [ɛskinã'si], cynancie [sinã'si], n.f. quinsy.
esquisse [ɛs'kis], n.f. sketch, outline, rough draft or plan.
esquisser [ɛski'se], v.t. to sketch, to outline.
esquiver [ɛski've], v.t. to avoid, to elude, to duck; to dodge. s'esquiver, v.r. to escape; to give the slip.
essai [ɛ'sɛ], n.m. trial; attempt; experiment, testing; (Rugby) try; (Lit.) essay.
essaim [ɛ'sɛ̃], n.m. swarm; (fig.) crowd, host.
essaimer [ɛsɛ'me], v.i. to swarm; to hive off.
essarter [ɛsar'te], v.t. to clear, to grub (land).
essayage [ɛsɛ'ja:ʒ], n.m. trying, testing; trying-on (of clothes).
essayer [ɛsɛ'je], v.t. (conjug. like PAYER) to try; to try on; to attempt; to assay.—v.i. to try, to make an attempt. s'essayer, v.r. to try one's strength or skill.
essayeur [ɛsɛ'jœ:r], n.m. (fem. -euse) assayer; (cloth) fitter.
essayiste [ɛsɛ'jist], n. essayist.
essence [ɛ'sã:s], n.f. essence; gasoline; attar (of roses).
essentiel [ɛsã'sjɛl], a. (fem. -elle) essential, material.—n.m. essential, main point.
essentiellement [ɛsãsjɛl'mã], adv. essentially, absolutely, above all.
essieu [ɛ'sjø], n.m. (pl. -eux) axle-tree; spindle; pin (of a block); écartement des essieux, wheel base (motor); essieu moteur, driving-shaft.
essor [ɛ'sɔ:r], n.m. flight, soaring; (fig.) impulse, vigor.
essorer [ɛsɔ're], v.t. to hang in the air to dry, to wring out (washing).
essoreuse [ɛsɔ'rø:z], n.f. wringer, mangle.
essoriller [ɛsɔri'je], v.t. to cut the ears (of a dog etc.); to crop.
essoufflement [ɛsuflə'mã], n.m. panting, breathlessness.
essouffler [ɛsu'fle], v.t. to wind (horses etc.). s'essouffler, v.r. to be out of breath; to be winded.
essuie-glaces [ɛsɥi'glas], n.m. pl. windshield wipers.
essuie-main(s) [ɛsɥi'mɛ̃], n.m. inv. hand towel.
essuie-pieds [ɛsɥi'pje], n.m. inv. doormat.
essuyage [ɛsɥi'ja:ʒ], n.m. wiping, drying.
essuyer [ɛsɥi'je], v.t. (conjug. like EMPLOYER) to wipe; to dry; to sustain, to endure, to undergo. s'essuyer, v.r. to dry oneself; s'essuyer les mains, la figure etc., to dry one's hands, one's face etc.
est [ɛst], n.m. east.
estacade [ɛsta'kad], n.f. breakwater; pier or boom made of timbers.
estafette [ɛsta'fɛt], n.f. courier, express messenger; dispatch rider.
estafilade [ɛstafi'lad], n.f. cut, gash; slash, rent.
estaminet [ɛstami'nɛ], n.m. coffee house or room; tavern.
estampage [ɛstã'pa:ʒ], n.m. stamping (of metal etc.).
estampe [ɛs'tã:p], n.f. print, engraving.
estamper [ɛstã'pe], v.t. to stamp, to punch.
estampeur [ɛstã'pœ:r], a. (fem. -euse) stamp-

ing.—n.m. (fem. -euse) stamper.—n.f. (-euse) stamping machine.
estampillage [ɛstãpi'ja:ʒ], n.m. stamping, marking.
estampille [ɛstã'pi:j], n.f. stamp, mark, trade mark.
estampiller [ɛstãpi'je], v.t. to stamp, to mark.
esthétique [ɛste'tik], a. esthetic.—n.f. esthetics.
Esthonie [ɛstɔ'ni], l', f. Estonia.
esthonien [ɛstɔ'njɛ̃], a. (fem. -enne) Estonian.—n.m. Estonian (language); (Esthonien, fem. -enne) Estonian (person).
estimable [ɛsti'mabl], a. estimable.
estimateur [ɛstima'tœ:r], n.m. (fem. -trice) appraiser, valuer.
estimation [ɛstima'sjɔ̃], n.f. estimation, appraising, valuation, estimate.
estime [ɛs'tim], n.f. esteem, regard, estimation; (Naut.) reckoning.
estimer [ɛsti'me], v.t. to estimate, to value, to assess; to esteem; to deem. s'estimer, v.r. to esteem oneself; to deem oneself.
estival [ɛsti'val], a. (m. pl. -aux) estival, summer (plant, resort etc.).
estivant [ɛsti'vã], n.m. (fem. -e) summer visitor.
estomac [ɛstɔ'ma], n.m. stomach; (fig.) pluck.
estompage [ɛstɔ̃'pa:ʒ], n.m. (Drawing) stumping.
estompe [ɛs'tɔ̃:p], n.f. (Drawing) stump.
estomper [ɛstɔ̃'pe], v.t. (Drawing) to stump; to shade off, to blur. s'estomper, v.r. to become blurred.
Estonie [ESTHONIE].
estonien [ESTHONIEN].
estrade [ɛs'trad], n.f. platform, stand, stage.
estragon [ɛstra'gɔ̃], n.m. (Bot.) tarragon.
estropié [ɛstrɔ'pje], a. crippled, lame, disabled.—n.m. (fem. -ée) cripple.
estropier [ɛstrɔ'pje], v.t. to cripple, to maim, to disable; (fig.) to distort, to mangle.
estuaire [ɛs'tɥe:r], n.m. estuary.
esturgeon [ɛstyr'ʒɔ̃], n.m. sturgeon.
et [e], conj. and.
étable [e'tabl], n.f. shed (for oxen, sheep, goats etc.); stall; pigsty, sty.
établi [eta'bli], n.m. bench (tailor's etc.).
établir [eta'bli:r], v.t. to fix, to erect, to set up; to establish, to found; to assert. s'établir, v.r. to establish oneself; to take up one's residence; to settle down; to set up in business.
établissement [etablis'mã], n.m. establishment, setting up; placing, erecting; proving; imposition (of taxes).
étage [e'ta:ʒ], n.m. storey, floor, flight (of stairs); (fig.) stage; tier; (Geol., Mining) layer, stratum.
étager [eta'ʒe], v.t. (conjug. like MANGER) to dispose in tiers. s'étager, v.r. to rise tier upon tier.
étagère [eta'ʒɛ:r], n.f. whatnot, set of shelves, shelf.
étai [e'te], n.m. stay, shore, prop, strut.
étaiement [ÉTAYAGE].
étain [e'tɛ̃], n.m. tin; pewter.
étal [e'tal], n.m. (pl. -aux or -als) butcher's stall, butcher's shop.
étalage [eta'la:ʒ], n.m. laying out of goods for sale; goods exposed for sale; shop window, frontage; (fig.) showing off.

143

étalager [etala'ʒe], v.t. (conjug. like MANGER) to display (goods) for sale.

étalagiste [etala'ʒist], n. stall keeper; window dresser.

étale [e'tal], a. slack (of water or wind).

étalement [etal'mã], n.m. display, parade; staggering (of holidays).

étaler [eta'le], v.t. to expose for sale; to spread out; to display; (Naut.) to stem (current); to weather (gale). **s'étaler**, v.r. to stretch oneself out, to sprawl; to show off.

étalon (1) [eta'lɔ̃], n.m. stallion.

étalon (2) [eta'lɔ̃], n.m. standard (of weights and measures).

étalonnage [etalɔ'naːʒ], **étalonnement** [etalɔn'mã], n.m. standardization; stamping (of weights etc.); gauging.

étalonner [etalɔ'ne], v.t. to standardize; to gauge.

étalonneur [etalɔ'nœːr], n.m. inspector of weights and measures.

étamage [eta'maːʒ], n.m. tinning; quick-silvering (of glass).

étamer [eta'me], v.t. to tin; to quicksilver.

étameur [eta'mœːr], n.m. tinner; silverer (of mirrors).

étamine (1) [eta'min], n.f. sieve, strainer; (Naut.) bunting.

étamine (2) [eta'min], n.f. (Bot.) stamen.

étampe [e'tɑ̃ːp], n.f. die; punch.

étamper [etɑ̃'pe], v.t. to punch (horse-shoes etc.); to stamp (sheet metal etc.).

étanche [e'tɑ̃ːʃ], a. water-tight, air-tight etc.

étanchement [etɑ̃ʃ'mã], n.m. stanching, stopping; slaking; quenching.

étancher [etɑ̃'ʃe], v.t. to stanch, to stop; to render water-tight; (fig.) to quench.

étang [e'tɑ̃], n.m. pond, mere, pool.

étape [e'tap], n.f. halting-place, stage, station; day's march.

état [e'ta], n.m. state, case, condition; circumstance, predicament; statement; list, estimate; profession.

étatique [eta'tik], a. nationalized.

étatiser [etati'ze], v.t. to nationalize.

étatisme [eta'tism], n.m. State socialism, State control, nationalization.

état-major [etama'ʒɔːr], n.m. (pl. **états-majors**) (Mil.) staff, general staff.

étau [e'to], n.m. (pl. **-aux**) (Tech.) vise.

étayage [etɛ'jaːʒ], **étayement** [etɛj'mã], **étaiement** [etɛ'mã], n.m. staying, shoring, supporting.

étayer [etɛ'je], v.t. (conjug. like PAYER) to stay, to shore; to support (a theory etc.).

été [e'te], n.m. (pl. **-s**) summer; (C) **Été des Sauvages**, Indian summer.

éteignoir [etɛ'nwaːr], n.m. extinguisher (for candles).

éteindre [e'tɛ̃ːdr], v.t. irr. (conjug. like CRAINDRE) to put out, to extinguish; to appease; to destroy. **s'éteindre**, v.r. to be extinguished, to be put out; to die out; to become extinct.

éteint [e'tɛ̃], a. extinguished; extinct; (fig.) dull.

étendard [etɑ̃'daːr], n.m. standard, banner, flag.

étendre [e'tɑ̃ːdr], v.t. to extend, to spread out; to stretch; to dilute; to prolong; to lay (down) (a person). **s'étendre**, v.r. to stretch oneself out; to reach, to extend; to dwell on.

étendu [etɑ̃'dy], a. outstretched, outspread; extensive; diluted.

étendue [etɑ̃'dy], n.f. extent; scope, length.

éternel [etɛr'nɛl], a. (fem. **-elle**) eternal, everlasting.—n.m. (**l'Éternel**) God, the Eternal.

éternellement [etɛrnɛl'mã], adv. eternally.

éterniser [etɛrni'ze], v.t. to perpetuate. **s'éterniser**, v.r. to be perpetuated, to last forever.

éternité [etɛrni'te], n.f. eternity.

éternuement or **éternûment** [etɛrny'mã], n.m. sneezing, sneeze.

éternuer [etɛr'nɥe], v.i. to sneeze.

éternueur [etɛr'nɥœːr], n.m. (fem. **-euse**) sneezer.

éteule [e'tœːl], n.f. stubble.

éther [e'tɛːr], n.m. ether.

éthéré [ete're], a. ethereal.

éthériser [eteri'ze], v.t. to etherize.

Éthiopie [etjɔ'pi], l', f. Ethiopia.

éthiopien [etjɔ'pjɛ̃], a. (fem. **-enne**) Ethiopian.—n.m. (**Éthiopien**, fem. **-enne**) Ethiopian (person).

éthique [e'tik], a. ethic(al).—n.f. ethics, morals.

ethnique [ɛt'nik], a. ethnic(al).

ethnographe [ɛtnɔ'graf], n. ethnographer.

ethnographie [ɛtnɔgra'fi], n.f. ethnography.

ethnographique [ɛtnɔgra'fik], a. ethnographic.

ethnologie [ɛtnɔlɔ'ʒi], n.f. ethnology.

ethnologique [ɛtnɔlɔ'ʒik], a. ethnological.

ethnologue [ɛtnɔ'lɔg], **ethnologiste** [ɛtnɔlɔ'ʒist], n. ethnologist.

éthologie [etɔlɔ'ʒi], n.f. ethology.

éthyle [e'tiːl], n.m. ethyl.

étiage [e'tjaːʒ], n.m. low-water mark; (fig.) level.

Étienne [e'tjɛn], m. Stephen.

étincelant [etɛ̃s'lã], a. sparkling, glittering, glistening.

étinceler [etɛ̃s'le], v.i. (conjug. like APPELER) to sparkle, to flash; to gleam, to glitter.

étincelle [etɛ̃'sɛl], n.f. spark, flash; brilliance.

étincellement [etɛ̃sɛl'mã], n.m. sparkling, twinkling, scintillation.

étiolement [etjɔl'mã], n.m. etiolation, sickliness (of plants etc.); paleness, emaciation.

étioler [etjɔ'le], v.t. to etiolate (plants); (fig.) to enervate. **s'étioler**, v.r. to become etiolated (of plants); (fig.) to waste away.

étique [e'tik], a. consumptive; emaciated.

étiqueter [etik'te], v.t. (conjug. like APPELER) to label, to ticket.

étiquette [eti'kɛt], n.f. ticket, label, tag; etiquette.

étirage [eti'raːʒ], n.m. stretching.

étirer [eti're], v.t. to stretch; to lengthen. **s'étirer**, v.r. to stretch one's limbs.

étisie [eti'zi], n.f. consumption.

étoffe [e'tɔf], n.f. material; stuff, cloth; quality, worth; (C) **étoffe du pays**, home-spun.

étoffé [etɔ'fe], a. stuffed full; upholstered; stout, substantial.

étoffer [etɔ'fe], v.t. to stuff; to upholster.

étoile [e'twal], n.f. star; (fig.) fate, destiny; blaze (on horse's head); star (crack in glass).

étoilé [etwa'le], a. starry, star-shaped.

étoiler [etwa'le], v.t. to star, to stud with stars; to crack (of glass). **s'étoiler**, v.r. to star, to crack (of glass).

étole [e'tɔl], *n.f.* stole.

étonnamment [etɔna'mɑ̃], *adv.* astonishingly, wonderfully, amazingly.

étonnant [etɔ'nɑ̃], *a.* astonishing, wonderful, marvellous.

étonnement [etɔn'mɑ̃], *n.m.* astonishment, amazement; wonder; crack, fissure.

étonner [etɔ'ne], *v.t.* to astonish, to amaze, to astound; to shock; to cause to crack. **s'étonner**, *v.r.* to be astonished, to wonder; to become cracked.

étouffant [etu'fɑ̃], *a.* suffocating, sultry, close.

étouffement [etuf'mɑ̃], *n.m.* suffocation.

étouffer [etu'fe], *v.t.* to suffocate, to choke, to smother; (*fig.*) to stifle, to hush up; to deaden (*sound etc.*).—*v.i.* to choke, to suffocate. **s'étouffer**, *v.r.* to be choking, to be suffocated; to swelter.

étoupe [e'tup], *n.f.* tow, oakum.

étouper [etu'pe], *v.t.* to stop (*with tow or oakum*); to caulk.

étoupiller [etupi'je], *v.t.* to prime (*a friction tube*).

étourderie [eturdə'ri], *n.f.* heedlessness, thoughtlessness; blunder.

étourdi [etur'di], *a.* giddy, thoughtless, heedless.—*n.m.* (*fem.* **-e**) madcap.

étourdiment [eturdi'mɑ̃], *adv.* heedlessly, thoughtlessly.

étourdir [etur'di:r], *v.t.* to stun, to deafen, to make giddy; to din; to astound. **s'étourdir**, *v.r.* to divert one's thoughts; to try to forget something.

étourdissant [eturdi'sɑ̃], *a.* deafening, stunning, astounding.

étourdissement [eturdis'mɑ̃], *n.m.* dizziness, giddiness; stupefaction; shock.

étourneau [etur'no], *n.m.* (*pl.* **-eaux**) starling; (*fig.*) giddy fellow.

étrange [e'trɑ̃:ʒ], *a.* strange, odd, queer.

étrangement [etrɑ̃ʒ'mɑ̃], *adv.* strangely, queerly, extraordinarily.

étranger [etrɑ̃'ʒe], *a.* (*fem.* **-ère**) foreign; strange; unknown; irrelevant.—*n.m.* (*fem.* **-ère**) foreigner, alien; stranger; *à l'étranger*, abroad.

étrangeté [etrɑ̃ʒ'te], *n.f.* strangeness, oddness.

étranglé [etrɑ̃'gle], *a.* strangled; restricted, scanty, too narrow.

étranglement [etrɑ̃glə'mɑ̃], *n.m.* strangling; garotting; constriction.

étrangler [etrɑ̃'gle], *v.t.* to strangle, to choke, to stifle; to constrict, to confine; (*fig.*) to smother, to suppress.—*v.i.* to be choked, to be short of breath. **s'étrangler**, *v.r.* to strangle oneself; to choke.

étrangleur [etrɑ̃'glœ:r], *n.m.* (*fem.* **-euse**) strangler; garotter.

être [ɛ:tr], *v.i. irr.* to be, to exist; to belong (*à*); to stand; to take part (*à*); to be a member (*de*).—*n.m.* being, existence; creature.

étreindre [e'trɛ̃:dr], *v.t. irr.* (*conjug. like* CRAINDRE) to embrace, to clasp, to grip.

étreinte [e'trɛ̃:t], *n.f.* embrace, hug; grip.

étrenne [e'trɛn], *n.f.* New Year's gift (*usually in pl.*); gift, present.

étrenner [etrɛ'ne], *v.t.* to give a New Year's gift; to handsel; to try or put on for the first time; to buy the first lot from.

étrier [etri'e], *n.m.* stirrup; (*Surg.*) caliper.

étrille [e'tri:j], *n.f.* curry-comb.

étriller [etri'je], *v.t.* to curry, to comb (*a horse*); (*fig.*) to fleece; to drub.

étriper [etri'pe], *v.t.* to gut (*an animal*).

étriqué [etri'ke], *a.* scanty, narrow, curtailed.

étriquer [etri'ke], *v.t.* to shorten, to curtail, to make too small.

étrivière [etri'vjɛ:r], *n.f.* stirrup leather.

étroit [e'trwa], *a.* narrow, tight, strait; limited; (*fig.*) strict, rigorous.

étroitement [etrwat'mɑ̃], *adv.* narrowly, tightly; intimately, closely.

étroitesse [etrwa'tes], *n.f.* narrowness, straitness; tightness, closeness.

Étrurie [etry'ri], **l'**, *f.* Etruria.

étrusque [e'trysk], *a.* Etruscan.—*n.m.* Etruscan (*language*).—*n.* (**Étrusque**) Etruscan (*person*).

étude [e'tyd], *n.f.* study; room for study; time of preparation; office, practice (*of attorneys*); essay, article.

étudiant [ety'djɑ̃], *n.m.* (*fem.* **-e**) student; undergraduate.

étudié [ety'dje], *a.* studied; affected.

étudier [ety'dje], *v.t.* to study, to learn; to practice (*music*); to rehearse (*a play*); to observe.—*v.i.* to study, to learn; to practice (*music*). **s'étudier**, *v.r.* to make (*it*) one's study, to school oneself.

étui [e'tɥi], *n.m.* case, box, sheath.

étuve [e'ty:v], *n.f.* sweating room; stove; drying room; incubator.

étuvée [ety've], *n.f.* stew.

étuver [ety've], *v.t.* to stew; (*Med.*) to bathe, to foment.

étymologie [etimɔlɔ'ʒi], *n.f.* etymology.

étymologique [etimɔlɔ'ʒik], *a.* etymological.

étymologiste [etimɔlɔ'ʒist], *n.* etymologist.

eucharistie [økaris'ti], *n.f.* eucharist.

eucharistique [økaris'tik], *a.* eucharistic.

eugénique [øʒe'nik], *n.f.*, **eugénisme** [øʒe'nism], *n.m.* eugenics.

euh [ø], *int.* aha! oh! hum!

eunuque [ø'nyk], *n.m.* eunuch.

euphémique [øfe'mik], *a.* euphemistic.

euphémisme [øfe'mism], *n.m.* euphemism.

euphonie [øfɔ'ni], *n.f.* euphony.

euphonique [øfɔ'nik], *a.* euphonious.

Euphrate [ø'frat], **l'**, *m.* the Euphrates.

euphuïsme [øfy'ism], *n.m.* euphuism.

eurasien [øra'zjɛ̃], *a.* (*fem.* **-enne**) Eurasian.—*n.m.* (**Eurasien**, *fem.* **-enne**) Eurasian (*person*).

Euripide [øri'pid], *m.* Euripides.

Europe [ø'rɔp], *f.* (*Myth.*) Europa; *l'Europe*, (*Geog.*) Europe.

européaniser [øropeani'ze], *v.t.* to Europeanize.

européen [øropé'ɛ̃], *a.* (*fem.* **-éenne**) European.—*n.m.* (**Européen**, *fem.* **-éenne**) European (*person*).

euthanasie [øtana'zi], *n.f.* euthanasia.

eux [ø], *pron. pers. m. pl.* (*fem.* **-elles**) they; them.

évacuant [eva'kɥɑ̃], **évacuatif** [evakɥa'tif] (*fem.* **-tive**), *a.* and *n.m.* evacuant.

évacuation [evakɥa'sjɔ̃], *n.f.* evacuation; ejection.

évacué [eva'kɥe], *n.m.* (*fem.* **-ée**) evacuee.

évacuer [eva'kɥe], *v.t.* to evacuate; to throw off, to eject, to clear. **s'évacuer**, *v.r.* to discharge (*into*).

145

évadé [eva'de], *a.* and *n.m.* (*fem.* **-ée**) escaped (*person*); escapée.

évader (s') [seva'de], *v.r.* to escape; to get away *or* out of (*de*).

évaluable [eva'lɥabl], *a.* appraisable.

évaluateur [evalɥa'tœ:r], *n.m.* (*fem.* **-trice**) valuer, appraiser.

évaluation [evalɥa'sjɔ̃], *n.f.* valuation, estimate.

évaluer [eva'lɥe], *v.t.* to value, to estimate, to appreciate.

évangélique [evɑ̃ʒe'lik], *a.* evangelical.

évangéliser [evɑ̃ʒeli'ze], *v.t.* to evangelize, to preach the Gospel to.

évangélisme [evɑ̃ʒe'lism], *n.m.* evangelism.

évangéliste [evɑ̃ʒe'list], *n.m.* evangelist.

évangile [evɑ̃'ʒil], *n.m.* Gospel.

évanouir (s') [seva'nwi:r], *v.r.* to faint, to swoon, to lose consciousness; (*fig.*) to vanish, to disappear.

évanouissement [evanwis'mɑ̃], *n.m.* swoon, fainting fit; disappearance; (*Math.*) cancelling out.

évaporatif [evapɔra'tif], *a.* (*fem.* **-tive**) evaporative.

évaporation [evapɔra'sjɔ̃], *n.f.* evaporation.

évaporé [evapɔ're], *a.* and *n.m.* (*fem.* **-ée**) frivolous, thoughtless (person).

évaporer [evapɔ're], *v.t.* to evaporate; (*fig.*) to exhale, to give vent to; **évaporer son chagrin**, to give vent to one's grief. **s'évaporer**, *v.r.* to evaporate; (*fig.*) to get giddy.

évasé [eva'ze], *a.* wide, bell-shaped; flared (*skirt*).

évasement [evaz'mɑ̃], *n.m.* width, widening (*at the mouth of a vase etc.*); flare (*of a skirt*).

évaser [eva'ze], *v.t.* to widen (*an opening*); to flare (*a skirt*). **s'évaser**, *v.r.* to be widened; to extend, to spread.

évasif [eva'zif], *a.* (*fem.* **-sive**) evasive.

évasion [eva'zjɔ̃], *n.f.* escape, flight; evasion; escapism.

évasivement [evaziv'mɑ̃], *adv.* evasively.

évêché [eve'ʃe], *n.m.* bishopric, episcopate, see; bishop's palace.

éveil [e've:j], *n.m.* awakening; warning, hint, alarm.

éveillé [eve'je], *a.* wide-awake, lively, sprightly; sharp, intelligent.

éveiller [eve'je], *v.t.* to awaken, to rouse; to excite, to enliven. **s'éveiller**, *v.r.* to wake up; to become animated.

événement [even'mɑ̃], *n.m.* event, occurrence; result; climax; emergency.

évent [e'vɑ̃], *n.m.* open air; vent hole, air hole; (*fig.*) flatness, vapidness.

éventail [evɑ̃'ta:j] *n.m.* (*pl.* **éventails**) fan; fan-light.

éventaire [evɑ̃'tɛ:r], *n.m.* flat tray (*carried by hawkers*); street stall.

éventé [evɑ̃'te], *a.* fanned, aired; flat, stale (*beer etc.*); (*fig.*) giddy, thoughtless.

éventer [evɑ̃'te], *v.t.* to fan; to winnow(*grain*); to air; to let (*wine etc.*) get flat; to get wind of; to divulge. **s'éventer**, *v.r.* to fan oneself; to evaporate; to become flat; to be divulged.

éventrer [evɑ̃'tre], *v.t.* to disembowel, to gut (*fish etc.*); to rip up, to break open. **s'éventrer**, *v.r.* to rip one's bowels open; to commit hara-kiri.

éventualité [evɑ̃tɥali'te], *n.f.* contingency, eventuality.

éventuel [evɑ̃'tɥɛl], *a.* (*fem.* **-elle**) contingent, possible.

éventuellement [evɑ̃tɥɛl'mɑ̃], *adv.* possibly; on occasion.

évêque [e've:k], *n.m.* bishop.

évertuer (s') [sever'tɥe], *v.r.* to strive, to exert *or* bestir oneself.

éviction [evik'sjɔ̃], *n.f.* eviction, ejectment.

évidemment [evida'mɑ̃], *adv.* evidently.

évidence [evi'dɑ̃:s], *n.f.* obviousness, clearness; conspicuousness.

évident [evi'dɑ̃], *a.* evident, plain, clear, obvious.

évider [evi'de], *v.t.* to hollow, to groove, to scoop out.

évier [e'vje], *n.m.* sink.

évincer [evɛ̃'se], *v.t.* (*conjug. like* COMMENCER) to evict, to eject, to oust.

éviscérer [evise're], *v.t.* (*conjug. like* CÉDER) to disembowel.

évitable [evi'tabl], *a.* avoidable.

évitement [evit'mɑ̃], *n.m.* (*Rail.*) siding, shunting; by-pass.

éviter [evi'te], *v.t.* to shun, to avoid, to evade; to abstain from.

évocateur [evɔka'tœ:r], *a.* (*fem.* **-trice**) evocative.

évocation [evɔka'sjɔ̃], *n.f.* evocation; recollection.

évolué [evɔ'lɥe], *a.* highly civilized.

évoluer [evɔ'lɥe], *v.i.* to evolve; to develop.

évolution [evɔly'sjɔ̃], *n.f.* evolution.

évoquer [evɔ'ke], *v.t.* to evoke; to allude to.

exacerbation [egzasɛrba'sjɔ̃], *n.f.* exacerbation.

exacerber [egzasɛr'be], *v.t.* to exacerbate.

exact [eg'zakt], *a.* exact, correct; punctual.

exactement [egzaktə'mɑ̃], *adv.* exactly, accurately; punctually.

exaction [egzak'sjɔ̃], *n.f.* exaction, impost, extortion.

exactitude [egzakti'tyd], *n.f.* exactness, accuracy; punctuality.

exagération [egzaʒera'sjɔ̃], *n.f.* exaggeration; overrating.

exagérer [egzaʒe're], *v.t.* (*conjug. like* CÉDER) to exaggerate, to magnify.

exaltation [egzalta'sjɔ̃], *n.f.* exaltation; extolling.

exalté [egzal'te], *a.* exalted, feverish.—*n.m.* (*fem.* **-ée**) enthusiast, fanatic.

exalter [egzal'te], *v.t.* to exalt, to magnify; to excite, to inflame. **s'exalter**, *v.r.* to become excited, to be elated.

examen [egza'mɛ̃], *n.m.* examination; inspection; research.

examinateur [egzamina'tœ:r], *n.m.* (*fem.* **-trice**) examiner.

examiner [egzami'ne], *v.t.* to examine, to inspect, to survey; to discuss, to investigate. **s'examiner**, *v.r.* to examine *or* search oneself; to observe each other attentively.

exaspération [egzaspera'sjɔ̃], *n.f.* exasperation, aggravation.

exaspérer [egzaspe're], *v.t.* (*conjug. like* CÉDER) to exasperate, to incense, to inflame; to aggravate (*pain etc.*). **s'exaspérer**, *v.r.* to become exasperated *or* incensed; to become aggravated (*pain etc.*).

exaucer [ɛgzo'se], v.t. (conjug. like COMMENCER) to hearken to, to grant.
excavateur [ɛkskava'tœ:r], n.m. excavator, digging machine.
excavation [ɛkskava'sjɔ̃], n.f. excavation.
excaver [ɛkska've], v.t. to excavate, to hollow out.
excédant [ɛkse'dɑ̃], a. exceeding, excessive; unbearable.
excédent [ɛkse'dɑ̃], n.m. surplus, excess.
excéder [ɛkse'de], v.t. (conjug. like CÉDER) to exceed, to surpass, to rise above (in level, price etc.); (fig.) to wear out, to tire out.
excellemment [ɛksɛla'mɑ̃], adv. excellently, surpassingly.
Excellence [ɛksɛ'lɑ̃:s], f. (title) Excellency.
excellence [ɛksɛ'lɑ̃:s], n.f. excellence; par excellence, pre-eminently, above all.
excellent [ɛksɛ'lɑ̃], a. excellent; delightful.
excellentissime [ɛksɛlɑ̃ti'sim], a. most excellent.
exceller [ɛksɛ'le], v.i. to excel, to be eminent; to surpass.
excentricité [ɛksɑ̃trisi'te], n.f. eccentricity.
excentrique [ɛksɑ̃'trik], a. eccentric, odd.
excepté [ɛksɛp'te], prep. except, excepting, but.
excepter [ɛksɛp'te], v.t. to except.
exception [ɛksɛp'sjɔ̃], n.f. exception.
exceptionnel [ɛksɛpsjɔ'nɛl], a. (fem. -elle) exceptional; rare, infrequent.
excès [ɛk'sɛ], n.m. inv. excess; (pl.) riot, outrages, violence.
excessif [ɛksɛ'sif], a. (fem. -ive) excessive, exorbitant; intemperate.
excessivement [ɛksɛsiv'mɑ̃], adv. excessively, to excess.
excise [ɛk'si:z], n.f. excise; excise office.
excitabilité [ɛksitabili'te], n.f. excitability.
excitable [ɛksi'tabl], a. excitable.
excitant [ɛksi'tɑ̃], a. exciting.—n.m. (Med.) excitant.
excitateur [ɛksita'tœ:r], a. (fem. ~~~) provocative.—n.m. (~~~ ~~~ -trice) instigator.
excitation [ɛks~~~ ~~~ -trice) instigator.
~~~ ...sita'sjɔ̃], n.f. exciting, excitation; excitement.
exciter [ɛksi'te], v.t. to excite, to stir up, to rouse; to stimulate, to animate; to instigate, to prompt; to irritate. s'exciter, v.r. to excite oneself, to work oneself up; to encourage each other; to be excited.
exclamation [ɛksklama'sjɔ̃], n.f. exclamation; point d'exclamation, exclamation mark.
exclamer (s') [sɛkskla'me], v.r. to exclaim, to cry out; to protest.
exclure [ɛks'kly:r], v.t. irr. (conjug. like CONCLURE) to exclude, to debar, to shut out; to bar; to be incompatible with.
exclusif [ɛkskly'zif], a. (fem. -sive) exclusive; intolerant.
exclusion [ɛkskly'zjɔ̃], n.f. exclusion.
exclusivement [ɛksklyziv'mɑ̃], adv. exclusively.
excommunication [ɛkskɔmynika'sjɔ̃], n.f. excommunication.
excommunié [ɛkskɔmy'nje], a. excommunicated.—n.m. (fem. -ée) excommunicated person.
excommunier [ɛkskɔmy'nje], v.t. to excommunicate.
excrément [ɛkskre'mɑ̃], n.m. excrement.
excréter [ɛkskre'te], v.t. (conjug. like CÉDER) to excrete.

excrétion [ɛkskre'sjɔ̃], n.f. excretion.
excroissance [ɛkskrwa'sɑ̃:s], n.f. excrescence (tumor etc.).
excursion [ɛkskyr'sjɔ̃], n.f. excursion, ramble, tour, trip; raid; (fig.) digression.
excursionniste [ɛkskyrsjɔ'nist], n. tripper.
excusable [ɛksky'zabl], a. excusable, pardonable.
excuse [ɛks'ky:z], n.f. excuse, (pl.) apology.
excuser [ɛksky'ze], v.t. to excuse, to pardon; to bear with; to apologize for. s'excuser, v.r. to excuse or exculpate oneself; to apologize; to decline; qui s'excuse, s'accuse, excuses indicate a guilty conscience.
exécrable [ɛgze'krabl], a. execrable; abominable.
exécrablement [ɛgzekrabla'mɑ̃], adv. execrably.
exécration [ɛgzekra'sjɔ̃], n.f. execration.
exécrer [ɛgze'kre], v.t. (conjug. like CÉDER) to execrate, to abhor.
exécutable [ɛgzeky'tabl], a. feasible, practicable.
exécutant [ɛgzeky'tɑ̃], n.m. (fem. -e) performer, player (esp. of music).
exécuter [ɛgzeky'te], v.t. to execute, to perform, to accomplish; to carry out, to fulfil. s'exécuter, v.r. to be performed, to be done, to take place; to yield, to comply, to submit; allons, exécutez-vous, come, do the needful.
exécuteur [ɛgzeky'tœ:r], n.m. (fem. -trice) executor, executrix; exécuteur (des hautes œuvres), executioner.
exécutif [ɛgzeky'tif], a. (fem. -tive) executive.—n.m. the executive.
exécution [ɛgz~~~ ky'sjɔ̃], n.f. execution, accomplishment, performance; fulfilment; (St. Exch.) ~~~, suspension. (of debtor).
exemplaire [ɛgza'plɛ:r], a. exemplary.—n.m. model, pattern; copy (of printed books, engravings etc.); specimen.
exemplairement [ɛgzɑ̃plɛr'mɑ̃], adv. in an exemplary manner.
exemple [ɛg'zɑ̃:pl], n.m. example, pattern, model; precedent, parallel, instance; à l'exemple de, in imitation of; par exemple, for instance; upon my word! sans exemple, unparalleled.
exempt [ɛg'zɑ̃], a. exempt, free (from).
exempté [ɛgzɑ̃'te], a. and n.m. (fem. -ée) exempt(ed) (person).
exempter [ɛgzɑ̃'te], v.t. to exempt, to free; to dispense, to exonerate.
exemption [ɛgzɑ̃'sjɔ̃], n.f. exemption, immunity; dispensation.
exercer [ɛgzɛr'se], v.t. (conjug. like COMMENCER) to exercise, to train; to fulfil (an office etc.); to follow, to practice (a trade or profession); (fig.) to try (one's patience etc.). s'exercer, v.r. to exercise, to practice; to exert oneself.
exercice [ɛgzɛr'sis], n.m. exercise, practice, use; (Customs) inspection; (Administration) financial year; (Mil.) drill.
exerciseur [ɛgzɛrsi'zœ:r], n.m. (Gym.) chest expander.
exhalaison [ɛgzalɛ'zɔ̃], n.f. exhalation, effluvium.
exhalation [ɛgzala'sjɔ̃], n.f. exhalation.

147

exhaler

exhaler [egza'le], v.t. to send forth, to exhale; to give vent to, to emit. **s'exhaler**, v.r. to be emitted, to be exhaled; to give vent to.

exhausser [egzo'se], v.t. to raise, to make higher.

exhaustif [egzos'tif], a. (fem. **-tive**) exhaustive.

exhaustion [egzos'tjɔ̃], n.f. exhaustion.

exhiber [egzi'be], v.t. to exhibit (in a law court); to produce, to show. **s'exhiber**, v.r. (pej.) to show off.

exhibition [egzibi'sjɔ̃], n.f. producing, show, exhibiting, exhibition.

exhilarant [egzila'rɑ̃], a. exhilarating.

exhortation [egzɔrta'sjɔ̃], n.f. exhortation.

exhorter [egzɔr'te], v.t. to exhort, to encourage.

exhumation [egzyma'sjɔ̃], n.f. exhumation, disinterment.

exhumer [egzy'me], v.t. to exhume, to disinter; (fig.) to rake up.

exigeant [egzi'ʒɑ̃], a. exacting, hard to please.

exigence [egzi'ʒɑ̃:s], n.f. unreasonableness; exigency; demand, requirement.

exiger [egzi'ʒe], v.t. (conjug. like MANGER) to exact, to require, to demand.

exigu [egzi'gy], a. (fem. **-uë**) very small; scanty, slender, slight.

exiguïté [egziguï'te], n.f. scantiness, slenderness, slightness.

exil [eg'zil], n.m. exile, banishment.

exilé [egzi'le], a. exiled.—n.m. (fem. **-ée**) exile.

exiler [egzi'le], v.t. to exile, to banish. **s'exiler**, v.r. to go into exile.

existant [egzis'tɑ̃], a. existing, in being, existent; extant.

existence [egzis'tɑ̃:s], n.f. existence; subsistence, living; (pl.) (Comm.) stock on hand.

existentialisme [egzistɑ̃sja'lism], n.m. existentialism.

exister [egzis'te], v.i. to exist, to live; to be extant.

exocet [egzɔ'sɛ], n.m. flying fish.

exode [eg'zɔd], n.m. exodus.

exonération [egzɔnera'sjɔ̃], n.f. exoneration.

exonérer [egzɔne're], v.t. (conjug. like CÉDER) to exonerate, to discharge.

exorable [egzɔ'rabl], a. lenient, merciful.

exorbitant [egzɔrbi'tɑ̃], a. exorbitant.

exorciser [egzɔrsi'ze], v.t. to exorcize.

exorde [eg'zɔrd], n.m. exordium, beginning (of a speech etc.).

exotique [egzɔ'tik], a. exotic; foreign, outlandish.

expansif [ekspɑ̃'sif], a. (fem. **-sive**) expansive; (fig.) unreserved, open-hearted.

expansion [ekspɑ̃'sjɔ̃], n.f. expansion; (fig.) unreservedness.

expatriation [ekspatria'sjɔ̃], n.f. expatriation; self-banishment.

expatrier [ekspatri'e], v.t. to expatriate, to exile. **s'expatrier**, v.r. to leave one's country.

expectant [ekspɛk'tɑ̃], a. expectant.

expectative [ekspɛkta'ti:v], n.f. expectation, hope, expectancy.

expectoration [ekspɛktɔra'sjɔ̃], n.f. expectoration; sputum.

expectorer [ekspɛktɔ're], v.t. to expectorate, to spit.

expédient [ekspe'djɑ̃], a. expedient, fit, meet.—n.m. expedient, device; shift.

expédier [ekspe'dje], v.t. to dispatch, to send off, to forward; to do quickly; to clear (at the customs); to draw up (a deed etc.).

expéditeur [ekspedi'tœr], n.m. (fem. **-trice**) sender (by post); shipper, consigner.

expéditif [ekspedi'tif], a. (fem. **-tive**) expeditious, quick.

expédition [ekspedi'sjɔ̃], n.f. expedition, dispatch; shipment; thing sent; performance; (Law) copy (of a deed etc.).

expéditionnaire [ekspedisjɔ'nɛːr], a. expeditionary.—n. sender, shipper; commission-agent; copying clerk.

expérience [ekspe'rjɑ̃:s], n.f. experience; experiment, test.

expérimental [eksperimɑ̃'tal], a. (m.pl. **-aux**) experimental.

expérimenté [eksperimɑ̃'te], a. experienced.

expérimenter [eksperimɑ̃'te], v.t. to try out, to test; to experience.

expert [eks'pɛːr], a. expert, skillful.—n.m. connoisseur; valuer, surveyor; expert; **expert comptable**, C. P. A., accountant.

expertement [ekspɛrt'mɑ̃], adv. expertly skilfully.

expertise [eksper'ti:z], n.f. survey, valuation; appraisal.

expertiser [eksperti'ze], v.t. to make a survey of; to appraise, to value, to assess.

expiation [ekspja'sjɔ̃], n.f. expiation, atonement.

expiatoire [ekspja'twa:r], a. expiatory.

expier [eks'pje], v.t. to expiate, to atone for.

expirant [ekspi'rɑ̃], a. expiring, dying.

expiration [ekspira'sjɔ̃], n.f. expiration.

expirer [ekspi're], v.t. to breathe out; exhale.—v.i. to expire, to come to an end.

explicable [ekspli'kabl], a. explicable.

explicatif [eksplika'tif], a. (fem. **-tive**) explicative, explanatory.

explication [eksplika'sjɔ̃], n.f. explanation; interpretation; meaning.

explicite [ekspli'sit], a. explicit, clear, express.

explicitement [eksplisit'mɑ̃], adv. explicitly, clearly.

expliquer [ekspli'ke], v.t. to explain, to expound; to interpret; to make known. **s'expliquer**, v.r. to explain oneself; to be explained.

exploit [eks'plwa], n.m. exploit, achievement, feat; (Law) writ, process.

exploitable [eksplwa'tabl], a. workable; (Law) distrainable.

exploitant [eksplwa'tɑ̃], n.m. operator (of mines etc.); farmer, grower.

exploitation [eksplwata'sjɔ̃], n.f. working, improving (of lands etc.); employing, using; taking advantage of, exploitation.

exploiter [eksplwa'te], v.t. to work, to improve, to cultivate; to use; to exploit, to take (unfair) advantage of.

exploiteur [eksplwa'tœr], n.m. (fem. **-euse**) exploiter, person who takes advantage (of others).

explorateur [eksplɔra'tœr], a. (fem. **-trice**) exploratory.—n.m. (fem. **-trice**) explorer.

exploration [ɛksplɔrɑ'sjɔ̃], *n.f.* exploration.
explorer [ɛksplɔ're], *v.t.* to explore.
exploser [ɛksplo'ze], *v.i.* to explode, to blow up.
explosible [ɛksplo'zibl], *a.* explosive.
explosif [ɛksplo'zif], *a.* (*fem.* **-sive**) and *n.m.* explosive.
explosion [ɛksplo'zjɔ̃], *n.f.* explosion; (*fig.*) outbreak.
exportateur [ɛkspɔrta'tœːr], *a.* (*fem.* **-trice**) exporting.—*n.m.* (*fem.* **-trice**) exporter.
exportation [ɛkspɔrta'sjɔ̃], *n.f.* exportation, export.
exporter [ɛkspɔr'te], *v.t.* to export.
exposant [ɛkspo'zɑ̃], *n.m.* (*fem.* **-e**) exhibitor; (*Law*) petitioner.—*n.m.* (*Math.*) exponent.
exposé [ɛkspo'ze], *a.* exposed, on view; dangerous (*position*).—*n.m.* statement, explanation; account, report.
exposer [ɛkspo'ze], *v.t.* to expose, to show, to exhibit; to lay bare; to state, to explain; to endanger.—*v.i.* to explain; to exhibit. **s'exposer**, *v.r.* to expose oneself; to be liable.
exposition [ɛkspozi'sjɔ̃], *n.f.* exhibition; exposure; situation, aspect; explanation, account.
exprès [ɛks'prɛs], *a.* (*fem.* **-presse**) express, formal, positive.—[ɛks'prɛ], *adv.* expressly, on purpose.—*n.m.* express (*messenger*).
express [ɛks'prɛs], *a.* (*Rail.*) express.—*n.m.* express train.
expressément [ɛksprɛsɛ'mɑ̃], *adv.* expressly, positively.
expressif [ɛksprɛ'sif], *a.* (*fem.* **-ive**) expressive.
expression [ɛksprɛ'sjɔ̃], *n.f.* expression; expressiveness.
exprimer [ɛkspri'me], *v.t.* to express; to press *or* squeeze out; to utter; to betoken. **s'exprimer**, *v.r.* to express oneself.
expropriation [ɛksprɔpriɑ'sjɔ̃], *n.f.* expropriation, dispossession, compulsory purchase.
exproprier [ɛksprɔpri'e], *v.t.* to expropriate, to dispossess; to requisition (*buildings*).
expulser [ɛkspyl'se], *v.t.* to expel, to turn out; to evict.
expulsion [ɛkspyl'sjɔ̃], *n.f.* expulsion; (*Law*) ejection.
expurger [ɛkspyr'ʒe], *v.t.* (*conjug. like* MANGER) to expurgate, to bowdlerize (*a book*).
exquis [ɛks'ki], *a.* exquisite, nice, refined.
exquisement [ɛkskiz'mɑ̃], *adv.* exquisitely.
exsangue [ɛk'sɑ̃ːɡ], *a.* bloodless, anaemic.
extase [ɛks'taːz], *n.f.* ecstasy, rapture.
extasier (**s'**) [ɛksta'zje], *v.r.* to be enraptured, to go into raptures.
extatique [ɛksta'tik], *a.* ecstatic, rapturous.
extenseur [ɛkstɑ̃'sœːr], *a.* extensor.—*n.m.* (*Anat.*) extensor; chest-expander.
extension [ɛkstɑ̃'sjɔ̃], *n.f.* extension, stretching; extent; increase.
exténuant [ɛkste'nɥɑ̃], *a.* extenuating.
exténuation [ɛkstenɥɑ'sjɔ̃], *n.f.* extenuation, debility.
exténuer [ɛkste'nɥe], *v.t.* to extenuate, to enfeeble.

extérieur [ɛkste'rjœːr], *a.* exterior, external, outward; foreign.—*n.m.* outward appearance; abroad.
extérieurement [ɛksterjœr'mɑ̃], *adv.* externally, outwardly.
exterminateur [ɛkstɛrminɑ'tœːr], *a.* (*fem.* **-trice**) exterminating, destroying.—*n.m.* (*fem.* **-trice**) destroyer, exterminator.
extermination [ɛkstɛrminɑ'sjɔ̃], *n.f.* extermination.
exterminer [ɛkstɛrmi'ne], *v.t.* to exterminate, to destroy.
externat [ɛkstɛr'na], *n.m.* day school.
externe [ɛks'tɛrn], *a.* external, exterior, outer.—*n.* day scholar.
extincteur [ɛkstɛ̃k'tœːr], *a.* (*fem.* **-trice**) extinguishing (*fire*).—*n.m.* fire extinguisher.
extinction [ɛkstɛ̃k'sjɔ̃], *n.f.* extinction, destruction; liquidation; quelling; quenching (*of thirst*); slaking (*of lime*).
extinguible [ɛkstɛ̃'ɡibl], *a.* extinguishable.
extirpateur [ɛkstirpa'tœːr], *n.m.* extirpator, destroyer; (*Agric.*) scarifier, weeder.
extirpation [ɛkstirpa'sjɔ̃], *n.f.* extirpation.
extirper [ɛkstir'pe], *v.t.* to extirpate.
extorquer [ɛkstɔr'ke], *v.t.* to extort, to wrest.
extorsion [ɛkstɔr'sjɔ̃], *n.f.* extortion.
extra [ɛks'tra], *n.m. inv.* extra.
extra-conjugal [ɛkstrakɔ̃ʒy'ɡal], *a.* (*m.pl.* **-aux**) extra-marital.
extracteur [ɛkstrak'tœːr], *n.m.* extractor.
extraction [ɛkstrak'sjɔ̃], *n.f.* extraction; origin, descent.
extrader [ɛkstra'de], *v.t.* to extradite.
extradition [ɛkstradi'sjɔ̃], *n.f.* extradition.
extraire [ɛks'trɛːr], *v.t. irr.* (*conjug. like* TRAIRE) to extract, to take out; to make extracts from.
extrait [ɛks'trɛ], *n.m.* extract; selection; abstract; certificate.
extraordinaire [ɛkstraɔrdi'nɛːr], *a.* extraordinary, unusual.—*n.m.* extraordinary thing.
extraordinairement [ɛkstraɔrdinɛr'mɑ̃], *adv.* extraordinarily, unusually; oddly.
extrapolation [ɛkstrapɔlɑ'sjɔ̃], *n.f.* (*Math.*) extrapolation.
extra-scolaire [ɛkstrasko'lɛːr], *a.* out-of-school (*activities*).
extravagamment [ɛkstravaga'mɑ̃], *adv.* extravagantly, unreasonably.
extravagance [ɛkstrava'ɡãːs], *n.f.* extravagance, folly.
extravagant [ɛkstrava'ɡɑ̃], *a.* and *n.m.* (*fem.* **-e**) extravagant (person).
extravaguer [ɛkstrava'ɡe], *v.i.* to talk wildly.
extrême [ɛks'trɛːm], *a.* extreme, utmost; excessive.—*n.m.* extreme *or* utmost point.
extrêmement [ɛkstrɛm'mɑ̃], *adv.* extremely.
Extrême-Orient [ɛkstrɛmɔ'rjɑ̃], *l'*, *m.* Far East.
extrémiste [ɛkstre'mist], *n.* extremist, die-hard.
extrémité [ɛkstremi'te], *n.f.* extremity, end; last moment; (*fig.*) border, brink.
exubérance [ɛɡzybe'rɑ̃ːs], *n.f.* exuberance.
exubérant [ɛɡzybe'rɑ̃], *a.* exuberant, luxuriant.
exultation [ɛɡzylta'sjɔ̃], *n.f.* exultation, rapture.

149

F, f

F

F, f (1) [εf], *n.m.* the sixth letter of the alphabet.
f. (2) or **fr.**, (*abbr.*) franc.
fa [fa], *n.m.* (*Mus.*) fa; F.
fable [fɑːbl], *n.f.* fable; story, tale; (*fig.*) untruth; byword.
fablier [fɑbli'e], *n.m.* book of fables; fabulist.
fabricant [fabri'kɑ̃], *n.m.* (*fem.* -**e**) manufacturer, maker.
fabricateur [fabrika'tœːr], *n.m.* (*fem.* -**trice**) fabricator; counterfeiter; forger.
fabrication [fabrika'sjɔ̃], *n.f.* fabrication, manufacture.
fabrique [fa'brik], *n.f.* building and maintenance (*esp. of churches*); factory; fabrication.
fabriquer [fabri'ke], *v.t.* to manufacture, to make; to fabricate.
fabuleusement [fabyløz'mɑ̃], *adv.* fabulously; (*fig.*) incredibly.
fabuleux [faby'lø], *a.* (*fem.* -**euse**) fabulous, fictitious; (*fig.*) incredible.
fabuliste [faby'list], *n.* fabulist.
façade [fa'sad], *n.f.* façade, front (*of an edifice*); (*fig.*) appearance.
face [fas], *n.f.* face; front; side (*of a record*); (*fig.*) state, appearance; turn (*of affairs*); **en face de**, opposite.
facétie [fase'si], *n.f.* facetiousness; jest, joke.
facétieusement [fasesjøz'mɑ̃], *adv.* facetiously.
facétieux [fase'sjø], *a.* (*fem.* -**euse**) facetious, humorous.
facette [fa'sɛt], *n.f.* facet, face.
fâcher [fa'ʃe], *v.t.* to anger, to offend, to displease; **être fâché avec**, to be on bad terms with; **fâché** (*contre*), angry (*with*); **fâché** (*de*), sorry. **se fâcher**, *v.r.* to get angry, to be offended.
fâcherie [fa'ʃri], *n.f.* angry feeling; quarrel.
fâcheusement [faʃøz'mɑ̃], *adv.* unfortunately, unpleasantly; inopportunely, disagreeably; awkwardly.
fâcheux [fa'ʃø], *a.* (*fem.* -**euse**) troublesome, vexatious; unfortunate; cross.—*n.m.* (*fem.* -**euse**) troublesome or disagreeable person or thing, pesterer, bore.
facial [fa'sjal], *a.* (*m. pl.* -**aux**) facial.
facile [fa'sil], *a.* easy; facile; fluent; ready, quick; weak.
facilement [fasil'mɑ̃], *adv.* easily, readily.
facilité [fasili'te], *n.f.* facility, ease; readiness; (*pl.*) easy terms (*for payment*).
faciliter [fasili'te], *v.t.* to facilitate, to make easy.
façon [fa'sɔ̃], *n.f.* make, shape, fashion; making, workmanship; (*fig.*) manner; appearance; sort; affectation; fuss; (*pl.*) ceremony.
faconde [fa'kɔ̃ːd], *n.f.* talkativeness, loquacity.
façonné [faso'ne], *a.* figured (*of materials*); wrought.
façonnement [fason'mɑ̃], **façonnage** [faso'naːʒ], *n.m.* fashioning, making.
façonner [faso'ne], *v.t.* to make, to fashion, to form; to work, to mold; to accustom, to use (*to discipline etc.*).
façonnier [faso'nje], *a.* (*fem.* -**ière**) ceremonious, affected.—*n.m.* custom tailor.
fac-similé [faksimi'le], *n.m.* facsimile.

factage [fak'ta:ʒ], *n.m.* porterage, carriage.
facteur [fak'tœːr], *n.m.* (*fem.* -**trice**) maker (*of musical instruments*); agent; postman; railway porter; (*Math., Biol.*) factor.
factice [fak'tis], *a.* factitious, artificial; unnatural.
factieux [fak'sjø], *a.* (*fem.* -**euse**) factious, mutinous.—*n.m.* (*fem.* -**euse**) rebel.
faction [fak'sjɔ̃], *n.f.* watch, sentry duty; faction.
factionnaire [faksjɔ'nɛːr], *n.m.* sentry.
factorerie [faktɔrɔ'ri], *n.f.* trading depot, factory (*in a colony etc.*).
facture [fak'tyːr], *n.f.* composition, workmanship (*of music, verse etc.*); (*Comm.*) bill (*of sale*), invoice.
facturer [fakty're], *v.t.* to invoice.
facultatif [fakylta'tif], *a.* (*fem.* -**tive**) optional; **arrêt facultatif**, request stop.
faculté [fakyl'te], *n.f.* faculty, ability, power; quality; option, right; (*pl.*) mental faculties.
fadaise [fa'dɛːz], *n.f.* trifle, stuff, nonsense, twaddle.
fade [fad], *a.* insipid, tasteless, dull; (*fig.*) flat, stale.
fadement [fad'mɑ̃], *adv.* insipidly, tastelessly; mawkishly.
fadeur [fa'dœːr], *n.f.* insipidity, tastelessness; (*fig.*) pointlessness.
fagot [fa'go], *n.m.* faggot, bundle of sticks etc.
fagoter [fago'te], *v.t.* to tie into faggots; (*fig.*) to jumble together; to dress in a slovenly manner; **comme le voilà fagoté**, what a sight he looks. **se fagoter**, *v.r.* to dress in a slovenly manner.
faible [fɛːbl], *a.* and *n.* weak, feeble (person). —*n.m.* weak part; defect, failing; partiality, weakness (*for*).
faiblement [fɛblɔ'mɑ̃], *adv.* weakly, feebly.
faiblesse [fɛ'blɛs], *n.f.* weakness, feebleness; faintness; deficiency; backwardness; defect; partiality.
faiblir [fɛ'bliːr], *v.i.* to become weak, to flag, to yield, to abate, to relax.
faïence [fa'jɑ̃ːs], *n.f.* crockery, earthenware.
faïencier [fajɑ̃'sje], *n.m.* (*fem.* -**ière**) dealer in or maker of crockery.
faille [faːj], *n.f.* (*Geol.*) fault.
failli [fa'ji], *a.* and *n.m.* (*fem.* -**e**) bankrupt, insolvent (person).
faillibilité [fajibili'te], *n.f.* fallibility.
faillible [fa'jibl], *a.* fallible.
faillir [fa'jiːr], *v.i. irr.* to err, to transgress; to yield; to fail; to be on the point of; **j'ai failli tomber**, I nearly fell.
faillite [fa'jit], *n.f.* bankruptcy, insolvency; **faire faillite**, to become bankrupt.
faim [fɛ̃], *n.f.* hunger, appetite; (*fig.*) longing; **avoir faim**, to be hungry.
faine [fɛːn], *n.f.* beechnut; beechmast.
fainéant [fɛne'ɑ̃], *a.* idle, lazy.—*n.m.* (*fem.* -**e**) idler.
fainéanter [fɛneɑ̃'te], *v.i.* (*colloq.*) to be idle, to loaf.
fainéantise [fɛneɑ̃'tiːz], *n.f.* idleness, laziness, sloth.
faire (1) [fɛːr], *v. irr.* (*The most frequently used verb in the language; faire not only translates to do or to make, but, followed by a noun or an infinitive, it may take the place of practically any verb; followed by an adjective*

or an adverb it forms many current idioms.)

I. *v.t.* to do; to make; to form; to be; *cela fait mon affaire*, this is exactly what I want; *cela fait beaucoup*, that makes a great difference; *cela fait rien*, that makes no difference; *faire accueil à*, to welcome; *faire attention*, to pay attention; *faire bâtir*, to have built; *faire cas de*, to have a high opinion of; (*Motor.*) *faire du 50 à l'heure*, to do 50 kilometres an hour; *faire le mort*, to sham dead; *faire part de*, to inform; to announce; *faire peu de cas de*, to set little store by; *faire ses dents*, to cut one's teeth; *faire une promenade*, to take a walk; *faire venir*, to send for; *faire voir*, to show; *faites-le entrer*, show him in; *il ne fait que d'arriver*, he has only just arrived; *je n'ai que faire de lui*, I am in no way interested in him; *qu'est-ce que cela vous fait?* what is that to you? *que faire?* what is to be done? *se laisser faire*, to offer no resistance.

II. *v.i.* to do; to mean, to signify, to look; to fit, to suit; to deal (*at cards*); to arrange, to manage; *avoir à faire*, to have work to do; *c'en est fait de*, it is all up with.

III. *v. impers.* to be; *il fait beau*, it is fine; *quel temps fait-il?* what sort of weather is it?

IV. *se faire*, *v.r.* to be done, to be made; to happen, to become; to pretend to be; to have, make *or* get oneself; to be used (*à*), to accustom oneself (*à*); to improve; *cela ne se fait pas*, that is not done.

faire (2) [fɛːr], *n.m.* doing, making; (*Paint. etc.*) execution, style.

faire-part [fɛr'paːr], *n.m. inv.* *un faire-part* or *une lettre de faire-part de décès* or *de mariage*, notification of death, wedding-card.

faisable [fə'zabl], *a.* practicable, feasible.

faisan [fə'zɑ̃], *n.m.* pheasant.

faisandé [fəzɑ̃'de], *a.* gamy, high.

faisandeau [fəzɑ̃'do], *n.m.* (*pl.* **-eaux**) young pheasant.

faisceau [fɛ'so], *n.m.* (*pl.* **-eaux**) bundle; sheaf (*of arrows etc.*); pile (*of arms etc.*); (*fig.*) union; (*Elec.*) beam; (*Antiq., pl.*) fasces.

faiseur [fə'zœːr], *n.m.* (*fem.* **-euse**) maker; doer; charlatan, quack.

fait [fɛ, fɛt], *a.* made; done; fit, qualified; dressed, got up; full grown; mature.—*n.m.* act, deed; fact, actual event; case, matter point in business; *tout à fait*, quite.

faîte [fɛːt], *n.m.* top, pinnacle; ridge, coping (*of a building*); (*fig.*) zenith, height.

faits divers [fɛdi'vɛr], *n.m. pl.* news items, news in brief.

faix [fɛ], *n.m. inv.* weight, burden, load.

falaise [fa'lɛːz], *n.f.* cliff.

fallacieusement [falasjøz'mɑ̃], *adv.* fallaciously, falsely.

fallacieux [fala'sjø], *a.* (*fem.* **-euse**) fallacious, deceptive.

falloir [fa'lwaːr], *v. impers. irr.* to be necessary, to be obligatory, proper *or* expedient (*should*, *must*); to be needful, to be wanting *or* lacking; *comme il faut*, properly, well-bred (*of people*); *peu s'en*

faut, very nearly; *tant s'en faut*, far from it.

falot [fa'lo], *n.m.* large hand-lantern.

falsification [falsifika'sjɔ̃], *n.f.* falsification; adulteration, debasement.

falsifier [falsi'fje], *v.t.* to falsify; to alter (*texts etc.*); to adulterate (*milk*, *metals*); to tamper with.

faluche [fa'lyʃ], *n.f.* student's beret.

famé [fa'me], *a. used only in* **bien** or **mal** *famé*, of good *or* evil repute.

famélique [fame'lik], *a.* starving.—*n.* starveling.

fameux [fa'mø], *a.* (*fem.* **-euse**) famous, celebrated; first-rate; (*iron. adj. before noun*) perfect.

familial [fami'ljal], *a.* (*m. pl.* **-aux**) pertaining to family.

familiariser [familjari'ze], *v.t.* to accustom to, to familiarize. **se familiariser**, *v.r.* to familiarize oneself (*avec*); to become accustomed; to grow familiar.

familiarité [familjari'te], *n.f.* familiarity, familiar terms, intimacy; (*pl.*) liberties.

familier [fami'lje], *a.* (*fem.* **-ière**) familiar, intimate; free; homely.—*n.m.* familiar.

familièrement [familjɛr'mɑ̃], *adv.* familiarly.

famille [fa'miːj], *n.f.* family, kindred, kin; race, tribe; (*fig.*) set.

famine [fa'min], *n.f.* famine, dearth.

fanal [fa'nal], *n.m.* (*pl.* **-aux**) signal light; ship's lantern.

fanatique [fana'tik], *a.* fanatical.—*n.* fanatic, enthusiast.

fanatiquement [fanatik'mɑ̃], *adv.* fanatically.

fanatisme [fana'tism], *n.m.* fanaticism.

faner [fa'ne], *v.t.* to toss *or* ted (*hay*); to cause to fade; to tarnish. **se faner**, *v.r.* to fade, to droop, to wither; to tarnish.

faneur [fa'nœːr], *n.m.* (*fem.* **-euse**) haymaker. —*n.f.* (**-euse**) haymaking machine.

fanfare [fɑ̃'faːr], *n.f.* flourish (*of trumpets*), fanfare; brass band.

fanfaron [fɑ̃fa'rɔ̃], *a.* (*fem.* **-onne**) blustering, swaggering, boasting.—*n.m.* (*fem.* **-onne**) blusterer, swaggerer; braggart.

fanfreluche [fɑ̃frə'lyʃ], *n.f.* bauble, gewgaw.

fange [fɑ̃ːʒ], *n.f.* mire, mud, dirt; vileness.

fangeux [fɑ̃'ʒø], *a.* (*fem.* **-euse**) miry, muddy, dirty.

fanon [fa'nɔ̃], *n.m.* dewlap (*oxen*); fetlock (*horse*); horny strip (*in whales*); (*Mil.*) pennon (*of lance*).

fantaisie [fɑ̃tɛ'zi], *n.f.* imagination; fancy; whim, caprice; (*Mus.*) fantasia.

fantaisiste [fɑ̃tɛ'zist], *a.* whimsical, fantastic. —*n.* whimsical painter, writer *or* other artist.

fantasmagorie [fɑ̃tasmagɔ'ri], *n.f.* phantasmagoria.

fantasque [fɑ̃'task], *a.* fantastic, whimsical; strange, odd.

fantassin [fɑ̃ta'sɛ̃], *n.m.* foot soldier, infantry-man.

fantastique [fɑ̃tas'tik] *a.* fantastic, fanciful. —*n.m.* uncanny.

fantastiquement [fɑ̃tastik'mɑ̃], *adv.* fantastically.

fantoche [fɑ̃'tɔʃ], *n.m.* marionette, puppet.

fantôme [fɑ̃'toːm], *n.m.* phantom, specter, ghost.

faon [fã], *n.m.* fawn, calf of deer.

faquin [fa'kɛ̃], *n.m.* cad, rascal.

farandole [farã'dɔl], *n.f.* farandole (*Provençal dance*).

farce [fars], *n.f.* stuffing, force-meat; farce; buffoonery; practical joke; prank.

farceur [far'sœːr], *a.* (*fem.* **-euse**) waggish, facetious.—*n.m.* (*fem.* **-euse**) practical joker; humbug.

farcir [far'siːr], *v.t.* to stuff with force-meat etc.; to cram.

fard [faːr], *n.m.* paint (*for the complexion*), rouge, make-up; (*fig.*) varnish, disguise; *sans fard*, plainly, frankly.

fardeau [far'do], *n.m.* (*pl.* **-eaux**) burden, load; mash (*for brewing*); (*Mining*) mass.

farder [far'de], *v.t.* to paint (*the face*), to make up; (*fig.*) to varnish, to gloss over. **se farder**, *v.r.* to paint one's face, to make up. (C) **fardoches** [far'dɔʃ], *n.f. pl.* brushwood.

farfadet [farfa'dɛ], *n.m.* goblin, elf.

farfouiller [farfu'je], *v.i.* (*fam.*) to rummage.

faribole [fari'bɔl], *n.f.* idle story; trifle.

farine [fa'rin], *n.f.* flour; meal.

farineux [fari'nø], *a.* (*fem.* **-euse**) mealy, farinaceous; white with flour.

farouche [fa'ruʃ], *a.* wild; fierce; sullen; shy.

fascicule [fasi'kyl], *n.m.* fascicle.

fascinateur [fasina'tœːr], *a.* (*fem.* **-trice**) fascinating.

fascination [fasina'sjɔ̃], *n.f.* fascination.

fasciner [fasi'ne], *v.t.* to fascinate.

fascisme [fa'ʃism], *n.m.* fascism.

fasciste [fa'ʃist], *a.* and *n.* fascist.

faste [fast], *a.* favourable, lucky.—*n.m.* (*used only in sing.*) pomp, ostentation.

fastidieusement [fastidjøz'mã], *adv.* tediously.

fastidieux [fasti'djø], *a.* (*fem.* **-euse**) irksome, tedious.

fastueusement [fastɥøz'mã], *adv.* ostentatiously, pompously; splendidly.

fastueux [fas'tɥø], *a.* (*fem.* **-euse**) ostentatious, pompous, showy; stately.

fat [fat], *a.* conceited, vain, foppish.—*n.m.* fop, coxcomb.

fatal [fa'tal], *a.* fatal; inevitable; *une femme fatale*, a vamp.

fatalement [fatal'mã], *adv.* fatally; inevitably.

fatalisme [fata'lism], *n.m.* fatalism.

fataliste [fata'list], *n.* fatalist.

fatalité [fatali'te], *n.f.* fatality.

fatigant [fati'gã], *a.* fatiguing, tiring, wearisome.

fatigue [fa'tig], *n.f.* fatigue, weariness; toil, hardship; *habits de fatigue*, working clothes.

fatigué [fati'ge], *a.* fatigued, tired; (*fig.*) worn out.

fatiguer [fati'ge], *v.t.* to fatigue; to tire.—*v.i.* to tire; to be fatiguing. **se fatiguer**, *v.r.* to tire oneself out, to get tired, to be jaded.

fatras [fa'trɑ], *n.m.* jumble; rubbish, trash.

fatuité [fatɥi'te], *n.f.* fatuity, self-conceit.

faubourg [fo'buːr], *n.m.* outskirts, suburb.

faubourien [fobu'rjɛ̃], *a.* (*fem.* **-enne**) suburban, working-class; common.—*n.m.* (*fem.* **-enne**) person living in the suburbs; (*pej.*) common person.

fauchage [fo'ʃaːʒ], *n.m.* mowing.

fauchaison [foʃɛ'zɔ̃], *n.f.* mowing time.

fauché [fo'ʃe], *a.* mown; (*slang*) broke.

faucher [fo'ʃe], *v.t.* to mow, to reap.

faucheur [fo'ʃœːr], *n.m.* (*fem.* **-euse**) mower, reaper.—*n.f.* (**-euse**) (*mechanical*) mower.

faucille [fo'siːj], *n.f.* sickle, reaping-hook.

faucon [fo'kɔ̃], *n.m.* falcon, hawk.

fauconnerie [fokɔn'ri], *n.f.* falconry.

fauconnier [fokɔ'nje], *n.m.* falconer.

faufiler [fofi'le], *v.t.* to tack, to baste (*needlework*). **se faufiler**, *v.r.* to insinuate oneself, to sneak in; to find a way in.

faune (1) [foːn], *n.m.* faun.

faune (2) [foːn], *n.f.* (*Zool.*) fauna.

faussaire [fo'sɛːr], *n.* forger.

fausse [fos], [FAUX].

faussement [fos'mã], *adv.* falsely, wrongfully.

fausser [fo'se], *v.t.* to bend; to falsify, to pervert; to break, to force or strain (*a lock*).

fausset [fo'sɛ], *n.m.* (*Mus.*) falsetto.

fausseté [fos'te], *n.f.* falsity, falsehood; duplicity.

faute [foːt], *n.f.* want; defect; fault, mistake, error; *faute de*, for want of.

fauteuil [fo'tœːj], *n.m.* arm-chair; chair (*speaker's, president's seat*).

fauteur [fo'tœːr], *n.m.* abettor, favorer.

fautif [fo'tif], *a.* (*fem.* **-tive**) faulty, at fault, defective.

fauve [foːv], *a.* fawn-colored, tawny.—*n.m.* wild animal; *Les Fauves*, group of French painters at the beginning of this century.

fauvette [fo'vɛt], *n.f.* warbler.

faux (1) [fo], *n.f. inv.* scythe.

faux (2) [fo], *a.* (*fem.* **fausse**) false, untrue, wrong; base, counterfeit, forged (*coinage*); sham; insincere; (*Mus.*) out of tune; *faire un faux pas*, to stumble; (*fig.*) to make a slip.—*n.m.* falsehood; error; forgery.—*adv.* falsely, erroneously; (*Mus.*) out of tune.

faux-filet [fofi'lɛ], *n.m.* sirloin.

faux-fuyant [fofɥi'jã], *n.m.* subterfuge, evasion.

faux-monnayeur [fomɔnɛ'jœːr], *n.m.* counterfeiter.

faveur [fa'vœːr], *n.f.* favor, boon; grace; vogue; (*narrow*) silk ribbon; *à la faveur de*, by means of; *en faveur de*, on behalf of.

favorable [favɔ'rabl], *a.* favorable, propitious.

favorablement [favɔrablə'mã], *adv.* favorably.

favori [favɔ'ri], *a.* and *n.m.* (*fem.* **-ite**) favorite. —*n.m.* (*pl.*) side whiskers.

favoriser [favɔri'ze], *v.t.* to favor, to befriend; to assist, to protect.

favoritisme [favɔri'tism], *n.m.* favoritism.

fébrile [fe'bril], *a.* febrile, feverish.

fécond [fe'kɔ̃], *a.* fruitful, prolific; copious, abundant, fertile.

fécondation [fekɔ̃da'sjɔ̃], *n.f.* impregnation; fertilization.

féconder [fekɔ̃'de], *v.t.* to make fruitful, to fertilize.

fécondité [fekɔ̃di'te], *n.f.* fecundity, fruitfulness, fertility.

fécule [fe'kyl], *n.f.* faecula, starch.

féculent [feky'lã], *a.* feculent.—*n.m.* starchy food.

fédéral [fede'ral], *a.* (*m. pl.* **-aux**) federal.

fédéralisme [federa'lism], *n.m.* federalism.

fédéraliste [federa'list], *a.* and *n.* federalist.

fédération [federɑˈsjɔ̃], *n.f.* federation, alliance.

fédéré [fedeˈre], *a.* federate, confederate; amalgamated.

fédérer (se) [səfedeˈre], *v.r.* (*conjug. like* CÉDER) to federate, to band together.

fée [fe], *n.f.* fairy, fay.

féerie [feaˈri], *n.f.* enchantment; fairy scene; fairy-land.

féerique [feaˈrik], *a.* fairy-like; wonderful.

feindre [fɛ̃:dr], *v.t. irr* (*conjug. like* CRAINDRE) to feign, to simulate, to sham, to pretend.—*v.i.* to feign, to sham.

feint [fɛ̃], *a.* feigned, pretended, sham.

feinte [fɛ̃:t], *n.f.* feint; pretence, dissimulation.

feld-maréchal [fɛldmareˈʃal], *n.m.* (*pl.* -**aux**) field marshal.

feldspath [fɛlsˈpat], *n.m.* feldspar.

fêlé [fɛˈle], *a.* cracked (*of glass*); (*fig.*) crack-brained.

fêler [fɛˈle], *v.t.* and **se fêler**, *v.r.* to crack (*of glass etc.*).

félicitation [felisitɑˈsjɔ̃], *n.f.* felicitation, congratulation.

félicité [felisiˈte], *n.f.* felicity, bliss.

féliciter [felisiˈte], *v.t.* to congratulate, to felicitate. **se féliciter**, *v.r.* to congratulate oneself.

félin [feˈlɛ̃], *a.* and *n.m.* (*fem.* -**e**) feline.

félon [feˈlɔ̃], *a.* (*fem.* -**onne**) disloyal, traitorous.—*n.m.* (*fem.* -**onne**) traitor, caitiff.

félonie [feloˈni], *n.f.* (*Feud.*) felony, treason.

fêlure [fɛˈly:r], *n.f.* crack, fissure.

femelle [fəˈmɛl], *a.* female, feminine, she-.—*n.f.* female, (*pej.*) woman.

féminin [femiˈnɛ̃], *a.* feminine, female, womanish, womanly, effeminate.—*n.m.* (*Gram.*) feminine.

femme [fam], *n.f.* woman; married woman; wife; female attendant; lady.

femme-agent [famaˈʒɑ̃], *n.f.* police-woman.

femmelette [famˈlɛt], *n.f.* silly, weak woman; effeminate man.

femme-soldat [famsɔlˈda], *n.f.* service-woman.

fémur [feˈmy:r], *n.m.* femur, thigh-bone.

fenaison [fənɛˈzɔ̃], *n.f.* hay time, hay-making.

fendiller (se) [səfɑ̃diˈje], *v.r.* to be covered with small cracks, to crack, to split.

fendre [fɑ̃:dr], *v.t.* to cleave, to split, to crack, to cut open; to plough (*the sea*). **se fendre**, *v.r.* to burst asunder, to split, to be ready to burst.

fendu [fɑ̃ˈdy], *a.* cleft, split, cloven.

fenêtre [fəˈnɛ:tr], *n.f.* window, casement.

fenil [fəˈni], *n.m.* hayloft.

fenouil [fəˈnu:j], *n.m.* fennel.

fente [fɑ̃:t], *n.f.* slit, chink, cleft: gap. crevice.

féodal [feoˈdal], *a.* (*m. pl.* -**aux**) feudal.

féodalisme [feodaˈlism], *n.m.* feudalism.

fer [fɛ:r], *n.m.* iron; iron tool; horseshoe; head, point, etc.; (*fig.*) sword, brand; (*Golf*) club; (*pl.*) irons, chains, fetters; **fer battu** or **forgé**, wrought iron; **fil de fer**, wire.

fer-blanc [fɛrˈblɑ̃], *n.m.* (*pl.* **fers-blancs**) tin, tin plate.

férié [feˈrje], *a.* holiday; **jour férié**, holiday, general holiday, bank holiday.

férir [feˈri:r], *v.t. used only in* **sans coup férir**, without striking a blow.

ferler [fɛrˈle], *v.t.* to furl (*sails*).

fermage [fɛrˈma:ʒ], *n.m.* rent (*of a farm*).

fermail [fɛrˈma:j], *n.m.* clasp, buckle.

ferme (1) [fɛrm], *a.* firm; fixed, stable; strong, stout, stiff, steady; resolute.—*adv.* firmly, fast, hard.

ferme (2) [fɛrm], *n.f.* farm, farmhouse, farmstead; farming (*of taxes*); letting out on lease.

ferme (3) [fɛrm], *n.f.* framework of beams.

fermement [fɛrməˈmɑ̃], *adv.* firmly, steadily; resolutely.

ferment [fɛrˈmɑ̃], *n.m.* ferment, leaven.

fermentation [fɛrmɑ̃tɑˈsjɔ̃], *n.f.* fermentation, working; (*fig.*) ferment.

fermenter [fɛrmɑ̃ˈte], *v.i.* to ferment, to rise, to work.

fermer [fɛrˈme], *v.t.* to shut, to close; to fasten; to turn off (*water, gas etc.*); to put an end to (*a discussion etc.*); to enclose.—*v.i.* to shut, to be shut. **se fermer**, *v.r.* to shut, to close, to be closed; to lock.

fermeté [fɛrməˈte], *n.f.* firmness; steadiness; resolution.

fermeture [fɛrməˈty:r], *n.f.* closing, shutting; **fermeture à glissière**, zip fastener.

fermier [fɛrˈmje], *n.m.* (tenant) farmer.

fermière [fɛrˈmjɛ:r], *n.f.* farmer's wife.

fermoir [fɛrˈmwa:r], *n.m.* clasp, fastener.

féroce [feˈrɔs], *a.* ferocious, fierce, savage.

férocement [ferɔsˈmɑ̃], *adv.* ferociously.

férocité [ferɔsiˈte], *n.f.* ferocity, fierceness.

ferraille [fɛˈra:j], *n.f.* old iron, scrap iron.

ferrailler [fɛraˈje], *v.i.* (*Spt.*) to fence clumsily; (*fig.*) to squabble.

ferrailleur [fɛraˈjœ:r], *n.m.* dealer in old iron, scrap merchant; (*Spt.*) clumsy fencer.

ferrant [fɛˈrɑ̃], *a.* **maréchal ferrant**, farrier, shoeing-smith.

ferré [fɛˈre], *a.* bourd, shod etc., with iron; metalled; (*colloq.*) skilled; **voie ferrée**, railway.

ferrer [fɛˈre], *v.t.* to bind, hoop, etc., with iron; to shoe (*a horse etc.*).

ferret [fɛˈrɛ], *n.m.* tag (*of a lace*).

ferronnerie [fɛrɔnˈri], *n.f.* iron foundry; ironmongery; wrought iron.

ferronnier [fɛrɔˈnje], *n.m.* (*fem.* -**ière**) ironmonger, iron worker.

ferroviaire [fɛrɔˈvjɛ:r], *a.* pertaining to railways.

ferrure [fɛˈry:r], *n.f.* iron work; shoeing (*of a horse etc.*).

fertile [fɛrˈtil], *a.* fertile, fruitful.

fertilement [fɛrtilˈmɑ̃], *adv.* fertilely, abundantly.

fertilisant [fɛrtiliˈzɑ̃], *a.* fertilizing.

fertiliser [fɛrtiliˈze], *v.t.* to fertilize, to manure.

fertilité [fɛrtiliˈte], *n.f.* fertility, fruitfulness.

féru [feˈry], *a.* smitten; keen on (*something or someone*).

férule [feˈryl], *n.f.* (*Sch.*) cane, ferule, rod; stroke, cut.

fervent [fɛrˈvɑ̃], *a.* fervent.—*n.m.* (*fem.* -**e**) enthusiast, devotee, fan.

ferveur [fɛrˈvœ:r], *n.f.* fervor, ardor.

fesse [fɛs], *n.f.* buttock, rump; (*pl.*) bottom.

fessée [fɛˈse], *n.f.* spanking.

fesse-mathieu [fɛsmaˈtjø], *n.m.* (*pl.* **fesse-mathieux**) miser, skinflint.

fesser [fɛˈse], *v.t.* to spank, to smack.

153

fessier [fɛ'sje], *n.m.* buttocks, bottom.
festin [fɛs'tɛ̃], *n.m.* feast, banquet.
*****festiner** [fɛsti'ne], *v.i.* to banquet, to carouse.
festival [fɛsti'val], *n.m.* festival.
festivité [fɛstivi'te], *n.f.* festivity.
feston [fɛs'tɔ̃], *n.m.* festoon; scallop.
festonner [fɛstɔ'ne], *v.t.* to festoon; to cut in festoons, to scallop.
festoyer [fɛstwa'je], *v.t.* (*conjug. like* EM-PLOYER) to entertain, to feast.
fête [fɛːt], *n.f.* holiday, festival; saint's day; feast; birthday; festivity, merry-making.
fête-Dieu [fɛːt'djø], *n.f.* Corpus Christi day.
fêter [fɛ'te], *v.t.* to keep (as a holiday); to entertain, to feast.
fétiche [fe'tiʃ], *n.m.* fetish.
fétide [fe'tid], *a.* fetid, rank, offensive.
fétidité [fetidi'te], *n.f.* fetidity, offensive smell.
fétu [fe'ty], *n.m.* straw; (*fig.*) pin, rap.
feu (1) [fø], *n.m.* (*pl.* **feux**) fire; burning; heat; discharge of fire-arms; fire-place; (*fig.*) light; brilliancy; passion; vivacity; *crier 'au feu'*, to cry 'fire!'; *faire feu*, to fire; *feu d'artifice*, fireworks; *feu de joie*, bonfire; *feux de position*, (*Motor.*) parking lights; *le coin du feu*, the fire-side; *prendre feu*, to catch fire.
feu (2) [fø], *a.* late, deceased.
feuillage [fœ'jaːʒ], *n.m.* foliage, leaves.
feuille [fœːj], *n.f.* leaf; sheet (*of paper, metal etc.*); newspaper; list; foil (*of mirrors*).
feuillet [fœ'jɛ], *n.m.* leaf (*of a book*).
feuilleter [fœj'te], *v.t.* (*conjug. like* APPELER) to turn over (*of a book*); to peruse rapidly; *gâteau feuilleté*, flaky puff.
feuillu [fœ'jy], *a.* leafy.
feutrage [fø'traːʒ], *n.m.* felting.
feutre [føːtr], *n.m.* felt; felt hat.
feutrer [fø'tre], *v.t.* to felt; to pad, to pack.
feutrier [føtri'e], *n.m.* (*fem.* **-ière**) felt maker.
fève [fɛːv], *n.f.* bean, broad bean.
février [fevri'e], *n.m.* February.
fez [fɛːz], *n.m. inv.* fez (*Turkish cap*).
fi! [fi], *int.* fie!
fiacre [fjakr], *n.m.* hackney-coach, cab.
fiançailles [fjɑ̃'saːj], *n.f.* (*used only in pl.*) betrothal, engagement.
fiancé [fjɑ̃'se], *n.m.* (*fem.* **-ée**) betrothed, fiancé, fiancée.
fiancer [fjɑ̃'se], *v.t.* (*conjug. like* COMMENCER) to betroth, to affiance. **se fiancer**, *v.r.* to become engaged to each other.
fiasco [fjas'ko], *n.m. inv.* fiasco, failure.
fibre [fibr], *n.f.* fiber, filament; (*fig.*) feeling.
fibreux [fi'brø], *a.* (*fem.* **-euse**) fibrous, stringy.
ficeler [fis'le], *v.t.* (*conjug. like* APPELER) to bind or tie up with string; to do up; to dress up.
ficeleur [fis'lœːr], *n.m.* (*fem.* **-euse**) packer.
ficelle [fi'sɛl], *n.f.* string, packthread, twine; (*fig.*) dodge.
fiche [fiʃ], *n.f.* peg, pin (*for a hinge etc.*); (*Teleph.*) plug; small card; (*Whist*) booby prize; (*colloq.*) slip of paper, memo.
ficher [fi'ʃe], *v.t.* to drive in, to fasten in. **se ficher**, *v.r.* (*colloq.*) to laugh at (*de*).
fichier [fi'ʃje], *n.m.* card index (*cabinet*).
fichoir [fi'ʃwaːr], *n.m.* clothespin.
fichtre! [fiʃtr], *int.* (*colloq.*) dash it! hang it!
fichu (1) [fi'ʃy], *n.m.* neckerchief.

fichu (2) [fi'ʃy], *a.* sorry, pitiful; got up (*dressed*); (*slang*) done for.
fictif [fik'tif], *a.* (*fem.* **-tive**) supposed, fictitious.
fiction [fik'sjɔ̃], *n.f.* fiction; fable.
fictivement [fiktiv'mɑ̃], *adv.* fictitiously.
fidèle [fi'dɛl], *a.* faithful, loyal, true.—*n.* faithful friend etc.; (*pl.*) worshippers, faithful.
fidèlement [fidɛl'mɑ̃], *adv.* faithfully, truly.
fidélité [fideli'te], *n.f.* fidelity, faithfulness, loyalty; accuracy.
fief [fjɛf], *n.m.* fief, fee.
fieffé [fje'fe], *a.* (*colloq.*) arrant, downright.
fiel [fjɛl], *n.m.* gall; (*fig.*) hatred, bitterness, rancour.
fier [fje], *v.t.* to trust, to entrust. **se fier**, *v.r.* to trust to or in, to depend upon (*à*).
fier [fjɛːr], *a.* (*fem.* **fière**) proud, haughty; bold; (*colloq.*) fine, capital.
fièrement [fjɛr'mɑ̃], *adv.* proudly, arrogantly, haughtily; boldly.
fierté [fjɛr'te], *n.f.* pride, arrogance; dignity.
fièvre [fjɛːvr], *n.f.* fever, feverishness; (*fig.*) restlessness, excitement.
fiévreux [fje'vrø], *a.* (*fem.* **-euse**) feverish; (*fig.*) restless.—*n.m.* (*fem.* **-euse**) fever patient.
fifre [fifr], *n.m.* fife; fifer.
figé [fi'ʒe], *a.* stiff, cold, set (*features, smile etc.*).
figement [fiʒ'mɑ̃], *n.m.* congealment, coagulation, curdling.
figer [fi'ʒe], *v.t.* and **se figer**, *v.r.* (*conjug. like* MANGER) to congeal, to coagulate, to curdle.
figue [fig], *n.f.* fig.
figuier [fi'gje], *n.m.* fig tree.
figurant [figy'rɑ̃], *n.m.* (*fem.* **-e**) (*Theat., Cine.*) figurant; extra.
figuratif [figyra'tif], *a.* (*fem.* **-tive**) figurative.
figurativement [figyrativ'mɑ̃], *adv.* figuratively.
figure [fi'gyːr], *n.f.* figure, shape; face, appearance; symbol, type.
figuré [figy're], *a.* figured; figurative.
figurer [figy're], *v.t.* to figure, to represent.—*v.i.* to figure, to appear. **se figurer**, *v.r.* to imagine, fancy or picture to oneself.
figurine [figy'rin], *n.f.* figurine, statuette.
fil [fil], *n.m.* thread; wire; yarn; (*cutting*) edge; grain, vein (*in stones etc.*); course (*of a stream etc.*); chain, series; *de fil en aiguille*, one thing leading to another; *donner un coup de fil*, to give a ring; *être au bout du fil*, to be speaking (*on the phone*); *fil à coudre*, sewing thread; *fil de la Vierge*, gossamer; *laine deux fils*, two-ply wool.
filage [fi'laːʒ], *n.m.* spinning.
filament [fila'mɑ̃], *n.m.* filament, thread.
filamenteux [filamɑ̃'tø], *a.* (*fem.* **-euse**) thready, stringy.
filandière [filɑ̃'djɛːr], *n.f.* spinner.
filandreux [filɑ̃'drø], *a.* (*fem.* **-euse**) fibrous, stringy, thready.
filant [fi'lɑ̃], *a.* flowing; ropy; shooting (*of stars*).
filasse [fi'las], *n.f.* harl, tow (*of flax, hemp etc.*); oakum.
filateur [fila'tœːr], *n.m.* spinning-mill owner; spinner.

filature [fila'ty:r], *n.f.* spinning-mill; spinning; shadowing (*by a detective*).

file [fil], *n.f.* file; *à la file*, one after another; *prendre la file*, to take one's place in the line.

filé [fi'le], *a.* drawn out, sustained.—*n.m.* gold *or* silver thread.

filer [fi'le], *v.t.* to spin; (*fig.*) to carry on; to spin out (*a story etc.*); (*Naut.*) to pay out (*a rope*); to trail, to shadow,—*v.i.* to become ropy; to go, to travel; to shoot (*of stars*); to flare (*of a lamp etc.*); to take oneself off; *filer à l'anglaise*, to take French leave; *filer doux*, to sing small.

filet [fi'le], *n.m.* slender thread, string; net; (*Rail.*) rack; filament, fiber; (*Bot., Arch. etc.*) fillet; drop (*of water etc.*); (*fig.*) streak; trickle, streamlet; snaffle-bridle; (*fig.*) snare.

fileur [fi'lœ:r], *n.m.* (*fem.* -**euse**) spinner; wire-drawer.

filial [fi'ljal], *a.* (*m. pl.* -**aux**) filial.

filiale [fi'ljal], *n.f.* subsidiary company, branch.

filiation [filja'sjɔ̃], *n.f.* filiation; (*fig.*) connection, relationship.

filière [fi'ljɛ:r], *n.f.* draw-plate; screw-plate; (*Carp.*) purlin; (*fig.*) channel, series.

filigrane [fili'gran], *n.m.* filigree, filigree work; water-mark (*in paper*); embossing.

filigraner [filigra'ne], *v.t.* to work in filigree; to emboss.

fille [fi:j], *n.f.* daughter; girl, young unmarried woman; maiden; servant-maid; *arrière-petite-fille*, great-granddaughter; *belle-fille*, daughter-in-law, stepdaughter; *jeune fille*, girl; *petite-fille*, granddaughter; *vieille fille*, old maid.

fillette [fi'jet], *n.f.* little girl; lass.

filleul [fi'jœl], *n.m.* godson.

filleule [fi'jœl], *n.f.* goddaughter.

film [film], *n.m.* film; *film fixe*, film strip.

filmer [fil'me], *v.t.* to film.

filon [fi'lɔ̃], *n.m.* metallic vein; (*fig.*) good job; tip.

filou [fi'lu], *n.m.* pickpocket, thief; swindler.

filouter [filu'te], *v.t.* to steal; to cheat, to swindle.

filouterie [filu'tri], *n.f.* picking pockets; swindling, cheating.

fils [fis], *n.m. inv.* son, male child; offspring; *arrière-petit-fils*, great-grandson; *beau-fils*, stepson, son-in-law; *petit-fils*, grandson.

filtrage [fil'tra:ʒ], *n.m.* filtering, straining.

filtrant [fil'trɑ̃], *a.* filtering, straining; *bout filtrant*, filter-tip.

filtration [filtra'sjɔ̃], *n.f.* filtration, straining; percolation.

filtre (1) [filtr], *n.m.* filter; cup of filtered coffee; *filtre à café*, percolator.

filtre (2) [PHILTRE].

filtrer [fil'tre], *v.t.* to filter, to strain.—*v.i.* and se **filtrer**, *v.r.* to filter; to percolate.

filure [fi'ly:r], *n.f.* texture of a spun fabric.

fin (1) [fɛ̃], *n.f.* end, conclusion, close; death; destination; aim, design.

fin (2) [fɛ̃], *a.* fine, thin, slender; delicate; refined, polite; acute; cunning.—*n.m.* sharp fellow; main point.—*n.f.* (-**e**) type of liqueur brandy.

final [fi'nal], *a.* final, last, ultimate.

finale [fi'nal], *n.m.* (*Mus.*) finale.—*n.f.* (*Spt.*) final.

finalement [final'mɑ̃], *adv.* finally, lastly.

finalité [finali'te], *n.f.* finality.

finance [fi'nɑ̃:s], *n.f.* ready money; (*pl.*) (*public*) finances, exchequer, treasury.

financer [finɑ̃'se], *v.t.* (*conjug. like* COMMENCER) to finance—*v.i.* to lay out money.

financier [finɑ̃'sje], *a.* (*fem.* -**ière**) financial. —*n.m.* financier.

financièrement [finɑ̃sjɛr'mɑ̃], *adv.* financially.

finaud [fi'no], *a.* sly, artful, cunning.—*n.m.* (*fem.* -**e**) sly, artful person.

fine [fin], [FIN (2)].

finement [fin'mɑ̃], *adv.* finely, delicately; ingeniously; artfully.

finesse [fi'nɛs], *n.f.* fineness; delicacy; ingenuity; finesse, artifice, slyness.

finette [fi'nɛt], *n.f.* thin material of wool *or* cotton, flannelette.

fini [fi'ni], *a.* finished, ended.—*n.m.* finish, high finish, perfection.

finir [fi'ni:r], *v.t.* to finish, to complete; to end, to terminate.—*v.i.* to end, to conclude, to be over; to expire.

finissage [fini'sa:ʒ], *n.m.* finishing touches.

finissant [fini'sɑ̃], *a.* declining, dying.

finlandais [fɛ̃lɑ̃'dɛ], *a.* Finnish.—*n.m.* Finnish (*language*); (**Finlandais**, *fem.* -**aise**) Finn.

Finlande [fɛ̃'lɑ̃:d], **la**, *f.* Finland.

finnois [fi'nwa], *a.* Finnish.—*n.m.* Finnish (*language*); (**Finnois**, *fem.* -**oise**) Finn.

fiole [fjɔl], *n.f.* phial.

firmament [firma'mɑ̃], *n.m.* firmament, sky.

fisc [fisk], *n.m.* public treasury, fisc.

fiscal [fis'kal], *a.* (*m. pl.* -**aux**) fiscal, financial.

fissible [fi'sibl], *a.* fissile (*of radio-active materials*).

fission [fi'sjɔ̃], *n.f.* fission, splitting (*of atom*); *fission de l'atome*, nuclear fission.

fissure [fi'sy:r], *n.f.* fissure, crack, rent.

fissurer (se) [safisy're], *v.r.* to become fissured.

five-o'clock [faivo'klɔk], *n.m.* afternoon tea.

fixation [fiksa'sjɔ̃], *n.f.* fixation, fixing; settlement; rating, assessment.

fixe [fiks], *a.* fixed; settled; appointed, regular. —*n.m.* fixed salary.—*int.* (*Mil.*) eyes front! steady!

fixement [fiksa'mɑ̃], *adv.* fixedly, steadily.

fixer [fik'se], *v.t.* to fix, to fasten; to settle; to establish; to stare at; to attract. se **fixer**, *v.r.* to be fixed; to settle down.

fixité [fiksi'te], *n.f.* fixity, stability.

flac [flak], *int.* slap! bang! plop!—*n.m.* anti-aircraft gunfire, flak.

flaccidité [flaksidi'te], *n.f.* flaccidity.

flacon [fla'kɔ̃], *n.m.* bottle; decanter; phial.

flagellant [flaʒɛl'lɑ̃], *n.m.* flagellant.

flagellation [flaʒɛla'sjɔ̃], *n.f.* flagellation, flogging.

flageller [flaʒɛl'le], *v.t.* to flagellate, to scourge, to flog; (*fig.*) to lash with words.

flageoler [flaʒɔ'le], *v.i.* to tremble, to shake (*of legs*).

flageolet [flaʒɔ'lɛ], *n.m.* flageolet (*music*); (*small*) green kidney bean.

flagorner [flagɔr'ne], *v.t.* to flatter servilely, to toady to.

flagornerie [flagɔrnəˈri], *n.f.* sycophancy, base flattery.

flagorneur [flagɔrˈnœːr], *n.m.* (*fem.* -euse) sycophant, toady.

flagrant [flaˈgrã], *a.* flagrant, gross; *en flagrant délit*, red-handed.

flair [flɛːr], *n.m.* (*Hunt.*) nose; (*fig.*) perspicacity.

flairer [flɛˈre], *v.t.* to smell, to scent; (*colloq.*) to smell of; to find out.

flamand [flaˈmã], *a.* Flemish.—*n.m.* Flemmish (*language*); (**Flamand**, *fem.* -**ande**) Fleming.

flamant (rose) [flaˈmã(roːz)], *n.m.* flamingo.

flambant [flãˈbã], *a.* blazing, flaming; (*pop.*) smart, flashy; *flambant neuf*, brand new.

flambeau [flãˈbo], *n.m.* (*pl.* -**eaux**) torch, link; candle, candlestick.

flambée [flãˈbe], *n.f.* blaze.

flamber [flãˈbe], *v.t.* to singe; to fumigate, to disinfect.—*v.i.* to blaze, to flame, to flare.

flamboiement [flãbwaˈmã], *n.m.* flaming, blaze.

flamboyant [flãbwaˈjã], *a.* flaming, blazing; flashing.

flamboyer [flãbwaˈje], *v.i.* (*conjug. like* EMPLOYER) to flame, to blaze, to flare.

flamme [flaːm], *n.f.* flame; (*fig.*) fire; glow; ardor, passion.

flammèche [flaˈmɛʃ], *n.f.* flake of fire, spark.

flammer [flaˈme], *v.t.* to singe (*material*).

flan [flã], *n.m.* (*baked*) custard tart; flan.

flanc [flã], *n.m.* flank, side; (*fig.*) womb, bowels.

flancher [flãˈʃe], *v.i.* (*fam.*) to give in, to rat, to scab; (*Motor.*) to stop, to break down.

flandrin [flãˈdrɛ̃], *n.m.* (*colloq.*) *un grand flandrin*, a long, lanky fellow.

flanelle [flaˈnɛl], *n.f.* flannel.

flâner [flaˈne], *v.i.* to lounge, to stroll, to loaf.

flânerie [flaˈnri], *n.f.* lounging; stroll; loafing.

flâneur [flaˈnœːr], *n.m.* (*fem.* -**euse**) stroller; lounger, loafer.

flanquer [flãˈke], *v.t.* to flank; (*Mil.*) to defend, to guard; (*colloq.*) to deal (*a blow*); to fling. **se flanquer**, *v.r.* *se flanquer par terre*, to throw oneself down.

flaque [flak], *n.f.* small pool, puddle.

flash [flaʃ], *n.m.* (*Phot.*) flash-light; (*Cine.*) flash.

flasque (1) [flask], *a.* limp, slack, flabby, flaccid.

flasque (2) [flask], *n.f.* powder horn.

flatter [flaˈte], *v.t.* to stroke, to caress; to flatter; to soothe; to cajole. **se flatter**, *v.r.* to flatter oneself; to pride oneself; to hope, to expect.

flatterie [flaˈtri], *n.f.* flattery, adulation.

flatteur [flaˈtœːr], *a.* (*fem.* -**euse**) flattering, complimentary.—*n.m.* (*fem.* -**euse**) flatterer.

flatteusement [flatøzˈmã], *adv.* flatteringly.

flatulence [flatyˈlãːs], *n.f.* flatulence, wind.

flatulent [flatyˈlã], *a.* flatulent, windy.

fléau [fleˈo], *n.m.* (*pl.* **fléaux**) flail; (*fig.*) scourge, plague; beam (*of a balance*).

flèche [flɛʃ], *n.f.* arrow, dart; shaft; (*Arch.*) slender spire; *faire flèche de tout bois*, to leave no stone unturned.

fléchette [fleˈʃɛt], *n.f.* dart (*game*).

fléchir [fleˈʃiːr], *v.t.* to bend, to bow; (*fig.*) to move, to persuade.—*v.i.* to bend, to bow, to yield; to stagger.

fléchissement [fleʃisˈmã], *n.m.* bending, giving way.

flegmatique [flɛgmaˈtik], *a.* (*Med.*) phlegmatic; (*fig.*) stolid, sluggish.

flegme [flɛgm], *n.m.* phlegm; (*fig.*) coolness, impassivity.

flet [flɛ], **flétan** [fleˈtã], *n.m.* **grand flétan**, halibut; *petit flétan* or *flet*, flounder.

flétrir [fleˈtriːr], *v.t.* to wither; (*fig.*) to blight, to tarnish, to blemish. **se flétrir**, *v.r.* to fade, to wither.

flétrissant [fletriˈsã], *a.* dishonoring, blighting.

flétrissure [fletriˈsyːr], *n.f.* fading, withering, stigma, disgrace.

fleur [flœːr], *n.f.* flower, blossom; bloom; (*fig.*) best, pick; surface; *à fleur d'eau*, at water level; *à fleur de peau*, superficially; *yeux à fleur de tête*, prominent *or* goggle eyes.

fleurer [flœˈre], *v.i.* to smell, to exhale.

fleuret [flœˈrɛ], *n.m.* (*Fenc.*) foil; miner's drill.

fleurette [flœˈrɛt], *n.f.* little flower, floweret; amorous discourse, gallant speech.

fleuri [flœˈri], *a.* flowery; florid.

fleurir [flœˈriːr], *v.t.* to decorate with flowers. —*v.i.* to flower, to blossom; to flourish. **se fleurir**, *v.r.* to adorn oneself with flowers.

fleurissant [flœriˈsã], *a.* blossoming, blooming.

fleuriste [flœˈrist], *a.* and *n.* florist; artificial flower maker *or* seller.

fleuron [flœˈrã], *n.m.* carved *or* painted flower; (*fig.*) flower work; jewel.

fleuve [flœːv], *n.m.* river (*flowing into the sea*), large stream.

flexibilité [flɛksibiliˈte], *n.f.* flexibility, pliancy.

flexible [flɛkˈsibl], *a.* flexible, pliable, supple.

flexion [flɛkˈsjã], *n.f.* flexion, bending.

flibuster [flibysˈte], *v.i.* to buccaneer, to filibuster, to freeboot.

flibusterie [flibysˈtri], *n.f.* filibustering; robbery, theft.

flibustier [flibysˈtje], *n.m.* buccaneer, pirate; filibuster.

flirt [flœrt], *n.m.* flirtation, flirting.

flirter [flœrˈte], *v.i.* to flirt.

floc [flɔk], *n.m.* tuft, tassel.—*int.* flop!

floche [flɔʃ], *a.* flossy, shaggy.

flocon [flɔˈkã], *n.m.* flock, tuft; flake (*of snow*).

floconneux [flɔkɔˈnø], *a.* (*fem.* -**euse**) flaky.

floraison [flɔrɛˈzã], *n.f.* efflorescence, flowering.

floral [flɔˈral], *a.* (*m. pl.* -**aux**) floral.

flore [flɔːr], *n.f.* flora.

florentin [flɔrãˈtɛ̃], *a.* Florentine.

florin [flɔˈrɛ̃], *n.m.* florin.

florir [flɔˈriːr], [FLEURIR]

florissant [flɔriˈsã], *a.* prosperous, flourishing.

floriste [flɔˈrist], *n.* florist.

flot [flo], *n.m.* wave, billow; (*fig.*) tide, flood; crowd; (*pl.*) sea, stream, torrent.

flottage [flɔˈtaːʒ], *n.m.* floating of wood, rafting.

flottaison [flɔtɛˈzã], *n.f.* floating.

flottant [flɔˈtã], *a.* floating, waving; (*fig.*) irresolute.

flotte [flɔt], *n.f.* fleet; navy.

flottement [flɔtˈmã], *n.m.* floating; (*fig.*) wavering, irresolution.

flotter [flɔ'te], *v.i.* to float; to flutter (*of flag*); to be irresolute.

flotteur [flɔ'tœːr], *n.m.* raftsman; fishing-float; cable-buoy.

flottille [flɔ'tiːj], *n.f.* flotilla.

flou [flu], *a.* hazy, soft, blurred, out of focus. —*n.m.* softness, haziness (*of outlines*); (*Dress.*) looseness.

fluctuation [flyktɥa'sjɔ̃], *n.f.* fluctuation.

fluctuer [flyk'tɥe], *v.i.* to fluctuate.

fluctueux [flyk'tɥø], *a.* (*fem.* **-euse**) fluctuating, agitated, boisterous.

fluet [flɥɛ], *a.* (*fem.* **-ette**) slender, thin, slim.

fluide [flɥ'id], *a.* fluid (*liquid*).—*n.m.* fluid.

fluidité [flɥidi'te], *n.f.* fluidity.

fluorescence [flyɔrɛ'sãːs], *n.f.* fluorescence.

fluorescent [flyɔrɛ'sã], *a.* fluorescent.

fluorure [flyɔ'ryːr], *n.m.* fluoride.

flûte [flyt], *n.f.* flute; long French roll; tall glass (*for champagne*).

flûté [fly'te], *a.* soft, fluted, fluty (*of a voice*).

flûtiste [fly'tist], *n.* flautist, flute player.

fluvial [fly'vjal], *a.* (*m. pl.* **-aux**) fluvial.

flux [fly], *n.m.* flux, flow, flood, rising.

fluxion [flyk'sjɔ̃], *n.f.* inflammation, swelling.

foc [fɔk], *n.m.* (*Naut.*) jib.

focal [fɔ'kal], *a.* (*m. pl.* **-aux**) focal.

foi [fwa], *n.f.* faith, belief; trust; fidelity, honor; proof, testimony.

foie [fwa], *n.m.* liver.

foin [fwɛ̃], *n.m.* hay.

foire [fwaːr], *n.f.* fair (*market*); fairing.

fois [fwa], *n.f. inv.* time (*turn, occasion*); **une fois**, once; **trois fois**, three times.

foison [fwa'zɔ̃], *n.f.* plenty, abundance.

foisonner [fwazɔ'ne], *v.i.* to abound, to increase, to multiply.

fol [fɔl], [FOU].

folâtre [fɔ'laːtr], *a.* playful, gay, frolicsome.

folâtrer [fɔla'tre], *v.i.* to play, to sport, to frolic.

folâtrerie [fɔlatrə'ri], *n.f.* frolic, prank, gambol.

foliacé [fɔlja'se], *a.* (*Bot.*) foliaceous.

foliation [fɔlja'sjɔ̃], *n.f.* foliation.

folichon [fɔli'fɔ̃], *a.* (*fam.*) frolicsome, waggish, wanton.

folie [fɔ'li], *n.f.* madness, distraction, folly; foolery, jest; mania; hobby.

folio [fɔ'ljo], *n.m.* folio.

folle [fɔl], [FOU].

follement [fɔl'mã], *adv.* madly, foolishly.

follet [fɔ'lɛ], *a.* (*fem.* **-ette**) wanton, playful, frolicsome; **feu follet**, will o' the wisp.

fomentation [fɔmãta'sjɔ̃], *n.f.* fomentation.

fomenter [fɔmã'te], *v.t.* to foment; (*fig.*) to feed, to excite.

foncé [fɔ̃'se], *a.* dark, deep (*of color*).

foncer [fɔ̃'se], *v.t.* (*conjug. like* COMMENCER) to fit a bottom to (*a cask etc.*); to sink (*wells etc.*); to deepen (*colors*). —*v.i.* to dash, to swoop (*sur*).

foncier [fɔ̃'sje], *a.* (*fem.* **-ière**) landed; based on *or* derived from land; (*fig.*) thorough.—*n.m.* land tax.

foncièrement [fɔ̃sjɛr'mã], *adv.* thoroughly, completely, fundamentally.

fonction [fɔ̃k'sjɔ̃], *n.f.* function, office; occupation.

fonctionnaire [fɔ̃ksjɔ'nɛːr], *n.m.* civil servant, officer, official.

fonctionnel [fɔ̃ksjɔ'nɛl], *a.* (*fem.* **-elle**) functional.

fonctionnement [fɔ̃ksjɔn'mã], *n.m.* operation, working, action.

fonctionner [fɔ̃ksjɔ'ne], *v.i.* to work, to act, to operate.

fond [fɔ̃], *n.m.* bottom; bed, ground; farther end; foundation; (*fig.*) essence; basis; subject matter; (*Paint.*) background; (*Theat.*) back-cloth.

fondage [fɔ̃'daːʒ], *n.m.* casting, smelting.

fondamental [fɔ̃damã'tal], *a.* (*m. pl.* **-aux**) fundamental, essential

fondamentalement [fɔ̃damãtal'mã], *adv.* fundamentally, essentially, radically.

fondant [fɔ̃'dã], *a.* melting, dissolving; luscious.—*n.m.* fondant (*sweetmeat*); flux (*for metals*).

fondateur [fɔ̃da'tœːr], *n.m.* (*fem.* **-trice**) founder; promoter.

fondation [fɔ̃da'sjɔ̃], *n.f.* foundation; groundwork; founding; endowment.

fondé [fɔ̃'de], *a.* founded, well-founded; (*Fin.*) consolidated.—*n.m.* proxy.

fondement [fɔ̃d'mã], *n.m.* foundation; basis, ground, cause.

fonder [fɔ̃'de], *v.t.* to lay the foundation of, to establish; to institute; to base; to endow. **se fonder**, *v.r.* to rely *or* rest (*upon*), to be founded (*sur*).

fonderie [fɔ̃'dri], *n.f.* foundry; smelting-house; casting.

fondeur [fɔ̃'dœːr], *n.m.* founder, caster, smelter.

fondre [fɔ̃:dr], *v.t.* to melt; to dissolve; to smelt; to cast.—*v.i.* to melt; to pounce (*sur*); to vanish; to blow (*of a fuse*); **fondre en larmes**, to burst into tears. **se fondre**, *v.r.* to melt; to dissolve; to be cast; to blend; to diminish, to melt away.

fondrière [fɔ̃dri'ɛːr], *n.f.* bog, quagmire; rut, pothole; slough.

fonds [fɔ̃], *n.m.* land, soil; landed property; funds, capital; business assets; (*pl.*) funds, stocks etc.

fondue [fɔ̃'dy], *n.f.* dish of melted cheese and eggs.

fongicide [fɔ̃ʒi'sid], *a.* fungicide.

fongoïde [fɔ̃gɔ'id], *a.* fungoid.

fongueux [fɔ̃'gø], *a.* (*fem.* **-euse**) fungous.

fongus [fɔ̃'gys], *n.m.* (*Med.*) fungus.

fontaine [fɔ̃'tɛːn], *n.f.* fountain, spring; cistern.

fonte [fɔ̃:t], *n.f.* melting, smelting; cast-iron; casting; holster (*of saddles*).

fonts [fɔ̃], *n.m. pl. (no sing.)* font.

football [fut'bol], *n.m.* Association Football.

footballeur [futba'lœːr], *n.m.* football player.

footing [fu'tiŋ], *n.m.* walking (*for training or exercise*).

forage [fɔ'raːʒ], *n.m.* boring, drilling; sinking (*of well*).

forain [fɔ'rɛ̃], *a.* non-resident, travelling, itinerant; **marchand forain**, hawker, pedlar.

forban [fɔr'bã], *n.m.* pirate, corsair, free-booter.

forçat [fɔr'sa], *n.m.* convict.

force [fɔrs], *n.f.* strength, might, power; authority; violence, constraint; vigor; resolution; skill; (*pl.*) troops, forces.— *adv.* a great deal, a great many.

forcé [fɔrˈse], *a*. forced, compulsory; unnatural, strained, far-fetched.

forcément [fɔrseˈmã], *adv*. forcibly; necessarily, inevitably.

forcené [fɔrsəˈne], *a*. mad, furious; passionate, infuriated.—*n.m.* (*fem.* **-ée**) mad person.

forceps [fɔrˈsɛps], *n.m. inv.* forceps.

forcer [fɔrˈse], *v.t.* (*conjug. like* COMMENCER) to force; to compel; to impel; to strain; to break open; to storm; to outrage. **se forcer**, *v.r.* to strain oneself; to do violence to one's feelings.

forer [fɔˈre], *v.t.* to bore, to drill, to perforate.

forestier [fɔrɛsˈtje], *a.* (*fem.* **-ière**) pertaining to forests.—*n.m.* ranger, keeper, forester.

foret [fɔˈrɛ], *n.m.* borer, drill.

forêt [fɔˈrɛ], *n.f.* forest; woodland.

forfaire [fɔrˈfɛːr], *v.t. irr.* to forfeit (*a fief*).—*v.i.* (*used only in inf.*, *p.p.* (**forfait** (1) *and compound tenses*) to fail (*in one's duty*); to trespass, to be false to.

forfait (2) [fɔrˈfɛ], *n.m.* crime, heinous offence.

forfait (3) [fɔrˈfɛ], *n.m.* contract.

forfaiture [fɔrfɛˈtyːr], *n.f.* forfeiture; breach of duty.

forfanterie [fɔrfãˈtri], *n.f.* romancing, bragging, boasting.

forge [fɔrʒ], *n.f.* forge, smithy; iron-works.

forger [fɔrˈʒe], *v.t.* (*conjug. like* MANGER) to forge, to hammer; (*fig.*) to invent, to fabricate. **se forger**, *v.r.* to imagine, to conjure up, to fancy.

forgeron [fɔrʒəˈrɔ̃], *n.m.* smith, blacksmith.

formaliser (**se**) [səfɔrmaliˈze], *v.r.* to take exception *or* offence (*de*).

formalisme [fɔrmaˈlism], *n.m.* formalism.

formaliste [fɔrmaˈlist], *a.* formal, precise.—*n.* formalist; quibbler.

formalité [fɔrmaliˈte], *n.f.* formality; form, ceremony.

format [fɔrˈma], *n.m.* format (*size, shape etc., of a book*).

formateur [fɔrmaˈtœːr], *a.* (*fem.* **-trice**) formative, creative.

formation [fɔrmaˈsjɔ̃], *n.f.* formation; education; (*Geol.*) structure.

forme [fɔrm], *n.f.* form, shape, figure; etiquette; crown (*of a hat*).

formé [fɔrˈme], *a.* formed, mature.

formel [fɔrˈmɛl], *a.* (*fem.* **-elle**) formal; express, precise.

formellement [fɔrmɛlˈmã], *adv.* formally; expressly, precisely, strictly.

former [fɔrˈme], *v.t.* to form, to frame; to make up; to bring up; to train; to mold. **se former**, *v.r.* to be formed; to take shape.

formidable [fɔrmiˈdabl], *a.* formidable, fearful; (*fam.*) terrific

Formose [fɔrˈmoːz], **la**, *f.* Formosa, Taiwan.

formule [fɔrˈmyl], *n.f.* formula, form; model; recipe.

formuler [fɔrmyˈle], *v.t.* to formulate; to detail; (*Med.*) to write (*a prescription*).

fort [fɔːr], *a.* strong, sturdy; powerful; clever; plentiful; shocking; painful; high (*wind*); heavy (*ground, rain*).—*n.m.* strong part; stronghold, fort; strength; depth, heat, height; centre.—*adv.* very, very much, extremely; hard.

fortement [fɔrtəˈmã], *adv.* strongly, vigorously; much, exceedingly.

forteresse [fɔrtəˈrɛs], *n.f.* fortress, stronghold.

fortifiant [fɔrtiˈfjã], *a.* strengthening, bracing.—*n.m.* (*Med.*) tonic.

fortification [fɔrtifikaˈsjɔ̃], *n.f.* fortification; fort, redoubt.

fortifier [fɔrtiˈfje], *v.t.* to strengthen, to invigorate; to fortify; to confirm. **se fortifier**, *v.r.* to fortify oneself, to grow strong.

fortuit [fɔrˈtɥi], *a.* fortuitous, casual.

fortuitement [fɔrtɥitˈmã], *adv.* fortuitously, casually, by chance.

fortune [fɔrˈtyn], *n.f.* fortune, chance, hazard, risk; success, luck; wealth.

fortuné [fɔrtyˈne], *a.* fortunate, lucky; happy; well-to-do.

fosse [foːs], *n.f.* hole, pit; grave; (*Hort.*) trench.

fossé [foˈse], *n.m.* ditch, drain, trench; moat.

fossette [foˈsɛt], *n.f.* dimple.

fossile [foˈsil], *a.* fossilized.—*n.m.* fossil.

fossiliser [fosiliˈse], *v.t.* to fossilize. **se fossiliser**, *v.r.* to become fossilized.

fossoyage [foswaˈjaːʒ], *n.m.* ditching; grave-digging.

fossoyer [foswaˈje], *v.t.* (*conjug. like* EMPLOYER) to ditch, to dig a trench round.

fossoyeur [foswaˈjœːr], *n.m.* grave digger; sexton beetle.

fou [fu], *a.* (*before vowels* **fol**, *fem.* **folle**) mad, demented; wild, foolish; tremendous.—*n.m.* (*fem.* **folle**) madman, madwoman.—*n.m.* jester, fool; (*Chess*) bishop.

foudre (1) [fudr], *n.f.* lightning; thunder, thunderbolt; (*fig.*) sudden calamity; **coup de foudre**, clap of thunder.—*n.m.* (*fig.*) **un foudre de guerre**, a great captain; **un foudre d'éloquence**, a mighty speaker.

foudre (2) [fudr], *n.m.* large cask, tun.

foudroiement [fudrwaˈmã], *n.m.* striking, blasting (*by thunder or lightning*); (*fig.*) destruction.

foudroyant [fudrwaˈjã], *a.* a thundering; terrible, crushing (*news*).

foudroyer [fudrwaˈje], *v.t.* (*conjug. like* EMPLOYER) to strike (*thunder or lightning*); to riddle with shot; (*fig.*) to blast, to crush.—*v.i.* to thunder; (*fig.*) to fulminate.

fouet [fwɛ], *n.m.* whip; lash; whipping, slating (*criticism*).

fouetter [fwɛˈte], *v.t.* to whip, to flog; to beat (*eggs etc.*); to flick; (*fig.*) to excite.—*v.i.* to beat, to patter (*of hail, rain*).

fougeraie [fuʒˈrɛ], *n.f.* fern patch, fernery.

fougère [fuˈʒɛːr], *n.f.* fern.

fougue [fug], *n.f.* ardor, impetuosity; fire, spirit, mettle; (*Naut.*) mizzen-top.

fougueux [fuˈgø], *a.* (*fem.* **-euse**) fiery, impetuous, ardent, passionate, high-mettled.

fouille [fuːj], *n.f.* excavation, digging; search.

fouiller [fuˈje], *v.t.* to excavate; (*fig.*) to pry into, to rummage, to ransack; to search; to think out (*problems etc.*).—*v.i.* to dig, to search; (*fig.*) to rummage.

fouillis [fuˈji], *n.m.* medley, jumble; confused mass (*of foliage etc.*).

fouine (1) [fwin], *n.f.* marten.

fouine (2) [fwin], *n.f.* pitchfork; fish spear.

fouiner [fwi'ne], *v.i.* (*colloq.*) to nose about, to ferret; to slink off.

fouir [fwi:r], *v.t.* to dig; to burrow.

fouissement [fwis'mã], *n.m.* digging; burrowing.

fouisseur [fwi'sœ:r], *a.* (*fem.* -**euse**) burrowing (*animal*).

foulage [fu'la:ʒ], *n.m.* fulling; treading, pressing (*of grapes*).

foulant [fu'lã], *a.* pressing; forcing; *pompe foulante*, force pump.

foulard [fu'la:r], *n.m.* silk neckerchief; scarf.

foule [ful], *n.f.* crowd, throng, multitude; mob.

foulée [fu'le], *n.f.* tread (*of steps*); stride (*of a horse* or *runner*).

fouler [fu'le], *v.t.* to tread; to trample down; to press; to oppress; to sprain (*ankle*).—*v.i.* (*Print.*) to press. **se fouler**, *v.r.* **se fouler le pied**, to sprain one's foot.

fouleur [fu'lœ:r], *n.m.* (*fem.* -**euse**) fuller; wine presser.

foulure [fu'ly:r], *n.f.* sprain, wrench, strain.

four [fu:r], *n.m.* oven; bakehouse; furnace; kiln; *des petits fours*, fancy biscuits, small cakes.

fourbe [furb], *a.* cheating, deceitful.—*n.* cheat, swindler, impostor.

fourberie [furbə'ri], *n.f.* cheating, knavery, imposture, deceit.

fourbir [fur'bi:r], *v.t.* to furbish, to polish.

fourbisseur [furbi'sœ:r], *n.m.* furbisher; sword-cutler.

fourbissure [furbi'sy:r], *n.f.* furbishing, polishing.

fourbu [fur'by], *a.* foundered, run down (*of horses*); dead tired (*of persons*).

fourbure [fur'by:r], *n.f.* foundering, inflammation of the feet.

fourche [furʃ], *n.f.* pitchfork, (garden) fork, fork (*of roads*).

fourchée [fur'ʃe], *n.f.* pitchforkful.

fourcher [fur'ʃe], *v.i.* to fork; to divide. **se fourcher**, *v.r.* to fork, to branch off.

fourchetée [furʃ'te], *n.f.* table-forkful.

fourchette [fur'ʃet], *n.f.* table fork; breast bone (*of birds*).

fourchu [fur'ʃy], *a.* forked; cloven; furcate.

fourgon (1) [fur'gõ], *n.m.* van, truck, freight or baggage car.

fourgon (2) [fur'gõ], *n.m.* poker, fire-iron (*for ovens etc.*).

fourgonner [furgɔ'ne], *v.i.* to poke the fire (*of an oven*); (*colloq.*) to poke, to rummage.

fourmi [fur'mi], *n.f.* ant.

fourmilière [furmi'lje:r], *n.f.* ant hill, ants' nest; (*fig.*) swarm; crowd.

fourmillement [furmij'mã], *n.m.* tingling, pins and needles; swarming.

fourmiller [furmi'je], *v.i.* to swarm, to be full (*de*); to have pins and needles (*in one's limbs etc.*).

fournaise [fur'nɛ:z], *n.f.* (*Lit.*) furnace; (*fig.*) oven.

fourneau [fur'no], *n.m.* (*pl.* -**eaux**) stove, cooker, cooking range; furnace.

fournée [fur'ne], *n.f.* batch, baking; kilnful (*of bricks*).

fournil [fur'ni], *n.m.* bakehouse.

fourniment [furni'mã], *n.m.* (*Mil.*) equipment.

fournir [fur'ni:r], *v.t.* to furnish, to supply, to stock, to provide; to make up (*a sum of money*).—*v.i.* to contribute (*à*); to suffice.

fournisseur [furni'sœ:r], *n.m.* army contractor; purveyor; tradesman.

fourniture [furni'ty:r], *n.f.* furnishing; supply, provision; equipment.

fourrage [fu'ra:ʒ], *n.m.* fodder; forage; foraging party.

fourrager [fura'ʒe], *v.t.* (*conjug. like* MANGER) to ravage; to upset.—*v.i.* to forage; to plunder, to ravage; (*fig.*) to rummage.

fourrageur [fura'ʒœ:r], *n.m.* forager; (*fig.*) marauder; rummager.

fourré [fu're], *a.* thick, furry; wooded; (*fig.*) underhand (*of a blow etc.*).—*n.m.* thicket, brake.

fourreau [fu'ro], *n.m.* (*pl.* -**eaux**) sheath, case; scabbard; cover; tight-fitting or sheath dress.

fourrer [fu're], *v.t.* to line with fur; to poke; to cram, to stuff. **se fourrer**, *v.r.* to thrust oneself in, to intrude; to wrap oneself up warmly.

fourreur [fu'rœ:r], *n.m.* furrier.

fourrier [fu'rje], *n.m.* quartermaster-sergeant; (*fig.*) harbinger.

fourrière [fu'rjɛ:r], *n.f.* pound (*for vehicles, strayed animals*).

fourrure [fu'ry:r], *n.f.* fur, furred gown.

fourvoyer [furvwa'je], *v.t.* (*conjug. like* EMPLOYER) to lead astray, to mislead; (*fig.*) to baffle. **se fourvoyer**, *v.r.* to go astray, to lose one's way; (*fig.*) to blunder badly.

fox (1) [foks], *n.m.* fox terrier.

fox (2) [foks], *n.m.* foxtrot.

foyer [fwa'je], *n.m.* hearth; fire; fire box (*of an engine*); (*fig.*) home, family; (*Theat.*) foyer; focus, source.

frac [frak], *n.m.* frock coat.

fracas [fra'ka], *n.m.* noise, din; disturbance; fuss.

fracasser [fraka'se], *v.t.* to break into pieces, to shatter. **se fracasser**, *v.r.* to crash to pieces.

fraction [frak'sjõ], *n.f.* breaking; fraction, portion.

fractionnaire [fraksjɔ'nɛ:r], *a.* fractional.

fracture [frak'ty:r], *n.f.* breaking (*with violence*), rupture; (*Surg.*) fracture.

fracturer [frakty're], *v.t.* to break, to smash; (*Surg.*) to fracture. **se fracturer**, *v.r.* to fracture oneself; to be fractured.

fragile [fra'ʒil], *a.* fragile, brittle; frail.

fragilité [fraʒili'te], *n.f.* fragility, brittleness; frailty.

fragment [frag'mã], *n.m.* fragment, piece, remnant.

fragmentaire [fragmã'tɛ:r], *a.* fragmentary.

fragmentation [fragmãta'sjõ], *n.f.* fragmenting, fragmentation.

fragmenter [fragmã'te], *v.t.* to reduce to fragments.

fragrance [fra'grã:s], *n.f.* fragrance.

fragrant [fra'grã], *a.* fragrant.

frai [frɛ], *n.m.* fraying; spawning (*of fish*).

fraîche [frɛʃ], [FRAIS (1).]

fraîchement [frɛʃ'mã], *adv.* coolly, freshly; newly, recently.

fraîcheur [frɛ'ʃœ:r], *n.f.* coolness, freshness, coldness; ruddiness; brilliancy.

fraîchir [frɛ'ʒi:r], *v.i.* to freshen; to get cool.

159

frais

frais (1) [frɛ], *a.* (*fem.* **fraîche**) cool; fresh; new; youthful; ruddy; new-laid (*of eggs*).—*n.m.* coolness, freshness; cool spot.—*adv.* freshly, newly, recently, just.

frais (2) [frɛ], *n.m.* (*used only in pl.*) expense, expenses; charge, charges, cost, outlay; *menus frais*, petty expenses; *sans frais*, free of charge.

fraise (1) [frɛːz], *n.f.* strawberry; strawberry mark, birthmark; ruff.

fraise (2) [frɛːz], *n.f.* fraise (*tool for enlarging a drill hole etc.*); (dentist's) drill.

fraiser [frɛˈze], *v.t.* to plait, to ruffle; to countersink.

fraisier [frɛˈzje], *n.m.* strawberry plant; strawberry grower.

framboise [frɑ̃ˈbwaːz], *n.f.* raspberry.

framboiser [frɑ̃bwaˈze], *v.t.* to give a raspberry flavor to.

framboisier [frɑ̃bwaˈzje], *n.m.* raspberry-bush.

franc (1) [frɑ̃], *n.m.* franc (*French coin*); new franc (*of 1960*).

franc (2) [frɑ̃], *a.* (*fem.* **franche**) free; exempt; frank, candid, sincere; clear.—*adv.* frankly, openly, sincerely; clean; quite, completely.

franc (3) [frɑ̃], *a.* (*fem.* **franque**) Frankish.—*n.m.* Frankish (*language*); (**Franc,** *fem.* **Franque**) Frank.

français [frɑ̃ˈsɛ], *a.* French.—*n.m.* French (*language*); (**Français,** *fem.* **-aise**) Frenchman, Frenchwoman.

France [frɑ̃ːs], **la,** *f.* France.

franche [frɑ̃ʃ], [FRANC (2)].

franchement [frɑ̃ʃˈmɑ̃], *adv.* frankly, sincerely; plainly; boldly.

franchir [frɑ̃ˈʃiːr], *v.t.* to leap, to jump over; to clear; to pass over; to surmount.

franchise [frɑ̃ˈʃiːz], *n.f.* exemption, immunity; freedom (*of a city*); (*fig.*) frankness, sincerity.

franchissable [frɑ̃ʃiˈsabl], *a.* passable, capable of being crossed.

franchissement [frɑ̃ʃisˈmɑ̃], *n.m.* leaping over, crossing.

francisation [frɑ̃sizaˈsjɔ̃], *n.f.* Gallicizing of foreign word; registration as a French ship.

franciscain [frɑ̃sisˈkɛ̃], *a.* and *n.m.* (*fem.* **-e**) Franciscan, grey friar, Franciscan nun.

franciser [frɑ̃siˈze], *v.t.* to Gallicize; to Frenchify. **se franciser,** *v.r.* to become French or Frenchified.

franc-maçon [frɑ̃maˈsɔ̃], *n.m.* (*pl.* **francs-maçons**) freemason.

franc-maçonnerie [frɑ̃masɔnˈri], *n.f.* freemasonry.

franco [frɑ̃ˈko], *adv.* free of charge; prepaid.

François [frɑ̃ˈswa], *m.* Francis.

Françoise [frɑ̃ˈswaːz], *f.* Frances.

francophile [frɑ̃koˈfil], *a.* and *n.* Francophile.

francophobe [frɑ̃koˈfob], *a.* and *n.* Francophobe.

franc-parler [frɑ̃parˈle], *n.m.* frankness or freedom of speech.

franc-tireur [frɑ̃tiˈrœːr], *n.m.* franc-tireur; sniper.

frange [frɑ̃ːʒ], *n.f.* fringe.

franger [frɑ̃ˈʒe], *v.t.* (*conjug. like* MANGER) to fringe.

franque [frɑ̃k], [FRANC (3)].

frappant [fraˈpɑ̃], *a.* striking, impressive.

frappé [fraˈpe], *a.* struck, astounded; iced (*of liquids etc.*); (*fig.*) powerful.

frappement [frapˈmɑ̃], *n.m.* striking, stamping; clapping (*of hands*).

frapper [fraˈpe], *v.t.* to strike, to slap, to hit; to make an impression on, to affect; to surprise, to frighten; to ice (*liquids*).—*v.i.* to knock, to rap. **se frapper,** *v.r.* to strike oneself; to strike each other; to be impressed.

frappeur [fraˈpœːr], *a.* (*fem.* **-euse**) striking, rapping.—*n.m.* (*fem.* **-euse**) beater, striker.

frasque [frask], *n.f.* prank, escapade.

fraternel [fraterˈnɛl], *a.* (*fem.* **-elle**) fraternal, brotherly.

fraternellement [fraternɛlˈmɑ̃], *adv.* fraternally.

fraternisation [fraternizaˈsjɔ̃], *n.f.* fraternization.

fraterniser [fraterniˈze], *v.t.* to fraternize.

fraternité [fraterniˈte], *n.f.* fraternity, brotherhood.

fratricide [fratriˈsid], *a.* fratricidal.—*n.m.* fratricide.

fraude [froːd], *n.f.* fraud, deceit.

frauder [froˈde], *v.t.* to defraud.—*v.i.* to smuggle.

fraudeur [froˈdœːr], *n.m.* (*fem.* **-euse**) defrauder; smuggler.

frauduleusement [frodyløzˈmɑ̃], *adv.* fraudulently.

frauduleux [frodyˈlø], *a.* (*fem.* **-euse**) fraudulent.

frayer [frɛˈje], *v.t.* to trace out, to open out; to make (*a way etc.*); to rub against, to graze.—*v.i.* to wear away; to spawn (*of fish*); (*fig.*) to frequent, to be on good terms (*avec*). **se frayer,** *v.r.* to open for oneself; to prepare or carve out (*a way*) for oneself.

frayeur [frɛˈjœːr], *n.f.* fright, terror, fear.

fredaine [frəˈdɛn], *n.f.* (*colloq.*) frolic, prank; freak.

Frédéric [fredeˈrik], *m.* Frederick.

Frédérique [fredeˈrik], *f.* Frederica.

fredon [frəˈdɔ̃], *n.m.* song, refrain.

fredonnement [frədɔnˈmɑ̃], *n.m.* humming.

fredonner [frədɔˈne], *v.t.*, *v.i.* to hum.

frégate [freˈgat], *n.f.* frigate; frigate bird; (*Navy*) *capitaine de frégate,* commander.

frein [frɛ̃], *n.m.* bit, bridle; curb, check; brake.

freinage [frɛˈnaːʒ], *n.m.* braking.

freiner [frɛˈne], *v.t.* to brake; to curb.

frelatage [frəlaˈtaːʒ], *n.m.* **frelatement** [frəlatˈmɑ̃], *n.m.*, **frelaterie** [frəlaˈtri], **frelatation** [frəlataˈsjɔ̃], *n.f.* adulteration.

frelater [frəlaˈte], *v.t.* to adulterate.

frêle [frɛːl], *a.* frail, fragile, weak.

frelon [frəˈlɔ̃], *n.m.* hornet.

freluquet [frəlyˈkɛ], *n.m.* conceited young man, puppy.

frémir [freˈmiːr], *v.i.* to quiver, to shudder, to tremble; to vibrate; to rustle.

frémissant [fremiˈsɑ̃], *a.* quivering, trembling.

frémissement [fremisˈmɑ̃], *n.m.* quivering, trembling, shuddering; thrill, vibration; rustling.

frênaie [frɛˈnɛ], *n.f.* ash grove.

frêne [frɛːn], *n.m.* ash, ash tree.

frénésie [freneˈzi], *n.f.* frenzy, madness.

frénétique [frene'tik], *a.* frantic, frenzied.—*n.* raving, frantic person.

frénétiquement [frenetik'mā], *adv.* frantically.

fréquemment [freka'mā], *adv.* frequently.

fréquence [fre'kā:s], *n.f.* frequency.

fréquent [fre'kā], *a.* frequent.

fréquentation [frekāta'sjɔ̃], *n.f.* frequentation, company.

fréquenter [frekā'te], *v.t.* to frequent, to keep company with; to haunt.—*v.i.* to associate (*chez*); to be a frequent caller (*at*).

frère [frɛːr], *n.m.* brother; fellow member; monk.

fresque [frɛsk], *n.f.* fresco.

fret [frɛ], *n.m.* freight, cargo.

fréter [fre'te], *v.t.* (*conjug. like* CÉDER) to charter; to freight; to hire (*a car*).

fréteur [fre'tœːr], *n.m.* freighter, charterer.

frétillant [freti'jā], *a.* wriggling, lively; frisky.

frétillement [fretij'mā], *n.m.* wriggling; frisking.

frétiller [freti'je], *v.i.* to wriggle, to jump about; to frisk.

fretin [frə'tɛ̃], *n.m.* fry, young fish; (*fig.*) trash.

freudien [frø'djɛ̃], *a.* (*fem.* **-enne**) Freudian.

freux [frø], *n.m. inv.* (*Orn.*) rook.

friable [fri'abl], *a.* friable; crisp, short.

friand [fri'ā], *a.* dainty, nice; partial to; appetizing.

friandise [friā'diːz], *n.f.* daintiness; dainty, titbit.

fricassée [frika'se], *n.f.* fricassee.

fricasser [frika'se], *v.t.* to fricassee.

friche [friʃ], *n.f.* waste or fallow land.

fricot [fri'ko], *n.m.* (*colloq.*) ragout, stew.

fricoter [friko'te], *v.t.* to squander.—*v.i.* to cook.

fricoteur [friko'tœːr], *n.m.* (*fem.* **-euse**) feaster; fast liver.

friction [frik'sjɔ̃], *n.f.* friction, rubbing.

frictionner [friksjɔ'ne], *v.t.* to rub.

frigide [fri'ʒid], *a.* frigid.

frigidité [friʒidi'te], *n.f.* frigidity.

frigorifier [frigɔri'fje], *v.t.* to chill, to freeze (*meat etc.*).

frileux [fri'lø], *a.* (*fem.* **-euse**) chilly; susceptible to cold.—*n.m.* redbreast, robin.

frimas [fri'ma], *n.m.* *rime, hoar-frost.

frime [frim], *n.f.* (*pop.*) show, pretence, sham.

fringant [frɛ̃'gā], *a.* brisk, frisky; smart.

fringuer [frɛ̃'ge], *v.i.* to skip; to prance (*of a horse*).

fripe [frip], *n.f.* rag, scrap (*of cloth etc.*).

friper [fri'pe], *v.t.* to crumple, to rumple. **se friper**, *v.r.* to become rumpled or shabby.

friperie [fri'pri], *n.f.* frippery, old clothes; junk shop.

fripier [fri'pje], *n.m.* (*fem.* **-ière**) dealer in old clothes, furniture etc.

fripon [fri'pɔ̃], *a.* (*fem.* **-onne**) cheating, rascally.—*n.m.* (*fem.* **-onne**) rogue, cheat.

friponnerie [fripɔn'ri], *n.f.* cheating, roguery, knavery.

friquet [fri'kɛ], *n.m.* tree sparrow.

frire [friːr], *v.t., v.i. irr.* to fry.

frisage [fri'zaːʒ], *n.m.* curling, frizzing (*of hair etc.*).

frise [friːz], *n.f.* (*Arch. etc.*) frieze.

friser [fri'ze], *v.t.* to curl, to frizz (*hair*); to graze; to border upon.—*v.i.* to curl. **se friser**, *v.r.* to curl; to curl one's hair.

frisson [fri'sɔ̃], *n.m.* shiver, shudder; thrill.

frissonnant [frisɔ'nā], *a.* shuddering, shivering.

frissonnement [frisɔn'mā], *n.m.* shivering, shudder; thrill.

frissonner [frisɔ'ne], *v.i.* to shiver, to shudder; to feel a thrill; to tremble.

frisure [fri'zyːr], *n.f.* crisping; curling.

frit [fri], *a.* fried.—*n.f.* **des frites**, chips, French fried potatoes.

friture [fri'tyːr], *n.f.* frying; fried fish etc.; grease (*for frying*).

frivole [fri'vɔl], *a.* frivolous, trifling; futile.

frivolité [frivɔli'te], *n.f.* frivolity; trifle.

froc [frɔk], *n.m.* cowl, monk's gown.

froid [frwa], *a.* cold; (*fig.*) indifferent, lifeless; reserved.—*n.m.* cold, coldness; chilliness; (*fig.*) unconcern, dullness; reserve.

froidement [frwad'mā], *adv.* coldly, frigidly; dispassionately.

froideur [frwa'dœːr], *n.f.* coldness; chilliness; (*fig.*) indifference, coolness.

froidure [frwa'dyːr], *n.f.* coldness (*of the weather*); cold; (*fig.*) winter.

froissement [frwas'mā], *n.m.* rumpling; bruising; (*fig.*) clash; slight, affront, annoyance.

froisser [frwa'se], *v.t.* to rumple; to crease; to bruise slightly; (*fig.*) to offend, to wound. **se froisser**, *v.r.* to become bruised (*of a muscle*); to take offence.

froissure [frwa'syːr], *n.f.* crease; bruise.

frôlement [frol'mā], *n.m.* grazing; rustle.

frôler [fro'le], *v.t.* to graze, to touch slightly in passing; to brush past.

fromage [frɔ'maːʒ], *n.m.* cheese; (*fig.*) **un (bon) fromage**, a nice soft job.

fromagerie [frɔmaʒ'ri], *n.f.* cheese farm or dairy; cheese trade.

fromageux [frɔma'ʒø], *a.* (*fem.* **-euse**) cheesy.

froment [frɔ'mā], *n.m.* wheat.

fronce [frɔ̃:s], *n.f.* gather, pucker (*in needlework etc.*); crease (*in paper*).

froncement [frɔ̃s'mā], *n.m.* contraction, knitting (*of the brows etc.*); (*fig.*) frown.

froncer [frɔ̃'se], *v.t.* (*conjug. like* COMMENCER) to contract; to wrinkle; to purse (*the lips*); to gather (*needlework*); **froncer les sourcils**, to frown. **se froncer**, *v.r.* to contract, to pucker; to wrinkle.

frondaison [frɔ̃dɛ'zɔ̃], *n.f.* foliation; foliage.

fronde [frɔ̃:d], *n.f.* sling; frond; (*Surg.*) bandage.

fronder [frɔ̃'de], *v.t.* to sling, to fling with a sling; to banter; to jeer at.

frondeur [frɔ̃'dœːr], *n.m.* (*fem.* **-euse**) slinger; censurer, fault-finder; rioter.

front [frɔ̃], *n.m.* forehead, brow; face; (*fig.*) boldness, impudence; (*Polit.*) **Front populaire**, Popular Front.

frontal [frɔ̃'tal], *a.* (*m. pl.* **-aux**) (*Anat.*) frontal.—*n.m.* headband.

frontière [frɔ̃'tjɛ:r], *n.f.* frontier, border.

frontispice [frɔ̃tis'pis], *n.m.* frontispiece; title page.

fronton [frɔ̃'tɔ̃], *n.m.* (*Arch.*) fronton, pediment.

frottage [frɔ'taːʒ], *n.m.* rubbing; polishing.

161

frottée

---

frottée [frɔ'te], *n.f.* (*colloq.*) drubbing.
frottement [frɔt'mɑ̃], *n.m.* rubbing, friction; (*fig.*) interaction.
frotter [frɔ'te], *v.t.* to rub; to polish; (*fig.*) to pommel, to warm (*the ears of*).—*v.i.* to rub. **se frotter**, *v.r.* to rub oneself; to provoke, to meddle (*à*).
frotteur [frɔ'tœːr], *n.m.* (*fem.* **-euse**) rubber; scrubber; floor polisher.
frottoir [frɔ'twaːr], *n.m.* rubbing cloth; (*Elec.*) brush (*of dynamo*).
frou-frou [fru'fru], *n.m.* (*pl.* **-frous**) rustling (*of silk etc.*).
fructification [fryktifika'sjɔ̃], *n.f.* fructification.
fructifier [frykti'fje], *v.i.* to fructify, to bear fruit; (*fig.*) to thrive.
fructueusement [fryktɥøz'mɑ̃], *adv.* fruitfully, profitably.
fructueux [fryk'tɥø], *a.* (*fem.* **-euse**) fruitful, profitable.
frugal [fry'gal], *a.* (*m. pl.* **-aux**) frugal.
frugalement [frygal'mɑ̃], *adv.* frugally.
frugalité [frygali'te], *n.f.* frugality.
fruit [frɥi], *n.m.* fruit; (*fig.*) offspring; advantage, utility; (*pl.*) fruits; result.
fruiterie [frɥi'tri], *n.f.* fruit loft; fruit trade.
fruitier [frɥi'tje], *a.* (*fem.* **-ière**) fruit-bearing.—*n.m.* (*fem.* **-ière**) fruiterer, greengrocer.
fruste [fryst], *a.* worn, defaced; unpolished (*person*).
frustration [frystra'sjɔ̃], *n.f.* frustration.
frustrer [frys'tre], *v.t.* to defraud; to frustrate, to disappoint; to baffle.
fuchsia [fyk'sja], *n.m.* fuchsia.
fugace [fy'gas], *a.* fugitive, fleeting, transient.
fugitif [fyʒi'tif], *a.* (*fem.* **-tive**) fugitive, fleeting.—*n.m.* (*fem.* **-tive**) fugitive, runaway.
fugue [fyg], *n.f.* fugue; (*colloq.*) flight, escapade.
fuir [fɥiːr], *v.t. irr.* to fly, to avoid; to shun.—*v.i.* to fly, to flee, to run away; to elude; to leak. **se fuir**, *v.r.* to fly from oneself; to shun *or* avoid each other.
fuite [fɥit], *n.f.* flight, escaping; avoiding; evasion, shift; leakage.
fulgurant [fylgy'rɑ̃], *a.* flashing, vivid, sharp.
fulguration [fylgyra'sjɔ̃], *n.f.* (*Chem.*) fulguration; lightning.
fuligineux [fyliʒi'nø], *a.* (*fem.* **-euse**) fuliginous.
fulminant [fylmi'nɑ̃], *a.* fulminant, fulminating.
fulminer [fylmi'ne], *v.t.* to fulminate, to send forth (*maledictions or religious decrees*).—*v.i.* to explode; (*fig.*) to storm, to thunder, to inveigh (*against*).
fumage [fy'maːʒ], *n.m.*, **fumaison** [fymɛ'zɔ̃], *fumure* [fy'myːr], *n.f.* manuring, spreading of dung on land.
fumant [fy'mɑ̃], *a.* smoking, reeking, fuming.
fumé [fy'me], *a.* smoked; manured.
fumée [fy'me], *n.f.* smoke; steam; fume, reek; phantom, dream.
fumer [fy'me], *v.t.* to smoke (*a cigarette etc.*); to smoke-dry; to manure.—*v.i.* to smoke; to reek, to steam; (*fig.*) to fret, to fume.
fumerolle [fym'rɔl], *n.f.* fumarole.
fumet [fy'mɛ], *n.m.* flavor (*of meat*); bouquet (*of wines*); (*fig.*) raciness; (*Hunt.*) scent.

fumeur [fy'mœːr], *n.m.* (*fem.* **-euse** (1)) smoker.
fumeux [fy'mø], *a.* (*fem.* **-euse** (2)) smoky, fumy; hazy (*of brain, ideas etc.*).
fumier [fy'mje], *n.m.* manure, dung, dunghill; (*fig.*) trash.
fumigateur [fymiga'tœːr], *n.m.* fumigator.
fumigation [fymiga'sjɔ̃], *n.f.* fumigation.
fumiger [fymi'ʒe], *v.t.* (*conjug. like* MANGER) to fumigate.
fumiste [fy'mist], *n.m.* stove *or* chimney repairer; (*fig.*) practical joker; humbug, trickster.
fumisterie [fymis'tri], *n.f.* (*fig.*) practical joke.
fumoir [fy'mwaːr], *n.m.* smoking shed (*for curing fish etc.*); smoking room.
fumure [FUMAGE].
funèbre [fy'nɛbr], *a.* funeral; funereal, mournful; dismal.
funérailles [fyne'raːj], *n.f. pl.* funeral ceremonies, obsequies.
funéraire [fyne'rɛːr], *a.* funeral; funereal.
funeste [fy'nɛst], *a.* fatal, deadly; (*fig.*) disastrous; distressing.
funestement [fynɛst'mɑ̃], *adv.* fatally, disastrously.
funiculaire [fyniky'lɛːr], *a.* funicular.—*n.m.* funicular railway.
fur [fyːr], *n.m.*, *used only in the expression* **au fur et à mesure** (*que*), gradually (as), in proportion (as).
furet [fy'rɛ], *n.m.* ferret; inquisitive, prying person.
fureter [fyr'te], *v.i.* (*conjug. like* AMENER) to ferret, to hunt with a ferret; (*fig.*) to rummage.
fureteur [fyr'tœːr], *n.m.* (*fem.* **-euse**) ferreter; (*fig.*) Nosey Parker.
fureur [fy'rœːr], *n.f.* rage, fury; passion, frenzy.
furibond [fyri'bɔ̃], *a.* furious, raging, wild.—*n.m.* (*fem.* **-e**) furious person.
furie [fy'ri], *n.f.* fury, rage; ardour, intensity.
furieusement [fyrjøz'mɑ̃], *adv.* furiously.
furieux [fy'rjø], *a.* (*fem.* **-euse**) furious; mad, fierce, impetuous; (*colloq.*) monstrous.—*n.m.* (*fem.* **-euse**) mad person.
furoncle [fy'rɔ̃ːkl], *n.m.* (*Med.*) furuncle, boil.
furtif [fyr'tif], *a.* (*fem.* **-tive**) furtive, stealthy, secret.
furtivement [fyrtiv'mɑ̃], *adv.* furtively.
fusain [fy'zɛ̃], *n.m.* spindle-tree; charcoal (*for drawing*).
fuseau [fy'zo], *n.m.* (*pl.* **-eaux**) spindle; distaff.
fusée [fy'ze], *n.f.* spindleful; spindle (*of axle*); (*Motor.*) stub axle; (*Mil. etc.*) fuse; rocket; (*Vet.*) splint.
fuselage [fyz'laːʒ], *n.m.* framework, fuselage (*of an aeroplane*).
fuselé [fyz'le], *a.* slender, tapering (*fingers*); streamlined.
fuser [fy'ze], *v.i.* to spirt; to liquefy, to dissolve, to fuse.
fusibilité [fyzibili'te], *n.f.* fusibility.
fusible [fy'zibl], *a.* fusible.—*n.m.* (*Elec.*) fuse.
fusil [fy'zi], *n.m.* gun, rifle; steel (*for sharpening knives*).
fusilier [fyzi'lje], *n.m.* fusilier; **fusilier marin**, marine.
fusillade [fyzi'jad], *n.f.* discharge of musketry, fusillade; execution by shooting.

fusiller [fyzi'je], *v.t.* to shoot (down); to execute by shooting.

fusil-mitrailleur [fyzimitra'jœ:r], *n.m.* sub-machine gun.

fusion [fy'zjɔ̃], *n.f.* fusion, melting; (*fig.*) blending, merger.

fusionner [fyzjɔ'ne], *v.t., v.i.* to amalgamate, to unite, to merge; to blend.

fustigation [fystiga'sjɔ̃], *n.f.* fustigation, whipping, flogging.

fustiger [fysti'ʒe], *v.t.* (*conjug. like* MANGER) to flog, to whip.

fût [fy], *n.m.* stock (*of a gun or pistol*); shaft (*of a column*); cask; barrel (*of a drum*).

futaie [fy'tɛ], *n.f.* forest of high trees; high forest tree.

futaille [fy'ta:j], *n.f.* cask, barrel.

futaine [fy'tɛ:n], *n.f.* fustian.

futé [fy'te], *a.* (*colloq.*) sharp, cunning, sly.

futile [fy'til], *a.* futile, frivolous, trifling.

futilité [fytili'te], *n.f.* futility; trifle.

futur [fy'ty:r], *a.* future.—*n.m.* (*Gram.*) future.—*n.m.* (*fem.* -**e**) intended husband *or* wife.

futurisme [fyty'rism], *n.m.* futurism.

futuriste [fyty'rist], *a.* futuristic.—*n.* futurist.

fuyant [fɥi'jɑ̃], *a.* flying, fleeing, retreating; receding (*of the forehead etc.*); fleeting.—*n.m.* perspective.

fuyard [fɥi'ja:r], *a.* and *n.m.* (*fem.* -**e**) fugitive, runaway.

G

G, g [ʒe], *n.m.* the seventh letter of the alphabet.

gabardine [gabar'din], *n.f.* gabardine.

gabare [ga'ba:r], *n.f.* lighter, flat-bottomed barge; store ship.

gabarier [gaba'rje], *n.m.* lighterman.

gabelle [ga'bɛl], *n.f.* gabelle, salt tax.

gâche (1) [ga:ʃ], *n.f.* staple, wall hook.

gâche (2) [ga:ʃ], *n.f.* trowel; (baker's) spatula.

gâcher [ga'ʃe], *v.t.* to mix (*mortar*); (*fig.*) to bungle, to botch.

gâchette [ga'ʃɛt], *n.f.* tumbler, sear (*of a gun-lock*); follower, catch (*of a lock*); (*fam.*) trigger.

gâcheur [ga'ʃœ:r], *n.m.* mason's helper; (*fig.*) bungler.

gâchis [ga'ʃi], *n.m.* wet mortar; sludge; (*fig.*) mess.

gaélique [gae'lik], *a.* Gaelic.—*n.m.* Gaelic (*language*).

gaffe [gaf], *n.f.* boat-hook, gaff; (*fam.*) gross blunder, howler.

gaffer [ga'fe], *v.t.* to hook with a gaff.—*v.i.* (*fam.*) to blunder; (*Row.*) to catch a crab.

gage [ga:ʒ], *n.m.* pawn, pledge; security, deposit; stake, token; (*pl.*) wages.

gager [ga'ʒe], *v.t.* (*conjug. like* MANGER) to wager, to bet, to stake; to pay wages to; to engage.

gageur [ga'ʒœ:r], *n.m.* (*fem.* -**euse**) bettor, one who wagers, punter.

gageure [ga'ʒy:r], *n.f.* wager, stake.

gagnant [ga'ɲɑ̃], *a.* winning.—*n.m.* (*fem.* -**e**) winner.

gagne-pain [gaɲ'pɛ̃], *n.m. inv.* livelihood, daily bread; bread-winner.

gagner [ga'ɲe], *v.t.* to gain, to earn; to win; to deserve; to prevail upon, to gain over; to allure; to seize; to overtake.—*v.i.* to spread; to gain (*à*); to improve. **se gagner**, *v.r.* to be gained; to be contagious.

gai [ge], *a.* gay, merry; exhilarating; vivid (*of colors*).

gaiement *or* **gaîment** [ge'mɑ̃], *adv.* gaily, merrily, cheerfully; briskly, willingly.

gaieté *or* **gaîté** [ge'te], *n.f.* gaiety, cheerfulness, good humor.

gaillard (1) [ga'ja:r], *n.m.* (*Naut.*) castle; **gaillard d'arrière**, quarter-deck; **gaillard d'avant**, forecastle.

gaillard (2) [ga'ja:r], *a.* strong; jolly, lively; wanton; gallant.—*n.m.* (*fem.* -**e**) lively, merry, strapping fellow *or* girl.

gaillardement [gajardə'mɑ̃], *adv.* joyously, merrily; boldly.

gaillardise [gajar'di:z], *n.f.* sprightliness, liveliness, jollity; broad language, risky story.

gaîment [GAIEMENT].

gain [gɛ̃], *n.m.* gain, profit; earnings; winnings.

gaine [gɛ:n], *n.f.* sheath; foundation garment; case (*of a clock etc.*).

gaîté [GAIETÉ].

gala [ga'la], *n.m.* gala.

galamment [gala'mɑ̃], *adv.* gallantly, courteously; gracefully, handsomely.

galant [ga'lɑ̃], *a.* attentive to ladies; elegant; correct, courteous; complimentary, flattering; **c'est un galant homme**, he is a man of honor; **femme galante**, courtesan.—*n.m.* gallant; sweetheart, suitor; **faire le galant**, to court the ladies.

galanterie [galɑ̃'tri], *n.f.* politeness; gallantry (*towards the ladies*); intrigue, love affair.

galantin [galɑ̃'tɛ̃], *n.m.* fop, coxcomb.

galbe [galb], *n.m.* graceful curve *or* contour.

gale [gal], *n.f.* scabies; itch; scab; mange.

galène [ga'lɛ:n], *n.f.* galena; **poste à galène**, crystal set.

galère [ga'lɛ:r], *n.f.* galley; (*pl.*) galleys, imprisonment with hard labor.

galerie [gal'ri], *n.f.* gallery; corridor; picture gallery; (*Theat.*) upper circle, gallery; (*fig.*) spectators; (*Mining*) drift.

galérien [gale'rjɛ̃], *n.m.* galley slave, convict.

galet [ga'lɛ], *n.m.* pebble, shingle; friction roller.

galetas [gal'ta], *n.m. inv.* garret, attic; (*fig.*) hole, hovel.

galette [ga'lɛt], *n.f.* broad thin cake; sea biscuit.

galeux [ga'lø], *a.* (*fem.* -**euse**) itchy; scabby; mangy; **brebis galeuse**, (*fig.*) black sheep.

Galilée [gali'le], *m.* Galileo.

Galilée [gali'le], *f.* Galilee.

galimatias [galima'tja], *n.m.* balderdash, rigmarole.

galion [ga'ljɔ̃], *n.m.* galleon.

galiote [ga'ljɔt], *n.f.* galliot, half galley.

galle [gal], *n.f.* gall.

Galles, le Pays de [ləpeida'gal], *m.* Wales.

gallican [gali'kɑ̃], *a.* gallican.
gallicisme [gali'sism], *n.m.*Gallicism, French idiom.
gallois [ga'lwa], *a.* Welsh.—*n.m.* Welsh (*language*); (**Gallois**, *fem.* **-oise**) Welshman, Welshwoman.
galoche [ga'lɔʃ], *n.f.* clog.
galon [ga'lɔ̃], *n.m.* braid; lace; (*pl.*) (*Mil.*) bands *or* stripes (*officers and N.C.O.s*).
galonner [galɔ'ne], *v.t.* to lace, to adorn with gold *or* silver lace.
galonnier [galɔ'nje], *n.m.* gold *or* silver lace maker.
galop [ga'lo], *n.m.* gallop, galloping.
galopade [galɔ'pad], *n.f.* galloping, gallop.
galoper [galɔ'pe], *v.t.* to gallop (*a horse etc.*); to run after.—*v.i.* to gallop; (*fig.*) to run on.
galopin [galɔ'pɛ̃], *n.m.* errand boy; (*fig.*) urchin, rogue, imp.
galvanique [galva'nik], *a.* galvanic.
galvaniser [galvani'ze], *v.t.* to galvanize; (*fig.*) to stimulate.
galvanisme [galva'nism], *n.m.* galvanism.
galvanomètre [galvanɔ'mɛ:tr], *n.m.* galvanometer.
galvanoplastie [galvanɔplas'ti], *n.f.* electroplating.
galvauder [galvo'de], *v.t.* to muddle; to lower, to dishonor.
gambade [gɑ̃'bad], *n.f.* skip, gambol.
gambader [gɑ̃ba'de], *v.i.* to skip, to gambol, to romp, to frisk about.
Gambie [gɑ̃'bi], **la**, *f.* Gambia.
gambit [gɑ̃'bi], *n.m.* gambit.
gamelle [ga'mɛl], *n.f.* (*Mil.*, *Naut.*) mess tin *or* pot; (*fig.*) company-mess.
gamète [ga'mɛt], *n.m.* (*Biol.*) gamete.
gamin [ga'mɛ̃], *n.m.* boy, youngster, urchin.
gamine [ga'min], *n.f.* hoyden, chit of a girl.
gamme [gam], *n.f.* gamut, scale.
gammée [ga'me], *a. used in* '**croix gammée**', swastika.
ganache [ga'naʃ], *n.f.* lower jaw (*of a horse*); (*colloq.*) booby, blockhead.
gandin [gɑ̃'dɛ̃], *n.m.* dandy, swell.
gang [gɑ̃g], *n.m.* gang (*of thieves*).
Gange [gɑ̃:ʒ], **le**, *m.* Ganges.
gangrène [gɑ̃'grɛːn], *n.f.* gangrene; (*fig.*) corruption.
gangrené .[gɑ̃grə'ne], *a.* gangrened; (*fig.*) cankered, corrupt.
gangrener [gɑ̃grə'ne], *v.t.* (*conjug. like* AMENER) to gangrene, to mortify; (*fig.*) to corrupt.
gangreneux [gɑ̃grə'nø], *a.* (*fem.* **-euse**) gangrenous, cankered.
gangster [gɑ̃gs'tɛːr], *n.m.* gangster.
ganse [gɑ̃:s], *n.f.* braid; cord, twist; edging; string.
gant [gɑ̃], *n.m.* glove, gauntlet.
gantelet [gɑ̃'tlɛ], *n.m.* gauntlet; hand-leather; (*Surg.*) glove bandage.
ganter [gɑ̃'te], *v.t.* to glove, to put gloves on; (*fig.*) to fit, to suit. **se ganter**, *v.r.* to put on one's gloves.
ganterie [gɑ̃'tri], *n.f.* glove-making; glove trade; glove shop.
gantier [gɑ̃'tje], *n.m.* (*fem.* **-ière**) glover.
garage [ga'ra:ʒ], *n.m.* parking, storing away; (*Rail.*) shunting; siding; (*on rivers, canals etc.*) putting into wet dock; (*Motor. etc.*) garage; (*Row.*) boat-house.

garagiste [gara'ʒist], *n.m.* garage keeper; garage mechanic *or* owner.
garance [ga'rɑ̃:s], *a.* madder-colored. —*n.f.* madder; madder root.
garant [ga'rɑ̃], *n.m.* (*fem.* **-e**) guarantor, surety.—*n.m.* guaranty, voucher, proof.
garanti [garɑ̃'ti], *a.* guaranteed, warranted.
garantie [garɑ̃'ti], *n.f.* guarantee, guaranty; indemnity; security; voucher, pledge.
garantir [garɑ̃'tiːr], *v.t.* to guarantee, to vouch for; to ensure; to indemnify; to protect, to shield. **se garantir**, *v.r.* to secure oneself, to preserve oneself.
garantisseur [garɑ̃ti'sœ:ʀ], *n.m.* warranter.
garçon [gar'sɔ̃], *n.m.* boy, lad; bachelor; workman; porter; waiter; stable boy; steward (*on ship*).
garçonnet [garsɔ'ne], *n.m.* little boy.
garçonnière [garsɔ'njɛ:r], *n.f.* bachelor's flat.
garde [gard], *n.f.* keeping; defense, guard; custody, watch; heed; nurse; hilt (*of sword*).—*n.m.* guard, guardsman, keeper, warder; watchman.
garde-à-vous [garda'vu], *n.m. inv.* (*Mil.*) position at attention.
garde-barrière [gardba'rjɛ:r], *n.m.* (*pl. unchanged or* **gardes-barrières**) (*Rail.*) signalman at level crossing.
garde-boue [gard'bu], *n.m. inv.* mudguard.
garde-cendre(s) [gard'sɑ̃:dr], *n.m. inv.* fender, fire guard.
garde-chasse [gard'ʃas], *n.m.* (*pl. unchanged or* **gardes-chasses**) game-keeper.
garde-chiourme [gard'ʃjurm], *n.m.* (*pl. unchanged or* **gardes-chiourme**) overseer of convict gangs; warder.
garde-corps [gard'kɔ:r], *n.m. inv.* rail, handrail; (*Naut.*) life-line.
garde-côte(s) [gard'kot], *n.m.* (*pl.* **garde-côtes** *or* **gardes-côtes**) guard ship, coast guard.
garde-crotte [gard'krɔt], *n.m. inv.* mudguard.
garde-feu [gard'fø], *n.m.* (*pl. unchanged or* **garde-feux**) fire-guard; fender.
garde-fou [gard'fu], *n.m.* (*pl.* **-fous**) parapet; railings.
garde-frein [gard'frɛ̃], *n.m.* (*pl.* **garde-freins** *or* **gardes-freins**) brakeman.
garde-magasin [gardmaga'zɛ̃], *n.m.* (*pl. unchanged or* **gardes-magasins**) warehouse keeper, storekeeper.
garde-malade [gardma'lad], *n.* (*pl. unchanged or* **gardes-malades**) sick-nurse, attendant.
garde-manger [gardmɑ̃'ʒe], *n.m. inv.* larder, pantry, meat safe.
garde-meuble(s) [gard'mœbl], *n.m. inv.* furniture repository.
garde-pêche [gard'pɛ:ʃ], *n.m.* (*pl.* **gardes-pêche**) river keeper, water bailiff.
garde-port [gard'pɔ:r], *n.m.* (*pl.* **gardes-port** *or* **gardes-ports**) harbor-master.
garder [gar'de], *v.t.* to keep, to preserve; to retain; to watch over, to take care of, to nurse; to guard, to defend; to observe (*silence etc.*); to keep up. **se garder**, *v.r.* to keep, to last; to beware, to take care not to; to refrain (**de**); to guard.
garderie [gardə'ri], *n.f.* day nursery.

garde-robe (1) [gard'rɔb], *n.m.* (*pl.* **-robes**) apron; overall.

garde-robe (2) [gard'rɔb], *n.f.* (*pl.* **-robes**) wardrobe (*cupboard for clothes*).

gardeur [gar'dœːr], *n.m.* (*fem.* **-euse**) herdboy *or* -girl, keeper.

gardien [gar'djɛ̃], *a.* (*fem.* **-enne**) tutelary, guardian.—*n.m.* (*fem.* **-enne**) guardian, keeper, door-keeper; trustee; *gardien de but*, goalkeeper.

gardon [gar'dɔ̃], *n.m.* roach.

gare! (1) [gaːr], *int.* beware! take care! look out!

gare (2) [gaːr], *n.f.* railway station, terminus; (*wet*) dock; *gare routière*, coach station.

garenne [ga'rɛn], *n.f.* warren.

garer [ga're], *v.t.* to side-track (*a train*); to garage, to park. **se garer**, *v.r.* to keep *or* get out of the way; to take cover; to park.

Gargantua [gargã'tɥa], *n.m.* Gargantua; glutton.

gargantuesque [gargã'tɥɛsk], *a.* gluttonous.

gargariser (se) [səgargari'ze], *v.r.* to gargle.

gargarisme [garga'rism], *n.m.* gargle, gargling.

gargote [gar'gɔt], *n.f.* cheap eating-house, cook-shop.

gargotier [gargɔ'tje]. *n.m.* (*fem.* **-ière**) keeper of a cook-shop; bad cook.

gargouille [gar'guːj], *n.f.* gargoyle, waterspout.

gargouillement [garguj'mã], *n.m.* rumbling (*in the stomach*); gurgling, bubbling (*of water*).

gargouiller [gargu'je], *v.i.* to rumble, to gurgle.

gargouillis [gargu'ji], *n.m.* gurgling (*of water*).

gargousse [gar'gus], *n.f.* cannon cartridge; *papier à gargousse*, cartridge paper.

garnement [garnə'mã], *n.m.* scapegrace, scamp, (*young*) rogue.

garni [gar'ni], *a.* furnished; trimmed, garnished.—*n.m.* furnished lodgings *or* house.

garnir [gar'niːr], *v.t.* to furnish, to stock; to trim, to garnish, to adorn; to fill. **se garnir**, *v.r.* to furnish *or* provide oneself (*with*).

garnison [garni'zɔ̃], *n.f.* garrison, station.

garnissage [garni'saːʒ], **garnissement** [garnis'mã], *n.m.* trimming (*of clothes etc.*).

garnisseur [garni'sœːr], *n.m.* (*fem.* **-euse**) trimmer.

garniture [garni'tyːr], *n.f.* furniture, trimmings; ornaments.

garrot (1) [ga'ro], *n.m.* withers (*of a horse etc.*).

garrot (2) [ga'r], *n.m.* tightener, garrot; (*Surg.*) tourniquet.

garrotte [ga'rɔt], *n.f.* garrotting, strangulation.

garrotter [garɔ'te], *v.t.* to tie down, to pinion; to strangle.

gars [gɑ], *n.m.* lad, stripling, young fellow.

Gascogne [gas'kɔɲ], **la**, *f.* Gascony; **le Golfe de Gascogne**, the Bay of Biscay.

gascon [gas'kɔ̃], *a.* (*fem.* **-onne**) Gascon.—*n.m.* Gascon (*dialect*); (**Gascon**, *fem.* **-onne**) Gascon (*person*); (*fig.*) boaster, braggart.

gasconnade [gaskɔ'nad], *n.f.* gasconade, boast, brag.

gasconner [gaskɔ'ne], *v.i.* to speak with a Gascon accent; to brag.

gaspillage [gaspi'jaːʒ], *n.m.* waste, squandering.

gaspiller [gaspi'je], *v.t.* to waste, to squander.

gaspilleur [gaspi'jœːr], *a.* (*fem.* **-euse**) wasting, squandering.—*n.m.* (*fem.* **-euse**) waster, squanderer, spendthrift.

gastrique [gas'trik], *a.* gastric.

gastrite [gas'trit], *n.f.* gastritis.

gastro-entérite [gastroãte'rit], *n.f.* gastroenteritis.

gâté [gɑ'te], *a.* marred, damaged, tainted; (*fig.*) spoiled.

gâteau [gɑ'to], *n.m.* (*pl.* **-eaux**) cake.

gâte-métier [gɑtme'tje], *n.m.* (*pl. unchanged* or **gâte-métiers**) underseller.

gâte-papier [gɑtpa'pje], *n. inv.* scribbler, poor writer.

gâter [gɑ'te], *v.t.* to spoil, to damage, to injure, to mar; to corrupt. **se gâter**, *v.r.* to taint, to spoil, to get spoiled; to break up (*of weather*).

gâterie [gɑ'tri], *n.f.* spoiling (*of children*), foolish indulgence.

gâte-sauce [gɑt'soːs], *n.m.* (*pl. unchanged* or **gâte-sauces**) scullion; (*colloq.*) bad cook.

gâteux [gɑ'tø], *a.* and *n.m.* (*fem.* **-euse**) idiot.

gauche [goːʃ], *a.* left; (*fig.*) crooked, ugly; clumsy.—*n.f.* left hand, left side; (*Mil.*) left wing, left flank.

gauchement [goʃ'mã], *adv.* awkwardly, clumsily.

gaucher [go'ʃe], *a.* and *n.m.* (*fem.* **-ère**) left-handed (person).

gaucherie [go'ʃri], *n.f.* awkwardness, clumsiness.

gauchir [go'ʃiːr], *v.t.* to warp.—*v.i.* to turn aside; to flinch; to become warped; (*fig.*) to dodge.

gaudriole [godri'ɔl], *n.f.* broad joke, coarse jest.

gaufrage [go'fraːʒ], *n.m.* goffering.

gaufre [go:fr], *n.f.* wafer, waffle (*thin cake*); honeycomb.

gaufrer [go'fre], *v.t.* to goffer.

gaufrette [go'frɛt], *n.f.* small wafer.

gaufreur [go'frœːr], *n.m.* (*fem.* **-euse**) gofferer.

gaufrier [gofri'e], *n.m.* waffle iron.

gaufrure [go'fryːr], *n.f.* goffering.

Gaule [goːl], **la**, *f.* Gaul.

gaule [goːl], *n.f.* pole, switch, long stick.

gauler [go'le], *v.t.* to beat (*trees*) with a long pole; to knock down (*fruit*).

gaullisme [go'lism], *n.m.* policy *or* partisanship of General de Gaulle.

gaulliste [go'list], *a.* and *n.* follower of General de Gaulle.

gaulois [go'lwa], *a.* Gaulish, Gallic; (*fig.*) free.—*n.m.* Gallic (*language*); (**Gaulois**, *fem.* **-oise**) Gaul (*person*).

gausser (se) [səgo'se], *v.r.* (*colloq.*) to banter, to chaff.

Gauthier [go'tje], *m.* Walter.

gave (1) [ga'v], *n.m.* torrent, mountain stream (*in the Pyrenees*).

gave (2) [ga'v], *n.f.* crop (*of birds*).

gaver [ga've], *v.t.* (*colloq.*) to cram, to gorge.

gavotte [ga'vɔt], *n.f.* gavotte (*dance*).

gavroche [ga'vrɔʃ], *n.m.* Parisian urchin.

gaz [gɑːz], *n.m.* gas; *bec de gaz*, gas burner.

gaze

gaze [gɑːz], *n.f.* gauze.
gazé [gɑ'ze], *a.* covered with gauze, veiled; softened, toned down; (*Mil.*) gassed (*soldier*).
gazelle [ga'zɛl], *n.f.* gazelle.
gazer (1) [gɑ'ze], *v.t.* to cover with gauze; (*fig.*) to veil, to tone down.
gazer (2) [gɑ'ze], *v.t.* (*Mil.*) to gas (*men*).
gazette [ga'zɛt], *n.f.* gazette, newspaper; (*fig.*) gossipmonger.
gazeux [gɑ'zø], *a.* (*fem.* **-euse**) gaseous; aerated.
gazier (1) [gɑ'zje], *n.m.* gas-fitter.
gazier (2) [gɑ'zje], *n.m.* (*fem.* **-ière**) gauze maker.
gazolène [gɑzɔ'lɛn], **gazoléine** [gɑzɔle'in], **gazoline** [gɑzɔ'lin], *n.f.* gasoline.
gazomètre [gɑzɔ'mɛtr], *n.m.* gasometer.
gazon [gɑ'zɔ̃], *n.m.* grass; sod, turf; lawn.
gazonnant [gɑzɔ'nɑ̃], *a.* producing grass; grassy.
gazonner [gɑzɔ'ne], *v.t.* to cover with turf, to turf.
gazonneux [gɑzɔ'nø], *a.* (*fem.* **-euse**) turfy, swarded.
gazouillement [gazuj'mɑ̃], *n.m.* chirping, warbling (*of birds*); babbling (*of a brook etc.*); prattle.
gazouiller [gazu'je], *v.i.* to chirp, to warble; to twitter; to prattle; to babble.
gazouillis [gazu'ji], *n.m.* warbling, twittering.
geai [ʒɛ], *n.m.* jay.
géant [ʒe'ɑ̃], *a.* gigantic.—*n.m.* (*fem.* **-e**) giant.
geignard [ʒɛ'naːr], *a.* always whining, querulous.
geignement [ʒɛɲ'mɑ̃], *n.m.* moan, whine.
geindre [ʒɛ̃ːdr], *v.i. irr.* (*conjug. like* CRAINDRE) to moan, to whine, to fret, to complain.
gel [ʒɛl], *n.m.* frost, freezing.
gélatine [ʒela'tin], *n.f.* gelatine.
gélatiner [ʒelati'ne], *v.t.* to gelatinize.
gélatineux [ʒelati'nø], *a.* (*fem.* **-euse**) gelatinous.
gelé [ʒə'le], *a.* frozen, cold.
gelée [ʒə'le], *n.f.* frost; jelly; aspic.
geler [ʒə'le], *v.t., v.i.* (*conjug. like* AMENER) and **se geler**, *v.r.* to freeze.
gélignite [ʒeli'nit], *n.f.* gelignite.
gelinotte [ʒəli'nɔt], *n.f.* grouse (*bird*).
gémir [ʒe'miːr], *v.i.* to groan, to moan; to lament; (*fig.*) to suffer.
gémissant [ʒemi'sɑ̃], *a.* groaning, moaning; lamenting.
gémissement [ʒemis'mɑ̃], *n.m.* groan, moan; (*fig.*) lament, cooing.
gemme [ʒɛm], *n.f.* gem; resin; (*Bot.*) bud.
gemmer [ʒɛ'me], *v.t.* to bud.
gênant [ʒɛ'nɑ̃], *a.* troublesome, inconvenient, embarrassing.
gencive [ʒɑ̃'siːv], *n.f.* gum (*of the teeth*).
gendarme [ʒɑ̃'darm], *n.m.* gendarme (*armed policeman*); constable; virago (*woman*).
gendarmerie [ʒɑ̃darm'ri], *n.f.* gendarmery (*armed police*); constabulary; barracks (*of gendarmes*).
gendre [ʒɑ̃ːdr], *n.m.* son-in-law.
gêne [ʒɛːn], *n.f.* constraint, uneasiness, annoyance; difficulty; financial difficulties, penury.
gêné [ʒɛ'ne], *a.* constrained, ill at ease; hard up.

généalogie [ʒenealɔ'ʒi], *n.f.* genealogy; pedigree.
généalogique [ʒenealɔ'ʒik], *a.* genealogical.
généalogiste [ʒenealɔ'ʒist], *n.m.* genealogist.
gêner [ʒɛ'ne], *v.t.* to constrain, to constrict; to impede; to obstruct; to thwart, to restrain; to inconvenience, to embarrass; to annoy. **se gêner**, *v.r.* to constrain oneself, to put oneself out.
général [ʒene'ral], *a.* (*m. pl.* **-aux**) general, universal; vague.—*adv. phr.* **en général**, in general.—*n.m.* (*Mil.*) general.
générale [ʒene'ral], *n.f.* general's wife; drumbeat (*to give alarm of fire etc.*).
généralement [ʒeneral'mɑ̃], *adv.* generally, in general.
généralisation [ʒeneraliza'sjɔ̃], *n.f.* generalization.
généraliser [ʒenerali'ze], *v.t.* to generalize.
généralissime [ʒenerali'sim], *n.m.* generalissimo, commander-in-chief of allied armies.
généralité [ʒenerali'te], *n.f.* generality.
générateur [ʒenera'tœːr], *a.* (*fem.* **-trice**) generating, generative.—*n.m.* generator.
génératif [ʒenera'tif], *a.* (*fem.* **-tive**) generative.
génération [ʒenera'sjɔ̃], *n.f.* generation; procreation.
générer [ʒene're], *v.t.* (*conjug. like* CÉDER) to generate.
généreusement [ʒenerøz'mɑ̃], *adv.* generously, bountifully, nobly, bravely.
généreux [ʒene'rø], *a.* (*fem.* **-euse**) generous, liberal, bountiful; noble; courageous.
générique [ʒene'rik], *a.* generic.—*n.m.* (*Ciné.*) credits.
générosité [ʒenerozi'te], *n.f.* generosity, liberality; magnanimity.
Gênes [ʒɛːn], *f.* Genoa.
genèse [ʒə'nɛz], *n.f.* genesis.
genêt [ʒə'nɛ], *n.m.* (*Bot.*) broom.
genette [ʒə'nɛt], *n.f.* genet, civet cat.
gêneur [ʒɛ'nœːr], *n.m.* (*fem.* **-euse**) intruder; spoil-sport.
Genève [ʒə'nɛv], *f.* Geneva.
genevois [ʒən'vwa], *a.* Genevese.
genévrier [ʒenevri'e], *n.m.* juniper tree.
génie [ʒe'ni], *n.m.* genius; spirit, nature, bent, talent; (*Mil.*) corps of engineers.
genièvre [ʒə'njɛːvr], *n.m.* juniper berry; juniper tree; gin.
génisse [ʒe'nis], *n.f.* heifer.
génital [ʒeni'tal], *a.* (*m. pl.* **-aux**) genital.
génitif [ʒeni'tif], *n.m.* (*Gram.*) genitive.
génocide [ʒeno'sid], *n.m.* genocide.
génois [ʒe'nwa], *a.* Genoese.
genou [ʒə'nu], *n.m.* (*pl.* **-oux**) knee; (*Mech.*) ball and socket; (*pl.*) lap.
genouillère [ʒanu'jɛːr], *n.f.* knee piece (*of armor*); top (*of a high boot*); knee-cap; ball-and-socket joint.
genre [ʒɑ̃ːr], *n.m.* genus; species, kind, sort; fashion, style; (*Gram.*) gender.
gens [ʒɑ̃], *n.m. pl.* (*but adjectives directly preceding the word take the feminine form*) people, persons, folk; men, hands; servants.
gent [ʒɑ̃], *n.f.* brood, race, tribe.
gentiane [ʒɑ̃'sjan], *n.f.* (*Bot.*) gentian.
gentil (1) [ʒɑ̃'ti], *n.m.* Gentile.
gentil (2) [ʒɑ̃'ti], *a.* (*fem.* **-ille**) noble, gentle; pretty, nice, graceful; amiable, pleasing.

gentilhomme [ʒɑ̃tiˈjɔm], *n.m.* (*pl.* **gentils-hommes**) nobleman, gentleman.
gentillesse [ʒɑ̃tiˈjɛs], *n.f.* kindness, sweetness (*of temperament*); prettiness, gracefulness; pretty thing, thought etc.
gentiment [ʒɑ̃tiˈmɑ̃], *adv.* prettily, gracefully, like a good boy *or* girl.
génuflexion [ʒenyflɛkˈsjɔ̃], *n.f.* genuflexion.
géocentrique [ʒeosɑ̃ˈtrik], *a.* geocentric.
Geoffroy [ʒɔˈfrwa], *m.* Geoffrey, Jeffrey.
géographe [ʒeoˈgraf], *n.m.* geographer.
géographie [ʒeograˈfi], *n.f.* geography.
géographique [ʒeograˈfik], *a.* geographical.
geôle [ʒoːl], *n.f.* jail, prison.
geôlier [ʒoˈlje], *n.m.* jailer.
géologie [ʒeoloˈʒi], *n.f.* geology.
géologique [ʒeoloˈʒik], *a.* geological.
géologue [ʒeoˈlɔg], *n.m.* geologist.
géométral [ʒeɔmeˈtral], *a.* (*m. pl.* **-aux**) geometrical.
géomètre [ʒeoˈmɛtr], *n.m.* geometrician; geometer.
géométrie [ʒeɔmeˈtri], *n.f.* geometry.
géométrique [ʒeɔmeˈtrik], *a.* geometrical.
Georges [ʒɔrʒ], *m.* George.
gérance [ʒeˈrɑ̃ːs], *n.f.* management, managership; editorship.
géranium [ʒeraˈnjɔm], *n.m.* geranium.
gérant [ʒeˈrɑ̃], *n.m.* (*fem.* **-e**) manager; editor; *rédacteur gérant*, managing editor.
gerbe [ʒɛrb], *n.f.* sheaf, bundle; bunch of flowers.
gerber [ʒɛrˈbe], *v.t.* to make up *or* bind into sheaves.
gerbier [ʒɛrˈbje], *n.m.* cornstack.
gerce [ʒɛrs], *n.f.* chap, crack.
gercé [ʒɛrˈse], *a.* chapped (*hands*).
gercer [ʒɛrˈse], *v.t., v.i.,* (*conjug. like* COMMENCER) and **se gercer**, *v.r.* to chap, to crack.
gerçure [ʒɛrˈsyːr], *n.f.* chap, crack; chink, cleft.
gérer [ʒeˈre], *v.t.* (*conjug. like* CÉDER) to manage, to administer.
gerfaut [ʒɛrˈfo], *n.m.* gerfalcon.
germain [ʒɛrˈmɛ̃], *a.* german, first (*of cousins etc.*); (*Law*) full (*brother etc.*).
germanique [ʒɛrmaˈnik], *a.* Germanic.
germe [ʒɛrm], *n.m.* germ, embryo; seed; bud, sprout, shoot; (*fig.*) origin.
germer [ʒɛrˈme], *v.i.* to shoot, to sprout, to germinate.
germination [ʒɛrminaˈsjɔ̃], *n.f.* germination.
gésier [ʒeˈzje], *n.m.* gizzard.
***gésir** [ʒeˈziːr], *v.i. irr.* to lie; *ci-gît*, here lies.
gestation [ʒɛstaˈsjɔ̃], *n.f.* gestation.
gestatoire [ʒɛstaˈtwaːr], *a.* gestatory.
geste [ʒɛst], *n.m.* gesture, action; sign.
gesticulateur [ʒɛstikylaˈtœːr], *n.m.* (*fem.* **-trice**) gesticulator.
gesticulation [ʒɛstikylaˈsjɔ̃], *n.f.* gesticulation.
gesticuler [ʒɛstikyˈle], *v.i.* to gesticulate.
gestion [ʒɛsˈtjɔ̃], *n.f.* management, administration.
geyser [geˈzɛːr], *n.m.* geyser.
Ghana [gaˈna], **le**, *m.* Ghana.
ghetto [geˈto], *n.m.* Jewish quarter, ghetto.
gibbeux [ʒiˈbø], *a.* (*fem.* **-euse**) gibbous, hump-backed.
gibbon [ʒiˈbɔ̃], *n.m.* gibbon (*ape*).
gibbosité [ʒiboziˈte], *n.f.* gibbosity; hump.

gibecière [ʒibˈsjɛːr], *n.f.* game bag, satchel; juggler's pocket.
gibelet [ʒiˈblɛ], *n.m.* gimlet.
giberne [ʒiˈbɛrn], *n.f.* cartridge box *or* pouch.
gibet [ʒiˈbɛ], *n.m.* gibbet, gallows.
gibier [ʒiˈbje], *n.m.* (*Hunt.*) game.
giboulée [ʒibuˈle], *n.f.* sudden shower, hail storm.
gibus [ʒiˈbyːs], *n.m. inv.* gibus (*crush-hat, opera hat*).
giclage [ʒiˈklaːʒ], *n.m.* spraying; *carburateur à giclage*, jet carburetor.
giclée [ʒiˈkle], *n.f.* squirt, spirt.
gicleur [ʒiˈklœːr], *n.m.* spray nozzle, jet.
gicler [ʒiˈkle], *v.i.* to spout, to squirt.
gifle [ʒifl], *n.f.* slap in the face, box on the ear.
gifler [ʒiˈfle], *v.t.* to slap in the face, to box the ears of.
gigantesque [ʒigɑ̃ˈtɛsk], *a.* gigantic, colossal.
gigot [ʒiˈgo], *n.m.* leg of mutton.
gigue [ʒig], *n.f.* shank, leg, haunch (*of venison*); jig (*dance*).
gilet [ʒiˈlɛ], *n.m.* waistcoat; vest.
Gilles [ʒil], *m.* Giles.
gingembre [ʒɛ̃ˈʒɑ̃ːbr], *n.m.* ginger.
gingivite [ʒɛ̃ʒiˈvit], *n.f.* gingivitis.
ginguet [ʒɛ̃ˈgɛ], *a.* (*fem.* **-ette**) (*colloq.*) weak, worthless, scanty.—*n.m.* thin wine.
girandole [ʒirɑ̃ˈdɔl], *n.f.* girandole, epergne.
giration [ʒiraˈsjɔ̃], *n.f.* gyration.
giratoire [ʒiraˈtwaːr], *a.* gyratory.
girofle [ʒiˈrɔfl], *n.m.* clove.
giroflée [ʒiroˈfle], *n.f.* gillyflower, stock; *giroflée jaune*, wallflower.
giron [ʒiˈrɔ̃], *n.m.* lap; (*fig.*) bosom.
girouette [ʒiˈrwɛt], *n.f.* weathercock, vane.
gisant [ʒiˈzɑ̃], *a.* lying (*ill, dead etc.*); outstretched [GÉSIR].
gisement [ʒizˈmɑ̃], *n.m.* (*Geol. etc.*) lie (*of strata*); layer, bed; (*Naut.*) bearing (*of coast etc.*).
gitan [ʒiˈtɑ̃], *n.m.* (*fem.* **-e**) gipsy.
gîte [ʒit], *n.m.* home, lodging; refuge; lair (*of deer*); (*Min.*) seam, layer.—*n.f.* (*Naut.*) list.
gîter [ʒiˈte], *v.t.* to lodge, to house; to put up, to shelter.—*v.i.* to lie, to lodge; (*Naut.*) to list; to run aground. **se gîter**, *v.r.* to lodge, to sleep.
givrage [ʒiˈvraːʒ], *n.m.* (*Av.*) frosting, icing.
givre [ʒiˈvr], *n.m.* hoar-frost, *rime.
givré [ʒiˈvre], *a.* rimed, rimy.
glabre [glɑːbr], *a.* (*Bot.*) glabrous, smooth, without down; hairless.
glaçage [glaˈsaːʒ], *n.m.* frosting, glazing.
glaçant [glaˈsɑ̃], *a.* freezing; icy, chilling.
glace [glas], *n.f.* ice; ice cream; glass, plate glass; mirror; carriage window; flaw (*in a diamond etc.*); icing (*on cakes etc.*).
glacé [glaˈse], *a.* frozen, freezing; icy-cold; iced; glazed; glossy (*paper*); candied.
glacer [glaˈse], *v.t.* (*conjug. like* COMMENCER) to freeze; to ice; (*fig.*) to paralyze; to glaze. —*v.i.* and **se glacer**, *v.r.* to freeze.
glaciaire [glaˈsjɛːr], *a.* of glaciers, glacial.
glacial [glaˈsjal], *a.* frozen, glacial, icy.
glaciale [glaˈsial], *n.f.* (*Bot.*) ice-plant.
glacier [glaˈsje], *n.m.* glacier, field of ice; ice-cream vendor.
glaçon [glaˈsɔ̃], *n.m.* block of ice; floe; ice cube; *petit glaçon*, icicle.
gladiateur [gladjaˈtœːr], *n.m.* gladiator.

glaïeul [gla'jœl], *n.m.* gladiolus; iris.
glaire [glɛːr], *n.f.* glair, white of egg; phlegm, mucus.
glaise [glɛːz], *a.* clayey.—*n.f.* clay, loam; potter's earth.
glaiseux [glɛ'zø], *a.* (*fem.* **-euse**) clayey, loamy.
glaisière [glɛ'zjɛːr], *n.f.* clay pit.
glaive [glɛːv], *n.m.* sword, blade, steel.
gland [glɑ̃], *n.m.* acorn; tassel.
glande [glɑ̃ːd], *n.f.* (*Anat.*) gland; (*pop.*) tumor; kernel.
glanduleux [glɑ̃dy'lø], *a.* (*fem.* **-euse**) glandulous, glandular.
glaner [gla'ne], *v.t.*, *v.i.* to glean.
glaneur [gla'nœːr], *n.m.* (*fem.* **-euse**) gleaner.
glapir [gla'piːr], *v.i.* to yelp (*of puppies etc.*); to screech, to scream (*of persons*).
glapissant [glapi'sɑ̃], *a.* yelping; screeching, shrill.
glapissement [glapis'mɑ̃], *n.m.* yelping; screeching.
glas [glɑ], *n.m.* knell.
glauque [gloːk], *a.* glaucous, sea-green.
glèbe [glɛb], *n.f.* glebe; land, soil.
glissade [gli'sad], *n.f.* sliding, slide; slipping.
glissant [gli'sɑ̃], *a.* slippery; (*fig.*) ticklish, delicate.
glissement [glis'mɑ̃], *n.m.* slipping, sliding, gliding; (*Polit.*) landslide.
glisser [gli'se], *v.t.* to slip, to slide; to insinuate.—*v.i.* to slip, to slide; to glide. **se glisser**, *v.r.* to slip, to slide, to creep, to steal, to insinuate oneself (*dans*).
glissière [gli'sjɛːr], *n.f.* slide; **porte à glissière**, sliding door.
glissoire [gli'swaːr], *n.f.* slide on ice.
global [glɔ'bal], *a.* (*m. pl.* **-aux**) in a mass, entire; **somme globale**, lump sum.
globe [glɔb], *n.m.* globe, sphere, orb; glass shade.
globulaire [glɔby'lɛːr], *a.* globular.
globule [glɔ'byl], *n.m.* globule.
gloire [glwaːr], *n.f.* glory, fame.
gloriette [glɔ'rjɛt], *n.f.* arbor, summer-house.
glorieusement [glɔrjøz'mɑ̃], *adv.* gloriously.
glorieux [glɔ'rjø], *a.* (*fem.* **-euse**) glorious; vainglorious.—*n.m.* braggart, boaster.
glorification [glɔrifika'sjɔ̃], *n.f.* glorification.
glorifier [glɔri'fje], *v.t.* to glorify, to honor. **se glorifier**, *v.r.* to glory in, to boast (*de*).
gloriole [glɔ'rjɔl], *n.f.* vainglory, petty vanity.
glose [gloːz], *n.f.* gloss; criticism; comment; parody.
gloser [glo'ze], *v.t.* to gloss; to criticize.—*v.i.* to carp, to find fault.
gloseur [glo'zœːr], *n.m.* (*fem.* **-euse**) carper, fault-finder.
glossaire [glɔ'sɛːr], *n.m.* glossary, vocabulary.
glouglou [glu'glu], *n.m.* gurgling, gurgle.
glouglouter [gluglu'te], *v.i.* to gurgle.
gloussement [glus'mɑ̃], *n.m.* clucking.
glousser [glu'se], *v.i.* to cluck (*of hens*).
glouton [glu'tɔ̃], *a.* (*fem.* **-onne**) gluttonous, greedy.—*n.m.* (*fem.* **-onne**) glutton.
gloutonnement [glutɔn'mɑ̃], *adv.* gluttonously, greedily.
gloutonnerie [gluton'ri], *n.f.* gluttony, greediness.
glu [gly], *n.f.* bird-lime, glue.
gluant [gly'ɑ̃], *a.* glutinous, sticky; slimy.

glucose [gly'koːz], *n.m.* glucose.
glutineux [glyti'nø], *a.* (*fem.* **-euse**) glutinous, viscous.
glycérine [glise'rin], *n.f.* glycerine.
glycine [gli'sin], *n.f.* wistaria.
gnome [gno:m], *n.m.* (*fem.* **gnomide**) gnome.
gnou [gnu], *n.m.* gnu.
gobelet [gɔ'blɛ], *n.m.* goblet, mug; dice box; **tour de gobelet**, juggler's trick.
gobelin [gɔ'blɛ̃], *n.m.* goblin, imp.
gobe-mouches [gɔb'muʃ], *n.m.* *inv.* fly-catcher (*bird*); fly-trap (*plant*); (*fig.*) simpleton.
gober [gɔ'be], *v.t.* to gulp down, to swallow; (*colloq.*) to believe easily; to have a liking for (*a person*).
(C) **godendard** [gɔdɑ̃'daːr], *n.m.* cross-cut saw, whip-saw, two-handle saw.
goder [gɔ'de], *v.i.* to crease to bag (*of clothes*), to pucker (*of needlework etc.*).
godiche [gɔ'diʃ], *a.* clumsy, boobyish, simple.
godille [gɔ'diːj], *n.f.* stern oar; scull.
goéland [gɔe'lɑ̃], *n.m.* gull, sea-gull.
goélette [gɔe'lɛt], *n.f.* schooner.
goémon [gɔe'mɔ̃], *n.m.* seaweed.
gogo [gɔ'go] (*in adv. phr.*) **à gogo**, galore.
goguenard [gɔg'naːr], *a.* bantering, jeering, mocking, scoffing.—*n.m.* (*fem.* **-e**) banterer, jeerer, chaffer.
goguenarder [gɔgnar'de], *v.i.* to jeer, to banter, to chaff.
goguette [gɔ'gɛt], *n.f.* **être en goguette**, to be in a merry mood, to be on the spree.
goinfre [gwɛ̃:fr], *n.m.* (*fam.*) guzzler, gormandizer.
goinfrer [gwɛ̃'fre], *v.i.* to gorge, to gormandize.
goinfrerie [gwɛ̃frə'ri], *n.f.* gluttony.
goître [gwa:tr], *n.m.* goitre; wen.
goitreux [gwa'trø], *a.* (*fem.* **-euse**) goitrous.—*n.m.* (*fem.* **-euse**) goitrous person, (*colloq.*) imbecile, idiot.
golfe [gɔlf], *n.m.* gulf, bay.
gommage [gɔ'maːʒ], *n.m.* gumming.
gomme [gɔm], *n.f.* gum; rubber; eraser.
gommer [gɔ'me], *v.t.* to gum; to rub out.
gommeux [gɔ'mø], *a.* (*fem.* **-euse**) gummy.
gommier [gɔ'mje], *n.m.* gum tree.
gond [gɔ̃], *n.m.* hinge; **hors des gonds**, unhinged, (*fig.*) enraged, beside oneself.
gondole [gɔ̃'dɔl], *n.f.* gondola; car or gondola (*of a balloon etc.*); eye-bath.
gondoler [gɔ̃dɔ'le], *v.i.* to bulge; to warp (*of wood*); to buckle.
gondolier [gɔ̃dɔ'lje], *n.m.* gondolier.
gonflement [gɔ̃flə'mɑ̃], *n.m.* swelling, inflation.
gonfler [gɔ̃'fle], *v.t.* to swell, to inflate; to pump up (*a tire*); to puff up.—*v.i.* to swell, to be swollen. **se gonfler**, *v.r.* to swell, to be swollen, to be puffed up; (*fam.*) to swank.
gonfleur [gɔ̃'flœːr], *n.m.* air-pump, inflator.
gong [gɔ̃:g], *n.m.* gong.
gorge [gɔrʒ], *n.f.* throat, gullet; bosom, neck; defile, strait; (*Bot.*) mouth; (*Arch., Fort.*) gorge; **avoir mal à la gorge**, to have a sore throat; **avoir la gorge serrée**, to have a lump in one's throat; **rendre gorge**, to refund, to pay up; **faire des gorges chaudes**, to gloat over.
gorge-de-pigeon [gɔrʒdəpi'ʒɔ̃], *a.* *inv.* iridescent, shot (*of colors*).

gorgée [gɔr'ʒe], *n.f.* draft; gulp; *petite gorgée*, sip.

gorger [gɔr'ʒe], *v.t.* (*conjug. like* MANGER) to gorge, to cram. **se gorger**, *v.r.* to gorge oneself.

gorille [gɔ'ri:j], *n.m.* gorilla.

gosier [go'zje], *n.m.* throat, gullet; (*fig.*) voice.

gosse [gɔs], *n.* (*fam.*) brat, urchin, kid.

gothique [go'tik], *a.* Gothic.—*n.f.* (*Print.*) Old English.

gouache [gwaʃ], *n.f.* gouache; painting in this.

goudron [gu'drɔ], *n.m.* tar.

goudronnage [gudrɔ'na:ʒ], *n.m.* tarring.

goudronner [gudrɔ'ne], *v.t.* to tar.

goudronneux [gudrɔ'nø], *a.* (*fem.* **-euse**) tarry.

gouffre [gufr], *n.m.* gulf, abyss, pit.

gouge [gu:ʒ], *n.f.* gouge.

goujat [gu'ʒa], *n.m.* (*fig.*) cad, vulgar fellow.

goujon [gu'ʒɔ], *n.m.* gudgeon (*pin or fish*).

goule [gul], *n.f.* ghoul.

goulet [gu'lɛ], *n.m.* narrow entrance (*to a harbour etc.*); inlet; mouth, neck (*of a bottle etc.*); gully, gorge (*between mountains etc.*).

goulot [gu'lo], *n.m.* neck (*of a bottle etc.*).

goulu [gu'ly], *a.* gluttonous, greedy.—*n.m.* (*fem.* **-e**) glutton, greedy person.

goulûment [guly'mã], *adv.* greedily.

goupille [gu'pi:j], *n.f.* (cotter) pin, peg, bolt.

goupiller [gupi'je], *v.t.* to pin, to bolt.

gourd [gu:r], *a.* benumbed, numb.

gourde [gurd], *n.f.* gourd; flask, wineskin.

gourdin [gur'dɛ], *n.m.* cudgel, club, thick stick.

gourmade [gur'mad], *n.f.* smack in the face.

gourmand [gur'mã], *a.* greedy.—*n.m.* (*fem.* **-e**) glutton.

gourmander [gurmã'de], *v.t.* to chide, to reprimand; to prune (*trees*).

gourmandise [gurmã'di:z], *n.f.* gluttony, greediness; (*pl.*) sweetmeats.

gourmé [gur'me], *a.* stiff, stuck-up, formal, solemn.

gourmer [gur'me], *v.t.* to box, to thump; to curb (*a horse*). **se gourmer**, *v.r.* to thump, to pummel each other.

gourmet [gur'mɛ], *n.m.* connoisseur in wines etc.; epicure.

gourmette [gur'mɛt], *n.f.* bit, curb chain.

gousse [gus], *n.f.* shell, pod, husk; *gousse d'ail*, clove of garlic.

gousset [gu'sɛ], *n.m.* armpit; fob, (waistcoat-) pocket; gusset (*of a shirt etc.*); bracket.

goût [gu], *n.m.* taste, flavor, relish; savor; inclination, liking; style, manner; *chacun à son goût*, every man to his taste; *chacun son goût*, tastes differ; *viande de haut goût*, highly seasoned meat.

goûter [gu'te], *v.t.* to taste, to try; to like; to enjoy; to feel.—*v.i.* to taste; to try; to have a snack.—*n.m.* a snack taken between lunch and dinner (*the equivalent of English tea*).

goutte (1) [gut], *n.f.* drop, small quantity; sip, dram; (*Arch.*, *Pharm.*) drop.—*adv. phr. ne . . . goutte*, *n'entendre goutte*, not to hear *or* understand in the least; *n'y voir goutte*, not to make it out at all.

goutte (2) [gut], *n.f.* gout.

gouttelette [gu'tlɛt], *n.f.* small drop, drip.

goutter [gu'te], *v.i.* to drip.

goutteux [gu'tø], *a.* and *n.m.* (*fem.* **-euse**) gouty (person).

gouttière [gu'tjɛ:r], *n.f.* gutter of a roof; shoot, spout (*for rain water*); cradle splint.

gouvernable [guvɛr'nabl], *a.* governable, manageable.

gouvernail [guvɛr'na:j], *n.m.* rudder, helm.

gouvernant [guvɛr'nã], *a.* governing, ruling.—*n.m.* governor, ruler.—*n.f.* (**-e**) governor's wife; governess; housekeeper (*of bachelor*).

gouverne [gu'vɛrn], *n.f.* guidance, guide, direction; (*pl.*) (*Av.*) rudders and ailerons.

gouvernement [guvɛrnə'mã], *n.m.* government, rule, sway; management; governorship.

gouvernemental [guvɛrnəmã'tal], *a.* (*m. pl.* **-aux**) governmental.

gouverner [guvɛr'ne], *v.t.* to control, to govern, to direct, to steer; to rule, to command; to manage, to regulate.—*v.i.* to steer, to answer the helm.

gouverneur [guvɛr'nœ:r], *n.m.* governor; manager; tutor.

grabat [gra'ba], *n.m.* pallet, litter (*of straw etc.*), trundle bed.

grabuge [gra'by:ʒ], *n.m.* (*fam.*) wrangling, squabble, brawl.

grâce [grɑ:s], *n.f.* grace, favor, mercy, forgiveness; gracefulness, elegance; (*pl.*) thanks; (*Myth.*) *les Grâces*, the Graces.

graciable [gra'sjabl], *a.* pardonable.

gracier [gra'sje], *v.t.* to pardon, to reprieve.

gracieusement [grasjøz'mã], *adv.* graciously, kindly, gracefully.

gracieuseté [grasjøz'te], *n.f.* graciousness, kindness; act of courtesy; gratuity.

gracieux [gra'sjø], *a.* (*fem.* **-euse**) graceful, gracious, obliging.

gracilité [grasili'te], *n.f.* slimness, slenderness.

gradation [gradɑ'sjɔ], *n.f.* gradation; climax.

grade [grad], *n.m.* grade, rank; degree; *monter en grade*, to be promoted.

gradé [gra'de], *n.m.* (*Mil.*) non-commissioned officer.

gradin [gra'dɛ], *n.m.* step; tier.

graduation [gradɥa'sjɔ], *n.f.* graduation; scale.

gradué [gra'dɥe], *a.* graduated; progressive (*exercises*).—*n.m.* (*fem.* **-ée**) graduate (*of a university*).

graduel [gra'dɥɛl], *a.* (*fem.* **-elle**) gradual.

graduellement [gradɥɛl'mã], *adv.* gradually.

graduer [gra'dɥe], *v.t.* to graduate, to proportion.

graillon [grɑ'jɔ], *n.m.* smell of burnt meat *or* fat; (*pl.*) scraps (*of meat etc.*) from a meal.

grain (1) [grɛ], *n.m.* grain, berry; bead; jot, bit; *avoir un grain*, to have a bee in one's bonnet; *grain de beauté*, mole, beauty-spot; *grain de café*, coffee bean; *grain de poivre*, peppercorn; *grain de raisin*, grape.

grain (2) [grɛ], *n.m.* (*Naut.*) squall.

graine [grɛn], *n.f.* seed; breed; *c'est une mauvaise graine*, he is a bad lot.

grainetier [grɛn'tje], **grainier** [grɛ'nje], *n.m.* (*fem.* **-ière**) seedsman, seedswoman; grain and seed dealer.

graissage [grɛ'sa:ʒ], *n.m.* greasing, oiling, lubrication.

169

graisse [grɛːs], n.f. fat, grease.
graisser [grɛ'se], v.t. to grease; to make greasy; to lubricate, to oil.
graisseur [grɛ'sœːr], n.m. greaser, oiler.
graisseux [grɛ'søɔ], a. (fem. -euse) greasy; oily; fatty.
grammaire [gra'mɛːr], n.f. grammar.
grammairien [gramɛ'rjɛ̃], n.m. (fem. -enne) grammarian.
grammatical [gramati'kal]. a. (m. pl. -aux) grammatical.
grammaticalement [gramatikal'mɑ̃], adv. grammatically.
gramme [gram], n.m. gramme or gram.
grand [grɑ̃], a. great; large, big; high, tall; wide, spacious; grown-up; capital (of letters); broad (of daylight); grand, noble.—adv. voir grand, to have big ideas; en grand, on a large scale; (of portraits) full length.—n.m. the grand, the sublime.—n.m. (fem.-e) great person; grown-up person; grand d'Espagne, Spanish grandee; (pl.) the great, the great people; (sch.) the big (or senior) boys or girls.
(C) **grand-bois** [grɑ̃'bwa], n.m. virgin forest.
grand-duc [grɑ̃'dyk], n.m. (pl. grands-ducs) grand duke; eagle-owl.
grand-duché [grɑ̃dy'ʃe], n.m. (pl. grands-duchés) grand duchy.
grande-duchesse [grɑ̃ddy'ʃɛs], n.f. (pl. grandes-duchesses) grand duchess.
grandement [grɑ̃d'mɑ̃], adv. greatly, extremely, very much; grandly, nobly, handsomely.
grandeur [grɑ̃'dœːr], n.f. extent, size; height; length; breadth; bulk; greatness, magnitude; tallness; grandeur, magnificence; grace, highness (titles).
grandiose [grɑ̃'djoːz], a. grandiose.
grandir [grɑ̃'diːr], v.t. to increase; to magnify.—v.i. to grow; to grow (tall, big, up etc.). se grandir, v.r. to make oneself appear taller; to grow taller; to raise oneself, to rise.
grandissement [grɑ̃dis'mɑ̃], n.m. growth, increase; rise; (Opt.) magnification.
grand-maman [grɑ̃ma'mɑ̃], n.f. (pl. -mamans) granny.
grand-mère [grɑ̃'mɛːr], n.f. (pl. -mères) grandmother.
grand-père [grɑ̃'pɛːr], n.m. (pl. grands-pères) grandfather.
grand-route [grɑ̃'rut], n.f. (pl. -routes) high-road, main road.
grand-rue [grɑ̃'ry], n.f. (pl. -rues) high street, main street.
grange [grɑ̃ːʒ], n.f. barn.
granit [gra'nit, gra'ni], **granite** [gra'nit], n.m. granite.
granulaire [grany'lɛːr], a. granular.
granule [gra'nyl], n.m. granule.
granulé [grany'le], a. granulated, granular.
graphique [gra'fik], a. graphic.—n.m. diagram; graph.
graphiquement [grafik'mɑ̃], adv. graphically.
graphite [gra'fit], n.m. graphite; plumbago.
grappe [grap], n.f. bunch (of grapes, currants etc.); cluster (of fruit etc.); (Artill.) grape-shot.
grappillage [grapi'jaːʒ], n.m. vine gleaning or pickings.

grappiller [grapi'je], v.t. to glean.—v.i. to glean; to get pickings, to make a little profit.
grappilleur [grapi'jœːr], n.m. (fem. -euse) gleaner; petty thief, profiteer.
grappin [gra'pɛ̃], n.m. grapnel, grappling iron; grab.
gras [grɑ], a. (fem. grasse) fat; fleshy, corpulent; greasy, oily, unctuous; rich; broad, indecent; eaux grasses, dishwater; faire la grasse matinée, to get up late; mardi gras, Shrove Tuesday; matières grasses, fats.—n.m. fat, fat part (of meat etc.); meat, flesh; meat diet.
gras-double [grɑ'dubl], n.m. tripe.
grassement [grɑs'mɑ̃], adv. plentifully, liberally; in affluence.
grasseyement [grasɛj'mɑ̃], n.m. exaggerated rolling of uvular r.
grasseyer [grasɛ'je], v.i. to roll one's r's.
grassouillet [grasu'jɛ], a. (fem. -ette) (fam.) plump, chubby.
gratification [gratifika'sjɔ̃], n.f. gratuity, extra pay, reward.
gratifier [grati'fje], v.t. to confer (a favor) on; to ascribe.
gratin [gra'tɛ̃], n.m. burnt part; au gratin, (Cook.) dressed with crust of bread-crumbs.
gratis [gra'tis], adv. gratis, for nothing.
gratitude [grati'tyd], n.f. gratitude.
gratte-ciel [grat'sjɛl], n.m. inv. skyscraper.
grattelle [gra'tɛl], n.f. rash, itching.
gratte-papier [gratpa'pje], n.m. inv. scribbler, pen pusher.
gratter [gra'te], v.t. to scratch; to scrape. se gratter, v.r. to scratch oneself.
grattoir [gra'twaːr], n.m. scraper; eraser, paint scraper.
gratuit [gra'tɥi], a. free (of charge); gratuitous.
gratuité [gratɥi'te], n.f. gratuitousness.
gratuitement [gratɥit'mɑ̃], adv. for nothing; gratuitously.
gravats [gra'va], n.m. pl. rubbish, debris (of a building).
grave [graːv], a. heavy, grave, serious; weighty; dangerous; low, deep (of voice); (Mus.) low-pitched.
gravé [gra've], a. pitted; engraved.
graveleux [gra'vlø], a. (fem. -euse) gravelly, sandy, gritty; (fig.) smutty.
gravelle [gra'vɛl], n.f. (Path.) gravel.
gravement [grav'mɑ̃], adv. gravely, seriously.
graver [gra've], v.t. to engrave; to impress, to imprint. se graver, v.r. to be engraved, to be impressed or imprinted.
graveur [gra'vœːr], n.m. engraver.
gravier [gra'vje], n.m. gravel, grit; (Path.) gravel.
gravir [gra'viːr], v.t. to clamber up, to climb, to ascend.
gravitation [gravita'sjɔ̃], n.f. gravitation.
gravité [gravi'te], n.f. gravity; seriousness, solemnity; weight, importance.
graviter [gravi'te], v.i. to gravitate.
gravure [gra'vyːr], n.f. engraving, print; illustration (in book).
gré [gre], n.m. will, wish; liking, pleasure; mind, taste; accord, consent bon gré mal gré or de gré ou de force, willy nilly; de bon gré, willingly; de mauvais gré, unwillingly; savoir (bon) gré, to be thankful; vendre de gré à gré, to sell by private contract.

grèbe [grɛb], *n.m.* (Orn.) grebe.
grec [grɛk], *a.* (*fem.* **grecque**) Greek; Grecian.—*n.m.* Greek (*language*); (**Grec**, *fem.* **Grecque**) Greek (*person*).
Grèce [grɛs], **la**, *f.* Greece.
gredin [grə'dɛ̃], *n.m.* rascal, scoundrel.
gréer [gre'e], *v.t.* to rig.
greffe (1) [grɛf], *n.m.* (*Law*) registry, record office.
greffe (2) [grɛf], *n.f.* graft; grafting.
greffer [grɛ'fe], *v.t.* to graft.
greffier [grɛ'fje], *n.m.* registrar, recorder, clerk of the court.
greffoir [grɛ'fwa:r], *n.m.* grafting knife.
greffon [grɛ'fɔ̃], *n.m.* graft, scion, slip.
grégaire [gre'gɛ:r], **grégarien** [grega'rjɛ̃] (*fem.* **-enne**), *a.* gregarious.
grêle (1) [grɛ:l], *a.* slender, slim; shrill.
grêle (2) [grɛ:l], *n.f.* hail; hailstorm.
grêlé [grɛ'le], *a.* ravaged by hail; pockmarked.
grêler [grɛ'le], *v. impers.* to hail.—*v.t.* to ravage, ruin *or* spoil by hail.
grêlon [grɛ'lɔ̃], *n.m.* hailstone.
grelot [grə'lo], *n.m.* small (*round*) bell.
grelotter [grəlɔ'te], *v.i.* to tremble, to shake, to shiver (*with cold, fear*); to tinkle.
grenade [grə'nad], *n.f.* pomegranate; (*Mil.*) grenade.
grenadier [grəna'dje], *n.m.* pomegranate tree; (*Mil.*) grenadier.
grenadine [grəna'din], *n.f.* grenadine (*silk or syrup*).
grenat [grə'na], *n.m.* garnet.—*a.* garnet-red.
grener [grə'ne], *v.t.* (*conjug. like* AMENER) to granulate; to grain (*leather etc.*); (*Engr.*) to stipple.—*v.i.* to seed, to run to seed.
grènetis [grɛn'ti], *n.m.* milling, milled edge.
grenier [grə'nje], *n.m.* loft; attic; corn loft, granary.
grenouille [grə'nu:j], *n.f.* frog.
grenu [grə'ny], *a.* full of grains, roughgrained.
grès [grɛ], *n.m.* sandstone, stoneware.
grésil [gre'zi], *n.m.* sleet.
grésillement [grezij'mã], *n.m.* pattering (*like sleet*); shrivelling, crackling; chirping.
grésiller [grezi'je], *v. impers.* to sleet, to patter.—*v.t.* to shrivel up.—*v.i.* to crackle.
grève [grɛ:v], *n.f.* strand, beach of sand *or* shingle; strike of workmen; **grève du zèle**, slowdown (strike).
grever [grə've], *v.t.* (*conjug. like* AMENER) to wrong, to injure; to burden; to encumber (*with debt etc.*).
gréviste [gre'vist], *n.* striker.
gribouillage [gribu'ja:ʒ], **gribouillis** [gribu'ji], *n.m.* (*Paint.*) daub; scrawl.
gribouiller [gribu'je], *v.t., v.i.* to daub; to scrawl, to scribble.
gribouilleur [gribu'jœ:r], *n.m.* (*fem.* **-euse**) dauber; scrawler, scribbler.
grief [gri'ɛf], *n.m.* wrong, injury, grievance.
grièvement [griɛv'mã], *adv.* grievously, gravely.
grièveté [griɛv'te], *n.f.* gravity, seriousness.
griffade [gri'fad], *n.f.* clawing, scratch.
griffe [grif], *n.f.* claw, talon; (*pl.*) clutches; paper-clip, clamp; **griffe d'asperge**, root of asparagus.
griffer [gri'fe], *v.t.* to claw, to scratch (*of cats etc.*); to stamp (*with signature etc.*).

griffon [gri'fɔ̃], *n.m.* griffin; griffon.
griffonnage [grifɔ'na:ʒ], *n.m.* scrawl, scribble.
griffonner [grifɔ'ne], *v.t.* to scrawl, to scribble.
griffonneur [grifɔ'nœ:r], *n.m.* (*fem.* **-euse**) scrawler, scribbler.
grignoter [griɲɔ'te], *v.t.* to nibble; (*fig.*) to get pickings out of.
gril [gri], *n.m.* gridiron, grill.
grillade [gri'jad], *n.f.* grilling, broiling; grill, grilled steak.
grillage [gri'ja:ʒ], *n.m.* grilling, broiling, toasting; wire guard *or* mesh; light iron railing.
grille [gri:j], *n.f.* railing, grating; grill; iron gate *or* bars; (*Elec.*) grid.
grille-pain [grij'pɛ̃], *n.m. inv.* toaster.
griller (1) [gri'je], *v.t.* to broil, to grill (*meat*); to roast (*coffee*); to toast (*bread*).—*v.i.* to broil, to be burned up *or* scorched; to burn out (*electric bulbs*); (*fig.*) to be itching (*to do something*). **se griller**, *v.r.* to be scorched, to be parched.
griller (2) [gri'je], *v.t.* to enclose with iron rails.
grillon [gri'jɔ̃], *n.m.* cricket.
grimaçant [grima'sã], *a.* grimacing, grinning; (*fig.*) gaping, ill-fitting.
grimace [gri'mas], *n.f.* grimace, wry face; (*fig.*) (*pl.*) affectations, airs and graces.
grimacer [grima'se], *v.i.* (*conjug. like* COMMENCER) to make faces, to grimace, to grin; to simper; to pucker.
grimer (**se**) [səgri'me], *v.r.* to make up.
grimpant [grɛ̃'pã], *a.* climbing, creeping (*of plants*).
grimper [grɛ̃'pe], *v.i.* to climb, to clamber up; to creep up (*of plants*).
grimpeur [grɛ̃'pœ:r], *a.* (*fem.* **-euse**) climbing, twining.—*n.m.* (*fem.* **-euse**) (*Orn.*) climber.
grincement [grɛ̃s'mã], *n.m.* gnashing, grinding (*of the teeth etc.*); grating.
grincer [grɛ̃'se], *v.i.* (*conjug. like* COMMENCER) to grind, to gnash, to grate.
grincheux [grɛ̃'ʃø], *a.* (*fem.* **-euse**) illtempered, peevish, crabbed, surly.—*n.m.* (*fem.* **-euse**) grumbler.
gringalet [grɛ̃ga'lɛ], *n.m.* weak, puny man.
griotte [gri'ɔt], *n.f.* morello cherry.
grippage [gri'pa:ʒ], **grippement** [grip'mã], *n.m.* friction (*of two surfaces*); seizing, jamming (*of bearing*).
grippe [grip], *n.f.* influenza, flu; (*colloq.*) dislike.
grippé [gri'pe], *a.* shrunk, contracted (*of the face*); ill with influenza; run hot, seized up (*of motors*).
gripper [gri'pe], *v.t.* to pounce upon, to clutch, to seize.—*v.i.* to run hot, to seize up, to jam. **se gripper**, *v.r.* to shrivel, to shrink.
grippe-sou [grip'su], *n.m.* (*pl. unchanged* or **grippe-sous**) miser, money-grubber.
gris [gri], *a.* grey; grey-haired; dull (*of the weather*); (*fig.*) tipsy; **papier gris**, brown paper.—*n.m.* grey.
grisaille [gri'za:j], *n.f.* sketch *or* painting in tones of grey; greyness (*of weather*).
grisâtre [gri'za:tr], *a.* grayish.
griser [gri'ze], *v.t.* to give a gray tint to; to intoxicate. **se griser**, *v.r.* to get tipsy.
grisette [gri'zɛt], *n.f.* gray gown; (*Orn.*) whitethroat.

grison [gri'zɔ̃], a. (fem. **-onne**) gray, gray-haired.—n.m. (colloq.) gray-beard (old man); donkey.

grisonnant [grizɔ'nɑ̃], a. turning gray.

grisonner [grizɔ'ne], v.i. to grow gray (of hair etc.).

grisou [gri'zu], n.m. fire-damp.

grive [gri:v], n.f. thrush.

grivelé [gri'vle], a. speckled.

grivois [gri'vwa], a. loose, broad, obscene.

grivoiserie [grivwaz'ri], n.f. smutty story.

Groenland [grɔɛn'lɑ̃d], le, m. Greenland.

groenlandais [grɔɛnlɑ̃dɛ], a. of Greenland.—n.m. (**Groenlandais**, fem. **-aise**) Greenlander.

grognard [grɔ'ɲa:r], a. grumbling, growling.—n. grumbler, grouser; veteran of Napoleon's Old Guard.

grognement [grɔɲ'mɑ̃], n.m. grunt, grunting; growling, grumbling.

grogner [grɔ'ɲe], v.i. to grunt; to growl, to grumble, to grouse.

grognon [grɔ'ɲɔ̃], a. (fem. **-onne**, but usu. unchanged) grumbling, querulous.—n.m. (fem. **-onne**) grumbler, growler.

groin [grwɛ̃], n.m. snout (of a hog).

grommeler [grɔm'le], v.t., v.i. (conjug. like APPELER) to mutter, to grumble.

grondant [grɔ̃'dɑ̃], a. scolding; roaring, rumbling.

grondement [grɔ̃d'mɑ̃], n.m. rumbling, growling, snarling; roar.

gronder [grɔ̃'de], v.t. to chide, to scold.—v.i. to growl, to mutter; to snarl, to rumble, to roar.

gronderie [grɔ̃d'dri], n.f. scolding, chiding.

grondeur [grɔ̃'dœ:r], a. (fem. **-euse**) grumbling, scolding.—n.m. (fem. **-euse**) scold; grumbler.

grondin [grɔ̃'dɛ̃], n.m. (Ichth.) gurnard, gurnet.

groom [grum], n.m. page, (U.S.) bell-boy; stable lad.

gros [gro], a. (fem. **grosse** (I)) big, large, bulky, stout; coarse; pregnant; loud (of laughter); gruff (of the voice); substantial; foul (of the weather); high (of the sea etc.); dark, deep (in color); (Cine.) **gros plan**, close-up.—n.m. large or main part; bulk, mass; main body (of an army); **en gros et en détail**, wholesale and retail.—adv. much.

groseille [gro'zɛ:j], n.f. currant; **groseille à maquereau**, gooseberry.

groseillier [groze'je], n.m. currant bush.

grosse (I) [gros], [GROS].

grosse (2) [gros], n.f. gross (twelve dozen).

grossement [gros'mɑ̃], adv. grossly, coarsely.

grossesse [gro'sɛs], n.f. pregnancy.

grosseur [gro'sœ:r], n.f. size, bulk; bigness; swelling, tumor.

grossier [gro'sje], a. (fem. **-ière**) gross, coarse, thick; plain, common; rough, rude, unpolished, unmannerly, boorish.

grossièrement [grosjɛr'mɑ̃], adv. coarsely, rudely, roughly, uncouthly.

grossièreté [grosjɛr'te], n.f. coarseness, grossness; rudeness; coarse language.

grossir [gro'si:r], v.t. to make bigger or greater.—v.i. to grow bigger; to put on weight.

grossissant [grosi'sɑ̃], a. magnifying.

grossissement [grosis'mɑ̃], n.m. magnifying, magnifying power; increase; exaggeration.

grosso-modo [grɔsɔmɔ'do], adv. summarily.

grotesque [grɔ'tɛsk], a. and n.m. grotesque.

grotte [grɔt], n.f. grotto, cave.

grouillant [gru'jɑ̃], a. stirring, swarming, crawling.

grouillement [gruj'mɑ̃], n.m. stirring, swarming; rumbling (of the intestines).

grouiller [gru'je], v.i. to stir, to move; to swarm; to rumble (of the intestines).

groupe [grup], n.m. group, party (of people); cluster (of stars); clump (of trees etc.).

groupement [grup'mɑ̃], n.m. grouping.

grouper [gru'pe], v.t. to group. **se grouper**, v.r. to form groups, to gather.

gruau [gry'o], n.m. flour of wheat; **gruau d'avoine**, groats; oatmeal; **tisane de gruau**, gruel.

grue [gry], n.f. (Orn., Eng.) crane.

gruger [gry'ʒe], v.t. (conjug. like MANGER) to crunch; to eat, to devour.

grume [grym], n.f. bark (of tree); **bois de** or **en grume**, wood with the bark on.

grumeau [gry'mo], n.m. (pl. **-eaux**) clot, small lump.

grumeler (se) [səgry'mle], v.r. (conjug. like APPELER) to clot.

grumeleux [gry'mlø], a. (fem. **-euse**) clotted, rough.

gruyère [gry'jɛ:r], n.m. Gruyère cheese.

guano [gwa'no], n.m. guano.

Guatémala [gwatema'la], le, m. Guatemala.

guatémaltèque [gwatemal'tɛk], a. Guatemalan.—n. (**Guatémaltèque**) Guatemalan (person).

gué [ge], n.m. ford.

guéable [ge'abl], a. fordable.

guéer [ge'e], v.t. to ford.

guenille [gə'ni:j], n.f. rag, tatter; (pl.) tattered clothes.

guenilleux [gəni'jø], a. (fem. **-euse**) tattered, ragged.

guenon [gə'nɔ̃], n.f. monkey, ape; she-monkey; (fig.) fright, ugly woman.

guépard [ge'pa:r], n.m. cheetah.

guêpe [gɛ:p], n.f. wasp.

guêpier [gɛ:'pje], n.m. wasps' nest; bee-eater (bird); scrape, difficulty.

guère [gɛ:r], adv. but little, not much, not very; not long; hardly, scarcely.

guères (poet.) [GUÈRE].

guéret [ge'rɛ], n.m. ploughed but unsown land; fallow land; (pl., poet.) fields.

guéridon [geri'dɔ̃], n.m. (small) round table.

guérilla [geri'ja], n.f. guerrilla war or troops.

guérir [ge'ri:r], v.t. to heal, to cure.—v.i. to heal, to heal up; to recover, to be cured.

guérison [geri'zɔ̃], n.f. recovery, healing, cure.

guérissable [geri'sabl], a. curable.

guérisseur [geri'sœ:r], n.m. (fem. **-euse**) healer, faith healer; quack.

guérite [ge'rit], n.f. sentry box; look-out turret.

Guernesey [gɛrnə'zɛ], f. Guernsey.

guerre [gɛ:r], n.f. war; warfare, hostilities; strife.

guerrier [ge'rje], a. (fem. **-ière**) warlike, martial.—n.m. (fem. **-ière**) warrior, fighting man or woman.

guerroyant [gɛrwa'jɑ̃], a. bellicose, pugnacious.

guerroyer [gɛrwa'je], v.i. (conjug. like EMPLOYER) to make war, to wage war.

guet [gɛ], n.m. watch; watching; *au guet*, on the look-out.

guet-apens [gɛta'pɑ̃], n.m. (pl. *guets-apens*) ambush; trap.

guêtre [gɛːtr], n.f. gaiter; *grandes guêtres*, leggings; *petites guêtres*, spats.

guetter [gɛ'te], v.t. to lie in wait for, to watch for, to waylay.

guetteur [gɛ'tœːr], n.m. signalman, look-out man.

gueulard [gœ'laːr], a. (pop.) bawling, mouthing; gluttonous; hard-mouthed (of horses). —n.m. (fem. -e) bawler; glutton.—n.m. mouth of a furnace.

gueule [gœl], n.f. mouth (of animals); (vulg.) mouth, face, mug (of human).

gueule-de-lion [gœlda'ljɔ̃], n.f. (pl. *gueules-de-lion*) antirrhinum.

gueule-de-loup [gœlda'lu], n.f. (pl. *gueules-de-loup*) snapdragon; chimney cowl.

gueuler [gœ'le], v.i. (pop.) to bawl.

gueuse (1) [gøːz], n.f. pig iron.

gueuser [gø'ze], v.t., v.i. to beg.

gueuserie [gø'zri], n.f. beggary; destitution; (fig.) trash.

gueux [gø], a. (fem. -euse) poor, destitute; wretched.—n.m. beggar, tramp; knave, rascal.—n.f. (-euse (2)) wench, bitch.

gui [gi], n.m. mistletoe.

guichet [gi'ʃɛ], n.m. wicket gate (of prison); spyhole (of door); position at counter (banks, post office), pay desk; ticket office (railways).

guichetier [giʃ'tje], n.m. turnkey.

guide [gid], n.m. guide; guide-book.—n.f. girl scout; rein.

guider [gi'de], v.t. to guide, to lead; to direct.

guidon [gi'dɔ̃], n.m. (Mil.) guidon; (Navy) burgee; (fore)sight, bead (of fire-arms); reference mark (in a book); handle-bar (of bicycle).

guigner [gi'ne], v.t. to peer or peep at; to ogle; to covet.—v.i. to peep, to peer.

guignol [gi'nɔl], n.m. Punch; puppet show, Punch and Judy show.

guignolet [giɲɔ'lɛ], n.m. cherry brandy.

guignon [gi'nɔ̃], n.m. bad luck, ill-luck.

Guillaume [gi'joːm], m. William.

guillemet [gij'mɛ], n.m. quotation mark, inverted comma.

guillemot [gij'mo], n.m. (Orn.) guillemot.

guilleret [gij'rɛ], a. (fem. -ette) brisk, lively.

guilleri [gij'ri], n.m. chirping (of sparrows).

guillotine [gijɔ'tin], n.f. guillotine; *fenêtre à guillotine*, sash-window.

guillotiner [gijɔti'ne], v.t. to guillotine.

guimauve [gi'moːv], n.f. marsh-mallow.

guimbarde [gɛ̃'bard], n.f. Jew's harp; (collog.) rickety old vehicle, boneshaker.

guimpe [gɛ̃ːp], n.f. stomacher; wimple (for nuns etc.).

guindé [gɛ̃'de], a. stiff, forced, unnatural; formal (of style).

guindeau [gɛ̃'do], n.m. (pl. -eaux) windlass.

guinder [gɛ̃'de], v.t. to hoist; to strain, to force. *se guinder*, v.r. to hoist oneself up; to be strained, to be forced.

Guinée [gi'ne], la, f. Guinea.

guinéen [gine'ɛ̃], a. (fem. -éenne) Guinean.— n.m. (**Guinéen**, fem. -éenne) Guinean (person).

guingan [gɛ̃'gɑ̃], n.m. gingham.

guingois [gɛ̃'gwa], n.m. crookedness; *de guingois*, awry, askew.

guinguette [gɛ̃'gɛt], n.f. small suburban tavern (usually with pleasure garden).

guirlande [gir'lɑ̃ːd], n.f. garland, wreath.

guise [giːz], n.f. manner, way, guise; fancy; *en guise de*, by way of.

guitare [gi'taːr], n.f. guitar.

guitariste [gita'rist], n. guitarist, guitar player.

gustatif [gysta'tif], a. (fem. -tive) gustatory.

gustation [gysta'sjɔ̃], n.f. tasting, gustation.

guttural [gyty'ral], a. (m. pl. -aux) guttural.

guyanais [gɥija'nɛ], a. (fem. -aise) Guyanese. —n.m. (**Guyanais**, fem. -aise) Guyanese (person).

Guyane [gɥi'jan], la, f. Guyana.

gymnase [ʒim'naːz], n.m. gymnasium.

gymnaste [ʒim'nast], n. gymnast.

gymnastique [ʒimnas'tik], a. gymnastic.— n.f. gymnastics.

gynécologie [ʒinekɔlɔ'ʒi], n.f. gynecology.

gynécologiste [ʒinekɔlɔ'ʒist], **gynécologue** [ʒinekɔ'lɔg], n. gynecologist.

gypse [ʒips], n.m. gypsum; plaster of Paris.

gyroscope [ʒirɔs'kɔp], n.m. gyroscope.

H

[In words marked thus † the h is 'aspirated'.]

H, h [aʃ], n.m. or f. the eighth letter of the alphabet. H is mute or aspirated. The so-called aspirated h is a graphic symbol which indicates that there is neither elision nor liaison; e.g. *la halle* [la'al], *les halles* [le'al]; *l'heure H*, (Mil.) zero hour.

habile [a'bil], a. able, clever; capable; skilful; sharp, cunning.

habilement [abil'mɑ̃], adv. cleverly, skilfully.

habileté [abil'te], n.f. ability, skill, cleverness.

habilité [abili'te], a. entitled, qualified.—n.f. (Law) competency, qualification.

habiliter [abili'te], v.t. to qualify, to enable, to entitle.

habillage [abi'jaːʒ], n.m. dressing; trussing (poultry).

habillant [abi'jɑ̃], a. dressy or suiting well (of clothes etc.).

habillé [abi'je], a. dressed, clad, decked out.

habillement [abij'mɑ̃], n.m. clothes, dress, attire.

habiller [abi'je], v.t. to dress; to make clothes for; to become, to fit; to wrap up; (Cook.) to truss (fowls, fish etc.); (fig.) to adorn. *s'habiller*, v.r. to dress; to have one's clothes made.

habilleur [abi'jœːr], n.m. (fem. -euse) (Theat.) dresser.

habit

habit [a'bi], *n.m.* clothes; dress coat; *habit complet,* suit of clothes.
habitable [abi'tabl], *a.* habitable.
habitant [abi'tɑ̃], *n.m.* (*fem.* **-e**) inhabitant, resident; occupier; denizen; (*C*) farmer.
habitation [abitɑ'sjɔ̃], *n.f.* habitation, residence, abode.
habiter [abi'te], *v.t.* to inhabit, to dwell in, to live in; to frequent; *habiter un lieu,* to live in a place.—*v.i.* to inhabit, to dwell, to reside; *habiter avec,* (*Law*) to cohabit.
habitude [abi'tyd], *n.f.* habit, custom, practice; *d'habitude,* usually.
habitué [abi'tɥe], *n.m.* (*fem.* **-ée**) frequenter, customer.
habituel [abi'tɥɛl], *a.* (*fem.* **-elle**) habitual, usual.
habituellement [abitɥɛl'mɑ̃], *adv.* habitually, usually.
habituer [abi'tɥe], *v.t.* to accustom. **s'habituer,** *v.r.* to accustom oneself; to get used (*à*).
†**hâbler** [a'ble], *v.i.* to brag, to boast.
†**hâblerie** [ɑblə'ri], *n.f.* bragging, boasting.
†**hâbleur** [a'blœːr], *n.m.* (*fem.* **-euse**) braggart, boaster.
†**hache** [aʃ], *n.f.* axe, hatchet.
†**haché** [a'ʃe], *a.* chopped up, mixed; (*fig.*) abrupt.
†**hacher** [a'ʃe], *v.t.* to chop, to cut to pieces; to hash, to mince; to hack; to cross-hatch.
†**hachis** [a'ʃi], *n.m.* minced meat, hash.
†**hachoir** [a'ʃwaːr], *n.m.* chopping board; chopping knife; mincer.
†**hachure** [a'ʃyːr], *n.f.* (*Engr.*) hatching, hachure.
†**hagard** [a'gaːr], *a.* wild-looking, haggard.
†**haie** [ɛ], *n.f.* hedge, hedgerow; hurdle; row, line.
†**haillon** [ɑ'jɔ̃], *n.m.* rag, tatter.
†**haine** [ɛːn], *n.f.* hate, hatred; dislike; spite.
†**haineusement** [ɛnøz'mɑ̃], *adv.* hatefully, spitefully.
†**haineux** [ɛ'nø], *a.* (*fem.* **-euse**) hating, spiteful.
†**haïr** [a'iːr], *v.t. irr.* to hate, to detest, to loathe.
†**haire** [ɛːr], *n.f.* hair shirt.
†**haïssable** [ai'sabl], *a.* hateful, odious.
Haïti [ai'ti], *m.* or *f.* Haiti.
†**haïtien** [ai'sjɛ̃], *a.* (*fem.* **-enne**) Haitian.—*n.m.* (**Haïtien,** *fem.* **-enne**) Haitian (*person*).
†**halage** [a'laːʒ], *n.m.* towage, hauling.
†**hale** [aːl], *n.m.* tow-line, tow-rope.
†**hâle** [ɑːl], *n.m.* heat of the sun; sunburn.
†**hâlé** [ɑ'le], *a.* sunburnt; tanned; swarthy.
haleine [a'lɛn], *n.f.* breath, wind.
†**haler** [a'le], *v.t.* (*Naut.*) to haul, to tow.
†**hâler** [ɑ'le], *v.t.* to tan, to burn (*of the sun*). **se hâler,** *v.r.* to become sunburnt or tanned.
†**haletant** [al'tɑ̃], *a.* out of breath, panting.
†**haleter** [al'te], *v.i.* (*conjug. like* AMENER) to pant, to gasp for breath.
†**hall** [ɔl], *n.m.* large entrance hall (*of hotel, station*).
†**halle** [al], *n.f.* market; market hall, market-place.
†**hallebarde** [al'bard], *n.f.* halberd; *pleuvoir des hallebardes,* to rain cats and dogs.
†**hallebardier** [albar'dje], *n.m.* halberdier.
†**hallier** [a'lje], *n.m.* thicket, coppice.

hallucination [alysinɑ'sjɔ̃], *n.f.* hallucination, delusion.
halluciné [alysi'ne], *a.* hallucinated; (*fig.*) deluded.—*n.m.* (*fem.* **-ée**) person suffering from delusions.
halluciner [alysi'ne], *v.t.* to hallucinate; (*fig.*) to delude.
†**halo** [a'lo], *n.m.* halo; (*Phot.*) halation.
†**halot** [a'lo], *n.m.* rabbit-burrow.
†**halte** [alt], *n.f.* halt; stand, stop; halting-place.—*int.* halt! stop!
haltère [al'tɛːr], *n.m.* dumb-bell.
†**hamac** [a'mak], *n.m.* hammock.
†**hameau** [a'mo], *n.m.* (*pl.* **-eaux**) hamlet.
hameçon [am'sɔ̃], *n.m.* hook, fish-hook; bait.
†**hampe** [ɑ̃ːp], *n.f.* staff (*of a lance, flag etc.*); stem, flower stalk.
hamster [ams'tɛːr], *n.m.* hamster.
hanche [ɑ̃ːʃ], *n.f.* hip; haunch (*of horse*).
handicap [ɑ̃di'kap], *n.m.* handicap.
†**hangar** [ɑ̃'gaːr], *n.m.* outhouse, shed, cart shed; hangar (*for airplanes*).
†**hanneton** [an'tɔ̃], *n.m.* May-bug, cockchafer; (*fig.*) thoughtless person.
†**hanter** [ɑ̃'te], *v.t.* to haunt; to frequent.
†**hantise** [ɑ̃'tiːz], *n.f.* obsession.
†**happer** [a'pe], *v.t.* to snap up, to snatch; to seize.
†**happeur** [a'pœːr], *n.m.* paper-clip.
†**haquenée** [ak'ne], *n.f.* hack, quiet horse; (*fig.*) ungainly woman.
†**haquet** [a'kɛ], *n.m.* dray.
†**harangue** [a'rɑ̃ːg], *n.f.* harangue, speech; (*boring*) address.
†**haranguer** [arɑ̃'ge], *v.t., v.i.* to harangue.
†**harangueur** [arɑ̃'gœːr], *n.m.* (*fem.* **-euse**) haranguer, orator, speechifier.
†**haras** [a'rɑ], *n.m.* stud, breeding-stud.
†**harasser** [ara'se], *v.t.* to harass, to tire out, to weary.
†**harceler** [arsə'le], *v.t.* (*conjug. like* APPELER) to worry, to pester, to torment, to harass.
†**harde** [ard], *n.f.* herd (*of deer etc.*); leash (*for hounds*).
†**hardes** [ard], *n.f.* (*used only in pl.*) wearing apparel, attire; worn clothes.
†**hardi** [ar'di], *a.* bold, daring, fearless; rash; impudent.
†**hardiesse** [ar'djɛs], *n.f.* boldness, daring; rashness; assurance, impudence.
†**hardiment** [ardi'mɑ̃], *adv.* boldly, daringly; impudently.
harem [a'rɛm], *n.m.* harem.
†**hareng** [a'rɑ̃], *n.m.* herring.
†**harengère** [arɑ̃'ʒɛːr], *n.f.* fish-wife.
†**harenguet** [arɑ̃'gɛ], *n.m.* sprat.
†**hargneux** [ar'nø], *a.* (*fem.* **-euse**) cross, cross-grained, peevish, surly.
†**haricot** [ari'ko], *n.m.* kidney bean; *haricot de mouton,* Irish stew; *haricots d'Espagne,* scarlet runners; *haricots verts,* French beans.
†**haridelle** [ari'dɛl], *n.f.* jade, hack; (*fig.*) gawky woman.
†**harle** [arl], *n.m.* (*Orn.*) merganser.
harmonica [armɔni'ka], *n.m.* harmonica, mouth-organ.
harmonie [armɔ'ni], *n.f.* harmony; concord; (*Mus.*) harmonics.
harmonieusement [armɔnjøz'mɑ̃], *adv.* harmoniously.

harmonieux [armɔ'njø], *a.* (*fem.* **-euse**) harmonious; musical, melodious; in keeping; blending (*of colors*).
harmonique [armɔ'nik], *a.* harmonic.—*n.f.* harmonics.
harmoniser [armɔni'ze], *v.t.* and **s'harmoniser**, *v.r.* to harmonize.
harmonium [armɔ'njɔm], *n.m.* harmonium.
†**harnachement** [arnaʃ'mã], *n.m.* harness, trappings.
†**harnacher** [arna'ʃe], *v.t.* to harness; to rig out.
†**harnais** [ar'nɛ], *n.m.* harness; horse-trappings; armor; equipment, tackle.
†**haro** [a'ro], *n.m.* hue and cry.
†**harpagon** [arpa'gɔ̃], *n.m.* miser, skinflint.
†**harpe** [arp], *n.f.* harp.
†**harper** [ar'pe], *v.t.* to grasp, to clutch.
†**harpie** [ar'pi], *n.f.* harpy, vixen, shrew.
†**harpiste** [ar'pist], *n.* harpist.
†**harpon** [ar'pɔ̃], *n.m.* harpoon.
†**harponner** [arpɔ'ne], *v.t.* to harpoon.
†**hasard** [a'za:r], *n.m.* chance; hazard; risk, danger; **à tout hasard**, on the off chance; **au hasard**, at random; **par hasard**, by chance.
†**hasardé** [azar'de], *a.* hazarded, ventured; hazardous, bold.
†**hasarder** [azar'de], *v.t.* to hazard, to risk, to venture. **se hasarder**, *v.r.* to hazard, to venture, to take the risk.
†**hasardeusement** [azardøz'mã], *adv.* hazardously.
†**hasardeux** [azar'dø], *a.* (*fem.* **-euse**) venturesome, daring; hazardous, unsafe.
†**hâte** [ɑːt], *n.f.* hurry, haste; **à la hâte**, in a hurry.
†**hâter** [ɑ'te], *v.t.* to hasten, to forward, to hurry, to urge on; to expedite; to force (*fruit*). **se hâter**, *v.r.* to make haste, to hurry.
†**hâtif** [ɑ'tif], *a.* (*fem.* **-tive**) forward; precocious, premature; (*Hort.*) early.
†**hâtivement** [ɑtiv'mã], *adv.* early, prematurely; hastily.
†**hauban** [o'bã], *n.m.* (*Naut.*) shroud, guy, stay.
†**hausse** [oːs], *n.f.* lift, block (*for raising anything*); (*Comm.*) rise, advance; (back) sight (*of a rifle*).
†**haussement** [os'mã], *n.m.* raising, lifting; **haussement d'épaules**, shrugging of the shoulders.
†**hausser** [o'se], *v.t.* to raise, to lift up; to increase; to shrug; (*Comm.*) to advance.—*v.i.* to rise; to get higher; to increase. **se hausser**, *v.r.* to be raised, to rise; to raise oneself; to clear up (*of the weather*); to increase.
†**haussier** [o'sje], *n.m.* (*St. Exch.*) bull.
†**haussière** [o'sjɛːr], *n.f.* hawser.
†**haut** [o], *a.* high, tall, lofty; elevated; upper; principal; eminent; haughty; loud (*of sound*); **lire à haute voix**, to read aloud; **pousser les hauts cris**, to complain loudly.—*n.m.* height; top, summit; upper part; **d'en haut**, from above.—*n.f.* (*colloq.*) **la haute**, the wealthy, the upper crust.—*adv.* high; loud, aloud, loudly; haughtily; **ainsi qu'il a été dit plus haut**, as has already been said; **parlez plus haut**, speak louder.—*adv. phr.* **en haut**, upstairs.

†**hautain** [o'tɛ̃], *a.* haughty, proud.
†**hautainement** [otɛn'mã], *adv.* haughtily, superciliously, proudly.
†**hautbois** [o'bwa], *n.m.* hautboy, oboe; oboe player.
†**haut-de-forme** [od'fɔrm], *n.m.* (*pl.* **hauts-de-forme**) top hat.
†**hautement** [ot'mã], *adv.* boldly, resolutely, proudly; aloud.
†**hauteur** [o'tœːr], *n.f.* height, elevation, altitude; depth; rising ground; haughtiness, arrogance; pitch (*of the voice etc.*); (*Naut.*) bearing; **être à la hauteur de quelqu'un**, to be a match for someone; **être à la hauteur d'une tâche**, to be equal to a task.
†**haut-fond** [o'fɔ̃], *n.m.* (*pl.* **hauts-fonds**) shoal, shallow.
†**haut-le-corps** [ol'kɔːr] *n.m. inv.* spring, bound; start.
†**haut-le-pied** [ol'pje], *a. inv.* **cheval haut-le-pied**, spare horse; **locomotive haut-le-pied**, engine running light.
†**haut-parleur** [opar'lœːr], *n.m.* (*pl.* **-parleurs**) loud-speaker; amplifier.
†**Havane** [a'van], **la**, *f.* Havana.
†**havane** [a'van], *a.* brown, tan.—*n.m.* Havana cigar.
†**hâve** [ɑːv], *a.* pale, wan, emaciated.
†**havre** [ɑːvr], *n.m.* haven, harbor, port.
†**havresac** [ɑvrə'sak], *n.m.* knapsack, pack.
†**Haye** [ɛ],**La**, *f.* The Hague.
†**hé!** [e], *int.* hoy! (*for calling, warning etc.*); why! well! I say! (*emphat.*).
†**heaume** [oːm], *n.m.* helmet.
hebdomadaire [ɛbdɔma'dɛːr], *a.* weekly.—*n.m.* weekly newspaper.
hébergement [ebɛrʒə'mã], *n.m.* lodging.
héberger [ebɛr'ʒe], *v.t.* (*conjug. like* MANGER) to lodge.
hébété [ebe'te], *a.* dazed, stupid, bewildered.
hébéter [ebe'te], *v.t.* (*conjug. like* CÉDER) to make stupid, to besot.
hébraïque [ebra'ik], *a.* Hebrew, Hebraic.
hébreu [e'brø], *a.* (*fem.* **hébraïque**) Hebrew.—*n.m.* Hebrew (*language*); (**Hébreu**, *fem.* **Juive**, *pl.* **Hébreux**) Hebrew (*person*).
hécatombe [eka'tɔ̃:b], *n.f.* hecatomb.
hectare [ɛk'taːr], *n.m.* hectare (*2 acres, 1 rood, 35 perches or 2.471 1 acres*).
hectogramme [ɛktɔ'gram], **hecto** [ɛk'to], *n.m.* hectogramme (*3.527 oz. avoirdupois*).
hectolitre [ɛktɔ'litr], *n.m.* hectolitre (*22.009668 imperial gallons*).
hectomètre [ɛktɔ'mɛtr], *n.m.* hectometre (*109.936 yds.*).
hégire [e'ʒiːr], *n.f.* Hegira (*Mohammedan era*).
†**hein!** [ɛ̃], *int.* (*before a sentence*) hey! what! (*after a sentence* = **n'est-ce pas**) isn't it etc.?
hélas! [e'lɑːs], *int.* alas!
Hélène [e'lɛn], *f.* Helen.
héler [e'le], *v.t.* (*conjug. like* CÉDER) to hail, to call (*a taxi, a boat etc.*).
hélice [e'lis], *n.f.* screw; propeller.
hélicoptère [elikɔp'tɛːr], *n.m.* helicopter.
héliport [eli'pɔːr], *n.m.* heliport, helicopter landing-ground.
hélium [e'ljɔm], *n.m.* helium.
helvétique [ɛlve'tik], *a.* Helvetic, Helvetian, Swiss.
hémisphère [emis'fɛːr], *n.m.* hemisphere.

hémisphérique

hémisphérique [emisfe′rik], *a.* hemispheric.
hémistiche [emis′tiʃ], *n.m.* hemistich.
hémoglobine [emɔglɔ′bin], *n.f.* hemoglobin.
hémophylie [emɔfi′li], *n.f.* hemophilia.
hémorragie [emɔra′ʒi], *n.f.* hemorrhage.
hémorroïdes [emɔrɔ′id], *n.f. pl.* hemorrhoids, piles.
†**henné** [ɛ′ne], *n.m.* (*Bot.*) henna.
†**hennir** [ɛ′niːr], *v.i.* to neigh, to whinny.
†**hennissement** [enis′mã], *n.m.* neighing.
Henri [ã′ri], *m.* Henry.
hépatique [epa′tik], *a.* hepatic.—*n.f.* (*Bot.*) liverwort.
hépatite [epa′tit], *n.f.* hepatitis (*inflammation of the liver*); (*Min.*) hepatite (*liver stone*).
heptagone [ɛpta′gɔn], *a.* heptagonal.—*n.m.* heptagon.
héraldique [eral′dik], *a.* heraldic.—*n.f.* heraldry.
†**héraut** [e′ro], *n.m.* herald.
herbacé [erba′se], *a.* (*Bot.*) herbaceous.
herbage [ɛr′baːʒ], *n.m.* herbage, grass-land; pasture.
herbager [ɛrba′ʒe] *v.t.* (*conjug. like* MANGER) to graze (*cattle*).
herbe [ɛrb], *n.f.* herb, grass, wort; *blé en herbe*, grain in the blade; *brin d'herbe*, blade of grass; *fines herbes*, herbs for seasoning; *mauvaise herbe*, weed; (*fig.*) scamp.
herbette [ɛr′bɛt], *n.f.* (*Poet.*) short grass, green-sward.
herbeux [ɛr′bø], *a.* (*fem.* -euse) grassy, herbous.
herbicide [ɛrbi′sid], *a.* weed-killing.—*n.m.* weed-killer.
herbivore [ɛrbi′vɔːr], *a.* herbivorous.—*n.m.* herbivore.
herboriste [ɛrbɔ′rist], *n.* herbalist, dealer in medicinal herbs.
herbu [er′by], *a.* grassy, covered with grass.
Hercule [ɛr′kyl], *m.* Hercules.
hercule [ɛr′kyl], *n.m.* man of herculean strength; strong-arm man.
herculéen [ɛrkyle′ɛ̃], *a.* (*fem.* -éenne) herculean.
†**hère** [ɛːr], *n.m.* un *pauvre hère*, a sorry fellow, a poor devil.
héréditaire [eredi′tɛːr], *a.* hereditary.
hérédité [eredi′te], *n.f.* hereditary transmission, inheritance *or* succession, hereditary right; heredity.
hérésie [ere′zi], *n.f.* heresy.
hérétique [ere′tik], *a.* heretical.—*n.* heretic.
†**hérissé** [eri′se], *a.* bristling, on end; rough, shaggy; (*Bot.*) hairy, prickly.
†**hérissement** [eris′mã], *n.m.* bristling, shagginess.
†**hérisser** [eri′se], *v.t.* to bristle, to erect. **se hérisser**, *v.r.* to stand on end, to bristle up; to be bristling with.
†**hérisson** [eri′sõ], *n.m.* hedgehog; (*fig.*) cross-grained person; *hérisson de mer*, sea-urchin.
héritage [eri′taːʒ], *n.m.* heritage, inheritance, legacy.
hériter [eri′te], *v.t.* to inherit.—*v.i.* to inherit, to be heir (*de*); to succeed.
héritier [eri′tje], *n.m.* (*fem.* -lère) heir, heiress.
hermétique [erme′tik], *a.* hermetic, air-tight, water-tight.

hermétiquement [ɛrmetik′mã], *adv.* hermetically.
hermine [ɛr′min], *n.f.* ermine.
hermitage [ɛrmi′taːʒ], [ERMITAGE].
†**herniaire** [ɛr′njɛːr], *a.* hernial; *bandage herniaire*, truss.
†**hernie** [ɛr′ni], *n.f.* hernia, rupture.
héroïne [erɔ′in], *n.f.* heroine; (*Chem.*) heroin.
héroïque [erɔ′ik], *a.* heroic.
héroïquement [erɔik′mã], *adv.* heroically.
héroïsme [erɔ′ism], *n.m.* heroism.
†**héron** [e′rõ], *n.m.* heron.
†**héros** [e′ro], *n.m.* hero.
†**hersage** [ɛr′saːʒ], *n.m.* harrowing.
†**herse** [ɛrs], *n.f.* harrow; portcullis,*herse; (*pl.*) (*Theat.*) battens, lights (*above stage*).
†**hersé** [ɛr′se], *a.* harrowed; (*Her.*) represented with a herse.
†**herser** [ɛr′se], *v.t.* to harrow.
hésitant [ezi′tã], *a.* hesitating, wavering.
hésitation [ezita′sjõ], *n.f.* hesitation.
hésiter [ezi′te], *v.i.* to hesitate, to falter, to pause, to waver.
†**hessois** [ɛ′swa], *a.* Hessian.—*n.m.* (**Hessois,** *fem.* -oise**) Hessian (*person*).
hétéroclite [eterɔ′klit], *a.* heteroclite, anomalous; irregular.
hétérodoxe [eterɔ′dɔks], *a.* heterodox.
hétérodyne [eterɔ′din], *a.* and *n.f.* (*Rad.*) heterodyne.
hétérogène [eterɔ′ʒɛːn], *a.* heterogeneous; incongruous.
†**hêtre** [ɛːtr], *n.m.* beech, beech tree.
heure [œːr], *n.f.* hour; o'clock; time of day; moment; (*pl.*) primer (*prayer-book*); *heures d'affluence* or *de pointe*, rush hours, peak periods; (*nouvelles de la*) *dernière heure*, latest news; *quelle heure est-il?* what time is it? *tout à l'heure*, in a few minutes, just now; *de bonne heure*, early.
heureusement [œrøz′mã], *adv.* happily, luckily, fortunately; successfully.
heureux [œ′rø], *a.* (*fem.* -euse) happy, blissful; blessed, lucky; successful; pleasing; delighted.
†**heurt** [œːr], *n.m.* blow; knock, shock, collision; bruise.
†**heurté** [œr′te], *a.* abrupt, harsh, jerky (*of style*).
†**heurtement** [œrtə′mã], *n.m.* clash, collision; hiatus.
†**heurter** [œr′te], *v.t.* to knock against, to strike against; to jostle; to shock, to offend; to jar with.—*v.i.* to strike, to knock, to hit. **se heurter**, *v.r.* to strike *or* hit oneself; to strike against each other; to jostle each other, to clash.
hiatus [ja′tyːs], *n.m.* hiatus; gap.
hibernal [iber′nal], *a.* (*m. pl.* -aux) hibernal.
hibernant [iber′nã], *a.* hibernating.
hibernation [iberna′sjõ], *n.f.* hibernation.
hiberner [iber′ne], *v.i.* to hibernate.
†**hibou** [i′bu], *n.m.* (*pl.* -oux) owl; (*fig.*) moper.
†**hic** [ik], *n.m.* knot, difficulty, rub.
†**hideur** [i′dœːr], *n.f.* hideousness.
†**hideusement** [idøz′mã], *adv.* hideously.
†**hideux** [i′dø], *a.* (*fem.* -euse) hideous, frightful, shocking.
hier [jɛːr], *adv.* yesterday; *avant-hier*, the day before yesterday; *hier matin*, yesterday morning; *hier (au) soir*, last night.

176

†**hiérarchie** [jerar'ʃi], *n.f.* hierarchy.
†**hiérarchique** [jerar'ʃik], *a.* hierarchical.
hiératique [jera'tik], *a.* hieratic.
hiéroglyphe [jerɔ'glif], *n.m.* hieroglyph.
hiéroglyphique [jerɔgli'fik], *a.* hieroglyphical.
Hilaire [i'lɛːr], *m.* Hilary.
hilarant [ila'rɑ̃], *a.* screamingly funny, rollicking; *gaz hilarant*, laughing-gas.
hilare [i'laːr], *a.* hilarious.
hilarité [ilari'te], *n.f.* hilarity, mirth, laughter.
hindou [ɛ̃'du], *a.* Hindu; Indian (*of India*).—*n.m.* (**Hindou**, *fem.* **-oue**) Hindu; Indian (*of India*).
hindouisme [ɛ̃du'ism], *n.m.* Hinduism.
hindoustani [ɛ̃dusta'ni], *n.m.* Hindustani, Urdu (*language*).
hippique [i'pik], *a.* hippic; *concours hippique*, horse show.
hippodrome [ipɔ'drɔm], *n.m.* hippodrome, circus; race-course.
hippopotame [ipɔpɔ'tam], *n.m.* hippopotamus.
hirondelle [irɔ̃'dɛl], *n.f.* swallow.
hirsute [ir'syt], *a.* hirsute, hairy; shaggy, dishevelled; (*fig.*) boorish.
†**hisser** [i'se], *v.t.* to hoist, to lift, to run up, to raise. **se hisser**, *v.r.* to raise, hoist *or* lift oneself up.
histoire [is'twaːr], *n.f.* history; tale, story; idle story, untruth, falsehood; trifle; (*pl.*) fuss.
historien [istɔ'rjɛ̃], *n.m.* historian.
historier [istɔ'rje], *v.t.* to illustrate, to embellish, to adorn.
historiette [istɔ'rjɛt], *n.f.* little story, short tale.
historiographe [istɔrjɔ'graf], *n.* historiographer.
historique [istɔ'rik], *a.* historic(al).—*n.m.* historical account.
historiquement [istɔrik'mɑ̃], *adv.* historically.
histrion [istri'jɔ̃], *n.m.* histrion, actor; mountebank.
histrionique [istriɔ'nik], *a.* histrionic.
hitlérien [itle'rjɛ̃], *a.* (*fem.* **-enne**) Hitlerite.
hitlérisme [itle'rism], *n.m.* Hitlerism.
hiver [i'vɛːr], *n.m.* winter.
hivernage [ivɛr'naːʒ], *n.m.* winter season, winter-time; wintering place.
hivernal [ivɛr'nal], *a.* (*m. pl.* **-aux**) wintry.
hiverner [ivɛr'ne], *v.t.* (*Agric.*) to winter-fallow.—*v.i.* to winter.
†**hobereau** [ɔ'bro], *n.m.* (*pl.* **-eaux**) hobby (*bird*); country squire, squireen.
†**hochement** [ɔʃ'mɑ̃], *n.m.* shaking, tossing, wagging (*of the head*).
†**hochequeue** [ɔʃ'kø], *n.m.* (*Orn.*) wagtail.
†**hocher** [ɔ'ʃe], *v.t.* to shake, to toss; to wag (*the tail etc.*).
†**hochet** [ɔ'ʃɛ], *n.m.* rattle (*for children*); (*fig.*) toy, bauble, plaything.
†**hockey** [ɔ'kɛ], *n.m.* hockey; (*C*) hockey, hockey stick; *hockey sur glace*, ice hockey.
†**holà!** [ɔ'la], *int.* stop! hold on! hallo, there!—*n.m.* stop, end; *mettre le holà*, to put a stop to (*a quarrel*).
†**hollandais** [ɔlɑ̃'dɛ], *a.* Dutch.—*n.m.* Dutch (*language*); (**Hollandais**, *fem.* **-aise**) Dutchman, Dutchwoman.

---

†**Hollande** [ɔ'lɑ̃ːd], **la**, *f.* Holland, the Netherlands.
holocauste [ɔlɔ'koːst], *n.m.* holocaust, burnt offering; sacrifice.
†**homard** [ɔ'maːr], *n.m.* lobster.
homélie [ɔme'li], *n.f.* homily, familiar sermon.
homéopathe [ɔmeɔ'pat], *a.* homeopathic.—*n.* homoeopath.
homéopathie [ɔmeɔpa'ti], *n.f.* homeopathy.
homéopathique [ɔmeɔpa'tik], *a.* homeopathic.
Homère [ɔ'mɛːr], *m.* Homer.
homérique [ɔme'rik], *a.* Homeric.
homicide [ɔmi'sid], *a.* murderous.—*n.m.* homicide, manslaughter.—*n.* murderer.
hommage [ɔ'maːʒ], *n.m.* homage; respect; service; acknowledgment; token, gift; (*pl.*) respects.
homme [ɔm], *n.m.* man; (*colloq.*) husband, old man.
homme-grenouille [ɔmgrə'nuːj], *n.m.* (*pl.* **hommes-grenouilles**) frogman.
homme-sandwich [ɔmsɑ̃'dwitʃ], *n.m.* (*pl.* **hommes-sandwich(e)s**) sandwich man.
homogène [ɔmɔ'ʒɛːn], *a.* homogeneous.
homogénéité [ɔmɔʒenei'te], *n.f.* homogeneity.
homonyme [ɔmɔ'nim], *a.* homonymous.—*n.m.* homonym; namesake.
†**Honduras** [ɔ̃dy'ras], **le**, *m.* Honduras.
†**hondurien** [ɔ̃dy'rjɛ̃], *a.* (*fem.* **-enne**) Honduran.—*n.m.* (**Hondurien**, *fem.* **-enne**) Honduran (*person*).
†**hongre** [ɔ̃ːgr], *a.* gelded.—*n.m.* gelding.
†**hongrer** [ɔ̃'gre], *v.t.* to geld (*a horse*).
†**Hongrie** [ɔ̃'gri], **la**, *f.* Hungary.
†**hongrois** [ɔ̃'grwa], *a.* Hungarian.—*n.m.* Hungarian (*language*); (**Hongrois**, *fem.* **-oise**) Hungarian (*person*).
bonnête [ɔ'nɛːt], *a.* honest, upright; modest (*of women*); respectable; decorous; proper; handsome; reasonable.—*n.m.* honesty, probity.
bonnêtement [ɔnɛt'mɑ̃], *adv.* honestly, honorably; virtuously; becomingly; handsomely; suitably; reasonably.
honnêteté [ɔnɛt'te], *n.f.* honesty, integrity; modesty, chastity, virtue; propriety; respectability.
honneur [ɔ'nœːr], *n.m.* honor; virtue; integrity; repute; credit; distinction; respect; (*Cards*) honor.
†**honnir** [ɔ'niːr], *v.t.* to dishonor, to disgrace, to cover with shame.
honorabilité [ɔnɔrabili'te], *n.f.* honor, respectability.
honorable [ɔnɔ'rabl], *a.* honorable; respectable, creditable; suitable.
honorablement [ɔnɔrablə'mɑ̃], *adv.* honorably, respectably, creditably; nobly.
honoraire [ɔnɔ'rɛːr], *a.* honorary, titular.—*n.m.* (*pl.*) honorarium, fee.
honorer [ɔnɔ're], *v.t.* to honor; to do credit to, to be an honor to; *honorer une traite*, to meet a bill. **s'honorer**, *v.r.* to do oneself honor; to acquire honor; to deem it an honor; to pride oneself.
honorifique [ɔnɔri'fik], *a.* honorary, titular, gratuitous.

†**honte** [3:t], *n.f.* shame; disgrace, infamy; reproach; scandal; *avoir honte de*, to be ashamed of; *mauvaise honte* or *fausse honte*, self-consciousness, bashfulness.

†**honteusement** [3tœz'mā], *adv.* shamefully, disgracefully; infamously.

†**honteux** [3'tø], *a.* (*fem.* -**euse**) ashamed; bashful, shy; shameful, disgraceful.

hôpital [opi'tal], *n.m.* (*pl.* -**aux**) hospital.

†**hoquet** [ɔ'kɛ], *n.m.* hiccup.

hoqueter [ɔk'te], *v.i.* (*conjug. like* APPELER) to hiccup.

horaire [ɔ'rɛ:r], *a.* hourly; horary, horal.—*n.m.* time-table, schedule.

†**horde** [ɔrd], *n.f.* horde; pack; rabble.

horizon [ɔri'zɔ̃], *n.m.* horizon, sky-line.

horizontal [ɔrizɔ̃'tal], *a.* (*m. pl.* -**aux**) horizontal.

horizontalement [ɔrizɔ̃tal'mā], *adv.* horizontally.

horloge [ɔr'lɔ:ʒ], *n.f.* clock; time-keeper.

horloger [ɔrlɔ'ʒe], *a.* (*fem.* -**ère**) pertaining to clock-making.—*n.m.* (*fem.* -**ère**) clockmaker, watch-maker.

horlogerie [ɔrlɔ'ʒri], *n.f.* watch- and clockmaking; clocks and watches.

hormis [ɔr'mi], *prep.* except, excepting, but.

hormone [ɔr'mɔn], *n.f.* hormone.

horoscope [ɔrɔs'kɔp], *n.m.* horoscope.

horreur [ɔ'rœ:r], *n.f.* horror, dread; detestation; enormity.

horrible [ɔ'ribl], *a.* horrible, dreadful; hideous, frightful, shocking.

horriblement [ɔriblə'mā], *adv.* horribly, awfully.

horrifier [ɔri'fje], *v.t.* to horrify.

horrifique [ɔri'fik], *a.* hair-raising.

horripilant [ɔripi'lā], *a.* exasperating.

horripiler [ɔripi'le], *v.t.* to horripilate; to exasperate.

†**hors** [ɔ:r], *prep.* out of, outside of; beyond, past; but, except, save; *hors d'affaire*, out of danger; *hors de combat*, disabled; *hors de doute*, beyond doubt; *hors d'ici!* away with you! out of my sight! *hors de prix*, exorbitant; *hors de service*, unserviceable, out of order; *hors la loi*, outlawed.

†**hors-bord** [ɔr'bɔr], *n.m. inv.* outboard; speed-boat.

†**hors-caste** [ɔr'kast], *a. and n. inv.* outcaste, untouchable.

†**hors-d'œuvre** [ɔr'dœ:vr], *n.m. inv.* (*Arch.*) outwork, outbuilding; (*Lit.*) digression, episode; (*Cook.*) dish served at the beginning of a meal.

†**hors-jeu** [ɔr'ʒø], *n.m. inv.* (*Ftb.*) off-side.

†**hors-la-loi** [ɔrla'lwa], *n.m. inv.* outlaw.

hortensia [ɔrtā'sja], *n.m.* hydrangea.

horticulteur [ɔrtikyl'tœ:r], *n.m.* horticulturist.

horticultural [ɔrtikylty'ral], *a.* (*m. pl.* -**aux**) horticultural.

horticulture [ɔrtikyl'tyr], *n.f.* horticulture.

hospice [ɔs'pis], *n.m.* refuge; asylum; almshouse.

hospitalier [ɔspita'lje], *a.* (*fem.* -**ière**) hospitable.—*n.m.* (*fem.* -**ière**) hospitaller.

hospitalièrement [ɔspitaljɛr'mā], *adv.* hospitably.

hospitalité [ɔspitali'te], *n.f.* hospitality.

hostellerie [ɔstɛl'ri], *n.f.* inn.

hostie [ɔs'ti], *n.f.* (*Jewish Ant.*) offering, victim, sacrifice; (*R.-C. Ch.*) host.

hostile [ɔs'til], *a.* hostile, adverse.

hostilement [ɔstil'mā], *adv.* hostilely, adversely.

hostilité [ɔstili'te], *n.f.* hostility, enmity.

hôte [o:t], *n.m.* (*fem.* -**esse**) host, hostess; landlord, innkeeper; guest; lodger; occupier, inmate.

hôtel [o'tɛl], *n.m.* town mansion, large house; hotel, inn; *hôtel de ville*, town hall; *hôtel des ventes*, auction mart; *hôtel meublé*, furnished lodgings, lodging-house.

hôtelier [otə'lje], *n.m.* (*fem.* -**ière**) innkeeper, host, hostess.

hôtellerie [otɛl'ri], *n.f.* inn, hotel; hotel trade.

hôtesse [o'tɛs], [HÔTE].

†**hotte** [ɔt], *n.f.* basket (*carried on the back*); dosser, hod.

†**hottée** [ɔ'te], *n.f.* basketful.

†**hottentot** [ɔtā'to], *a.* Hottentot.—*n.m.* (Hottentot, *fem.* -**e**) Hottentot (*person*).

†**houage** [wa:ʒ], *n.m.* hoeing.

†**houblon** [u'blɔ̃], *n.m.* (*Bot.*) hop.

†**houblonnière** [ublɔ'njɛ:r], *n.f.* hop field.

†**houe** [u], *n.f.* hoe.

†**houer** [u'e], *v.t.* to hoe.

†**houille** [u:j], *n.f.* coal.

†**houiller** [u'je], *a.* (*fem.* -**ère**) coal-bearing. —*n.f.* (-**ère**) coal mine, colliery.

†**houilleur** [u'jœ:r], *n.m.* collier, coal miner.

†**houilleux** [u'jø], *a.* (*fem.* -**euse**) containing coal.

†**houle** [ul], *n.f.* swell, surge.

†**houlette** [u'lɛt], *n.f.* (shepherd's) crook; crosier.

†**houleux** [u'lø], *a.* (*fem.* -**euse**) swelling, rough (*of sea*).

†**houppe** [up], *n.f.* tuft; top-knot; tassel.

†**houppé** [u'pe], *a.* tufted, crested.

†**houppelande** [u'plā:d], *n.f.* overcoat, cloak.

†**houpper** [u'pe], *v.t.* to tuft; to comb (*wool*).

†**houppette** [u'pɛt], *n.f.* powder puff.

†**hourdage** [ur'da:ʒ], †**hourdis** [ur'di], *n.m.* rough-walling; pugging.

†**hourder** [ur'de], *v.t.* to rough-wall; to pug.

†**hourdis** [HOURDAGE].

†**hourra** [u'ra], *n.m.* hurrah.

†**houspiller** [uspi'je], *v.t.* to manhandle; to rough-house; to abuse.

†**housse** [us], *n.f.* housing, horse-cloth; dust-sheet, loose cover.

†**housser** [u'se], *v.t.* to cover up.

†**houssine** [u'sin], *n.f.* switch; riding-whip.

†**houssiner** [usi'ne], *v.t.* to switch; to beat.

†**houx** [u], *n.m.* holly, holly tree.

†**hoyau** [wa'jo], *n.m.* (*pl.* -**aux**) mattock, grubbing-hoe.

†**huard** [ɥa:r], *n.m.* osprey; sea-eagle.

†**hublot** [y'blo], *n.m.* (*Naut.*) side-light, port-hole.

†**huche** [yʃ], *n.f.* kneading trough; bread pan.

†**hue!** [y], *int.* gee! gee up!

†**huée** [ɥe], *n.f.* whoop, shouting; hooting, booing.

†**huer** [ɥe], *v.t.* to shout after; to hoot at, to boo.—*v.i.* to boo.

†**huguenot** [yg'no], *a.* Huguenot.—*n.m.* (**Huguenot**, *fem.* **-e**) Huguenot (*person*).
huilage [ɥi'la:ʒ], *n.m.* oiling.
huile [ɥil], *n.f.* oil.
huiler [ɥi'le], *v.t.* to oil; to anoint with oil; to lubricate.—*v.i.* (*Bot.*) to exude oil.
huilerie [ɥil'ri], *n.f.* oil works.
huileux [ɥi'lø], *a.* (*fem.* **-euse**) oily, greasy.
huilier [ɥi'lje], *n.m.* cruet-stand; oil merchant.
†***huis** [ɥi], *n.m.* door; **à huis clos**, behind closed doors, in camera.
huisserie [ɥis'ri], *n.f.* door frame.
huissier [ɥi'sje], *n.m.* usher; gentleman-usher; door-keeper; sheriff's officer, bailiff.
†**huit** [ɥit], *a.* and *n.m.* eight; eighth.
†**huitaine** [ɥi'tɛn], *n.f.* eight days, week.
†**huitième** [ɥi'tjɛm], *a.* eighth.—*n.m.* eighth, eighth part.
†**huitièmement** [ɥitjɛm'mã], *adv.* eighthly.
huître [ɥitr], *n.f.* oyster; (*fig.*) blockhead, dunce.
huîtrier [ɥit'rje], *n.m.* (*Orn.*) oyster-catcher.
huîtrière [ɥitri'ɛ:r], *n.f.* oyster bed.
hululer (ULULER).
humain [y'mɛ̃], *a.* human; humane, benevolent.—*n.m.* humanity, mankind.
humainement [ymɛn'mã], *adv.* humanly; humanely.
humaniser [ymani'ze], *v.t.* to humanize, to civilize. **s'humaniser**, *v.r.* to become humanized.
humanisme [yma'nism], *n.m.* humanism.
humaniste [yma'nist], *a.* and *n.* humanist; classical scholar.
humanitaire [ymani'tɛ:r], *a.* and *n.* humanitarian.
humanité [ymani'te], *n.f.* humanity; human nature; mankind.
humble [œ̃:bl], *a.* humble, meek, modest.
humblement [œ̃mblə'mã], *adv.* humbly, meekly.
humectant [ymɛk'tã], *a.* refreshing, moistening.—*n.m.* humectant.
humectation [ymɛkta'sjɔ̃], *n.f.* moistening.
humecter [ymɛk'te], *v.t.* to damp, to moisten, to refresh. **s'humecter**, *v.r.* to be moistened; to refresh oneself.
†**humer** [y'me], *v.t.* to inhale.
humeur [y'mœ:r], *n.f.* humor; temperament, disposition; mood, fancy; ill-humor.
humide [y'mid], *a.* damp, wet, moist, humid.
humidité [ymidi'te], *n.f.* humidity, moisture, dampness.
humiliant [ymi'ljã], *a.* humiliating, degrading.
humiliation [ymilja'sjɔ̃], *n.f.* humiliation, abasement.
humilier [ymi'lje], *v.t.* to humble, to humiliate. **s'humilier**, *v.r.* to humble *or* abase oneself.
humilité [ymili'te], *n.f.* humility, meekness, lowliness.
humoriste [ymɔ'rist], *a.* humorous.—*n.* humorist.
humoristique [ymɔris'tik] *a.* humorous (*writer etc.*).
humour [y'mur], *n.m.* humor.
humus [y'mys], *n.m.* humus, mold.
†**hune** [yn], *n.f.* (*Naut.*) top.
†**hunier** [y'nje], *n.m.* topsail.
†**huppe** [yp], *n.f.* hoopoe; tuft, crest.

†**huppé** [y'pe], *a.* tufted, crested (*of birds*); (*colloq.*) well off, smartly dressed.
†**hurlement** [yrlə'mã], *n.m.* howling; howl, roar, yell.
†**hurler** [yr'le], *v.i.* to howl, to yell; to roar; **hurler avec les loups**, to do as others do.
†**hurleur** [yr'lœ:r], *a.* (*fem.* **-euse** howling.—*n.m.* (*fem.* **-euse**) howler.
hurluberlu [yrlyber'ly], *n.* hare-brained person, harum-scarum.
†**hussard** [y'sa:r], *n.m.* hussar.
†**hutte** [yt], *n.f.* hut, cabin, shanty.
hyacinthe [ja'sɛ̃:t], *n.f.* jacinth; hyacinth.
hybride [i'brid], *a.* and *n.m.* hybrid, mongrel.
hydrangée [iurɑ̃'ʒe], *n.f.* (*Bot.*) hydrangea.
hydrater [idra'te], *v.t.* to hydrate.
hydraulique [idro'lik], *a.* hydraulic.—*n.f.* hydraulics.
hydravion [idra'vjɔ̃], *n.m.* flying boat, sea-plane.
hydre [idr], *n.f.* hydra.
hydro-électrique [idroelɛk'trik], *a.* hydro-electric.
hydrogène [idrɔ'ʒɛ:n], *n.m.* hydrogen.
hydrophobe [idrɔ'fɔb], *a.* and *n.* hydrophobic (person).
hydrophobie [idrɔfɔ'bi], *n.f.* hydrophobia, rabies.
hydropique [idrɔ'pik], *a.* and *n.* dropsical (person).
hydropisie [idrɔpi'zi], *n.f.* dropsy.
hydroplane [idrɔ'plan], *n.m.* hydroplane.
hydroscope [idrɔs'kɔp], *n.m.* water diviner.
hyène [jɛ:n], *n.f.* hyena.
hygiène [i'ʒjɛ:n], *n.f.* hygiene.
hygiénique [iʒje'nik], *a.* hygienic; sanitary.
hymen [i'mɛn], **hyménée** [ime'ne], *n.m.* hymen, marriage, wedlock.
hymnaire [im'nɛ:r], *n.m.* hymn book, hymnal.
hymne [imn], *n.m.* (*patriotic*) song, anthem.—*n.f.* hymn.
hyperbole [iper'bɔl], *n.f.* hyperbole, exaggeration; (*Math.*) hyperbola.
hyperbolique [iperbɔ'lik], *a.* hyperbolic.
hypermétrope [iperme'trɔp], *a.* long-sighted.
hypersensible [ipersã'sibl], *a.* over-sensitive.
hypertension [ipertã'sjɔ̃], *n.f.* high blood pressure.
hypnose [ip'no:z], *n.f.* hypnosis.
hypnotique [ipnɔ'tik], *a.* and *n.m.* hypnotic.
hypnotiser [ipnɔti'ze], *v.t.* to hypnotize; to fascinate.
hypnotiseur [ipnɔti'zœ:r], *n.m.* (*fem.* **-euse**) hypnotist.
hypnotisme [ipnɔ'tism], *n.m.* hypnotism.
hypocondriaque [ipɔkɔ̃'driak], *a.* and *n.* hypochondriac.
hypocondrie [ipɔkɔ̃'dri], *n.f.* hypochondria.
hypocrisie [ipɔkri'zi], *n.f.* hypocrisy.
hypocrite [ipɔ'krit], *a.* hypocritical.—*n.* hypocrite.
hypodermique [ipɔdɛr'mik], *a.* hypodermic, under the skin.
hypotension [ipotã'sjɔ̃], *n.f.* low blood pressure.
hypothécaire [ipɔte'kɛ:r], *a.* on mortgage.
hypothèque [ipɔ'tɛk], *n.f.* mortgage.
hypothéquer [ipɔte'ke], *v.t.* (*conjug. like* CÉDER) to mortgage.
hypothèse [ipɔ'tɛ:z], *n.f.* hypothesis, supposition.

hypothétique [ipɔte'tik], a. hypothetical.
hystérie [iste'ri], n.f. hysteria.
hystérique [iste'rik], a. hysteric, hysterical.

I

I, i [i], n.m. the ninth letter of the alphabet.
iceberg [is'bɛrg], n.m. iceberg.
ici [i'si], adv. here, in this place; hither; now, this time.
iconoclaste [ikɔnɔ'klast], a. iconoclastic.—n. iconoclast.
iconolâtrie [ikɔnɔla'tri], n.m. image-worshipper.
iconolâtrie [ikɔnɔla'tri], n.f. image-worship.
idéal [ide'al], a. (m. pl. **-aux**) ideal; unreal, imaginary.—n.m. (pl. **-als** or **-aux**) ideal.
idéalement [ideal'mɑ̃], adv. ideally.
idéaliser [ideali'ze], v.t. to idealize.
idéalisme [idea'lism], n.m. idealism.
idéaliste [idea'list], a. idealistic.—n. idealist.
idée [i'de], n.f. idea; notion; conception; opinion; plan; fancy; sketch, suggestion.
idem [i'dɛm], adv. idem, ditto.
identification [idɑ̃tifika'sjɔ̃], n.f. identification.
identifier [idɑ̃ti'fje], v.t. to identify. **s'identifier**, v.r. to identify oneself.
identique [idɑ̃'tik], a. identical, the same.
identiquement [idɑ̃tik'mɑ̃], adv. identically.
identité [idɑ̃ti'te], n.f. identity.
idéologie [ideɔlɔ'ʒi], n.f. ideology.
idéologique [ideɔlɔ'ʒik], a. ideological.
idéologue [ideɔ'lɔg], n.m. ideologist.
ides [id], n.f. pl. Ides (15 March etc.).
idiomatique [idjɔma'tik], a. idiomatic.
idiome [i'djo:m], n.m. idiom, dialect.
idiosyncrasie [idjɔsɛ̃kra'zi], n.f. idiosyncrasy.
idiot [i'djo], a. idiotic, absurd.—n.m. (fem. **-e**) idiot, imbecile, fool.
idiotie [idjɔ'si], n.f. idiocy, imbecility.
idiotisme [idjɔ'tism], n.m. (Gram.) idiom; (Path.) idiocy.
idolâtre [idɔ'lɑ:tr], a. idolatrous.—n. idolater.
idolâtrer [idɔla'tre], v.t. to idolize, to dote upon.
idolâtrie [idɔla'tri], n.f. idolatry.
idole [i'dɔl], n.f. idol.
idylle [i'dil], n.f. idyll.
idyllique [idi'lik], a. idyllic.
if [if], n.m. yew, yew tree.
igloo or **iglou** [i'glu], n.m. igloo.
ignare [i'na:r], a. illiterate, ignorant.—n. dunce, ignoramus.
igné [ig'ne], a. igneous.
ignifuge [igni'fy:ʒ], a. fire-resisting, fireproof; **grenade ignifuge**, fire extinguisher.
ignifuger [ignify'ʒe], v.t. (conjug. like MANGER) to fireproof.
ignition [igni'sjɔ̃], n.f. ignition.
ignoble [i'nɔbl], a. ignoble; vile, base; beastly, filthy.
ignoblement [inɔblə'mɑ̃], adv. ignobly, vilely, basely.

ignominie [inɔmi'ni], n.f. ignominy, shame, dishonor.
ignominieusement [inɔminjøz'mɑ̃], adv. ignominiously.
ignominieux [inɔmi'njø], a. (fem. **-euse**) ignominious.
ignorance [inɔ'rɑ̃:s], n.f. ignorance; error, mistake, blunder.
ignorant [ino'rɑ̃], a. ignorant, illiterate, unlearned.—n.m. (fem. **-e**) ignoramus.
ignorer [ino're], v.t. to be ignorant of, not to know, not to be aware of. **s'ignorer**, v.r. not to know oneself; to be ignorant of one's own capabilities.
iguane [i'gwan], n.m. iguana.
il [il], pron. m. (pl. **ils**) he; it; there; (pl.) they.
île [il], n.f. island, isle.
illégal [ille'gal], a. (m. pl. **-aux**) illegal, unlawful.
illégalement [illegal'mɑ̃], adv. illegally.
illégalité [illegali'te], n.f. illegality.
illégitime [illeʒi'tim], a. illegitimate; unlawful, unjust.
illégitimement [illeʒitim'mɑ̃], adv. illegitimately, unlawfully.
illégitimité [illeʒitimi'te], n.f. illegitimacy; unlawfulness; spuriousness.
illettré [ille'tre], a. and n.m. (fem. **-ée**) illiterate, unlettered (person).
illicite [illi'sit], a. illicit, unlawful.
illicitement [illisit'mɑ̃], adv. illicitly, unlawfully.
illimitable [illimi'tabl], a. illimitable.
illimité [illimi'te], a. unlimited, unbounded, boundless.
illisibilité [illizibili'te], n.f. illegibility.
illisible [illi'zibl], a. illegible.
illisiblement [illiziblə'mɑ̃], adv. illegibly.
illogique [illɔ'ʒik], a. illogical.
illogiquement [illɔʒik'mɑ̃], adv. illogically.
illuminant [illymi'nɑ̃], a. illuminating.—n.m. illuminant.
illuminateur [illymina'tœ:r], n.m. illuminator, enlightener.
illumination [illymina'sjɔ̃], n.f. illumination.
illuminé [illymi'ne], a. illuminated, enlightened.—n.m. (fem. **-ée**) visionary, fanatic.
illuminer [illymi'ne], v.t. to illuminate, to illumine, to light up; to enlighten (the mind etc.). **s'illuminer**, v.r. to light or brighten up.
illusion [illy'zjɔ̃], n.f. illusion, self-deception, delusion; fallacy, chimera.
illusionner [illyzjɔ'ne], v.t. to delude, to deceive.
illusionniste [illyzjɔ'nist], n.m. conjurer.
illusoire [illy'zwa:r], a. illusive, illusory, delusive.
illusoirement [illyzwar'mɑ̃], adv. illusively.
illustration [illystra'sjɔ̃], n.f. illustriousness, renown; explanation; illustration.
illustre [il'lystr], a. illustrious, famous.
illustrer [illys'tre], v.t. to do honor to; to illustrate, to make clear. **s'illustrer**, v.r. to win fame.
illustrissime [illystri'sim], a. most illustrious.
îlot [i'lo], n.m. islet (in sea); holm (in river); block (of houses).
ilote [i'lɔt], n.m. helot.
ils [il], pl. pron. [IL].
image [i'ma:ʒ], n.f. image; likeness; picture; statue.

impardonnable

imaginable [imaʒiˈnabl], *a.* imaginable.
imaginaire [imaʒiˈnɛːr], *a.* imaginary, visionary, unreal, fantastic.
imaginatif [imaʒinaˈtif], *a.* (*fem.* **-tive**) imaginative.
imagination [imaʒinaˈsjɔ̃], *n.f.* imagination; conception, thought; fancy.
imaginer [imaʒiˈne], *v.t.* to imagine, to conceive; to fancy, to suppose; to devise. **s'imaginer**, *v.r.* to imagine oneself; to imagine, to fancy; to surmise.
imbécile [ɛ̃beˈsil], *a.* imbecile; foolish, idiotic.—*n.* imbecile, idiot; fool.
imbécilement [ɛ̃besilˈmɑ̃], *adv.* foolishly.
imbécillité [ɛ̃besiliˈte], *n.f.* imbecility, idiocy; stupidity.
imberbe [ɛ̃ˈbɛrb], *a.* beardless; (*fig.*) green.
imbiber [ɛ̃biˈbe], *v.t.* to imbibe; to imbue; to steep. **s'imbiber**, *v.r.* to imbibe, to drink in.
imbroglio [ɛ̃brɔˈljo], *n.m.* imbroglio, intricacy.
imbu [ɛ̃ˈby], *a.* imbued, saturated.
imbuvable [ɛ̃byˈvabl], *a.* undrinkable.
imitable [imiˈtabl], *a.* imitable.
imitateur [imitaˈtœːr], *a.* (*fem.* **-trice**) imitative.—*n.m.* (*fem.* **-trice**) imitator.
imitatif [imitaˈtif], *a.* (*fem.* **-tive**) imitative.
imitation [imitaˈsjɔ̃], *n.f.* imitation.
imiter [imiˈte], *v.t.* to imitate, to copy; to mimic; to resemble.
immaculé [immakyˈle], *a.* immaculate, spotless.
immanent [immaˈnɑ̃], *a.* immanent.
immangeable [ɛ̃mɑ̃ˈʒabl, imɑ̃ˈʒabl], *a.* uneatable.
immanquable [ɛ̃mɑ̃ˈkabl], *a.* infallible, certain, sure.
immanquablement [ɛ̃mɑ̃kablǝˈmɑ̃], *adv.* infallibly, certainly, without fail.
immatériel [immateˈrjɛl], *a.* (*fem.* **-elle**) immaterial, incorporeal.
immatriculation [immatrikylaˈsjɔ̃], *n.f.* matriculation; registering; enrolment; (*Motor.*) **plaque d'immatriculation**, license plate.
immatriculé [immatrikyˈle], *a.* registered; matriculated.
immatriculer [immatrikyˈle], *v.t.* to matriculate; to register.
immaturité [immatyriˈte], *n.f.* unripeness; immaturity.
immédiat [immeˈdja], *a.* immediate.
immédiatement [immedjatˈmɑ̃], *adv.* immediately.
immémorial [immemɔˈrjal], *a.* (*m. pl.* **-aux**) immemorial.
immense [imˈmɑ̃ːs], *a.* immense, immeasurable; boundless, huge.
immensément [immɑ̃seˈmɑ̃], *adv.* immensely.
immensité [immɑ̃siˈte], *n.f.* immensity.
immerger [immɛrˈʒe], *v.t.* (*conjug. like* MANGER) to immerse, to plunge.
immérité [immeriˈte], *a.* undeserved, unmerited, unjust.
immersion [immɛrˈsjɔ̃], *n.f.* immersion; submergence; committal to the deep.
immesurable [immǝzyˈrabl], *a.* unmeasurable, immeasurable.
immeuble [imˈmœbl], *a.* fixed, real (*of estate*).—*n.m.* real estate; property; premises.

immigrant [immiˈgrɑ̃], *a.* and *n.m.* (*fem.* **-e**) immigrant.
immigration [immigraˈsjɔ̃], *n.f.* immigration.
immigrer [immiˈgre], *v.i.* to immigrate.
imminence [immiˈnɑ̃ːs], *n.f.* imminence.
imminent [immiˈnɑ̃], *a.* imminent, impending.
immiscer (s') [simmiˈse], *v.r.* (*conjug. like* COMMENCER) to interfere.
immobile [immɔˈbil], *a.* motionless, still; (*fig.*) firm, immovable, unshaken.
immobilier [immɔbiˈlje], *a.* (*fem.* **-ière**) real, landed (*of estate*); **agent immobilier**, real estate agent; **société immobilière**, building society.
immobilisation [immɔbilizaˈsjɔ̃], *n.f.* immobilization; (*Law*) conversion of movable property into real estate.
immobiliser [immɔbiliˈze], *v.t.* to immobilize; to convert into real estate, to tie up (*capital*).
immobilité [immɔbiliˈte], *n.f.* immobility, immovability.
immodération [immɔderaˈsjɔ̃], *n.f.* immoderation.
immodéré [immɔdeˈre], *a.* immoderate, excessive, violent.
immodérément [immɔdereˈmɑ̃], *adv.* immoderately, intemperately; excessively.
immodeste [immɔˈdɛst], *a.* immodest, indecent.
immodestement [immɔdɛstǝˈmɑ̃], *adv.* immodestly.
immodestie [immɔdɛsˈti], *n.f.* immodesty.
immolation [immɔlaˈsjɔ̃], *n.f.* immolation; (*fig.*) sacrifice.
immoler [immɔˈle], *v.t.* to immolate, to sacrifice; to slay. **s'immoler**, *v.r.* to immolate or sacrifice oneself.
immonde [imˈmɔ̃ːd], *a.* unclean, impure.
immondice [immɔ̃ˈdis], *n.f.* (*usu. in pl.*) filth, dirt; rubbish.
immoral [immɔˈral], *a.* (*m. pl.* **-aux**) immoral.
immoralité [immɔraliˈte], *n.f.* immorality.
immortaliser [immɔrtaliˈze], *v.t.* to immortalize. **s'immortaliser**, *v.r.* to immortalize oneself.
immortalité [immɔrtaliˈte], *n.f.* immortality.
immortel [immɔrˈtɛl], *a.* (*fem.* **-elle**) immortal, everlasting.
immuable [imˈmɥabl], *a.* immutable, unalterable, unchangeable.
immuablement [immɥablǝˈmɑ̃], *adv.* immutably, unalterably, unchangeably.
immunisation [immynizaˈsjɔ̃], *n.f.* (*Med.*) immunization.
immuniser [immyniˈze], *v.t.* to immunize.
immunité [immyniˈte], *n.f.* immunity; privilege; exemption.
immutabilité [immytabiliˈte], *n.f.* immutability, unchangeableness, fixity.
impact [ɛ̃ˈpakt], *n.m.* impact; hit.
impaction [ɛ̃pakˈsjɔ̃], *n.f.* (*Surg.*) impaction.
impair [ɛ̃ˈpɛːr], *a.* odd, uneven.—*n.m.* blunder, bloomer.
impalpabilité [ɛ̃palpabiliˈte], *n.f.* impalpability.
impalpable [ɛ̃palˈpabl], *a.* impalpable.
impardonnable [ɛ̃pardɔˈnabl], *a.* unpardonable, unforgivable.

181

imparfait

imparfait [ɛpar'fɛ], a. imperfect, incomplete, defective.—n.m. (Gram.) imperfect (tense).

imparfaitement [ɛparfɛt'mɑ̃], adv. imperfectly.

imparité [ɛpari'te], n.f. imparity, inequality; oddness.

impartageable [ɛparta'ʒabl], a. indivisible.

impartial [ɛpar'sjal], a. (m. pl. -aux) impartial.

impartialement [ɛparsjal'mɑ̃], adv. impartially, even-handedly.

impartialité [ɛparsjali'te], n.f. impartiality.

impasse [ɛ̃'pɑːs], n.f. blind alley, cul-de-sac; deadlock, dilemma.

impassibilité [ɛpasibili'te], n.f. impassibility, insensibility.

impassible [ɛpa'sibl], a. impassive, unmoved.

impassiblement [ɛpasiblə'mɑ̃], adv. impassively, impassibly.

impatiemment [ɛpasja'mɑ̃], adv. impatiently, eagerly.

impatience [ɛpa'sjɑ̃ːs], n.f. impatience; restlessness; eagerness, longing.

impatient [ɛpa'sjɑ̃], a. impatient; anxious, restless, eager.

impatientant [ɛpasjɑ̃'tɑ̃], a. provoking, vexing, tiresome.

impatienter [ɛpasjɑ̃'te], v.t. to make impatient, to put out of patience; to provoke. **s'impatienter**, v.r. to lose one's patience; to fret, to worry.

impayable [ɛpɛ'jabl], a. invaluable, priceless; inimitable, extraordinarily funny.

impayé [ɛpɛ'je], a. unpaid.

impeccabilité [ɛpɛkabili'te], n.f. impeccability.

impeccable [ɛpɛ'kabl], a. impeccable, faultless.

impécunieux [ɛpeky'njø], a. (fem. -euse) impecunious.

impénétrabilité [ɛpenetrabili'te], n.f. impenetrability, imperviousness.

impénétrable [ɛpene'trabl], a. impenetrable, impervious; inscrutable.

impénitence [ɛpeni'tɑ̃ːs], n.f. impenitence, obduracy.

impénitent [ɛpeni'tɑ̃], a. and n.m. (fem. -e) impenitent, obdurate (person).

impératif [ɛpera'tif], a. (fem. -tive) imperative, peremptory.—n.m. (Gram.) imperative.

impérativement [ɛperativ'mɑ̃], adv. imperatively.

impératrice [ɛpera'tris], n.f. empress.

imperceptible [ɛpɛrsɛp'tibl], a. imperceptible, unperceivable.

imperceptiblement [ɛpɛrsɛptiblə'mɑ̃], adv. imperceptibly.

imperfectible [ɛpɛrfɛk'tibl], a. imperfectible.

imperfection [ɛpɛrfɛk'sjɔ̃], n.f. imperfection, defect, flaw.

impérial [ɛpe'rjal], a. (m. pl. -aux) imperial.

impériale [ɛpe'rjal], n.f. top, outside (of a coach); imperial (small beard under the lip).

impérieusement [ɛperjøz'mɑ̃], adv. imperiously.

impérieux [ɛpe'rjø], a. (fem. -euse) imperious, supercilious, haughty, lordly.

impérissable [ɛperi'sabl], a. imperishable.

impérissablement [ɛperisablə'mɑ̃], adv. imperishably.

impéritie [ɛperi'si], n.f. incapacity, incompetence.

imperméabilité [ɛpɛrmeabili'te], n.f. impermeability.

imperméable [ɛpɛrme'abl], a. impermeable, impervious.—n.m. raincoat, mackintosh.

impersonnalité [ɛpɛrsɔnali'te], n.f. impersonality.

impersonnel [ɛpɛrsɔ'nɛl], a. (fem. -elle) impersonal.—n.m. (Gram.) impersonal verb.

impersonnellement [ɛpɛrsɔnɛl'mɑ̃], adv. impersonally.

impertinemment [ɛpɛrtina mɑ̃], adv. impertinently.

impertinence [ɛpɛrti'nɑ̃ːs], n.f. impertinence, insolence; silliness.

impertinent [ɛpɛrti'nɑ̃], a. impertinent, insolent, pert.—n.m. (fem. -e) impertinent, saucy person.

imperturbabilité [ɛpɛrtyrbabili'te], n.f. imperturbability.

imperturbable [ɛpɛrtyr'babl], a. imperturbable.

imperturbablement [ɛpɛrtyrbablə'mɑ̃], adv. imperturbably.

impétigo [ɛpeti'go]. n.m. (Med.) impetigo.

impétueusement [ɛpetɥøz'mɑ̃], adv. impetuously.

impétueux [ɛpe'tɥø], a. (fem. -euse) impetuous, vehement, violent.

impétuosité [ɛpetɥozi'te], n.f. impetuosity, vehemence; impetus.

impie [ɛ̃'pi], a. impious, godless; irreligious. —n. impious, ungodly or irreligious person.

impiété [ɛpje'te], n.f. impiety, godlessness.

impitoyable [ɛpitwa'jabl], a. pitiless, merciless, ruthless; unrelenting.

impitoyablement [ɛpitwajablə'mɑ̃], adv. pitilessly.

implacabilité [ɛplakabili'te], n.f. implacability.

implacable [ɛpla'kabl], a. implacable.

implacablement [ɛplakablə'mɑ̃], adv. implacably.

implantation [ɛplɑ̃tɑ'sjɔ̃], n.f. implantation.

implanter [ɛplɑ̃'te], v.t. to implant; to plant. **s'implanter**, v.r. to be implanted, fixed, rooted or lodged.

implication [ɛplika'sjɔ̃], n.f. implication, involving; discrepancy.

implicite [ɛpli'sit], a. implicit.

implicitement [ɛplisit'mɑ̃], adv. implicitly.

impliquer [ɛpli'ke], v.t. to implicate, to involve, to entangle; to imply.

implorateur [ɛplɔra'tœːr], n.m. (fem. -trice) implorer, supplicant.

imploration [ɛplɔra'sjɔ̃], n.f. supplication, imploration.

implorer [ɛplɔ're], v.t. to implore, to entreat, to beseech; to crave.

imployable [ɛplwa'jabl], a. unbending.

impoli [ɛpɔ'li], a. impolite, discourteous, uncivil, rude.

impoliment [ɛpɔli'mɑ̃], adv. impolitely, discourteously.

impolitesse [ɛpɔli'tɛs], n.f. impoliteness, incivility; rudeness.

impolitique [ɛpɔli'tik], a. impolitic, ill-advised.

impudence

impolitiquement [ɛ̃pɔlitik'mã], *adv.* unwisely.

impopulaire [ɛ̃pɔpy'lɛːr], *a.* unpopular.

impopularité [ɛ̃pɔpylari'te], *n.f.* unpopularity.

importable [ɛ̃pɔr'tabl], *a.* importable.

importance [ɛ̃pɔr'tãːs], *n.f.* importance, consequence; authority, credit; self-conceit.

important [ɛ̃pɔr'tã], *a.* important, of consequence, weighty.—*n.m.* the essential, the main point; (*fem.* -e) person of importance.

importateur [ɛ̃pɔrta'tœːr], *a.* (*fem.* -trice) importing.—*n.m.* (*fem.* -trice) importer.

importation [ɛ̃pɔrta'sjɔ̃], *n.f.* importation; (*pl.*) imports.

importer [ɛ̃pɔr'te], *v.t.* to import; (*fig.*) to introduce.—*v.i.* to import, to be of moment, to matter; **n'importe**, no matter, never mind; **n'importe où**, anywhere; **n'importe qui**, anyone; **n'importe quoi**, anything; **peu importe**, it does not much matter; **venez n'importe quand**, come when you like.

importun [ɛ̃pɔr'tœ̃], *a.* importunate, tiresome, obtrusive, irksome.—*n.m.* (*fem.* -e) tiresome person; intruder, bore.

importuner [ɛ̃pɔrty'ne], *v.t.* to importune, to pester; to inconvenience; to tease.

importunité [ɛ̃pɔrtyni'te], *n.f.* importunity.

imposable [ɛ̃po'zabl], *a.* taxable.

imposant [ɛ̃po'zã], *a.* imposing, impressive, striking.

imposer [ɛ̃po'ze], *v.t.* to lay on (*hands*); to impose, to tax; to force (*à*).—*v.i.* or **en imposer**, to awe, to overawe. **s'imposer**, *v.r.* to assert oneself; to thrust oneself (*upon somebody*); to be indispensable.

imposition [ɛ̃pozi'sjɔ̃], *n.f.* imposition, laying on (*of hands*); tax, assessment.

impossibilité [ɛ̃pɔsibili'te], *n.f.* impossibility.

impossible [ɛ̃po'sibl], *a.* impossible.—*n.m.* one's utmost, a great deal.

imposte [ɛ̃'pɔst], *n.f.* (*Arch.*) impost, fanlight.

imposteur [ɛ̃pɔs'tœːr], *n.m.* impostor, cheat.

imposture [ɛ̃pɔs'tyːr], *n.f.* imposture, deception.

impôt [ɛ̃'po], *n.m.* tax, duty, impost; **percevoir les impôts**, to collect the taxes.

impotence [ɛ̃po'tãːs], *n.f.* helplessness, infirmity.

impotent [ɛ̃po'tã], *a.* infirm, crippled.—*n.m.* (*fem.* -e) cripple, helpless invalid.

impraticabilité [ɛ̃pratikabili'te], *n.f.* impracticability.

impraticable [ɛ̃prati'kabl], *a.* impracticable; impassable; unmanageable.

imprécation [ɛ̃preka'sjɔ̃], *n.f.* imprecation, curse.

imprécatoire [ɛ̃preka'twaːr], *a.* imprecatory.

imprécis [ɛ̃pre'si], *a.* unprecise, indefinite (*words*); (*Mil.*) inaccurate (*fire*).

imprécision [ɛ̃presi'zjɔ̃], *n.f.* lack of precision, vagueness (*of statement*); looseness (*of terms*); (*Mil.*) inaccuracy (*in firing*).

imprégnation [ɛ̃preɲa'sjɔ̃], *n.f.* impregnation.

imprégner [ɛ̃pre'ɲe], *v.t.* (*conjug. like* CÉDER) to impregnate; (*fig.*) to imbue. **s'imprégner**, *v.r.* to become impregnated; to be imbued.

imprenable [ɛ̃prə'nabl] *a.* impregnable.

impressif [ɛ̃prɛ'sif], *a.* (*fem.* -ive) impressive, striking.

impression [ɛ̃prɛ'sjɔ̃], *n.f.* impression; mark, stamp; print; edition; **faute d'impression**, misprint.

impressionnable [ɛ̃prɛsjɔ'nabl], *a.* impressionable, sensitive.

impressionnant [ɛ̃prɛsjɔ'nã], *a.* impressive.

impressionner [ɛ̃prɛsjɔ'ne], *v.t.* to move, to affect, to impress.

impressionnisme [ɛ̃prɛsjɔ'nism], *n.m.* impressionism.

impressionniste [ɛ̃prɛsjɔ'nist], *a.* and *n.* impressionist.

imprévisible [ɛ̃previ'zibl], *a.* unforeseeable.

imprévoyance [ɛ̃prevwa'jãːs], *n.f.* want of foresight, improvidence.

imprévoyant [ɛ̃prevwa'jã], *a.* improvident.

imprévu [ɛ̃pre'vy], *a.* unforeseen, unexpected.

imprimable [ɛ̃pri'mabl], *a.* fit to be printed.

imprimé [ɛ̃pri'me], *n.m.* printed book, paper, document etc.; **service des imprimés**, book post.

imprimer [ɛ̃pri'me], *v.t.* to imprint, to impress, to stamp; to print; to instil; to impart. **s'imprimer**, *v.r.* to be printed.

imprimerie [ɛ̃prim'ri], *n.f.* printing; printing office, printing establishment.

imprimeur [ɛ̃pri'mœːr], *n.m.* printer; (*Print.*) press-man.

improbabilité [ɛ̃prɔbabili'te], *n.f.* improbability, unlikelihood.

improbable [ɛ̃prɔ'babl], *a.* improbable, unlikely.

improbablement [ɛ̃prɔbablə'mã], *adv.* improbably.

improbité [ɛ̃prɔbi'te], *n.f.* improbity, dishonesty.

improductible [ɛ̃prɔdyk'tibl], *a.* unproducible.

improductif [ɛ̃prɔdyk'tif], *a.* (*fem.* -tive) unproductive, idle.

impromptu [ɛ̃prɔ̃p'ty], *a. inv.* impromptu, extemporary.—*n.m.* impromptu.—*adv.* offhand, extempore.

imprononçable [ɛ̃prɔnɔ̃'sabl], *a.* unpronounceable (*word*).

impropre [ɛ̃'prɔpr], *a.* improper, wrong; unfit.

improprement [ɛ̃prɔprə'mã], *adv.* improperly.

impropriété [ɛ̃prɔprie'te], *n.f.* impropriety; unfitness.

improvisateur [ɛ̃prɔviza'tœːr], *n.m.* (*fem.* -trice) improviser, extemporary speaker.

improvisation [ɛ̃prɔviza'sjɔ̃], *n.f.* improvisation; (*Mus.*) voluntary.

improviser [ɛ̃prɔvi'ze], *v.t.* to improvise, to extemporize.

improviste (à l') [alɛ̃prɔ'vist], *adv. phr.* all of a sudden, unawares, unexpectedly.

imprudemment [ɛ̃pryda'mã], *adv.* imprudently, indiscreetly.

imprudence [ɛ̃pry'dãːs], *n.f.* imprudence, rashness; indiscretion.

imprudent [ɛ̃pry'dã], *a.* imprudent, foolhardy, unwise, incautious.

impudemment [ɛ̃pyda'mã], *adv.* impudently, shamelessly.

impudence [ɛ̃py'dãːs], *n.f.* impudence, shamelessness.

183

impudent

impudent [ɛ̃py'dɑ̃]. *a.* impudent, shameless, saucy.—*n.m.* *(fem.* **-e)** impudent person.
impudeur [ɛ̃py'dœ:r], *n.f.* immodesty. indecency; effrontery.
impudicité [ɛ̃pydisi'te], *n.f.* impudicity, immodesty, lewdness.
impudique [ɛ̃py'dik], *a.* unchaste, lewd, immodest.
impudiquement [ɛ̃pydik'mɑ̃], *adv.* immodestly, unchastely, lewdly.
impuissance [ɛ̃pɥi'sɑ̃:s], *n.f.* impotence, incapacity, powerlessness.
impuissant [ɛ̃pɥi'sɑ̃], *a.* impotent, powerless, unable.
impulsif [ɛ̃pyl'sif], *a.* *(fem.* **-sive)** impulsive.
impulsion [ɛ̃pyl'sjɔ̃], *n.f.* impulsion, impulse; impetus; motive.
impunément [ɛ̃pyne'mɑ̃], *adv.* with impunity.
impuni [ɛ̃py'ni], *a.* unpunished.
impunité [ɛ̃pyni'te], *n.f.* impunity.
impur [ɛ̃'py:r], *a.* impure, foul; unchaste, immodest; unclean.
impurement [ɛ̃pyr'mɑ̃], *adv.* impurely; immodestly.
impureté [ɛ̃pyr'te], *n.f.* impurity, foulness; immodesty; obscenity.
imputabilité [ɛ̃pytabili'te], *n.f.* imputability.
imputable [ɛ̃py'tabl], *a.* imputable, chargeable; to be deducted.
imputation [ɛ̃pyta'sjɔ̃], *n.f.* imputation, charge; deduction.
imputer [ɛ̃py'te], *v.t.* to impute, to attribute; to deduct.
imputrescible [ɛ̃pytre'sibl], *a.* not liable to putrefaction; rot-proof.
inabordable [inabɔr'dabl], *a.* inaccessible, unapproachable.
inabrité [inabri'te], *a.* unsheltered, open.
inabrogé [inabrɔ'ʒe], *a.* unrepealed.
inacceptable [inaksɛp'tabl], *a.* unacceptable.
inaccessibilité [inaksɛsibili'te], *n.f.* inaccessibility.
inaccessible [inaksɛ'sibl], *a.* inaccessible.
inaccordable [inakɔr'dabl], *a.* irreconcilable; unallowable, inadmissible.
inaccoutumé [inakuty'me], *a.* unaccustomed, unusual.
inachevé [inaʃ've], *a.* unfinished.
inactif [inak'tif], *a.* *(fem.* **-tive)** inactive; inert, indolent.
inaction [inak'sjɔ̃], *n.f.* inaction; indolence, inertness.
inactivement [inaktiv'mɑ̃], *adv.* inactively.
inactivité [inaktivi'te], *n.f.* inactivity.
inadaptation [inadapta'sjɔ̃], *n.f.* maladjustment.
inadapté [inadap'te], *a.* maladjusted.—*n.m.* *(fem.* **-ée)** social misfit.
inadmissible [inadmi'sibl], *a.* inadmissible.
inadmission [inadmi'sjɔ̃], *n.f.* non-admission.
inadvertance [inadvɛr'tɑ̃:s], *n.f.* inadvertence, oversight.
inaliénable [inalje'nabl], *a.* inalienable.
inaliéné [inalje'ne], *a.* unalienated.
inalliable [ina'ljabl], *a.* that cannot be alloyed; incompatible.
inaltérable [inalte'rabl], *a.* unalterable, invariable.
inamical [inami'kal], *a.* *(m. pl.* **-aux)** unfriendly.

inamovibilité [inamɔvibili'te], *n.f.* irremovability, fixity of tenure.
inamovible [inamɔ'vibl], *a.* irremovable, permanent; built in.
inanimé [inani'me], *a.* inanimate, lifeless.
inanité [inani'te], *n.f.* inanity, emptiness.
inanition [inani'sjɔ̃], *n.f.* inanition, starvation.
inapaisé [inapɛ'ze], *a.* unappeased; unquenched.
inaperçu [inapɛr'sy], *a.* unperceived, unobserved, unnoticed.
inapparent [inapa'rɑ̃], *a.* unapparent; inconspicuous.
inapplicable [inapli'kabl], *a.* inapplicable.
inappliqué [inapli'ke], *a.* inattentive, heedless.
inappréciable [inapre'sjabl], *a.* inappreciable; invaluable.
inappréciablement [inapresjablə'mɑ̃], *adv.* inappreciably.
inapprécié [inapre'sje], *a.* unappreciated.
inapprêté [inaprɛ'te], *a.* unprepared, undressed, uncooked.
inapprochable [inaprɔ'ʃabl], *a.* unapproachable.
inapte [i'napt], *a.* inapt, unfit, unqualified.
inaptitude [inapti'tyd], *n.f.* inaptitude, unfitness; disqualification.
inarticulé [inartiky'le], *a.* inarticulate.
inassouvi [inasu'vi], *a.* unsatiated.
inassouvissable [inasuvi'sabl], *a.* insatiable.
inattaquable [inata'kabl], *a.* unassailable; *(fig.)* unimpeachable, irreproachable.
inattendu [inatɑ̃'dy], *a.* unexpected, unforeseen; unhoped for.
inattentif [inatɑ̃'tif], *a.* *(fem.* **-tive)** inattentive, unmindful.
inattention [inatɑ̃'sjɔ̃], *n.f.* inattention, carelessness; *faute d'inattention*, slip.
inaudible [ino'dibl], *a.* inaudible.
inaugural [inogy'ral], *a.* *(m. pl.* **-aux)** inaugural.
inauguration [inogyra'sjɔ̃], *n.f.* inauguration.
inaugurer [inogy're], *v.t.* to inaugurate, to open; to usher in.
inavouable [ina'vwabl], *a.* unavowable; shameful.
incalculable [ɛ̃kalky'labl], *a.* incalculable, numberless.
incandescence [ɛ̃kɑ̃dɛ'sɑ̃:s], *n.f.* incandescence.
incandescent [ɛ̃kɑ̃dɛ'sɑ̃], *a.* incandescent.
incapable [ɛ̃ka'pabl], *a.* incapable, unable *(de)*; unfit, incompetent.
incapacité [ɛ̃kapasi'te], *n.f.* incapacity, incapability; inability, unfitness; incompetence, disability; disqualification, *(Mil.)* disablement; *frapper d'incapacité*, to incapacitate.
incarcération [ɛ̃karsera'sjɔ̃], *n.f.* incarceration.
incarcérer [ɛ̃karse're], *v.t. (conjug. like* CÉDER) to incarcerate, to imprison.
incarnat [ɛ̃kar'na], *a.* flesh-colored, rosy.—*n.m.* carnation, flesh-color.
incarnation [ɛ̃karna'sjɔ̃], *n.f.* incarnation.
incarné [ɛ̃kar'ne], *a.* incarnate; ingrowing *(nail).*

incarner [ɛ̃kar'ne], *v.t.* to incarnate, to embody. **s'incarner**, *v.r.* to become incarnate; to grow in (*of nails*).
incartade [ɛ̃kar'tad], *n.f.* thoughtless insult; prank, folly.
incassable [ɛ̃ka'sabl], *a.* unbreakable.
incendiaire [ɛ̃sɑ̃'djɛ:r], *a.* and *n.* incendiary.
incendie [ɛ̃sɑ̃'di], *n.m.* fire, conflagration.
incendié [ɛ̃sɑ̃'dje], *a.* burnt-out, gutted.— *n.m.* (*fem.* **-ée**) sufferer by fire.
incendier [ɛ̃sɑ̃'dje], *v.t.* to set fire to, to burn down.
incertain [ɛ̃sɛr'tɛ̃], *a.* uncertain; unsettled, inconstant; vague.
incertitude [ɛ̃sɛrti'tyd], *n.f.* uncertainty, doubt, suspense; instability, fickleness.
incessamment [ɛ̃sɛsa'mɑ̃], *adv.* immediately, at once; incessantly.
incessant [ɛ̃sɛ'sɑ̃], *a.* incessant, ceaseless, unremitting.
inceste [ɛ̃'sɛst], *a.* incestuous.—*n.m.* incest. —*n.* incestuous person.
incestueusement [ɛ̃sɛstɥøz'mɑ̃], *adv.* incestuously.
incestueux [ɛ̃sɛs'tɥø], *a.* (*fem.* **-euse**) incestuous.—*n.m.* (*fem.* **-euse**) incestuous person.
incidemment [ɛ̃sida'mɑ̃], *adv.* incidentally.
incidence [ɛ̃si'dɑ̃:s], *n.f.* incidence.
incident [ɛ̃si'dɑ̃], *a.* incidental; incident.— *n.m.* incident, occurrence.
incinération [ɛ̃sinera'sjɔ̃], *n.f.* incineration; cremation.
incinérer [ɛ̃sine're], *v.t.* (*conjug. like* CÉDER) to incinerate; to cremate.
inciser [ɛ̃si'ze], *v.t.* to make an incision in, to notch, to gash; to tap (*a tree*).
incisif [ɛ̃si'zif], *a.* (*fem.* **-sive**) sharp, cutting, incisive.—*n.f.* (**-sive**) incisive tooth, incisor.
incision [ɛ̃si'zjɔ̃], *n.f.* incision.
incitation [ɛ̃sita'sjɔ̃], *n.f.* incitement, instigation; (*Med.*) stimulus.
inciter [ɛ̃si'te], *v.t.* to incite, to instigate, to induce.
incivil [ɛ̃si'vil], *a.* uncivil, unmannerly.
incivilement [ɛ̃sivil'mɑ̃], *adv.* uncivilly.
incivilisé [ɛ̃sivili'ze], *a.* uncivilized.
incivilité [ɛ̃sivili'te], *n.f.* incivility; rude remark.
inclémence [ɛ̃kle'mɑ̃:s], *n.f.* inclemency.
inclément [ɛ̃kle'mɑ̃], *a.* inclement.
inclinaison [ɛ̃kline'zɔ̃], *n.f.* inclination; incline, gradient; pitch, slant.
inclination [ɛ̃klina'sjɔ̃], *n.f.* bow. bending; proneness, propensity; attachment, passion.
incliner [ɛ̃kli'ne], *v.t.* to incline, to slope; to bow; to bend; (*fig.*) to dispose, to turn.— *v.i.* to incline, to lean; to be inclined (*à* or *vers*). **s'incliner**, *v.r.* to incline, to lean; to bow to bend, to yield.
inclure [ɛ̃'kly:r] *v.t. irr.* (*conjug. like* CONCLURE *but p.p.* **inclus**) to include, to enclose, to insert.
inclus [ɛ̃'kly], *a.* enclosed included.
inclusif [ɛ̃kly'zif], *a.* (*fem.* **-sive**) inclusive.
inclusion [ɛ̃kly'zjɔ̃], *n.f.* enclosing; inclusion.
inclusivement [ɛ̃klyziv'mɑ̃], *adv.* inclusively.
incognito [ɛ̃kɔɲi'to], *adv.* incognito.
incohérence [ɛ̃kɔe'rɑ̃:s], *n.f.* incoherence.
incohérent [ɛ̃kɔe'rɑ̃], *a.* incoherent.
incolore [ɛ̃kɔ'lɔ:r], *a.* colorless.
incomber [ɛ̃kɔ̃'be], *v.i.* to be incumbent (*on anyone*).

incombustible [ɛ̃kɔ̃bys'tibl], *a.* incombustible, fire-proof.
incomestible [ɛ̃kɔmɛs'tibl], *a.* inedible.
incommode [ɛ̃kɔ'mɔd], *a.* inconvenient, uncomfortable; annoying, disagreeable.
incommodé [ɛ̃kɔmɔ'de], *a.* indisposed, unwell, poorly.
incommodément [ɛ̃kɔmɔde'mɑ̃], *adv.* incommodiously, inconveniently.
incommoder [ɛ̃kɔmɔ'de], *v.t.* to inconvenience, to trouble; to disturb, to annoy; to make unwell.
incommodité [ɛ̃kɔmɔdi'te], *n.f.* inconvenience, incommodiousness; annoyance; indisposition.
incommunicable [ɛ̃kɔmyni'kabl], *a.* incommunicable.
incomparable [ɛ̃kɔpa'rabl], *a.* incomparable, unequalled, peerless.
incomparablement [ɛ̃kɔparabla'mɑ̃], *adv.* incomparably.
incompatibilité [ɛ̃kɔpatibili'te], *n.f.* incompatibility.
incompatible [ɛ̃kɔpa'tibl], *a.* incompatible, inconsistent.
incompétence [ɛ̃kɔpe'tɑ̃:s] *n.f.* incompetence.
incompétent [ɛ̃kɔpe'tɑ̃], *a.* imcompetent.
incomplet [ɛ̃kɔ̃'plɛ], *a.* (*fem.* **-ète**) incomplete.
incomplètement [ɛ̃kɔ̃plɛt'mɑ̃], *adv.* incompletely.
incompréhensible [ɛ̃kɔ̃preɑ̃'sibl], *a.* incomprehensible, inscrutable.
incompréhension [ɛ̃kɔ̃preɑ̃'sjɔ̃], *n.f.* lack of understanding; obtuseness.
incompressible [ɛ̃kɔ̃prɛ'sibl], *a.* incompressible.
incompris [ɛ̃kɔ̃'pri], *a.* and *n.m.* (*fem.* **-e**) misunderstood, unappreciated (person).
inconcevable [ɛ̃kɔ̃s'vabl], *a.* inconceivable, unthinkable.
inconcevablement [ɛ̃kɔ̃svabla'mɑ̃], *adv.* inconceivably.
inconciliable [ɛ̃kɔ̃si'ljabl], *a.* irreconcilable, incompatible.
inconduite [ɛ̃kɔ̃'dɥit], *n.f.* misconduct.
inconfort [ɛ̃kɔ̃'fɔ:r], *n.m.* discomfort, lack of comfort.
inconfortable [ɛ̃kɔfɔr'tabl], *a.* uncomfortable.
incongru [ɛ̃kɔ̃'gry], *a.* incongruous, improper, unseemly.
incongruité [ɛ̃kɔ̃gryi'te], *n.f.* incongruity, impropriety.
incongrûment [ɛ̃kɔ̃gry'mɑ̃], *adv.* incongruously, improperly.
inconnu [ɛ̃kɔ'ny], *a.* unknown.—*n.m.* the unknown.—*n.m.* (*fem.* **-e**) stranger. —*n.f.* (**-e**) (*Math.*) unknown quantity.
inconquis [ɛ̃kɔ̃'ki], *a.* unconquered.
inconsciemment [ɛ̃kɔ̃sja'mɑ̃], *adv.* unconsciously, unawares.
inconscience [ɛ̃kɔ̃'sjɑ̃:s], *n.f.* unconsciousness; failure to realize.
inconscient [ɛ̃kɔ̃'sjɑ̃], *a.* unconscious.—*n.m.* the unconscious.
inconséquemment [ɛ̃kɔ̃seka'mɑ̃], *adv.* inconsistently, inconsequentially.
inconséquence [ɛ̃kɔ̃se'kɑ̃:s], *n.f.* inconsistency, inconsequence.
inconséquent [ɛ̃kɔ̃se'kɑ̃], *a.* inconsistent; inconsequential.

185

inconsidéré [ɛ̃kɔ̃side're], *a.* inconsiderate, thoughtless.

inconsistance [ɛ̃kɔ̃sis'tɑ̃:s], *n.f.* inconsistency.

inconsistant [ɛ̃kɔ̃sis'tɑ̃], *a.* inconsistent.

inconsolable [ɛ̃kɔ̃sɔ'labl], *a.* disconsolate; inconsolable.

inconsolablement [ɛ̃kɔ̃sɔlablə'mɑ̃], *adv.* disconsolately, inconsolably.

inconsolé [ɛ̃kɔ̃sɔ'le], *a.* unconsoled, uncomforted.

inconstamment [ɛ̃kɔ̃sta'mɑ̃], *adv.* inconstantly; unsteadily.

inconstance [ɛ̃kɔ̃s'tɑ̃:s], *n.f.* inconstancy, fickleness; instability.

inconstant [ɛ̃kɔ̃'stɑ̃], *a.* inconstant, fickle; changeable; unsettled, unsteady.—*n.m.* (*fem.* **-e**) fickle person.

inconstitutionnel [ɛ̃kɔ̃stitysjɔ'nɛl], *a.* (*fem.* **-elle**) unconstitutional.

incontestable [ɛ̃kɔ̃tɛs'tabl], *a.* incontestable, indisputable.

incontestablement [ɛ̃kɔ̃testablə'mɑ̃], *adv.* incontestably.

incontesté [ɛ̃kɔ̃tɛs'te], *a.* uncontested, unquestioned, undisputed.

incontinence [ɛ̃kɔ̃ti'nɑ̃:s], *n.f.* incontinence.

incontinent (1) [ɛ̃kɔ̃ti'nɑ̃], *a.* incontinent, unchaste.

incontinent (2) [ɛ̃kɔ̃ti'nɑ̃], *adv.* at once, immediately, forthwith.

incontrôlable [ɛ̃kɔ̃tro'labl], *a.* that cannot be checked *or* verified.

inconvenance [ɛ̃kɔ̃v'nɑ̃:s], *n.f.* impropriety, unseemliness; indecorum; *quelle inconvenance !* how very improper!

inconvenant [ɛ̃kɔ̃v'nɑ̃], *a.* improper, unbecoming, unseemly.

inconvénient [ɛ̃kɔ̃ve'njɑ̃], *n.m.* inconvenience, harm; drawback, objection.

inconvertible [ɛ̃kɔ̃vɛr'tibl], *a.* unconvertible.

incorporation [ɛ̃kɔrpɔrɑ'sjɔ̃], *n.f.* incorporation.

incorporer [ɛ̃kɔrpɔ're], *v.t.* to incorporate, to embody; to fuse, **s'incorporer**, *v.r.* to be embodied; to unite, to be blended.

incorrect [ɛ̃kɔ'rɛkt], *a.* incorrect, inaccurate.

incorrectement [ɛ̃kɔrɛktə'mɑ̃], *adv.* incorrectly, inaccurately.

incorrection [ɛ̃kɔrɛk'sjɔ̃], *n.f.* incorrectness, inaccuracy.

incorrigible [ɛ̃kɔri'ʒibl], *a.* incorrigible.

incorrigiblement [ɛ̃kɔriʒiblə'mɑ̃], *adv.* incorrigibly.

incorruptible [ɛ̃kɔryp'tibl], *a.* incorruptible, unbribable.

incrédibilité [ɛ̃kredibili'te], *n.f.* incredibility.

incrédule [ɛ̃kre'dyl], *a.* incredulous, unbelieving.—*n.* unbeliever, infidel.

incrédulité [ɛ̃kredyli'te], *n.f.* incredulity, unbelief.

incriminer [ɛ̃krimi'ne], *v.t.* to incriminate, to accuse.

incroyable [ɛ̃krwa'jabl], *a.* incredible, past belief.

incroyablement [ɛ̃krwajablə'mɑ̃], *adv.* incredibly.

incroyance [ɛ̃krwa'jɑ̃:s], *n.f.* unbelief.

incroyant [ɛ̃krwa'jɑ̃], *a.* unbelieving.—*n.m.* (*fem.* **-e**) unbeliever.

incruster [ɛ̃krys'te], *v.t.* to encrust, to inlay. **s'incruster**, *v.r.* to become encrusted.

incubateur [ɛ̃kyba'tœ:r], *a.* (*fem.* **-trice**) incubating.—*n.m.* incubator.

incubation [ɛ̃kyba'sjɔ̃], *n.f.* incubation, hatching.

incuber [ɛ̃ky'be], *v.t.* to incubate.

inculcation [ɛ̃kylka'sjɔ̃], *n.f.* inculcation.

inculpation [ɛ̃kylpɑ'sjɔ̃], *n.f.* indictment, charge.

inculpé [ɛ̃kyl'pe], *n.m.* (*fem.* **-ée**) defendant, accused.

inculper [ɛ̃kyl'pe], *v.t.* to indict, to inculpate, to charge.

inculquer [ɛ̃kyl'ke], *v.t.* to inculcate, to impress.

inculte [ɛ̃'kylt], *a.* uncultivated; untilled; unpolished; unkempt.

incultivable [ɛ̃kylti'vabl], *a.* untillable, uncultivable.

incultivé [ɛ̃kylti've], *a.* uncultivated; (*fig.*) uncultured.

incurable [ɛ̃ky'rabl], *a. and n.* incurable.

incurablement [ɛ̃kyrablə'mɑ̃], *adv.* incurably.

incurie [ɛ̃ky'ri], *n.f.* carelessness, heedlessness; negligence.

incursion [ɛ̃kyr'sjɔ̃], *n.f.* incursion, inroad, irruption; expedition.

incurver [ɛ̃kyr've], *v.t.* to curve (*something*) inwards.

Inde [ɛ̃:d], *f.* India; ***les Indes**, the Indies; **les Indes occidentales**, the West Indies.

indécemment [ɛ̃desa'mɑ̃], *adv.* indecently.

indécence [ɛ̃de'sɑ̃:s], *n.f.* indecency, impropriety.

indécent [ɛ̃de'sɑ̃], *a.* indecent; unseemly.

indéchiffrable [ɛ̃deʃi'frabl], *a.* undecipherable, illegible; obscure, incomprehensible.

indéchirable [ɛ̃deʃi'rabl], *a.* untearable.

indécis [ɛ̃de'si], *a.* undecided, doubtful; irresolute.

indécision [ɛ̃desi'zjɔ̃], *n.f.* indecision, irresolution.

indécrottable [ɛ̃dekrɔ'tabl], *a.* uncleanable; (*fig.*) incorrigible.

indéfendable [ɛ̃defɑ̃'dabl], *a.* indefensible, untenable.

indéfini [ɛ̃defi'ni], *a.* indefinite, unlimited.

indéfiniment [ɛ̃defini'mɑ̃], *adv.* indefinitely.

indéfinissable [ɛ̃defini'sabl], *a.* undefinable; nondescript.

indéfrichable [ɛ̃defri'ʃabl], *a.* unclearable (*of land*).

indéfrisable [ɛ̃defri'zabl], *n.f.* permanent wave.

indélébile [ɛ̃dele'bil], *a.* indelible, ineffaceable.

indélicat [ɛ̃deli'ka], *a.* indelicate; unhandsome.

indélicatement [ɛ̃delikat'mɑ̃], *adv.* indelicately; unhandsomely.

indélicatesse [ɛ̃delika'tɛs], *n.f.* tactlessness; unscrupulousness; objectionable action.

indémaillable [ɛ̃dema'jabl], *a.* run-proof (*stocking*).

indemne [ɛ̃'dɛmn], *a.* uninjured.

indemnisation [ɛ̃dɛmniza'sjɔ̃], *n.f.* indemnification, compensation.

indemniser [ɛ̃dɛmni'ze], *v.t.* to indemnify; to make good.

indemnité [ɛ̃dɛmni'te], *n.f.* indemnity; *indemnité de charges de famille*, family allowance; *indemnité de chômage*, unemployment benefit; *indemnité de vie chère*, cost of living bonus.
indéniable [ɛ̃de'njabl], *a.* undeniable; self-evident.
indépendamment [ɛ̃depɑ̃da'mɑ̃], *adv.* independently.
indépendance [ɛ̃depɑ̃'dɑ̃:s], *n.f.* independence.
indépendant [ɛ̃depɑ̃'dɑ̃], *a.* independent.
indescriptible [ɛ̃dɛskrip'tibl], *a.* indescribable.
indésirable [ɛ̃dezi'rabl], *a.* and *n.* undesirable.
indestructible [ɛ̃dɛstryk'tibl], *a.* indestructible.
indéterminable [ɛ̃detɛrmi'nabl], *a.* indeterminable.
indétermination [ɛ̃detɛrminɑ'sjɔ̃], *n.f.* indetermination, irresolution.
indéterminé [ɛ̃detɛrmi'ne], *a.* undetermined, irresolute.
index [ɛ̃'dɛks], *n.m. inv.* fore-finger; index.
indicateur [ɛ̃dika'tœ:r], *a.* (*fem.* **-trice**) indicating, indicatory.—*n.m.* indicator, guide; time-table; (*fem.* **-trice**) (*fig.*) informer.
indicatif [ɛ̃dika'tif], *a.* (*fem.* **-tive**) indicative.—*n.m.* (*Gram.*) indicative mood; call-sign; signature tune.
indication [ɛ̃dika'sjɔ̃], *n.f.* indication, information; sign, mark.
indice [ɛ̃'dis], *n.m.* indication, sign, mark, clue.
indicible [ɛ̃di'sibl], *a.* inexpressible, unspeakable, indescribable.
indiciblement [ɛ̃disiblə'mɑ̃], *adv.* inexpressibly.
indien [ɛ̃'djɛ̃], *a.* (*fem.* **-enne**) Indian.—*n.m.* (**Indien**, *fem.* **-enne**) Indian (*person*).—*n.f.* (**-enne**) printed calico, printed cotton.
indifféremment [ɛ̃difera'mɑ̃], *adv.* indifferently; alike.
indifférence [ɛ̃dife'rɑ̃:s], *n.f.* indifference, unconcern.
indifférent [ɛ̃dife'rɑ̃], *a.* indifferent, immaterial; unconcerned, heedless.—*n.m.* (*fem.* **-e**) indifferent person.
indigence [ɛ̃di'ʒɑ̃:s], *n.f.* indigence, poverty, need.
indigène [ɛ̃di'ʒɛ:n], *a.* indigenous, native.—*n.* native.
indigent [ɛ̃di'ʒɑ̃], *a.* indigent, needy.—*n.m.* (*fem.* **-e**) pauper, destitute person.
indigéré [ɛ̃diʒe're], *a.* undigested, crude.
indigeste [ɛ̃di'ʒɛst], *a.* indigestible; undigested.
indigestion [ɛ̃diʒɛs'tjɔ̃], *n.f.* indigestion, surfeit.
indignation [ɛ̃diɲɑ'sjɔ̃], *n.f.* indignation.
indigne [ɛ̃'diɲ], *a.* unworthy; infamous, worthless.
indigné [ɛ̃di'ɲe], *a.* indignant; shocked.
indignement [ɛ̃diɲə'mɑ̃], *adv.* unworthily; scandalously.
indigner [ɛ̃di'ɲe], *v.t.* to render indignant; to shock. **s'indigner**, *v.r.* to be indignant; to be shocked.
indignité [ɛ̃diɲi'te], *n.f.* unworthiness, worthlessness; indignity; infamy.

indigo [ɛ̃di'go], *a. inv.* and *n.m.* indigo.
indigotier [ɛ̃digɔ'tje], *n.m.* indigo plant *or* manufacturer.
indiquer [ɛ̃di'ke], *v.t.* to indicate, to point out; to mention; to denote; to appoint, to recommend; to outline.
indirect [ɛ̃di'rɛkt], *a.* indirect; circumstantial (*of evidence*); collateral (*of heirs*).
indirectement [ɛ̃dirɛktə'mɑ̃], *a.* indirectly.
indiscipline [ɛ̃disi'plin], *n.f.* indiscipline, insubordination.
indiscipliné [ɛ̃disipli'ne], *a.* undisciplined.
indiscret [ɛ̃dis'krɛ], *a.* (*fem.* **-ète**) indiscreet, inconsiderate; inquisitive; tell-tale.—*n.m.* (*fem.* **-ète**) babbler.
indiscrètement [ɛ̃diskrɛt'mɑ̃], *adv.* indiscreetly, inconsiderately.
indiscrétion [ɛ̃diskre'sjɔ̃], *n.f.* indiscretion; unwariness.
indiscutable [ɛ̃disky'tabl], *a.* incontestable, indisputable, obvious.
indispensable [ɛ̃dispɑ̃'sabl], *a.* indispensable.
indispensablement [ɛ̃dispɑ̃sablə'mɑ̃], *adv.* indispensably.
indisponible [ɛ̃dispɔ'nibl], *a.* unavailable.
indisposé [ɛ̃dispo'ze], *a.* unwell; unfriendly.
indisposer [ɛ̃dispo'ze], *v.t.* to indispose, to make unwell; to disincline, to set against (*contre*).
indisposition [ɛ̃dispozi'sjɔ̃], *n.f.* indisposition; disinclination.
indisputé [ɛ̃dispy'te], *a.* unquestioned.
indissoluble [ɛ̃disɔ'lybl], *a.* indissoluble.
indissolublement [ɛ̃disɔlyblə'mɑ̃], *adv.* indissolubly.
indistinct [ɛ̃dis'tɛ̃:kt], *a.* indistinct.
indistinctement [ɛ̃distɛ̃ktə'mɑ̃], *adv.* indistinctly.
individu [ɛ̃divi'dy], *n.m.* individual; (*colloq.*) fellow.
individualisme [ɛ̃dividɥa'lism], *n.m.* individualism.
individualiste [ɛ̃dividɥa'list], *a.* individualistic.—*n.* individualist.
individualité [ɛ̃dividɥali'te], *n.f.* individuality.
individuel [ɛ̃divi'dɥɛl], *a.* (*fem.* **-elle**) individual.
individuellement [ɛ̃dividɥɛl'mɑ̃], *adv.* individually.
indivis [ɛ̃divi'ze], *a.* undivided.
indivisément [ɛ̃divize'mɑ̃], *adv.* jointly.
indivisibilité [ɛ̃divizibili'te], *n.f.* indivisibility.
indivisible [ɛ̃divi'zibl], *a.* indivisible.
indivisiblement [ɛ̃diviziblə'mɑ̃], *adv.* indivisibly.
indivision [ɛ̃divi'zjɔ̃], *n.f.* joint possession.
Indochine [ɛ̃dɔ'ʃin], **l'**, *f.* Indo-China.
indochinois [ɛ̃dɔʃi'nwa], *a.* Indo-Chinese.—*n.m.* (**Indochinois**, *fem.* **-oise**) Indo-Chinese (*person*).
indocile [ɛ̃dɔ'sil], *a.* indocile, unmanageable.
indocilité [ɛ̃dɔsili'te], *n.f.* indocility, intractability.
indolemment [ɛ̃dɔla'mɑ̃], *adv.* indolently.
indolence [ɛ̃dɔ'lɑ̃:s], *n.f.* indolence, sloth.
indolent [ɛ̃dɔ'lɑ̃], *a.* indolent, slothful.—*n.m.* (*fem.* **-e**) sluggard.
indolore [ɛ̃dɔ'lɔ:r], *a.* painless.
indomptable [ɛ̃dɔ̃'tabl], *a.* indomitable, untamable; unmanageable.

indompté [ɛ̃dɔ̃'te], *a.* untamed, wild; unsubdued.

Indonésie [ɛ̃dɔne'zi], *l'*, *f.* Indonesia.

indonésien [ɛ̃dɔne'zjɛ̃], *a.* Indonesian.—*n.m.* Indonesian (*language*); (**Indonésien**, *fem.* **-enne**) Indonesian (*person*).

indou [HINDOU].

indu [ɛ̃'dy], *a.* undue, unseasonable, late.

indubitable [ɛ̃dybi'tabl], *a.* indubitable, certain.

indubitablement [ɛ̃dybitablə'mɑ̃], *adv.* undoubtedly.

inductif [ɛ̃dyk'tif], *a.* (*fem.* **-tive**) inductive.

induction [ɛ̃dyk'sjɔ̃], *n.f.* induction, inference.

induire [ɛ̃'dɥiːr], *v.t. irr.* (*conjug. like* CONDUIRE) to induce, to lead; to infer.

indulgence [ɛ̃dyl'ʒɑ̃ːs], *n.f.* indulgence, leniency.

indulgent [ɛ̃dyl'ʒɑ̃], *a.* indulgent, forbearing.

indûment [ɛ̃dy'mɑ̃] *adv.* unduly.

industrialiser [ɛ̃dystriali'ze], *v.t.* to industrialize.

industrialisme [ɛ̃dystria'lism], *n.m.* industrialism.

industrie [ɛ̃dys'tri], *n.f.* skill, ingenuity; business; manufacturing; industry, work; *chevalier d'industrie*, swindler, sharper; *industrie de base* or *industrie clef*, key industry.

industriel [ɛ̃dystri'ɛl], *a.* (*fem.* **-elle**) industrial, manufacturing.—*n.m.* manufacturer, mill owner.

industrieusement [ɛ̃dystriøz'mɑ̃], *adv.* ingeniously, skilfully; industriously.

industrieux [ɛ̃dystri'ø], *a.* (*fem.* **-euse**) ingenious, skilful; industrious.

inébranlable [inebrɑ̃'labl], *a.* immovable; firm, resolute.

inébranlablement [inebrɑ̃lablə'mɑ̃], *adv.* immovably, steadily; resolutely.

inédit [ine'di], *a.* unpublished; new.

ineffable [inɛ'fabl], *a.* ineffable, inexpressible, unutterable.

ineffaçable [inɛfa'sabl], *a.* indelible, ineffaceable.

inefficace [inɛfi'kas], *a.* ineffectual, ineffective.

inefficacité [inɛfikasi'te], *n.f.* inefficacy, ineffectiveness.

inégal [ine'gal], *a.* (*m. pl.* **-aux**) unequal; rough; (*fig.*) ill-matched; irregular.

inégalement [inegal'mɑ̃], *adv.* unequally, unevenly.

inégalité [inegali'te], *n.f.* inequality; unevenness; irregularity.

inélégance [inele'gɑ̃ːs], *n.f.* inelegance.

inélégant [inele'gɑ̃], *a.* inelegant.

inéligible [ineli'ʒibl], *a.* ineligible.

inéluctable [inelyk'tabl], *a.* unavoidable; unescapable.

inénarrable [inena'rabl], *a.* untellable; incredible.

inepte [i'nɛpt], *a.* foolish, silly, inept, absurd.

ineptie [inɛp'si], *n.f.* ineptitude, foolishness, absurdity.

inépuisable [inepɥi'zabl], *a.* inexhaustible.

inépuisablement [inepɥizablə'mɑ̃], *adv.* inexhaustibly.

inéquitable [ineki'tabl], *a.* unfair.

inerte [i'nɛrt], *a.* inert, sluggish, inactive.

inertie [inɛr'si], *n.f.* inertia; indolence.

inespéré [inɛspe're], *a.* unhoped for, unexpected.

inestimable [inɛsti'mabl], *a.* inestimable.

inévitable [inevi'tabl], *a.* inevitable, unavoidable.

inévitablement [inevitablə'mɑ̃], *adv.* inevitably, unavoidably.

inexact [inɛg'zakt], *a.* inexact, inaccurate, incorrect.

inexactement [inɛgzaktə'mɑ̃], *adv.* inaccurately, incorrectly.

inexactitude [inɛgzakti'tyd], *n.f.* incorrectness; inaccuracy, slip.

inexcusable [inɛksky'zabl], *a.* inexcusable, unwarrantable.

inexécutable [inɛgzeky'tabl], *a.* impracticable.

inexercé [inɛgzɛr'se], *a.* untrained.

inexistant [inɛgzis'tɑ̃], *a.* non-existent.

inexorable [inɛgzɔ'rabl], *a.* inexorable, inflexible; pitiless.

inexorablement [inɛgzɔrablə'mɑ̃], *adv.* inexorably.

inexpérience [inɛkspe'rjɑ̃ːs], *n.f.* inexperience.

inexpérimenté [inɛksperimɑ̃'te], *a.* inexperienced; untried (*of things*).

inexplicable [inɛkspli'kabl], *a.* inexplicable, unaccountable.

inexpliqué [inɛkspli'ke], *a.* unexplained.

inexploitable [inɛksplwa'tabl], *a.* unworkable, useless.

inexploité [inɛksplwa'te], *a.* uncultivated (*of land*); unworked (*of mines etc.*); untapped (*resources*).

inexploré [inɛksplɔ're], *a.* unexplored.

inexplosible [inɛksplɔ'zibl], *a.* unexplosive.

inexpressible [inɛksprɛ'sibl], *a.* inexpressible.

inexpressif [inɛkspre'sif], *a.* (*fem.* **-ive**) inexpressive, lacking expression.

inexprimable [inɛkspri'mabl], *a.* inexpressible, unspeakable.

inextinguible [inɛkstɛ̃'gibl], *a.* inextinguishable; unquenchable (*thirst, fire*); irrepressible (*laughter*).

inextricable [inɛkstri'kabl], *a.* inextricable.

inextricablement [inɛkstrikablə'mɑ̃], *adv.* inextricably.

infaillibilité [ɛ̃fajibili'te], *n.f.* infallibility.

infaillible [ɛ̃fa'jibl], *a.* infallible.

infailliblement [ɛ̃fajiblə'mɑ̃], *adv.* infallibly.

infaisable [ɛ̃fə'zabl], *a.* impracticable.

infamant [ɛ̃fa'mɑ̃], *a.* infamous, ignominious.

infâme [ɛ̃'faːm], *a.* infamous; squalid, sordid.—*n.* infamous person, wretch.

infamie [ɛ̃fa'mi], *n.f.* infamy, ignominy; baseness.

infant [ɛ̃'fɑ̃], *n.m.* (*fem.* **-e**) infante, infanta (*Spanish prince* or *princess*).

infanterie [ɛ̃fɑ̃'tri], *n.f.* infantry.

infanticide [ɛ̃fɑ̃ti'sid], *n.m.* infanticide.—*n.* child-murderer.

infantile [ɛ̃fɑ̃'til], *a.* infantile.

infatigable [ɛ̃fati'gabl], *a.* indefatigable, untiring.

infatuation [ɛ̃fatɥa'sjɔ̃], *n.f.* infatuation.

infatuer [ɛ̃fa'tɥe], *v.t.* to infatuate. **s'infatuer**, *v.r.* to become infatuated.

infécond [ɛ̃fe'kɔ̃], *a.* unfruitful, barren, sterile.

infécondité [ɛ̃fekɔ̃di'te], *n.f.* unfruitfulness, barrenness, sterility.

infect [ɛ̃'fɛkt], *a.* infected, foul, noisome, stinking.

infectant [ɛ̃fɛk'tɑ̃], *a.* infecting.

infecter [ɛ̃fɛk'te], *v.t.* to infect, to contaminate; to taint.—*v.i.* to stink.

infectieux [ɛ̃fɛk'sjø], *a.* (*fem.* **-euse**) infectious.

infection [ɛ̃fɛk'sjɔ̃], *n.f.* infection; infectious disease; stench; *foyer d'infection*, hotbed of disease.

inférence [ɛ̃fe'rɑ̃:s], *n.f.* conclusion, inference.

inférer [ɛ̃fe're], *v.t.* (*conjug. like* CÉDER) to infer, to conclude.

inférieur [ɛ̃fe'rjœ:r], *a.* inferior, lower.— *n.m.* (*fem.* **-e**) inferior; subordinate.

infériorité [ɛ̃ferjori'te], *n.f.* inferiority.

infernal [ɛ̃fɛr'nal], *a.* (*m. pl.* **-aux**) infernal, hellish.

infernalement [ɛ̃fɛrnal'mɑ̃], *adv.* infernally.

infertile [ɛ̃fɛr'til], *a.* infertile, unfruitful; sterile, barren.

infertilité [ɛ̃fɛrtili'te], *n.f.* unfruitfulness.

infester [ɛ̃fɛs'te], *v.t.* to infest, to overrun; to haunt.

infidèle [ɛ̃fi'dɛl], *a.* unfaithful, disloyal; unbelieving.—*n.* unfaithful person; infidel.

infidèlement [ɛ̃fidɛl'mɑ̃], *adv.* unfaithfully; inaccurately.

infidélité [ɛ̃fideli'te], *n.f.* infidelity; unbelief; dishonesty.

infiltration [ɛ̃filtra'sjɔ̃], *n.f.* infiltration.

infiltrer (s') [sɛ̃fil'tre], *v.r.* to infiltrate, to percolate.

infime [ɛ̃'fim], *a.* lowest (*of ranks*); tiny.

infini [ɛ̃fi'ni], *a.* infinite, boundless.—*n.m.* infinite, infinity.

infiniment [ɛ̃fini'mɑ̃], *adv.* infinitely, without end; exceedingly, extremely.

infinité [ɛ̃fini'te], *n.f.* infinity, infiniteness; (*fig.*) crowd; no end.

infinitif [ɛ̃fini'tif], *a.* (*fem.* **-tive**) and *n.m.* infinitive (*mood*).

infirme [ɛ̃'firm], *a.* crippled, invalid; infirm; feeble.—*n.* invalid, cripple.

infirmerie [ɛ̃firm'ri], *n.f.* infirmary, sick ward; (*sch.*) sanatorium, sick-bay.

infirmier [ɛ̃fir'mje], *n.m.* (*fem.* **-ière**) hospital attendant; nurse.

infirmité [ɛ̃firmi'te], *n.f.* infirmity, weakness, failing.

inflammable [ɛ̃fla'mabl], *a.* inflammable.

inflammation [ɛ̃flama'sjɔ̃], *n.f.* inflammation.

inflammatoire [ɛ̃flama'twa:r], *a.* inflammatory.

inflation [ɛ̃fla'sjɔ̃], *n.f.* inflation, swelling.

inflexible [ɛ̃flɛk'sibl], *a.* inflexible; unyielding, unbending.

inflexiblement [ɛ̃flɛksibl'mɑ̃], *adv.* inflexibly.

inflexion [ɛ̃flɛk'sjɔ̃], *n.f.* inflexion; modulation, variation.

infliction [ɛ̃flik'sjɔ̃], *n.f.* infliction.

infliger [ɛ̃fli'ʒe], *v.t.* (*conjug. like* MANGER) to inflict, to impose.

influence [ɛ̃fly'ɑ̃:s], *n.f.* influence; sway, power, authority.

influencer [ɛ̃flyɑ̃'se], *v.t.* (*conjug. like* COMMENCER) to influence, to sway, to bias.

influent [ɛ̃fly'ɑ̃], *a.* influential.

influenza [ɛ̃flyɑ̃'za], *n.f.* influenza.

influer [ɛ̃fly'e], *v.i.* to have an influence (*sur, on*).

informateur [ɛ̃fɔrma'tœ:r], *n.m.* (*fem.* **-trice**) informant.

information [ɛ̃fɔrma'sjɔ̃], *n.f.* inquiry; information; (*pl.*) news (bulletin).

informe [ɛ̃'fɔrm], *a.* shapeless; misshapen; crude, imperfect.

informer [ɛ̃fɔr'me], *v.t.* to inform, to acquaint, to apprise. **s'informer**, *v.r.* to inquire, to make inquiries, to investigate.

infortune [ɛ̃fɔr'tyn], *n.f.* misfortune, adversity.

infortuné [ɛ̃fɔrty'ne], *a.* unfortunate, unhappy, ill-fated, wretched.—*n.m.* (*fem.* **-ée**) unfortunate, unhappy or wretched person.

infraction [ɛ̃frak'sjɔ̃], *n.f.* infringement, breach, violation.

infranchissable [ɛ̃frɑ̃ʃi'sabl], *a.* insurmountable, insuperable.

infra-rouge [ɛ̃fra'ruʒ], *a.* infra-red.

infréquenté [ɛ̃frekɑ̃'te], *a.* unfrequented.

infructueusement [ɛ̃fryktɥøz'mɑ̃], *adv.* fruitlessly, to no purpose, in vain.

infructueux [ɛ̃fryk'tɥø], *a.* (*fem.* **-euse**) unfruitful, vain, unavailing.

infus [ɛ̃'fy], *a.* infused, innate, native (*of knowledge etc.*).

infuser [ɛ̃fy'ze], *v.t.* to infuse, to instill; to steep.

infusion [ɛ̃fy'zjɔ̃], *n.f.* infusion, decoction.

ingambe [ɛ̃'gɑ̃:b], *a.* nimble, brisk, active.

ingénier (s') [sɛ̃ʒe'nje], *v.r.* to tax one's ingenuity, to contrive.

ingénieur [ɛ̃ʒe'njœ:r], *n.m.* engineer.

ingénieusement [ɛ̃ʒenjøz'mɑ̃], *adv.* ingeniously.

ingénieux [ɛ̃ʒe'njø], *a.* (*fem.* **-euse**) ingenious, clever, witty.

ingéniosité [ɛ̃ʒenjozi'te], *n.f.* ingenuity; cleverness.

ingénu [ɛ̃ʒe'ny], *a.* ingenuous; guileless, unsophisticated; simple, artless.—*n.m.* (*fem.* **-e**) ingenuous person, artless or simpleminded person.

ingénuité [ɛ̃ʒenɥi'te], *n.f.* ingenuousness.

ingénument [ɛ̃ʒeny'mɑ̃], *adv.* ingenuously.

ingérence [ɛ̃ʒe'rɑ̃:s], *n.f.* interference, meddling.

ingérer (s') [sɛ̃ʒe're], *v.r.* (*conjug. like* CÉDER) to meddle with, to interfere, to obtrude.

inglorieux [ɛ̃glɔ'rjø], *a.* (*fem.* **-euse**) inglorious.

ingouvernable [ɛ̃guvɛr'nabl], *a.* ungovernable, uncontrollable.

ingrat [ɛ̃'gra], *a.* unthankful, ungrateful; thankless, unprofitable.

ingratitude [ɛ̃grati'tyd], *n.f.* ingratitude, thanklessness.

ingrédient [ɛ̃gre'djɑ̃], *n.m.* ingredient.

inguérissable [ɛ̃geri'sabl], *a.* incurable.

inhabile [ina'bil], *a.* unskillful, unskilled, inexpert.

inhabilement [inabil'mɑ̃], *adv.* unskillfully.

inhabileté [inabil'te], *n.f.* unskillfulness, incompetence, inability.

inhabitable [inabi'tabl], *a.* uninhabitable.

inhabité [inabi'te], *a.* uninhabited.

inhabitué [inabi'tɥe], *a.* unaccustomed, unused.

inhalation [inalɑ'sjɔ̃], *n.f.* inhalation.
inhaler [ina'le], *v.t.* to inhale.
inharmonieux [inarmɔ'njø], *a.* (*fem.* -euse) inharmonious, unmusical.
inhérent [ine'rã], *a.* inherent.
inhospitalier [inɔspita'lje], *a.* (*fem.* -ière) inhospitable; (*fig.*) unfriendly, forbidding.
inhumain [iny'mɛ̃], *a.* inhuman, cruel.
inhumainement [inymɛn'mã], *adv.* inhumanly.
inhumanité [inymani'te], *n.f.* inhumanity, cruelty.
inhumation [inymɑ'sjɔ̃], *n.f.* inhumation, interment.
inhumer [iny'me], *v.t.* to bury, to inter.
inimaginable [inimaʒi'nabl], *a.* unimaginable, inconceivable.
inimitable [inimi'tabl], *a.* inimitable.
inimitié [inimi'tje], *n.f.* enmity, antipathy, aversion.
ininflammable [inɛ̃fla'mabl], *a.* non-inflammable, fire-proof.
inintelligemment [inɛ̃tɛliʒa'mã], *adv.* unintelligently.
inintelligence [inɛ̃tɛli'ʒã:s], *n.f.* lack of intelligence.
inintelligent [inɛ̃tɛli'ʒã], *a.* unintelligent.
inintelligible [inɛ̃tɛli'ʒibl], *a.* unintelligible.
inintéressant [inɛ̃tɛrɛ'sã], *a.* uninteresting.
ininterrompu [inɛ̃tɛrɔ̃'py], *a.* uninterrupted.
inique [i'nik], *a.* iniquitous; unrighteous.
iniquement [inik'mã], *adv.* iniquitously.
iniquité [iniki'te], *n.f.* iniquity, unrighteousness; injustice.
initial [ini'sjal], *a.* (*m. pl.* -aux) initial.
initiale [ini'sjal], *n.f.* initial.
initialement [inisjal'mã], *adv.* initially.
initiateur [inisja'tœ:r], *n.m.* (*fem.* -trice) initiator.
initiation [inisja'sjɔ̃], *n.f.* initiation.
initiative [inisja'ti:v], *n.f.* initiative.
initier [ini'sje], *v.t.* to initiate, to admit.
injecté [ɛ̃ʒɛk'te], *a.* injected; bloodshot; creosoted.
injecter [ɛ̃ʒɛk'te], *v.t.* to inject.
injection [ɛ̃ʒɛk'sjɔ̃], *n.f.* injection.
injonction [ɛ̃ʒɔ̃k'sjɔ̃], *n.f.* injunction, order.
injudicieux [ɛ̃ʒydi'sjø], *a.* (*fem.* -euse) injudicious.
injure [ɛ̃'ʒy:r], *n.f.* injury; insult; (*pl.*) abuse, abusive language; slander.
injurier [ɛ̃ʒy'rje], *v.t.* to abuse, to insult.
injurieux [ɛ̃ʒy'rjø], *a.* (*fem.* -euse) wrongful; abusive, insulting.
injuste [ɛ̃'ʒyst], *a.* unjust, unfair, wrong.
injustement [ɛ̃ʒystə'mã], *adv.* unjustly, wrongly.
injustice [ɛ̃ʒys'tis], *n.f.* injustice; wrong.
injustifiable [ɛ̃ʒysti'fjabl], *a.* unjustifiable.
injustifié [ɛ̃ʒysti'fje], *a.* unjustified, groundless.
inlassable [ɛ̃lɑ'sabl], *a.* untirable.
inné [in'ne], *a.* innate, inborn.
innocemment [inɔsa'mã], *adv.* innocently.
innocence [inɔ'sã:s], *n.f.* innocence; inoffensiveness; simplicity.
innocent [inɔ'sã], *a.* innocent; harmless, inoffensive; guileless, simple.—*n.m.* (*fem.* -e) simpleton; idiot.
innocenter [inɔsã'te], *v.t.* to acquit.
innombrable [innɔ̃'brabl], *a.* innumerable, numberless.

innombrablement [inɔ̃brablə'mã], *adv.* innumerably.
innovateur [innɔva'tœ:r], *n.m.* (*fem.* -trice) innovator.
innovation [innɔvɑ'sjɔ̃], *n.f.* innovation.
innover [innɔ've], *v.t.* to make innovations.
inobservable [inɔpsɛr'vabl], *a.* inobservable.
inobservance [inɔpsɛr'vã:s], inobservation [inɔpsɛrvɑ'sjɔ̃], *n.f.* non-observance.
inobservé [inɔpsɛr've], *a.* unobserved, unnoticed.
inoccupé [inɔky'pe], *a.* unoccupied; idle; vacant.
inoculateur [inɔkyla'tœ:r], *n.m.* (*fem.* -trice) inoculator.
inoculation [inɔkylɑ'sjɔ̃], *n.f.* inoculation.
inoculer [inɔky'le], *v.t.* to inoculate.
inodore [inɔ'dɔ:r], *a.* odorless.
inoffensif [inɔfã'sif], *a.* (*fem.* -sive) inoffensive; innocuous.
inoffensivement [inɔfãsiv'mã], *adv.* inoffensively.
inofficiel [inɔfi'sjɛl], *a.* (*fem.* -elle) unofficial.
inofficiellement [inɔfisjɛl'mã], *adv.* unofficially.
inondation [inɔ̃dɑ'sjɔ̃], *n.f.* inundation, flood, deluge.
inonder [inɔ̃'de], *v.t.* to inundate, to overflow; (*fig.*) to overrun.
inopérant [inɔpe'rã], *a.* inoperative; inefficient.
inopiné [inɔpi'ne], *a.* unforeseen, unexpected, sudden.
inopinément [inɔpine'mã], *adv.* unawares, unexpectedly, suddenly.
inopportun [inɔpɔr'tœ̃], *a.* inopportune, untimely.
inorganique [inɔrga'nik], *a.* inorganic.
inoubliable [inu'bljabl], *a.* unforgettable.
inoublié [inu'blje], *a.* unforgotten, well-remembered.
inouï [i'nwi], *a.* unheard of, unprecedented.
inoxydable [inɔksi'dabl], *a.* rustless, stainless.
inqualifiable [ɛ̃kali'fjabl], *a.* unspeakable.
inquiet [ɛ̃'kjɛ], *a.* (*fem.* -ète) anxious; restless.
inquiétant [ɛ̃kje'tã], *a.* disquieting, alarming.
inquiéter [ɛ̃kje'te], *v.t.* (*conjug. like* CÉDER) to disquiet; to worry; to disturb. s'inquiéter, *v.r.* to be anxious, to be uneasy; to worry.
inquiétude [ɛ̃kje'tyd], *n.f.* anxiety, uneasiness, concern.
inquisiteur [ɛ̃kizi'tœ:r], *a.* inquisitorial; inquisitive.—*n.m.* inquisitor.
inquisitif [ɛ̃kizi'tif], *a.* (*fem.* -tive) inquisitive.
inquisition [ɛ̃kizi'sjɔ̃], *n.f.* inquisition.
insaisissable [ɛ̃sɛzi'sabl], *a.* unseizable, imperceptible.
insalubre [ɛ̃sa'lybr], *a.* insalubrious, unhealthy, unwholesome.
insalubrement [ɛ̃salybrə'mã], *adv.* insalubriously, unhealthily.
insalubrité [ɛ̃salybri'te], *n.f.* insalubrity, unhealthiness.
insanité [ɛ̃sani'te], *n.f.* insanity.
insatiabilité [ɛ̃sasjabili'te], *n.f.* insatiability.
insatiable [ɛ̃sa'sjabl], *a.* insatiable.
insciemment [ɛ̃sja'mã], *adv.* unwittingly.
inscription [ɛ̃skrip'sjɔ̃], *n.f.* inscription; registration, enrolment; matriculation.

inscrire [ɛs'kri:r], *v.t. irr. (conjug. like* ÉCRIRE) to inscribe, to set down, to register. **s'inscrire**, *v.r.* to inscribe oneself; to enter one's name; to register, to enroll.

inscrutable [ɛskry'tabl], *a.* inscrutable, unfathomable.

insecte [ɛ̃'sɛkt], *n.m.* insect.

insecticide [ɛ̃sɛkti'sid], *a.* insecticidal.—*n.m.* insecticide.

insectivore [ɛ̃sɛkti'vɔ:r], *a.* insectivorous.

insécurité [ɛ̃sekyri'te], *n.f.* insecurity.

insémination [ɛ̃semina'sjɔ̃], *n.f.* insemination *(cows, ewes etc.).*

inséminer [ɛ̃semi'ne], *v.t.* to inseminate.

insensé [ɛ̃sɑ̃'se], *a.* insane, mad; foolish, senseless.—*n.m. (fem. -ée)* madman, mad woman, maniac.

insensibiliser [ɛ̃sɑ̃sibili'ze], *v.t.* to anesthetize.

insensibilité [ɛ̃sɑ̃sibili'te], *n.f.* insensibility; callousness.

insensible [ɛ̃sɑ̃'sibl], *a.* insensible, unconscious; hard-hearted, insensitive.

insensiblement [ɛ̃sɑ̃sibləmɑ̃], *adv.* insensibly; gradually, imperceptibly.

inséparable [ɛ̃sepa'rabl], *a.* inseparable.—*n.m. (pl.) (Orn.)* love-birds.

inséparablement [ɛ̃separabləmɑ̃], *adv.* inseparably.

insérer [ɛ̃se're], *v.t. (conjug. like* CÉDER) to insert, to put in.

insertion [ɛ̃sɛr'sjɔ̃], *n.f.* insertion.

insidieusement [ɛ̃sidjøz'mɑ̃], *adv.* insidiously.

insidieux [ɛ̃si'djø], *a. (fem. -euse)* insidious.

insigne [ɛ̃'siɲ], *a.* distinguished; conspicuous; notorious.—*n.m.* badge, mark; *(pl.)* insignia.

insignifiance [ɛ̃siɲi'fjɑ̃:s], *n.f.* insignificance.

insignifiant [ɛ̃siɲi'fjɑ̃], *a.* insignificant, trivial.

insincère [ɛ̃sɛ̃'sɛ:r], *a.* insincere.

insinuant [ɛ̃si'nɥɑ̃], *a.* insinuating; ingratiating.

insinuation [ɛ̃sinɥa'sjɔ̃], *n.f.* insinuation, hint, innuendo.

insinuer [ɛ̃si'nɥe], *v.t.* to insinuate; to hint, to suggest. **s'insinuer**, *v.r.* to insinuate oneself *(dans)*, to creep *or* worm one's way *(into).*

insipide [ɛ̃si'pid], *a.* insipid, tasteless; dull.

insipidité [ɛ̃sipidi'te], *n.f.* insipidity.

insistance [ɛ̃sis'tɑ̃:s], *n.f.* insistence, persistence.

insister [ɛ̃sis'te], *v.i.* to insist, to lay stress *(sur).*

insociable [ɛ̃sɔ'sjabl], *a.* unsociable; difficult to live with.

insolation [ɛ̃sɔla'sjɔ̃], *n.f.* insolation, sunstroke.

insolemment [ɛ̃sɔla'mɑ̃], *adv.* insolently.

insolence [ɛ̃sɔ'lɑ̃:s], *n.f.* insolence, impertinence.

insolent [ɛ̃sɔ'lɑ̃], *a.* insolent, impudent, rude.—*n.m. (fem. -e)* insolent person.

insolite [ɛ̃sɔ'lit], *a.* unusual, unwonted.

insolubilité [ɛ̃sɔlybili'te], *n.f.* insolubility.

insoluble [ɛ̃sɔ'lybl], *a.* insoluble.

insolvabilité [ɛ̃sɔlvabili'te], *n.f.* insolvency.

insolvable [ɛ̃sɔl'vabl], *a.* insolvent.

insomnie [ɛ̃sɔm'ni], *n.f.* insomnia.

insondable [ɛ̃sɔ̃'dabl], *a.* unfathomable.

insonore [ɛ̃sɔ'nɔ:r], *a.* sound-proof.

insouciance [ɛ̃su'sjɑ̃:s], *n.f.* carelessness, thoughtlessness.

insouciant [ɛ̃su'sjɑ̃], **insoucieux** [ɛ̃su'sjø] *(fem. -euse),* *a.* careless, thoughtless; unconcerned, easy-going.

insoumis [ɛ̃su'mi], *a.* unsubdued; refractory, unruly.—*n.m. (Mil.)* defaulter.

insoumission [ɛ̃sumi'sjɔ̃], *n.f.* insubordination.

insoutenable [ɛ̃sut'nabl], *a.* indefensible; unbearable.

inspecter [ɛ̃spɛk'te], *v.t.* to inspect, to survey, to scan.

inspecteur [ɛ̃spɛk'tœ:r], *n.m. (fem. -trice)* inspector, superintendent, surveyor.

inspection [ɛ̃spɛk'sjɔ̃], *n.f.* inspection, survey; superintendence; **faire l'inspection de,** to inspect; **passer à l'inspection,** to undergo inspection.

inspirateur [ɛ̃spira'tœ:r], *a. (fem. -trice)* inspiring; *(Anat.)* inspiratory.—*n.m. (fem. -trice)* inspirer.

inspiration [ɛ̃spira'sjɔ̃], *n.f.* inspiration; suggestion; inhaling.

inspiré [ɛ̃spi're], *a.* and *n.m. (fem. -ée)* inspired (person).

inspirer [ɛ̃spi're], *v.t.* to inspire, to breathe in; *(fig.)* to suggest, to instill. **s'inspirer,** *v.r.* to draw one's inspiration *(de).*

instabilité [ɛ̃stabili'te], *n.f.* instability, fickleness.

instable [ɛ̃'stabl], *a.* unstable; unsteady, wobbly.

installation [ɛ̃stala'sjɔ̃], *n.f.* installation; equipment.

installer [ɛ̃sta'le], *v.t.* to install; to inaugurate, to establish. **s'installer,** *v.r.* to install oneself; to settle.

instamment [ɛ̃sta'mɑ̃], *adv.* earnestly, urgently.

instance [ɛ̃s'tɑ̃:s], *n.f.* entreaty; urgency, earnestness; *(Law)* instance; *(pl.)* entreaties.

instant (1) [ɛ̃s'tɑ̃], *n.m.* instant, moment; **à l'instant,** in an instant, immediately.

instant (2) [ɛ̃s'tɑ̃], *a.* pressing, urgent; imminent.

instantané [ɛ̃stɑ̃ta'ne], *a.* instantaneous.—*n.m.* snapshot.

instantanément [ɛ̃stɑ̃tane'mɑ̃], *adv.* instantaneously.

instar (à l') [alɛs'ta:r], *prep. phr.* **à l'instar de,** like; in imitation of.

instigateur [ɛ̃stiga'tœ:r], *n.m. (fem. -trice)* instigator.

instigation [ɛ̃stiga'sjɔ̃], *n.f.* instigation.

instiller [ɛ̃sti'le], *v.t.* to instil.

instinct [ɛ̃s'tɛ̃], *n.m.* instinct.

instinctif [ɛ̃stɛ̃k'tif], *a. (fem. -tive)* instinctive.

instinctivement [ɛ̃stɛ̃ktiv'mɑ̃], *adv.* instinctively.

instituer [ɛ̃sti'tɥe], *v.t.* to institute, to establish.

institut [ɛ̃sti'ty], *n.m.* institution; institute; order *(of monks).*

instituteur [ɛ̃stity'tœ:r], *n.m. (fem. -trice)* teacher, schoolmaster, schoolmistress *(in primary schools);* **institutrice (particulière),** governess.

institution [ɛ̃stity'sjɔ̃], *n.f.* institution; establishment; *(Law)* appointment.

instructeur [ɛ̃stryk'tœːr], *n.m.* instructor, drill-master.

instructif [ɛ̃stryk'tif], *a.* (*fem.* **-tive**) instructive.

instruction [ɛ̃stryk'sjɔ̃], *n.f.* instruction, tuition, education, learning; (*Law*) inquiry, examination; (*pl.*) directions.

instruire [ɛs'trɥiːr], *v.t.* irr. (*conjug. like* CONDUIRE) to instruct, to teach, to educate; to inform (*de*). **s'instruire**, *v.r.* to instruct, inform *or* improve oneself.

instruit [ɛ̃'strɥi], *a.* instructed, informed; aware; educated.

instrument [ɛ̃stry'mɑ̃], *n.m.* instrument, tool; document.

instrumental [ɛ̃strymɑ̃'tal], *a.* (*m. pl.* **-aux**) instrumental.

instrumentiste [ɛ̃strymɑ̃'tist], *n.* instrumentalist.

insu [ɛ̃'sy], *prep. phr.* **à l'insu de**, unknown to; **à mon insu**, unknown to me.

insubmersible [ɛ̃sybmɛr'sibl], *a.* unsinkable.

insubordination [ɛ̃sybɔrdina'sjɔ̃], *n.f.* insubordination.

insubordonné [ɛ̃sybɔrdɔ'ne], *a.* insubordinate.

insuccès [ɛ̃syk'sɛ], *n.m. inv.* failure, lack of success.

insuffisamment [ɛ̃syfiza'mɑ̃], *adv.* insufficiently.

insuffisance [ɛ̃syfi'zɑ̃ːs], *n.f.* insufficiency.

insuffisant [ɛ̃syfi'zɑ̃], *a.* insufficient, inadequate.

insulaire [ɛ̃sy'lɛːr], *a.* insular.—*n.* islander.

insularité [ɛ̃sylari'te], *n.f.* insularity.

insuline [ɛ̃sy'lin], *n.f.* insulin.

insultant [ɛ̃syl'tɑ̃], *a.* insulting.

insulte [ɛ̃'sylt], *n.f.* insult.

insulter [ɛ̃syl'te], *v.t.* to insult, to affront.

insupportable [ɛ̃sypɔr'tabl], *a.* intolerable, unbearable.

insupportablement [ɛ̃sypɔrtablə'mɑ̃], *adv.* intolerably, unbearably.

insurgé [ɛ̃syr'ʒe], *p.a.* and *n.m.* (*fem.* **-ée**) rebel, insurgent.

insurger (s') [sɛ̃syr'ʒe], *v.r.* (*conjug. like* MANGER) to revolt, to rebel.

insurmontable [ɛ̃syrmɔ̃'tabl], *a.* insurmountable, insuperable.

insurrection [ɛ̃syrɛk'sjɔ̃], *n.f.* insurrection, rising.

intact [ɛ̃'takt], *a.* intact, entire, whole.

intangible [ɛ̃tɑ̃'ʒibl], *a.* intangible.

intarissable [ɛ̃tari'sabl], *a.* inexhaustible.

intégral [ɛ̃te'gral], *a.* (*m. pl.* **-aux**) integral, whole, entire.

intégrale [ɛ̃te'gral], *n.f.* (*Math.*) integral.

intégralement [ɛ̃tegral'mɑ̃], *adv.* integrally, entirely, in full.

intègre [ɛ̃'tɛgr], *a.* honest, upright, just.

intègrement [ɛ̃tegrə'mɑ̃], *adv.* honestly, uprightly.

intégrer [ɛ̃te'gre], *v.t.* (*conjug. like* CÉDER) to integrate. **s'intégrer**, *v.r.* to combine into; to form an integral part of.

intégrité [ɛ̃tegri'te], *n.f.* integrity, uprightness, probity.

intellect [ɛ̃te'lɛkt], *n.m.* intellect, understanding.

intellectuel [ɛ̃tɛlɛk'tɥɛl], *a.* (*fem.* **-elle**) and *n.m.* (*fem.* **-elle**) intellectual.

intellectuellement [ɛ̃tɛlɛktɥɛl'mɑ̃], *adv.* intellectually.

intelligemment [ɛ̃tɛliʒa'mɑ̃] *adv.* intelligently.

intelligence [ɛ̃tɛli'ʒɑ̃ːs], *n.f.* intelligence, intellect; clear comprehension; cleverness, skill, ability; mutual understanding; **avec intelligence**, skilfully, cleverly; **en bonne intelligence avec**, on good terms with; **être d'intelligence avec**, to be in collusion with.

intelligent [ɛ̃tɛli'ʒɑ̃], *a.* intelligent; bright, clever, sharp.

intelligible [ɛ̃tɛli'ʒibl], *a.* intelligible; distinct, clear.

intelligiblement [ɛ̃tɛliʒiblə'mɑ̃], *adv.* intelligibly, clearly.

intempérance [ɛ̃tɑ̃pe'rɑ̃ːs], *n.f.* intemperance, insobriety.

intempérant [ɛ̃tɑ̃pe'rɑ̃], *a.* intemperate.

intempérie [ɛ̃tɑ̃pe'ri], *n.f.* (*usu. in pl.*) inclemency (*of the weather*).

intempestif [ɛ̃tɑ̃pɛs'tif], *a.* (*fem.* **-tive**) unseasonable, untimely.

intenable [ɛ̃tə'nabl], *a.* untenable; insufferable.

intendance [ɛ̃tɑ̃'dɑ̃ːs], *n.f.* stewardship (*of an estate*); (*Mil.*) commissariat; the Army Service Corps.

intendant [ɛ̃tɑ̃'dɑ̃], *n.m.* intendant, steward; major-domo; (*Mil.*) administrative officer (*having the rank of a general*).

intense [ɛ̃'tɑ̃ːs], *a.* intense, violent; severe.

intensité [ɛ̃tɑ̃si'te], *n.f.* intensity, violence, severity.

intensivement [ɛ̃tɑ̃siv'mɑ̃], *adv.* intensively.

intenter [ɛ̃tɑ̃'te], *v.t.* (*Law*) **intenter une action** *or* **un procès à** *or* **contre quelqu'un**, to enter *or* bring an action against someone.

intention [ɛ̃tɑ̃'sjɔ̃], *n.f.* intention; (*Law*) intent; purpose; **à l'intention de**, for the sake of; **avec intention**, on purpose; **avoir l'intention de**, to intend to; **sans intention**, unintentionally.

intentionné [ɛ̃tɑ̃sjɔ'ne], *a.* intentioned, disposed, meaning.

intentionnel [ɛ̃tɑ̃sjɔ'nɛl], *a.* (*fem.* **-elle**) intentional.

inter [ɛ̃'tɛr], *n.m.* (*Ftb.*) inside-forward.

interaction [ɛ̃tɛrak'sjɔ̃], *n.f.* interaction.

intercaler [ɛ̃tɛrka'le], *v.t.* to intercalate; to interpolate; (*Elec.*) to switch in.

intercéder [ɛ̃tɛrse'de], *v.i.* (*conjug. like* CÉDER) to intercede, to plead.

intercepter [ɛ̃tɛrsɛp'te], *v.t.* to intercept.

intercession [ɛ̃tɛrsɛ'sjɔ̃], *n.f.* intercession; mediation.

intercontinental [ɛ̃tɛrkɔ̃tinɑ̃'tal], *a.* (*m. pl.* **-aux**) intercontinental.

interdépartemental [ɛ̃tɛrdepartəmɑ̃'tal], *a.* (*m. pl.* **-aux**) interdepartmental.

interdiction [ɛ̃tɛrdik'sjɔ̃], *n.f.* interdiction, prohibition.

interdire [ɛ̃tɛr'diːr], *v.t.* irr. (*conjug. like* MÉDIRE) to interdict, to prohibit; to forbid; to suspend; (*fig.*) to confound, to nonplus.

interdit [ɛ̃tɛr'di], *a.* forbidden, prohibited; (*fig.*) abashed, confused; **entrée interdite**, no admittance; **passage interdit**, no thoroughfare.—*n.m.* interdict.—*n.m.* (*fem.* **-e**) person interdicted.

intéressant [ɛ̃terɛ'sɑ̃], *a.* interesting; attractive (*price*).
intéressé [ɛ̃terɛ'se], *a.* interested; selfish.—*n.m.* (*fem.* **-ée**) interested party.
intéresser [ɛ̃terɛ'se], *v.t.* to interest; to concern, to affect. **s'intéresser**, *v.r.* to take an interest in, to be interested (*à*).
intérêt [ɛ̃te're], *n.m.* interest, concern; share.
interférence [ɛ̃terfe'rɑ̃:s], *n.f.* interference; (*pl.*) (*Rad.*, *Tel.*) interference.
interférer [ɛ̃terfe're], *v.i.* (*conjug. like* CÉDER) to interfere.
intérieur [ɛ̃te'rjœ:r], *a.* inner, inward, internal, interior; inland.—*n.m.* interior; home, private life; *à l'intérieur*, inside; *Ministre de l'Intérieur*, Home Secretary.
interlocuteur [ɛ̃tɛrlɔky'tœ:r], *n.m.* (*fem.* **-trice**) speaker (*in a conversation*).
interloquer [ɛ̃tɛrlɔ'ke], *v.t.* to nonplus, to disconcert.
intermède [ɛ̃tɛr'mɛd], *n.m.* interlude.
intermédiaire [ɛ̃tɛrme'djɛ:r], *a.* intermediate, intervening.—*n.m.* medium, agency; intermediary, middleman, agent.
interminable [ɛ̃tɛrmi'nabl], *a.* interminable, endless.
intermission [ɛ̃tɛrmi'sjɔ̃], *n.f.* intermission, pause.
intermittence [ɛ̃tɛrmi'tɑ̃:s], *n.f.* intermission, cessation.
intermittent [ɛ̃tɛrmi'tɑ̃], *a.* intermittent.
internat [ɛ̃tɛr'na], *n.m.* boarding school; house-surgeonship (*of hospitals*).
international [ɛ̃tɛrnasjɔ'nal], *a.* (*m. pl.* **-aux**) international.
interne [ɛ̃'tɛrn], *a.* internal, inward, resident.—*n.* boarder (*in schools*).
interné [ɛ̃tɛr'ne], *a.* interned.—*n.m.* (*fem.* **-ée**) internee.
interner [ɛ̃tɛr'ne], *v.t.* to intern.
interpellation [ɛ̃tɛrpɛla'sjɔ̃], *n.f.* interpellation.
interpeller [ɛ̃tɛrpə'le], *v.t.* to hail, to call upon, to challenge; (*Polit.*) to interpellate.
interplanétaire [ɛ̃tɛrplane'tɛ:r], *a.* interplanetary.
interpoler [ɛ̃tɛrpɔ'le], *v.t.* to interpolate.
interposer [ɛ̃tɛrpɔ'ze], *v.t.* to interpose. **s'interposer**, *v.r.* to interpose, to come between.
interprétation [ɛ̃tɛrpreta'sjɔ̃], *n.f.* interpretation; rendering (*of a play*).
interprète [ɛ̃tɛr'prɛt], *n.* interpreter, expounder; artist, actor, actress.
interpréter [ɛ̃tɛrpre'te], *v.t.* (*conjug. like* CÉDER) to interpret, to explain; to construe.
interrègne [ɛ̃tɛr'rɛɲ], *n.m.* interregnum.
interrogateur [ɛ̃tɛrɔga'tœr], *n.m.* (*fem.* **-trice**) interrogator, questioner, examiner.
interrogatif [ɛ̃tɛrɔga'tif], *a.* (*fem.* **-tive**) interrogative.
interrogation [ɛ̃tɛrɔga'sjɔ̃], *n.f.* interrogation, question; *point d'interrogation*, question mark.
interrogatoire [ɛ̃tɛrɔga'twa:r], *n.m.* examination.
interroger [ɛ̃tɛrɔ'ʒe], *v.t.* (*conjug. like* MANGER) to interrogate, to question; to examine.
interrompre [ɛ̃te'rɔ̃:pr], *v.t.* (*conjug. like* RÔMPRE) to interrupt, to break off; to stop.
interrupteur [ɛ̃tɛryp'tœ:r], *a.* and *n.m.* (*fem.*

-trice) interrupting; interrupter.—*n.m.* (*Elec.*) switch, cut-out.
interruption [ɛ̃tɛryp'sjɔ̃], *n.f.* interruption; (*Elec.*) disconnection.
interscolaire [ɛ̃tɛrskɔ'lɛ:r], *a.* inter-school (*competition etc.*).
intersection [ɛ̃tɛrsɛk'sjɔ̃], *n.f.* intersection.
interstice [ɛ̃tɛr'stis], *n.m.* interstice, chink, crack.
intervalle [ɛ̃tɛr'val], *n.m.* interval; distance, gap; *dans l'intervalle*, in the meantime.
intervenir [ɛ̃tɛrvə'ni:r], *v.i. irr.* (*conjug. like* TENIR) to intervene, to interfere; to happen.
intervention [ɛ̃tɛrvɑ̃'sjɔ̃], *n.f.* intervention, interference.
interversion [ɛ̃tɛrvɛr'sjɔ̃], *n.f.* inversion.
intervertir [ɛ̃tɛrvɛr'ti:r], *v.t.* to invert, to reverse.
intestin [ɛ̃tɛs'tɛ̃], *a.* intestine; internal, domestic, civil.—*n.m.* intestine.
intimation [ɛ̃tima'sjɔ̃], *n.f.* notification.
intime [ɛ̃'tim], *a.* intimate, inmost, secret; close.—*n.* intimate.
intimement [ɛ̃tim'mɑ̃], *adv.* intimately.
intimider [ɛ̃timi'de], *v.t.* to intimidate, to frighten.
intimité [ɛ̃timi'te], *n.f.* intimacy, closeness.
intitulé [ɛ̃tity'le], *a.* entitled.—*n.m.* title (*of deeds, books etc.*).
intituler [ɛ̃tity'le], *v.t.* to entitle, to call, to name. **s'intituler**, *v.r.* to entitle or call oneself.
intolérable [ɛ̃tɔle'rabl], *a.* intolerable, insufferable.
intolérablement [ɛ̃tɔlerablə'mɑ̃], *adv.* unbearably.
intolérance [ɛ̃tɔle'rɑ̃:s], *n.f.* intolerance.
intolérant [ɛ̃tɔle'rɑ̃], *a.* intolerant.
intonation [ɛ̃tɔna'sjɔ̃], *n.f.* intonation; pitch.
intoxicant [ɛ̃tɔksi'kɑ̃], *a.* poisonous.
intoxication [ɛ̃tɔksika'sjɔ̃], *n.f.* poisoning.
intoxiquer [ɛ̃tɔksi'ke], *v.t.* to poison.
intraduisible [ɛ̃traduj'zibl], *a.* untranslatable.
intraitable [ɛ̃trɛ'tabl], *a.* intractable, unmanageable.
intransigeant [ɛ̃trɑ̃zi'ʒɑ̃], *a.* intransigent, uncompromising.—*n.m.* (*fem.* **-e**) intransigent, diehard.
intransitif [ɛ̃trɑ̃zi'tif], *a.* (*fem.* **-tive**) (*Gram.*) intransitive.
intraversable [ɛ̃travɛr'sabl], *a.* impassable.
intrépide [ɛ̃tre'pid], *a.* intrepid, dauntless, fearless.
intrigant [ɛ̃tri'gɑ̃], *a.* intriguing.—*n.m.* (*fem.* **-e**) intriguer, schemer.
intrigue [ɛ̃'trig], *n.f.* intrigue; plot (*of a novel etc.*).
intrigueur [ɛ̃tri'gœ:r], *n.m.* (*fem.* **-euse**) intriguer, plotter.
intrinsèque [ɛ̃trɛ̃'sɛk], *a.* intrinsic.
introduction [ɛ̃trɔdyk'sjɔ̃], *n.f.* introduction; preamble.
introductoire [ɛ̃trɔdyk'twa:r], *a.* introductory, preliminary.
introduire [ɛ̃trɔ'dɥi:r], *v.t. irr.* (*conjug. like* CONDUIRE) to show or bring in, to introduce. **s'introduire**, *v.r.* to get in, to find one's way in; to intrude.
introniser [ɛ̃troni'ze], *v.t.* to install, to enthrone; (*fig.*) to establish (*a fashion*).
introspectif [ɛ̃trɔspɛk'tif], *a.* (*fem.* **-tive**) introspective.

introuvable [ɛ̃tru'vabl], *a.* not to be found; matchless.
introverti [ɛ̃trɔvɛr'ti], *a.* introverted.—*n.m.* (*fem.* -e) introvert.
intrus [ɛ̃'try], *a.* intruding, intruded.—*n.m.* (*fem.* -e) intruder.
intrusion [ɛ̃try'zjɔ̃], *n.f.* intrusion.
intuitif [ɛ̃tɥi'tif], *a.* (*fem.* -tive) intuitive.
intuition [ɛ̃tɥi'sjɔ̃], *n.f.* intuition.
inusable [iny'zabl], *a.* durable, everlasting.
inusité [inyzi'te], *a.* unused; unusual; obsolete.
inutile [iny'til], *a.* useless, unnecessary.
inutilement [inytil'mɑ̃], *adv.* uselessly, to no purpose, needlessly.
inutilisable [inytili'zabl], *a.* that cannot be utilized, worthless.
inutilité [inytili'te], *n.f.* uselessness; useless thing.
invaincu [ɛ̃vɛ̃'ky], *a.* unvanquished, unconquered.
invalidation [ɛ̃valida'sjɔ̃], *n.f.* invalidation.
invalide [ɛ̃va'lid], *a.* disabled, crippled, infirm, invalid; (*Law*) not valid.—*n.* invalid, pensioner; *Hôtel des Invalides,* the veterans hospital of France.
invalider [ɛ̃vali'de], *v.t.* to invalidate, to annul.
invariable [ɛ̃va'rjabl], *a.* invariable, unchangeable.
invariablement [ɛ̃varjablə'mɑ̃], *adv.* invariably.
invasion [ɛ̃va'zjɔ̃], *n.f.* invasion; inroad.
invective [ɛ̃vɛk'ti:v], *n.f.* invective, (*pl.*) abuse.
invectiver [ɛ̃vɛkti've] *v.t.* to abuse.—*v.i.* to inveigh against, to revile (*contre*).
inventaire [ɛ̃vɑ̃'tɛ:r], *n.m.* inventory; stocktaking.
inventer [ɛ̃vɑ̃'te], *v.t.* to invent, to devise; to find out; to imagine; to forge.
inventeur [ɛ̃vɑ̃'tœ:r], *n.m.* (*fem.* -trice) inventor.
inventif [ɛ̃vɑ̃'tif], *a.* (*fem.* -tive) inventive.
invention [ɛ̃vɑ̃'sjɔ̃], *n.f.* invention; inventiveness; device, trick; falsehood; *brevet d'invention,* patent.
inventorier [ɛ̃vɑ̃tɔ'rje], *v.t.* to draw up an inventory of; to schedule, to catalogue.
inversable [ɛ̃vɛr'sabl], *a.* that cannot be upset.
inverse [ɛ̃'vɛrs], *a.* inverse, inverted.—*n.m.* reverse, contrary.
inversement [ɛ̃vɛrs'mɑ̃], *adv.* inversely.
invertébré [ɛ̃vɛrte'bre], *a.* and *n.m.* (*fem.* -ée) invertebrate.
inverti [ɛ̃vɛr'ti], *a.* inverted, reversed.
investigateur [ɛ̃vɛstiga'tœ:r], *a.* (*fem.* -trice) searching, inquiring.—*n.m.* (*fem.* -trice) investigator.
investigation [ɛ̃vɛstiga'sjɔ̃], *n.f.* investigation, inquiry.
investir [ɛ̃vɛs'ti:r], *v.t.* to invest; to surround, to lay siege to.
investiture [ɛ̃vɛsti'ty:r], *n.f.* investiture.
invétéré [ɛ̃vete're], *a.* inveterate.
invincibilité [ɛ̃vɛ̃sibili'te], *n.f.* invincibility.
invincible [ɛ̃vɛ̃'sibl], *a.* invincible, unconquerable.
inviolable [ɛ̃vjɔ'labl], *a.* inviolable.
inviolé [ɛ̃vjɔ'le], *a.* inviolate.
invisible [ɛ̃vi'zibl], *a.* invisible.

invisiblement [ɛ̃viziblə'mɑ̃], *adv.* invisibly.
invitation [ɛ̃vita'sjɔ̃], *n.f.* invitation.
invité [ɛ̃vi'te], *n.m.* (*fem.* -ée) guest.
inviter [ɛ̃vi'te], *v.t.* to invite, to request; to incite, to tempt.
invocation [ɛ̃vɔka'sjɔ̃], *n.f.* invocation.
involontaire [ɛ̃vɔlɔ̃'tɛ:r], *a.* involuntary, unwilling.
involontairement [ɛ̃vɔlɔ̃tɛr'mɑ̃], *adv.* involuntarily.
invoquer [ɛ̃vɔ'ke], *v.t.* to invoke, to call upon; to appeal to.
invraisemblable [ɛ̃vrɛsɑ̃'blabl], *a.* unlikely, improbable.
invraisemblablement [ɛ̃vrɛsɑ̃blablə'mɑ̃], *adv.* improbably.
invraisemblance [ɛ̃vrɛsɑ̃'blɑ̃:s], *n.f.* unlikelihood, improbability.
invulnérable [ɛ̃vylne'rabl], *a.* invulnerable.
iode [jɔd], *n.m.* iodine.
ion [jɔ̃], *n.m.* (*Phys.*) ion.
ionisation [jɔniza'sjɔ̃], *n.f.* ionization.
ionosphère [jɔnɔs'fɛ:r], *n.f.* ionosphere.
iota [jɔ'ta], *n.m.* iota, jot, tittle.
Irak [i'rak], l', *m.* Iraq.
irakien [ira'kjɛ̃], *a.* (*fem.* -enne) Iraqi.—*n.m.* (**Irakien**, *fem.* -enne) Iraqi (*person*).
Iran [i'rɑ̃], l', *m.* Iran.
iranien [ira'njɛ̃], *a.* (*fem.* -enne) Iranian.—*n.m.* (**Iranien**, *fem.* -enne) Iranian (*person*).
irascibilite [irasibili'te], *n.f.* irascibility.
irascible [ira'sibl], *a.* irascible, irritable.
iridescence [iride'sɑ̃:s], *n.f.* iridescence.
iridescent [iride'sɑ̃], *a.* iridescent.
iris [i'ri:s], *n.m. inv.* iris; rainbow.
irisé [iri'ze], *a.* rainbow-colored, iridescent.
irlandais [irlɑ̃'dɛ], *a.* Irish.—*n.m.* Irish (*language*); (**Irlandais**, *fem.* -aise) Irishman, Irishwoman.
Irlande [ir'lɑ̃d], l', *f.* Ireland.
ironie [irɔ'ni], *n.f.* irony, mockery, raillery.
ironique [irɔ'nik], *a.* ironical.
irradiation [irradja'sjɔ̃], *n.f.* irradiation.
irradier [irra'dje], *v.t.* to radiate through; (*C*) to broadcast.
irraisonnable [irrɛzɔ'nabl], *a.* irrational.
irraisonnablement [irrɛzɔnablə'mɑ̃], *adv.* irrationally.
irrationnel [irrasjɔ'nɛl], *a.* (*fem.* -elle) irrational.
irrationnellement [irrasjɔnɛl'mɑ̃], *adv.* irrationally.
irréalisable [irreali'zabl], *a.* impossible, impracticable.
irréconciliable [irrekɔ̃si'ljabl], *a.* irreconcilable.
irrécusable [irreky'zabl], *a.* unexceptionable, unimpeachable.
irréductible [irredyk'tibl], *a.* irreducible; (*fig.*) unyielding.
irréel [irre'ɛl], *a.* (*fem.* -éelle) unreal.—*n.m.* unreality.
irréfléchi [irrefle'fi], *a.* thoughtless, inconsiderate.
irréflexion [irreflɛk'sjɔ̃], *n.f.* thoughtlessness, heedlessness.
irréfutable [irrefy'tabl], *a.* irrefutable.
irrégularité [irregylari'te], *n.f.* irregularity.
irrégulier [irregy'lje], *a.* (*fem.* -ière) irregular.
irrégulièrement [irregyljɛr'mɑ̃], *adv.* irregularly.

irréligieux [irreli'ʒjø], *a.* (*fem.* **-euse**) irreligious.

irrémédiable [irreme'djabl], *a.* irremediable, irreparable, irretrievable.

irrémédiablement [irremedjablə'mã], *adv.* irremediably, irreparably.

irrémissible [irremi'sibl], *a.* irremissible, unpardonable.

irremplaçable [irrãpla'sabl], *a.* irreplaceable.

irréparable [irrepa'rabl], *a.* irreparable.

irrépressible [irrepre'sibl], *a.* irrepressible.

irréprochable [irreprɔ'ʃabl], *a.* irreproachable.

irrésistible [irrezis'tibl], *a.* irresistible.

irrésistiblement [irrezistiblə'mã], *adv.* irresistibly.

irrésolu [irrezɔ'ly], *a.* irresolute, wavering.

irrésolument [irrezɔly'mã], *adv.* irresolutely.

irrésolution [irrezɔly'sjɔ̃], *n.f.* irresolution, indecision.

irrespectueusement [irrɛspɛktɥøz'mã], *adv.* disrespectfully.

irrespectueux [irrɛspɛk'tɥø], *a.* (*fem.* **-euse**) disrespectful.

irresponsabilité [irrɛspɔsabili'te], *n.f.* irresponsibility.

irresponsable [irrɛspɔ'sabl], *a.* irresponsible.

irrétrécissable [irretresi'sabl], *a.* unshrinkable.

irrévérence [irreve'rã:s], *n.f.* irreverence, disrespect.

irrévocable [irrevɔ'kabl], *a.* irrevocable.

irrévocablement [irrevɔkablə'mã], *adv.* irrevocably.

irrigateur [irriga'tœ:r], *n.m.* watering engine; garden hose.

irrigation [irriga'sjɔ̃], *n.f.* irrigation.

irriguer [irri'ge], *v.t.* to irrigate, to water.

irritabilité [irritabili'te], *n.f.* irritability.

irritable [irri'tabl], *a.* irritable.

irritant [irri'tã], *a.* irritating, provoking.

irritation [irrita'sjɔ̃], *n.f.* irritation, exasperation.

irriter [irri'te], *v.t.* to irritate, to incense, to anger; to provoke, to excite. **s'irriter**, *v.r.* to grow angry; to become irritated.

irruption [irryp'sjɔ̃], *n.f.* irruption, raid; overflow, flood; **faire irruption dans**, to invade.

Isaïe [iza'i], *m.* Isaiah.

Islam [is'lam], *n.m.* Islam.

islandais [islã'dɛ], *a.* Icelandic.—*n.m.* Icelandic (*language*); (**Islandais,** *fem.* **-aise**) Icelander.

Islande [is'lãd], *l'*, *f.* Iceland.

isobare [izɔ'bar], *n.* isobar.

isocèle *or* **isoscèle** [izɔ'sɛl], *a.* (*Geom.*) isosceles.

isolant [izɔ'lã], *a.* insulating; **bouteille isolante,** vacuum flask.

isolateur [izɔla'tœ:r], *a.* (*fem.* **-trice**) insulating.—*n.m.* insulator.

isolation [izɔla'sjɔ̃], *n.f.* insulation; isolation.

isolé [izɔ'le], *a.* isolated; lonely, solitary; detached; insulated; apart.

isolement [izɔl'mã], *n.m.* loneliness, isolation; insulation.

isolément [izɔle'mã], *adv.* separately.

isoler [izɔ'le], *v.t.* to isolate; to insulate; to detach; to separate.

isotope [izɔ'tɔp], *n.m.* isotope.

Israël [isra'ɛl], *l'*, *m.* Israel.

israélien [israe'ljɛ̃], *a.* (*fem.* **-enne**) Israel(i). —*n.m.* (**Israélien,** *fem.* **-enne**) Israeli (*person*).

issu [i'sy], *a.* born, descended, sprung from.

issue [i'sy], *n.f.* issue, outlet; escape; (*fig.*) end, event.

isthme [ism], *n.m.* isthmus.

Italie [ita'li], *l'*, *f.* Italy.

italien [ita'ljɛ̃], *a.* (*fem.* **-enne**) Italian.— *n.m.* Italian (*language*); (**Italien,** *fem.* **-enne**) Italian (*person*).

italique [ita'lik], *a.* and *n.m.* italic.

itinéraire [itine'rɛ:r], *a.* pertaining to roads etc.—*n.m.* itinerary, route; guide-book.

itinérant [itine'rã], *a.* itinerant.

ivoire [i'vwa:r], *n.m.* ivory; (*fig.*) whiteness; **la Côte d'Ivoire,** Ivory Coast.

ivraie [i'vrɛ], *n.f.* darnel, tare.

ivre [i:vr], *a.* drunk; intoxicated; (*fig.*) transported; **ivre mort,** dead drunk.

ivresse [i'vrɛs], *n.f.* drunkenness, intoxication; (*fig.*) frenzy, rapture.

ivrogne [i'vrɔɲ], *a.* drunken.—*n.* drunkard.

ivrognerie [ivrɔ'ɲri], *n.f.* habitual drunkenness.

J

J, j [ʒi], *n.m.* the tenth letter of the alphabet.

jabot [ʒa'bo], *n.m.* crop (*of a bird*); frill (*of a shirt or blouse*); jabot.

jaboter [ʒabɔ'te], *v.i.* (*colloq.*) to prattle, to chatter.

jacasser [ʒaka'se], *v.i.* to chatter (*of the magpie*); (*fig.*) to chatter, to jabber.

jachère [ʒa'ʃɛ:r], *n.f.* fallow.

jacinthe [ʒa'sɛ̃:t], *n.f.* jacinthe; hyacinth.

Jacques [ʒɑ:k], *m.* James.

jade [ʒad], *n.m.* jade.

jadis [ʒɑ'dis], *adv.* of old, formerly.

jaguar [ʒa'gwa:r], *n.m.* jaguar.

jaillir [ʒa'ji:r], *v.i.* to spout, to gush; to shoot out *or* up.

jaillissant [ʒaji'sã], *a.* spouting, gushing.

jaillissement [ʒajis'mã], *n.m.* gushing, spouting, flashing.

jais [ʒɛ], *n.m.* jet.

jalon [ʒa'lɔ̃], *n.m.* levelling staff, surveying staff; (*fig.*) landmark, beacon.

jalonnement [ʒalɔn'mã], *n.m.* (*Land surveying*) staking out, marking out.

jalonner [ʒalɔ'ne], *v.t.* to mark *or* stake out.—*v.i.* to place land marks etc.

jalousement [ʒaluz'mã], *adv.* jealously.

jalouser [ʒalu'ze], *v.t.* to be jealous of, to envy.

jalousie [ʒalu'zi], *n.f.* jealousy, envy; Venetian blind; (*Bot.*) sweet william.

jaloux [ʒa'lu], *a.* (*fem.* **-ouse**) jealous; envious; desirous, anxious.—*n.m.* (*fem.* **-ouse**) jealous person.

jamaïquain [ʒamaïˈkɛ̃], a. Jamaican.—n.m. (**Jamaïquain**, *fem.* **-aine**) Jamaican (*person*).

Jamaïque [ʒamaˈik], la, *f.* Jamaica.

jamais [ʒaˈmɛ], *adv.* (*neg.*) never, (*affirm.*) ever; **à jamais**, for ever; **jamais de la vie**, not on your life!; **mieux vaut tard que jamais**, better late than never.

jambage [ʒɑ̃ˈbaːʒ], *n.m.* jamb (*of a door etc.*); down-stroke, pot-hook (*in writing*).

jambe [ʒɑ̃ːb], *n.f.* leg; shank; **courir à toutes jambes**, to run as fast as one can; **prendre ses jambes à son cou**, to take to one's heels.

jambière [ʒɑ̃ˈbjɛːr], *n.f.* legging, leg guard.

jambon [ʒɑ̃ˈbɔ̃], *n.m.* ham.

jamboree [ʒɑ̃bɔˈri], *n.m.* jamboree.

jante [ʒɑ̃ːt], *n.f.* felloe, rim (*of a wheel*).

janvier [ʒɑ̃ˈvje], *n.m.* January.

Japon [ʒaˈpɔ̃], le, *m.* Japan.

japonais [ʒapɔˈnɛ], *a.* Japanese.—*n.m.* Japanese (*language*); (**Japonais**, *fem.* **-aise**) Japanese (*person*).

japper [ʒaˈpe], *v.i.* to yelp, to yap.

jaquette [ʒaˈkɛt], *n.f.* morning coat, tail coat; woman's jacket; dust cover (*of book*).

jardin [ʒarˈdɛ̃], *n.m.* garden.

jardinage [ʒardiˈnaːʒ], *n.m.* gardening; garden produce.

jardiner [ʒardiˈne], *v.i.* to garden.

jardinier [ʒardiˈnje], *a.* (*fem.* **-ière**) (of the) garden.—*n.m.* (*fem.* **-ière**) gardener.—*n.f.* (**-ière**) flower-stand, jardinière.

jardiniste [ʒardiˈnist], *n.* landscape-gardener.

jargon [ʒarˈgɔ̃], *n.m.* jargon, gibberish; lingo.

jarre [ʒaːr], *n.f.* jar.

jarret [ʒaˈrɛ], *n.m.* ham (*of man*); hough, hock (*of horse*).

jarretière [ʒarˈtjɛr], *n.f.* (lady's) garter.

jars (1) [ʒaːr], *n.m.* gander.

jars (2) [ʒaːr], *n.m.* (another form of **jargon**) slang.

jaser [ʒaˈze], *v.i.* to chatter, to gossip.

jaserie [ʒazˈri], *n.f.* chatter; gossip.

jaseur [ʒaˈzœːr], *a.* (*fem.* **-euse**) talkative.—*n.m.* (*fem.* **-euse**) chatterer, chatterbox.

jasmin [ʒasˈmɛ̃], *n.m.* jasmine.

jaspe [ʒasp], *n.m.* jasper.

jasper [ʒasˈpe], *v.t.* to marble, to vein, to variegate.

jaspure [ʒasˈpyːr], *n.f.* marbling, veining.

jatte [ʒat], *n.f.* bowl, platter; dog's bowl.

jauge [ʒoːʒ], *n.f.* gauge; (*Naut.*) tonnage.

jaugeage [ʒoˈʒaːʒ], *n.m.* gauging.

jauger [ʒoˈʒe], *v.t.* (*conjug. like* MANGER) to gauge, to measure the capacity of; (*Naut.*) to draw (*so many feet of water*).

jaunâtre [ʒoˈnɑːtr], *a.* yellowish.

jaune [ʒoːn], *a.* yellow; **rire jaune**, to give a sickly smile.—*n.m.* yellow; **jaune d'œuf**, egg yolk.

jaunir [ʒoˈniːr], *v.t.* to make yellow, to dye yellow.—*v.i.* to grow yellow, to turn yellow.

jaunissant [ʒoniˈsɑ̃], *a.* turning yellow, yellowing; ripening.

jaunisse [ʒoˈnis], *n.f.* jaundice.

javanais [ʒavaˈnɛ], *a.* Javanese.—*n.m.* (**Javanais**, *fem.* **-aise**) Javanese (*person*).

javeau [ʒaˈvo], *n.m.* (*pl.* **-eaux**) sandbank.

javeline [ʒaˈvlin], *n.f.* javelin.

javelle [ʒaˈvɛl], *n.f.* swathe, loose sheaf.

javelot [ʒaˈvlo], *n.m.* javelin.

jazz [(d)ʒɑːz], *n.m.* jazz.

je [ʒə], (**j'**, *before a vowel sound*), *pron.* I.

Jean [ʒɑ̃], *m.* John [JEANNOT].

Jeanne [ʒɑ(ː)n], *f.* Joan, Jane, Jean.

Jeannot [ʒaˈno], *m.* Johnny, Jock.

jeep [(d)ʒip], *n.f.* jeep.

jésuite [ʒeˈzɥit], *a.* Jesuit.—*n.m.* (**Jésuite**) Jesuit.

Jésus [ʒeˈzy], *m.* Jesus.

jet [ʒɛ], *n.m.* casting, cast, throw; jet, gush, spurt (*of water*); sudden ray (*of light*); casting (*of metal*); shoot, sprout (*of plants*); spout (*of pump etc.*); new swarm (*of bees*); **arme de jet**, missile weapon.

jetée [ʒəˈte], *n.f.* jetty, pier; breakwater.

jeter [ʒəˈte], *v.t.* (*conjug. like* APPELER) to throw, to fling, to hurl; to throw up; to throw down, to knock down; to throw out; to mold; to shoot out; to send forth; to empty; to discharge. **se jeter**, *v.r.* to throw oneself, to fling oneself; to fall upon (*attack*); to flow (*of rivers etc.*).

jeton [ʒəˈtɔ̃], *n.m.* token, counter; voucher.

jeu [ʒø], *n.m.* (*pl.* **jeux**) play, sport; game; fun; gambling; (*fig.*) stake; manner of playing; performance (*of players*); (*Mach.*) working; clearance; play.

jeudi [ʒøˈdi], *n.m.* Thursday.

jeun (à) [aˈʒœ̃], *adv.* fasting, sober, on an empty stomach.

jeune [ʒœn], *a.* young, youthful; junior, new, early, unripe, green.—*n.* young person or animal.

jeûne [ʒøːn], *n.m.* fasting; fast, abstinence.

jeûner [ʒøˈne], *v.i.* to fast.

jeunesse [ʒœˈnɛs], *n.f.* youth, young days; youthfulness; freshness, prime; young people.

jeunet [ʒœˈnɛ], *a.* (*fem.* **-ette**) (*colloq.*) very young.

jiu-jitsu [(d)ʒyʒiˈtsy], *n.m.* ju-jitsu.

joaillerie [ʒwajˈri], *n.f.* jeweller's trade or business; jewelry, jewels.

joaillier [ˈʒwaˈje], *n.m.* (*fem.* **-ière**) jeweller.

jobard [ʒoˈbaːr], *n.m.* (*colloq.*) sucker, mug, fool.

jockey [ʒoˈke], *n.m.* jockey.

jocrisse [ʒoˈkris], *n.m.* dolt, simpleton.

joie [ʒwa], *n.f.* joy, happiness, joyfulness, gladness; glee, mirth.

joignant [ʒwaˈɲɑ̃], *a.* and *prep.* next to, adjoining.

joindre [ʒwɛ̃ːdr], *v.t. irr.* (*conjug. like* CRAINDRE) to join, to put together, to unite, to combine; to add; to meet; to overtake.—*v.i.* to join, to meet. **se joindre**, *v.r.* to join, to be joined, to be united; to be adjoining, to be adjacent; to be added.

joint [ʒwɛ̃], *a.* joined, united; added.—*n.m.* joint; seam, junction.

jointé [ʒwɛ̃ˈte], *a.* jointed.

jointure [ʒwɛ̃ˈtyːr], *n.f.* joint, jointing, articulation.

joli [ʒoˈli], *a.* pretty, pleasing, neat; fine, nice.—*n.m.* what is pretty; **le joli de la chose c'est que . . .**, the best of the thing is that . . .

joliment [ʒoliˈmɑ̃], *adv.* prettily, (*iron.*) nicely, finely; (*colloq.*) awfully, jolly, much, very.

jonc [ʒɔ̃], *n.m.* (*Bot.*) rush; cane, Malacca cane; keeper, guard (*ring*).

jonchée [ʒɔ̃ˈʃe], *n.f.* strewing (*of flowers*).
joncher [ʒɔ̃ˈʃe], *v.t.* to strew; to heap; to scatter.
jonction [ʒɔ̃kˈsjɔ̃], *n.f.* junction, joining.
jongler [ʒɔ̃ˈgle], *v.i.* to juggle.
jonglerie [ʒɔ̃gləˈri], *n.f.* juggling.
jongleur [ʒɔ̃ˈglœːr], *n.m.* juggler; (*fig.*) trickster.
jonque [ʒɔ̃k], *n.f.* junk (*Chinese vessel*).
jonquille [ʒɔ̃ˈkiːj], *n.f.* jonquil.—*a. inv.* and *n.m.* pale yellow, jonquil (*color*).
Jordanie [ʒɔrdaˈni], **la**, *f.* Jordan.
jordanien [ʒɔrdaˈnjɛ̃], *a.* Jordanian.—*n.m.* (**Jordanien**, *fem.* **-enne**) Jordanian (*person*).
Joseph [ʒɔˈzef], *m.* Joseph.
jouable [ʒwabl], *a.* playable.
joue [ʒu]. *n.f.* cheek; *coucher* or *mettre en joue,* to take aim at.
jouer [ʒwe], *v.t.* to play; to stake; to gamble away; to move (*a piece*); to perform, to act; to pretend to be, to imitate; to ridicule; to deceive.—*v.i.* to play, to amuse oneself; to speculate (*on the funds*); to work, to work loose (*of machinery etc.*); to act, to perform. **se jouer,** *v.r.* to sport, to play; to make game (*of*); to make light of.
jouet [ʒwe], *n.m.* plaything, toy; laughing-stock, jest, sport.
joueur [ʒwœːr], *n.m.* (*fem.* **-euse**) player; gambler; speculator; performer (*on an instrument*).
joufflu [ʒuˈfly], *a.* chubby, chubby-cheeked.
joug [ʒu(g)], *n.m.* yoke; bondage, slavery.
jouir [ʒwiːr], *v.i.* to enjoy, to revel; to be in possession (*de*).
jouissance [ʒwiˈsãːs], *n.f.* enjoyment; possession, use; delight; interest payable.
jouissant [ʒwiˈsã], *a.* enjoying, in possession (*de*).
joujou [ʒuˈʒu], *n.m.* (*pl.* **-oux**) plaything, toy.
jour [ʒuːr], *n.m.* day, daylight; light; daybreak; day time; opening, gap; *broderie à jours,* open-work embroidery; *donner le jour à,* to give birth to; *plat du jour,* today's special; *se faire jour,* to force one's way through; *un jour de fête,* a holiday.
Jourdain [ʒurˈdɛ̃], **le,** *m.* Jordan (*river*).
journal [ʒurˈnal], *n.m.* (*pl.* **-aux**) journal, diary; newspaper; (*Comm.*) day-book.
journalier [ʒurnaˈlje], *a.* (*fem.* **-ière**) daily, diurnal.—*n.m.* journeyman, day laborer.
journalisme [ʒurnaˈlism], *n.m.* journalism.
journaliste [ʒurnaˈlist], *n.* journalist.
journée [ʒurˈne], *n.f.* day (time), day's work *or* wages; day's journey; battle; historic day; *toute la journée,* all day long (long).
journellement [ʒurnɛlˈmã], *adv.* daily, every day.
joute [ʒut], *n.f.* joust, tilting match; contest; (*C*) game.
jouter [ʒuˈte], *v.i.* to joust, to tilt.
jouteur [ʒuˈtœːr], *n.m.* tilter; (*fig.*) antagonist, adversary.
jovial [ʒɔˈvjal], *a.* (*m. pl.* **-aux**) jovial, jolly, merry.
jovialement [ʒɔvjalˈmã], *adv.* jovially.
jovialité [ʒɔvjaliˈte], *n.f.* joviality, jollity.
joyau [ʒwaˈjo], *n.m.* (*pl.* **-aux**) jewel.
joyeusement [ʒwajøzˈmã], *adv.* cheerfully, joyfully.
joyeuseté [ʒwajøzˈte], *n.f.* (*fam.*) joke, jest.

joyeux [ʒwaˈjø], *a.* (*fem.* **-euse**) joyful, merry; cheerful.
jubilaire [ʒybiˈlɛːr], *a.* jubilee; (*fig.*) of fifty years' standing (*of persons etc.*).
jubilant [ʒybiˈlã], *a.* jubilant, delighted.
jubilation [ʒybilaˈsjɔ̃], *n.f.* jubilation, rejoicing.
jubilé [ʒybiˈle], *n.m.* jubilee; (*fig.*) golden wedding.
jubiler [ʒybiˈle], *v.i.* to jubilate, to exult.
jucher [ʒyˈʃe], *v.i.* to roost, to perch; to lodge (*at the top of a house etc.*); to perch (*oneself*); to go to roost; to perch (*oneself*). **se jucher,** *v.r.* to go to roost; to perch (*oneself*).
juchoir [ʒyˈʃwaːr], *n.m.* roosting-place, perch.
judaïque [ʒydaˈik], *a.* Judaical, Jewish.
judaïsme [ʒydaˈism], *n.m.* Judaism.
judas [ʒyˈda], *n.m.* Judas, traitor; peep-hole (*in a door etc.*).
Judée [ʒyˈde], **la,** *f.* Judaea.
judicature [ʒydikaˈtyːr], *n.f.* judicature, magistracy.
judiciaire [ʒydiˈsjɛːr], *a.* judiciary, judicial; legal.
judiciairement [ʒydisjɛrˈmã], *adv.* judicially, by authority of justice.
judicieusement [ʒydisjøzˈmã], *adv.* judiciously, discreetly.
judicieux [ʒydiˈsjø], *a.* (*fem.* **-euse**) judicious, wise, discreet.
juge [ʒyːʒ], *n.m.* judge; magistrate, justice; (*pl.*) bench.
jugé [ʒyˈʒe], *a.* judged.—*n.m. au jugé,* at a guess.
jugement [ʒyʒˈmã], *n.m.* judgment; opinion; trial; sentence; good sense; *jugement arbitral,* award; *jugement provisoire,* decree nisi; *jugement définitif,* decree absolute.
juger [ʒyˈʒe], *v.t.* (*conjug. like* MANGER) to judge; to try; to pass sentence on; to consider, to think.—*v.i.* to judge (*de*); to give judgment, to deem. **se juger,** *v.r.* to judge oneself; to deem oneself; to be judged.
jugulaire [ʒygyˈlɛːr], *a.* (*Anat.*) jugular.—*n.f.* jugular vein; chin strap.
juguler [ʒygyˈle], *v.t.* to strangle; (*fig.*) to torment; to fleece.
juif [ʒɥif], *a.* (*fem.* **juive**) Jewish.—*n.m.* (**Juif**, *fem.* **Juive**) Jew, Jewess.
juillet [ʒɥiˈje], *n.m.* July.
juin [ʒɥɛ̃], *n.m.* June.
juiverie [ʒɥiˈvri], *n.f.* ghetto (*Jews' quarter*).
jujube [ʒyˈʒyb], *n.f.* jujube (*fruit*).—*n.m.* or *pâte de jujube,* jujube (*lozenge*).
julep [ʒyˈlɛp], *n.m.* julep.
julienne [ʒyˈljɛn], *n.f.* julienne (*vegetable soup*).
jumeau [ʒyˈmo], *a.* (*fem.* **-elle**, *m. pl.* **-eaux**) twin; double (*of fruit etc.*).—*n.m.* twin (brother).
jumelage [ʒymˈlaːʒ], *n.m.* twinning (*of towns etc.*).
jumelé [ʒymˈle], *a.* twin, in couples; *maison jumelée,* semi-detached house; (*horse racing*) *pari jumelé,* each-way bet.
jumelle [ʒyˈmɛl], *n.f.* twin (sister); (*pl.*) binoculars; *jumelles de campagne,* field glasses; *jumelles de théâtre,* opera glasses; *jumelles de manchettes,* cuff links.
jument [ʒyˈmã], *n.f.* mare.
jungle [ʒɔ̃ːgl], *n.f.* jungle.
jupe [ʒyp], *n.f.* skirt.

Jupiter [ʒypi'tɛr], *m.* Jupiter, Jove.

jupon [ʒy'pɔ̃], *n.m.* petticoat.

juré [ʒy're], *a.* sworn.—*n.m.* juror, juryman.

jurement [ʒyr'mɑ̃], *n.m.* oath; swearing.

jurer [ʒy're], *v.t.* to swear by; to swear, to vow, to take an oath that; to blaspheme.—*v.i.* to swear, to take an oath; to blaspheme; *(fig.)* to contrast, to jar, to clash (*of colors etc.*).

juridiction [ʒyridik'sjɔ̃], *n.f.* jurisdiction; department, province.

juridique [ʒyri'dik], *a.* juridical, judicial, legal.

juridiquement [ʒyridik'mɑ̃], *adv.* juridically, judicially.

jurisprudence [ʒyrispry'dɑ̃s], *n.f.* jurisprudence.

juriste [ʒy'rist], *n.m.* jurist.

juron [ʒy'rɔ̃], *n.m.* oath, curse, swear word.

jury [ʒy'ri], *n.m.* jury; board, committee.

jus [ʒy], *n.m.* juice; gravy.

jusque or ***jusques** [ʒysk], *prep.* even to, as far as; till, until; down to; up to.

juste [ʒyst], *a.* just, equitable; fair, legitimate, lawful; proper, fit; exact; well-fitting; tight; *au plus juste prix*, at the lowest price; *un homme juste*, a righteous man.—*n.m.* upright man, virtuous man; what is just.— *adv.* just, exactly, precisely; *(Mus.)* true.

justement [ʒystə'mɑ̃], *adv.* justly, precisely; justifiably.

justesse [ʒys'tɛs], *n.f.* justness, exactness, precision, accuracy; appropriateness.

justice [ʒys'tis], *n.f.* justice; righteousness, probity; fairness, impartiality; reason; courts of justice, judges; *palais de justice*, law court.

justifiable [ʒysti'fjabl], *a.* justifiable; warrantable.

justification [ʒystifika'sjɔ̃], *n.f.* justification, vindication, proof.

justifier [ʒysti'fje], *v.t.* to justify, to vindicate, to make good. **se justifier**, *v.r.* to justify, clear or vindicate oneself.

jute [ʒyt], *n.m.* jute.

juteux [ʒy'tø], *a.* (*fem.* **-euse**) juicy.

juvénile [ʒyve'nil], *a.* juvenile, youthful.

juvénilement [ʒyvenil'mɑ̃], *adv.* boyishly, in a juvenile manner.

juxtaposer [ʒykstapo'ze], *v.t.* to place side by side. **se juxtaposer**, *v.r.* to be in juxtaposition.

juxtaposition [ʒykstapozi'sjɔ̃], *n.f.* juxtaposition.

K

K, k [kɑ], *n.m.* the eleventh letter of the alphabet; *Échelle K* (*viz. Kelvin*), absolute scale (*of temperature*).

kakatoès [kakato'ɛs], [CACATOIS].

kaki [ka'ki], *a. inv.* khaki (*color*).

kaléidoscope [kaleidɔs'kɔp], *n.m.* kaleidoscope.

kangourou [kɑ̃gu'ru], *n.m.* kangaroo.

kaolin [kaɔ'lɛ̃], *n.m.* kaolin, porcelain clay, china clay.

kapok or **kapoc** [ka'pɔk], *n.m.* kapok.

kascher or **kacher** [ka'ʃɛr], **kachir** [ka'ʃir], *a.* (*Jew. Relig.*) kosher.

kayac [ka'jak], *n.m.* kayak.

Kénia [ke'nja], **le**, *m.* Kenya.

képi [ke'pi], *n.m.* kepi, military cap; peak cap.

kermesse [kɛr'mɛs], *n.f.* kermis (*in the Netherlands*); kermesse; village fair.

kérosène [kero'zɛːn], *n.m.* kerosene, coal oil.

kidnapper [kidna'pe], *v.t.* to kidnap.

kilo [ki'lo], *n.m.* (*abbr.*) kilogramme.

kilocycle [kilɔ'sikl], *n.m.* kilocycle.

kilogramme [kilɔ'gram], *n.m.* kilogramme (*2.2 lb. avoirdupois*).

kilomètre [kilɔ'mɛtr], *n.m.* kilometre (*1093.6 yards*).

kilowatt [kilɔ'wat], *n.m.* kilowatt.

kimono [kimɔ'no], *n.m.* kimono.

kiosque [kjɔsk], *n.m.* kiosk; (*Naut.*) house; *kiosque à journaux*, newspaper stand; *kiosque à musique*, bandstand.

klakson or **klaxon** [klak'sɔ̃], *n.m.* klaxon, hooter, horn.

kleptomane [klɛptɔ'man], *a.* and *n.* kleptomaniac.

kleptomanie [klɛptɔma'ni], *n.f.* kleptomania.

kola or **cola** [kɔ'la], *n.m.* kola.

Kominform [kɔmɛ̃'fɔrm], *n.m.* Cominform.

Komintern [kɔmɛ̃'tɛrn], *n.m.* Comintern.

Koweit [kɔ'weit], **le**, *m.* Kuwait.

kyrielle [ki'rjɛl], *n.f.* litany; (*fig.*) long string (*of words etc.*), long tedious story.

kyste [kist], *n.m.* (*Path.*) cyst.

L

L, l [ɛl], *n.m.* or *f.* the twelfth letter of the alphabet.

l', *art.* and *pron.* (*by elision of* **le** *or* **la**) the; him, her, it.

la (1) [la], *art.* and *pron. f.* the; her, it.

la (2) [la], *n.m.* (*Mus.*) la; the note A.

là [la], *adv.* and *int.* there, thither; then (*of time*); *çà et là*, here and there; *là là*, now now! there! there now! *là où*, where; *par là*, that way.

là-bas [la'ba], *adv.* there, over there.

labbe [lab], *n.m.* (*Orn.*) skua.

label [la'bɛl], *n.m.* (*Ind.*) label; brand, mark.

labeur [la'bœːr], *n.m.* labor, work, toil.

laboratoire [labɔra'twaːr], *n.m.* laboratory.

laborieusement [labɔrjøz'mɑ̃], *adv.* laboriously; painfully.

laborieux [labɔ'rjø], *a.* (*fem.* **-euse**) laborious, hard-working.

labour [la'buːr], *n.m.* ploughing, tillage; arable land.

labourable [labu'rabl], *a.* arable.

labourage [labu'raːʒ], *n.m.* tillage, ploughing; dressing.

labourer [labu're], *v.t.* to plough, to till; to dig, to turn up; to dress; to toil through.

laboureur [labu'rœːr], *n.m.* husbandman, plowman.

laboureuse [labu'røːz], *n.f.* tractor plow.

laburne [la'byrn], *n.m.* laburnum.

labyrinthe [labi'rɛ̃ːt], *n.m.* labyrinth, maze.

lac [lak], *n.m.* lake.

laçage [la'saːʒ], *n.m.* lacing.

lacer [la'se], *v.t.* (*conjug. like* COMMENCER) to lace.

lacération [laseru'sjɔ̃], *n.f.* laceration.

lacérer [lase're], *v.t.* (*conjug. like* CÉDER) to lacerate, to tear.

lacet [la'sɛ], *n.m.* lace, shoe-lace; noose; bow-string (*or strangling*); winding, hairpin bend (*of road etc.*); (*pl.*) toils.

lâche [lɑːʃ], *a.* loose, slack; faint-hearted, cowardly; base, mean, shameful.—*n.* coward, craven; dastard.—*adv.* loosely.

lâché [lɑ'ʃe], *a.* slovenly, slipshod.

lâchement [lɑʃ'mɑ̃], *adv.* in a dastardly *or* cowardly manner; loosely; shamefully.

lâcher [lɑ'ʃe], *v.t.* to loosen, to slacken; to let go, to release; to unbind; to blurt out; to let fly, to discharge; to let down (*someone*).—*v.i.* to slacken, to become loose; to slip; (*Spt.*) to give up.

lâcheté [lɑʃ'te], *n.f.* cowardice; baseness, meanness.

lacis [la'si], *n.m.* network.

laconique [lakɔ'nik], *a.* laconic.

laconiquement [lakɔnik'mɑ̃], *adv.* laconically.

lacs [lɑ], *n.m. inv.* string; noose; trap; *lacs d'amour*, love-knot.

lacté [lak'te], *a.* lacteous, milky; *la voie lactée*, the Milky Way.

lacune [la'kyn], *n.f.* gap, break, hiatus, blank.

là-dedans [lad'dɑ̃], *adv.* in there.

là-dehors [lad'ɔːr], *adv.* outside.

là-dessous [la'tsu], *adv.* under there.

là-dessus [la'tsy], *adv.* on that; thereupon.

ladite [la'dit], [LEDIT].

ladre [lɑːdr], *a.* leprous; (*fig.*) mean, sordid, stingy; unfeeling.—*n.m.* (*fem.* -esse) leper; (*fig.*) sordid person.

ladrerie [ludrə'ri], *n.f.* sordid avarice, stinginess.

lagune [la'gyn], *n.f.* lagoon.

là-haut [la'o], *adv.* up there; upstairs.

lai [lɛ]. *n.m.* lay (*poem, song*).

laïc [LAÏQUE].

laid [lɛ], *a.* ugly, unsightly; unseemly, unbecoming.—*n.m.* ugliness; (*fam.* -e) ugly person, creature etc.; naughty boy *or* girl.

laidement [lɛd'mɑ̃], *adv.* in an ugly way.

laideron [lɛd'rɔ̃], *n.m.* (*fem.* -onne) ugly creature.

laideur [lɛ'dœːr], *n.f.* ugliness, uncomeliness; unseemliness.

laie [lɛ], *n.f.* path (*in a forest*).

lainage [lɛ'naːʒ], *n.m.* woollens, woollen goods.

laine [lɛn], *n.f.* wool; *laine filée*, yarn; *laine peignée*, worsted; *tapis de haute laine*, thick-pile carpet; *tout laine*, pure wool.

lainerie [lɛn'ri], *n.f.* woollen goods, woollens; wool trade, shop etc.

laineux [lɛ'nø], *a.* (*fem.* -euse) woolly, fleecy.

lainier [lɛ'nje], *a.* (*fem.* -ière) of wool, woollen.—*n.m.* (*fem.* -ière) wool merchant; wool worker.

laïque or **laïc** [la'ik], *a.* lay, secular.—*n.* layman, lay person.

laisse [lɛːs], *n.f.* string, leash, lead.

laisser [lɛ'se], *v.t.* to leave, to quit; to leave behind, to part with; to bequeath; to permit, to let, to allow; to let alone; to leave off; to give up. **se laisser**, *v.r.* to allow oneself, to let oneself.

laisser-aller [lɛsea'le], *n.m.* unconstraint, negligence; slovenliness; indolence.

laisser-faire [lɛse'fɛːr], *n.m.* non-interference.

laissez-passer [lɛsɛpa'se], *n.m. inv.* permit, leave, pass.

lait [lɛ], *n.m.* milk; *au lait*, with milk; *lait de chaux*, whitewash; *lait de poule*, egg-flip; *petit-lait* or *lait clair*, whey.

laitage [lɛ'taːʒ], *n.m.* milk puddings; milk products.

laiterie [lɛt'ri], *n.f.* dairy, dairy-farm.

laiteux [lɛ'tø], *a.* (*fem.* -euse) lacteous, milky.

laitier [lɛ'tje], *a.* (*fem.* -ière) pertaining to milk; having milk, milch (*of cows*).—*n.m.* (*fem.*-ière) milkman; milkmaid, dairy maid. —*n.f.* (-ière) milch cow; milk truck *or* cart.

laiton [lɛ'tɔ̃], *n.m.* brass, latten.

laitue [lɛ'ty], *n.f.* lettuce.

lama [la'ma], *n.m.* lama (*priest*); llama.

lambeau [lɑ̃'bo], *n.m.* (*pl.* -eaux) shred; rag; fragment, scrap.

lambin [lɑ̃'bɛ̃], *a.* slow, dawdling.—*n.m.* (*fem.* -e) dawdler, slowcoach.

lambiner [lɑ̃bi'ne], *v.i.* to dawdle, to dilly-dally.

lambrequin [lɑ̃brə'kɛ̃], *n.m.* valance, cut-out, pelmet.

lambris [lɑ̃'bri] *n.m.* panelling; wainscot; ceiling; (*fig.*) mansion, palace; canopy.

lambrissage [lɑ̃bri'saːʒ], *n.m.* wainscoting, panelling.

lambrisser [lɑ̃bri'se], *v.t.* to panel, to wainscot.

lame [lam], *n.f.* thin plate, leaf of metal; foil; knife (*of mower etc.*), blade; (*fig.*) sword; wave, billow.

lamé [la'me], *a.* spangled with gold or silver.

lamentable [lamɑ̃'tabl], *a.* lamentable, sad, distressing; pitiful.

lamentablement [lamɑ̃tablə'mɑ̃], *adv.* woefully.

lamentation [lamɑ̃ta'sjɔ̃], *n.f.* lamentation, wailing; lament; whining.

lamenter (se) [səlamɑ̃'te], *v.r.* to lament, to bewail.

laminage [lami'naːʒ], *n.m.* laminating; rolling (*of gold etc.*).

laminer [lami'ne], *v.t.* to laminate, to roll.

laminoir [lami'nwaːr], *n.m.* flattening mill; rolling mill.

lampe [lɑ̃ːp], *n.f.* lamp; (*Rad. Tel.*) tube; *lampe de bord*, (*Motor.*) dashboard light; *lampe de poche*, electric flashlight.

lampion [lɑ̃'pjɔ̃], *n.m.* illumination lamp, fairy-light; Chinese lantern; (*slang*) cocked hat.

lampiste [lɑ̃'pist], *n.m.* lamp maker; lamp lighter.

lampisterie [lɑ̃pis'tri], *n.f.* lamp room.

lamproie [lɑ̃'prwa], *n.f.* lamprey.

lance [lɑ̃ːs], *n.f.* lance, spear; staff, flagstaff; nozzle (*of a fire-hose*).

lance-flammes [lɑ̃s'flam], *n.m. inv.* flame-thrower.

lancement [lɑ̃s'mɑ̃], *n.m.* throwing, darting; launching, launch.

lance-pierres [lɑ̃s'pjɛːr], *n.m. inv.* catapult.

lancer [lɑ̃'se], *v.t.* (*conjug. like* COMMENCER) to fling, to hurl, to throw; to launch; to shoot forth, to dart; to issue (*a warrant etc.*). **se lancer**, *v.r.* to dart, to spring; to rush, to fly; to launch out; (*fig.*) to make a start.

lancette [lɑ̃'sɛt], *n.f.* lancet.

lancier [lɑ̃'sje], *n.m.* lancer.

lancinant [lɑ̃si'nɑ̃], *a.* shooting (*of pains*).

lande [lɑ̃ːd], *n.f.* waste land, moor, heath.

langage [lɑ̃'gaːʒ], *n.m.* language; speech, diction.

lange [lɑ̃ːʒ], *n.m.* diaper; swaddling-cloth; (*pl.*) swaddling clothes.

langoureusement [lɑ̃gurøz'mɑ̃], *adv.* languishingly, languidly.

langoureux [lɑ̃gu'rø], *a.* (*fem.* **-euse**) languishing, languid.

langouste [lɑ̃'gust], *n.f.* spiny lobster.

langoustine [lɑ̃gus'tin], *n.f.* large Brittany prawn; Dublin Bay prawn.

langue [lɑ̃ːg], *n.f.* tongue; language; strip (*of land*); **avoir la langue bien pendue** or **bien affilée**, to have the gift of the gab; **avoir la langue liée**, to be tongue-tied.

languette [lɑ̃'gɛt], *n.f.* small tongue; tongue-like strip; partition; tongue (*of instruments*); index (*of a balance*); tongue (*of shoe*).

langueur [lɑ̃'gœːr], *n.f.* apathy, languor; weakness, weariness; debility.

languir [lɑ̃'giːr], *v.i.* to languish, to pine away; to droop; to linger; to flag.

languissant [lɑ̃gi'sɑ̃], *a.* languid, languishing, pining; (*Comm.*) dull, inactive.

lanière [la'njɛːr], *n.f.* thong, lash.

lanoline [lanɔ'lin], *n.f.* lanoline.

lanterne [lɑ̃'tɛrn], *n.f.* lantern; street lamp; (*Arch.*) skylight; dawdler; **lanterne vénitienne**, Chinese lantern.

lanterner [lɑ̃tɛr'ne], *v.i.* to dawdle, to trifle away one's time.

Laos [laɔs], **le**, *m.* Laos.

laotien [laɔ'sjɛ̃], *a.* (*fem.* **-enne**) Laotian.—*n.m.* (**Laotien**, *fem.* **-enne**) Laotian (*person*).

lapement [lap'mɑ̃], *n.m.* lapping.

laper [la'pe], *v.t., v.i.* to lap (up).

lapidaire [lapi'dɛːr], *a.* and *n.m.* lapidary.

lapidation [lapida'sjɔ̃], *n.f.* lapidation, stoning.

lapider [lapi'de], *v.t.* to lapidate, to stone to death; (*fig.*) to pelt, to abuse.

lapin [la'pɛ̃], *n.m.* rabbit.

lapis [la'piːs], **lapis lazuli** [lapislazy'li], *n.m. inv.* lapis lazuli.

lapon [la'pɔ̃], *a.* (*fem.* **-onne**) Lapp.—*n.m.* Lappish (*language*); (**Lapon**, *fem.* **-onne**) Laplander.

Laponie [lapɔ'ni], **la**, *f.* Lapland.

laps (1) [laps], *n.m.* lapse (*of time*).

laps (2) [laps], *a.* +lapsed, fallen into heresy.

lapsus [lap'syːs], *n.m. inv.* slip, mistake.

laquais [la'kɛ], *n.m. inv.* lackey, footman.

laque [lak], *n.f.* lacquer, lac, lake (*paint*).—*n.m.* lacquer.

laquelle [la'kɛl], [LEQUEL].

laquer [la'ke], *v.t.* to lacquer, to japan.

larcin [lar'sɛ̃], *n.m.* larceny, pilfering; petty theft; **larcin littéraire**, plagiarism.

lard [laːr], *n.m.* fat (*esp. of pigs*); bacon; **flèche de lard**, flitch of bacon; **tranche de lard**, rasher of bacon.

larder [lar'de], *v.t.* to lard; to pink, to run through, to pierce.

lardon [lar'dɔ̃], *n.m.* thin slice of bacon; (*fam.*) child, kid, brat.

large [larʒ], *a.* broad, wide; large, great, extensive; generous, liberal; lax, loose.—*n.m.* breadth, width; offing, open sea; **au large !** keep off! sheer off! **au large de Dieppe**, off Dieppe.

largement [larʒə'mɑ̃], *adv.* largely, abundantly; fully; liberally.

largesse [lar'ʒɛs], *n.f.* largess, bounty, munificence.

largeur [lar'ʒœːr], *n.f.* breadth, width; amplitude.

larme [larm], *n.f.* tear; drop; **fondre en larmes**, to burst into tears.

larmoiement [larmwa'mɑ̃], *n.m.* watering of the eyes.

larmoyant [larmwa'jɑ̃], *a.* weeping, in tears; tearful, whining.

larmoyer [larmwa'je], *v.i.* (*conjug. like* EMPLOYER) to shed tears; to whine, to snivel; to water (*of the eyes*).

larron [la'rɔ̃], *n.m.* thief.

larve [larv], *n.f.* larva, grub.

laryngite [larɛ̃'ʒit], *n.f.* laryngitis.

larynx [la'rɛ̃ːks], *n.m. inv.* larynx.

las! (1) [lɑ], *int.* alas!

las (2) [lɑ], *a.* (*fem.* **lasse**) tired, weary, fatigued; bored; disgusted.

lascif [la'sif], *a.* (*fem.* **-cive**) lascivious, lewd, wanton.

lascivement [lasiv'mɑ̃], *adv.* lasciviously.

lassant [lɑ'sɑ̃], *a.* tiresome, wearisome, tedious.

lasser [lɑ'se], *v.t.* to tire, to weary, to fatigue, to wear out. **se lasser**, *v.r.* to tire, to grow tired, to be wearied.

lassitude [losi'tyd], *n.f.* lassitude, weariness.

lasso [la'so], *n.m.* lasso.

latent [la'tɑ̃], *a.* latent, concealed, secret.

latéral [late'ral], *a.* (*m. pl.* **-aux**) lateral, side.

latéralement [lateral'mɑ̃], *adv.* laterally.

latin [la'tɛ̃], *a.* Latin.—*n.m.* Latin (*language*); **latin de cuisine**, dog Latin.—*n.m.* (**Latin**, *fem.* **-ine**) Latin (*person*).

latitude [lati'tyd], *n.f.* latitude; room, space, margin.

latte [lat], *n.f.* lath.

latter [la'te], *v.t.* to lath.

lattis [la'ti], *n.m.* lathing, lath-work; laths.

laudanum [loda'nɔm], *n.m.* laudanum.

laudatif [loda'tif], *a.* (*fem.* **-tive**) laudatory.

lauréat [lɔre'a], *a.* laureate.—*n.m.* (*fem.* **-e**) prize-winner.

laurier [lɔ'rje], *n.m.* laurel, bay tree; (*fig.*) glory, honor.

lavable [la'vabl], *a.* washable.

lavabo [lava'bo], *n.m.* wash-basin; wash-stand; (*pl.*) conveniences.

lavage [la'vaːʒ], *n.m.* washing; dilution.

lavande [la'vɑ̃ːd], *n.f.* lavender.

lavandière [lavɑ̃'djɛːr], *n.f.* laundress, washerwoman; (*Orn.*) gray wagtail.

lavasse [la'vas], *n.f.* washy soup *or* wine.

lave [laːv], *n.f.* lava.

lavé [la've], *a.* washed out, faint.

lave-dos [lav′do], *n.m. inv.* back brush.
lavement [lav′mã], *n.m.* (*Med.*) enema.
laver [la′ve], *v.t.* to wash, to cleanse; to purify; to expiate; *laver à grande eau*, to swill; *laver la vaisselle*, to wash up; *machine à laver*, washing machine. **se laver**, *v.r.* to wash, to wash oneself; to clear oneself (*of an accusation*).
lavette [la′vɛt], *n.f.* dish mop.
laveur [la′vœːr], *n.m.* (*fem.* **-euse**) washer, scourer; *laveuse de vaisselle*, scullery maid.
lavoir [la′vwaːr], *n.m.* wash house.
laxatif [laksa′tif], *a.* (*fem.* **-tive**) laxative, opening.—*n.m.* laxative.
layette [lɛ′jɛt], *n.f.* box; baby's trousseau *or* outfit.
le [lǝ], *art.* and *pron. m.* the; him, it; so; *je le crois*, I think so.
lécher [le′ʃe], *v.t.* (*conjug. like* CÉDER) to lick; to lick up; (*fig.*) to labor, to polish, to elaborate, to overdo; *lécher les vitrines*, to go window-shopping.
leçon [lǝ′sɔ̃], *n.f.* lesson; reading (*of a text*).
lecteur [lɛk′tœːr], *n.m.* (*fem.* **-trice**) reader, lector.
lecture [lɛk′tyːr], *n.f.* reading; perusal.
ledit [lǝ′di], *a.* (*fem.* **ladite**, *pl.* **lesdit(e)s**) the (afore)said, the same.
légal [le′gal], *a.* (*m. pl.* **-aux**) legal, lawful, legitimate.
légalement [legal′mã], *adv.* legally, lawfully.
légaliser [legali′ze], *v.t.* to legalize.
légalité [legali′te], *n.f.* legality, lawfulness.
légataire [lega′tɛːr], *n.* legatee.
légation [lega′sjɔ̃], *n.f.* legateship; legation.
légendaire [leʒã′dɛːr], *a.* and *n.m.* legendary.
légende [le′ʒãːd], *n.f.* legend; inscription; caption; key (*to map etc.*).
léger [le′ʒe], *a.* (*fem.* **-ère**) light; slight; buoyant; fleet, fast; nimble; fickle; faint; thoughtless.
légèrement [leʒɛr′mã], *adv.* lightly, slightly; swiftly; thoughtlessly.
légèreté [leʒɛr′te], *n.f.* lightness; swiftness; fickleness; frivolity; thoughtlessness.
légiférer [leʒife′re], *v.i.* (*conjug. like* CÉDER) to legislate.
légion [le′ʒjɔ̃], *n.f.* legion; great number, host.
légionnaire [leʒjɔ′nɛːr], *n.m.* legionary; member of the Legion of Honor; soldier of the Foreign Legion.
législateur [leʒisla′tœːr], *a.* (*fem.* **-trice**) legislative, lawgiving.—*n.m.* (*fem.* **-trice**) legislator.
législatif [leʒisla′tif], *a.* (*fem.* **-tive**) legislative.
législation [leʒislɑ′sjɔ̃], *n.f.* legislation.
législature [leʒisla′.yːr], *n.f.* legislature.
légitime [leʒi′tim], *a.* lawful, legitimate, rightful; justifiable.
légitimement [leʒitim′mã], *adv.* legitimately, lawfully; justifiably.
légitimer [leʒiti′me], *v.t.* to legitimate; to justify; to recognize.
légitimité [leʒitimi′te], *n.f.* legitimacy, lawfulness.
legs [lɛ], *n.m.* legacy, bequest.
léguer [le′ge], *v.t.* (*conjug. like* CÉDER) to leave by will; to bequeath.
légume [le′gym], *n.m.* vegetable.—*n.f. pl.* (*fam.*) *les grosses légumes*, the bigwigs.

légumier [legy′mje], *a.* (*fem.* **-ière**) of vegetables.—*n.m.* vegetable dish.
lendemain [lãd′mɛ̃], *n.m.* morrow, next day, day after.
lent [lã], *a.* slow, tardy; backward; sluggish, slack.
lentement [lãt′mã], *adv.* slowly, tardily; sluggishly.
lenteur [lã′tœːr], *n.f.* slowness; tardiness.
lenticulaire [lãtiky′lɛːr], **lenticulé** [lãtiky′le], *a.* lenticular.
lentille [lã′tiːj], *n.f.* lentil; lens; (*pl.*) freckles; *lentille d'eau*, duckweed.
léonin [leɔ′nɛ̃], *a.* leonine.
léopard [leɔ′paːr], *n.m.* leopard.
lèpre [lɛpr], *n.f.* leprosy.
lépreux [le′prø], *a.* (*fem.* **-euse**) leprous.—*n.m.* (*fem.* **-euse**) leper.
léproserie [lepro′zri], *n.f.* leper hospital.
lequel [lǝ′kɛl], *pron. m.* (*fem.* **laquelle**, *m. pl.* **lesquels**, *f. pl.* **lesquelles**) who, whom, that, which; (*inter.*) which one, which?
les [le], *art.* and *pron. pl.* the; them.
lèse-majesté [lɛzmaʒɛs′te], *n.f.* high treason, lese-majesty.
léser [le′ze], *v.t.* (*conjug. like* CÉDER) to wrong; to injure, to hurt.
lésine [le′zin], *n.f.* niggardliness, stinginess.
lésiner [lezi′ne], *v.i.* to be stingy *or* mean; to haggle.
lésinerie [lezin′ri], *n.f.* stinginess, meanness.
lésion [le′zjɔ̃], *n.f.* (*Law*) wrong, injury; (*Surg.*) lesion.
lessive [lɛ′siːv], *n.f.* wash, linen washed *or* to be washed, washing.
leste [lɛst], *a.* brisk, nimble, active; light; smart; sharp; improper, free.
lestement [lɛst′mã], *adv.* briskly; cleverly; flippantly; freely.
lester [lɛs′te], *v.t.* to ballast. **se lester**, *v.r.* (*fam.*) to take in ballast; to line one's stomach.
léthargie [letar′ʒi], *n.f.* lethargy.
léthargique [letar′ʒik], *a.* lethargic.
lette [lɛt], **letton** [lɛ′tɔ̃] (*fem.* **-onne**), *a.* Latvian.—*n.m.* Latvian (*language*); (**Lette, Letton,** *fem.* **-onne**) Latvian (*person*).
Lettonie [lɛtɔ′ni], **la,** *f.* Latvia.
lettre [lɛtr], *n.f.* letter, note; (*Print.*) character, type; (*pl.*) literature, letters; *les belles-lettres*, humanities; *lettre de change*, bill of exchange; *lettre d'envoi*, covering letter; *lettre de voiture*, way-bill.
lettré [le′tre], *a.* cultured, literate, well-read; literary.—*n.m.* (*fem.* **-ée**) scholar.
leur [lœːr], *a. poss.* their.—*poss. pron. le leur, la leur* *or* *les leurs*, theirs.—*pers. pron.* to them, them.
leurre [lœːr], *n.m.* lure, decoy; bait; snare, trap.
leurrer [lœ′re], *v.t.* to lure, to entice; to decoy; to ensnare. **se leurrer**, *v.r.* to delude oneself.
levage [lǝ′vaːʒ], *n.m.* raising, lifting.
levain [lǝ′vɛ̃], *n.m.* leaven; (*fig.*) germ.
levant [lǝ′vã], *a.* rising.—*n.m.* east; rising sun; Levant.
levantin [lǝvã′tɛ̃], *a.* Levantine.—*n.m.* (**Levantin,** *fem.* **-ine**) Levantine (*person*).
levé [lǝ′ve], *a.* lifted up, raised; up, out of bed.

levée [lə've], *n.f.* raising, lifting; levying; gathering (*crop, fruit etc.*); collection (*post-office*); embankment; swell (*of the sea*); (*Cards*) trick.

lever [lə've], *v.t.* (*conjug. like* AMENER) to lift, to lift up, to raise; to heave; to pull up; to weigh (*anchor*); to take away; to take out; to collect; to levy.—*v.i.* to come up; to spring up, to rise. **se lever,** *v.r.* to rise, to get up; to stand up; to heave (*of the sea*); to clear up (*of the weather*).

lever [lə've], *n.m.* rising, getting up; levee (*of king*).

levier [lə'vje], *n.m.* lever; crowbar, handspike.

levraut [lə'vro], *n.m.* leveret, young hare.

lèvre [lɛːvr], *n.f.* lip; rim.

lévrier [levri'e], *n.m.* greyhound.

levure [lə'vyːr], *n.f.* yeast.

lexique [lɛk'sik], *n.m.* lexicon; abridged dictionary.

lézard [le'zaːr], *n.m.* lizard.

lézarde [le'zard], *n.f.* crevice, crack, chink.

lézardé [lezar'de], *a.* cracked (*of walls etc.*).

lézarder [lezar'de], *v.t.* to crack (*walls etc.*). **se lézarder,** *v.r.* to crack, to become cracked.

liais [ljɛ], *n.m.* lias; blue limestone.

liaison [ljɛ'zɔ̃], *n.f.* joining; connection, acquaintance; intimacy; (*Mil.*) liaison.

liane [ljan], *n.f.* liana, tropical creeper.

liant [ljɑ̃], *a.* supple, flexible; affable, sociable.—*n.m.* suppleness; sociability; gentleness.

liard [ljaːr], *n.m.* liard (*half-farthing*).

liasse [ljas], *n.f.* bundle, file (*of papers*); wad (*of banknotes*).

Liban [li'bɑ̃], **le,** *m.* Lebanon.

libanais [liba'nɛ], *a.* Lebanese.—*n.m.* (**Libanais,** *fem.* **-aise**) Lebanese (*person*).

libation [liba'sjɔ̃], *n.f.* libation; (*fig.*) potation.

libelle [li'bɛl], *n.m.* libel, lampoon.

libellé [libɛl'le], *a.* drawn up, specified.—*n.m.* wording, contents.

libellule [libɛl'lyl], *n.f.* dragon-fly.

libéral [libe'ral], *a.* (*m. pl.* **-aux**) liberal, generous, bountiful; (*Polit.*) liberal.

libéralement [liberal'mɑ̃], *adv.* liberally, bountifully, generously.

libéralisme [libera'lism], *n.m.* liberalism.

libéralité [liberali'te], *n.f.* generosity, open-handedness.

libérateur [libera'tœːr], *n.m.* (*fem.* **-trice**) deliverer, liberator, rescuer.

libération [libera'sjɔ̃], *n.f.* liberation, deliverance; rescue, discharge.

libéré [libe're], *a.* liberated discharged.

libérer [libe're], *v.t.* (*conjug. like* CÉDER) to liberate, to free; to discharge. **se libérer,** *v.r.* to free oneself, to clear oneself (*de*); to pay off one's debts.

Libéria [libe'rja], **le,** *m.* Liberia.

libérien [libe'rjɛ̃], *a.* (*fem.* **-enne**) Liberian.—*n.m.* (**Libérien,** *fem.* **-enne**) Liberian (*person*).

liberté [liber'te], *n.f.* liberty, freedom, ease.

libertin [liber'tɛ̃], *a.* libertine, licentious; dissolute.—*n.m.* (*fem.* **-e**) libertine, rake.

libertinage [liberti'naːʒ], *n.m.* libertinism, debauchery.

libraire [li'brɛːr], *n.* bookseller; *libraire-éditeur,* publisher and bookseller.

librairie [librɛ'ri], *n.f.* book trade; bookseller's shop.

libre [libr], *a.* free; at liberty; independent; undisciplined, unconfined; bold, broad; exempt; irregular (*of verse*).

libre-échange [librɛ'ʃɑ̃ːʒ], *n.m.* free trade.

libre-échangiste [librɛʃɑ̃'ʒist], *n.m.* (*pl.* **libre-échangistes**) free-trader.

librement [librə'mɑ̃], *adv.* freely, without restraint; boldly.

librettiste [librɛ'tist], *n.m.* librettist.

Libye [li'bi], **la,** *f.* Libya.

libyen [li'bjɛ̃], *a.* (*fem.* **-enne**) Libyan.—*n.m.* (**Libyen,** *fem.* **-enne**) Libyan (*person*).

lice [lis], *n.f.* lists, tilt yard.

licence [li'sɑ̃ːs], *n.f.* license, leave, permission; licentiousness; licentiate's degree.

licencié [lisɑ̃'sje], *a.* licentiate; (*C*) *épicier licencié,* licensed grocer.—*n.m.* (*fem.* **-ée**) licenciate.

licenciement [lisɑ̃si'mɑ̃], *n.m.* disbanding.

licencier [lisɑ̃'sje], *v.t.* to disband (*troops*); to declare redundant, to lay off; to dismiss.

licencieusement [lisɑ̃sjøz'mɑ̃], *adv.* licentiously, dissolutely.

licencieux [lisɑ̃'sjø], *a.* (*fem.* **-euse**) licentious, dissolute.

licite [li'sit], *a.* licit, lawful, allowable.

licitement [lisit'mɑ̃], *adv.* lawfully, licitly.

licol [LICOU].

licorne [li'kɔrn], *n.f.* unicorn.

licou [li'ku], **licol** [li'kɔl], *n.m.* halter.

licteur [lik'tœːr], *n.m.* (*Rom. Ant.*) lictor.

lie [li], *n.f.* lees, dregs; (*fig.*) scum, refuse.

liège [ljɛːʒ], *n.m.* cork; cork tree.

lien [ljɛ̃], *n.m.* bond, tie, link; (*pl.*) bonds, shackles.

lier [lje], *v.t.* to fasten, to tie; to bind, to tie up; to join, to connect (*avec*); to engage in; (*Mus.*) to slur; to thicken (*a sauce etc.*). **se lier,** *v.r.* to become acquainted; to thicken (*of sauce etc.*).

lierre [ljɛːr], *n.m.* ivy.

lieu [ljø], *n.m.* (*pl.* **lieux**) place, spot; position; cause; (*pl.*) premises, apartments; *au lieu de,* instead of; *avoir lieu,* to take place; *lieu commun,* commonplace.

lieue [ljø], *n.f.* league (*4 kilometres, 2½ miles*).

lieur [ljœːr], *n.m.* (*fem.* **-euse**) (*Agric.*) binder (*person*).—*n.f.* (**-euse**) binder (*machine*).

lieutenance [ljøt'nɑ̃ːs], *n.f.* lieutenancy.

lieutenant [ljøt'nɑ̃], *n.m.* lieutenant; right-hand man.

lièvre [ljɛːvr], *n.m.* hare.

liftier [lif'tje], *n.m.* (*fem.* **-ière**) elevator operator.

ligament [liga'mɑ̃], *n.m.* ligament.

ligature [liga'tyːr], *n.f.* ligature.

ligaturer [ligaty're], *v.t.* to ligature, to splice.

lignage [li'ɲaːʒ], *n.m.* lineage.

ligne [liɲ], *n.f.* line; row; path, way; cord; fishing line; order.

lignée [li'ɲe], *n.f.* issue, progeny, offspring.

ligoter [ligɔ'te], *v.t.* to bind, to tie up.

ligue [lig], *n.f.* league, confederacy.

liguer [li'ge], *v.t.* to unite in a league. **se liguer,** *v.r.* to league, to combine.

ligueur [li'gœːr], *n.m.* (*fem.* **-euse**) leaguer; plotter.

lilas [li'la], *a. inv.* lilac-colored. —*n.m.* lilac.

lilliputien [lilipy'sjɛ̃], *a.* (*fem.* **-enne**) Lilliputian.

limace [li'mas], *n.f.* slug; Archimedean screw.

limaçon [lima'sɔ̃], *n.m.* snail.

limbe [lɛ̃:b], *n.m.* (*Math., Bot. etc.*) limb; (*Astron.*) border, halo; (*pl.*) limbo.

lime (1) [lim], *n.f.* file.

lime (2) [lim], *n.f.* lime, citron.

limer [li'me], *v.t.* to file, to smooth.

limeur [li'mœ:r], *n.m.* (*fem.* **-euse**) filer.— *n.f.* (**-euse**) finishing tool *or* machine.

limier [li'mje], *n.m.* bloodhound; (*fig.*) police spy, detective.

liminaire [limi'nɛ:r], *a.* prefatory.

limitatif [limita'tif], *a.* (*fem.* **-tive**) limiting, restrictive.

limitation [limita'sjɔ̃], *n.f.* limitation.

limite [li'mit], *n.f.* limit, boundary; border; landmark.

limiter [limi'te], *v.t.* to limit, to bound; to confine.

limitrophe [limi'trɔf], *a.* neighboring, bordering.

limon [li'mɔ̃], *n.m.* silt, ooze, mud; shaft (*of a carriage*); sour lime (*fruit*).

limonade [limɔ'nad], *n.f.* lemonade.

limonadier [limɔna'dje], *n.m.* (*fem.* **-ière**) seller of lemonade.

limoneux [limɔ'nø], *a.* (*fem.* **-euse**) muddy, turbid, slimy; alluvial.

limonier [limɔ'nje], *n.m.* carriage horse; lime tree.

limonière [limɔ'njɛ:r], *n.f.* pair of shafts (*of wagon etc.*); wagon with two shafts.

limousin [limu'zɛ̃], *n.m.* stonemason.

limousine [limu'zin], *n.f.* limousine (*car*); coarse woollen cloak.

limpide [lɛ̃'pid], *a.* limpid, clear.

limpidité [lɛ̃pidi'te], *n.f.* limpidity.

lin [lɛ̃], *n.m.* flax; **graine de lin**, linseed; **huile de lin**, linseed oil; **toile de lin**, linen cloth.

linceul [lɛ̃'sœl], *n.m.* winding-sheet, shroud.

linéaire [line'ɛ:r], *a.* linear.

linéal [line'al], *a.* (*m. pl.* **-aux**) lineal, in a direct line.

linéament [linea'mã], *n.m.* lineament, feature; (*fig.*) trace, vestige.

linge [lɛ̃:ʒ], *n.m.* linen; piece, rag.

linger [lɛ̃'ʒe], *n.m.* (*fem.* **-ère**) linen dealer; maker of linen goods; seamstress (*of same*). —*n.f.* (**-ère**) wardrobe woman.

lingerie [lɛ̃'ʒri], *n.f.* linen trade; linen room; linen goods.

lingot [lɛ̃'go], *n.m.* ingot; bullion.

lingue [lɛ̃:g], *n.f.* (*Ichth.*) ling.

linguiste [lɛ̃'gɥist], *n.* linguist.

linguistique [lɛ̃gɥis'tik], *a.* linguistic.—*n.f.* linguistics.

linier [li'nje], *a.* (*fem.* **-ière**) of flax *or* linen.— *n.f.* (**-ière**) flax field.

linoléum [linɔle'ɔm], *n.m.* linoleum.

linon [li'nɔ̃], *n.m.* lawn (*fine linen*).

linot [li'no], *n.m.*, **linotte** [li'nɔt], *n.f.* linnet.

linotype [linɔ'tip], *n.f.* linotype.

linotypiste [linɔti'pist], *n.* linotype operator.

linteau [lɛ̃'to], *n.m.* (*pl.* **-eaux**) lintel.

lion [ljɔ̃], *n.m.* (*fem.* **lionne**) lion, lioness; (*fig.*) a bold, brave fellow.

lionceau [ljɔ̃'so], *n.m.* (*pl.* **-eaux**) young lion, lion's cub.

lippe [lip], *n.f.* thick lower lip; pouting lip.

lippu [li'py], *a.* thick-lipped.

liquéfaction [likefak'sjɔ̃], *n.f.* liquefaction.

liquéfiable [like'fjabl], *a.* liquefiable.

liquéfier [like'fje], *v.t.* and **se liquéfier**, *v.r.* to liquefy.

liqueur [li'kœ:r], *n.f.* liquid; liqueur, cordial; (*Chem.*) spirit.

liquidateur [likida'tœ:r], *n.m.* liquidator.

liquidation [likida'sjɔ̃], *n.f.* liquidation; settlement (*of debts etc.*); winding up (*of a business*); clearance sale.

liquide [li'kid], *a.* liquid; clear, net (*of money*).—*n.m.* liquid, fluid; drink.

liquider [liki'de], *v.t.* to liquidate, to settle; to wind up; to sell off; (*fam.*) to get rid of.

liquidité [likidi'te], *n.f.* liquidity, fluidity.

liquoreux [likɔ'rø], *a.* (*fem.* **-euse**) luscious, sweet.

liquoriste [likɔ'rist], *n.m.* wine and spirit merchant.

lire [li:r], *v.t. irr.* to read, to peruse, to study.

lis [lis], *n.m.* lily.

liseré [lizə're], *n.m.* piping; border, edge.

liserer [lizə're], *v.t. (conjug. like* CÉDER*)* to trim (*a dress etc.*) with piping.

liseron [liz'rɔ̃], **liset** [li'zɛ], *n.m.* (*Bot.*) convolvulus.

liseur [li'zœ:r], *n.m.* (*fem.* **-euse**) reader.

lisibilité [lizibili'te], *n.f.* legibility, readableness.

lisible [li'zibl], *a.* legible, readable.

lisiblement [liziblə'mã], *adv.* legibly.

lisière [li'zjɛ:r], *n.f.* selvedge, edge (*of cloth etc.*); border, verge, outskirts.

lissage [li'sa:ʒ], *n.m.* smoothing, glossing.

lisse (1) [lis], *a.* smooth; sleek; glossy.—*n.m.* smoothness, gloss.

lisse (2) [lis], *n.f.* rail, railing (*of ship*).

lisser [li'se], *v.t.* to smooth, to polish.

lisseur [li'sœ:r], *n.m.* (*fem.* **-euse**) polisher.

liste [list], *n.f.* list, roll; catalogue; schedule.

lit [li], *n.m.* bed; layer (*of clay, mortar*); direction, set (*of tide, current*); (*fig.*) marriage.

litanie [lita'ni], *n.f.* (*fig.*) rigmarole; (*pl.*) litany.

litée [li'te], *n.f.* litter (*of animals*).

literie [li'tri], *n.f.* bedding.

lithographe [litɔ'graf], *n.m.* lithographer.

lithographie [litɔgra'fi], *n.f.* lithography; lithograph.

lithographier [litɔgra'fje], *v.t.* to lithograph.

lithographique [litɔgra'fik] *a.* lithographic.

Lithuanie [LITUANIE].

lithuanien [LITUANIEN].

litière [li'tjɛ:r], *n.f.* stable litter; litter (*for carrying sick persons etc.*).

litigant [liti'gã], *a.* litigant.

litige [li'ti:ʒ], *n.m.* litigation, legal dispute; (*fig.*) strife.

litigieux [liti'sjø], *a.* (*fem.* **-euse**) litigious, given to lawsuits.

litre [litr], *n.m.* litre (*1.76 pints*).

littéraire [lite'rɛ:r], *a.* literary; **propriété littéraire**, copyright.

littérairement [literɛr'mã], *adv.* in a literary manner *or* way.

littéral [lite'ral], *a.* (*m. pl.* **-aux**) literal.

littéralement [literal'mã], *adv.* literally, word for word.

littérateur [litera'tœ:r], *n.m.* literary man, author, man of letters.

littérature [litera'ty:r], *n.f.* literature.

littoral [lit⊃'ral], *a.* (*m. pl.* **-aux**) littoral, coastal.—*n.m.* littoral, seaboard.
Lituanie [litɥa'ni], **la,** *f.* Lithuania.
lituanien [litɥa'njɛ̃], *a.* Lithuanian.—*n.m.* Lithuanian (*language*); (**Lituanien**, *fem.* **-enne**) Lithuanian (*person*).
liturgie [lityr'ʒi], *n.f.* liturgy.
liturgique [lityr'ʒik], *a.* liturgic, liturgical.
liturgiste [lityr'ʒist], *n.* liturgist.
livide [li'vid], *a.* livid, ghastly.
lividité [lividi'te], *n.f.* lividness.
livrable [li'vrabl], *a.* deliverable.
livraison [livrɛ'zɔ̃], *n.f.* delivery (*of goods*); part, number, issue (*of a magazine etc.*).
livre (1) [li:vr], *n.m.* book; register, account book.
livre (2) [li:vr], *n.f.* pound (*1. 1 lb. avoirdupois*); *livre sterling*, pound sterling.
livrée [li'vre], *n.f.* livery; livery servants.
livrer [li'vre], *v.t.* to deliver; to give up, to hand over; to betray (*a secret*). **se livrer**, *v.r.* to give oneself up (*à*); to surrender; to devote oneself; to entrust oneself to; to indulge in (*a vice*).
livret [li'vrɛ], *n.m.* little book; memorandum book; libretto.
livreur [li'vrœ:r], *n.m.* (*fem.* **-euse**) deliverer (*of goods*); delivery man, van man.—*n.f.* (**-euse**) delivery van.
lobe [lɔb], *n.m.* lobe (*of ear, liver etc.*).
lobélie [lɔbe'li], *n.f.* (*Bot.*) lobelia.
local [lɔ'kal], *a.* (*m. pl.* **-aux**) local.—*n.m.* place, premises; quarters.
localement [lɔkal'mã], *adv.* locally.
localisation [lɔkaliza'sjɔ̃], *n.f.* localization.
localiser [lɔkali'ze], *v.t.* to localize. **se localiser**, *v.r.* to become localized.
localité [lɔkali'te], *n.f.* locality.
locataire [lɔka'tɛ:r], *n.* tenant, lodger, occupier.
location [lɔka'sjɔ̃], *n.f.* letting out; hiring, renting; (*Theat.*) booking of seat.
lock-out [lɔ'kaut], *n.m. inv.* lock-out.
lock-outer [lɔkau'te], *v.t.* to lock-out.
locomoteur [lɔkɔmɔ'tœ:r], *a.* (*fem.* **-trice**) locomotor.
locomotif [lɔkɔmɔ'tif], *a.* (*fem.* **-tive**) locomotive.—*n.f.* (**-tive**) locomotive, engine.
locomotion [lɔkɔmɔ'sjɔ̃], *n.f.* locomotion.
locomotive [LOCOMOTIF].
locuste [lɔ'kyst], *n.f.* locust.
locution [lɔky'sjɔ̃], *n.f.* locution, expression, form of speech; term, phrase.
logarithme [lɔga'ritm], *n.m.* logarithm.
loge [lɔ:ʒ], *n.f.* hut; lodge; (*Theat.*) box, dressing room; stand, stall; (*kennel*); booth.
logeable [lɔ'ʒabl], *a.* tenantable, fit to live in.
logement [lɔʒ'mã], *n.m.* lodgings; dwelling; house-room, accommodation; quarters.
loger [lɔ'ʒe], *v.t.* (*conjug. like* MANGER) to lodge; to put up, to accommodate, to house; to quarter; to stable.—*v.i.* to lodge, to live; to put up. **se loger**, *v.r.* to lodge, to take up one's abode; to lodge itself.
logette [lɔ'ʒɛt], *n.f.* small lodge.
logeur [lɔ'ʒœ:r], *n.m.* (*fem.* **-euse**) lodging-house keeper.
logicien [lɔʒi'sjɛ̃], *n.m.* (*fem.* **-enne**) logician.
logique [lɔ'ʒik], *a.* logical.—*n.f.* logic.
logiquement [lɔʒik'mã], *adv.* logically.
logis [lɔ'ʒi], *n.m.* (*rare*) house, dwelling.

loi [lwa], *n.f.* law, statute, act; rule.
loin [lwɛ̃], *adv.* far, at a distance; remote, distant; *au loin*, far away, far and wide; *de loin*, from afar, from a distance; *de loin en loin*, at long intervals.
lointain [lwɛ̃'tɛ̃], *a.* remote, far off, distant.—*n.m.* distance, distant prospect.
loir [lwa:r], *n.m.* dormouse.
loisible [lwa'zibl], *a.* optional, lawful, allowable.
loisir [lwa'zi:r], *n.m.* leisure, spare time.
lombes [lɔ̃:b], *n.m. pl.* (*Anat.*) lumbar region, loins.
londonien [lɔ̃dɔ'njɛ̃], *a.* (*fem.* **-enne**) of or pertaining to London.—*n.m.* (**Londonien**, *fem.* **-enne**) Londoner.
Londres ['lɔ̃dra], *f.* London.
long [lɔ̃], *a.* (*fem.* **longue**) long; slow, tedious; diffuse, drawn out.—*n.m.* length; extent; (*tout*) *au long*, in full; *de long en large*, up and down, to and fro.—*n.f. à la longue*, in the long run.—*adv.* much, great deal.
longanimité [lɔ̃ganimi'te], *n.f.* longanimity, forbearance, long-suffering.
long-courrier [lɔ̃ku'rje], *n.m.* (*pl.* **-courriers**) ocean-going ship.
longe (1) [lɔ̃:ʒ], *n.f.* tether, leading-rein; thong.
longe (2) [lɔ̃:ʒ], *n.f. longe de veau*, loin of veal.
longer [lɔ̃'ʒe], *v.t.* (*conjug. like* MANGER) to go, to run along; to skirt; to extend along.
longévité [lɔ̃ʒevi'te], *n.f.* longevity.
longitude [lɔ̃ʒi'tyd], *n.f.* longitude.
longitudinal [lɔ̃ʒitydi'nal], *a.* (*m. pl.* **-aux**) longitudinal.
longitudinalement [lɔ̃ʒitydinal'mã], *adv.* lengthwise.
longtemps [lɔ̃'tã], *adv.* long, a long while.
longuement [lɔ̃g'mã], *adv.* long, a long time, for a great while.
longueur [lɔ̃'gœ:r], *n.f.* length, extent in time; slowness; prolixity.
longue-vue [lɔ̃g'vy], *n.f.* (*pl.* **longues-vues**) telescope, spy-glass.
lopin [lɔ'pɛ̃], *n.m.* small piece or share; *lopin de terre*, plot of ground.
loquace [lɔ'kwas], *a.* loquacious, talkative.
loquacement [lɔkwas'mã], *adv.* talkatively, loquaciously.
loquacité [lɔkwasi'te], *n.f.* loquacity, talkativeness.
loque [lɔk], *n.f.* rag, tatter.
loquet [lɔkɛ], *n.m.* latch; *fermé au loquet*, on the latch.
loqueteau [lɔk'to], *n.m.* (*pl.* **-eaux**) small latch.
loqueteux [lɔk'to], *a.* (*fem.* **-euse**) in rags.—*n.m.* (*fem.* **-euse**) ragged person.
lorgner [lɔr'ɲe], *v.t.* to leer at, to ogle.
lorgnette [lɔr'ɲɛt], *n.f.* field or opera glasses.
lorgnon [lɔr'ɲɔ̃], *n.m.* (*sometimes pl.*) eyeglasses; lorgnette.
lorry [lɔ'ri], *n.m.* (*Rail.*) trolley, repair or construction car.
lors [lɔ:r], *adv.* then; *depuis* or *dès lors*, from that time, since then; *lors de*, at the time of; *lors même que*, even though; *pour lors*, then, at the time; so, therefore.
lorsque [lɔrsk, 'lɔrskə], *conj.* when; at the time *or* moment of.

losange [lɔ'zɑ̃:ʒ], *n.m.* diamond-shape, lozenge.

losangé [lɔzɑ̃'ʒe], *a.* in lozenges.

lot [lo], *n.m.* lot; portion, share; prize (*in a lottery*); (*fig.*) fate.

loterie [lɔ'tri], *n.f.* lottery, raffle.

lotion [lo'sjɔ̃], *n.f.* lotion; ablution.

lotir [lɔ'ti:r], *v.t.* to divide into lots, to portion off.

lotissement [lɔtis'mɑ̃], *n.m.* dividing into lots; building plot.

loto [lɔ'to], *n.m.* lotto (*game of chance*); bingo.

lotus [lɔ'ty:s], *n.m. inv.* lotus.

louable [lwabl], *a.* laudable, praiseworthy, commendable.

louablement [lwablə'mɑ̃], *adv.* commendably.

louage [lwa:ʒ], *n.m.* letting out, hiring, renting; hire.

louange [lwɑ̃:ʒ], *n.f.* praise, commendation, eulogy.

louanger [lwɑ̃'ʒe], *v.t.* (*conjug. like* MANGER) to praise, to flatter, to extol.

louangeur [lwɑ̃'ʒœ:r], *a.* (*fem.* **-euse**) laudatory, eulogistic.—*n.m.* (*fem.* **-euse**) praiser, flatterer.

louche (1) [luʃ], *n.f.* (*soup*) ladle; scoop; countersink bit.

louche (2) [luʃ], *a.* squint-eyed; dubious; ambiguous; suspicious, shady.

loucher [lu'ʃe], *v.i.* to squint.

loucheur [lu'ʃœ:r], *a.* (*fem.* **-euse**) squinting.—*n.m.* (*fem.* **-euse**) squinter.

louer (1) [lwe], *v.t.* to let *or* hire out; to lease, to rent; to hire; to book. **se louer** (1), *v.r.* to hire oneself out; to be let *or* rented.

louer (2) [lwe], *v.t.* to praise, to commend, to extol. **se louer** (2), *v.r.* to praise oneself; to rejoice.

loueur [lwœ:r], *n.m.* (*fem.* **-euse**) hirer, letter out.

lougre [lugr], *n.m.* lugger.

Louis [lwi], *m.* Lewis, Louis.

louis [lwi], *n.m. inv.* louis (*a French coin worth 20 gold francs*).

loup [lu], *n.m.* wolf; black velvet mask.

loup-cervier [luscr'vje] *n.m.* (*pl.* **loups-cerviers**) lynx; (*fig.*) profiteer.

loupe (1) [lup], *n.f.* magnifying glass.

loupe (2) [lup], *n.f.* wen; gnarl (*on trees*).

louper [lu'pe], *v.t.* (*pop.*) to botch (*a piece of work*); (*Exam.*) to fail; to miss (*train*).

loupeux [lu'pø], *a.* (*fem.* **-euse**) wenny, knobby.

loup-garou [luga'ru], *n.m.* (*pl.* **loups-garous**) wer(e)wolf; bugbear.

lourd [lu:r], *a.* heavy, clumsy; stupid; sultry.

lourdaud [lur'do], *a.* loutish.—*n.m.* (*fem.* **-e**) blockhead.

lourdement [lurdə'mɑ̃], *adv.* heavily; clumsily.

lourdeur [lur'dœ:r], *n.f.* heaviness; clumsiness; stupidity; sultriness.

loutre [lutr], *n.f.* otter; otter fur.

louve [lu:v], *n.f.* she-wolf.

louveteau [luv'to], *n.m.* (*pl.* **-eaux**) wolf cub.

louveterie [luv'tri], *n.f.* wolf-hunting equipage; wolf hunting.

louvetier [luv'tje], *n.m.* wolf hunter.

louvoyer [luvwa'je], *v.i.* (*conjug. like* EM-PLOYER) to tack, to tack about; (*fig.*) to maneuver, to dodge.

lover [lɔ've], *v.t.* to coil (*rope etc.*). **se lover**, *v.r.* to coil up (*of snakes*).

loyal [lwa'jal], *a.* (*m. pl.* **-aux**) fair, honest, upright; loyal; (*Comm.*) unadulterated.

loyalement [lwajal'mɑ̃] *adv.* fairly, honestly; loyally.

loyauté [lwajo'te], *n.f.* honesty, fairness; loyalty, faithfulness.

loyer [lwa'je], *n.m.* hire, rent.

lubie [ly'bi] *n.f.* crotchet, whim, fad.

lubrifiant [lybri'fjɑ̃], ɔ. lubricating.—*n.m.* lubricant.

lubrification [lybrifika'sjɔ̃], *n.f.* lubrication.

lubrifier [lybri'tje], *v.t.* to lubricat⁻

Luc [lyk], *m.* Luke.

lucarne [ly'karn], *n.f.* dormer window, skylight.

lucide [ly'sid], *a.* lucid, clear.

lucidement [lysid'mɑ̃], *adv.* lucidly.

lucidité [lysidi'te], *n.f.* lucidity, clearness.

luciole [ly'sjɔl], *n.f.* (*Ent.*) fire-fly; winged glow-worm.

lucratif [lykra'tif], *a.* (*fem.* **-tive**) lucrative.

lucre [lykr], *n.m.* lucre, gain.

lueur [lɥœ:r], *n.f.* glimmer, gleam; flash.

luffa [ly'fa], *n.m.* or *f.* loofah.

lugubre [ly'gybr], *a.* lugubrious, doleful, dismal.

lugubrement [lygybrə'mɑ̃], *adv.* ominously; dismally.

lui [lɥi], *pers. pron.* he, it; to him, to her, to it.

luire [lɥi:r], *v.i. irr.* to shine; to glitter, to gleam, to glisten; to dawn.

luisant [lɥi'zɑ̃], *a.* glistening, glittering, bright; glossy.—*n.m.* gloss, shine.

lumbago [lœba'go], *n.m.* lumbago.

lumière [ly'mjɛ:r], *n.f.* light; daylight, day; (*fig.*) enlightenment; knowledge, wisdom.

luminaire [lymi'nɛ:r], *n.m.* luminary, light.

lumineux [lymi'nø], *a.* (*fem.* **-euse**) luminous; bright.

lunaire [ly'nɛ:r], *a.* lunar.

lunatique [lyna'tik], *a.* fantastical, whimsical.—*n.* incalculable *or* whimsical person.

lundi [lœ'di], *n.m.* Monday.

lune [lyn], *n.f.* moon.

lunetier [lyn'tje], *n.m.* (*fem.* **-ière**) spectacle maker; optician.

lunette [ly'nɛt], *n.f.* telescope, field glass; (*pl.*) spectacles.

lupin [ly'pɛ̃], *n.m.* (*Bot.*) lupin(e).

lupus [ly'pys], *n.m.* lupus.

luron [ly'rɔ̃], *n.m.* (*fem.* **-onne**) jolly fellow, gay dog; carefree type of girl.

lustrage [lys'tra:ʒ], *n.m.* glossing.

lustral [lys'tral], *a.* (*m. pl.* **-aux**) lustral.

lustration [lystra'sjɔ̃], *n.f.* lustration.

lustre (1) [lystr], *n.m.* luster, brilliancy, brightness; (*fig.*) distinction; chandelier.

lustre (2) [lystr], *n.m.* (*Rom. Ant.*) lustrum, space of five years.

lustré [lys'tre], *a.* glossy, shiny.

lustrer [lys'tre], *v.t.* to give a luster *or* gloss to, to glaze.

lustrine [lys'trin], *n.f.* lustering, cotton luster.

luth [lyt], *n.m.* lute.

luthérien [lyte'rjɛ̃], *a.* Lutheran.—*n.m.* (**Luthérien**, *fem.* **-enne**) Lutheran (*person*).

205

lutin

lutin [ly'tɛ̃], *a.* roguish, sprightly.—*n.m.* goblin, sprite, elf, imp.

lutiner [lyti'ne], *v.t.* to plague, to tease, to pester.—*v.i.* to be mischievous, to play the imp.

lutrin [ly'trɛ̃], *n.m.* music lectern *or* desk; choir.

lutte [lyt], *n.f.* wrestling; struggle, contest, strife; *de bonne lutte*, by fair play; *de haute lutte*, by force.

lutter [ly'te], *v.i.* to wrestle; to struggle, to contend.

lutteur [ly'tœːr], *n.m.* (*fem.* **-euse**) wrestler.

luxation [lyksa'sjɔ̃], *n.f.* luxation, dislocation.

luxe [lyks], *n.m.* luxury; profusion; extravagance, excess.

Luxembourg [lyksɑ̃'buːr], **le**, *m.* Luxembourg.

luxembourgeois [lyksɑ̃bur'ʒwa], *a.* (of) Luxembourg.—*n.m.* (**Luxembourgeois**, *fem.* **-oise**) citizen of Luxembourg.

luxer [lyk'se], *v.t.* to luxate, to dislocate.

luxueusement [lyksyøz'mɑ̃], *a.* luxuriously, sumptuously, richly.

luxueux [lyk'sɥø], *a.* (*fem.* **-euse**) luxurious; magnificent, rich, sumptuous.

luxure [lyk'syːr], *n.f.* lust.

luxuriance [lyksy'rjɑ̃ːs], *n.f.* luxuriance.

luxuriant [lyksy'rjɑ̃], *a.* luxuriant.

luxurieux [lyksy'rjø], *a.* (*fem.* **-euse**) lustful, lecherous.

lycée [li'se], *n.m.* French grammar *or* high school.

lycéen [lise'ɛ̃], *n.m.* (*fem.* **-éenne**) grammar-school pupil.

lymphatique [lɛ̃fa'tik], *a.* lymphatic.

lymphe [lɛ̃ːf] *n.f.* lymph; (*Bot.*) sap.

lynchage [lɛ̃'ʃaːʒ], *n.m.* lynching.

lyncher [lɛ̃'ʃe], *v.t.* to lynch.

lynx [lɛ̃ːks], *n.m. inv.* lynx.

Lyon [ljɔ̃], *m.* Lyons.

lyre [liːr], *n.f.* lyre; (*fig.*) poetry.

lyrique [li'rik], *a.* lyric, lyrical.

lyrisme [li'rism], *n.m.* lyric poetry; poetic fire.

M

M m [ɛm], *n.m. or f.* the thirteenth letter of the alphabet; *M*, 1000; *M. MM.*, abbr. of *Monsieur, Messieurs*.

m' [ME].

ma [ma], *a. poss. f.* [MON].

macabre [ma'kaːbr], *a.* gruesome, macabre, deathly, ghastly; *la danse macabre*, the dance of death.

macadam [maka'dam], *n.m.* macadam.

macadamiser [makadami'ze], *v.t.* to macadamize.

macaque [ma'kak], *n.m.* macaco (*monkey*).

macaron [maka'rɔ̃], *n.m.* macaroon.

macaroni [makarɔ'ni], *n.m.* macaroni.

Macédoine [mase'dwan], **la**, *f.* Macedonia.

macédoine [mase'dwan], *n.f.* vegetable hotchpotch; fruit salad; (*fig.*) medley, hotchpotch.

macédonien [masedɔ'njɛ̃], *a.* Macedonian.—*n.m.* (**Macédonien**, *fem.* **-enne**) Macedonian (*person*).

macération [masera'sjɔ̃], *n.f.* maceration.

macérer [mase're], *v.t.* (*conjug. like* CÉDER) to macerate; (*fig.*) to mortify.—*v.i.* to soak. **se macérer**, *v.r.* to macerate one's body; (*fig.*) to mortify oneself.

mâcher [mɑ'ʃe], *v.t.* to chew, to masticate; *ne pas mâcher ses mots*, not to mince matters.

machiavélique [makjave'lik], *a.* Machiavellian.

machiavélisme [makjave'lism], *n.m.* Machiavellism.

machiavéliste [makjave'list], *n.* Machiavellian.

machinal [maʃi'nal], *a.* (*m. pl.* **-aux**) mechanical, automatic, instinctive.

machinalement [maʃinal'mɑ̃], *adv.* mechanically, automatically, instinctively.

machinateur [maʃina'tœːr], *n.m.* (*fem.* **-trice**) plotter, schemer.

machination [maʃina'sjɔ̃], *n.f.* machination, plot, scheme.

machine [ma'ʃin], *n.f.* machine, engine, piece of machinery; apparatus; scheme, plot; *machine à coudre*, sewing machine; *machine à écrire*, typewriter; *machine à laver*, washing machine; *machine pneumatique*, air pump.

machine-outil [maʃinu'ti], *n.f.* (*pl.* **machines-outils**) machine tool.

machiner [maʃi'ne], *v.t.* to contrive, to plot.

machiniste [maʃi'nist], *n.m.* machinist, engine man; (*Theat.*) scene shifter.

mâchoire [mɑ'ʃwaːr], *n.f.* jaw; jawbone.

mâchonner [maʃɔ'ne], *v.t.* to chew with difficulty; to munch; to mumble; to champ (*the bit*).

mâchurer [maʃy're], *v.t.* to daub, to smudge; to bruise.

maçon [ma'sɔ̃], *n.m.* mason, bricklayer; freemason.

maçonnage [masɔ'naːʒ], *n.m.* mason's work, stonework.

maçonner [masɔ'ne], *v.t.* to build; to wall up.

maçonnerie [masɔn'ri], *n.f.* masonry, mason's work, stone work; freemasonry.

maçonnique [masɔ'nik], *a.* masonic.

macule [ma'kyl], *n.f.* stain, spot.

maculer [maky'le], *v.t.* to blot, to spot.

Madagascar [madagas'kaːr], **le**, *n.m.* Malagasy Republic.

madame [ma'dam], *n.f.* (*pl.* **mesdames**) madam, ma'am; Mrs.; your ladyship.

madécasse [made'kas], *a.* Madagascan.—*n.* (**Madécasse**) Madagascan (*person*).

madeleine [ma'dlɛn], *n.f.* shell-shaped sponge-cake; early pear.

Madelon [ma'dlɔ̃], *f.* Maud.

mademoiselle [madmwa'zɛl], *n.f.* (*pl.* **mesdemoiselles**) Miss; young lady.

Madère [ma'dɛːr], **la**, *f.* Madeira.

madère [ma'dɛːr], *n.m.* Madeira wine.

madone [ma'dɔn], *n.f.* Madonna.

madré [mɑ'dre], *a.* veined, mottled; (*fig.*) cunning, sly, sharp.—*n.m.* (*fem.* **-ée**) cunning, sharp *or* sly person.

madrier [madri'e], *n.m.* thick plank.

maestria [maɛs'tria], *n.f.* masterliness; *avec maestria*, in a masterly manner.

magasin [maga'zɛ̃], *n.m.* warehouse, store-house; shop, store; magazine (*of fire-arm, camera etc.*).

(C) **magasiner** [magazi'ne], *v.i.* to shop.

magasinier [magazi'nje], *n.m.* warehouse keeper, storeman.

magazine [maga'zin], *n.m.* magazine (*usu. illustrated*).

mage [ma:ʒ], *n.m.* mage, magus; seer; *les rois mages*, the three wise men.

magicien [maʒi'sjɛ̃], *n.m.* (*fem.* **-enne**) magician, wizard, sorcerer, sorceress.

magie [ma'ʒi], *n.f.* magic.

magique [ma'ʒik], *a.* magic(al).

magister [maʒis'tɛ:r], *n.m.* village school-master; pedant.

magistral [maʒis'tral], *a.* (*m. pl.* **-aux**) magisterial; masterly, authoritative, sovereign.

magistralement [maʒistral'mɑ̃], *adv.* magisterially; in a masterly fashion.

magistrat [maʒis'tra], *n.m.* magistrate, justice; civic officer.

magistrature [maʒistra'ty:r], *n.f.* magistracy; bench.

magnanime [maɲa'nim], *a.* magnanimous, high-minded.

magnanimement [maɲanim'mɑ̃], *adv.* magnanimously.

magnanimité [maɲanimi'te], *n.f.* magnanimity.

magnat [mag'na], *n.m.* magnate.

magnésie [maɲe'zi], *n.f.* magnesia.

magnétique [maɲe'tik], *a.* magnetic.

magnétiser [maɲeti'ze], *v.t.* to magnetize.

magnétiseur [maɲeti'zœ:r], *n.m.* magnetizer.

magnétisme [maɲe'tism], *n.m.* magnetism; (*fig.*) attraction.

magnétophone [maɲeto'fɔn], *n.m.* (*Reg. trade mark*) tape recorder.

magnificence [maɲifi'sɑ̃:s], *n.f.* magnificence, splendor.

magnifier [maɲi'fje], *v.t.* to magnify, to glorify.

magnifique [maɲi'fik], *a.* magnificent, splendid; gorgeous.

magnifiquement [maɲifik'mɑ̃], *adv.* magnificently.

magot [ma'go], *n.m.* magot, ape; grotesque figure (*of china*); (*fig.*) ugly person; (*fam.*) hoard, hidden savings.

Mahomet [mao'mɛ], *m.* Mohammed.

mahométan [maome'tɑ̃], *a.* Mohammedan. —*n.m.* (**Mahométan.** *fem.* **-ane**) Mohammedan (*person*).

mahométisme [maome'tism], *n.m.* Mohammedanism.

mai [mɛ], *n.m.* May; maypole.

maigre [mɛ:gr], *a.* meager, lean, thin; poor, scanty; barren; fasting; *repas maigre*, meatless meal; *maigre repas*, slender meal.

maigrement [mɛgrə'mɑ̃], *adv.* meagerly, poorly; sparingly.

maigreur [mɛ'grœ:r], *n.f.* leanness, meagerness; thinness, poorness, barrenness.

maigrir [mɛ'gri:r], *v.i.* to grow thin, to lose weight.

mail [ma:j], *n.m.* mall (*game, promenade, avenue of trees*).

maille [mɑ:j], *n.f.* mesh; ring of cable; link of mail; stitch.

maillé [mɑ'je], *a.* stitched; mailed.

mailler [mɑ'je], *v.t.* to make with meshes, to lattice; to mail.

maillet [mɑ'jɛ], *n.m.* mallet.

maillon [mɑ'jɔ̃], *n.m.* link (*of chain*).

maillot [mɑ'jo], *n.m.* swaddling-band; swaddling clothes; pair of tights (*for theatre*); bathing suit, (*Spt.*) jersey, vest; *enfant au maillot*, baby in arms.

main [mɛ̃], *n.f.* hand; handwriting; lead, deal (*at cards*); handle; quire (*of paper*); *à la main*, in his or her hand, by hand; *à la portée de la main*, within reach; *à main armée*, by force of arms, armed; *à pleines mains*, by handfuls, liberal; *vol à main armée*, armed robbery.

main-d'œuvre [mɛ̃'dœ:vr], *n.f.* (*pl.* **mains-d'œuvre**) man-power, labor; workmanship.

main-forte [mɛ̃'fɔrt], *n.f.* assistance, help.

maint [mɛ̃], *a.* many; *maintes fois*, many a time.

maintenant [mɛ̃t'nɑ̃], *adv.* now, at this moment, at present, nowadays.

maintenir [mɛ̃t'ni:r], *v.t. irr.* (*conjug. like* TENIR) to uphold, to sustain; to maintain; to enforce. **se maintenir,** *v.r.* to keep up; to subsist; to hold out, to stand one's ground; to remain in force.

maintien [mɛ̃'tjɛ̃], *n.m.* maintenance, keeping up; deportment; attitude.

maire [mɛ:r], *n.m.* mayor.

mairesse [mɛ'rɛs], *n.f.* mayoress.

mairie [mɛ'ri], *n.f.* mayoralty; town hall.

mais [mɛ], *conj.* but; why.

maïs [ma'is], *n.m.* maize, Indian corn.

maison [mɛ'zɔ̃], *n.f.* house; home; house-keeping; family; (*Comm.*) firm; *à la maison*, at home.

maisonnée [mɛzo'ne], *n.f.* (*fam.*) whole house *or* family, household.

maisonnette [mɛzo'nɛt], *n.f.* small house, cottage, lodge.

maître [mɛ:tr], *n.m.* master; ruler, lord; proprietor, landlord; teacher, tutor; (*Naut.*) chief petty officer; *coup de maître*, masterly stroke; *maître chanteur*, black-mailer.

maître-autel [mɛtro'tɛl], *n.m.* (*pl.* **maîtres-autels**) high altar.

maîtresse [mɛ'trɛs], *a.* chief, leading, main.— *n.f.* mistress; ruler, lady; proprietress; teacher; sweetheart.

maîtrise [mɛ'tri:z], *n.f.* mastery; control; music school (*in a cathedral*).

maîtriser [mɛtri'ze], *v.t.* to master, to control; to lord (it) over.

majesté [maʒɛs'te], *n.f.* majesty; stateliness.

majestueusement [maʒɛstɥøz'mɑ̃], *adv.* majestically.

majestueux [maʒɛs'tɥø], *a.* (*fem.* **-euse**) majestic.

majeur [ma'ʒœ:r], *a.* major, greater; superior, main, chief, most important; of full age.— *n.m.* (*fem.* **-e**) a male *or* female of full age, major.—*n.m.* middle finger.

majolique [maʒo'lik], *n.f.* majolica.

major [ma'ʒo:r], *n.m.* major; medical officer.

majordome [maʒor'dom], *n.m.* major-domo.

majorer [maʒo're], *v.t.* to raise (*the price*).

majorité [maʒori'te], *n.f.* majority.

majuscule [maʒys'kyl], *a.* capital, large.— *n.f.* capital letter.

mal

mal [mal], *n.m.* (*pl.* **maux**) evil, ill; harm; pain, ache, sickness; hardship, misfortune; trouble; repugnance.—*adv.* wrong, badly; *mal à propos*, improperly.

malade [ma'lad], *a.* sick, ill; unhealthy.—*n.* sick person, invalid; patient.

maladie [mala'di], *n.f.* illness, sickness, malady.

maladif [mala'dif], *a.* (*fem.* **-dive**) sickly, puny, ailing, unhealthy.

maladivement [maladiv'mɑ̃], *adv.* morbidly.

maladresse [mala'drɛs], *n.f.* awkwardness, clumsiness; blunder.

maladroit [mala'drwa], *a.* and *n.m.* (*fem.* **-e**) awkward, clumsy, stupid (person).

maladroitement [maladrwat'mɑ̃], *adv.* clumsily.

malais [ma'lɛ], *a.* Malay, Malayan, Malaysian.—*n.m.* Malay (*language*); (**Malais**, *fem.* **-aise**) Malay, Malayan, Malaysian (*person*).

malaise [ma'lɛːz] *n.m.* uneasiness, discomfort; indisposition.

malaisé [malɛ'ze], *a.* hard, difficult, rough, arduous.

malaisément [malɛze'mɑ̃], *adv.* with difficulty, painfully.

Malaisie [malɛ'zi], **la**, *f.* Malaysia.

malappris [mala'pri], *a.* unmannerly, ill-bred.—*n.m.* (*fem.* **-e**) ill-bred person, lout.

malard [ma'laːr], *n.m.* mallard, wild drake.

malaria [mala'rja], *n.f.* malaria.

malart [MALARD].

malavisé [malavi'ze], *a.* ill-advised, imprudent, unwise, indiscreet.

malaxer [malak'ze], *v.t.* to mix, knead *or* work up; to massage.

malbâti [malbɑ'ti], *a.* ill-shaped, gawky.—*n.m.* (*fem.* **-e**) ill-favored person.

malchance [mal'ʃɑ̃ːs], *n.f.* ill-luck, mishap, mischance.

malchanceux [malʃɑ̃'sø], *a.* (*fem.* **-euse**) unlucky.

mâle [mɑːl], *a.* male; manly, virile; masculine.—*n.m.* male; cock.

malédiction [maledik'sjɔ̃], *n.f.* malediction, curse.

maléfice [male'fis], *n.m.* evil spell, sorcery.

maléfique [male'fik], *a.* harmful, malefic, baleful.

malencontre [malɑ̃'kɔ̃ːtr], *n.f.* mishap, mischance.

malencontreusement [malɑ̃kɔ̃trøz'mɑ̃], *adv.* unluckily, untowardly.

malencontreux [malɑ̃kɔ̃'trø], *a.* (*fem.* **-euse**) unlucky, untoward.

mal-en-point [malɑ̃'pwɛ̃], *adv.* badly off; in a sorry plight.

malentendu [malɑ̃tɑ̃'dy], *n.m.* misunderstanding, misapprehension, mistake.

malfaçon [malfa'sɔ̃], *n.f.* bad work; malpractice, illicit profit.

malfaire [mal'fɛːr], *v.i.* (*used only in the inf.*) to do evil.

malfaisant [malfə'zɑ̃], *a.* mischievous; spiteful, malevolent.

malfaiteur [malfɛ'tœːr], *n.m.* (*fem.* **-trice**) malefactor, evil-doer; offender; thief.

malfamé [malfa'me], *a.* ill-famed, of bad repute.

malformation [malfɔrma'sjɔ̃], *n.f.* malformation.

malgache [mal'gaʃ], *a.* Madagascan,—*n.* (**Malgache**) Malagasy, Madagascan.

malgracieusement [malgrasjøz'mɑ̃], *adv.* ungraciously, rudely, uncivilly.

malgracieux [malgra'sjø], *a.* (*fem.* **-euse**) rude, ungracious, uncivil.

malgré [mal'gre], *prep.* in spite of, notwithstanding.

malhabile [mala'bil], *a.* unskilled, awkward.

malhabilement [malabil'mɑ̃], *adv.* unskilfully, awkwardly.

malhabileté [malabil'te], *n.f.* unskilfulness, awkwardness, clumsiness.

malheur [ma'lœːr], *n.m.* unhappiness, misfortune, bad luck; mischance; calamity, disaster; woe, adversity; poverty.

malheureusement [malœrøz'mɑ̃], *adv.* unfortunately.

malheureux [malœ'rø], *a.* (*fem.* **-euse**) unfortunate, unlucky; unsuccessful; unpleasant; unhappy, miserable, wretched.—*n.m.* (*fem.* **-euse**) unhappy person.

malhonnête [malɔnɛːt], *a.* dishonest; uncivil, rude.—*n.* rude person.

malhonnêtement [malɔnɛt'mɑ̃], *adv.* dishonestly; rudely.

malhonnêteté [malɔnɛt'te], *n.f.* rudeness, incivility; dishonesty.

malice [ma'lis], *n.f.* malice, spite; mischievousness; prank, trick.

malicieusement [malisjøz'mɑ̃], *adv.* maliciously; mischievously; slyly.

malicieux [mali'sjø], *a.* (*fem.* **-euse**) malicious, spiteful; mischievous; roguish.

malignement [maliɲ'mɑ̃], *adv.* malignantly; maliciously.

malignité [maliɲi'te], *n.f.* malignity, spite.

malin [ma'lɛ̃], *a.* (*fem.* **maligne**) malicious, mischievous; malignant; waggish, roguish; cunning, clever.—*n.m.* (*fem.* **maligne**) malignant *or* malicious person.—*n.m.* devil, evil spirit, fiend.

maline [ma'lin], *n.f.* spring tide.

malingre [ma'lɛ̃ːgr], *a.* sickly, weakly, puny.

malintentionné [malɛ̃tɑ̃sjɔ'ne], *a.* evil-minded, ill-disposed.

malle [mal], *n.f.* trunk, box; mail car, mail boat.

malléabilité [maleabili'te], *n.f.* malleability; pliability.

malléable [male'abl], *a.* malleable.

malle-poste [mal'pɔst], *n.f.* (*pl.* **malles-poste(s)**) mail car.

mallette [ma'lɛt], *n.f.* small case, suitcase, attaché-case.

malmener [malmə'ne], *v.t.* (*conjug. like* AMENER) to ill-treat, to handle roughly; to abuse.

malodorant [malɔdɔ'rɑ̃], *a.* malodorous, ill-smelling.

malotru [malɔ'try], *a.* coarse, uncouth, vulgar.—*n.m.* (*fem.* **-e**) ill-bred person; lout.

Malouines [ma'lwin], **les îles**, *f. pl.* the Falkland Islands.

malpeigné [malpɛ'ɲe], *a.* unkempt.—*n.m.* (*fem.* **-ée**) unkempt *or* dirty person.

malplaisant [malplɛ'zɑ̃], *a.* unpleasant, disagreeable.

malpropre [mal'prɔpr], *a.* slovenly, dirty; dishonest; unfit (à).

malproprement [malprɔprə'mɑ̃], *adv.* in a slovenly way, dirtily; improperly.

malpropreté [malprɔprə'te], *n.f.* dirtiness.
malsain [mal'sɛ̃], *a.* unhealthy; unwholesome, injurious.
malséant [malse'ã], *a.* unbecoming, unseemly, improper.
malsonnant [malsɔ'nã], *a.* ill-sounding; offensive.
malt [malt], *n.m.* malt.
maltais [mal'tɛ], *a.* Maltese.—*n.m.* Maltese (*language*); (**Maltais**, *fem.* **-aise**) Maltese (*person*).
Malte [malt], **la**, *f.* Malta.
maltraiter [maltrɛ'te], *v.t.* to ill-use, to maltreat, to abuse.
malveillamment [malvɛja'mã], *adv.* malevolently.
malveillance [malvɛ'jã:s], *n.f.* malevolence, ill-will, malice.
malveillant [malvɛ'jã], *a.* malevolent, malignant, ill-disposed, spiteful.—*n.m.* (*fem.* **-e**) evil-minded person.
malversation [malvɛrsa'sjɔ̃], *n.f.* malversation, peculation, embezzlement.
maman [ma'mã], *n.f.* mamma, mummy.
mamelle [ma'mɛl], *n.f.* breast; udder.
mamelon [mam'lɔ̃], *n.m.* nipple, teat; dug (*of animals*); pap, hillock, knoll.
mameluk [mam'luk], *n.m.* Mameluke.
mammouth [ma'mut], *n.m.* mammoth.
manant [ma'nã], *n.m.* peasant, clodhopper.
manche (1) [mã:ʃ], *n.m.* handle; neck (*of violin etc.*).
manche (2) [mã:ʃ], *n.f.* sleeve; hose; channel; (*Spt.*) rubber, game, heat.
Manche [mã:ʃ], **la**, *f.* The (English) Channel. *Les Îles de la Manche*, the Channel Islands.
manchette [mã'ʃɛt], *n.f.* cuff; ruffle; wristband.
manchon [mã'ʃɔ̃], *n.m.* muff.
manchot [mã'ʃo], *a.* one-handed, one-armed.—*n.m.* penguin; (*fem.* **-e**) one-handed, one-armed person.
mandarin [mãda'rɛ̃], *a.* and *n.m.* (*fem.* **-ine** (1)) mandarin.
mandarine (2) [mãda'rin], *n.f.* tangerine.
mandat [mã'da], *n.m.* mandate, authority; warrant, writ; money order, order.
mandataire [mãda'tɛ:r], *n.m.* mandatory; proxy, attorney, agent.
mandchou [mãt'ʃu], *a.* Manchu(rian).—*n.m.* Manchu(rian) (*language*); (**Mandchou**, *fem.* **-oue**) Manchu(rian) (*person*).
Mandchourie [mãtʃu'ri], **la**, *f.* Manchuria.
mandement [mãd'mã], *n.m.* mandate; bishop's letter.
mander [mã'de], *v.t.* to write, to send word, to inform; to send for.
mandoline [mãdɔ'lin], *n.f.* mandolin.
mandoliniste [mãdɔli'nist], *n.* mandolin player.
manège [ma'nɛ:ʒ], *n.m.* horsemanship, riding school; merry-go-round; (*fig.*) trick, intrigue.
mânes [mɑ:n], *n.m. pl.* manes, shades.
manette [ma'nɛt], *n.f.* hand lever, grip; (*Hort.*) trowel.
mangeable [mã'ʒabl], *a.* eatable, edible.
mangeoire [mã'ʒwa:r], *n.f.* manger, crib.
manger [mã'ʒe], *v.t.* (*see Verb Tables*) to eat; (*fig.*) to squander, to run through.—*v.i.* to eat; to feed.—*n.m.* eating; victuals, food.

se manger, *v.r.* to eat each other; to hurt each other; to be edible.
mangeur [mã'ʒœ:r], *n.m.* (*fem.* **-euse**) eater; spendthrift.
mangouste [mã'gust], *n.f.* mongoose.
maniable [ma'njabl], *a.* easy to handle; tractable, supple, pliable.
maniaque [ma'njak], *a.* eccentric, having a mania.—*n.* crank, faddist.
manicure [mani'ky:r], [MANUCURE].
manie [ma'ni], *n.f.* mania; fad, hobby; inveterate habit, craze.
maniement [mani'mã], *n.m.* handling; management, use.
manier [ma'nje], *v.t.* to handle; to touch; to use, to wield; to manage, to govern.
manière [ma'njɛ:r], *n.f.* manner, way, style; sort; affectation; (*pl.*) manners; *de manière à*, so as to; *de quelle manière*, how; *manière d'être*, bearing, attitude.
maniéré [manje're], *a.* affected, unnatural, forced.
maniérisme [manje'rism], *n.m.* mannerism.
manifestation [manifɛsta'sjɔ̃], *n.f.* manifestation; (*Polit.*) demonstration.
manifeste [mani'fɛst], *a.* manifest, obvious.—*n.m.* manifesto.
manifestement [manifɛstə'mã], *adv.* manifestly.
manifester [manifɛs'te], *v.t.* to manifest, to display, to show.—*v.i.* to attend a (*political*) demonstration. **se manifester**, *v.r.* to manifest oneself, to make oneself known.
manigance [mani'gã:s], *n.f.* (*fam.*) maneuver, intrigue.
manigancer [manigã'se], *v.t.* (*conjug. like* COMMENCER) to contrive, to plot.
Manille [ma'ni:j], **la**, *f.* Manila.
manipulateur [manipyla'tœ:r], *n.m.* (*fem.* **-trice**) manipulator.
manipulation [manipyla'sjɔ̃], *n.f.* manipulation.
manipuler [manipy'le], *v.t.* to manipulate; (*Teleg.*) to operate.
manivelle [mani'vɛl], *n.f.* crank; handle.
manne (1) [ma:n], *n.f.* manna.
manne (2) [ma:n], *n.f.* hamper, flat basket.
mannequin (1) [man'kɛ̃], *n.m.* small hamper.
mannequin (2) [man'kɛ̃], *n.m.* lay figure; tailor's dummy; model girl; mannequin.
manœuvre [ma'nœ:vr], *n.f.* working; drilling (*of soldiers*); maneuver; scheme; move; (*Rail.*) marshalling.—*n.m.* unskilled workman, laborer.
manœuvrer [manœ'vre], *v.t.* to maneuver; to work (*a machine*); to shunt (*trains*).
manœuvrier [manœvri'e], *a.* (*fem.* **-ière**) highly trained.—*n.m.* expert seaman; tactician.
manoir [ma'nwa:r], *n.m.* manor; country house.
manouvrier [manuvri'e], *n.m.* (*fem.* **-ière**) day laborer.
manquant [mã'kã], *a.* missing, absent, wanting.—*n.m.* (*fem.* **-e**) absentee, defaulter.—*n.m.* (*pl.*) shortages, deficiencies.
manque [mã:k], *n.m.* want, lack; defect; deficiency.
manqué [mã'ke], *a.* missed; defective; unsuccessful, abortive.
manquement [mãkə'mã], *n.m.* omission, oversight; failure; breach.

manquer [mɑ̃'ke], v.t. to miss, to lose; to spoil.—v.i. to miss, to fail; to be wanting; to be deficient; to slip; to misfire; to go bankrupt; to miscarry.

mansarde [mɑ̃'sard], n.f. roof window, dormer; garret.

mansardé [mɑ̃sar'de], a. with attics.

mansuétude [mɑ̃sɥe'tyd], n.f. mildness, gentleness, forbearance.

mante (1) [mɑ̃:t], n.f. mantle (woman's).

mante (2) [mɑ̃:t], n.f. mantis; *mante religieuse*, praying mantis.

manteau [mɑ̃'to], n.m. (pl. **-eaux**) cloak, mantle; overcoat; (fig.) pretence.

mantille [mɑ̃'ti:j], n.f. mantilla.

manucure [many'ky:r], **manicure** [mani'ky:r], n. manicure (person), manicurist.

manuel [ma'nɥɛl], a. (fem. **-elle**) manual, portable.—n.m. manual, textbook.

manuellement [manɥɛl'mɑ̃], adv. by hand, manually.

manufacture [manyfak'ty:r], n.f. manufacture, making; factory, mill, works.

manufacturer [manyfakty're], v.t. to manufacture.

manufacturier [manyfakty'rje], a. (fem. **-ière**) manufacturing.—n.m. manufacturer.

manuscrit [manys'kri], a. handwritten.—n.m. manuscript.

manutention [manytɑ̃'sjɔ̃], n.f. management, administration; manipulation; handling (of goods etc.); army bakery.

mappemonde [map'mɔ̃:d], n.f. map of the world, planisphere.

maquereau [ma'kro], n.m. (pl. **-eaux**) mackerel.

maquette [ma'kɛt], n.f. (Sculp.) small rough model (in clay, wax etc.); (Paint.) rough sketch; lay figure; (Theat., Cine.) model.

maquignon [maki'ɲɔ̃], n.m. (fem. **-onne**) horse dealer, jobber.

maquignonnage [makiɲɔ'na:ʒ], n.m. horse-dealing; underhand work, jobbery.

maquignonner [makiɲɔ'ne], v.t. to jockey to bishop (a horse for sale); to job.

maquillage [maki'ja:ʒ], n.m. make-up.

maquiller [maki'je], v.t. to make up; to fake up. **se maquiller**, v.r. to make up or paint oneself.

maquilleur [maki'jœ:r], n.m. (fem. **-euse**) (Theat.) maker-up; faker (of paintings etc.).

maquis [ma'ki], n.m. inv. scrub (in Corsica); (1941-44) underground forces.

maquisard [maki'za:r], n.m. free fighter in the maquis.

maraîcher [marɛ'ʃe], a. (fem. **-ère**) of market gardening.—n.m. market gardener.

marais [ma'rɛ], n.m. marsh, fen, bog, swamp.

marasme [ma'rasm], n.m. emaciation; (fig.) depression; stagnation, slump.

marâtre [ma'ra:tr], n.f. stepmother; (fig.) harsh mother.

maraudage [maro'da:ʒ], n.m. marauding.

maraude [ma'ro:d], n.f. pilfering.

marauder [maro'de], v.i. to pilfer, to go scrounging.

maraudeur [maro'dœ:r], n.m. (fem. **-euse**) marauder; plunderer.

marbre [marbr], n.m. marble.

marbré [mar'bre], a. marbled.

marbrer [mar'bre], v.t. to marble, to vein.

marbrerie [marbrə'ri], n.f. marble-cutting; marble works.

marbrier [marbri'e], a. (fem. **-ière**) of marble.—n.m. marble cutter, marble polisher; dealer in marble.—n.f. (-ière) marble quarry.

marbrure [mar'bry:r], n.f. marbling; mottling (on the skin).

marc [ma:r], n.m. residuum (of fruit etc. squeezed, boiled or strained); dregs, grounds.

Marc [mark], m. Mark.

marchand [mar'ʃɑ̃], a. saleable, trading.—n.m. (fem. **-e**) dealer, tradesman, shop-keeper; merchant; *marchand des quatre saisons*, hawker of fruits etc.; *marchand au détail*, retail merchant; *marchand en gros*, wholesale dealer.

marchandage [marʃɑ̃'da:ʒ], n.m. bargaining, haggling; piece-work.

marchander [marʃɑ̃'de], v.t. to bargain for; to haggle over; (fig.) to spare; to grudge.—v.i. to haggle; to hesitate.

marchandeur [marʃɑ̃'dœ:r], n.m. (fem. **-euse**) bargainer, haggler; contractor on small scale.

marchandise [marʃɑ̃'di:z], n.f. merchandise; goods, wares, commodities.

marche (1) [marʃ], n.f. walk; gait; march, journey; procession; movement; conduct; *marche arrière*, reversing (of a car); *mettre en marche*, to set going.

marche (2) [marʃ], n.f. step, stair; treadle.

marché [mar'ʃe], n.m. market; market-place; bargain, purchase; price, rate; contract; *à bon marché*, cheaply; *bon marché*, cheap, cheapness.

marchepied [marʃə'pje], n.m. step (of a coach, altar etc.); step-ladder; running-board.

marcher [mar'ʃe], v.i. to walk; to progress; to step, to tread; to march; to run, to ply; to work (of a machine).

marcheur [mar'ʃœ:r], n.m. (fem. **-euse**) walker.

mardi [mar'di], n.m. Tuesday; *mardi gras*, Shrove Tuesday.

mare [ma:r], n.f. pool, pond.

marécage [mare'ka:ʒ], n.m. marsh, bog, fen, swamp.

marécageux [mareka'ʒø], a. (fem. **-euse**) marshy, swampy, boggy.

maréchal [mare'ʃal], n.m. (pl. **-aux**) marshal, field marshal.

maréchalerie [mareʃal'ri], n.f. farriery, smithy.

maréchal-ferrant [mareʃalfɛ'rɑ̃], n.m. (pl. **maréchaux-ferrants**) farrier, shoeing smith.

marée [ma're], n.f. tide, flood; fresh sea-fish.

marelle [ma'rɛl], n.f. hopscotch.

mareyeur [marɛ'jœ:r] n.m. fish dealer, fish-salesman.

margarine [marga'rin], n.f. margarine.

marge [marʒ], n.f. margin, border, edge; (fig.) freedom, latitude, scope; means.

margelle [mar'ʒɛl], n.f. curb, edge (of a well etc.).

Marguerite [margə'rit], f. Margaret.

marguerite [margə'rit], n.f. daisy.

marguillier [margi'je], n.m. churchwarden.

mari [ma'ri], n.m. husband.

mariable [ma'rjabl], a. marriageable.

mariage [ma'rja:ʒ], *n.m.* marriage; matrimony; wedding; union, blending.

Marie [ma'ri], *f.* Mary, Maria.

marié [ma'rje], *a.* married.—*n.m.* (*fem.* **-ée**) married man; bridegroom; married woman; bride.

marier [ma'rje], *v.t.* to give in marriage, to marry off; to match. **se marier**, *v.r.* to marry, to get married (*avec*).

marieur [ma'rjœ:r] *n.m.* (*fem.* **-euse**) matchmaker.

marin [ma'rɛ̃], *a.* marine; sea-going.—*n.m.* sailor.

marinade [mari'nad], *n.f.* pickle, souse.

marine [ma'rin], *n.f.* sea service; Admiralty; navy.

mariner [mari'ne], *v.t.* to pickle, to souse.

marinier [mari'nje], *a.* (*fem.* **-ière** (1)) *officiers mariniers*, petty officers.—*n.m.* bargeman, lighter-man.—*n.f.* (**-ière**) (*Swim.*) side stroke.

marinière (2) [mari'njɛ:r], *n.f.* (*Cook.*) onion sauce.

marionnette [marjɔ'nɛt], *n.f.* puppet, marionette; (*pl.*) puppet show.

marital [mari'tal], *a.* (*m. pl.* **-aux**) marital.

maritalement [marital'mɑ̃], *adv.* maritally, as man and wife.

maritime [mari'tim], *a.* maritime, naval.

marmaille [mar'ma:j], *n.f.* (*colloq.*) brats.

marmelade [marmə'lad], *n.f.* compote; (*fig.*) jelly, soup.

marmite [mar'mit], *n.f.* cooking pot.

marmiteux [marmi'tø], *a.* (*fem.* **-euse**) pitiful, wretched, miserable.—*n.m.* (*fem.* **-euse**) poor devil.

marmiton [marmi'tɔ̃], *n.m.* scullion.

marmonner [marmɔ'ne], *v.t.* to mutter.

marmoréen [marmɔre'ɛ̃], *a.* (*fem.* **-éenne**) marmorean.

marmot [mar'mo], *n.m.* kid, brat, urchin.

marmotte [mar'mɔt], *n.f.* marmot.

marmotter [marmɔ'te], *v.t., v.i.* to mutter, to mumble.

marmouset [marmu'zɛ], *n.m.* grotesque figure; young monkey (*little boy*); fire-dog.

marne [marn], *n.f.* marl, chalk, clay.

maruer [mar'ne], *v.t.* to marl.

marneux [mar'nø], *a.* (*fem.* **-euse**) marly.

marnière [mar'njɛ:r], *n.f.* marlpit.

Maroc [ma'rɔk], **le**, *m.* Morocco.

marocain [marɔ'kɛ̃], *a.* Moroccan.—*n.m.* (**Marocain**, *fem.* **-aine**) Moroccan (*person*).

maroquin [marɔ'kɛ̃], *n.m.* morocco leather.

maroquiner [marɔki'ne], *v.t.* to morocco.

maroquinerie [marɔkin'ri], *n.f.* morocco leather manufacture *or* factory.

maroquinier [marɔki'nje], *n.m.* morocco leather tanner.

marotte [ma'rɔt], *n.f.* cap and bells; hairdresser's dummy head; (*fig.*) fancy, hobby.

marquant [mar'kɑ̃], *a.* conspicuous, striking.

marque [mark], *n.f.* mark, imprint, stamp; cipher, trade mark, make; badge, sign, token; proof; distinction.

marqué [mar'ke], *a.* marked, conspicuous, obvious; determined.

marquer [mar'ke], *v.t.* to mark; to stamp; to brand; to indicate; to denote; to testify; to score.—*v.i.* to mark, to be remarkable; to show off.

marqueter [markə'te], *v.t.* (*conjug. like* APPELER) to speckle, to spot; to inlay.

marqueterie [markə'tri], *n.f.* marquetry, inlaid work, inlaying.

marqueur [mar'kœ:r], *n.m.* (*fem.* **-euse**) marker; scorer.

marquis [mar'ki], *n.m.* marquess, marquis.

marquise [mar'ki:z], *n.f.* marchioness; marquee, glass porch *or* roof.

marraine [ma'rɛn], *n.f.* godmother; sponsor.

marron (1) [ma'rɔ̃], *a. inv.* maroon, chestnut-color.—*n.m.* chestnut; cracker (*fireworks*); *marron d'Inde*, horse chestnut.

marron (2) [ma'rɔ̃] *a.* (*fem.* **-onne**) fugitive, runaway (*of slaves*); (*Comm.*) unlicensed; unqualified (*doctor etc.*).

marronnier [marɔ'nje], *n.m.* chestnut tree; *marronnier d'Inde*, horse chestnut tree.

mars [mars], *n.m.* March.

Marseillaise [marsɛ'jɛ:z], *n.f.* Marseillaise (*French national anthem*).

marsouin [mar'swɛ̃], *n.m.* porpoise.

marte [MARTRE].

marteau [mar'to], *n.m.* (*pl.* **-eaux**) hammer; *marteau de porte*, knocker; *marteau pneumatique*, pneumatic drill.

marteau-pilon [martopi'lɔ̃], *n.m.* (*pl.* **marteaux-pilons**) steam hammer.

martelage [martə'la:ʒ], *n.m.* hammering; marking (*of trees*).

martelé [martə'le], *a.* hammered; (*Mus.*) brilliant and distinct.

marteler [martə'le], *v.t.* (*conjug. like* AMENER) to hammer; to mark (*trees*).

Marthe [mart], *f.* Martha.

martial [mar'sjal], *a.* (*m. pl.* **-aux**) martial, warlike, soldierly.

martinet (1) [marti'nɛ], *n.m.* (*Orn.*) swift, martlet.

martinet (2) [marti'nɛ], *n.m.* tilt hammer; cat-o'-nine-tails.

martingale [martɛ̃'gal], *n.f.* martingale; *jouer la martingale*, to play double or quits.

martin-pêcheur [martɛpɛ'ʃœ:r], *n.m.* (*pl.* **martins-pêcheurs**) kingfisher; *martin-pêcheur d'Australie*, laughing jackass.

martre [martr], *n.f.* marten.

martyr [mar'ti:r], *n.m.* (*fem.* **martyre** (1)) martyr.

martyre (2) [mar'ti:r], *n.m.* martyrdom.

martyriser [martiri'ze], *v.t.* to martyrize; to torment, to torture.

marxisme [mark'sism], *n.m.* Marxism.

marxiste [mark'sist], *a.* and *n.* Marxist.

mascarade [maska'rad], *n.f.* masquerade.

mascotte [mas'kɔt], *n.f.* mascot, charm.

masculin [masky'lɛ̃], *a.* masculine, male.—*n.m.* (*Gram.*) masculine.

masculiniser [maskylini'ze], *v.t.* to make masculine.

masculinité [maskylini'te], *n.f.* masculinity.

masque [mask], *n.m.* mask; (*fig.*) blind, cloak, pretence; masquerader, mummer; (*Fenc.*) face guard.

masqué [mas'ke], *a.* masked; disguised; concealed; *virage masqué*, blind corner.

masquer [mas'ke], *v.t.* to mask; to cloak, to disguise; to conceal.

massacrant [masa'krɑ̃], *a.* used chiefly in *être d'une humeur massacrante*, to be in an awful temper.

massacre [ma'sakr], *n.m.* massacre, butchery, slaughter; (*fig.*) havoc, waste.
massacrer [masa'kre], *v.t.* to massacre, to butcher, to murder, to slaughter; (*fig.*) to bungle.
massacreur [masa'krœːr], *n.m.* (*fem.* **-euse**) slaughterer, slayer; (*fig.*) bungler.
massage [ma'saːʒ], *n.m.* massage.
masse (1) [mas], *n.f.* mass, heap, lump; mob; stock; (*Elec.*) ground.
masse (2) [mas], *n.f.* sledge-hammer.
massepain [mas'pɛ̃], *n.m.* marzipan.
masser [ma'se], *v.t.* to mass (*troops etc.*); to massage.
masseur [ma'sœːr], *n.m.* (*fem.* **-euse**) masseur, masseuse.
massier [ma'sje], *n.m.* mace bearer.
massif [ma'sif], *a.* (*fem.* **-ive**) massive, bulky, massy, solid; lumpish, heavy.—*n.m.* clump (*of trees, flowers etc.*); solid mass or block (*of masonry*); (*Geog.*) massif.
massivement [masiv'mɑ̃], *adv.* massively, heavily, solidly.
massiveté [masiv'te], *n.f.* massiveness.
massue [ma'sy], *n.f.* club (*weapon*).
mastic [mas'tik], *n.m.* mastic; cement; putty; filling (*for teeth*); plastic wood.
masticage [masti'kaːʒ], *n.m.* cementing, puttying; filling.
mastication [mastika'sjɔ̃], *n.f.* mastication, chewing.
mastiquer (1) [masti'ke], *v.t.* to masticate.
mastiquer (2) [masti'ke], *v.t.* to putty, to cement.
mastodonte [masto'dɔ̃ːt], *n.m.* mastodon.
mastoïde [masto'id], *a.* mastoid.
masure [ma'zyːr], *n.f.* hovel, tumbledown cottage.
mat (1) [mat], *n.m.* (*Chess*) mate.
mat (2) [mat], *a.* mat, dull, unpolished; dull-sounding; heavy, sodden.
mât [mo], *n.m.* mast; pole.
matador [mata'dɔːr], *n.m.* matador.
matamore [mata'mɔːr], *n.m.* blusterer, braggart.
match [matʃ], *n.m.* (*pl.* **matches**) (*Spt.*) match; *match nul*, draw.
matelas [ma'tlɑ], *n.m.* mattress; pad, cushion; *toile à matelas*, ticking.
matelasser [matla'se], *v.t.* to stuff, to pad.
matelot [ma'tlo], *n.m.* sailor, seaman.
matelote [ma'tlɔt], *n.f.* sailor's wife; fish stew.
mater (1) [ma'te], *v.t.* to checkmate; to bring down, to subdue.
mater (2) [ma'te], *v.t.* to make mat or dull, to deaden.
matérialiser [materjali'ze], *v.t.* to materialize.
matérialisme [materja'lism], *n.m.* materialism.
matérialiste [materja'list], *a.* materialistic.—*n.* materialist.
matériaux [mate'rjo], *n.m. pl.* materials.
matériel [mate'rjɛl], *a.* (*fem.* **-elle**) material; gross, rough; heavy, dull.—*n.m.* material, working stock, implements, plant.
matériellement [materjɛl'mɑ̃], *adv.* materially; positively; sensually.
maternel [matɛr'nɛl], *a.* (*fem.* **-elle**) maternal, motherly; *école maternelle*, nursery school.
maternité [matɛrni'te], *n.f.* maternity.

mathématicien [matemati'sjɛ̃], *n.m.* (*fem.* **-enne**) mathematician.
mathématique [matema'tik], *a.* mathematical.—*n.f.* (*usu. in pl.*) mathematics.
mathématiquement [matematik'mɑ̃], *adv.* mathematically.
matière [ma'tjɛːr], *n.f.* matter; material; subject matter; cause, motive; contents; *matière première*, raw material.
matin [ma'tɛ̃], *n.m.* morning, forenoon; prime, dawn.—*adv.* early, early in the morning.
mâtin [mo'tɛ̃], *n.m.* mastiff; big mongrel dog.
matinal [mati'nal], *a.* (*m. pl.* **-aux**) morning, early; early-rising.
matinée [mati'ne], *n.f.* morning, forenoon; afternoon performance, matinée.
matines [ma'tin], *n.f. pl.* matins.
matineux [mati'nø], *a.* (*fem.* **-euse**) rising early.
matois [ma'twa], *a.* cunning, artful, sly.—*n.m.* (*fem.* **-e**) cunning person, sly dog.
matoisement [matwaz'mɑ̃], *adv.* cunningly, slyly.
matoiserie [matwaz'ri], *n.f.* cunning; wile.
matou [ma'tu], *n.m.* tom-cat; (*fam.*) curmudgeon.
matraque [ma'trak], *n.f.* bludgeon; truncheon.
matriarcal [matriar'kal], *a.* (*m. pl.* **-aux**) matriarchal.
matriarcat [matriar'ka], *n.m.* matriarchy.
matrice [ma'tris], *n.f.* womb, matrix.
matricide [matri'sid], *a.* matricidal.—*n.* matricide (*person*).—*n.m.* matricide (*crime*).
matricule [matri'kyl], *n.f.* register, roll; matriculation.—*n.m.* regimental number (*of a soldier*); number (*of a rifle etc.*).
matrimonial [matrimo'njal], *a.* (*m. pl.* **-aux**) matrimonial.
Matthieu [ma'tjø], *m.* Matthew.
maturation [matyra'sjɔ̃], *n.f.* maturation.
mâture [mo'tyːr], *n.f.* masting, masts and spars.
maturité [matyri'te], *n.f.* maturity, ripeness.
maudire [mo'diːr], *v.t. irr.* to curse; to detest.
maudissable [modi'sabl], *a.* execrable, detestable.
maudit [mo'di], *a.* cursed, accursed; wretched.
maugréer [mogre'e], *v.i.* to fret and fume, to curse and swear.
maure [MORE].
Maurice [mo'ris], *m.* Maurice; *l'île Maurice*, Mauritius.
Mauritanie [morita'ni], **la**, *f.* Mauritania.
mauritanien [morita'njɛ̃], *a.* (*fem.* **-enne**) Mauritanian.—*n.m.* (**Mauritanien**, *fem.* **-enne**) Mauritanian (*person*).
mausolée [mozo'le], *n.m.* mausoleum.
maussade [mo'sad], *a.* sulky, sullen, cross; disagreeable, dull.
maussadement [mosad'mɑ̃], *adv.* disagreeably, sullenly, peevishly.
maussaderie [mosa'dri], *n.f.* sullenness, sulkiness.
mauvais [mo've], *a.* bad, ill, evil; naughty, mischievous; hurtful; wrong; unpleasant; wretched; nasty.—*n.m.* bad.—*adv.* bad, badly, wrong.
mauve [moːv], *a.* mauve.—*n.f.* (*Bot.*) mallow.

maxillaire [maksi'lɛ:r], *a.* maxillary.—*n.m.* jaw-bone.

maxime [mak'sim], *n.f.* maxim.

maximum [maksi'nɔm], *a.* (*fem.* **maxima**) maximum.—*n.m.* (*pl.* **maxima** or **maximums**) maximum; acme.

mayonnaise [majɔ'nɛ:z], *n.f.* mayonnaise.

mazout [ma'ʒut], *n.m.* fuel oil.

me [mə], *pron. pers.* me; to me.

méandre [me'ɑ̃:dr], *n.m.* meander, winding.

mécanicien [mekani'sjɛ̃], *n.m.* mechanic; engine driver, (*Am.*) engineer; *ingénieur mécanicien*, mechanical engineer.

mécanique [meka'nik], *a.* mechanical.—*n.f.* mechanics; mechanism, machinery; machine.

mécaniquement [mekanik'mɑ̃], *adv.* mechanically.

mécanisation [mekaniza'sjɔ̃], *n.f.* mechanization.

mécaniser [mekani'ze], *v.t.* to mechanize.

mécanisme [meka'nism], *n.m.* mechanism, machinery.

méchamment [meʃa'mɑ̃], *adv.* wickedly; maliciously.

méchanceté [meʃɑ̃s'te], *n.f.* wickedness; spitefulness; naughtiness.

méchant [me'ʃɑ̃], *a.* wicked, evil, bad; spiteful, malicious; naughty; paltry; vicious (*of an animal*); nasty.—*n.m.* (*fem.* **-e**) wicked person, evil-doer; naughty child.

mèche [mɛ:ʃ], *n.f.* wick (*of candle*); fuse; bit, drill; worm (*of screws*); lock (*of hair*).

mécompte [me'kɔ̃:t], *n.m.* miscalculation; mistake; disappointment.

méconnaissable [mekɔnɛ'sabl], *a.* unrecognizable.

méconnaissance [mekɔnɛ'sɑ̃:s], *n.f.* misappreciation, misreading; ingratitude.

méconnaître [mekɔ'nɛ:tr], *v.t. irr.* (*conjug. like* CONNAÎTRE) not to recognize; to disown; to disregard, to ignore; to misjudge. **se méconnaître**, *v.r.* to forget oneself.

méconnu [mekɔ'ny], *a.* unrecognized, unacknowledged; ignored, disowned.

mécontent [mekɔ̃'tɑ̃], *a.* displeased, dissatisfied.—*n.m.* (*fem.* **-e**) malcontent.

mécontentement [mekɔ̃tɑ̃t'mɑ̃], *n.m.* dissatisfaction, discontent.

mécontenter [mekɔ̃tɑ̃'te], *v.t.* to displease.

Mecque [mɛk], **la**, *f.* Mecca.

mécréant [mekre'ɑ̃], *n.m.* (*fem.* **-e**) unbeliever, infidel.

médaille [me'da:j], *n.f.* medal; (*Arch.*) medallion.

médaillé [meda'je], *a.* with a medal as a reward; having a badge (*of hawker, porter etc.*).—*n.m.* (*fem.* **-ée**) holder of a medal.

médaillon [meda'jɔ̃], *n.m.* medallion; locket.

médecin [med'sɛ̃], *n.m.* physician, doctor; *faire venir le médecin*, to send for the doctor.

médecine [med'sin], *n.f.* medicine.

médiateur [medja'tœ:r], *a.* (*fem.* **-trice**) mediatory.—*n.m.* (*fem.* **-trice**) mediator.

médiation [medja'sjɔ̃], *n.f.* mediation.

médical [medi'kal], *a.* (*m. pl.* **-aux**) medical.

médicament [medika'mɑ̃], *n.m.* medicine, drug.

médicamenter [medikamɑ̃'te], *v.t.* to physic, to doctor.

médication [medika'sjɔ̃], *n.f.* medication.

médicinal [medisi'nal], *a.* (*m. pl.* **-aux**) medicinal.

médiéval [medje'val], *a.* (*m. pl.* **-aux**) medi(a)eval.

médiocre [me'djɔkr], *a.* mediocre, middling; moderate.—*n.m.* mediocrity.

médiocrement [medjɔkrə'mɑ̃], *adv.* middlingly, indifferently; poorly; barely.

médiocrité [medjɔkri'te], *n.f.* mediocrity.

médire [me'di:r], *v.i. irr.* to slander, to speak ill of, to traduce.

médisance [medi'zɑ̃:s], *n.f.* slander, scandal.

médisant [medi'zɑ̃], *a.* slanderous, scandalous.—*n.m.* (*fem.* **-e**) slanderer, scandalmonger.

méditatif [medita'tif], *a.* (*fem.* **-tive**) meditative, pensive.

méditation [medita'sjɔ̃], *n.f.* meditation.

méditer [medi'te], *v.t.* to meditate, to think over; to plan.—*v.i.* to meditate, to muse.

méditerrané [mediterra'ne], *a.* inland; *la* (*Mer*) *Méditerranée*, the Mediterranean (Sea).

méditerranéen [mediterrane'ɛ̃], *a.* (*fem.* **-enne**) Mediterranean.

médium [me'djɔm], *n.m.* medium.

médoc [me'dɔk], *n.m.* or *vin de Médoc*, Médoc (*claret*).

meeting [mi'tiŋ], *n.m.* (*Polit., Spt.*) meeting.

méfait [me'fɛ], *n.m.* misdeed, crime.

méfiance [me'fjɑ̃:s], *n.f.* mistrust, distrust, suspicion.

méfiant [me'fjɑ̃], *a.* distrustful, suspicious.

méfier (**se**) [same'fje], *v.r.* to mistrust, to distrust, to be suspicious of (*de*).

mégaphone [mega'fɔn], *n.m.* megaphone.

mégarde [me'gard], *n.f.* inadvertence; *par mégarde*, inadvertently.

mégère [me'ʒɛ:r], *n.f.* shrew, vixen.

mégot [me'go], *n.m.* (*pop.*) cigar stump, cigarette end.

meilleur [mɛ'jœ:r], *a.* better; preferable; *le meilleur*, the best; *meilleur marché*, cheaper; *de meilleure heure*, earlier.—*n.m.* best.

mélancolie [melɑ̃kɔ'li], *n.f.* melancholy, sadness, gloom, dejection.

mélancolique [melɑ̃kɔ'lik], *a.* melancholy; dismal, gloomy.

mélancoliquement [melɑ̃kɔlik'mɑ̃], *adv.* gloomily.

mélange [me'lɑ̃:ʒ], *n.m.* mixture, mingling; blending (*of tea*); medley, mash (*for brewing*).

mélanger [melɑ̃'ʒe], *v.t.* and **se mélanger**, *v.r.* (*conjug. like* MANGER) to mix, to mingle, to blend.

mélasse [me'las], *n.f.* molasses treacle.

mêlé [mɛ'le], *a.* mixed; miscellaneous.

mêlée [mɛ'le], *n.f.* conflict, fray; scramble, scuffle, free fight.

mêler [mɛ'le], *v.t.* to mingle, to mix; to blend; to jumble; to entangle, to involve; to shuffle (*cards*). **se mêler**, *v.r.* to mingle to blend, to intermingle; to trouble oneself (*de*); to interfere (*de*); to have a hand in; to get entangled, to get mixed up (*dans*); *mêlez-vous de vos affaires*, mind your own business.

mélèze [me'lɛ:z], *n.m.* larch.

mélodie [melɔ'di], *n.f.* melody; melodiousness.

mélodieusement [melɔdjøz'mã], *adv.* tunefully.

mélodieux [melɔ'djø], *a.* (*fem.* **-euse**) melodious, musical, tuneful.

mélodramatique [melɔdrama'tik], *a.* melodramatic.

mélodrame [melɔ'dram], *n.m.* melodrama.

melon [mə'lɔ̃], *n.m.* melon; derby (hat).

membrane [mã'bran], *n.f.* membrane; web (*of duck's foot etc.*).

membraneux [mãbra'nø], *a.* (*fem.* **-euse**) membranous.

membre [mã:br], *n.m.* limb; member.

membrure [mã'bry:r], *n.f.* limbs, frame (*of a person etc.*); ribs, timbers (*of a ship*).

même [mɛ:m], *a.* same; self, self-same, very same; **moi-même**, myself.—*adv.* even, also; **à même de**, in a position to, able to; **de même**, likewise; **quand même**, even though; **tout de même**, all the same.

mémoire (1) [me'mwa:r], *n.f.* memory; remembrance; commemoration; fame; **de mémoire** from memory; **de mémoire d'homme**, within living memory.

mémoire (2) [me'mwa:r], *n.m.* memorandum, bill, statement of account; (*Sci., Lit.*) treatise; memorial; (*pl.*) memoirs.

mémorable [memɔ'rabl], *a.* memorable.

mémorandum [memɔrã'dɔm], *n.m.* memorandum; notebook.

mémorial [memɔ'rjal], *n.m.* (*pl.* **-aux**) memorial; memoirs; (*Comm.*) daybook.

menaçant [mɔna'sã], *a.* menacing, threatening.

menace [mɔ'nas], *n.f.* menace, threat.

menacer [mɔna'se], *v.t.* (*conjug. like* COMMENCER) to threaten, to menace; to forebode; to impend.

ménage [me'na:ʒ], *n.m.* housekeeping; household, family, married couple; household equipment; economy; **faire bon ménage**, to live happily together; **faire des ménages**, to do housework by the day; **femme de ménage**, housemaid.

ménagement [menaʒ'mã], *n.m.* regard, circumspection, caution, discretion.

ménager [mena'ʒe], *v.t.* (*conjug. like* MANGER) to be sparing of, to save; to be careful of, to treat with caution, to humor; to procure; to contrive. **se ménager**, *v.r.* to take care of oneself; to spare oneself.—*a.* (*fem.* **-ère**) thrifty, sparing, frugal; household.—*n.f.* (**-ère**) housewife, housekeeper; cruet stand; tableware.

ménagerie [menaʒ'ri], *n.f.* menagerie.

mendiant [mã'djã], *n.m.* (*fem.* **-e**) beggar, mendicant.

mendicité [mãdisi'te], *n.f.* begging, mendicity.

mendier [mã'dje], *v.t.* to beg for.—*v.i.* to beg.

mener [mə'ne], *v.t.* (*conjug. like* AMENER) to guide, to conduct, to lead; to drive (*a carriage*); to steer (*a boat etc.*); to bring, to take; to manage.—*v.i.* to lead, to conduct, to go.

ménestrel [menɛs'trɛl], *n.m.* minstrel.

meneur [mə'nœ:r], *n.m.* (*fem.* **-euse**) driver, leader; agitator, ringleader.

méningite [menɛ̃'ʒit], *n.f.* meningitis.

menotte [mɔ'nɔt], *n.f.* (*colloq.*) little hand (*of a child*); (*pl.*) handcuffs.

menotter [mɔnɔ'te], *v.t.* to handcuff.

mensonge [mã'sɔ̃:ʒ], *n.m.* lie, falsehood, untruth.

mensonger [mãsɔ̃'ʒe], *a.* (*fem.* **-ère**) lying, untrue, false.

menstruation [mãstrɥa'sjɔ̃], *n.f.* menstruation.

menstrues [mã'stry], *n.f. pl.* menses, periods.

mensualité [mãsɥali'te], *n.f.* monthly payment.

mensuel [mã'sɥɛl], *a.* (*fem.* **-elle**) monthly.

mensuellement [mãsɥɛl'mã], *adv.* monthly.

mensuration [mãsyra'sjɔ̃], *n.f.* measurement.

mental [mã'tal], *a.* (*m. pl.* **-aux**) mental.

mentalement [mãtal'mã], *adv.* mentally.

mentalité [mãtali'te], *n.f.* mentality.

menteur [mã'tœ:r], *a.* (*fem.* **-euse**) lying, false, deceitful.—*n.m.* (*fem.* **-euse**) liar, story-teller.

menthe [mã:t], *n.f.* mint.

mention [mã'sjɔ̃], *n.f.* mention; (*sch.*) **reçu avec mention**, passed with distinction.

mentionner [mãsjɔ'ne], *v.t.* to mention, to name.

mentir [mã'ti:r], *v.i. irr.* (*conjug. like* SENTIR) to lie, to tell a lie or untruth.

menton [mã'tɔ̃], *n.m.* chin.

mentor [mã'tɔ:r], *n.m.* mentor, guide, tutor.

menu [mə'ny], *a.* slender, spare, thin, small; petty.—*n.m.* minute detail, particulars; menu, bill of fare; **par le menu**, in detail.—*adv.* small, fine, minutely, in small pieces; **hacher menu**, to mince.

menuet [mə'nɥɛ], *n.m.* minuet.

menuiser [mənɥi'ze], *v.t.* to saw, cut etc. (*wood*).—*v.i.* to do carpenter's work.

menuiserie [mənɥiz'ri], *n.f.* woodwork, joinery, carpentry.

menuisier [mənɥi'zje], *n.m.* joiner, carpenter.

méprendre (**se**) [same'prã:dr], *v.r. irr.* (*conjug. like* PRENDRE) to mistake, to be mistaken.

mépris [me'pri], *n.m.* contempt, scorn.

méprisable [mepri'zabl], *a.* contemptible, despicable.

méprisant [mepri'zã], *a.* contemptuous, scornful.

méprise [me'pri:z], *n.f.* mistake, misunderstanding.

mépriser [mepri'ze], *v.t.* to despise, to scorn.

mer [mɛ:r], *n.f.* sea; **aller au bord de la mer**, to go to the seaside; **en pleine mer**, on the open sea; **mal de mer**, seasickness.

mercantile [merkã'til], *a.* mercantile, commercial; (*fig.*) mercenary.

mercenaire [mersə'nɛ:r], *a.* mercenary, venal.—*n.m.* mercenary, hireling.

mercerie [mersə'ri], *n.f.* mercery (store).

merci [mer'si], *n.f.* (*no pl.*) mercy, discretion, will.—*n.m.* thanks.—*int.* thank you, thanks.

mercier [mer'sje], *n.m.* (*fem.* **-ière**) dealer in notions.

mercredi [merkrə'di], *n.m.* Wednesday; **mercredi des Cendres**, Ash Wednesday.

mercure [mer'ky:r], *n.m.* mercury, quicksilver.

mercuriel [merky'rjɛl], *a.* (*fem.* **-elle**) mercurial.

mère [mɛ:r], *n.f.* mother; dam (*of animals*); (*fig.*) cause, reason.

méridien [meri'djɛ̃], *a.* (*fem.* **-enne**) and *n.m.* meridian.—*n.f.* (**-enne**) siesta.

méridional [meridjɔ'nal], *a.* (*m. pl.* **-aux**) meridional, southern.—*n.m.* (*fem.* **-e**) person of the Midi, southerner.

meringue [mə'rɛ̃ːg], *n.f.* meringue (*confection*).

mérinos [meri'nɔːs], *n.m.* merino sheep; merino wool; merino (*material*).

merise [mə'riːz], *n.f.* wild cherry.

merisier [məri'zje], *n.m.* wild-cherry tree.

méritant [meri'tɑ̃], *a.* meritorious, worthy.

mérite [me'rit], *n.m.* merit, worth; desert.

mériter [meri'te], *v.t.* to deserve, to merit; to earn.—*v.i.* to be deserving (*de*).

méritoire [meri'twaːr], *a.* meritorious.

méritoirement [meritwar'mɑ̃], *adv.* meritoriously, deservingly.

merlan [mɛr'lɑ̃], *n.m.* whiting.

merle [mɛrl], *n.m.* blackbird.

merluche [mɛr'lyʃ], *n.f.* hake; dried cod.

merveille [mɛr've:j], *n.f.* wonder, marvel, prodigy; *à merveille*, wonderfully well.

merveilleusement [mɛrvejœz'mɑ̃], *adv.* wonderfully, admirably.

merveilleux [mɛrve'jø], *a.* (*fem.* **-euse**) wonderful, marvellous.—*n.m.* the wonderful, the marvellous part.

mes [me], *pl.* [MON].

mésalliance [meza'ljɑ̃ːs], *n.f.* misalliance, bad match.

mésallier [meza'lje], *v.t.* to marry off (*somebody*) badly; (*fig.*) to disparage. **se mésallier**, *v.r.* to marry beneath one.

mésange [me'zɑ̃ːʒ], *n.f.* (*Orn.*) tit.

mésangette [mezɑ̃'ʒɛt], *n.f.* bird trap.

mésaventure [mezavɑ̃'tyːr], *n.f.* mischance, misadventure, misfortune.

mésentente [mezɑ̃'tɑ̃ːt], *n.f.* misunderstanding; disagreement.

mésestime [mezɛs'tim], *n.f.* low esteem.

mésestimer [mezɛsti'me], *v.t.* to underestimate, to underrate.

mésintelligence [mezɛ̃teli'ʒɑ̃ːs], *n.f.* misunderstanding, variance, disagreement.

mesmérisme [mɛsme'rism], *n.m.* mesmerism.

mesquin [mɛs'kɛ̃], *a.* shabby; paltry; mean.

mesquinement [mɛskin'mɑ̃], *adv.* shabbily, meanly.

mesquinerie [mɛskin'ri], *n.f.* meanness, shabbiness.

mess [mɛs], *n.m. inv.* (*Mil.*) mess.

message [me'saːʒ], *n.m.* message.

messager [mesa'ʒe], *n.m.* (*fem.* **-ère**) messenger; carrier; (*fig.*) forerunner.

messagerie [mesa'ʒri], *n.f.* shipping office; carriage of goods; goods department; parcels office; *messageries maritimes*, shipping service.

messe [mɛs], *n.f.* (*R.-C. Ch.*) mass.

messéance [mese'ɑ̃ːs], *n.f.* unseemliness, impropriety.

messéant [mese'ɑ̃], *a.* unseemly, unbecoming, improper.

messeigneurs [mesɛ'ɲœːr], *pl.* [MONSEIGNEUR].

Messie [me'si], *m.* Messiah.

messieurs [me'sjø], *pl.* [MONSIEUR].

mesurable [məzy'rabl], *a.* measurable.

mesurage [məzy'raːʒ], *n.m.* measurement, measuring.

mesure [mə'zyːr], *n.f.* measure; gauge, standard; measurement, extent, limit; (*fig.*)

moderation; dimension; (*Mus.*) bar; (*Pros.*) metre; *à mesure que*, in proportion as, as; *outre mesure*, excessively; *se mettre en mesure de*, to prepare to, to get ready to.

mesuré [məzy're], *a.* measured, regular; cautious.

mesurer [məzy're], *v.t.* to measure; to proportion; to calculate; to compare, to consider. **se mesurer**, *v.r.* to try one's strength; (*fig.*) to vie, to contend, to cope.

mesureur [məzy'rœːr], *n.m.* measurer; meter.

mésusage [mezy'zaːʒ], *n.m.* misuse, abuse.

mésuser [mezy'ze], *v.i.* to misuse, to abuse (*de*).

métabolisme [metabɔ'lism], *n.m.* metabolism.

métairie [mete'ri], *n.f.* land, small farm.

métal [me'tal], *n.m.* (*pl.* **-aux**) metal.

métallique [meta'lik], *a.* metallic.

métallurgie [metalyr'ʒi], *n.f.* metallurgy.

métallurgiste [metalyr'ʒist], *n.m.* metallurgist.

métamorphose [metamɔr'foːz], *n.f.* metamorphosis, transformation.

métaphore [meta'fɔːr], *n.f.* metaphor.

métaphorique [metafɔ'rik], *a.* metaphorical.

métaphoriquement [metafɔrik'mɑ̃], *adv.* metaphorically.

métaphysique [metafi'zik], *a.* metaphysical. —*n.f.* metaphysics.

métatarse [meta'tars], *n.m.* (*Anat.*) metatarsus.

métayage [mete'jaːʒ], *n.m.* metayage.

métayer [mete'je], *n.m.* (*fem.* **-ère**) small farmer.

météo [mete'o], *n.f.* (*fam.*) meteorology; weather report; meteorological office.

météore [mete'ɔːr], *n.m.* meteor.

météorique [meteɔ'rik], *a.* meteoric.

météorite [meteɔ'rit], *n.m.* or *f.* meteorite.

météorologie [meteɔrɔlɔ'ʒi], *n.f.* meteorology.

météorologique [meteɔrɔlɔ'ʒik], *a.* meteorological.

météorologiste [meteɔrɔlɔ'ʒist], **météorologue** [meteɔrɔ'lɔg], *n.* meteorologist.

méthane [me'tan], *n.m.* marsh gas, methane.

méthode [me'tɔd], *n.f.* method, system; way.

méthodique [metɔ'dik], *a.* methodical, systematic.

méthodiquement [metɔdik'mɑ̃], *adv.* methodically.

méthodisme [metɔ'dism], *n.m.* Methodism.

méthodiste [metɔ'dist], *a.* and *n.* Methodist.

méticuleusement [metikyløz'mɑ̃], *adv.* meticulously.

méticuleux [metiky'lø], *a.* (*fem.* **-euse**) meticulous, fastidious.

méticulosité [metikylɔzi'te], *n.f.* meticulousness.

métier [me'tje], *n.m.* trade, business, calling, craft, profession; loom, frame; *arts et métiers*, arts and crafts; *corps de métier*, corporation, guild; *gens de métier*, professionals; *homme de métier*, craftsman; *métier manuel*, handicraft.

métis [me'tiːs], *a.* (*fem.* **-isse**) half-caste, cross-bred; hybrid (*plant*); mongrel (*dog*).— *n.m.* (*fem.* **-isse**) half-caste; mongrel (*dog*).

métissage [meti'saːʒ], *n.m.* cross-breeding.

métisser [meti'se], *v.t.* to cross-breed.

215

métrage [me'tra:ʒ], *n.m.* measurement (*in metres*); (*Ciné.*) **court métrage**, short film.
mètre [mɛtr], *n.m.* metre (1.09 *yards*); rule, measure (*of 1 metre*); (*Pros.*) metre.
métrer [me'tre], *v.t.* (*conjug. like* CÉDER) to measure (*by the metre*).
métreur [me'trœːr], *n.m.* quantity surveyor.
métrique [me'trik], *a.* metric (*system etc.*); (*Pros.*) metrical.—*n.f.* scansion.
métro [me'tro], *n.m.* (*colloq. abbr. of* **chemin de fer métropolitain**) the underground (railway), the tube (*in Paris*), (*Am.*) the subway.
métropole [metrɔ'pɔl], *n.f.* mother country; metropolis.
métropolitain [metrɔpɔli'tɛ̃], *a.* metropolitan.—*n.m.* metropolitan, archbishop; underground railway, subway.
mets [mɛ], *n.m.* dish, food, viands.
mettable [mɛ'tabl], *a.* fit to be worn, wearable.
metteur [mɛ'tœːr], *n.m.* **metteur en scène**, (*Theat.*) producer, (*Ciné.*) director.
mettre [mɛtr], *v.t. irr.* to put, to set, to place; to put on, to wear; to employ; to contribute, to expend; to suppose, to imagine; **mettre en marche** or **en mouvement**, to start up, to set going; **mettre quelqu'un en état de**, to enable someone to; **mettre un habit**, to put on a coat. **se mettre**, *v.r.* to put or place oneself; to dress; to begin (à); to take to; **se mettre à parler**, to begin to speak; **se mettre à table**, to sit down to table; **se mettre bien**, to dress well; **se mettre en route**, to start.
meuble [mœbl], *a.* movable; **biens meubles**, (*Law*) personal property.—*n.m.* piece of furniture; (*pl.*) furniture.
meublé [mœ'ble], *a.* furnished.—*n.m.* a furnished room or flat.
meubler [mœ'ble], *v.t.* to furnish; to stock, to store. **se meubler**, *v.r.* to furnish one's home.
meule [mø:l], *n.f.* millstone, grindstone; (*Agric.*) stack, rick (*of grain, hay etc.*); (*Hort.*) hotbed.
meunerie [møn'ri], *n.f.* miller's trade; (*collect.*) millers.
meunier [mø'nje], *n.m.* miller; chub (*fish*).
meunière [mø'njɛːr], *n.f.* miller's wife.
meurtre [mœrtr], *n.m.* murder.
meurtrier [mœrtri'e], *a.* (*fem.* **-ière**) murdering, murderous, deadly; killing.—*n.m.* (*fem.* **-ière** (1)) murderer, murderess.
meurtrière (2) [mœrtri'ɛːr], *n.f.* (*Fort.*) loophole.
meurtrir [mœr'triːr], *v.t.* to bruise, to make black and blue.
meurtrissure [mœrtri'syːr], *n.f.* bruise.
meute [mø:t], *n.f.* pack (*of hounds etc.*).
mévendre [me'vɑ̃:dr], *v.t.* to sell at a loss.
mévente [me'vɑ̃:t], *n.f.* selling at a loss; slump.
mexicain [mɛksi'kɛ̃], *a.* Mexican.—*n.m.* (**Mexicain** *fem.* **-aine**) Mexican (*person*).
Mexico [mɛksi'ko], *m.* Mexico City.
Mexique [mɛk'sik], **le**, *m.* Mexico.
mi [mi], *n.m.* (*Mus.*) mi; the note E.
mi- [mi], *comb. form.* half, demi-; semi-; mid, middle; **à mi-chemin**, half-way; **à mi-corps**, up to the waist; **à mi-côte**, half-way

up the hill; **à mi-jambe**, half-way up the leg; **la mi-août**, the middle of August.
miaou [mjau], *n.m. inv.* (*fam.*) mew, miaow; cat.
miaulement [mjol'mɑ̃], *n.m.* mewing.
miauler [mjo'le], *v.i.* to mew; to caterwaul.
mica [mi'ka], *n.m.* mica.
miche [miʃ], *n.f.* round loaf.
Michel [mi'ʃɛl], *m.* Michael; **la Saint-Michel**, Michaelmas.
Michel-Ange [mikɛl'ɑ̃:ʒ], *m.* Michelangelo.
Micheline [miʃ'lin], *n.f.* rail-car, autorail.
micro [mi'kro], *n.m.* (*fam. abbr. of* **microphone**) mike.
microbe [mi'krɔb], *n.m.* microbe.
microcosme [mikrɔ'kɔsm], *n.m.* microcosm.
microfilm [mikrɔ'film], *n.m.* microfilm.
micromètre [mikrɔ'mɛtr], *n.m.* micrometer.
micro-organisme [mikrɔɔrga'nism], *n.m.* micro-organism.
microphone [mikrɔ'fɔn], *n.m.* microphone.
microscope [mikrɔs'kɔp], *n.m.* microscope.
microscopique [mikrɔskɔ'pik], *a.* microscopic.
midi [mi'di], *n.m.* noon, midday, twelve o'clock (*in the day*); meridian; south; **le Midi (de la France)**, the South of France.
midinette [midi'nɛt], *n.f.* (*fam.*) young dressmaker or milliner in Paris.
mie [mi], *n.f.* crumb; soft part of loaf.
miel [mjɛl], *n.m.* honey; **lune de miel**, honeymoon.
miellé [mjɛ'le], *a.* honeyed; like honey; (*fig.*) sweet, bland.
miellée [mjɛ'le], **miellure** [mjɛ'ly:r], *n.f.* honeydew.
mielleusement [mjɛløz'mɑ̃], *adv.* sweetly, blandly, honey-like.
mielleux [mjɛ'lo], *a.* (*fem.* **-euse**) honeyed; sweet, bland.
mien [mjɛ̃], *a. poss. and pron. poss.* (*fem.* **mienne**) mine; **le mien, la mienne, les miens, les miennes**, mine, my own.
miette [mjɛt], *n.f.* crumb, bit, morsel.
mieux [mjø], *adv.* better; correctly; more agreeably, more comfortably etc.; rather, more; **faute de mieux**, for want of better; **mieux vaut tard que jamais**, better late than never; **tant mieux**, so much the better; **valoir mieux**, to be better, to be worth more.—*n.m.* best thing; improvement.
mièvre [mjɛːvr], *a.* finical, affected; delicate (*child*), fragile.
mièvrerie [mjɛvra'ri], **mièvreté** [mjɛvra'te], *n.f.* affectation.
mignard [mi'na:r], *a.* delicate, pretty, dainty; mincing, affected.
mignardement [minardə'mɑ̃], *adv.* delicately, daintily; mincingly.
mignarder [minar'de], *v.t.* to fondle, to pet; to indulge.
mignardise [minar'di:z], *n.f.* delicacy, prettiness, daintiness; affectation, mincing ways.
mignon [mi'nɔ̃], *a.* (*fem.* **-onne**) delicate, pretty, dainty; sweet; neat, tiny.—*n.m.* (*fem.* **-onne**) darling, pet, favorite.
mignonnement [minɔn'mɑ̃], *adv.* daintily, prettily.
migraine [mi'grɛːn], *n.f.* sick headache; migraine.

migrateur [migra´tœːr], *a.* (*fem.* **-trice**) migratory.

migration [migro´sjɔ̃], *n.f.* migration.

migratoire [migra´twaːr], *a.* migratory.

mijoter [miʒɔ´te], *v.t.*, *v.i.* to cook slowly, to stew; to simmer; (*fig.*) to plot, to brew.

mil (1) [MILLE (2)].

mil (2) [mil], *n.m.* millet.

milan [mi´lɑ̃], *n.m.* kite (*bird*).

milice [mi´lis], *n.f.* militia; (*fig.*) troops, soldiery.

milicien [mili´sjɛ̃], *n.m.* militiaman.

milieu [mi´ljø], *n.m.* (*pl.* **-eux**) middle, midst; heart, center; mean; environment, ~~~~dings; *au beau milieu*, in the very surrou~~~~ middle.

militaire [mili´tɛːr], *a.* military.—*n.m.* soldier.

militairement [militɛr´mɑ̃], *adv.* in a soldier-like manner.

militant [mili´tɑ̃], *a.* militant.

militer [mili´te], *v.i.* to militate (*pour* or *contre*).

(*C*) **millage** [mi´la:ʒ], *n.m.* mileage.

mille (1) [mil], *n.m.* mile (*English, American mile, 1609.35 metres*).

mille (2) [mil], *a. inv.* and *n.m. inv.* (**mil** in *dates of the Christian era*) thousand, a thousand, one thousand.

millénaire [mille´nɛːr], *a.* millenary.—*n.m.* millennium.

mille-pattes [mil´pat], *n.m. inv.* centipede.

millésime [mille´zim], *n.m.* date (*on a coin, monument etc.*).

millet [mi´jɛ], *n.m.* millet, millet grass.

milliard [mi´ljaːr], *n.m.* one thousand millions, (*Am.*) one billion.

milliardaire [miljar´dɛːr], *a.* and *n.* multi-millionaire(ss).

millibar [milli´bar], *n.m.* (*Meteor.*) millibar.

millième [mi´ljɛm], *a.* and *n.m.* thousandth.

millier [mi´lje], *n.m.* thousand.

milligramme [milli´gram], *n.m.* milligramme (*.0154 grain*).

millimètre [milli´mɛtr], *n.m.* millimetre (*.03937 in.*).

million [mi´ljɔ̃], *n.m.* million.

millionième [miljo´njɛːm], *a.* and *n.m.* millionth.

millionnaire [miljo´nɛːr], *a.* and *n.* millionaire(ss).

mime [mim], *n.m.* mime; mimic.

mimer [mi´me], *v.t.*, *v.i.* to mimic, to mime.

mimi [mi´mi], *n.m.* (*Childish*) cat, pussy; darling, ducky.

mimique [mi´mik], *a.* mimic, mimetic.—*n.f.* art of mimicry.

mimosa [mimo´za], *n.m.* mimosa.

minable [mi´nabl], *a.* (*colloq.*) seedy, shabby.

minaret [mina´rɛ], *n.m.* minaret.

minauder [mino´de], *v.i.* to smirk, to simper.

minauderie [mino´dri], *n.f.* affected *or* mincing manners, simpering, smirking.

minaudier [mino´dje], *a.* (*fem.* **-ière**) affected, lackadaisical.—*n.m.* (*fem.* **-ière**) affected person.

mince [mɛ̃:s], *a.* thin, slender, slim; puny, slight, trivial; scanty, small.—*int.* (*pop.*) *ah ! mince !* or *mince alors !* my word ! well, I never !

minceur [mɛ̃´sœːr], *n.f.* slenderness, slimness.

mine (1) [min], *n.f.* look, bearing; face, expression; appearance, aspect; (*pl.*) airs.

mine (2) [min], *n.f.* (*Min.*) mine; (*fig.*) source, store.

mine (3) [min], *n.f.* (*Mil., Pyro.*) mine.

miner [mi´ne], *v.t.* to mine, to undermine, to sap; to wear away.

minerai [min´rɛ], *n.m.* ore.

minéral [mine´ral], *a.* (*m. pl.* **-aux**) mineral. —*n.m.* (*pl.* **-aux**) mineral; ore.

minéralogie [mineralɔ´ʒi], *n.f.* mineralogy.

minéralogique [mineralɔ´ʒik], *a.* mineralogical.

minéralogiste [mineralɔ´ʒist], *n.* mineralogist.

Minerve [mi´nɛrv], *f.* Minerva.

minet [mi´nɛ], *n.m.* (*fem.* **-ette**) (*colloq.*) puss, kitten.

mineur (1) [mi´nœːr], *n.m.* miner, pitman; (*Mil.*) sapper.

mineur (2) [mi´nœːr], *a.* lesser, minor; under age.—*n.m.* (*fem.* **-e**) minor; (*Law*) infant.

miniature [minja´tyːr], *n.f.* miniature. —*n.m.* miniature painter.

miniaturiste [minjaty´rist], *a.* of miniatures.

minier [mi´nje], *a.* (*fem.* **-ière**) pertaining to mines, mining.—*n.f.* (**-ière**) open mine.

minime [mi´nim], *a.* very small, trifling.

minimum [mini´mɔm], *a.* (*usu. inv.*) minimum.—*n.m.* (*pl.* **minimums** *or* **minima**) minimum.

ministère [minis´tɛːr], *n.m.* ministry; department; minister's office; offices, services; administration.

ministériel [ministe´rjɛl], *a.* (*fem.* **-elle**) ministerial.

ministre [mi´nistr], *n.m.* (*Polit., Ch.*) minister; clergyman.

minois [mi´nwa] *n.m. inv.* pretty face; looks, appearance.

minoritaire [minɔri´tɛːr], *a.* minority.

minorité [minɔri´te], *n.f.* minority; (*Law*) infancy.

Minorque [mi´nork], *f.* Minorca.

minoterie [minɔ´tri] *n.f.* flour mill; flour trade.

minotier [minɔ´tje], *n.m.* flour dealer, grain dealer.

minuit [mi´nɥi], *n.m.* midnight.

minuscule [minys´kyl], *a.* small (*of letters*), minute, tiny.—*n.f.* small letter.

minute [mi´nyt], *n.f.* minute (*of time*), moment, instant; rough draft; minute, record; *minute !* (*fam.*) just a moment !

minuter [miny´te], *v.t.* to record; to time.

minuterie [minyt´ri], *n.f.* time switch.

minutie [miny´si], *n.f.* trifle, (*pl.*) minutiae.

minutieusement [minysjøz´mɑ̃], *adv.* minutely.

minutieux [miny´sjø], *a.* (*fem.* **-euse**) minute; meticulous.

mioche [mjɔʒ], *n.* (*colloq.*) brat, urchin.

mi-parti [mipar´ti], *a.* bipartite, half and half.

mirabelle [mira´bɛl], *n.f.* yellow variety of plum.

miracle [mi´ra:kl], *n.m.* miracle; (*fig.*) wonder; *à miracle*, wonderfully well.

miraculeusement [mirakyløz´mɑ̃], *adv.* miraculously; wonderfully.

miraculeux [miraky´lø], *a.* (*fem.* **-euse**) miraculous; wonderful, marvellous.

mirage [mi'ra:ʒ], *n.m.* mirage; (*Naut.*) looming; (*fig.*) shadow.

mire [mi:r], *n.f.* land-surveyor's pole; (*Artill.*) aim; sight (*of fire-arms*).

mirer [mi're], *v.t.* to aim at; to have in view, to look at; to covet, **se mirer**, *v.r.* to look at oneself; to admire oneself; to be reflected.

mirliton [mirli'tɔ̃], *n.m.* reed pipe.

mirobolant [mirɔbɔ'lɑ̃], *a.* (*colloq.*) wonderful, prodigious.

miroir [mi'rwa:r], *n.m.* mirror, looking-glass.

miroitant [mirwa'tɑ̃], *a.* reflecting (*like a mirror*), glistening.

miroité [mirwa'te], *a.* shot, shiny; dappled (*of horses*).

miroitement [mirwat'mɑ̃], *n.m.* reflection of the light by polished surfaces; sheen, brilliancy.

miroiter [mirwa'te], *v.i.* to reflect light, to shine, to glisten, to shimmer.

mis [mi], *p.p.* [METTRE] **bien** or **mal mis**, well or badly dressed.

misaine [mi'zɛn], *n.f.* **mât de misaine**, foremast; **voile de misaine**, foresail.

misanthrope [mizɑ̃'trɔp], *n.* misanthrope.

misanthropie [mizɑ̃trɔ'pi], *n.f.* misanthropy.

misanthropique [mizɑ̃trɔ'pik], *a.* misanthropic.

miscellanées [misɛla'ne], *n.f. pl.* miscellanea, miscellany.

mise [mi:z], *n.f.* placing; stake; investment; bidding (*at auctions*); capital; dress; **mise en marche**, starting; starting-handle; **mise en marche automatique**, self-starter; **mise en scène**, (*Theat.*) production, (*Cine.*) direction.

misérable [mize'rabl], *a.* miserable, pitiable; worthless; despicable.—*n.* wretch, miserable person; miscreant.

misérablement [mizerablə'mɑ̃], *adv.* miserably.

misère [mi'zɛ:r], *n.f.* misery, wretchedness, distress; poverty; trouble; trifling thing.

miséreux [mize'rø], *a.* and *n.m.* (*fem.* **-euse**) poor, destitute; seedy looking (person).

miséricorde [mizeri'kɔrd], *n.f.* mercy, pardon, grace.

miséricordieux [mizerikɔr'djø], *a.* (*fem.* **-euse**) merciful, compassionate.

missel [mi'sɛl], *n.m.* missal, mass book.

mission [mi'sjɔ̃], *n.f.* mission.

missionnaire [misjɔ'nɛ:r], *n.* missionary.

missive [mi'si:v], *a.f.* and *n.f.* missive.

mistral [mis'tral], *n.m.* mistral (*cold north wind in southern France*).

mitaine [mi'tɛn], *n.f.* mitten.

mite [mit], *n.f.* mite; moth; **mangé des mites**, moth-eaten.

mité [mi'te], *a.* moth-eaten, maggoty.

mi-temps [mi'tɑ̃], *n.f.* (*Ftb.*) half-time.

miteux [mi'tø], *a.* (*fem.* **-euse**) full of mites; (*fig.*) shabby, poverty-stricken.

mitigation [mitigɑ'sjɔ̃], *n.f.* mitigation.

mitiger [miti'ʒe], *v.t.* (*conjug. like* MANGER) to mitigate, to alleviate, to modify.

mitonner [mitɔ'ne], *v.t.* to coddle, to fondle; to nurse.—*v.i.* to let slices of bread simmer in the broth, to simmer.

mitoyen [mitwa'jɛ̃], *a.* (*fem.* **-enne**) middle; intermediate; party, joint; **mur mitoyen**, party wall.

mitraille [mi'tra:j], *n.f.* grape-shot.

mitrailler [mitra'je], *v.t., v.i.* to machine-gun.

mitraillette [mitra'jɛt], *n.f.* Tommy gun.

mitrailleuse [mitra'jø:z], *n.f.* machine gun.

mitre [mitr], *n.f.* miter.

mitré [mi'tre], *a.* mitered.

mitron [mi'trɔ̃], *n.m.* journeyman baker; pastry-cook's boy.

mixte [mikst], *a.* mixed.

mixture [miks'ty:r], *n.f.* mixture.

mobile [mɔ'bil], *a.* mobile, movable; unsteady, variable.—*n.m.* body in motion, mover, motive power.

mobilier [mɔbi'lje], *a.* (*fem.* **-ière**) movable; personal (*of property*).—*n.m.* furniture.

mobilisation [mɔbiliza'sjɔ̃], *n.f.* mobilization; liquidation (*of capital*).

mobiliser [mɔbili'ze], *v.t.* (*Law*) to liquidate; (*Mil.*) to mobilize.

mobilité [mɔbili'te], *n.f.* mobility; variability; instability.

mode (1) [mɔd], *n.f.* fashion; manner, way, custom; (*pl.*) millinery.

mode (2) [mɔd], *n.m.* (*Mus. etc.*) mode; (*Gram.*) mood; method; **mode d'emploi**, directions for use.

modelage [mɔ'dla:ʒ], *n.m.* modelling.

modèle [mɔ'dɛl], *a.* exemplary.—*n.m.* model; pattern, design.

modelé [mɔ'dle], *n.m.* (*Sculp., Paint.*) relief; reproduction.

modeler [mɔ'dle], *v.t.* (*conjug. like* AMENER) to model; to shape; to mold (*clay*). **se modeler**, *v.r.* to model oneself (*sur*).

modeleur [mɔ'dlœ:r], *n.m.* modeller.

modérateur [mɔdera'tœ:r], *a.* (*fem.* **-trice**) moderating.—*n.m.* (*fem.* **-trice**) moderator.—*n.m.* (*Mech.*) regulator.

modération [mɔdera'sjɔ̃], *n.f.* moderation; abatement.

modéré [mɔde're], *a.* moderate, reasonable.—*n.m.* (*fem.* **-e**) (*Polit.*) moderate.

modérément [mɔdere'mɑ̃], *adv.* moderately, in moderation.

modérer [mɔde're], *v.t.* (*conjug. like* CÉDER) to moderate, to mitigate; to restrain. **se modérer**, *v.r.* to keep one's temper; to restrain oneself.

moderne [mɔ'dɛrn], *a.* modern, up-to-date.—*n.m.* modern style.

modernisation [mɔderniza'sjɔ̃], *n.f.* modernization.

moderniser [mɔderni'ze], *v.t.* to modernize.

modeste [mɔ'dɛst], *a.* modest, unassuming; quiet; simple.

modestement [mɔdɛstə'mɑ̃], *adv.* modestly, quietly, simply.

modestie [mɔdɛs'ti], *n.f.* modesty, simplicity.

modicité [mɔdisi'te], *n.f.* smallness; modicum.

modification [mɔdifikɑ'sjɔ̃], *n.f.* modification.

modifier [mɔdi'fje], *v.t.* to modify, to change, to alter. **se modifier**, *v.r.* to become modified.

modique [mɔ'dik], *a.* moderate; small.

modiquement [mɔdik'mɑ̃], *adv.* moderately.

modiste [mɔ'dist], *n.* modiste, milliner.

modulation [mɔdylɑ'sjɔ̃], *n.f.* modulation; (*Rad.*) **modulation de fréquence**, very high frequency, V.H.F.

moduler [mɔdy'le], *v.t.* to modulate.
moelle [mwal], *n.f.* marrow (*of bone*); (*Bot.*) pith.
moelleusement [mwalœz'mɑ̃], *adv.* softly; (*Paint.*) with mellowness.
moelleux [mwa'lø], *a.* (*fem.* **-euse**) full of marrow; pithy; soft; mellow.—*n.m.* softness; mellowness.
moellon [mwa'lɔ̃], *n.m.* rubble; building stone.
mœurs [mœrs], *n.f. pl.* morals; manners, habits, ways, customs; *certificat de bonne vie et mœurs,* certificate of good character.
Mogol [mɔ'gɔl], *m.* Mogul.
moi [mwa], *pron. pers.* I; me, to me; *moi-même,* myself.—*n.m.* self, ego.
moignon [mwa'ɲɔ̃], *n.m.* stump (*of limbs, trees etc.*).
moindre [mwɛ̃:dr], *a.* lesser; least.
moine [mwan], *n.m.* monk, friar; bed-warmer.
moineau [mwa'no], *n.m.* (*pl.* **-eaux**) sparrow.
moins [mwɛ̃], *adv.* less; fewer (*de* or *que*); not so; *à moins de* (or *que*), unless; *du moins,* at least, at any rate; *les moins de seize ans,* the under sixteens.—*prep.* less, minus.—*n.m.* (*Math.*) minus sign; (*Print.*) dash.
moire [mwar], *n.f.* watering; moire, watered silk.
moiré [mwa're], *a.* watered, moiré.—*n.m.* watered effect.
moirer [mwa're], *v.t.* to moiré, to give a watered appearance to.
mois [mwa], *n.m.* month; monthly allowance, month's pay.
Moïse [mɔ'i:z], *m.* Moses.
moisi [mwa'zi], *a.* moldy, musty.—*n.m.* moldiness, mustiness.
moisir [mwa'zi:r], *v.t.* to make moldy or musty.—*v.i.* and **se moisir,** *v.r.* to grow moldy or musty.
moisissure [mwazi'sy:r], *n.f.* moldiness, mustiness, mildew.
moisson [mwa'sɔ̃], *n.f.* harvest, harvest time.
moissonner [mwasɔ'ne], *v.t.* to reap, to gather in, to mow.
moissonneur [mwasɔ'nœ:r], *n.m.* (*fem.* **-euse**) reaper, harvester.—*n.f.* (**-euse**) reaping machine.
moissonneuse-batteuse [mwasɔ'nøzba'tø:z] *n.f.* (*pl.* **moissonneuses-batteuses**) combine harvester.
moite [mwat], *a.* moist, damp; clammy.
moiteur [mwa'tœ:r], *n.f.* moistness, dampness.
moitié [mwa'tje], *n.f.* half; (*colloq.*) better half, wife.—*adv.* half; *à moitié fait,* half done; *trop cher de moitié,* too dear by half.
moka [mɔ'ka], *n.m.* mocha (*coffee* or *cake*).
mol [mɔl], [MOU].
molaire [mɔ'lɛ:r], *a.* molar.—*n.f.* molar (tooth).
môle [mo:l], *n.m.* mole, pier.
moléculaire [mɔleky'lɛ:r], *a.* molecular.
molécule [mɔle'kyl], *n.f.* molecule.
molestation [mɔlɛsta'sjɔ̃], *n.f.* molestation, annoyance.
molester [mɔlɛs'te], *v.t.* to molest, to trouble.

mollasse [mɔ'las], *a.* flabby; spineless.
molle [mɔl], [MOU].
mollement [mɔl'mɑ̃], *adv.* softly; feebly; indolently.
mollesse [mɔ'lɛs], *n.f.* softness; flabbiness; slackness; indolence.
mollet [mɔ'lɛ], *a.* (*fem.* **-ette**) soft; light (*of bread*).—*n.m.* calf (*of the leg*).
molletière [mɔl'tjɛ:r], *n.f.* legging, puttee.
molleton [mɔl'tɔ̃], *n.m.* thick flannel, duffel.
mollir [mɔ'li:r], *v.i.* to soften; to mellow (*of fruit*); to slacken, to give way.
mollusque [mɔ'lysk], *n.m.* mollusc.
molosse [mɔ'lɔs], *n.m.* mastiff, watch-dog.
môme [mo:m], *n.* (*pop.*) brat, urchin.
moment [mɔ'mɑ̃], *n.m.* moment, instant; favorable occasion; *au moment de,* just as; *du moment que,* since.
momentané [mɔmɑ̃ta'ne], *a.* momentary.
momentanément [mɔmɑ̃tane'mɑ̃], *adv.* momentarily.
momie [mɔ'mi], *n.f.* mummy; (*fig.*) old fogy.
momifier [mɔmi'fje], *v.t.* to mummify.
mon [mɔ̃], *a.poss.m.* (*fem.* **ma,** *pl.* **mes**) my.
monarchie [mɔnar'ʃi], *n.f.* monarchy.
monarchique [mɔnar'ʃik], *a.* monarchical.
monarchiste [mɔnar'ʃist], *a.* and *n.* monarchist.
monarque [mɔ'nark], *n.m.* monarch.
monastère [mɔnas'tɛ:r], *n.m.* monastery, convent.
monastique [mɔnas'tik], *a.* monastic.
monceau [mɔ̃'so], *n.m.* (*pl.* **-eaux**) heap, pile.
mondain [mɔ̃'dɛ̃], *a.* worldly, mundane.—*n.m.* (*fem.* **-e**) worldly person.
mondanité [mɔ̃dani'te], *n.f.* worldliness; (*pl.*) social events.
monde [mɔ̃:d], *n.m.* world; universe; mankind; people; society; company, set; men; customers; *tout le monde,* everybody.
monder [mɔ̃'de], *v.t.* to cleanse; to hull (*barley*), to blanch (*almonds*).
mondial [mɔ̃'djal], *a.* (*m. pl.* **-aux**) world, world-wide.
monétaire [mɔne'tɛ:r], *a.* monetary.
mongol [mɔ̃'gɔl], *a.* Mongolian.—*n.m.* Mongolian (*language*); (**Mongol,** *fem.* **-ole**) Mongol(ian) (*person*).
Mongolie [mɔ̃gɔ'li], **la,** *f.* Mongolia.
Monique [mɔ'nik], *f.* Monica.
moniteur [mɔni'tœ:r], *n.m.* (*fem.* **-trice**) (*sch.*) prefect, monitor; instructor.
monnaie [mɔ'nɛ], *n.f.* coin, money; change; mint; money forte, hard currency; *monnaie légale,* legal tender.
monnayage [mɔnɛ'ja:ʒ], *n.m.* coining, minting.
monnayer [mɔnɛ'je], *v.t.* (*conjug. like* PAYER) to coin into money, to mint; (*fig.*) to make money out of, to sell.
monnayeur [mɔnɛ'jœ:r], *n.m.* coiner, minter; *faux monnayeur,* counterfeiter, forger.
monochrome [mɔnɔ'krom], *a.* monochrome.
monocle [mɔ'nɔkl], *n.m.* monocle, eyeglass.
monogramme [mɔnɔ'gram], *n.m.* monogram.
monologue [mɔnɔ'lɔg], *n.m.* monologue, soliloquy.
monopole [mɔnɔ'pɔl], *n.m.* monopoly.
monopoliser [mɔnɔpɔli'ze], *v.t.* to monopolize.
monorail [mɔnɔ'ra:j], *a.* and *n.m.* monorail.

monosyllabe

monosyllabe [mɔnɔsil'lab], *a.* monosyllabic. —*n.f.* monosyllable.

monosyllabique [mɔnɔsilla'bik], *a.* monosyllabic.

monotone [mɔnɔ'tɔn], *a.* monotonous.

monotonie [mɔnɔtɔ'ni], *n.f.* monotony.

monseigneur [mɔ̃sɛɲpœːr], *n.m.* (*pl.* **messeigneurs** *or* **nosseigneurs**) my lord; your Grace; your Royal *or* Imperial Highness.

monsieur [mɔ'sjø, msjø], *n.m.* (*pl.* **messieurs**) sir; gentleman; Mr.

monstre [mɔ̃:str], *a.* (*fam.*) huge.—*n.m.* monster.

monstrueusement [mɔ̃strɥøz'mɑ̃], *adv.* monstrously, prodigiously.

monstrueux [mɔ̃s'trɥø], *a.* (*fem.* -**euse**) monstrous, prodigious.

monstruosité [mɔ̃strɥozi'te], *n.f.* monstrosity.

mont [mɔ̃], *n.m.* hill, mount, mountain.

montage [mɔ̃'ta:ʒ], *n.m.* carrying up; mounting; assembling; (*Cine.*) editing (*of film*); (*Ind.*) **châine de montage,** assembly line.

montagnard [mɔ̃ta'ɲaːr], *a.* mountain, highland.—*n.m.* (*fem.* -**e**) mountaineer, highlander.

montagne [mɔ̃'taɲ], *n.f.* mountain; hill.

montagneux [mɔ̃ta'ɲø], *a.* (*fem.* -**euse**) mountainous, hilly.

montant (1) [mɔ̃'tɑ̃], *n.m.* upright (*of a ladder etc.*); post (*of door etc.*); (*Naut.*) stanchion; amount, sum total; rising tide; high flavor, pungency; (*Ftb.*) goal post.

montant (2) [mɔ̃'tɑ̃], *a.* rising; ascending; flowing, coming in; high-necked (*of dresses*).

monte [mɔ̃:t], *n.f.* mounting, mount (*of a jockey*); serving (*of animals*), covering season.

monte-charge [mɔ̃t'farʒ], *n.m. inv.* hoist, goods lift; (*Am.*) freight elevator.

montée [mɔ̃'te], *n.f.* gradient, slope; ascent; (*Arch. etc.*) height.

monter [mɔ̃'te], *v.t.* to mount, to ascend, to go up: to walk, ride, row etc. up; to get up on, to ride; to raise; to wind up; to equip; to make up; to rouse.—*v.i.* (*with aux.* AVOIR *or* ÊTRE *according as action or condition is meant*) to go (*or* come) up, to mount; to climb; to rise; to increase; to amount. **se monter,** *v.r.* to amount, to rise; to get excited; to supply oneself with (*en*).

monteur [mɔ̃'tœːr], *n.m.* (*fem.* -**euse**) setter, mounter (*of jewels, machinery etc.*); (*Cine.*) (film-)editor.

monticule [mɔ̃ti'kyl], *n.m.* hillock, knoll.

montoir [mɔ̃'twaːr], *n.m.* horse-block; *côté du montoir,* near side; *côté hors montoir,* off side.

montre (1) [mɔ̃:tr], *n.f.* show-case, shop-window; show, display, exhibition.

montre (2) [mɔ̃:tr], *n.f.* watch.

montre-bracelet [mɔ̃trabras'lɛ], *n.f.* (*pl.* **montres-bracelets**) wrist watch.

montrer [mɔ̃'tre], *v.t.* to show, to display; to demonstrate; to teach; to indicate. **se montrer,** *v.r.* to show oneself; to appear; to prove oneself to be, to turn out.

montreur [mɔ̃'trœːr], *n.m.* (*fem* -**euse**) showman, exhibitor.

montueux [mɔ̃'tɥø], *a.* (*fem.* -**euse**) hilly.

220

monture [mɔ̃'tyːr], *n.f.* animal for riding, mount; setting (*of gems etc.*); frame.

monument [mɔny'mɑ̃], *n.m.* monument; memorial.

monumental [mɔnymɑ̃'tal], *a.* (*m. pl.* -**aux**) monumental.

moquer (se) [səmɔ'ke], *v.r.* (*de*) to mock, to jeer, to laugh at; to make fun of.

moquerie [mɔ'kri], *n.f.* mockery, derision; jest.

moquette [mɔ'kɛt], *n.f.* carpet; fitted carpet; velvet pile.

moqueur [mɔ'kœːr], *a.* (*fem.* -**euse**) mocking, jeering, derisive.—*n.m.* (*fem.* -**euse**) mocker, scoffer; wag.

moral [mɔ'ral], *a.* (*m. pl.* -**aux**) moral; mental.—*n.m.* mind, mental faculties, spirit, morale.

morale [mɔ'ral], *n.f.* ethics, moral philosophy; morals, morality; rebuke, lecture; moral (*of a story etc.*).

moralement [mɔral'mɑ̃], *adv.* morally.

moraliste [mɔra'list], *a.* and *n.* moralist.

moralité [mɔrali'te], *n.f.* morality; morals.

morbide [mɔr'bid], *a.* morbid.

morbleu! [mɔr'blø], *int.* the devil! hang it!

morceau [mɔr'so], *n.m.* (*pl.* -**eaux**) bit, piece, morsel, fragment.

morceler [mɔrs'le], *v.t.* (*conjug. like* APPELER) to parcel out, to cut up.

mordant [mɔr'dɑ̃], *a.* biting; cutting, sarcastic.—*n.m.* mordant; pungency, keenness.

mordiller [mɔrdi'je], *v.t.* to nibble, to bite at.

mordoré [mɔrdɔ're], *a.* and *n.m.* reddish brown.

mordre [mɔrdr], *v.t.* to bite; to gnaw; to eat into.—*v.i.* to bite, to nibble; to take hold; to succeed; to criticize. **se mordre,** *v.r.* to bite oneself; *s'en mordre les doigts,* to repent of a thing.

more [mɔːr], **moresque** [mɔ'rɛsk], *a.* Moorish.—*n.* (**More**) Moor; Negro.

morfondre [mɔr'fɔ̃dr], *v.t.* to chill. **se morfondre,** *v.r.* to be chilled, to shiver; to kick one's heels; (*fig.*) to mope.

morfondu [mɔrfɔ̃'dy], *a.* chilled, shivering, benumbed.

morganatique [mɔrgana'tik], *a.* morganatic.

morgue (1) [mɔrg], *n.f.* haughtiness, arrogance.

morgue (2) [mɔrg], *n.f.* morgue, mortuary.

moribond [mɔri'bɔ̃], *a.* moribund, dying.— *n.m.* (*fem.* -**e**) person in a dying state.

moricaud [mɔri'ko], *a.* dark, darkish.—*n.m.* (*fem.* -**e**) (*pej.*) blackamoor, (*pej.*) Negro.

morigéner [mɔriʒe'ne], *v.t.* (*conjug. like* CÉDER) to scold, to reprimand.

mormon [mɔr'mɔ̃], *a.* Mormon.—*n.m.* (**Mormon,** *fem.* -**e**) Mormon (*person*).

morne [mɔrn], *a.* gloomy, dejected, dreary.

morose [mɔ'roːz], *a.* morose, sullen, surly.

morosité [mɔrozi'te], *n.f.* moroseness, sullenness, surliness.

Morphée [mɔr'fe], *m.* Morpheus.

morphine [mɔr'fin], *n.f.* morphia.

morphologie [mɔrfɔlɔ'ʒi], *n.f.* morphology.

mors [mɔːr], *n.m. inv.* bit (*of a bridle*); (*fig.*) curb, check.

morse (1) [mɔrs], *n.m.* morse, walrus.

morse (2) [mɔrs], *n.m.* Morse (code).

morsure [mɔr'syːr], *n.f.* bite. biting.

mort [mɔːr], *a.* dead; lifeless, inanimate; dormant; stagnant; out (*of a candle etc.*); *nature morte*, still life; *au point mort*, at a standstill, in neutral (gear) (*of a car*).—*n.m.* (*fem.* **-e**) dead person, corpse.—*n.m.* dummy (*at cards*).—*n.f.* death; *à mort*, mortally, to the death.

mortalité [mɔrtali'te], *n.f.* mortality.

mort-bois [mɔr'bwa], *n.m.* (*no pl.*) brushwood, undergrowth.

morte-eau [mɔr'to], *n.f.* (*pl.* **mortes-eaux**) neap tide.

mortel [mɔr'tɛl], *a.* (*fem.* **-elle**) mortal, deadly; grievous.—*n.m.* (*fem.* **-elle**) mortal.

mortellement [mɔrtɛl'mɑ̃], *adv.* fatally, deadly.

morte-saison [mɔrtsɛ'zɔ̃], *n.f.* (*pl.* **mortes-saisons**) slack time, off season.

mortier [mɔr'tje], *n.m.* mortar (*cement, artillery, vessel*).

mortifiant [mɔrti'fjɑ̃], *a.* mortifying, humiliating.

mortification [mɔrtifika'sjɔ̃], *n.f.* mortification, humiliation.

mortifier [mɔrti'fje], *v.t.* to mortify; to humiliate. **se mortifier**, *v.r.* to mortify oneself.

mort-né [mɔr'ne], *a.* and *n.m.* (*fem.* **mort-née**, *pl.* **mort-nés, mort-nées**) stillborn (*child*).

mortuaire [mɔr'tɥɛːr], *a.* mortuary; *drap mortuaire*, pall.

morue [mɔ'ry], *n.f.* cod, codfish; *huile de foie de morue*, cod-liver oil.

morveux [mɔr'vø], *a.* (*fem.* **-euse**) snotty; *qui se sent morveux se mouche*, if the cap fits, wear it.

mosaïque [mɔza'ik], *a.* and *n.f.* mosaic.

Moscou [mɔs'ku], **le**, *m.* Moscow.

mosquée [mɔs'ke], *n.f.* mosque.

mot [mo], *n.m.* word; remark, saying, sentence; motto; note; (*Mil.*) parole, watchword; *au bas mot*, at the least; *bon mot*, witticism; *mots croisés*, crossword.

motel [mɔ'tɛl], *n.m.* motel.

moteur [mɔ'tœːr], *a.* (*fem.* **-trice**) motive, driving.—*n.m.* mover; motor; engine; motive power.

motif [mɔ'tif], *a.* (*fem.* **-tive**) moving, inciting.—*n.m.* motive, incentive; cause; (*Mus. etc.*) motif, design.

motion [mɔ'sjɔ̃], *n.f.* (*Polit.*) motion.

motiver [mɔti've], *v.t.* to justify; to allege as a motive; to be the cause of, to bring about.

moto [mɔ'to], *n.f.* (*fam.*) motor bike.

motocyclette [mɔtosi'klɛt], *n.f.* motor-cycle.

motte [mɔt], *n.f.* clod; *motte de beurre*, pat of butter.

motus! [mɔ'ty:s], *int.* (*colloq.*) mum's the word!

mou [mu], *a.* (**mol** before vowel or *h* mute, *fem.* **molle**) soft; limp; flabby; weak; slack, sluggish, indolent.—*n.m.* soft part of thing; slack (*of a rope*); lights (*of animals*).

mouchard [mu'ʃaːr], *n.m.* sneak, *esp.* police spy, nark, informer.

moucharder [muʃar'de], *v.t., v.i.* to inform (*on*), to spy (*on*); to sneak.

mouche [muʃ], *n.f.* fly; patch (*on the face*), beauty spot; button (*of foil*); bull's-eye (*of a target*); river passenger-steamer.

(C) **mouche à feu** [muʃa'fø], *n.f.* firefly.

moucher [mu'ʃe], *v.t.* to wipe the nose of; to snuff. **se moucher**, *v.r.* to blow one's nose.

moucheron [muʃ'rɔ̃], *n.m.* gnat, very small fly.

moucheté [muʃ'te], *a.* spotted, speckled, flecked; capped (*of foils*).

moucheter [muʃ'te], *v.t.* (*conjug. like* APPELER) to spot, to speckle, to fleck; to cap (*foils*).

mouchoir [mu'ʃwaːr], *n.m.* handkerchief.

moudre [mudr], *v.t. irr.* to grind, to crush.

moue [mu], *n.f.* pout; *faire la moue*, to pout.

mouette [mwɛt], *n.f.* gull, sea-mew.

moufle [mufl], *n.f.* mitten; tackle-block.

mouillage [mu'jaːʒ], *n.m.* soaking, wetting; anchorage.

mouillé [mu'je], *a.* wet, watery; liquid (*of the letter l*); at anchor.

mouiller [mu'je], *v.t.* to wet, to moisten.—*v.i.* to drop anchor; to moor.

moulage [mu'laːʒ], *n.m.* molding, casting; mold, cast; grinding, milling.

moule (1) [mul], *n.m.* mold, matrix; pattern.

moule (2) [mul], *n.f.* mussel.

moulé [mu'le], *a.* molded, cast; well-formed; *lettre moulée*, block letter.

mouler [mu'le], *v.t.* to cast, to mold; to shape. **se mouler**, *v.r.* to model oneself (*sur*).

mouleur [mu'lœːr], *n.m.* molder.

moulin [mu'lɛ̃], *n.m.* mill; grinder; (*Geol.*) pothole; *jeter son bonnet par-dessus les moulins*, to throw off all restraint.

moulinet [muli'nɛ], *n.m.* small mill; winch; turnstile; fishing reel.

moulu [mu'ly], *a.* ground; bruised.

moulure [mu'lyːr], *n.f.* (*Arch.*) molding.

mourant [mu'rɑ̃], *a.* dying, expiring; fading.—*n.m.* (*fem.* **-e**) dying person.

mourir [mu'riːr], *v.i. irr.* (*with aux.* ÊTRE) to die, to expire; to perish; to stop, to go out (*of fire*); to be out (*at play*). **se mourir**, *v.r.* (*Poet., only used in pres. and imp. indic.*) to be dying.

mouron [mu'rɔ̃], *n.m.* (*Bot.*) *mouron rouge*, scarlet pimpernel; *mouron des oiseaux*, chickweed.

mousquet [mus'kɛ], *n.m.* musket; *mousquet à pierre*, flintlock.

mousquetaire [muska'tɛːr], *n.m.* musketeer.

mousse (1) [mus], *a.* blunt (*of tools*).

mousse (2) [mus], *n.f.* moss; froth, foam; lather; whipped cream.

mousse (3) [mus], *n.m.* ship's boy.

mousseline [mus'lin], *n.f.* muslin.

mousser [mu'se], *v.i.* to froth, to foam; to sparkle (*of wine*).

mousseux [mu'sø], *a.* (*fem.* **-euse**) foaming, frothy; sparkling (*of wine etc.*).

mousson [mu'sɔ̃], *n.f.* monsoon.

moussu [mu'sy], *a.* mossy.

moustache [mus'taʃ], *n.f.* moustache; whiskers (*of animals*).

moustiquaire [musti'kɛːr], *n.f.* mosquito net.

moustique [mus'tik], *n.m.* mosquito.

moût [mu], *n.m.* must (*wine not fermented*); wort (*of beer*).

moutarde [mu'tard], *n.f.* mustard.

221

moutardier [mutar′dje], *n.m.* mustard pot; mustard maker.

mouton [mu′tõ], *n.m.* sheep; mutton; sheep-skin (*leather*); ram; (*fig.*) ninny; (*slang*) decoy, prison spy; (*pl.*) white-crested waves; *revenons à nos moutons*, let us return to the subject.

moutonné [muto′ne], *a.* fleecy, curled; white with foam (*of the sea*).

moutonner [muto′ne], *v.t.* to make woolly *or* fleecy; to curl, to frizzle.—*v.i.* to be ruffled, to foam.

moutonneux [muto′nø], *a.* (*fem.* **-euse**) fleecy; foaming (*of waves*).

moutonnier [muto′nje], *a.* (*fem.* **-ière**) sheep-like.

mouvant [mu′vã], *a.* moving, shifting; unstable.

mouvement [muv′mã], *n.m.* movement, motion; march; animation, bustle; emotion, commotion; spirit, impulse; (*Mus.*) time; (*Mil.*) maneuver.

mouvementé [muvmã′te], *a.* animated, lively; undulating (*ground*).

mouvoir [mu′vwa:r], *v.t. irr.* to move, to stir; to prompt. **se mouvoir**, *v.r.* to move, to stir.

moyen [mwa′jɛ̃], *a.* (*fem.* **-enne**) mean, middle, medium; average.—*n.m.* means; way, manner, medium; (*pl.*) resources; talents.

moyennant [mwajɛ′nã], *prep.* by means of; in consideration of.—*conj. phr.* **moyennant que**, on condition that.

moyenne [mwa′jɛn], *n.f.* average; (*sch.*) passing mark.

moyeu [mwa′jø], *n.m.* (*pl.* **-eux**) nave (*of cartwheel*); hub (*of bicycle*).

muable [mɥabl], *a.* mutable, changeable.

mucosité [mykozi′te], *n.f.* mucus.

mucus [my′ky:s], *n.m.* mucus.

mue [my], *n.f.* molting; skin, slough; mew, coop (*cage*).

muer [mɥe], *v.i.* to molt, to cast *or* slough horns etc.; to break (*of the voice*).

muet [mɥɛ], *a.* (*fem.* **muette**) dumb, mute; silent (*of letters*); blank (*of maps*).—*n.m.* (*fem.* **muette** (1)) dumb man *or* woman.

muette (2) [mɥɛt], *n.f.* mews; hunting lodge.

mufle [myfl], *n.m.* snout, muzzle (*of animals*); (*pop.*) beast, cad.

muflier [myfli′e], *n.m.* (*Bot.*) antirrhinum.

mugir [my′ʒi:r], *v.i.* to bellow, to low; (*fig.*) to roar; to sough (*of the wind*).

mugissement [myʒis′mã], *n.m.* bellowing, lowing, roaring; soughing (*of the wind*).

muguet [my′gɛ], *n.m.* lily of the valley.

mulâtre [my′lɑ:tr], *a.* and *n.m.* (*fem. inv. or* **-esse**) mulatto, half-caste.

mule [myl], *n.f.* mule, slipper; she-mule.

mulet [my′lɛ], *n.m.* he-mule; mullet.

muletier [myl′tje], *a.* (*fem.* **-ière**) pertaining to mules.—*n.m.* muleteer.

mulot [my′lo], *n.m.* field-mouse.

multicolore [myltiko′lo:r], *a.* many-colored; motley; variegated.

multiforme [mylti′fɔrm], *a.* multiform.

multilatéral [myltilate′ral], *a.* (*m. pl.* **-aux**) multilateral.

multiple [myl′tipl], *a.* multiple; multifarious.—*n.m.* multiple.

multiplicateur [myltiplika′tœ:r], *a.* (*fem.* **-trice**) multiplying.—*n.m.* (*Arith.*) multiplier, multiplicator.

multiplication [myltiplika′sjõ], *n.f.* multiplication; gearing (-ratio).

multiplicité [myltiplisi′te], *n.f.* multiplicity.

multiplié [myltipli′e], *a.* multiplied; manifold; frequent.

multiplier [myltipli′e], *v.t., v.i.* to multiply; to gear up to. **se multiplier**, *v.r.* to multiply; to be repeated.

multitude [mylti′tyd], *n.f.* multitude; crowd.

muni [my′ni], *a.* supplied, provided (*de*); fortified.

municipal [mynisi′pal], *a.* (*m. pl.* **-aux**) municipal.—*n.m.* soldier of the municipal guard.

municipalité [mynisipali′te], *n.f.* municipality; town council and staff.

munificence [mynifi′sã:s], *n.f.* bounty, munificence.

munificent [mynifi′sã], *a.* bountiful.

munir [my′ni:r], *v.t.* to provide, to supply; to arm, to secure. **se munir**, *v.r.* to provide oneself, to be provided (*de*).

munitions [myni′sjõ], *n.f. pl.* ammunition, munitions; military stores.

muqueux [my′kø], *a.* (*fem.* **-euse** (1)) mucous.

muqueuse (2) [my′kø:z], *n.f.* mucous membrane.

mur [my:r], *n.m.* wall; *le mur du son*, the sound barrier.

mûr [my:r], *a.* ripe, mature, matured.

murage [my′ra:ʒ], *n.m.* walling.

muraille [my′ra:j], *n.f.* thick, high wall; (*pl.*) ramparts.

mural [my′ral], *a.* (*m. pl.* **-aux**) mural; *peinture murale*, mural.

mûre [my:r], *n.f.* mulberry.

mûrement [myr′mã], *adv.* maturely.

murer [my′re], *v.t.* to wall in, to brick up; (*fig.*) to screen.

mûrier [my′rje], *n.m.* mulberry tree, bramble bush.

mûrir [my′ri:r], *v.t.* to ripen, to mature.—*v.i.* to ripen, to grow ripe, to mature.

murmurant [myrmy′rã], *a.* murmuring; babbling; grumbling.

murmure [myr′my:r], *n.m.* murmur; grumbling; whispering, babbling; soughing (*of the wind*).

murmurer [myrmy′re], *v.t.* to mutter, to whisper.—*v.i.* to murmur, to whisper; to grumble; to gurgle, to prattle, to babble; to sough.

musard [my′za:r], *a.* loitering, dawdling.—*n.m.* (*fem.* **-e**) (*colloq.*) loiterer, dawdler.

musarder [myzar′de], *v.i.* to dawdle.

musarderie [myzar′dri], **musardise** [myzar′di:z], *n.f.* loitering, dawdling, trifling.

musc [mysk], *n.m.* musk deer, musk.

muscade [mys′kad], *n.f.* nutmeg; juggler's ball.

muscadier [myska′dje], *n.m.* nutmeg tree.

muscat [mys′ka], *a.* and *n.m.* muscat (grape), muscadine; dried muscatel wine; variety of pear.

muscle [myskl], *n.m.* muscle.

musculaire [mysky′lɛ:r], *a.* muscular.

musculeux [mysky′lø], *a.* (*fem.* **-euse**) muscular, brawny.

muse [my:z], *n.f.* muse.

museau [my'zo], *n.m.* (*pl.* **-eaux**) muzzle, snout, nose.

musée [my'ze], *n.m.* museum, art gallery.

museler [myz'le], *v.t.* (*conjug. like* APPELER) to muzzle; (*fig.*) to gag, to silence.

muselière [myz'ljɛːr], *n.f.* muzzle.

musellement [myzɛl'mã], *n.m.* muzzling; (*fig.*) gagging, silencing.

muser [my'ze], *v.i.* to loiter, to moon, to dawdle.

musette [my'zɛt], *n.f.* bagpipe; (*Mil.*) haversack; nosebag (*for horses*).

muséum [myze'ɔm], *n.m.* natural history museum.

musical [myzi'kal], *a.* (*m. pl.* **-aux**) musical.

musicalement [myzikal'mã], *adv.* musically.

musicien [myzi'sjɛ̃], *n.m.* (*fem.* **-enne**) musician.

musique [my'zik], *n.f.* music; band, musicians.

musoir [my'zwaːr], *n.m.* pier head, jetty head.

musqué [mys'ke], *a.* musked, perfumed; (*fig.*) affected (*language etc.*).

musquer [mys'ke], *v.t.* to perfume with musk.

musulman [myzyl'mã], *a.* Moslem.—*n.m.* (**Musulman,** *fem.* **-ane**) Moslem (*person*).

mutabilité [mytabili'te], *n.f.* mutability, changeableness.

mutation [myta'sjɔ̃], *n.f.* change; (*Biol.*) mutation.

muter [my'te], *v.t.* (*Mil.*, *Adm.*) to transfer.

mutilateur [mytila'tœːr], *n.m.* (*fem.* **-trice**) mutilator, maimer, defacer.

mutilation [mytila'sjɔ̃], *n.f.* mutilation, maiming.

mutiler [myti'le], *v.t.* to mutilate, to maim; (*fig.*) to disfigure.

mutin [my'tɛ̃], *a.* obstinate; fractious; pert.—*n.m.* (*fem.* **-e**) mutineer, rebel.

mutiné [myti'ne], *a.* mutinous, riotous.

mutiner (**se**) [samyti'ne], *v.r.* to mutiny.

mutinerie [mytin'ri], *n.f.* unruliness; mutiny, riot; pertness.

mutisme [my'tism], *n.m.* dumbness; speechlessness.

mutualité [mytuali'te], *n.f.* mutuality.

mutuel [my'tuɛl], *a.* (*fem.* **-elle**) mutual, reciprocal; *société de secours mutuels,* mutual benefit society.

mutuellement [mytuɛl'mã], *adv.* mutually.

myope [mjɔp], *a.* myopic, short-sighted.—*n.* short-sighted person.

myopie [mjɔ'pi], *n.f.* myopia, short-sightedness.

myosotis [mjɔzɔ'tiː], *n.m.* myosotis, forget-me-not.

myriade [mi'rjad], *n.f.* myriad.

myrrhe [miːr], *n.f.* myrrh.

myrte [mirt], *n.m.* myrtle.

myrtille [mir'tiːj], *n.f.* bilberry.

mystère [mis'tɛːr], *n.m.* mystery; secret; (*fig.*) fuss.

mystérieusement [misterjøz'mã], *adv.* mysteriously.

mystérieux [miste'rjø], *a.* (*fem.* **-euse**) mysterious.

mysticisme [misti'sism], *n.m.* mysticism.

mystificateur [mistifika'tœːr], *a.* (*fem.* **-trice**) mystifying, hoaxing.—*n.m.* (*fem.* **-trice**) mystifier, hoaxer.

mystification [mistifika'sjɔ̃], *n.f.* hoax.

mystifier [misti'fje], *v.t.* to mystify; to hoax.

mystique [mis'tik], *a.* mystical, mystic.—*n.* mystic.

mythe [mit], *n.m.* myth; fable, fiction.

mythique [mi'tik], *a.* mythical.

mythologie [mitɔlɔ'ʒi], *n.f.* mythology.

mythologique [mitɔlɔ'ʒik], *a.* mythological.

mythologiste [mitɔlɔ'ʒist], **mythologue** [mitɔ'lɔg], *n.* mythologist.

myxomatose [miksɔma'toːz], *n.f.* myxomatosis.

N

N, n [ɛn], *n.m.* the fourteenth letter of the alphabet.

nabab [na'bab], *n.m.* nabob.

nacelle [na'sɛl], *n.f.* wherry, skiff; gondola (*of airship etc.*).

nacre [nakr], *n.f.* mother-of-pearl.

nacré [na'kre], *a.* nacreous, pearly.

nage [naːʒ], *n.f.* swimming; rowing, sculling; (*fam.*) *être en nage,* to be bathed in perspiration.

nageoire [na'ʒwaːr], *n.f.* fin (*of a fish*).

nager [na'ʒe], *v.i.* (*conjug. like* MANGER) to swim; to float; to row.

nageur [na'ʒœːr], *a.* (*fem.* **-euse**) swimming. —*n.m.* (*fem.* **-euse**) swimmer; rower, oarsman.

naguère [na'gɛːr], *adv.* lately, not long ago.

naïade [na'jad], *n.f.* naiad, water nymph.

naïf [na'if], *a.* (*fem.* **naïve**) naïve, artless, ingenuous, unaffected; simple.

nain [nɛ̃], *a.* dwarfish.—*n.m.* (*fem.* **-e**) dwarf.

naissance [nɛ'sãːs], *n.f.* birth; descent; (*fig.*) beginning, dawn, rise.

naissant [nɛ'sã], *a.* new-born, in its infancy; beginning, rising.

naître [nɛːtr], *v.i. irr.* (*with aux.* ÊTRE) to be born, (*fig.*) to originate; to dawn.

naïvement [naiv'mã], *adv.* naïvely, ingenuously, artlessly.

naïveté [naiv'te], *n.f.* artlessness, simplicity, naïvety.

nantir [nã'tiːr], *v.t.* to give as a pledge, to secure; (*fig.*) to furnish. **se nantir,** *v.r.* to provide oneself (*de*); to take possession (*de*).

nantissement [nãtis'mã], *n.m.* security, pledge.

naphte [naft], *n.m.* naphtha.

napolitain [napɔli'tɛ̃], *a.* Neapolitan.—*n.m.* (**Napolitain,** *fem.* **-aine**) Neapolitan (*person*).

nappe [nap], *n.f.* table-cloth, cover; sheet (*of water etc.*).

napperon [na'prɔ̃], *n.m.* tray cloth; doily.

narcisse [nar'sis], *n.m.* (*Bot.*) narcissus.

narcotique [narkɔ'tik], *a.* and *n.m.* narcotic.

narcotisme [narkɔ'tism], *n.m.* narcotism.

narguer [nar'ge], *v.t.* to defy, to flout.

narine [na'rin], *n.f.* nostril.
narquois [nar'kwa], *a.* cunning, sly; chaffing.
narquoisement [narkwaz'mã], *adv.* slyly, quizzingly.
narrateur [nara'tœ:r], *n.m.* (*fem.* **-trice**) narrator, relater.
narratif [nara'tif], *a.* (*fem.* **-tive**) narrative.
narration [nara'sjõ], *n.f.* narration, narrative.
narrer [na're], *v.t.* to narrate, to tell.
nasal [na'zal], *a.* (*m. pl.* **-aux**) nasal.
nasalement [nazal'mã], *adv.* nasally, with a nasal sound.
naseau [na'zo], *n.m.* (*pl.* **-eaux**) nostril (*of animals*).
nasillant [nazi'jã], *a.* speaking through the nose.
nasillard [nazi'ja:r], *a.* snuffling, nasal.
nasillement [nazij'mã], *n.m.* speaking through the nose, snuffling; twang.
nasiller [nazi'je], *v.i.* to speak through the nose, to snuffle.
nasse [nɑ:s], *n.f.* bow net, weir, eel pot.
natal [na'tal], *a.* (*m. pl.* **-als** (*rare*)) natal, native.
natalité [natali'te], *n.f.* birth-rate.
natation [nata'sjõ], *n.f.* swimming.
natif [na'tif], *a.* (*fem.* **-tive**) native; natural. —*n.m.* native.
nation [na'sjõ], *n.f.* nation.
national [nasjo'nal], *a.* (*m. pl.* **-aux**) national.
nationalement [nasjonal'mã], *adv.* nationally.
nationalisation [nasjonaliza'sjõ], *n.f.* nationalization.
nationaliser [nasjonali'ze], *v.t.* to nationalize.
nationaliste [nasjona'list], *n.* nationalist.
nationalité [nasjonali'te], *n.f.* nationality.
nativité [nativi'te], *n.f.* nativity, birth.
natte [nat], *n.f.* mat, matting (*of straw*); plait.
natter [na'te], *v.t.* to mat; to plait, to twist.
naturalisation [natyraliza'sjõ], *n.f.* naturalization; taxidermy.
naturaliser [natyrali'ze], *v.t.* to naturalize; to stuff (*animal*).
naturalisme [natyra'lism], *n.m.* naturalness; naturalism.
naturaliste [natyra'list], *a.* naturalistic.—*n.* naturalist; taxidermist.
nature [na'ty:r], *n.f.* nature; kind, sort; temperament; life, life-size; *de nature à*, likely to; *dessiner d'après nature*, to draw from life; *nature morte*, still life; *payer en nature*, to pay in kind.
naturel [naty'rɛl], *a.* (*fem.* **-elle**) natural; native, innate; artless, plain; *enfant naturel*, illegitimate child.—*n.m.* (*fem.* **-elle**) native (*of a country*).—*n.m.* disposition, nature; genuineness, simplicity.
naturellement [natyrɛl'mã], *adv.* naturally. —*int.* of course!
naturiste [naty'rist], *a.* a naturistic.—*n.* naturist.
naufrage [no'fra:3], *n.m.* shipwreck.
naufragé [nofra'3e], *a.* shipwrecked, wrecked. —*n.m.* (*fem.* **-ée**) shipwrecked person, castaway.
nauséabond [nozea'bõ], *a.* nauseating, loathsome, disgusting.
nausée [no'ze], *n.f.* nausea, sickness; (*fig.*) loathing, disgust.
nauséeux [noze'ø], *a.* (*fem.* **-éeuse**) nauseating.

nautique [no'tik], *a.* nautical.
naval [na'val] *a.* (*m. pl.* **-als**) naval, nautical.
navet [na'vɛ], *n.m.* turnip.
navette [na'vɛt], *n.f.* incense box; weaver's shuttle; (*Bot.*) rape; *faire la navette*, to run a shuttle service.
navigabilité [navigabili'te], *n.f.* airworthiness, seaworthiness.
navigable [navi'gabl], *a.* navigable; seaworthy, airworthy.
navigateur [naviga'tœ:r], *n.m.* navigator.— *a.m.* seafaring; swimming (*birds etc.*).
navigation [naviga'sjõ], *n.f.* navigation; voyage, sailing.
naviguer [navi'ge], *v.i.* to navigate; to row, to sail etc.
navire [na'vi:r], *n.m.* vessel, ship.
navrant [na'vrã], *a.* heartrending, harrowing, distressing.
navrer [na'vre], *v.t.* to distress, to rend (*the heart*).
nazaréen [nazare'ɛ̃], *a.* (*fem.* **-éenne**) of Nazareth.—*n.m.* (**Nazaréen**, *fem.* **-éenne**) Nazarene; Nazarite.
nazi [na'zi], *a.* Nazi.—*n.* (**Nazi**) Nazi.
nazisme [na'zism], *n.m.* Nazism.
ne [nə], *adv.* no, not.
né [ne], *a.* born.
néanmoins [neã'mwɛ̃], *adv.* nevertheless, however, for all that.
néant [ne'ã], *n.m.* naught, nothingness; nil.
nébuleux [neby'lø], *a.* (*fem.* **-euse**) cloudy, misty, nebulous; (*fig.*) obscure.—*n.f.* (**-euse**) nebula.
nébulosité [nebylozi'te], *n.f.* patch of haze.
nécessaire [nese'sɛ:r], *a.* necessary; inevitable.—*n.m.* the needful; necessities (*of life etc.*); dressing-case, work-box.
nécessairement [nesesɛr'mã], *adv.* necessarily; inevitably, of course.
nécessité [nesesi'te], *n.f.* necessity; need, want.
nécessiter [nesesi'te], *v.t.* to necessitate; to compel, to oblige.
nécessiteux [nesesi'tø], *a.* (*fem.* **-euse**) necessitous, needy.—*n.m.* (*fem.* **-euse**) pauper.
nécrologe [nekro'lo:3], *n.m.* obituary list; death roll.
nécrologie [nekrolo'3i], *n.f.* necrology, obituary.
nécrologique [nekrolo'3ik], *a.* necrological.
nécromancie [nekromã'si], *n.f.* necromancy.
nécromancien [nekromã'sjɛ̃], *n.m.* (*fem.* **-enne**) necromancer.
nécropole [nekro'pol], *n.f.* necropolis.
nectar [nɛk'ta:r], *n.m.* nectar.
néerlandais [neɛrlã'dɛ], *a.* Dutch.—*n.m.* Dutch (*language*); (**Néerlandais**, *fem.* **-aise**) Dutchman, Dutchwoman.
nef [nɛf], *n.f.* nave (*of a church*).
néfaste [ne'fast], *a.* inauspicious; disastrous.
nèfle [nɛfl], *n.f.* medlar.
néflier [ne'flje], *n.m.* medlar tree.
négatif [nega'tif], *a.* (*fem.* **-tive**) negative.— *n.m.* (*Phot.*) negative.—*n.f.* (**-tive**) negative, refusal.
négation [nega'sjõ], *n.f.* negation; (*Gram.*) negative.
négativement [negativ'mã], *adv.* negatively.

négligé [negli'ʒe], *a.* neglected, unnoticed; careless; slovenly.—*n.m.* undress, negligee.

négligeable [negli'ʒabl], *a.* negligible; trifling, unimportant.

négligemment [negliʒa'mɑ̃], *adv.* nonchalantly; negligently.

négligence [negli'ʒɑ̃:s], *n.f.* negligence, neglect, oversight.

négligent [negli'ʒɑ̃], *a.* negligent, careless.—*n.m.* (*fem.* **-e**) negligent person.

négliger [negli'ʒe], *v.t.* (*conjug. like* MANGER) to neglect; to omit. **se négliger**, *v.r.* to neglect oneself; to be careless.

négoce [ne'gɔs], *n.m.* trade, business; trafficking.

négociabilité [negɔsjabili'te], *n.f.* negotiability.

négociable [negɔ'sjabl], *a.* negotiable, transferrable.

négociant [negɔ'sjɑ̃], *n.m.* (*fem.* **-e**) merchant (*wholesale*).

négociateur [negɔsja'tœ:r], *n.m.* (*fem.* **-trice**) negotiator, transactor.

négociation [negɔsja'sjɔ̃], *n.f.* negotiation, transaction.

négocier [negɔ'sje], *v.t.* to negotiate.—*v.i.* to trade.

nègre [nɛ:gr], *a.* and *n.m.* (*fem.* **négresse**) (*pej.*) Negro; (*pl.*) (*pej.*) blacks.

négrier [negri'e], *n.m.* slave ship; slaver; slave dealer.

négrillon [negri'jɔ̃], *n.m.* (*fem.* **-onne**) (*pej.*) little Negro, Negro boy or girl.

neige [nɛ:ʒ], *n.f.* snow; **boule de neige**, snowball.

neiger [nɛ'ʒe], *v. impers.* (*conjug. like* MANGER) to snow.

neigeux [nɛ'ʒø], *a.* (*fem.* **-euse**) snowy, snow-covered.

nénuphar [neny'fa:r], *n.m.* water lily.

néon [ne'ɔ̃], *n.m.* neon.

néo-zélandais [neozelɑ̃'dɛ], *a.* New Zealand (*butter, cheese etc.*).—*n.m.* (**Néo-Zélandais**, *fem.* **-aise**) New Zealander.

Népal [ne'pa:l], le, *m.* Nepal.

népalais [nepa'lɛ], *a.* Nepalese.—*n.m.* (**Népalais**, *fem.* **-aise**) Nepalese (*person*).

népotisme [nepɔ'tism], *n.m.* nepotism.

nerf [nɛ:r], *n.m.* nerve; sinew; fortitude, strength.

nerveusement [nɛrvøz'mɑ̃], *adv.* impatiently; nervously.

nerveux [nɛr'vø], *a.* (*fem.* **-euse**) nervous; excitable; muscular.

nervosité [nɛrvozi'te], *n.f.* nervousness.

nervure [nɛr'vy:r], *n.f.* (*Bot. etc.*) nervure, nerve; (*Arch.*) molding; (*Carp.*) rib, fillet; (*Bookb.*) tapes, cording; (*Needlework*) piping.

net [nɛt], *a.* (*fem.* **nette**) clean; pure; clear, distinct; flat, frank, pointblank; net (*of prices*).—*n.m.* fair copy; **mettre au net**, to make a fair copy.—*adv.* clean off, at once; flatly, point-blank.

nettement [nɛt'mɑ̃], *adv.* cleanly; clearly; plainly, flatly.

netteté [nɛt'te], *n.f.* cleanness; clearness; distinctness.

nettoiement [nɛtwa'mɑ̃], **nettoyage** [nɛtwa'ja:ʒ], *n.m.* cleaning; clearing; wiping.

nettoyer [nɛtwa'je], *v.t.* (*conjug. like* EMPLOYER) to clean; to wipe; to rid (*de*).

neuf (1) [nœf], *a.* and *n.m.* nine, ninth.

neuf (2) [nœf], *a.* (*fem.* **neuve**) new, brand-new; young, raw.—*n.m.* something new.

neurologie [nœrɔlɔ'ʒi], *n.f.* neurology.

neutralisation [nøtraliza'sjɔ̃], *n.f.* neutralization.

neutraliser [nøtrali'ze], *v.t.* to neutralize. **se neutraliser**, *v.r.* to neutralize each other.

neutralité [nøtrali'te], *n.f.* neutrality.

neutre [nø:tr], *a.* and *n.m.* neuter; neutral.

neutron [nø'trɔ̃], *n.m.* neutron.

neuvième [nœ'vjɛm], *a.* and *n.* ninth.

neveu [nə've], *n.m.* (*pl.* **-eux**) nephew; (*pl. poet.*) descendants.

névralgie [nevral'ʒi], *n.f.* neuralgia.

névralgique [nevral'ʒik], *a.* neuralgic.

névrite [ne'vrit], *n.f.* neuritis.

névritique [nevri'tik], *a.* neuritic.

névrose [ne'vro:z], *n.f.* neurosis, nervous disorder.

névrosé [nevro'ze], *a.* and *n.m.* (*fem.* **-ée**) neurotic.

nez [ne], *n.m. inv.* nose; face; scent (*of dogs etc.*).

ni [ni], *conj.* nor, neither . . . nor; (*after* **sans**, **sans que**, *etc.*) either . . . or.

niable [njabl], *a.* deniable.

niais [njɛ], *a.* silly, foolish.—*n.m.* (*fem.* **-e**) ninny, simpleton.

niaisement [njɛz'mɑ̃], *adv.* foolishly.

niaiser [njɛ'ze], *v.i.* to play the fool.

niaiserie [njɛz'ri], *n.f.* foolishness; nonsense.

Nicaragua [nikara'gwa], le, *m.* Nicaragua.

nicaraguayen [nikaragwa'jɛ̃], *a.* (*fem.* **-enne**) Nicaraguan.—*n.m.* (**Nicaraguayen**, *fem.* **-enne**) Nicaraguan (*person*).

niche [niʃ], *n.f.* niche, nook; recess; kennel; (*fam.*) prank.

nichée [ni'ʃe], *n.f.* nestful (*of young birds*); brood (*of animals, children etc.*).

nicher [ni'ʃe], *v.t.* to lodge, to put.—*v.i.* to build a nest; to nestle. **se nicher**, *v.r.* to nest, to nestle; to hide oneself.

nickel [ni'kɛl], *n.m.* nickel.

nickelage [ni'kla:ʒ], *n.m.* nickel-plating.

nickeler [ni'kle], *v.t.* (*conjug. like* APPELER) to nickel-plate.

Nicolas [nikɔ'la], *m.* Nicholas.

nicotine [nikɔ'tin], *n.f.* nicotine.

nid [ni], *n.m.* nest; berth, post.

nièce [njɛs], *n.f.* niece.

nier [nje], *v.t.* to deny; to repudiate, to disown.

nigaud [ni'go], *a.* (*colloq.*) silly, simple.—*n.m.* (*fem.* **-e**) booby, simpleton.

Nigéria [niʒe'rja], le, *m.* Nigeria.

nigérien [niʒe'rjɛ̃], *a.* (*fem.* **-enne**) Nigerian.—*n.m.* (**Nigérien**, *fem.* **-enne**) Nigerian (*person*).

nihilisme [nii'lism], *n.m.* nihilism.

nihiliste [nii'list], *a.* nihilistic.—*n.* nihilist.

Nil [nil], le, *m.* the Nile.

nimbe [nɛ̃:b], *n.m.* nimbus, halo.

nippe [nip], *n.f. usu. pl.* (*colloq.*) old clothes, togs.

nipper [ni'pe], *v.t.* (*colloq.*) to fit out, to rig out. **se nipper**, *v.r.* to rig oneself out.

nippon [ni'pɔ̃], *a.* Japanese.—*n.m.* (**Nippon**, *fem.* **-one**) Japanese (*person*).

nitrate [ni'trat], *n.m.* nitrate.

nitre [nitr], *n.m.* nitre, saltpeter.

nitrique [ni'trik], *a.* nitric.

nitrogène [nitrɔ'ʒɛn], n.m. nitrogen.
niveau [ni'vo], n.m. (pl. -eaux) level; standard; *passage à niveau*, level crossing.
niveler [ni'vle], v.t. (conjug. like APPELER) to level, to flatten (out).
niveleur [ni'vlœːr], a. (fem. -euse) levelling. —n.m. (fem. -euse) leveller.
nivellement [nivɛl'mɑ̃], n.m. levelling.
nobiliaire [nɔbi'ljɛːr], a. of the nobility, nobiliary.
noble [nɔbl], a. noble; great, high, exalted.— n. noble, nobleman, noblewoman.
noblement [nɔblə'mɑ̃], adv. nobly; honorably.
noblesse [nɔ'blɛs], n.f. nobility; nobleness, loftiness.
noce [nɔs], n.f. wedding; wedding party; (colloq.) jollification.
noceur [nɔ'sœːr], n.m. (fem. -euse) gay dog, gay woman, rake.
nocif [nɔ'sif], a. (fem. -cive) injurious, noxious.
noctambule [nɔktɑ̃'byl], a. noctambulant, noctambulous.—n. sleep-walker.
noctambulisme [nɔktɑ̃by'lism], n.m. noctambulism, sleep-walking.
nocturne [nɔk'tyrn], a. nocturnal, nightly.— n.m. (Mus.) nocturne.
Noël [nɔ'ɛl], n.m. Christmas, Yule-tide; (noël) Christmas carol.
nœud [nø], n.m. knot; bow; difficulty, intricacy; (fig.) tie; bond.
noir [nwaːr], a. black; swarthy; gloomy, dismal; foul; *bête noire*, pet aversion.— n.m. black (color); (fem. -e) Negro.
noirâtre [nwa'roːtr], a. blackish.
noiraud [nwa'ro], a. dark, swarthy-looking.
noirceur [nwar'sœːr], n.f. blackness; baseness; foul deed.
noircir [nwar'siːr], v.t. to blacken; to sully; to defame; to darken.—v.i. and se noircir, v.r. to blacken, to darken, to grow black or dark.
noircissure [nwarsi'syːr], n.f. black spot, smudge.
noire (2) [nwaːr], n.f. (Mus.) crotchet.
noisetier [nwaz'tje], n.m. hazel (tree or bush).
noisette [nwa'zɛt], n.f. hazel-nut.
noix [nwa], n.f. inv. walnut; nut.
nom [nɔ̃], n.m. name; fame, celebrity; noun.
nomade [nɔ'mad], a. nomad, nomadic, wandering.—n. nomad.
nombre [nɔ̃:br], n.m. number; quantity; numbers.
nombrer [nɔ̃'bre], v.t. to number, to reckon.
nombreux [nɔ̃'brø], a. (fem. -euse) numerous; harmonious (prose, style).
nombril [nɔ̃'bri], n.m. navel.
nomenclature [nɔmɑ̃kla'tyːr], n.f. nomenclature; list, catalogue.
nominal [nɔmi'nal], a. (m. pl. -aux) nominal.
nominalement [nɔminal'mɑ̃], adv. nominally.
nominatif [nɔmina'tif], a. (fem. -tive) and n.m. nominative.
nomination [nɔmina'sjɔ̃], n.f. nomination; appointment.
nominativement [nɔminativ'mɑ̃], adv. by name.
nommé [nɔ'me], a. named, called; appointed.
nommément [nɔme'mɑ̃], adv. namely, particularly, especially.

nommer [nɔ'me], v.t. to name, to call; to mention; to nominate, to appoint. se nommer, v.r. to state one's name; to be called.
non [nɔ̃], adv. no, not.
non-activité [nɔ̃naktivi'te], n.f. state of being unattached or unemployed
nonagénaire [nɔnaʒe'nɛːr], a. ninety years of age.—n. nonagenarian.
non-agression [nɔ̃nagrɛ'sjɔ̃], n.f. non-aggression.
nonce [nɔ̃:s], n.m. nuncio.
nonchalamment [nɔ̃ʃala'mɑ̃], adv. nonchalantly, carelessly, heedlessly.
nonchalance [nɔ̃ʃa'lɑ̃:s], n.f. carelessness, heedlessness, nonchalance.
nonchalant [nɔ̃ʃa'lɑ̃], a. nonchalant, careless; listless.—n.m. (fem. -e) such a person.
non-lieu [nɔ̃'ljø], n.m. (Law) no true bill.
nonne [nɔn], n.f. nun.
nonobstant [nɔnɔps'tɑ̃], prep. notwithstanding, in spite of.—adv. nevertheless.
nonpareil [nɔ̃pa'rɛːj], a. (fem. -eille) nonpareil, matchless.
non-sens [nɔ̃'sɑ̃:s], n.m. meaningless sentence, translation, or action.
nord [nɔːr], a. inv. north, *Pôle nord*, North Pole.—n.m. north; north-wind; *nord-est*, north-east; *nord-ouest*, north-west.
nordique [nɔr'dik], a. Nordic, Scandinavian. —n. (Nordique) Nordic, Scandinavian (person).
normal [nɔr'mal], a. (m. pl. -aux) normal; (Geom.) perpendicular.
normalement [nɔrmal'mɑ̃], adv. normally.
normalien [nɔrma'ljɛ̃], n.m. (fem. -enne) training-college student or ex-student.
normalité [nɔrmali'te], n.f. normality.
normand [nɔr'mɑ̃], a. Norman.—n.m. (Normand, fem. -ande) Norman (person).
Normandie [nɔrmɑ̃'di], la, f. Normandy.
norme [nɔrm], n.f. norm, average.
Norvège [nɔr'veːʒ], la, f. Norway.
norvégien [nɔrve'ʒjɛ̃], a. (fem. -enne) Norwegian.—n.m. Norwegian (language); (Norvégien, fem. -enne) Norwegian (person).
nos [no], pl. [NOTRE].
nostalgie [nɔstal'ʒi], n.f. nostalgia, homesickness.
nostalgique [nɔstal'ʒik], a. nostalgic; sad.
notabilité [nɔtabili'te], n.f. respectability; person of note.
notable [nɔ'tabl], a. notable, of influence.— n. notable, person of note.
notablement [nɔtablə'mɑ̃], adv. notably.
notaire [nɔ'tɛːr], n.m. notary; solicitor.
notamment [nɔta'mɑ̃], adv. specially, more particularly.
notariat [nɔta'rja], n.m. profession, business or function of notary.
notation [nɔta'sjɔ̃], n.f. notation.
note [nɔt], n.f. note, memorandum; mark; statement; bill.
noter [nɔ'te], v.t. to note; to mark; to note down; to observe, to notice.
notice [nɔ'tis], n.f. notice, account; review (of a book); notification.
notification [nɔtifika'sjɔ̃], n.f. notification, notice, intimation.
notifier [nɔti'fje], v.t. to notify; to intimate.
notion [no'sjɔ̃], n.f. notion, idea; (pl.) elements, rudiments.

notoire [nɔ'twa:r], *a.* notorious; well-known.

notoirement [nɔtwar'mɑ̃], *adv.* notoriously.

notoriété [nɔtɔrje'te], *n.f.* notoriety (*of fact*); repute (*of person*).

notre [nɔtr], *a. poss.* (*pl.* **nos**) our.

nôtre [no:tr], *pron. poss.* (*pl.* **nôtres**) ours; our own; our things, friends, relatives etc.

noué [nwe], *a.* knotty, tied; rickety.

nouer [nwe], *v.t.* to tie, to knot; (*fig.*) to devise; to establish. **se nouer**, *v.r.* to be twisted *or* tied; to fasten oneself.

noueux [nu'ø], *a.* (*fem.* **-euse**) knotty, gnarled.

nougat [nu'ga], *n.m.* nougat; almond cake.

nouilles [nu:j], *n.f. pl.* noodles, spaghetti.

nourri [nu'ri], *a.* nourished, fed; full, rich, copious; brisk (*fire*).

nourrice [nu'ris], *n.f.* nurse; wet-nurse; (*Motor.*, *Av.*) feed-tank.

nourricier [nuri'sje], *a.* (*fem.* **-ière**) life-giving, nourishing; producing food.—*n.m.* (*fem.* **-ière**) foster parent.

nourrir [nu'ri:r], *v.t.* to nourish, to feed; to keep, to maintain; to nurse; to foster; to rear; to cherish. **se nourrir** *v.r.* to feed, to live upon.

nourrissage [nuri'sa:ʒ], *n.m.* rearing, feeding (*of cattle*).

nourrissant [nuri'sɑ̃], *a.* nutritious; nourishing; sustaining.

nourrisseur [nuri'sœ:r], *n.m.* cow keeper; stock raiser.

nourrisson [nuri'sɔ̃], *n.m.* (*fem.* **-onne**) infant; foster child; nursling.

nourriture [nuri'ty:r], *n.f.* nourishment, food; livelihood.

nous [nu], *pers. pron.* we; us; to us; ourselves; each other.

nouveau [nu'vo] (*before a vowel or unaspirated* h, **nouvel**), *a.* (*fem.* **-elle** (1)) new; recent, novel; additional; inexperienced.—*n.m.* (*pl.* **-eaux**) new, something new; **à nouveau**, afresh; **de nouveau**, again.

nouveau-né [nuvo'ne], *n.m.* (*fem.* **nouveau-née**, *pl.* **nouveau-né(e)s**) new-born child.

nouveauté [nuvo'te], *n.f.* novelty; change, innovation; (*pl.*) fancy articles; (*fig.*) new book, new play.

nouvelle (2) [nu'vɛl], *n.f.* (*often in pl.*) news, tidings; short story, short novel.

nouvellement [nuvɛl'mɑ̃], *adv.* newly, lately, recently.

Nouvelle-Zélande [nuvɛlze'lɑ̃:d], **la**, *f.* New Zealand.

nouvelliste [nuvɛ'list], *n.* newswriter; short story writer.

novateur [nɔva'tœ:r], *a.* (*fem.* **-trice**) innovating.—*n.m.* (*fem.* **-trice**) innovator.

novembre [nɔ'vɑ̃:br], *n.m.* November.

novice [nɔ'vis], *a.* ɪovice, inexperienced.—*n.* novice, probationer.

noviciat [nɔvi'sja], *n.m.* noviciate.

noyade [nwa'jad], *n.f.* drowning.

noyau [nwa'jo], *n.m.* (*pl.* **-aux**) stone (*of fruit*), nucleus; core (*of statues, casts etc.*).

noyé [nwa'je], *a.* drowned.—*n.m.* (*fem.* **-ée**) drowned person.

noyer (1) [nwa'je], *n.m.* walnut tree; walnut (*wood*).

noyer (2) [nwa'je], *v.t.* (*conjug. like* EMPLOYER) to drown; to swamp; to deluge. **se noyer**, *v.r.* to be drowned; to be plunged (*dans*).

nu [ny], *a.* naked, nude, bare; uncovered; unadorned; destitute.—*n.m.* the nude, nudity.

nuage [nɥa:ʒ], *n.m.* cloud; mist; (*fig.*) gloom, dejection.

nuageux [nɥa'ʒø], *a.* (*fem.* **-euse**) cloudy, overcast.

nuance [nɥɑ̃:s], *n.f.* shade, hue; gradation; tinge.

nuancer [nɥɑ̃'se], *v.t.* (*conjug. like* COMMENCER) to shade; to vary slightly.

nubile [ny'bil], *a.* nubile, marriageable.

nubilité [nybili'te], *n.f.* nubility, marriageable age.

nucléaire [nykle'ɛ:r], *a.* nuclear.

nudité [nydi'te], *n.f.* nudity, nakedness.

nuée [nɥe], *n.f.* cloud; (*fig.*) swarm, host, multitude, flock.

nues [ny], *n.f. pl.* (*Poet.*) skies.

nuire [nɥi:r], *v.i. irr.* to be hurtful, to jeopardize, to harm (**à**).

nuisible [nɥi'zibl], harmful, noxious, prejudicial.

nuit [nɥi], *n.f.* night, night-time; darkness; *il fait nuit*, it is dark; *nuit blanche*, sleepless night.

nuitamment [nɥita'mɑ̃], *adv.* by night, in the night.

nul [nyl], *a.* (*fem.* **nulle**) no, not any; void, null.—*pron.* no one, nobody, not one.

nullement [nyl'mɑ̃], *adv.* not at all, by no means.

nullifier [nyli'fje], *v.t.* to nullify.

nullité [nyli'te], *n.f.* nullity; nonentity; (*fig.*) incapacity.

numéraire [nyme'rɛ:r], *a.* legal (*of coin*).—*n.m.* metallic currency, cash.

numéral [nyme'ral], *a.* (*m. pl.* **-aux**) numeral.

numérateur [nymera'tœ:r], *n.m.* (*Arith.*) numerator.

numération [nymera'sjɔ̃], *n.f.* numeration, notation.

numérique [nyme'rik], *a.* numerical.

numériquement [nymerik'mɑ̃], *adv.* numerically.

numéro [nyme'ro], *n.m.* number.

numérotage [nymerɔ'ta:ʒ], *n.m.*, **numérotation** [nymerɔta'sjɔ̃], *n.f.* numbering.

numéroter [nymerɔ'te], *v.t.* to number.

numismate [nymis'mat], **numismatiste** [nymisma'tist], *n.* numismatist.

numismatique [nymisma'tik], *a.* numismatic.—*n.f.* numismatics.

nuptial [nyp'sjal], *a.* (*m. pl.* **-aux**) nuptial, bridal.

nuque [nyk], *n.f.* nape (*of the neck*).

nutritif [nytri'tif], *a.* (*fem.* **-tive**) nutritious, nourishing.

nutrition [nytri'sjɔ̃], *n.f.* nutrition.

nylon [ni'lɔ̃], *n.m.* nylon; *des bas nylon*, nylon stockings.

nymphe [nɛ̃:f], *n.f.* nymph.

O

O, o [o], *n.m.* the fifteenth letter of the alphabet.

ô! [o] *int.* oh!

oasis [oa'zi:s], *n.f. inv.* oasis.
obéir [ɔbe'i:r], *v.i.* to obey; to comply, to yield, to submit (*à*).
obéissance [ɔbei'sã:s], *n.f.* obedience; allegiance.
obéissant [ɔbei'sã], *a.* obedient; docile.
obélisque [ɔbe'lisk], *n.m.* obelisk, needle.
obérer [ɔbe're], *v.t.* (*conjug. like* CÉDER) to encumber *or* involve in debt.
obèse [ɔ'bɛ:z], *a.* obese, stout.
obésité [ɔbezi'te], *n.f.* obesity, stoutness.
obituaire [ɔbitɥɛ:r], *a.* and *n.m.* obituary, register of deaths; mortuary.
objecter [ɔbʒɛk'te], *v.t.* to object; to allege.
objecteur [ɔbʒɛk'tœ:r], *n.m.* objector.
objectif [ɔbʒɛk'tif], *a.* (*fem.* -**tive**) objective. —*n.m.* objective, aim; lens; (*Mil.*) target.
objection [ɔbʒɛk'sjɔ̃], *n.f.* objection.
objectivement [ɔbʒɛktiv'mã], *adv.* objectively.
objectivité [ɔbʒɛktivi'te], *n.f.* objectivity.
objet [ɔb'ʒɛ], *n.m.* object; subject, matter; aim; (*pl.*) articles, goods.
obligation [ɔbliga'sjɔ̃], *n.f.* obligation; (*Law*) bond; (*Comm.*) debenture.
obligatoire [ɔbliga'twa:r], *a.* compulsory, obligatory, incumbent.
obligatoirement [ɔbligatwar'mã], *adv.* compulsorily.
obligeamment [ɔbliʒa'mã], *adv.* obligingly.
obligeance [ɔbli'ʒã:s], *n.f.* obligingness; kindness.
obligeant [ɔbli'ʒã] *a.* obliging, kind, helpful.
obliger [ɔbli'ʒe], *v.t.* (*conjug. like* MANGER) to oblige, to bind; to compel; to gratify. **s'obliger**, *v.r.* to put oneself under an obligation.
oblique [ɔ'blik], *a.* oblique, slanting; (*fig.*) indirect, underhand.
obliquement [ɔblik'mã], *adv.* obliquely, indirectly; unfairly.
obliquer [ɔbli'ke], *v.i.* to slant, to swerve.
obliquité [ɔbliki'te], *n.f.* obliquity.
oblitération [ɔblitera'sjɔ̃], *n.f.* obliteration.
oblitérer [ɔblite're], *v.t.* (*conjug. like* CÉDER) to obliterate; to cancel (*stamps*).
oblong [ɔ'blɔ̃], *a.* (*fem.* -**ue**) oblong.
obole [ɔ'bɔl] *n.f.* obolus; (*fig.*) farthing, mite.
obscène [ɔp'sɛːn], *a.* obscene.
obscénité [ɔpseni'te], *n.f.* obscenity, lewdness.
obscur [ɔps'ky:r], *a.* obscure; dark, gloomy; (*fig.*) humble; mean.
obscurcir [ɔpskyr'si:r], *v.t.* to obscure, to darken, to dim; to tarnish. **s'obscurcir**, *v.r.* to grow dim.
obscurcissement [ɔpskyrsis'mã], *n.m.* darkening; (*Mil.*) black-out.
obscurément [ɔpskyre'mã], *adv.* obscurely, dimly.
obscurité [ɔpskyri'te], *n.f.* obscurity, darkness.
obséder [ɔpse'de], *v.t.* (*conjug. like* CÉDER) to beset; to haunt, to importune, to obsess.
obsèques [ɔp'sɛk], *n.f. pl.* obsequies, funeral.
obséquieusement [ɔpsekjøz'mã], *adv.* obsequiously.
obséquieux [ɔpse'kjø], *a.* (*fem.* -**euse**) obsequious, fawning.
observable [ɔpsɛr'vabl], *a.* observable.
observance [ɔpsɛr'vã:s], *n.f.* observance.

observateur [ɔpsɛrva'tœ:r], *a.* (*fem.* -**trice**) observant.—*n.m.* (*fem.* -**trice**) observer, onlooker.
observation [ɔpsɛrva'sjɔ̃], *n.f.* observation; observance; remark.
observatoire [ɔpsɛrva'twa:r], *n.m.* observatory; look-out.
observer [ɔpsɛr've], *v.t.* to observe, to notice; to watch; to remark; to perform. **s'observer**, *v.r.* to be circumspect, to be on one's guard; to observe each other.
obsession [ɔpsɛ'sjɔ̃], *n.f.* obsession.
obstacle [ɔps'takl], *n.m.* obstacle, bar, hindrance.
obstination [ɔpstina'sjɔ̃], *n.f.* obstinacy, stubbornness, wilfulness.
obstiné [ɔpsti'ne], *a.* obstinate, self-willed, stubborn; persistent.
obstinément [ɔpstine'mã], *adv.* obstinately, stubbornly.
obstiner (s') [sɔpsti'ne], *v.r.* to be obstinately resolved (*à*), to insist, to persist.
obstructif [ɔpstryk'tif], *a.* (*fem.* -**tive**) obstructive.
obstruction [ɔpstryk'sjɔ̃], *n.f.* obstruction; stoppage.
obstruer [ɔpstrɥ'e], *v.t.* to obstruct, to block.
obtempérer [ɔptãpe're], *v.i.* to obey, to comply (*à*).
obtenir [ɔptə'ni:r], *v.t. irr.* (*conjug. like* TENIR) to obtain, to procure, to get. **s'obtenir**, *v.r.* to be obtained; to be obtainable.
obtention [ɔptã'sjɔ̃], *n.f.* obtaining, getting.
obturer [ɔpty're], *v.t.* to seal, to obturate; to fill (*gap*), to fill (*a tooth etc.*).
obtus [ɔp'ty], *a.* obtuse; dull, blunt.
obus [ɔ'by], *n.m.* (*Artill.*) shell.
obusier [ɔby'zje], *n.m.* howitzer.
obvier [ɔb'vje], *v.i.* to obviate, to prevent (*à*).
occasion [ɔka'zjɔ̃], *n.f.* opportunity, occasion; cause; bargain, job lot; *livres d'occasion*, second-hand books.
occasionnel [ɔkazjɔ'nɛl], *a.* (*fem.* -**elle**) occasional.
occasionnellement [ɔkazjɔnɛl'mã], *adv.* occasionally.
occasionner [ɔkazjɔ'ne], *v.t.* to occasion, to cause.
occident [ɔksi'dã], *n.m.* west.
occidental [ɔksidã'tal], *a.* (*m. pl.* -**aux**) occidental, western.
Occidentaux [ɔksidã'to], *n.m. pl.* natives *or* inhabitants of the western countries, members of the western *bloc*.
occulte [ɔ'kylt], *a.* occult.
occupant [ɔky'pã], *a.* occupying.—*n.m.* (*fem.* -**e**) occupant, occupier.
occupation [ɔkypa'sjɔ̃], *n.f.* occupation; occupancy; capture.
occupé [ɔky'pe], *a.* occupied, busy, engaged; seized.
occuper [ɔky'pe], *v.t.* to occupy; to employ; to inhabit. **s'occuper**, *v.r.* to occupy oneself; to be busy; to look after; to see to (*de*).
occurrence [ɔky'rã:s], *n.f.* occurrence; event; *en l'occurrence*, under the circumstances.
océan [ɔse'ã], *n.m.* ocean, high sea.
océanique [ɔsea'nik], *a.* oceanic.
ocre [ɔkr], *n.f.* ochre.
octane [ɔk'tan], *n.m.* octane.
octave [ɔk'ta:v], *n.f.* octave.

octavo [ɔkta'vo], *adv.* eighthly.—*n.m.* octavo.

octobre [ɔk'tɔbr], *n.m.* October.

octogénaire [ɔktɔʒe'nɛːr], *a.* and *n.* octo-genarian.

octogone [ɔktɔ'gɔn], *a.* octagonal, eight-sided.—*n.m.* octagon.

octroi [ɔk'trwa], *n.m.* grant, concession; town dues, toll; toll house or office.

octroyer [ɔktrwa'je], *v.t. (conjug. like* EM-PLOYER) to grant, to concede.

oculaire [ɔky'lɛːr], *a.* ocular; *témoin oculaire*, eyewitness.—*n.m.* eye-piece.

oculiste [ɔky'list], *n.m.* oculist.

odalisque [ɔda'lisk], *n.f.* odalisque.

ode [ɔd], *n.f.* ode.

odeur [ɔ'dœːr], *n.f.* odor, smell; scent.

odieusement [ɔdjøz'mɑ̃], *adv.* odiously, hatefully.

odieux [ɔ'djø], *a. (fem.* **-euse**) odious, hateful, loathsome.—*n.m.* odiousness, hatefulness.

odorant [ɔdɔ'rɑ̃], *a.* fragrant, sweet-smelling.

odorat [ɔdɔ'ra], *n.m.* smell, sense of smell.

odoriférant [ɔdɔrife'rɑ̃], *a.* sweet-smelling.

Odyssée [ɔdi'se], *n.f.* Odyssey.

œil [œːj], *n.m. (pl.* **yeux**) eye; look; luster; bud; dint, hole (*in bread, cheese*); *des yeux à fleur de tête*, prominent eyes; *d'un coup d'œil*, at a glance; *en un clin d'œil*, in the twinkling of an eye.

œil-de-bœuf [œjdə'bœf], *n.m. (pl.* **œils-de-bœuf**) round or oval window.

œillade [œ'jad], *n.f.* glance; ogle, leer; wink.

œillère [œ'jɛːr], *n.f.* blinker; canine tooth; eye bath.

œillet [œ'jɛ], *n.m.* eyelet; (*Bot.*) dianthus, pink; *œillet des fleuristes*, carnation; *œillet de poète*, sweet william; *petit œillet d'Inde*, French marigold.

œuf [œf], *n.m. (pl.* **œufs**) egg; ovum; spawn, roe (*of fish*).

œuvre [œːvr], *n.f.* work; performance; production; (*pl.*) works (*of an author*).—*n.m.* (*no pl.*) work (*of an author, painter, musician etc.*)

œuvrer [œ'vre], [OUVRER].

offensant [ɔfɑ̃'sɑ̃], *a.* offensive, insulting.

offense [ɔ'fɑ̃ːs], *n.f.* offense; injury, wrong, trespass.

offensé [ɔfɑ̃'se], *n.m. (fem.* **-ée**) offended party.

offenser [ɔfɑ̃'se], *v.t.* to offend; to sin against; to hurt, to injure (*feelings*); to shock. *s'offenser*, *v.r.* to be offended, to take offense.

offenseur [ɔfɑ̃'sœːr], *n.m.* offender.

offensif [ɔfɑ̃'sif], *a. (fem.* **-sive**) offensive.—*n.f.* (**-sive**) offensive (*attack*).

offensivement [ɔfɑ̃siv'mɑ̃], *adv.* offensively.

office [ɔ'fis], *n.m.* office; duty; employment; service; Divine worship.—*n.f.* servants' hall, pantry, larder.

officiant [ɔfi'sjɑ̃], *a.* officiating.—*n.m.* officiating priest.

officiel [ɔfi'sjɛl], *a. (fem.* **-elle**) official, formal.

officiellement [ɔfisjɛl'mɑ̃], *adv.* officially.

officier (1) [ɔfi'sje], *v.i.* to officiate (*at divine service*).

officier (2) [ɔfi'sje], *n.m.* officer.

officieusement [ɔfisjøz'mɑ̃], *adv.* officiously.

officieux [ɔfi'sjø], *a. (fem.* **-euse**) officious, semi-official; obliging.—*n.m. (fem.* **-euse**) busybody.

offrande [ɔ'frɑ̃ːd], *n.f.* offertory; offering.

offre [ɔfr], *n.f.* offer, tender.

offrir [ɔ'friːr], *v.t. (conjug. like* OUVRIR) to offer, to tender; to present, to give. *s'offrir*, *v.r.* to offer oneself; to present itself.

offusquer [ɔfys'ke], *v.t.* to obscure; to dazzle; to offend. *s'offusquer*, *v.r.* (*rare*) to become darkened; (*fig.*) to take offense.

ogival [ɔʒi'val], *a.* (*m. pl.* **-aux**) (*Arch.*) pointed; gothic.

ogive [ɔ'ʒiːv], *n.f.* ogive, pointed arch; nose (*of missile, rocket*).

ogre [ɔgr], *n.m. (fem.* **-esse**) ogre, ogress.

oh! [o], *int.* O! ho!

ohm [om], *n.m.* ohm.

oie [wa], *n.f.* goose; (*fig.*) simpleton.

oignon [ɔ'ɲɔ̃], *n.m.* onion; bulb; bunion.

oindre [wɛ̃ːdr], *v.t. irr.* to anoint.

oiseau [wa'zo], *n.m. (pl.* **-eaux**) bird; hod; (*colloq.*) fellow, chap; *à vol d'oiseau*, as the crow flies.

oiseau-mouche [wazo'muʃ], *n.m.* (*pl.* **oiseaux-mouches**) humming-bird.

oiselet [wa'zlɛ], *n.m.* small bird.

oiseleur [wa'zlœːr], *n.m.* bird-catcher; fowler.

oiselier [waz'lje], *n.m.* bird seller; bird fancier.

oiseux [wa'zø], *a. (fem.* **-euse**) idle, useless, trifling.

oisif [wa'zif], *a. (fem.* **-sive**) idle, unoccupied; lying dead (*money*).—*n.m. (fem.* **-sive**) idler.

oisillon [wazi'jɔ̃], *n.m.* young bird, fledg(e)ling.

oisivement [waziv'mɑ̃], *adv.* idly.

oisiveté [waziv'te], *n.f.* idleness; hours of ease.

oison [wa'zɔ̃], *n.m.* gosling; (*fig.*) simpleton.

oléagineux [ɔleaʒi'nø], *a. (fem.* **-euse**) oleaginous, oily.

oléoduc [ɔleɔ'dyk], *n.m.* pipeline.

oligarchie [ɔligar'ʃi], *n.f.* oligarchy.

oligarchique [ɔligar'ʃik], *a.* oligarchical.

oligarque [ɔli'gark], *n.* oligarch.

olivâtre [ɔli'vɑːtr], *a.* olivaceous, olive-hued; sallow.

olive [ɔ'liːv], *a. inv.* olive-colored.—*n.f.* olive.

Olivier [ɔli'vje], *m.* Oliver.

olivier [ɔli'vje], *n.m.* olive tree; olive wood.

olographe [ɔlɔ'graf], *a.* holograph(ic) (*will*).

Olympe [ɔ'lɛ̃ːp], *n.m.* Olympus; (*fig.*) heaven.

olympien [ɔlɛ̃'pjɛ̃], *a. (fem.* **-enne**) Olympian. —*n.m.* (**Olympien**, *fem.* **-enne**) Olympian.

olympique [ɔlɛ̃'pik], *a.* Olympic.

ombrage [ɔ̃'braːʒ], *n.m.* shade; umbrage, suspicion.

ombrager [ɔ̃bra'ʒe], *v.t. (conjug. like* MANGER) to shade; (*fig.*) to protect.

ombrageux [ɔ̃bra'ʒø], *a. (fem.* **-euse**) skittish (*of horses*); suspicious, touchy.

ombre [ɔ̃ːbr], *n.f.* shadow; shade; darkness; ghost; *à l'ombre*, in the shade.

ombré [ɔ̃'bre], *a.* tinted, shaded.

ombrelle [ɔ̃'brɛl], *n.f.* parasol, sunshade.

ombrer [ɔ̃'bre], *v.t.* to shade; to darken.

ombreux [ɔ̃'brø], *a. (fem.* **-euse**) shady.

omelette [ɔm'lɛt], *n.f.* omelet(te).

omettre [ɔ'mɛtr], *v.t. irr. (conjug. like* METTRE) to omit.

omission [ɔmi'sjɔ̃], *n.f.* omission.

omnibus [ɔmni'byːs], *a.* suitable for all; *train omnibus*, slow train, local train. —*n.m. inv.* omnibus, bus.

229

omnipotence

omnipotence [ɔmnipɔ'tũːs], *n.f.* omnipotence.

omnipotent [ɔmnipɔ'tũ], *a.* omnipotent.

omnivore [ɔmni'vɔːr], *a.* omnivorous.—*n.m.* omnivore.

omoplate [ɔmɔ'plat], *n.f.* shoulder-blade; scapula.

on [ɔ̃], *indef. pron.* one, they, we, you, people, men, somebody.

once (1) [ɔ̃ːs], *n.f.* ounce (*weight*).

once (2) [ɔ̃ːs], *n.f.* ounce, snow leopard.

oncle [ɔ̃ːkl], *n.m.* uncle.

onction [ɔ̃k'sjɔ̃], *n.f.* unction, anointing; (*fig.*) unctuousness.

onctueusement [ɔ̃ktɥøz'mɑ̃], *adv.* unctuously.

onctueux [ɔ̃k'tɥø], *a.* (*fem.* **-euse**) unctuous, oily.

onctuosité [ɔ̃ktɥɔzi'te], *n.f.* unctuousness; smoothness.

onde [ɔ̃ːd], *n.f.* wave, billow; (*fig.*) sea.

ondé [ɔ̃'de], *a.* undulating, wavy; watered (*of silk etc.*).

ondée [ɔ̃'de], *n.f.* shower (*of rain*).

ondoyant [ɔ̃dwa'jɑ̃], *a.* undulating; (*fig.*) changeable.

ondoyer [ɔ̃dwa'je], *v.t.* (*conjug. like* EMPLOYER) to baptize privately.—*v.i.* to undulate; to ripple (*water*).

ondulant [ɔ̃dy'lɑ̃], *a.* undulating; waving, flowing.

ondulation [ɔ̃dyla'sjɔ̃], *n.f.* undulation; wave (*of hair*).

ondulé [ɔ̃dy'le], *a.* rolling, undulating; waved (*hair*); corrugated (*iron*).

onduler [ɔ̃dy'le], *v.t.* to wave (*hair*).—*v.i.* to undulate; to ripple.

onduleux [ɔ̃dy'lø], *a.* (*fem.* **-euse**) sinuous, wavy.

onéreux [ɔne'rø], *a.* (*fem.* **-euse**) burdensome, onerous; expensive.

ongle [ɔ̃ːgl], *n.m.* nail (*of fingers, claws etc.*); claw, talon; hoof.

onglée [ɔ̃'gle], *n.f.* numbness of the fingers (*from cold*).

onglet [ɔ̃'gle], *n.m.* miter, miter-joint.

onglier [ɔ̃'glje], *n.m.* manicure case; (*pl.*) (*curved*) nail scissors.

onguent [ɔ̃'gɑ̃], *n.m.* ointment, salve.

ongulé [ɔ̃gy'le], *a.* hoofed, ungulate.

onyx [ɔ'niks], *a.* and *n.m. inv.* onyx.

onze [ɔ̃ːz], *a.* and *n.m.* eleven, eleventh.

onzième [ɔ̃'zjɛm], *a.* and *n.m.* eleventh.

onzièmement [ɔ̃zjɛm'mɑ̃], *adv.* eleventhly, in the eleventh place.

opacité [ɔpasi'te], *n.f.* opacity; (*fig.*) darkness.

opale [ɔ'pal], *n.f.* opal.

opalescence [ɔpalɛ'sɑ̃ːs], *n.f.* opalescence.

opalescent [ɔpalɛ'sɑ̃], *a.* opalescent.

opaque [ɔ'pak], *a.* opaque.

opéra [ɔpe'ra], *n.m.* opera; opera house.

opéra-bouffe [ɔpera'buf], *n.m.* comic opera; musical comedy.

opérateur [ɔpera'tœːr], *n.m.* (*fem.* **-trice**) operator; operative.

opératif [ɔpera'tif], *a.* (*fem.* **-tive**) operative.

opération [ɔpera'sjɔ̃], *n.f.* operation, working, performance; (*Comm.*) transaction.

opératoire [ɔpera'twaːr], *a.* operative, surgical.

opérer [ɔpe're], *v.t.* (*conjug. like* CÉDER) to operate, to bring about, to perform; to

operate upon.—*v.i.* to work, to operate.

s'opérer, *v.r.* to take place, to be brought about.

opérette [ɔpe'rɛt], *n.f.* operetta, light opera.

ophtalmie [ɔftal'mi], *n.f.* ophthalmia.

ophtalmique [ɔftal'mik], *a.* ophthalmic.

opiner [ɔpi'ne], *v.i.* to opine, to give *or* be of opinion; to speak.

opiniâtre [ɔpi'njaːtr], *a.* stubborn. obstinate. —*n.* stubborn person.

opiniâtrement [ɔpinjatrə'mɑ̃], *adv.* doggedly.

opiniâtrer (s') [sɔpinja'tre], *v.r.* to be obstinate, to insist.

opiniâtreté [ɔpinjatrə'te], *n.f.* obstinacy.

opinion [ɔpi'njɔ̃], *n.f.* opinion; judgment, view; (*pl.*) votes.

opium [ɔ'pjɔm], *n.m.* opium.

opossum [ɔpɔ'sɔm], *n.m.* opossum.

opportun [ɔpɔr'tœ̃], *a.* opportune, timely; expedient.

opportunément [ɔpɔrtyne'mɑ̃], *adv.* seasonably.

opportunisme [ɔpɔrty'nism], *n.m.* opportunism.

opportuniste [ɔpɔrty'nist], *a.* and *n.* opportunist.

opportunité [ɔpɔrtyni'te], *n.f.* opportuneness, expediency.

opposant [ɔpo'zɑ̃], *a.* opposing, adverse.— *n.m.* (*fem.* **-e**) opponent, adversary.

opposé [ɔpo'ze], *a.* opposite, contrary.—*n.m.* the opposite, the reverse, the contrary.

opposer [ɔpo'ze], *v.t.* to oppose; to object; to urge. **s'opposer**, *v.r.* to be opposed *or* contrary (*à*), to set oneself against, to resist.

opposition [ɔpozi'sjɔ̃], *n.f.* opposition, resistance; contrast.

oppresser [ɔprɛ'se], *v.t.* (*fig.*) to depress; *to oppress.

oppresseur [ɔprɛ'sœːr], *a.m.* oppressive.— *n.m.* oppressor.

oppressif [ɔprɛ'sif], *a.* (*fem.* **-ive**) oppressive.

oppression [ɔprɛ'sjɔ̃], *n.f.* oppression.

oppressivement [ɔprɛsiv'mɑ̃], *adv.* tyrannically, oppressively (*person*).

opprimant [ɔpri'mɑ̃], *a.* oppressing.

opprimé [ɔpri'me], *a.* oppressed.—*n.m.* (*fem.* **-ée**) the oppressed.

opprimer [ɔpri'me], *v.t.* to oppress, to crush.

opprobre [ɔ'prɔbr], *n.m.* opprobrium, shame, disgrace.

opter [ɔp'te], *v.i.* to choose, to decide.

opticien [ɔpti'sjɛ̃], *n.m.* optician.

optimisme [ɔpti'mism], *n.m.* optimism.

optimiste [ɔpti'mist], *a.* optimistic.—*n.* optimist.

option [ɔp'sjɔ̃], *n.f.* option, choice.

optique [ɔp'tik], *a.* optic, optical.—*n.f.* optics; perspective.

opulence [ɔpy'lɑ̃ːs], *n.f.* opulence, wealth.

opulent [ɔpy'lɑ̃], *a.* opulent, wealthy.

or (1) [ɔːr], *n.m.* gold; (*Her.*) or.

or (2) [ɔːr], *conj.* but, now; well.

oracle [ɔ'raːkl], *n.m.* oracle.

orage [ɔ'raːʒ], *n.m.* storm; thunder-storm; (*fig.*) tumult, disorder.

orageusement [ɔraʒøz'mɑ̃], *adv.* tempestuously; boisterously.

orageux [ɔra'ʒø], *a.* (*fem.* **-euse**) stormy, tempestuous, restless.

oraison [ɔrɛ'zɔ̃], *n.f.* speech, oration; prayer.
oral [ɔ'ral], *a.* (*m. pl.* **-aux**) oral, by word of mouth.
oralement [ɔral'mɑ̃], *adv.* orally, by word of mouth.
orange [ɔ'rɑ̃:ʒ], *n.f.* orange (*fruit*).—*a. inv.* and *n.m.* orange (*color*).
orangé [ɔrɑ̃'ʒe], *a.* orange(-colored).
orangeade [ɔrɑ̃'ʒad], *n.f.* orangeade, orange squash.
oranger [ɔrɑ̃'ʒe], *n.m.* orange tree.
orangerie [ɔrɑ̃'ʒri], *n.f.* orange house; orange grove, orangery.
orang-outan(g) [ɔrɑ̃u'tɑ̃], *n.m.* (*pl.* **orangs-outans**) orang-utan.
orateur [ɔra'tœ:r], *n.m.* (*fem.* **-trice**) orator, speaker.
oratoire [ɔra'twa:r], *a.* oratorical; oratorial.—*n.m.* oratory; private chapel.
orbe [ɔrb], *n.m.* orb, orbit; globe; sphere; coil (*snake*).
orbite [ɔr'bit], *n.f.* orbit; (*Anat.*) socket; (*fig.*) sphere (*of action*).
Orcades [ɔr'kad], **les**, *f. pl.* the Orkneys.
orchestral [ɔrkɛs'tral], *a.* (*m. pl.* **-aux**) orchestral.
orchestration [ɔrkɛstra'sjɔ̃], *n.f.* scoring, orchestration.
orchestre [ɔr'kɛstr], *n.m.* orchestra; band.
orchestrer [ɔrkɛs'tre], *v.t.* to score, to orchestrate.
orchidée [ɔrki'de], *n.f.* orchid; (*pl.*) Orchidaceae.
ordinaire [ɔrdi'nɛ:r], *a.* ordinary, common, usual.—*n.m.* ordinary practice; usual fare.
ordinairement [ɔrdinɛr'mɑ̃], *adv.* usually.
ordinal [ɔrdi'nal], *a.* (*m. pl.* **-aux**) ordinal.
ordination [ɔrdina'sjɔ̃], *n.f.* ordination.
ordonnance [ɔrdɔ'nɑ̃:s], *n.f.* order, ordinance, regulation; disposition, arrangement; (*Med.*) prescription.—*n.* (*usu. fem.*) (*Mil.*) orderly.
ordonnateur [ɔrdɔna'tœ:r], *a.* (*fem.* **-trice**) ordaining, ordering.—*n.m.* (*fem.* **-trice**) organizer, manager; master of ceremonies.
ordonné [ɔrdɔ'ne], *a.* ordered; tidy; ordained (*priest*).
ordonner [ɔrdɔ'ne], *v.t.* to order, to regulate; to direct, to command; to ordain; (*Med.*) to prescribe.
ordre [ɔrdr], *n.m.* order, command; class, tribe; (*pl.*) holy orders.
ordure [ɔr'dy:r], *n.f.* filth, dirt; (*pl.*) sweepings, refuse, garbage.
ordurier [ɔrdy'rje], *a.* (*fem.* **-ière**) filthy, ribald, lewd.
oreille [ɔ'rɛ:j], *n.f.* ear; hearing; flange; handle (*of a vase etc.*); *avoir l'oreille basse*, to be cres'fallen; *avoir mal aux oreilles*, to have ear-ache; *faire la sourde oreille*, to turn a deaf ear; *prêter l'oreille à*, to listen to.
oreiller [ɔrɛ'je], *n.m.* pillow.
oreillons [ɔrɛ'jɔ̃], *n.m. pl.* mumps.
orfèvre [ɔr'fɛ:vr], *n.m.* goldsmith, silversmith.
orfraie [ɔr'frɛ], *n.f.* osprey.
organdi [ɔrgɑ̃'di], *n.m.* organdie.
organe [ɔr'gan], *n.m.* organ; voice; agent, agency; spokesman.
organique [ɔrga'nik], *a.* organic.

organisateur [ɔrganiza'tœ:r], *a.* (*fem.* **-trice**) organizing.—*n.m.* (*fem.* **-trice**) organizer.
organisation [ɔrganiza'sjɔ̃], *n.f.* organization; (*fig.*) set-up; constitution.
organisé [ɔrgani'ze], *a.* organized.
organiser [ɔrgani'ze], *v.t.* to organize; to get up, to arrange. **s'organiser**, *v.r.* to become organized.
organisme [ɔrga'nism], *n.m.* organism.
organiste [ɔrga'nist], *n.* organist.
orge [ɔrʒ], *n.f.* barley; (*masc. in orge mondé*, hulled barley, *and orge perlé*, pearl barley).
orgelet [ɔrʒ'lɛ], *n.m.* sty (*in the eye*).
orgie [ɔr'ʒi], *n.f.* orgy; (*fig.*) profusion.
orgue [ɔrg], *n.m.* (*fem. in pl.*) (*Mus.*) organ.
orgueil [ɔr'gœ:j], *n.m.* pride; arrogance.
orgueilleusement [ɔrgœjøz'mɑ̃], *adv.* proudly, haughtily.
orgueilleux [ɔrgœ'jø], *a.* (*fem.* **-euse**) proud, haughty, arrogant.—*n.m.* (*fem.* **-euse**) proud and haughty person.
orient [ɔ'rjɑ̃], *n.m.* East, Orient; rise; water (*of pearls*).
oriental [ɔrjɑ̃'tal], *a.* (*m. pl.* **-aux**) oriental, eastern.—*n.m.* (*fem.* **-e**) oriental (*person*).
orientation [ɔrjɑ̃ta'sjɔ̃], *n.f.* orientation.
orienter [ɔrjɑ̃'te], *v.t.* to orientate; to set (*a map*) by the compass; (*fig.*) to guide; (*Naut.*) to trim (*sails*). **s'orienter**, *v.r.* to take one's bearings, to ascertain one's position; (*fig.*) to see what one is about.
orifice [ɔri'fis], *n.m.* orifice, aperture, hole.
originaire [ɔriʒi'nɛ:r], *a.* originally (*coming*) from; native (*de*); primitive.
originairement [ɔriʒinɛr'mɑ̃], *adv.* originally, primitively.
original [ɔriʒi'nal], *a.* (*m. pl.* **-aux**) original; singular, odd, peculiar, quaint.—*n.m.* original manuscript, drawing etc. (*not a copy*).—*n.m.* (*fem.* **-e**) queer person, character, oddity.
originalement [ɔriʒinal'mɑ̃], *adv.* originally; singularly, oddly.
originalité [ɔriʒinali'te], *n.f.* originality; eccentricity.
origine [ɔri'ʒin], *n.f.* origin, source; descent, derivation, extraction; *d'origine*, authentic; vintage (*wine*).
originel [ɔriʒi'nɛl], *a.* (*fem.* **-elle**) original, primitive.
originellement [ɔriʒinɛl'mɑ̃], *adv.* originally.
orignal [ɔri'nal], *n.m.* elk (*of Canada*), moose.
Orion [ɔ'rjɔ̃], *n.m.* (*Astron.*) Orion.
oripeau [ɔri'po], *n.m.* (*pl.* **-eaux**) tinsel; foil; (*pl.*) tawdry finery; (*more usually*) rags.
orme [ɔrm], *n.m.* elm.
ormeau [ɔr'mo], *n.m.* (*pl.* **-eaux**) young elm.
orné [ɔr'ne], *a.* ornate.
ornement [ɔrnə'mɑ̃], *n.m.* ornament, embellishment.
ornemental [ɔrnəmɑ̃'tal], *a.* (*m. pl.* **-aux**) ornamental.
ornementation [ɔrnəmɑ̃ta'sjɔ̃], *n.f.* ornamentation.
orner [ɔr'ne], *v.t.* to adorn, to decorate, to deck, to embellish. **s'orner**, *v.r.* to adorn oneself; to be adorned.
ornière [ɔr'njɛ:r], *n.f.* rut.
ornithologie [ɔrnitɔlɔ'ʒi], *n.f.* ornithology.
ornithologiste [ɔrnitɔlɔ'ʒist], **ornithologue** [ɔrnitɔ'lɔg], *n.m.* ornithologist.

Orphée

Orphée [ɔr'fe], *m.* Orpheus.
orphelin [ɔrfə'lɛ̃], *a.* and *n.m.* (*fem.* **-e**) orphan.
orphelinat [ɔrfəli'na], *n.m.* orphanage.
orphéon [ɔrfe'ɔ̃], *n.m.* male-voice choir.
ort [ɔːr], *a. inv.* and *adv.* (*Comm.*) gross, gross weight.
orteil [ɔr'tɛːj], *n.m.* toe, *esp.* the big toe.
orthodoxe [ɔrtɔ'dɔks], *a.* orthodox.
orthodoxie [ɔrtɔdɔk'si], *n.f.* orthodoxy.
orthographe [ɔrtɔ'graf], *n.f.* orthography, spelling.
orthopédie [ɔrtɔpe'di], *n.f.* orthopedics.
ortie [ɔr'ti], *n.f.* nettle.
orvet [ɔr'vɛ], *n.m.* slow-worm.
os [ɔs; *pl.* o], *n.m. inv.* bone.
oscillation [ɔsi'lɑ], *a.* oscillating.
oscillation [ɔsila'sjɔ̃], *n.f.* oscillation, vibration.
oscillatoire [ɔsila'twaːr], *a.* oscillatory.
osciller [ɔsi'le], *v.i.* to oscillate, to swing, to vibrate; (*fig.*) to fluctuate.
oscillographe [ɔsilɔ'graf], *n.m.* (*Elec.*) oscillograph.
osé [o'ze], *a.* bold, daring.
oseille [o'zɛj], *n.f.* sorrel.
oser [o'ze], *v.t., v.i.* to dare, to venture.
oseraie [oz're], *n.f.* osier bed.
osier [o'zje] *n.m.* osier, withy, wicker.
osselet [ɔs'lɛ], *n.m.* knuckle bone (*of sheep*); ossicle (*of ear*).
ossements [ɔs'mɑ̃], *n.m. pl.* bones (*of the dead*).
osseux [ɔ'sø], *a.* (*fem.* **-euse**) bony, osseous.
ossification [ɔsifika'sjɔ̃], *n.f.* ossification.
ossifier [ɔsi'fje], *v.t.* to ossify. **s'ossifier**, *v.r.* to become ossified.
ossuaire [ɔ'sɥɛːr], *n.m.* ossuary, charnel-house.
ostensible [ɔstɑ̃'sibl], *a.* open; above-board.
ostensiblement [ɔstɑ̃siblə'mɑ̃], *adv.* openly, publicly.
ostensoir [ɔstɑ̃'swaːr], *n.m.* monstrance.
ostentation [ɔstɑ̃ta'tœːr], *a.* (*fem.* **-trice**) ostentatious.
ostentation [ɔstɑ̃ta'sjɔ̃], *n.f.* ostentation, show.
ostraciser [ɔstrasi'ze], *v.t.* to ostracize.
ostracisme [ɔstra'sism], *n.m.* ostracism.
ostréiculture [ɔstreikyl'tyːr], *n.f.* oyster culture.
otage [ɔ'taːʒ], *n.m.* hostage; pledge.
ôter [o'te], *v.t.* to take away; to remove; to take off; to deprive of; to deduct; to rid of. **s'ôter**, *v.r.* to remove oneself, to get away; to rid oneself; *ôtez-vous de mon chemin*, stand aside.
ou [u], *conj.* or, either, else; *ou bien*, or else; *ou . . . ou*, either . . . or.
où [u], *adv.* where; whither; at which, in which, to which, through which; when, that; *par où?* which way?
ouais! [wɛ], *int.* well now! my word!
ouate [wat], *n.f.* **l'ouate** or **la ouate**, wadding, padding; cotton-wool.
ouater [wa'te], *v.t.* to wad, to pad; to coddle.
oubli [u'bli], *n.m.* forgetfulness; oblivion; oversight, slip; pardon.
oubliable [u'bljabl], *a.* liable or deserving to be forgotten.
oublier [u'blje], *v.t.* to forget, to omit, to

neglect; to pardon. **s'oublier**, *v.r.* to forget oneself; to be forgotten.
oubliettes [u'bljɛt], *n.f. pl.* oubliette, trapdungeon.
oublieux [u'bljø], *a.* (*fem.* **-euse**) forgetful, unmindful.
ouest [wɛst], *a. inv.* westerly, western.—*n.m.* west.
ouf! [uf], *int.* oh! (*of relief*).
Ouganda [ugɑ̃'da], **l'**, *m.* Uganda.
oui [wi], *adv.* yes.—*n.m.* yes.
ouï [wi], *p.p.* [OUÏR].
ouï-dire [wi'diːr], *n.m. inv.* hearsay.
ouïe [wi], *n.f.* *hearing; hole (*of a violin etc.*); (*pl.*) gills (*of fish*).
ouïr [wiːr], *v.t. irr.* (*rarely used except in the infinitive and compound tenses*) to hear; *j'ai ouï dire*, I have heard say.
ouragan [ura'gɑ̃], *n.m.* hurricane; (*fig.*) storm.
ourdir [ur'diːr], *v.t.* to warp (*cloth*); (*fig.*) to weave, to plot, to concoct.
ourdissage [urdi'saːʒ], *n.m.* warping.
ourdou [ur'du], *n.m.* Urdu (*language*), Hindustani.
ourler [ur'le], *v.t.* to hem; *ourler à jour*, to hemstitch.
ourlet [ur'lɛ], *n.m.* hem.
ours [urs], *n.m.* bear.
ourse [urs], *n.f.* she-bear.
oursin [ur'sɛ̃], *n.m.* sea-urchin.
ourson [ur'sɔ̃], *n.m.* bear cub.
outil [u'ti], *n.m.* tool, implement.
outillage [uti'jaːʒ], *n.m.* stock of tools; equipment.
outillé [uti'je], *a.* furnished with tools.
outiller [uti'je], *v.t.* to furnish with tools; to equip.
outrage [u'traːʒ], *n.m.* outrage, gross insult; injury, wrong.
outrageant [utra'ʒɑ̃], *a.* outrageous; insulting, abusive.
outrager [utra'ʒe], *v.t.* (*conjug. like* MANGER) to outrage; to insult, to offend.
outrageusement [utraʒøz'mɑ̃], *adv.* insultingly.
outrageux [utra'ʒø], *a.* (*fem.* **-euse**) outrageous.
outrance [u'trɑ̃s], *n.f.* extreme; excess; *à outrance*, to the death.
outre (1) [utr], *n.f.* goatskin or leather bottle.
outre (2) [utr], *adv.* further, beyond; *en outre*, besides; *passer outre*, to go on, to take no notice of a thing.—*prep.* beyond; besides, in addition to; *outre que*, besides.
outré [u'tre], *a.* exaggerated, strained, excessive; incensed.
outrecuidance [utrəkyi'dɑ̃s], *n.f.* presumption.
outrecuidant [utrəkyi'dɑ̃], *a.* presumptuous, bumptious.
outre-Manche [utrə'mɑ̃ːʃ], *adv.* across the Channel.
outremer [utrə'mɛːr], *n.m.* ultramarine (*color*).
outre-mer [utrə'mɛːr], *adv.* overseas.
outrepasser [utrəpa'se], *v.t.* to go beyond, to transgress.
outrer [u'tre], *v.t.* to overdo; to exaggerate.
ouvert [u'vɛːr], *a.* open; unfortified (*of towns*); (*fig.*) frank.

ouvertement [uvɛrtə'mã]. *adv.* openly, frankly.

ouverture [uvɛr'ty:r], *n.f.* opening; aperture, gap, hole; (*Mus.*) overture; (*Arch.*) span, width (*of a doorway etc.*); (*Av.*) (parachute) drop.

ouvrable [u'vrabl], *a.* working, workable; *jour ouvrable*, working day.

ouvrage [u'vra:ʒ], *n.m.* work, piece of work; performance, workmanship.

ouvragé [uvra'ʒe], *a.* wrought, figured.

ouvrager [uvra'ʒe], *v.t.* (*conjug. like* MANGER) to work, to figure.

ouvrant [u'vrã], *a.* opening.

ouvré [u'vre], *a.* wrought; diapered, figured.

ouvre-boîte [uvrə'bwa:t], *n.m.* (*pl.* -boîtes) can opener.

ouvrer [u'vre], *v.t.* to work (*material*); to diaper (*linen*).—*v.i.* to work.

ouvrier [uvri'e], *a.* (*fem.* -ière) operative, working.—*n.m.* (*fem.* -ière) workman, (female) worker, hand, operative; laborer.

ouvrir [u'vri:r], *v.t. irr.* to open, to unlock; to sharpen (*the appetite*); to broach (*opinions etc.*).—*v.i.* to open; to expand. **s'ouvrir**, *v.r.* to open; to open for oneself; to open one's mind.

ouvroir [u'vrwa:r], *n.m.* charity workshop; workroom.

ovaire [ɔ'vɛ:r], *n.m.* ovary.

ovalaire [ɔva'lɛ:r], *a.* (*Anat.*) oval.

ovale [ɔ'val], *a.* and *n.m.* oval.

ovation [ɔva'sjɔ̃], *n.f.* ovation.

ovoïde [ɔvɔ'id], *a.* ovoid, egg-shaped.

ovule [ɔ'vyl] *n.m.* ovule.

oxalique [ɔksa'lik], *a.* oxalic.

oxyacétylénique [ɔksiasetile'nik], *a.* oxy-acetylene (*welding etc.*).

oxyde [ɔk'sid], *n.m.* oxide.

oxyder [ɔksi'de], *v.t.* to oxidize.

oxygène [ɔksi'ʒɛ:n], *n.m.* oxygen.

oxygéné [ɔksiʒe'ne], *a. eau oxygénée*, hydrogen peroxide.

ozone [ɔ'zɔn], *n.m.* ozone.

P

P, p [pe], *n.m.* the sixteenth letter of the alphabet.

pacage [pa'ka:ʒ], *n.m.* pasture land; *droit de pacage*, grazing rights.

pacificateur [pasifika'tœ:r], *a.* (*fem.* -trice) pacifying, peace-making.—*n.m.* (*fem.* -trice) peacemaker.

pacification [pasifika'sjɔ̃], *n.f.* pacification.

pacifier [pasi'fje], *v.t.* to pacify, to appease.

pacifique [pasi'fik], *a.* pacific, peaceful.

pacifiquement [pasifik'mã], *adv.* peaceably, quietly.

pacifisme [pasi'fism], *n.m.* pacifism.

pacifiste [pasi'fist], *a.* and *n.* pacifist.

pacotille [pako'ti:j], *n.f.* goods carried free of charge by passengers *or* seamen; shoddy goods; pack, bale.

pacte [pakt], *n.m.* compact, contract, pact, agreement; *pacte de préférence*, preference clause.

pactiser [pakti'ze], *v.i.* to covenant, to make a compact (*avec*).

paf! [paf], *int.* slap! bang!

pagaie [pa'gɛ], *n.f.* paddle (*for canoe etc.*).

pagaïe or **pagaille** [pa'gaj], *n.f.* hurry; disorder; *en pagaïe*, (*pop.*) higgledy-piggledy.

paganisme [paga'nism], *n.m.* paganism.

pagayer [page'je], *v.t.*, *v.i.* (*conjug. like* PAYER) to paddle.

page (1) [pa:ʒ], *n.m.* page (boy).

page (2) [pa:ʒ], *n.f.* page (*of a book*).

pagode [pa'gɔd], *n.f.* pagoda.

paiement [PAYEMENT].

païen [pa'jɛ̃], *a.* and *n.m.* (*fem.* -enne) pagan, heathen.

paillard [pa'ja:r], *a.* lecherous, lewd.—*n.m.* (*fem.* -e) wanton, sensual person, bawd.

paillasse (1) [pa'jas], *n.f.* straw mattress.

paillasse (2) [pa'jas], *n.m.* clown, buffoon.

paillasson [paja'sɔ̃], *n.m.* straw mat; doormat.

paille [pa:j], *a. inv.* straw-colored. —*n.f.* straw; flaw (*in gems, metals etc.*); *botte de paille*, bale of straw.

paillé [pa'je], *a.* straw-colored; faulty (*of metals etc.*).

pailler (1) [pa'je], *n.m.* farm yard; heap *or* stack of straw.

pailler (2) [pa'je], *v.t.* to mulch (*plants*).

pailleter [paj'te], *v.t.* (*conjug. like* APPELER) to spangle.

paillette [pa'jɛt], *n.f.* spangle; flaw (*in a gem*); *savon en paillettes*, soap flakes.

paillis [pa'ji], *n.m.* mulch.

paillon [pa'jɔ̃], *n.m.* large spangle, tinsel; wisp of straw; straw wrapper (*for bottle*).

pain [pɛ̃], *n.m.* bread; loaf; cake (*of soap etc.*); (*pop.*) blow, punch; *pain grillé*, toast; *un pain*, a loaf; *un petit pain*, a roll.

pair [pɛ:r], *a.* equal, even (*of numbers*).—*n.m.* peer; equal; mate (*of birds*); par, equality; *au pair*, at par, even (*with*), 'au pair'; *de pair*, on a par; *hors* (*de*) *pair*, beyond comparison.

paire [pɛ:r], *n.f.* pair, brace, couple.

pairesse [pɛ'rɛs], *n.f.* peeress.

pairie [pɛ'ri], *n.f.* peerage.

paisible [pe'zibl], *a.* peaceful, quiet, calm.

paisiblement [pezibls'mã], *adv.* peacefully.

paître [pɛ:tr], *v.t.*, *v.i. irr.* to graze, to feed.

paix [pɛ], *n.f.* peace; quiet; stillness; rest.—*int.* be quiet!

Pakistan [pakis'tã], **le**, *m.* Pakistan.

pakistanais [pakista'nɛ], *a.* Pakistani.—*n.m.* (**Pakistanais**, *fem.* -aise) Pakistani (*person*).

paladin [pala'dɛ̃], *n.m.* paladin, champion.

palais (1) [pa'lɛ], *n.m.* palace; (*fig.*) the bar, the law; *palais de justice*, law-courts.

palais (2) [pa'lɛ], *n.m.* palate, roof (*of the mouth*).

palan [pa'lã], *n.m.* tackle, pulley block.

pale [pal], *n.f.* blade (*of oar, propeller etc.*); sluice, flood-gate.

pâle [pɑ:l], *a.* pale, wan, pallid, ghastly.

palefrenier [palfrə'nje], *n.m.* groom, ostler.

palefroi [pal'frwa], *n.m.* palfrey.

Palestine [palɛs'tin], **la**, *f.* Palestine.

palestinien [palɛsti'njɛ̃], *a.* (*fem.* -enne) Palestinian.

233

palet

palet [pa'lɛ], *n.m.* quoit.
palette [pa'lɛt], *n.f.* paddle (*of paddle-wheel*); bat (*ping-pong*); palette (*of painter*).
pâleur [pa'lœːr], *n.f.* pallor, wanness.
pâli [pa'li], *a.* grown pale.
palier [pa'lje], *n.m.* landing (*on a staircase*), floor; stage, degree; level stretch; *vitesse en palier*, speed on the flat.
pâlir [pa'liːr], *v.t.* to make pale, to bleach.— *v.i.* to (grow, turn *or* become) pale; to grow dim.
palis [pa'li], *n.m.* stake, pale; paling, enclosure.
palissade [pali'sad], *n.f.* palisade, paling; wooden fence; hedgerow; stockade.
palissader [palisa'de], *v.t.* to palisade; to stockade; to fence in.
pâlissant [pali'sɑ̃], *a.* turning pale, fading.
pallier [pa'lje], *v.t.* to palliate, to excuse.
palmarès [palma'rɛːs], *n.m. inv.* prize list, list of honors.
palme [palm], *n.f.* palm, palm branch; palm tree; (*fig.*) victory, triumph.
palmé [pal'me], *a.* palmate; web-footed.
palmier [pal'mje], *n.m.* palm tree, palm.
palombe [pa'lɔ̃ːb], *n.f.* wood pigeon, ring-dove.
palonnier [palɔ'nje], *n.m.* pole (*of a coach*); (*Motor.*) compensator (*of brake*); (*Av.*) rudder bar.
pâlot [pa'lo], *a.* (*fem.* **-otte**) palish, rather pale.
palourde [pa'luːrd], *n.f.* clam.
palpable [pal'pabl], *a.* palpable.
palpablement [palpablə'mɑ̃], *adv.* palpably.
palper [pal'pe], *v.t.* to feel, to touch; (*colloq.*) to pocket.
palpitant [palpi'tɑ̃], *a.* palpitating; thrilling.
palpitation [palpita'sjɔ̃], *n.f.* palpitation; throbbing; thrill, flutter.
palpiter [palpi'te], *v.i.* to palpitate, to throb; to quiver, to flutter.
paludéen [palyde'ɛ̃], *a.* (*fem.* **-éenne**) paludal, marshy.
pâmer [pɑ'me], *v.i.* and **se pâmer**, *v.r.* to swoon.
pâmoison [pɑmwa'zɔ̃], *n.f.* swoon, fainting fit.
pamphlet [pɑ̃'flɛ], *n.m.* satirical booklet, lampoon.
pamphlétaire [pɑ̃fle'tɛːr], *n.* pamphleteer.
pamplemousse [pɑ̃plə'mus], *n.m. or f.* grapefruit.
pampre [pɑ̃ːpr], *n.m.* vine branch.
pan (1) [pɑ̃], *n.m.* flap, coat tails, panel (*of dress*); side, section (*of a wall etc.*); *pan de ciel*, stretch *or* patch of sky; *pan de mur*, bare wall, piece of wall.
pan! (2) [pɑ̃], *int.* slap! bang! smack!
panacée [pana'se], *n.f.* panacea.
panache [pa'naʃ], *n.m.* plume, bunch of feathers etc.; (*fig.*) show, swagger.
panaché [pana'ʃe], *a.* plumed, tufted; striped; (*colloq.*) variegated, motley; *glace panachée*, mixed ice-cream.
panacher [pana'ʃe], *v.t.* to plume; to streak, to variegate, to mix.
panais [pa'nɛ], *n.m.* parsnip.
Panama [pana'ma], **le**, *m.* Panama.
panama [pana'ma], *n.m.* panama hat.
panamien [pana'mjɛ̃], *a.* (*fem.* **-enne**) Panama(nian).—*n.m.* (**Panamien**, *fem.* **-enne**) Panamanian (*person*).

234

panaris [pana'ri], *n.m.* whitlow.
pancarte [pɑ̃'kart], *n.f.* large placard *or* bill.
pancréas [pɑ̃kre'aːs], *n.m. inv.* pancreas; sweetbread.
panda [pɑ̃'da], *n.m.* panda.
pandémonium [pɑ̃demɔ'njɔm], *n.m.* pandemonium.
pandit [pɑ̃'di], *n.m.* pundit.
Pandore [pɑ̃'dɔːr], *f.* Pandora.
pané [pa'ne], *a.* covered *or* fried, in bread-crumbs.
panégyrique [paneʒi'rik], *n.m.* panegyric.
paner [pa'ne], *v.t.* to cover with breadcrumbs.
panier [pa'nje], *n.m.* basket, hamper, pannier; hoop-petticoat; *le dessus du panier*, the pick of the basket; *panier à salade*, (*wire*) salad washer; (*slang*) black Maria; *panier percé*, spendthrift.
panique [pa'nik], *a.* and *n.f.* panic.
panne [pan], *n.f.* plush; fat, lard; purlin; breakdown, mishap; *panne d'allumage*, (*Motor.*) ignition trouble; *rester en panne* (*Motor.*) to have a breakdown.
panneau [pa'no], *n.m.* (*pl.* **-eaux**) panel; snare, trap; (*Naut.*) hatch; (*Hort.*) glass frame.
panoplie [panɔ'pli], *n.f.* panoply; trophy (*of arms*).
panorama [panɔra'ma], *n.m.* panorama.
panoramique [panɔra'mik], *a.* panoramic.
pansage [pɑ̃'saːʒ], *n.m.* grooming (*of horses etc.*).
panse [pɑ̃ːs], *n.f.* belly, paunch.
pansement [pɑ̃s'mɑ̃], *n.m.* dressing (*of wounds*); *pansement sommaire*, first aid; dressing.
panser [pɑ̃'se], *v.t.* to dress (*wounds*); to groom (*a horse*).
pansu [pɑ̃'sy], *a.* and *n.m.* (*fem.* **-e**) pot-bellied (person); bulging.
pantalon [pɑ̃ta'lɔ̃], *n.m.* (pair of) trousers; *pantalon de femme*, women's drawers, panties.
pantelant [pɑ̃'tlɑ̃], *a.* panting, gasping.
panteler [pɑ̃'tle], *v.i.* (*conjug. like* APPELER) to gasp, to pant.
panthère [pɑ̃'tɛːr], *n.f.* panther.
pantin [pɑ̃'tɛ̃], *n.m.* nonentity, puppet; (*fig.*) jumping-jack.
pantois [pɑ̃'twa], *a.* (*fig.*) astonished, flabbergasted.
pantomime [pɑ̃tɔ'mim], *a.* pantomimic.— *n.f.* dumb-show, pantomime.—*n.m.* pantomime (actor).
pantoufle [pɑ̃'tufl], *n.f.* slipper; *en pantoufles*, slipshod.
paon [pɑ̃], *n.m.* peacock; emperor moth; (*fig.*) vain person.
paonne [pan], *n.f.* peahen.
papa [pa'pa], *n.m.* papa, daddy.
papal [pa'pal], *a.* (*m. pl.* **-aux**) papal.
papauté [papo'te], *n.f.* papacy.
pape [pap], *n.m.* pope.
paperasse [pa'pras], *n.f.* useless papers, documents; red tape; paper work.
paperasser [papra'se], *v.i.* to rummage among old papers; to scribble.
paperasserie [papras'ri], *n.f.* red tape.
paperassier [papra'sje], *a.* (*fem.* **-ière**) red-tape; formal.—*n.m.* (*fem.* **-lère**) everlasting scribbler; rummager through old papers.

papeterie [pap'tri], *n.f.* paper mill, paper trade; stationery; stationer's shop; stationery case.

papetier [papə'tje], *a.* (*fem.* **-ière**) paper (*industry etc.*).—*n.m.* (*fem.* **-ière**) paper maker; stationer.

papier [pa'pje], *n.m.* paper; *papier buvard*, blotting paper; *papier d'emballage*, brown paper; *papier de verre*, glass-paper, sand-paper; *papier hygiénique*, toilet paper.

papillon [papi'jɔ̃], *n.m.* butterfly.

papillonner [papijɔ'ne], *v.i.* to flutter about, to hover; (*fig.*) to trifle, to flirt.

papillotage [papijɔ'ta:ʒ], *n.m.* blinking (*of the eyes*); dazzle, glitter, tinsel (*of style*).

papillote [papi'jɔt], *n.f.* curl paper; bonbon; *fer à papillotes*, curling irons; *papillotes à pétard*, Christmas crackers.

papilloter [papijɔ'te], *v.t.* to put (*hair etc.*) in paper.—*v.i.* to blink; to dazzle, to be gaudy.

papisme [pa'pism], *n.m.* papism, popery.

papiste [pa'pist], *a.* popish.—*n.* papist.

papou [pa'pu], *a.* Papuan.—*n.m.* (**Papou**, *fem.* **-oue**) Papuan (*person*).

Papouasie [papwa'zi], **la**, *f.* Papua.

papyrus [papi'ry:s], *n.m.* papyrus.

pâque [pɑ:k], *n.f.* Passover (*among Jews*).

paquebot [pak'bo], *n.m.* packet boat, steamer, liner.

pâquerette [pɑ'krɛt], *n.f.* daisy.

Pâques [pɑ:k], *n.m.* Easter.

paquet [pa'kɛ], *n.m.* package, bundle, parcel; packet; (*fig.*) clumsy lout.

paqueter [pak'te], *v.t.* (*conjug. like* APPELER) to make into a packet, parcel etc.

par [pa:r], *prep.* by, through, out of, from; about, in, into; for, for the sake of.

parabole [para'bɔl], *n.f.* parabola; parable.

parabolique [parabɔ'lik], *a.* parabolic.

parachutage [paraʃy'ta:ʒ], *n.m.* parachuting; parachute landing.

parachute [para'ʃyt], *n.m.* parachute; *sauter en parachute*, to bale out.

parachuter [paraʃy'te], *v.t., v.i.* to parachute, to drop (by parachute).

parachutiste [paraʃy'tist], *n.* parachutist, paratrooper.

parade [pa'rad], *n.f.* parade, show, display; pageantry; (*Fenc.*) parry.

parader [para'de], *v.i.* to show off.

paradis [para'di], *n.m.* paradise; (*Theat.*) upper gallery, the gods.

paradoxal [paradɔk'sal], *a.* (*m. pl.* **-aux**) paradoxical.

paradoxe [para'dɔks], *n.m.* paradox.

parafe or **paraphe** [pa'raf], *n.m.* paraph; flourish (*after one's signature*); initials and flourish.

parafer or **parapher** [para'fe], *v.t.* to paraph, to put one's flourish, dash or initials to.

paraffine [para'fin], *n.f.* paraffin, paraffin wax; *huile de paraffine*, liquid paraffin.

parage [pa'ra:ʒ], *n.m.* extraction, descent, lineage; (*usually in pl.*) localities, latitudes, waters; *dans ces parages*, in these parts.

paragraphe [para'graf], *n.m.* paragraph.

Paraguay [para'gwɛ], **le**, *m.* Paraguay.

paraguayen [paragwɛ'jɛ̃], *a.* (*fem.* **-enne**)

Paraguayan.—*n.m.* (**Paraguayen**, *fem.* **-enne**) Paraguayan (*person*).

paraître [pa'rɛ:tr], *v.i. irr.* (*conjug. like* CON-NAÎTRE) to appear, to come into sight; to make a show, to seem, to look like; to come out, to be published; *à ce qu'il paraît*, as it would seem.

parallèle [para'lɛl], *a.* parallel.—*n.f.* parallel line.—*n.m.* parallel, comparison; (*Geog.*) parallel of latitude.

parallèlement [paralɛl'mɑ̃], *adv.* in a parallel way *or* direction.

parallélogramme [paralelɔ'gram], *n.m.* parallelogram.

paralysateur [paraliza'tœ:r] (*fem.* **-trice**), **paralysant** [parali'zɑ̃], *a.* paralysing.

paralyser [parali'ze], *v.t.* to paralyse.

paralysie [parali'zi], *n.f.* paralysis, palsy.

paralytique [parali'tik], *a.* and *n.* paralytic.

parangon [parɑ̃'gɔ̃], *n.m.* model, paragon; comparison; flawless precious stone.

paranoïa [parano'ja], *n.f.* (*Med.*) paranoia.

parapet [para'pɛ], *n.m.* parapet.

paraphrase [para'frɑ:z], *n.f.* paraphrase, amplification.

paraphraser [parafrɑ'ze], *v.t.* to paraphrase; to amplify.

parapluie [para'plɥi], *n.m.* umbrella.

parasite [para'zit], *a.* parasitic; superfluous; extraneous.—*n.m.* parasite; (*fig.*) hanger-on; (*pl.*) (*Rad.*) atmospherics.

parasol [para'sɔl], *n.m.* sunshade.

paratonnerre [paratɔ'nɛ:r], *n.m.* lightning-conductor.

paratyphoïde [paratifɔ'id], *a.* and *n.f.* (*Med.*) paratyphoid (fever).

paravent [para'vɑ̃], *n.m.* folding screen; (*fig.*) screen.

parbleu! [par'blø], *int.* by Jove! why, of course!

parc [park], *n.m.* park; pen; *parc à huîtres*, oyster-bed; *parc d'attractions*, carnival.

parcage [par'ka:ʒ], *n.m.* folding (*of sheep*); penning (*of cattle*); parking (*of cars*).

parcellaire [parsɛ'lɛ:r], *a.* by small portions, by lots, in detail.

parcelle [par'sɛl], *n.f.* portion; particle; piece (*of land*).

parceller [parsɛ'le], *v.t.* to portion *or* parcel out.

parce que [parsə'kə, pars'kə], *conj.* because, as.—*n.m. inv.* **les pourquoi et les parce que**, the whys and the wherefores.

parchemin [parʃə'mɛ̃], *n.m.* parchment; (*fam.*) diploma; (*pl.*) titles of nobility.

parcimonie [parsimɔ'ni], *n.f.* parsimony.

parcimonieusement [parsimɔnjøz'mɑ̃], *adv.* parsimoniously.

parcimonieux [parsimɔ'njø] *a.* (*fem.* **-euse**) parsimonious, stingy.

(C) **parcomètre** [parko'mɛtr], *n.m.* parking meter.

parcourir [parku'ri:r], *v.t. irr.* (*conjug. like* COURIR) to travel through to run over *or* through, to scour; to look over; to peruse, to glance through (*a book*).

parcours [par'ku:r], *n.m.* line, course, road, way; route (*of bus*); distance; course (*golf*).

par-dessous [pardə'su], *prep.* and *adv.* under, beneath, underneath.

par-dessus [pardə'sy], *prep.* and *adv.* over, above.

pardessus [pardə'sy], *n.m.* overcoat.
pardon [par'dɔ̃], *n.m.* pardon, forgiveness; pilgrimage (*in Brittany*); **pardon !** excuse me!
pardonnable [pardɔ'nabl] *a.* pardonable, excusable.
pardonner [pardɔ'ne], *v.t.* to pardon, to forgive; to overlook; to excuse.
paré [pa're], *a.* adorned, got up; dressed.
pare-boue [par'bu], *n.m. inv.* fender.
pare-brise [par'briːz], *n.m. inv.* windshield (*of motor-car*).
pare-chocs [par'ʃɔk], *n.m. inv.* bumper (*of car*).
pare-étincelles [paretɛ̃'sɛl], *n.m. inv.* fire-screen, fire-guard.
pareil [pa'rɛːj], *a.* (*fem.* **-eille**) like, equal, similar; such, like that; same, identical.— *n.m.* (*fem.* **-eille**) similar *or* equal person. —*n.m.* equal, fellow.—*n.f.* (**-eille**) the like, tit for tat.
pareillement [parɛj'mã], *adv.* in like manner; likewise, also.
parement [par'mã], *n.m.* ornament; facing (*of dress*); cuff (*of sleeves*); (*Build.*) curb-stone.
parent [pa'rã], *n.m.* (*fem.* **-e**) relative, kinsman, kinswoman; (*pl.*) parents, relations, relatives; *être parent*, to be related; *parents par alliance*, related by marriage.
parenté [parã'te], *n.f.* relationship, kinship; relatives, kith and kin.
parenthèse [parã'tɛːz], *n.f.* parenthesis, digression; (*Print.*) bracket.
parer [pa're], *v.t.* to adorn, to set off, to embellish; to attire, to trim; (*Box.*) to parry; to shelter, to guard.—*v.i.* to fend, to guard (*against*). **se parer,** *v.r.* to adorn oneself; to deck oneself out; to screen *or* guard oneself, to ward off.
pare-soleil [parsɔ'lɛːj], *n.m. inv.* (*Motor.*) sun visor.
paresse [pa'rɛs], *n.f.* idleness, sloth, laziness, indolence.
paresser [parɛ'se], *v.i.* to idle, to fritter away one's time.
paresseusement [parɛsøz'mã], *adv.* lazily, idly.
paresseux [parɛ'sø], *a.* (*fem.* **-euse**) lazy, idle, slothful.—*n.m.* (*fem.* **-euse**) sluggard, lazy person.—*n.m.* (*Zool.*) sloth.
parfaire [par'fɛːr], *v.t.v. irr.* (*conjug. like* FAIRE) to complete, to perfect.
parfait [par'fɛ], *a.* perfect, faultless; complete, full.—*n.m.* perfection; (*Gram.*) perfect; *un parfait au café*, a coffee ice-cream.
parfaitement [parfɛt'mã], *adv.* perfectly, completely; exactly, just so, decidedly.
parfilage [parfi'laːʒ], *n.m.* unravelling.
parfois [par'fwa], *adv.* sometimes, occasionally.
parfum [par'fœ̃], *n.m.* perfume, odor, scent.
parfumer [parfy'me], *v.t.* to perfume, to sweeten; to scent; to fumigate. **se parfumer** *v.r.* to use perfume, to scent oneself.
parfumerie [parfym'ri], *n.f.* perfumery.
pari [pa'ri], *n.m.* bet, wager, stake; *pari mutuel*, totalizator; (*fam.*) tote.
paria [pa'rja], *n.m.* pariah, outcast.

parier [pa'rje], *v.t.* to bet, to stake.
parieur [pa'rjœːr], *n.m.* (*fem.* **-euse**) bettor; backer.
parisien [pari'zjɛ̃], *a.* (*fem.* **-enne**) Parisian.— *n.m.* (**Parisien,** *fem.* **-enne**) Parisian (*person*).
parité [pari'te], *n.f.* parity, likeness, equality; (*Fin.*) par.
parjure [par'ʒyːr], *a.* perjured.—*n.m.* perjury, false oath.—*n.* perjurer.
parjurer (se) [səparʒy're], *v.r.* to perjure oneself.
parking [par'kiŋ], *n.m.* parking place, parking lot.
parlant [par lã], *a.* speaking; (*colloq.*) talkative.
parlement [parlə'mã], *n.m.* parliament.
parlementaire [parləmã'tɛːr], *a.* parliamentary.—*n.m.* bearer of a flag of truce; parliamentarian.
parlementer [parləmã'te], *v.i.* to parley, to come to terms.
parler [par'le], *v.t.* to speak, to talk.—*v.i.* to speak, to talk; to discourse, to converse, to treat (*de*); (*pop.*) *tu parles !* you're telling me! **se parler,** *v.r.* to be spoken; to talk to oneself; to talk to each other.—*n.m.* speech.
parleur [par'lœːr], *n.m.* (*fem.* **-euse**) glib talker.
parloir [par'lwaːr], *n.m.* parlor (*of convent, school, prison*).
parmentier [parmã'tje], *a.* and *n.m.* *potage parmentier*, thick potato soup.
parmesan [parmə'zã], *n.m.* Parmesan (*cheese*).
parmi [par'mi], *prep.* among, amongst, amid, amidst.
parodie [parɔ'di], *n.f.* parody.
parodier [parɔ'dje], *v.t.* to parody, to burlesque.
paroi [pa'rwa], *n.f.* wall; partition; inner surface; lining; (*Theat.*) flat.
paroisse [pa'rwas], *n.f.* parish; (*collect.*) parishioners.
paroissial [parwa'sjal], *a.* (*m. pl.* **-aux**) parochial, parish.
paroissien [parwa'sjɛ̃], *n.m.* (*fem.* **-enne**) parishioner.—*n.m.* prayer book.
parole [pa'rɔl], *n.f.* (spoken) word; speech, utterance, voice; eloquence; promise; parole; *engager sa parole*, to pledge one's word; *manquer à sa parole*, to break one's word; *tenir parole*, to keep one's word.
paroxysme [parɔk'sism], *n.m.* paroxysm; culminating point.
parpaing [par'pɛ̃], *n.m.* (*Build.*) through stone, bondstone.
parquer [par'ke], *v.t.* to fold, to pen; to enclose; (*Motor.*) to park.—*v.i.* to be penned up (*of cattle etc.*). **se parquer,** *v.r.* to be placed in an enclosure.
parquet [par'kɛ], *n.m.* well (*of a court of justice*); prosecuting magistrates; (inlaid) floor.
parquetage [parkə'taːʒ], *n.m.* making a floor; flooring.
parqueter [parkə'te], *v.t.* (*conjug. like* APPELER) to floor, to lay a floor.
parqueterie [parkə'tri], *n.f.* floor-making; inlaid flooring.

parrain [pa'rɛ̃], n.m. godfather, sponsor; proposer.
parricide [pari'sid], a. parricidal.—n. parricide (person).—n.m. parricide crime).
parsemer [parsə'me], v.t. (conjug. like AMENER) to strew, to sprinkle; to be strewn on, to stud, to spangle.
parsi [par'si], a. Parsee.—n.m. (**Parsi**, fem. **-ie**) Parsee (person).
part [pa:r], n.f. share, part; concern, interest; place (where); à part, aside; apart from; de part en part, through and through; de toutes parts, on all sides; dites-lui de ma part, tell him from me; nulle part, nowhere; quelque part, somewhere (or other).
partage [par'ta:ʒ], n.m. sharing, share; partition.
partageable [parta'ʒabl], a. divisible into shares.
partageant [parta'ʒɑ̃], n.m. (fem. -e) (Law) sharer.
partager [parta'ʒe], v.t. (conjug. like MANGER) to divide, to share out; to participate in; to endow.—v.i. to share, to receive a share. se partager, v.r. to divide, to be divided.
partance [par'tɑ̃:s], n.f. (Naut.) sailing, departure; en partance pour, bound for.
partant [par'tɑ̃], adv. consequently, hence, therefore.—n.m. (Turf) starter.
partenaire [partə'nɛ:r], n. (Spt. etc.) partner.
parterre [par'tɛ:r], n.m. flower bed; (Theat.) pit.
parti [par'ti], n.m. (Polit.) party; part, cause; resolution, course; profit, advantage; match (marriage); (Mil.) detachment; parti pris, set purpose; rank prejudice; le parti conservateur, the Conservative party; le parti travailliste, the Labour party.
partial [par'sjal], a. (m. pl. -aux) partial, biased.
partialement [parsjal'mɑ̃], adv. partially, with partiality.
partialité [parsjali'te], n.f. partiality, bias.
participant [partisi'pɑ̃], a. participating.—n.m. (fem. -e) participant, sharer.
participation [partisipa'sjɔ̃], n.f.participation, share.
participe [parti'sip], n.m. (Gram.) participle.
participer [partisi'pe], v.i. to participate in, to share in; to be a party to (à); to partake of (de).
particularité [partikylari'te], n.f. peculiarity; particular circumstance.
particule [parti'kyl], n.f. particle.
particulier [partiky'lje], a. (fem. -ière) particular, peculiar; private; special; singular; personal.—n.m. (fem. -ière) private person, individual; (colloq.) fellow.
particulièrement [partikyljɛr'mɑ̃], adv. particularly, especially.
partie [par'ti], n.f. part (of a whole); line of business; party, amusement; game, match; client; opponent; (Law) party; (Comm.) parcel; partie nulle, drawn game.
partiel [par'sjɛl], a. (fem. -elle) partial.
partiellement [parsjɛl'mɑ̃], adv. partially, in part.
partir [par'ti:r], v.i. irr. (with aux. ÊTRE) to set out, to start, to depart, to leave; to rise (of birds); to proceed, to emanate (from); to go

off (of firearms); à partir d'aujourd'hui, from this day forward.
partisan [parti'zɑ̃], n.m. (fem. -e) partisan.
partition [parti'sjɔ̃], n.f. (Her.) partition; (Mus.) score.
partout [par'tu], adv. everywhere, on all sides.
parure [pa'ry:r]. n.f. attire, dress, finery, ornament.
parvenir [parvə'ni:r], v.i. irr. (conjug. like TENIR but with aux. ÊTRE) to attain, to reach; to succeed; to get; to arrive; to rise in the world.
parvenu [parvə'ny], n.m. (fem. -e) upstart, self-made person.
parvis [par'vi], n.m. parvis, open space (in front of a church); (Poet.) hall, temple.
pas (1) [pɑ], n.m. inv. step, pace; footprint; gait; dance; precedence; threshold; step of stair; strait, pass; thread (of screw); aller à pas mesurés, to proceed with circumspection; au pas, at a walking pace; in step; faire un faux pas, to stumble, (fig.) to blunder; le pas de Calais, the Straits of Dover; pas à pas, slowly, little by little.
pas (2) [pɑ], adv. no; not; pas du tout, not at all.
pascal [pas'kal], a. (m. pl. -aux) paschal.
passable [pɑ'sabl], a. passable, tolerable; (fig.) middling, so-so.
passablement [pɑsablə'mɑ̃], adv. fairly, passably.
passade [pɑ'sad], n.f. short stay; (fig.) passing fancy.
passage [pɑ'sa:ʒ], n.m. passage, transit; thoroughfare; arcade; crossing (on railway etc.); passage clouté, pedestrian crossing.
passager [pɑsa'ʒe], a. (fem. -ère) passing, transitory, short-lived; migratory.—n.m.(fem. -ère) passenger (by sea or air); passer-by.
passagèrement [pɑsaʒɛr'mɑ̃], adv. transiently.
passant [pɑ'sɑ̃], a. much-frequented.—n.m. (fem. -e) passer-by, wayfarer.
passavant [pɑsa'vɑ̃], n.m. pass, permit; (Naut.) gangway.
passe [pɑs], n.f. passing, passage; permit, pass; situation, state; (Fenc.) thrust; channel, narrow passage (of harbors, rivers etc.); stake (at play); (Ftb.) pass; être dans une mauvaise passe, to be in a fix; en passe de, in a fair way to.
passé [pɑ'se], a. past, bygone; faded, worn, withered.—n.m. past, past life, time past.— prep. after, beyond.
passée [pɑ'se], n.f. (Hunt.) flight, passage (of woodcock etc.).
passefiler [pɑsfi'le], v.t. to darn.
passement [pɑs'mɑ̃], n.m. lace (of gold, silk etc.).
passe-partout [pɑspar'tu], n.m. inv. master key; latch-key; passe-partout (frame); cross-cut saw.
passeport [pɑs'pɔ:r], n.m. passport.
passer [pɑ'se], v.t. (takes the auxiliary AVOIR or ÊTRE according as action or condition is implied) to pass; to cross, to go over; to transport; to strain (liquids); to sift (flour); to put on (wearing apparel); to omit; to waive; to allow; to spend (time); to take (an examination).—v.i. to pass to pass on;

to pass away; to die; to pass for; to fade. **se passer**, *v.r.* to pass, to pass away; to fade; to happen; to do without (*de*).

passereau [pas'ro], *n.m.* (*pl.* **-eaux**) sparrow.

passerelle [pas'rɛl], *n.f.* foot bridge; (*Naut.*) bridge, gangway.

passe-temps [pas'tā], *n.m.* inv. pastime, hobby.

passeur [pa'sœːr], *n.m.* (*fem.* **-euse**) ferryman, ferrywoman.

passibilité [pasibili'te], *n.f.* liability.

passible [pa'sibl], *a.* passible; liable (*to*).

passif [pa'sif], *a.* (*fem.* **-ive**) passive; (*Comm.*) on debit side.—*n.m.* (*Gram.*) passive; (*Comm.*) liabilities.

passion [pa'sjɔ̃], *n.f.* suffering, agony; passion, *esp.* love; (*fig.*) fondness.

passionnant [pasjɔ'nā], *a.* exciting, thrilling.

passionné [pasjɔ'ne], *a.* a passionate, impassioned, very fond of (*de*).

passionnel [pasjɔ'nɛl], *a.* (*fem.* **-elle**) *crime passionnel*, crime due to jealous love.

passionnément [pasjɔne'mā], *adv.* passionately, fondly.

passionner [pasjɔ'ne], *v.t.* to impassion, to interest deeply. **se passionner**, *v.r.* to be passionately fond of; to become enamored of.

passivement [pasiv'mā], *adv.* passively.

passiveté [pasiv'te], **passivité** [pasivi'te], *n.f.* passivity.

passoire [pa'swaːr], *n.f.* strainer.

pastel [pas'tɛl], *n.m.* pastel, crayon.

pastèque [pas'tɛk], *n.f.* water-melon.

pasteur [pas'tœːr], *n.m.* pastor, (*Protestant*) minister; clergyman.

pasteurisation [pastœriza'sjɔ̃], *n.f.* pasteurization.

pasteuriser [pastœri'ze], *v.t.* to pasteurize.

pastiche [pas'tiʃ], *n.m.* pastiche; (*Mus.*) medley.

pastille [pas'tij], *n.f.* pastille; lozenge; rubber patch (*for tubes of tire*).

pastoral [pasto'ral] *a.* (*m. pl.* **-aux**) pastoral. —*n.f.* (**-e**) pastoral (*play or poem*).

patapouf [pata'puf], *int. faire patapouf*, to fall flat.—*n.m. gros patapouf*, fat fellow, fatty.

patate [pa'tat], *n.f.* sweet potato.

patati [pata'ti], *only used in the phrase, et patati et patata*, and so on and so forth.

patatras! [pata'tra], *int.* crack! slap! bang!

pataud [pa'to], *a.* awkward, clumsy.—*n.m.* (*fem.* **-e**) pup with large paws; (*fig.*) lout, clumsy person.

patauger [pato'ʒe], *v.i.* (*conjug. like* MANGER) to splash, to flounder.

pâte [paːt], *n.f.* paste; dough, batter; (*fig.*) kind sort; (*Print.*) pie.

pâté [pa'te], *n.m.* pie, pasty, patty; blot (*of ink*); block (*of buildings*); (*Print.*) pie.

pâtée [pa'te], *n.f.* mash (*to fatten poultry*); mess (*for dogs or cats*).

patelin [pa'tlɛ̃], *a.* smooth-tongued, wheedling.—*n.m.* (*fem.* **-e**) wheedler.—*n.m.* (*fam.*) village.

patent [pa'tā], *a.* patent; obvious, manifest.

patenté [patā'te], *a.* licensed.—*n.m.* (*fem.* **-ée**) licensed dealer.

patenter [patā'te], *v.t.* to license.

patère [pa'tɛːr], *n.f.* coat hook; curtain hook.

paternel [patɛr'nɛl], *a.* (*fem.* **-elle**) paternal, fatherly.

paternité [patɛrni'te], *n.f.* paternity, fatherhood.

pâteux [pa'tø], *a.* (*fem.* **-euse**) pasty, clammy, sticky.

pathétique [pate'tik], *a.* pathetic, moving.— *n.m.* pathos.

pathétiquement [patetik'mā], *adv.* pathetically.

pathologie [patɔlɔ'ʒi], *n.f.* pathology.

pathologiste [patɔlɔ'ʒist], *n.m.* pathologist.

pathos [pa'tɔːs], *n.m.* bathos; (*fig.*) bombast.

patiemment [pasja'mā], *adv.* patiently.

patience [pa'sjāːs], *n.f.* patience, endurance.

patient [pa'sjā], *a.* patient, enduring, forbearing.—*n.m.* (*fem.* **-e**) sufferer; (*Med.*) patient.

patienter [pasjā'te], *v.i.* to be patient.

patin [pa'tɛ̃], *n.m.* skate; flange (*of rail*); skid (*of airplane*); shoe (*of brake*); *patins à roulettes*, roller skates.

patinage [pati'naːʒ], *n.m.* skating; skidding (*of locomotive, car etc.*).

patine [pa'tin], *n.f.* patina (*of bronze*).

patiner [pati'ne], *v.i.* to skate; to skid (*of wheels*).

patinette [pati'nɛt], *n.f.* scooter.

patineur [pati'nœːr], *n.m.* (*fem.* **-euse**) skater.

patinoire [pati'nwaːr], *n.f.* skating rink.

pâtir [pa'tiːr], *v.i.* to suffer; to be in distress.

pâtisser [pati'se], *v.t.*, to knead (*flour*).—*v.i.* to knead; to make pastry.

pâtisserie [patis'ri], *n.f.* pastry, fancy cake; pastry-cook's shop *or* business.

pâtissier [pati'sje], *n.m.* (*fem.* **-ière**) pastrycook.—*a.f.* **-ière** *crème pâtissière*, custard.

patois [pa'twa], *n.m. inv.* patois, provincial dialect; brogue; jargon.

patouiller [patu'je], [PATAUGER].

patraque [pa'trak], *a.* seedy, broken-down.— *n.f.* broken-down person *or* machine.

pâtre [paːtr], *n.m.* herdsman, shepherd.

patriarcal [patriar'kal], *a.* (*m. pl.* **-aux**) patriarchal.

patriarche [patri'arʃ], *n.m.* patriarch.

Patrice [pa'tris], *m.* Patrick.

patrice [pa'tris], *n.m.* patrician.

patricien [patri'sjɛ̃], *a.* and *n.m.* (*fem.* **-enne**) patrician.

patrie [pa'tri], *n.f.* native land, fatherland.

patrimoine [patri'mwan], *n.m.* patrimony, inheritance.

patriote [patri'ɔt], *a.* patriotic (*person*).—*n.* patriot.

patriotique [patriɔ'tik], *a.* patriotic (*song, speech etc.*).

patriotisme [patriɔ'tism], *n.m.* patriotism.

patron (1) [pa'trɔ̃], *n.m.* pattern, model.

patron (2) [pa'trɔ̃], *n.m.* (*fem.* **-onne**) patron; master, mistress, employer; proprietor; (*colloq.*) boss; (*Naut.*) skipper, coxswain.

patronage [patrɔ'naːʒ], *n.m.* patronage.

patronat [patrɔ'na], *n.m.* management.

patronner [patrɔ'ne], *v.t.* to patronize; to support.

patrouille [pa'truːj], *n.f.* patrol.

patrouiller [patru'je], *v.i.* to patrol.

patrouilleur [patru'jœːr], *n.m.* (*Naut.*) patrol boat.

patte [pat], *n.f.* paw (*of quadruped*); foot (*of bird*); leg (*of insect*); bracket, cramp; flap (*of pocket etc.*); tab, strap (*of clothes*); (*fig.*) claws, clutches.

pâturage [pɑty'ra:ʒ], n.m. pasture.

pâture [pɑ'ty:r], n.f. food (for animals); pasture; fodder.

pâturer [pɑty're], v.t. to graze on.—v.i. to pasture, to graze, to feed.

pâturon or paturon [pɑty'rɔ̃], n.m. pastern.

paume [po:m], n.f. palm (of the hand); jeu de paume, (court) tennis, 'real' tennis.

paupérisme [pope'rism], n.m. pauperism.

paupière [po'pjɛ:r], n.f. eyelid; (fig.) eye(s).

pause [po:z], n.f. pause, stop; (Mus.) rest.

pauser [po'ze], v.i. to pause.

pauvre [po:vr], a. poor, needy; wretched, paltry, mean.—n.m. poor person pauper; beggar.

pauvrement [povrə'mɑ̃], adv. poorly, wretchedly.

pauvresse [po'vrɛs], n.f. poor woman, beggar-woman.

pauvret [po'vrɛ], n.m. (fem. -ette) poor creature, poor little thing.

pauvreté [povrə'te], n.f. poverty; wretchedness; sorry thing.

pavage [pa'va:ʒ], n.m. paving; pavement.

pavane [pa'van], n.f. pavan (dance).

pavaner (se) [sapava'ne], v.r. to strut, to stalk proudly.

pavé [pa've], a. paved.—n.m. paving stone; paved part of road; (fig.) road, street(s).

pavement [pav'mɑ̃], n.m. paving; flooring.

paver [pa've], v.t. to pave.

paveur [pa'vœ:r], n.m. pavior.

pavillon [pavi'jɔ̃], n.m. pavilion, tent; summerhouse; detached house; wing (of a house), outhouse, lodge; (Naut.) flag.

pavoiser [pavwa'ze], v.t. to deck with flags, to dress (ship).

pavot [pa'vo], n.m. poppy.

payable [pe'jabl], a. payable.

payant [pe'jɑ̃], a. paying; to be paid for.—n.m. (fem. -e) payer.

paye [pɛ:j], paie [pɛ], n.f. pay, wages.

payement or paiement [pɛ'mɑ̃], n.m. payment.

payer [pe'je], v.t. (see Verb Tables) to pay (for); to reward; to expiate, to atone for.—se payer, v.r. to be paid or satisfied; to treat oneself to.

payeur [pe'jœ:r], n.m. (fem. -euse) payer; pay-clerk; (Mil.) pay-master.

pays [pe'i], n.m. inv. country, land; region, district; fatherland, home; avoir le mal du pays, to be home-sick; pays perdu, out-of-the-way place.

paysage [pei'za:ʒ], n.m. landscape, scenery.

paysagiste [peiza'ʒist], n. a. and n.m. landscape (painter).

paysan [pei'zɑ̃], a. (fem. -anne) rustic.—n.m. (fem. -anne) peasant, country man, country woman; farmer.

paysannerie [peizan'ri], n.f. rusticity; peasantry.

Pays-Bas [pei'bɑ], les, m.pl. the Netherlands.

péage [pe'a:ʒ], n.m. toll; toll house.

péan or pæan [pe'ɑ̃], n.m. pæan, song of triumph or joy.

peau [po], n.f. (pl. peaux) skin; hide; peel, rind.

Peau-Rouge [po'ru:ʒ], n. (pl. Peaux-Rouges) Redskin, Red Indian.

peccadille [pɛka'di:j], n.f. peccadillo.

pêche (1) [pɛ:ʃ], n.f. peach.

pêche (2) [pɛ:ʃ], n.f. fishing, angling.

péché [pe'ʃe], n.m. sin, transgression.

pécher [pe'ʃe], v.i. (conjug. like CÉDER) to sin, to transgress; to offend; to be deficient.

pêcher (1) [pe'ʃe], n.m. peach tree.

pêcher (2) [pe'ʃe], v.t. to fish for; to drag out; (fig.) to get hold of.—v.i. to fish, to angle.

pécheresse [peʃ'rɛs], [PÉCHEUR].

pêcherie [pɛʃ'ri], n.f. fishing ground, fishery.

pécheur [pe'ʃœ:r], n.m. (fem. -eresse) sinner.

pêcheur [pe'ʃœ:r], n.m. (fem. -euse) fisher, fisherman, fisherwoman.

pécore [pe'kɔ:r], n.f. stupid creature, blockhead; esp. silly girl.

pécule [pe'kyl], n.m. savings; earnings (of a prisoner).

pécuniaire [peky'njɛ:r], a. pecuniary.

pédagogie [pedago'ʒi], n.f. pedagogy.

pédagogue [peda'gog], n. pedagogue.

pédale [pe'dal], n.f. pedal; treadle.

pédaler [peda'le], v.i. to pedal; (colloq.) to cycle.

pédant [pe'dɑ̃], a. pedantic.—n.m. (fem. -e) pedant.

pédanterie [pedɑ̃'tri], n.f. pedantry.

pédantesque [pedɑ̃'tɛsk], a. pedantic.

pédantisme [pedɑ̃'tism], n.m. pedantry.

pédestre [pe'dɛstr], a. pedestrian, on foot.

pédestrement [pedɛstrə'mɑ̃], adv. on foot.

pédicure [pedi'ky:r], n. chiropodist.

Pégase [pe'ga:z], m. Pegasus.

peignage [pe'ɲa:ʒ], n.m. combing, woolcombing.

peigne [pɛɲ], n.m. comb.

peigné [pe'ɲe], a. combed; (fig.) arranged.—n.m. worsted.

peigner [pe'ɲe], v.t. to comb; to card; (fig.) to polish (style). se peigner, v.r. to comb one's hair.

peignoir [pe'ɲwa:r], n.m. dressing-gown; (Am.) bath-robe.

peindre [pɛ̃:dr], v.t. irr. (conjug. like CRAINDRE) to paint, to portray; to represent, to express; se faire peindre, to sit for one's portrait. se peindre, v.r. to paint oneself; to be represented.

peine [pɛn], n.f. punishment, penalty; pain, grief, sorrow; anxiety; trouble; difficulty; reluctance; à peine, hardly, scarcely; un homme de peine, an unskilled laborer.

peiné [pe'ne], a. pained, grieved; labored; elaborate.

peiner [pe'ne], v.t. to pain, to trouble, to grieve; (fig.) to elaborate.—v.i. to labor, to toil; to be reluctant.

peintre [pɛ̃:tr], n.m. painter.

peinture [pɛ̃'ty:r], n.f. painting; picture; description, appearance; paint, color.

péjoratif [peʒora'tif], a. (fem. -tive) pejorative.

Pékin [pe'kɛ̃], m. Peking.

pékinois [peki'nwa], a. Pekinese.—n.m. Pekinese (dog); (Pékinois, fem. -oise) Pekinese (person).

pelage [pə'la:ʒ], n.m. hair, fur, coat (of animal).

pelé [pə'le], a. bald; which has lost its hair (animals).—n.m. (fem. -ée) bald-headed person.

pêle-mêle [pɛl'mɛl], adv. pell-mell, higgledy-piggledy.—n.m. inv. disorder, jumble.

peler [pə'le], *v.t.* (*conjug. like* AMENER) to skin, to peel.—*v.i.* to peel off (*of the skin etc.*). **se peler,** *v.r.* to come off, to peel.

pèlerin [pɛl'rɛ̃], *n.m.* (*fem.* **-ine** (1)) pilgrim; peregrine falcon; basking shark.

pèlerinage [pɛlri'na:ʒ], *n.m.* pilgrimage.

pèlerine (2) [pɛl'rin], *n.f.* tippet, cape (*with hood*).

pélican [peli'kɑ̃], *n.m.* pelican.

pelisse [pə'lis], *n.f.* pelisse; fur-lined coat.

pelle [pɛl], *n.f.* shovel, scoop, blade (*of an oar*); (*fam.*) spill, cropper.

pelletée [pɛl'te], *n.f.* shovelful.

pelleter [pɛl'te], *v.t.* (*conjug. like* APPELER) to shovel.

pelletier [pɛl'tje], *n.m.* (*fem.* **-ière**) furrier.

pellicule [peli'kyl], *n.f.* pellicle; (*Phot.*) film; (*pl.*) scurf (*of scalp*), dandruff.

pelotage [pələ'ta:ʒ], *n.m.* winding skeins into balls; (*Billiards, Ten.*) warmup.

pelote [pə'lɔt], *n.f.* ball; ball of thread; pellet; pin-cushion; (*Spt.*) *pelote basque*, pelota.

peloter [pələ'te], *v.t.* to make *or* wind into a ball.—*v.i.* (*Spt.*) to warm up.

peloton [pələ'tɔ̃], *n.m.* ball; cluster (*of bees*); (*Mil.*) squad; (*Racing*) bunch (*of runners*).

pelotonner [pələtɔ'ne], *v.t.* to wind into balls. **se pelotonner,** *v.r.* to roll oneself up; to curl up.

pelouse [pə'lu:z], *n.f.* lawn, greensward.

peluche [pə'lyʃ], *n.f.* plush.

peluché [pəly'ʃe], *a.* shaggy.

pelucher [pəly'ʃe], *v.i.* to become shaggy, to wear rough.

pelucheux [pəly'ʃø], *a.* (*fem.* **-euse**) shaggy; fluffy.

pelure [pə'ly:r], *n.f.* paring; peel, skin; rind.

pénal [pe'nal], *a.* (*m. pl.* **-aux**) penal.

pénaliser [penali'ze], *v.t.* to penalize.

pénalité [penali'te] *n.f.* penal law; penalty.

pénates [pe'nat], *n.m. pl.* penates, household gods; (*fig.*) home.

penaud [pə'no], *a.* abashed, sheepish, crest-fallen.

penchant [pɑ̃'ʃɑ̃], *a.* inclined, sloping, lean-ing.—*n.m.* declivity, slope; inclination, bent.

pencher [pɑ̃'ʃe], *v.t.* to incline, to bend.—*v.i.* to lean; to tilt, to slope. **se pencher,** *v.r.* to bend, to stoop; to slope, to be inclined.

pendable [pɑ̃'dabl], *a.* deserving hanging, abominable.

pendaison [pɑ̃dɛ'zɔ̃], *n.f.* hanging (*on the gallows*), death by hanging.

pendant [pɑ̃'dɑ̃], *a.* pendent, hanging; pend-ing; depending.—*n.m.* thing hanging, pendant; counterpart.—*prep.* during; for; *pendant que,* while.

pendard [pɑ̃'da:r], *n.m.* (*fem.* **-e**) (*colloq.*) rascal, rogue, jade.

pendeloque [pɑ̃'dlɔk], *n.f.* ear-drop; pen-dant.

pendiller [pɑ̃di'je], *v.i.* to hang loose, to dangle.

pendre [pɑ̃:dr], *v.t.* to hang, to hang up, to suspend.—*v.i.* to hang; to dangle, to droop. **se pendre,** *v.r.* to hang oneself.

pendu [pɑ̃'dy], *a.* hanging; hanged; hung.—*n.m.* (*fem.* **-e**) one that has been hanged.

pendule [pɑ̃'dyl], *n.f.* clock, time-piece.—*n.m.* pendulum.

pêne [pɛ:n], *n.m.* bolt (*of a lock*).

pénétrabilité [penetrabili'te], *n.f.* penetra-bility.

pénétrable [pene'trabl], *a.* penetrable.

pénétrant [pene'trɑ̃], *a.* penetrating; pierc-ing, keen; acute; impressive.

pénétration [penetra'sjɔ̃], *n.f.* penetration; acuteness, shrewdness.

pénétré [pene'tre], *a.* penetrated; moved, impressed.

pénétrer [pene'tre], *v.t.* (*conjug. like* CÉDER) to penetrate, to go through; to pierce; to pervade; to fathom; to impress, to affect.—*v.i.* to penetrate (*dans*); to reach (*à*). **se pénétrer,** *v.r.* to penetrate each other; to be impressed.

pénible [pe'nibl], *a.* painful, laborious; troublesome.

péniblement [peniblə'mɑ̃], *adv.* laboriously.

pénicilline [penisi'lin], *n.f.* penicillin.

péninsulaire [penɛ̃sy'lɛ:r], *a.* peninsular.

péninsule [penɛ̃'syl], *n.f.* peninsula.

pénitence [peni'tɑ̃:s], *n.f.* penitence, repen-tance; penance; punishment.

pénitencier [penitɑ̃'sje], *a.* penitentiary.—*n.m.* penitentiary, reformatory.

pénitent [peni'tɑ̃], *a.* penitent, repentant.—*n.m.* (*fem.* **-e**) penitent.

pénitentiaire [penitɑ̃'sjɛ:r], *a.* penitentiary.

penne [pɛn], *n.f.* tail feather, wing feather.

penniforme [peni'fɔrm], *a.* penniform.

pennon [pe'nɔ̃], *n.m.* pennon.

pénombre [pe'nɔ̃:br], *n.f.* penumbra; semi-darkness, half-light.

pensée [pɑ̃'se], *n.f.* thought; opinion; idea, conception; meaning; (*Bot.*) pansy.

penser [pɑ̃'se], *v.t.* to think, to think of (*à or de*).—*v.i.* to think, to reflect, to consider; to expect; to take heed, to take care.—*n.m.* (*poet.*) inward reasoning, thought.

penseur [pɑ̃'sœ:r], *a.* (*fem.* **-euse**) thinking, thoughtful.—*n.m.* (*fem.* **-euse**) thinker.

pensif [pɑ̃'sif], *a.* (*fem.* **-sive**) pensive, thoughtful.

pension [pɑ̃'sjɔ̃], *n.f.* board and lodging; boarding house; boarding school; pension, allowance, annuity.

pensionnaire [pɑ̃sjɔ'nɛ:r], *n.* boarder; school-boy *or* -girl; pensioner, resident.

pensionnat [pɑ̃sjɔ'na], *n.m.* private boarding school.

pensionné [pɑ̃sjɔ'ne], *a.* pensioned.—*n.m.* (*fem.* **-ée**) pensioner.

pensionner [pɑ̃sjɔ'ne], *v.t.* to pension, to grant a pension to.

pensum [pɛ̃'sɔm], *n.m.* imposition, extra task (*at school*).

pente [pɑ̃:t], *n.f.* declivity, slope; acclivity, ascent; gradient; pitch (*of roofs*); (*fig.*) propensity, bent.

Pentecôte [pɑ̃t'ko:t], *n.f.* Pentecost, Whitsun-tide.

pénultième [penyl'tjɛm], *a.* last but one, penultimate.

pénurie [peny'ri], *n.f.* scarcity, dearth; penury, want.

pépier [pe'pje], *v.i.* to chirp, to cheep.

pépin [pe'pɛ̃], *n.m.* pip (*of apple etc.*); stone (*of grape*).

pépinière [pepi'njɛ:r], *n.f.* nursery (*of trees*).

pépiniériste [pepinje'rist], *n.m.* nurseryman.

pépite [pe'pit], *n.f.* nugget (*of gold*).

pepsine [pɛp'sin], *n.f.* pepsine.

peptique [pɛp'tik], a. peptic.
percale [pɛr'kal], n.f. cotton cambric, percale.
percaline [pɛrka'lin], n.f. glazed calico or lining, percaline.
perçant [pɛr'sɑ̃], a. piercing; sharp; shrill, acute.
perce [pɛrs], n.f. piercer, borer.
percé [pɛr'se], a. pierced, bored, in holes.
percée [pɛr'se], n.f. opening, cutting (in a wood), vista, glade; (fig.) break-through.
percement [pɛrsə'mɑ̃], n.m. piercing, boring, perforation.
perce-neige [pɛrs'nɛ:ʒ], n.f. inv. snowdrop.
perce-oreille [pɛrsɔ'rɛ:j], n.m. (pl. -oreilles) earwig.
percepteur [pɛrsɛp'tœ:r], n.m. collector of taxes.
perceptible [pɛrsɛp'tibl], a. collectible; perceptible.
perceptiblement [pɛrsɛptiblə'mɑ̃], adv. perceptibly.
perceptif [pɛrsɛp'tif], a. (fem. -tive) perceptive.
perception [pɛrsɛp'sjɔ̃], n.f. perception; collecting; receipt; collectorship, collector's office.
percer [pɛr'se], v.t. (conjug. like COMMENCER) to pierce, to bore, to drill; to make an opening; to tunnel; to wet through (of rain etc.).—v.i. to pierce through, to come through; to transpire; to manifest itself. **se percer**, v.r. to pierce oneself, to be pierced.
perceur [pɛr'sœ:r], n.m. (fem. -euse) borer.— n.f. (-euse) boring machine, drill.
percevoir [pɛrsə'vwa:r], v.t. irr. (conjug. like RECEVOIR) to collect (taxes etc.); (Phil.) to perceive.
perche [pɛrʃ], n.f. perch, pole; (Ichth.) perch.
perché [pɛr'ʃe], a. perched, perched up, roosting.
percher [pɛr'ʃe], v.i. and **se percher**, v.r. to perch, to roost.
percheur [pɛr'ʃœ:r], a. (fem. -euse) perching, roosting (of birds).
perchoir [pɛr'ʃwa:r], n.m. roost.
perclus [pɛr'kly], a. crippled, impotent.
percolateur [pɛrkɔla'tœ:r], n.m. percolator.
percussion [pɛrky'sjɔ̃], n.f. percussion.
percutant [pɛrky'tɑ̃], a. producing percussion; (colloq.) fabulous.
percuter [pɛrky'te], v.t. to strike; to percuss. —v.i. to crash.
perdable [pɛr'dabl], a. losable.
perdant [pɛr'dɑ̃], a. losing.—n.m. (fem. -e) loser.
perdition [pɛrdi'sjɔ̃], n.f. perdition.
perdre [pɛrdr], v.t. to lose, to be deprived of; to waste, to ruin, to corrupt, to lead astray. —v.i. to lose, to be a loser; to leak. **se perdre**, v.r. to be lost; to lose one's way, to be bewildered; to disappear.
perdreau [pɛr'dro], n.m. (pl. -eaux) young partridge.
perdrix [pɛr'dri], n.f. inv. partridge.
perdu [pɛr'dy], a. lost; ruined; spoilt; stray; obsolete; out of the way; bewildered; **salle des pas perdus**, waiting hall (in courts of law).
père [pɛ:r], n.m. father; sire.

pérégrination [peregrina'sjɔ̃], n.f. peregrination.
péremptoire [perɑ̃p'twa:r], a. peremptory.
péremptoirement [perɑ̃ptwar'mɑ̃], adv. peremptorily.
pérennité [pereni'te], n.f. perpetuity.
perfectibilité [pɛrfɛktibili'te], n.f. perfectibility.
perfectible [pɛrfɛk'tibl], a. perfectible.
perfection [pɛrfɛk'sjɔ̃], n.f. perfection; faultlessness; completeness.
perfectionnement [pɛrfɛksjɔn'mɑ̃], n.m. improvement, perfecting.
perfectionner [pɛrfɛksjɔ'ne], v.t. to perfect; to improve. **se perfectionner**, v.r. to perfect oneself; to improve.
perfide [pɛr'fid], a. perfidious, treacherous, false.—n. perfidious or treacherous person.
perfidement [pɛrfid'mɑ̃], adv. perfidiously, falsely, treacherously.
perfidie [pɛrfi'di], n.f. perfidy, treachery.
perforage [pɛrfɔ'ra:ʒ], n.m. boring, perforation.
perforant [pɛrfɔ'rɑ̃], a. perforating, penetrating.
perforateur [pɛrfɔra'tœ:r], a. (fem. -trice (1)) perforative.—n.m. perforator.
perforation [pɛrfɔra'sjɔ̃], n.f. perforation.
perforatrice [pɛrfɔra'tris], n.f. drilling machine.
perforer [pɛrfɔ're], v.t. to perforate, to bore, to drill.
péricliter [perikli'te], v.i. to be in jeopardy.
péril [pe'ril], n.m. peril, danger, hazard, risk.
périlleusement [perijøz'mɑ̃], adv. perilously.
périlleux [peri'jø], a. (fem. -euse) perilous, dangerous.
périmé [peri'me], a. out-of-date, no longer valid.
période [pe'rjɔd], n.f. period of time, era; (Gram.) period, sentence; (Mus.) phrase.— n.m. pitch, summit, degree, acme.
périodicité [perjɔdisi'te], n.f. periodicity.
périodique [perjɔ'dik], a. periodic, periodical.—n.m. periodical.
périodiquement [perjɔdik'mɑ̃], adv. periodically.
péripétie [peripe'si], n.f. sudden turn of fortune; (pl.) vicissitudes.
périr [pe'ri:r], v.i. to perish, to die; to be wrecked; to decay.
périscope [peris'kɔp], n.m. periscope.
périssable [peri'sabl], a. perishable.
péristyle [peris'til], a. and n.m. peristyle.
péritoine [peri'twan], n.m. peritoneum.
péritonite [perito'nit], n.f. peritonitis.
perle [pɛrl], n.f. pearl; bead, bugle (for bracelets, necklaces etc.); (fig.) gem, jewel, the best.
perlé [pɛr'le], a. pearled, set with pearls; pearly.
perler [pɛr'le], v.t. to bead, to form into beads; to pearl.—v.i. to form beads (of sweat etc.).
perlier [pɛr'lje], a. (fem. -ière) of pearl.
permanence [pɛrma'nɑ̃:s], n.f. permanence; headquarters (of a political party).
permanent [pɛrma'nɑ̃], a. permanent, lasting.
permanente [pɛrma'nɑ̃:t], n.f. (Hairdressing) permanent wave.

perméabilité [pɛrmeabili'te], *n.f.* permeability.

perméable [pɛrme'abl], *a.* permeable, pervious (*to*).

permettre [pɛr'mɛtr], *v.t. irr.* (*conjug. like* METTRE) to permit, to allow; to enable, to afford room for. **se permettre**, *v.r.* to permit oneself; to indulge, to venture, to take the liberty (*de*).

permis [pɛr'mi], *a.* allowed, permitted, lawful.—*n.m.* permission, leave; permit, license, pass.

permission [pɛrmi'sjɔ̃], *n.f.* permission, leave, permit.

permutant [pɛrmy'tɑ̃], *n.m.* permuter, exchanger.

permutation [pɛrmyta'sjɔ̃], *n.f.* permutation, exchange; (*Mil.*) transfer.

permuter [pɛrmy'te], *v.t.* to exchange, to permute, to transpose.

pernicieusement [pɛrnisjøz'mɑ̃], *adv.* perniciously, mischievously, injuriously.

pernicieux [pɛrni'sjø], *a.* (*fem.* **-euse**) pernicious, mischievous, hurtful.

péronnelle [perɔ'nɛl], *n.f.* pert hussy, saucy baggage.

péroraison [perɔrɛ'zɔ̃], *n.f.* peroration.

pérorer [perɔ're], *v.i.* to hold forth, to speechify.

péroreur [perɔ'rœːr], *n.m.* (*fem.* **-euse**) speechifier, spouter.

Pérou [pe'ru], **le**, *m.* Peru.

perpendiculaire [pɛrpādiky'lɛːr], *a.* and *n.f.* perpendicular.

perpendiculairement [pɛrpādikylɛr'mā], *adv.* perpendicularly.

perpétration [pɛrpetra'sjɔ̃], *n.f.* perpetration.

perpétrer [pɛrpe'tre], *v.t.* (*conjug. like* CÉDER) to perpetrate, to commit.

perpétuation [pɛrpetɥa'sjɔ̃], *n.f.* perpetuation.

perpétuel [pɛrpe'tɥɛl], *a.* (*fem.* **-elle**) perpetual, permanent; for life.

perpétuellement [pɛrpetɥɛl'mā], *adv.* perpetually; everlastingly.

perpétuer [pɛrpe'tɥe], *v.t.* to perpetuate. **se perpétuer**, *v.r.* to be perpetuated, to continue.

perpétuité [pɛrpetɥi'te], *n.f.* perpetuity; *à perpétuité*, for ever, for life.

perplexe [pɛr'plɛks], *a.* perplexed, embarrassed, irresolute; perplexing.

perplexité [pɛrplɛksi'te], *n.f.* perplexity.

perquisition [pɛrkizi'sjɔ̃], *n.f.* perquisition, search; investigation.

perquisitionner [pɛrkizisjɔ'ne], *v.i.* to make a search.

perron [pɛ'rɔ̃], *n.m.* steps (*before a house*).

perroquet [perɔ'kɛ] *n.m.* parrot.

perruche [pɛ'ryʃ], *n.f.* parakeet, budgerigar; (*pop.*) hen-parrot.

perruque [pɛ'ryk], *n.f.* wig, periwig.

perruquier [pɛry'kje], *n.m.* wig-maker; (*obs.*) hair-dresser, barber.

persan [pɛr'sā], *a.* Persian.—*n.m.* Persian (*language*); (**Persan**, *fem.* **-ane**) Persian (*person*).

Perse [pɛrs], **la**, *f.* Persia.

perse [pɛrs], *n.f.* chintz.

persécuter [pɛrseky'te], *v.t.* to persecute; (*fig.*) to bore, to dun.

persécuteur [pɛrseky'tœːr], *a.* (*fem.* **-trice**) persecuting; troublesome.—*n.m.* (*fem.* **-trice**) persecutor; troublesome person.

persécution [pɛrseky'sjɔ̃], *n.f.* persecution; annoyance, importunity.

persévérance [pɛrseve'rɑ̃ːs], *n.f.* perseverance; firmness, steadiness.

persévérant [pɛrseve'rā], *a.* persevering; steady, resolute.

persévérer [pɛrseve're], *v.i.* (*conjug. like* CÉDER) to persevere; to be steadfast; to persist.

persienne [pɛr'sjɛn], *n.f.* Venetian shutter.

persiflage [pɛrsi'flaːʒ], *n.m.* banter, chaff, persiflage.

persifler [pɛrsi'fle], *v.t.*, *v.i.* to rally, to banter, to chaff.

persifleur [pɛrsi'flœːr], *a.* (*fem.* **-euse**) bantering, chaffing.—*n.m.* (*fem.* **-euse**) banterer, tease.

persil [pɛr'si], *n.m.* parsley.

persillé [pɛrsi'je], *a.* spotted; blue-molded (*cheese*).

persique [pɛr'sik], *a.* ancient Persian; *le Golfe Persique*, Persian Gulf.

persistance [pɛrsis'tɑ̃ːs], *n.f.* persistence.

persistant [pɛrsis'tā], *a.* persistent.

persister [pɛrsis'te], *v.i.* to persist.

personnage [pɛrsɔ'naːʒ], *n.m.* personage, person; (*Theat.*) character, part.

personnalité [pɛrsɔnali'te], *n.f.* personality, personal character; person; selfishness.

personne [pɛr'sɔn], *n.f.* person; own self; appearance.—*pron. indef.* anyone, no one, nobody.

personnel [pɛrsɔ'nɛl], *a.* (*fem.* **-elle**) personal; selfish.—*n.m.* personnel, staff.

personnellement [pɛrsɔnɛl'mā], *adv.* personally.

personnification [pɛrsɔnifika'sjɔ̃], *n.f.* personification.

personnifier [pɛrsɔni'fje], *v.t.* to personify; to embody.

perspectif [pɛrspɛk'tif], *a.* (*fem.* **-tive**) perspective.—*n.f.* (**-tive**) perspective; view, prospect, distance, vista.

perspicace [pɛrspi'kas], *a.* perspicacious, shrewd.

perspicacité [pɛrspikasi'te], *n.f.* perspicacity, insight.

persuader [pɛrsɥa'de], *v.t.* to persuade; to convince, to satisfy. **se persuader**, *v.r.* to persuade *or* convince oneself; to be persuaded.

persuasible [pɛrsɥa'zibl], *a.* persuadable.

persuasif [pɛrsɥa'zif], *a.* (*fem.* **-sive**) persuasive; convincing.

persuasion [pɛrsɥa'zjɔ̃], *n.f.* persuasion; conviction, belief, opinion.

persuasivement [pɛrsɥaziv'mā], *adv.* persuasively.

perte [pɛrt], *n.f.* loss; waste; ruin, fall, doom; *à perte*, at a loss; *en pure perte*, in vain.

pertinemment [pɛrtina'mā], *adv.* pertinently.

pertinence [pɛrti'nāːs], *n.f.* pertinence.

pertinent [pɛrti'nā], *a.* pertinent, relevant.

pertuis [pɛr'tɥi], *n.m.* opening, sluice; straits.

perturbateur [pɛrtyrba'tœːr], *a.* (*fem.* **-trice**) disturbing.—*n.m.* (*fem.* **-trice**) disturber.

perturbation [pɛrtyrba'sjɔ̃], *n.f.* perturbation, disturbance.

perturber [pɛrtyr'be], *v.t.* to perturb, to disturb.

péruvien [pery'vjɛ̃], *a.* (*fem.* -**enne**) Peruvian.—*n.m.* (**Péruvien**, *fem.* -**enne**) Peruvian (*person*).

pervenche [pɛr'vɑ̃:ʃ], *n.f.* (*Bot.*) periwinkle.

pervers [pɛr'vɛːr], *a.* perverse, wicked, depraved.—*n.m.* (*fem.* -**e**) perverse person; wrongdoer.

perversion [pɛrvɛr'sjɔ̃], *n.f.* perversion.

perversité [pɛrvɛrsi'te], *n.f.* perverseness.

pervertir [pɛrvɛr'tiːr], *v.t.* to pervert.

pervertissement [pɛrvɛrtis'mɑ̃], *n.m.* perversion.

pervertisseur [pɛrvɛrti'sœːr], *a.* (*fem.* -**euse**) perverting.—*n.m.* (*fem.* -**euse**) perverter, corrupter.

pesage [pə'zaːʒ], *n.m.* weighing; (*Turf.*) weighing-in room; paddock (*on racecourse*), the enclosure.

pesamment [pəza'mɑ̃], *adv.* heavily, ponderously; clumsily.

pesant [pə'zɑ̃], *a.* heavy, ponderous; unwieldy; sluggish.—*n.m.* weight.—*adv.* in weight.

pesanteur [pəzɑ̃'tœːr], *n.f.* weight; heaviness; unwieldiness, dullness, ponderousness; (*Phys.*) gravity.

pesée !pə'ze], *n.f.* weighing.

pèse-lettre [pɛz'lɛtr], *n.m.* (*pl.* -**lettres**) letter-scales.

peser [pə'ze], *v.t.* (*conjug. like* AMENER) to weigh; (*fig.*) to ponder, to estimate.—*v.i.* to weigh; to be heavy; to be of importance; to lie heavy; to dwell (*sur*).

peseur [pə'zœːr], *n.m.* (*fem.* -**euse**) weigher.

pessimisme [pɛsi'mism], *n.m.* pessimism.

pessimiste [pɛsi'mist], *a.* pessimistic.—*n.* pessimist.

peste [pɛst], *n.f.* plague, pestilence; (*fig.*) pest, bore, nuisance.—*int.* the deuce! hang it!

pester [pɛs'te], *v.i.* to inveigh, to storm, to rave.

pestiféré [pɛstife're], *a.* and *n.m.* (*fem.* -**ée**) plague-stricken (person).

pestilence [pɛsti'lɑ̃ːs], *n.f.* pestilence.

pestilent [pɛsti'lɑ̃], *a.* pestilent.

pestilentiel [pɛstilɑ̃'sjɛl], *a.* (*fem.* -**elle**) pestilential.

pétale [pe'tal], *n.m.* petal.

pétarade [peta'rad], *n.f.* cracking (*noise*); back-fire (*of car*).

pétard [pe'taːr], *n.m.* petard; cracker (*firework*); (*Rail.*) detonator, fog signal.

pétaudière [peto'djɛːr], *n.f.* noisy *or* disorderly assembly.

pétillant [peti'jɑ̃], *a.* crackling; sparkling.

pétillement [petij'mɑ̃], *n.m.* crackling; sparkling.

pétiller [peti'je], *v.i.* to crackle (*of burning wood*); to sparkle.

petiot [pə'tjo], *a.* (*fam.*) tiny, wee.—*n.m.* (*fem.* -**e**) little one; darling.

petit [pə'ti], *a.* little, small; short; very young; petty, slight; shabby; humble.— *n.m.* (*fem.* -**e**) little child, little one; young one; whelp, pup, kitten, cub.

petite-fille [pətit'fij], *n.f.* (*pl.* **petites-filles**) granddaughter.

petitement [pətit'mɑ̃], *adv.* in small quantity; not much, poorly, meanly.

petitesse [pəti'tɛs], *n.f.* smallness, littleness; insignificance; meanness; narrowness.

petit-fils [pəti'fis], *n.m.* (*pl.* **petits-fils**) grandson.

pétition [peti'sjɔ̃], *n.f.* petition, request.

pétitionnaire [petisjɔ'nɛːr], *n.* petitioner.

pétitionnement [petisjɔn'mɑ̃], *n.m.* petitioning.

pétitionner [petisjɔ'ne], *v.i.* to make a request, to petition.

petit-lait [pəti'lɛ], *n.m.* whey.

petits-enfants [pətizɑ̃'fɑ̃], *n.m. pl.* grandchildren.

pétrel [pe'trɛl], *n.m.* petrel.

pétri [pe'tri], *a.* kneaded.

pétrifiant [petri'fjɑ̃], *a.* petrifying.

pétrification [petrifika'sjɔ̃], *n.f.* petrifaction.

pétrifier [petri'fje], *v.t.* to petrify. **se pétrifier,** *v.r.* to turn into stone.

pétrin [pe'trɛ̃], *n.m.* kneading trough; (*fig.*) scrape.

pétrir [pe'triːr], *v.t.* to knead; (*fig.*) to mold, to form.

pétrissable [petri'sabl], *a.* that can be kneaded; (*fig.*) yielding, pliant.

pétrissage [petri'saːʒ], **pétrissement** [petris'mɑ̃], *n.m.* kneading; (*fig.*) forming.

pétrisseur [petri'sœːr], *n.m.* (*fem.* -**euse**) kneader.—*n.f.* (-**euse**) kneading-machine.

pétrole [pe'trɔl], *n.m.* petroleum, (mineral) oil; kerosene.

pétrolier [petrɔ'lje], *a.* (*fem.* -**ière**) pertaining to oil.—*n.m.* oil tanker.

pétulance [pety'lɑ̃ːs], *n.f.* liveliness, ebulliency; friskiness.

pétulant [pety'lɑ̃], *a.* lively, ebullient, frisky.

pétunia [pety'nja], *n.m.* petunia.

peu [pø], *adv.* little, not much; few, not many; not very.—*n.m.* little; bit.

peuplade [pœ'plad], *n.f.* clan, tribe, horde.

peuple [pœpl], *a.* plebeian, common, vulgar. —*n.m.* people, nation; the people, the multitude, the lower classes.

peuplé [pœ'ple], *a.* heavily populated, populous.

peuplement [pœplə'mɑ̃], *n.m.* peopling; stocking of a poultry yard, pond etc.

peupler [pœ'ple], *v.t.* to people; to stock with animals etc.; to populate; to throng.—*v.i.* to multiply, to breed. **se peupler,** *v.r.* to become peopled; to be populated.

peuplier [pœ'plje], *n.m.* poplar.

peur [pœːr], *n.f.* fear, dread, terror; apprehension; **avoir peur,** to be afraid; **de peur de,** for fear of.

peureusement [pœrøz'mɑ̃], *adv.* timorously.

peureux [pœ'rø], *a.* (*fem.* -**euse**) fearful, timid, timorous.—*n.m.* (*fem.* -**euse**) timid person.

peut-être [pø'tɛːtr], *adv.* perhaps, maybe.

phalange [fa'lɑ̃ːʒ], *n.f.* phalanx; (*poet.*) army, host.

phalène [fa'lɛːn], *n.f.* moth.

pharaon [fara'ɔ̃], *n.m.* Pharaoh.

phare [faːr], *n.m.* lighthouse; beacon; (*Motor.*) head-light.

pharisien [fari'zjɛ̃], *n.m.* Pharisee; (*fig.*) hypocrite; self-righteous person.

pharmaceutique [farmasø'tik], *a.* pharmaceutical.—*n.f.* pharmaceutics.

pharmacie

pharmacie [farma'si], *n.f.* pharmacy, druggist's shop, dispensary; medicine chest.

pharmacien [farma'sjɛ̃], *n.m.* (*fem.* **-enne**) pharmacist.

phase [fɑːz], *n.f.* phasis (*of planet*); phase; aspect, period.

phénicien [feni'sjɛ̃], *a.* (*fem.* **-enne**) Phoenician.—*n.m.* (**Phénicien**, *fem.* **-enne**) Phoenician (*person*).

phénix [fe'niks], *n.m.* phoenix; paragon.

phénoménal [fenɔme'nal], *a.* (*m. pl.* **-aux**) phenomenal; (*colloq.*) extraordinary.

phénomène [fenɔ'mɛːn], *n.m.* phenomenon; (*colloq.*) remarkable person *or* thing; freak.

philanthrope [filɑ̃'trɔp], *n.* philanthropist.

philanthropie [filɑ̃trɔ'pi], *n.f.* philanthropy.

philanthropique [filɑ̃trɔ'pik], *a.* philanthropic.

philatélie [filate'li], *n.f.* philately, stamp collecting.

philatéliste [filate'list], *n.* stamp collector.

Philippe [fi'lip], *m.* Philip.

philippine [fili'pin], *a.* Philippine, Filipino. —*n.* (**Philippine**) Filipino (*person*).

Philippines [fili'pin], **les**, *f. pl.* Philippines, Philippine Islands.

Philistin [filis'tɛ̃], *n.m.* (*fem.* **-e**) Philistine, person of vulgar taste.

philosophale [filɔzɔ'fal], *a.* **la pierre philosophale**, the philosopher's stone.

philosophe [filɔ'zɔf], *a.* philosophical.—*n.* philosopher.

philosopher [filɔzɔ'fe], *v.i.* to philosophize.

philosophie [filɔzɔ'fi], *n.f.* philosophy; class in French school roughly equivalent to English sixth.

philosophique [filɔzɔ'fik], *a.* philosophical.

philosophiquement [filɔzɔfik'mɑ̃], *adv.* philosophically.

philtre *or* **filtre** [filtr], *n.m.* philtre.

phlébite [fle'bit], *n.f.* phlebitis.

phlegmatique [FLEGMATIQUE].

phobie [fɔ'bi], *n.f.* phobia, morbid dread.

phonétique [fɔne'tik], *a.* phonetic.—*n.f.* phonetics.

phonique [fɔ'nik], *a.* phonic.

phonographe [fɔnɔ'graf], *n.m.* phonograph, gramophone.

phonographie [fɔnɔgra'fi], *n.f.* phonography, sound recording.

phonographique [fɔnɔgra'fik], *a.* phonographic.

phoque [fɔk], *n.m.* (*Zool.*) seal.

phosphate [fɔs'fat], *n.m.* phosphate.

phosphore [fɔs'fɔːr], *n.m.* phosphorus.

phosphorescence [fɔsfɔre'sɑ̃ːs], *n.f.* phosphorescence.

phosphorescent [fɔsfɔre'sɑ̃], *a.* phosphorescent.

phosphoreux [fɔsfɔ'rø], *a.m.* phosphorous.

phosphorique [fɔsfɔ'rik], *a.* phosphoric.

photo [fɔ'to], *n.f. abbr.* [PHOTOGRAPHIE].

photocopie [fɔtɔkɔ'pi], *n.f.* photocopy, photostat.

photogénique [fɔtɔʒe'nik], *a.* photogenic.

photographe [fɔtɔ'graf], *n.* photographer.

photographie [fɔtɔgra'fi], *n.f.* photography; photograph.

photographier [fɔtɔgra'fje], *v.t.* to photograph.

photographique [fɔtɔgra'fik], *a.* photo-

graphic; **appareil photographique**, camera.

photogravure [fɔtɔgra'vyːr], *n.f.* photogravure.

phrase [frɑːz], *n.f.* sentence; (*Mus.*) phrase; **phrase toute faite**, commonplace, stock phrase.

phraséologie [frazeɔlɔ'zi], *n.f.* phraseology.

phraser [frɑ'ze], *v.t.* to express in phrases; (*Mus.*) to phrase.—*v.i.* to phrase.

phraseur [frɑ'zœːr], *n.m.* (*fem.* **-euse**) (*fam.*) verbose writer *or* talker.

phtisie [fti'zi], *n.f.* phthisis, consumption.

phtisique [fti'zik], *a.* consumptive.—*n.* consumptive person.

physicien [fizi'sjɛ̃], *n.m.* (*fem.* **-enne**) physicist.

physionomie [fizjɔnɔ'mi], *n.f.* physiognomy, countenance, aspect, look.

physionomiste [fizjɔnɔ'mist], *n.* physiognomist.

physiothérapie [fizjɔtera'pi], *n.f.* (*Med.*) physiotherapy.

physiothérapiste [fizjɔtera'pist], *n.* physiotherapist.

physique [fi'zik], *a.* physical, material, bodily.—*n.f.* physics.—*n.m.* physique, natural constitution; outward appearance.

physiquement [fizik'mɑ̃], *adv.* physically.

piaffer [pja'fe], *v.i.* to paw the ground, to prance (*of horses*).

piaffeur [pja'fœːr], *a.* (*fem.* **-euse**) pawing, prancing.—*n.m.* (*fem.* **-euse**) pawer, prancer.

piailler [pja'je], *v.i.* to cheep (*of small birds*); (*fig.*) to squall; to rant.

piaillerie [pjaj'ri], *n.f.* cheeping; squealing.

piailleur [pja'jœːr], *n.m.* (*fem.* **-euse**) cheeper; squaller.

pianiste [pja'nist], *n.* pianist.

piano [pja'no], *n.m.* piano, pianoforte; **piano à queue**, grand piano.

piaulement [pjol'mɑ̃], *n.m.* whining, puling; cheeping (*of chickens*).

piauler [pjo'le], *v.i.* to cheep (*of chickens etc.*); (*fig.*) to pule, to whine.

pic [pik], *n.m.* pick, pickaxe; gaff; peak (*of a mountain*); woodpecker.

pick-up [pi'kœp], *n.m. inv.* record player.

picoté [piko'te], *a.* pricked, marked.

picotement [pikɔt'mɑ̃], *n.m.* pricking, tingling.

picoter [pikɔ'te], *v.t.* to cause to tingle; to prick; to peck (*of birds*).

picvert *or* **pivert** [pi've:r], *n.m.* green woodpecker.

pie [pi], *a. inv.* and *n.* piebald (horse).—*n.f.* magpie.

pièce [pjɛs], *n.f.* piece; patch; cask (*of wine etc.*); head (*of cattle, poultry etc.*); apartment, room; piece of ordnance, cannon; (*Theat.*) play; coin; joint (*of meat*).

pied [pje], *n.m.* foot; footing; footprint, track; leg (*of furniture*); stand, rest; stalk (*of plants*).

pied-à-terre [pjeta'te:r], *n.m. inv.* occasional lodging.

pied-de-biche [pjed'bif], *n.m.* (*pl.* **pieds-de-biche**) bell-pull; (*Surg.*) forceps; nailclench.

piédestal [pjedes'tal], *n.m.* (*pl.* **-aux**) pedestal.

piège [pjɛːʒ], *n.m.* trap, snare.
piéger [pje'ʒe], *v.t.* (*conjug. like* CÉDER) to trap (*animals*); (*Mil.*) to set a booby trap.
pie-grièche [pigri'ɛʃ], *n.f.* (*pl.* **pies-grièches**) (*Orn.*) shrike; (*fig.*) shrew.
pierraille [pjɛ'raːj], *n.f.* rubble, ballast.
Pierre [pjɛːr], *m.* Peter.
pierre [pjɛːr], *n.f.* stone; (*Path.*) calculus.
pierreries [pjɛr'ri], *n.f. pl.* precious stones, gems.
pierreux [pjɛ'rø], *a.* (*fem.* **-euse**) stony, flinty, gritty, gravelly; calculous.
pierrot [pjɛ'ro], *n.m.* pierrot, merry-andrew; house sparrow.
piété [pje'te], *n.f.* piety, godliness; affection.
piétinement [pjetin'mɑ̃], *n.m.* stamping, trampling.
piétiner [pjeti'ne], *v.t.* to tread *or* trample under foot.—*v.i.* to stamp; to paw the ground (*of horses*).
piéton [pje'tɔ̃], *n.m.* (*fem.* **-onne**) pedestrian.
piètre [pjɛtr], *a.* poor, paltry, pitiful.
piètrement [pjɛtrə'mɑ̃], *adv.* pitifully, wretchedly.
pieu [pjø], *n.m.* (*pl.* **pieux** (1)) stake, pile, post.
pieusement [pjøz'mɑ̃], *adv.* piously, devoutly; obediently; reverently.
pieuvre [pjœːvr], *n.f.* octopus, poulpe.
pieux (2) [pjø], *a.* (*fem.* **pieuse**) pious, godly.
pigeon [pi'ʒɔ̃], *n.m.* pigeon, dove; (*slang*) dupe, gull.
pigeonneau [piʒɔ'no], *n.m.* (*pl.* **-eaux**) young pigeon, squab.
pigeonnier [piʒɔ'nje], *n.m.* pigeon house, dove-cot.
pigment [pig'mɑ̃], *n.m.* (*Anat.*) pigment.
pignon [pi'ɲɔ̃], *n.m.* gable end; pinion; kernel (*of fir cone*).
pilaire [pi'lɛːr], *a.* pilous, pilose.
pilastre [pi'lastr], *n.m.* (*Arch.*) pilaster.
pilchard [pil'ʃaːr], *n.m.* pilchard.
pile [pil], *n.f.* pile, heap; pier (*of a bridge etc.*); mole (*masonry*); (*Elec.*) battery; reverse (*of coins*); **pile atomique**, atomic pile.
piler [pi'le], *v.t.* to pound, to crush, to powder.
pileur [pi'lœːr], *n.m.* (*fem.* **-euse** (1)) pounder, beater.
pileux [pi'lø], *a.* (*fem.* **-euse** (2)) pilous, hairy.
pilier [pi'lje], *n.m.* pillar, column, post; (*fig.*) supporter, prop.
pillage [pi'jaːʒ], *n.m.* pillage, plunder; (*fig.*) pilfering.
pillard [pi'jaːr], *a.* plundering; predatory.—*n.m.* (*fem.* **-e**) pillager, plunderer.
piller [pi'je], *v.t.* to pillage, to plunder; to ransack; to pilfer.
pillerie [pij'ri], *n.f.* pillage, plunder; extortion.
pilleur [pi'jœːr], *n.m.* (*fem.* **-euse**) pillager, plunderer, pilferer.
pilon [pi'lɔ̃], *n.m.* pestle; rammer, stamper; wooden leg.
pilonnage [pilɔ'naːʒ], *n.m.* ramming, pounding, stamping, milling.
pilonner [pilɔ'ne], *v.t.* to ram, to pound, to mill; to stamp (*ore*).
pilori [pilɔ'ri], *n.m.* pillory.
pilorier [pilɔ'rje], *v.t.* to pillory.
pilotage [pilɔ'taːʒ], *n.m.* (*Civ. Eng.*) pile-driving; (*Naut.*) piloting.
pilote [pi'lɔt], *n.m.* pilot; guide; pilot fish.

piloter [pilɔ'te], *v.t.* to pile, to drive piles into; (*Naut., Av.*) to pilot; (*fig.*) to guide.
pilotis [pilɔ'ti], *n.m.* pilework.
pilule [pi'lyl], *n.f.* pill.
pimbêche [pɛ̃'bɛʃ], *n.f.* uppish and impertinent woman.
piment [pi'mɑ̃], *n.m.* pimento, allspice.
pimenter [pɛ̃'pɑ̃], *v.t.* to flavor with pimento.
pimpant [pɛ̃'pɑ̃], *a.* natty, spruce, smart.
pin [pɛ̃], *n.m.* pine tree; **pomme de pin**, fir cone.
pinacle [pi'nakl], *n.m.* pinnacle.
pince [pɛ̃ːs], *n.f.* pinching, nipping; hold, grip; pincers, pliers, forceps; tongs, clip; crowbar (*lever*); toe (*of a horse's foot*); claw (*of a lobster etc.*).
pincé [pɛ̃'se], *a.* affected, stiff, prim.
pinceau [pɛ̃'so], *n.m.* (*pl.* **-eaux**) paint-brush.
pincée [pɛ̃'se], *n.f.* pinch (*of snuff, salt etc.*).
pince-nez [pɛ̃s'ne], *n.m. inv.* pince-nez, (*folding*) eye glasses.
pince-notes [pɛ̃s'nɔt], *n.m. inv.* paper clip.
pincer [pɛ̃'se], *v.t.* (*conjug. like* COMMENCER) to pinch, to nip; to grip; to bite (*of cold etc.*); to pluck (*a musical instrument*); (*Naut.*) to hug (*the wind*).
pince-sans-rire [pɛ̃ssɑ̃'riːr], *n.m. inv.* sly *or* malicious person, dry joker.
pincette(s) [pɛ̃'sɛt], *n.f.* (*pl.*) tongs; tweezers, nippers.
pinçure [pɛ̃'syːr], *n.f.* pinching; crease in cloth.
pingouin [pɛ̃'gwɛ̃], *n.m.* auk.
pingre [pɛ̃ːgr], *a.* avaricious, stingy.—*n.* miser, skinflint.
pinson [pɛ̃'sɔ̃], *n.m.* finch, chaffinch.
pintade [pɛ̃'tad], *n.f.* guinea fowl.
piochage [pjɔ'jaːʒ], *n.m.* digging; (*fig.*) working, fagging.
pioche [pjɔʃ], *n.f.* pickaxe.
piocher [pjɔ'ʃe], *v.t.* to dig.—*v.i.* to dig; (*fig.*) to fag, to work hard, to grind
piocheur [pjɔ'ʃœːr], *n.m.* (*fem.* **-euse**) digger; (*slang*) hard-working student, grind. —*n.f.* (**-euse**) (*Civ. Eng.*) excavator.
piolet [pjɔ'lɛ], *n.m.* piolet, ice axe.
pion [pjɔ̃], *n.m.* pawn (*at chess*); piece (*at checkers*);(*Sch. slang*) assistant teacher.
pionnier [pjɔ'nje], *n.m.* pioneer.
pipe [pip], *n.f.* pipe; tobacco-pipe; pipe (*cask*).
pipeau [pi'po], *n.m.* (*pl.* **-eaux**) pipe, reed-pipe; bird-call; limed twig, snare.
pipée [pi'pe], *n.f.* bird-catching (*with a bird-call*); (*fig.*) deceit, trickery.
piper [pi'pe], *v.t.* to catch (*birds*) with a bird-call etc.; (*fig.*) to trick, to decoy.
pipeur [pi'pœːr], *a.* (*fem.* **-euse**) cheating, deceitful.—*n.m.* (*fem.* **-euse**) one who decoys birds; cheat, trickster (*at play*).
piquant [pi'kɑ̃], *a.* prickling, stinging; pungent; biting; cutting, keen; piquant, pointed; smart.—*n.m.* prickle; quill (*of porcupine*); pungency, point, piquancy.
pique [pik], *n.f.* pike (*weapon*); pique, spite, quarrel.—*n.m.* (*Cards*) spade(s).
piqué [pi'ke], *a.* quilted, pinked; worm-eaten; sour (*wine*).—*n.m.* quilting; piqué; nose-dive; **bombardement en piqué**, dive-bombing.

pique-nique

pique-nique [pik'nik], *n.m.* (*pl.* **-niques**) picnic.

piquer [pi'ke], *v.t.* to prick; to sting; to goad, to spur; to puncture; to bite (*of insects*); to quilt; to lard; to prick off; to excite, to stimulate; to nettle, to rouse; (*Med.*) to inject.—*v.i.* to turn sour (*of wine etc.*). **se piquer**, *v.r.* to prick oneself; to be offended, to be piqued; to pride oneself; to turn sour.

piquet [pi'kɛ], *n.m.* peg, stake; (*Mil.*) picket; piquet (*card game*).

piqueter [pik'te], *v.t.* (*conjug. like* APPELER) to mark out with stakes *or* pegs; to mark with little points.

piquette [pi'kɛt], *n.f.*, **piqueton** [pik'tɔ̃], *n.m.* thin wine.

piqueur (1) [pi'kœːr], *n.m.* outrider; overseer (*of workmen*); stud groom; huntsman.

piqueur (2) [pi'kœːr], *n.m.* (*fem.* **-euse**) stitcher.

piqûre [pi'kyːr], *n.f.* prick; sting; bite; puncture; (*Needlework*) quilting, stitching; (*Med.*) injection, shot.

pirate [pi'rat], *n.m.* pirate; (*fig.*) extortioner, plagiarist.

pirater [pira'te], *v.i.* to commit piracy.

piraterie [pira'tri], *n.f.* piracy; act of piracy *or* plagiarism.

pire [piːr], *a.* and *n.m.* worse; the worst.

pirogue [pi'rɔg], *n.f.* pirogue, dug-out, canoe.

pirouette [pi'rwɛt], *n.f.* pirouette, whirligig.

pirouetter [pirwe'te], *v.i.* to pirouette, to whirl about.

pis (1) [pi], *n.m.* udder, dug (*of cow*).

pis (2) [pi], *adv.* and *n.m.* worse.—*n.m. inv.* **pis-aller**, the worst, last resource, make-shift.

pisciculture [pisikyl'tyːr], *n.f.* fish culture.

piscine [pi'sin], *n.f.* piscina; swimming pool.

pissenlit [pisɑ̃'li], *n.m.* dandelion.

pistache [pis'taʃ], *n.f.* pistachio, pistachio nut.

pistachier [pista'ʃje], *n.m.* pistachio tree.

piste [pist], *n.f.* track, footprint, trail, scent; course, race-course.

pistolet [pistɔ'lɛ], *n.m.* pistol; spray gun.

piston [pis'tɔ̃], *n.m.* piston; sucker (*of a pump*); press button; (*Mus.*) cornet.

pitance [pi'tɑ̃ːs], *n.f.* pittance; allowance (*of food*), dole.

piteusement [pitøz'mɑ̃], *adv.* piteously, woe-fully, sadly.

piteux [pi'tø], *a.* (*fem.* **-euse**) piteous, piti-able, woeful.

pitié [pi'tje], *n.f.* pity, compassion; object of pity.

piton [pi'tɔ̃], *n.m.* eye-bolt, screw-ring, ring-bolt; peak (*of mountain*).

pitoyable [pitwa'jabl], *a.* pitiful, piteous; paltry.

pitoyablement [pitwajablə'mɑ̃], *adv.* piti-fully.

pittoresque [pitɔ'rɛsk], *a.* picturesque; graphic.—*n.m.* the picturesque, pictur-esqueness.

pittoresquement [pitɔrɛsk'mɑ̃], *adv.* pic-turesquely.

pivert [PICVERT].

pivoine [pi'vwan], *n.m.* bullfinch.—*n.f.* peony.

pivot [pi'vo], *n.m.* pivot, pin, spindle, hinge.

pivoter [pivɔ'te], *v.i.* to pivot, to turn on a pivot, to revolve, to turn.

placage [pla'kaːʒ], *n.m.* plating (*metal-work*); veneering (*of wood*); (*Lit.*) patchwork.

placard [pla'kaːr], *n.m.* placard, poster, bill; (*Print.*) slip; cupboard (*in a wall*).

placarder [plakar'de], *v.t.* to placard, to post up.

place [plas], *n.f.* place; room; seat; stead; post, job, situation; town; public square; **faire place**, to make room; **retenir des places**, to book seats; **sur place**, on the spot.

placement [plas'mɑ̃], *n.m.* placing; sale; employment; investment.

placer [pla'se], *v.t.* (*conjug. like* COMMENCER) to place, to put; to find a place *or* situation for; to invest; to deposit; to sell. **se placer** *v.r.* to place oneself; to find a job.

placet [pla'sɛ], *n.m.* petition, address.

placide [pla'sid], *a.* placid, calm.

placidement [plasid'mɑ̃], *adv.* placidly, calmly.

placidité [plasidi'te], *n.f.* placidity.

plafond [pla'fɔ̃], *n.m.* ceiling.

plafonnage [plafɔ'naːʒ], *n.m.* ceiling (*action, work*); (*Av.*) visibility.

plafonner [plafɔ'ne], *v.t.* to ceil, to put a ceiling to.—*v.i.* to reach the highest point (*of prices etc.*); (*Av.*) to fly at the ceiling; (*Motor.*) to travel at maximum speed.

plafonneur [plafɔ'nœːr], *n.m.* plasterer.

plafonnier [plafɔ'nje], *n.m.* ceiling light.

plage [plaːʒ], *n.f.* beach, shore; sea-side resort.

plagiaire [pla'ʒjɛːr], *a.* and *n.* plagiarist.

plagiat [pla'ʒja], *n.m.* plagiarism.

plagier [pla'ʒje], *v.t.* to plagiarize.

plaid [plɛd], *n.m.* plaid, travelling rug.

plaidant [plɛ'dɑ̃], *a.* pleading, litigant.

plaider [plɛ'de], *v.t.* to defend; to allege.—*v.i.* to go to law, to litigate; to plead, to argue.

plaideur [plɛ'dœːr], *n.m.* (*fem.* **-euse**) liti-gant, suitor.

plaidoirie [plɛdwa'ri], *n.f.* pleading; coun-sel's speech.

plaidoyer [plɛdwa'je], *n.m.* speech for the defence, counsel's address.

plaie [plɛ], *n.f.* wound; sore; (*fig.*) plague; evil.

plaignant [plɛ'ɲɑ̃], *a.* complaining; **la partie plaignante**, the plaintiff.—*n.m.* (*fem.* **-e**) plaintiff, prosecutor.

plain [plɛ̃], *a.* plain, even, flat, level.

plaindre [plɛ̃ːdr], *v.t. irr.* (*conjug. like* CRAINDRE) to pity, to be sorry for. **se plaindre**, *v.r.* to complain; to grumble.

plaine [plɛn], *n.f.* plain; flat country.

plain-pied (de) [dəplɛ̃'pje], *adv. phr.* on a level; (*fig.*) without difficulty.

plainte [plɛ̃ːt], *n.f.* complaint; plaint; lam-entation, wail; plaint at law.

plaintif [plɛ̃'tif], *a.* (*fem.* **-tive**) plaintive, complaining; querulous.

plaintivement [plɛtiv'mɑ̃], *adv.* dolefully; querulously.

plaire [plɛːr], *v.i. irr.* to please; to be pleasant *or* agreeable (*à*); **s'il vous plaît**, please. **se plaire**, *v.r.* to delight, to take pleasure; to like.

plaisamment [plɛza'mɑ̃], *adv.* humorously, amusingly; ludicrously.

plaisance [plɛ'zɑ̃ːs], *n.f.* pleasure.

plaisant [plɛ'zɑ̃], *a.* humorous, amusing, funny; (*iron.*) odd, strange.—*n.m.* jester, wag; the funny side; *un mauvais plaisant*, a practical joker.

plaisanter [plɛzɑ̃'te], *v.i.* to chaff, to banter. —*v.i.* to jest, to joke.

plaisanterie [plɛzɑ̃'tri], *n.f.* jest, joke, witticism; mockery, trifle.

plaisir [plɛ'ziːr], *n.m.* pleasure; delight; diversion, entertainment; favor.

plan [plɑ̃], *a.* even, level, flat.—*n.m.* plane; plan; drawing; scheme, project; (*Paint.*) ground.

planche [plɑ̃ːʃ], *n.f.* board, plank; shelf; (*Engr.*) plate; (*Gard.*) bed, border.

planchéiage [plɑ̃ʃe'jaːʒ], *n.m.* boarding, planking; flooring.

planchéier [plɑ̃ʃe'je], *v.t.* to board over, to floor.

plancher [plɑ̃'ʃe], *n.m.* floor, deck planking.

planchette [plɑ̃'ʃɛt], *n.f.* small board; (*Math.*) plane table.

plancton [plɑ̃k'tɔ̃], *n.m.* plankton.

plane [plan], *n.f.* drawing-knife; planisher.

plané [pla'ne], *a.* soaring, gliding; *un vol plané*, gliding descent.

planer [pla'ne], *v.t.* to make smooth, to plane. —*v.i.* to hover, to soar; to look down (*on*) (*sur*); (*Av.*) to glide.

planétaire [plane'tɛːr], *a.* planetary.

planète [pla'nɛːt], *n.f.* planet.

planeur [pla'nœːr], *n.m.* planisher; glider (*airplane*).

planeuse [pla'nøːz], *n.f.* planing machine.

planification [planifika'sjɔ̃], *n.f.* (*Polit. Econ.*) planning.

planifier [plani'fje], *v.t.* to plan.

plant [plɑ̃], *n.m.* young plant, seedling; slip; sapling; plantation.

plantation [plɑ̃ta'sjɔ̃], *n.f.* planting; plantation.

plante [plɑ̃ːt], *n.f.* plant; *la plante du pied*, (*Anat.*) the sole of the foot.

planter [plɑ̃'te], *v.t.* to plant; to set, to drive in; to set up, to erect. *se planter*, *v.r.* to station oneself.

planteur [plɑ̃'tœːr], *n.m.* planter.

planteuse [plɑ̃'tøːz], *n.f.* potato-planting machine.

plantoir [plɑ̃'twaːr], *n.m.* dibble.

planton [plɑ̃'tɔ̃], *n.m.* (*Mil.*) orderly.

plantureusement [plɑ̃tyrøz'mɑ̃], *adv.* copiously, abundantly, luxuriantly.

plantureux [plɑ̃ty'rø], *a.* (*fem.* -**euse**) plentiful, copious; fertile.

plaquage [pla'kaːʒ], *n.m.* (*Ftb.*) rugby tackle.

plaque [plak], *n.f.* plate, slab; plaque; badge, star; *plaque tournante*, (*Rail.*) turn-table.

plaqué [pla'ke], *a.* plated, covered with.

plaquer [pla'ke], *v.t.* to plate (*metal*); to veneer (*wood*); (*Ftb.*) to tackle.

plaquette [pla'kɛt], *n.f.* small thin book; small plate; thin slab.

plasticité [plastisi'te], *n.f.* plasticity.

plastique [plas'tik], *a.* plastic.—*n.m.* plastics. —*n.f.* plastic art; figure.

plastron [plas'trɔ̃], *n.m.* breast-plate; fencing pad; shirt front.

plastronner [plastrɔ'ne], *v.i.* to strut, to swagger.

plat (1) [pla], *a.* flat; level; regular, (*fig.*) dull, insipid.—*n.m.* flat part, side; flat racing.

plat (2) [pla], *n.m.* dish (*the vessel and the food*), (*Naut.*) mess; course (*of a meal*).

platane [pla'tan], *n.m.* plane tree, platan.

plateau [pla'to], *n.m.* (*pl.* -**eaux**) scale (*of a balance*); tray; table-land, plateau; turn-table (*of gramophone*).

plate-bande [plat'bɑ̃ːd], *n.f.* (*pl.* **plates-bandes**) border, flower bed.

plate-forme [plat'fɔrm], *n.f.* (*pl.* **plates-formes**) platform (*of a bus etc.*).

platement [plat'mɑ̃], *adv.* flatly, dully.

platine [pla'tin], *n.f.* lock (*of fire-arms*); plate (*of lock, watch, machine*); platen (*of typewriter*).—*n.m.* platinum.

platiné [plati'ne], *a.* platinum-plated; platinum-colored (*of hair*).

platitude [plati'tyd], *n.f.* platitude; flatness, dullness.

Platon [pla'tɔ̃], *m.* Plato.

platonique [plato'nik], *a.* Platonic.

platonisme [plato'nism], *n.m.* Platonism.

plâtrage [plɑ'traːʒ], *n.m.* plaster work, plastering.

plâtras [plɑ'trɑ], *n.m.* debris of plaster work; rubbish.

plâtre [plɑːtr], *n.m.* plaster.

plâtré [plɑ'tre], *a.* plastered.

plâtrer [plɑ'tre], *v.t.* to plaster; (*fig.*) to patch up, to disguise.

plâtreux [Lplɑ'trø], *a.* (*fem.* -**euse**) chalky.

plâtrier [plɑtri'je], *n.m.* plasterer.

plâtrière [plɑtri'jɛːr], *n.f.* chalk pit; plaster kiln.

plâtroir [plɑ'trwaːr], *n.m.* plasterer's trowel.

plausibilité [plozibili'te], *n.f.* plausibility.

plausible [plo'zibl], *a.* a plausible (*never of person*).

plausiblement [plozibla'mɑ̃], *adv.* plausibly.

plèbe [plɛb], *n.f.* common people.

plébéien [plebe'jɛ̃], *a.* and *n.m.* (*fem.* -**enne**) plebeian.

plébiscite [plebi'sit], *n.m.* plebiscite.

plein [plɛ̃], *a.* full; fraught (*de*); filled, replete; entire, whole; thorough; copious; solid; *en plein air*, in the open air; *en plein hiver*, in the heart of winter.—*n.m.* full part; plenum.—*adv.* full.

pleinement [plɛn'mɑ̃], *adv.* fully, entirely, thoroughly.

plénier [ple'nje], *a.* (*fem.* -**ière**) plenary; full, complete.

plénipotentiaire [plenipotɑ̃'sjɛːr], *a.* and *n.m.* plenipotentiary.

plénitude [pleni'tyd], *n.f.* plenitude, fullness.

pleur [plœːr], *n.m.* (*poet.*) tear; lament.

pleurard [plœ'raːr], *a.* a whimpering, tearful.— *n.m.* (*fem.* -**e**) whimperer, blubberer.

pleurer [plœ're], *v.t.* to weep, to bewail, to mourn, to deplore the loss of.—*v.i.* to weep, to cry, to shed tears; to mourn; to run (*of the eyes*); to drip (*of a tap*).

pleurésie [plœre'zi], *n.f.* pleurisy.

pleureur [plœ'rœːr], *a.* (*fem.* -**euse**) whimpering, tearful; *saule pleureur*, weeping willow.—*n.m.* (*fem.* -**euse**) whimperer, weeper.—*n.f.* (-**euse**) paid mourner.

pleurnichement [plœrniʃ'mã], *n.m.* whimpering, snivelling.

pleurnicher [plœrni'ʃe], *v.i.* to whimper, to whine, to snivel.

pleurnicheur [plœrni'ʃœːr], *a.* (*fem.* **-euse**) whimpering, snivelling.—*n.m.* (*fem.* **-euse**) whimperer, sniveller.

pleutre [pløːtr], *n.m.* contemptible fellow.

pleuvoir [plœ'vwaːr], *v. impers. irr.* to rain; *il pleut à verse* or *à seaux*, it is pouring in buckets; *pleuvoir des hallebardes*, to rain cats and dogs.

pli [pli], *n.m.* fold; wrinkle; coil; bend; undulation, depression; cover, envelope; habit; (*Cards*) trick; *mise en pli*, setting (*the hair*); *sous pli recommandé*, in a registered envelope; *un faux pli*, a crease.

pliable [pli'jabl], *a.* pliable, flexible, supple.

pliage [pli'jaːʒ], **pliement** [pli'mã], *n.m.* folding.

pliant [pli'jã], *a.* pliant, docile; folding, collapsible.—*n.m.* folding chair, deck chair.

plie [pli], *n.f.* plaice.

plier [pli'je], *v.t.* to fold, to fold up; to bend.—*v.i.* to bend, to bow; to give way. **se plier**, *v.r.* to bow, to bend, to yield.

plieur [pli'jœːr], *n.m.* (*fem.* **-euse**) folder.—*n.f.* (**-euse**) folding-machine.

plinthe [plẽːt], *n.f.* plinth; skirting-board.

plissage [pli'saːʒ], *n.m.* pleating, kilting.

plissé [pli'se], *a.* kilted, pleated.—*n.m.* kilting, pleats.

plissement [plis'mã], *n.m.* folding, doubling over; crumpling.

plisser [pli'se], *v.t.* to fold; to crumple, to wrinkle; to pleat.—*v.i.* and **se plisser**, *v.r.* to be wrinkled, to pucker.

plissure [pli'syːr], *n.f.* pleating; pleats.

ploiement [plwa'mã], *n.m.* folding, bending.

plomb [plõ], *n.m.* lead; bullet, shot; plumb-line; sinker; custom-house seal; fuse; *à plomb*, vertically.

plombage [plõ'baːʒ], *n.m.* leading, plumbing, filling (*of teeth*).

plombagine [plõba'ʒin], *n.f.* plumbago, blacklead, graphite.

plomber [plõ'be], *v.t.* to cover with lead, to seal; to fill (*a tooth*); to plumb.

plomberie [plõ'bri], *n.f.* plumber's shop; plumbing; lead-making; lead works.

plombier [plõ'bje], *n.m.* lead worker; plumber.

plongée [plõ'ʒe], *n.f.* slope; dive.

plongeoir [plõ'ʒwaːr], *n.m.* diving-board.

plongeon [plõ'ʒõ], *n.m.* plunge, dive; (*Orn.*) diver.

plonger [plõ'ʒe], *v.t.* (*conjug. like* MANGER) to plunge, to dip, to immerse; to throw, to involve.—*v.i.* to dive, to plunge; to submerge (*of submarine*); to pitch (*of ships*). **se plonger**, *v.r.* to be plunged; to immerse oneself (*in*).

plongeur [plõ'ʒœːr], *a.* (*fem.* **-euse**) plunging, diving (*bird*).—*n.m.* (*fem.* **-euse**) diver; dish washer (*in hotels etc.*).

ploutocrate [pluto'krat], *n.m.* plutocrat.

ploutocratie [plutokra'si], *n.f.* plutocracy.

ploutocratique [plutokra'tik], *a.* plutocratic.

ployable [plwa'jabl], *a.* pliable, flexible.

ployer [plwa'je], *v.t.* (*conjug. like* EMPLOYER) to bend; to fold up.—*v.i.* and **se ployer**,

v.r. to bend, to be folded; to yield, to give way.

pluie [plɥi], *n.f.* rain; (*fig.*) shower.

plumage [ply'maːʒ], *n.m.* plumage, feathers.

plumassier [plyma'sje], *n.m.* (*fem.* **-lère**) feather merchant *or* dresser.

plume [plym], *n.f.* feather; plume; quill, pen; nib.

plumeau [ply'mo], *n.m.* (*pl.* **-eaux**) feather broom; feather duster.

plumée [ply'me], *n.f.* penful (*of ink*); plucking (*of poultry*).

plumer [ply'me], *v.t.* to pluck, to plume; (*fig.*) to fleece.

plumet [ply'mɛ], *n.m.* plume.

plumetis [plym'ti], *n.m.* feather-stitch.

plumier [ply'mje], *n.m.* pen box, pen tray.

plupart [ply'paːr], *n.f. la plupart*, most, most part, the majority (*de*), most people.

pluralité [plyrali'te], *n.f.* plurality; pluralism.

pluriel [ply'rjɛl], *a.* (*fem.* **-elle**) plural.—*n.m.* plural.

plus [ply], *adv.* more, -er (*que*, than); -est, the most; also, moreover, further, besides; (*with ne*) no more, no longer, never again; *de plus*, besides, moreover.—*n.m.* the most, the maximum; the more.

plusieurs [ply'zjœːr], *a. pl.* and *pron. indef.* several, some.

plus-que-parfait [plyskəpar'fɛ], *n.m.* pluperfect.

plutonium [plyto'njɔm], *n.m.* plutonium.

plutôt [ply'to], *adv.* rather, sooner (*que*).

pluvial [ply'vjal], *a.* (*m. pl.* **-aux**) pluvial, of rain, rainy.

pluvier [ply'vje], *n.m.* plover.

pluvieux [ply'vjø], *a.* (*fem.* **-euse**) rainy, wet, pluvious.

pluviomètre [plyvjɔ'mɛtr], *n.m.* rain gauge.

pluviosité [plyvjozi'te], *n.f.* rainfall.

pneu [pnø], *n.m.* (*pl.* **pneus**) *fam. abbr.* [PNEUMATIQUE].

pneumatique [pnøma'tik], *a.* pneumatic.—*n.m.* tire; express letter (*in Paris*).—*n.f.* pneumatics.

pneumonie [pnømɔ'ni], *n.f.* pneumonia.

pochade [pɔ'ʃad], *n.f.* rough sketch; (*fig.*) hurried piece of writing etc.

poche [pɔʃ], *n.f.* pocket; pouch; sack, bag; wrinkle (*in clothes*); crop (*of a bird*).

pocher [pɔ'ʃe], *v.t.* to poach (*eggs*); to give a black eye to; to stencil; to make a rough sketch of.—*v.i.* to become baggy, to bag.

pochet [pɔ'ʃɛ], *n.m.* nosebag (*of horse*).

pochette [pɔ'ʃɛt], *n.f.* small pocket; small net; folder, jacket (*containers*); fancy handkerchief.

pochoir [pɔ'ʃwaːr], *n.m.* stencil.

podagre [pɔ'dagr], *a.* gouty.—*n.f.* gout.—*n.* gouty person.

podomètre [pɔdɔ'mɛtr], *n.m.* pedometer.

poêle [pwaːl], *n.f.* frying pan.—*n.m.* stove; pall (*at a funeral*).

poêlée [pwa'le], *n.f.* panful.

poêlon [pwa'lõ], *n.m.* small saucepan.

poème [pɔ'ɛːm], *n.m.* poem.

poésie [pɔe'zi], *n.f.* poetry, verse; poem.

poète [pɔ'ɛːt], *n.m.* poet.

poétesse [pɔe'tɛs], *n.f.* poetess.

poétique [pɔe'tik], *a.* poetical.—*n.f.* poetics.

poétiquement [pɔetik'mã], *adv.* poetically.

poétiser [pɔeti'ze], *v.t.* to make poetical, to idealize, to poeticize.

pogrom [pɔ'grɔm], *n.m.* pogrom.

poids [pwɑ], *n.m. inv.* weight; heaviness; gravity; load; (*fig.*) importance, consequence; **les poids lourds**, heavy vehicles.

poignant [pwa'nɑ̃], *a.* poignant; sharp, acute, keen.

poignard [pwa'na:r], *n.m.* dagger.

poignarder [pwaɲar'de], *v.t.* to stab; to knife; (*fig.*) to grieve to the heart.

poigne [pwaɲ], *n.f.* (*colloq.*) grasp, grip; (*fig.*) strength.

poignée [pwa'ne], *n.f.* handful; handle, hilt; shake (*of the hand*).

poignet [pwa'nɛ], *n.m.* wrist; wristband, cuff.

poil [pwal], *n.m.* hair (*of animals*); hair (*of persons, other than that of the head*); (*fig.*) beard; nap (*of cloth, of hats etc.*); *à contre-poil*, against the grain.

pollu [pwa'ly], *a.* hairy, shaggy.

poinçon [pwɛ̃'sɔ̃], *n.m.* punch; point, stiletto; awl, stamp, die.

poinçonnage [pwɛ̃sɔ'na:ʒ], **poinçonnement** [pwɛ̃sɔn'mɑ̃], *n.m.* stamping, punching.

poinçonner [pwɛ̃sɔ'ne], *v.t.* to punch, to stamp.

poinçonneuse [pwɛ̃sɔ'nø:z], *n.f.* stamping *or* punching machine.

poindre [pwɛ̃:dr], *v.i. irr.* to dawn, to break; (*fig.*) to appear.

poing [pwɛ̃], *n.m.* fist, hand; (*fig.*) force, brute strength; (*fig.*) *dormir à poings fermés*, to sleep like a log.

point [pwɛ̃], *adv.* (*used with negative*) no, not at all; none (*more emphatic than* pas).—*n.m.* point; speck; dot, mark; (*Sch.*) mark; full stop; hole (*of a strap etc.*); (*Needlework*) stitch; matter, question; particular; state, case; degree; place; *à point*, in the nick of time; well done (*of meat*); *en tout point*, in every respect; *sur ce* or *en ce point*, on that score.

pointage [pwɛ̃'ta:ʒ], **pointement** [pwɛ̃t'mɑ̃], *n.m.* pointing, levelling (*of guns*); checking; scrutiny (*of votes*), tally.

pointe [pwɛ̃:t], *n.f.* point (*sharp end*); tip, head (*of an arrow etc.*); nose (*of a bullet*); cape; peak; etching needle; nail, tack; (*Print.*) bodkin; (*fig.*) dash, flavor; pungency, sharpness; witticism.

pointement [POINTAGE].

pointer [pwɛ̃'te], *v.t.* to point, to aim (*a gun etc.*); to pierce, to stab, to prick; to mark; to tally, to scrutinize (*votes*); to prick up (*ears etc.*); to sharpen.—*v.i.* to point; to spring, to soar; to rear; to sprout.

pointeur [pwɛ̃'tœ:.], *n.m.* (*fem.* **-euse**) pointer, marker, checker; (*Artill.*) gun layer.

pointillage [pwɛ̃ti'ja:ʒ], **pointillement** [pwɛ̃tij'mɑ̃], *n.m.* dotting, stippling; dotted line.

pointillé [pwɛ̃ti'je], *n.m.* stipple drawing *or* engraving; dotted line.

pointiller [pwɛ̃ti'je], *v.t.* to dot, to stipple; (*fig.*) to tease.—*v.i.* to bicker, to cavil.

pointilleux [pwɛ̃ti'jø], *a.* (*fem.* **-euse**) cavilling, captious; fastidious.

pointu [pwɛ̃'ty], *a.* pointed, sharp; (*fig.*) subtle, captious.

pointure [pwɛ̃'ty:r], *n.f.* (*Print.*) point; size, number (*of shoes, gloves etc.*).

poire [pwa:r], *n.f.* pear; bulb (*rubber*).

poiré [pwa're], *n.m.* perry.

poireau [pwa'ro], **porreau** [pɔ'ro], *n.m.* (*pl.* **-eaux**) leek; wart.

poirée [pwa're], *n.f.* white beet.

poirier [pwa'rje], *n.m.* pear tree.

pois [pwa], *n.m. inv.* pea, peas.

poison [pwa'zɔ̃], *n.m.* poison.

poissard [pwa'sa:r], *a.* vulgar, low.

poisser [pwa'se], *v.t.* to pitch; to make sticky.

poisseux [pwa'sø], *a.* (*fem.* **-euse**) pitchy, gluey, sticky.

poisson [pwa'sɔ̃], *n.m.* fish; *poisson d'avril*, April fool.

poissonnerie [pwasɔn'ri], *n.f.* fishmarket; fish shop.

poissonneux [pwasɔ'nø], *a.* (*fem.* **-euse**) abounding in fish.

poissonnier [pwasɔ'nje], *n.m.* (*fem.* **-ière**) fishmonger, fishwife.—*n.f.* (**-ière**) fishkettle.

poitrail [pwa'tra:j], *n.m.* breast (*of a horse*); breast piece (*of harness*).

poitrinaire [pwatri'nɛ:r], *a.* and *n.* consumptive.

poitrine [pwa'trin], *n.f.* chest, breast; breasts; lungs; brisket.

poivrade [pwa'vrad], *n.f.* pepper sauce.

poivre [pwa:vr], *n.m.* pepper.

poivrer [pwa'vre], *v.t.* to pepper.

poivrier [pwavri'je], *n.m.* pepper plant; pepper box.

poivrière [pwavri'jɛ:r], *n.f.* pepper plantation; (*Fort.*) corner turret; pepper box.

poix [pwa], *n.f.* pitch; shoemakers' wax.

polaire [pɔ'lɛ:r], *a.* polar.

polariser [pɔlari'ze], *v.t.* to polarize.

pôle [po:l], *n.m.* (*Astron., Geog.*) pole.

polémique [pɔle'mik], *a.* polemical.—*n.f.* polemics, controversy.

poli [pɔ'li], *a.* polished, glossy, sleek; polite, civil; refined.—*n.m.* polish, finish, gloss.

police [pɔ'lis], *n.f.* police; police regulations; insurance policy; *agent de police*, police constable.

policer [pɔli'se], *v.t.* (*conjug. like* COMMENCER) to establish law and order in; to civilize, to polish, to refine.

polichinelle [pɔliʃi'nɛl], *n.m.* Punch; buffoon; Punch and Judy show.

policier [pɔli'sje], *a.* (*fem.* **-ière**) pertaining to the police; *roman policier*, detective story.—*n.m.* policeman; detective.

policlinique [pɔlikli'nik], *n.f.* out-patients' department.

poliment [pɔli'mɑ̃], *adv.* politely.

poliomyélite [pɔljomje'lit], *n.f.* poliomyelitis.

polir [pɔ'li:r], *v.t.* to polish, to burnish; (*fig.*) to civilize, to refine. *se polir*, *v.r.* to become polished; to become refined.

polissage [pɔli'sa:ʒ], **polissement** [pɔlis'mɑ̃], *n.m.* polishing, finishing.

polisseur [pɔli'sœ:r], *n.m.* (*fem.* **-euse**) polisher.

polissoir [pɔli'swa:r], *n.m.* polisher (*tool*).

polisson [pɔli'sɔ̃], *a.* (*fem.* **-onne**) loose, naughty, licentious, smutty.—*n.m.* (*fem.* **-onne**) mischievous child, scamp; loose person.

polissonner [pɔlisɔ'ne], *v.i.* to run about the streets (*of children*).

polissonnerie [pɔlisɔn'ri], *n.f.* smutty joke, lewd act.

polissure [pɔli'syːr], *n.f.* polishing.

politesse [pɔli'tɛs], *n.f.* politeness, civility, polite attention; compliment.

politicien [pɔliti'sjɛ̃], *n.m.* (*fem.* **-enne**) (*usu. pej.*) politician.

politique [pɔli'tik], *a.* political; (*fig.*) politic, prudent, wise.—*n.f.* politics; policy, discretion.—*n.m.* politician, statesman.

politiquement [pɔlitik'mɑ̃], *adv.* politically; (*fig.*) shrewdly.

polka [pɔl'ka], *n.f.* polka.

pollen [pɔl'lɛn], *n.m.* pollen.

pollinisation [pɔliniza'sjɔ̃], *n.f.* pollinization.

polluer [pɔl'lɥe], *v.t.* to pollute; to defile; to profane.

pollution [pɔly'sjɔ̃], *n.f.* pollution; profanation.

polo [pɔ'lo], *n.m.* polo.

Pologne [pɔ'lɔɲ], la, *f.* Poland.

polonais [pɔlɔ'nɛ], *a.* Polish.—*n.m.* Polish (*language*); (**Polonais**, *fem.* **-aise**) Pole.— *n.f.* (**-aise**) Polonaise (*dress, dance, tune*).

poltron [pɔl'trɔ̃], *a.* (*fem.* **-onne**) cowardly, chicken-hearted. — *n.m.* (*fem.* **-onne**) coward, poltroon.

poltronnerie [pɔltrɔn'ri], *n.f.* cowardice, poltroonery.

polycopier [pɔlikɔ'pje], *v.t.* to cyclostyle.

polygamie [pɔliga'mi], *n.f.* polygamy.

polyglotte [pɔli'glɔt], *a.* and *n.* polyglot.

polytechnique [pɔlitɛk'nik], *a.* polytechnic.

pommade [pɔ'mad], *n.f.* pomade; ointment.

pomme [pɔm], *n.f.* apple; ball, knob; head (*of a cabbage, lettuce, walking-stick etc.*); (*pop.*) head, nut; **pomme de pin**, fir cone; **pomme de terre**, potato.

pommé [pɔ'me], *a.* grown to a round head; (*colloq.*) complete, downright.

pommeau [pɔ'mo], *n.m.* (*pl.* **-eaux**) pommel (*of a saddle, sword etc.*); head, knob.

pommelé [pɔm'le], *a.* dappled, mottled.

pommeler (se) [sapɔ'mle], *v.r.* (*conjug. like* APPELER) to become dappled.

pommer [pɔ'me], *v.i.* and **se pommer**, *v.r.* to grow to a firm round head (*of cabbage, lettuce etc.*).

pommette [pɔ'mɛt], *n.f.* apple-like ball or knob; cheek bone; (*C*) crab apple.

pommier [pɔ'mje], *n.m.* apple tree.

pompe [pɔ̃ːp], *n.f.* pomp, ceremony; display; pump, inflator; **pompe à incendie**, fire-engine.

pomper [pɔ̃'pe], *v.t.* to pump; (*fig.*) to suck up.—*v.i.* to pump.

pompeusement [pɔ̃pøz'mɑ̃], *adv.* solemnly, with pomp.

pompeux [pɔ̃'pø], *a.* (*fem.* **-euse**) stately, solemn; pompous.

pompier [pɔ̃'pje], *a. inv.* conventional (*art, style*).—*n.m.* fireman.

pompiste [pɔ̃'pist], *n.* pump attendant (*at gas pump etc.*).

pompon [pɔ̃'pɔ̃], *n.m.* pompon, top-knot.

pomponner [pɔ̃pɔ'ne], *v.t.* to ornament with pompons, to deck out. **se pomponner**, *v.r.* to dress oneself up.

ponce [pɔ̃ːs], *n.f.* pumice; (*Drawing*) pounce.

ponceau (1) [pɔ̃'so], *n.m.* (*pl.* **-eaux**) small bridge, culvert.

ponceau (2) [pɔ̃'so], *a.* poppy-red.—*n.m.* (*pl.* **-eaux**) corn poppy.

Ponce Pilate [pɔ̃spi'lat], *m.* Pontius Pilate.

poncer [pɔ̃'se], *v.t.* (*conjug. like* COMMENCER) to pumice; (*Drawing*) to pounce.

poncif [pɔ̃'sif], *n.m.* pounced drawing; (*fig.*) commonplace piece of work.

ponctualité [pɔ̃ktɥali'te], *n.f.* punctuality.

ponctuation [pɔ̃ktɥa'sjɔ̃], *n.f.* punctuation.

ponctué [pɔ̃k'tɥe], *a.* punctuated; dotted; **ligne ponctuée**, dotted line.

ponctuel [pɔ̃k'tɥɛl], *a.* (*fem.* **-elle**) punctual, exact.

ponctuellement [pɔ̃ktɥɛl'mɑ̃], *adv.* punctually.

ponctuer [pɔ̃k'tɥe], *v.t.* to punctuate; to point.

pondéré [pɔ̃de're], *a.* poised, calm, self-controlled.

pondérer [pɔ̃de're], *v.t.* (*conjug. like* CÉDER) to poise, to balance.

pondeur [pɔ̃'dœːr], *a.* (*fem.* **-euse**) good laying (*of poultry etc.*); (*colloq.*) productive. —*n.f.* (**-euse**) good layer.

pondre [pɔ̃ːdr], *v.t.* to lay (*eggs*).

poney [pɔ'ne], *n.m.* pony.

pont [pɔ̃], *n.m.* bridge; deck; **Ponts et Chaussées**, (*France*) Department of Bridges and Highways.

ponte (1) [pɔ̃ːt], *n.f.* laying of eggs.

ponte (2) [pɔ̃ːt], *n.m.* better; (*fam.*) V.I.P.

ponté [pɔ̃'te], *a.* decked (*of ship*); **non ponté**, open (*boat*).

ponter [pɔ̃'te], *v.i.* to punt, to gamble.

pontet [pɔ̃'tɛ], *n.m.* trigger guard; saddle-tree.

pontife [pɔ̃'tif], *n.m.* pontiff.

pontifier [pɔ̃ti'fje], *v.i.* (*fam.*) to act or speak solemnly or pompously; to pontificate, to lay down the law.

pont-levis [pɔ̃l'vi], *n.m.* (*pl.* **ponts-levis**) drawbridge.

ponton [pɔ̃'tɔ̃], *n.m.* bridge of boats; pontoon.

popeline [pɔ'plin], *n.f.* poplin.

populace [pɔpy'las], *n.f.* populace, mob, rabble.

populacier [pɔpyla'sje], *a.* (*fem.* **-ière**) low, vulgar.

populaire [pɔpy'lɛːr], *a.* popular; common. —*n.m.* populace, rabble.

populairement [pɔpylɛr'mɑ̃], *adv.* popularly.

populariser [pɔpylari'ze], *v.t.* to popularize.

popularité [pɔpylari'te], *n.f.* popularity.

population [pɔpyla'sjɔ̃], *n.f.* population.

populeux [pɔpy'lø], *a.* (*fem.* **-euse**) populous.

porc [pɔːr], *n.m.* pig; swine; pork.

porcelaine [pɔrsa'lɛn], *n.f.* porcelain, china, chinaware.

porcelet [pɔrsa'lɛ], *n.m.* young pig, piglet.

porc-épic [pɔrke'pik], *n.m.* (*pl.* **porcs-épics**) porcupine; (*Am.*) hedgehog.

porche [pɔrʃ], *n.m.* porch.

porcher [pɔr'ʃe], *n.m.* (*fem.* **-ère**) swineherd.

porcherie [pɔrʃ'ri], *n.f.* pigsty, piggery.

porcin [pɔr'sɛ̃], *a.* porcine.—*n.m.* (*pl.*) pigs.

pore [pɔːr], *n.m.* pore.

poreux [pɔ'rø], *a.* (*fem.* **-euse**) porous.

pornographie [pɔrnɔgra'fi], *n.f.* pornography.

pornographique [pɔrnɔgra'fik], *a.* pornographic.

porphyre [pɔr'fiːr], n.m. porphyry.
porphyriser [pɔrfiri'ze], v.t. to porphyrize; to pulverize.
porreau [POIREAU].
port (1) [pɔːr], n.m. haven, harbor, port; sea-port town; **arriver à bon port**, to arrive safely; (fig.) to end happily; **port d'escale**, port of call.
port (2) [pɔːr], n.m. carrying; carriage; postage; bearing, gait; (Naut.) tonnage.
portable [pɔr'tabl], a. portable; wearable.
portage [pɔr'taːʒ], n.m. carriage, transport.
portail [pɔr'taːj], n.m. (pl. **-s**) portal, front gate (of a church etc.).
portant [pɔr'tɑ̃], a. bearing, carrying; **être bien portant**, to be in good health.
portatif [pɔrta'tif], a. (fem. **-tive**) portable.
porte [pɔrt], n.f. doorway, gateway; door; gate; entrance; eye (of hooks etc.); defile.
porté [pɔr'te], a. carried; inclined, prone, disposed (à); projected (of shadows).
porte-à-faux [pɔrta'fo], n.m. inv. overhang; **en porte-à-faux**, overhanging; unsteady.
porte-affiches [pɔrta'fiʃ], n.m. inv. advertising board.
porte-avions [pɔrta'vjɔ̃], n.m. inv. aircraft carrier.
porte-bagages [pɔrtba'gaːʒ], n.m. inv. luggage rack.
porte-billets [pɔrtbi'jɛ], n.m. inv. note case; (Am.) bill-fold.
porte-bonheur [pɔrtbɔ'nœːr], n.m. inv. good-luck charm; mascot.
porte-bouteilles [pɔrtbu'teːj], n.m. inv. bottle rack, wine bin.
porte-chapeaux [pɔrtʃa'po], n.m. inv. hat-stand.
porte-cigarettes [pɔrtsiga'rɛt], n.m. inv. cigarette case.
porte-clefs [pɔrta'kle], n.m. inv. key ring.
porte-couteau [pɔrtku'to], n.m. inv. knife rest.
porte-crayon [pɔrtakrɛ'jɔ̃], n.m. inv. pencil case.
porte-documents [pɔrtdɔky'mɑ̃], n.m. inv. dispatch case.
porte-drapeau [pɔrtdra'po], n.m. inv. ensign, color bearer.
portée [pɔr'te], n.f. brood, litter; reach (of the hand, arm etc.); hearing; range, shot; scope; capacity; import, significance; bearing; resting-point; (Mus.) stave.
porte-étendard [pɔrtetɑ̃'daːr], n.m. inv. standard bearer.
porte-fenêtre [pɔrtfɔ'nɛːtr], n.f. (pl. **portes-fenêtres**) French window.
portefeuille [pɔrta'fœːj], n.m. wallet; (fig.) portfolio; office.
porte-flambeau [pɔrtflɑ̃'bo], n.m. inv. torch bearer, linkman.
porte-jupe [pɔrta'ʒyp], n.m. inv. skirt-hanger.
porte-livres [pɔrta'liːvr], n.m. inv. book rest.
porte-malheur [pɔrtma'lœːr], n.m. inv. bird of ill omen, bearer of ill luck.
portemanteau [pɔrtmɑ̃'to], n.m. (pl. **-eaux**) coat stand, coat rail; peg.
porte-masse [pɔrta'mas], n.m. inv. mace bearer.
porte-mine(s) [pɔrta'min], n.m. inv. mechanical pencil.

porte-monnaie [pɔrtmɔ'nɛ], n.m. inv. purse.
porte-musique [pɔrtmy'zik], n.m. inv. music case.
porte-parapluies [pɔrtpara'plɥi], n.m. inv. umbrella stand.
porte-parole [pɔrtpa'rɔl], n.m. inv. mouthpiece, spokesman.
porte-plume [pɔrta'plym], n.m. inv. penholder.
porte-queue [pɔrta'kø], n.m. inv. train bearer; swallowtail butterfly.
porter [pɔr'te], v.t. to carry, to bear, to support; to endure; to bring, to take; to wear; to deal (blows etc.); to turn (the eyes etc.); to entertain (affection etc.); to incline; to produce; to declare, to show.—v.i. to bear; to rest, to lie; to take effect; to hit; to reach; to carry (of a gun etc.); (Naut.) to stand, to bear off; to be with young (of animals). **se porter**, v.r. to go, to repair, to move; to resort, to flock; to be inclined or disposed, to tend; to be, to do (of health); to be worn; to present oneself, to stand forth; to turn, to be directed.
porte-rame [pɔrt'ram], n.m. inv. oarlock.
porte-serviette(s) [pɔrtsɛr'vjɛt], n.m. inv. towel rail.
porteur [pɔr'tœːr], n.m. (fem. **-euse**) porter, carrier, bearer; holder; sleeper (on railway track).
porte-voix [pɔrt'vwa], n.m. inv. megaphone.
portier [pɔr'tje], n.m. (fem. **-ière** (1)) porter, door-keeper.
portière (2) [pɔr'tjɛːr], n.f. door-curtain, door (of vehicle).
portion [pɔr'sjɔ̃], n.f. portion, part, share, allowance.
portionner [pɔrsjɔ'ne], v.t. to share out.
portique [pɔr'tik], n.m. portico; porch.
porto [pɔr'to], n.m. port (wine).
portrait [pɔr'trɛ], n.m. portrait, likeness, picture.
portraitiste [pɔrtrɛ'tist], n. portrait painter.
portugais [pɔrty'gɛ], a. Portuguese.—n.m. Portuguese (language); (**Portugais**, fem. **-aise**) Portuguese (person).
Portugal [pɔrty'gal], **le**, m. Portugal.
pose [poːz], n.f. laying, setting; pose, posture, attitude; posing, affectation; sitting (for one's portrait etc.); hanging (of bells); (Mil.) posting (of sentries); (Phot.) (time) exposure.
posé [po'ze], a. laid, set, poised; bearing, resting; sedate, staid, sober; **cela posé**, this being granted.
posément [poze'mɑ̃], adv. calmly; sedately.
poser [po'ze], v.t. to put, to put in (a lock, a window pane); to place, to lay down; to hang; to suppose, to grant; to post (sentries etc.); to lay down, to state; (Mus.) to pitch; to sit (for portrait); **poser une question**, to ask a question.—v.i. to lie, to rest (sur); to stand, to pose, to sit (for one's portrait); to show off. **se poser**, v.r. to perch (of birds etc.); to come down, to land (plane); to set up (en), to play the part (en).
poseur [po'zœːr], n.m. (Rail.) track layer.—n.m. (fem. **-euse**) (colloq.) poseur, snob, prig.
positif [pozi'tif], a. (fem. **-tive**) positive, certain; practical, actual, matter-of-fact.—n.m. positive reality; certainty, fact; (Phot., Ciné., Gram.) positive.

position [pozi'sjɔ̃], n.f. position, situation; status, standing; case, state, circumstances.
positivement [pozitiv'mɑ̃], adv. positively, exactly.
possédé [pose'de], a. possessed—n.m. (fem. -ée) person possessed, madman, maniac.
posséder [pose'de], v.t. (conjug. like CÉDER) to possess, to be possessed of, to own; to be master of; to be conversant with; to dominate; (fig.) to deceive. se posséder (a person); (pop.) to deceive.—v.r. se posséder, v.r. to master one's passions, to contain oneself.
possesseur [pose'sœːr], n.m. possessor, owner, occupier.
possessif [pose'sif], a. (fem. -ive) possessive. —n.m. (Gram.) possessive adjective or pronoun.
possession [pose'sjɔ̃], n.f. possession; property.
possibilité [posibili'te], n.f. possibility; (pl.) facilities.
possible [po'sibl], a. possible.—n.m. possibility; au possible, extremely; je ferai tout mon possible, I'll do the best I can.
postal [pos'tal], a. (m. pl. -aux) postal, of the post.
poste (1) [post], n.m. post, station; guardhouse; place, employment, post; (Naut.) berth; (Teleph.) extension; entry (in books); poste de radio, radio set; poste d'incendie, fire station.
poste (2) [post], n.f. post (relay); post stage; postal service; post office, mail; bureau de poste, post office.
poster [pos'te], v.t. to station, to post (sentry or letter).
postérieur [poste'rjœːr], a. posterior, later; behind.—n.m. (colloq.) posterior.
postérieurement [posterjœr'mɑ̃], adv. subsequently.
postérité [posteri'te], n.f. posterity.
posthume [pos'tym], a. posthumous.
postiche [pos'tiʃ], a. superadded; false, artificial.—n.m. wig.
postier [pos'tje], n.m. (fem. -ière) postoffice employee.
postillon [posti'jɔ̃], n.m. postilion; post boy.
postscolaire [postskɔ'lɛːr], a. continuation (class); enseignement postscolaire, adult education.
post-scriptum [postskrip'tɔm] (abbr. P.S.), n.m. inv. postscript.
postulant [posty'lɑ̃], n.m. (fem. -e) candidate, applicant; postulant.
postuler [posty'le], v.t. to solicit, to apply for.—v.i. (Law) to act on behalf of a client.
posture [pos'tyːr], n.f. posture, attitude, situation.
pot [po], n.m. pot; jug, tankard, flagon, can, jar; (C) half a gallon.
potable [po'tabl], a. drinkable (water).
potage [po'taːʒ], n.m. soup.
potager (1) [pota'ʒe], n.m. kitchen garden; kitchen stove.
potager (2) [pota'ʒe], a. (fem. -ère) culinary; jardin potager, kitchen garden.
potasse [po'tas], n.f. potash.
potassium [pota'sjɔm], n.m. potassium.
pot-au-feu [poto'fø], n.m. inv. beef boiled with carrots etc.; broth of this.
pot-de-vin [pod'vɛ̃], n.m. (pl. pots-de-vin) gratuity; bribe; hush money.

poteau [po'to], n.m. (pl. -eaux) post, stake.
potée [po'te], n.f. potful; (colloq.) swarm (of children etc.); putty; (Metal.) molding.
potelé [po'tle], a. plump, chubby.
potence [po'tɑ̃ːs], n.f. gallows, gibbet; bracket; crutch; gibier de potence, jail-bird.
potentat [potɑ̃'ta], n.m. potentate.
potentiel [potɑ̃'sjɛl], a. (fem. -elle) potential. —n.m. potentiality.
potentiellement [potɑ̃sjɛl'mɑ̃], adv. potentially.
poterie [po'tri], n.f. pottery, earthenware.
poterne [po'tɛrn], n.f. postern.
potiche [po'tiʃ], n.f. China or Japan porcelain vase.
potier [po'tje], n.m. potter.
potin [po'tɛ̃], n.m. pinchbeck; (pl.) gossip.
potion [po'sjɔ̃], n.f. potion, draft.
potiron [poti'rɔ̃], n.m. pumpkin.
pou [pu], n.m. (pl. poux) louse.
pouah! [pwa], int. ugh! disgusting!
poubelle [pu'bɛl], n.f. dustbin; (Am.) ashcan.
pouce [pus], n.m. thumb; big toe; inch; un morceau sur le pouce, a snack; (C) faire du pouce, to hitch-hike.
poucet [pu'sɛ], n.m. le petit Poucet, Tom Thumb.
pouding [pu'diŋ], n.m. plum pudding.
poudre [pudr], n.f. powder; gunpowder; dust; sucre en poudre, powdered sugar.
poudrer [pu'dre], v.t. to powder, to sprinkle with powder.
poudrerie [pudrə'ri], n.f. gunpowderfactory; (C) blizzard.
poudreux [pu'drø], a. (fem. -euse) dusty, powdery.
poudrier [pudri'e], n.m. (powder) compact.
poudrière [pudri'ɛːr], n.f. powder mill, magazine; sand box.
poudroyer [pudrwa'je], v.i. (conjug. like EMPLOYER) to rise in dust; to be dusty (of roads etc.).
pouf! (1) [puf], int. plop! flop! phew!
pouf (2) [puf], n.m. ottoman (seat), pouf; blurb(advertisement).
pouffer [pu'fe], v.i. pouffer de rire, to burst out laughing, to guffaw.
pouilleux [pu'jø], a. and n.m. (fem. -euse) lousy; wretched, mean (person).
poulailler [pula'je], n.m. hen house; (of persons) poulterer; (Theat.) gods, gallery.
poulain [pu'lɛ̃], n.m. foal, colt.
poularde [pu'lard], n.f. fat pullet.
poulbot [pul'bo], n.m. Paris street urchin.
poule [pul], n.f. hen; fowl; pool (at games); eliminating round (in a competition).
poulet [pu'lɛ], n.m. chicken; love letter.
poulette [pu'lɛt], n.f. pullet.
pouliche [pu'liʃ], n.f. filly.
poulie [pu'li], n.f. (Naut.) block.
pouliner [puli'ne], v.i. to foal (of mares).
poulinière [puli'njɛːr], a.f. and n.f. (jument) poulinière, brood mare.
poulpe [pulp], n.m. octopus, devil-fish.
pouls [pu], n.m. pulse; se tâter le pouls, to feel one's pulse.
poumon [pu'mɔ̃], n.m. lung; poumon d'acier, iron lung.

préambule [pr~~...~~] ~~...~~ face.

préau [pre'~~o~~], ~~...~~ rn, poop.
~~...~~ pe~~...~~ *f.* doll; puppet; tailor's dummy.

poupin [pu'pɛ̃], *a.* fresh-colored; rosy.

poupon [pu'pɔ̃], *n.m. (fem.* -**onne**) baby; plump, chubby-cheeked boy *or* girl.

pouponnière [pupɔ'njɛːr], *n.f. (public)* day nursery.

pour [puːr], *prep.* for; on account of; on behalf of; as regards, as for; in order; although.—*n.m.* for, pro.

pourboire [puːr'bwaːr], *n.m.* tip, gratuity.

pourceau [puːr'so], *n.m. (pl.* -**eaux**) hog, pig, swine.

pour-cent [puːr'sɑ̃], **pourcentage** [pursɑ̃ 'taːʒ], *n.m.* percentage.

pourchasser [purʃa'se], *v.t.* to pursue, to chase, to badger.

pourfendre [puːr'fɑ̃ːdr], *v.t.* to cleave asunder.

pourlécher [purle'ʃe], *v.t. (conjug. like* CÉDER) to lick all over. **se pourlécher,** *v.r.* to lick one's lips.

pourparler [purpar'le], *n.m. (usu. in pl.)* parley, negotiations; talks.

pourpoint [puːr'pwɛ̃], *n.m.* doublet.

pourpre [purpr], *a.* purple, dark red.—*n.f.* purple *(stuff); (fig.)* sovereign dignity; cardinalate.—*n.m.* purple, crimson *(color).*

pourpré [puːr'pre], *a.* purple.

pourquoi [puːr'kwa], *adv.* and *conj.* why, wherefore; **pourquoi pas?** why not?—*n.m. inv.* the reason why.

pourri [pu'ri], *a.* rotten; **temps pourri,** muggy weather.—*n.m.* the rotten part; rottenness.

pourrir [pu'riːr], *v.t.* to make rotten, to corrupt.—*v.i.* to rot; *(fig.)* to perish. **se pourrir,** *v.r.* to become rotten, to go bad.

pourrissable [puri'sabl], *a.* perishable.

pourrissant [puri'sɑ̃], *a.* rotting, causing rot.

pourriture [puri'tyːr], *n.f.* rot, rottenness, putrefaction; *(fig.)* corruption.

poursuite [puːr'sɥit], *n.f.* pursuit, chase; prosecution; *(Law)* suit, proceedings.

poursuivable [pursɥi'vabl], *a.* actionable.

poursuivant [pursɥi'vɑ̃], *a.* suing, prosecuting.—*n.m.* suitor.—*n.m. (fem.* -**e**) prosecutor, plaintiff.

poursuivre [puːr'sɥiːvr], *v.t. irr. (conjug. like* SUIVRE) to pursue; to seek; to persecute; to haunt; to go on with; to follow up; *(Law)* to sue, to prosecute.—*v.i.* to pursue, to go on, to continue. **se poursuivre,** *v.r.* to continue, to follow its course.

pourtant [puːr'tɑ̃], *adv.* however, yet, still, nevertheless.

pourtour [puːr'tuːr], *n.m.* periphery, circumference; aisle *(in a theatre etc.);* precincts *(of cathedral).*

pourvoi [puːr'vwa], *n.m. (Law)* appeal.

pourvoir [puːr'vwaːr], *v.t. irr.* to invest with, to appoint; to provide, to supply, to endow. —*v.i. (followed by* à) to see to, to attend to, to provide for; to make an appointment to. **se pourvoir,** *v.r.* to provide oneself; to appeal.

pourvoyeur [purvwa'jœːr], *n.m. (fem.* -**euse**) purveyor, provider, caterer.

pourvu que [puːr'vykə], *conj. phr.* provided that, provided.

poussée [pu'se], *n.f. ~~...~~* *(of arches etc.) ~~...~~*

pousse-pousse [pus'pus], ~~...~~ sting ~~...~~ *(carriage or man.)*

pousser [pu'se], *v.t.* to push, ~~...~~ shove; to drive on; to carry on, to ext~~...~~ to grow, to send forth *(of plants etc.);* to urge, to provoke; to assist, to help on; to utter, to heave *(a sigh etc.);* to deal *(a blow etc.).*—*v.i.* to sprout, to shoot *(of plants);* to grow *(of the hair, nails etc.);* to push on, to go on; to bulge; to be broken-winded *(of horses).* **se pousser,** *v.r.* to push forward, to push oneself forward; to push each other, to jostle.

poussette [pu'sɛt], *n.f.* go-cart; movement in dancing.

poussier [pu'sje], *n.m.* coal dust, screenings.

poussière [pu'sjɛːr], *n.f.* dust; spray *(of water).*

poussiéreux [pusje'rø], *a. (fem.* -**euse**) dusty.

poussif [pu'sif], *a. (fem.* -**ive**) shortwinded.

poussin [pu'sɛ̃], *n.m.* chick, chicken just hatched.

poussinière [pusi'njɛːr], *n.f.* chicken-coop; incubator.

poutre [putr], *n.f.* beam; girder.

poutrelle [pu'trɛl], *n.f.* small beam.

pouvoir [pu'vwaːr], *v.t. irr.* to be able to do.— *v.i.* to be able *(can etc.);* to have power; to be allowed *(may etc.); (impers.)* to be possible; **il peut arriver que,** it may happen that; **il se peut que,** it is possible that; **on ne peut plus,** *(followed by adj.)* exceedingly; **sauve qui peut,** every man for himself.—*n.m.* power; might; authority; command, government.

prairie [pre'ri], *n.f.* meadow, grass-land, grass field; *(U.S.)* prairie.

praline [pra'lin], *n.f.* burnt almond.

praliner [prali'ne], *v.t.* to brown in sugar *(like burnt almonds).*

praticabilité [pratikabili'te], *n.f.* practicability, feasibility.

praticable [prati'kabl], *a.* practicable, feasible; passable *(of roads);* accessible; *(Theat.)* real, usable.

praticien [prati'sjɛ̃], *a. (fem.* -**enne**) practicing.—*n.m. (fem.* -**enne**) practitioner.

pratiquant [prati'kɑ̃], *a.* church-going.— *n.m. (fem.* -**e**) church-goer.

pratique [pra'tik], *a.* practical; experienced. —*n.f.* practice; execution; method; experience; usage; custom *(of tradesman),* practice *(of attorneys, physicians etc.);* customer; *(pl.)* dealings.

pratiquement [pratik'mɑ̃], *adv.* in actual fact, practically; in a practical way.

pratiquer [prati'ke], *v.t.* to practice, to exercise; to frequent; to tamper with, to bribe; to obtain; *(Arch.)* to contrive. **se pratiquer,** *v.r.* to be in use, to be practiced.

pré [pre], *n.m.* meadow.

préalable [prea'labl], *a.* preliminary; previous.—*n.m.* **au préalable,** previously, first of all.

préalablement [prealabla'mɑ̃], *adv.* previously, first, to begin with.

pré- **prédécéder** [predese'de], *v.i. (conjug. like* ~~...~~ *of arches etc.).* **prédecease** *(someone).*

prédestiné, ~~...~~ **prédestined.**

253

convent or prison; play- ground.

préavis [prea'vi], *n.m. inv.* (previous) notice.

précaire [pre'kɛːr], *a.* precarious; uncertain.

précairement [prekɛr'mã], *adv.* precariously.

précaution [preko'sjɔ̃], *n.f.* precaution; caution, care.

précautionner [prekosjo'ne], *v.t.* to warn, to caution. **se précautionner,** *v.r.* to take precautions.

précédemment [preseda'mã], *adv.* before, previously.

précédent [prese'dã], *a.* preceding, former.— *n.m.* precedent.

précéder [prese'de], *v.t.* (*conjug. like* CÉDER) to precede, to go before; to take precedence (*of*).

précepte [pre'sɛpt], *n.m.* precept, rule.

précepteur [presɛp'tœːr], *n.m.* (*fem.* **-trice**) tutor, teacher.

prêche [prɛːʃ], *n.m.* sermon (*Protestant*); Protestant church.

prêcher [prɛ'ʃe], *v.t.* to preach; to exhort; to extol, to praise.—*v.i.* to preach.

prêcheur [prɛ'ʃœːr], *n.m.* (*fem.* **-euse**) preacher.

précieusement [presjøz'mã], *adv.* preciously; carefully; affectedly.

précieux [pre'sjø], *a.* (*fem.* **-euse**) precious, valuable; affected.—*n.m.* affectation.—*n.m.* (*fem.* **-euse**) affected person.

préciosité [presjozi'te], *n.f.* affectation.

précipice [presi'pis], *n.m.* precipice.

précipitamment [presipita'mã], *adv.* precipitately, hurriedly, rashly.

précipitation [presipita'sjɔ̃], *n.f.* haste, hurry; (*Chem.*) precipitation.

précipité [presipi'te], *a.* precipitated, hurled; precipitate, hasty, sudden.—*n.m.* (*Chem.*) precipitate.

précipiter [presipi'te], *v.t.* to precipitate, to hurl; to hasten, to accelerate; (*Chem.*) to precipitate. **se précipiter,** *v.r.* to precipitate, throw *or* hurl oneself; to rush forward, to spring forth, to dart.

précis [pre'si], *a.* fixed, precise, exact; formal, terse, concise.—*n.m.* summary, abstract.

précisément [presize'mã], *adv.* precisely, exactly; quite; just so.

préciser [presi'ze], *v.t.* to state precisely, to specify.

précision [presi'zjɔ̃], *n.f.* precision, preciseness.

précité [presi'te], *a.* afore-mentioned.

précoce [pre'kɔs], *a.* precocious, early, forward.

précocité [prekɔsi'te], *n.f.* precocity.

préconçu [prekɔ̃'sy], *a.* preconceived.

préconiser [prekɔni'ze], *v.t.* to advocate, to recommend.

préconnaissance [prekɔnɛ'sãːs], *n.f.* foreknowledge.

précurseur [prekyr'sœːr], *n.m.* forerunner, precursor, harbinger.

prédateur [preda'tœːr], *a.* (*fem.* **-trice**) (*Ent.*) predatory.

shoot, sprout.

prédestiné [pre... *n.m.* inv. (*fam.*) ...], *a.* predetermined.—*n.m.* (*fem.* **-ée**) one of the elect.

prédicateur [predika'tœːr], *n.m.* (*fem.* **-trice**) preacher.

prédiction [predik'sjɔ̃], *n.f.* prediction, forecast.

prédilection [prediłɛk'sjɔ̃], *n.f.* predilection, preference.

prédire [pre'diːr], *v.t. irr.* (*conjug. like* MÉDIRE) to predict, to foretell.

prédisposer [predispo'ze], *v.t.* to predispose.

prédisposition [predispozi'sjɔ̃], *n.f.* predisposition.

prédominance [predɔmi'nãːs], *n.f.* predominance, ascendancy.

prédominant [predɔmi'nã], *a.* predominant.

prédominer [predɔmi'ne], *v.t.* to prevail over. —*v.i.* to predominate.

prééminence [preemi'nãːs], *n.f.* pre-eminence.

prééminent [preemi'nã], *a.* pre-eminent.

préemption [preãp'sjɔ̃], *n.f.* pre-emption.

préfabriqué [prefabri'ke], *a.* prefabricated.

préface [pre'fas], *n.f.* preface; foreword.

préfecture [prefɛk'tyːr], *n.f.* prefecture; **préfecture de police,** Paris police headquarters.

préférable [prefe'rabl], *a.* preferable.

préférablement [preferablə'mã], *adv.* preferably.

préféré [prefe'ʁe], *a.* favorite.

préférence [prefe'rãːs], *n.f.* preference.

préférer [prefe're], *v.t.* (*conjug. like* CÉDER) to prefer.

préfet [pre'fɛ], *n.m.* prefect; chief administrator of a department in France; **préfet de police,** chief commissioner of Parisian police.

préhensile [preã'sil], *a.* prehensile.

préhistorique [preisto'rik], *a.* prehistoric.

préjudice [preʒy'dis], *n.m.* detriment, injury, damage, prejudice.

préjudiciable [preʒydi'sjabl], *a.* prejudicial, detrimental.

préjudicier [preʒydi'sje], *v.i.* to be prejudicial *or* detrimental.

préjugé [preʒy'ʒe], *n.m.* presumption, prejudice; (*Law*) precedent.

préjuger [preʒy'ʒe], *v.t.* (*conjug. like* MANGER) to prejudge.

prélasser (se) [saprela'se], *v.r.* to strut, to stalk along.

prélat [pre'la], *n.m.* prelate.

prélèvement [prelɛv'mã], *n.m.* deduction; sample; (*Med.*) swab.

prélever [prela've], *v.t.* (*conjug. like* AMENER) to deduct; to appropriate.

préliminaire [prelimi'nɛːr], *a.* and *n.m.* preliminary.

prélude [pre'lyd], *n.m.* prelude.

prématuré [prematy're], *a.* premature, untimely.

prématurément [prematyre'mã], *adv.* prematurely.

préméditation [premedita'sjɔ̃], *n.f.* premeditation.

préméditer [premedi'te], *v.t.* to premeditate.

prémices [pre'mis], *n.f. pl.* first-fruits; *(fig.)* beginning.

premier [prə'mje], *a.* *(fem.* **-ière)** first; foremost, best, chief; former *(of two)*; early, pristine, primeval; *(Arith.)* prime; *au premier abord,* at first sight; *le premier rang,* the front rank; *matières premières,* raw materials.—*n.m.* *(fem.* **-ière)** chief, head, leader.—*n.m.* first floor; first of the month etc.—*n.f.* **(-ière)** *(Theat.)* first night.

premièrement [prəmjɛr'mɑ̃], *adv.* firstly, in the first place.

prémonition [premɔni'sjɔ̃], *n.f.* premonition.

prémunir [premy'ni:r], *v.t.* to forewarn, to caution, to secure beforehand. **se prémunir,** *v.r.* to provide *(contre).*

prenant [prə'nɑ̃], taking, prehensile; *(fig.)* fascinating; *partie prenante,* payee.

prendre [prɑ̃:dr], *v.t. irr.* to take; to take up; to snatch; to seize; to capture; to contract, to catch *(a cold etc.);* to choose; to fetch; to assume; to collect *(votes etc.);* to help oneself to; to conduct *(an affair etc.);* to entertain *(a feeling etc.);* **en prendre à son aise,** to take it easy; *prendre pour dit,* to take for granted; *que je t'y prenne un peu !* just let me catch you at it!—*v.i.* to take; to take root; to congeal, to freeze; to curdle *(of milk etc.);* to succeed; to begin to burn. **se prendre,** *v.r.* to be taken, to be caught; to catch; to freeze; to congeal *(of liquids);* to begin.

preneur [prə'nœ:r], *n.m.* *(fem.* **-euse)** taker; lessee; purchaser; catcher *(of animals).*

prénom [pre'nɔ̃], *n.m.* Christian name.

prénommé [prenɔ'me], *a.* and *n.m.* *(fem.* **-ée)** (the) above-named, aforesaid; named.

préoccupation [preɔkypa'sjɔ̃], *n.f.* preoccupation; anxiety, concern.

préoccupé [preɔky'pe], *a.* preoccupied, absorbed; worried.

préoccuper [preɔky'pe], *v.t.* to engross, to preoccupy; to worry. **se préoccuper,** *v.r.* to see to, to be engaged in *(de),* to be anxious about.

préparateur [prepara'tœ:r], *n.m.* *(fem.* **-trice)** preparer, assistant *(in laboratory or in a dispensing druggist's).*

préparatif(s) [prepara'tif], *n.m. sing.* or *pl.* preparation.

préparation [prepara'sjɔ̃], *n.f.* preparation; *sans préparation,* extempore.

préparatoire [prepara'twa:r], *a.* preparatory.

préparer [prepa're], *v.t.* to prepare, to make ready; to fit; to make up, to manufacture. **se préparer,** *v.r.* to prepare, to prepare oneself, to get ready.

prépondérance [prepɔ̃de'rɑ̃:s], *n.f.* preponderance.

prépondérant [prepɔ̃de'rɑ̃], *a.* preponderant; *voix prépondérante,* casting-vote.

préposé [prepo'ze], *n.m.* *(fem.* **-ée)** officer in charge, superintendent, agent.

préposer [prepo'ze], *v.t.* to set over, to appoint to, to put in charge of.

préposition [prepozi'sjɔ̃], *n.f.* preposition.

prérogative [preroga'ti:v], *n.f.* prerogative.

près [pre], *adv.* by, near, hard by; nearly, almost, about; on the point of; *à beaucoup près,* by a great deal; *à cela près,* with that exception; *à peu près,* pretty near, nearly so; *de près,* close, near; *tout près,* very near.—*prep.* *(usu. près de)* near, close to.

présage [pre'za:ʒ], *n.m.* presage, omen, foreboding.

présager [preza'ʒe], *v.t. (conjug. like* MANGER*)* to presage, to portend.

pré-salé [presa'le], *n.m.* *(pl.* **prés-salés)** salt-marsh sheep *or* mutton.

presbyte [prɛz'bit], *a.* long-sighted.—*n.* long-sighted person.

presbytère [prɛzbi'tɛ:r], *n.m.* parsonage, vicarage, rectory; presbytery *(R.-C. Ch.).*

presbytérien [prɛzbite'rjɛ̃], *a.* and *n.m.* *(fem.* **-enne)** Presbyterian.

presbytie [prɛzbi'si], *n.f.* far- *or* long-sightedness.

prescience [pre'sjɑ̃:s], *n.f.* prescience, foreknowledge.

prescription [prɛskrip'sjɔ̃], *n.f.* prescription; regulation.

prescrire [prɛs'kri:r], *v.t. irr. (conjug. like* ÉCRIRE*)* to prescribe, to stipulate; *(Law)* to bar.

préséance [prese'ɑ̃:s], *n.f.* precedence.

présence [pre'zɑ̃:s], *n.f.* presence, attendance, appearance; *mettre en présence,* to bring face to face.

présent [pre'zɑ̃], *a.* present; *présent !* here! —*n.m.* present, present time; gift; *dès à présent,* from now on.

présentable [prezɑ̃'tabl], *a.* presentable, fit to be seen.

présentation [prezɑ̃ta'sjɔ̃], *n.f.* presentation, introduction.

présentement [prezɑ̃t'mɑ̃], *adv.* now, at present.

présenter [prezɑ̃'te], *v.t.* to present, to offer; to show; to introduce. **se présenter,** *v.r.* to present oneself, to appear.

préservateur [prezɛrva'tœ:r], *a.* *(fem.* **-trice)** preservative.

préservatif [prezɛrva'tif], *a.* *(fem.* **-tive)** preservative.

préservation [prezɛrva'sjɔ̃], *n.f.* preservation.

préserver [prezɛr've], *v.t.* to preserve; to defend, to keep safe; *le ciel m'en préserve !* heaven forbid! **se préserver,** *v.r.* to preserve oneself, to guard against.

présidence [prezi'dɑ̃:s], *n.f.* presidency, chairmanship.

président [prezi'dɑ̃], *n.m.* president *(of tribunal),* presiding judge; speaker *(of the House of Commons),* chairman.

présidente [prezi'dɑ̃:t], *n.f.* lady president; president's wife.

présider [prezi'de], *v.t.* to preside over, to be president *or* chairman of.—*v.i.* to preside, to be president, to be in the chair.

présomptif [prezɔ̃p'tif], *a.* *(fem.* **-tive)** presumptive, apparent, presumed *(of heirs).*

présomption [prezɔ̃p'sjɔ̃], *n.f.* presumption, self-conceit.

présomptueusement [prezɔ̃ptyøz'mɑ̃], *adv.* presumptuously.

présomptueux [prezɔ̃p'tyø], *a.* *(fem.* **-euse)** presumptuous.

presque [prɛsk], *adv.* almost, nearly, all but; hardly, scarcely; *presque jamais,* hardly ever; *presque plus (de),* scarcely any left; *presque rien,* hardly anything.

presqu'île [prɛs'kil], *n.f.* peninsula.
pressage [prɛ'saːʒ], *n.m.* pressing.
pressant [prɛ'sɑ̃], *a.* pressing, urgent, earnest.
presse [prɛs], *n.f.* throng, crowd; hurry; urgency; (*Navy*) press-gang; press (*newspapers*); printing-press.
pressé [prɛ'se], *a.* pressed; crowded; close, thick; in haste, hurried; urgent; eager; very busy; (*fig.*) condensed, concise.
presse-citron [prɛssi'trɔ̃], *n.m.* (*pl. unchanged or* -**citrons**) lemon-squeezer.
pressée [prɛ'se], *n.f.* pressing, pressure; pressful (*of print etc.*).
pressentiment [prɛsɑ̃ti'mɑ̃], *n.m.* presentiment; foreboding.
pressentir [prɛsɑ̃'tiːr], *v.t. irr.* (*conjug. like* SENTIR) to have a presentiment of; to sound.
presse-papiers [prɛspa'pje], *n.m. inv.* paper-weight.
presse-purée [prɛspy're], *n.m. inv.* potato masher.
presser [prɛ'se], *v.t.* to press, to squeeze; to tread down; to crowd; to hasten; to entreat, to urge.—*v.i.* to be urgent. **se presser**, *v.r.* to press, to squeeze, to crowd; to make haste, to hurry.
pression [prɛ'sjɔ̃], *n.f.* pressure.
pressoir [prɛ'swaːr], *n.m.* press (*wine etc.*).
pressurer [prɛsy're], *v.t.* to press (*grapes, apples etc.*); (*fig.*) to squeeze money etc. out of; to oppress.
pressureur [prɛsy'rœːr], *n.m.* (*fem.* -**euse**) presser (*of fruit etc.*); (*fig.*) squeezer, sponger; oppressor.
prestance [prɛs'tɑ̃ːs], *n.f.* commanding appearance, fine presence.
prestation [prɛsta'sjɔ̃], *n.f.* taking (*of an oath*); prestation (*payment of toll etc.*).
preste [prɛst], *a.* agile, nimble; smart.
prestement [prɛstə'mɑ̃], *adv.* nimbly, quickly.
prestesse [prɛs'tɛs], *n.f.* agility, quickness.
prestidigitateur [prɛstidiʒita'tœːr], *n.m.* conjurer, juggler.
prestidigitation [prɛstidiʒita'sjɔ̃], *n.f.* conjuring, sleight of hand.
prestige [prɛs'tiːʒ], *n.m.* marvel; illusion, magic spell; prestige.
prestigieux [prɛsti'ʒjø], *a.* (*fem.* -**euse**) marvellous, amazing.
(C) **presto** [prɛs'to], *n.m.* pressure cooker.
présumer [prezy'me], *v.t.* to presume, to suppose.
présure [pre'zyːr], *n.f.* rennet.
prêt (1) [prɛ], *a.* ready, prepared.
prêt (2) [prɛ], *n.m.* loan; (*Mil.*) pay.
prétantaine [pretɑ̃'tɛn], *n.f. courir la prétantaine*, to gad about.
prêté [prɛ'te], *a.* lent.
prétendant [pretɑ̃'dɑ̃], *n.m.* (*fem.* -**e**) claimant.—*n.m.* suitor; pretender (*to the throne*).
prétendre [pre'tɑ̃ːdr], *v.t.* to claim, to lay claim to; to mean; affirm.—*v.i.* to lay claim (*to*); to aspire (*à*).
prétendu [pretɑ̃'dy], *a.* pretended, supposed, sham, so-called, would-be.—*n.m.* (*fem.* -**e**) future husband *or* wife.
prétentieux [pretɑ̃'sjø], *a.* (*fem.* -**euse**) pretentious, assuming.
prétention [pretɑ̃'sjɔ̃], *n.f.* pretension, claim; intention, wish; expectation.

prêter [prɛ'te], *v.t.* to lend; to impart; to attribute; to bestow.—*v.i.* to give, to stretch; to invite, to give rise to. **se prêter**, *v.r.* to give way; to lend oneself or itself; to countenance, to favor.
prêteur [prɛ'tœːr], *n.m.* (*fem.* -**euse**) lender.
prétexte [pre'tɛkst], *n.m.* pretext, pretence; plea.
prétexter [pretɛks'te], *v.t.* to allege (*as pretext*), to pretend, to feign.
prétoire [pre'twaːr], *n.m.* (*Rom. Ant.*) praetorium.
prétorien [preto'rjɛ̃], *a.* (*fem.* -**enne**) praetorian.
prêtre [prɛːtr], *n.m.* priest.
prêtresse [prɛ'trɛs], *n.f.* priestess.
prêtrise [prɛ'triːz], *n.f.* priesthood.
preuve [prœːv], *n.f.* proof; evidence, testimony.
preux [prø], *a. inv.* gallant, doughty, valiant.—*n.m.* valiant knight.
prévaloir [preva'lwaːr], *v.i. irr.* (*conjug. like* VALOIR) to prevail. **se prévaloir**, *v.r.* to take advantage, to avail oneself; to boast.
prévaricateur [prevarika'tœːr], *a.* (*fem.* -**trice**) dishonest, unjust.—*n.m.* (*fem.* -**trice**) betrayer of trust.
prévarication [prevarika'sjɔ̃], *n.f.* betrayal of trust, maladministration of justice.
prévariquer [prevari'ke], *v.i.* to betray one's trust.
prévenance [prev'nɑ̃ːs], *n.f.* (*pl.*) kind attentions.
prévenant [prev'nɑ̃], *a.* obliging, kind; prepossessing, engaging.
prévenir [prev'niːr], *v.t. irr.* (*conjug. like* TENIR) to precede; to forestall; to prevent; to prepossess, to predispose; to warn. **se prévenir**, *v.r.* to be prejudiced.
préventif [prevɑ̃'tif], *a.* (*fem.* -**tive**) preventive.
prévention [prevɑ̃'sjɔ̃], *n.f.* prepossession, prejudice; suspicion; accusation.
préventivement [prevɑ̃tiv'mɑ̃], *adv.* by way of prevention; while awaiting trial.
prévenu [prev'ny], *a.* forestalled, anticipated; prejudiced; accused.—*n.m.* (*fem.* -**e**) the accused.
prévisible [previ'zibl], *a.* foreseeable.
prévision [previ'zjɔ̃], *n.f.* forecast; estimate, expectation.
prévoir [pre'vwaːr], *v.t. irr.* to foresee, to anticipate.
prévôt [pre'vo], *n.m.* provost.
prévôté [prevo'te], *n.f.* provostship; military police.
prévoyance [prevwa'jɑ̃ːs], *n.f.* foresight, forethought, prudence.
prévoyant [prevwa'jɑ̃], *a.* provident, prudent, careful.
prié [pri'je], *a.* invited (*to a feast etc.*).
prie-Dieu [pri'djø], *n.m. inv.* praying-stool.
prier [pri'je], *v.t.* to pray, to beseech; to request; to invite.
prière [pri'jɛːr], *n.f.* prayer; request, entreaty; invitation.
prieur [pri'jœːr], *n.m.* prior (*superior of a convent*).
prieure [pri'jœːr], *n.f.* prioress.
prieuré [prijœ're], *n.m.* priory.
primaire [pri'mɛːr], *a.* primary.

primat [pri'ma], *n.m.* primate, metropolitan.
primauté [primo'te], *n.f.* primacy, priority, pre-eminence; the lead (*at cards, dice etc.*).
prime [prim], *a.* first.—*n.f.* premium; subsidy; (*Mil.*) bounty; bonus, prize; (*Fenc.*) prime; (*Comm.*) free gift; **certificat de primes**, debenture; **faire prime**, to be at a premium.
primer [pri'me], *v.t.* to surpass, to excel.—*v.i.* to play first, to lead (*at games*); to excel.
primeur [pri'mœ:r], *n.f.* early vegetables, fruit, flowers, etc.; early sentiment, love etc.; freshness, bloom.
primevère [prim'vɛ:r], *n.f.* (*Bot.*) primula, primrose, cowslip.
primitif [primi'tif], *a.* (*fem.* **-tive**) first, early, primitive, aboriginal; pristine.—*n.m.* (*Gram., Paint.*) primitive.
primitivement [primitiv'mã], *adv.* primitively, originally.
primo [pri'mo], *adv.* first, in the first place.
primordial [primor'djal], *a.* (*m. pl.* **-aux**) primordial.
prince [prɛ̃:s], *n.m.* prince.
princeps [prɛ̃'sɛps], *a. inv.* **édition princeps**, first edition.
princesse [prɛ̃'sɛs], *n.f.* princess.
princier [prɛ̃'sje], *a.* (*fem.* **-ière**) princely, like a prince.
principal [prɛ̃si'pal], *a.* (*m. pl.* **-aux**) principal, chief, most important.—*n.m.* chief thing, principal point; principal, capital (*money*); headmaster (*of a collège*); (*pl.*) chief personages (*of a town etc.*).
principalement [prɛ̃sipal'mã], *adv.* principally, chiefly.
principauté [prɛ̃sipo'te], *n.f.* principality, princedom.
principe [prɛ̃'sip], *n.m.* beginning, source, basis; principle; (*pl.*) principles, rudiments; **dès le principe**, from the very first; **en principe**, as a rule.
printanier [prɛ̃ta'nje], *a.* (*fem.* **-ière**) spring-like, vernal; (*fig.*) youthful, early.
printemps [prɛ̃'tã], *n.m.* spring, spring-time; (*fig.*) prime, bloom.
priorité [priori'te], *n.f.* priority.
pris [pri], *a.* taken, caught, seized; frozen.
prisable [pri'zabl], *a.* estimable, worthy of esteem.
prise [pri:z], *n.f.* taking, capture; prize; hold, purchase; grip; quarrel; dose; pinch (*of snuff etc.*); (*pl.*) fighting.
priser (1) [pri'ze], *v.t., v.i.* to (take) snuff.
priser (2) [pri'ze], *v.t.* to appraise, to estimate; to esteem.
priseur [pri'zœ:r], *n.m.* **commissaire priseur**, auctioneer, valuer.
prismatique [prisma'tik], *a.* prismatic.
prisme [prism], *n.m.* prism.
prison [pri'zɔ̃], *n.f.* prison, jail; imprisonment.
prisonnier [prizo'nje], *n.m.* (*fem.* **-ière**) prisoner.
privation [priva'sjɔ̃], *n.f.* privation; want, need.
privauté [privo'te], *n.f.* extreme familiarity or liberty.
privé [pri've], *a.* and *n.m.* (*fem.* **-ée**) private; familiar, intimate; tame (*of animals*).

priver [pri've], *v.t.* to deprive, to bereave; to tame (*animals etc.*). **se priver**, *v.r.* to deprive or stint oneself; to abstain (*de*).
privilège [privi'lɛ:ʒ], *n.m.* privilege; license; prerogative, grant.
privilégié [privile'ʒje], *a.* privileged; licensed; entitled to preference (*of creditors*); preference (*of shares*).—*n.m.* (*fem.* **-ée**) privileged person.
privilégier [privile'ʒje], *v.t.* to privilege; to license.
prix [pri], *n.m. inv.* price, cost, value; rate, return; reward, prize; stakes (*race for prize*); **à prix d'argent**, for money; **à vil prix**, dirt cheap; **prix coûtant**, cost price; **prix de gros**, wholesale price; **remporter le prix**, to carry off the prize.
probabilité [probabili'te], *n.f.* probability, likelihood.
probable [pro'babl], *a.* probable, likely, credible.
probablement [probabla'mã], *adv.* probably.
probant [pro'bã], *a.* convincing, conclusive.
probation [proba'sjɔ̃], *n.f.* (*Eccles.*) probation.
probe [prob], *a.* honest, upright.
probité [probi'te], *n.f.* probity, honesty, integrity.
problématique [problema'tik], *a.* problematical; questionable, doubtful.
problématiquement [problematik'mã], *adv.* problematically.
problème [pro'blɛm], *n.m.* problem.
procédé [prose'de], *n.m.* behavior, proceeding, conduct; process, operation; (*Billiards*) cue tip.
procéder [prose'de], *v.i.* (*conjug. like* CÉDER) to proceed, to arise, to originate (*de*); to behave.
procédure [prose'dy:r], *n.f.* procedure; proceedings.
procès [pro'sɛ], *n.m.* lawsuit, action, trial; (*Anat.*) process.
procession [prosɛ'sjɔ̃], *n.f.* procession.
processionnel [prosɛsjo'nɛl], *a.* (*fem.* **-elle**) processional.
procès-verbal [prosɛvɛr'bal], *n.m.* (*pl.* **-verbaux**) official report; minute of proceedings; police report.
prochain [pro'ʃɛ̃], *a.* near, nearest, next.—*n.m.* neighbor, fellow creature.
prochainement [proʃɛn'mã], *adv.* shortly, soon.
proche [proʃ], *a.* near, neighboring; nigh, approaching.—*prep.* and *adv.* near, nigh; **de proche en proche**, gradually.—*n.m.* (*usu. in pl.*) near relation, kin, kindred.
proclamation [proklama'sjɔ̃], *n.f.* proclamation.
proclamer [prokla'me], *v.t.* to proclaim, to announce, to publish; to disclose.
proclivité [proklivi'te], *n.f.* proclivity, slope.
procréateur [prokrea'tœ:r], *a.* (*fem.* **-trice**) procreative.—*n.m.* (*fem.* **-trice**) procreator.
procréation [prokrea'sjɔ̃], *n.f.* procreation.
procréer [prokre'e], *v.t.* to procreate, to beget.
procurateur [prokyra'tœ:r], *n.m.* (*Hist.*) procurator.
procuration [prokyra'sjɔ̃], *n.f.* procuration, power of attorney, proxy (*deed*).

257

procurer [prɔky're], *v.t.* to procure, to obtain. **se procurer,** *v.r.* to procure, to get for oneself.

procureur [prɔky'rœːr], *n.m.* (*fem.* **procuratrice**) attorney, procurator, proxy.

prodigalement [prɔdigal'mɑ̃], *adv.* prodigally, extravagantly.

prodigalité [prɔdigali'te], *n.f.* prodigality, lavishness.

prodige [prɔ'diːʒ], *n.m.* prodigy, marvel.

prodigieusement [prɔdiʒjøz'mɑ̃], *adv.* prodigiously.

prodigieux [prɔdi'ʒjø], *a.* (*fem.* **-euse**) prodigious, wonderful; stupendous.

prodigue [prɔ'dig], *a.* prodigal, lavish; wasteful.—*n.* prodigal, spendthrift.

prodiguer [prɔdi'ge], *v.t.* to be prodigal of; to waste, to squander. **se prodiguer,** *v.r.* to make oneself cheap; not to spare oneself.

prodrome [prɔ'droːm], *n.m.* introduction, preface, preamble.

producteur [prɔdyk'tœːr], *a.* (*fem.* **-trice**) productive.—*n.m.* (*fem.* **-trice**) producer.

productif [prɔdyk'tif], *a.* (*fem.* **-tive**) productive.

production [prɔdyk'sjɔ̃], *n.f.* production; produce, product (*of nature*); yield, output.

productivité [prɔdyktivi'te], *n.f.* productivity; productiveness.

produire [prɔ'dɥiːr], *v.t. irr.* (*conjug. like* CONDUIRE) to produce; to bear; to exhibit; to introduce. **se produire,** *v.r.* to put oneself forward; to occur, to happen.

produit [prɔ'dɥi], *n.m.* produce, product, production; proceeds.

proéminence [prɔemi'nɑ̃ːs], *n.f.* prominence; protuberance.

proéminent [prɔemi'nɑ̃], *a.* prominent, protuberant.

profanateur [prɔfana'tœːr], *n.m.* (*fem.* **-trice**) profaner.

profanation [prɔfana'sjɔ̃], *n.f.* profanation.

profane [prɔ'fan], *a.* profane; secular.—*n.* profane person; outsider; layman.

profaner [prɔfa'ne], *v.t.* to profane, to desecrate; to defile.

proférer [prɔfe're], *v.t.* (*conjug. like* CÉDER) to utter, to pronounce.

professer [prɔfe'se], *v.t.* to profess; to exercise, to practice; to teach, to lecture on. —*v.i.* to lecture, to teach.

professeur [prɔfe'sœːr], *n.m.* (*fem.* **femme professeur**) professor, lecturer (*at university*); teacher in secondary schools.

profession [prɔfe'sjɔ̃], *n.f.* profession, declaration; calling, business.

professionnel [prɔfesjɔ'nɛl], *a.* and *n.m.* (*fem.* **-elle**) (*Spt. etc.*) professional.

professoral [prɔfesɔ'ral], *a.* (*m. pl.* **-aux**) professorial.

professorat [prɔfesɔ'ra], *n.m.* professorship, lectureship; mastership (*of lycée or collège*).

profil [prɔ'fil], *n.m.* profile, side view; outline; (*Drawing*) section.

profiler [prɔfi'le], *v.t.* to represent *or* show in profile. **se profiler,** *v.r.* to appear in profile, to be outlined.

profit [prɔ'fi], *n.m.* profit, gain; benefit, utility, use; (*pl.*) perquisites.

profitable [prɔfi'tabl], *a.* profitable, advantageous.

profiter [prɔfi'te], *v.i.* to profit, to gain, to benefit; to take advantage of (*de*).

profiteur [prɔfi'tœːr], *n.m.* (*fem.* **-euse**) (*pej.*) profiteer.

profond [prɔ'fɔ̃], *a.* deep; profound; vast; sound (*of sleep etc.*); downright; dark (*of night etc.*).—*n.m.* depth, abyss.

profondément [prɔfɔ̃de'mɑ̃], *adv.* deeply, profoundly, greatly; soundly.

profondeur [prɔfɔ̃'dœːr], *n.f.* depth; profundity; penetration; extent.

profus [prɔ'fy], *a.* profuse.

profusément [prɔfyze'mɑ̃], *adv.* profusely.

profusion [prɔfy'zjɔ̃], *n.f.* profusion.

progéniture [prɔʒeni'tyːr], *n.f.* progeny.

prognostique [prɔgnɔs'tik], *a.* (*Med.*) prognostic.

programmation [prɔgrama'sjɔ̃], *n.f.* programming.

programme [prɔ'gram], *n.m.* (*Theat. etc.*) program; (*sch.*) curriculum, syllabus.

progrès [prɔ'grɛ], *n.m.* progress; advancement, improvement, development.

progresser [prɔgrɛ'se], *v.i.* to progress, to get on.

progressif [prɔgrɛ'sif], *a.* (*fem.* **-ive**) progressive.

progression [prɔgrɛ'sjɔ̃], *n.f.* progression.

progressiste [prɔgrɛ'sist], *a.* progressive.— *n.* progressist, progressive.

progressivement [prɔgrɛsiv'mɑ̃], *adv.* progressively.

prohiber [prɔi'be], *v.t.* to forbid, to prohibit.

prohibitif [prɔibi'tif], *a.* (*fem.* **-tive**) prohibitive, exorbitant.

prohibition [prɔibi'sjɔ̃], *n.f.* prohibition.

proie [prwa], *n.f.* prey, prize, booty.

projecteur [prɔʒɛk'tœːr], *n.m.* searchlight; projector; floodlight.

projectile [prɔʒɛk'til], *a.* and *n.m.* projectile, missile.

projection [prɔʒɛk'sjɔ̃], *n.f.* projection; (*Cine.*) **appareil de projection,** projector.

projectionniste [prɔʒɛksjɔ'nist], *n.* (*Cine.*) projectionist.

projet [prɔ'ʒɛ], *n.m.* project, plan, idea; rough draft; **homme à projets,** schemer.

projeter [prɔʒ'te], *v.t.* (*conjug. like* APPELER) to project, to throw; to delineate, to plan, to design; to contemplate, to intend.—*v.i.* to scheme, to form projects. **se projeter,** *v.r.* to project, to stand out.

prolétaire [prɔle'tɛːr], *a.* and *n.m.* proletarian.

prolétariat [prɔleta'rja], *n.m.* proletariat.

prolifique [prɔli'fik], *a.* prolific.

prolixe [prɔ'liks], *a.* verbose.

prologue [prɔ'lɔg], *n.m.* prologue.

prolongation [prɔlɔ̃ga'sjɔ̃], *n.f.* prolongation; extension.

prolongement [prɔlɔ̃ʒ'mɑ̃], *n.m.* prolongation, extension.

prolonger [prɔlɔ̃'ʒe], *v.t.* (*conjug. like* MANGER) to prolong, to lengthen, to protract; to draw out. **se prolonger,** *v.r.* to be protracted; to extend; to continue.

promenade [prɔm'nad], *n.f.* walk; walking; promenade; drive, excursion, pleasure trip.

promener [prɔm'ne], *v.t.* to take out for a walk, for a drive, for a ride, for an airing; to cast (*one's eyes*) over; to run or pass (*one's hand, fingers*) over. **se promener,** *v.r.* to walk, to go for a walk, ramble, drive, row, sail etc.; to stroll.

promeneur [prɔm'nœːr], *n.m.* (*fem.* **-euse**) walker; rider; person taking a drive.

promenoir [prɔm'nwaːr], *n.m.* covered walk; promenade (*in a concert hall etc.*).

promesse [prɔ'mɛs], *n.f.* promise; promissory note.

promettre [prɔ'mɛtr], *v.t. irr.* (*conjug. like* METTRE) to promise; to forebode.—*v.i.* to be promising. **se promettre**, *v.r.* to promise oneself; to purpose; to promise each other.

promis [prɔ'mi], *a.* promised; intended, engaged.—*n.m.* (*fem.* **-e**) fiancé *or* fiancée.

promiscuité [prɔmiskɥi'te], *n.f.* promiscuity.

promontoire [prɔmɔ̃'twaːr], *n.m.* promontory, headland.

promoteur [prɔmɔ'tœːr], *n.m.* (*fem.* **-trice**) promoter.

promotion [prɔmo'sjɔ̃], *n.f.* promotion, preferment.

promouvoir [prɔmu'vwaːr], *v.t. irr.* (*conjug. like* MOUVOIR) to promote, to advance.

prompt [prɔ̃], *a.* prompt, quick, active; sudden, swift; hasty.

promptement [prɔ̃t'mã], *adv.* promptly.

promptitude [prɔ̃ti'tyːd], *n.f.* promptitude, promptness; suddenness; hastiness.

promulgation [prɔmylga'sjɔ̃], *n.f.* promulgation.

promulguer [prɔmyl'ge], *v.t.* to promulgate.

prône [proːn], *n.m.* sermon (*at Mass*); (*fig.*) lecture, rebuke.

prôner [pro'ne], *v.t.* to lecture, to sermonize; to extol.—*v.i.* to sermonize.

prôneur [pro'nœːr], *n.m.* (*fem.* **-euse**) long-winded preacher.

pronom [prɔ'nɔ̃], *n.m.* (*Gram.*) pronoun.

prononçable [prɔnɔ̃'sabl], *a.* pronounceable.

prononcé [prɔnɔ̃'se], *a.* pronounced, decided, marked; (*Paint. etc.*) prominent; broad (*of speech*).—*n.m.* judgment delivered, sentence.

prononcer [prɔnɔ̃'se], *v.t.* (*conjug. like* COMMENCER) to pronounce, to utter, to say, to declare; to pass (*a verdict etc.*).—*v.i.* to declare one's sentiments, to decide with authority. **se prononcer**, *v.r.* to declare oneself, to express one's opinion, to give a verdict; to be pronounced.

prononciation [prɔnɔ̃sja'sjɔ̃], *n.f.* pronunciation; utterance.

pronostic [prɔnɔs'tik], *n.m.* prognostic; prognostication; (*Med.*) prognosis; weather forecast; (*racing*) tip.

propagande [prɔpa'gãːd], *n.f.* propaganda.

propagandiste [prɔpagã'dist], *n.* propagandist.

propagateur [prɔpaga'tœːr], *a.* (*fem.* **-trice**) propagating, spreading.—*n.m.* (*fem* **-trice**) propagator.

propagation [prɔpaga'sjɔ̃], *n.f.* propagation, spreading, diffusion.

propager [prɔpa'ʒe], *v.t.* (*conjug. like* MANGER) to propagate, to spread abroad, to diffuse. **se propager**, *v.r.* to be propagated, to spread.

propension [prɔpã'sjɔ̃], *n.f.* propensity, tendency.

prophète [prɔ'fɛːt], *n.m.* prophet, seer.

prophétesse [prɔfe'tɛs], *n.f.* prophetess.

prophétie [prɔfe'si], *n.f.* prophecy, prophesying.

prophétique [prɔfe'tik], *a.* prophetic.

prophétiser [prɔfeti'ze], *v.t.* to prophesy, to foretell.

propice [prɔ'pis], *a.* propitious, favorable.

propitiation [prɔpisja'sjɔ̃], *n.f.* propitiation.

propitiatoire [prɔpisja'twaːr], *a.* propitiatory.

proportion [prɔpɔr'sjɔ̃], *n.f.* proportion, ratio.

proportionné [prɔpɔrsjɔ'ne], *a.* proportioned, suited.

proportionnel [prɔpɔrsjɔ'nɛl], *a.* (*fem.* **-elle**) proportional.

proportionner [prɔpɔrsjɔ'ne], *v.t.* to proportion, to adjust, to adapt.

propos [prɔ'po], *n.m.* talk, words; remark; purpose, resolution; (*pl.*) idle remarks, tittle-tattle; *à propos*, apt, to the purpose; by the way; *à propos de*, with respect to; *à quel propos?* what about? *de propos délibéré*, of set purpose; *mal à propos*, ill-timed; *propos de table*, table-talk; *venir fort à propos*, to come in the nick of time.

proposer [prɔpo'ze], *v.t.* to propose; to propound, to move; to designate, to set up.—*v.i.* to propose. **se proposer**, *v.r.* to propose oneself; to intend, to have in view.

proposeur [prɔpo'zœːr], *n.m.* (*fem.* **-euse**) proposer, propounder.

proposition [prɔpozi'sjɔ̃], *n.f.* proposal; proposition; motion; (*Gram.*) clause.

propre [prɔpr], *a.* own; very, same, selfsame; proper; appropriate, suitable; good, right, correct; clean, neat, tidy; *le mot propre*, the right word; *peu propre*, inappropriate; dirty.—*n.m.* characteristic, property; proper sense; (*Law*) real property.

propre à rien [prɔpra'rjɛ̃], *n. inv.* good for nothing.

proprement [prɔprə'mã], *adv.* properly, correctly; cleanly, neatly.

propret [prɔ'prɛ], *a.* (*fem.* **-ette**) spruce, neat, tidy.

propreté [prɔprə'te], *n.f.* cleanliness; neatness.

propriétaire [prɔprie'tɛːr], *n.* owner, proprietor, proprietress; landlord, householder.

propriété [prɔprie'te], *n.f.* property; estate; characteristic; *propriété littéraire*, copyright.

propulser [prɔpyl'se], *v.t.* (*Naut., Av.*) to propel.

propulseur [prɔpyl'sœːr], *n.m.* propeller.

propulsif [prɔpyl'sif], *a.* (*fem.* **-sive**) propelling, propellent.

propulsion [prɔpyl'sjɔ̃], *n.f.* propulsion.

prorogation [prɔrɔga'sjɔ̃], *n.f.* adjournment, prorogation (*of Parliament etc.*); extension.

proroger [prɔrɔ'ʒe], *v.t.* (*conjug. like* MANGER) to prolong the time of; to prorogue (*Parliament etc.*).

prosaïque [prɔza'ik], *a.* prosaic; banal; prosy.

prosaïquement [prɔzaik'mã], *adv.* prosaically.

prosateur [prɔza'tœːr], *n.m.* prose writer.

proscription [prɔskrip'sjɔ̃], *n.f.* proscription.

proscrire [prɔs'kriːr], *v.t. irr.* (*conjug. like* ÉCRIRE) to proscribe, to outlaw; to banish.

259

proscrit

proscrit [prɔs'kri], *a.* proscribed, forbidden.
—*n.m.* (*fem.* **-e**) proscribed person, outlaw;
exile.

prose [proːz], *n.f.* prose.

prosodie [prɔzɔ'di], *n.f.* prosody.

prospecter [prɔspɛk'te], *v.t.* to prospect (*for
oil, minerals*).

prospecteur [prɔspɛk'tœːr], *n.m.* prospector.

prospectus [prɔspɛk'tyːs], *n.m. inv.* prospectus; handbill.

prospère [prɔs'pɛːr], *a.* prosperous, thriving.

prospérer [prɔspe're], *v.i.* (*conjug. like*
CÉDER) to prosper, to be prosperous, to
thrive.

prospérité [prɔsperi'te], *n.f.* prosperity.

prostate [prɔs'tat], *n.f.* (*Anat.*) prostate.

prosternation [prɔstɛrna'sjɔ̃], *n.f.*, **pros-
ternement** [prɔstɛrnə'mã], *n.m.* prostration,
obeisance.

prosterner [prɔstɛr'ne], *v.t.* to prostrate. **se
prosterner**, *v.r.* to prostrate oneself, to
bow low.

prostituée [prɔsti'tɥe], *n.f.* prostitute.

prostituer [prɔsti'tɥe], *v.t.* to prostitute. **se
prostituer**, *v.r.* to prostitute oneself.

prostitution [prɔstity'sjɔ̃], *n.f.* prostitution.

prostration [prɔstra'sjɔ̃], *n.f.* prostration.

protagoniste [prɔtagɔ'nist], *n.m.* protagonist.

protecteur [prɔtɛk'tœːr], *a.* (*fem.* **-trice**)
protective; patronizing.—*n.m.* (*fem.* **-trice**)
protector, protectress; patron, patroness.—
n.m. (*Eng.*) guard (*for machine tool*).

protection [prɔtɛk'sjɔ̃], *n.f.* protection,
shelter; support, patronage.

protectorat [prɔtɛktɔ'ra], *n.m.* protectorate.

protégé [prɔte'ʒe], *n.m.* (*fem.* **-ée**) favorite,
dependant.

protéger [prɔte'ʒe], *v.t.* (*conjug. like* ASSIÉGER)
to protect, to defend; to patronize, to
favor.

protège-vue [prɔtɛʒ'vy], *n.m. inv.* eye-shade.

protéine [prɔte'in], *n.f.* protein.

protestant [prɔtɛs'tã], *a.* and *n.m.* (*fem.* **-e**)
Protestant.

protestantisme [prɔtɛstã'tism], *n.m.* Protestantism.

protestation [prɔtɛsta'sjɔ̃], *n.f.* protestation,
protest.

protester [prɔtɛs'te], *v.t.* to protest, to
affirm.—*v.i.* to protest.

protocole [prɔtɔ'kɔl], *n.m.* protocol.

proton [prɔ'tɔ̃], *n.m.* proton.

protoplasma [prɔtɔplas'ma], **protoplasme**
[prɔtɔ'plasm], *n.m.* protoplasm.

prototype [prɔtɔ'tip], *n.m.* prototype.

protubérance [prɔtybe'rãːs], *n.f.* protuberance.

protubérant [prɔtybe'rã], *a.* protuberant.

proue [pru], *n.f.* prow, stem, bows (*of ship*).

prouesse [pru'ɛs], *n.f.* prowess, valor; feat.

prouver [pru've], *v.t.* to prove; to substantiate; to show.

provenance [prɔv'nãːs], *n.f.* origin, source;
(*pl.*) produce, commodities.

provençal [prɔvã'sal], *a.* (*m. pl.* **-aux**)
Provençal.—*n.m.* Provençal (*language*);
(**Provençal**, *fem.* **-ale**) Provençal (*person*).

provenir [prɔv'niːr], *v.i. irr.* (*conjug. like*
TENIR *but with aux.* ÊTRE) to issue, proceed,
spring, originate *or* come from (*de*).

proverbe [prɔ'vɛrb], *n.m.* proverb, saying.

proverbial [prɔvɛr'bjal], *a.* (*m. pl.* **-aux**)
proverbial.

providence [prɔvi'dãːs], *n.f.* providence.

providentiel [prɔvidã'sjɛl], *a.* (*fem.* **-elle**)
providential.

provigner [prɔvi'ɲe], *v.t.* to layer (*vines*).

provin [prɔ'vɛ̃], *n.m.* layer (*of a vine*).

province [prɔ'vɛ̃ːs], *n.f.* province, shire;
country; **en province**, in the country, in
the provinces.

provincial [prɔvɛ̃'sjal], *a.* (*m. pl.* **-aux**)
provincial; countrified.—*n.m.* (*fem.* **-e**)
provincial, country person.

proviseur [prɔvi'zœːr], *n.m.* headmaster (*of
a lycée*).

provision [prɔvi'zjɔ̃], *n.f.* provision, stock,
store, supply; deposit; (*Comm.*) reserve
funds.

provisionnel [prɔvizjɔ'nɛl], *a.* (*fem.* **-elle**)
provisional.

provisoire [prɔvi'zwaːr], *a.* provisional,
temporary.—*n.m.* provisional nature (*of
something*).

provisoirement [prɔvizwar'mã], *adv.* provisionally, temporarily.

provocant [prɔvɔ'kã], *a.* provoking, provocative; exciting.

provocateur [prɔvɔka'tœːr], *a.* (*fem.* **-trice**)
provoking, provocative; **agent provoca-
teur**, agent hired to instigate a riot etc.—
n.m. (*fem.* **-trice**) provoker; aggressor.

provocation [prɔvɔka'sjɔ̃], *n.f.* provocation.

provoquer [prɔvɔ'ke], *v.t.* to provoke, to
incite, to call forth; to instigate.

proximité [prɔksimi'te], *n.f.* proximity, nearness.

prude [pryd], *a.* prudish.—*n.f.* prude.

prudemment [pryda'mã], *adv.* prudently,
discreetly, cautiously.

prudence [pry'dãːs], *n.f.* carefulness, prudence.

prudent [pry'dã], *a.* prudent, discreet; advisable.

pruderie [pry'dri], *n.f.* prudery, prudishness.

prud'homme [pry'dɔm], *n.m.* upright,
honest man; (*Ind.*) arbitrator.

pruine [prɥin], *n.f.* bloom (*on fruits*).

prune [pryn], *n.f.* plum.

pruneau [pry'no], *n.m.* (*pl.* **-eaux**) prune.

prunelle (1) [pry'nɛl], *n.f.* sloe; sloe gin.

prunelle (2) [pry'nɛl], *n.f.* pupil, apple (*of the
eye*), eyeball.

prunellier [prynɛ'lje], *n.m.* sloe tree, black-
thorn.

prunier [pry'nje], *n.m.* plum tree.

Prusse [prys], la, *f.* Prussia.

prussien [pry'sjɛ̃], *a.* (*fem.* **-enne**) Prussian.
—*n.m.* (**Prussien**, *fem.* **-enne**) Prussian
(*person*).

prussique [pry'sik], *a.* (*Chem.*) prussic.

psalmiste [psal'mist], *n.m.* psalmist.

psalmodie [psalmɔ'di], *n.f.* psalmody, inton-
ing; (*fig.*) sing-song.

psalmodier [psalmɔ'dje], *v.t., v.i.* to recite,
to chant (*as the psalms*); to read *or* recite in a
sing-song manner.

psaume [psoːm], *n.m.* psalm.

psautier [pso'tje], *n.m.* psalter, psalm book.

pseudonyme [psødɔ'nim], *a.* pseudonymous.
—*n.m.* pseudonym, nom-de-plume.

psychanalyse [psikana'liːz], *n.f.* psycho-
analysis.

psychanalyste [psikana'list], *n.m.* psycho-analyst.

psychiatre [psi'kja:tr], *n.m.* psychiatrist.

psychiatrie [psikja'tri], *n.f.* psychiatry.

psychologie [psikɔlɔ'ʒi], *n.f.* psychology.

psychologique [psikɔlɔ'ʒik], *a.* psychological.

psychologue [psikɔ'lɔg], *n.* psychologist.

puant [pɥɑ̃], *a.* stinking; foul.

puanteur [pɥɑ̃'tœːr], *n.f.* stench, stink.

pubère [py'bɛːr], *a.* pubescent, puberal.

puberté [pybɛr'te], *n.f.* puberty.

public [py'blik], *a.* (*fem.* **-ique**) public; notorious; *la chose publique*, the common weal, the State.—*n.m.* public.

publication [pyblika'sjɔ̃], *n.f.* publication; publishing, proclamation.

publiciste [pybli'sist], *n.m.* publicist, journalist.

publicité [pyblisi'te], *n.f.* publicity; advertising.

publier [py'blje], *v.t.* to publish, to make public, to proclaim; to issue.

publiquement [pyblik'mã], *adv.* in public.

puce (1) [pys], *a. inv.* puce, puce-colored.

puce (2) [pys], *n.f.* flea.

puceron [pys'rɔ̃], *n.m.* plant louse, greenfly.

pudeur [py'dœːr], *n.f.* modesty; bashfulness, shame; reserve.

pudibond [pydi'bɔ̃], *a.* bashful; prudish.

pudicité [pydisi'te], *n.f.* modesty, chastity.

pudique [py'dik], *a.* chaste, modest; bashful.

pudiquement [pydik'mã], *adv.* modestly.

puer [pɥe], *v.t.* (*fam.*) to smell of, to reek of.—*v.i.* to stink.

puéril [pɥe'ril], *a.* juvenile, childish, puerile.

puérilement [pɥeril'mã], *adv.* childishly.

puérilité [pɥerili'te], *n.f.* puerility, childishness.

pugilat [pyʒi'la], *n.m.* pugilism, boxing.

pugiliste [pyʒi'list], *n.m.* pugilist, boxer.

pugnace [pyg'nas], *a.* pugnacious.

pugnacité [pygnasi'te], *n.f.* pugnacity.

puîné [pɥi'ne], *a.* (*fem.* **-ée**) younger (*brother or sister*).

puis [pɥi], *adv.* then, afterwards, after that, next; besides.

puisage [pɥi'za:ʒ], **puisement** [pɥiz'mã], *n.m.* drawing up; drawing water.

puisard [pɥi'za:r], *n.m.* cesspool; sump, water-sump.

puisatier [pɥiza'tje], *n.m.* well-sinker; shaft-sinker (*in mining*).

puisement [PUISAGE].

puiser [pɥi'ze], *v.t.* to draw, to fetch up (*a liquid*); (*fig.*) to imbibe.

puisque [pɥisk], *conj.* since, as, seeing that.

puissamment [pɥisa'mã], *adv.* powerfully; extremely, very.

puissance [pɥi'sã:ə], *n.f.* power; force; dominion, sway; influence.

puissant [pɥi'sã], *a.* powerful, mighty; lusty, stout; strong.

puits [pɥi], *n.m. inv.* well; pit, shaft.

pullulation [pylyla'sjɔ̃], *n.f.*, **pullulement** [pylyl'mã], *n.m.* pullulation, swarming.

pulluler [pyly'le], *v.i.* to multiply, to pullulate, to swarm.

pulmonaire [pylmɔ'nɛːr], *a.* pulmonary; *phthisie pulmonaire*, consumption.

pulmonique [pylmɔ'nik], *a.* and *n.* consumptive.

pulpe [pylp], *n.f.* pulp.

pulper [pyl'pe], *v.t.* to pulp.

pulpeux [pyl'pø], *a.* (*fem.* **-euse**) pulpous, pulpy.

pulsatif [pylsa'tif], *a.* (*fem.* **-tive**) pulsatory, throbbing.

pulsation [pylsa'sjɔ̃], *n.f.* beating of the pulse, pulsation, throbbing.

pulvérin [pylve'rɛ̃], *n.m.* spray (*from waterfalls*).

pulvérisateur [pylveriza'tœːr], *n.m.* pulverizator, vaporizer; spray, atomiser.

pulvérisation [pylveriza'sjɔ̃], *n.f.* pulverization.

pulvériser [pylveri'ze], *v.t.* to reduce to powder or dust, to pulverize; to atomize; (*fig.*) to annihilate.

pulvérulent [pylvery'lã], *a.* pulverulent, powdery.

puma [py'ma], *n.m.* puma, cougar.

pumicin [pymi'sɛ̃], *n.m.* palm oil.

punaise [py'nɛːz], *n.f.* bug; thumbtack.

punch [pɛ̃:ʃ], *n.m.* (*Box.*) punch; punch (*beverage*).

punique [py'nik], *a.* Punic.

punir [py'niːr], *v.t.* to punish, to chastise.

punissable [pyni'sabl], *a.* punishable.

punisseur [pyni'sœːr], *a.* (*fem.* **-euse**) punishing, avenging.—*n.m.* (*fem.* **-euse**) punisher; avenger.

punitif [pyni'tif], *a.* (*fem.* **-tive**) punitive.

punition [pyni'sjɔ̃], *n.f.* punishment.

pupille [py'pil], *n.* ward, minor in charge of guardian.—*n.f.* pupil (*of the eye*).

pupitre [py'pitr], *n.m.* desk; music stand.

pur [py:r], *a.* pure, unalloyed; unadulterated; unblemished; innocent, chaste; mere, sheer; neat (*of liquor*); *en pure perte*, to no purpose.

purée [py're], *n.f.* mash, purée, thick soup.

purement [pyr'mã], *adv.* purely; merely.

pureté [pyr'te], *n.f.* purity, guilelessness, innocence; chastity.

purgatif [pyrga'tif], *a.* (*fem.* **-tive**) purgative, purging.—*n.m.* (*Med.*) purgative.

purgation [pyrga'sjɔ̃], *n.f.* purgation, purge.

purgatoire [pyrga'twa:r], *n.m.* purgatory.

purge [pyrʒ], *n.f.* purge; cleansing; disinfection.

purger [pyr'ʒe], *v.t.* (*conjug. like* MANGER) to purge; to cleanse, to purify. **se purger**, *v.r.* to purge oneself; to clear oneself (*of*).

purificateur [pyrifika'tœːr], *a.* (*fem.* **-trice**) purifying.—*n.m.* (*fem.* **-trice**) purifier.

purification [pyrifika'sjɔ̃], *n.f.* purification.

purifier [pyri'fje], *v.t.* to purify, to cleanse; to refine (*metals etc.*). **se purifier**, *v.r.* to purify oneself, to become refined.

puritain [pyri'tɛ̃], *a.* and *n.m.* (*fem.* **-e**) Puritan, puritan.

puritanisme [pyrita'nism], *n.m.* puritanism.

purpurin [pyrpy'rɛ̃], *a.* purplish.

pur-sang [pyr'sã], *n.m. inv.* thoroughbred.

pus [py], *n.m.* pus, matter.

pusillanime [pyzila'nim], *a.* pusillanimous, faint-hearted.

pusillanimité [pyzilanimi'te], *n.f.* pusillanimity.

pustule [pys'tyl], *n.f.* pustule, pimple, blotch.

putatif [pyta'tif], *a.* (*fem.* **-tive**) putative, reputed, supposed.

putativement [pytativ'mã], *adv.* reputedly.

putois [py'twa], *n.m.* polecat, skunk.

putréfaction [pytrefak'sjɔ̃], *n.f.* putrefaction; putrescence.

putréfier [pytre'fje], *v.t.* to putrefy; to rot. **se putréfier**, *v.r.* to putrefy; to rot; to decompose.

putride [py'trid], *a.* putrid.

pygmée [pig'me], *n.m.* pygmy.

pyjama [piʒa'ma], *n.m.* pajamas.

pylône [pi'lo:n], *n.m.* pylon; mast.

pyorrhée [pjɔ're], *n.f.* pyorrhœa.

pyramidal [pirami'dal], *a.* (*m. pl.* **-aux**) pyramidal.

pyramide [pira'mid], *n.f.* pyramid.

python [pi'tɔ̃], *n.m.* python (*snake*).

Q

Q, q [ky] *n.m.* the seventeenth letter of the alphabet.

qu' [k], *elision* [QUE].

quadragénaire [kwadraʒe'nɛːr], *a.* forty years of age.—*n.* person forty years old.

quadrangle [kwa'drɑ̃:gl], *n.m.* quadrangle.

quadrangulaire [kwadrɑ̃gy'lɛːr], *a.* quadrangular, four-cornered.

quadrillage [kadri'ja:ʒ], *n.m.* checker-work, pattern in squares; map grid.

quadrille [ka'dri:j], *n.m.* quadrille (*card game*); quadrille (*dance*); check (*in tapestry*).

quadrillé [kadri'je], *a.* checkered (*of cloth*); ruled in squares (*of paper*).

quadriréacteur [kwadrireak'tœːr], *n.m.* four-engined jet plane.

quadrupède [kwadry'pɛd], *a.* and *n.m.* quadruped.

quadruple [kwa'drypl], *a.* quadruple, four-fold.

quadruplé [kwadry'ple], *n.m.* (*fem.* **-ée**) quadruplet, (*fam.*) quad.

quadrupler [kwadry'ple], *v.t., v.i.* to quadruple, to increase fourfold.

quai [ke], *n.m.* quay, wharf, pier; embankment (*along river*); platform (*railway*).

qualifiable [kali'fjabl], *a.* qualifiable, characterized (*as*).

qualification [kalifika'sjɔ̃], *n.f.* title; designation, qualification.

qualifié [kali'fje], *a.* qualified; named.

qualifier [kali'fje], *v.t.* to qualify; to style. **se qualifier**, *v.r.* to style oneself; to qualify (*for*).

qualité [kali'te], *n.f.* quality; property; excellence; talent; qualification; title; *en qualité de*, in the capacity of.

quand [kɑ̃], *adv.* when, whenever, what time; while.—*conj.* though; *quand même*, even though; all the same.

quant [kɑ̃], *adv.* (*followed by à*) as for, with regard to.

quant-à-soi [kɑ̃ta'swa], *n.m.* reserve, dignity.

quantième [kɑ̃'tjɛm], *n.m.* which (*day of the month etc.*).

quantité [kɑ̃ti'te], *n.f.* quantity; abundance, plenty; variety.

quarantaine [karɑ̃'tɛn], *n.f.* about forty; age of forty; quarantine.

quarante [ka'rɑ̃t], *a.* and *n.m.* forty.

quarantième [karɑ̃'tjɛm], *a.* and *n.* fortieth.

quart [kaːr], *a.* fourth.—*n.m.* quarter, fourth part; point (*of the compass*); quart (*measure*); (*Mil.*) tin cup; (*Naut.*) watch.

quarte [kart], *n.f.* (*Mus.*) fourth; (*Fenc., Piquet*) carte.

quartier [kar'tje], *n.m.* quarter, fourth part; piece, part; ward, district; gammon; (*Mil.*) quarters, barracks.

quartier-maître [kar'je'mɛ:tr], *n.m.* (*pl.* **quartiers-maîtres**) (*Naut.*) leading seaman.

quarto [kwar'to], *adv.* fourthly, in the fourth place.

quartz [kwa:rts], *n.m.* quartz.

quasi [ka'zi], *adv.* almost, as if, quasi.

quasiment [kazi'mɑ̃], *adv.* (*dial.*) almost, nearly, as you might say.

quaternaire [kwater'nɛːr], *a.* quaternary.

quatorze [ka'tɔrz], *a.* and *n.m.* fourteen; fourteenth.

quatorzième [kator'zjɛm], *a.* and *n.* fourteenth.

quatrain [ka'trɛ̃], *n.m.* quatrain.

quatre ['katrə, katr], *a.* and *n.m. inv.* four, fourth.

quatre-temps [katrə'tɑ̃], *n.m. pl.* Ember days.

quatre-vingtième [katrəvɛ̃'tjɛm], *a.* and *n.m.* eightieth.

quatre-vingt(s) [katrə'vɛ̃], *a.* and *n.m.* eighty.

quatrième [ka'trjɛm], *a.* and *n.* fourth.—*n.m.* fourth floor, fourth storey. —*n.f.* (*Piquet*) quart.

quatrièmement [katrjɛm'mɑ̃], *adv.* fourthly.

quatuor [kwaty'ɔr], *n.m.* (*Mus.*) quartet.

que (1) [kə, k], *pron. rel.* whom, that; which; what? on which; *qu'est-ce que c'est?* what is it?

que (2) [kə, k], *conj.* that; than; than that; as, if, whether; when; without; yet; lest; in order that; oh that, may; let; before; so; only, but; *afin que*, in order that; *attendez qu'il vienne*, wait till he comes; *de sorte que*, so that.—*adv.* how, how much, how many; why, wherefore?

quel [kɛl], *a.* (*fem.* **quelle**) what, which, what sort of.

quelconque [kɛl'kɔ̃:k], *a. indef.* any; any whatsoever; mediocre.

quelque ['kɛlkə, kɛlk], *adj.* some, any; a few; whatever, whatsoever.—*adv.* however, howsoever; some, about.

quelquefois [kɛlkə'fwa], *adv.* sometimes.

quelqu'un [kɛl'kœ̃], *pron. indef. m.* someone, somebody; anyone, anybody.—*n.m.* (*fem.* **quel-qu'une**, *pl.* **quelques-uns, quelques-unes**, one (or other), some.

quémander [kemɑ̃'de], *v.t., v.i.* to beg, to solicit.

quémandeur [kemɑ̃'dœːr], *n.m.* (*fem.* **-euse**) importunate beggar.

qu'en-dira-t-on [kɑ̃dira'tɔ̃], *n.m. inv.* public talk, tittle-tattle.

quenelle [kə'nɛl], *n.f.* forcemeat *or* fish ball.

quenotte [kə'nɔt], *n.f.* (*colloq.*) tooth (*of young children*).

quenouille [kə'nuːj], *n.f.* distaff; bed-post.

querelle [kǝ'rɛl], *n.f.* quarrel; row, brawl; feud; cause of dispute; *chercher querelle à*, to pick a quarrel with.

quereller [kǝrɛ'le], *v.t.* to quarrel with; to scold. **se quereller**, *v.r.* to quarrel, to wrangle, to have words.

querelleur [kǝrɛ'lœːr], *a.* (*fem.* **-euse**) quarrelsome.—*n.m.* (*fem.* **-euse**) quarreller, wrangler.

quérir [ke'riːr], *v.t.* to fetch (*employed only in the infinitive with aller, envoyer, venir*).

questeur [kɥɛs'tœːr], *n.m.* quaestor.

question [kɛs'tjɔ̃], *n.f.* question, interrogation; query, point, issue; rack, torture.

questionnaire [kɛstjɔ'nɛːr], *n.m.* questionnaire; book of questions.

questionner [kɛstjɔ'ne], *v.t.* to question, to interrogate.

questionneur [kɛstjɔ'nœːr], *a.* (*fem.* **-euse**) inquisitive.—*n.m.* (*fem.* **-euse**) questioner.

questure [kɥɛs'tyːr], *n.f.* quaestorship; quaestors' office.

quête [kɛːt], *n.f.* quest, search; collection, offertory; (*Hunt.*) beating about.

quêter [kɛ'te], *v.t.* to look for, to seek, to go in quest of, to gather.—*v.i.* to beg.

quêteur [kɛ'tœːr], *n.m.* (*fem.* **-euse**) collector; mendicant (friar).

queue [kø], *n.f.* tail; stalk; stem; end; rear; billiard cue; handle; train (*of robes etc.*); queue, line.

queue-d'aronde [køda'rɔ̃ːd], *n.f.* (*pl.* **queues-d'aronde**) dovetail.

qui [ki], *pron. rel.* and *inter.* who, that, whom, which; whoever, whomsoever, whatever; what; some.

quiconque [ki'kɔ̃ːk], *pron. indef.* whoever, whosoever; whomsoever; whichever.

quiétude [kɥie'tyd], *n.f.* quietude.

quignon [ki'ɲɔ̃], *n.m.* hunch, chunk, hunk (*of bread*).

quille [kiːj], *n.f.* keel; skittle, ninepin.

quiller [ki'je], *v.i.* to throw for partners or for first play (*at skittles*).

quillier [ki'je], *n.m.* skittle alley.

quincaillerie [kɛ̃kaj'ri], *n.f.* ironmongery, hardware.

quincaillier [kɛ̃ka'je], *n.m.* hardware dealer.

quinconce [kɛ̃'kɔ̃ːs], *n.m.* quincunx.

quine [kin], *n.m.* two fives (*at trictrac*); five winning numbers (*in a lottery*).

quinine [ki'nin], *n.f.* quinine.

quinquagénaire [kɥɛ̃kwaʒe'nɛːr], *a.* fifty years old.—*n.* person of fifty.

quinquennal [kɥɛ̃kɥe'nal], *a.* (*m. pl.* **-aux**) quinquennial.

quinquet [kɛ̃'kɛ], *n.m.* Argand lamp.

quinquina [kɛ̃ki'na], *n.m.* Peruvian bark.

quintal [kɛ̃'tal], *n.m.* (*pl.* **-aux**) quintal, hundredweight; 100 kilogr.

quinte [kɛ̃ːt], *n.f.* (*Mus.*) fifth; (*Piquet*) quint; (*fig.*) freak, whim; (*Fenc.*) quinte; *quinte de toux*, fit of coughing.

quintessence [kɛ̃te'sɑ̃ːs], *n.f.* quintessence; (*fig.*) pith, essential part.

quintette [kɛ̃'tɛt], *n.m.* quintet.

quinteux [kɛ̃'tø], *a.* (*fem.* **-euse**) whimsical, crotchety; jibbing (*of a horse*).

quintuple [kɛ̃'typl], *a.* and *n.m.* quintuple.

quintuplé [kɛ̃ty'ple], *n.m.* quintuplet.

quintupler [kɛ̃ty'ple], *v.t.* to quintuple.

quinzaine [kɛ̃'zɛn], *n.f.* about fifteen; fortnight.

quinze [kɛ̃ːz], *a.* and *n.m.* fifteen; fifteenth.

quinzième [kɛ̃'zjɛm], *a.* and *n.* fifteenth.

quinzièmement [kɛ̃zjɛm'mɑ̃], *adv.* fifteenthly, in the fifteenth place.

quiproquo [kipro'ko], *n.m.* mistake; substitution.

quittance [ki'tɑ̃ːs], *n.f.* receipt, discharge.

quittancer [kitɑ̃'se], *v.t.* (*conjug. like* COMMENCER) to receipt.

quitte [kit], *a.* discharged (*from debt*); clear, free.

quitter [ki'te], *v.t.* to leave; to discharge; to give up; to leave off, to lay aside; to depart (*life*); *ne quittez pas !* (*Teleph.*) hold the line! **se quitter**, *v.r.* to part company, to separate.

qui va là? [kiva'la], *inter. phr.* who goes there?

qui-vive [ki'viːv], *n.m.* who goes there? (*challenge of a sentry*); *être sur le qui-vive*, to be on the alert.

quoi [kwa], *pron. rel.* and *inter.* which; what; *il n'y a pas de quoi*, don't mention it! *le je ne sais quoi*, the indefinable something; *quoi que*, whatever.—*int.* what!

quoique ['kwakǝ], *conj.* although, though.

quolibet [kɔli'bɛ], *n.m.* gibe, jeer.

quote-part [kɔt'paːr], *n.f.* (*pl.* **quotes-parts**) quota, portion, share.

quotidien [kɔti'djɛ̃], *a.* (*fem.* **-enne**) daily, quotidian.—*n.m.* daily (newspaper).

quotidiennement [kɔtidjɛn'mɑ̃], *adv.* daily.

quotient [kɔ'sjɑ̃], *n.m.* quotient.

quotité [kɔti'te], *n.f.* (*Fin.*) quota, share; proportion.

R

R, r [ɛːr], *n.m.* the eighteenth letter of the alphabet.

rabâchage [rabɑ'ʃaːʒ], *n.m.* tiresome repetition; drivel.

rabâcher [rabɑ'ʃe], *v.t.*, *v.i.* to repeat (*the same thing*) over and over again.

rabâcheur [rabɑ'ʃœːr], *n.m.* (*fem.* **-euse**) eternal repeater, twaddler.

rabais [ra'bɛ], *n.m. inv.* abatement, reduction; discount.

rabaissement [rabɛs'mɑ̃], *n.m.* lowering, depreciation; (*fig.*) humiliation.

rabaisser [rabɛ'se], *v.t.* to lower; to abate, to lessen; to depreciate; to humble, to disparage.

rabat [ra'ba], *n.m.* clerical or academic band, Geneva bands; beating (*for game*).

rabat-joie [raba'ʒwa], *n.m. inv.* damper, wet blanket, spoil-sport.

rabattage [raba'taːʒ], *n.m.* cutting down, diminution; beating (*for game*).

rabattre [ra'batr], *v.t.* (*conjug. like* BATTRE) to beat down, to bring or cut down; to smooth down; to humble; (*Hunt.*) to beat up; to abate.—*v.i.* to reduce one's pretensions. **se**

263

rabattre, *v.t.* to turn off, to change one's road; to come down; to fall back on.

rabbin [ra'bɛ̃], *n.m.* rabbi.

rabbinique [rabi'nik], *a.* rabbinical.

rabique [ra'bik], *a.* rabid, rabic.

râble [rɑ:bl], *n.m.* back (*of hare, rabbit etc.*); fire rake.

râblé [rɑ'ble], *a.* broad-backed; (*fig.*) vigorous, strapping.

rabonnir [rabɔ'ni:r], *v.t., v.i.* to improve (*wine*).

rabot [ra'bo], *n.m.* plane.

rabotage [rabɔ'ta:ʒ], **rabotement** [rabɔt 'mɑ̃], *n.m.* planing.

raboter [rabɔ'te], *v.t.* to plane; (*fig.*) to polish; (*slang*) to pilfer, to filch.

raboteur [rabɔ'tœ:r], *n.m.* planer.

raboteuse (1) [rabɔ'tø:z], *n.f.* planing machine.

raboteux [rabɔ'tø], *a.* (*fem.* **-euse** (2)) knotty; rough, rugged, uneven; (*fig.*) harsh (*of style*).

rabougri [rabu'gri], *a.* stunted, dwarfed.

rabougrir [rabu'gri:r], *v.t.* to stunt.

raboutir [rabu'ti:r], **rabouter** [rabu'te], *v.t.* to join end to end, to join on.

rabrouer [rabru'e], *v.t.* to snub, to rebuke sharply.

rabroueur [rabru'œ:r], *n.m.* (*fem.* **-euse**) snappish person, scold.

racaille [ra'kɑ:j], *n.f.* rabble, riffraff; rubbish, trash.

raccommodage [rakɔmɔ'da:ʒ], *n.m.* mending, repairing; darning.

raccommodement [rakɔmɔd'mɑ̃], *n.m.* reconciliation.

raccommoder [rakɔmɔ'de], *v.t.* to mend, to repair; to darn; to patch; to set right, to correct; to reconcile. **se raccommoder**, *v.r.* to be reconciled.

raccommodeur [rakɔmɔ'dœ:r], *n.m.* (*fem.* **-euse**) mender.

raccompagner [rakɔpa'ɲe], *v.t.* to accompany back.

raccord [ra'kɔ:r], *n.m.* joining, fitting; joint, connection.

raccordement [rakɔrdə'mɑ̃], *n.m.* joining, union, junction; levelling; *voie de raccordement*, loop *or* junction line.

raccorder [rakɔr'de], *v.t.* to join, to unite, to connect. **se raccorder**, *v.r.* to fit together, to blend.

raccourci [rakur'si], *a.* shortened, abridged. —*n.m* abridgment, epitome; short cut.

raccourcir [rakur'si:r], *v.t.* to shorten, to curtail, to abridge.—*v.i.* to become shorter; to take a short cut. **se raccourcir**, *v.r.* to grow shorter, to contract, to shrink.

raccourcissement [rakursis'mɑ̃], *n.m.* shortening, abridgment, shrinking.

raccoutrage [raku'tra:ʒ], **raccoutrement** [rakutrə'mɑ̃], *n.m.* mending (*of clothes etc.*).

raccoutrer [raku'tre], *v.t.* to mend, to repair (*garment*).

raccoutumer (se) [sərakuty'me], *v.r.* to re-accustom oneself, to get used to again.

raccroc [ra'kro], *n.m.* chance, lucky stroke (*esp. at billiards*), fluke.

raccrocher [rakrɔ'ʃe], *v.t.* to hook up again, to hang up again; (*colloq.*) to recover.—*v.t.* to make flukes (*at play*); (*Teleph.*) to ring off. **se raccrocher**, *v.r.* to cling; to retrieve one's losses; to grasp *or* snatch at.

race [ras], *n.f.* race; stock, breed; family, ancestry; generation; *un cheval de race*, a thoroughbred horse.

rachat [ra'ʃa], *n.m.* repurchase, redemption.

rachetable [raʃ'tabl], *a.* redeemable.

racheter [raʃ'te], *v.t.* (*conjug. like* AMENER) to buy back, to repurchase; to redeem; to ransom; to compensate; to atone for. **se racheter**, *v.r.* to redeem oneself; to be made up for.

rachitique [raʃi'tik], *a.* rachitic, rickety.—*n.* rickety person.

rachitis [raʃi'tis], **rachitisme** [raʃi'tism], *n.m.* rachitis, rickets; (*Bot.*) blight.

racial [ra'sjal], *a.* (*m. pl.* **-aux**) racial.

racine [ra'sin], *n.f.* root; (*fig.*) principle, origin.

racisme [ra'sism], *n.m.* racialism, racism.

raciste [ra'sist], *a.* racial.—*n.* racialist, racist.

raclage [rɑ'kla:ʒ], *n.m.* scraping, raking.

racle [rɑ:kl], *n.f.* scraper.

raclée [rɑ'kle], *n.f.* (*fam.*) thrashing, hiding.

racler [rɑ'kle], *v.t.* to scrape, to rake; to rasp.

racleur [rɑ'klœ:r], *n.m.* (*fem.* **-euse**) scraper; (*fam.*) bad violinist.

racloir [rɑ'klwa:r], *n.m.* scraper, road scraper.

raclure [rɑ'kly:r], *n.f.* scrapings.

racolage [rakɔ'la:ʒ], *n.m.* impressing; recruiting.

racoler [rakɔ'le], *v.t.* to enlist.

racoleur [rakɔ'lœ:r], *n.m.* tout.

racontable [rakɔ'tabl], *a.* relatable.

racontar [rakɔ'ta:r], *n.m.* gossip, tittle-tattle.

raconter [rakɔ'te], *v.t.* to relate, to tell, to narrate.

raconteur [rakɔ'tœ:r], *n.m.* (*fem.* **-euse**) story-teller, narrator, raconteur.

racornir [rakɔr'ni:r], *v.t.* to harden; to dry up, to shrivel up. **se racornir**, *v.r.* to grow hard; to shrivel up; to grow callous.

racornissement [rakɔrnis'mɑ̃], *n.m.* hardening.

racquit [ra'ki], *n.m.* winning back.

racquitter [raki'te], *v.t.* to indemnify, to recoup. **se racquitter**, *v.r.* to retrieve one's losses.

radar [ra'dar], *n.m.* radar.

radariste [rada'rist], *n.* radar operator.

rade [rad], *n.f.* (*Naut.*) roads, roadstead.

radeau [ra'do], *n.m.* (*pl.* **-eaux**) raft.

radiance [ra'djɑ̃:s], *n.f.* radiance, luster.

radiant [ra'djɑ̃], *a.* radiant.

radiateur [radja'tœ:r], *a.* (*fem.* **-trice**) radiating.—*n.m.* radiator.

radiation [radja'sjɔ̃], *n.f.* radiation, irradiation; obliteration.

radical [radi'kal], *a.* (*m. pl.* **-aux**) radical; complete.—*n.m.* radical; root.

radicalement [radikal'mɑ̃], *adv.* radically.

radicalisme [radika'lism], *n.m.* radicalism.

radier (1) [ra'dje], *n.m.* floor *or* apron (*of docks, locks, basins etc.*); invert (*of tunnel*).

radier (2) [ra'dje], *v.t.* to strike out, to erase.—*v.i.* to radiate, to beam (*with satisfaction*).

radieux [ra'djø], *a.* (*fem.* **-euse**) radiant, beaming, shining.

radio [ra'djo], *n.f.* broadcasting, radio; radio set; radiography.—*n.m.* radio message; radio operator.

radio-actif [radjoak'tif], *a.* (*fem.* **-tive**) radio-active.

radio-activité [radjoaktivi'te], *n.f.* radio-activity.

radiodiffuser [radjɔdify'ze], *v.t.* to broadcast.

radiodiffusion [radjɔdify'zjɔ̃], *n.f.* broadcasting.

radiographie [radjɔgra'fi], *n.f.* radiography.

radio-reporter [radjɔrapɔr'tɛːr], *n.m.* commentator.

radis [ra'di], *n.m.* radish.

radium [ra'djɔm], *n.m.* radium.

radotage [radɔ'taːʒ], *n.m.* nonsense, drivel; dotage.

radoter [radɔ'te], *v.i.* to talk idly, to talk drivel; to dote.

radoteur [radɔ'tœːr], *n.m.* (*fem.* **-euse**) driveller; dotard.

radoucir [radu'siːr], *v.t.* to soften; to appease, to pacify. **se radoucir**, *v.r.* to grow milder; to soften, to be appeased, to relent, to relax.

radoucissement [radusis'mɑ̃], *n.m.* softening; getting milder (*of the weather*); mitigation, appeasement.

rafale [ra'fal], *n.f.* squall; gust of wind; (*Mil.*) burst of fire.

raffermir [rafɛr'miːr], *v.t.* to make firm, to secure, to strengthen; to confirm. **se raffermir**, *v.r.* to grow stronger; to be established; to improve in strength *or* health.

raffermissement [rafɛrmis'mɑ̃], *n.m.* hardening; securing; strengthening; confirmation.

raffinage [rafi'naːʒ], *n.m.* refining.

raffiné [rafi'ne], *a.* refined, delicate; subtle, clever; polished.—*n.m.* (*fem.* **-ée**) exquisite, sophisticated person.

raffinement [rafin'mɑ̃], *n.m.* refinement, affectation.

raffiner [rafi'ne], *v.t.* to refine.—*v.i.* to split hairs. **se raffiner**, *v.r.* to become refined.

raffinerie [rafin'ri], *n.f.* refinery.

raffineur [rafi'nœːr], *n.m.* (*fem.* **-euse**) refiner.

raffoler [rafɔ'le], *v.i.* to dote, to be passionately fond (*de*).

rafistolage [rafisto'laːʒ], *n.m.* (*colloq.*) patching up, mending.

rafistoler [rafistɔ'le], *v.t.* to mend, to patch up.

rafle [rɑːfl], *n.f.* clean sweep (*by thieves*); raid, round-up in the streets by police.

rafler [rɑ'fle], *v.t.* to sweep off, to carry off; to round up (*of police*).

rafraîchir [rafrɛ'ʃiːr], *v.t.* to cool; to refresh, to restore, to renew; to rub up; to trim.—*v.i.* to cool; to freshen. **se rafraîchir**, *v.r.* to cool, to take refreshment; to be refreshed, to rest.

rafraîchissant [rafrɛʃi'sɑ̃], *a.* cooling, refreshing; laxative.

rafraîchissement [rafrɛʃis'mɑ̃], *n.m.* cooling; (*pl.*) cool drinks.

ragaillardir [ragaiar'diːr], *v.t.* to enliven, to cheer up, to buck up.

rage [raːʒ], *n.f.* rabies; hydrophobia; violent pain; rage, fury; passion; mania.

rager [ra'ʒe], *v.i.* (*conjug. like* MANGER) (*colloq.*) to be in a passion; to be angry, to fume.

rageur [ra'ʒœːr], *a.* and *n.m.* (*fem.* **-euse**) ill-tempered (person).

ragot [ra'go], *a.* thick-set.—*n.m.* tittle-tattle.

ragoût [ra'gu], *n.m.* ragout; stew; (*fig.*) relish.

ragoûtant [ragu'tɑ̃], *a.* relishing, savory, (*fig.*) inviting, tempting.

ragoûter [ragu'te], *v.t.* to restore the appetite of; to stimulate, to stir up.

ragrafer [ragra'fe], *v.t.* to reclasp, to hook again.

ragréer [ragre'e], *v.t.* to give the finishing touch to (*wall, building*); to renovate (*building*).

ragrément *or* **ragréement** [ragre'mɑ̃], *n.m.* finishing; restoration, renovation.

rai [RAIS].

raid [rɛd], *n.m.* long-distance run *or* flight; raid; **un raid aérien**, an air-raid.

raide [rɛd], *a.* stiff, rigid; taut; steep; firm; rapid.—*adv.* quickly, swiftly, suddenly.

raideur [rɛ'dœːr], *n.f.* stiffness; inflexibility; steepness; harshness.

raidillon [rɛdi'jɔ̃], *n.m.* stiff ascent.

raidir [rɛ'diːr], *v.t.* to stiffen; to tighten; to make inflexible.—*v.i.* and **se raidir**, *v.r.* to stiffen; to be inflexible; (*fig.*) to harden oneself (*contre*).

raidissement [rɛdis'mɑ̃], *n.m.* stiffening, tautening.

raie [rɛ], *n.f.* line, stroke; stripe; parting (*of hair*); (*Ichth.*) ray, skate.

raifort [rɛ'fɔːr], *n.m.* horse-radish.

rail [rɑːj, raːj], *n.m.* (*Rail.*) rail.

railler [rɑ'je], *v.t.* to chaff; to scoff at.—*v.i.* to banter, to jest. **se railler**, *v.r.* to jest, to mock, to make game (*de*).

raillerie [rɑj'ri], *n.f.* raillery, bantering; jesting.

railleur [rɑ'jœːr], *a.* (*fem.* **-euse**) bantering, joking; jeering, scoffing.—*n.m.* (*fem.* **-euse**) banterer, joker; scoffer.

rainette [rɛ'nɛt], *n.f.* (*Zool.*) tree toad.

rainure [rɛ'nyːr], *n.f.* groove, rabbet, slot.

rais *or* **rai** [rɛ], *n.m.* spoke (*of a wheel*); ray (*of light*).

raisin [rɛ'zɛ̃], *n.m.* grapes; **des raisins secs**, raisins.

raisiné [rɛzi'ne], *n.m.* grape jam.

raison [rɛ'zɔ̃], *n.f.* reason; sense, judgment; satisfaction; justice, right; proof, ground; motive; **avoir raison**, to be right.

raisonnable [rɛzɔ'nabl], *a.* rational, reasonable, sensible; just, right; adequate, moderate, fair.

raisonnablement [rɛzɔnabla'mɑ̃], *adv.* reasonably, sensibly; fairly, justly; moderately; tolerably.

raisonné [rɛzɔ'ne], *a.* rational, intelligent; systematic; classified, analytical.

raisonnement [rɛzɔn'mɑ̃], *n.m.* reasoning, argument.

raisonner [rɛzɔ'ne], *v.t.* to study; to talk *or* discourse upon.—*v.i.* to reason; to argue; to answer, to murmur. **se raisonner**, *v.r.* to reason with oneself.

raisonneur [rɛzɔ'nœːr], *a.* (*fem.* **-euse**) reasoning; argumentative.—*n.m.* (*fem.* **-euse**) reasoner, logician; argufier, pertinacious answerer.

rajeunir [raʒœ'niːr], *v.t.* to rejuvenate; to make look young *or* younger; to renew; to modernize.—*v.i.* to grow young again. **se**

rajeunir, *v.r.* to make oneself look young again.

rajeunissant [raʒœni'sã], *a.* that makes one look younger, rejuvenating.

rajeunissement [raʒœnis'mã], *n.m.* rejuvenation; renewal, renovation.

rajouter [raʒu'te], *v.t.* to add again; to add more of.

rajustement [raʒystə'mã], *n.m.* readjustment, setting in order; (*fig.*) reconciliation.

rajuster [raʒys'te], *v.t.* to readjust; (*fig.*) to settle, to reconcile. **se rajuster**, *v.r.* to readjust *or* straighten one's dress; to be reconciled.

râle (1) [rɑːl], *râlement* [rɑːl'mã], *n.m.* rattling in the throat; death rattle.

râle (2) [rɑːl], *n.m.* (Orn.) rail.

ralenti [ralã'ti], *a.* slower.—*n.m.* (*Cine.*) slow motion; *tourner au ralenti*, (*Motor.*) to idle.

ralentir [ralã'tiːr], *v.t.*, *v.i.* to slow down, to ease up; to lessen, to moderate. **se ralentir**, *v.r.* to slacken, to slow up; to abate, to relax.

ralentissement [ralãtis'mã], *n.m.* slackening; decrease; cooling (*of zeal*).

râler [rɑ'le], *v.i.* to be at one's last gasp.

ralliement [rali'mã], *n.m.* rallying, rally; winning over; *mot de ralliement*, (*Mil.*) password.

rallier [ra'lje], *v.t.* to rally; to rejoin; to win over. **se rallier**, *v.r.* to rally; to join.

rallonge [ra'lõːʒ], *n.f.* lengthening-piece, leaf; *table à rallonges*, draw-table.

rallongement [ralõʒ'mã], *n.m.* lengthening, extension.

rallonger [ralõ'ʒe], *v.t.* (*conjug. like* MANGER) to lengthen; to let out (*skirt*).

rallumer [raly'me], *v.t.* to relight; to re-kindle; to revive. **se rallumer**, *v.r.* to light again; (*fig.*) to rekindle.

rallye [ra'li], *n.m.* (*Motor.*) race meeting, rally.

ramage [ra'maːʒ], *n.m.* floral pattern (*on materials*); chirping, warbling (*of birds*); (*fig.*) prattle (*of children*).

ramaigrir [ramɛ'griːr], *v.t.* to make lean *or* thin again.—*v.i.* to grow thin again.

ramaigrissement [ramɛgris'mã], *n.m.* emaciation, leanness.

ramas [ra'mɑ], *n.m. inv.* heap, disorderly collection; set, troop, lot, rabble.

ramassé [rama'se], *a.* thick-set, stocky; compact.

ramasser [rama'se], *v.t.* to collect, to gather; to pick up, to take up. **se ramasser**, *v.r.* to assemble, to gather together; to roll itself up (*of an animal*); to crouch; to pick oneself up (*after a spill*).

ramasseur [rama'sœːr], *n.m.* (*fem.* **-euse**) gatherer, collector.

ramassis [rama'si], [RAMAS].

rame [ram], *n.f.* scull, oar; (*Hort.*) stick, prop; (*Manuf.*) tenter frame; ream (*of paper*); made-up train *or* portion of train; *une rame de Métro*, an Underground train, a subway train.

ramé [ra'me], *a.* supported with sticks (*of peas*), staked (*of plants*).

rameau [ra'mo], *n.m.* (*pl.* **-eaux**) bough, small branch (*of a tree*); subdivision.

ramée [ra'me], *n.f.* green boughs, green arbor.

ramener [ram'ne], *v.t.* (*conjug. like* AMENER) to bring back; to take home; to restore; to reclaim; to recall.

ramer (1) [ra'me], *v.t.* to stick (*peas*), to stake (*plants*).

ramer (2) [ra'me], *v.i.* to row, to scull.

rameur [ra'mœːr], *n.m.* (*fem.* **-euse**) rower.

ramier [ra'mje], *n.m.* wood pigeon, ring dove.

ramification [ramifika'sjõ], *n.f.* ramification.

ramifier [rami'fje], *v.t.* to ramify. **se ramifier**, *v.r.* to ramify, to divide.

ramille [ra'miːj], *n.f.*, *ramillon* [rami'jõ], *n.m.* twig.

ramollir [ramɔ'liːr], *v.t.* to soften, (*fig.*) to enervate, to unman. **se ramollir**, *v.r.* to soften; (*fig.*) to relent.

ramollissant [ramɔli'sã], *a.* softening, emollient.

ramollissement [ramɔlis'mã], *n.m.* softening.

ramonage [ramɔ'naːʒ], *n.m.* chimney sweeping.

ramoner [ramɔ'ne], *v.t.* to sweep (*a chimney*).

ramoneur [ramɔ'nœːr], *n.m.* chimney sweeper, sweep.

rampant [rã'pã], *a.* creeping, crawling; (*fig.*) cringing, servile.

rampe [rãːp], *n.f.* banister; flight of stairs; slope, ramp, incline, gradient; (*Theat.*) footlights.

rampement [rãp'mã], *n.m.* creeping, crawling.

ramper [rã'pe], *v.i.* to creep, to crawl; (*fig.*) to crouch, to grovel.

ramure [ra'myːr], *n.f.* branches, boughs; antlers (*of a stag*).

rancart [rã'kaːr], *n.m. mettre au rancart*, to throw aside; to cast off; to put on the shelf.

rance [rãːs], *a.* rancid, rank.—*n.m.* rancidness.

ranci [rã'si], *a.* rancid.

rancidité [rãsidi'te], *rancissure* [rãsi'syːr], *n.f.*, **rancissement** [rãsis'mã], *n.m.* rancidity.

rancir [rã'siːr], *v.i.* to grow rancid.

rancœur [rã'kœːr], *n.f.* rancor, bitterness.

rançon [rã'sõ], *n.f.* ransom.

rançonnement [rãsɔn'mã], *n.m.* ransoming; (*fig.*) extortion.

rançonner [rãsɔ'ne], *v.t.* to ransom; (*fig.*) to fleece.

rancune [rã'kyn], *n.f.* rancor, spite, grudge, malice.

rancunier [rãky'nje], *a.* and *n.m.* (*fem.* **-ière**) rancorous, spiteful (person).

randonnée [rãdɔ'ne], *n.f.* outing, run, ramble, tour.

rang [rã], *n.m.* row, line; order, class; rank.

rangé [rã'ʒe], *a.* tidy; steady; *en bataille rangée*, in a pitched battle.

rangée [rã'ʒe], *n.f.* row, range, line, tier, set.

rangement [rãʒ'mã], *n.m.* arranging, putting in order.

ranger [rã'ʒe], *v.t.* (*conjug. like* MANGER) to put in order, to set to rights; to draw up; to arrange; to range; to rank; to reduce, to subdue. **se ranger**, *v.r.* to make room, to make way (*for*); to draw up (*of carriages*, *troops etc.*), to pull up (*at curb*); to fall in (*of soldiers*).

ranimer [rani'me], *v.t.* to restore to life, to revive; to rouse, to enliven; to cheer up. **se ranimer**, *v.r.* to revive, to brighten up, to be enlivened; to cheer up.

Raoul [ra'ul], *m.* Ralph.

rapace [ra'pas], *a.* rapacious; grasping (*of person*).—*n.m.* rapacious bird, bird of prey.

rapacement [rapas'mã], *adv.* rapaciously.

rapacité [rapasi'te], *n.f.* rapacity; cupidity.

râpage [rɑ'pa:ʒ], *n.m.* rasping; grating.

rapatriement [rapatri'mã], *n.m.* repatriation.

rapatrier [rapatri'je], *v.t.* to repatriate; (*dial.*) to reconcile.

râpe [rɑ:p], *n.f.* grater; rasp; stalk (*of grapes*).

râpé [rɑ'pe], *a.* grated; rasped; threadbare (*of clothes*).

râper [rɑ'pe], *v.t.* to grate (*cheese*), to rasp; to make threadbare.

rapetassage [rapta'sa:ʒ], *n.m.* patching up, mending, cobbling.

rapetasser [rapta'se], *v.t.* to patch, to mend, to cobble.

rapetasseur [rapta'sœ:r], *n.m.* (*fem.* -euse) piecer, patcher, cobbler; (*fig.*) compiler, adapter.

rapetissement [raptis'mã], *n.m.* shortening, shrinking; (*fig.*) belittling.

rapetisser [rapti'se], *v.t.* to shorten, to make smaller; (*fig.*) to belittle.—*v.i.* to grow less, to shorten, to shrink.

raphia [ra'fja], *n.m.* raffia.

rapide [ra'pid], *a.* rapid, quick, fast; sudden; steep.—*n.m.* rapid; fast train.

rapidement [rapid'mã], *adv.* rapidly, swiftly; steeply.

rapidité [rapidi'te], *n.f.* rapidity, speed; steepness.

rapiéçage [rapje'sa:ʒ], **rapiècement** [rapjɛs'mã], *n.m.* piecing, patching.

rapiécer [rapje'se], (*see Verb Tables*), **rapiéceter** [rapjɛs'te] (*conjug. like* AMENER), *v.t.* to piece, to patch.

rapière [ra'pjɛ:r], *n.f.* rapier.

rapin [ra'pɛ̃], *n.m.* art student; (*fig.*) dauber.

rapine [ra'pin], *n.f.* rapine, robbery; plunder; graft.

rapiner [rapi'ne], *v.t., v.i.* to pillage, to plunder.

rapineur [rapi'nœ:r], *n.m.* (*fem.* -euse) plunderer, pillager, pilferer.

rappareiller [rapare'je], **rapparier** [rapa'rje], *v.t.* to match, to complete.

rappel [ra'pɛl], *n.m.* recall, reminder, call (*to order*); tattoo, assembly; revocation; back pay; (*Theat.*) curtain call.

rappeler [ra'ple], *v.t.* (*conjug. like* APPELER) to call back, to recall; to restore (*to life etc.*); to muster; to retract; to recall to mind; to remind. **se rappeler**, *v.r.* to recollect, to remember.

rapport [ra'pɔ:r], *n.m.* revenue, profit; produce, productiveness; report, account, information, tale; return, statement; resemblance, conformity; agreement; connection; communication; proportion; reimbursement; *faire un rapport*, to draw up a report; *maison de rapport*, tenement house; *sous tous les rapports*, in every respect.

rapporter [rapɔr'te], *v.t.* to bring back; to bring home; to yield; to retrieve (*of dog*); to refund; to recall; to give an account of; to attribute.—*v.i.* to retrieve (*of dog*); (*sch.*) to tell tales; to be profitable. **se rapporter**, *v.r.* to agree, to correspond, to tally; to be related.

rapporteur [rapɔr'tœ:r], *n.m.* (*fem.* -euse) tale-bearer; reporter.—*n.m.* (*Geom.*) protractor.

rapprendre [ra'prã:dr], *v.t.* irr. (*conjug. like* PRENDRE) to learn anew; to teach again.

rapprochement [raprɔʃ'mã], *n.m.* drawing closer, bringing together; reconciliation; junction; comparison.

rapprocher [raprɔ'ʃe], *v.t.* to bring near again; to bring together; to reconcile; to compare. **se rapprocher**, *v.r.* to come near again; to draw nearer; to be brought together; to become reconciled; to approximate (*de*).

rapsodie [rapsɔ'di], *n.f.* rhapsody.

rapt [rapt], *n.m.* abduction; kidnapping.

raquette [ra'kɛt], *n.f.* racket, battledore; snow-shoe.

rare [ra:r], *a.* rare, uncommon; scarce; thin, scanty.

raréfaction [rarefak'sjɔ̃], *n.f.* rarefaction.

raréfiant [rare'fjã], *a.* rarefying.

raréfier [rare'fje], *v.t.* to rarefy. **se raréfier**, *v.r.* to become rare; to become rarefied.

rarement [rar'mã], *adv.* rarely, seldom.

rarissime [rari'sim], *a.* very rare, most rare.

ras [rɑ], *a.* close-shaven, shorn; bare, smooth, open, flat, low; (*fig.*) *faire table rase*, to sweep away all preconceptions; *rase campagne*, open country.—*n.m.* short-nap cloth; level; raft; race (*of a mill*) [RAZ].

rasade [rɑ'zad], *n.f.* brimful glass (*of wine*).

rasant [rɑ'zã], *a.* shaving, grazing; sweeping; (*fam.*) boring.

raser [ra'ze], *v.t.* to shave; to demolish; to graze, to skim over; (*fam.*) to bore. **se raser**, *v.r.* to shave, to be shaved.

rasoir [rɑ'zwa:r], *n.m.* razor; (*fam.*) bore.

rassasiant [rasa'zjã], *a.* satiating, filling (*food*).

rassasiement [rasazi'mã], *n.m.* satiety.

rassasier [rasa'zje], *v.t.* to satisfy, to fill; to satiate; to surfeit. **se rassasier**, *v.r.* to be cloyed; to take one's fill.

rassemblement [rasãblə'mã], *n.m.* assembly, muster, crowd, mob; political group.

rassembler [rasã'ble], *v.t.* to gather together, to collect; to put together; to assemble. **se rassembler**, *v.r.* to assemble, to congregate, to muster.

rasseoir [ra'swa:r], *v.t.* irr. (*conjug. like* ASSEOIR) to seat again, to reseat; to replace; to calm, to compose. **se rasseoir**, *v.r.* to sit down again; to settle (*of liquids*); to become composed again.

rasséréner [rasere'ne], *v.t.* (*conjug. like* CÉDER) to clear up; to restore serenity to. **se rasséréner**, *v.r.* to clear up; to recover one's serenity.

rassis [ra'si], *a.* settled; calm, staid, sedate, stale.

rassortiment [rasɔrti'mã], **réassortiment** [reasɔrti'mã], *n.m.* rematching (*of colors, materials etc.*), resorting; restocking.

rassortir [rasɔr'tiːr], **réassortir** [reasɔr'tiːr], *v.t.* to sort *or* match again; to stock (*a shop etc.*).

rassurant [rasy'rā], *a.* tranquillizing; encouraging, reassuring.

rassurer [rasy're], *v.t.* to make firm; to strengthen; to tranquillize, to reassure. **se rassurer**, *v.r.* to be reassured; to reassure oneself; to clear up (*of the weather*); *rassurez-vous*, set your mind at rest.

rat [ra], *n.m.* rat; *rat des champs*, field mouse; *rat d'hôtel*, hotel thief.

ratafia [rata'fja], *n.m.* ratafia.

ratatiné [ratati'ne], *a.* shrivelled, shrunken.

ratatiner (se) [saratati'ne], *v.r.* to shrink, to shrivel up.

rate (1) [rat], *n.f.* spleen.

rate (2) [rat], *n.f.* female rat.

râteau [ra'to], *n.m.* (*pl. -eaux*) rake.

râtelage [rat'laːʒ], *n.m.* raking.

râtelée [rat'le], *n.f.* rakeful, raking.

râteler [rat'le], *v.t.* (*conjug. like* APPELER) to rake.

râteleur [rat'lœːr], *n.m.* (*fem. -euse*) raker.

râtelier [rata'lje], *n.m.* rack; set of teeth, denture.

rater [ra'te], *v.t.* to miss; (*fig.*) to fail to obtain.—*v.i.* to misfire, to miss (*one's shot*); (*fig.*) to miscarry.

ratière [ra'tjeːr], *n.f.* rat trap.

ratification [ratifika'sjɔ̃], *n.f.* ratification.

ratifier [rati'fje], *v.t.* to ratify.

ratine [ra'tin], *n.f.* ratteen, petersham (*cloth*).

ration [ra'sjɔ̃], *n.f.* ration, allowance.

rationaliser [rasjonali'ze], *v.t.* to rationalize.

rationalisme [rasjona'lism], *n.m.* rationalism.

rationaliste [rasjona'list], *a.* and *n.* rationalist.

rationalité [rasjonali'te], *n.f.* rationality.

rationnel [rasjo'nɛl], *a.* (*fem. -elle*) rational.

rationnement [rasjon'mā], *n.m.* rationing.

rationner [rasjo'ne], *v.t.* to ration.

ratissage [rati'saːʒ], *n.m.* scraping; raking.

ratisser [rati'se], *v.t.* to rake; to scrape.

ratissoire [rati'swaːr], *n.f.* scraper, light rake, hoe.

ratissure [rati'syːr], *n.f.* scrapings.

raton [ra'tɔ̃], *n.m.* little rat; (*fig.*) little pet, darling.

rattacher [rata'ʃe], *v.t.* to refasten; to attach; (*fig.*) to link. **se rattacher**, *v.r.* to be attached *or* connected; to be linked up (*with*).

ratteindre [ra'tɛ̃ːdr], *v.t. irr.* (*conjug. like* CRAINDRE) to retake, to catch again; to overtake.

rattendrir [ratɑ̃'driːr], *v.t.* to soften again.

rattraper [ratra'pe], *v.t.* to catch again, to retake; to overtake; to recover. **se rattraper**, *v.r.* to catch hold (*à*); to be caught again; to make up for one's losses.

rature [ra'tyːr], *n.f.* erasure.

raturer [raty're], *v.t.* to erase.

raucité [rosi'te], *n.f.* raucity, hoarseness.

rauque [roːk], *a.* hoarse, raucous, rough.

ravage [ra'vaːʒ], *n.m.* ravage, havoc.

ravager [rava'ʒe], *v.t.* (*conjug. like* MANGER) to ravage, to lay waste; to spoil, to ruin.

ravageur [rava'ʒœːr], *n.m.* (*fem. -euse*) ravager, spoiler.

ravalement [raval'mā], *n.m.* scraping and

pointing (*of a wall*); rough-casting; repainting.

ravaler [rava'le], *v.t.* to swallow again; (*fig.*) to disparage; to point (*stonework*); to rough-cast (*wall*). **se ravaler**, *v.r.* to debase oneself, to lower oneself.

ravaudage [ravo'daːʒ], *n.m.* mending (*of old clothes etc.*).

ravauder [ravo'de], *v.t.* to mend, to darn; (*dial.*) to scold.

ravaudeur [ravo'dœːr], *n.m.* (*fem. -euse*) mender (*of stockings, old clothes etc.*).

rave [raːv], *n.f.* (*Bot.*) *grosse rave*, French turnip; *petite rave*, radish.

ravenelle [rav'nɛl], *n.f.* wallflower.

ravi [ra'vi], *a.* carried away, enraptured, delighted.

ravier [ra'vje], *n.m.* radish dish.

ravière [ra'vjɛːr], *n.f.* radish bed.

ravigote [ravi'gɔt], *n.f.* ravigote sauce.

ravigoter [ravigo'te], *v.t.* to revive, to refresh, to buck up. **se ravigoter**, *v.r.* to recover one's spirits, to perk up.

ravilir [ravi'liːr], *v.t.* to degrade, to lower.

ravin [ra'vɛ̃], *n.m.* ravine; gully.

ravine [ra'vin], *n.f.* mountain torrent; small gully.

ravinement [ravin'mā], *n.m.* hollowing out *or* furrowing (*by waters*).

raviner [ravi'ne], *v.t.* to channel, to furrow.

ravir [ra'viːr], *v.t.* to carry off, to ravish; (*fig.*) to charm, to enrapture.

raviser (se) [sɔravi'ze], *v.r.* to change one's mind; to think better of it.

ravissant [ravi'sā], *a.* ravishing, delightful, charming.

ravissement [ravis'mā], *n.m.* carrying off; *rape; rapture, delight.

ravisseur [ravi'sœːr], *n.m.* (*fem. -euse*) ravisher; kidnapper.

ravitaillement [ravitaj'mā], *n.m.* revictualling; supplying; supplies; food.

ravitailler [ravita'je], *v.t.* to provision; to supply.

raviver [ravi've], *v.t.* to revive, to cheer; to freshen up (*colors*).

ravoir [ra'vwaːr], *v.t.* (*usu. in infin.*) to get back again, to recover.

rayé [rɛ'je], *a.* striped (*garment*); rifled (*gun*); scratched (*glass*); struck off (*a list*).

rayer [rɛ'je], *v.t.* (*conjug. like* PAYER) to scratch (*dishes etc.*); to streak, to stripe; to erase; (*Artill.*) to rifle.

rayon [rɛ'jɔ̃], *n.m.* ray; beam, gleam; radius; spoke (*of a wheel*); shelf; department (*of a shop*); *rayon de miel*, honeycomb.

rayonnant [rɛjo'nā], *a.* radiant, beaming.

rayonne [rɛ'jɔn], *n.f.* rayon.

rayonnement [rɛjon'mā], *n.m.* radiance; radiation.

rayonner [rɛjo'ne], *v.i.* to radiate; to shine, to beam; to sparkle.

rayure [rɛ'jyːr], *n.f.* stripe; streak, scratch; rifling (*of fire-arms*); erasure.

raz *or* **ras** [ra], *n.m. inv.* race (*a violent current*); *raz de marée*, tidal wave.

razzia [ra'zja], *n.f.* (*Algerian*) razzia, raid, inroad, foray.

ré [re], *n.m.* (*Mus.*) re, D.

réabonnement [reabon'mā], *n.m.* renewed subscription.

réabonner (se) [səreabɔ'ne], *v.r.* to renew one's subscription.

réacteur [reak'tœ:r], *n.m.* reactor; (*Av.*) jet engine.

réaction [reak'sjɔ̃], *n.f.* reaction; *les avions à réaction,* jet aircraft.

réactionnaire [reaksjɔ'nɛ:r], *a.* and *n.* reactionary.

réactionner [reaksjɔ'ne], *v.t.* to sue again.—*v.i.* (*St. Exch.*) to react against a rise.

réadmettre [read'mɛtr], *v.t. irr.* (*conjug. like* METTRE) to admit again, to readmit.

réadmission [readmi'sjɔ̃], *n.f.* readmission.

réagir [rea'ʒi:r], *v.i.* to react.

réajourner [reaʒur'ne], *v.t.* to readjourn.

réalisable [reali'zabl], *a.* realizable; feasible.

réalisateur [realiza'tœ:r], *n.m.* (*Cine.*) film director.

réalisation [realiza'sjɔ̃], *n.f.* realization; achievement; conversion into money; clearance sale.

réaliser [reali'ze], *v.t.* to realize; to achieve; to convert into money. **se réaliser,** *v.r.* to be realized, to come true.

réalisme [rea'lism], *n.m.* realism.

réaliste [rea'list], *a.* realistic.—*n.* realist.

réalité [reali'te], *n.f.* reality.

réapparaître [reapa'rɛ:tr], *v.i. irr.* (*conjug. like* CONNAÎTRE) to reappear.

réapparition [reapari'sjɔ̃], *n.f.* reappearance.

réarmement [rearma'mɑ̃], *n.m.* rearmament.

réarmer [rear'me], *v.t.* to rearm; (*Navy*) to refit.

réassortiment [RASSORTIMENT].

rebaisser [rabɛ'se], *v.t.* to lower again.

rébarbatif [rebarba'tif], *a.* (*fem.* **-tive**) stern, surly, forbidding.

rebâtir [rabɑ'tir], *v.t.* to rebuild.

rebattre [rə'batr], *v.t.* (*conjug. like* BATTRE) to beat again; to repeat; to shuffle (*cards*) again.

rebattu [rəba'ty], *a.* hackneyed, trite.

rebelle [rə'bɛl], *a.* rebellious; disobedient; unyielding; refractory.—*n.* rebel.

rebeller (se) [sərəbɛ'le], *v.r.* to rebel, to revolt.

rébellion [rebɛ'ljɔ̃], *n.f.* rebellion; resistance.

rebiffer (se) [sərəbi'fe], *v.r.* (*fam.*) to bridle up, to kick over the traces.

reblanchir [rəblɑ̃'ʃi:r], *v.t.* to bleach again; to whitewash again.

reboire [rə'bwa:r], *v.t. irr.* (*conjug. like* BOIRE) to drink again.

reboisement [rəbwaz'mɑ̃], *n.m.* retimbering, reforestation.

reboiser [rəbwa'ze], *v.t.* to retimber, to reforest.

rebond [rə'bɔ̃], *n.m.* rebound; bounce (*of ball*).

rebondi [rəbɔ̃'di], *a.* plump, chubby.

rebondir [rəbɔ̃'di:r], *v.i.* to rebound; to bounce.

rebondissement [rəbɔ̃dis'mɑ̃], *n.m.* rebounding; bounce.

rebord [rə'bɔ:r], *n.m.* edge, brink; sill (*of window*); border, hem.

reborder [rəbɔr'de], *v.t.* to border again, to re-hem.

rebouillir [rəbu'ji:r], *v.i. irr.* (*conjug. like* BOUILLIR) to boil again.

rebours [rə'bu:r], *a.* cross-grained (*wood*); intractable (*horse*).—*n.m.* wrong side (*of*

material *etc.*); wrong way (*of the grain*); contrary, reverse; *à rebours* or *au rebours* the wrong way, against the grain, backwards.

reboutage [rəbu'ta:ʒ], *n.m.* bone-setting.

rebouter [rəbu'te], *v.t.* to set (*bones*).

rebouteur [rəbu'tœ:r], **rebouteux** [rəbu'tø], *n.m.* (*fem.* **-euse**) bone setter.

reboutonner [rəbutɔ'ne], *v.t.* to rebutton. **se reboutonner,** *v.r.* to button up one's clothes again.

rebroussement [rəbrus'mɑ̃], *n.m.* turning back, turning up.

rebrousse-poil (à) [arəbrus'pwal], *adv. phr.* against the grain; the wrong way.

rebrousser [rəbru'se], *v.t.* to turn up (*the hair*); *rebrousser chemin,* to turn back.

rebuffade [rəby'fad], *n.f.* rebuff, repulse; snub.

rébus [re'by:s], *n.m.* rebus; riddle.

rebut [rə'by], *n.m.* repulse, rebuff; refuse, rubbish; scum.

rebutant [rəby'tɑ̃], *a.* repulsive, disgusting, forbidding.

rebuter [rəby'te], *v.t.* to repulse, to rebuff, to reject, to snub; to disgust. **se rebuter,** *v.r.* to become discouraged.

récalcitrant [rekalsi'trɑ̃], *a.* refractory, recalcitrant; rebellious.

récalcitrer [rekalsi'tre], *v.i.* to kick (*of horses*); (*fig.*) to be refractory.

recaler [rəka'le], *v.t.* to wedge up again, to refix; (*Sch.*) to fail (*s. o. in an examination*).

récapitulation [rekapityly'sjɔ̃], *n.f.* recapitulation, summing up; summary.

récapituler [rekapity'le], *v.t.* to recapitulate, to sum up; (*colloq.*) to recap.

recel [rə'sɛl], **recèlement** [rəsɛl'mɑ̃], *n.m.* receiving of stolen goods.

receler [rəs'le] (*conjug. like* AMENER), **recéler** [rəse'le] (*conjug. like* CÉDER), *v.t.* to receive (*stolen goods*); to embezzle; to conceal from justice; to contain.

receleur [rəs'lœ:r], *n.m.* (*fem.* **-euse**) receiver of stolen goods, fence.

récemment [resa'mɑ̃], *adv.* recently, newly.

recensement [rəsɑ̃s'mɑ̃], *n.m.* census; return, inventory; verification.

recenser [rəsɑ̃'se], *v.t.* to take the census of; to record; to verify.

recenseur [rəsɑ̃'sœ:r], *n.m.* (*fem.* **-euse**) census taker; enumerator.

recension [rəsɑ̃'sjɔ̃], *n.f.* recension; collation (*of books etc.*).

récent [re'sɑ̃], *a.* recent, new, fresh, late.

receper [rəsə'pe] (*conjug. like* AMENER), **recéper** [rəse'pe] (*conjug. like* CÉDER), *v.t.* to cut back; to clear (*a wood*).

récépissé [resepi'se], *n.m.* receipt, acknowledgment (*for documents, papers etc.*).

réceptacle [resɛp'takl], *n.m.* receptacle; repository.

récepteur [resɛp'tœ:r], *a.* (*fem.* **-trice**) receiving; *poste récepteur,* receiving set. —*n.m.* receiver; reservoir (*in a machine, etc.*); receiving instrument (*of telegraphs*).

réception [resɛp'sjɔ̃], *n.f.* receiving; receipt; admission; (*hotel*) reception desk; reception, party.

réceptionnaire [resɛpsjɔ'nɛ:r], *a.* receiving. —*n.* receiver, receiving clerk; consignee.

réceptionniste [resɛpsjɔ'nist], *n.* receptionist.

recette [rə'sɛt], *n.f.* receipts, returns; takings; (*Cook.*) recipe; receiver's office; **faire recette**, to be a hit (*of a play*).

recevable [rəsə'vabl], *a.* receivable, admissible.

receveur [rəsə'vœːr], *n.m.* (*fem.* **-euse**) receiver, collector (*of taxes etc.*); (bus) conductor.

recevoir [rəsə'vwaːr], *v.t. irr.* to receive, to accept, to take; to let in, to admit; to welcome; to entertain.—*v.i.* to receive, to be at home to visitors.

rechange [rə'ʃãːʒ], *n.m.* change (*of anything*), replacement; spare things; (*Comm.*) reexchange; **roue de rechange**, spare wheel.

rechanter [rəʃã'te], *v.t.* to sing again; to retell.

rechaper [rəʃa'pe], *v.t.* to retread (*a tire*).

réchapper [reʃa'pe], *v.i.* to escape; **réchapper d'une maladie**, to recover from an illness.

recharge [rə'ʃarʒ], *n.f.* fresh *or* second charge.

rechargement [rəʃarʒə'mã], *n.m.* reloading, relading; reballasting.

recharger [rəʃar'ʒe], *v.t.* (*conjug. like* MANGER) to load again; to recharge.

réchaud [re'ʃo], *n.m.* small portable stove; chafing dish; dish warmer.

réchauffage [reʃo'faːʒ], *n.m.* warming up again, reheating.

réchauffé [reʃo'te], *n.m.* dish *or* food warmed up again; rehash, stale stuff *or* news.

réchauffer [reʃo'fe], *v.t.* to warm up, to reheat; to reanimate, to stir up. **se réchauffer**, *v.r.* to warm oneself, to get warm.

réchauffoir [reʃo'fwaːr], *n.m.* plate warmer, hot plate.

rechausser [rəʃo'se], *v.t.* to put shoes *or* stockings on (*a person*) again; (*Build.*) to underpin.

rêche [rɛːʃ], *a.* rough (*to the taste, touch etc.*); (*fig.*) sour, crabbed (*of persons*).

recherche [rə'ʃɛrʃ], *n.f.* search, pursuit, inquiry, investigation; research; (*fig.*) studied elegance *or* refinement, affectation.

recherché [rəʃɛr'ʃe], *a.* choice, exquisite; affected; far-fetched; in great demand.

rechercher [rəʃɛr'ʃe], *v.t.* to seek again; to seek, to search for; to investigate, to pry into; to desire; to court, to woo.

rechigné [rəʃi'ɲe], *a.* sour-faced, surly, crabbed.

rechignement [rəʃiɲə'mã], *n.m.* sulking, sullenness.

rechigner [rəʃi'ɲe], *v.i.* to look sulky, sullen, grim etc; to balk (*at something*).

rechute [rə'ʃyt], *n.f.* relapse, set-back.

rechuter [rəʃy'te], *v.i.* to have a relapse; to backslide.

récidive [resi'diːv], *n.f.* recidivism; second offence.

récidiver [residi've], *v.i.* to repeat the offence; to relapse; to recur (*of disease*).

récidiviste [residi'vist], *n.* recidivist, old lag.

récif [re'sif], *n.m.* reef (*of rocks*).

récipé [resi'pe], *n.m.* recipe, prescription.

récipient [resi'pjã], *n.m.* container, receptacle; reservoir.

réciprocité [resiprɔsi'te], *n.f.* reciprocity, reciprocation.

réciproque [resi'prɔk], *a.* reciprocal, mutual.

réciproquement [resiprɔk'mã], *adv.* reciprocally, mutually; vice versa.

récit [re'si], *n.m.* recital, account, story narrative, report.

récital [resi'tal], *n.m.* (*pl.* **-als**) musical recital.

récitant [resi'tã], *a.* (*Mus.*) solo (*instrument, voice*).—*n.m.* (*fem.* **-e**) soloist; narrator.

récitateur [resita'tœːr], *n.m.* (*fem.* **-trice**) reciter, repeater.

récitatif [resita'tif], *n.m.* (*Mus.*) recitative.

récitation [resita'sjã], *n.f.* recitation, reciting; repetition.

réciter [resi'te], *v.t.* to recite, to rehearse; to repeat, to say; to tell, to relate, to recount.

réclamant [rekla'mã], *a.* claiming.—*n.m.* (*fem.* **-e**) claimant.

réclamation [reklama'sjã], *n.f.* claim, request, demand; complaint.

réclame [re'klaːm], *n.f.* advertisement; publicity; (*Print.*) catch-word; blurb.

réclamer [rekla'me], *v.t.* to crave, to entreat; to beseech; to claim.—*v.i.* to object, to complain; to protest (*contre*). **se réclamer**, *v.r.* to refer to.

reclus [rə'kly], *a.* shut up, secluded.—*n.m.* (*fem.* **-e**) recluse; monk, nun.

reclusion [rəkly'zjã], **réclusion** [rekly'zjã], *n.f.* reclusion, confinement; (*Law*) solitary confinement (*with hard labor*).

recoin [rə'kwɛ̃], *n.m.* corner, nook; **coins et recoins**, nooks and crannies.

récolte [re'kɔlt], *n.f.* harvest, crop, vintage.

récolter [rekɔl'te], *v.t.* to reap, to gather in; to get in.

recommandable [rəkɔmã'dabl], *a.* respectable; commendable.

recommandation [rəkɔmãda'sjã], *n.f.* recommendation; reference; (*fig.*) esteem; (*Post*) registration.

recommander [rəkɔmã'de], *v.t.* to recommend; to enjoin; to request; to commend; (*Post*) to register. **se recommander**, *v.r.* to recommend oneself; to refer to.

recommencement [rəkɔmãs'mã], *n.m.* recommencement, fresh start.

recommencer [rəkɔmã'se], *v.t.*, *v.i.* (*conjug. like* COMMENCER) to recommence, to begin again; to do (*it*) again.

récompense [rekɔ'pãːs], *n.f.* reward, recompense; prize; compensation; **en récompense de**, in return for.

récompenser [rekɔpã'se], *v.t.* to reward; to compensate; to repay.

recomposer [rəkɔpo'ze], *v.t.* to recompose.

recomposition [rəkɔpozi'sjã], *n.f.* recomposition.

réconciliable [rekɔ̃si'ljabl], *a.* reconcilable.

réconciliateur [rekɔ̃silja'tœːr], *n.m.* (*fem.* **-trice**) reconciler.

réconciliation [rekɔ̃silja'sjã], *n.f.* reconciliation.

réconcilier [rekɔ̃si'lje], *v.t.* to reconcile. **se réconcilier**, *v.r.* to be(come) reconciled; (*colloq.*) to make it up.

reconduire [rəkɔ̃'dɥiːr], *v.t. irr.* (*conjug. like* CONDUIRE) to lead back, to see home; to show out.

reconduite [rəkɔ̃'dɥit], *n.f.* showing out, seeing out, seeing home.

réconfort [rekɔ̃'fɔːr], *n.m.* comfort, relief.

réconforter [rekɔ̃fɔr'te], *v.t.* to comfort, to cheer up; to fortify.

reconnaissable [rəkɔnɛ'sabl], *a.* recognizable.

reconnaissance [rəkɔnɛ'sãːs], *n.f.* recognition; discovery; gratitude, thankfulness; survey; acknowledgment, confession; reward; recognizance; pawn ticket; (*Mil.*) reconnaissance.

reconnaissant [rəkɔnɛ'sã], *a.* grateful, thankful.

reconnaître [rəkɔ'nɛːtr], *v.t. irr.* (*conjug. like* CONNAÎTRE) to recognize, to identify; to discover; to acknowledge, to admit; to be grateful for; to reconnoitre. **se reconnaître**, *v.r.* to recognize oneself; to be recognizable; to make out where one is.

reconquérir [rəkɔ̃ke'riːr], *v.t. irr.* (*conjug. like* ACQUÉRIR) to reconquer; to regain.

reconstituer [rəkɔ̃sti'tɥe], *v.t.* to reconstitute, to restore.

reconstitution [rəkɔ̃stity'sjɔ̃], *n.f.* reconstitution, reorganization; reconstruction (*of a murder*).

reconstruction [rəkɔ̃stryk'sjɔ̃], *n.f.* reconstruction, rebuilding.

reconstruire [rəkɔ̃s'trɥiːr], *v.t. irr.* (*conjug. like* CONDUIRE) to rebuild, to reconstruct; to rehabilitate.

recopier [rəkɔ'pje], *v.t.* to make a copy of.

recoquillement [rəkɔkij'mã], *n.m.* curling up, dog('s)-earing (*of pages of book*).

recoquiller [rəkɔki'je], *v.t.* to turn up *or* back. **se recoquiller**, *v.r.* to curl up, to shrivel.

record [rə'kɔːr], *n.m.* record (*in sports etc.*).

recorder [rəkɔr'de], *v.t.* to learn by heart; to tie up again.

recors [rə'kɔːr], *n.m.* local magistrate's helper.

recoucher [rəku'ʃe], *v.t.* to put to bed again; to lay down again. **se recoucher**, *v.r.* to go to bed again, to lie down again.

recoudre [rə'kudr], *v.t. irr.* (*conjug. like* COUDRE) to sew again, to sew up.

recoupement [rəkup'mã], *n.m.* (*Build.*) offset; cross-checking.

recouper [rəku'pe], *v.t.* to cut again; to cross-check.

recourbé [rəkur'be], *a.* curved, bent (back).

recourber [rəkur'be], *v.t.* to bend back, to bend round. **se recourber**, *v.r.* to be curved, to bend.

recourir [rəku'riːr], *v.i. irr.* (*conjug. like* COURIR) to run again; to resort (*à*); (*Law*) to appeal

recours [rə'kur], *n.m.* recourse; (*fig.*) resource, remedy; (*Law*) appeal.

recousu [rəku'zy], *a.* sewn *or* stitched again.

recouvrement [rəkuvrə'mã], *n.m.* recovery, regaining; recovering (*of debts etc.*); covering up, overlapping; cap (*of a watch*).

recouvrer [rəku'vre], *v.t.* to recover, to retrieve, to collect.

recouvrir [rəku'vriːr], *v.t. irr.* (*conjug. like* OUVRIR) to cover up, to cover over, to overlay; to hide. **se recouvrir**, *v.r.* to cover oneself again; to cloud over.

recracher [rəkra'ʃe], *v.t.* to spit out again; to disgorge.—*v.i.* to spit again.

récréatif [rekrea'tif], *a.* (*fem.* -**tive**) recreative, entertaining.

récréation [rekrea'sjɔ̃], *n.f.* recreation, amusement; (*Sch.*) playtime, break.

recréer [rəkre'e], *v.t.* to re-create, to create again.

récréer [rekre'e], *v.t.* to entertain; to amuse. **se récréer**, *v.r.* to amuse oneself, to take recreation.

recrépir [rəkre'piːr], *v.t.* to give a fresh coat of plaster to; to repoint (*a wall*); (*fig.* and *fam.*) to paint (*one's face*); to recast.

recrépissement [rəkrepis'mã], **recrépissage** [rəkrepi'saːʒ], *n.m.* replastering; repatching.

récrier (se) [sərekri'je], *v.r.* to exclaim, to cry out; to protest (*contre*); to be amazed.

récrimination [rekrimina'sjɔ̃], *n.f.* recrimination.

récriminatoire [rekrimina'twaːr], *a.* recriminatory.

récriminer [rekrimi'ne], *v.i.* to recriminate.

récrire [re'kriːr], *v.t. irr.* (*conjug. like* ÉCRIRE) to rewrite; to write back.

recroqueviller (se) [sərəkrɔkvi'je], *v.r.* to curl up, to shrivel.

recru [rə'kry], *a.* tired out, worn out.

recrudescence [rəkrydɛ'sãːs], *n.f.* recrudescence.

recrudescent [rəkrydɛ'sã], *a.* recrudescent.

recrue [rə'kry], *n.f.* recruiting; recruit.

recrutement [rəkryt'mã], *n.m.* recruiting, recruitment.

recruter [rəkry'te], *v.t.* to recruit; to enroll. **se recruter**, *v.r.* to be recruited.

recruteur [rəkry'tœːr], *n.m.* recruiter; recruiting officer.

rectangle [rɛk'tãːgl], *n.m.* rectangle.

rectangulaire [rɛktãgy'lɛːr], *a.* rectangular, right-angled.

recteur [rɛk'tœːr], *n.m.* rector, vice-chancellor (*of a University*); parish priest (*in Brittany*).

rectifiable [rɛkti'fjabl], *a.* rectifiable.

rectification [rɛktifika'sjɔ̃], *n.f.* rectification; adjustment.

rectifier [rɛkti'fje], *v.t.* to rectify; to adjust; to reform.

rectiligne [rɛkti'liɲ], *a.* rectilinear.

rectitude [rɛkti'tyd], *n.f.* rectitude, uprightness.

recto [rɛk'to], *n.m.* first page of a leaf, right-hand page, recto.

rectorat [rɛktɔ'ra], *n.m.* rectorship.

reçu [rə'sy], *a.* received; admitted, recognized; *être reçu* (*à un examen*), to pass (an examination).—*n.m.* receipt.

recueil [rə'kœːj], *n.m.* collection, selection; anthology.

recueillement [rəkœj'mã], *n.m.* meditation; peaceful contemplation.

recueilli [rəkœ'ji], *a.* meditative, calm, rapt.

recueillir [rəkœ'jiːr], *v.t. irr.* (*conjug. like* CUEILLIR) to gather, to collect; to reap; to receive; to shelter. **se recueillir**, *v.r.* to collect one's thoughts; to be plunged in meditation.

recuire [rə'kɥiːr], *v.t. irr.* (*conjug. like* CONDUIRE) to cook again.

recuit [rə'kɥi], *a.* cooked, baked *or* roasted again.

recul [rə'kyl], *n.m.* recoil (*of cannon*), kick (*of rifle*); backing (*of horse, car*).

reculade [rəky'lad], *n.f.* falling back, retreat.

reculé [rəky'le], *a.* distant, remote.

reculement [rəkȳl'mā], *n.m.* drawing back, backing (*of carriages etc.*); breech (*of saddles*).

reculer [rəky'le], *v.t.* to draw back, to move back, to back; (*fig.*) to put off, to defer.—*v.i.* to go back, to draw back, to retreat; to recoil; to give way. **se reculer**, *v.r.* to draw back, to become more remote.

reculons (à) [arəky'lɔ̃], *adv. phr.* backwards.

récupérage [rekype'ra:ʒ], *n.m.*, **récupération** [rekyperɑ'sjɔ̃], *n.f.* recovery, recuperation.

récupérer [rekype're], *v.t.* (*conjug. like* CÉDER) to recover, to retrieve, to recuperate.

récurer [reky're], *v.t.* to scour, to clean.

récusable [reky'zabl], *a.* (*Law*) exceptionable, doubtful (*of witnesses etc.*).

récusation [rekyzɑ'sjɔ̃], *n.f.* (*Law*) challenge; exception.

récuser [reky'ze], *v.t.* to challenge, to object to (*witnesses, jurors etc.*); to reject. **se récuser**, *v.r.* to excuse oneself, to decline; to decline, to give a decision (*of judges, jurors etc.*).

rédacteur [redak'tœ:r], *n.m.* (*fem.* **-trice**) writer, inditer (*of deed*); clerk (*in public office*); **rédacteur en chef**, editor.

rédaction [redak'sjɔ̃], *n.f.* drawing up (*deeds etc.*); wording; editing (*periodicals*); essay.

reddition [redi'sjɔ̃], *n.f.* surrender; rendering (*of accounts*).

rédempteur [redãp'tœ:r], *a.* (*fem.* **-trice**) redeeming, redemptory.—*n.m.* redeemer, savior.

rédemption [redãp'sjɔ̃], *n.f.* redemption; redeeming.

redescendre [rədɛ'sã:dr], *v.t.* (*with aux.* AVOIR) to carry or take down again.—*v.i.* (*with aux.* ÊTRE) to come, go or step down again.

redevable [rəd'vabl], *a.* indebted, owing.

redevance [rəd'vã:s], *n.f.* rent, due, tax.

redevenir [rədəv'ni:r], *v.i. irr.* (*conjug. like* TENIR, *but with aux.* ÊTRE) to become again.

redevoir [rəd(ə)'vwa:r], *v.t. irr.* (*conjug. like* DEVOIR) to owe still.

rédiger [redi'ʒe], *v.t.* (*conjug. like* MANGER) to draw up, to draft; to edit.

redingote [rədɛ̃'gɔt], *n.f.* frock coat.

redire [rə'di:r], *v.t. irr.* (*conjug. like* DIRE) to repeat, to reveal.—*v.i.* to criticize; *trouver à redire à*, to find fault with.

redondance [rədɔ̃'dã:s], *n.f.* superfluity of words, redundancy.

redondant [rədɔ̃'dã], *a.* redundant.

redonner [rədɔ'ne], *v.t.* to give back again, to restore.—*v.i.* to fall again; to begin again; to charge again.

redoublé [rədu'ble], *a.* redoubled, increased.

redoublement [rədublə'mã], *n.m.* redoubling, increase; (*Med.*) paroxysm.

redoubler [rədu'ble], *v.t.* to redouble, to reiterate; to increase; to reline (*dress*).—*v.i.* to increase, to redouble.

redoutable [rədu'tabl], *a.* formidable, redoubtable.

redoute [rə'dut], *n.f.* redoubt.

redouter [rədu'te], *v.t.* to dread, to fear.

redressement [rədrɛs'mã], *n.m.* straightening; rectification, redress.

redresser [rədrɛ'se], *v.t.* to make straight; to set up again; to put right; (*colloq.*) to rebuke. **se redresser**, *v.r.* to become

272

straight again; to right itself (*of a ship etc.*); to be redressed; *redressez-vous*, sit up.

redû [rə'dy], *n.m.* balance due.

réducteur [redyk'tœ:r], *a.* (*fem.* **-trice**) reducing.—*n.m.* (*Chem.*) reducer.

réductible [redyk'tibl], *a.* reducible.

réduction [redyk'sjɔ̃], *n.f.* reduction; subjugation; allowance.

réduire [re'dɥi:r], *v.t. irr.* (*conjug. like* CONDUIRE) to reduce, to diminish; to subdue; to compel, to oblige. **se réduire**, *v.r.* to be reduced, to diminish, to abate, to vanish; to be subdued; to amount to.

réduit [re'dɥi], *a.* reduced; dimmed (*of light*).—*n.m.* retreat, nook; hovel; (*Fort.*) keep.

réédification [reedifikɑ'sjɔ̃], *n.f.* rebuilding.

réédifier [reedi'fje], *v.t.* to rebuild.

rééducatif [reedyka'tif], *a.* (*fem.* **-tive**) **thérapie rééducative**, occupational therapy.

réel [re'ɛl], *a.* (*fem.* **-elle**) real, actual; genuine.—*n.m.* reality.

réélection [reelɛk'sjɔ̃], *n.f.* re-election.

réélire [ree'li:r], *v.t. irr.* (*conjug. like* LIRE) to re-elect.

réellement [reɛl'mã], *adv.* really, in reality.

réembobiner [reãbɔbi'ne], *v.t.* to rewind.

réemploi [reã'plwa], *n.m.* re-employment.

réexpédier [reɛkspe'dje], *v.t.* to send on, to (re)forward; to send back.

refaçonner [rəfasɔ'ne], *v.t.* to make again, to refashion.

réfaction [refak'sjɔ̃], *n.f.* rebate, allowance.

refaire [rə'fɛ:r], *v.t. irr.* (*conjug. like* FAIRE) to do again, to remake; to recommence; to do up; to deal again (*at cards*); to revive; (*slang*) to cheat. **se refaire**, *v.r.* to recover one's strength; to recoup oneself.

refait [rə'fɛ], *a.* set up, done again; (*slang*) *j'ai été refait(e)*, I have been had.—*n.m.* drawn game.

réfection [refɛk'sjɔ̃], *n.f.* repairs (*to buildings etc.*).

réfectoire [refɛk'twa:r], *n.m.* refectory, dining room or hall (*in college, convent etc.*).

refend [rə'fã], *n.m.* splitting, sawing, dividing; *mur de refend*, partition wall.

refendre [rə'fã:dr], *v.t.* to cleave or split again; to quarter (*timber*); to saw (*stone*) into slabs.

référence [refe'rã:s], *n.f.* reference.

referendum [refərã'dɔm], **référendum** [referã'dɔm], *n.m.* referendum.

référer [refe're], *v.t.* (*conjug. like* CÉDER) to refer; to ascribe.—*v.i.* to refer; *en référer à*, to refer to. **se référer**, *v.r.* to refer, to have reference; to leave it (*à*); to trust (*à*).

refermer [rəfɛr'me], *v.t.* to shut again; to close up. **se refermer**, *v.r.* to shut itself; to close up; to heal up (*of wound*).

réfléchi [refle'ʃi], *a.* reflected; deliberate; reflective, thoughtful; wary; (*Gram.*) reflexive.

réfléchir [refle'ʃi:r], *v.t.* to reflect, to throw back; to reverberate.—*v.i.* to reflect, to consider, to ponder. **se réfléchir**, *v.r.* to be reflected.

réfléchissant [refleʃi'sã], *a.* reflecting.

réflecteur [reflɛk'tœ:r], *a.* reflecting.—*n.m.* reflector.

reflet [rə'flɛ], *n.m.* reflection, reflex; reflected light.

refléter [rəfle'te], *v.t.* (*conjug. like* CÉDER) to reflect (*light etc.*).—*v.i.* and **se refléter**, *v.r.* to be reflected.

refleurir [rəflœ'ri:r], *v.i.* to blossom again.

réflexe [re'flɛks], *a.* and *n.m.* reflex.

réflexion [reflɛk'sjɔ̃], *n.f.* reflection; thought, consideration.

refluer [rə'flɥe], *v.i.* to reflow, to ebb; (*fig.*) to swing back.

reflux [rə'fly], *n.m.* reflux, ebb; flowing back.

refondre [rə'fɔ̃:dr], *v.t.* to refound (*metal*), to melt down again, to cast again; (*fig.*) to remodel.

refonte [rə'fɔ̃:t], *n.f.* refounding, recasting; recoining; remodelling.

réformateur [reforma'tœ:r], *a.* (*fem.* **-trice**) reforming.—*n.m.* (*fem.* **-trice**) reformer.

réformation [reforma'sjɔ̃], *n.f.* reformation.

réforme [re'form], *n.f.* reform, reformation, amendment; (*Mil.*) reduction, discharge.

réformé [refor'me], *a.* reformed; (*Mil.*) invalided out of the service.

réformer [refor'me], *v.t.* to reform, to improve; (*Mil.*) to invalid. **se réformer**, *v.r.* to reform, to mend one's ways.

reformer [rəfor'me], *v.t.* to form again. **se reformer**, *v.r.* to form anew, to re-form (*of troops etc.*).

réformiste [refor'mist], *a.* and *n.* reformist.

refoulement [rəful'mɑ̃], *n.m.* driving back; (*Psych.*) inhibition, repression.

refouler [rəfu'le], *v.t.* to drive back; to compress; to suppress; to expel (*aliens*); to stem (*the tide*).—*v.i.* to ebb, to flow back; **la marée refoule**, the tide is ebbing.

réfractaire [refrak'tɛ:r], *a.* refractory, obstinate, rebellious; **terre réfractaire**, fireproof clay.—*n.m.* defaulter.

réfracter [refrak'te], *v.t.* to refract. **se réfracter**, *v.r.* to be refracted.

réfraction [refrak'sjɔ̃], *n.f.* refraction.

refrain [rə'frɛ̃], *n.m.* refrain, chorus; (*fig.*) constant theme.

réfréner [refre'ne], *v.t.* (*conjug. like* CÉDER) to curb, to control (*passions*); to bridle, to restrain.

réfrigérant [refriʒe'rɑ̃], *a.* refrigerant, cooling.—*n.m.* refrigerator.

réfrigérateur [refriʒera'tœ:r], *n.m.* refrigerating chamber, refrigerator; (*colloq.*) fridge; (*Am.*) icebox.

réfrigération [refriʒera'sjɔ̃], *n.f.* refrigeration.

réfrigérer [refriʒe're], *v.t.* (*conjug. like* CÉDER) to chill, to freeze (*food etc.*).

refroidir [rəfrwa'di:r], *v.t.* to cool, to chill.—*v.i.* to cool, to become cold. **se refroidir**, *v.r.* to cool, to grow cold; to catch cold; to slacken, to relax.

refroidissement [rəfrwadis'mɑ̃], *n.m.* cooling, refrigeration; coldness; chill, cold.

refuge [rə'fy:ʒ], *n.m.* refuge, shelter; (street-)island; lay-by.

réfugié [refy'ʒje], *n.m.* (*fem.* **-ée**) refugee.

réfugier (se) [sərefy'ʒje], *v.r.* to take refuge; (*fig.*) to have recourse (*to*) (*dans*).

refus [rə'fy], *n.m. inv.* refusal, denial.

refuser [rəfy'ze], *v.t.* to refuse, to deny, to decline, to reject.—*v.i.* to refuse and to decline.

se refuser, *v.r.* to deny oneself; to shun; to resist.

réfuter [refy'te], *v.t.* to refute, to disprove.

regagner [rəga'ne], *v.t.* to regain, to recover, to retrieve; to rejoin, to reach.

regain [rə'gɛ̃], *n.m.* aftermath; second crop; (*fig.*) revival, new lease (*of life*).

régal [re'gal], *n.m.* feast, entertainment, treat.

régalade [rega'lad], *n.f.* giving a treat, regaling; blazing fire.

régalant [rega'lɑ̃], *a.* pleasant, entertaining.

régaler [rega'le], *v.t.* to regale, to treat, to entertain. **se régaler**, *v.r.* to regale oneself; to enjoy oneself; to entertain *or* treat each other.

regard [rə'ga:r], *n.m.* look; glance; gaze, notice, attention; inspection hole; (*pl.*) eyes; **au regard de**, in comparison with; **d'un seul regard**, at one glance; **en regard**, opposite; **un regard de côté**, a sidelong glance.

regardant [rəgar'dɑ̃], *a.* particular, meticulous; stingy, niggardly.

regarder [rəgar'de], *v.t.* to look at, to behold; to look into, to consider; to face, to be opposite; to concern; **cela vous regarde**, that concerns you.—*v.i.* to look; to mind, to pay heed. **se regarder**, *v.r.* to look at oneself; to look at each other; to look upon oneself (*comme*); to consider one another (*comme*); to face each other.

regarnir [rəgar'ni:r], *v.t.* to furnish again; to retrim (*dress*); to re-cover (*furniture*) etc.

régate [re'gat], *n.f.* regatta, boat race.

régence [re'ʒɑ̃:s], *n.f.* regency.

régénérateur [reʒenera'tœ:r], *a.* (*fem.* **-trice**) regenerating.—*n.m.* regenerator.

régénération [reʒenera'sjɔ̃], *n.f.* regeneration; reclamation (*of land*).

régénérer [reʒene're], *v.t.* (*conjug. like* CÉDER) to regenerate.

régent [re'ʒɑ̃], *a.* and *n.m.* (*fem.* **-e**) regent.

régenter [reʒɑ̃'te], *v.t.* to domineer, to lord it over.

régie [re'ʒi], *n.f.* administration; (*public*) corporation; excise.

regimbement [rəʒɛ̃bə'mɑ̃], *n.m.* kicking (*of horses*); resistance, recalcitrance.

regimber [rəʒɛ̃'be], *v.i.* to kick (*of horses*); (*fig.*) to resist, to jib.

régime [re'ʒim], *n.m.* regimen; diet; form of government; rules, regulations; régime, system; speed (*of motor etc.*); bunch (*of bananas etc.*).

régiment [reʒi'mɑ̃], *n.m.* regiment.

régimentaire [reʒimɑ̃'tɛ:r], *a.* regimental.

région [re'ʒjɔ̃], *n.f.* region; district.

régional [reʒjo'nal], *a.* (*m. pl.* **-aux**) local.

régir [re'ʒi:r], *v.t.* to govern, to rule; to administer.

régisseur [reʒi'sœ:r], *n.m.* manager, steward; (*Theat.*) stage manager.

registre [rə'ʒistr], *n.m.* register; account book; damper (*in chimneys*).

réglable [re'glabl], *a.* adjustable.

réglage [re'gla:ʒ], *n.m.* ruling (*of paper*); regulating, adjusting, tuning.

règle [rɛgl], *n.f.* ruler, rule; order, regularity; model.

réglé [re'gle], *a.* regular, steady; ruled; paid.

273

règlement [rɛglə'mɑ̃], *n.m.* regulation; settlement (*of accounts*).

réglementaire [rɛgləmɑ̃'tɛːr], *a.* according to regulations, lawful; usual.

réglementer [rɛglɑ̃mɑ̃'te], *v.t.* to regulate.— *v.i.* to make regulations.

régler [re'gle], *v.t.* (*conjug. like* CÉDER) to rule (*paper etc.*); to regulate, to order, to adjust, to time (*a watch etc.*); to settle (*an account*). **se régler**, *v.r.* to regulate oneself, to be regulated; to be guided (*sur*).

régleur [re'glœːr], *n.m.* (*fem.* **-euse**) regulator (*of clocks etc.*).

réglisse [re'glis], *n.f.* liquorice.

réglure [re'glyːr], *n.f.* ruling (*of paper*).

régnant [re'nɑ̃], *a.* reigning; (*fig.*) prevailing, predominant.

règne [rɛɲ], *n.m.* reign; prevalence, vogue; (*Nat. Hist.*) kingdom.

régner [re'ɲe], *v.i.* (*conjug. like* CÉDER) to reign, to rule; to prevail, to be in fashion.

regonfler [rəgɔ̃'fle], *v.t.* to swell again; to pump up (*tire*).—*v.i.* to swell again.

regorgeant [rəgɔr'ʒɑ̃], *a.* overflowing; abounding.

regorger [rəgɔr'ʒe], *v.t.* (*conjug. like* MANGER) to regurgitate, to disgorge.—*v.i.* to overflow, to run over; to be crammed (*with*); to be plentiful, to abound.

régressif [regrɛ'sif], *a.* (*fem.* **-ive**) regressive, retrogressive.

régression [regrɛ'sjɔ̃], *n.f.* regression, recession; retrogression; (*fig.*) decline.

regret [rə'grɛ], *n.m.* regret; *à regret*, with reluctance.

regrettable [rəgrɛ'tabl], *a.* regrettable, deplorable.

regrettablement [rəgrɛtablə'mɑ̃], *adv.* regrettably.

regretter [rəgrɛ'te], *v.t.* to regret; to grieve; to be sorry for, to repent; to miss.

régularisation [regylariza'sjɔ̃], *n.f.* putting in order, regularization.

régulariser [regylari'ze], *v.t.* to put in order, to regularize.

régularité [regylari'te], *n.f.* regularity.

régulateur [regyla'tœːr], *a.* (*fem.* **-trice**) regulating.—*n.m.* regulator; (*Eng. etc.*) governor.

régulier [regy'lje], *a.* (*fem.* **-ière**) regular; steady, exact.—*n.m.* regular (*monk, soldier etc.*).

régulièrement [regyljɛr'mɑ̃], *adv.* regularly.

régurgitation [regyrʒita'sjɔ̃], *n.f.* regurgitation.

régurgiter [regyrʒi'te], *v.t.* to regurgitate.

réhabilitation [reabilita'sjɔ̃], *n.f.* rehabilitation.

réhabiliter [reabili'te], *v.t.* to rehabilitate; to reinstate. **se réhabiliter**, *v.r.* to rehabilitate oneself, to recover one's good name.

rehaussement [rəos'mɑ̃], *n.m.* raising; heightening, enhancing; increase of value (*of coin*).

rehausser [rəo'se], *v.t.* to raise; to heighten, to enhance; to raise the value of; to enrich; to set off.

réimposer [reɛ̃po'ze], *v.t.* to reassess (*tax*); (*Print.*) to reimpose.

réimpression [reɛ̃prɛ'sjɔ̃], *n.f.* reprinting, reprint.

réimprimer [reɛ̃pri'me], *v.t.* to print again, to reprint.

rein [rɛ̃], *n.m.* kidney; (*pl.*) loins, back.

réincarnation [reɛ̃karna'sjɔ̃], *n.f.* reincarnation.

reine [rɛːn], *n.f.* queen.

reine-claude [rɛːn'kloːd], *n.f.* (*pl.* **reines-claude**) greengage.

reine-des-prés [rɛːnde'pre], *n.f.* (*pl.* **reines-des-prés**) meadowsweet.

réinstallation [reɛ̃stala'sjɔ̃], *n.f.* reinstallment, re-establishment.

réinstaller [reɛ̃sta'le], *v.t.* to reinstall.

réintégration [reɛ̃tegra'sjɔ̃], *n.f.* reinstatement.

réintégrer [reɛ̃te'gre], *v.t.* (*conjug. like* CÉDER) to reinstate.

réitératif [reitera'tif], *a.* (*fem.* **-tive**) reiterative.

réitération [reitera'sjɔ̃], *n.f.* reiteration, repetition.

réitérer [reite're], *v.t.* (*conjug. like* CÉDER) to reiterate, to repeat.

rejaillir [rəʒa'jiːr], *v.i.* to gush, to spurt out; to spring, to spout; (*fig.*) to flash; to reflect; to rebound.

rejaillissement [rəʒajis'mɑ̃], *n.m.* gushing out; spouting, springing; reflection, flashing; rebound.

réjection [reʒɛk'sjɔ̃], *n.f.* rejection.

rejet [rə'ʒɛ], *n.m.* rejection; throwing out; young shoot, sprout.

rejeter [rəʒ'te], *v.t.* (*conjug. like* APPELER) to throw again; to throw back; to tilt back (*one's hat*); to repel; to throw away; to throw up (*of plants*); to reject; to deny.— *v.i.* to shoot (*of plants*). **se rejeter**, *v.r.* to have recourse to; to fall back (*upon*).

rejeton [rəʒ'tɔ̃], *n.m.* shoot, sprout; (*fig.*) scion.

rejoindre [rə'ʒwɛ̃ːdr], *v.t. irr.* (*conjug. like* CRAINDRE) to rejoin, to join; to reunite; to overtake, to catch up. **se rejoindre**, *v.r.* to reunite; to meet; to catch each other up again.

rejouer [rə'ʒwe], *v.t., v.i.* to play again, to replay.

réjoui [re'ʒwi], *a.* and *n.m.* (*fem.* **-e**) jovial, joyous, merry (person).

réjouir [re'ʒwiːr], *v.t.* to rejoice, to delight, to cheer. **se réjouir**, *v.r.* to be *or* to make merry; to rejoice, to be delighted (*de*).

réjouissance [reʒwi'sɑ̃ːs], *n.f.* rejoicing; (*pl.*) merry-making.

réjouissant [reʒwi'sɑ̃], *a.* cheering; diverting, amusing.

relâchant [rəla'ʃɑ̃], *a.* relaxing; laxative, loosening.—*n.m.* (*Med.*) laxative.

relâche (1) [rə'laːʃ], *n.m.* intermission, discontinuance, respite; relaxation; (*Theat.*) suspension of performance; *relâche ce soir*, no performance this evening.

relâche (2) [rə'laːʃ], *n.f.* (*Naut.*) putting into a port; port of call.

relâché [rəla'ʃe], *a.* a lax, relaxed; loose, remiss.

relâchement [rəlaʃ'mɑ̃], *n.m.* slackening; slackness; laxity (*of morals*); looseness (*of bowels*).

relâcher [rəla'ʃe], *v.t.* to slacken, to loosen, to relax; to release, to unbend (*the mind etc.*); to yield, to abate.—*v.i.* (*Naut.*) to put into port. **se relâcher**, *v.r.* to grow slack *or* loose; to abate; to relax, to unbend.

relais [rə'lɛ], *n.m.* relay (*fresh horses*); stage; shift (*of workmen*).

relancer [rəlɑ̃'se], *v.t.* (*conjug. like* COMMENCER) to throw back; (*Ten.*) to return (*the ball*); (*Cards*) to raise (*a bid*); (*fig.*) to harry (*someone*).

relaps [rə'laps], *a.* relapsed, relapsed into heresy.—*n.m.* (*fem.* **-e**) relapsed heretic.

rélargir [relar'ʒiːr], *v.t.* to widen, to let out (*clothes etc.*).

relater [rələ'te], *v.t.* to state, to tell.

relatif [rələ'tif], *a.* (*fem.* **-tive**) relative; relating (*à*).

relation [rələ'sjɔ̃], *n.f.* relation, account; statement; respect; connection; communication, correspondence; (*pl.*) connections.

relativement [rəlativ'mɑ̃], *adv.* relatively.

relativité [rəlativi'te], *n.f.* relativity.

relaxation [rəlaksa'sjɔ̃], *n.f.* release; relaxation (*of muscles*).

relaxer [rəlak'se], *v.t.* to release (*a prisoner*); to relax (*muscles*).

relayer [rəlɛ'je] *v.t.* (*conjug. like* PAYER) to take the place of, to relieve; (*Elec. Eng., Rad., Teleg. etc.*) to relay.—*v.i.* to change horses. **se relayer**, *v.r.* to relieve each other; to work in shifts.

rélégation [relega'sjɔ̃], *n.f.* relegation; deportation (*of convict*).

reléguer [rəle'ge], *v.t.* (*conjug. like* CÉDER) to deport (*for life*); to shut up; to relegate, to consign (*à*). **se reléguer**, *v.r.* to shut oneself up.

relent [rə'lɑ̃], *a.* moldy, musty.—*n.m.* mustiness, moldiness.

relève [rə'lɛːv], *n.f.* (*Mil.*) relief.

relevé [rəl've], *a.* raised, erect; exalted, lofty; refined; highly seasoned.—*n.m.* abstract; statement, return; survey.

relèvement [rələv'mɑ̃], *n.m.* raising again; recovery (*of business*); relieving (*of sentry*); raise, increase (*of salary*); (*Naut.*) bearing.

relever [rəl've], *v.t.* (*conjug. like* AMENER) to raise again, to lift up again; to turn up; to restore; to relieve (*troops*), to change (*sentry*); to raise (*prices, salary*); (*Naut.*) to take the bearings of.—*v.i.* to recover; to turn up; to depend. **se relever**, *v.r.* to rise again; to get up, to pick oneself up; to recover; to be raised; to relieve each other.

relief [rə'ljɛf], *n.m.* relief, embossment; enhancement; (*pl.*) scraps (*from the table*).

relier [rə'lje], *v.t.* to connect; to hoop (*casks*); to bind (*books*).

relieur [rə'ljœːr], *n.m.* (*fem.* **-euse**) binder, book-binder.

religieusement [rəliʒjøz'mɑ̃], *adv.* religiously; scrupulously.

religieux [rəli'ʒjø], *a.* (*fem.* **-euse**) religious, strict.—*n.m.* (*fem.* **-euse**) monk, nun.

religion [rəli'ʒjɔ̃], *n.f.* religion.

reliquaire [rəli'kɛːr], *n.m.* reliquary, shrine.

reliquat [rəli'ka], *n.m.* balance, remainder (*of an account*); after-effects (*of a disease etc.*).

relique [rə'lik], *n.f.* relic (*of a saint*).

relire [rə'liːr], *v.t. irr.* (*conjug. like* LIRE) to re-read.

reliure [rə'ljyːr], *n.f.* binding (*of books*).

relouer [rəlu'e], *v.t.* to relet; to sub-let.

reluire [rəlɥiːr], *v.i. irr.* (*conjug. like* LUIRE) to shine, to glitter.

reluisant [rəlɥi'zɑ̃], *a.* gleaming, shining, glittering.

reluquer [rəly'ke], *v.t.* (*colloq.*) to ogle, to leer at; (*fig.*) to have an eye on.

remâcher [rəmɑ'ʃe], *v.t.* to chew again; (*fig.*) to turn over in one's mind.

remailler [rəmɑ'je], *v.t.* to repair the meshes (*of fishing nets etc.*); to mend a run (*in stocking*).

remaniement or **remaniment** [rəmani'mɑ̃], *n.m.* (*Polit.*) shakeup; handling again, touching up; repairing; changing.

remanier [rəma'nje], *v.t.* to handle again; to remodel; to adapt, to revise.

remariage [rəma'rjaːʒ], *n.m.* re-marriage.

remarier [rəma'rje], *v.t.* to remarry. **se remarier**, *v.r.* to marry again, to remarry.

remarquable [rəmar'kabl], *a.* remarkable, notable.

remarquablement [rəmarkablə'mɑ̃], *adv.* remarkably.

remarque [rə'mark], *n.f.* remark; notice.

remarquer [rəmar'ke], *v.t.* to mark again; to notice; to distinguish; **faire remarquer**, to point out. **se remarquer**, *v.r.* to be remarked.

remballer [rɑ̃ba'le], *v.t.* to pack up again.

rembarquement [rɑ̃barkə'mɑ̃], *n.m.* re-embarkation.

rembarquer [rɑ̃bar'ke], *v.t.* to re-embark, to ship again. **se rembarquer**, *v.r.* to go on board again.

rembarrer [rɑ̃ba're], *v.t.* to repulse; to snub; (*fam.*) to tell someone off.

remblai [rɑ̃'blɛ], *n.m.* filling up; embankment.

remblayer [rɑ̃blɛ'je], *v.t.* (*conjug. like* PAYER) to embank, to fill up (*with earth*).

remboîter [rɑ̃bwa'te], *v.t.* to fit in again; to reassemble; to reset (*a bone*).

rembourrage [rɑ̃bu'raːʒ], **rembourrement** [rɑ̃bur'mɑ̃], *n.m.* stuffing, padding.

rembourrer [rɑ̃bu're], *v.t.* to stuff, to pad; to upholster.

remboursable [rɑ̃bur'sabl], *a.* repayable; redeemable.

remboursement [rɑ̃bursə'mɑ̃], *n.m.* re-imbursement, repayment.

rembourser [rɑ̃bur'se], *v.t.* to repay; to reimburse; to redeem (*an annuity etc.*).

rembruni [rɑ̃bry'ni], *a.* dark, gloomy.

rembrunir [rɑ̃bry'niːr], *v.t.* to darken; to cloud over; (*fig.*) to sadden. **se rembrunir**, *v.r.* to grow darker; to become cloudy *or* gloomy.

remède [rə'mɛd], *n.m.* remedy, medicine.

remédiable [rəme'djabl], *a.* remediable.

remédier [rəme'dje], *v.i.* to remedy, to cure (*à*).

remêler [rəmɛ'le], *v.t.* to mix again, to reshuffle.

remembrement [rəmɑ̃brə'mɑ̃], *n.m.* consolidation (*of land*).

remémoratif [rəmemɔra'tif], *a.* (*fem.* **-tive**) commemorative.

remémorer [rəmemɔ're], *v.t.* to bring (*a thing*) to someone's mind. **se remémorer**, *v.r.* to recollect.

275

remerciement or **remercîment** [rəmɛrsi'mɑ̃], *n.m.* thanking; (*pl.*) thanks; *faire des remerciements*, to thank.

remercier [rəmɛr'sje], *v.t.* to thank; to dismiss; *non, je vous remercie*, no, thank you.

remettre [rə'mɛtr], *v.t. irr.* (*conjug. like* METTRE) to put back; to put on again; to lay down again; to make well again; to deliver; to postpone; to entrust; to forgive; to remember; (*Ten.*) (*balle*) *à remettre*, let (ball); *je vous remets*, I remember your face; *remettre dans l'esprit*, to remind. **se remettre,** *v.r.* to recover (*oneself*); to resume, to start again; to recollect; to refer; to improve (*of weather*).

réminiscence [remini'sɑ̃:s], *n.f.* reminiscence.

remis [rə'mi], *a.* put back, put off, postponed.

remisage [rəmi'za:ʒ], *n.m.* housing, putting away (*vehicle*).

remise [rə'mi:z], *n.f.* delivery; remittance; discount; commission; delay; coach house, mews, shed.

remiser [rəmi'ze], *v.t.* to put up, to put away (*vehicle*); to house; (*colloq.*) to put by.

rémissible [remi'sibl], *a.* remissible, pardonable.

rémission [remi'sjɔ̃], *n.f.* remission, forgiveness.

remmener [rɑ̃m'ne], *v.t.* (*conjug. like* AMENER) to take back, to lead back.

remodeler [rəmɔ'dle], *v.t.* (*conjug. like* AMENER) to remodel.

remontage [rəmɔ̃'ta:ʒ], *n.m.* going up; winding up (*of clock etc.*); assembling; refitting (*of parts of machinery*); restocking (*of shop*).

remonte [rə'mɔ̃:t], *n.f.* remounting, going upstream; run (*of fish*); (*Mil.*) remount.

remonter [rəmɔ̃'te], *v.t.* (*with aux.* AVOIR *or* ÊTRE *according as action or condition is meant*) to go up again; to take up again; to raise; to stock; to wind up (*clock etc.*); to re-string (*instruments*).—*v.i.* to go up again; to go back; to rise *or* increase (*in value etc.*); to date back; to remount (*cavalry*). **se remonter,** *v.r.* to take in a fresh supply (*de*); to be wound up (*of watches etc.*); to recover one's strength *or* spirits.

remontoir [rəmɔ̃'twa:r], *n.m.* winder, key (*of clock, watch*).

remontrance [rəmɔ̃'trɑ̃:s], *n.f.* remonstrance.

remontrer [rəmɔ̃'tre], *v.t.* to show again; to point out; to represent.—*v.i. en remontrer*, (*fig.*) to give advice.

remordre [rə'mɔrdr], *v.t.* to bite again.—*v.i.* to try again.

remords [rə'mɔ:r], *n.m.* remorse.

remorquage [rəmɔr'ka:ʒ], *n.m.* towing, hauling.

remorque [rə'mɔrk], *n.f.* towing; tow; tow-line; trailer (*car*).

remorquer [rəmɔr'ke], *v.t.* to tow, to haul.

remorqueur [rəmɔr'kœ:r], *a.* (*fem.* **-euse**) towing, hauling.—*n.m.* tug-boat, tug.

rémoulade [remu'lad], *n.f.* sharp sauce.

rémouleur [remu'lœ:r], *n.m.* knife-grinder.

remous [rə'mu], *n.m.* eddy; back-wash (*of ship*); slip-stream.

rempailler [rɑ̃pɑ'je], *v.t.* to re-seat (*a straw-bottomed chair*); to re-stuff with straw.

rempailleur [rɑ̃pɑ'jœ:r], *n.m.* (*fem.* **-euse**) chair mender.

rempaqueter [rɑ̃pak'te], *v.t.* (*conjug. like* APPELER) to pack up again.

rempart [rɑ̃'pa:r], *n.m.* rampart; (*fig.*) bulwark.

remplaçable [rɑ̃pla'sabl], *a.* replaceable.

remplaçant [rɑ̃pla'sɑ̃], *n.m.* (*fem.* **-e**) substitute; locum.

remplacement [rɑ̃plas'mɑ̃], *n.m.* replacing, replacement.

remplacer [rɑ̃pla'se], *v.t.* (*conjug. like* COMMENCER) to take the p'ce of, to replace; to reinvest. **se remplacer,** *v.r.* to be replaced.

rempli [rɑ̃'pli], *a.* filled, full.—*n.m.* tuck, take-up.

remplier [rɑ̃pli'je], *v.t.* to make a tuck in; to turn in.

remplir [rɑ̃'pli:r], *v.t.* to refill, to replenish; to fill, to fill up; to fill in (*form*); to cram; to supply; to occupy (*time etc.*); to fulfil. **se remplir,** *v.r.* to fill oneself; to become full.

remplissage [rɑ̃pli'sa:ʒ], *n.m.* filling, filling up (*of casks etc.*); (*fig.*) rubbish, padding.

remploi [rɑ̃'plwa], *n.m.* reinvestment.

remployer [rɑ̃plwa'je], *v.t.* (*conjug. like* EMPLOYER) to use again; to reinvest.

remplumer [rɑ̃ply'me], *v.t.* to feather again. **se remplumer,** *v.r.* to get new feathers; (*fig.*) to retrieve one's losses; to get plump again.

rempocher [rɑ̃pɔ'ʃe], *v.t.* to put (*something*) back in one's pocket.

remporter [rɑ̃pɔr'te], *v.t.* to carry *or* take back; to carry off, to take away with one; to get; to win.

rempoter [rɑ̃pɔ'te], *v.t.* to repot.

remuant [rə'mɥɑ̃], *a.* restless; bustling; (*fam.*) on the go.

remue-ménage [rəmyme'na:ʒ], *n.m. inv.* stir, disturbance, bustle.

remuement or **remûment** [rəmy'mɑ̃], *n.m.* stir, stirring; removal; disturbance.

remuer [rə'mɥe], *v.t.* to move, to stir; to rouse; to turn up; to shake.—*v.i.* and **se remuer,** *v.r.* to stir, to move; to fidget.

rémunérateur [remynera'tœ:r], *a.* (*fem.* **-trice**) remunerative, profitable.—*n.m.* (*fem.* **-trice**) rewarder.

rémunération [remynera'sjɔ̃], *n.f.* remuneration, reward.

rémunératoire [remynera'twa:r], *a.* remunerative.

rémunérer [remyne're], *v.t.* (*conjug. like* CÉDER) to remunerate; to reward.

renâcler [rənɑ'kle], *v.i.* to snort; (*fam.*) to turn up one's nose; to balk (*at something*).

renaissance [rənɛ'sɑ̃:s], *n.f.* rebirth; renaissance.

renaissant [rənɛ'sɑ̃], *a.* springing up again, reviving.

renaître [rə'nɛ:tr], *v.i. irr.* (*conjug. like* NAÎTRE, *but no p.p.*) to be born again; to grow again; to appear again; to revive.

rénal [re'nal], *a.* (*m. pl.* **-aux**) (*Anat.*) renal.

renard [rə'na:r], *n.m.* fox; (*fig.*) sly fellow; (*pop.*) strikebreaker.

renarde [rə'nard], *n.f.* vixen.

renardeau [rənar'do], *n.m.* (*pl.* **-eaux**) fox cub.

Renaud [rə'no], *m.* Reginald.

renchéri [rãʃe'ri], *a.* particular, over-nice (*of a person*).—*n.m.* (*fem.* **-e**) fastidious person; *faire le renchéri*, to put on airs.

renchérir [rãʃe'ri:r], *v.t.* to raise the price of. —*v.i.* to get dearer, to rise in price; *renchérir sur*, to improve upon.

renchérissement [rãʃeris'mã], *n.m.* rise in price.

rencogner (se) [sərãkɔ'ɲe], *v.r.* to retreat,to crouch in a corner.

rencontre [rã'kɔ̃:tr], *n.f.* meeting, encounter; duel; accidental meeting, discovery etc.; collision; chance, coincidence.

rencontrer [rãkɔ̃'tre], *v.t.* to meet, to meet with; to light upon, to encounter. **se rencontrer**, *v.r.* to meet, to meet each other; to be met with; to agree, to coincide.

rendement [rãd'mã], *n.m.* produce, yield, output; efficiency (*of a machine etc.*); (*Spt.*) handicap; (*Comm.*) return, profit.

rendez-vous [rãde'vu], *n.m. inv.* rendezvous, appointment; engagement; place of meeting.

rendormir [rãdɔr'mi:r], *v.t. irr.* (*conjug. like* SENTIR) to put to sleep again. **se rendormir**, *v.r.* to fall asleep again.

rendre [rã:dr], *v.t.* to return, to restore, to give back; to repay; to deliver; to give up; to pay; to produce; to reward; to carry; to eject; to emit; to express; to translate; *rendre visite*, to pay a visit.—*v.i.* to lead (*of roads*); to be lucrative; to function, to work. **se rendre**, *v.r.* to go; to resort; to make oneself, to render oneself; to become; to surrender, to give up; to be worn out.

rendu [rã'dy], *a.* rendered, delivered; exhausted, tired out; arrived.—*n.m.* return, tit for tat.

rendurcir [rãdyr'si:r], *v.t.* to make harder. **se rendurcir**, *v.r.* to become harder.

rêne [rɛ:n], *n.f.* rein.

renégat [rɛne'ga], *a.* and *n.m.* (*fem.* **-e**) renegade, turncoat.

rêner [rɛ'ne], *v.t.* to bridle (*a horse*).

renfermé [rãfɛr'me], *a.* **personne renfermée**, close, uncommunicative person.— *n.m. odeur de renfermé*, fustiness; musty smell; *sentir le renfermé*, to smell close, fusty *or* stuffy.

renfermer [rãfɛr'me], *v.t.* to shut up; to contain; to include, to comprise; to conceal. **se renfermer**, *v.r.* to shut oneself up; to confine oneself.

renfiler [rãfi'le], *v.t.* to thread, to string again.

renflammer [rãfla'me], *v.t.* to rekindle. **se renflammer**, *v.r.* to flare up again.

renflé [rã'fle], *a.* swollen, swelling; (*Bot.*) inflated.

renflement [rãflə'mã], *n.m.* swelling, bulge.

renfler [rã'fle], *v.t., v.i.* to swell.

renflouage [rãflu'a:ʒ], **renflouement** [rãflu 'mã], *n.m.* refloating (*a ship*).

renflouer [rãflu'e], *v.t.* to refloat, to raise (*a ship*); (*fig.*) to salvage (*firm, company etc.*).

renfoncement [rãfɔ̃s'mã], *n.m.* cavity, hollow, recess.

renfoncer [rãfɔ̃'se], *v.t.* (*conjug. like* COMMENCER) to drive deeper; to pull (*a hat etc.*) further on.

renforçage [rãfɔr'sa:ʒ], *n.m.* strengthening.

renforcé [rãfɔr'se], *a.* downright, regular; reinforced.

renforcement [rãfɔrsə'mã], *n.m.* strengthening; reinforcement.

renforcer [rãfɔr'se], *v.t.* (*conjug. like* COMMENCER) to strengthen, to reinforce; to increase. **se renforcer**, *v.r.* to gather strength, to grow stronger; (*Mil.*) to be reinforced.

renfort [rã'fɔ:r], *n.m.* reinforcement; (*fig.*) help, aid, relief; strengthening-piece.

renfrogné [rãfrɔ'ɲe], *a.* frowning, scowling, surly.

renfrognement [rãfrɔɲə'mã], *n.m.* frown, scowl.

renfrogner (se) [sərãfrɔ'ɲe], *v.r.* to frown.

rengagement [rãgaʒ'mã], *n.m.* re-engagement; (*Mil.*) re-enlistment.

rengager [rãga'ʒe], *v.t.* (*conjug. like* MANGER) to re-engage.—*v.i.* (*Mil.*) to re-enlist. **se rengager**, *v.r.* to re-engage; to begin afresh; to re-enlist.

rengaine [rã'gɛ:n], *n.f.* catch phrase; (*fam.*) hackneyed story; popular tune.

rengainer [rãgɛ'ne], *v.t.* to sheathe, to put up (*one's sword*); to withdraw, to put away.

rengorgement [rãgɔrʒə'mã], *n.m.* swaggering, puffing out the neck (*of peacock*).

rengorger (se) [sərãgɔr'ʒe], *v.r.* to carry one's head high; (*fig.*) to give oneself airs.

reniable [rə'njabl], *a.* deniable.

reniement *or* **reniment** [rəni'mã], *n.m.* denying, disowning.

renier [rə'nje], *v.t.* to disown (*son, friend etc.*); to deny (*God, doctrine*).

reniflement [rəniflə'mã], *n.m.* sniffling, snuffing, snivelling.

renifler [rəni'fle], *v.i.* to sniff, to snivel; (*fig.*) to turn up one's nose (*sur*); to hang back.

renne [rɛn], *n.m.* reindeer.

renom [rə'nɔ̃], *n.m.* renown, fame, reputation.

renommé [rənɔ'me], *a.* renowned, famed.

renommée [rənɔ'me], *n.f.* renown, fame reputation; rumor.

renommer [rənɔ'me], *v.t.* to name again, to re-elect; to make famous, to praise.

renoncement [rənɔ̃s'mã], *n.m.* renouncement; renunciation.

renoncer [rənɔ̃'se], *v.t.* (*conjug. like* COMMENCER) to renounce, to disclaim, to disown.—*v.i.* to give up, to renounce (*à*).

renonciation [rənɔ̃sja'sjɔ̃], *n.f.* renunciation, self-denial.

renoncule [rənɔ̃'kyl], *n.f.* (*Bot.*) ranunculus, buttercup, crowfoot.

renouer [rənu'e], *v.t.* to tie again, to knot again; to put together; to resume.—*v.i.* to resume relations (*avec*).

renouveau [rənu'vo], *n.m.* (*pl.* **-eaux**) (*poet.*) spring.

renouvelable [rənu'vlabl], *a.* renewable.

renouveler [rənu'vle], *v.t.* (*conjug. like* APPELER) to renew; to renovate; to revive; to recommence, to repeat. **se renouveler**, *v.r.* to be renewed, to be revived, to occur again.

renouvellement [rənuvɛl'mã], *n.m.* renewal, revival, renovation; increase.

rénovateur [renova'tœ:r], *a.* (*fem.* **-trice**) renovating.—*n.m.* (*fem.* **-trice**) renovator, restorer.

rénovation [renɔvɑ'sjɔ̃], *n.f.* renovation, renewal.

renseignement [rɑ̃sɛɲ'mɑ̃], *n.m.* (piece of) information, (piece of) intelligence, account; (*pl.*) information; references; *bureau de renseignements*, information bureau, inquiry office.

renseigner [rɑ̃sɛ'ɲe], *v.t.* to give information to; to direct. **se renseigner**, *v.r.* to seek information, to make inquiries.

rente [rɑ̃:t], *n.f.* yearly income; revenue; stock, funds.

renté [rɑ̃'te], *a.* of independent means; endowed (*of hospital etc.*).

renter [rɑ̃'te], *v.t.* to allow a yearly income to, to endow (*public services etc.*).

rentier [rɑ̃'tje], *n.m.* (*fem.* **-ière**) stockholder; person of independent means.

rentrant [rɑ̃'trɑ̃], *a.* re-entering, returning; (*Av.*) retractable.—*n.m.* recess (*in a wall*); (*fem.* **-e**) new player.

rentré [rɑ̃'tre], *a.* returned; suppressed; depressed.

rentrée [rɑ̃'tre], *n.f.* re-entrance; return, home-coming; reopening (*of schools etc.*); reappearance; ingathering (*of crops etc.*); receipt, collection.

rentrer [rɑ̃'tre], *v.t.* (*aux.* AVOIR) to take in, to bring in; to suppress.—*v.i.* (*aux.* ÊTRE) to re-enter, to go in again; to return home; to join again; to reopen (*of schools etc.*).

renversable [rɑ̃vɛr'sabl], *a.* liable to be upset; reversible.

renversant [rɑ̃vɛr'sɑ̃], *a.* (*colloq.*) amazing, stunning.

renverse [rɑ̃'vɛrs], *n.f. à la renverse*, backwards.

renversé [rɑ̃vɛr'se], *a.* thrown down, thrown back; upside-down.

renversement [rɑ̃vɛrsə'mɑ̃], *n.m.* reversing; overturning, overthrow; turning upside down; confusion; subversion.

renverser [rɑ̃vɛr'se], *v.t.* to turn upside down, to upset; to reverse; to knock over; to spill (*a liquid*); to destroy; to confuse; to turn (*the brain*); (*fam.*) to astound; to rout; (*Arith., Mus.*) to invert. **se renverser**, *v.r.* to fall back; to fall down; to capsize; to be spilt.

renvoi [rɑ̃'vwa], *n.m.* sending back, return; dismissal; referring (*to a committee etc.*).

renvoyer [rɑ̃vwa'je], *v.t. irr.* (*conjug. like* ENVOYER) to send again; to send back, to return; to dismiss; to refer; to postpone; to throw back; to reflect (*light, heat etc.*); to reverberate (*sound*). **se renvoyer**, *v.r.* to be sent back or returned; to send from one to the other.

réoccupation [reɔkypɑ'sjɔ̃], *n.f.* reoccupation.

réoccuper [reɔky'pe], *v.t.* to reoccupy.

réorganisation [reɔrganizɑ'sjɔ̃], *n.f.* re-organization.

réorganiser [reɔrgani'ze], *v.t.* to reorganize.

réouverture [reuvɛr'ty:r], *n.f.* reopening (*of a theatre*).

repaire (1) [rə'pɛ:r], *n.m.* haunt (*of criminals*); den, lair (*of animals*).

repaire (2) [REPÈRE].

repaître [rə'pɛ:tr], *v.t. irr.* (*conjug. like* PAÎTRE) to feed, to nourish. **se repaître**, *v.r.*

to feed on, to feast on; to delight in, to indulge in.

répandre [re'pɑ̃:dr], *v.t.* to pour out, to shed; to spill; to scatter; to distribute; to exhale; to spread abroad. **se répandre**, *v.r.* to be poured out, to be shed, to be spilt; to be spread; to be exhaled; to be spread abroad; to be current; to go into society.

répandu [repɑ̃'dy], *a.* spilt, shed; wide-spread.

réparable [repa'rabl], *a.* reparable; rectifiable.

reparaître [rəpar'rɛ:tr], *v.i. irr.* (*conjug. like* CONNAÎTRE) to reappear.

réparateur [repara'tœ:r], *a.* (*fem.* **-trice**) restorative, refreshing.—*n.m.* (*fem.* **-trice**) repairer, restorer.

réparation [reparɑ'sjɔ̃], *n.f.* repairing, mending; amends; compensation; *en réparation*, under repair.

réparer [repa're], *v.t.* to repair, to mend; to make amends for, to make up for.

répareur [repa'rœ:r], *n.m.* (*fem.* **-euse**) repairer.

reparler [rəpar'le], *v.i.* to speak again.

repartie [rəpar'ti], *n.f.* repartee, retort.

repartir (1) [rəpar'ti:r], *v.t., v.i.* (*conjug. like* SENTIR) to answer, to retort.

repartir (2) [rəpar'ti:r], *v.i. irr.* (*conjug. like* SENTIR, *but with aux.* ÊTRE) to set out again, to go away again.

répartir [repar'ti:r], *v.t.* to divide, to distribute; to assess.

répartissable [reparti'sabl], *a.* divisible; assessable.

répartiteur [reparti'tœ:r], *n.m.* (*fem.* **-trice**) distributor; assessor (*of taxes etc.*).

répartition [reparti'sjɔ̃], *n.f.* distribution; assessment.

repas [rə'pɑ], *n.m. inv.* meal, repast.

repassage [rəpɑ'sa:ʒ], *n.m.* repassing; grinding, sharpening (*of cutlery*); ironing (*of linen etc.*).

repasser [rəpɑ'se], *v.t.* (*aux.* AVOIR) to pass again; to cross again; to think over; to sharpen, to grind (*tools*); to iron; to repeat; to look over again.—*v.i.* (*aux.* ÊTRE) to pass again; to go, come, call etc., again.

repasseur [rəpɑ'sœ:r], *n.m.* (*fem.* **-euse**) (*Ind.*) examiner; grinder.—*n.f.* (**-euse**) ironer (*person or machine*).

repavage [rəpa'va:ʒ], **repavement** [rəpav'mɑ̃], *n.m.* repaving.

repaver [rəpa've], *v.t.* to repave.

repêchage [rəpɛ'ʃa:ʒ], *n.m.* rescuing; (*Spt.*) *épreuve de repêchage*, supplementary heat; (*Sch.*) second chance (*for candidate who has failed an examination*).

repêcher [rəpɛ'ʃe], *v.t.* to fish up or out again; (*fig.*) to recover, to retrieve.

repeindre [rə'pɛ̃:dr], *v.t. irr.* (*conjug. like* CRAINDRE) to repaint.

repenser [rəpɑ̃'se], *v.t., v.i.* to think over; to think again (*of*).

repentance [rəpɑ̃'tɑ̃:s], *n.f.* repentance, contrition.

repentant [rəpɑ̃'tɑ̃], *a.* repentant.

repenti [rəpɑ̃'ti], *a.* penitent.

repentir [rəpɑ̃'ti:r], *n.m.* repentance, contrition, regret.

repentir (se) [sərəpɑ̃'ti:r], *v.r. irr.* (*conjug. like* SENTIR) to repent; to rue (*de*).

repérage [rəpe'ra:ʒ], *n.m.* locating; (*Cine.*) synchronization; (*Mil.*) spotting.

répercussion [repɛrky'sjɔ̃], *n.f.* repercussion, reverberation.

répercuter [repɛrky'te], *v.t.* to reverberate, to echo; to reflect. **se répercuter**, *v.r.* to be reflected (*light*); to reverberate (*sound*); (*fig.*) to have repercussions.

repère or **repaire** [rə'pɛ:r], *n.m.* mark; benchmark; (*fig.*) landmark.

repérer [rəpe're], *v.t.* (*conjug. like* CÉDER) to locate, to spot; to make a guiding mark upon. **se repérer**, *v.r.* to find one's bearings.

répertoire [repɛr'twa:r], *n.m.* table, list, catalogue; repertory.

répéter [repe'te], *v.t.* (*conjug. like* CÉDER) to repeat, to tell again; to rehearse; to reflect; (*Law*) to demand back. **se répéter**, *v.r.* to be repeated; to repeat oneself.

répétiteur [repeti'tœ:r], *n.m.* (*fem.* **-trice**) private teacher, tutor.

répétition [repeti'sjɔ̃], *n.f.* repetition; recurrence; private lesson; (*Theat.*) rehearsal.

repétrir [rəpe'tri:r], *v.t.* to remold; to re-fashion.

repeupler [rəpœ'ple], *v.t.* to repeople; to restock. **se repeupler**, *v.r.* to be repeopled; to be restocked.

repiquage [rəpi'ka:ʒ], *n.m.* transplanting, pricking *or* planting out (again); repairing (*of road*).

repiquer [rəpi'ke], *v.t.* to prick again; to prick out; to transplant; to repair (*road*).

répit [re'pi], *n.m.* respite; (*fig.*) rest, breathing space.

replacement [rəplas'mã], *n.m.* replacing, putting *or* setting back; reinvestment (*of funds*).

replacer [rəpla'se], *v.t.* (*conjug. like* COMMENCER) to replace, to put in place again; to bring back; to reinvest (*funds*). **se replacer**, *v.r.* to find oneself a new situation.

replanir [rəpla'ni:r], *v.t.* to plane down (*wood*).

replanter [rəplã'te], *v.t.* to replant.

replâtrer [rəplɑ'tre], *v.t.* to replaster; to patch up (*temporarily*).

replet [rə'plɛ], *a.* (*fem.* **-ète**) obese, stout; (*fam.*) pudgy.

réplétion [reple'sjɔ̃], *n.f.* stoutness; repletion, surfeit.

repli [rə'pli], *n.m.* fold, crease; (*fig.*) winding, coil, meander (*of river*); (*Mil.*) withdrawal.

repliable [rəpli'jabl], *a.* folding, collapsible.

replier [rəpli'je], *v.t.* to fold again, to fold up; to bend back; to coil (*a rope etc.*). **se replier**, *v.r.* to twist oneself, to writhe, to wind, to coil; (*Mil.*) to retreat.

réplique [re'plik], *n.f.* reply, answer, retort; (*Mus.*) repeat; (*Theat.*) cue.

répliquer [repli'ke], *v.t.*, *v.i.* to reply, to retort.

replonger [rəplɔ̃'ʒe], *v.t.* (*conjug. like* MANGER) to plunge again, to dip again.— *v.i.* and **se replonger**, *v.r.* to plunge again; to dive again.

répondant [repɔ̃'dã], *n.m.* candidate (*at an examination*); bail, surety.

répondre [re'pɔ̃:dr], *v.t.* to answer, to reply. —*v.i.* to answer, to reply; to write back; to come up (*à*); to correspond; to re-echo; to be answerable (*de*); to pledge oneself

(*pour*); **je vous en réponds**, take my word for it.

répons [re'pɔ̃], *n.m.* response (*in church*).

réponse [re'pɔ̃:s], *n.f.* answer, reply, response.

report [rə'pɔ:r], *n.m.* (*Book-keeping*) carrying forward, bringing forward; amount brought forward.

reportage [rəpɔr'ta:ʒ], *n.m.* (*Journ.*) reporting; feature article.

reporter (1) [rəpɔr'tɛ:r], *n.m.* (*Journ.*) reporter.

reporter (2) [rəpɔr'te], *v.t.* to carry back; to take back; (*Book-keeping*) to carry forward. **se reporter**, *v.r.* to go back; to refer; **se reporter à**, please refer to.

repos [rə'po], *n.m.* rest, repose; sleep; quiet; resting place; **en repos**, at rest; (*Mil.*) **repos !** stand at ease!

reposant [rəpo'zã], *a.* restful, refreshing.

reposé [rəpo'ze], *a.* rested, refreshed; quiet, calm, cool.

reposer [rəpo'ze], *v.t.* to place again, to lay again, to replace; to rest (*on anything*); to refresh.—*v.i.* to rest, to lie down; to sleep; to be at rest. **se reposer**, *v.r.* to rest, to lie down; to settle down; to alight again (*of birds*); **se reposer sur**, to rely on.

reposoir [rəpo'zwa:r], *n.m.* resting place; pause.

repoussant [rəpu'sã], *a.* repulsive, loathsome.

repoussé [rəpu'se], *a.* chased (*silver*), embossed.

repousser [rəpu'se], *v.t.* to push back, to repel; to spurn, to reject; to rebuff; to shoot out (*branches etc.*) again; **repousser du cuir**, to emboss leather; **repousser du cuivre**, to chase copper.—*v.i.* to recoil; to spring up again (*of plants etc.*); to grow again (*of hair*); to be repulsive.

repoussoir [rəpu'swa:r], *n.m.* (*Paint.*) foil.

répréhensible [repreã'sibl], *a.* reprehensible.

répréhension [repreã'sjɔ̃], *n.f.* reprehension, reproof.

reprendre [rə'prã:dr], *v.t.* *v.i.* irr. (*conjug. like* PRENDRE) to recover, to recapture; to take up again; to reprove; to repair.—*v.i.* to take root again; to freeze again; to close up again (*of wounds etc.*); to begin again, to return to; to improve; to reply; to resume. **se reprendre**, *v.r.* to correct oneself; to be caught again; to begin again.

représaille [repre'za:j], *n.f.* (*usu. pl.*) reprisal; **user de représailles**, to retaliate.

représentant [rəprezã'tã], *n.m.* (*fem.* **-e**) representative.

représentatif [rəprezãta'tif], *a.* (*fem.* **-tive**) representative.

représentation [rəprezãta'sjɔ̃], *n.f.* representation; performance; show; remonstrance; agency.

représenter [rəprezã'te], *v.t.* to present again; to show, to produce; to represent; to resemble; to act (*a play*); to be the representative of.—*v.i.* to have an imposing appearance; to make a good show. **se représenter**, *v.r.* to present oneself again; to picture to oneself; to occur.

répressible [repre'sibl], *a.* repressible.

répressif [repre'sif], *a.* (*fem.* **-ive**) repressive.

répression [repre'sjɔ̃], *n.f.* repression.

réprimande [repri'mã:d], *n.f.* reprimand, rebuke.

réprimander [reprimã'de], *v.t.* to reprimand, to reprove.

réprimant [repri'mã], *a.* repressive.

réprimer [repri'me], *v.t.* to repress, to restrain.

repris [rə'pri], *a.* retaken, taken up again; reset (*of a bone*).—*n.m.* **repris de justice**, old offender, (*fam.*) old lag.

reprisage [rəpri'za:ʒ], *n.m.* darn; darning.

reprise [rə'pri:z], *n.f.* resumption; recapture, recovery; revival; darn; (*Mus.*) repetition; refrain (*of a song*); (*Fib. etc.*) second half; (*Fenc.*) bout; (*Box.*) round; **à plusieurs reprises**, several times, repeatedly.

repriser [rəpri'ze], *v.t.* to darn.

réprobateur [reprɔba'tœ:r], *a.* (*fem.* **-trice**) reproving.

réprobation [reprɔba'sjɔ̃], *n.f.* reprobation.

reprochable [rəprɔ'ʃabl], *a.* reproachable.

reproche [rə'prɔʃ], *n.m.* reproach.

reprocher [rəprɔ'ʃe], *v.t.* to reproach, to upbraid; to taunt. **se reprocher**, *v.r.* to reproach oneself; to blame oneself.

reproducteur [rəprɔdyk'tœ:r], *a.* (*fem.* **-trice**) reproductive.

reproductif [rəprɔdyk'tif], *a.* (*fem.* **-tive**) reproductive.

reproduction [rəprɔdyk'sjɔ̃], *n.f.* reproduction; copy.

reproduire [rəprɔ'dɥi:r], *v.t.* irr. (*conjug. like* CONDUIRE) to reproduce; to reprint. **se reproduire**, *v.r.* to reproduce; to breed; to recur.

réprouvable [repru'vabl], *a.* censurable, reprehensible.

réprouvé [repru've], *a.* and *n.m.* (*fem.* **-ée**) reprobate.

réprouver [repru've], *v.t.* to disapprove of; (*Theol.*) to condemn.

reps [rɛps], *n.m.* rep (*silk or woollen fabric*).

reptile [rɛp'til], *a.* creeping, crawling.—*n.m.* reptile.

repu [rə'py], *a.* and *p.p.* of **repaître**, full, satiated.

républicain [repybli'kɛ̃], *a.* and *n.m.* (*fem.* **-e**) republican.

republier [rəpybli'je], *v.t.* to republish.

république [repy'blik], *n.f.* republic; commonwealth.

répudiation [repydja'sjɔ̃], *n.f.* repudiation.

répudier [repy'dje], *v.t.* to repudiate.

répugnance [repy'ɲɑ̃:s], *n.f.* repugnance; reluctance.

répugnant [repy'ɲɑ̃], *a.* repugnant.

répugner [repy'ɲe], *v.i.* to be repugnant; to feel repugnance; to clash with.

répulsif [repyl'sif], *a.* (*fem.* **-sive**) repulsive, repellent; (*fig.*) disgusting.

répulsion [repyl'sjɔ̃], *n.f.* repulsion; (*fig.*) aversion, disgust.

réputation [repyta'sjɔ̃], *n.f.* reputation; character; fame.

réputé [repy'te], *a.* well-known.

réputer [repy'te], *v.t.* to repute, to consider, to deem.

requérant [rəke'rɑ̃], *n.m.* (*fem.* **-e**) plaintiff, petitioner.

requérir [rəke'ri:r], *v.t.* irr. (*conjug. like* ACQUÉRIR) to request; to require; to claim; to requisition.

requête [rə'kɛ:t], *n.f.* request, petition, demand.

requiem [rekɥi'ɛm], *n.m.* requiem.

requin [rə'kɛ̃], *n.m.* shark.

requis [rə'ki], *a.* required, requisite, necessary.

réquisition [rekizi'sjɔ̃], *n.f.* requisition; summons; levy.

réquisitionner [rekizisjɔ'ne], *v.t.* to requisition, to commandeer.

rescapé [rɛska'pe], *a.* and *n.m.* (*fem.* **-ée**) survivor of a disaster.

rescousse [rɛs'kus], *n.f.* **venir** (**aller**) **à la rescousse**, to come (to go) to the rescue.

réseau [re'zo], *n.m.* (*pl.* **-eaux**) net; network; (*fig.*) web, tangle; (*Rail.*, *Elec. etc.*) network, system.

réséda [reze'da], *n.m.* reseda; mignonette.

réservation [rezɛrva'sjɔ̃], *n.f.* reservation, reserving; booking (*of seats*).

réserve [re'zɛrv], *n.f.* reserve; reservation, caution; modesty; stock, store; preserve (*for game*).

réservé [rezɛr've], *a.* reserved; cautious.

réserver [rezɛr've], *v.t.* to reserve; to keep (**pour**). **se réserver**, *v.r.* to reserve for oneself; to reserve oneself, to wait.

réserviste [rezɛr'vist], *n.m.* (*Mil.*) reservist.

réservoir [rezɛr'vwa:r], *n.m.* reservoir; tank, cistern, well.

résidant [rezi'dɑ̃], *a.* resident.

résidence [rezi'dɑ̃:s], *n.f.* residence, dwelling.

résident [rezi'dɑ̃], *n.m.* (*fem.* **-e**) resident.

résidentiel [rezidɑ̃'sjɛl], *a.* (*fem.* **-elle**) residential.

résider [rezi'de], *v.i.* to reside, to dwell.

résidu [rezi'dy], *n.m.* residue; remainder.

résiduaire [rezi'dɥɛ:r], *a.* waste.

résignation [reziɲa'sjɔ̃], *n.f.* resignation.

résigné [rezi'ɲe], *a.* resigned, submissive.

résigner [rezi'ɲe], *v.t.* to resign, to give up. **se résigner**, *v.r.* to resign oneself, to submit.

résiliation [rezilja'sjɔ̃], *n.f.*, **résiliement** or **résiliment** [rezili'mɑ̃], *n.m.* cancelling, annulment.

résilience [rezi'ljɑ̃:s], *n.f.* resilience (*in metals*).

résilier [rezi'lje], *v.t.* to cancel, to annul.

résille [re'zi:j], *n.f.* hair net.

résine [re'zin], *n.f.* resin, rosin.

résineux [rezi'nø], *a.* (*fem.* **-euse**) resinous.

résistance [rezis'tɑ̃:s], *n.f.* resistance, opposition; **la Résistance**, the Resistance Movement (1940-45).

résistant [rezis'tɑ̃], *a.* unyielding; resistant, tough.—*n.m.* (*fem.* **-e**) member of the Resistance Movement.

résister [rezis'te], *v.i.* to resist, to withstand (**à**).

résistible [rezis'tibl], *a.* resistible.

résistivité [rezistivi'te], *n.f.* (*Elec.*) resistivity.

résolu [rezɔ'ly], *a.* resolved, resolute, determined; solved.

résoluble [rezɔ'lybl], *a.* soluble.

résolument [rezɔly'mɑ̃], *adv.* resolutely, boldly.

résolution [rezɔly'sjɔ̃], *n.f.* resolution, solution; decision, determination; resolve.

résonance [rezɔ'nɑ̃:s], *n.f.* resonance.

résonnant [rezɔ'nɑ̃], *a.* resonant, resounding, sonorous.

résonnement [rezɔn'mã], *n.m.* resounding, re-echoing.
résonner [rezɔ'ne], *v.i.* to resound, to reverberate, to re-echo.
résoudre [re'zu:dr], *v.t. irr.* to resolve; to dissolve; to solve; to decide upon; to cancel; to persuade. **se résoudre,** *v.r.* to resolve; to determine; to be resolved, to be solved; to dissolve.
respect [rɛs'pɛ], *n.m.* respect, regard, reverence.
respectabilité [rɛspɛktabili'te], *n.f.* respectability.
respectable [rɛspɛk'tabl], *a.* respectable.
respectablement [rɛspɛktablə'mã], *adv.* respectably.
respecter [rɛspɛk'te], *v.t.* to respect, to revere; to spare.
respectif [rɛspɛk'tif], *a. (fem.* -**tive**) respective.
respectivement [rɛspɛktiv'mã], *adv.* respectively.
respectueusement [rɛspɛktɥøz'mã], *adv.* respectfully, deferentially.
respectueux [rɛspɛk'tɥø], *a. (fem.* -**euse**) respectful, deferential.
respirable [rɛspi'rabl], *a.* respirable, breathable.
respirateur [rɛspira'tœ:r], *a.m.* respiratory. —*n.m.* respirator.
respiration [rɛspira'sjɔ̃], *n.f.* respiration, breathing.
respiratoire [rɛspira'twa:r], *a.* respiratory, breathing.
respirer [rɛspi're], *v.t.* to breathe; *(fig.)* to express; to long for.—*v.i.* to breathe; to catch one's breath, to rest.
resplendir [rɛsplã'di:r], *v.i.* to shine brightly; to glitter.
resplendissant [rɛsplãdi'sã], *a.* resplendent, glittering.
resplendissement [rɛsplãdis'mã], *n.m.* splendor, refulgence.
responsabilité [rɛspɔ̃sabili'te], *n.f.* responsibility, liability.
responsable [rɛspɔ̃'sabl], *a.* responsible, accountable.
resquillage [rɛski'ja:ʒ], *n.m.,* **resquille** [rɛs'ki:j], *n.f. (slang)* gate-crashing; **entrer à la resquille,** to gate-crash.
resquiller [rɛski'je], *v.i.* to gate-crash; to wangle.
ressac [rə'sak], *n.m.* surf.
ressaisir [rəsɛ'zi:r], *v.t.* to seize again. **se ressaisir,** *v.r.* to regain one's self-control.
ressasser [rəsa'se], *v.t. (fig.)* to scrutinize; *(fig.)* to repeat tediously, to harp on.
ressaut [rə'so], *n.m.* projection; abrupt fall, dip.
ressauter [rəso'te], *v.t.* to leap over again.—*v.i.* to leap again; *(Arch.)* to project.
ressemblance [rəsã'blã:s], *n.f.* resemblance, likeness.
ressemblant [rəsã'blã], *a.* like, similar.
ressembler [rəsã'ble], *v.i.* to look like, to resemble (à). **se ressembler,** *v.r.* to be like each other; to look alike.
ressemelage [rəsəm'la:ʒ], *n.m.* resoling *(of shoes).*
ressemeler [rəsəm'le], *v.t. (conjug. like* APPELER) to re-sole *(shoes etc.).*
ressenti [rəsã'ti], *a.* felt; *(Paint.)* strongly expressed.

ressentiment [rəsãti'mã], *n.m.* resentment.
ressentir [rəsã'ti:r], *v.t. irr. (conjug. like* SENTIR) to feel, to experience; to manifest; to resent. **se ressentir,** *v.r.* to feel the effects *(de);* to be felt.
resserrement [rəsɛr'mã], *n.m.* contraction, tightening; restriction.
resserrer [rəsɛ're], *v.t.* to tighten; to pen in; to restrain; to abridge; to close up; to lock up again. **se resserrer,** *v.r.* to contract, to be contracted; to confine oneself; to curtail one's expenses.
ressort (1) [rə'sɔ:r], *n.m.* spring; elasticity; energy, activity, strength; means.
ressort (2) [rə'sɔ:r], *n.m.* extent of jurisdiction; *(fig.)* department, line.
ressortir (1) [rəsɔr'ti:r], *v.i. irr. (conjug. like* SENTIR, *but with aux.* ÊTRE) to go or come out again; *(fig.)* to stand out; to result *(de);* **faire ressortir,** to throw into relief.
ressortir (2) [rəsɔr'ti:r], *v.i.* to be under the jurisdiction of, to be dependent on.
ressortissant [rəsɔrti'sã], *n.m. (fem.* -**e**) national.
ressource [rə'surs], *n.f.* resource, resort, expedient, shift; *(pl.)* resources; **il n'y a point de ressource,** there's no help for it; **ressources personnelles,** private means.
ressouvenir [rəsuv'ni:r], *n.m.* remembrance, recollection, reminiscence.
ressouvenir (se) [sərəsuv'ni:r], *v.r. irr. (conjug. like* TENIR, *but with aux.* ÊTRE) to recollect, to remember.
ressuscitation [resysita'sjɔ̃], *n.f.* resuscitation, revival.
ressusciter [resysi'te], *v.t.* to resuscitate; to revive *(a custom etc.).*—*v.i.* to come to life again.
restant [rɛs'tã], *a.* remaining, left.—*n.m.* remainder, rest.
restaurant [rɛsto'rã], *n.m.* restaurant; restorative.
restaurateur [rɛstora'tœ:r], *n.m. (fem.* -**trice**) restorer; restaurant keeper.
restauration [rɛstora'sjɔ̃], *n.f.* restoration, repair.
restaurer [rɛsto're], *v.t.* to restore; to refresh. **se restaurer,** *v.r.* to take refreshment; to build up one's strength *(after illness).*
reste [rɛst], *n.m.* rest, remainder; trace, vestige; *(pl.)* remnants, relics; remains; **au reste** or **du reste,** besides, moreover; **de reste,** over and above; **et le reste,** and so on, and so forth; **être en reste,** to be in arrears; **les restes,** remnants *(of meal);* mortal remains.
rester [rɛs'te], *v.i. (aux.* ÊTRE) to remain; to stay; to last; to pause; **rester court,** to stop short.
restituable [rɛsti'tɥabl], *a.* repayable, returnable.
restituer [rɛsti'tɥe], *v.t.* to restore; to return, to refund.
restitution [rɛstity'sjɔ̃], *n.f.* restitution; restoration.
restreindre [rɛs'trɛ̃:dr], *v.t. irr. (conjug. like* CRAINDRE) to restrict; to limit; to restrain. **se restreindre,** *v.r.* to restrain oneself; to curtail one's expenses.
restreint [rɛs'trɛ̃], *a.* restricted, limited.
restrictif [rɛstrik'tif], *a. (fem.* -**tive**) restrictive.

281

restriction [rɛstrik'sjɔ̃], *n.f.* restriction, restraint; *restriction mentale*, mental reservation.

restringent [rɛstrɛ̃'ʒɑ̃], *a.* and *n.m.* (*Med.*) astringent.

résultant [rezyl'tɑ̃], *a.* resulting.

résultat [rezyl'ta], *n.m.* result.

résulter [rezyl'te], *v.i.* to result.

résumé [rezy'me], *n.m.* recapitulation, summary; *en résumé*, to sum up.

résumer [rezy'me], *v.t.* to summarize. **se résumer**, *v.r.* to recapitulate, to sum up.

résurrection [rezyrɛk'sjɔ̃], *n.f.* resurrection; revival.

rétablir [reta'bliːr], *v.t.* to re-establish, to restore; to repair; to recover; to retrieve. **se rétablir**, *v.r.* to recover one's health; to be restored.

rétablissement [retablis'mɑ̃], *n.m.* re-establishment, restoration; repair; recovery.

retailler [rɑtɑ'je], *v.t.* to cut again, to prune again.

rétamer [reta'me], *v.t.* to tin over again; to resilver.

rétameur [reta'mœːr], *n.m.* tinker.

retaper [rɑtɑ'pe], *v.t.* (*colloq.*) to do up (*a hat etc.*), to straighten (*bedclothes*). **se retaper**, *v.r.* (*fam.*) to buck up.

retard [rɑ'taːr], *n.m.* delay; slowness (*of a clock etc.*); *être en retard*, to be late.

retardataire [rɑtarda'tɛːr], *a.* in arrears, late; backward.—*n.m.* late-comer; defaulter.

retardement [rɑtardə'mɑ̃], *n.m.* delay, retardment.

retarder [rɑtar'de], *v.t.* to retard, to delay; to defer (*payment*); to set back (*clocks and watches*).—*v.i.* to lose time; to be slow (*of clocks and watches*); to be behind the times.

retenir [rɑt'niːr] *v.t. irr.* (*conjug. like* TENIR) to hold back; to retain; to detain; to remember; to reserve; to hold in, to restrain; to engage; to prevent; to get hold of again; (*Arith.*) to carry. **se retenir**, *v.r.* to control oneself; to refrain; to catch hold.

retenteur [rɑtɑ̃'tœːr], *a.* (*fem.* **-trice**) retaining.

rétentif [retɑ̃'tif], *a.* (*fem.* **-tive**) retentive.

rétention [retɑ̃'sjɔ̃], *n.f.* reservation.

retentir [rɑtɑ̃'tiːr], *v.i.* to resound, to re-echo, to ring.

retentissant [rɑtɑ̃ti'sɑ̃], *a.* resounding, echoing; ringing, loud; (*fig.*) famous.

retentissement [rɑtɑ̃tis'mɑ̃], *n.m.* resounding, echo; ringing; (*fig.*) fame, celebrity.

retenu [rɑt'ny], *a.* reserved, cautious, wary.

retenue [rɑt'ny], *n.f.* discretion, circumspection, caution; detention; (*Comm.*) deduction; guy rope.

réticence [reti'sɑ̃ːs], *n.f.* reserve, silence; concealment (*of some particular*).

rétif [re'tif], *a.* (*fem.* **-tive**) restive; stubborn.

rétine [re'tin], *n.f.* retina (*of the eye*).

retirable [rɑti'rabl], *a.* withdrawable.

retiré [rɑti're], *a.* retired, secluded; in retirement.

retirement [rɑtir'mɑ̃], *n.m.* contraction; shrinking.

retirer [rɑti're], *v.t.* to draw again; to pull back, to withdraw; to take away; to retract; to derive. **se retirer**, *v.r.* to retire, to withdraw; to subside (*of waters*); to contract.

retombée [rɑtɔ̃'be], *n.f.* fall, fall-out;

retombée de particules radioactives, radio-active fall-out.

retomber [rɑtɔ̃'be], *v.i.* (*aux.* ÊTRE) to fall again; to have a relapse; to subside.

retordre [rɑ'tordr], *v.t.* to twist again; to twist (*silk, thread etc.*).

rétorquer [retor'ke], *v.t.* to retort.

retors [rɑ'toːr], *a.* twisted; artful, cunning, crafty.—*n.m.* twisted thread; crafty person.

retouche [rɑ'tuʃ], *n.f.* retouching, touching up.

retoucher [rɑtu'ʃe], *v.t.* to retouch; to touch up.

retour [rɑ'tuːr], *n.m.* return; repetition, recurrence; sending back; (*fig.*) change; reverse; turning, winding; (*Law*) reversion; *billet d'aller et retour*, return ticket.

retourne [rɑ'turn], *n.f.* trump card.

retourner [rɑtur'ne], *v.t.* (*aux.* AVOIR) to turn, to turn up, to turn over, round, about etc.; to send back.—*v.i.* (*aux.* ÊTRE) to return, to go again, to go back (*again*); to recoil upon; to turn up (*cards*). **se retourner**, *v.r.* to turn, to turn round, to look round.

retracer [rɑtra'se], *v.t.* (*conjug. like* COMMENCER) to trace again, to retrace; to relate. **se retracer**, *v.r.* to recall to mind; to recur, to be retraced (*in mind*).

rétracter [retrak'te], *v.t.* and **se rétracter** *v.r.* to retract; to recant.

retrait [rɑ'trɛ], *a.* shrunk (*of grain, wood etc.*).—*n.m.* shrinkage; recess (*in wall*), closet; withdrawal.

retraite [rɑ'trɛt], *n.f.* retreat, retiring; privacy; refuge; haunt; retirement (*from office*); superannuation; retiring pension; *battre en retraite*, to beat a retreat.

retraité [rɑtrɛ'te], *a.* superannuated, retired, pensioned off.

retraiter [rɑtrɛ'te], *v.t.* to retire, to pension off.

retranchement [rɑtrɑ̃ʃ'mɑ̃], *n.m.* retrenchment, curtailment; (*Mil.*) entrenchment.

retrancher [rɑtrɑ̃'ʃe], *v.t.* to retrench, to curtail, to cut short; to cut out; to abridge; (*Arith.*) to subtract; (*Mil.*) to entrench. **se retrancher**, *v.r.* to restrain oneself; to curtail one's expenses; (*Mil.*) to entrench oneself; (*fig.*) to fall back upon.

rétrécir [retre'siːr], *v.t.* to take in, to contract; to narrow, to limit.—*v.i.* and **se rétrécir**, *v.r.* to grow narrower; to shrink, to contract.

rétrécissement [retresis'mɑ̃], *n.m.* narrowing; shrinking.

retremper [rɑtrɑ̃'pe], *v.t.* to soak again; to temper again; (*fig.*) to strengthen. **se retremper**, *v.r.* to be strengthened or invigorated.

rétribuer [retri'bɥe], *v.t.* to remunerate.

rétribution [retriby'sjɔ̃], *n.f.* payment, reward.

rétroactif [retroak'tif], *a.* (*fem.* **-tive**) retro-active.

rétroaction [retroak'sjɔ̃], *n.f.* retroaction; (*Rɑd. Teleg.*) feed-back.

rétrograde [retro'grad], *a.* retrograde; backward.

rétrograder [retrogra'de], *v.i.* to retrograde, to go back; (*Mil.*) to fall back.

rétrogressif [retrogrɛ'sif], *a.* (*fem.* **-ive**) retrogressive.

rétrogression [retrɔgrɛ'sjɔ̃], n.f. retrogression.

rétrospectif [retrɔspɛk'tif], a. (fem. -tive) retrospective.

retroussé [ratru'se], a. turned up; tucked up; *nez retroussé*, turned-up nose, snub nose.

retrousser [ratru'se], v.t. to turn up, to roll up (trousers); to tuck up; to cock (one's hat). **se retrousser**, v.r. to tuck up one's skirt or other garment.

retroussis [ratru'si], n.m. cock (of a hat); top (of a shoe); facing (of a uniform).

retrouver [ratru've], v.t. to find again, to regain, to recover. **se retrouver**, v.r. to find each other again; to be oneself again.

rétroviseur [retrovi'zœːr], n.m. (Motor.) rearview mirror.

rets [rɛ], n.m. inv. net; (fig.) snare, toils.

réunion [rey'njɔ̃], n.f. reunion; reconciliation; junction; meeting, assembly, gathering; reception.

réunir [rey'niːr], v.t. to reunite, to join again, to bring together again, to reconcile; to connect; to collect. **se réunir**, v.r. to assemble again, to reunite; to meet; to amalgamate.

réussi [rey'si], a. successful, brilliant.

réussir [rey'siːr], v.i. to carry out well, to accomplish, to perform successfully.—v.i. to succeed, to be successful, to prosper, to thrive; to pass (Exam.).

réussite [rey'sit], n.f. success; (happy) issue or result; (Cards) solitaire.

revaloir [rava'lwaːr], v.t. irr. (conjug. like VALOIR) to return like for like, to be even with.

revanche [ra'vɑ̃ːʃ], n.f. revenge; return match.

rêvasser [rɛva'se], v.i. to day-dream, to muse.

rêvasserie [rɛvas'ri], n.f. day-dreams; idle musing.

rêvasseur [rɛva'sœːr], n.m. (fem. -euse) (colloq.) dreamer, muser.

rêve [rɛːv], n.m. dream; day-dream, illusion.

revêche [ra'vɛːʃ], a. rough; cross, ill-natured, cantankerous.

réveil [re'vɛːj], n.m. waking, awaking; alarm clock; (Mil.) reveille.

réveille-matin [revɛjma'tɛ̃], n.m. inv. alarm clock.

réveiller [revɛ'je], v.t. to awake, to arouse; to recall. **se réveiller**, v.r. to awake, to wake up; to be roused; to revive.

réveillon [revɛ'jɔ̃], n.m. midnight repast, esp. Christmas Eve revel.

réveillonner [revɛjɔ'ne], v.i. to take part in a *réveillon*.

révélateur [revela'tœːr], a. (fem. -trice) revealing, tell-tale.—n.m. (fem. -trice) revealer, informer.—n.m. (Phot.) developer.

révélation [revela'sjɔ̃], n.f. revelation, disclosure.

révéler [reve'le], _____ _____ (conjug. like CÉDER) to reveal, to disclose; to betray; (Phot.) to develop. **se révéler**, v.r. to reveal oneself; to prove (to be).

revenant [rav'nɑ̃], a. pleasing, prepossessing. —n.m. ghost.

revendeur [ravɑ̃'dœːr], n.m. (fem. -euse) retail dealer, dealer in old clothes etc.

revendicable [ravɑ̃di'kabl], a. claimable.

revendicateur [ravɑ̃dika'tœːr], n.m. (fem. -trice) claimant.

revendication [ravɑ̃dika'sjɔ̃], n.f. claim, demand.

revendiquer [ravɑ̃di'ke], v.t. to claim.

revendre [ra'vɑ̃ːdr], v.t. to sell again, to resell.

revenir [rav'niːr], v.i. irr. (conjug. like TENIR but with aux. ÊTRE) to come again, to come back, to return; to reappear, to haunt, to walk (of ghosts); to recur; to recover; to amount, to cost; to retract; to please.

revente [ra'vɑ̃ːt], n.f. resale.

revenu [rav'ny], n.m. revenue, income.

revenue [rav'ny], n.f. young wood, after-growth.

rêver [rɛ've], v.t. to dream, to dream of.—v.i. to dream; to have day-dreams; to muse.

réverbérant [reverbe'rɑ̃], a. reverberating.

réverbération [reverbera'sjɔ̃], n.f. reverberation; reflection (of light, heat).

réverbère [rever'bɛːr], n.m. reflector; street lamp.

réverbérer [reverbe're], v.t., v.i. (conjug. like CÉDER) to reverberate; to reflect (light, heat).

reverdir [raver'diːr], v.t. to make green again, to revive.—v.i. to become green again; (fig.) to grow young again.

reverdissement [raverdis'mɑ̃], n.m. growing green again.

révéremment [revera'mɑ̃], adv. reverently.

révérence [reve'rɑ̃ːs], n.f. reverence; bow, curtsy.

révérenciel [reverɑ̃'sjɛl], a. (fem. -elle) reverential.

révérencieusement [reverɑ̃sjøz'mɑ̃]. adv. reverentially.

révérencieux [reverɑ̃'sjø], a. (fem. -euse) ceremonious, obsequious.

révérend [reve'rɑ̃], a. reverend.

révérendissime [reverɑ̃di'sim], a. most reverend, right reverend.

révérer [reve're], v.t. (conjug. like CÉDER) to revere.

rêverie [rɛ'vri], n.f. reverie, musing, dreaming.

revers [ra'vɛːr], n.m. back, reverse; facing (of clothes); lapel (of a coat); turn-up (of trousers); top (of shoes); (Ten.) back-hand stroke; misfortune, set back.

reverser [raver'se], v.t. to pour out again; to pour back; to transfer; to pay back.

réversible [rever'sibl], a. reversible; revertible.

réversion [rever'sjɔ̃], n.f. reversion.

reversoir [raver'swaːr], n.m. weir.

revêtement [ravet'mɑ̃], n.m. facing (of masonry etc.); surface (of road).

revêtir [rave'tiːr], v.t. irr. (conjug. like VÊTIR) to give clothes to, to dress; to put on; to assume; to cover; (fig.) to invest or endow with. **se revêtir**, _____ _____ to clothe oneself; to put on, to assume.

rêveur [rɛ'vœːr], a. (fem. -euse) dreaming; (fig.) pensive, dreamy.—n.m. (fem. -euse) dreamer; muser.

revient [ra'vjɛ̃], n.m. **prix de revient**, net cost.

revirement [ravir'mɑ̃], n.m. tacking about; (fig.) sudden change.

revirer [ravi're], v.i. to tack, to put about; (fig.) to change sides.

revisable [rəvi'zabl], **révisable** [revi'zabl], *a.* revisable.

reviser [rəvi'ze], **réviser** [revi'ze], *v.t.* to revise, to review, to examine; to overhaul (*engine*).

reviseur [rəvi'zœːr], **réviseur** [revi'zœːr], *n.m.* reviser, examiner; auditor; proof-reader.

revision [rəvi'zjɔ̃], **révision** [revi'zjɔ̃], *n.f.* revision, review; overhaul (*of engine*).

revivifier [rəvivi'fje], *v.t.* to revivify, to regenerate, to revive.

revivre [rə'viːvr], *v.t. irr.* (*conjug. like* VIVRE) to relive.—*v.i.* to come to life again, to live again.

révocable [revɔ'kabl], *a.* revocable; removable (*of an official*).

révocation [revɔka'sjɔ̃], *n.f.* revocation (*of will*), repeal; dismissal (*of an official*).

revoici [rəvwa'si], **revoilà** [rəvwa'la], *adv.* (*colloq.*) **me revoici**, here I am again; **le revoilà**, there he is again.

revoir [rə'vwaːr], *v.t. irr.* (*conjug. like* VOIR) to see again; to meet again; to revise, to review. **se revoir**, *v.r.* to see *or* meet each other again.—*n.m. inv.* **au revoir**, good-bye (*for the present*).

revoler (1) [rəvɔ'le], *v.t.* to steal again.

revoler (2) [rəvɔ'le], *v.i.* to fly again; to fly back.

révoltant [revɔl'tɑ̃], *a.* revolting, shocking.

révolte [re'vɔlt], *n.f.* revolt, rebellion.

révolté [revɔl'te], *n.m.* (*fem.* **-ée**) rebel; mutineer.

révolter [revɔl'te], *v.i.* to stir up, to rouse; to shock, to disgust. **se révolter**, *v.r.* to revolt, to rebel; to be indignant, to be shocked.

révolu [revɔ'ly], *a.* accomplished, completed; elapsed.

révolution [revɔly'sjɔ̃], *n.f.* revolution.

révolutionnaire [revɔlysjɔ'nɛːr], *a.* revolutionary.—*n.* revolutionary; revolutionist.

révolutionner [revɔlysjɔ'ne], *v.t.* to revolutionize.

revolver [revɔl'vɛːr], *n.m.* revolver.

révoquer [revɔ'ke], *v.t.* to dismiss (*an official etc.*); to recall (*an ambassador etc.*); to repeal, to cancel.

revue [rə'vy], *n.f.* review, survey; revision; magazine; review (*critical article*); (*Mil.*) review; (*Theat.*) revue.

révulsion [revyl'sjɔ̃], *n.f.* revulsion.

rez [re], *prep.* on a level with, even with.

rez-de-chaussée [redʃo'se], *n.m. inv.* ground-level; ground floor.

rhabillage [rabi'jaːʒ], *n.m.* mending, overhaul.

rhabiller [rabi'je], *v.t.* to dress again; to mend.

rhétori- [retɔ'ri] **-cien** [retɔri'sjɛ̃], *n.m.* rhetorician.

rhétorique [retɔ'rik], *n.f.* rhetoric.

Rhin [rɛ̃], **le**, *m.* the Rhine.

rhinocéros [rinɔse'rɔs], *n.m. inv.* rhinoceros.

rhododendron [rɔdɔdɛ̃'drɔ̃], *n.m.* rhododendron.

rhombe [rɔ̃b], *a.* rhombic.—*n.m.* rhomb; rhombus.

rhubarbe [ry'barb], *n.f.* rhubarb.

rhum [rɔm], *n.m.* rum.

rhumatisant [rymati'zɑ̃], *a.* suffering from rheumatism, rheumatic.—*n.m.* (*fem.* **-e**) sufferer from rheumatism.

rhumatismal [rymatis'mal], *a.* (*m. pl.* **-aux**) rheumatic.

rhumatisme [ryma'tism], *n.m.* rheumatism.

rhume [rym], *n.m.* cold (*illness*).

riant [ri'jɑ̃], *a.* smiling, cheerful, pleasant, pleasing.

ribambelle [ribɑ̃'bɛl], *n.f.* (*colloq.*) swarm, string, lot.

ribaud [ri'bo], *a.* and *n.m.* (*fem.* **-e**) ribald.

ribauderie [ribod'ri], *n.f.* ribaldry.

ricanement [rikan'mɑ̃], *n.m.* sneering, sneer; mocking laughter.

ricaner [rika'ne], *v.i.* to sneer, to snigger.

ricaneur [rika'nœːr], *a.* (*fem.* **-euse**) sneering, derisive.—*n.m.* (*fem.* **-euse**) sneerer.

Richard [ri'ʃaːr], *m.* Richard.

richard [ri'ʃaːr], *n.m.* (*fam.* and *pej.*) moneyed person, capitalist.

riche [riʃ], *a.* rich, wealthy; copious; valuable. —*n.* rich person.

richement [riʃ'mɑ̃], *adv.* richly; splendidly.

richesse [ri'ʃɛs], *n.f.* riches, wealth; copiousness; richness.

richissime [riʃi'sim], *a.* (*colloq.*) rolling in money.

ricin [ri'sɛ̃], *n.m.* castor-oil plant.

ricocher [rikɔ'ʃe], *v.i.* to rebound; to ricochet.

ricochet [rikɔ'ʃe], *n.m.* rebound (*on the water*); (*Artill.*) ricochet; (*fig.*) chain (*of events*).

rictus [rik'tyːs], *n.m. inv.* grin; rictus.

ride [rid], *n.f.* wrinkle; ripple.

ridé [ri'de], *a.* wrinkled; rippling; corrugated.

rideau [ri'do], *n.m.* (*pl.* **-eaux**) curtain; screen (*of trees etc.*).

rider [ri'de], *v.t.* to wrinkle; to corrugate; to shrivel; to ruffle (*water*). **se rider**, *v.r.* to be wrinkled; to shrivel up; to ripple (*of water*).

ridicule [ridi'kyl], *a.* ridiculous.—*n.m.* ridicule; ridiculousness.

ridiculement [ridikyl'mɑ̃], *adv.* ridiculously.

ridiculiser [ridikyli'ze], *v.t.* to ridicule, to make fun of.

rien [rjɛ̃], *n.m.* trifle, mere nothing.—*indef. pron.* nothing, nought, not anything; anything.

rieur [ri'jœːr], *a.* (*fem.* **rieuse**) laughing, joking.

rigide [ri'ʒid], *a.* rigid, stiff; strict, severe.

rigidement [riʒid'mɑ̃], *adv.* rigidly, strictly.

rigidité [riʒidi'te], *n.f.* rigidity, stiffness; strictness, severity.

rigole [ri'gɔl], *n.f.* trench, small ditch *or* channel; gutter.

rigoler [rigɔ'le], *v.i.* (*pop.*) to laugh; to have fun; to joke.

rigorisme [rigɔ'rism], *n.m.* rigorism, austerity.

rigoriste [rigɔ'rist], *a.* over-severe.—*n.* rigorist, stickler.

rigoureusement [rigurøz'mɑ̃], *adv.* rigorously, severely, strictly.

rigoureux [rigu'rø], *a.* (*fem.* **-euse**) rigorous, harsh; strict; stern; inclement.

rigueur [ri'gœːr], *n.f.* rigor, strictness; precision; severity; inclemency; **à la rigueur**, at a pinch; if necessary; **de rigueur**, indispensable, compulsory.

rimailler [rima'je], *v.i.* to write doggerel.

rimailleur [rimɑ´jœːr], *n.m.* (*fem.* **-euse**) sorry rhymer, rhymester.

rime [rim], *n.f.* rhyme; (*fig.*) verse.

rimer [ri´me], *v.i.* to rhyme; to write verses.

rimeur [ri´mœːr], *n.m.* rhymer, versifier.

rinçage [rɛ̃´sa:ʒ], *n.m.* rinsing, washing.

rincer [rɛ̃´se], *v.t.* (*conjug. like* COMMENCER) to rinse, to wash. **se rincer**, *v.r.* to rinse.

ripaille [ri´paːj], *n.f.* feasting, junketing.

riposte [ri´pɔst], *n.f.* (*Fenc.*) ripost, return; (*fig.*) retort, repartee.

riposter [ripɔs´te], *v.i.* (*Fenc.*) to ripost, to parry and thrust; (*fig.*) to make a smart reply.

rire [riːr], *v.i. irr.* to laugh; to smile; to be favorable; to joke; to mock. **se rire**, *v.r.* to make sport, to scoff (*de*).—*n.m.* laughter, laughing.

ris [ri], *n.m. inv.* laugh, smile, laughter; (*Naut.*) reef (*of sails*); sweetbread.

risée [ri´ze], *n.f.* laugh, laughter; mockery; laughing-stock.

risette [ri´zɛt], *n.f.* pleasant little laugh, smile.

risible [ri´zibl], *a.* comical, laughable; ridiculous.

risiblement [rizibla´mɑ̃], *adv.* laughably, ludicrously.

risque [risk], *n.m.* risk, hazard.

risqué [ris´ke], *a.* risky; *une plaisanterie risquée*, a doubtful joke.

risquer [ris´ke], *v.t.* to risk, to venture; (*fam.*) to chance. **se risquer**, *v.r.* to risk, to venture.

risque-tout [riska´tu], *n.m. inv.* (*colloq.*) dare-devil.

rissole [ri´sɔl], *n.f.* rissole.

rissoler [risɔ´le], *v.t.* (*Cook.*) to brown.

ristourne [ris´turn], *n.f.* refund; rebate.

rit *or* **rite** [rit], *n.m.* rite.

ritournelle [ritur´nɛl], *n.f.* (*Mus.*) ritornello, flourish.

rituel [ri´tɥɛl], *a.* (*fem.* **-elle**) ritual.—*n.m.* ritual (*prayer book*).

rivage [ri´va:ʒ], *n.m.* shore, strand, beach; bank, waterside.

rival [ri´val], *a.* (*m. pl.* **-aux**) rival, competitive.—*n.m.* (*pl.* **-e, -es, -aux**) rival.

rivaliser [rivali´ze], *v.i.* to rival, to vie, to compete.

rivalité [rivali´te], *n.f.* rivalry, emulation.

rive [riːv], *n.f.* bank, shore (*of rivers, lakes etc.*); (*fig.*) seashore; border.

rivement [riv´mɑ̃], *n.m.* riveting.

river [ri´ve], *v.t.* to clinch, to rivet.

riverain [ri´vrɛ̃], *a.* riparian; bordering (*on rivers or woods*).—*n.m.* (*fem.* **-e**) riverside resident; borderer.

rivet [ri´vɛ], *n.m.* rivet; clinch.

rivetage [riv´ta:ʒ], *n.m.* riveting.

riveter [riv´te], *v.t.* (*conjug. like* APPELER) to rivet.

riveteur [riv´tœːr], **riveur** [ri´vœːr], *n.m.* riveter.

rivière [ri´vjɛːr], *n.f.* river, stream.

rivoir [ri´vwaːr], *n.m.* or **rivoire** [ri´vwaːr], *n.f.* riveting hammer *or* machine.

rivure [ri´vyːr], *n.f.* clinching, riveting.

rixe [riks], *n.f.* fight, scuffle; brawl, affray.

riz [ri], *n.m.* rice.

rizière [ri´zjɛːr], *n.f.* rice field, paddy field, rice plantation; rice swamp.

robe [rɔb], *n.f.* gown, dress, frock; robe;

long robe (*lawyers*), the cloth (*clergy*); coat (*of certain animals*); skin, husk, peel (*of certain fruits etc.*).

robinet [rɔbi´ne], *n.m.* tap; cock; *ouvrir* (*fermer*) *le robinet*, to turn on (off) the tap.

robot [rɔ´bo], *a. inv. avion robot*, pilotless plane; *fusée, satellite robot*, unmanned rocket, satellite.—*n.m.* automaton, robot.

robuste [rɔ´byst], *a.* robust, sturdy; hardy, strong.

robustement [rɔbystə´mɑ̃], *adv.* robustly, athletically.

robustesse [rɔbys´tɛs], *n.f.* robustness, strength, vigor.

roc [rɔk], *n.m.* rock.

rocaille [rɔ´kaːj], *n.f.* rock work, grotto work.

rocailleux [rɔka´jø], *a.* (*fem.* **-euse**) pebbly, stony, rugged, rough.

roche [rɔʃ], *n.f.* rock; boulder; stony mass.

rocher [rɔ´ʃe], *n.m.* rock, crag.

rochet [rɔ´ʃɛ], *n.m.* rochet (*surplice*); ratchet.

rocheux [rɔ´ʃø], *a.* (*fem.* **-euse**) rocky, stony.

rococo [rɔkɔ´ko], *a. inv. rococo*: antiquated.—*n.m.* rococo, antiquated style.

rodage [rɔ´da:ʒ], *n.m.* grinding in; polishing; *en rodage*, breaking in (*engine*).

roder [rɔ´de], *v.t.* to break in (*car*); to grind, to polish.

rôder [ro´de], *v.i.* to prowl.

rôdeur [ro´dœːr], *a.* (*fem.* **-euse**) prowling.—*n.m.* (*fem.* **-euse**) prowler; vagrant.

rodomontade [rɔdɔmɔ̃´tad], *n.f.* bluster, swagger.

Rodrigue [rɔ´drig], *m.* Roderick.

rogaton [rɔga´tɔ̃], *n.m.* (*pl.*) scraps, odds and ends.

Roger [rɔ´ʒe], *m.* Roger; *c'est un vrai Roger Bontemps*, he is a happy-go-lucky sort of chap.

rogner [rɔ´ɲe], *v.t.* to cut, to pare, to crop; to clip, to prune.

rogneux [rɔ´ɲø], *a.* (*fem.* **-euse**) mangy, scabby.

rognon [rɔ´ɲɔ̃], *n.m.* kidney (*as food*).

rognure [rɔ´ɲyːr], *n.f.* a paring, a clipping; (*pl.*) scraps, refuse, leavings.

rogue [rɔg], *a.* arrogant, haughty.

roi [rwa], *n.m.* king.

roitelet [rwa´tlɛ], *n.m.* petty king; wren.

rôle [roːl], *n.m.* roll; list, roster, catalogue; (*Theat.*) part, character.

romain [rɔ´mɛ̃], *a.* a Roman.—*n.m.* (**Romain**, *fem.* **-aine**) Roman (*person*).

roman (1) [rɔ´mɑ̃], *a.* Romance, Romanic.

roman (2) [rɔ´mɑ̃], *n.m.* novel, romance, fiction.

romance [rɔ´mɑ̃:s], *n.f.* (*Mus.*) ballad, sentimental song.

romancier [rɔmɑ̃´sje], *n.m.* (*fem.* **-ière**) novelist.

romanesque [rɔma´nɛsk], *a.* romantic.—*n.m.* the romantic.

roman-feuilleton [rɔmɑ̃fœj´tɔ̃], *n.m.* (*pl.* **romans-feuilletons**) newspaper serial (story).

romantique [rɔmɑ̃´tik], *a.* romantic.—*n.m.* romanticist.

romantiquement [rɔmɑ̃tik´mɑ̃], *adv.* romantically.

romantisme [rɔmɑ̃´tism], *n.m.* (*Lit. Hist.*) romanticism.

285

romarin [rɔma'rɛ̃], *n.m.* rosemary.
rompre [rɔ̃:pr], *v.t.* (*see Verb Tables*) to break, to snap; to break off; to dissolve; to break in; to divert; to interrupt. —*v.i.* to break; to fall out. **se rompre**, *v.r.* to break off, to snap.
rompu [rɔ̃'py], *a.* broken, snapped; broken in.
romsteck [rɔm'stɛk], *n.m.* rump steak.
ronce [rɔ̃:s], *n.f.* bramble, blackberry bush.
ronceraie [rɔ̃s'rɛ], *n.f.* brake, brambly ground.
ronchonner [rɔ̃ʃɔ'ne], *v.i.* (*fam.*) to grumble.
rond [rɔ̃], *a.* round; plump, rotund; frank; even (*of money* or *accounts*).—*adv.* normally, true (*of motor*).—*n.m.* round, ring, orb, circle, disk.
ronde [rɔ̃:d], *n.f.* round; patrol; beat; (*Mus.*) whole note; roundelay; round-hand (*writing*).
rondeau [rɔ̃'do], *n.m.* (*pl.* **-eaux**) rondeau (*French poem*); (*Mus.*) rondo; roller.
rondelet [rɔ̃d'lɛ], *a.* (*fem.* **-ette**) roundish, plump, pudgy.
rondelle [rɔ̃'dɛl], *n.f.* rondelle, washer; rundle, ring.
rondement [rɔ̃d'mɑ̃], *adv.* roundly; briskly; frankly, bluntly.
rondeur [rɔ̃'dœ:r], *n.f.* roundness, rotundity; fullness; plain dealing.
rondin [rɔ̃'dɛ̃], *n.m.* round log; cudgel.
rond-point [rɔ̃'pwɛ̃], *n.m.* (*pl.* **ronds-points**) (*Arch.*) apsis; circle (*place where several roads etc. meet*); traffic circle.
ronflant [rɔ̃'flɑ̃], *a.* snoring; humming, whirring; sonorous.
ronflement [rɔ̃flə'mɑ̃], *n.m.* snoring; roaring, rumbling; boom; snorting (*of horses*).
ronfler [rɔ̃'fle], *v.i.* to snore; to snort (*of horses*); to roar (*cannon, thunder etc.*); to boom; to peal (*organs*); to hum (*spinning-tops*).
ronfleur [rɔ̃'flœ:r], *n.m.* (*fem.* **-euse**) snorer.
rongeant [rɔ̃'ʒɑ̃], *a.* gnawing, corroding; (*fig.*) tormenting.
ronger [rɔ̃'ʒe], *v.t.* (*conjug. like* MANGER) to gnaw, to nibble; to consume, to corrode; to prey upon (*the mind etc.*); **ronger son frein,** to champ the bit. **se ronger,** *v.r.* to fret.
rongeur [rɔ̃'ʒœ:r], *a.* (*fem.* **-euse**) gnawing, biting; corroding; consuming.—*n.m.* (*Zool.*) rodent.
ronron [rɔ̃'rɔ̃], *n.m.* purr, purring.
ronronner [rɔ̃rɔ'ne], *v.i.* to purr, to hum.
roquet [rɔ'kɛ], *n.m.* pug dog; cur, mongrel.
rosace [ro'zas], *n.f.* (*Arch.*) rose; rose window.
rosage [ro'za:ʒ], *n.m.* rhododendron; azalea.
rosaire [ro'zɛ:r], *n.n .* (*R.-C. Ch.*) rosary.
rosâtre [ro'za:tr], *a.* pinkish.
rosbif [rɔs'bif], *n.m.* roast beef.
rose [ro:z], *a.* rosy; pink, rose-colored. —*n.f.* rose; rose window; **rose trémière**, holly-hock.—*n.m.* rose-color, pink.
rosé [ro'ze], *a.* rosy, roseate; **vin rosé,** light-red wine.
roseau [ro'zo], *n.m.* (*pl.* **-eaux**) reed.
rosée [ro'ze], *n.f.* dew.
roselière [rozə'ljɛ:r], *n.f.* reed bed.
roséole [roze'ɔl], *n.f.* scarlet rash; German measles.
roser [ro'ze], *v.t.* to make pink.

roseraie [roz'rɛ], *n.f.* rosery, rose garden.
rosette [ro'zɛt], *n.f.* small rose; rosette.
rosier [ro'zje], *n.m.* rose tree, rose-bush.
rosière [ro'zjɛ:r], *n.f.* rose queen; queen of the May.
rosiériste [rozje'rist], *n.* rose grower.
rosse [rɔs], *a.* bad, malicious.—*n.f.* old horse; (*fig.* and *fam.*) worthless *or* nasty person.
rossée [rɔ'se], *n.f.* shower of blows, thrashing.
rosser [rɔ'se], *v.t.* (*colloq.*) to thrash, to beat up.
rossignol [rɔsi'ɲɔl], *n.m.* nightingale; pick-lock, skeleton key; (*Carp.*) wedge; (*fig.*) un-saleable article (*in a shop*).
rot [ro], *n.m.* (*pop.*) belch, eructation.
rôt [ro], *n.m.* roast, roast meat.
rotarien [rota'rjɛ̃], *n.m.* member of a Rotary Club.
rotateur [rota'tœ:r], *a.* (*fem.* **-trice**) (*Anat.*) rotatory.—*n.m.* (*Anat.*) rotator.
rotatif [rota'tif], *a.* (*fem.* **-tive**) rotary.
rotation [rota'sjɔ̃], *n.f.* rotation.
rotatoire [rota'twa:r], *a.* rotatory.
roter [ro'te], *v.i.* to belch.
rôti [ro'ti], *n.m.* roast, roast meat.
rôtie [ro'ti], *n.f.* slice of toast.
rôtir [ro'ti:r], *v.t., v.i.* to roast; to broil; to toast (*bread etc.*); (*fig.*) to parch.
rôtissage [roti'sa:ʒ], *n.m.* roasting.
rôtisserie [rotis'ri], *n.f.* cook-shop.
rôtisseur [roti'sœ:r], *n.m.* (*fem.* **-euse**) cook-shop keeper.
rôtissoire [roti'swa:r], *n.f.* roaster, Dutch oven.
rotonde [ro'tɔ̃:d], *n.f.* rotunda; long sleeve-less cloak.
rotondité [rotɔ̃di'te], *n.f.* rotundity; plump-ness.
rotor [ro'tɔ:r], *n.m.* rotor.
roturier [roty'rje], *a.* (*fem.* **-ière**) plebeian; vulgar, mean.—*n.m.* (*fem.* **-ière**) commoner.
rouage [rwa:ʒ], *n.m.* wheelwork; cog-wheel; machinery; (*Horol.*) movement.
rouan [rwɑ̃], *a.* (*fem.* **rouanne**) roan (*of horses, cattle etc.*).—*n.m.* roan horse.
roublard [ru'bla:r], *a.* and *n.m.* (*fem.* **-e**) (*fam.*) wily, crafty (person).
rouble [rubl], *n.m.* rouble (*Russian coin*).
roucoulement [rukul'mɑ̃], *n.m.* cooing; gurgling (*of babies*).
roucouler [ruku'le], *v.t., v.i.* to coo.
roue [ru], *n.f.* wheel; paddle-wheel; **faire la roue,** to spread (out) its tail (*of peacocks etc.*); to show off; **mettre** *or* **jeter des bâtons dans les roues,** to put spokes into the wheel (*of*), to interfere.
roué [rwe], *a.* cunning, sharp, artful; ex-hausted.—*n.m.* rake, profligate; (*fem.* **-ée**) cunning *or* unscrupulous person.
rouelle [rwɛl], *n.f.* round slice (*meat*).
rouer [rwe], *v.t.* to break upon the wheel; **rouer de coups,** to beat unmercifully.
rouerie [ru'ri], *n.f.* piece of knavery, trick, sharp practice.
rouet [rwɛ], *n.m.* spinning-wheel.
rouge [ru:ʒ], *a.* red; red-hot; bloodshot.—*n.m.* rouge; redness.—*n.* (*fam.*) left-winger, communist.
rougeâtre [ru'ʒa:tr], *a.* reddish.
rougeaud [ru'ʒo], *a.* (*colloq.*) red-faced, ruddy.—*n.m.* (*fem.* **-e**) red-faced person.

rouge-gorge [ruʒˈgɔrʒ], *n.m.* (*pl.* **rouges-gorges**) red-breast, robin redbreast.

rougeole [ruˈʒɔl], *n.f.* measles.

rougeoyer [ruʒwaˈje], *v.i.* (*conjug. like* EMPLOYER) to turn red; to glow.

rouget [ruˈʒɛ], *a.* (*fem.* **-ette**) reddish.—*n.m.* (*Ichth.*) red mullet.

rougeur [ruˈʒœːr], *n.f.* redness; flush, glow, blush.

rougir [ruˈʒiːr], *v.t.* to redden, to tinge with red.—*v.i.* to redden, to grow red, to color, to blush.

rouille [ruːj], *n.f.* rust, rustiness; (*Agric.*) mildew, blight.

rouillé [ruˈje], *a.* rusty; blighted (*of grain*).

rouiller [ruˈje], *v.t.*, *v.i.* to rust; to blight; to impair. **se rouiller**, *v.r.* to rust; to grow rusty; to be impaired.

rouilleux [ruˈjø], *a.* (*fem.* **-euse**) rust-colored.

rouillure [ruˈjyːr], *n.f.* rustiness; (*Agric.*) rust.

rouir [rwiːr], *v.t.* to steep, to soak, to ret.

rouissage [rwiˈsaːʒ], *n.m.* steeping, retting.

roulade [ruˈlad], *n.f.* roll, rolling down; (*Mus.*) trill.

roulage [ruˈlaːʒ], *n.m.* rolling; haulage, carriage (*in wagons etc.*); road traffic.

roulant [ruˈlɑ̃], *a.* rolling; travelling (*crane*); easy (*of roads*); (*Print.*) at work.

rouleau [ruˈlo], *n.m.* (*pl.* **-eaux**) roll; roller; rolling-pin; coil (*rope*).

roulement [rulˈmɑ̃], *n.m.* rolling, roll; rumbling, rattle; rotation; *par roulement*, in rotation; *roulement à billes*, ball-bearing.

rouler [ruˈle], *v.t.* to roll; to roll up; to wind up; to revolve; (*colloq.*) to cheat; (*Golf*) *coup roulé*, putt.—*v.i.* to roll, to roll along; to revolve; to ride (*en*); to ramble; to keep going. **se rouler**, *v.r.* to roll; to tumble, to wallow.

roulette [ruˈlɛt], *n.f.* small wheel; roller, castor, truckle; roulette (*game*).

roulier [ruˈlje], *a.* carrying (*trade*).—*n.m.* wagoner, carter, carrier.

roulis [ruˈli], *n.m.* rolling, roll (*waves or ships*), lurch.

roulotte [ruˈlɔt], *n.f.* gipsy van; (*Motor.*) trailer.

roumain [ruˈmɛ̃], *a.* Rumanian.—*n.m.* Rumanian (*language*); (**Roumain,** *fem.* **-aine**) Rumanian (*person*).

Roumanie [rumaˈni], **la,** *f.* Rumania.

roupie [ruˈpi], *n.f.* rupee.

roupiller [rupiˈje], *v.i.* (*colloq.*) to doze, to snooze.

rouquin [ruˈkɛ̃], *a.* (*pop.*) ginger-haired, carroty-haired.

roussâtre [ruˈsɑːtr], *a.* reddish, russet.

rousseur [ruˈsœːr], *n.f.* redness.

roussi [ruˈsi], *a.* browned, scorched.—*n.m.* burnt smell; burning.

roussir [ruˈsiːr], *v.t.*, *v.i.* to redden; to singe, to scorch; *faire roussir*, to brown (*meat etc.*).

roussissage [rusiˈsaːʒ], **roussissement** [rusisˈmɑ̃], *n.m.* reddening; browning; scorching.

routage [ruˈtaːʒ], *n.m.* sorting (*of mail*).

route [rut], *n.f.* road, way; route, path, course; track (*of a ship etc.*); highway.

router [ruˈte], *v.t.* to sort (*mail*).

routier [ruˈtje], *a.* (*fem.* **-ière**) of roads; *carte routière*, road map.—*n.m.* truck driver; (*fig.*) old hand; road racer (*cyclist*).

routine [ruˈtin], *n.f.* routine, habit, practice.

routinier [rutiˈnje], *a.* (*fem.* **-ière**) routine, following a routine.—*n.m.* (*fem.* **-ière**) person following a routine; stick-in-the-mud.

rouvrir [ruˈvriːr], *v.t.*, *v.i.* irr. (*conjug. like* OUVRIR) to reopen.

roux [ru], *a.* (*fem.* **rousse**) reddish; red-haired, sandy.—*n.m.* (*fem.* **rousse**) red-haired *or* sandy person.—*n.m.* reddish color.

royal [rwaˈjal], *a.* (*m. pl.* **-aux**) royal; regal, kingly.

royalement [rwajalˈmɑ̃], *adv.* royally; regally.

royalisme [rwajaˈlism], *n.m.* royalism.

royaliste [rwajaˈlist], *a.* and *n.* royalist.

royaume [rwaˈjoːm], *n.m.* kingdom, realm; *le Royaume-Uni*, the United Kingdom.

royauté [rwajoˈte], *n.f.* royalty, kingship, monarchy.

ruade [rɥad], *n.f.* kick (*by horse etc.*); lashing out.

Ruanda [RWANDA].

ruban [ryˈbɑ̃], *n.m.* ribbon; (*fig.*) strip; tape.

rubané [rybaˈne], *a.* covered with ribbons.

rubaner [rybaˈne], *v.t.* to trim with ribbons; to cut into ribbons.

rubanerie [rybanˈri], *n.f.* ribbon-weaving; ribbon trade.

rubéole [rybeˈɔl], *n.f.* rubeola, German measles.

rubescent [rybeˈsɑ̃], *a.* reddish; growing red.

rubicond [rybiˈkɔ̃], *a.* rubicund.

rubis [ryˈbi], *n.m. inv.* ruby.

rubrique [ryˈbrik], *n.f.* red chalk; (*pl.*) rubric; (*fig.*) heading (*of article*).

ruche [ryʃ], *n.f.* hive; (*Needlework*) frilling, ruche.

ruchée [ryˈʃe], *n.f.* hiveful.

rucher [ryˈʃe], *n.m.* stand *or* shed for bee-hives; apiary.

rucher (2) [ryˈʃe], *v.t.* (*Needlework*) to ruche, to frill.

rude [ryd], *a.* harsh, rough, rugged; violent; severe; uncouth; churlish; arduous, difficult.

rudement [rydˈmɑ̃], *adv.* roughly, harshly, severely, violently; (*pop.*) awfully, very.

rudesse [ryˈdɛs], *n.f.* roughness, coarseness; ruggedness, uncouthness; harshness; unkindness.

rudiment [rydiˈmɑ̃], *n.m.* rudiment; primer.

rudimentaire [rydimɑ̃ˈtɛːr], *a.* rudimentary.

rudoiement [rydwaˈmɑ̃], *n.m.* bullying, brow-beating.

rudoyer [rydwaˈje], *v.t.* (*conjug. like* EMPLOYER) to treat roughly; to bully, to ill-treat.

rue [ry], *n.f.* street; rue (*plant*).

ruée [rɥe], *n.f.* rush; onslaught.

ruelle [rɥɛl], *n.f.* lane, alley.

ruer [rɥe], *v.i.* to kick (*of horses etc.*). **se ruer**, *v.r.* to throw oneself, to rush (*sur*).

rugby [rygˈbi], *n.m.* rugby football, rugger.

rugir [ryˈʒiːr], *v.i.* to roar, to bellow.

rugissant [ryʒiˈsɑ̃], *a.* roaring.

rugissement [ryʒisˈmɑ̃], *n.m.* roaring, roar.

rugosité [rygoziˈte], *n.f.* rugosity, roughness.

rugueux [ryˈgø], *a.* (*fem.* **-euse**) rugose, rough.

ruine

ruine [rɥin], *n.f.* ruin; decay, destruction.
ruiner [rɥi'ne], *v.t.* to ruin, to lay waste; to destroy; to spoil. **se ruiner**, *v.r.* to ruin oneself; to fall into decay.
ruineux [rɥi'nø], *a.* (*fem.* **-euse**) ruinous
ruisseau [rɥi'so], *n.m.* (*pl.* **-eaux**) brook, stream; gutter.
ruisselant [rɥi'slɑ̃], *a.* streaming, dripping.
ruisseler [rɥi'sle], *v.i.* (*conjug. like* APPELER) to run, to be very wet, to stream (with) (*de*).
rumeur [ry'mœːr], *n.f.* clamor, uproar; (*fig.*) report, rumor.
ruminant [rymi'nɑ̃], *a.* ruminant, ruminating.—*n.m.* ruminant.
rumination [rymina'sjɔ̃], *n.f.* rumination (*chewing the cud*).
ruminer [rymi'ne], *v.t.* to ruminate on; (*fig.*) to think over.—*v.i.* to ruminate, to chew the cud; (*fig.*) to ponder, to muse.
rupture [ryp'tyːr], *n.f.* breaking, rupture; annulment; hernia.
rural [ry'ral], *a.* (*m. pl.* **-aux**) rural, rustic.
ruse [ryːz], *n.f.* guile, cunning; trick, wile, ruse.
rusé [ry'ze], *a.* artful, crafty, sly.—*n.m.* (*fem.* **-ée**) artful, crafty or sly person.
ruser [ry'ze], *v.i.* to use deceit, craft or guile.
russe [rys], *a.* Russian.—*n.m.* Russian (*language*).—*n.* (**Russe**) Russian (*person*).
Russie [ry'si], **la**, *f.* Russia.
rustaud [rys'to], *a.* rustic, boorish, uncouth.—*n.m.* (*fem.* **-e**) rustic, clodhopper
rusticité [rystisi'te], *n.f.* rusticity, simplicity.
rustique [rys'tik], *a.* rustic, rural; homely, simple.
rustiquement [rystik'mɑ̃], *adv.* rustically; boorishly, uncouthly.
rustre [rystr], *a.* boorish, rude.—*n.m.* boor, lout.
rutabaga [rytaba'ga], *n.m.* rutabaga, Swedish turnip.
rutilant [ryti'lɑ̃], *a.* glowing, gleaming, rutilant.
rutiler [ryti'le], *v.i.* to glow, to gleam (*red*).
Rwanda, Ruanda [rwɑ̃'da], **le**, *m.* Rwanda.
rythme [ritm], *n.m.* rhythm.
rythmique [rit'mik], *a.* rhythmical.

S

S, s [ɛs], *n.m.* the nineteenth letter of the alphabet.
s' [s], *elision*, [SE].
sa [sa], [SON (1)].
sabbat [sa'ba], *n.m.* Sabbath.
sable [saːbl], *n.m.* sand; gravel; (*Zool., Her.*) sable.
sablé [sa'ble], *a.* covered with sand or gravel.
sabler [sa'ble], *v.t.* to sand, to gravel; (*fig.*) to drink off.
sableux [sa'blø], *a.* (*fem.* **-euse**) sandy.
sablier [sabli'je], *n.m.* sand-glass, hour-glass; egg-timer.
sablière [sabli'jɛːr], *n.f.* sand pit; gravel pit.

288

sablon [sa'blɔ̃], *n.m.* fine sand, scouring sand.
sablonner [sablɔ'ne], *v.t.* to scour with sand.
sablonneux [sablɔ'nø], *a.* (*fem.* **-euse**) sandy, gritty.
sablonnière [sablɔ'njɛːr], *n.f.* sand pit.
sabord [sa'boːr], *n.m.* (*Naut.*) port-hole.
saborder [sabɔr'de], *v.t.* to scuttle.
sabot [sa'bo], *n.m.* sabot, clog; hoof (*of horse etc.*); trig (*of carriages*); *dormir comme un sabot*, to sleep like a top.
sabotage [sabɔ'taːʒ], *n.m.* sabotage.
saboter [sabɔ'te], *v.t.* (*colloq.*) to bungle; to damage wilfully, to sabotage.
saboteur [sabɔ'tœːr], *n.m.* (*fem.* **-euse**) bungler; saboteur.
sabotier [sabɔ'tje], *n.m.* (*fem.* **-ière**) sabot maker.
sabre [saːbr], *n.m.* saber; broadsword.
sabrer [sa'bre], *v.t.* to strike or cut with a saber, to saber; (*colloq.*) to hurry over, to botch.
sabreur [sa'brœːr], *n.m.* swashbuckler; (*colloq.*) botcher.
sac (1) [sak], *n.m.* sack, bag; pouch (*of certain animals*).
sac (2) [sak], *n.m.* sack (*plunder*), pillage.
saccade [sa'kad], *n.f.* jerk, jolt.
saccadé [saka'de], *a.* jerky, broken, abrupt, irregular.
saccader [saka'de], *v.t.* to jerk.
saccage [sa'kaːʒ], *n.m.* upset, confusion; pillage.
saccager [saka'ʒe], *v.t.* (*conjug. like* MANGER) to sack, to plunder; (*fig.*) to play havoc with.
saccharine [saka'rin], *n.f.* saccharine.
sacerdoce [saser'dɔs], *n.m.* priesthood.
sacerdotal [saserdɔ'tal], *a.* (*m. pl.* **-aux**) sacerdotal.
sachée [sa'ʃe], *n.f.* sackful, bagful.
sachet [sa'ʃɛ], *n.m.* small bag, sachet.
sacoche [sa'kɔʃ], *n.f.* (*Mil.*) saddle-bag; money-bag; tool-bag.
sacramental [sakramɑ̃'tal] (*m. pl.* **-aux**), **sacramentel** [sakramɑ̃'tɛl] (*fem.* **-elle**), *a.* sacramental.
sacre [sakr], *n.m.* anointing and coronation of a king; consecration of a bishop.
sacré [sa'kre], *a.* holy, consecrated; sacred, inviolable.
sacrebleu! [sakrə'blø], *int.* confound it! curse it!
sacrement [sakrə'mɑ̃], *n.m.* sacrament, *esp.* matrimony.
sacrer [sa'kre], *v.t.* to anoint, to crown; to consecrate.—*v.i.* to curse and swear.
sacrificateur [sakrifika'tœːr], *n.m.* (*fem.* **-trice**) sacrificer.
sacrificatoire [sakrifika'twaːr], *a.* sacrificial.
sacrifice [sakri'fis], *n.m.* sacrifice; renunciation.
sacrifier [sakri'fje], *v.t.* to sacrifice; to devote; to give up.—*v.i.* to sacrifice.
sacrilège [sakri'lɛːʒ], *a.* sacrilegious.—*n.m.* sacrilege.
sacrilègement [sakrilɛʒ'ma], *adv.* sacrilegiously.
sacripant [sakri'pɑ̃], *n.m.* rascal, scoundrel.
sacristain [sakris'tɛ̃], *n.m.* sacristan, sexton.
sacristie [sakris'ti], *n.f.* sacristy, vestry; church plate.
sacristine [sakris'tin], *n.f.* vestry nun, sacristine.

sacro-saint [sakrɔ'sɛ̃], *a.* sacrosanct.
sadique [sa'dik], *a.* sadistic.—*n.* sadist.
sadisme [sa'dism], *n.m.* sadism.
saducéen [sadyse'ɛ̃], *a.* (*fem.* **-éenne**) Sadducean.—*n.m.* (*fem.* **-éenne**) Sadducee.
safran [sa'frɑ̃], *n.m.* saffron; crocus.
safrané [safra'ne], *a.* saffron-colored.
saga [sa'ga], *n.f.* saga.
sagace [sa'gas], *a.* sagacious, shrewd.
sagacité [sagasi'te], *n.f.* sagacity.
sage [sa:ʒ], *a.* wise; sage, sensible, prudent; sober, well-behaved, good; virtuous, modest; gentle (*of animals*).—*n.m.* wise man, sage.
sage-femme [saʒ'fam], *n.f.* (*pl.* **sages-femmes**) midwife.
sagement [saʒ'mɑ̃], *adv.* wisely; prudently; soberly, steadily.
sagesse [sa'ʒɛs], *n.f.* wisdom; prudence; steadiness; chastity; good behavior (*of children*); gentleness (*of animals*).
sagittaire [saʒi'tɛ:r], *n.m.* (*Rom. Ant.*) archer; (*Astron.*) Sagittarius.
sagou [sa'gu], *n.m.* sago.
sagouier [sagu'je] or (*preferably*) **sagoutier** [sagu'tje], *n.m.* sago tree.
sagouin [sa'gwɛ̃], *n.m.* squirrel-monkey; (*fem.* **-e**) (*fig.*) slovenly fellow *or* woman.
Sahara [saa'ra], **le**, *m.* the Sahara.
saignant [sɛ'ɲɑ̃], *a.* bleeding, bloody; underdone (*of meat*).
saignée [sɛ'ɲe], *n.f.* blood-letting, phlebotomy; small of the arm; (*fig.*) drain on the purse.
saignement [sɛɲə'mɑ̃], *n.m.* bleeding.
saigner [sɛ'ɲe], *v.t.* to bleed; to stick (*an animal*); (*fig.*) to drain.—*v.i.* to bleed. **se saigner**, *v.r.* to bleed oneself; to drain oneself *or* one's purse.
saigneux [sɛ'ɲø], *a.* (*fem.* **-euse**) bloody.
saillant [sa'jɑ̃], *a.* jutting out, projecting; (*fig.*) striking, remarkable.—*n.m.* (*Fort.*) salient.
saillie [sa'ji], *n.f.* start, sudden spurt; sally; (*fig.*) witticism; projection.
saillir [sa'ji:r], *v.i.* to gush (*of liquids*); to ripple (*of muscles*).
sain [sɛ̃], *a.* hale, healthy; sound; sane; **sain et sauf**, safe and sound.
saindoux [sɛ̃'du], *n.m. inv.* lard.
sainement [sɛn'mɑ̃], *adv.* wholesomely; healthily, soundly; judiciously.
sainfoin [sɛ̃'fwɛ̃], *n.m.* sainfoin.
saint [sɛ̃], *a.* holy, sacred; godly, saintly; sanctified, consecrated.—*n.m.* (*fem.* **-e**) saint; patron saint.
saintement [sɛ̃t'mɑ̃], *adv.* sacredly; piously, religiously.
sainteté [sɛ̃tə'te], *n.f.* holiness, sanctity, sacredness, saintliness; **Sa Sainteté le Pape**, His Holiness the Pope.
saisi [sɛ'zi], *a.* seized, possessed, struck (*de*).
saisie [sɛ'zi], *n.f.* (*Law*) seizure, distraint, execution.
saisir [sɛ'zi:r], *v.t.* to seize, to take hold of; to understand; (*fig.*) to impress, to shock, to startle; to distrain. **se saisir**, *v.r.* to seize, to catch hold (*de*); to take possession (*de*); to arrest.
saisissable [sɛzi'sabl], *a.* distrainable, seizable.
saisissant [sɛzi'sɑ̃], *a.* keen, sharp, piercing (*of cold*); striking, impressive.

saisissement [sɛzis'mɑ̃], *n.m.* shock, violent impression, seizure.
saison [sɛ'zɔ̃], *n.f.* season; **marchand des quatre saisons**, street vendor (*of produce*).
saisonnier [sɛzɔ'nje], *a.* (*fem.* **-ière**) seasonal.
salade [sa'lad], *n.f.* salad, herb grown for salad; (*fig.*) medley, confusion.
saladier [sala'dje], *n.m.* salad bowl.
salage [sa'la:ʒ], *n.m.* salting.
salaire [sa'lɛ:r], *n.m.* wages, pay, hire; reward.
salaison [salɛ'zɔ̃], *n.f.* salting; salt provisions; curing (*of bacon etc.*).
salamalec [salama'lɛk], *n.m.* (*used chiefly in pl.*) salaam; (*fig.*) exaggerated politeness.
salamandre [sala'mɑ̃:dr], *n.f.* salamander; slow-combustion stove.
salant [sa'lɑ̃], *a.m.* **marais salant**, salt-marsh.
salarié [sala'rje], *a.* paid, wage-earning.—*n.m.* (*fem.* **-ée**) wage-earner.
salarier [sala'rje], *v.t.* to pay, to give wages to.
salaud [sa'lo], *n.m.* (*fem.* **-e**) (*pop.* and *rude*) sloven, dirty person, slut; **quel salaud!** dirty beast! dirty dog!
sale [sal], *a.* dirty; nasty, foul; coarse, obscene; squalid.
salé [sa'le], *a.* salted, salt; briny; (*fig.*) keen, biting; coarse; spicy.—*n.m.* salt pork; **du petit salé**, pickled pork.
salement [sal'mɑ̃], *adv.* dirtily; nastily.
saler [sa'le], *v.t.* to salt; (*fig.*) to overcharge for; to fleece (*customers*).
saleté [sal'te], *n.f.* dirtiness, filthiness; filth, dirt; dirty trick; obscenity.
saleur [sa'lœ:r], *n.m.* (*fem.* **-euse**) salter, curer.
salière [sa'ljɛ:r], *n.f.* salt-cellar; salt box; eye-pit (*in horses*).
salin [sa'lɛ̃], *a.* salt, saline, briny.—*n.m.* salt works; salt marsh.
saline [sa'lin], *n.f.* salt marsh, salt mine, salt pit.
salinier [sali'nje], *n.m.* owner of salt works; salt worker *or* vendor.
salique [sa'lik], *a.* **loi salique**, Salic law.
salir [sa'li:r], *v.t.* to dirty, to soil; to taint, to sully. **se salir**, *v.r.* to get dirty; to sully one's reputation.
salissant [sali'sɑ̃], *a.* that soils *or* gets dirty easily; dirty (*of job, work etc.*).
salive [sa'li:v], *n.f.* saliva, spittle.
saliver [sali've], *v.i.* to salivate.
salle [sal], *n.f.* hall; large room; gallery (*of museum*); ward (*in hospitals*); (*Theat.*) house; **salle à manger**, dining room; **salle d'attente**, waiting room; **salle de bain(s)**, bathroom; **salle de spectacle**, playhouse.
saloir [sa'lwa:r], *n.m.* salt box; salting-tub.
salon [sa'lɔ̃], *n.m.* drawing-room, parlor; lounge; saloon; exhibition (*art*); (*pl.*) world of fashion.
salopette [salɔ'pɛt], *n.f.* overall, dungarees.
salpêtrage [salpɛ'tra:ʒ], *n.m.* saltpeter-making; nitrification.
salpêtre [sal'pɛ:tr], *n.m.* saltpeter.
salpêtrer [salpɛ'tre], *v.t.* to cover with saltpeter.
salpêtrerie [salpɛtrə'ri], *n.f.* saltpeter-works.

salpêtreux [salpɛ'trø], *a.* (*fem.* **-euse**) saltpetrous.

salpêtrière [salpɛtri'jɛːr], *n.f.* saltpeter works.

salsepareille [salspa'rɛːj], *n.f.* sarsaparilla.

saltimbanque [saltɛ̃'bɑ̃ːk], *n.m.* mountebank, buffoon; (*fig.*) humbug.

salubre [sa'lybr], *a.* salubrious, healthy (*climate*).

salubrité [salybri'te], *n.f.* salubrity, healthfulness, wholesomeness.

saluer [sa'lɥe], *v.t.* to salute, to bow to; to greet; to cheer; to proclaim. **se saluer**, *v.r.* to bow to *or* salute each other.

salure [sa'lyːr], *n.f.* saltness, salinity.

salut [sa'ly], *n.m.* safety; salvation; welfare; escape; salutation, greeting; hail, cheers.

salutaire [saly'tɛːr], *a.* salutary, advantageous, beneficial.

salutairement [salytɛr'mɑ̃], *adv.* beneficially.

salutation [salyta'sjɔ̃], *n.f.* salutation, greeting; (*pl.*) compliments.

Salvador [salva'dɔr], **le, m.** El Salvador.

salvadorègne [salvadɔ'rɛɲ], *a.* Salvadorean. —*n.* (**Salvadorègne**) Salvadorean (*person*).

salve [salv], *n.f.* salvo, volley; salute (*of artillery*).

samedi [sam'di], *n.m.* Saturday.

sanatorium [sanatɔ'rjɔm], *n.m.* sanatorium.

sanctifiant [sɑ̃kti'fjɑ̃], *a.* sanctifying.

sanctificateur [sɑ̃ktifika'tœːr], *a.* (*fem.* **-trice**) sanctifying.—*n.m.* sanctifier.

sanctification [sɑ̃ktifika'sjɔ̃], *n.f.* sanctification.

sanctifier [sɑ̃kti'fje], *v.t.* to sanctify, to hallow.

sanction [sɑ̃k'sjɔ̃], *n.f.* sanction; approbation; penalty.

sanctionner [sɑ̃ksjɔ'ne], *v.t.* to sanction, to approve; to penalize.

sanctuaire [sɑ̃k'tɥɛːr], *n.m.* sanctuary (*of the temple etc.*), shrine; chancel (*of church*).

sandale [sɑ̃'dal], *n.f.* sandal; fencing shoe.

sandalier [sɑ̃da'lje], *n.m.* sandal-maker.

sandow [sɑ̃'dɔf], *n.m.* chest-expander; rubber shock-absorber.

sandwich [sɑ̃'dwitʃ], *n.m.* (*pl.* **sandwichs** or **sandwiches**) sandwich.

sang [sɑ̃], *n.m.* blood; race; kindred; *pur sang*, thoroughbred.

sang-froid [sɑ̃'frwa], *n.m.* coolness, composure, sang-froid.

sanglade [sɑ̃'glad], *n.f.* lash, cut (*with a whip*).

sanglant [sɑ̃'glɑ̃], *a.* bloody, bleeding; (*fig.*) biting, outrageous.

sangle [sɑ̃ːgl], *n.f.* strap, belt; saddle-girth; *lit de sangle*, camp bed.

sangler [sɑ̃'gle], *v.t.* to girth, to strap; to lace too tightly; to deal (*a slashing blow*). **se sangler**, *v.r.* to lace oneself tightly.

sanglier [sɑ̃'glje], *n.m.* wild boar.

sanglot [sɑ̃'glo], *n.m.* sob.

sangloter [sɑ̃glɔ'te], *v.i.* to sob.

sang-mêlé [sɑ̃mɛ'le], *n.m. inv.* half-caste.

sangsue [sɑ̃'sy], *n.f.* leech; (*fig.*) extortioner.

sanguin [sɑ̃'gɛ̃], *a.* of blood; full-blooded; blood-red.

sanguinaire [sɑ̃gi'nɛːr], *a.* sanguinary, bloody, blood-thirsty.

sanitaire [sani'tɛːr], *a.* sanitary.

sans [sɑ̃], *prep.* without; free from; but for, had it not been for, were it not for; *cela va sans dire*, of course; *sans abri, sans gîte, sans logis*, homeless; *sans cela*, otherwise; *sans quoi*, otherwise.

sans-atout [sɑ̃za'tu], *n.m.* no trumps.

sans-cœur [sɑ̃'kœːr], *n. inv.* heartless, unfeeling person.

sanscrit [sɑ̃s'kri], *n.m.* Sanskrit.

sans-façon [sɑ̃fa'sɔ̃], *n.m.* bluntness; off-handedness.

sans-gêne [sɑ̃'ʒɛːn], *n.m.* unceremoniousness, coolness; (*fam.*) cheek.

sansonnet [sɑ̃sɔ'nɛ], *n.m.* (*Orn.*) starling.

sans-patrie [sɑ̃pa'tri], *n. inv.* stateless person.

sans-souci [sɑ̃su'si], *a.* carefree, happy-go-lucky.—*n. inv.* (*colloq.*) carefree, easy-going person.—*n.m. inv.* free-and-easy manners.

sans-travail [sɑ̃tra'vaj], *n.m. inv.* *les sans-travail*, the unemployed.

santal [sɑ̃'tal], *n.m.* (*pl.* **-als**) sandalwood, santal.

santé [sɑ̃'te], *n.f.* health, healthiness; state of health.

saoul [suːl].

sape [sap], *n.f.* sapping, undermining; mine; trench.

saper [sa'pe], *v.t.* to sap, to undermine.

sapeur [sa'pœːr], *n.m.* sapper.

sapeur-pompier [sapœrpɔ̃'pje], *n.m.* (*pl.* **sapeurs-pompiers**) fireman.

sapeur-télégraphiste [sapœrtelegra'fist], *n.m.* (*pl.* **sapeurs-télégraphistes**) soldier of the signal corps; (*pl.*) (*fam.*) signals.

saphir [sa'fiːr], *n.m.* sapphire.

sapin [sa'pɛ̃], *n.m.* fir, fir tree; (*bois de*) *sapin*, deal.

sapinette [sapi'nɛt], *n.f.* spruce.

sapinière [sapi'njɛːr], *n.f.* fir wood, fir plantation.

sarabande [sara'bɑ̃ːd], *n.f.* saraband (*dance*); (*fam.*) song-and-dance.

sarcasme [sar'kasm], *n.m.* sarcasm, sarcastic remark.

sarcastique [sarkas'tik], *a.* sarcastic.

sarcelle [sar'sɛl], *n.f.* (*Orn.*) teal.

sarclage [sar'klaːʒ], *n.m.* weeding.

sarcler [sar'kle], *v.t.* to weed; to hoe; (*fig.*) to extirpate.

sarcleur [sar'klœːr], *n.m.* (*fem.* **-euse**) weeder.

sarcloir [sar'klwaːr], *n.m.* hoe.

sarcophage (1) [sarkɔ'faːʒ], *n.m.* sarcophagus.

sarcophage (2) [sarkɔ'faːʒ], *n.f.* (*Ent.*) blow-fly.

Sardaigne [sar'dɛɲ], **la,** *f.* Sardinia.

sarde [sard], *a.* Sardinian.—*n.* (**Sarde**) Sardinian (*person*).

sardine [sar'din], *n.f.* sardine.

sardinerie [sardin'ri], *n.f.* sardine packing and curing factory.

sardinier [sardi'nje], *n.m.* (*fem.* **-ière**) sardine fisher; sardine packer *or* curer. —*n.m.* sardine net; sardine boat.

sardoine [sar'dwan], *n.f.* sardonyx.

sardonique [sardɔ'nik], *a.* sardonic.

sarigue [sa'rig], *n.* sarigue (*opossum*).

sarment [sar'mɑ̃], *n.m.* vine shoot, vine branch.

sarmenteux [sarmɑ̃'tø], *a.* (*fem.* **-euse**) branchy, climbing; rambling (*of roses*).

sarrasin [sara'zɛ̃], *n.m.* buckwheat.

sarrau [sa'ro], *n.m.* (*pl.* **-aux**) smock frock; child's blouse.

sas [sɑ], *n.m. inv.* sieve, screen; (*Naut.*) floating chamber (*of submarine*).

Satan [sa'tɑ̃], *m.* Satan.

satané [sata'ne], *a.* (*colloq.*) devilish, confounded.

satanique [sata'nik], *a.* satanic, diabolical.

sataniquement [satanik'mɑ̃], *adv.* fiendishly, diabolically.

satellite [satɛ'lit], *a.* satellite.—*n.m.* satellite.

satiété [sasje'te], *n.f.* satiety, repletion.

satin [sa'tɛ̃], *n.m.* satin.

satiné [sati'ne], *a.* satin-like, satiny; glazed (*of paper etc.*).

satiner [sati'ne], *v.t.* to satin; to glaze (*paper etc.*).—*v.i.* to look like satin.

satire [sa'tiːr], *n.f.* satire; lampoon.

satirique [sati'rik], *a.* satirical.—*n.m.* satirist.

satiriquement [satirik'mɑ̃], *adv.* satirically.

satiriser [satiri'ze], *v.t.* to satirize.

satisfaction [satisfak'sjɔ̃], *n.f.* satisfaction; gratification; atonement.

satisfaire [satis'fɛːr], *v.t. irr.* (*conjug. like* FAIRE) to satisfy; to gratify; to answer; to give satisfaction to, to make amends to.—*v.i.* to be satisfactory (*à*); to fulfil (*à*). **se satisfaire,** *v.r.* to satisfy oneself, to indulge oneself.

satisfaisant [satisfa'zɑ̃], *a.* satisfactory.

satisfait [satis'fɛ], *a.* satisfied, contented, pleased.

saturant [saty'rɑ̃], *a.* saturating.

saturation [satyra'sjɔ̃], *n.f.* saturation.

saturer [saty're], *v.t.* to saturate; (*fig.*) to surfeit.

saturnales [satyr'nal], *n.f. pl.* saturnalia.

Saturne [sa'tyrn], *m.* Saturn.

satyre [sa'tiːr], *n.m.* satyr.

sauce [soːs], *n.f.* sauce; *sauce blanche*, melted butter.

saucé [so'se], *a.* soused, wet through.

saucer [so'se], *v.t.* (*conjug. like* COMMENCER) to dip in sauce; to sop, to souse.

saucière [so'sjɛːr], *n.f.* sauce dish.

saucisse [so'sis], *n.f.* (*fresh*) sausage.

saucisson [sosi'sɔ̃], *n.m.* large dry sausage; salami.

sauf (1) [sof], *a.* (*fem.* **sauve**) safe; unhurt, unscathed; *sain et sauf*, safe and sound.

sauf (2) [sof], *prep.* save, except; unless.

sauf-conduit [sofkɔ̃'dɥi], *n.m.* (*pl.* **-conduits**) safe-conduct.

sauge [soːʒ], *n.f.* sage (*herb*).

saugrenu [sogra'ny], *a.* absurd, ridiculous, preposterous.

saulaie [so'lɛ], *n.f.* willow grove.

saule [soːl], *n.m.* willow.

saumâtre [so'mɑːtr], *a.* brackish, briny.

saumon [so'mɔ̃], *n.m.* salmon.

saumoné [somo'ne], *a.* salmon-colored; *truite saumonée*, salmon trout.

saumurage [somy'raːʒ], *n.m.* pickling (*in brine*), brining.

saumure [so'myːr], *n.f.* brine, pickle.

saumuré [somy're], *a.* pickled, brined.

saunage [so'naːʒ], *n.m.*, **saunaison** [sonɛ'zɔ̃], *n.f.* salt-making; salt trade.

sauner [so'ne], *v.i.* to make salt.

saunerie [son'ri], *n.f.* saltworks.

saunier [so'nje], *n.m.* salt-maker; salt merchant.

saunière [so'njɛːr], *n.f.* salt bin.

saupoudrage [sopu'draːʒ], *n.m.* salting; sprinkling, powdering.

saupoudrer [sopu'dre], *v.t.* to sprinkle with salt, pepper etc.; to powder, to sprinkle.

saur or **sor** [soːr], *a.m.* smoked and salted; red (*of herrings*).

saure [sor], *a.* yellowish-brown; sorrel (*of horses*); red, smoked (*of herrings*).

saurer [so're], *v.t.* to smoke (*herrings*).

saurin [so'rɛ̃], *n.m.* freshly smoked herring, bloater.

saurisserie [soris'ri], *n.f.* kippering factory.

saut [so], *n.m.* leap, jump, hop, bound; *de plein saut*, at once, suddenly; *saut périlleux*, somersault.

sautage [so'taːʒ], *n.m.* exploding (*mines*).

saut-de-mouton [sodmu'tɔ̃], *n.m.* (*pl.* **sauts-de-mouton**) overpass.

saute [sot], *n.f.* (*Naut.*) sudden shift *or* change (*of wind*).

sauté [so'te], *a.* fried, tossed in the pan.

saute-mouton [sotmu'tɔ̃], *n.m.* leap-frog (*game*).

sauter [so'te], *v.t.* to leap over; to leave out, to skip; to toss in the pan.—*v.i.* to leap, to jump; to explode; to spring; to blow out (*of fuse*).

sauterelle [so'trɛl], *n.f.* grasshopper, locust.

sauterie [sot'ri], *n.f.* (*fam.*) informal dance, hop.

saute-ruisseau [sotrɥi'so], *n.m. inv.* messenger boy (*in offices*).

sauteur [so'tœːr], *a.* (*fem.* **-euse**) jumping, leaping.—*n.m.* (*fem.* **-euse**) leaper, jumper; vaulter.

sautillant [soti'jɑ̃], *a.* hopping, skipping.

sautiller [soti'je], *v.i.* to hop, to skip, to jump about.

sautoir [so'twaːr], *n.m.* Saint Andrew's cross.

sauvage [so'vaːʒ], *a.* savage, wild; uncivilized; brutal; shy; unsociable.—*n.* savage; unsociable person.

sauvagement [sovaʒ'mɑ̃], *adv.* wildly, savagely; barbarously, fiercely.

sauvageon [sovɑ'ʒɔ̃], *n.m.* (*Agric.*) wild stock (*for grafting*); briar (*of roses*).

sauvagerie [sovaʒ'ri], *n.f.* unsociableness; shyness; wildness.

sauvagesse [sova'ʒɛs], *n.f.* uncivilized woman; hoyden.

sauvagin [sova'ʒɛ̃], *a.* fishy (*in taste, smell, etc.*).—*n.m.* fishy taste *or* smell.—*n.f.* (*-e*) wild waterfowl.

sauvegarde [sov'gard], *n.f.* safe-keeping, safeguard; safe-conduct; (*Naut.*) life-line.

sauvegarder [sovgar'de], *v.t.* to watch over, to protect, to safeguard.

sauve-qui-peut [sovki'pø], *n.m. inv.* headlong flight, stampede; every man for himself.

sauver [so've], *v.t.* to save, to rescue; to preserve; to exempt; to conceal. **se sauver,** *v.r.* to escape, to make off; (*fam.*) to abscond; to take refuge.

sauvetage [sov'taːʒ], *n.m.* salvage; life-saving, rescue; *appareil de sauvetage*, rescue apparatus, fire escape; *bouée de*

sauvetage, life buoy; *canot de sauve-tage*, life-boat; *ceinture de sauvetage*, life belt.
sauveteur [sov'tœːr], *n.m.* rescuer, lifeboat man.
sauveur [so'vœːr], *a.* saving, redeeming.—*n.m.* saver, deliverer; Saviour.
savamment [sava'mã], *adv.* learnedly; knowingly.
savane [sa'van], *n.f.* savanna; (C) swamp.
savant [sa'vã], *a.* learned, expert (*en*); scholarly; clever.—*n.m.* (*fem.* -e) scholar, scientist.
savarin [sava'rɛ̃], *n.m.* round, hollow cake.
savate [sa'vat], *n.f.* old shoe; clumsy person.
savetier [sav'tje], *n.m.* cobbler; (*fig.*) bungler.
saveur [sa'vœːr], *n.f.* savor, flavor, relish.
savoir [sa'vwaːr], *v.t. irr.* to know, to be aware of; to understand; to know how (*can*), to be able. **se savoir**, *v.r.* to get known.—*n.m.* knowledge, learning, scholarship.
savoir-faire [savwar'fɛːr], *n.m.* tact; savoir-faire; cleverness.
savoir-vivre [savwar'viːvr], *n.m.* good manners, good breeding.
savon [sa'vɔ̃], *n.m.* soap; (*colloq.*) scolding.
savonnage [savɔ'naːʒ], *n.m.* soaping, washing with soap.
savonner [savɔ'ne], *v.t.* to soap; to lather; (*colloq.*) to scold. **se savonner**, *v.r.* to be washable, to wash (*of fabrics*); to lather (*oneself*).
savonnerie [savɔn'ri], *n.f.* soap manufacture; soap trade; soap works.
savonnette [savɔ'nɛt], *n.f.* cake of toilet soap.
savonneux [savɔ'nø], *a.* (*fem.* -euse) soapy.
savourer [savu're], *v.t.* to savor, to relish; (*fig.*) to enjoy.
savoureusement [savurøz'mã], *adv.* with relish.
savoureux [savu'rø], *a.* (*fem.* -euse) savory, tasty (*dish*); racy (*story*).
savoyard [savwa'jaːr], *a.* of Savoy.—*n.m.* (**Savoyard**, *fem.* -**arde**) Savoyard (*person*); *petit Savoyard*, little chimney-sweep.
saxifrage [saksi'fraːʒ], *a.* saxifragous.—*n.f.* saxifrage.
saxon [sak'sɔ̃], *a.* (*fem.* -**onne**) Saxon.—*n.m.* (**Saxon**, *fem.* -**onne**) Saxon (*person*).
saxophone [saksɔ'fɔn], *n.m.* saxophone.
saynète [sɛ'nɛt], *n.f.* playlet, sketch.
scabieux [ska'bjø], *a.* (*fem.* -**euse**) scabious, scabby.—*n.f.* (-**euse**) scabious (*plant*).
scabreux [ska'brø], *a.* (*fem.* -**euse**) scabrous, rugged, rough; (*fig.*) dangerous, difficult, ticklish; improper.
scalp [skalp], *n.m.* scalp (*of an enemy*).
scalpel [skal'pɛl], *n.m.* scalpel.
scalper [skal'pe], *v.t.* to scalp.
scandale [skã'dal], *n.m.* scandal; shame, dismay, disgust.
scandaleusement [skãdaløz'mã], *adv.* scandalously.
scandaleux [skãda'lø], *a.* (*fem.* -**euse**) scandalous.
scandaliser [skãdali'ze], *v.t.* to scandalize, to shock. **se scandaliser**, *v.r.* to be shocked.
scander [skã'de], *v.t.* to scan; to stress (*a phrase*).
scandinave [skãdi'naːv], *a.* Scandinavian.—*n.* (**Scandinave**) Scandinavian (*person*).
Scandinavie [skãdina'vi], **la,** *f.* Scandinavia.

292

scansion [skã'sjɔ̃], *n.f.* scansion.
scaphandre [ska'fãːdr], *n.m.* diving suit.
scaphandrier [skafãdri'je], *n.m.* diver.
scapulaire [skapy'lɛːr], *a.* and *n.m.* scapular.
scarabée [skara'be], *n.m.* scarabaeus (*beetle*); scarab.
scarlatine [skarla'tin], *a.* and *n.f.* (*fièvre*) *scarlatine*, scarlet fever.
sceau [so], *n.m.* (*pl.* **sceaux**) seal; (*fig.*) sanction; *mettre le sceau à*, to seal, (*fig.*) to complete.
scélérat [sele'ra], *a.* wicked, villainous, criminal, vile.—*n.m.* (*fem.* -**e**) scoundrel, villain, miscreant, jade.
scélératesse [selera'tɛs], *n.f.* villainy.
scellé [sɛ'le], *n.m.* seal.
scellement [sɛl'mã], *n.m.* sealing; fastening.
sceller [sɛ'le], *v.t.* to put an official seal on, to seal; (*Build.*) to fasten; (*fig.*) to ratify.
scénario [sena'rjo], *n.m.* (*pl.* **scénarios** or **scénarii**) scenario (*of ballet etc.*); film script.
scénariste [sena'rist], *n.* script writer, scenario writer.
scène [sɛːn], *n.f.* stage; scenery; (*colloq.*) scene, quarrel.
scénique [se'nik], *a.* scenic, theatrical; *indications scéniques*, stage directions.
scepticisme [sɛpti'sism], *n.m.* scepticism.
sceptique [sɛp'tik], *a.* sceptical.—*n.* sceptic.
sceptre [sɛptr], *n.m.* sceptre; (*fig.*) sway, dominion.
schah [ʃa], *n.m.* shah (*of Persia*).
scheik or **cheik** [ʃɛk], *n.m.* sheik.
schéma [ʃe'ma], **schème** [ʃɛm], *n.m.* diagram; rough sketch.
schématique [ʃema'tik], *a.* diagrammatic; *dessin schématique*, draft, diagram.
schibboleth [ʃibɔ'lɛt], *n.m.* catchword, shibboleth.
schisme [ʃism], *n.m.* schism.
schiste [ʃist], *n.m.* schist, slaty rock, shale.
schizophrène [skizɔ'frɛn], *a.* and *n.* schizophrenic.
schizophrénie [skizɔfre'ni], *n.f.* schizophrenia.
schnorkel [ʃnɔr'kɛl], *n.m.* snorkel; submarine's air-tube.
schooner [sku'nœːr], *n.m.* schooner.
sciage [sja'ʒ], *n.m.* sawing.
sciatique [sja'tik], *a.* sciatic.—*n.m.* sciatic nerve.—*n.f.* sciatica.
scie [si], *n.f.* saw; (*pop.*) bore, nuisance.
sciemment [sja'mã], *adv.* wittingly, knowingly.
science [sjã's], *n.f.* science, knowledge, learning; skill.
scientifique [sjãti'fik], *a.* scientific.
scientifiquement [sjãtifik'mã], *adv.* scientifically.
scier [sje], *v.t.* to saw; to cut down.—*v.i.* (*Row.*) to back water.
scierie [si'ri], *n.f.* sawmill.
scieur [sjœːr], *n.m.* sawyer.
scinder [sɛ̃'de], *v.t.* to divide, to split up.
scintillant [sɛ̃ti'jã], *a.* scintillating; twinkling.
scintillation [sɛ̃tija'sjɔ̃], *n.f.*, **scintillement** [sɛ̃tij'mã], *n.m.* scintillation, sparkling; twinkling.
scintiller [sɛ̃ti'je], *v.i.* to scintillate, to sparkle; to twinkle (*of star*); to flicker.

scion [sjø], *n.m.* scion, shoot.
scission [si'sjɔ̃], *n.f.* scission; split, secession.
scissure [si'sy:r], *n.f.* fissure, crack, cleft.
sciure [sjy:r], *n.f.* **sciure de bois**, sawdust.
sclérose [skle'ro:z], *n.f.* sclerosis.
scolaire [skɔ'lɛ:r], *a.* of schools; **année scolaire**, school year.
scolarité [skɔlari'te], *n.f.* course of study; school attendance.
scolastique [skɔlas'tik], *a.* scholastic.—*n.m.* scholastic; schoolman.—*n.f.* scholasticism.
scolastiquement [skɔlastik'mɑ̃], *adv.* scholastically.
scooter [sku'tɛ:r], *n.m.* motor-scooter; **autos scooters**, 3-wheeled delivery vehicles.
scorbut [skɔr'byt], *n.m.* scurvy.
scorbutique [skɔrby'tik], *a.* and *n.* scorbutic.
scorie [skɔ'ri], *n.f.* scoria, slag, dross.
scorifier [skɔri'fje], *v.t.* to scorify.
scorpion [skɔr'pjɔ̃], *n.m.* scorpion.
scout [skut], *a.* of scouting.—*n.m.* (boy) scout.
scoutisme [sku'tism], *n.m.* scouting, boy-scout movement.
scratch [skratʃ], *n.* (*Spt.*) **être** or **partir scratch**, to start at scratch.
scratcher [skrat'ʃe], *v.t.* (*Spt.*) to scratch (*horse, competitor etc.*).
scribe [skrib], *n.m.* scribe; copyist.
script [skript], *n.m.* script (*film or play*).
scriptural [skripty'ral], *a.* (*m. pl.* **-aux**) scriptural.
scrofule [skrɔ'fyl], *n.f.* scrofula, king's evil.
scrofuleux [skrɔfy'lø], *a.* and *n.m.* (*fem.* **-euse**) scrofulous (person).
scrupule [skry'pyl], *n.m.* scruple, qualm, doubt; scrupulousness.
scrupuleusement [skrypyløz'mɑ̃], *adv.* scrupulously.
scrupuleux [skrypy'lø], *a.* (*fem.* **-euse**) scrupulous, strict, punctilious.
scrutateur [skryta'tœ:r], *a.* (*fem.* **-trice**) searching, scrutinizing.—*n.m.* (*fem.* **-trice**) investigator, scrutinizer; scrutineer, teller (*of a ballot etc.*).
scruter [skry'te], *v.t.* to scrutinize, to investigate.
scrutin [skry'tɛ̃], *n.m.* ballot, balloting, poll.
sculpter [skyl'te], *v.t.* to sculpture, to carve.
sculpteur [skyl'tœ:r], *n.m.* sculptor, carver.
sculptural [skylty'ral], *a.* (*m. pl.* **-aux**) sculptural.
sculpture [skyl'ty:r], *n.f.* sculpture, carving.
se [sə], **s'** [s], *pron. irr.* oneself, himself, herself, itself, themselves; to oneself etc.; one another, each other; **cela se peut**, that may be.
séance [se'ɑ̃:s], *r f.* seat (*right to sit*); session, duration, meeting; sitting (*for one's portrait etc.*); seance; **être en séance**, to be in session; **lever la séance**, to close the meeting; **séance tenante**, there and then, forthwith.
séant [se'ɑ̃], *a.* a sitting; fitting, seemly, becoming.—*n.m.* sitting posture; seat.
seau [so], *n.m.* (*pl.* **seaux**) pail, bucket.
sébile [se'bil], *n.f.* small wooden bowl (*used by beggars*); pan (*in gold mining*).
sec [sɛk], *a.* (*fem.* **sèche**) dry, arid; withered; lean; plain; unfeeling, sharp; **à pied sec**, dry-shod; **coup sec**, sharp stroke; **perte**

sèche, dead loss.—*n.m.* dryness.—*adv.* dryly, sharply.
sécateur [seka'tœ:r], *n.m.* (*Gard.*) pruning-shears; secateurs.
seccotine [sɛkɔ'tin], *n.f.* (*reg. trade ma.k*) Seccotine.
sécession [sesɛ'sjɔ̃], *n.f.* secession.
séchage [se'ʃa:ʒ], *n.m.* drying.
sèchement [sɛʃ'mɑ̃], *adv.* dryly; curtly.
sécher [se'ʃe], *v.t.* (*conjug. like* CÉDER) to dry; to dry up; to cure.—*v.i.* to dry; to wither; to pine away. **se sécher**, *v.r.* to dry oneself; to dry (*of a thing*).
sécheresse [se'ʃrɛs], *n.f.* dryness; drought; (*fig.*) sharpness.
séchoir [se'ʃwa:r], *n.m.* drying room; clothes-horse; clothes airer; hair dryer.
second [sə'gɔ̃, zgɔ̃], *a.* second.—*n.m.* (*fem.* **-e**) second, assistant.—*n.m.* second floor.—*n.f.* (**-e**) second class; (*Sch.*) fifth grade; second (*of time*).
secondaire [səgɔ̃'dɛ:r], *a.* secondary; accessory.
secondairement [səgɔ̃dɛr'mɑ̃], *adv.* secondarily.
secondement [səgɔ̃d'mɑ̃], *adv.* secondly.
seconder [səgɔ̃'de], *v.t.* to second, to assist; to back (up); to support; to promote.
secouement [səku'mɑ̃], **secouage** [sə'kwa:ʒ], *n.m.* shaking, jogging, jolting.
secouer [sə'kwe], *v.t.* to shake, to jolt; to shake off; to shock; to rouse. **se secouer**, *v.r.* to shake oneself, to bestir oneself.
secourable [səku'rabl], *a.* helpful, helping; relievable.
secourir [səku'ri:r], *v.t. irr.* (*conjug. like* COURIR) to succor, to assist, to help, to relieve.
secourisme [səku'rism], *n.m.* first aid.
secouriste [səku'rist], *n.* qualified first-aider.
secours [sə'ku:r], *n.m.* help, assistance, aid; rescue; **appeler police secours**, to call police emergency; **au secours !** help!
secousse [sə'kus], *n.f.* shake, shock; blow, concussion; jerk, jolt.
secret [sə'krɛ], *a.* (*fem.* **-ète**) secret, private, hidden; reserved.—*n.m.* secret; secrecy, privacy, mystery.
secrétaire [səkre'tɛ:r], *n.* secretary.—*n.m.* writing desk.
secrétariat [səkreta'rja], *n.m.* secretaryship; secretary's office; secretariat.
secrètement [səkrɛt'mɑ̃], *adv.* secretly, in secret, inwardly.
sécréter [sekre'te], *v.t.* (*conjug. like* CÉDER) to secrete (*of glands etc.*).
sécréteur [sekre'tœ:r], *a.* (*fem.* **-euse** or **-trice**) secretory.
sécrétion [sekre'sjɔ̃], *n.f.* secretion.
sectaire [sɛk'tɛ:r], *a.* sectarian.—*n.* sectary.
sectateur [sɛkta'tœ:r], *n.m.* (*fem.* **-trice**) follower, votary.
secte [sɛkt], *n.f.* sect.
secteur [sɛk'tœ:r], *n.m.* sector, section; district.
section [sɛk'sjɔ̃], *n.f.* section; division.
sectionnement [sɛksjɔn'mɑ̃], *n.m.* division into parts.
sectionner [sɛksjɔ'ne], *v.t.* to divide into sections; to cut short.
séculaire [seky'lɛ:r], *a.* secular, coming once in a century; ancient; time-honored.

séculier [seky'lje], *a.* (*fem.* **-ière**) secular, lay; temporal, worldly.—*n.m.* layman.

secundo [sagɔ'do], *adv.* secondly.

sécurité [sekyri'te], *n.f.* security, safety.

sédatif [seda'tif], *a.* (*fem.* **-tive**) and *n.m.* sedative.

sédentaire [sedɑ̃'tɛːr], *a.* sedentary; settled, stationary.

sédiment [sedi'mɑ̃], *n.m.* sediment.

sédimentaire [sedimɑ̃'tɛːr], *a.* sedimentary.

séditieusement [sedisjøz'mɑ̃], *adv.* seditiously.

séditieux [sedi'sjø], *a.* (*fem.* **-euse**) seditious; mutinous.—*n.m.* rebel, mutineer.

sédition [sedi'sjɔ̃], *n.f.* sedition, mutiny, riot.

séducteur [sedyk'tœːr], *a.* (*fem.* **-trice**) seductive; enticing, alluring.—*n.m.* (*fem.* **-trice**) seducer, enticer.

séduction [sedyk'sjɔ̃], *n.f.* seduction; allurement; bribing.

séduire [se'dɥiːr], *v.t. irr.* (*conjug. like* CONDUIRE) to seduce; to beguile; to charm; to fascinate; to bribe.

séduisant [sedɥi'zɑ̃], *a.* seductive, alluring; fascinating; tempting.

segment [sɛg'mɑ̃], *n.m.* segment.

ségrégation [segrega'sjɔ̃], *n.f.* segregation.

seigle [sɛgl], *n.m.* rye.

seigneur [sɛ'ɲœːr], *n.m.* lord; lord of the manor, squire; nobleman; **le Seigneur**, the Lord.

seigneurial [sɛɲœ'rjal], *a.* (*m. pl.* **-aux**) manorial; lordly.

seigneurie [sɛɲœ'ri], *n.f.* lordship; manor.

sein [sɛ̃], *n.m.* breast, bosom; (*fig.*) heart, midst; womb.

seine [sɛːn], *n.f.* seine, (fishing-) net.

séisme [se'ism], *n.m.* earthquake.

seize [sɛːz], *a.* and *n.* sixteen, sixteenth.

seizième [sɛ'zjɛm], *a.* and *n.* sixteenth.

séjour [se'ʒuːr], *n.m.* stay, abode, sojourn; place where one sojourns.

séjourner [seʒur'ne], *v.i.* to stay, to sojourn.

sel [sɛl], *n.m.* salt; (*fig.*) wit, pungency; (*pl.*) smelling salts.

sélecteur [selɛk'tœːr], *a.* (*fem.* **-trice**) selecting; selective.

sélection [selɛk'sjɔ̃], *n.f.* selection.

sélectivité [selɛktivi'te], *n.f.* selectivity.

sellage [sɛ'laːʒ], *n.m.* saddling.

selle [sɛl], *n.f.* saddle; bowel movement.

seller [sɛ'le], *v.t.* to saddle.

sellerie [sɛl'ri], *n.f.* saddlery; harness room.

sellette [sɛ'lɛt], *n.f.* stool of repentance; shoeblack's box; (*Naut.*) slung cradle.

sellier [sɛ'lje], *n.m.* saddler.

selon [sa'lɔ̃], *prep.* according to; **c'est selon**, that depends; **selon moi**, in my opinion; **selon que**, according as.

semailles [sa'maːj], *n.f. pl.* seeds; sowing; sowing time.

semaine [sa'mɛn], *n.f.* week; week's work; week's money.

semainier [samɛ'nje], *n.m.* (*fem.* **-ière**) person on duty for the week.—*n.m.* (*Ind.*) time-sheet; weekly output.

sémaphore [sema'fɔːr], *n.m.* semaphore, signal post.

semblable [sɑ̃'blabl], *a.* like, similar, alike.—*n.* like; fellow, match, equal.—*n.m.* fellow creature.

semblablement [sɑ̃blabla'mɑ̃], *adv.* likewise, also.

semblant [sɑ̃'blɑ̃], *n.m.* appearance, semblance, look; pretence; **faire semblant**, to pretend.

sembler [sɑ̃'ble], *v.i.* to seem, to appear.

semé [sa'me], *a.* sowed, sown; strewn (*de*).

semelle [sa'mɛl], *n.f.* sole (*of boots, shoes etc.*); foot (*of stockings*); length of a foot.

semence [sa'mɑ̃ːs], *n.f.* seed; semen; (*fig.*) cause.

semer [sa'me], *v.t.* (*conjug. like* AMENER) to sow; to scatter, to strew; to sprinkle.

semestre [sa'mɛstr], *n.m.* half-year, six months.

semestriel [samɛstri'ɛl], *a.* (*fem.* **-elle**) half-yearly.

semeur [sa'mœːr], *n.m.* (*fem.* **-euse**) sower; (*fig.*) disseminator.

semi-circulaire [samisirky'lɛːr], *a.* semi-circular.

sémillance [semi'jɑ̃ːs], *n.f.* sprightliness, liveliness.

sémillant [semi'jɑ̃], *a.* brisk, lively, sprightly.

semi-mensuel [samimɑ̃'sɥɛl], *a.* (*fem.* **-elle**) fortnightly.

séminaire [semi'nɛːr], *n.m.* seminary, theological college; specialized course.

semis [sa'mi], *n.m.* sowing; seed bed; seedlings.

sémitique [semi'tik], *a.* Semitic.

sémitisme [semi'tism], *n.m.* Semitism.

semi-ton [sami'tɔ̃], *n.m.* (*pl.* **-tons**) semi-tone.

semoir [sa'mwaːr], *n.m.* seed bag; seed drill.

semonce [sa'mɔ̃ːs], *n.f.* rebuke, reprimand, lecture.

semoncer [samɔ̃'se], *v.t.* (*conjug. like* COMMENCER) to reprimand, to lecture.

semoule [sa'mul], *n.f.* semolina.

sempiternel [sɛ̃piter'nɛl], *a.* (*fem.* **-elle**) sempiternal, everlasting.

sénat [se'na], *n.m.* senate; senate building.

sénateur [sena'tœːr], *n.m.* senator.

sénatorial [senatɔ'rjal], *a.* (*m. pl.* **-aux**) senatorial.

séné [se'ne], *n.m.* senna.

seneçon [san'sɔ̃], *n.m.* groundsel.

Sénégal [sene'gal], **le**, *m.* Senegal.

sénégalais [senega'le], *a.* Senegalese.—*n.m.* (**Sénégalais**, *fem.* **-aise**) Senegalese (*person*).

Sénèque [se'nɛk], *m.* Seneca.

*****sénestre** [se'nɛstr], **senestre** [sa'nɛstr], *a.* left, (*Her.*) sinister.

sénile [se'nil], *a.* senile.

sénilité [senili'te], *n.f.* senility, old age.

senne [sɛn], [SEINE].

sens [sɑ̃ːs], *n.m. inv.* sense; senses, feelings; intelligence; consciousness; meaning; opinion; way, direction; **à contre-sens**, in a wrong sense; **à double sens**, with double meaning; **sens dessus dessous**, upside down; **sens interdit**, no entry.

sensation [sɑ̃sa'sjɔ̃], *n.f.* sensation, feeling.

sensationnel [sɑ̃sasjɔ'nɛl], *a.* (*fem.* **-elle**) sensational.

sensé [sɑ̃'se], *a.* sensible, intelligent.

sensément [sɑ̃se'mɑ̃], *adv.* sensibly, judiciously.

sensibilité [sɑ̃sibili'te], *n.f.* sensibility, sensitiveness, feeling; compassion.

sensible [sã'sibl], *a.* sensitive, susceptible, sympathetic; tender; sore (*skin etc.*); perceptible, noticeable, tangible.

sensiblement [sãsiblə'mã], *adv.* appreciably; feelingly, deeply; obviously; considerably.

sensiblerie [sãsiblə'ri], *n.f.* sentimentality; (*fam.*) sob stuff.

sensitif [sãsi'tif], *a.* (*fem.* **-tive**) sensitive; sensory.—*n.f.* (**-tive**) sensitive plant.

sensitivité [sãsitivi'te], *n.f.* sensitivity.

sensualiste [sãsɥa'list], *a.* sensual.—*n.* sensualist.

sensualité [sãsɥali'te], *n.f.* sensuality.

sensuel [sã'sɥɛl], *a.* (*fem.* **-elle**) sensual.—*n.m.* (*fem.* **-elle**) sensualist.

sensuellement [sãsɥɛl'mã], *adv.* sensually.

sentence [sã'tã:s], *n.f.* maxim; sentence, judgment, verdict.

sentencieusement [sãtãsjøz'mã], *adv.* sententiously.

sentencieux [sãtã'sjø], *a.* (*fem.* **-euse**) sententious.

senteur [sã'tœ:r], *n.f.* smell; scent, perfume; *pois de senteur*, sweet pea.

senti [sã'ti], *a.* felt, experienced.

sentier [sã'tje], *n.m.* path, footpath; *sentier battu*, beaten track.

sentiment [sãti'mã], *n.m.* feeling; sensation; sentiment; affection, *esp.* love; perception, sense; opinion.

sentimental [sãtimã'tal], *a.* (*m. pl.* **-aux**) sentimental.

sentimentalement [sãtimãtal'mã], *adv.* sentimentally.

sentimentaliste [sãtimãta'list], *n.* sentimentalist.

sentimentalité [sãtimãtali'te], *n.f.* sentimentality.

sentinelle [sãti'nɛl], *n.f.* sentinel, sentry.

sentir [sã'ti:r], *v.t. irr.* to feel; to guess; to perceive; to smell; to savor of; to seem.—*v.i.* to smell. **se sentir**, *v.r.* to feel oneself, to feel; to be conscious; to feel the effects (*de*); to be perceived, felt etc.

seoir (1) [swa:r], *v.i. irr.* (*only used in pres. p.* **séant** *and p.p.* **sis**) to sit, to be sitting.

seoir (2) [swa:r], *v.i. irr.* (*pres. p.* **seyant**, *no p.p.*) to suit, to become.

Séoudite [seu'dit], [ARABIE].

séparable [sepa'rabl], *a.* separable.

séparation [separa'sjɔ̃], *n.f.* separation, parting.

séparé [sepa're], *a.* separate; distinct.

séparément [separe'mã], *adv.* separately; apart.

séparer [sepa're], *v.t.* to separate, to part; to sever. **se séparer**, *v.r.* to separate, to part; to divide.

sépia [se'pja], *n.f.* sepia.

sept [sɛt], *a.* and *n.m. inv.* seven; seventh.

septembre [sɛp'tã:br], *n.m.* September.

septénaire [sɛpte'nɛ:r], *a.* and *n.m.* septenary.

septennal [sɛpte'nal], *a.* (*m. pl.* **-aux**) septennial.

septentrion [sɛptãtri'ɔ̃], *n.m.* north.

septentrional [sɛptãtrio'nal], *a.* (*m. pl.* **-aux**) north, northern.

septicémie [sɛptise'mi], *n.f.* (*Med.*) septicemia, blood poisoning.

septième [sɛ'tjɛm], *a.* and *n.* seventh.

septique [sɛp'tik], *a.* septic.

septuagénaire [sɛptɥaʒe'nɛ:r], *a.* and *n.* septuagenarian.

sépulcral [sepyl'kral], *a.* (*m. pl.* **-aux**) sepulchral.

sépulcre [se'pylkr], *n.m.* sepulcher.

sépulture [sepyl'ty:r], *n.f.* burial, interment; burial place, tomb.

séquelle [se'kɛl], *n.f.* (*pl.*) after-effects (*of illness*).

séquence [se'kã:s], *n.f.* sequence.

séquestration [sekɛstra'sjɔ̃], *n.f.* sequestration.

séquestre [se'kɛstr], *n.m.* sequestration; sequestrator; depository.

séquestrer [sekɛs'tre], *v.t.* to sequester, to sequestrate; to shut up illegally. **se séquestrer**, *v.r.* to sequester oneself.

sequin [sə'kɛ̃], *n.m.* sequin (*gold coin*).

sérail [se'ra:j], *n.m.* seraglio.

séraphin [sera'fɛ̃], *n.m.* seraph.

séraphique [sera'fik], *a.* seraphic.

serbe [sɛrb], *a.* Serbian.—*n.* (**Serbe**) Serb. **Serbie** [sɛr'bi], **la**, *f.* Serbia.

serein [sə'rɛ̃], *a.* serene, placid, calm.—*n.m.* (*poet.*) night dew.

sérénade [sere'nad], *n.f.* serenade.

sérénité [sereni'te], *n.f.* serenity, calmness; equanimity.

séreux [se'rø], *a.* (*fem.* **-euse**) serous, watery.

serf [sɛrf], *a.* (*fem.* **serve**) in bondage, servile.—*n.m.* (*fem.* **serve**) serf, bondsman, bondswoman.

serge [sɛrʒ], *n.f.* serge.

sergent [sɛr'ʒã], *n.m.* sergeant; *sergent de ville*, police constable.

séricicole [serisi'kɔl], *a.* silk-producing.

sériciculteur [serisikyl'tœ:r], *n.m.* silk grower.

sériciculture [serisikyl'ty:r], *n.f.* silk culture.

série [se'ri], *n.f.* series; succession; run; (*Spt.*) heat; *fabrication en série*, mass production.

sérieusement [serjøz'mã], *adv.* seriously, gravely.

sérieux [se'rjø], *a.* (*fem.* **-euse**) serious, grave; earnest; real, true.—*n.m.* seriousness, importance, gravity.

serin [sə'rɛ̃], *n.m.* canary; (*fig.*) duffer, fool.

seriner [səri'ne], *v.t.* to din (*something*) into someone.

seringue [sə'rɛ̃:g], *n.f.* syringe, squirt.

seringuer [sərɛ̃'ge], *v.t.* to syringe, to squirt; to inject.

serment [sɛr'mã], *n.m.* oath, promise, solemn declaration; (*pl.*) swearing.

sermon [sɛr'mɔ̃], *n.m.* sermon; lecture.

sermonner [sɛrmɔ'ne], *v.t., v.i.* to sermonize, to lecture, to reprimand.

sermonneur [sɛrmɔ'nœ:r], *n.m.* (*fem.* **-euse**) sermonizer, preacher, fault-finder.

sérosité [serozi'te], *n.f.* serosity, wateriness.

serpe [sɛrp], *n.f.* bill-hook.

serpent [sɛr'pã], *n.m.* serpent, snake; *serpent à sonnettes*, rattlesnake.

serpenter [sɛrpã'te], *v.i.* to meander, to wind.

serpentin [sɛrpã'tɛ̃], *a.* serpentine.—*n.m.* paper streamer.

serpette [sɛr'pɛt], *n.f.* pruning knife.

serpolet [sɛrpo'lɛ], *n.m.* wild thyme.

serrage [sɛ'ra:ʒ], *n.m.* tightening, pressing.

serre [sɛ:r], *n.f.* squeeze, pressure; talon, claw (*of birds*); clip; hot-house, greenhouse, conservatory.

serré [sɛ're], *a.* close; compact; tight; clenched; (*fam.*) close-fisted.

serre-frein(s) [sɛr'frɛ̃], *n.m. inv.* (*Rail.*) brakeman.

serre-livres [sɛ:r'livr], *n.m. inv.* book ends.

serrement [sɛr'mɑ̃], *n.m.* pressing, squeezing; **serrement de cœur**, pang (*of grief*); **serrement de main**, handshake.

serre-papiers [sɛrpa'pje], *n.m. inv.* paper clip; file (*for papers*); set of pigeon-holes (*for papers*).

serrer [sɛ're], *v.t.* to press, to squeeze; to fasten, to lock; to grip; to condense, to put close together; to press; to close (*the ranks*); to clench (*one's fist, teeth etc.*). **se serrer**, *v.r.* to press each other close; to sit, lie or stand close together; to stint oneself.

serre-tête [sɛr'tɛ:t], *n.m. inv.* headband; crash helmet.

serrure [sɛ'ry:r], *n.f.* lock.

serrurier [sɛry'rje], *n.m.* locksmith.

sérum [se'rɔm], *n.m.* serum.

servage [sɛr'va:ʒ], *n.m.* servitude, bondage.

servant [sɛr'vɑ̃], *a.m.* serving; in waiting.—*n.m.* (*Artill.*) gunner.

servante [sɛr'vɑ̃:t], *n.f.* maid-servant; servant-girl; dinner wagon.

serveur [sɛr'vœ:r], *n.m.* (*fem.* **-euse**) (*Ten.*) server; waiter, barman; (*Cards*) dealer.

serviable [sɛr'vjabl], *a.* willing, obliging.

service [sɛr'vis], *n.m.* service; attendance; duty; function; divine service.

serviette [sɛr'vjɛt], *n.f.* napkin, serviette; towel; briefcase.

servile [sɛr'vil], *a.* servile, menial; slavish.

servilement [sɛrvil'mɑ̃], *adv.* servilely, slavishly.

servir [sɛr'vi:r], *v.t. irr.* (*conjug. like* SENTIR) to serve, to attend; to serve up; to be of service to; to assist.—*v.i.* to serve, to be of use; to serve up a meal. **se servir**, *v.r.* to serve oneself; to be served up (*of dishes*); **servez-vous**, help yourself.

serviteur [sɛrvi'tœ:r], *n.m.* servant, man-servant.

servitude [sɛrvi'tyd], *n.f.* servitude, slavery.

ses [se], [SON].

session [sɛ'sjɔ̃], *n.f.* session, sitting; term (*of law courts etc.*).

seuil [sœ:j], *n.m.* threshold; door-step; shelf (*of ocean bed*).

seul [sœl], *a.* alone; single, only, sole; mere, bare.—*n.m.* one only, the only one.

seulement [sœl'mɑ̃], *adv.* only; but; solely, merely.

sève [sɛ:v], *n.f.* sap; (*fig.*) pith, vigor, strength.

sévère [se'vɛ:r], *a.* severe, stern, austere; strict.

sévèrement [sevɛr'mɑ̃], *adv.* severely, sternly; strictly.

sévérité [severi'te], *n.f.* severity; strictness; purity.

séveux [se'vø], *a.* (*fem.* **-euse**) (*Bot.*) sappy; (*fig.*) vigorous.

sévices [se'vis], *n.m. pl.* (*Law*) cruelty, ill-treatment.

sévir [se'vi:r], *v.i.* to deal severely (*contre*); to rage (*of war etc.*).

sevrage [sə'vra:ʒ], *n.m.* weaning.

sevrer [sə'vre], *v.t.* (*conjug. like* AMENER) to wean; (*fig.*) to deprive (*de*).

sexagénaire [sɛkzaʒe'nɛ:r], *a.* and *n.* sexagenarian.

sexe [sɛks], *n.m.* sex.

sextant [sɛks'tɑ̃], *n.m.* sextant.

sextuple [sɛks'typl], *a.* and *n.m.* sextuple, six-fold.

sexualité [sɛksuali'te], *n.f.* sexuality.

sexuel [sɛk'sɥɛl], *a.* (*fem.* **-elle**) sexual.

shampooing [ʃɑ̃'pwɛ̃], *n.m.* shampoo, hair-wash.

shérif [ʃe'rif], *n.m.* sheriff.

short [ʃɔrt], *n.m.* (*Cost.*) shorts.

shunt [ʃœ:t], *n.m.* (*Elec.*) shunt.

shunter [ʃœ:'te], *v.t.* to shunt.

si (1) [si], *conj.* if; whether; supposing, what if.

si (2) [si], *adv.* so, so much, however much; yes.

si (3) [si], *n.m. inv.* (*Mus.*) si; the note B.

Siam [sjam], **le**, *m.* Thailand, Siam.

siamois [sja'mwa], *a.* Siamese.—*n.m.* Siamese (*language*); (**Siamois**, *fem.* **-oise**) Siamese (*person*).

Sibérie [sibe'ri], **la**, *f.* Siberia.

sibérien [sibe'rjɛ̃], *a.* (*fem.* **-enne**) Siberian. —*n.m.* (**Sibérien**, *fem.* **-enne**) Siberian (*person*).

sibilant [sibi'lɑ̃], *a.* sibilant, hissing.

siccatif [sika'tif], *a.* (*fem.* **-tive**) siccative, drying.

Sicile [si'sil], **la**, *f.* Sicily.

sicilien [sisi'ljɛ̃], *a.* (*fem.* **-enne**) Sicilian.—*n.m.* (**Sicilien**, *fem.* **-enne**) Sicilian (*person*).

sidérurgie [sideryr'ʒi], *n.f.* iron and steel industry.

siècle [sjɛkl], *n.m.* century; age, period.

siège [sjɛ:ʒ], *n.m.* seat; bench (*of a court of justice*); headquarters (*of society etc.*); (*Eccles.*) see; siege.

siéger [sje'ʒe], *v.i.* (*conjug. like* ASSIÉGER) to sit (*of assemblies, courts etc.*); to hold one's see (*of bishops*); to be seated; (*fig.*) to lie (*of a thing*); to have one's headquarters (*of business, society*).

sien [sjɛ̃], *pron. poss. 3rd pers. sing.* (*fem.* **sienne**) his, hers, its, one's.—*n.m.* one's own (*property, work etc.*).

Sienne [sjɛn], *f.* Sienna.

Sierra-Leone [sjɛrale'ɔn], **le**, *m.* Sierra Leone.

sieste [sjɛst], *n.f.* siesta.

sifflant [si'flɑ̃], *a.* hissing; whistling; wheezing.

sifflement [siflə'mɑ̃], *n.m.* hissing, hiss; whistling, whistle; whizzing; wheezing.

siffler [si'fle], *v.t.* to whistle; to hiss.—*v.i.* to hiss; to whistle; to whizz; to wheeze.

sifflet [si'flɛ], *n.m.* whistle (*instrument and sound*); catcall; hiss; (*colloq.*) windpipe.

siffleur [si'flœ:r], *a.* (*fem.* **-euse**) whistling, piping (*of birds*); wheezing (*of horses*).—*n.m.* (*fem.* **-euse**) whistler; hisser.

sigle [sigl], *n.m.* initial letter; group of initial letters used as abbreviation of phrase (*U.N. etc.*).

signal [si'nal], *n.m.* (*pl.* **-aux**) signal.

signalé [sina'le], *a.* signal, remarkable, conspicuous.

signalement [sinal'mɑ̃], *n.m.* description (*of a man etc.*), particulars.

signaler [siɲa'le], *v.t.* to signal; to give the description of; to point out, to mark out; to signalize. **se signaler**, *v.r.* to signalize *or* distinguish oneself.

signaleur [siɲa'lœːr], *n.m.* signalman; (*Mil.*) signaller.

signalisateur [siɲaliza'tœːr], *n.m.*(*Motor.*) directional signal.

signataire [siɲa'tɛːr], *n.* signer, subscriber, signatory.

signature [siɲa'tyːr], *n.f.* signature; signing.

signe [siɲ], *n.m.* sign; mark, indication; badge; omen; *faire signe de la main,* to beckon; *signe de la tête,* nod.

signer [si'ne], *v.t., v.i.* to sign, to subscribe. **se signer**, *v.r.* to cross oneself.

signet [si'nɛ], *n.m.* signet; book mark; signet ring.

significatif [siɲifika'tif], *a.* (*fem.* **-tive**) significant.

signification [siɲifika'sjɔ̃], *n.f.* signification, meaning; (*Law*) legal notice.

significativement [siɲifikativ'mã], *adv.* significantly.

signifier [siɲi'fje], *v.t.* to signify, to mean; to notify, to intimate; (*Law*) to serve.

silence [si'lɑ̃ːs], *n.m.* silence; stillness; secrecy; (*Mus.*) rest.

silencieusement [silãsjøz'mã], *adv.* silently.

silencieux [silã'sjø], *a.* (*fem.* **-euse**) silent; still.—*n.m.* (*Motor.*) muffler.

silex [si'lɛks], *n.m.* silex, flint.

silhouette [si'lwɛt], *n.f.* silhouette; outline, profile.

silice [si'lis], *n.f.* (*Chem.*) silica, flint.

sillage [si'jaːʒ], *n.m.* wake, wash; slip-stream.

sillon [si'jɔ̃], *n.m.* furrow made by plow; seed drill; (*fig.*) track, wake (*of a ship etc.*); wrinkle.

sillonner [sijo'ne], *v.t.* to furrow; to streak.

silo [si'lo], *n.m.* silo (*pit or tower for preserving fodder*).

silotage [silo'taːʒ], *n.m.* silage.

simagrée [sima'gre], *n.f.* pretence, affectation; (*pl.*) fuss.

simiesque [si'mjɛsk], *a.* ape-like, apish (*face*).

similaire [simi'lɛːr], *a.* similar.

similarité [similari'te], *n.f.* similarity, likeness.

similitude [simili'tyd], *n.f.* similitude, resemblance; simile.

simoun [si'muːn], *n.m.* simoom, simoon.

simple [sɛ̃ːpl], *a.* simple, single; easy; only, mere; common, plain; private (*soldier*); simple-minded, silly; natural.—*n.m.* that which is simple; (*Ten.*) singles; *simple dames,* women's singles.

simplement [sɛ̃plə'mã], *adv.* simply.

simplet [sɛ̃'plɛ], *a.* (*fem.* **-ette**) naïve, simple; (*fam.*) a bit off; (*Am.*) green.—*n.m.* (*fem.* **-ette**) simpleton, silly.

simplicité [sɛ̃plisi'te], *n.f.* simplicity; artlessness; silliness.

simplification [sɛ̃plifika'sjɔ̃], *n.f.* simplification.

simplifier [sɛ̃pli'fje], *v.t.* to simplify.

simulacre [simy'lakr], *n.m.* image; phantom; semblance, sham.

simulé [simy'le], *a.* feigned, sham.

simuler [simy'le], *v.t.* to feign, to sham.

simultané [simylta'ne], *a.* simultaneous.

simultanément [simyltane'mã], *adv.* simultaneously.

sincère [sɛ̃'sɛːr], *a.* sincere, frank; honest.

sincèrement [sɛ̃sɛr'mã], *adv.* sincerely, honestly.

sincérité [sɛ̃seri'te], *n.f.* sincerity.

sinécure [sine'kyːr], *n.f.* sinecure.

Singapour [sɛ̃ga'puːr], *m.* Singapore.

singe [sɛ̃ːʒ], *n.m.* ape, monkey; hoist; (*Mil. slang*) bully beef.

singer [sɛ̃'ʒe], *v.t.* (*conjug. like* MANGER) to ape, to mimic.

singerie [sɛ̃'ʒri], *n.f.* monkey house; grimace; antic; mimicry.

singeur [sɛ̃'ʒœːr], *a.* (*fem.* **-euse**) aping, mimicking.—*n.m.* (*fem.* **-euse**) ape, mimic.

singulariser [sɛ̃gylari'ze], *v.t.* to singularize; to make conspicuous. **se singulariser**, *v.r.* to make oneself conspicuous.

singularité [sɛ̃gylari'te], *n.f.* singularity; peculiarity.

singulier [sɛ̃gy'lje], *a.* (*fem.* **-ière**) singular; peculiar; odd.—*n.m.* (*Gram.*) singular.

singulièrement [sɛ̃gyljɛr'mã], *adv.* singularly, oddly.

sinistre [si'nistr], *a.* sinister; dismal; evil.— *n.m.* disaster, calamity.

sinistré [sinis'tre], *a.* affected by disaster (*shipwreck, fire etc.*).—*n.m.* (*fem.* **-ée**) victim of disaster; casualty.

sinon [si'nɔ̃], *conj.* otherwise, if not, else; except, unless; *sinon que,* except that.

sinueux [si'nɥø], *a.* (*fem.* **-euse**) sinuous, winding.

sinuosité [sinɥozi'te], *n.f.* sinuosity, winding.

sinus [si'nyːs], *n.m. inv.* sine; (*Anat.*) sinus.

sinusite [siny'zit], *n.f.* sinusitis.

siphon [si'fɔ̃], *n.m.* siphon; (*Naut.*) waterspout.

sire [siːr], *n.m.* sire (*title of kings and emperors*).

sirène [si'rɛn], *n.f.* siren, mermaid; horn, fog-horn.

sirocco [siro'ko], *n.m.* sirocco.

sirop [si'ro], *n.m.* syrup.

siroter [siro'te], *v.t.* to sip; (*pop.*) to tipple.

sirupeux [siry'pø], *a.* (*fem.* **-euse**) syrupy.

sis [si], *a.* seated, situated [SEOIR (1)].

Sisyphe [si'zif], *m.* Sisyphus.

site [sit], *n.m.* site (*situation with regard to scenery etc.*); *un beau site,* a beauty spot.

sitôt [si'to], *adv.* so soon, as soon; *sitôt dit, sitôt fait,* no sooner said than done; *sitôt que,* as soon as.

situation [sitɥa'sjɔ̃], *n.f.* situation, site, position; state of affairs, predicament.

situé [si'tɥe], *a.* situated, lying.

situer [si'tɥe], *v.t.* to place.

six [si *before a consonant,* siz *before a vowel* sis *at the end of a sentence*], *a.* six; sixth.— [sis], *n.m.* six; sixth; sixth day.

sixième [si'zjɛm], *a.* and *n.* sixth.—*n.m.* sixth (part); sixth floor.—*n.f.* (*in France*) sixth class, (*in England*) first form (*of upper school*).

ski [ski], *n.m.* ski; *faire du ski,* to go in for skiing; *ski nautique,* water-skiing.

slave [slav], *a.* Slav, Slavonic.—*n.* (**Slave**) Slav (*person*).

slip [slip], *n.m.* (*Cost.*) trunks, briefs; *slip de bain,* (swimming) trunks.

slovène

slovène [slɔ'vɛn], *a.* Slovenian.—*n.* **(Slovène)** Slovene.

smoking [smɔ'kiŋ], *n.m.* dinner jacket.

snob [snɔb], *a.* (*fam.*) swanky.—*n.m.* person who tries to be always in the swim.

snobisme [snɔ'bism], *n.m.* affected up-to-dateness.

sobre [sɔbr], *a.* (*of persons*) abstemious, temperate, moderate; (*of colors, style etc.*) sober, quiet, unadorned.

sobrement [sɔbrə'mɑ̃], *adv.* soberly, moderately.

sobriété [sɔbrie'te], *n.f.* sobriety; abstemiousness (*in food and drink*).

sobriquet [sɔbri'kɛ], *n.m.* nickname.

soc [sɔk], *n.m.* ploughshare.

sociabilité [sɔsjabili'te], *n.f.* sociability, good fellowship.

sociable [sɔ'sjabl], *a.* sociable, companionable.

sociablement [sɔsjablə'mɑ̃], *adv.* sociably.

social [sɔ'sjal], *a.* (*m. pl.* **-aux**) social; **siège social**, registered office; head office.

socialement [sɔsjal'mɑ̃], *adv.* socially.

socialisme [sɔsja'lism], *n.m.* socialism.

socialiste [sɔsja'list], *a.* and *n.* socialist.

sociétaire [sɔsje'tɛːr], *n.* associate, member; partner; shareholder.

société [sɔsje'te], *n.f.* society, association; community; firm; partnership; **société anonyme**, incorporated company.

sociologie [sɔsjɔlɔ'ʒi], *n.f.* sociology.

sociologiste [sɔsjɔlɔ'ʒist], **sociologue** [sɔsjɔ'lɔg], *n.* sociologist.

socle [sɔkl], *n.m.* socle, pedestal, stand, base.

socque [sɔk], *n.m.* clog, patten.

Socrate [sɔ'krat], *m.* Socrates.

sœur [sœːr], *n.f.* sister; nun.

sœurette [sœ'rɛt], *n.f.* (*colloq.*) little sister, sis(s).

sofa [sɔ'fa], *n.m.* sofa, settee.

soi [swa], **soi-même** [swa'mɛm], *impers. pron. 3rd pers. sing.* oneself, itself; self.

soi-disant [swadi'zɑ̃], *a. inv.* self-styled, would-be, so-called.

soie [swa], *n.f.* silk; silken hair; bristle (*of hogs*); **papier de soie**, tissue paper.

soierie [swa'ri], *n.f.* silks, silk goods; silk-trade; silk-factory.

soif [swaf], *n.f.* thirst; **avoir soif**, to be thirsty.

soigné [swa'ɲe], *a.* carefully done; neat, smart; (*colloq.*) first-rate.

soigner [swa'ɲe], *v.t.* to take care of, to look after; to nurse. **se soigner**, *v.r.* to take care of oneself.

soigneusement [swaɲøz'mɑ̃], *adv.* carefully.

soigneux [swa'ɲø], *a.* (*fem.* **-euse**) careful; solicitous.

soi-même [sɔi].

soin [swɛ̃], *n.m.* care; attendance; (*pl.*) attentions, pains, trouble.

soir [swaːr], *n.m.* evening; night.

soirée [swa're], *n.f.* evening (*duration*); evening party.

soit [swat, swa], *adv.* be it so, well and good, granted; let us say.—*conj.* either, or; whether.

soixantaine [swasɑ̃'tɛn], *n.f.* about sixty.

soixante [swa'sɑ̃ːt], *a.* and *n.m.* sixty.

soixantième [swasɑ̃'tjɛːm], *a.* and *n.* sixtieth.

298

sol [sɔl], *n.m.* ground; soil; earth.

solaire [sɔ'lɛːr], *a.* solar.

soldat [sɔl'da], *n.m.* soldier; **simple soldat**, private; **les simples soldats**, the rank and file.

soldatesque [sɔlda'tɛsk], *n.f.* (*usu. pej.*) soldiery.

solde (1) [sɔld], *n.f.* (*Mil.*) pay.

solde (2) [sɔld], *n.m.* balance (*between debit and credit*); clearance sale; (*pl.*) sale bargains, reductions.

solder (1) [sɔl'de], *v.t.* to pay (*soldiers*) to have in one's pay.

solder (2) [sɔl'de], *v.t.* to settle (*an account*); to sell off, to clear.

sole [sɔl], *n.f.* sole (*of animal's foot*); sole (*fish*).

solécisme [sɔle'sism], *n.m.* solecism.

soleil [sɔ'lɛːj], *n.m.* sun; sunshine; (*fig.*) star; catherine wheel (*firework*); sunflower.

solennel [sɔla'nɛl], *a.* (*fem.* **-elle**) solemn.

solennellement [sɔlanɛl'mɑ̃], *adv.* solemnly.

solenniser [sɔlani'ze], *v.t.* to solemnize.

solennité [sɔlani'te], *n.f.* solemnity.

solénoïde [sɔleno'id], *n.m.* solenoid.

solidaire [sɔli'dɛːr], *a.* jointly and separately liable.

solidairement [sɔlidɛr'mɑ̃], *adv.* jointly and severally.

solidariser [sɔlidari'ze], *v.t.* to render jointly liable.

solidarité [sɔlidari'te], *n.f.* joint and separate liability; solidarity, fellowship.

solide [sɔ'lid], *a.* solid; strong; substantial, sound; reliable.—*n.m.* solid, solid body.

solidement [sɔlid'mɑ̃], *adv.* solidly; firmly; soundly.

solidification [sɔlidifikɑ'sjɔ̃], *n.f.* solidification.

solidifier [sɔlidi'fje], *v.t.* and **se solidifier**, *v.r.* to solidify.

solidité [sɔlidi'te], *n.f.* solidity; strength; stability; soundness.

soliloque [sɔli'lɔk], *n.m.* soliloquy.

soliste [sɔ'list], *a.* solo.—*n.* soloist.

solitaire [sɔli'tɛːr], *a.* solitary, single, alone; lonely, desert.—*n.m.* lonely person, recluse; solitaire (*diamond* or *game*).

solitairement [sɔlitɛr'mɑ̃], *adv.* solitarily, alone.

solitude [sɔli'tyd], *n.f.* solitude, loneliness; desert.

solive [sɔ'liːv], *n.f.* joist.

soliveau [sɔli'vo], *n.m.* (*pl.* **-eaux**) small joist.

sollicitation [sɔlisita'sjɔ̃], *n.f.* solicitation; pull (*of magnet*).

solliciter [sɔlisi'te], *v.t.* to incite; to solicit, to entreat; to call into action; to attract (*of magnet*).

sollicitude [sɔlisi'tyd], *n.f.* solicitude, care; concern.

solo [sɔ'lo], *a. inv.* solo.—*n.m.* (*pl.* **solos** or **soli**) solo.

solstice [sɔls'tis], *n.m.* solstice.

solubilité [sɔlybili'te], *n.f.* solubility.

soluble [sɔ'lybl], *a.* soluble.

solution [sɔly'sjɔ̃], *n.f.* solution; resolution; (*Law*) discharge; **solution de continuité**, interruption, break, fault.

solvabilité [sɔlvabili'te], *n.f.* solvency.

solvable [sɔl'vabl], *a.* solvent.

solvant [sɔl'vɑ̃], *n.m.* solvent.

somali [sɔmaˈli], a. Somali.—n.m. Somali (language).—n. (**Somali**) Somali (person); **Côte Française des Somalis**, French Somaliland.

Somalie [sɔmaˈli], **la**, f. Somalia, Somaliland.

sombre [sɔ̃:br], a. dark, somber, gloomy; dim; overcast; melancholy.

sombrer [sɔ̃ˈbre], v.i. (Naut.) to founder.

sombrero [sɔ̃breˈro], n.m. sombrero.

sommaire [sɔˈmɛ:r], a. summary, concise; scanty.—n.m. summary, abstract.

sommairement [sɔmɛrˈmã], adv. summarily; hastily.

sommation [sɔmaˈsjɔ̃], n.f. summons, demand; (Mil.) challenge.

somme [sɔm], n.f. sum, total; amount; summary; burden.—n.m. nap; **faire un somme**, to have forty winks.

sommeil [sɔˈmɛːj], n.m. sleep; **avoir sommeil**, to be sleepy.

sommeiller [sɔmɛˈje], v.i. to slumber; to doze.

sommelier [sɔmɔˈlje], n.m. butler, cellarman, wine waiter.

sommellerie [sɔmɛlˈri], n.f. butler's pantry.

sommer [sɔˈme], v.t. to summon, to call upon; to sum up.

sommet [sɔˈmɛ], n.m. top, summit; acme; crown (of the head etc.).

sommier (1) [sɔˈmje], n.m. pack horse; box mattress; wind chest (of organ); (Arch.) cross-beam.

sommier (2) [sɔˈmje], n.m. cash book, register.

sommité [sɔmiˈte], n.f. summit, top; head, principal; chief point; prominent person.

somnambule [sɔmnãˈbyl], a. somnambulistic.—n. sleepwalker.

somnambulisme [sɔmnãbyˈlism], n.m. somnambulism, sleep-walking.

somnolence [sɔmnɔˈlã:s], n.f. somnolence.

somnolent [sɔmnɔˈlã], a. somnolent, sleepy.

somptuaire [sɔ̃pˈtɥɛ:r], a. sumptuary.

somptueusement [sɔ̃ptɥøzˈmã], adv. sumptuously.

somptueux [sɔ̃pˈtɥø], a. (fem. **-euse**) sumptuous; magnificent.

somptuosité [sɔ̃ptɥoziˈte], n.f. sumptuousness.

son (1) [sɔ̃], a. (fem. **sa**, pl. **ses**) his, her, its; one's.

son (2) [sɔ̃], n.m. sound.

son (3) [sɔ̃], n.m. bran; **tache de son**, freckle.

sonate [sɔˈnat], n.f. sonata.

sondage [sɔ̃ˈda:ʒ], n.m. sounding; (Mining) boring.

sonde [sɔ̃:d], n.f. sounding-line, lead; (Surg. etc.) probe; (Mining) drill, boring machine.

sonder [sɔ̃ˈde], v.t. to sound; to taste; to search, to fathom, to investigate.

sondeur [sɔ̃ˈdœ:r], n.m. (Naut.) leadsman; (Mining) driller, borer.

songe [sɔ̃:ʒ], n.m. dream; dreaming.

songe-creux [sɔ̃ʒˈkrø], n.m. inv. dreamer, visionary.

songer [sɔ̃ˈʒe], v.t. (conjug. like MANGER) to dream; (fig.) to imagine; to think of.—v.i. to dream; (fig.) to day-dream; to think; to mean, to intend, to propose.

songerie [sɔ̃ˈʒri], n.f. dreaming; musing; day-dreaming.

songeur [sɔ̃ˈʒœ:r], a. (fem. **-euse**) thoughtful, dreamy.—n.m. (fem. **-euse**) dreamer.

sonique [sɔˈnik], a. sonic.

sonnant [sɔˈnã], a. sounding; sonorous.

sonner [sɔˈne], v.t., v.i. to sound; to ring, to toll, to strike (of clocks etc.).

sonnerie [sɔnˈri], n.f. ring, ringing (of bells); bells, chimes; striking part (of a clock etc.); (Mil.) bugle call.

sonnet [sɔˈnɛ], n.m. sonnet.

sonnette [sɔˈnɛt], n.f. small bell; hand bell.

sonneur [sɔˈnœ:r], n.m. bell ringer.

sonore [sɔˈnɔ:r], a. resonant; clear; **ondes sonores**, sound waves.

sonorité [sɔnɔriˈte], n.f. resonance.

sophisme [sɔˈfism], n.m. sophism, fallacy.

sophiste [sɔˈfist], a. sophistical.—n. sophist.

sophistiqué [sɔfistiˈke], a. sophisticated; affected.

soporifique [sɔpɔriˈfik], a. soporific; (fig.) tedious.—n.m. soporific.

soprano [sɔpraˈno], n. (pl. **soprani** or **sopranos**) soprano, treble.

sorbet [sɔrˈbɛ], n.m. sherbet.

sorbier [sɔrˈbje], n.m. mountain ash, rowan tree.

sorcellerie [sɔrsɛlˈri], n.f. sorcery, witchcraft.

sorcier [sɔrˈsje], n.m. (fem. **-ière**) sorcerer, wizard, sorceress, witch.

sordide [sɔrˈdid], a. sordid, filthy; mean, vile.

sordidement [sɔrdidˈmã], adv. sordidly.

Sorlingues [sɔrˈlɛ̃:g], **les**, f. pl. the Scilly Isles.

sornette [sɔrˈnɛt], n.f. (usu. in pl.) idle talk, small talk.

sort [sɔ:r], n.m. fate, destiny; lot; condition; fortune; chance; spell, charm; **au sort**, by lot; **le sort en est jeté**, the die is cast; **tirer au sort**, to draw lots; to toss.

sortable [sɔrˈtabl], a. suitable.

sortablement [sɔrtablaˈmã], adv. suitably.

sortant [sɔrˈtã], a. outgoing, retiring, leaving (office etc.); drawn (of numbers in lotteries).—n.m. person going out; person leaving office etc.; **les entrants et les sortants**, the incomers and outgoers.

sorte [sɔrt], n.f. sort, kind, species; manner, way; **de la sorte**, thus, in that way; **de sorte que** or **en sorte que**, so that.

sortie [sɔrˈti], n.f. going or coming out; exit, way out; outing, trip; exportation; sortie; (colloq.) outburst, attack; **droit de sortie**, export duty; **jour de sortie**, day off, holiday.

sortilège [sɔrtiˈlɛ:ʒ], n.m. sorcery, magic; spell, charm.

sortir [sɔrˈti:r], v.t. irr. (conjug. like SENTIR with aux. AVOIR) to bring out, to take out; to pull out, to extricate.—v.i. (with aux. ÊTRE) to go out, to come out, to come forth, to emerge; to make one's exit; to leave, to depart; to swerve; to wander (from a subject); to proceed, to result; to spring, to come up; to sally forth; to burst forth; to escape; (Paint. etc.) to stand out; to be in relief.—n.m. going out, leaving; rising.

sosie [sɔˈzi], n.m. double, counterpart.

sot [sɔ], a. (fem. **sotte**) stupid, silly, foolish; (fig.) embarrassed, sheepish.—n.m. (fem. **sotte**) fool, ass, idiot.

sottement [sɔtˈmã], adv. stupidly; foolishly.

299

sottise [sɔ'tiːz], *n.f.* silliness, folly; foolish trick, nonsense; insult; (*pl.*) abusive language.

sou [su], *n.m.* sou (*copper coin worth 5 centimes*); copper, penny.

soubresaut [subrə'so], *n.m.* sudden leap *or* bound; plunge (*of a horse*); start; jolt.

soubresauter [subrə'sote], *v.i.* to start, to jump, to plunge.

soubrette [su'brɛt], *n.f.* lady's maid, waiting-woman.

souche [suʃ], *n.f.* stump, stock, stub, stem; (*fig.*) blockhead; founder (*of a family etc.*); origin; chimney-stack; counterfoil; tally; *faire souche*, to found a family.

souci (1) [su'si], *n.m.* care, anxiety.

souci (2) [su'si], *n.m.* (*Bot.*) marigold.

soucier (**se**) [səsu'sje], *v.r.* to care, to mind, to be concerned, to be anxious (*de*).

soucieux [su'sjø], *a.* (*fem.* **-euse**) anxious, full of care; pensive, thoughtful.

soucoupe [su'kup], *n.f.* saucer.

soudage [su'daːʒ], *n.m.* soldering, welding; (*fig.*) reconciliation.

soudain [su'dɛ̃], *a.* sudden, unexpected.—*adv.* suddenly.

soudainement [sudɛn'mɑ̃], *adv.* suddenly, all of a sudden.

soudaineté [sudɛn'te], *n.f.* suddenness.

Soudan [su'dɑ̃], **le**, *n.m.* the Sudan.

soudanais [suda'nɛ], *a.* Sudanese.—*n.m.* (**Soudanais**, *fem.* **-aise**) Sudanese (*person*).

soude [sud], *n.f.* soda.

souder [su'de], *v.t.* to solder, to braze, to weld; (*fig.*) to unite. **se souder**, *v.r.* to be soldered *or* welded; to knit (*of bones*).

soudeur [su'dœːr], *n.m.* welder.

soudoyer [sudwa'je], *v.t.* (*conjug. like* EMPLOYER) to keep in one's pay; to hire; to bribe.

soudure [su'dyːr], *n.f.* solder; soldering, welding; *soudure autogène*, oxyacetylene welding.

soue [su], *n.f.* pigsty.

soufflage [su'flaːʒ], *n.m.* glass-blowing.

soufflant [su'flɑ̃], *a.* blowing.

souffle [sufl], *n.m.* breath, breathing; puff (*of wind etc.*); (*fig.*) inspiration, influence.

soufflé [su'fle], *a.* soufflé (*of pastry etc.*); exaggerated (*reputation*).—*n.m.* soufflé (*light dish*).

soufflement [suflə'mɑ̃], *n.m.* blowing.

souffler [su'fle], *v.t.* to blow, to blow out; to inflate; to whisper; (*Theat.*) to prompt; to huff (*at checkers*); (*Naut.*) to sheathe.—*v.i.* to blow, to breathe; to pant, to puff; (*fig.*) to breathe a word etc.; *souffler aux oreilles de quelqu'un*, to whisper in someone's ear.

soufflerie [suflə'ri], *n.f.* bellows (*of an organ*); wind-tunnel.

soufflet [su'flɛ], *n.m.* pair of bellows; box on the ear, slap in the face; affront.

souffleter [suflə'te], *v.t.* (*conjug. like* APPELER) to slap in the face, to box the ears of; (*fig.*) to insult.

souffleur [su'flœːr], *a.* (*fem.* **-euse**) blowing, puffing.—*n.m.* (*fem.* **-euse**) blower; (*Theat.*) prompter.—(*C*) *n.f.* (**-euse**) snow blower.

souffrance [su'frɑ̃ːs], *n.f.* suffering, pain; suspense; (*Law*) sufferance; *en souffrance*, awaiting delivery; in abeyance.

souffrant [su'frɑ̃], *a.* suffering; unwell; long-suffering.

souffre-douleur [sufrədu'lœːr], *n.m. inv.* drudge; butt, laughing-stock.

souffreteux [sufrə'tø], *a.* (*fem.* **-euse**) needy; poorly, sickly, weakly.

souffrir [su'friːr], *v.t. irr.* (*conjug. like* OUVRIR) to suffer; to bear, to endure, to undergo, to sustain; to stand, to tolerate; to admit of; *faire souffrir*, to pain; to grieve.—*v.i.* to suffer, to be in pain; to be pained; to be injured.

soufre [sufr], *n.m.* sulphur, brimstone.

souhait [swɛ], *n.m.* wish, desire; *à souhait*, to one's heart's content, as one would have it.

souhaitable [swɛ'tabl], *a.* desirable.

souhaiter [swɛ'te], *v.t.* to desire, to wish for.

souiller [su'je], *v.t.* to soil, to dirty; to stain, to blemish, to sully; to defile. **se souiller**, *v.r.* to soil oneself, to get dirty; to tarnish one's good name.

souillon [su'jɔ̃], *n.* sloven, slut; scullion.

souillure [su'jyːr], *n.f.* spot, stain; blot, blemish; contamination.

soûl *or* **saoul** [su], *a.* glutted, surfeited (*de*); drunk; satiated, heartily sick (*de*).—*n.m.* fill, bellyful; *tout son soûl*, to one's heart's content.

soulagement [sulaʒ'mɑ̃], *n.m.* relief, alleviation; solace, help.

soulager [sula'ʒe], *v.t.* (*conjug. like* MANGER) to relieve, to ease; to alleviate, to allay; to soothe, to comfort. **se soulager**, *v.r.* to relieve oneself; to help each other.

soûlard [su'laːr], *a.* drunken.—*n.m.* (*fem.* **-e**) drunkard, sot.

soûler [su'le], *v.t.* to fill, to glut; to make drunk. **se soûler**, *v.r.* to gorge; to get drunk.

soûlerie [sul'ri], *n.f.* drinking bout, 'binge'.

soulèvement [sulɛv'mɑ̃], *n.m.* heaving; swelling (*of sea waves etc.*); rising (*of the stomach*); (*fig.*) insurrection, revolt.

soulever [sul've], *v.t.* (*conjug. like* AMENER) to raise, to lift up; to heave; to take up; (*fig.*) to excite, to stir up; to sicken; to rouse the indignation of. **se soulever**, *v.r.* to raise oneself, to rise; to heave, to swell; to rise in insurrection.

soulier [su'lje], *n.m.* shoe; *être dans ses petits souliers*, to be ill at ease; *souliers ferrés*, hobnailed boots.

soulignement [sulin'mɑ̃], *n.m.* underlining.

souligner [suli'ne], *v.t.* to underline; (*fig.*) to emphasize.

soumettre [su'mɛtr], *v.t. irr.* (*conjug. like* METTRE) to subdue, to subject; to submit, to refer; to subordinate. **se soumettre**, *v.r.* to submit, to yield; to comply, to assent (*à*).

soumis [su'mi], *a.* submissive.

soumission [sumi'sjɔ̃], *n.f.* submission, compliance, obedience; subjection; mark of respect; bid for a contract etc.

soumissionner [sumisjɔ'ne], *v.t.* to bid for.

soupape [su'pap], *n.f.* valve; *soupape de sûreté*, safety-valve.

soupçon [sup'sɔ̃], *n.m.* suspicion; surmise, conjecture; (*fig.*) slight taste, dash, touch.

soupçonner [supsɔ'ne], *v.t.* to suspect; to surmise.

soupçonneux [supsɔ'nø], a. (fem. -euse) suspicious.

soupe [sup], n.f. soup; sop; *c'est une soupe au lait*, he has a quick temper; *trempé comme une soupe*, drenched to the skin.

soupente [su'pɑ̃:t], n.f. straps (of a horse); loft, garret.

souper [su'pe], v.i. to sup, to have supper. —n.m. supper.

soupeser [supə'ze], v.t. (conjug. like AMENER) to weigh in one's hand, to try the weight of.

soupière [su'pjɛ:r], n.f. soup tureen.

soupir [su'pi:r], n.m. sigh; breath, gasp; (Mus.) quarter rest.

soupirail [supi'ra:j], n.m. (pl. -aux) air-hole, ventilator.

soupirant [supi'rɑ̃], a. sighing.—n.m. wooer, lover.

soupirer [supi're], v.t. to breathe forth, to sigh out.—v.i. to sigh; to gasp; to long.

souple [supl], a. supple, pliant, flexible, yielding; docile.

souplesse [su'plɛs], n.f. suppleness, flexibility; compliance, pliancy; versatility; toughness.

souquenille [suk'ni:j], n.f. smock frock; (shabby) old garment.

source [surs], n.f. spring, source, fountain.

sourcier [sur'sje], n.m. (fem. -ière) water-diviner.

sourcil [sur'si], n.m. eyebrow; brow; *froncer le sourcil*, to frown.

sourciller [sursi'je], v.i. to knit one's brows, to frown; to wince.

sourcilleux [sursi'jø], a. (fem. -euse) haughty, proud, supercilious; frowning; uneasy.

sourd [su:r], a. deaf; (fig.) dull; insensible; hollow, muffled (of sound); underhand.—n.m. (fem. -e) deaf person.

sourdement [surdə'mɑ̃], adv. indistinctly; with a hollow voice; in an underhand manner.

sourdine [sur'din], n.f. mute (of a musical instrument); damper (of a piano etc.); *en sourdine*, secretly, on the sly.

sourd-muet [sur'mɥe], a. and n.m. (fem. **sourde-muette**) deaf-and-dumb (person), deaf-mute.

sourdre [surdr], v.i. to spring, to gush, to well; (fig.) to result.

souriant [su'rjɑ̃], a. smiling.

souricière [suri'sjɛ:r], n.f. mouse-trap.

sourire [su'ri:r], v.i. irr. (conjug. like RIRE) to smile; to be agreeable, to delight, to please; to be propitious.—n.m. smile; *large sourire*, grin; *sourire affecté*, smirk.

souris [su'ri], a. inv. mouse-colored.—n.f. mouse; mouse-color; knuckle (of a leg of mutton).

sournois [sur'nwa], a. artful, cunning, sly.—n.m. (fem. -e) sneak.

sournoisement [surnwaz'mɑ̃], adv. cunningly, slyly.

sournoiserie [surnwaz'ri], n.f. slyness, cunning; underhand trick.

sous [su], prep. under, beneath, below; on, upon; with; in; by; *affirmer sous serment*, to swear under oath; *sous dix jours*, within ten days; *sous peu*, in a short time.

sous-alimentation [suzalimɑ̃ta'sjɔ̃], n.f. malnutrition.

sous-alimenté [suzalimɑ̃'te], a. underfed.

sous-chef [su'ʃef], n.m. deputy head-clerk; assistant manager.

souscripteur [suskrip'tœ:r], n.m. subscriber; (Comm.) underwriter.

souscription [suskrip'sjɔ̃], n.f. subscription; signature.

souscrire [sus'kri:r], v.t. irr. (conjug. like ÉCRIRE) to subscribe, to sign.—v.i. to consent, to agree (à).

sous-développé [sudevlɔ'pe], a. underdeveloped (country).

sous-dit [su'di], a. undermentioned.

sous-entendre [suzɑ̃'tɑ̃:dr], v.t. not to express fully, to hint, to imply.

sous-entendu [suzɑ̃tɑ̃'dy], n.m. thing understood, implication.

sous-entente [suzɑ̃'tɑ̃:t], n.f. mental reservation.

sous-lieutenant [suljøt'nɑ̃], n.m. second-lieutenant; *sous-lieutenant aviateur*, pilot officer.

sous-louer [su'lwe], v.t. to sub-let.

sous-main [su'mɛ̃], n.m. inv. writing pad; *en sous-main*, behind the scenes.

sous-marin [suma'rɛ̃], a. and n.m. submarine.

sous-off [su'zɔf], abbr. fam. of **sous-officier** [suzɔfi'sje], n.m. non-commissioned officer, N.C.O.

sous-ordre [su'zɔrdr], n.m. inv. subordinate.

sous-préfet [supre'fɛ], n.m. subprefect, under-sheriff.

sous-produit [suprɔ'dɥi], n.m. by-product.

sous-secrétaire [susəkrə'tɛ:r], n. under-secretary.

soussigné [susi'ne], a. undersigned; *nous soussignés certifions*, we, the undersigned, certify.

sous-sol [su'sɔl], n.m. subsoil; basement.

sous-titre [su'titr], n.m. sub-title.

soustraction [sustrak'sjɔ̃], n.f. taking away, subtraction.

soustraire [sus'trɛ:r], v.t. irr. (conjug. like TRAIRE) to take away, to withdraw, to screen; (Arith.) to subtract. *se soustraire*, v.r. to escape, to flee, to avoid; to withdraw oneself; to be subtracted.

sous-traitant [sutrɛ'tɑ̃], n.m. subcontractor.

soutache [su'taʃ], n.f. braid.

soutane [su'tan], n.f. cassock; (fig.) the cloth.

soute [sut], n.f. (Naut.) store-room; (Av.) luggage bay, bomb bay.

soutenable [sut'nabl], a. sustainable; tenable.

soutènement [sutɛn'mɑ̃], n.m. (Arch.) support.

soutenir [sut'ni:r], v.t. irr. (conjug. like TENIR) to hold up, to support, to sustain, to keep up, to prop up; (fig.) to maintain, to uphold; to countenance; to afford (an expense); to endure. *se soutenir*, v.r. to support oneself; to hold oneself up; to bear up, to hold out; to stand firm; to succeed; to continue; to sustain one another.

soutenu [sut'ny], a. sustained; unremitting, unceasing, constant; lofty, elevated.

souterrain [sute'rɛ̃], a. underground; (fig.) underhand.—n.m. underground vault, cavern; (Rail.) tunnel; underground passage.

soutien [su'tjɛ̃], *n.m.* support, prop, stay, staff.

soutien-gorge [sutjɛ̃'gɔrʒ], *n.m. inv.* brassiere.

soutirer [suti're], *v.t.* to draw off, to rack (*liquors*); (*fig.*) to worm out (*à*), to extract (*money, information*).

souvenir [suv'ni:r], *n.m.* recollection; reminder, souvenir, keepsake.—*v. impers. irr.* (*conjug. like* TENIR *but with aux.* ÊTRE) to occur to the mind; *il m'en souvient*, I remember it. **se souvenir**, *v.r.* to remember, to call to mind, to recollect.

souvent [su'vã], *adv.* often, frequently.

souverain [su'vrɛ̃], *a.* sovereign, supreme; highest, extreme; infallible.—*n.m.* (*fem.* **-e**) sovereign (*monarch*).—*n.m.* sovereign (*coin*).

souverainement [suvrɛn'mã], *adv.* in the extreme; supremely.

souveraineté [suvrɛn'te], *n.f.* sovereignty, dominion.

soviet [so'vjɛt], *n.m.* soviet.

soviétique [sɔvje'tik], *a.* **l'Union des Républiques socialistes soviétiques** (*U.R.S.S.*), the Union of Soviet Socialist Republics (*U.S.S.R.*).—*n.* (**Soviétique**) Soviet citizen.

soyeux [swa'jø], *a.* (*fem.* **-euse**) silky, silken.

spacieusement [spasjøz'mã], *adv.* spaciously.

spacieux [spa'sjø], *a.* (*fem.* **-euse**) spacious, wide, roomy.

spahi [spa'i], *n.m.* spahi (*Algerian native trooper*).

sparadrap [spara'dra], *n.m.* sticking plaster.

Sparte [spart], la, *f.* Sparta.

spartiate [spar'sjat], *a.* Spartan.—*n.* (**Spartiate**) Spartan (*person*).

spasme [spasm], *n.m.* spasm.

spasmodique [spasmo'dik], *a.* spasmodic.

spasmodiquement [spasmɔdik'mã], *adv.* spasmodically.

spatule [spa'tyl], *n.f.* spatula.

speaker [spi'kœ:r], *n.m.* (*fem.* **speakerine**) (*Rad.*) announcer.

spécial [spe'sjal], *a.* (*m. pl.* **-aux**) special, especial, particular; professional.

spécialement [spesjal'mã], *adv.* especially, particularly.

spécialisation [spesjaliza'sjɔ̃], *n.f.* specialization.

spécialiser [spesjali'ze], *v.t.* to specialize.

spécialiste [spesja'list], *n.* specialist, expert.

spécialité [spesjali'te], *n.f.* peculiarity, specialty; patent medicine.

spécieux [spe'sjø], *a.* (*fem.* **-euse**) specious, plausible.

spécification [spesifika'sjɔ̃], *n.f.* specification.

spécifier [spesi'fje], *v.t.* to specify.

spécifique [spesi'fik], *a.* and *n.m.* specific.

spécifiquement [spesifik'mã], *adv.* specifically.

spécimen [spesi'mɛn], *n.m.* specimen.

spectacle [spɛk'takl], *n.m.* spectacle, scene, sight; theatre; play, performance; show; *se donner en spectacle*, to make an exhibition of oneself.

spectaculaire [spɛktaky'lɛ:r], *a.* spectacular.

spectateur [spɛkta'tœ:r], *n.m.* (*fem.* **-trice**) spectator, looker-on.

spectral [spɛk'tral], *a.* (*m. pl.* **-aux**) spectral.

spectre [spɛktr], *n.m.* specter, ghost; spectrum.

spéculateur [spekyla'tœ:r], *n.m.* (*fem.* **-trice**) speculator.

spéculatif [spekyla'tif], *a.* (*fem.* **-tive**) speculative.

spéculation [spekyla'sjɔ̃], *n.f.* speculation.

spéculativement [spekylativ'mã], *adv.* in a speculative manner.

spéculer [speky'le], *v.i.* to speculate.

sperme [spɛrm], *n.m.* sperm, seed.

sphaigne [sfɛ:ɲ], *n.f.* sphagnum moss.

sphère [sfɛ:r], *n.f.* sphere, orb, globe; (*fig.*) circle.

sphérique [sfe'rik], *a.* spherical.

sphinx [sfɛ̃:ks], *n.m.* sphinx.

spinal [spi'nal], *a.* (*m. pl.* **-aux**) spinal.

spiral [spi'ral], *a.* (*m. pl.* **-aux**) spiral.—*n.m.* hair-spring (*of watch*).

spirale [spi'ral], *n.f.* spiral.

spirite [spi'rit], *a.* spiritualistic.—*n.* spiritualist.

spiritisme [spiri'tism], *n.m.* spiritualism.

spiritualisme [spiritɥa'lism], *n.m.* spiritualism.

spiritualiste [spiritɥa'list], *a.* and *n.* spiritualist.

spirituel [spiri'tɥɛl], *a.* (*fem.* **-elle**) spiritual; intellectual; witty, shrewd, lively, intelligent.

spirituellement [spiritɥɛl'mã], *adv.* spiritually; wittily, cleverly.

spiritueux [spiri'tɥø], *a.* (*fem.* **-euse**) spirituous.—*n.m.* spirit, spirituous liquor.

spleen [splin], *n.m.* spleen; (*fam.*) *avoir le spleen*, to be in the dumps.

splendeur [splã'dœ:r], *n.f.* splendor, brilliance; magnificence.

splendide [splã'did], *a.* sumptuous, magnificent.

splendidement [splãdid'mã], *adv.* splendidly.

spoliateur [spɔlja'tœ:r], *a.* (*fem.* **-trice**) despoiling.—*n.m.* (*fem.* **-trice**) spoiler, despoiler.

spoliation [spɔlja'sjɔ̃], *n.f.* spoliation.

spolier [spɔ'lje], *v.t.* to despoil, to plunder.

spongieux [spɔ̃'sjø], *a.* (*fem.* **-euse**) spongy.

spontané [spɔ̃ta'ne], *a.* spontaneous.

spontanéité [spɔ̃taneʤ'te], *n.f.* spontaneity.

spontanément [spɔ̃tane'mã], *adv.* spontaneously.

sporadique [spɔra'dik], *a.* sporadic.

spore [spɔ:r], *n.f.* spore.

sport [spɔ:r], *n.m.* games, outdoor games; *faire du sport*, to play games.

sportif [spɔr'tif], *a.* (*fem.* **-tive**) sporting; *réunion sportive*, athletics meeting.—*n.m.* (*fem.* **-tive**) athlete; devotee of out-door games; sportsman, sportswoman.

spumeux [spy'mø], *a.* (*fem.* **-euse**) spumy.

square [skwa:r], *n.m.* residential square with enclosed garden.

squelette [skə'lɛt], *n.m.* skeleton; carcass, frame (*of a ship*).

squelettique [skəlɛ'tik], *a.* lanky.

stabilisateur [stabiliza'tœ:r], *a.* (*fem.* **-trice**) stabilizing.—*n.m.* (*Av., Naut.*) stabilizer.

stabiliser [stabili'ze], *v.t.* to stabilize.

stabilité [stabili'te], *n.f.* stability, durability.

stable [sta:bl], *a.* stable, firm; durable, lasting, permanent.

stade [stad], *n.m.* sports ground, stadium; (*fig.*) stage, period.

stage [sta:ʒ], *n.m.* term of probation, study, residence etc.; training course; (*fig.*) probation.

stagiaire [sta'ʒjɛ:r], *n.* probationer, trainee.

stagnant [stag'nɑ̃], *a.* stagnant, at a standstill.

stagnation [stagna'sjɔ̃], *n.f.* stagnation.

stagner [stag'ne], *v.i.* to stagnate.

stalactite [stalak'tit], *n.f.* stalactite.

stalagmite [stalag'mit], *n.f.* stalagmite.

stalle [stal], *n.f.* stall; box (*for horses*) (*Theat.*) stall, seat.

stance [stɑ̃:s], *n.f.* stanza.

stand [stɑ̃:d], *n.m.* rifle range; shooting gallery; stall, stand (*at exhibitions etc.*).

standard [stɑ̃'da:r], *n.m.* (*in house* or *office*) switchboard; standard (*of living*).

standardiser [stɑ̃dardi'ze], *v.t.* to standardize.

standardiste [stɑ̃dar'dist], *n.* switchboard operator.

star [sta:r], *n.f.* (*Cine.*) star.

starlette [star'lɛt], *n.f.* starlet.

starter [star'tɛ:r], *n.m.* (*Motor.*) choke; (*Racing*) starter.

station [sta'sjɔ̃], *n.f.* station, standing; stop (*of bus etc.*); taxi stand; resort.

stationnaire [stasjo'nɛ:r], *a.* stationary.

stationnement [stasjon'mɑ̃], *n.m.* stationing, standing; parking; *stationnement interdit*, no parking, no standing.

stationner [stasjo'ne], *v.i.* to stop, to stand, to park (*of cars*).

statique [sta'tik], *a.* static.—*n.f.* statics.

statisticien [statisti'sjɛ̃], *n.m.* statistician.

statistique [statis'tik], *a.* statistical.—*n.f.* statistics.

statuaire [sta'tɥɛ:r], *a.* statuary.—*n.* sculptor.—*n.f.* statuary (*art*).

statue [sta'ty], *n.f.* statue.

statuer [sta'tɥe], *v.t.* to decree, to resolve, to ordain.—*v.i.* to give a ruling.

statuette [sta'tɥɛt], *n.f.* statuette.

stature [sta'ty:r], *n.f.* stature, height.

statut [sta'ty], *n.m.* statute, ordinance, by-law; status.

statutaire [staty'tɛ:r], *a.* statutory.

stellaire [stɛl'lɛ:r], *a.* stellar, starry.

stencil [stɛn'sil], *n.m.* stencil.

sténo [ste'no], *abbr. of* **sténographe** or **sténographie**.

sténo-dactylo(graphe) [stenodakti'lo('graf)], *n.* shorthand typist.

sténographe [steno'graf], *n.* stenographer, shorthand writer.

sténographie [stenogra'fi], *n.f.* stenography, shorthand.

sténographier [stenogra'fje], *v.t.* to take down in shorthand.

stentor [stɑ̃'tɔ:r], *n.m.* stentor; *d'une voix de stentor*, in a stentorian voice.

steppe [stɛp], *n.f.* steppe.

stéréoscope [stereɔs'kɔp], *n.m.* stereoscope.

stéréotypé [stereɔti'pe], *a.* stereotyped, hackneyed.

stérile [ste'ril], *a.* sterile, barren; (*fig.*) fruitless, vain.

stérilisant [sterili'zɑ̃], *a.* sterilizing.—*n.m.* sterilizing agent.

stérilisation [steriliza'sjɔ̃], *n.f.* sterilization.

stériliser [sterili'ze], *v.t.* to sterilize.

stérilité [sterili'te], *n.f.* sterility, barrenness.

sterling [stɛr'liŋ], *a. inv.* and *n.m.* sterling.

stéthoscope [stetɔs'kɔp], *n.m.* stethoscope.

stigmate [stig'mat], *n.m.* scar, stigma, stain; brand.

stigmatiser [stigmati'ze], *v.t.* to stigmatize, to brand.

stimulant [stimy'lɑ̃], *a.* stimulating.—*n.m.* stimulant; stimulus; incentive.

stimulation [stimylɑ'sjɔ̃], *n.f.* stimulation.

stimuler [stimy'le], *v.t.* to stimulate; to excite, to rouse.

stipendiaire [stipɑ̃'djɛ:r], *a.* and *n.m.* stipendiary, mercenary.

stipendié [stipɑ̃'dje], *a.* hired.—*n.m.* stipendiary, hireling.

stipendier [stipɑ̃'dje], *v.t.* to hire, to keep on the payroll.

stipulation [stipylɑ'sjɔ̃], *n.f.* stipulation.

stipuler [stipy'le], *v.t.* to stipulate; to contract.

stock [stɔk], *n.m.* (*Comm.*) stock.

stocker [stɔ'ke], *v.t.* to stock; to stockpile.

stockiste [stɔ'kist], *n.m.* warehouseman; dealer; agent (*for a certain make of car*); service station (*with spare parts*).

stoïcien [stɔi'sjɛ̃], *a.* stoic, stoical.—*n.m.* (*fem.* **-enne**) stoic.

stoïcisme [stɔi'sism], *n.m.* stoicism.

stoïque [stɔ'ik], *a.* stoic, stoical.—*n.* stoic.

stoïquement [stɔik'mɑ̃], *adv.* stoically.

stop [stɔp], *int.* stop!—*n.m.* (*Motor.*) stop-light.

stoppage [stɔ'pa:ʒ], *n.m.* invisible mending; stoppage (*of motion, current*).

stopper [stɔ'pe], *v.t.* to mend invisibly; to stop.—*v.i.* to stop (*of a train, steamboat etc.*).

store [stɔ:r], *n.m.* (*spring-roller*) blind.

strabisme [stra'bism], *n.m.* squinting.

strangulation [strɑ̃gylɑ'sjɔ̃], *n.f.* strangulation.

strapontin [strapɔ̃'tɛ̃], *n.m.* folding seat, tip-up seat.

strass or **stras** [stras], *n.m.* strass, paste jewels.

stratagème [strata'ʒɛm], *n.m.* stratagem.

strate [strat], *n.f.* stratum.

stratégie [strate'ʒi], *n.f.* strategy.

stratégique [strate'ʒik], *a.* strategic.

stratégiquement [strateʒik'mɑ̃], *adv.* strategically.

stratégiste [strate'ʒist], *n.m.* strategist.

stratosphère [stratɔs'fɛ:r], *n.f.* stratosphere.

strict [strikt], *a.* strict, precise; severe.

strictement [striktə'mɑ̃], *adv.* strictly; severely.

strident [stri'dɑ̃], *a.* strident, jarring.

strié [stri'e], *a.* striate, streaked; corrugated; scored.

strontium [strɔ̃'sjɔm], *n.m.* strontium.

strophe [strɔf], *n.f.* strophe; stanza.

structural [strykty'ral], *a.* (*m. pl.* **-aux**) structural.

structure [stryk'ty:r], *n.f.* structure; form, make.

strychnine [strik'nin], *n.f.* strychnin(e).

stuc [styk], *n.m.* stucco.

stucage [sty'ka:ʒ], *n.m.* stucco-work.

studieusement [stydjøz'mɑ̃], *adv.* studiously.

studieux [stu'djø], *a.* (*fem.* **-euse**) studious.

studio [sty'djo], *n.m.* (*Cine.*) film studio; (*Rad.*, *Tel.*) broadcasting studio; one-room flat.

stupéfaction [stypefak'sjɔ̃], n.f. stupefaction, amazement.

stupéfait [stype'fɛ], a. amazed, dumbfounded.

stupéfiant [stype'fjɑ̃], a. stupefactive; amazing, astounding.—n.m. narcotic.

stupéfier [stype'fje], v.t. to stupefy, to astound, to dumbfound.

stupeur [sty'pœːr], n.f. stupor; amazement.

stupide [sty'pid], a. stunned; stupid, foolish, dull.

stupidement [stypid'mɑ̃], adv. stupidly.

stupidité [stypidi'te], n.f. stupidity.

style (1) [stil], n.m. style.

style (2) [stil], n.m. stylus.

stylé [sti'le], a. stylate; (colloq.) trained, taught, clever.

styler [sti'le], v.t. to train, to form, to school.

stylet [sti'le], n.m. stiletto; (Surg.) probe.

stylo [sti'lo], abbr. of stylographe [stilɔ'graf], n.m. fountain pen; stylo à bille, ballpoint pen.

stylomine [stilo'min], n.m. mechanical pencil.

styptique [stip'tik], a. and n.m. styptic.

su (1) [sy], n.m. knowledge; au vu et au su de tout le monde, as everybody knows.

su (2) [sy], p.p. [SAVOIR].

suaire [sɥɛːr], n.m. winding sheet, shroud.

suant [sɥɑ̃], a. sweating, in a sweat.

suave [sɥaːv], a. sweet, agreeable; suave, bland; soft.

suavement [sɥav'mɑ̃], adv. suavely; sweetly.

suavité [sɥavi'te], n.f. suavity; sweetness.

subalterne [sybal'tɛrn], a. and n. subaltern, subordinate; inferior.

subdiviser [sybdivi'ze], v.t. to subdivide. se subdiviser, v.r. to be subdivided.

subdivision [sybdivi'zjɔ̃], n.f. subdivision.

subir [sy'biːr], v.t. to support; to go through, to undergo, to suffer; to submit to.

subit [sy'bit], a. sudden, unexpected.

subitement [sybit'mɑ̃], adv. suddenly, all of a sudden.

subjectif [sybʒɛk'tif], a. (fem. -tive) subjective.

subjection [sybʒɛk'sjɔ̃], n.f. subjection.

subjectivement [sybʒɛktiv'mɑ̃], adv. subjectively.

subjonctif [sybʒɔ̃k'tif], a. (fem. -tive) and n.m. subjunctive.

subjugation [sybʒyga'sjɔ̃], n.f. subjugation.

subjuguer [sybʒy'ge], v.t. to subjugate, to subdue.

sublimation [syblima'sjɔ̃], n.f. sublimation.

sublime [sy'blim], a. lofty, sublime, splendid. —n.m. the sublime.

sublimement [syblim'mɑ̃], adv. sublimely.

submerger [sybmɛr'ʒe], v.t. (conjug. like MANGER) to submerge, to swamp, to flood; (fig.) to overwhelm.

submersible [sybmɛr'sibl], a. submersible. —n.m. submarine (boat).

submersion [sybmɛr'sjɔ̃], n.f. submersion.

subordination [sybɔrdina'sjɔ̃], n.f. subordination.

subordonné [sybɔrdɔ'ne], a. and n.m. (fem. -ée) subordinate, dependent.

subordonner [sybɔrdɔ'ne], v.t. to subordinate.

suborner [sybɔr'ne], v.t. to suborn, to bribe.

suborneur [sybɔr'nœːr], a. (fem. -euse)

suborning, bribing.—n.m. (fem. -euse suborner, briber.

subreptice [sybrɛp'tis], a. surreptitious.

subrepticement [sybrɛptis'mɑ̃], adv. surreptitiously.

subséquemment [sybseka'mɑ̃], adv. subsequently.

subséquent [sybse'kɑ̃], a. subsequent.

subside [syb'sid], n.m. subsidy; (colloq.) aid.

subsidiaire [sybsi'djɛːr], a. subsidiary, auxiliary.

subsidiairement [sybsidjɛr'mɑ̃], adv. further, also, additionally.

subsistance [sybzis'tɑ̃ːs], n.f. subsistence, sustenance, maintenance; (pl.) provisions.

subsistant [sybzis'tɑ̃], a. subsisting, existing

subsister [sybzis'te], v.i. to subsist, to stand; to hold good; to exist, to live.

substance [sybs'tɑ̃ːs], n.f. substance.

substantiel [sybstɑ̃'sjɛl], a. (fem. -elle) substantial.

substantiellement [sybstɑ̃sjɛl'mɑ̃], adv. substantially.

substantif [sybstɑ̃'tif], a. (fem. -tive) substantive.—n.m. (Gram.) noun.

substituer [sybsti'tɥe], v.t. to substitute; (Law) to entail.

substitut [sybsti'ty], n.m. substitute, deputy (to someone).

substitution [sybstity'sjɔ̃], n.f. substitution; (Law) entail.

subterfuge [sybtɛr'fyːʒ], n.m. subterfuge, evasion, shift.

subtil [syb'til], a. subtile, tenuous; penetrating; acute, keen, sharp; cunning; fine-spun, subtle.

subtilement [sybtil'mɑ̃], adv. subtly, craftily.

subtiliser [sybtili'ze], v.t. to subtilize, to refine; (colloq.) to sneak, to steal.

subtilité [sybtili'te], n.f. subtlety, fineness; acuteness; shrewdness.

suburbain [sybyr'bɛ̃], a. suburban.

subvenir [sybvə'niːr], v.i. irr. (conjug. like TENIR) to be helpful; to supply, to provide.

subvention [sybvɑ̃'sjɔ̃], n.f. subsidy, aid.

subventionner [sybvɑ̃sjɔ'ne], v.t. to subsidize, to make a grant to.

subversif [sybvɛr'sif], a. (fem. -sive) subversive.

subversion [sybvɛr'sjɔ̃], n.f. subversion, overthrow.

suc [syk], n.m. juice; (fig.) essence, quintessence.

succéder [sykse'de], v.i. (conjug. like CÉDER) to succeed, to follow after (à). se succéder, v.r. to succeed each other.

succès [syk'sɛ], n.m. success.

successeur [syksɛ'sœːr], n.m. successor.

successif [syksɛ'sif], a. (fem. -ive) successive, in succession.

succession [syksɛ'sjɔ̃], n.f. succession; inheritance; heritage, estate.

successivement [syksɛsiv'mɑ̃], adv. successively, in succession.

succinct [syk'sɛ̃], a. succinct, concise.

succinctement [syksɛt'mɑ̃], adv. succinctly, briefly.

succion [syk'sjɔ̃], n.f. suction.

succomber [sykɔ̃'be], v.i. to sink, to faint; to yield, to succumb; to fail; to die.

succulence [syky'lɑ̃ːs], n.f. succulence.

succulent [syky'lɑ̃], a. succulent, juicy; rich.

succursale [sykyr'sal], *n.f.* branch (*of a bank etc.*).

sucement [sys'mã], *n.m.* sucking, suck.

sucer [sy'se], *v.t.* (*conjug. like* COMMENCER) to suck, to suck in; to imbibe.

sucette [sy'sɛt], *n.f.* lollipop; pacifier (*for baby*).

suceur [sy'sœ:r], *a.* (*fem.* -**euse**) sucking.— *n.m.* sucker; nozzle (*of a vacuum cleaner*).

suçoir [sy'swa:r], *n.m.* sucker.

sucre [sykr], *n.m.* sugar; *sucre cristallisé*, granulated sugar; *sucre d'orge*, barley-sugar; *sucre en poudre*, powdered sugar.

sucré [sy'kre], *a.* sugared, sweet, sugary; (*fig.*) demure, prim.

sucrer [sy'kre], *v.t.* to sugar, to sweeten.

sucrerie [sykrə'ri], *n.f.* sugar refinery; (*pl.*) sweets.

sucrier [sykri'e], *n.m.* sugar bowl; sugar maker.

sud [syd], *a. inv.* south, southerly (*of the wind*).—*n.m.* south; south wind.

sud-est [sy'dɛst], *a. inv.* and *n.m.* south-east.

Sudètes [sy'dɛt], **les**, *m. pl.* Sudetenland.

sud-ouest [sy'dwɛst], *a. inv.* and *n.m.* south-west.

Suède [sɥɛd], **la**, *f.* Sweden.

suède [sɥɛd], *n.m.* suede (*glove leather*).

suédois [sɥe'dwa], *a.* Swedish.—*n.m.* Swedish (*language*); (**Suédois**, *fem.* -**oise**) Swede.

suée [sɥe], *n.f.* sweating.

suer [sɥe], *v.t.* to sweat.—*v.i.* to sweat, to perspire; (*fig.*) to toil, to drudge; to ooze (*of walls*).

sueur [sɥœ:r], *n.f.* sweat, perspiration; (*pl.*) labor, toil.

suffire [sy'fi:r], *v.i. irr.* to suffice, to be sufficient; to be adequate; *cela suffit*, that's enough. **se suffire**, *v.r.* to provide for oneself.

suffisamment [syfiza'mã], *adv.* sufficiently.

suffisance [syfi'zã:s], *n.f.* sufficiency, adequacy; conceit, self-sufficiency.

suffisant [syfi'zã], *a.* sufficient; conceited.— *n.m.* (*fem.* -**e**) conceited person.

suffixe [sy'fiks], *n.m.* suffix.

suffocant [syfɔ'kã], *a.* suffocating, choking.

suffocation [syfɔka'sjõ], *n.f.* suffocation.

suffoquer [syfɔ'ke], *v.t.* to suffocate, to choke.—*v.i.* to choke.

suffrage [sy'fra:ʒ], *n.m.* suffrage, vote; approbation, commendation.

suggérer [sygʒe're], *v.t.* (*conjug. like* CÉDER) to suggest.

suggestif [sygʒɛs'tif], *a.* (*fem.* -**tive**) suggestive; erotic.

suggestion [sygʒɛs'tjõ], *n.f.* suggestion, hint, instigation.

suicide [sɥi'sid], *n.m.* suicide.

suicidé [sɥisi'de], *n.m.* (*fem.* -**ée**) suicide.

suicider (**se**) [səsɥisi'de], *v.r.* to commit suicide.

suie [sɥi], *n.f.* soot.

suif [sɥif], *n.m.* tallow.

suintement [sɥɛt'mã], *n.m.* oozing, sweating.

suinter [sɥɛ'te], *v.i.* to ooze, to sweat (*of walls etc.*); to leak, to run (*of vessels*).

Suisse [sɥis], **la**, *f.* Switzerland.

suisse [sɥis], *a.* Swiss.—*n.m.* porter (*of a mansion*); church officer; (**Suisse**, *fem.* **Suissesse**) Swiss (*person*).

suite [sɥit], *n.f.* the rest; retinue, attendants; sequel, continuation; series; set; connection; result; *à la suite*, after, behind; *de suite*, consecutively; *et ainsi de suite*, and so on; *tout de suite*, immediately.

suivant [sɥi'vã], *prep.* according to; in the direction of; *suivant que*, as, according as. —*a.* next, following, subsequent.—*n.m.* (*fem.* -**e**) follower, attendant.—*n.f.* (-**e**) lady's maid.

suivi [sɥi'vi], *a.* followed; connected; consistent; popular.

suivre [sɥi:vr], *v.t. irr.* to follow; to be next to; to attend; to observe; to pursue; to practise (*a profession etc.*).—*v.i.* to follow; to come after; to result; to ensue; *à faire suivre*, to be forwarded; *à suivre*, to be continued. **se suivre**, *v.r.* to follow each other, to be continuous.

sujet [sy'ʒɛ], *a.* (*fem.* -**ette**) subject, subjected, liable, exposed; apt, addicted, inclined (*à*).—*n.m.* subject; topic; cause.

sujétion [syʒe'sjõ], *n.f.* subjection, servitude; constraint.

sulfate [syl'fat], *n.m.* sulphate.

sulfureux [sylfy'rø], *a.* (*fem.* -**euse**) sulphurous, sulphureous.

sulfurique [sylfy'rik], *a.* sulphuric (*acid*).

sultan [syl'tã], *n.m.* sultan.

sultane [syl'tan], *n.f.* sultana, sultaness.

sumac [sy'mak], *n.m.* sumac.

superbe [sy'pɛrb], *a.* proud, arrogant; superb; stately; lofty; vainglorious.—*n.* proud person.—*n.f.* arrogance; vainglory.

superbement [sypɛrbə'mã], *adv.* haughtily, superbly.

supercarburant [sypɛrkarby'rã], *n.m.* high-octane gasolene.

supercherie [sypɛrʃə'ri], *n.f.* deceit, fraud.

superficie [sypɛrfi'si], *n.f.* area, surface; (*fig.*) superficiality.

superficiel [sypɛrfi'sjɛl], *a.* (*fem.* -**elle**) superficial; shallow.

superficiellement [sypɛrfisjɛl'mã], *adv.* superficially.

superfin [sypɛr'fɛ], *a.* superfine, of superior quality.

superflu [sypɛr'fly], *a.* superfluous; unnecessary.—*n.m.* superfluity, excess.

superfluité [sypɛrflɥi'te], *n.f.* superfluity.

supérieur [sype'rjœ:r], *a.* superior; upper, higher.—*n.m.* (*fem.* -**e**) superior.

supérieurement [syperjœr'mã], *adv.* in a superior manner; superlatively.

supériorité [syperjori'te], *n.f.* superiority.

superlatif [sypɛrla'tif], *a.* (*fem.* -**tive**) superlative.—*n.m.* (*Gram.*) superlative.

superlativement [sypɛrlativ'mã], *adv.* superlatively.

superposer [sypɛrpo'ze], *v.t.* to superpose; to superimpose.

superposition [sypɛrpozi'sjõ], *n.f.* superposition; superimposition.

supersonique [sypɛrso'nik], *a.* supersonic.

superstitieusement [sypɛrstisjøz'mã], *adv.* superstitiously.

superstitieux [sypɛrsti'sjø], *a.* (*fem.* -**euse**) superstitious.

superstition [sypɛrsti'sjõ], *n.f.* superstition.

superstructure [sypɛrstryk'ty:r], *n.f.* superstructure; right of way (*of railway*).

supin [sy'pɛ], *n.m.* (*Gram.*) supine.

305

supplantation [syplāta'sjɔ̃], *n.f.* supplantation; supersession.

supplanter [syplā'te], *v.t.* to supplant, to oust, to supersede.

suppléance [syple'ā:s], *n.f.* substitution, deputyship.

suppléant [syple'ā], *a.* and *n.m.* (*fem.* **-e**) substitute, assistant, deputy, understudy.

suppléer [syple'e], *v.t.* to supply, to fill up; to take the place of.—*v.i.* to make up the deficiency, to compensate for (*à*).

supplément [syple'mā], *n.m.* supplement; additional price, excess fare.

supplémentaire [syplemā'te:r], *a.* supplementary, supplemental, additional, extra.

suppliant [sypli'ā], *a.* suppliant, beseeching. —*n.m.* (*fem.* **-e**) suppliant, supplicant, petitioner.

supplication [syplika'sjɔ̃], *n.f.* supplication, entreaty.

supplice [sy'plis], *n.m.* corporal punishment; torture; (*fig.*) torment, ordeal; *être au supplice*, to be upon the rack.

supplicié [sypli'sje], *n.m.* (*fem.* **-ée**) executed criminal.

supplicier [sypli'sje], *v.t.* to put to death, to execute.

supplier [sypli'e], *v.t.* to beseech, to entreat, to beg.

supplique [sy'plik], *n.f.* petition, entreaty.

support [sy'pɔ:r], *n.m.* support, prop; rest, stand, bracket.

supportable [sypɔr'tabl], *a.* supportable, bearable, tolerable.

supportablement [sypɔrtablə'mā], *adv.* tolerably.

supporter (1) [sypɔr'tœ:r], *n.m.* (*Spt.*) supporter, partisan.

supporter (2) [sypɔr'te], *v.t.* to support, to uphold; to endure, to suffer; to stand. **se supporter**, *v.r.* to be borne; to bear with each other.

supposable [sypo'zabl], *a.* supposable.

supposé [sypo'ze], *a.* pretended, forged, assumed; reputed.

supposer [sypo'ze], *v.t.* to suppose; to admit, to imply; to conjecture; to forge (*a will*).

supposition [sypozi'sjɔ̃], *n.f.* supposition; substitution; forgery.

suppôt [sy'po], *n.m.* agent, tool, abettor.

suppressif [sypre'sif], *a.* (*fem.* **-ive**) suppressive.

suppression [sypre'sjɔ̃], *n.f.* suppression; cancelling (*of passage*); concealment.

supprimer [sypri'me], *v.t.* to suppress; to omit; to abolish, to cancel.

suppuration [sypyra'sjɔ̃], *n.f.* suppuration.

suppurer [sypy're], *v.i.* to suppurate, to run.

supputation [sypyt'a'sjɔ̃], *n.f.* computation, calculation.

supputer [sypy'te], *v.t.* to calculate, to compute, to reckon.

suprématie [syprema'si], *n.f.* supremacy.

suprême [sy'prɛ:m], *a.* supreme, highest; last.

suprêmement [syprɛmə'mā], *adv.* supremely.

sur (1) [syr], *prep.* on, upon; over; in; towards; about; concerning; out of.

sur (2) [sy:r], *a.* sour, tart.

sûr [sy:r], *a.* sure, certain; safe, secure; firm, steady; trustworthy; *à coup sûr*, for certain; *en lieu sûr*, in a place of safety; *je suis sûr de vous*, I can depend on you; *sûr et certain*, positive.

surabondamment [syrabɔ̃da'mā], *adv.* superabundantly.

surabondance [syrabɔ̃'dā:s], *n.f.* superabundance; glut.

surabondant [syrabɔ̃'dā], *a.* superabundant.

surabonder [syrabɔ̃'de], *v.i.* to superabound; to be glutted (*de*).

suraigu [syre'gy], *a.* (*fem.* **-ë**) overshrill; very acute (*inflammation*).

suralimenté [syralimā'te], *a.* overfed.

suralimenter [syralimā'te], *v.t.* to overfeed, to feed up; (*Motor.*) to supercharge.

suranné [syra'ne], *a.* expired; superannuated, antiquated.

surcharge [syr'farʒ], *n.f.* overloading; (*stamp*) surcharge; excess.

surcharger [syrfar'ʒe], *v.t.* (*conjug. like* MANGER) to overload, to overtax; (*fig.*) to overwhelm; to oppress; *surcharger d'impôts*, to overtax.

surchauffer [syrfo'fe], *v.t.* to overheat.

surclasser [syrkla'se], *v.t.* to outclass.

surcompresseur [syrkɔ̃pre'sœ:r], *n.m.* supercharger.

surcompression [syrkɔ̃pre'sjɔ̃], *n.f.* supercharging.

surcomprimé [syrkɔ̃pri'me], *a.* supercharged.

surcroît [syr'krwa], *n.m.* addition, increase; surplus, excess.

surcuit [syr'kɥi], *a.* overdone.

surdité [syrdi'te], *n.f.* deafness.

sureau [sy'ro], *n.m.* (*pl.* **-eaux**) elder (tree).

surélever [syrel've], *v.t.* (*conjug. like* AMENER) to raise higher; (*Golf*) to tee.

sûrement [syr'mā], *adv.* surely, certainly, to be sure; safely.

surenchère [syrā'fe:r], *n.f.* higher bid, outbidding.

surenchérir [syrā'fe'ri:r], *v.i.* to overbid, to bid higher.

surestimation [syrɛstima'sjɔ̃], *n.f.* overestimate, overvaluation.

surestimer [syrɛsti'me], *v.t.* to overestimate; to overrate.

sûreté [syr'te], *n.f.* safety, security; warranty; *la Sûreté*, Criminal Investigation Department.

surexcitation [syrɛksita'sjɔ̃], *n.f.* excitement, overexcitement.

surexciter [syrɛksi'te], *v.t.* to overexcite.

surexposer [syrɛkspo'ze], *v.t.* (*Phot.*) to overexpose.

surexposition [syrɛkspozi'sjɔ̃], *n.f.* (*Phot.*) overexposure.

surface [syr'fas], *n.f.* surface; outside.

surfaire [syr'fe:r], *v.t. irr.* (*conjug. like* FAIRE) to ask too much for; to overrate, to overpraise.

surfin [syr'fɛ̃], *a.* (*Comm.*) superfine.

surgir [syr'ʒi:r], *v.i.* to rise, to surge; to loom up.

surgissement [syrʒis'mā], *n.m.* upheaval.

surhomme [sy'rɔm], *n.m.* superman.

surhumain [syry'mɛ̃], *a.* superhuman.

surintendant [syrɛ̃tā'dā], *n.m.* superintendent, overseer; steward (*of large estate*).

surintendante [syrɛ̃tā'dā:t], *n.f.* woman superintendent; superintendent's wife.

surir [sy'ri:r], *v.i.* to turn sour.

sur-le-champ [syrlə'fā], *adv.* at once.

surlendemain [syrlɑ̃d'mɛ̃], *n.m.* two days after.

surmenage [syrmə'naːʒ], *n.m.* excess fatigue; overworking.

surmener [syrmə'ne], *v.t.* (*conjug. like* AMENER) to overwork, to overtire. **se surmener,** *v.r.* to overwork.

surmontable [syrmɔ̃'tabl], *a.* surmountable, superable.

surmonter [syrmɔ̃'te], *v.t.* to surmount; to overcome, to surpass.

surmultiplication [syrmyltiplika'sjɔ̃], *n.f.* (*Motor.*) overdrive.

surnager [syrna'ʒe], *v.i.* (*conjug. like* MANGER) to float on the surface; (*fig.*) to survive.

surnaturel [syrnaty'rɛl], *a.* (*fem.* **-elle**) supernatural.—*n.m.* supernatural.

surnaturellement [syrnatyrɛl'mɑ̃], *adv.* supernaturally.

surnom [syr'nɔ̃], *n.m.* nickname.

surnommer [syrnɔ'me], *v.t.* to nickname.

surnuméraire [syrnyme'rɛːr], *a.* and *n.m.* supernumerary.

surpasser [syrpa'se], *v.t.* to surpass, to excel, to outdo, to exceed.

surpeuplé [syrpœ'ple], *a.* overpopulated.

surpeuplement [syrpœplə'mɑ̃], *n.m.* overpopulation, overcrowding.

surplis [syr'pli], *n.m. inv.* surplice.

surplomb [syr'plɔ̃], *n.m.* overhang (*of buildings*); **en surplomb,** overhanging.

surplomber [syrplɔ̃'be], *v.t., v.i.* to overhang.

surplus [syr'ply], *n.m. inv.* surplus, remainder, excess.

surpoids [syr'pwa], *n.m.* overweight, excess weight.

surprenant [syrprə'nɑ̃], *a.* surprising, astonishing.

surprendre [syr'prɑ̃ːdr], *v.t. irr.* (*conjug. like* PRENDRE) to surprise, to catch; to overhear; to entrap; to intercept. **se surprendre,** *v.r.* to surprise oneself; to catch oneself (*napping etc.*).

surprise [syr'priːz], *n.f.* surprise; amazement.

surproduction [syrprɔdyk'sjɔ̃], *n.f.* overproduction.

surréalisme [syrrea'lism], *n.m.* surrealism.

surréaliste [syrrea'list], *a.* and *n.* surrealist.

sursaut [syr'so], *n.m.* start, jump.

sursauter [syrso'te], *v.i.* to start up; *faire sursauter (quelqu'un),* to startle (someone).

surseoir [syr'swaːr], *v.t., v.i. irr.* to suspend, to delay, to postpone.

sursis [syr'si], *n.m.* delay, respite, reprieve.

surtaxe [syr'taks], *n.f.* surtax; surcharge.

surtaxer [syrtak'se], *v.t.* to overtax.

surtout [syr'tu], *adv.* above all, chiefly.—*n.m.* overcoat; centrepiece (*for table*).

surveillance [syrvɛ'jɑ̃ːs], *n.f.* supervision; surveillance.

surveillant [syrvɛ'jɑ̃], *n.m.* (*fem.* **-e**) inspector, superintendent; supervisor.

surveiller [syrvɛ'je], *v.t.* to superintend, to inspect; to watch, to supervise.

survenir [syrvə'niːr], *v.i. irr.* (*conjug. like* TENIR, *but with aux.* ÊTRE) to arrive or happen unexpectedly; to drop in.

survêtement [syrvɛt'mɑ̃], *n.m.* (*Spt.*) track suit.

survivant [syrvi'vɑ̃], *a.* surviving.—*n.m.* (*fem.* **-e**) survivor.

survivre [syr'viːvr], *v.i. irr.* (*conjug. like* VIVRE) to survive, to outlive someone (*à*). **se survivre,** *v.r.* to live or exist again.

survoler [syrvɔ'le], *v.t.* to fly over (*of aircraft*).

sus [sys], *prep.* upon; **en sus,** over and above. —*int.* courage! come on!

susceptibilité [syssɛptibili'te], *n.f.* susceptibility; irritability.

susceptible [syssɛp'tibl], *a.* susceptible, capable; likely to; touchy; irascible.

susciter [sysi'te], *v.t.* to raise up, to set up; to create; to arouse, to instigate.

suscription [syskrip'sjɔ̃], *n.f.* superscription, address.

susdit [sys'di], *a.* and *n.m.* (*fem.* **-e**) aforesaid.

suspect [sys'pɛkt, sys'pɛ], *a.* suspected, suspicious, suspect, doubtful.—*n.m.* suspect.

suspecter [syspɛk'te], *v.t.* to suspect.

suspendre [sys'pɑ̃ːdr], *v.t.* to suspend, to hang up; to delay, to defer.

suspendu [syspɑ̃'dy], *a.* suspended, hung up; in suspense.

suspens [sys'pɑ̃], *adv. phr.* **en suspens,** in suspense; (*person*) in doubt; (*thing*) in abeyance.

suspension [syspɑ̃'sjɔ̃], *n.f.* suspension, interruption; hanging lamp.

suspicion [syspi'sjɔ̃], *n.f.* suspicion.

susurration [sysyra'sjɔ̃], *n.f.*, **susurrement** [sysyr'mɑ̃], *n.m.* susurration, whispering, murmur; rustling.

suttée [sy'te], **suttie** [sy'ti], *n.f.* suttee.

suture [sy'tyːr], *n.f.* suture; joint; stitching.

Suzanne [sy'zan], *f.* Susan.

suzerain [syz'rɛ̃], *a.* paramount, suzerain.— *n.m.* (*fem.* **-e**) suzerain, lord or lady paramount.

suzeraineté [syzrɛn'te], *n.f.* suzerainty.

svastika [zvasti'ka], *n.m.* swastika.

svelte [zvɛlt], *a.* slender, slim.

sveltesse [zvɛl'tɛs], *n.f.* slenderness, slimness.

sybarite [siba'rit], *a.* sybaritic.—*n.* sybarite, voluptuary.

sycomore [sikɔ'mɔːr], *n.m.* sycamore.

sycophante [sikɔ'fɑ̃ːt], *a.* sycophantic.—*n.m.* informer; hypocrite, impostor; sycophant, (*fam.*) toady.

syllabe [sil'lab], *n.f.* syllable.

syllabique [silla'bik], *a.* syllabic.

syllogisme [sillɔ'ʒism], *n.m.* syllogism.

sylphe [silf], *n.m.*, **sylphide** [sil'fid], *n.f.* sylph.

sylvain [sil'vɛ̃], *n.m.* sylvan.

sylvestre [sil'vɛstr], *a.* sylvan, growing in woods.

Sylvie [sil'vi], *f.* Sylvia.

symbole [sɛ̃'bɔl], *n.m.* symbol, sign, emblem; creed.

symbolique [sɛ̃bɔ'lik], *a.* symbolic, symbolical.

symboliser [sɛ̃bɔli'ze], *v.t.* to symbolize.

symbolisme [sɛ̃bɔ'lism], *n.m.* symbolism.

symétrie [sime'tri], *n.f.* symmetry.

symétrique [sime'trik], *a.* symmetrical.

symétriquement [simetrik'mɑ̃], *adv.* symmetrically.

sympathie [sɛ̃pa'ti], *n.f.* liking, fellow feeling.

sympathique [sɛ̃pa'tik], *a.* congenial, likeable.

sympathisant [sɛ̃pati'zɑ̃], *a.* sympathizing.—*n.m.* (*Pol.*) fellow traveller.
sympathiser [sɛ̃pati'ze], *v.i.* to get on well together.
symphonie [sɛ̃fɔ'ni], *n.f.* symphony.
symptomatique [sɛ̃ptɔma'tik], *a.* symptomatic.
symptôme [sɛ̃p'to:m], *n.m.* symptom; indication, sign; token.
synagogue [sina'gɔg], *n.f.* synagogue.
synchronisation [sɛ̃krɔniza'sjɔ̃], *n.f.* synchronization.
synchroniser [sɛ̃krɔni'ze], *v.t.* to synchronize.
syncope [sɛ̃'kɔp], *n.f.* syncope, swoon, fainting fit; (*Mus.*) syncopation.
syndic [sɛ̃'dik], *n.m.* syndic, trustee; assignee (*in bankruptcy*).
syndicalisme [sɛ̃dika'lism], *n.m.* **syndicalisme ouvrier**, trade-unionism.
syndicaliste [sɛ̃dⁱka'list], *a.* and *n.* trade-unionist.
syndicat [sɛ̃di'ka], *n.m.* syndicate, trusteeship; **syndicat d'initiative**, tourists' information bureau; **syndicat ouvrier**, trade union.
synonyme [sinɔ'nim], *a.* synonymous.—*n.m.* synonym.
syntaxe [sɛ̃'taks], *n.f.* syntax.
synthétique [sɛ̃te'tik], *a.* synthetic.
syriaque [si'rjak], *a.* Syriac.—*n.m.* Syriac (*language*).
Syrie [si'ri], **la**, *f.* Syria.
syrien [si'rjɛ̃], *a.* Syrian.—*n.m.* Syrian (*language*); (**Syrien**, *fem.* **-enne**) Syrian (*person*).
systématique [sistema'tik], *a.* systematic(al).
systématiquement [sistematik'mɑ̃], *adv.* systematically.
système [sis'tɛm], *n.m.* system, scheme, plan; device.

T

T, t [te], *n.m.* the twentieth letter of the alphabet.
t' [t], *elision* [TE].
ta [ta], [TON (1)].
tabac [ta'ba], *n.m.* tobacco; snuff.
tabatière [taba'tjɛ:r], *n.f.* snuff box.
tabernacle [taber'nakl], *n.m.* tent; tabernacle.
table [tabl], *n.f.* table · board (*food, fare*); mess (*of officers etc.*); slab; face (*of anvil etc.*); table of contents etc.; **faire table rase**, to make a clean sweep; **mettre** or **dresser la table**, to lay the table.
tableau [ta'blo], *n.m.* (*pl.* **-eaux**) picture, painting, tableau; scene; description; list; blackboard.
tablée [ta'ble], *n.f.* company at table.
tablette [ta'blɛt], *n.f.* shelf; tablet; slab, bar (*of chocolate*); (*Pharm.*) lozenge; note-book.
tablier [ta'blje], *n.m.* apron (*in all senses*); chess or checker board.
tabou [ta'bu], *a.* and *n.m.* taboo.

tabouret [tabu'rɛ], *n.m.* stool, foot-stool.
tabourin [tabu'rɛ̃], *n.m.* chimney cowl.
tabulateur [tabyla'tœ:r], *n.m.* tabulator; (*Teleph.*) dial.
tachant [ta'ʃɑ̃], *a.* easily soiled.
tache [taʃ], *n.f.* spot, stain; (*fig.*) blot.
tâche [ta:ʃ], *n.f.* task, job.
tacher [ta'ʃe], *v.t.* to stain, to spot; (*fig.*) to taint.
tâcher [ta'ʃe], *v.i.* to try, to endeavor, to strive.
tacheter [taʃ'te], *v.t.* (*conjug. like* APPELER) to fleck, to speckle, to mottle.
tacite [ta'sit], *a.* tacit, implied.
tacitement [tasit'mɑ̃], *adv.* tacitly.
taciturne [tasi'tyrn], *a.* taciturn.
taciturnité [tasityrni'te], *n.f.* taciturnity.
tact [takt], *n.m.* feeling, touch; tact.
tacticien [takti'sjɛ̃], *n.m.* tactician.
tactile [tak'til], *a.* tactile.
tactilité [taktili'te], *n.f.* tactility.
tactique [tak'tik], *a.* tactical.—*n.f.* tactics; (*fig.*) stratagem, move.
taffetas [taf'ta], *n.m.* taffeta.
taie (1) [tɛ], *n.f.* **taie d'oreiller**, pillow-case.
taie (2) [tɛ], *n.f.* film, speck (*in the eye*).
taillade [ta'jad], *n.f.* slash, gash, cut.
taillader [taja'de], *v.t.* to slash, to cut, to gash.
taillant [ta'jɑ̃], *n.m.* edge (*of a knife etc.*).
taille [ta:j], *n.f.* cutting, cut, fashion; edge (*of a sword*); height, stature; waist, figure; (*Hort.*) pruning; **de taille à**, quite capable of.
taillé [ta'je], *a.* cut, carved; well-built (*person*).
taille-crayon [tajkrɛ'jɔ̃], *n.m.* (*pl.* **-crayons**) pencil sharpener.
taille-ongles [taj'ɔ̃:gl], *n.m. inv.* nail clippers.
tailler [ta'je], *v.t.* to cut, to cut out; to carve; to hew; to prune; to sharpen; to shape; to deal (*cards*).
tailleur [ta'jœ:r], *n.m* tailor; cutter; hewer; (*woman's two-piece*) suit.
tailleuse [ta'jø:z], *n.f.* tailoress.
taillis [ta'ji], *n.m. inv.* copse; brushwood.
tain [tɛ̃], *n.m.* foil; silvering (*for mirrors*).
taire [tɛ:r], *v.t. irr.* to say nothing of, to pass over in silence; to suppress; to keep dark. **se taire**, *v.r.* to be silent; to remain unsaid.
talc [talk], *n.m.* talc, talcum powder.
talent [ta'lɑ̃], *n.m.* talent; (*fig.*) ability.
talion [ta'ljɔ̃], *n.m.* talion, retaliation.
talisman [talis'mɑ̃], *n.m.* talisman.
taloche [ta'lɔʃ], *n.f.* cuff, thump, buffet.
talocher [talɔ'ʃe], *v.t.* to cuff, to box (*someone's*) ears.
talon [ta'lɔ̃], *n.m.* heel; counterfoil, stub.
talonner [talɔ'ne], *v.t.* to be close on the heels of; to press hard, to spur.—*v.i.* (*Naut.*) to ground; (*Ftb.*) to heel out (*of the scrum*).
talonneur [talɔ'nœ:r], *n.m.* (*Ftb.*) hooker.
talus [ta'ly], *n.m.* slope, ramp; embankment.
talutage [taly'ta:ʒ], *n.m.* sloping, embanking.
tamarin [tama'rɛ̃], *n.m.* tamarind.
tamaris [tama'ris], **tamarisc** [tama'risk], *n.m.* tamarisk.
tambour [tɑ̃'bu:r], *n.m.* drum; drummer; embroidery frame; (*Anat.*) tympanum; **tambour de ville**, town crier.
tambourin [tɑ̃bu'rɛ̃], *n.m.* Provençal tabor.
tambourinage [tɑ̃buri'na:ʒ], *n.m.* drumming.
tambouriner [tɑ̃buri'ne] *v.t.* to advertise.—*v.i.* to drum, to tattoo.

tambour-major [tābûrma'ʒɔ:r], *n.m.* (*pl.* **tambours-majors**) drum major.

tamis [ta'mi], *n.m. inv.* sieve, sifter, strainer.

tamisage [tami'za:ʒ], *n.m.* sifting, straining.

Tamise [ta'mi:z], **la**, *f.* the Thames.

tamiser [tami'ze], *v.t.* to sift, to strain; to filter.

tamiseur [tami'zœːr], *n.m.* (*fem.* **-euse**) sifter.

tampon [tɑ̃'pɔ̃], *n.m.* stopper; plug; bung; buffer; pad (*used in engraving etc.*).

tamponnement [tɑ̃pɔn'mɑ̃], *n.m.* plugging, stopping; (*Rail.*) head-on collision.

tamponner [tɑ̃pɔ'ne], *v.t.* to plug, to stop up; to run into (*another train etc.*). **se tamponner**, *v.r.* to collide.

tan [tɑ̃], *a. inv.* tan(-colored). —*n.m.* tan; tanner's bark.

tancer [tɑ̃'se], *v.t.* (*conjug. like* COMMENCER) to rate, to lecture, to scold.

tanche [tɑ̃:ʃ], *n.f.* tench.

tandem [tɑ̃'dɛm], *n.m.* tandem.

tandis [tɑ̃'di] **que**, *conj. phr.* while; whereas.

tangage [tɑ̃'ga:ʒ], *n.m.* pitching (*of ship, airplane*).

tangent [tɑ̃'ʒɑ̃], *a.* tangential.—*n.f.* (**-e**) tangent.

tangible [tɑ̃'ʒibl], *a.* tangible.

tangiblement [tɑ̃ʒiblə'mɑ̃], *adv.* tangibly.

tangue [tɑ̃:g], *n.f.* slimy sand (*used as manure*).

tanguer [tɑ̃'ge], *v.i.* (*Naut.*) to pitch.

tanière [ta'njɛ:r], *n.f.* den, hole, lair (*of beasts*).

tank [tɑ̃k], *n.m.* (*Mil.*) tank.

tannage [ta'na:ʒ], *n.m.* tanning.

tannant [ta'nɑ̃], *a.* tanning; (*pop.*) tiresome, annoying.

tanné [ta'ne], *a.* tanned, sunburnt (*skin*); tawny.—*n.m.* tan (*color*).

tanner [ta'ne], *v.t.* to tan; (*pop.*) to tease; to beat.

tannerie [tan'ri], *n.f.* tan-yard, tannery.

tanneur [ta'nœːr], *n.m.* tanner.

tant [tɑ̃], *adv.* so much, such; so many; as much, as many; to such a degree, so; so far; so long, as long; *tant bien que mal*, somehow or other, after a fashion; *tant pis*, too bad, never mind.

tantaliser [tɑ̃tali'ze], *v.t.* to tantalize.

tante [tɑ̃:t], *n.f.* aunt; (*pop.*) pawnbroker, 'uncle'.

tantôt [tɑ̃'to], *adv.* presently, by and by, anon; soon; a little while ago, just now; sometimes.

Tanzanie [tɑ̃za'ni], **la**, *f.* Tanzania.

taon [tɑ̃], *n.m.* botfly, gadfly, cleg.

tapage [ta'pa:ʒ], *n.m.* noise, uproar, row; (*colloq.*) show.

tapageur [tapa'ʒœːr], *a.* (*fem.* **-euse**) rackety, boisterous, noisy; flashy.—*n.m.* (*fem.* **-euse**) noisy person, blusterer.

tape [tap], *n.f.* rap, slap, tap, thump.

taper [ta'pe], *v.t.* to hit, to slap; to smack, to tap.—*v.i.* to hit, to stamp; to strum; to beat down (*of sun*).

tapinois [tapi'nwa], *only in* **en tapinois**, *adv. phr.* stealthily, slyly.

tapioca [tapjɔ'ka], *n.m.* tapioca.

tapir (se) [səta'pi:r], *v.r.* to squat, to crouch, to cower, to lurk.

tapis [ta'pi], *n.m.* carpet, rug; cover cloth (*for tables etc.*).

tapis-brosse [tapi'brɔs], *n.m.* (*pl.* **-brosses**) door-mat.

tapisser [tapi'se], *v.t.* to hang with tapestry; to cover; to deck, to adorn; to paper; to carpet.

tapisserie [tapis'ri], *n.f.* tapestry, hangings; wallpaper; upholstery.

tapissier [tapi'sje], *n.m.* (*fem.* **-ière**) upholsterer; tapestry worker.

tapoter [tapɔ'te], *v.t.* to pat, to tap; to strum.

taquin [ta'kɛ̃], *a.* teasing.—*n.m.* (*fem.* **-e**) tease, teasing person.

taquiner [taki'ne], *v.t.* to tease, to plague.

taquinerie [takin'ri], *n.f.* teasing; teasing disposition.

tard [ta:r], *adv.* late.—*n.m.* late hour.

tarder [tar'de], *v.i.* to delay; to tarry, to loiter; to be long; (*impers.*) to long (*de*).

tardif [tar'dif], *a.* (*fem.* **-dive**) tardy, late; slow, belated; backward.

tardivement [tardiv'mɑ̃], *adv.* tardily, slowly, belatedly.

tare [ta:r], *n.f.* tare; (*Comm.*) waste, damage; (*fig.*) blemish, defect.

taré [ta're], *a.* damaged, spoiled; disreputable.

tarentule [tarɑ̃'tyl], *n.f.* tarantula.

tarer [ta're], *v.t.* to injure, to damage, to spoil; (*Comm.*) to tare. **se tarer**, *v.r.* to spoil, to deteriorate.

targuer (se) [sətar'ge], *v.r.* to boast, to brag.

tarif [ta'rif], *n.m.* tariff, rate, scale of prices.

tarifer [tari'fe], *v.t.* to tariff, to price, to rate.

tarir [ta'ri:r], *v.t.* to dry up; to exhaust.—*v.i.* to dry up; to be exhausted; to cease. **se tarir**, *v.r.* to dry up.

tarissable [tari'sabl], *a.* exhaustible.

tarissement [taris'mɑ̃], *n.m.* exhausting, drying up.

tartan [tar'tɑ̃], *n.m.* tartan, plaid.

tarte [tart], *n.f.* tart; flan.

tartelette [tar'tlɛt], *n.f.* tartlet.

tartine [tar'tin], *n.f.* slice of bread (*with butter, jam etc.*).

tartufe [tar'tyf], *n.m.* hypocrite.

tas [tɑ̃], *n.m. inv.* heap, pile; (*fig.*) lot, set (*of persons etc.*).

Tasmanie [tasma'ni], **la**, *f.* Tasmania.

tasmanien [tasma'njɛ̃], *a.* Tasmanian.—*n.m.* (**Tasmanien**, *fem.* **-enne**) Tasmanian (*person*).

tasse [tɑ̃:s], *n.f.* cup.

tassement [tas'mɑ̃], *n.m.* settling, sinking, subsidence.

tasser [tɑ̃'se], *v.t.* to heap *or* pile up; to compress, to squeeze, to cram.—*v.i.* to grow thick. **se tasser**, *v.r.* to sink, to settle, to subside; to huddle together (*of persons*).

tâter [ta'te], *v.t.* to feel; to try, to taste; to sound, to test.—*v.i.* to taste, to try (*de* or *à*). **se tâter**, *v.r.* to examine oneself.

tatillon [tati'jɔ̃], *a.* (*fem.* **-onne**) niggling, finical.

tâtonnement [tɑ̃tɔn'mɑ̃], *n.m.* groping.

tâtonner [tɑ̃tɔ'ne], *v.i.* to feel one's way, to grope.

tâtons (à) [ata'tɔ̃], *adv. phr.* gropingly.

tatouage [ta'twa:ʒ], *n.m.* tattooing.

tatouer [ta'twe], *v.t.* to tattoo.

taudis [to'di], *n.m.* hovel, slum, hole.

taupe [to:p], *n.f.* mole; moleskin.

taupier [to'pje], *n.m.* mole catcher.
taupière [to'pjɛ:r], *n.f.* mole trap.
taupinière [topi'njɛ:r], **taupinée** [topi'ne], *n.f.* mole-hill; hillock, knoll.
taure [to:r], *n.f.* heifer.
taureau [to'ro], *n.m.* (*pl.* **-eaux**) bull; (*Astron.*) Taurus.
taux [to], *n.m. inv.* price, rate; rate of interest.
taverne [ta'vɛrn], *n.f.* tavern, café, restaurant.
tavernier [taver'nje], *n.m.* (*fem.* **-ière**) innkeeper.
taxation [taksa'sjɔ̃], *n.f.* taxation; fixing of prices.
taxe [taks], *n.f.* tax; duty, rate; fixing of prices; controlled price.
taxer [tak'se], *v.t.* to tax; to rate, to fix the price of; to accuse (*de*).
taxi [tak'si], *n.m.* taxi (-cab).
taxiphone [taksi'fɔn], *n.m.* public telephone booth.
Tchécoslovaquie [tʃekɔslɔva'ki], **la**, *f.* Czechoslovakia.
tchèque [tʃɛk], *a.* Czech.—*n.m.* Czech (*language*).—*n.* (**Tchèque**) Czech (*person*).
te [tə, t], *pron. obj.* *thee, you.
technicien [tɛkni'sjɛ̃], *n.m.* (*fem.* **-enne**) technician.
technique [tɛk'nik], *a.* technical.—*n.f.* technique.
techniquement [tɛknik'mã], *adv.* technically.
technologie [tɛknɔlɔ'ʒi], *n.f.* technology.
technologique [tɛknɔlɔ'ʒik], *a.* technological.
technologue [tɛknɔ'lɔg], *n.m.* technologist.
teck or **tek** [tɛk], *n.m.* teak, teak-wood.
teigne [tɛɲ], *n.f.* tinea (*moth*); tinea (*skin disease, such as ringworm*).
teigneux [tɛ'ɲø], *a.* (*fem.* **-euse**) scurvy.—*n.m.* (*fem.* **-euse**) scurfy person.
teindre [tɛ̃:dr], *v.t. irr.* (*conjug. like* CRAINDRE) to dye, to stain.
teint [tɛ̃], *n.m.* dye, color; complexion; hue.
teinte [tɛ̃:t], *n.f.* tint, color, shade, hue; (*fig.*) smack, touch.
teinter [tɛ̃'te], *v.t.* to tint; to give a color to.
teinture [tɛ̃'ty:r], *n.f.* dye; dyeing; color, hue; (*Pharm.*) tincture.
teinturerie [tɛ̃ty'ri], *n.f.* dyeing; dye works; dry cleaning.
teinturier [tɛ̃ty'rje], *n.m.* (*fem.* **-ière**) dyer; dry cleaner.
tek [TECK].
tel [tɛl], *a.* (*fem.* **telle**) such; like, similar.—*pron. indef.* such a one; **M. un tel**, Mr. So-and-so.
télécommande [telekɔ'mã:d], *n.f.* remote control.
télécommunications [telekɔmynika'sjɔ̃], *n.f. pl.* telecommunications.
télégramme [tele'gram], *n.m.* telegram.
télégraphe [tele'graf], *n.m.* telegraph.
télégraphie [telegra'fi], *n.f.* telegraphy; **télégraphie sans fil**, wireless telegraphy.
télégraphier [telegra'fje], *v.t., v.i.* to telegraph; to wire, to cable.
télégraphique [telegra'fik], *a.* telegraphic.
télégraphiste [telegra'fist], *n.* telegraphist.
téléguidé [telegi'de], *a.* guided; **engin téléguidé**, guided missile.
téléimprimeur [teleɛ̃pri'mœ:r], **téléscripteur** [teleskrip'tœr], *n.m.* teleprinter.
télémètre [tele'mɛtr], *n.m.* rangefinder.

télépathie [telepa'ti], *n.f.* telepathy.
télépathique [telepa'tik], *a.* telepathic.
téléphérique [telefe'rik], *a.* and *n.m.* teleferic.
téléphone [tele'fɔn], *n.m.* telephone; **un coup de téléphone**, a telephone call.
téléphoner [telefɔ'ne], *v.t., v.i.* to telephone, to ring up.
téléphonique [telefɔ'nik], *a.* **cabine téléphonique**, telephone booth.
téléphoniste [telefɔ'nist], *n.* telephone operator.
télescope [telɛs'kɔp], *n.m.* telescope.
télescopique [telɛskɔ'pik], *a.* telescopic.
télescripteur [teleskrip'tœ:r], [TÉLÉIMPRIMEUR].
télespectateur [telespɛkta'tœ:r], *n.m.* (*fem.* **-trice**) televiewer.
téléviser [televi'ze], *v.t.* to televise.
téléviseur [televi'zœ:r], *n.m.* television (receiving-)set.
télévision [televi'zjɔ̃], *n.f.* television.
tellement [tɛl'mã], *adv.* so, in such a manner; so much, so far.
téméraire [teme'rɛ:r], *a.* rash, reckless.—*n.* reckless person, daredevil.
témérairement [temerɛr'mã], *adv.* rashly, recklessly.
témérité [temeri'te], *n.f.* temerity.
témoignage [temwa'ɲa:ʒ], *n.m.* testimony, evidence, witness; testimonial; (*fig.*) token, mark, proof.
témoigner [temwa'ɲe], *v.t.* to testify; to show, to prove, to be the sign of.—*v.i.* to testify, to give evidence (*de*).
témoin [te'mwɛ̃], *n.m.* witness, evidence, proof, mark; second (*in duels*).
tempe [tã:p], *n.f.* (*Anat.*) temple.
tempérament [tãpera'mã], *n.m.* constitution, temperament; temper; (*fig.*) moderation, compromise; **à tempérament**, by instalments.
tempérance [tãpe'rã:s], *n.f.* temperance.
température [tãpera'ty:r], *n.f.* temperature.
tempéré [tãpe're], *a.* temperate (*of climate*); limited, constitutional (*of governments*); restrained, sober (*of style*).
tempérer [tãpe're], *v.t.* (*conjug. like* CÉDER) to temper, to moderate, to allay, to assuage, to check. **se tempérer**, *v.r.* to become mild (*of the weather*).
tempête [tã'pɛ:t], *n.f.* storm, tempest.
tempêter [tãpɛ'te], *v.i.* to storm, to bluster, to fume.
tempétueusement [tãpetɥøz'mã], *adv.* tempestuously, violently.
tempétueux [tãpe'tɥø], *a.* (*fem.* **-euse**) tempestuous, boisterous, stormy.
temple [tã:pl], *n.m.* temple; French Protestant church.
templier [tãpli'e], *n.m.* Knight Templar.
temporaire [tãpɔ'rɛ:r], *a.* temporary.
temporairement [tãpɔrɛr'mã], *adv.* temporarily, provisionally.
temporel [tãpɔ'rɛl], *a.* (*fem.* **-elle**) temporal.
temporisateur [tãpɔriza'tœ:r], *a.* (*fem.* **-trice**) procrastinating, temporizing.—*n.m.* (*fem.* **-trice**) temporizer, procrastinator.
temporisation [tãpɔriza'sjɔ̃], *n.f.* temporizing, procrastination.
temporiser [tãpɔri'ze], *v.i.* to temporize, to delay.

temps [tā], *n.m. inv.* time, while, period, term; occasion; season; weather; (*Gram.*) tense; *à temps*, in time; *avec le temps*, in course of time; *dans le temps*, formerly; *en temps et lieu*, in proper time and place.

tenable [tə'nabl], *a.* tenable; bearable.

tenace [tə'nas], *a.* tenacious, adhesive, sticky.

ténacité [tenasi'te], *n.f.* tenacity, toughness; retentiveness (*of memory*).

tenaille [tə'naːj], *n.f.* (*usu. in pl.*) pincers, nippers, pliers.

tenailler [tənɑ'je], *v.t.* to torture with red-hot pincers; (*fig.*) to torture.

tenant [tə'nā], *a.* *séance tenante*, during the sitting; forthwith, then and there.—*n.m.* titlist (*at a tournament*); (*fig.*) champion, defender.

tendance [tā'dāːs], *n.f.* tendency; leaning, bent, inclination.

tendancieux [tādā'sjø], *a.* (*fem.* -**euse**) tendentious; insinuating, suggestive.

tendeur [tā'dœːr], *n.m.* (*fem.* -**euse**) spreader, layer, setter (*of snares*); wire-stretcher.

tendoir [tā'dwaːr], *n.m.* clothes-line.

tendon [tā'dɔ̃], *n.m.* tendon, sinew.

tendre (1) [tāːdr], *a.* tender, soft; delicate, sensitive; affectionate; moving; early, young, new.

tendre (2) [tāːdr], *v.t.* to stretch, to strain; to bend (*a bow etc.*); to spread, to lay, to set; to hold out; to pitch (*tents*); to hang (*tapestry etc.*).—*v.i.* to lead; to tend, to conduce.

tendrement [tādrə'mā], *adv.* tenderly, affectionately.

tendresse [tā'drɛs], *n.f.* tenderness, fondness; (*pl.*) endearments.

tendron [tā'drɔ̃], *n.m.* shoot (*of plants*).

tendu [tā'dy], *a.* stretched, held out; tight, tense; strained.

ténèbres [te'nɛːbr], *n.f.* (*used only in pl.*) darkness, night, gloom.

ténébreusement [tenebrøz'mā], *adv.* darkly, gloomily; secretly.

ténébreux [tene'brø], *a.* (*fem.* -**euse**) dark, gloomy, overcast; obscure, mysterious.

teneur (1) [tə'nœːr], *n.f.* tenor, terms, text; purport.

teneur (2) [tə'nœːr], *n.m.* (*fem.* -**euse**) holder; *teneur de livres*, book-keeper.

ténia [te'nja], *n.m.* tapeworm.

tenir [tə'niːr], *v.t. irr.* to hold, to have hold of; to have, to possess; to seize; to occupy; to keep, to follow; to retain; to perform; to consider.—*v.i.* to hold; to adhere, to stick; to hold together; to cling; to prize (*à*); to be attached *or* related (*à*); to be contiguous; to depend, to result (*de*); to be held (*of fairs, markets, assemblies etc.*); to take after; to savor; to persist; to resist; to be anxious (*à*). **se tenir**, *v.r.* to hold fast, to remain; to adhere; to consider oneself; to contain oneself, to refrain.

tennis [te'nis], *n.m.* lawn tennis.

tenon [tə'nɔ̃], *n.m.* tenon; bolt (*of fire-arms*).

ténor [te'nɔːr], *n.m.* (*Mus.*) tenor.

tension [tā'sjɔ̃], *n.f.* tension, strain; tenseness; (*Elec.*) voltage.

tentacule [tāta'kyl], *n.m.* tentacle, feeler.

tentant [tā'tā], *a.* tempting.

tentateur [tāta'tœːr], *a.* (*fem.* -**trice**) tempting.—*n.m.* (*fem.* -**trice**) tempter, temptress.

tentation [tāta'sjɔ̃], *n.f.* temptation.

tentative [tāta'tiːv], *n.f.* attempt, trial, endeavor.

tente [tāːt], *n.f.* tent, pavilion; (*Naut.*) awning.

tenter [tā'te], *v.t.* to attempt, to try; to tempt.

tenture [tā'tyːr], *n.f.* hangings, tapestry; wall-paper; paper-hanging.

ténu [te'ny], *a.* tenuous, thin, slender.

tenue [tə'ny], *n.f.* holding (*of assemblies etc.*); session; attitude (*of a person*); behavior, bearing; dress; keeping (*of books*); *grande tenue*, (*Mil.*) full dress; *petite tenue*, undress.

ténuité [tenɥi'te], *n.f.* tenuity, thinness; (*fig.*) insignificance.

tenure [tə'nyːr], *n.f.* tenure.

ter [tɛːr], *adv.* thrice; for the third time.

térébenthine [terebā'tin], *n.f.* turpentine.

térébinthe [tere'bɛ̃ːt], *n.m.* turpentine tree, terebinth.

tergiversation [tɛrʒivɛrsa'sjɔ̃], *n.f.* tergiversation, evasion.

tergiverser [tɛrʒivɛr'se], *v.i.* to waver, to beat about the bush.

terme [tɛrm], *n.m.* term; termination, end; limit, boundary; time; three months; quarter's rent; expression; (*pl.*) state, conditions, terms; *avant terme*, prematurely.

terminaison [tɛrminɛ'zɔ̃], *n.f.* termination, ending.

terminer [tɛrmi'ne], *v.t.* to bound, to limit; to terminate, to conclude. **se terminer**, *v.r.* to terminate; to be bounded.

terminus [tɛrmi'nys], *n.m.* terminus (*of railway*).

terne [tɛrn], *a.* dull, dim; wan; spiritless.

ternir [tɛr'niːr], *v.t.* to dull, to deaden; to tarnish. **se ternir**, *v.r.* to tarnish, to grow dull; to fade (*of colors*).

ternissure [tɛrni'syːr], *n.f.* tarnishing, fading; stain.

terrain [tɛ'rɛ̃], *n.m.* piece of ground; soil, earth; site; field, course.

terrassant [tɛra'sā], *a.* crushing (*news etc.*).

terrasse [tɛ'ras], *n.f.* terrace; flat roof, balcony.

terrassement [tɛras'mā], *n.m.* earthwork, embankment; ballasting.

terrasser [tɛra'se], *v.t.* to embank; to throw to the ground; to beat; to confound, to dismay.

terrassier [tɛra'sje], *n.m.* digger, excavator, laborer; earthwork contractor.

terre [tɛːr], *n.f.* earth; land; ground, soil; dominion, territory; grounds, estate, property; (*C*) farm.

terreau [tɛ'ro], *n.m.* (*pl.* -**eaux**) compost.

Terre-Neuve [tɛr'nœːv], *f.* Newfoundland.

terre-neuve [tɛr'nœːv], *n.m. inv.* Newfoundland dog.

terrer [tɛ're], *v.t.* to earth up (*a tree etc.*). *v.i.* to burrow. **se terrer**, *v.r.* to dig oneself in.

terrestre [tɛ'rɛstr], *a.* terrestrial, earthly.

terreur [tɛ'rœːr], *n.f.* terror; awe, dread.

terreux [tɛ'rø], *a.* (*fem.* -**euse**) terreous, earthy; dirty; dull (*of colors*); ashen (*of the face*).

terrible [tɛ'ribl], *a.* terrible, dreadful; unmanageable (*of children*).

terriblement [tɛriblə'mā], *adv.* terribly; (*colloq.*) with a vengeance.

terrier [tɛ'rje], *n.m.* burrow, hole; earth (*of fox*); terrier (*dog*).

terrifier [tɛri'fje], *v.t.* to terrify, to dismay.

terrine [tɛ'rin], *n.f.* earthen pan, dish; potted meat.

territoire [tɛri'twa:r], *n.m.* territory, district

territorial [tɛrito'rjal], *a.* (*m. pl.* **-aux**) territorial.

terroir [tɛ'rwa:r], *n.m.* soil, ground; *goût de terroir*, raciness (*of style*); native tang (*of wine*).

terroriser [tɛrɔri'ze], *v.t.* to terrorize.

terrorisme [tɛrɔ'rism], *n.m.* terrorism.

terroriste [tɛrɔ'rist], *n.m.* terrorist.

tertiaire [tɛr'sjɛ:r], *a.* tertiary.

tertre [tɛrtr], *n.m.*, knoll, hillock.

tes [te], [TON (1)].

tesson [tɛ's3], *n.m.* potsherd, fragment of broken glass etc.

test [tɛst], *n.m.* shell; trial, test.

testacé [tɛsta'se]. *a.* testaceous.—*n.m.* testacean.

testament [tɛsta'mā], *n.m.* will.

tester [tɛs'te], *v.t.* to test.—*v.i.* to make one's will.

testimonial [tɛstimɔ'njal], *a.* (*m. pl.* **-aux**) testifying, testimonial

tétanos [teta'nɔs], *n.m.* tetanus, lock-jaw.

têtard [tɛ'ta:r], *n.m.* tadpole.

tête [tɛ:t], *n.f.* head; head-piece; face; beginning; top; van, vanguard; (*fig.*) brains, sense, judgment; presence of mind; *en tête*, in one's head; in front, ahead; *mal de tête*, headache; *tête de mort*, skull.

tête-à-tête [tɛta'tɛ:t], *n.m. inv.* tête-à-tête, private interview or conversation; settee (*for two*).

téter [te'te], *v.t.* (*conjug. like* CÉDER) to suck.

têtière [tɛ'tjɛ:r], *n.f.* infant's cap; head-stall (*of a bridle*); antimacassar.

tétin [te'tɛ̃], *n.m.* nipple, teat; breast.

téton [te't3], *n.m.* teat; (*fam.*) breast.

tétrarque [te'trark], *n.m.* tetrarch.

tétras [te'tra], *n.m. inv.* (*Orn.*) grouse.

têtu [te'ty], *a.* headstrong, stubborn, obstinate.

teutonique [tøtɔ'nik], *a.* teutonic.

texte [tɛkst], *n.m.* text; theme, matter, subject; passage (*of Scripture*).

textile [tɛks'til], *a.* and *n.m.* textile.

textuel [tɛks'tɥɛl], *a.* (*fem.* **-elle**) textual, word for word.

textuellement [tɛkstɥɛl'mā], *adv.* textually.

texture [tɛks'ty:r], *n.f.* texture; disposition.

thaïlandais [tailã'de], *a.* Thai.—*n.m.* Thai (*language*); (**Thaï**, **andais**, *fem.* **-aise**) Thai (*person*).

Thaïlande [tai'lã:d], **la**, *f.* Thailand, Siam.

thé [te], *n.m.* tea; tea party.

théâtral [tea'tral], *a.* (*m. pl.* **-aux**) theatrical.

théâtre [te'a:tr], *n.m.* theatre, playhouse; stage; plays (*collection*); scene; *coup de théâtre*, striking event.

théerie [te'ri], *n.f.* tea plantation.

théière [te'jɛ:r], *n.f.* teapot.

théisme [te'ism], *n.m.* theism.

thème [tɛːm], *n.m.* topic, subject, theme; (*sch.*) prose, composition.

théodolite [teɔdɔ'lit], *n.m.* theodolite.

théologie [teɔlɔ'ʒi], *n.f.* theology; divinity.

théologien [teɔlɔ'ʒjɛ̃], *n.m.* theologian.

théorème [teɔ'rɛm], *n.m.* theorem.

théorie [teɔ'ri], *n.f.* theory, speculation.

théorique [teɔ'rik], *a.* theoretical.

théoriquement [teɔrik'mā], *adv.* theoretically.

théoriser [teɔri'ze], *v.t.*, *v.i.* to theorize.

théoriste [teɔ'rist], *n.* theorist.

Thérèse [te'rɛ:z], *f.* Theresa.

thermal [tɛr'mal], *a.* (*m. pl.* **-aux**) thermal; *eaux thermales*, hot springs.

thermomètre [tɛrmɔ'mɛtr], *n.m.* thermometer.

thermos [tɛr'mɔs], *n.m.* thermos (flask).

thermostat [termo'sta], *n.m.* thermostat.

thésauriser [tezɔri'ze], *v.t.* to treasure.—*v.i.* to hoard treasure.

thèse [tɛ:z], *n.f.* thesis, proposition.

thibaude [ti'bo:d], *n.f.* hair-cloth, coarse drugget.

Thomas [tɔ'ma], *m.* Thomas.

thon [t3], *n.m.* tunny-fish.

thoracique [tɔra'sik], *a.* thoracic.

thorax [tɔ'raks], *n.m.* thorax, chest.

thrombose [tr3'bo:z], *n.f.* thrombosis.

thym [tɛ̃], *n.m.* thyme.

thyroïde [tiro'id], *a.* thyroid.

tiare [tja:r], *n.f.* tiara.

Tibet [ti'bɛ], **le** *m.* Tibet.

tibétain [tibe'tɛ̃], *a.* Tibetan.—*n.m.* Tibetan (*language*); (**Tibétain**, *fem.* **-aine**) Tibetan (*person*).

tibia [ti'bja], *n.m.* (*Anat.*) tibia, shin-bone.

tic [tik], *n.m.* tic, twitching; bad habit.

ticket [ti'kɛ], *n.m.* ticket (*for bus, underground etc., but not railways*).

tiède [tjɛd], *a.* lukewarm, tepid, mild; (*fig.*) indifferent.

tièdement [tjɛd'mā], *adv.* with indifference.

tiédeur [tje'dœ:r], *n.f.* lukewarmness; (*fig.*) indifference.

tiédir [tje'di:r], *v.t.* to take the chill off, to tepefy.—*v.i.* to cool, to grow lukewarm.

tien [tjɛ̃], *pron. poss. m.* (*fem.* **tienne**) *thine*, yours.—*n.* (*pl.*) **les tiens**, your relations and friends.

tiens! [tjɛ̃], *2nd sing. imper.* [TENIR], *int.* well hello! look here! here! really? you don't say so!

tierce (1) [tjɛrs], *n.f.* a third (*of time*); tierce (*at cards etc.*).

tiers [tj:ɛr], *a.* (*fem.* **tierce** (2)) third.—*n.m.* third person, third party; (*fig.*) stranger; third part.

tige [ti:ʒ], *n.f.* stem, stalk; trunk (*of tree*); straw(*of grain*); shank (*of a key, anchor etc.*); stock (*of a family*).

tignasse [ti'nas], *n.f.* old wig; (*pop.*) mop, shock (*of hair*).

tigre [tigr], *n.m.* (*fem.* **-esse**) tiger, tigress.

tigrer [ti'gre], *v.t.* to stripe, to spot, to speckle.

tillac [ti'jak], *n.m.* deck.

tilleul [ti'jœl], *n.m.* lime tree, linden tree.

timbale [tɛ̃'bal], *n.f.* kettledrum, timbal; metal cup or mug; kitchen mold.

timbre [tɛ̃:br], *n.m.* bell, clock chime; sound, tone; stamp; stamp duty; postmark.

timbré [tɛ̃:bre], *a.* stamped; (*fam.*) cracked.

timbre-poste [tɛ̃brə'pɔst], *n.m.* (*pl.* **timbres-poste**) postage stamp.

timbrer [tɛ̃'bre], v.t. to stamp; to stick a stamp on (a letter).

timide [ti'mid], a. shy, bashful, self-conscious; timid.

timidement [timid'mɑ̃], adv. shyly; timidly.

timidité [timidi'te], n.f. shyness, bashfulness; timidity.

timon [ti'mɔ̃], n.m. pole (of a carriage, cart etc.); shaft; beam (of a plough); (Naut.) helm, tiller; (fig.) direction, government.

timonerie [timɔn'ri], n.f. steerage, steering.

timonier [timɔ'nje], n.m. steersman, helmsman; wheel horse.

timoré [timɔ're], a. timorous, fearful.

Timothée [timɔ'te], m. Timothy.

tine [tin], n.f. tub, water cask.

tintamarre [tɛ̃ta'ma:r], n.m. hubbub, uproar, hurly-burly, din.

tintement [tɛ̃t'mɑ̃], n.m. ringing sound, tinkling; tolling; singing or buzzing (in the ears etc.).

tinter [tɛ̃'te], v.t. to ring, to toll; to sound (a knell etc.); (Naut.) to prop, to support.—v.i. to ring, to toll; to tinkle, to jingle; to tingle.

tintouin [tɛ̃'twɛ̃], n.m. (fam.) anxiety, trouble.

tique [tik], n.f. cattle tick, dog tick.

tiquer [ti'ke], v.i. to have a tic, to twitch.

tiqueté [tik'te], a. speckled, spotted.

tiqueture [tik'ty:r], n.f. mottling, speckles.

tir [ti:r], n.m. shooting; firing, fire; shooting gallery, rifle range.

tirade [ti'rad], n.f. passage (of prose or verse); tirade.

tirage [ti'ra:ʒ], n.m. drawing, hauling, towing; tow-path; (fig.) difficulties; working off; printing, circulation (of newspaper); drawing (of a lottery); focal length (of camera).

tiraillement [tiraj'mɑ̃], n.m. pulling, hauling about; twinge, pain; (fig.) jarring, wrangling, vexation.

tirailler [tira'je], v.t. to pull about; to tease, to pester.—v.i. to shoot wildly; to skirmish. **se tirailler**, v.r. to pull each other about.

tirailleur [tiru'jœ:r], n.m. sharpshooter; skirmisher.

tirant [ti'rɑ̃], n.m. purse-string; boot-strap; (Carp. etc.) tie-beam; brace (of a drum); *tirant d'eau*, ship's draft.

tire [ti:r], n.f. pull.

tiré [ti're], a. drawn; fatigued.—n.m. (Comm.) drawee (of a bill).

tire-bouchon [tirbu'ʃɔ̃], n.m. (pl. -bouchons) corkscrew; ringlet (of hair).

tire-bouton [tirbu'tɔ̃], n.m. (pl. -boutons) button-hook.

tire-d'aile (à) [atir'dɛl], adv. phr. at full speed (of a bird flying).

tire-larigot (à) [atirlari'go], adv. phr. (fam.) to one's heart's content.

tirelire [tir'li:r], n.f. money box.

tirer [ti're], v.t. to draw, to pull; to take out, to extract; to tap (liquors); to stretch, to tighten; to receive, to reap; to infer; to put on; to get; to shoot, to fire; (Print.) to print.—v.i. to draw, to pull; to fire; to tend, to border, to verge (sur). **se tirer**, v.r. to extricate oneself; to get out; to recover (from illness).

tiret [ti're], n.m. hyphen, dash.

tiretaine [tir'tɛːn], n.f. linsey-woolsey.

tireur [ti'rœ:r], n.m. (fem. -euse) one who draws; marksman, sharpshooter.

tiroir [ti'rwa:r], n.m. drawer (in a table etc.); slide, slide-valve (steam engine).

tisane [ti'zan], n.f. infusion of herbs etc.

tison [ti'zɔ̃], n.m. brand, fire-brand; (fig.) embers.

tisonner [tizɔ'ne], v.t., v.i. to poke (the fire).

tisonnier [tizɔ'nje], n.m. poker, fire iron.

tissage [ti'sa:ʒ], n.m. weaving; cloth mill.

tisser [ti'se], v.t. to weave; *métier à tisser* weaving-loom.

tisserand [tis'rɑ̃], n.m. (fem. -e) weaver.

tissu [ti'sy], a. woven.—n.m. material, fabric; tissue.

tissure [ti'sy:r], n.f. tissue, texture.

titan [ti'tɑ̃], n.m. Titan, titan.

titanesque [tita'nɛsk], **titanique** [tita'nik], a. titanic, Titanic.

titillant [titil'lɑ̃], a. titillating, tickling.

titillation [titilla'sjɔ̃], n.f. titillation, tickling.

titiller [titil'le], v.t., v.i. to titillate, to tickle.

titre [titr], n.m. title, style, denomination; title page; head, heading; right, claim, reason; voucher; title deed; *titre de circulation*, (railway) ticket or pass; *à bon titre* or *à juste titre*, deservedly, justly.

titrer [ti'tre], v.t. to give a title to.

titubant [tity'bɑ̃], a. staggering.

titubation [tityba'sjɔ̃], n.f. reeling, staggering.

tituber [tity'be], v.i. to stagger, to reel.

titulaire [tity'lɛ:r], a. titular.—n. titular incumbent, holder, chief.

toast [tost], n.m. toast, health; toast(ed bread); *porter un toast* (à quelqu'un), to toast (someone).

toboggan [tɔbɔ'gɑ̃], n.m. toboggan.

toc [tɔk], int. tap, rap.—n.m. rap, knock (at a door etc.).

tocsin [tɔk'sɛ̃], n.m. tocsin, alarm bell.

toge [tɔ:ʒ], n.f. toga; (fig.) robe, gown (of a judge etc.).

Togo [tɔ'go], le, m. Togo.

togolais [tɔgɔ'lɛ], a. of Togo.—n.m. (**Togolais**, fem. **-aise**) native of Togo.

tohu-bohu [tɔybɔ'y], n.m. chaos; (fig.) confusion; jumble, hubbub.

toi [twa], pron. pers. *thou, *thee, you.

toile [twal], n.f. linen, cloth; canvas; sail; painting, picture; web; *toile cirée*, oil-cloth; *toile d'araignée*, cobweb, spider's web.

toilette [twa'lɛt], n.f. doily; toilet set; dressing table, wash-stand; dress, attire; *cabinet de toilette*, dressing room; *grande toilette*, full dress; *les toilettes*, toilets.

toise [twa:z], n.f. fathom; fathom measure; (fig.) measure, standard.

toiser [twa'ze], v.t. to measure; to survey; (fig.) to eye from head to foot.

toiseur [twa'zœ:r], n.m. measurer; quantity surveyor.

toison [twa'zɔ̃], n.f. fleece; (fig.) mop, thick head of hair.

toit [twa], n.m. roof, house-top; top, roof (of a mine); (fig.) house, home; *toit à cochons* pigsty.

toiture [twa'ty:r], n.f. roofing, roof.

tôle [to:l], n.f. sheet iron; plate of steel; *tôle ondulée*, corrugated iron.

313

tolérable [tɔle'rabl], *a.* tolerable, bearable; middling.

tolérablement [tɔlerablə'mã], *adv.* tolerably.

tolérance [tɔle'rãːs], *n.f.* tolerance, toleration; endurance, forbearance; indulgence; tolerance (*in coins*).

tolérant [tɔle'rã], *a.* tolerant.

tolérer [tɔle're], *v.t.* (*conjug. like* CÉDER) to tolerate, to allow; to endure, to bear; to wink at.

tomate [tɔ'mat], *n.f.* tomato.

tombal [tɔ̃'bal], *a.* (*m. pl.* **-aux**) pertaining to a tomb; *pierre tombale*, tombstone.

tombe [tɔ̃ːb], *n.f.* tomb, grave; tombstone.

tombeau [tɔ̃'bo], *n.m.* (*pl.* **-eaux**) tomb, grave; (*fig.*) sepulcher, death.

tombée [tɔ̃'be], *n.f.* fall (*of night etc.*).

tomber [tɔ̃'be], *v.i.* (*with aux.* ÊTRE) to fall, to fall down; to sink; to decay, to droop; to abate; to sag; to fall into; to meet, to light (upon) (*sur*); *laisser tomber*, to drop; *tomber amoureux (de)*, to fall in love (with); *tomber bien* or *mal*, to come at the right or wrong moment; *tomber d'accord*, to agree; *tomber malade*, to fall ill.

tombereau [tɔ̃'bro], *n.m.* (*pl.* **-eaux**) tip-cart.

tombola [tɔ̃bɔ'la], *n.f.* tombola; raffle.

tome [toːm], *n.m.* volume, tome.

ton (1) [tɔ̃], *a. poss. m.* (*fem.* **ta**, *pl.* **tes**) *thy, your.

ton (2) [tɔ̃], *n.m.* tone; intonation, accent; tint; (*fig.*) manner, style; breeding; (*Mus.*) pitch, key.

tondaison [TONTE].

tondeur [tɔ̃'dœːr], *n.m.* (*fem.* **-euse**) shearer, clipper.—*n.f.* (**-euse**) shearing machine, clipper; *tondeuse (de gazon)*, lawn-mower.

tondre [tɔ̃ːdr], *v.t.* to shear, to clip, to crop; to cut, to mow, to trim.

tondu [tɔ̃'dy], *a.* shorn.

tonique [tɔ'nik], *a.* tonic; stressed.—*n.m.* (*Med.*) tonic.—*n.f.* (*Mus.*) keynote.

tonnage [tɔ'naːʒ], *n.m.* tonnage; displacement.

tonne [tɔn], *n.f.* tun (*wooden vessel*); ton (*20 cwt., approx. 1000 kil.*).

tonneau [tɔ'no], *n.m.* (*pl.* **-eaux**) tun (*cask*); tun (*measure*); ton [TONNE]; (*colloq.*) drunkard; *mettre un tonneau en perce*, to broach a cask; *tonneau percé*, (*fig.*) spendthrift.

tonnelier [tɔnə'lje], *n.m.* cooper.

tonnelle [tɔ'nɛl], *n.f.* arbor, bower.

tonnellerie [tɔnɛl'ri], *n.f.* cooperage.

tonner [tɔ'ne], *v.i.* to thunder; (*fig.*) to inveigh.

tonnerre [tɔ'nɛːr], *n.m.* thunder, thunderbolt; *coup* or *éclat de tonnerre*, clap of thunder.

tonsure [tɔ̃'syːr], *n.f.* tonsure.

tonsuré [tɔ̃sy're], *a.m.* tonsured, shaven.—*n.m.* cleric, priest.

tonte [tɔ̃ːt], **tondaison** [tɔ̃dɛ'zɔ̃], *n.f.* sheepshearing, clipping.

tonture [tɔ̃'tyːr], *n.f.* shearings, clippings; flock (*of cloth*); (*Naut.*) sheer.

top [tɔp], *n.m.* time signal; *les tops*, the pips.

topaze [tɔ'paːz], *n.f.* topaz.

toper [tɔ'pe], *v.i.* to agree; *tope là!* done! agreed!

topinambour [tɔpinã'buːr], *n.m.* Jerusalem artichoke.

topographe [tɔpɔ'graf], *n.m.* topographer.

topographie [tɔpɔgra'fi], *n.f.* topography.

topographique [tɔpɔgra'fik], *a.* topographical.

toquade or **tocade** [tɔ'kad], *n.f.* (*colloq.*) infatuation, whim, fad, craze.

toque [tɔk], *n.f.* toque; jockey's cap; magistrate's cap.

toqué [tɔ'ke], *a.* (*fam.*) cracked, touched; infatuated.

torche [tɔrʃ], *n.f.* torch; twist (*of straw etc.*); pad (*on head*).

torcher [tɔr'ʃe], *v.t.* to wipe, to clean; (*fig.*) to polish off. **se torcher**, *v.r.* to wipe oneself.

torchère [tɔr'ʃɛːr], *n.f.* torch-holder, tall candelabrum, hall lamp.

torchis [tɔr'ʃi], *n.m.* loam; *mur de torchis*, mud wall.

torchon [tɔr'ʃɔ̃], *n.m.* duster, house-cloth, dish-cloth.

tordage [tɔr'daːʒ], *n.m.* twisting, twist.

tordeur [tɔr'dœːr], *n.m.* (*fem.* **-euse**) twister (*of wool etc.*); throwster (*of silk*).

tordoir [tɔr'dwaːr], *n.m.* mangle, wringer.

tordre [tɔrdr], *v.t.* to twist, to wring; to contort, to disfigure. **se tordre**, *v.r.* to twist; to writhe.

tordu [tɔr'dy], *a.* twisted, distorted.

toréador [tɔrea'dɔːr], *n.m.* toreador, bullfighter.

tornade [tɔr'nad], *n.f.* tornado.

torpédo [tɔrpe'do], *n.f.* (*Motor.*) touring car.

torpeur [tɔr'pœːr], *n.f.* torpor.

torpide [tɔr'pid], *a.* torpid.

torpille [tɔr'piːj], *n.f.* torpedo (*numb-fish*); (*Navy, Av.*) torpedo.

torpiller [tɔrpi'je], *v.t.* to torpedo.

torpilleur [tɔrpi'jœːr], *n.m.* torpedo boat.

torréfier [tɔre'fje], *v.t.* to torrefy, to roast (*coffee*).

torrent [tɔ'rã], *n.m.* torrent, stream; flood (*of tears etc.*); flow (*of words etc.*).

torrentiel [tɔrã'sjɛl], **torrentueux** [tɔrã'tɥø], *a.* (*fem.* **-elle**, **-euse**) torrential; impetuous.

torride [tɔ'rid], *a.* torrid.

tors [tɔr], *a.* (*fem.* **torse** (1) or **torte**) twisted, wreathed, contorted; wry, crooked.—*n.m.* twisting (*of ropes etc.*); torsion.

torsade [tɔr'sad], *n.f.* twisted fringe or cord; bullion (*on epaulets etc.*).

torse (2) [tɔrs], *n.m.* torso, trunk, bust.

torsion [tɔr'sjɔ̃], *n.f.* torsion, twisting.

tort [tɔːr], *n.m.* wrong, injustice; harm, injury, mischief, offence; prejudice, detriment; *à tort ou à raison*, rightly or wrongly; *avoir tort*, to be wrong.

torticolis [tɔrtikɔ'li], *n.m.* wryneck, stiff neck; crick (*in the neck*).

tortiller [tɔrti'je], *v.t.* to twist.—*v.i.* to wriggle, to shuffle; to prevaricate. **se tortiller**, *v.r.* to wriggle, to writhe.

tortionnaire [tɔrsjɔ'nɛːr], *n.m.* executioner, torturer.

tortu [tɔr'ty], *a.* crooked, tortuous; *jambes tortues*, bandy legs.

tortue [tɔr'ty], *n.f.* tortoise; *tortue de mer*, turtle.

tortueux [tɔr'tɥø], *a.* (*fem.* **-euse**) tortuous, winding, crooked; (*fig.*) artful, crafty.

torture [tɔr'ty:r], *n.f.* torture; the rack.

torturer [tɔrty're], *v.t.* to torture, to put on the rack.

tôt [to], *adv.* soon, quickly; early; *au plus tôt* or *le plus tôt possible*, as soon as possible; *tôt ou tard*, sooner or later.

total [tɔ'tal], *a.* (*m. pl.* **-aux**) total, whole, entire; utter.—*n.m.* whole, total, sum total.

totalement [tɔtal'mã], *adv.* totally, wholly, utterly, completely.

totalisateur [tɔtaliza'tœ:r], *n.m.* calculating-machine; totalisator.

totaliser [tɔtali'ze], *v.t.* to tot up, to total up.

totalitaire [tɔtali'tɛ:r], *a.* totalitarian.

totalitarisme [tɔtalita'rism], *n.m.* totalitarianism.

totalité [tɔtali'te], *n.f.* totality, whole.

touage [twa:ʒ], *n.m.* towage, towing, warping.

toucan [tu'kã], *n.m.* toucan.

touchant [tu'ʃã], *a.* touching, moving, affecting.—*n.m.* the moving, affecting or impressive part.—*prep.* concerning, with regard to.

touche [tuʃ], *n.f.* touch; assay, trial; (*Paint. etc.*) manner, style; key (*of piano, typewriter etc.*); stop (*of organ*); (*Fishing*) nibble, bite; (*Fenc. etc.*) hit; drove of cattle; *pierre de touche*, touchstone.

touche-à-tout [tuʃa'tu], *a. inv.* meddling.—*n. inv.* meddler; jack-of-all-trades.

toucher [tu'ʃe], *v.t.* to touch; to handle, to feel, to finger; to assay, to try (*precious metals etc.*); to receive (*money*); to hit; to offend; to move, to affect; to whip, to drive (*animals*); to play on (*a musical instrument*); to express, to describe; to allude to; to concern, to regard; *toucher un chèque*, to cash a check.—*v.i.* to touch, to meddle (*à*); to reach; to play (*on a musical instrument*); to draw near, to be related, to be like; to concern; (*Naut.*) to go aground. **se toucher**, *v.r.* to touch, to touch each other; to be adjoining.—*n.m.* touch, feeling.

toue [tu], *n.f.* barge.

touée [tu'e], *n.f.* towing, warping; towline.

touer [tu'e], *v.t.* to tow, to warp.

toueur [tu'œ:r], *n.m.* towboat, tug.

touffe [tuf], *n.f.* tuft, clump, bunch, wisp.

touffer [tu'fe], *v.t.* to arrange in tufts.—*v.i.* to grow in a tuft or tufts.

touffu [tu'fy], *a.* tufted, bushy, leafy; full, thick; labored (*of style*).

toujours [tu'ʒu:r], *adv.* always, ever, for ever; still; all the same, nevertheless, at least; *toujours est-il que* .., still, the fact remains that . . . .

toupet [tu'pɛ], *n.m.* tuft of hair; forelock; front, foretop (*on a horse*); (*colloq.*) effrontery, cheek, impudence.

toupie [tu'pi], *n.f.* top, spinning-top.

toupiller [tupi'je], *v.i.* to spin, to whirl round and round.

tour (1) [tu:r], *n.f.* tower; (*Chess*) rook, castle.

tour (2) [tu:r], *n.m.* turn, winding; revolution; circumference, circuit; twist, strain; tour, trip; trick; feat; *à tour de rôle*, in turn; *tour de force*, feat of strength; *tour de reins*, sprain in the back.

tour (3) [tu:r], *n.m.* lathe.

tourangeau [turã'ʒo], *a.* (*fem.* **-elle**, *m. pl.* **-eaux**) of Touraine.—*n.m.* (**Tourangeau**, *fem.* **-elle**) native of Touraine.

tourbe [turb], *n.f.* mob, rabble; peat, turf.

tourbeux [tur'bø], *a.* (*fem.* **-euse**) peaty.

tourbillon [turbi'jõ], *n.m.* whirlwind; whirlpool, eddy; (*fig.*) hurly-burly, bustle.

tourbillonner [turbijo'ne], *v.i.* to whirl, to eddy; to swirl.

tourelle [tu'rɛl], *n.f.* turret; gun turret; *tourelle de veille*, conning tower.

touret [tu're], *n.m.* wheel (*of a lathe etc.*); angler's reel.

tourie [tu'ri], *n.f.* carboy.

tourillon [turi'jõ], *n.m.* axle; axle-tree, arbor; spindle, pivot.

tourisme [tu'rism], *n.m.* touring, tourism.

touriste [tu'rist], *n.* tourist.

tourment [tur'mã], *n.m.* torment, torture; anguish, pain; agony of mind.

tourmente [tur'mã:t], *n.f.* tempest, storm; (*fig.*) disturbance, turmoil.

tourmenter [turmã'te], *v.t.* to torment, to torture, to rack; to distress, to harass; to worry; to jolt; to toss. **se tourmenter**, *v.r.* to be uneasy, to fret; to warp (*of wood*); to labor hard (*of a ship*).

tourmenteur [turmã'tœ:r], *a.* (*fem.* **-euse**) torturing, tormenting.—*n.m.* (*fem.* **-euse**) torturer, tormentor.

tournailler [turna'je], *v.i.* (*colloq.*) to prowl round.

tournant [tur'nã], *a.* turning, winding; *plaque tournante*, turn-table; *pont tournant*, swing-bridge.—*n.m.* turn, turning, bend; street corner; (*fig.*) indirect means; turning-point.

tourné [tur'ne], *a.* turned, shaped; expressed; sour, spoilt; *avoir l'esprit mal tourné*, to be cross-grained.

tournebroche [turnə'brɔʃ], *n.m.* roasting-jack; turnspit.

tourne-disques [turnə'disk], *n.m. inv.* record player.

tournedos [turnə'do], *n.m. inv.* filet mignon.

tournée [tur'ne], *n.f.* round, turn, visit, journey; circuit.

tournemain (en un) [ãnœ̃turnə'mɛ̃], *adv. phr.* in a trice.

tourner [tur'ne], *v.t.* to turn; to turn round, to revolve, to twirl; to wind; (*Cine.*) to shoot (*a film*); to convert; to interpret; to shape.—*v.i.* to turn, to turn round, to revolve; to turn out; to change; to ripen; to spoil, to curdle (*of liquids*). **se tourner**, *v.r.* to turn round; to turn; to change.

tournesol [turnə'sɔl], *n.m.* turnsole, sunflower; (*Chem.*) litmus.

tourneur [tur'nœ:r], *n.m.* turner.

tournevent [turnə'vã], *n.m.* cowl (*for chimney*).

tournevis [turnə'vis], *n.m.* screwdriver.

tourniole [tur'njɔl], *n.f.* whitlow.

tourniquet [turni'ke], *n.m.* turnstile; swivel; (*Surg.*) tourniquet.

tournoi [tur'nwa], *n.m.* tournament.

tournoiement [turnwa'mã], *n.m.* turning round, whirling, swirling; dizziness.

tournoyer [turnwa'je], *v.i.* (*conjug. like* EMPLOYER) to turn round and round, to wind; to eddy; (*fig.*) to beat about the bush, to shilly-shally.

tournure [tur′ny:r], *n.f.* turn, direction, course; figure, shape; (*fig.*) cast (*of mind, style etc.*); phrase, construction (*of language*); **les choses commencent à prendre une mauvaise tournure,** things are beginning to look bad.

tourte [turt], *n.f.* covered pie; round loaf.

tourtereau [turtə′ro], *n.m.* (*pl.* **-eaux**) young turtle-dove; (*pl.*) (*fam.*) lovers.

tourterelle [turtə′rɛl], *n.f.* turtle-dove.

Toussaint [tu′sɛ̃], **la,** *f.* All Saints' Day.

tousser [tu′se], *v.i.* to cough.

tout [tu; *liaison-form,* tut], *a.* (*m. pl.* **tous**) all; whole, the whole of; every; each; any; **tous les jours,** every day; **toutes les fois que,** as often as, every time that; **tout le monde,** all the world, everybody.—*pron. indef.* (*m. pl. pronounced* tu:s) all, everything; (*pl.*) all men; **à tout prendre,** on the whole; **comme tout,** exceedingly, extremely; **du tout,** not at all; **en tout,** in all, on the whole.—*n.m.* whole, the whole; the chief point, only thing.—*adv.* wholly, entirely, quite, thoroughly; all, altogether; although, however, for all; **parler tout haut,** to speak aloud; **tout à coup,** suddenly; **tout à fait,** quite, entirely; **tout à l'heure,** just now; presently; **tout à vous,** sincerely yours; **tout beau** or **tout doux,** softly, gently, not so fast; **tout de bon,** in earnest; **tout de suite,** immediately; **tout nu,** stark naked.

toutefois [tut′fwa], *adv.* yet, nevertheless, however, still.

toute-puissance [tutpɥi′sɑ̃:s], *n.f.* omnipotence, almighty power.

tout-puissant [tupɥi′sɑ̃], *a.* (*fem.* **toute-puissante**) almighty. — *n.m.* (**Tout-Puissant**) the Almighty.

toux [tu], *n.f. inv.* cough.

toxémie [tɔkse′mi], *n.f.* (*Med.*) toxemia, blood poisoning.

toxique [tɔk′sik], *a.* toxic, poisonous.—*n.m.* poison.

tracas [tra′kɑ], *n.m.* bustle, turmoil, disturbance; worry, annoyance.

tracassement [trakas′mɑ̃], *n.m.* worrying.

tracasser [traka′se], *v.t.* to worry, to pester. **se tracasser,** *v.r.* to worry.

tracasserie [trakas′ri], *n.f.* worry, pestering, annoyance, vexation; (*pl.*) bickering.

tracassier [traka′sje], *a.* (*fem.* **-ière**) pestering, worrying, annoying; fussy; mischief-making.—*n.m.* (*fem.* **-ière**) pesterer, busybody; troublesome person, mischief-maker.

trace [tras], *n.f.* trace, track, footprint; spoor, trail; mark, impression, vestige; outline, sketch.

tracé [tra′se], *n.m.* outline, sketch (*of figure*); marking out; laying out (*of grounds etc.*); direction.

tracement [tras′mɑ̃], *n.m.* tracing, laying out (*of grounds, roads etc.*).

tracer [tra′se], *v.t.* (*conjug. like* COMMENCER) to trace, to draw, to trace out; to sketch; to portray; to lay out (*grounds, roads etc.*); (*fig.*) to set forth, to mark out.—*v.i.* to spread roots (*of trees*); to burrow (*of moles*).

trachée [tra′ʃe], *n.f.* trachea, air vessel.

trachée-artère [traʃear′tɛ:r], *n.f.* (*pl.* **trachées-artères**) trachea, windpipe.

tract [trakt], *n.m.* tract, leaflet (*for propaganda*).

tracteur [trak′tœ:r], *n.m.* tractor, traction engine.

traction [trak′sjɔ̃], *n.f.* traction; pulling; draft. t; **traction avant,** front-wheel drive.

tradition [tradi′sjɔ̃], *n.f.* tradition; (*Law*) delivery.

traditionnel [tradisjɔ′nɛl], *a.* (*fem.* **-elle**) traditional.

traducteur [tradyk′tœ:r], *n.m.* (*fem.* **-trice**) translator.

traduction [tradyk′sjɔ̃], *n.f.* translation, (*sch.*) crib, pony.

traduire [tra′dɥi:r], *v.t. irr.* (*conjug. like* CONDUIRE) to translate; to interpret, to construe; to convey, to express; to indicate, to denote.

traduisible [tradɥi′zibl], *a.* translatable.

trafic [tra′fik], *n.m.* traffic; trading, trade; dealings.

trafiquant [trafi′kɑ̃], *n.m.* (*fem.* **-e**) trafficker.

trafiquer [trafi′ke], *v.i.* to traffic, to trade, to deal (*de*).

tragédie [traʒe′di], *n.f.* tragedy.

tragédien [traʒe′djɛ̃], *n.m.* (*fem.* **-enne**) tragedian.

tragique [tra′ʒik], *a.* tragic, tragical.—*n.m.* tragedy, tragic art; tragic writer.

trahir [tra′i:r], *v.t.* to betray; to deceive; to divulge, to reveal. **se trahir,** *v.r.* to betray oneself; to betray each other.

trahison [trai′zɔ̃], *n.f.* treachery, treason, perfidy; breach of faith.

train [trɛ̃], *n.m.* pace, rate; train, suite, attendants; way, manner; noise, clatter, dust; carriage; quarters (*of a horse etc.*); (*Rail.*) train; **à fond de train,** at full speed; **être en train de faire quelque chose,** to be (in the act of) doing something; **train de maison,** style of living; **train de marchandises,** freight train; **train omnibus,** slow or local train.

traînage [trɛ′na:ʒ], *n.m.* dragging, drawing; sledging, sleighing.

traînant [trɛ′nɑ̃], *a.* dragging, trailing (*dress*); drawling (*voice*); shuffling (*gait*).

traînard [trɛ′na:r], *n.m.* straggler, laggard; slow-coach.

traîne [trɛ:n], *n.f.* dragging, being dragged or drawn; train (*of a dress etc.*).

traîneau [trɛ′no], *n.m.* (*pl.* **-eaux**) sledge, sleigh; drag-net.

traînée [trɛ′ne], *n.f.* train (*of gunpowder etc.*); trail, track.

traîner [trɛ′ne], *v.t.* to drag, to draw; to track; to spin out, to drag out, to protract; to drawl; to put off.—*v.i.* to trail, to draggle, to lag; to droop; to languish, to flag; to lie about; to loiter, to linger, to be protracted. **se traîner,** *v.r.* to crawl along, to creep; to lag, to drag oneself along.

train-train [trɛ̃′trɛ̃], *n.m.* (*colloq.*) routine, regular course.

traire [trɛ:r], *v.t. irr.* to milk; to draw (*milk*).

trait [trɛ], *n.m.* arrow, dart, bolt, shaft; thunderbolt; stroke, hit; trace (*of harness*); leash (*for dogs*); turn (*of the scale*); draft, gulp; dash (*of the pen etc.*); flash (*of light*); stroke, touch; trait, feature, lineament; act, deed; prime move (*at chess, draughts etc.*); *avoir trait à*, to have reference to; *boire à longs traits*, to drink long draughts of; *d'un seul trait*, at one gulp; *trait de génie*, stroke of genius, (*fam.*) brain-wave; *trait d'union*, hyphen.

traite [trɛt], *n.f.* stage, journey, stretch; milking; (*Comm.*) draft, bill; *traite des noirs*, slave trade.

traité [trɛ'te], *n.m.* treatise, tract, dissertation; treaty; agreement.

traitement [trɛt'mã], *n.m.* treatment; (*Ind.*) processing; reception; salary, pay.

traiter [trɛ'te], *v.t.* to treat; (*Ind.*) to process; to entertain; to use, to behave to; to discuss, to handle; to call, to style; to negotiate; to execute, to do.—*v.i.* to treat, to negotiate.

traiteur [trɛ'tœːr], *n.m.* restaurant keeper; caterer.

traître -[trɛ:tr], *a.* (*fem.* **-esse**) treacherous, perfidious.—*n.m.* (*fem.* **-esse**) treacherous person, traitor, traitress.

traîtreusement [trɛtrøz'mã], *adv.* treacherously.

traîtrise [trɛ'tri:z], *n.f.* treachery.

trajectoire [traʒɛk'twa:r], *a.* and *n.f.* trajectory.

trajet [tra'ʒɛ], *n.m.* passage, journey, crossing, voyage; (*Med.*) course.

trame [tram], *n.f.* weft, woof; plot, conspiracy; course, progress, thread.

tramer [tra'me], *v.t.* to weave; (*fig.*) to plot, to contrive, to hatch.

tramontane [tramɔ̃'tan], *n.f.* tramontane, north wind; north; North Star.

tramway [tra'mwɛ], *n.m.* trolley car.

tranchant [trã'ʃã], *a.* sharp, cutting; (*fig.*) trenchant, decisive; salient, prominent.—*n.m.* edge.

tranche [trã:ʃ], *n.f.* slice, chop; slab; edge (*of a book*); *doré sur tranche*, gilt-edged (*of a book*); *tranche de lard*, rasher of bacon.

tranchée [trã'ʃe], *n.f.* trench, cutting; (*pl.*) colic.

trancher [trã'ʃe], *v.t.* to cut; to cut off; to slice; to decide, to determine, to settle.—*v.i.* to cut; to decide; to set up for; to affect; to be glaring (*of colors*).

tranchoir [trã'ʃwa:r], *n.m.* trencher, cutting-board.

tranquille [trã'kil], *a.* quiet, calm, tranquil, placid, peaceful; undisturbed (*in mind etc.*); *soyez tranquille*, set your mind at ease.

tranquillement [trãkil'mã], *adv.* peacefully, quietly.

tranquillisant [trãkili'zã], *a.* tranquillizing. —*n.m.* tranquillizer.

tranquilliser [trãkili'ze], *v.t.* to tranquillize, to make easy, to soothe. **se tranquilliser**, *v.r.* to become tranquil, to calm down.

tranquillité [trãkili'te], *n.f.* tranquillity, quiet, peace.

transaction [trãzak'sjɔ̃], *n.f.* transaction, arrangement.

transalpin [trãzal'pɛ̃], *a.* transalpine.

transatlantique [trãzatlã'tik], *a.* transatlantic.—*n.m.* liner; deck chair.

transborder [trãsbɔr'de], *v.t.* to tranship.

transbordeur [trãsbɔr'dœːr], *n.m.* transporter; *pont transbordeur*, transporter bridge.

transcendant [trãsã'dã], *a.* transcendent.

transcription [trãskrip'sjɔ̃], *n.f.* transcription, transcript, copy.

transcrire [trã'skri:r], *v.t. irr.* (*conjug. like* ÉCRIRE) to transcribe, to copy out.

transe [trã:s], *n.f.* fright, apprehension; trance.

transférable [trãsfe'rabl], *a.* transferable.

transférer [trãsfe're], *v.t.* (*conjug. like* CÉDER) to transfer, to transport, to convey, to move.

transfert [trãs'fe:r], *n.m.* transfer.

transfiguration [trãsfigyra'sjɔ̃], *n.f.* transfiguration.

transfigurer [trãsfigy're], *v.t.* to transfigure. **se transfigurer**, *v.r.* to be transfigured.

transformateur [trãsfɔrma'tœːr], *n.m.* (*Elec.*) transformer.

transformation [trãsfɔrma'sjɔ̃], *n.f.* transformation.

transformer [trãsfɔr'me], *v.t.* to transform; to change, to convert. **se transformer**, *v.r.* to be transformed.

transfuge [trãs'fy:ʒ], *n.m.* deserter; fugitive; turncoat.

transgresser [trãsgrɛ'se], *v.t.* to transgress, to infringe, to contravene.

transgression [trãsgrɛ'sjɔ̃], *n.f.* transgression.

transhumance [trãzy'mã:s], *n.f.* transhumance.

transi [trã'zi], *a.* chilled, benumbed.

transiger [trãzi'ʒe], *v.i.* (*conjug. like* MANGER) to compound, to compromise, to come to terms (*avec*).

transir [trã'zi:r], *v.t.* to chill, to benumb; to paralyse.—*v.i.* to be chilled; to be paralyzed (*with fear etc.*).

transissement [trãzis'mã], *n.m.* chill, numbness; shivering (*with terror etc.*).

transistor [trãzis'tɔr], *n.m.* transistor.

transit [trã'zit], *n.m.* transit.

transitaire [trãzi'te:r], *a.* pertaining to the transit of goods.

transitif [trãzi'tif], *a.* (*fem.* **-tive**) transitive.

transition [trãzi'sjɔ̃], *n.f.* transition.

transitoire [trãzi'twa:r], *a.* transitory.

translation [trãsla'sjɔ̃], *n.f.* transfer(ring), relaying.

translucide [trãsly'sid], *a.* translucent.

translucidité [trãslysidi'te], *n.f.* translucence.

transmarin [trãsma'rɛ̃], *a.* transmarine, oversea.

transmetteur [trãsmɛ'tœːr], *n.m.* (*Rad.*) transmitter.

transmettre [trãs'mɛtr], *v.t. irr.* (*conjug. like* METTRE) to transmit, to convey, to send on; to transfer.

transmigration [trãsmigra'sjɔ̃], *n.f.* transmigration.

transmigrer [trãsmi'gre], *v.i.* to transmigrate.

transparence [trãspa'rã:s], *n.f.* transparency.

transparent [trãspa'rã], *a.* transparent.—*n.m.* paper ruled with black lines; transparency.

transpercer [trãspɛr'se], *v.t.* (*conjug. like* COMMENCER) to pierce through; to run through (*with a sword etc.*), to transfix.

transpiration [trãspira'sjɔ̃], *n.f.* perspiration, perspiring.

transpirer [trãspi're], *v.i.* to perspire; to ooze out; to transpire.

transplanter [trăsplă'te], *v.t.* to transplant.
transport [trɑ̀s'pɔ:r], *n.m.* carriage, conveyance; transport, removal; transfer, assignment; (*fig.*) rapture, ecstasy; transport ship; *transport au cerveau*, stroke, fit of delirium.
transportation [trăspɔrta'sjɔ̃], *n.f.* transportation.
transporté [trăspɔr'te], *n.m.* (*fem.* **-ée**) deported person, convict.
transporter [trăspɔr'te], *v.t.* to convey, to transport; to transfer; to banish; to enrapture. **se transporter**, *v.r.* to transport oneself, to go.
transporteur [trăspɔr'tœ:r], *n.m.* carrier, conveyor.
transposer [trăspo'ze], *v.t.* to transpose.
transposition [trăspozi'sjɔ̃], *n.f.* transposition.
transrhénan [trăsre'nɑ̃], *a.* from beyond the Rhine.
transsubstantiation [trăssybstɑ̃sja'sjɔ̃], *n.f.* transubstantiation.
transvaser [trăsva'ze], *v.t.* to decant.
transversal [trɑ̀zvɛr'sal], *a.* (*m.pl.* **-aux**) transversal, transverse.
trapèze [tra'pɛ:z], *n.m.* trapezium; trapeze.
trappe [trap], *n.f.* trap door; trap, pitfall; curtain, register (*of chimney*).
trappeur [tra'pœ:r], *n.m.* trapper.
trappiste [tra'pist], *a.* and *n.m.* Trappist.
trapu [tra'py], *a.* squat, dumpy, thick-set, stocky.
traquer [tra'ke], *v.t.* (*Hunt.*) to beat for game; to enclose, to encircle; to track down.
travail [tra'va:j], *n.m.* (*pl.* **-aux**) labor, work; toil; travail; piece of work; workmanship; occupation; study; *cabinet de travail*, study (*room*); *travaux forcés*, hard labor.
travaillé [travo'je], *a.* worked, wrought; labored, elaborate; laboring (*under*).
travailler [travo'je], *v.t.* to work, to work at; to do with care; to fashion; to till (*the ground*).—*v.i.* to labor, to work; to study; to strive; to ferment (*of wines*); to warp (*of wood*). **se travailler**, *v.r.* to torment oneself; to be overwrought.
travailleur [travo'jœ:r], *a.* (*fem.* **-euse**) industrious, hard-working; painstaking.— *n.m.* (*fem.* **-euse**) workman, laborer; hard-working person.
travailliste [travo'jist], *a.* Labour, Socialist. —*n.* member of the Labour Party.
travée [tra've], *n.f.* (*Arch.*) bay; truss (*of bridges*); (*Av.*) rib (*of wing*).
travers [tra'vɛ:r], *n.m.* breadth; fault, failing; oddity; (*Naut.*) side, broadside; *à travers*, across; *au travers de*, through; *de travers*, obliquely, awry, askew; *en travers*, across, crosswise; *à tort et à travers*, at random.
traverse [tra'vɛrs], *n.f.* cross-bar, cross-piece; cross-road, short cut; (*Rail.*) tie; (*pl.*) (*fig.*) setbacks.
traversée [traver'se], *n.f.* passage, crossing.
traverser [traver'se], *v.t.* to cross, to go over *or* through, to traverse; to get through *or* across; to run through (*with a sword etc.*); to lie across; to span; to intersect; to penetrate; to thwart.

traversier [traver'sje], *a.* (*fem.* **-ière**) cross-; that plies across.
traversin [traver'sɛ̃], *n.m.* bolster; (*Carp. etc.*) cross-beam; (*Naut.*) stretcher (*in boats*).
travesti [travɛs'ti], *a.* disguised; travestied, parodied.
travestir [travɛs'ti:r], *v.t.* to disguise, to travesty; (*fig.*) to misrepresent.
travestissement [travɛstis'mɑ̃], *n.m.* disguise; travesty.
trébuchant [treby'ʃɑ̃], *a.* of full weight (*of coins*); stumbling.
trébucher [treby'je], *v.i.* to stumble, to slip; to err; (*fig.*) to turn the scale.
trébuchet [treby'ʃɛ], *n.m.* bird trap; assay-balance.
tréfiler [trefi'le], *v.t.* to wire-draw.
trèfle [trɛfl], *n.m.* trefoil, clover; (*Cards*) clubs; *trèfle blanc*, shamrock.
tréfonds [tre'fɔ̃], *n.m.* subsoil; (*fig.*) bottom; heart.
treillage [trɛ'ja:ʒ], *n.m.* trellis(-work), lattice-work.
treille [trɛ:j], *n.f.* vine trellis; shrimp net.
treillis [trɛ'ji], *n.m.* trellis, lattice; coarse canvas etc., sackcloth.
treizaine [trɛ'zɛn], *n.f.* baker's dozen.
treize [trɛ:z], *a.* and *n.m.* thirteen; thirteenth.
treizième [trɛ'zjɛm], *a.* and *n.* thirteenth (part).
tréma [tre'ma], *n.m.* dieresis.
tremblant [trɑ̃'blɑ̃], *a.* trembling, quivering; flickering (*of light etc.*).
tremble [trɑ̃:bl], *n.m.* aspen.
tremblé [trɑ̃'ble], *a.* wavy (*of lines*); shaky (*of writing*).
tremblement [trɑ̃blə'mɑ̃], *n.m.* trembling, shaking, quaking, trepidation, tremor; flickering (*of light*); (*Mus.*) tremolo; *tremblement de terre*, earthquake.
trembler [trɑ̃'ble], *v.i.* to tremble, to shake, to shiver; to quake, to fear; to flutter (*of wings*).
tremblotant [trɑ̃blo'tɑ̃], *a.* trembling, tremulous (*of sound etc.*); shivering, quivering, fluttering.
tremblotement [trɑ̃blɔt'mɑ̃], *n.m.* trembling, shivering.
trembloter [trɑ̃blɔ'te], *v.i.* to tremble (*of sound*); to quiver, to shiver; to flutter (*of wings*); to flicker (*of light*).
trémousser [tremu'se], *v.t.* to bestir, to move about, to flutter.—*v.i.* to shake, to stir. **se trémousser**, *v.r.* to flutter *or* frisk about; to bestir oneself.
trempage [trɑ̃'pa:ʒ], *n.m.* steeping, soaking; (*Print.*) wetting.
trempe [trɑ̃:p], *n.f.* temper (*of steel etc.*); (*fig.*) character, stamp, quality.
tremper [trɑ̃'pe], *v.t.* to soak, to steep, to wet, to drench; to temper (*iron, steel etc.*); to dilute (*wine etc.*).—*v.i.* to soak, to be steeped; to be implicated (*in a crime*).
tremplin [trɑ̃'plɛ̃], *n.m.* spring-board, diving board; trampoline.
trentaine [trɑ̃'tɛn], *n.f.* about thirty; age of thirty.
trente [trɑ̃:t], *a.* and *n.m.* thirty; thirtieth.
trentième [trɑ̃'tjɛm], *a.* and *n.* thirtieth (part).

318

trépan [tre'pɑ̃], *n.m.* trepan (*instrument*); trepanning.

trépaner [trepa'ne], *v.t.* to trepan.

trépas [tre'pɑ], *n.m. inv.* (*poet.*) decease, death.

trépassé [trepa'se], *n.m.* (*fem.* **-ée**) dead person.

trépasser [trepa'se], *v.i.* to depart this life, to pass away.

trépidant [trepi'dɑ̃], *a.* vibrating; (*fig.*) agitated, hectic.

trépidation [trepida'sjɔ̃], *n.f.* trepidation, trembling; agitation.

trépied [tre'pje], *n.m.* trivet; tripod.

trépignement [trepiɲ'mɑ̃], *n.m.* stamping (*of feet*).

trépigner [trepi'ɲe], *v.i.* to stamp, to stamp one's foot.

très [trɛ], *adv.* very; most; very much.

trésor [tre'zɔ:r], *n.m.* treasure; treasury; exchequer; thesaurus.

trésorerie [trezɔr'ri], *n.f.* treasury; treasurership.

trésorier [trezɔ'rje], *n.m.* treasurer; (*Mil.*) paymaster.

tressage [trɛ'sa:ʒ], *n.m.* plaiting, braiding.

tressaillement [trɛsaj'mɑ̃], *n.m.* start, bound, thrill, shudder; flutter.

tressaillir [trɛsa'jir], *v.i. irr.* (*conjug. like* ASSAILLIR) to start, to thrill; to quake, to tremble, to shudder.

tresse [trɛs], *n.f.* tress, plait (*of hair*); braid.

tresser [trɛ'se], *v.t.* to weave, to plait, to braid; to wreathe.

tréteau [tre'to], *n.m.* (*pl.* **-eaux**) trestle; (*pl.*) stage.

treuil [trœːj], *n.m.* windlass; winch.

trêve [trɛːv], *n.f.* truce.

tri [tri], *n.m.* sorting (*of letters etc.*).

triage [tri'ja:ʒ], *n.m.* picking, sorting; choice, selection.

triangle [tri'jɑ̃:gl], *n.m.* triangle.

triangulaire [trijɑ̃gy'lɛːr], *a.* triangular.

tribord [tri'bɔːr], *n.m.* (*Naut.*) starboard.

tribu [tri'by], *n.f.* tribe.

tribulation [tribyla'sjɔ̃], *n.f.* tribulation.

tribun [tri'bœ̃], *n.m.* tribune; (*fig.*) democratic leader.

tribunal [triby'nal], *n.m.* (*pl.* **-aux**) tribunal, bench; court of justice.

tribune [tri'byn], *n.f.* tribune (*rostrum*); hustings; gallery.

tribut [tri'by], *n.m.* tribute; grant, contribution; *duty; (*fig.*) debt.

tributaire [triby'tɛːr], *a.* dependent (*upon*).—*n.m.* tributary.

tricher [tri'ʃe], *v.t., v.i.* to cheat, to trick.

tricherie [triʃ'ri], *n.f.* cheating, trick, trickery.

tricheur [tri'ʃœːr], *n.m.* (*fem.* **-euse**) cheat, trickster.

tricolore [trikɔ'lɔːr], *a.* tricolored.

tricorne [tri'kɔrn], *a.* three-cornered.—*n.m.* three-cornered hat.

tricot [tri'ko], *n.m.* knitting; jersey, jumper, (*fam.*) woolly; *tricot de corps*, vest.

tricotage [trikɔ'ta:ʒ], *n.m.* knitting.

tricoter [trikɔ'te], *v.t., v.i.* to knit.

trictrac [trik'trak], *n.m.* tric-trac (*form of backgammon*).

tricycle [tri'sikl], *n.m.* three-wheeled vehicle; tricycle.

trident [tri'dɑ̃], *n.m.* trident.

triennal [triɛ'nal], *a.* (*m. pl.* **-aux**) triennial.

trier [tri'je], *v.t.* to pick, to choose, to sort, to select; to route (freight cars).

trieur [tri'jœːr], *n.m.* (*fem.* **-euse**) sorter, picker.

trigonométrie [trigɔnɔme'tri], *n.f.* trigonometry.

trille [tri:j], *n.m.* quaver, trill.

triller [tri'je], *v.t.* to trill, to quaver.

trillion [tri'ljɔ̃], *n.m.* (*since 1948 = 1 followed by 18 ciphers*) trillion, one million billion(s); (*Am.*) quintillion.

trilogie [trilɔ'ʒi], *n.f.* trilogy.

trimbaler [trɛ̃ba'le], *v.t.* (*fam.*) to drag or lug about (*parcels*); to trail (*children*) about. **se trimbaler**, *v.r.* (*pop.*) to traipse round.

trimer [tri'me], *v.i.* (*pop.*) to drudge, to wear oneself out.

trimestre [tri'mɛstr], *n.m.* quarter (*three months*); quarter's pay; (*Sch.*) term.

trimestriel [trimɛstri'ɛl], *a.* (*fem.* **-elle**) quarterly.

tringle [trɛ̃:gl], *n.f.* rod.

Trinité [trini'te], *n.f.* Trinity; *la Trinité*, Trinity Sunday; (*l'Île de*) *la Trinité*, Trinidad.

trinquer [trɛ̃'ke], *v.i.* to clink glasses (*before drinking*); to drink to one another's health; (*pop.*) to suffer, to be hurt.

trio [tri'o], *n.m.* trio.

triomphal [triɔ̃'fal], *a.* (*m. pl.* **-aux**) triumphal.

triomphalement [triɔ̃fal'mɑ̃], *adv.* triumphantly.

triomphant [triɔ̃'fɑ̃], *a.* triumphant.

triomphe [tri'ɔ̃:f], *n.m.* triumph.

triompher [triɔ̃'fe], *v.i.* to triumph; to overcome; to exult; to excel.

triparti [tripar'ti], **tripartite** [tripar'tit], *a.* tripartite.

tripe [trip], *n.f.* tripe; imitation velvet, velveteen (*also called tripe de velours*).

triperie [trip'ri], *n.f.* tripe shop.

triple [tripl], *a.* and *n.m.* treble, triple, threefold.

tripler [tri'ple], *v.t., v.i.* to treble, to triple.

triplicata [triplika'ta], *n.m. inv.* triplicate.

tripode [tri'pɔd], *a.* and *n.m.* tripod.

tripot [tri'po], *n.m.* gambling den; house of ill fame.

tripotage [tripɔ'ta:ʒ], *n.m.* mess; underhand dealing; chore.

tripoter [tripɔ'te], *v.t.* to meddle with; to speculate in.—*v.i.* to make mischief, to mess about; to act in an underhand way.

tripoteur [tripɔ'tœːr], *n.m.* (*fem.* **-euse**) mischief-maker, shady speculator.

trique [trik], *n.f.* (*fam.*) cudgel, stick, bludgeon.

trisaïeul [triza'jœl], *n.m.* (*pl.* **-aïeuls**) great-great-grandfather.

trisaïeule [triza'jœl], *n.f.* great-great-grandmother.

triste [trist], *a.* sorrowful, mournful, sad, melancholy, dejected; dull, dreary, dismal; poor, sorry (*of persons*); mean, paltry.

tristement [tristə'mɑ̃], *adv.* sadly.

tristesse [tris'tɛs], *n.f.* sadness; melancholy; dreariness.

triton [tri'tɔ̃], *n.m.* triton, newt.

trivial [tri'vjal], *a.* (*m. pl.* **-aux**) vulgar, trifling; trite, hackneyed.—*n.m.* vulgarity.

trivialité [trivjali'te], *n.f.* vulgarity; triteness.
troc [trɔk], *n.m.* trade, barter, swap.
troène [trɔ'ɛn], *n.m.* privet.
troglodyte [trɔglɔ'dit], *n.m.* troglodyte.
trogne [trɔɲ], *n.f.* reddish *or* bloated face.
trognon [trɔ'ɲɔ̃], *n.m.* core (*of a pear or apple*); stump (*of a cabbage*).
Troie [trwa], *f.* Troy.
trois [trwa], *a.* and *n.m. inv.* three; third.
troisième [trwa'zjɛm], *a.* third.—*n.* third.— *n.m.* third floor.
troisièmement [trwazjɛm'mã], *adv.* thirdly.
trombe [trɔ̃:b], *n.f.* waterspout.
tromblon [trɔ̃'blɔ̃], *n.m.* blunderbuss.
trombone [trɔ̃'bɔn], *n.m.* trombone; paper clip (*of wire*).
trompe [trɔ̃:p], *n.f.* *trump, horn; proboscis, trunk (*of elephants*).
tromper [trɔ̃'pe], *v.t.* to deceive, to impose upon; to delude; to cheat, to take in; to betray, to be unfaithful to (*wife, husband*). **se tromper**, *v.r.* to be mistaken, to make a mistake, to deceive oneself.
tromperie [trɔ̃'pri], *n.f.* cheat, fraud; illusion, delusion.
trompeter [trɔ̃pə'te], *v.t.* (*conjug. like* APPELER) to trumpet abroad.
trompette [trɔ̃'pɛt], *n.f.* trumpet.—*n.m.* trumpeter.
trompeur [trɔ̃'pœ:r], *a.* (*fem.* **-euse**) deceitful; false, misleading.—*n.m.* (*fem.* **-euse**) deceiver, cheat, impostor; betrayer.
trompeusement [trɔ̃pøz'mã], *adv.* deceitfully, deceptively.
tronc [trɔ̃], *n.m.* trunk, bole (*of tree*); stock; poor box.
tronçon [trɔ̃'sɔ̃], *n.m.* broken piece, fragment, stump.
tronçonner [trɔ̃sɔ'ne], *v.t.* to cut into pieces.
trône [troːn], *n.m.* throne.
trôner [tro'ne], *v.i.* to sit on a throne; (*fig.*) to lord it.
tronquer [trɔ̃'ke], *v.t.* to mutilate, to truncate; (*fig.*) to garble, to mangle.
trop [tro], *adv.* too much, too, over, too many; **de trop**, too much, too many; **être de trop**, to be in the way, not to be wanted; **par trop**, excessively.—*n.m.* excess, superfluity.
trophée [tro'fe], *n.m.* trophy.
tropical [trɔpi'kal], *a.* (*m. pl.* **-aux**) tropical.
tropique [trɔ'pik], *n.m.* tropic.
trop-plein [trɔ'plɛ̃], *n.m.* (*pl.* **-pleins**) overflow, waste; surplus, excess.
troquer [trɔ'ke], *v.t.* to trade, to barter, to exchange.
trot [tro], *n.m.* trot.
trotte-menu [trɔtmə'ny] *a. inv.* running with little steps, pitter-pattering.
trotter [trɔ'te], *v.i.* to trot; to run about, to toddle (*children*).
trotteur [trɔ'tœːr], *n.m.* (*fem.* **-euse**) trotter. —*n.f.* (**-euse**) second hand (*of watch*).
trottin [trɔ'tɛ̃], *n.m.* errand girl.
trottiner [trɔti'ne], *v.i.* to go at a jog-trot; to toddle along.
trottinette [trɔti'nɛt], *n.f.* (*child's*) scooter.
trottoir [trɔ'twaːr], *n.m.* foot-path, pavement, (*Am.*) sidewalk; **le bord du trottoir**, the curb.
trou [tru], *n.m.* hole; gap; orifice, mouth; **boucher un trou**, to stop a gap, to pay a

debt; **trou d'air**, air pocket; **trou de la serrure**, keyhole; **trou du souffleur**, (*Theat.*) prompter's box.
troubadour [truba'duːr], *n.m.* troubadour.
troublant [tru'blã], *a.* disturbing, troubling.
trouble [trubl], *a.* thick, muddy, turbid, cloudy; dull.—*adv.* dimly, confusedly.— *n.m.* confusion, disorder, disturbance; perplexity, uneasiness; dispute, quarrel; (*pl.*) disturbances, dissensions.
trouble-fête [trublə'fɛːt], *n.m. inv.* kill-joy.
troubler [tru'ble], *v.t.* to disturb, to make thick, to make muddy: to muddle, to turn; to confuse, to agitate; to perplex, to disconcert; to trouble; to interrupt; to ruffle, to annoy; to dim, to dull. **se troubler**, *v.r.* to grow thick, to become muddy; to be confused, to be disconcerted; to become cloudy; to become confused.
trouée [tru'e], *n.f.* opening, gap, breach; pass.
trouer [tru'e], *v.t.* to bore, to make a hole in. **se trouer**, *v.r.* to get holes in it.
trouille [truːj], *n.f.* (*vulg.*) fear.
troupe [trup], *n.f.* troop, band; crew, gang, set; company (*of actors*); flock, crowd; (*pl.*) troops, forces.
troupeau [tru'po], *n.m.* (*pl.* **-eaux**) flock, herd, drove.
troupier [tru'pje], *n.m.* soldier.
trousse [truːs], *n.f.* bundle, truss; (*Surg.*) case of instruments; case for razors, toilet articles etc; **je suis à ses trousses**, I am after him.
troussé [tru'se], *a.* tucked up; **bien troussé**, well set up, neat, dapper.
trousseau [tru'so], *n.m.* (*pl.* **-eaux**) bunch (*of keys*); trousseau; outfit, kit.
trousser [tru'se], *v.t.* to tuck up, to turn up, to pin up; to truss; to dispatch (*business etc.*). **se trousser**, *v.r.* to tuck up one's clothes.
trouvaille [tru'vaːj], *n.f.* godsend, windfall; find.
trouvé [tru've], *a.* found; **bien trouvé**, felicitous; **enfant trouvé**, foundling.
trouver [tru've], *v.t.* to find, to discover, to meet with, to hit upon; to detect; to find out; to deem, to judge; **trouver à dire** or **à redire à**, to find fault with; **trouver bon**, to think fit; **trouver mauvais**, to blame, to be displeased with; **vous trouvez?** you think so, do you? **se trouver**, *v.r.* to find oneself; to be, to exist; to feel; to prove, to turn out; **se trouver mal**, to faint.
truand [try'ã], *a.* vagrant.—*n.m.* (*fem.* **-e**) vagrant, beggar, tramp; crook.
truc (1) [tryk], *n.m.* knack, dodge, trick; (*Theat.*) machinery; (*pop.*) thing, thingumajig, gadget.
truc (2) *or* **truck** [tryk], *n.m.* (*Rail.*) flatcar.
trucheman *or* **truchement** [tryʃ'mã], *n.m.* interpreter; go-between.
truculent [tryky'lã], *a.* truculent.
truelle [try'ɛl], *n.f.* trowel; **truelle à poisson**, slice of fish.
truffe [tryf], *n.f.* truffle.
truie [truɪj], *n.f.* sow.
truite [truɪt], *n.f.* trout.
truité [truɪ'te], *a.* spotted, speckled.
trumeau [try'mo], *n.m.* (*pl.* **-eaux**) pier; pier glass; leg of beef.

tsar [tsa:r], *n.m.* Tsar.

tsigane [TZIGANE].

tu [ty], *pron.* *thou, you.

tuant [ty'ã], *a.* killing, tiresome, laborious.

tube [tyb], *n.m.* tube, pipe; (*Anat.*) duct.

tuberculeux [tybɛrky'lø], *a.* (*fem.* **-euse**) tuberculous.

tuberculose [tybɛrky'lo:z], *n.f.* tuberculosis.

tubulaire [tyby'lɛ:r], *a.* tubular.

tuer [tɥe], *v.t.* to kill, to slay; to slaughter, to butcher; to tire to death; to while away. **se tuer**, *v.r.* to kill oneself, to be killed; (*fig.*) to wear oneself out.

tuerie [ty'ri], *n.f.* slaughter, butchery; slaughter-house.

tue-tête (à) [aty'tɛ:t], *adv. phr.* at the top of one's voice.

tueur [tɥœ:r], *n.m.* (*fem.* **-euse**) killer, thug.

tuile [tɥil], *n.f.* tile.

tuilerie [tɥil'ri], *n.f.* tile-works; **les Tuileries**, the Tuileries (*before 1871 a Royal palace, now a garden in Paris*).

tulipe [ty'lip], *n.f.* tulip.

tulle [tyl], *n.m.* tulle, net.

tumeur [ty'mœ:r], *n.f.* tumor, swelling.

tumulte [ty'mylt], *n.m.* tumult, uproar; hubbub.

tumultueux [tymyl'tɥø], *a.* (*fem.* **-euse**) tumultuous, riotous.

tunique [ty'nik], *n.f.* tunic; envelope, film.

Tunisie [tyni'zi], **la**, *f.* Tunisia.

tunisien [tyni'ʒjɛ̃], *a.* Tunisian.—*n.m.* (**Tunisien**, *fem.* **-enne**) Tunisian (*person*).

tunnel [ty'nɛl], *n.m.* tunnel.

turban [tyr'bã], *n.m.* turban.

turbine [tyr'bin], *n.f.* turbine.

turbopropulseur [tyrbopropyl'sœ:r], *n.m.* turbo-prop.

turboréacteur [tyrboreak'tœ:r], *n.m.* jet engine; turbo-jet.

turbot [tyr'bo], *n.m.* turbot.

turbulence [tyrby'lã:s], *n.f.* turbulence.

turbulent [tyrby'lã], *a.* turbulent, boisterous; rowdy.

turc [tyrk], *a.* (*fem.* **turque**) Turkish.—*n.m.* Turkish (*language*); (**Turc**, *fem.* **Turque**) Turk.

turelure [tyr'ly:r], *n.f.* fol-de-rol (*burden of a song*).

turf [tyrf], *n.m.* the turf, horse racing.

turpitude [tyrpi'tyd], *n.f.* turpitude, baseness, ignominy.

turque [TURC].

Turquie [tyr'ki], **la**, *f.* Turkey.

turquoise [tyr'kwa:z], *a.* and *n.f.* turquoise.

tussor [ty'so:r], *n.m.* tussore (*silk*).

tutelle [ty'tɛl], *n.f.* tutelage, guardianship; (*Polit.*) trusteeship.

tuteur [ty'tœ:r], *n.m.* (*fem.* **tutrice**) guardian, trustee, protector.—*n.m.* (*Hort.*) stake.

tutoiement or tutoîment [tytwa'mã], *n.m.* addressing a person as 'tu', 'theeing and thouing'.

tutoyer [tytwa'je], *v.t.* (*conjug. like* EMPLOYER) to be on intimate terms with. **se tutoyer**, *v.r.* to be on familiar terms.

tutrice [ty'tris], [TUTEUR].

tuyau [tɥi'jo], *n.m.* (*pl.* **-aux**) pipe; tube; (chimney) flue; shaft, funnel; stalk (*of grain*); nozzle (*of bellows etc.*); stem (*of a tobacco pipe*); **tuyau d'arrosage**, garden hose; **tuyau d'incendie**, fire hose; **tuyau de poêle**, stove-pipe.

tuyautage [tɥijo'ta:ʒ], *n.m.* frilling, fluting; tubing.

tuyauter [tɥijo'te], *v.t.* to goffer, to frill.

tuyauterie [tɥijo'tri], *n.f.* system of pipes; plumbing; pipe trade.

tympan [tɛ̃'pã], *n.m.* ear-drum, tympanum; tympan; spandrel.

type [tip], *n.m.* type; model, pattern; symbol, emblem; standard; (*Astron.*) plan, drawing; (*colloq.*) guy, chap, fellow.

typhoïde [tifɔ'id], *a.* typhoid.

typhon [ti'fɔ̃], *n.m.* typhoon.

typhus [ti'fy:s], *n.m.* typhus.

typique [ti'pik], *a.* typical; characteristic.

typographe [tipɔ'graf], *n.m.* typographer.

typographie [tipɔgra'fi], *n.f.* typography.

tyran [ti'rã], *n.m.* tyrant.

tyrannie [tira'ni], *n.f.* tyranny.

tyrannique [tira'nik], *a.* tyrannical.

tyranniser [tirani'ze], *v.t.* to tyrannize, to oppress.

tzar [TSAR].

tzigane or tsigane [tsi'gan], *a.* and *n.* gipsy.

U

U, u [y], *n.m.* the twenty-first letter of the alphabet.

ubiquité [ybikɥi'te], *n.f.* ubiquity.

Ukraine [y'krɛn], **l'**, *f.* the Ukraine.

ukrainien [ykrɛ'njɛ̃], *a.* Ukrainian.—*n.m.* (**Ukrainien**, *fem.* **-enne**) Ukrainian (*person*).

ulcère [yl'sɛ:r], *n.m.* ulcer.

ulcéré [ylse're], *a.* ulcerated; (*fig.*) embittered.

ulcérer [ylse're], *v.t.* (*conjug. like* CÉDER) to ulcerate; (*fig.*) to embitter, to incense.

ultérieur [ylte'rjœ:r], *a.* ulterior, further, later, subsequent.

ultérieurement [ylterjœr'mã], *adv.* later on.

ultimatum [ultima'tɔm], *n.m.* ultimatum.

ultime [yl'tim], *a.* last, final, ultimate.

ultra-sonore [yltrasɔ'nɔ:r], *a.* supersonic.

ultra-violet [yltravjɔ'lɛ], *a.* (*fem.* **-ette**) ultra-violet.

ululer [yly'le], *v.i.* to ululate, to hoot.

Ulysse [y'lis], *m.* Ulysses.

umbre [ɔ̃:br], **omble** [ɔ̃:bl], **ombre** [ɔ̃:br], *n.m.* grayling (*fish*).

un [œ̃], *a.* and *art. indef.* (*fem.* **une**) one, the first; single; a, an; any, a certain.—*pron. indef.* one thing; one; **c'est tout un**, it is all one; **les uns disent oui, les autres disent non**, some say yes, others say no; **les uns et les autres**, all, all together; **l'un et l'autre**, both; **l'un ou l'autre**, the one or the other; **l'un vaut l'autre**, one is as good as the other; **un à un**, one by one.—*n.m.* one.

unanime [yna'nim], *a.* unanimous.

unanimement [ynanim'mã], *adv.* unanimously.

unanimité [ynanimi'te], *n.f.* unanimity.

uni [y'ni], *a.* united; smooth, even, level; uniform; plain, unaffected.

unicorne [yni'kɔrn], *n.m.* unicorn.

unième [y'njɛm], *a.* (*in compounds only*) first; *vingt et unième*, 21st.

unification [ynifika'sjɔ̃], *n.f.* unification.

unifier [yni'fje], *v.t.* to unify, to unite; to amalgamate.

uniforme [yni'fɔrm], *a.* uniform.—*n.m.* uniform, regimentals.

uniformément [yniforme'mɑ̃], *adv.* uniformly.

uniformité [yniformi'te], *n.f.* uniformity.

unilatéral [ynilate'ral], *a.* (*m. pl.* **-aux**) unilateral.

uniment [yni'mɑ̃], *adv.* evenly, smoothly; plainly.

union [y'njɔ̃], *n.f.* union; concord, agreement; mixture; marriage.

unique [y'nik], *a.* only, sole; single, unique, unparalleled; odd, singular; *fils unique*, only son; *sens unique*, one way (*street*).

uniquement [ynik'mɑ̃], *adv.* solely.

unir [y'ni:r], *v.t.* to unite, to join; to smooth, to level; to pair. **s'unir**, *v.r.* to unite, to join together.

unisson [yni'sɔ̃], *n.m.* unison; (*fig.*) harmony, concert.

unité [yni'te], *n.f.* unity; unit; (*fig.*) concord, agreement.

univers [yni'vɛ:r], *n.m.* inv. universe.

universalité [yniversali'te], *n.f.* universality; sum total, whole.

universel [yniver'sɛl], *a.* (*fem.* **-elle**) universal; residuary (*of legacies*).

universellement [yniversɛl'mɑ̃], *adv.* universally.

universitaire [yniversi'tɛ:r], *a.* of the university, academic.—*n.* teacher, professor.

université [yniversi'te], *n.f.* university.

uranium [yra'njom], *n.m.* uranium.

urbain [yr'bɛ̃], *a.* urban.

urbanisme [yrba'nism], *n.m.* town-planning.

urbaniste [yrba'nist], *n.m.* town-planner.

urbanité [yrbani'te], *n.f.* urbanity.

urgence [yr'ʒɑ̃:s], *n.f.* urgency; emergency; *d'urgence*, urgently, immediately.

urgent [yr'ʒɑ̃], *a.* urgent, pressing.

urinaire [yri'nɛ:r], *a.* urinary.

urine [y'rin], *n.f.* urine.

uriner [yri'ne], *v.i.* to urinate, to make water.

urinoir [yri'nwa:r], *n.m.* (public) urinal.

urne [yrn], *n.f.* urn; *urne électorale*, ballot box.

Ursule [yr'syl], *f.* Ursula.

urticaire [yrti'kɛ:r], *n.f.* nettle rash; urticaria.

Uruguay [yry'gɛ], l', *m.* Uruguay.

uruguayen [yrygɛ'jɛ̃], *a.* Uruguayan.—*n.m.* (**Uruguayen**, *fem.* **-enne**) Uruguayan (*person*).

us [ys, yz], *n.m. pl.* *les us et coutumes*, the ways and customs.

usage [y'za:ʒ], *n.m.* custom, practice, usage; use; wear (*of clothes etc.*); *avoir de l'usage*, to have breeding; *hors d'usage*, out of use; *faire de l'usage* or *faire un bon usage*, to last or wear a long time.

usagé [yza'ʒe], *a.* used, worn, second-hand.

usager [yza'ʒe], *n.m.* user; *les usagers de la route*, road-users.

usé [y'ze], *a.* worn-out, threadbare; stale, trite, hackneyed.

user [y'ze], *v.t.* to use up, to consume; to wear out; to spend, to waste.—*v.i.* to make use of. **s'user**, *v.r.* to wear oneself out; to wear away.

usine [y'zin], *n.f.* works, mills, factory.

usinier [yzi'nje], *n.m.* manufacturer, mill owner.

usité [yzi'te], *a.* used, usual, in common use.

ustensile [ystɑ̃'sil], *n.m.* utensil; tool, implement.

usuel [y'zɥɛl], *a.* (*fem.* **-elle**) usual, customary, ordinary.

usuellement [ysɥɛl'mɑ̃], *adv.* habitually, ordinarily.

usure [y'zy:r], *n.f.* usury, excessive interest; wear and tear.

usurier [yzy'rje], *a.* (*fem.* **-ière**) usurious.—*n.m.* (*fem.* **-ière**) usurer.

usurpateur [yzyrpa'tœ:r], *a.* (*fem.* **-trice**) usurping.—*n.m.* (*fem.* **-trice**) usurper.

usurpation [yzyrpa'sjɔ̃], *n.f.* usurpation; encroachment.

usurper [yzyr'pe], *v.t.* to usurp; to encroach upon.

ut [yt], *n.m.* (*Mus.*) ut, do, the note C.

utérus [yte'rys], *n.m.* uterus, womb.

utile [y'til], *a.* useful, serviceable; advantageous, expedient, beneficial; *en temps utile*, in due or good time.—*n.m.* utility, usefulness.

utilement [ytil'mɑ̃], *adv.* usefully.

utilisation [ytiliza'sjɔ̃], *n.f.* use, utilization.

utiliser [ytili'ze], *v.t.* to use, to find use for, to employ.

utilité [ytili'te], *n.f.* utility, usefulness; benefit, profit, service, avail.

utopie [yto'pi], *n.f.* utopia.

utopique [yto'pik], *a.* utopian.

V

V, v [ve], *n.m.* the twenty-second letter of the alphabet.

vacance [va'kɑ̃:s], *n.f.* vacancy; (*pl.*) vacation, holiday; recess (*of parliament etc.*).

vacant [va'kɑ̃], *a.* vacant; unoccupied, empty.

vacarme [va'karm], *n.m.* hubbub, uproar, fuss.

vacation [vaka'sjɔ̃], *n.f.* attendance, sitting (*of public officers etc.*); day's sale (*at auctions*); vacation (*of courts*).

vaccin [vak'sɛ̃], *n.m.* vaccine.

vaccination [vaksina'sjɔ̃], *n.f.* inoculation, vaccination.

vacciner [vaksi'ne], *v.t.* to inoculate, to vaccinate; to immunize.

vache [vaʃ], *n.f.* cow; cow-hide.

vacher [va'ʃe], *n.m.* (*fem.* **-ère**) cow-herd.

vacherie [va'ʃri], *n.f.* cow-house, byre.

vacillant [vasi'jɑ̃], *a.* vacillating, wavering, flickering; shaky, uncertain, unsteady.

vacillation [vasija'sjɔ̃], *n.f.* wobbling, flickering.

vaciller [vasi'je], *v.i.* to vacillate; to waver, to stagger; to flicker (*of light etc.*).

vacuité [vakɥi'te], *n.f.* vacuity, emptiness.

vacuum [va'kɥɔm], *n.m.* vacuum.

va-et-vient [vae'vjɛ̃]. *n.m. inv.* reciprocating motion, swing, see-saw motion, oscillation; (*fig.*) coming and going.

vagabond [vaga'bɔ̃], *a.* and *n.m.* (*fem.* **-e**) vagabond, vagrant.

vagabondage [vagabɔ̃'daːʒ], *n.m.* vagrancy.

vagabonder [vagabɔ̃'de], *v.i.* to be a vagabond; to roam; (*fig.*) to flit from one thing to another.

vagin [va'ʒɛ̃], *n.m.* (*Anat.*) vagina.

vagir [va'ʒiːr], *v.i.* to wail, to pule (*of infants*).

vague (1) [vag], *n.f.* wave, billow.

vague (2) [vag], *a.* vague, indeterminate, uncertain; faint, indistinct, hazy; empty, vacant; *terres vagues*, waste-land; *terrain vague*, vacant site, piece of waste ground. —*n.m.* vagueness, looseness, uncertainty; empty space.

vaguement [vag'mɑ̃], *adv.* vaguely, dimly.

vaguer [va'ge], *v.i.* to ramble, to wander, to stray.

vaillamment [vaja'mɑ̃], *adv.* valiantly.

vaillance [va'jɑ̃ːs], *n.f.* valor, bravery.

vaillant [va'jɑ̃], *a.* valiant, brave, gallant; stout (*heart*); *n'avoir pas un sou vaillant*, to be penniless.

vain [vɛ̃], *a.* vain, fruitless, ineffectual; empty, hollow; trifling; vainglorious; conceited; *en vain*, vainly, in vain.

vaincre [vɛ̃:kr], *v.t. irr.* to vanquish, to conquer, to overcome, to defeat; to outdo, to surpass; *se laisser vaincre*, to give way to, to yield.

vaincu [vɛ̃'ky], *a.* conquered, vanquished. —*n.m.* (*fem.* **-e**) conquered person, loser.

vainement [vɛn'mɑ̃], *adv.* vainly, in vain.

vainqueur [vɛ̃'kœːr], *a.* conquering, victorious.—*n.m.* vanquisher, conqueror, victor; prize winner.

vairon [vɛ'rɔ̃], *n.m.* minnow.

vaisseau [vɛ'so], *n.m.* (*pl.* **-eaux**) vessel, receptacle; ship; large covered space (*of a building*); (*Anat.*, *Bot.*) vessel, tube, duct; (*pl.*) shipping.

vaisselle [vɛ'sɛl], *n.f.* plates and dishes; plate (*of gold* or *silver*); *faire la vaisselle*, to wash up.

val [val], *n.m.* (*pl.* **vals** or **vaux**) narrow valley, vale, dale.

valable [va'labl], *a.* valid, good.

valet [va'lɛ]. *n.m.* footman, valet, manservant; jack (*at cards*); door weight; holdfast; *valet de chambre*, valet; *valet de chiens*, whipper-in; *valet de ferme*, farm worker.

valeter [val'te], *v.i.* (*conjug. like* APPELER) to cringe, to dance attendance.

valétudinaire [valetydi'nɛːr], *a.* valetudinary.—*n.* valetudinarian, invalid.

valeur [va'lœːr], *n.f.* value, worth, price; consideration; import, meaning; valor, bravery; (*pl.*) bills, paper, stocks, shares, securities.

valeureusement [valœrøz'mɑ̃], *adv.* bravely, courageously.

valeureux [valœ'rø], *a.* (*fem.* **-euse**) brave, courageous, gallant.

valide [va'lid], *a.* valid, good; healthy, able-bodied.—*n.* person in good health.

valider [vali'de], *v.t.* to make valid; to ratify, to validate.

validité [validi'te], *n.f.* validity; availability (*of a ticket*).

valise [va'liːz], *n.f.* suit-case; valise, portmanteau.

vallée [va'le], *n.f.* valley.

vallon [va'lɔ̃], *n.m.* small valley, vale, dale.

valoir [va'lwaːr], *v.t. irr.* to yield, to bring in; to procure, to furnish.—*v.i.* to be worth, to be as good as, to be equal to; to deserve, to merit; *autant vaut*, to all intents and purposes; *à valoir*, on account; *faire valoir son droit*, to assert one's right; *se faire valoir*, to boast; *vaille que vaille*, for better or worse; *valoir mieux*, to be better.

valse [vals], *n.f.* waltz.

valser [val'se], *v.i.* to waltz.

valve [valv], *n.f.* valve; electron tube.

vampire [vɑ̃'piːr], *n.m.* vampire.

van [vɑ̃], *n.m.* (*Agric.*) winnowing basket.

vandale [vɑ̃'dal], *n.* vandal.

vandalisme [vɑ̃da'lism], *n.m.* vandalism.

vanille [va'niːj], *n.f.* vanilla.

vanité [vani'te], *n.f.* vanity, conceit.

vaniteux [vani'tø], *a.* (*fem.* **-euse**) vainglorious, vain.

vannage [va'naːʒ], *n.m.* winnowing.

vanne [van], *n.f.* sluice, sluice gate.

vanneau [va'no], *n.m.* (*pl.* **-eaux**) lapwing, peewit.

vanner [va'ne], *v.t.* to winnow, to fan, to sift; (*pop.*) to tire out.

vannerie [van'ri], *n.f.* basket-making, basket trade.

vanneur [va'nœːr], *a.* (*fem.* **-euse**) winnowing.—*n.m.* (*fem.* **-euse**) winnower.—*n.f.* (**-euse**) winnowing machine.

vannier [va'nje], *n.m.* (*fem.* **-iere**) basket-maker.

vannure [va'nyːr], *n.f.* chaff.

vantard [vɑ̃'taːr], *a.* boastful, boastful, bragging.—*n.m.* (*fem.* **-e**) boaster, braggart.

vantardise [vɑ̃tar'diːz], *n.f.* boasting, bragging.

vanter [vɑ̃'te], *v.t.* to praise, to commend, to extol. **se vanter**, *v.r.* to boast, to pride oneself on (*de*).

vanterie [vɑ̃'tri], *n.f.* boasting, bragging.

va-nu-pieds [vany'pje], *n. inv.* ragamuffin.

vapeur [va'pœːr], *n.f.* vapor; steam; haze, mist; *à la vapeur* or *à toute vapeur*, at full speed.—*n.m.* steamer, steamship.

vaporeux [vapɔ'rø], *a.* (*fem.* **-euse**) vaporous; steamy, hazy.

vaquer [va'ke], *v.i.* to be vacant; to attend, to devote oneself (*à*).

varech or **varec** [va'rɛk], *n.m* sea-wrack, sea-weed.

variabilité [varjabili'te], *n.f.* variability, changeableness.

variable [va'rjabl], *a.* variable, fickle, unsettled.—*n.f.* (*Math.*) variable.

variant [va'rjɑ̃], *a.* variable, fickle.—*n.f.* (**-e**) variant (*reading* or *interpretation*).

variation [varja'sjɔ̃], *n.f.* variation.

varice [va'ris], *n.f.* varix, varicose vein.

varier [va'rje], *v.t.* to vary, to change; to variegate.—*v.i.* to vary, to be changeable; to disagree.

variété [varje'te], *n.f.* variety, diversity, change; (*pl.*) miscellanea.

variole [va'rjɔl], *n.f.* smallpox.

Varsovie [varsɔ'vi], *f.* Warsaw.

vase (1) [vɑːz], *n.m.* vase, vessel.

vase (2) [vɑːz], *n.f.* slime, mud, mire, ooze.

vaseline [vaz'lin], *n.f.* petroleum jelly, Vaseline (*reg. trade mark*).

vaseux [va'zø], *a.* (*fem.* **-euse**) slimy, muddy, miry.

vasistas [vazis'tɑːs], *n.m. inv.* transom, fan-light (*over a door* or *a window*).

vassal [va'sal], *n.m.* (*fem.* **-e**, *m. pl.* **-aux**) vassal.

vaste [vast], *a.* vast, wide, spacious.

vastement [vastə'mɑ̃], *adv.* vastly, widely.

Vatican [vati'kɑ̃], le, *m.* the Vatican.

va-tout [va'tu], *n.m. inv.* one's all (*at cards*); *jouer son va-tout*, to stake one's all.

vaudeville [vod'vil], *n.m.* vaudeville; light form of comedy.

vau-l'eau (**à**) [avo'lo], *adv. phr.* with the current, down-stream; to rack and ruin.

vaurien [vo'rjɛ̃], *n.m.* (*fem.* **-enne**) good-for-nothing, scamp; rogue.

vautour [vo'tuːr], *n.m.* vulture.

vautre [voːtr], *n.m.* boar-hound.

vautrer (**se**) [sovo'tre], *v.r.* to wallow; to sprawl.

veau [vo], *n.m.* (*pl.* **veaux**) calf; (*Cook.*) veal; calf-skin, calf leather; (*fig.*) slow-witted fellow; *veau marin*, seal, seal-skin.

vedette [və'dɛt], *n.f.* vedette, mounted sentinel; scout; observation post, watch-tower; (*Theat.*) star.

végétal [veʒe'tal], *a.* (*m. pl.* **-aux**) vegetable.—*n.m.* (*pl.* **-aux**) vegetable, plant.

végétarien [veʒeta'rjɛ̃], *a.* and *n.m.* (*fem.* **-enne**) vegetarian.

végétation [veʒeta'sjɔ̃], *n.f.* vegetation; (*pl.*) adenoids.

végéter [veʒe'te], *v.i.* (*conjug. like* CÉDER) to vegetate.

véhémence [vee'mɑ̃ːs], *n.f.* vehemence.

véhément [vee'mɑ̃], *a.* vehement, impetuous, hot, passionate.

véhiculaire [veiky'lɛːr], *a.* vehicular.

véhicule [vei'kyl], *n.m.* vehicle; medium.

veille [vɛːj], *n.f.* sleeplessness, watching; being awake; vigil; eve, day before; point, verge; (*pl.*) midnight work; *être à la veille de*, to be on the point of; *la veille de Noël*, Christmas Eve.

veillée [vɛ'je], *n.f.* time from supper to bed-time, evening (*in company*); sitting up to work etc. in company; night attendance (*upon a sick person*).

veiller [vɛ'je], *v.t.* to watch by, to nurse, to look after, to sit up with.—*v.i.* to sit up, to watch; to attend, to take care, to have an eye (**à**).

veilleur [vɛ'jœːr], *n.m.* (*fem.* **-euse**) watcher; *veilleur de nuit*, night watchman.—*n.f.* (**-euse**) night-light.

veinard [vɛ'naːr], *a.* and *n.m.* (*fem.* **-e**) (*pop.*) lucky (person), lucky dog.

veine [vɛːn], *n.f.* vein; (*Geol. etc.*) seam; (*pop.*) good luck; *avoir de la veine*, to be in luck; *en veine de*, in the mood for; *un coup de veine*, a fluke.

veiné [vɛ'ne], *a.* veined, veiny.

veineux [vɛ'nø], *a.* (*fem.* **-euse**) veined, veiny; venous (*system, blood*).

vélin [ve'lɛ̃], *n.m.* vellum.

velléité [vɛlei'te], *n.f.* passing fancy, wish, whim.

vélo [ve'lo], *n.m.* (*fam.*) bike.

vélocité [velɔsi'te], *n.f.* velocity.

vélodrome [velɔ'drɔm], *n.m.* cycle-racing track.

vélomoteur [velɔmɔ'tœːr], *n.m.* motorbike.

velours [və'luːr], *n.m.* velvet; *velours à côtes*, corduroy; *velours de coton*, velveteen.

velouté [vəlu'te], *a.* velvet, velvety, velvet-like; soft and smooth to the palate (*of wines*).—*n.m.* velvet pile; softness; bloom (*of fruit*); smooth rich soup *or* sauce; *velouté de laine*, velours.

velu [və'ly], *a.* hairy, shaggy, rough.—*n.m.* shagginess.

vélum [ve'lɔm], *n.m.* awning.

venaison [vənɛ'zɔ̃], *n.f.* venison.

vénal [ve'nal], *a.* (*m. pl.* **-aux**) venal, mercenary.

vénalité [venali'te], *n.f.* venality.

venant [və'nɑ̃], *a.* coming, thriving.—*n.m.* comer; *tout-venant*, unsorted (*of produce*).

vendable [vɑ̃'dabl], *a.* saleable, marketable.

vendange [vɑ̃'dɑ̃ːʒ], *n.f.* vintage, grape gathering.

vendanger [vɑ̃dɑ̃'ʒe], *v.t.* (*conjug. like* MANGER) to gather in the grapes from; (*fig.*) to ravage, to spoil.—*v.i.* to pick (*the grapes*); (*fig.*) to make illicit profits.

vendangeur [vɑ̃dɑ̃'ʒœːr], *n.m.* (*fem.* **-euse**) vintager, grape gatherer.

vendéen [vɑ̃de'ɛ̃], *a.* (*fem.* **-éenne**) Vendean.

vendetta [vɛ̃de'ta], *n.f.* vendetta.

vendeur [vɑ̃'dœːr], *n.m.* (*fem.* **-euse**) vendor, seller, dealer; salesman, shop assistant.

vendre [vɑ̃ːdr], *v.t.* to sell; (*fig.*) to betray; *à vendre*, for sale. **se vendre**, *v.r.* to sell one-self; to be sold; to go off (*well etc.*).

vendredi [vɑ̃drə'di], *n.m.* Friday; *le Vendredi saint*, Good Friday.

vené [və'ne], *a.* high (*of meat*).

vénéneux [vene'nø], *a.* (*fem.* **-euse**) poison-ous (*when eaten*).

vénérable [vene'rabl], *a.* venerable.

vénération [venera'sjɔ̃], *n.f.* veneration.

vénérer [vene're], *v.t.* (*conjug. like* CÉDER) to venerate, to hold in reverence.

vénerie [ven'ri], *n.f.* venery, hunting.

veneur [və'nœːr], *n.m.* huntsman.

Vénézuéla [venezye'la], le, *m.* Venezuela.

vénézuélien [venezye'ljɛ̃], *a.* (*fem.* **-enne**) Venezuelan.—*n.m.* (**Vénézuélien**, *fem.* **-enne**) Venezuelan (*person*).

vengeance [vɑ̃'ʒɑ̃ːs], *n.f.* vengeance, revenge.

venger [vɑ̃'ʒe], *v.t.* (*conjug. like* MANGER) to revenge, to avenge. **se venger**, *v.r.* **se venger de quelqu'un**, to revenge oneself on someone.

vengeur [vɑ̃'ʒœːr], *a.* (*fem.* **-eresse**) revenge-ful, avenging.—*n.m.* (*fem.* **-eresse**) avenger, revenger.

véniel [ve'njɛl], *a.* (*fem.* **-elle**) venial.

venimeux [vəni'mø], *a.* (*fem.* **-euse**) com-municating poison (*from outside*), venomous (*snake etc.*); (*fig.*) malignant, harmful.

venin [vəˈnɛ̃], *n.m.* venom, poison; (*fig.*) spite, malice.

venir [vəˈniːr], *v.i. irr.* (*conjug. like* TENIR, *but with aux.* ÊTRE) to come, to be coming; to arrive; to reach; to occur, to happen; to grow, to grow up; to thrive; to issue, to arise; to be descended; **d'où vient cela?** what is the cause of that? **en venir aux mains**, to come to blows; **faire venir le médecin**, to send for the doctor; **il va et vient**, he goes in and out; **je ne ferai qu'aller et venir**, I will not stay, I shall come straight back; **le voilà qui vient**, here he comes; **où voulez-vous en venir?** what are you getting at? **s'en venir**, to come away; **si ma lettre venait à se perdre**, if my letter should happen to go astray; **venir à bout de**, to master; **venir de**, to come from, (*followed by an infinitive,* to have just)—**je viens de le voir**, I have just seen him; **je venais de le quitter**, I had just left him).

Venise [vəˈniːz], *f.* Venice.

vent [vɑ̃], *n.m.* wind; breeze; breath, breathing; (*Med.*) (*pl.*) flatulence; (*Hunt.*) scent; (*fig.*) vanity, emptiness; **autant en emporte le vent**, all that is idle talk; **avoir vent de**, to get wind of; **coup de vent**, gust of wind; (*colloq.*) **dans le vent**, 'with it'; **en plein vent**, in the open air; **il fait du vent**, it is windy.

vente [vɑ̃t], *n.f.* sale; selling, auction; felling *or* cutting (*of timber*); **en vente**, for sale, on sale; **vente aux enchères**, sale at auction.

venter [vɑ̃ˈte], *v.i.* (*usu. impers.*) to blow, to be windy.

venteux [vɑ̃ˈtø], *a.* (*fem.* **-euse**) windy, gusty.

ventilateur [vɑ̃tilaˈtœːr], *n.m.* ventilator, fan, blower.

ventilation [vɑ̃tilaˈsjɔ̃], *n.f.* ventilation, airing.

ventiler [vɑ̃tiˈle], *v.t.* to ventilate, to air; (*fig.*) to discuss.

ventosité [vɑ̃toziˈte], *n.f.* flatulence.

ventouse [vɑ̃ˈtuːz], *n.f.* cupping-glass; vent, air-hole; sucker (*of leech*); nozzle (*of vacuum cleaner*).

ventre [vɑ̃ːtr], *n.m.* belly, abdomen; stomach; womb; bowels, one's inside; bulge; **à plat ventre**, flat on one's face; **ventre à terre**, at full speed; **j'ai mal au ventre**, I have a stomach ache.

ventrière [vɑ̃triˈɛːr], *n.f.* abdominal belt; sling, brace; girth (*of horse*).

ventriloque [vɑ̃triˈlɔk], *n.m.* ventriloquist.

ventriloquie [vɑ̃trilɔˈki], *n.f.* ventriloquy.

ventru [vɑ̃ˈtry], *a.* big-bellied, corpulent; bulging.—*n.m.* (*fem.* **-e**) pot-bellied person.

venu [vəˈny], *a.* come; done; come up, grown; **bien venu** [BIENVENU]; **enfant bien venu**, well-grown child; **mal venu**, unwelcome; open to censure.—*n.m.* (*fem.* **-e**) **le dernier venu**, the last arrival; **le premier venu** *or* **la première venue**, the first comer, anyone.—*n.f.* (**-e**) coming, arrival, advent; growth.

Vénus [veˈnys], *f.* Venus.

vêpres [vɛːpr], *n.f. pl.* vespers.

ver [vɛːr], *n.m.* worm; maggot, mite; moth; **mangé** *or* **rongé des vers**, worm-eaten; **nu comme un ver**, stark naked; **ver blanc**, grub; **ver à soie**, silkworm; **ver luisant**, glow-worm; **ver solitaire**, tapeworm.

véracité [verasiˈte], *n.f.* veracity.

véranda [verɑ̃ˈda], *n.f.* veranda.

verbal [vɛrˈbal], *a.* (*m. pl.* **-aux**) verbal.

verbalement [vɛrbalˈmɑ̃], *adv.* verbally; (*colloq.*) by word of mouth.

verbaliser [vɛrbaliˈze], *v.i.* to draw up a written statement.

verbe [vɛrb], *n.m.* verb; (*Theol.*) **le Verbe**, the Word.

verbeux [vɛrˈbø], *a.* (*fem.* **-euse**) verbose.

verbiage [vɛrˈbjaːʒ], *n.m.* verbiage.

verbosité [vɛrboziˈte], *n.f.* verbosity.

verdâtre [vɛrˈdɑːtr], *a.* greenish.

verdelet [vɛrdˈlɛ], *a.* (*fem.* **-ette**) greenish; tart (*of wine*); hale (*of old people*).

verdeur [vɛrˈdœːr], *n.f.* greenness, sap (*of wood*); tartness, harshness (*of wine*); vigor; spryness (*of old people*); (*fig.*) crudeness (*of language*).

verdict [vɛrˈdikt], *n.m.* verdict, finding.

verdier [vɛrˈdje], *n.m.* greenfinch; verderer, ranger.

verdir [vɛrˈdiːr], *v.t.* to make *or* paint green.—*v.i.* to turn green.

verdoyant [vɛrdwaˈjɑ̃], *a.* verdant, green.

verdoyer [vɛrdwaˈje], *v.i.* (*conjug. like* EMPLOYER) to become green.

verdure [vɛrˈdyːr], *n.f.* verdure; greenery; pot-herbs.

verdurier [vɛrdyˈrje], *n.m.* (*fem.* **-ière**) greengrocer, fruit and vegetable grocer.

véreux [veˈrø], *a.* (*fem.* **-euse**) worm-eaten, maggoty; rotten; (*fig.*) suspect; insecure (*of bills etc.*).

verge [vɛːrʒ], *n.f.* rod, wand; shaft, pin; shank (*of an anchor etc.*); (*C*) yard (*measure*).

verger [vɛrˈʒe], *n.m.* orchard.

vergeté [vɛrʒaˈte], *a.* streaky.

vergette [vɛrˈʒɛt], *n.f.* clothes brush; bundle of rods, switch.

verglacé [vɛrglaˈse], *a.* covered with glazed frost; icy.

verglas [vɛrˈgla], *n.m.* thin coating of ice, frost after a thaw *or* rain; glazed frost.

vergne [vɛrɲ], **verne** [vɛrn], *n.m.* alder (*tree*).

vergogne [vɛrˈgɔɲ], *n.f.* shame; **sans vergogne**, shameless(ly).

vergue [vɛrg], *n.f.* yard (*for sail*).

véridicité [veridisiˈte], *n.f.* veracity, truthfulness.

véridique [veriˈdik], *a.* veracious, truthful.

vérificateur [verifikaˈtœːr], *n.m.* verifier, examiner, inspector; (*Eng.*) calipers, gauge; **vérificateur des comptes**, auditor.

vérification [verifikaˈsjɔ̃], *n.f.* verification, auditing, probate.

vérifier [veriˈfje], *v.t.* to verify, to inspect, to examine, to audit; to prove.

vérin [veˈrɛ̃], *n.m.* (*Eng.*) jack.

véritable [veriˈtabl], *a.* true, genuine, real; staunch, downright, thorough.

véritablement [veritablˈmɑ̃], *adv.* truly, in reality, indeed.

vérité [veriˈte], *n.f.* truth, verity, truthfulness; **à la vérité**, indeed, it is true, I admit; **dire la vérité**, to speak the truth; **en vérité**, indeed, truly.

verjus [vɛrˈʒy], *n.m.* verjuice; sour grapes.

verjuté [vɛrʒyˈte], *a.* sharp, tart, acid.

325

vermeil [vɛr'mɛːj], *a.* (*fem.* **-eille**) vermilion, ruddy, rosy.—*n.m.* vermeil, silver-gilt.
vermicelle [vɛrmi'sɛl], *n.m.* vermicelli.
vermiculaire [vɛrmiky'lɛːr], *a.* vermicular, worm-shaped.
vermillon [vɛrmi'jɔ̃], *a. inv.* and *n.m.* vermilion.
vermine [vɛr'min], *n.f.* vermin (*only insects such as fleas, lice etc.*); (*fig.*) rabble.
vermoulu [vɛrmu'ly], *a.* worm-eaten.
vermoulure [vɛrmu'lyːr], *n.f.* worm hole, rottenness caused by worms (*in wood*).
vermout(h) [vɛr'mut], *n.m.* vermouth.
vernaculaire [vɛrnaky'lɛːr], *a.* and *n.m.* vernacular.
vernal [vɛr'nal], *a.* (*m. pl.* **-aux**) vernal, spring-like.
vernier [vɛr'nje], *n.m.* vernier, sliding scale.
vernir [vɛr'niːr], *v.t.* to varnish; to glaze, to polish.
vernis [vɛr'ni], *n.m.* varnish, polish, glaze.
vernissage [vɛrni'saːʒ], *n.m.* varnishing; private view (*of art exhibition*).
vernisser [vɛrni'se], *v.t.* to glaze (*pottery etc.*).
vérole [ve'rol], *n.f.* **petite vérole**, smallpox; **petite vérole volante**, chicken pox.
véronal [vero'nal], *n.m.* (*Chem.*) veronal, barbitone.
Véronique [vero'nik], *f.* Veronica.
véronique [vero'nik], *n.f.* veronica, speedwell.
verrat [vɛ'ra], *n.m.* boar.
verre [vɛːr], *n.m.* glass; **verre à eau** or **verre gobelet**, tumbler; **verre à vin**, wine glass; **verre de vin**, glass of wine.
verrerie [vɛr'ri], *n.f.* glass-works; glass-ware.
verrier [vɛ'rje], *n.m.* glass-maker.
verrière [vɛ'rjɛːr], *n.f.* stained-glass window.
verroterie [vɛrɔ'tri], *n.f.* small glass-ware, glass beads.
verrou [vɛ'ru], *n.m.* bolt, bar.
verrouiller [vɛru'je], *v.t.* to bolt. **se verrouiller**, *v.r.* to bolt oneself in.
verrue [vɛ'ry], *n.f.* wart; **verrue plantaire**, verruca.
vers (1) [vɛːr], *n.m. inv.* verse, line (*of poetry*).
vers (2) [vɛːr], *prep.* towards, to; about; **vers (les) quatre heures**, about four o'clock.
versable [vɛr'sabl], *a.* apt to overturn, liable to upset.
versage [vɛr'saːʒ], *n.m.* emptying, tipping; (*Agric.*) first ploughing (*of fallow land*).
versant (1) [vɛr'sɑ̃], *a.* liable to be overturned.
versant (2) [vɛr'sɑ̃], *n.m.* declivity, side, slope; watershed.
versatile [vɛrsa'til], *a.* inconstant, changeable.
versatilité [vɛrsatili'te], *n.f.* inconstancy.
verse (à) [a'vɛrs], *adv.* abundantly; **il pleut à verse**, it is pouring down rain.
versé [vɛr'se], *a.* spilt; well versed, conversant.
versement [vɛrsə'mɑ̃], *n.m.* payment; deposit.
verser [vɛr'se], *v.t.* to pour, to pour out; to discharge, to empty; to shed, to spill; to pay in, to deposit; to overturn, to upset; to lay (*grain*).—*v.i.* to overturn, to upset (*of vehicles*); to be laid flat (*of standing grain*).
verset [vɛr'sɛ], *n.m.* (*Bibl. etc.*) verse.

versificateur [vɛrsifika'tœːr], *n.m.* (*fem.* **-trice**) versifier.
versification [vɛrsifika'sjɔ̃], *n.f.* versification.
versifier [vɛrsi'fje], *v.t., v.i.* to versify.
version [vɛr'sjɔ̃], *n.f.* version; (*Sch.*) translation.
verso [vɛr'so], *n.m.* verso, back, left-hand page.
vert [vɛːr], *a.* green; sharp, harsh (*of things*); tart (*of wine*); raw; sour; (*fig.*) vigorous, robust; spicy (*of stories*).—*n.m.* green, green color; green food; sharpness (*of wine etc.*); (*Golf*) (putting-)green.
vert-de-gris [vɛrdə'gri], *n.m.* verdigris.
vertèbre [vɛr'tɛːbr], *n.f.* vertebra.
vertébré [vɛrte'bre], *a.* and *n.m.* vertebrate.
vertement [vɛrtə'mɑ̃], *adv.* sharply; harshly, severely.
vertical [vɛrti'kal], *a.* (*m. pl.* **-aux**) vertical.
verticalement [vɛrtikal'mɑ̃], *adv.* vertically.
vertige [vɛr'tiːʒ], *n.m.* dizziness, giddiness, vertigo; (*fig.*) madness, intoxication.
vertigineux [vɛrtiʒi'nø], *a.* (*fem.* **-euse**) dizzy, giddy; (*fig.*) breath-taking.
vertigo [vɛrti'go], *n.m.* staggers; (*fig.*) whim.
vertu [vɛr'ty], *n.f.* virtue, chastity; property, faculty, quality; efficacy, force.
vertueusement [vɛrtɥøz'mɑ̃], *adv.* virtuously.
vertueux [vɛr'tɥø], *a.* (*fem.* **-euse**) virtuous, chaste.
verve [vɛrv], *n.f.* warmth, animation, verve, spirit, zest.
verveine [vɛr'vɛn], *n.f.* vervain, verbena.
vésicule [vezi'kyl], *n.f.* vesicle, bladder; **vésicule biliaire**, gall bladder.
vespasienne [vɛspa'zjɛn], *n.f.* public urinal; public convenience.
vessie [vɛ'si], *n.f.* bladder.
veste [vɛst], *n.f.* jacket.
vestiaire [vɛs'tjɛːr], *n.m.* cloakroom; changing room; robing room (*for judges*); hat-and-coat rack.
vestibule [vɛsti'byl], *n.m.* vestibule, lobby, hall.
vestige [vɛs'tiːʒ], *n.m.* footprint, vestige, sign, mark; trace, remains.
veston [vɛs'tɔ̃], *n.m.* jacket, coat; **complet veston**, business suit.
Vésuve [ve'zyːv], **le,** *m.* Vesuvius.
vêtement [vɛt'mɑ̃], *n.m.* garment; (*pl.*) dress, clothes; (*poet.*) raiment; **vêtements de dessous**, underwear.
vétéran [vete'rɑ̃], *n.m.* veteran; (*Sch.*) boy who stays in a grade a second year.
vétérinaire [veteri'nɛːr], *a.* veterinary.—*n.m.* veterinary surgeon.
vétille [ve'tiːj], *n.f.* trifle, bagatelle.
vétiller [veti'je], *v.i.* to trifle; to split hairs.
vétilleux [veti'jø], *a.* (*fem.* **-euse**) particular, finicky.
vêtir [vɛ'tiːr], *v.t. irr.* to clothe; to array, to dress; to put on. **se vêtir**, *v.r.* to dress oneself.
véto [ve'to], *n.m.* veto.
vêtu [vɛ'ty], *a.* dressed, clothed, arrayed.
vétuste [ve'tyst], *a.* old, antiquated; dilapidated, worn out.
vétusté [vetys'te], *n.f.* antiquity, old age, decay.

veuf [vœf], *a.* (*fem.* **veuve**) widowed.—*n.m.* widower.—*n.f.* (**veuve**) widow.

veule [vœːl], *a.* feckless, weak, feeble.

veuvage [vœˈvaːʒ]. *n.m.* widowhood, widowerhood.

vexant [vɛkˈsã], *a.* vexing, provoking.

vexer [vɛkˈse], *v.t.* to vex, to plague, to annoy.

viable [vjabl], *a.* likely to live, viable; fit for traffic.

viaduc [vjaˈdyk], *n.m.* viaduct.

viager [vjaˈʒe], *a.* (*fem.* **-ère**) for life, during life; **rente viagère**, life annuity.

viande [vjãːd], *n.f.* meat; **menue viande**, fowl and game; **grosse viande**, butcher's meat.

vibrant [viˈbrã], *a.* vibrating; vibrant, resonant.

vibration [vibrɑˈsjɔ̃], *n.f.* vibration.

vibrer [viˈbre], *v.i.* to vibrate.

vicaire [viˈkɛːr], *n.m.* curate (*of a parish*).

vicariat [vikaˈrja], *n.m.*, **vicairie** [vikɛˈri], *n.f.* curacy; vicariate.

vice [vis], *n.m.* fault, defect, flaw, blemish; vice, viciousness.

vice-amiral [visamiˈral], *n.m.* (*pl.* **-aux**) vice admiral; second ship of a fleet.

vice-roi [visˈrwa], *n.m.* (*pl.* **vice-rois**) viceroy.

vicié [viˈsje], *a.* vitiated, depraved, corrupted; foul (*of air etc.*).

vicier [viˈsje], *v.t.* to vitiate, to taint, to corrupt.

vicieusement [visjøzˈmã], *adv.* viciously.

vicieux [viˈsjø], *a.* (*fem.* **-euse**) vicious, faulty, defective.

vicinal [visiˈnal], *a.* (*m. pl.* **-aux**) local, connecting (*of roads*); **chemin vicinal**, by-road.

vicissitude [visisiˈtyd], *n.f.* vicissitude, change.

vicomte [viˈkɔ̃ːt], *n.m.* viscount.

vicomtesse [vikɔ̃ˈtɛs], *n.f.* viscountess.

victime [vikˈtim], *n.f.* victim; sufferer; casualty.

Victoire [vikˈtwaːr], **Victoria** [viktɔˈrja], *f.* Victoria.

victoire [vikˈtwaːr], *n.f.* victory.

victorieux [viktɔˈrjø], *a.* (*fem.* **-euse**) victorious.

victuaille [vikˈtɥaːj], *n.f.* (*colloq.*) provisions.

vidange [viˈdãːʒ], *n.f.* emptying; draining off; night soil; **tonneau en vidange**, broached cask.

vidanger [vidãˈʒe], *v.t.* (*conjug. like* MANGER) to empty, to clean out, to drain, to blow off.

vidangeur [vidãˈʒœːr], *n.m.* scavenger.

vide [vid], *a.* empty; void, vacant, blank; destitute.—*n.m.* empty space, blank; vacuum; gap, hole; emptiness.—*adv. phr.* **à vide**, empty.

vidé [viˈde], *a.* emptied, exhausted.

vider [viˈde], *v.t.* to empty; to drain; to hollow out; to draw (*poultry*); to gut (*fish*); to vacate; to decide, to settle.

vie [vi], *n.f.* life; lifetime; existence, days; vitality: livelihood, living; food, subsistence; spirit, animation; noise; **être en vie**, to be alive; **le coût de la vie**, the cost of living; **niveau de vie**, standard of living.

vieil [vjɛj], [VIEUX].

viellard [vjɛˈjaːr], *n.m.* old man.

vieille [vjɛj], [VIEUX].

vieillerie [vjɛjˈri], *n.f.* (*usu. pl.*) old things, old clothes, old lumber, rubbish; obsolete ideas.

vieillesse [vjɛˈjɛs], *n.f.* old age; oldness.

vieillir [vjɛˈjiːr], *v.t.* to make old; to make look old.—*v.i.* to grow old; to become obsolete.

vieillissant [vjɛjiˈsã], *a.* growing old.

vieillot [vjɛˈjo], *a.* (*fem.* **-otte**) oldish.

vielle [vjɛl], *n.f.* *hurdy-gurdy.

Vienne [vjɛn], *f.* Vienna.

viennois [vjɛˈnwa], *a.* Viennese.—*n.m.* (**Viennois**, *fem.* **-oise**) Viennese (*person*).

vierge [vjɛrʒ], *a.* virgin, virginal, maiden; pure, untrodden; unwrought; free (*from*).—*n.f.* virgin, maid; (*Astron.*) Virgo.

Viet-Nam [vjɛtˈnam], **le**, *m.* Vietnam.

vietnamien [vjɛtnaˈmjɛ̃], *a.* (*fem.* **-enne**) Vietnamese.—*n.m.* Vietnamese (*language*); (**Vietnamien**, *fem.* **-enne**) Vietnamese (*person*).

vieux [vjø], *a.* (*before a vowel or* h *mute*, **vieil**, *fem.* **vieille**) old, aged, advanced in years; ancient, venerable; **vieux jeu**, old-fashioned.—*n.m.* (*fem.* **vieille**) old man, old woman; **la retraite des vieux**, old-age pension; **mon vieux**, (a term of endearment) old friend, old chap.

vif [vif], *a.* (*fem.* **vive**) alive, live, living; quick; lively, brisk, sprightly, animated, fiery, mettlesome, ardent, eager; hasty; keen; sharp, violent (*of pain etc.*); bracing (*of air etc.*); vivid, bright (*of colors*). —*n.m.* the quick (*live flesh*); living person; **être pris sur le vif**, to be very lifelike; **piquer au vif**, to sting to the quick.

vif-argent [vifarˈʒã], *n.m.* quicksilver.

vigie [viˈʒi], *n.f.* look-out man; look-out (*station* or *ship*); (*Rail.*) seat on the top of trainmen's car.

vigilance [viʒiˈlãːs], *n.f.* vigilance.

vigilant [viʒiˈlã], *a.* vigilant, watchful.

vigile [viˈʒil], *n.f.* vigil, eve.

vigne [viɲ], *n.f.* vine; vineyard; **vigne vierge**, wild grape; Virginia creeper.

vigneron [viɲəˈrɔ̃], *n.m.* (*fem.* **-onne**) vine dresser, wine grower.

vignette [viˈɲɛt], *n.f.* vignette; (*pop.*) meadow-sweet.

vignoble [viˈɲɔbl], *n.m.* vineyard.

vigoureusement [vigurøzˈmã], *adv.* vigorously, energetically.

vigoureux [viguˈrø], *a.* (*fem.* **-euse**) vigorous, energetic; stout, stalwart.

vigueur [viˈgœːr], *n.f.* vigor, strength; force, power, energy; **entrer en vigueur**, to come into force (*of laws etc.*).

vil [vil], *a.* vile, base, mean; abject, low; worthless; **à vil prix**, dirt cheap.

vilain [viˈlɛ̃], *a.* ugly; unsightly; pitiful; nasty; sordid, wretched; naughty (*of a child*); **un vilain tour**, a dirty trick; **vilain temps**, vile weather.—*n.m.* (*fem.* **-e**) *villein (*bondman*); nasty fellow; (*childish*) naughty boy or girl.

vilainement [vilɛnˈmã], *adv.* uglily; basely, shamefully, deplorably.

vilebrequin [vilbrəˈkɛ̃], *n.m.* brace, wimble; (*Mech.*) crankshaft.

vilement [vilˈmã], *adv.* vilely, basely.

vilenie [vil'ni], *n.f.* nastiness, foulness; vile action; stinginess, meanness; (*pl.*) offensive words.

vileté [vil'te], *n.f.* cheapness, low price; vileness; mean action.

vilipender [vilipā'de], *v.t.* to vilify; to disparage.

villa [vil'la], *n.f.* villa.

village [vi'la:ʒ], *n.m.* village.

villageois [vila'ʒwa], *a.* rustic.—*n.m.* (*fem.* -e) villager.

ville [vil], *n.f.* town, city; *être en ville*, to be out (*not at home*); *hôtel de ville*, town hall; *ville d'eaux*, spa.

villégiature [vileʒia'ty:r], *n.f.* sojourn in the country; *en villégiature*, staying in the country.

vin [vɛ̃], *n.m.* wine; *à bon vin point d'enseigne*, good wine needs no bush; *vin de Bordeaux rouge*, claret; *vin de marque*, vintage wine; *vin mousseux*, sparkling wine; *vin ordinaire*, dinner wine.

vinaigre [vi'nɛ:gr], *n.m.* vinegar.

vinaigrer [vinɛ'gre], *v.t.* to season with vinegar.

vindicatif [vɛ̃dika'tif], *a.* (*fem.* -tive) vindictive, revengeful.

vingt [vɛ̃], *a.* and *n.m. inv.* twenty, score; twentieth.

vingtaine [vɛ̃'tɛ:n], *n.f.* a score, about twenty.

vingt-et-un [vɛ̃tɛ'œ̃], *n.m.* twenty-one (*card game*).

vingtième [vɛ̃'tjɛ:m], *a.* and *n.* twentieth.

vinicole [vini'kɔl], *a.* wine-growing, wine-producing.

viol [vjɔl], *n.m.* rape (*Law*).

violateur [vjɔla'tœ:r], *a.* (*fem.* -trice) violating, transgressing, infringing.—*n.m.* (*fem.* -trice) violator, infringer, breaker.

violation [vjɔla'sjɔ̃], *n.f.* violation, breach, infringement.

violâtre [vjɔ'lɑ:tr], *a.* purplish.

viole [vjɔl], *n.f.* viol.

violemment [vjɔla'mɑ̃], *adv.* violently.

violence [vjɔ'lɑ̃:s], *n.f.* violence; (*Law*) duress; (*fig.*) stress, fury.

violent [vjɔ'lɑ̃], *a.* violent; strong (*of suspicion etc.*); (*colloq.*) excessive; *c'est par trop violent*, it really is too bad.

violenter [vjɔlɑ̃'te], *v.t.* to offer *or* do violence to, to force; to constrain; to violate.

violer [vjɔ'le], *v.t.* to violate; to outrage, to transgress.

violet [vjɔ'lɛ], *a.* (*fem.* -ette) violet-colored, purple.—*n.m.* violet(color). —*n.f.* (-ette) (*Bot.*) violet.

violier [vjɔ'lje], *n.m.* wallflower, gillyflower.

violon [vjɔ'lɔ̃], *n.m.* violin, fiddle; violinist, fiddler; (*pop.*) lock-up, cells (*prison*).

violoncelle [vjɔlɔ̃'sɛl], *n.m.* violoncello, cello.

violoncelliste [vjɔlɔ̃sɛ'nist], *n.* violoncellist, cellist.

violoniste [vjɔlɔ'nist], *n.* violinist.

viorne [vjɔrn], *n.f.* viburnum.

vipère [vi'pɛ:r], *n.f.* viper, adder.

virage [vi'ra:ʒ], *n.m.* turning, cornering; turn, bend, corner; (*Naut.*) tacking; *virage incliné*, bank; *virage en épingle à cheveux*, hair-pin bend.

virago [vira'go], *n.f.* virago, termagant.

virée [vi're], *n.f.* turning; winding.

virement [vir'mɑ̃], *n.m.* turning; (*Naut.*) veering about, tacking; (*Book-keeping*) clearing, transfer; *banque de virement*, clearing-bank.

virer [vi're], *v.t.* to transfer, to clear (*a sum o money*).—*v.i.* to turn, to turn about; (*Naut.*) to tack, to veer about.

vireux [vi'rø], *a.* (*fem.* -euse) poisonous, noxious, nauseous.

virginal [virʒi'nal], *a.* (*m. pl.* -aux) virginal, maidenly.

Virginie [virʒi'ni], *f.* Virginia; (*Geog.*) *La Virginie*, Virginia.

virginité [virʒini'te], *n.f.* virginity, maidenhood.

virgule [vir'gyl], *n.f.* comma; *point et virgule*, semi-colon.

viril [vi'ril], *a.* virile, male; manly.

virilement [viril'mɑ̃], *adv.* like a man; in a manly way.

virilité [virili'te], *n.f.* virility; manhood.

virole [vi'rɔl], *n.f.* ferrule.

virtuel [vir'tɥɛl], *a.* (*fem.* -elle) virtual.

virtuellement [virtɥɛl'mɑ̃], *adv.* virtually; potentially.

virtuose [vir'tɥo:z], *n.* virtuoso.

virtuosité [virtɥozi'te], *n.f.* virtuosity.

virulence [viry'lɑ̃:s], *n.f.* virulence.

virulent [viry'lɑ̃], *a.* virulent.

virus [vi'ry:s], *n.m.* virus.

vis [vis], *n.f. inv.* screw; *escalier à vis*, spiral staircase.

visa [vi'za], *n.m.* visa, signature, endorsement (*on passports etc.*).

visage [vi'za:ʒ], *n.m.* face, visage, countenance; aspect, look, air; *à deux visages*, double-faced; *à visage découvert*, openly, barefacedly; *avoir bon visage*, to look well.

vis-à-vis [viza'vi], *prep. phr.* opposite, over against; towards, in relation to; *vis-à-vis de l'église*, opposite the church.—*adv. phr.* opposite.—*n.m. inv.* vis-à-vis (*in dancing etc.*); person opposite (*at table etc.*).

viscère [vi'sɛ:r], *n.m.* any of the viscera *or* vital organs.

viscosité [viskozi'te], *n.f.* viscosity, viscidity stickiness.

visée [vi'ze], *n.f.* aim, end; design, plan.

viser [vi'ze], *v.t.* to aim at; to allude to; to pursue; to endorse.—*v.i.* to aim, to take aim; to aspire (*à*).

viseur [vi'zœ:r], *n.m.* (*Phot.*) view finder.

visibilité [vizibili'te], *n.f.* visibility.

visible [vi'zibl], *a.* visible; evident, manifest, obvious.

visiblement [vizibla'mɑ̃], *adv.* visibly, obviously.

visière [vi'zjɛ:r], *n.f.* visor (*of a helmet*); peak (*of caps etc.*), eye shade; sight (*on fire-arms*).

vision [vi'zjɔ̃], *n.f.* vision, sight; dream, phantom, fancy.

visionnaire [vizjɔ'nɛ:r], *a.* visionary, fanciful. —*n.* seer; dreamer, visionary.

visite [vi'zit], *n.f.* visit; call; visitation (*of a bishop etc.*); examination, inspection; search; *droit de visite*, right of search; *faire la visite des bagages*, to examine luggage; *faire une visite* or *rendre visite*, to pay a visit.

visiter [vizi'te], *v.t.* to visit (*patients, clients etc.*); to visit (*cathedral etc.*); to search, to examine, to inspect.

visiteur [vizi'tœ:r], *n.m.* (*fem.* **-euse**) visitor, caller; inspector, searcher.

vison [vi'zɔ̃], *n.m.* mink (*animal*).

visqueux [vis'kø], *a.* (*fem.* **-euse**) viscous, sticky; slimy; clammy.

visser [vi'se], *v.t.* to screw, to screw on, up *or* down. **se visser**, *v.r.* to fix *or* attach oneself firmly.

visserie [vi'sri], *n.f.* screws, nuts and bolts.

Vistule [vis'tyl], **la**, *f.* the Vistula.

visuel [vi'zɥɛl], *a.* (*fem.* **-elle**) visual.

vital [vi'tal], *a.* (*m. pl.* **-aux**) vital; (*fig.*) essential.

vitalement [vital'mɑ̃], *adv.* vitally.

vitalité [vitali'te], *n.f.* vitality.

vitamine [vita'min], *n.f.* vitamin.

vite [vit], *a.* swift, quick, speedy, rapid.— *adv.* quick, quickly, fast, rapidly, expeditiously; *vite !* quick! look sharp!

vitesse [vi'tɛs], *n.f.* quickness, rapidity, celerity, swiftness, speed; (*Motor.*) gear; *à grande* or *à toute vitesse*, at full speed; *boîte de vitesse*, gear box; *changement de vitesse*, change of gear; *gagner (quelqu'un) de vitesse*, to outrun (someone).

Viti [vi'ti], **les Îles**, *f.pl.* the Fiji Islands.

viticole [viti'kɔl], *a.* pertaining to vine culture, viticultural.

viticulture [vitikyl'ty:r], *n.f.* vine-growing.

vitrage [vi'tra:ʒ], *n.m.* glazing; glass windows.

vitrail [vi'tra:j], *n.m.* (*pl.* **-aux**) stained-glass window.

vitre [vitr], *n.f.* pane of glass; window.

vitré [vi'tre], *a.* glazed, of glass; (*Anat. etc.*) vitreous; *porte vitrée*, glass door.

vitrer [vi'tre], *v.t.* to furnish with glass windows, to glaze.

vitreux [vi'trø], *a.* (*fem.* **-euse**) vitreous, glassy.

vitrier [vitri'e], *n.m.* glass-maker; glazier.

vitrine [vi'trin], *n.f.* shop window; show-case.

vitriol [vitri'ɔl], *n.m.* vitriol.

vitupération [vitypera'sjɔ̃], *n.f.* vituperation.

vitupérer [vitype're], *v.t.* (*conjug. like* CÉDER) to vituperate, to reprimand.

vivace [vi'vas], *a.* long-lived, perennial (*of plants*); inveterate, deep-rooted.

vivacité [vivasi'te], *n.f.* vivacity, liveliness, sprightliness; spirit, life, ardor.

vivant [vi'vɑ̃], *a.* living, alive; lively, animated; *langue vivante*, modern language; *portrait vivant*, lifelike portrait.—*n.m.* life, lifetime; *de son vivant*, in his lifetime.— *n.m.* (*fem.* **-e**) living person.

vivat! [vi'vat], *int.* and *n.m.* hurrah! huzza!

vivement [viv'mɑ̃], *adv.* quickly, briskly, sharply, vigorously; eagerly; keenly, acutely; smartly, angrily; spiritedly.

viveur [vi'vœ:r], *n.m.* (*fem.* **-euse**) rake, gay dog, person who leads a fast life.

vivier [vi'vje], *n.m.* fish pond.

vivifiant [vivi'fjɑ̃], *a.* vivifying, quickening; refreshing, invigorating.

vivifier [vivi'fje], *v.t.* to vivify, to quicken; to give life to; to enliven, to revive.

vivisection [vivisɛk'sjɔ̃], *n.f.* vivisection.

(C) **vivoir** [vi'vwa:r], *n.m.* living room.

vivoter [vivɔ'te], *v.i.* to live poorly, - to scrape along.

vivre [vi:vr], *v.i. irr.* to live, to be alive; to subsist, to live on, to be maintained; to board, to take one's meals; to behave; to last; *vive la France !* long live France! *qui vive?* who goes there ? *il ne sait pas vivre*, he has no manners.—*n.m.* living, board, food; (*pl.*) provisions, victuals, rations.

vocable [vɔ'kabl], *n.m.* vocable, word, name.

vocabulaire [vɔkaby'lɛ:r], *n.m.* vocabulary.

vocal [vɔ'kal], *a.* (*m. pl.* **-aux**) vocal.

vocation [vɔka'sjɔ̃], *n.f.* vocation, calling, call; inclination; bent, talent.

vociférant [vɔsife'rɑ̃], *a.* vociferous.

vociférer [vɔsife're], *v.t.* (*conjug. like* CÉDER) to vociferate, to bawl.

vœu [vø], *n.m.* (*pl.* **vœux**) vow; prayer, wish, desire; vote, suffrage.

vogue [vɔg], *n.f.* vogue, fashion; credit, craze; *avoir de la vogue*, to be in fashion.

voguer [vɔ'ge], *v.i.* to move forward by rowing (*of a galley etc.*); to sail, to float, to move along.

voici [vwa'si], *prep.* see here, behold; here is, here are, this is, these are; ago, past; *le voilà, me voici*, there he is, here I am; *monsieur que voici*, this gentleman; *voici trois mois que je suis à l'hôpital*, I have been in hospital for the past three months.

voie [vwa], *n.f.* way, road; line, path, track; (*fig.*) organ, medium, channel, course; conveyance; gauge, breadth (*between the wheels of carriages*); load; (*Chem.*) process; *être en voie de*, to be in a fair way to; *voie d'eau*, (*Naut.*) leak; *voie ferrée*, railway track; *voie libre*, line clear.

voilà [vwa'la], *prep.* there, behold, there now, there is, there are, that is; *ah ! vous voilà*, oh! there you are! *voilà une heure qu'il parle*, he has been speaking for an hour.

voile (1) [vwal], *n.m.* veil; (*fig.*) cover, mask, disguise, show, pretence.

voile (2) [vwal], *n.f.* sail; canvas; (*fig.*) ship; *faire voile*, to sail, to set sail.

voilé [vwa'le], *a.* rigged; veiled; clouded, dull, dim; (*wheel*) buckled, out of true.

voiler [vwa'le], *v.t.* to veil; to cover, to cloak, to blind, to disguise; to conceal; to buckle (*wheel*).—*v.i.* and **se voiler**, *v.r.* to wear a veil; to cloud over (*of the sky*); to buckle (*of a wheel*).

voilier [vwa'lje], *n.m.* sail maker; sailing ship.

voir [vwa:r], *v.t. irr.* to see; to behold; to witness; to look at, to observe, to view; to inspect, to superintend; to overlook; to visit; to frequent; *faire voir*, to show, to let see; *voyons !* let us see! now then!—*v.i.* to see, to look, to watch; to have one's sight; *voir à* or *voir à ce que*, to see to it that. **se voir**, *v.r.* to see oneself; to see each other; to visit each other; to be obvious.

voire [vwa:r], *adv.* and even, and indeed.

voirie [vwa'ri], *n.f.* roads, system of roads; commission of public streets and highways; refuse dump.

voisin [vwa'zɛ̃], *a.* bordering, adjacent, next; next door, neighboring. —*n.m.* (*fem.* **-e**) neighbor.

voisinage [vwazi'na:ʒ], *n.m.* neighbourhood; vicinity, proximity, nearness; neighbours.

voiturage [vwaty'ra:ʒ], *n.m.* carriage, cartage (*of goods etc.*).

voiture [vwa'ty:r], *n.f.* vehicle, conveyance; carriage; coach; cart, car; cart-load; *descendre de voiture*, to alight from a carriage; *en voiture!* take your seats! *se promener en voiture* or *aller en voiture*, to drive; *voiture d'enfant*, perambulator, baby-carriage, (*fam.*) pram.

voiturer [vwaty're], *v.t.* to carry, to convey, to cart.

voiturier [vwaty'rje], *n.m.* carrier, carter.

voix [vwa], *n.f. inv.* voice; tone, sound; vote, suffrage; opinion, judgment; singer; *à demi-voix*, in a low voice; *à haute voix*, in a loud voice; *de vive voix*, by word of mouth.

vol (1) [vɔl], *n.m.* flying, soaring; flight; flock (*of birds*); spread (*of wings*); *au vol*, on the wing; *à vol d'oiseau*, as the crow flies.

vol (2) [vɔl], *n.m.* theft, robbery, stealing, larceny; stolen goods; *vol à l'étalage*, shoplifting; *vol avec effraction*, burglary.

volage [vɔ'la:ʒ], *a.* fickle, inconstant, flighty.

volaille [vɔ'la:j], *n.f.* poultry, fowls; *marchand de volaille*, poulterer.

volant [vɔ'lɑ̃], *a.* flying; loose, floating; movable, portable.—*n.m.* shuttlecock; flounce (*of a dress*); flywheel (*of machinery*); steering-wheel (*of a car*); sail (*of a windmill*).

volatil [vɔla'til], *a.* (*Chem.*) volatile; (*fig.*) volatile (*of temperament*).

volatile [vɔla'til], *a.* winged.—*n.m.* winged creature, bird.

vol-au-vent [vɔlo'vɑ̃], *n.m. inv.* vol-au-vent, puff-pie.

volcan [vɔl'kɑ̃], *n.m.* volcano.

volcanique [vɔlka'nik], *a.* volcanic, fiery.

volée [vɔ'le], *n.f.* flight (*of birds etc.*); flock, covey; brood; bevy; volley (*of guns*); shower (*of blows*); thrashing; peal (*of bells*); *à la volée*, flying, as it flies, in the air; (*fig.*) rashly, at random; *sonner à toute volée*, to ring a full peal; *volée d'escalier*, flight of stairs.

voler (1) [vɔ'le], *v.i.* to fly; to take wing, to soar; *entendre voler une mouche*, to hear a pin drop.

voler (2) [vɔ'le], *v.t.* to steal, to rob; to fleece, to plunder; (*fig.*) to embezzle, to usurp.—*v.i.* to steal.

volerie [vɔl'ri], *n.f.* robbery; pilfering.

volet [vɔ'le], *n.m.* (window-)shutter; dovecot; (*Av.*) flap.

voleter [vɔl'te], *v.i.* (*conjug. like* APPELER) to flutter.

voleur [vɔ'lœ:r], *n.m.* (*fem.* -euse) thief, robber; plunderer, extortioner; stealer; *au voleur!* stop thief!

volière [vɔ'lje:r], *n.f.* aviary, large bird-cage.

volontaire [vɔlɔ̃'tɛ:r], *a.* voluntary, willing; intended, intentional; spontaneous; obstinate, wilful.—*n.* volunteer.

volontairement [vɔlɔ̃tɛr'mɑ̃], *adv.* voluntarily; wilfully.

volonté [vɔlɔ̃'te], *n.f.* will; (*pl.*) whims, caprices; *avoir de la bonne volonté*, to be willing; *à volonté*, at pleasure, at will; *dernières volontés*, last will and testament; *faire ses quatre volontés*, (*colloq.*)

to do as one pleases; *mauvaise volonté* illwill; unwillingness.

volontiers [vɔlɔ̃'tje], *adv.* willingly, gladly with pleasure.

volt [vɔlt], *n.m.* (*Elec.*) volt.

voltage [vɔl'ta:ʒ], *n.m.* voltage.

volte-face [vɔlt'fas], *n.f. inv.* turning round; *faire volte-face*, to face about; (*fig.*) to reverse one's opinions completely.

voltige [vɔl ti:ʒ], *n.f.* slack-rope gymnastics, flying-trapeze exercises.

voltigeant [vɔlti'ʒɑ̃], *a.* fluttering, hovering.

voltigement [vɔlti'ʒ mɑ̃], *n.m.* tumbling; fluttering.

voltiger [vɔlti'ʒe], *v.i.* (*conjug. like* MANGER) to flutter, to fly about, to hover.

voltigeur [vɔlti'ʒœ:r], *n.m.* vaulter; light-infantry soldier, rifleman.

voltmètre [vɔlt'mɛtr], *n.m.* voltmeter.

volubilis [vɔlybi'lis], *n.m.* convolvulus.

volubilité [vɔlybili'te], *n.f.* volubility, fluency glibness.

volume [vɔ'lym], *n.m.* volume; bulk, size mass.

volumineux [vɔlymi'nø], *a.* (*fem.* -euse) voluminous, bulky.

volupté [vɔlyp'te], *n.f.* voluptuousness, sensual pleasure.

voluptueux [vɔlyp'tɥø], *a.* (*fem.* -euse) voluptuous, sensual.—*n.m.* (*fem.* -euse) voluptuary.

volute [vɔ'ly:t], *n.f.* volute; scroll.

vomir [vɔ'mi:r], *v.t.* to vomit, to throw up, (*fig.*) to belch forth.—*v.i.* to vomit, to be sick.

vomissement [vɔmis'mɑ̃], *n.m.* vomit(ing).

vorace [vɔ'ras], *a.* voracious, ravenous.

voracité [vɔrasi'te], *n.f.* voracity.

vos [vo], [VOTRE].

votant [vɔ'tɑ̃], *n.m.* (*fem.* -e) voter.

vote [vɔt], *n.m.* vote; division, voting, poll.

voter [vɔ'te], *v.i.* to vote; to pass (*a bill*).

votif [vɔ'tif], *a.* (*fem.* -tive) votive.

votre [vɔtr], *a. poss.* (*pl.* **vos**) your.

vôtre [vo:tr], *pron.poss.* (*m. sing.* **le vôtre**, *fem. sing.* **la vôtre**, *pl.* **les vôtres**) yours.—*n.* your own, your own property; (*pl.*) your relations, friends etc.; your pranks, tricks.

vouer [vwe], *v.t.* to devote, to dedicate; to vow, to swear. **se vouer**, *v.r.* to devote oneself.

vouloir [vu'lwa:r], *v.t. irr.* to want; to desire, to wish, to require; to consent; to please; to choose; to determine; to try, to attempt; to admit, to grant; to mean; *en vouloir à quelqu'un*, to bear someone a grudge; *oui, je (le) veux bien*, yes, I am willing; *que veut dire cela?* what does that mean? *que voulez-vous?* what do you want? what can I do for you? what cae you expect? *veuillez me dire*, please tell me.—*n.m.* will; *bon vouloir*, goodwill, *mauvais vouloir*, illwill.

voulu [vu'ly], *a.* wished desired, required, requisite; due, received; deliberate, studied.

vous [vu], *pron. pers.* you; to you.

voûte [vut], *n.f.* arch, vault. (*fig.*) roof, canopy; *clef de voûte*, keystone.

voûté [vu'te], *a.* vaulted, curved.

voûter [vu'te], *v.t.* to vault, to arch over; to bend. **se voûter**, *v.r.* to arch to vault; to be bent, to stoop.

vouvoyer [vuvwa'je], *v.t.* (*conjug. like* EM-PLOYER) to say *vous* instead of *tu* when addressing somebody.

voyage [vwa'ja:ʒ], *n.m.* travel; journey, voyage, trip; visit; (*pl.*) travels; *bon voyage !* pleasant journey to you! *être en voyage,* to be travelling.

voyager [vwaja'ʒe], *v.i.* (*conjug. like* MANGER) to travel, to journey.

voyageur [vwaja'ʒœ:r], *a.* (*fem.* -euse) travelling, migrating; *commis voyageur,* commercial traveller; *oiseau voyageur,* migratory bird; *pigeon voyageur,* carrier pigeon.—*n.m.* (*fem.* -euse) traveller; passenger.

voyant [vwa'jɑ̃], *a.* gaudy, showy (*of colors*).—*n.m.* (*fem.* -e) seer, clairvoyant.

voyelle [vwa'jɛl], *n.f.* vowel.

voyou [vwa'ju], *n.m.* (*fam.*) guttersnipe, hooligan; loafer.

vrac (en) [ɑ̃'vrak], *adv. phr.* in bulk, loose, pell-mell.

vrai [vrɛ], *a.* true, real, genuine; right, proper, fit; downright, arrant.—*int.* truly, really, in truth!—*n.m.* truth; *à vrai dire,* to tell the truth, as a matter of fact.

vraiment [vrɛ'mɑ̃], *adv.* truly, in truth; indeed, really!

vraisemblable [vrɛsɑ̃'blabl], *a.* likely, probable.—*n.m.* probability, likelihood.

vraisemblance [vrɛsɑ̃'blɑ̃:s], *n.f.* probability, likelihood, verisimilitude.

vrille [vri:j], *n.f.* gimlet, borer, piercer; (*Bot.*) tendril; (*Av.*) tail-spin.

vriller [vri'je], *v.t.* to bore.—*v.i.* to ascend spirally.

vrillette [vri'jɛt], *n.f.* death-watch beetle.

vrombir [vrɔ̃'bi:r], *v.i.* to buzz, to hum, to whirr, to purr, to throb.

vu [vy], *a.* considered, regarded; seen, observed.—*prep.* considering, in view of.—*n.m.* sight, examination, inspection; (*Law*) preamble.—*conj. phr. vu que,* seeing that, whereas.

vue [vy], *n.f.* sight, eyesight; eyes; view, survey, inspection; prospect; appearance; light, window; design; *à perte de vue,* as far as the eye can reach, out of sight; *à vue d'œil,* visibly.

Vulcain [vyl'kɛ̃], *m.* Vulcan.

vulcaniser [vylkani'ze], *v.t.* to vulcanize.

vulgaire [vyl'gɛ:r], *a.* vulgar, common.—*n.m.* the common herd.

vulgairement [vylgɛr'mɑ̃], *adv.* vulgarly, commonly.

vulgariser [vylgari'ze], *v.t.* to popularize.

vulgarité [vylgari'te], *n.f.* vulgarity.

vulnérabilité [vylnerabili'te], *n.f.* vulnerability.

vulnérable [vylne'rabl], *a.* vulnerable.

W

W, w [dubla've], *n.m.* this twenty-third letter of the alphabet is used only in borrowed words.

wagon [va'gɔ̃], *n.m.* (*Rail.*) car, coach; freight car.

wagon-lit [vagɔ̃'li], *n.m.* (*pl.* **wagons-lits**) sleeping-car, sleeper.

wagonnet [vagɔ'nɛ], *n.m.* tip-truck.

wallon [wa'lɔ̃], *a.* (*fem.* -**onne**) Walloon.—*n.m.* Walloon (*language*); (**Wallon,** *fem.* -**onne**) Walloon (*person*).

warrant [va'rɑ̃], *n.m.* warrant.

warranter [varɑ̃'te], *v.t.* to warrant, to guarantee, to certify.

water [wa'tɛr], **les W.C.** [lɛvɛ'se], *n.m. pl.* water closet, lavatory, toilet.

watt [wat], *n.m.* (*Elec.*) watt.

wattman [wat'man], *n.m.* (*pl.*-**men**) motorman.

week-end [wik'ɛnd], *n.m.* (*pl.* **week-ends**) week-end.

whisky [wis'ki], *n.m.* whisky.

whist [wist], *n.m.* whist.

wigwam [wig'wam], *n.m.* wigwam.

wolfram [vɔl'fram], *n.m.* wolfram (*tungsten ore*).

X

X, x [iks], *n.m.* the twenty-fourth letter of the alphabet; *rayons X,* X-rays.

xénophobe [ksenɔ'fɔb], *a.* and *n.* xenophobe.

xérès [kse'rɛs], *n.m.* sherry (*wine*).

xylophone [ksilɔ'fɔn], *n.m.* (*Mus.*) xylophone.

Y

Y, y [i grɛk], *n.m.* the twenty-fifth letter of the alphabet.

y [i], *adv.* there; thither; within, at home; *ça y est !* that's it! *il y a,* there is, there are; *je l'y ai vu,* I saw him there; *j'y suis,* I follow you, I get you; *y compris,* included.—*pron.* by, for, in, at *or* to him, her, it *or* them.

yacht [jɔt, jak], *n.m.* yacht.

Yémen [je'mɛn], **le,** *m.* Yemen.

yéménite [jema'nit], *a.* Yemeni.—*n.* (**Yéménite**) Yemeni (*person*).

yeuse [jø:z], *n.f.* ilex, holm oak.

yeux [jø:], [ŒIL].

yodler [jɔ'dle], *v.i.* (*Mus.*) to yodel.

yogi *or* **yogui** [jo'gi], *n.m.* yogi.

yole [jɔl], *n.f.* yawl, gig.

yougoslave [jugɔs'lav], *a.* Yugoslav.—*n.m.* Yugoslav (*language*).—*n.* (**Yougoslave**) Yugoslav (*person*).

Yougoslavie [jugɔsla'vi], **la,** *f.* Yugoslavia.

youyou [ju'ju], *n.m.* dinghy.

Z

Z, z [zed], *n.m.* the twenty-sixth letter of the alphabet.
Zambie [zã'bi], **la,** *f.* Zambia.
zèbre [zɛːbr], *n.m.* zebra.
zébré [ze'bre], *a.* striped like the zebra.
zèle [zɛːl], *n.m.* zeal, warmth, ardor, enthusiasm.
zélé [ze'le], *a.* zealous.
zélote [ze'lɔt], *n.m.* zealot.
zénith [ze'nit], *n.m.* zenith.
zéphire, zéphyr or **zéphyre** [ze'fiːr], *n.m.* zephyr, gentle breeze.
zéro [ze'ro], *n.m.* nought; zero (*of the thermometer*); (*fig.*) a mere cipher, nonentity.
zeste [zɛst], *n.m.* woody skin dividing sections of a walnut; peel (*of orange, lemon etc.*), rind; (*fig.*) straw, fig, nothing.
zézaiement or **zézayement** [zezɛ(j)'mã]
n.m. ·lisping, lisp (*incorrect pronunciation of* [z] *instead of* [ʒ]).
zézayer [zeze'je], *v.i.* (*conjug. like* PAYER) to lisp.
zibeline [zi'blin], *n.f.* sable.
zigzag [zig'zag], *n.m.* zigzag; *éclair en zig-zag*, forked lightning.
zinc [zɛ̃ːg], *n.m.* zinc; (*slang*) bar or counter of a bistro.
zingaro [zɛ̃ga'ro], *n.m.* (*pl.* **zingari**) gipsy.
zinguer [zɛ̃'ge], *v.t.* to cover with zinc; to zinc.
zizanie [ziza'ni], *n.f.* tare, *darnel; (*fig.*) discord, bickering.
zodiaque [zɔ'djak], *n.m.* zodiac.
zone [zoːn], *n.f.* zone, belt, area.
zoo [zo'o], *n.m.* (*fam.*) zoo.
zoologie [zɔɔlɔ'ʒi], *n.f.* zoology.
zoologique [zɔɔlɔ'ʒik], *a.* zoological.
zoologiste [zɔɔlɔ'ʒist], *n.* zoologist.
zouave [zwaːv], *n.m.* Zouave (*soldier*).
zut! [zyt], *int.* (*fam.*) (*to convey anger, scorn, disappointment, flat refusal*); *zut! zut alors! non, zut!* be blowed! no go! never! bother!

A, a (1) [ei]. première lettre de l'alphabet; (*Mus.*) la, *m.*; *a.m.*, du matin.

a (2) [ei, ə], **an** [æn, ən] (*before vowel*), *indef. art.* un, *m.*, une, *f.*; *a shilling a pound*, un shilling la livre; *three a day*, trois par jour.

aback [ə'bæk], *adv.* en arrière; (*fig.*) à l'improviste, au dépourvu.

abacus ['æbakəs], *n.* (*pl.* **abaci** ['æbəkai]) (*Arch., Math.*) abaque, *m.*

abaft [ə'bɑ:ft], *adv.* sur l'arrière, en arrière.— *prep.* en arrière de, à l'arrière de.

abandon [ə'bændən], *v.t.* abandonner; délaisser, quitter; renoncer à, se désister de. —*n.* abandon, *m.*; désinvolture, *f.*

abandoned [ə'bændənd], *a.* abandonné; dépravé.

abandonment [ə'bændənmənt], *n.* abandonnement; délaissement; abandon, *m.*

abase [ə'beis], *v.t.* abaisser; ravaler.

abasement [ə'beismənt], *n.* abaissement; ravalement, *m.*; humiliation, *f.*

abash [ə'bæʃ], *v.t.* déconcerter, décontenancer; interdire, confondre.

abate [ə'beit], *v.t.* diminuer; rabattre; affaiblir, atténuer; amortir; calmer, apaiser. —*v.i.* diminuer; s'affaiblir; se calmer, s'apaiser (*temps etc.*); tomber, baisser, s'abattre (*vent etc.*).

abatement [ə'beitmənt], *n.* diminution, réduction, *f.*; rabais; affaiblissement, adoucissement; apaisement, *m.*

abbacy ['æbəsi], *n.* dignité d'abbé, *f.*

abbess ['æbes], *n.* abbesse, *f.*

abbey ['æbi], *n.* abbaye, *f.*

abbot ['æbət], *n.* abbé, supérieur (*d'abbaye*), *m.*

abbreviate [ə'bri:vieit], *v.t.* abréger; raccourcir.

abbreviation [əbri:vi'eiʃən], *n.* abréviation, *f.*

abdicate ['æbdikeit], *v.t.*, *v.i.* abdiquer.

abdication [æbdi'keiʃən], *n.* abdication, *f.*

abdomen [æb'doumən, 'æbdəmən], *n.* abdomen, bas-ventre, *m.*

abdominal [æb'dɔminəl], *a.* abdominal.

abduct [æb'dʌkt], *v.t.* détourner, enlever (*clandestinement ou par force*).

abduction [æb'dʌkʃən], *n.* abduction, *f.*, enlèvement (*de mineur etc.*), détournement, *m.*

abductor [æb'dʌktə], *n.* (*Anat.*) abducteur; (*Law*) ravisseur, *m*

abed [ə'bed], *adv.* au lit, couché.

aberration [æbə'reiʃən], *n.* aberration, *f.*; éloignement, écart, égarement, *m.*; erreur (*de jugement*), *f.*

abet [ə'bet], *v.t.* soutenir, encourager (*à un crime*); *to aid and abet*, être le complice.

abetment [ə'betmənt], **abetting** [ə'betiŋ], *n.* encouragement (*à un crime*), *m.*

abettor [ə'betə], *n.* instigateur (*d'un crime*), *m.*; complice, *m.*, *f.*

abeyance [ə'beiəns], *n.* vacance; suspension, *f.*; *in abeyance*, en suspens; *to fall into abeyance*, tomber en désuétude.

abhor [əb'hɔ:], *v.t.* abhorrer, détester.

abhorrence [əb'hɔrəns], *n.* horreur, *f.*

abhorrent [əb'hɔrənt], *a.* odieux, répugnant (à).

abide [ə'baid], *v.t. irr.* attendre; supporter; subir, souffrir.—*v.i.* demeurer, rester; séjourner; durer; *to abide by* (*a decision etc.*), rester fidèle à; *to abide by* (*the laws etc.*), se conformer à.

abiding [ə'baidiŋ], *a.* constant, immuable.

ability [ə'biliti], *n.* capacité, *f.*; pouvoir; talent, *m.*; habileté, *f.*

abject ['æbdʒekt], *a.* abject, bas, vil.

abjection [æb'dʒekʃən], **abjectness** ['æbdʒektnis], *n.* abjection, misère, *f.*

abjectly ['æbdʒektli], *adv.* d'une manière abjecte.

abjure [æb'dʒuə], *v.t.* abjurer; renoncer à, renier.

ablative ['æblətiv], *a.* and *n.* (*Gram.*) ablatif, *m.*

ablaze [ə'bleiz], *a.* en feu, en flammes; (*fig.*) enflammé.

able [eibl], *a.* capable (*de*), à même (*de*); habile; *to be able to*, pouvoir.

able-bodied ['eiblbɔdid], *a.* fort, robuste, vigoureux.

ablution [ə'blu:ʃən], *n.* ablution, *f.*

ably ['eibli], *adv.* habilement, avec talent.

abnegation [æbni'geiʃən], *n.* abnégation, renonciation, *f.*; désaveu, *m.*

abnormal [æb'nɔ:məl], *a.* anormal.

abnormality [æbnɔ:'mæliti], *n.* anomalie, difformité, *f.*

abnormally [æb'nɔ:məli], *adv.* anormalement.

aboard [ə'bɔ:d], *adv.* à bord (*de*).

abode (1) [ə'boud], *n.* demeure, habitation, *f.*; séjour, *m.*

abode (2) [ə'boud], *past and p.p.* [ABIDE].

abolish [ə'bɔliʃ], *v.t.* abolir; supprimer.

abolishment [ə'bɔliʃmənt], **abolition** [æbə'liʃən], *n.* abolition, suppression, *f.*; abolissement, *m.*

abominable [ə'bɔminəbl], *a.* abominable, infâme, détestable.

abominably [ə'bɔminəbli], *adv.* abominablement.

abominate [ə'bɔmineit], *v.t.* abominer, détester.

abomination [əbɔmi'neiʃən], *n.* abomination, horreur, *f.*

aboriginal [æbə'ridʒinəl], *a.* aborigène, primitif.—*n.* aborigène, *m.*, *f.*

aborigine [æbə'ridʒini], *n.* aborigène, *m.*, *f.*

abortion [ə'bɔːʃən], *n.* avortement (*acte*); avorton (*embryon*), *m.*

abortive [ə'bɔːtiv], *a.* abortif, manqué; avorté.

abortively [ə'bɔːtivli], *adv.* avant terme; (*fig.*) sans résultat, sans succès.

abortiveness [ə'bɔːtivnis], *n.* (*fig.*) insuccès, *m.*

abound [ə'baund], *v.i.* abonder (*de ou en*), regorger (*de*).

abounding [ə'baundiŋ], *a.* abondant.

about [ə'baut], *prep.* autour de; auprès de; sur; vers; environ; touchant, au sujet de, à l'égard de; à peu près; sur le point de; dans, par; *about that*, là-dessus, à ce sujet; *about two o'clock*, vers (les) deux heures; *what is it all about?* de quoi s'agit-il?—*adv.* tout autour, à l'entour, à la ronde; çà et là; *to be about to*, être sur le point de.

above [ə'bʌv], *prep.* au-dessus de, par-dessus; en amont de; plus de; au delà de; *above all*, surtout, par-dessus tout; *above board*, ouvertement, franchement.—*adv.* en haut; là-haut; au-dessus; ci-dessus.

abrasion [ə'breiʒən], *n.* abrasion, écorchure, *f.*

abrasive [ə'breisiv], *a.* and *n.* abrasif, *m.*

abreast [ə'brest], *adv.* de front, à côté l'un de l'autre; (*fig.*) de pair avec.

abridge [ə'bridʒ], *v.t.* abréger, raccourcir; restreindre, priver; *abridged edition* (*of book*), édition réduite, *f.*

abridgment [ə'bridʒmənt], *n.* abrégé, précis, *m.*; réduction, diminution, *f.*

abroad [ə'brɔːd], *adv.* à l'étranger; au loin, de tous côtés; *to get abroad*, se répandre (*nouvelles*).

abrogate ['æbrogeit], *v.t.* abroger.

abrogation [æbro'geiʃən], *n.* abrogation, *f.*

abrupt [ə'brʌpt], *a.* brusque; brisé, saccadé; précipité, soudain; abrupt, escarpé, à pic.

abruptly [ə'brʌptli], *adv.* brusquement, tout à coup.

abruptness [ə'brʌptnis], *n.* précipitation; (*fig.*) brusquerie, rudesse, *f.*; escarpement, *m.*

abscess ['æbses], *n.* abcès, dépôt, *m.*

abscond [əb'skɔnd], *v.i.* se soustraire (*furtivement*) aux poursuites de la justice); disparaître; (*fam.*) décamper.

absconder [əb'skɔndə], *n.* fugitif, *m.*; (*Law*) contumace, *m.*, *f.*

absence ['æbsəns], *n.* absence, *f.*; éloignement, *m.*; absence d'esprit, distraction, *f.*; manque, *m.*

absent ['æbsənt], *a.* absent.—[æb'sent], *v.r. to absent oneself*, s'absenter.

absentee [æbsən'tiː], *n.* absent, manquant, *m.*

absenteeism [æbsən'tiːizm], *n.* absentéisme, *m.*

absent-minded ['æbsənt'maindid], *a.* distrait.

absinthe ['æbsinθ], *n.* absinthe, *f.*

absolute ['æbsəluːt], *a.* absolu, illimité; irrévocable (*décret*); véritable.

absolutely [æbsə'luːtli], *adv.* absolument.

absolution [æbsə'luːʃən], *n.* absolution; (*R.-C. Ch.*) absoute, *f.*

absolve [əb'zɔlv], *v.t.* absoudre (*de*); délier, décharger, dégager, affranchir.

absorb [əb'sɔːb], *v.t.* absorber; amortir (*un choc*).

absorbent [əb'sɔːbənt], *a.* and *n.* absorbant, *m.*

absorption [əb'sɔːpʃən], *n.* absorption, *f.*; absorbement, amortissement, *m.*

abstain [əb'stein], *v.i.* s'abstenir (*de*).

abstainer [əb'steinə], *n.* buveur d'eau, *m.*, abstème, *m.*, *f.*; *total abstainer*, personne qui ne boit jamais d'alcool, *f.*

abstemious [əb'stiːmiəs], *a.* tempérant, sobre.

abstemiously [əb'stiːmiəsli], *adv.* sobrement, avec modération.

abstemiousness [əb'stiːmiəsnis], *n.* abstinence; modération, sobriété, *f.*

abstention [əb'stenʃən], *n.* abstention, *f.*

abstinence ['æbstinəns], *n.* abstinence, *f.*

abstinent ['æbstinənt], *a.* abstinent, sobre.

abstract (1) [æb'strækt], *v.t.* soustraire dérober, détourner; faire abstraction de; résumer, abréger.

abstract (2) ['æbstrækt], *a.* abstrait.—*n.* abrégé, résumé, précis, *m.*; analyse, *f.*; (*Comm.*) relevé, *m.*

abstracted [æb'stræktid], *a.* séparé; distrait, rêveur, pensif; soustrait, dérobé.

abstractedness [æb'stræktidnis], *n.* caractère abstrait, *m.*; préoccupation, *f.*

abstraction [æb'strækʃən], *n.* soustraction, distraction; abstraction; préoccupation, *f.*

abstractly ['æbstræktli], *adv.* abstractivement, d'une manière abstraite.

abstruse [æb'struːs], *a.* caché; abstrus, obscur.

absurd [əb'səːd], *a.* absurde.

absurdity [əb'səːditi], *n.* absurdité, *f.*

absurdly [əb'səːdli], *adv.* absurdement.

abundance [ə'bʌndəns], *n.* abondance, grande quantité, *f.*; grand nombre, *m.*; (*fig.*) prospérité, *f.*

abundant [ə'bʌndənt], *a.* abondant.

abundantly [ə'bʌndəntli], *adv.* abondamment, en abondance, à foison.

abuse (1) [ə'bjuːz], *v.t.* abuser de; maltraiter; médire de; injurier, dire des injures à; séduire.

abuse (2) [ə'bjuːs], *n.* abus, *m.*; insultes, injures, *f. pl.*

abuser [ə'bjuːzə], *n.* détracteur; séducteur; trompeur, *m.*

abusive [ə'bjuːsiv], *a.* abusif; injurieux.

abusively [ə'bjuːsivli], *adv.* abusivement; injurieusement.

abusiveness [ə'bjuːsivnis], *n.* langage injurieux *ou* grossier, *m.*

abut [ə'bʌt], *v.i.* aboutir (à); (*Build.*) s'appuyer (*contre*).

abysmal [ə'bizməl], *a.* sans fond; (*ignorance*) profonde.

abyss [ə'bis], *n.* abîme, gouffre, *m.*

Abyssinia [æbi'sinjə], l'Abyssinie, l'Éthiopie, *f.*

Abyssinian [æbi'sinjən], *a.* abyssinien.—*n.* Abyssinien (*personne*), *m.*

acacia [ə'keiʃə], *n.* acacia, *m.*

academic [ækə'demik], *a.* **academical** [ækə'demikəl], *a.* académique, universitaire, classique, scolaire.

academician [əkædə'miʃən], *n.* académicien, *m.*

academy [ə'kædəmi], *n.* académie (*société savante*); école libre, *f.*, pensionnat, *m.*, institution, *f.*

acanthus [ə'kænθəs], *n.* acanthe, *f.*

accede [æk'siːd], *v.i.* accéder, consentir (à); monter (*sur le trône*).

accelerate [æk'seləreit], *v.t.* accélérer; hâter.—*v.i.* s'accélérer.

acceleration [ækselə'reiʃən], *n.* accélération, *f.*

accelerator [æk'seləreitə], *n.* accélérateur, *m.*

accent (1) [æk'sent], *v.t.* accentuer.

accent (2) ['æksənt], *n.* accent, *m.*

accentuate [æk'sentjueit], *v.t.* accentuer.

accept [ək'sept], *v.t.* accepter, agréer, admettre.

acceptability [əkseptə'biliti], **acceptableness** [ək'septəblnis], *n.* acceptabilité, *f.*; droit au bon accueil, *m.*

acceptable [ək'septəbl], *a.* acceptable; agréable.

acceptance [ək'septəns], *n.* acceptation, *f.*; accueil favorable, *m.*

acceptation [æksep'teiʃən], *n.* acception, *f.*, sens (*d'un mot*), *m.*

access ['ækses], *n.* accès, abord, *m.*; entrée, admission, *f.*

accessible [æk'sesibl], *a.* accessible, abordable.

accession [æk'seʃən], *n.* acquisition; augmentation, addition, *f.*, accroissement; avènement (*au trône etc.*), *m.*

accessory [æk'sesəri], *a.* accessoire.—*n.* accessoire (*chose*), *m.*; complice (*personne*), *m.*, *f.*

accidence ['æksidəns], *n.* morphologie, *f.*; rudiments (*de grammaire*), *m. pl.*

accident ['æksidənt], *n.* accident, *m.*, avarie, *f.*, hasard; incident; malheur, *m.*

accidental [æksi'dentəl], *a.* accidentel, fortuit.

accidentally [æksi'dentəli], *adv.* accidentellement; par hasard.

acclaim [ə'kleim], *v.t.* acclamer, applaudir à; proclamer.—*n.* acclamation, *f.*

acclamation [æklə'meiʃən], *n.* acclamation, *f.*

acclimatation [əklaimə'teiʃən], **acclimation** [æklai'meiʃən], *n.* acclimatement, *m.*; acclimatation, *f.*

acclimatization [əklaimətai'zeiʃən], *n.* acclimatation, *f.*

acclimatize [ə'klaimətaiz], *v.t.* acclimater; *to become acclimatized*, s'acclimater; s'accoutumer.

acclivity [ə'kliviti], *n.* montée, côte, rampe, *f.*

accolade [æko'leid], *n.* accolade, *f.*

accommodate [ə'kɔmədeit], *v.t.* accommoder, ajuster; loger, recevoir; fournir; obliger (*par*), servir (*de*).

accommodating [ə'kɔmədeitiŋ], *a.* accommodant, obligeant; complaisant.

accommodation [əkɔmə'deiʃən], *n.* ajustement, accommodement, *m.*; complaisance; convenance, *f.*; logement, *m.*; facilités, *f.pl.*

accompaniment [ə'kʌmpnimənt], *n.* accompagnement, *m.*

accompanist [ə'kʌmpənist], *n.* (*Mus.*) accompagnateur, *m.*, accompagnatrice, *f.*

accompany [ə'kʌmpəni], *v.t.* accompagner; reconduire (*à sa voiture etc.*).

accomplice [ə'kʌmplis], *n.* complice, *m.*, *f.*, compère, *m.*

accomplish [ə'kʌmpliʃ], *v.t.* accomplir, achever; effectuer; réaliser (*une prédiction etc.*).

accomplished [ə'kʌmpliʃt], *a.* accompli, achevé; parfait.

accomplishment [ə'kʌmpliʃmənt], *n.* accomplissement, *m.*; exécution, *f.*; (*usu. pl.*) arts d'agrément, talents, *m.pl.*

accord [ə'kɔːd], *v.t.* accorder, concéder.—*v.i.* s'accorder, être d'accord.—*n.* accord, consentement, *m.*; *of one's own accord*, de son propre gré, spontanément; *with one accord*, d'un commun accord.

accordance [ə'kɔːdəns], *n.* accord, rapport, *m.*; conformité, *f.*

according [ə'kɔːdiŋ], *a.* conforme (*à*); *according as*, selon que, suivant que; *according to*, selon, suivant, conformément à, d'après.

accordingly [ə'kɔːdiŋli], *adv.* en conséquence; donc, aussi.

accordion [ə'kɔːdiən], *n.* accordéon, *m.*

accost [ə'kɔst], *v.t.* accoster, aborder.

account [ə'kaunt], *n.* compte; mémoire, rapport, exposé, compte rendu, *m.*; relation, *f.*, récit. *m.*; raison; cause; (*fig.*) considération, valeur, *f.*; cas, poids, *m.*; *by all accounts*, au dire de tout le monde; *current account*, compte courant; *on account of*, à cause de; *to keep accounts*, tenir les livres.—*v.t.* compter; estimer (*de*), regarder (*comme*), tenir (*pour*).—*v.i.* *to account for*, rendre compte de, expliquer; répondre de, rendre raison de.

accountable [ə'kauntəbl], *a.* responsable; comptable.

accountancy [ə'kauntənsi], *n.* comptabilité, *f.*

accountant [ə'kauntənt], *n.* comptable, agent comptable, *m.*; *chartered accountant*, expert comptable, *m.*

account book [ə'kauntbuk], *n.* livre de comptes, *m.*

accouter [ə'kuːtə], *v.t.* habiller, équiper; accoutrer (*un chevalier etc.*).

accouterment [ə'kuːtəmənt], *n.* harnachement; équipement (*du soldat*), *m.*

accredit [ə'kredit], *v.t.* accréditer.

accretion [ə'kriːʃən], *n.* accroissement, *m.*

accrue [ə'kruː], *v.i.* provenir, résulter (*de*); s'accumuler.

accumulate [ə'kjuːmjuleit], *v.t.* accumuler, entasser; amonceler.—*v.i.* s'accumuler, s'amonceler.

accumulation [əkjuːmju'leiʃən], *n.* accumulation, *f.*; amoncellement, amas, entassement, *m.*

accumulative [ə'kjuːmjulətiv], *a.* (*chose*) qui s'accumule; (*personne*) qui accumule, thésauriseur.

accumulator [ə'kjuːmjuleitə], *n.* accumulateur, *m.*

accuracy ['ækjurisi], **accurateness** ['ækjuritnis], *n.* exactitude, justesse; précision, *f.*; soin, *m.*

accurate ['ækjurit], *a.* exact, juste, correct, précis.

accurately ['ækjuritli], *adv.* exactement, avec justesse.

accurateness [ACCURACY].

accursed [ə'kəːsid], *a.* maudit; détestable, exécrable.

accusation [ækju'zeiʃən], *n.* accusation, *f.*

accusative [ə'kjuːzətiv], *a.* and *n.* (*Gram.*), accusatif, *m.*

accusatory [ə'kjuːzətri], *a.* accusateur.

accuse [ə'kjuːz], *v.t.* accuser.

accuser [ə'kjuːzə], *n.* accusateur, *m.*

accustom [ə'kʌstəm], *v.t.* accoutumer, habituer.

ace [eis], *n.* as; (*fig.*) point, iota, *m.*; *within an ace of*, à deux doigts de.

acerb [ə'səːb], *a.* acerbe, aigre.

acerbity [ə'səːbiti], *n.* acerbité, aigreur; (*fig.*) âpreté, sévérité, *f.*

acetic [ə'siːtik, ə'setik], *a.* acétique.

acetylene [ə'setili:n], *n.* acétylène, *m.*

ache [eik], *n.* mal, *m.*; douleur, *f.*; **headache**, mal de tête; **toothache**, mal de dents.—*v.i.* faire mal; *(fig.)* souffrir *(de)*; **my head aches,** j'ai mal à la tête.

achieve [ə'tʃi:v], *v.t.* exécuter, accomplir; remporter *(une victoire)*; atteindre *(à).*

achievement [ə'tʃi:vmənt], *n.* exploit, fait d'armes; accomplissement, succès, *m.*; réalisation, *f.*

aching ['eikiŋ], *a.* endolori, douloureux; **an aching heart,** un cœur dolent.

acid ['æsid], *a.* and *n.* acide, *m.*; **acid drops,** bonbons acidulés, *m.pl.*

acidity [ə'siditi], *n.* acidité, *f.*

acknowledge [æk'nɔlidʒ], *v.t.* reconnaître; avouer, confesser; accuser réception de *(lettre)*; répondre à.

acknowledgment [æk'nɔlidʒmənt], *n.* reconnaissance, *f.*; aveu; accusé de réception, *m.*; remerciements, *m.pl.*

acme ['ækmi], *n.* comble, faîte; apogée, *m.*

acolyte ['ækolait], *n.* acolyte, *m.*

aconite ['ækonait], *n. (Bot.)* aconit, *m.*

acorn ['eikɔ:n], *n.* gland, *m.*

acoustic [ə'ku:stik], *a.* acoustique.—*n. (pl.)* acoustique, *f.*

acquaint [ə'kweint], *v.t.* informer *(de)*; faire savoir à, faire part à; **to be acquainted with,** connaître, savoir.

acquaintance [ə'kweintəns], *n.* connaissance *(de)*; personne de ma *(sa etc.)* connaissance, *f.*

acquainted [ə'kweintid], *a.* connu; instruit *(de)*, familier *(avec).*

acquiesce [ækwi'es], *v.i.* acquiescer *(à)*; accéder *(à).*

acquiescence [ækwi'esəns], *n.* acquiescement; consentement, *m.*

acquiescent [ækwi'esənt], *a.* résigné, soumis; consentant.

acquire [ə'kwaiə], *v.t.* acquérir, obtenir, gagner.

acquirement [ə'kwaiəmənt], *n.* acquisition; connaissance, *f.*

acquisition [ækwi'ziʃən], *n.* acquisition, *f.*

acquisitive [ə'kwizitiv], *a.* âpre au gain.

acquit [ə'kwit], *v.t.* régler *(une dette)*; absoudre, acquitter *(un accusé)*; acquitter *(d'un devoir)*; **to acquit oneself well,** faire son devoir.

acquittal [ə'kwitəl], *n.* acquittement, *m.*

acre ['eikə], *n.* arpent, *m.*, acre, *f.*

acreage ['eikəridʒ], *n.* superficie, *f.*

acrid ['ækrid], *a.* âcre; *(fig.)* acerbe.

acridity [æ'kriditi], *n.* âcreté, *f.*

acrimonious [ækri'mouniəs], *a.* acrimonieux.

acrimoniously [ækri'mouniəsli], *adv.* avec aigreur, avec acrimonie.

acrimony ['ækriməni], *n.* acrimonie, aigreur, *f.*

acrobat ['ækrəbæt], *n.* acrobate, *m.*, *f.*

acrobatic [ækrə'bætik], *a.* acrobatique.—*n. (pl.)* acrobatie, *f.*

acropolis [ə'krɔpəlis], *n.* acropole, *f.*

across [ə'krɔs, ə'krɔ:s], *prep.* à travers, sur; **to come across,** rencontrer.—*adv.* à travers, en travers; de l'autre côté; **across the street,** de l'autre côté de la rue.

acrostic [ə'krɔstik], *n.* acrostiche, *m.*

act [ækt], *n.* acte, *m.*, loi; action, *f.*; **in the act,** sur le fait; **in the act of doing it,** en

train de le faire; **in the very act,** en flagrant délit.—*v.t.* jouer, représenter; feindre, contrefaire.—*v.i.* agir *(en, sur etc.)*; se conduire; se comporter; opérer.

acting ['æktiŋ], *a.* qui agit; suppléant; *(Comm.)* gérant; **acting manager,** directeur gérant, *m.*—*n. (Theat.)* jeu, *m.*; *(fig.)* feinte, *f.*

action ['ækʃən], *n.* action, *f.*, fait; *(Law)* procès, *m.*; bataille, *f.*

actionable ['ækʃənəbl], *a.* actionnable, sujet à procès.

activate ['æktiveit], *v.t.* activer; rendre radioactif.

active ['æktiv], *a.* actif, agile, alerte.

actively ['æktivli], *adv.* activement.

activity [æk'tiviti], *n.* activité, *f.*

actor ['æktə], *n.* acteur, comédien, *m.*

actress ['æktris], *n.* actrice, comédienne, *f.*

actual ['æktjuəl], *a.* réel, véritable, effectif.

actuality [æktju'æliti], *n.* réalité, *f.*

actually ['æktjuəli], *adv.* réellement, en effet, positivement, véritablement; à vrai dire.

actuarial [æktju'eəriəl], *a.* actuariel.

actuary ['æktjuəri], *n.* actuaire, *m.*

actuate ['æktjueit], *v.t.* mettre en action; pousser, animer.

acuity [ə'kjuiti], *n.* acuité, *f.*

acumen [ə'kju:mən], *n.* finesse, pénétration, *f.*

acute [ə'kju:t], *a.* aigu, pointu, fin; *(fig.)* violent, poignant; perçant, pénétrant.

acutely [ə'kju:tli], *adv.* vivement; avec finesse.

acuteness [ə'kju:tnis], *n.* acuité; intensité; finesse, pénétration, *f.*

adage ['ædidʒ], *n.* adage, proverbe, *m.*

adamant ['ædəmənt], *a.* inflexible, intransigeant.—*n.* diamant, *m.*

adamantine [ædə'mæntain], *a.* adamantin, inflexible.

adapt [ə'dæpt], *v.t.* adapter, approprier, ajuster *(à).*

adaptability [ədæptə'biliti], *n.* faculté d'adaptation, souplesse, *f.*

adaptable [ə'dæptəbl], *a.* adaptable, qui peut s'adapter.

adapter [ə'dæptə], *n. (Elec.)* raccord, *m.*

add [æd], *v.t.* ajouter, joindre; additionner.

adder ['ædə], *n.* vipère, *f.*

addict ['ædikt], *n.* personne adonnée à *(stupéfiants etc.)*, *f.*—[ə'dikt], *v.i.* s'adonner, se livrer *(à).*

addictedness [ə'diktidnis], *n.* attachement, goût *(pour)*, penchant *(à)*, *m.*

addiction [ə'dikʃən], *n.* attachement, goût *(pour)*, penchant *(à)*, *m.*

addition [ə'diʃən], *n.* addition, *f.*; surcroît, supplément, accroissement, *m.*

additional [ə'diʃənəl], *a.* additionnel, supplémentaire, de plus.

additionally [ə'diʃənəli], *adv.* par addition, en sus, de plus, en outre.

addle [ædl], *v.t.* rendre couvi, corrompre; *(fig.)* brouiller *(le cerveau).*—*a.* couvi *(œuf)*; pourri; *(fig.)* stérile.

addle-headed ['ædl'hedid], *a.* à cerveau vide, écervelé, à l'esprit brouillon.

address [ə'dres], *n.* adresse; habileté; dextérité; allocution, *f.*, discours; *(fig.)* abord, *m.*—*v.t.* adresser *(une lettre)*; adresser la parole à, aborder *(quelqu'un)*; *(Golf)* **to address the ball,** viser la balle.

addressee [ædre'si:], *n.* destinataire, *m.*, *f.*

adduce [ə'dju:s], *v.t.* alléguer; apporter, avancer, produire.

Adela ['ædilə]. Adèle, *f.*

Adelaide ['ædəleid]. Adélaïde, *f.*

adenoid ['ædinɔid], *a.* adénoïde.—*n.* (*pl.*) adénite, *f.*; végétations, *f. pl.*

adept [æ'dept], *a.* adepte, habile, versé (*dans*).—*n.* adepte, *m.*, *f.*

adequacy ['ædikwəsi], **adequateness** ['ædi kwitnis], *n.* juste proportion, suffisance, *f.*

adequate ['ædikwit], *a.* proportionné, suffisant (*à*), compétent.

adequately ['ædikwitli], *adv.* en juste proportion, suffisamment, convenablement.

adequateness [ADEQUACY].

adhere [əd'hiə], *v.i.* adhérer, s'attacher, s'en tenir (*à*).

adherence [əd'hiərəns], *n.* adhérence, *f.*, attachement, *m.*

adherent [əd'hiərənt], *n.* adhérent, *m.*

adhesion [əd'hi:ʒən], *n.* adhésion, *f.*

adhesive [əd'hi:siv], *a.* adhésif, tenace; gommé, agglutinant.

adieu [ə'dju:], *adv.* and *n.* adieu, *m.*; *to bid someone adieu*, faire ses adieux à quelqu'un.

adipose ['ædipous], *a.* adipeux.

adjacency [ə'dʒeisənsi], *n.* contiguïté, *f.*, voisinage, *m.*

adjacent [ə'dʒeisənt], *a.* adjacent, contigu (*à*), avoisinant.

adjectival [ædʒək'taivəl], *a.* comme adjectif.

adjectivally [ædʒək'taivəli], *adv.* adjectivement.

adjective ['ædʒəktiv], *a.* and *n.* adjectif, *m.*

adjoin [ə'dʒɔin], *v.t.* adjoindre, joindre; toucher, se joindre à.—*v.i.* se toucher, être contigu.

adjoining [ə'dʒɔiniŋ], *a.* adjacent, avoisinant, contigu (*à*).

adjourn [ə'dʒə:n], *v.t.* ajourner, différer, remettre.—*v.i.* s'ajourner, lever la séance.

adjournment [ə'dʒə:nmənt], *n.* ajournement, *m.*; remise, *f.*

adjudge [ə'dʒʌdʒ], *v.t.* adjuger; juger, condamner; (*fig.*) estimer.

adjudicate [ə'dʒu:dikeit], *v.t.* adjuger; prononcer.

adjudication [ədʒu:di'keiʃən], *n.* jugement, *m.*; décision, *f.*, arrêt, *m.*

adjudicator [ə'dʒu:dikeitə], *n.* juge, arbitre, *m.*, *f.*

adjunct ['ædʒʌŋkt], *a.* adjoint, accessoire.—*n.* accessoire; adjoint, *m.*

adjure [ə'dʒuə], *v.t.* adjurer.

adjust [ə'dʒʌst], *v.t.* ajuster, régler, arranger.

adjustable [ə'dʒʌstəbl], *a.* réglable.

adjustment [ə'dʒʌstmənt], *n.* ajustement, arrangement, accord, *m.*; mise au point, *f.*, réglage, *m.*

adjutant ['ædʒutənt], *n.* capitaine adjudant major; major de la garnison, *m.*

administer [əd'ministə], *v.t.* administrer, gérer, régir; faire prêter (*un serment*).

administrate [əd'ministreit], *v.t.* administrer; régir.

administration [ədminis'treiʃən], *n.* administration, *f.*, gouvernement, *m.*

administrative [əd'ministrətiv], *a.* administratif.

administrator [əd'ministreitə], *n.* administrateur; (*Law*) curateur, *m.*

admirable ['ædmərəbl], *a.* admirable.

admirably ['ædmərəbli], *adv.* admirablement, à ravir, à merveille.

admiral ['ædmərəl], *n.* amiral, *m.*; *rear admiral*, contre-amiral, *m.*; *vice admiral*, vice-amiral, *m.*

admiralty ['ædmərəlti], *n.* amirauté, *f.*; Ministère de la Marine (*en France*), *m.*; *Board of Admiralty*, conseil d'amirauté, *m.*; *First Lord of the Admiralty*, ministre de la marine, *m.*

admiration [ædmə'reiʃən], *n.* admiration, *f.*; étonnement, *m.*

admire [əd'maiə], *v.t.* admirer; aimer; s'étonner de.—*v.i.* s'étonner.

admirer [əd'maiərə], *n.* admirateur, *m.*, admiratrice, *f.*

admissible [əd'misibl], *a.* admissible.

admission [əd'miʃən], *n.* admission, entrée, *f.*; accès; aveu, *m.*, concession, *f.*

admit [əd'mit], *v.t.* admettre, laisser entrer; avouer, reconnaître; tolérer.—*v.i.* *to admit of*, comporter, permettre; souffrir.

admittance [əd'mitəns], *n.* accès, *m.*; admission, entrée, *f.*; *no admittance*, défense d'entrer.

admittedly [əd'nitidli], *adv.* de l'aveu général; il est vrai que.

admixture [əd'mikstʃə], *n.* mélange, *m.*

admonish [əd'mɔniʃ], *v.t.* avertir, exhorter; reprendre, réprimander.

admonishment [əd'mɔniʃmənt], **admonition** [ædmə'niʃən], *n.* admonition, *f.*, avertissement, *m.*; remontrance, réprimande, *f.*

ado [ə'du:], *n.* bruit, fracas, *m.*, façons, cérémonies, *f.pl.*, embarras, *m.*, peine, difficulté, *f.*; *much ado about nothing*, beaucoup de bruit pour rien; *without any more ado*, sans plus de façons.

adolescence [ædo'lesəns], *n.* adolescence, *f.*

adolescent [ædo'lesənt], *a.* and *n.* adolescent, *m.*

Adolphus [ə'dɔlfəs]. Adolphe, *m.*

adopt [ə'dɔpt], *v.t.* adopter.

adopted [ə'dɔptid], **adoptive** [ə'dɔptiv], *a.* adoptif, adopté, d'adoption.

adoption [ə'dɔpʃən], *n.* adoption, *f.*

adoptive [ADOPTED].

adorable [ə'dɔ:rəbl], *a.* adorable.

adorably [ə'dɔ:rəbli], *adv.* d'une manière adorable, adorablement.

adoration [ædo'reiʃən], *n.* adoration, *f.*

adore [ə'dɔ:], *v.t.* adorer.

adorer [ə'dɔ:rə], *n.* adorateur, *m.*

adoringly [ə'dɔ:riŋli], *adv.* avec adoration.

adorn [ə'dɔ:n], *v.t.* orner; parer, embellir; (*fig.*) faire l'ornement de.

adornment [ə'dɔ:nmənt], *n.* ornement, *m.*, parure; ornementation, *f.*

Adrian ['eidriən]. Adrien, *m.*

Adriatic Sea [eidri'ætik'si:]. la mer Adriatique, l'Adriatique, *f.*

adrift [ə'drift], *adv.* en ou à la dérive; à l'abandon.

adroit [ə'drɔit], *a.* adroit, habile.

adroitly [ə'drɔitli], *adv.* adroitement.

adroitness [ə'drɔitnis], *n.* adresse, dextérité, *f.*

adulate ['ædjuleit], *v.t.* aduler.

adulation [ædju'leiʃən], *n.* adulation, *f.*

adulatory ['ædjuleitəri], *a.* adulateur.

adult [ə'dʌlt, 'ædʌlt], *a.* and *n.* adulte, *m.*, *f.*

adulterate [ə'dʌltəreit], *v.t.* adultérer, frelater, falsifier, sophistiquer; (*fig.*) corrompre.
adulteration [ədʌltə'reiʃən], *n.* falsification, sophistication, *f.*, frelatage, *m.*
adulterator [ə'dʌltəreitə], *n.* frelateur, falsificateur. *m.*
adulterer [ə'dʌltərə], *n.* adultère, *m.*
adulteress [ə'dʌltəris], *n.* (femme) adultère, *f.*
adulterous [ə'dʌltərəs], *a.* adultère; (*fig.*) altéré, faux.
adultery [ə'dʌltəri], *n.* adultère, *m.*
advance [əd'vɑːns], *v.t.* avancer, faire avancer; élever, hausser, augmenter.—*v.i.* avancer, s'avancer, se porter en avant.—*n.* mouvement en avant, *m.*; avance (*de fonds*), *f.*; avancement, progrès, *m.*; *in advance*, d'avance.
advance guard [əd'vɑːnsgɑːd], *n.* avant-garde, *f.*
advancement [əd'vɑːnsmənt], *n.* avancement, progrès, *m.*; (*Comm.*) avance, *f.*
advantage [əd'vɑːntidʒ], *n.* avantage; profit, intérêt, *m.*; *to have the advantage*, avoir le dessus; *to take advantage of*, profiter de; *to take advantage of someone's kindness*, abuser de la bonté de quelqu'un.
advantageous [ædvən'teidʒəs], *a.* avantageux (*à* ou *de*).
advantageously [ædvən'teidʒəsli], *adv.* avantageusement.
Advent [' ædvənt]. (*Eccles.*) l'Avent, *m.*
advent ['ædvənt], *n.* venue, *f.*
adventitious [ædven'tiʃəs], *a.* adventice, fortuit.
adventure [əd'ventʃə], *n.* aventure, entreprise hasardeuse, *f.*—*v.t.* aventurer, hasarder.—*v.i.* s'aventurer, se hasarder.
adventurer [əd'ventʃərə], *n.* aventurier, *m.*
adventuress [əd'ventʃəris], *n.* aventurière, *f.*
adventurous [əd'ventʃərəs], *a.* aventureux, hardi.
adventurously [əd'ventʃərəsli], *adv.* aventureusement.
adverb ['ædvəːb], *n.* adverbe, *m.*
adverbial [əd'vəːbjəl], *a.* adverbial.
adverbially [əd'vəːbjəli], *adv.* adverbialement.
adversary ['ædvəsəri], *n.* adversaire, *m.*, *f.*
adverse ['ædvəːs], *a.* adverse, contraire (*à*); défavorable.
adversely ['ædvəsli], *adv.* d'une manière hostile, malheureusement.
adversity [əd'vəːsiti], *n.* adversité, *f.*
advert [əd'vəːt], *v.i.* faire allusion (*à*); parler (*de*).
advertise ['ædvətaiz], *v.t.* annoncer, faire annoncer, afficher, faire de la publicité pour.
advertisement [əd'vəːtizmənt], *n.* annonce (*journal*), publicité, réclame, *f.*; avis, *m.*; *classified advertisements*, petites annonces, *f.pl.*
advertiser ['ædvətaizə], *n.* personne qui fait des annonces, *f.*; journal d'annonces, *m.*
advertising ['ædvətaiziŋ], *n.* publicité, réclame, *f.*; *advertising agency*, agence de publicité, *f.*
advice [əd'vais], *n.* avis, conseil, *m.*; *if you take my advice*, si vous m'en croyez; *to take advice*, prendre conseil (*de*), consulter (*un médecin etc.*).

advisable [əd'vaizəbl], *a.* judicieux, convenable (*pour* ou *de*); opportun.
advisability [ədvaizə'biliti], *n.* convenance, utilité, opportunité, *f.*
advise [əd'vaiz], *v.t.* conseiller; donner avis (*de*); prévenir (*de*); annoncer.—*v.i.* délibérer, prendre conseil, consulter.
advisedly [əd'vaizidli], *adv.* avec réflexion, de propos délibéré.
adviser [əd'vaizə], *n.* conseiller, *m.*
advisory [əd'vaizəri], *a.* consultatif.
advocacy ['ædvəkəsi], *n.* profession d'avocat; défense, *f.*, plaidoyer, *m.*
advocate ['ædvəkət], *n.* avocat, défenseur; intercesseur, *m.*—['ædvəkeit], *v.t.* défendre, plaider; soutenir, appuyer, préconiser.
adze [ædz], *n.* herminette, doloire; aissette, *f.* —*v.t.* entailler à l'herminette, doler.
Aegean Sea [iː'dʒiːənsiː]. la mer Égée, *f.*
aegis ['iːdʒis], *n.* égide, *f.*
Aeneas [iː'niːas]. Énée, *m.*
Aeneid [iː'niːid]. l'Énéide, *f.*
aeon ['iːan], *n.* éternité, *f.*, éon, *m.*
aerate ['εəreit], *v.t.* aérer; gazéifier.
aeration [εə'reiʃən], *n.* aération, *f.*
aerial ['εəriəl], *a.* aérien.—*n.* antenne, *f.*
aerie, aery, eyrie, eyry ['εəri, 'iəri], *n.* aire, *f.*
aerobatics [εərə'bætiks], *n.pl.* acrobaties aériennes, *f.pl.*
aerodrome ['εərodroum], *n.* aérodrome, *m.*
aerodynamic ['εərodai'næmik], *a.* aérodynamique.—*n.* (*pl.*) aérodynamique, *f.*
aerolite ['εərolait], **aerolith** ['εəroliθ], *n.* aérolithe, bolide, *m.*
aeronaut ['εərɔnɔːt], *n.* aéronaute, *m.*, *f.*
aeronautic [εərɔ'nɔːtik], *a.* aéronautique.
aeroplane ['εəroplein], *n.* aéroplane, avion, *m.*
aerostat ['εərostæt], *n.* aérostat, *m.*
Aeschylus ['iːskiləs]. Eschyle, *m.*
Aesop ['iːsɔp]. Ésope, *m.*
aesthete ['iːsθiːt], *n.* esthète, *m.*, *f.*
aesthetic [iːs'θetik], **aesthetical** [iːs'θetikəl], *a.* esthétique.
aesthetically [iːs'θetikəli], *adv.* esthétiquement.
aestival [iːs'taivəl], *a.* estival.
aether [ETHER].
afar [ə'fɑː], *adv.* loin, de loin, au loin.
affability [æfə'biliti], **affableness** ['æfəblnis], *n.* affabilité, *f.*
affable ['æfəbl], *a.* affable, doux, gracieux.
affably ['æfəbli], *adv.* affablement, avec affabilité.
affair [ə'fεə], *n.* affaire, *f.*
affect [ə'fekt], *v.t.* affecter; intéresser, toucher, émouvoir.
affectation [æfek'teiʃən], *n.* affectation, *f.*; **affectedness** [ə'fektidnis], *n.* affectation, *f.*
affected [ə'fektid], *a.* disposé (*pour etc.*); affecté, précieux; maniéré, prétentieux (*style*).
affecting [ə'fektiŋ], *a.* touchant, émouvant, attendrissant.
affection [ə'fekʃən], *n.* affection, *f.*, amour; goût, attachement, penchant, *m.*; maladie, *f.*
affectionate [ə'fekʃənit], *a.* affectueux, affectionné.
affectionately [ə'fekʃənitli], *adv.* affectueusement.
affiance [ə'faiəns], *v.t.* fiancer.—*n.* fiançailles, *f.pl.*

affianced [əˈfaiənst], a. fiancé.

affidavit [æfiˈdeivit], n. déclaration par écrit sous serment, attestation, f.

affiliate [əˈfilieit], v.t. affilier; attribuer, rattacher (à).

affiliation [əfiliˈeiʃən], n. affiliation, f.

affinity [əˈfiniti], n. affinité, f.

affirm [əˈfəːm], v.t. affirmer.

affirmation [æfəˈmeiʃən], n. affirmation, f.

affirmative [əˈfəːmətiv], a. affirmatif.—n. affirmative, f.

affirmatively [əˈfəːmətivli], adv. affirmativement.

affix [əˈfiks], v.t. apposer, attacher (à).

afflatus [əˈfleitəs], n. souffle, m., inspiration, f.

afflict [əˈflikt], v.t. affliger (de); tourmenter.

afflicting [əˈfliktiŋ], a. affligeant.

affliction [əˈflikʃən], n. affliction; calamité, f., malheur, m.

affluence [ˈæfluəns], n. opulence, affluence; abondance, f., concours (de personnes), m.

affluent [ˈæfluənt], a. opulent, riche; affluent.

afford [əˈfɔːd], v.t. donner, fournir, accorder; avoir les moyens de, pouvoir.

afforestation [əfɔrisˈteiʃən], n. boisement; reboisement, m.

affranchise [əˈfræntʃaiz], v.t. affranchir.

affray [əˈfrei], n. bagarre, échauffourée, f.

affright [əˈfrait], v.t. effrayer.

affront [əˈfrʌnt], n. affront, m., insulte, injure, f., outrage, m.—v.t. affronter, offenser, insulter.

afield [əˈfiːld], adv. aux champs, à la campagne; **to go far afield**, aller très loin.

afire [əˈfaiə], adv. en feu.

aflame [əˈfleim], adv. en flammes.

afloat [əˈflout], adv. à flot; (fig.) en circulation.

afoot [əˈfut], adv. à pied; en marche, en route; (fig.) sur pied; en train.

afore [əˈfɔː], adv. précédemment, auparavant; par devant.

aforementioned [əˈfɔːmenʃənd], a. mentionné plus haut, susdit, précité.

aforesaid [əˈfɔːsed], a. susdit, ledit, susnommé.

aforethought [əˈfɔːθɔːt], a. **with malice aforethought**, avec intention criminelle.

afraid [əˈfreid], a. effrayé, pris de peur; **I am afraid not**, je crains que non; **I am afraid she's gone**, je crains bien qu'elle ne soit partie; **to be afraid of**, avoir peur de.

afresh [əˈfreʃ], adv. de nouveau, de plus belle.

Africa [ˈæfrikə]. l'Afrique, f.

African [ˈæfrikən], a. africain.—n. Africain (personne), m.

aft [ɑːft], a. arrière, de l'arrière.—adv. (Naut.) à l'arrière.

after [ˈɑːftə], a. subséquent, ultérieur, futur; arrière.—prep. après; sur, à la suite de; selon, d'après.—adv. après, d'après, ensuite.—conj. après que.

aftercrop [ˈɑːftəkrɔp], n. seconde récolte, f.; regain, m.

aftereffects [ˈɑːftərifekts], n. pl. suites, f. pl., répercussion, f.

afterlife [ˈɑːftəlaif], n. suite de la vie, f.; au-delà, m.

aftermath [ˈɑːftəmæθ], n. regain, m.; (fig.) suites, f.pl.

afternoon [ɑːftəˈnuːn], n. après-midi, m. ou f.

afterthought [ˈɑːftəθɔːt], n. réflexion après coup, f.

afterward [ˈɑːftəwəd], **afterwards** [ˈɑːftəwədz], adv. après, ensuite, plus tard.

again [əˈgein], adv. encore; encore une fois, de nouveau; **again and again**, à plusieurs reprises; **as much again**, encore autant; **never again**, jamais plus.

against [əˈgeinst], prep. contre; vis-à-vis; vers; pour.

agape [əˈgeip], adv. bouche bée.

agate [ˈægeit], n. agate, f.

Agatha [ˈægəθə]. Agathe, f.

age [eidʒ], n. âge, m.; époque, f.; **of age**, majeur; **under age**, mineur; **Middle Ages**, moyen âge.—v.t., v.i. vieillir.

aged [ˈeidʒid, (after prefix) eidʒd], a. vieux, âgé; **middle-aged**, entre deux âges.

ageless [ˈeidʒlis], a. toujours jeune.

agency [ˈeidʒənsi], n. action, entremise; (Comm.) agence, f.

agenda [əˈdʒendə], n. ordre du jour; programme, m.

agent [ˈeidʒənt], n. représentant, agent, mandataire, m.

agglomerate [əˈglɔməreit], v.t. agglomérer.—v.i. s'agglomérer.—a. aggloméré.

agglomeration [əglɔməˈreiʃən], n. agglomération, f.

aggrandize [əˈgrændaiz], v.t. agrandir.

aggrandizement [əˈgrændizmənt], n. agrandissement, m.

aggravate [ˈægrəveit], v.t. aggraver; exagérer; (colloq.) agacer, pousser à bout, exaspérer.

aggravation [ægrəˈveiʃən], n. aggravation; circonstance aggravante, f., agacement, m.

aggregate [ˈægrigit], a. collectif, global, réuni.—n. masse, f.; ensemble, m., somme totale, f.—[ˈægrigeit], v.t. rassembler.

aggregation [ægriˈgeiʃən], n. agrégation, f., assemblage, m.

aggression [əˈgreʃən], n. agression, f.

aggressive [əˈgresiv], a. agressif.

aggressiveness [əˈgresivnis], n. caractère agressif, m.

aggressor [əˈgresə], n. agresseur, m.

aggrieve [əˈgriːv], v.t. chagriner, affliger; blesser, léser.

aghast [əˈgɑːst], a. consterné, ébahi, médusé, tout pantois.

agile [ˈædʒail], a. agile, leste.

agility [əˈdʒiliti], n. agilité, f.

agio [ˈædʒiou], n. prix du change, agio, m.

agiotage [ˈædʒətidʒ], n. agiotage, m.

agitate [ˈædʒiteit], v.t. agiter, exciter; remuer, troubler.

agitation [ædʒiˈteiʃən], n. agitation; discussion, f., examen, m.

agitator [ˈædʒiteitə], n. agitateur; meneur, m.

aglow [əˈglou], a. enflammé, resplendissant.

agnostic [ægˈnɔstik], a. and n. agnosticiste, agnostique, m., f.

agnosticism [ægˈnɔstisizm], n. agnosticisme, m.

ago [əˈgou], adv. passé, il y a; **two days ago**, il y a deux jours.

agog [əˈgɔg], adv. excité, impatient, empressé; en train, en l'air; **to be all agog**, avoir la tête montée.

agonize [ˈægənaiz], v.t. torturer, mettre au supplice.—v.i. souffrir l'agonie, être au supplice.

agonizing ['ægənaiziŋ], a. atroce, déchirant.

agony ['ægəni], n. douleur, angoisse, f., paroxysme, m.

agrarian [ə'grɛəriən], a. agraire.

agree [ə'gri:], v.i. s'accorder (à ou avec); être d'accord; consentir (à); convenir (de); être conforme (à).

agreeable [ə'gri:əbl], a. agréable, aimable; conforme (à); consentant.

agreeably [ə'gri:əbli], adv. agréablement; conformément (à).

agreed [ə'gri:d], a. convenu, d'accord; *it's agreed*, c'est entendu.

agreement [ə'gri:mənt], n. accord, m.; convention, f., contrat, pacte, marché, m.; conformité, f.

agricultural [ægri'kʌltʃərəl], a. agricole, d'agriculture.

agriculture ['ægrikʌltʃə], n. agriculture, f.

agriculturist [ægri'kʌltʃərist], n. agriculteur, agronome, m.

aground [ə'graund], adv. échoué; à terre.

ague ['eigju:], n. fièvre intermittente, f.

ahead [ə'hed], adv. en avant; (fig.) en tête; *go ahead!* en avant! vas-y! *straight ahead*, tout droit; *ahead of time*, en avance.

aid [eid], v.t. aider, assister; secourir; *to aid each other*, s'entr'aider.—n. aide, assistance, f.; secours, concours, subside, m.; *with the aid of*, à l'aide de.

aide-de-camp [eiddə'kɑ̃], n. aide de camp, m.

aigrette [ei'gret], n. aigrette, f.

ail [eil], v.t. faire mal à; chagriner; *what ails him?* qu'est-ce qu'il a?—v.i. être souffrant.

aileron ['eilərɔn], n. aileron, m.

ailing ['eiliŋ], a. souffrant, indisposé, mal portant.

ailment ['eilmənt], n. mal, malaise, m., indisposition, f.

aim [eim], v.t. viser; diriger, lancer (un coup etc.).—v.i. viser (à); aspirer (à); avoir pour but (de).—n. point de mire, but, objet, dessein, m.; visée, f.; *to take aim at*, viser, coucher en joue.

aimless ['eimlis], a. sans but, sans objet.

air [ɛə], n. air; vent, m., brise; (fig.) mine, expression, f.; *in the air*, en l'air; *in the open air*, en plein air.—v.t. aérer, donner de l'air à, mettre à l'air; sécher.

air- [ɛə], see also **aero-** .

airborne ['ɛəbɔːn], a. (Av.) aéroporté.

air-conditioned ['ɛəkəndiʃənd], a. climatisé.

air conditioning ['ɛəkəndiʃəniŋ], n. climatisation, f.

air cooling ['ɛəku:liŋ], n. refroidissement par air, m.

aircraft ['ɛəkrɑːft], n. avion, m.; les avions, m.pl.

aircrew ['ɛəkru:], n. équipage (d'avion), m.

airfield ['ɛəfiːld], n. terrain d'aviation, m.

air hostess ['ɛəhoustis], n. hôtesse de l'air, f.

airily ['ɛərili], adv. allègrement, légèrement.

airiness ['ɛərinis], n. situation aérée; (fig.) légèreté, vivacité, désinvolture, f.

airing ['ɛəriŋ], n. aérage, m., exposition à l'air, f., éventage, m.; promenade, f.

airlift ['ɛəlift], n. pont aérien, m.

airline ['ɛəlain], n. ligne aérienne, f.

airliner ['ɛəlainə], n. avion de ligne, m.

air mail ['ɛəmeil], n. poste aérienne, f.

airman ['ɛəmən], n. aviateur, m.

air mattress ['ɛəmætris], n. matelas à air, m.

air pocket ['ɛəpɔkit], n. (Av.) trou d'air, m.

airport ['ɛəpɔːt], n. aéroport, m.

airship ['ɛəʃip], n. dirigeable, m.

airsickness ['ɛəsiknis], n. mal de l'air, m.

airstrip ['ɛəstrip], n. piste d'atterrissage, f.

airtight ['ɛətait], a. imperméable à l'air, hermétique.

airworthy ['ɛəwəːði], a. navigable.

airy ['ɛəri], a. ouvert à l'air; aérien, aéré; (fig.) léger, dégagé, gai, enjoué, insouciant; *airy words*, paroles en l'air, f.pl.

aisle [ail], n. bas-côté, passage, m.

ajar [ə'dʒɑː], a. entr'ouvert, entrebâillé.

akimbo [ə'kimbou], adv. appuyé sur la hanche; *with one's arms akimbo*, les poings sur les hanches.

akin [ə'kin], a. allié (à); parent (de); (fig.) qui a rapport (avec).

alabaster ['æləbɑːstə], a. d'albâtre.—n. albâtre, m.

alacrity [ə'lækriti], n. alacrité, f., empressement, m., promptitude, f.

Alan, Allan, Allen ['ælən], Alain, m.

alarm [ə'lɑːm], n. alarme, alerte, f.; réveil (réveille-matin), m.—v.t. alarmer; effrayer, faire peur à.

alarm bell [ə'lɑːmbel], n. cloche d'alarme, f., tocsin, m.

alarm clock [ə'lɑːmklɔk], n. réveille-matin, m.

alarming [ə'lɑːmiŋ], a. alarmant.

alarmingly [ə'lɑːmiŋli], adv. d'une manière alarmante.

alarmist [ə'lɑːmist], n. alarmiste, m., f.

alas! [ə'læs], int. hélas!

Albania [æl'beinjə], l'Albanie, f.

Albanian [æl'beinjən], a. albanais.—n. Albanais (personne), m.

albatross ['ælbətrɔs], n. albatros, m.

albeit [ɔːl'biːit], conj. quoique, bien que (with subj.).

albino [æl'biːnou], a. and n. albinos, m., f.

album ['ælbəm], n. album, m.

albumen [æl'bjuːmin], n. albumen; blanc d'œuf, m.; albumine, f.

albuminous [æl'bjuːminəs], a. albumineux.

alburnum [æl'bəːnəm], n. aubier, m.

alchemic [æl'kemik], **alchemical** [æl'kemikəl], a. alchimique.

alchemist ['ælkimist], n. alchimiste, m.

alchemistic [ælki'mistik], **alchemistical** [ælki'mistikəl], a. d'alchimiste, alchimique.

alchemy ['ælkimi], n. alchimie, f.

alcohol ['ælkəhɔl], n. alcool, m. [see **spirit**]

alcoholic [ælkə'hɔlik], a. and n. alcoolique, m., f.

alcoholism ['ælkəhɔlizm], n. alcoolisme, m.

Alcoran [ælkə'rɑːn], le Coran, le Koran.

alcove ['ælkouv], n. alcôve; niche, f., enfoncement, m.

alder ['ɔːldə], n. aune, vergne, m.

alder grove ['ɔːldəgrouv], n. aunaie, f.

alderman ['ɔːldəmən], n. (pl. **-men** [men]) conseiller municipal, alderman, échevin, m.

ale [eil], n. ale, bière, f.

alehouse ['eilhaus], n. taverne, f.

alembic [ə'lembik], n. alambic, m.

alert [ə'ləːt], a. alerte, vigilant, éveillé.—n. alerte, f.; *on the alert*, sur le qui-vive.

alertness [ə'lə:tnis], n. vigilance, promptitude, prestesse, f.

Alexander [ælig'zɑ:ndə]. Alexandre, m.

alexandrine [ælig'zɑ:ndrin], n. (Pros.) alexandrin, m.

alfresco [æl'freskou], adv. en plein air.

algebra ['ældʒəbrə], n. algèbre, f.

algebraic [ældʒə'breiik], **algebraical** [ældʒə'breiikəl], a. algébrique.

Algeria [æl'dʒiəriə]. l'Algérie, f.

Algerian [æl'dʒiəriən], a. algérien.—n. Algérien (personne), m.

Algiers [æl'dʒiəz]. Alger, m.

alias ['eiliəs], n. nom d'emprunt ou de rechange, m.—adv. dit, autrement nommé, alias.

alibi ['ælibai], n. alibi, m.

alien ['eiljən], a. étranger (à); éloigné (de).—n. étranger, m.

alienate ['eiljəneit], v.t. aliéner (de).

alienation [eiljə'neiʃən], n. aliénation, f.

alienist ['eiljənist], n. aliéniste, m., f.

alight [ə'lait], a. allumé, embrasé.—v.i. descendre; mettre pied à terre; s'abattre (oiseau etc.); atterrir (aviateur), amerrir (sur l'eau).

align [ALINE].

alike [ə'laik], adv. également; de même, de la même manière; à la fois.—a. semblable, pareil; to be alike, se ressembler.

aliment ['ælimənt], n. aliment, m.

alimentary [æli'mentəri], a. alimentaire.

alimony ['æliməni], n. pension alimentaire, f.

aline, align [ə'lain], v.t. aligner; dresser.—v.i. s'aligner.

alinement, alignment [ə'lainmənt], n. alignement, m.

alive [ə'laiv], a. en vie, vivant; vif, éveillé; au monde; animé, sensible (à); dead or alive, mort ou vif; to be alive with, grouiller de, fourmiller de; alive to, sensible à; while alive, de son vivant.

alkali ['ælkəlai], n. alcali, m.

Alkoran [ALCORAN].

all [ɔːl], a. tout, tous; all of you, vous tous; for all that, malgré cela; it is all the same to me, cela m'est égal; with all speed, au plus vite, à toute vitesse.—adv. tout, entièrement; all at once, tout à coup, tout d'un coup; all the better, tant mieux; not at all, point du tout.—n. and pron. tout, m.; above all, surtout; all but, presque; all aboard! en voiture!

allay [ə'lei], v.t. apaiser, adoucir, calmer.

allegation [ælə'geiʃən], n. allégation, f.

allege [ə'ledʒ], v.t. alléguer, prétendre (that, que).

allegiance [ə'li:dʒəns], n. fidélité; obéissance, f.

allegorical [ælə'gɔrikəl], a. allégorique.

allegorically [ælə'gɔrikəli], adv. allégoriquement.

allegory ['æləgəri], n. allégorie, f.

allelujah [æli'lu:jə], n. and int. alléluia, m..

allergic [ə'lə:dʒik], a. (Med.) allergique.

allergy ['ælədʒi], n. allergie, f.

alleviate [ə'li:vieit], v.t. alléger, soulager, adoucir.

alleviation [əli:vi'eiʃən], n. allégement, adoucissement, soulagement, m.

alley ['æli], n. ruelle (d'une ville); allée (jardin),

f.; blind alley, impasse, f., cul de sac; m.

All Fools' Day [ɔːl'fuːlzdei]. le Ier avril.

alliance [ə'laiəns], n. alliance, f.

allied [ə'laid, ə'laid], a. allié; parent, voisin (de).

alligator ['æligeitə], n. alligator, caïman, m.

alliteration [əlitə'reiʃən], n. allitération, f.

alliterative [ə'litərətiv], a. allitératif.

allocate ['æləkeit], v.t. allouer, assigner.

allocation [ælo'keiʃən], n. allocation, f.

allot [ə'lɔt], v.t. assigner, donner en partage; répartir.

allotment [ə'lɔtmənt], r partage, lot, lotissement, m., portion; distribution, f.; lopin de terre, jardin ouvrier, m.

allow [ə'lau], v.t. permettre, autoriser; accorder, allouer; admettre, reconnaître; to allow someone to do something, permettre à quelqu'un de faire quelque chose.

allowable [ə'lauəbl], a. permis, admissible, légitime.

allowance [ə'lauəns], n. pension, rente; allocation; ration; remise, réduction; indulgence, indemnité, f.; to make allowance for, tenir compte de; to put on short allowance, rationner.

alloy [ə'lɔi], n. alliage, mélange, m.—v.t. allier; (fig.) altérer, diminuer, corrompre.

All Saints' Day [ɔːl'seintsdei]. la Toussaint, f.

All Souls' Day [ɔːl'soulzdei]. Jour des Morts, m.

allude [ə'lju:d], v.i. faire allusion (à).

allure [ə'ljuə], v.t. amorcer, attirer, séduire, inviter (à).

allurement [ə'ljuəmənt], n. amorce, f., appât, charme, attrait, m.

alluring [ə'ljuəriŋ], a. attrayant, séduisant.

alluringly [ə'ljuəriŋli], adv. d'une manière séduisante.

allusion [ə'lju:ʒən], n. allusion, f.

allusive [ə'lju:siv], a. allusif, plein d'allusions.

allusively [ə'lju:sivli], adv. par allusion.

alluvia [ə'lju:viə], n.pl. terres d'alluvion, f.pl., alluvion, f.

alluvial [ə'lju:viəl], a. alluvial, d'alluvion.

alluvium [ə'lju:viəm], n. alluvion, f.

ally [ə'lai], v.t. allier.—v.i. s'allier (à ou avec).—['ælai, ə'lai], n. allié, confédéré, m.

almanac ['ɔːlmənæk], n. almanach, m.

almighty [ɔːl'maiti], a. tout-puissant; the Almighty, le Tout-Puissant.

almond ['ɑːmənd], n. amande, f.; burnt almond, praline, f.

almond-tree ['ɑːməndtriː], n. amandier, m.

almost ['ɔːlmoust], adv. presque, à peu près; I almost fell, j'ai failli tomber.

alms [ɑːmz], n. aumône, f.; to give alms, faire l'aumône.

almshouse ['ɑːmzhaus], n. maison de retraite, f., asile, m.

aloe ['ælou], n. aloès, m.; bitter aloes, amer d'aloès, m.

aloft [ə'lɔft], adv. en haut, en l'air; (Naut.) dans la mâture.

alone [ə'loun], a. seul, solitaire; leave me alone, laissez-moi tranquille.

along [ə'lɔŋ], adv. and prep. le long de; all along (time), tout le temps; (place) tout le long du chemin; along with, avec; come along, venez donc; get along with you, allez-vous en, allez-vous promener.

alongside

alongside [ə'lɒŋsaid], *adv.* bord à bord; bord à quai.—*prep.* à côté de.
aloof [ə'luːf], *a.* distant.—*adv.* au loin, (*Naut.*) au large; éloigné, à l'écart; *to keep aloof,* se tenir à l'écart.
aloofness [ə'luːfnis], *n.* attitude distante, *f.*
aloud [ə'laud], *adv.* à haute voix, haut.
alpaca [æl'pækə], *n.* alpaga (*tissu*); alpaca (*animal*), *m.*
alphabet ['ælfəbet], *n.* alphabet; abécédaire (*livre d'enfant*), *m.*
alphabetic [ælfə'betik], **alphabetical** [ælfə 'betikəl], *a.* alphabétique.
alphabetically [ælfə'betikəli], *adv.* alphabétiquement.
alpine ['ælpain], *a.* alpin; des Alpes, alpestre.
alpinist ['ælpinist], *n.* alpiniste, *m., f.*
Alps [ælps]. les Alpes, *f. pl.*
already [ɔːl'redi], *adv.* déjà.
Alsatian [æl'seiʃən], *a.* alsacien.—*n.* (*chien*) chien-loup; (*personne*) Alsacien, *m.*
also ['ɔːlsou], *adv.* aussi, également.
altar ['ɔːltə], *n.* autel, *m.*; **high altar,** maître-autel, *m.*
altar cloth ['ɔːltəklɔθ], *n.* nappe d'autel, *f.*
altar screen ['ɔːltəskriːn], *n.* retable, *m.*
alter ['ɔːltə], *v.t.* changer, modifier; retoucher, corriger.—*v.i.* changer, se changer.
alteration [ɔːltə'reiʃən], *n.* changement, *m.,* modification, *f.*
altercation [ɔːltə'keiʃən], *n.* altercation, dispute, *f.*
alternate ['ɔːltəneit], *v.t.* alterner, faire alternativement.—*v.i.* alterner; se succéder; *alternating current,* courant alternatif, *m.*—['ɔːltənit], *a.* alternatif; alternant; *alternate rhymes,* rimes croisées, *f. pl.*
alternately [ɔːl'təːnitli], *adv.* alternativement, tour à tour.
alternative [ɔːl'təːnətiv], *a.* alternatif.—*n.* alternative; autre solution, *f.*
alternatively [ɔːl'təːnətivli], *adv.* alternativement, tour à tour.
alternator ['ɔːltəneitə], *n.* (*Elec.*) alternateur, *m.*
although [ɔːl'ðou], *conj.* quoique, bien que (*with subj.*).
altimeter [ælti'miːtə], *n.* altimètre, *m.*
altitude ['æltitjuːd], *n.* altitude, élévation, hauteur, *f.*
alto ['æltou], *n.* alto, *m.*
altogether [ɔːltə'geðə], *adv.* tout à fait, entièrement.
altruistic [æltru'istik], *a.* altruiste.
alum ['æləm], *n.* alun, *m.*
aluminum [æ'luːminəm], *n.* aluminium, *m.*
always [ɔːl'weiz], *adv.* toujours.
***amain** [ə'mein], *adv.* avec force, de toutes ses forces.
amalgam [ə'mælgəm], *n.* amalgame, *m.*
amalgamate [ə'mælgəmeit], *v.t.* amalgamer; (*Comm.*) fusionner.—*v.i.* s'amalgamer; (*Comm.*) fusionner.
amalgamation [əmælgə'meiʃən], *n.* amalgamation, *f.*; (*fig.*) amalgame, fusionnement, *m.*
amanuensis [əmænju'ensis], *n.* (*pl.* **amanuenses** [əmænju'ensiːz]) secrétaire, *m., f.*
amaranth ['æmərænθ], *n.* amarante, *f.*
amass [ə'mæs], *v.t.* amasser.
amateur ['æmətə:, 'æmətjuə], *n.* amateur, *m.*

amateurish [æmə'tə:riʃ, 'æmətjuəriʃ], *a.* d'amateur.
amateurism ['æmətə:rizm, 'æmətjuərizm], *n.* (*Spt.*) amateurisme, *m.*
amatory ['æmətəri], *a.* d'amour, amoureux.
amaze [ə'meiz], *v.t.* étonner, confondre, stupéfier; *to be amazed,* s'étonner.
amazement [ə'meizmənt], **amazedness** [ə'meizidnis], *n.* étonnement, *m.,* stupeur, stupéfaction, *f.*
amazing [ə'meiziŋ], *a.* étonnant.
Amazon ['æməzən], **the.** l'Amazone, *m.*
amazon ['æməzən], *n.* amazone, *f.*
ambassador [æm'bæsədə], *n.* ambassadeur, *m.*
ambassadress [æm'bæsədris], *n.* ambassadrice, *f.*
amber ['æmbə], *a.* d'ambre; *amber light* (*traffic*), feu orange, *m.*—*n.* ambre, *m.*
amber-colored ['æmbəkʌləd], *a.* ambré.
ambergris ['æmbəgris], *n.* ambre gris, *m.*
ambidexter [æmbi'dekstə], *a.* and *n.* ambidextre, *m., f.*
ambidextrous [æmbi'dekstrəs], *a.* ambidextre.
ambient ['æmbiənt], *a.* ambiant.
ambiguity [æmbi'gju:iti], **ambiguousness** [æm'bigjuəsnis], *n.* ambiguïté; équivoque, *f.*
ambiguous [æm'bigjuəs], *a.* ambigu; équivoque; douteux.
ambiguously [æm'bigjuəsli], *adv.* ambigument, d'une manière équivoque.
ambit ['æmbit], *n.* tour, circuit, *m.*; (*fig.*) étendue, portée, *f.*
ambition [æm'biʃən], *n.* ambition, *f.*
ambitious [æm'biʃəs], *a.* ambitieux.
ambitiously [æm'biʃəsli], *adv.* ambitieusement.
amble [æmbl], *v.i.* aller (à) l'amble (*cheval*); (*fig.*) trottiner, aller son chemin, déambuler.—*n.* amble, *m.*
Ambrose ['æmbrouz]. Ambroise, *m.*
ambrosia [æm'brouziə], *n.* ambroisie, *f.*
ambulance ['æmbjuləns], *n.* ambulance, *f.*; hôpital militaire, *m.*
ambulant ['æmbjulənt], *a.* ambulant.
ambulatory ['æmbʌsəleit], *a.* ambulatoire.
ambuscade [æmbəs'keid], *n.* embuscade, *f.*; *to lay an ambuscade for,* dresser une embuscade à.—*v.t.* embusquer; mettre en embuscade.
ambush ['æmbuʃ], *n.* embuscade, *f.,* guet-apens, *m.*—*v.t.* embusquer.
Amelia [ə'miːliə]. Amélie, *f.*
ameliorate [ə'miːljəreit], *v.t.* améliorer.—*v.i.* s'améliorer.
amelioration [əmiːljə'rəiʃən], *n.* amélioration, *f.*
amen [ɑː'men], *int.* amen, ainsi soit-il.
amenable [ə'miːnəbl], *a.* responsable, comptable; docile, soumis, sujet (à).
amend [ə'mend], *v.t.* amender, corriger; réformer.—*v.i.* s'amender, se corriger.
amendment [ə'mendmənt], *n.* modification, *f.,* amendement, *m.,* amélioration, *f.*
amends [ə'mendz], *n. pl.* dédommagement, *m.,* compensation, réparation, *f.*; *to make amends for,* dédommager de, faire réparation de.
amenity [ə'miːniti, ə'meniti], *n.* aménité, *f.* agrément, *m.*
America [ə'merikə]. l'Amérique, *f.*

342

American [ə'merikən], *a.* américain.—*n.* Américain (*personne*), *m.*

amethyst ['æmiθist], *n.* améthyste, *f.*

amiability [eimjə'biliti], **amiableness** ['eimjəblnis], *n.* amabilité, *f.*

amiable ['eimjəbl], *a.* aimable.

amiably ['eimjəbli], *adv.* aimablement, avec amabilité.

amicable ['æmikəbl], *a.* amical; *amicable settlement,* arrangement à l'amiable, *m.*

amicably ['æmikəbli], *adv.* amicalement; à l'amiable.

amid [ə'mid], *prep.* au milieu de; parmi.

amidships [ə'midʃips], *adv.* (*Naut.*) par le travers.

amidst [ə'midst], [AMID].

amiss [ə'mis], *adv.* mal, en mauvaise part; (*unseasonably*) mal à propos.

amity ['æmiti], *n.* amitié, *f.*

ammeter ['æmitə], *n.* ampèremètre, *m.*

ammonia [ə'mouniə], *n.* ammoniaque, *f.*

ammunition [æmju'niʃən], *n.* munitions de guerre; cartouches, *f.pl.*

amnesia [æm'ni:ziə], *n.* amnésie, *f.*

amnesty ['æmnəsti], *n.* amnistie, *f.*—*v.t.* amnistier.

amoeba [ə'mi:bə], *n.* (*pl.* **amoebae** [ə'mi:bai], **amoebas** [ə'mi:bəz]) amibe, *f.*

amok [AMUCK].

among [ə'mʌŋ], **amongst** [ə'mʌŋst], *prep.* entre, parmi; au milieu de, chez, avec; *among other things,* entre autres choses; *from among,* d'entre.

amorous ['æmərəs], *a.* amoureux; porté à l'amour.

amorously ['æmərəsli], *adv.* amoureusement.

amorousness ['æmərəsnis], *n.* tempérament amoureux, *m.,* tendance à l'amour, *f.*

amorphous [ə'mɔ:fəs], *a.* amorphe.

amount [ə'maunt], *n.* montant, total, *m.,* somme; quantité; (*fig.*) valeur, *f.,* résultat, *m.*; *to the amount of,* jusqu'à la concurrence de.—*v.i.* s'élever, se monter (à); revenir (à), se réduire (à); *that amounts to the same thing,* cela revient au même.

amour [ə'muə], *n.* intrigue amoureuse, *f.*

ampere ['æmpɛə], *n.* (*Elec.*) ampère, *m.*

amphibian [æm'fibiən], *n.* amphibie, *m.*

amphibious [æm'fibiəs], *a.* amphibie.

amphitheater [æmfi'θiətə], *n.* amphithéâtre, *m.*

amphitheatrical [æmfiθi'ætrikəl], *a.* amphithéâtral, d'amphithéâtre.

amphora ['æmfərə], *n.* amphore, *f.*

ample [æmpl], *a.* ample, large, abondant, copieux; très suffisant.

ampleness ['æmplnis], *n.* ampleur; grandeur, *f.*

amplification [æmplifi'keiʃən], *n.* amplification, *f.*

amplifier ['æmplifaiə], *n.* (*Rad.*, *Tel.*) amplificateur, *m.*

amplify ['æmplifai], *v.t.* amplifier; exagérer.

amplitude ['æmplitju:d], *n.* amplitude, étendue, largeur, *f.*

amply ['æmpli], *adv.* amplement.

amputate ['æmpjuteit], *v.t.* amputer.

amputation [æmpju'teiʃən], *n.* amputation, *f.*

amuck [ə'mʌk], **amock**, **amok** [ə'mɔk], *adv.* *to run amuck,* devenir fou furieux.

amulet ['æmjulit], *n.* amulette, *f.*

amuse [ə'mju:z], *v.t.* amuser, divertir; *to be amused at,* s'amuser *ou* se divertir de.

amusement [ə'mju:zmənt], *n.* amusement, divertissement, *m.*

amusing [ə'mju:ziŋ], *a.* amusant, divertissant.

amusingly [ə'mju:ziŋli], *adv.* d'une manière amusante.

Amy ['eimi]. Aimée, *f.*

an [ʌ (2)].

anachronism [ə'nækrənizm], *n.* anachronisme, *m.*

anachronistic [ənækrə'nistik], *a.* anachronique.

anaconda [ænə'kɔndə], *n.* anaconda, eunecte, *m.*

anaemia [ə'ni:miə], *n.* anémie, *f.*

anaemic [ə'ni:mik], *a.* anémique.

anaesthesia [ænəs'θi:ziə], *n.* anesthésie, *f.*

anaesthetic [ænəs'θetik], *a.* and *n.* anesthésique, *m.*

anaesthetist [ə'ni:sθətist], *n.* anesthésiste, *m.,* *f.*

anaesthetize [ə'ni:sθətaiz], *v.t.* anesthésier.

anagram ['ænəgræm], *n.* anagramme, *f.*

analgesia [ænæl'dʒi:ziə], *n.* analgésie, analgie, *f.*

analogical [ænə'lɔdʒikəl], *a.* analogique.

analogism [ə'nælədʒizm], *n.* (*Phil.*) analogisme, *m.*

analogous [ə'næləgəs], *a.* analogue.

analogy [ə'nælədʒi], *n.* analogie, *f.*

analysis [ə'nælisis], *n.* analyse, *f.*

analyst ['ænəlist], *n.* analyste, *m.,* *f.*

analytic [ænə'litik], **analytical** [ænə'litikəl], *a.* analytique.

analytically [ænə'litikəli], *adv.* analytiquement.

analyze ['ænəlaiz], *v.t.* analyser, faire l'analyse de.

anarchism ['ænəkizm], *n.* anarchisme, *m.*

anarchist ['ænəkist], *a.* and *n.* anarchiste, *m.,* *f.*

anarchy ['ænəki], *n.* anarchie, *f.*

anathema [ə'næθimə], *n.* anathème, *m.*

anathematize [ə'næθimətaiz], *v.t.* anathématiser, frapper d'anathème; maudire.

anatomical [ænə'tɔmikəl], *a.* anatomique.

anatomically [ænə'tɔmikəli], *adv.* anatomiquement.

anatomist [ə'nætəmist], *n.* anatomiste, *m.,* *f.*

anatomize [ə'nætəmaiz], *v.t.* anatomiser.

anatomy [ə'nætəmi], *n.* anatomie, *f.*

ancestor ['ænsəstə], *n.* aïeul, *m.*

ancestors ['ænsəstəz], *n.pl.* ancêtres, pères, aïeux, *m.pl.*

ancestral [æn'sestrəl], *a.* ancestral, d'ancêtres, de ses ancêtres; héréditaire.

ancestry ['ænsəstri], *n.* ancêtres, *m.pl.*; race, origine, naissance, *f.,* lignage, *m.*

anchor ['æŋkə], *n.* ancre, *f.*; *sheet anchor,* maîtresse ancre, (*fig.*) ancre de miséricorde; *to ride at anchor,* être à l'ancre; *to weigh anchor,* lever l'ancre.—*v.t.* mouiller, ancrer.—*v.i.* ancrer, s'ancrer, jeter l'ancre, mouiller; (*fig.*) se fixer.

anchorage ['æŋkəridʒ], *n.* mouillage, ancrage, *m.*; retraite (*d'anachorète*)

anchoret ['æŋkəret], **anchorite** ['æŋkərait], *n.* anachorète, ermite, *m.,* *f.*

anchovy [æn'tʃouvi, 'æntʃəvi], *n.* anchois, *m.*

ancient ['einʃənt], *a.* ancien; antique.—*n.* ancien, *m.*; **the Ancient of Days**, l'Éternel, *m.*

anciently ['einʃəntli], *adv.* anciennement.

ancillary [æn'siləri], *a.* ancillaire, subordonné, auxiliaire.

and [ænd], *conj.* et; **and so on**, et ainsi de suite; **better and better**, de mieux en mieux; **carriage and pair**, voiture à deux chevaux, *f.*; **go and see**, allez voir.

Andes ['ændi:z], *the.* les Andes, *f.pl.*

andiron ['ændaiən], *n.* landier; chenet, *m.*

Andrew ['ændru:]. André, *m.*

anecdote ['ænikdout], *n.* anecdote, *f.*

anecdotal [ænik'doutl], *a.* anecdotique.

anemone [ə'neməni], *n.* anémone, *f.*

*anent** [ə'nent], *prep.* touchant.

aneroid ['ænərɔid], *a.* and *n.* anéroïde, *m.*

anes-, see **anaes-**.

aneurism ['ænjurizm], *n.* anévrisme, *m.*

anew [ə'nju:], *adv.* de nouveau.

angel ['eindʒəl], *n.* ange, *m.*

Angela ['ændʒələ]. Angèle, *f.*

angelic [æn'dʒelik], **angelical** [æn'dʒelikəl], *a.* angélique.

angelica [æn'dʒelikə], *n.* angélique, *f.*

angelus ['ændʒələs], *n.* angélus, *m.*

anger ['æŋgə], *n.* colère, *f.*; emportement; courroux, *m.*—*v.t.* fâcher, irriter, mettre en colère.

angina [æn'dʒainə], *n.* (*Path.*) angine, *f.*

angle (1) [æŋgl], *n.* angle; coin, *m.*

angle (2) [æŋgl], *v.i.* pêcher à la ligne.

angled [æŋgld], *a.* à angles; **right-angled**, rectangulaire.

angler ['æŋglə], *n.* pêcheur à la ligne, *m.*; (*Ichth.*) baudroie, *f.*; crapaud de mer, *m.*

Anglican ['æŋglikən], *a.* anglican.—*n.* Anglican, *m.*

Anglicism ['æŋglisizm], *n.* anglicisme, *m.*

Anglicize ['æŋglisaiz], *v.t.* angliciser.

angling ['æŋgliŋ], *n.* pêche à la ligne, *f.*

Anglophil(e) ['æŋglof(a)il], *n.* anglophile, *a.,f.*

Anglo-Saxon ['æŋglo'sæksən], *a.* anglo-saxon.—*n.* Anglo-Saxon, *m.*

angrily ['æŋgrili], *adv.* en colère, avec colère.

angry ['æŋgri], *a.* en colère, fâché, irrité (*contre ou about*), courroucé; **to be angry with**, être en colère contre, en vouloir à.

anguish ['æŋgwiʃ], *n.* angoisse, douleur, *f.*—*v.t.* angoisser, navrer de douleur.

angular ['æŋgjulə], *a.* angulaire, angulé; anguleux; maigre, décharné.

angularity [æŋgju'læriti], *n.* angularité, *f.*

angularly ['æŋgjuləli], *adv.* angulairement.

anile ['einail], *a.* de vieille femme, débile.

aniline ['ænilain], *n.* (*Chem.*) aniline, *f.*

anility [ə'niliti], *n.* seconde enfance, *f.*, radotage, *m.*

animadversion [ænimæd'və:ʃən], *n.* animadversion, censure, critique, *f.*

animadvert [ænimæd'və:t], *v.i.* **to animadvert upon**, critiquer, censurer.

animal ['æniməl], *a.* and *n.* animal, *m.*

animalism ['æniməlizm], **animality** [æni'mæliti], *n.* animalité, *f.*

animalize ['æniməlaiz], *v.t.* animaliser.

animate ['ænimeit], *v.t.* animer (*de*).—['ænimit], *a.* animé.

animated ['ænimeitid], *a.* animé, vif.

animatedly ['ænimeitidli], *adv.* vivement.

animating ['ænimeitiŋ], *a.* qui anime, qui ranime.

animation [æni'meiʃən], *n.* animation, vivacité, vie, *f.*

animator ['ænimeitə], *n.* animateur, *m.*

animosity [æni'mɔsiti], *n.* animosité, *f.*

animus ['æniməs], *n.* animosité, hostilité, *f.*; esprit (*de*), *m.*

anise ['ænis], *n.* anis, *m.*

aniseed ['ænisi:d], *n.* graine d'anis, *f.*

ankle [æŋkl], *n.* cheville du pied, *f.*

ankle bone ['æŋklboun], *n.* astragale, *m.*

ankle deep ['æŋkldi:p], *adv.* jusqu'aux chevilles.

Anna ['ænə]. Anne, *f.*

annalist ['ænəlist], *n.* annaliste, *m.*, *f.*

annals ['ænəlz], *n.pl.* annales, *f.pl.*

Ann(e) [æn]. Anne, *f.*

anneal [ə'ni:l], *v.t.* détremper; adoucir (*acier etc.*), recuire (*verre*).

annealing [ə'ni:liŋ], *n.* recuite, *f.*

annex [ə'neks], *v.t.* annexer, joindre (*à*).—['æneks], *n.* annexe, *f.*

annexation [ænek'seiʃən], *n.* annexation, *f.*

annexed [ə'nekst], *a.* ci-joint, annexé.

annihilate [ə'naiileit], *v.t.* anéantir, annihiler.

annihilation [ənaii'leiʃən], *n.* anéantissement, *m.*, annihilation, *f.*

annihilator [ə'naiileitə], *n.* annihilateur, *m.*

anniversary [æni'və:səri], *a.* and *n.* anniversaire, *m.*

Anno Domini ['ænou'dɔminai], (*abbr.* **A.D.** [ei'di:]). l'an du Seigneur; l'an de grâce; ap. J.-C.

annotate ['ænoteit], *v.t.* annoter.

annotation [æno'teiʃən], *n.* annotation, *f.*

annotator ['ænoteitə], *n.* annotateur, *m.*

announce [ə'nauns], *v.t.* annoncer, proclamer.

announcement [ə'naunsmənt], *n.* annonce, *f.*, avis, *m.*; lettre de faire-part, *f.*

announcer [ə'naunsə], *n.* annonciateur; (*Theat.*) compère, *m.*, commère, *f.*; (*Rad., Tel.*) speaker, *m.*, speakerine, *f.*

annoy [ə'nɔi], *v.t.* gêner; incommoder, ennuyer, importuner; contrarier, tracasser.

annoyance [ə'nɔiəns], *n.* ennui, désagrément, chagrin, *m.*; contrariété, *f.*

annoying [ə'nɔiiŋ], *a.* ennuyeux, contrariant, vexant.

annoyingly [ə'nɔiiŋli], *adv.* ennuyeusement.

annual ['ænjuəl], *a.* annuel.—*n.* annuaire, *m.*

annually ['ænjuəli], *adv.* annuellement, tous les ans.

annuitant [ə'njuitənt], *n.* bénéficiaire d'une pension *ou* d'une rente viagère, *m.*, *f.*

annuity [ə'njuiti], *n.* annuité, rente annuelle, pension, *f.*; **life annuity**, rente viagère, *f.*

annul [ə'nʌl], *v.t.* annuler.

annuler [ə'nʌlə], *a.* annulaire.

annulet ['ænjulit], *n.* annelet, filet, *m.*

annulment [ə'nʌlmənt], *n.* annulation, *f.*; **decree of annulment**, décret abolitif, *m.*

Annunciation [ənʌnsi'eiʃən], *the.* (*Eccles.*) l'Annonciation, *f.*

annunciation [ənʌnsi'eiʃən], *n.* annonce, proclamation, *f.*, avis, *m.*

anode ['ænoud], *n.* (*Elec.*) anode, *f.*

anodyne ['ænədain], *a.* anodin, calmant.—*n.* anodin (*remède*), *m.*

anoint [ə'nɔint], *v.t.* oindre.

anointed [ə'nɔintid], a. oint; *the Lord's Anointed*, l'Oint du Seigneur, m.

anomalous [ə'nɔmələs], a. anomal, irrégulier.

anomaly [ə'nɔməli], n. anomalie, f.

anon [ə'nɔn], adv. tout à l'heure, bientôt; à l'instant.

anonymity [ænə'nimiti], n. anonymat, m.

anonymous [ə'nɔniməs], a. anonyme.

anonymously [ə'nɔniməsli], adv. anonymement.

another [ə'nʌðə], a. and pron. autre, un autre; encore un; *one another*, l'un l'autre, les uns les autres.

answer ['ɑːnsə], v.t. répondre; répondre à; satisfaire, suffire à.—v.i. faire réponse; répondre (de ou pour); raisonner; réussir.— n. réponse; solution (d'un problème), f.

answerable ['ɑːnsərəbl], a. susceptible de réponse; responsable (for, de).

ant [ænt], n. fourmi, f.

antagonism [æn'tægənizm], n. antagonisme, m., opposition, f.

antagonist [æn'tægənist], n. antagoniste, m.,f.

antagonistic [æntægə'nistik], a. opposé (à); antagonique.

antagonize [æn'tægənaiz], v.t. eveiller l'antagonisme (de).

Antarctic [ænt'ɑːktik], a. antarctique.—n. Antarctique, m.

ant-eater ['ænti:tə], n. fourmilier, m.

antecedence [ænti'si:dəns], n. antériorité, f.

antecedent [ænti'si:dənt], a. and n. antécédent, m.

ante-chamber ['æntitʃeimbə], n. antichambre, f.

antediluvian [æntidi'lu:viən], a. and n. antédiluvien, m.

antelope ['æntiloup], n. antilope, f.

ante-meridiem [æntimə'ridiəm], (abbr. **a.m.** [ei'em]), adv. avant midi; *at 11 a.m.*, à onze heures du matin.

ante-natal ['ænti'neitəl], a. prénatal.

antenna [æn'tenə], n. (pl. **antennae** [æn'teni:]) antenne, f.

antepenult [æntipi'nʌlt], **antepenultimate** [æntipi'nʌltimit], a. and n. antépénultième, f.

anterior [æn'tiəriə], a. antérieur.

anteroom ['æntiru:m], n. antichambre, f.

anthem ['ænθəm], n. hymne (national), m.; antienne, f.

ant-hill ['ænthil], n. fourmilière, f.

anthology [æn'θɔlədʒi], n. anthologie, chrestomathie, f.

Anthony ['æntəni]. Antoine, m.

anthracite ['ænθrəsait], n. anthracite, m.

anthrax ['ænθræks], n. (Med.) anthrax, m.

anthropoid ['ænθrəpɔid], a. and n. anthropoïde, m.

anthropological [ænθrəpə'lɔdʒikəl], a. anthropologique.

anthropologist [ænθrə'pɔlədʒist], n. anthropologiste, anthropologue, m.,f.

anthropology [ænθrə'pɔlədʒi], n. anthropologie, f.

anti-aircraft [ænti'ɛəkrɑːft], a. contre-avion, antiaérien.

antibiotic [æntibai'ɔtik], a. and n. antibiotique, m.

antic ['æntik], n. bouffonnerie, farce, f.

Antichrist ['æntikraist], n. antéchrist, m.

antichristian ['ænti'kristjən], a. and n. antichrétien, m.

anticipate [æn'tisipeit], v.t. anticiper; prévenir, devancer; s'attendre à, prévoir, envisager; jouir d'avance de; se promettre.

anticipation [æntisi'peiʃən], n. anticipation, f.; avant-goût, m.; attente, f.

anticipatory [æn'tisipətri], a. par anticipation.

anticlerical [ænti'klerikəl], a. and n. anticlérical, m.

anticlericalism [ænti".lerikəlizm], n. anticléricalisme, m.

anti-climax [ænti'klaimæks], n. anticlimax, m.

anti-clockwise [COUNTER-CLOCKWISE].

anticyclone [ænti'saikloun], n. anticyclone, m.

anti-dazzle ['ænti'dæzl], a. anti-aveuglant; (Motor) *anti-dazzle head lights*, pharescode, m.pl.

antidote ['æntidout], n. antidote, contrepoison, m.

anti-freeze ['æntifri:z], n. anti-gel, m.

Antilles [æn'tili:z], the. les Antilles, f.pl.

antimacassar [æntimə'kæsə], n. têtière, f.

antimony ['æntiməni], n. antimoine, m.

antinomy [æn'tinəmi], n. antinomie, f.

antipathetic [æntipə'θetik], **antipathetical** [æntipə'θetikəl], a. antipathique.

antipathy [æn'tipəθi], n. antipathie, aversion, f.

antiphony [æn'tifəni], n. contre-chant, m.

antiphrasis [æn'tifrəsis], n. antiphrase, f.

antipodal [æn'tipədəl], a. antipodal.

antipodes [æn'tipədi:z], n. pl. antipodes, m.pl.

anti-pope ['æntipoup], n. antipape m.

antiquarian [ænti'kwɛəriən], a. d'antiquaire; archéologique.—n. antiquaire, m.

antiquary ['æntikwəri], n. archéologue n. antiquaire, m.

antiquated ['æntikweitid], a. vieilli, vétuste; suranné, démodé.

antique [æn'ti:k], a. antique, ancien.—n. *the antique*, l'antique, m.; *an antique*, un objet antique, une antiquité.

antiquity [æn'tikwiti], n. antiquité; ancienneté, f.

antirrhinum [ænti'rainəm], n. antirrhine, f.

anti-Semitism [ænti'semitizm], n. antisémitisme, m.

antiseptic [ænti'septik], a. and n. antiseptique, m.

anti-tank [ænti'tæŋk], a. anti-chars.

antithesis [æn'tiθisis], n. antithèse, f.

antithetic [ænti'θetik], **antithetical** [ænti'θetikəl], a. antithétique.

antler ['æntlə], n. andouiller, bois (de cerf), m.

Antony ['æntəni]. Antoine, m.

Antwerp ['æntwə:p]. Anvers, m.

anvil ['ænvil], n. enclume, f.; (fig.) *on the anvil*, sur le métier, en préparation.

anxiety [æŋ'zaiəti], n. anxiété, inquiétude, sollicitude, f.; désir, m.

anxious ['æŋkʃəs], a. inquiet, soucieux, plein de sollicitude (pour); désireux (de); *to be anxious to*, désirer vivement (de), tenir à.

anxiously ['æŋkʃəsli], adv. anxieusement, avec anxiété, avec inquiétude.

345

any ['eni], *a.* and *pron.* du, de la, etc.; en; aucun; quelque; n'importe lequel; *any man*, tout homme; *any others*, d'autres; *at any rate*, en tout cas; *I haven't any*, je n'en ai pas; *scarcely any*, presque pas.

anybody ['enibɔdi]. **anyone** [eniwʌn], *pron.* quelqu'un, chacun, qui que ce soit, n'importe qui, tout le monde; *I didn't see anybody*, je n'ai vu personne.

anyhow ['enihau], **anyway** ['eniwei], *adv.* de toute façon, de quelque manière que ce soit, en tout cas, quand même.

anyone [ANYBODY].

anything ['eniθiŋ], *pron.* quelque chose, *m.*, quoi que ce soit, n'importe quoi; *not to say anything*, ne rien dire.

anyway [ANYHOW].

anywhere ['eniwɛə], *adv.* quelque part, dans quelque endroit que ce soit, n'importe où; *not anywhere*, nulle part.

apace [ə'peis], *adv.* vite, à grands pas.

apanage *or* **appanage** ['æpənidʒ], *n.* apanage, *m.*

apart [ə'pɑːt], *adv.* à part; de côté, séparément.

apartheid [ə'pɑːtheit], *n.* (*en Afrique du Sud*) ségrégation, *f.*

apartment [ə'pɑːtmənt], *n.* chambre; pièce (*d'un appartement*), *f.*; logement; (*Am.*) appartement; (*pl.*) appartement, *m.*

apathetic [æpə'θetik], *a.* apathique.

apathy ['æpəθi], *n.* apathie, *f.*

ape [eip], *n.* singe, *m.*, guenon, *f.*—*v.t.* singer.

aperient [ə'piəriənt], **aperitive** [ə'peritiv], *a.* and *n.* laxatif, *m.*

aperture ['æpətjuə], *n.* ouverture, *f.*; orifice, *m.*

apex ['eipeks], *n.* (*pl.* **apices** ['eipisiːz], **apexes** ['eipeksiz]) sommet, *m.*, pointe, *f.*

aphorism ['æfərizm], *n.* aphorisme, *m.*

apiary ['eipiəri], *n.* rucher, *m.*

apiece [ə'piːs], *adv.* la pièce; par tête, par personne, chacun.

apish ['eipiʃ], *a.* de singe, simiesque; *apish trick*, singerie, *f.*

apocalypse [ə'pɔkəlips], *n.* apocalypse, *f.*

apocalyptic [əpɔkə'liptik], **apocalyptical** [əpɔkə'liptikəl], *a.* apocalyptique.

Apocrypha [ə'pɔkrifə], *n.pl.* les Apocryphes, *m.pl.*

apocryphal [ə'pɔkrifəl], *a.* apocryphe.

apogee ['æpədʒiː], *n.* apogée, *m.*

apologetic [əpɔlə'dʒetik], **apologetical** [əpɔlə'dʒetikəl], *a.* qui s'excuse, qui regrette; *he was quite apologetic about it*, il s'en excusa vivement.

apologetically [əpɔlə'dʒetikəli], *adv.* pour s'excuser, en s'excusant.

apologia [æpə'loudʒiə], *n.* apologie; justification, *f.*

apologist [ə'pɔlədʒist], *n.* apologiste, *m.*, *f.*

apologize [ə'pɔlədʒaiz], *v.i.* s'excuser, faire des excuses (*de* ou *auprès de*).

apologue ['æpəlɔg], *n.* apologue, *m.*

apology [ə'pɔlədʒi], *n.* excuses, *f.pl.*, apologie, *f.*

apoplectic ['æpə'plektik], *a.* apoplectique; *apoplectic stroke*, coup de sang, *m.*

apoplexy ['æpəpleksi], *n.* apoplexie, *f.*; *a fit of apoplexy*, congestion cérébrale, *f.*

apostasy [ə'pɔstəsi], *n.* apostasie, *f.*

apostate [ə'pɔsteit], *a.* and *n.* apostat, *m.*

apostle [ə'pɔsl], *n.* apôtre, *m.*; *the Acts of the Apostles*, les Actes des Apôtres, *m.pl.*

apostolic [æpəs'tɔlik], **apostolical** [æpəs'tɔlikəl], *a.* apostolique.

apostrophe [ə'pɔstrəfi], *n.* apostrophe, *f.*

apostrophize [ə'pɔstrəfaiz], *v.t.* apostropher.

apothecary [ə'pɔθikəri], *n.* apothicaire; pharmacien, *m.*

apotheosis [əpɔθi'ousis], *n.* apothéose, *f.*

appal [ə'pɔːl], *v.t.* épouvanter, consterner.

appalling [ə'pɔːliŋ], *a.* épouvantable, effrayant.

appallingly [ə'pɔːliŋli], *adv.* épouvantablement.

appanage [APANAGE].

apparatus [æpə'reitəs], *n.* appareil, dispositif, *m.*

apparel [ə'pærəl], *v.t.* vêtir; parer.—*n.* habillement, vêtement, *m.*

apparent [ə'pærənt], *a.* évident, manifeste, apparent; *heir apparent*, héritier présomptif, *m.*

apparently [ə'pærəntli], *adv.* en apparence, apparemment.

apparition [æpə'riʃən], *n.* apparition, *f.*

appeal [ə'piːl], *v.i.* appeler, en appeler (*de*), faire appel (*à*); (*Law*) se pourvoir en cassation, réclamer (*contre* ou *à*); (*fig.*) attirer, séduire.—*n.* appel, attrait, *m.*; *Court of Appeal*, cour de cassation, *f.*

appealing [ə'piːliŋ], *a.* suppliant, attrayant, séduisant.

appear [ə'piə], *v.i.* paraître, apparaître; se montrer, se présenter (*à*).

appearance [ə'piərəns], *n.* apparition; apparence, figure, mine, *f.*; air, aspect, *m.*; (*Law*) comparution, *f.*; *at first appearance*, au premier abord, au premier coup d'œil.

appeasable [ə'piːzəbl], *a.* qu'on peut apaiser.

appease [ə'piːz], *v.t.* apaiser, pacifier.

appeasement [ə'piːzmənt], *n.* apaisement, adoucissement, *m.*; conciliation, *f.*

appellant [ə'pelənt], *a.* and *n.* (*Law*) appelant, *m.*

appellation [æpə'leiʃən], *n.* nom, *m.*, appellation, dénomination, *f.*

append [ə'pend], *v.t.* apposer, attacher (*à*).

appendage [ə'pendidʒ], *n.* accessoire, apanage, *m.*

appendant [ə'pendənt], *a.* accessoire, attaché, annexé (*à*).

appendicitis [əpendi'saitis], *n.* appendicite, *f.*

appendix [ə'pendiks], *n.* (*pl.* **appendixes** [ə'pendiksiz], **appendices** [ə'pendisiːz]) appendice, *m.*

appertain [æpə'tein], *v.i.* appartenir (*à*).

appetite ['æpitait], *n.* appétit; (*fig.*) désir, *m.*, soif, *f.*

appetize ['æpitaiz], *v.t.* mettre en appétit.

appetizer ['æpitaizə], *n.* apéritif, *m.*

appetizing ['æpitaiziŋ], *a.* appétissant.

applaud [ə'plɔːd], *v.t.*, *v.i.* applaudir (*à*).

applause [ə'plɔːz], *n.* applaudissements, *m.pl.*

apple [æpl], *n.* pomme, *f.*; *apple of the eye*, prunelle, *f.*

apple pie ['æpl'pai], *n.* tourte aux pommes, *f.*

apple-sauce ['æpl'sɔːs], *n.* compote de pommes, *f.*

apple tart ['æpl'tɑːt], *n.* tarte aux pommes, *f.*

apple tree ['æpltriː], *n.* pommier, *m.*

appliance [ə'plaiəns], *n.* instrument, appareil, dispositif, *m.*

applicability [æplikə'biliti], **applicableness** ['æplikəblnis], *n.* applicabilité, *f.*

applicable ['æplikəbl], *a.* applicable.

applicant ['æplikant], *n.* postulant, candidat; (*Law*) demandeur, *m.*

application [æpli'keiʃən], *n.* application; sollicitation, demande, *f.*; usage, *m.*; *for external application*, usage externe; *on application*, sur demande; *to make application to*, s'adresser à, faire une demande à.

apply [ə'plai], *v.t.* appliquer (à); *to apply the brake*, freiner; serrer le frein.—*v.i.* s'adresser (à); s'appliquer, être applicable; *to apply for* (a job), faire une demande (d'emploi); *to apply to*, s'adresser à *ou* chez.

appoint [ə'pɔint], *v.t.* arrêter, désigner, fixer; nommer; installer, équiper; *at the appointed hour*, à l'heure convenue; *a well-appointed house*, une maison bien installée.

appointment [ə'pɔintmənt], *n.* nomination, *f.*; décret, arrêt; établissement; emploi; rendez-vous, *m.*; convocation, *f.*

apportion [ə'pɔːʃən], *v.t.* partager, répartir, assigner.

apportionment [ə'pɔːʃənmənt], *n.* répartition, *f.*, partage, *m.*

apposite ['æpəzait], *a.* juste; à propos; approprié, convenable (à).

appositely ['æpəzaitli], *adv.* convenablement, justement, à propos.

appositeness ['æpəzaitnis], *n.* à-propos, *m.*, opportunité, *f.*

appraisal [APPRAISEMENT].

appraise [ə'preiz], *v.t.* priser, évaluer, estimer.

appraisement [ə'preizmənt], **appraisal** [ə'preizəl], *n.* évaluation, estimation; expertise, *f.*

appraiser [ə'preizə], *n.* commissaire-priseur, expert, *m.*

appreciable [ə'priːʃəbl], *a.* appréciable, sensible.

appreciably [ə'priːʃəbli], *adv.* sensiblement.

appreciate [ə'priːʃieit], *v.t.* apprécier, estimer.—*v.i.* (*Comm. etc.*) augmenter de valeur.

appreciation [əpriːʃi'eiʃən], *n.* appréciation; hausse de valeur, *f.*

appreciative [ə'priːʃiətiv], *a.* appréciateur.

apprehend [æpri'hend], *v.t.* comprendre; prendre, saisir, arrêter, appréhender; craindre.

apprehension [æpri'henʃən], *n.* appréhension; arrestation, prise de corps; crainte, inquiétude, *f.*

apprehensive [æpri'hensiv], *a.* intelligent, prompt à saisir; appréhensif, inquiet.

apprentice [ə'prentis], *n.* apprenti, *m.*—*v.t.* mettre en apprentissage.

apprenticeship [ə'prentisʃip], *n.* apprentissage, *m.*

apprise [ə'praiz], *v.t.* prévenir, informer, instruire.

approach [ə'proutʃ], *n.* approche, *f.*; abord, accès; rapprochement, *m.*; (*Math.*) approximation, *f.*—*v.t.* approcher de, s'approcher de, aborder; (*fig.*) pressentir, tâter (*quelqu'un*).—*v.i.* approcher, s'approcher.

approachable [ə'proutʃəbl], *a.* abordable, accessible.

approbation [æpro'beiʃən], *n.* approbation, *f.*; *on approbation*, à condition, à l'essai.

appropriate [ə'prouprieit], *v.t.* approprier, affecter (à); s'approprier; s'emparer de.—[ə'proupriət], *a.* approprié; propre, convenable (à).

appropriately [ə'proupriətli], *adv.* à juste titre; convenablement.

appropriateness [ə'proupriətnis], *n.* convenance, *f.*, à-propos, *m.*, justesse, *f.*

appropriation [əproupri'eiʃən], *n.* application, destination, appropriation, *f.*; crédit (*budgétaire*), *m.*

approval [ə'pruːvəl], *n.* approbation, *f.*; *on approval*, à condition.

approve [ə'pruːv], *v.t.* approuver; trouver bon (*que, with subj.*).

approver [ə'pruːvə], *n.* approbateur, *m.*

approving [ə'pruːviŋ], *n.* approbateur, approbatif.

approvingly [ə'pruːviŋli], *adv.* avec approbation, d'un air approbateur.

approximate [ə'prɔksimeit], *v.t.* rapprocher.—*v.i.* se rapprocher (de).—[ə'prɔksimit], *a.* approximatif.

approximately [ə'prɔksimitli], *adv.* approximativement, à peu près.

approximation [əprɔksi'meiʃən], *n.* approximation, *f.*; rapprochement, *m.*

appulse [ə'pʌls], *n.* choc, *m.*

appurtenance [ə'pəːtinəns], *n.* appartenance, dépendance, *f.*; (*pl.*) accessoires, *m.pl.*

appurtenant [ə'pəːtinənt], *a.* appartenant (à), dépendant (de).

apricot ['eiprikət], *n.* abricot, *m.*

apricot tree ['eiprikɔttriː], *n.* abricotier, *m.*

April ['eipril], avril, *m.*; *to make an April fool of*, donner un poisson d'avril à.

apron ['eiprən], *n.* tablier, *m.*; (*Av.*) aire de manœuvre *ou* d'atterrissage, *f.*

apron stage ['eiprənsteidʒ], *n.* avant-scène, *f.*

apse [æps], **apsis** ['æpsis], *n.* (*pl.* **apses** ['æpsiz], **apsides** [æp'saidiːz]) abside; (*Astron.*) apside, *f.*

apt [æpt], *a.* sujet, enclin, porté (à); propre, convenable (à); capable; juste (*mot*).

aptitude ['æptitjuːd], **aptness** ['æptnis], *n.* aptitude, disposition, *f.*

aptly ['æptli], *adv.* à propos; convenablement.

aqua fortis [ækwə'fɔːtis], *n.* eau-forte, *f.*

aquamarine [ækwəmə'riːn], *n.* aigue-marine, *f.*

aqua regia [ækwə'riːdʒiə], *n.* eau régale, *f.*

aquarium [ə'kwɛəriəm], *n.* aquarium, *m.*

aquatic [ə'kwɔtik, ə'kwætik], *a.* aquatique.

aquatics [ə'kwætiks], **aquatic sports** [ə'kwætikspɔːts], *n.pl.* sports nautiques, *m.pl.*

aqua vitae [ækwə'vaitiː], *n.* eau de vie, *f.*

aqueduct ['ækwidʌkt], *n.* aqueduc, *m.*

aqueous ['eikwiəs], *a.* aqueux.

aquiline ['ækwilain], *a.* aquilin, d'aigle.

Arab ['ærəb], *a.* arabe.—*n.* Arabe, *m.,f.*

arabesque [ærə'besk], *a.* and *n.* arabesque, *f.*

Arabia [ə'reibiə], l'Arabie, *f.*; *Saudi Arabia*, l'Arabie Séoudite.

Arabian [ə'reibiən], *a.* arabe.

347

Arabic

Arabic ['ærəbik], *a.* arabe, arabique; *Arabic figures*, chiffres arabes, *m.pl.—n.* arabe (*langue*), *m.*

arable ['ærəbl], *a.* arable, labourable.

arbalest ['aːbəlest], *n.* arbalète, *f.*

arbiter ['aːbitə], *n.* arbitre, *m.*, *f.*

arbitrament [aː'bitrəmənt], *n.* arbitrage, *m.*, arbitration, *f.*; jugement, *m.*

arbitrarily ['aːbitrərəli], *adv.* arbitrairement.

arbitrary ['aːbitrəri], *a.* arbitraire.

arbitrate ['aːbitreit], *v.t.*, *v.i.* arbitrer, décider.

arbitration [aːbi'treiʃən], *n.* arbitrage, *m.*

arbitrator ['aːbitreitə], *n.* arbitre, *m.*, *f.*

arbor ['aːbə], *n.* berceau, *m.*, tonnelle, *f.*

arbutus [aː'bjuːtəs], *n.* arbousier, *m.*

arc [aːk], *n.* arc, *m.*

arcade [aː'keid], *n.* arcade, *f.*; passage, *m.*

arch [aːtʃ], *a.* moqueur, malin, espiègle; grand, maître, archi-, insigne, fieffé.—*n.* arche, *f.*; arc, cintre, *m.*, voûte, *f.*; *pointed arch*, ogive, *f.*; *triumphal arch*, arc de triomphe.—*v.t.* voûter, cintrer, arquer.

archaeological [aːkiə'lɔdʒikəl], *a.* archéologique.

archaeologist [aːki'ɔlədʒist], *n.* archéologue, *m.*, *f.*

archaeology [aːki'ɔlədʒi], *n.* archéologie, *f.*

archaic [aː'keiik], *a.* archaïque.

archaism ['aːkeiizm], *n.* archaïsme, *m.*

archangel [aː'keindʒəl], *n.* archange, *m.*

archbishop [aːtʃ'biʃəp], *n.* archevêque, *m.*

archbishopric [aːtʃ'biʃəprik], *n.* archevêché, *m.*

archdeacon [aːtʃ'diːkən], *n.* archidiacre, *m.*

archduchess [aːtʃ'dʌtʃis], *n.* archiduchesse, *f.*

archduchy [aːtʃ'dʌtʃi], *n.* archiduché, *m.*

archduke [aːtʃ'djuːk], *n.* archiduc, *m.*

archer ['aːtʃə], *n.* archer, *m.*; (*Astron.*) *the Archer*, Sagittaire, *m.*

archery ['aːtʃəri], *n.* tir à l'arc, *m.*

archetype ['aːkitaip], *n.* archétype; étalon (*mesure*), *m.*

archiepiscopal [aːkiə'piskəpəl], *a.* archiépiscopal.

archipelago [aːki'peləgou], *n.* archipel, *m.*

architect ['aːkitekt], *n.* architecte; (*fig.*) artisan, *m.*

architectural [aːki'tektʃərəl], *a.* architectural.

architecture ['aːkitektʃə], *n.* architecture, *f.*

archives ['aːkaivz], *n. pl.* archives, *f.pl.*

archivist ['aːkivist], *n.* archiviste, *m.*, *f.*

archly ['aːtʃli], *adv.* avec espièglerie, d'un air malin.

archness ['aːtʃnis], *n.* malice, espièglerie, *f.*

arc light ['aːklæmp], *n.* lampe à arc, *f.*

Arctic ['aːktik], *a.* arctique.

ardent ['aːdənt], *a.* ardent; *ardent spirits*, spiritueux, *m.pl.*

ardently ['aːdəntli], *adv.* ardemment, avec ardeur.

ardor ['aːdə], *n.* ardeur, *f.*

arduous ['aːdjuəs], *a.* ardu, rude, pénible, difficile.

arduously ['aːdjuəsli], *adv.* difficilement, péniblement.

arduousness ['aːdjuəsnis], *n.* difficulté, *f.*

area ['ɛəriə], *n.* étendue; aire, surface, superficie; région, zone; courette d'entrée (*devant la maison*), *f.*; *area steps*, escalier de service, *m.*; *postal area*, zone postale, *f.*

arena [ə'riːnə], *n.* arène, *f.*

argent ['aːdʒənt], *a.* argenté.—*n.* (*Her.*) argent, *m.*

Argentina [aːdʒən'tiːnə]. l'Argentine, la République Argentine, *f.*

Argentine ['aːdʒəntain], *a.* argentin.—*n.* Argentin, *m.*; *the Argentine* [ARGENTINA].

Argentinian [aːdʒən'tinjən], *a.* argentin.—*n.* Argentin (*personne*), *m.*

argil ['aːdʒil], *n.* argile, *f.*

argonaut ['aːgənɔːt], *n.* argonaute, *m.*

argosy ['aːgəsi], *n.* caraque, *f.*

argue ['aːgjuː], *v.t.* discuter; soutenir; (*fig.*) dénoter, indiquer, accuser.—*v.i.* argumenter (*contre*), raisonner (*sur*), discuter (*avec*); (*Law*) plaider.

argument ['aːgjumənt], *n.* argument, raisonnement, *m.*; discussion, dispute; thèse, *f.*; *for argument's sake*, à titre d'exemple.

argumentative [aːgju'mentətiv], *a.* raisonneur; disposé à argumenter.

aria ['aːriə], *n.* aria, *f.*

arid ['ærid], *a.* aride.

aridity [ə'riditi], **aridness** ['æridnis], *n.* aridité, *f.*

aright [ə'rait], *adv.* correctement; bien.

arise [ə'raiz], *v.i. irr.* (*conjug. like* RISE) se lever; s'élever; survenir, se présenter; provenir, résulter (*de*); *if the question arises*, le cas échéant.

aristocracy [æris'tɔkrəsi], *n.* aristocratie, *f.*

aristocrat ['æristəkræt], *n.* aristocrate, *m.*, *f.*

aristocratic [æristə'krætik], *a.* aristocratique.

arithmetic [ə'riθmətik], *n.* arithmétique, *f.*, calcul, *m.*

arithmetical [æriθ'metikəl], *a.* arithmétique.

arithmetically [æriθ'metikəli], *adv.* arithmétiquement.

arithmetician [æriθmə'tiʃən], *n.* arithméticien, *m.*

ark [aːk], *n.* arche, *f.*; *Noah's ark*, l'arche de Noé.

arm [aːm], *n.* bras, *m.*; arme (*à feu*), *f.*; (*pl.*) (*Her.*) armes, armoiries, *f.pl.*; *arm in arm*, bras dessus bras dessous; *with arms folded*, les bras croisés; *with open arms*, à bras ouverts.—*v.t.* armer; s'armer (*de*); prendre les armes.

armada [aː'maːdə], *n.* armada, *f.*

armadillo [aːmə'dilou], *n.* tatou, *m.*

armament ['aːməmənt], *n.* armement, *m.*, armée, flotte, *f.*; *armaments race*, course aux armements, *f.*

armature ['aːmətjuə], *n.* armature, *f.*, induit, *m.*

arm band ['aːmbænd], *n.* brassard, *m.*

arm-chair ['aːmtʃɛə], *n.* fauteuil, *m.*

Armenia [aː'miːniə], l'Arménie, *f.*

Armenian [aː'miːniən], *a.* arménien.—*n.* arménien (*langue*); Arménien (*personne*), *m.*

armful ['aːmful], *n.* brassée, *f.*

arm-hole ['aːmhoul], *n.* emmanchure, entournure, *f.*

armistice ['aːmistis], *n.* armistice, *m.*

armless ['aːmlis], *a.* sans bras.

armlet ['aːmlit], *n.* brassard; bracelet; petit bras (*de mer*), *m.*

armor ['aːmə], *n.* armure, *f.*; blindés, *m.pl.*—*v.t.* cuirasser, blinder.

armored ['aːməd], *a.* cuirassé, blindé.

armorer ['aːmərə], *n.* armurier, *m.*

armorial [ɑːˈmɔːriəl], *a.* armorial; *armorial bearings,* armoiries, *f.pl.*

armor plate [ˈɑːməˈpleit], *n.* plaque de blindage, *f.*

armor-plated [ˈɑːməˈpleitid], *a.* cuirassé, blindé.

armory [ˈɑːməri], *n.* arsenal, *m.*; salle d'armes; armurerie, *f.*

armpit [ˈɑːmpit], *n.* aisselle, *f.*

army [ˈɑːmi], *n.* armée; *(fig.)* foule, multitude, *f.*; *the Salvation Army,* l'Armée du Salut.

Arnold [ˈɑːnəld]. 'Arnaud, *m.*

aroma [əˈroumə], *n.* arome *ou* arôme; bouquet *(de vin), m.*

aromatic [ærəˈmætik], *a.* aromatique.

around [əˈraund], *prep.* autour de; *(colloq.)* environ, vers, à peu près.—*adv.* autour, à l'entour, aux alentours.

arouse [əˈrauz], *v.t.* réveiller, éveiller; exciter, provoquer.

arraign [əˈrein], *v.t.* accuser, poursuivre en justice, attaquer.

arraignment [əˈreinmənt], *n.* mise en accusation, *f.*

arrange [əˈreindʒ], *v.t.* arranger, régler, disposer, distribuer; organiser.

arrangement [əˈreindʒmənt], *n.* arrangement, *m.*, disposition, organisation, *f.*, dispositif, *m.*

arrant [ˈærənt], *a.* insigne, achevé, fieffé.

arrantly [ˈærəntli], *adv.* notoirement, impudemment.

array [əˈrei], *v.t.* ranger, déployer; revêtir, parer.—*n.* ordre, rang; étalage; appareil, *m.*

arrear [əˈriə], *n.* arriéré, *m.*; *(pl.)* arrérages, *m.pl.*; *to be in arrears,* être en retard, avoir de l'arriéré.

arrest [əˈrest], *v.t.* arrêter; fixer; suspendre. —*n.* arrestation, prise de corps, *f.*; arrêt, *m.*, suspension, *f.*

arresting [əˈrestiŋ], *a.* frappant, qui arrête l'attention.

arrival [əˈraivəl], *n.* arrivée, *f.*; arrivage *(de marchandises etc.), m.*; *arrival platform,* quai d'arrivée, débarcadère, *m.*

arrive [əˈraiv], *v.i.* arriver *(à)*; parvenir *(à).*

arrogance [ˈærəgəns], *n.* arrogance, *f.*

arrogant [ˈærəgənt], *a.* arrogant.

arrogantly [ˈærəgəntli], *adv.* arrogamment.

arrogate [ˈærəgeit], *v.t.* attribuer injustement; *to arrogate to oneself,* s'arroger.

arrogation [ærəˈgeiʃən], *n.* prétention, usurpation, *f.*

arrow [ˈærou], *n.* flèche, *f.*; *(fig.)* trait, *m.*— *v.t.* indiquer par des flèches.

arrow-root [ˈærouruːt], *n.* arrow-root, *m.*

arsenal [ˈɑːsənəl], *n.* arsenal, *m.*

arsenic [ˈɑːsenik], *a.* arsénique.—[ˈɑːsənik], *n.* arsenic, *m.*

arson [ˈɑːsən], *n.* incendie volontaire, *m.*

art [ɑːt], *n.* art, *m.*; adresse, habileté, *f.*; *faculty of arts,* faculté des lettres, *f.*; *fine arts,* beaux-arts, *m.pl.*; *school of art,* école de dessin, académie, *f.*

arterial [ɑːˈtiəriəl], *a.* artériel; *arterial road,* route à grande circulation, *f.*

artery [ˈɑːtəri], *n.* artère, *f.*

artesian [ɑːˈtiːʒən], *a.* artésien.

artful [ˈɑːtful], *a.* rusé, fin, artificieux.

artfully [ˈɑːtfuli], *adv.* avec artifice, artificieusement, adroitement.

artfulness [ˈɑːtfulnis], *n.* ruse, finesse, *f.*, artifice, *m.*

arthritic [ɑːˈθritik], *a.* arthritique.

arthritis [ɑːˈθraitis], *n.* arthrite, *f.*

artichoke [ˈɑːtitʃouk], *n.* *Chinese artichoke,* crosne (du Japon), *m.*; *globe artichoke,* artichaut, *m.*; *Jerusalem artichoke,* topinambour, *m.*

article [ˈɑːtikl], *n.* article; objet; statut, *m.*— *v.t.* engager par contrat; placer *(chez un avoué)* comme clerc; *articled clerk,* clerc d'avoué, *m.*

articulate [ɑːˈtikjuleit], *v.t., v.i.* articuler; énoncer, parler distinctement.—[ɑːˈtikjulit], *a.* articulé.

artifice [ˈɑːtifis], *n.* artifice, *m.*, ruse, finesse, *f.*

artificer [ɑːˈtifisə], *n.* artisan, ouvrier, mécanicien, *m.*

artificial [ɑːtiˈfiʃəl], *a.* artificiel; factice.

artificiality [ɑːtifiʃiˈæliti], *n.* nature artificielle, *f.*

artificially [ɑːtiˈfiʃəli], *adv.* artificiellement.

artillery [ɑːˈtiləri], *n.* artillerie, *f.*

artilleryman [ɑːˈtilərimən], *n.* (*pl.* -men [men]) artilleur, *m.*

artisan [ɑːtiˈzæn], *n.* artisan, ouvrier, *m.*

artist [ˈɑːtist], *n.* artiste, *m.,f.*

artistic [ɑːˈtistik], *a.* artistique.

artistically [ɑːˈtistikli], *adv.* artistement, avec art.

artless [ˈɑːtlis], *a.* ingénu, naïf; sans art, naturel.

artlessly [ˈɑːtlisli], *adv.* ingénument, naïvement; sans art.

artlessness [ˈɑːtlisnis], *n.* naïveté; simplicité, *f.*

as [æz], *conj.* comme; tel que; à titre de; aussi . . . que; à mesure que; en, pour; parce que; *as big as,* aussi gros que; *as cold as charity,* froid comme le marbre; *as for,* quant à, pour; *as he advanced,* à mesure qu'il avançait; *as I was walking,* comme il marchait; *as if,* comme si; *as it were,* pour ainsi dire; *as much as,* autant que, tant que; *as yet,* jusqu'à présent, encore; *as you were,* (Mil.) au temps! be that as it may, quoi qu'il en soit; *do as you wish,* faites comme vous voudrez; *rich as she is,* toute riche qu'elle est; *she was dressed as a page,* elle était habillée en page; *that's as may be,* c'est selon; *to act as,* agir en.

asbestos [æzˈbestəs], *n.* asbeste, amiante, *m.*

ascend [əˈsend], *v.t.* monter; gravir, faire l'ascension de; remonter *(un fleuve).*—*v.i.* monter (*à ou sur*); remonter; s'élever *(montagne etc.).*

ascendancy [əˈsendənsi], *n.* ascendant, *m.*; supériorité, influence, *f.*

ascendant [əˈsendənt], *a.* ascendant; supérieur.—*n.* ascendant, *m.*; supériorité, *f.*, dessus, *m.*

Ascension [əˈsenʃən], *n.* (*Eccles.*) Ascension, *f.*; *Ascension Day,* jour de l'Ascension, *m.*

ascent [əˈsent], *n.* ascension; élévation, montée, pente, *f.*

ascertain [æsəˈtein], *v.t.* s'assurer, s'informer de, constater, vérifier.

ascetic [əˈsetik], *a.* ascétique.—*n.* ascète, ascétique, *m.,f.*

asceticism [əˈsetisizm], *n.* ascétisme, *m.*

349

ascribable [ə'skraibəbl], a. attribuable, imputable.

ascribe [ə'skraib], v.t. attribuer, imputer (à).

aseptic [æ'septik], a. and n. aseptique, m.

asexual [æ'seksjuəl], a. asexué, asexuel.

ash (1) [æʃ], a. de frêne.—n. frêne (arbre); bâton, m.; **mountain ash**, sorbier, m.

ash (2) [æʃ], n. cendre, f.; cendres, f.pl.

ashamed [ə'ʃeimd], a. honteux, confus; **to be ashamed of**, avoir honte de.

ash bin, pit ['æʃbin, -pit], n. cendrier, m.

ashcan ['æʃkæn], n. (Am.) boîte à ordures, f.

ashen (1) [æʃn], a. de frêne.

ashen (2) [æʃn], a. cendré; gris pâle.

ashore [ə'ʃɔː], adv. à terre; échoué (navire); **to go ashore**, débarquer.

ash pit [ASH BIN].

ashtray ['æʃtrei], n. cendrier, m.

Ash Wednesday [æʃ'wenzdi]. mercredi des Cendres, m.

ashy ['æʃi], a. cendré; gris pâle.

Asia ['eiʃə]. l'Asie, f.

Asia Minor ['eiʃə'mainə]. l'Asie-Mineure, f.

Asiatic [eiʃi'ætik], (Asian ['eiʃən], a. asiatique. —n. Asiatique (personne), m.,f.

aside [ə'said], adv. de côté; (Theat.) à part; à l'écart.—n. (Theat.) aparté, m.

asinine ['æsinəin], a. d'âne; sot.

ask [ɑːsk], v.t. demander, prier (de); inviter (à); s'informer, se renseigner; poser (une question); **to ask in**, prier d'entrer; **to ask someone to do something**, demander à quelqu'un de faire quelque chose; **to ask to see**, demander à voir.

askance [ə'skɑːns], adv. de travers, obliquement.

askew [ə'skjuː], adv. de côté, de biais.

aslant [ə'slɑːnt], adv. obliquement, de biais, de côté, en travers.

asleep [ə'sliːp], a. endormi; **to be asleep**, dormir; **to fall asleep**, s'endormir.

asp (1) [æsp], **aspic** ['æspik], n. aspic, m.

asp (2) [æsp], **aspen** ['æspən], n. tremble, m.

asparagus [əs'pærəgəs], n. asperges, f.pl.

aspect ['æspekt], n. aspect, m.; exposition, f.; **to have a southern aspect**, être exposé au midi.

aspen ['æspən], a. de tremble.—n. [ASP (2)].

asperity [æs'periti], n. aspérité, âpreté, rudesse, f.

aspersion [æs'pəːʃən], n. calomnie, f.; **to cast aspersions on**, répandre des calomnies sur.

asphalt ['æsfælt], a. d'asphalte.—n. asphalte, m.

asphyxia [æs'fiksiə], n. asphyxie, f.

asphyxiate [æs'fiksieit], v.t. asphyxier.

aspic [ASP (1)].

aspirant [ə'spaiərənt], n. aspirant, candidat, m.

aspirate ['æspireit], v.t. aspirer.—['æspirit], a. aspiré.

aspiration [æspi'reiʃən], n. aspiration, f.

aspire [ə'spaiə], v.i. aspirer (à), ambitionner.

aspirin ['æspirin], n. aspirine, f.

asquint [ə'skwint], adv. de travers, en louchant.

ass [æs], n. âne, m.; **he is a silly ass**, il est bête à manger du foin; **she-ass**, ânesse, f.; **to make an ass of oneself**, agir sottement; **young ass**, ânon, m.

assail [ə'seil], v.t. assaillir, attaquer.

assailant [ə'seilənt], n. assaillant, m.

assassin [ə'sæsin], n. assassin (politique), m.

assassinate [ə'sæsineit], v.t. assassiner.

assassination [əsæsi'neiʃən], n. assassinat, m.

assault [ə'sɔːlt], n. assaut, m., attaque brusquée; (Law) tentative de voie de fait, f.; **assault and battery**, voies de fait, f.pl.; **indecent assault**, outrage aux mœurs, m. —v.t. assaillir, attaquer.

assay [ə'sei], n. épreuve, vérification, f.; essai, m.—v.t. essayer.

assemble [ə'sembl], v.t. assembler, réunir.— v.i. s'assembler, se réunir.

assembly [ə'sembli], n. assemblée, réunion, f.; assemblage (d'une machine), m.; **assembly line**, chaîne de montage, f.

assent [ə'sent], v.i. donner son assentiment (à), admettre.—n. assentiment, consentement, m.

assert [ə'səːt], v.t. affirmer, prétendre, soutenir; revendiquer, faire valoir (ses droits etc.).

assertion [ə'səːʃən], n. assertion, revendication, f.

assertive [ə'səːtiv], a. assertif.

assertively [ə'səːtivli], adv. d'un ton péremptoire.

assess [ə'ses], v.t. répartir, fixer; imposer; évaluer.

assessment [ə'sesmənt], n. imposition, répartition, assiette; évaluation, f.

assessor [ə'sesə], n. assesseur; répartiteur, m.

asset ['æset], n. avoir; avantage, m.

assets ['æsets], n.pl. actif, m; **assets and liabilities**, actif et passif, m.; **personal assets**, biens meubles, m.pl.; **real assets**, biens immobiliers, m.pl.

asseverate [ə'sevəreit], v.t. affirmer solennellement.

assiduity [æsi'djuːiti], n. assiduité, f.

assiduous [ə'sidjuəs], a. assidu.

assiduously [ə'sidjuəsli], adv. assidûment.

assign [ə'sain], v.t. assigner, attribuer; transférer (à).—n. (Law) ayant droit, m.

assignation [æsig'neiʃən], n. attribution, assignation, cession, f.; rendez-vous, m.

assignee [æsi'niː], n. cessionnaire, m., f.; syndic (de faillite), m.

assimilate [ə'simileit], v.t. assimiler.—v.i. s'assimiler.

assimilation [əsimi'leiʃən], n. assimilation, f.

assist [ə'sist], v.t. aider; **to assist each other**, s'entr'aider.

assistance [ə'sistəns], n. assistance, aide, f.; secours, concours, m.

assistant [ə'sistənt], a. qui aide, auxiliaire.— n. aide; adjoint; commis (dans une boutique), m.; **assistant examiner**, examinateur adjoint, m.; **assistant manager**, sous-directeur, m.

assizes [ə'saiziz], n. pl. assises, f.pl.

associate [ə'souʃieit], v.t. associer (avec ou à). —v.i. s'associer (avec ou à); **to associate with**, fréquenter.—[ə'souʃiit], a. associé.— n. associé, m.; complice, m., f.

association [əsousi'eiʃən], n. association, f.; souvenir, m.

assort [ə'sɔːt], v.t. assortir.

assorted [ə'sɔːtid], a. assorti.

assortment [ə'sɔːtmənt], n. assortiment, m.; classification, f.

assuage [ə'sweidʒ], v.t. adoucir, apaiser, calmer, soulager.—v.i. s'apaiser, se calmer.

assume [ə'sju:m], v.t. prendre sur soi, s'arroger, s'attribuer; assumer (une responsabilité); supposer, présumer; se donner; affecter.

assuming [ə'sju:miŋ], a. arrogant, présomptueux, prétentieux; **assuming that,** en supposant que.

assumption [ə'sʌmpʃən], n. supposition; prétention, f.; (Eccles.) **the Assumption,** l'Assomption (de la Sainte Vierge), f.

assurance [ə'ʃuərəns], n. assurance, f.

assure [ə'ʃuə], v.t. assurer.

assuredly [ə'ʃuəridli], adv. assurément, à coup sûr.

Assyria [ə'siriə], l'Assyrie, f.

Assyrian [ə'siriən], a. assyrien.—n. assyrien (langue); Assyrien (personne), m.

aster ['æstə], n. (Bot., Biol.) aster, m.

asterisk ['æstərisk], n. astérisque, m.

astern [ə'stə:n], adv. (Naut.) à l'arrière, sur l'arrière; **to go astern,** culer.

asteroid ['æstərɔid], n. astéroïde, m.

asthma ['æsθmə], n. asthme, m.

asthmatic [æsθ'mætik], a. asthmatique.

astigmatism [ə'stigmətizm], n. astigmatisme, m.

astir [ə'stə:], a. en mouvement, agité, en émoi; debout.

astonish [ə'stɔniʃ], v.t. étonner.

astonishing [ə'stɔniʃiŋ], a. étonnant.

astonishment [ə'stɔniʃmənt], n. étonnement, m.

astound [ə'staund], v.t. étonner, ébahir, étourdir.

astounding [ə'staundiŋ], a. renversant, abasourdissant.

astray [ə'strei], adv. égaré, (fig.) dévoyé; **to go astray,** s'égarer.

astride [ə'straid], adv. à califourchon; **astride upon,** à cheval sur.

astringent [ə'strindʒənt], a. and n. astringent, m.

astrologer [ə'strɔlədʒə], n. astrologue, m.,f.

astrology [ə'strɔlədʒi], n. astrologie, f.

astronaut ['æstrənɔ:t], n. astronaute, m.,f.

astronomer [ə'strɔnəmə], n. astronome, m.,f.

astronomic [æstrə'nɔmik], **astronomical** [æstrə'nɔmikəl], a. astronomique.

astronomy [ə'strɔnəmi], n. astronomie, f.

astute [ə'stju:t], a. fin, avisé; rusé, astucieux.

astuteness [ə'stju:tnis], n. astuce, sagacité, f.

asunder [ə'sʌndə], adv. en deux.

asylum [ə'sailəm], n. asile, refuge; hospice, m.

at [æt], prep. à, en, dans; après; **at first,** d'abord; **at hand,** sous la main; **at home,** chez soi; **at last,** enfin; **at least,** (quantity) au moins; (fig.) d'i moins; **at once,** tout de suite; à la fois; **at school,** à l'école; **at the same time,** en même temps; **at work,** à l'ouvrage.

atheism ['eiθiizm], n. athéisme, m.

atheist ['eiθiist], n. athée, m., f.

atheistic [eiθi'istik], a. athée, athéistique.

Athens ['æθənz], Athènes, f.

athirst [ə'θə:st], a. altéré, assoiffé.

athlete ['æθli:t], n. athlète, m., f.

athletic [æθ'letik], a. athlétique.

athletics [æθ'letiks], n. pl. l'athlétisme, m.

Atlantic [ət'læntik], a. atlantique.—n. l'(Océan) Atlantique, m.

atlas ['ætləs], n. atlas, m.

atmosphere ['ætməsfiə], n. atmosphère, f.

atmospheric [ætməs'ferik], **atmospherical** [ætməs'ferikəl], a. atmosphérique.

atmospherics [ætməs'feriks], n. pl. (Rad.) parasites, m.pl.

atoll ['ætɔl], n. atoll, atoll, m.

atom ['ætəm], n. atome, m.; **atom bomb,** bombe atomique, f.

atomic [ə'tɔmik], a. atomique.

atomize ['ætəmaiz], v.t. pulvériser, vaporiser.

atomizer ['ætəmaizə], n. pulvérisateur, m.

atone [ə'toun], v.t., v.i. expier; racheter.

atonement [ə'tounmənt], n. expiation, f.

atop [ə'tɔp], adv. au sommet, en haut.

atrocious [ə'trouʃəs], a. atroce.

atrociously [ə'trouʃəsli], adv. atrocement.

atrocity [ə'trɔsiti], n. atrocité, f.

atrophy ['ætrəfi], n. atrophie, f.—v.t. atrophier.—v.i. s'atrophier.

attach [ə'tætʃ], v.t. attacher, lier (à).

attachable [ə'tætʃəbl], a. qu'on peut attacher.

attaché case [ə'tæʃikeis], n. mallette, f.

attachment [ə'tætʃmənt], n. attachement, m.

attack [ə'tæk], v.t. attaquer.—n. attaque, f., accès, assaut, m.

attacker [ə'tækə], n. agresseur, m.

attain [ə'tein], v.t. atteindre, parvenir à.

attainable [ə'teinəbl], a. qu'on peut atteindre.

attainment [ə'teinmənt], n. acquisition, f.; talent, m.; (pl.) connaissances, f.pl.

attaint [ə'teint], v.t. accuser; condamner; flétrir, dégrader.

attempt [ə'tempt], v.t. tenter, essayer tâcher (de).—n. tentative, f., essai, effort; attentat, m.

attend [ə'tend], v.t. s'occuper de; soigner (un malade); servir; assister (à).—v.i. faire attention, écouter; assister (à); servir; s'appliquer (à).

attendance [ə'tendəns], n. service, m.; assistance (à une réunion); présence; fréquentation (scolaire), f.; soins (pour un malade), m.pl.

attendant [ə'tendənt], a. qui suit.—n. assistant, aide; serviteur, m.

attention [ə'tenʃən], n. attention, f.; (pl.) soins, m.pl.

attentive [ə'tentiv], a. attentif (à), assidu (auprès de).

attentively [ə'tentivli], adv. attentivement.

attest [ə'test], v.t. attester.

attic ['ætik], n. mansarde, f., grenier, m.

attire [ə'taiə], v.t. vêtir, parer.—n. vêtements m.pl., costume, m.; parure, f., atours, m.pl.

attitude ['ætitju:d], n. attitude, pose, f.

attorney [ə'tə:ni], n. (Am.) avoué; mandataire, m.; **power of attorney,** procuration, f. [see **prosecutor**]

attorney general [ə'tə:ni'dʒenərəl], n. procureur-général, m.

attract [ə'trækt], v.t. attirer.

attraction [ə'trækʃən], n. attraction, f.; (pl.) attraits, appas, m.pl.

attractive [ə'træktiv], a. attrayant, séduisant; attractif (de l'aimant etc.).

attractiveness [ə'træktivnis], n. attrait, charme, m.

attributable [ə'tribjutəbl], a. attribuable.

attribute [ə'tribju:t], v.t. attribuer, imputer (à).—['ætribju:t], n. attribut, m., qualité, f.

attrition [ə'triʃən], *n.* attrition, *f.*; *war of attrition*, guerre d'usure, *f.*
attune [ə'tjuːn], *v.t.* accorder.
auburn ['ɔːbən], *a.* châtain roux.
auction ['ɔːkʃən], *n.* enchère, *f.*—*v.t.* vendre aux enchères.
auctioneer [ɔːkʃə'niə], *n.* commissaire-priseur, *m.*
auction-room ['ɔːkʃənruːm], *n.* salle des ventes, *f.*
audacious [ɔː'deiʃəs], *a.* audacieux.
audaciously [ɔː'deiʃəsli], *adv.* audacieusement.
audacity [ɔː'dæsiti], *n.* audace, *f.*
audible ['ɔːdibl], *a.* qu'on peut entendre, audible; distinct, intelligible.
audibly ['ɔːdibli], *adv.* de manière à être entendu.
audience ['ɔːdjəns], *n.* auditoire, *m.*, assistance, audience, *f.*
audio-visual ['ɔːdjo'vizjuəl], *a.* audio-visuel.
audit ['ɔːdit], *v.t.* apurer, vérifier (*des comptes*).—*n.* apurement, *m.*, vérification de comptes, *f.*; *audit office*, cour des comptes, *f.*
audition [ɔː'diʃən], *n.* audition, *f.*—*v.t.* (*fam.*) auditionner.
auditor ['ɔːditə], *n.* vérificateur; expert comptable, *m.*
auger ['ɔːgə], *n.* tarière, *f.*
aught [ɔːt], *n.* quelque chose; quoi que ce soit, *m.*; *for aught I know*, pour autant que je sache.
augment [ɔːg'ment], *v.t.* augmenter, accroître.
augur ['ɔːgə], *v.t., v.i.* augurer, présager.—*n.* augure, *m.*
augury ['ɔːgjuri], *n.* augure, *m.*
August ['ɔːgəst], *n.* août, *m.*; *in August*, en août.
august [ɔː'gʌst], *a.* auguste, imposant.
auk [ɔːk], *n.* (*Orn.*) pingouin, *m.*
aunt [ɑːnt], *n.* tante, *f.*
auntie ['ɑːnti], *n.* (*colloq.*) tata, *f.*
aura ['ɔːrə], *n.* exhalaison, *f.*, effluve, *m.*
aural ['ɔːrəl], *a.* de l'oreille.
Aurora [ɔː'rɔːrə], *n.* aurore, *f.*; *Aurora Borealis*, aurore boréale.
auspice ['ɔːspis], *n.* (*usu. in pl.*) auspice, *m.*
auspicious [ɔː'spiʃəs], *a.* de bon augure, propice.
auspiciously [ɔː'spiʃəsli], *adv.* sous d'heureux auspices.
austere [ɔːs'tiə], *a.* austère; âpre.
austerity [ɔːs'teriti], *n.* austérité, *f.*
Australasia [ɔːstrə'leiʃiə], l'Australasie, *f.*
Australia [ɔːs'treiliə], l'Australie, *f.*
Australian [ɔːs'treiliən], *a.* australien.—*n.* Australien (*personne*), *m.*
Austria ['ɔːstriə], l'Autriche, *f.*
Austrian ['ɔːstriən], *a.* autrichien.—*n.* Autrichien (*personne*), *m.*
authentic [ɔː'θentik], *a.* authentique.
authentically [ɔː'θentikli], *adv.* authentiquement.
authenticate [ɔː'θentikeit], *v.t.* authentiquer, constater.
authenticated [ɔː'θentikeitid], *a.* authentique, avéré.
authenticity [ɔːθen'tisiti], *n.* authenticité, *f.*
author ['ɔːθə], *n.* auteur, *m.*
authoress ['ɔːθəris], *n.* femme auteur, femme écrivain, *f.*

authoritative [ɔː'θɔritətiv], *a.* d'autorité; autorisé; autoritaire, impérieux.
authority [ɔː'θɔriti], *n.* autorité; autorisation, *f.*, mandat, *m.*
authorization [ɔːθərai'zeiʃən], *n.* autorisation, *f.*
authorize ['ɔːθəraiz], *v.t.* autoriser.
authorship ['ɔːθəʃip], *n.* qualité d'auteur; (*colloq.*) paternité, *f.*
autobiographer [ɔːtəbai'ɔgrəfə], *n.* autobiographe, *m.*, *f.*
autobiography [ɔːtəbai'ɔgrəfi], *n.* autobiographie, *f.*
autocracy [ɔː'tɔkrəsi], *n.* autocratie, *f.*
autocrat ['ɔːtəkræt], *n.* autocrate, *m.*, *f.*
auto-cycle ['ɔːtosaikl], *n.* cyclomoteur, *m.*
autograph ['ɔːtəgrɑːf], *n.* autographe, *m.*—*v.t.* signer, autographier.
autogyro [ɔːto'dʒairou], *n.* autogyre, *m.*
automatic [ɔːtə'mætik], *a.* automatique.
automatically [ɔːtə'mætikli], *adv.* automatiquement; machinalement.
automation [ɔːtə'meiʃən], *n.* automation, *f.*
automaton [ɔː'tɔmətən], *n.* (*pl.* **automata** [ɔː'tɔmətə]) automate, *m.*
automobile ['ɔːtəməbiːl], *n.* (*Am.*) automobile, auto, voiture, *f.*
autonomous [ɔː'tɔnəməs], *a.* autonome.
autonomy [ɔː'tɔnəmi], *n.* autonomie, *f.*
autopsy ['ɔːtɔpsi, ɔː'tɔpsi], *n.* autopsie, *f.*
autumn ['ɔːtəm], *n.* automne, *m.* ou *f.*
autumnal [ɔː'tʌmnəl], *a.* automnal, d'automne.
auxiliary [ɔːg'ziljəri], *a.* and *n.* auxiliaire, *m.*
avail [ə'veil], *v.t., v.i.* profiter, servir; *to avail oneself of*, se servir de.—*n.* service, avantage, *m.*, utilité, *f.*; *of what avail is it?* à quoi bon?
available [ə'veiləbl], *a.* disponible; valable.
avalanche ['ævəlɑːnʃ], *n.* avalanche, *f.*
avarice ['ævəris], *n.* avarice, *f.*
avaricious [ævə'riʃəs], *a.* avare, avaricieux.
avenge [ə'vendʒ], *v.t.* venger; *to avenge oneself*, se venger (*de* ou *sur*).
avenger [ə'vendʒə], *n.* vengeur, *m.*
avenging [ə'vendʒiŋ], *a.* vengeur.—*n.* vengeance, *f.*
avenue ['ævənjuː], *n.* avenue, *f.*
aver [ə'vəː], *v.t.* affirmer.
average ['ævəridʒ], *a.* commun, moyen.—*n.* moyenne, *f.*, prix moyen, terme moyen, *m.*; (*Naut.*) avarie, *f.*; *on an average*, en moyenne.—*v.t.* établir la moyenne de; atteindre une moyenne de.
averse [ə'vəːs], *a.* opposé (*à*), ennemi (*de*).
aversely [ə'vəːsli], *adv.* à contre-cœur.
aversion [ə'vəːʃən], *n.* répugnance, aversion, *f.*; *it is his pet aversion*, c'est sa bête noire.
avert [ə'vəːt], *v.t.* détourner, écarter.
aviary ['eiviəri], *n.* volière, *f.*
aviation [eivi'eiʃən], *n.* aviation, *f.*
aviator ['eivieitə], *n.* aviateur, *m.*
avid ['ævid], *a.* avide.
avidly ['ævidli], *adv.* avec avidité, avidement.
avoid [ə'void], *v.t.* éviter.
avoidable [ə'voidəbl], *a.* évitable.
avoidance [ə'voidəns], *n.* action d'éviter, *f.*
avoirdupois [ævədə'poiz], *n.* poids du commerce, *m.*
avow [ə'vau], *v.t.* avouer, confesser, déclarer.

352

avowal [əˈvauəl], n. aveu, m.
avowedly [əˈvauidli], adv. de son propre aveu.
await [əˈweit], v.t. attendre.
awake [əˈweik], v.t. irr. éveiller, réveiller.—v.i. s'éveiller, se réveiller.—a. éveillé; attentif.
awaken [əˈweikən], v.t. éveiller, réveiller.
awakening [əˈweikniŋ], n. réveil, m.
award [əˈwɔːd], v.t. décerner, adjuger.—n. décision, f., jugement, m., sentence; (Sch.) récompense, f.
aware [əˈweə], a. qui sait; instruit; *to be aware of*, savoir, avoir connaissance de; *not to be aware of*, ignorer.
awareness [əˈweənis], n. conscience, f.
away [əˈwei], adv. absent; loin, au loin; *away with you!* allez-vous en! *far away*, au loin; *right away*, immédiatement.
awe [ɔː], n. crainte, terreur, f., respect, m.
awe-inspiring [ˈɔːinspaiəriŋ], a. terrifiant.
awestruck [ˈɔːstrʌk], a. frappé de terreur.
awful [ˈɔːful], a. terrible, redoutable, effroyable; solennel; *what awful weather!* quel temps affreux!
awfully [ˈɔːfuli], adv. horriblement, terriblement; (fam.) diablement.
awhile [əˈwail], adv. un instant, un peu.
awkward [ˈɔːkwəd], a. gauche, maladroit; embarrassant.
awkwardly [ˈɔːkwədli], adv. gauchement, maladroitement.
awkwardness [ˈɔːkwədnis], n. gaucherie, maladresse, f.
awl [ɔːl], n. alène, f.; poinçon, m.
awning [ˈɔːniŋ], n. tente, banne, bâche, f.
awry [əˈrai], a. and adv. de travers.
axe [æks], n. hache, cognée, f.
axiom [ˈæksiəm], n. axiome, m.
axiomatic [æksiəˈmætik], a. axiomatique.
axis [ˈæksis], n. (pl. **axes** [ˈæksiːz]) axe, m.
axle [æksl], n. arbre, essieu, m.; (Motor.) *rear axle*, pont arrière, m.
ay, aye [ai], adv. oui, c'est vrai; *aye, aye!* (Naut.) bon quart!—n. *ayes and noes*, voix pour et contre, f.pl.
azalea [əˈzeiliə], n. (Bot.) azalée, f.
Azores [əˈzɔːz], the. les Açores, f.pl.
azote [əˈzout], n. (Chem.) azote, m.
azure [ˈæʒuə, ˈeiʒə], a. d'azur.—n. azur, m.

B

B, b [biː]. deuxième lettre de l'alphabet; (Mus.) si, m.
baa [bɑː], v.i. bêler.—n. bêlement, m.
babble [bæbl], v.i. babiller; gazouiller, jaser; (fig.) murmurer (ruisseau).—n. babil, caquet, m.; (fig.) murmure, m., jaserie, f.
babbler [ˈbæblə], n. babillard, m.
babbling [ˈbæbliŋ], a. babillard, bavard.
babe [beib], n. enfant nouveau-né, petit enfant, m.
Babel [ˈbeibəl]. Babel, f.

baboon [bəˈbuːn], n. babouin, m.
baby [ˈbeibi]. n. bébé, m.; *baby grand (piano)*, piano à demi-queue, m.; *baby linen*, layette, f. [*carriage*, see pram]
babyhood [ˈbeibihud], n. première enfance, f.
babyish [ˈbeibiiʃ], a. enfantin.
bacchanalia [bækəˈneiliə], n.pl. bacchanales, f.pl.
bacchanalian [bækəˈneiliən], a. bachique.—n. ivrogne, m.
bachelor [ˈbætʃələ], n. célibataire, vieux garçon; bachelier (ès lettres), m.
back [bæk], a. arrière, de derrière; *a back street*, une petite rue.—n. dos, m., reins, m.pl.; envers (d'un tissu); verso (d'une page etc.); fond (d'une salle etc.); (Ftb.) arrière; revers (d'une colline etc.); derrière (d'une maison etc.); dossier (d'une chaise), m.; *at the back of*, derrière; *back to back*, dos à dos; *on the back of* (a letter etc.), au verso.—adv. en arrière, de retour, rentré; *a few years back*, il y a quelques années; *to be back*, être de retour; *to call back*, rappeler; *to come back*, revenir.—v.t. soutenir; (Betting) jouer (un cheval); faire reculer.—v.i. reculer.
backbite [ˈbækbait], v.t. médire de, calomnier.
backbiting [ˈbækbaitiŋ], n. médisance, f.
backbone [ˈbækboun], n. épine dorsale, f.
back door [ˈbækˈdɔː], n. porte de derrière, f.
backer [ˈbækə], n. partisan, second; parieur pour, m.
back-fire [ˈbækˈfaiə], v.i. (Motor.) pétarader.
backgammon [ˈbækˈgæmən], n. trictrac, m.
back garden [ˈbækˈgɑːdn], n. jardin de derrière, m.
background [ˈbækgraund], n. arrière-plan, fond, m.
back room [ˈbækˈruːm], n. chambre de derrière, f.
backside [ˈbækˈsaid], n. (pop.) derrière, m.
backslide [ˈbækslaid], v.i. retomber dans le vice ou le péché.
backstage [ˈbækˈsteidʒ], adv. derrière la scène; dans les coulisses.
backstairs [ˈbækˈstɛəz], n. escalier de service, m.
backward [ˈbækwəd], a. arriéré; en retard; en arrière; lent, tardif.
backward(s) [ˈbækwəd(z)], adv. à reculons; en arrière; à la renverse.
backwoodsman [ˈbækwudzmən], n. (pl. **-men** [men]) défricheur de forêts, m.
back-yard [ˈbækˈjɑːd], n. cour de derrière, f.
bacon [ˈbeikən], n. lard, m.
bacterium [bækˈtiəriəm], n. (pl. **bacteria** [bækˈtiəriə]) bactérie, f.
bad [bæd], a. mauvais; méchant (enfant etc.); gâté (aliment etc.); malade; *that is too bad*, c'est trop fort.
badge [bædʒ], n. insigne, m.; plaque, f.; (Mil.) écusson; brassard, m.
badger [ˈbædʒə], n. blaireau, m.—v.t. harceler.
badly [ˈbædli], adv. mal; grièvement, fort, beaucoup.
badness [ˈbædnis], n. méchanceté, f.; mauvais état, m.
baffle [bæfl], v.t. déjouer; confondre.

353

bag [bæg], *n.* sac; cornet (*papier*), *m.*; ***game bag***, gibecière, *f.*; ***with bag and baggage***, avec armes et bagages.—*v.t.* mettre en sac; abattre (*du gibier*); (*colloq.*) s'emparer de; (*slang*) chiper.—*v.i.* bouffer (*pantalon*).

baggage ['bægidʒ], *n.* (*chiefly Am.*) bagages, *m.pl.*

bagpipes ['bægpaips], *n. pl.* cornemuse, *f.*

bail (1) [beil], *n.* caution, *f.*; ***on bail***, sous caution.

bail (2) [beil], *v.t.* vider l'eau d' (*un bateau*), écoper.—*v.i. to bail out*, (*Av.*) sauter en parachute.

bailiff ['beilif], *n.* huissier, *m.*; ***farm bailiff***, régisseur, *m.*

bait [beit], *v.t.* amorcer (*un hameçon*); (*fig.*) harceler, tourmenter.—*n.* amorce, *f.*; appât, leurre, *m.*

baize [beiz], *n.* serge, *f.*; ***green baize***, tapis vert, *m.*

bake [beik], *v.t., v.i.* cuire au four.

bakehouse ['beikhaus], *n.* fournil, *m.*, boulangerie, *f.*

Bakelite ['beikəlait], *n.* bakélite (*reg. trade mark*), *f.*

baker ['beikə], *n.* boulanger, *m.*

bakery ['beikəri], *n.* boulangerie, *f.*

baking ['beikiŋ], *n.* cuisson; fournée, *f.*

balance ['bæləns], *n.* balance, *f.*; équilibre; balancier (*d'une pendule*), *m.*—*v.t.* équilibrer, balancer; ***to balance up***, arrêter.

balance-sheet ['bælənsʃi:t], *n.* bilan, *m.*

balance-weight ['bælənsweit], *n.* contre-poids, *m.*

balcony ['bælkəni], *n.* balcon, *m.*

bald [bɔ:ld], *a.* chauve; (*fig.*) plat, sec (*style*).

baldly ['bɔ:ldli], *adv.* pauvrement, platement, sèchement.

baldness ['bɔ:ldnis], *n.* calvitie; (*fig.*) platitude, *f.*

bale (2) [beil], *n.* balle, *f.*, ballot, *m.*—*v.t.* emballer.

baleful ['beilful], *a.* sinistre, funeste.

balefully ['beilfuli], *adv.* d'une manière funeste.

balk, baulk [bɔ:k], *n.* poutre, bille; (*Billiards*) ligne de départ, *f.*—*v.t.* frustrer, contrarier, déjouer.

Balkan ['bɔ:lkən], *a.* balkanique.

Balkans ['bɔ:lkənz], ***the*** les Balkans, les États Balkaniques, *m.pl.*

ball (1) [bɔ:l], *n.* balle; boule (*de neige*); pelote, *f.*, peloton (*de laine, de ficelle*); boulet (*de canon*), *m.*; (*Billiards*) bille; (*Cook.*) boulette, *f.*; ballon (*plein d'air*), *m.*; prunelle (*d'œil*), *f.*; ***ball-point pen***, stylo à bille, *m.*

ball (2) [bɔ:l], *n.* bal, *m.*; ***fancy-dress ball***, bal masqué.

ballad ['bæləd], *n.* (*Mus.*) romance; ballade, *f.*

ballast ['bæləst], *n.* lest, (*Rail.*) ballast, *m.*; ***in ballast***, sur lest.—*v.t.* lester; (*Rail.*) ensabler.

ballerina [bælə'ri:nə], *n.* ballerine, *f.*

ballet ['bælei], *n.* ballet, *m.*

balloon [bə'lu:n], *n.* ballon, aérostat, *m.*—*v.i.* se ballonner.

ballot ['bælət], *n.* boule, *f.*; bulletin, scrutin, *m.*; ***by ballot***, au scrutin.—*v.i.* voter au scrutin.

ballot box ['bælətbɔks], *n.* urne électorale, *f.*

ballot (paper) ['bælətpeipə], *n.* bulletin de vote, *m.*

354

balm [ba:m], *n.* baume, *m.*; mélisse, *f.*—*v.t.* parfumer.

balmy ['ba:mi], *a.* embaumé, parfumé.

balsam ['bɔ:lsəm], *n.* baume, *m.*

Baltic ['bɔ:ltik], ***the*** la Baltique, *f.*

balustrade [bæləs'treid], *n.* balustrade, *f.*

bamboo [bæm'bu:], *n.* bambou, *m.*

bamboozle [bæm'bu:zl], *v.t.* (*colloq.*) tromper, duper, enjôler.

ban [bæn], *n.* ban, *m.*; interdiction, *f.*; (*Eccles.*) interdit, *m.*—*v.t.* interdire, proscrire.

banal [bə'næl, 'beinəl], *a.* banal.

banality [bə'næliti], *n.* banalité, *f.*

banana [bə'na:nə], *n.* banane, *f.*

banana tree [bə'na:nətri:], *n.* bananier, *m.*

band (1) [bænd], *n.* bande, *f.*, lien; ruban, *m.*; raie, *f.*—*v.t.* bander.

band (2) [bænd], *n.* bande, troupe; (*Mil.*) musique, *f.*; orchestre, *m.*; ***brass band***, fanfare, *f.*—*v.t.* liguer, réunir en troupe.—*v.i.* se liguer.

bandage ['bændidʒ], *n.* bandeau; (*Surg.*) bandage, pansement, *m.*

bandbox ['bændbɔks], *n.* carton (*de modiste*), *m.*

bandit ['bændit], *n.* bandit, *m.*

bandmaster ['bændma:stə], *n.* chef de musique, *m.*

bandoleer, bandolier [bændə'liə], *n.* bandoulière, *f.*

bandsman ['bændzmən], *n.* (*pl.* ***-men*** [men]) musicien, *m.*

bandstand ['bændstænd], *n.* kiosque à musique, *m.*

bandy ['bændi], *v.t.* renvoyer; échanger; se renvoyer; ***to bandy words***, se renvoyer des paroles.—*v.i.* se disputer.

bandy-legged ['bændilegd], *a.* bancal.

bane [bein], *n.* poison; (*fig.*) fléau, *m.*

baneful ['beinful], *a.* pernicieux, funeste, nuisible.

bang [bæŋ], *n.* coup, grand bruit, *m.*, détonation, *f.*—*v.t.* frapper violemment, taper; ***to bang a door***, claquer une porte.—*int.* pan! paf! boum!

bangle ['bæŋgl], *n.* porte-bonheur, bracelet, *m.*

banish ['bæniʃ], *v.t.* bannir, exiler.

banishment ['bæniʃmənt], *n.* bannissement, exil, *m.*

bank (1) [bæŋk], *n.* rivage, bord, *m.*; berge, rive; terrasse, *f.*, remblai, talus; banc (*de sable, de gazon etc.*), *m.*; digue, *f.*; carreau (*de mine*), *m.*—*v.t.* terrasser, remblayer.

bank (2) [bæŋk], *n.* (*Comm.*) banque, *f.*; ***savings bank***, caisse d'épargne, *f.*—*v.t.* encaisser (*de l'argent*).

banker ['bæŋkə], *n.* banquier, *m.*

banking ['bæŋkiŋ], *n.* banque, *f.*

bank note ['bæŋknout], *n.* billet de banque, *m.*

bankrupt ['bæŋkrʌpt], *a.* failli, en faillite; (*fig.*) ruiné.—*v.t.* mettre en faillite, ruiner.—*n.* banqueroutier, failli, *m.*; ***to go bankrupt***, faire faillite.

bankruptcy ['bæŋkrʌptsi], *n.* banqueroute, faillite, *f.*

banner ['bænə], *n.* bannière, *f.*

bannock ['bænək], *n.* (*grosse*) galette d'avoine, *f.*

banns [bænz], *n.pl.* ***banns of marriage***, bans de mariage, *m.pl.*

banquet ['bæŋkwit], *n.* banquet; *festin, *m.*

banter ['bæntə], *v.t.* railler, badiner.—*n.* badinage, *m.*, raillerie, *f.*

baptism ['bæptizm], *n.* baptême, *m.*

baptismal [bæp'tizməl], *a.* baptismal.

baptist ['bæptist], *n.* baptiste, *m.*, *f.*

baptize [bæp'taiz], *v.t.* baptiser.

bar (1) [bɑ:], *n.* barre, *f.*; (*Law etc.*) barreau, parquet, *m.*; (*fig.*) barrière; buvette, *f.*, comptoir, bar (*de café, hôtel etc.*); (*Law*) banc des accusés, *m.*; (*Mus.*) mesure; tablette (*de chocolat*), *f.*; **to be admitted to the bar,** être reçu avocat.—*v.t.* barrer, empêcher; exclure.

bar (2) [BARRING].

barb [bɑ:b], *n.* barbillon, dardillon (*hameçon*), *m.*; pointe (*flèche*); barbe, arête (*blé*), *f.*

Barbados [bɑ:'beidəs]. la Barbade, *f.*

barbarian [bɑ:'bɛəriən], *a.* and *n.* barbare, *m.*, *f.*

barbaric [bɑ:'bærik], *a.* barbare.

barbarism ['bɑ:bərizm], *n.* barbarie, *f.*; (*Gram.*) barbarisme, *m.*

barbarity [bɑ:'bæriti], *n.* barbarie, cruauté, *f.*

barbarous ['bɑ:bərəs], *a.* barbare.

barbecue ['bɑ:bəkju:], *n.* grand gril; grand pique-nique (en plein air), *m.*—*v.t.* rôtir à la broche.

barbed [bɑ:bd], *a.* barbelé; (*fig.*) acéré; **barbed wire,** fil de fer barbelé, *m.*

barbel ['bɑ:bəl], *n.* (*Ichth.*) barbeau, *m.*

barber ['bɑ:bə], *n.* coiffeur, *m.*

Barcelona [bɑ:sə'lounə]. Barcelone, *f.*

bard [bɑ:d], *n.* barde, trouvère, *m.*

bare [bɛə], *a.* nu, découvert; (*fig.*) seul, simple; pauvre.—*v.t.* découvrir, dépouiller; mettre à nu.

bareback ['bɛəbæk], *adv.* à dos nu.

barefaced ['bɛəfeist], *a.* à visage découvert; éhonté, sans déguisement.

barefoot ['bɛəfut], *a.* nu-pieds, les pieds nus.

bareheaded ['bɛə'hedid], *a.* nu-tête, la tête nue.

barely ['bɛəli], *adv.* à peine; tout juste, simplement, seulement; pauvrement.

bareness ['bɛənis], *n.* nudité; misère, *f.*

bargain ['bɑ:gin], *n.* marché, *m.*, affaire; occasion, *f.*; **into the bargain,** par-dessus le marché; **it is a bargain,** c'est convenu; **to strike a bargain,** conclure un marché. —*v.i.* marchander, faire marché.

barge [bɑ:dʒ], *n.* chaland, *m.*; péniche, *f.*— *v.i.* **to barge into,** se heurter contre, bousculer.

bargee [bɑ:'dʒi:], **bargeman** ['bɑ:dʒmən] (*pl.* **-men** [men]), *n.* batelier, *m.*

baritone ['bæritoun], *a.* de baryton.—*n.* baryton, *m.*

bark (1) [bɑ:k], *n.* écorce, *f.*; tan, *m.*

bark (2) [bɑ:k], *n.* aboiement, *m.*—*v.i.* aboyer.

bark (3), **barque** [bɑ:k], *n.* trois-mâts, *m.*

barking ['bɑ:kiŋ], *n.* aboiement, *m.*

barley ['bɑ:li], *n.* orge, *f.*

barmaid ['bɑ:meid], *n.* barmaid, *f.*

barman ['bɑ:mən], *n.* (*pl.* **-men** [men]) barman, *m.*

barmy ['bɑ:mi], *a.* (*colloq.*) fou, toqué.

barn [bɑ:n], *n.* grange, *f.*; (*Am.*) étable, *f.*

barnacle ['bɑ:nəkl], *n.* barnache (*oie*), *f.*; balane, anatife (*crustacé*), *m.*

barometer [bə'rɔmitə], *n.* baromètre, *m.*

barometric [bæro'metrik], *a.* barométrique.

baron ['bærən], *n.* baron, *m.*; **baron of beef,** double aloyau, *m.*

baroness ['bærənis], *n.* baronne, *f.*

baronet ['bærənet], *n.* baronnet, *m.*

baronial [bə'rouniəl], *a.* baronnial, seigneurial.

barony ['bærəni], *n.* baronnie, *f.*

barouche [bə'ru:ʃ], *n.* calèche, *f.*

barque [BARK (3)].

barrack ['bærək], *n.* (*usu. in pl.*) caserne, *f.*; quartier (*pour la cavalerie*), *m.*

barrage ['bæridʒ, 'bærɑ:ʒ], *n.* barrage, *m.*

barrel ['bærəl], *n.* baril, *m.*; gonne, caque (*de poissons etc.*), *f.*; corps (*de pompe*); cylindre, tambour (*de machine*); canon (*de fusil*), *m.* —*v.t.* embariller, entonner, mettre en baril, encaquer.

barrel organ ['bærəlɔ:gən], *n.* orgue de Barbarie, *m.*

barren ['bærən], *a.* stérile; infertile (*terre*).

barrenness ['bærənnis], *n.* stérilité, *f.*

barricade [bæri'keid], *n.* barricade, *f.*—*v.t.* barricader.

barrier ['bæriə], *n.* barrière, *f.*

barring ['bɑ:riŋ], **bar** (2) [bɑ:], *prep.* excepté, hormis, sauf.

barrister ['bæristə], *n.* avocat, *m.*

barrow ['bærou], *n.* brouette, *f.*

barrow-boy ['bæroubɔi], *n.* (*fam.*) marchand des quatre saisons, *m.*

barter ['bɑ:tə], *n.* échange, troc; trafic, *m.*— *v.t.* troquer, échanger.—*v.i.* échanger, faire échange.

basalt [bə'sɔ:lt], *n.* basalte, *m.*

base (1) [beis], *a.* bas, vil, indigne, méprisable; illégitime (*enfant*); de mauvais aloi; non précieux, faux (*monnaie*).

base (2) [beis], *n.* base, *f.*, fondement; fond, *m.*—*v.t.* fonder (*sur*); asseoir (*l'impôt*).

baseball ['baisbɔ:l], *n.* (*Spt.*) base-ball, *m.*

baseless ['beislis], *a.* sans fondement.

basely ['beisli], *adv.* bassement, lâchement.

basement ['beismənt], *n.* sous-sol, *m.*

baseness ['beisnis], *n.* bassesse, lâcheté, *f.*

bashful ['bæʃful], *a.* timide, intimidé.

bashfully ['bæʃfuli], *adv.* timidement, en rougissant.

bashfulness ['bæʃfulnis], *n.* timidité, fausse honte, *f.*

basic ['beisik], *a.* (*Chem.*) basique; de base.

basilica [bə'zilikə], *n.* basilique, *f.*

basilisk ['bæzilisk], *n.* basilic, *m.*

basin ['beisən], *n.* bassin; bol, *m.*; cuvette, *f.*

basis ['beisis], *n.* (*pl.* **bases** ['beisi:z]) base, *f.* fondement, *m.*

bask [bɑ:sk], *v.i.* se chauffer.

basket ['bɑ:skit], *n.* panier, *m.*, corbeille, *f.*

basketball ['bɑ:skitbɔ:l], *n.* (*Spt.*) basketball, (*fam.*) basket, *m.*

Basle [bɑ:l]. Bâle, *f.*

bas-relief [bɑ:rə'li:f], *n.* bas-relief, *m.*

bass (1) [beis], *n.* (*Mus.*) basse; basse-taille, *f.*; **double bass,** contre-basse, *f.*

bass (2) [bæs], *n.* (*Ichth.*) bar, *m.*; perche, *f.*

bassinet [bæsi'net], *n.* bercelonnette, *f.*, moise, *m.*

bassoon [bə'su:n], *n.* basson, *m.*

bastard ['bæstəd], *a.* bâtard; (*fig.*) faux.—*n.* bâtard, *m.*, bâtarde, *f.*; (*pop.*) salaud, *m.*

baste [beist], *v.t.* arroser (*viande*); (*fig.*) bâtonner; (*Needlework*) bâtir.

bastion

bastion ['bæstiən], n. bastion, m.
bat (1) [bæt], n. (Cricket) batte, f.; *off his own bat*, de sa propre initiative.—v.i. être au guichet.
bat (2) [bæt], n. (Zool.) chauve-souris, f.
Batavian [bə'teiviən], a. batave.—n. Batave (personne), m., f.
batch [bætʃ], n. fournée (pain); (fig.) troupe, bande, f.; tas; lot, m.
bate [beit], v.t. rabattre, rabaisser.
bath [ba:θ], n. bain, m.; baignoire, f.; *shower bath*, douche, f.—v.t. donner un bain à, baigner.—v.i. prendre un bain.
bathe [beið], v.t. baigner; tremper, mouiller. —v.i. se baigner.—n. baignade, f.
bather ['beiðə], n. baigneur, m., baigneuse, f.
bathing ['beiðiŋ], n. baignade, f.; bains, m.pl.
bathing suit ['beiðiŋsju:t], n. costume de bain, maillot, m.
bathos ['beiθɔs], n. pathos, m., enflure, f.
bathroom ['ba:θrum], n. salle de bains(s), f.
batman ['bætmən], n. (pl. -men [men]) ordonnance, brosseur, m.
baton ['bætən], n. bâton, m.; baguette, f.
batsman ['bætsmən], n. (Cricket) batteur, m.
battalion [bə'tæliən], n. bataillon, m.
batten ['bætən], n. volige, latte, f.—v.t. fermer; (Carp.) voliger.—v.i. s'engraisser.
batter ['bætə], v.t. battre en brèche; battre; délabrer, ébranler, démolir.—n. pâte, f.
battered ['bætəd], a. délabré.
battering-ram ['bætəriŋræm], n. bélier, m.
battery ['bætəri], n. batterie (Elec.) pile, batterie, f., accumulateur, m.; action de battre en brèche, f.; (Law) voies de fait, f.pl.
battle [bætl], n. bataille, f., combat, m.; *pitched battle*, bataille rangée; *to give battle*, livrer bataille.—v.i. lutter, combattre; (colloq.) bataîller.
battle-axe ['bætlæks], n. hache d'armes, f.
battledore ['bætldɔ:], n. raquette, f.
battle dress ['bætldres], n. tenue de campagne, f.
battle-field ['bætlfi:ld], n. champ de bataille, m.
battlement ['bætlmənt], n. créneau, m.
battleship ['bætlʃip], n. cuirassé, m.
bauble ['bɔ:bl], n. babiole, fanfreluche, f.; *fool's bauble*, marotte, f.
baulk [bɔ:lk].
bauxite ['bɔ:ksait, 'bouzait], n. bauxite, f.
Bavaria [bə'veəriə], la Bavière, f.
Bavarian [bə'veəriən], a. bavarois.—n. Bavarois (personne).
bawdy ['bɔ:di], a. obscène, paillard.
bawl [bɔ:l], v.i. crier, brailler.
bay (1) [bei], a. bai (cheval).
bay (2) [bei], n. baie, f., golfe m.; (Arch.) baie, f.
bay (3) [bei], n. (Bot.) baie, f.; laurier, m.
bay (4) [bei], n. abois, m.pl.; *at bay*, aux abois.—v.i. aboyer.
bayonet ['beiənit], n. baïonnette, f.—v.t. tuer ou percer à coups de baïonnette.
bay window ['beiwindou], n. fenêtre en saillie ou à baie, f.
bazaar [bə'zɑ:], n. bazar, m.; vente de charité, f.
bazooka [bə'zu:kə], n. bazooka, m.
be [bi:], v.i. irr. être; exister; subsister; y

avoir, se trouver; avoir; faire; devoir, falloir; *be it so*, soit; *be that as it may*, quoi qu'il en soit; *how is it that . . .?* comment se fait-il que . . .? *I was to*, je devais; *to be better*, valoir mieux; se porter mieux; *to be mistaken*, se tromper; *to be right*, avoir raison.
beach [bi:tʃ], n. plage, grève, f., rivage, m.— v.t. échouer.
beacon ['bi:kən], n. phare, fanal, m.; balise, f. —v.t. baliser, éclairer.
bead [bi:d], n. grain (de chapelet, de bracelet, de collier); globule, m.; *string of beads*, collier, chapelet, m.; *to tell one's beads*, égrener son chapelet.
beadle [bi:dl], n. bedeau; appariteur, m.
beagle [bi:gl], n. chien briquet, bigle, m.
beak [bi:k], n. bec, m.; bigorne (enclume), f.; (Naut.) éperon, m.
beaker ['bi:kə], n. gobelet, m., coupe, f.
beakful ['bi:kful], n. becquée, f.
beam [bi:m], n. poutre, f.; timon (charrue, voiture etc.); rayon (lumière); large sourire (de joie etc.), m.—v.t. lancer, darder (des rayons).—v.i. rayonner.
beaming ['bi:miŋ], a. rayonnant, radieux.— n. rayonnement, m.
bean [bi:n], n. fève, f.; haricot; grain (de café), m.; *French beans*, haricots verts; *kidney beans*, haricots, soissons.
bear (1) [bɛə], n. ours; (St. Exch.) joueur à la baisse, baissier, m.; *polar bear*, ours blanc.
bear (2) [bɛə], v.t. irr. porter, soutenir; endurer, supporter, souffrir; subir; avoir, produire (fruits etc.); enfanter; donner naissance à; y tenir; remporter.—v.i. endurer, souffrir; porter, peser; avoir rapport (à); appuyer; porter (sur); rapporter.
bearable ['bɛərəbl], a. supportable.
beard [biəd], n. barbe, f.—v.t. braver, défier.
bearded ['biədid], a. barbu.
beardless ['biədlis], a. imberbe.
bearer ['bɛərə], n. porteur; (Arch.) support, m.
bearing ['bɛəriŋ], n. rapport; maintien, port, m., conduite, relation, f., aspect, m., portée, face, f.; (Arch.) support; (Mech.) coussinet, m.; *ball bearings*, roulement à billes, m.; *to take one's bearings*, s'orienter.
bearskin ['bɛəskin], n. (Mil.) bonnet d'oursin, m.
beast [bi:st], n. bête, f.; (fig.) animal, cochon, m.
beastliness ['bi:stlinis], n. saleté, saloperie, f.
beastly ['bi:stli], a. bestial; sale, malpropre, dégoûtant.
beat [bi:t], v.t. irr. battre; frapper; piler, broyer; l'emporter sur; fouetter (pluie, neige etc.); se frapper (la poitrine etc.); *beat it!* fiche-moi le camp! *that beats all*, cela dépasse tout; *to beat a retreat*, battre en retraite.—v.i. battre; être agité.—n. coup, battement; son; itinéraire, m.; ronde (d'un agent de police), f., parcours (facteurs etc.), m.; (Hunt.) battue; (Mus.) mesure, f., temps, m.; *beat of the drum*, batterie de tambour, f. [see **whisk**]
beaten [bi:tn], a. battu.
beater ['bi:tə], n. batteur (Spt.) rabatteur, m.; batte (instrument), f. [see **whisk**]
beating ['bi:tiŋ], n. battement, m.; rossée, f.; coups, m.pl.; batterie, f.; roulement (tambour etc.), m.

beau [bou], n. (pl. **beaux** [bouz]) petit-maître; prétendant (amant), m.
beauteous ['bju:tiəs], a. (Poet.) beau.
beauteously ['bju:tiəsli], adv. avec beauté.
beautiful ['bju:tiful], a. très beau; (colloq.) magnifique.
beautifully ['bju:tifuli], adv. admirablement.
beautify ['bju:tifai], v.t. embellir, orner.—v.i. s'embellir.
beauty ['bju:ti], n. beauté (personne et qualité), f.
beauty spot ['bju:tispɔt], n. mouche, f., grain de beauté; site pittoresque, m.
beaver ['bi:və], n. castor; chapeau de castor, m.

becalm [bi'ka:m], v.t. *apaiser, calmer; abriter (navire).
because [bi'kɔz], conj. parce que; **because of**, à cause de.
beck (1) [bek], n. signe (du doigt etc.), m.—v.i. faire signe (du doigt etc.).
beck (2) [bek], n. ruisseau, m.
beckon ['bekən], v.t. faire signe à, appeler.—v.i. faire signe (à).
become [bi'kʌm], v.t. irr. (conjug. like COME) aller bien à, convenir à, être propre à.—v.i. devenir, commencer à être.
becoming [bi'kʌmiŋ], a. bienséant, convenable, qui va bien, attrayant.
becomingly [bi'kʌmiŋli], adv. avec bienséance.
bed [bed], n. lit, m.; couche; (Geol.) assise, f.; encaissement (rue); parterre, m., plate-bande (fleurs), f.; carré, m.—v.t. coucher, mettre au lit; loger, fixer, enfoncer; parquer (huîtres).—v.i. coucher, se coucher.
bedaub [bi'dɔ:b], v.t. barbouiller.
*bed-chamber [BEDROOM].
bedclothes ['bedklouðz], n.pl. les draps et les couvertures, m.pl.
bedding ['bediŋ], n. literie; litière (pour animaux), f.
bedeck [bi'dek], v.t. parer (de).
bedfellow ['bedfelou], n. camarade de lit, m.
*bedizen [bi'daizn], v.t. attifer, parer.
bedraggle [bi'drægl], v.t. crotter, traîner dans la boue.
bedridden ['bedridn], a. alité.
bedroom ['bedru:m], *bed-chamber [bed tʃeimbə], n. chambre (à coucher), f.
bedside ['bedsaid], n. ruelle, f., chevet, bord du lit, m.
bed-spread ['bedspred], n. couvrelit, dessus de lit, m.
bedstead ['bedsted], n. lit, bois de lit, m.; couchette, f.
bee [bi:], n. abeille, f.; **to have a bee in one's bonnet**, avoir une araignée dans le plafond.
beech [bi:tʃ], n. hêtre, m.
beef [bi:f], n. bœuf (viande); (pl. **beeves** [bi:vz]) bœuf (animal), m.
beef-steak ['bi:f'steik], n. bifteck, m.
beehive ['bi:haiv], n. ruche, f.
bee-line ['bi:lain], n. ligne droite, f.; **in a bee-line**, à vol d'oiseau; **to make a bee-line for**, se diriger tout droit vers.
Beelzebub [bi'elzəbʌb], Belzébuth, m.
beer [biə], n. bière, f.; **glass of beer**, bock, m.
beet [bi:t], n. betterave, f.
beetle (1) [bi:tl], n. coléoptère, scarabée, escarbot, m.

beetle (2) [bi:tl], n. maillet, m., mailloche; batte, f., battoir (de laveuse), m.; hie, demoiselle (d'un paveur), f.; mouton (à enfoncer les pieux), m.
beetle (3) [bi:tl], v.i. surplomber.—a. en surplomb.
beets ['bi:tz], n. betterave rouge, f.
beet-sugar [bi:t'ʃugə], n. sucre de betterave, m.

befall [bi'fɔ:l], v.t., v.i. irr. (conjug. like FALL) arriver, survenir (à).
befit [bi'fit], v.t. convenir à.
befitting [bi'fitiŋ], a. convenable à.
before [bi'fɔ:], adv. avant (temps, ordre etc.); auparavant, en avant; plus haut; jusqu'alors, naguère, jusqu'ici.—prep. devant (endroit); avant (temps etc.); **before going there**, avant d'y aller.—conj. avant que (with subj.).
beforehand [bi'fɔ:hænd], adv. à l'avance, d'avance.
befriend [bi'frend], v.t. seconder, aider, secourir; devenir l'ami de (quelqu'un).
beg [beg], v.t. mendier (demander l'aumône); demander, prier (de).—v.i. mendier.
beget [bi'get], v.t. irr. engendrer; (fig.) produire, causer.
beggar ['begə], n. mendiant, m., mendiante, f.; gueux, m., gueuse, f.—v.t. appauvrir, ruiner; (fig.) épuiser.
beggarly ['begəli], a. chétif, pauvre, misérable.
beggary ['begəri], n. mendicité, misère, f.
begging ['begiŋ], n. mendicité, f.
begin [bi'gin], v.t. irr. commencer; entamer, débuter; se mettre à.—v.i. commencer (by, with, par); **begin afresh**, recommencer.
beginner [bi'ginə], n. commençant; débutant, m.
beginning [bi'giniŋ], n. commencement, début, m., origine, f.
begone! [bi'gɔn], int. va-t'en! allez-vous-en!
begonia [bi'gounjə], n. (Bot.) bégonia, m.
begrudge [bi'grʌdʒ], v.t. envier; refuser (à).
begrudgingly [bi'grʌdʒiŋli], adv. à contre-cœur.
beguile [bi'gail], v.t. tromper, séduire; (fig.) passer (le temps).
behalf [bi'ha:f], n. faveur, part, f.; **on behalf of**, au nom de.
behave [bi'heiv], v.i. se comporter, se conduire; **well-behaved**, sage.
behavior [bi'heivjə], n. conduite, tenue, f.; comportement, m.; manières, f.pl.
behead [bi'hed], v.t. décapiter.
behest [bi'hest], n. commandement, ordre, m.
behind [bi'haind], adv. derrière, par derrière, en arrière.—prep. derrière, en arrière de; après, en retard de.—n. (colloq.) derrière, m.
behindhand [bi'haindhænd], a. and adv. en arrière, en retard.
behold [bi'hould], v.t. irr. (conjug. like HOLD) voir, regarder.—int. voyez! voici! voilà!
beholden [bi'houldən], a. redevable (à).
behoove [bi'houv], v.i.impers. incomber à; **it behooves**, il faut, il convient.
beige [beiʒ], a. and n. beige, m.
being ['bi:iŋ], n. être, m.; existence, f.; **in being**, existant, vivant.—pres.p. [BE] étant; **for the time being**, pour le moment.
Beirut [bei'ru:t], Beyrouth, m.
belated [bi'leitid], a. attardé; tardif.

belch [beltʃ], *v.t.*, *v.i.* roter, éructer; *to belch forth*, vomir; *to belch out flames*, vomir des flammes.—*n.* rot, *m.*, éructation, *f.*

beleaguer [bi'li:gə], *v.t.* assiéger, investir.

belfry ['belfri], *n.* clocher, beffroi, *m.*

Belgian ['beldʒən], *a.* belge.—*n.* Belge (*personne*), *m.*, *f.*

Belgium ['beldʒəm]. la Belgique, *f.*

belie [bi'lai], *v.t.* démentir.

belief [bi'li:f], *n.* croyance, *f.*; credo, *m.*

believable [bi'li:vəbl], *a.* croyable.

believe [bi'li:v], *v.t.* croire.—*v.i.* croire (*en* ou *à*); *I believe not*, je crois que non, je ne le crois pas; *I believe so*, je crois que oui, je le crois.

believer [bi'li:və], *n.* croyant, *m.*

bell [bel], *n.* cloche, clochette, *f.*; grelot (*de chevaux etc.*), *m.*; sonnette (*de maison*), *f.*; timbre (*horloge, bicyclette*); (*Arch.*) vase, *m.*

belle [bel], *n.* belle, beauté, *f.*

bellicose ['belikous], *a.* belliqueux.

belligerent [bi'lidʒərənt], *a.* and *n.* belligérant, *m.*

bellow ['belou], *v.i.* beugler; mugir (*mer*); gronder (*tonnerre*).—*n.* beuglement, *m.*

bellows ['belouz], *n.pl.* soufflet, *m.*

bell ringer ['belriŋə], *n.* sonneur, *m.*

bell rope ['belroup], *n.* corde de cloche, *f.*

bell tower ['beltauə], *n.* campanile; clocher, *m.*

belly ['beli], *n.* ventre, *m.*—*v.i.* bomber, s'enfler, se gonfler.

belong [bi'lɔŋ], *v.i.* appartenir, être (*à*).

belongings [bi'lɔŋiŋz], *n.pl.* effets, *m.pl.*, affaires, *f.pl.*

beloved [bi'lʌvd, bi'lʌvid], *a.* cher, chéri, bien-aimé.

below [bi'lou], *prep.* sous, au-dessous de; en aval de.—*adv.* au-dessous, dessous, en bas; *here below*, ici-bas.

belt [belt], *n.* ceinture, *f.*; ceinturon; baudrier, *m.*; (*Mach.*) courroie, *f.*; *green belt*, zone verte, *f.*—*v.t.* ceindre, entourer.

bemoan [bi'moun], *v.t.* pleurer, déplorer.—*v.i.* gémir (*sur*).

bemuse [bi'mju:z], *v.t.* stupéfier.

bench [bentʃ], *n.* banc; gradin, *m.*; banquette, *f.*; établi (*de menuisier*); siège, tribunal, *m.*

bend [bend], *v.t. irr.* plier; courber, faire plier; incliner, tendre (*un arc*); fléchir (*le genou*); (*fig.*) appliquer.—*v.i.* plier, ployer; se courber, se pencher, s'incliner; s'appliquer (*à*); tourner; fléchir.—*n.* courbure, *f.*; coude, (*Motor.*) tournant, virage, *m.*

beneath [bi'ni:θ], *prep.* sous, au-dessous de.—*adv.* au-dessous, en bas.

Benedict ['benidikt]. Benoît, *m.*

benediction [beni'dikʃən], *n.* bénédiction, *f.*

benefaction [beni'fækʃən], *n.* bienfait, *m.*

benefactor ['benifæktə], *n.* bienfaiteur, *m.*

benefactress ['benifæktris], *n.* bienfaitrice, *f.*

benefice ['benifis], *n.* bénéfice, *m.*

beneficence [bə'nefisəns], *n.* bienfaisance, *f.*

beneficial [beni'fiʃəl], *a.* salutaire, avantageux.

beneficiary [beni'fiʃəri], *a.* and *n.* bénéficiaire, *m.*, *f.*

benefit ['benifit], *n.* bienfait, profit; bénéfice, *m.*; indemnité (*de chômage etc.*), *f.*—*v.t.* faire du bien à.—*v.i.* profiter.

Benelux ['benilʌks]. Bénélux, *m.*

benevolence [bə'nevələns], *n.* bienveillance, *f.*

benevolent [bə'nevələnt], *a.* bienveillant, bienfaisant.

benighted [bi'naitid], *a.* anuité, surpris par la nuit; (*fig.*) ignorant.

benign [bi'nain], *a.* bénin, *m.*, bénigne (*maladie, médecine etc.*), *f.*; bienfaisant (*personne*); doux, affable.

benignant [bi'nignant], *a.* bon, bienveillant.

bent (1) [bent], *past* and *p.p.* [BEND].

bent (2) [bent], *a.* courbé, plié; *bent on*, résolu à.—*n.* penchant, *m.*, disposition, tendance, *f.*

benumb [bi'nʌm], *v.t.* engourdir.

benzene ['benzi:n], *n.* benzène, *m.*

benzine ['benzi:n], *n.* benzine, *f.*

bequeath [bi'kwi:ð], *v.t.* léguer.

bequest [bi'kwest], *n.* legs, *m.*

bereave [bi'ri:v], *v.t. irr.* priver (*de*).

bereavement [bi'ri:vmənt], *n.* privation, perte, *f.*; deuil, *m.*

beret ['berei], *n.* béret, *m.*

Bermuda(s) [bə:'mju:də(z)], (**the**). les (Îles) Bermudes, *f.pl.*

berry ['beri], *n.* baie, *f.*; grain, *m.*

berth [bə:θ], *n.* mouillage; lit, *m.*, couchette, *f.*; poste, *m.*, place, *f.*, emploi, *m.*—*v.t.* amarrer à quai.—*v.i.* mouiller.

Bertha ['bə:θə]. Berthe, *f.*

beseech [bi'si:tʃ], *v.t. irr.* supplier, implorer.

beset [bi'set], *v.t. irr.* (*conjug. like* SET) obséder, entourer, assaillir.

besetting [bi'setiŋ], *a.* habituel, obsesseur.

beside [bi'said], *prep.* à côté de, auprès de; hors, hormis, excepté.

besides [bi'saidz], *prep.* outre, hors, hormis, excepté.—*adv.* d'ailleurs, du reste, en outre, de plus.

besiege [bi'si:dʒ], *v.t.* assiéger.

besmear [bi'smiə], *v.t.* barbouiller; souiller.

besmirch [bi'smə:tʃ], *v.t.* tacher, salir.

besom ['bi:zəm], *n.* balai, *m.*

bespatter [bi'spætə], *v.t.* éclabousser, couvrir de boue.

bespeak [bi'spi:k], *v.t. irr.* (*conjug. like* SPEAK) commander; retenir; annoncer, dénoter, accuser.

best [best], *a.* and *n.* le meilleur, la meilleure, le mieux; *at best*, au mieux, tout au plus; *best man* (*at weddings*), garçon d'honneur, *m.*; *to do one's best*, faire de son mieux; *to have the best of it*, avoir le dessus; *to make the best of it*, tirer le meilleur parti; *to the best of my belief*, autant que je sache.—*adv.* le mieux.

bestial ['bestial], *a.* bestial, de bête.

bestir [bi'stə:], *v.t.* remuer, mettre en mouvement.

bestow [bi'stou], *v.t.* donner, accorder.

bestrew [bi'stru:], *v.t. irr.* (*conjug. like* STREW) joncher (*de*), parsemer (*de*).

bestride [bi'straid], *v.t. irr.* (*conjug. like* STRIDE) enjamber, enfourcher (*un cheval*); être à cheval sur.

bet [bet], *n.* pari, *m.*, gageure, *f.*—*v.t.*, *v.i.* parier.

betake [bi'teik], *v.r. irr.* (*conjug. like* TAKE) *to betake oneself to*, se mettre à, s'en aller à, avoir recours à.

bethink [bi'θiŋk], *v.t. irr.* (*conjug. like* THINK) s'aviser (*de*); *to bethink oneself of*, se rappeler.

Bethlehem ['beθlihem, 'beθliəm]. Bethléem, *m.*

betide [bi'taid], *v.t.* **woe betide you,** malheur à vous.—*v.i.* arriver, advenir.

betimes [bi'taimz], *adv.* de bonne heure.

betoken [bi'toukn], *v.t.* annoncer, présager.

betray [bi'trei], *v.t.* trahir; tromper; révéler; faire tomber, entraîner.

betrayal [bi'treiəl], *n.* trahison, perfidie, *f.*

betrayer [bi'treiə], *n.* traître, *m.*

betroth [bi'trouð], *v.t.* fiancer.

betrothal [bi'trouðəl], *n.* fiançailles, *f.pl.*

betrothed [bi'trouðd], *a.* and *n.* fiancé, *m.* fiancée, *f.*

better ['betə], *a.* meilleur; *to get the better of,* l'emporter sur.—*adv.* mieux; *better late than never,* mieux vaut tard que jamais; *better and better,* de mieux en mieux; *for better for worse,* vaille que vaille; *I had better,* je ferais mieux; *so much the better!* tant mieux!—*n.* meilleur; supérieur, *m.*—*v.t.* améliorer, avancer.

betterment ['betəmənt], *n.* amélioration, *f.*

betting ['betiŋ], *n.* paris, *m.pl.*

Betty ['beti]. Babette, *f.*

between [bi'twi:n], *prep.* entre.

*****betwixt** [bi'twikst], *prep.* entre; *betwixt and between,* entre les deux.

bevel ['bevəl], *a.* de biais, en biseau.—*n.* fausse équerre (*outil*), *f.*—*v.t.* tailler en biseau.—*v.i.* biaiser.

beverage ['bevəridʒ], *n.* boisson, *f.*; *****breuvage, *m.*

bevy ['bevi], *n.* volée; troupe, compagnie, *f.*

bewail [bi'weil], *v.t.* pleurer, lamenter.

bewailing [bi'weiliŋ], *n.* lamentation, *f.*

beware [bi'weə], *v.i.* se garder (*de*); prendre garde (*à*); se méfier (*de*).

bewilder [bi'wildə], *v.t.* égarer, embarrasser.

bewildering [bi'wildəriŋ], *a.* déroutant, ahurissant.

bewilderment [bi'wildəmənt], *n.* égarement, *m.*

bewitch [bi'witʃ], *v.t.* ensorceler.

bewitching [bi'witʃiŋ], *a.* enchanteur, séduisant.

beyond [bi'jɔnd], *prep.* par delà, au delà de; au-dessus de; outre, hors de.—*adv.* là-bas. —*n.* au-delà, *m.*

bias ['baiəs], *a.* and *adv.* de biais, de travers.—*n.* biais, *m.*, pente, *f.*; penchant, parti pris, préjugé, *m.*—*v.t.* décentrer (*boule*); faire pencher; prévenir; influencer.

biased ['baiəst], *a.* décentré; partial, prédisposé.

bib (1) [bib], *n.* bavette, *f.*

bib (2) [bib], *n.* tacaud (*poisson*), *m.*

Bible [baibl], *n.* Bible, *f.*

biblical ['biblikəl], *a.* biblique.

biceps ['baiseps], *n.* (*Anat.*) biceps, *m.*

bicker ['bikə], *v.i.* se quereller, se chamailler.

bickering ['bikəriŋ], *n.* bisbille, *f.*, querelles, *f.pl.*

bicycle ['baisikl], *n.* bicyclette, *f.*; (*pop.*) vélo, *m.*, bécane, *f.*

bid [bid], *v.t.* irr. ordonner, dire, commander (*de*); inviter (*à*); offrir, enchérir; *to bid good-bye to,* dire adieu à.—*n.* enchère, *f.*

bidder ['bidə], *n.* enchérisseur, acheteur, *m.*

bidding ['bidiŋ], *n.* commandement, ordre, *m.*; invitation, prière, *f.*; enchères, *f.pl.*

bide [baid], *v.t.* irr. *archaic except in* **to bide one's time,** attendre le bon moment.

biennial [bai'eniəl], *a.* biennal; (*Bot.*) bisannuel.

biennially [bai'eniəli], *adv.* tous les deux ans.

bier [biə], *n.* civière, *f.*, corbillard, *m.*

big [big], *a.* gros; grand, vaste; enceinte, grosse (*d'enfant*), pleine (*bête*); (*fig.*) fier, hautain.

bigamist ['bigəmist], *n.* bigame, *m.*, *f.*

bigamy ['bigəmi], *n.* bigamie, *f.*

bigness ['bignis], *n.* grosseur, grandeur, *f.*

bigot ['bigət], *n.* bigot, cagot, *m.*, fanatique, *m.*, *f.*

bigoted ['bigətid], *a.* bigot.

bigotry ['bigətri], *n.* bigoterie, *f.*, sectarisme, fanatisme, *m.*

bigwig ['bigwig], *n.* (*fam.*) gros bonnet, *m.*

bike [baik], *n.* (*colloq.*) vélo, *m.*, bécane, *f.*

bikini [bi'ki:ni], *n.* (*Cost.*) bikini, *m.*

bile [bail], *n.* bile, *f.*

bilge [bildʒ], *n.* (*Naut.*) sentine, *f.*; (*colloq.*) bêtises, *f.pl.*

bilge water ['bildʒwɔ:tə], *n.* eau de la cale, *f.*

bilingual [bai'liŋgwəl], *a.* bilingue.

bilious ['biljəs], *a.* bilieux.

bill (1) [bil], *n.* bec (*d'oiseau*), *m.*

bill (2) [bil], *n.* hallebarde, *f.*

bill (3) [bil], *n.* mémoire, compte, *m.*; facture (*invoice*), note (*hôtels etc.*), addition (*restaurants*); (*Comm.*) note, *f.*; billet, effet, *m.*; (*Banking*) lettre de change, *f.*; (*Parl.*) projet de loi, *m.*; affiche, *f.*, placard, *m.*; *bill of fare,* menu, *m.*, carte, *f.*; *bill of health,* patente de santé, *f.*; *post no bills!* défense d'afficher!

billet ['bilit], *n.* bûche, *f.*; (*Mil.*) billet de logement, *m.*—*v.t.*, *v.i.* loger chez l'habitant.

bill-hook ['bilhuk], *n.* serpe, *f.*, vouge, *m.*

billiard ['biljəd], *a.* de billard.

billiard ball ['biljədbɔ:l], *n.* bille, *f.*

billiards ['biljədz], *n.pl.* billard, *m.*; *to play a game of billiards,* faire une partie de billard.

billiard table ['biljədteibl], *n.* billard, *m.*

billion ['biliən], *n.* (*since 1948*) billion; (*Am.*) milliard, *m.*

billow ['bilou], *n.* grande vague, lame, *f.*—*v.i.* s'élever en vagues, rouler.

billowy ['biloui], *a.* houleux.

bill-sticker ['bilstikə], *n.* afficheur, colleur d'affiches, *m.*

billy goat ['biligout], *n.* bouc, *m.*

bin [bin], *n.* huche, *f.*, bac; coffre, *m.*

binary ['bainəri], *a.* binaire.

bind [baind], *v.t.* irr. lier; obliger; resserrer; border (*chaussures etc.*); garrotter; serrer; rendre constipé; relier (*livres*); *to be bound to,* être tenu de.—*n.* (*pop.*) *that's a bind,* quelle scie!

binder ['baində], *n.* lieur; relieur, *m.*; bande, attache, *f.*

binding ['baindiŋ], *a.* obligatoire; (*Med.*) astringent.—*n.* reliure, *f.*; bandeau, galon, *m.*, bordure, *f.*

bindweed ['baindwi:d], *n.* liseron, *f.*

binge [bindʒ], *n.* (*pop.*) bombe, *f.*; *to be on a binge,* faire la bombe.

binoculars [bi'nɔkjuləz], *n.pl.* jumelles, *f.pl.*

binomial [bai'noumiəl], *a.* (*Alg.*) binôme.

biochemist [baio'kemist], *n.* biochimiste, *m.*

biochemistry [baio'kemistri], *n.* biochimie, *f.*

biographer [bai'ɔgrəfə], n. biographe, m.
biography [bai'ɔgrəfi], n. biographie, f.
biologist [bai'ɔlədʒist], n. biologiste, biologue, m.
biology [bai'ɔlədʒi], n. biologie, f.
biped ['baiped], n. bipède, m.
birch [bɔːtʃ], n. bouleau, m.; verges, f.pl.; *silver birch*, bouleau blanc.—v.t. fouetter.
bird [bɔːd], n. oiseau; (*pop.*) type, m.; *little bird*, oiselet, m.
bird cage ['bɔːdkeidʒ], n. cage d'oiseau, f.
bird-lime ['bɔːdlaim], n. glu, f.
bird's-eye view ['bɔːdzai'vjuː], n. vue à vol d'oiseau, f.
bird's nest ['bɔːdznest], n. nid d'oiseau, m.
birth [bɔːθ], n. naissance, f.; enfantement, m.; (*fig.*) origine, source, f.
birth control ['bɔːθkɔntroul], n. limitation des naissances, f.
birthday ['bɔːθdei], n. anniversaire, m.
birthplace ['bɔːθpleis], n. lieu de naissance, pays natal, m.
birth rate ['bɔːθreit], n. natalité, f.
birthright ['bɔːθrait], n. droit d'aînesse, m.
Biscay ['biskei]. la Biscaye, f.; *the Bay of Biscay*, le Golfe de Gascogne, m.
biscuit ['biskit], n. biscuit, m.
bisect [bai'sekt], v.t. couper en deux.
bishop ['biʃəp], n. évêque; (*Chess*) fou, m.
bishopric ['biʃəprik], n. évêché, m.
bit (1) [bit], n. morceau, m.; pièce (*de monnaie*), f.; (*colloq.*) brin, bout, peu, m.; mèche (*outil*); (*Naut.*) bitte, f.; mors (*de bride*), m.
bit (2) [bit], past [BITE].
bitch [bitʃ], n. chienne; femelle (*in compounds*), f.
bite [bait], n. morsure; piqûre, f.; coup de dent, m., bouchée; (*Fishing*) touche, f.—v.t. irr. mordre; piquer; ronger; (*fig.*) attraper, pincer, couper (*vent*).—v.i. mordre.
biting ['baitiŋ], a. mordant, piquant; coupant (*vent*).
bitter ['bitə], a. amer, acerbe; (*fig.*) acharné, mordant, aigre.—n. amer, m.
bitterly ['bitəli], adv. avec amertume; amèrement.
bittern ['bitən], n. butor, m.
bitterness ['bitənis], n. amertume, aigreur, âpreté, f.
bitumen [bi'tjuːmən], n. bitume, m.
bivouac ['bivuæk], n. bivouac, m.—v.i. bivouaquer.
blab [blæb], v.i. jaser, bavarder.—n. bavard, m.
black [blæk], a. noir; (*fig.*) obscur, sombre, triste.—v.t. noircir; cirer (*chaussures*).—n. noir, m.
black-ball ['blækbɔːl], n. boule noire, f.—v.t. rejeter au scrutin.
black beetle ['blæk'biːtl], n. cafard, m., blatte, f.
blackberry ['blækbəri], n. mûre (sauvage), f.
blackbird ['blækbɔːd], n. merle, m.
blackboard ['blækbɔːd], n. tableau noir, m.
black currant ['blæk'kʌrənt], n. cassis, m.
blacken ['blækən], v.t., v.i. noircir.
blackguard ['blæɡɑːd], n. polisson, gredin, vaurien, m.
blacking ['blækiŋ], n. cirage (*chaussures*); noircissement, m.
blackish ['blækiʃ], a. noirâtre.
black lead [blæk'led], n. mine de plomb, f.

blackleg ['blækleg], n. (*Gambling*) escroc; (*Strikes*) renard, jaune, m.
blackmail ['blækmeil], n. chantage, m.—v.t. faire chanter.
blackmailer ['blækmeilə], n. maître-chanteur, m.
black market [blæk'mɑːkit], n. marché noir, m.
blackness ['blæknis], n. noirceur, f.
black-out ['blækaut], n. extinction des lumières, f.; black-out, m.
blacksmith ['blæksmiθ], n. forgeron, m.
bladder ['blædə], n. vessie; (*Bot.*) vésicule, f.
blade [bleid], n. lame (*de couteau etc.*), f.; brin (*d'herbe*), m.; pelle (*d'un aviron*); pale (*d'hélice*), f.; (*fig.*) gaillard (*personne*), m.
blain [blein], n. pustule, f.
blame [bleim], n. blâme, m.; faute, f.—v.t. blâmer, s'en prendre à; censurer, reprocher.
blameless ['bleimlis], a. innocent, sans tache.
blanch [blɑːntʃ], v.t. blanchir; pâlir; faire pâlir; monder (*amandes*).—v.i. blanchir; pâlir.
blancmange [blə'mɔnʒ], n. blanc-manger, m.
bland [blænd], a. doux, aimable, affable.
blandish ['blændiʃ], v.t. caresser, flatter, cajoler.
blandishment ['blændiʃmənt], n. flatterie, f.
blank [blæŋk], a. blanc, en blanc; (*fig.*) vide, confus, déconcerté.—n. blanc; (*Lotteries*) billet blanc; (*fig.*) vide, m., lacune, f.
blanket ['blæŋkit], n. couverture, f.
blare [blɛə], v.t. faire retentir.—v.i. sonner (*comme une trompette*), cuivrer.—n. sonnerie, f.
blaspheme [blæs'fiːm], v.t., v.i. blasphémer.
blasphemer [blæs'fiːmə], n. blasphémateur, m.
blasphemous ['blæsfəməs], a. blasphématoire.
blasphemy ['blæsfəmi], n. blasphème, m.
blast [blɑːst], n. vent, coup de vent; son (*d'un instrument à vent*), m.; explosion, f.—v.t. flétrir, brûler; détruire, ruiner; faire sauter.—int. sacrebleu!
blast furnace ['blɑːstfəːnis], n. haut fourneau, m.
blasting ['blɑːstiŋ], a. destructeur.—n. coup de mine, m., explosion, f.
blatant ['bleitənt], a. bruyant, criard.
blatantly ['bleitəntli], adv. avec une vulgarité criarde.
blaze (1) [bleiz], n. flamme; flambée, f.; feu; (*fig.*) éclat, m.; étoile (*de cheval*), f.—v.i. être en flammes; flamber, brûler.
blaze (2) [bleiz], blazon (1) ['bleizən], v.t. proclamer; *to blaze abroad*, répandre, crier par-dessus les toits.
blazing ['bleiziŋ], a. flambant; enflammé, embrasé; (*fig.*) brillant.
blazon (2) ['bleizən], n. blason, m.—v.t. blasonner.
bleach [bliːtʃ], v.t., v.i. blanchir; (*Hairdressing*) oxygéner.—n. agent de blanchiment, m., eau de javel; (*Hairdressing*) oxygénée, f.
bleak [bliːk], a. ouvert, sans abri; froid; désert; triste, morne.
bleakness ['bliːknis], n. exposition découverte, f.; froid, m.; tristesse, f.; aspect morne, m.
blear [bliə], **bleary** ['bliəri], a. larmoyant.
bleat [bliːt], v.i. bêler.—n. bêlement, m.

bleed [bli:d], *v.t. irr.* saigner; (*colloq.*) débourser.—*v.i.* saigner; pleurer (*vignes etc.*).
bleeding ['bli:diŋ], *a.* saignant.—*n.* saignement, *m.*; (*Surg.*) saignée, *f.*
blemish ['blemiʃ], *v.t.* tacher, flétrir.—*n.* tache, flétrissure, *f.*, défaut, *m.*
blend [blend], *v.t.* mêler, mélanger; fondre.—*v.i.* se fondre, se marier (*à ou avec*).—*n.* mélange, *m.*
bless [bles], *v.t.* bénir; rendre heureux, réjouir.
blessed [blest, 'blesid], *a.* béni, saint; bienheureux.
blessedness ['blesidnis], *n.* béatitude, félicité, *f.*, bonheur, *m.*
blessing ['blesiŋ], *n.* bénédiction, *f.*; bonheur, bien, *m.*
blight [blait], *v.t.* flétrir (*vent*); brouir (*soleil*); (*fig.*) frustrer, détruire.—*n.* brouissure (*des fleurs et des fruits*); rouille (*du blé etc.*); (*fig.*) flétrissure, *f.*
blind [blaind], *a.* aveugle; obscur; *blind alley,* impasse, *f.*; *blind in one eye,* borgne; *blind side,* côté faible, *m.*—*n.* store (*fenêtre*); abat-jour, *m.*; banne (*de boutique*); persienne (*à l'extérieur*), *f.*; (*fig.*) voile, *m.*; *Venetian blind,* jalousie, *f.*—*v.t.* aveugler; (*fig.*) éblouir.
blindfold ['blaindfould], *v.t.* bander les yeux à.—*a.* les yeux bandés.
blindly ['blaindli], *adv.* aveuglément.
blind-man's buff ['blaindmænz'bʌf], *n.* colin-maillard, *m.*
blindness ['blaindnis], *n.* cécité, *f.*; aveuglement, *m.*
blink [bliŋk], *v.i.* clignoter, cligner des yeux; vaciller (*lumière*).—*n.* clignotement, *m.*
blinker ['bliŋkə], *n.* œillère (*de ch/val*), *f.*
bliss [blis], *n.* félicité, béatitude, *f.*
blissful ['blisful], *a.* bienheureux.
blister ['blistə], *n.* ampoule, bulle; cloque (*peinture*), *f.*—*v.i.* faire venir des ampoules à.—*v.i.* se couvrir d'ampoules; se cloquer (*peinture*).
blithe [blaið], **blithesome** ['blaiðsəm], *a.* gai, joyeux.
blitz [blits], *n.* bombardement aérien (*2me guerre mondiale*), *m.*
blizzard ['blizəd], *n.* tempête de neige, *f.*
bloat [blout], *v.t.* gonfler, bouffir, enfler.
bloater ['bloutə], *n.* hareng saur, *m.*
blob [blɔb], *n.* goutte (*d'eau*), *f.*; pâté (*d'encre*), *m.*
block [blɔk], *n.* bloc, *m.*, bille, *f.*; billot; (*fig.*) obstacle, *m.*; *block of houses,* pâté de maisons, *m.*; *block of flats,* immeuble, *m.* —*v.t.* bloquer; *to block up,* fermer, boucher.
blockade [blɔ'keid], *n.* blocus, *m.*—*v.t.* bloquer.
blockhead ['blɔkhed], *n.* imbécile, sot, *m.*
bloke [blouk], *n.* (*pop.*) type, *m.*
blond(e) [blɔnd], *a.* and *n.* blond, *m.*
blood [blʌd], *n.* sang, *m.*; (*fig.*) parenté, *f.*; tempérament, *m.*; race (*de cheval*), *f.*
blood group ['blʌdgru:p], *n.* groupe sanguin, *m.*
bloodhound ['blʌdhaund], *n.* limier, *m.*
bloodless ['blʌdlis], *a.* exsangue; pâle.
bloodshed ['blʌdʃed], *n.* effusion de sang, *f.*
bloodshot ['blʌdʃɔt], *a.* injecté de sang.

bloodthirsty ['blʌdθə:sti], *a.* sanguinaire.
bloody ['blʌdi], *a.* sanglant, ensanglanté, sanguinaire.
bloom [blu:m], *n.* fleur, *f.*; duvet, velouté (*de fruit*), *m.*; (*Metal.*) loupe, *f.*—*v.i.* fleurir; (*fig.*) être éclatant.
blooming ['blu:miŋ], *a.* fleurissant; (*pop.*) sacré, satané.—*n.* floraison, *f.*
blossom ['blɔsəm], *n.* fleur, *f.*—*v.i.* fleurir; être en fleur; *to blossom out,* s'épanouir.
blossoming ['blɔsəmiŋ], *n.* floraison, *f.*
blot [blɔt], *n.* tache, *f.*; pâté (*d'encre*), *m.*—*v.t.* tacher, salir; faire un pâté sur; sécher (*avec papier buvard*); *to blot out,* rayer, effacer.—*v.i.* boire (*papier*).
blotch [blɔtʃ], *n.* pustule, tache, *f.*
blotchy ['blɔtʃi], *a.* tacheté.
blotting paper ['blɔtiŋpeipə], *n.* papier buvard, *m.*
blouse [blauz], *n.* blouse; chemisette, *f.*; corsage, chemisier, *m.*
blow (1) [blou], *n.* coup, *m.*; *to come to blows,* en venir aux mains.
blow (2) [blou], *v.t. irr.* souffler; sonner (*un instrument à vent*); faire sauter (*plomb*); *to blow away,* chasser; *to blow out,* éteindre (*une lumière*); faire sauter (*la cervelle*); *to blow up,* faire sauter; gonfler (*un pneu*). —*v.i.* souffler; faire du vent; sauter (*plomb*); claquer (*ampoule électrique*); *to blow up,* sauter, éclater.
blow (3) [blou], *v.i.* s'épanouir (*fleurs*).
blower ['blouə], *n.* souffleur; rideau de cheminée, *m.*
blow-lamp ['bloulæmp], *n.* lampe à souder, *f.*
blubber ['blʌbə], *n.* graisse de baleine, *f.*
bludgeon ['blʌdʒən], *n.* gourdin, *m.*; trique, *f.*
blue [blu:], *a.* bleu.—*n.* bleu; azur, *m.*—*v.t.* bleuir.
blue-bell ['blu:bel], *n.* jacinthe des prés, *f.*
blueness ['blu:nis], *n.* couleur bleue, *f.*
blue-print ['blu:print], *n.* dessin négatif; (*fam.*) bleu, projet, *m.*
bluestocking ['blu:stɔkiŋ], *n.* bas bleu, *m.*
bluff (1) [blʌf], *a.* escarpé, accore; brusque (*personne*).—*n.* à-pic, *m.*, falaise, *f.*, escarpement, *m.*
bluff (2) [blʌf], *n.* bluff (*feinte*), *m.*—*v.t.* bluffer.
bluffness ['blʌfnis], *n.* rudesse, brusquerie, *f.*
bluish ['blu:iʃ], *a.* bleuâtre.
blunder ['blʌndə], *n.* bévue, étourderie, balourdise, *f.*—*v.t.* embrouiller.—*v.i.* faire une bévue.
blunderbuss ['blʌndəbʌs], *n.* tromblon, *m.*
blunderer ['blʌndərə], *n.* maladroit, étourdi, *m.*
blundering ['blʌndəriŋ], *a.* maladroit.
blunt [blʌnt], *a.* émoussé; (*fig.*) brusque, bourru.—*v.t.* émousser, épointer; (*fig.*) amortir.
bluntly ['blʌntli], *adv.* brusquement, carrément.
bluntness ['blʌntnis], *n.* état émoussé, *m.*; brusquerie, *f.*
blur [blə:], *v.t.* tacher, barbouiller; (*fig.*) brouiller.
blurt [blə:t], *v.t. to blurt out,* laisser échapper.
blush [blʌʃ], *v.i.* rougir.—*n.* rougeur, *f.*; *at the first blush,* au premier abord.
blushing ['blʌʃiŋ], *a.* rougissant.

bluster ['blʌstə], *v.i.* tempêter, crier (*contre*), fanfaronner.—*n.* fracas, tapage, *m.*, fanfaronnade, fureur (*d'une tempête*), *f.*
blusterer ['blʌstərə], *n.* fanfaron, *m.*, bravache, *m.*, *f.*
blustering ['blʌstəriŋ], *a.* orageux; bruyant; bravache.
boa ['bouə], *n.* boa, *m.*
boar [bɔ:], *n.* verrat, *m.*; **wild boar**, sanglier, *m.*
board [bɔ:d], *n.* planche, *f.*; écriteau, *m.*; table, pension, *f.*; conseil, *m.*, administration, *f.*; (*Bookb.*) carton; (*Tailors*) établi, (*Naut.*) bord; (*Chess*) échiquier, *m.*; **Board of Trade**, ministère du commerce, *m.*; **on board**, à bord.—*v.t.* planchéier; nourrir; (*Naut.*) aborder; **to board out**, mettre en pension.—*v.i.* se mettre en pension.
boarder ['bɔ:də], *n.* pensionnaire; interne, *m.*, *f.*
boarding ['bɔ:diŋ], *n.* planchéiage, plancher, *m.*; table, pension, *f.*; (*Naut.*) abordage, *m.*
boarding house ['bɔ:diŋhaus], *n.* pension de famille, *f.*
boarding school ['bɔ:diŋsku:l], *n.* pensionnat, internat, *m.*
boast [boust], *v.i.* se vanter, se glorifier.—*n.* vanterie, *f.*
boaster ['boustə], *n.* vantard, *m.*
boastful ['boustful], *a.* vantard.
boat [bout], *n.* bateau, canot, *m.*, barque, *f.*
boating ['boutiŋ], *n.* canotage, *m.*
boatman ['boutmən], *n.* batelier, *m.*
boatswain, bosun [bousn], *n.* maître d'équipage, *m.*
bob [bɔb], *n.* (*Hairdressing*) perruque ronde; lentille (*d'un pendule*); secousse, *f.*; coup, *m.*, tape; petite révérence, *f.*—*v.t.* écourter (*la queue*); secouer, ballotter, balancer.—*v.i.* pendiller, osciller, s'agiter; **to bob up**, revenir à la surface.
bobbin ['bɔbin], *n.* bobine, *f.*
bode [boud], *v.t.*, *v.i.* présager; **to bode well** (*ill*), être de bon (mauvais) augure.
bodice ['bɔdis], *n.* corsage, *m.*
bodiless ['bɔdilis], *a.* sans corps.
bodily ['bɔdili], *a.* corporel, matériel.—*adv.* corporellement; entièrement, en masse.
boding ['boudiŋ], *n.* présage, pressentiment, *m.*
bodkin ['bɔdkin], *n.* poinçon; passe-lacet, *m.*
body ['bɔdi], *n.* corps; fond; cœur, centre; gros (*d'une armée*), *m.*; bande, troupe; nef (*d'une église*); personne; sève (*de vin*), carrosserie (*d'un véhicule*), *f.*; corsage (*d'une robe*), *m.*
body-guard ['bɔdiga:d], *n.* garde du corps, *m.*
body-work ['bɔdiwə:k], *n.* carrosserie, *f.*
boffin ['bɔfin], *n.* (*fam.*) savant, inventeur, *m.*
bog [bɔg], *n.* marécage, *m.*, fondrière, *f.*; **to get bogged down**, s'embourber.
boggle ['bɔgl], *v.i.* hésiter (à); reculer (*devant*).
boggy ['bɔgi], *a.* marécageux.
bogie ['bougi], *n.* (*Rail.*) bogie, *m.*
bogus ['bougəs], *a.* faux, simulé.
boil (1) [bɔil], *v.t.* faire bouillir; faire cuire à l'eau.—*v.i.* bouillir; bouillonner; **to boil over**, déborder.
boil (2) [bɔil], *n.* (*Med.*) furoncle, clou, *m.*

boiled [bɔild], *a.* bouilli, cuit à l'eau; **a boiled egg**, un œuf à la coque.
boiler ['bɔilə], *n.* chaudière, *f.*; réservoir à eau chaude, *m.*
boiler house ['bɔiləhaus], *n.* salle des chaudières, *f.*
boiler maker ['bɔiləmeikə], *n.* chaudronnier, *m.*
boiler suit ['bɔiləsju:t], *n.* bleus, *m.pl.*
boiling ['bɔiliŋ], *a.* en ébullition.—*n.* bouillonnement, *m.*
boisterous ['bɔistərəs], *a.* orageux, violent; bruyant, turbulent.
boisterously ['bɔistərəsli], *adv.* impétueusement; violemment; bruyamment.
boisterousness ['bɔistərəsnis], *n.* impétuosité, turbulence; violence, *f.*
bold [bould], *a.* hardi; audacieux, téméraire; impudent, effronté; saillant, net.
bold-faced ['bouldfeist], *a.* impudent, effronté.
boldly ['bouldli], *adv.* hardiment, intrépidement; impudemment.
boldness ['bouldnis], *n.* hardiesse, audace; assurance, effronterie, *f.*
bole [boul], *n.* tronc, fût (*d'un arbre*), *m.*
Bolivia [bə'liviə], la Bolivie, *f.*
Bolivian [bə'liviən], *a.* bolivien.—*n.* Bolivien (*personne*), *m.*
bollard ['bɔləd], *n.* (*Naut.*) pieu d'amarrage, *m.*
Bolshevik ['bɔlʃivik], *a.* bolchevik.—*n.* Bolchevik, *m.*
Bolshevism ['bɔlʃivizm], *n.* bolchevisme, *m.*
bolster ['boulstə], *n.* traversin; coussin, *m.*—*v.t.* mettre un traversin sous, (*fig.*) appuyer, soutenir.
bolt [boult], *n.* verrou; pêne; (*Tech.*) boulon, *m.*, cheville, *f.*; (*fig.*) trait, *m.*, fleche; fuite, *f.*; **thunder-bolt**, éclair, *m.*—*v.t.* verrouiller; fermer au verrou; gober, avaler (*to swallow*).—*v.i.* décamper, filer; s'emporter, s'emballer (*cheval*).
bomb [bɔm], *n.* bombe, *f.*—*v.t.* bombarder.
bombard [bɔm'ba:d], *v.t.* bombarder.
bombardier [bɔmbə'diə], *n.* bombardier, *m.*
bombardment [bɔm'ba:dmənt], *n.* bombardement, *m.*
bombast ['bɔmbæst], *n.* emphase, enflure, *f.*, boursouflage, *m.*
bombastic [bɔm'bæstik], *a.* enflé, ampoulé.
bomber ['bɔmə], *n.* avion de bombardement, *m.*
bombing ['bɔmiŋ], *n.* bombardement, *m.*
bona fide [bounə'faidi], *a.* sérieux, de bonne foi.
bond [bɔnd], *n.* lien, *m.*; liaison, *f.*; engagement, *m.*; obligation, *f.*; (*Fin.*) bon, *m.*; **in bonds**, dans les fers.—*v.t.* entreposer; **bonded goods**, marchandises entreposées, *f.pl.*
bondage ['bɔndidʒ], *n.* esclavage, *m.*, servitude, *f.*
bond-holder ['bɔndhouldə], *n.* obligataire, *m.*, *f.*, porteur d'obligation, *m.*
bondman ['bɔndmən], **bondsman** ['bɔndzmən], *n.* (*pl.* **-men** [men]) serf, esclave, *m.*
bondwoman ['bɔndwumən], **bondswoman** ['bɔndzwumən], *n.* (*pl.* **-women** [wimin]) esclave, *f.*
bone [boun], *n.* os, *m.*; arête (*de poisson*); baleine (*whale bone*); ivoire (*des dents*), *f.*; (*pl.*) ossements, *m.pl.*; **bone of contention**, pomme de discorde, *f.*—*v.t.* désosser.

bonfire ['bɔnfaiə], *n.* feu de joie *ou* de jardin, *m.*

bonnet ['bɔnit], *n.* chapeau (*de femme*); bonnet (*d'un Écossais*).

bonny ['bɔni], *a.* gentil, joli, joyeux, gai.

bonus ['bounəs], *n.* boni, *m.*; prime, *f.*

bony ['bouni], *a.* osseux; plein d'arêtes (*poisson*).

boo [bu:], *v.t., v.i.* huer.—*n.* huée, *f.*—*int.* hou!

booby ['bu:bi], *n.* nigaud, benêt, *m.*

booby trap ['bu:bitræp], *n.* attrape-nigaud, *m.*; (*Mil.*) mine-piège, *f.*

book [buk], *n.* livre, livret; registre; bouquin (*vieux livre*), *m.*; **exercise book**, cahier, *m.* —*v.t.* retenir, réserver; enregistrer, inscrire.

bookbinder ['bukbaində], *n.* relieur, *m.*

bookbinding ['bukbaindiŋ], *n.* reliure, *f.*

book-case ['bukkeis], *n.* bibliothèque, *f.*

booking office ['bukiŋɔfis], *n.* bureau d'enregistrement; guichet (*de gare etc.*), *m.*

bookish ['bukiʃ], *a.* studieux; livresque (*style*).

book-keeper ['bukki:pə], *n.* teneur de livres, *m.*

book-keeping ['bukki:piŋ], *n.* comptabilité, *f.*

book lover ['buklʌvə], *n.* bibliophile, *m., f.*

bookseller ['bukselə], *n.* libraire, *m., f.*

bookshelf ['bukʃelf], *n.* rayon (*de bibliothèque*), *m.*

book-shop ['bukʃɔp], (*Am.*) **bookstore** ['buksto:], *n.* librairie, *f.*

book-stall ['buksto:l], *n.* (*Rail.*) bibliothèque, *f.*, étalage de livres, *m.*

boom [bu:m], *n.* (*Naut.*) bout-dehors, *m.*; chaîne (*des ports etc.*); (*Cine.*) perche, *f.*; grondement, retentissement, *m.*; (*fig., Comm.*) grande (*et rapide*) hausse, *f.*—*v.i.* gronder, retentir; (*Comm.*) être en hausse, prospérer.

boomerang ['bu:məræŋ], *n.* boumerang, *m.*

boon (1) [bu:n], *n.* bienfait, *m.*; faveur, *f.*; bien, avantage, *m.*

boon (2) [bu:n], *a.* gai, joyeux.

boor [buə], *n.* rustre, *m.*

boorish ['buəriʃ], *a.* rustre, grossier.

boost [bu:st], *v.t.* (*Am.*) pousser (*par derrière*); lancer; (*Elec.*) survolter.

boot (1) [bu:t], *n.* chaussure, bottine, botte, *f.*

boot (2) [bu:t], *n.* (*used only in*) **to boot**, en sus, par-dessus le marché.

booth [bu:ð], *n.* baraque, tente, cabine, *f.*

booty ['bu:ti], *n.* butin, *m.*

borax ['bɔ:ræks], *n.* borax, *m.*

border ['bɔ:də], *n.* bord, *m.*; bordure (*de vêtement etc.*); frontière (*d'un pays*), *f.*; (*Gard.*) parterre, *m.*, platebande, *f.*—*v.t.* border.—*v.i.* about'ir, toucher (*à*); avoisiner.

bordering ['bɔ:dəriŋ], *a.* contigu, voisin.

border-line ['bɔ:dəlain], *a.* indéterminé.—*n.* ligne de démarcation, *f.*

bore (1) [bɔ:], *v.t.* percer, forer; sonder, creuser; (*fig.*) ennuyer, embêter.—*v.i.* percer.—*n.* trou; calibre; (*fig.*) fâcheux (*personne*); ennui (*chose*); mascaret (*d'un fleuve*), *m.*

bore (2) [bɔ:], *past* [BEAR].

boredom ['bɔ:dəm], *n.* ennui, *m.*

born [bɔ:n], *a.* né; **to be born**, naître.

borough ['bʌrə], *n.* bourg, *m.*, ville, *f.*

borrow ['bɔrou], *v.t.* emprunter (*à*).

borrower ['bɔrouə], *n.* emprunteur, *m.*

bosh [bɔʃ], *n.* blague, farce, *f.*; bêtises, *f.pl.* galimatias, *m.*

bosom ['buzəm], *n.* sein; (*fig.*) cœur, *m.*

boss (1) [bɔs], *n.* bosse, *f.*; moyeu (*d'une roue*), *m.*

boss (2) [bɔs], *n.* patron, chef, contremaître, *m.*—*v.t.* diriger, contrôler; régenter.

bosun [BOATSWAIN].

botanic [bɔ'tænik], **botanical** [bɔ'tænikəl] *a.* botanique.

botanist ['bɔtənist], *n.* botaniste, *m., f.*

botany ['bɔtəni], *n.* botanique, *f.*

botch [bɔtʃ], *n.* pustule, *f.*; (*fig.*) ravaudage, replâtrage, travail mal fait, *m.*—*v.t.* ravauder, replâtrer, saboter.

both [bouθ], *a.* and *pron.* tous les deux, tous deux, l'un et l'autre.—*conj.* tant, à la fois.

bother ['bɔðə], *v.t.* ennuyer, tracasser; (*colloq.*) embêter.—*n.* ennui, tracas, embêtement, *m.*

bottle ['bɔtl], *n.* bouteille, *f.*; flacon; biberon (*d'enfant*), *m.*; botte (*de foin*), *f.*; **hot water bottle**, bouillotte, *f.*—*v.t.* mettre en bouteille.

bottle-neck ['bɔtlnek], *n.* goulot; embouteillage (*de circulation routière*), *m.*

bottling ['bɔtliŋ], *n.* mise en bouteilles, *f.*

bottom ['bɔtəm], *n.* fond; bas; dessous, pied; derrière, *m.*; base; (*Naut.*) carène, *f.*

bottomless ['bɔtəmlis], *a.* sans fond.

boudoir ['bu:dwa:], *n.* boudoir, *m.*

bough [bau], *n.* branche, *f.*, rameau, *m.*

boulder ['bouldə], *n.* grosse pierre, *f.* bloc, *m.*

bounce [bauns], *v.i.* sauter, (re)bondir. —*n.* saut, (re)bond, *m.*

bouncer ['baunsə], *n.* (*pop.*) expulseur, videur, *m.*

bound (1) [baund], *n.* bond, saut *m.*—*v.i.* bondir, sauter.

bound (2) [baund], *n.* borne, limite, *f.*—*v.t.* borner, limiter.

bound (3) [baund], *a.* (*Naut.*) allant (*à*), en partance (*pour*).

bound (4) [baund], *past* and *p.p.* [BIND].

boundary ['baundri], *n.* limite, borne, frontière, *f.*

bounden ['baundən], *a.* obligatoire, impérieux.

boundless ['baundlis], *a.* sans bornes; illimité.

bounteous ['bauntiəs], **bountiful** ['bauntiful], *a.* libéral, généreux; abondant.

bounty ['baunti], *n.* bonté, générosité, libéralité, *f.*; don, *m.*

bouquet [bu'kei], *n.* bouquet, *m.*

bourne, bourn [bɔ:n], *n.* borne, frontière, limite, *f.*; terme, but, *m.*

bout [baut], *n.* tour, *m.*, partie, *f.*; accès, *m.*, crise, *f.*

bovine ['bouvain], *a.* bovin.

bow (1) [bau], *v.t.* courber, plier, fléchir, incliner.—*v.i.* se courber, s'incliner; saluer; se soumettre (*à*).—*n.* salut, *m.*, révérence, *f.*

bow (2) [bau], *n.* (*Naut.*) avant, bossoir, *m.*

bow (3) [bou], *n.* arc; archet (*de violon*); nœud (*rubans*), *m.*

bowels ['bauəlz], *n.pl.* entrailles, *f.pl.*, intestins, boyaux, *m.pl.*; (*fig.*) compassion, *f.*

bower ['bauə], *n.* berceau de verdure, *m.*, tonnelle, *f.*

bowl

bowl [boul], *n.* bol, vase, *m.*, coupe; jatte, *f.*; fourneau (*d'une pipe*), *m.*; boule (*sphère*), *f.*; (*pl.*) boules, *f.pl.*; **to play** (**at**) **bowls**, jouer aux boules.—*v.i.* rouler, faire rouler; (*Cricket*) lancer, bôler.

bow-legged ['bouleg(i)d], *a.* à jambes arquées, bancal.

bowler(-hat) ['boulə(hæt)], *n.* chapeau melon, *m.*

bowsprit ['bousprit], *n.* (*Naut.*) beaupré, *m.*

bow tie ['bou'tai], *n.* nœud carré, *m.*

bow window ['bou'windou], *n.* fenêtre en saillie, *f.*

box (1) [bɔks], *n.* boîte, *f.*; coffret (*petit*); coffre (*grand*), *m.*, caisse; malle; (*Theat.*) loge, *f.*; buis (*arbre*), *m.*—*v.t.* enfermer dans une boîte, emboîter, encaisser.

box (2) [bɔks], *v.t.* souffleter, gifler.—*v.i.* boxer.—*n.* soufflet, *m.*, gifle, *f.*

boxer ['bɔksə], *n.* boxeur, pugiliste, *m.*

boxing ['bɔksiŋ], *n.* la boxe, *f.*

box office ['bɔksɔfis], *n.* (*Theat.*) bureau de location, *m.*

boy [bɔi], *n.* garçon, petit garçon; fils, *m.*

boycott ['bɔikɔt], *v.t.* boycotter.

boycotting ['bɔikɔtiŋ], *n.* boycottage, *m.*

boyhood ['bɔihud], *n.* enfance, adolescence, *f.*

boyish ['bɔiiʃ], *a.* puéril; d'enfant, enfantin.

boy scout ['bɔi'skaut], *n.* (jeune) éclaireur, scout, *m.*

bra [brɑː], (*pop.*) [BRASSIÈRE].

brace [breis], *n.* couple (*gibier*); paire (*pistolets*), *f.*; vilebrequin (*outil*), *m.*; (*pl.*) bretelles, *f.pl.*—*v.t.* lier, serrer, attacher; (*fig.*) fortifier.

bracelet ['breislit], *n.* bracelet, *m.*

bracing ['breisiŋ], *a.* fortifiant, tonifiant.

bracken ['brækən], *n.* fougère, *f.*

bracket ['brækit], *n.* console, applique, *f.*, tasseau, *m.*; accolade, *f.*; bras (*pour une lampe etc.*), *m.*; (*Print.*) parenthèse, *f.*

brackish ['brækiʃ], *a.* saumâtre.

bradawl ['brædɔːl], *n.* poinçon, *m.*

brag [bræg], *v.i.* se vanter.—*n.* fanfaronnade, vanterie, *f.*

braggart ['brægət], *n.* fanfaron, *m.*

braid [breid], *n.* tresse; soutache, ganse, *f.*; lacet; galon, *m.*—*v.t.* tresser, natter, soutacher.

braille [breil], *n.* braille, *m.*

brain [brein], *n.* cerveau (*organe*), *m.*; cervelle (*substance*), *f.*; (*fig.*) jugement, esprit, *m.*; tête, *f.*

brainless ['breinlis], *a.* sans cervelle; stupide.

brainy ['breini], *a.* intelligent.

braise [breiz], *v.t.* braiser.

brake (1) [breik], *n.* fourré, hallier, *m.*, fougère (*thicket*), *f.*

brake (2) [breik], *n.* frein; *m.*; **to put on the brake**, serrer le frein.—*v.t.*, *v.i.* freiner.

braking ['breikiŋ], *n.* freinage, *m.*

bramble ['bræmbl], *n.* ronce, *f.*

bran [bræn], *n.* son, *m.*

branch [brɑːntʃ], *n.* branche, *f.*, rameau, *m.*; succursale (*d'une banque etc.*), *f.*—*v.i.* **to branch off**, s'embrancher, bifurquer; **to branch out**, se ramifier.

brand [brænd], *n.* brandon, tison; fer chaud, stigmate, *m.*; flétrissure (*d' infamie*); (*Comm.*) marque, *f.*—*v.t.* marquer au fer chaud; flétrir; (*fig.*) stigmatiser (*de*).

brandish ['brændiʃ], *v.t.* brandir.

brand-new ['brænd'njuː], *a.* tout (flambant) neuf.

brandy ['brændi], *n.* eau-de-vie, *f.*, cognac, *m.*

brash [bræʃ], *a.* effronté, présomptueux.

brass [brɑːs], *n.* cuivre jaune, laiton; (*fig.*) toupet, *m.*, effronterie, *f.*

brassière ['bræsjɛə], *n.* soutien-gorge, *m.*

brat [bræt], *n.* marmot, bambin, *m.*

bravado [brə'vɑːdou], *n.* bravade, *f.*

brave [breiv], *a.* courageux, brave, vaillant; (*fig.*) fameux, excellent.—*v.t.* braver, défier.

bravely ['breivli], *adv.* courageusement, bravement.

bravery ['breivəri], *n.* bravoure, *f.*, courage, *m.*

brawl [brɔːl], *n.* dispute, rixe, querelle, *f.*; bruit, tapage, *m.*—*v.i.* brailler, disputer.

brawler ['brɔːlə], *n.* tapageur; braillard, querelleur, *m.*

brawn [brɔːn], *n.* pâté de cochon, fromage de tête, *m.*; (*fig.*) muscles, *m.pl.*

brawny ['brɔːni], *a.* charnu, musculeux.

bray (1) [brei], *v.t.* broyer, piler.

bray (2) [brei], *v.i.* braire (*ânes etc.*); (*fig.*) résonner.—*n.* braiment, *m.*

brazen ['breizən], *a.* d'airain; (*fig.*) effronté, impudent.—*v.t.* **to brazen it out**, payer d'effronterie.

brazen-faced ['breizənfeist], *a.* à front d'airain; effronté.

brazier ['breiziə], *n.* chaudronnier, *m.*

Brazil [brə'zil]. le Brésil, *m.*

Brazilian [brə'ziljən], *a.* brésilien.—*n.* Brésilien (*personne*), *m.*

Brazil nut [brə'zilnʌt], *n.* noix du Brésil, *f.*

breach [briːtʃ], *n.* brèche, rupture; (*fig.*) violation, infraction, *f.*—*v.t.* battre en brèche.

bread [bred], *n.* pain, *m.*; **brown bread**, pain bis; **stale bread**, pain rassis.

breadcrumb ['bredkrʌm], *n.* miette, *f.*; (*pl.*) (*Cook.*) chapelure, *f.*, gratin, *m.*

breadth [bredθ], *n.* largeur, *f.*

bread-winner ['bredwinə], *n.* soutien de famille, *m.*

break [breik], *v.t. irr.* casser; briser; rompre; violer, enfreindre; ruiner; défricher (*terrain inculte*); (*fig.*) faire part de, communiquer (*une nouvelle*); amortir (*un choc*); **to break through the sound barrier**, franchir le mur du son.—*v.i.* se casser, se briser, se rompre, casser, rompre; éclater (*tempête etc.*); (*Comm.*) faire faillite; poindre (*jour*); changer (*temps*); **to break away**, se détacher; (*Mil.*) rompre les rangs; (*Box.*) cesser le corps-à-corps; **to break down**, s'abattre, se délabrer, s'effondrer, s'écrouler; (*Motor.*) tomber en panne; défaillir, s'altérer (*santé*); fondre en larmes; **to break in**, pénétrer dans; (*Motor.*) roder; **to break into**, entamer; éclater en; **to break loose**, s'échapper, s'évader; (*fig.*) s'émanciper; **to break off**, rompre, s'arrêter; **to break out**, éclater, se déclarer (*maladie*); jaillir, paraître, s'échapper; **to break up**, se disperser; entrer en vacances; **to break with**, rompre avec.—*n.* rupture, brisure, fracture; trouée, fente; (*fig.*) interruption, *f.*; changement (*de temps*); arrêt (*dans un voyage*), *m.*; (*Sch.*) récréation, *f.*; **break of day**, point du jour, *m.*

breakage ['breikidʒ], *n.* rupture, cassure; (*Comm.*) casse, *f.*

breakdown ['breikdaun], *n.* (*Motor., Mech.*) panne; (*fig.*) débâcle, *f.*; **nervous breakdown**, dépression nerveuse, *f.*

breaker ['breikə], *n.* infracteur, briseur; violateur; brisant (*mer*), *m.*

breakfast ['brekfəst], *n.* petit déjeuner, *m.*—*v.i.* prendre le petit déjeuner.

breakwater ['breikwɔ:tə], *n.* brise-lames, *m.*, digue, jetée, *f.*

bream [bri:m], *n.* (*Ichth.*) brème, *f.*

breast [brest], *n.* sein, *m.*, poitrine, *f.*; (*fig.*) cœur, *m.*, âme, conscience, *f.*; poitrail (*d'un cheval*), *m.*

breastplate ['brestpleit], *n.* cuirasse, *f.*

breath [breθ], *n.* haleine, respiration, *f.*, souffle, *m.*; (*fig.*) vie, existence, *f.*; **to be out of breath**, être hors d'haleine *ou* tout essoufflé.

breathe [bri:ð], *v.t.* respirer, souffler; **to breathe in**, aspirer; **to breathe one's last**, rendre le dernier soupir; **to breathe out**, exhaler.—*v.i.* respirer; souffler, reprendre haleine.

breathing-space ['bri:ðiŋ'speis], *n.* temps de respirer, relâche, répit, *m.*

breathless ['breθlis], *a.* hors d'haleine, essoufflé, haletant.

breech [bri:tʃ], *n.* culasse (*fusil*), *f.*—*v.t.* culotter.

breeches ['britʃiz], *n.pl.* culotte, *f.*

breed [bri:d], *v.t. irr.* élever; faire naître.—*v.i.* multiplier, se reproduire.—*n.* race, *f.*

breeder ['bri:də], *n.* éleveur, *m.*

breeding ['bri:diŋ], *n.* élevage (*de bestiaux etc.*), *m.*; reproduction; éducation, *f.*; **good breeding**, politesse, *f.*, savoir-vivre, *m.*

breeze [bri:z], *n.* (forte) brise, *f.*, vent assez fort, *m.*

breezy ['bri:zi], *a.* frais; jovial.

brevity ['breviti], *n.* brièveté, concision, *f.*

brew [bru:], *v.t.* brasser; faire une infusion; (*fig.*) tramer, machiner.—*v.i.* faire de la bière; (*fig.*) se préparer, se tramer, couver.

brewer ['bru:ə], *n.* brasseur, *m.*

brewery ['bru:əri], *n.* brasserie, *f.*

bribe [braib], *n.* présent (*dans le but de corrompre*); pot-de-vin, *m.*—*v.t.* gagner, corrompre, acheter.

bribery ['braibəri], *n.* corruption, *f.*

brick [brik], *a.* de briques, en briques.—*n.* brique, *f.*; (*fig.*) brave garçon, bon enfant, *m.*

brickbat ['brikbæt], *n.* briqueton, *m.*

brick kiln ['brikkiln], *n.* four à briques, *m.*

bricklayer ['brikleiə], *n.* maçon, *m.*

bridal [braidl], *a.* nuptial, de noces.—*n.* fête nuptiale, noce, *f.*

bride [braid], *n.* nouvelle mariée, mariée, *f.*

bridegroom ['braidgru:m], *n.* nouveau marié, *m.*

bridesmaid ['braidzmeid], *n.* demoiselle d'honneur, *f.*

bridge [bridʒ], *n.* pont, *m.*; passerelle (*de navire etc.*), *f.*; chevalet (*d'instrument à cordes*); dos (*du nez*); (*Cards*) bridge, *m.*—*v.t.* jeter un pont sur; (*fig.*) combler (*une lacune*).

bridge-head ['bridʒhed], *n.* tête de pont, *f.*, point d'appui, *m.*

Bridget ['bridʒit]. Brigitte, *f.*

bridle [braidl], *n.* bride, *f.*; (*fig.*) frein, *m.*—*v.t.* brider; (*fig.*) mettre un frein à.—*v.i.* redresser la tête, se rebiffer.

brief [bri:f], *a.* bref, court; (*fig.*) concis.—*n.* abrégé; dossier, *m.*—*v.t.* confier une cause à; donner des instructions à.

brief-case ['bri:fkeis], *n.* serviette, *f.*

briefly ['bri:fli], *adv.* brièvement, en peu de mots.

brier ['braiə], *n.* bruyère, *f.*; églantier, *m.*; (*pl.*) ronces, *f.pl.*

brig [brig], *n.* (*Naut.*) brick, *m.*

brigade [bri'geid], *n.* brigade, *f.*

brigadier [brigə'diə], *n.* général de brigade, *m.*

brigand ['brigənd], *n.* brigand, *m.*

brigantine ['brigənti:n], *n.* brigantin, *m.*

bright [brait], *a.* brillant; poli; clair, lumineux; éclatant, vif; (*fig.*) joyeux, intelligent.

brighten [braitn], *v.t.* faire briller; éclaircir, égayer; polir; (*fig.*) illustrer, embellir; dégourdir.—*v.i.* s'éclaircir; briller, étinceler.

brightly ['braitli], *adv.* brillamment, avec éclat.

brightness ['braitnis], *n.* brillant, *m.*; clarté, *f.*; éclat, *m.*; (*fig.*) joie, vivacité; intelligence, *f.*

brill [bril], *n.* (*Ichth.*) barbue, *f.*

brilliance ['briljəns], **brilliancy** ['briljənsi], *n.* lustre, éclat, *m.*

brilliant ['briljənt], *a.* brillant, éclatant.—*n.* brillant (*diamant*), *m.*

brilliantly ['briljəntli], *adv.* brillamment, avec éclat.

brim [brim], *n.* bord, *m.*—*v.i.* être plein jusqu'au bord; **brimming over**, débordant.

brimful ['brimful], *a.* rempli jusqu'au bord, tout plein.

brimstone ['brimstən], *n.* soufre, *m.*

brindle(d) [brindl(d)], *a.* tacheté, bringé.

brine [brain], *n.* saumure, *f.*

bring [briŋ], *v.t. irr.* apporter (*choses*); amener (*personnes et animaux*); conduire; porter (*to carry*); transporter; réduire (*to reduce*); (*fig.*) mettre; **to bring about**, amener, causer, opérer, provoquer; **to bring down**, descendre, abattre; **to bring forth**, produire, mettre au monde, mettre bas; **to bring forward**, amener, avancer; **to bring in**, faire entrer, rapporter; **to bring into play**, mettre en œuvre; **to bring off**, tirer d'affaire, sauver; conduire à bien, réussir; **to bring on**, amener, occasionner; **to bring to again**, faire reprendre connaissance à; **to bring together**, réunir, assembler, réconcilier; **to bring up**, nourrir, élever.

brink [briŋk], *n.* bord, *m.*

briny ['braini], *a.* saumâtre, salé; (*fig.*) amer.

brisk [brisk], *a.* vif; (*fig.*) animé, actif, gai, frais, dispos.

briskly ['briskli], *adv.* vivement.

briskness ['brisknis], *n.* vivacité; activité, *f.*

bristle [brisl], *n.* soie, *f.*; poil raide, *m.*—*v.i.* se hérisser (*de*); se raidir (*contre*).

bristling ['brisliŋ], **bristly** ['brisli], *a.* hérissé (*de*); (*Bot.*) poilu.

Britain ['britən]. la Grande-Bretagne, *f.*

Britannic [bri'tænik], *a.* (*rare*) britannique.

British ['britiʃ], *a.* britannique; **the British**, les Anglais, les Britanniques, *m.pl.*

Brittany

Brittany ['britəni]. la Bretagne, *f.*
brittle [britl], *a.* fragile, cassant.
brittleness ['britlnis], *n.* fragilité, *f.*
broach [broutʃ], *n.* broche, *f.*—*v.t.* embrocher; mettre (*un tonneau*) en perce; introduire, entamer (*un sujet*).
broad [brɔːd], *a.* large, grand, gros, vaste; (*fig.*) libre, grossier, hardi; peu voilé (*allusion*); prononcé (*accent*).
broadcast ['brɔːdkɑːst], *a.* à la volée; radiodiffusé.—*v.t. irr.* semer (*du grain*) à la volée; répandre (*une nouvelle*); radiodiffuser.—*n.* émission, *f.*
broadcaster ['brɔːdkɑːstə], *n.* speaker, *m.*
broadcasting ['brɔːdkɑːstiŋ], *n.* radiodiffusion, *f.*; **broadcasting station**, poste émetteur, *m.*
broaden [brɔːdn], *v.t.* élargir.—*v.i.* s'élargir, s'étendre.
broadly ['brɔːdli], *adv.* largement.
broad-minded ['brɔːd'maindid], *a.* tolérant, à l'esprit large.
broadness ['brɔːdnis], *n.* largeur; (*fig.*) grossièreté, *f.*
broadside ['brɔːdsaid], *n.* (*Naut.*) côté, flanc, *m.*; bordée, *f.*
brocade [broʹkeid], *n.* brocart, *m.*
brogue (1) [broug], *n.* accent irlandais, *m.*
brogue (2) [broug], *n.* brogue (*chaussure*), *f.*
broil (1) [brɔil], *n.* querelle, *f.*, tumulte, *m.*
broil (2) [brɔil], *v.t.* griller.—*v.i.* se griller.
broken ['broukən], *a.* cassé, brisé, rompu; (*fig.*) navré; entrecoupé, décousu (*discours etc.*); accidenté (*terrain*); interrompu (*sommeil*); délabré (*santé*).
broker ['broukə], *n.* courtier; brocanteur (*articles d'occasion*), *m.*; **ship broker**, courtier maritime; **stockbroker**, agent de change, *m.*
brokerage ['broukəridʒ], *n.* courtage, *m.*
bromide ['broumaid], *n.* bromure, *m.*
bromine ['broumi:n, 'broumain], *n.* brome, *m.*
bronchia ['brɔŋkiə], *n.pl.* bronches, *f.pl.*
bronchial ['brɔŋkiəl], *a.* bronchial.
bronchitis [brɔŋ'kaitis], *n.* bronchite, *f.*
bronze [brɔnz], *n.* bronze, *m.*
bronzed [brɔnzd], *a.* bronzé, basané.
brooch [broutʃ], *n.* broche, *f.*
brood [bruːd], *v.i.* couver; **to brood over**, rêver à, ruminer.—*n.* couvée, *f.*
broody ['bruːdi], *a.* couveuse (*poule*); distrait (*personne*).
brook (1) [bruk], *n.* ruisseau, *m.*
brook (2) [bruk], *v.t.* (*always neg.*) souffrir; avaler, digérer.
broom [bruːm], *n.* balai; genêt (*plante*), *m.*
broth [brɔθ], *n.* bouillon, potage, *m.*
brother ['brʌðə], *n.* (*pl.* **brothers** ['brʌðəz], *rhet.* **brethren** ['breðrin]) frère, *m.*; **brother in arms**, frère d'armes; **foster brother**, frère de lait.
brotherhood ['brʌðəhud], *n.* fraternité; confrérie, confraternité, *f.*
brother-in-law ['brʌðərinlɔː], *n.* beau-frère, *m.*
brotherly ['brʌðəli], *a.* fraternel.
brow [brau], *n.* front; sourcil; (*fig.*) sommet, *m.*
browbeat ['braubi:t], *v.t. irr.* (*conjug. like* BEAT) intimider, rudoyer.
brown [braun], *a.* brun; sombre, rembruni; châtain (*chevelure*); (*Cook.*) rissolé; **brown bread**, pain bis, *m.*; **brown study**, rêverie, *f.*; **brown sugar**, sucre brut, *m.*—

n. brun, *m.*—*v.t.* brunir; (*Cook.*) rissoler, faire dorer.
brownie ['brauni], *n.* jeannette, *f.*
brownish ['brauniʃ], *a.* brunâtre.
browse [brauz], *v.i.* brouter.
bruise [bruːz], *v.t.* meurtrir, contusionner; écraser, froisser.—*n.* meurtrissure, contusion, *f.*
brunette [bruːʹnet], *a.* and *n.* brune, *f.*
brunt [brʌnt], *n.* choc, *m.*; violence, fureur, *f.*; **to bear the brunt of**, faire tous les frais de.
brush [brʌʃ], *n.* brosse, *f.*; balai; pinceau, *m.*; (*fig.*) escarmouche; queue (*d'un renard*), *f.*—*v.t.* brosser; balayer; (*fig.*) effleurer, raser.
brush-maker ['brʌʃmeikə], *n.* brossier, *m.*
brushwood ['brʌʃwud], *n.* broussailles, *f.pl.*, fourré, *m.*
brusque [brusk], *a.* brusque.
Brussels [brʌslz]. Bruxelles, *f.*; **Brussels sprouts**, choux de Bruxelles, *m.pl.*
brutal [bruːtl], *a.* brutal, cruel, inhumain.
brutality [bruːʹtæliti], *n.* brutalité, cruauté, *f.*
brutally ['bruːtəli], *adv.* brutalement.
brute [bruːt], *a.* brut, insensible; sauvage; brutal (*animaux*).—*n.* animal, *m.*, brute, bête, *f.*, brutal, *m.*
bubble [bʌbl], *n.* bulle; (*fig.*) chimère, illusion; duperie, *f.*—*v.i.* bouillonner; pétiller (*vin*).
bubonic [bjuːʹbɔnik], *a.* bubonique.
buccaneer [bʌkəʹniə], *n.* boucanier, flibustier, *m.*
buck [bʌk], *n.* daim; chevreuil; mâle (*lièvre ou lapin*); (*fig.*) gaillard, beau, élégant, *m.*
bucket ['bʌkit], *n.* seau; baquet, *m.*
buckle [bʌkl], *n.* boucle, agrafe, *f.*—*v.t.* boucler, agrafer.—*v.i.* se boucler; se courber.
buckler ['bʌklə], *n.* bouclier, *m.*
buckram ['bʌkrəm], *n.* bougran, *m.*
buckwheat ['bʌkwiːt], *n.* sarrasin, blé noir, *m.*
bucolic [bjuːʹkɔlik], *a.* bucolique.—*n.* poème bucolique, *m.*
bud [bʌd], *n.* bourgeon, bouton; (*fig.*) germe, *m.*—*v.t.* écussonner.—*v.i.* bourgeonner.
Buddha ['budə], *n.* Bouddha, *m.*
Buddhism ['budizm], *n.* bouddhisme, *m.*
Buddhist ['budist], *n.* bouddhiste, *m., f.*
budge [bʌdʒ], *v.t.* bouger.—*v.i.* bouger, se remuer.
budgerigar [bʌdʒəriʹgɑː], *n.* (*Orn.*) perruche inséparable, *f.*
budget ['bʌdʒit], *n.* sac; (*Fin.*) budget, *m.*
buff [bʌf], *a.* de couleur chamois.—*n.* buffle, *m.*, peau de buffle; couleur chamois, *f.*—*v.t.* polir au buffle.
buffalo ['bʌfəlou], *n.* buffle, *m.*
buffer ['bʌfə], *n.* tampon, amortisseur, *m.*
buffet (1) [buʹfei], *n.* buffet (*sideboard*); buffet (*meal*), *m.*
buffet (2) ['bʌfit], *v.t.* frapper à coups de poing, souffleter.—*v.i.* se battre à coups de poing.—*n.* soufflet, coup de poing, *m.*
buffoon [bʌʹfuːn], *n.* bouffon, *m.*
buffoonery [bʌʹfuːnəri], *n.* bouffonnerie, *f.*
bug [bʌg], *n.* punaise, *f.*, insecte, *m.*
bugle [bjuːgl], *n.* cor de chasse; (*Mil.*) clairon, *m.*
bugler ['bjuːglə], *n.* clairon, *m.*
build [bild], *v.t. irr.* bâtir, faire bâtir, construire; (*fig.*) édifier, fonder, baser.—*n.* construction; forme, carrure, taille, *f.*

builder ['bɪldə], n. constructeur, entrepreneur de maçonnerie, m.

building ['bɪldɪŋ], n. construction, f.; édifice, bâtiment, m.; *building and loan association*, société immobilière, f.

bulb [bʌlb], n. bulbe, oignon, m.; cuvette (de thermomètre); poire (en caoutchouc); (Elec.) ampoule, lampe, f.

bulbous ['bʌlbəs], a. bulbeux.

Bulgaria [bʌl'gɛəriə], la Bulgarie, f.

Bulgarian [bʌl'gɛəriən], a. bulgare.—n. bulgare (langue), m.; Bulgare (personne), m., f.

bulge [bʌldʒ], n. bombement, m., bosse, f.—v.t., v.i. faire saillie, bomber.

bulging ['bʌldʒiŋ], a. bombé.

bulk [bʌlk], n. volume, m., grosseur; masse, f., gros, m.; (Naut.) charge, f.; *in bulk*, en bloc, en gros.

bulkhead ['bʌlkhed], n. cloison étanche, f.

bulky ['bʌlki], a. gros, encombrant.

bull (1) [bul], n. taureau; (St. Exch.) haussier, m.

bull (2) [bul], n. bulle (du Pape), f.

bulldog ['buldɔg], n. bouledogue, m.

bulldozer ['buldouzə], n. bulldozer, m.

bullet ['bulit], n. balle, f.

bulletin ['bulitin], n. bulletin, communiqué, m. [*bulletin board*, see notice-board]

bullet-proof ['bulitpru:f], a. à l'épreuve des balles.

bullfinch ['bulfintʃ], n. (Orn.) bouvreuil, m.

bullion ['buljən], n. or ou argent en lingots, m.

bullock ['bulək], n. bœuf, bouvillon, m.

bull's-eye ['bulzai], n. centre, noir (d'une cible); œil-de-bœuf (fenêtre), m.

bully ['buli], n. matamore, bravache, m.; brute, f.—v.t. malmener, intimider.—v.i. faire le matamore.

bulrush ['bulrʌʃ], n. (Bot.) jonc, m.

bulwark ['bulwək], n. rempart, m.; (Naut.) pavois, m.

bumble-bee ['bʌmblbi:], n. bourdon, m.

bump [bʌmp], n. bosse, f.; heurt, cahot, coup, choc, m.—v.t. frapper, cogner.—v.i. se cogner, se heurter.

bumper ['bʌmpə], n. rasade, f., rouge-bord; (Motor.) pare-choc, m.

bumpkin ['bʌmpkin], n. rustre, lourdaud, m.

bumpy ['bʌmpi], a. cahoteux (route).

bun [bʌn], n. petit pain rond(au lait);chignon (coiffure), m.

bunch [bʌntʃ], n. botte, f.; bouquet, m., gerbe (de fleurs); grappe (de raisins), f.; régime (de bananes); trousseau (de clefs), m.

bundle [bʌndl], n. paquet; ballot; faisceau; fagot (de bois etc.), m.; liasse (de papiers), f.—v.t. empaqueter.

bung [bʌŋ], n. bondon, tampon, m.—v.t. boucher.

bungalow ['bʌŋgəlou], n. maison sans étage, f.

bung-hole ['bʌŋhoul], n. bonde, f.

bungle [bʌŋgl], v.t. bousiller, gâcher, rater.—v.i. s'y prendre gauchement, faire de la mauvaise besogne.—n. bousillage; gâchis, m.

bungler ['bʌŋglə], n. maladroit, savetier, bousilleur, m.

bungling ['bʌŋgliŋ], a. maladroit, gauche.

bunion ['bʌnjən], n. oignon (de pied), m.

bunk [bʌŋk], n. (Naut.) couchette, f.

bunker ['bʌŋkə], n. soute (à charbon); (Golf) banquette, f.

bunting ['bʌntiŋ], n. étamine, f.; (Orn.) bruant, m.; (fig.) drapeaux, pavillons, m.pl.

buoy [bɔi], n. bouée, f.; *life buoy*, bouée de sauvetage; *mooring buoy*, coffre d'amarrage, m.—v.t. to buoy up, soutenir sur l'eau; (fig.) encourager.

buoyancy ['bɔiənsi], n. légèreté, f.; élan, m.; vivacité, animation, f.

buoyant ['bɔiənt], a. léger, flottant; animé, vif.

burble [bə:bl], v.i. murmurer, bafouiller.—n. murmure, m.

burden [bə:dn], n. fardeau, m.; charge, f.; poids; refrain (d'une chanson), m.—v.t. charger.

burdensome ['bə:dnsəm], a. pesant, lourd; ennuyeux.

bureau [bjuə'rou], n. bureau, m.

bureaucracy [bjuə'rɔkrəsi], n. bureaucratie, f.

bureaucrat ['bjuərokræt], n. bureaucrate, m., f.

bureaucratic [bjuəro'krætik], a. bureaucratique.

burgess ['bə:dʒis], n. bourgeois, citoyen, électeur, m.

burgh ['bʌrə], n. (Sc.) bourg, m.

burglar ['bə:glə], n. cambrioleur, m.

burglary ['bə:gləri], n. vol avec effraction; cambriolage, m.

burgle [bə:gl], v.t., v.i. cambrioler.

burgomaster ['bə:gəma:stə], n. bourgmestre, m.

burial ['beriəl], n. enterrement, m., obsèques, f.pl.; inhumation, f.

burlesque [bə:'lesk], a. and n. burlesque, m.—v.t. parodier, travestir.

burliness ['bə:linis], ɴ. grosseur, corpulence, f.

burly ['bə:li], a. de forte carrure.

Burma(h) [bə:mə]. la Birmanie, f.

Burmese [bə:'mi:z], a. birman.—n. birman (langue); Birman (personne), m.

burn [bə:n], v.t. irr. brûler; cuire (briques etc.); incendier.—v.i. brûler; (fig.) brûler, être impatient de.—n. brûlure, f.

burner ['bə:nə], n. brûleur; bec (de gaz etc.), m.

burning ['bə:niŋ], a. en feu; brûlant, ardent.—n. brûlure, f.; incendie, m.

burnish ['bə:niʃ], v.t. brunir, polir.

burrow ['bʌrou], n. terrier, trou, m.—v.t. creuser.—v.i. se terrer; (fig.) se cacher.

bursar ['bə:sə], n. économe, intendant; trésorier; boursier, m.

bursary ['bə:səri], n. bourse (d'études), f.

burst [bə:st], v.t. irr. crever; faire éclater; fendre; rompre.—v.i. crever, éclater; sauter; jaillir; s'élancer; éclore (bourgeon); to burst into tears, fondre en larmes; to burst out laughing, éclater de rire.—n. éclat, éclatement, m., explosion; rupture, hernie, f.

bury ['beri], v.t. enterrer, ensevelir; (fig.) enfoncer; cacher.

bus [bʌs], n. autobus, m.

bus conductor ['bʌskəndʌktə], n. receveur (d'autobus), m.

bush [buʃ], n. buisson; fourré, m.

bushel ['buʃl], n. boisseau, m.

bushy ['buʃi], a. buissonneux; touffu.

367

busily ['bizili], *adv.* activement; avec empressement.

business ['biznis], *n.* affaire, occupation, *f.,* devoir; état, métier, *m.*; affaires, *f.pl.,* commerce, *m.*; *what business is that of yours ?* est-ce que cela vous regarde ? *you have no business here,* vous n'avez que faire ici; *business suit,* complet veston, *m.*

businesslike ['biznislaik], *a.* pratique, régulier, méthodique; franc, droit, sérieux.

buskin ['baskin], *n.* brodequin; *(fig.)* cothurne, *m.*

bust [bast], *n. (Sculp.)* buste, *m.*; gorge *(de femme)*; *(Art)* bosse, *f.*

bustard ['bastəd], *n. (Orn.)* outarde, *f.*

bustle [basl], *n.* mouvement; bruit, *m.,* confusion, activité, agitation, *f.—v.i.* se remuer, s'empresser.

bustling ['baslin], *a.* empressé, affairé, remuant; bruyant.

busy ['bizi], *a.* affairé, occupé, empressé, diligent.—*v.r.* *to busy oneself,* s'occuper.

busybody ['bizibɔdi], *n.* officieux, *m.*

but [bat], *conj.* mais, que; sauf que; qui ne; *but that,* sans que.—*adv.* ne . . . que; seulement; *all but,* presque.—*prep.* sans, excepté, à part.

butcher ['butʃə], *n.* boucher, *m.*; *butcher's shop,* boucherie, *f.—v.t.* égorger, massacrer.

butchery ['butʃəri], *n.* boucherie, tuerie, *f.,* massacre, carnage, *m.*

butler ['batlə], *n.* maître d'hôtel, *m.*

butt (1) [bat], *n.* bout, *m.*; crosse *(d'un fusil)*; masse *(d'une queue de billard), f.*

butt (2) [bat], *n.* cible, *f.*; *(fig.)* point de mire; plastron *(personne), m.*

butt (3) [bat], *n.* coup de tête, *m.—v.t.* cosser, frapper de la tête *(animal).*

butt (4) [bat], *n.* barrique, *f.*

butter ['batə], *n.* beurre, *m.—v.t.* beurrer.

buttercup ['batəkap], *n.* bouton d'or, *m.*

butter dish ['batədiʃ], *n.* beurrier, *m.*

butterfly ['batəflai], *n.* papillon, *m.*

buttermilk ['batəmilk], *n.* petit-lait, *m.*

buttery ['batəri], *a.* de beurre, graisseux.—*n.* dépense, *f.*

buttock ['batək], *n.* fesse; croupe *(de cheval)*; culotte *(de bœuf), f.*

button ['batn], *n.* bouton, *m.—v.t.* boutonner. —*v.i.* se boutonner.

buttonhole ['batnhoul], *n.* boutonnière, *f.—v.t.* accrocher *(quelqu'un).*

button-hook ['batnhuk], *n.* tire-bouton, *m.*

buttress ['batris], *n.* contrefort, éperon, *m.*; *flying buttress,* arc-boutant, *m.—v.t.* arcbouter.

buxom ['baksəm], *a.* plein de santé et d'entrain; rondelette et fraîche *(femme).*

buy [bai], *v.t. irr.* acheter; prendre *(billet)*; corrompre, acheter *(quelqu'un)*; *to buy up,* accaparer.

buyer ['baiə], *n.* acheteur, acquéreur, *m.*

buying ['baiin], *n.* achat, *m.*

buzz [baz], *v.i.* bourdonner.—*n.* bourdonnement; brouhaha *(de conversation), m.*

buzzard ['bazəd], *n. (Orn.)* buse, *f.*

buzzer ['bazə], *n.* trompe, *f.*; vibreur, appel vibré, *m.*

by [bai], *prep.* par; de; à; sur; près de, auprès de, à côté de; en *(with participles)*; *by far,* de beaucoup; *by no means,* nullement; *by sight,* de vue.—*adv.* près; passé.

by-election ['baiilekʃən], *n.* élection partielle, *f.*

bygone ['baigɔn], *a.* passé, d'autrefois.

by-pass ['baipɑːs], *n.* route d'évitement, déviation, *f.—v.t.* contourner, éviter *(une ville).*

by-play ['baiplei], *n.* jeu de scène, jeu muet, *m.*

by-product ['baiprɔdakt], *n.* sous-produit, *m.*

byre ['baiə], *n.* étable à vaches, *f.*

bystander ['baistændə], *n.* spectateur, assistant, *m.*

byword ['baiwəːd], *n.* dicton, proverbe, *m.*; *(fig.)* risée, *f.*

C

C, c [siː]. troisième lettre de l'alphabet; *(Mus.)* ut, do, *m.*

cab [kæb], *n.* fiacre, taxi, *m.*

cabal [kə'bæl], *n.* cabale, *f.—v.i.* cabaler.

cabbage ['kæbidʒ], *n.* chou, *m.*

cabin ['kæbin], *n.* cabine, chambre *(pour officiers etc.)*; *(Av.)* carlingue; cabane, case, hutte, *f.*

cabin boy ['kæbinbɔi], *n.* mousse, *m.*

cabinet ['kæbinit], *n.* meuble à tiroirs; classeur; cabinet; ministère, *m.*

cabinet-maker ['kæbinit'meikə], *n.* ébéniste, *m., f.*

cable [keibl], *n.* câble; câblogramme, *m.—v.t.* câbler, télégraphier.

cablegram ['keiblgræm], *n.* câblogramme, *m.*

caboose [kə'buːs], *n. (Naut.)* cuisine, cambuse, *f.*

cackle [kækl], *n.* caquet, *m.—v.i.* caqueter; *(fig.)* ricaner, glousser; cacarder *(oie).*

cackling ['kæklin], *n.* caquetage, *m.*

cactus ['kæktəs], *n.* cactus, *m.*

cad [kæd], *n.* goujat, *m.*; canaille, *f.*

cadaverous [kə'dævərəs], *a.* cadavéreux.

caddie ['kædi], *n. (Golf)* cadet, *m.—v.i.* servir de cadet.

caddy ['kædi], *n.* boîte à thé, *f.*

cadet [kə'det], *n.* cadet; élève-officier (d'une école militaire *ou* d'une école navale), *m.*

cadge [kædʒ], *v.t., v.i.* colporter; quémander; écornifler.

cage [keidʒ], *n.* cage, *f.—v.t.* mettre en cage.

Cairo ['kaiərou]. le Caire, *m.*

cajole [kə'dʒoul], *v.t.* cajoler, enjôler.

cake [keik], *n.* gâteau, *m.*; masse, croûte *(matière solidifiée), f.*; *cake of soap,* savonnette, *f.—v.i.* se cailler, se prendre, se coller.

calamitous [kə'læmitəs], *a.* calamiteux, désastreux, funeste.

calamity [kə'læmiti], *n.* calamité, *f.,* désastre, malheur, *m.*

calculate ['kælkjuleit], *v.t.* calculer; compter; évaluer.

calculation [kælkju'leiʃən], *n.* calcul, compte, *m.*

calculus ['kælkjuləs], *n.* (*Med.*) calcul; (*Math.*) calcul infinitésimal, *m.*
Caledonia [kæli'douniə]. la Calédonie, *f.*
calendar ['kæləndə], *n.* calendrier, *m.*; (*Law*) liste, *f.*
calender ['kæləndə], *n.* calandre, *f.*
calends ['kæləndz], *n.pl.* calendes, *f.pl.*
calf [kɑːf], *n.* (*pl.* **calves** [kɑːvz]) veau; mollet (*de la jambe*), *m.*
calibre ['kælibə], *n.* calibre; (*Tech.*) compas, *m.*
calibrate ['kælibreit], *v.t.* calibrer, graduer.
calico ['kælikou], *n.* indienne, *f.*
California [kæli'fɔːniə]. la Californie, *f.*
caliph ['keilif], *n.* calife, *m.*
calk [kɔːk], *v.t.* ferrer à glace (*cheval etc.*).
call [kɔːl], *n.* appel, cri, *m.*; voix, *f.*; (*Naut.*) sifflet, *m.*; (*fig.*) obligation, *f.*, devoir, *m.*; demande, invitation; visite, *f.*; coup de téléphone, *m.*; **within call**, à portée de voix.—*v.t.* appeler; nommer, qualifier (*de*); convoquer; rappeler; **to be called Peter**, s'appeler Pierre; **to call for**, demander, exiger; aller chercher; **to call in**, faire rentrer; **to call in a doctor**, faire venir un médecin; **to call off**, rappeler, rompre, décommander; **to call out**, appeler, crier; **to call to mind**, se rappeler; **to call up**, faire monter; réveiller; appeler sous les drapeaux, mobiliser.—*v.i.* appeler, crier; venir *ou* aller (*chez*), rendre visite (*à*); (*Naut.*) toucher (*à*); **to call at**, passer par, s'arrêter à; **to call on**, inviter, prier, rendre visite à; **to call upon**, faire appel (*à quelqu'un*).
call-box ['kɔːlbɔks], *n.* cabine téléphonique, *f.*
call-boy ['kɔːlbɔi], *n.* (*Theat.*) avertisseur, *m.*
caller ['kɔːlə], *n.* visiteur, *m.*; (*Teleph.*) celui *ou* celle qui appelle, *m.*, *f.*
calling ['kɔːliŋ], *n.* appel, *m.*; profession, vocation, *f.*, métier, état, *m.*
callipers ['kælipəz], *n.* compas de calibre, *m.*
callous ['kæləs], *a.* calleux, endurci; insensible.
callously ['kæləsli], *adv.* durement, impitoyablement.
callousness ['kæləsnis], *n.* insensibilité, *f.*, endurcissement, *m.*
callow ['kælou], *a.* sans plume; (*fig.*) jeune, novice.
call-up ['kɔːlʌp], *n.* (*Mil.*) appel sous les drapeaux, *m.*
calm [kɑːm], *a.* and *n.* calme, *m.*—*v.t.* calmer, apaiser.
calmly ['kɑːmli], *adv.* avec calme, tranquillement.
calorie ['kæləri], *n.* calorie, *f.*
calumniate [kə'lʌmnieit], *v.t.* calomnier.
calumnious [kə'lʌmniəs], *a.* calomnieux.
calumny ['kæləmni], *n.* calomnie, *f.*
calvary ['kælvəri], *n.* calvaire; chemin de la croix, *m.*
calve [kɑːv], *v.i.* vêler.
calves [kɑːvz]. *n.pl.* [CALF].
calyx ['keiliks, 'kæliks], *n.* calice, *m.*
cam [kæm], *n.* (*Mech.*) came, *f.*
camber ['kæmbə], *n.* cambrure, *f.*
Cambodia [kæm'boudiə]. le Cambodge, *m.*
Cambodian [kæm'boudiən], *a.* cambodgien.—*n.* cambodgien (*langue*); Cambodgien (*personne*), *m.*
cambric ['keimbrik], *n.* batiste, *f.*

camel ['kæməl], *n.* chameau, *m.*
camellia [kə'miːljə], *n.* camélia, *m.*
camel hair ['kæməlhɛə], *n.* poil de chameau, *m.*
cameo ['kæmiou], *n.* camée, *m.*
camera ['kæmərə], *n.* appareil (photographique), *m.*; **movie camera**, (ciné)caméra, *f.*
cameraman ['kæmərəmæn], *n.* (*pl.* **cameramen** ['kæmərəmen]) photographe (*de presse*); (*Cine. Tel.*) opérateur, cameraman, *m.*
camouflage ['kæmuflɑːʒ], *n.* camouflage, *m.*—*v.t.* camoufler.
camp [kæmp], *n.* camp, *m.*; **to break up a camp**, lever un camp; **to pitch a camp**, établir un camp.—*v.i.* camper.
campaign [kæm'pein], *n.* campagne, *f.*—*v.i.* faire campagne.
campaigner [kæm'peinə], *n.* vieux soldat, *m.*
campanile [kæmpə'niːli], *n.* campanile, *m.*
campanula [kæm'pænjulə], *n.* (*Bot.*) campanule, *f.*
camp bed ['kæmpbed], *n.* lit de camp, *m.*
camper ['kæmpə], *n.* campeur, *m.*
camphor ['kæmfə], *n.* camphre, *m.*
camping ['kæmpiŋ], *n.* (*Mil.*) campement; camping, *m.*; **to go camping**, faire du camping.
can (1) [kæn], *n.* pot, broc, bidon, *m.*; boîte en fer blanc, *f.*—*v.t.* mettre en boîte.
can (2) [kæn], *v. aux. irr.* (*inf.* **to be able**) pouvoir (*to be able*); savoir (*to know how to*); **he can read**, il sait lire; **I can do it**, je peux *ou* je sais le faire.
Canada ['kænədə]. le Canada, *m.*
Canadian [kə'neidiən], *a.* canadien.—*n.* Canadien (*personne*), *m.*
canal [kə'næl], *n.* canal, *m.*
canary [kə'nɛəri], *n.* (*Orn.*) serin, *m.*
cancel ['kænsəl], *v.t.* annuler; effacer, biffer, rayer; oblitérer (*un timbre*); décommander; (*Comm.*) résilier.
cancellation [kænsə'leiʃən], *n.* annulation; résiliation, oblitération, *f.*
cancer ['kænsə], *n.* cancer, *m.*
cancerous ['kænsərəs], *a.* cancéreux.
candelabrum [kændi'lɑːbrəm], **candelabra** [kændi'lɑːbrə], *n.* candélabre, *m.*
candid ['kændid], *a.* sincère, franc.
candidate ['kændidit], *n.* aspirant, candidat, *m.*
candidature ['kænditʃə], *n.* candidature, *f.*
candidly ['kændidli], *adv.* franchement, de bonne foi.
candle ['kændl], *n.* chandelle; bougie; (*fig.*) lumière, *f.*; (*Ch.*) cierge, *m.*
Candlemas ['kændlməs]. la Chandeleur, *f.*
candlestick ['kændlstik], *n.* chandelier; bougeoir, *m.*
candle wax ['kændlwæks], *n.* suif, *m.*
candor ['kændə], *n.* franchise, sincérité, bonne foi, *f.*
candy ['kændi], *n.* candi, *m.*; (*Am.*) bonbons, *m.pl.*
cane [kein], *n.* canne, *f.*
canine ['kænain, 'keinain], *a.* canin, de chien.
caning ['keiniŋ], *n.* coups de canne, *m.pl.*, râclée, *f.*

369

canister ['kænistə], *n.* boîte en fer blanc; boîte à thé, *f.*

canker ['kæŋkə], *n.* chancre; (*fig.*) ver rongeur; fléau, *m.—v.t.* ronger; (*fig.*) corrompre, empoisonner.—*v.i.* se ronger; (*fig.*) se gangrener, se corrompre.

canned [kænd], *a.* (*Am.*) conservé en boîtes (*fruits etc.*); (*fam.*) enregistré (*musique*).

cannibal ['kænibəl], *n.* cannibale, anthropophage, *m., f.*

cannibalism ['kænibəlizm], *n.* cannibalisme, *m.*

cannon ['kænən], *n.* canon; (*Billiards*) carambolage, *m.—v.i.* caramboler.

cannonade [kænə'neid], *n.* cannonade, *f.*

cannon ball ['kænənbɔ:l], *n.* boulet de canon, *m.*

canoe [kə'nu:], *n.* canoë, *m.*; périssoire; pirogue, *f.*

canoeist [kə'nu:ist], *n.* canoëiste, *m., f.*

canon ['kænən], *n.* chanoine; canon (*règle*), *m.*

canonical [kə'nɔnikl], *a.* canonique.

canonization [kænənai'zeifən], *n.* canonisation, *f.*

canonize ['kænənaiz], *v.t.* canoniser.

can opener ['kænoupənə], *n.* (*Am.*) ouvre-boîte, *m.*

canopy ['kænəpi], *n.* dais; (*Arch.*) baldaquin, *m.*; voûte (*du ciel*), *f.*

cant (1) [kænt], *n.* cant, langage hypocrite, *m.*; afféterie; hypocrisie, *f.—v.i.* parler avec afféterie ou avec affectation

cant (2) [kænt], *n.* (*Arch.*) pan coupé, *m.—v.t.* pousser, jeter de côté, incliner.

cantankerous [kæn'tæŋkərəs], *a.* acariâtre, revêche, bourru.

cantankerousness [kæn'tæŋkərəsnis], *n.* humeur acariâtre, *f.*

cantata [kæn'tɑ:tə], *n.* cantate, *f.*

canteen [kæn'ti:n], *n.* cantine, *f.*; restaurant; bidon (*boîte*), *m.*; **canteen of cutlery**, ménagère, *f.*

canter ['kæntə], *n.* petit galop, *m.—v.i.* aller au petit galop.

canticle ['kæntikl], *n.* cantique, *m.*

cantilever ['kæntiliːvə], *n.* (*Arch.*) encorbellement, modillon, *m.*

canto ['kæntou], *n.* chant, *m.*

canton ['kæntən], *n.* canton, *m.*

cantonment [kæn'tu:mənt], *n.* cantonnement, *m.*

canvas ['kænvəs], *n.* toile, *f.*; tableau, *m.*, peinture; voile, toile à voiles, *f.*; **under canvas**, sous la tente.

canvass ['kænvəs], *n.* débat, *m.*, discussion; sollicitation de suffrages, *f.—v.t.* agiter, discuter; solliciter.—*v.i.* solliciter des suffrages; faire la place.

canvasser ['kænvəsə], *n.* agent électoral; (*Comm.*) représentant, *m.*

canvassing ['kænvəsiŋ], *n.* propagande électorale; (*Comm.*) prospection, *f.*

canyon ['kænjən], *n.* gorge, *f.*, défilé, *m.*

cap [kæp], *n.* bonnet (*de femme*), *m.*; casquette (*d'homme*); barrette (*d'un cardinal*); capsule, amorce (*d'armes à feu*), *f.*; (*Phot.*) chapeau (*d'un objectif etc.*); capuchon (*d'un stylo*), *m.* —*v.t.* coiffer, couvrir; (*fig.*) couronner, surpasser.

capability [keipə'biliti], *n.* capacité, *f.*

capable ['keipəbl], *a.* capable; susceptible (*de*); compétent.

capacious [kə'peifəs], *a.* ample, vaste, spacieux.

capaciousness [kə'peifəsnis], *n.* capacité, étendue, *f.*

capacitate [kə'pæsiteit], *v.t.* rendre capable de.

capacity [kə'pæsiti], *n.* capacité, *f.*; **in the capacity of**, en qualité de.

cap-à-pie [kæpə'pi:], *adv.* de pied en cap.

caparison [kə'pærizn], *n.* caparaçon, *m.—v.t.* caparaçonner.

cape (1) [keip], *n.* cap, promontoire, *m.*

cape (2) [keip], *n.* pèlerine, cape (*manteau*), *f.*

caper (1) ['keipə], *n.* bond, entrechat, *m.—v.i.* cabrioler; bondir, sauter.

caper (2) ['keipə], *n.* (*Bot.*) câpre, *f.*

capillary [kə'piləri], *a.* capillaire.

capital ['kæpitl], *a.* capital; (*collog.*) excellent; (*Print.*) majuscule.—*n.* capital, *m.*, capitaux, *m.pl.*; capitale (*ville*), *f.*; (*Comm.*) fonds; (*Arch.*) chapiteau, *m.*; (*Print.*) majuscule, *f.*

capitalism ['kæpitəlizm], *n.* capitalisme, *m.*

capitalist ['kæpitəlist], *n.* capitaliste, *m., f.*

capitalize ['kæpitəlaiz], *v.t.* capitaliser.

capitally ['kæpitəli], *adv.* principalement; admirablement, à merveille.

capitulate [kə'pitjuleit], *v.i.* capituler.

capitulation [kəpitju'leifən], *n.* capitulation, *f.*

capon ['keipən], *n.* chapon, *m.*

caprice [kə'pri:s], *n.* caprice, *m.*

capricious [kə'prifəs], *a.* capricieux.

capriciously [kə'prifəsli], *adv.* capricieusement.

capsize [kæp'saiz], *v.t.* faire chavirer.—*v.i.* chavirer (*bateau*).

capstan ['kæpstən], *n.* cabestan, *m.*

capsule ['kæpsju:l], *n.* capsule, *f.*

captain ['kæptin], *n.* capitaine, *m.*

caption ['kæpfən], *n.* arrestation; saisie (*choses*), *f.*; en-tête (*d'un chapitre etc.*), *m.*, légende (*d'une photographie etc.*), *f.*; (*Cine.*) sous-titre, *m.*

captious ['kæpfəs], *a.* insidieux, chicaneur.

captiousness ['kæpfəsnis], *n.* esprit de chicane; sophisme, *m.*

captivate ['kæptiveit], *v.t.* captiver; charmer, séduire.

captivating ['kæptiveitiŋ], *a.* enchanteur, séduisant.

captive ['kæptiv], *a.* captif.—*n.* captif, prisonnier, *m.*

captivity [kæp'tiviti], *n.* captivité, *f.*

capture ['kæptfə], *n.* capture; prise, arrestation, *f.—v.t.* capturer, prendre, arrêter.

car [kɑ:], *n.* (*Motor.*) auto, voiture, *f.*; (*Rail.*) wagon; (*Lit.*) char, chariot, *m.*; nacelle (*d'un ballon*), *f.*; **dining car**, wagon-restaurant, *m.*; **sleeping car**, wagon-lit, *m.* **[freight car**, see van]

caramel ['kærəmel], *n.* caramel, *m.*

carat ['kærət], *n.* carat, *m.*

caravan [kærə'væn, 'kærəvæn], *n.* caravane; roulotte, *f.*

caravanserai [kærə'vænsərai], *n.* caravansérail, *m.*

caraway ['kærəwei], *n.* (*Bot.*) carvi, cumin des prés, *m.*

carbide ['kɑ:baid], *n.* carbure, *m.*

carbine ['kɑ:bain], *n.* carabine, *f.*

carbohydrate [kɑ:bou'haidreit], *n.* hydrate de carbone, *m.*

carbolic [ka:ˈbɔlik], *a.* phénique.
carbon [ˈka:bən], *n.* (*Chem.*) carbone; (*Elec.*) charbon, *m.*
carbonic [ka:ˈbɔnik], *a.* carbonique.
carboniferous [ka:bəˈnifərəs], *a.* carbonifère.
carboy [ˈka:bɔi], *n.* tourie, bonbonne, *f.*
carbuncle [ˈka:bʌŋkl], *n.* escarboucle, *f.*; (*Med.*) charbon, furoncle, *m.*
carburation [ka:bjuˈreiʃən], *n.* carburation, *f.*
carburetor [ka:bjuˈreta], *n.* carburateur, *m.*
carcase, carcass [ˈka:kəs], *n.* carcasse, *f.*; cadavre, *m.*
card [ka:d], *n.* carte à jouer; fiche, carte; (*Manuf.*) carde, *f.*—*v.t.* carder.
cardboard [ˈka:dbɔ:d], *n.* carton, *m.*
cardiac [ˈka:diæk], *a.* cardiaque.
cardigan [ˈka:digən], *n.* gilet de tricot, *m.*
cardinal [ˈka:dinl], *a.* cardinal, fondamental. —*n.* cardinal, *m.*
card index [ˈka:dindeks], *n.* fichier, *m.*—*v.t.* encarter.
cardiograph [ˈka:diogræf, -gra:f], *n.* cardiographe, *m.*
card-sharper [ˈka:dʃa:pə], *n.* grec, fileur de cartes, *m.*
card table [ˈka:dteibl], *n.* table de jeu, *f.*
care [kɛə], *n.* soin; souci, *m.*; sollicitude; précaution, attention, *f.*; *care of* (*abbr.* c/o), aux bons soins de, chez; *to take care of,* avoir soin de, s'occuper de.—*v.i.* se soucier, s'inquiéter (*de*); *I dont care!* cela m'est égal! je m'en moque!
career [kəˈriə], *n.* carrière, course, *f.*—*v.i.* courir rapidement.
carefree [ˈkɛəfriː], *a.* libre de soucis; insouciant.
careful [ˈkɛəful], *a.* soigneux, attentif; prudent, économe; soucieux.
carefully [ˈkɛəfuli], *adv.* soigneusement, avec soin.
carefulness [ˈkɛəfulnis], *n.* attention, *f.*; soin, *m.*
careless [ˈkɛəlis], *a.* insouciant, nonchalant; négligent (*de*).
carelessly [ˈkɛəlisli], *adv.* nonchalamment, négligemment.
carelessness [ˈkɛəlisnis], *n.* insouciance, nonchalance; négligence, *f.*
caress [kəˈres], *n.* caresse, *f.*—*v.t.* caresser.
caretaker [ˈkɛəteikə], *n.* gardien, *m.*, concierge, *m.*, *f.*
cargo [ˈka:gou], *n.* cargaison, *f.*, chargement, *m.*
cargo boat [ˈka:goubout], *n.* cargo, *m.*
Caribbean [kæriˈbi:ən], *a.* antillais; *Caribbean Sea,* la mer des Antilles, *f.*—*n.* *the Caribbean,* les Antilles, *f.pl.*
caribou [ˈkæriˈbu:], *n.* caribou, *m.*
caricature [kærikəˈtjuə], *n.* caricature, charge, *f.*—*v.t.* caricaturer, faire la charge de.
carking [ˈka:kiŋ], *a.* cuisant (*souci*); rongeur.
carmine [ˈka:main], *a.* and *n.* carmin, *m.*
carnage [ˈka:nidʒ], *n.* carnage, *m.*
carnal [ˈka:nl], *a.* charnel.
carnally [ˈka:nəli], *adv.* charnellement.
carnation [ka:ˈneiʃən], *n.* (*Bot.*) œillet; incarnat, *m.*, carnation (*couleur*), *f.*
carnival [ˈka:nivl], *n.* carnaval, *m.*

carnivorous [ka:ˈnivərəs], *a.* carnivore, carnassier.
carol [ˈkærəl], *n.* chanson, *f.*, chant, *m.*; *Christmas carol,* noël, *m.*—*v.i.* chanter.
carousal [kəˈrauzəl], *n.* orgie, débauche, ripaille, *f.*; festin, *m.*
carouse [kəˈrauz], *v.i.* boire, faire la fête.
carp (1) [ka:p], *n.* (*Ichth.*) carpe, *f.*
carp (2) [ka:p], *v.i.* critiquer, chicaner (*sur*).
car-park [ˈka:pa:k], *n.* parc de stationnement, *m.*
carpenter [ˈka:pintə], *n.* menuisier, charpentier, *m.*
carpentry [ˈka:pintri], *n.* grosse menuiserie, charpenterie, *f.*
carpet [ˈka:pit], *n.* tapis, *m.*; *fitted carpet,* moquette, *f.*—*v.t.* garnir de tapis, tapisser.
carpet sweeper [ˈka:pitswi:pə], *n.* balai mécanique, *m.*
carping [ˈka:piŋ], *a.* chicanier, pointilleux.
carpingly [ˈka:piŋli], *adv.* en glosant; malignement.
carriage [ˈkæridʒ], *n.* voiture, *f.*; équipage; (*Rail.*) wagon, *m.*, voiture, *f.*; port, factage (*de paquets etc.*); affût (*de canon*), *m.*; (*Comm.*) frais de transport, *m.pl.*; (*fig.*) maintien, *m.*, tenue, démarche, *f.*
carriageway [ˈkæridʒwei], *n.* *dual carriageway,* route à double circulation, *f.*
carrier [ˈkæriə], *n.* camionneur; porteur, messager; (*Cycl.*) porte-bagages, *m.*; *aircraft carrier,* porte-avions, *m.inv.*; *carrier pigeon,* pigeon voyageur, *m.*
carrion [ˈkæriən], *n.* charogne, *f.*
carrion crow [ˈkæriənˈkrou], *n.* corbeau, *m.*, corbine, *f.*
carrot [ˈkærət], *n.* carotte, *f.*
carry [ˈkæri], *v.t.* porter; emporter; rapporter (*chien*); mener, conduire, entraîner; faire voter, adopter; (*Arith.*) retenir; *to carry away,* emporter, enlever, emmener: *to carry off,* emporter, enlever, remporter; *to carry on,* poursuivre, continuer; *to carry out,* porter dehors; mettre à exécution; *to carry through,* mener à bonne fin. —*v.i.* porter (*sons*).
cart [ka:t], *n.* charrette, *f.*; (*Mil.*) fourgon, *m.*; carriole (*de paysan*), *f.*—*v.t.* charrier, transporter, voiturer.
cartage [ˈka:tidʒ], *n.* charriage, transport, *m.*
carte [ka:t], *n.* carte, *f.*; menu, *m.*
carter [ˈka:tə], *n.* charretier, roulier, voiturier, *m.*
cart horse [ˈka:thɔ:s], *n.* cheval de trait, *m.*
cartilage [ˈka:tilidʒ], *n.* cartilage, *m.*
cart-load [ˈka:tloud], *n.* charretée, *f.*
carton [ˈka:tən], *n.* carton, *m.*; petite boîte en carton, *f.*
cartoon [ka:ˈtu:n], *n.* carton, *m.*; (*Polit.*) caricature, *f.*; dessin humoristique; (*Cine.*) dessin animé, *m.*
cartoonist [ka:ˈtu:nist], *n.* caricaturiste, *m.*, *f.*
cartridge [ˈka:tridʒ], *n.* cartouche, *f.*
cartridge paper [ˈka:tridʒpeipə], *n.* (*Ind.*) papier à cartouche, *m.*
cartridge pouch [ˈka:tridʒpautʃ], *n.* cartouchière, giberne, *f.*
cart shed [ˈka:tʃed], *n.* hangar, *m.*
cartwright [ˈka:trait], *n.* charron, *m.*
carve [ka:v], *v.t.* sculpter, tailler; graver, ciseler; découper (*viande etc.*).

carver

carver ['kɑːvə], n. découpeur; (Art.) sculpteur, graveur, ciseleur, m.

carving ['kɑːviŋ], n. découpage (de viande), m.; (Art) sculpture, gravure, ciselure, f.

cascade [kæs'keid], n. cascade, f.—v.i. tomber en cascade, cascader.

case (1) [keis], n. cas, état, m.; question; (Law) cause, affaire, f.; (Med.) malade, blessé, m.; **in any case**, en tout cas; **in case**, dans le cas où.

case (2) [keis], n. étui, fourreau, m.; caisse (d'emballage), f.; écrin (à bijoux), m.—v.t. enfermer; emballer; encaisser.

casemate ['keismeit], n. casemate, f.—v.t. casemater.

casement ['keismənt], n. châssis de fenêtre, m.

cash [kæʃ], n. argent, numéraire, m.; espèces (argent), f.pl.; **cash down**, argent comptant; **cash on delivery**, contre remboursement; **to pay cash**, payer en espèces; **to sell for cash**, vendre au comptant.—v.t. toucher, encaisser (chèque, mandat-poste); changer (billet); **to cash in on**, tirer profit de, tirer parti de.

cash-book ['kæʃbuk], n. livre de caisse, m.

cash box ['kæʃbɔks], n. caisse, f.

cash-desk ['kæʃdesk], n. caisse, f.

cashier (1) [kæ'ʃiə], n. caissier, m.

cashier (2) [kæ'ʃiə], v.t. (Mil.) casser, dégrader.

cashmere ['kæʃmiə], n. cachemire, m.

cash register ['kæʃrɛdʒistə], n. caisse enregistreuse, f.

cask [kɑːsk], n. fût, baril, m., barrique, f., tonneau, m.

casket ['kɑːskit], n. écrin, m., cassette, f.

Caspian (Sea) ['kæspiən(siː)], the. la mer Caspienne, f.

cassock ['kæsək], n. soutane, f.

cast [kɑːst], v.t. irr. jeter; se dépouiller de (arbre, animal); (Metal.) couler, fondre; (Theat.) distribuer les rôles; **to cast a glance at**, jeter un regard sur; **to cast aside**, mettre de côté, rejeter; **to cast down**, jeter par terre, abattre, décourager; **to cast its slough**, faire peau neuve; **to cast off**, rejeter, repousser, abandonner.—v.i. se jeter; se déjeter (arbre).—a. fondu.—n. coup, jet; moule, m.; (Metal.) fonte; (Theat.) distribution des rôles, f.; rôles, acteurs, m.pl.; (fig.) nuance, tournure, f., air, caractère, m.; (Sculp.) statuette, figure, f., plâtre, m.

castanet [kæstə'net], n. castagnette, f.

castaway ['kɑːstəwei], a. rejeté.—n. naufragé, m.

caste [kɑːst], n. caste, f.

castigate ['kæstigeit], v.t. châtier, punir; critiquer sévèrement.

castigation [kæsti'geiʃən], n. châtiment, m., correction, discipline, f.

casting ['kɑːstiŋ], n. (Metal.) coulée, fonte, f., moulage, m.; (Theat.) distribution des rôles, f.

cast-iron ['kɑːst'aiən], a. en fonte; (fig.) de fer, rigide.—n. fonte, f.

castle [kɑːsl], n. château, château fort, m.; (Chess) tour, f.; **castles in the air**, châteaux en Espagne.

castor [kɑːstə], n. roulette (de meuble); poivrière, f.; (pair of) **castors**, huilier, m.

castor oil ['kɑːstər'oil], n. huile de ricin, f.

castrate [kæs'treit], v.t. châtrer.

casual ['kæʒjuəl], a. fortuit, accidentel, casuel, de passage; insouciant.

casually ['kæʒjuəli], adv. fortuitement, par hasard; négligemment.

casualty ['kæʒjuəlti], n. accident; accidenté (personne), m.; (pl.) (Mil.) pertes, f.pl.

cat [kæt], n. chat; (Mil., Navy) fouet, martinet (à neuf queues), m.; **tom-cat**, matou, m.

catacombs ['kætəkuːmz], n.pl. catacombes, f.pl.

catalepsy ['kætəlepsi], n. catalepsie, f.

catalogue ['kætələg], n. catalogue, m., liste, f.

catamaran [kætəmə'ræn], n. catamaran, m.

catapult ['kætəpult], n. catapulte, f.; lance-pierre (jouet), m.

cataract ['kætərækt], n. cataracte, f.

catarrh [kə'tɑː], n. catarrhe, m.

catastrophe [kə'tæstrəfi], n. catastrophe, f.; désastre, m.

catch [kætʃ], v.t. irr. attraper, prendre, saisir; (colloq.) pincer; frapper (l'œil etc.); **to catch a cold**, s'enrhumer; **to catch on**, avoir du succès, réussir; **to catch up**, atteindre, rattraper.—v.i. s'accrocher (à), se prendre (à).—n. prise; attrape; (fig.) aubaine, belle affaire, f.; cliquet (d'une roue); crampon (d'une porte); mentonnet (d'un loquet), m.

catching ['kætʃiŋ], a. contagieux; communicatif (rire); facile à retenir (air).—n. prise, capture, f.

catechism ['kætəkizm], n. catéchisme, m.

categorical [kætə'gɔrikəl], a. catégorique.

categorically [kætə'gɔrikəli], adv. catégoriquement.

category ['kætəgəri], n. catégorie, f.

cater ['keitə], v.i. pourvoir (à).

caterer ['keitərə], n. pourvoyeur, fournisseur, m.

caterpillar ['kætəpilə], n. chenille, f.; **caterpillar tractor**, tracteur à chenilles, m.

cathedral [kə'θiːdrəl], n. cathédrale, f.

catholic ['kæθəlik], a. universel; éclectique; catholique.

catkin ['kætkin], n. (Bot.) chaton, m.

cattiness ['kætinis], **cattishness** ['kætiʃnis], n. méchanceté, sournoiserie, f.

cattish ['kætiʃ], **catty** ['kæti], a. méchant, sournois, rosse.

cattle [kætl], n. bétail, m., bestiaux, m.pl.

Caucasus ['kɔːkəsəs], the. le Caucase, m.

cauldron ['kɔːldrən], n. chaudron, m., chaudière, f.

cauliflower ['kɔliflauə], n. chou-fleur, m.

caulk [kɔːk], v.t. calfater (navire).

cause [kɔːz], n. raison, cause, f., motif, sujet m.—v.t. causer, être cause de; occasionner, provoquer (un accident).

causeway ['kɔːzwei], n. chaussée, f.

caustic ['kɔːstik], a. caustique, corrosif; (fig.) mordant.

cauterize ['kɔːtəraiz], v.t. cautériser.

cautery ['kɔːtəri], n. cautère, m.

caution ['kɔːʃən], n. avis (avertissement), m.; précaution, prévoyance, prudence; caution, garantie, f.—v.t. avertir, aviser (de); réprimander.

cautious ['kɔːʃəs], a. circonspect, prudent, en garde.

372

cautiously [ˈkɔːʃəsli], *adv.* avec précaution, prudemment.
cavalcade [kævəlˈkeid], *n.* cavalcade, *f.*
cavalier [kævəˈliə], *a.* cavalier, désinvolte.—*n.* cavalier, *m.*
cavalry [ˈkævəlri], *n.* cavalerie, *f.*
cave [keiv], *n.* caverne, *f.*, antre, souterrain, *m.*—*v.t.* creuser.—*v.i.* **to cave in**, céder, s'affaisser, s'effondrer (*édifice*).
cavern [ˈkævən], *n.* caverne, *f.*
cavernous [ˈkævənəs], *a.* caverneux.
caviare [kæviˈɑː], *n.* caviar, *m.*
cavil [ˈkævil], *v.i.* chicaner (*sur*).
cavilling [ˈkæviliŋ], *a.* chicaneur.—*n.* chicanerie, *f.*
cavity [ˈkæviti], *n.* cavité, *f.*
cavort [kəˈvɔːt], *v.i.* cabrioler.
caw [kɔː], *v.i.* croasser.
cawing [ˈkɔːiŋ], *n.* croassement, *m.*
cease [siːs], *v.t.* cesser; faire cesser.—*v.i.* cesser, discontinuer.
ceaseless [ˈsiːslis], *a.* incessant, continuel.
ceaselessly [ˈsiːslisli], *adv.* sans cesse.
Cecilia [səˈsiliə], Cécile, *f.*
cedar [ˈsiːdə], *n.* cèdre, *m.*
cede [siːd], *v.t.*, *v.i.* (*Law*) céder.
cedilla [səˈdilə], *n.* (*Gram.*) cédille, *f.*
ceiling [ˈsiːliŋ], *n.* plafond, *m.*
celebrate [ˈselibreit], *v.t.* célébrer, fêter.
celebrated [ˈselibreitid], *a.* célèbre, fameux.
celebration [seliˈbreiʃən], *n.* célébration, *f.*
celebrity [səˈlebriti], *n.* célébrité, *f.*
celerity [səˈleriti], *n.* célérité, vitesse, *f.*
celery [ˈseləri], *n.* céleri, *m.*
celestial [səˈlestjəl], *a.* céleste.
celibacy [ˈselibəsi], *n.* célibat, *m.*
celibate [ˈselibit], *a.* and *n.* célibataire, *m.*, *f.*
cell [sel], *n.* cellule, case; alvéole (*d'abeilles*), *f.*; compartiment; cachot; (*Elec.*) élément, *m.*, pile, *f.*
cellar [ˈselə], *n.* cave, *f.*; cellier, caveau, *m.*
cello [ˈtʃelou], *n.* (*abbr. of* **violoncello**) violoncelle, *m.*
cellophane [ˈseləfein], *n.* cellophane, *f.*
celluloid [ˈseljuloid], *n.* celluloïd, celluloïde, *m.*
Celt [kelt, selt], *n.* Celte, *m.*, *f.*
Celtic [ˈkeltik, ˈseltik], *a.* celtique.
cement [siˈment], *n.* ciment, *m.*—*v.t.* cimenter; (*fig.*) consolider, fortifier.
cement mixer [siˈmentmiksə], *n.* bétonnière, *f.*
cemetery [ˈsemətri], *n.* cimetière, *m.*
cenotaph [ˈsenotæf, -tɑːf], *n.* cénotaphe, *m.*
censer [ˈsensə], *n.* encensoir, *m.*
censor [ˈsensə], *n.* censeur, *m.*—*v.t.* soumettre à des coupures; censurer.
censorious [senˈsɔːriəs], *a.* critique, hargneux.
censorship [ˈsensəʃip], *n.* censure, *f.*; fonctions de censeur, *f.pl.*
censure [ˈsenʃə], *n.* censure, critique, *f.*, blâme, *m.*—*v.t.* censurer, critiquer, blâmer.
census [ˈsensəs], *n.* recensement, *m.*
cent [sent], *n.* cent, *m.*; sou (*pièce de monnaie*), *m.*; **ten per cent**, dix pour cent.
centaur [ˈsentɔː], *n.* centaure, *m.*
centenarian [sentiˈnɛəriən], *n.* centenaire, *m.*, *f.*
centenary [senˈtiːnəri], *a.* and *n.* centenaire, *m.*
centennial [senˈteniəl], *a.* de cent ans, séculaire.

center [ˈsentə], *n.* centre; milieu; (*fig.*) foyer, *m.*—*v.t.* placer au centre; concentrer.—*v.i.* se concentrer.
centesimal [senˈtesiməl], *a.* centésimal.—*n.* centième, *m.*
centigrade [ˈsentigreid], *a.* centigrade.
centipede [ˈsentipiːd], *n.* scolopendre, *f.*, mille-pattes, *m.*
central [ˈsentrəl], *a.* central; **central heating**, chauffage central, *m.*
centralization [sentrəlaiˈzeiʃən], *n.* centralisation, *f.*
centralize [ˈsentrəlaiz], *v.t.* centraliser.
centrifugal [senˈtrifjugəl], *a.* centrifuge.
centripetal [senˈtripitl], *a.* centripète.
centuple [ˈsentjupl], *a.* and *n.* centuple, *m.*—*v.t.* centupler.
centurion [senˈtjuəriən], *n.* centurion, (*Bibl.*) centenier, *m.*
century [ˈsentʃuri], *n.* siècle, *m.*
ceramic [səˈræmik], *a.* céramique.
ceramics [səˈræmiks], *n.pl.* céramique, *f.*
cereal [ˈsiəriəl], *a.* and *n.* céréale, *f.*
cerebral [ˈserəbrəl], *a.* cérébral.
ceremonial [seriˈmouniəl], *a.* de cérémonie.—*n.* cérémonie, étiquette, *f.*, cérémonial, *m.*
ceremonially [seriˈmouniəli], *adv.* rituellement.
ceremonious [seriˈmouniəs], *a.* cérémonieux.
ceremoniously [seriˈmouniəsli], *adv.* cérémonieusement.
ceremony [ˈseriməni], *n.* cérémonie, solennité, *f.*; **without ceremony**, sans façon.
cerise [səˈriːs], *a.* and *n.* cerise (*couleur*), *m.*
certain [ˈsəːtin], *a.* certain, sûr; **he is certain to do it**, il le fera certainement; **to make certain of something**, s'assurer de quelque chose.
certainly [ˈsəːtinli], *adv.* certainement.
certainty [ˈsəːtinti], *n.* certitude; chose certaine, *f.*
certificate [səˈtifikit], *n.* certificat; diplôme, brevet; concordat (*de faillite*); acte (*de naissance, de mariage ou de mort*), *m.*
certify [ˈsəːtifai], *v.t.* certifier; notifier, donner avis à.
certitude [ˈsəːtitjuːd], *n.* certitude, *f.*
cessation [seˈseiʃən], *n.* cessation, suspension, *f.*
cession [ˈseʃən], *n.* cession, *f.*
cesspit [ˈsespit], **cesspool** [ˈsespuːl], *n.* puisard, *m.*, fosse d'aisances, *f.*; (*fig.*) sentine, *f.*
Ceylon [siˈlɔn], le Ceylan, *m.*
Ceylonese [siləˈniːz], *a.* cingalais.—*n.* Cingalais (*personne*), *m.*
chafe [tʃeif], *v.t.* échauffer, irriter; érailler (*un câble*).—*v.i.* frotter; s'user, s'érailler (*un câble*); s'irriter; s'enflammer.
chafer (1) [ˈtʃeifə], *n.* hanneton (*insecte*), *m.*
chafer (2) [tʃeifə], *n.* réchaud (*plat*), *m.*
chafing dish [ˈtʃeifiŋdiʃ], *n.* réchaud (*de table*), *m.*
chaff [tʃɑːf], *n.* menue paille; (*colloq.*) plaisanterie, raillerie, blague, *f.*—*v.t.* blaguer, taquiner, se moquer de.
chaffinch [ˈtʃæfintʃ], *n.* (*Orn.*) pinson, *m.*
chagrin [ʃæˈgriːn], *n.* chagrin; dépit, *m.*—*v.t.* chagriner, vexer.
chain [tʃein], *n.* chaîne; chaînée, *f.*—*v.t.* enchaîner. [**chain store**, see **multiple**]

chair [tʃɛə], *n.* chaise, *f.*; siège, *m.*; chaire (à l'université), *f.*; fauteuil (d'un président), *m.*; **arm-chair**, fauteuil; **deck chair**, chaise longue, transat(lantique), *m.*; **rocking chair**, fauteuil à bascule; **wheel chair**, fauteuil roulant; **to be in the chair**, présider.

chairman [ˈtʃɛəmən], *n.* président, *m.*

chalice [ˈtʃælis], *n.* calice, *m.*, coupe, *f.*

chalk [tʃɔːk], *n.* craie, *f.*, calcaire; crayon (pour dessiner), *m.*—*v.t.* blanchir avec de la craie; marquer *ou* écrire à la craie.

chalk pit [ˈtʃɔːkpit], *n.* carrière de craie, *f.*

chalky [ˈtʃɔːki], *a.* crayeux, crétacé, calcaire.

challenge [ˈtʃælindʒ], *n.* défi, cartel, *m.*; (*fig.*) provocation, demande; (*Law*) récusation, *f.*; (*Mil.*) qui-vive; (*Spt.*) challenge, *m.*—*v.t.* défier; contester; (*Law*) récuser.

challenger [ˈtʃælindʒə], *n.* auteur d'un cartel; provacateur, agresseur, champion; (*Spt.*) challenger, *m.*

chamber [ˈtʃeimbə], *n.* chambre; salle, pièce, *f.*, cabinet, *m.*; (*Artill.*) âme, *f.*; (*pl.*) bureaux, *m.pl.*, étude, *f.*

chamberlain [ˈtʃeimbəlin], *n.* chambellan; camérier (du Pape), *m.*

chamber-maid [ˈtʃeimbəmeid], *n.* femme de chambre, *f.*

chamber music [ˈtʃeimbəmjuːzik], *n.* musique de chambre, *f.*

chameleon [kəˈmiːljən], *n.* caméléon, *m.*

chamfer [ˈtʃæmfə], *n.* chanfrein, *m.*—*v.t.* chanfreiner, biseauter.

chamois [ˈʃæmwɑː], *n.* chamois, *m.*

chamois leather [ˈʃæmiˈleðə], *n.* chamois, *m.*, peau de chamois, *f.*

champ [tʃæmp], *v.t.* ronger, mâcher.—*v.i.* ronger son frein.

champagne [ʃæmˈpein], *n.* champagne, vin de Champagne, *m.*

champion [ˈtʃæmpiən], *n.* champion, *m.*—*v.t.* soutenir, défendre.

championship [ˈtʃæmpiənʃip], *n.* championnat, *m.*

chance [tʃɑːns], *a.* accidentel, de hasard.—*n.* chance, *f.*, hasard, sort, *m.*; **by chance**, par hasard; **to stand a chance of**, avoir des chances de.—*v.t.* risquer.—*v.i.* arriver par hasard, venir à.

chancel [ˈtʃɑːnsəl], *n.* sanctuaire, chœur, *m.*

chancellery [ˈtʃɑːnsələri], *n.* chancellerie, *f.*

chancellor [ˈtʃɑːnsələ], *n.* chancelier, *m.*

chancery [ˈtʃɑːnsəri], *n.* cour de la chancellerie, *f.*

chandelier [ʃændiˈliə], *n.* lustre, *m.*

chandler [ˈtʃɑːndlə], *n.* marchand *ou* fabricant de chandelles, *m.*; **corn-chandler**, marchand de blé; **ship chandler**, approvisionneur de navires, *m.*

change [tʃeindʒ], *n.* changement, *m.*; phase (de la lune); monnaie (espèces), *f.*; **change of life**, retour d'âge, *m.*; **changes of life**, vicissitudes, *f.pl.*; **for a change**, pour changer.—*v.t.* changer; modifier; donner la monnaie de.—*v.i.* changer (de); se renouveler (la lune); **to change for the better**, s'améliorer.

changeable [ˈtʃeindʒəbl], *a.* changeant, variable, inconstant.

changer [ˈtʃeindʒə], *n.* changeur, *m.*

channel [ˈtʃænl], *n.* canal; lit (de rivière), *m.*; passe (de port), *f.*; (*Naut.*) détroit, *m.*;

(*fig.*) voie, *f.*, moyen, *m.*, entremise, *f.*; **the Channel Islands**, les îles Anglo-normandes, *f.pl.*; **the English Channel**, la Manche, *f.*—*v.t.* creuser.

chant [tʃɑːnt], *n.* chant, plain-chant, *m.*—*v.t.*, *v.i.* chanter.

chaos [ˈkeiɔs], *n.* chaos, *m.*

chaotic [keiˈɔtik], *a.* chaotique.

chap (1) [tʃæp], *v.t.* gercer.—*v.i.* gercer, se gercer.—*n.* gerçure, crevasse (dans la peau etc.), *f.*

chap (2) [tʃæp], *n.* garçon, gaillard, type, *m.*; **old chap**, (collog.) mon vieux.

chap (3) [tʃæp], **chop** (1) [tʃɔp], *n.* mâchoire, bouche; bajoue (de cochon), *f.*

chapel [tʃæpl], *n.* chapelle, *f.*

chaperon [ˈʃæpəroun], *n.* chaperon, *m.*—*v.t.* chaperonner.

chap-fallen [ˈtʃæpfɔːlən], *a.* (fam.) penaud, abattu, consterné.

chaplain [ˈtʃæplin], *n.* aumônier, *m.*

chaplet [ˈtʃæplit], *n.* chapelet, *m.*, guirlande, *f.*

chapter [ˈtʃæptə], *n.* chapitre, *m.*

chapter house [ˈtʃæptəhaus], *n.* chapitre, *m.*

char (1) [tʃɑː], *v.t.* carboniser.—*v.i.* se carboniser.

char (2) [tʃɑː], *v.i.* faire des ménages.—*n.* (pop. abbr. of CHARWOMAN) femme de ménage, *f.*

character [ˈkæriktə], *n.* caractère; (*Theat.*) rôle, personnage; genre, *m.*, nature, qualité, réputation, *f.*; certificat (de mœurs); (*fig.*) personnage, type, *m.*; **a bad character**, un mauvais sujet; **he is quite a character**, c'est un vrai original; **out of character**, déplacé.

characteristic [kæriktəˈristik], *a.* caractéristique.—*n.* trait caractéristique, *m.*

charade [ʃəˈrɑːd], *n.* charade, *f.*

charcoal [ˈtʃɑːkoul], *n.* charbon de bois, *m.*

charge [tʃɑːdʒ], *v.t.* charger, accuser (de); faire payer; (fig.) adjurer; ordonner à.—*v.i.* (*Mil.*) charger.—*n.* charge, *f.*; prix, *m.*; garde, *f.*; soin; ordre, commandement; (*Law*) acte d'accusation, *m.*, accusation, *f.*; mandement (d'un évêque); résumé (d'un juge), *m.*; (*pl.*) frais, dépens, *m.pl.*; **free of charge**, gratis; **the officer in charge**, l'officier commandant, *m.*; **to take charge of**, se charger de.

chargeable [ˈtʃɑːdʒəbl], *a.* à charge (à); accusable (de).

charger [ˈtʃɑːdʒə], *n.* grand plat; cheval de bataille; (*Elec.*) chargeur, *m.*

charily [ˈtʃɛərili], *adv.* avec précaution, frugalement.

chariot [ˈtʃæriət], *n.* char, chariot, *m.*

charioteer [tʃæriəˈtiə], *n.* conducteur de chariot, *m.*

charitable [ˈtʃæritəbl], *a.* de charité; charitable.

charitably [ˈtʃæritəbli], *adv.* charitablement.

charity [ˈtʃæriti], *n.* charité, bienveillance; aumône, *f.*

charlatan [ˈʃɑːlətən], *n.* charlatan, *m.*

charm [tʃɑːm], *n.* charme, *m.*; breloque (trinket), *f.*, porte-bonheur, *m.* inv.; (*pl.*) attraits, *m.pl.*—*v.t.* charmer, enchanter.

charmer [ˈtʃɑːmə], *n.* enchanteur, charmeur, *m.*

charming [ˈtʃɑːmiŋ], *a.* enchanteur, charmant; ravissant.

charnel ['tʃɑːnəl], *a.* de charnier.
charnel house ['tʃɑːnəlhaus], *n.* charnier, ossuaire, *m.*
chart [tʃɑːt], *n.* carte marine, *f.*—*v.t.* porter sur une carte.
charter ['tʃɑːtə], *n.* charte, *f.*, acte, *m.*; **on charter**, loué, affrété.—*v.t.* établir par un acte; (*Comm.*) fréter, affréter; **chartered accountant**, expert comptable, *m.*; **chartered plane**, avion-taxi, *m.*
charwoman ['tʃɑːwumən], *n.* (*pl.* **-women** [wimin]) femme de journée, femme de ménage, *f.*
chary ['tʃɛəri], *a.* prudent, économe.
chase (1) [tʃeis], *n.* chasse; poursuite, *f.*—*v.t.* chasser, poursuivre; **to chase away**, chasser.
chase (2) [tʃeis], *v.t.* (*Metal.*) ciseler.
chasm [kæzm], *n.* abîme; chasme; vide énorme, *m.*, brèche, fissure, *f.*
chassis ['ʃæsi], *n.* (*Motor.*) châssis, *m.*
chaste [tʃeist], *a.* chaste, pudique; pur (*language*); de bon goût.
chasten ['tʃeisn], *v.t.* châtier; purifier.
chastise [tʃæs'taiz], *v.t.* châtier.
chastisement ['tʃæstizmənt], *n.* châtiment, *m.*
chastity ['tʃæstiti], *n.* chasteté, pureté, *f.*
chasuble ['tʃæzjubl], *n.* chasuble, *f.*
chat [tʃæt], *n.* causerie; (*colloq.*) causette, *f.*, entretien, *m.*—*v.i.* causer, bavarder; (*colloq.*) faire la causette.
chattel [tʃætl], *n.* bien meuble, *m.*; **goods and chattels**, biens et effets, *m.pl.*
chatter ['tʃætə], *v.i.* jaser, bavarder; jacasser (*singes etc.*); babiller; claquer (*dents*).—*n.* caquetage, *m.*, jaserie, *f.*
chatterbox ['tʃætəbɔks], *n.* moulin à paroles, jaseur, babillard, *m.*
chattering ['tʃætəriŋ], *n.* jaserie, *f.*; claquement (*des dents*), *m.*
chatty ['tʃæti], *a.* causeur, bavard.
chauffeur ['ʃoufə, ʃou'fəː], *n.* chauffeur, *m.*
cheap [tʃiːp], *a.* (à) bon marché; peu coûteux; de peu de valeur; **dirt cheap**, pour rien, à vil prix.
cheapen ['tʃiːpən], *v.t.* faire baisser le prix de; **to cheapen oneself**, se déprécier.
cheaper ['tʃiːpə], *a.* (à) meilleur marché.
cheaply ['tʃiːpli], *adv.* à bon marché, à bon compte.
cheapness ['tʃiːpnis], *n.* bon marché, bas prix, *m.*
cheat [tʃiːt], *n.* fourberie, tromperie, *f.*; trompeur; (*Cards etc.*) tricheur, *m.*—*v.t.* tromper; (*Cards etc.*) tricher.
cheating ['tʃiːtiŋ], *n.* tromperie; (*Cards etc.*) tricherie, *f.*
check [tʃek], *v.t.* réprimer; arrêter; contenir; (*Comm.*) vérifier; enregistrer (*bagages etc.*); contrôler (*comptes*); (*Chess*) faire échec à.—*n.* échec, obstacle; (*Comm.*) bon; (*Am.*) [CHEQUE] carreau, damier (*dessin*); (*Chess*) échec, *m.* [**checkroom**, see **luggage**]
checking ['tʃekiŋ], *n.* répression, *f.* contrôle, *m.*
checkmate ['tʃekmeit], *n.* échec et mat, *m.*—*v.t.* mettre échec et mat, mater.
cheek [tʃiːk], *n.* joue; bajoue (*cochon*); (*fig.*) impudence, *f.*, front, toupet, *m.*; **cheek by jowl**, côte à côte.—*v.t.* narguer.
cheek-bone ['tʃiːkboun], *n.* pommette, *f.*
cheeky ['tʃiːki], *a.* impudent, effronté.

cheep [tʃiːp], *n.* piaulement, *m.*—*v.i.* piauler.
cheer [tʃiə], *n.* chère (*aliment etc.*); gaieté, *f.*, courage, *m.*; acclamation, *f.*, applaudissement, hourra, vivat, *m.*—*v.t.* égayer, réjouir, animer; applaudir, acclamer.—*v.i.* se réjouir; applaudir.
cheerful ['tʃiəful], *a.* joyeux, gai; riant (*paysage etc.*).
cheerfully ['tʃiəfuli], *adv.* gaiement, joyeusement.
cheerfulness ['tʃiəfulnis], *n.* gaieté, allégresse, bonne humeur, *f.*
cheerily ['tʃiərili], *adv.* gaiement.
cheering ['tʃiəriŋ], *a.* consolant, encourageant.—*n.* applaudissements, *m.pl.*
cheerio! ['tʃiəriou], *int.* (*fam.*) (*good-bye*) à bientôt! (*when drinking*) à votre santé!
cheerless ['tʃiəlis], *a.* triste, morne.
cheery ['tʃiəri], *a.* gai, joyeux, réjoui.
cheese [tʃiːz], *n.* fromage, *m.*
cheese-paring ['tʃiːzpɛəriŋ], *n.* (*fig.*) économie de bouts de chandelle, *f.*
cheetah, chetah ['tʃiːtə], *n.* guépard, *m.*
chef [ʃef], *n.* chef (cuisinier), *m.*
chemical ['kemikəl], *a.* chimique.
chemically ['kemikli], *adv.* chimiquement.
chemicals ['kemikəlz], *n.pl.* produits chimiques, *m.pl.*
chemise [ʃi'miːz], *n.* chemise de femme, *f.*
chemist ['kemist], *n.* (*scientist*) chimiste, *m.*, *f.*; (*druggist*) pharmacien, *m.*; **chemist's shop**, pharmacie, *f.*
chemistry ['kemistri], *n.* chimie, *f.*
cheque [tʃek], *n.* chèque, *m.*; **traveller's cheque**, chèque de voyage, *m.*
cheque-book ['tʃekbuk], *n.* carnet de chèques, *m.*
cherish ['tʃeriʃ], *v.t.* chérir; soigner; nourrir, entretenir (*de l'espoir etc.*).
cherry ['tʃeri], *n.* cerise, *f.*
cherry tree ['tʃeritri:], *n.* cerisier, *m.*
cherub ['tʃerəb], *n.* (*pl.* **cherubs** [tʃerəbz], **cherubim** [tʃerəbim]) chérubin, *m.*
cherubic [tʃə'ruːbik], *a.* de chérubin, angélique.
chess [tʃes], *n.* échecs, *m.pl.*
chess-board [tʃesbɔːd], *n.* échiquier, *m.*
chessman ['tʃesmən], *n.* (*pl.* **chessmen** ['tʃesmen]) pièce, *f.*; **a set of chessmen**, un jeu d'échecs.
chest [tʃest], *n.* coffre, *m.*, caisse; (*Anat.*) poitrine, *f.*; poitrail (*de cheval*), *m.*; **chest of drawers**, commode, *f.*
chestnut ['tʃesnʌt], *a.* châtain, marron (*couleur*); alezan (*cheval*).—*n.* marron, *m.*; châtaigne, *f.*
chestnut tree ['tʃesnʌttriː], *n.* châtaignier (*Spanish chestnut*); marronnier (d'Inde) (*horse chestnut*), *m.*
chevalier [ʃevə'liə], *n.* chevalier, *m.*
chevron ['ʃevrən], *n.* chevron, *m.*
chew [tʃuː], *v.t.* mâcher; (*fig.*) **to chew over**, ruminer.
chick [tʃik], *n.* poussin; (*fig.*) poulet, *m.*
chicken [tʃikin], *n.* poussin; poulet, *m.*
chicken-hearted ['tʃikin'hɑːtid], *a.* peureux, poltron.
chicken pox ['tʃikinpɔks], *n.* varicelle, *f.*
chickweed ['tʃikwiːd], *n.* mouron des oiseaux, *m.*

375

chicory ['tʃikəri], *n.* chicorée (*assaisonnement ou pour remplacer le café*); endive (*légume*). *f.*

chide [tʃaid], *v.t.* gronder, blâmer.

chief [tʃi:f], *a.* principal.—*n.* chef, *m.*; partie principale, *f.*; (*fam.*) **the chief**, le patron, *m.*

chiefly ['tʃi:fli], *adv.* surtout, principalement.

chieftain ['tʃi:ftən], *n.* chef de clan, *m.*

chiffon ['ʃifɔn], *n.* chiffon, *m.*

chiffonier [ʃifə'niə], *n.* chiffonnier, *m.*

chilblain ['tʃilblein], *n.* engelure, *f.*

child [tʃaild], *n.* (*pl.* **children** ['tʃildrən]) enfant, *m.*; **with child**, enceinte.

child-bed ['tʃaildbed], *n.* couches, *f.pl.*

child-birth ['tʃaildbə:θ], *n.* enfantement, *m.*

childhood ['tʃaildhud], *n.* enfance, *f.*

childish ['tʃaildiʃ], *a.* enfantin; puéril.

childishness ['tʃaildiʃnis], *n.* puérilité, *f.*; enfantillage, *m.*

Chile ['tʃili]. le Chili, *m.*

Chilean ['tʃiliən], *a.* chilien.—*n.* Chilien (*personne*).

chill [tʃil], *a.* froid; glacé.—*n.* froid; refroidissement, frisson, *m.*; **to catch a chill**, prendre froid.—*v.t.* refroidir; (*fig.*) glacer; décourager.

chilli ['tʃili], *n.* piment, *m.*

chilliness ['tʃilinis], *n.* froid, frisson, *m.*; froideur, *f.*

chilly ['tʃili], *a.* un peu froid (*chose*); frileux (*personne ou temps*).

chime [tʃaim], *n.* carillon, *m.*—*v.t., v.i.* carillonner.

chimera [kai'miərə], *n.* chimère, *f.*

chimney ['tʃimni], *n.* cheminée, *f.*

chimney corner ['tʃimni'kɔ:nə], *n.* coin du feu, *m.*

chimney piece ['tʃimnipi:s], *n.* chambranle *ou* manteau de cheminée, *m.*; (*colloq.*) cheminée, *f.*

chimney pot ['tʃimnipɔt], *n.* tuyau de cheminée, *m.*

chimney sweep ['tʃimniswi:p], *n.* ramoneur, *m.*

chimpanzee [tʃimpæn'zi:], *n.* chimpanzé, *m.*

chin [tʃin], *n.* menton, *m.*

China ['tʃainə]. la Chine, *f.*

china ['tʃainə], *n.* porcelaine, *f.*

Chinese [tʃai'ni:z], *a.* chinois, de Chine.—*n.* chinois (*langue*); Chinois (*personne*), *m.*

chink [tʃiŋk], *n.* crevasse, fente, lézarde, *f.*; son, tintement, (*slang*) argent, *m.*—*v.t.* crevasser; faire sonner.—*v.i.* se fendiller; sonner.

chintz [tʃints], *n.* (*Tex.*) indienne, *f.*

chip [tʃip], *n.* copeau, fragment, éclat (*de bois*); (*Cards*) jeton, *m.*; (*pl., Cook.*) (pommes de terre) frites, *f.pl.*—*v.t.* tailler; railler.—*v.i.* s'écorner; s'écailler (*porcelaine etc.*).

chiropodist [ki'rɔpədist], *n.* pédicure, *m.,f.*

chirp [tʃə:p], *v.i.* pépier, gazouiller; crier (*insectes*).—*n.* gazouillement, pépiement; cri (*insectes*), *m.*

chirpy ['tʃə:pi], *a.* (*colloq.*) gai, réjoui.

chirrup ['tʃirəp], [CHIRP].

chisel [tʃizl], *n.* ciseau, *m.*—*v.t.* ciseler.

chit [tʃit], *n.* marmot, bambin; billet (*lettre*), *m.*

chitchat ['tʃittʃæt], *n.* caquet, babillage, *m.*

chivalrous ['ʃivalrəs], *a.* chevaleresque.

chivalry ['ʃivalri], *n.* chevalerie, *f.*

chives [tʃaivz], *n.pl.* ciboulette, *f.*

chlorate ['klɔ:reit], *n.* (*Chem.*) chlorate, *m.*

chlorinate ['klɔ:rineit], *v.t.* verduniser (*eau potable*).

chlorine ['klɔ:ri:n], *n.* chlore, *m.*

chloroform ['klɔrəfɔ:m], *n.* chloroforme, *m.* —*v.t.* chloroformer.

chlorophyll ['klɔrəfil], *n.* chlorophylle, *f.*

choc-ice ['tʃɔkais], *n.* chocolat glacé, *m.*

chock-full [tʃɔk'ful], (*fam.*) **chock-a-block** ['tʃɔkə'blɔk], *a.* plein comme un œuf, comble.

chocolate ['tʃɔkəlit], *n.* chocolat, *m.*

choice [tʃɔis], *a.* choisi; de choix; recherché; fin (*vin*).—*n.* choix, *m.*; élite, *f.*; assortiment, *m.*

choir ['kwaiə], *n.* chœur, *m.*

choke [tʃouk], *v.t.* étouffer, suffoquer; engorger.—*v.i.* s'engorger.—*n.* étranglement (*de voix*); (*Motor.*) starter, *m.*

choking ['tʃoukiŋ], *a.* étouffant.—*n.* étouffement, *m.*, suffocation, *f.*

choky ['tʃouki], *a.* étouffant, suffoquant.

choler ['kɔlə], *n.* colère, bile, *f.*

cholera ['kɔlərə], *n.* choléra, *m.*

choleric ['kɔlərik], *a.* colérique, irascible.

choose [tʃu:z], *v.t. irr.* choisir; élire; préférer; vouloir.

chop (1) [CHAP].

chop (2) [tʃɔp], *v.t.* couper en morceaux, hacher; trafiquer, troquer; **to chop down**, abattre.—*v.i.* trafiquer, troquer; (*Naut.*) tourner (*vent*); clapoter (*mer*); **chopping block**, hachoir, billot, *m.*—*n.* tranche; côtelette (*de mouton*); (*colloq., pl.*) gueule, *f.*

chopper ['tʃɔpə], *n.* couperet, *m.*

chopping ['tʃɔpiŋ], *n.* coupe, action de couper, *f.*

choppy ['tʃɔpi], *a.* crevassé, haché; clapoteux (*mer*).

choral ['kɔ:rəl], *a.* choral, en *ou* de chœur.

chord [kɔ:d], *n.* corde, *f.*; (*Mus.*) accord, *m.*

chores [tʃɔ:z], *n.pl.* corvées domestiques, *f.pl.*

chorister ['kɔristə], *n.* choriste, *m.*; enfant de chœur, *m.,f.*

chorus ['kɔ:rəs], *n.* chœur; refrain, *m.*

Christ [kraist]. le Christ, *m.*

christen [krisn], *v.t.* baptiser.

Christendom ['krisndəm], *n.* chrétienté, *f.*

christening ['krisniŋ], *n.* baptême, *m.*

Christian ['kristjən], *a. and n.* chrétien, *m.*; **Christian name**, prénom, *m.*

Christianity [kristi'æniti], *n.* christianisme, *m.*

Christmas ['krisməs]. Noël, *m.*, la fête de Noël, *f.*; **Christmas carol**, chant de Noël, *m.*; **Christmas Eve**, la veille de Noël, *f.*

Christmas box ['krisməsbɔks], *n.* étrennes, *f.pl.*

Christopher ['kristəfə]. Christophe, *m.*

chrome [kroum], *n.* bichromate de potasse, *m.*; **chrome leather**, cuir chromé, *m.*

chromium ['kroumiəm], *n.* chrome, *m.*

chronic ['krɔnik], *a.* chronique.

chronicle ['krɔnikl], *n.* chronique, *f.*

chronicler ['krɔniklə], *n.* chroniqueur, *m.*

chronological [krɔnə'lɔdʒikəl], *a.* chronologique.

chrysalis ['krisəlis], *n.* chrysalide, *f.*

chrysanthemum [kri'sænθəmʌm], *n.* chrysanthème, *m.*

chub [tʃʌb], *n.* (*Ichth.*) chabot, chevesne, *m.*

chubby ['tʃʌbi], *a.* joufflu; potelé (*mains*).

chuck (1) [tʃʌk], *n.* gloussement, *m.*—*v.i.* glousser.

chuck (2) [tʃʌk], *n.* petite tape sous le menton, *f.*

chuckle [tʃʌkl], *v.i.* rire tout bas, rire sous cape (*de*).—*n.* rire étouffé, gloussement, *m.*

chum [tʃʌm], *n.* copain, *m.*

chummy [tʃʌmi], *a.* intime.

chump [tʃʌmp], *n.* tronçon (*de bois*); (*colloq.*) idiot, *m.*; **chump chop**, côtelette de gigot, *f.*

chunk [tʃʌŋk], *n.* gros morceau, *m.*

church [tʃəːtʃ], *n.* église, *f.*; (*Protestant*) temple, *m.*

churchwarden [ˈtʃəːtʃwɔːdn], *n.* marguillier, *m.*

churchyard [ˈtʃəːtʃjaːd], *n.* cimetière, *m.*

churl [tʃəːl], *n.* rustre, manant, ladre, *m.*

churlish [ˈtʃəːliʃ], *a.* grossier, rude, ladre.

churlishly [ˈtʃəːliʃli], *adv.* grossièrement.

churlishness [ˈtʃəːliʃnis], *n.* grossièreté, *f.*

churn [tʃəːn], *n.* baratte, *f.*; *milk churn*, bidon à lait, *m.*—*v.i.* baratter.

chute [ʃuːt], *n.* chute (*d'eau*); glissière, piste (*de luges*), *f.*

Cicero [ˈsisərou]. Cicéron, *m.*

cider [ˈsaidə], *n.* cidre, *m.*

cigar [siˈgaː], *n.* cigare, *m.*

cigarette [sigəˈret], *n.* cigarette, *f.*

cinder [ˈsində], *n.* cendre, *f.*; (*pl.*) escarbilles (*de charbon*), *f.pl.*

Cinderella [sindəˈrelə]. Cendrillon, *f.*

cine-camera [ˈsiniˌkæmərə], *n.* (ciné)caméra, *f.*

cinema [ˈsinimə], *n.* cinéma, *m.*

cinnamon [ˈsinəmən], *n.* cannelle, *f.*

cipher [ˈsaifə], *n.* zéro; chiffre, *m.*—*v.t.*, *v.i.* chiffrer; calculer.

circle [səːkl], *n.* cercle, *m.*; (*fig.*) coterie, *f.*—*v.t.* entourer (*de*).—*v.i.* tournoyer.

circlet [ˈsəːklit], *n.* petit cercle, anneau *m.*

circuit [ˈsəːkit], *n.* rotation, révolution, *f.*; tour; circuit, *m.*, circonférence; tournée (*de juge* etc.), *f.*

circuitous [səːˈkjuːitəs], *a.* détourné, sinueux.

circular [ˈsəːkjulə], *a.* circulaire.—*n.* circulaire, *f.*, bulletin, *m.*

circulate [ˈsəːkjuleit], *v.t.* mettre en circulation, faire circuler; répandre.—*v.i.* circuler.

circulating [ˈsəːkjuleitiŋ], *a.* circulant.

circulation [səːkjuˈleiʃən], *n.* circulation, *f.*; tirage (*d'un journal* etc.), *m.*

circumference [səːˈkʌmfərəns], *n.* circonférence, périphérie, *f.*

circumflex [ˈsəːkəmfleks], *a.* (*Gram.*) circonflexe.

circumlocution [səːkəmləˈkjuːʃən], *n.* circonlocution, *f.*

circumscribe [ˈsəːkəmskraib], *v.t.* circonscrire.

circumspect [ˈsəːkəmspekt], *a.* circonspect.

circumstance [ˈsəːkəmstæns], *n.* circonstance, *f.*; état, *m.*; (*pl.*) moyens, *m.pl.*; *in straitened circumstances*, dans la gêne; *in easy circumstances*, dans l'aisance; *under no circumstances*, en aucun cas.

circumstantial [səːkəmˈstænʃəl], *a.* circonstancié, minutieux; indirect (*témoignage*).

circumvent [səːkəmˈvent], *v.t.* circonvenir.

circumvention [səːkəmˈvenʃən], *n.* circonvention, *f.*

circus [ˈsəːkəs], *n.* cirque; rond-point (*de rues*), *m.*

cistern [ˈsistən], *n.* citerne, *f.*, réservoir, *m.*

citadel [ˈsitədl], *n.* citadelle, *f.*

citation [saiˈteiʃən], *n.* citation, *f.*

cite [sait], *v.t.* citer; sommer (*de*).

citizen [ˈsitizn], *n.* citoyen, bourgeois; habitant, *m.*

citron [ˈsitrən], *n.* cédrat, *m.*

city [ˈsiti], *n.* ville; cité, *f.* [see **town** etc.]

civet [ˈsivit], *n.* civette, *f.*

civic [ˈsivik], *a.* civique.

civil [ˈsivl], *a.* civil; municipal; honnête, poli; *civil servant*, fonctionnaire, *m.*; *in the Civil Service*, dans l'administration.

civilian [siˈviljən], *n.* bourgeois, civil, *m.*

civility [siˈviliti], *n.* civilité, politesse, *f.*

civilization [siviˌlaiˈzeiʃən], *n.* civilisation, *f.*

civilize [ˈsivilaiz], *v.t.* civiliser.

claim [kleim], *v.t.* demander, prétendre (*à*), réclamer, revendiquer.—*n.* demande, *f.*; titre, droit, *m.*

claimant [ˈkleimənt], *n.* réclamateur, prétendant, *m.*

clam [klæm], *n.* peigne (*bivalve*), *m.*, palourde, *f.*

clamber [ˈklæmbə], *v.i.* grimper (*sur* ou *à*).

clammy [ˈklæmi], *a.* visqueux, pâteux; moite (*mains*).

clamor [ˈklæmə], *n.* clameur, *f.*, bruit, *m.*—*v.i.* crier, vociférer.

clamorous [ˈklæmərəs], *a.* bruyant; criard.

clamp [klæmp], *n.* crampon; (*Carp.*) serre-joints, *m.*—*v.t.* cramponner; serrer; entasser.

clan [klæn], *n.* clan, *m.*; clique, coterie, *f.*

clandestine [klænˈdestin], *a.* clandestin.

clang [klæŋ], **clank** [klæŋk], *n.* cliquetis, son métallique, *m.*—*v.t.* faire résonner.—*v.i.* résonner.

clap [klæp], *n.* coup, *m.*; claque, *f.*; battement de mains; coup (*de tonnerre*), *m.*—*v.t.* claquer, frapper, battre (*mains*, *ailes* etc.); applaudir.—*v.i.* claquer ou battre des mains; applaudir.

clapper [ˈklæpə], *n.* applaudisseur; battant (*d'une cloche*); claquet (*d'un moulin*), *m.*

clapping [ˈklæpiŋ], *n.* battement des mains, *m.*, applaudissements, *m.pl.*

Clara [ˈklɛərə], **Clare** [klɛə]. Claire, *f.*

claret [ˈklærət], *n.* vin de Bordeaux rouge, *m.*

clarify [ˈklærifai], *v.t.* clarifier.—*v.i.* se clarifier.

clarinet [klæriˈnet], *n.* clarinette, *f.*

clarion [ˈklæriən], *n.* clairon, *m.*

clarity [ˈklæriti], *n.* clarté, *f.*

clash [klæʃ], *v.t.* faire résonner (*en frappant*); choquer, heurter.—*v.i.* résonner, se heurter; (*fig.*) être aux prises (*avec*), s'opposer.—*n.* fracas, choc, conflit; cliquetis (*d'armes* etc.), *m.*

clasp [klɑːsp], *n.* fermoir, *m.*; agrafe, *f.*; (*fig.*) embrassement, *m.*, étreinte, *f.*—*v.t.* agrafer; serrer, presser.

clasp knife [ˈklɑːspnaif], *n.* couteau de poche, *m.*

class [klɑːs], *n.* classe, *f.*; (*Sch.*) cours; genre, *m.*, catégorie, *f.*—*v.t.* classer.

classic [ˈklæsik], *a.* and *n.* classique, *m*; *to study classics*, faire ses humanités *f.pl.*

classical [ˈklæsikəl], *a.* classique.

classification [klæsifiˈkeiʃən], *n.* classification, *f.*

classify ['klæsifai], *v.t.* classifier.
classroom ['klɑːsruːm], *n.* salle de classe, classe, *f.*
clatter ['klætə], *n.* bruit, tapage, fracas (*de ferraille etc.*), tintamarre, *m.*—*v.i.* faire du bruit, claquer.
clause [klɔːz], *n.* clause; proposition, *f.*
clavicle ['klævikl], *n.* (*Anat.*) clavicule, *f.*
claw [klɔː], *n.* griffe; (*Zool.*) serre; pince (*de crabes*), *f.*—*v.t.* griffer; déchirer; égratigner; (*fig.*) railler, gronder.
clay [klei], *n.* argile, terre glaise, glaise, *f.*—*v.t.* (*Agric.*) glaiser; terrer (*sucre*).
clayey ['kleii], *a.* argileux.
clean [kliːn], *a.* propre; blanc (*linge*); ciré (*chaussures*); (*fig.*) net, droit.—*adv.* entièrement, tout à fait, droit, raide.—*v.t.* nettoyer; décrotter, cirer (*chaussures*); écurer (*égouts, canaux etc.*).
cleaner ['kliːnə], *n.* nettoyeur (*personne*), *m.*
cleaning ['kliːniŋ], *n.* nettoyage, nettoiement, *m.*; **dry cleaning**, nettoyage à sec.
cleanliness ['klenlinis], **cleanness** ['kliːnnis], *n.* propreté, *f.*
cleanly ['klenli], *a.* propre; (*fig.*) pur.— ['kliːnli], *adv.* proprement, nettement.
cleanness [CLEANLINESS].
cleanse [klenz], *v.t.* nettoyer; curer (*égouts etc.*); (*fig.*) purifier.
cleansing ['klenziŋ], *n.* nettoiement, nettoyage, *m.*; (*fig.*) purification, *f.*
clear [kliə], *a.* clair; net, évident; sûr; innocent, sans tache.—*adv.* clair.—*v.t.* éclaircir; clarifier (*liquides*); faire évacuer (*salle etc.*); déblayer (*débris etc.*); gagner (*profit etc.*); (*Agric.*) défricher; (*fig.*) acquitter; (*Customs*) passer.—*v.i.* s'éclaircir; **to clear off**, s'en aller, filer; **to clear out**, se retirer; **to clear up**, élucider (*problème, mystère*); s'éclaircir, se rasséréner (*temps*).
clearance ['kliərəns], *n.* dégagement; déblaiement (*débris*), *m.*; levée (*du courrier*), *f.*; (*Naut.*) congé; (*Customs*) dédouanement, *m.*; **clearance sale**, solde, *m.*; liquidation, *f.*
clear-cut ['kliəkʌt], *a.* net, d'une grande netteté.
clear-headed ['kliə'hedid], *a.* à l'esprit clair.
clearing ['kliəriŋ], *n.* éclaircissement; débrouillement; acquittement; (*Customs*) dédouanement; défrichement (*de terrain*), *m.*; éclaircie (*de forêt*), *f.*; déblaiement (*débris*), *m.*
clearing-house ['kliəriŋhaus], *n.* (*Rail.*) bureau de liquidation, *m.*; (*Banking*) banque de virement, *f.*
clearly ['kliəli], *adv.* nettement, clairement, évidemment.
clearness ['kliənis], *n.* clarté, netteté, pureté, *f.*
cleavage ['kliːvidʒ], *n.* clivage, *m.*; fissure, scission, *f.*
cleave [kliːv], *v.t. irr.* fendre, se fendre; **in a cleft stick**, (*fig.*) dans une impasse.
clef [klef], *n.* (*Mus.*) clef, *f.*
cleft [kleft], *n.* fente, fissure, crevasse, *f.*
clemency ['klemənsi], *n.* clémence; douceur (*du temps*), *f.*
clement ['klemənt], *a.* doux, clément.
clench [klentʃ], *v.t.* river (*clous etc.*); serrer (*poing*).
Cleopatra [kliə'pætrə]. Cléopâtre, *f.*
clergy ['kləːdʒi], *n.* clergé, *m.*

clergyman ['kləːdʒimən], *n.* (*pl.* **-men** [men]) ecclésiastique; (*R.-C. Ch.*) prêtre, abbé, curé; (*Protestant*) ministre, pasteur, *m.*
cleric ['klerik], *n.* ecclésiastique, prêtre, *m.*
clerical ['klerikal], *a.* clérical; **clerical error**, faute de copiste, *f.*
clerk [klɑːk], *n.* (*Law*) clerc; (*Eccles.*) ecclésiastique; (*Comm.*) commis; (*Civil Service*) employé, *m.* [see **shop-assistant**]
clerkship ['klɑːkʃip], *n.* place de clerc, place de commis, *f.*
clever ['klevə], *a.* adroit, habile, (*colloq.*) malin; intelligent; bien fait; **to be clever at**, être fort en.
cleverly ['klevəli], *adv.* habilement, adroitement, avec adresse.
cleverness ['klevənis], *n.* habileté, dextérité, adresse; intelligence, *f.*
click [klik], *v.i.* faire tic-tac, cliqueter.—*n.* bruit sec, clic; cliquetis; déclic, *m.*
client ['klaiənt], *n.* client, *m.*
clientele [kliːɑ̃'tel], *n.* clientèle, *f.*
cliff [klif], *n.* falaise, *f.*; rocher escarpé, *m.*
climate ['klaimit], *n.* climat, *m.*
climatic [klai'mætik], *a.* climatique.
climax ['klaimæks], *n.* gradation, *f.*; (*fig.*) comble, apogée, *m.*
climb [klaim], *v.t.* escalader, gravir, monter.—*v.i.* grimper; monter (*sur*); (*fig.*) s'élever.—*n.* ascension, montée, *f.*
climber ['klaimə], *n.* grimpeur, *m.*; alpiniste, *m., f.*; **social climber**, arriviste, *m., f.*
clime [klaim], *n.* (*poet.*) climat; pays, *m.*
clinch [klintʃ], *v.t.* river (*clous*); **to clinch an argument**, confirmer un argument.—*n.* (*Box.*) corps à corps, *m.*
cling [kliŋ], *v.i. irr.* se cramponner, s'attacher, s'accrocher (*à*); coller (*à*) (*robe*).
clinic ['klinik], *n.* clinique, *f.*
clinical ['klinikal], *a.* clinique.
clink [kliŋk], *n.* tintement, cliquetis, *m.*—*v.t.* faire tinter.—*v.i.* tinter.
clinker ['kliŋkə], *n.* mâchefer, *m.*
clip [klip], *v.t.* couper (*à ciseaux*); tondre (*chiens, chevaux*); écorcher, estropier (*paroles*); contrôler (*billets*).—*n.* tonte, *f.*; pince-notes, *m.*
clipper ['klipə], *n.* rogneur; (*Naut.*) fin voilier, *m.*
clippers ['klipəz], *n.pl.* tondeuse, *f.*
clique [kliːk], *n.* coterie, *f.*
cloak [klouk], *n.* manteau; (*fig.*) voile, masque, prétexte, *m.*—*v.t.* couvrir d'un manteau, (*fig.*) masquer, voiler, cacher.
cloak-room ['kloukruːm], *n.* (*Rail.*) consigne, *f.*; (*Theat.*) vestiaire, *m.*
clock [klɔk], *n.* horloge (*grand*); pendule (*petit*), *f.*; **alarm clock**, réveille-matin, *m.*—*v.i.* (*Ind.*) **to clock in** or **out**, pointer à l'arrivée *ou* au départ.
clock-maker ['klɔkmeikə], *n.* horloger, *m.*
clockwise ['klɔkwaiz], *adv.* dans le sens des aiguilles d'une montre.
clockwork ['klɔkwəːk], *a.* mécanique.—*n.* mouvement, mécanisme d'horlogerie; (*fig.*) travail régulier, *m.*
clod [klɔd], *n.* motte de terre, *f.*
clodhopper ['klɔdhɔpə], *n.* rustre; manant, *m.*
clog [klɔg], *n.* sabot, *m.*—*v.t.* obstruer.—*v.i.* se boucher, s'obstruer.

cloister ['klɔistə], n. cloître, m.
close (I) [klouz], v.t. fermer; clore, terminer.
—v.i. se fermer; clore, se terminer, conclure, finir.—n. fin, conclusion, clôture, f.
close (2) [klous], a. clos, bien fermé; serré;
lourd (temps); (fig.) mystérieux.—adv. près;
de près; close by, tout près; close to, près
de.
close-fisted ['klous'fistid], a. avare.
closely ['klousli], adv. de près; étroitement;
secrètement.
closeness ['klousnis], n. proximité; exactitude;
lourdeur (temps); intimité, f.
closet ['klɔzit], n. cabinet; boudoir, m.;
garde-robe, armoire, f.—v.t. to be closeted
with, être en tête-à-tête avec.
close-up ['klousʌp], n. (Cine.) gros plan, m.
closing ['klouziŋ], a. dernier, final.—n.
clôture, fermeture (de magasin); fin, conclusion, f.
closure ['klouʒə], n. clôture, fermeture, f.
clot [klɔt], n. grumeau, caillot, m.—v.i. se
cailler, se figer.
cloth [klɔːθ], n. drap (de laine ou tissu d'or ou
d'argent), m.; toile (de lin), f.; table-cloth,
nappe, f., tapis (de laine), m.
clothe [klouð], v.t. habiller, (re)vêtir.
clothes [klouðz], n.pl. habits, vêtements,
m.pl., hardes, f.pl.; bed-clothes, draps et
couvertures, m.pl.
clothing ['klouðiŋ], n. vêtement, habillement,
m.; vêtements, m.pl.
cloud [klaud], n. nuage, m.; (poet.) nue; (fig.)
nuée, f.; every cloud has a silver lining,
après la pluie le beau temps; to be under a
cloud, être mal vu du monde.—v.t. couvrir
de nuages; obscurcir; (fig.) assombrir.—
v.i. se couvrir (de nuages).
cloudburst ['klaudbəːst], n. trombe, rafale de
pluie, f.
cloudless ['klaudlis], a. sans nuage.
cloudy ['klaudi], a. nuageux, couvert; trouble
(liquides); (fig.) ténébreux.
clout [klaut], n. torchon, linge, m.; gifle, tape,
f.—v.t. rapetasser; taper, souffleter.
clove [klouv], n. clou de girofle, m.; clove of
garlic, gousse d'ail, f.
cloven [klouvn], a. fendu; fourchu; to show
the cloven foot, laisser voir le bout de
l'oreille.
clover ['klouvə], n. trèfle, m.
clown [klaun], n. rustre, manant, m. (Theat.)
bouffon, clown, m.
cloy [klɔi], v.t. écœurer, rassasier.
club [klʌb], n. massue, f.; (Golf) club (instrument), m.; crosse, f.; cercle, club, m., association, f.; (Cards) trèfle, m.—v.t. frapper avec
une massue.—v.i. ˙e cotiser, s'associer.
club-foot ['klʌbfut], n. pied bot, m.
club-house ['klʌbhaus], n. cercle; pavillon
(de golf etc.), m.
cluck [klʌk], v.i. glousser.
clucking ['klʌkiŋ], n. gloussement, m.
clue [kluː], n. fil, indice, signe, m.; idée, f.
clueless ['kluːlis], a. (fam.) to be clueless,
ne savoir rien de rien.
clump [klʌmp], n. masse, f., gros bloc; (fig.)
groupe, m.; clump of trees, bouquet
d'arbres, m.
clumsily ['klʌmzili], adv. gauchement, maladroitement.

clumsiness ['klʌmzinis], n. gaucherie, maladresse, f.
clumsy ['klʌmzi], a. gauche, maladroit; mal
fait (chose).
cluster ['klʌstə], n. grappe (de raisin), f.;
bouquet (de fleurs); régime (de bananes);
nœud (de diamants), m.—v.i. se former en
grappes; se grouper.
clutch [klʌtʃ], v.t. saisir, empoigner.—n.
griffe, serre, étreinte, f.; (Motor.) embrayage, m.; couvée (d'œufs), f.
clutter ['klʌtə], n. fracas, vacarme; encombrement, désordre, m.—v.t. to clutter up,
encombrer.
coach [koutʃ], n. voiture, f., carrosse, m.;
(Rail.) voiture, f., wagon; autocar, car;
(Sch.) répétiteur; (Spt.) entraîneur, m.—
v.t. entraîner; préparer aux examens.
coaching ['koutʃiŋ], n. (Spt.) entraînement
(d'équipe), m.; (Sch.) répétitions, f.pl.
coachman ['koutʃmən], n. (pl. -men
[men]) cocher, m.
coachwork ['koutʃwəːk], n. carrosserie, f.
coagulate [kou'ægjuleit], v.t. coaguler.—v.i.
se coaguler.
coal [koul], n. charbon, m.; houille, f.; live
coal, charbon ardent.—v.t. charbonner.—
v.i. s'approvisionner de charbon (navire).
coal cellar ['koulselə], n. cave à charbon, f.
coalesce [kouə'les], v.i. s'unir, se fondre,
fusionner.
coal-field ['koulfiːld], n. bassin houiller, m.
coalition [kouə'liʃən], n. coalition, f.
coal mine ['koulmain], n. mine de charbon,
houillère, f.
coal miner ['koulmainə], n. mineur, m.
coal scuttle ['koulskʌtl], n. seau à charbon,
m.
coarse [kɔːs], a. gros, grossier.
coarseness ['kɔːsnis], n. grossièreté, f.
coast [koust], n. côte, plage, f., rivage, littoral,
m.—v.t. côtoyer.—v.i. côtoyer, suivre la
côte; caboter; planer (oiseau); (Motor.)
rouler au débrayé.
coastal ['koustəl], a. côtier.
coaster ['koustə], n. caboteur, m.
coast guard ['koustgɑːd], n. garde-côte, m.
coast-line ['koustlain], n. littoral, m.
coat [kout], n. habit; enduit (de goudron etc.),
m.; robe (de certains animaux); (Mil.)
tunique; (Paint.) couche, f.; coat of mail,
cotte de mailles, f.; double breasted coat,
veston croisé, m.—v.t. revêtir; enduire (de).
coat hanger ['kouthæŋə], n. cintre, m.;
porte-vêtements, m. inv.
coax [kouks], v.t. amadouer, cajoler, flatter.
co-axial [kou'æksiəl], a. coaxial.
coaxing ['kouksiŋ], n. cajolerie, f., enjôlement, m.
cob [kɔb], n. bidet, goussant (cheval); épi (de
maïs), m.
cobalt ['koubɔːlt], n. cobalt, m.
cobble [kɔbl], v.t. saveter, raccommoder;
paver en cailloutis.—n. galet rond, pavé m.
cobbler ['kɔblə], n. cordonnier, m.
cobnut ['kɔbnʌt], n. aveline, f.
cobra ['koubrə], n. cobra, m.
cobweb ['kɔbweb], n. toile d'araignée, f.
cocaine [ko'kein], n. cocaïne, f.
cochineal ['kɔtʃiniːl], n. cochenille, f.

cock [kɔk], *n.* coq; mâle (*de petits oiseaux*); robinet (*tap*); chien (*de fusil*); tas, meulon (*de foin*), *m.*; **black-cock**, coq de bruyère; **cock-and-bull story**, coq-à-l'âne, *m.*—*v.t.* relever; retrousser; armer (*fusil*); **cocked hat**, chapeau à cornes, *m.*

cockade [kɔ'keid], *n.* cocarde, *f.*

cock-a-doodle-doo ['kɔkədu:dl'du:], *n.* coquerico, cocorico, *m.*

cockatoo [kɔkə'tu:], *n.* kakatoès, cacatois, *m.*

cockatrice ['kɔkətri:s], *n.* basilic, *m.*

cockchafer ['kɔktʃeifə], *n.* hanneton, *m.*

cock-crow ['kɔkkrou], *n.* chant du coq; (*fig.*) point du jour, *m.*

cockerel ['kɔkərəl], *n.* jeune coq, *m.*

cock-eyed ['kɔkaid], *a.* de biais, de travers.

cockle [kɔkl], *n.* bucarde, *f.*

cock-pit ['kɔkpit], *n.* arène des combats de coqs; (*Av.*) carlingue, *f.*

cockroach ['kɔkroutʃ], *n.* blatte, *f.*

cockscomb ['kɔkskoum], *n.* crête de coq, *f.*; [COXCOMB].

cocksure ['kɔkʃuə], *a.* sûr et certain, outrecuidant.

cocktail ['kɔkteil], *n.* cocktail, *m.*; **cocktail party**, cocktail.

cocky ['kɔki], *a.* effronté, suffisant.

coco ['koukou], *n.* coco, *m.*

cocoa ['koukou], *n.* cacao, *m.*

coconut, cocoa-nut ['koukənʌt], *n.* coco, *m.*, noix de coco, *f.*

cocoon [kə'ku:n], *n.* cocon, *m.*

cod [kɔd], *n.* morue, *f.*; cabillaud (*morue fraiche*), *m.*

coddle [kɔdl], *v.t.* mitonner; dorloter, choyer.

code [koud], *n.* code, *m.*—*v.t.* coder; chiffrer.

codicil ['kɔdisil], *n.* codicille, *m.*

codify ['koudifai], *v.t.* codifier.

cod-liver oil ['kɔdlivər'ɔil], *n.* huile de foie de morue, *f.*

co-education ['kouedju'keiʃən], *n.* enseignement mixte, *m.*

co-educational ['kouedju'keiʃənəl], *a.* (*Sch.*) mixte.

coefficient [koui'fiʃənt], *n.* coefficient, *m.*

coerce [kou'ə:s], *v.t.* forcer, contraindre.

coercion [kou'ə:ʃən], *n.* coercition, contrainte, *f.*

coexist [kouig'zist], *v.i.* coexister.

coexistence [kouig'zistəns], *n.* coexistence, *f.*

coffee ['kɔfi], *n.* café, *m.*; **white coffee**, café au lait.

coffee bean ['kɔfibi:n], *n.* grain de café, *m.*

coffee house ['kɔfihaus], *n.* café, *m.*

coffee mill ['kɔfimil], **coffee grinder** ['kɔfi graində], *n.* moulin à café, *m.*

coffee-pot ['kɔfipɔt], *n.* cafetière, *f.*

coffer ['kɔfə], *n.* coffre; caisson; sas *m.*

coffin ['kɔfin], *n.* cercueil, *m.*, bière, *f.*

cog [kɔg], *n.* dent, *f.*

cogency ['koudʒənsi], *n.* force, puissance, *f.*

cogent ['koudʒənt], *a.* puissant, fort.

cogged [kɔgd], *a.* denté, à dents.

cogitate ['kɔdʒiteit], *v.t.* penser (à.)—*v.i.* méditer, penser.

cogitation [kɔdʒi'teiʃən], *n.* réflexion, pensée, méditation, *f.*

cognate ['kɔgneit], *a.* de la même famille; analogue.

cognizance ['kɔgnizəns], *n.* connaissance, *f.*; (*Her.*) insigne, *m.*

cognomen [kɔg'noumən], *n.* surnom; nom de guerre, sobriquet, *m.*

cog-wheel ['kɔgwi:l], *n.* roue d'engrenage, *f.*

cohabit [kou'hæbit], *v.i.* cohabiter.

cohabitation [kouhæbi'teiʃən], *n.* cohabitation, *f.*

coherence [kou'hiərəns], *n.* cohésion, cohérence, *f.*

coherent [kou'hiərənt], *a.* cohérent; conséquent.

coherently [kou'hiərəntli], *adv.* d'une manière cohérente.

cohesion [kou'hi:ʒən], *n.* cohésion, *f.*

cohesive [kou'hi:siv], *a.* cohésif.

cohort ['kouhɔ:t], *n.* cohorte, *f.*

coil [kɔil], *n.* rouleau (*de cheveux etc.*); repli (*de serpents*), *m.*; (*Elec.*) bobine, *f.*—*v.t.* replier, enrouler.—*v.i.* se replier, s'enrouler.

coin [kɔin], *n.* pièce de monnaie, *f.*—*v.t.* monnayer; forger, fabriquer, inventer.

coinage ['kɔinidʒ], *n.* monnayage, *m.*, monnaie; (*fig.*) fabrication, *f.*

coincide [kouin'said], *v.i.* s'accorder, coïncider (*avec*).

coincidence [kou'insidəns], *n.* coïncidence, *f.*

coincidental [kouinsi'dentl], *a.* de coïncidence.

coiner ['kɔinə], *n.* monnayeur; faux monnayeur, *m.*

coition [kou'iʃən], *n.* coït, *m.*

coke [kouk], *n.* coke, *m.*

colander ['kʌləndə], *n.* passoire, *f.*

cold [kould], *a.* froid; **it is cold**, il fait froid; **to be cold** (*of people*), avoir froid.—*n.* froid; rhume (*maladie*), refroidissement; frisson (*sensation*), *m.*; **to catch cold**, s'enrhumer.

coldly ['kouldli], *adv.* froidement.

cole [koul], *n.* chou marin, *m.*

colic ['kɔlik], *n.* colique, *f.*

collaborate [kə'læbəreit], *v.i.* collaborer.

collaboration [kəlæbə'reiʃən], *n.* collaboration, *f.*

collaborator [kə'læbəreitə] *n.* collaborateur, *m.*

collapse [kə'læps], *v.i.* s'affaisser, s'écrouler, s'effondrer.—*n.* affaissement, *m.*, débâcle, *f.*

collapsible [kə'læpsibl], *a.* pliant, démontable.

collar ['kɔlə], *n.* collier (*de chien, de cheval, de décoration*); col (*de chemise*); collet (*de pardessus*), *m.*; collerette (*de dames*), *f.*—*v.t.* colleter, prendre au collet.

collar-bone ['kɔləboun], *n.* clavicule, *f.*

collar stud ['kɔləstʌd], *n.* bouton de col, *m.*

collate [kə'leit], *v.t.* collationner, comparer.

collateral [kə'lætərəl], *a.* collatéral.

collation [kə'leiʃən], *n.* collation, *f.*; don, présent; repas froid, *m.*

colleague ['kɔli:g], *n.* collègue, confrère, *m.*

collect (1) [kə'lekt], *v.t.* recueillir; ramasser; collectionner; percevoir, encaisser (*impôts*); recouvrer (*dettes*); quêter; faire la levée (*du courrier*).—*v.i.* s'amasser.

collect (2) ['kɔlikt], *n.* collecte; (*courte*) prière, *f.*

collected [kə'lektid], *a.* rassemblé; (*fig.*) recueilli, calme, tranquille.

collection [kə'lekʃən], *n.* collection, *f.*; assemblage, rassemblement, *m.*; collecte, quête; levée (*du courrier*), *f.*

collective [kə'lektiv], *a.* collectif.

collector [kə'lektə], *n.* collecteur; collection-neur; percepteur (*impôts*); quêteur (*aumône*); receveur (*douane*), *m.*

college [kɔlidʒ], *n.* collège (d'Université), *m.*; école, *f.*

collide [kə'laid], *v.i.* se heurter.

collier [kɔliə], *n.* mineur; (*Naut.*) (bateau) charbonnier, *m.*

colliery [kɔljəri], *n.* houillère, mine de charbon, *f.*

collision [kə'liʒən], *n.* collision, *f.*, choc, *m.*

colloquial [kə'loukwiəl], *a.* de la conversation, familier; **colloquial French**, français parlé, *m.*

colloquialism [kə'loukwiəlizm], *n.* expression familière, *f.*

colloquy [kɔləkwi], *n.* colloque, entretien, *m.*

collusion [kə'lu:ʒən], *n.* collusion, connivence, *f.*

Colombia [kə'lʌmbiə]. la Colombie, *f.*

colon (1) [koulən], *n.* (*Anat.*) côlon, *m.*

colon (2) [koulən], *n.* (*Gram.*) deux points, *m.pl.*

colonel [kə:nl], *n.* colonel, *m.*

colonial [kə'lounjəl], *a.* colonial.

colonist [kɔlənist], *n.* colon, *m.*

colonization [kɔlənai'zeiʃən], *n.* colonisation, *f.*

colonize [kɔlənaiz], *v.t.* coloniser.

colony [kɔləni], *n.* colonie, *f.*

color [kʌlə], *n.* couleur, *f.*; (*fig.*) prétexte, *m.*, apparence, *f.*; (*pl.*) (*Mil.*) drapeau; (*Navy*) pavillon, *m.*; **to be off color**, être pâle, n'être pas bien en train; **with the colors**, sous les drapeaux.—*v.t.* colorer; colorier, enluminer (*gravure etc.*).—*v.i.* rougir (*personne*); se colorer (*chose*).

Colorado-beetle [kɔlərə'dou'bi:tl], *n.* doryphore, *m.*

color-blind [kʌləblaind], *a.* daltonien.

color-blindness [kʌləblaindnis], *n.* daltonisme, *m.*

colored [kʌləd], *a.* coloré; colorié; de couleur.

colorful [kʌləful], *a.* coloré, pittoresque.

coloring [kʌlərin], *n.* coloris, *m.*; couleur, *f.*

colorless [kʌləlis], *a.* sans couleur.

colossal [kə'lɔsl], *a.* colossal.

Colosseum [kɔlə'si:əm]. Colisée, *m.*

colossus [kə'lɔsəs], *n.* (*pl.* **colossi** [kə'lɔsai], **colossuses** [kə'lɔsəsiz]) colosse, *m.*

colt [koult], *n.* poulain, *m.*; (*fig.*) novice, *m.*

Columbus [kə'lʌmbəs]. Colomb, *m.*

column [kɔləm], *n.* colonne, *f.*

coma [koumə], *n.* coma; assoupissement, *m.*

comb [koum], *n.* peigne, *m.*; étrille (*chevaux*); crête (*coq*), *f.*; rayon (*miel*) *m.*—*v.t.* peigner; étriller (*cheval*).

combat [kɔmbæt], *n.* combat, *m.*—*v.t.*, *v.i.* combattre.

combatant [kɔmbətənt], *n.* combattant, *m.*

combination [kɔmbi'neiʃən], *n.* combinaison, *f.*; association, coalition, *f.*; concours (*de circonstances*), *m.*

combine [kəm'bain], *v.t.* combiner; réunir; allier.—*v.i.* se combiner; se coaliser (*avec*); s'unir (*à*); se syndiquer.—[kɔmbain], *n.* (*Comm.*) cartel, *m.*

combine-harvester [kɔmbain'ha:vistə], *n.* moissonneuse-batteuse, *f.*

combustion [kəm'bʌstʃən], *n.* combustion, *f.*

come [kʌm], *v.i. irr.* venir; arriver, parvenir; se présenter, advenir, se faire; devenir; **come in!** entrez! **come on!** allons! **to come back**, revenir; **to come down**, descendre; **to come for**, venir chercher; **to come forward**, s'avancer; **to come home**, rentrer; **to come in**, entrer; **to come off**, se détacher; **to come out**, sortir; **to come up**, monter.

comedian [kə'mi:diən], *n.* comédien, *m.*

comedy [kɔmidi], *n.* comédie, *f.*

comeliness [kʌmlinis], *n.* aspect gracieux, *m.*; agréments, *m.pl.*

comely [kʌmli], *a.* avenant.

comer [kʌmə], *n.* venant; venu, *m.*; **first comer**, premier venu; **newcomer**, nouveau venu.

comet [kɔmit], *n.* comète, *f.*

comfort [kʌmfət], *n.* réconfort; bien-être, agrément, confort, *m.*; aise(s); aisance, *f.*; **to take comfort**, se consoler.—*v.t.* réconforter, soulager; consoler.

comfortable [kʌmfətəbl], *a.* à son aise; agréable, confortable.

comfortably [kʌmfətəbli], *adv.* à son aise, confortablement.

comforter [kʌmfətə], *n.* consolateur (*le Saint Esprit*); cache-nez (*foulard*), *m.*; couvre-pieds (*inv.*) piqué, *m.*

comfortless [kʌmfətlis], *a.* sans consolation; désolé, triste.

comic [kɔmik], **comical** [kɔmikəl], *a.* comique, drôle.

comically [kɔmikli], *adv.* comiquement.

coming [kʌmin], *n.* venue; arrivée; approche, *f.*

comma [kɔmə], *n.* virgule, *f.*; **inverted commas**, guillemets, *m.pl.*

command [kə'ma:nd], *n.* ordre, commandement; pouvoir, *m.*; autorité, *f.*—*v.t.* commander; posséder; inspirer (*respect*).

commandant [kɔməndænt], *n.* commandant, *m.*

commandeer [kɔmən'diə], *v.t.* réquisitionner.

commander [kə'ma:ndə], *n.* commandant; commandeur (*décoration*); (*Navy*) capitaine (*de frégate etc.*), *m.*

commander-in-chief [kəma:ndərin'tʃi:f], *n.* généralissime, commandant en chef, *m.*

commanding [kə'ma:ndin], *a.* commandant; imposant (*important*); qui domine (*surplombant*); impérieux (*de commandement*).

commandment [kə'ma:ndmənt], *n.* commandement (*de Dieu*), *m.*

commando [kə'ma:ndou], *n.* (*Mil.*) corps franc, commando, *m.*

commemorate [kə'meməreit], *v.t.* célébrer, solenniser; commémorer.

commemoration [kəmemə'reiʃən], *n.* célébration, commémoration, *f.*; souvenir, *m.*

commence [kə'mens], *v.t.*, *v.i.* commencer.

commencement [kə'mensmənt], *n.* commencement, début, *m.*

commend [kə'mend], *v.t.* confier (*à*); recommander; louer.

commendable [kə'mendəbl], *a.* louable.

commendation [kɔmen'deiʃən], *n.* éloge, *m.*, louange, *f.*

comment [kɔment], *n.* commentaire, *m.*—*v.i.* commenter.

commentary ['kɔməntəri], *n.* commentaire, *m.*; *running commentary*, radio-reportage (*d'un match*), *m.*

commerce ['kɔmə:s], *n.* commerce, *m.*

commercial [kə'mə:ʃəl], *a.* commercial, de commerce; commerçant (*ville etc.*); *commercial traveller*, commis voyageur, *m.*—*n.* (*Tel.*) film publicitaire, *m.*

commingle [kɔ'miŋgl], *v.t.* mêler ensemble, mêler.—*v.i.* se mêler ensemble *ou* avec; se fondre (*dans ou en*).

commissariat [kɔmi'sɛəriət], *n.* commissariat, *m.*, intendance, *f.*

commission [kə'miʃən], *n.* commission, *f.*; (*Mil.*) brevet; (*Law*) mandat, *m.*—*v.t.* charger, commissionner.

commissionaire [kəmiʃə'nɛə], *n.* portier (*de magasin*); chasseur (*d'hôtel*); commissionnaire, *m.*

commissioner '[kə'miʃənə], *n.* commissaire, *m.*

commit [kə'mit], *v.t.* commettre; confier, livrer, consigner; engager.

committee [kə'miti], *n.* comité, *m.*; (*Parl.*) commission, *f.*

commode [kə'moud], *n.* commode, *f.*

commodious [kə'moudjəs], *a.* spacieux.

commodity [kə'mɔditi], *n.* marchandise, denrée, *f.*, produit, *m.*

commodore ['kɔmədɔ:], *n.* (*Navy*) chef de division, *m.*; *air-commodore*, général de brigade, *m.*

common ['kɔmən], *a.* commun; ordinaire; vulgaire; (*fig.*) trivial; (*Mil.*) simple.—*n.* commune, *f.*; communal, *m.*; bruyère, lande, *f.*; *House of Commons*, Chambre des Communes, *f.*

commoner ['kɔmənə], *n.* bourgeois, roturier, *m.*

commonly ['kɔmənli], *adv.* ordinairement.

commonplace ['kɔmənpleis], *a.* banal, commun, trivial.—*n.* lieu commun, *m.*, banalité, *f.*

commonweal ['kɔmən'wi:l], *n.* le bien public, *m.*

commonwealth ['kɔmənwelθ], *n.* la chose publique, *f.*, l'État, *m.*; *the (British) Commonwealth*, le Commonwealth (britannique).

commotion [kə'mouʃən], *n.* secousse, agitation, *f.*, tumulte, *m.*

communal [kə'mju:nəl], *a.* communal.

commune (1) [kə'mju:n], *v.i.* parler, converser, s'entretenir (*avec*).

commune (2) ['kɔmju:n], *n.* commune, *f.*

communicate [kə'mju:nikeit], *v.t.* communiquer.—*v.i.* se communiquer.

communication [kəmju:ni'keiʃən], *n.* communication, *f.*

communion [kə'mju:njən], *n.* (*Eccles.*) communion, *f.*; commerce, *m.*

communiqué [kə'mju:nikei], *n.* communiqué, *m.*

Communism ['kɔmjunizm], *n.* communisme, *m.*

Communist ['kɔmjunist], *a.* and *n.* communiste, *m.*, *f.*

community [kə'mju:niti], *n.* communauté, société, *f.*

commutator ['kɔmjuteitə], *n.* commutateur, *m.*

compact (1) ['kɔmpækt], *n.* pacte, contrat; poudrier (*de dame*), *m.*

compact (2) [kəm'pækt], *a.* compact, serré, bien lié; concis.—*v.t.* rendre compact, unir.

companion [kəm'pænjən], *n.* compagnon, *m.*, compagne; dame *ou* demoiselle de compagnie (*to a lady*), *f.*; pendant (*mobilier*), *m.*

companionship [kəm'pænjənʃip], *n.* camaraderie; compagnie, *f.*

company ['kʌmpəni], *n.* compagnie; société, corporation; troupe (*acteurs*), *f.*; (*Naut.*) équipage, *m.*; *we have company today*, nous avons du monde aujourd'hui.

comparable ['kɔmpərəbl], *a.* comparable.

comparative [kəm'pærətiv], *a.* comparatif.

comparatively [kəm'pærətivli], *adv.* relativement, comparativement.

compare [kəm'pɛə], *v.t.* comparer.—*v.i.* être comparable à, rivaliser.

comparison [kəm'pærisən], *n.* comparaison, *f.*

compartment [kəm'pɑ:tmənt], *n.* compartiment, *m.*

compass ['kʌmpəs], *n.* compas; circuit, cercle, *m.*; boussole; portée (*atteinte*); étendue (*de la voix*), *f.*; *a pair of compasses*, un compas.—*v.t.* faire le tour de, entourer; accomplir; *to compass about*, environner.

compassion [kəm'pæʃən], *n.* compassion, pitié, *f.*

compassionate [kəm'pæʃənit], *a.* compatissant.

compatible [kəm'pætəbl], *a.* compatible (*avec*).

compatriot [kəm'pætriət], *n.* compatriote, *m.*, *f.*

compel [kəm'pel], *v.t.* contraindre, forcer (*de*), obliger (*à ou de*).

compelling [kəm'peliŋ], *a.* compulsif, irrésistible.

compensate ['kɔmpənseit], *v.t.* dédommager (*de*); compenser.—*v.i.* *to compensate for*, remplacer, racheter.

compensation [kɔmpən'seiʃən], *n.* dédommagement, *m.*; compensation, *f.*

compete [kəm'pi:t], *v.i.* concourir (*pour*), faire concurrence (*à*); disputer, rivaliser.

competence ['kɔmpitəns], *n.* capacité, aptitude; (*fig.*) aisance (*fortune*), *f.*

competent ['kɔmpitənt], *a.* compétent (*pour*), capable (*de*).

competently ['kɔmpitəntli], *adv.* avec compétence; suffisamment.

competition [kɔmpi'tiʃən], *n.* (*Comm.*) concurrence, *f.*; concours, *m.*

competitive [kəm'petitiv], *a.* compétitif, de concurrence; *competitive examination*, concours, *m.*

competitor [kəm'petitə], *n.* compétiteur; (*Comm.*) concurrent, *m.*

compile [kəm'pail], *v.t.* compiler, composer.

complacent [kəm'pleisənt], *a.* suffisant, de suffisance.

complacently [kəm'pleisəntli], *adv.* avec un air *ou* ton suffisant.

complain [kəm'plein], *v.i.* se plaindre (*de*).

complaint [kəm'pleint], *n.* plainte; maladie, *f.*, mal (*illness*), *m.*; réclamation, *f.*; *to lodge a complaint*, porter plainte.

complaisance [kəm'pleizəns], *n.* complaisance, *f.*

complement ['kɔmplimənt], *n.* complément, *m.*

complementary [kɔmpli'mentəri], *a.* complémentaire.

complete [kəm'pli:t], *a.* complet, entier; achevé.—*v.t.* compléter, achever; (*fig.*) accomplir; remplir (*une fiche*).

completely [kəm'pli:tli], *adv.* complètement.

completion [kəm'pli:ʃən], *n.* achèvement, accomplissement, *m.*; perfection, *f.*

complex ['kɔmpleks], *a.* and *n.* complexe, *m.*

complexion [kəm'plekʃən], *n.* teint, *m.*; couleur, *f.*; caractère, *m.*; **to put a different complexion on**, présenter sous un autre jour.

complexity [kəm'pleksiti], *n.* complexité, *f.*

compliance [kəm'plaiəns], *n.* acquiescement, *m.*; obéissance, *f.*; **in compliance with**, conformément à.

complicate ['kɔmplikeit], *v.t.* compliquer; embrouiller.

complicated ['kɔmplikeitid], *a.* compliqué.

complication [kɔmpli'keiʃən], *n.* complication, *f.*

compliment ['kɔmplimənt], *n.* compliment, *m.*; (*pl.*) salutations, *f.pl.*, hommages (*à une dame*), *m.pl.*—[kɔmpli'ment], *v.t.* complimenter, féliciter.

complimentary [kɔmpli'mentəri], *a.* flatteur; en hommage; **complimentary ticket**, billet de faveur, *m.*

comply [kəm'plai], *v.i.* se soumettre, se conformer; accéder (*à*).

component [kəm'pounənt], *a.* constituant, composant.—*n.* (*Mech.*) composant, *m.*

compose [kəm'pouz], *v.t.* composer; écrire; rédiger, arranger; calmer.

composed [kəm'pouzd], *a.* composé; calme.

composer [kəm'pouzə], *n.* auteur; (*Mus.*) compositeur, *m.*

composite ['kɔmpəzit], *a.* composé; (*Arch.*) composite.

composition [kɔmpə'ziʃən], *n.* composition; (*Sch.*) rédaction, *f.*; **French composition**, thème français, *m.*

compositor [kəm'pɔzitə], *n.* (*Print.*) compositeur, *m.*

compost ['kɔmpɔst], *n.* compost, terreau, *m.*

composure [kəm'pouʒə], *n.* calme, *m.*

compound ['kɔmpaund], *a.* and *n.* composé, *m.*; **compound interest**, intérêts composés, *m.pl.*—[kəm'paund], *v.t.* composer; mêler, combiner; (*Comm.*) atermoyer.—*v.i.* s'arranger.

comprehend [kɔmpri'hend], *v.t.* comprendre.

comprehensible [kɔmpri'hensibl], *a.* compréhensible.

comprehension [kɔmpri'henʃən], *n.* compréhension, *f.*

comprehensive [kɔmpri'hensiv], *a.* étendu, compréhensif; **comprehensive study**, étude d'ensemble, *f.*

compress [kɔmpres], *n.* compresse, *f.*—[kəm'pres], *v.t.* comprimer; (*fig.*) resserrer.

comprise [kɔm'praiz], *v.t.* contenir, renfermer, comporter.

compromise ['kɔmprəmaiz], *n.* compromis, arrangement, *m.*—*v.t.* compromettre.—*v.i.* transiger.

compromising ['kɔmprəmaiziŋ], *a.* compromettant.

compulsion [kəm'pʌlʃən], *n.* contrainte, *f.*

compulsorily [kəm'pʌlsərili], *adv.* par force, forcément.

compulsory [kəm'pʌlsəri], *a.* forcé, obligatoire.

compute [kəm'pju:t], *v.t.* calculer, supputer.

computer [kəm'pju:tə], *n.* machine à calculer, *f.*; ordinateur, *m.*

comrade ['kɔmrid], *n.* camarade, compagnon, *m.*

comradeship ['kɔmridʃip], *n.* camaraderie, *f.*

concave ['kɔnkeiv], *a.* concave, creux.

conceal [kən'si:l], *v.t.* cacher; (*fig.*) dissimuler; celer *ou* céler (*à*).

concealment [kən'si:lmənt], *n.* dissimulation, *f.*; secret, mystère, *m.*; retraite, cachette, *f.*

concede [kən'si:d], *v.t.* concéder, accorder, admettre.—*v.i.* faire des concessions.

conceit [kən'si:t], *n.* suffisance, vanité, *f.*

conceited [kən'si:tid], *a.* suffisant, vaniteux.

conceivable [kən'si:vəbl], *a.* concevable, imaginable.

conceive [kən'si:v], *v.t.* concevoir; imaginer.—*v.i.* concevoir, devenir enceinte (*femme*).

concentrate ['kɔnsəntreit], *v.t.* concentrer.—*v.i.* se concentrer.

concentration [kɔnsən'treiʃən], *n.* concentration, *f.*

conception [kən'sepʃən], *n.* conception, idée, *f.*

concern [kən'sə:n], *n.* intérêt; soin, souci, *m.*, anxiété; (*Comm.*) entreprise; (*fig.*) affaire, *f.*—*v.t.* concerner, regarder; intéresser; inquiéter.

concerning [kən'sə:niŋ], *prep.* touchant, concernant, en ce qui concerne, à l'égard de.

concert [kən'sə:t], *v.t.* concerter.—*v.i.* se concerter.—['kɔnsət], *n.* concert; accord, *m.*

concerto [kən'tʃə:tou], *n.* (*Mus.*) concerto, *m.*

concession [kən'seʃən], *n.* concession, *f.*

concessionary [kən'seʃənəri], *a.* concessionnaire.

conch [kɔŋk], *n.* conque, *f.*

conciliate [kən'silieit], *v.t.* concilier.

conciliation [kənsili'eiʃən], *n.* conciliation, *f.*

conciliator [kən'silieitə], *n.* conciliateur, *m.*

conciliatory [kən'siljətri], *a.* conciliant, conciliatoire.

concise [kən'sais], *a.* concis.

concisely [kən'saisli], *adv.* succinctement.

conclude [kən'klu:d], *v.t.* conclure; terminer, achever; estimer.

concluding [kən'klu:diŋ], *a.* final, dernier.

conclusion [kən'klu:ʒən], *n.* conclusion, fin; décision, *f.*

conclusive [kən'klu:siv], *a.* concluant; conclusif.

concoct [kən'kɔkt], *v.t.* confectionner; inventer, préparer; machiner (*un plan*), tramer.

concoction [kən'kɔkʃən], *n.* confection (*d'un plat*); potion; (*fig.*) machination (*complot*), *f.*

concord ['kɔŋkɔ:d], *n.* concorde, harmonie, *f.*; (*Mus.*) accord, *m.*

concourse ['kɔŋkɔ:s], *n.* concours, *m.*, affluence, foule; réunion, *f.*

concrete ['kɔŋkri:t], *a.* concret.—*n.* béton; bétonnage, *m.*; **reinforced concrete**, béton armé.—*v.t.* bétonner.

concubine ['kɔŋkjubain], *n.* concubine, *f.*

concur [kən'kə:], *v.i.* s'accorder, être d'accord (*avec*).

concurrence [kən'kʌrəns], *n.* assentiment; concours, *m.*

concurrent [kən'kʌrənt], *a.* qui concourt, qui s'accorde, concourant.

concurrently [kən'kʌrəntli], *adv.* concurremment.

concussion [kən'kʌʃən], *n.* secousse, *f.*; choc, *m.*; (*Med.*) commotion, *f.*

condemn [kən'dem], *v.t.* condamner (*à*); déclarer coupable; blâmer.

condemnation [kɔndem'neiʃən], *n.* condamnation, censure, *f.*, blâme, *m.*

condensation [kɔnden'seiʃən], *n.* condensation, *f.*

condense [kən'dens], *v.t.* condenser; (*fig.*) resserrer, abréger.

condenser [kən'densə], *n.* condenseur; (*Phys.*) condensateur, *m.*

condescend [kɔndə'send], *v.i.* condescendre, daigner (*à*).

condescension [kɔndə'senʃən], *n.* condescendance, *f.*; acte de condescendance, *m.*

condiment ['kɔndimənt], *n.* assaisonnement, condiment, *m.*

condition [kən'diʃən], *n.* condition, *f.*, état, *m.*—*v.t.* conditionner.

conditional [kən'diʃənəl], *a.* conditionnel.

conditionally [kən'diʃənəli], *adv.* conditionnellement.

condole [kən'doul], *v.i.* prendre part à la douleur (*de*), exprimer ses condoléances.

condolence [kən'douləns], *n.* condoléance, *f.*

condone [kən'doun], *v.t.* excuser, pardonner.

condor ['kɔndə], *n.* condor, *m.*

conduce [kən'dju:s], *v.i.* contribuer (*à*).

conducive [kən'dju:siv], *a.* qui contribue (*à*).

conduct ['kɔndʌkt], *n.* conduite; direction, *f.*; *safe conduct*, sauf-conduit, *m.*—[kən'dʌkt], *v.t.* conduire (*à*); diriger, mener.

conductor [kən'dʌktə], *n.* receveur (d'autobus); (*Am.*) (*Rail.*) chef de train; (*Mus.*) chef d'orchestre; (*Phys.*) conducteur, *m.*; *lightning-conductor*, paratonnerre, *m.*

conductress [kən'dʌktris], *n.* receveuse (d'autobus), *f.*

conduit ['kʌndit, 'kɔndit], *n.* conduit; tuyau, *m.*

cone [koun], *n.* cône; (*Bot.*) strobile, *m.*, pomme de pin, *f.*; *ice-cream cone*, cornet de glace, *m.*

confection [kən'fekʃən], *n.* bonbon, *m.*, friandise, *f.*

confectioner [kən'fekʃənə], *n.* confiseur, *m.*

confectionery [kən'fekʃənəri], *n.* confiserie, *f.*, bonbons, *m.pl.*

confederacy [kən'fedərəsi], *n.* confédération (*d'États*); ligue (*de conspirateurs*), *f.*

confederate [kən'fedərit], *a.* confédéré.—*n.* confédéré, *m.*, complice, *m.*, *f.*

confederation [kɔnfedə'reiʃən], *n.* confédération, *f.*

confer [kən'fə:], *v.t.* conférer, accorder.—*v.i.* conférer (*de*).

conference ['kɔnfərəns], *n.* conférence, *f.*, congrès, *m.*

confess [kən'fes], *v.t.* confesser, avouer.—*v.i.* se confesser.

confessed [kən'fest], *a.* reconnu, confessé, avoué.

confessedly [kən'fesidli], *adv.* de son propre aveu.

confession [kən'feʃən], *n.* confession, *f.*, aveu, *m.*

confessor [kən'fesə], *n.* confesseur, *m.*

confidant ['kɔnfidænt], *n.* confident, *m.*

confide [kən'faid], *v.t.* confier (*à*).—*v.i.* se confier, se fier (*à*).

confidence ['kɔnfidəns], *n.* confiance; hardiesse; assurance; confidence (*secret*), *f.*

confident ['kɔnfidənt], *a.* confiant, certain, sûr; assuré.

confidential [kɔnfi'denʃəl], *a.* de confiance (*personne*); confidentiel (*chose*).

confidentially [kɔnfi'denʃəli], *adv.* de confiance; confidentiellement.

confidently ['kɔnfidəntli], *adv.* avec confiance.

confine [kən'fain], *v.t.* confiner, enfermer; retenir; limiter; *to be confined* (*of woman*), faire ses couches, accoucher.—['kɔnfain], *n.* (*usu. in pl.*) confins, *m.pl.*; (*fig.*) limite, borne, *f.*

confinement [kən'fainmənt], *n.* emprisonnement, *m.*; (*Mil.*) arrêts, *m.pl.*; accouchement, *m.*, couches (*de femme*), *f.pl.*

confirm [kən'fə:m], *v.t.* confirmer; affermir.

confirmation [kɔnfə'meiʃən], *n.* confirmation, *f.*, affermissement, *m.*

confirmed [kən'fə:md], *a.* invétéré, fieffé, incorrigible.

confiscate ['kɔnfiskeit], *v.t.* confisquer.

confiscation [kɔnfis'keiʃən], *n.* confiscation, *f.*

conflagration [kɔnflə'greiʃən], *n.* conflagration, *f.*, incendie, *m.*

conflict ['kɔnflikt], *n.* conflit, *m.*; (*fig.*) lutte, contradiction, *f.*—[kən'flikt], *v.i.* s'entrechoquer, lutter (*contre*); être en conflit (*avec*).

conflicting [kən'fliktiŋ], *a.* en conflit, contradictoire.

confluence ['kɔnfluəns], *n.* confluent; concours, *m.*; (*Path.*) confluence, *f.*

conform [kən'fɔ:m], *v.t.* conformer.—*v.i.* se conformer.

conformity [kən'fɔ:miti], *n.* conformité, *f.*; *in conformity with*, conformément (*à*).

confound [kən'faund], *v.t.* confondre; (*fig.*) bouleverser; embarrasser; *confound it!* zut!

confounded [kən'faundid], *a.* maudit, sacré.

confoundedly [kən'faundidli], *adv.* terriblement, furieusement, diablement.

confront [kən'frʌnt], *v.t.* confronter; affronter, faire face à.

confuse [kən'fju:z], *v.t.* rendre confus, embrouiller; (*fig.*) déconcerter.

confused [kən'fju:zd], *a.* confus; embrouillé.

confusedly [kən'fju:zidli], *adv.* confusément.

confusion [kən'fju:ʒən], *n.* confusion, *f.*, désordre; (*fig.*) embarras, *m.*

confute [kən'fju:t], *v.t.* réfuter.

congeal [kən'dʒi:l], *v.t.* congeler, glacer, geler, figer.—*v.i.* se congeler, se geler, se figer.

congenial [kən'dʒi:niəl], *a.* de la même nature; sympathique (*à* ou *avec*); qui convient (*à*); *a congenial task*, une tâche agréable.

conger ['kɔŋgə], *n.* (*Ichth.*) congre, *m.*, anguille de mer, *f.*

congest [kən'dʒest], *v.t.* entasser; engorger; *to become congested*, se congestionner; s'embouteiller (*rues*).

congestion [kən'dʒestʃən], *n.* amoncellement, *m.*; (*Path.*) congestion, *f.*; encombrement (*des rues*), *m.*

conglomerate [kən'gləməreit], *v.t.* conglomérer.—*v.i.* se conglomérer.—[kən'gləmərit], *n.* (*Geol.*) conglomérat, *m.*

conglomeration [kəngləmə'reiʃən], *n.* conglomération, *f.*

Congo ['kəngou]. le Congo, *m.*

Congolese [kəngo'li:z], *a.* congolais.—*n.* Congolais (*personne*).

congratulate [kən'grætjuleit], *v.t.* féliciter.

congratulation [kəngrætju'leiʃən], *n.* félicitation, *f.*

congregate ['kəngrigeit], *v.t.* rassembler.—*v.i.* se rassembler.

congregation [kəngri'geiʃən], *n.* (*Eccles.*) congrégation, *f.*, fidèles, *m.pl.*; assemblée, *f.*, auditoire, *m.*, assistance, *f.*

congress ['kəngres], *n.* congrès, *m.*

congressional [kəŋ'greʃənl], *a.* congressionnel.

congressman ['kəngresmən], *n.* (*pl.* -men [men]) (*U.S.*) membre du Congrès, *m.*

conic ['kənik], **conical** ['kənikəl], *a.* conique.

conifer ['kounifə], *n.* conifère, *m.*

coniferous [ko'nifərəs], *a.* conifère.

conjecture [kən'dʒektʃə], *v.t., v.i.* conjecturer.—*n.* conjecture, *f.*

conjugal ['kəndʒugəl], *a.* conjugal.

conjugate ['kəndʒugeit], *v.t.* conjuguer.

conjugation [kəndʒu'geiʃən], *n.* conjugaison, *f.*

conjunction [kən'dʒʌŋkʃən], *n.* conjonction, *f.*

conjure ['kʌndʒə], *v.t.* ensorceler; escamoter; *to conjure up*, évoquer.

conjurer, conjuror ['kʌndʒərə], *n.* escamoteur, prestidigitateur, illusionniste, *m.*

conjuring ['kʌndʒəriŋ], *n.* prestidigitation, *f.*, escamotage, *m.*

connect [kə'nekt], *v.t.* lier, joindre, rattacher, unir (*à*); accoupler.—*v.i.* se lier; faire correspondance (*trains*).

connected [kə'nektid], *a.* joint, uni, lié; cohérent; en relations.

connection (connexion) [kə'nekʃən], *n.* connexion, liaison, suite, *f.*; rapport, *m.*; (*Rail.*) correspondance, *f.*; (*Elec.*) contact, *m.*; (*Comm.*) clientèle, *f.*; (*pl.*) parents, *m.pl.*; *in connection with*, à propos de.

connivance [kə'naivəns], *n.* connivence, *f.*

connive [kə'naiv], *v.i.* *to connive at*, fermer les yeux sur, être de connivence dans.

connoisseur [kənə'sə:], *n.* connaisseur, *m.*

connubial [kə'nju:biəl], *a.* conjugal.

conquer ['kəŋkə], *v.t.* vaincre, dompter; conquérir.—*v.i.* vaincre, remporter la victoire.

conqueror ['kəŋkərə], *n.* vainqueur, conquérant, *m.*

conquest ['kəŋkwesʼ], *n.* conquête, *f.*

conscience ['kənʃəns], *n.* conscience, *f.*; *conscience money*, restitution anonyme, *f.*

conscientious [kənʃi'enʃəs], *a.* consciencieux; de conscience; *conscientious objector*, objecteur de conscience, *m.*

conscientiously [kənʃi'enʃəli], *adv.* consciencieusement.

conscious ['kənʃəs], *a.* conscient; *to be conscious*, avoir sa connaissance; *to be conscious of*, avoir conscience de.

consciously ['kənʃəsli], *adv.* sciemment, en connaissance de cause.

consciousness ['kənʃəsnis], *n.* conscience; connaissance, *f.*

conscript ['kənskript], *a.* and *n.* conscrit, *m.*—[kən'skript], *v.t.* enrôler (par la conscription).

conscription [kən'skripʃən], *n.* conscription, *f.*

consecrate ['kənsikreit], *v.t.* consacrer (*une église*); bénir (*pain*); sacrer (*évêque, roi*); *consecrated ground*, terre sainte, *f.*

consecration [kənsi'kreiʃən], *n.* consécration; canonisation, *f.*; sacre (*d'évêque, de roi etc.*), *m.*

consecutive [kən'sekjutiv], *a.* consécutif.

consent [kən'sent], *v.i.* consentir (*à*).—*n.* consentement; accord, *m.*

consequence ['kənsikwəns], *n.* conséquence, suite, *f.*, effet, *m.*; importance, *f.*

consequent ['kənsikwənt], *a.* résultant; (*Log.*) conséquent.—*n.* conséquent, *m.*

consequential [kənsi'kwenʃəl], *a.* conséquent, logique; (*fig.*) suffisant, important.

consequently ['kənsikwəntli], *adv.* and *conj.* par conséquent.

conservative [kən'sə:vətiv], *a.* and *n.* conservateur, *m.*

conservatory [kən'sə:vətri], *n.* conservatoire (*théâtre, musique*), *m.*; (*Hort.*) serre, *f.*

consider [kən'sidə], *v.t.* considérer, examiner; estimer.—*v.i.* considérer, réfléchir (*à*).

considerable [kən'sidərəbl], *a.* considérable, grand, important.

considerably [kən'sidərəbli], *adv.* considérablement.

considerate [kən'sidərit], *a.* modéré, indulgent; attentif, plein d'égards; prévenant.

consideration [kənsidə'reiʃən], *n.* considération, *f.*, examen, *m.*; égards, *m.pl.*; récompense, *f.*, dédommagement, *m.*; *to take into consideration*, tenir compte de.

considering [kən'sidəriŋ], *prep.* eu égard à, étant donné, vu.—*conj.* vu que, attendu que, étant donné que.

consign [kən'sain], *v.t.* consigner, livrer, confier (*à*); (*Comm.*) expédier.

consignment [kən'sainmənt], *n.* expédition, *f.*, envoi, *m.*

consist [kən'sist], *v.i.* consister (*en*); *to consist of*, se composer (*de*).

consistency [kən'sistənsi], *n.* consistance, suite, *f.*, esprit de suite; accord, *m.*, harmonie; stabilité, *f.*

consistent [kən'sistənt], *a.* consistant; compatible (*avec*), conséquent.

consistently [kən'sistəntli], *adv.* d'une manière conséquente, conséquemment.

consolation [kənsə'leiʃən], *n.* consolation, *f.*

console [kən'soul], *v.t.* consoler (*de*).

consolidate [kən'səlideit], *v.t.* consolider.—*v.i.* se consolider; *consolidated annuities*, (*abbr.*) *consols*, consolidés, *m.pl.*

consolidation [kənsəli'deiʃən], *n.* consolidation, *f.*

consoling [kən'souliŋ], *a.* consolant, consolateur.

consonant ['kənsənənt], *a.* consonant, conforme (*à*).—*n.* (*Phon.*) consonne, *f.*

consort ['kənsɔ:t], *n.* compagnon, *m.*, compagne, *f.*; époux, *m.*, épouse, *f.*—[kən'sɔ:t], *v.i.* s'associer (*à*); *to consort with*, fréquenter.

conspicuous [kən'spikjuəs], *a.* bien visible, en évidence; remarquable, éminent.
conspicuously [kən'spikjuəsli], *adv.* visiblement, manifestement, éminemment.
conspiracy [kən'spirəsi], *n.* conspiration, conjuration, *f.*
conspirator [kən'spirətə], *n.* conspirateur; conjuré, *m.*
conspire [kən'spaiə], *v.i.* conspirer, comploter (*contre*); (*fig.*) se réunir (*pour*).
constable ['kʌnstəbl], *n.* gouverneur (*de château*); agent de police, *m.*; **chief constable**, commissaire de police, *m.*
constabulary [kən'stæbjulari], *n.* police; gendarmerie, *f.*
constancy ['kɔnstənsi], *n.* constance, fermeté, fidélité; régularité, *f.*
constant ['kɔnstənt], *a.* stable, constant, fidèle; continu.
constantly ['kɔnstəntli], *adv.* constamment, invariablement.
constellation [kɔnstə'leiʃən], *n.* constellation, *f.*
consternation [kɔnstə'neiʃən], *n.* consternation, *f.*, atterrement, *m.*
constipation [kɔnsti'peiʃən], *n.* constipation, *f.*
constituency [kən'stitjuənsi], *n.* circonscription électorale, *f.*, électeurs, *m.pl.*
constituent [kən'stitjuənt], *a.* constituant.—*n.* constituant; (*Polit.*) commettant, électeur, *m.*
constitute ['kɔnstitju:t], *v.t.* constituer, faire.
constitution [kɔnsti'tju:ʃən], *n.* constitution, *f.*, tempérament, *m.*
constitutional [kɔnsti'tju:ʃənəl], *a.* constitutionnel.—*n.* promenade de santé, *f.*
constrain [kən'strein], *v.t.* contraindre, forcer; retenir; gêner.
constraint [kən'streint], *n.* contrainte, gêne, *f.*
constrict [kən'strikt], *v.t.* resserrer, étrangler; brider.
construct [kən'strʌkt], *v.t.* construire, bâtir.
construction [kən'strʌkʃən], *n.* construction, *f.*; bâtiment, *m.*; (*fig.*) interprétation, *f.*, sens, *m.*
constructive [kən'strʌktiv], *a.* constructif; implicite.
construe [kən'stru:], *v.t.* traduire mot-à-mot; (*fig.*) expliquer, interpréter.
consul ['kɔnsəl], *n.* consul, *m.*
consular ['kɔnsjulə], *a.* consulaire.
consulate ['kɔnsjulit], **consulship** ['kɔnsəlʃip], *n.* consulat, *m.*
consult [kən'sʌlt], *v.t.* consulter.—*v.i.* délibérer.
consultation [kɔnsəl'teiʃən], *n.* consultation, délibération, *f.*
consume [kən'sju:m], *v.t.* consumer, dissiper, dévorer; gaspiller; consommer (*to use*).
consumer [kən'sju:mə], *n.* consommateur; abonné (*de gaz etc.*), *m.*; **consumer goods**, biens de consommation, *m.pl.*
consummate ['kɔnsəmeit], *v.t.* consommer, achever, accomplir.—[kən'sʌmit], *a.* consommé, complet, achevé, fieffé.
consummation [kɔnsə'meiʃən], *n.* consommation, fin, *f.*; (*fig.*) comble, *m.*
consumption [kən'sʌmpʃən], *n.* consommation; phtisie, consomption (*maladie*), *f.*
consumptive [kən'sʌmptiv], *a.* poitrinaire, phtisique, tuberculeux.

contact ['kɔntækt], *n.* contact, rapport, *m.*—*v.t.* contacter, se mettre en relation avec, entrer en contact avec.
contagion [kən'teidʒən], *n.* contagion, *f.*
contagious [kən'teidʒəs], *a.* contagieux.
contain [kən'tein], *v.t.* contenir; retenir, renfermer.
container [kən'teinə], *n.* récipient, réservoir, *m.*; (*Comm.*) boîte, *f.*
contaminate [kən'tæmineit], *v.t.* souiller, contaminer.
contamination [kəntæmi'neiʃən], *n.* souillure, contamination, *f.*
contemplate ['kɔntəmpleit], *v.t.* contempler; méditer, projeter.—*v.i.* songer, méditer.
contemplation [kɔntəm'pleiʃən], *n.* contemplation; méditation, *f.*; projet, *m.*
contemplative [kən'templətiv], *a.* contemplatif; pensif.
contemporaneous [kəntempə'reinjəs], *a.* contemporain.
contemporary [kən'tempərəri], *a.* and *n.* contemporain, *m.*
contempt [kən'tempt], *n.* mépris, dédain, *m.*
contemptible [kən'temptəbl], *a.* méprisable, à dédaigner.
contemptuous [kən'temptjuəs], *a.* méprisant, dédaigneux.
contend [kən'tend], *v.i.* lutter, combattre; contester; prétendre (*que*).
contender [kən'tendə], *n.* compétiteur, concurrent, *m.*
content (1) [kən'tent], *a.* content, satisfait; **to be content with**, se contenter de.—*n.* contentement, *m.*—*v.t.* contenter, satisfaire.
content (2) ['kɔntent], *n.* contenu, *m.*; **table of contents**, table des matières, *f.*
contented [kən'tentid], *a.* satisfait, content (*de*).
contentedly [kən'tentidli], *adv.* avec contentement.
contention [kən'tenʃən], *n.* dispute, lutte, *f.*, débat, *m.*; prétention, *f.*; **bone of contention**, pomme de discorde, *f.*
contentious [kən'tenʃəs], *a.* contentieux, litigieux, querelleur.
contentiousness [kən'tenʃəsnis], *n.* humeur querelleuse, *f.*
contentment [kən'tentmənt], *n.* contentement, *m.*
conterminous [kən'tə:minəs], *a.* limitrophe, voisin (*de*); attenant (*à*).
contest ['kɔntest], *n.* lutte, *f.*, combat; concours, *m.*—[kən'test], *v.t.*, *v.i.* contester, disputer.
contestant [kən'testənt], *n.* contestant, concurrent, *m.*
context ['kɔntekst], *n.* contexte, *m.*; **in this context**, à ce sujet.
contiguity [kɔnti'gju:iti], *n.* contiguïté, *f.*
contiguous [kən'tigjuəs], *a.* contigu, attenant (*à*).
continence ['kɔntinəns], *n.* continence, chasteté; (*fig.*) retenue, *f.*
continent (1) ['kɔntinənt], *a.* continent, chaste; (*fig.*) modéré, retenu.
continent (2) ['kɔntinənt], *n.* continent, *m.*
continental [kɔnti'nentl], *a.* and *n.* continental, *m.*
contingence [kən'tindʒəns], **contingency** [kən'tindʒənsi], *n.* éventualité, *f.*, cas imprévu, *m.*

contingent [kən'tindʒənt], *a.* contingent, fortuit, imprévu.—*n.* (*Mil.*) contingent, *m.*

contingently [kən'tindʒəntli], *adv.* éventuellement, fortuitement.

continual [kən'tinjuəl], *a.* continuel.

continually [kən'tinjuəli], *adv.* continuellement.

continuance [kən'tinjuəns], *n.* continuation; durée, *f.*

continuation [kəntinju'eiʃən], *n.* continuation, durée, *f.*

continue [kən'tinju:], *v.t.* continuer; prolonger; reprendre; perpétuer.—*v.i.* continuer; demeurer; durer.

continued [kən'tinju:d], *a.* continu, suivi; à suivre (*feuilleton*); **to be continued**, à suivre.

continuity [kənti'nju:iti], *n.* continuité, *f.*

continuous [kən'tinjuəs], *a.* continu.

continuously [kən'tinjuəsli], *adv.* continûment, sans interruption.

contort [kən'tɔ:t], *v.t.* tordre, contourner, défigurer.

contorted [kən'tɔ:tid], *a.* tordu, contourné, défiguré.

contortion [kən'tɔ:ʃən], *n.* contorsion, (*Anat.*) luxation, *f.*

contortionist [kən'tɔ:ʃənist], *n.* contorsionniste, *m., f.*

contour ['kəntuə], *n.* contour, tracé (*de niveau*), *m.*

contra ['kəntrə], *prep.* contre; (*Comm.*) d'autre part.

contraband ['kəntrəbænd], *a.* de contrebande.—*n.* contrebande, *f.*

contraception [kəntrə'sepʃən], *n.* procédés anticonceptionnels, *m.pl.*

contraceptive [kəntrə'septiv], *a.* anticonceptionnel.—*n.* procédé *ou* appareil anticonceptionnel, *m.*

contract [kən'trækt], *v.t.* contracter (*dans tous les sens*); abréger; (*fig.*) resserrer; rider, froncer (*les sourcils etc.*); prendre (*habitude*).—*v.i.* se contracter, se resserrer, se rétrécir; (*Comm.*) traiter (*pour*), contracter, entreprendre, soumissionner; **to contract out of something**, renoncer à *ou* se dégager de quelquechose par contrat.—['kəntrækt], *n.* contrat; pacte, *m.*, convention; adjudication, *f.*

contractible [kən'træktəbl], *a.* contractile.

contraction [kən'trækʃən], *n.* contraction, *f.*, rétrécissement; raccourcissement; retrait (*métaux*), *m.*; (*Math.*) abréviation, *f.*

contractor [kən'træktə], *n.* contractant; entrepreneur (*constructeur*); fournisseur (*aux forces armées*); adjudicataire (*concesseur*), *m.*

contradict [kəntrə'dikt], *v.t.* contredire, démentir.

contradiction [kəntrə'dikʃən], *n.* contradiction, incompatibilité, *f.*, démenti (*négation*), *m.*

contradictory [kəntrə'diktəri], *a.* contradictoire.

contralto [kən'træltou], *n.* (*Mus.*) contralto, contralte, *m.*

contrariety [kəntrə'raiəti], *n.* contrariété, opposition, *f.*

contrarily ['kəntrərili], *adv.* contrairement, en sens contraire.

contrary ['kəntrəri], *a.* contraire, opposé; (*fam.*) [kən'treəri], contrariant (*personne*).—*n.* contraire, *m.*; **on the contrary**, au contraire.—*adv.* contrairement (à); à l'encontre (*de*).

contrast ['kəntra:st], *n.* contraste, *m.*—[kən'tra:st], *v.t.* faire contraster; mettre en contraste.—*v.i.* contraster, faire contraste.

contravene [kəntrə'vi:n], *v.t.* contrevenir à, enfreindre.

contravention [kəntrə'venʃən], *n.* contravention, infraction, *f.*

contribute [kən'tribju't], *v.t.* contribuer, payer.—*v.i.* contribuer (à).

contribution [kəntri'bju:ʃən], *n.* contribution, *f.*

contributor [kən'tribjutə], *n.* contribuant; (*Journ.*) collaborateur, *m.*

contributory [kən'tribjutəri], *a.* contribuant.

contrite ['kəntrait], *a.* contrit, pénitent.

contritely ['kəntraitli], *adv.* avec contrition.

contriteness ['kəntraitnis], **contrition** [kən'triʃən], *n.* contrition, pénitence, *f.*

contrivance [kən'traivəns], *n.* invention; combinaison, idée, *f.*; artifice, *m.*

contrive [kən'traiv], *v.t.* inventer, imaginer; pratiquer, ménager.—*v.i.* s'arranger (*pour*), trouver moyen (*de*); parvenir (à).

contriver [kən'traivə], *n.* inventeur, *m.*, inventrice, *f.*

contriving [kən'traiviŋ], *a.* ingénieux.

control [kən'troul], *n.* autorité (*supérieure*); surveillance; (*Tech.*) commande, *f.*; **out of control**, désemparé; **remote control**, télécommande, *f.*—*v.t.* diriger, régler; gouverner, commander; **to control oneself**, se dominer, se retenir.

controller [kən'troulə], *n.* contrôleur, *m.*

controversial [kəntrə'və:ʃəl], *a.* sujet à controverse, polémique.

controversy ['kəntrəvə:si], *n.* controverse, polémique, *f.*; différend, *m.*

controvert ['kəntrəvə:t], *v.t.* controverser, disputer.

contumacious [kəntju'meiʃəs], *a.* obstiné, récalcitrant, opiniâtre; (*Law*) contumace.

contumaciousness [kəntju'meiʃəsnis], **contumacy** ['kəntjuməsi], *n.* obstination, opiniâtreté; (*Law*) contumace, *f.*

contumelious [kəntju'mi:liəs], *a.* injurieux, outrageant.

contumely ['kəntjuməli], *n.* injure, *f.*, outrage, *m.*, honte, *f.*

contuse [kən'tju:z], *v.t.* contusionner.

contusion [kən'tju:ʃən], *n.* contusion, meurtrissure, *f.*

conundrum [kə'nʌndrəm], *n.* énigme, devinette, *f.*

convalesce [kənvə'les], *v.i.* être en convalescence.

convalescence [kənvə'lesəns], *n.* convalescence, *f.*

convalescent [kənvə'lesənt], *a.* and *n.* convalescent, *m.*, convalescente, *f.*

convection [kən'vekʃən], *n.* convection, *f.*

convene [kən'vi:n], *v.t.* convoquer, réunir, assembler.—*v.i.* s'assembler, se réunir.

convenience [kən'vi:niəns], *n.* commodité, convenance, *f.*

convenient [kən'vi:niənt], *a.* commode, convenable.

387

conveniently [kən'vi:niəntli], *adv.* commodément, convenablement, sans inconvénient.

convent ['kɔnvənt], *n.* couvent, *m.*

conventicle [kən'ventikl], *n.* conventicule, *m.*

convention [kən'venʃən], *n.* convention; assemblée, *f.*; (*pl.*) convenances *f.pl.*

conventional [kən'venʃənəl], *a.* conventionnel, de convention.

conventual [kən'ventjuəl], *a.* conventuel.—*n.* conventuel, religieux, *m.*, religieuse, *f.*

converge [kən'və:dʒ], *v.i.* converger.

conversant [kən'və:sənt], *a.* versé (*dans*); familier (*avec*), au courant de.

conversation [kɔnvə'seiʃən], *n.* conversation, *f.*, entretien, *m.*

conversational [kɔnvə'seiʃənəl], *a.* de conversation.

conversationalist [kɔnvə'seiʃənəlist], *n.* causeur, *m.*

converse [kən'və:s], *v.i.* causer, converser, s'entretenir.—['kɔnvə:s], *n.* entretien, *m.*, conversation; (*Math.*) réciproque, *f.*

conversely ['kɔnvə:sli], *adv.* réciproquement.

conversion [kən'və:ʃən], *n.* conversion, *f.*

convert [kən'və:t], *v.t.* convertir, transformer; faire servir.—['kɔnvə:t], *n.* converti, *m.*, convertie, *f.*

converter [kən'və:tə], *n.* convertisseur, *m.*

convertible [kən'və:tibl], *a.* convertible (*chose*); convertissable (*personne*); (*Motor.*) décapotable.

convex ['kɔnveks], *a.* convexe.

convey [kən'vei], *v.t.* transporter (*marchandises etc.*); porter, conduire, amener; transmettre (*son etc.*); présenter (*remerciements etc.*); donner (*idée etc.*); communiquer (*nouvelle etc.*); céder (*propriété etc.*).

conveyable [kən'veiəbl], *a.* transportable; exprimable.

conveyance [kən'veiəns], *n.* transport, *m.*; transmission, *f.*; véhicule, *m.*; (*Law*) cession, *f.*

conveyor [kən'veiə], *n.* porteur, voiturier; (appareil) transporteur; conducteur (électrique), *m.*; **conveyor belt**, chaîne de montage, *f.*

convict [kən'vikt], *v.t.* condamner, déclarer coupable; convaincre (*quelqu'un de son erreur etc.*).—['kɔnvikt], *n.* forçat, *m.*

conviction [kən'vikʃən], *n.* conviction, persuasion; (*Law*) condamnation, *f.*

convince [kən'vins], *v.t.* convaincre, persuader.

convincing [kən'vinsiŋ], *a.* convaincant; persuasif.

convincingly [kən'vinsiŋli], *adv.* d'une manière convaincante.

convivial [kən'viviəl], *a.* joyeux, jovial.

conviviality [kənvivi'æliti], *n.* franche gaieté, *f.*; (*pl.*) joyeux repas, *m.pl.*

convocation [kɔnvə'keiʃən], *n.* convocation; (*Eccles.*) assemblée, *f.*, synode, *m.*

convoke [kən'vouk], *v.t.* convoquer, assembler.

convolvulus [kən'vɔlvjuləs], *n.* (*pl.* **convolvuli** [kən'vɔlvjulai]) volubilis, liseron, *m.*, belle-de-jour, *f.*

convoy ['kɔnvɔi], *n.* convoi, *m.*, escorte, *f.*

convulse [kən'vʌls], *v.t.* convulser; (*fig.*) ébranler, bouleverser.

convulsion [kən'vʌlʃən], *n.* convulsion; (*fig.*) commotion, *f.*

convulsive [kən'vʌlsiv], *a.* convulsif.

cony, coney ['kouni], *n.* lapin, *m.*

coo [ku:], *v.i.* roucouler.

cooing ['ku:iŋ], *n.* roucoulement, *m.*

cook [kuk], *n.* cuisinier, *m.*, cuisinière, *f.*; (*Naut.*) coq, *m.*; **head cook**, chef, *m.*—*v.t.* cuire, faire cuire.—*v.i.* cuire; faire la cuisine, cuisiner.

cooker ['kukə], *n.* cuisinière (*appareil*), *f.*; fruit à cuire, *m.*; **pressure cooker**, cocotte-minute, *f.*

cookery ['kukəri], *n.* cuisine (*art*), *f.*

cooking ['kukiŋ], *n.* cuisine; cuisson, *f.*

cool [ku:l], *a.* frais, (*fig.*) calme, tranquille; peu gêné.—*n.* frais, *m.*, fraîcheur, *f.*—*v.t.* rafraîchir; refroidir; (*fig.*) calmer.—*v.i.* se refroidir; refroidir; **to cool down**, se calmer, s'apaiser.

cooling ['ku:liŋ], *a.* rafraîchissant, calmant; **cooler**, refroidisseur, *m.*

coolly ['ku:lli], *adv.* fraîchement; (*fig.*) de sangfroid, tranquillement.

coolness ['ku:lnis], *n.* fraîcheur, *f.*, frais, *m.*; (*fig.*) froideur (*indifférence*), *f.*; sang-froid; sans-gêne (*insolence*), *m.*

coop [ku:p], *n.* cage à poules, mue, *f.*—*v.t.* mettre en mue; **to coop up**, enfermer étroitement, claquemurer.

cooper ['ku:pə], *n.* tonnelier, *m.*

co-operate [kou'ɔpəreit], *v.i.* coopérer, concourir (à).

co-operation [kouɔpə'reiʃən], *n.* coopération, *f.*; concours, *m.*

co-operative [kou'ɔpərətiv], *a.* coopérant, coopératif.

co-opt [kou'ɔpt], *v.t.* coopter.

co-ordinate [kou'ɔ:dineit], *v.t.* coordonner.—[kou'ɔ:dinit], *a.* du même rang, égal; (*Math.*) coordonné.

coot [ku:t], *n.* (*Orn.*) foulque, *f.*

cop [kɔp], *n.* cime, *f.*, sommet, *m.*; huppe, aigrette (*d'oiseau*), *f.*; (*slang*) flic (*agent de police*), *m.*

copartner [kou'pa:tnə], *n.* associé, *m.*

copartnership [kou'pa:tnəʃip], *n.* société en nom collectif, *f.*

cope (1) [koup], *n.* chaperon, *m.*, chape (*vêtement sacerdotal*), *f.*—*v.t.* couvrir, chaperonner.

cope (2) [koup], *v.i.* se débrouiller; **to cope with**, tenir tête à; venir à bout de.

Copenhagen [koupən'heigən], Copenhague, *f.*

copier ['kɔpiə], **copyist** ['kɔpiist], *n.* copiste, *m.*, *f.*; (*fig.*) imitateur, *m.*

coping ['koupiŋ], *n.* faîte (*d'un édifice*); couronnement (*d'un mur*), *m.*

copious ['koupiəs], *a.* abondant, copieux.

copiously ['koupiəsli], *adv.* copieusement, abondamment.

copiousness ['koupiəsnis], *n.* abondance, *f.*

copper ['kɔpə], *a.* de cuivre, en cuivre.—*n.* cuivre (rouge), *m.*; chaudière (*boiler*), *f.*; (*slang*) flic (*agent de police*), *m.*; (*pl.*) petite monnaie, *f.*—*v.t.* cuivrer; (*Naut.*) doubler en cuivre.

copper-beech ['kɔpə'bi:tʃ], *n.* hêtre rouge, *m.*

copper-smith ['kɔpəsmiθ], *n.* chaudronnier, *m.*

coppice ['kɔpis], **copse** [kɔps], *n.* taillis, *m.*

copy ['kɔpi], *n.* copie, *f.*; exemple (*d'écriture*); exemplaire (*livre*); numéro (*journal*); modèle (*de dessin*), *m.*; **rough copy**, brouillon, *m.*—*v.t.* copier; imiter. [**copy editor**, see **sub-editor**]

copy-book ['kɔpibuk], *n.* cahier d'écriture, *m.*

copyist [COPIER].

copyright ['kɔpirait], *n.* droits d'auteur, *m.pl.*; propriété littéraire, *f.*

coquet [ko'ket], *v.i.* faire des coquetteries (*à*); faire la coquette (*avec*).

coquette [ko'ket], *n.* coquette, *f.*

coquetry ['koukətri], *n.* coquetterie, *f.*

coquettish [ko'ketiʃ], *a.* coquet, en coquette; provocant (*sourire*).

coquettishly [kə'ketiʃli], *adv.* d'un air provocant.

coral ['kɔrəl], *a.* de corail.—*n.* corail, *m.*

cord [kɔːd], *n.* corde, *f.*, cordon; cordage, *m.*, ganse, *f.*; (*fig.*) lien, *m.*—*v.t.* corder.

cordial ['kɔːdiəl], *a.* cordial.—*n.* cordial, *m.*, liqueur, *f.*

cordiality [kɔːdi'æliti], *n.* cordialité, *f.*

cordially ['kɔːdiəli], *adv.* cordialement.

cordon ['kɔːdən], *n.* cordon, *m.*—*v.t.* **to cordon off**, isoler par un cordon (*de police*).

corduroy ['kɔːdjurɔi], *n.* velours à côtes, *m.*

core [kɔː], *n.* cœur; noyau (*d'un moule*); (*fig.*) milieu, centre, *m.*; (*Naut.*) âme (*de corde*), *f.*; trognon (*de pomme*), *m.*—*v.t.* vider (*une pomme*); creuser, évider (*un moule*).

co-respondent [kouris'pɔndənt], *n.* complice, *m.*, *f.*, co-défendeur (*en adultère*), *m.*

corgi, corgy ['kɔːgi], *n.* basset gallois, *m.*

cork [kɔːk], *n.* liège; bouchon (*à bouteille etc.*), *m.*—*v.t.* boucher.

corkscrew ['kɔːkskru], *n.* tire-bouchon, *m.*; **corkscrew staircase**, escalier en colimaçon, *m.*

cork-tipped ['kɔːk'tipt], *a.* à bouts de liège (*cigarettes*).

corm [kɔːm], *n.* (*Bot.*) bulbe, *m.*

cormorant ['kɔːmərənt], *n.* cormoran; (*fig.*) rapace, affameur, *m.*

corn (1) [kɔːn], *n.* grain, *m.*; céréales, *f.pl.*; blé, *m.*; (*Am.*) **corn**, maïs, *m.*—*v.t.* saler (*bœuf*).

corn (2) [kɔːn], *n.* cor (au pied), *m.*

corn-chandler ['kɔːntʃɑːndlə], *n.* blatier, marchand de blé, *m.*

corn-crake ['kɔːnkreik], *n.* râle de genêt, *m.*

cornea ['kɔːniə], *n.* (*Anat.*) cornée, *f.*

corned beef ['kɔːnd'biːf], *n.* bœuf salé, bœuf de conserve, *m.*

corner ['kɔːnə], *n.* coin, angle, *m.*; encoignure, *f.*; (*fig.*) monopole, accaparement, *m.*; **blind corner**, tournant (*ou virage*) masqué, *m.*—*v.t.* (*Comm.*) accaparer; (*fig.*) pousser dans un coin, acculer.—*v.i.* prendre un virage, virer.

corner-stone ['kɔːnəstoun], *n.* pierre angulaire, *f.*

cornet ['kɔːnit], *n.* cornet (*à pistons*), *m.*

cornfield ['kɔːnfiːld], *n.* champ de maïs, *m.*

cornflakes ['kɔːnfleiks], *n.pl.* paillettes de maïs, *f.pl.*

corn-flower ['kɔːnflauə], *n.* bluet, *m.*

cornice ['kɔːnis], *n.* corniche, *f.*

corn-poppy ['kɔːnpɔpi], *n.* coquelicot, *m.*

cornstarch ['kɔːnstɑːtʃ], *n.* farine de maïs, *f.*

corollary ['kɔːrələri], *n.* corollaire, *m.*

coronation [kɔrə'neiʃən], *n.* couronnement, sacre, *m.*

coroner ['kɔrənə], *n.* coroner, *m.*

coronet ['kɔrənit], *n.* (petite) couronne, *f.*

corporal ['kɔːpərəl], *a.* corporel.—*n.* caporal (*infanterie*); brigadier (*cavalerie*), *m.*

corporate ['kɔːpərit], *a.* érigé en corporation; de corporation.

corporately ['kɔːpəritli], *adv.* collectivement.

corporation [kɔːpə'reiʃən], *n.* corporation, *f.*; conseil municipal, *m.*, municipalité (*d'une ville*), *f.*

corporeal [kɔː'pɔːriəl], *a.* corporel, matériel.

corps [kɔː], *n.inv.* corps, *m.*, formation, *f.*

corpse [kɔːps], *n.* cadavre, *m.*

corpulence ['kɔːpjuləns], **corpulency** ['kɔːpjulənsi], *n.* corpulence, *f.*, embonpoint, *m.*

corpulent ['kɔːpjulənt], *a.* corpulent, gros, gras.

corpuscle ['kɔːpʌsl], *n.* corpuscule, globule, *m.*

correct [kə'rekt], *a.* correct, exact, juste; (*fig.*) convenable, en règle; pur, bon (*style*); bien élevé (*personne*); comme il faut.—*v.t.* corriger, rectifier, reprendre; punir.

correction [kə'rekʃən], *n.* correction; punition, *f.*

correctly [kə'rektli], *adv.* correctement, exactement, justement.

correctness [kə'rektnis], *n.* exactitude, justesse; pureté (*de style*), *f.*

correlate ['kɔrileit], *v.t.* mettre en corrélation. —*v.i.* correspondre.

correlation [kɔri'leiʃən], *n.* corrélation, *f.*

correspond [kɔris'pɔnd], *v.i.* correspondre (*à* ou *avec*); répondre (*à*); s'accorder (*avec*); être conforme (*à*).

correspondence [kɔris'pɔndəns], *n.* correspondance, *f.*, rapport, *m.*

correspondent [kɔris'pɔndənt], *a.* conforme, qui se rapporte (*à*).—*n.* correspondant, *m.*

corridor ['kɔridɔː], *n.* corridor; couloir, *m.*

corroborate [kə'rɔbəreit], *v.t.* corroborer, confirmer.

corroboration [kərɔbə'reiʃən], *n.* corroboration, confirmation, *f.*; **in corroboration of**, à l'appui de.

corrode [kə'roud], *v.t.* corroder, ronger; (*fig.*) détruire.—*v.i.* se corroder.

corrosion [kə'rouʒən], *n.* corrosion; (*fig.*) destruction, *f.*

corrosive [kə'rouziv], *a.* corrosif; (*fig.*) rongeur.—*n.* corrosif, *m.*

corrugate ['kɔrugeit], *v.t.* rider, plisser, froncer; onduler; **corrugated iron**, tôle ondulée, *f.*—*v.i.* se plisser, se froncer.

corrupt [kə'rʌpt], *v.t.* corrompre.—*v.i.* se corrompre.—*a.* corrompu, dépravé, vicié.

corruption [kə'rʌpʃən], *n.* corruption; (*fig.*) altération (*d'un texte etc.*), *f.*

corruptive [kə'rʌptiv], *a.* corruptif.

corruptly [kə'rʌptli], *adv.* par corruption.

corsair ['kɔːsɛə], *n.* corsaire, *m.*

corset ['kɔːsit], *n.* corset, *m.*

corset-maker ['kɔːsitmeikə], *n.* corsetier, *m.* corsetière, *f.*

Corsica ['kɔːsikə], la Corse, *f.*

Corsican ['kɔːsikən], *a.* corse.—*n.* Corse (*personne*), *m.*, *f.*

corslet [ˈkɔːslit], n. corselet m.
cortège [kɔːˈteiʒ], n. cortège (funèbre), m., procession; suite, f.
cortisone [ˈkɔːtizoun], n. cortisone, f.
coruscate [ˈkɔrəskeit], v.i. scintiller, briller.
corvette [kɔːˈvet], n. (Naut.) corvette, f.
cosh [kɔʃ], n. matraque, f.—v.t. matraquer.
cosily [ˈkouzili], adv. à l'aise, bien au chaud, douillettement.
cosmetic [kɔzˈmetik], a. and n. cosmétique, m.
cosmic [ˈkɔzmik], **cosmical** [ˈkɔzmikəl], a. cosmique.
cosmopolitan [kɔzmoˈpɔlitən], a. and n. cosmopolite, m., f.
cosmos [ˈkɔzmɔs], n. cosmos, m.
cosset [ˈkɔsit], v.t. dorloter, choyer.
cost [kɔst], n. prix; frais, m., dépense, f.; (Comm.) cout, m.; (Law, pl.) dépens, m.pl.; *at any cost, at all costs*, à tout prix; *cost of living*, coût de la vie.—v.i. irr. coûter; *cost what it may*, coûte que coûte.
coster [ˈkɔstə], **costermonger** [ˈkɔstəmʌŋgə], n. marchand des quatre saisons, m.
costive [ˈkɔstiv], a. constipé.
costliness [ˈkɔstlinis], n. haut prix, prix élevé, m.
costly [ˈkɔstli], a. coûteux, de prix; somptueux.
costume [ˈkɔstjuːm], n. costume, m.
cosy [ˈkouzi], a. chaud, confortable, douillet; commode et petit (appartement).—n. (*tea) cosy*, couvre-théière, m.
cot [kɔt], n. cabane, chaumière, f.; bercail, parc (à moutons); petit lit, lit d'enfant, m.
coterie [ˈkoutəri], n. coterie, clique, f.
cottage [ˈkɔtidʒ], n. chaumière; villa, f.
cotter pin, see **split pin**.
cotton [ˈkɔtn], n. coton, m.
cotton mill [ˈkɔtnmil], n. filature de coton, f.
cotton plant [ˈkɔtnplɑːnt], **cotton bush** [ˈkɔtnbuʃ], n. cotonnier, m.
cotton-spinning [ˈkɔtnspiniŋ], n. filage du coton, m.
cotton-wool [ˈkɔtnˈwul], n. ouate, f.
couch [kautʃ], n. canapé, divan, m.—v.t. coucher; (fig.) rédiger, exprimer.—v.i. se coucher; se tapir.
cougar [ˈkuːgə], n. couguar, puma, m.
cough [kɔf], n. toux, f.; *whooping cough*, coqueluche, f.—v.i. tousser.
coughing [ˈkɔfiŋ], n. toux, f.; *fit of coughing*, quinte de toux, f.
council [ˈkaunsil], n. conseil; (Eccles.) concile, m.
councilor [ˈkaunsilə], n. conseiller, m.
counsel [ˈkaunsəl], n. conseil, avis; dessein; avocat, m.—v.t. conseiller.
counsellor [ˈkaunsə.ə], n. conseiller; avocat, m.
count (1) [kaunt], n. comte (titre), m.
count (2) [kaunt], n. calcul, compte, total, m.—v.t. compter; (fig.) regarder, considérer; *to count on or upon*, compter sur.
countenance [ˈkauntinəns], n. figure, mine, f., air, m.; (fig.) approbation, f., appui, m.; *to give countenance to*, favoriser, encourager; *to keep one's countenance*, garder son sérieux; *to put out of countenance*, décontenancer.—v.t. appuyer, encourager, favoriser; être en faveur de.

counter [ˈkauntə], n. calculateur; compteur (instrument); (Cards etc.) jeton; comptoir (de magasin), m.—adv. contre, contrairement (à), à l'encontre (de).—v.t., v.i. parer; contrer.
counteract [kauntəˈrækt], v.t. contrecarrer, contre-balancer, neutraliser.
counteraction [kauntəˈrækʃən], n. action contraire, opposition, résistance, f.
counter-clockwise [ˈkauntəˈklɔkwaiz], **anti-clockwise** [ˈæntiˈklɔkwaiz], adv. dans le sens contraire des aiguilles d'une montre.
counter-espionage [ˈkauntərˈespiɔnɑːʒ], n. contre-espionnage, m.
counterfeit [ˈkauntəfiːt], a. contrefait, imité faux.—n. contrefaçon; fausse pièce, fausse monnaie; imitation, f.—v.t. contrefaire, imiter; feindre.—v.i. feindre.
counterfoil [ˈkauntəfɔil], n. talon (de registre), m., souche, f.
countermand [kauntəˈmɑːnd], v.t. contremander.—n. contremandement, m.
counterpane [ˈkauntəpein], n. couvre-pied, couvre-lit, m.
counterpart [ˈkauntəpɑːt], n. contre-partie, f.; pendant, m.
countess [ˈkauntis], n. comtesse, f.
counting [ˈkauntiŋ], n. compte; dépouillement (elections), m.
counting house [ˈkauntiŋhaus], n. bureau, comptoir, m., caisse, f.
countless [ˈkauntlis], a. innombrable, sans nombre.
countrified [ˈkʌntrifaid], a. (devenu) campagnard ou provincial.
country [ˈkʌntri], n. pays, m.; contrée; région; campagne (opposée à la ville); province (opposée à la capitale); patrie (fatherland), f.; *across country*, à travers champs; *in open country*, en rase campagne; *in the country*, à la campagne.
countryman [ˈkʌntrimən], n. (pl. -men [men]) paysan, campagnard, m.; *fellow countryman*, compatriote, m.
countryside [ˈkʌntrisaid], n. campagne, f.; paysage, m.
country-woman [ˈkʌntriwumən], n. (pl. -women [wimin]) paysanne, f.
county [ˈkaunti], n. comté, m.; *county council*, conseil général, m.; *county seat*, chef-lieu m.
couple [kʌpl], n. couple, f.; couple (mâle et femelle), m.—v.t. coupler, accoupler; atteler; joindre.—v.i. s'accoupler.
couplet [ˈkʌplit], n. couplet, distique, m.
coupling [ˈkʌpliŋ], n. accouplement, m.
coupon [ˈkuːpɔn], n. coupon; bon, m.
courage [ˈkʌridʒ], n. courage, m.
courageous [kəˈreidʒəs], a. courageux.
courageously [kəˈreidʒəsli], adv. courageusement.
courier [ˈkuriə], n. courrier, m.
course [kɔːs], n. cours, m.; carrière, voie, suite, f.; lit (d'une rivière); genre (de vie); service (de repas); courant (durée); (Racing) terrain de course; hippodrome, m.; (Naut.) route, f.; (Med., pl.) règles, f.pl.; *in due course*, en temps voulu; *of course*, naturellement, bien entendu.—v.t. courir; faire courir; chasser (le lièvre).—v.i. courir; circuler (sang).
courser [ˈkɔːsə], n. coureur, coursier, m.

court [kɔːt], *n.* cour, *f.*; tribunal, *m.*; impasse, *f.*, passage (*petite rue*); (*Ten.*) court, *m.*—*v.t.* faire sa cour à, courtiser; rechercher; briguer.

courteous [ˈkɔːtiəs], *a.* courtois, poli.

courteously [ˈkɔːtiəsli], *adv.* courtoisement, poliment.

courtesan [kɔːtiˈzæn], *n.* courtisane, *f.*

courtesy [ˈkɔːtəsi], *n.* courtoisie, politesse, *f.*

court-house [ˈkɔːthaus], *n.* palais de justice, *m.*

courtier [ˈkɔːtiə], *n.* courtisan, homme de cour, *m.*

courtliness [ˈkɔːtlinis] *n.* élégance, politesse, *f.*

courtly [ˈkɔːtli], *a.* poli, élégant, courtois.

court-martial [ˈkɔːtˈmɑːʃəl], *n.* conseil de guerre, *m.*—*v.t.* faire passer en conseil de guerre.

courtship [ˈkɔːtʃip], *n.* cour, *f.*

courtyard [ˈkɔːtjɑːd], *n.* cour (*de maison*), *f.*

cousin [kʌzn], *n.* cousin, *m.*

cove [kouv], *n.* anse, crique, *f.*

covenant [ˈkʌvənənt], *n.* convention, *f.*, pacte, contrat, *m.*—*v.t.* stipuler par contrat. —*v.i.* convenir (*de*), s'engager (à).

Coventry [ˈkovəntri, ˈkʌvəntri]. (*colloq.*) **to send to Coventry**, mettre en quarantaine.

cover [ˈkʌvə], *v.t.* couvrir; voiler, déguiser; cacher.—*n.* couverture; cloche (*d'un plat etc.*); enveloppe (*d'une lettre etc.*); housse (*d'une chaise*), *f.*; couvercle (*d'une casserole etc.*); couvert (*gibier*); (*fig.*) voile, abri, *m.*; **under cover of**, sous la protection de, à la faveur de.

covering [ˈkʌvərin], *n.* couverture; enveloppe; housse (*de chaise*), *f.*; habits (*vêtements*), *m.pl.*; **covering letter**, lettre d'envoi, *f.*

coverlet [ˈkʌvəlit], *n.* couvre-pied, couvre-lit, *m.*

covert [ˈkʌvəːt], *a.* couvert, caché, secret.—*n.* couvert, abri; gîte, *m.*, tanière, *f.*

covertly [ˈkʌvəːtli], *adv.* secrètement, en cachette.

covet [ˈkʌvit], *v.t.* convoiter, désirer ardemment.

covetous [ˈkʌvitəs], *a.* avide, avaricieux, cupide.

covetously [ˈkʌvitəsli], *adv.* avec convoitise, avidement.

covetousness [ˈkʌvitəsnis], *n.* convoitise, cupidité, *f.*

covey [ˈkʌvi], *n.* compagnie (*de perdrix*), *f.*

cow (1) [kau], *n.* vache, *f.*

cow (2) [kau], *v.t.* intimider, dompter.

coward [ˈkauəd], *n.* lâche, poltron, *m.*, poltronne, *f.*

cowardice [ˈkauədis], **cowardliness** [ˈkauədlinis], *n.* couardise, poltronnerie, lâcheté, *f.*

cowardly [ˈkauədli], *a.* couard, lâche, poltron. —*adv.* lâchement.

cowboy [ˈkauboi], *n.* jeune vacher; (*Am.*) cowboy, *m.*

cower [ˈkauə], *v.i.* s'accroupir, se blottir, se tapir.

cowherd [ˈkauhəːd], *n.* vacher, *m.*

cowhide [ˈkauhaid], *n.* peau de vache, *f.*

cowl [kaul], *n.* capuchon; (*Naut., Av.*) capot, tabourin (*de cheminée*), *m.*

cow-shed [ˈkauʃed], *n.* vacherie, étable à vaches, *f.*

cowslip [ˈkauslip], *n.* primevère, *f.*, coucou, *m.*

coxcomb, cockscomb [ˈkɔkskoum], *n.* petit-maître, freluquet, fat, *m.*

coxswain [ˈkɔksn], *n.* patron de chaloupe; (*Row.*) barreur, *m.*

coy [kɔi], *a.* timide, réservé.

coyly [ˈkɔili], *adv.* timidement, avec réserve.

coyness [ˈkɔinis], *n.* timidité, réserve, *f.*

coyote [kɔiˈjouti], *n.* loup de prairie, coyote, *m.*

cozen [kʌzn], *v.t.* duper, tromper.

crab [kræb], *n.* crabe, cancre; (*Astron.*) cancer, *m.*

crab apple [ˈkræbæpl], ꞏ. pomme sauvage, *f.*

crabbed [kræbd], *a.* acariâtre, revêche, bourru.

crab tree [ˈkræbtriː], *n.* pommier sauvage, *m.*

crabwise [ˈkræbwaiz], *adv.* comme un crabe, de biais.

crack [kræk], *v.t.* fendre; fêler (*porcelaine etc.*); gercer (*la peau etc.*); casser (*noix etc.*); faire claquer (*fouet*); faire sauter (*bouteille de vin*); faire, lâcher (*plaisanterie*); (*fig.*) rompre, briser.—*v.i.* se fendre, se lézarder; se gercer (*la peau etc.*); claquer (*fouet*); se fêler (*verre etc.*); muer (*la voix*).—*a.* fameux, d'élite; **to be a crack shot**, être un fin tireur.—*n.* fente, crevasse, fissure; détonation (*de fusil*); lézarde, fêlure (*verre*), *f.*; craquement (*bruit*); claquement (*d'un fouet*), *m.*; mue (*de la voix*); hâblerie (*boast*), *f.*

crack-brained [ˈkrækbreind], *a.* (*fam.*) timbré, fou.

cracked [krækd], *a.* fendu, fêlé; (*fig.*) timbré.

cracker [ˈkrækə], *n.* vantard; pétard (*feu d'artifice*); (*Am.*) biscuit, *m.*; **nut-crackers**, casse-noix, *m.inv.*

crackle [krækl], *v.i.* pétiller, craqueter, crépiter.

crackling [ˈkræklin], *n.* pétillement, crépitement; (*fig.*) rissolé (*de rôti de porc*), *m.*

cracknel [ˈkræknəl], *n.* craquelin, *m.*, croquignole, *f.*

cradle [kreidl], *n.* berceau; (*Naut.*) ber, *m.*— *v.t.* bercer; endormir (*en berçant*).

cradle-song [ˈkreidlsɔŋ], *n.* berceuse, *f.*

craft [krɑːft], *n.* métier (*trade*); ruse, astuce (*cunning*); (*Naut.*) embarcation, *f.*, bâtiment, *m.*

craftily [ˈkrɑːftili], *adv.* sournoisement, avec ruse.

craftiness [ˈkrɑːftinis], *n.* artifice, *m.*, ruse, astuce, *f.*

craftsman [ˈkrɑːftsmən], *n.* (*pl.* **-men** [men]) artisan; artiste dans son métier, *m.*

craftsmanship [ˈkrɑːftsmənʃip], *n.* habileté technique, exécution, *f.*

crafty [ˈkrɑːfti], *a.* rusé, astucieux.

crag [kræg], *n.* rocher escarpé, rocher à pic, *m.*

craggy [ˈkrægi], *a.* rocailleux, escarpé, abrupt.

crake [kreik], *n.* (*Orn.*) râle, *m.*

cram [kræm], *v.t.* fourrer, remplir, bourrer; préparer, chauffer (*étudiants*).—*v.i.* se bourrer, s'empiffrer; (*fig.*) piocher, bûcher.

crammer [ˈkræmə], *n.* préparateur; (*colloq.*) colleur, *m.*

cramp [kræmp], *n.* crampe, (*Tech.*) crampon, *m.*; (*fig.*) gêne, entrave, *f.*—*v.t.* cramponner; resserrer; (*fig.*) gêner, entraver, restreindre.

cramped [kræmpt], *a.* gêné; **to be cramped** (*for space*), être très à l'étroit.

cranberry ['krænbəri], *n.* (*Bot.*) canneberge, *f.*

crane [krein], *n.* (*Orn.*, *Tech.*) grue, *f.*—*v.t.* allonger, tendre (*le cou*).

cranial ['kreiniəl], *a.* crânien.

cranium ['kreiniəm], *n.* crâne, *m.*

crank [kræŋk], *n.* manivelle, *f.*; coude, *m.*; (*fig.*) maniaque, excentrique, *m.*, *f.*, original (*personne*), *m.*

crankshaft ['kræŋkʃɑːft], *n.* arbre de manivelle; (*Motor.*) vilebrequin, *m.*

cranky ['kræŋki], *a.* capricieux, fantasque; impatient.

crannied ['krænid], *a.* crevassé, lézardé.

cranny ['kræni], *n.* crevasse, fente, lézarde, fissure, *f.*

crape [kreip], *n.* crêpe, *m.*

crash [kræʃ], *v.t.* fracasser, briser.—*v.i.* éclater, retentir; se tamponner (*deux autos etc.*).—*n.* fracas, grand bruit, *m.*; (*Motor.*) collision; (*fig.*) débâcle, ruine; faillite, *f.*

crash helmet ['kræʃhelmit], *n.* casque, *m.*

crash landing ['kræʃ'lændiŋ], *n.* (*Av.*) atterrissage brutal; crash, *m.*

crass [kræs], *a.* crasse, grossier, stupide.

crate [kreit], *n.* caisse à claire-voie, *f.*—*v.t.* emballer.

crater ['kreitə], *n.* cratère, *m.*

cruvat [krə'væt], *n.* cravate, *f.*

crave [kreiv], *v.t.* implorer, solliciter; (*fig.*) soupirer après.

craven [kreivn], *a.* and *n.* lâche, poltron, *m.*

craving ['kreiviŋ], *n.* désir ardent.

crawfish [CRAYFISH].

crawl [krɔːl], *v.i.* ramper, se traîner; *to crawl with*, grouiller de.—*n.* mouvement traînant; (*Swim.*) crawl, *m.*

crawling ['krɔːliŋ], *a.* rampant; grouillant, fourmillant (*de*).

crayfish ['kreifiʃ], **crawfish** ['krɔːfiʃ], *n.* écrevisse (*d'eau douce*), *f.*; *sea crayfish*, langouste, *f.*

crayon ['kreiən], *n.* crayon, pastel, fusain, *m.*—*v.t.* crayonner, dessiner au pastel.

craze [kreiz], *v.t.* craqueler (*porcelaine*); frapper de folie, rendre fou.—*n.* folie; (*fig.*) passion folle; toquade, *f.*

crazed [kreizd], *a.* craquelé (*porcelaine*); fou, dément.

crazily ['kreizili], *adv.* follement.

craziness ['kreizinis], *n.* délabrement, *m.*; démence, folie, *f.*

crazy ['kreizi], *a.* délabré; (*fam.*) fou, toqué.

creak [kriːk], *v.i.* crier, craquer, grincer.—*n.* cri, grincement, *m.*

creaking ['kriːkiŋ], *a.* qui crie, qui craque.—*n.* cri, grincement, *m.*

cream [kriːm], *n.* crème, *f.*—*v.i.* crémer, mousser.

cream-color(ed) [kriːmkʌlə(d)], *a.* crème.

creamery ['kriːməri], *n.* crémerie, *f.*

cream pitcher ['kriːmpitʃə], *n.* pot à crème, *m.*

creamy ['kriːmi], *a.* crémeux; de crème.

crease [kriːs], *n.* pli, faux pli, *m.*—*v.t.* faire des plis à, plisser, chiffonner, friper.—*v.i.* se plisser; se friper.

create [kriː'eit], *v.t.* créer, faire naître; produire, engendrer, occasionner; faire.

creation [kriː'eiʃən], *n.* création; nature, *f.*, univers, *m.*; dernière mode, *f.*

creative [kriː'eitiv], *a.* créateur.

creator [kriː'eitə], *n.* créateur, *m.*

creature ['kriːtʃə], *n.* créature, personne, *f.*, être; animal, *m.*

crèche [kreiʃ], *n.* crèche, *f.*

credence ['kriːdəns], *n.* créance, croyance, foi, *f.*; *to give credence to*, ajouter foi à.

credentials [kri'denʃəlz], *n.pl.* lettres de créance, *f.pl.*

credibility [kredi'biliti], *n.* crédibilité, *f.*

credible ['kredibl], *a.* croyable, digne de foi.

credibly ['kredibli], *adv.* d'une manière digne de foi; *to be credibly informed*, tenir de bonne source.

credit ['kredit], *n.* croyance, foi; (*fig.*) influence; réputation, *f.*; mérite, honneur; (*Comm.*) crédit, *m.*; *on credit*, à crédit; *to do credit to*, faire honneur à.—*v.t.* ajouter foi à, croire à; faire honneur à; (*Comm.*) faire crédit à.

creditable ['kreditəbl], *a.* honorable, estimable.

creditably ['kreditəbli], *adv.* honorablement.

creditor ['kreditə], *n.* créancier; (*Book-keeping*) créditeur, avoir, *m.*

credulity [kre'djuːliti], **credulousness** ['kredjuləsnis], *n.* crédulité, *f.*

credulous ['kredjuləs], *a.* crédule.

creed [kriːd], *n.* credo, *m.*; (*fig.*) profession de foi; croyance, foi, *f.*

creek [kriːk], *n.* ruisseau, *m.*

creel [kriːl], *n.* panier de pêche, *m.*

creep [kriːp], *v.i.* *irr.* se traîner, ramper, se glisser.

creeper ['kriːpə], *n.* reptile, *m.*; plante grimpante, *f.*; *tree creeper*, (*Orn.*) grimpereau, *m.*

creeping ['kriːpiŋ], *a.* rampant, grimpant; qui fait frissonner.—*n.* fourmillement (*sensation*), *m.*

creepy ['kriːpi], *a.* horrifique, qui donne la chair de poule; rampant.

cremate [kri'meit], *v.t.* incinérer.

cremation [kri'meiʃən], *n.* crémation, incinération, *f.*

crematorium [kremə'tɔːriəm], *n.* crématorium, *m.*

Creole ['kriːoul], *n.* créole.—*n.* Créole, *m.*, *f.*

creosote ['kriːəsout], *n.* créosote, *f.*

crêpe [kreip], *n.* crêpe blanc (*ou* clair), *m.*

crescent ['kresənt], *a.* croissant.—*n.* croissant, *m.*, demi-lune; rue en demi-cercle, *f.*

cress [kres], *n.* cresson, *m.*

crest [krest], *n.* cimier, *m.*; crête (*d'un coq ou d'une montagne*), huppe (*d'un oiseau*); aigrette (*de paon*), *f.*; (*Her.*) écusson, *m.*; armoiries, *f.pl.*

crestfallen ['krestfɔːlən], *a.* abattu, découragé, l'oreille basse.

Cretan ['kriːtən], *a.* crétois.—*n.* Crétois, *m.*

Crete [kriːt], la Crète, la Candie, *f.*

crevasse [krə'væs], *n.* crevasse (*d'un glacier*), *f.*—*v.i.* se crevasser.

crevice ['krevis], *n.* crevasse, lézarde, fente (*mur*); fissure (*rocher*), *f.*—*v.t.* crevasser, lézarder, fissurer.

crew (1) [kruː], *n.* bande, troupe, *f.*; (*Naut.*) équipage, *m.*

crew (2) [kruː], *past* [CROW (2)].

crib [krib], *n.* lit d'enfant, *m.*; crèche, mangeoire, *f.*; (*collog.*) livre de corrigés, *m.*—*v.t.* chiper; copier (*sur*).

crick [krik], *n.* crampe, *f.*, effort, torticolis, *m.*
—*v.t.* **to crick one's neck**, se donner le torticolis.

cricket (1) ['krikit], *n.* (*Ent.*) grillon, *m.*

cricket (2) ['krikit], *n.* cricket (*jeu*), *m.*; (*colloq.*) **that's not cricket**, ça ne se fait pas, ce n'est pas loyal.

crier ['kraiə], *n.* crieur; huissier (*d'une cour*), *m.*

crime [kraim], *n.* crime, *m.*

Crimea [krai'miːə]. la Crimée, *f.*

criminal ['kriminl], *a.* and *n.* criminel, *m.*

criminologist [krimi'nɔlədʒist], *n.* criminaliste, *m.*, *f.*

criminology [krimi'nɔlədʒi], *n.* criminologie, *f.*

crimp [krimp], *v.t.* gaufrer; friser; boucler (*les cheveux*).

crimson ['krimzn], *a.* and *n.* cramoisi; pourpre, *m.*—*v.t.* teindre en cramoisi.—*v.i.* devenir cramoisi.

cringe [krindʒ], *v.i.* faire des courbettes; s'humilier, ramper.

cringing ['krindʒiŋ], *a.* craintif; obséquieux. —*n.* basse servilité, *f.*

crinkle [kriŋkl], *v.t.* froisser; former en zigzag.—*v.i.* serpenter, aller en zigzag.—*n.* sinuosité, *f.*; pli, *m.*; fronce, *f.*

crinkly ['kriŋkli], *a.* ratatiné.

cripple [kripl], *n.* boiteux; estropié, *m.*—*v.t.* estropier; (*fig.*) paralyser.

crisis ['kraisis], *n.* (*pl.* **crises** ['kraisiːz]) crise, *f.*; dénouement, *m.*

crisp [krisp], *a.* croquant, croustillant (*pâtisserie etc.*); crépu, frisé (*cheveux*).—*v.t.* friser (*cheveux etc.*); crêper (*tissu*).—*v.i.* se crêper.

crispness ['krispnis], *n.* qualité de ce qui est croquant *ou* cassant; frisure; netteté (*style etc.*), *f.*

criss-cross ['kriskrɔs], *a.* entrecroisé, croisé, en croix.—*n.* croisement, *m.*—*v.t.* entrecroiser.—*v.i.* s'entrecroiser.

criterion [krai'tiəriən], *n.* critérium, *m.*

critic ['kritik], *n.* critique; censeur, *m.*; **dramatic critic**, critique de théâtre.

critical ['kritikl], *a.* critique, (*fig.*) difficile, délicat.

critically ['kritikli], *adv.* d'une manière critique; avec soin; **critically ill**, dangereusement malade.

criticism ['kritisizm], *n.* critique, appréciation, censure, *f.*

criticize ['kritisaiz], *v.t.* critiquer, faire la critique de, censurer.—*v.i.* faire de la critique.

croak [krouk], *v.i.* coasser (*grenouille*); croasser (*freux*); (*fig.*) gronder, grogner.—*n.* coassement (*grenouille*); croassement (*freux*); (*fig.*) grognement, *m.*

croaker ['kroukə], *n.* grognon, *m.*; (*fig.*) pessimiste, *m.*, *f.*

croaky ['krouki] *a.* enroué, rauque.

crochet ['krouʃei], *n.* ouvrage au crochet, *m.* —*v.t.*, *v.i.* broder au crochet.

crock [krɔk], *n.* cruche, *f.*; pot de terre, *m.*; (*fam.*) **old crock**, vieux clou, tacot (*bicyclette, auto etc.*); vieux débris, croulant (*personne*), *m.*

crockery ['krɔkəri], *n.* faïence, vaisselle, *f.*

crocodile ['krɔkədail], *n.* crocodile, *m.*; (*fig.*) procession, *f.*

crocus ['kroukəs], *n.* safran, crocus, *m.*

croft [krɔft], *n.* petit clos, *m.*, petite ferme, *f.*

crofter ['krɔftə], *n.* petit cultivateur, *m.*

crone [kroun], *n.* vieille femme, vieille, *f.*

crony ['krouni], *n.* vieux camarade; copain, compère, *m.*

crook [kruk], *n.* courbure; houlette (*de berger*); crosse (*d'evêque*), *f.*; (*fig.*) escroc (*personne*), *m.*; **by hook or by crook**, coûte que coûte, par un moyen ou par un autre.—*v.t.* courber; (*fig.*) pervertir.—*v.i.* se courber.

crook-backed ['krukbæˑt], *a.* bossu, voûté.

crooked ['krukid], *a.* courbé, crochu, tortueux; tortu; (*fig.*) malhonnête.

crookedly ['krukidli], *adv.* tortueusement, de travers.

crookedness ['krukidnis], *n.* nature tortueuse; difformité, *f.*; (*fig.*) travers, *m.*, perversité, *f.*

croon [kruːn], *v.i.* chantonner, fredonner.

crooner ['kruːnə], *n.* fredonneur, chanteur de charme, *m.*

crop [krɔp], *n.* récolte, moisson; cueillette (*de fruits*), *f.*; jabot (*d'un oiseau*), *m.*; coupe (*cheveux*), *f.*; **hunting crop**, fouet (*de chasse*), *m.*; **second crop**, regain, *m.*—*v.t.* tondre; couper; écourter (*chevaux*); brouter (*l'herbe*).

crosier, crozier ['krouziə], *n.* crosse (*d'évêque*), *f.*

cross [krɔs], *a.* en travers, de travers; fâcheux, contraire; maussade, de mauvaise humeur, fâché.—*n.* croix, *f.*; (*fig.*) malheur, *m.*; traverse, *f.*; croisement (*dans la reproduction*), *m.*; **criss-cross**, croisé, en croix.—*v.t.* croiser; marquer d'une croix, barrer (*un chèque*); (*fig.*) franchir; contrarier; **to cross off** or **out**, effacer, rayer, biffer; **to cross oneself**, faire le signe de la croix.—*v.i.* être mis en travers; faire la traversée; se croiser (*lettres*).

crossbow ['krɔsbou], *n.* arbalète, *f.*

cross-breed ['krɔsbriːd], *n.* race croisée, *f.*; métis, *m.*—*v.t.* croiser.

cross-country ['krɔs'kʌntri], *a.* à travers champs; (*Racing*) **cross-country running**, cross, *m.*

cross-examination ['krɔsigzæmi'neiʃən], *n.* contre-interrogatoire, *m.*

cross-examine ['krɔsig'zæmin], *v.t.* interroger; (*Law*) contre-interroger.

crossing ['krɔsiŋ], *n.* traversée (*de la mer*), *f.*; passage; carrefour, croisement (*de routes*); croisement (*animaux*), *m.*; **pedestrian crossing**, passage clouté.

crossly ['krɔsli], *adv.* de travers; avec mauvaise humeur.

crossness ['krɔsnis], *n.* mauvaise humeur, méchanceté, *f.*

cross-roads ['krɔsroudz], *n.pl.* carrefour, *m.*

crossword ['krɔswɔːd], *n.* **crossword (puzzle)**, mots croisés, *m.pl.*

crotchet ['krɔtʃit], *n.* lubie, *f.*, caprice, *m.*, marotte; (*Mus.*) noire, *f.*

crotchety ['krɔtʃiti], *a.* capricieux, d'humeur difficile.

crouch [krautʃ], *v.i.* se tapir, se blottir.

crouching ['krautʃiŋ], *a.* accroupi, tapi.

croup [kruːp], *n.* croupe (*animaux*), *f.*; croupion (*oiseaux*); (*Path.*) croup, *m.*

crow (1) [krou], n. corneille. f.; **as the crow flies**, à vol d'oiseau; **crow's nest**, (Naut.) hune, f.

crow (2) [krou], v.i. irr. chanter (coq).—n. chant du coq, m.

crow-bar ['krouba:], n. pince, f.; levier, m.

crowd [kraud], n. foule, cohue, f.—v.t. serrer, encombrer; presser.—v.i. se presser en foule, se serrer.

crown [kraun], n. couronne; crête, f., sommet; écu (pièce de monnaie); fond (d'un chapeau), m.—v.t. couronner; combler.

crozier [CROSIER].

crucial ['kru:ʃəl], a. crucial; (fig.) définitif, décisif.

crucible ['kru:sibl], n. creuset, m.

crucifix ['kru:sifiks], n. crucifix, m.

crucifixion [kru:si'fikʃən], n. crucifiement, m., crucifixion, f.

crucify ['kru:sifai], v.t. crucifier.

crude [kru:d], a. cru; (fig.) informe, indigeste; grossier; brut.

crudely ['kru:dli], adv. crûment.

crudeness ['kru:dnis], crudity ['kru:diti], n. crudité, nature informe, f.

cruel ['kru:əl], a. cruel.

cruelly ['kru:əli], adv. cruellement.

cruelty ['kru:əlti], n. cruauté, inhumanité, f.

cruet ['kru:it], n. burette, f.

cruet stand ['kru:itstænd], n. huilier, m.

cruise [kru:z], n. croisière, course, f.—v.i. croiser, faire la course; marauder (taxi).

cruiser ['kru:zə], n. croiseur, m.

crumb [krʌm], n. mie; miette, f.—v.t. émietter.

crumble [krʌmbl], v.t. émietter; (fig.) pulvériser, broyer.—v.i. s'émietter; tomber en poussière; **to crumble down**, tomber en ruine, s'écrouler.

crump [krʌmp], n. coup violent, m.; chute, f.

crumpet ['krʌmpit], n. sorte de petite crêpe, crêpe bretonne (pour le thé), f.

crumple [krʌmpl], v.t. chiffonner, froisser.—v.i. se rider, se chiffonner.

crunch [krʌntʃ], v.t. croquer; broyer, écraser.—v.i. crisser, s'écraser.—n. coup de dent; grincement; crissement, m.

crupper ['krʌpə], n. croupe; croupière, f.

crusade [kru:'seid], n. croisade, f.

crusader [kru:'seidə], n. croisé, m.

crush [krʌʃ], n. écrasement, choc, m.; foule, cohue, f.—v.t. écraser, broyer; froisser (une robe); (fig.) accabler, anéantir.—v.i. s'écraser.

crushing ['krʌʃiŋ], a. écrasant; (fig.) foudroyant.—n. broiement, écrasement, m.

crust [krʌst], n. croûte, f., croûton, m.—v.i. s'encroûter.

crustily ['krʌstili], adv. d'une manière morose.

crusty ['krʌsti], a. couvert d'une croûte; (fig.) bourru, hargneux.

crutch [krʌtʃ], n. béquille, f.

crux [krʌks], n. nœud (d'une question), m.; crise, f.

cry [krai], n. cri, m.—v.t. crier.—v.i. pleurer; crier; s'écrier.

crying ['kraiiŋ], n. larmes, f.pl., pleurs, m.pl.; cri, m., cris, m.pl.

crypt [kript], n. crypte, f.

cryptic ['kriptik], a. secret; énigmatique.

crystal [kristl], a. de cristal.—n. cristal, m.

crystallize ['kristəlaiz], v.t. cristalliser.—v.i. se cristalliser; **crystallized fruits**, fruits glacés, m.pl.

cub [kʌb], n. petit (d'une bête sauvage); ourson (ours); lionceau (lion); louveteau (loup); renardeau (renard), m.

Cuba ['kju:bə], le Cuba, m.

Cuban ['kju:bən], a. cubain.—n. Cubain, m.

cubby-hole ['kʌbihoul], n. retraite, f.; placard, m.; niche, f.

cube [kju:b], n. cube, m.

cubicle ['kju:bikl], n. compartiment, m. cabine, f.

cubit ['kju:bit], n. coudée, f.

cuckoo ['kuku:], n. coucou, m.

cucumber ['kju:kʌmbə], n. concombre, m.

cud [kʌd], n. bol alimentaire, m.; **to chew the cud**, ruminer.

cuddle [kʌdl], v.t. serrer (tendrement) dans ses bras; étreindre.—v.i. s'étreindre (amoureusement); se blottir; se peloter.

cudgel ['kʌdʒəl], n. bâton, gourdin, m.—v.t. bâtonner.

cue [kju:], n. queue de billard; (Theat.) réplique, f.; (fig.) avis, mot, indice, m.

cuff (1) [kʌf], v.t. souffleter, calotter, battre.—n. calotte, taloche, f.

cuff (2) [kʌf], n. manchette (d'une manche), f.; parement (d'un pardessus); poignet (d'une robe), m.

cuff link ['kʌfliŋk], n. bouton de manchette, m.

cuirass [kwi'ræs], n. cuirasse, f.

cuirassier ['kwi'ræsiə], n. cuirassier, m.

culinary ['kʌlinəri], a. de cuisine, culinaire.

cull [kʌl], v.t. recueillir, cueillir; (fig.) choisir.

culminate ['kʌlmineit], v.i. se terminer (en), finir (par); (Astron.) culminer.

culmination [kʌlmi'neiʃən], n. point culminant, apogée, m.; (Astron.) culmination, f.

culpable ['kʌlpəbl], a. coupable.

culprit ['kʌlprit], n. accusé; inculpé, m.; coupable, m., f.

cult [kʌlt], n. culte, m.

cultivate ['kʌltiveit], v.t. cultiver.

cultivation [kʌlti'veiʃən], n. culture, f.

cultivator ['kʌltiveitə], n. cultivateur, m.

cultural ['kʌltʃərəl], a. agricole, cultural; culturel.

culture ['kʌltʃə], n. culture; (fig.) instruction éducation, f.

cultured ['kʌltʃəd], a. cultivé.

culvert ['kʌlvə:t], n. ponceau, petit aqueduc, m.

cumber ['kʌmbə], v.t. embarrasser, encombrer (de).—n. embarras, obstacle, m.

cumbersome ['kʌmbəsəm], cumbrous ['kʌmbrəs], a. embarrassant, gênant.

cumulate ['kju:mjuleit], v.t. accumuler, cumuler.

cunning ['kʌniŋ], a. fin, rusé, adroit, astucieux.—n. finesse, ruse, astuce, f.

cunningly ['kʌniŋli], adv. avec finesse, adroitement; par ruse.

cup [kʌp], n. tasse, coupe, f.; gobelet; (Bot. etc.) calice, m.; (Med.) ventouse, f.—v.t. (Med.) appliquer des ventouses à.

cupbearer ['kʌpbɛərə], n. échanson, m.

cupboard ['kʌbəd], n. armoire (pour vêtements etc.), f.; placard (dans un mur), m.

cupidity [kju:'piditi], n. cupidité, f.

cupola ['kju:pələ], n. coupole, f.

cur [kə:], *n.* chien bâtard; roquet; (*fig.*) malotru, *m.*, vilaine bête, *f.*

curable ['kjuərəbl], *a.* guérissable.

curate ['kjuərit], *n.* vicaire, desservant, *m.*

curator [kjuə'reitə], *n.* administrateur; conservateur (*de musée*), *m.*

curb [kə:b], *n.* gourmette, *f.*; (*fig.*) frein, *m.*; [KERB].—*v.t.* gourmer; (*fig.*) réprimer, contenir, brider; freiner.

curd [kə:d], *n.* caillé, lait caillé, *m.*—*v.t.* cailler, figer.

curdle ['kə:dl], *v.t.* cailler, figer.—*v.i.* se cailler, se figer.

cure [kjuə], *n.* guérison, *f.*; remède, *m.*; (*Eccles.*) cure, *f.*—*v.t.* guérir; sécher (*foin etc.*); mariner (*poisson etc.*); saler (*viande etc.*); (*fig.*) corriger.

curfew ['kə:fju:], *n.* couvre-feu, *m.*

curio ['kjuəriou], *n.* curiosité, *f.*; bibelot, *m.*

curiosity [kjuəri'ositi], *n.* curiosité, *f.*

curious ['kjuəriəs], *a.* curieux; (*fig.*) remarquable, singulier.

curiously ['kjuəriəsli], *adv.* curieusement.

curl [kə:l], *n.* boucle (*de cheveux*); moue (*de lèvres*); spirale (*de fumée*); ondulation, *f.*—*v.t.* boucler, friser, (*fig.*) faire onduler.—*v.i.* friser; se replier (*serpent etc.*); s'entrelacer (*vignes etc.*); tourbillonner (*fumée*); onduler (*vagues*); **to curl up,** s'enrouler, se pelotonner (*chat*).

curled ['kə:ld], *a.* frisé.

curlew ['kə:lju:], *n.* (*Orn.*) courlis, *m.*

curly ['kə:li], *a.* frisé, bouclé.

curmudgeon [kə:'mʌdʒən], *n.* ladre, pingre; bourru, *m.*

currant ['kʌrənt], *n.* groseille (*à grappes*), *f.*; **black currant,** cassis, *m.*; (*dried*) **currants,** raisins de Corinthe, *m.pl.*

currant bush ['kʌrəntbuʃ], *n.* groseillier, *m.*

currency ['kʌrənsi], *n.* circulation (*d'argent etc.*); monnaie, *f.*; cours; crédit, *m.*, vogue, *f.*

current ['kʌrənt], *a.* courant; actuel; admis, reçu; **current events,** actualités, *f.pl.*—*n.* courant; cours d'eau, *m.*

currently ['kʌrəntli], *adv.* couramment; généralement.

curriculum [kə'rikjuləm], *n.* (*Sch.*) programme, plan d'études, *m.*

currier ['kʌriə], *n.* corroyeur, *m.*

curry (1) ['kʌri], *v.t.* corroyer (*cuir*); étriller (*un cheval*); (*fig.*) rosser.

curry (2) ['kʌri], *v.t.* (*Cook.*) apprêter au cari.—*n.* cari, *m.*

curry-comb ['kʌrikoum], *n.* étrille, *f.*

curse [kə:s], *n.* malédiction, *f.*; (*fig.*) fléau, malheur, *m.*—*v.t.* maudire; (*fig.*) affliger.—*v.i.* jurer; (*colloq.*) sacrer.

cursed [kə:sid], *a.* maudit, exécrable.

cursorily ['kə:sərili], *adv.* rapidement, superficiellement.

cursory ['kə:səri], *a.* rapide, superficiel; général.

curt [kə:t], *a.* brusque, bref, sec.

curtail [kə:'teil], *v.t.* retrancher, raccourcir, abréger.

curtailment [kə:'teilmənt], *n.* raccourcissement, *m.*, réduction, *f.*

curtain [kə:tn], *n.* rideau, *m.*; toile, *f.*—*v.t.* garnir de rideaux; (*fig.*) voiler.

curtly ['kə:tli], *adv.* brusquement, sèchement.

curtsy, or **curtsey** ['kə:tsi], *n.* révérence, *f.*—*v.i.* faire la révérence.

curve [kə:v], *n.* courbe, *f.*—*v.t.* courber; cintrer.—*v.i.* se courber.

curvet [kə:'vet], *v.i.* faire des courbettes; sauter, gambader.—*n.* courbette, *f.*

cushion ['kuʃən], *n.* coussin, *m.*; (*Billiards*) bande, *f.*—*v.t.* garnir de coussins; amortir.

custard ['kʌstəd], *n.* crème (au lait), *f.*; flan, *m.*

custodian [kʌs'toudiən], *n.* gardien; conservateur, *m.*

custody ['kʌstədi], *n.* garde; prison, détention, *f.*

custom ['kʌstəm], *n.* coutume, habitude, *f.*, usage, *m.*; pratique (*d'une boutique*), *f.*; achalandage (*d'un magasin*), *m.*; (*pl.*) douane, *f.*; droits (*taxes*), *m.pl.*

customarily ['kʌstəmərili], *adv.* ordinairement, d'habitude.

customary ['kʌstəməri], *a.* ordinaire, d'usage.

customer ['kʌstəmə], *n.* chaland, client, *m.*; pratique, *f.*; (*colloq.*) individu, *m.*

customs officer ['kʌstəmzɔfisə], *n.* douanier, *m.*

cut [kʌt], *n.* coup, *m.*; coupure (*place cut open*); coupe (*de vêtements, cheveux, cartes à jouer*); taille (*forme*), façon, tournure (*silhouette*); (*Engr.*) gravure, planche, *f.*; chemin de traverse (*raccourci*); (*Ten. etc.*) coup tranchant, *m.*—*v.t.* irr. couper, trancher; fendre; rogner; se rogner (*les ongles*); piquer, percer; faire (*une dent*); **to cut down,** abattre; réduire; **to cut out,** tailler, découper; **to cut short,** abréger; interrompre, couper la parole à; **to be cut up,** être blessé; avoir de la peine.—*v.i.* couper; se couper; percer (*dent*).

cute [kju:t], *a.* rusé, fin; (*Am.*) attirant (*enfant, fille*); amusant (*chose, truc*).

cuticle ['kju:tikl], *n.* cuticule, *f.*

cutler ['kʌtlə], *n.* coutelier, *m.*

cutlery ['kʌtləri], *n.* coutellerie, *f.*

cutlet ['kʌtlit], *n.* côtelette; escalope, *f.*

cut-price ['kʌtprais], *n.* prix réduit, *m.*

cutter ['kʌtə], *n.* coupeur; coupoir (*outil*); (*Naut.*) cutter, cotre, *m.*

cutting ['kʌtiŋ], *a.* incisif; (*fig.*) piquant, tranchant, mordant.—*n.* incision; rognure (*morceau*); coupe (*bois, cartes, cheveux etc.*); (*Hort.*) bouture, *f.*

cyanide ['saiənaid], *n.* cyanure, *m.*

cycle [saikl], *n.* cycle, *m.*; bicyclette, *f.*, vélo, *m.*—*v.i.* aller à bicyclette.

cyclone ['saikloun], *n.* cyclone, *m.*

cygnet ['signit], *n.* jeune cygne, *m.*

cylinder ['silində], *n.* cylindre, *m.*

cymbal ['simbəl], *n.* cymbale, *f.*

cynic ['sinik], *n.* cynique; sceptique, *m.*, *f.*

cynical ['sinikl], *a.* cynique.

cynically ['sinikli], *adv.* cyniquement.

cynicism ['sinisizm], *n.* cynisme, *m.*

cynosure ['sainəʃuə], *n.* (*fig.*) point de mire, *m.*

cypress ['saiprəs], *n.* cyprès, *m.*

Cyprian ['sipriən], *a.* cypriote.—*n.* Cypriote, *m.*, *f.*

Cypriot ['sipriət], *n.* Cypriote, *m.*, *f.*

Cyprus ['saiprəs], *n.* la Chypre, *f.*

cyst [sist], *n.* (*Anat. etc.*) kyste, *m.*

czar [TSAR].

Czech [tʃek], *a.* tchèque.—*n.* tchèque (*langue*), *m.*; Tchèque (*personne*), *m.*, *f.*

Chechoslovak [tʃeko'slouvæk], *a.* tchécoslovaque.—*n.* tchécoslovaque (*langue*), *m.*; Tchécoslovaque (*personne*), *m.*, *f.*

Czechoslovakia [tʃekoslo'vækiə], la Tchécoslovaquie, *f.*

D

D, d [di:]. quatrième lettre de l'alphabet; (*Mus.*) ré, *m.*

dab [dæb], *n.* coup léger, *m.*; tape; éclaboussure, tache, *f.*; (*slang*) adepte, *m.*; (*Ichth.*) limande, *f.*—*v.t.* toucher légèrement; éponger à petits coups.

dabble [dæbl], *v.t.* humecter; éclabousser.— *v.i.* barboter, patauger; **to dabble in,** se mêler de.

dace [deis], *n.* (*Ichth.*) vandoise, *f.*, dard, *m.*

dachshund ['dækshund], *n.* basset allemand, *m.*

dad [dæd], **daddy** ['dædi], *n.* papa, *m.*

dado ['deidou], *n.* lambris (*de mur*), *m.*

daffodil ['dæfədil], *n.* jonquille, *f.*, narcisse des prés, *m.*

daft [dɑ:ft], *a.* niais, sot, à moitié fou.

dagger ['dægə], *n.* poignard, *m.*, dague, *f.*

dahlia ['deiliə], *n.* (*Bot.*) dahlia, *m.*

daily ['deili], *a.* journalier, quotidien.—*n.* (*journal*) quotidien, *m.*; femme de ménage, *f.*—*adv.* journellement, tous les jours.

daintily ['deintili], *adv.* délicatement; avec délicatesse.

daintiness ['deintinis], *n.* délicatesse, *f.*, goût difficile, *m.*

dainty ['deinti], *a.* friand; délicat, difficile.— *n.* friandise, *f.*

dairy ['dɛəri], *n.* laiterie, *f.*

dairy farm ['dɛərifɑ:m], *n.* ferme laitière, *f.*

dairy-man ['dɛərimən], *n.* (*pl.* **-men** [men]) nourrisseur; crémier, *m.*

dais [deis, 'deiis], *n.* estrade, *f.*

daisy ['deizi], *n.* marguerite, pâquerette, *f.*

dale [deil], *n.* vallon, *m.*; vallée, *f.*

dalliance ['dæliəns], *n.* folâtrerie, *f.*; badinage, *m.*; caresses, *f.pl.*

dally ['dæli], *v.i.* folâtrer, perdre son temps; tarder; (*fig.*) badiner (*avec*).

dam (1) [dæm], *n.* mère (*animaux*), *f.*

dam (2) [dæm], *n.* digue (*d'un canal*), *f.*; barrage (*d'une rivière*), *m.*—*v.t.* diguer, barrer.

damage ['dæmidʒ], *n.* dommage; tort, dégât; (*fig.*) préjudice, détriment, *m.*; (*pl.*) (*Law*) dommages-intérêts, *m.pl.*—*v.t.* endommager; avarier (*en transportant*); (*fig.*) faire tort à, nuire à.—*v.i.* s'endommager.

damask ['dæməsk], *n.* damas; (*color*) damassé, *m.*

dame [deim], *n.* (*poet.*) dame, *f.*

damn [dæm], *v.t.* damner; (*fig.*) condamner, désapprouver.

damnation [dæm'neiʃən], *n.* damnation, *f.*

damnatory ['dæmnətəri], *a.* condamnatoire.

damned [dæmd], *a.* damné, maudit, exécrable.

damning ['dæmin], *a.* écrasant (*témoignage*).

damp [dæmp], *a.* humide; moite; (*fig.*) triste, abattu.—*n.* or **dampness** ['dæmpnis], humidité; (*fig.*) tristesse, *f.*—*v.t.* rendre humide; (*fig.*) décourager.

damper ['dæmpə], *n.* éteignoir; (*Piano*) étouffoir; (*fig.*) rabat-joie, *m.*

•**damsel** ['dæmzəl], *n.* jeune fille, demoiselle, *f.*

damson ['dæmzən], *n.* prune de Damas, *f.*

dance [dɑ:ns], *n.* danse, *f.*; bal, *m.*—*v.t.* danser; faire danser.—*v.i.* danser.

dancer ['dɑ:nsə], *n.* danseur, *m.*, danseuse, *f.*

dandelion ['dændilaiən], *n.* (*Bot.*) pissenlit, *m.*

dandle [dændl], *v.t.* dorloter, bercer.

dandruff ['dændrʌf], *n.* pellicules, *f.pl.*

dandy ['dændi], *n.* dandy, élégant, petit-maître, *m.*

Dane [dein], *n.* Danois (*personne*), *m.*

danger ['deindʒə], *n.* danger, péril, *m.*

dangerous ['deindʒərəs], *a.* dangereux.

dangerously ['deindʒərəsli], *adv.* dangereusement.

dangle [dæŋgl], *v.t.* laisser pendre, balancer. —*v.i.* pendiller, baller.

Danish ['deiniʃ], *a.* danois.—*n.* danois (*langue*).

dank [dæŋk], *a.* humide et froid.

Danube ['dænju:b], **the.** le Danube, *m.*

dapper ['dæpə], *a.* petit et vif, pimpant; soigné (*homme*).

dapple [dæpl], *v.t.* tacheter, pommeler.—*v.i.* se pommeler, se tacheter.—*a.* or **dappled** [dæpld], pommelé, truité, miroité.

dare [dɛə], *v.t.* défier, braver; provoquer.— *v.i.* oser; **I dare say!** sans doute; je le crois bien.

dare-devil ['dɛədevəl], *a.* and *n.* cassecou, *m.*

daring ['dɛərin], *a.* audacieux, hardi, cassecou.—*n.* hardiesse, audace, *f.*

dark [dɑ:k], *a.* obscur, sombre, noir; foncé (*couleur*); brun, basané (*teint*); (*fig.*) secret, mystérieux.—*n.* ténèbres, *f.pl.*, obscurité, *f.*; **after dark,** à la nuit close.

darken ['dɑ:kən], *v.t.* obscurcir; brunir (*teint*) (*Paint.*) assombrir (*couleurs*).—*v.i.* s'obscurcir; s'assombrir.

darkening ['dɑ:knin], *n.* obscurcissement, assombrissement, *m.*

darkness ['dɑ:knis], *n.* obscurité, *f.*, ténèbres, *f.pl.*, teint brun (*du visage*), *m.*

darling ['dɑ:lin], *a.* and *n.* chéri, mignon, bien-aimé, *m.*; **my darling,** (*colloq.*) mon ange, mon chou, *m.*, ma chérie, *f.*

darn [dɑ:n], *n.* reprise, *f.*—*v.t.* repriser.

darning ['dɑ:nin], *n.* reprise, *f.*

dart [dɑ:t], *n.* dard, trait, *m.*; fléchette, *f.*; élan soudain, *m.*—*v.t.* darder, lancer (*contre*).—*v.i.* se lancer, s'élancer (*sur*).

dash [dæʃ], *n.* choc, coup, *m.*; impétuosité, *f.*, entrain, cran; élan soudain; tiret; trait (*de plume*); (*fig.*) soupçon (*petite quantité*), *m.*— *v.t.* jeter; heurter, briser; abattre.—*v.i.* se briser; se précipiter.—*int.* zut!

dash-board ['dæʃbɔ:d], *n.* (*Motor.*) tableau de bord, *m.*

dashing ['dæʃin], *a.* fougueux, brillant; pimpant, élégant.

dastard ['dæstəd], *n.* lâche ignoble, *m.*

dastardly ['dæstədli] *a.* lâche.

date (1) [deit], *n.* date, échéance, *f.*, millésime (*de pièce de monnaie*); (*Am. pop.*) rendez-vous, *m.*; *up to date*, à la page, à jour.—*v.t.* dater.—*v.i.* dater (*de*).

date (2) [deit], *n.* datte (*fruit*), *f.*

date palm ['deitpɑ:m], *n.* dattier, *m.*

dative ['deitiv], *a.* and *n.* datif, *m.*

datum ['deitəm], *n.* (*pl.* **data** ['deitə]) donnée, *f.*

daub [dɔ:b], *v.t.* barbouiller, enduire; (*fig.*) déguiser (*vérité*).—*n.* barbouillage, *m.*; (*Paint.*) croûte, *f.*

daughter ['dɔ:tə], *n.* fille, *f.*

daughter-in-law ['dɔ:tərinlɔ:], *n.* belle-fille, bru, *f.*

daunt [dɔ:nt], *v.t.* effrayer, intimider, décourager.

dauntless ['dɔ:ntlis], *a.* intrépide.

dauphin ['dɔ:fin], *n.* dauphin, *m.*

David ['deivid]. David, *m.*

davit ['dævit], *n.* (*Naut.*) bossoir, *m.*

dawdle [dɔ:dl], *v.i.* flâner, muser.

dawdler ['dɔ:dlə], *n.* flâneur, musard, *m.*

dawn [dɔ:n], *v.i.* poindre, paraître; (*fig.*) naître, percer.—*n.* aube, *f.*, point du jour, *m.*; aurore, *f.*

day [dei], *n.* jour, *m.*; journée (*de travail etc.*); (*fig.*) bataille, victoire, *f.*; *at the present day*, de nos jours; *every day*, tous les jours; *the day after*, le lendemain; *the day before*, la veille; *today*, aujourd'hui.

day boarder ['deibɔ:də], *n.* demi-pensionnaire, *m.f.*

day-book ['deibuk], *n.* journal, *m.*

day boy ['deibɔi], **day girl** ['deigə:l], *n.* externe, *m.f.*

day-break ['deibreik], *n.* [DAWN.]

daylight ['deilait], *n.* lumière du jour, *f.*

daze [deiz], *v.t.* éblouir; hébéter.—*n.* stupéfaction, *f.*; *in a daze*, hébété.

dazzle [dæzl], *v.t.* éblouir, aveugler.

dazzling ['dæzliŋ], *a.* éblouissant.

deacon ['di:kən], *n.* diacre, *m.*

dead [ded], *a.* mort; inanimé; inerte, insensible; éventé (*boisson alcoolique*); mat (*couleur*); au rebut (*lettres*); *dead drunk*, ivremort; *dead loss*, perte sèche, *f.*; (*fig.*) crétin (*personne*), *m.*; *dead march* marche funèbre, *f.*; *dead stop*, halte subite, *f.*; *dead weight*, poids mort, *m.*; *for a dead certainty*, à coup sûr.—*n.* cœur (*de l'hiver*), fort, *m.*; *at dead of night*, au plus profond de la nuit.

dead-beat ['ded'bi:t], *a.* éreinté, épuisé.

deaden [dedn], *v.t.* amortir; émousser (*les sens*); éventer (*boisson alcoolique*); assourdir (*son*).

dead-end ['ded'end], *n.* cul-de-sac, *m.*; impasse, *f.*

deadlock ['dedlɔk], *n.* situation sans issue; impasse, *f.*

deadly ['dedli], *a.* mortel, à mort; meurtrier.—*adv.* mortellement.

deadness ['dednis], *n.* mort, *f.*; (*fig.*) engourdissement, *m.*, froideur, *f.*

deaf [def], *a.* sourd; (*fig.*) insensible.

deafen [defn], *v.t.* rendre sourd, assourdir.

deafening ['defniŋ], *a.* assourdissant.

deaf-mute ['def'mju:t], *n.* sourd-muet, *m.*

deafness ['defnis], *n.* surdité, *f.*

deal (1) [di:l], *n.* quantité; (*Cards*) donne; affaire, *f.*, marché, *m.*; *a great* or *good*

deal, beaucoup (*de*); *by a good deal*, à beaucoup près.—*v.t.* irr. distribuer; (*Cards*) donner; porter, asséner (*coups*).—*v.i.* agir, traiter, en user (*avec*).

deal (2) [di:l], *n.* bois blanc, bois (*de sapin*), *m.*

dealer ['di:lə], *n.* marchand; (*Cards*) donneur, *m.*

dealing ['di:liŋ], *n.* conduite, *f.*; procédé, *m.*, affaire, *f.*; (*pl.*) relations, *f.pl.*, rapports, *m.pl.*

dean [di:n], *n.* doyen, *m.*

dear [diə], *a.* cher; précieux; (*fig.*) joli, gentil, charmant.—*adv.* cher; chèrement, beaucoup.—*n.* cher; cher ami, *m.*—*int.* *oh dear!* mon Dieu!

dearth [də:θ], *n.* disette, *f.*

death [deθ], *n.* mort, *f.*; (*poet.*) trépas; (*Law*) décès, *m.*

death duties ['deθdju:tiz], *n.pl.* droits de succession, *m.pl.*

death rate ['deθreit], *n.* taux de mortalité, *m.*

death rattle ['deθrætl], *n.* râle, *m.*

death throes ['deθθrouz], *n.pl.* agonie, *f.*

debar [di'bɑ:], *v.t.* exclure, priver (*de*).

debase [di'beis], *v.t.* avilir, abaisser; abâtardir; (*Chem.*) adultérer; (*Coin.*) altérer.

debasement [di'beismənt], *n.* abaissement, avilissement, *m.*; (*Coin.*) altération, dépréciation, *f.*

debasing [di'beisiŋ], *a.* avilissant.

debatable [di'beitəbl], *a.* contestable.

debate [di'beit], *n.* débat, *m.*; discussion, *f.*—*v.t.* débattre, discuter, disputer.—*v.i.* délibérer (*sur*); contester (*avec*).

debauch [di'bɔ:tʃ], *n.* débauche, *f.*—*v.t.* débaucher, corrompre, pervertir.

debauchery [di'bɔ:tʃəri], *n.* débauche, *f.*

debenture [di'bentʃə], *n.* obligation, *f.*

debilitate [di'biliteit], *v.t.* débiliter, affaiblir, anémier.

debilitation [dibili'teiʃən], *n.* débilitation, *f.*, affaiblissement, *m.*

debility [di'biliti], *n.* débilité, faiblesse, *f.*

debit ['debit], *n.* débit, *m.*—*v.t.* débiter (*de*).

debonair [debə'nɛə], *a.* jovial; de caractère enjoué; élégant.

debouch [di'bu:ʃ], *v.i.* déboucher.

débris, debris ['debri:], *n.* débris, *m.pl.*

debt [det], *n.* dette, *f.*; dettes, *f.pl.*; créance, *f.*

debtor ['detə], *n.* débiteur, *m.*

debutante ['deibjutɑ:t], *n.* débutante (*à la cour*), *f.*

decade ['dekeid], *n.* décade; décennie, *f.*

decadence ['dekədəns], *n.* décadence, *f.*

decadent ['dekədənt], *a.* décadent.

decamp [di'kæmp], *v.i.* décamper; lever le camp.

decant [di'kænt], *v.t.* décanter, verser.

decanter [di'kæntə], *n.* carafe, *f.*

decapitate [di'kæpiteit], *v.t.* décapiter.

decapitation [dikæpi'teiʃən], *n.* décapitation, *f.*

decay [di'kei], *n.* décadence; pourriture; ruine; carie (*de dent*), *f.*—*v.i.* tomber en décadence; dépérir (*plante*); se carier (*dent*).

decease [di'si:s], *n.* (*Law*) décès, *m.*—*v.i.* décéder.

deceased [di'si:st], *a.* décédé, feu.—*n.* défunt, *m.*

deceit [di'si:t], *n.* supercherie, fourberie, tromperie, ruse, *f.*

deceitful [di'si:tful], *a.* trompeur; décevant (*choses*).
deceive [di'si:v], *v.t.* tromper, abuser.
deceiver [di'si:və], *n.* imposteur, trompeur, *m.*
decelerate [di:'seləreit], *v.t.*, *v.i.* ralentir.
December [di'sembə], décembre, *m.*
decency ['di:sənsi], *n.* bienséance, *f.*, convenances, *f.pl.*; décence (*modestie*), *f.*
decennial [di'senjəl], *a.* décennal.
decent ['di:sənt], *a.* bienséant, décent; propre, convenable; gentil.
decently ['di:səntli], *adv.* décemment; convenablement.
decentralization ['di:sentrəlai'zeiʃən], *n.* décentralisation, *f.*, régionalisme, *m.*
decentralize [di:'sentrəlaiz], *v.t.* décentraliser.
deception [di'sepʃən], *n.* tromperie, fraude, duperie, *f.*
deceptive [di'septiv], *a.* trompeur.
decibel ['desibel], *n.* décibel, *m.*
decide [di'said], *v.t.* décider; décider de.—*v.i.* se décider.
decided [di'saidid], *a.* décidé, prononcé; positif; résolu.
decidedly [di'saididli], *adv.* décidément; positivement.
decimal ['desiməl], *a.* décimal; **decimal point**, virgule, *f.*—*n.* (*fraction*) décimale, *f.*
decimate ['desimeit], *v.t.* décimer.
decipher [di'saifə], *v.t.* déchiffrer.
decision [di'siʒən], *n.* décision; (*fig.*) résolution, fermeté, *f.*
decisive [di'saisiv], *a.* décisif; concluant.
decisively [di'saisivli], *adv.* décisivement.
deck [dek], *n.* (*Naut.*) pont; tillac (*navire marchand*); plan (*avion*), *m.*—*v.t.* parer (*de*); orner.
deck chair ['dek'tʃɛə], *n.* transat(lantique), *m.*
declaim [di'kleim], *v.t.*, *v.i.* déclamer (*contre*).
declamatory [di'klæmətəri], *a.* déclamatoire.
declaration [deklə'reiʃən], *n.* déclaration; proclamation, *f.*
declare [di'klɛə], *v.t.* déclarer; (*fig.*) annoncer, affirmer.—*v.i.* se déclarer, se prononcer (*pour*).
decline [di'klain], *v.t.* pencher, incliner; refuser.—*v.i.* pencher; décliner; baisser (*prix*).—*n.* déclin, *m.*, décadence (*Path.*) maladie de langueur, *f.*
declutch [di:'klʌtʃ], *v.i.* débrayer.
decode [di:'koud], *v.t.* déchiffrer.
decompose [di:kəm'pouz], *v.t.* décomposer.—*v.i.* se décomposer.
decompression [di:kəm'preʃən], *n.* décompression, *f.*
decontaminate [di:kən'tæmineit], *v.t.* désinfecter.
decontrol [di:kən'troul], *v.t.* rendre libre de nouveau, libérer (*prix, loyers etc.*).—*n.* libération (*prix, loyers etc.*), *f.*
decorate ['dekəreit], *v.t.* décorer; orner.
decoration [dekə'reiʃən], *n.* décoration, *f.*; ornement, *m.*
decorator ['dekəreitə], *n.* décorateur, *m.*
decorous ['dekərəs, di'kɔ:rəs], *a.* bienséant, convenable.
decorously ['dekərəsli, di'kɔ:rəsli], *adv.* convenablement.

decorum [di'kɔ:rəm], *n.* bienséance, *f.*, décorum, *m.*
decoy [di'kɔi], *v.t.* leurrer, amorcer.—*n.* leurre; piège, *m.*
decrease ['di:kri:s], *n.* décroissement, *m.*; diminution; décrue (*eau*), *f.*—[di'kri:s], *v.t.* faire décroître.—*v.i.* diminuer; décroître.
decree [di'kri:], *n.* décret; (*Law*) arrêt, *m.*—*v.t.* arrêter, décréter.
decrepit [di'krepit], *a.* décrépit, caduc.
decry [di'krai], *v.t.* décrier, dénigrer.
dedicate ['dedikeit], *v.t.* dédier (*à*); consacrer (*à*).
dedication [dedi'keiʃən], *n.* dédicace, *f.*
deduce [di'dju:s], *v.t.* déduire, inférer (*de*).
deduct [di'dʌkt], *v.t.* déduire, rabattre.
deduction [di'dʌkʃən], *n.* déduction, *f.*
deed [di:d], *n.* action, *f.*; fait, exploit; (*Law*) titre, *m.*
deem [di:m], *v.t.* juger; penser, estimer.
deep [di:p], *a.* profond, extrême; foncé (*couleur*); grave (*son*); (*fig.*) rusé.—*n.* (*poet.*) océan, *m.*
deepen ['di:pən], *v.t.* approfondir; assombrir.—*v.i.* devenir plus profond ou plus foncé.
deep-freeze ['di:p'fri:z], *n.* réfrigérateur à basse température, *m.*
deeply ['di:pli], *adv.* profondément; extrêmement.
deep-rooted ['di:p'ru:tid], **deep-seated** ['di:p'si:tid], *a.* profond, enraciné.
deer [diə], *n.* cervidé, *m.*; **fallow deer**, daim, *m.*, daine, *f.*; **red deer**, cerf, *m.*
deface [di'feis], *v.t.* défigurer; mutiler.
defamation [defə'meiʃən], *n.* diffamation, *f.*
defame [di'feim], *v.t.* diffamer.
default [di'fɔ:lt], *n.* défaut, manque, *m.*; (*Law*) contumace, *f.*
defaulter [di'fɔ:ltə], *n.* délinquant; (*Mil.*) réfractaire; (*Law*) défaillant, *m.*
defeat [di'fi:t], *n.* défaite, déroute, *f.*—*v.t.* battre, vaincre; (*fig.*) annuler, déjouer.
defeatism [di'fi:tizm], *n.* défaitisme, *m.*
defeatist [di'fi:tist], *a.* and *n.* défaitiste, *m.*, *f.*
defect [di'fekt], *n.* défaut, *m.*; imperfection, *f.*
defective [di'fektiv], *a.* défectueux, imparfait.
defend [di'fend], *v.t.* défendre (*de*), protéger (*contre*).
defender [di'fendə], *n.* défenseur, *m.*
defense[di'fens],*n.*défense,*f.*[see **war-office**]
defensible [di'fensəbl], *a.* défendable; (*fig.*) soutenable.
defensive [di'fensiv], *a.* défensif.—*n.* défensive, *f.*
defer [di'fə:], *v.t.* différer, remettre.—*v.i.* différer; déférer (*à*).
deference ['defərəns], *n.* déférence, *f.*
deferential [defə'renʃəl] *a.* de déférence, respectueux.
deferment [di'fə:mənt], *n.* (*Mil.*) sursis, *m.*
defiance [di'faiəns], *n.* défi, *m.*
defiant [di'faiənt], *a.* défiant.
deficiency [di'fiʃənsi], *n.* défaut, *m.*; insuffisance, *f.*
deficient [di'fiʃənt], *a.* défectueux; insuffisant.
deficit ['defisit], *n.* déficit, *m.*
defile (1) [di:'fail], *n.* défilé, *m.*
defile (2) [di'fail], *v.t.* souiller; déshonorer.
define [di'fain], *v.t.* définir; déterminer.
definite ['definit], *a.* déterminé; (*Gram.*) défini.

definitely ['definitli], *adv.* absolument, nettement, d'une manière déterminée.

definition [defi'niʃən], *n.* définition, *f.*

deflate [di'fleit], *v.t.* dégonfler.

deflation [di'fleiʃən], *n.* dégonflement, *m.*; déflation monétaire, *f.*

deflect [di'flekt], *v.t.* faire dévier, détourner. —*v.i.* dévier.

deforestation [di:foris'teiʃən], *n.* déboisement, *m.*

deform [di'fɔ:m], *v.t.* déformer, défigurer.

deformation [di:fɔ:'meiʃən], *n.* déformation, *f.*

deformed [di'fɔ:md], *a.* difforme.

deformity [di'fɔ:miti], *n.* difformité; laideur, *f.*

defraud [di'frɔ:d], *v.t.* frauder.

defray [di'frei], *v.t.* défrayer; payer.

deft [deft], *a.* adroit, habile.

deftly ['deftli], *adv.* adroitement, lestement.

defunct [di'fʌŋkt], *a.* défunt, trépassé, décédé.—*n.* défunt, *m.*

defy [di'fai], *v.t.* défier, braver.

degeneracy [di'dʒenərəsi], **degeneration** [didʒenə'reiʃən], *n.* dégénérescence, *f.*

degenerate [di'dʒenərit], *a.* and *n.* dégénéré, *m.*—[di'dʒenəreit], *v.i.* dégénérer, s'abâtardir (*dans* ou *en*).

degradation [degrə'deiʃən], *n.* dégradation, *f.*; (*fig.*) avilissement, *m.*

degrade [di'greid], *v.t.* dégrader; (*fig.*) avilir.

degrading [di'greidiŋ], *a.* dégradant, avilissant.

degree [di'gri:], *n.* degré; rang, ordre, *m.*; qualité, *f.*; *university degree*, grade universitaire, *m.*

de-ice [di:'ais], *v.t.*, *v.i.* dégivrer.

deify ['di:ifai], *v.t.* déifier.

deign [dein], *v.t.*, *v.i.* daigner.

deity ['di:iti], *n.* divinité; (*Myth.*) déité, *f.*

dejected [di'dʒektid], *a.* abattu, triste.

dejection [di'dʒekʃən], *n.* abattement, *m.*

delay [di'lei], *n.* délai, retard, *m.*—*v.t.* différer; remettre.—*v.i.* tarder.

delegacy ['deligəsi], *n.* délégation, *f.*

delegate [di'deligit], *n.* délégué, *m.*—['deligeit], *v.t.* déléguer.

delegation [deli'geiʃən], *n.* délégation, *f.*

delete [di'li:t], *v.t.* effacer, rayer, biffer.

deletion [di'li:ʒən], *n.* rature, *f.*, grattage, *m.*

deliberate [di'libərit], *a.* délibéré, prémédité; réfléchi.—[di'libəreit], *v.i.* délibérer.

deliberately [di'libəritli], *adv.* à dessein; lentement.

deliberation [dilibə'reiʃən], *n.* délibération, *f.*

delicacy ['delikəsi], *n.* délicatesse; friandise (*a titbit*), *f.*

delicate ['delikit], *a.* délicat.

delicious [di'liʃəs], *a.* délicieux.

deliciously [di'liʃəsli], *adv.* délicieusement.

delight [di'lait], *n.* délices, *f.pl.*, plaisir, *m.*—*v.t.* plaire à, réjouir, enchanter; *to be delighted to*, être enchanté de.—*v.i.* se plaire à.

delightful [di'laitful], *a.* délicieux; charmant (*personne*).

delineate [di'linieit], *v.t.* esquisser, dessiner; (*fig.*) décrire.

delinquency [di'liŋkwənsi], *n.* délit, *m.*; *juvenile delinquency*, délinquance juvénile, *f.*

delinquent [di'liŋkwənt], *n.* délinquant, *m.*; *juvenile delinquent*, jeune délinquant.

delirious [di'liriəs], *a.* en délire; délirant.

delirium [di'liriəm], *n.* délire; (*fig.*) transport de joie, *m.*

deliver [di'livə], *v.t.* délivrer, sauver; distribuer (*lettres etc.*); remettre (*lettre, paquet etc.*); livrer (*marchandises*), prononcer (*un discours*); (faire) accoucher (*femme*).

deliverance [di'livərəns], *n.* délivrance, *f.*

deliverer [di'livərə], *n.* libérateur, sauveur, *m.*

delivery [di'livəri], *n.* délivrance, remise, *f.*; débit, *m.*, diction (*d'un discours*); livraison (*de marchandises*); distribution (*du courrier*), *f.*; (*Med.*) accouchement, *m.*; *payment on delivery*, livraison contre remboursement.

delivery van [də'livərivæn], *n.* camion de livraison, *m.*; camionnette, *f.*.

dell [del], *n.* vallon, *m.*

delta ['deltə], *n.* delta, *m.*

delude [di'lju:d], *v.t.* tromper, abuser.

deluge ['delju:dʒ], *n.* déluge, *m.*—*v.t.* inonder.

delusion [di'lju:ʒən], *n.* illusion, erreur, *f.*

delve [delv], *v.t.*, *v.i.* bêcher, creuser; (*fig.*) sonder.

demagnetize [di:'mægnitaiz], *v.t.* démagnétiser.

demagogue ['deməgɔg], *n.* démagogue, *m.*, *f.*

demand [di'mɑ:nd], *n.* exigence; réclamation; demande, requête, *f.*; *in great demand*, très demandé, très recherché; *on demand*, sur demande; *supply and demand*, l'offre et la demande, *f.*—*v.t.* exiger; réclamer; demander.

demarcation [di:mɑ:'keiʃən], *n.* démarcation, *f.*; *line of demarcation*, ligne de démarcation, *f.*

demean [di'mi:n], *v.i.* se comporter, se conduire; (*colloq.*) s'abaisser, se dégrader.

demeanor [di'mi:nə], *n.* conduite, *f.*, maintien, *m.*; tenue, *f.*

demented [di'mentid], *a.* fou, dément.

demi ['demi], *prep.* demi, à demi.

demigod ['demigɔd], *n.* demi-dieu, *m.*

demise [di'maiz], *n.* décès, *m.*, mort, *f.*—*v.t.* léguer; céder à bail.

demi-semiquaver ['demi'semikweivə], *n.* (*Mus.*) triple croche, *f.*

demister [di'mistə], *n.* (*Motor.*) appareil antibuée, *m.*

demobilization [di:moubilai'zeiʃən], *n.* démobilisation, *f.*

demobilize [di:'moubilaiz], *v.t.* démobiliser.

democracy [di'mɔkrəsi], *n.* démocratie, *f.*

democrat ['deməkræt], *n.* démocrate, *m.*, *f.*

democratic [demə'krætik], *a.* démocratique.

democratically [demə'krætikəli], *adv.* démocratiquement.

demolish [di'mɔliʃ], *v.t.* démolir.

demolition [demə'liʃən], *n.* démolition, *f.*

demon ['di:mən], *n.* démon, diable, *m.*

demonstrate ['demənstreit], *v.t.* démontrer. —*v.i.* (*Polit.*) manifester.

demonstration [demən'streiʃən], *n.* démonstration; (*Polit.*) manifestation, *f.*

demonstrative [di'mɔnstrətiv], *a.* démonstratif.

demoralize [di:'mɔrəlaiz], *v.t.* démoraliser.

demote [di'mout], *v.t.* (*Mil.*) réduire à un grade inférieur, rétrograder.

demur [di'mə:], *n.* hésitation, objection, *f.*— *v.i.* hésiter, temporiser.

399

demure

demure [di'mjuə], *a.* réservé, posé; d'une modestie affectée.

demurely [di'mjuəli], *adv.* d'un air posé; avec une modestie affectée.

den [den], *n.* antre; repaire (*de voleurs etc.*), *m.*; loge (*de ménagerie*), *f.*; (*fig.*) bouge, taudis; (*colloq.*) cabinet de travail, *m.*

denationalize [di:'næʃnəlaiz], *v.t.* dénationaliser.

denial [di'naiəl], *n.* déni, *m.*, dénégation, *f.*

denier ['deniə], *n.* (*Hosiery*) denier, *m.*; *a 15-denier stocking*, un bas 15 deniers.

denigrate ['denigreit], *v.t.* noircir, dénigrer.

Denis [DENNIS].

denizen ['denizn], *n.* citoyen, habitant, *m.*

Denmark ['denmɑːk]. le Danemark, *m.*

Dennis ['denis]. Denis, *m.*

denomination [dinɔmi'neiʃən], *n.* dénomination, *f.*; culte, *m.*, secte, *f.*

denominational [dinɔmi'neiʃənl], *a.* confessionnel (*école*).

denote [di'nout], *v.t.* dénoter, marquer, indiquer; signifier.

denounce [di'nauns], *v.t.* dénoncer.

dense [dens], *a.* dense, épais; compact; stupide.

densely ['densli], *adv.* en masse.

density ['densiti], *n.* densité, épaisseur, *f.*

dent [dent], *n.* renfoncement, *m.*, bosselure; coche, *f.*—*v.t.* bosseler, cabosser.

dental [dentl], *a.* dentaire, (*Phon.*) dental; *dental surgeon*, chirurgien dentiste, *m.*

dentifrice ['dentifris], *n.* dentifrice, *m.*

dentist ['dentist], *n.* dentiste, *m.*, *f.*

dentistry ['dentistri], *n.* dentisterie, *f.*

denture ['dentʃə], *n.* dentier; (*fam.*) râtelier, *m.*

denude [di'njuːd], *v.t.* dénuder; (*fig.*) dénuer.

denunciation [dinʌnsi'eiʃən], *n.* dénonciation, *f.*

deny [di'nai], *v.t.* nier, démentir; (*Law*) dénier, renier; refuser.

deodorant [di:'oudərənt], **deodorizer** [di:'oudəraizə], *n.* désinfectant, désinfecteur, désodorisant, *m.*

depart [di'pɑːt], *v.t.* quitter.—*v.i.* partir, s'en aller, se retirer, s'éloigner; (*fig.*) mourir.

departed [di'pɑːtid], *a.* mort, défunt; passé, évanoui.—*n. the departed*, le défunt, *m.*, les trépassés, *m.pl.*

department [di'pɑːtmənt], *n.* département, service; (*Polit.*) bureau; comptoir, rayon (*de boutique*), *m.*; *department store*, grand magasin, *m.*

departmental [di:pɑːt'mentl], *a.* départemental.

departure [di'pɑːtʃə], *n.* départ; éloignement, *m.*; déviation; (*fig.*) mort, *f.*

depend [di'pend], *v.i.* dépendre (*de*); compter (*sur*), se reposer (*sur*).

dependable [di'pendəbl], *a.* digne de confiance; sûr.

dependent [di'pendənt], *a.* dépendant; (*Law*) à la charge de; (*Gram.*) subordonné; *dependent relatives*, parents à charge, *m.pl.*

depict [di'pikt], *v.t.* peindre, dépeindre.

deplete [di'pliːt], *v.t.* amoindrir, épuiser.

deplorable [di'plɔːrəbl], *a.* déplorable; pitoyable (*lamentable*).

deplore [di'plɔː], *v.t.* déplorer.

deploy [di'plɔi], *v.t.* (*Mil.*) déployer.—*v.i.* se déployer.

depopulate [di:'pɔpjuleit], *v.t.* dépeupler.—*v.i.* se dépeupler.

deport [di'pɔːt], *v.t.* déporter, expulser; *to deport oneself*, se comporter.

deportment [di'pɔːtmənt], *n.* tenue, conduite, *f.*, manières, *f.pl.*

depose [di'pouz], *v.t.*, *v.i.* déposer (*de*).

deposit [di'pɔzit], *n.* dépôt; (*Banking*) versement; gage, nantissement, *m.*, arrhes, *f.pl.*, caution, *f.*; (*Geol.*) gisement, gîte, *m.*; *deposit account*, compte de dépôt, *m.*—*v.t.* déposer; verser.

deposition [depə'ziʃən, di:pə'ziʃən], *n.* déposition, *f.*; dépôt, *m.*

depositor [di'pɔzitə], *n.* (*Comm.*) déposant, *m.*

depository [di'pɔzitri], *n.* dépôt; garde-meubles, *m.*

depot ['depou], *n.* dépôt, *m.*; (*Am.*) ['di:pou] gare, *f.*

deprave [di'preiv], *v.t.* dépraver, corrompre.

depraved [di'preivd], *a.* dépravé, corrompu.

depravity [di'præviti], *n.* dépravation, *f.*

deprecate ['deprikeit], *v.t.* désapprouver, désavouer. s'opposer à.

deprecatingly ['deprikeitiŋli], *adv.* avec désapprobation.

deprecative ['deprikeitiv], **deprecatory** ['deprikeitəri], *a.* de déprécation.

depreciate [di'priːʃieit], *v.t.* déprécier.—*v.i.* se déprécier.

depreciation [dipriːʃi'eiʃən], *n.* dépréciation, *f.*

depress [di'pres], *v.t.* baisser, abaisser; abattre; accabler, décourager.

depressed [di'prest], *a.* abattu; bas.

depression [di'preʃən], *n.* abaissement, *m.*; dépression; (*Comm.*) crise, *f.*

deprivation [depri'veiʃən], *n.* privation, perte, *f.*

deprive [di'praiv], *v.t.* priver (*de*); déposséder.

depth [depθ], *n.* profondeur, *f.*; enfoncement (*recoin*); fort (*des saisons*), *m.*; *in the depth of winter*, au cœur ou au plus fort de l'hiver, *m.*; *to get out of one's depth*, perdre pied.

depth charge ['depθtʃɑːdʒ], *n.* grenade sous-marine, *f.*

deputation [depju'teiʃən], *n.* députation, délégation, *f.*

depute [di'pjuːt], *v.t.* députer, déléguer.

deputize ['depjutaiz], *v.i.* remplacer quelqu'un.

deputy ['depjuti], *n.* député, délégué; adjoint, *m.*

derail [di:'reil], *v.t.* (*Rail.*) dérailler.

derailment [di:'reilmənt], *n.* déraillement, *m.*

derange [di'reindʒ], *v.t.* déranger.

derangement [di'reindʒmənt], *n.* dérangement, *m.*

derelict ['derilikt], *a.* délaissé, abandonné.

deride [di'raid], *v.t.* tourner en dérision, se moquer de.

derision [di'riʒən], *n.* dérision, moquerie, *f.*

derisive [di'raisiv], *a.* dérisoire.

derivation [deri'veiʃən], *n.* dérivation; origine, *f.*

derivative [di'rivativ], *n.* (*Gram.*) dérivé, *m.*

derive [di'raiv], *v.t.* dériver.—*v.i.* venir, dériver (*de*).

400

derogatory [di'rɔgətəri], *a.* péjoratif, déroga-toire, dérogeant (*à*).
derrick ['derik], *n.* grue, *f.*; derrick, *m.*
dervish ['də:viʃ], *n.* derviche, *m.*
descend [di'send], *v.i.* descendre, tomber; s'abaisser; *to be descended from*, descendre de; *to descend upon*, tomber sur.
descendant [di'sendənt], *n.* descendant, *m.*
descendent [di'sendənt], *a.* descendant, qui descend, provenant (*de*).
descent [di'sent], *n.* descente; chute, pente; descendance, naissance, origine (*lignée*), *f.*
describe [dis'kraib], *v.t.* décrire, dépeindre, peindre.
description [dis'kripʃən], *n.* description; désignation (*d'une personne*), *f.*; (*Law*) signalement, *m.*; (*colloq.*) qualité, sorte, espèce, *f.*
descriptive [dis'kriptiv], *a.* descriptif.
descry [dis'krai], *v.t.* découvrir, apercevoir; aviser; reconnaître.
desecrate ['desəkreit], *v.t.* profaner.
desecration [desə'kreiʃən], *n.* profanation, *f.*
desert (1) [di'zə:t], *n.* mérite, *m.*; mérites, *m.pl.*
desert (2) ['dezət], *a.* désert; solitaire.—*n.* désert, *m.*; solitude, *f.*
desert (3) [di'zə:t], *v.t.* abandonner, déserter.
deserted [di'zə:tid], *a.* abandonné, désert.
deserter [di'zə:tə], *n.* déserteur, *m.*
desertion [di'zə:ʃən], *n.* désertion, *f.*, aban-don, *m.*
deserve [di'zə:v], *v.t.* mériter, être digne de.
deservedly [di'zə:vidli], *adv.* à bon droit, justement.
deserving [di'zə:viŋ], *a.* de mérite, méritoire.
desiccated ['desikeitid], *a.* desséché.
design [di'zain], *n.* dessein, projet; dessin (*drawing*); (*Manuf.*) modèle, *m.*; *by design*, à dessein.—*v.t.* projeter, se proposer de; dessiner.
designedly [di'zainidli], *adv.* à dessein.
designer [di'zainə], *n.* inventeur; auteur; architecte; dessinateur (*draftsman*), *m.*
designing [di'zainiŋ], *a.* artificieux, intrigant.
designate ['dezigneit], *v.t.* désigner, nom-mer.—['dezignit], *a.* désigné, nommé.
desirable [di'zaiərəbl], *a.* désirable, à sou-haiter.
desire [di'zaiə], *n.* désir, *m.*; prière, demande, *f.*—*v.t.* désirer, souhaiter; prier.
desirous [di'zaiərəs], *a.* désireux (*de*), em-pressé (*à*); *to be desirous of*, avoir envie de.
desist [di'zist], *v.i.* se désister, cesser (*de*).
desk [desk], *n.* pupitre (*école*); bureau (*meuble*), *m.*; caisse (*boutique*); chaire (*de professeur*), *f.*
desolate ['desəlit], *a.* désolé, inhabité, soli-taire, dévasté.
desolation [desə'leiʃən], *n.* désolation, *f.*
despair [dis'peə], *n.* désespoir, *m.*—*v.i.* désespérer (*de*).
despatch [DISPATCH].
desperado [despə'reidou, despə'ra:dou], *n.* désespéré, *m.*
desperate ['despərit], *a.* désespéré; furieux, forcené; acharné, terrible.
desperately ['despəritli], *adv.* désespéré-ment; (*fig.*) excessivement.

desperation [despə'reiʃən], *n.* désespoir, *m.*; fureur, *f.*, acharnement, *m.*
despicable ['dispikəbl], *a.* méprisable.
despise [dis'paiz], *v.t.* mépriser, dédaigner.
despite [dis'pait], *n.* (*Lit.*) dépit, *m.*—*prep.* en dépit de, malgré.
despoil [dis'pɔil], *v.t.* dépouiller.
despondency [dis'pɔndənsi], *n.* abattement, désespoir, *m.*
despondent [dis'pɔndənt], *a.* découragé, abattu.
despot ['despɔt], *n.* despote, *m.*, *f.*
despotic [des'pɔtik], *a.* despotique.
despotism ['despətizm], *n.* despotisme, *m.*
dessert [di'zə:t], *n.* dessert, *m.*
destination [desti'neiʃən], *n.* destination, *f.*
destine ['destin], *v.t.* destiner, désigner.
destiny ['destini], *n.* destin, *m.*, destinée, *f.*
destitute ['destitju:t], *a.* dépourvu, destitué; indigent.
destitution [desti'tju:ʃən], *n.* dénuement, abandon, *m.*, indigence, *f.*
destroy [dis'trɔi], *v.t.* détruire, ruiner.
destroyer [dis'trɔiə], *n.* (*Naut.*) contre-torpilleur, *m.*
destroying [dis'trɔiiŋ], *a.* destructeur, des-tructif.
destruction [dis'trʌkʃən], *n.* destruction, *f.*, anéantissement, *m.*; ruine, *f.*
destructive [dis'trʌktiv], *a.* destructeur; funeste, fatal (*à*).
desultorily ['desəltərili], *adv.* à bâtons rompus, sans suite.
desultory ['desəltəri], *a.* à bâtons rompus, décousu, sans suite.
detach [di'tætʃ], *v.t.* détacher (*de*); isoler; *to become detached*, se détacher.
detachable [di'tætʃəbl], *a.* démontable, détachable.
detached [di'tætʃt], *a.* détaché, isolé.
detachment [di'tætʃmənt], *n.* détachement, *m.*
detail ['di:teil], *n.* détail, *m.*—[di'teil], *v.t.* détailler; (*Mil.*) désigner (*pour*).
detain [di'tein], *v.t.* retenir; détenir; (*Law*) empêcher.
detect [di'tekt], *v.t.* découvrir; détecter.
detection [di'tekʃən], *n.* découverte, *f.*
detective [di'tektiv], *n.* agent de la (police de) sûreté, policier, détective, *m.*; *a detective story*, un roman policier.
detention [di'tenʃən], *n.* action de retenir; (*Law*) détention; (*Sch.*) consigne, *f.*
deter [di'tə:], *v.t.* détourner, empêcher (*de*); dissuader (*de*).
detergent [di'tə:dʒənt], *a.* and *n.* détersif, détergent, *m.*
deteriorate [di'tiəriəreit], *v.i.* se détériorer.
deterioration [ditiəriə'reiʃən], *n.* détériora-tion, *f.*; dépérissement, *m.*
determination [ditə:mi'neiʃən], *n.* déter-mination, décision, *f.*
determine [di'tə:min], *v.t.* déterminer, décider.—*v.i.* se déterminer, se décider, résoudre.
determined [di'tə:mind], *a.* résolu, obstiné.
deterrent [di'terənt], *a.* préventif.—*n.* arme préventive, *f.*
detest [di'test], *v.t.* détester.
detestable [di'testəbl], *a.* détestable; (*fig.*) odieux.
detestation [di:tes'teiʃən], *n.* détestation, *f.*

dethrone

dethrone [di'θroun], *v.t.* détrôner.
detonation [detə'neiʃən], *n.* détonation, *f.*
detonator ['detəneitə], *n.* détonateur, *m.*
detour [di'tuə], *n.* déviation, *f.*
detract [di'trækt], *v.t.* enlever, ôter (à); dénigrer.—*v.i.* déroger (à).
detriment ['detrimənt], *n.* détriment, préjudice, *m.*
detrimental [detri'mentl], *a.* préjudiciable, nuisible (à).
deuce [dju:s], *n.* (*Cards*) deux; (*Ten.*) à deux; à égalité; (*collog.*) diable, diantre, *m.*
Deuteronomy [dju:tə'ronəmi]. Deutéronome, *m.*
devaluation [di:vælju'eiʃən], *n.* dévaluation, *f.*
devalue [di:'vælju], **devaluate** [di:'væljueit], *v.t.* dévaluer, déprécier.
devastate ['devəsteit], *v.t.* dévaster.
devastation [devəs'teiʃən], *n.* dévastation, *f.*
develop [di'veləp], *v.t.* développer.
developer [di'veləpə], *n.* (*Phot.*) révélateur, *m.*
development [di'veləpmənt], *n.* développement, *m.*
deviate ['di:vieit], *v.i.* dévier, se dévier; s'écarter (*de*).
deviation [di:vi'eiʃən], *n.* déviation, *f.*, écart, *m.*
device [di'vais], *n.* dessein, moyen, stratagème; dispositif, mécanisme, *m.*; devise (*motto*), *f.*
devil [devl], *n.* diable, démon, *m.*; **daredevil**, téméraire, *m.*, *f.*—*v.t.* griller et poivrer; **devil-may-care**, étourdi, *m.*
devilish ['devliʃ], *a.* maudit, diabolique.
devilment ['devilmənt], **deviltry** ['devil tri], *n.* diablerie, *f.*
devious ['di:viəs], *a.* détourné, écarté; (*fig.*) errant.
devise [di'vaiz], *v.t.* imaginer, inventer; tramer, machiner.
devitalize [di:'vaitəlaiz], *v.t.* dévitaliser.
devoid [di'void], *a.* exempt, dénué (*de*).
devote [di'vout], *v.t.* dévouer, consacrer (à).
devoted [di'voutid], *a.* dévoué, consacré.
devotee [devo'ti:], *n.* dévot; passionné, *m.*, fanatique, *m.*, *f.*
devotion [di'vouʃən], *n.* dévotion, *f.*; dévouement, *m.*
devour [di'vauə], *v.t.* dévorer.
devout [di'vaut], *a.* dévot, pieux, fervent.
devoutly [di'vautli], *adv.* dévotement.
dew [dju:], *n.* rosée, *f.*
dewdrop ['dju:drop], *n.* goutte de rosée, *f.*
dewlap ['dju:læp], *n.* fanon, *m.*
dewy ['dju:i], *a.* (couvert) de rosée.
dexterity [deks'teriti], *n.* dextérité, adresse, *f.*
dexterous ['dekstrəs], *a.* adroit; habile.
diabetes [daiə'bi:ti:z], *n.* diabète, *m.*
diabetic [daiə'betik], *a. and n.* diabétique, *m.*, *f.*
diabolic [daiə'bolik], **diabolical** [daiə'bolikl], *a.* diabolique.
diadem ['daiədem], *n.* diadème, *m.*
diæresis [dai'iərəsis], *n.* (*pl.* **diæreses** [dai'iərəsi:z]) tréma, *m.*
diagnose [daiəg'nouz], *v.t.* diagnostiquer.
diagnosis [daiəg'nousis], *n.* diagnose, *f.*; diagnostic, *m.*
diagonal [dai'ægənəl], *a.* diagonal.—*n.* diagonale, *f.*

diagram ['daiəgræm], *n.* diagramme, schéma, *m.*, épure, *f.*
diagrammatic [daiəgrə'mætik], *a.* schématique.
dial ['daiəl], *n.* cadran, *m.*; **sun-dial**, cadran solaire.—*v.t.* (*Teleph.*) composer (*un numéro*).
dialect ['daiəlekt], *n.* dialecte, patois; (*fig.*) langage, *m.*
dialogue ['daiəlog], *n.* dialogue; entretien, *m.*
diameter [dai'æmitə], *n.* diamètre, *m.*
diamond ['daiəmənd], *n.* diamant; (*Cards*) carreau, *m.*
diamond cutter ['daiəməndkʌtə], *n.* lapidaire, *m.*
diamond-shaped ['daiəməndʃeipt], *a.* en losange.
Diana [dai'ænə]. (*Myth.*) Diane, *f.*
diaper ['daiəpə], *n.* linge ouvré, *m.*; (*Am.*) serviette hygiénique, couche (*d'enfant*), *f.*
diarrhoea [daiə'ri:ə], *n.* diarrhée, *f.*
diary ['daiəri], *n.* journal (particulier); agenda, *m.*
diatribe ['daiətraib], *n.* diatribe, *f.*
dice [dais], *n.pl.* dés, *m.pl.*—*v.i.* jouer aux dés.
dicky ['diki], *n.* faux plastron (de chemise), *m.*
dictate [dik'teit], *v.t.* dicter.—*v.i.* commander (à).—['dikteit], *n.* précepte, ordre, *m.*
dictation [dik'teiʃən], *n.* dictée, *f.*
dictator [dik'teitə], *n.* dictateur, *m.*
dictatorial [diktə'tɔ:riəl], *a.* dictatorial; impérieux.
dictatorship [dik'teitəʃip], *n.* dictature, *f.*
diction ['dikʃən], *n.* diction, *f.*; débit, *m.*
dictionary ['dikʃənri], *n.* dictionnaire, *m.*
dictum ['diktəm], *n.* (*pl.* **dicta** ['diktə]) dicton, *m.*
diddle [didl], *v.t.* (*collog.*) duper, rouler.
die (1) [dai], *n.* (*pl.* **dies** [daiz]) coin (*pour estamper*).
die (2) [dai], *n.* (*pl.* **dice** [dais]) dé (à jouer), *m.*; (*fig.*) chance, *f.*
die (3) [dai], *v.i.* mourir; (*fig.*) s'éteindre; **to die down**, s'apaiser, se calmer; **to die of**, mourir de; **to die out**, s'éteindre, disparaître, s'oublier.
die-hard ['daihɑ:d], *n.* intransigeant, *m.*
diet ['daiət], *n.* diète, *f.*, régime, *m.*; diète (*assemblée*), *f.*—*v.t.* mettre à la diète, mettre au régime.—*v.i.* faire diète, être au régime.
dietetics [daiə'tetiks], *n.pl.* diététique, *f.*
differ ['difə], *v.i.* différer (*de*); se quereller (*avec*).
difference ['difrəns], *n.* différence; dispute, *f.*; différend (*de valeur*), *m.*; **to split the difference**, partager le différend.
different ['difrənt], *a.* différent.
differentiate [difə'renʃieit], *v.t.* différencier, distinguer.
differently ['difrəntli], *adv.* différemment, autrement.
difficult ['difikəlt], *a.* difficile; malaisé.
difficulty ['difikəlti], *n.* difficulté; peine, *f.*, embarras; (*pl.*) embarras pécuniaires, *m.*
diffidence ['difidəns], *n.* défiance (*de soi*), modestie, timidité, *f.*
diffident ['difidənt], *a.* timide, hésitant.
diffidently ['difidəntli], *adv.* avec hésitation, timidement.
diffuse [di'fju:s], *a.* répandu, étendu; diffus, verbeux (*style*).—[di'fju:z], *v.t.* répandre.
diffusely [di'fju:sli], *adv.* diffusément.

dig [dig]. *v.t. irr.* creuser; bêcher; piocher.— *v.i.* bêcher, piocher; faire des fouilles.—*n.* coup (*de coude*); (*colloq.*) coup de patte, *m.*

digest [di'dʒest], *v.t.* digérer (*aliment etc.*); résumer.—*v.i.* digérer.—['daidʒest], *n.* sommaire, abrégé, *m.*

digestion [di'dʒestʃən], *n.* digestion, *f.*

digestive [di'dʒestiv], *a.* and *n.* digestif, *m.*

digger ['digə], *n.* terrassier; mineur; fouilleur (*archéologue*); (*pop.*) Australien, *m.*

digging ['digiŋ], *n.* fouille, *f.,* creusement, *m.*; (*pl.*) (*pop.*) (*abbr.* **digs** [digz]) logement, *m.*

dignified ['dignifaid], *a.* plein de dignité, digne; noble.

dignify ['dignifai], *v.t.* honorer, élever, illustrer.

dignitary ['dignitri], *n.* dignitaire, *m., f.*

dignity ['digniti], *n.* dignité, *f.*

digress [dai'gres], *v.i.* faire une digression; s'écarter (*de*).

digression [dai'greʃən], *n.* digression, *f.*

dike or **dyke** [daik], *n.* digue, *f.,* fossé, *m.*

dilapidated [di'læpideitid], *a.* délabré.

dilapidation [dilæpi'deiʃən], *n.* délabrement, *m.*

dilate [dai'leit], *v.t.* dilater, élargir, étendre.— *v.i.* se dilater.

dilatory ['dilətəri], *a.* négligent, lent.

dilemma [di'lemə, dai'lemə], *n.* dilemme; (*fig.*) embarras, *m.*; **on the horns of a dilemma**, enfermé dans un dilemme.

diligence ['dilidʒəns], *n.* diligence, assiduité, *f.*

diligent ['dilidʒənt], *a.* diligent, appliqué.

dilute [dai'lju:t, di'lju:t], *v.t.* délayer; diluer; couper (*vin*); (*fig.*) affaiblir.—*a.* dilué, mitigé.

dilution [dai'lju:ʃən, di'lju:ʃən], *n.* dilution (*liquides*), *f.*; délayement; (*fig.*) affaiblissement, *m.*

dim [dim], *a.* obscur, trouble; blafard; terne (*lumière*); indécis.—*v.t.* obscurcir; ternir.

dimension [di'menʃən, dai'menʃən], *n.* dimension, étendue, *f.*

dimensional [di'menʃənəl, dai'menʃənəl], *a.* dimensionnel; (*Cine.*) **three-dimensional (3-D) film**, film en relief, *m.*

diminish [di'miniʃ], *v.t.* diminuer; abaisser. —*v.i.* diminuer.

diminutive [di'minjutiv], *a.* diminutif, minuscule.

dimly ['dimli], *adv.* obscurément, indistinctement, faiblement, à peine; sans éclat.

dimness ['dimnis], *n.* obscurcissement, *m.*; obscurité; faiblesse (*de vue*), *f.*

dimple ['dimpl], *n.* fossette, *f.*—*v.i.* (*fig.*) se rider (*eau etc.*).

din [din], *n.* vacarme, tapage, fracas; cliquetis (*d'armes etc.*), *m.*

dine [dain], *v.i.* dîner (*de*).

diner ['dainə], *n.* dîneur, *m.*

dinghy ['diŋgi], *n.* (*Naut.*) youyou, canot, *m.*

dinginess ['dindʒinis], *n.* couleur terne, *f.*; aspect sale, *m.*

dingy ['dindʒi], *a.* terne; sale; défraîchi.

dining car ['dainiŋkɑ:], *n.* wagon-restaurant, *m.*

dining room ['dainiŋrum], *n.* salle à manger, *f.*

dinner ['dinə], *n.* dîner, *m.*

dinner jacket ['dinədʒækit], *n.* smoking, *m.*

dint (1) [dint], *n.* force, *f.,* pouvoir, *m.*; **by dint of**, à force de.

dint (2) [dint], [DENT].

diocese ['daiəsis], *n.* diocèse, *m.*

dioxide [dai'ɔksaid], *n.* (*Chem.*) bioxyde, *m.*

dip [dip], *v.t.* plonger (*dans*); tremper, mouiller; (*Motor.*) mettre en code (*phares*).—*v.i.* plonger; **to dip into**, s'engager dans, feuilleter (*un livre*).—*n.* plongeon, *m.*, baignade, *f.*

diphtheria [dif'θiəriə], *n.* diphtérie, *f.*

diphthong ['difθɔŋ], *n.* diphtongue, *f.*

diploma [di'ploumə], *n.* diplôme, *m.*

diplomacy [di'plouməsi], *n.* diplomatie, *f.*

diplomat ['dipləmæt], **diplomatist** [di'ploumətist], *n.* diplomate, *m., f.*

diplomatic [diplo'mætik], *a.* diplomatique.

dip-stick ['dipstik], *n.* (*Motor.*) réglette-jauge, *f.*

dire ['daiə], *a.* terrible, affreux; cruel.

direct [di'rekt, dai'rekt], *a.* direct, droit; exprès, clair.—*adv.* (*colloq.*) directement.— *v.t.* diriger; ordonner, charger (*de*); indiquer, donner des renseignements à; (*Theat.*) mettre en scène.

direction [di'rekʃən], *n.* direction, *f.*; ordre, *m.,* instruction, *f.*; sens, côté, *m.*; adresse (*d'une lettre*), *f.*

directional signal [di'rekʃənəl 'signəl], *n.* (*Motor.*) clignotant, *m.*

directly [di'rektli], *adv.* directement.

director [di'rektə], *n.* directeur, administrateur, gérant; (*Cine.*) réalisateur, *m.*

directory [di'rektəri], *n.* directoire; (*Postal, Teleph.*) annuaire, *m.*

direful ['daiəful], *a.* terrible, affreux.

dirge [də:dʒ], *n.* chant funèbre, *m.*

dirt [də:t], *n.* saleté; crasse; boue, fange; ordure, *f.*

dirtily ['də:tili], *adv.* salement; (*fig.*) vilainement.

dirtiness ['də:tinis], *n.* saleté; (*fig.*) bassesse, *f.*

dirty ['də:ti], *a.* sale, malpropre, crasseux; (*fig.*) bas, vilain.—*v.t.* salir, crotter; (*fig.*) souiller.

disability [disə'biliti], *n.* incapacité, *f.*

disable [dis'eibl], *v.t.* rendre incapable, mettre hors d'état (*de*).

disabled [dis'eibld], *a.* hors de service; (*Mil.*) hors de combat; **disabled ex-service men**, mutilés de guerre, *m.pl.*

disadvantage [disad'vɑ:ntidʒ], *n.* désavantage, inconvénient, *m.*; perte, *f.*

disagree [disə'gri:], *v.i.* différer, ne pas s'accorder; **my dinner disagreed with me**, mon dîner m'a fait mal.

disagreeable [disə'gri:əbl], *a.* désagréable; fâcheux.

disagreeableness [disə'gri:əblnis], *n.* désagrément, *m.,* nature désagréable, *f.*

disagreeably [disə'gri:əbli], *adv.* désagréablement.

disagreement [disə'gri:mənt], *n.* différence, *f.,* désaccord; différend, *m.*; brouille, *f.*

disallow [disə'lau], *v.t.* désapprouver; refuser, défendre.

disappear [disə'piə], *v.i.* disparaître.

disappearance [disə'piərəns], *n.* disparition, *f.*

disappoint [disə'pɔint], *v.t.* désappointer, décevoir.

disappointing [disə'pɔintiŋ], *a.* décevant.

disappointment [disə'pɔintmənt], *n.* désappointement, *m.*; déception, *f.*; contretemps, *m.*

disapprobation [disæpro'beiʃən], **disapproval** [disə'pruːvəl], *n.* désapprobation, *f.*

disapprove [disə'pruːv], *v.t.* désapprouver.— *v.i.* **to disapprove of,** désapprouver.

disarm [dis'ɑːm], *v.t.* désarmer.

disarmament [dis'ɑːməmənt], *n.* désarmement, *m.*

disarrange [disə'reindʒ], *v.t.* déranger.

disarray [disə'rei], *v.i.* mettre en désarroi *ou* en désordre.—*n.* désarroi, désordre, *m.*

disaster [di'zɑːstə], *n.* désastre, malheur, *m.*

disastrous [di'zɑːstrəs], *a.* désastreux.

disavow [disə'vau], *v.t.* désavouer.

disband [dis'bænd], *v.t.* licencier, congédier; disperser.—*v.i.* se disperser.

disbelief [disbi'liːf], *n.* incrédulité, *f.*

disbelieve [disbi'liːv], *v.t.* ne pas croire, refuser de croire.

disbeliever [disbi'liːvə], *n.* incrédule, *m.*, *f.*

disc [DISK].

discard [dis'kɑːd], *v.t.* mettre de côté; congédier; écarter; éliminer; (*Cards*) faire son écart.—['diskɑːd], *n.* (*Cards*) écart, *m.*

discern [di'səːn, di'zəːn], *v.t.* discerner, distinguer.

discerning [di'səːniŋ, di'zəːniŋ], *a.* judicieux, éclairé, attentif.

discernment [di'səːnmənt, di'zəːnmənt], *n.* discernement, jugement, *m.*

discharge [dis'tʃɑːdʒ], *n.* déchargement, *m.*; décharge (*arme à feu etc.*); mise en liberté (*d'un prisonnier*, *f.*); accomplissement (*d'un devoir*), *m.*; réhabilitation (*d'un failli*); quittance (*récépissé*), *f.*; congé (*d'employé*); (*Mil.*) congé définitif; (*Med.*) écoulement, *m.*—*v.t.* décharger; congédier (*employé*); libérer (*de prison*); acquitter (*dette*); décharger (*arme à feu*); remplir (*devoir*); (*Mil., Navy*) congédier; (*Law*) quitter.—*v.i.* suppurer (*blessure etc.*).

disciple [di'saipl], *n.* disciple, *m.*

disciplinarian [disipli'nɛəriən], *a.* disciplinaire.—*n.* personne rigide pour la discipline, *f.*

disciplinary ['disiplinəri], *a.* disciplinaire.

discipline ['disiplin], *n.* discipline, *f.*—*v.t.* discipliner.

disclaim [dis'kleim], *v.t.* désavouer, renier, nier.

disclose [dis'klouz], *v.t.* découvrir, révéler.

disclosure [dis'klouʒə], *n.* révélation, découverte, *f.*

discolor [dis'kʌlə], *v.t.* décolorer.

discomfort [dis'kʌmfət], *n.* incommodité, *f.*, inconfort, malaise, *m.*; gêne, *f.*

discompose [diskəm'pouz], *v.t.* déranger, troubler.

discomposure [diskəm'pouʒə], *n.* trouble, désordre, *m.*, agitation, *f.*

disconcert [diskən'səːt], *v.t.* déconcerter.

disconnect [diskə'nekt], *v.t.* désunir, séparer; (*Elec.*) débrancher; (*Mach.*) désembrayer.

disconnected [diskə'nektid], *a.* débrayé; déconnecté; (*fig.*) décousu.

disconsolate [dis'kɔnsəlit], *a.* inconsolable, désolé.

discontent [diskən'tent], *n.* mécontentement, *m.*

discontented [diskən'tentid], *a.* mécontent (*de*).

discontinue [diskən'tinjuː], *v.t., v.i.* discontinuer; cesser de.

discord ['diskɔːd], *n.* discorde; (*Mus.*) dissonance, *f.*

discordant [dis'kɔːdənt], *a.* discordant; (*fig.*) en désaccord.

discount ['diskaunt], *n.* escompte; rabais, *m.* **at a discount,** au rabais, en baisse.—[dis'kaunt], *v.t.* escompter; (*fig.*) décompter, rabattre.—*v.i.* faire l'escompte.

discourage [dis'kʌridʒ], *v.t.* décourager, détourner.

discouragement [dis'kʌridʒmənt], *n.* découragement, *m.*

discouraging [dis'kʌridʒiŋ], *a.* décourageant.

discourse (1) ['diskɔːs], *n.* discours, entretien; (*fig.*) langage, propos, *m.*—[dis'kɔːs], *v.i.* discourir, s'entretenir, traiter (*de*).

discourteous [dis'kəːtiəs], *a.* impoli.

discourtesy [dis'kəːtisi], *n.* impolitesse, *f.*

discover [dis'kʌvə], *v.t.* découvrir; révéler, montrer.

discovery [dis'kʌvəri], *n.* découverte, *f.*

discredit [dis'kredit], *n.* discrédit, *m.*; honte, *f.*—*v.t.* ne pas croire; déshonorer.

discreditable [dis'kreditəbl], *a.* peu honorable; honteux.

discreet [dis'kriːt], *a.* discret, prudent, circonspect, sage.

discreetly [dis'kriːtli], *adv.* discrètement, sagement, prudemment.

discrepancy [dis'krepənsi], *n.* désaccord, *m.*

discretion [dis'kreʃən], *n.* discrétion, prudence, sagesse, *f.*; jugement, discernement, *m.*

discriminate [dis'krimineit], *v.t.* discriminer, distinguer.—*v.i.* faire des distinctions.

discriminating [dis'krimineitiŋ], *a.* discriminatoire, distinctif.

discrimination [diskrimi'neiʃən], *n.* discrimination, *f.*, discernement, *m.*

discuss [dis'kʌs], *v.t.* discuter, débattre.

discussion [dis'kʌʃən], *n.* discussion, *f.*, débat, *m.*

disdain [dis'dein], *n.* dédain, mépris, *m.*—*v.t.* dédaigner, mépriser.

disdainful [dis'deinful], *a.* dédaigneux, méprisant.

disease [di'ziːz], *n.* maladie, *f.*, mal; (*fig.*) vice, *m.*

diseased [di'ziːzd], *a.* malade; (*fig.*) dérangé.

disembark [disim'bɑːk], *v.t., v.i.* débarquer.

disembarkation [disembɑː'keiʃən], *n.* débarquement, *m.*

disembodied [disim'bɔdid], *a.* désincarné.

disembowel [disim'bauəl], *v.t.* éventrer.

disengage [disin'geidʒ], *v.t.* dégager; (*Tech.*) débrayer.—*v.i.* se dégager.

disengaged [disin'geidʒd], *a.* dégagé; libre.

disentangle [disin'tæŋgl], *v.t.* démêler, débrouiller.

disentanglement [disin'tæŋglmənt], *n.* débrouillement, *m.*

disestablish [disis'tæbliʃ], *v.t.* séparer (*l'Église de l'État*).

disestablishment [disis'tæbliʃmənt], *n.* séparation de l'Église et de l'État, *f.*

disfavor [dis'feivə], *n.* défaveur, *f.*

disfigure [dis'figə], *v.t.* défigurer, enlaidir.

disfigurement [dis'figəmənt], *n.* action de défigurer; difformité, *f.*

disfranchisement [dis'frænt∫izinənt], *n.* privation *ou* perte des privilèges électoraux, *f.*

disgorge [dis'gɔːdʒ], *v.t.* dégorger, rendre, vomir.—*v.i.* rendre gorge.

disgrace [dis'greis], *n.* disgrâce, honte, *f.*, déshonneur, *m.*—*v.t.* disgracier; déshonorer.

disgraceful [dis'greisful], *a.* honteux; déshonorant, ignoble.

disgracefully [dis'greisfuli], *adv.* honteusement.

disgruntled [dis'grʌntld], *a.* mécontent; de mauvaise humeur.

disguise [dis'gaiz], *n.* déguisement, travestissement, *(fig.)* masque, voile, *m.*—*v.t.* déguiser; *(fig.)* cacher, voiler.

disguised [dis'gaizd], *a.* déguisé.

disgust [dis'gʌst], *n.* dégoût, *m.*, aversion, *f.*; ennui, *m.*—*v.t.* dégoûter *(de)*; écœurer.

disgusting [dis'gʌstiŋ], *a.* dégoûtant.

dish [di∫], *n.* (*pl.* **dishes** ['di∫iz]) plat *(vaisselle)*; mets *(aliment)*, *m.*; *(pl.)* vaisselle, *f.*—*v.t.* dresser, servir, apprêter; *(colloq.)* enfoncer.

dish-cloth ['di∫klɔθ], *n.* torchon, *m.*

dishearten [dis'hɑːtn], *v.t.* décourager.

disheartening [dis'hɑːtniŋ], *a.* décourageant.

dishevel [di'∫evəl], *v.t.* ébouriffer.

dishevelled [di'∫evəld], *a.* dépeigné, ébouriffé.

dishonest [dis'ɔnist], *a.* malhonnête.

dishonestly [dis'ɔnistli], *adv.* malhonnêtement.

dishonesty [dis'ɔnisti], *n.* improbité, malhonnêteté, *f.*

dishonor [dis'ɔnə], *n.* déshonneur, *m.*—*v.t.* déshonorer; avilir; *(Comm.)* **dishonored check,** chèque impayé, *m.*

dishonorable [dis'ɔnərəbl], *a.* sans honneur; honteux *(chose).*

dishonorably [dis'ɔnərəbli], *adv.* malhonnêtement.

disillusion [disi'ljuːʒən], *v.t.* désillusionner.—*n.*, *also* **disillusionment** [disi'ljuːʒənmənt], désillusionnement, *n.*

disinclination [disinkli'nei∫ən], *n.* éloignement, *m.*; aversion, *f.*

disinclined [disin'klaind], *a.* peu disposé.

disinfect [disin'fekt], *v.t.* désinfecter.

disinfectant [disin'fektənt], *n.* désinfectant, *m.*

disingenuous [disin'dʒenjuəs], *a.* sans franchise, de mauvaise foi, dissimulé.

disingenuously [disin'dʒenjuəsli], *adv.* de mauvaise foi.

disingenuousness [disin'dʒenjuəsnis], *n.* dissimulation, mauvaise foi, fausseté, *f.*

disinherit [disin'herit], *v.t.* déshériter.

disinheritance [disin'heritəns], *n.* déshéritement, *m.*

disintegrate [dis'intigreit], *v.t.* désagréger; désintégrer.—*v.i.* se désagréger, se désintégrer.

disintegration [disinti'grei∫ən], *n.* désagrégation; désintégration, *f.*

disinter [disin'tə], *v.t.* déterrer, exhumer.

disinterested [dis'intrəstid], *a.* désintéressé.

disjointed [dis'dʒɔintid], *a.* désarticulé, disloqué; *(fig.)* décousu, sans suite *(style etc.).*

disjointedly [dis'dʒɔintidli], *adv.* d'une manière décousue *ou* incohérente.

disk [disk], *n.* disque, *m.*; *(Med.)* **slipped disk,** hernie discale, *f.*

dislike [dis'laik], *v.t.* ne pas aimer; avoir du dégoût pour.—*n.* aversion, *f.*; dégoût, *m.*

dislocate ['dislokeit], *v.t.* disloquer, démettre; déboîter *(os etc.).*

dislodge [dis'lɔdʒ], *v.t.* déloger; déplacer.

disloyal [dis'lɔiəl], *a.* perfide, déloyal.

disloyalty [dis'lɔiəlti], *n.* défection *(de)*, déloyauté, perfidie, *f.*

dismal ['dizməl], *a.* sombre, morne, triste.

dismally ['dizməli] *adv.* lugubrement, tristement.

dismantle [dis'mæntl], *v.t.* dévêtir; démonter *(machine).*

dismay [dis'mei], *n.* effroi, *m.*, terreur épouvante, *f.*—*v.t.* effarer, épouvanter, consterner.

dismiss [dis'mis], *v.t.* renvoyer *(de)*; congédier; quitter *(sujet etc.)*; rejeter *(appel etc.)*; chasser *(pensées etc.).*

dismissal [dis'misəl], *n.* renvoi; congé; *(Law)* acquittement, *m.*

dismount [dis'maunt], *v.t.* démonter.—*v.i.* descendre de cheval.

disobedience [diso'biːdiəns], *n.* désobéissance, *f.*

disobedient [diso'biːdiənt], *a.* désobéissant.

disobey [diso'bei], *v.t.* désobéir à.

disobliging [diso'blaidʒiŋ], *a.* désobligeant.

disorder [dis'ɔːdə], *n.* désordre; dérèglement, *m.*; maladie *(Med.)*, *f.*—*v.t.* déranger, troubler.

disordered [dis'ɔːdəd], *a.* en désordre, dérangé; malade.

disorderly [dis'ɔːdəli], *a.* en désordre, déréglé; vicieux; tumultueux.

disorganization [disɔːgəni'zei∫ən], *n.* désorganisation, *f.*

disorganize [dis'ɔːgənaiz], *v.t.* désorganiser.

disown [dis'oun], *v.t.* désavouer, nier.

disparage [dis'pæridʒ], *v.t.* déprécier, ravaler, dénigrer.

disparagement [dis'pæridʒmənt], *n.* dénigrement, déshonneur, reproche, *m.*; honte, *f.*, tort, *m.*

disparaging [dis'pæridʒiŋ], *a.* dénigrant, injurieux.

disparagingly [dis'pæridʒiŋli], *adv.* avec mépris.

dispassionate [dis'pæ∫ənit], *a.* calme; impartial.

dispatch, despatch [dis'pæt∫], *v.t.* dépêcher, expédier; achever.—*n.* dépêche, *f.*, envoi, *m.*; promptitude, *f.*; **mentioned in dispatches,** cité à l'ordre du jour.

dispel [dis'pel], *v.t.* dissiper, chasser.

dispensary [dis'pensəri], *n.* dispensaire, *m.*; pharmacie, *f.*

dispensation [dispən'sei∫ən], *n.* dispensation, *f.*; *(fig.)* bienfait, don, *m.*

dispense [dis'pens], *v.t.* distribuer, dispenser, administrer; *(Pharm.)* préparer *(médecine)*; **to dispense with,** se passer de.

dispenser [dis'pensə], *n.* dispensateur, pharmacien, *m.*

dispersal [dis'pəːsəl], *n.* dispersion, *f.*

disperse [dis'pəːs], *v.t.* disperser; dissiper.—*v.i.* se disperser.

dispirited [dis'piritid], *a.* découragé, abattu.

displace [dis'pleis], *v.t.* déplacer; destituer (*d'un emploi*).

displacement [dis'pleismənt], *n.* déplacement, *m.*

display [dis'plei], *n.* exposition, parade, *f.*; (*fig.*) étalage, *m.*—*v.t.* montrer, exposer, étaler.

displease [dis'pli:z], *v.t.* déplaire à; fâcher.

displeased [dis'pli:zd], *a.* mécontent, offensé (*de*).

displeasing [dis'pli:ziŋ], *a.* désagréable.

displeasure [dis'pleʒə], *n.* déplaisir; courroux, *m.*

disport [dis'pɔːt], *v.t.* **to disport oneself**, s'amuser, se divertir.

disposal [dis'pouzəl], *n.* disposition; vente, cession (*sale*), *f.*

dispose [dis'pouz], *v.t.* disposer; porter (*à croire*); **to dispose of**, céder, vendre, se défaire de, se débarrasser de.

disposition [dispə'ziʃən], *n.* disposition, *f.*; caractère, naturel, *m.*

dispossess [dispə'zes], *v.t.* déposséder (*de*).

disproportionate [disprə'pɔːʃənit], *a.* disproportionné.

disprove [dis'pru:v], *v.t.* réfuter.

dispute [dis'pju:t], *n.* différend; conflit, *m.*; **beyond dispute**, sans contredit.—*v.t.* disputer, discuter.

disqualification [diskwɔlifi'keiʃən], *n.* incapacité, *f.*

disqualify [dis'kwɔlifai], *v.t.* rendre incapable (*de*).

disquiet [dis'kwaiət], *n.* inquiétude, *f.*

disregard [disri'gɑːd], *n.* insouciance, indifférence, *f.*—*v.t.* négliger, faire peu de cas de.

disrepair [disri'pɛə], *n.* délabrement, *m.*

disreputable [dis'repjutəbl], *a.* de mauvaise réputation; compromettant, déshonorant (*chose*).

disrepute [disri'pju:t], *n.* discrédit, déshonneur, *m.*; mauvaise réputation, *f.*

disrespect [disris'pekt], *n.* manque de respect, irrespect, *m.*

disrespectful [disris'pektful], *a.* irrespectueux.

disrobe [dis'roub], *v.t.* déshabiller, dévêtir.—*v.i.* se déshabiller.

disrupt [dis'rʌpt], *v.t.* rompre.

dissatisfaction [dissætis'fækʃən], *n.* mécontentement, *m.*

dissatisfied [dis'sætisfaid], *a.* mécontent (*de*).

dissect [di'sekt], *v.t.* disséquer.

dissection [di'sekʃən], *n.* dissection, *f.*

dissemble [di'sembl], *v.t.* dissimuler, déguiser, cacher.—*v.i.* dissimuler, feindre.

disseminate [di'semineit], *v.t.* disséminer, répandre, propager.

dissension [di'senʃən], *n.* dissension, *f.*; **to sow dissension**, semer la zizanie.

dissent [di'sent], *n.* dissentiment, *m.*; (*Relig.*) dissidence, *f.*—*v.i.* différer (*de*); différer de sentiment (*avec*).

dissenter [di'sentə], *n.* dissident, *m.*, nonconformiste, *m.*, *f.*

disservice [dis'sə:vis], *n.* mauvais service, *m.*

dissever [di'sevə], *v.t.* séparer (*de*).

dissimilar [di'similə], *a.* dissemblable (*à*); différent (*de*).

dissimulate [di'simjuleit], *v.t.* dissimuler.

dissipate ['disipeit], *v.t.* dissiper.—*v.i.* se dissiper.

dissociate [di'souʃieit], *v.t.* désassocier, dissocier.

dissolute ['disəlu:t], *a.* dissolu.

dissolve [di'zɔlv], *v.t.* dissoudre; désunir; supprimer; résoudre (*doute etc.*).—*v.i.* se dissoudre.

dissonance ['disənəns], *n.* dissonance; discordance, *f.*

dissuade [di'sweid], *v.t.* dissuader (*de*).

distaff ['distɑːf], *n.* quenouille, *f.*; **the distaff side**, le côté maternel.

distance ['distəns], *n.* distance, *f.*; éloignement, lointain, *m.*; (*fig.*) réserve, *f.*

distant ['distənt], *a.* éloigné, lointain; (*fig.*) réservé, froid.

distaste [dis'teist], *n.* dégoût, *m.*, aversion (*pour*), *f.*

distasteful [dis'teistful], *a.* désagréable, offensant.

distemper [dis'tempə], *n.* maladie (*de chien*), (*Paint.*) détrempe, *f.*—*v.t.* peindre en détrempe.

distend [dis'tend], *v.t.* étendre; dilater, enfler.—*v.i.* se détendre.

distil [dis'til], *v.t.*, *v.i.* distiller.

distillation [disti'leiʃən], *n.* distillation, *f.*

distiller [dis'tilə], *n.* distillateur, *m.*

distillery [dis'tiləri], *n.* distillerie, *f.*

distinct [dis'tiŋkt], *a.* distinct; exprès, clair, net.

distinction [dis'tiŋkʃən], *n.* distinction; (*Sch.*) mention, *f.*

distinctive [dis'tiŋktiv], *a.* distinctif.

distinctly [dis'tiŋktli], *adv.* distinctement, clairement; (*fig.*) indéniablement.

distinguish [dis'tiŋgwiʃ], *v.t.* distinguer (*de*).

distinguished [dis'tiŋgwiʃt], *a.* distingué; **a distinguished man**, un homme éminent.

distort [dis'tɔːt], *v.t.* tordre, contourner; décomposer (*les traits*); (*fig.*) torturer, défigurer.

distorted [dis'tɔːtid], *a.* tordu, décomposé; (*fig.*) torturé.

distortion [dis'tɔːʃən], *n.* contorsion, déformation, *f.*

distract [dis'trækt], *v.t.* distraire, détourner (*de*); tourmenter.

distracted [dis'træktid], *a.* bouleversé, fou, hors de soi.

distracting [dis'træktiŋ], *a.* atroce, déchirant, affolant.

distraction [dis'trækʃən], *n.* distraction, *f.*, trouble, *m.*, confusion; démence, folie, *f.*; **to drive to distraction**, mettre hors de soi.

distraught [dis'trɔːt], *a.* affolé, éperdu.

distress [dis'tres], *n.* détresse, affliction, peine, *f.*, chagrin, *m.*; misère (*pauvreté*), *f.*—*v.t.* affliger, désoler.

distressed [dis'trest], *a.* affligé, malheureux; dans la misère (*pauvre*).

distressing [dis'tresiŋ], *a.* affligeant, désolant; pénible.

distribute [dis'tribju:t], *v.t.* distribuer.

distribution [distri'bju:ʃən], *n.* distribution, répartition, *f.*

district ['distrikt], *n.* contrée, région, *f.*, arrondissement, district; quartier (*de ville*); (*Postal*) secteur, *m.*

distrust [dis'trʌst], *n.* méfiance, *f.*—*v.t.* se méfier de.

distrustful [dis'trʌstful], *a.* défiant; méfiant, soupçonneux.

disturb [dis'tə:b], *v.t.* troubler; déranger.

disturbance [dis'tə:bəns], *n.* trouble, *m.*; confusion, émeute, *f.*; bruit, tapage; désordre, *m.*

disuse [dis'ju:s], *n.* désuétude, *f.*

disused [dis'ju:zd], *a.* hors d'usage.

ditch [ditʃ], *n.* fossé, *m.*—*v.t.* (*pop.*) abandonner.—*v.i.* creuser un fossé.

dither ['diðə], *n. to be all of a dither,* être tout agité.—*v.i.* trembler, trembloter, hésiter.

ditto ['ditou], *adv.* idem; (*Comm.*) dito.

ditty ['diti], *n.* chanson, chansonnette, *f.*

diurnal [dai'ə:nəl], *a.* journalier, du jour; (*Med.*) quotidien.

divan [di'væn], *n.* divan, *m.*

dive [daiv], *v.i.* plonger.—*n.* plongeon, *m.*; (*pop.*) boîte de nuit, *f.*

diver ['daivə], *n.* plongeur; plongeon (*oiseau*), *m.*

diverge [dai'və:dʒ], *v.i.* diverger (*de*).

divergent [dai'və:dʒənt], *a.* divergent.

diverse [dai'və:s], *a.* divers, varié.

diversify [dai'və:sifai], *v.t.* diversifier; varier (*couleurs*).

diversion [dai'və:ʃən], *n.* divertissement, amusement, *m.*; diversion, distraction, *f.*

diversity [dai'və:siti], *n.* diversité, variété, *f.*

divert [dai'və:t], *v.t.* divertir, réjouir; distraire; dévier, détourner (*de*).

diverting [dai'və:tiŋ], *a.* divertissant, amusant.

divest [di'vest, dai'vest], *v.t.* dépouiller (*de*).

divide [di'vaid], *v.t.* diviser; partager.—*v.i.* se diviser.

dividend ['dividend], *n.* dividende, *m.*

dividers [di'vaidəz], *n. pl.* compas à pointes sèches, *m.*

divine [di'vain], *a.* divin; (*fam.*) adorable.—*n.* théologien, ecclésiastique, *m.*—*v.t.* deviner, pressentir.

diving ['daiviŋ], *n.* plongement, plongeon, *m.*

diving board ['daiviŋbɔ:d], *n.* plongeoir, *m.*

divinity [di'viniti], *n.* divinité; théologie, *f.*

divisible [di'vizibl], *a.* divisible.

division [di'viʒən], *n.* division, *f.*, partage, *m.*; scission, *f.*; vote, *m.*

divorce [di'vɔ:s], *n.* divorce, *m.*; séparation, *f.*—*v.t.* séparer; divorcer avec.—*v.i.* se séparer (*de*).

divorcee [divɔ:'si:], *n.* divorcé, *m.*, divorcée, *f.*

divulge [dai'vʌldʒ, di'vʌldʒ], *v.t.* divulguer, publier.

dizziness ['dizinis], *n.* vertige, étourdissement, *m.*

dizzy ['dizi], *a.* étourdi; vertigineux (*élévation*).

do [du:], *v.t. irr.* faire; rendre (*service, justice etc.*); finir (*achever*); (*Cook.*) cuire; (*collog.*) duper; *done!* c'est entendu! *done to a turn,* cuit à point; *he is done for,* c'en est fait de lui; *it can't be done,* pas moyen; *overdone,* trop cuit (*viande*); *to be doing well,* faire de bonnes affaires, réussir; *to do over,* enduire (*de*), couvrir (*de*); *to do up,* empaqueter, emballer, remettre en état, remettre à neuf; *underdone,* saignant (*viande*); *well done!* bravo! *what is to be done?* que faire?—*v.i.* se porter, se conduire; aller, convenir

(*faire l'affaire*); suffire (*répondre à un besoin*); finir (*terminer*); *how do you do?* comment allez-vous? *to do away with,* supprimer, se défaire de, faire disparaître; *to do by,* agir envers; *to do without,* se passer de.—*n.* duperie; soirée, réception, *f.*

docile ['dousail], *a.* docile.

docility [dou'siliti], *n.* docilité, *f.*

dock [dɔk], *v.t.* écourter; rogner (*comptes etc.*); (*Naut.*) mettre dans le bassin.—*v.i.* entrer aux docks.—*n.* bassin, dock, *m.*; (*Bot.*) patience, *f.*; (*Law*) banc des accusés, *m.*

docker ['dɔkə], *n.* déchargeur, docker, *m.*

docket ['dɔkit], *n.* étiquette, fiche, *f.*—*v.t.* étiqueter; enregistrer.

doctor ['dɔktə], *n.* docteur, médecin, *m.*—*v.t.* soigner, droguer; (*fig.*) altérer; frelater (*vin*).

doctrinaire [dɔktri'nɛə], *a.* doctrinaire.

doctrinal [dɔk'trainəl], *a.* doctrinal.

doctrine ['dɔktrin], *n.* doctrine, *f.*

document ['dɔkjumənt], *n.* document, titre, *m.*—*v.t.* munir de documents.

documentary [dɔkju'mentəri], *a.* justificatif, authentique.—*n.* (*Cine.*) documentaire, *m.*

documentation [dɔkjumen'teiʃən], *n.* documentation, *f.*

dodge [dɔdʒ], *v.t.* éviter; esquiver.—*v.i.* s'esquiver; (*fig.*) ruser, faire des détours.—*n.* tour, détour, *m.*; (*fig.*) ruse, ficelle, *f.*

dodger ['dɔdʒə], *n.* rusé, malin, finaud, *m.*

doe [dou], *n.* daine, *f.*

doer ['du:ə], *n.* faiseur; auteur, *m.*

doff [dɔf], *v.t.* tirer, enlever, ôter.

dog [dɔg], *n.* chien; (*facet.*) coquin, gaillard, *m.*; *lucky dog!* quel veinard!—*v.t.* suivre à la piste; harceler, épier.

dog days ['dɔgdeiz], *n.pl.* canicule, *f.*

dogged ['dɔgid], *a.* obstiné; acharné.

doggedly ['dɔgidli], *adv.* avec acharnement.

doggedness ['dɔgidnis], *n.* obstination, *f.* acharnement, *m.*

doggerel ['dɔgərəl], *n.* vers burlesques, vers de mirliton, *m.pl.*

doggie ['dɔgi], *n.* (*Childish*) tou-tou, *m.*

doggo ['dɔgou], *adv. to lie doggo,* se tenir coi.

dogma ['dɔgmə], *n.* dogme, *m.*

dogmatic [dɔg'mætik], *a.* dogmatique.

dogmatism ['dɔgmətizm], *n.* dogmatisme, *m.*

doily ['dɔili], *n.* serviette de dessert, *f.*, napperon, *m.*

doing ['du:iŋ], *n.* (*usu. in pl.*) faits, *m.pl.*; actions, *f.pl.*, exploits, *m.pl.*

dole [doul], *n.* aumône, *f.*, partage, *m.*; allocation de chômage, *f.*—*v.t. to dole out,* distribuer, répartir avec parcimonie.

doleful ['doulful], *a.* plaintif, lugubre.

doll [dɔl], *n.* poupée, *f.*—*v.r. to doll oneself up,* se pomponner.

dollar ['dɔlə], *n.* dollar, *m.*

dolphin ['dɔlfin], *n.* dauphin, *m.*

dolt [doult], *n.* lourdaud, sot, butor, *m.*

domain [do'mein], *n.* domaine, *m.*

dome [doum], *n.* dôme, *m.*

domestic [də'mestik], *a.* de famille; domestique (*animaux*).—*n.* domestique, *m.*,*f.*, servante, *f.*

domesticate [də'mestikeit], *v.t.* domestiquer, apprivoiser; (*fig.*) rendre casanier.

domesticated [də'mestikeited], *a.* casanier (*personnes*); apprivoisé (*animaux*).
domicile ['dɔmisail, 'dɔmisil], *n.* domicile, *m.*
dominance ['dɔminəns], *n.* dominance, *f.*
dominant ['dɔminənt], *a.* dominant.
dominate ['dɔmineit], *v.t.* dominer sur.—*v.i.* dominer; prévaloir, prédominer.
domination [dɔmi'neiʃən], *n.* domination, *f.*
domineer [dɔmi'niə], *v.i.* dominer (*sur.*).
domineering [dɔmi'niəriŋ], *a.* impérieux, autoritaire.
Dominican [dɔ'minikən], *a.* dominicain.—*n.* Dominicain (*personne*), *m.*; **Dominican nun**, Dominicaine, *f.*
dominie ['dɔmini], *n.* (*Sc.*) maître d'école, *m.*
dominion [dɔ'miniən], *n.* domination, autorité, *f.*; empire, *m.*; (*pl.*) états, *m.pl.*
domino ['dɔminou], *n.* domino (*capuchon, jeu*), *m.*
don [dɔn], *n.* don (*titre*); (*fig.*) grand seigneur; (*Univ.*) professeur d'université, *m.*—*v.t.* mettre, endosser.
donate [do'neit], *v.t.* faire un don de.
donation [do'neiʃən], *n.* donation, *f.*, don, *m.*
donkey ['dɔŋki], *n.* âne, baudet, *m.*
donor ['dounə], *n.* donateur, *m.*
doodle [du:dl], *v.i.* griffonner.—*n.* griffonnage, *m.*
doom [du:m], *v.t.* condamner (*à*); (*fig.*) destiner (*à*).—*n.* jugement; destin funeste, *m.*; perte, ruine, *f.*
doomsday ['du:mzdei], *n.* jour du jugement dernier, *m.*
door [dɔ:], *n.* porte; portière (*d'une voiture*), *f.*; **folding doors**, porte à deux battants; **next door**, à côté; **indoors**, à la maison; **out of doors**, dehors; **behind closed doors**, à huis clos.
door-bell ['dɔ:bel], *n.* sonnette, *f.*
door-keeper ['dɔ:ki:pə], *n.* concierge, portier (*d'une maison*); gardien (*des monuments publics*), *m.*
doorman ['dɔ:mən], *n.* portier, *m.*
door mat ['dɔ:mæt], *n.* paillasson, *m.*
door-step ['dɔ:step], *n.* seuil de la porte, pas de (la) porte, *m.*
door-way ['dɔ:wei], *n.* entrée, porte, *f.*
dope [doup], *n.* drogue, *f.*, narcotique, *m.*—*v.t.* droguer.
dormant ['dɔ:mənt], *a.* dormant; assoupi.
dormer window ['dɔ:məwindou], *n.* lucarne, *f.*
dormitory ['dɔ:mitri], *n.* dortoir, *m.*
dormouse ['dɔ:maus], *n.* (*pl.* **dormice** ['dɔ:mais]) loir, *m.*
Dorothy ['dɔrəθi], Dorothée, *f.*
dose [dous], *n.* dose, *f.*—*v.t.* médicamenter; doser.
dossier ['dɔsjei], *n.* dossier, *m.*
dot [dɔt], *n.* point, *m.*—*v.t.* marquer d'un point, marquer avec des points; (*Paint.*) pointiller.
dotage ['doutidʒ], *n.* seconde enfance, *f.*, radotage, *m.*
dote [dout], *v.i.* radoter; raffoler (*de*).
double [dʌbl], *a.* double, en deux; **bent double**, voûté.—*n.* double, pendant, sosie; (*Mil.*) pas de course, *m.*—*adv.* double; au double; **to fold double**, plier en deux.—*v.t.* doubler; serrer (*poings*).—*v.i.* doubler;

user de ruse; **to double back**, revenir sur ses pas.
double bed ['dʌbl'bed], *n.* lit à deux places, *m.*
double-breasted ['dʌblbrestid], *a.* croisé.
double-cross ['dʌbl'krɔs], *v.t.* duper, tromper.
double-dealing ['dʌbl'di:liŋ], *n.* duplicité, *f.*
double decker ['dʌbl'dekə], *n.* autobus à impériale, *m.*
double-room ['dʌbl'ru:m], *n.* chambre pour deux personnes, *f.*
doubt [daut], *n.* doute, *m.*; hésitation, *f.*; **beyond a doubt**, sans aucun doute.—*v.t.* douter de.—*v.i.* douter; soupçonner.
doubtful ['dautful], *a.* douteux, incertain.
doubtless ['dautlis], *adv.* sans doute.
dough [dou], *n.* pâte, *f.*
dough-nut ['dounʌt], *n.* pet-de-nonne, *m.*
doughty ['dauti], *a.* vaillant, preux.
dour ['duə], *a.* (*Sc.*) austère et froid.
douse [daus], *v.t.* plonger dans l'eau; éteindre.
dove [dʌv], *n.* colombe, *f.*; pigeon, *m.*
dove-cot(e) ['dʌvkɔt, 'dʌvkout], *n.* colombier, *m.*
Dover ['douvə], Douvres, *m.*; **the Straits of Dover**, le Pas-de-Calais, *m.*
dowager ['dauədʒə], *n.* douairière, *f.*
dowdy ['daudi], *a.f.* gauche et mal mise, mal fagotée.
dowel ['dauəl], *n.* (*Carp.*) goujon, *m.*
down (1) [daun], *n.* duvet (*poil follet*), *m.*; dune (*colline*), *f.*
down (2) [daun], *adv.* en bas; à bas; bas, à terre; tombé, apaisé (*vent*); couché (*soleil*); à plat (*pneu*); en baisse (*prix*); (*fig.*) sur le déclin; **to go down**, descendre.—*prep.* en bas de; vers le bas de.
downcast ['daunkɔ:st], *a.* abattu.
downfall ['daunfɔ:l], *n.* chute; (*fig.*) débâcle, *f.*
downhill ['daunhil], *a.* incliné; en pente.—['daun'hil], *adv.* en descendant.
downpour ['daunpɔ:], *n.* averse, *f.*
downright ['daunrait], *a.* direct; franc.—*adv.* net, tout à fait.
downstairs [daun'steəz], *adv.* en bas (de l'escalier).
downtrodden ['dauntrɔdn], *a.* opprimé.
downward ['daunwəd], *a.* de haut en bas, qui descend, descendant.—*adv.* (*also* **downwards** ['daunwədz]) en bas, en descendant en aval.
downy ['dauni] *a.* de duvet, duveteux.
dowry ['dauri], *n.* dot, *f.*
doze [douz], *v.i.* s'assoupir, sommeiller, être assoupi.—*n.* petit somme, *m.*
dozen [dʌzn], *n.* douzaine, *f.*
drab [dræb], *a.* gris sale, brun terne; (*fig.*) terne, décoloré.—*n.* (*fig.*) traînée (*femme*), *f.*
draft [drɑ:ft], *v.t.* dessiner, rédiger; (*Mil.*) détacher.—*n.* dessin (*esquisse*); brouillon (*projet*), *m.*; (*Comm.*) traite, *f.*; (*Mil.*) détachement, *m.*
draft ['drɑ:ft], *n.* tirage; trait; courant d'air; coup (*boisson*); dessin (*esquisse*); coup de filet (*de pêcheur*); tirant (*d'un navire*), *m.*; (*Med.*) potion, *f.*; (*pl.*) jeu de dames, *m.*
draft-board ['drɑ:ftbɔ:d], *n.* damier, *m.*
draft-horse ['drɑ:ftbɔ:s], *n.* cheval de trait, *m.*
draftsman ['drɑ:ftsmən], *n.* (*pl.* **-men** [men]) dessinateur, *m.*
drafty ['drɑ:fti], *a.* plein de courants

d'air.

drag [dræg], *v.t.* traîner, tirer; (*Naut.*) draguer; *to drag away from*, entraîner, arracher de; *to drag on*, entraîner; (*fig.*) traîner en longueur; *to drag out*, faire sortir de force.—*v.i.* se traîner; traîner; chasser (*ancre*).

draggle [drægl], *v.t.* traîner dans la boue.

drag-net ['drægnet], *n.* seine, *f.*, chalut, *m.*

dragoman ['drægomən], *n.* drogman, *m.*

dragon ['drægən], *n.* dragon, *m.*

dragon-fly ['drægənflai], *n.* demoiselle, libellule, *f.*, agrion, *m.*

dragoon [drə'gu:n], *n.* (*Mil.*) dragon, *m.*—*v.t.* (*fig.*) forcer par des mesures violentes.

drain [drein], *v.t.* faire écouler; dessécher; drainer; (*fig.*) épuiser; vider (*verre etc.*).—*v.i.* s'écouler.—*n.* tranchée, *f.*, égout, *m.*

drainage ['dreinidʒ], **draining** ['dreiniŋ] *n.* écoulement; (*Agric.*) drainage, *m.*

draining-board ['dreiniŋbɔːd], *n.* égouttoir, *m.*

drake [dreik], *n.* canard, *m.*

dram [dræm], *n.* (*Pharm.*) drachme, *f.*

drama ['drɑːmə], *n.* drame; (*fig.*) théâtre, *m.*

dramatic [drə'mætik], **dramatical** [drə'mætikəl], *a.* dramatique.

dramatist ['drɑːmətist, 'dræmətist], *n.* auteur dramatique, *m.*, dramaturge, *m.*, *f.*

dramatize ['drɑːmətaiz, 'dræmətaiz], *v.t.* dramatiser.

drape [dreip], *v.t.* draper, tendre (*de*).—*n.* (*Am.*) rideau, *m.*

draper ['dreipə], *n.* drapier; marchand de drap, *m.*

drapery ['dreipəri], *n.* draperie, *f.*

drastic ['dræstik], *a.* énergique, radical, brutal.

draw [drɔː], *v.t. irr.* tirer; traîner; dessiner (*tableau etc.*); toucher (*rations, appointements etc.*); arracher (*dent*); puiser (*eau etc.*); (*fig.*) attirer (*à* ou *sur*); *to draw lots for*, tirer au sort.—*v.i.* dessiner; dessiner (*au crayon*); (*Spt.*) faire partie nulle *ou* match nul.—*n.* tirage (*au sort*), *m.*; attraction; (*Spt.*) partie nulle, *f.*

drawback ['drɔːbæk], *n.* mécompte, désavantage, inconvénient, *m.*

drawbridge ['drɔːbridʒ], *n.* pont-levis, *m.*

drawer ['drɔːə], *n.* tireur (*d'un chèque*); puiseur (*d'eau*); tiroir (*meuble*); (*pl.*) caleçon (*vêtement*), *m.*; *chest of drawers*, commode, *f.*

drawing ['drɔːiŋ], *n.* tirage; dessin (*croquis*), *m.*

drawing board ['drɔːiŋbɔːd], *n.* planche à dessin, *f.*

drawing-pin ['drɔːiŋpin], *n.* punaise (*pour le dessin*), *f.*

drawing room ['drɔːiŋru:m], *n.* salon, *m.*; (*Court*) réception, *f.*

drawl [drɔːl], *v.i.* parler d'une voix traînante.—*n.* voix traînante *f.*

drawling ['drɔːliŋ], *a.* traînant.

drawn [drɔːn], *a.* indécis, égal (*bataille etc.*); tiré, nu (*épée*); *drawn game*, partie nulle, *f.*

dray [drei], *n.* camion, haquet, *m.*

dread [dred], *a.* redoutable, terrible, auguste.—*n.* terreur, crainte, *f.*—*v.t.* craindre, redouter.

dreadful ['dredful]. *a.* affreux, terrible, épouvantable.

dreadfully ['dredfuli], *adv.* terriblement, affreusement.

dream [driːm], *n.* songe, rêve, *m.*; *day-dream*, rêverie, *f.*—*v.t. irr.* rêver.—*v.i.* rêver; (*fig.*) s'imaginer.

dreamer ['driːmə], *n.* rêveur, *m.*; (*fig.*) visionnaire, *m.*, *f.*

dreamy ['driːmi], *a.* rêveur; chimérique, visionnaire.

drear [driə], **dreary** ['driəri], *a.* triste, morne, lugubre.

drearily ['driərili], *adv.* tristement, lugubrement.

dreariness ['driərinis], *n.* tristesse, *f.*, aspect morne, *m.*

dredge (1) [dredʒ], *n.* drague, *f.*—*v.t.*, *v.i.* draguer.

dredge (2) [dredʒ], *v.t.* saupoudrer (*de farine etc.*).

dredger (1) ['dredʒə], *n.* dragueur (*bateau*), *m.*

dredger (2) ['dredʒə], *n.* saupoudreuse, *f.*

dregs [dregz], *n.pl.* lie, *f.*

drench [drentʃ], *v.t.* tremper, mouiller (*de*); noyer (*de*).

dress [dres], *v.t.* habiller, vêtir, parer, orner; panser (*blessure etc.*); apprêter (*aliments etc.*); (*Mil.*) aligner; (*Navy*) pavoiser.—*v.i.* s'habiller; faire sa toilette; (*Mil.*) s'aligner.—*n.* habillement, *m.*; robe (*de femme*); mise, toilette; (*Mil.*) tenue, *f.*; *dress rehearsal*, répétition générale, *f.*; *evening dress*, tenue de soirée, *f.*

dress circle ['dres'sə:kl], *n.* (*Theat.*) fauteuils de balcon, *m.pl.*

dresser ['dresə], *n.* habilleur (*personne*); dressoir (*de cuisine*), *m.*

dressing ['dresiŋ], *n.* toilette, *f.*, habillement; pansement (*de blessure etc.*), *m.*; (*Cook.*) assaisonnement, *m.*; (*Agric.*) fumure, *f.*, engrais, *m.*

dressing case ['dresiŋkeis], *n.* mallette de toilette, *f.*

dressing gown ['dresiŋgaun], *n.* robe de chambre, *f.*, peignoir, *m.*

dressing room ['dresiŋru:m], *n.* cabinet de toilette, *m.*

dressing table ['dresiŋteibl], *n.* coiffeuse, table de toilette, *f.*

dressmaker ['dresmeikə], *n.* couturière, *f.*

dressmaking ['dresmeikiŋ], *n.* confections pour dames, *f.pl.*, couture, *f.*

dressy ['dresi], *a.* élégant, chic, coquet (*personne*); habillé (*robe*).

dribble [dribl], *v.t.* laisser dégoutter, laisser tomber goutte à goutte; (*Ftb.*) dribbler.—*v.i.* tomber goutte à goutte, dégoutter; baver; (*Ftb.*) dribbler.

drier ['draiə], *comp. a.* [DRY].—*n.* [DRYER].

drift [drift], *n.* monceau; tourbillon, *m.*, rafale, *f.*; objet flottant, *m.*; (*fig.*) tendance; (*Naut.*) dérive, *f.*—*v.t.* chasser, pousser; amonceler.—*v.i.* dériver, aller à la dérive, flotter; s'amonceler, s'amasser.

drifter ['driftə], *n.* (*Naut.*) chalutier, *m.*

drill [dril], *n.* foret, *m.*, mèche, *f.*; (*Agric.*) sillon; (*Mil.*) exercice, *m.*, manœuvre, *f.*—*v.t.* forer, percer; (*Mil.*) exercer.—*v.i.* (*Mil.*) faire l'exercice.

drilling ['drilin], *n.* forage; (*Dent.*) fraisage; (*Mil.*) exercice, *m.*

drink [drink], *n.* boisson; (*fig.*) ivresse (*drunkenness*), *f.*—*v.t., v.i.* irr. boire.

drinker ['drinkə], *n.* buveur; ivrogne, *m.*

drinking ['drinkin], *a.* potable; à boire.—*n.* boire, *m.*; ivrognerie, *f.*, alcoolisme, *m.*

drinking fountain ['drinkinfauntin], *n.* fontaine publique, *f.*

drip [drip], *v.t.* faire dégoutter.—*v.i.* dégoutter, tomber goutte à goutte.—*n.* goutte, *f.*; égout, *m.*

dripping ['dripiŋ], *n.* graisse de rôti, *f.*; (*pl.*) gouttes, *f.pl.*

drive [draiv], *v.t.* irr. pousser; chasser; enfoncer (*clou etc.*); mener, conduire (*voiture, cheval etc.*); forcer, réduire (*à*); **to drive away**, chasser, éloigner; **to drive back**, repousser; **to drive in**, faire entrer, enfoncer; **to drive out**, faire sortir, chasser.—*v.i.* conduire; aller en voiture; **to drive at**, tendre à, vouloir en venir à; **to drive up**, arriver (en voiture).—*n.* promenade *ou* course en voiture; grande avenue *ou* allée, *f.*

drivel [drivl], *n.* bave, *f.*—*v.i.* baver; (*fig.*) radoter.

driver ['draivə], *n.* cocher (*d'un carrosse*); voiturier (*d'une charrette*); (*Rail.*) mécanicien; (*Motor. etc.*) chauffeur, conducteur, *m.*

driving ['draiviŋ], *n.* action de conduire, *f.*; percement (*d'un tunnel*), *m.*

driving license ['draiviŋlaisəns], *n.* permis de conduire, *m.*

driving test ['draiviŋtest], *n.* examen pour permis de conduire, *m.*

drizzle [drizl], *v.i.* bruiner.—*n.* bruine, pluie fine, *f.*

droll [droul], *a.* plaisant, drôle.

drollery ['drouləri], *n.* plaisanterie, drôlerie, farce, *f.*

dromedary ['drʌmədəri, 'drɔmədəri], *n.* dromadaire, *m.*

drone [droun], *n.* (*Ent., Mus.*) faux-bourdon; (*fig.*) frelon; fainéant (*personne*); bourdonnement (*son*), *m.*—*v.i.* bourdonner.

droning ['drouniŋ], *a.* bourdonnant.—*n.* bourdonnement, *m.*

droop [dru:p], *v.t.* laisser tomber, laisser pendre.—*v.i.* languir, se pencher, tomber, pencher; (*fig.*) s'affaiblir.

drooping ['dru:piŋ], *a.* languissant, abattu; penché.—*n.* abattement, *m.*, langueur, *f.*

drop [drɔp], *n.* goutte; chute (*descente*), *f.*; pendant (*bijou*), *m.*—*v.t.* laisser tomber; jeter (*l'ancre*); sauter (*une maille*); déposer (*quelqu'un*) quelque part; laisser échapper (*prononcer*); abandonner (*lâcher*).—*v.i.* tomber goutte à goutte; dégoutter (*de*); échapper (*glisser*); **to drop behind**, se laisser dépasser, rester en arrière; **to drop in**, entrer en passant; **to drop out**, se retirer.

dropsy ['drɔpsi], *n.* hydropisie, *f.*

dross [drɔs], *n.* scorie, crasse, *f.*; (*fig.*) rebut, *m.*

drought [draut], *n.* sécheresse, *f.*

drove (1) [drouv], *n.* troupeau (*en marche*), *m.*; (*fig.*) foule (*en marche*), *f.*

drove (2) [drouv], *past* [DRIVE].

drover ['drouvə], *n.* conducteur de bestiaux, bouvier, *m.*

drown [draun], *v.t.* noyer; (*fig.*) submerger; étouffer (*bruit*).—*v.i.* se noyer.

drowsily ['drauzili], *adv.* comme endormi; (*fig.*) avec indolence.

drowsiness ['drauzinis], *n.* assoupissement, *m.*

drowsy ['drauzi], *a.* assoupi; somnolent; lourd, stupide.

drub [drʌb], *v.t.* rosser, battre.

drubbing ['drʌbiŋ], *n.* volée (de coups), *f.*

drudge [drʌdʒ], *n.* homme (*ou femme*) de peine, souffre-douleur, *m.*, *f.*—*v.i.* travailler sans relâche, peiner.

drudgery ['drʌdʒəri], *n.* travail pénible, *m.*; corvée, vile besogne, *f.*

drug [drʌg], *n.* drogue, *f.*—*v.t.* droguer; (*fig.*) empoisonner.

drug addict ['drʌgædikt], *n.* toxicomane, *m.*, *f.*

druggist ['drʌgist], *n.* (*Am.*) pharmacien, *m.*

drug store ['drʌgstɔ:], *n.* (*Am.*) pharmacie, *f.*

druid ['dru:id], *n.* druide, *m.*

drum [drʌm], *n.* tambour, *m.*; caisse, *f.*; tympan (*de l'oreille*), *m.*—*v.t.* (*Mil.*) **to drum out**, dégrader.—*v.i.* battre du tambour (*sur*); (*fig.*) tinter.

drum major ['drʌmmeidʒə], *n.* tambour-major, *m.*

drummer ['drʌmə], *n.* tambour (*homme*), *m.*

drum-stick ['drʌmstik], *n.* baguette de tambour, *f.*

drunk [drʌŋk], *a.* ivre, gris, soûl.

drunkard ['drʌŋkəd], *n.* ivrogne, *m.*

drunkenness ['drʌŋkənnis], *n.* ivresse; ivrognerie, *f.*

dry [drai], *a.* sec, desséché; aride; altéré; (*fig.*) caustique; ennuyeux.—*v.t.* sécher; dessécher.—*v.i.* sécher; **to dry up**, tarir; se taire.

dry-dock ['draidɔk], *n.* bassin de radoub, *m.*, cale sèche, *f.*

dryer, drier ['draiə], *n.* (*Ind. etc.*) séchoir; (*Paint.*) siccatif, dessiccatif, *m.*

dryness ['drainis], *n.* sécheresse, aridité, *f.*

dry-shod ['draiʃɔd], *a.* and *adv.* à pied sec.

dual ['dju:əl], *a.* double; **dual carriage-way**, route à double circulation, *f.*—*n.* duel, *m.*

dub [dʌb], *v.t.* armer chevalier; (*colloq.*) qualifier, baptiser; (*Cine.*) doubler (*film*).

dubiety [dju:'baiəti], **dubiousness** ['dju:biəsnis], *n.* doute, *m.*, incertitude, *f.*

dubious ['dju:biəs], *a.* douteux, incertain.

dubiously ['dju:biəsli], *adv.* douteusement.

duchess ['dʌtʃis], *n.* duchesse, *f.*

duchy ['dʌtʃi], *n.* duché, *m.*

duck (1) [dʌk], *n.* cane, *f.*; canard; (*colloq.*) chou (*mot tendre*), *m.*

duck (2) [dʌk], *n.* (*Box.*) esquive, *f.*—*v.t.* plonger dans l'eau.—*v.i.* plonger; baisser la tête subitement; (*Box.*) esquiver.

duck (3) [dʌk], *n.* toile à voile, *f.*; (*pl.*) pantalon blanc, *m.*

ducking ['dʌkiŋ], *n.* plongeon; (*Naut.*) baptême de la ligne, *m.*

duckling ['dʌkliŋ], *n.* caneton, *m.*

duck-weed ['dʌkwi:d], *n.* lentille d'eau, *f.*

duct [dʌkt], *n.* conduit; (*Anat.*) canal, *m.*

dudgeon ['dʌdʒən], *n.* colère, *f.*; **in high dudgeon**, fort en colère.

due [dju:], *a.* dû; convenable, propre, juste; (*Comm.*) échu; (*fig.*) requis, voulu; *to fall due*, échoir.—*n.* dû; (*pl.*) droit, impôt, *m.*, redevance, *f.*—*adv.* droit, directement.
duel ['dju:əl], *n.* duel, *m.*, (*fig.*) lutte, *f.*
duellist ['dju:alist], *n.* duelliste, *m.*
duenna [dju:'enə], *n.* duègne, *f.*
duet [dju:'et], *n.* duo, *m.*
duke [dju:k], *n.* duc, *m.*
dukedom ['dju:kdəm], *n.* duché, *m.*; dignité de duc, *f.*
dull [dʌl], *a.* lourd, hébété, stupide (*personne*); lourd, gris, sombre (*temps*); sourd (*son*); triste (*morne*); émoussé (*moins aigu*); terne (*couleur*); ennuyeux.—*v.t.* hébéter; émousser (*rendre moins aigu*); ternir (*ôter l'éclat de*); engourdir (*de froid*).—*v.i.* s'hébéter; s'engourdir; s'émousser.
dullard ['dʌləd], *n.* âne, lourdaud (*personne*), *m.*
dullness ['dʌlnis], *n.* lenteur, *f.*; assoupissement, ennui; manque d'éclat, *m.*, faiblesse (*de son*), *f.*
dully ['dʌli], *adv.* lourdement, tristement.
duly ['dju:li], *adv.* dûment, justement.
dumb [dʌm], *a.* muet, réduit au silence; (*Am.*) stupide.
dumb-bells ['dʌmbelz], *n.pl.* haltères, *m.pl.*
dumbfound [dʌm'faund], *v.t.* confondre, abasourdir, interdire.
dumbly ['dʌmli], *adv.* en silence.
dumbness ['dʌmnis], *n.* mutisme; (*fig.*) silence, *m.*
dumb show ['dʌmʃou], *n.* pantomime, *f.*, jeu muet, *m.*
dummy ['dʌmi], *n.* muet, *m.*, muette, *f.*; mannequin, objet imité; (*fig.*) homme de paille; (*Cards*) mort, *m.*
dump [dʌmp], *v.t.* déposer, décharger, déverser.—*n.* tas; dépotoir, *m.*
dumpling ['dʌmpliŋ], *n.* pâte cuite, *f.*
dumpy ['dʌmpi], *a.* trapu, gros et court.
dun (1) [dʌn], *a.* brun foncé; bai (*cheval*).
dun (2) [dʌn], *n.* créancier importun, *m.*—*v.t.* importuner.
dunce [dʌns], *n.* ignorant, âne, sot, *m.*
dune [dju:n], *n.* dune, *f.*
dung [dʌŋ], *n.* crotte, *f.*; crottin; (*Agric.*) fumier, *m.*
dung cart ['dʌŋka:t], *n.* tombereau à fumier, *m.*
dungeon ['dʌndʒən], *n.* cachot, *m.*
dunghill ['dʌŋhil], *n.* fumier, *m.*
duodenal [dju:o'di:nl], *a.* (*Anat.*) duodénal: *duodenal ulcer*, ulcère au duodénum, *m.*
dupe [dju:p], *n.* dupe, *f.*—*v.t.* duper, tromper.
duplicate ['dju:plikit], *a.* double.—*n.* double, duplicata, *m.*—['dju:plikeit], *v.t.* doubler, copier.
duplicity [dju:'plisiti], *n.* duplicité, mauvaise foi, *f.*
durability [djuərə'biliti], **durableness** ['djuərəblnis], *n.* solidité, durabilité, *f.*
durable ['djuərəbl], *a.* durable.
duration [dju'reiʃən], *n.* durée, *f.*
during ['djuəriŋ], *prep.* pendant, durant.
dusk [dʌsk], *n.* crépuscule, *m.*; obscurité, *f.*
duskiness ['dʌskinis], *n.* obscurité, teinte sombre, *f.*
dusky ['dʌski], *a.* foncé, sombre; noiraud, noirâtre.
dust [dʌst], *n.* poussière; poudre, *f.*; (*fig.*)

cendres (des morts), *f.pl.*; *sawdust*, sciure, *f.*—*v.t.* épousseter.
dust-bin ['dʌstbin], *n.* boîte à ordures, poubelle, *f.*
dust-cart ['dʌstka:t], *n.* tombereau, *m.*
duster ['dʌstə], *n.* torchon, chiffon, *m.*
dustman ['dʌstmən], *n.* (*pl.* **-men** [men]) boueur, *m.*
dusty ['dʌsti], *a.* poussiéreux, couvert de poussière; poudreux.
Dutch [dʌtʃ], *a.* hollandais, de Hollande.—*n.* hollandais (*langue*), *m.*; *the Dutch*, les Hollandais, *m.pl.*
Dutchman ['dʌtʃmən], *n.* (*pl.* **-men** [men]) Hollandais, *m.*
Dutchwoman ['dʌtʃwumən], *n.* (*pl.* **-women** [wimin]) Hollandaise, *f.*
duteous ['dju:tiəs], **dutiful** ['dju:tiful], *a.* obéissant, soumis.
dutifully ['dju:tifuli], *adv.* avec soumission, respectueusement.
duty ['dju:ti], *n.* (*pl.* **duties** ['dju:tiz]) devoir; (*Customs*) droit; (*Mil. etc.*) service, *m.*; *on duty*, de service, de garde, en faction.
dwarf [dwɔ:f], *a.* and *n.* nain, *m.*, naine, *f.*—*v.t.* rapetisser; (*Hort.*) rabougrir.
dwell [dwel], *v.i.* *irr.* demeurer, habiter; rester; *to dwell on*, insister sur.
dweller ['dwelə], *n.* habitant, *m.*, habitante, *f.*
dwelling ['dweliŋ], *n.* habitation, demeure, *f.*
dwindle [dwindl], *v.i.* diminuer, s'amoindrir; dépérir.
dye [dai], *v.t.* teindre.—*v.i.* teindre, se teindre.—*n.* teinture, teinte; couleur, nuance, *f.*; (*fig.*) caractère, *m.*
dyeing ['daiiŋ], *n.* teinture, *f.*
dyer ['daiə], *n.* teinturier, *m.*, teinturière, *f.*
dye-works ['daiwə:ks], *n.pl.* teinturerie, *f.*
dying ['daiiŋ], *a.* mourant, moribond; suprême, dernier.
dyke [DIKE].
dynamic [dai'næmik], **dynamical** [dai'næmikəl], *a.* dynamique.
dynamics [dai'næmiks], *n.pl.* dynamique, *f.*
dynamite ['dainəmait], *n.* dynamite, *f.*—*v.t.* dynamiter.
dynamo ['dainəmou], *n.* dynamo, *f.*
dynasty ['dinəsti], *n.* dynastie, *f.*
dysentery ['disəntri], *n.* dysenterie, *f.*
dyspepsia [dis'pepsiə], *n.* dyspepsie, *f.*
dyspeptic [dis'peptik], *a.* dyspepsique, dyspeptique.

E

E, e [i:], cinquième lettre de l'alphabet; (*Mus.*) mi, *m.*
e-, see also **ae-.**
each [i:tʃ], *a.* chaque.—*pron.* chacun, *m.*, chacune, *f.*: *each other*, l'un l'autre, les uns les autres.
eager ['i:gə], *a.* vif, ardent (*à*); impatient (*de*); désireux; empressé (*à* ou *de*).
eagerly ['i:gəli], *adv.* ardemment; impatiemment.

eagerness ['i:gənis], *n.* ardeur, *f.*; empressement, *m.*

eagle [i:gl], *n.* aigle, *m.*, *f.*

eaglet ['i:glit], *n.* aiglon, *m.*

ear [iə], *n.* oreille, *f.*; épi (*de blé*), *m.*—*v.i.* monter en épi.

ear-ache ['iəreik], *n.* mal d'oreille, *m.*

ear-drum ['iədrʌm], *n.* tympan, tambour de l'oreille, *m.*

earl [ə:l], *n.* comte, *m.*

earldom ['ə:ldəm], *n.* comté, *m.*

earliness ['ə:linis], *n.* heure peu avancée; précocité (*de fruits*), *f.*

early ['ə:li], *a.* matinal; matineux (*personne*); ancien; précoce, hâtif (*fruit etc.*).—*adv.* de bonne heure, de bon matin; de grand matin; tôt.

ear-mark ['iəmɑ:k], *v.t.* (*fig.*) réserver, mettre de côté.

earn [ə:n], *v.t.* gagner, acquérir; (*fig.*) mériter.

earnest (1) ['ə:nist], *a.* sérieux, empressé, sincère.

earnest (2) ['ə:nist], *n.* gage, *m.*, garantie, *f.*, arrhes, *f.pl.*

earnestly ['ə:nistli], *adv.* sérieusement, avec empressement.

earnestness ['ə:nistnis], *n.* ardeur, *f.*, empressement; sérieux, *m.*

earnings ['ə:ninz], *n.pl.* gain, *m.*; gages, *m.pl.*

ear-phones ['iəfəunz], *n.pl.* casque, *m.*

ear-ring ['iəriŋ], *n.* boucle d'oreille, *f.*

earth [ə:θ], *n.* terre, *f.*; terrier (*de renard etc.*), *m.*—*v.t.* enterrer, enfouir, couvrir de terre; (*Elec.*) joindre à la terre.

earthen ['ə:θən], *a.* de terre.

earthenware ['ə:θənweə], *n.* poterie, vaisselle de terre, faïence, *f.*

earthly ['ə:θli], *a.* terrestre.

earthquake ['ə:θkweik], *n.* tremblement de terre, *m.*

earthy ['ə:θi], *a.* de terre, terreux.

earwig ['iəwig], *n.* perce-oreille, *m.*

ease [i:z], *n.* aisance, aise; facilité; tranquillité, *f.*, repos; (*fig.*) abandon; soulagement (*de douleur*), *m.*—*v.t.* soulager, mettre à l'aise; (*fig.*) tranquilliser, calmer.

easel [i:zl], *n.* chevalet, *m.*

easily ['i:zili], *adv.* facilement, sans peine; aisément.

east [i:st], *a.* d'est, d'orient; oriental.—*n.* est, orient; levant, *m.*

Easter ['i:stə], Pâques, *m.*

easterly ['i:stəli], *a.* d'est.—*adv.* vers l'orient, vers l'est.

eastern ['i:stən], *a.* d'est, d'orient, oriental.

eastward ['i:stwəd], *adv.* vers l'est, vers l'orient.

easy ['i:zi], *a.* facile; aisé; confortable; tranquille; naturel (*style*); à l'aise; *easy chair*, fauteuil, *m.*—*adv.* doucement.

easy-going ['i:zigouiŋ], *a.* accommodant, peu exigeant.

eat [i:t], *v.t.*, *v.i. irr.* manger; ronger (*corroder*); *to eat away*, consumer, ronger; *to eat up*, manger, achever de manger.

eatable ['i:təbl], *a.* mangeable, comestible.—*n.* comestible, *m.*; (*pl.*) vivres, *m.pl.*

eating ['i:tiŋ], *n.* action de manger, *f.*; manger, *m.*

eaves [i:vz], *n.* avance du toit, *f.*; gouttières, *f.pl.*

412

eavesdrop ['i:vzdrɔp], *v.i.* écouter aux portes.

eavesdropper ['i:vzdrɔpə], *n.* écouteur aux portes, *m.*

ebb [eb], *v.i.* baisser; décliner, refluer, se retirer.—*n.* reflux; (*fig.*) déclin, *m.*, décadence, *f.*

ebb tide ['ebtaid], *n.* jusant, *m.*

ebony ['ebəni], *a.* d'ébène.—*n.* ébène, *f.*, bois d'ébène, *m.*

ebony tree ['ebənitri:], *n.* ébénier, *m.*

ebullience [i'bʌliəns], **ebulliency** [i'bʌliənsi], *n.* ébullition, effervescence, *f.*

ebullient [i'bʌliənt], *a.* en ébullition, bouillonnant; (*fig.*) exubérant, pétulant.

ebullition [ebə'liʃən], *n.* ébullition; (*fig.*) effervescence, *f.*, transport, *m.*

eccentric [ek'sentrik], *a.* excentrique; désaxé; (*fig.*) singulier.

eccentricity [eksen'trisiti], *n.* excentricité, *f.*

ecclesiastic [ikli:zi'æstik], *a.* and *n.* ecclésiastique, *m.*

echo ['ekou], *n.* écho, *m.*—*v.t.* répercuter; (*fig.*) répéter.—*v.i.* faire écho; retentir, résonner (*de*).

eclipse [i'klips], *n.* éclipse, *f.*—*v.t.* éclipser; (*fig.*) surpasser.—*v.i.* s'éclipser.

economic [i:kə'nɔmik], **economical** [i:kə'nɔmikl], *a.* économique (*chose*); économe, ménager (*personne*).

economically [i:kə'nɔmikəli], *adv.* économiquement.

economics [i:kə'nɔmiks], *n.pl.* économie politique, *f.*

economist [i'kɔnəmist], *n.* économiste, *m.*, *f.*

economize [i'kɔnəmaiz], *v.t.* économiser.—*v.i.* user d'économie.

economy [i'kɔnəmi], *n.* économie, *f.*; système, *m.*; *planned economy*, économie planifiée.

ecstasy ['ekstəsi], *n.* extase, *f.*, transport, *m.*

ecstatic [eks'tætik], **ecstatical** [eks'tætikl], *a.* extatique, d'extase.

Ecuador [ekwə'dɔ:]. (la République de) l'Équateur, *f.*

Ecuadorean [ekwə'dɔ:riən], *a.* équatorien.—*n.* Équatorien (*personne*), *m.*

eczema ['eksimə], *n.* eczéma, *m.*

eddy ['edi], *n.* remous (*eau*); tourbillon (*vent*), *m.*—*v.i.* tourbillonner.

Eden ['i:dən]. Éden, *m.*

edge [edʒ], *n.* bord (*marge*); fil, tranchant (*de couteau etc.*), *m.*; lisière (*d'une forêt etc.*), *f.*; cordon (*d'une pièce de monnaie*); tranche (*d'un livre*), *f.*—*v.t.* affiler, aiguiser; border (*entourer*).—*v.i. to edge away*, s'éloigner graduellement.

edged [edʒd], *a.* tranchant; bordé.

edgeways ['edʒweiz], **edgewise** ['edʒwaiz], *adv.* de côté, de champ.

edging ['edʒiŋ], *n.* bordure, *f.*

edible ['edibl], *a.* comestible, bon à manger.

edict ['i:dikt], *n.* édit, *m.*

edifice ['edifis], *n.* édifice, *m.*

edify ['edifai], *v.t.* édifier.

Edinburgh ['edinbrə]. Édimbourg, *m.*

edit ['edit], *v.t.* éditer, rédiger.

edition [i'diʃən], *n.* édition, *f.*

editor ['editə], *n.* compilateur, annotateur; (*Journ.*) rédacteur en chef, directeur, *m.*

editorial [edi'tɔ:riəl], *a.* de rédacteur.—*n.* article de fond, éditorial, *m.*

Edmund ['edmənd]. Edmond, *m.*
educate ['edjukeit], *v.t.* élever; instruire.
education [edju'keiʃən], *n.* éducation, *f.*; enseignement, *m.*; instruction, *f.*
Edward ['edwəd]. Édouard, *m.*
eel [i:l], *n.* anguille, *f.*
eerie ['iəri], *a.* étrange, mystérieux.
eeriness ['iərinis], *n.* étrangeté surnaturelle, *f.*
efface [i'feis], *v.t.* effacer.
effect [i'fekt], *n.* effet, *m.*; (*pl.*) effets, biens, *m.pl.*; *in effect*, en effet; *to carry into effect*, accomplir, exécuter, mettre à effet; *to no effect*, en vain, sans résultat; *to take effect*, faire son effet, opérer; (*Law*) entrer en vigueur.—*v.t.* effectuer, exécuter, accomplir.
effective [i'fektiv], *a.* effectif; efficace.
effectively [i'fektivli], *adv.* effectivement; efficacement.
effeminacy [i'feminəsi], *n.* mollesse, nature efféminée, *f.*
effeminate [i'feminit], *a.* efféminé.
effervesce [efə'ves], *v.i.* être en effervescence; mousser (*boisson*).
effervescence [efə'vesəns], *n.* effervescence, *f.*
effervescent [efə'vesənt], **effervescing** [efə'vesiŋ], *a.* effervescent; mousseux; gazeux (*eau minérale*).
effete [i'fi:t], *a.* usé; stérile, épuisé, caduc.
efficacious [efi'keiʃəs], *a.* efficace.
efficacy ['efikəsi], *n.* efficacité, *f.*
efficiency [i'fiʃənsi], *n.* efficacité; bonne condition, *f.*; (*Mach.*) rendement, *m.*
efficient [i'fiʃənt], *a.* efficace (*remède*); capable, compétent (*personne*).
efficiently [i'fiʃəntli], *adv.* efficacement.
effigy ['efidʒi], *n.* effigie, *f.*
effloresce [eflo'res], *v.i.* s'effleurir.
efflorescence [eflo'resəns], *n.* efflorescence; (*Bot.*) floraison, *f.*
efflorescent [eflo'resənt], *a.* efflorescent; (*Bot.*) fleurissant.
effluvium [i'flu:viəm], *n.* (*pl.* **effluvia** [i'flu:viə]) exhalaison, *f.*, effluve, *m.*
effort ['efət], *n.* effort, *m.*
effortless ['efətlis], *a.* sans effort.
effrontery [i'frʌntəri], *n.* effronterie, *f.*
effulgence [i'fʌldʒəns], *n.* splendeur, *f.*, éclat, *m.*
effulgent [i'fʌldʒənt], *a.* resplendissant, éclatant.
effusion [i'fju:ʒən], *n.* effusion, *f.*, épanchement, *m.*
effusive [i'fju:siv], *a.* expansif; (*fig.*) excessif, exubérant.
egg [eg], *n.* œuf, *m.*; *boiled egg*, œuf à la coque; *fried egg*, œuf sur le plat; *hard-boiled egg*, œuf dur; *new-laid egg*, œuf frais.—*v.t.* pousser (*à*).
egg cup ['egkʌp], *n.* coquetier, *m.*
egg-shell ['egʃel], *n.* coquille d'œuf, *f.*
eglantine ['egləntain], *n.* églantier, *m.*; églantine (*fleur*), *f.*
egoism ['egouizm], *n.* égoïsme, *m.*
egoist ['egouist], *n.* égoïste, *m.*, *f.*
egotism ['egətizm], *n.* égotisme, culte du moi, *m.*
egotist ['egətist], *n.* égotiste, *m.*, *f.*
egregious [i'gri:dʒəs], *a.* insigne, énorme; fameux.

egress ['i:gres], *n.* sortie, issue, *f.*
Egypt ['i:dʒipt]. l'Égypte, *f.*
Egyptian [i'dʒipʃən], *a.* égyptien.—*n.* Egyptien (*personne*), *m.*
eider ['aidə], **eider duck** ['aidədʌk], *n.* eider, *m.*
eiderdown ['aidədaun], *n.* édredon, *m.*
eight [eit], *a.* huit.
eighteen ['eiti:n], *a.* dix-huit.
eighteenth ['eiti:nθ], *a.* dix-huitième; dix-huit (*roi etc.*).—*n.* dix-huitième (*fraction*), *m.*
eighth [eitθ], *a.* huitième; huit (*roi etc.*).—*n.* huitième (*fraction*), *m.*; (*Mus.*) octave, *f.*
eightieth ['eitiiθ], *a.* quatre-vingtième.—*n.* quatre-vingtième (*fraction*), *m.*
eighty ['eiti], *a.* quatre-vingts.
Eire ['ɛərə]. l'Irlande, *f.*
either ['aidə, 'i:ðə], *pron.* l'un ou l'autre, *m.*, l'une ou l'autre, *f.*; l'un d'eux, *m.*, l'une d'elles, *f.*; (*used negatively*) ni l'un ni l'autre, *m.*, ni l'une ni l'autre, *f.*—*conj.* ou, soit.—*adv.* non plus.
ejaculate [i'dʒækjuleit], *v.t.* pousser (*un cri*).—*v.i.* s'écrier; éjaculer.
ejaculation [idʒækju'leiʃən], *n.* cri, *m.* exclamation; éjaculation, *f.*
eject [i'dʒekt], *v.t.* rejeter; émettre (*flammes*); chasser, expulser.
ejection [i'dʒekʃən], **ejectment** [i'dʒektmənt], *n.* expulsion, éjection; (*Law*) éviction, *f.*
eke [i:k], *v.t. to eke out*, allonger; suppléer à, augmenter; ménager; *to eke out a living*, se faire un maigre pitance.
elaborate [i'læbərit], *a.* élaboré, soigné; compliqué.—[i'læbəreit], *v.t.* élaborer.
elaboration [ilæbə'reiʃən], *n.* élaboration, *f.*
elapse [i'læps], *v.i.* s'écouler.
elastic [i'læstik], *a.* and *n.* élastique, *m.*
elasticity [elæs'tisiti], *n.* élasticité, *f.*
elate [i'leit], *v.t.* élever, exalter, transporter.
elation [i'leiʃən], *n.* transport de joie, *m.*, exaltation, ivresse, *f.*
elbow ['elbou], *n.* coude, *m.*—*v.t.* coudoyer, pousser du coude.
elder (1) ['eldə], *n.* sureau (*arbre*), *m.*
elder (2) ['eldə], *a.* aîné, plus âgé; plus ancien.—*n.* aîné; ancien, *m.*
elderly ['eldəli], *a.* d'un certain âge.
eldest ['eldist], *a.* le plus âgé, l'aîné.
Eleanor ['elinə]. Éléonore, *f.*
elect [i'lekt], *a.* élu, choisi, nommé.—*n.* élu, *m.*—*v.t.* élire, nommer, choisir; (*fig.*) se décider à.
election [i'lekʃən], *n.* élection, *f.*
electioneer [ilekʃə'niə], *v.i.* solliciter des votes, travailler les électeurs.
electioneering [ilekʃə'niəriŋ], *n.* manœuvres électorales, *f.pl.*
elective [i'lektiv], *a.* électif; électoral.
elector [i'lektə], *n.* électeur, votant, *m.*
electric [i'lektrik], **electrical** [i'lektrikəl], *a.* électrique; *electric shock*, secousse électrique, *f.*
electrician [elek'triʃən, ilek'triʃən], *n.* électricien, *m.*
electricity [elek'trisiti, ilek'trisiti], *n.* électricité, *f.*
electrify [i'lektrifai], *v.t.* électriser; électrifier.
electrocute [i'lektrokju:t], *v.t.* électrocuter.
electron [i'lektrɔn] *n.* électron *m.*

413

electronic [elek'trɔnik, ilek'trɔnik], *a.* électronique.

electronics [elek'trɔniks, ilek'trɔniks], *n.* électronique, *f.*

electro-plate [i'lektroupleit], *n.* argenture électrique, *f.*—*v.t.* plaquer, argenter.

elegance ['eligəns], *n.* élégance, *f.*

elegant ['eligənt], *a.* élégant, chic.—*n.* élégant, beau, *m.*

elegantly ['eligəntli], *adv.* élégamment.

elegiac [eli'dʒaiək], *a.* élégiaque.—*n.* vers élégiaque, *m.*

elegist ['elidʒist], *n.* poète élégiaque, *m.*

elegy ['elidʒi], *n.* élégie, *f.*

element ['elimənt], *n.* élément, *m.*; (*pl.*) rudiments, *m.pl.*

elemental [eli'mentl], **elementary** [eli'mentri], *a.* élémentaire.

elephant ['elifənt], *n.* éléphant, *m.*

elephantine [eli'fæntain], *a.* éléphantin.

elevate ['eliveit], *v.t.* élever; hausser, exalter, exciter.

elevation [eli'veiʃən], *n.* élévation; hauteur, altitude, *f.*

elevator ['eli'veitə], *n.* (*Anat. etc.*) élévateur; (*Am.*) [LIFT].

eleven [i'levn], *a.* onze; **the eleven,** les apôtres, *m.pl.*; (*Spt.*) le onze, *m.*

eleventh [i'levnθ], *a.* onzième; onze (*roi etc.*). —*n.* onzième (*fraction*), *m.*

elf [elf], *n.* (*pl.* **elves** [elvz]) esprit follet, lutin, elfe, *m.*

elfin ['elfin], *a.* des lutins, des elfes.—*n.* gamin, bambin, *m.*

elicit [i'lisit], *v.t.* faire sortir, tirer (*de*); déduire, découvrir, faire avouer (*à*).

elide [i'laid], *v.t.* (*Gram.*) élider.—*v.i.* s'élider.

eligible ['elidʒibl], *a.* éligible; convenable (*pour*); acceptable.

eliminate [i'limineit], *v.t.* éliminer, supprimer.

eliminating [i'limineitiŋ], *a.* éliminateur, éliminatoire.

elimination [ilimi'neiʃən], *n.* élimination, *f.*

elision [i'liʒən], *n.* élision, *f.*

elixir [i'liksə], *n.* élixir, *m.*

Elizabeth [i'lizəbəθ]. Élisabeth, *f.*

elk [elk], *n.* (*Zool.*) élan, *m.*

ell [el], *n.* aune, *f.*

Ellen ['elin]. Hélène, *f.*

ellipse [i'lips], *n.* ellipse, *f.*

elliptic [i'liptik], **elliptical** [i'liptikəl], *a.* elliptique.

elm [elm], *n.* orme, *m.*

elocution [elo'kju:ʃən], *n.* élocution, diction, *f.*

elocutionist [elo'kju:ʃənist], *n.* déclamateur, *m.*

elongate ['i:lɔŋgeit], *v.t.* allonger, prolonger.

elongation [i:lɔŋ'geiʃən], *n.* allongement, prolongement, *m.*; (*Surg.*) élongation, *f.*

elope [i'loup], *v.i.* s'enfuir (*avec un amant*).

elopement [i'loupmənt], *n.* fuite, *f.,* enlèvement, *m.*

eloquence ['eləkwəns], *n.* éloquence, *f.*

eloquent ['eləkwənt], *a.* éloquent.

eloquently ['eləkwəntli], *adv.* éloquemment.

else [els], *adv.* autrement, ou bien, ailleurs.— *a.* autre; **anywhere else,** n'importe où ailleurs; **everything else,** tout le reste; **nobody else,** personne d'autre; **nothing**

else, rien d'autre; **someone (somebody) else,** quelqu'un d'autre.

elsewhere ['elswεə], *adv.* ailleurs, autre part.

Elsie ['elsi]. Élise, *f.*

elucidate [i'lju:sideit], *v.t.* expliquer, éclaircir, élucider.

elucidation [ilju:si'deiʃən], *n.* éclaircissement, *m.,* élucidation, explication, *f.*

elude [i'lju:d], *v.t.* éluder, éviter, échapper à.

elusion [i'lju:ʒən], *n.* subterfuge, *m.,* réponse évasive, *f.*

elusive [i'lju:siv], *a.* artificieux (*réponse*); fuyant, insaisissable (*personne*).

elves [ELF].

emaciate [i'meiʃieit], *v.t.* amaigrir.—*v.i.* maigrir, s'amaigrir.

emaciated [i'meiʃieitid], *a.* amaigri, maigre, décharné.

emaciation [imeiʃi'eiʃən], *n.* amaigrissement, *m.,* maigreur, *f.*

emanate ['eməneit], *v.i.* émaner.

emancipate [i'mænsipeit], *v.t.* affranchir, émanciper (*de*).

emancipation [imænsi'peiʃən], *n.* affranchissement, *m.,* émancipation, *f.*

emasculate [i'mæskjuleit], *v.t.* châtrer; (*fig.*) affaiblir, efféminer.

embalm [im'bɑ:m], *v.t.* embaumer.

embalmer [im'bɑ:mə], *n.* embaumeur, *m.*

embalming [im'bɑ:miŋ], *n.* embaumement, *m.*

embank [im'bæŋk], *v.t.* endiguer, remblayer; encaisser (*canal etc.*).

embankment [im'bæŋkmənt], *n.* levée, *f.;* terrassement, talus; (*Rail.*) remblai; quai (*rivière, canal*), *m.*

embarcation [EMBARKATION].

embargo [im'bɑ:gou], *n.* embargo, *m.*—*v.t.* mettre l'embargo sur; défendre, interdire.

embark [im'bɑ:k], *v.t.* embarquer.—*v.i.* s'embarquer (*sur*); (*fig.*) s'engager (*dans*).

embarkation or **embarcation** [embɑ:'keiʃən], *n.* embarquement, *m.*

embarrass [im'bærəs], *v.t.* embarrasser, gêner.

embarrassment [im'bærəsmənt], *n.* embarras, *m.;* (*fig.*) perplexité; gêne (*manque d'argent*), *f.*

embassy ['embəsi], *n.* ambassade, *f.*

embellish [im'beliʃ], *v.t.* embellir, orner (*avec*).

embellishment [im'beliʃmənt], *n.* embellissement, ornement, *m.*

ember ['embə], *n.* braise, cendre ardente, *f.*

embezzle [im'bezl], *v.t.* détourner; s'approprier frauduleusement (*des fonds*).

embezzlement [im'bezlmənt], *n.* détournement, *m.*

embezzler [im'bezlə], *n.* détourneur (*de fonds*), *m.*

embitter [im'bitə], *v.t.* rendre amer; (*fig.*) empoisonner; aigrir.

emblazon [im'bleizn], *v.t.* blasonner (*de*); (*fig.*) publier, proclamer.

emblem ['embləm], *n.* emblème, *m.;* (*Her.*) devise, *f.*

embodiment [im'bɔdimənt], *n.* incarnation; personnification; (*Mil.*) incorporation, *f.*

embody [im'bɔdi], *v.t.* incarner; (*Mil. etc.*) incorporer (*dans*); (*fig.*) personnifier.

embolden [im'bouldn], *v.t.* enhardir.

emboss [im'bɔs], *v.t.* bosseler, relever en bosse; gaufrer (*papier*).

embossing [im'bɔsiŋ], *n.* bosselage; gaufrage, *m.*

embrace [im'breis], *n.* embrassement, *m.*,
étreinte, *f.*—*v.t.* embrasser, étreindre; (*fig.*)
accepter; comprendre.

embrocation [embrə'keiʃən], *n.* émbroca-
tion, *f.*

embroider [im'brɔidə], *v.t.* broder.

embroidery [im'brɔidəri], *n.* broderie, *f.*

embroil [im'brɔil], *v.t.* brouiller, embrouiller.

embryo ['embriou], *n.* embryon, germe, *m.*

emend [i'mend], *v.t.* corriger; (*Law*) émender.

emendation [i:men'deiʃən], *n.* correction,
émendation, *f.*

emerald ['emərəld], *n.* émeraude, *f.*

emerge [i'mə:dʒ], *v.i.* surgir; sortir (*de*);
ressortir.

emergency [i'mə:dʒənsi], *n.* circonstance
critique; crise, *f.*, cas imprévu, *m.*; *in case
of emergency*, en cas d'urgence; *emergency exit*, sortie de secours, *f.*

emery ['eməri], *n.* émeri, *m.*; *emery cloth*,
toile d'émeri, *f.*

emetic [i'metik], *n.* émétique, *m.*

emigrant ['emigrənt], *n.* émigrant; (*Fr. Hist.*)
émigré, *m.*

emigrate ['emigreit], *v.i.* émigrer.

emigration [emi'greiʃən], *n.* émigration, *f.*

Emily ['emili], Émilie, *f.*

eminence ['eminəns], *n.* éminence, colline;
(*fig.*) grandeur, distinction, *f.*

eminent ['eminənt], *a.* éminent; distingué,
illustre.

eminently ['eminəntli], *adv.* éminemment,
par excellence.

emissary ['emisəri], *n.* émissaire, messager,
m.

emission [i'miʃən], *n.* émission, *f.*

emit [i'mit], *v.t.* jeter; exhaler, dégager;
(*Fin.*) émettre.

emolument [i'mɔljumənt], *n.* (*usu. pl.*)
émoluments, *m.pl.*, rémunération, *f.*; (*fig.*)
profit, *m.*

emotion [i'mouʃən], *n.* émotion, *f.*

emotional [i'mouʃənəl], *a.* porté à l'émotion,
émotif.

emperor ['empərə], *n.* empereur. *m.*

emphasis ['emfəsis], *n.* (*pl.* **emphases**
['emfəsi:z]) force, énergie, emphase, *f.*;
accent, *m.*

emphasize ['emfəsaiz], *v.t.* appuyer sur;
accentuer, souligner.

emphatic [im'fætik], *a.* fort, énergique;
expressif; accentué, emphatique; (*fig.*)
positif.

emphatically [im'fætikəli], *adv.* avec force,
énergiquement; positivement.

empire ['empaiə], *n.* empire, *m.*

empiric [em'pirik], *n.* empirique; charlatan,
m.—*a.* (*also* **empirical** [em'pirikəl]) empirique, guidé par l'expérience.

employ [im'plɔi], *v.t.* employer; se servir de.
—*n.* emploi, *m.*; occupation, *f.*

employee [im'plɔii:], *n.* employé, *m.*

employer [im'plɔiə], *n.* patron; employeur,
m.

employment [im'plɔimənt], *n.* emploi, *m.*,
occupation, *f.*

emporium [em'pɔ:riəm], *n.* entrepôt; (*fam.*)
grand magasin, *m.*

empower [em'pauə], *v.t.* autoriser (*à*), mettre
à même (*de*).

empress ['empris], *n.* impératrice, *f.*

emptiness ['emptinis], *n.* vide, *m.*; (*fig.*)
vanité, *f.*, néant, *m.*

empty ['empti], *a.* vide, à vide; désert (*rues
etc.*); (*fig.*) vain, stérile.—*v.t.* vider, décharger.—*v.i.* se vider.

emu ['i:mju:], *n.* (*Orn.*) émeu, *m.*

emulate ['emjuleit], *v.t.* rivaliser avec;
imiter.

emulation [emju'leiʃən], *n.* émulation,
rivalité, *f.*

emulsion [i'mʌlʃən], *n.* émulsion, *f.*

enable [i'neibl], *v.t.* mettre à même (*de*);
mettre en état (*de*); permettre (*de*).

enact [i'nækt], *v.t.* ordonner, arrêter; rendre
(*loi*); jouer, faire (*un rôle*).

enactment [i'næktmənt], *n.* loi, ordonnance,
f., décret, *m.*

enamel [i'næml], *n.* émail, *m.*—*v.t.* émailler
(*de*).—*v.i.* peindre en émail.

enamelling [i'næməliŋ], *n.* émaillure, *f.*;
émaillage, *m.*

enamor [i'næmə], *v.i.* (*used now only in
p.p.*) *to be enamored of*, être épris de.

encamp [in'kæmp], *v.t.*, *v.i.* camper.

encase [in'keis], *v.t.* encaisser, enfermer.

enchain [in'tʃein], *v.t.* enchaîner.

enchant [in'tʃɑ:nt], *v.t.* enchanter; (*fig.*)
charmer, ravir (*de*).

enchanter [in'tʃɑ:ntə], *n.* enchanteur, *m.*

enchanting [in'tʃɑ:ntiŋ], *a.* enchanteur,
ravissant, charmant.

enchantment [in'tʃɑ:ntmənt], *n.* enchantement, charme, *m.*, fascination, *f.*

enchantress [in'tʃɑ:ntris], *n.* enchanteresse, *f.*

encircle [in'sə:kl], *v.t.* ceindre, entourer (*de*),
encercler.

enclose [in'klouz], *v.t.* enclore; entourer,
environner; renfermer; envoyer sous le
même pli (*lettre etc.*).

enclosed [in'klouzd], *a.* entouré, environné;
inclus, ci-inclus, sous ce pli (*paquet, lettre
etc.*).

enclosure [in'klou3ə], *n.* clôture; enceinte
(*espace clos*), *f.*; contenu (*objet renfermé*), *m.*

encomium [en'koumjəm], *n.* éloge, *m.*,
louange, *f.*

encompass [in'kʌmpəs], *v.t.* entourer, environner; renfermer.

encore [ɔŋ'kɔ:], *n.* and *int.* bis.—*v.t.* bisser.

encounter [in'kauntə], *n.* rencontre, *f.*;
combat, *m.*, lutte, *f.*—*v.t.* rencontrer,
aborder; (*fig.*) éprouver, essuyer.

encourage [in'kʌridʒ], *v.t.* encourager.

encouragement [in'kʌridʒmənt], *n.* encouragement, *m.*

encroach [in'kroutʃ], *v.i.* empiéter (*sur*);
abuser (*de*).

encroachment [in'kroutʃmənt], *n.* empiétement, *m.*, usurpation, *f.*

encumber [in'kʌmbə], *v.t.* encombrer,
accabler, embarrasser (*de*); grever (*un
héritage*).

encumbrance [in'kʌmbrəns], *n.* encombrement, embarras, *m.*; (*Law*) hypothèque, *f.*

encyclopaedia [insaiklə'pi:diə], *n.* encyclopédie, *f.*

encyclopaedic [insaiklə'pi:dik], *a.* encyclo-
pédique.

end [end], *n.* fin; extrémité, *f.*, bout; but, objet; (*fig.*) dessein, *m.*, issue, *f.*; *at an end*, fini, terminé; *big end*, (*Motor.*) tête de bielle, *f.*; *from end to end*, d'un bout à l'autre; *in the end*, à la fin; *three days on end*, trois jours de suite; *to be at a loose end*, être désœuvré, se trouver sans avoir rien à faire; *to draw to an end*, tirer *ou* toucher à sa fin; *to make an end of*, en finir avec; *to make both ends meet*, joindre les deux bouts.—*v.t.* finir, terminer, achever.—*v.i.* finir, se terminer (*en*); cesser (*de*); aboutir (*à*).

endanger [in'deindʒə], *v.t.* mettre en danger, compromettre, risquer.

endear [in'diə], *v.t.* rendre cher (*à*).

endearing [in'diəriŋ], *a.* tendre, affectueux.

endearment [in'diəmənt], *n.* charme, *m.*; (*pl.*) caresses, *f.pl.*

endeavor [in'devə], *n.* effort, *m.*, tentative, *f.* —*v.i.* tâcher, essayer, tenter (*de*), chercher (*à*).

ending [endiŋ], *n.* fin, conclusion; (*Gram.*) terminaison, *f.*

endive [endiv], *n.* chicorée; escarole, *f.*

endless [endlis], *a.* sans fin; éternel, perpétuel, interminable.

endlessly [endlisli], *adv.* à l'infini, sans cesse.

endorse [in'dɔ:s], *v.t.* endosser; viser (*passeport*); (*fig.*) sanctionner, approuver.

endorsement [in'dɔ:smənt], *n.* suscription, *f.*; (*Comm.*) endossement (*signature au dos*); visa (*de passeport*), *m.*; (*fig.*) sanction, *f.*

endow [in'dau], *v.t.* doter (*de*); (*fig.*) douer (*de*).

endowment [in'daumənt], *n.* dotation, *f.*

endurable [in'djuərəbl], *a.* supportable, endurable.

endurance [in'djuərəns], *n.* endurance; souffrance, patience, *f.*

endure [in'djuə], *v.t.* supporter, souffrir, endurer.—*v.i.* durer; endurer, souffrir.

enduring [in'djuəriŋ], *a.* endurant, qui endure, patient; durable, qui dure (*permanent*).

endways [endweiz], **endwise** [endwaiz], *adv.* debout, de champ; bout à bout (*horizontalement*).

enema [enimə, i'ni:mə], *n.* lavement, *m.*

enemy [enəmi], *n.* ennemi, *m.*

energetic [enə'dʒetik], *a.* énergique.

energy [enədʒi], *n.* énergie, *f.*

enervate [enəveit], *v.t.* affaiblir, énerver.

enfeeble [in'fi:bl], *v.t.* affaiblir.

enfold [in'fould], *v.t.* envelopper.

enforce [in'fɔ:s], *v.t.* donner de la force à; faire respecter; faire exécuter; forcer.

enforcement [in'fɔ:smənt], *n.* mise en vigueur, exécution, *f.*

enfranchise [in'fræntʃaiz], *v.t.* affranchir (*un esclave*); donner le droit de vote à.

enfranchisement [in'fræntfizmənt], *n.* affranchissement, *m.*; admission au suffrage, *f.*

engage [in'geidʒ], *v.t.* engager; retenir, prendre (*réserver*); louer (*prendre à louage*); arrêter (*un marché*); occuper (*attention etc.*); (*fig.*) en venir aux mains avec.—*v.i.* s'engager (*à*); livrer combat.

engaged [in'geidʒd], *a.* fiancé (*futur époux*);

occupé (*pris par le travail*); pas libre (*téléphone, cabinets*); aux prises (*combat*).

engagement [in'geidʒmənt], *n.* engagement, *m.*; occupation, *f.*; fiançailles, *f.pl.*; combat, *m.*

engaging [in'geidʒiŋ], *a.* engageant, attrayant.

engender [in'dʒendə], *v.t.* engendrer, faire naître, causer.

engine [endʒin], *n.* machine, *f.*, moteur, *m.*; (*Rail.*) locomotive, *f.*; *fire engine*, pompe à incendie, *f.*; *steam engine*, machine à vapeur.

engine-driver [endʒindraivə], *n.* (*Rail.*) mécanicien, *m.*

engineer [endʒi'niə], *n.* ingénieur; (*Manuf.*) constructeur-mécanicien; (*Mil.*) soldat du génie; (*pl.*) le génie, *m.*

engineering [endʒi'niəriŋ], *n.* art de l'ingénieur, *m.*; *civil engineering*, génie civil, *m.*; *electrical engineering*, technique électrique, *f.*

England [ingglənd]. l'Angleterre, *f.*

English [ingglif], *a.* anglais; de l'Angleterre; *the English Channel*, la Manche, *f.*—*n.* anglais (*langue*), *m.*; *the English*, les Anglais, *m.pl.*

Englishman [inglifmən], *n.* (*pl.* -men [men]) Anglais, *m.*

Englishwoman [inglifwumən], *n.* (*pl.* -women [wimin]) Anglaise, *f.*

engrave [in'greiv], *v.t.* graver.

engraver [in'greivə], *n.* graveur, *m.*

engraving [in'greiviŋ], *n.* gravure; *copperplate engraving*, taille-douce, *f.*

engross [in'grous], *v.t.* grossoyer (*copier*); accaparer (*monopoliser*); absorber, occuper (*l'esprit*).

engulf [in'gʌlf], *v.t.* engouffrer; (*fig.*) engloutir.

enhance [in'hɑ:ns], *v.t.* enchérir, renchérir; (*fig.*) rehausser.

enhancement [in'hɑ:nsmənt], *n.* hausse, *f.*; (*fig.*) rehaussement, *m.*

enigma [i'nigmə], *n.* énigme, *f.*

enigmatic [enig'mætik], **enigmatical** [enig'mætikəl], *a.* énigmatique, obscur.

enjoin [in'dʒɔin], *v.t.* enjoindre; prescrire (*à*).

enjoy [in'dʒɔi], *v.t.* jouir de, posséder; goûter; *to enjoy oneself*, s'amuser.

enjoyable [in'dʒɔiəbl], *a.* agréable.

enjoyment [in'dʒɔimənt], *n.* jouissance (*de*) *f.*; plaisir, *m.*

enkindle [in'kindl], *v.t.* enflammer; (*fig.*) exciter.

enlace [in'leis], *v.t.* enlacer.

enlarge [in'lɑ:dʒ], *v.t.* agrandir, étendre, dilater.—*v.i.* grandir, s'agrandir.

enlargement [in'lɑ:dʒmənt], *n.* agrandissement (*also Phot.*), *m.*; augmentation, *f.*

enlighten [in'laitn], *v.t.* éclairer; (*fig.*) éclaircir.

enlightenment [in'laitnmənt], *n.* éclaircissement, *m.*; lumières, *f.pl.*

enlist [in'list], *v.t.* enrôler, engager.—*v.i.* s'engager.

enlistment [in'listmənt], *n.* engagement, enrôlement, *m.*

enliven [in'laivn], *v.t.* égayer, animer.

enmity [enmiti], *n.* inimitié; animosité, haine, hostilité, *f.*

ennoble [i'noubl], *v.t.* anoblir; (*fig.*) ennoblir.

ennoblement [i'noublmənt], *n.* anoblissement; (*fig.*) ennoblissement, *m.*

enormity [i'nɔ:miti], **enormousness** [i'nɔ:məsnis], *n.* énormité, *f.*

enormous [i'nɔ:məs], *a.* énorme; (*fig.*) atroce, monstrueux.

enormously [i'nɔ:məsli], *adv.* énormément.

enough [i'nʌf], *a.* and *adv.* assez; *large enough,* assez grand; *more than enough,* plus qu'il n'en faut.

enquire [INQUIRE].

enrage [in'reidʒ], *v.t.* faire enrager; exaspérer.

enrapture [in'ræptʃə], *v.t.* transporter, ravir.

enrich [in'ritʃ], *v.t.* enrichir.

enrichment [in'ritʃmənt], *n.* enrichissement, *m.*

enroll [in'roul], *v.t.* enrôler, enregistrer, inscrire.—*v.i.* s'enrôler, se faire inscrire.

enrollment [in'roulmənt], *n.* enrôlement, *m.*, inscription, *f.*

ensconce [in'skɔns], *v.t.* cacher; *to ensconce oneself,* se cacher (*dans*), se blottir.

enshrine [in'ʃrain], *v.t.* enchâsser (*dans*).

enshroud [in'ʃraud], *v.t.* mettre dans un linceul; (*fig.*) couvrir.

ensign ['ensain, (*R. Navy*) 'ensin], *n.* enseigne, *f.*, drapeau; (*Mil.*) porte-drapeau (*personne*), *m.*

enslave [in'sleiv], *v.t.* asservir; (*fig.*) captiver.

ensnare [in'snɛə], *v.t.* prendre au piège; (*fig.*) attraper séduire.

ensue [in'sju:], *v.i.* s'ensuivre.

ensuing [in'sju:iŋ], *a.* suivant; prochain.

ensure [in'ʃuə], *v.t.* assurer; garantir.

entail [en'teil], *v.t.* substituer (*à*); (*fig.*) entraîner; impliquer.

entangle [in'tæŋgl], *v.t.* emmêler, enchevêtrer; empêtrer (*les pieds*); (*fig.*) embrouiller.

entanglement [in'tæŋglmənt], *n.* embrouillement, embarras, *m.*

enter ['entə], *v.t.* entrer dans, pénétrer; inscrire (*nom etc.*); enregistrer (*paquet*).—*v.i.* entrer; s'engager (*dans*).

enteritis [entə'raitis], *n.* entérite, *f.*

enterprise ['entəpraiz], *n.* entreprise, hardiesse, *f.*; esprit d'entreprise, *m.*

entertain [entə'tein], *v.t.* recevoir (*des invités*); divertir, amuser (*distraire*); concevoir (*idée etc.*); accepter (*proposition*).—*v.i.* recevoir (*invités*).

entertainer [entə'teinə], *n.* (*Theat. etc.*) diseur, *m.*, diseuse, *f.*, comique, *m.*, *f.*; hôte, *m.*, hôtesse, *f.*

entertainment [entə'teinmənt], *n.* hospitalité, *f.*; accueil (*reception*); festin, *m.*, fête, *f.*; divertissement, spectacle (*amusement*), *m.*

enthrall [in'θrɔ:l], *v.t.* asservir, assujettir; (*fig.*) ravir.

enthuse [in'θju:z], *v.i.* s'enthousiasmer de *ou* pour.

enthusiasm [in'θju:ziæzm], *n.* enthousiasme, *m.*

enthusiast [in'θju:ziæst], *n.* enthousiaste, *m.*, *f.*

enthusiastic [inθju:zi'æstik], *a.* enthousiaste.

entice [in'tais], *v.t.* attirer; entraîner (*dans*); séduire (*à*).

enticement [in'taismənt], *n.* appât, charme, *m.*; tentation, *f.*

enticer [in'taisə], *n.* tentateur, séducteur, *m.*

enticing [in'taisiŋ], *a.* séduisant, attrayant, tentant.

entire [in'taiə], *a.* entier, complet.

entirely [in'taiəli], *adv.* entièrement, complètement, tout entier.

entirety [in'taiəti], *n.* totalité; intégrité, *f.*

entitle [in'taitl], *v.t.* intituler, appeler; donner droit à.

entity ['entiti], *n.* entité, *f.*, être de raison, *m.*

entomb [in'tu:m], *v.t.* ensevelir.

entrails ['entreilz], *n.pl.* entrailles, *f.pl.*

entrance (1) ['entrəns], *n.* entrée, *f.*; commencement, début (*de carrière*), *m.*; (*fig.*) initiation, *f.*

entrance (2) [in'trɑ:ns], *v.t.* extasier, ravir.

entrancing [in'trɑ:nsiŋ], *a.* prenant; ravissant.

entrant ['entrənt], *n.* inscrit (*de concours*), *m.*; inscrite, *f.*; débutant (*dans une profession nouvelle*), *m.*, débutante, *f.*

entrap [in'træp], *v.t.* prendre au piège, attraper (*dans*).

entreat [in'tri:t], *v.t.* supplier, prier instamment (*de*).

entreaty [in'tri:ti], *n.* prière; supplication, (*pl.*) sollicitation, *f.*, instances, *f.pl.*

entrust [in'trʌst], *v.t.* charger (*de*).

entry ['entri], *n.* entrée; inscription (*enregistrement*); (*Book-keeping*) écriture, *f.*, article, *m.*; (*Customs*) déclaration d'entrée, *f.*; *no entry,* sens interdit, passage interdit.

entwine [in'twain], *v.t.* enlacer, entortiller.—*v.i.* s'enlacer, s'entortiller.

enumerate [i'nju:məreit], *v.t.* énumérer, dénombrer.

enunciate [i'nʌnsieit], *v.t.* énoncer; prononcer.—*v.i.* articuler.

envelop [in'veləp], *v.t.* envelopper (*de* ou *dans*).

envelope ['enviloup, 'ɔnviloup], *n.* enveloppe, *f.*

envenom [in'venəm], *v.t.* envenimer; exaspérer (*aigrir*).

envious ['enviəs], *a.* envieux (*de*).

environ [in'vaiərən], *v.t.* environner (*de*).

environment [in'vaiərənmənt], *n.* milieu, entourage, environnement, *m.*

environs [in'vaiərənz], *n.pl.* environs, *m.pl.*

envisage [in'vizidʒ], *v.t.* envisager.

envoy ['envɔi], *n.* envoyé, *m.*

envy ['envi], *n.* envie, *f.*—*v.t.* envier, porter envie à.

epaulet(te) ['epɔ:let], *n.* épaulette, *f.*

ephemeral [i'femərəl], *a.* éphémère.

epic ['epik], *a.* épique; (*fig.*) légendaire.—*n.* épopée, *f.*, poème épique, *m.*

epicure ['epikjuə], *n.* gourmet, *m.*, gastronome, *m.*, *f.*

epidemic [epi'demik], *a.* épidémique.—*n.* épidémie, *f.*

epigram ['epigræm], *n.* épigramme, *f.*

epilepsy ['epilepsi], *n.* épilepsie, *f.*

epileptic [epi'leptik], *a.* and *n.* épileptique, *m.*, *f.*

epilogue ['epilɔg], *n.* épilogue, *m.*

episcopacy [i'piskəpəsi], *n.* épiscopat, *m.*

episcopal [i'piskəpəl], *a.* épiscopal.

episode ['episoud], *n.* épisode, *m.*

epistle [i'pisl], *n.* épître, *f.*

epitaph ['epitɑ:f], *n.* épitaphe, *f.*

epithet ['epiθet], *n.* épithète, *f.*

epitome [i'pitəmi], *n.* épitomé, abrégé, précis, *m.*

epitomize [i'pitəmaiz], *v.t.* faire un abrégé de; être une image en petit de.

epoch ['i:pɔk], *n.* époque, *f.*

equable ['ekwəbl], *a.* uniforme, égal.

equal ['i:kwəl], *a.* égal; (*fig.*) impartial, juste; *equal to*, de force à, à la hauteur de.—*n.* égal, *m.*, égale, *f.*; (*pl.*) pareils, égaux, *m.pl.* —*v.t.* égaler, être égal à.

equality [i'kwɔliti], *n.* égalité, *f.*

equalize ['i:kwəlaiz], *v.t.* égaliser; compenser.

equally ['i:kwəli], *adv.* également, pareillement.

equanimity [i:kwə'nimiti], *n.* égalité d'âme, équanimité, *f.*

equation [i'kweiʃən], *n.* équation, *f.*

equator [i'kweitə], *n.* équateur, *m.*

equatorial [ekwə'tɔ:riəl], *a.* équatorial, de l'équateur.

equerry ['ekwəri], *n.* écuyer, *m.*

equestrian [i'kwestriən], *a.* équestre.—*n.* cavalier; (*Circus*) écuyer, *m.*

equilibrium [i:kwi'libriəm], *n.* équilibre, *m.*

equine ['i:kwain, 'ekwain], *a.* du cheval, équin.

equinox ['i:kwinɔks], *n.* équinoxe, *m.*

equip [i'kwip], *v.t.* équiper; (*Tech.*) outiller.

equipment [i'kwipmənt], *n.* équipement, matériel, outillage, *m.*

equitable ['ekwitəbl], *a.* équitable, juste.

equity ['ekwiti], *n.* équité, justice, *f.*

equivalent [i'kwivələnt], *a.* équivalent (*à*); *to be equivalent to*, être équivalent à, équivaloir à.—*n.* équivalent, *m.*

equivocal [i'kwivəkl], *a.* équivoque, ambigu.

equivocate [i'kwivəkeit], *v.i.* user d'équivoque, équivoquer.

era ['iərə], *n.* ère, *f.*

eradicate [i'rædikeit], *v.t.* déraciner; (*fig.*) exterminer.

erase [i'reiz], *v.t.* raturer, effacer, rayer.

eraser [i'reizə], *n.* grattoir, *m.*, gomme à effacer, *f.*

erasure [i'reiʒə], *n.* grattage, *m.*, rature, *f.*

*ere [eə], *conj.* avant que; plutôt que.—*prep.* avant.

erect [i'rekt], *a.* debout, droit, élevé.—*v.t.* ériger, dresser; (*fig.*) établir.

erection [i'rekʃən], *n.* construction, érection, élévation; (*fig.*) fondation, *f.*

ermine ['ə:min], *a.* d'hermine.—*n.* hermine, *f.*

erode [i'roud], *v.t.* éroder, ronger.

erosion [i'rouʒən], *n.* érosion, *f.*

erotic [i'rɔtik], *a.* érotique.

err [ə:], *v.i.* s'écarter, s'égarer (*de*); (*fig.*) se tromper.

errand ['erənd], *n.* message, *m.*, commission, course, *f.*

errand boy ['erəndbɔi], *n.* petit commissionnaire; saute-ruisseau (*de bureau*), chasseur (*dans un restaurant*), *m.*

erratic [i'rætik], *a.* erratique; errant, excentrique; irrégulier; inégal.

erroneous [i'rouniəs], *a.* erroné, faux.

erroneously [i'rouniəsli], *adv.* à faux, à tort.

error ['erə], *n.* erreur, faute, *f.*, écart, *m.*

erudite ['erudait], *a.* érudit, savant.

erudition [eru'diʃən], *n.* érudition, *f.*

erupt [i'rʌpt], *v.i.* faire éruption (*volcan*); percer (*dent*).

eruption [i'rʌpʃən], *n.* éruption, *f.*

erysipelas [eri'sipiləs], *n.* érysipèle, *m.*

escalade [eskə'leid], *n.* escalade, *f.*—*v.t.* escalader.

escalate ['eskəleit], *v.i.* escalader.

escalation [eskə'leiʃən], *n.* escalade, *f.*

escalator ['eskəleitə], *n.* escalier roulant, *m.*

escapade [eskə'peid], *n.* escapade, *f.*

escape [is'keip], *n.* évasion; fuite (*gaz*); (*fig.*) délivrance, *f.*; *fire escape*, échelle de sauvetage, *f.*; *to have a narrow escape*, l'échapper belle.—*v.t.* échapper à; éviter.—*v.i.* (s')échapper; s'évader (*de prison*).

escarpment [is'kɑ:pmənt], *n.* escarpement, talus, *m.*

eschew [is'tʃu:], *v.t.* éviter; renoncer à.

escort [is'kɔ:t], *v.t.* escorter.—['eskɔ:t], *n.* escorte, *f.*; cavalier, *m.*

escutcheon [is'kʌtʃən], *n.* écusson, *m.*

Eskimo ['eskimou], *a.* esquimau.—*n.* Esquimau (*personne*), *m.*

especial [is'peʃəl], *a.* spécial, particulier.

especially [is'peʃəli], *adv.* spécialement, surtout.

esplanade [esplə'neid], *n.* esplanade, promenade, *f.*

espouse [is'pauz], *v.t.* épouser; (*fig.*) adopter.

espy [is'pai], *v.t.* apercevoir, aviser, épier.

essay ['esei], *n.* essai; effort, *m.*; (*Sch.*) composition, dissertation, *f.*—[e'sei], *v.t.* essayer (*de*).

essence ['esəns], *n.* essence, *f.*

essential [i'senʃəl], *a.* essentiel.—*n.* (*also pl.*) essentiel, *m.*

essentially [i'senʃəli], *adv.* essentiellement.

establish [is'tæbliʃ], *v.t.* établir, fonder; (*fig.*) confirmer; prouver.

establishment [is'tæbliʃmənt], *n.* établissement, *m.*; maison; (*fig.*) confirmation, *f.*

estate [is'teit], *n.* état, rang (*condition*), *m.* propriété, *f.*, bien (*immeuble*), *m.*

estate agent [is'teiteidʒənt], *n.* agent immobilier, *m.*

estate duty [is'teitdju:ti], *n.* droits de succession, *m.pl.*

esteem [is'ti:m], *n.* estime, considération, *f.* —*v.t.* estimer, regarder comme.

estimate ['estimit], *n.* évaluation, *f.*, calcul, devis, *m.*; (*fig.*) appréciation, *f.*—['estimeit] *v.t.* estimer, apprécier; évaluer, calculer.

Estonia [es'touniə], l'Esthonie, *f.*

Estonian [es'touniən], *a.* esthonien.—*n.* esthonien (*langue*); Esthonien (*personne*), *m.*

estrange [is'treindʒ], *v.t.* aliéner, éloigner (*de*).

estrangement [is'treindʒmənt], *n.* aliénation, *f.*, éloignement, *m.*, brouille, *f.*

estuary ['estjuəri], *n.* estuaire, *m.*

etching ['etʃiŋ], *n.* gravure à l'eau-forte, *f.*

eternal [i'tə:nl], *a.* and *n.* éternel, *m.*

eternity [i'tə:niti], *n.* éternité, *f.*

ether ['i:θə], *n.* éther, *m.*

ethereal [i'θiəriəl], *a.* éthéré; céleste.

ethic ['eθik], **ethical** ['eθikəl], *a.* éthique; moral.

ethics ['eθiks], *n.pl.* morale, éthique, *f.*

Ethiopia [i:θi'oupiə], l'Éthiopie, *f.*

Ethiopian [i:θi'oupiən], *a.* éthiopien.—*n.* Éthiopien (*personne*), *m.*

etiquette ['etiket], *n.* étiquette, *f.*, convenances, *f.pl.*

Etruria [i'truəriə], l'Étrurie, *f.*

Etruscan [i'trʌskən], a. étrusque.—n. étrusque (langue); Étrusque (personne), m.; f.
etymology [eti'mɒlədʒi], n. étymologie, f.
eucharist ['ju:kərist], n. eucharistie, f.
eulogium [ju:'loudʒiəm], eulogy ['ju:lədʒi], n. éloge, panégyrique, m.
eulogize ['ju:lədʒaiz], v.t. louer, faire l'éloge de.
eunuch ['ju:nək], n. eunuque, m.
euphemism ['ju:fimizm], n. euphémisme, m.
euphony ['ju:fəni], n. euphonie, f.
Eurasian [juə'reiʒən], a. eurasien.—n. Eurasien (personne), m.
Europe ['juərəp], l'Europe, f.
European [juərə'pi:ən], a. européen.—n. Européen (personne), m.
euthanasia [ju:θə'neiziə], n. euthanasie, f.
evacuate [i'vækjueit], v.t. évacuer.
evacuation [ivækju'eiʃən], n. évacuation, f.
evade [i'veid], v.t. éluder, esquiver, éviter, se soustraire à; échapper à, déjouer (la loi).
evaluate [i'væljueit], v.t. évaluer.
evaporate [i'væpəreit], v.t. faire évaporer.—v.i. s'évaporer.
evaporation [ivæpə'reiʃən], n. évaporation, f.
evasion [i'veiʒən], n. subterfuge, m.; échappatoire, défaite, f.
eve [i:v], n. veille, f.; on the eve of, à la veille de.
even (1) [i:vn], n. (Poet.) soir, m.
even (2) [i:vn], a. égal; régulier (respiration, pouls); uni (lisse); de niveau (avec); pair (numéro).—adv. même, aussi bien; précisément.—v.t. égaler, égaliser; niveler.
evening ['i:vniŋ], a. du soir; evening dress, tenue de soirée, f.—n. soir, m.; soirée, f.; (fig.) déclin, m.
evenly ['i:vnli], adv. également; de niveau; (fig.) impartialement.
evenness ['i:vnnis], n. égalité; régularité; sérénité, f.
evensong ['i:vnsɒŋ], n. chant du soir, m.; vêpres, m.pl.
event [i'vent], n. événement, m.; issue, f.; at all events, en tout cas, dans tous les cas; in the event of, au cas où.
even-tempered ['i:vntempəd], a. calme, placide, égal.
eventful [i'ventful], a. mouvementé.
eventual [i'ventjuəl], a. éventuel, aléatoire; final, définitif.
eventually [i'ventjuəli], adv. finalement, à la fin, par la suite.
ever ['evə], adv. toujours; jamais; ever since, depuis; for ever, à jamais.
evergreen ['evəgri:n], a. toujours vert.—n. arbre toujours vert, m.
everlasting [evə'la:stiŋ], a. éternel, perpétuel.—n. éternité, f.; éternel, m.
everlastingly [evə'la:stiŋli], adv. éternellement.
evermore [evə'mɔ:], adv. toujours; éternellement.
every ['evri], a. chaque, tout, tous les; every one, chacun, m., chacune, f., tous, pl.
everybody [EVERYONE].
everyday ['evridei], a. quotidien; ordinaire; de tous les jours.
everyone ['evriwʌn], everybody ['evribɒdi], n. tout le monde, m.
everything ['evriθiŋ], n. tout, m.
everywhere ['evriweə], adv. partout.

evict [i'vikt], v.t. évincer, expulser.
eviction [i'vikʃən], n. éviction, expulsion, f.
evidence ['evidəns], n. évidence; preuve, f., témoignage; témoin (personne), m.—v.t. montrer, prouver, démontrer.
evident ['evidənt], a. évident, visible.
evidently ['evidəntli], adv. évidemment.
evil [i:vl], a. mauvais; malheureux, malfaisant, méchant (esprit etc.).—n. mal; malheur, m., calamité, f.—adv. mal.
evil-doer ['i:vldu:ə], n. malfaiteur, méchant, m.
evil-speaking ['i:vl'spi:kiŋ], n. médisance, f.
evince [i'vins], v.t. montrer, manifester, démontrer.
evoke [i'vouk], v.t. évoquer; susciter.
evolution [i:və'lu:ʃən], n. évolution, f.
evolve [i'vɒlv], v.t. dérouler; développer.—v.i. se dérouler; se développer.
ewe [ju:], n. brebis, f.
ewer ['ju:ə], n. aiguière, f., broc, m.
exact [ig'zækt], v.t. exiger, extorquer.—a. exact, précis.
exaction [ig'zækʃən], n. exaction, f.
exactitude [ig'zæktitju:d], exactness [ig'zæktnis], n. exactitude, f.
exactly [ig'zæktli], adv. exactement, précisément, au juste; juste.
exaggerate [ig'zædʒəreit], v.t. exagérer.
exaggeration [igzædʒə'reiʃən], n. exagération, f.
exalt [ig'zɔ:lt], v.t. exalter, élever; (fig.) louer.
exaltation [egzɔ:l'teiʃən], n. exaltation, élévation, f.
examination [igzæmi'neiʃən], n. examen, m.; inspection, vérification, f.; (Law) interrogatoire (de prisonniers), m.; audition (de témoins), f.; to pass an examination, réussir à un examen; to sit (for) an examination, passer un examen.
examine [ig'zæmin], v.t. examiner; visiter; (Law) interroger.
examiner [ig'zæminə], n. examinateur; (Law) juge d'instruction, m.
example [ig'za:mpl], n. exemple, m.; for example, par exemple.
exasperate [ig'za:spəreit], v.t. exaspérer; irriter, aigrir.
exasperation [igza:spə'reiʃən], n. exaspération, irritation, f.
excavate ['ekskəveit], v.t. creuser, excaver.
excavation [ekskə'veiʃən], n. excavation, f.; fouilles, f.pl.
excavator ['ekskəveitə], n. piocheuse-défonceuse, f.
exceed [ik'si:d], v.t. excéder, dépasser; (fig.) surpasser.
exceeding [ik'si:diŋ], a. grand, extrême.
exceedingly [ik'si:diŋli], adv. très, fort, extrêmement.
excel [ik'sel], v.t. surpasser, l'emporter sur.—v.i. exceller, se distinguer (à).
excellence ['eksələns], n. excellence, supériorité, f.
excellent ['eksələnt], a. excellent.
excellently ['eksələntli], adv. excellemment, parfaitement.
except [ik'sept], v.t. excepter; exclure (de).—prep. excepté, à l'exception de, hors, sauf.—conj. à moins que, à moins de.
excepting [ik'septiŋ], prep. excepté, hormis.

exception [ik'sepʃən], *n.* exception; objection, *f.*; *to take exception to*, se formaliser de.

exceptionable [ik'sepʃənəbl], *a.* blâmable, à critiquer.

exceptional [ik'sepʃənəl], *a.* exceptionnel.

exceptionally [ik'sepʃənəli], *adv.* exceptionnellement.

excerpt ['eksə:pt], *n.* extrait, *m.*, citation, *f.*

excess [ik'ses], *n.* excès; excédent (*poids*), *m.*

excessive [ik'sesiv], *a.* excessif, extrême; immodéré.

excessively [ik'sesivli], *adv.* excessivement, à l'excès.

exchange [iks'tʃeindʒ], *n.* échange; (*Comm.*) change, *m.*; Bourse (*édifice*), *f.*; *bill of exchange*, lettre de change, *f.*; *rate of exchange*, taux du change, *m.*; *telephone exchange*, central téléphonique, *m.*—*v.t.* échanger, changer (*contre* ou *pour*).

exchequer [iks'tʃekə], *n.* trésor; Ministère des Finances, *m.*

excisable [ek'saizəbl], *a.* imposable; sujet aux droits de l'accise.

excise ['eksaiz], *n.* (*England*) excise, *f.*; (*France*) contributions indirectes, *f.pl.*, régie, *f.*

excise-man ['eksaizmən], *n.* (*pl.* -men [men]) préposé *ou* employé de la régie, *m.*

excitable [ik'saitəbl], *a.* excitable, impressionnable.

excite [ik'sait], *v.t.* exciter; irriter; émouvoir; (*fig.*) provoquer.

excitement [ik'saitmənt], *n.* émoi, *m.*, surexcitation; émotion, agitation, *f.*

exciting [ik'saitiŋ], *a.* émouvant, passionnant, palpitant.

exclaim [iks'kleim], *v.i.* s'écrier, se récrier, s'exclamer.

exclamation [eksklə'meiʃən], *n.* exclamation, *f.*, cri, *m.*

exclude [iks'klu:d], *v.t.* exclure (*de*); proscrire.

excluding [iks'klu:diŋ], *prep.* sans compter.

exclusion [iks'klu:ʒən], *n.* exclusion, *f.*

exclusive [iks'klu:siv], *a.* exclusif.

excommunicate [ekskə'mju:nikeit], *v.t.* excommunier.

excrement ['ekskrimənt], *n.* excrément, *m.*

excrescence [iks'kresəns], *n.* excroissance, *f.*

excruciate [iks'kru:ʃieit], *v.t.* tourmenter, torturer.

excruciating [iks'kru:ʃieitiŋ], *a.* atroce, affreux, horrible.

exculpate ['ekskʌlpeit], *v.t.* disculper, justifier.

excursion [iks'kə:ʃən], *n.* excursion, randonnée; (*fig.*) digression, *f.*

excusable [iks'kju:zəbl], *a.* excusable.

excuse [iks'kju:s], *n.* excuse, *f.*; prétexte, *m.*; *to find an excuse*, chercher des excuses; *to make excuses*, s'excuser.—[eks'kju:z], *v.t.* excuser, pardonner; *excuse me!* pardon! *to be excused from duty*, être exempt de service.

execrable ['eksikrəbl], *a.* exécrable.

execrate ['eksikreit], *v.t.* exécrer, maudire.

execute ['eksikju:t], *v.t.* exécuter, accomplir; remplir (*un ordre*); *to execute a deed*, signer un contrat.

execution [eksi'kju:ʃən], *n.* exécution, *f.*; accomplissement supplice, *m.*

executioner [eksi'kju:ʃənə], *n.* bourreau, *m.*

executive [ig'zekjutiv], *a.* exécutif.—*n.* pouvoir exécutif; (*Comm.*) directeur, *m.*

executor [ig'zekjutə], *n.* exécuteur testamentaire, *m.*

exemplar [ig'zemplə], *n.* modèle, exemplaire, *m.*

exemplary [ig'zempləri], *a.* exemplaire; modèle.

exemplify [ig'zemplifai], *v.t.* démontrer par des exemples, illustrer; donner un exemple de.

exempt [ig'zempt, eg'zemt], *v.t.* exempter (*de*).—*a.* exempt.

exemption [ig'zempʃən], *n.* exemption, *f.*

exercise ['eksəsaiz], *n.* exercice; (*Sch.*) thème, devoir, *m.*—*v.t.* exercer; promener (*un chien*).—*v.i.* s'exercer; (*Mil.*) faire l'exercice.

exercise book ['eksəsaizbuk], *n.* cahier (*de devoirs*), *m.*

exert [ig'zə:t], *v.t.* déployer; mettre en œuvre; exercer (*influence, pression etc.*); *to exert oneself*, faire des efforts (*pour*).

exertion [ig'zə:ʃən], *n.* effort, *m.*

exhale [eks'heil], *v.t.* exhaler, émettre.

exhaust [ig'zɔ:st], *v.t.* épuiser.—*n.* échappement, *m.*

exhausted [ig'zɔ:stid], *a.* épuisé.

exhaustion [ig'zɔ:stʃən], *n.* épuisement, *m.*

exhaustive [ig'zɔ:stiv], *a.* qui épuise; (*fig.*) complet.

exhaust pipe [ig'zɔ:stpaip], *n.* (*Motor.*) tuyau d'échappement, *m.*

exhibit [ig'zibit], *v.t.* montrer; exposer; (*fig.*) exhiber.—*n.* objet exposé, *m.*

exhibition [eksi'biʃən], *n.* exposition; représentation, *f.*, spectacle, *m.*; (*Univ.*) bourse, *f.*

exhibitioner [eksi'biʃənə], *n.* (*Univ.*) boursier, *m.*

exhibitor [ig'zibitə], *n.* exposant, *m.*

exhilarate [ig'ziləreit], *v.t.* réjouir, égayer.

exhilarating [ig'ziləreitiŋ], *a.* qui égaye, réjouissant.

exhilaration [igzilə'reiʃən], *n.* réjouissance, gaieté, joie de vivre, *f.*

exhort [ig'zɔ:t], *v.t.* exhorter (*à*).

exhortation [egzɔ:'teiʃən], *n.* exhortation, *f.*

exhume [eks'hju:m], *v.t.* exhumer, déterrer.

exile ['eksail], *n.* exil; exilé (*personne*), *m.*—*v.t.* exiler.

exist [ig'zist], *v.i.* exister.

existence [ig'zistəns], *n.* existence, *f.*; être, *m.*

exit ['eksit], *n.* sortie, *f.*—*v.i.* (*Theat.*) il (elle) sort.

exodus ['eksədəs], *n.* exode, *m.*

exonerate [ig'zɔnəreit], *v.t.* décharger, exempter, exonérer, justifier.

exorbitant [ig'zɔ:bitənt], *a.* exorbitant, excessif, exagéré.

exotic [eg'zɔtik], *a.* exotique.

expand [iks'pænd], *v.t.* étendre, faire épanouir; amplifier; dilater (*gaz*).—*v.i.* se dilater; s'épanouir; se développer.

expanse [iks'pæns], *n.* étendue, *f.*

expansion [iks'pænʃən], *n.* expansion, *f.*

expatiate [eks'peiʃieit], *v.i.* s'étendre (*sur*).

expatriate [eks'peitrieit], *v.t.* expatrier, bannir.

expect [iks'pekt], *v.t.* attendre; s'attendre à, compter sur (*choses*); espérer; *she is expecting*, elle attend un bébé; *to know what to expect*, savoir à quoi s'en tenir.

expectant [iks'pektənt], *a.* expectant.
expectation [ekspek'teiʃən], *n.* attente, espérance; expectative; probabilité, *f.*
expedience [iks'pi:diəns], **expediency** [iks'pi:diənsi], *n.* convenance, utilité, opportunité, *f.*
expedient [iks'pi:diənt], *a.* convenable, à propos, utile, opportun.—*n.* expédient, *m.*
expedite ['ekspədait], *v.t.* expédier, hâter, accélerer.
expedition [ekspə'diʃən], *n.* expédition, *f.*; promptitude, *f.*
expeditious [ekspi'diʃəs], *a.* expéditif, prompt.
expel [iks'pel], *v.t.* expulser, chasser; (*Sch.*) renvoyer.
expend [iks'pend], *v.t.* dépenser; (*fig.*) employer.
expenditure [iks'penditʃə], *n.* dépense, *f.*, dépenses, *f.pl.*; (*fig.*) sacrifice, *m.*
expense [iks'pens], *n.* dépense, *f.*; dépens, frais, *m.pl.*; *at any expense*, à tout prix; *incidental expenses*, faux frais; *to clear one's expenses*, faire ses frais.
expensive [iks'pensiv], *a.* coûteux, cher (*chose*); dépensier (*personne*).
expensively [iks'pensivli], *adv.* à grands frais.
experience [iks'piəriəns], *n.* expérience, *f.*; sentiment, *m.*—*v.t.* éprouver, faire l'expérience de.
experienced [iks'piəriənst], *a.* éprouvé, expérimenté.
experiment [eks'perimənt], *n.* expérience, *f.*—*v.i.* expérimenter.
experimental [eksperi'mentl], *a.* expérimental.
expert ['ekspə:t], *a.* expert, habile.—*n.* expert, *m.*
expiate ['ekspieit], *v.t.* expier.
expiation [ekspi'eiʃən], *n.* expiation, *f.*
expiration [ekspi'reiʃən], **expiry** [iks'paiəri], *n.* expiration; fin, *f.*, terme, *m.*
expire [iks'paiə], *v.i.* expirer, mourir.
explain [iks'plein], *v.t.* expliquer.—*v.i.* s'expliquer.
explanation [eksplə'neiʃən], *n.* explication, *f.*
explanatory [iks'plænətri], *a.* explicatif.
explicit [iks'plisit], *a.* explicite, formel; franc.
explode [iks'ploud], *v.t.* faire éclater; faire sauter (*mine*); (*fig.*) discréditer; *exploded theory*, théorie abandonnée, *f.*—*v.i.* éclater, sauter, faire explosion.
exploit ['eksploit], *n.* exploit, haut fait, *m.*—[iks'ploit], *v.t.* exploiter.
exploitation [eksploi'teiʃən], *n.* exploitation, *f.*
exploration [eksplɔ:'reiʃən], *n.* exploration, *f.*; (*fig.*) examen, *m.*
explore [iks'plɔ:], *v.t.* explorer; (*fig.*) examiner.
explorer [iks'plɔ:rə], *n.* explorateur, *m.*
explosion [iks'plouʒən], *n.* explosion, *f.*
explosive [iks'plousiv], *a.* and *n.* explosif, *m.*
exponent [eks'pounənt], *n.* (*Math.*) exposant, *f.* (*fig.*) représentant, *m.*
export ['ekspɔ:t], *n.* exportation; marchandise exportée, *f.*—[eks'pɔ:t], *v.t.* exporter, *f.*
expose [iks'pouz], *v.t.* exposer; (*fig.*) révéler, découvrir, démasquer.
expostulate [iks'pɔstjuleit], *v.i.* faire des remontrances (*à*).
exposure [iks'pouʒə], *n.* exposition (*aux*

intempéries, à un danger), *f.*; étalage (*de marchandises*); esclandre, *m.*; (*Phot.*) pose, *f.*; *to die of exposure*, mourir de froid.
expound [iks'paund], *v.t.* expliquer, exposer.
express [iks'pres], *a.* exprès; formel, explicite; *by express delivery*, par exprès.—*n.* exprès (*messager*); train express, *m.*—*v.t.* exprimer.
expression [iks'preʃən], *n.* expression, *f.*
expressive [iks'presiv], *a.* expressif.
expressly [iks'presli], *adv.* expressément, formellement.
expropriate [eks'prouprieit], *v.t.* exproprier.
expulsion [iks'pʌlʃən], *n.* expulsion, *f.*
expurgate ['ekspə:geit], *v.t.* corriger, expurger (*livre*).
exquisite ['ekskwizit], *a.* exquis; vif, extrême (*douleur*); raffiné, délicat.
exquisitely ['ekskwizitli], *adv.* d'une manière exquise; parfaitement.
ex-service man [eks'sə:vismən], *n.* (*pl.* -men [men]) ancien combattant, *m.*
extant [ek'stænt], *a.* qui existe encore.
extempore [eks'tempəri], *a.* improvisé.—*adv.* impromptu, sans préparation.
extemporize [eks'tempəraiz], *v.t.* improviser.
extend [iks'tend], *v.t.* étendre; prolonger; tendre (*la main*); *to extend a welcome*, souhaiter la bienvenue.—*v.i.* s'étendre; se prolonger (*temps*).
extension [iks'tenʃən], *n.* extension; étendue, prolongation (*de temps*), *f.*; (*Teleph.*) poste, *m.*; (*Elec.*) [FLEX].
extensive [iks'tensiv], *a.* étendu, vaste; ample.
extensively [iks'tensivli], *adv.* d'une manière étendue; bien, très, au loin.
extent [iks'tent], *n.* étendue, *f.*; (*fig.*) degré, point, *m.*; *to a certain extent*, jusqu'à un certain point; *to the extent of*, jusqu'à.
extenuate [eks'tenjueit], *v.t.* atténuer, amoindrir.
extenuating [eks'tenjueitiŋ], *a.* (*Law*) atténuant.
exterior [eks'tiəriə], *a.* extérieur, en dehors.—*n.* extérieur, *m.*
exterminate [iks'tə:mineit], *v.t.* exterminer; extirper.
extermination [ikstə:mi'neiʃən], *n.* extermination, *f.*
external [eks'tə:nl], *a.* extérieur; externe (*étudiant etc.*).
extinct [iks'tiŋkt], *a.* éteint; qui n'existe plus (*espèce etc.*); aboli.
extinguish [iks'tiŋgwiʃ], *v.t.* éteindre; (*fig.*) éclipser.
extinguisher [iks'tiŋgwiʃə], *n.* extincteur (*appareil*), *m.*
extirpate ['ekstə:peit], *v.t.* extirper.
extol [iks'toul], *v.t.* exalter, vanter.
extort [iks'tɔ:t], *v.t.* extorquer, arracher.
extortion [iks'tɔ:ʃən], *n.* extorsion, *f.*
extortionate [iks'tɔ:ʃənit], *a.* extorsionnaire, exorbitant.
extra ['ekstrə], *a.* en sus; supplémentaire. *extra charge*, prix en sus, supplément, *m.*—*n.* supplément; (*Cine.*) figurant, *m.*—*adv.* en sus, de plus; *extra strong*, extra-solide.
extract ['ekstrækt], *n.* extrait; concentré (*de viande etc.*), *m.*—[iks'trækt], *v.t.* extraire, tirer (*de*); arracher (*dent*) à.

extraction [iks'trækʃən], *n.* extraction; origine, *f.*

extraneous [eks'treinjəs], *a.* étranger (*à*); non-essentiel.

extraordinarily [iks'trɔːdnrili], *a.* extraordinairement.

extraordinary [iks'trɔːdnri], *a.* extraordinaire, rare.

extravagance [iks'trævəgəns], *n.* extravagance; prodigalité, *f.*, gaspillage, *m.*

extravagant [iks'trævəgənt], *a.* extravagant (*immodéré*); prodigue, dépensier; exorbitant (*prix*).

extravagantly [iks'trævəgəntli], *adv.* d'une manière extravagante.

extreme [iks'triːm], *a.* extrême.—*n.* extrémité, *f.*; extrême, *m.*

extremely [iks'triːmli], *adv.* extrêmement, au dernier degré.

extremist [iks'triːmist], *n.* extrémiste, *m.*, *f.*; ultra, *m.*

extremity [iks'tremiti], *n.* extrémité, *f.*, extrême; bout, *m.*

extricate ['ekstrikeit], *v.t.* débarrasser, dégager; **to extricate oneself**, se tirer d'affaire.

extrovert ['ekstrəvɔːt], *n.* extroverti, *m.*

exuberance [ig'zjuːbərəns], *n.* exubérance, surabondance, *f.*

exuberant [ig'zjuːbərənt], *a.* exubérant, surabondant.

exude [ek'sjuːd], *v.t.* faire exsuder.—*v.i.* exsuder.

exult [ig'zʌlt], *v.i.* se réjouir, exulter (*de*).

exultant [ig'zʌltənt], *a.* joyeux, triomphant.

exultation [egzʌl'teiʃən], *n.* triomphe, *m.*, exultation, *f.*

eye [ai], *n.* œil; trou (*d'une aiguille*), (*Bot.*) œil, bouton, *m.*; (*Needlework*) porte; (*fig.*) vue, *f.*; **black eye**, œil poché; **blind in one eye**, borgne; **in the twinkling of an eye**, en un clin d'œil; **to keep an eye on**, surveiller.—*v.t.* regarder; lorgner.

eyeball ['aibɔːl], *n.* bulbe de l'œil, *m.*

eyebrow ['aibrau], *n.* sourcil, *m.*

eyed [aid], *a.* **blue-eyed**, aux yeux bleus.

eyeglass ['aiglɑːs], *n.* monocle (*un seul verre*); lorgnon, pince-nez (*double*), *m.*

eye-hole ['aihoul], *n.* orbite; petit judas, *m.*

eyelash ['aileʃ], *n.* cil, *m.*

eyelet ['ailit], *n.* œillet, *m.*

eyelid ['ailid], *n.* paupière, *f.*

eyesight ['aisait], *n.* vue, *f.*

eyesore ['aisɔː], *n.* chose qui blesse l'œil, *f.*, objet d'aversion, *m.*

eye-witness ['aiwitnis], *n.* témoin oculaire, *m.*

eyrie, eyry [AERIE].

F

F, f [ef]. sixième lettre de l'alphabet; (*Mus.*) fa, *m.*

fable [feibl], *n.* fable, *f.*, conte, *m.*

fabric ['fæbrik], *n.* construction, *f.*; édifice, ouvrage, *m.*; étoffe, *f.*; (*fig.*) système, *m.*

fabricate ['fæbrikeit], *v.t.* fabriquer, inventer, contrefaire.

fabrication [fæbri'keiʃən], *n.* fabrication, *f.*

fabulous ['fæbjuləs], *a.* fabuleux.

face [feis], *n.* figure, *f.*; visage, *m.*; face, surface (*des choses*); (*fig.*) apparence, *f.*, état, *m.*; mine, physionomie, *f.*; front (*insolence*), *m.*; façade, *f.*, devant (*front*), *m.*; facette (*d'un diamant*), *f.*; cadran (*de pendule*), *m.*; **face to face**, vis-à-vis; **to make faces at**, faire des grimaces à.—*v.t.* faire face à, affronter; mettre un revers à, parer (*vêtements*); revêtir (*mur etc.*); donner sur (*maison etc.*).—*v.i.* prendre un faux dehors; (*Mil.*) faire front; **face about!** volte-face!

facet ['fæsit], *n.* facette, *f.*—*v.t.* facetter.

facetious [fə'siːʃəs], *a.* facétieux.

facetiously [fə'siːʃəsli], *adv.* facétieusement.

facetiousness [fə'siːʃəsnis], *n.* plaisanterie, *f.*

facial ['feiʃəl], *a.* facial.

facile ['fæsail], *a.* facile; complaisant.

facility [fə'siliti], *n.* facilité, *f.*

facilitate [fə'siliteit], *v.t.* faciliter.

facing ['feisiŋ], *n.* parement de (*vêtements*); revers, *m.*

facsimile [fæk'simili], *n.* fac-similé, *m.*

fact [fækt], *n.* fait, *m.*; **as a matter of fact, in fact,** en effet; **in point of fact,** au fait; **matter-of-fact man,** homme positif, *m.*

faction ['fækʃən], *n.* faction; (*fig.*) discorde, dissension, *f.*

factor ['fæktə], *n.* agent; facteur, *m.*

factory ['fæktri], *n.* usine, fabrique, *f.*; (*obs.*) comptoir (*d'outre-mer*) *m.*

faculty ['fækəlti], *n.* faculté, *f.*, pouvoir, talent, *m.*

fad [fæd], *n.* marotte, manie, *f.*

fade [feid], *v.t.* flétrir, faire flétrir.—*v.i.* se faner, se flétrir; disparaître, périr.

fag [fæg], *v.t.* forcer à piocher; fatiguer, éreinter; **fagged out,** éreinté.—*v.i.* travailler dur, piocher (*à*).—*n.* fatigue, peine, corvée, *f.*; (*pop.*) cigarette, *f.*

fag end ['fægend], *n.* (*pop.*) mégot (*de cigarette*), *m.*

faggot ['fægət], *n.* fagot, *m.*

fail [feil], *v.t.* manquer à, abandonner.—*v.i.* faillir; manquer (*to miss*); échouer (*ne pas réussir*); (*Comm.*) faire faillite.—*n.* manque, insuccès, *m.*

failing ['feiliŋ], *n.* défaut, *m.*, faute; (*Comm.*) faillite, *f.*—*prep.* à défaut de.

failure ['feiljə], *n.* manque, défaut (*want*); échec; insuccès, *m.*, affaire manquée, *f.*, fiasco, *m.*; chute (*d'une pièce etc.*); (*Comm.*) faillite, *f.*; **he is a failure,** c'est un raté.

***fain** [fein], *adv.* avec plaisir, volontiers.

faint [feint], *a.* faible; affaibli; languissant; découragé; timide.—*v.i.* s'évanouir, défaillir.—*n.* évanouissement, *m.*

faint-hearted ['feinthɑːtid], *a.* timide, sans courage, découragé.

fainting ['feintiŋ], *n.* évanouissement, *m.*, défaillance, *f.*

faintly ['feintli], *adv.* faiblement; mollement.

faintness ['feintnis], *n.* faiblesse, *f.*

fair [fɛə], *a.* beau; favorable (*vent*); clair (*teint*); blond (*cheveux etc.*); juste, équitable;

(*fig.*) assez bon, passable; *fair play*, franc jeu, *m.*; *fair price*, juste prix, *m.*; *that is not fair* (*at games*), cela n'est pas de jeu.—*adv.* bien; de bonne foi, honorablement.—*n.* foire (*marché*), *f.*

fairly ['fɛəli], *adv.* bien; loyalement; doucement; avec justesse; de bonne foi; passablement, assez.

fairness ['fɛənis], *n.* beauté; couleur blonde (*des cheveux*); blancheur (*du teint*); équité, impartialité, *f.*

fairy ['fɛəri], *a.* des fées, féerique.—*n.* fée, *f.*

fairy tale ['fɛəriteil], *n.* conte de fées, *m.*

faith [feiθ], *n.* foi, croyance; (*fig.*) fidélité *f.*—*int.* ma foi! en vérité!

faithful ['feiθful], *a.* fidèle.

faithfully ['feiθfuli], *adv.* fidèlement; *yours faithfully* (*lettre d'affaires*), veuillez agréer mes salutations distinguées.

faithfulness ['feiθfulnis], *n.* fidélité, *f.*

faithless ['feiθlis], *a.* sans foi, infidèle.

faithlessness ['feiθlisnis], *n.* infidélité; déloyauté, *f.*

fake [feik], *v.t., v.i.* truquer, maquiller.

falcon ['fɔːlkən], *n.* faucon, *m.*

fall [fɔːl], *v.i. irr.* tomber; s'abaisser; baisser, diminuer; *to fall away from*, abandonner, quitter; *to fall back* tomber en arrière; (*Mil.*) reculer; *to fall down*, tomber par terre; *to fall for*, tomber amoureux de; *to fall for it*, s'y laisser prendre; *to fall in*, s'écrouler; se mettre en rangs, s'aligner; *to fall off*, tomber; diminuer; *to fall out*, tomber; se brouiller; (*Mil.*) *fall out!* rompez vos rangs! *to fall through*, échouer; *to fall to*, se mettre à; *to fall under*, être compris sous; tomber sous; *to fall upon*, tomber sur, attaquer; incomber à.—*n.* chute, *f.*; (*Am.*) automne, *m.* ou *f.*; tombée (*de la nuit*); baisse (*de prix*), *f.*; éboulement (*de terre*), *m.*; chute, cascade (*de rivières etc.*); décrue (*des eaux*); diminution (*de quantité*), *f.*

fallacy ['fæləsi], *n.* erreur, fausseté, illusion, *f.*

fallible ['fæləbl], *a.* faillible.

fall-out ['fɔːlaut], *n.* retombées radioactives, *f.pl.*

fallow ['fæləu], *a.* en jachère; (*fig.*) inculte; fauve (*daim etc.*).—*n.* jachère, friche, *f.*

false [fɔːls], *a.* faux, perfide, déloyal; infidèle; prétendu; illegal (*détention*).

falsehood ['fɔːlshud], *n.* mensonge, *m.*

falsely ['fɔːlsli], *adv.* faussement.

falseness ['fɔːlsnis], *n.* fausseté; perfidie, *f.*

falsetto [fɔːl'setou], *n.* (*Mus.*) voix de fausset, *f.*

falsify ['fɔːlsifai], *v.t.* falsifier; fausser.

falter ['fɔːltə], *v.i.* hésiter; bégayer; chanceler.

faltering ['fɔːltəriŋ], *n.* hésitation, *f.*

fame [feim], *n.* gloire, renommée, *f.*

famed [feimd], *a.* renommé.

familiar [fə'miliə], *a.* familier, intime; de la famille; *to be familiar with*, être familier avec, connaître.—*n.* ami intime; esprit familier, *m.*

familiarity [fəmili'æriti], *n.* familiarité, *f.*

familiarly [fə'miliəli], *adv.* familièrement, sans cérémonie.

family ['fæmili], *a.* de famille, de la famille.—*n.* famille, *f.*

famine ['fæmin], *n.* famine, disette, *f.*

famished ['fæmiʃt], *a.* affamé.

famous ['feiməs], *a.* fameux, célèbre.

famously ['feiməsli], *adv.* fameusement; (*fig.*) prodigieusement.

fan [fæn], *n.* éventail; ventilateur; (*colloq.*) admirateur enthousiaste (*d'un artiste* ou *d'un sport*), *m.*—*v.t.* éventer; souffler (*feu*); (*Agric.*) vanner; (*fig.*) exciter, activer.

fanatic [fə'nætik], *a. and n.* fanatique, *m., f.*

fanatical [fə'nætikəl], *a.* fanatique.

fanaticism [fə'nætisizm], *n.* fanatisme, *m.*

fancied ['fænsid], *a.* imaginaire, imaginé; (*Turf*) bien coté (*cheval*).

fancier ['fænsiə], *n.* amateur (*de*), *m.*

fanciful ['fænsiful], *a.* fantasque, capricieux.

fancy ['fænsi], *a.* de fantaisie.—*n.* fantaisie, imagination; idée, *f.*, caprice, goût (*pour*), *m.*, envie (*de*), *f.*—*v.t.* s'imaginer, se figurer; avoir du goût pour.—*v.i.* s'imaginer, se figurer; figurer; *just fancy!* figurez-vous!

fancy dress ['fænsidres], *n.* travesti, *m.*; *fancy-dress ball*, bal costumé, *m.*

fane [fein], *n.* temple, édifice sacré, *m.*

fanfare ['fænfɛə], *n.* fanfare, *f.*

fang [fæŋ], *n.* croc (*de chien*), *m.*; racine (*d'une dent*); défense (*de sanglier*); (*fig.*) griffe, *f.*

fantastic [fæn'tæstik], *a.* fantastique; fantasque (*personne*).

fantasy ['fæntəsi], *n.* fantaisie, *f.*

far [fɑː], *a.* (*comp.* **farther**, **further**; *superl.* **farthest**, **furthest**) lointain, éloigné, reculé; *the Far East*, l'extrême Orient, *m.* —*adv.* loin, au loin; bien, fort, beaucoup; *as far as*, aussi loin que, jusqu'à; *by far*, de beaucoup; *far and wide*, de tous côtés; *how far?* jusqu'où?

far-away ['fɑːrəwei], *a.* rêveur (*regard*); lointain.

farce [fɑːs], *n.* farce, *f.*

farcical ['fɑːsikl], *a.* burlesque; (*fig.*) drôle.

fare [fɛə], *v.i.* aller; se porter; se nourrir, vivre.—*n.* prix de la course; prix de la place, *m.*, place, *f.*; voyageur (*personne*), *m.*; chère (*aliment*), *f.*; prix de la fare, menu, *m.*, carte du jour, *f.*; *return fare*, aller et retour, *m.*; *single fare*, billet simple, *m.*

farewell ['fɛəwel, fɛə'wel], *a.* d'adieu.—*n.* adieu, *m.*

far-fetched [fɑː'fetʃt], *a.* recherché; tiré par les cheveux.

farm [fɑːm], *n.* ferme, *f.*—*v.t.* affermer; prendre à ferme; exploiter.

farmer ['fɑːmə], *n.* fermier, métayer; cultivateur, *m.*

farm-house ['fɑːmhaus], *n.* ferme, *f.*

farming ['fɑːmiŋ], *n.* agriculture, exploitation agricole, *f.*

farm-yard ['fɑːmjɑːd], *n.* basse-cour, *f.*

Faroe ['fɛərou] **Islands**, les îles Féroé, *f.pl.*

far-reaching [fɑː'riːtʃiŋ], *a.* d'une grande portée.

farrier ['færiə], *n.* maréchal ferrant, *m.*

farther [FURTHER].

farthest [FURTHERMOST].

fascinate ['fæsineit], *v.t.* fasciner; charmer, séduire.

fascinating ['fæsineitiŋ], *a.* fascinateur, enchanteur, séduisant.

fascination [fæsi'neiʃən], *n.* fascination, *f.*, charme, *m.*

fascism ['fæsizm], *n.* fascisme, *m.*

fascist ['fæʃist], *a. and n.* fasciste, *m., f.*

fashion ['fæʃən], n. façon, forme; mode, f.; le grand monde, m.; *after a fashion*, tant bien que mal; *in fashion*, à la mode; *to set the fashion*, donner le ton.—v.t. façonner, former.

fashionable ['fæʃnəbl], a. à la mode, élégant, de bon ton, (*fam.*) chic.

fashionably ['fæʃnəbli], adv. à la mode, élégamment.

fast (1) [fɑːst], n. jeûne, m.—v.i. jeûner.

fast (2) [fɑːst], a. ferme, fixe (*solide*); fidèle (*constant*); bon teint (*couleur*); serré (*nœud*); (*Naut.*) amarré (*fixé*); bien fermé (*porte*); vite, rapide; en avance (*horloge etc.*); (*fig.*) dissolu; *to make fast*, assujettir, fermer (*porte, fenêtre*); (*Naut.*) amarrer.—adv. ferme (*stable*); vite, rapidement (*avec célérité*); fort (*pluie*); *to hold fast*, tenir bon; *to stand fast*, ne pas broncher.

fasten [fɑːsn], v.t. attacher, fixer; lier; fermer (*fenêtre, porte etc.*).—v.i. s'attacher (à); se fermer.

fastener ['fɑːsnə], **fastening** ['fɑːsniŋ], n. attache; agrafe (*de robe*); fermeture, f.

fastidious [fæs'tidiəs], a. difficile; dédaigneux; délicat; exigeant.

fastness ['fɑːstnis], n. fermeté; vitesse; place forte (*forteresse*); légèreté de conduite, f.

fat [fæt], a. gras; gros (*personne*); (*fig.*) riche, fertile.—n. gras, m.; graisse; (*fig.*) substance, f.; (*pl.*) matières grasses, f.pl.

fatal [feitl], a. fatal, funeste; mortel.

fatality [fə'tæliti], n. fatalité, f.; accident mortel, m.

fatally ['feitəli], adv. fatalement, mortellement.

fate [feit], n. destin, sort, m.

fated ['feitid], a. destiné.

fateful ['feitful], a. fatal; décisif.

fat-head ['fæthed], n. (*colloq.*) nigaud, m.

father ['fɑːðə], n. père, m.; (*pl.*) pères, ancêtres, aïeux, m.pl.; *godfather*, parrain, m.; *grandfather*, grand-père, m.; *stepfather*, beau-père, m.

father-in-law ['fɑːðərinlɔː], n. beau-père, m.

fatherland ['fɑːðəlænd], n. pays natal, m., patrie, f.

fatherly ['fɑːðəli], a. paternel, de père.

fathom ['fæðəm], n. toise; (*Naut.*) brasse (= 6 pieds = 1 m. 829); (*fig.*) portée, profondeur, f.—v.t. sonder; (*fig.*) approfondir.

fatigue [fə'tiːg], n. fatigue; (*Mil.*) corvée, f.—v.t. fatiguer, lasser.

fatiguing [fə'tiːgiŋ], a. fatigant.—pres.p. fatiguant.

fatten [fætn], v.t. engraisser; (*fig.*) enrichir.

fattening ['fætniŋ], a. engraissant.—n. engraissement, m.

fatty ['fæti], a. graisseux.

fatuous ['fætjuəs], a. sot; béat.

fatuousness ['fætjuəsnis], n. fatuité, f.

fault [fɔːlt], n. faute, f.; défaut, vice, m.; (*Geol.*) faille, f.

faultless ['fɔːltlis], a. sans défaut, sans faute, impeccable.

faultlessly ['fɔːltlisli], adv. irréprochablement.

faultlessness ['fɔːltlisnis], n. perfection, f.

faulty ['fɔːlti], a. fautif, blâmable, défectueux.

favor ['feivə], n. faveur, f., bonnes grâces, f.pl.; bienfait, m.; grâce (*permission*), f.;

couleurs, faveurs (*rubans*), f.pl.; (*Comm.*) honorée, f.—v.t. favoriser, honorer (*de*).

favorable ['feivərəbl], a. favorable.

favorably ['feivərəbli], adv. favorablement.

favorite ['feivərit], a. favori, préféré.—n. favori, m.

fawn [fɔːn], n. faon, m.—v.i. *to fawn upon*, caresser, flatter.

fawning ['fɔːniŋ], a. flatteur, servile.—n. caresse, flatterie, f.

fear [fiə], n. crainte, peur; inquiétude, f.; *for fear of*, de peur de.—v.t. craindre, redouter, avoir peur de.—v.i. craindre, avoir peur.

fearful ['fiəful], a. craintif, timide; terrible, affreux, effrayant.

fearless ['fiəlis], a. sans peur, intrépide.

fearlessly ['fiəlisli], adv. sans crainte, avec intrépidité.

feasible ['fiːzəbl], a. faisable, praticable.

feast [fiːst], n. festin, m.; fête, f.; régal, m.—v.t. fêter, régaler.—v.i. faire festin, se régaler.

feat [fiːt], n. exploit, fait, haut fait, m.

feather ['feðə], n. plume; penne (*aile et queue d'oiseau*), f.; (*Mil.*) plumet, m.—v.t. orner d'une plume; *to feather one's nest*, faire sa pelote.

feature ['fiːtʃə], n. trait, m. (*pl.*) visage, m. figure; (*fig.*) spécialité, f.

February ['februari], n. février, m.

feckless ['feklis], a. faible, veule.

fecundity [fə'kanditi], n. fécondité, f.

federal ['fedərəl], a. fédéral.

federate ['fedəriti], a. fédéré.—['fedəreit], v.t. fédérer.—v.i. se fédérer.

federation [fedə'reiʃən], n. fédération, f.

fee [fiː], n. honoraires, m.pl., cachet, salaire; (*Eccles.* etc.) droit, m.

feeble [fiːbl], a. faible; débile.

feebleness ['fiːblnis], n. faiblesse, f.

feebly ['fiːbli], adv. faiblement.

feed [fiːd], n. nourriture; pâture, f., pâturage (*pour bestiaux*), m.—v.t. irr. nourrir; donner à manger à; paître, faire paître (*bestiaux*); (*pop.*) *to be fed up*, en avoir marre.—v.i. se nourrir; paître (*animaux*).

feed-back ['fiːdbæk], n. (*Rad.*) rétro-action, f.

feeding ['fiːdiŋ], n. nourriture; pâture (*pour bestiaux*), f.

feeding bottle ['fiːdiŋbɔtl], n. biberon, m.

feel [fiːl], v.t. irr. tâter, toucher, sentir; éprouver; *to feel one's way*, avancer à tâtons.—v.i. sentir, se sentir; se trouver; *to feel cold*, avoir froid; *to feel like doing something*, avoir envie de faire quelque chose.—n. toucher; attouchement; tact, m.

feeler ['fiːlə], n. antenne (*d'insecte*), f.; (*fig.*) ballon d'essai, m.

feeling ['fiːliŋ], a. tendre, touchant.—n. toucher; sentiment, m. sensibilité, émotion, f.

feet [FOOT].

feign [fein], v.t. feindre, simuler.—v.i. feindre, faire semblant (*de*).

feigned [feind], a. feint, simulé.

feint [feint], n. feinte, f.—v.i. feinter.

felicitate [fi'lisiteit], v.t. féliciter.

felicitation [filisi'teiʃən], n. félicitation, f.

felicity [fi'lisiti], n. félicité, f., bonheur, m.

fell (1) [fel], v.t. abattre, assommer, terrasser.

fell (2) [fel], *past* [FALL].
fellow ['felou], *n.* compagnon, camarade, confrère; associé, membre; pendant, pareil (*choses*); (*colloq.*) garçon; individu, type, *m.*; *good fellow*, brave type.
fellow citizen ['felou'sitizn], *n.* concitoyen, *m.*
fellow countryman ['felou'kʌntrimən], *n.* (*pl. -men* [men]) compatriote, *m.*
fellow feeling ['felou'fi:liŋ], *n.* sympathie, *f.*
fellowship ['felouʃip], *n.* société, association; camaraderie, *f.*
fellow traveller ['felou'trævlə], *n.* compagnon de voyage; (*Polit.*) sympathisant communiste, communisant, *m.*
felon ['felən], *a.* félon, traître.—*n.* criminel, *m.*
felony ['feləni], *n.* crime, *m.*
felt (1) [felt], *n.* feutre, chapeau de feutre, *m.*; *roofing felt*, carton bitumé, *m.*
felt (2) [felt], *past* [FEEL].
female ['fi:meil], *a.* féminin, de femme; femelle (*animaux*); *a female friend*, une amie.—*n.* femme; jeune personne; femelle (*animaux*), *f.*
feminine ['feminin], *a.* féminin.
fen [fen], *n.* marais, marécage, *m.*
fence [fens], *n.* clôture, enceinte; palissade, barrière; (*Turf*) haie; (*Spt.*) escrime (à l'épée); (*slang*) défense. *f.*; (*slang*) receleur (*d'objets volés*), *m.*; *to sit on the fence*, (*fig.*) ne pas s'engager, ménager la chèvre et le chou.—*v.t.* enclore, mettre une clôture à, palissader; (*fig.*) protéger.—*v.i.* faire des armes.
fencing ['fensiŋ], *n.* (*Spt.*) escrime; enceinte, clôture, *f.*
fencing master ['fensiŋmɑːstə], *n.* maître d'armes, *m.*
fend [fend], *v.t. to fend off*, parer.—*v.i. to fend for oneself*, se débrouiller, veiller à ses intérêts.
fender ['fendə], *n.* garde-feu, *m.*; (*Naut.*) défense, *f.*; (*Am. Motor.*) pare-boue, *m.*
ferment ['fə:mənt], *n.* ferment, *m.*; fermentation, *f.*—[fə:'ment], *v.t.* faire fermenter.—*v.i.* fermenter.
fermentation [fə:mən'teiʃən], *n.* fermentation, *f.*
fern [fə:n], *n.* fougère, *f.*
ferocious [fə'rouʃəs], *a.* féroce.
ferociously [fə'rouʃəsli], *adv.* avec férocité.
ferocity [fə'rɔsiti], *n.* férocité, *f.*
ferret ['ferit], *n.* furet, *m.*—*v.t. to ferret out*, dépister, dénicher.
ferrule ['feru:l], *n.* virole (*anneau*), *f.*
ferry ['feri], *v.t.* passer en bac.—*n.* bac, passage, *m.*; *air ferry*, avion transbordeur, *m.*
ferry-boat ['feribout], *n.* bac, bateau transbordeur de trains, *m.*
fertile ['fə:tail], *a.* fertile, fécond.
fertility [fə'tiliti], *n.* fertilité, fécondité, *f.*
fertilize ['fə:tilaiz], *v.t.* fertiliser.
fertilizer ['fə:tilaizə], *n.* fertilisant, engrais, *m.*
fervent ['fə:vənt], *a.* ardent, fervent, vif.
fervently ['fə:vəntli], *adv.* ardemment, avec ferveur.
fester ['festə], *v.i.* s'ulcérer; (*fig.*) se corrompre.—*n.* abcès, *m.*, pustule, *f.*
festival ['festivl], *a.* de fête, joyeux.—*n.* fête, *f.*; (*Mus., Theat.*) festival, *m.*
festive ['festiv], *a.* de fête, joyeux.

festivity [fes'tiviti], *n.* fête, *f.*; réjouissances, *f.pl.*
festoon [fes'tu:n], *n.* feston, *m.*—*v.t.* festonner (*de*).
fetch [fetʃ], *v.t.* chercher, aller chercher; apporter (*choses*); amener (*personnes etc.*); rapporter (*prix*).—*n.* ruse, *f.*; tour, *m.*
fête [feit], *n.* fête, *f.*—*v.t.* fêter.
fetlock ['fetlɔk], *n.* fanon (*de cheval*), *m.*
fetter ['fetə], *v.t.* entraver, enchaîner.
fetters ['fetəz], *n.pl.* (*fig.*) fers, *m.pl.*, chaînes; entraves (*de cheval*), *f.pl.*
fettle [fetl], *v.t.* arranger, préparer.—*n.* bon état, *m.*
feud [fju:d], *n.* querelle; vendetta, *f.*
feudal ['fju:dl], *a.* féodal.
feudalism ['fju:dlizm], *n.* féodalité *f.*
fever ['fi:və], *n.* fièvre, *f.*
feverish ['fi:vəriʃ], *a.* fiévreux; (*fig.*) fébrile.
few [fju:], *a.* peu de; *a few*, quelques.—*n.* peu de gens, *m.pl.*; *a few*, quelques-uns, *m.pl.*, quelques-unes, *f.pl.*
fewer ['fju:ə], *a.* moins (*de*); moins nombreux.
fiasco [fi'æskou], *n.* fiasco, four, *m.*
fib [fib], *n.* petit mensonge, *m.*—*v.i.* mentir.
fibber ['fibə], *n.* menteur, *m.*
fibre ['faibə], *n.* fibre, *f.*
fibrositis [faibrə'saitis], *n.* (*Med.*) cellulite, *f.*
fibrous ['faibrəs], *a.* fibreux.
fickle [fikl], *a.* volage, inconstant.
fickleness ['fiklnis], *n.* inconstance, légèreté, *f.*
fiction ['fikʃən], *n.* fiction, *f.*; *works of fiction*, romans, *m.pl.*
fictitious [fik'tiʃəs], *a.* fictif, imaginaire; (*fig.*) faux, factice.
fiddle [fidl], *n.* violon; (*pej.*) crincrin, *m.*; (*pop.*) resquille, combine, *f.*—*v.i.* jouer du violon; (*fig.*) niaiser (*baguenauder*); (*pop.*) resquiller.
fiddler ['fidlə], *n.* joueur de violon; ménétrier, *m.*
fiddlesticks! ['fidlstiks], *int.* bah! quelle blague!
fidelity [fi'deliti], *n.* fidélité, *f.*
fidget ['fidʒit], *n.* agitation, *f.*; être remuant (*personne*), *m.*—*v.i.* se remuer, s'agiter.
fidgety ['fidʒiti], *a.* remuant, agité; ennuyeux (*gênant*).
field [fi:ld], *n.* champ; pré, *m.*, prairie; (*Mil.*) campagne, *f.*; champ de bataille, *m.*; (*Turf etc.*) courants, *m.pl.*; *in the scientific field*, dans le domaine des sciences.—*v.t.* (*Cricket*) arrêter (*une balle*); réunir (*équipe*).—*v.i.* (*Cricket*) tenir le champ.
field-day ['fi:lddei], *n.* (*Mil.*) jour de manœuvres; (*fig.*) jour de grand succès, *m.*
field marshal ['fi:ldmɑ:ʃl], *n.* maréchal, *m.*
fiend [fi:nd], *n.* démon, *m.*
fiendish ['fi:ndiʃ], *a.* diabolique, infernal.
fierce [fiəs], *a.* féroce, farouche, furieux.
fiercely ['fiəsli], *adv.* férocement, furieusement.
fierceness ['fiəsnis], *n.* violence, fureur, brutalité, *f.*; (*fig.*) acharnement, *m.*
fieriness ['faiərinis], *n.* fougue, ardeur, *f.*
fiery ['faiəri], *a.* de feu; (*fig.*) ardent, fougueux.
fife [faif], *n.* fifre, *m.*
fifteen [fif'ti:n], *a. and n.* quinze, *m.*
fifteenth [fif'ti:nθ], *a.* quinze (*jour du mois, roi etc.*).—*n.* quinzième (*fraction*), *m.*

425

fifth [fifθ], *a.* cinquième; cinq (*jour du mois, roi etc.*); **Charles the Fifth**, Charles-Quint.—*n.* cinquième (*fraction*), *m.*; (*Mus.*) quinte, *f.*

fiftieth ['fiftiəθ], *a.* cinquantième.—*n.* cinquantième (*fraction*), *m.*

fifty ['fifti], *a.* and *n.* cinquante, *m.*; **about fifty**, une cinquantaine.

fig [fig], *n.* figue, *f.*; figuier (*arbre*), *m.*

fight [fait], *v.t. irr.* se battre avec, combattre; livrer (*une bataille*).—*v.i.* se battre; combattre (*avec*).—*n.* combat, *m.*, bataille; (*fig.*) lutte, *f.*

fighter ['faitə], *n.* combattant, *m.*; (*pej.*) batailleur; (*Av.*) chasseur, *m.*

fighting ['faitiŋ], *n.* combat, *m.*; lutte, *f.*

figment ['figmənt], *n.* fiction, invention, *f.*

figurative ['figjuərətiv], *a.* figuré; figuratif.

figuratively ['figjuərətivli], *adv.* au figuré; figurativement.

figure ['figə], *n.* figure; taille, tournure (*d'une personne*), *f.*; dessin (*sur un tissu*) (*Arith.*) chiffre, *m.*; **figure of speech**, figure de rhétorique, métaphore; (*fam.*) façon de parler, *f.*; **to cut a figure**, faire figure.—*v.t.* figurer, former; façonner; (*fig.*) imaginer; **to figure out**, calculer.—*v.i.* figurer.

figure-head ['figəhed], *n.* (*Naut.*) figure de proue, *f.*; (*fig.*) homme de paille; prête-nom, *m.*

Fiji ['fi:dʒi:], **the Fiji Islands**, les îles Fidji *ou* Viti, *f.pl.*

filament ['filəmənt], *n.* filament, *m.*

filbert ['filbət], *n.* aveline, grosse noisette, *f.*

filch [filtʃ], *v.t.* escamoter, filouter, chiper.

file [fail], *n.* lime (*outil*), liasse, *f.*, dossier, classeur (*de papiers*), *m.*; liste; collection (*de journaux*); (*Mil.*) file; (*Theat. etc.*) queue, *f.*; **card-index file**, fichier, *m.*—*v.t.* limer, affiler; mettre en liasse; (*Law*) déposer (*une requête etc.*); **to file away**, classer.—*v.i.* (*Mil.*) marcher à la file; **to file off** or **past**, défiler.

filial ['filiəl], *a.* filial.

filibuster ['filibʌstə], *n.* flibustier, *m.*

filing ['failiŋ], *n.* limage, *m.*; mise en liasse, *f.*, classement, *m.*; (*pl.*) limaille, *f.*

filing cabinet ['failiŋkæbinit], *n.* cartonnier, classeur, *m.*

fill [fil], *v.t.* emplir, remplir; combler (*jusqu'au bord*); occuper; rassasier; **to fill a tooth**, plomber une dent.—*v.i.* se remplir, s'emplir.—*n.* suffisance, *f.*; (*colloq.*) **one's fill**, tout son soûl.

fillet ['filit], *n.* bandeau; filet (*de poisson*), *m.*

filling ['filiŋ], *a.* rassasiant.—*n.* plombage, *m.*

filling station ['filiŋ'steiʃən], *n.* poste d'essence, *m.*

filly ['fili], *n.* pouliche, *f.*

film [film], *n.* taie (*devant les yeux*), pellicule; (*Anat.*) tunique, *f.*; (*fig.*) nuage, voile, *m.*; (*Phot.*) pellicule, couche sensible, *f.*; (*Cine.*) film, *m.*; **film script**, scénario, script, *m.*; **film star**, vedette de cinéma, *f.*—*v.t.* couvrir d'une tunique, d'une pellicule etc.; filmer, mettre à l'écran.—*v.i.* tourner un film.

film-strip ['filmstrip], *n.* film fixe, *m.*

filter ['filtə], *n.* filtre, *m.*—*v.t.* filtrer.

filter tip ['filtə'tip], *n.* bout filtrant, *m.*

filth [filθ], *n.* ordure, saleté; (*fig.*) corruption, *f.*

filthy ['filθi], *a.* sale, immonde; (*fig.*) obscène, infect.

fin [fin], *n.* nageoire, *f.*; aileron (*de requin*), *m.*; (*Naut., Av.*) dérive; (*Motor.*) ailette (*de radiateur*), *f.*

final [fainl], *a.* final, dernier; décisif.—*n.* (*Spt.*) finale, *f.*

finally ['fainəli], *adv.* enfin, finalement; définitivement.

finance ['fainæns, fai'næns], *n.* finance, *f.*

financial [fai'nænʃəl], *a.* financier.

financier [fai'nænsiə], *n.* financier, *m.*

finch [fintʃ], *n.* (*Orn.*) pinson, *m.*

find [faind], *v.t. irr.* trouver; estimer; (*Law*) déclarer (*coupable*); prononcer (*un verdict*); (*fig.*) pourvoir; **to find out**, trouver, découvrir, inventer, résoudre; démasquer; **to find out about**, se renseigner sur; découvrir la vérité de.—*n.* découverte, trouvaille, *f.*

finding ['faindiŋ], *n.* (*Law*) verdict, *m.*

fine (1) [fain], *n.* amende, *f.*—*v.t.* mettre à l'amende.

fine (2) [fain], *a.* fin; raffiné; subtil; beau (*à voir*); (*fig.*) bon, accompli; (*colloq.*) fameux; **it is fine**, il fait beau (*temps*).

fine arts [fain'ɑ:ts], *n.pl.* beaux arts, *m.pl.*

finely ['fainli], *adv.* fin, délicatement; élégamment; (*colloq.*) bien; (*iron.*) joliment.

fineness ['fainnis], *n.* finesse, délicatesse, *f.*

finery ['fainəri], *n.* parure, *f.*, beaux habits, *m.pl.*

finesse [fi'nes], *n.* finesse, *f.*

finger ['fiŋgə], *n.* doigt, *m.*; (*fig.*) main, *f.*—*v.t.* toucher, manier.—*v.i.* (*Mus.*) doigter.

fingering ['fiŋgəriŋ], *n.* maniement; (*Mus.*) doigté, *m.*

finger-nail ['fiŋgəneil], *n.* ongle de la main, *m.*

finger-print ['fiŋgəprint], *n.* empreinte digitale, *f.*

finger-stall ['fiŋgəstɔ:l], *n.* doigtier, *m.*

finical ['finikl], **finicking** ['finikiŋ], (*colloq.*) **finicky** ['finiki], *a.* précieux, méticuleux, vétilleux.

finish ['finiʃ], *v.t.* finir, terminer; achever; (*Tech.*) usiner.—*v.i.* cesser, finir, prendre fin.—*n.* fini, *m.*; (*fig.*) fin; (*Spt.*) arrivée, *f.*

finished ['finiʃt], *a.* fini; (*fig.*) parfait.

finishing ['finiʃiŋ], *a.* dernier; (*Spt.*) **finishing line**, ligne d'arrivée, *f.*

finite ['fainait], *a.* fini; borné.

Finland ['finlənd], la Finlande, *f.*

Finn [fin], *n.* Finlandais, Finnois, *m.*

Finnish ['finiʃ], *a.* finlandais.—*n.* finnois (*langue*), *m.*

fir [fə:], *n.* sapin; bois de sapin, *m.*

fir cone ['fə:koun], *n.* pomme de pin, *f.*

fire [faiə], *n.* feu; incendie (*accidentel*), *m.*; (*fig.*) ardeur, *f.*; **fire!** au feu! **to be on fire**, être en feu; **to catch fire**, prendre feu; **to hang fire**, faire long feu; **to miss fire**, rater; **to set on fire**, **to set fire to**, mettre le feu à.—*v.t.* mettre le feu à; embraser, incendier; tirer (*fusil*); (*pop.*) renvoyer.—*v.i.* prendre feu; tirer; (*Motor.*) donner; **fire!** (*Mil.*) feu!

fire alarm ['faiərəlɑ:m], *n.* avertisseur d'incendie, *m.*

fire-arms ['faiərɑ:mz], *n.pl.* armes à feu, *f.pl.*

fire brigade ['faiəbrigeid], *n.* (corps de) sapeurs pompiers, *m.*

fire engine ['faiərendʒin], *n.* pompe à incendie, *f.*

fire escape ['faiəriskeip], *n.* échelle de sauvetage, *f.*

fire extinguisher ['faiərikstiŋwiʃə], *n.* extincteur, *m.*

fire-fly ['faiəflai], *n.* luciole, *f.*

fire-guard ['faiəgɑ:d], *n.* garde-feu, *m.*

fireman ['faiəmən], *n.* (*pl.* -men [men]) pompier, *m.*

fireplace ['faiəpleis], *n.* cheminée, *f.*, foyer, âtre, *m.*

fireproof ['faiəpru:f], *a.* incombustible, ignifuge.

fireside ['faiəsaid], *n.* coin du feu; (*fig.*) foyer domestique, *m.*

fire station ['faiəsteiʃən], *n.* caserne de pompiers, *f.*

fireworks ['faiəwə:ks], *n.pl.* feu d'artifice, *m.*

firing ['faiəriŋ], *n.* action d'incendier, *f.*; chauffage (*heating*), *m.*; cuisson (*de poterie etc.*), *f.*; combustible (*fuel*); (*Mil.*) feu, tir, *m.*, fusillade, *f.*

firm [fə:m], *a.* ferme, solide; constant.—*n.* maison de commerce, raison sociale, firme, *f.*

firmament ['fə:məmənt], *n.* firmament, *m.*

firmly ['fə:mli], *adv.* fermement, solidement.

firmness ['fə:mnis], *n.* fermeté, solidité, *f.*

first [fə:st], *a.* premier; (*in compounds*) unième; **twenty-first**, vingt et unième.—*n.* (le) premier, *m.*, (la) première, *f.*—*adv.* premièrement; **at first**, d'abord.

first aid ['fə:st'eid], *n.* premiers secours, *m.pl.*; **first-aid post**, poste de secours, *m.*

first-born ['fə:stbɔ:n], *a.* premier-né, aîné.

first-class ['fə:st'klɑ:s], **first-rate** ['fə:st'reit], *a.* de premier ordre; de premier choix; (*colloq.*) de première force; **first-class compartment**, compartiment de première classe, *m.*

firth [fə:θ], *n.* (*Sc.*) estuaire, *m.*

fiscal ['fiskəl], *a.* fiscal.

fiscally ['fiskəli], *adv.* fiscalement.

fish [fiʃ], *n.* poisson, *m.*; **a pretty kettle of fish**, un beau gâchis; **a queer fish**, un drôle de type.—*v.t.* pêcher.—*v.i.* pêcher; **to fish for**, pêcher; (*fig.*) rechercher, quêter.

fish bone ['fiʃboun], *n.* arête, *f.*

fisher ['fiʃə], **fisherman** ['fiʃəmən] (*pl.* -men [men]), *n.* pêcheur, *m.*

fishery ['fiʃəri], *n.* pêche; pêcherie, *f.*

fish-hook ['fiʃhuk], *n.* hameçon, *m.*

fishing ['fiʃiŋ], *n.* pêche, *f.*; **to go fishing**, aller à la pêche.

fishing boat ['fiʃiŋbout], *n.* bateau de pêche, *m.*

fishing rod ['fiʃiŋrɔd], *n.* canne à pêche, *f.*

fish knife ['fiʃnaif], *n.* couteau à poisson, *m.*

fishmonger ['fiʃmʌŋgə], *n.* marchand de poisson, *m.*

fish-slice ['fiʃslais], *n.* truelle à poisson, *f.*

fishy ['fiʃi], *a.* de poisson, poissonneux; qui sent le poisson; (*slang*) louche, véreux.

fission ['fiʃən], *n.* (*Biol.*) fissiparité; (*Phys.*) fission, désintégration, *f.*; **nuclear fission**, fission nucléaire.

fissure ['fiʃə], *n.* fissure, fente, *f.*

fist [fist], *n.* poing, *m.*

fisted ['fistid], *a.* **close-fisted**, avare, dur à la détente.

fisticuffs ['fistikʌfs], *n.pl.* coups de poing, *m.pl.*

fit (1) [fit], *n.* accès (*de colère etc.*), *m.*; attaque (*de maladie*); convulsion, *f.*; **by fits and starts**, à bâtons rompus, par accès.

fit (2) [fit], *a.* propre, bon, convenable (*à*); juste, à propos; capable (*de*); en bonne santé, en forme; **to think fit**, juger convenable, juger bon.—*n.* ajustement (*de vêtements*), *m.*; (*fig.*) coupe, forme, *f.*—*v.t.* convenir à; aller à (*vêtements*); habiller; adapter, ajuster; **to fit out**, équiper, monter, armer (*un navire*).—*v.i.* convenir; s'adapter (*à*), aller bien (*vêtements*); **to fit in with**, s'accorder avec.

fitful ['fitful], *a.* agité; capricieux; irrégulier.

fitfully ['fitfuli], *adv.* par boutades; irrégulièrement.

fitly ['fitli], *adv.* à propos, convenablement.

fitness ['fitnis], *n.* convenance, *f.*; à-propos, *m.*; **physical fitness**, bonne forme, *f.*

fitter ['fitə], *n.* ajusteur; (*Dress.*) essayeur, *m.*

fitting ['fitiŋ], *a.* convenable, à propos, juste.—*n.* ajustement, essayage, *m.*, (*pl.*) garniture, *f.*

five [faiv], *a.* and *n.* cinq, *m.*

fix [fiks], *v.t.* fixer, attacher, arrêter, établir; (*colloq.*) réparer.—*v.i.* se fixer.—*n.* difficulté, impasse, *f.*, embarras, *m.*

fixation [fik'seiʃən], *n.* fixation, *f.*

fixed [fikst], *a.* fixe, fixé.

fixedly ['fiksidli], *adv.* fixement.

fixture ['fikstʃə], *n.* meuble à demeure, *m.*, agencements fixes, *m.pl.*; match, engagement (*prévu, annoncé*), *m.*

fizzy ['fizi], *a.* gazeux (*limonade etc.*), mousseux (*vin*).

flabby ['flæbi], *a.* flasque; mollasse (*personne*).

flag (1) [flæg], *v.i.* pendre mollement; se relâcher, faiblir; s'affaisser.

flag (2) [flæg], *n.* drapeau; (*Naut.*) pavillon; iris (*plante*); carreau, *m.*, dalle (*pierre*), *f.*—*v.t.* paver, dalleur; pavoiser.

flag day ['flægdei], *n.* jour de quête, *m.*

flag officer ['flægɔfisə], *n.* chef d'escadre, *m.*

flagon ['flægən], *n.* flacon, *m.*; burette (*d'église*), *f.*

flagrancy ['fleigrənsi], *n.* énormité, notoriété, *f.*

flagrant ['fleigrənt], *a.* flagrant, notoire, énorme.

flag-ship ['flægʃip], *n.* vaisseau amiral, *m.*

flagstaff ['flægstɑ:f], *n.* mât de pavillon, *m.*

flagstone ['flægstoun], *n.* dalle, *f.*

flail [fleil], *n.* fléau, *m.*

flair [flɛə], *n.* perspicacité, *f.*, flair, *m.*; aptitude (*à*), *f.*

flake [fleik], *n.* flocon, *m.*; écaille; étincelle, *f.*—*v.t.* former en flocons, écailler.—*v.i.* s'écailler.

flaky ['fleiki], *a.* floconneux; écaillé; feuilleté (*pâtisserie*).

flame [fleim], *n.* flamme, *f.*; feu, *m.*—*v.i.* flamber.

flaming ['fleimiŋ], *a.* flamboyant, flambant; (*fig.*) violent, ardent; (*pop.*) sacré.

flamingo [flə'miŋgou], *n.* (*Orn.*) flamant, *m.*

flan [flæn], *n.* flan, *m.*

Flanders ['flɑ:ndəz], la Flandre, *f.*

flange [flændʒ], *n.* bride, *f.*, rebord (*d'un tube etc.*); (*Tech.*) boudin (*de roue*), *m.*; (*Motor.*) ailette, collerette, *f.*

flank [flæŋk], *n.* flanc; côté, *m.*—*v.t.* flanquer (*de*); (*Mil.*) prendre en flanc.—*v.i.* border.

flannel [flænl], *a.* de flanelle.—*n.* flanelle, *f.*; (*pl.*) pantalon de flanelle, *m.*

flap [flæp], *v.t.* frapper légèrement; battre, agiter.—*v.i.* battre légèrement; (*fig.*, *pop.*) s'affoler.—*n.* battement (*d'aile*); claquement (*de voile*); petit coup (*de la main*), *m.*, tape, *f.*; battant (*d'une table etc.*), *m.*; patte (*d'une poche*), *f.*, pan (*d'un habit*); rabat (*d'une enveloppe*); (*fig.*, *pop.*) affolement, *m.*

flare [flɛə], *v.i.* flamboyer; s'évaser (*jupe*); **to flare up**, flamber; (*fig.*) se mettre en colère.—*n.* flamme, *f.*; (*Av.*) brûlot, *m.*

flash [flæʃ], *n.* éclair, éclat, jet de lumière; (*fig.*) trait; (*Mil.*) écusson, *m.*—*v.t.* faire jaillir, lancer.—*v.i.* luire, éclater, étinceler.

flashy ['flæʃi], *a.* voyant, clinquant; superficiel.

flask [flɑːsk], *n.* flacon, *m.*, gourde, *f.*

flat [flæt], *a.* plat; étendu (*à terre*); éventé (*vin etc.*); (*Comm.*) languissant; (*Mus.*) bémol; grave (*son*); (*fig.*) net, clair; fade, insipide (*goût*).—*n.* surface plane, *f.*; étage (*d'une maison*), appartement; (*Mus.*) bémol; (*Theat.*) châssis, *m.*

flat-iron ['flætaiən], *n.* fer à repasser, *m.*

flatly ['flætli], *adv.* à plat; (*fig.*) nettement, clairement.

flatten [flætn], *v.t.* aplatir, aplanir; éventer (*boisson alcoolique*); (*fig.*) abattre, attrister; (*Mus.*) rendre grave.—*v.i.* s'aplatir; s'éventer (*boisson alcoolique*).

flatter ['flætə], *v.t.* flatter.

flatterer ['flætərə], *n.* flatteur, *m.*

flattering ['flætəriŋ], *a.* flatteur.

flattery ['flætəri], *n.* flatterie, *f.*

flatulence ['flætjuləns], *n.* flatuosité; flatulence, *f.*

flatulent ['flætjulənt], *a.* flatueux.

flaunt [flɔːnt], *v.t.* faire parade de, étaler, déployer.—*v.i.* se pavaner, parader, flotter.—*n.* étalage, *m.*, parade, *f.*

flavor ['fleivə], *n.* saveur, *f.*; goût, fumet (*de viande*); arome (*de thé, café etc.*); bouquet (*de vin*), *m.*—*v.t.* donner du goût, un arome etc. à, assaisonner (*de*).

flavoring ['fleivəriŋ], *n.* assaisonnement, *m.*

flaw [flɔː], *n.* défaut, *m.*; félure; brèche, fente; paille (*de pierres précieuses*), *f.*

flawless ['flɔːlis], *a.* parfait, sans défaut.

flax [flæks], *a.* de lin.—*n.* lin, *m.*

flaxen ['flæksən], *a.* de lin; blond filasse (*cheveux*).

flay [flei], *v.t.* écorcher.

flaying ['fleiiŋ], *n.* écorchement, *m.*

flea [fliː], *n.* puce, *f.*

fleck [flek], *n.* tache, moucheture, marque, *f.*—*v.t.* moucheter, tacheter (*de*).

fledge(e)ling ['fledʒliŋ], *n.* oisillon, *m.*

flee [fliː], *v.t. irr.* fuir, éviter.—*v.i.* s'enfuir, se réfugier.

fleece [fliːs], *n.* toison, *f.*—*v.t.* tondre; (*fig.*) écorcher, plumer.

fleecy ['fliːsi], *a.* laineux, (*fig.*) floconneux.

fleet (1) [fliːt], *n.* flotte, *f.*; **the Home Fleet**, la flotte métropolitaine.

fleet (2) [fliːt], *a.* vite, rapide, leste.

fleeting ['fliːtiŋ], *a.* fugitif, passager.

Fleming ['flemiŋ], *n.* Flamand, *m.*

Flemish ['flemiʃ], *a.* flammand.—*n.* flamand (*langue*).

flesh [fleʃ], *n.* chair; viande (*meat*), *f.*; **in the flesh**, en chair et en os; **to put on flesh**, s'empâter, prendre de l'embonpoint.—*v.t.* (*Hunt.*) acharner; écharner (*peaux*).

fleshy ['fleʃi], *a.* charnu.

flex (1) [fleks], *n.* fil électrique, *m.*

flex (2) [fleks], *v.t.* fléchir.

flexibility [fleksi'biliti], *n.* flexibilité, souplesse, *f.*

flexible ['fleksibl], *a.* flexible, souple.

flick [flik], *n.* petit coup (*de fouet, de torchon*), *m.*; chiquenaude, *f.*; (*pl.*) (*pop.*) ciné, *m.*—*v.t.* effleurer; donner une chiquenaude à.

flicker ['flikə], *v.i.* trembloter, vaciller (*lumière*); ciller (*paupières*).

flickering ['flikəriŋ], *a.* vacillant, clignotant.—*n.* trémoussement; clignement, *m.*, vacillation, *f.*

flight [flait], *n.* vol, *m.*, volée (*d'oiseaux etc.*); fuite, *f.*; (*fig.*) élan, *m.*; (*Av.*) escadrille, *f.*; **flight of stairs**, escalier, *m.*; **flight of steps**, perron, *m.*; **in flight**, en déroute.

flightiness ['flaitinis], *n.* légèreté, étourderie, *f.*

flighty ['flaiti], *a.* étourdi, léger; volage.

flimsiness ['flimzinis], *n.* légèreté (*fig.*) mesquinerie, *f.*

flimsy ['flimzi], *a.* mollasse, léger, sans consistance.

flinch [flintʃ], *v.i.* reculer, céder.

fling [fliŋ], *v.t. irr.* jeter, lancer.—*n.* coup (*lancé*), *m.*; ruade (*de cheval*), *f.*; pas seul (*danse écossaise*); (*fig.*) essai; trait, coup de patte, *m.*, raillerie, *f.*

flint [flint], *n.* silex, *m.*, pierre à briquet; (*fig.*) roche, dureté, *f.*

flip [flip], *n.* petit coup, *m.*, chiquenaude, *f.*; flip (*boisson*), *m.*

flippancy ['flipənsi], *n.* ton léger; bavardage, *m.*

flippant ['flipənt], *a.* léger; désinvolte; cavalier (*manières, mine*).

flipper ['flipə], *n.* nageoire, *f.*

flirt [fləːt], *v.i.* faire la coquette, flirter (*femme*); conter fleurette (*homme*).—*n.* coquette, *f.*

flirtation [fləːˈteiʃən], *n.* coquetterie, *f.*, flirt, *m.*

flit [flit], *v.i.* fuir, voltiger; (*Sc.*) déménager.—*n.* **to do a moonlight flit**, déménager à la cloche de bois.

float [flout], *v.t.* faire flotter, (*fig.*) lancer.—*v.i.* flotter, surnager; **to float on one's back**, faire la planche.—*n.* train (*bois*); flotteur; char (*carnaval*), *m.*

floating ['floutiŋ], *a.* flottant; **floating capital**, fonds de roulement, *m.*; **floating dock**, bassin à flot, *m.*

flock [flɔk], *n.* troupeau, *m.*; bande, troupe, *f.*; ouailles (*paroissiens*), *f.pl.*; flocon, *m.*, bourre (*de laine etc.*), *f.*—*v.i.* s'attrouper, s'assembler.

floe [flou], *n.* nappe de glaçons flottants; banquise, *f.*

flog [flɔg], *v.t.* fouetter, flageller; (*pop.*) bazarder.

flogging ['flɔgiŋ], *n.* fouet, *m.*; flagellation, *f.*

flood [flʌd], *n.* déluge, *m.*; inondation, crue, *f.*; (*fig.*) cours d'eau, torrent, *m.*; marée, *f.*—*v.t.* inonder, submerger, noyer.

flood-light ['flʌdlait], *n.* projecteur, *m.*—*v.t.* illuminer (*un monument*) avec des projecteurs.

flood tide ['flʌdtaid], *n.* marée montante, *f.*

floor [flɔ:], *n.* plancher; carreau, parquet (*pavage*); étage (*storey*), *m.*—*v.t.* planchéier, parqueter; (*fig.*) terrasser, réduire au silence.

flooring ['flɔ:riŋ], *n.* plancher, parquet, *m.*

floorwalker, see **shop-walker**.

flop [flɔp], *int.* plouf!—*n.* (*Theat.*) four, *m.*

floral ['flɔ:rəl, 'flɔ:rəl], *a.* floral; *floral games*, jeux floraux, *m.pl.*

Florence ['flɔrəns]. Florence, *f.*

florid ['flɔrid], *a.* fleuri.

Florida ['flɔridə]. la Floride, *f.*

florist ['flɔrist], *n.* fleuriste, *m., f.*

floss [flɔs], *n.* bourre (*de soie*), *f.*; (*Metal.*) floss; (*Bot.*) duvet, *m.*

flotilla [flo'tilə], *n.* flottille, *f.*

flounder (1) ['flaundə], *n.* (*Ichth.*) flet, pétit flétan, *m.*

flounder (2) ['flaundə], *v.i.* se débattre; patauger.

flour ['flauə] *n.* farine; fécule (*des pommes de terre etc.*), *f.*

flourish ['flʌriʃ], *n.* éclat, *m.*; fleur de rhétorique, *f.*; panache (*manières, geste*); moulinet, tour, *m.*; (*Mus.*) fioriture; fanfare (*trompettes*), *f.*; (*Fenc.*) fleuret; brandir (*épée etc.*).—*v.i.* fleurir; parafer; brandir (*épée etc.*).—*v.i.* fleurir; venir bien (*plantes*); prospérer.

flourishing ['flʌriʃiŋ], *a.* florissant.

flout [flaut], *v.t.* railler; se moquer de.—*n.* moquerie, raillerie, *f.*

flow [flou], *v.i.* s'écouler, couler; monter (*marée*); (*fig.*) découler (*de*).—*n.* écoulement; flux; (*fig.*) épanchement, *m.*

flower ['flauə], *n.* fleur; (*fig.*) élite, *f.*—*v.i.* fleurir, être en fleur.

flower-bed ['flauəbed], *n.* plate-bande, *f.*, parterre, *m.*

flowered ['flauəd], *a.* figuré; fleuri.

flower garden ['flauəgɑ:dn], *n.* jardin d'agrément, *m.*

flower-pot ['flauəpɔt], *n.* pot à fleurs, *m.*

flowing ['flouiŋ], *a.* coulant; (*fig.*) naturel.—*n.* cours, écoulement, *m.*

flown [floun], *a.* envolé; *high-flown*, gonflé, outré (*style*).

flu [flu:], (*colloq.*) [INFLUENZA].

fluctuate ['flʌktjueit], *v.i.* balancer, flotter, varier.

fluctuating ['flʌktjueitiŋ], *a.* flottant; incertain; variable.

fluctuation [flʌktju'eiʃən], *n.* fluctuation, *f.*; (*fig.*) balancement, doute, *m.*

flue [flu:], *n.* tuyau de cheminée; carneau (*d'un fourneau*), *m.*

fluency ['flu:ənsi], *n.* facilité (*de parole*), *f.*

fluent ['flu:ənt], *a.* coulant, courant; facile.

fluently ['flu:əntli], *adv.* couramment, avec facilité.

fluff [flʌf], *n.* duvet, *m.*, peluches, *f.pl.*

fluid ['flu:id], *a.* and *n.* fluide, liquide, *m.*

fluke [flu:k], *n.* patte (*d'ancre*), *f.*; carrelet (*poisson*); (*fig.*) coup de raccroc, *m.*

flunkey ['flʌŋki], *n.* laquais, (*colloq.*) sycophante, *m.*

flurry ['flʌri], *n.* agitation, *f.*, désordre, émoi, *m.*—*v.t.* agiter, ahurir.

flush [flʌʃ], *a.* frais, plein de vigueur; à fleur, au ras (*de niveau*); *flush with the ground*, à ras de terre.—*n.* rougeur, *f.*; transport, *m.*; chasse d'eau, *f.*; (*Cards*), flush, *m.*—*v.t.* faire rougir; laver à grande eau; (*Hunt.*) lever; (*fig.*) animer.—*v.i.* rougir; partir tout à coup.

fluster ['flʌstə], *v.t.* déconcerter, agiter, ahurir.—*n.* agitation, *f.*

flute [flu:t], *n.* flûte, *f.*

fluted ['flu:tid], *a.* cannelé.

flutter ['flʌtə], *n.* trémoussement, émoi, *m.*; agitation, *f.*; battement d'ailes, *m.*—*v.t.* mettre en désordre, agiter, ahurir.—*v.i.* battre des ailes; s'agiter; palpiter.

flux [flʌks], *n.* flux, courant; (*Metal.*) fondant, *f.*

fly (1) [flai], *n.* (*pl.* **flies** [flaiz]) (*Ent.*) mouche, *f.*

fly (2) [flai], *v.t. irr.* faire voler; fuir, éviter.—*v.i.* voler, s'envoler, se sauver, prendre la fuite, fuir s'enfuir; *to fly into a passion*, s'emporter, se mettre en colère; *to fly over*, survoler.—*a.* (*pop.*) malin.

flyer ['flaiə], *n.* aviateur, *m.*

flying ['flaiiŋ], *a.* volant; *flying squad*, brigade mobile, *f.*

flying boat ['flaiiŋbout], *n.* hydravion, *m.*

flying buttress ['flaiiŋbʌtris], *n.* arc-boutant, *m.*

fly-over ['flaiouvə], *n.* enjambement, *m.*

fly-paper ['flaipeipə], *n.* papier tue-mouches, *m.*

fly-past ['flaipɑ:st], *n.* défilé aérien, *m.*

foal [foul], *n.* poulain, *m.*, pouliche, *f.*—*v.i.* pouliner, mettre bas.

foam [foum], *n.* écume; bave; mousse, *f.*—*v.i.* écumer; moutonner (*mer*); baver (*animaux*).

foaming ['foumiŋ], *a.* écumant.

fob [fɔb], *n.* gousset (*de pantalon*), *m.*—*v.t.* (*fam.*) *to fob someone off with something*, refiler quelque chose à quelqu'un.

fo'c'sle ['fouksl], [FORECASTLE].

focus ['foukəs], *n.* (*pl.* **foci** ['fousai], **focuses** ['foukəsiz]) foyer, *m.*—*v.t.* mettre au point.

fodder ['fɔdə], *n.* fourrage, *m.*, pâture, *f.*; *cannon fodder*, chair à canon, *f.*

foe [fou], *n.* ennemi, adversaire, *m.*

fog [fɔg], *n.* brouillard, *m.*; (*fig.*) perplexité, *f.*; *sea fog*, brume, *f.*

fog-bound ['fɔgbaund], *a.* enveloppé de brouillard; arrêté par le brouillard.

foggy ['fɔgi], *a.* brumeux; (*fig.*) sombre; *it is foggy*, il fait du brouillard.

fogy, fogey ['fougi], *n.* ganache, vieille perruque, *f.*

foil [fɔil], *n.* feuille de métal, *f.*; tain (*de miroir*), *m.*; défaite, *f.*, échec (*check*); contraste, repoussoir (*set off*); (*Fenc.*) fleuret, *m.*—*v.t.* déjouer, faire échouer; frustrer.

fold (1) [fould], *v.t.* plier, ployer; envelopper; serrer; *to fold one's arms*, croiser les bras.—*n.* pli, repli, *m.*; *threefold*, triple; *twofold*, double.

fold (2) [fould], *n.* parc (*à moutons*), *m.*, bergerie, *f.*—*v.t. to fold sheep*, parquer des moutons.

folder ['fouldə], *n.* chemise (*à documents*), *f.*; dépliant, prospectus, *m.*

folding ['fouldiŋ], *a.* pliant; brisé, à deux battants (*porte*).
foliage ['fouliidʒ], *n.* feuillage, *m.*
folio ['fouliou], *n.* in-folio, *m.*; page, *f.*, folio, *m.*
folk(s) [fouk(s)], *n.* (*pl.*) gens, *m.pl.*, *f.pl.*, personnes, *f.pl.*
folklore ['fouklɔː], *n.* folklore, *m.*, légendes, traditions populaires, *f.pl.*
folk song ['fouksɔŋ], *n.* chanson populaire, *f.*
follow ['folou], *v.t.* suivre; poursuivre; observer, imiter; exercer (*une profession*).—*v.i.* s'ensuivre, résulter; *as follows*, comme suit.
follower ['folouə], *n.* suivant; partisan; compagnon; (*colloq.*) amoureux, *m.*
following ['folouiŋ], *a.* suivant.—*n.* suite, *f.*, parti, *m.*
folly ['foli], *n.* folie, sottise, bêtise, *f.*
foment [fo'ment], *v.t.* fomenter.
fond [fond], *a.* passionné (*pour*); fou (*de*); indulgent (*pour*); doux, cher (*espoir*); vain, sot; *to be* (*passionately*) *fond of*, aimer (à la folie).
fondle [fondl], *v.t.* câliner, caresser.
fondly ['fondli], *adv.* tendrement.
fondness ['fondnis], *n.* tendresse; affection, *f.*; penchant, goût, *m.*
font [font], *n.* fonts baptismaux, *m.pl.*
food [fuːd], *n.* nourriture, *f.*, aliment *m.*; vivres, *m.pl.*; denrées, *f.pl.*; pâture (*pour animaux*), *f.*
food-stuffs ['fuːdstʌfs], *n.pl.* comestibles, *m.pl.*
fool [fuːl], *n.* sot; insensé, imbécile, niais, *m.*; dupe, *f.*, fou (*bouffon*), *m.*; *to make a fool of*, se moquer de; *to make a fool of oneself*, se rendre ridicule, se faire moquer de soi.—*v.t.* duper; (*colloq.*) se moquer de.—*v.i.* faire la bête; *you are fooling*, vous plaisantez; vous blaguez.
foolery ['fuːləri], *n.* folie, sottise; niaiserie, *f.*
foolhardy ['fuːlhɑːdi], *a.* téméraire.
foolish ['fuːliʃ], *a.* sot insensé, bête, ridicule.
foolishly ['fuːliʃli], *adv.* follement, sottement.
foolishness ['fuːliʃnis], *n.* folie, sottise, *f.*
foolproof ['fuːlpruːf], *a.* indéréglable.
foot [fut], *n.* (*pl.* **feet** [fiːt]) pied, *m.*; patte (*d' insectes etc.*); base (*de colonne*), *f.*; bas (*d'une page*), *m.*; (*Mil.*) infanterie, *f.*; *on foot*, à pied.
football ['futbɔːl], *n.* ballon; football (*jeu*), *m.*
foot-bridge ['futbridʒ], *n.* passerelle, *f.*
footfall ['futfɔːl], *n.* pas, bruit de pas, *m.*
foothold ['futhould], *n.* prise pour le pied, *f.*; (*fig.*) point d'appui, *m.*
footing ['futiŋ], *n.* pied, point d'appui; établissement, *m.*; position, *f.*; *on an equal footing*, sur un pied d'égalité.
footlights ['futlaits], *n.pl.* (*Theat.*) rampe, *f.*
footman ['futmən], *n.* (*pl.* **-men** [men]) laquais, valet de pied, *m.*
footnote ['futnout], *n.* note au bas de la page, apostille, *f.*
foot-path ['futpɑːθ], *n.* sentier; trottoir (*de rue*), *m.*
foot-print ['futprint] *n.* empreinte du pied, *f.*
foot soldier ['futsouldʒə], *n.* fantassin, *m.*
footstep ['futstep], *n.* pas, *m.*; trace, *f.*; vestige, *m.*
footstool ['futstuːl], *n.* tabouret, *m.*
footwear ['futwɛə], *n.* chaussures, *f.pl.*

fop [fɔp], *n.* fat, *m.*
foppery ['fɔpəri], *n.* affectation, fatuité, *f.*
foppish ['fɔpiʃ], *a.* affecté sot, fat.
for [fɔː], *prep.* pour, par; de, à, vers, pendant; depuis; en place de, en lieu de; en faveur de; à cause de, pour le compte de; malgré; pour avoir; pour que (*with subj.*).—*conj.* car.
forage ['fɔridʒ], *n.* fourrage, *m.*—*v.i.* fourrager.
*****forasmuch** [fɔrəz'mʌtʃ], *conj.* **forasmuch as**, d'autant que, vu que.
foray ['fɔrei], *n.* incursion, razzia, *f.*, raid, *m.*
forbear (1) [FOREBEAR].
forbear (2) [fɔː'bɛə], *v.t.* *irr.* cesser; épargner, supporter.—*v.i.* s'abstenir, se garder (*de*).
forbearance [fɔː'bɛərəns], *n.* patience; indulgence, *f.*
forbid [fɔ'bid], *v.t.* *irr.* défendre, interdire (*de*); empêcher (*de*); *God forbid !* à Dieu ne plaise!
forbidding [fɔ'bidiŋ], *a.* rebutant, repoussant.
force [fɔːs], *n.* force; violence; efficacité; valeur, *f.*; (*Mil.*, *pl.*) forces, *f.pl.*, armée, *f.*; *in force*, (*Law*) en vigueur.—*v.t.* forcer, contraindre (*à ou de*); violenter.
forced [fɔːst], *a.* forcé, contraint; guindé (*style*).
forcedly ['fɔːsidli], *adv.* de force.
forceps ['fɔːseps], *n.pl.* (*Surg.*) pince, *f.*, forceps, *m.*
forcible ['fɔːsibl], **forceful** ['fɔːsful], *a.* fort; énergique.
forcibly ['fɔːsibli], *adv.* par force; fortement.
ford [fɔːd], *n.* gué, *m.*—*v.t.* passer à gué, guéer.
fore! (1) [fɔː], *int.* (*Golf*) gare devant!
fore (2) [fɔː], *a.* antérieur; de devant; (*Naut.*) de misaine; *fore and aft*, (*Naut.*) de l'avant à l'arrière.—*adv.* d'avance; (*Naut.*) de l'avant.
forearm (1) [fɔːr'ɑːm], *v.t.* prémunir.
forearm (2) ['fɔːrɑːm], *n.* avant-bras, *m.*
forebear ['fɔːbɛə], *n.* aïeul, ancêtre, *m.*
forebode [fɔː'boud], *v.t.* présager, prédire, pressentir.
foreboding [fɔː'boudiŋ], *n.* présage, pressentiment, *m.*
forecast ['fɔːkɑːst], *n.* prévoyance, prévision, *f.*; pronostic, *m.*; *weather forecast*, prévisions météorologiques, *f.pl.*—*v.t.* prévoir; pronostiquer.
forecastle [fouksl, 'fɔːkɑːsl], *n.* gaillard d'avant, *m.*
fore-court ['fɔːkɔːt], *n.* avant-cour, *f.*
forefather ['fɔːfɑːðə], *n.* aïeul, ancêtre, *m.*
forefinger ['fɔːfiŋgə], *n.* index, *m.*
forego [fɔː'gou], *v.t.* précéder, aller devant.
foregone [fɔː'gɔːn], *a.* prévu, résolu, décidé d'avance.
foreground ['fɔːgraund], *n.* premier plan, *m.*
forehead ['fɔrid], *n.* front, *m.*
foreign ['fɔrin], *a.* étranger; *Foreign Office*, Ministère des Affaires Étrangères, *m.*
foreigner ['fɔrinə], *n.* étranger, *m.*
foreland ['fɔːland], *n.* promontoire, cap, *m.*
foreleg ['fɔːleg], *n.* patte de devant, *f.*
forelock ['fɔːlɔk], *n.* goupille, *f.*; toupet, *m.*
foreman ['fɔːmən], *n.* (*pl.* **-men** [men]) chef (*d'un jury*); contremaître; chef d'atelier *ou* d'équipe; brigadier, *m.*
foremast ['fɔːmɑːst], *n.* mât de misaine, *m.*

foremost ['fɔ:moust], *a.* premier; en tête, au premier rang; *first and foremost*, tout d'abord.

forenoon ['fɔːˈnuːn], *n.* matin, *m.*, matinée, *f.*

forensic [fɔˈrensik], *a.* **forensic medicine**, médecine légale, *f.*

forerunner ['fɔːrʌnə], *n.* précurseur, *m.*

foresee [fɔːˈsiː], *v.t. irr. (conjug. like* SEE) prévoir.

foreseeable [fɔːˈsiːəbl], *a.* prévisible.

foreshore ['fɔːʃɔː], *n.* plage, *f.*

foreshorten [fɔːˈʃɔːtn], *v.t. (Paint.)* dessiner en raccourci.

foreshortening [fɔːˈʃɔːtniŋ], *n.* raccourci, *m.*

foresight ['fɔːsait], *n.* prévoyance, *f.*; guidon *(d'arme à feu)*, *m.*; *lack of foresight*, imprévoyance, *f.*

forest ['fɔrist], *a.* de forêt, forestier.—*n.* forêt, *f.*

forestall [fɔːˈstɔːl], *v.t.* anticiper, devancer.

forester ['fɔristə], *n.* garde forestier; habitant d'une forêt, *m.*

forestry ['fɔristri], *n.* sylviculture, *f.*

foretaste ['fɔːteist], *n.* avant-goût, *m.*; anticipation, *f.*

foretell [fɔːˈtel], *v.t. irr. (conjug. like* TELL) prédire.

forethought ['fɔːθɔːt], *n.* prévoyance, prescience, *f.*

forewarn [fɔːˈwɔːn], *v.t.* prévenir, avertir.

foreword ['fɔːwəːd], *n.* préface, *f.*; avant-propos, *m.*

forfeit ['fɔːfit], *a.* confisqué; *(fig.)* perdu.—*n.* amende *(à payer)*; forfaiture, confiscation, *f.*; *(Games)* gage, *m.*—*v.t.* forfaire *(à)*; confisquer; perdre.

forfeiture ['fɔːfitʃə], *n.* forfaiture, confiscation; perte, déchéance, *f.*

forgather [fɔːˈgæðə], *v.i.* s'assembler, se réunir.

forge [fɔːdʒ], *n.* forge, *f.*—*v.t.* forger; contrefaire *(monnaie etc.)*, fabriquer *(document etc.)*.—*v.i.* commettre un faux; *to forge ahead*, pousser de l'avant.

forger ['fɔːdʒə], *n.* faussaire; faux-monnayeur, *m.*

forgery ['fɔːdʒəri], *n.* falsification; contrefaçon, *f.*; faux, *m.*

forget [fɔˈget], *v.t., v.i. irr.* oublier.

forgetful [fɔˈgetful], *a.* oublieux.

forgetfulness [fɔˈgetfulnis], *n.* oubli, manque de mémoire, *m.*; négligence, *f.*

forget-me-not [fɔˈgetminɔt], *n.* myosotis, *m.*

forgive [fɔˈgiv], *v.t. irr. (conjug. like* GIVE) pardonner, faire grâce de; pardonner à.

forgiveness [fɔˈgivnis], *n.* pardon, *m.*; clémence, grâce, *f.*

forgiving [fɔˈgiviŋ], *a.* clément, miséricordieux.

forgo [fɔːˈgou], *v.t. irr. (conjug. like* GO) renoncer à, s'abstenir de; se refuser à.

fork [fɔːk], *n.* fourchette; fourche; bifurcation *(de rues)*; pointe *(d'une flèche etc.)*, *f.*; zigzag *(d'éclair)*, *m.*—*v.t.* enlever avec une fourche.—*v.i.* fourcher; bifurquer.

forked [fɔːkt], *a.* fourchu; *(Bot.)* bifurqué.

forlorn [fɔˈlɔːn], *a.* abandonné, désespéré, délaissé.

forlornness [fɔˈlɔːnnis], *n.* délaissement, abandon; état désespéré, *m.*

form [fɔːm], *n.* forme, figure; formalité, *f.*; banc *(siège)*, *m.*; *(Sch.)* classe, *f.*; gîte *(de lièvre)*;

imprimé *(fiche)*, *m.*—*v.t.* former, faire; façonner.—*v.i.* se former; se giter *(lièvres)*.

formal ['fɔːməl], *a.* formel; pointilleux; affecté, cérémonieux. formaliste.

formality [fɔːˈmæliti], *n.* formalité, cérémonie, *f.*

formally ['fɔːməli], *adv.* avec formalité, en forme, formellement.

formation [fɔːˈmeiʃən], *n.* formation, *f.*; ordre, *m.*

formative ['fɔːmətiv], *a.* formatif, formateur, plastique.

former ['fɔːmə], *a.* précédent, passé; ancien; premier *(de deux)*.—*pron.* celui-là, celle-là. —*n.* moule, *m.*

formerly ['fɔːməli], *adv.* autrefois, auparavant; jadis.

formidable ['fɔːmidəbl], *a.* formidable, redoutable.

formless ['fɔːmlis], *a.* informe, sans forme.

Formosa [fɔːˈmouzə]. Formose, *f.*

formula ['fɔːmjulə], *n. (pl.* **formulæ** ['fɔːmjul(a)i]) formule, *f.*

forsake [fɔˈseik], *v.t. irr.* délaisser, abandonner.

forsaking [fɔˈseikiŋ], *n.* délaissement, abandon, *m.*

***forsooth** [fɔˈsuːθ], *adv.* en vérité ma foi.

forswear [fɔːˈsweə], *v.t. irr. (conjug. like* SWEAR) abjurer, répudier.—*v.i.* se parjurer.

fort [fɔːt], *n.* fort, *m.*, forteresse, *f.*

forth [fɔːθ], *adv.* en avant; au dehors; *and so forth*, et ainsi de suite.

forthcoming [fɔːθˈkʌmiŋ], *a.* tout prêt, prêt à paraître; prochain, à venir.

forthright [fɔːˈθrait], *a.* franc, carré, brutal.

forthwith [fɔːθˈwið], *adv.* incontinent, aussitôt, sur-le-champ, tout de suite.

fortieth ['fɔːtiiθ], *a.* quarantième.—*n.* quarantième *(fraction)*, *m.*

fortification [fɔːtifiˈkeiʃən], *n.* fortification, *f.*

fortify ['fɔːtifai], *v.t.* fortifier; munir *(de)*.

fortifying ['fɔːtifaiiŋ], *a. (fig.)* réconfortant, fortifiant.

fortitude ['fɔːtitjuːd], *n.* force d'âme, *f.* courage, *m.*

fortnight ['fɔːtnait], *n.* quinze jours, *m.pl.*, quinzaine, *f.*

fortnightly ['fɔːtnaitli], *a.* bimensuel.—*adv.* tous les quinze jours.

fortress ['fɔːtris], *n.* forteresse, place forte, *f.*

fortuitous [fɔːˈtjuːitəs], *a.* fortuit.

fortuitously [fɔːˈtjuːitəsli], *adv.* fortuitement, par hasard.

fortunate ['fɔːtʃənit, 'fɔːtjunit], *a.* heureux, fortuné.

fortunately ['fɔːtʃənitli], *adv.* heureusement.

fortune ['fɔːtʃən], *n.* fortune, *f.*, sort *(lot)*, destin, *m.*; *by good fortune*, par bonheur.

fortune hunter ['fɔːtʃənhʌntə], *n.* aventurier, coureur de dots, *m.*

fortune-teller ['fɔːtʃəntelə], *n.* diseur de bonne aventure, *m.*

forty ['fɔːti], *a.* quarante; *she must be nearly forty*, elle doit friser la quarantaine.

forward ['fɔːwəd], *a.* avancé; *(fig.)* empressé *(de)*, ardent *(à)*; précoce *(fruits etc.)*; présomptueux.—*n. (Ftb.)* avant, *m.*—*adv.* en avant; en évidence.—*v.t.* avancer, hâter; *(Comm.)* envoyer, expédier; faire suivre *(lettre)*.

forwardness ['fɔːwədnis], *n.* empressement; progrès, *m.*; précocité *(fruits etc.)*; hardiesse; effronterie, *f.*

fossil ['fɔsil] *a.* and *n.* fossile, *m.*

foster ['fɔstə], *v.t.* élever, nourrir; *(fig.)* encourager.

foster brother ['fɔstəbrʌðə], *n.* frère de lait, *m.*

foster child ['fɔstətʃaild], *n.* nourrisson, *m.*

foster father ['fɔstəfɑːðə], *n.* père nourricier, *m.*

foster mother ['fɔstəmʌðə], *n.* mère nourricière, *f.*

foster sister ['fɔstəsistə], *n.* sœur de lait, *f.*

foul [faul], *a.* sale, malpropre, immonde, trouble, bourbeux *(eau)*; grossier *(langage)*; *by fair means or foul,* de gré ou de force; *foul air,* air vicié, *m.*; *foul play,* trahison, *f.—n.* (Spt.) coup-bas, *m.—v.t.* salir, souiller, troubler; encrasser *(arme à feu)*; *(Naut.)* aborder; s'engager *(cordes)*.

foully ['faulli], *adv.* salement, honteusement.

foul-mouthed ['faulmauðd], *a.* grossier.

foulness ['faulnis], *n.* saleté, impureté; turpitude, noirceur, *f.*

found (1) [faund], *past* and *p.p.* [FIND].

found (2) [faund], *v.t.* fonder, établir; fondre *(to cast)*.

foundation [faun'deiʃən], *n.* fondement, *m.*, fondation; *(fig.)* base, source, *f.*

founder (1) ['faundə], *n.* fondateur, auteur; *(Metal.)* fondeur, *m.*

founder (2) ['faundə], *v.t.* surmener *(un cheval).—v.i.* (Naut.) sombrer, couler bas; broncher *(un cheval); (fig.)* échouer.

foundered ['faundəd], *a.* courbatu *(cheval)*; sombré *(navire)*.

foundling ['faundliŋ], *n.* enfant trouvé, *m.*

foundry ['faundri], *n.* fonderie, *f.*

fount [faunt], *n.* fontaine, *(fig.)* cause, source, *f.*

fountain ['fauntin], *n.* fontaine, source, *f.*; jet d'eau, *m.*

fountain-head ['fauntinhed], *n.* source, origine, *f.*

fountain pen ['fauntinpen], *n.* stylo, *m.*

four [fɔː], *a.* and *n.* quatre, *m.*; *carriage and four,* voiture à quatre chevaux, *f.*; *on all fours,* à quatre pattes.

four-engined ['fɔːrendʒind], *a.* (Av.) quadrimoteur.

four-fold ['fɔːfould], *a.* quatre fois, quatre fois autant, quadruple.

four-footed ['fɔːfutid], *a.* quadrupède, à quatre pieds.

fourteen ['fɔːtiːn], *a.* and *n.* quatorze, *m.*

fourteenth ['fɔːtiːnθ], *a.* quatorzième; quatorze *(date; rois etc.).—n.* quatorzième *(fraction)*, *m.*

fourth [fɔːθ], *a.* quatrième; quatre *(date, roi etc.).—n.* quart *(fraction)*, *m.*; *(Mus.)* quarte, *f.*

fowl [faul], *n.* oiseau, *m.*, poule *(hen)*; (Cook.) volaille, *f.*

fowler ['faulə], *n.* oiseleur, *m.*

fowl-house ['faulhaus], *n.* poulailler, *m.*

fowling piece ['fauliŋpiːs], *n.* fusil de chasse, *m.*

fox [fɔks], *n.* (*pl.* **foxes** ['fɔksiz]) renard; *(fig.)* rusé, *m.*

foxglove ['fɔksglʌv], *n.* digitale, *f.*

foxy ['fɔksi], *a.* de renard, rusé; roux *(red)*.

fraction ['frækʃən], *n.* fraction, *f.*

fractious ['frækʃəs], *a.* revêche, maussade, hargneux, de mauvaise humeur.

fracture ['fræktʃə], *n.* fracture, cassure, *f.— v.t.* casser, rompre; *(Surg.)* fracturer.

fragile ['frædʒail], *a.* fragile.

fragility [frə'dʒiliti], *n.* fragilité, *f.*

fragment ['frægmənt], *n.* fragment, éclat, *m.*

fragrance ['freigrəns], *n.* odeur suave, *f.*, parfum, *m.*

fragrant ['freigrənt], *a.* odoriférant, parfumé.

frail [freil], *a.* frêle, fragile, faible.—*n.* cabas, panier d'emballage, *m.*

frailty ['freilti], *n.* faiblesse fragilité, *f.*

frame [freim], *n.* charpente, *f.*; châssis *(de fenêtre etc.)*, chambranle *(de porte)*, *m.*; *(fig.)* forme, *f.*; cadre *(de tableau etc.)*, *m.*; disposition *(d'esprit)*, *f.—v.t.* former, construire; encadrer; inventer.

framer ['freimə], *n.* encadreur, *m.*; *(fig.)* auteur *(d'un projet)*, *m.*

France [frɑːns], la France, *f.*

Frances ['frɑːnsis], Françoise, *f.*

franchise ['fræntʃaiz], *n.* franchise, *f.*, droit de vote, *m.*

Francis ['frɑːnsis], François, Francis, *m.*

Franciscan [fræn'siskən], *a.* and *n.* Franciscain, *m.*

frank [fræŋk], *a.* franc, sincère, libéral; libre. —*v.t.* affranchir.

frankincense ['fræŋkinsens], *n.* encens, *m.*

frankly ['fræŋkli], *adv.* franchement.

frankness ['fræŋknis], *n.* franchise, sincérité, *f.*

frantic ['fræntik], *a.* frénétique, forcené, furieux.

frantically ['fræntikəli], *adv.* follement, avec frénésie.

fraternal [frə'təːnəl], *a.* fraternel.

fraternity [frə'təːniti], *n.* fraternité, confrérie, *f.*

fraud [frɔːd], *n.* imposteur *(personne)*, *m.*; *(also* **fraudulence** ['frɔːdjuləns]) fraude, supercherie, *f.*, dol, *m.*

fraudulent ['frɔːdjulənt], *a.* frauduleux, de mauvaise foi.

fraught [frɔːt], *a.* rempli, plein *(de)*; riche, fertile *(en)*.

fray (1) [frei], *n.* échauffourée, mêlée, bagarre, *f.*

fray (2) [frei], *v.t.* érailler, effilocher.—*v.i.* s'érailler.

fraying ['freiiŋ], *n.* éraillure, *f.*

freak [friːk], *n.* caprice, *m.*; bizarrerie, *f.*; monstre, *m.*; bigarrure, *f.—v.t.* bigarrer, tacheter *(de)*.

freakish ['friːkiʃ], *a.* bizarre, fantasque, capricieux.

freckle ['frekl], *n.* tache de rousseur, tache de son, *f.—v.t.* tacheter.

Frederick ['fredrik], Frédéric, *m.*

free [friː], *a.* libre; exempt; sincère, franc; gratuit; aisé, dégagé; *delivered free,* rendu franco à domicile; *free and easy,* sans façon.—*adv.* gratis.—*v.t.* délivrer, libérer.

freebooter ['friːbuːtə], *n.* maraudeur, flibustier, *m.*

freedman ['friːdmən], *n.* (*pl.* -**men** [men]) affranchi, *m.*

freedom ['friːdəm], *n.* liberté; indépendance; aisance; bourgeoisie *(d'une ville)*, *f.*

freehold ['fri:hould], *n.* propriété foncière libre, *f.*

free-holder ['fri:houldə], *n.* propriétaire foncier, *m.*

freely ['fri:li], *adv.* librement, sans contrainte, gratuitement; libéralement.

freeman ['fri:mən], *n.* (*pl.* **-men** [men]) citoyen, homme libre, *m.*

freemason ['fri:meisn], *n.* franc-maçon, *m.*

freemasonry ['fri:meisnri], *n.* franc-maçonnerie, *f.*

freestone ['fri:stoun], *n.* pierre de taille, *f.*

freestyle ['fri:stail], *n.* nage libre, *f.*

freethinker ['fri:'θiŋkə], *n.* esprit fort, libre penseur, *m.*

free trade ['fri:'treid], *n.* libre-échange, *m.*; **free-trade area**, zone de libre-échange, *f.*

free-trader ['fri:'treidə], *n.* libre-échangiste, *m.*, *f.*

freeze [fri:z], *v.t. irr.* geler; (*Fin.*) bloquer (*prix, salaires*).—*v.i.* se geler, se glacer.

freezing ['fri:ziŋ], *a.* glacial.—*n.* congélation, *f.*; (*Fin.*) blocage, *m.*

freight [freit], *n.* cargaison, *f.*, chargement; fret (*cost*), *m.*—*v.t.* fréter.

French [frentʃ], *a.* français; **French window**, porte-fenêtre, *f.*—*n.* français (*langue*), *m.*; **the French**, les Français, *m.pl.*

Frenchman ['frentʃmən], *n.* (*pl.* **-men** [men]) Français, *m.*

Frenchwoman ['frentʃwumən], *n.* (*pl.* **-women** [wimin]) Française, *f.*

frenzy ['frenzi], *n.* frénésie, *f.*; délire, *m.*

frequence ['fri:kwəns], **frequency** ['fri:kwənsi], *n.* fréquence; répétition fréquente, *f.*; *V.H.F.*, modulation de fréquence, *f.*

frequent ['fri:kwənt], *a.* fréquent, très répandu; rapide (*pouls*).—[fri'kwent], *v.t.* fréquenter; hanter.

frequently ['fri:kwəntli], *adv.* fréquemment, souvent.

fresco ['freskou], *n.* fresque, *f.*

fresh [freʃ], *a.* frais; récent, nouveau; (*fig.*) vigoureux; novice, vert; **fresh water**, eau douce, *f.*

freshen ['freʃən], *v.t.* rafraîchir.—*v.i.* se rafraîchir.

freshly ['freʃli], *adv.* fraîchement; récemment, depuis peu.

freshman ['freʃmən], *n.* (*pl.* **-men** [men]) étudiant de première année, bizuth, *m.*

freshness ['freʃnis], *n.* fraîcheur, *f.*; (*fig.*) nouveauté, *f.*

freshwater ['freʃwɔ:tə], *a.* d'eau douce *ou* de rivière.

fret [fret], *n.* fermentation; (*fig.*) agitation de l'âme, *f.*—*v.t.* frotter (*contre*); ronger, écorcher (*excorier*); chagriner, irriter; découper.—*v.i.* se chagriner, s'inquiéter; s'user, s'érailler.

fretful ['fretful], *a.* chagrin, maussade; agité, inquiet.

fretfulness ['fretfulnis], *n.* mauvaise humeur, irritation, *f.*

fretsaw ['fretsɔ:], *n.* scie à découper, *f.*

fretwork ['fretwə:k], *n.* ouvrage à claire-voie, découpage, *m.*

friable ['fraiəbl], *a.* friable.

friar ['fraiə], *n.* moine, *m.*

friction ['frikʃən], *n.* frottement, *m.*; (*Med.*) friction, *f.*

Friday ['fraid(e)i], vendredi, *m.*; **Good Friday**, vendredi saint.

friend [frend], *n.* ami, *m.*, amie, *f.*

friendless ['frendlis], *a.* sans ami, délaissé.

friendliness [frendlinis], *n.* bienveillance, *f.*

friendly ['frendli], *a.* d'ami, amical; bienveillant (*pour*).

friendship ['frendʃip], *n.* amitié, *f.*

frieze [fri:z], *a.* de frise.—*n.* frise, *f.*

frigate ['frigit], *n.* frégate, *f.*

fright [frait], *n.* effroi, *m.*, épouvante, frayeur, *f.*

frighten [fraitn], *v.t.* épouvanter, effrayer, faire peur à.

frightful ['fraitful], *a.* épouvantable, effroyable, affreux.

frightfulness ['fraitfulnis], *n.* horreur, frayeur, *f.*

frigid ['fridʒid], *a.* froid, glacial.

frigidity [fri'dʒiditi], **frigidness** ['fridʒidnis], *n.* frigidité, froideur, *f.*

frill [fril], *n.* volant, *m.*, ruche, *f.*, jabot (*de chemise*), *m.*; **without frills**, sans façons.—*v.t.* plisser, froncer; rucher.

fringe [frindʒ], *n.* frange; crépine, *f.*; bord, *m.*; bordure, *f.*; effilé, *m.*—*v.t.* franger, border.

frippery ['fripəri], *n.* parure sans valeur, *f.*; clinquant, *m.*

frisk [frisk], *n.* gambade, *f.*—*v.i.* sautiller, gambader, frétiller.

friskiness ['friskinis], *n.* folâtrerie, gaieté, vivacité, *f.*

frisky ['friski], *a.* vif, enjoué, folâtre; fringant (*cheval*).

fritter ['fritə], *n.* (*Cook.*) beignet, *m.*—*v.t.* couper en morceaux, morceler; **to fritter away** (*one's time ou money*), gaspiller *ou* dissiper (son temps *ou* son argent).

frivolity [fri'voliti], *n.* frivolité, *f.*

frivolous ['frivələs], *a.* frivole.

frivolousness ['frivələsnis], *n.* frivolité, *f.*

frizz [friz], **frizzle** [frizl], *v.t.* friser, crêper.—*v.i.* frisotter (*cheveux*).—*n.* frisure, *f.*

frizzy ['frizi], *a.* frisottant, crêpé.

fro [frou], *adv.* en s'éloignant; **to go to and fro**, aller et venir.

frock [frok], *n.* robe d'enfant, robe, *f.*; froc (*de moine*), *m.*

frock coat ['frokkout], *n.* redingote, *f.*

frog [frog], *n.* grenouille, *f.*

frogman ['frogmən], *n.* (*pl.* **-men** [men]) homme-grenouille, *m.*

frolic ['frolik], *n.* espièglerie, *f.*, ébats, *m.pl.*, gambades, *f.pl.*—*v.i.* folâtrer, gambader.

frolicsome ['froliksəm], *a.* folâtre, espiègle.

from [from], *prep.* de; depuis, dès, à partir de; par (*à cause de*); d'après (*selon*); par suite de, en conséquence de (*en raison de*); de la part de (*comme représentant de*); **as from**, à partir de (*telle ou telle date*); **from above**, d'en haut; **from afar**, de loin; **from behind**, de derrière; **from hence**, d'ici; **from thence**, de là; **from . . . till**, depuis . . . jusqu'à; **from you**, de votre part.

front [frʌnt], *n.* devant, *m.*; face, façade (*d'un édifice*); audace, *f.*, front, *m.*—*v.t.* faire face à; s'opposer à; donner sur.

frontage ['frʌntidʒ], *n.* façade, devanture (*de magasin*), *f.*

front door ['frʌnt'dɔ:], *n.* porte d'entrée, *f.*

frontier

frontier ['frʌntiə], *a.* and *n.* frontière, *f.*

frontispiece ['frʌntispi:s], *n.* frontispice, *m.*

frost [frɔst], *n.* gelée, *f.*, gel, *m.*; *glazed frost*, verglas, *m.*; *ground frost*, gelée blanche; *hoar-frost*, givre, *m.*—*v.t.* glacer; damasquiner.

frost-bite ['frɔstbait], *n.* gelure, froidure, *f.*

frosted ['frɔstid], *a.* givré; dépoli (*verre*).

frosty ['frɔsti], *a.* de gelée; glacé; (*fig.*) froid.

froth [frɔθ], *n.* écume; mousse (*de boisson*), *f.* —*v.i.* écumer; mousser.

frothy ['frɔθi], *a.* écumeux; écumant; mousseux; (*fig.*) vain, frivole.

frown [fraun], *n.* froncement de sourcil, *m.* —*v.i.* froncer les sourcils; être contraire (*à*); (*fig.*) *to frown upon*, désapprouver.

frowning ['fraunin], *a.* rechigné, renfrogné; (*fig.*) menaçant.

frowzy ['frauzi], *a.* sale, malpropre.

frozen [frouzn], *a.* glacé, gelé; (*Fin.*) bloqué.

fructify ['frʌktifai], *v.t.* fertiliser, féconder.— *v.i.* fructifier.

frugal ['fru:gl], *a.* frugal, économe, ménager.

frugality [fru:'gæliti], *n.* économie, frugalité, *f.*

fruit [fru:t], *a.* à fruit, fruitier.—*n.* fruit, *m.*; fruits, *m.pl.*; (*fig.*) avantage, profit, *m.*; *first fruits*, prémices, *f.pl.*

fruiterer ['fru:tərə], *n.* fruitier, *m.*

fruitful ['fru:tful], *a.* fertile; (*fig.*) fécond.

fruitfully ['fru:tfuli], *adv.* fertilement, abondamment.

fruitfulness ['fru:tfulnis], *n.* fertilité; (*fig.*) fécondité, *f.*

fruition [fru:'iʃən], *n.* jouissance, réalisation, *f.*

fruitless ['fru:tlis], *a.* stérile; (*fig.*) infructueux, inutile.

frump [frʌmp], *n.* femme désagréable et mal habillée, *f.*

frustrate [frʌs'treit], *v.t.* frustrer, rendre inutile, déjouer.

frustration [frʌs'treiʃən], *n.* frustration, *f.*, insuccès, *m.*

fry (1) [frai], *n.* fretin, frai (*petits poissons*), *m.*

fry (2) [frai], *n.* (*Cook.*) friture, *f.*—*v.t.* frire, faire frire, sauter; *fried eggs*, œufs au plat, *m.pl.*—*v.i.* frire.

frying pan ['fraiinpæn], *n.* poêle à frire, *f.*

fuchsia ['fju:ʃə], *n.* fuchsia, *m.*

fuddle ['fʌdl], *v.t.* griser; hébéter.—*v.i.* se griser.

fudge [fʌdʒ], *int.* bah!—*n.* blague, faribole, *f.*; fondant américain (*bonbon*), *m.*

fuel ['fjual], *n.* combustible, *f.*; (*fig.*) aliment, *m.*

fuel-oil ['fjualɔil], *n.* mazout, *m.*

fugitive ['fju:dʒitiv], *a.* fugitif; fuyard, passager.—*n.* fugitif, transfuge, déserteur; (*Mil.*) fuyard, *m.*

fugue [fju:g], *n.* (*Mus.*) fugue, *f.*

fulcrum ['fʌlkrəm], *n.* (*pl.* **fulcra** ['fʌlkrə]) point d'appui, *m.*

fulfil [ful'fil], *v.t.* accomplir, réaliser; satisfaire.

fulfilment [ful'filmənt], *n.* exécution, *f.*, accomplissement, *m.*

full [ful], *a.* plein, rempli; comble, replet, gras; entier, complet; ample; (*fig.*) repu; (*Gram.*) *full stop*, point, *m.*; *full up!* (*autobus etc.*) complet!—*adv.* tout à fait, entièrement; parfaitement.—*n.* plein; comble, *m.*, satiété, *f.*; soûl, *m.*

full-back ['fulbæk], *n.* (*Ftb.*) arrière, *m.*

full-blown ['fulbloun], *a.* épanoui; (*fig.*) dans tout son éclat.

full-bodied ['fulbɔdid], *a.* gros, replet; corsé (*vin*).

fuller ['fulə], *n.* foulon, *m.*

full-faced ['ful'feist], *a.* au visage plein.

full-length ['ful'lenθ], *a.* en pied (*portrait*).

fullness ['fulnis], *n.* plénitude, abondance; ampleur, *f.*

fully ['fuli], *adv.* pleinement, entièrement, tout à fait; parfaitement.

fulmar ['fulmə], *n.* (*Orn.*) fulmar, *m.*

fulminate ['fʌlmineit], *v.t.*, *v.i.* fulminer.

fulsome ['fulsəm], *a.* excessif, écœurant, servile; gonflé (*style*).

fumble ['fʌmbl], *v.t.* manier maladroitement. —*v.i.* farfouiller; tâtonner.

fumbler ['fʌmblə], *n.* maladroit, *m.*

fume [fju:m], *n.* fumée, vapeur; (*fig.*) colère, *f.*—*v.t.* fumer.—*v.i.* fumer, s'exhaler; (*fig.*) être en colère.

fumigate ['fju:migeit], *v.t.* fumiger; désinfecter.

fun [fʌn], *n.* amusement, *m.*, plaisanterie, drôlerie, *f.*

function ['fʌŋkʃən], *n.* fonction, *f.*, métier, *m.*; cérémonie, réception, *f.*—*v.i.* fonctionner, marcher.

fund [fʌnd], *n.* fonds, *m.*; caisse, *f.*

fundamental [fʌndə'mentl], *a.* fondamental. —*n.*(*pl.*) principe fondamental, *m.*

funeral ['fju:nərəl], *a.* funèbre, funéraire.— *n.* enterrement, convoi funèbre, *m.*, funérailles, obsèques, *f.pl.*

funereal [fju:'niəriəl], *a.* funèbre; lugubre.

fungus ['fʌŋgəs], *n.* (*pl.* **fungi** ['fʌndʒai]) champignon; (*Med.*) fongus, *m.*

funk [fʌŋk], *n.* peur, *f.*—*v.t.* éviter, avoir peur de.

funnel [fʌnl], *n.* entonnoir; tuyau, *m.*; cheminée (*de bateau à vapeur*), *f.*

funny ['fʌni], *a.* amusant, drôle, comique; bizarre.

fur [fə:], *n.* fourrure, *f.*; gibier à poil; (*fig.*) dépôt, *m.*, incrustation, *f.*—*v.t.* fourrer, garnir de fourrure.—*v.i.* s'incruster, s'encrasser (*la langue*).

furbish ['fə:biʃ], *v.t.* fourbir.

furious ['fjuəriəs], *a.* furieux, acharné.

furiously ['fjuəriəsli], *adv.* avec fureur, avec acharnement.

furl [fə:l], *v.t.* (*Naut.*) ferler, serrer.

furlong ['fə:lɔŋ], *n.* furlong (*le huitième d'un mille anglais, 201 mètres*), *m.*

furlough ['fə:lou], *n.* (*Mil.*) congé, *m.*

furnace ['fə:nis], *n.* fournaise, *f.*; fourneau (*d'une forge*); foyer (*de locomotive*), *m.*; *blast furnace*, haut fourneau.

furnish ['fə:niʃ], *v.t.* fournir, garnir, pourvoir (*de*); meubler.

furnisher ['fə:niʃə], *n.* fournisseur, marchand de meubles, *m.*

furnishing ['fə:niʃiŋ], *n.* ameublement, *m.*, garniture, *f.*

furniture ['fə:nitʃə], *n.* meubles, *m.pl.* mobilier, ameublement; équipage, *m.*; *a piece of furniture*, un meuble.

furrier ['fʌriə], *n.* fourreur, pelletier, *m.*

furrow ['fʌrou], *n.* sillon, raie; ride; rainure, *f.* —*v.t.* sillonner, rider (*la figure*).

furry ['fə:ri], *a.* fourré.

434

further ['fəːðə], *v.t.* avancer; faciliter, favoriser, seconder.—*a.* (*also* **farther** ['fɑːðə]) plus éloigné, ultérieur; autre, nouveau; *further end*, extrémité, *f.*—*adv.* (*also* **farther** ['fɑːðə]) plus loin; de plus, en outre, davantage, encore; ultérieurement; au delà.

furtherance ['fəːðərəns], *n.* avancement; progrès, *m.*

furthermore ['fəːðəmɔː], *adv.* de plus, en outre, d'ailleurs.

furthermost ['fəːðəmoust], **furthest** ['fəːðist], **farthest** ['fɑːðist], *a.* le plus éloigné; le plus reculé.—*adv.* and *n.* le plus loin.

furtive ['fəːtiv], *a.* furtif.

furtively ['fəːtivli], *adv.* furtivement, à la dérobée.

fury ['fjuəri], *n.* furie, fureur, *f.*; acharnement, *m.*

furze [fəːz], *n.* ajonc, genêt épineux, *m.*

fuse [fjuːz], *v.t.* fondre, liquéfier.—*v.i.* se fondre.—*n.* mèche, fusée, *f.*; (*Elec.*) fusible, plomb, *m.*; *the fuse has gone*, le plomb a sauté.

fuselage ['fjuːzilɑːʒ, 'fjuːzilidʒ], *n.* fuselage, *m.*

fuse wire ['fjuːzwaiə], *n.* fil fusible, *m.*

fusible ['fjuːzibl], *a.* fusible.

fusilier [fjuːziˈliə], *n.* fusilier, *m.*

fusillade [fjuːziˈleid], *n.* fusillade, *f.*

fusion ['fjuːʒən], *n.* fusion, *f.*

fuss [fʌs], *n.* fracas, embarras, *m.*, façons, *f.pl.*

fussily ['fʌsili], *adv.* avec embarras.

fussy ['fʌsi], *a.* qui fait des embarras; affairé.

fustian ['fʌstjən], *n.* futaine, *f.*; (*fig.*) galimatias, *m.*

fusty ['fʌsti], *a.* qui sent le renfermé *ou* le moisi.

futile ['fjuːtail], *a.* futile, vain, frivole.

futility [fjuːˈtiliti], *n.* futilité, *f.*

future ['fjuːtʃə], *a.* futur, à venir.—*n.* avenir; (*Gram.*) futur, *m.*

fuzz [fʌz], *n.* bourre, *f.*, duvet (*de couverture*); flou (*de photographie*), *m.*

fuzzy ['fʌzi], *a.* duveteux, floconneux; bouffant, moutonné (*cheveux*); flou (*photographie*).

G

G, g [dʒiː]. septième lettre de l'alphabet; (*Mus.*) sol, *m.*

gab [gæb], *n.* faconde, *f.*, bagout, *m.*; *to have the gift of the gab*, (*colloq.*) avoir la langue bien pendue.

gabardine [GABERDINE].

gabble [gæbl], *v.i.* parler très vite, bredouiller; caqueter, jacasser.—*n.* bredouillement; caquet, *m.*

gaberdine, gabardine [gæbəˈdiːn], *n.* gabardine, *f.*

gable [geibl], *n.* pignon, gable, *m.*

gadfly ['gædflai], *n.* taon, *m.*

gadget ['gædʒit], *n.* instrument, accessoire; truc, machin, *m.*

gaff [gæf], *n.* gaffe, *f.*—*v.t.* gaffer (*poisson*).

gag [gæg], *n.* bâillon, *m.*; (*Theat.*) plaisanterie, *f.*; (*Cine.*) gag, *m.*—*v.t.* bâillonner.

gage [geidʒ], *n.* gage, *m.*, assurance, *f.*

gaggle [gægl], *n.* troupeau d'oies, *m.*

gaiety ['geiiti], *n.* gaieté, *f.*; éclat, *m.*

gaily ['geili], *adv.* gaiement, joyeusement.

gain [gein], *n.* gain, profit, avantage, *m.*—*v.t.* gagner, acquérir; remporter (*victoire*); atteindre.—*v.i.* avancer (*montre etc.*).

gainings ['geiniŋz], *n.pl.* gains, profits, *m.pl.*

gainsay [geinˈsei, geinˈsei], *v.t.* contredire.

gait [geit], *n.* démarche, allure, *f.*

gaiter ['geitə], *n.* guêtre *f.*

gala ['geilə, 'gɑːlə], *n.* gala, *m.*; fête, *f.*

galaxy ['gæləksi], *n.* voie lactée, galaxie, *f.*; (*fig.*) assemblage brillant, *m.*

gale [geil], *n.* coup de vent, *m.*, tempête, *f.*

Galilee ['gælili:]. la Galilée, *f.*

gall [gɔːl], *n.* fiel, *m.*; écorchure (*plaie*); noix de galle, galle (*d'arbres etc.*); (*fig.*) rancune, *f.*, chagrin, *m.*—*v.t.* écorcher; (*fig.*) fâcher.

gallant ['gælənt], *a.* brave, intrépide; [gəˈlænt] galant.—*n.* brave; preux; [gəˈlænt] galant; amant, *m.*

gallantry ['gæləntri], *n.* vaillance; galanterie, *f.*

gall bladder ['gɔːlblædə], *n.* vésicule biliaire, *f.*

galleon ['gæliən], *n.* galion, *m.*

gallery ['gæləri], *n.* galerie, *f.*; (*Theat.*) balcon, *m.*; (*Parl.*) tribune publique, *f.*

galley ['gæli], *n.* galère; (*Naut.*) cuisine, *f.*

galley slave ['gælisleiv], *n.* galérien, *m.*

Gallic ['gælik], *a.* gaulois.

galling ['gɔːliŋ], *a.* irritant, vexant.

gallon ['gælən], *n.* gallon (*quatre litres et demi*), *m.*

gallop ['gæləp], *n.* galop, *m.*—*v.i.* galoper, aller au galop.

gallows ['gæləuz], *n.* potence, *f.*

galvanize ['gælvənaiz], *v.t.* galvaniser.

Gambia ['gæmbiə]. la Gambie, *f.*

gamble [gæmbl], *v.i.* jouer de l'argent.

gambler ['gæmblə], *n.* joueur, *m.*

gambling ['gæmbliŋ], *n.* jeu, *m.*

gambol [gæmbl], *n.* gambade, *f.*; ébats, *m.pl.*—*v.i.* gambader, folâtrer.

game (1) [geim], *a.* estropié (*jambe, bras etc.*).

game (2) [geim], *a.* courageux.—*n.* jeu, *m.*, partie, *f.*; *drawn game*, partie nulle; *to make game of*, se moquer de.—*v.i.* jouer de l'argent.

game (3) [geim], *n.* gibier, *m.*

game bag ['geimbæg], *n.* carnassière, *f.*

game-keeper ['geimkiːpə], *n.* garde-chasse, *m.*

gamester ['geimstə], *n.* joueur, *m.*

gammon ['gæmən], *n.* quartier de lard fumé, *m.*—*v.t.* saler et fumer (*jambon*).

gamut ['gæmət], *n.* (*Mus.*) gamme, *f.*

gander ['gændə], *n.* jars, *m.*

gang [gæŋ], *n.* bande, troupe, brigade, équipe (*d'ouvriers*), *f.*

ganger ['gæŋə], *n.* chef d'équipe; cantonnier, *m.*

Ganges ['gændʒiːz]. le Gange, *m.*

gangrene ['gæŋgriːn], *n.* gangrène, *f.*

gangster ['gæŋstə], *n.* (*Am.*) bandit, gangster, *m.*

gangway ['gæŋwei], *n.* passage, *m.*; (*Naut.*) passerelle (*pour débarquer*), coupée, *f.*

gannet ['gænit], *n.* (*Orn.*) fou, *m.*

gaol [JAIL].
gap [gæp], *n.* brèche, ouverture, *f.*, trou, *m.*; (*fig.*) lacune; trouée (*dans une forêt*), *f.*
gape [geip], *v.i.* bâiller; s'entr'ouvrir (*porte etc.*); (*fig.*) bayer; **to gape at**, regarder bouche bée.—*n.* bâillement, *m.*
gaping ['geipiŋ], *a.* béant.—*n.* bâillement, *m.*
garage ['gæra:ʒ], *n.* garage, *m.*—*v.t.* garer.
garb [ga:b], *n.* costume, habit, habillement, *m.*
garbage ['ga:bidʒ], *n.* entrailles, issues; (*Am.*) ordures, *f.pl.* [see also **dust-bin** *etc.*]
garble [ga:bl], *v.t.* mutiler, tronquer (*citation etc.*), altérer.
garden [ga:dn], *n.* jardin, *m.*—*v.i.* jardiner.
garden-city ['ga:dn'siti], *n.* cité-jardin, *f.*
gardener ['ga:dnə], *n.* jardinier, *m.*
gardenia [ga:'di:njə], *n.* gardenia, *m.*
gardening ['ga:dniŋ], *n.* jardinage, *m.*
gargle [ga:gl], *v.i.* se gargariser.—*n.* gargarisme, *m.*
gargoyle ['ga:goil], *n.* gargouille, *f.*
garish ['gɛəriʃ], *a.* éclatant, voyant.
garland ['ga:lənd], *n.* guirlande, *f.*—*v.t.* enguirlander.
garlic ['ga:lik], *n.* ail, *m.*
garment ['ga:mənt], *n.* vêtement, *m.*
garner ['ga:nə], *n.* grenier, *m.*—*v.t.* mettre en grenier, engranger; (*fig.*) amasser.
garnet ['ga:nit], *n.* grenat, *m.*
garnish ['ga:niʃ], *v.t.* garnir, orner de.—*n.* garniture, *f.*
garret ['gærət], *n.* galetas, *m.*, mansarde, soupente, *f.*
garrison ['gærisən], *n.* garnison, *f.*—*v.t.* mettre garnison dans; mettre en garnison.
garrotte [gə'rɔt], *n.* garrotte, *f.*—*v.t.* garrotter.
garrulity [gə'ru:liti], *n.* garrulité, loquacité, *f.*
garrulous ['gæruləs], *a.* babillard, loquace.
garter [ga:tə], *n.* jarretière, *f.*; (*Am.*) support-chaussette, *m.*
gas [gæs], *n.* (*pl.* **gases** ['gæsiz]) gaz, *m.*; **laughing gas**, gaz hilarant.—*v.t.* gazer; intoxiquer par un gaz. [see **petrol**]
gas cooker ['gæs'kukə], *n.* réchaud à gaz, four à gaz.
gaseous ['geisiəs], *a.* gazeux.
gash [gæʃ], *n.* balafre, estafilade, entaille, *f.*—*v.t.* balafrer, taillader.
gas-holder ['gæshouldə], **gasometer** [gæ'sɔmitə], *n.* gazomètre, *m.*
gas mask ['gæsma:sk], *n.* masque à gaz, *m.*
gasometer [GAS-HOLDER].
gasp [ga:sp], *v.i.* respirer avec peine.—*n.* respiration haletante, *f.*; sursaut (*de surprise*), soupir convulsif, *m.*
gasping ['ga:spiŋ], *a.* haletant.—*n.* respiration haletante, *f.*
gas stove ['gæsstouv], *n.* fourneau à gaz, *m.*
gastric ['gæstrik], *a.* gastrique.
gastronomy [gæs'trɔnəmi], *n.* gastronomie, *f.*
gate [geit], *n.* porte; barrière (*de péage*); grille (*en fer forgé*), *f.*
gate-keeper ['geitki:pə], *n.* portier; (*Rail.*) garde-barrière, *m.*
gate-post ['geitpoust], *n.* montant de porte, *m.*
gateway ['geitwei], *n.* porte, porte cochère, *f.*; portail (*grand*); guichet (*petit*), *m.*
gather ['gæðə], *v.t.* ramasser; assembler; recueillir (*réunir*); cueillir (*fruits etc.*); (*fig.*)

conclure; (*Dress.*) froncer.—*v.i.* se rassembler, se réunir, s'assembler; s'amasser. —*n.* pli, froncis, *m.*
gatherer ['gæðərə], *n.* cueilleur; percepteur (*des contributions directes*); vendangeur (*de raisins*), *m.*
gathering ['gæðəriŋ], *n.* rassemblement, *m.*; assemblée, réunion; perception (*des contributions directes*); récolte (*de fruits etc.*), *f.*: (*Dress.*) froncis; (*Med.*) abcès, *m.*
gaudiness ['gɔ:dinis], *n.* faste, faux brillant, *m.*
gaudy ['gɔ:di], *a.* éclatant; criard, fastueux, de mauvais goût.
gauge [geidʒ], *v.t.* jauger, mesurer; (*fig.*) juger.—*n.* jauge, mesure, *f.*; calibre, *m.*; (*Rail.*) voie, *f.*
Gaul [gɔ:l], la Gaule, *f.*
Gauls [gɔ:lz], **the.** les Gaulois, *m.pl.*
gaunt [gɔ:nt], *a.* maigre, décharné.
gauntlet ['gɔ:ntlit], *n.* gantelet, *m.*
gauze [gɔ:z], *n.* gaze, *f.*
gawk [gɔ:k], *n.* sot, maladroit, *m.*
gawky ['gɔ:ki], *a.* dégingandé.
gay [gei], *a.* gai, réjoui, joyeux; pimpant.
gayety [GAIETY].
gayly [GAILY].
gaze [geiz], *v.i.* regarder fixement.—*n.* regard fixe *ou* attentif, *m.*
gazelle [gə'zel], *n.* gazelle, *f.*
gazette [gə'zet], *n.* gazette, *f.*; bulletin officiel, *m.*—*v.t.* publier *ou* annoncer dans le journal officiel.
gazetteer [gæzi'tiə], *n.* dictionnaire géographique, gazetier, *m.*
gear [giə], *n.* appareil, attirail; harnais (*d'un cheval*), *m.*; (*colloq.*) vêtements; (*Naut.*) apparaux, *m.pl.*; (*Mach.*) engrenage, *m.*; (*Motor.*) vitesse, *f.*; (*Motor.*) **bottom**, **first** or **low gear**, première, *f.*; **neutral gear**, point mort, *m.*; **in top gear**, en prise.
gear-box ['giəbɔks], *n.* boîte de changement de vitesse, *f.*
geese [GOOSE].
gelatine ['dʒeləti:n], *n.* gélatine, *f.*
gelatinous [dʒe'lætinəs], *a.* gélatineux.
gelding ['geldiŋ], *n.* cheval hongre, *m.*
gem [dʒem], *n.* pierre précieuse, *f.*, joyau, *m.*
gender ['dʒendə], *n.* genre, *m.*
genealogical [dʒi:niə'lɔdʒikl], *a.* généalogique.
genealogist [dʒi:ni'ælədʒist], *n.* généalogiste, *m.*, *f.*
genealogy [dʒi:ni'ælədʒi], *n.* généalogie, *f.*
general ['dʒenərəl], *a.* général, commun.—*n.* général, *m.*
generalize ['dʒenrəlaiz], *v.t.* généraliser.
generally ['dʒenrəli], *adv.* en général, ordinairement, généralement.
generate ['dʒenəreit], *v.t.* produire, engendrer.
generation [dʒenə'reiʃən], *n.* génération, famille; production, *f.*; âge, *m.*
generator ['dʒenəreitə], *n.* générateur, *m.*; **electricity generator**, génératrice, *f.*
generic [dʒə'nerik], **generical** [dʒe'nerikəl], *a.* générique.
generosity [dʒenə'rɔsiti], *n.* générosité, magnanimité, libéralité, *f.*
generous ['dʒenərəs], *a.* généreux; (*fig.*) abondant, riche (*en*).

generously ['dʒenərəsli], *adv.* généreusement.
genesis ['dʒenəsis], *n.* genèse, *f.*
genetics [dʒə'netiks], *n.* génétique, *f.*
Geneva [dʒə'ni:və]. Genève, *f.*
genial ['dʒi:niəl], *a.* bon; affable; cordial,
joyeux.
geniality [dʒi:ni'æliti], *n.* bonne humeur,
nature sympathique, gaieté, *f.*, entrain, *m.*
genially ['dʒi:niəli], *adv.* avec bonté, d'un air
affable.
genie ['dʒi:ni], *n.* (*Myth.*) génie, djinn, *m.*
genitive ['dʒenitiv], *n.* (*Gram.*) génitif, *m.*
genius ['dʒi:niəs], *n.* génie, *m.*
Genoa ['dʒenouə]. Gênes, *f.*
genteel [dʒen'ti:l], *a.* (*now often iron.*) de bon
ton, comme il faut, distingué.
gentility [dʒen'tiliti], *n.* bon ton, *m.*, distinction, *f.*
gentle ['dʒentl], *a.* doux, aimable; paisible;
modéré (*pente etc.*).
gentlefolk ['dʒentlfouk], *n.pl.* personnes de
bon ton, *f.pl.*, gens comme il faut, *m.pl.*
gentleman ['dʒentlmən], *n.* (*pl.* gentlemen
[-men]) monsieur, *m.*; homme comme il faut,
galant homme, homme bien né, *m.*
gentlemanly ['dʒentlmənli], *a.* distingué, de
bon ton, comme il faut.
gentleness ['dʒentlnis], *n.* douceur, bonté, *f.*
gentlewoman ['dʒentlwumən], *n.* (*pl.*
-women ['wimin]) dame *ou* jeune fille de
bonne famille, *f.*
gently ['dʒentli], *adv.* doucement.
genuine ['dʒenjuin], *a.* pur, vrai, véritable,
authentique, naturel; sincère.
genuinely ['dʒenjuinli], *adv.* purement,
sincèrement, authentiquement.
genuineness ['dʒenjuinnis], *n.* authenticité;
sincérité, *f.*
genus ['dʒi:nəs], *n.* (*pl.* genera ['dʒenərə])
genre, *m.*
Geoffrey ['dʒefri]. Geoffroi, *m.*
geographer [dʒi'ogrəfə], *n.* géographe, *m.*, *f.*
geographical [dʒiə'græfikl], *a.* géographique.
geography [dʒi'ogrəfi], *n.* géographie, *f.*
geology [dʒi'olədʒi], *n.* géologie, *f.*
geometry [dʒi'omitri], *n.* géométrie, *f.*
George [dʒɔ:dʒ]. Georges, *m.*
geranium [dʒə'reiniəm], *n.* (*Bot.*) géranium, *m.*
germ [dʒə:m], *n.* germe, *m.*
German ['dʒə:mən], *a.* allemand.—*n.* allemand (*langue*); Allemand (*personne*), *m.*
Germany ['dʒə:məni]. l'Allemagne, *f.*
germinate ['dʒə:mineit], *v.i.* germer;
pousser, *f.*
gesticulate [dʒes'tikjuleit], *v.i.* gesticuler.
gesticulation [dʒestikju'leiʃən], *n.* gesticulation, *f.*
gesture ['dʒestʃə], *n.* geste, *m.*, action, *f.*—*v.i.*
gesticuler.
get [get], *v.t. irr.* (se) procurer, acquérir,
obtenir; recevoir; remporter (*to gain*);
gagner (*to earn*); avoir; acheter (*to buy*);
arriver à, atteindre (*to reach*); aller chercher
(*to fetch*); trouver (*to find*); faire, se faire
(*to induce, make, cause etc.*); attraper,
s'attirer (*to catch etc.*); **to get hold of**,
s'emparer de, saisir, obtenir.—*v.i.* se
mettre (*en*); devenir, se faire (*to become*);
aller (*to go*); **to get about**, sortir, prendre
de l'exercice; **to get at**, arriver à; attaquer;
atteindre; **to get away**, s'en aller, se

sauver, échapper (*à*); **to get back**, revenir,
regagner; recouvrer; **to get in**, entrer,
faire entrer, rentrer; **to get off**, s'en tirer,
s'échapper; descendre; ôter, enlever; **to
get on**, avancer, réussir, faire des progrès;
monter sur; **to get out**, sortir, s'en tirer,
faire sortir; **to get over**, passer, surmonter, vaincre; se consoler de; **to get rid
of**, se débarrasser de; **to get through**,
passer par, parcourir; réussir (*à un examen*);
to get up, se lever, monter, faire monter,
lever; préparer.
gewgaw ['gju:gɔ:], *n.* babiole, bagatelle, *f.*,
colifichet, *m.*
geyser ['gi:zə], *n.* chauffe-bain; (*Geol.*) geyser,
m.
Ghana ['gɑ:nə]. le Ghana, *m.*
Ghanaian [gɑ:'neiən], *a.* du Ghana.—*n.*
citoyen(ne) du Ghana, *m.*, *f.*
ghastliness ['gɑ:stlinis], *n.* pâleur, *f.*; aspect
effrayant, *m.*
ghastly ['gɑ:stli], *a.* pâle, pâle comme la
mort; horrible; affreux.
gherkin ['gə:kin], *n.* cornichon, *m.*
ghetto ['getou], *n.* ghetto, *m.*
ghost [goust], *n.* revenant, fantôme, spectre,
m.; ombre, *f.*; **the Holy Ghost**, le Saint-
Esprit.
ghostly ['goustli], *a.* spirituel; de spectre.
ghoul [gu:l], *n.* goule, *f.*
ghoulish ['gu:liʃ], *a.* de goule.
ghyll [gɪLL (2)].
giant ['dʒaiənt], *a.* de géant.—*n.* géant, *m.*
gibber ['dʒibə], *v.i.* baragouiner.
gibberish ['dʒibəriʃ], *n.* baragouin, charabia,
m.
gibbet ['dʒibit], *n.* potence, *f.*, gibet, *m.*
gibe [dʒaib], *v.t., v.i.* railler, se moquer (*de*).—
n. sarcasme, *m.*; raillerie, moquerie, *f.*
giblets ['dʒiblits], *n.pl.* abatis, *m.pl.*
giddily ['gidili], *adv.* étourdiment, à l'étour-
die.
giddiness ['gidinis], *n.* vertige, *m.*; (*fig.*)
étourderie, *f.*
giddy ['gidi], *a.* étourdi; (*fig.*) volage; vertigineux; **I feel giddy**, la tête me tourne; **that
makes me feel giddy**, cela me donne le
vertige.
gift [gift], *n.* don, présent, cadeau; (*fig.*)
talent, *m.*; **Christmas gifts**, étrennes,
f.pl.—*v.t.* douer, doter (*de*).
gifted ['giftid], *a.* doué, de talent.
gigantic [dʒai'gæntik], *a.* gigantesque, de
géant.
giggle [gigl], *v.i.* rire nerveusement, rire un
peu bêtement.—*n.* ricanement, petit rire
bête, *m.*
gild [gild], *v.t.* dorer; (*fig.*) embellir.
gilding ['gildiŋ], *n.* dorure, *f.*
Giles [dʒailz]. Gilles, *m.*
gill (1) [gil], *n.* (*usu. pl.*) ouïe (*de poisson*), *f.*
gill (2), ghyll [gil], *n.* ravin boisé; ruisseau
(*du ravin*), *m.*
gill (3) [dʒil], *n.* treize centilitres, *m.pl.*
gillyflower ['dʒiliflauə], *n.* giroflée, *f.*
gilt [gilt], *a.* doré.—*n.* dorure, *f.*
gilt-edged ['gilted3d], *a.* **gilt-edged securities**, valeurs de tout repos, *f.pl.*
gimcrack ['dʒimkræk], *n.* pacotille, camelote,
f.
gimlet ['gimlit], *n.* vrille, *f.*
gimmick ['gimik], *n.* machin; tour (*artifice*), *m.*

gin (1) [dʒin], n. trébuchet, piège, m.
gin (2) [dʒin], n. genièvre, gin (liquor), m.
ginger ['dʒindʒə], n. gingembre; (fam.) poil de carotte (personne aux cheveux roux), m.
gingerbread ['dʒindʒəbred], n. pain d'épice, m.
gingerly ['dʒindʒəli], adv. tout doucement, délicatement.
gipsy, gypsy ['dʒipsi], n. bohémien, tzigane, m., bohémienne, f.
giraffe [dʒi'rɑ:f], n. girafe, f.
gird [gə:d], v.t. irr. ceindre (de); entourer (de).
girder ['gə:də], n. poutre, solive, traverse, f.
girdle [gə:dl], n. ceinture, f.; ceinturon, m.; gaine, f.—v.t. ceinturer.
girl [gə:l], n. fille, jeune fille; jeune personne, f.
girlish ['gə:liʃ], a. de jeune fille.
girl scout [gə:l'skaut], n. éclaireuse, f.
girth [gə:θ], n. sangle, f.; tour, m., circonférence, f.
gist [dʒist], n. fond, fin mot; point principal, m., substance (d'un discours), f.
give [giv], v.t. irr. donner; livrer, rendre, accorder; faire (réponse, crédit, compliment, amitiés etc.); remettre; porter (un coup etc.); pousser (un gémissement etc.); émettre (un son); to give away, donner; trahir; to give up, abandonner, renoncer à.—v.i. céder; plier (se courber); prêter (s'allonger); give and take, donnant donnant; to give in, céder; to give oneself up, se rendre; to give way, céder, se relâcher.
given [givn], a. adonné, porté à; donné; given these difficulties, étant donné ces difficultés.
giver ['givə], n. donneur, m.
gizzard ['gizəd], n. gésier, m.
glacial ['gleiʃəl], a. glacial, glaciaire.
glacier ['glæsiə], n. glacier, m.
glad [glæd], a. content, aise, bien aise; heureux (de).
gladden [glædn], v.t. réjouir.
glade [gleid], n. clairière, percée, f.
gladiator ['glædieitə], n. gladiateur, m.
gladiolus [glædi'oulas], n. (pl. gladioli [glædi'oulai]) glaïeul, m.
gladly ['glædli], adv. volontiers, avec plaisir.
glamorous ['glæmərəs], a. charmeur, ensorcelant.
glamour ['glæmə], n. charme, prestige, éclat, m.
glance [glɑ:ns], n. ricochet, coup en biais; regard, coup d'œil, m.—v.i. jeter un coup d'œil (sur); étinceler; to glance off, ricocher.
gland [glænd], n. (Anat.) glande, f.
glare [gleə], n. éclat, m., lueur, f.; regard irrité ou farouche, m.—v.i. éblouir; luire; regarder d'un air furieux.
glaring ['gleəriŋ], a. voyant, éblouissant; choquant; manifeste.
glass [glɑ:s], a. de verre.—n. (pl. glasses ['glɑ:siz]) verre, m.; vitre (de fenêtre), f.; (pl.) lunettes, f. pl.; cut glass, cristal taillé, m.; field glasses, jumelles, f. pl.; looking glass, miroir, m.; magnifying glass, loupe, f.; stained glass, vitraux, m. pl.; (weather-)glass, baromètre, m.
glass-maker ['glɑ:smeikə], n. verrier, m.

glass-ware ['glɑ:swɛə], n. verrerie, f.
glassy ['glɑ:si], a. vitreux, transparent.
glaze [gleiz], v.t. vitrer; vernir.
glazier ['gleiziə], n. vitrier, m.
glazing ['gleiziŋ], n. vitrage (de fenêtres); vernissage (de peintures), m.
gleam [gli:m], n. rayon, m., lueur, f.—v.i. briller, luire (de).
gleaming ['gli:miŋ], a. miroitant, luisant.
glean [gli:n], v.t. glaner.
gleaner ['gli:nə], n. glaneur, m.
glebe [gli:b], n. glèbe, terre, f., sol, m.
glee [gli:], n. joie, gaieté, f.
gleeful ['gli:ful], a. joyeux, gai.
glen [glen], n. vallon, ravin, m.
glib [glib], a. coulant, délié, volubile.
glibly ['glibli], adv. avec volubilité; doucereusement.
glide [glaid], v.i. couler, glisser; se glisser (dans).—n. glissade, f.; (Av.) vol plané, m.
glider ['glaidə], n. (Av.) planeur, m.
glimmer ['glimə], n. lueur, f., faible rayon, m.—v.i. entre-luire, luire faiblement; poindre (l'aube).
glimpse [glimps], n. coup d'œil, m., vue rapide, f.; to catch a glimpse of, entrevoir.
glint [glint], n. trait de lumière, m., lueur, f.—v.i. luire par moments.
glisten [glisn], glister ['glistə] glitter ['glitə], v.i. reluire, scintiller, chatoyer.—n. éclat, lustre, m.
gloaming ['gloumiŋ], n. crépuscule, m.
gloat [glout], v.i. dévorer ou couver des yeux; (fig.) se régaler de.
global [gloubl], a. global; global war, conflit mondial, m.
globe [gloub], n. globe, m.
globule ['glɔbju:l], n. globule, m.
gloom [glu:m], gloominess ['glu:minis], n. obscurité, f., ténèbres, f. pl.; (fig.) tristesse, f.
gloomily ['glu:mili], adv. obscurément; d'un air triste, lugubrement.
gloomy ['glu:mi], a. sombre, obscur; morne, triste.
glorify ['glɔ:rifai], v.t. glorifier.
glorious ['glɔ:riəs], a. glorieux; illustre, superbe.
glory ['glɔ:ri], n. gloire, f.; (Paint.) auréole, f.—v.i. se glorifier (de).
gloss [glɔs], n. lustre; apprêt, m.; (fig.) glose, f., commentaire, m.—v.i. gloser, interpréter; lustrer; to gloss over, glisser sur.
glossary ['glɔsəri], n. glossaire, m.
glossiness ['glɔsinis], n. lustre, brillant, glacé, m.
glossy ['glɔsi], a. lustré, brillant, luisant.
glove [glʌv], n. gant, m.
glover ['glʌvə], n. gantier, m.
glow [glou], v.i. brûler (de); briller; (fig.) s'échauffer.—n. lueur rouge, f.; (fig.) feu, éclat, m., splendeur, f.
glowing ['glouiŋ], a. embrasé; ardent, chaleureux.
glow-worm ['glouwə:m], n. ver luisant, m.
glue [glu:], n. colle-forte, f.—v.t. coller.
glum [glʌm], a. maussade, de mauvaise humeur, morne.
glut [glʌt], v.t. gorger, rassasier; engorger (le marché).—n. surabondance, f., excès, m.
glutton [glʌtn], n. gourmand, goinfre, m.

gluttonous ['glʌtənəs], *a.* gourmand, glouton, vorace.

gluttony ['glʌtəni], *n.* gloutonnerie, *f.*

glycerine ['glisəri:n], *n.* glycérine, *f.*

gnarled [nɑ:ld], *a.* noueux.

gnash [næʃ], *v.t.* grincer.—*v.i.* grincer des dents.

gnashing ['næʃiŋ], *n.* grincement, *m.*

gnat [næt], *n.* cousin, moucheron, *m.*

gnaw [nɔ:], *v.t.* ronger.

gnawing ['nɔ:iŋ], *a.* rongeant, rongeur.—*n.* rongement, *m.*

gnome [noum], *n.* gnome, *m.*

gnu [nu:], *n.* gnou, *m.*

go [gou], *v.i. irr.* aller, se rendre; marcher, passer; s'en aller, partir (*to leave*); disparaître; devenir (*to become*); s'égarer; *to go astray*, s'égarer; *to go away*, s'en aller, partir; *to go back*, retourner, s'en retourner, reculer; *to go backward*, aller à reculons, reculer; *to go down*, descendre; se coucher (*soleil*); tomber; *to go off*, partir (*fusil*); s'en aller; *to go on*, aller, avancer, continuer; se passer; *to go through*, passer par, traverser; subir, souffrir; *to go to sleep*, s'endormir; *to go without*, se passer de; *to let go*, lâcher prise.—*n.* mode, vogue, *f.*; (*fig.*) entrain, coup, essai, *m.*

goad [goud], *n.* aiguillon, *m.*—*v.t.* aiguillonner; (*fig.*) stimuler.

goal [goul], *n.* but; terme, *m.*

goal-keeper ['goulki:pə], *n.* (*Ftb.*) gardien de but, *m.*

goat [gout], *n.* chèvre, *f.*; *he-goat*, bouc, *m.*

gobble [gɔbl], *v.t.* gober, avaler.—*v.i.* glouglouter (*dindon*).

goblet ['gɔblit], *n.* gobelet, *m.*

goblin ['gɔblin], *n.* lutin, *m.*

God [gɔd], Dieu, *m.*

god [gɔd], *n.* dieu, *m.*

godchild ['gɔdtʃaild], *n.* filleul, *m.*, filleule, *f.*

goddaughter ['gɔdɔ:tə], *n.* filleule, *f.*

goddess ['gɔdis], *n.* déesse, *f.*

godfather ['gɔdfɑ:ðə], *n.* parrain, *m.*

Godfrey ['gɔdfri]. Godefroi, *m.*

godless ['gɔdlis], *a.* athée, impie.

godliness ['gɔdlinis], *n.* piété, *f.*

godly ['gɔdli], *a.* pieux, dévot.

godmother ['gɔdmʌðə], *n.* marraine, *f.*

godsend ['gɔdsend], *n.* aubaine, trouvaille, *f.*

godson ['gɔdsʌn], *n.* filleul, *m.*

godspeed [gɔd'spi:d], *n.* succès, *m.*

goffer ['gɔfə], *v.t.* gaufrer.

goggle [gɔgl], *v.i.* rouler de gros yeux; *goggle eyes*, des yeux en boules de loto, *m.pl.*

goggles [gɔglz], *n.pl.* lunettes (protectrices), *f.pl.*

going ['gouiŋ], *n.* marche, démarche, allée, *f.*, départ, *m.*

goitre ['gɔitə], *n.* (*Med.*) goitre, *m.*

gold [gould], *a.* d'or, en or.—*n.* or, *m.*

golden [gouldn], *a.* d'or.

goldfinch ['gouldfintʃ], *n.* chardonneret, *m.*

goldfish ['gouldfiʃ], *n.* poisson rouge, *m.*

goldsmith ['gouldsmiθ], *n.* orfèvre, *m.*

golf [gɔlf, gɔf], *n.* golf, *m.*

golf club ['gɔlfklʌb], *n.* club de golf (*société ou instrument*), *m.*

golf course ['gɔlfkɔ:s], *n.* terrain de golf, *m.*

gondola ['gɔndələ], *n.* gondole; nacelle (*de ballon*), *f.*

gondolier [gɔndə'liə], *n.* gondolier, *m.*

gone [gɔ:n, gɔn], *a.* allé, parti; perdu, disparu; passé, écoulé; adjugé (*aux enchères*).

gong [gɔŋ], *n.* gong; timbre (*d'une horloge*), *m.*

good [gud], *a.* bon; de bien, honnête, convenable, avantageux; valide, solide; (*colloq.*) sage; *good luck*, bonheur, *m.*, bonne chance, *f.*; *to make good*, exécuter; compenser, indemniser; assurer.—*n.* bien, bon, avantage, profit, *m.*; *for good (and all)*, pour (tout) de bon; *what's the good of?* à quoi bon? (*pl.*) effets, biens, *m.pl.*, marchandises, *f.pl.*—*adv.* bien.—*int.* bon! bien! c'est très bien!

good-bye! [gud'bai], *int.* adieu! *good-bye for the present*, au revoir.

good-for-nothing [gudfə'nʌθiŋ], *n.* vaurien, *m.*

Good Friday [gud'fraid(e)i]. vendredi saint, *m.*

good-humored ['gud'hju:məd], *a.* de bonne humeur, enjoué, gai.

good-natured ['gud'neitʃəd], *a.* d'un bon naturel, bon, bienveillant.

goodness ['gudnis], *n.* bonté; probité, *f.*; *thank goodness!* Dieu merci!

goodwill [gud'wil], *n.* bienveillance, bonne volonté, bonté; (*Comm.*) clientèle, *f.*

goose [gu:s], *n.* (*pl.* **geese** [gi:s]) oie, *f.*; (*fig.*) imbécile, nigaud, *m.*

gooseberry ['guzbri], *n.* groseille à maquereau, *f.*

gooseberry bush ['guzbribuʃ], *n.* groseillier, *m.*

goose flesh ['gu:sfleʃ], *n.* chair de poule, *f.*

gore [gɔ:], *n.* sang, sang caillé, *m.*—*v.t.* donner un coup de corne à.

gorge [gɔ:dʒ], *n.* gorge, *f.*; gosier, *m.*—*v.t.* gorger, avaler, rassasier.—*v.i.* se gorger (*de*).

gorgeous ['gɔ:dʒəs], *a.* magnifique, splendide, fastueux.

gorilla [gə'rilə], *n.* gorille, *m.*

gorse [gɔ:s], *n.* ajonc, *m.*

gory ['gɔ:ri], *a.* sanglant, couvert de sang.

gosling ['gɔzliŋ], *n.* oison, *m.*

gospel ['gɔspəl], *n.* évangile, *m.*

gossamer ['gɔsəmə], *n.* fil de la Vierge, *m.*

gossip ['gɔsip], *n.* commère, *f.*, causeur (*personne*), *m.*; causerie, *f.*, commérage, *m.*—*v.i.* bavarder, faire des commérages.

gossip writer ['gɔsipraitə], *n.* (*Journ.*) échotier, *m.*

Goth [gɔθ], *n.* Goth; (*fig.*) barbare, *m.*

Gothic ['gɔθik], *a.* gothique, ogival.

gouge [gaudʒ], *n.* gouge, *f.*—*v.t.* gouger; *to gouge out*, arracher (*l'œil etc.*).

gourd [guəd], *n.* gourde, calebasse, *f.*

gout [gaut], *n.* goutte, *f.*

gouty ['gauti], *a.* goutteux.

govern ['gʌvən], *v.t.* gouverner, régir, diriger.

governess ['gʌvənis], *n.* institutrice, gouvernante, *f.*

government ['gʌvənmənt], *n.* gouvernement, *m.*, administration, *f.*, régime, *m.*

governor ['gʌvənə], *n.* gouverneur, gouvernant; directeur (*d'une institution*); (*Mech.*) régulateur, *m.*

gown [gaun], *n.* robe, *f.*; *dressing gown*, peignoir, *m.*, robe de chambre, *f.*; *night-gown*, chemise de nuit, *f.*

grab [græb], *v.t.* empoigner, saisir (d'un geste brusque).

439

grace

grace [greis], *n.* grâce; faveur, *f.*; pardon; (*Mus.*) agrément; bénédicité (*avant le repas*), *m.*; grâces (*après le repas*), *f.pl.*—*v.t.* orner, embellir; illustrer, honorer (*de*).
graceful ['greisful], *a.* gracieux, bien fait, élégant.
gracefully ['greisfuli], *adv.* gracieusement, élégamment.
gracefulness ['greisfulnis], *n.* grâce, *f.*
graceless ['greislis], *a.* sans grâce; dépravé.
gracious ['greiʃəs], *a.* gracieux, clément, bon, favorable, bénin.
graciously ['greiʃəsli], *adv.* gracieusement, avec bonté, favorablement.
graciousness ['greiʃəsnis], *n.* bonté, grâce, *f.*
grade [greid], *n.* grade; degré, rang, *m.*—*v.t.* classer; calibrer; graduer.
grading ['greidiŋ], *n.* classement; calibrage, *m.*; graduation, *f.*
gradient ['greidiənt], *n.* (*Rail.*) rampe, inclinaison, *f.*
gradual ['grædjuəl], *a.* graduel, par degrés, gradué.
gradually ['grædjuəli], *adv.* graduellement, par degrés, peu à peu.
graduate ['grædjueit], *v.t.* graduer.—*v.i.* être reçu à un examen d'enseignement supérieur.—['grædjuit], *n.* gradué, *m.*
graduation [grædju'eiʃən], *n.* graduation; (*Univ.*) remise d'un diplôme, *f.*
graft (1) [grɑ:ft], *v.t.* greffer, enter (*sur*).—*n.* greffe, *f.*
graft (2) [grɑ:ft], *n.* (*colloq.*) corruption, *f.*
grafting ['grɑ:ftiŋ], *n.* greffe, *f.*
grafting knife ['grɑ:ftiŋnaif], *n.* greffoir, *m.*
grain [grein], *n.* grain, *m.*; céréales; fibres (*de bois*), *f.pl.*; **against the grain**, contre le fil, (*fig.*) à contre-cœur, à rebrousse-poil.
gram, gramme [græm], *n.* gramme, *m.*
grammar ['græmə], *n.* grammaire, *f.*
grammar school ['græməsku:l], *n.* école primaire, *f.*
grammatical [grə'mætikəl], *a.* grammatical; de grammaire, *f.*
gramophone ['græməfoun], *n.* gramophone; phonographe, *m.*
grampus ['græmpəs], *n.* épaulard, *m.*
granary ['grænəri], *n.* grenier, *m.*
grand [grænd], *a.* grand, magnifique, sublime, grandiose; **grand (piano)**, piano à queue, *m.*
grandchild ['græntʃaild], *n.* (*pl.* **grandchildren** ['græntʃildrən]) petit-fils, *m.*, petite-fille, *f.*
granddaughter ['grændɔ:tə], *n.* petite-fille, *f.*
grandee [græn'di:], *n.* grand d'Espagne, *m.*
grandeur ['grændjə], *n.* grandeur, *f.*, éclat, *m.*
grandfather ['grænfɑ:ðə], *n.* grand-père, *m.*
grandiloquence [græn'diləkwəns], *n.* langage pompeux, *m.*; emphase, grandiloquence, *f.*
grandiloquent [græn'diləkwənt], *a.* pompeux, enflé, grandiloquent.
grandly ['grændli], *adv.* grandement, avec éclat.
grandmother ['grænmʌðə], *n.* grand-mère, *f.*
grandson ['grænsʌn], *n.* petit-fils, *m.*
grandstand ['grændstænd], *n.* tribune, *f.*
grange [greindʒ], *n.* manoir (avec ferme), *m.*
granite ['grænit], *n.* granit, *m.*
grant [grɑ:nt], *v.t.* accorder, concéder; convenir, avouer, admettre.—*n.* aide, bourse; concession, *f.*

440

granulate ['grænjuleit], *v.t.* grener, granuler.—*v.i.* se granuler.
granule ['grænju:l], *n.* granule, *m.*
grape [greip], *n.* grain de raisin, *m.*; (*pl.*) raisins, *m.pl.*; **a bunch of grapes**, une grappe de raisin.
grape-fruit ['greipfru:t], *n.* pamplemousse, *m.*
grape-shot ['greipʃɔt], *n.* mitraille, *f.*
graph [grɑ:f], *n.* (*Math.*) courbe, *f.*; graphique, *m.*—*v.t.* graphiquer.
graphic ['græfik], *a.* graphique, pittoresque.
graph paper ['grɑ:fpeipə], *n.* papier quadrillé, *m.*
graphite ['græfait], *n.* graphite, *m.*
grapnel ['græpnəl], *n.* grappin, *m.*
grapple ['græpl], *n.* grappin, *m.*; lutte, *f.*—*v.t.* accrocher; grappiner.—*v.i.* en venir aux prises; lutter (*contre*).
grasp [grɑ:sp], *v.t.* empoigner, saisir, serrer; embrasser; vouloir se saisir de.—*n.* prise, étreinte, poignée; (*fig.*) portée; compréhension, *f.*; **within one's grasp**, à la portée de la main.
grasping ['grɑ:spiŋ], *a.* avide, cupide, avare.
grass [grɑ:s], *n.* herbe, *f.*; gazon, herbage, *m.*
grasshopper ['grɑ:shɔpə], *n.* sauterelle, *f.*
grassy ['grɑ:si], *a.* herbeux, couvert de gazon, verdoyant.
grate [greit], *n.* grille, *f.*; foyer (*âtre*), *m.*—*v.t.* râper; frotter.—*v.i.* crisser (*sur ou contre*).
grateful ['greitful], *a.* reconnaissant; (*fig.*) agréable.
gratefully ['greitfuli], *adv.* avec reconnaissance; (*fig.*) agréablement.
grater ['greitə], *n.* râpe, *f.*
gratification [grætifi'keiʃən], *n.* satisfaction, *f.*; plaisir, *m.*; gratification, récompense, *f.*
gratify ['grætifai], *v.t.* satisfaire, faire plaisir à; récompenser.
gratifying ['grætifaiiŋ], *a.* agréable; (*fig.*) flatteur.
grating ['greitiŋ], *a.* grinçant, discordant, choquant, désagréable.—*n.* grille, *f.*, grillage; grincement (*bruit*), *m.*
gratis ['greitis], *adv.* gratuitement, gratis, pour rien.
gratitude ['grætitju:d], *n.* gratitude, reconnaissance, *f.*
gratuitous [grə'tju:itəs], *a.* gratuit; (*fig.*) volontaire; bénévole.
gratuitously [grə'tju:itəsli], *adv.* gratuitement; (*fig.*) sans motif.
gratuity [grə'tju:iti], *n.* don, présent, *m.* gratification, *f.*; pourboire, *m.*
grave (1) [greiv], *n.* tombe, fosse, *f.*; tombeau, *m.*
grave (2) [greiv], *a.* grave, sérieux.
grave (3) [greiv], *v.t.* graver, tailler, ciseler.
grave-digger ['greivdigə], *n.* fossoyeur, *m.*
gravel ['grævl], *n.* gravier, sable, *m.*—*v.t.* sabler.
gravely ['greivli], *adv.* gravement, sérieusement.
graven [greivn], *a.* gravé, taillé, ciselé.
graver ['greivə], *n.* graveur; burin (*instrument*), *m.*
gravity ['græviti], *n.* gravité, *f.*; air sérieux, *m.*; pesanteur, *f.*
gravy ['greivi], *n.* jus (*de viande*), *m.*; sauce, *f.*
gravy boat, see **sauce boat**.

gray (*Am.*) [GREY].*.

graze [greiz], *v.t.* effleurer, raser, frôler; érafler, écorcher (*la peau*).—*v.i.* paître, brouter.—*n.* écorchure, éraflure, *f.*

grease [gri:s], *n.* graisse, *f.*—*v.t.* graisser.

greasiness ['gri:sinis, 'gri:zinis], *n.* état graisseux, *m.*; (*fig.*) onctuosité, *f.*

greasy ['gri:si, 'gri:zi], *a.* gras, graisseux; (*fig.*) onctueux.

great [greit], *a.* grand; considérable; important, principal; gros (*de*); **a great deal** (*of*), **a great many** (*of*), beaucoup (de).

great-coat ['greitkout], *n.* pardessus, *m.*; (*Mil.*) capote, *f.*

great-grandparents ['greitgrændpɛərənts], *n.pl.* arrière-grands-parents, *m.pl.*

greatly ['greitli], *adv.* grandement, fort, beaucoup, de beaucoup.

greatness ['greitnis], *n.* grandeur; sublimité; force, *f.*

Grecian ['gri:ʃən], *a.* grec, de Grèce.—*n.* Helléniste (*pers.*), *m.f.*

Greece [gri:s]. la Grèce, *f.*

greed [gri:d], **greediness** ['gri:dinis], *n.* cupidité, avidité; gourmandise, *f.*

greedily ['gri:dili], *adv.* avidement.

greedy ['gri:di], *a.* cupide, avide; glouton.

Greek [gri:k], *a.* grec, de Grèce.—*n.* grec (*langue*); Grec (*personne*), *m.*

green [gri:n], *a.* vert; (*fig.*) frais, nouveau; novice.—*n.* vert, *m.*; verdure, *f.*; gazon, *m.*; (*pl.*) légumes verts, *m.pl.*

greenfinch ['gri:nfintʃ], *n.* verdier, *m.*

greengage ['gri:ngeidʒ], *n.* reine-claude, *f.*

greengrocer ['gri:ngrousə], *n.* fruitier, marchand de légumes, *m.*

greenhorn ['gri:nho:n], *n.* blanc-bec, niais, *m.*

greenhouse ['gri:nhaus], *n.* serre, *f.*

greenish ['gri:niʃ], *a.* verdâtre.

Greenland ['gri:nlənd]. le Groenland, *m.*

greet [gri:t], *v.t.* saluer, accueillir.

greeting ['gri:tiŋ], *n.* salutation, *f.*, salut, *m.*; (*pl.*) compliments, *m.pl.*

gregarious [gri'gɛəriəs], *a.* grégaire.

Gregory ['gregəri]. Grégoire, *m.*

grenade [grə'neid], *n.* grenade, *f.*

grenadier [grenə'diə], *n.* grenadier, *m.*

grey [grei], *a.* gris.

greyhound ['greihaund], *n.* lévrier, *m.*

greyish ['greiiʃ], *a.* grisâtre.

grid [grid], **gridiron** ['gridaiən], *n.* gril, *m.*

grief [gri:f], *n.* douleur, tristesse, peine, *f.*; chagrin, *m.*

grievance ['gri:vəns], *n.* grief, *m.*; injustice, *f.*

grieve [gri:v], *v.t.* chagriner, attrister, faire de la peine à.—*v.i.* se chagriner, s'affliger.

grievous ['gri:vəs], *a.* lourd, douloureux, grave, affligeant; atroce.

grievously ['gri:vəsli], *adv.* grièvement, cruellement.

grill [gril], *v.t.* griller, faire griller.—*n.* gril, *m.*; grillade; viande grillée, *f.*

grim [grim], *a.* farouche, féroce; lugubre, effrayant; sinistre.

grimace [gri'meis], *n.* grimace; (*pl.*) grimacerie, *f.*—*v.i.* grimacer.

grime [graim], *n.* saleté, noirceur, *f.*

grimly ['grimli], *adv.* d'un air farouche *ou* sinistre.

grimness ['grimnis], *n.* air renfrogné, air farouche, *m.*

grimy ['graimi], *a.* sale, noirci, encrassé.

grin [grin], *n.* grimace, *f.*, ricanement, *m.*—*v.i.* ricaner, grimacer.

grind [graind], *v.t. irr.* moudre; broyer; aiguiser, repasser (*couteau etc.*); grincer (*dents*); (*fig.*) opprimer.

grinder ['graində], *n.* repasseur, émouleur; broyeur, *m.*; dent molaire, *f.*

grinding ['graindiŋ], *n.* broiement, grincement (*des dents etc.*); repassage (*de couteaux*), *m.*; (*fig.*) oppression, *f.*

grindstone ['graindstoun], *n.* meule, *f.*

grip [grip], *n.* prise, étreinte, *f.*, serrement, *m.*—*v.t.* empoigner, saisir, serrer.

gripe [graip], *v.t.* saisir; opprimer; donner la colique à.—*v.i.* avoir la colique.—*n.* saisine; (*pl.*) colique, *f.*

griping ['graipiŋ], *a.* (*fig.*) cuisant, affreux; avare (*pingre*).—*n.* colique, *f.*

grisly ['grizli], *a.* hideux, affreux, horrible.

grist [grist], *n.* blé à moudre, *m.*, mouture, *f.*; (*fig.*) gain, profit, *m.*

gristle ['grisl], *n.* cartilage, *m.*

grit [grit], *n.* grès, sable; (*fig.*) courage, *m.*

gritty ['griti], *a.* graveleux.

grizzled ['grizld], *a.* grison, grisâtre.

grizzly ['grizli], *a.* grisâtre; **grizzly bear**, ours gris d'Amérique, *m.*

groan [groun], *n.* gémissement, grognement, *m.*—*v.i.* gémir, grogner.

grocer ['grousə], *n.* épicier, *m.*

grocery ['grousəri], *n.* épicerie, *f.*

groggy ['grogi], *a.* gris, pochard; titubant; aux jambes faibles (*cheval*).

groin [groin], *n.* aine, *f.*; (*Arch.*) arête, *f.*

groom [gru:m], *n.* palefrenier, valet d'écurie, *m.*—*v.t.* panser; **well-groomed**, bien soigné, *m.*

groove [gru:v], *n.* rainure, rayure, cannelure; (*fig.*) ornière (*rut*), *f.*—*v.t.* creuser, canneler.

grope [group], *v.i.* tâtonner.

gropingly ['groupiŋli], *adv.* à tâtons.

gross [grous], *a.* gros; grossier, rude; (*Comm.*) brut; (*fig.*) flagrant, énorme.—*n.* gros, *m.*, grosse; masse, *f.*

grossly ['grousli], *adv.* grossièrement; d'une manière flagrante.

grossness ['grousnis], *n.* grossièreté; énormité, *f.*

grotto ['grotou], *n.* grotte, *f.*

grotesque [gro'tesk], *a.* grotesque.

ground (1) [graund], *past* and *p.p.* [GRIND] and *a.* broyé, moulu; aiguisé (*affilé*).

ground (2) [graund], *n.* terre, *f.*; terrain (*plot*); sol (*soil*), *m.*; fond (*de tableau, de dessin textile etc.*); (*fig.*) fondement, sujet, motif, *m.*, cause, *f.*; (*pl.*) terrains, *m.pl.*; sédiment, marc de café, *m.*—*v.t.* fonder, baser, établir, appuyer (*sur*).—*v.i.* échouer.

grounded ['graundid], *a.* fondé, établi; **well-grounded**, bien fondé.

ground floor ['graund'flɔ:], *n.* rez-de-chaussée, *m.*

groundless ['graundlis], *a.* sans fondement.

groundlessly ['graundlisli], *adv.* sans fondement.

group [gru:p], *n.* groupe, peloton, *m.*—*v.t.* grouper.

grouping ['gru:piŋ], *n.* groupement, *m.*

grouse (1) [graus], *n.* (*Orn.*) tétras; coq de bruyère, *m.*

grouse (2) [graus], *v.i.* grogner, grincher.

grove [grouv], *n.* bocage, bosquet, *m.*

grovel [grɔvl], *v.i.* ramper, se vautrer.

grovelling [grɔvliŋ], *a.* rampant, abject, vil. —*n.* bassesse, *f.*

grow [grou], *v.t. irr.* cultiver.—*v.i.* croître, pousser; s'accroître; devenir, se faire (*to become*); **to grow up**, croître, grandir, arriver à maturité.

grower [ˈgrouə], *n.* cultivateur, producteur, *m.*

growing [ˈgrouiŋ], *a.* croissant.—*n.* croissance; culture, *f.*

growl [graul], *v.i.* grogner, gronder.—*n.* grognement, grondement, *m.*

grown-up [ˈgrounʌp], *a.* fait, grand.—*n.* adulte, *m., f.*

growth [grouθ], *n.* croissance, *f.*; produit, cru, *m.*, récolte (*produce*), *f.*; (*fig.*) progrès, *m.*

grub [grʌb], *n.* larve, *f.*, ver blanc, *m.*—*v.t.* défricher, fouiller.—*v.i.* bêcher, creuser.

grubby [ˈgrʌbi], *a.* véreux; (*fig.*) sale.

grudge [grʌdʒ], *n.* rancune, animosité, *f.*; **to bear a grudge against**, en vouloir à.—*v.t.* donner à contre-cœur.

grudgingly [ˈgrʌdʒiŋli], *adv.* à contre-cœur; de mauvaise grâce.

gruel [ˈgruəl], *n.* gruau, *m.*

gruesome [ˈgruːsəm], *a.* macabre, horrible, lugubre.

gruff [grʌf], *a.* bourru, rude, rébarbatif.

grumble [grʌmbl], *v.i.* se plaindre, grogner, grommeler (*contre* ou *de*).

grumbler [ˈgrʌmblə], *n.* grondeur, grogneur, *m.*

grumbling [ˈgrʌmbliŋ], *n.* grognement, *m.*

grunt [grʌnt], *v.i.* grogner.—*n.* grognement, *m.*

guarantee [gærənˈtiː], *n.* garant, *m.*, caution, garantie, *f.*—*v.t.* garantir.

guard [gɑːd], *n.* garde; défense, protection, *f.*; garde (*personne*), (*Rail.*) conducteur, chef de train, *m.*—*v.t.* garder, défendre, protéger, veiller sur.—*v.i.* se garder, se prémunir (*contre*).

guarded [ˈgɑːdid], *a.* prudent, circonspect; réservé.

guardedly [ˈgɑːdidli], *adv.* avec circonspection, avec réserve.

guardian [ˈgɑːdjən], *n.* gardien, tutélaire.—*n.* gardien; tuteur (*de jeunes*), *m.*

guardianship [ˈgɑːdjənʃip], *n.* tutelle, protection, *f.*

guard-room [ˈgɑːdrum], *n.* corps de garde, *m.*, salle de police, *f.*

Guatemala [gwætəˈmɑːlə]. le Guatemala, *m.*

gudgeon [ˈgʌdʒən], *n.* goujon; (*Mech.*) tourillon, *m.*; (*fig.*) dupe, *f.*

guess [ges], *v.t., v.i.* deviner, conjecturer.—*n.* conjecture, *f.*

guest [gest], *n.* invité, *m.*, convive, *m., f.*; hôte, *m.*

guffaw [gəˈfɔː], *n.* gros rire, *m.*—*v.i.* pouffer de rire.

guidance [ˈgaidəns], *n.* conduite, direction, *f.*

guide [gaid], *n.* guide, conducteur, *m.*; **Girl Guide**, éclaireuse, *f.*—*v.t.* conduire, guider; diriger; **guided missile**, (*Mil.*) engin téléguidé, *m.*

guild [gild], *n.* corporation, guilde, *f.*

guildhall [ˈgildhɔːl], *n.* hôtel de ville, *m.*

guile [gail], *n.* astuce, *f.*, artifice, *m.*

guilt [gilt], *n.* culpabilité, *f.*

guiltily [ˈgiltili], *adv.* criminellement.

guiltless [ˈgiltlis], *a.* innocent.

guilty [ˈgilti], *a.* coupable; **the guilty party**, le coupable; **to find guilty**, (*Law*) déclarer coupable; **to plead guilty**, s'avouer coupable.

Guinea [ˈgini]. la Guinée, *f.*

guinea [ˈgini], *n.* guinée, *f.*

guinea fowl [ˈginifaul], *n.* pintade, *f.*

guinea pig [ˈginipig], *n.* cochon d'Inde, *m.*

guise [gaiz], *n.* guise, façon, apparence, *f.*; costume, *m.*, dehors, *m.pl.*

guitar [giˈtɑː], *n.* guitare, *f.*

gulf [gʌlf], *n.* golfe; (*fig.*) gouffre, *m.*

gull [gʌl], *n.* mouette, *f.*, goéland; (*fig.*) jobard, *m.*—*v.t.* duper, flouer.

gullet [ˈgʌlit], *n.* gosier, *m.*

gullible [ˈgʌlibl], *a.* crédule.

gully [ˈgʌli], *n.* ravin, *m.*

gulp [gʌlp], *v.t.* avaler, gober.—*n.* goulée, gorgée, *f.*, trait, *m.*; **at a gulp**, d'un trait.

gum [gʌm], *n.* gomme; (*Anat.*) gencive, *f.*

gumboil [ˈgʌmbɔil], *n.* abcès aux gencives, *m.*

gumption [ˈgʌmpʃən], *n.* (*colloq.*) sens pratique, *m.*, jugeotte, *f.*

gum tree [ˈgʌmtriː], *n.* gommier, *m.*; (*fig.*) **up a gum tree**, dans le pétrin.

gun [gʌn], *n.* canon, *m.*; pièce d'artillerie, bouche à feu, *m.*; fusil (*non rayé*); (*Am.*) revolver, *m.*; **machine gun**, mitrailleuse *f.*

gunboat [ˈgʌnbout], *n.* canonnière, *f.*

guncarriage [ˈgʌnkæridʒ], *n.* affût (de canon), *m.*

gunnel [GUNWALE].

gunner [ˈgʌnə], *n.* canonnier, servant, artilleur, *m.*

gunnery [ˈgʌnəri], *n.* artillerie, *f.*; tir au canon, *m.*

gunpowder [ˈgʌnpaudə], *n.* poudre à canon, *f.*

gunshot [ˈgʌnʃɔt], *n.* portée de fusil (*distance*), *f.*; coup de canon (*discharge*); coup de feu (*blessure*), *m.*

gunwale [ˈgʌnl], *n.* (*Naut.*) plat-bord, *m.*

gurgle [gəːgl], *v.i.* faire glouglou; gargouiller.

gush [gʌʃ], *n.* jaillissement, *m.*; effusion, *f.*, jet; débordement (*de sentiments*), *m.*—*v.i.* jaillir; (*fig.*) être sentimental à l'excès.

gusher [ˈgʌʃə], *n.* (*Min.*) puits jaillissant, *m.*

gushing [ˈgʌʃiŋ], *a.* jaillissant; bouillonnant; (*fig.*) expansif, empressé.

gusset [ˈgʌsit], *n.* gousset, *m.*

gust [gʌst], *n.* coup de vent, *m.*, bouffée, rafale, *f.*

gusty [ˈgʌsti], *a.* orageux, venteux.

gut [gʌt], *n.* boyau, intestin, *m.*; corde à boyau (*fabriqué*), *f.*; (*pl.*) (*fam.*) intestins, *m.pl.*, ventre; courage, cran, *m.*—*v.t.* éventrer, vider; (*fig.*) détruire.

gutter [ˈgʌtə], *n.* gouttière (*d'une maison*), *f.*; ruisseau, caniveau (*dans la rue*), *m.*—*v.i.* couler.

guttersnipe [ˈgʌtəsnaip], *n.* gamin, voyou, *m.*

guttural [ˈgʌtərəl], *a.* guttural.

guy [gai], *n.* épouvantail, *m.*; (*Naut.*) corde soutien, *f.*, guide; (*Am.*) type, individu, *m.*

Guyana [giˈɑːnə], la Guyane, *f.*

guzzle [gʌzl], *v.t., v.i.* bouffer (*aliment*), lamper (*boisson*).

gym [dʒim], [GYMNASIUM].

gymkhana [dʒimˈkɑːnə], *n.* gymkhana, *m.*

gymnasium [dʒimˈneiziəm], *n.* gymnase, *m.*

gymnast ['dʒimnæst], *n.* gymnaste, *m.*, *f.*
gymnastic [dʒim'næstik], *a.* gymnastique.—*n.*(*pl.*) gymnastique, *f.*
gypsum ['dʒipsəm], *n.* gypse, *m.*
gypsy [GIPSY].
gyrate [dʒai'reit], *v.i.* tournoyer.
gyration [dʒai'reiʃən], *n.* mouvement giratoire, *m.*

H

H, h [eitʃ]. huitième lettre de l'alphabet, *m.* ou *f.*; *H-bomb*, [HYDROGEN].
haberdasher ['hæbədæʃə], *n.* confectionneur et chemisier, *m.*
haberdashery ['hæbədæʃəri], *n.* confection pour hommes, *f.*
habit ['hæbit], *n.* habitude, coutume, *f.*; (*pl.*) mœurs, *f.pl.*; *riding habit*, amazone, *f.*; *to be in the habit of*, avoir coutume de.—*v.t.* vêtir.
habitable ['hæbitəbl], *a.* habitable.
habitation [hæbi'teiʃən], *n.* habitation, demeure, *f.*
habitual [hə'bitjuəl], *a.* habituel.
habitually [hə'bitjuəli], *adv.* habituellement, d'habitude.
habituate [hə'bitjueit], *v.t.* habituer, accoutumer.
hack [hæk], *v.t.* hacher, couper, ébrécher; (*fig.*) massacrer, écorcher.
hack (2) [hæk], *n.* cheval de louage, *m.*; rosse (*cheval sans force*), *f.*; (*fig.*) écrivassier à gages, *m.*
hackney ['hækni], *n.* *hackney carriage*, fiacre, *m.*
hackneyed ['hæknid], *a.* banal, rebattu; *hackneyed phrase*, cliché, *m.*
haddock ['hædək], *n.* (*Ichth.*) aiglefin, *m.*
Hades ['heidi:z]. les Enfers, *m.pl.*
haemoglobin [hi:mə'gloubin], *n.* hémoglobine, *f.*
haemorrhage ['heməridʒ], *n.* hémorrhagie, *f.*
haft [ha:ft], *n.* manche, *m.*, poignée, *f.*
hag [hæg], *n.* vieille sorcière; (*pop.*) vieille fée, *f.*
haggard ['hægəd], *a.* hagard, farouche, égaré.
haggle [hægl], *v.i.* marchander.
Hague [heig], **The.** La Haye, *f.*
hail (1) [heil], *n.* grêle, *f.*—*v.i.* grêler.
hail (2) [heil], *n.* salut, appel, *m.*—*int.* salut!—*v.t.* saluer; (*Naut.*) héler; *to hail a taxi*, héler *ou* appeler un taxi; *to hail from*, venir de.
hailstone ['heilstoun], *n.* grêlon, *m.*
hailstorm ['heilstɔ:m], *n.* tempête de grêle, *f.*
hair [hɛə], *n.* cheveu (*a single hair*), *m.*; cheveux, *m.pl.*, chevelure (*head of hair*), *f.*; poil (*on the body, on animals etc.*), crin (*horsehair*), *m.*; soies (*bristles*), *f.pl.*; *to do one's hair*, se coiffer; *to split hairs*, chicaner sur les mots.
hair-brush ['hɛəbrʌʃ], *n.* brosse à cheveux, *f.*
hair-cut ['hɛəkʌt], *n.* coupe de cheveux, *f.*
hairdresser ['hɛədresə], *n.* coiffeur, *m.*
hairless ['hɛəlis], *a.* chauve, sans cheveux; sans poil (*animal*).

hair net ['hɛənet], *n.* résille, *f.*
hairy ['hɛəri], *a.* velu, chevelu, poilu.
Haiti [hai'i:ti]. Haïti, *m.* ou *f.*
Haitian [hai'i:ʃən], *a.* haïtien.—*n.* Haïtien (*personne*), *m.*
hake [heik], *n.* (*Ichth.*) merluche, *f.*, (*fam.*) colin, *m.*
halberd ['hælbəd], *n.* hallebarde, *f.*
hale [heil], *a.* robuste, sain, bien portant; *to be hale and hearty*, avoir bon pied, bon œil.
half [ha:f], *a.* demi.—*n.* (*pl.* **halves** [ha:vz]) moitié, *f.*, demi, *m.*, *half an hour*, une demi-heure, *f.*; (*pop.*) *not half!* tu parles!—*adv.* à demi, à moitié.
half-back ['ha:fbæk], *n.* (*Ftb.*) demi, *m.*
half brother ['ha:fbrʌðə], *n.* demi-frère, frère utérin, frère consanguin, *m.*
half-caste ['ha:fka:st], *n.* métis, *m.*
half fare ['ha:f'fɛə], *n.* demi-place, *f.*, demi-tarif, *m.*
half holiday ['ha:f'hɔlidi], *n.* demi-congé, *m.*
half pay ['ha:f'pei], *n.* demi-solde, *f.*
half time ['ha:f'taim], *n.* (*Spt.*) la mi-temps, *f.*
half-way ['ha:f'wei], *adv.* à mi-chemin; *half-way up the hill*, à mi-côte.
half-witted ['ha:f'witid], *a.* niais, sot, idiot.
half year ['ha:f'jiə], *n.* semestre, *m.*
halibut ['hælibət], *n.* (*Ichth.*) flétan, *m.*
hall [hɔ:l], *n.* salle, *f.*; vestibule (*entrance-hall*); château, manoir (*seat*); réfectoire (*dining hall*); hôtel de ville (*town hall*), *m.*; *hall porter*, concierge, *m.*
hall-mark ['hɔ:lmɑ:k], *n.* poinçon de contrôle, *m.*—*v.t.* contrôler.
hallo! [hə'lou], *int.* holà! hé!
hallow ['hælou], *v.t.* sanctifier, consacrer.
hallucinate [hə'lju:sineit], *v.t.* halluciner.
hallucination [həlju:si'neiʃən], *n.* hallucination; (*fig.*) déception, illusion, *f.*
halo ['heilou], *n.* (*Astron.*) halo, *m.*; (*Paint.*) auréole, *f.*
halt (1) [hɔ:lt], *n.* halte, *f.*; arrêt; clochement, *m.*—*v.i.* faire halte.—*int.* halte-là!
***halt** (2) [hɔ:lt], *a.* boiteux, estropié.
halter ['hɔ:ltə], *n.* licou, *m.*, longe (*à cheval*); corde (*du gibet*), *f.*
halve [ha:v], *v.t.* diviser en deux.
ham [hæm], *n.* jambon; jarret (*humain*), *m.*
hamlet ['hæmlit], *n.* hameau, *m.*
hammer ['hæmə], *n.* marteau; chien (*de fusil*), *m.*; *to bring under the hammer*, mettre aux enchères.—*v.t.* marteler, forger.—*v.i.* marteler.
hammock ['hæmək], *n.* hamac, *m.*
hamper (1) ['hæmpə], *n.* panier, *m.*, manne, *f.*
hamper (2) ['hæmpə], *v.t.* empêtrer, embarrasser, gêner.
hamstring ['hæmstriŋ], *n.* tendon du jarret, *m.*—*v.t. irr.* (*conjug. like* STRING) couper le jarret à; (*fig.*) couper les moyens à.
hand [hænd], *n.* main; palme (*mesure de 4 pouces*); signature; écriture (*calligraphie*), *f.*; (*Cards*) jeu, *m.*; aiguille (*d'une montre etc.*), *f.*; ouvrier, employé, *m.*; *at hand*, sous la main; *off-hand*, sur-le-champ; *second-hand*, d'occasion.—*v.t.* passer, donner, remettre; donner la main à; conduire, guider; *to hand about* or *round*, faire passer de main en main, faire circuler; *to hand down*, transmettre; *to hand over*, remettre, céder.

handbag

handbag ['hændbæg], *n.* sac à main, *m.*
hand bell ['hændbel], *n.* sonnette, clochette, *f.*
handbook ['hændbuk], *n.* manuel; guide, *m.*
handcuff ['hændkʌf], *n.* menotte, *f.*—*v.t.* mettres les menottes à.
handful ['hændful], *n.* poignée, *f.*; (*fig.*) petit nombre, peu, *m.*
handicap ['hændikæp], *n.* handicap, *m.*— *v.t.* handicaper.
handicraft ['hændikraːft], *n.* métier, travail manuel, *m.*
handiwork ['hændiwəːk], *n.* ouvrage, travail manuel, *m.*
handkerchief ['hæŋkətʃif], *n.* mouchoir, *m.*
handle ['hændl], *n.* manche, *m.*; poignée (*d'une epée etc.*), *f.*; bouton (*d'une porte*), *m.*; anse (*d'une cruche*); queue (*d'une poêle*), *f.*; **starting handle**, (*Motor.*) manivelle (de mise en marche), *f.*—*v.t.* manier; toucher à, manipuler.
handle-bar ['hændlbaː], *n.* guidon (*de bicyclette*), *m.*
handling ['hændliŋ], *n.* maniement, traitement, *m.*
handmaid ['hændmeid], *n.* servante, *f.*
handrail ['hændreil], *n.* garde-fou, *m.*, rampe, main courante, *f.*
handshake ['hændʃeik], *n.* poignée de main, *f.*, serrement de main, *m.*
handsome ['hænsəm], *a.* beau, élégant; (*fig.*) gracieux.
handsomely ['hænsəmli], *adv.* joliment, élégamment; généreusement.
handwriting ['hændraitiŋ], *n.* écriture, *f.*
handy ['hændi], *a.* adroit (*personne*); commode; à portée de la main.
hang [hæŋ], *v.t. irr.* pendre, suspendre; accrocher (*à*); tendre, tapisser (*de*); laisser pendre, pencher, baisser (*la tête etc.*); poser (*portes etc.*); **hang it!** fichtre! **go and be hanged**, va-t'en au diable! *to* **hang fire**, faire long feu; (*fig.*) vaciller.— *v.i.* pendre, être suspendu; s'accrocher, se pendre; baisser, se pencher (*à*); *to* **hang about**, rôder autour de; *to* **hang over**, être suspendu sur, surplomber.
hangar ['hæŋə], *n.* (*Av.*) hangar, *m.*
hang-dog ['hændɔg], *n.* **hang-dog look**, mine patibulaire, *f.*
hanger-on ['hæŋə'rɔn], *n.* dépendant, parasite, *m.*
hanging ['hæŋiŋ], *a.* suspendu.—*n.* suspension, pendaison; pose (*papier de tenture*), *f.*; collage, *m.*; (*pl.*) tapisserie, tenture, *f.*
hangman ['hæŋmən], *n.* (*pl.* **-men** [men]) bourreau, *m.*
hank [hæŋk], *n.* poignée, *f.*, écheveau, *m.*
hanker ['hæŋkə], *v.i. to* **hanker after**, désirer ardemment.
hankering ['hæŋkəriŋ], *n.* grande envie, *f.*, vif désir, *m.*
haphazard [hæp'hæzəd], *a.* au petit bonheur, fortuit.—*n.* hasard, sort, *m.*
haply ['hæpli], *adv.* par hasard; peut-être.
happen ['hæpən], *v.i.* arriver, advenir, se passer; se trouver par hasard.
happily ['hæpili], *adv.* heureusement, par bonheur.
happiness ['hæpinis], *n.* bonheur, *m.*
happy ['hæpi], *a.* heureux, content.
harass ['hærəs], *v.t.* harasser, harceler.

harbinger ['haːbindʒə], *n.* avant-coureur, précurseur, *m.*
harbor ['haːbə], *n.* port, havre; (*fig.*) refuge, asile, gîte, *m.*—*v.t.* héberger, recéler, donner asile à; (*fig.*) entretenir, nourrir.— *v.i.* se réfugier.
hard [haːd], *a.* dur, ferme; (*fig.*) malaisé, difficile; pénible, rude, rigoureux; dur à la détente (*pingre*); **hard frost**, forte gelée, *f.*; **hard labor**, travaux forcés, *m.pl.*; **hard up**, à court (d'argent).—*adv.* dur, rudement, péniblement; fort, ferme.
harden [haːdn], *v.t.* durcir; (*fig.*) endurcir (*à*).—*v.i.* s'endurcir, devenir dur.
hardening ['haːdniŋ], *n.* durcissement; (*fig.*) endurcissement, *m.*; trempe (*d'acier*), *f.*
hardihood ['haːdihud], *n.* hardiesse, audace, intrépidité, *f.*
hardily ['haːdili], *adv.* durement, hardiment.
hardiness ['haːdinis], *n.* hardiesse, *f.*; tempérament robuste, *m.*; (*fig.*) effronterie, assurance, *f.*
hardly ['haːdli], *adv.* durement, rudement, mal; à peine, guère (*presque pas*); **hardly ever**, presque jamais.
hardness ['haːdnis], *n.* dureté, solidité; difficulté; crudité (*d'eau*), *f.*
hardship ['haːdʃip], *n.* fatigue, peine, privation, *f.*; (*pl.*) épreuves, souffrances, *f.pl.*
hardware ['haːdwɛə], *n.* quincaillerie, *f.*
hardy ['haːdi], *a.* hardi, courageux; fort; de pleine terre (*plantes*).
hare [hɛə], *n.* lièvre, *m.*
hare-brained ['hɛəbreind], *a.* écervelé, étourdi.
hare-lip ['hɛəlip], *n.* bec-de-lièvre, *m.*
hark [haːk], *v.i.* écouter, prêter l'oreille.—*int.* écoutez!
harlequin ['haːlikwin], *n.* arlequin, *m.*
harm [haːm], *n.* tort, dommage, mal, *m.*— *v.t.* nuire à, faire du mal à.
harmful ['haːmful], *a.* nuisible, malfaisant, nocif.
harmless ['haːmlis], *a.* innocent, inoffensif.
harmonic [haː'mɔnik], *a.* harmonique; harmonieux.—*n.(pl.)* harmonique, *f.*
harmonious [haː'mounias], *a.* harmonieux; mélodieux.
harmonize ['haːmənaiz], *v.t.* rendre harmonieux, accorder, harmoniser.—*v.i.* s'harmoniser; (*fig.*) s'accorder.
harmony ['haːməni], *n.* harmonie, *f.*; accord, *m.*
harness ['haːnis], *n.* harnais, harnachement, *m.*—*v.t.* harnacher; atteler (*à une voiture*).
harp [haːp], *n.* harpe, *f.*; **jew's harp**, guimbarde, *f.*—*v.i.* jouer de la harpe; *to* **harp on one string**, rabâcher toujours la même chose.
harpist ['haːpist], *n.* harpiste, *m., f.*
harpoon [haː'puːn], *n.* harpon, *m.*—*v.t.* harponner.
harpsichord ['haːpsikɔːd], *n.* clavecin, *m.*
harridan ['hæridən], *n.* chipie, mégère, *f.*
harrow ['hærou], *n.* herse, *f.*—*v.t.* herser; (*fig.*) torturer.
harrowing ['hærouiŋ], *a.* navrant.—*n.* hersage; (*fig.*) déchirement, *m.*
Harry ['hæri]. Henri, *m.*
harry ['hæri], *v.t.* harceler; piller.
harsh [haːʃ], *a.* âpre, rude, dur; discordant.
harshly ['haːʃli], *adv.* durement, sévèrement.

harshness ['ha:∫nis], n. âpreté; discordance, f.

harum-scarum ['hɛərəm'skɛərəm], a. écervelé, étourdi.

harvest ['ha:vist], n. moisson (de blé); récolte (de fruits etc.); vendange (de raisins), f.—v.t. moissonner; récolter; vendanger.

harvester. see combine-harvester.

hash [hæ∫], n. hachis, m.—v.t. hacher, hacher menu; (fig.) plagier.

hasp [hæsp, ha:sp], n. loquet, m.

hassock ['hæsək], n. coussin (pour les genoux ou les pieds), m.

haste [heist], n. hâte, précipitation, f., emportement, m.; diligence, f.; in haste, à la hâte; to make haste, se hâter, se dépêcher.—v.i. or hasten [heisn], se hâter, se dépêcher, s'empresser.

hasten [heisn], v.t. hâter, dépêcher.

hastily ['heistili], adv. à la hâte; brusquement.

hastiness ['heistinis], n. hâte, précipitation, f.; emportement, m.

hasty ['heisti], a. rapide, précipité; inconsidéré, emporté.

hat [hæt], n. chapeau, m.; bowler-hat, chapeau melon; felt hat, feutre, m.; soft felt hat, chapeau mou; straw hat, chapeau de paille; top hat, chapeau haut de forme.

hatch (1) [hæt∫], n. (pl. hatches ['hæt∫iz]) couvée (de poulets); éclosion (d'œufs); porte coupée (dans le mur); (Naut.) écoutille, f.; (pl.) panneaux des écoutilles, m.pl.—v.t. couver (incuber); faire éclore; (fig.) tramer, produire.—v.i. éclore.

hatch (2) [hæt∫], v.t. hacher (un dessin).

hatchet ['hæt∫it], n. cognée, hachette, haché, f.

hate [heit], n. haine, f.—v.t. haïr, détester.

hateful ['heitful], a. odieux, détestable.

hatred ['heitrid], n. haine, f.

hat stand ['hætstænd], n. porte-chapeaux, m. inv.

hatter ['hætə], n. chapelier, m.

haughtily ['hɔ:tili], adv. hautainement, avec arrogance.

haughtiness ['hɔ:tinis], n. arrogance, f.

haughty ['hɔ:ti], a. hautain, arrogant.

haul [hɔ:l], n. tirage, remorquage; coup de filet, m.—v.t. tirer, remorquer, haler; charrier, transporter.

haulage ['hɔ:lidʒ], n. camionnage, roulage; remorquage, m.

hauler ['hɔ:lə], n. camionneur, m.

haunch [hɔ:nt∫], n. hanche (d'un animal), f., cuissot (de venaison), m.

haunt [hɔ:nt], n. retraite, f.; repaire (de voleurs etc.), m.—v.t. hanter, fréquenter; (fig.) obséder.

Havana [hə'vænə]. 1a Havane, f.

have [hæv], v.t. and aux. irr. avoir; tenir, posséder; contenir; prendre; faire; I had rather, j'aimerais mieux; I have it, j'y suis; to have to, devoir, falloir, avoir à.

haven [heivn], n. havre, port; (fig.) asile, m.

haversack ['hævəsæk], n. (Mil.) musette, f.; havresac, m.

havoc ['hævək], n. dégât, ravage, m.

hawk [hɔ:k], n. faucon, m.—v.t. chasser au faucon; colporter (vendre).

hawker ['hɔ:kə], n. colporteur, m.

hawser ['hɔ:zə], n. haussière, f., grelin, m.

hawthorn ['hɔ:θɔ:n], n. aubépine, f.

hay [hei], n. foin, m.

hay fever ['hei'fi:və], n. rhume des foins, m.

hay-making ['heimeikiŋ], n. fenaison, f.

hayrick ['heirik], haystack ['heistæk], n. meule de foin, f.

hazard ['hæzəd], n. hasard, danger, risque, m.—v.t. hasarder, risquer.—v.i. se hasarder, s'aventurer.

hazardous ['hæzədəs], a. hasardeux, risqué, dangereux.

haze [heiz], n. petite brume; (fig.) obscurité, f.

hazel [heizl], a. noisette.—n. noisetier, coudrier, m.

hazel-nut ['heizlnʌt], n. noisette, f.

hazily ['heizili], adv. indistinctement.

hazy ['heizi], a. brumeux; to have hazy notions, avoir des idées vagues.

he [hi:], pron. il, celui, lui; he and I, lui et moi; he that or he who, celui qui.

he- [hi:], pref. mâle.

head [hed], a. premier, principal, en chef.—n. tête, f.; chef, avant, m.; proue (de navire), f.; haut bout (d'une table); chevet (d'un lit), m.; chute (d'eau), f.; pièces (de gibier), f.pl.; source (d'une rivière), f.; (fig.) sujet, chapitre, m.—v.t. conduire, diriger.—v.i. to head for, (Naut.) mettre le cap sur; se diriger vers, s'avancer vers.

headache ['hedeik], n. mal de tête, m., migraine, f.

head-dress ['heddres], n. coiffure, f.

heading ['hediŋ], n. titre, en-tête, m.

headland ['hedlənd], n. cap, promontoire, m.

head-light ['hedlait], n. (Motor.) phare, m.

headline ['hedlain], n. (Journ.) titre, sous-titre, m.

headlong ['hedlɔŋ], adv. la tête la première; (fig.) tête baissée.—a. précipité, irréfléchi.

headmaster ['hed'ma:stə], n. principal, directeur, proviseur, m.

head-mistress ['hed'mistris], n. directrice, f.

head-phone ['hedfoun], n. (Teleph.) écouteur, m.

head-quarters ['hed'kwɔ:təz], n.pl. quartier général, m.

headstone ['hedstoun], n. pierre tombale, f.

headstrong ['hedstrɔŋ], a. opiniâtre, obstiné, entêté.

headway ['hedwei], n. progrès, m.; to make headway, avancer, progresser.

heady ['hedi], a. capiteux (boisson).

heal [hi:l], v.t. guérir; (fig.) apaiser.—v.i. guérir, se guérir; se cicatriser.

healing ['hi:liŋ], a. curatif; (fig.) salutaire.—n. guérison, f.

health [helθ], n. santé, f.; toast, m.; National Health Service, sécurité sociale, f.; bill of health, patente de santé, f.

healthily ['helθili], adv. en santé; sainement.

healthy ['helθi], a. bien portant, en bonne santé; sain, salubre.

heap [hi:p], n. tas, monceau, amas, m.—v.t. entasser, amonceler.

hear [hiə], v.t. irr. entendre; entendre dire; écouter (faire attention à); (fig.) apprendre; to hear it said, entendre dire.—v.i. entendre; entendre parler; écouter; recevoir des nouvelles, avoir des nouvelles (de); hear! hear! très bien! bravo!

445

hearing

hearing ['hiəriŋ], *n.* ouïe (*sens auditif*); audition (*de témoins*), *f.*; **hard of hearing**, dur d'oreille; **within hearing**, à portée de la voix.
hearken [hɑːkn], *v.i.* écouter.
hearsay ['hiəsei], *n.* ouï-dire, *m.*
hearse [həːs], *n.* corbillard, *m.*
heart [hɑːt], *n.* cœur; (*fig.*) courage; centre, *m.*
heart attack ['hɑːtətæk], *n.* crise cardiaque, *f.*
heart-breaking ['hɑːtbreikiŋ], *a.* qui fend le cœur, navrant.
heart-broken ['hɑːtbroukən], *a.* qui a le cœur brisé.
heartburn ['hɑːtbəːn], *n.* brûlures d'estomac, aigreurs, *f.pl.*
hearten [hɑːtn], *v.t.* encourager, animer.
heart failure ['hɑːtfeiljə], *n.* arrêt du cœur, *m.*
heartfelt ['hɑːtfelt], *a.* qui vient du cœur.
hearth [hɑːθ], *n.* âtre, foyer, *m.*
heartily ['hɑːtili], *adv.* cordialement, de bon cœur; de bon appétit (*manger*).
heartiness ['hɑːtinis], *n.* cordialité; vigueur (*de l'appétit*), *f.*
heartless ['hɑːtlis], *a.* sans cœur, sans pitié.
hearty ['hɑːti], *a.* sincère, cordial; abondant, bon (*repas*).
heat [hiːt], *n.* chaleur; (*fig.*) ardeur; colère (*courroux*); (*Racing*) épreuve, *f.*—*v.t.* chauffer, échauffer.—*v.i.* s'échauffer.
heated ['hiːtid], *a.* chaud; échauffé; animé.
heath [hiːθ], *n.* bruyère, lande; brande (*plante*), *f.*
heathen [hiːðn], *a. and n.* païen, *m.*
heather ['heðə], *n.* bruyère, brande, *f.*
heating ['hiːtiŋ], *n.* chauffage, *m.*
heave [hiːv], *n.* effort (*pour soulever*), *m.*, secousse, *f.*; soulèvement, *m.*—*v.t. irr.* lever; élever; soulever; pousser (*un soupir*).—*v.i.* se soulever; palpiter, battre (*sein, cœur etc.*).
heaven [hevn], *n.* ciel, *m.*, cieux, *m.pl.*
heavenly ['hevnli], *a.* céleste, divin.
heavily ['hevili], *adv.* pesamment, lourdement; fortement.
heaviness ['hevinis], *n.* pesanteur, lourdeur; (*fig.*) tristesse, *f.*
heavy ['hevi], *a.* lourd, pesant; (*fig.*) gros; triste.
Hebrew ['hiːbruː], *a.* hébreu, *m.*; hébraïque, *f.*—*n.* hébreu (*langue*); Hébreu, Juif (*personne*), *m.*
heckle [hekl], *v.t.* embarrasser de questions, harasser (*en public*).
hectic ['hektik], *a.* hectique; agité, fiévreux.
hedge [hedʒ], *n.* haie, *f.*—*v.t.* entourer d'une haie.—*v.i.* (*fig.*) éviter de se compromettre.
hedgehog ['hedʒhɔg], *n.* hérisson, *m.*
hedge sparrow ['hedʒspærou], *n.* mouchet, *m.*, fauvette d'hiver, *f.*
heed [hiːd], *n.* attention, *f.*, soin, *m.*—*v.t.* faire attention à, prendre garde à, écouter.
heedless ['hiːdlis], *a.* étourdi, inattentif, insouciant.
heedlessly ['hiːdlisli], *adv.* négligemment; étourdiment.
heel [hiːl], *n.* talon, *m.*; **to be down at heel**, traîner la savate; **to cool one's heels**, faire antichambre.—*v.i.* **to heel over**, (*Naut.*) donner de la bande.
hefty ['hefti], *a.* (*fam.*) solide, costaud.

heifer ['hefə], *n.* génisse, *f.*
height [hait], *n.* hauteur, élévation; taille, *f.*; (*fig.*) comble, faîte, *m.*; **the height of summer**, le cœur *ou* le fort de l'été.
heighten [haitn], *v.t.* rehausser, relever.
heinous ['heinəs], *a.* atroce.
heir [ɛə], *n.* héritier, *m.*
heiress ['ɛəris], *n.* héritière, *f.*
heirloom ['ɛəluːm], *n.* meuble *ou* bijou (de famille), *m.*
Helen ['helin], (*Myth.*) Hélène, *f.*
helicopter ['helikɔptə], *n.* hélicoptère, *m.*
helium ['hiːliəm], *n.* (*Chem.*) hélium, *m.*
hell [hel], *n.* enfer, *m.*
hellish ['heliʃ], *a.* infernal, d'enfer.
hello! [he'lou], **hullo!** [hʌ'lou], *int.* holà! allô! (*au téléphone*); tiens! (*surprise*).
helm (1) [helm], *n.* (*Naut.*) gouvernail, timon, *m.*, barre, *f.*
helm (2) [helm], *n.* (*poet.*) heaume (*casque*), *m.*
helmet ['helmit], *n.* casque, *m.*
helmsman ['helmzmən], *n.* (*pl.* **-men** [men]) timonier, *m.*
help [help], *n.* secours, *m.*; aide, assistance, *f.*; remède (*recours*), *m.*; **help!** au secours!—*v.t.* aider, secourir, assister; servir (*à table*); empêcher (*prevent*); éviter (*avoid*); **help yourself** (*at table*), servez-vous; **how can I help it?** que voulez-vous que j'y fasse? **how can it be helped?** qu'y faire? **I can't help it**, je n'y puis rien; **I cannot help saying**, je ne puis m'empêcher de dire.—*v.i.* aider, servir, contribuer.
helper ['helpə], *n.* aide, *m.*, *f.*
helpful ['helpful], *a.* utile; secourable.
helpless ['helplis], *a.* faible, impuissant; sans appui.
helplessly ['helplisli], *adv.* faiblement; sans ressource.
helter-skelter ['heltə'skeltə], *adv.* pêle-mêle; en pagaille.
helve [helv], *n.* manche, *m.*
hem [hem], *n.* ourlet, bord, *m.*—*v.t.* ourler, border; **to hem in**, entourer.
hemisphere ['hemisfiə], *n.* hémisphère, *m.*
hemlock ['hemlɔk], *n.* ciguë, *f.*
hemorrhage [HAEMORRHAGE]
hemp [hemp], *n.* (*Bot.*) chanvre, *m.*; (*fig.*) corde, *f.*
hen [hen], *n.* poule; femelle (*d'oiseau*), *f.*
hence [hens], *adv.* d'ici; de là, ainsi (*pour cela*); désormais (*temps*).
henceforth ['hensfɔːθ], **henceforward** [hens'fɔːwəd], *adv.* désormais, dorénavant, à l'avenir.
henchman ['hentʃmən], *n.* (*pl.* **-men** [men]) écuyer, valet; (*fig.*) partisan, *m.*
hen house ['henhaus], *n.* poulailler, *m.*
hen-pecked ['henpekt], *a.* gouverné par sa femme.
Henry ['henri]. Henri, *m.*
her [həː], *pers. pron.* elle, la, lui.—*poss. 'a.* son, sa, ses.—*dem. pron.* celle, *f.*
herald ['herəld], *n.* héraut; (*fig.*) avant-coureur, précurseur, *m.*—*v.i.* annoncer.
heraldry ['herəldri], *n.* science héraldique, *f.*, blason, *m.*
herb [həːb], *n.* herbe, *f.*; **pot-herbs**, herbes potagères, *f.pl.*; **sweet herbs**, fines herbes, *f.pl.*
herbaceous [həː'beiʃəs], *a.* herbacé.
herbage ['həːbidʒ], *n.* herbage, *m.*

446

herbalist ['hɔ:bɔlist], n. herboriste, m., f.

Hercules ['hɔ:kjuli:z]. Hercule, m.

herd [hɔ:d], n. troupeau, m., troupe, f.—v.t. garder.—v.i. vivre en troupeau.

herdsman ['hɔ:dzmɔn], n. (pl. -men [men]) bouvier, m.

here [hiɔ], adv. ici; voici, que voici; here! présent! here and there, çà et là; here they are, les voici; I am here, me voici; this one here, celui-ci.

hereafter [hiɔr'ɑ:ftɔ], adv. désormais; dans la vie à venir.—n. l'au-delà, m.

hereby [hiɔ'bai], adv. par ce moyen, par là.

hereditary [hi'reditɔri], a. héréditaire.

heredity [hi'rediti], n. hérédité, f.

heresy ['herisi], n. hérésie, f.

heretic ['heretik], n. hérétique, m., f.

heretical [hi'retikɔl], a. hérétique.

heretofore [hiɔtu'fɔ:], adv. jadis, jusqu'ici.

hereupon [hiɔrɔ'pɔn], adv. là-dessus.

herewith [hiɔ'wið], adv. ci-joint.

heritage ['heritidʒ], n. héritage, m.

hermetic [hɔ:'metik], a. hermétique.

hermetically [hɔ:'metikli], adv. hermétiquement.

hermit ['hɔ:mit], n. ermite, m.

hero ['hiɔrou], n. (pl. heroes ['hiɔrouz]) héros, m.

heroic [hi'rouik], heroical [-ɔl], a. héroïque.

heroine ['hɔrouin], n. héroïne, f.

heroism ['hɔrouizm], n. héroïsme, m.

heron ['herɔn], n. héron, m.

herring ['heriŋ], n. hareng, m.; red herring, hareng saur; (fig.) diversion, f.

hers [hɔ:z], pron. le sien, m., la sienne, f., les siens, m.pl., les siennes, f.pl.; a friend of hers, une de ses amies, f.

herself [hɔ:'self], pron. elle-même, elle; (reflexive) se; by herself, toute seule.

hesitant ['hezitɔnt], a. hésitant.

hesitate ['heziteit], v.i. hésiter.

hesitation [hezi'teiʃɔn], n. hésitation, f.

heterodox ['hetɔrɔdɔks], a. hétérodoxe.

heterogeneous [hetɔrɔ'dʒi:niɔs], a. hétérogène.

hew [hju:], v.t. irr. tailler, couper.

hewer ['hjuɔ], n. tailleur (de pierre); piqueur (de charbon); fendeur (de bois), m.

hexagon ['heksɔgɔn], n. hexagone, m.

heyday ['heidei], n. beaux jours, m.pl.

hiatus [hai'eitɔs], n. hiatus, m.; (fig.) lacune, f.

hibernate ['haibɔneit], v.i. hiverner, hiberner.

hiccough, hiccup ['hikʌp], n. hoquet, m.— v.i. avoir le hoquet.

hidden [hidn], a. caché, secret; (fig.) occulte.

hide (1) [haid], n. peau, f., cuir, m.

hide (2) [haid], v.t. irr. cacher; enfouir (en terre); hide-and-seek, cache-cache, m.— v.i. se cacher, se tenir caché.

hideous ['hidiɔs], a. hideux, affreux.

hiding (1) ['haidiŋ], n. (colloq.) rossée, raclée, f.; to give someone a good hiding, tanner le cuir à quelqu'un.

hiding (2) ['haidiŋ], n. in hiding, caché; hiding place, cachette, f.

hie [hai], v.i. se hâter, se rendre (à).

hierarchy ['haiɔrɑ:ki], n. hiérarchie, f.

high [hai], a. haut, élevé; (fig.) grand; sublime; fier, altier; faisandé (gibier); avancé (viande); from on high, d'en haut; high road, grand-route, f.; high street, grand-

rue, f.; it is high time, il est grand temps. —adv. haut, hautement; grandement; fort; to run high, s'échauffer (sentiments).

highbrow ['haibrau], a. and n. (fam.) intellectuel, m.

higher ['haiɔ], comp. a. plus haut, plus élevé; supérieur.

highest ['haiist], superl. a. le plus haut, le plus élevé; at the highest, au comble.

high-flown ['haifloun], a. enflé; ampoulé (style).

high-handed ['hai'hændid], a. arbitraire, tyrannique.

Highland ['hailɔnd], a. de la Haute Écosse.

highland ['hailɔnd], a. des montagnes.

Highlander ['hailɔndɔ], n. montagnard de l'Écosse.

Highlands ['hailɔndz], the. les hautes terres d'Écosse, f.pl., la haute Écosse, f.

highlands ['hailɔndz], n.pl. pays montagneux, m.

highlight ['hailait], n. point culminant, (fam.) clou, m.

highly ['haili], adv. hautement; fortement.

Highness ['hainis], n. Altesse (titre), f.

highness ['hainis], n. hauteur, f.

high-pitched ['haipitʃt], a. aigu (son).

high-sounding ['haisaundiŋ], a. pompeux; ronflant (style).

high-spirited ['haispiritid], a. fougueux, plein de cœur.

highway ['haiwei], n. grand chemin, m., grand-route, f.

highwayman ['haiweimɔn], n. (pl. -men [men]) voleur de grand chemin, m.

hike [haik], n. excursion à pied, f.—v.i. aller à pied, vagabonder; faire des excursions à pied.

hiker ['haikɔ], n. touriste à pied, m., f.

hilarious [hi'leɔriɔs], a. gai, joyeux.

hilarity [hi'læriti], n. hilarité, f.

hill [hil], n. colline, montagne, f., coteau, m., butte; côte, f.

hillock ['hilɔk], n. monticule, m., butte, f.

hilly ['hili], a. montagneux, accidenté.

hilt [hilt], n. poignée, garde, f.

him [him], pers. pron. le, lui.—dem. pron. celui.

himself [him'self], pron. lui-même, lui; (reflexive) se; by himself, tout seul.

hind (1) [haind], n. (Zool.) biche, f.

hind (2) [haind], a. de derrière, postérieur, arrière.

hinder ['hindɔ], v.t. empêcher, gêner, embarrasser, retarder.

hindrance ['hindrɔns], n. empêchement, obstacle, m.

Hindu [hin'du:], a. hindou.—n. Hindou, m.

hinge [hindʒ], n. gond, m.; paumelle; charnière (butt hinge), f.; (fig.) pivot, m.

hint [hint], n. insinuation, allusion, f.; (fig.) soupçon, m.; conseils, m.pl.; broad hint, allusion évidente; to take the hint, comprendre à demi-mot.—v.i. donner à entendre (à), insinuer, suggérer.

hip [hip], n. hanche, f.

hippopotamus [hipɔ'pɔtɔmɔs], n. (pl. hippopotami [hipɔ'pɔtɔmai], hippopotamuses [hipɔ'pɔtɔmɔsɔz]) hippopotame, m.

hire ['haiɔ], n. louage, prix de louage; salaire, m., gages, m.pl.; for hire, à louer, libre (taxi).—v.t. louer; engager, employer.

hireling ['haiɔliŋ], a. and n. mercenaire, m.

447

hire-purchase

hire-purchase [ˈhaiəˈpəːtʃəs], *n.* vente à tempérament, location-vente, *f.*
hirsute [ˈhəːsjuːt], *a.* velu, hirsute.
his [hiz], *a.* son, sa, ses.—*pron.* le sien, *m.*, la sienne, *f.*, les siens, *m.pl.*, les siennes, *f.pl.*; **a friend of his,** un de ses amis; **it is his,** c'est à lui.
hiss [his], *v.t., v.i.* siffler.—*n.* sifflement; sifflet, *m.*
hissing [ˈhisiŋ], *a.* sifflant.—*n.* sifflement, *m.*
historian [hisˈtɔːriən], *n.* historien, *m.*
historic [hisˈtɔrik], **historical** [hisˈtɔrikəl], *a.* historique.
history [ˈhistəri], *n.* histoire, *f.*
hit [hit], *v.t. irr.* frapper, heurter; atteindre (*le but*); donner (*un coup*); toucher.—*v.i.* frapper, frapper (*contre*).—*n.* coup, *m.*, chance, trouvaille; (*fig.*) invention, *f.*; (*Theat.*) succès, *m.*
hitch [hitʃ], *v.t.* accrocher, attacher; (*Naut.*) nouer, amarrer.—*n.* accroc, *m.*; entrave, *f.*; empêchement; (*Naut.*) nœud, *m.*
hitch-hike [ˈhitʃhaik], *v.i.* faire de l'auto-stop.
hither [ˈhiðə], *adv.* ici; **hither and thither,** çà et là.
hitherto [hiðəˈtuː], *adv.* jusqu'ici.
hive [haiv], *n.* ruche, *f.*; (*fig.*) essaim (*swarm*), *m.*
hoard [hɔːd], *n.* monceau, amas (*secret*); trésor, *m.*—*v.t.* amasser, accumuler.—*v.i.* thésauriser.
hoarding [ˈhɔːdiŋ], *n.* accumulation, *f.*; panneau-réclame, *m.*
hoar-frost [ˈhɔːfrɔst], *n.* gelée blanche, *f.*, givre, *m.*
hoarse [hɔːs], *a.* enroué, rauque.
hoary [ˈhɔːri], *a.* blanc; aux cheveux gris *ou* blancs.
hoax [houks], *n.* mystification, *f.*; mauvais tour (*brimade*); canard (*fausse nouvelle*), *m.*—*v.t.* mystifier; attraper.
hob [hɔb], *n.* plaque (*de l'âtre*), *f.*
hobble [hɔbl], *v.t.* entraver.—*v.i.* clocher, clopiner; aller clopin clopant.—*n.* clochement, *m.*, difficulté, *f.*, embarras, *m.*; entrave, *f.*
hobby [ˈhɔbi], *n.* marotte (*manie*), distraction, *f.*, passe-temps, *m.*
hobby-horse [ˈhɔbihɔːs], *n.* cheval de bois, dada, *m.*
hobgoblin [hɔbˈgɔblin], *n.* lutin, *m.*
hobnob [ˈhɔbnɔb], *v.i.* trinquer ensemble.
hobo [ˈhoubou], *n.* (*Am.*) chemineau, *m.*
hock [hɔk], *n.* jarret (*d'un cheval*); vin du Rhin, *m.*
hockey [ˈhɔki], *n.* hockey, *m.*
ho. key stick [ˈhɔkistik], *n.* crosse de hockey, *f.*
hoe [hou], *n.* houe, binette, *f.*; **Dutch hoe,** sarcloir, *m.*—*v.t., v.i.* houer; biner, sarcler.
hog [hɔg], *n.* cochon; goret; (*Comm.*) porc, pourceau; (*fam.*) glouton, *m.*
hogshead [ˈhɔgzhed], *n.* muid, *m.*; barrique de 240 litres (*tonneau*), *f.*
hoist [hɔist], *v.t.* hisser; guinder (*avec un treuil*); lever; arborer (*un drapeau*).—*n.* grue, *f.*, palan, *m.*
hold [hould], *n.* prise, *f.*; soutien (*appui*), *m.*; garde (*custody*); place forte (*fortresse*); (*Naut.*) cale, *f.*; **to take hold of,** prendre, saisir; **to let go one's hold,** lâcher prise.—*v.t. irr.* tenir, retenir; arrêter; garder, maintenir; occuper, avoir; contenir (*to contain*);

regarder comme; célébrer; **to hold back,** retenir, cacher; **to hold fast,** tenir ferme, tenir bon; **to hold off,** tenir à distance; **to hold over,** remettre, ajourner; **to hold up,** lever, soulever, soutenir; arrêter, retarder.—*v.i.* tenir; se maintenir, durer; supporter; adhérer (*à*); rester; s'arrêter; être vrai; **hold on,** arrêtez! (*Teleph.*) ne quittez pas! **hold tight !** ne lâchez pas! **to hold back,** se tenir en arrière, hésiter; **to hold fast,** tenir ferme; **to hold forth,** haranguer, pérorer; **to hold on,** s'accrocher à; persévérer, poursuivre.
hold-all [ˈhouldɔːl], *n.* enveloppe de voyage, *f.*
holder [ˈhouldə], *n.* personne qui tient, *f.*; (*Spt.*) tenant, locataire, *m.*; poignée, anse, *f.*, manche, *m.*, (*in compound words*) porte-; (*Fin.*) titulaire, *m.*
holding [ˈhouldiŋ], *n.* possession, tenure; ferme, *f.*
hold-up [ˈhouldʌp], *n.* arrêt de la circulation, *m.*; panne, *f.*; hold-up, *m.*
hole [houl], *n.* trou; antre, *m.*, caverne, *f.*; orifice, *m.*, ouverture, *f.*
holiday [ˈhɔlidei], *a.* de fête, de congé; de vacances.—*n.* fête, *f.*, jour de fête, jour férié, (*Sch. etc.*) congé, *m.*, (*pl.*) vacances, *f.pl.*; **bank holiday,** fête légale; **on holiday,** en vacance(s).
holiness [ˈhoulinis], *n.* sainteté, *f.*
Holland [ˈhɔlənd], la Hollande, *f.*
hollow [ˈhɔlou], *a.* creux; vide; sourd (*son*).—*n.* creux, *m.*, cavité, *f.*; bas-fond, *m.*—*v.t.* creuser, évider.
holly [ˈhɔli], *n.* houx, *m.*
hollyhock [ˈhɔlihɔk], *n.* rose trémière, *f.*
holster [ˈhoulstə], *n.* fonte (*de selle*), *f.*; étui (*de revolver*), *m.*
holy [ˈhouli], *a.* saint, sacré; bénit; **Holy Ghost,** le Saint-Esprit; **Holy Land,** la Terre Sainte; **holy water,** eau bénite, *f.*; **Holy Week,** la semaine sainte, *f.*
homage [ˈhɔmidʒ], *n.* hommage, *m.*
home [houm], *a.* de la maison, domestique; (*fig.*) qui porte (*coup*).—*n.* foyer domestique, chez-soi; logis, *m.*, maison, *f.*, intérieur, *m.*; (*fig.*) demeure, *f.*; pays, *m.*, patrie (*pays natal*), *f.*; **at home,** chez soi, à la maison; **Home Office,** Ministère de l'Intérieur, *m.*; **to make oneself at home,** faire comme chez soi.—*adv.* chez soi, au logis, à la maison; dans son pays; (*fig.*) directement; **to bring home to,** faire admettre à; **homing pigeon,** pigeon voyageur, *m.*
home-coming [ˈhoumkamiŋ], *n.* retour au foyer, *m.*
homeland [ˈhoumlænd], *n.* patrie, *f.*; pays natal, *m.*
homeliness [ˈhoumlinis], *n.* caractère domestique, *m.*; simplicité; rusticité, *f.*
homely [ˈhoumli], *a.* du ménage; simple, sans façon, (*Am.*) laid.
Homer [ˈhoumə]. Homère, *m.*
home-sick [ˈhoumsik], *a.* qui a le mal du pays, nostalgique.
home-sickness [ˈhoumsiknis], *n.* mal du pays, *m.*, nostalgie, *f.*
homestead [ˈhoumsted], *n.* manoir, *m.*, ferme, *f.*
homeward(s) [ˈhoumwəd(z)], *adv.* vers la maison; vers son pays.

448

homework ['houmwə:k], n. devoirs, m.pl.
homicide ['homisaid], n. homicide, m.
homogeneous [homə'dʒi:niəs], a. and n. homosexuel, m.
homosexual [houmo'seksjuəl], a. and n. homosexuel, m.
Honduran [hon'djuərən], a. hondurien.—n. Hondurien (personne), m.
Honduras [hon'djuərəs]. l'Honduras, m.
hone [houn], n. pierre à aiguiser. f.—v.t. aiguiser.
honest ['onist], a. honnête, loyal, probe, de bonne foi, sincère; **honest man**, homme de bien, honnête homme, m.
honestly ['onistli], adv. honnêtement, sincèrement.
honesty ['onisti], n. honnêteté, probité, bonne foi, sincérité, f.
honey ['hʌni], n. miel, m.; (fig.) (Am.) chérie, f., ange, m.
honeycomb ['hʌnikoum], n. rayon de miel, m.
honeymoon ['hʌnimu:n], n. lune de miel, f.
honeysuckle ['hʌnisakl], n. chèvrefeuille, m.
honorary ['onərəri], a. honoraire.
honor ['onə], n. honneur, m.; (fig.) dignité, estime, f.—v.t. honorer (de); faire honneur à, faire bon accueil à (une facture).
honorable ['onərəbl], a. honorable, d'honneur.
hood [hud], n. capuchon, m.; coiffe; capote (de voiture), f.; (Am. Motor.) [BONNET].
hoodwink ['hudwiŋk], v.t. bander les yeux à; (fig.) tromper.
hoof [hu:f, huf], n. (pl. **hooves** [hu:vz]) sabot, m.
hook [huk], n. crochet, croc; hameçon (pour pêcher), m.; faucille (sickle), f.; **hook and eye**, agrafe et porte, m.—v.t. accrocher; agrafer; attraper.
hooked [hukt], a. crochu, recourbé; aquilin (nez).
hooligan ['hu:ligən], n. voyou, m.
hooliganism ['hu:ligənizm], n. voyouterie, f.
hoop [hu:p], n. cercle; cerceau, m.; huppe (d'oiseau); jante (de roue), f.; panier (de robe); (Croquet) arceau, m.—v.t. cercler; (fig.) entourer.
hoot [hu:t], v.t., v.i. hululer (hibou); huer; (Motor.) klaxonner.
hooter ['hu:tə], n. (colloq.) sirène d'usine, f. klaxon, m.
hop (1) [hop], n. saut, sautillement; bal populaire, m.—v.i. sauter, sautiller; (pop.) to **hop it**, ficher le camp.
hop (2) [hop], n. (Bot.) houblon, m.
hop-field ['hopfi:ld], n. houblonnière, f.
hopscotch ['hopskotʃ], n. marelle, f.
hope [houp], n. espérance, f., espoir, m., attente, f.—v.t. espérer, s'attendre à.—v.i. espérer.
hopeful ['houpful], a. plein d'espérance; qui promet beaucoup; encourageant.
hopefully ['houpfuli], adv. avec espoir, avec confiance; si tout va bien.
hopeless ['houplis], a. vain (effort); non valable (excuse); inextricable (difficulté); inconsolable (douleur); irrémédiable (mal); inutile (négociation); incorrigible (personne); désespéré (situation).
hopelessly ['houplisli], adv. sans espoir.
hopper ['hopə], n. trémie (d'un moulin), f.; (Agric.) semoir, m.

horizon [hə'raizən], n. horizon, m.
horizontal [hori'zontl], a. horizontal.
hormone ['hɔ:moun], n. hormone, f.
horn [hɔ:n], a. de corne.—n. corne, f.; bois (de cerf), m.; coupe (à boire); (Ent.) antenne f.; (Mus.) cor, cornet, m.;(Motor.)klaxon, m.
hornet ['hɔ:nit], n. frelon, m.
horrible ['horibl], a. horrible, affreux.
horribly ['horibli], adv. horriblement, affreusement.
horrid ['horid], a. affreux, horrible.
horrific [hə'rifik], a. horrifique.
horrify ['horifai], v.t. horrifier.
horror ['horə], n. horreur, f.
horse [hɔ:s], n. cheval, m., chevaux, m.pl.; (Mil.) cavalerie, f.; chevalet (pour scier), séchoir (pour le linge), m.
horseback ['hɔ:sbæk], n. dos de cheval, m.; **on horseback**, à cheval.
horseblock ['hɔ:sblok], n. montoir, m.
horse chestnut ['hɔ:s'tʃesnʌt], n. marron d'Inde; marronnier d'Inde (arbre), m.
horse dealer ['hɔ:sdi:lə], n. maquignon, m.
horse doctor ['hɔ:sdoktə], n. vétérinaire, m.
horse-fly ['hɔ:sflai], n. taon, m.
horseman ['hɔ:smən], n. (pl. **-men** [men]) cavalier; écuyer, m.
horsemanship ['hɔ:smənʃip], n. équitation, f.; manège, m.
horse-play ['hɔ:splei], n. jeu de mains, m.
horse-power ['hɔ:spauə], n. cheval-vapeur, m.
horseshoe ['hɔ:ʃʃu:], a. en fer à cheval.—n. fer de cheval; fer à cheval, m.
horsewhip ['hɔ:swip], n. cravache, f.—v.t. cravacher.
horticulture ['hɔ:tikʌltʃə], n. horticulture, f.
hose [houz], n. bas, m.pl.; tuyau d'arrosage, boyau, m.
hosiery ['houʒəri], n. bonneterie, f.
hospitable ['hospitəbl], a. hospitalier.
hospital ['hospitl], n. hôpital, m., infirmerie, f.; hospice, m.
hospitality [hospi'tæliti], n. hospitalité, f.
host [houst], n. hôte, hôtelier, aubergiste, m.; armée, foule; (R.-C. Ch.) hostie, f.
hostage ['hostidʒ], n. otage, m.
hostel ['hostəl], n. hôtel ou foyer pour les étudiants etc., m.; **youth hostel**, auberge de la jeunesse, f.
hostess ['houstis, 'houstes], n. hôtesse, f.
hostile ['hostail], a. hostile, ennemi; (fig.) opposé (à).
hostility [hos'tiliti], n. hostilité, f.
hot [hot], a. chaud, ardent; brûlant, piquant; épicé (plat, sauce); (fig.) vif, violent, échauffé; **boiling hot**, tout bouillant; **to be hot**, avoir chaud (personne); faire chaud (temps), être chaud (chose).
hotbed ['hotbed], n. couche, f.
hotel [ho'tel], n. hôtel, m.
hot-headed ['hot'hedid], a. violent, fougueux.
hot-house ['hothaus], n. serre, f.
hotly ['hotli], adv. avec chaleur, avec acharnement.
hotness ['hotnis], n. chaleur; (fig.) passion, violence, f.
hot-water bottle [hot'wo:təbotl], n. bouillotte, f.
hough [hok], n. jarret (d'animal), m.
hound [haund], n. chien de chasse, m.—v.t. chasser; (fig.) traquer; exciter.

449

hour ['auə], *n.* heure, *f.*; *an hour ago*, il y a une heure; *an hour and a half*, une heure et demie; *a quarter of an hour*, un quart d'heure; *half an hour*, une demi-heure.

hourly ['auəli], *a.* continuel, d'heure en heure, à l'heure.—*adv.* d'heure en heure.

house [haus], *n.* maison, *f.*, logis, *m.*, demeure, habitation, *f.*; ménage (*household*), *m.*; famille; (*Parl.*) chambre; (*Theat.*) salle, *f.*; *a country house*, une maison de campagne; *a nobleman's house*, un hôtel; *house full*, (*Theat.*) salle comble; *public house*, café, *m.*, brasserie, *f.*—[hauz], *v.t.* loger, héberger; garer (*une voiture*); rentrer (*blé etc.*); faire rentrer (*bestiaux etc.*).

house agent ['hauseidʒənt], *n.* agent de location, agent immobilier, *m.*

house-breaker ['hausbreikə], *n.* cambrioleur (*voleur*); démolisseur (*ouvrier*), *m.*

house-breaking ['hausbreikiŋ], *n.* vol avec effraction, *m.*

household ['haushould], *a.* de ménage, domestique.—*n.* maison, *f.*, ménage, *m.*, famille, *f.*

householder ['haushouldə], *n.* chef de famille, chef de maison, *m.*

housekeeper ['hauski:pə], *n.* femme de charge, ménagère, *f.*; concierge, *m.*, *f.*

housekeeping ['hauski:piŋ], *n.* ménage, *m.*

housemaid ['hausmeid], *n.* bonne à tout faire, *f.*

house surgeon ['haussə:dʒən], *n.* interne (en chirurgie), *m.*

housewife ['hauswaif], *n.* ménagère, *f.*

housework ['hauswə:k], *n.* travaux ménagers, *m.pl.*; *to do the housework*, faire le ménage.

housing ['hauziŋ], *n.* logement, *m.*; rentrée, *f.*, rentrage, *m.*; (*Tech.*) enchâssure, *f.*

hovel ['hɔvl], *n.* appentis, *m.*, bicoque, *f.*, taudis, *m.*, masure, *f.*

hover ['hɔvə], *v.i.* planer; hésiter.

how [hau], *adv.* comment, de quelle façon; combien; comme, que; *how are you?* comment allez-vous? *how far*, jusqu'où; *how many, how much*, combien de; *how old are you?* quel âge avez-vous?

however [hau'evə], *conj.* cependant, pourtant, du reste, d'ailleurs, toutefois.—*adv.* de quelque manière que; quelque . . . que; *however rich he may be*, quelque riche qu'il soit, tout riche qu'il est; *however that may be*, quoi qu'il en soit.

howl [haul], *n.* hurlement, cri; mugissement, *m.*—*v.i.* hurler, crier; mugir.

howler ['haulə], *n.* faute grossière, bévue, *f.*

howling ['hauliŋ], *a.* hurlant; *a howling success*, un succès fou.—*n.* hurlement, *m.*

hoyden ['hɔidn], *n.* garçon manqué (*se dit d'une jeune fille*), *m.*

hub [hʌb], *n.* moyeu, *m.*; (*fig.*) centre, *m.*

hubbub ['hʌbʌb], *n.* vacarme, brouhaha, tintamarre, *m.*

hub cap ['hʌbkæp], *n.* (*Motor.*) enjoliveur, *m.*

huddle ['hʌdl], *v.t.* entasser pêle-mêle, (*fig.*) brouiller, confondre ensemble.—*v.i.* se mêler, se presser les uns contre les autres; (*fig.*) se confondre.—*n.* tas confus, fouillis, méli-mélo, ramassis, *m.*

hue [hju:], *n.* couleur, teinte, nuance; huée,

clameur, *f.*; *to raise a hue and cry after*, crier haro sur, élever un tollé contre.

huff [hʌf], *n.* emportement, accès de colère, *m.* —*v.t.* froisser; (*checkers*) souffler.—*v.i.* se gonfler, se mettre en colère.

hug [hʌg], *v.t.* embrasser, étreindre; étouffer (*en serrant*).—*n.* embrassement, *m.*, étreinte, *f.*

huge [hju:dʒ], *a.* vaste, immense, énorme.

hulk [hʌlk], *n.* carcasse (*d'un navire*), *f.*, ponton; (*pl.*) bagne, *m.*

hulking ['hʌlkiŋ], *a.* gros, lourd.

hull [hʌl], *n.* coque (*d'un navire*); cosse, gousse (*de pois, fèves etc.*); écale (*de noix*), *f.*—*v.t.* écaler (*noix*); écosser (*fèves*).

hullo [HELLO].

hum [hʌm], *v.t.*, *v.i.* fredonner (*personne*); bourdonner (*abeilles*); *to hum and ha(w)*, bredouiller.—*n.* bourdonnement; brouhaha (*de conversation*), *m.*

human ['hju:mən], *a.* humain.

humane [hju:'mein], *a.* humain, compatissant.

humanist ['hju:mənist], *n.* humaniste, *m.*, *f.*

humanity [hju:'mæniti], *n.* humanité, *f.*

humanly ['hju:mənli], *adv.* humainement.

humble ['hʌmbl], *a.* humble; modeste.—*v.t.* humilier, abaisser, mortifier.

humble-bee ['hʌmblbi:], *n.* bourdon, *m.*

humbly ['hʌmbli], *adv.* humblement, avec humilité; modestement.

humbug ['hʌmbʌg], *n.* blague, farce, *f.*, charlatanisme; blagueur, farceur, charlatan, *m.*

humdrum ['hʌmdrʌm], *a.* monotone, assommant.

humid ['hju:mid], *a.* humide.

humidity [hju:'miditi], *n.* humidité, *f.*

humiliate [hju:'milieit], *v.t.* humilier, abaisser.

humiliating [hju:'milieitiŋ], *a.* humiliant.

humiliation [hju:mili'eiʃən], *n.* humiliation, *f.*

humility [hju:'militi], *n.* humilité, *f.*

humming ['hʌmiŋ], *n.* bourdonnement, fredonnement; (*fig.*) murmure, *m.*

humming-bird ['hʌmiŋbə:d], *n.* oiseau-mouche, colibri, *m.*

humor ['hju:mə], *n.* humeur, disposition, *f.*; humour. *m.*—*v.t.* complaire à, laisser faire.

humorist ['hju:mərist], *n.* humoriste, *m.*, *f.*, personne spirituelle, *f.*

humorous ['hju:mərəs], *a.* humoristique; plaisant, drôle, comique.

hump [hʌmp], *n.* bosse, *f.*; *to have the hump*, (*slang*) être maussade.

humpbacked ['hʌmpbækt], *a.* bossu.

hunch [hʌntʃ], *n.* gros morceau (*de pain, de fromage*), *m.*; bosse (*du dos*), (*fig., fam.*) idée, *f.*, soupçon, *m.*; *to have a hunch that*, soupçonner que.

hunchback ['hʌntʃbæk], *n.* bossu, *m.*

hundred ['hʌndrəd], *a.* cent.—*n.* cent, *m.*; centaine, *f.*; canton, district, *m.*

hundredth ['hʌndrətθ], *a.* centième.—*n.* centième (*fraction*), *m.*

hundredweight ['hʌndrədweit], *n.* quintal, *m.*

Hungarian [hʌŋ'gɛəriən], *a.* hongrois.—*n.* hongrois (*langue*); Hongrois (*personne*), *m.*

Hungary ['hʌŋgəri], la Hongrie, *f.*

hunger ['hʌŋgə], *n.* faim, *f.*—*v.i.* avoir faim; être affamé (*de*).

hungrily ['hʌŋgrili], *adv.* avidement.

hungry ['hʌŋgri], *a.* affamé, qui a faim; maigre (*terre etc.*); *to be hungry*, avoir faim.

hunk [hʌŋk], *n.* gros morceau (*de gâteau, de fromage*), *m.*

hunt [hʌnt], *v.t.* chasser à courre; (*fig.*) poursuivre, chercher.—*v.i.* chasser, aller à la chasse.—*n.* chasse à courre, *f.*

hunter ['hʌntə], *n.* chasseur; cheval de chasse, *m.*

hunting ['hʌntiŋ], *n.* chasse; (*fig.*) recherche, *f.*

huntress ['hʌntris], *n.* chasseuse; (*poet.*) chasseresse, *f.*

huntsman ['hʌntsmən], *n.* (*pl.* -men [men]) veneur, piqueur, *m.*

hurdle [hə:dl], *n.* claie, *f.*; (*Spt.*) obstacle, *m.*, haie, *f.*; *hurdle race*, course de haies, *f.*

hurdy-gurdy ['hə:di'gə:di], *n.* vielle, *f.*

hurl [hə:l], *v.t.* lancer (avec force), précipiter, jeter.

hurly-burly ['hə:li'bə:li], *n.* tintamarre, brouhaha, tohu-bohu, *m.*

hurrah [hu'rɑ:], **hurray** [hu'rei], *n.* hourra, *m.*

hurricane ['hʌrikən], *n.* ouragan, *m.*

hurried ['hʌrid], *a.* précipité, pressé; fait à la hâte.

hurriedly ['hʌridli], *adv.* précipitamment, à la hâte.

hurry ['hʌri], *n.* hâte, précipitation, *f.*; (*fig.*) tumulte, confusion, *f.*; *to be in a hurry*, être pressé.—*v.t.* hâter, presser, précipiter.—*v.i.* se hâter, se dépêcher, se presser.

hurt [hə:t], *n.* mal, *m.*, blessure, *f.*; (*fig.*) tort, *m.*—*v.t. irr.* faire mal à, (*fig.*) nuire à, offenser, blesser; *to hurt oneself*, se faire du mal.—*v.i.* faire du mal; faire mal.

hurtful ['hə:tful], *a.* nuisible (*à*).

hurtle [hə:tl], *v.t.* lancer.—*v.i.* se précipiter; se heurter.

husband ['hʌzbənd], *n.* mari, époux, *m.*—*v.t.* ménager, économiser.

husbandman ['hʌzbəndmən], *n.* (*pl.* -men [men]) laboureur, cultivateur, *m.*

husbandry ['hʌzbəndri], *n.* agriculture, industrie agricole; économie, *f.*

hush [hʌʃ], *n.* silence, calme, *m.*—*int.* chut! paix!—*v.t.* taire, faire taire; (*fig.*) calmer.—*v.i.* se taire, faire silence.

husk [hʌsk], *n.* cosse, gousse (*de pois etc.*), *f.*; brou, *m.*, écale (*de noix*); balle, pellicule (*de grain*), *f.*

huskiness ['hʌskinis], *n.* enrouement (*de la voix*), *m.*

husky ['hʌski], *a.* cossu; rauque, enroué (*voix*); (*colloq.*) costaud, fort.—*n.* chien esquimau, *m.*

hussar [hu'zɑ:], *n.* hussard, *m.*

hussy ['hʌsi], *n.* friponne, coquine, *f.*

hustle ['hʌsl], *v.t.* bousculer, presser, pousser.—*v.i.* se presser, se dépêcher.

hut [hʌt], *n.* hutte, cabane; (*Mil.*) baraque, *f.*

hutch [hʌtʃ], *n.* huche, *f.*; clapier (*de lapin*), *m.*

hyacinth ['haiəsinθ], *n.* (*Bot.*) jacinthe, *f.*

hybrid ['haibrid], *a.* and *n.* hybride, *m.*

hydrangea [hai'drændʒə, hai'dreindʒə], *n.* (*Bot.*) hortensia, *m.*

hydrant ['haidrənt], *n.* prise d'eau, *f.*; *fire hydrant*, bouche d'incendie, *f.*

hydraulic [hai'drɔ:lik], *a.* hydraulique.

hydrochloric [haidrə'klɔrik], *a.* (*acide*) chlorhydrique.

hydrogen ['haidridʒən], *n.* hydrogène, *m.*; *hydrogen bomb* or (*fam.*) *H-bomb*, bombe à hydrogène, bombe H, *f.*

hydrophobia [haidro'foubiə], *n.* hydrophobie, rage, *f.*

hyena [hai'i:nə], *n.* hyène, *f.*

hygiene ['haidʒi:n], *n.* hygiène, *f.*

hygienic [hai'dʒi:nik], *a.* hygiénique.

hymn [him], *n.* (*Eccles.*) hymne, *m.* ou *f.*, cantique, *m.*

hymn book ['himbuk], **hymnal** [himnl], *n.* hymnaire, *m.*

hyperbola [hai'pə:bələ], *n.* (*Geom.*) hyperbole, *f.*

hyperbole [hai'pə:bəli], *n.* (*Gram.*) hyperbole, *f.*

hyphen ['haifən], *n.* trait d'union, *m.*

hypnosis [hip'nousis], *n.* hypnose, *f.*

hypnotism ['hipnətizm], *n.* hypnotisme, *m.*

hypnotist ['hipnətist], *n.* hypnotiste, *m.*, *f.*

hypocrisy [hi'pɔkrisi], *n.* hypocrisie, *f.*

hypocrite ['hipəkrit], *n.* hypocrite, *m.*, *f.*

hypocritical [hipə'kritikl], *a.* hypocrite.

hypothesis [hai'pɔθisis], *n.* (*pl.* **hypotheses** [hai'pɔθisi:z]) hypothèse, *f.*

hysteria [his'tiəriə], *n.*, **hysterics** [his'teriks], *n.pl.* crise de nerfs, attaque de nerfs, *f.*

hysterical [his'terikəl], *a.* hystérique.

I

I (1), **i** [ai]. neuvième lettre de l'alphabet, *m.*

I (2) [ai], *pron.* je; moi.

ibex ['aibeks], *n.* bouquetin, *m.*

ibis ['aibis], *n.* (*Orn.*) ibis, *m.*

ice [ais], *n.* glace, *f.*—*v.t.* glacer (*gâteau*); frapper (*vin*).—*v.i.* (*Av.*) *to ice up*, givrer.

ice axe ['aisæks], *n.* piolet, *m.*

iceberg ['aisbə:g], *n.* iceberg, *m.*

ice-bound ['aisbaund], *a.* pris dans *ou* bloqué par les glaces.

ice-box ['aisbɔks], *n.* glacière, *f.*

ice-breaker ['aisbreikə], *n.* brise-glace, *m.*

ice cream ['ais'kri:m], *n.* glace, *f.*

iced [aist], *a.* glacé; frappé (*vin etc.*); *iced lollypop*, sucette, *f.*

ice-floe ['aisflou], *n.* banc de glace, *m.*

Iceland ['aisland]. l'Islande, *f.*

Icelander ['aislandə], *n.* Islandais, *m.*

Icelandic [ais'lændik], *a.* islandais, d'Islande.

ice pack, see **pack-ice**.

icicle ['aisikl], *n.* petit glaçon, *m.*

icing ['aisiŋ], *n.* glacé; frappage (*de vin*), *m.*

icon ['aikɔn], *n.* icone, *f.*

icy ['aisi], *a.* glacé, glacial; *icy road*, route verglacée, *f.*

idea [ai'diə], *n.* idée, *f.*

ideal [ai'diəl], *a.* and *n.* idéal, *m.*

idealism [ai'diəlizm], *n.* idéalisme, *m.*

idealist [ai'diəlist], *n.* idéaliste, *m.*, *f.*

ideally [ai'diəli], *adv.* idéalement, *m.*

identical [ai'dentikl], *a.* identique.

identification [aidentifi'keiʃən], *n.* identification, *f.*

identify

identify [ai'dentifai], *v.t.* identifier *(avec)*; reconnaître.
identity [ai'dentiti], *n.* identité, *f.*
idiocy ['idiəsi], *n.* idiotie, *f.*
idiom ['idiəm], *n.* idiome; idiotisme, *m.*
idiomatic [idiə'mætik], *a.* idiomatique.
idiot ['idiət], *n.* idiot, *m.*; imbécile, *m., f.*
idiotic [idi'ɔtik], *a.* idiot, d'imbécile.
idle [aidl], *a.* oisif, paresseux *(indolent)*; désœuvré *(inactif)*; en chômage *(personne sans travail)*, en repos *(machine)*; *(fig.)* inutile, frivole; **idle fellow**, fainéant, paresseux, *m.*; **idle talk**, balivernes, *f.pl.*—*v.t.* **to idle away**, perdre, gaspiller.—*v.i.* nê rien faire, faire le paresseux, fainéanter; *(Motor.)* tourner au ralenti.
idleness ['aidlnis], *n.* paresse; oisiveté; *(fig.)* inutilité, *f.*; désœuvrement, *m.*
idler ['aidlə], *n.* oisif, fainéant, paresseux, *m.*
idly ['aidli], *adv.* dans l'oisiveté, en paresseux; inutilement.
idol ['aidl], *n.* idole, *f.*
idolater [ai'dɔlətə], **idolatress** [ai'dɔlətris], *n.* idolâtre, *m., f.*
idolatry [ai'dɔlətri], *n.* idolâtrie, *f.*
idolize ['aidəlaiz], *v.t.* idolâtrer.
idyllic [ai'dilik, i'dilik], *a.* idyllique.
if [if], *conj.* si, quand, quand même; *even if*, même si, quand même; *if necessary*, s'il le faut, au besoin; *if not*, sinon, si ce n'est.
igloo ['iglu:], *n.* hutte de neige, *f.*; igloo *(des Esquimaux)*, *m.*
ignite [ig'nait], *v.t.* allumer.—*v.i.* prendre feu
ignition [ig'niʃən], *n.* ignition, *f.*; *(Motor.)* allumage, *m.*; *ignition key*, clé de contact, *f.*
ignoble [ig'noubl], *a.* roturier; ignoble.
ignominious [ignə'miniəs], *a.* ignominieux.
ignominy ['ignəmini], *n.* ignominie, *f.*
ignoramus [ignə'reiməs], *n.* ignorant, *(fam.)* âne bâté, *m.*
ignorance ['ignərəns], *n.* ignorance, *f.*
ignorant ['ignərənt], *a.* ignorant.
ignore [ig'nɔ:], *v.t.* feindre d'ignorer; ne tenir aucun compte de.
ill [il], *a.*; malade *(santé)*; mauvais, méchant.—*n.* mal, *m.*—*adv.* mal; peu; *it ill becomes you*, il vous sied mal.
ill-bred [il'bred], *a.* mal élevé.
illegal [i'li:gəl], *a.* illégal; illicite.
illegible [i'ledʒibl], *a.* illisible.
illegitimate [ilə'dʒitimit], *a.* illégitime; naturel *(enfant)*.
ill-fated [il'feitid], *a.* infortuné, malheureux.
ill-feeling [il'fi:liŋ], *n.* ressentiment, *m.*
ill-gotten [il'gɔtn], *a.* mal acquis.
ill-health [il'helθ], *n.* mauvaise santé, *f.*
illicit [i'lisit], *a.* illicite.
ill-informed [ilin'fɔ:md], *a.* mal renseigné.
illiteracy [i'litərəsi] *n.* analphabétisme, *m.*
illiterate [i'litərit], *a.* and *n.* illettré, *m.*
ill-mannered [il'mænəd], *a.* malappris.
ill-natured [il'neitʃəd], *a.* méchant, d'un mauvais naturel.
illness ['ilnis], *n.* maladie, indisposition, *f.*
illogical [i'lɔdʒikl], *a.* illogique, peu logique.
ill-tempered [il'tempəd], *a.* maussade, de mauvaise humeur.
ill-treat [il'tri:t], *v.t.* maltraiter.
illuminate [i'lju:mineit], *v.t.* illuminer, éclairer; enluminer *(un livre)*.
illumination [ilju:mi'neiʃən], *n.* illumination; enluminure *(de livres etc.)*, *f.*

452

illusion [i'lu:ʒən, i'lju:ʒən], *n.* illusion, *f.*
illustrate ['iləstreit], *v.t.* illustrer; *(fig.)* expliquer; orner, embellir.
illustration [iləs'treiʃən], *n.* illustration; explication, *f.*; éclaircissement, *m.*
illustrative [i'lʌstrətiv], *a.* explicatif.
illustrious [i'lʌstriəs], *a.* illustre, célèbre.
ill-will [il'wil], *n.* mauvais vouloir, *m.*; rancune, *f.*
I'm [aim] *(=I am)* [BE].
image ['imidʒ], *n.* image, *f.*; *(fig.)* portrait, *m.*
imagery ['imidʒri], *n.* images, *f.pl.*; langage figuré, *m.*
imaginable [i'mædʒinəbl], *a.* imaginable.
imaginary [i'mædʒinri], *a.* imaginaire.
imagination [imædʒi'neiʃən], *n.* imagination; conception, idée, *f.*
imagine [i'mædʒin], *v.t.* imaginer; s'imaginer, se figurer.
imbecile ['imbisi:l], *a.* and *n.* faible d'esprit, *m., f.*
imbecility [imbi'siliti], *n.* faiblesse d'esprit, *f.*
imbibe [im'baib], *v.t.* imbiber, absorber; *(fig.)* puiser.
imbue [im'bju:], *v.t.* imprégner, teindre; *(fig.)* pénétrer, douer *(de)*.
imbued [im'bju:d], *a.* imbu, pénétré *(de)*.
imitate ['imiteit], *v.t.* imiter.
imitation [imi'teiʃən], *n.* imitation; *(Comm.)* contrefaçon, *f.*
imitative ['imitətiv], *a.* imitatif, imitateur.
immaculate [i'mækjulit], *a.* sans tache, immaculé.
immaterial [imə'tiəriəl], *a.* immatériel; peu important.
immature [imə'tjuə], *a.* pas mûr; prématuré.
immeasurable [i'meʒərəbl], *a.* infini; incommensurable.
immeasurably [i'meʒərəbli], *adv.* outre mesure, infiniment.
immediate [i'mi:djit], *a.* immédiat; urgent, très pressé *(sur enveloppe)*.
immediately [i'mi:djitli], *adv.* immédiatement, tout de suite, sur-le-champ.—*conj.* aussitôt que, dès que.
immense [i'mens], *a.* immense.
immensely [i'mensli], *adv.* immensément.
immensity [i'mensiti], *n.* immensité, *f.*
immerse [i'mə:s], *v.t.* plonger, immerger.
immigrant ['imigrənt], *a.* and *n.* immigrant, *m.*
immigrate ['imigreit], *v.i.* immigrer.
immigration [imi'greiʃən], *n.* immigration, *f.*
imminent ['iminənt], *a.* imminent.
immobilize [i'moubilaiz], *v.t.* immobiliser.
immodest [i'mɔdist], *a.* immodeste, peu modeste, impudique.
immoral [i'mɔrl], *a.* immoral; dissolu.
immorality [imə'ræliti], *n.* immoralité, *f.*
immortal [i'mɔ:tl], *a.* immortel.
immortality [imɔ:'tæliti], *n.* immortalité, *f.*
immortalize [i'mɔ:təlaiz], *v.t.* immortaliser, rendre immortel.
immovable [i'mu:vəbl], *a.* fixe, immuable, inébranlable.
immutable [i'mju:təbl], *a.* immuable.
imp [imp], *n.* diablotin, petit démon; petit diable *(gamin)*, *m.*
impact ['impækt], *n.* choc, impact, *m.*—[im'pækt], *v.t.* serrer, encastrer.
impair [im'pɛə], *v.t.* altérer, affaiblir.

impale [im'peil], *v.t.* empaler.
impalpable [im'pælpəbl], *a.* impalpable; intangible.
impart [im'pɑːt], *v.t.* accorder, donner; communiquer.
impartial [im'pɑːʃl], *a.* impartial, désintéressé.
impartially [im'pɑːʃəli], *adv.* impartialement.
impassable [im'pɑːsəbl], *a.* impraticable, infranchissable.
impassioned [im'pæʃənd], *a.* passionné.
impassive [im'pæsiv], *a.* impassible, insensible.
impatience [im'peiʃəns], *n.* impatience, *f.*
impatient [im'peiʃənt], *a.* impatient; (*fig.*) emporté.
impatiently [im'peiʃəntli], *adv.* impatiemment.
impeach [im'piːtʃ], *v.t.* accuser; attaquer.
impeachment [im'piːtʃmənt], *n.* mise en accusation; accusation, *f.*
impeccable [im'pekəbl], *a.* impeccable.
impecunious [impi'kjuːniəs], *a.* besogneux.
impede [im'piːd], *v.t.* empêcher; retarder, gêner.
impediment [im'pedimənt], *n.* empêchement, obstacle, *m.*; (*fig.*) difficulté, *f.*
impel [im'pel], *v.t.* pousser (à); forcer (de).
impelling [im'peliŋ], *a.* impulsif, moteur.
impend [im'pend], *v.i.* être suspendu sur, menacer; être imminent.
impending [im'pendiŋ], *a.* imminent, menaçant.
impenetrable [im'penitrəbl], *a.* impénétrable; (*fig.*) insensible.
impenitent [im'penitənt], *a.* impénitent.
imperative [im'perətiv], *a.* impératif; (*fig.*) obligatoire.—*n.* (*Gram.*) impératif, *m.*
imperceptible [impə'septibl], *a.* imperceptible, insensible.
imperceptibly [impə'septibli], *adv.* imperceptiblement.
imperfect [im'pəːfikt], *a.* imparfait; incomplet; (*Gram.*) imparfait.—*n.* (*Gram.*) imparfait, *m.*
imperfection [impə'fekʃən], *n.* imperfection, *f.*
imperfectly [im'pəːfiktli], *adv.* imparfaitement.
imperial [im'piəriəl], *a.* impérial; (*fig.*) princier.
imperil [im'peril], *v.t.* mettre en danger, hasarder.
imperious [im'piəriəs], *a.* impérieux.
imperishable [im'periʃəbl], *a.* impérissable.
impersonal [im'pəːsənl], *a.* impersonnel.
impersonate [im'pəːsəneit], *v.t.* personnifier; (*Theat.*) représenter, jouer le rôle de.
impertinence [im'pəːtinəns], *n.* impertinence, insolence, *f.*
impertinent [im'pəːtinənt], *a.* impertinent, insolent; hors de propos.
impertinently [im'pəːtinəntli], *adv.* d'un ton insolent; mal à propos.
imperturbable [impə'təːbəbl], *a.* imperturbable.
impervious [im'pəːviəs], *a.* imperméable, impénétrable; (*fig.*) inaccessible.
impetuous [im'petjuəs], *a.* impétueux.
impetus ['impitəs], *n.* impulsion, *f.*; élan, essor, *m.*

impinge [im'pindʒ], *v.i.* se heurter (à ou *contre*); empiéter (*sur*).
impious ['impiəs], *a.* impie.
impiously ['impiəsli], *adv.* en impie, avec impiété.
impish ['impiʃ], *a.* espiègle, malicieux.
implacable [im'plækəbl], *a.* implacable, acharné.
implant [im'plɑːnt], *v.t.* implanter; (*fig.*) imprimer, inculquer.
implement ['implimənt], *n.* outil; instrument; ustensile, *m.*—['impliment], *v.t.* exécuter; accomplir.
implicate ['implikeit], *v.t.* impliquer.
implication [impli'keiʃən], *n.* implication, *f.*; **by implication**, implicitement.
implicit [im'plisit], *a.* implicite; (*fig.*) aveugle.
implied [im'plaid], *a.* implicite, tacite.
implore [im'plɔː], *v.t.* implorer, conjurer, supplier (*de*).
imply [im'plai], *v.t.* impliquer, signifier, vouloir dire; donner à entendre (*suggérer*).
impolite [impə'lait], *a.* impoli.
impoliteness [impə'laitnis], *n.* impolitesse, *f.*
import ['impɔːt], *n.* portée, signification, *f.*, sens, *m.*; importance; (*Comm.*) importation, *f.*—[im'pɔːt], *v.t.* importer; introduire; signifier.
importance [im'pɔːtəns], *n.* importance, *f.*
important [im'pɔːtənt], *a.* important.
importer [im'pɔːtə], *n.* importateur, *m.*
importunate [im'pɔːtjunit], *a.* importun; pressant.
importune [impɔː'tjuːn], *v.t.* importuner.
impose [im'pouz], *v.t.* imposer.—*v.i.* en imposer (à).
imposing [im'pouziŋ], *a.* imposant.
imposition [impə'ziʃən], *n.* impôt (*taxe*), *m.*; imposture (*tromperie*), *f.*; (*Sch.*) pensum, *m.*
impossibility [impɔsi'biliti], *n.* impossibilité, *f.*
impossible [im'pɔsibl], *a.* impossible.
impostor [im'pɔstə], *n.* imposteur, *m.*
imposture [im'pɔstʃə], *n.* imposture, tromperie, *f.*
impotence ['impətəns], **impotency** ['impətənsi], *n.* impuissance, *f.*
impotent ['impətənt], *a.* impuissant, faible.
impound [im'paund], *v.t.* mettre en fourrière; (*fig.*) enfermer, confisquer.
impoverish [im'pɔvəriʃ], *v.t.* appauvrir.
impracticable [im'præktikəbl], *a.* impossible, impraticable; intraitable (*personne*).
imprecation [impri'keiʃən], *n.* imprécation, *f.*
impregnable [im'pregnəbl], *a.* imprenable; (*fig.*) inébranlable.
impregnate [im'pregneit], *v.t.* imprégner (*de*); féconder.
impress [im'pres], *v.t.* imprimer (à); faire bien comprendre (*quelque chose à quelqu'un*); pénétrer (*de*); impressionner.
impression [im'preʃən], *n.* impression, empreinte, *f.*; (*fig.*) idée, *f.*
impressive [im'presiv], *a.* impressionnant, frappant, touchant, émouvant.
impressiveness [im'presivnis], *n.* force, puissance, grandeur, *f.*
imprint [im'print], *v.t.* imprimer, empreindre.—['imprint], *n.* empreinte, *f.*

imprison

imprison [im'prizn], *v.t.* emprisonner, enfermer.

imprisonment [im'priznmənt], *n.* emprisonnement, *m.*, détention, *f.*

improbability [improbə'biliti], *n.* improbabilité; invraisemblance, *f.*

improbable [im'probəbl], *a.* improbable, invraisemblable.

impromptu [im'promptju:], *a.* impromptu, improvisé.—*adv.* par improvisation, impromptu.

improper [im'propə], *a.* inconvenant; peu propre (*à*), impropre (*langage*).

improperly [im'propəli], *adv.* d'une manière peu convenable; à tort, mal à propos.

impropriety [impro'praiəti], *n.* inconvenance (*de conduite*); impropriété (*de langage*), *f.*

improve [im'pru:v], *v.t.* améliorer, perfectionner (*invention etc.*); faire avancer; utiliser; bonifier (*terre etc.*); embellir (*rendre plus beau*); exploiter (*cultiver*).—*v.i.* s'améliorer; se perfectionner; se bonifier (*vin etc.*); faire des progrès; (*Comm.*) hausser; augmenter de prix; *to improve upon,* améliorer, perfectionner, surpasser.

improvement [im'pru:vmənt], *n.* amélioration, *f.*; perfectionnement; progrès, avancement (*en connaissances*), *m.*

improvident [im'providənt], *a.* imprévoyant.

improvisation [improvai'zeiʃən], *n.* improvisation, *f.*

improvise ['improvaiz], *v.t.* improviser.

imprudence [im'pru:dəns], *n.* imprudence, *f.*

imprudent [im'pru:dənt], *a.* imprudent.

imprudently [im'pru:dəntli], *adv.* imprudemment.

impudence ['impjudəns], *n.* impudence, effronterie, *f.*

impudent ['impjudənt], *a.* impudent, effronté.

impudently ['impjudəntli], *adv.* impudemment, effrontément.

impugn [im'pju:n], *v.t.* attaquer, contester; (*fig.*) mettre en doute.

impulse ['impʌls], **impulsion** [im'pʌlʃən], *n.* impulsion, *f.*, mouvement; (*fig.*) élan, *m.*; *sudden impulse,* coup de tête, *m.*

impulsive [im'pʌlsiv], *a.* impulsif, primesautier.

impulsively [im'pʌlsivli], *adv.* par impulsion, par un mouvement involontaire.

impunity [im'pju:niti], *n.* impunité, *f.*; *with impunity,* impunément.

impure [im'pjuə], *a.* impur; impudique.

impurity [im'pjuəriti], *n.* impureté; impudicité, *f.*

imputation [impju'teiʃən], *n.* imputation, accusation, *f.*

impute [im'pju:t], *v t.* imputer, attribuer (*à*).

in [in], *prep.* en, dans; à; par; pour; sur; avec; chez, parmi (*en compagnie de*); *he will do it in one hour,* il fera cela en une heure; *he will start in one hour,* il partira dans une heure; *in bed,* au lit; *in England,* en Angleterre; *in Japan,* au Japon; *in Paris,* à Paris; *in spite of,* malgré; *in spring,* au printemps; *in summer (autumn, winter),* en été (automne, hiver); *in the morning,* le matin; *in the U.S.A.,* aux États-Unis; *one in ten,* un sur dix; *to be clothed in,* être vêtu de.—*adv.* dedans, au dedans, rentré; chez soi, à la maison, y (*at home*); élu (*vainqueur aux élections*); au pouvoir (*parti politique*); *all in,* las, fatigué. —*n. to know all the ins and outs of a matter,* connaître les tenants et les aboutissants d'une affaire.

inability [inə'biliti], *n.* impuissance, incapacité, *f.*

inaccessible [inæk'sesibl], *a.* inaccessible; inabordable (*à*).

inaccuracy [in'ækjurəsi], *n.* inexactitude, *f.*

inaccurate [in'ækjurit], *a.* inexact.

inaction [in'ækʃən], *n.* inaction, inertie, *f.*

inactive [in'æktiv], *a.* inactif; inerte (*choses*).

inactivity [inæk'tiviti], *n.* inactivité, *f.*

inadequacy [in'ædikwəsi], *n.* insuffisance, imperfection, *f.*

inadequate [in'ædikwit], *a.* insuffisant; imparfait, défectueux, incomplet.

inadequately [in'ædikwitli], *adv.* insuffisamment.

inadmissible [inəd'misibl], *a.* inadmissible.

inadvertence [inəd'və:təns], **inadvertency** [inəd'və:tənsi], *n.* inadvertance, *f.*

inadvertent [inəd'və:tənt], *a.* négligent, inattentif.

inadvertently [inəd'və:təntli], *adv.* par inadvertance.

inalienable [in'eiliənəbl], *a.* inaliénable; inséparable.

inane [i'nein], *a.* vide; (*fig.*) inepte, absurde.

inanimate [in'ænimit], *a.* inanimé; mort.

inanition [inə'niʃən], *n.* inanition, *f.*

inanity [i'næniti], *n.* inanité, *f.*

inapplicable [in'æplikəbl], *a.* inapplicable.

inappreciable [inə'pri:ʃəbl], *a.* inappréciable, insensible.

inappropriate [inə'proupriit], *a.* peu propre, qui ne convient pas.

inapt [in'æpt], *a.* inapte, impropre, peu propre (*à*).

inarticulate [ina:'tikjulit], *a.* inarticulé, qui s'exprime peu clairement.

inartistic [ina:'tistik], *a.* peu artistique.

inasmuch [inəz'mʌtʃ], *adv.* vu que, attendu que, d'autant que.

inattention [inə'tenʃən], *n.* inattention; distraction, *f.*

inattentive [inə'tentiv], *a.* inattentif, distrait; négligent.

inattentively [inə'tentivli], *adv.* sans attention, négligemment.

inaudible [in'ɔ:dibl], *a.* imperceptible, qu'on ne peut entendre.

inaudibly [in'ɔ:dibli], *adv.* à ne pouvoir être entendu.

inaugural [in'ɔ:gjurəl], *a.* inaugural.

inaugurate [in'ɔ:gjureit], *v.t.* inaugurer.

inauspicious [inɔ:'spiʃəs], *a.* malheureux, peu propice.

inauspiciously [inɔ:'spiʃəsli], *adv.* sous de mauvais auspices.

inborn ['inbɔ:n], **inbred** ['inbred], *a.* inné, naturel.

incalculable [in'kælkjuləbl], *a.* incalculable.

incapable [in'keipəbl], *a.* incapable (*de*).

incapacitate [inkə'pæsiteit], *v.i.* rendre incapable (*de*).

incarcerate [in'ka:səreit], *v.t.* incarcérer, mettre en prison.

incarnate [in'ka:nit], *a.* incarné.

incautious [in'kɔ:ʃəs], *a.* inconsidéré, imprudent.

454

incendiarism [in'sendjərizm], *n.* crime d'incendie, *m.*

incendiary [in'sendjəri], *a.* and *n.* incendiaire, *m., f.*

incense ['insens], *n.* encens, *m.*—[in'sens], *v.t.* irriter, exaspérer (*contre*).

incentive [in'sentiv], *a.* excitant, stimulant.— *n.* motif, stimulant, encouragement, *m.*

inception [in'sepʃən], *n.* commencement, *m.*

incessant [in'sesənt]. *a.* incessant; continuel.

incest ['insest], *n.* inceste, *m.*

inch [intʃ], *n.* pouce (*2,539 centimètres*), *m.*

incident ['insidənt], *a.* qui arrive; particulier. —*n.* incident, événement, *m.*

incidental [insi'dentl], *a.* fortuit, accidentel; accessoire; *incidental expenses*, faux frais, *m.pl.*

incidentally [insi'dentli], *adv.* fortuitement, par hasard; soit dit en passant.

incinerate [in'sinəreit], *v.t.* incinérer.

incipient [in'sipiənt], *a.* naissant, qui commence.

incise [in'saiz], *v.t.* inciser, graver.

incision [in'siʒən], *n.* incision, *f.*

incisive [in'saisiv], *a.* incisif.

incite [in'sait], *v.t.* inciter, stimuler; encourager (*à*).

incitement [in'saitmənt], *n.* encouragement, motif, stimulant, *m.*

incivility [insi'viliti], *n.* incivilité, impolitesse, *f.*

inclemency [in'klemənsi], *n.* inclémence, *f.*; intempéries, *f.pl.*, rigueur (*du temps etc.*), *f.*

inclement [in'klemənt], *a.* inclément; rigoureux.

inclination [inkli'neiʃən], *n.* inclinaison, pente; inclination (*de la tête* ou *du corps*), *f.*; penchant, goût (*disposition*), *m.*

incline ['inklain], *n.* pente; (*Rail.*) rampe, *f.* —[in'klain], *v.t.* incliner, (faire) pencher; (*fig.*) porter, disposer (*à*).—*v.i.* incliner, s'incliner, pencher; (*fig.*) être porté (*à*).

inclined [in'klaind], *a.* incliné; enclin (*à*); porté, disposé (*à*).

include [in'klu:d], *v.t.* comprendre, renfermer.

included [in'klu:did], *a.* compris, y compris.

including [in'klu:diŋ], *prep.* comprenant, y compris.

inclusion [in'klu:ʒən], *n.* inclusion, *f.*

inclusive [in'klu:siv], *a.* inclusif; qui renferme, qui comprend; *inclusive of*, y compris.

incoherence [inko'hiərəns], *n.* incohérence, *f.*

incoherent [inko'hiərənt], *a.* incohérent.

incombustible [inkəm'bʌstibl], *a.* incombustible.

income ['inkəm], *n.* revenu, *m.*; *private income*, rente, *f.*, rentes, *f.pl.*

income tax ['inkəmtæks], *n.* impôt sur le revenu, *m.*

incommode [inkə'moud], *v.t.* incommoder, gêner, déranger.

incommodious [inkə'moudjəs], *a.* incommode.

incomparable [in'kɔmprəbl], *a.* incomparable.

incompatible [inkəm'pætibl], *a.* incompatible.

incompetence [in'kɔmpitəns], *n.* incompétence, insuffisance; incapacité, *f.*

incompetent [in'kɔmpitənt], *a.* incompétent, incapable.

incompetently [in'kɔmpitəntli], *adv.* avec incompétence.

incomplete [inkəm'pli:t], *a.* imparfait, inachevé, incomplet.

incompletely [inkəm'pli:tli], *adv.* incomplètement, imparfaitement.

incomprehensibility [inkəmprihensi'biliti], *n.* incompréhensibilité, *f.*

incomprehensible [inkəmpri'hensibl], *a.* incompréhensible.

inconceivable [inkən'si:vəbl], *a.* inconcevable.

inconclusive [inkən'klu:siv], *a.* qui n'est pas concluant.

incongruity [inkɔŋ'gru:iti], *n.* désaccord, *m.*, incongruité; inconvenance, *f.*

incongruous [in'kɔŋgruəs], *a.* incongru, inconvenant, (*fig.*) disparate.

inconsequence [in'kɔnsikwəns], *n.* inconséquence; fausse déduction, *f.*

inconsequent [in'kɔnsikwənt], *a.* inconséquent.

inconsiderable [inkən'sidərəbl], *a.* petit, insignifiant; de peu d'importance.

inconsiderate [inkən'sidərit], *a.* inconsidéré, irréfléchi; sans égards pour les autres.

inconsistency [inkən'sistənsi], *n.* inconséquence; contradiction, *f.*

inconsistent [inkən'sistənt], *a.* incompatible (*avec*), contradictoire (*à*); inconséquent.

inconsistently [inkən'sistəntli], *adv.* avec un manque de continuité.

inconspicuous [inkən'spikuəs], *a.* peu apparent, peu remarquable; discret.

inconstancy [in'kɔnstənsi], *n.* inconstance, *f.*; caractère changeant, *m.*

inconstant [in'kɔnstənt], *a.* inconstant, volage, changeant.

incontestable [inkən'testəbl], *a.* incontestable, irrécusable.

incontrovertible [inkɔntrə'və:tibl], *a.* incontestable, indisputable.

inconvenience [inkən'vi:niəns], *n.* inconvénient; embarras, dérangement, *m.*—*v.t.* déranger, incommoder, gêner.

inconvenient [inkən'vi:niənt], *a.* incommode, gênant.

inconveniently [inkən'vi:niəntli], *adv.* incommodément, mal.

incorporate [in'kɔ:pəreit], *v.t.* incorporer, former en société.—*v.i.* s'incorporer.

incorporated, see **joint-stock**.

incorrect [inkə'rekt], *a.* incorrect, inexact.

incorrectly [inkə'rektli], *adv.* incorrectement; inexactement.

incorrectness [inkə'rektnis], *n.* incorrection; inexactitude, *f.*

incorrigible [in'kɔridʒibl], *a.* incorrigible.

incorrupt [inkə'rʌpt], *a.* incorrompu, pur.

incorruptible [inkə'rʌptibl], *a.* incorruptible.

increase [in'kri:s], *v.t.* augmenter, agrandir, accroître.—*v.i.* croître, s'accroître; augmenter.—['inkri:s], *n.* augmentation (*de prix*), *f.*, accroissement (*de vitesse*); (*fig.*) produit, *m.*; crue (*de rivière*), *f.*

increasing [in'kri:siŋ], *a.* croissant.

increasingly [in'kri:siŋli], *adv.* de plus en plus.

incredible [in'kredibl], *a.* incroyable.

incredibly [in'kredibli], adv. incroyablement, d'une manière incroyable.
incredulity [inkrə'dju:liti], n. incrédulité, f.
incredulous [in'kredjuləs], a. incrédule.
increment ['inkrimənt], n. augmentation, f.; produit, m.
incriminate [in'krimineit], v.t. incriminer.
incubate ['inkjubeit], v.t. couver.
incubation [inkju'beiʃən], n. incubation, f.
incubator ['inkjubeitə], n. couveuse artificielle, f.
incubus ['inkjubəs], n. incube, cauchemar, (fig.) grand poids, m.
inculcate ['inkʌlkeit], v.t. inculquer (à).
incumbent [in'kʌmbənt], a. couché (sur); imposé, obligatoire; to be incumbent on, incomber à; to feel it incumbent on one to do, se faire un devoir de.—n. titulaire, bénéficier, m.
incur [in'kə:], v.t. encourir (blâme), s'attirer (colère); faire (dettes).
incurable [in'kjuərəbl], a. incurable, inguérissable.—n. incurable, m., f.
incursion [in'kə:ʃən], n. incursion, irruption, f.
indebted [in'detid], a. endetté; redevable (de).
indebtedness [in'detidnis], n. dette, obligation, f.
indecency [in'di:sənsi], n. indécence, f.
indecent [in'di:sənt], a. indécent.
indecently [in'di:səntli], adv. indécemment.
indecision [indi'siʒən], n. irrésolution, f.
indecisive [indi'saisiv], a. peu décisif, indécis.
indecorous [in'dekərəs], a. inconvenant.
indecorousness [in'dekərəsnis], indecorum [indi'kɔ:rəm], n. manque de décorum, m., inconvenance, f.
indeed [in'di:d], adv. en effet, en vérité; vraiment; à dire vrai, à la vérité.—int. vraiment! allons donc!
indefatigable [indi'fætigəbl], a. infatigable.
indefensible [indi'fensibl], a. indéfendable, inexcusable.
indefinable [indi'fainəbl], a. indéfinissable.
indefinite [in'definit], a. indéfini, vague.
indefinitely [in'definitli], adv. indéfiniment, vaguement.
indelible [in'delibl], a. indélébile, ineffaçable.
indelibly [in'delibli], adv. d'une manière indélébile, ineffaçablement.
indelicacy [in'delikəsi], n. indélicatesse, grossièreté, inconvenance, f.
indelicate [in'delikit], a. indélicat, grossier, inconvenant.
indemnify [in'demnifai], v.t. dédommager, indemniser (de).
indemnity [in'demniti], n. dédommagement, m.; indemnité, f.
indent [in'dent], v.t. denteler; ébrécher, échancrer.—v.i. to indent for, réquisitionner.—n. dentelure, bosselure, f.
indented [in'dentid], a. dentelé; échancré.
indenture [in'dentʃə], n. titre; (esp. pl.) contrat d'apprentissage, m.—v.t. mettre en apprentissage.
independence [indi'pendəns], independency [indi'pendənsi], n. indépendance, f.
independent [indi'pendənt], a. indépendant; libre.
independently [indi'pendəntli], adv. indépendamment; dans l'indépendance.
indescribable [indi'skraibəbl], a. indicible, indescriptible.

indestructible [indi'strʌktibl], a. indestructible.
index ['indeks], n. (pl. indexes ['indeksiz], indices ['indisi:z]) indice, signe, indicateur; index (d'un livre), m.; aiguille (d'une montre etc.), f.; (Anat.) index, doigt indicateur; (Math.) exposant, m.
India ['indjə], l'Inde, f.
Indian ['indjən], a. indien; des Indiens; de l'Inde, des Indes; Indian corn, maïs, m.—n. Indien (personne), m.; Red Indian, Peau-Rouge, m., f.
India rubber ['indjə'rʌbə], n. caoutchouc, m.
indicate ['indikeit], v.t. indiquer.
indication [indi'keiʃən], n. indication, f., signe, indice, m.
indicative [in'dikativ], a. and n. indicatif, m.
indicator ['indikeitə], n. indicateur, m.
indict [in'dait], v.t. inculper, mettre en accusation.
indictment [in'daitmənt], n. accusation; mise en accusation, f.
Indies ['indiz], the. les Indes, f.pl.; the West Indies, les Antilles, f.pl.
indifference [in'difrəns], n. indifférence, apathie, f.
indifferent [in'difrənt], a. indifférent; impartial; passable, médiocre.
indifferently [in'difrəntli], adv. indifféremment; médiocrement.
indigence ['indidʒəns], n. indigence, f.
indigent ['indidʒənt], a. nécessiteux, indigent.
indigenous [in'didʒinəs], a. du pays, indigène.
indigestible [indi'dʒestibl], a. indigeste.
indigestion [indi'dʒestʃən], n. indigestion, dyspepsie, f.
indignant [in'dignənt], a. indigné (de); plein d'indignation.
indignantly [in'dignəntli], adv. avec indignation.
indignation [indig'neiʃən], n. indignation, f.
indignity [in'digniti], n. indignité, f.; outrage, affront, m.
indigo ['indigou], n. indigo, m.
indirect [indi'rekt], a. indirect; (fig.) oblique, insidieux.
indiscreet [indis'kri:t], a. indiscret, irréfléchi, imprudent.
indiscreetly [indis'kri:tli], adv. indiscrètement.
indiscretion [indis'kreʃən], n. indiscrétion, imprudence, f.
indiscriminate [indis'kriminit], a. confus, sans distinction; aveugle.
indiscriminately [indis'kriminitli], adv. sans distinction, à tort et à travers, aveuglément.
indispensable [indis'pensəbl], a. indispensable, nécessaire.
indispose [indis'pouz], v.t. indisposer (contre), déranger, détourner (de).
indisposed [indis'pouzd], a. souffrant.
indisposition [indispə'ziʃən], n. indisposition, f.; malaise, m.
indisputable [indis'pju:təbl], a. incontestable, indiscutable.
indisputably [indis'pju:təbli], adv. incontestablement.
indissoluble [indi'sɔljubl], a. indissoluble.
indistinct [indis'tiŋkt], a. indistinct, confus, imprécis, vague.

indistinctly [indis'tiŋktli], *adv.* indistincte-ment, confusément, vaguement.
indistinguishable [indis'tiŋgwiʃəbl], *a.* in-distinct, imperceptible.
indite [in'dait], *v.t.* rédiger.
individual [indi'vidjuəl], *a.* individuel; seul, unique.—*n.* individu, particulier, *m.*
individuality [individju'æliti], *n.* individua-lité, personnalité, *f.*
individually [indi'viduəli], *adv.* individuelle-ment.
indivisible [indi'vizibl], *a.* indivisible.
indoctrinate [in'dɔktrineit], *v.t.* instruire; endoctriner.
indolence ['indələns], *n.* indolence, paresse, *f.*
indolent ['indələnt], *a.* indolent, paresseux.
indolently ['indələntli], *adv.* indolemment, nonchalamment.
indomitable [in'dɔmitəbl], *a.* indomptable.
Indonesia [indo'ni:ziə], l'Indonésie, *f.*
Indonesian [indo'ni:ziən], *a.* indonésien.—*n.* indonésien (*langue*); Indonésien (*personne*), *m.*
indoors [in'dɔ:z], *adv.* à la maison, au dedans.
indubitable [in'dju:bitəbl], *a.* indubitable, incontestable.
induce [in'dju:s], *v.t.* porter, persuader, induire, pousser (*à*); amener, causer, pro-duire.
inducement [in'dju:smənt], *n.* raison, tenta-tion, *f.*, motif, mobile, *m.*
induction [in'dʌkʃən], *n.* installation; induc-tion, *f.*
indulge [in'dʌldʒ], *v.t.* satisfaire; avoir trop d'indulgence pour; (*fig.*) flatter, caresser (*une espérance etc.*).—*v.i.* se laisser aller, se livrer à, s'abandonner (*à*).
indulgence [in'dʌldʒəns], *n.* faveur, *f.*, plaisir, agrément, *m.*; (*R.-C. Ch.*) indul-gence, *f.*
indulgent [in'dʌldʒənt], *a.* indulgent, facile, complaisant.
industrial [in'dʌstriəl], *a.* industriel, de l'industrie.
industrialist [in'dʌstriəlist], *n.* industriel, *m.*
industrious [in'dʌstriəs], *a.* travailleur; dili-gent, laborieux.
industriously [in'dʌstriəsli], *adv.* assidûment, diligemment.
industry ['indəstri], *n.* travail, *m.*, diligence, assiduité, *f.*; (*fig.*) empressement, *m.*; industrie (*production*), *f.*
inebriate [i'ni:brieit], *v.t.* enivrer.—[i'ni:briit], *a.* enivré.—*n.* ivrogne, *m.*, *f.*
inebriation [ini:bri'eiʃən], **inebriety** [ini'braiəti], *n.* ivresse, ébriété, *f.*
inedible [in'edibl], *a.* immangeable; non comestible.
ineffaceable [in'efəbl], *a.* ineffable.
ineffaceable [ini'feisəbl], *a.* ineffaçable, in-délébile.
ineffective [ini'fektiv], *a.* inefficace, sans effet.
ineffectual [ini'fektjuəl], *a.* inefficace, inutile, vain; incapable.
ineffectually [ini'fektjuəli], *adv.* inutilement, sans effet.
inefficacious [inefi'keiʃəs], *a.* inefficace.
inefficiency [ini'fiʃənsi], *n.* inefficacité, in-capacité, incompétence, *f.*
inefficient [ini'fiʃənt], *a.* inefficace; incapable.

ineligible [in'elidʒibl], *a.* inéligible; peu propre (*à*).
inept [in'ept], *a.* inepte, sot, absurde, peu propre (*à*).
inequality [ini'kwɔliti], *n.* inégalité, dis-parité, *f.*
inert [i'nɔ:t], *a.* inerte.
inertia [i'nɔ:ʃə], *n.* inertie, inactivité, *f.*
inestimable [in'estiməbl], *a.* inestimable; incalculable.
inevitable [in'evitəbl], *a.* inévitable; fatal.
inevitably [in'evitəbli], *adv.* inévitablement.
inexact [inig'zækt], *a.* inexact.
inexcusable [iniks'kju:zəbl], *a.* inexcusable, sans excuse.
inexhaustible [inig'zɔ:stibl], *a.* inépuisable.
inexorable [in'eksərəbl], *a.* inexorable, inflexible.
inexpedient [iniks'pi:djənt], *a.* inopportun, mal à propos.
inexpensive [iniks'pensiv], *a.* peu coûteux, bon marché.
inexperience [iniks'piəriəns], *n.* inexpérience, *f.*
inexperienced [iniks'piəriənst], *a.* inexpéri-menté, sans expérience.
inexplicable [in'eksplikəbl], *a.* inexplicable.
inexpressible [iniks'presibl], *a.* inexprimable, indicible.
inextricable [in'ekstrikəbl], *a.* inextricable.
infallible [in'fælibl], *a.* infaillible, imman-quable.
infamous ['infəməs], *a.* infâme.
infamy ['infəmi], *n.* infamie, *f.*
infancy ['infənsi], *n.* première enfance, *f.*, bas âge, *m.*
infant ['infənt], *a.* en bas âge, dans l'enfance; petit; (*fig.*) naissant, qui commence.—*n.* enfant en bas âge, nourrisson, bébé; (*Law*) mineur, *m.*
infantile ['infəntail], *a.* enfantin, d'enfant.
infantry ['infəntri], *n.* infanterie, *f.*
infant-school ['infənt'sku:l], *n.* école mater-nelle, *f.*
infatuate [in'fætjueit], *v.t.* infatuer, entêter, affoler; **to become infatuated with,** s'engouer de, s'amouracher de.
infatuation [infætju'eiʃən], *n.* engouement, *m.*; infatuation; (*fam.*) toquade, *f.*
infect [in'fekt], *v.t.* infecter (*de*).
infection [in'fekʃən], *n.* infection, contagion, *f.*
infectious [in'fekʃəs], *a.* infect; contagieux, infectieux.
infectiousness [in'fekʃəsnis], *n.* nature con-tagieuse, contagion, *f.*
infer [in'fə:], *v.t.* inférer; (*fig.*) supposer.
inference ['infərəns], *n.* conséquence, conclu-sion, déduction, *f.*
inferior [in'fiəriə], *a.* inférieur; subordonné.—*n.* inférieur, *m.*
inferiority [infiəri'ɔriti], *n.* infériorité, *f.*
infernal [in'fə:nəl], *a.* infernal, d'enfer; (*fig.*) diabolique.
inferno [in'fə:nou], *n.* enfer; brasier, *m.*
infest [in'fest], *v.t.* infester.
infidel ['infidəl], *a.* and *n.* infidèle; incrédule, *m.*, *f.*
infidelity [infi'deliti], *n.* infidélité; déloyauté (*d'un serviteur*), *f.*
infiltrate ['infiltreit], *v.i.* s'infiltrer (*dans*); pénétrer.

457

infinite ['infinit], *a.* and *n.* infini, *m.*
infinitely ['infinitli], *adv.* infiniment, à l'infini; fort.
infinitive [in'finitiv], *a.* and *n.* infinitif, *m.*
infinity [in'finiti], *n.* infinité; immensité, *f.*
infirm [in'fə:m], *a.* infirme, faible; *(fig.)* inconstant, irrésolu.
infirmary [in'fə:məri], *n.* hôpital, *m.*, infirmerie, *f.*
infirmity [in'fə:miti], *n.* infirmité, faiblesse, *f.*
inflame [in'fleim], *v.t.* enflammer; *(fig.)* exciter.—*v.i.* s'enflammer.
inflammable [in'flæməbl], *a.* inflammable.
inflammation [inflə'meiʃən], *n.* inflammation, fluxion, *f.*
inflammatory [in'flæmətri], *a.* inflammatoire; *(fig.)* incendiaire.
inflate [in'fleit], *v.t.* enfler, gonfler.
inflated [in'fleitid], *a.* enflé, gonflé; exagéré; boursouflé *(style)*.
inflation [in'fleiʃən], *n.* enflure, *f.*, gonflement, *m.*; inflation (monétaire), *f.*
inflect [in'flekt], *v.t.* fléchir; varier, moduler *(la voix)*.
inflection [in'flekʃən], *n.* inflexion, modulation, *f.*
inflexible [in'fleksibl], *a.* inflexible.
inflict [in'flikt], *v.t.* infliger, faire *(une peine)*.
infliction [in'flikʃən], *n.* infliction; *(fig.)* peine, *f.*
influence ['influəns], *n.* influence *(sur)*, *f.*, empire, *m.*—*v.t.* influencer; influer *(sur)*.
influential [influ'enʃəl], *a.* influent, qui a de l'influence.
influenza [influ'enzə], *n.* influenza, grippe, *f.*
influx ['inflʌks], *n.* affluence; invasion; embouchure, *f.*
inform [in'fə:m], *v.t.* informer, instruire, renseigner, avertir; faire savoir à; **to inform against**, dénoncer.
informal [in'fə:məl], *a.* sans cérémonie, simple.
informality [infə:'mæliti], *n.* manque de cérémonie, *m.*; simplicité, *f.*
informally [in'fə:məli], *adv.* sans cérémonie, sans façon.
informant [in'fə:mənt], *n.* correspondant; informateur, *m.*
information [infə'meiʃən], *n.* renseignements, *m.pl.*; **piece of information**, renseignement, avis, *m.*, nouvelle, *f.*; savoir, *m.*; *(Law)* dénonciation, *f.*
informative [in'fə:mətiv], *a.* instructif; éducatif.
informer [in'fə:mə], *n.* délateur, dénonciateur, *m.*
infraction [in'frækʃən], *n.* infraction, contravention, *f.*
infra-red [infrə'red], *a.* infra-rouge.
infrequent [in'fri:kwənt], *a.* rare.
infringe [in'frindʒ], *v.t.* enfreindre, violer, transgresser.
infringement [in'frindʒmənt], *n.* infraction, violation; contrefaçon *(d'un brevet)*, *f.*
infuriate [in'fjuərieit], *v.t.* rendre furieux.
infuriated [in'fjuərieitid], *a.* furieux, en fureur.
infuse [in'fju:z], *v.t.* infuser; faire infuser; macérer; *(fig.)* inspirer *(à)*.
infusion [in'fju:ʒən], *n.* infusion, *f.*
ingenious [in'dʒi:niəs], *a.* ingénieux, habile.

ingeniously [in'dʒi:niəsli], *adv.* ingénieusement; spirituellement.
ingeniousness [in'dʒi:niəsnis], **ingenuity** [indʒi'nju:iti], *n.* ingéniosité, habileté, *f.*
ingenuous [in'dʒenjuəs], *a.* ingénu; naïf; candide.
ingenuously [in'dʒenjuəsli], *adv.* ingénument, naïvement.
ingenuousness [in'dʒenjuəsnis], *n.* ingénuité, naïveté, *f.*
inglorious [in'glɔːriəs], *a.* obscur; inconnu; honteux.
ingloriously [in'glɔːriəsli], *adv.* sans gloire; honteusement.
ingoing ['ingouin], *a.* entrant, nouveau.—*n.* entrée, *f.*
ingot ['ingət], *n.* lingot, *m.*
ingrained [in'greind], *a.* encrassé; *(fig.)* enraciné, invétéré.
ingratiate [in'greiʃieit], *v.t.* insinuer *(dans)*; **to ingratiate oneself with**, s'insinuer dans les bonnes grâces de.
ingratitude [in'grætitju:d], *n.* ingratitude, *f.*
ingredient [in'gri:diənt], *n.* ingrédient; élément, *m.*
ingrowing ['ingrouin], *a.* incarné *(ongle)*.
inhabit [in'hæbit], *v.t.* habiter; habiter *(dans)*.
inhabitable [in'hæbitəbl], *a.* habitable.
inhabitant [in'hæbitənt], *n.* habitant, *m.*
inhabited [in'hæbitid], *a.* habité.
inhalation [inhə'leiʃən], *n.* inhalation; inspiration, *f.*
inhale [in'heil], *v.t.* aspirer; respirer, humer.
inherent [in'hiərənt], *a.* inhérent, naturel *(à)*.
inherit [in'herit], *v.t.* hériter *(de)*.—*v.i.* hériter.
inheritance [in'heritəns], *n.* héritage, patrimoine, *m.*
inheritance tax, see **death-duties**.
inhibit [in'hibit], *v.t.* arrêter, empêcher interdire.
inhibition [inhi'biʃən], *n.* interdiction; *(Psych.)* inhibition, *f.*
inhospitable [in'hɔspitəbl], *a.* inhospitalier.
inhuman [in'hju:mən], *a.* inhumain; dénaturé; cruel.
inhumanity [in'hju:mæniti], *n.* inhumanité; brutalité, *f.*
inhumation [inhju'meiʃən], *n.* inhumation, *f.*, enterrement, *m.*
inimical [i'nimikl], *a.* hostile, ennemi; contraire *(à)*.
inimitable [i'nimitəbl], *a.* inimitable.
iniquitous [i'nikwitəs], *a.* inique, injuste.
iniquity [i'nikwiti], *n.* iniquité, *f.*
initial [i'niʃəl], *a.* initial; premier.—*n.* initiale, *f.*—*v.t.* mettre ses initiales à.
initially [i'niʃəli], *adv.* au commencement.
initiate [i'niʃieit], *v.t.* initier *(à ou dans)*; amorcer, commencer.
initiation [iniʃi'eiʃən], *n.* initiation, *f.*
initiative [i'niʃiətiv], *n.* initiative, *f.*
inject [in'dʒekt], *v.t.* injecter; faire une piqûre.
injection [in'dʒekʃən], *n.* injection; *(Med.)* piqûre, *f.*
injudicious [indʒu'diʃəs], *a.* peu judicieux, malavisé, imprudent.
injudiciously [indʒu'diʃəsli], *adv.* peu judicieusement, imprudemment.
injunction [in'dʒʌnkʃən], *n.* injonction; recommandation, *f.*

injure ['indʒə], *v.t.* nuire à, faire tort à, léser; endommager (*to damage*); faire mal à, blesser.

injured ['indʒəd], *a.* offensé; blessé; *the injured*, les blessés, les accidentés, *m.pl.*

injurious [in'dʒuəriəs], *a.* nuisible, préjudiciable (à).

injuriously [in'dʒuəriəsli], *adv.* à tort.

injury ['indʒəri], *n.* tort, mal; dégât, dommage (*à des marchandises*), *m.*; (*Med.*) lésion, blessure, *f.*

injustice [in'dʒʌstis], *n.* injustice, *f.*

ink [iŋk], *n.* encre, *f.*; *India ink*, encre de Chine.—*v.t.* tacher *ou* barbouiller d'encre.

inkling ['iŋkliŋ], *n.* soupçon, vent (*d'une affaire*), *m.*

inkstand ['iŋkstænd], *n.* encrier de bureau, *m.*

ink-well ['iŋkwel], *n.* encrier, *m.*

inky ['iŋki], *a.* d'encre; taché d'encre.

inlaid [in'leid], *a.* incrusté, marqueté.

inland ['inlənd], *a.* intérieur, de l'intérieur.—*n.* intérieur (*d'un pays*), *m.*

inlay ['inlei], *n.* marqueterie, incrustation, *f.*—[in'lei], *v.t. irr.* (*conjug. like* LAY) marqueter, incruster.

inlet ['inlit], *n.* entrée, *f.*, passage, *m.*, voie, *f.*; petit bras de mer, *m.*

inmate ['inmeit], *n.* habitant, *m.*, locataire (*dans une maison*); interne, pensionnaire (*dans une maison de santé*), *m.*, *f.*

inmost ['inmoust], *a.* le plus profond, le plus secret.

inn [in], *n.* auberge, *f.*; hôtel, *m.*; hôtellerie, *f.*; *to put up at an inn*, descendre à une auberge.

innate [i'neit], *a.* inné; foncier.

innavigable [i'nævigəbl], *a.* innavigable.

inner ['inə], *a.* intérieur, de l'intérieur; (*fig.*) interne, secret.

innermost ['inəmoust], *a.* le plus intérieur, le plus reculé.

innkeeper ['inki:pə], *n.* aubergiste, *m.*, *f.*, hôtelier, *m.*

innocence ['inəsəns], *n.* innocence, *f.*

innocent ['inəsənt], *a.* innocent; permis, légitime.

innocently ['inəsəntli], *adv.* innocemment.

innocuous [i'nɔkjuəs], *a.* innocent, inoffensif.

innovate ['inoveit], *v.i.* innover.

innovation [ino'veiʃən], *n.* innovation, *f.*, changement, *m.*

innuendo [inju'endou], *n.* insinuation, allusion malveillante, *f.*

innumerable [i'nju:mərəbl], *a.* innombrable, sans nombre.

inoculate [i'nɔkjuleit], *v.t.* inoculer, vacciner.

inoculation [inɔkju'leiʃən], *n.* inoculation, *f.*, vaccin, *m.*

inodorous [in'oudərəs], *a.* inodore.

inoffensive [ino'fensiv], *a.* inoffensif.

inopportune [in'ɔpətju:n], *a.* inopportun, intempestif, mal à propos.

inopportunely [in'ɔpətju:nli], *adv.* inopportunément, mal à propos.

inordinate [i'nɔ:dinit], *a.* démesuré, immodéré.

inordinately [i'nɔ:dinitli], *adv.* démesurément, immodérément.

inorganic [inɔ:'gænik], *a.* inorganique.

inquest ['inkwest], *n.* enquête (*après une mort subite*), *f.*

inquire [in'kwaiə], *v.t.* demander.—*v.i.* s'enquérir, s'informer (*de*); s'adresser (*à ou chez*).

inquiring [in'kwaiəriŋ], *a.* investigateur, curieux.

inquiry [in'kwaiəri], *n.* demande, investigation, recherche, *f.*; (*pl.*) informations, *f.pl.* renseignements, *m.pl.*, (*Law*) enquête, *f.*

inquisition [inkwi'ziʃən], *n.* recherche, investigation, *f.*; (*R.-C. Ch.*) inquisition, *f.*

inquisitive [in'kwizitiv], *a.* curieux.

inroad ['inroud], *n.* incursion, invasion, *f.*; (*fig.*) empiétement (*sur*), *m.*

insalubrious [insæ'lju:briəs], *a.* insalubre.

insane [in'sein], *a.* fou, aliéné; dérangé; (*fig.*) insensé.

insanitary [in'sænitəri], *a.* insalubre, malsain.

insanity [in'sæniti], *n.* folie, démence, *f.*

insatiable [in'seiʃəbl], *a.* insatiable.

insatiate [in'seiʃiit], *a.* insatiable; inassouvi.

inscribe [in'skraib], *v.t.* inscrire; dédier (à).

inscription [in'skripʃən], *n.* inscription, *f.*; titre (*title*), *m.*; dédicace (*dedication*), *f.*

inscrutable [in'skru:təbl], *a.* inscrutable, impénétrable.

insect ['insekt], *n.* insecte, *m.*

insecticidal [in'sektisaidl], *a.* insecticide.

insecticide [in'sektisaid], *n.* insecticide, *m.*

insecure [insi'kjuə], *a.* en danger; chanceux, hasardeux; peu sûr, mal assuré.

insecurely [insi'kjuəli], *adv.* sans sûreté, en danger.

insecurity [insi'kjuəriti], *n.* manque de sûreté; danger, péril, *m.*; incertitude, *f.*

insensible [in'sensibl], *a.* imperceptible; insignifiant; inconscient (*unconscious*); sans connaissance.

insensibly [in'sensibli], *adv.* insensiblement, peu à peu.

insensitive [in'sensitiv], *a.* insensible.

inseparable [in'sepərəbl], *a.* inséparable.

insert [in'sə:t], *v.t.* insérer, faire insérer (*dans*).

insertion [in'sə:ʃən], *n.* insertion; interpolation, *f.*

inshore [in'ʃɔ:], *a.* and *adv.* près du rivage.

inside ['insaid], *a.* intérieur, d'intérieur.—*n.* dedans, intérieur, *m.*; *inside out*, à l'envers; [in'said] entrailles, *f.pl.*—[in'said], *adv.* à l'intérieur, en dedans.—[in'said], *prep.* en, dans, à l'intérieur de.

insidious [in'sidiəs], *a.* insidieux, captieux, perfide.

insight ['insait], *n.* perspicacité, pénétration, *f.*

insignia [in'signiə], *n.pl.* insignes, *m.pl.*

insignificance [insig'nifikəns], *n.* insignifiance, *f.*, peu d'importance, *m.*

insignificant [insig'nifikənt], *a.* insignifiant.

insincere [insin'siə], *a.* peu sincère, faux, hypocrite.

insincerely [insin'siəli], *adv.* de mauvaise foi, hypocritement.

insincerity [insin'seriti], *n.* manque de sincérité, *m.*, fausseté, *f.*

insinuate [in'sinjueit], *v.t.* insinuer, glisser (*dans*); donner à entendre.—*v.i.* s'insinuer, se glisser (*dans*).

insinuation [insinju'eiʃən], *n.* insinuation, *f.*

insipid [in'sipid], *a.* insipide, fade.

insipidity [insi'piditi], *n.* insipidité, fadeur, *f.*

insist [in'sist], *v.i.* insister (*sur ou* à); persister; vouloir absolument.

insistence [in'sistəns], *n.* insistance, *f.*

insistent

insistent [in'sistənt], *a.* insistant.
insobriety [inso'braiəti], *n.* intempérance, *f.*
insolence ['insələns], *n.* insolence; effronterie, *f.*
insolent ['insələnt], *a.* insolent.
insolently ['insələntli], *adv.* insolemment.
insoluble [in'sɔljubl], *a.* insoluble.
insolvency [in'sɔlvənsi], *n.* insolvabilité, faillite, *f.*
insolvent [in'sɔlvənt], *a.* insolvable, en faillite.
insomnia [in'sɔmniə], *n.* insomnie, *f.*
insomuch [inso'mʌtʃ], *adv.* au point (*que*), à un tel point (*que*), tellement (*que*).
inspect [in'spekt], *v.t.* inspecter, examiner, visiter.
inspection [in'spekʃən], *n.* inspection, revue, *f.*, contrôle, examen, *m.*; surveillance, *f.*
inspector [in'spektə], *n.* inspecteur, *m.*
inspiration [inspi'reiʃən], *n.* inspiration, *f.*; encouragement, *m.*
inspire [in'spaiə], *v.t.* inspirer, souffler (*dans*); animer (*de*).—*v.i.* aspirer.
inspiring [in'spaiəriŋ], *a.* inspirateur; qui donne du courage; qui élève l'esprit.
instability [instə'biliti], *n.* instabilité, *f.*
install [in'stɔ:l], *v.t.* installer; monter (*appareil, machine*).
installation [instə'leiʃən], *n.* installation, *f.*; montage (*de machine, équipement*), *m.*
installment [inso'stɔ:lmənt], *n.* installation, *f.*; (*Comm.*) accompte, versement (*partiel*); épisode (*de feuilleton*), *m.*
installment plan, see **hire-purchase**.
instance ['instəns], *n.* requête, demande, *f.*; exemple, *m.*, occasion, *f.*, cas, *m.*; **for instance**, par exemple; **in the first instance**, en premier lieu.—*v.t.* citer comme exemple.
instant ['instənt], *a.* instant, pressant, immédiat; courant (*mois*).—*n.* instant, moment, *m.*
instantaneous [instən'teiniəs], *a.* instantané.
instantaneously [instən'teiniəsli], *adv.* instantanément.
instantly ['instəntli], *adv.* à l'instant; tout de suite; sur-le-champ.
instead [in'sted], *adv.* à la place; **instead of**, au lieu de.
instep ['instep], *n.* cou-de-pied, *m.*
instigate ['instigeit], *v.t.* exciter, inciter, pousser (à).
instigation [insti'geiʃən], *n.* instigation, *f.*
instill [in'stil], *v.t.* instiller; (*fig.*) inspirer (à).
instillation [insti'leiʃən], *n.* instillation; (*fig.*) inspiration, *f.*
instinct ['instiŋkt], *n.* instinct, *m.*
instinctive [in'stiŋktiv], *a.* instinctif; (*fig.*) spontané.
instinctively [in'stiŋktivli], *adv.* d'instinct, instinctivement.
institute ['institju:t], *n.* institut, *m.*—*v.t.* instituer, établir; intenter (*un procès*).
institution [insti'tju:ʃən], *n.* institution, *f.*, établissement, *m.*
instruct [in'strʌkt], *v.t.* instruire, enseigner; charger (*de*).
instruction [in'strʌkʃən], *n.* instruction, *f.*, enseignement, *m.*
instructive [in'strʌktiv], *a.* instructif.
instructor [in'strʌktə], *n.* (*Mil.*) instructeur; précepteur, *m.*

instructress [in'strʌktris], *n.* préceptrice, monitrice, *f.*
instrument ['instrumənt], *n.* instrument; (*fig.*) agent, *m.*
instrumental [instru'mentl], *a.* instrumental; **to be instrumental in**, contribuer à.
insubordinate [insə'bɔ:dinit], *a.* insubordonné; indocile.
insubordination [insəbɔ:di'neiʃən], *n.* insubordination; insoumission, *f.*
insufferable [in'sʌfərəbl], *a.* insupportable, intolérable.
insufficiency [insə'fiʃənsi], *n.* insuffisance, *f.*
insufficient [insə'fiʃənt], *a.* insuffisant.
insufficiently [insə'fiʃəntli], *adv.* insuffisamment.
insular ['insjulə], *a.* insulaire; (*fig.*) borné, rétréci.
insularity [insju'læriti], *n.* insularité, *f.*
insulate ['insjuleit], *v.t.* isoler; calorifuger.
insulation [insju'leiʃən], *n.* isolement, *m.*; (*Phys.*) isolation, *f.*
insulator ['insjuleitə], *n.* isolateur, isoloir, *m.*
insulin ['insjulin], *n.* insuline, *f.*
insult [in'sʌlt], *v.t.* insulter, faire insulte à, injurier.—['insʌlt], *n.* insulte, injure, *f.*, affront, *m.*
insulting [in'sʌltiŋ], *a.* insultant, outrageux, injurieux.
insultingly [in'sʌltiŋli], *adv.* insolemment, injurieusement.
insuperable [in'sju:pərəbl], *a.* insurmontable, invincible.
insupportable [insə'pɔ:təbl], *a.* insupportable, intolérable.
insuppressible [insə'presibl], *a.* irrépressible, irrésistible, inextinguible (*rire*).
insurance [in'ʃuərəns], *n.* assurance, *f.*; **fire insurance**, assurance contre l'incendie; **life insurance**, assurance sur la vie.
insure [in'ʃuə], *v.t.* assurer, faire assurer; (*fig.*) garantir.
insurgent [in'sə:dʒənt], *a. and n.* insurgé, *m.*
insurmountable [insə'mauntəbl], *a.* insurmontable, infranchissable.
insurrection [insə'rekʃən], *n.* insurrection, *f.* soulèvement, *m.*
intact [in'tækt], *a.* intact, indemne.
intangible [in'tændʒibl], *a.* intangible.
integer ['intədʒə], *n.* entier, nombre entier, *m.*
integral ['intəgrəl], *a.* intégral; **an integral part**, une partie intégrante.—*n.* totalité, *f.*, tout, *m.*
integrate ['intigreit], *v.t.* compléter, rendre entier.
integrity [in'tegriti], *n.* intégrité, probité, *f.*
intellect ['intilekt], *n.* intelligence, *f.*, esprit, *m.*
intellectual [inti'lektjuəl], *a.* intellectuel; intelligent.—*n.* intellectuel, *m.*
intellectually [inti'lektjuəli], *adv.* intellectuellement.
intelligence [in'telidʒəns], *n.* intelligence, *f.*, esprit; renseignement, avis, *m.*; nouvelle, *f.*
intelligent [in'telidʒənt], *a.* intelligent.
intelligently [in'telidʒəntli], *adv.* intelligemment, avec intelligence.
intelligibility [intelidʒi'biliti], *n.* intelligibilité, clarté, *f.*
intelligible [in'telidʒibl], *a.* intelligible.

intemperance [in'tempərəns], *n.* intempérance, *f.*

intemperate [in'tempərit], *a.* démesuré, immodéré; intempérant; violent, emporté (*langage*).

intend [in'tend], *v.t.* se proposer de, avoir l'intention de, compter, vouloir; destiner (*à*); vouloir dire.

intended [in'tendid], *a.* projeté; intentionnel; *to be intended for*, être destiné à.

intense [in'tens], *a.* intense, véhément; (*fig.*) opiniâtre, très sérieux; vif, fort, aigu (*douleur etc.*).

intensely [in'tensli], *adv.* avec intensité, vivement, fortement.

intenseness [in'tensnis], **intensity** [in 'tensiti], *n.* intensité; force, violence, *f.*

intensify [in'tensifai], *v.t.* rendre plus vif, intensifier.

intensive [in'tensiv], *a.* intensif.

intent [in'tent], *a.* attentif, absorbé (*par*); déterminé (*à*); fixe (*regard*).—*n.* dessein, but; sens, *m.*, intention, portée, *f.*; *to all intents and purposes*, à tous égards.

intention [in'tenʃən], *n.* intention, *f.*; dessein, but, *m.*

intentional [in'tenʃənəl], *a.* intentionnel, fait à dessein.

intentionally [in'tenʃənəli], *adv.* avec intention, à dessein, exprès.

intently [in'tentli], *adv.* attentivement.

intentness [in'tentnis], *n.* attention, force d'application, *f.*

inter [in'tə:], *v.t.* enterrer, inhumer, ensevelir.

intercede [intə'si:d], *v.i.* intercéder (*auprès de*).

intercept [intə'sept], *v.t.* intercepter; arrêter; (*fig.*) surprendre.

interchange [intə'tʃeindʒ], *v.t.* échanger.—['intətʃeindʒ], *n.* échange, *m.*, succession; (*fig.*) variété, *f.*

intercourse ['intəkɔ:s], *n.* commerce, *m.*, relations, *f.pl.*, rapports, *m.pl.*

interdict [intə'dikt], *v.t.* interdire, interdire à, défendre à.—['intədikt], *n.* or **interdiction** [intə'dikʃən], interdit, *m.*, défense, interdiction, *f.*

interest ['intrəst], *v.t.* intéresser; *to be interested in*, s'intéresser à.—*n.* intérêt, *m.*; protection, *f.*, crédit, *m.*

interested ['intrəstid], *a.* intéressé.

interesting ['intrəstiŋ], *a.* intéressant.

interfere [intə'fiə], *v.i.* intervenir, se mêler (*de*); *to interfere with*, se mêler de, gêner, contrarier, déranger.

interference [intə'fiərəns], *n.* intervention, *f.*; (*Rad.*) brouillage, *m.*

interim ['intərim], *a.* provisoire.—*n.* intérim, intervalle, *m.*; *in the interim*, en attendant.

interior [in'tiəriə], *a.* and *n.* intérieur, *m.*; *interior angle*, angle interne, *m.*

interject [intə'dʒekt], *v.t.* interjecter; s'écrier (*en conversation*).

interjection [intə'dʒekʃən], *n.* interjection, *f.*

interlace [intə'leis], *v.t.* entrelacer.

interlacing [intə'leisiŋ], *n.* entrelacement, *m.*

interleave [intə'li:v], *v.t.* interfolier (*de*).

interloper ['intəloupə], *n.* intrus, *m.*

interlude ['intəlu:d], *n.* intermède, *m.*

intermediary [intə'mi:diəri], *a.* and *n.* intermédiaire, *m.*

intermediate [intə'mi:djit], *a.* intermédiaire, moyen.

interment [in'tə:mənt], *n.* enterrement, *m.*, inhumation, *f.*

interminable [in'tə:minəbl], *a.* interminable.

intermingle [intə'miŋgl], *v.t.* entremêler.—*v.i.* s'entremêler.

intermission [intə'miʃən], *n.* interruption momentanée, *f.*; relâche, intervalle;(*Theat.*) entr'acte, *m.*

intermittent [intə'mitənt], *a.* intermittent.

intermittently [intə'mitəntli], *adv.* par intervalles.

intern [in'tə:n], *v.t.* interner.

intern ['intə:n], *n.* (*Med.*) interne, *m.*, *f.*

internal [in'tə:nl], *a.* interne, intérieur.

international [intə'næʃənl], *a.* international.—*n.* (joueur) international, *m.*

internecine [intə'ni:sain], *a.* meurtrier.

internee [intə:'ni:], *n.* interné, *m.*

internment [in'tə:nmənt], *n.* internement, *m.*; *internment camp*, camp de concentration, camp de prisonniers, *m.*

interplanetary [intə'plænətəri], *a.* interplanétaire.

interpolate [in'tə:poleit], *v.t.* interpoler; intercaler.

interpose [intə'pouz], *v.t.* interposer.—*v.i.* s'interposer, intervenir.

interpret [in'tə:prit], *v.t.* interpréter; expliquer.

interpretation [intə:pri'teiʃən], *n.* interprétation, *f.*

interpreter [in'tə:pritə], *n.* interprète, *m.*, *f.*

interracial [intə'reiʃəl], *a.* interracial.

interrogate [in'terəgeit], *v.t.* interroger, questionner.

interrogation [interə'geiʃən], *n.* interrogation, question, *f.*

interrogative [intə'rɔgətiv], *a.* interrogatif, interrogateur.

interrupt [intə'rʌpt], *v.t.* interrompre.

interruption [intə'rʌpʃən], *n.* interruption, *f.*; (*fig.*) obstacle, *m.*

intersect [intə'sekt], *v.t.* entrecouper; (*Geom.*) couper.—*v.i.* (*Geom.*) se couper, se croiser.

intersection [intə'sekʃən], *n.* intersection, *f.*

intersperse [intə'spə:s], *v.t.* entremêler (*de*); parsemer (*de*).

interstice [in'tə:stis], *n.* interstice; intervalle, *m.*

intertwine [intə'twain], *v.t.* entrelacer.—*v.i.* s'entrelacer.

interval ['intəvəl], *n.* intervalle, *m.*

intervene [intə'vi:n], *v.i.* intervenir, s'interposer; survenir, arriver (*événements*); s'écouler (*temps*).

intervening [intə'vi:niŋ], *a.* intervenant (*personnes*); intermédiaire (*espace, endroits, temps etc.*).

intervention [intə'venʃən], *n.* intervention, *f.*

interview ['intəvju:], *n.* entrevue; (*Journ.*) interview, *f.*—*v.t.* avoir une entrevue avec; (*Journ.*) interviewer.

interviewer ['intəvju:ə], *n.* interviewer, *m.*

interweave [intə'wi:v], *v.t.* irr. (*conjug. like* WEAVE) entrelacer; entremêler.

intestate [in'testit], *a.* intestat.

intestine [in'testin], *a.* and *n.* intestin, *m.*

intimacy ['intiməsi], *n.* intimité, *f.*

intimate ['intimit], *a.* intime, lié.—['intimeit], *v.t.* donner à entendre; intimer (*à*).

intimately ['intimitli], *adv.* intimement.
intimation [inti'meiʃən], *n.* avis, *m.*, indication, *f.*
intimidate [in'timideit], *v.t.* intimider.
intimidation [intimi'deiʃən], *n.* intimidation, *f.*
into ['intu], *prep.* dans, en, à, entre.
intolerable [in'tɔlərəbl], *a.* intolérable, insupportable.
intolerance [in'tɔlərəns], *n.* intolérance, *f.*
intolerant [in'tɔlərənt], *a.* intolérant.
intonation [intɔ'neiʃən], *n.* intonation, *f.*
intone [in'toun], *v.t., v.i.* psalmodier; entonner.
intoxicant [in'tɔksikənt], *n.* boisson alcoolique, *f.*
intoxicate [in'tɔksikeit], *v.t.* enivrer (*de*).
intoxicated [in'tɔksikeitid], *a.* ivre; (*fig.*) enivré (*de*).
intoxicating [in'tɔksikeitiŋ], *a.* enivrant.
intoxication [intɔksi'keiʃən], *n.* ivresse, *f.*; (*fig.*) enivrement, *m.*
intractability [intræktə'biliti], *n.* naturel intraitable, *m.*, indocilité, *f.*
intractable [in'træktəbl], *a.* intraitable, indocile.
intransigence [in'trænsidʒəns, in'traːnsidʒəns], *n.* intransigeance, *f.*
intransigent [in'trænsidʒənt, in'traːnsidʒənt], *a.* intransigeant.
intransitive [in'trænsitiv, in'traːnsitiv], *a.* intransitif.
intrepid [in'trepid], *a.* intrépide.
intricacy ['intrikəsi], *n.* embrouillement, *m.*; complication, *f.*, dédale, *m.*
intricate ['intrikit], *a.* embrouillé; embarrassé; obscur; compliqué.
intrigue [in'triːg], *n.* intrigue, *f.*—*v.t.* intriguer.—*v.i.* intriguer, s'intriguer.
intriguing [in'triːgiŋ], *a.* intrigant, qui excite la curiosité.
intrinsic [in'trinsik], intrinsical [in'trinsikəl], *a.* intrinsèque.
introduce [intrə'djuːs], *v.t.* introduire, faire entrer; présenter (*personnes*), faire connaître (*à*).
introduction [intrə'dakʃən], *n.* introduction; présentation; recommandation (*par lettre*), *f.*; avant-propos (*de livre*), *m.*
introductory [intrə'daktəri], *a.* introductoire, préliminaire.
introspection [intrə'spekʃən], *n.* introspection, *f.*
introspective [intrə'spektiv], *a.* introspectif; qui s'analyse.
introvert ['introvɔːt], *n.* introverti, *m.*
intrude [in'truːd], *v.i.* s'introduire, se faufiler, se fourrer; **to intrude on**, importuner, déranger.
intruder [in'truːdə], *n.* intrus, *m.*
intrusion [in'truːʒən], *n.* intrusion, importunité; (*fig.*) usurpation, *f.*, empiètement, *m.*
intuition [intju'iʃən], *n.* intuition, *f.*
intuitive [in'tjuːitiv], *a.* intuitif, d'intuition.
inundate ['inandeit], *v.t.* inonder (*de*).
inundation [inan'deiʃən], *n.* inondation, *f.*, débordement, *m.*
inure [i'njuə], *v.t.* habituer, endurcir, rompre.
invade [in'veid], *v.t.* envahir.
invader [in'veidə], *n.* envahisseur, *m.*
invading [in'veidiŋ], *a.* envahissant; d'invasion.

invalid ['invəliːd], *a.* malade, infirme; [in'vælid], (*Law*) invalide, de nul effet.—*n.* malade, *m.*, *f.*, personne malade, *f.*—*v.t.* **to invalid out** (*of the army*), réformer.
invalidate [in'vælideit], *v.t.* invalider, casser.
invaluable [in'væljuəbl], *a.* inestimable, sans prix.
invariable [in'vɛəriəbl], *a.* invariable, constant, uniforme.
invariably [in'vɛəriəbli], *adv.* invariablement; constamment.
invasion [in'veiʒən], *n.* invasion, *f.*, envahissement, *m.*; (*fig.*) violation, *f.*
invective [in'vektiv], *n.* invective, *f.*
inveigh [in'vei], *v.i.* invectiver (*contre*).
inveigle [in'viːgl, in'veigl], *v.t.* séduire, attirer, entraîner.
invent [in'vent], *v.t.* inventer.
invention [in'venʃən], *n.* invention, *f.*
inventive [in'ventiv], *a.* inventif.
inventor [in'ventə], *n.* inventeur, *m.*
inventory ['invəntri], *n.* inventaire, *m.*
inverse [in'vɔːs], *a.* inverse.
inversely [in'vɔːsli], *adv.* en sens inverse, inversement.
inversion [in'vɔːʃən], *n.* inversion, *f.*
invert [in'vɔːt], *v.t.* tourner sens dessus dessous, renverser.
invertebrate [in'vɔːtibrit], *a.* and *n.* invertébré, *m.*
invest [in'vest], *v.t.* vêtir, revêtir (*de*); (*Mil.*) investir, bloquer; placer (*argent*).
investigate [in'vestigeit], *v.t.* rechercher, examiner; enquêter sur.
investigation [investi'geiʃən], *n.* investigation, recherche, enquête, *f.*
investigator [in'vestigeitə], *n.* investigateur, *m.*; **private investigator**, détective privé, *m.*
investment [in'vestmənt], *n.* placement (*d'argent*), *m.*; (*Mil.*) investissement, *m.*
investor [in'vestə], *n.* actionnaire, *m.*, *f.*, personne qui place ses fonds, *f.*
inveterate [in'vetərit], *a.* invétéré, enraciné; acharné.
invidious [in'vidiəs], *a.* odieux; désagréable, ingrat (*tâche*).
invigorate [in'vigəreit], *v.t.* fortifier; donner de la vigueur à.
invigorating [in'vigəreitiŋ], *a.* fortifiant, vivifiant, tonifiant.
invincible [in'vinsibl], *a.* invincible.
inviolable [in'vaiələbl], *a.* inviolable.
inviolate [in'vaiəlit], *a.* inviolé, pur, intact.
invisible [in'vizibl], *a.* invisible.
invitation [invi'teiʃən], *n.* invitation, *f.*
invite [in'vait], *v.t.* inviter, engager (*à*); (*fig.*) appeler, provoquer.
inviting [in'vaitiŋ], *a.* attrayant, appétissant, tentant.
invoice ['invɔis], *n.* facture, *f.*—*v.t.* facturer.
invoke [in'vouk], *v.t.* invoquer.
involuntarily [in'vɔləntərili], *adv.* involontairement.
involuntary [in'vɔləntəri], *a.* involontaire.
involve [in'vɔlv], *v.t.* envelopper (*to envelop*); compromettre, impliquer, entraîner (*to entail*); comprendre, renfermer (*to comprise*); embarrasser, entortiller (*to entangle*).
involved [in'vɔlvd], *a.* embrouillé, entortillé, compliqué.
invulnerable [in'vʌlnərəbl], *a.* invulnérable.

inward ['inwəd], *a.* intérieur, interne.—*adv.* (*also* **inwards** ['inwədz]) en dedans, intérieurement.

inwardly ['inwədli], *adv.* intérieurement, intimement.

iodine ['aiədi:n, 'aiədain], *n.* iode, *m.*

ion ['aiən], *n.* ion, *m.*

ionosphere [ai'ɔnəsfiə], *n.* ionosphère, *f.*

iota [ai'outə], *n.* iota; rien, *m.*

Iran [i'rɑːn]. l'Iran, *m.*

Iranian [i'reiniən, ai'reiniən], *a.* iranien, *m.*—*n.* Iranien (*personne*), *m.*

Iraq, Irak [i'rɑːk]. l'Irak, *m.*

Iraqi [i'rɑːki], *a.* irakien.—*n.* Irakien (*personne*), *m.*

irascible [i'ræsibl], *a.* irascible.

irate [ai'reit], *a.* courroucé, irrité.

ire ['aiə], *n.* colère, *f.*, courroux, *m.*

Ireland ['aiələnd]. l'Irlande, *f.*

Irene [ai'riːni, ai'riːn]. Irène, *f.*

iridescent [iri'desənt], *a.* iridescent, irisé; chatoyant.

iris ['aiəris], *n.* (*pl.* **irises** ['aiərisiz]) iris, *m.*

Irish ['aiəriʃ], *a.* irlandais.—*n.* irlandais (*langue*), *m.*; **the Irish**, les Irlandais, *m.pl.*

Irishman ['aiəriʃmən], *n.* (*pl.* **-men** [men]) Irlandais, *m.*

Irishwoman ['aiəriʃwumən], *n.* (*pl.* **-women** [wimin]) Irlandaise, *f.*

irk [əːk], *v.t.* peiner, affliger; ennuyer.

irksome ['əːksəm], *a.* ingrat, ennuyeux.

iron ['aiən], *n.* fer à repasser, *m.*

iron ['aiən], *a.* de fer, en fer.—*n.* fer, *m.*; **cast iron**, fonte, *f.*; **corrugated iron**, tôle ondulée, *f.*; **sheet iron**, tôle, *f.*; **wrought iron**, fer forgé.—*v.t.* repasser (*linge etc.*).

ironic [ai'rɔnik], **ironical** [ai'rɔnikəl], *a.* ironique.

ironing ['aiəniŋ], *a.* à repasser.—*n.* repassage, *m.*

ironing board ['aiəniŋbɔːd], *n.* planche à repasser, *f.*

ironmonger ['aiənmʌŋgə], *n.* quincaillier, *m.*

ironmongery ['aiənmʌŋgəri], *n.* quincaillerie, *f.*

iron ore ['aiən'ɔː], *n.* minerai de fer, *m.*

iron-works ['aiənwəːks], *n.pl.* forges, *f.pl.*; usine métallurgique, *f.*

irony ['aiərəni], *n.* ironie, *f.*

irradiate [i'reidieit], *v.t.* rayonner sur; éclairer.—*v.i.* rayonner.

irrational [i'ræʃənl], *a.* irraisonnable, déraisonnable; (*Math.*) irrationnel.

irreclaimable [iri'kleiməbl], *a.* incorrigible, invétéré.

irreconcilable [irekən'sailəbl], *a.* irréconciliable (*avec*); incompatible (*avec*); implacable.

irrecoverable [iri'k vərəbl], *a.* irrécouvrable; irréparable.

irredeemable [iri'diːməbl], *a.* irrachetable; irrémédiable.

irreducible [iri'djuːsibl], *a.* irréductible.

irreformable [iri'fɔːməbl], *a.* inaltérable, irréformable.

irrefutable [i'refjutəbl], *a.* irréfutable.

irregular [i'regjulə], *a.* irrégulier, anormal; déréglé.

irregularity [iregju'læriti], *n.* irrégularité, *f.*, dérèglement, *m.*

irregularly [i'regjuləli], *adv.* irrégulièrement.

irrelevant [i'reləvənt], *a.* hors de propos, non pertinent; inapplicable (*a*).

irreligious [iri'lidʒəs], *a.* irréligieux.

irremediable [iri'miːdiəbl], *a.* irrémédiable, sans remède.

irremovable [iri'muːvəbl], *a.* inébranlable, immuable; inamovible.

irreparable [i'repərəbl], *a.* irréparable.

irreplaceable [iri'pleisəbl], *a.* irremplaçable.

irrepressible [iri'presibl], *a.* irrépressible; inextinguible (*rire*).

irreproachable [iri'proutʃəbl], *a.* irréprochable, sans tache.

irresistible [iri'zistibl], *a.* irrésistible.

irresolute [i'rezoljuːt], *a.* irrésolu, indécis.

irresolutely [i'rezoljuːtli], *adv.* irrésolument, avec hésitation.

irresolution [irezo'ljuːʃən], **irresoluteness** [i'rezoljuːtnis], *n.* irrésolution, indécision, *f.*

irrespective [iris'pektiv], *a.* indépendant (*de*), sans égard (*pour*); **irrespective of**, indépendamment de.

irrespectively [iris'pektivli], *adv.* indépendamment (*de*), sans égard (*pour*).

irresponsibility [irisponsi'biliti], *n.* irresponsabilité, étourderie, *f.*

irresponsible [iris'ponsibl], *a.* irresponsable; irréfléchi, étourdi.

irretrievable [iri'triːvəbl], *a.* irréparable, irrémédiable.

irreverence [i'revərəns], *n.* irrévérence, *f.*, manque de respect, *m.*

irreverent [i'revərənt], *a.* irrévérencieux.

irrevocable [i'revəkəbl], *a.* irrévocable.

irrigate ['irigeit], *v.t.* arroser, irriguer.

irrigation [iri'geiʃən], *n.* arrosement, *m.* irrigation, *f.*

irritability [irita'biliti], *n.* irritabilité, *f.*

irritable ['iritəbl], *a.* irritable.

irritate ['iriteit], *v.t.* irriter; **to be irritated**, s'irriter.

irritation [iri'teiʃən], *n.* irritation, *f.*

irruption [i'rʌpʃən], *n.* irruption, *f.*

Isabel ['izəbel], **Isabella** [izə'belə]. Isabelle, *f.*

island ['ailənd], *n.* île, *f.*; refuge (*au centre de la rue*), *m.*

islander ['ailəndə], *n.* insulaire, *m.*, *f.*

isle [ail], *n.* île, *f.*

islet ['ailit], *n.* îlot, *m.*

isobar ['aisobɑː], *n.* isobare, *f.*

isolate ['aisəleit], *v.t.* isoler.

isolated ['aisəleitid], *a.* isolé, seul.

isolation [aisə'leiʃən], *n.* isolement, *m.*

isosceles [ai'sɔsəliːz], *a.* isocèle, isoscèle.

Israel ['izreil]. l'Israel, *m.*

Israeli [iz'reili], *a.* israélien.—*n.* Israélien (*personne*), *m.*

issue ['isjuː; 'iʃjuː], *n.* issue, sortie (*egress*), *f.*; écoulement (*d'eau etc.*), *m.*; distribution (*envoi*); émission (*de billets de banque, timbres-poste*); publication (*de livres etc.*), *f.*; résultat (*conséquence*), *m.*; enfants, *m.pl.* (*Law*) question, *f.*; **at issue**, en question.—*v.t.* publier; expédier, distribuer; émettre (*billets de banque*).—*v.i.* sortir, jaillir (*de*); (*fig.*) provenir.

isthmus ['isməs], *n.* isthme, *m.*

it [it], *pron.* il, *m.*, elle, *f.*; (*accusatif*) le, *m.*, la, *f.*; (*datif*) lui, (*impersonnel*) il, ce, cela.

Italian [i'tæljən], *a.* italien.—*n.* italien (*langue*); Italien (*personne*), *m.*

italic [i'tælik], *a.* italique.—*n.* (*pl.*) italiques, *m.pl.*
italicize [i'tælisaiz], *v.t.* mettre *ou* imprimer en italiques.
Italy ['itəli]. l'Italie, *f.*
itch [itʃ], *n.* démangeaison; gale (*maladie*), *f.*—*v.i.* démanger.
item ['aitəm]. *n.* article; détail, *m.*, rubrique, *f.*; *item of news*, nouvelle, *f.*—*adv.* item, de plus.
itinerant [i'tinərənt], *a.* ambulant.
itinerary [i'tinərəri], *n.* itinéraire, *m.*
its [its], *poss. a.* son, *m.*, sa, *f.*; ses, *m.pl.*
itself [it'self], *pron.* lui, *m.*, elle, *f.*, soi, lui-même, *m.*, elle-même, *f.*, soi-même, *m.*; (*reflexive*) se.
ivory ['aivəri], *a.* d'ivoire.—*n.* ivoire, *m.*
ivy ['aivi], *n.* lierre, *m.*

J

J, j [dʒei]. dixième lettre de l'alphabet, *m.*
jabber ['dʒæbə], *v.i.* jaboter, baragouiner.—*n.* bavardage, baragouinage, *m.*
jack [dʒæk], *n.* chevalet (*de scieur*); cric (*pour auto*); (*Cards*) valet; (*Bowls*) cochonnet, *m.*—*v.t.* **to jack up**, soulever avec un cric.
jackal ['dʒækɔːl], *n.* chacal, *m.*
jackanapes ['dʒækəneips], *n.* singe; fat, *m.*
jackass ['dʒækæs], *n.* âne, baudet, bourriquet; (*fig.*) idiot, *m.*
jackdaw ['dʒækdɔː], *n.* choucas, *m.*
jacket ['dʒækit], *n.* veste, *f.*; veston, *m.*; (*Tech.*) chemise, enveloppe, jaquette, *f.*
jack-in-the-box ['dʒækinðəbɔks], *n.* boîte à surprise, *f.*
jack-tar ['dʒæk'tɑː], *n.* marin, *m.*
jade (1) [dʒeid]. *n.* rosse; haridelle; (*fig.*) coquine (*femme*), *f.*—*v.t.* surmener, harasser, éreinter.
jade (2) [dʒeid]. *n.* (*Min.*) jade, *m.*
jaded ['dʒeidid], *a.* surmené, éreinté.
jagged [dʒægid], **jaggy** ['dʒægi], *a.* dentelé, ébréché.
jaguar ['dʒægjuə], *n.* jaguar, *m.*
jail [dʒeil], *n.* prison, geôle, *f.*
jailer ['dʒeilə], *n.* geôlier, *m.*
jam [dʒæm], *n.* confitures, *f.pl.*; encombrement, embouteillage (*de circulation*), *m.*—*v.t.* serrer, presser, bloquer; (*Rad.*) brouiller.—*v.i.* se coincer.
jamming ['dʒæmin], *n.* coincement; (*Rad.*) brouillage, *m.*
Jamaica [dʒə'meikə]. la Jamaïque, *f.*
Jamaican [dʒə'meikən], *a.* jamaïquain.—*n.* Jamaïquain (*personne*).
James [dʒeimz]. Jacques, *m.*
Jane [dʒein]. Jeanne, *f.*
jangle [dʒængl], *v.t.* choquer avec bruit; (*fig.*) agacer (*nerfs*).—*v.i.* faire un bruit de ferraille.
janitor ['dʒænitə], *n.* portier, concierge, *m.*
January ['dʒænjuəri], *n.* janvier, *m.*
Japan [dʒə'pæn]. le Japon, *m.*

japan [dʒə'pæn], *n.* laque, vernis, *m.*—*v.* laquer; vernir.
Japanese [dʒæpə'niːz], *a.* japonais.—*n.* japonais (*langue*); Japonais (*personne*), *m.*
jar (1) [dʒɑː], *v.t.* remuer, secouer; ébranler.—*v.i.* être discordant (*instrument de musique*); heurter, s'entrechoquer (*être en conflit*); jurer (*couleurs*); (*fig.*) se disputer.—*n.* son discordant, choc, *m.*; querelle, *f.*
jar (2) [dʒɑː], *n.* jarre, cruche (*faïence*), *f.*, bocal (*verre*), *m.*
jargon ['dʒɑːgən], *n.* jargon, *m.*
jarring ['dʒɑːrin], *a.* discordant; en conflit.—*n.* son discordant, *m.*; querelles, *f.pl.*
jasmine ['dʒæzmin], *n.* jasmin, *m.*
jasper ['dʒæspə], *n.* jaspe, *m.*
jaundice ['dʒɔːndis], *n.* jaunisse, *f.*
jaundiced ['dʒɔːndist], *a.* qui a la jaunisse; (*fig.*) prévenu (*contre*).
jaunt [dʒɔːnt], *n.* petite promenade *ou* excursion, *f.*—*v.i.* faire une petite promenade *ou* excursion.
jauntily ['dʒɔːntili], *adv.* avec insouciance, légèrement.
jauntiness ['dʒɔːntinis], *n.* légèreté, *f.*, enjouement, *m.*
jaunty ['dʒɔːnti], *a.* léger, enjoué, sémillant.
javelin ['dʒævəlin], *n.* javeline, *f.*, javelot, *m.*
jaw [dʒɔː], *n.* mâchoire, *f.*; (*fig.*, *pl.*) portes, *f.pl.*; bras, *m.pl.*, étreintes, *f.pl.*
jawbone ['dʒɔːboun], *n.* mâchoire, *f.*
jay [dʒei], *n.* geai, *m.*
jay-walker ['dʒeiwɔːkə], *n.* piéton distrait, *m.*
jazz [dʒæz], *n.* jazz, *m.*
jealous ['dʒeləs], *a.* jaloux.
jealously ['dʒeləsli], *adv.* jalousement; par jalousie.
jealousy ['dʒeləsi], *n.* jalousie, *f.*
jean [dʒiːn], *n.* coutil, treillis; (*pl.*) pantalon (*de coutil*), *m.*
jeep [dʒiːp], *n.* jeep, *f.*
jeer [dʒiə], *n.* raillerie, moquerie, *f.*—*v.t.* railler, huer, se moquer de.—*v.i.* railler, se moquer, goguenarder.
jeering ['dʒiərin], *a.* railleur, moqueur, goguenard.—*n.* raillerie, moquerie, *f.*
jeeringly ['dʒiərinli], *adv.* en raillant, d'un ton moqueur.
jelly ['dʒeli], *n.* gelée, *f.*
jelly-fish ['dʒelifiʃ], *n.* méduse, *f.*
jennet ['dʒenit], *n.* genet (*d'Espagne*), *m.*
jeopardize ['dʒepədaiz], *v.t.* hasarder, risquer, mettre en danger.
jeopardy ['dʒepədi], *n.* danger, hasard, *m.*
jerk [dʒəːk], *n.* saccade, secousse, *f.*—*v.t.* donner une poussée à; jeter.
jerkily ['dʒəːkili], *adv.* par saccades.
jerkin ['dʒəːkin], *n.* pourpoint; paletot (*de cuir*), *m.*
jerky ['dʒəːki], *a.* saccadé, irrégulier.
jersey ['dʒəːzi], *n.* vareuse de laine, *f.*, maillot, tricot, *m.*
jest [dʒest], *n.* plaisanterie, facétie, *f.*, bon mot, *m.*; risée (*objet de rire*), *f.*—*v.i.* plaisanter (*de ou avec*), badiner (*sur*).
jester ['dʒestə], *n.* plaisant, railleur; bouffon, fou, *m.*
jesting ['dʒestin], *a.* pour rire, badin.—*n.* raillerie, plaisanterie, *f.*, badinage, *m.*
jestingly ['dʒestinli], *adv.* en plaisantant, pour rire.
Jesuit ['dʒezjuit], *n.* Jésuite, *m.*

Jesus ['dʒiːzəs]. Jésus, *m*.

jet [dʒet], *n*. jet, jet d'eau; (*Min*.) jais, *m*.; *jet engine*, turbo-réacteur, *m*.; *jet plane*, avion à réaction, *m*.—*v.i*. s'élancer; gicler.

jet-black ['dʒet'blæk], *a*. noir comme du jais.

jetsam ['dʒetsəm], *n*. marchandise jetée à la mer, *f*., épaves, *f.pl*.

jettison ['dʒetisən], *n*. jet à la mer, *m*.—*v.t*. jeter par-dessus bord.

jetty ['dʒeti], *n*. jetée, *f*.

Jew [dʒuː], *n*. Juif, *m*.

jewel ['dʒuːəl], *n*. joyau, bijou, *m*.; pierre précieuse, *f*.; (*pl*.) pierreries, *f.pl*.; rubis (*de montre*), *m.pl*.—*v.t*. orner de bijoux.

jeweler ['dʒuːələ], *n*. joaillier, bijoutier, *m*.

jewelry ['dʒuːəlri], *n*. joaillerie, bijouterie, *f*.

Jewess ['dʒuːis], *n*. Juive, *f*.

Jewish ['dʒuːiʃ], *a*. juif, des Juifs.

Jewry ['dʒuːri], *n*. Juiverie, *f*.

jib [dʒib], *n*. (*Naut*.) foc, *m*.—*v.i*. reculer; regimber.

jiffy ['dʒifi], *n*. *in a jiffy*, en un clin d'œil.

jig [dʒig], *n*. gigue (*danse*), *f*., gabarit, *m*.—*v.t*. danser la gigue.

jilt [dʒilt], *n*. coquette, *f*.—*v.t*. planter là; abandonner, (*fam*.) plaquer (*un amoureux*).

jingle ['dʒiŋgl], *n*. tintement (*de cloches*); cliquetis (*de verres, métaux etc*.), *m*.—*v.t*. faire tinter, faire cliqueter.—*v.i*. tinter (*grelots etc*.); s'entrechoquer (*verres etc*.).

jingo ['dʒiŋgou], *n*. chauvin, *m*.; *by jingo!* par exemple!

jingoism ['dʒiŋgouizm], *n*. chauvinisme, *m*.

jinx [dʒiŋks], *n*. porte-guigne, *m*.

Joan [dʒoun]. Jeanne, *f*.; *Joan of Arc*, Jeanne d'Arc.

job [dʒɔb], *n*. travail, ouvrage, *m*.; tâche, pièce, besogne, affaire, *f*.; emploi, *m*.; *job lot*, solde, *m*., occasion, *f*.; *that's just the job*, cela fait juste l'affaire.—*v.t*. louer; tripoter.—*v.i*. travailler à la tâche; (*Comm*.) agioter, spéculer.

jobber ['dʒɔbə], *n*. ouvrier à la tâche; (*Comm*.) agioteur, coulissier; exploiteur, *m*.

jobbing ['dʒɔbiŋ], *a*. *jobbing gardener*, jardinier à la journée, *m*.—*n*. ouvrage à la tâche; (*Comm*.) agiotage; tripotage, *m*.

jockey ['dʒɔki], *n*. jockey, *m*.

jocose [dʒo'kous], *a*. plaisant, jovial.

jocular ['dʒɔkjulə], *a*. plaisant, facétieux.

jocularly ['dʒɔkjuləli], *adv*. facétieusement.

jocund ['dʒɔkənd], *a*. joyeux, enjoué, gai.

jog [dʒɔg], *v.t*. pousser d'un coup de coude; secouer, cahoter; (*fig*.) rafraîchir (*la mémoire*).—*v.i*. se mouvoir; marcher lentement; *to jog along*, aller doucement.—*n*. secousse légère, *f*., cahot; coup de coude, *m*.; *jog trot*, petit trot, *m*.

John [dʒɔn]. Jean, *m*.; *Johnnie*, (*colloq*.) Jeannot, *m*.

join [dʒɔin], *v.t*. joindre, unir; associer (*à*); rejoindre (*rattraper*); relier (*rues etc*.); *will you join us?* voulez-vous être des nôtres ?—*v.i*. se joindre, s'unir; s'inscrire; s'associer; prendre part (*à*).

joiner ['dʒɔinə], *n*. menuisier, *m*.

joinery ['dʒɔinəri], *n*. menuiserie, *f*.

joint [dʒɔint], *a*. commun, ensemble, réuni.—*n*. jointure, *f*., joint, *m*.; pièce, *f*.; rôti (*de viande*), *m*.; phalange (*du doigt*), *f*.; charnière (*de porte*); soudure; (*Anat*.) articulation, *f*.; (*Bot*.) nœud, *m*.; (*slang*) boîte, *f*.; *out of*

joint, disloqué, (*fig*.) dérangé; *to put one's arm out of joint*, se démettre le bras.—*v.t*. couper aux jointures; joindre.

jointed ['dʒɔintid], *a*. articulé, jointé; séparé.

jointly ['dʒɔintli], *adv*. conjointement.

joint stock ['dʒɔintstɔk], *n*. capital, fonds commun, *m*.; *joint-stock bank*, banque par actions, *f*.; *joint-stock company*, société anonyme, *f*.

joist [dʒɔist], *n*. solive, poutre, poutrelle, *f*.

joke [dʒouk], *n*. bon mot, mot pour rire, *m*., plaisanterie, (*fam*.) blague, *f*.; *a practical joke*, une farce, un mauvais tour; *to crack a joke*, dire un bon mot.—*v.i*. plaisanter sur, railler de.—*v.i*. plaisanter, badiner; rire de.

joker ['dʒoukə], *n*. plaisant, farceur; (*Cards*) joker, *m*.

joking ['dʒoukiŋ], *n*. plaisanterie, farce, *f*.

jokingly ['dʒoukiŋli], *adv*. en plaisantant, pour rire.

jollification [dʒɔlifi'keiʃən], *n*. partie de plaisir, *f*.

jollity ['dʒɔliti], *n*. joie, gaieté, *f*.

jolly ['dʒɔli], *a*. gai, joyeux, gaillard, réjoui.

jolt [dʒoult], *n*. cahot, choc, *m*.—*v.t*. cahoter.—*v.i*. faire des cahots.

Jonah ['dʒounə]. Jonas, *m*.—*n*. porte-malheur, *m*.

jonquil ['dʒɔŋkwil], *n*. (*Bot*.) jonquille, *f*.

Jordan ['dʒɔːdən]. le Jourdain (*rivière*), *m*.; la Jordanie (*pays*), *f*.

Jordanian [dʒɔː'deiniən], *a*. jordanien.—*n*. Jordanien (*personne*), *m*.

jostle [dʒɔsl], *v.t*. pousser, bousculer; (*Spt*.) gêner (*un concurrent*).—*v.i*. jouer des coudes.

jot [dʒɔt], *n*. iota, brin, *m*.—*v.t*. *to jot down*, noter, prendre note de.

journal ['dʒəːnəl], *n*. journal, *m*.; revue, *f*.

journalism ['dʒəːnəlizm], *n*. journalisme, *m*.

journalist ['dʒəːnəlist], *n*. journaliste, *m*., *f*.

journey ['dʒəːni], *n*. voyage; trajet (*distance*), *m*.; *a pleasant journey to you!* bon voyage! *on the journey*, en route; *to go on a journey*, faire un voyage.—*v.i*. voyager.

journeyman ['dʒəːnimən], *n*. (*pl*. *-men* [men]) garçon, ouvrier, *m*.

joust [dʒaust, dʒuːst], *n*. joute, *f*.—*v.t*. jouter.

Jove [dʒouv]. Jupiter, *m*.; *by Jove!* bigre! mâtin!

jovial ['dʒouviəl], *a*. joyeux, gai.

joviality [dʒouvi'æliti], *n*. humeur joviale, jovialité, *f*.

jowl [dʒaul], *n*. joue; hure (*de saumon*), *f*.; *cheek by jowl*, côte à côte.

joy [dʒɔi], *n*. joie, *f*.; *to wish someone joy*, féliciter quelqu'un.—*v.i*. se réjouir (*de ou avec*).

joyful ['dʒɔiful], *a*. joyeux.

joyfully ['dʒɔifuli], *adv*. joyeusement.

joyfulness ['dʒɔifulnis], *n*. allégresse, joie, *f*.

joyous ['dʒɔiəs], *a*. joyeux.

jubilant ['dʒuːbilənt], *a*. réjoui; jubilant.

jubilation [dʒuːbi'leiʃən], *n*. réjouissances de triomphe, *f.pl*., jubilation, *f*.

jubilee ['dʒuːbiliː], *n*. jubilé, *m*.

Judaea [dʒuː'diə]. la Judée, *f*.

Judaism ['dʒuːdeiizm], *n*. judaïsme, *m*.

judge [dʒʌdʒ], *n.* juge; (*fig.*) connaisseur, *m.*; *to be a judge of*, se connaître à *ou* en.—*v.t.* juger; discerner, considérer.

judgment [ˈdʒʌdʒmənt], *n.* jugement; arrêt, *m.*, sentence, *f.*; (*fig.*) avis, sens, *m.*, opinion, *f.*

judicature [ˈdʒuːdikətʃə], *n.* judicature, justice; cour de justice, *f.*

judicial [dʒuːˈdiʃl], *a.* judiciaire, juridique.

judicious [dʒuːˈdiʃəs], *a.* judicieux, prudent.

judiciously [dʒuːˈdiʃəsli], *adv.* judicieusement.

judo [ˈdʒuːdou], *n.* jiu-jitsu, (*fam.*) judo, *m.*

jug [dʒʌg], *n.* broc, *m.*; cruche, *f.*; *water jug*, pot à eau, *m.*—*v.t.* faire un civet de (*lièvre*); *jugged hare*, civet de lièvre, *m.*

juggle [dʒʌgl], *v.t.* jouer, duper, escamoter.—*v.i.* faire des tours de passe-passe; (*fig.*) escamoter.—*n.* jonglerie, *f.*; escamotage, tour de passe-passe, *m.*

juggler [ˈdʒʌglə], *n.* jongleur; escamoteur; (*fig.*) charlatan, *m.*

juggling [ˈdʒʌgliŋ], *n.* jonglerie, *f.*, escamotage, *m.*

jugular [ˈdʒʌgjulə], *a.* and *n.* jugulaire, *f.*

juice [dʒuːs], *n.* jus; suc, *m.*

juicy [ˈdʒuːsi], *a.* juteux; succulent.

ju-jitsu [dʒuːˈdʒitsu], *n.* jiu-jitsu, *m.*

jukebox [ˈdʒuːkbɔks], *n.* phonographe à sous, jukebox, *m.*

Julian [ˈdʒuːliən], Julien, *m.*

Juliet [ˈdʒuːliət], Juliette, *f.*

July [dʒuːˈlai], juillet, *m.*

jumble [dʒʌmbl], *v.t.* jeter pêle-mêle, mêler ensemble, confondre.—*n.* pêle-mêle, méli-mélo, *m.*, confusion, *f.*; *jumble sale*, vente de charité, *f.*

jump [dʒʌmp], *n.* saut; bond; sursaut, *m.*; *high jump*, saut en hauteur, *broad jump*, saut en longueur.—*v.t.* sauter, franchir d'un bond; sauter de; faire sauter; (*fam.*) *to jump the queue*, resquiller (dans une queue).—*v.i.* sauter; se jeter, se précipiter (*sur*); *to jump at*, accepter avec empressement.

jumper (1) [ˈdʒʌmpə], *n.* sauteur, *m.*

jumper (2) [ˈdʒʌmpə], *n.* chandail, jersey, jumper, *m.*

jumpy [ˈdʒʌmpi], *a.* nerveux.

junction [ˈdʒʌŋkʃən], *n.* jonction, *f.*; (*Rail.*) embranchement, *m.*

juncture [ˈdʒʌŋktʃə], *n.* jointure, *f.*; moment critique, *m.*

June [dʒuːn], juin, *m.*

jungle [dʒʌŋgl], *n.* jungle, *f.*; fourré, *m.*

junior [ˈdʒuːniə], *a.* jeune, cadet.—*n.* cadet, inférieur en âge, *m.*

juniper [ˈdʒuːnipə], *n.* genièvre, *m.*

junk (1) [dʒʌŋk], *n.* jonque (*navire*), *f.*

junk (2) [dʒʌŋk], *n.* objets de rebut, *m.pl.*

junket [ˈdʒʌŋkit], *n.* lait caillé, *m.*; jonchée (*fromage*), talmouse (*gâteau*), *f.*—*v.t.* régaler.—*v.i.* se régaler.

jurisdiction [dʒuərisˈdikʃən], *n.* juridiction, *f.*

jurisprudence [dʒuərisˈpruːdəns], *n.* jurisprudence, *f.*

jurist [ˈdʒuərist], *n.* juriste, *m.*, *f.*

juror [ˈdʒuərə], *n.* juré, *m.*

jury [ˈdʒuəri], *n.* jury, *m.*

juryman [ˈdʒuərimən], *n.* (*pl.* **-men** [men]) juré, *m.*

just [dʒʌst], *a.* juste, équitable.—*adv.* juste, justement, précisément; tout, tout juste, seulement, un peu; *he has just gone out*, il vient de sortir; *just now*, à l'instant, tout à l'heure; *just so*, précisément.

justice [ˈdʒʌstis], *n.* justice, *f.*; juge (*magistrat*), *m.*; *Justice of the Peace*, juge de paix; *to do justice to*, (*fig.*) faire honneur à (*un repas etc.*).

justifiable [dʒʌstiˈfaiəbl], *a.* justifiable, légitime.

justification [dʒʌstifiˈkeiʃən], *n.* justification, *f.*

justify [ˈdʒʌstifai], *v.t.* justifier, autoriser, permettre; *to feel justified in*, se croire autorisé à, croire devoir.

justly [ˈdʒʌstli], *adv.* exactement, justement; à bon droit.

jut [dʒʌt], *v.i.* avancer, faire saillie.

jute [dʒuːt], *n.* jute, *m.*

jutting [ˈdʒʌtiŋ], *a.* en saillie, saillant.

juvenile [ˈdʒuːvənail], *a.* jeune; juvénile, de jeunesse; *juvenile delinquent*, jeune délinquant, *m.*—*n.* jeune, *m.*, *f.*; adolescent, *m.*

juxtaposition [dʒʌkstəpəˈziʃən], *n.* juxtaposition, *f.*; *in juxtaposition*, juxtaposé.

K

K, k [kei]. onzième lettre de l'alphabet, *m.*

kale, kail [keil], *n.* (Sc.) chou, *m.*; *sea kale*, chou marin.

kaleidoscope [kəˈlaidəskoup], *n.* kaléidoscope, *m.*

kangaroo [kæŋgəˈruː], *n.* kangourou, *m.*

Katharine, Katherine [ˈkæθərin]. Catherine, *f.*

keel [kiːl], *n.* quille; carène, *f.*

keen [kiːn], *a.* affilé, aigu, aiguisé; (*fig.*) vif, ardent; amer, mordant (*acerbe*); pénétrant, perçant (*brisant la surface de*); dévorant (*appétit*).

keenly [ˈkiːnli], *adv.* vivement, ardemment, âprement.

keenness [ˈkiːnnis], *n.* finesse (*de tranchant*); (*fig.*) subtilité; vivacité, ardeur, *f.*, empressement; mordant (*de troupes*), *m.*, âpreté (*du froid*), *f.*

keep [kiːp], *v.t.* irr. tenir, retenir, garder; maintenir, conserver (*ne pas perdre*); avoir (*volaille etc.*); entretenir (*subvenir aux besoins de*); nourrir (*avoir en pension*); avoir à son service; (*fig.*) observer, célébrer, fêter; garantir, protéger; remplir; continuer; *keep it up!* continuez! *to keep away*, éloigner, tenir éloigné; *to keep back*, retenir, garder, tenir en réserve; retarder; *to keep from*, préserver de, empêcher de; *to keep in*, tenir enfermé, retenir; *to keep on*, continuer; *to keep out*, ne pas admettre, écarter, éloigner; *to keep to*, s'en tenir à; *to keep up*, tenir levé, soutenir; continuer; entretenir.—*v.i.* se tenir; rester, demeurer (*ne pas cesser d'être*); se garder, se conserver (*durer*); (*fig.*) se garder, s'abstenir; *to keep away*, se tenir éloigné; *to keep back*, se tenir en arrière; *to keep* (*doing, saying, telling* etc.), ne pas cesser de; *to keep silent*, se taire; *to keep up with*, aller de pair avec.—*n.* donjon, réduit (*forteresse*), *m.*; nourriture, *f.*; entretien (*subsistance*), *m.*

keeper ['ki:pə], *n.* garde; gardien; surveillant, *m.*

keeping ['ki:piŋ], *n.* garde, surveillance; conservation; (*fig.*) harmonie, *f.*

keepsake ['ki:pseik], *n.* souvenir, *m.*

keg [keg], *n.* caque (*de hareng*), *f.*, petit baril, *m.*

ken [ken], *n.* vue; portée, *f.*

kennel [kenl], *n.* chenil, *m.*; niche, *f.*

Kenya ['kenjə], le Kénya, *m.*

kept [kept], *a.* entretenu.—*p.p.* [KEEP].

kerb [kə:b], *n.* bordure (*de trottoir*), margelle (*de puits*), *f.* (*Am.* **curb**.)

kerb-stone ['kə:bstoun], *n.* bordure (*de trottoir*), *f.*, parement, *m.*

***kerchief** ['kə:tʃif], *n.* fichu, *m.*

kernel [kə:nl], *n.* graine, amande, *f.*, pignon (*de pomme de pin*); noyau (*de drupe*); (*fig.*) fond, essentiel, *m.*

kerosene ['kerosi:n], *n.* kérosène; pétrole lampant, *m.*

kestrel ['kestrəl], *n.* crécerelle, *f.*

ketch [ketʃ], *n.* (*Naut.*) quaiche, *f.*, ketch, *m.*

kettle [ketl], *n.* bouilloire, *f.*; chaudron (*bassine à confitures*), *m.*; *a pretty kettle of fish*, un beau gâchis.

kettledrum ['ketldrəm], *n.* timbale, *f.*

key [ki:], *n.* clef, clé, *f.*; (*Arith.* etc.) corrigé; (*Mus.*) ton, *m.*; touche (*sur le piano* etc.), *f.*; *under lock and key*, sous clef.

key-board ['ki:bɔ:d], *n.* clavier, *m.*

keyhole ['ki:houl], *n.* trou de la serrure, *m.*

key-note ['ki:nout], *n.* tonique; (*fig.*) idée maîtresse, *f.*

key-stone ['ki:stoun], *n.* clef de voûte, *f.*

khaki ['ka:ki], *n.* kaki, *m.*

khan [ka:n], *n.* kan, khan, *m.*

kick [kik], *n.* coup de pied; recul (*d'un fusil*), *m.*; ruade (*d'animal*), *f.*; (*Ftb.*) *free kick*, coup franc, *m.*—*v.t.* donner un coup de pied à; frapper *ou* pousser du pied (*Ftb.*) botter; *to kick out*, chasser à coups de pied; *to kick up a row*, faire du tapage.—*v.i.* donner des coups de pied; ruer, regimber (*animal*); reculer (*fusil*).

kick-off ['kikɔf], *n.* (*Ftb.*) coup d'envoi, *m.*

kid [kid], *a.* de chevreau; *kid gloves*, gants de chevreau, *m.pl.*—*n.* chevreau; (*colloq.*) enfant, gosse, *m.*—*v.t.* (*fam.*) en conter à; *no kidding !* sans blague!

kidnap ['kidnæp], *v.t.* enlever.

kidney ['kidni], *n.* rein; rognon (*d'animal*), *m.*

kidney bean ['kidni'bi:n], *n.* haricot, *m.*

kill [kil], *v.t.* tuer; faire mourir; abattre (*assassiner*).

killer ['kilə], *n.* tueur, *m.*

killing ['kiliŋ], *a.* mortel; assommant (*travail*). —*n.* tuerie, boucherie, *f.*, massacre, *m.*

kiln [kiln], *n.* four, *m.*

kilogram ['kiləgræm], *n.* kilogramme, *m.*

kilometer ['kiləmi:tə], *n.* kilomètre, *m.*

kilowatt ['kilowot], *n.* kilowatt, *m.*

kin [kin], *n.* parenté, *f.*; parent, allié, *m.*; *next of kin*, le plus proche parent.

kind [kaind], *a.* bon, bienveillant, bienfaisant; obligeant, complaisant (*accommodant*); *my kind regards to him*, faites-lui toutes mes amitiés; *will you be so kind as to*, voulez-vous avoir la bonté de.—*n.* genre, *m.*, sorte, espèce, *f.*; *in kind*, en nature.

kindergarten ['kindəga:tn], *n.* école maternelle, *f.*

kindhearted ['kaind'ha:tid], *a.* bon, bienveillant.

kindle [kindl], *v.t.* allumer, enflammer; (*fig.*) éveiller, exciter.—*v.i.* s'allumer, s'enflammer.

kindliness ['kaindlinis], *n.* bienveillance, bonté, *f.*

kindly ['kaindli], *a.* bon, bienveillant, favorable.—*adv.* avec bienveillance.

kindness ['kaindnis], *n.* bienveillance, bonté, *f.*; bienfait, *m.*

kindred ['kindrid], *a.* de même nature.—*n.* parenté, *f.*; parents, *m.pl.*

kinema ['kinimə], [CINEMA].

king [kiŋ], *n.* roi, *m.*; (*checkers*) dame, *f.*

kingdom ['kiŋdəm], *n.* royaume, *f.*; (*fig.*) empire; (*Nat. Hist.*) règne, *m.*; *the United Kingdom*, le Royaume-Uni.

kingfisher ['kiŋfiʃə], *n.* (*Orn.*) martin-pêcheur, *m.*

kingly ['kiŋli], *a.* de roi, royal.

kink [kiŋk], *n.* nœud; (*colloq.*) point faible, défaut, *m.*

kinsman ['kinzmən], *n.* (*pl.* **-men** [men]) parent, allié, *m.*

kiosk ['ki:ɔsk], *n.* kiosque, *m.*; *telephone kiosk*, cabine téléphonique, *f.*

kirk [kə:k], *n.* église d'Écosse, *f.*

kiss [kis], *n.* baiser, *m.*—*v.t.*, *v.i.* embrasser; *to kiss* (*each other*), s'embrasser.

kit [kit], *n.* petit équipement, *m.*, effets, *m.pl.*; trousse, *f.*; outils (*d'un ouvrier*), *m.pl.*

kit bag ['kitbæg], *n.* sac, *m.*

kitchen ['kitʃin], *n.* cuisine, *f.*

kitchen garden ['kitʃinga:dn], *n.* jardin potager, *m.*

kitchen utensils ['kitʃinju:tenslz], *n.pl.* batterie de cuisine, *f.*

kite [kait], *n.* milan (*oiseau*); cerf-volant (*jouet*), *m.*

kith [kiθ], *n.* *kith and kin*, parents et amis, *m.pl.*

kitten [kitn], *n.* chaton, petit chat, *m.*

knack [næk], *n.* adresse, *f.*, tour de main, *m.*

knapsack ['næpsæk], *n.* havresac, *m.*

knave [neiv], *n.* fripon, coquin; (*Cards*) valet, *m.*

knavery ['neivəri], *n.* friponnerie, coquinerie, *f.*

knavish ['neiviʃ], *a.* fripon; malin.

knead [ni:d], *v.t.* pétrir.

knee [ni:], *n.* genou, *m.*

knee breeches ['ni:britʃiz], *n.pl.* culotte courte, *f.*

knee-cap ['ni:kæp], *n.* genouillère; (*Anat.*) rotule, *f.*

kneel [ni:l], *v.i.* irr. s'agenouiller.

knell [nel], *n.* glas, *m.*

knickers ['nikəz], *n.* culotte (*de femme*), *f.*

knick-knack ['niknæk], *n.* brimborion, *m.*, babiole, *f.*; colifichet, bibelot, *m.*

knife [naif], *n.* (*pl.* **knives** [naivz]) couteau, *m.*; (*Tech.*) coupoir; (*Surg.*) scalpel, bistouri, *m.*; *carving knife*, couteau à découper; *pen-knife*, canif, *m.*—*v.t.* poignarder.

knife-grinder ['naifgraində], *n.* rémouleur, *m.*

knight [nait], *n.* chevalier; (*Chess*) cavalier, *m.*—*v.t.* créer chevalier.

knighthood ['naithud], *n.* chevalerie, *f.*

knightly ['naitli], *a.* chevaleresque, de chevalier.

knit [nit], *v.t.* tricoter; froncer (*les sourcils*); (*fig.*) joindre, attacher, lier.

knitting ['nitiŋ], *n.* tricot, *m.*

knitting needle ['nitiŋni:dl], *n.* aiguille à tricoter, *f.*

knives [KNIFE].

knob [nɔb], *n.* bosse, *f.*; bouton (*de porte*), *m.*

knock [nɔk], *v.t.* frapper, heurter, cogner; *to knock about*, bousculer, malmener; *to knock down*, renverser, assommer; adjuger (*aux enchères*).—*v.i. to knock about*, rouler sa bosse, aller de par le monde; *to knock off*, cesser le travail.—*n.* coup, choc; cognement, *m.*

knocker ['nɔkə], *n.* marteau (*de porte*), *m.*

knocking ['nɔkiŋ], *n.* coups, *m.pl.*

knoll [noul], *n.* monticule, tertre, *m.*, butte, *f.*

knot [nɔt], *n.* nœud; groupe (*de personnes etc.*), *m.*; (*fig.*) difficulté, *f.*, embarras, *m.*—*v.t.* nouer; lier; (*fig.*) embrouiller.—*v.i.* faire des nœuds; se nouer.

knotted ['nɔtid], *a.* noueux.

knotty ['nɔti], *a.* noueux; (*fig.*) dur (*difficile*); embrouillé, compliqué.

know [nou], *v.t. irr.* savoir, apprendre (*to learn*); connaître (*to be acquainted with*); reconnaître (*to recognize*); *to know by heart*, savoir par cœur; *to know by sight*, connaître de vue; *to know someone*, connaître quelqu'un; *to know something*, savoir quelque chose.—*n. to be in the know*, être dans le secret.

know-how ['nouhau], *n.* savoir-faire, *m.*

knowing ['nouiŋ], *a.* intelligent, instruit; fin, malin.

knowingly ['nouiŋli], *adv.* sciemment; avec ruse.

knowledge ['nɔlidʒ], *n.* connaissance, science, *f.*; savoir, *m.*; *not to my knowledge*, pas que je sache; *without my knowledge*, à mon insu.

knowledgeable ['nɔlidʒəbl], *a.* bien informé.

knuckle [nʌkl], *n.* jointure, articulation du doigt, *f.*; jarret (*de viande*), *m.*—*v.i. to knuckle under*, se soumettre, mettre les pouces.

knuckle-bone ['nʌklboun], *n.* osselet, *m.*

Korea [kə'ri:ə], la Corée, *f.*

Korean [kə'ri:ən], *a.* coréen.—*n.* coréen (*langue*); Coréen (*personne*), *m.*

Kuwait [ku'weit]. le Koweit, *m.*

L

L, l [el]. douzième lettre de l'alphabet, *m.*

la [lɑ:], *n.* (*Mus.*) la, *m.*

lab [læb], *n.* (*fam.*) labo, *m.*

label [leibl], *n.* étiquette, *f.*; (*Ind.*) label, *m.*—*v.t.* étiqueter; (*fig.*) désigner sous le nom de.

labor ['leibə], *n.* travail, labeur, *m.*, peine, *f.*; ouvrage (*piece of work*); travail d'enfant (*accouchement*), *m.*; *hard labor*, travaux forcés, *m.pl.*; *manual labor*, main-d'œuvre, *f.*; *the Labor Party*, le parti travailliste.—*v.t.* travailler; (*fig.*) élaborer.—*v.i.* travailler; souffrir, peiner; chercher (à), s'efforcer (*de*); *to labor under a delusion*, être dans l'erreur.

laboratory [lə'bɔrətəri, 'læbrətəri], *n.* laboratoire, *m.*

laborer ['leibərə], *n.* manœuvre, homme de peine, *m.*

labor-exchange ['leibəriks'tʃeindʒ], *n.* bureau de placement (*municipal ou d'état*), *m.*

laborious [lə'bɔ:riəs], *a.* laborieux, pénible.

laboriously [lə'bɔ:riəsli], *adv.* laborieusement, péniblement.

labor-saving ['leibəseiviŋ], *a. labor-saving device*, économiseur de travail, *m.*

Labrador ['læbrədɔ:]. le Labrador, *m.*

labrador ['læbrədɔ:], *n.* chien de Labrador, *m.*

laburnum [lə'bə:nəm], *n.* faux ébénier, cytise, *m.*

labyrinth ['læbirinθ], *n.* labyrinthe, *m.*

lace [leis], *n.* dentelle, *f.*, point, galon; lacet (*cordon*); ruban (*bande*), *m.*; *shoelace*, lacet de bottine.—*v.t.* lacer (*ses souliers*); garnir de dentelle, galonner (*orner de dentelle*); (*fig.*) orner.

lacerate ['læsəreit], *v.t.* déchirer, lacérer.

laceration [læsə'reiʃən], *n.* déchirure, lacération, *f.*

lachrymose ['lækrimous], *a.* larmoyant.

lacing ['leisiŋ], *n.* lacement, *m.*

lack [læk], *n.* manque, besoin, défaut, *m.*; *for lack of*, faute de.—*v.t.* manquer de.—*v.i.* manquer.

lackey ['læki], *n.* laquais, *m.*

lacking ['lækiŋ], *a.* manquant (*de*), dépourvu (*de*).

laconic [lə'kɔnik], *a.* laconique.

lacquer ['lækə], *n.* laque, *m.*

lad [læd], *n.* garçon, jeune homme; gaillard, *m.*

ladder ['lædə], *n.* échelle, *f.*; démaillage (*d'un bas*) *m.*; *ladder-proof*, indémaillable (*bas*).—*v.t.* démailler (*un bas*).

lade [kid], *v.t.* (*Naut.*) charger.

laden [leidn], *a.* chargé.

lading ['leidiŋ], *n.* chargement, *m.*; *bill of lading*, connaissement, *m.*

ladle [leidl], *n.* louche, cuiller à pot, *f.*

lady ['leidi], *n.* (*pl.* **ladies** ['leidiz]) dame, *f.*; *young lady*, demoiselle, *f.*

lady-bird ['leidibə:d], *n.* coccinelle, bête à bon Dieu, *f.*

lady-killer ['leidikilə], *n.* bourreau des cœurs, *m.*

lady-like ['leidilaik], *a.* de dame, comme il faut, qui a l'air distingué.

lag [læg], *v.i.* se traîner; traîner (*choses*).—*n.* retard, *m.*

laggard ['lægəd], *n.* traînard, lambin, *m.*

lager ['lɑ:gə], *n.* bière blonde (*allemande*), *f.*

lagoon [lə'gu:n], *n.* lagune, *f.*

lair [lɛə], *n.* repaire, antre, *m.*

laird [lɛəd], *n.* (*Sc.*) propriétaire, châtelain, *m.*

laity ['leiiti], *n.* laïques, *m.pl.*

lake [leik], *n.* lac, *m.*; laque (*couleur*), *f.*
lamb [læm], *n.* agneau, *m.*—*v.i.* agneler.
lambkin ['læmkin], *n.* agnelet, petit agneau, *m.*
lame [leim], *a.* boiteux, estropié (*infirme*); (*fig.*) défectueux, imparfait; *a lame excuse*, une piètre excuse; *a lame man*, un boiteux.—*v.t.* estropier.
lamely ['leimli], *adv.* en boitant; (*fig.*) imparfaitement, mal.
lameness ['leimnis], *n.* claudication, *f.*; clochement, boitement, *m.*; (*fig.*) faiblesse (*d'une excuse*), *f.*
lament [lə'ment], *v.t.* se lamenter sur, pleurer; s'affliger de.—*v.i.* se lamenter, pleurer.—*n.* lamentation, complainte, plainte, *f.*
lamentable ['læməntəbl], *a.* lamentable, pitoyable.
lamentation [læmən'teiʃən], *n.* lamentation, plainte, jérémiade, *f.*
lamented [lə'mentid], *a.* regretté (*feu*).
lamp [læmp], *n.* lampe; lanterne (*carrosse etc.*); (*fig.*) lumière, *f.*; *street lamp*, réverbère, *m.*
lampoon [læm'pu:n], *n.* satire, *f.*, libelle, *m.*
lamp-post ['læmppoust], *n.* lampadaire, *m.*
lamp shade ['læmpʃeid], *n.* abat-jour, *m.*
lance [lɑ:ns], *n.* lance, *f.*—*v.t.* percer d'un coup de lance; (*Surg.*) donner un coup de lancette à, percer.
lance corporal ['lɑ:ns'kɔ:pərəl], *n.* soldat de première classe, *m.*
lancer ['lɑ:nsə], *n.* lancier, *m.*
lancet ['lɑ:nsit], *n.* lancette; (*Arch.*) ogive, *f.*
land [lænd], *n.* terre, *f.*; pays (*territoire*), *m.*; (*Law*) bien-fonds, *m.*; *Holy Land*, la Terre Sainte.—*v.t.* mettre à terre, prendre (*poisson*); débarquer.—*v.i.* débarquer (*à ou sur*), aborder; (*fig.*) arriver; (*Av.*) atterrir.
landed ['lændid], *a.* foncier; territorial.
landing ['lændiŋ], *n.* palier (*d'escalier*), *m.*; (*Naut.*) débarquement; (*Av.*) atterrissage, *m.*
landing ground ['lændiŋgraund], *n.* terrain d'atterrissage, *m.*
landing stage ['lændiŋsteidʒ], *n.* débarcadère, *m.*
landing strip ['lændiŋstrip], *n.* piste d'atterrissage, *f.*
landlady ['lændleidi], *n.* propriétaire (*d'une maison*), logeuse (*d'un meuble*); aubergiste, hôtesse (*d'une auberge*), *f.*
landlord ['lændlɔ:d], *n.* propriétaire, hôte, hôtelier, aubergiste (*d'une auberge*), *m.*
landlubber ['lændlʌbə], *n.* marin d'eau douce, *m.*
landmark ['lændmɑ:k], *n.* borne, limite, *f.*; point de repère, *m.*
landowner ['lændounə], *n.* propriétaire foncier, *m.*
landscape ['lændskeip], *n.* paysage, *m.*; vue, *f.*
landscape garden ['lændskeip'gɑ:dən], *n.* jardin paysager, *m.*
land tax ['lændtæks], *n.* impôt foncier, *m.*
lane [lein], *n.* ruelle, *f.*, passage, *m.*; voie (*d'autoroute*), *f.*; chemin vicinal (*de campagne*), *m.*
language ['læŋgwidʒ], *n.* langage, *m.*, langue, expression, *f.*; *modern languages*, langues vivantes, *f.pl.*
languid ['læŋgwid], *a.* languissant.

languish ['læŋgwiʃ], *v.i.* languir.
languishing ['læŋgwiʃiŋ], *a.* languissant, langoureux.
languor ['læŋgə], *n.* langueur, *f.*
laniard [LANYARD].
lank [læŋk], *a.* efflanqué; maigre; décharné; fluet, grêle.
lanky ['læŋki], *a.* grand et maigre; *lanky fellow*, grand flandrin, *m.*
lantern ['læntən], *n.* lanterne, *f.*; (*Mil.*) falot; (*Naut.*) fanal, phare, *m.*; *Chinese lantern*, lanterne vénitienne; *dark lantern*, lanterne sourde; *lantern jaws*, joues creuses, *f.pl.*
lanyard ['lænjəd], *n.* (*Naut.*) ride, *f.*; (*Artill.*) (cordon) tire-feu, *m.*
Laos [laus]. le Laos, *m.*
Laotian ['lauʃən], *a.* laotien.—*n.* laotien (*langue*); Laotien (*personne*), *m.*
lap (1) [læp], *n.* pan (*de manteau etc.*); giron, *m.*; (*fig.*) genoux, *m.pl.*; sein; (*Racing*) tour de piste, *m.*; *in the lap of*, au sein de.—*v.i.* se replier.
lap (2) [læp], *v.t.* (*Racing*) prendre un tour (*à*).
lap (3) [læp], *v.t.* laper (*boire*).—*v.i.* laper; clapoter (*vagues*).
lap dog ['læpdɔg], *n.* bichon, petit chien, *m.*
lapel [lə'pel], *n.* revers (*d'habit*), *m.*
lapidary ['læpidəri], *a.* and *n.* lapidaire, *m.*—*v.t.* lapider.
lapidation [læpi'deiʃən], *n.* lapidation, *f.*
Lapland ['læplənd]. la Laponie, *f.*
Laplander ['læpləndə], *n.* Lapon, *m.*
Lapp [læp], *a.* lapon.—*n.* lapon (*langue*); Lapon (*personne*), *m.*
lapse [læps], *n.* cours, laps (*temps*), *m.*; faute, erreur, *f.*; manquement, écart, manque (*divergence*), *m.*—*v.i.* s'écouler; tomber, faillir, manquer (*à*).
lapsed [læpst], *a.* périmé; caduc (*contrat, testament*).
lapwing ['læpwiŋ], *n.* vanneau, *m.*
larceny ['lɑ:səni], *n.* larcin, vol, *m.*
larch [lɑ:tʃ], *n.* (*Bot.*) mélèze, *m.*
lard [lɑ:d], *n.* saindoux, *m.*—*v.t.* larder (*de*).
larder ['lɑ:də], *n.* garde-manger, *m.*
large [lɑ:dʒ], *a.* grand, gros; étendu, considérable; fort; *as large as life*, grandeur nature; *at large*, en liberté, libre; en général.
largely ['lɑ:dʒli], *adv.* amplement, largement; au long, en grande partie.
largeness ['lɑ:dʒnis], *n.* grandeur, étendue, ampleur, *f.*
largess(e) ['lɑ:dʒes], *n.* largesse, libéralité, *f.*
lark [lɑ:k], *n.* alouette; (*fig.*) escapade, *f.*
larkspur ['lɑ:kspə:], *n.* pied-d'alouette, *m.*
larva ['lɑ:və], *n.* (*pl.* **larvae** ['lɑ:vi:]) larve, *f.*
laryngitis [lærin'dʒaitis], *n.* laryngite, *f.*
larynx ['læriŋks], *n.* (*pl.* **larynges** [læ'rindʒiz]) larynx, *m.*
lascar ['læskə], *n.* matelot indien, *m.*
lascivious [lə'siviəs], *a.* lascif.
lash [læʃ], *n.* coup de fouet; (*fig.*) coup, trait, *m.*; *eyelash* [EYE].—*v.t.* cingler, fouetter; châtier; lier, attacher (*to tie*).
lashing ['læʃiŋ], *a.* cinglant, fouettant.—*n.* coups de fouet, *m.pl.*; (*Naut.*) ligne d'amarrage, *f.*
lass [læs], *n.* (*Sc.*) jeune fille, *f.*
lassitude ['læsitju:d], *n.* lassitude, *f.*

last (1) [lɑːst], *a*. dernier, passé; ***last but one***, avant-dernier; ***last night***, hier soir; ***last week***, la semaine dernière; ***the last time***, la dernière fois; ***this day last week***, il y a aujourd'hui huit jours.—*n*. bout, *m*., fin, *f*.; *at last*, à la fin, enfin; *to the last*, jusqu'au bout, jusqu'à la fin.—*v.i*. durer.

last (2) [lɑːst], *n*. forme (*pour chaussures*), *f*.

lasting ['lɑːstiŋ], *a*. durable, permanent.

lastly ['lɑːstli], *adv*. en dernier lieu, enfin.

latch [lætʃ], *n*. loquet, *m*.—*v.t*. fermer au loquet.

latchkey ['lætʃkiː], *n*. passe-partout, *m*., clef de la maison, *f*.

late [leit], *a*. tard; en retard; tardif (*fruits, légumes etc*.); avancé (*heure*); ancien, ex-(*autrefois*); feu (*décédé*); récent, dernier (*depuis peu*); *the late king*, feu le roi; *to be late*, être en retard.—*adv*. tard; sur la fin; récemment, depuis peu; *at latest*, au plus tard; *better late than never*, mieux vaut tard que jamais; *of late*, récemment; *to be getting late*, (*impers*.) se faire tard.

lately ['leitli], *adv*. dernièrement, récemment.

lateness ['leitnis], *n*. retard, *m*.; heure avancée, *f*., temps avancé, *m*.; tardiveté, *f*.

latent ['leitənt], *a*. caché, secret, latent.

later ['leitə], *a*. postérieur, ultérieur.—*adv*. plus tard.

lateral ['lætərəl], *a*. de côté, latéral.

latest ['leitist], *a*. dernier; *at the latest*, au plus tard.

lath [lɑːθ], *n*. latte, *f*.

lathe [leið], *n*. tour, *m*.

lather ['læðə, 'lɑːðə], *n*. mousse; (*fig*.) écume, *f*.—*v.t*. savonner; (*colloq*.) rosser.

Latin ['lætin], *a*. latin.—*n*. latin (*langue*), *m*.

Latin-American ['lætinəmerikən], *a*. latino-américain.—*n*. Latino-Américain (*personne*), *m*.

latish ['leitiʃ], *a*. un peu tard, un peu en retard.—*adv*. un peu tard.

latitude ['lætitjuːd], *n*. latitude; étendue (*breadth*), *f*.

latter ['lætə], *a*. dernier; moderne, récent; *the latter*, ce dernier, celui-ci, *m*.

lattice ['lætis], *n*. trellis, treillage, *m*.

Latvia ['lætviə], la Lettonie, *f*.

Latvian ['lætviən], *a*. lette, letton.—*n*. lette, letton (*langue*), *m*.; Lette, *m*., *f*., Letton, *m*. (*personne*).

laud [lɔːd], *v.t*. louer, célébrer.

laudable ['lɔːdəbl], *a*. louable, digne de louanges.

laugh [lɑːf], *n*. rire, *m*., risée (*moquerie*), *f*.; *loud laugh*, gros rire, éclat de rire, *m*.—*v.i*. rire; *to burst out laughing*, éclater de rire; *to laugh at*, se moquer de.

laughable ['lɑːfəbl], *a*. risible.

laughing ['lɑːfiŋ], *a*. rieur, enjoué; *it is no laughing matter*, il n'y a pas de quoi rire.

laughing-stock ['lɑːfiŋstɔk], *n*. risée, *f*.

laughingly ['lɑːfiŋli], *adv*. en riant.

laughter ['lɑːftə], *n*. rire, *m*., rires, *m.pl*.; risée, moquerie, *f*.; *burst of laughter*, éclat de rire, *m*.

launch [lɔːntʃ], *v.t*. lancer; mettre à la mer.—*v.i*. se lancer, se jeter.—*n*. lancement, *m*.; chaloupe (*bateau*), vedette, *f*.

launching ['lɔːntʃiŋ], *n*. (*Naut*.) mise à l'eau,

470

f., lancement, *m*.; *launching pad*, piste de lancement, *f*.

launder ['lɔːndə], *v.t*. blanchir; lessiver (*linge*).

launderette [lɔːndəˈret], *n*. laverie automatique, *f*.

laundress ['lɔːndris], *n*. blanchisseuse, *f*.

laundromat ['lɔːndromæt], (*Am*.) [LAUN-DERETTE].

laundry ['lɔːndri], *n*. buanderie; blanchisserie, *f*.; linge à blanchir, *m*.

laurel ['lɔrəl], *n*. laurier, *m*.

lava ['lɑːvə], *n*. lave, *f*.

lavatory ['lævət(ə)ri], *n*. water-closet, *m*., les lavabos, les water, *m.pl*.

lavender ['lævəndə], *n*. lavande, *f*.

lavish ['læviʃ], *a*. prodigue.—*v.t*. prodiguer.

lavishly ['læviʃli], *adv*. prodigalement.

lavishness ['læviʃnis], *n*. prodigalité, *f*.

law [lɔː], *n*. loi, *f*.; droit, *m*.; *Law Courts*, Palais de Justice, *m*.

lawful ['lɔːful], *a*. légitime, licite, permis.

lawfully ['lɔːfuli], *adv*. légitimement.

lawless ['lɔːlis], *a*. sans loi; (*fig*.) sans frein, déréglé.

lawlessness ['lɔːlisnis], *n*. désordre, *m*. licence, *f*.

lawn (1) [lɔːn], *n*. pelouse, *f*.

lawn (2) [lɔːn], *n*. linon (*tissu*), *m*.

lawn mower ['lɔːnmouə], *n*. tondeuse de gazon, *f*.

lawsuit ['lɔːsjuːt], *n*. procès, *m*.

lawyer ['lɔːjə], *n*. homme de loi; avocat; (*solicitor*) notaire (*notary*), *m*.

lax [læks], *a*. lâche, mou, flasque; (*fig*.) relâché, négligent.

laxative ['læksətiv], *a*. and *n*. laxatif, *m*.

laxity ['læksiti], **laxness** ['læksnis], *n*. relâchement, *m*.; flaccidité, *f*.; manque d'exactitude, *m*.

lay (1) [lei], *past* [LIE (2)].

lay (2) [lei], *v.t*. *irr*. placer, mettre, poser; coucher, étendre (*de tout son long*); faire; parier (*pari*); pondre (*œuf*); tendre, dresser (*piège*); abattre (*poussière*); calmer, apaiser (*rendre tranquille*); *to lay aside*, mettre de côté; *to lay claim to*, prétendre à; *to lay down*, mettre bas, poser (*principe*); *to lay down one's life for*, donner sa vie pour; *to lay hold of*, s'emparer de; *to lay in*, faire provision de; *to lay on*, appliquer, (*fam*.) arranger; *to lay out*, arranger; ensevelir (*cadavre*); disposer (*jardin etc*.); *to lay siege to*, assiéger; *to lay up*, mettre de côté, faire garder la chambre à; *to lay waste*, dévaster.—*v.i*. pondre (*œufs*).

lay (3) [lei], *n*. lai, *m*., chanson, *f*., chant, *m*.

lay (4) [lei], *a*. lai, laïque.

layer ['leiə], *n*. couche, *f*., lit (*strate*), *m*.; (*Geol*.) assise; (*Hort*.) marcotte, *f*.; provin (*de vigne*), *m*.; pondeuse (*poule*), *f*.

laying ['leiiŋ], *n*. mise, pose; ponte (*d'œufs*), *f*.

layman ['leimən], *n*. (*pl*. **-men** [men]) laïque, profane, séculier, *m*.

lay-out ['leiaut], *n*. dessin, tracé, *m*.; disposition, *f*.

Lazarus ['læzərəs], Lazare, *m*.

laze [leiz], *v.i*. *to laze about*, baguenauder.

lazily ['leizili], *adv*. lentement; en paresseux.

laziness ['leizinis], *n*. paresse, oisiveté, *f*.

lazy ['leizi], *a*. paresseux, indolent; *lazy fellow*, fainéant, *m*.

lea [li:], *n.* (*poet.*) prairie, *f.*

lead (1) [led], *n.* plomb (*métal*), *m.*; (*Naut.*) sonde; (*Print.*) interligne; mine de plomb (*pour des crayons*), *f.*;**black lead**, mine de plomb.

lead (2) [li:d], *v.t. irr.* mener, guider, conduire; porter, faire, induire (*à*); entraîner (*à ou dans*); **to lead astray**, égarer; **to lead back**, ramener, reconduire; **to lead in**, introduire; **to lead out**, emmener; **to lead someone to believe**, faire croire à quelqu'un; **to lead up to**, amener.—*v.i.* conduire, mener; (*Spt.*) jouer le premier. —*n.* conduite, direction, *f.*, commandement, *m.*; laisse (*chien*), *f.*; (*Spt.*) début; (*Theat.*) premier rôle, *m.*, vedette, *f.*; (*Elec.*) conducteur, *m.*

leader [li:də], *n.* conducteur, guide, chef, meneur; (*Journ.*) article de fond, éditorial; (*Polit.*) chef de parti, leader, *m.*

leadership ['li:dəʃip], *n.* conduite, direction, *f.*; qualités de chef, *f.pl.*

leading ['li:diŋ], *a.* premier, principal; **leading article**, article de fond, *m.*—*n.* conduite, direction, *f.*

leaf [li:f], *n.* (*pl.* **leaves** [li:vz]) feuille, *f.*; feuillet (*livre etc.*); battant (*porte*), *m.*; rallonge (*table*), *f.*; **to turn over a new leaf**, (*fig.*) changer de conduite; **to turn over the leaves of**, feuilleter.

leaflet ['li:flit], *n.* feuillet, imprimé, prospectus, *m.*

leafy ['li:fi], *a.* feuillu, couvert de feuilles.

league [li:g], *n.* ligue; lieue (*3 miles*), *f.*

leak [li:k], *n.* fuite, perte d'eau; (*Naut.*) voie d'eau, *f.*; **to spring a leak**, (*Naut.*) faire eau.—*v.i.* fuir, couler, faire eau; prendre l'eau (*chaussures*); **to leak out**, s'éventer.

leakage ['li:kidʒ], *n.* coulage, *m.*; fuite, *f.*

leaky ['li:ki], *a.* qui coule; (*Naut.*) qui fait eau.

lean (1) [li:n], *a.* and *n.* maigre, *m.*

lean (2) [li:n], *v.t. irr.* appuyer, faire pencher, incliner.—*v.i.* s'appuyer, s'incliner, se pencher; **to lean back against**, s'adosser à; **to lean out**, se pencher au dehors.

leaning ['li:niŋ], *a.* penché.—*n.* penchant, *m.*; (*fig.*) tendance, *f.*

leanness ['li:nnis], *n.* maigreur, *f.*

lean-to ['li:ntu:], *n.* appentis, *m.*

leap [li:p], *n.* saut, bond, *m.*—*v.t. irr.* sauter, franchir.—*v.i.* sauter, bondir; s'élancer, se précipiter.

leap-frog ['li:pfrɔg], *n.* saute-mouton, *m.*

leap year ['li:pjiə], *n.* année bissextile, *f.*

learn [lə:n], *v.t. irr.* apprendre.—*v.i.* apprendre, s'instruire.

learned ['lə:nid], *a.* savant, instruit, érudit; **learned man**, savant, *m.*; **learned profession**, profession libérale, *f.*

learner ['lə:nə], *n.* élève, commençant, apprenti, *m.*; **learner driver**, élève chauffeur.

learning ['lə:niŋ], *n.* science, instruction, *f.*, savoir, *m.*, connaissances, *f.pl.*; érudition, *f.*

lease [li:s], *n.* bail, *m.*—*v.t.* louer, donner à bail; prendre à bail.

leasehold ['li:should], *a.* à bail.—*n.* tenure par bail, *f.*

leash [li:ʃ], *n.* laisse, *f.*—*v.t.* mener en laisse, attacher.

least [li:st], *a.* le moindre, le plus petit.—*adv.* le moins; **at least**, au moins, du moins; **not in the least**, point du tout, nullement.

leather ['leðə], *a.* de cuir.—*n.* cuir, *m.*; **upper leather**, empeigne, *f.*—*v.t.* (*colloq.*) étriller, rosser.

leave [li:v], *n.* permission, *f.*, congé; adieu, *m.*; **on leave**, en congé (*un mois ou plus*), en permission (*moins d'un mois*); **with your leave**, avec votre permission.—*v.t. irr.* laisser; quitter, partir de (*s'en aller de*); cesser (*de*); **he left the house**, il quitta la maison, il partit de la maison; **he left the pen on the table**, il laissa le stylo sur la table; **to be left**, rester; **to leave about**, laisser traîner; **to leave alone**, laisser tranquille; **to leave off**, cesser (*de*); **to leave out**, supprimer, omettre, oublier. —*v.i.* partir, quitter; cesser.

leaven [levn], *n.* levain, *m.*—*v.t.* faire lever.

leaves [LEAF].

leave-taking ['li:vteikiŋ], *n.* adieux, *m.pl.*

leavings ['li:viŋz], *n.pl.* restes, *m.pl.*

Lebanese ['lebəni:z], *a.* libanais.—*n.* Libanais (*personne*), *m.*

Lebanon ['lebənən]. le Liban, *m.*

lecherous ['letʃərəs], *a.* lascif, libertin, lubrique.

lecherousness ['letʃərəsnis], **lechery** ['letʃəri], *n.* lasciveté, *f.*

lectern ['lektə:n], *n.* lutrin, *m.*

lecture ['lektʃə], *n.* conférence (*sur*), leçon (*de*), *f.*; (*fig.*) sermon, *m.*, semonce, *f.*—*v.t.* faire un cours à; (*fig.*) sermonner, semoncer. —*v.i.* faire un cours (*de*), faire une conférence (*sur*).

lecturer ['lektʃərə], *n.* conférencier; maître de conférences, *m.*

lecture room ['lektʃəru:m], *n.* salle de conférences, *f.*

ledge [ledʒ], *n.* rebord, bord, *m.*; (*Arch.*) saillie, *f.*

ledger ['ledʒə], *n.* grand livre, *m.*

lee [li:], *a.* sous le vent.—*n.* (*Naut.*) côté sous le vent, *m.*

leech [li:tʃ], *n.* sangsue, *f.*

leek [li:k], *n.* poireau, *m.*

leer [liə], *n.* œillade, *f.*; regard de côté, *m.*—*v.i.* lorgner.

lees [li:z], *n.pl.* lie, *f.*

leeward ['lu:əd], *a.* and *adv.* (*Naut.*) sous le vent.

lee-way ['li:wei], *n.* dérive; (*fig.*) marge, *f.*

left (1) [left], *past* and *p.p.* [LEAVE].

left (2) [left], *a.* and *n.* gauche, *f.*; **on the left**, à gauche.

left-handed ['left'hændid], *a.* gaucher; à gauche (*vis*); (*fig.*) gauche.

left-overs ['leftouvez], *n.pl.* restes (*d'un repas*), *m.pl.*

leg [leg], *n.* jambe; patte (*d'oiseau, d'insecte etc.*); tige (*bottines*); cuisse (*volaille*), *f.*; pied (*meuble*); gigot (*mouton*); trumeau (*bœuf*), *m.*; branche (*compas*), *f.*; **to pull someone's leg**, se moquer de quelqu'un.

legacy ['legəsi], *n.* legs, *m.*

legal ['li:gl], *a.* légal, judiciaire, juridique.

legality [li'gæliti], *n.* légalité, *f.*

legalize ['li:gəlaiz], *v.t.* légaliser, (*fig.*) autoriser.

legally ['li:gəli], *adv.* légalement.

legation [li'geiʃən], *n.* légation, *f.*

legend ['ledʒənd], *n.* légende, *f.*

legendary ['ledʒəndri], *a.* légendaire, fabuleux.

legged [legd, 'legid], *a.* à jambes, à pieds;

four-legged, à quatre pattes; **two-legged**, à deux jambes, bipède.

leggings ['legiŋz], *n.pl.* jambières, guêtres, *f.pl.*

legibility [ledʒi'biliti], *n.* lisibilité, netteté d'écriture, *f.*

legible ['ledʒibl], *a.* lisible.

legion ['liːdʒən], *n.* légion, *f.*; **the Foreign Legion**, la Légion (étrangère).

legislate ['ledʒisleit], *v.t.* légiférer, faire des lois.

legislation [ledʒis'leiʃən], *n.* législation, *f.*

legislative ['ledʒislətiv], *a.* législatif.

legitimate [li'dʒitimit], *a.* légitime; juste, correct.

leisure ['leʒə], *n.* loisir, *m.*; **at leisure**, de loisir; **at one's leisure**, à loisir; **you are at leisure to come or not**, il vous est loisible de venir ou non.

leisurely ['leʒəli], *a.* sans hâte, mesuré.—*adv.* à loisir.

lemon ['lemən], *n.* citron, limon, *m.*

lemonade [lemə'neid], *n.* citron pressé, *m.*

lemon squash ['lemən'skwɔʃ], *n.* citronnade, *f.*

lemon-squeezer ['lemən'skwiːzə], *n.* presse-citrons, *m.inv.*

lem on tree ['leməntriː], *n.* citronnier, *m.*

lend [lend], *v.t. irr.* prêter; (*fig.*) donner.

lender ['lendə], *n.* prêteur, *m.*

lending ['lendiŋ], *n.* prêt, *m.*; **lending library** bibliothèque de prêt, *f.*

length [leŋθ], *n.* longueur, étendue, *f.*; degré, point (*extrémité*), *m.*; durée (*temps*), *f.*; **at full length**, tout au long (*non abrégé*); en toutes lettres (*mots*); de tout son; long (*personnes*); **at great length**, longuement; **at length**, enfin; **full length**, de grandeur nature; **two feet in length**, deux pieds de longueur ou de long.

lengthen ['leŋθən], *v.t.* allonger, étendre; prolonger (*temps*).—*v.i.* s'allonger, s'étendre; se prolonger (*temps*); (*colloq.*) rallonger (*journées etc.*).

lengthening ['leŋθniŋ], *n.* allongement, *m.*; prolongation (*de temps*), *f.*; accroissement (*des journées*), *m.*

lengthways ['leŋθweiz], **lengthwise** ['leŋθwaiz], *adv.* en longueur, en long.

lengthy ['leŋθi], *a.* un peu long, ennuyeux.

leniency ['liːniənsi], *n.* douceur, clémence, indulgence (*pour*), *f.*

lenient ['liːniənt], *a.* doux, indulgent (*à, envers ou pour*).

leniently ['liːniəntli], *adv.* avec douceur, avec indulgence.

lens [lenz], *n.* (*pl.* **lenses**, ['lenziz]) (*Opt.*) lentille, loupe, *f.*

Lent [lent]. le carême, *m.*

lentil ['lentil], *n.* lentille, *f.*

leonine ['liːənain], *a.* de lion, léonin.

leopard ['lepəd], *n.* léopard, *m.*

leper ['lepə], *n.* lépreux, *m.*

leprosy ['leprəsi], *n.* lèpre, *f.*

leprous ['leprəs], *a.* lépreux.

less [les], *a.* moindre, plus petit, inférieur; **to grow less**, diminuer.—*adv.* moins; **less and less**, de moins en moins; **no less**, rien moins, pas moins; **so much the less**, d'autant moins; **the less . . . the more . . .**, moins . . . plus . . . .—*n.* moins; moindre, *m.*

lessee [le'siː], *n.* locataire à bail, *m., f.*

lessen [lesn], *v.t.* diminuer, amoindrir, rapetisser, rabaisser (*to lower*); ralentir (*la vitesse*).—*v.i.* diminuer, s'amoindrir.

lesser ['lesə], *a.* moindre, plus petit.

lesson [lesn], *n.* leçon, *f.*

lest [lest], *conj.* de peur que, de crainte que (*followed by* ne *with subj.*).

let (1) [let], *v.t. irr.* laisser, permettre à (*donner la permission à*); souffrir que (*with subjunctive*); faire (*causer*); louer (*maison*); **let him come**, qu'il vienne; **let me see**, voyons; **let us go**, allons; **to let alone**, laisser tranquille; **to let down**, descendre, faire descendre, baisser, rabattre; **to let fall**, laisser tomber; **to let go**, lâcher; **to let in**, faire entrer; **to let know**, faire savoir à; **to let off**, laisser échapper; tirer (*arme à feu*); **to let out**, faire sortir, laisser sortir; élargir (*vêtements*).

let (2) [let], *n.* empêchement; obstacle, délai, *m.*; (*Tennis*) (balle) à remettre.

lethal ['liːθl], *a.* mortel, fatal.

lethargic [lə'θɑːdʒik], *a.* léthargique.

lethargy ['leθədʒi], *n.* léthargie, *f.*

letter ['letə], *n.* lettre, *f.*; (*pl.*, *fig.*) belles-lettres, *f.pl.*; **registered letter**, lettre recommandée.

letter box ['letəbɔks], *n.* boîte aux lettres, *f.*

letter-card ['letəkɑːd], *n.* carte-lettre, *f.*

lettered ['letəd], *a.* lettré, savant.

letteri g ['letəriŋ], *n.* titre, *m.*

letting ['letiŋ], *n.* louage, *m.*; **letting out**, location, *f.*; agrandissement (*de vêtement*), *m.*

lettuce ['letis], *n.* laitue, *f.*

let-up ['letʌp], *n.* diminution, *f.*

Levant [lə'vænt], **the.** le Levant, *m.*

Levantine [li'væntain], *a.* du Levant, levantin.—*n.* Levantin (*personne*), *m.*; **levantine** (*soie*), *f.*

level ['levl], *a.* de niveau (*avec*), au niveau (*de*); uni (*surface*); égal (*à*); **level crossing**, passage à niveau, *m.*—*n.* niveau, *m.*; surface unie, *f.*; **at ministerial level**, à l'échelon ministériel.—*v.t.* aplanir, niveler, mettre de niveau; braquer, pointer (*arme à feu*); porter (*coup*).—*v.i.* viser, mettre en joue, pointer.

level-headed ['levlhedid], *a.* équilibré, de sens rassis.

levelling ['levliŋ], *n.* nivellement; pointage (*de fusil*), *m.*

lever ['liːvə], *n.* levier, *m.*; **hand lever** manette, *f.*

leveret ['levərit], *n.* levraut, *m.*

levity ['leviti], *n.* légèreté, *f.*; manque de sérieux, *m.*

levy ['levi], *n.* levée; perception (*d'impôts*), *f.*—*v.t.* lever; imposer (*amende etc.*).

lewd [ljuːd], *a.* impudique, lascif.

lexicon ['leksikn], *n.* lexique, dictionnaire, *m.*

liability [laiə'biliti], *n.* responsabilité; tendance, *f.*; danger, *m.*; (*Comm.*) (*pl.*) engagements, *m.pl.*, passif, *m.*; **assets and liabilities**, actif et passif, *m.*

liable ['laiəbl], *a.* sujet (*à*), exposé (*à*), responsable (*de*).

liar ['laiə], *n.* menteur, *m.*

libel [laibl], *n.* libelle, écrit diffamatoire, *m.*—*v.t.* diffamer.

libelous ['laibələs], *a.* diffamatoire.

liberal ['libərəl], *a.* libéral, généreux; prodigue, abondant.—*n.* (*Polit.*) Libéral, *m.*

liberality [libə'ræliti], *n.* libéralité, *f.*

liberate ['libəreit], v.t. libérer, rendre libre; délivrer (de).

liberation [libə'reiʃən], n. mise en liberté, f., élargissement (de prisonniers); affranchissement, m.; libération, délivrance, f.

liberator ['libəreitə], n. libérateur, m.

Liberia [lai'biəriə]. le Libéria, m.

Liberian [lai'biəriən], a. libérien.—n. Libérien (personne), m.

liberty ['libəti], n. liberté, f.; privilèges, m.pl., franchises, f.pl.

librarian [lai'brɛəriən], n. bibliothécaire, m.,f.

library ['laibrəri], n. bibliothèque, f.; **film library**, cinémathèque, f.; **record library**, discothèque, f.

Libya ['libiə]. la Lybie, f.

Libyan ['libiən], a. libyen.—n. Libyen (personne), m.

lice [LOUSE].

license [lai'saisns], n. licence, liberté; permission, f., permis; certificat; (fig.) dérèglement, m.; autorisation (de prédicateur), f.; brevet (de libraire), m.; (Comm.) patente, f.; **driving license**, permis de conduire; **gun license**, permis de port d'armes; permis de chasse; **marriage license**, dispense de bans, f. [see **number-plate**]

license ['laisəns], v.t. autoriser, accorder un permis à.

licensed ['laisənst], a. autorisé; breveté; (Comm.) patenté.

licentious [lai'senʃəs], a. licencieux.

lichen ['laikən], n. lichen, m.

lick [lik], v.t. lécher; laper (boire); (slang) rosser (battre).—n. coup de langue, m.

licking ['likiŋ], n. (slang) coups, m.pl., raclée, f.

licorice [LIQUORICE].

lid [lid], n. couvercle, m.; paupière (d'œil), f.

lie (1) [lai], n. mensonge; démenti, m.; **to give the lie to**, donner un démenti à; **white lie**, mensonge pieux.—v.i. mentir.

lie (2) [lai], v.i. irr. être couché, se coucher; reposer, être, être situé, se trouver; s'appuyer (se soutenir); rester (to remain); consister; **here lies**, ci-gît; **lie down!** (à un chien) couche! **to lie about** (objets), traîner çà et là; **to lie down**, se coucher, se reposer.—n. gisement, m., position, situation, f.

lieutenant [lef'tenənt], n. lieutenant, m.

life [laif], n. (pl. **lives** [laivz]) vie, f.; homme vivant, m.; personne; (fig.) vie, âme, vivacité, f., entrain; mouvement; (Paint. etc.) naturel, m.; **a double life**, une vie double; **for life**, à vie, à perpétuité; **from life**, d'après nature; **high life**, le grand monde, m.; **never in my life**, jamais de ma vie; **pension for life**, pension viagère, f.; **prime of life**, fleur de l'âge, f.; **single life**, célibat, m.; **to come to life**, s'animer.

life belt ['laifbelt], n. ceinture de sauvetage, f.

life boat ['laifbout], n. canot de sauvetage, m.

life buoy ['laifbɔi], n. bouée de sauvetage, f.

lifeguard ['laifgɑːd], n. garde du corps, m.; (pl.) les Gardes du corps, m.pl.; sauveteur, m.

life-insurance ['laifinʃuərəns], n. assurance sur la vie, f.

lifeless ['laiflis], a. sans vie, inanimé.

lifelike ['laiflaik], a. comme un être vivant, d'après nature, vivant.

lifelong ['laiflɔŋ], a. de toute la vie.

life-size ['laifsaiz], a. de grandeur nature.

lifetime ['laiftaim], n. vie, f., vivant, m.; **in his** or **her lifetime**, de son vivant.

lift [lift], n. action de lever, élévation, f., effort; coup de main (aide); monte-charge (machine); ascenseur, m.—v.t. lever, soulever, hausser, soupeser (évaluer le poids de); (fig.) élever, relever.

lift man ['liftmən], n. (pl. **men** [men]) liftier, m.

light (1) [lait], n. lumière, f., jour (du soleil); clair (de la lune etc.), m.; clarté (de l'œil etc.); lueur, f.; (fig.) aspect, point de vue, m.; **electric light**, éclairage à l'électricité, m.; **it is light**, il fait jour; **light and shade**, clair-obscur, m.; **traffic lights**, feux de circulation, m.pl.; **will you give me a light?** voulez-vous me donner du feu?—v.t. irr. allumer; illuminer, éclairer (fenêtres etc.).—v.i. **to light up**, briller, s'enflammer.

light (2) [lait], v.i. **to light upon**, descendre ou tomber sur.

light (3) [lait], a. léger; (fig.) gai, frivole; clair (couleur etc.); blond (teint).

lighten (1) [laitn], v.t. éclairer, illuminer.—v.i éclairer; faire des éclairs.

lighten (2) [laitn], v.t. soulager, alléger (adoucir).

lightening ['laitniŋ], n. éclaircissement; allègement; soulagement, m.

lighter ['laitə], n. allumeur; briquet (pour cigarettes), m.; (Naut.) allège, gabare, f., chaland, m.

light-hearted [lait'hɑːtid], a. gai, réjoui.

light-heartedness [lait'hɑːtidnis], n. enjouement, m., gaieté, f.

lighthouse ['laithaus], n. phare, m.

lighting ['laitiŋ], n. éclairage, m.; **lighting-up time**, heure d'éclairage, f.

lightly ['laitli], adv. légèrement, à la légère; lestement, facilement, aisément; gaiement.

lightness ['laitnis], n. légèreté, f.

lightning ['laitniŋ], n. éclair, m., les éclairs, m.pl.; foudre, f.; **flash of lightning**, éclair.

lightning rod ['laitniŋrɔd], n. paratonnerre, m.

lights [laits], n.pl. mou (d'animal), m.

lightship ['laitʃip], n. bateau-feu, m.

like (1) [laik], a. semblable, tel, pareil; même, égal, *vraisemblable; **as like as not**, probablement; **that is something like!** à la bonne heure! **to be like**, ressembler à; **to feel like doing something**, avoir envie de faire quelque chose; **what is he like?** comment est-il?—prep. comme, semblable à, pareil à.—n. chose pareille, f., pareil, m.; même chose, f.; **the likes of you**, les gens de votre sorte, m.pl., f.pl.

like (2) [laik], v.t. aimer, aimer bien, trouver bon, trouver bien; vouloir (bien), désirer, être bien aise (de); **as you like**, comme il vous plaira, comme vous voudrez.—n. goût, m.; préférence, f.; **everyone has his likes and dislikes**, chacun son goût.

likeable ['laikəbl], a. sympathique, aimable.

likelihood ['laiklihud], n. probabilité, vraisemblance, f.

likely ['laikli], a. probable, vraisemblable.—adv. probablement, vraisemblablement.

liken [laikn], *v.t.* comparer (*à* ou *avec*).
likeness ['laiknis], *n.* ressemblance, *f.*; portrait, *m.*
likewise ['laikwaiz], *adv.* également, pareillement, de même, aussi.
liking ['laikiŋ], *n.* gré, goût, penchant, *m.*, inclination; amitié, *f.*
lilac ['lailək], *n.* lilas, *m.*
lily ['lili], *n.* lis, *m.*; *lily of the valley*, muguet, *m.*
limb [lim], *n.* membre (*du corps*); (*colloq.*) enfant terrible, *m.*; grosse branche (*d'arbre*), *f.*
limber (1) ['limbə], *a.* souple, flexible; (*fig.*) agile.—*v.i. to limber up*, se chauffer les muscles.
limber (2) ['limbə], *n.* avant-train, *m.*
limbo ['limbou], *n.* limbes, *m.pl.*
lime (1) [laim], *n.* (*Bot.*) lime, limette, *f.*; *lime juice*, jus de limette, *m.*; *lime tree*, tilleul (*linden*); limettier, *m.*
lime (2) [laim], *n.* chaux; glu (*pour prendre des oiseaux*), *f.*
limelight ['laimlait], *n.* (*Theat.*) les feux de la lampe, *m.pl.*; *to be in the limelight*, être en évidence.
limestone ['laimstoun], *n.* pierre à chaux, *f.*; (*Geol.*) calcaire, *m.*
limit ['limit], *n.* limite, borne, *f.*; (*fam.*) *that's the limit!* ça c'est le comble!—*v.t.* limiter, borner, restreindre.
limitation [limi'teiʃən], *n.* limitation, restriction, *f.*
limited ['limitid], *a.* limité, borné; (*Comm.*) anonyme.
limitless ['limitlis], *a.* sans limite.
limp [limp], *a.* mou, flasque, sans consistance.—*v.i.* boiter.
limpet ['limpit], *n.* lépas, *m.*, patelle, *f.*
limpid ['limpid], *a.* limpide.
linden [lindn], *n.* (*Bot.*) tilleul, *m.*
line (1) [lain], *n.* ligne; corde, *f.*, cordeau (*ficelle*), *m.*; file, *f.*, alignement (*rang*); trait (*écrit*), *m.*; raie (*bande*), *f.*; contour (*profil*), *m.*; ride (*pli du visage*); (*Rail.*) voie; lignée, race (*descendance*), *f.*; (*fig.*) genre d'affaires *etc.*); (*Pros.*) vers; mot, petit mot (*lettre brève*), *m.*; limite (*de territoire*), *f.*; *air-line*, ligne aérienne; (*Teleph.*) *hold the line!* ne quittez pas! *it is hard lines*, c'est dur; *not in my line*, pas de mon ressort.—*v.t.* ligner, régler; *to line up*, aligner. **[queue]**
line (2) [lain], *v.t.* doubler (*vêtement*); garnir (*de*); border (*de*).
lineage ['liniədʒ], *n.* lignée, race, famille, *f.*
lineal ['liniəl], *a.* linéaire.
lineally ['liniəli], *adv.* en ligne directe.
linear ['liniə], *a.* linéaire.
linen ['linin], *a.* de toile.—*n.* toile, toile de lin, *f.*, lin; linge (*habits*), *m.*
liner [lain], *n.* (*Naut.*) paquebot de ligne, transatlantique, *m.*
linesman ['lainzmən], *n.* (*pl.* **-men** [men]) (*Ftb.*) arbitre de touche, *m.*
linger ['liŋgə], *v.i.* traîner, tarder; hésiter.
lingering ['liŋgəriŋ], *a.* qui traîne, lent; languissant.—*n.* retard, *m.*, lenteur; hésitation, *f.*
lingo ['liŋgou], *n.* (*slang*) jargon, *m.*; langue, *f.*
linguist ['liŋgwist], *n.* linguiste, *m.*, *f.*
liniment ['linimənt], *n.* liniment, *m.*
lining ['lainiŋ], *n.* doublure; garniture (*de*

vêtement); coiffe (*de chapeau*), *f.*; (*Build.*) revêtement, *m.*
link [liŋk], *n.* chaînon, anneau; (*fig.*) lien; trait d'union, *m.*; *cuff links*, boutons de manchettes, *m.pl.*—*v.t.* lier, relier (*avec.*); enchaîner (*dans*); unir.—*v.i.* s'allier (*à*).
links [liŋks], *n.pl. golf links*, terrain de golf, *m.*
linnet ['linit], *n.* linotte, *f.*
linoleum [li'nouljəm], *n.* linoléum, *m.*
linotype ['lainotaip], *n.* linotype, *f.*
linseed ['linsi:d], *n.* graine de lin, *f.*; *linseed oil*, huile de lin, *f.*
lint [lint], *n.* charpie, *f.*
lintel [lintl], *n.* linteau, *m.*
lion ['laiən], *n.* lion, *m.*; (*fig.*) célébrité, *f.*; *lion's cub*, lionceau, *m.*
lioness ['laiənes], *n.* lionne, *f.*
lion tamer ['laiənteimə], *n.* dompteur de lions, *m.*
lip [lip], *n.* lèvre; babine (*de certains animaux*), *f.*; bord (*de choses*), *m.*; (*fig.*) impertinence, *f.*
lipstick ['lipstik], *n.* bâton de rouge, *m.*
liquefy ['likwifai], *v.t.* liquéfier.—*v.i.* se liquéfier.
liqueur [li'kjuə], *n.* liqueur, *f.*
liquid ['likwid], *a.* liquide; doux, coulant.—*n.* liquide, *m.*
liquidate ['likwideit], *v.t.* liquider.
liquidation [likwi'deiʃən], *n.* liquidation, *f.*, acquittement (*d'une dette*), *m.*
liquor ['likə], *n.* (*Chem.*) liqueur, solution; (*Am.*) boisson alcoolique, *f.*; (*Am.*) *hard liquor*, alcool, *m.*
liquorice ['likəris], *n.* réglisse, *f.*
Lisbon ['lizbən]. Lisbonne, *f.*
lisp [lisp], *v.t.*, *v.i.* dire (θ, ð) au lieu de (s, z); (*colloq.*) susurrer, zozoter.
lissom [lism], *a.* souple, leste.
list (1) [list], *n.* liste, *f.*, rôle, *m.*; *Army List*, annuaire de l'armée, *m.*—*v.t.* enrôler, enregistrer.
list (2) [list], *v.i.* (*Naut.*) donner de la bande.—*n.* (*Naut.*) bande, *f.*
listen [lisn], *v.i.* écouter.
listener ['lisnə], *n.* auditeur, *m.*
listless ['listlis], *a.* apathique.
listlessness ['listlisnis], *n.* apathie, *f.*
lists [lists], *n. pl.* lice, arène (*arena*), *f.*
litany ['litəni], *n.* litanie, *f.*
literal ['litərəl], *a.* littéral.
literally ['litərəli], *adv.* littéralement, à la lettre.
literary ['litərəri], *a.* littéraire; lettré (*personne*).
literature ['litritʃə], *n.* littérature, *f.*
lithe [laið], *a.* pliant, flexible, souple.
lithograph ['liθogra:f], *n.* lithographie, *f.*
lithographer [li'θɔgrəfə], *n.* lithographe, *m.*, *f.*
Lithuania [liθju'einiə]. la Lituanie, la Lithuanie, *f.*
Lithuanian [liθju'einiən], *a.* lituanien, lithuanien.—*n.* lituanien, lithuanien (*langue*); Lituanien, Lithuanien (*personne*), *m.*
litigant ['litigənt], *n.* plaideur, *m.*
litigate ['litigeit], *v.t.* plaider, disputer.—*v.i.* être en procès.
litigation [liti'geiʃən], *n.* litige; procès, *m.*
litre ['li:tə], *n.* litre, *m.*
litter ['litə], *n.* litière, civière (*véhicule*), *f.*; ordures, *f.pl.*, détritus, *m.pl.*; (*fig.*) fouillis, désordre, *m.*; portée (*d'animal*), *f.*—*v.t.*

joncher; jeter çà et là; (*fig.*) mettre en désordre; mettre bas (*animal*); salir; *to litter down* (*of horse*), faire la litière à.

litter bin ['litəbin], *n.* boîte à ordures, *f.*

little [litl], *a.* petit; minime, exigu; mesquin; *little one*, enfant, *m.*, *f.*, petit, *m.*—*n.* peu, *m.*; *to think little of*, faire peu de cas de.—*adv.* peu, un peu, pas beaucoup, peu de chose, peu de; *a little*, un peu; *as little as possible*, le moins possible; *little by little*, petit à petit, peu à peu; *little or none*, peu ou point.

littleness ['litlnis], *n.* petitesse, *f.*

liturgy ['litədʒi], *n.* liturgie, *f.*

live (1) [liv], *v.t.* mener (une vie).—*v.i.* vivre; résider, demeurer, habiter; *long live the Queen!* vive la Reine! *to live by*, vivre de; *to live down a scandal*, faire oublier un scandale avec le temps; *to live on*, se nourrir de.

live (2) [laiv], *a.* en vie, vivant; ardent, vif (*charbons*); *live rail*, rail conducteur, *m.*; *livestock*, bétail, *m.*; *live wire*, fil sous tension, *m.*

lived [livd], *a.* de vie; *long-lived*, qui vit longtemps, de longue vie.

livelihood ['laivlihud], *n.* vie, subsistance, *f.*; gagne-pain, *m.*

liveliness ['laivlinis], *n.* vivacité, gaieté, *f.*

livelong ['livlɔŋ], *a.* durable, long, sans fin; *the livelong day*, toute la sainte journée.

lively ['laivli], *a.* vif, gai, enjoué, animé; vivant (*endroit*).

liven [laivn], *v.t.* *to liven up*, animer.

liver (1) ['livə], *n.* *fast liver*, viveur, noceur, *m.*

liver (2) ['livə], *n.* (*Anat.*) foie, *m.*

livery ['livəri], *n.* livrée; pension (*de chevaux*), *f.*

lives [LIFE].

livestock ['laivstɔk], [LIVE (2)].

livid ['livid], *a.* livide, blême.

living ['liviŋ], *a.* en vie, vivant; vif.—*n.* vie, subsistance, existence, *f.*; genre de vie, *m.*, chère, *f.*; (*Eccles.*) bénéfice, *m.*, cure, *f.*

living room ['liviŋrum], *n.* salle de séjour, *f.*

lizard ['lizəd], *n.* lézard, *m.*

llama ['lɑːmə], *n.* lama, *m.*

lo! [lou], *int.* voici! voilà! voyez! regardez!

load [loud], *n.* charge, *f.*, fardeau; (*fig.*) chargement, *m.*; charretée (*cartful*), *f.*—*v.t.* charger; (*fig.*) combler, accabler (*de*).

loaf [louf], *n.* (*pl.* loaves [louvz]) pain (*long*), *m.*; miche (*rond*), *f.*—*v.i.* flâner, fainéanter; *to loaf about town*, battre le pavé.

loafer ['loufə], *n.* fainéant, batteur de pavé, *m.*

loam [loum], *n.* terre grasse, *f.*

loamy ['loumi], *a.* glaiseux.

loan [loun], *n.* emprunt; prêt, *m.*; *to raise a loan*, faire un emprunt.—*v.t.* prêter.

loath [louθ], *a.* fâché, peiné; *to be loath to*, faire à contre-cœur.

loathe [louð], *v.t.* détester.

loathing ['louðiŋ], *n.* dégoût, *m.*, aversion, *f.*

loathsome ['louðsəm], *a.* dégoûtant, odieux.

loaves [LOAF].

lobby ['lɔbi], *n.* couloir, *m.*; salle d'attente (*vestibule*); (*Theat.*) entrée, *f.*—*v.t.*, *v.i.* (*Polit.*) faire les couloirs.

lobe [loub], *n.* lobe, *m.*

lobelia [lo'biːliə], *n.* lobélie, *f.*

lobster ['lɔbstə], *n.* homard, *m.*

local ['loukəl], *a.* local; topographique.

locality [lo'kæliti], *n.* localité, *f.*

localize ['loukəlaiz], *v.t.* localiser.

locally ['loukəli], *adv.* localement.

locate [lo'keit], *v.t.* placer, localiser; repérer.

location [lo'keiʃən], *n.* situation, *f.*, emplacement, *m.*; location, *f.*; (*Cine.*) extérieurs, *m.pl.*

loch [lɔx], *n.* (*Sc.*) lac, *m.*

lock [lɔk], *n.* serrure; écluse (*de canal*); platine (*de fusil*); mèche, boucle (*de cheveux*), *f.*; flocon (*de laine*), *m.*; (*pl.*) cheveux, *m.pl.*; *dead-lock*, impasse, *f.*; *padlock*, cadenas, *m.*—*v.t.* fermer à clef; accrocher (*roues etc.*); *to lock in*, enfermer; *to lock up*, serrer, enfermer, mettre en prison.—*v.i.* fermer à clef.

locker ['lɔkə], *n.* armoire, *f.*; coffre, *m.*

locket ['lɔkit], *n.* médaillon, *m.*

lock-jaw ['lɔkdʒɔː], *n.* trisme, tétanos, *m.*

locksmith ['lɔksmiθ], *n.* serrurier, *m.*

locomotion [loukə'mouʃən], *n.* locomotion, *f.*

locomotive ['loukəmoutiv], *a.* locomotif.—*n.* locomotive, *f.*

locust (1) ['loukəst], *n.* sauterelle d'Orient, *f.*, criquet, *m.*

locust (2) ['loukəst], *n.* caroubier (*plante*), *m.*; *locust tree*, robinier, *m.*

lodge [lɔdʒ], *n.* loge (*de concierge*), *f.*; pavillon, *m.*; maisonnette (*de garde*), *f.*—*v.t.* loger; abriter; enfoncer (*mettre dans*); déposer (*placer*); implanter (*dans le cœur*); interjeter (*appel*); *to lodge a complaint*, porter plainte.—*v.i.* loger, se loger; s'arrêter, se fixer.

lodger ['lɔdʒə], *n.* locataire; pensionnaire, *m.*, *f.*

lodging ['lɔdʒiŋ], *n.* logement; appartement, *m.*; *to live in furnished lodgings*, loger en garni *ou* en meublé.

lodging house ['lɔdʒiŋhaus], *n.* hôtel garni, hôtel meublé, *m.*

loft [lɔft], *n.* grenier, *m.*; tribune, *f.*; pigeonnier, *m.*

loftily ['lɔftili], *adv.* haut, avec hauteur, pompeusement.

loftiness ['lɔftinis], *n.* élévation; hauteur, fierté, pompe; sublimité, *f.*

lofty ['lɔfti], *a.* haut, élevé; altier; sublime (*style*).

log [lɔg], *n.* bûche, *f.*; (*Naut.*) loch, *m.*; *to sleep like a log*, dormir comme une souche.

loganberry ['lougənberi], *n.* ronce-framboise, *f.*

logarithm ['lɔgəriðm], *n.* logarithme, *m.*

log-book ['lɔgbuk], *n.* journal *ou* livre de bord; (*Motor.*) carnet de route, *m.*

loggerhead ['lɔgəhed], *n.* lourdaud, *m.*; *to be at loggerheads*, être aux prises *ou* à couteaux tirés.

logic ['lɔdʒik], *n.* logique, *f.*

logical ['lɔdʒikəl], *a.* logique, de la logique.

loin [lɔin], *n.* longe (*de veau*), *f.*; filet (*de mouton*), *m.*; (*pl.*) reins, lombes, *m.pl.*

loiter ['lɔitə], *v.t.* perdre, gaspiller.—*v.i.* flâner, traîner; s'amuser en chemin.

loiterer ['lɔitərə], *n.* musard, flâneur, *m.*

loitering ['lɔitəriŋ], *n.* flânerie, *f.*

loll [lɔl], *v.t.* laisser pendre (*la langue*).—*v.i.* s'étaler, se pencher; pendre (*la langue*).

lolling ['lɔliŋ], *a.* étendu, étalé.
lollipop ['lɔlipɔp], *n.* sucre d'orge, *m.*, sucette, *f.*
lolly ['lɔli], *n.* (*fam.*) sucette; (*slang*) galette (*argent*), *f.*
London ['lʌndən]. Londres, *m.* ou *f.*
Londoner ['lʌndənə], *n.* Londonien, *m.*
lone [loun], *a.* seul, solitaire; délaissé.
loneliness ['lounlinis], *n.* solitude, *f.*; isolement, *m.*
lonely ['lounli], *a.* isolé; délaissé.
long (1) [lɔŋ], *v.i.* avoir bien envie, brûler (*de*); (*impers.*) tarder (*de*).
long (2) [lɔŋ], *a.* long; étendu, prolongé, allongé; *a long time*, longtemps, depuis longtemps, pendant longtemps; *in the long run*, à la longue; *to be three feet long*, avoir trois pieds de long, être long de trois pieds.—*n.* *the long and the short of*, le fort et le faible de.—*adv.* fort; longtemps, longuement; depuis longtemps; pendant longtemps; durant; *all night long*, tout le long de la nuit; *before long*, bientôt, avant peu, sous peu; *how long have you been here?* combien de temps y a-t-il que vous êtes ici? *long ago*, il y a longtemps, depuis longtemps; *not long after*, peu de temps après; *so long as*, tant que.
longer ['lɔŋgə], *a.* plus long.—*adv.* plus longtemps; de plus.
longing ['lɔŋiŋ], *n.* désir ardent, *m.*, envie, *f.*
longitude ['lɔndʒitjuːd], *n.* longitude, *f.*
long-sighted ['lɔŋsaitid], *a.* presbyte; (*fig.*) clairvoyant; *I am long-sighted*, j'ai la vue longue.
look [luk], *v.i.* regarder (*d'une fenêtre*); sembler, avoir l'air, paraître; donner sur (*maison etc.*); *look out!* attention! gare! *to look after*, soigner, s'occuper de; *to look away*, détourner ses regards; *to look back*, regarder en arrière; *to look down upon*, mépriser; *to look for*, chercher; *to look forward to*, attendre avec impatience; *to look in*, faire une petite visite, dire un petit bonjour à; *to look into*, examiner; *to look like*, ressembler à; *to look on*, regarder, considérer; *to look over*, jeter un coup d'œil sur, examiner.—*n.* regard, air, *m.*, apparence, mine, *f.*; coup d'œil, *m.*
looker-on ['lukər'ɔn], *n.* spectateur, *m.*
looking ['lukiŋ], *a.* à l'air . . .; à la mine . . .; *good-looking*, beau.
looking glass ['lukiŋglɑːs], *n.* miroir, *m.*, glace, *f.*
look-out ['lukaut], *n.* guet, *m.*, vigilance, vue, *f.*; (*Mil.*) guetteur, *m.*; (*Naut.*) vigie, *f.*; *to keep a look-out*, avoir l'œil au guet.
loom [luːm], *n.* métier à tisser, *m.*—*v.i.* apparaître indistinctement, surgir.
looming ['luːmiŋ], *a.* vague, estompé.
loop [luːp], *n.* boucle; bride (*pour bouton*), *f.*; (*Av.*) looping, *m.*
loop-hole ['luːphoul], *n.* meurtrière (*pour bouton*); (*fig.*) échappatoire, *f.*, faux-fuyant, *m.*
loose [luːs], *a.* délié, défait; branlant; (*fig.*) relâché, lâche (*mœurs*); vague; licencieux; libre; *loose cash*, menue monnaie, *f.*—*n.* *on the loose*, dissolu, dissipé.—*v.t.* délier, lâcher; (*fig.*) débrancher.
loosely ['luːsli], *adv.* librement, négligemment; licencieusement.

loosen ['luːsn], *v.t.* délier, détacher, défaire; desserrer; ébranler.—*v.i.* se délier; se défaire; se desserrer.
looseness ['luːsnis], *n.* état desserré, relâchement; caractère vague, *m.*
loot [luːt], *n.* butin; pillage, *m.*—*v.t.* piller.
looter ['luːtə], *n.* pillard, *m.*
lop [lɔp], *v.t.* élaguer, ébrancher.
lopsided ['lɔpsaidid], *a.* qui penche trop d'un côté, déjeté.
loquacious [lo'kweiʃəs], *a.* loquace.
lord [lɔːd], *n.* seigneur; (*fig.*) maître; lord (*titre anglais*); Monseigneur (*à un prince, noble, évêque etc.*), *m.*; *Our Lord*, notre Seigneur; *the Lord's Prayer*, l'oraison dominicale, *f.*; *the year of our Lord*, l'an de grâce, *f.*—*v.t.* *to lord it over*, dominer, faire le maître.
lordliness ['lɔːdlinis], *n.* hauteur, *f.*, orgueil, *m.*
lordling ['lɔːdliŋ], *n.* petit seigneur; hobereau, *m.*
lordly ['lɔːdli], *a.* de seigneur, noble; hautain, fier.
lore [lɔː], *n.* savoir, *m.*; science, *f.*
lorry ['lɔri], *n.* camion, *m.*
lose [luːz], *v.t. irr.* perdre; égarer; *to lose one's temper*, s'emporter; *to lose one's way*, s'égarer; *to lose sight of*, perdre de vue.—*v.i.* perdre (*de valeur*); retarder (*horloge etc.*).
loss [lɔs], *n.* perte, *f.*; (*Hunt.*) défaut, *m.*; extinction (*de voix*), *f.*; *at a loss*, dans l'embarras; *dead loss*, perte sèche.
lost [lɔst], *a.* perdu; égaré (*fourvoyé*); abîmé (*endommagé*).
lot [lɔt], *n.* sort, destin, *m.*, part; quantité, *f.*; tas (*de personnes*); lot (*à une vente*), *m.*; *a lot of*, beaucoup de; *to draw* ou *cast lots*, tirer au sort. [see plot]
lotion ['louʃən], *n.* lotion, *f.*
lottery ['lɔtəri], *n.* loterie, *f.*
loud [laud], *a.* haut; fort, grand; bruyant; retentissant; tapageur (*tumultueux*); criard (*couleurs*).
loudly ['laudli], *adv.* haut, fort, à haute voix; avec grand bruit, à grands cris.
loudness ['laudnis], *n.* force, *f.*, grand bruit, éclat, *m.*
loud-speaker [laud'spiːkə], *n.* (*Rad.*) haut-parleur, *m.*
Louisa [lu'iːzə], **Louise** [lu'iːz]. Louise, *f.*
lounge [laundʒ], *v.i.* flâner; être couché ou étendu ou appuyé paresseusement (*sur*).—*n.* promenoir; sofa (*canapé*); petit salon; hall (*d'hôtel*), *m.*; *lounge jacket*, veston, *m.*; *lounge suit*, complet veston, *m.*
lounger ['laundʒə], *n.* flâneur, *m.*
lour, lower (1) ['lauə], *v.i.* froncer les sourcils; s'assombrir, s'obscurcir (*du temps*); *the sky lours*, le temps se couvre.
louring, lowering (1) ['lauəriŋ], *a.* couvert, sombre; (*fig.*) menaçant.
louse [laus], *n.* (*pl.* lice [lais]) pou, *m.*
lousy ['lauzi], *a.* pouilleux; (*fig.*) bas, vil, sale.
lout [laut], *n.* rustre, butor, *m.*
loutish ['lautiʃ], *a.* rustre.
lovable ['lʌvəbl], *a.* digne d'être aimé; aimable.
love [lʌv], *v.t.* aimer, adorer.—*n.* amour, *m.*; affection; amitié, *f.*; ami (*mot tendre*), *m.*; (*Ten.*) zéro, rien, *m.*; *my love to all*, mes

amitiés à tous; *to be in love with*, être amoureux de.

love affair ['lʌvəfɛə], *n.* amourette, *f.*

love letter ['lʌvletə], *n.* billet doux, *m.*

loveliness ['lʌvlinis], *n.* amabilité; beauté, *f.*, charme, *m.*

lovely ['lʌvli], *a.* charmant, ravissant, séduisant, gracieux.

lover ['lʌvə], *n.* amant, amoureux; amateur (*de*), *m.*

lovesick ['lʌvsik], *a.* en mal d'amour.

loving ['lʌviŋ], *a.* aimant, affectueux, affectionné, tendre; d'amour (*choses*); *loving kindness*, bonté, miséricorde, *f.*

low (t) [lou], *a.* bas; petit; peu élevé, vulgaire; profond (*révérence*); (*fig.*) lent (*fièvre*); abattu (*humeur*); *at low water*, à marée basse; *in a low voice*, d'une voix basse.—*adv.* bas, en bas; à voix basse; profondément (*révérence*).

low (2) [lou], *v.i.* beugler.

low-brow ['loubrau], *a.* peu intellectuel.—*n.* philistin, *m.*

lower (1) [LOUR].

lower (2) ['louə], *a.* plus bas, inférieur; bas.—*v.t.* baisser, abaisser; descendre; rabaisser, humilier; diminuer, affaiblir.

lower class ['louəklɑːs], *n.* peuple, *m.*

lowering (1) [LOURING].

lowering (2) ['louəriŋ], *n.* abaissement, *m.*, diminution, *f.*

lowest ['louist], *a.* le plus bas, le dernier.

lowing ['louiŋ], *n.* mugissement, beuglement, *m.*

lowliness ['loulinis], *n.* humilité, *f.*

lowly ['louli], *a.* humble.—*adv.* humblement.

lowness ['lounis], *n.* situation basse, petitesse; faiblesse (*santé*); dépression (*prix*), *f.*; abaissement (*température*); abattement (*humeur*), découragement, *m.*; vulgarité, *f.*

loyal ['lɔiəl], *a.* fidèle, loyal.

loyalty ['lɔiəlti], *n.* fidélité, *f.*

lozenge ['lɔzindʒ], *n.* pastille, *f.*; (*Geom., Her. etc.*) losange, *m.*

lubber ['lʌbə], *n.* lourdaud, *m.*; *land-lubber*, marin d'eau douce, *m.*

lubricant ['luːbrikənt], *n.* lubrifiant, *m.*

lubricate ['luːbrikeit], *v.t.* lubrifier.

lubrication [luːbri'keiʃən], *n.* lubrication, *f.*

lucid ['luːsid], *a.* lucide; limpide, transparent.

lucidity [luː'siditi], **lucidness** ['luːsidnis], *n.* transparence, limpidité, lucidité, *f.*

luck [lʌk], *n.* chance, fortune, *f.*, bonheur, *m.*; *by good luck*, par bonheur; *by ill luck*, par malheur; *good luck*, bonne chance.

luckily ['lʌkili], *adv.* heureusement, par bonheur.

lucky ['lʌki], *a.* heureux; *to be lucky*, avoir de la chance; porter bonheur (*chose*).

lucrative ['luːkrətiv], *a.* lucratif.

lucre ['luːkə], *n.* lucre, *m.*

Lucy ['luːsi]. Lucie, *f.*

ludicrous ['luːdikrəs], *a.* risible, comique, ridicule.

luggage ['lʌgidʒ], *n.* bagage, *m.*, bagages, *m.pl.*; *left-luggage office*, consigne, *f.*

lugubrious ['luː'gjuːbriəs], *a.* lugubre.

lukewarm ['luːkwɔːm], *a.* tiède; (*fig.*) peu zélé.

lull [lʌl], *v.t.* bercer, endormir; calmer.—*v.i.* se calmer, s'apaiser.—*n.* moment de calme, *m.*; (*Naut.*) accalmie, *f.*

lullaby ['lʌləbai], *n.* berceuse, *f.*

lumbago [lʌm'beigou], *n.* lumbago, *m.*

lumber ['lʌmbə], *n.* vieilleries, *f.pl.*; (*Am.*) bois de charpente, *m.*—*v.t.* entasser sans ordre; remplir de fatras.—*v.i.* se traîner lourdement.

lumbering ['lʌmbəriŋ], *a.* lourd, encombrant.

lumberjack ['lʌmbədʒæk], *n.* bûcheron, *m.*

luminous ['luːminəs], *a.* lumineux.

lump [lʌmp], *n.* masse, *f.*; morceau, bloc (*piece*), *m.*—*v.t.* prendre en bloc; réunir ensemble.

lumpish ['lʌmpiʃ], *a.* gros, lourd, pesant.

lumpy ['lʌmpi], *a.* grumeleux.

lunacy ['luːnəsi], *n.* aliénation mentale, *f.*

lunar ['luːnə], *a.* lunaire.

lunatic ['luːnətik], *a.* de fou, d'aliéné.—*n.* aliéné; fou, *m.*, folle, *f.*

lunatic asylum ['luːnətikəsailəm], *n.* asile d'aliénés, *m.*

lunch [lʌntʃ], *n.* déjeuner (*vers midi*), *m.*—*v.i.* déjeuner.

lung [lʌŋ], *n.* (*usu. in pl.*) poumon; mou (*de veau*), *m.*; *iron lung*, poumon d'acier.

lunge [lʌndʒ], *n.* (*Fenc.*) botte, *f.*, coup droit, *m.*—*v.i.* porter une botte.

lupin ['ljuːpin], *n.* (*Bot.*) lupin, *m.*

lurch [ləːtʃ], *n.* embardée, *f.*, cahot; (*fig.*) embarras, *m.*; *to leave in the lurch*, planter là.—*v.i.* faire une embardée (*navire*).

lure [ljuə], *n.* leurre, appât, piège; (*fig.*) attrait, *m.*—*v.t.* leurrer, attirer, séduire.

lurid ['ljuərid], *a.* sombre, blafard; sensationnel.

lurk [ləːk], *v.i.* être aux aguets; se tenir caché.

luscious ['lʌʃəs], *a.* délicieux, savoureux; liquoreux (*vin*).

lusciousness ['lʌʃəsnis], *n.* nature succulente, douceur extrême; volupté, *f.*

lush [lʌʃ], *a.* luxuriant.

lust [lʌst], *n.* luxure, *f.*; désir lascif, *m.*; (*fig.*) convoitise, *f.*—*v.i.* désirer immodérément; *to lust after*, convoiter.

luster ['lʌstə], *n.* brillant, lustre; (*fig.*) éclat, *m.*, splendeur, *f.*

lustily ['lʌstili], *adv.* vigoureusement.

lustrous ['lʌstrəs], *a.* brillant, lustré.

lusty ['lʌsti], *a.* vigoureux, robuste, fort.

lute [ljuːt], *n.* luth, *m.*

Luxembourg ['lʌksəmbəːg]. le Luxembourg (*Duché*), *m.*

luxuriance [lʌg'zjuəriəns], *n.* exubérance, surabondance, luxuriance, *f.*

luxuriant [lʌg'zjuəriənt], *a.* exubérant, surabondant, luxuriant.

luxurious [lʌg'zjuəriəs], *a.* de luxe, somptueux, luxueux.

luxuriously [lʌg'zjuəriəsli], *adv.* avec luxe, somptueusement.

luxuriousness [lʌg'zjuəriəsnis], *n.* somptuosité, *f.*

luxury ['lʌkʃəri], *n.* luxe, *m.*, exubérance, *f.*; fin morceau; objet de luxe, *m.*

lying ['laiiŋ], *a.* menteur; mensonger (*choses*).—*n.* mensonge, *m.*

lymph [limf], *n.* lymphe, *f.*; vaccin, *m.*

lynch [lintʃ], *v.t.* lyncher (*exécuter sommairement*).

lynx [liŋks], *n.* lynx, *m.*

lyre ['laiə], *n.* lyre, *f.*
lyric ['lirik], *a.* lyrique.—*n.* poème lyrique, *m.*; (*pl.*) paroles (*d'une chanson*), *f.pl.*
lyrical ['lirikəl], *a.* lyrique.

M

M, m [em]. treizième lettre de l'alphabet, *m.*
macadam [mə'kædəm], *n.* macadam, *m.*
macaroni [mækə'rouni], *n.* macaroni, *m.*
macaroon [mækə'ru:n], *n.* macaron, *m.*
mace [meis], *n.* masse (*de cérémonie*), *f.*
mace-bearer ['meisbɛərə], *n.* massier, *m.*
Macedonia [mæsə'dounia]. la Macédoine, *f.*
Macedonian [mæsə'dounian], *a.* macédonien.
—*n.* Macédonien (*personne*), *m.*
macerate ['mæsəreit], *v.t.* macérer.
machine [mə'ʃi:n], *n.* machine, *f.*; (*fig.*) instrument; appareil (*avion*), *m.*
machine gun [mə'ʃi:ngʌn], *n.* mitrailleuse, *f.*
machinery [mə'ʃi:nəri], *n.* mécanique, *f.*, mécanisme, *m.*; machines, *f.pl.*
machine tool [mə'ʃi:ntu:l], *n.* machine-outil, *f.*
mackerel ['mækərəl], *n.* maquereau, *m.*
mackintosh ['mækintɔʃ], *n.* imperméable, *m.*
mad [mæd], *a.* fou, aliéné, insensé; affolé; furieux (*déchaîné*); enragé (*animal*).
Madagascan [mædə'gæskən], *a.* malgache.—*n.* Malgache (*personne*), *m.*, *f.*
Madagascar [mædə'gæskə]. Madagascar, *m.*
madam ['mædəm], *n.* madame, *f.*
madcap ['mædkæp], *a.* étourdi, fou.—*n.* fou, *m.*
madden [mædn], *v.t.* rendre fou; faire enrager.
maddening ['mædniŋ], *a.* à rendre fou, enrageant.
madder ['mædə], *n.* garance, *f.*
made [meid], *a.* fait, confectionné; **self-made man**, fils de ses œuvres, *m.*; **made up**, inventé (*histoire*); maquillé (*visage*).
Madeira [mə'diərə]. Madère, *f.*—*n.* madère (*vin*), *m.*
madly ['mædli], *adv.* follement, furieusement.
madman ['mædmən], *n.* (*pl.* **-men** [men]) aliéné, fou, *m.*
madness ['mædnis], *n.* démence, fureur, folie; rage (*d'animal*), *f.*
Madonna [mə'dɔnə]. la Madone, *f.*
maelstrom ['meilstroum, 'meilstrəm], *n.* (*Geog.*) malstrom; (*fig.*) tourbillon, *m.*
magazine [mægə'zi:n], *n.* magasin (*boutique*; *aussi chargeur d'arme à feu*); magazine, *m.*, revue (*périodique*), *f.*
magenta [mə'dʒentə], *a.* and *n.* magenta (*couleur*), *m.*
maggot ['mægət], *n.* larve, *f.*, ver, asticot, *m.*
magic ['mædʒik], *a.* magique.—*n.* magie, *f.*
magical ['mædʒikəl], *a.* magique.
magician [mə'dʒiʃən], *n.* magicien, *m.*
magisterial [mædʒis'tiəriəl], *a.* de maître; magistral.
magistrate ['mædʒistreit], *n.* magistrat, *m.*; **examining magistrate**, juge d'instruc-

tion, *m.*; **police court magistrate**, juge de paix, *m.*
magnanimity [mægnə'nimiti], *n.* magnanimité, *f.*
magnanimous [mæg'næniməs], *a.* magnanime.
magnate ['mægneit], *n.* magnat; grand; (*colloq.*) gros bonnet, *m.*
magnesia [mæg'ni:ʃə], *n.* magnésie, *f.*
magnesium [mæg'ni:ziəm], *n.* magnésium, *m.*
magnet ['mægnit], *n.* aimant, *m.*
magnetic [mæg'netik], *a.* aimanté; magnétique; (*fig.*) attirant.
magnetism ['mægnitizm], *n.* magnétisme, *m.*; (*Elec.*) aimantation, *f.*
magnetize ['mægnitaiz], *v.t.* aimanter; (*fig.*) magnétiser.
magneto [mæg'ni:tou], *n.* magnéto, *f.*
magnificence [mæg'nifisəns], *n.* magnificence, *f.*
magnificent [mæg'nifisənt], *a.* magnifique, superbe.
magnify ['mægnifai], *v.t.* magnifier, augmenter, grossir; (*fig.*) exalter.
magnifying ['mægnifaiiŋ], *a.* qui grossit; **magnifying glass**, loupe, *f.*
magnitude ['mægnitju:d], *n.* grandeur; importance, *f.*
magnolia [mæg'noulia], *n.* (*Bot.*) magnolia, magnolier, *m.*
magpie ['mægpai], *n.* pie, *f.*
mahogany [mə'hɔgəni], *n.* acajou, bois d'acajou, *m.*
maid [meid]. *n.* fille, jeune fille; vierge (*virgin*); bonne, servante, domestique, *f.*; **chambermaid**, fille de chambre; **kitchen maid**, fille de cuisine; **maid of all work**, bonne à tout faire; **maid of honor**, demoiselle d'honneur, *f.*
maiden [meidn], *a.* de fille, de jeune fille; virginal; (*fig.*) pur, neuf; **maiden aunt**, tante non mariée, *f.*; **maiden name**, nom de jeune fille, *m.*; **maiden speech**, premier discours (*d'un nouveau membre du Parlement*), *m.*; **maiden voyage**, premier voyage, *m.*—*n.* jeune fille, fille, *f.*
maidenly ['meidnli], *a.* de jeune fille; modeste, chaste.
mail (1) [meil], *n.* mailles (*armure*), *f.pl.*
mail (2) [meil], *n.* courrier, *m.*, dépêches (*lettres*), *f.pl.*—*v.t.* (*Am.*) mettre à la poste.
mail-bag ['meilbæg], *n.* sac postal, *m.*
mail train ['meiltrein], *n.* train-postal, *m.*
maim [meim], *v.t.* mutiler, estropier.
main (1) [mein], *a.* principal, premier; grand; important, essentiel.—*n.* gros, *m.*, plus grande partie, *f.*; principal océan, *m.*; **in the main**, pour la plupart, en général.
main (2) [mein], *n.* force, *f.*
main deck ['meindek], *n.* premier pont, *m.*
mainland ['meinlənd], *n.* continent, *m.*
mainly ['meinli], *adv.* principalement, surtout.
mainmast ['meinmɔ:st], *n.* grand mât, *m.*
mainstay ['meinstei], *n.* soutien, *m.*
maintain [mein'tein], *v.t.* maintenir; soutenir, alléguer; conserver; entretenir, nourrir (*subvenir aux besoins de*).
maintenance ['meintənəns], *n.* maintien, soutien; entretien, *m.*
maize [meiz], *n.* maïs, *m.*

majestic [mə'dʒestik], _a._ majestueux.

majesty ['mædʒəsti], _n._ majesté, _f._; _His_ or _Her Majesty_, Sa Majesté.

major ['meidʒə], _a._ plus grand, majeur.—_n._ commandant, _m._; (_Law_) personne majeure, _f._; _drum major_, tambour-major, _m._; _sergeant major_, adjudant, _m._

Majorca [mə'jɔːkə], Majorque, _f._

majority [mə'dʒɔriti], _n._ majorité, _f._

make [meik], _v.t. irr._ faire; créer, façonner, fabriquer, confectionner; rendre (_faire devenir_); forcer, contraindre (_obliger_); amasser, gagner (_argent_); _to make a mistake_, se tromper; _to make a noise_, faire du bruit; _to make believe_, faire accroire à; _to make fun of_, se moquer de; _to make good_, soutenir; réparer; dédommager de; _to make it up_, se raccommoder; _to make known_, faire connaître, faire savoir à; _to make out_, comprendre, déchiffrer, distinguer; _to make over to_, céder à; _to make sure of_, s'assurer de; _to make up_, compléter (_histoire_); arranger (_querelle_); régler (_comptes_); _to make up for_, suppléer à; rattraper (_temps_); _to make up one's mind_, se décider.—_v.i._ se diriger (_vers_); contribuer (_à_); faire (_comme si_); _to make believe_, faire semblant; _to make of_, comprendre; _to make off_, se sauver; _to make up_, se maquiller; _to make up for_, suppléer à; dédommager de, compenser.—_n._ façon, forme, tournure; fabrication, _f._

make-believe ['meikbiliːv], _n._ feinte, _f._, semblant, _m._

maker ['meikə], _n._ créateur, auteur; faiseur; (_Comm._) fabricant, _m._

makeshift ['meikʃift], _n._ pis aller, expédient, _m._

make-up ['meikʌp], _n._ contexture, _f._; maquillage (_du visage_), _m._

make-weight ['meikweit], _n._ supplément; (_fig._) remplissage, _m._

making ['meikiŋ], _n._ création; façon, fabrication, construction; confection (_de vêtements_), _f._

maladjusted [mælə'dʒʌstid], _a._ inadapté.

maladjustment [mælə'dʒʌstmənt], _n._ inadaptation, _f._

maladministration [mælədmɪnɪs'treiʃən], _n._ mauvaise administration, _f._

malady ['mælədi], _n._ maladie, _f._

malaria [mə'lɛəriə], _n._ malaria, _f._, paludisme, _m._

Malay [mə'lei], _a._ malais.—_n._ malais (_langue_); Malais (_personne_), _m._

Malaysia [mə'leiziə], la Malaisie, _f._

Malaysian [mə'leiziən], _a._ malais.—_n._ Malais (_personne_), _m._

malcontent ['mælkəntent], _a._ and _n._ mécontent, _m._

male [meil], _a._ mâle; masculin.—_n._ mâle, _m._

malediction [mæli'dikʃən], _n._ malédiction, _f._

malefactor ['mælifæktə], _n._ malfaiteur, _m._

malevolence [mə'levələns], _n._ malveillance, _f._

malevolent [mə'levələnt], _a._ malveillant.

Mali ['mɑːli], le Mali, _m._

malice ['mælis], _n._ malice; malveillance, méchanceté; rancune, _f._; _to bear malice_, vouloir du mal à, garder rancune à.

malicious [mə'liʃəs], _a._ malicieux, méchant.

maliciously [mə'liʃəsli], _adv._ méchamment.

maliciousness [mə'liʃəsnis], _n._ malice, malveillance, _f._

malign [mə'lain], _a._ malin; méchant.—_v.t._ diffamer, noircir.

malignant [mə'lignənt], _a._ malin, méchant.

malignantly [mə'lignəntli], _adv._ malignement, méchamment.

malignity [mə'ligniti], _n._ malignité, malveillance, _f._

malinger [mə'liŋgə], _v.i._ (_Mil._) faire le malade; tirer au flanc.

mall (1) [mɔːl], _n._ gros maillet, _m._

mall (2) [mæl], _n._ mail (_rue_), _m._

mallard ['mæləd], _n._ (_Orn._) canard sauvage, _m._

malleability [mæliə'biliti], _n._ malléabilité, _f._

malleable ['mæliəbl], _a._ malléable.

mallet ['mælit], _n._ maillet, _m._; tapette, _f._

mallow ['mælou], _n._ (_Bot._) mauve, _f._

malmsey ['muːmzi], _n._ malvoisie, _f._

malnutrition [mælnjuː'triʃən], _n._ sousalimentation, _f._

malpractice [mæl'præktis], _n._ malversation, _f._, méfait, _m._

malt [mɔːlt], _n._ malt, _m._—_v.t._ malter.

Malta ['mɔːltə], Malte, _f._

Maltese [mɔːl'tiːz], _a._ maltais.—_n._ Maltais (_personne_), _m._

maltreat [mæl'triːt], _v.t._ maltraiter.

maltreatment [mæl'triːtmənt], _n._ mauvais traitement, _m._

mammal ['mæməl], _n._ mammifère, _m._

mammoth ['mæməθ], _n._ mammouth, _m._

man [mæn], _n._ (_pl._ **men** [men]) homme; domestique, valet (_servant_), _m._; (_Chess_) pièce, _f._; (_Draughts_) pion, _m._; _the man in the street_, l'homme de la rue, le grand public.—_v.t._ garnir d'hommes; armer (_pompe, bateau_).

manacle ['mænəkl], _v.t._ mettre les menottes à.—_n._ (_pl._) menottes, _f.pl._

manage ['mænidʒ], _v.t._ diriger, mener, conduire; arranger (_choses_); gouverner, administrer, gérer; ménager (_habilement_); manier, dompter (_cheval_).—_v.i._ s'arranger (_pour_), parvenir à; venir à bout (_de_).

manageable ['mænidʒəbl], _a._ traitable, maniable.

management ['mænidʒmənt], _n._ conduite, administration; (_Comm._) gestion (_direction_), _f._; artifice, savoir-faire (_manège_), _m._

manager ['mænidʒə], _n._ directeur, administrateur; (_Comm._) gérant; (_Theat._) régisseur; (_Spt._) manager, _m._

manageress [mænidʒə'res], _n._ directrice, gérante, _f._

Manchuria [mæn'tʃuəriə], la Mandchourie, _f._

Manchu(rian) [mæn'tʃu(əriən)], _a._ mandchou.—_n._ mandchou (_langue_); Mandchou (_personne_), _m._

mandarin ['mændərin], _n._ mandarin, _m._; mandarine (_orange_), _f._

mandate ['mændeit], _n._ commandement, mandat; ordre, _m._

mandatory ['mændətəri], _a._ and _n._ mandataire, _m._

mandolin ['mændəlin], _n._ mandoline, _f._

mane [mein], _n._ crinière, _f._

maneuver, see manœuvre.

manfully ['mænfuli], _adv._ en homme, virilement, vaillamment.

manganese ['mæŋgəniːz], _n._ manganèse, _m._

mange

mange [meindʒ], n. gale (d'animaux), f.
manger ['meindʒə], n. mangeoire, crèche, f.
mangle [mæŋgl], v.t. déchirer, mutiler; calandrer (linge).—n. calandre, f.
mango ['mæŋgou], n. (Bot.) mangue, f.; manguier (arbre), m.
mangrove ['mæŋgrouv], n. (Bot.) mangle, f.; manglier, manguier (arbre), m.
mangy ['meindʒi], a. galeux.
man-handle ['mænhændl], v.t. manutentionner; (fig.) maltraiter.
man-hole ['mænhoul], n. bouche d'égout, f.
manhood ['mænhud], n. virilité, f.; âge viril, m.; nature humaine, f.
mania ['meinjə], n. folie, rage, manie, f.
maniac ['meiniæk], a. furieux, fou.—n. fou furieux, fou, m.; (fig.) maniaque, m., f.
maniacal [mə'naiəkl], a. furieux, fou.
manicure ['mænikjuə], n. soin des ongles, m. —v.t. soigner les ongles.
manicurist ['mænikjuərist], n. manucure, m., f.
manifest ['mænifest], v.t. manifester, témoigner, montrer; to manifest a cargo, déclarer une cargaison.—a. manifeste, évident.—n. manifeste, m.
manifestation [mænifes'teiʃən], n. manifestation, f.
manifesto [mæni'festou], n. manifeste, m.
manifold ['mænifould], a. divers, multiple; varié.
manikin ['mænikin], n. bout d'homme, mannequin, homuncule, m.
Manila [mə'nilə], Manille, f.
manipulate [mə'nipjuleit], v.t. manipuler.
mankind [mæn'kaind], n. genre humain, m., l'humanité, f.
manlike ['mænlaik], a. d'homme, viril; mâle; hommasse (femme).
manliness ['mænlinis], n. caractère viril, m.
manly ['mænli], a. d'homme, viril, mâle.
manna ['mænə], n. manne, f.
mannequin ['mænikin], n. (Dress.) mannequin, m.; mannequin parade, défilé de mannequins, m.
manner ['mænə], n. manière, f., air; genre, m., sorte, façon, espèce; coutume, habitude, f.; (pl.) mœurs, maint; as many as, autant que, jusqu'à (devant un numéro); how many? combien? many a time, maintes fois; so many, tant, tant de; too many, trop, trop de.—n. the many, la multitude, la foule, f.
mannerism ['mænərizm], n. air maniéré, maniérisme; tic, m.
mannerly ['mænəli], a. poli.
manning ['mæniŋ], n. armement, équipement, m.
mannish ['mæniʃ], a. hommasse.
manœuvre [mə'nuːvə], n. manœuvre, f.— v.t., v.i. manœuvrer.
manor ['mænə], n. seigneurie, f.; manoir, château seigneurial, m.
manorial [mə'nɔːriəl], a. seigneurial.
man-power ['mænpauə], n. main d'œuvre, f.
manse [mæns], n. presbytère, m.
mansion ['mænʃən], n. château (à la campagne); hôtel particulier (en ville), m.
manslaughter ['mænslɔːtə], n. (Law) homicide involontaire, m.
mantel [mæntl], mantelpiece ['mæntlpiːs], n. manteau ou dessus de cheminée, m., cheminée, f.

mantilla [mæn'tilə], n. mantille, f.
mantis ['mæntis], n. (Ent.) mante, f.; praying mantis, mante religieuse.
mantle [mæntl], n. manteau, m.—v.t. couvrir, voiler.
manual ['mænjuel], a. manuel, de la main.— n. manuel (livre); (Organ) clavier, m.
manufacture [mænju'fæktʃə], n. manufacture, confection, fabrication, f.; produits manufacturés, m.pl.—v.t. manufacturer, fabriquer.
manufacturer [mænju'fæktʃərə], n. fabricant, industriel, m.
manure [mə'njuə], n. engrais, fumier, m.— v.t. engraisser, fumer.
manuscript ['mænjuskript], a. and n. manuscrit, m.
Manx [mæŋks], a. de l'île de Man, mannois; Manx cat, chat sans queue, m.
many ['meni], a. beaucoup (de), bien (des); nombreux; plusieurs, maint; as many as, autant que, jusqu'à (devant un numéro); how many? combien? many a time, maintes fois; so many, tant, tant de; too many, trop, trop de.—n. the many, la multitude, la foule, f.
many-colored ['menikʌləd], a. multicolore.
many-sided ['meniˌsaidid], a. polygone; (fig.) complexe.
map [mæp], n. carte, carte géographique, f.; map of a town, plan d'une ville, m.; map of the world, mappemonde, f.—v.t. faire une carte ou un plan de, tracer.
maple [meipl], n. érable, m.
mar [maː], v.t. gâter, défigurer; (fig.) troubler.
marathon ['mærəθɔn], n. marathon, m.
marauder [mə'rɔːdə], n. maraudeur, malandrin, m.
marauding [mə'rɔːdiŋ], n. maraude, f. maraudage, m.
marble [maːbl], a. de marbre.—n. marbre, m.; bille (jouet), f.
marbled [maː'bld], a. marbré.
marbling ['maːbliŋ], n. marbrure, f.
March [maːtʃ], mars (mois), m.
march (1) [maːtʃ], n. (Mil.) marche, f.; (fig.) progrès, m; march past, défilé, m.—v.t. mettre en marche; emmener.—v.i. marcher, se mettre en marche; (fig.) avancer; to march past, défiler devant.
march (2) [maːtʃ], n. frontière, f.
marching ['maːtʃiŋ], a. de marche.—n. marche, f.
marchioness [maːʃə'nes], n. marquise, f.
mare [meə], n. jument, f.
Margaret ['maːgərit], Marguerite, f.
margarine ['maːgəriːn, 'maːdʒəriːn], n. margarine, f.
margin ['maːdʒin], n. marge (de papier etc.), f.; bord (de rivière, de lac), m.—v.t. border.
marginal ['maːdʒinəl], a. en marge; marginal.
marigold ['mærigould], n. (Bot.) souci, m.
marine [mə'riːn], a. marin, de mer; naval.— n. fusilier marin, m.; tell that to the marines, allez conter cela à d'autres.
mariner ['mærinə], n. marin, m.
maritime ['mæritaim], a. maritime.
Mark [maːk], Marc, m.
mark (1) [maːk], n. marque, f., signe, m.; em-

480

preinte; (*fig.*) distinction, importance, *f.*; témoignage (*d'estime*), *m.*; (*Sch.*) note, *f.*, point, *m.*; cible (*but*); croix (*signature*), *f.* —*v.t.* marquer, remarquer; (*Sch.*) noter; (*fig.*) observer, faire attention à.

mark (2) [maːk], *n.* marc (*pièce de monnaie*), *m.*

marked [maːkt], *a.* marqué, évident; prononcé (*accent*).

marker ['maːkə], *n.* marqueur; jeton (*au jeu*); signet (*de livre*), *m.*

market ['maːkit], *n.* marché, *m.*; halle, *f.*; débit (*vente*); cours (*prix*); (*Comm.*) débouché, *m.*—*v.t.* acheter au marché, vendre au marché.

market garden ['maːkit'gaːdn], *n.* jardin maraîcher, *m.*

market gardener ['maːkit'gaːdnə], *n.* maraîcher, *m.*

marking ['maːkiŋ], *n.* marquage, *m.*

marking ink ['maːkiŋiŋk], *n.* encre à marquer, *f.*

marksman ['maːksmən], *n.* (*pl.* **-men** [men]) bon tireur, *m.*

marksmanship ['maːksmənʃip], *n.* adresse au tir, *f.*

marl [maːl], *n.* marne, *f.*—*v.t.* marner.

marline-spike ['maːlinspaik], *n.* épissoir, *m.*

marmalade ['maːməleid], *n.* confiture d'oranges, *f.*

marmoset ['maːməzet], *n.* ouistiti, *m.*

marmot ['maːmət], *n.* marmotte, *f.*

maroon (1) [mə'ruːn], *n.* noir marron, *m.*— *v.t.* abandonner dans une île déserte.

maroon (2) [mə'ruːn], *a.* and *n.* marron pourpré (*couleur*), *m.*

marquee [maː'kiː], *n.* grande tente, *f.*

marquetry ['maːkətri], *n.* marqueterie, *f.*

marquis [MARQUESS].

marriage ['mæridʒ], *n.* mariage, *m.*; noces (*fêtes*), *f.pl.*

marriageable ['mæridʒəbl], *a.* mariable, nubile.

married ['mærid], *a.* marié; conjugal.

marrow ['mærou], *n.* moelle; (*fig.*) essence, *f.*; *vegetable marrow*, courgette, *f.*

marry ['mæri], *v.t.* marier (*donner ou unir en mariage*); se marier avec, épouser (*prendre pour époux*).—*v.i.* se marier.

Marseilles [maː'seilz], Marseille, *f.*

marsh [maːʃ], *n.* marais, *m.*

marshal ['maːʃl], *n.* maréchal.—*v.t.* ranger; mettre en ordre; classer.

marsh-mallow ['maːʃ'mælou], *n.* (*Bot.*) guimauve, *f.*; bonbon à la guimauve, *m.*

marshy ['maːʃi], *a.* marécageux.

mart [maːt], *n.* marché, entrepôt, *m.*

marten [maːtn], *n.* martre, *f.*; *beech marten*, fouine, *f.*

Martha ['maːθə], Marthe, *f.*

martial [maːʃl], *a.* martial; de guerre, de bataille; guerrier, belliqueux.

martin ['maːtin], *n.* martin, martinet, *m.*

martinet [maːti'net], *n.* officier strict sur la discipline, *m.*

Martinmas ['maːtinmæs], la Saint-Martin, *f.*

martyr ['maːtə], *n.* martyr, *m.*—*v.t.* martyriser.

martyrdom ['maːtədəm], *n.* martyre, *m.*

martyrize ['maːtəraiz], *v.t.* (*fam.*) faire souffrir, martyriser.

marvel [maːvl], *n.* merveille, *f.*—*v.i.* s'émerveiller, s'étonner.

marvellous ['maːv(i)ləs], *a.* merveilleux, étonnant.

marvellously ['maːv(i)ləsli], *adv.* à merveille.

Marxism ['maːksizm], *n.* Marxisme, *m.*

Marxist ['maːksist], *a.* marxiste.—*n.* Marxiste, *m.*, *f.*

Mary ['mɛəri]. Marie, *f.*

marzipan [maːzi'pæn], *n.* massepain, *m.*

mascot ['mæskət], *n.* mascotte, *f.*

masculine ['mæskjulin], *a.* mâle, d'homme; (*Gram.*) masculin; hommasse (*femme*).—*n.* masculin, *m.*

mash [mæʃ], *n.* mélange, *m.*, pâte, bouillie; mâche (*pour bestiaux*); pâtée (*pour chien, volaille*), *f.*—*v.t.* broyer; mélanger; (*Brewing*) brasser; *mashed potatoes*, purée de pommes de terre, *f.*

mask [maːsk], *n.* masque; loup (*de soie, de velours*), *m.*—*v.t.* masquer; déguiser.—*v.i.* se masquer.

mason [meisn], *n.* maçon, *m.*; *freemason*, franc-maçon, *m.*

masonic [mə'sɔnik], *a.* maçonnique.

masonry ['meisənri], *n.* maçonnerie, *f.*; *freemasonry*, franc-maçonnerie, *f.*

masquerade [mæskə'reid], *n.* mascarade *f.* —*v.i.* se masquer; *to masquerade as*, se faire passer pour.

mass (1) [mæs], *n.* masse, *f.*; amas, gros, *m.*; multitude, foule (*de gens*), *f.*—*v.t.* se masser; s'amonceler (*nuages*).

mass (2) [mæs, maːs], *n.* (R.-C. *Ch.*) messe, *f.*

massacre ['mæsəkə], *n.* massacre, *m.*—*v.t.* massacrer.

massive ['mæsiv], *a.* massif.

mass meeting ['mæs'miːtiŋ], *n.* assemblée en masse, *f.*, grand meeting, *m.*

mast [maːst], *n.* mât, *m.*; (*pl.*) mâts, *m.pl.*; mâture, *f.*; *half-mast*, à mi-mât, en berne.

master ['maːstə], *n.* maître, directeur, chef; (*Naut.*) patron, maître (*d'un navire*); patron (*d'ouvriers*); (*Sch. etc.*) maître d'école, professeur; (*fig.*) possesseur, *m.*—*v.t.* maîtriser, surmonter, dompter, vaincre; se rendre maître de; l'emporter sur.

masterful ['maːstəful], *a.* de maître, impérieux, dominateur.

master key ['maːstəkiː], *n.* passe-partout, *m.*

masterly ['maːstəli], *a.* de maître; magistral.

master-mind ['maːstəmaind], *n.* esprit supérieur, *m.*

masterpiece ['maːstəpiːs], *n.* chef-d'œuvre, *m.*

master-stroke ['maːstəstrouk], **master-touch** ['maːstətʌtʃ], *n.* coup de maître, *m.*

mastery ['maːstəri], *n.* empire, pouvoir, *m.*; supériorité, maîtrise, *f.*

masticate ['mæstikeit], *v.t.* mâcher.

mastication [mæsti'keiʃən], *n.* mastication, *f.*

mastiff ['mæstif], *n.* mâtin, *m.*

mastitis [mæs'taitis], *n.* mastite, *f.*

mastodon ['mæstədɔn], *n.* mastodonte, *m.*

mastoid ['mæstɔid], *a.* mastoïde.

mat [mæt], *n.* natte, *f.*; dessous de lampe, *m.*; *door mat*, paillasson, *m.*; *table mat*, dessous de plat, *m.*—*v.t.* natter, tresser.

match (1) [mætʃ], n. pareil, pendant, égal (*semblable*); mariage; parti (*futur époux*), m.; lutte (*concours*), f.; (*Spt.*) match, m., partie; course, f.; **to be a bad match**, aller mal ensemble (*choses*); **to be more than a match for**, être trop fort pour; **to make a good match**, faire un bon mariage.—v.t. assortir, appareiller, égaler, apparier (*deux choses*); se mesurer avec (*opposer*).—v.i. s'assortir, être pareil.

match (2) [mætʃ], n. allumette, f.

match-box ['mætʃbɔks], n. boîte d'allumettes *ou* à allumettes, f.

matchless ['mætʃlis], a. incomparable, sans pareil.

match-maker (1) ['mætʃmeikə], n. marieur, m.

match-maker (2) ['mætʃmeikə], n. fabricant d'allumettes, m.

mate (1) [meit], n. camarade, compagnon, m., compagne, f.; second (*de marine marchande*), m.—v.t. égaler, assortir, apparier; tenir compagnie avec; accoupler (*oiseaux*).—v.i. s'accoupler (*animaux*).

mate (2) [meit], n. (*Chess*) mat, m.—v.t. mater.

material [mə'tiəriəl], a. matériel; important. —n. matière, f.; étoffe, f., tissu (*textile*); matériel (*réserves*), m.; (*pl.*) matériaux, m.pl.; **raw materials**, matière première.

materialism [mə'tiəriəlizm], n. matérialisme, m.

materialist [mə'tiəriəlist], n. matérialiste, m., f.

materialistic [mətiəriə'listik], a. matérialiste.

materialize [mə'tiəriəlaiz], v.t. matérialiser. —v.i. se réaliser; se concrétiser.

materially [mə'tiəriəli], adv. matériellement; essentiellement.

maternal [mə'tə:nl], a. maternel.

maternity [mə'tə:niti], n. maternité, f.

mathematics [mæθə'mætiks], n.pl. mathématiques, f.pl.

Matilda [mə'tildə], Mathilde, f.

matins ['mætinz], n.pl. matines, f.pl.

matriarch ['meitriɑːk], n. matriarche, f.

matricide ['mætrisaid], n. matricide (*crime*), m.; matricide (*criminel*), m., f.

matrimonial [mætri'mouniəl], a. conjugal.

matrimony ['mætriməni], n. mariage, m., vie conjugale, f.

matron ['meitrən], n. matrone, mère de famille; infirmière en chef, f.

matronly ['meitrənli], a. de matrone; d'un certain âge; respectable.

matt [mæt], a. mat.

matter ['mætə], n. matière; chose, affaire, f.; fond; sujet; (*Med.*) pus, m.; (*fig.*) importance, f.; **as a matter of fact**, le fait est que; **what is the matter?** Nothing, qu'y a-t-il? Il n'y a rien; **what is the matter with you?** Nothing, qu'avez-vous? Je n'ai rien.—v.imp. importer; **it doesn't matter**, n'importe; **it doesn't matter very much**, ce n'est pas grand'chose; **it matters little**, peu importe; **what matter?** qu'importe?

matter-of-fact ['mætərəvfækt], a. pratique, positif.

Matthew ['mæθju], Mathieu, m.

mattock ['mætək], n. pioche, f.

mattress ['mætris], n. matelas, m.

mature [mə'tjuə], a. mûr, mûri.—v.t. mûrir, faire mûrir.—v.i. mûrir; (*Comm.*) échoir.

maturity [mə'tjuəriti], n. maturité; (*Comm.*) échéance, f.

matutinal [mætju'tainl], a. matutinal, du matin.

Maud [mɔːd], Madelon, f.

maudlin ['mɔːdlin], a. pleurard, pleurnichard.

maul [mɔːl], n. maillet, m.—v.t. rosser, rouer de coups.

maul-stick ['mɔːlstik], ٦. (*Paint.*) appuimain, m.

Mauritania [mɔri'teiniə], la Mauritanie, f.

Mauritanian [mɔri'teiniən], a. mauritanien. —n. Mauritanien (*personne*), m.

Mauritian [mə'riʃən], a. mauritien.—n. Mauritien (*personne*), m.

Mauritius [mə'riʃəs], l'Île Maurice, f.

mausoleum [mɔːsə'liːəm], n. mausolée, m.

mauve [mouv], a. mauve.

maw [mɔː], n. jabot (*d'oiseau*), m.; caillette (*de ruminant*), f.

mawkish ['mɔːkiʃ], a. fade, insipide; sottement sentimental.

maxim ['mæksim], n. maxime, f.

maximum ['mæksiməm], n. (*pl.* **maxima** ['mæksimə]) maximum, m.

May [mei], mai (*mois*), m.

may [mei], v.aux. irr. pouvoir, être autorisé à; **he may go**, il peut sortir; **it may be that**, il se peut que (*with subj.*); **it might be**, cela se pourrait; **maybe**, peut-être; **may I?** puis-je? **one might as well**, autant vaudrait; **that may be**, cela se peut; **that might be**, cela pourrait être; **you might have gone there**, vous auriez pu y aller.

may-blossom ['meiblɔsəm], n. aubépine, f.

May Day ['meidei], n. premier mai, m.

mayor [mɛə], n. maire, m.

maze [meiz], n. labyrinthe, dédale; (*fig.*) embarras, m.

mazy ['meizi], a. sinueux; (*fig.*) compliqué.

mazurka [mə'zəːkə], n. mazurka, f.

me [miː], pron. me, moi.

mead [miːd], n. hydromel; (*poet.*) pré (*champ*), m.

meadow ['medou], n. pré, m., prairie, f.

meager ['miːgə], a. maigre; pauvre.

meagerness ['miːgənis], n. maigreur; pauvreté, f.

meal (1) [miːl], n. repas, m.

meal (2) [miːl], n. farine, f.

mealy ['miːli], a. farineux, poudreux.

mealy-mouthed ['miːliˌmauðd], a. doucereux.

mean (1) [miːn], a. bas, méprisable, vil, abject; médiocre (*de peu de valeur*); mesquin; pauvre, humble; sordide; avare; **a mean trick**, un vilain tour.

mean (2) [miːn], a. moyen.—n. milieu, moyen terme, m.; (*Math.*) moyenne, f.; **golden mean**, le juste milieu.

mean (3) [miːn], v.t. irr. signifier, vouloir dire, entendre; se proposer de, avoir l'intention de, vouloir (*to intend*); destiner (*pour ou de*); **do you mean it?** le voulez-vous? **what does that word mean?** que veut dire ce mot? **what do you mean?** que voulez-vous dire?—v.i. vouloir, entendre; **to mean well**, avoir de bonnes intentions.

meander [mi'ændə], *n*. détour, méandre, *m*., sinuosité, *f*.—*v.i*. serpenter.

meandering [mi'ændəriŋ], *a*. onduleux, sinueux, tortueux.

meaning ['nii:niŋ], *a*. significatif; à intentions; **well-meaning**, bien intentionné.—*n*. signification, *f*., sens, *m*.; intention, *f*., dessein, *m*.; pensée (*idée*), *f*.; **double meaning**, double sens.

meaningless ['mi:niŋlis], *a*. qui n'a pas de sens, dénué de sens.

meanly ['mi:nli], *adv*. bassement; vilement; abjectement; pauvrement; médiocrement.

meanness ['mi:nnis], *n*. bassesse; pauvreté, mesquinerie; médiocrité, *f*.

means [mi:nz], *n*. moyen, *m*., voie, *f*.; moyens, *m.pl*., fortune, *f*., ressources, *f.pl*.

meantime ['mi:ntaim], **meanwhile** ['mi:nwail], *n*. and *adv*. **in the meantime**, dans l'intervalle, en attendant, cependant, sur ces entrefaites.

measles [mi:zlz], *n.pl*. rougeole, *f*.; **German measles**, rubéole, *f*.

measurable ['meʒərəbl], *a*. mesurable.

measure ['meʒə], *n*. mesure; (*fig*.) capacité, portée, *f*.; (*Parl*.) projet de loi, *m*.; assise (*de charbon*), *f*.—*v.t*. mesurer; arpenter (*terre*); prendre mesure à (*une personne pour vêtements*); (*fig*.) considérer, toiser, métrer; *this measures ten feet*, ceci a dix pieds de longueur.

measured ['meʒəd], *a*. mesuré; égal, cadencé.

measurement ['meʒəmənt], *n*. mesurage; arpentage (*de terre*), *m*.; mesure, dimension, *f*.

meat [mi:t], *n*. viande; nourriture, *f*., aliment (*manger*), *m*.

meat-safe ['mi:tseif], *n*. garde-manger, *m*.

meaty ['mi:ti], *a*. charnu; (*fig*.) bien rempli.

Mecca ['mekə]. la Mecque, *f*.

mechanic [mi'kænik], *n*. artisan, ouvrier mécanicien, *m*.; **garage mechanic**, garagiste, *m*.

mechanical [mi'kænikəl], *a*. mécanique; d'ouvrier; machinal (*fait sans intelligence*).

mechanically [mi'kænikli], *adv*. mécaniquement; machinalement (*sans intelligence*).

mechanics [mi'kæniks], *n.pl*. mécanique, *f*.

mechanism ['mekənizm], *n*. mécanisme, *m*.

mechanization [mekənai'zeiʃən], *n*. mécanisation, *f*.

mechanize ['mekənaiz], *v.t*. mécaniser; **mechanized farming**, motoculture, *f*.; **mechanized army**, armée motorisée, *f*.

medal [medl], *n*. médaille, *f*.

medallion [mi'dæljən], *n*. médaillon, *m*.

medallist ['medlist], *n*. médaillé (*honoré*), *m*.

meddle [medl], *v.i*. se mêler (*de*), toucher (*à*), s'immiscer (*dans*).

meddler ['medlə], *n*. intrigant; officieux, *m*.

meddlesome ['medlsəm], **meddling** ['medliŋ], *a*. intrigant; officieux.

mediaeval [medi'i:vəl], *a*. du moyen âge.

medial ['mi:diəl], *a*. moyen; (*Gram*.) médial.

mediate ['mi:dieit], *v.i*. s'entremettre; s'interposer (*dans*).

mediation [mi:di'eiʃən], *n*. médiation, entremise, *f*.

mediator ['mi:dieitə], *n*. médiateur, *m*.

medical ['medikəl], *a*. médical; de médecine (*école*); en médecine (*étudiant*); **medical**

officer, officier sanitaire, *m*.; *to take medical advice*, consulter un médecin.

medicament [me'dikəmənt], *n*. médicament, *m*.

medicinal [mə'disinl], *a*. médicinal.

medicine ['medsin], *n*. médecine, *f*., médicament; (*fig*.) remède, *m*.

medicine chest ['medsintʃest], *n*. pharmacie, *f*.

medicine man ['medsinmæn], *n*. sorcier, *m*.

mediocre ['mi:dioukə], *a*. médiocre.

mediocrity [mi:di'ɔkriti], *n*. médiocrité, *f*.

meditate ['mediteit], *v.t*. se proposer de, projeter.—*v.i*. méditer (*sur*).

meditation [medi'teiʃən], *n*. méditation, *f*.

Mediterranean [meditə'reiniən], *a*. méditerrané; méditerranéen.—*n*. la Méditerranée, *f*.

medium ['mi:djəm], *a*. moyen.—*n*. (*pl*. **media** ['mi:diə], **mediums** ['mi:djəmz]) milieu, moyen, *m*.; voie, entremise; (*Math*.) moyenne proportionnelle, *f*.; agent intermédiaire; (*Spiritualism*) médium, *m*.

medlar ['medlə], *n*. nèfle (*fruit*), *f*.; néflier (*arbre*), *m*.

medley ['medli], *a*. mêlé, hétéroclite.—*n*. mélange, *m*.; confusion, *f*.; (*Mus*.) pot pourri, *m*.

medulla [mi'dʌlə], *n*. médulle, moelle, *f*.

meed [mi:d], *n*. récompense; part (*portion*), *f*.

meek [mi:k], *a*. doux, humble, soumis.

meekly ['mi:kli], *adv*. avec douceur; humblement.

meekness ['mi:knis], *n*. douceur; humilité, *f*.

meet (1) [mi:t], *v.t. irr*. rencontrer, aller à la rencontre de; trouver, recevoir (*atteindre*); faire la connaissance de; faire face à, affronter (*braver*); se présenter devant (*paraître devant*); faire honneur à (*dette*); (*fig*.) satisfaire, remplir (*demande*).—*v.i*. se rencontrer; se voir; se réunir, s'assembler; se joindre (*s'unir*); *to meet half-way*, se faire des concessions mutuelles.—*n*. rendez-vous de chasse, *m*.

meet (2) [mi:t], *a*. propre, convenable.

meeting ['mi:tiŋ], *n*. rencontre; entrevue; assemblée, réunion, *f*., meeting, *m*.; séance (*session*), *f*.; confluent (*rivières*), *m*.; jonction (*routes*), *f*.

megaton ['megətɔn], *n*. mégatonne, *f*.

melancholy ['melənkəli], *a*. mélancolique, triste, affligeant.—*n*. mélancolie, tristesse, *f*.

mellifluous [mə'lifluəs], *a*. mielleux, doucereux.

mellow ['melou], *a*. mûr, fondant (*fruit*); moelleux, doux; gris (*à moitié ivre*); meuble (*terre*).—*v.t*. mûrir, faire mûrir; ameublir (*terre*); (*fig*.) adoucir.—*v.i*. mûrir; devenir meuble (*terre*); (*fig*.) s'adoucir.

mellowness ['melouis], *n*. maturité, *f*.; moelleux, *m*.; (*fig*.) douceur, *f*.

melodious [mə'loudiəs], *a*. mélodieux.

melodiously [mə'loudiəsli], *adv*. mélodieusement.

melodrama ['melədrɑ:mə], *n*. mélodrame, *m*.

melodramatic [melədrə'mætik], *a*. mélodramatique.

melody ['melədi], *n*. mélodie, *f*., air, *m*.

melon ['melən], *n*. melon, *m*.

melt [melt], *v.t*. fondre, faire fondre; (*fig*.) attendrir.—*v.i*. fondre, se fondre; (*fig*.) s'attendrir.

melting ['meltiŋ], *a.* qui fond; fondant (*glace*); (*fig.*) attendrissant.—*n.* fusion, fonte, *f.*; attendrissement, *m.*

melting pot ['meltiŋpɔt], *n.* creuset, *m.*

member ['memba], *n.* membre; (*Parl.*) député, *m.*

membered ['membad], *a.* membré; qui a des membres; *large-membered*, membru.

membership ['membaʃip], *n.* les membres d'une société etc., *m.pl.*

membrane ['membrəi], *n.* membrane, *f.*

memento [mə'mentou], *n.* souvenir, mémento, *m.*

memoir ['memwɑ:], *n.* mémoire, *m.*

memorable ['memərəbl], *a.* mémorable.

memorandum [memə'rændəm], *n.* (*pl.* **memoranda** [memə'rændə]) note, *f.*, mémorandum; (*Comm.*) bordereau, *m.*

memorial [mi'mɔ:riəl], *a.* commémoratif.—*n.* souvenir, mémoire; monument commémoratif, *m.*; requête, pétition, *f.*

memorize ['meməraiz], *v.t.* apprendre par cœur.

memory ['meməri], *n.* mémoire, *f.*; (*colloq.*) souvenir, *m.*; *in memory of*, en souvenir de; *to the best of my memory*, autant qu'il m'en souvient.

men [MAN].

menace ['menəs], *n.* menace, *f.*—*v.t.* menacer.

menagerie [mə'nædʒəri], *n.* ménagerie, *f.*

mend [mend], *v.t.* raccommoder, réparer; corriger, améliorer; *to mend one's ways*, rentrer dans le bon chemin.—*v.i.* s'améliorer, se corriger; se rétablir (*santé*); se remettre au beau (*temps*).

mendacious [men'deiʃəs], *a.* mensonger.

mendacity [men'dæsiti], *n.* mensonge, *m.*; duplicité, *f.*

mendicant ['mendikənt], *a.* and *n.* mendiant, *m.*

mendicity [men'disiti], *n.* mendicité, *f.*

mending ['mendiŋ], *n.* raccommodage; reprisage (*des bas*), *m.*; réparation, *f.*

menial ['mi:niəl], *a.* de domestique; (*fig.*) servile.—*n.* domestique, *m.*, *f.*; (*fig.*) valet, laquais, *m.*

meningitis [menin'dʒaitis], *n.* méningite, *f.*

mental [mentl], *a.* mental; *a mental case*, un aliéné.

mentality [men'tæliti], *n.* mentalité, *f.*; esprit, *m.*

mention ['menʃən], *n.* mention, indication, *f.*—*v.t.* dire, faire mention de, mentionner, parler de; citer; *don't mention it!* il n'y a pas de quoi! *not to mention*, sans compter.

menu ['menju], *n.* menu, *m.*, carte, *f.*

mercantile ['mə:kəntail], *a.* marchand, de commerce, commerçant; *mercantile marine*, marine marchande, *f.*

mercenary ['mə:sənri], *a.* mercenaire, vénal.—*n.* mercenaire, *m.*

merchandise ['mə:tʃəndaiz], *n.* marchandise, *f.*

merchant ['mə:tʃənt], *a.* marchand; commercial.—*n.* négociant, commerçant; marchand en gros, *m.*

merchantman ['mə:tʃəntmən] (*pl.* -men [men]), **merchant ship** ['mə:tʃəntʃip], *n.* navire marchand, *m.*

merchant marine ['mə:tʃənt mə'ri:n], *n.* marine marchande, *f.*

merciful ['mə:siful], *a.* miséricordieux.

merciless ['mə:silis], *a.* sans pitié, impitoyable.

mercurial [mə:'kjuəriəl], *a.* de Mercure; de mercure; (*fig.*) mercuriel, vif.

mercury ['mə:kjuəri], *n.* mercure, *m.*

mercy ['mə:si], *n.* miséricorde; pitié; grâce, indulgence (*pardon*), *f.*; *for mercy's sake*, par grâce; *recommendation to mercy*, recours en grâce, *m.*; *sisters of mercy*, sœurs de charité, *f.pl.*

mere (1) [miə], *n.* lac, étang, *m.*

mere (2) [miə], *a.* pur, simple, seul, rien que.

merely ['miəli], *adv.* simplement, seulement, rien que.

meretricious [meri'triʃəs], *a.* d'un éclat factice (*style*).

merge [mə:dʒ], *v.t.* fondre, amalgamer, absorber.—*v.i.* se perdre (*dans*).

merger ['mə:dʒə], *n.* fusion, *f.*

meridian [mə'ridiən], *a.* méridien; de midi.—*n.* méridien; (*fig.*) apogée, *m.*

merino [mə'ri:nou], *n.* mérinos, *m.*

merit ['merit], *n.* mérite, *m.*—*v.t.* mériter.

meritorious [meri'tɔ:riəs], *a.* méritoire (*choses*); méritant (*personnes*).

meritoriously [meri'tɔ:riəsli], *adv.* d'une manière méritoire.

mermaid ['mə:meid], *n.* sirène, *f.*

merrily ['merili], *adv.* joyeusement, gaiement.

merriment ['merimənt], *n.* gaieté, réjouissance, *f.*

merry ['meri], *a.* joyeux, gai, plaisant; un peu gris; *to make merry*, se réjouir, se divertir.

merry-go-round ['merigouraund], *n.* chevaux de bois, *m.pl.*; manège, *m.*

merry-making ['merimeikiŋ], *n.* réjouissance, fête, *f.*, divertissement, *m.*

mesh [meʃ], *n.* maille, *f.*; engrenage, *m.*

mesmerism ['mezmərizm], *n.* mesmérisme, magnétisme animal, *m.*

mesmerize ['mezməraiz], *v.t.* magnétiser; hypnotiser.

mess (1) [mes], *n.* gâchis, *m.*; saleté, *f.*; *to be in a fine mess*, être dans de beaux draps; *what a mess!* quel gâchis!—*v.t.* salir.—*v.i.* faire du gâchis.

mess (2) [mes], *n.* mets, plat; (*Mil.*) mess, *m.*; *mess tin*, gamelle (individuelle), *f.*—*v.t.* donner à manger à.—*v.i.* manger; manger ensemble.

message ['mesidʒ], *n.* message, *m.*, commission, *f.*

messenger ['mesəndʒə], *n.* messager; commissionnaire; coursier (*dans un bureau*); (*fig.*) avant-coureur, *m.*

Messiah [mə'saiə], *n.* Messie, *m.*

messmate ['mesmeit], *n.* camarade de table, *m.*

messy ['mesi], *a.* sale; graisseux, salissant.

metabolism [mə'tæbolizm], *n.* métabolisme, *m.*

metal [metl], *n.* métal; cailloutis, empierrement (*pour routes*), *m.*

metalled [metld], *a.* empierré.

metallic [mə'tælik], *a.* métallique.

metallurgy [me'tælədʒi], *n.* métallurgie, *f.*

metamorphosis [metəmɔ:'fəsis], *n.* métamorphose, *f.*

metaphor ['metəfə], *n.* métaphore, *f.*

metaphysical [metə'fizikl], *a.* métaphysique.

metaphysics [metə'fiziks], *n.pl.* métaphysique, *f.*

mete [mi:t], *v.t.* mesurer; *to mete out*, distribuer, décerner (*prix*); assigner (*punitions*).

meteor ['mi:tiə], *n.* météore, *m.*

meteoric [mi:ti'ɔrik], *a.* météorique.

meteorite ['mi:tiərait], *n.* météorite, *m.* ou *f.*

meteorological [mi:tiərə'lɔdʒikl], *a.* météorologique.

meteorologist [mi:tiə'rɔlədʒist], *n.* météorologiste, *m., f.*

meteorology [mi:tiə'rɔlədʒi], *n.* météorologie, *f.*

meter ['mi:tə], *n.* mesureur; compteur (*de gaz*), *m.*

method ['meθəd], *n.* méthode, *f.*; procédé, *m.*; modalité; (*fig.*) manière, *f.*, ordre, *m.*

methodical [mə'θɔdikəl], *a.* méthodique.

methylate ['meθileit], *v.t.* méthyler; *methylated spirit*, alcool à brûler, *m.*

meticulous [mə'tikjuləs], *a.* méticuleux.

meticulousness [mə'tikjuləsnis], *n.* méticulosité, *f.*

metre ['mi:tə], *n.* mètre; (*Pros.*) vers, *m.*, mesure, *f.*

metric ['metrik], *a.* métrique.

metrical ['metrikl], *a.* métrique; en vers.

metropolis [mə'trɔpəlis], *n.* capitale, métropole, *f.*

metropolitan [metrə'pɔlitən], *a.* de la capitale, métropolitain.

mettle [metl], *n.* courage, cœur, *m.*; fougue, ardeur, vivacité, *f.*; caractère, *m.*; *to put someone on his mettle*, piquer quelqu'un d'honneur.

mettled [metld], **mettlesome** ['metlsəm], *a.* fougueux, ardent, vif.

mew (1) [mju:], *n.* mue, cage, *f.*; (*pl.*) écuries, *f.pl.*; impasse, ruelle (*derrière les grandes maisons de ville*), *f.*—*v.t.* enfermer (*emprisonner*).

mew (2) [mju:], *v.i.* miauler (*chat*).

mew (3) [mju:], *n.* (*Orn.*) mouette, *f.*

mewing ['mju:iŋ], *n.* miaulement (*de chat*), *m.*

Mexican ['meksikn], *a.* mexicain.—*n.* Mexican (*personne*), *m.*

Mexico ['meksikou], le Mexique (*pays*); *Mexico City*, Mexico, *m.*

miasma [mi'æzmə], *n.* (*pl.* **miasmata** [mi'æzmətə]) miasme, *m.*

mica ['maikə], *n.* mica, *m.*

mice [MOUSE].

Michael [maikl]. Michel, *m.*

Michaelmas ['miklməs]. la Saint-Michel, *f.*

microbe ['maikroub], *n.* microbe, *m.*

microphone ['maikrəfoun], *n.* microphone, *m.*

microscope ['maikrəskoup], *n.* microscope, *m.*

microscopic [maikrə'skɔpik], *a.* microscopique.

mid [mid], *a.* du milieu, moyen.—*prep.* au milieu de.

mid-air [mid'eə], *n.* milieu de l'air, haut des airs, *m.*; *in mid-air*, entre ciel et terre.

midday ['middei], *a.* de midi.—*n.* midi, *m.*

middle [midl], *a.* du milieu, central; moyen; *Middle Ages*, Moyen Âge, *m.*; *middle class*, bourgeoisie, *f.*; *middle course*, moyen terme, *m.*—*n.* milieu, centre, *m.*; ceinture, *f.*

middle-aged ['midleidʒd], *a.* entre deux âges.

middle-man ['midlmæn], *n.* (*pl.* **-men** [men]) intermédiaire, tiers, *m.*

middling ['midliŋ], *a.* médiocre, passable, assez bien (*santé*); (*Comm.*) bon, ordinaire.

midget ['midʒit], *n.* nain, nabot, *m.*

midland ['midlənd], *a.* de l'intérieur, du centre.

Mid-Lent ['mid'lent], mi-carême, *f.*

midnight ['midnait], *a.* de minuit.—*n.* minuit, *m.*

midriff ['midrif], *n.* diaphragme, *m.*

midshipman ['midʃipmən], *n.* (*pl.* **-men** [men]) aspirant de marine, *m.*

midships ['midʃips], [AMIDSHIPS].

midst [midst], *n.* milieu; (*fig.*) fort, sein, cœur, *m.*—*prep.* au milieu de, parmi.

midstream ['midstri:m], *n.* milieu du courant; milieu du fleuve, *m.*

midsummer ['midsʌmə], *n.* milieu de l'été, cœur de l'été, *m.*; *Midsummer Day*, la Saint-Jean, *f.*

midway ['midwei], *a.* and *adv.* à mi-chemin; à mi-côte (*d'une colline*).

midwife ['midwaif], *n.* (*pl.* **midwives** ['midwaivz]) sage-femme, accoucheuse, *f.*

midwifery ['midwifri], *n.* obstétrique, *f.*

midwinter ['mid'wintə], *n.* fort de l'hiver, *m.*

mien [mi:n], *n.* mine, *f.*, air, *m.*

might (1) [mait], *past* [MAY].

might (2) [mait], *n.* force, puissance, *f.*

mightily ['maitili], *adv.* fortement, vigoureusement; extrêmement.

mighty ['maiti], *a.* fort, puissant; grand, important.—*adv.* fort, très, extrêmement.

mignonette [minjə'net], *n.* réséda, *m.*

migraine ['mi:grein], *n.* (*Med.*) migraine, *f.*

migrate [mai'greit], *v.i.* émigrer.

migration [mai'greiʃən], *n.* migration, *f.*

migratory ['maigrətəri], *a.* migratoire; migrateur.

milch [miltʃ], *a.* à lait, laitière.

mild [maild], *a.* doux; léger (*boisson, tabac etc.*); bénin.

mildew ['mildju:], *n.* rouille, moisissure, *f.*, taches d'humidité, *f.pl.*—*v.t.* gâter par l'humidité; souiller, tacher.

mildly ['maildli], *adv.* doucement, avec douceur; modérément.

mildness ['maildnis], *n.* douceur, *f.*

mile [mail], *n.* mille, *m.*

mileage ['mailidʒ], *n.* distance en milles, *f.*; prix par mille, *m.*

milestone ['mailstoun], *n.* borne milliaire, borne kilométrique, *f.*

militant ['militənt], *a.* militant.—*n.* activiste, *m., f.*

militarism ['militərizm], *n.* militarisme, *m.*

military ['militəri], *a.* militaire.—*n.* **the military**, les militaires, *m.pl.*, la troupe, *f.*

militate ['militeit], *v.i.* militer (*contre*).

militia [mi'liʃə], *n.* milice, *f.*

milk [milk], *n.* lait, *m.*; *milk and water*, lait coupé; (*fig.*) fade, insipide, sans caractère; *skim milk*, lait écrémé; *to come home with the milk*, rentrer à la première heure.—*v.t.* traire.

milk can [milkkæn], *n.* pot au lait, *m.*

milkiness ['milkinis], *n.* nature laiteuse; (*fig.*) douceur, *f.*

milkmaid ['milkmeid], *n.* laitière, *f.*

milkman ['milkmən], *n.* (*pl.* -**men** [men]) laitier, *m.*

milk pail ['milkpeil], *n.* séau à lait, *m.*

milksop ['milksɔp], *n.* (*colloq.*) poule mouillée, *f.*

milky ['milki], *a.* laiteux; *Milky Way*, voie lactée, *f.*

mill [mil], *n.* moulin, *m.*; filature, fabrique (*usine*), *f.—v.t.* moudre; (*Coin.*) estamper.— *v.i.* fourmiller (*foule*).

millenary ['milənari], *a.* millénaire.

millennium [mi'leniəm], *n.* millénaire, *m.*, mille ans; les temps messianiques, *m.pl.*

miller ['milə], *n.* meunier, *m.*

millet ['milit], *n.* millet, mil, *m.*

millimetre ['milimi:tə], *n.* millimètre, *m.*

milliner ['milinə], *n.* marchande de modes; modiste, *f.*

millinery ['milinri], *n.* modes, *f.pl.*

million ['miljən], *n.* million, *m.*

millionaire [miljə'nɛə], *n.* millionnaire, *m., f.*

millstone ['milstoun], *n.* meule de moulin, *f.*

mime [maim], *n.* mime, *m.—v.t.* mimer (*une scène*).—*v.i.* jouer par gestes.

mimic ['mimik], *a.* imitateur, mimique; imitatif (*animaux*).—*n.* mime, imitateur, *m.* —*v.t.* contrefaire, imiter.

mimicry ['mimikri], *n.* mimique, imitation, *f.*

minatory ['minətəri], *a.* menaçant.

mince [mins], *v.t.* hacher menu.—*v.i.* marcher à petits pas; minauder (*parler d'une façon affectée*).—*n.* hachis, haché, *m*

mincemeat ['minsmi:t], *n.* pâte d'épices, *f.*, mincemeat, *m.*

mince pie ['mins'pai], *n.* tartelette au mincemeat, *f.*

mincing ['minsiŋ], *a.* affecté, minaudier.

mind [maind], *n.* esprit, *m.*, intelligence; envie, *f.*, désir (*inclination*), *m.*; pensée, *f.*, avis (*opinion*); souvenir (*mémoire*), *m.*; songer à, faire attention à; regarder à (*s'occuper de*); se défier de (*se douter de*); obéir à, écouter (*se soumettre à*); soigner, garder (*veiller sur*); surveiller, observer (*étudier*); *mind your own business*, mêlez-vous de ce qui vous regarde; *never mind*, peu importe, tant pis.

minded ['maindid], *a.* disposé, enclin.

mindful ['maindful], *a.* attentif (à), soigneux (*de*); qui se souvient (*de*).

mindfulness ['maindfulnis], *n.* attention, *f.*

mindless ['maindlis], *a.* inattentif (à); sans esprit.

mine (1) [main], *pron.poss.* le mien, *m.*, la mienne, *f.*; les miens, *m.pl.*, les miennes, *f.pl.—a.* à moi; *a friend of mine*, un de mes amis.

mine (2) [main], *n.* mine, *f.—v.t.* miner, saper.

mine-layer ['mainleiə], *n.* (*Navy*) mouilleur de mines, *m.*

miner ['mainə], *n.* mineur, *m.*

mineral ['minərəl], *a.* and *n.* minéral, *m.*

mineralogy [minə'rælədʒi], *n.* minéralogie, *f.*

mine-sweeper ['mainswi:pə], *n.* (*Navy*) dragueur de mines, *m.*

mingle [miŋgl], *v.t.* mélanger, mêler.—*v.i.* se mêler, se mélanger (*avec, dans* ou *en*).

mingling ['miŋgliŋ], *n.* mélange, *m.*

miniature [mini(ə)tʃə], *a.* en miniature.—*n.* miniature, *f.*

minim ['minim], *n.* goutte; (*Mus.*) blanche, *f.*

minimum ['miniməm], *n.* (*pl.* **minima** ['minimə]) minimum, *m.*

mining ['mainiŋ], *a.* des mines; de mineur, minier.—*n.* travail dans les mines, *m.*

minion ['minjən], *n.* favori, *m.*, favorite, *f.*

minister ['ministə], *n.* ministre; (*Eccles.*) pasteur, *m.—v.t.* administrer; fournir.—*v.i.* servir (à); (*Eccles.*) officier à.

ministerial [minis'tiəriəl], *a.* de ministère, ministériel.

ministration [minis'treiʃən], *n.* ministère; service, *m.*

ministry ['ministri], *n.* ministère, département, *m.*

mink [miŋk], *n.* vison, *m.*

minnow ['minou], *n.* vairon, *m.*

minor ['mainə], *a.* moindre; secondaire; (*Mus., Geog. etc.*) mineur.—*n.* mineur, *m.*

Minorca [mi'nɔːkə]. Minorque, *f.*

minority [mai'nɔriti], *n.* minorité, *f.*

minster ['minstə], *n.* cathédrale, église abbatiale, *f.*

minstrel ['minstrəl], *n.* ménestrel; (*fam.*) poète, musicien, chanteur, *m.*

mint (1) [mint], *n.* menthe, *f.*; *peppermint*, menthe poivrée.

mint (2) [mint], *n.* *The Mint*, la Monnaie, *f.* —*v.t.* monnayer, frapper; (*fig.*) forger.

mintage ['mintidʒ], *n.* objet monnayé, *m.*

minting ['mintiŋ], *n.* monnayage, *m.*

minuet [minju'et], *n.* menuet, *m.*

minus ['mainəs], *prep.* moins; sans (*n'ayant pas de*).—*n.* moins, *m.*

minute (1) [mai'nju:t], *a.* menu, minuscule, très petit; minutieux.

minute (2) ['minit], *n.* minute, *f.*; instant, moment, *m.*; note, *f.*; (*pl.*) procès-verbal, compte-rendu (*d'une réunion*), *m.—v.t.* minuter, prendre note de.

minute-book ['minitbuk], *n.* journal, *m.*

minute hand ['minithænd], *n.* grande aiguille, *f.*

minutely [mai'nju:tli], *adv.* minutieusement; exactement; en détail.

minuteness [mai'nju:tnis], *n.* petitesse; exactitude, *f.*; détails minutieux, *m.pl.*

minx [miŋks], *n.* coquine, friponne, *f.*

miracle ['mirəkl], *n.* miracle, *m.*

miraculous [mi'rækjuləs], *a.* miraculeux.

mirage [mi'rɑːʒ], *n.* mirage, *m.*

mire [maiə], *n.* boue, bourbe, fange, vase, *f.*

miry ['maiəri], *a.* fangeux, bourbeux.

mirror ['mirə], *n.* miroir, *m.*, glace, *f.*; *rearview mirror*, rétroviseur, *m.* —*v.t.* refléter

mirth [mə:θ], *n.* gaieté, hilarité, *f.*, rire, *m.*

mirthful ['mə:θful], *a.* gai, joyeux.

misadventure [misəd'ventʃə], *n.* mésaventure, *f.*, contretemps, *m.*

misanthropist [mi'sænθrəpist], *n.* misanthrope, *m., f.*

misanthropy [mi'sænθrəpi], *n.* misanthropie, *f.*

misapplication [misæpli'keiʃən], *n.* mauvaise application, *f.*

misapply [misə'plai], *v.t.* mal appliquer, détourner (*fonds etc.*).

misapprehend [misæpri'hend], *v.t.* comprendre mal.

misapprehension [misæpri'henʃən], *n.* malentendu, *m.*, méprise, *f.*

misappropriate [misəˈprouprieit], v.t. détourner.

misappropriation [misəprouprˈeiʃən], n. détournement, mauvais emploi, m.

misbehave [misbiˈheiv], v.i. se conduire mal.

misbehavior [misbiˈheivjə], n. mauvaise conduite, f.

miscalculate [misˈkælkjuleit], v.t. calculer mal.

miscalculation [misˈkælkjuˈleiʃən], n. calcul erroné; mécompte, m.

miscarriage [misˈkæridʒ], n. insuccès, coup manqué, m.; fausse couche (de femme), f.

miscarry [misˈkæri], v.i. manquer, échouer; faire une fausse couche (femme).

miscellaneous [misiˈleinjəs], a. varié, divers; général; **miscellaneous news**, faits divers, m.pl.

miscellany [miˈseləni], n. (pl. **miscellanies** [miˈseləniz]) mélange, m.; mélanges (livre), m.pl.

mischance [misˈtʃɑːns], n. malheur, accident, m., mésaventure, infortune, f.

mischief [ˈmistʃif], n. mal, dommage, dégât, tort, m.

mischief-maker [ˈmistʃifmeikə], n. brouillon, m.

mischievous [ˈmistʃivəs], a. méchant, malicieux; malfaisant, mauvais, nuisible (chose); espiègle (enfant).

mischievously [ˈmistʃivəsli], adv. méchamment.

mischievousness [ˈmistʃivəsnis], n. méchanceté; espièglerie (d'enfant), f.

misconceive [miskənˈsiːv], v.t., v.i. mal concevoir, juger mal.

misconception [miskənˈsepʃən], n. malentendu, m.

misconduct [misˈkɔndʌkt], n. mauvaise conduite, f.—[miskənˈdʌkt], v.t. conduire mal; **to misconduct oneself**, se conduire mal.

misconstruction [miskənˈstrʌkʃən], n. fausse interprétation, f., contresens, m.

misconstrue [miskənˈstruː], v.t. mal interpréter.

miscount [misˈkaunt], v.t. compter mal.—v.i. faire une erreur de compte.—n. mécompte, m.

miscreant [ˈmiskriənt], n. mécréant, m; (fig.) misérable, m., f.

misdeal [misˈdiːl], v.t. maldonner.—n. maldonne, f.

misdeed [misˈdiːd], n. méfait, m.

misdemean [misdəˈmiːn], v.r. **to misdemean oneself**, se comporter mal.

misdemeanor [misdəˈmiːnə], n. délit, crime, m., offense, f.

misdirect [misdiˈrekt], v.t. mal diriger, renseigner mal; mettre une fausse adresse à (lettre).

misdoing [misˈduːiŋ], n. méfait, m.

miser [ˈmaizə], n. avare, m., f.

miserable [ˈmizərəbl], a. misérable, pitoyable, malheureux; mesquin (piètre).

miserliness [ˈmaizəlinis], n. avarice, f.

miserly [ˈmaizəli], a. d'avare, avare, sordide.

misery [ˈmizəri], n. misère, f.; (fig.) tourment; supplice, m.; **to put out of misery**, mettre fin aux souffrances (de).

misfire [misˈfaiə], v.i. rater; (Motor.) avoir des ratés.—n. raté d'allumage, m.

misfit [ˈmisfit], n. vêtement manqué; inadapté (personne), m.

misfortune [misˈfɔːtʃən], n. malheur, m., infortune, f.

misgiving [misˈgiviŋ], n. pressentiment, soupçon, doute, m.; inquiétude, f.

misgovern [misˈgʌvən], v.t. gouverner mal.

misgovernment [misˈgʌvənmənt], n. mauvais gouvernement, m.

misguided [misˈgaidid], a. malencontreux; peu judicieux; dévoyé.

mishandle [misˈhændl], v.t. manier mal, malmener.

mishap [misˈhæp], n. contretemps, malheur, m., mésaventure, f.

misinform [misinˈfɔːm], v.t. mal renseigner.

misinterpret [misinˈtəːprit], v.t. interpréter mal.

misjudge [misˈdʒʌdʒ], v.t. juger mal, méjuger.

mislay [misˈlei], v.t. irr. (conjug. like LAY) égarer.

mislead [misˈliːd], v.t. irr. (conjug. like LEAD) égarer; induire en erreur, fourvoyer; tromper.

misleading [misˈliːdiŋ], a. trompeur.

mismanage [misˈmænidʒ], v.t. diriger mal.—v.i. s'y prendre mal, s'arranger mal (pour).

mismanagement [misˈmænidʒmənt], n. mauvaise administration, f.

misnomer [misˈnoumə], n. faux nom, m.

misogynist [misˈɔdʒinist], n. misogyne, m.

misogyny [misˈɔdʒini], n. misogynie, f.

misplace [misˈpleis], v.t. mal placer; déplacer.

misprint [ˈmisprint], n. faute d'impression, f.—[misˈprint], v.t. imprimer incorrectement.

mispronounce [misprəˈnauns], v.t. prononcer mal.

mispronunciation [misprənʌnsiˈeiʃən], n. prononciation incorrecte, f.

misquote [misˈkwout], v.t. citer à faux.

misread [misˈriːd], v.t. irr. (conjug. like READ) mal lire, mal interpréter.

misrepresent [misrepriˈzent], v.t. représenter mal, dénaturer.

misrepresentation [misreprizenˈteiʃən], n. faux rapport, m.

misrule [misˈruːl], n. désordre; mauvais gouvernement, m.

miss (1) [mis], n. mademoiselle, demoiselle, f.

miss (2) [mis], n. manque, m.; perte (privation); erreur (méprise), f.; coup manqué, m.—v.t. manquer; omettre; s'apercevoir de l'absence de, regretter vivement, ne plus trouver; **I miss my friend very much**, mon ami me manque beaucoup.—v.i. manquer; ne pas réussir, échouer, se tromper; **to be missing**, être absent, manquer.

missal [misl], n. missel, m.

misshapen [misˈʃeipən], a. difforme.

missile [ˈmisail], a. de jet, de trait.—n. projectile, m.; **guided missile**, engin téléguidé, m.

missing [ˈmisiŋ], a. absent, perdu, disparu.

mission [ˈmiʃən], n. mission, f.

missionary [ˈmiʃənəri], a. des missions.—n. missionnaire, m., f.

missive [ˈmisiv], a. missive.—n. missive, lettre, f.

misspell [misˈspel], v.t. irr. (conjug. like SPELL) épeler mal.

misspelling [mis'speliŋ], *n.* faute d'orthographe, *f.*

misspend [mis'spend], *v.t.* irr. (*conjug. like* SPEND) employer mal; gaspiller.

misstate [mis'steit], *v.t.* rapporter incorrectement.

misstatement [mis'steitmənt], *n.* rapport erroné, *m.*

mist [mist], *n.* brume; buée (*sur une glace*), *f.*; *Scotch mist*, bruine, *f.*—*v.t.* couvrir (*une glace*) de buée.—*v.i.* se couvrir de buée.

mistake [mis'teik], *v.t.* (*conjug. like* TAKE) se tromper de *ou* sur, se méprendre à *ou* sur; prendre (*pour*).—*v.i.* se tromper, se méprendre, s'abuser.—*n.* erreur, méprise, faute; bévue (*erreur grossière*), *f.*; *to make a mistake*, se tromper.

mistaken [mis'teikən] *a.* qui se trompe; faux, erroné (*chose*).

mistimed [mis'taimd], *a.* inopportun.

mistletoe [mis'ltou], *n.* gui, *m.*

mistress ['mistris], *n.* maîtresse; patronne; institutrice (*d'école primaire*), *f.*; *headmistress*, directrice, *f.*

mistrust [mis'trʌst], *n.* méfiance, *f.*, soupçon, *m.*—*v.t.* se méfier de, soupçonner.

mistrustful [mis'trʌstful], *a.* méfiant.

misty ['misti], *a.* brumeux; vaporeux (*lumière*), (*fig.*) confus.

misunderstand [misʌndə'stænd], *v.t.* irr. (*conjug. like* STAND) mal comprendre, entendre mal, se méprendre sur.

misunderstanding [misʌndə'stændiŋ], *n.* malentendu (*manque de compréhension*), *m.*; mésintelligence (*querelle*), *f.*

misuse [mis'ju:s], *n.* abus, *m.*—[mis'ju:z], *v.t.* mésuser de; maltraiter (*faire du mal à*).

mite (1) [mait], *n.* (*Zool.*) mite, *f.*

mite (2) [mait], *n.* denier (*argent*); (*fig.*) rien, *m.*, obole, *f.*; (*fam.*) petit gosse, *m.*

miter ['maitə], *n.* mitre, *f.*

mitigate ['mitigeit], *v.t.* mitiger, adoucir, modérer.

mitigating ['mitigeitiŋ], *a.* adoucissant, atténuant.

mitigation [miti'geiʃən], *n.* mitigation, *f.*, adoucissement, *m.*

mitten [mitn], *n.* mitaine, *f.*

mix [miks], *v.t.* mêler, mélanger; couper (*boissons*); *to mix up*, mêler, embrouiller, confondre.—*v.i.* se mélanger, se mêler (*de*); s'associer (*à*).

mixed [mikst], *a.* mélangé, mêlé (*de*); mixte.

mixture ['mikstʃə], *n.* mélange, *m.*; (*Pharm.*) potion, mixture, *f.*

mix-up ['miksʌp], *n.* confusion, *f.*, embrouillement, *m.*; (*pop.*) pagaïe, *f.*

mizzen [mizn], *n.* artimon, *m.*

mizzen-mast ['mizn mɑ:st], *n.* mât d'artimon, *m.*

moan [moun], *n.* gémissement, *m.*, plainte; (*fig.*) lamentation, *f.*—*v.t.* gémir de *ou* sur; se lamenter sur.—*v.i.* gémir, (*fig.*) se lamenter; (*pop.*) grognonner.

moat [mout], *n.* fossé, *m.*, douve, *f.*

mob [mɔb], *n.* foule; populace, canaille, *f.*—*v.t.* houspiller, malmener; assiéger.

mobile ['moubail], *a.* mobile.

mobility [mou'biliti], *n.* mobilité; légèreté (*inconstance*), *f.*

mobilization [moubilai'zeiʃən], *n.* mobilisation, *f.*

mobilize ['moubilaiz], *v.t.* mobiliser.

mock [mɔk], *v.t.* se moquer de; narguer.—*v.i.* railler.—*a.* dérisoire; faux, simulé.

mocker ['mɔkə], *n.* moqueur, *m.*

mockery ['mɔkəri], *n.* moquerie, *f.*

mocking-bird ['mɔkiŋbə:d], *n.* oiseau moqueur, *m.*

mode [moud], *n.* mode, façon, manière, *f.*

model [mɔdl], *n.* modèle; mannequin, *m.*—*v.t.* modeler; (*Cloth.*) présenter des vêtements (*défilé de mannequins*).

moderate ['mɔdərit], *a.* modéré; modique, ordinaire, passable, médiocre.—['mɔdəreit], *v.t.* modérer, adoucir, tempérer.—*v.i.* se modérer.

moderately ['mɔdəritli], *adv.* modérément, passablement.

moderation [mɔdə'reiʃən], *n.* modération, *f.*

moderator ['mɔdəreitə], *n.* modérateur, *m.*

modern ['mɔdən], *a.* and *n.* moderne, *m.*, *f.*; *modern languages*, langues vivantes, *f.pl.*

modernize ['mɔdənaiz], *v.t.* moderniser.

modest ['mɔdist], *a.* modeste; pudique; modéré (*demandes etc.*).

modesty ['mɔdisti], *n.* modestie, *f.*

modicum ['mɔdikəm], *n.* petite portion, *f.*

modification [mɔdifi'keiʃən], *n.* modification, *f.*

modify ['mɔdifai], *v.t.* modifier.

modulate ['mɔdjuleit], *v.t.* moduler.

modulation [mɔdju'leiʃən], *n.* modulation, *f.*

mohair ['mouhɛə], *n.* poil de chèvre angora, mohair, *m.*

Mohammed [mo'hæməd]. Mahomet, *m.*

Mohammedan [mo'hæmədən], *a.* mahométan.—*n.* Mahométan, *m.*

Mohammedanism [mo'hæmədənizm], *n.* mahométisme, *m.*

moist [mɔist], *a.* moite, humide.

moisten [mɔisn], *v.t.* humecter; mouiller.

moisture ['mɔistʃə], **moistness** ['mɔistnis], *n.* moiteur, humidité, *f.*

mol-, see **moul-**.

molasses [mo'læsiz], *n.pl.* mélasse, *f.*

mole (1) [moul], *n.* taupe (*animal*), *f.*

mole (2) [moul], *n.* tache, *f.*, grain de beauté (*sur la peau*), *m.*

mole (3) [moul], *n.* môle (*jetée*), *m.*

molecular [mo'lekjulə], *a.* moléculaire.

molecule ['mɔlikju:l], *n.* molécule, *f.*

mole-hill ['moulhil], *n.* taupinière, *f.*

moleskin ['moulskin], *n.* peau de taupe, molesquine, *f.*, velours de coton, *m.*

molest [mo'lest], *v.t.* molester; vexer.

mollify ['mɔlifai], *v.t.* amollir; adoucir.

molten ['moulten], *a.* fondu.

moment ['moumənt], *n.* moment, instant, *m.*; (*fig.*) importance, *f.*; *at the present moment*, actuellement; *at this moment*, en ce moment; *not for a moment*, pour rien au monde; *of no moment*, d'aucune importance; *the moment that*, dès que, aussitôt que.

momentarily ['mouməntərili], *adv.* momentanément.

momentary ['mouməntəri], *a.* momentané.

momentous [mo'mentəs], *a.* important, d'une importance capitale.

momentum [mo'mentəm], *n.* (*Phys.*) force vive; vitesse acquise, *f.*; élan, *m.*

monarch ['mɔnək], *n.* monarque, *m.*

monarchy [ˈmɔnəki], n. monarchie, f.
monastery [ˈmɔnəstri], n. monastère, m.
monastic [məˈnæstik], a. monastique.
monasticism [məˈnæstisizm], n. mona-chisme, m.

Monday [ˈmʌndi], lundi, m.
monetary [ˈmʌnitəri], a. monétaire.
money [ˈmʌni], n. argent, m.; monnaie, f., espèces (*pièces*), f.pl.; *made of money*, cousu d'or; *ready money*, argent comp-tant; *to make money*, gagner de l'argent.
money box [ˈmʌnibɔks], n. tirelire, f.
money-changer [ˈmʌnitʃeindʒə], n. chan-geur, m.
moneyed [ˈmʌnid], a. riche.
money grubber [ˈmʌnigrʌbə], n. grippe-sou, m.
money-lender [ˈmʌnilendə], n. prêteur d'argent, m.
money market [ˈmʌniməːkit], n. bourse, f.
money order [ˈmʌniɔːdə], n. mandat, m.
Mongol [ˈmɔŋgɔl], a. mongol.—n. Mongol (*personne*), m.
Mongolia [mɔŋˈgouliə], la Mongolie, f.
Mongolian [mɔŋˈgouliən], a. mongol.—n. mongol (*langue*); Mongol (*personne*), m.
mongrel [ˈmʌŋgrəl], a. métis.—n. métis, m., métisse, f.
monitor [ˈmɔnitə], n. moniteur, m.
monk [mʌŋk], n. moine, m.
monkey [ˈmʌŋki], n. singe, m.; guenon, f.
monkey wrench [ˈmʌŋkirentʃ], n. clé an-glaise, f.
monocle [ˈmɔnəkl], n. monocle, m.
monogram [ˈmɔnəgræm], n. monogramme, m.
monologue [ˈmɔnələg], n. monologue, m.
monoplane [ˈmɔnəplein], n. monoplan, m.
monopoly [məˈnɔpəli], n. monopole, accapa-rement, m.
monorail [ˈmɔnəreil], n. monorail, m.
monotonous [məˈnɔtənəs], a. monotone.
monotonously [məˈnɔtənəsli], adv. avec monotonie.
monotony [məˈnɔtəni], n. monotonie, f.
monsoon [mɔnˈsuːn], n. mousson, f.
monster [ˈmɔnstə], n. monstre, m.
monstrosity [mɔnˈstrɔsiti], n. monstruosité, f.
monstrous [ˈmɔnstrəs], a. monstrueux; prodigieux.
month [mʌnθ], n. mois, m.; *calendar month*, mois civil; *the day of the month*, le quantième du mois, m.
monthly [ˈmʌnθli], a. mensuel, de tous les mois.—n. (*fam.*) revue mensuelle, f.—adv. tous les mois, par mois.
monument [ˈmɔnjumənt], n. monument, m.
monumental [mɔnjuˈmentl], a. monumental.
moo [muː], v.i. meugler, beugler.—n. meugle-ment, m.
mood [muːd], n. humeur, f.; (*Gram. etc.*) mode, m.
moody [ˈmuːdi], a. de mauvaise humeur, triste.
moon [muːn], n. lune, f.; *by the light of the moon*, au clair de la lune.—v.i. muser; *to moon about*, flâner.
moonbeam [ˈmuːnbiːm], n. rayon de lune, m.
moonlight [ˈmuːnlait], n. clair de lune, m.
moonlit [ˈmuːnlit], a. éclairé par la lune.

moonshine [ˈmuːnʃain], n. clair de lune, m.; (*fig.*) chimères, f.pl.
moonstrike [ˈmuːnstraik], n. alunissage, m.
moonstruck [ˈmuːnstrʌk], a. lunatique.
Moor [muə], n. Maure, m., f.
moor (1) [muə], n. lande, bruyère, f.; marais, m.
moor (2) [muə], v.t. amarrer.—v.i. s'amarrer.
moor hen [ˈmuəhen], n. poule d'eau, f.
moorings [ˈmuəriŋz], n. amarres, f.pl., mouillage, m.
moorland [ˈmuələnd], n. lande, bruyère, f., marais, m.
moose [muːs], n. élan du Canada, m.
moot [muːt], v.t. discuter, débattre, con-troverser.—a. *moot point*, question discu-table, f.
mop [mɔp], n. balai à laver, m.—v.t. nettoyer avec un balai, éponger; *to mop one's face*, s'éponger la figure.
mope [moup], v.i. s'ennuyer; être hébété.
moping [ˈmoupiŋ], a. triste, hébété.
moral [ˈmɔrəl], a. moral.—n. morale; moralité, f.; (*pl.*) mœurs, f.pl.
morale [mɔˈrɑːl], n. moral (*de militaires etc.*), m.
morality [məˈræliti], n. morale; moralité, f.
moralize [ˈmɔrəlaiz], v.i. moraliser.
morally [ˈmɔrəli], adv. moralement.
morass [məˈræs], n. marais, m., fondrière, f.
morbid [ˈmɔːbid], a. maladif, malsain, morbide.
morbidly [ˈmɔːbidli], adv. morbidement.
morbidity [mɔːˈbiditi], **morbidness** [ˈmɔː-bidnis], n. état maladif, état morbide, m.
more [mɔː], a. and adv. plus; plus de; plus nombreux; encore; davantage; *more and more*, de plus en plus; *more than*, plus que, plus de (*suivi d'un nombre*); *no more*, pas davantage; *no more of that!* arrêtez cela! *once more*, encore une fois; *some more*, encore un peu, davantage.
moreover [mɔːˈrouvə], adv. de plus, d'ail-leurs, en outre.
moribund [ˈmɔribʌnd], a. moribond.
Mormon [ˈmɔːmən], a. mormon.—n. Mor-mon (*personne*), m.
morn [mɔːn], n. (*poet.*) matin, m., aurore, f.
morning [ˈmɔːniŋ], n. matin, m.—n. matin, m., matinée, f.; *good morning*, bonjour, m.; *in the morning*, le matin; *the next morning*, le lendemain matin.
Moroccan [məˈrɔkən], a. marocain.—n. Marocain (*personne*), m.
Morocco [məˈrɔkou], le Maroc, m.
morocco leather [məˈrɔkouˈleðə], n. maro-quin, m.
moron [ˈmɔːrən], n. crétin, idiot, m.
morose [məˈrous], a. morose.
morphia [ˈmɔːfiə], **morphine** [ˈmɔːfiːn], n. morphine, f.
morrow [ˈmɔrou], n. (*poet.*) demain, lende-main, m.; *tomorrow*, demain.
morsel [ˈmɔːsl], n. morceau, m.
mortal [ˈmɔːtl], a. mortel, funeste (*fatal*); des mortels, humain (*terrestre*); à outrance, à mort (*combat*); *any mortal thing*, n'importe quoi.—n. mortel, m.
mortality [mɔːˈtæliti], n. mortalité; humanité, f.
mortally [ˈmɔːtəli], adv. mortellement, à mort.
mortar [ˈmɔːtə], n. mortier, m.

mortgage ['mɔːgidʒ], n. hypothèque, f.—
v.t. hypothéquer.
mortician [mɔːˈtiʃən], n. (Am.) entrepreneur
de pompes funèbres, m.
mortification [mɔːtifiˈkeiʃən], n. mortification; (Path.) gangrène, f.
mortify ['mɔːtifai], v.t. mortifier; (Path.)
faire gangrener.—v.i. se gangrener.
mortise ['mɔːtis], n. mortaise, f.—v.t. mor-
taiser.
mortuary ['mɔːtjuəri], a. mortuaire.—n.
morgue, f., dépôt mortuaire, m.
mosaic [moˈzeiik], a. and n. mosaïque, f.
Moscow ['mɔskou]. Moscou, m.
Moses ['mouziz]. Moïse, m.
Moslem ['mɔzlim, 'mɔzləm], a. musulman.—
n. Musulman (personne), m.
mosque [mɔsk], n. mosquée, f.
mosquito [mɔsˈkiːtou], n. moustique, m.
mosquito net [mɔsˈkiːtounet], n. moustiquaire, f.
moss [mɔs], n. mousse, f.; marais, m.; tourbière (bog), m.
moss-grown ['mɔsgroun], a. mossy ['mɔsi], a.
couvert de mousse, moussu.
moss rose ['mɔsrouz], n. rose moussue, f.
most [moust], a. le plus; le plus grand; *most
men*, la plupart des hommes; *the most
part*, la plus grande partie.—adv. le plus,
plus; très, fort; *a most valuable book*,
un livre des plus précieux; *most likely*,
très probablement.—n. la plupart, f.; le
plus grand nombre, m.
mostly ['moustli], adv. pour la plupart; le
plus souvent; principalement.
mote [mout], n. grain de poussière, m.; paille
(dans l'œil), f.
motel ['moutel], n. motel, m.
motet [mouˈtet], n. (Mus.) motet, m.
moth [mɔθ], n. (Ent.) lépidoptère; papillon de
nuit, m.; phalène; mite (de vêtements), f.
moth-eaten ['mɔθiːtn], a. mité.
mother ['mʌðə], n. mère; maternel; métropolitain (église); *mother tongue*, langue
maternelle, f.—n. mère; bonne mère, bonne
femme (terme familier), f.; *stepmother*,
belle-mère, f.—v.t. servir de mère à;
adopter; enfanter (quelque chose).
mother country ['mʌðəkʌntri], n. mère
patrie, f.
mother-in-law ['mʌðərinlɔː], n. belle-mère,
f.
motherly ['mʌðəli], a. maternel, de mère.—
adv. maternellement, en mère.
mother-of-pearl [mʌðərəvˈpɔːl], n. nacre, f.
motion ['mouʃən], n. mouvement; signe
(signal), m.; motion, proposition (à une
réunion); (Med.) selle, f.—v.t. faire signe (à).
motionless ['mouʃənlis], a. immobile.
motivate ['moutiveit], v.t. motiver (une
action).
motive ['moutiv], a. moteur, qui fait mouvoir;
motive power, force motrice, f.—n. motif,
mobile, m.
motley ['mɔtli], a. bigarré, mélangé.
motor ['moutə], n. moteur, m.—v.i. aller ou
voyager en auto.
motor-boat ['moutəbout], n. canot automobile, m.
motor car ['moutəkaː], n. automobile, auto,
voiture, f.
motor-cycle ['moutəsaikl], n. motocyclette, f.

motoring ['moutəriŋ], n. automobilisme, m.
motorist ['moutərist], n. automobiliste, m., f.
motorway ['moutəwei], n. autoroute, f.
mottle [mɔtl], v.t. madrer; marbrer.
motto ['mɔtou], n. (pl. **mottoes** ['mɔtouz])
devise, f.
mould (1) [mould], n. moisi (mousse); terreau
(humus), m.—v.i. se moisir.
mould (2) [mould], n. moule, m., forme, f.—
v.t. mouler; (fig.) pétrir.
moulder ['mouldə], v.i. se réduire en poudre
ou en poussière.
mouldiness ['mouldinis], n. moisissure, f.
moulding ['mouldiŋ], n. moulure, f.
mouldy ['mouldi], a. moisi.
moult [moult], v.i. muer.
moulting ['moultiŋ], n. mue, f.
mound [maund], n. butte, f., tertre, m.;
(Fort.) remparts, m.pl.
mount [maunt], n. mont, m., montagne;
monture (cheval); (Turf) monte, f.; (Phot.)
carton, m.—v.t. monter, monter sur.—v.i.
monter, s'élever; monter à cheval.
mountain ['mauntin], a. de montagne, des
montagnes, montagnard, montagneux (paysage).—n. montagne, f.
mountaineer [mauntiˈniə], n. montagnard,
m.; alpiniste, m., f.
mountaineering [mauntiˈniəriŋ], n. alpinisme, m.
mountainous ['mauntinəs], a. montagneux,
de montagnes; (fig.) énorme.
mountebank ['mauntibæŋk], n. charlatan, m.
mounted ['mauntid], a. monté, à cheval;
(Phot.) collé.
mounting ['mauntiŋ], n. montage, m., monture, f.; (Phot.) collage, m.
mourn [mɔːn], v.t. pleurer, déplorer.—v.i.
pleurer, se lamenter.
mourner ['mɔːnə], n. personne affligée, f.;
pleureur (professionnel), m., personne qui suit
le convoi, f.
mournful ['mɔːnful], a. triste, lugubre.
mourning ['mɔːniŋ], a. affligé, triste; de
deuil.—n. affliction, lamentation, f.; deuil
(vêtements), m.
mouse [maus], n. (pl. **mice** [mais]) souris, f.;
field mouse, mulot, m.
mouse-trap ['maustræp], n. souricière, f.
moustache [məˈstaːʃ], n. moustache, f.
mousy ['mausi], a. gris (couleur); timide.
mouth [mauθ], n. (pl. **mouths** [mauðz])
bouche, f.; gueule (de bête sauvage); embouchure (de rivière); ouverture, entrée, f.;
orifice (donnant accès); goulot (d'une bouteille), m.; by word of mouth, de vive voix.
—[mauð], v.t., v.i. crier.
mouthed [mauðd], a. a *foul-mouthed*, mal
embouché; *mealy-mouthed*, doucereux.
mouthful ['mauθful], n. bouchée; gorgée (de
vin), f.
mouthpiece ['mauθpiːs], n. embouchure, f.;
(fig.) interprète, porte-parole, m.
movable ['muːvəbl], a. mobile.—n. meuble,
m.
move [muːv], v.t. remuer; déplacer; mouvoir,
faire mouvoir, mettre en mouvement, faire
marcher, faire aller; transporter (marchandises etc.); (fig.) émouvoir, toucher, exciter,
pousser (à); proposer (que); (Chess) jouer;
to move forward, avancer; *to move out*,
déloger, sortir.—v.i. bouger, se remuer, se

mouvoir, se déplacer; se mettre en mouvement, aller, partir, marcher, s'avancer;
s'ébranler (*armée*); déménager (*changer de
résidence*); (*Chess*) jouer; **move on!**
circulez! *to move aside*, s'écarter; *to
move away*, s'éloigner; *to move back*,
reculer, se reculer; *to move in*, emménager;
to move off, s'éloigner, s'en aller; *to move
on*, avancer; *to move out*, sortir, déménager.—*n.* mouvement; coup; (*Chess*)
trait, *m.*; **masterly move**, coup de maître;
to be on the move, être en mouvement, se
remuer; *to get a move on*, se presser.

movement ['mu:vmənt], *n.* mouvement, *m.*
mover ['mu:və], *n.* moteur; mobile, *m.*; force
motrice, *f.*; déménageur, *m.*
movie ['mu:vi], *n.* (*Am.*) film, *m.*; **the
movies**, le cinéma, *m.*
moving ['mu:viŋ], *a.* mouvant, mobile; (*fig.*)
émouvant.—*n.* mouvement; déménagement
(*de mobilier*); déplacement (*changement de
place*), *m.*
movingly ['mu:viŋli], *adv.* d'une manière
émouvante.
mow [mou], *v.t. irr.* faucher; tondre.
mower ['mouə], *n.* faucheur (*personne*), *m.*;
faucheuse, tondeuse (*machine*), *f.*
Mr. ['mistə]. Monsieur (*abbr.* M.).
Mrs. ['misiz]. Madame (*abbr.* Mme.).
much [mʌtʃ], *adv.* beaucoup, bien, fort, très;
as much, autant; *how much?* combien
(*de*)? *much more*, pas grand'chose; *nothing
much*, pas grand'chose; *pretty much*, à
peu près; *so much*, tant; *so much more*,
d'autant plus; *so much the better*, tant
mieux; *to make much of*, faire grand cas
de; *too much*, trop (*de*).
muck [mʌk], *n.* fumier (*engrais*), *m.*; fange
(*boue*), (*fig.*) saleté, *f.*—*v.t.* fumer; salir.
muckiness ['mʌkinis], *n.* saleté, ordure, *f.*
mucky ['mʌki], *a.* sale, malpropre.
mucous ['mju:kəs], *a.* muqueux; *mucous
membrane*, muqueuse, *f.*
mucus ['mju:kəs], *n.* mucus, *m.*; mucosité, *f.*
mud [mʌd], *n.* boue, bourbe, vase, *f.*, limon,
m.
mudguard ['mʌdgɑ:d], *n.* garde-boue, *m.*
muddle [mʌdl], *v.t.* brouiller; troubler;
gâcher.—*v.i.* faire du gâchis.—*n.* confusion,
f., désordre, gâchis, *m.*
muddled [mʌdld], *a.* troublé; hébété.
muddler ['mʌdlə], *n.* brouillon, *m.*
muddy ['mʌdi], *a.* boueux, bourbeux; crotté.
muff [mʌf], *n.* manchon, *m.*—*v.t.* gâcher.
muffle [mʌfl], *v.t.* emmitoufler, affubler;
assourdir (*cloche*); voiler (*tambour*).—*n.*
moufle, *f.*
muffler ['mʌflə], *n.* cache-nez, *m.*; (*Motor.*)
pot d'échappemen', *m.*
mug [mʌg], *n.* pot, *m.*, tasse; (*slang*) gueule,
binette, *f.*; (*colloq.*) imbécile, *m., f.*
muggy ['mʌgi], *a.* humide, lourd.
mulberry ['mʌlbəri], *n.* mûre, *f.*; *mulberry
bush*, mûrier, *m.*
mulch [mʌltʃ], *n.* paillis, *m.*—*v.t.* pailler,
fumer.
mule [mju:l], *n.* mulet, *m.*, mule, *f.*
mulish ['mju:liʃ], *a.* de mulet; (*fig.*) têtu.
mull [mʌl], *v.t.* ruminer.—*v.t.* faire chauffer
et épicer; *mulled wine*, vin chaud épicé.
multicolored ['mʌltikʌləd], *a.* multicolore.

multifarious [mʌlti'fɛəriəs], *a.* varié, divers,
multiplié.
multi-millionaire ['mʌltimiljə'nɛə], *n.*
milliardaire, *m., f.*
multiple ['mʌltipl], *a. and n.* multiple, *m.*;
multiple store, maison à succursales, *f.*
multiplication [mʌltipli'keiʃən], *n.* multiplication, *f.*
multiplicity [mʌlti'plisiti], *n.* multiplicité, *f.*
multiply ['mʌltiplai], *v.t.* multiplier.—*v.i.*
multiplier, se multiplier.
multitude ['mʌltitju:d], *n.* multitude, *f.*
multitudinous [mʌlti'tju:dinəs], *a.* très nombreux, innombrable.
mum (1) [mʌm], *a.* muet.—*int.* bouche close!
chut!
mum (2) [mʌm], *n.* (*fam.*) maman, *f.*
mumble [mʌmbl], *v.i.* marmotter.
mumbler ['mʌmblə], *n.* marmotteur, *m.*
mummer ['mʌmə], *n.* mime (*acteur*), *m.*
mummify ['mʌmifai], *v.t.* momifier.
mummy (1) ['mʌmi], *n.* momie, *f.*
mummy (2), **mummie** ['mʌmi]. *n.* (*fam.*)
maman, *f.*
mumps [mʌmps], *n.pl.* (*Med.*) oreillons, *m.pl.*
munch [mʌntʃ], *v.t., v.i.* mâcher, croquer.
mundane ['mʌndein], *a.* mondain.
municipal [mju'nisipl], *a.* municipal.
municipality [mjunisi'pæliti], *n.* municipalité, *f.*
munificence [mju'nifisəns], *n.* munificence, *f.*
munificent [mju'nifisənt], *a.* libéral, généreux.
munition [mju'niʃən], *n.* munitions (*de
guerre*), *f.pl.*—*v.t.* approvisionner.
mural ['mjuərəl], *a.* mural.—*n.* peinture
murale, *f.*
murder ['mə:də], *n.* meurtre, homicide, *m.*;
wilful murder, meurtre avec préméditation, assassinat, *m.*—*v.t.* assassiner, tuer;
(*fig.*) écorcher (*une langue etc.*).
murderer ['mə:dərə], *n.* meurtrier, assassin,
m.
murderess ['mə:dəris], *n.* meurtrière, *f.*
murdering ['mə:dəriŋ], **murderous** ['mə:də
rəs], *a.* meurtrier, assassin.
murkiness ['mə:kinis], *n.* obscurité, *f.*
murky ['mə:ki], *a.* sombre, obscur, ténébreux.
murmur ['mə:mə], *n.* murmure, *m.*—*v.i.*
murmurer.
murmuring ['mə:məriŋ], *a.* murmurant,
murmurateur.—*n.* murmure, *m.*, mur-
mures, *m.pl.*
muscle [mʌsl], *n.* muscle, *m.*
muscular ['mʌskjulə], *a.* musculaire (*force*);
musculeux (*membres*).
Muse [mju:z], *n.* muse, *f.*
muse [mju:z], *v.i.* méditer (*sur*) rêver (*à*).—
n. muse, rêverie, méditation, *f.*
museum [mju'zi:əm], *n.* musée, *m.*
mushroom ['mʌʃrum], *n.* champignon, *m.*
music ['mju:zik], *n.* musique, *f.*
musical ['mju:zikəl], *a.* musical; (*fig.*) harmonieux, mélodieux; qui aime la musique.
musician [mju'ziʃən], *n.* musicien, *m.*
music stand ['mju:zikstænd], *n.* pupitre à
musique, *m.*
music stool ['mju:zikstu:l], *n.* tabouret de
piano, *m.*
musing ['mju:ziŋ], *n.* méditation; (*pl.*)
rêverie, *f.*

musk [mʌsk], *n.* musc, *m.*

musket [ˈmʌskit], *n.* fusil, mousquet, *m.*

musketeer [mʌskiˈtiə], *n.* mousquetaire, *m.*

musketry [ˈmʌskitri], *n.* mousqueterie, *f.*, tir, *m.*

musky [ˈmʌski], *a.* musqué, parfumé de musc.

Muslim [ˈmʌzlim], [MOSLEM].

muslin [ˈmʌzlin], *a.* de mousseline.—*n.* mousseline, *f.*

mussel [mʌsl], *n.* moule, *f.*

must (1) [mʌst], *v. aux.* falloir; devoir; *I must do it*, il faut que je le fasse; *you must know*, vous devez savoir.

must (2) [mʌst], *n.* moût (*de vin*), *m.*

mustard [ˈmʌstəd], *n.* moutarde, *f.*

muster [ˈmʌstə], *n.* appel, *m.*, revue, *f.*; rassemblement, *m.*; troupe, bande, *f.*; contrôles (*liste*), *m.pl.*—*v.t.* faire l'appel de; passer en revue; réunir, rassembler; se procurer; *to muster up courage*, prendre son courage à deux mains.—*v.i.* s'assembler, se réunir.

mustiness [ˈmʌstinis], *n.* moisi, *m.*

musty [ˈmʌsti], *a.* moisi; qui sent le renfermé.

mutability [mjuːtəˈbiliti], *n.* mutabilité, *f.*

mutation [mjuːˈteiʃən], *n.* mutation, *f.*

mute [mjuːt], *a.* and *n.* muet, *m.*—*v.t.* amortir (*les cordes d'un violon etc.*).

mutely [ˈmjuːtli], *adv.* en silence.

mutilate [ˈmjuːtileit], *v.t.* mutiler, estropier.

mutilated [ˈmjuːtileitid], *a.* mutilé.

mutilation [mjuːtiˈleiʃən], *n.* mutilation, *f.*

mutineer [mjuːtiˈniə], *n.* révolté, rebelle, mutin, *m.*

mutinous [ˈmjuːtinəs], *a.* rebelle, mutiné, mutin.

mutinously [ˈmjuːtinəsli], *adv.* séditieusement.

mutiny [ˈmjuːtini], *n.* mutinerie, sédition, révolte, *f.*—*v.i.* se mutiner, s'insurger.

mutter [ˈmʌtə], *v.t.*, *v.i.* marmotter.—*n.* marmottement, *m.*

muttering [ˈmʌtəriŋ], *a.* marmotteur, murmurant.—*n.* murmure, marmottement, marmottage, *m.*

mutton [mʌtn], *n.* mouton (*viande*), *m.*; *leg of mutton*, gigot, *m.*

mutton chop [ˈmʌtnˈtʃɔp], *n.* côtelette de mouton, *f.*

mutual [ˈmjuːtjuəl], *a.* mutuel, réciproque; *mutual friend*, ami commun, *m.*

mutually [ˈmjuːtjuəli], *adv.* mutuellement.

muzzle [mʌzl], *n.* museau (*d'animal*), *m.*; bouche, gueule (*de canon*), *f.*; bout (*de fusil etc.*), *m.*; muselière (*pour chien*), *f.*—*v.t.* museler.

muzzy [ˈmʌzi], *a.* brouillé, confus.

my [mai], *poss. a.* mon, *m.*, ma, *f.*, mes, *pl.*

myopic [maiˈɔpik], *a.* myope.

myriad [ˈmiriəd], *a.* (*poet.*) innombrable.—*n.* myriade, *f.*

myrrh [məː], *n.* myrrhe, *f.*

myrtle [məːtl], *n.* myrte, *m.*

myself [maiˈself], *pron.* me; moi-même; moi; *I consider myself*, je me crois.

mysterious [misˈtiəriəs], *a.* mystérieux.

mysteriously [misˈtiəriəsli], *adv.* mystérieusement.

mystery [ˈmistəri], *n.* mystère, *m.*

mystic [ˈmistik], *a.* and *n.* (*Theol.*) mystique, *m.*, *f.*

mysticism [ˈmistisizm], *n.* mysticisme, *m.*

mystify [ˈmistifai], *v.t.* envelopper de mystère, mystifier.

mystique [misˈtiːk], *n.* mystique, *f.*

myth [miθ], *n.* mythe, *m.*

mythical [ˈmiθikl], *a.* mythique.

mythology [miˈθɔlədʒi], *n.* mythologie, *f.*

N

N, n [en], quatorzième lettre de l'alphabet, *m.* ou *f.*

nab [næb], *v.t.* happer, saisir, pincer.

nag (1) [næg], *n.* bidet, petit cheval, *m.*

nag (2) [næg], *v.t.*, *v.i.* gronder, chamailler, criailler.

nagging [ˈnægiŋ], *a.* querelleur (*personne*); agaçant (*sensation*).

nail [neil], *n.* clou; ongle (*de griffes, de doigts*), *m.*—*v.t.* clouer; clouter.

nail brush [ˈneilbrʌʃ], *n.* brosse à ongles, *f.*

naïve [naiˈiːv], *a.* naïf, ingénu.

naked [ˈneikid], *a.* nu, à nu; à découvert, ouvert (*sans protection*); dégarni (*sans meubles*); *stark naked*, tout nu.

nakedness [ˈneikidnis], *n.* nudité, *f.*

name [neim], *n.* nom, (*fig.*) renom, *m.*, renommée, réputation, *f.*; *Christian name*, nom de baptême, prénom, *m.*; *maiden name*, nom de jeune fille; *what is your name?* comment vous appelezvous?—*v.t.* nommer, appeler; désigner; *to be named*, s'appeler, se nommer.

named [neimd], *a.* nommé, désigné.

nameless [ˈneimlis], *a.* sans nom, anonyme; inconnu.

namely [ˈneimli], *adv.* à savoir, c'est-à-dire.

namesake [ˈneimseik], *n.* homonyme, *m.*

nanny [ˈnæni], *n.* bonne d'enfant; (*childish*) nounou, *f.*

nap (1) [næp], *n.* somme (*sommeil*), *m.*; *afternoon nap*, sieste, *f.*; *to take a nap*, faire un somme; *to catch napping*, prendre au dépourvu.

nap (2) [næp], *n.* poil (*de tissu etc*), *m.*

nap (3) [næp], *n.* napoléon (*jeu*); tuyau certain (*courses de chevaux*), *m.*

nape [neip], *n.* nuque, *f.*

napkin [ˈnæpkin], *n.* serviette; couche (*de bébé*), *f.*

Napoleon [nəˈpouljən], Napoléon, *m.*

narcissus [naːˈsisəs], *n.* narcisse, *m.*

narcotic [naːˈkɔtik], *a.* and *n.* narcotique, *m.*

narrate [nəˈreit], *v.t.* raconter, narrer.

narration [nəˈreiʃən], *n.* narration, *f.*, récit, *m.*

narrative [ˈnærətiv], *a.* narratif.—*n.* récit, narré, *m.*

narrator [nəˈreitə], *n.* narrateur, *m.*

narrow [ˈnærou], *a.* étroit, resserré; à l'étroit, gêné; rétréci, limité, borné (*esprit*); *to have a narrow escape*, l'échapper belle.—*n.* (*pl.*) détroit, pas, *m.*—*v.t.* rétrécir, resserrer, limiter, borner.—*v.i.* se rétrécir, se resserrer.

narrowly [ˈnærouli], *adv.* étroitement, à l'étroit; de près.

narrow-minded ['nærou'maindid], *a.* à l'esprit étroit.
narrowness ['nærounis], *n.* étroitesse, *f.*
nasal [neizl], *a.* nasal, du nez.
nascent ['næsənt], *a.* naissant.
nastily ['nɑːstili], *adv.* salement, malproprement.
nastiness ['nɑːstinis], *n.* saleté; grossièreté, *f.*
nasturtium [nəs'təːʃəm], *n.* capucine, *f.*
nasty ['nɑːsti], *a.* sale, malpropre; (*fig.*) méchant, vilain; dégoûtant.
natal [neitl], *a.* natal, de naissance.
nation ['neiʃən], *n.* nation, *f.*
national ['næʃənl], *a.* national; ***national anthem**, hymne national, *m.*; ***national debt**, dette publique, *f.*; ***national insurance**, assurances sociales, *f.pl.*
nationalism ['næʃnəlizm], *n.* nationalisme, *m.*
nationality [næʃə'næliti], *n.* nationalité, *f.*
nationalization [næʃnəlai'zeiʃən], *n.* nationalisation (*d'une industrie*); (*Am.*) naturalisation (*d'une personne*), *f.*
nationalize ['næʃnəlaiz], *v.t.* nationaliser.
native ['neitiv], *a.* natif, naturel, indigène (*personne* ou *plante*); maternel (*langue etc.*); ***native land**, patrie, *f.*—*n.* natif (*d'une ville*); habitant (*d'une île*); naturel (*de tribu sauvage*); indigène (*des pays d'outremer*), *m.*; ***a native of England**, Anglais de naissance, *m.*; ***a native of Paris**, natif de Paris.
nativity [nə'tiviti], *n.* nativité; naissance, *f.*
natty ['næti], *a.* pimpant, propret, coquet.
natural ['nætʃərəl], *a.* naturel; réel; naïf, simple; (*Mus.*) bécarre.
naturalist ['nætʃərəlist], *n.* naturaliste, *m.,* *f.*
naturalization [nætʃərəlai'zeiʃən], *n.* naturalisation, *f.*
naturally ['nætʃərəli], *adv.* naturellement.
nature ['neitʃə], *n.* nature, *f.*; naturel (*disposition*), *m.*
naught [nɔːt], *n.* néant, rien; (*Arith.*) zéro, *m.*; ***to come to naught**, échouer.
naughtily ['nɔːtili], *adv.* par méchanceté.
naughtiness ['nɔːtinis], *n.* méchanceté, *f.*
naughty ['nɔːti], *a.* méchant, vilain.
nausea ['nɔːziə], *n.* nausée, *f.*
nauseating ['nɔːzieitiŋ], *a.* nauséabond, dégoûtant, écœurant.
nautical ['nɔːtikl], *a.* nautique; marin (*milles etc.*).
naval [neivl], *a.* naval; maritime; de la marine (de guerre); ***naval officer**, officier de marine, *m.*
nave (1) [neiv], *n.* nef (*d'église*), *f.*
nave (2) [neiv], *n.* moyeu (*de roue*), *m.*
navel [neivl], *n.* nombril, *m.*
navigable ['nævigəbl], *a.* navigable.
navigate ['nævigeit], *v.t.* gouverner.—*v.i.* naviguer.
navigation [nævi'geiʃən], *n.* navigation, *f.*
navigator ['nævigeitə], *n.* navigateur, *m.*
navvy ['nævi], *n.* terrassier, *m.*
navy ['neivi], *n.* marine de guerre, *f.*; ***Merchant Navy**, marine marchande.
navy blue ['neivi'bluː], *a.* and *n.* bleu marine, *m.inv.*
*****nay** [nei], *adv.* non; bien plus; et même, qui plus est; ***to say nay**, refuser.
Neapolitan [niə'pɔlitən], *a.* napolitain, de Naples.—*n.* Napolitain (*personne*), *m.*
neap tide ['niːp'taid], *n.* marée de morte eau, *f.*

near [niə], *a.* proche, rapproché; chiche (*parcimonieux*); cher (*bien-aimé*); fidèle (*intime*); de gauche (*left*).—*adv.* près, près de, de près; presque.—*prep.* près de, auprès de.—*v.t., v.i.* s'approcher de.
nearby ['niəbai], *a.,* [niə'bai], *adv.* tout près, tout proche.
nearly ['niəli], *adv.* de près; à peu près; presque; ***he was nearly drowned**, il faillit se noyer.
nearness ['niənis], *n.* proximité; parcimonie (*avarice*), *f.*
neat [niːt], *a.* propre, soigné, net; simple et élégant; pur, sec (*sans mélange*).
neatly ['niːtli], *adv.* proprement; nettement; adroitement (*habilement*).
neatness ['niːtnis], *n.* propreté, netteté, *f.*
nebula ['nebjulə], *n.* (*Astron.*) nébuleuse, *f.*
nebulous ['nebjuləs], *a.* nébuleux.
necessaries ['nesəsəriz], *n.pl.* nécessaire, *m.*
necessarily ['nesəsərili], *adv.* nécessairement, forcément.
necessary ['nesəsri], *a.* nécessaire.
necessitate [ni'sesiteit], *v.t.* nécessiter.
necessitous [ni'sesitəs], *a.* nécessiteux, dans le besoin.
necessity [ni'sesiti], *n.* nécessité, *f.*; besoin (*indigence*), *m.*; ***of necessity**, nécessairement, forcément.
neck [nek], *n.* cou; goulot (*de bouteille etc.*); manche (*de violon*); collet (*de viande*), *m.*; encolure (*d'une robe*), langue (*de terre*), *f.*; ***stiff neck**, torticolis, *m.*
neckerchief ['nekətʃif], *n.* foulard (*d'homme*), fichu (*de femme*), *m.*
necklace ['neklis], *n.* collier, *m.*
neck-tie ['nektai], *n.* cravate, *f.*
necromancy ['nekrəmænsi], *n.* nécromancie, *f.*
necropolis [ni'krɔpəlis], *n.* nécropole, *f.*
nectar ['nektə], *n.* nectar, *m.*
nectarine ['nektərin], *n.* brugnon, *m.*
need [niːd], *n.* besoin, *m.*; nécessité; indigence, *f.*; ***if need be**, le cas échéant; ***in case of need**, au besoin; ***to be in need**, être dans la misère; ***to be in need of** or ***to have need of***, avoir besoin de.—*v.t.* avoir besoin de; exiger.—*v.i.* avoir besoin; devoir, avoir (*à*); (*impers.*) falloir, être nécessaire.
needful ['niːdful], *a.* nécessaire; ***the needful**, le nécessaire, *m.*
needle [niːdl], *n.* aiguille, *f.*
needless ['niːdlis], *a.* inutile.
needlework ['niːdlwəːk], *n.* ouvrage à l'aiguille, *m.*; (*Sch.*) couture, *f.*
*****needs** [niːdz], *adv.* (*used only with* must) nécessairement, absolument; ***I must needs**, il faut absolument que je (*with subj.*).
needy ['niːdi], *a.* indigent, nécessiteux.
ne'er [nɛə], (*poet.*) [NEVER].
nefarious [ni'fɛəriəs], *a.* abominable, infâme.
negation [ni'geiʃən], *n.* négation, *f.*
negative ['negativ], *a.* négatif.—*n.* négative, *f.*; (*Phot.*) cliché, négatif, *m.*—*v.t.* rejeter.
neglect [ni'glekt], *n.* négligence, *f.*; oubli, *m.*—*v.t.* négliger.
neglected [ni'glektid], *a.* négligé.
neglectful [ni'glektful], *a.* négligent.
negligence ['neglidʒəns], *n.* négligence, *f.*
negligent ['neglidʒənt], *a.* négligent.

493

negligible ['neglidʒibl], *a.* négligeable.
negotiable [ni'gouʃiəbl], *a.* négociable.
negotiate [ni'gouʃieit], *v.t.*, *v.i.* négocier.
negotiation [nigouʃi'eiʃən], *n.* négociation, *f.*
negotiator [ni'gouʃieitə], *n.* négociateur, *m.*
Negress ['ni:gres], *n.* (*pej.*) noire, *f.*
Negro ['ni:grou], *n.* noir, *m.*, noire, *f.*
neigh [nei], *v.i.* hennir.—*n.* hennissement, *m.*
neighbor ['neibə], *n.* voisin; (*Bibl.*) prochain, *m.*
neighborhood ['neibəhud], *n.* voisinage, *m.*; alentours, environs, *m.pl.*; quartier, *m.*
neighboring ['neibəriŋ], *a.* voisin.
neighborly ['neibəli], *a.* de voisin, de bon voisin.
neighing ['neiiŋ], *n.* hennissement, *m.*
neither ['naiðə, 'ni:ðə], *a.* and *pron.* ni l'un ni l'autre, *m.*—*conj.* ni... ni... ne plus; *neither ... nor,* ni... ni.—*adv.* du reste, d'ailleurs.
nemesis ['nemisis], *n.* némésis, *f.*
neolithic [ni:ə'liθik], *a.* néolithique.
neon ['ni:ɔn], *a.* *neon light,* lampe au néon, *f.*—*n.* (*Chem.*) néon, *m.*
Nepal [nə'pɔ:l], le Népal, *m.*
Nepalese [nepə'li:z], *a.* népalais.—*n.* Népalais (*personne*), *m.*
nephew ['nefju, 'nevju], *n.* neveu, *m.*
nepotism ['nepətizm], *n.* népotisme, *m.*
Nero ['niərou], Néron, *m.*
nerve [nə:v], *n.* nerf; (*fig.*) courage, *m.*; audace, *f.*; (*pop.*) toupet, *m.*
nerve cell ['nə:vsel], *n.* cellule nerveuse, *f.*
nerveless ['nə:vlis], *a.* sans nerf; (*fig.*) sans vigueur.
nerve-racking ['nə:vrækiŋ], *a.* horripilant, énervant.
nervous ['nə:vəs], *a.* nerveux (*physiquement*); timide, craintif (*moralement*); *nervous breakdown,* dépression nerveuse, *f.*
nervousness ['nə:vəsnis], *n.* inquiétude, timidité; nervosité, *f.*
nest [nest], *n.* nid, *m.*; nichée (*couvée d'oiseaux*), *f.*; (*fig.*) repaire, *m.*; *nest of tables,* table gigogne, *f.*—*v.i.* nicher, faire un nid.
nestle [nesl], *v.i.* nicher, se nicher.
nestling ['nesliŋ], *n.* petit oiseau encore au nid, béjaune, *m.*
net [net], *a.* net; pur.—*n.* filet, rets, *m.*; résille (*à cheveux*), *f.*; tulle (*tissu*), *m.*—*v.t.* prendre dans un filet; (*Comm.*) rapporter net.
nether ['neðə], *a.* bas, inférieur.
Netherlands ['neðələndz], **the.** les Pays-Bas, *m.pl.*
nethermost ['neðəmoust], *a.* le plus bas.
netting ['netiŋ], *n.* filet, réseau; grillage (*de fil de fer*), *m.*
nettle [netl], *n.* ortie, *f.*—*v.t.* piquer, agacer, irriter.
nettlerash ['netlræʃ], *n.* urticaire, *f.*
network ['netwə:k], *n.* réseau, enchevêtrement, *m.*
neuralgia [nju'ræ1dʒə], *n.* névralgie, *f.*
neuritis [nju'raitis], *n.* névrite, *f.*
neurosis [nju'rousis], *n.* névrose, *f.*
neurotic [nju'rɔtik], *a.* and *n.* névrosé, *m.*, neurotique, *m.*, *f.*
neuter ['nju:tə], *a.* and *n.* neutre, *m.*
neutral ['nju:trəl], *a.* neutre; indifférent.—*n.* (*Motor.*) point-mort, *m.*
neutrality [nju'træliti], *n.* neutralité; indifférence, *f.*

neutralize ['nju:trəlaiz], *v.t.* neutraliser.
neutron ['nju:trɔn], *n.* neutron, *m.*
never ['nevə], *adv.* jamais; ne... jamais; *never mind!* peu importe!
nevermore [nevə'mɔ:], *adv.* ne... jamais plus, ne... plus jamais.
nevertheless [nevəðə'les], *conj.* néanmoins, cependant, pourtant.
new [nju:], *a.* neuf (*qui n'a pas servi*); nouveau (*récemment acquis, différent*); frais, récent (*arrivé depuis peu*); *brand-new,* flambant neuf, tout battant neuf; *New Year's Day,* le jour de l'an, *m.*
new-born ['nju:bɔ:n], *a.* nouveau-né; *new-born daughters,* filles nouveau-nées, *f.pl.*
new-comer ['nju:kʌmə], *n.* nouveau venu, *m.*
Newfoundland ['nju:fəndlænd, nju:'faundlənd]. la Terre-Neuve, *f.*—*n.* terre-neuve (*chien*), *m.*
New Guinea [nju:'gini]. la Nouvelle-Guinée, *f.*
new-laid ['nju:leid], *a.* frais (*œuf*).
newly ['nju:li], *adv.* nouvellement, fraîchement, récemment, de nouveau.
newness ['nju:nis], *n.* nouveauté, *f.*
New Orleans [nju:'ɔ:liənz]. la Nouvelle-Orléans, *f.*
news [nju:z], *n.* nouvelle, *f.*, nouvelles, *f.pl.*; (*Rad., Tel.*) bulletin d'informations, *m.*
news-agent ['nju:zeidʒənt], *n.* marchand de journaux, *m.*
newspaper ['nju:speipə], *n.* journal, *m.*
newt [nju:t], *n.* triton, *m.*, salamandre, *f.*
New Zealand [nju:'zi:lənd]. la Nouvelle-Zélande, *f.*—*a.* néo-zélandais.
New Zealander [nju:'zi:ləndə], *n.* Néo-Zélandais, *m.*
next [nekst], *a.* voisin, le plus voisin; le plus près; de côté; prochain (*dans l'avenir*); suivant (*dans le passé*); premier (*à la suite de*).—*adv.* après, ensuite, puis; *what next?* et après? ensuite?—*prep. next to,* à côté de.
nib [nib], *n.* bec (*de stylo*), *m.*; pointe (*d'outil*), *f.*
nibble [nibl], *v.t.* mordiller, grignoter; mordre à (*l'hameçon*); brouter (*l'herbe etc.*).—*n.* grignotement, *m.*; touche (*du poisson*), *f.*
Nicaragua [nikə'rægjuə]. le Nicaragua, *m.*
Nicaraguan [nikə'rægjuən], *a.* nicaraguayen.—*n.* Nicaraguayen (*personne*), *m.*
nice [nais], *a.* bon, agréable, friand; (*colloq.*) délicat, gentil, aimable, charmant, propre; exact, difficile, exigeant (*délicat*); *a nice child,* un enfant gentil, *m.*
nicely ['naisli], *adv.* bien, agréablement; délicatement; gentiment, aimablement; joliment; d'une manière recherchée.
nicety ['naisəti], *n.* (*pl.* **niceties** ['naisətiz]) délicatesse. finesse, *f.*; soin scrupuleux, *m.*; précision; exactitude, *f.*; (*pl.*) subtilités, finesses, *f.pl.*
niche [nitʃ], *n.* niche, *f.*
Nicholas ['nikələs]. Nicolas, *m.*
nick [nik], *n.* moment précis, *m.*; encoche, entaille (*coupure*), *f.*; (*Print.*) cran, *m.*; *in the nick of time,* fort à propos, à point nommé.
nickel [nikl], *n.* nickel, *m.*; (*Am.*) pièce de cinq cents, *f.*
nickname ['nikneim], *n.* sobriquet, surnom, *m.*—*v.t.* donner un sobriquet à.
nicotine ['nikəti:n], *n.* nicotine, *f.*

niece [niːs], *n.* nièce, *f.*

nifty ['nifti], *a.* (*fam.*) pimpant.

Niger [naiʤəǝ], **the.** le Niger, *m.*

Nigeria [naiʤiǝriǝ]. le Nigéria, *m.*

Nigerian [naiʤiǝriǝn], *a.* nigérien.—*n.* Nigérien (*personne*), *m.*

niggard ['nigǝd], *a.* and *n.* avare, ladre, *m.*

niggardliness ['nigǝdlinis], *n.* mesquinerie, ladrerie, *f.*

niggardly ['nigǝdli], *a.* mesquin, ladre, chiche.—*adv.* avec avarice, en avare.

niggle [nigl], *v.i.* tatillonner; fignoler.

nigh [nai], *adv.* près; presque; *to draw nigh*, approcher, s'approcher (*de*).

night [nait], *n.* nuit, *f.*; soir, *m.*; *first night*, première, *f.*

night-club ['naitklʌb], *n.* boîte de nuit, *f.*

night-dress ['naitdres], *n.* chemise de nuit, *f.*

night-fall ['naitfɔːl], *n.* tombée de la nuit, *f.*

nightie ['naiti], *colloq. abbr.* [NIGHT-DRESS].

nightingale ['naitiŋgeil], *n.* rossignol, *m.*

night-light ['naitlait], *n.* veilleuse, *f.*

nightly ['naitli], *a.* nocturne, de nuit.—*adv.* chaque nuit, toutes les nuits; tous les soirs.

nightmare ['naitmɛǝ], *n.* cauchemar, *m.*

night-time ['naittaim], *n.* nuit, *f.*; *in the night-time*, pendant la nuit.

night-watchman ['naitwɔtʃmǝn], *n.* (*pl.* **-men** [men]) veilleur de nuit, *m.*

nihilism ['naiilizm], *n.* nihilisme, *m.*

nil [nil], *n.* rien, néant, zéro, *m.*

Nile [nail], **the.** le Nil, *m.*

nimble [nimbl], *a.* agile, léger, leste.

nimbly ['nimbli], *adv.* agilement, lestement.

nine [nain], *a.* and *n.* neuf, *m.*

ninefold ['nainfould], *a.* neuf fois autant.

ninepins ['nainpinz], *n.pl.* quilles, *f.pl.*; jeu de quilles, *m.*

nineteen [nain'tiːn], *a.* and *n.* dix-neuf, *m.*

nineteenth [nain'tiːnθ], *a.* dix-neuvième; dix-neuf (*du mois ou souverains*) *m.* dix-neuvième (*fraction*), *m.*

ninetieth ['naintiiθ], *a.* quatre-vingt-dixième. —*n.* quatre-vingt-dixième (*fraction*), *m.*

ninety ['nainti], *a.* and *n.* quatre-vingt-dix, *m.*

ninny ['nini], *n.* nigaud, niais, *m.*

ninth [nainθ], *a.* neuvième; neuf (*du mois ou souverains*), *m.*—*n.* neuvième (*fraction*), *m.*

nip [nip], *n.* pincement, *m.*, pince, *f.*, serrement, *m.*; morsure; (*Hort.*) brûlure (par le froid), *f.*—*v.t.* pincer; mordre; (*Hort.*) brûler (par le froid); *to nip off*, couper, enlever le bout de.

nipper ['nipǝ], *n.* pince, *f.*; (*colloq.*) gamin, gosse, *m.*; (*pl.*) pincettes, pinces, *f.pl.*

nipple [nipl], *n.* mamelon, bout de sein, *m.*

nippy ['nipi], *a.* preste, rapide; perçant (*froid*).

nit [nit], *n.* lente, *f.*

nitrate ['naitreit], *n.* nitrate, *m.*

nitre ['naitǝ], *n.* nitre, *m.*

nitric ['naitrik], *a.* nitrique, azotique.

nitrogen ['naitrǝdʒǝn], *n.* azote, *m.*

nitwit ['nitwit], *n.* imbécile, *m.*, *f.*

no [nou], *a.* and *adv.* non, pas, ne . . . pas de, ne . . . point de; pas un, nul, aucun.—*n.* non, *m.*

Noah ['nouǝ]. Noé, *m.*

nob [nɔb], *n.* (*colloq.*) caboche, *f.*; gros bonnet, *m.*

nobility [no'biliti], *n.* noblesse, *f.*

noble [noubl], *a.* noble; illustre, grand; généreux.—*n.* noble, *m.*

nobleman ['noublmǝn], *n.* (*pl.* **-men** [men]) noble, gentilhomme, *m.*

nobly ['noubli], *adv.* noblement; superbement.

nobody ['noubǝdi], *pron.* personne, *m.*; *I know nobody*, je ne connais personne; *nobody else*, personne d'autre.—*n.* zéro, inconnu, *m.*

nocturnal [nɔk'tǝːnl], *a.* nocturne, de nuit.

nod [nɔd], *n.* signe de tête, *m.*; inclination de tête, *f.*—*v.i.* faire un signe de tête; s'incliner; sommeiller (*s'assoupir*).

noggin ['nɔgin], *n.* petit pot (*en étain*), *m.*

noise [nɔiz], *n.* bruit; tapage, fracas, vacarme; tintement (*de cloche*), bourdonnement (*d'insectes etc.*); (*fig.*) éclat, *m.*—*v.t.* ébruiter, publier, répandre.

noiseless ['nɔizlis], *a.* sans bruit; silencieux.

noiselessly ['nɔizlisli], *adv.* sans bruit.

noisily ['nɔizili], *adv.* bruyamment.

noisome ['nɔisǝm], *a.* malsain, infect, nuisible.

noisy ['nɔizi], *a.* bruyant; turbulent (*enfants*).

nomad ['noumæd], *n.* nomade, *m.*

nomadic [no'mædik], *a.* nomade, *m.*

nominal ['nɔminl], *a.* nominal; de nom; *nominal roll*, état nominatif, *m.*

nominally ['nɔminǝli], *adv.* de nom; nominalement.

nominate ['nɔmineit], *v.t.* nommer; désigner; présenter, proposer (*un candidat etc.*).

nomination [nɔmi'neiʃǝn], *n.* nomination; présentation, *f.*

nominative ['nɔminǝtiv], *a.* au nominatif, nominatif.—*n.* (*Gram.*) nominatif, *m.*

nominee [nɔmi'niː], *n.* personne nommée, *f.*

nonagenarian [nounǝdʒi'nɛǝriǝn], *a.* and *n.* nonagénaire, *m.*, *f.*

non-aggression [nɔnǝ'greʃǝn], *n.* non-agression, *f.*

non-alcoholic [nɔnælkǝ'hɔlik], *a.* non-alcoolique.

non-attendance [nɔnǝ'tendǝns], *n.* absence, *f.*

nonchalance ['nɔnʃǝlǝns], *n.* nonchalance, *f.*

non-combatant [nɔn'kɑmbǝtǝnt, nɔn'kɔmbǝtǝnt], *a.* and *n.* non-combattant, *m.*

non-commissioned [nɔnkǝ'miʃǝnd], *a.* sans brevet; *non-commissioned officer*, sous-officier, *m.*

non-committal [nɔnkǝ'mitl], *a.* qui n'engage à rien, diplomatique.

nonconformist [nɔnkǝn'fɔːmist], *a.* and *n.* dissident, *m.*, nonconformiste, *m.*, *f.*

nondescript ['nɔndiskript], *a.* indéfinissable, quelconque.—*n.* chose sans nom, chose indéfinissable, *f.*

none [nʌn], *a.* and *pron.* nul, nulle, *f.*, aucun, *m.*, aucune, *f.*, pas un, *m.*, pas une, *f.*, personne, *m.*—*adv.* pas, point; néant (*sur des bordereaux*).

nonentity [nɔ'nentiti], *n.* néant, *m.*; (*fig.*) nullité, *f.*, zéro, *m.*

nonesuch ['nʌnsʌtʃ], *a.* sans pareil, non-pareil.

non-existent ['nɔnig'zistǝnt], *a.* qui n'existe pas.

non-intervention ['nɔnintǝ'venʃǝn], *n.* non-intervention, *f.*

non-observance ['nɔnǝb'zǝːvǝns], *n.* inobservation, *f.*

non-payment ['nɔn'peimǝnt], *n.* non-payement, *m.*

nonplussed ['nɔn'plʌst], a. embarrassé, dérouté.

nonsense ['nɔnsəns], n. non-sens, m.; sottise, absurdité, f.; **nonsense!** allons donc! quelle sottise!

nonsensical [nɔn'sensikl], a. vide de sens, absurde.

non-skid ['nɔn'skid], a. antidérapant.

non-stop ['nɔn'stɔp], a. and adv. sans arrêt.

noodle [nuːdl], n. nigaud, benêt, sot, m.; (pl.) (Cook.) nouilles, f.pl.

nook [nuk], n. recoin, réduit, m.

noon [nuːn], n. midi, m.

noonday ['nuːndei], a. de midi.—n. midi, m.

noontide ['nuːntaid], n. heure de midi, f., midi, m.

noose [nuːs], n. nœud coulant, lacet, m.

nor [nɔː], conj. ni; ni . . . ne.

norm [nɔːm], n. norme, f.

normal [nɔːml], a. normal.

normally [nɔːml], adv. normalement.

Norman ['nɔːmən], a. normand.—n. Normand (personne), m.

Normandy ['nɔːməndi]. la Normandie, f.

north [nɔːθ], a. du nord, septentrional.—n. nord, septentrion, m.—adv. au nord.

north-east [nɔːθ'iːst], n. nord-est, m.

northerly ['nɔːðəli], a. septentrional, du nord. —adv. au nord, vers le nord.

northern ['nɔːðən], a. du nord; **northern lights**, aurore boréale, f.

northerner ['nɔːðənə], n. habitant du nord, m.

north-west [nɔːθ'west], n. nord-ouest, m.

Norway ['nɔːwei]. la Norvège, f.

Norwegian [nɔː'wiːdʒən], a. norvégien.—n. norvégien (langue); Norvégien (personne), m.

nose [nouz], n. nez; museau (d'animal); odorat (flair), m.; **Roman nose**, nez aquilin; **to blow one's nose**, se moucher; **to put someone's nose out of joint**, supplanter quelqu'un; **to turn up one's nose at**, faire fi de; **turned-up nose**, nez retroussé.—v.t. flairer.—v.i. **to nose about**, fureter.

nose-bag ['nouzbæg], n. musette (de cheval etc.), f.

nose-dive ['nouzdaiv], v.i. (Av.) piquer du nez.—n. piqué, m.

nosegay ['nouzgei], n. bouquet, m.

nostalgia [nɔs'tældʒiə], n. nostalgie, f., mal du pays, m.

nostril ['nɔstril], n. narine, f.; naseau (de cheval etc.), m.

nosy ['nouzi], a. (pop.) fouinard.

not [nɔt], adv. non; ne . . . pas, ne . . . point, pas, non pas; **not at all**, point du tout; **why not?** pourquoi pas?

notability [noutə'biliti], n. notabilité, f.

notable ['noutəbl], a. notable, insigne, remarquable.—n. notable, m., f.

notably ['noutəbli], adv. notamment (particulièrement).

notary ['noutəri], n. notaire, m.

notation [no'teiʃən], n. notation, f.

notch [nɔtʃ], n. encoche, entaille, brèche, f.— v.t. entailler, ébrécher.

note [nout], n. note, marque, f., signe, m.; lettre, f., billet, m.; marque (distinction), f.; **bank note**, billet de banque; **to take a note of**, prendre note de.—v.t. noter; remarquer.

notebook ['noutbuk], n. carnet, m.

noted ['noutid], a. distingué (personne); célèbre (chose).

notepaper ['noutpeipə], n. papier à lettres, m.

noteworthy ['noutwəːði], a. remarquable.

nothing ['nʌθin], n. rien, néant, m.; **a mere nothing**, (fig.) un zéro.—pron. (ne) . . . rien; **good-for-nothing**, bon à rien, m.; **nothing at all**, rien du tout; **to do nothing but**, ne faire que.—adv. en rien, nullement, aucunement.

nothingness ['nʌθiŋnis], n. néant, rien, m.

notice ['noutis], n. connaissance; attention, f.; préavis, m.; notice (article dans un journal); (Law) notification; annonce (dans un journal); affiche (avis placardé), f.; **a week's notice**, un préavis de huit jours; **at short notice**, à court délai; **to give notice**, avertir, donner congé; **to take notice of**, faire attention à, remarquer; **until further notice**, jusqu'à nouvel ordre.—v.t. prendre connaissance de, remarquer, s'apercevoir de.

noticeable ['noutisəbl], a. perceptible.

noticeably ['noutisəbli], adv. perceptiblement, sensiblement.

notice-board ['noutisbɔːd], n. écriteau, m.

notification [noutifi'keiʃən], n. notification, f., avis, avertissement, m.

notify ['noutifai], v.t. faire savoir, notifier.

notion ['nouʃən], n. notion, idée, f.

notoriety [noutə'raiəti], n. notoriété, f.

notorious [no'tɔːriəs], a. notoire.

notwithstanding [nɔtwið'stændiŋ], prep. malgré, nonobstant.—adv. néanmoins.

noun [naun], n. nom, substantif, m.

nourish ['nʌriʃ], v.t. nourrir; (fig.) entretenir.

nourishing ['nʌriʃiŋ], a. nourrissant, nutritif.

nourishment ['nʌriʃmənt], n. nourriture, alimentation, f.

Nova Scotia ['nouvə'skouʃə]. la Nouvelle-Écosse, f.

novel [nɔvl], a. nouveau, original.—n. roman, m.

novelist ['nɔvəlist], n. romancier, m.

novelty ['nɔvəlti], n. nouveauté, f.

November [no'vembə]. novembre, m.

novercal [no'vəːkl], a. de marâtre.

novice ['nɔvis], n. novice, m., f.

novitiate [no'viʃiit], n. noviciat, m.

now [nau], adv. maintenant, à présent, actuellement; alors, or, donc (raisonnement); **now and then**, de temps en temps; **now . . . now**, tantôt . . . tantôt; **now then!** eh bien!

nowadays ['nauədeiz], adv. aujourd'hui, de nos jours.

nowhere ['nouwɛə], adv. nulle part.

nowise ['nouwaiz], adv. en aucune manière.

noxious ['nɔkʃəs], a. nuisible.

nozzle [nɔzl], n. nez; bec, bout; (Motor. etc.) ajutage, m.; lance (de tuyau), f.

nuclear ['njuːkliə], a. nucléaire; **nuclear fission**, fission de l'atome, f.; **nuclear war**, guerre atomique, f.

nucleus ['njuːkliəs], n. noyau, m.

nude [njuːd], a. and n. nu, m.

nudge [nʌdʒ], n. coup de coude, m.—v.t. donner un coup de coude à, pousser du coude.

nugget ['nʌgit], n. pépite (d'or), f.

nuisance ['njuːsəns], n. peste, plaie, f., fléau, m.; (Law) dommage, m.

null [nʌl], *a.* nul; *null and void*, nul et non avenu.
nullify ['nʌlifai], *v.t.* annuler.
nullity ['nʌliti], *n.* nullité, *f.*
numb [nʌm], *a.* engourdi, transi.—*v.t.* engourdir (*par*).
number ['nʌmbə], *n.* nombre; chiffre (*de 0 à 9*); numéro (*d'une série*), *m.*; livraison (*de publications*), *f.*; (*fig., pl.*) nombres, *m.pl.*; *a number of*, plusieurs, une foule de (*gens*); *cardinal, ordinal, odd, ou even number*, nombre cardinal, ordinal, impair *ou* pair.—*v.t.* compter; numéroter (*en série*).
numberless ['nʌmbəlis], *a.* innombrable.
number-plate ['nʌmbəpleit], *n.* (*Motor.*) plaque d'immatriculation, *f.*
numbness ['nʌmnis], *n.* engourdissement, *m.*
numeral ['nju:mərəl], *a.* numéral.—*n.* lettre numérale, *f.*; chiffre, *m.*
numerical [nju'merikl], *a.* numérique.
numerous ['nju:mərəs], *a.* nombreux.
numskull ['nʌmskʌl], *n.* benêt, idiot, *m.*
nun [nʌn], *n.* religieuse, (*fam.*) nonne, *f.*
nunnery ['nʌnəri], *n.* couvent (*de religieuses*), *m.*
nuptial ['nʌpʃəl], *a.* nuptial, de noces.
nuptials ['nʌpʃəlz], *n.pl.* noces, *f.pl.*
nurse [nə:s], *n.* bonne d'enfant, *f.*; garde-malade, *m., f.*; infirmier, *m.*, infirmière, *f.* (*à l'hôpital*); *wet nurse*, nourrice, *f.*—*v.t.* nourrir, élever; soigner, garder (*les malades*).
nurse-maid ['nə:smeid], *n.* bonne d'enfant, *f.*
nursery ['nə:səri], *n.* chambre d'enfants; (*Hort.*) pépinière, *f.*; *nursery rhyme*, chanson d'enfants, *f.*
nursery-man ['nə:sərimən], *n.* (*pl.* **-men** [men]) pépiniériste, *m.*
nursery school ['nə:sərisku:l], *n.* école maternelle, *f.*
nursing home ['nə:siŋhoum], *n.* clinique, maison de santé, *f.*
nurture ['nə:tʃə], *n.* nourriture; éducation, *f.*—*v.t.* nourrir; élever.
nut [nʌt], *n.* noix (*du noyer etc.*); noisette (*du noisetier*), *f.*; (*Tech.*) écrou, *m.*
nut-brown ['nʌtbraun], *a.* châtain.
nut-cracker ['nʌtkrækə], *n.* casse-noix (*oiseau*), *m.*; (*pl.*) casse-noisettes, *m.pl.*
nutmeg ['nʌtmeg], *n.* muscade, *f.*
nutrient ['nju:triənt], *a.* nourrissant.
nutrition [nju'triʃən], *n.* nutrition; alimentation, *f.*
nutritious [nju'triʃəs], *a.* nourrissant, nutritif.
nutshell ['nʌtʃel], *n.* coquille de noix, *f.*
nut tree ['nʌttri:], *n.* noisetier, *m.*
nutty ['nʌti], *a.* qui a un goût de noisette; (*pop.*) fêlé, toqué.
nylon ['nailən], *n.* nylon, *m.*
nymph [nimf], *n.* nymphe, *f.*

O

O, o [ou], quinzième lettre de l'alphabet, *m.*
oaf [ouf], *n.* idiot, *m.*
oafish ['oufiʃ], *a.* stupide, idiot.

oak [ouk], *n.* chêne; bois de chêne, *m.*
oak apple ['oukæpl], *n.* pomme de chêne, *f.*
oak tree ['ouktri:], *n.* chêne, *m.*
oar [ɔ:], *n.* aviron, *m.*, rame, *f.*
oarlock, see **rowlock**.
oarsman ['ɔ:zmən], *n.* (*pl.* **-men** [men]) rameur, *m.*
oasis [ou'eisis], *n.* (*pl.* **oases** [ou'eisi:z]) oasis, *f.*
oatcake ['outkeik], *n.* galette d'avoine, *f.*
oaten [outn], *a.* d'avoine.
oath [ouθ], *n.* serment; juron, *m.*; *on oath*, sous serment; *to take an oath*, prêter serment.
oatmeal ['outmi:l], *n.* farine d'avoine, *f.*
oats [outs], *n.pl.* avoine, *f.*
obduracy ['ɔbdjurəsi], *n.* endurcissement, entêtement, *m.*
obdurate ['ɔbdjurit], *a.* endurci; obstiné, opiniâtre; impénitent.
obedience [o'bi:djənt], *a.* obéissance, soumission, *f.*
obedient [o'bi:djənt], *a.* obéissant, soumis.
obediently [o'bi:djəntli], *adv.* avec obéissance.
obeisance [o'beisəns], *n.* révérence, *f.*
obelisk ['ɔbəlisk], *n.* obélisque, *m.*
obese [o'bi:s], *a.* obèse.
obesity [o'bi:siti], *n.* obésité, *f.*
obey [o'bei], *v.t.* obéir à.—*v.i.* obéir.
obfuscate ['ɔbfʌskeit], *v.t.* offusquer, obscurcir.
obituary [ɔ'bitjuəri], *a.* obituaire; nécrologique.—*n.* nécrologie, *f.*
object (1) ['ɔbdʒikt], *n.* objet; but (*fin*), *m.*; considération, *f.*; (*Gram.*) régime, *m.*
object (2) [əb'dʒekt], *v.t.* objecter.—*v.i.* s'opposer (*à*).
objection [əb'dʒekʃən], *n.* objection, *f.*; obstacle, *m.*; (*Racing*) contestation, *f.*
objectionable [əb'dʒekʃənəbl], *a.* déplaisant; inadmissible.
objective [əb'dʒektiv], *a.* objectif.—*n.* objectif, but, *m.*
objectively [əb'dʒektivli], *adv.* objectivement.
oblation [o'bleiʃən], *n.* oblation, offrande, *f.*
obligation [ɔbli'geiʃən], *n.* obligation, *f.*; engagement, *m.*
obligatory [ɔ'bligətəri], *a.* obligatoire.
oblige [ə'blaidʒ], *v.t.* obliger; faire plaisir à.
obliging [ə'blaidʒiŋ], *a.* obligeant.
oblique [o'bli:k], *a.* oblique; indirect.
obliterate [ɔ'blitəreit], *v.t.* effacer, oblitérer.
obliteration [əblitə'reiʃən], *n.* oblitération, *f.*
oblivion [ɔ'bliviən], *n.* oubli, *m.*; *act of oblivion*, loi d'amnistie, *f.*
oblivious [ə'bliviəs], *a.* oublieux (*de*).
oblong ['ɔblɔŋ], *a.* oblong.—*n.* rectangle, *m.*
obnoxious [ɔb'nɔkʃəs], *a.* odieux, désagréable, déplaisant.
oboe ['oubou], *n.* hautbois, *m.*
obscene [ɔb'si:n], *a.* obscène, sale.
obscenity [ɔb'seniti], *n.* obscénité, *f.*
obscure [ɔb'skjuə], *a.* obscur; (*fig.*) caché.—*v.t.* obscurcir; voiler (*lumière*).
obscurely [ɔb'skjuəli], *adv.* obscurément.
obscurity [ɔb'skjuəriti], *n.* obscurité, *f.*
obsequies ['ɔbsikwiz], *n.pl.* obsèques, *f.pl.*
obsequious [ɔb'si:kwiəs], *a.* obséquieux.
obsequiousness [ɔb'si:kwiəsnis], *n.* soumission obséquieuse, *f.*

497

observance

observance [ǝb'zǝːvǝns], *n.* observance;
pratique, observation, *f.*
observant [ǝb'zǝːvǝnt], *a.* observateur.
observation [ɔbzǝ'veiʃǝn], *n.* observation, *f.*
observatory [ǝb'zǝːvǝtri], *n.* observatoire, *m.*
observe [ǝb'zǝːv], *v.t.* observer; remarquer;
faire remarquer.
observer [ǝb'zǝːvǝ], *n.* observateur, *m.*
obsess [ǝb'ses], *v.t.* obséder.
obsessed [ǝb'sest], *a.* obsédé.
obsession [ǝb'seʃǝn], *n.* obsession, *f.*
obsolete ['ɔbsǝliːt], *a.* vieilli, suranné; tombé
en désuétude.
obstacle ['ɔbstǝkl], *n.* obstacle, *m.*
obstetrics [ɔb'stetriks], *n.pl.* obstétrique, *f.*
obstinacy ['ɔbstinǝsi], *n.* obstination, opiniâtreté, *f.*; entêtement (*de caractère*), *m.*
obstinate ['ɔbstinit], *a.* obstiné, opiniâtre,
entêté; têtu (*enfant*).
obstinately ['ɔbstinitli], *adv.* obstinément.
obstreperous [ǝb'strepǝrǝs], *a.* turbulent,
tapageur; récalcitrant.
obstruct [ǝb'strʌkt], *v.t.* empêcher, retarder;
obstruer, encombrer, boucher.
obstruction [ǝb'strʌkʃǝn], *n.* empêchement,
obstacle, *m.*; (*Med., Polit.*) obstruction, *f.*;
encombrement (*circulation*), *m.*
obstructive [ǝb'strʌktiv], *a.* qui empêche,
(*Med.*) obstructif.
obtain [ǝb'tein], *v.t.* obtenir, gagner; se
procurer.—*v.i.* prévaloir.
obtainable [ǝb'teinǝbl], *a.* qu'on peut
obtenir, procurable.
obtrude [ǝb'truːd], *v.t.* imposer.—*v.i.* s'introduire de force; être importun.
obtrusive [ǝb'truːsiv], *a.* importun.
obtuse [ǝb'tjuːs], *a.* obtus; émoussé; stupide.
obtuseness [ǝb'tjuːsnis], *n.* (*fig.*) stupidité, *f.*
obverse ['ɔbvǝːs], *n.* face, *f.*, avers, obvers (*de
médaille etc.*), *m.*
obviate ['ɔbvieit], *v.t.* éviter, obvier à.
obvious ['ɔbviǝs], *a.* évident, clair.
obviously ['ɔbviǝsli], *adv.* évidemment.
occasion [ǝ'keiʒǝn], *n.* occasion, rencontre;
raison, cause, *f.*; besoin (*nécessité*), *m.*—*v.t.*
occasionner, causer.
occasional [ǝ'keiʒǝnl], *a.* occasionnel,
fortuit.
occasionally [ǝ'keiʒǝnǝli], *adv.* quelquefois,
de temps en temps.
occident ['ɔksidǝnt], *n.* occident, *m.*
occidental [ɔksi'dentl], *a.* occidental.
occult [ǝ'kʌlt], *a.* occulte.
occupant ['ɔkjupǝnt], *n.* occupant, *m.*; locataire (*de chambre louée*); titulaire (*d'un poste*),
m., *f.*
occupation [ɔkju'peiʃǝn], *n.* occupation, *f.*;
emploi, métier, *m.*; possession, *f.*
occupier ['ɔkjupaiǝ], *n.* occupant, *m.*; locataire (*de chambre louée*), *m.*, *f.*, habitant, *m.*
occupy ['ɔkjupai], *v.t.* occuper; employer;
habiter (*une maison*).
occur [ǝ'kǝː], *v.i.* arriver, avoir lieu, se produire; venir à l'esprit; *it occurred to me
that,* l'idée m'est venue que.
occurrence [ǝ'kʌrǝns], *n.* occurrence, rencontre, *f.*, événement, *m.*
ocean ['ouʃǝn], *a.* de l'océan.—*n.* océan, *m.*
oceanic [ousi'ænik], *a.* océanique.
ochre ['oukǝ], *n.* ocre, *f.*
o'clock [ǝ'klɔk], [CLOCK].
octagon ['ɔktǝgǝn], *n.* octogone, *m.*

octagonal [ɔk'tægǝnǝl], *a.* octogone, octo-
gonal.
octane ['ɔktein], *n.* octane, *m.*; **high-octane
fuel,** supercarburant, *m.*
octave ['ɔktiv], *n.* (*Mus., Eccles.*) octave, *f.*
octavo [ɔk'teivou], *n.* in-octavo, *m.*
octet(te) [ɔk'tet], *n.* (*Mus.*) octuor, *m.*
October [ɔk'toubǝ], octobre, *m.*
octogenarian [ɔktoudʒi'nɛǝriǝn], *a.* and *n.*
octogénaire, *m.*, *f.*
octopus ['ɔktǝpǝs], *n.* pieuvre, *f.*
ocular ['ɔkjulǝ], *a.* oculaire.
oculist ['ɔkjulist], *n.* oculiste, *m.*
odd [ɔd], *a.* impair; de surplus; d'appoint
(*argent*); dépareillé (*article isolé d'une collection*); étrange, singulier, bizarre; *odd
moments,* moments perdus, *m.pl.*; *odd
number,* nombre impair, *m.*
oddity ['ɔditi], *n.* bizarrerie, *f.*; original
(*personne*), *m.*
odd-looking ['ɔdlukiŋ], *a.* à la mine bizarre.
oddly ['ɔdli], *adv.* étrangement; bizarrement.
oddments ['ɔdmǝnts], *n.pl.* bric-à-brac, *m.*,
fins de séries, *f.pl.*
odds [ɔdz], *n.pl.* inégalité, *f.*; (*fig.*) avantage,
m., supériorité, *f.*; chances, *f.pl.*; *it makes
no odds,* cela ne fait rien; *odds and ends,*
petits bouts, *m.pl.*; *to be at odds with,*
être mal avec.
ode [oud], *n.* ode, *f.*
odious ['oudiǝs], *a.* odieux.
odium ['oudiǝm], *n.* détestation, *f.*
odor ['oudǝ], *n.* odeur, *f.*, parfum, *m.*; *in
bad odor,* en mauvaise odeur.
odorless ['oudǝlis], *a.* sans odeur.
odorous ['oudǝrǝs], *a.* odorant.
o'er ['ɔːǝ], (*poet.*) [OVER].
of [ɔv], *prep.* de; d'entre.
off [ɔf, ɔːf], *adv.* au loin, à distance; d'ici;
rompu, enlevé; fini; fermé (*électricité etc.*);
qui n'est plus frais (*aliments*); *day off,*
jour de congé, *m.*; *fifty yards off,* à cinquante pas; *I am off,* je m'en vais; *off and
on,* de temps à autre; *time off,* temps libre,
m.; *to be well off,* être dans l'aisance.—*a.
off day,* jour de congé, *m.*; *off side,* côté
droit, hors montoir; (*Ftb.*) hors-jeu; *off
white,* blanc teinté.—*prep.* de, de dessus;
éloigné de; (*Naut.*) au large de.
offal ['ɔfl], *n.* issues, *f.pl.*; abats, *m.pl.*; rebut,
m.
offence [ǝ'fens], *n.* agression; offense; injure;
violation (*d'une loi etc.*), *f.*, délit, crime, *m.*
offend [ǝ'fend], *v.t.* offenser, outrager;
blesser; violer (*transgresser*).—*v.i.* déplaire
(à); commettre une offense.
offender [ǝ'fendǝ], *n.* offenseur, *m.*; (*Law*)
délinquant, *m.*
offensive [ǝ'fensiv], *a.* offensant, désagréable;
choquant; offensif (*attaquant*).—*n.* offensive,
f.
offensively [ǝ'fensivli], *adv.* d'une manière
offensante; offensivement.
offensiveness [ǝ'fensivnis], *n.* nature offensante, *f.*
offer ['ɔfǝ], *v.t.* offrir, présenter, proposer à.—
v.i. s'offrir, se présenter à; essayer de.—*n.*
offre, *f.*
offering ['ɔfǝriŋ], *n.* offrande, *f.*; sacrifice, *m.*
off-hand ['ɔf'hænd], *adv.* au premier abord;
sans réflexion, sur-le-champ; cavalière-

ment.—*a.* brusque, cavalier; impromptu, improvisé.

off-handed ['ɔf'hændid], *a.* sans façon, sans gêne.

off-handedness ['ɔf'hændidnis], *n.* sans-façon, sans-gêne, *m.*

office ['ɔfis], *n.* bureau (*immeuble*), *m.*, agence, *f.*; cabinet (*du directeur*), *m.*; étude (*d'avoué etc.*), *f.*; office, emploi; ministère, *m.*, charge, *f.*, fonctions, *f.pl.*; (*pl.*) devoirs (*services*), *m.pl.*; (*pl.*) cabinet (of physician, dentist, lawyer), *m.*

officer ['ɔfisə], *n.* officier; fonctionnaire (*du gouvernement*); agent (*de police*), *m.*; **non-commissioned officer**, sous-officier, *m.*—*v.t.* fournir des officiers à; encadrer.

official [ə'fiʃəl], *a.* officiel.—*n.* fonctionnaire; employé, *m.*

officialdom [ə'fiʃəldəm], *n.* bureaucratie, *f.*

officially [ə'fiʃəli], *adv.* officiellement.

officiate [ə'fiʃieit], *v.i.* officier, desservir.

officious [ə'fiʃəs], *a.* officieux; importun.

officiousness [ə'fiʃəsnis], *n.* zèle officieux, *m.*

offing ['ɔfiŋ], *n.* (*Naut.*) **in the offing**, au large; (*fig.*) en perspective.

offset ['ɔfset], *v.t.* (*Comm.*) compenser; (*Tech.*) désaxer, décaler.

offshoot ['ɔfʃuːt], *n.* rejeton, *m.*

offspring ['ɔfspriŋ], *n.* enfants, descendants, *m.pl.*; (*fig.*) fruit, produit, *m.*

often ['ɔfn], ***oft** [ɔft], ***oftentimes** ['ɔfn taimz], ***oft-times** ['ɔfttaimz], *adv.* souvent, maintes fois.

ogle [ougl], *v.t.* lorgner; lancer des œillades à. —*n.* œillade, *f.*

ogler ['ouglə], *n.* lorgneur, *m.*

ogling ['ougliŋ], *n.* lorgnerie, *f.*, œillades, *f.pl.*

ogre ['ougə], *n.* ogre, *m.*

ogress ['ougris], *n.* ogresse, *f.*

oh! [ou], *int.* oh! hélas!

ohm [oum], *n.* (*Elec.*) ohm, *m.*

oil [ɔil], *n.* huile, *f.*; (*crude*) **oil**, pétrole (*brut*), *m.*; **fuel oil**, mazout, *m.*; **coal oil**, pétrole (*lampant*), *m.*—*v.t.* huiler; graisser; (*fig.*) délier (*la langue*).

oilcake ['ɔilkeik], *n.* tourteau, *m.*

oil-can ['ɔilkæn], *n.* burette, *f.*

oil-cloth ['ɔilklɔθ], *n.* toile cirée, *f.*

oil field ['ɔilfiːld], *n.* gisement pétrolifère, *m.*

oiliness ['ɔilinis], *n.* onctuosité, nature huileuse, *f.*

oil lamp ['ɔillæmp], *n.* lampe à huile *ou* à pétrole, *f.*

oil painting ['ɔilpeintiŋ], *n.* peinture à l'huile, *f.*

oilskin ['ɔilskin], *n.* toile cirée vernie, *f.*

oil stove ['ɔilstouv], *n.* réchaud à pétrole, *m.*

oil tanker ['ɔiltæŋkə], *n.* (*Naut.*) pétrolier; (*Motor.*) camion-citerne, *m.*

oil well ['ɔilwel], *n.* puits de pétrole, *m.*

oily ['ɔili], *a.* huileux; (*fig.*) oléagineux, onctueux.

ointment ['ɔintmənt], *n.* onguent, *m.*, pommade, *f.*

old [ould], *a.* vieux; âgé; ancien, antique; **how old are you?** quel âge avez-vous? **old man** (*chap, boy*), mon vieux, mon brave; **to grow old**, vieillir.

olden ['ouldən], *a.* vieux, ancien; **in olden times**, au temps jadis.

old-fashioned [ould'fæʃənd] *a.* démodé, suranné.

oldish ['ouldiʃ], *a.* un peu vieux, vieillot.

old maid ['ouldmeid], *n.* vieille fille, *f.*

oleaginous [ouli'ædʒinəs], *a.* oléagineux.

oleander [ouli'ændə], *n.* (*Bot.*) laurier-rose, oléandre, *m.*

oligarchy ['ɔligaːki], *n.* oligarchie, *f.*

olive ['ɔliv], *n.* olive, *f.*, olivier (*arbre*), *m.*

Oliver ['ɔlivə]. Olivier, *m.*

Olympian [o'limpiən], *a.* olympien.

Olympic [o'limpik], *a.* olympique; **the Olympic Games**, les jeux olympiques, *m.pl.*

Olympus [o'limpəs]. Olympe, *m.*

omega ['oumigə], *n.* oméga, *m.*

omelet(te) ['ɔmɔlit], *n.* omelette, *f.*

omen ['oumən], *n.* augure, *m.*

ominous ['ɔminəs], *a.* de mauvais augure, sinistre; menaçant.

ominously ['ɔminəsli], *adv.* de mauvais augure.

omission [o'miʃən], *n.* omission, *f.*

omit [o'mit], *v.t.* omettre; oublier.

omnipotence [ɔm'nipətəns], *n.* omnipotence, toute-puissance, *f.*

omnipotent [ɔm'nipətənt], *a.* tout-puissant, omnipotent.

omniscient [ɔm'nisiənt], *a.* omniscient.

omnivorous [ɔm'nivərəs], *a.* omnivore.

on [ɔn], *prep.* sur, dessus; à; de; en, dans; lors de, après; **on foot**, à pied; **on Monday**, lundi; **on purpose**, à dessein, exprès; **on the whole**, en somme.—*adv.* dessus; en avant, avant, avancé; toujours (*continuation*); de suite (*succession*); **and so on**, et ainsi de suite; **on and on**, sans cesse, interminablement; **play on**, continuez de jouer; **read on**, lisez toujours.

once [wʌns], *adv.* une fois, une seule fois; autrefois, jadis (*anciennement*); **at once**, sur-le-champ, tout de suite; **once upon a time there was**, il était une fois.

one [wʌn], *a.* un; seul, unique; un certain.— *n.* un, *m.*, une, *f.*—*pron.* on, l'on; vous (*accusatif*); celui, *m.*, celle, *f.*; quelqu'un; un homme, *m.*, une femme, *f.*

one-armed ['wʌnaːmd], *a.* manchot.

one-eyed ['wʌnaid], *a.* borgne.

onerous ['ɔnərəs], *a.* onéreux.

onerousness ['ɔnərəsnis], *n.* poids, *m.*, charge, *f.*

oneself [wʌn'self], *pron.* soi, soi-même; (*reflexive*) se.

one-sided ['wʌn'saidid], *a.* à un côté, à une face; (*fig.*) partial, unilatéral.

one-sidedness ['wʌn'saididnis], *n.* partialité, *f.*

one-way ['wʌnwei], *a.* **a one-way street**, rue à sens unique, *f.*; **one-way ticket**, billet simple, *m.*

onion ['ʌnjən], *n.* oignon, *m.*; **spring onion**, ciboule, *f.*

onion bed ['ʌnjənbed], *n.* oignonnière, *f.*

onlooker ['ɔnlukə], *n.* spectateur, *m.*

only ['ounli], *a.* seul; unique; **only child**, enfant unique, *m.*, *f.*—*adv.* seulement; rien que; uniquement; ne . . . que.—*conj.* mais.

onset ['ɔnset], *n.* assaut *m.*, attaque, charge, *f.*

onslaught ['ɔnslɔːt], *n.* attaque, *f.*; assaut, *m.*

onus ['ounəs], *n.* charge, responsabilité, obligation, *f.*

onward ['ɔnwəd], a. en avant; avancé, progressif.—adv. or onwards ['ɔnwədz], en avant.

onyx ['ɔniks], n. onyx, m.

ooze [u:z], n. limon, m.—v.i. suinter, filtrer; (fig.) s'ébruiter.

oozing ['u:ziŋ], n. suintement; (fig.) ébruitement, m.

oozy ['u:zi], a. vaseux, limoneux.

opal [oupl], n. opale, f.

opaque [o'peik], a. opaque; (fig.) épais.

opaqueness [o'peiknis], n. opacité, f.

open ['oupən], v.t. ouvrir; déboucher (une bouteille); (fig.) expliquer; commencer, entamer; révéler; décacheter (une lettre); défaire (un colis); inaugurer.—v.i. s'ouvrir; commencer.—a. ouvert, découvert, à découvert, nu, à nu; franc, sincère; libre; (fig.) clair; in the open (air), en plein air; on the open sea, en pleine mer.

opener ['oupnə], n. ouvreur, m.; tin-opener, ouvre-boîte, m.

open-handed ['oupən'hændid], a. libéral, généreux.

open-hearted ['oupən'ha:tid], a. franc.

opening ['oupniŋ], a. qui commence, d'inauguration; the opening chapter, le premier chapitre.—n. ouverture, embrasure, f.; commencement, début, m.; chance; éclaircie (dans une forêt etc.), f.

openly ['oupənli], adv. ouvertement; franchement.

open-minded ['oupən'maindid], a. sans parti pris, libéral, à l'esprit ouvert.

open-mouthed ['oupən'mauðd], a. bouche béante, bouche bée.

openness ['oupənnis], n. franchise, sincérité, candeur, f.

opera ['ɔpərə], n. opéra, m.

opera glass ['ɔprəglu:s], n. lorgnette, f.; (pl.) jumelles, f.pl.

opera hat ['ɔprəhæt], n. claque, m.

opera house ['ɔprəhaus], n. opéra, m.

operate ['ɔpəreit], v.t. opérer, effectuer.—v.i. opérer, agir; (Fin.) spéculer; to operate on someone for appendicitis, opérer quelqu'un de l'appendicite.

operatic [ɔpə'rætik], a. d'opéra.

operation [ɔpə'reiʃən], n. opération, action, f.

operative ['ɔpərətiv], a. actif, efficace; des ouvriers.—n. artisan, ouvrier, m.

operator ['ɔpəreitə], n. opérateur, m. telephone operator téléphoniste, m., f.; radio operator, radio, m.

operetta [ɔpə'retə], n. opérette, f.

opiate ['oupiit], a. opiacé.—n. opiat, m.

opinion [ə'pinjən], n. opinion, f., avis, sentiment, m.; idée, pensée; (Law) consultation, f.; in my opinion, à mon avis.

opinionated [ə'pinjəneitid], a. opiniâtre; têtu, imbu de ses opinions.

opium ['oupjəm], n. opium, m.

opossum [o'pɔsəm], n. opossum, m.; sarigue, f.

opponent [ə'pounənt], n. opposant, m., adversaire, m., f.

opportune ['ɔpətju:n], a. opportun, à propos.

opportunely ['ɔpətju:nli], adv. à propos.

opportunity [ɔpə'tju:niti], n. occasion, f.

oppose [ə'pouz], v.t. opposer; s'opposer à.

opposite ['ɔpəzit], a. opposé; vis-à-vis, contraire (à), en face.—n. opposé, contre-pied,

m.—adv. vis-à-vis, en face.—prep. en face de, vis-à-vis de.

opposition [ɔpə'ziʃən], n. opposition, résistance; concurrence (rivalité), f.; obstacle, m.

oppress [ə'pres], v.t. opprimer; accabler.

oppression [ə'preʃən], n. oppression, f.

oppressive [ə'presiv], a. accablant, oppressif; lourd.

oppressiveness [ə'presivnis], n. caractère oppressif, m., lourdeur, f.

oppressor [ə'presə], n. oppresseur, m.

opprobrious [ə'proubriəs], a. infamant; injurieux.

opprobrium [ə'proubriəm], n. opprobre, m.

opt [ɔpt], v.i. opter.

optic ['ɔptik], optical ['ɔptikəl], a. optique; d'optique.

optician [ɔp'tiʃən], n. opticien, m.

optimism ['ɔptimizm], n. optimisme, m.

optimist ['ɔptimist], n. optimiste, m., f.

optimistic [ɔpti'mistik], a. optimiste.

option ['ɔpʃən], n. option, f., choix, m.

optional ['ɔpʃənl], a. facultatif.

opulence ['ɔpjuləns], n. opulence, f.

opulent ['ɔpjulənt], a. opulent.

or [ɔ:], conj. ou; (negatively) ni; or else, ou bien, autrement.

oracle ['ɔrəkl], n. oracle, m.

oracular [ɔ'rækjulə], a. d'oracle; (fig.) dogmatique.

oral ['ɔ:rəl], a. oral.

orally ['ɔ:rəli], adv. oralement; par la bouche.

orange ['ɔrindʒ], n. orange; couleur orange, f.

orangery ['ɔrindʒəri], n. orangerie, f.

orange-tree ['ɔrindʒtri:], n. oranger, m.

orang-outang [o'ræŋu'tæŋ], n. orang-outang, m.

oration [o'reiʃən], n. allocution, f., discours, m.; funeral oration, oraison funèbre, f.

orator ['ɔrətə], n. orateur, m.

oratorical [ɔrə'tɔrikəl], a. oratoire.

oratorio [ɔrə'tɔ:riou], n. oratorio, m.

oratory ['ɔrətri], n. art oratoire, m., éloquence, f.; oratoire (chapelle), m.

orb [ɔ:b], n. globe; corps sphérique; orbe, m.

orbit ['ɔ:bit], n. orbe, m.; (Anat., Astron.) orbite, f.

orchard ['ɔ:tʃəd], n. verger, m.

orchestra ['ɔ:kistrə], n. orchestre, m. [see stall]

orchestral [ɔ:'kestrəl], a. d'orchestre, orchestral.

orchid ['ɔ:kid], n. orchidée, f.

ordain [ɔ:'dein], v.t. ordonner, décréter.

ordeal [ɔ:'di:əl], n. dure épreuve, f.

order ['ɔ:də], n. ordre; règlement, m.; décoration (insigne); (Mil.) consigne; classe, f., rang, m.; commande (de marchandises), f.; mandat (de payer), m.; in order that, afin que; in order to, afin de; money order, mandat-poste, m.—v.t. ordonner; régler; diriger (administrer); commander; prescrire (médecine).

ordering ['ɔ:dəriŋ], n. disposition, f., arrangement, m.

orderliness ['ɔ:dəlinis], n. bon ordre, m., méthode, f.

orderly ['ɔ:dəli], a. en bon ordre, méthodique, rangé.—n. (Mil.) planton, m.

ordinal ['ɔ:dinl], a. ordinal.

ordinance ['ɔ:dinəns], n. ordonnance, f.

ordinarily ['ɔːdinrili], *adv.* ordinairement, d'ordinaire.

ordinary ['ɔːdinri], *a.* ordinaire; moyen.— *n.* ordinaire, *m.*; table d'hôte, *f.*

ordination [ɔːdi'neiʃən], *n.* ordination, *f.*

ordnance ['ɔːdnəns], *n.* artillerie, *f.*; *ordnance map*, carte d'état major, *f.*

ore [ɔː], *n.* minerai, *m.*

organ ['ɔːgən], *n.* (*Anat. etc.*) organe; (*Mus.*) orgue, *m.*

organic [ɔː'gænik], *a.* organique; des organes.

organism ['ɔːgənizm], *n.* organisme, *m.*

organist ['ɔːgənist], *n.* organiste, *m.*, *f.*

organization [ɔːgənai'zeiʃən], *n.* organisation; œuvre, *f.*

organize ['ɔːgənaiz], *v.t.* organiser; aménager.

organizer ['ɔːgənaizə], *n.* organisateur, *m.*

orgy ['ɔːdʒi], *n.* orgie, *f.*

orient ['ɔːriənt], *n.* orient, *m.*

Oriental [ɔːri'entl], *a.* oriental, d'Orient.—*n.* natif de l'Orient, oriental, *m.*

orifice ['ɔrifis], *n.* orifice, *m.*, ouverture, *f.*

origin ['ɔridʒin], *n.* origine, source; provenance, *f.*

original [ə'ridʒinl], *a.* original, inédit (*nouveau*); primitif (*sens des mots etc.*).—*n.* original, *m.*

originality [əridʒi'næliti], *n.* originalité, *f.*

originally [ə'ridʒinəli], *adv.* originairement; originalement.

originate [ə'ridʒineit], *v.t.* faire naître, produire; (*fig.*) inventer.—*v.i.* tirer son origine (*de*), provenir de.

originator [ə'ridʒineitə], *n.* initiateur, auteur, *m.*

oriole ['ɔːrioul], *n.* (*Orn.*) loriot, *m.*

orison ['ɔrizn], *n.* oraison, prière, *f.*

Orkneys ['ɔːkniz], the. les Orcades, *f.pl.*

ornament ['ɔːnəmənt], *n.* ornement, *m.*—*v.t.* orner, décorer (*de*).

ornamental [ɔːnə'mentl], *a.* ornemental, d'ornement; d'agrément.

ornate [ɔː'neit], *a.* orné, élégant, paré.

ornately [ɔː'neitli], *adv.* avec ornement.

ornithologist [ɔːni'θɔlədʒist], *n.* ornithologiste, ornithologue, *m.*, *f.*

ornithology [ɔːni'θɔlədʒi], *n.* ornithologie, *f.*

orphan ['ɔːfən], *a.* and *n.* orphelin, *m.*

orphanage ['ɔːfənidʒ], *n.* état d'orphelin; orphelinat, *m.*

orthodox ['ɔːθədɔks], *a.* orthodoxe.

orthodoxy ['ɔːθədɔksi], *n.* orthodoxie, *f.*

orthographic [ɔːθə'græfik], *a.* orthographique.

orthography [ɔː'θɔgrəfi], *n.* orthographe, orthographie, *f.*

orthop(a)edic [ɔːθə'piːdik], *a.* orthopédique.

orthop(a)edist [ɔːθə'piːdist], *n.* orthopédiste, *m.*

orthop(a)edy ['ɔːθəpiːdi], *n.* orthopédie, *f.*

oscillate ['ɔsileit], *v.i.* osciller; (*fig.*) balancer, vaciller.

oscillation [ɔsi'leiʃən], *n.* oscillation, *f.*

oscillatory ['ɔsileitəri], *a.* oscillatoire.

osier ['ouʒiə], *n.* osier, *m.*

osier bed ['ouʒiəbed], *n.* oseraie, *f.*

osprey ['ɔsprei], *n.* (*Orn.*) orfraie, *f.*

osseous ['ɔsiəs], *a.* osseux.

ossicle ['ɔsikl], *n.* ossicule, osselet, *m.*

ossification [ɔsifi'keiʃən], *n.* ossification, *f.*

ossify ['ɔsifai], *v.t.* ossifier.—*v.i.* s'ossifier.

ostensible [ɔs'tensibl], *a.* prétendu.

ostensibly [ɔs'tensibli], *adv.* en apparence.

ostentation [ɔsten'teiʃən], *n.* ostentation, *f.*, faste, *m.*

ostentatious [ɔsten'teiʃəs], *a.* pompeux, fastueux.

osteopath ['ɔstiopæθ], *n.* ostéopathe, *m.*

ostler ['ɔslə], *n.* garçon d'écurie, *m.*

ostracism ['ɔstrəsizm], *n.* ostracisme, *m.*

ostracize ['ɔstrəsaiz], *v.t.* frapper d'ostracisme, exiler.

ostrich ['ɔstritʃ], *n.* autruche, *f.*

other ['ʌðə], *a.* autre; *every other day*, tous les deux jours; *other people*, d'autres, autrui.—*pron.* autre; autrui; *all the others*, tous les autres.

otherwise ['ʌðəwaiz], *adv.* autrement; sans quoi.

otter ['ɔtə], *n.* loutre, *f.*

ought [ɔːt], *v.aux.* devoir; falloir; *you ought to do it*, vous devriez le faire; *you ought to have seen*, il aurait fallu voir.

ounce (1) [auns], *n.* once (*poids*), *f.*

ounce (2) [auns], *n.* (*Zool.*) once, *f.*

our ['auə], *a.poss.* notre, *sing.*, nos, *pl.*

ours ['auəz], *pron.* le nôtre, *m.*, la nôtre, *f.*, les nôtres, *pl.*; à nous.

ourselves [auə'selvz], *pron.* nous-mêmes; nous.

oust [aust], *v.t.* évincer, déloger.

out [aut], *adv.* hors, dehors; sorti (*pas chez soi*); découvert, exposé (*dévoilé*); éteint (*feu etc.*); épuisé, fini (*tout vendu* ou *tout consumé*), jusqu'au bout; haut à voix (*parler*); dans l'erreur (*pas exact*); publié, paru (*livre*); épanoui (*fleur*); out externe.

outbid [aut'bid], *v.t. irr.* (*conjug. like* BID) enchérir sur, surenchérir.

outboard ['autbɔːd], *a. outboard motorboat*, hors-bord, *m.*

outbreak ['autbreik], *n.* éruption, explosion; épidémie, *f.*

outburst ['autbəːst], *n.* explosion, *f.*, transport, éclat, *m.*

outcast ['autkɑːst], *a.* expulsé, proscrit, rejeté.—*n.* proscrit, banni, paria, *m.*

outcome ['autkʌm], *n.* résultat, *m.*

outcry ['autkrai], *n.* clameur, *f.*, tollé, *m.*

outdated [aut'deitid], *a.* démodé.

outdo [aut'du], *v.t. irr.* (*conjug. like* DO) surpasser, exceller.

outdoor ['autdɔː], *a.* en plein air; externe.

outdoors [aut'dɔːz], *adv.* en plein air; hors de la maison.

outer ['autə], *a.* extérieur, du dehors, externe.

outermost ['autəmoust], *a.* le plus extérieur.

outfit ['autfit], *n.* attirail, équipement; trousseau, *m.*

outfitter ['autfitə], *n.* confectionneur et chemisier, *m.*

outflank [aut'flæŋk], *v.t.* déborder, tourner.

outgoing ['autgouiŋ], *a.* sortant, qui sort.— *n.* (*pl.*) dépenses, *f.pl.*

outgrow [aut'grou], *v.t. irr.* (*conjug. like* GROW) dépasser, surpasser.

outgrowth ['autgrouθ], *n.* excroissance; conséquence, *f.*

outhouse ['authaus], *n.* hangar, *m.*; dépendance, *f.*

outing ['autiŋ], *n.* excursion, promenade, *f.*

outlandish [aut'lændiʃ], *a.* étranger; bizarre; retiré.

outlast [aut'lɑːst], *v.t.* survivre à.

outlaw ['autlɔ:], *n.* proscrit, *m.*—*v.t.* mettre hors la loi, proscrire.
outlay ['autlei], *n.* dépense, *f.*, débours, *m.pl.*
outlet ['autlit], *n.* issue, sortie, *f.*; (*Comm.*) débouché, *m.*
outline ['autlain], *n.* contour, *m.*; profil, *m.*, ébauche, *f.*—*v.t.* esquisser.
outlive [aut'liv], *v.t.* survivre à.
outlook ['autluk], *n.* vue, perspective, *f.*
outlying ['autlaiiŋ], *a.* éloigné, détaché.
outnumber [aut'nʌmbə], *v.t.* surpasser en nombre.
out-of-date [autəv'deit], *a.* démodé, dépassé.
outpost ['autpoust], *n.* avant-poste, *m.*
outpour [aut'pɔ:], *v.t.* épancher, verser à flots.
outpouring ['autpɔ:riŋ], *n.* effusion, *f.*, épanchement, *m.*
outrage ['autreidʒ], *n.* outrage, *m.*—*v.t.* outrager.
outrageous [aut'reidʒəs], *a.* outrageux, outrageant.
outrageousness [aut'reidʒəsnis], *n.* nature outrageante, énormité, *f.*
outright ['autrait], *adv.* complètement; carrément (*à cœur ouvert*).
outrun [aut'rʌn], *v.t. irr.* (*conjug. like* RUN) dépasser à la course, gagner de vitesse.
outset ['autset], *n.* début, commencement, *m.*, *at the very outset*, dès l'origine.
outshine [aut'ʃain], *v.t. irr.* (*conjug. like* SHINE) surpasser en éclat, éclipser.
outside ['autsaid], *a.* extérieur, externe, du dehors.—*n.* dehors, extérieur, *m.*—[aut'said], *adv.* en dehors, à l'extérieur.—[aut'said], *prep.* hors de, à l'extérieur de.
outsider [aut'saidə], *n.* étranger, *m.*; (*Racing*) outsider, *m.*
outsize ['autsaiz], *a.* de grande taille, hors série.
outskirts ['autskə:ts], *n.pl.* bords, *m.pl.*; lisière (*d'un bois*), banlieue, *f.*, faubourg (*d'une ville*), *m.*
outspoken [aut'spoukən], *a.* franc, clair, carré.
outstanding [aut'stændiŋ], *a.* saillant, remarquable, excellent; non payé; en suspens (*affaires*).
outstretched [aut'stretʃt], *a.* étendu, déployé, tendu.
outstrip [aut'strip], *v.t.* devancer, distancer.
outward ['autwəd], *a.* extérieur, du dehors, externe; superficiel.—*adv.* or **outwards** ['autwədz], à l'extérieur; au dehors, extérieurement; *outward bound*, en partance.
outwardly ['autwədli], *adv.* extérieurement, à l'extérieur; (*fig.*) en apparence.
outweigh [aut'wei], *v.t.* peser plus que; l'emporter sur.
outwit [aut'wit], *v.t.* surpasser en finesse, duper.
oval [ouvl], *a.* and *n.* ovale, *m.*
ovary ['ouvəri], *n.* ovaire, *m.*
ovation [o'veiʃən], *n.* ovation, *f.*
oven [ʌvn], *n.* four, *m.*
over ['ouvə], *prep.* sur; par-dessus; au-dessus de; de l'autre côté de (*en face*); pendant (*au cours de*); *over there*, là-bas.—*adv.* d'un côté à l'autre; par-dessus, au-dessus; trop (*à l'excès*); plus de (*excédant*);

de reste (*surplus inemployé*); fini, terminé, fait; passé.
overact [ouvər'ækt], *v.t.* outrer, exagérer.
overall ['ouvrə:l], *a.* total.—*n.* blouse, *f.*; tablier, *m.*; (*pl.*) salopette, combinaison, *f.*
overawe [ouvər'ɔ:], *v.t.* intimider, imposer à.
overbalance [ouvə'bæləns], *v.t.* l'emporter sur.—*v.i.* perdre l'équilibre.
overbearing [ouvə'bɛəriŋ], *a.* impérieux, autoritaire.
overboard ['ouvəbɔ:d], *adv.* par-dessus bord.
overburden [ouvə'bə:dn], *v.t.* surcharger; accabler (*de*).
overcast ['ouvəkɑ:st], *a.* couvert, nuageux.
overcharge [ouvə'tʃɑ:dʒ], *v.t.* surcharger; faire payer trop cher.—*n.* prix excessif, *m.*
overcoat ['ouvəkout], *n.* pardessus, *m.*
overcome [ouvə'kʌm], *v.t. irr.* (*conjug. like* COME) surmonter, vaincre, accabler.—*v.i.* l'emporter.
over-confident ['ouvə'kɔnfidənt], *a.* trop confiant; présomptueux, téméraire.
overcrowd [ouvə'kraud], *v.t.* encombrer à l'excès, trop remplir.
overcrowding [ouvə'kraudiŋ], *n.* surpeuplement, *m.*
overdo [ouvə'du:], *v.t. irr.* (*conjug. like* DO) exagérer, outrer; faire trop cuire; harasser.
overdone [ouvə'dʌn], *a.* trop cuit; (*fig.*) exagéré.
overdose ['ouvədous], *n.* dose trop forte, *f.*
overdraw [ouvə'drɔ:], *v.t. irr.* (*conjug. like* DRAW) excéder; *to overdraw one's account*, tirer à découvert; tirer un chèque sans provision.
overdue [ouvə'dju:], *a.* en retard.
overestimate [ouvər'estimeit], *v.t.* évaluer trop haut.
overflow [ouvə'flou], *v.t.* inonder.—*v.i.* déborder, se déborder.—['ouvəflou], *n.* inondation, *f.*, débordement, *m.*
overflowing [ouvə'flouiŋ], *a.* qui déborde, trop plein.—*n.* débordement, *m.*
overgrown [ouvə'groun], *a.* couvert (*d'herbes, ronces*); trop grand, énorme.
overhang ['ouvəhæŋ], *n.* surplomb, *m.*—[ouvə'hæŋ], *v.t. irr.* (*conjug. like* HANG) pencher sur, surplomber; faire saillie.
overhanging ['ouvəhæŋiŋ], *a.* en surplomb.
overhaul [ouvə'hɔ:l], *v.t.* examiner, revoir; réviser, vérifier, démonter.—['ouvəhɔ:l], *n.* examen détaillé, *m.*
overhead [ouvə'hed], *adv.* par-dessus la tête, en haut.—*a.* aérien (*fil etc.*).—['ouvə hedz], *n.* (*pl.*) (*Comm.*) frais généraux, *m.pl.*
overhear [ouvə'hiə], *v.t. irr.* (*conjug. like* HEAR) entendre par hasard.
overheat [ouvə'hi:t], *v.t.* surchauffer.
overjoyed [ouvə'dʒɔid], *a.* transporté de joie, ravi.
overland ['ouvəlænd], *a.* and *adv.* par voie de terre.
overlap [ouvə'læp], *v.t.* recouvrir.—['ouvə læp], *n.* recouvrement, *m.*
overlapping [ouvə'læpiŋ], *n.* recouvrement, chevauchement, *m.*
overload [ouvə'loud], *v.t.* surcharger, surmener.
overlook [ouvə'luk], *v.t.* donner sur, dominer; surveiller (*diriger*); fermer les yeux sur (*passer sur*); oublier, négliger.

overlooking [ouvə'lukiŋ], *a.* donnant (*sur*).
overmuch ['ouvəmʌtʃ], *a.* excessif.—*n.* trop, *m.*—*adv.* par trop, excessivement.
overnight [ouvə'nait], *adv.* durant la nuit; hier soir; du jour au lendemain.
overpay [ouvə'pei], *v.t. irr. (conjug. like* PAY) payer trop.
overpower [ouvə'pauə], *v.t.* vaincre; accabler (*de*).
overpowering [ouvə'pauəriŋ], *a.* accablant, écrasant.
overproduction [ouvəprə'dʌkʃən], *n.* surproduction, *f.*
overrate [ouvə'reit], *v.t.* estimer trop haut.
overreach [ouvə'riːtʃ], *v.t.* tromper.—*v.i.* forger (*chevaux*); **to overreach oneself,** trop présumer de ses forces.
override [ouvə'raid], *v.t. irr. (conjug. like* RIDE) surmener, outrepasser.
overrule [ouvə'ruːl], *v.t.* dominer; (*Law*) rejeter.
overrun [ouvə'rʌn], *v.t. irr. (conjug. like* RUN) envahir, faire une irruption dans; infester (*de*).—*v.i.* déborder.
oversea ['ouvəsiː], **overseas** ['ouvəsiːz, ouvə siːz], *a.* and *adv.* d'outre-mer.
oversee [ouvə'siː], *v.t. irr. (conjug. like* SEE) surveiller.
overseer ['ouvəsiə], *n.* surveillant; contremaître (*d'usine etc.*), *m.*
overshadow [ouvə'ʃædou], *v.t.* ombrager; éclipser.
overshoes ['ouvəʃuːz], *n.pl.* caoutchoucs, *m.pl.*
overshoot [ouvə'ʃuːt], *v.t. irr. (conjug. like* SHOOT) dépasser.
oversight ['ouvəsait], *n.* inadvertance, *f.*, oubli, *m.*
oversleep [ouvə'sliːp], *v.i. irr. (conjug. like* SLEEP) dormir au delà de son heure.
overstate [ouvə'steit], *v.t.* exagérer.
overstatement [ouvə'steitmənt], *n.* exagération, *f.*
overstep [ouvə'step], *v.t.* dépasser.
overt ['ouvəːt], *a.* ouvert, manifeste.
overtake [ouvə'teik], *v.t. irr. (conjug. like* TAKE) rattraper; doubler, dépasser.
overtax [ouvə'tæks], *v.t.* surtaxer, surcharger.
overthrow [ouvə'θrou], *v.t. irr. (conjug. like* THROW) renverser; défaire, détruire.—['ouvəθrou], *n.* renversement, *m.*, défaite; destruction, *f.*
overtime ['ouvətaim], *n.* heures supplémentaires, *f.pl.*
overtop [ouvə'tɔp], *v.t.* s'élever au-dessus de, dépasser.
overture ['ouvətjuə], *n.* ouverture; offre, *f.*
overturn [ouvə'təːn], *v.t.* renverser; bouleverser.—*v.i.* verser.
overweening [ouvə'wiːniŋ], *a.* présomptueux, outrecuidant.
overweight ['ouvəweit], *n.* excédent, *m.*
overwhelm [ouvə'welm], *v.t.* accabler (*de*); combler (*de*) (*bontés etc.*).
overwhelming [ouvə'welmiŋ], *a.* accablant, écrasant.
overwork [ouvə'wəːk], *v.t.* surcharger de travail, surmener.—*n.* travail excessif; surmenage, *m.*
ovoid ['ouvoid], *a.* ovoïde.
owe [ou], *v.t.* devoir; être redevable à . . . de.

owing ['ouiŋ], *a.* dû (*à*); **owing to,** à cause de, grâce à.
owl [aul], *n.* hibou, *m.*; chouette, *f.*
owlet ['aulit], *n.* jeune hibou, *m.*
own (1) [oun], *a.* propre (*à soi*); **my own money,** mon argent; **to hold one's own,** se maintenir.—*v.t.* posséder, être propriétaire de (*avoir*).
own (2) [oun], *v.t.* avouer, confesser.
owner ['ounə], *n.* possesseur, *m.*, propriétaire, *m., f.*
ownership ['ounəʃip], *n.* propriété, *f.*
ox [ɔks], *n.* (*pl.* **oxen** ['ɔksən]) bœuf, *m.*
oxalic [ɔk'sælik], *a.* oxalique.
ox-fly ['ɔksflai], *n.* taon, *m.*
oxide ['ɔksaid], *n.* oxyde, *m.*
oxidization [ɔksidai'zeiʃən], *n.* oxydation, calcination, *f.*
oxidize ['ɔksidaiz], *v.t.* oxyder; calciner.
oxyacetylene [ɔksiə'setiliːn], *a.* oxyacétylénique.
oxygen ['ɔksidʒən], *n.* oxygène, *m.*
oxygenate ['ɔksidʒəneit], *v.t.* oxygéner.
oxygenous [ɔk'sidʒənəs], *a.* d'oxygène.
oyster ['ɔistə], *n.* huître, *f.*
oyster bed ['ɔistəbed], *n.* banc d'huîtres, *m.*
ozone [ou'zoun], *n.* ozone, *m.*

P

P, p [piː]. seizième lettre de l'alphabet, *m.*
pabulum ['pæbjuləm], *n.* aliment, *m.*, nourriture, *f.*
pace [peis], *n.* pas, *m.*; allure (*de cheval*), *f.*; train, *m.*; vitesse, *f.*; **to put someone through his paces,** mettre quelqu'un à l'épreuve.—*v.t.* arpenter; (*Spt.*) entraîner.—*v.i.* aller au pas, marcher.
pacific [pə'sifik], *a.* pacifique, paisible.—*n.* **the Pacific (Ocean),** le Pacifique, l'océan Pacifique, *m.*
pacification [pæsifi'keiʃən], *n.* pacification, *f.*
pacifier ['pæsifaiə], *n.* pacificateur, *m.*
pacifism ['pæsifizm], *n.* pacifisme, *m.*
pacifist ['pæsifist], *n.* pacifiste, *m., f.*
pacify ['pæsifai], *v.t.* pacifier, apaiser.
pack [pæk], *n.* paquet, ballot, *m.*; meute (*chiens de chasse*), *f.*; jeu (*de cartes*), *m.*—*v.t.* emballer, empaqueter.—*v.i.* s'assembler; se grouper; faire sa malle.
package ['pækidʒ], *n.* colis, paquet, *m.*
packer ['pækə], *n.* emballeur, *m.*
packet ['pækit], *n.* paquet; paquebot (*bateau*), *m.*
pack horse ['pækhɔːs], *n.* cheval de bât, *m.*
pack-ice ['pækais], *n.* glace de banquise, *f.*, pack, *m.*
packing ['pækiŋ], *n.* emballage, *m.*
pact [pækt], *n.* pacte, *m.*
pad [pæd], *n.* tampon; coussinet, *m.*; **writing pad,** sous-main, bloc de papier, *m.*—*v.t.* ouater; rembourrer.—*v.i.* aller à pied.
padding ['pædiŋ], *n.* ouate, bourre, *f.*

paddle

paddle [pædl], *n.* pagaie; aube (*de roue*), *f.*
—*v.t.* pagayer.—*v.i.* patauger.
paddle boat ['pædlbout], *n.* bateau à aubes,
m.
paddock ['pædək], *n.* enclos, pré, pâturage,
m.
padlock ['pædlɔk], *n.* cadenas, *m.*—*v.t.*
cadenasser, fermer au cadenas.
paean ['piːən], *n.* péan, *m.*
pagan ['peigən], *a.* and *n.* païen, *m.*
paganism ['peigənizm], *n.* paganisme, *m.*
page (1) [peidʒ], *n.* page (*garçon*), *m.*
page (2) [peidʒ], *n.* page (*de livre*), *f.*
pageant ['pædʒənt], *n.* spectacle pompeux,
cortège *ou* spectacle historique, *m.*
pageantry ['pædʒəntri], *n.* pompe, *f.*, faste,
apparat, *m.*
pagoda [pə'goudə], *n.* pagode, *f.*
paid [peid], *a.* payé, acquitté; affranchi
(*lettres*).
pail [peil], *n.* seau, *m.*
pailful ['peilful], *n.* (plein) seau, *m.*
pain [pein], *n.* douleur; peine (*effort*), *f.*; **on
pain of,** sous peine de; **to take pains,** se
donner de la peine.—*v.t.* faire mal à; (*fig.*)
faire de la peine à; affliger.
painful ['peinful], *a.* douloureux, pénible.
painless ['peinlis], *a.* sans douleur, indolore.
painstaking ['peinzteikiŋ], *a.* soigneux,
assidu.
paint [peint], *n.* couleur; peinture, *f.*; fard
(*pour le visage*), *m.*—*v.t.* peindre; farder (*le
visage*).—*v.i.* peindre; se farder.
painter (1) ['peintə], *n.* peintre, *m.*
painter (2) ['peintə], *n.* (*Naut.*) amarre, *f.*
painting ['peintiŋ], *n.* peinture, *f.*; tableau
(*picture*), *m.*
pair [pɛə], *n.* paire, *f.*; couple (*époux etc.*), *m.*
—*v.t.* accoupler.—*v.i.* s'accoupler.
pajamas [pi'dʒɑːməz], *n.pl.* pyjama, *m.*
Pakistan [pɑːki'stɑːn], le Pakistan, *m.*
Pakistani [pɑːki'stɑːni], *a.* pakistanais.—*n.*
Pakistanais (*personne*), *m.*
pal [pæl], *n.* (*colloq.*) camarade, copain, *m.*
palace ['pælis], *n.* palais, *m.*; **archbishop's
palace,** archevêché, *m.*; **bishop's palace,**
évêché, *m.*
palatable ['pælətəbl], *a.* agréable au goût.
palate ['pælit], *n.* palais; (*fig.*) goût, *m.*
palatial [pə'leiʃl], *a.* du palais, palatial;
grandiose.
palaver [pə'lɑːvə], *n.* palabre (*chez certains
peuples primitifs*), *f.*; verbiage, *m.*; flagornerie, *f.*—*v.i.* palabrer, faire des phrases.
pale (1) [peil], *a.* pâle, blême; (*fig.*) blafard
(*lumière*).—*v.i.* pâlir; (*fig.*) s'éclipser.
pale (2) [peil], *n.* pieu, palis, *m.*; limites
(*bornes*), *f.pl.*; **beyond the pale,** au ban de
la société.
pale-faced ['peilfeist], *a.* au teint pâle.
paleness ['peilnis], *n.* pâleur, *f.*
Palestine ['pælistain], la Palestine, *f.*
Palestinian [pælis'tinian], *a.* palestinien.
palette ['pælit], *n.* palette, *f.*
palfrey ['pɔːlfri], *n.* palefroi, *m.*
paling ['peiliŋ], *n.* palissade, *f.*
palisade [pæli'seid], *n.* palissade, *f.*—*v.t.*
palissader.
palish ['peiliʃ], *a.* un peu pâle, pâlot.
pall [pɔːl], *n.* poêle; (*fig.*) drap mortuaire;

voile (*de fumée etc.*), *m.*—*v.i.* devenir fade,
s'affadir.
pallet ['pælit], *n.* grabat, *m.*, paillasse, *f.*
palliate ['pælieit], *v.t.* pallier.
palliation [pæli'eiʃən], *n.* palliation, *f.*
palliative ['pæliətiv], *a.* and *n.* palliatif, *m.*
pallid ['pælid], *a.* pâle, blême, blafard.
pallor ['pælə], *n.* pâleur, *f.*
palm (1) [pɑːm], *n.* paume (*de main*), *f.*—*v.t.*
to palm off (*something on someone*), passer,
refiler (*quelque chose à quelqu'un*).
palm (2) [pɑːm], *n.* palmier (*arbre*), *m.*;
palme (*rameau*), *f.*; **Palm Sunday,**
dimanche des Rameaux, *m.*
palmist ['pɑːmist], *n.* chiromancien, *m.*
palmistry ['pɑːmistri], *n.* chiromancie, *f.*
palmy ['pɑːmi], *a.* beau, glorieux, heureux.
palpable ['pælpəbl], *a.* palpable; manifeste.
palpitate ['pælpiteit], *v.i.* palpiter.
palpitation [pælpi'teiʃən], *n.* palpitation, *f.*
palsied ['pɔːlzid], *a.* frappé de paralysie,
paralytique.
palsy ['pɔːlzi], *n.* paralysie, *f.*
palter ['pɔːltə], *v.i.* tergiverser, biaiser.
paltriness ['pɔːltrinis], *n.* mesquinerie, *f.*
paltry ['pɔːltri], *a.* mesquin, misérable.
pamper ['pæmpə], *v.t.* choyer, dorloter.
pamphlet ['pæmflit], *n.* brochure, *f.*; (*pej.*)
pamphlet, *m.*
pamphleteer [pæmfli'tiə], *n.* auteur de
brochures, *m.*; (*pej.*) pamphlétaire, *m.*, *f.*
pan [pæn], *n.* casserole, *f.*, poêlon, *m.*;
frying pan, poêle, *f.*
panacea [pænə'siːə], *n.* panacée, *f.*
Panama ['pænəmɑː], le Panama, *m.*
Panamanian [pænə'meiniən], *a.* panamanien.
—*n.* Panamanien (*personne*), *m.*
pancake ['pænkeik], *n.* crêpe, *f.*
pancreas ['pænkriəs], *n.* (*Anat.*) pancréas, *m.*
pandemonium [pændi'mouniəm], *n.* pandémonium, *m.*
pander ['pændə], *v.i.* se prêter à, se faire
complaisant pour.
pane [pein], *n.* carreau, *m.*, vitre, *f.*
panegyric [pæni'dʒirik], *a.* de panégyrique.—
n. panégyrique, *m.*
panegyrist [pæni'dʒirist], *n.* panégyriste, *m.*, *f.*
panel ['pænl], *n.* panneau, *m.*; liste (*de juré
etc.*), *f.*; **instrument panel,** tableau de
manœuvre, *m.*—*v.t.* diviser en panneaux;
lambrisser.
panelling ['pænliŋ], *n.* panneaux, *m.pl.*,
lambrissage, *m.*
pang [pæŋ], *n.* angoisse, vive douleur, *f.*;
serrement de cœur, *m.*
panic ['pænik], *a.* panique.—*n.* panique;
terreur panique, *f.*—*v.i.* s'affoler.
pannier ['pæniə], *n.* panier, *m.*, hotte, *f.*
panoply ['pænəpli], *n.* panoplie, armure
complète, *f.*
panorama [pænə'rɑːmə], *n.* panorama, *m.*
panoramic [pænə'ræmik], *a.* panoramique.
pansy ['pænzi], *n.* (*Bot.*) pensée, *f.*
pant [pænt], *n.* palpitation, *f.*, halètement, *m.*
—*v.i.* haleter, palpiter, panteler.
pantechnicon [pæn'teknikn], *n.* garde-
meuble, *m.*; voiture de déménagement, *m.*
pantheism ['pænθiːizm], *n.* panthéisme, *m.*
pantheist ['pænθiːist], *n.* panthéiste, *m.*, *f.*
pantheistic [pænθiː'istik], *a.* panthéistique.
panther ['pænθə], *n.* panthère, *f.*

pantile ['pæntail], n. tuile faitière ou flamande, f.

pantomime ['pæntəmaim], n. pantomime, f.

pantomimic [pæntə'mimik], a. pantomime.

pantry ['pæntri], n. office, f., garde-manger, m.

pants [pænts], n.pl. (colloq.) caleçon; (Am.) pantalon, m. **[panties,** see **knickers]**

pap [pæp], n. mamelle; bouillie (aliment), f.

papacy ['peipəsi], n. papauté, f.

papal ['peipəl], a. papal, du pape.

paper ['peipə], a. de papier.—n. papier, m.; feuille de papier, f.; journal; papier-monnaie, m.; billets, m.pl.; mémoire, m., étude (article); composition (d'examen), f.; (pl.) papiers, m.pl.; dossier, m.; **blotting paper,** papier buvard; **kraft paper,** papier gris.—v.t. tapisser (de papier).

paper-back ['peipəbæk], n. livre broché, m.

paper clip ['peipəklip], n. attache, f., trombone (de fil), m.

paper-hanger ['peipəhæŋə], n. colleur de papier, m.

paper-knife ['peipənaif], n. coupe-papier, m.

paper maker ['peipəmeikə], n. fabricant de papier, m.

paper mill ['peipəmil], n. papeterie, f.

paper trade ['peipətreid], n. papeterie, f.

papism ['peipizm], n. papisme, m.

papist ['peipist], n. papiste, m., f.

Papua [pə'puə]. la Papouasie, f.

Papuan [pə'puən], a. papou.—n. Papou (personne), m.

papyrus [pə'paiərəs], n. (pl. **papyri** [pə'paiərai]) papyrus, m.

par [pɑː], n. pair, m., égalité, (Golf) normale, f.; **at par,** au pair.

parable ['pærəbl], n. parabole, f.

parabola [pə'ræbələ], n. (Math.) parabole, f.

parachute ['pærə'ʃuːt], n. parachute, m.—v.t., v.i. parachuter.

parachutist ['pærə'ʃuːtist], n. parachutiste, m., f.

parade [pə'reid], n. parade, f.; étalage, m.; esplanade, f.; (Mil.) rassemblement, m.; procession, f.—v.t. faire parade de.—v.i. faire de la parade; (Mil.) parader.

paradise ['pærədais], n. paradis, m.

paradox ['pærədɒks], n. paradoxe, m.

paradoxical [pærə'dɒksikl], a. paradoxal.

paraffin ['pærəfin], n. (Chem.) paraffine, f.; **paraffin (oil),** pétrole (lampant), m.

paragon ['pærəgən], n. parangon; modèle, m.

paragraph ['pærəgrɑːf], n. paragraphe; alinéa, m.—v.t. diviser en paragraphes.

Paraguay ['pærəgwai]. le Paraguay, m.

Paraguayan [pærə'gwaiən], a. paraguayen.—n. Paraguayen (personne), m.

parakeet ['pærəkiːt], n. (Orn.) perruche, f.

parallel ['pærəlel], a. parallèle; (fig.) semblable, pareil.—n. ligne parallèle, f., parallèle, m.; (fig.) comparaison, f.—v.t. mettre en parallèle; (fig.) comparer (à); être pareil (à).

parallelism ['pærəlelizm], n. parallélisme, m.; (fig.) comparaison, f.

parallelogram [pærə'leləgræm], n. parallélogramme, m.

paralysis [pə'rælisis], n. paralysie, f.

paralytic [pærə'litik], a. and n. paralytique, m., f.

paralyze ['pærəlaiz], v.t. paralyser.

paramount ['pærəmaunt], a. souverain, suprême; **of paramount importance,** d'une importance capitale.—n. souverain, seigneur, m.

paramour ['pærəmuə], n. amant, m., maîtresse, f.

parapet ['pærəpit], n. (Fort.) parapet; garde-fou (sur un pont etc.), m.

paraphernalia [pærəfə'neiliə], n.pl. (Law) biens paraphernaux, m.pl.; équipage, attirail, m.

paraphrase ['pærəfreiz], n. paraphrase, f.—v.t. paraphraser.

parasite ['pærəsait], n. parasite, m.

parasitic [pærə'sitik], **parasitical** [pærə'sitikl], a. parasite, parasitique.

parasol [pærə'sɒl], n. ombrelle, f., parasol, m.

paratrooper ['pærətruːpə], n. (soldat) parachutiste, m.

parcel [pɑːsl], n. colis, paquet; lot, m.—v.t. morceler, diviser, partager; empaqueter.

parch [pɑːtʃ], v.t. brûler, dessécher (par la chaleur).—v.i. se brûler; se dessécher.

parchment ['pɑːtʃmənt], n. parchemin, m.

pardon [pɑːdn], n. pardon, m.; (Law) grâce, f.; **I beg your pardon?** plaît-il? pardon? comment?—v.t. pardonner (quelque chose à quelqu'un); **pardon me!** pardon! permettez!

pardonable ['pɑːdnəbl], a. excusable, pardonnable (acte); digne de pardon (personne).

pare [pɛə], v.t. peler (fruits etc.); éplucher; rogner (ongles etc.).

parent ['pɛərənt], a. mère.—n. père, m., mère, f.; (pl.) parents, les père et mère, m.pl.

parentage ['pɛərəntidʒ], n. parentage, m.; extraction, f.

parental [pə'rentl], a. des parents, du père, de la mère; paternel, maternel.

parenthesis [pə'renθisis], n. (pl. **parentheses** [pə'renθisiːz]) parenthèse, f.

parenthetic [pærən'θetik], **parenthetical** [pærən'θetikl], a. entre parenthèses.

pariah ['pæriə], n. paria, m.

paring ['pɛəriŋ], n. rognage; épluchage, m.

paring knife ['pɛəriŋ'naif], n. tranchet, m.

parish ['pæriʃ], a. de la commune; communal, vicinal (routes, impôts etc.); (Eccles.) de la paroisse, paroissial.—n. (Eccles.) paroisse; (civil) commune, f.

parishioner [pə'riʃənə], n. paroissien, m.

Parisian [pə'riziən], a. de Paris, parisien.—n. Parisien (personne), m.

parity ['pæriti], n. parité, f.; égalité (de rang etc.), f.

park [pɑːk], n. parc, m.—v.t. parquer, garer.—v.i. stationner.

parking ['pɑːkiŋ], n. stationnement, parcage, m. **[see car-park]**

parlance ['pɑːləns], n. parler, langage, m.; **in common parlance,** dans le langage ordinaire.

parley ['pɑːli], n. pourparlers, m.pl.—v.i. être ou entrer en pourparlers (avec); (Mil.) parlementer.

parliament ['pɑːləmənt], n. parlement, m.; (France) les Chambres, f.pl.

parliamentary [pɑːlə'mentəri], a. parlementaire, du parlement.

parlor ['pɑːlə], n. petit salon, parloir (de convent ou école), m.

parlous ['pɑːləs], a. alarmant, précaire.

parochial

parochial [pə'roukiəl], *a.* communal; (*Eccles.*) paroissial.

parody ['pærədi], *n.* parodie, *f.*—*v.t.* parodier.

parole [pə'roul], *n.* parole (d'honneur), *f.*

paroxysm ['pærəksizm], *n.* paroxysme, accès, *m.*

parquet ['pɑːkei, pɑː'ket], *n.* parquet, *m.*—*v.t.* parqueter.

parquetry ['pɑːkitri], *n.* parqueterie, *f.*

parricidal [pæri'saidl], *a.* parricide.

parricide ['pærisaid], *n.* parricide (*crime*), *m.*; parricide (*personne*), *m.*, *f.*

parrot ['pærət], *n.* (*Orn.*) perroquet, *m.*

parry ['pæri], *v.t.* parer, détourner; (*fig.*) éviter.

parse [pɑːz], *v.t.* analyser (grammaticalement).

parsimonious [pɑːsi'mouniəs], *a.* parcimonieux; pingre.

parsimony ['pɑːsiməni], *n.* parcimonie, épargne, *f.*

parsley ['pɑːsli], *n.* (*Bot.*) persil, *m.*

parsnip ['pɑːsnip], *n.* (*Bot.*) panais, *m.*

parson [pɑːsn], *n.* curé; (*Protestant*) pasteur, *m.*

parsonage ['pɑːsnidʒ], *n.* presbytère, *m.*, cure, *f.*

part [pɑːt], *n.* partie; part, portion, *f.*; (*Theat.*) rôle; parti (*dans une dispute etc.*), *m.*; région (*de ville, pays etc.*), *f.*, quartier (*de ville*); (*pl.*) talent, *m.*; **spare parts**, pièces de rechange, *f.pl.*—*v.t.* partager; séparer (*de*). —*v.i.* se séparer (*de*); se quitter; se rompre (*câble*).

partake [pɑː'teik], *v.t.*, *v.i. irr.* (*conjug. like* TAKE) prendre part à, participer à.

partaker [pɑː'teikə], *n.* participant, *m.*

partial [pɑːʃl], *a.* partial (*prévenu*), injuste; partiel (*en partie*).

partiality [pɑːʃi'æliti], *n.* partialité (*favoritisme*), *f.*; (*fig.*) goût, *m.*

partially ['pɑːʃəli], *adv.* partialement (*injustement*); en partie.

participant [pɑː'tisipənt], *a.* and *n.* participant, *m.*

participate [pɑː'tisipeit], *v.i.* participer (à).

participation [pɑːtisi'peiʃən], *n.* participation, *f.*

participle ['pɑːtisipl], *n.* participe, *m.*

particle [pɑːtikl], *n.* particule, molécule, parcelle, *f.*; atome, *m.*

particular [pə'tikjulə], *a.* particulier, spécial; méticuleux, pointilleux; exigeant (*difficile*). —*n.* particularité, *f.*, détail, *m.*; (*pl.*) renseignements, *m.pl.*; signalement, *m.*

particularity [pətikju'læriti], *n.* particularité, *f.*; détail, *m.*

particularize [pə'tikjuləraiz], *v.t.* particulariser.—*v.i.* préciser.

particularly [pə'tikjuləli], *adv.* particulièrement; principalement, surtout.

parting ['pɑːtiŋ], *a.* de séparation; d'adieu; dernier.—*n.* séparation; raie (*cheveux*), *f.*

partisan [pɑːti'zæn], *n.* partisan, *m.*

partition [pɑː'tiʃən], *n.* partage (*division*), *m.*; cloison (*dans une pièce etc.*), *f.*—*v.t.* partager, diviser.

partitive ['pɑːtitiv], *a.* and *n.* partitif, *m.*

partly ['pɑːtli], *adv.* en partie, partiellement.

partner ['pɑːtnə], *n.* (*Comm.*) associé; (*Dancing*) danseur, cavalier, *m.*; (*Cards, Spt.*) partenaire, *m.*, *f.*—*v.t.* s'associer à;

(*Spt.*) être le partenaire de.

partnership ['pɑːtnəʃip], *n.* association, *f.*

partridge ['pɑːtridʒ], *n.* (*Orn.*) perdrix, *f.*; **young partridge**, perdreau, *m.*

part-time ['pɑːttaim], *a.* and *n.* (emploi) à temps partiel, *m.*; **to be on part-time**, être en chômage partiel.

party ['pɑːti], *n.* parti (*politique*), *m.*; partie (*de plaisir*), *f.*; (*fig.*) réunion; réception, *f.*, groupe, *m.*; **to give a party**, recevoir du monde, donner une soirée.

party wall ['pɑːtiwɔːl], *n.* mur mitoyen, *m.*

pasha ['pɑːʃə], *n.* pacha, *m.*

pass [pɑːs], *v.t.* (*Motor.*) doubler.

pass [pɑːs], *v.t.* passer; passer par, passer devant; dépasser; devancer; faire passer; prononcer (*sur*); voter (*un projet de loi etc.*); **to pass an examination**, être reçu ou réussir à un examen.—*v.i.* passer, se passer, s'écouler (*temps*); mourir; (*Exam.*) être reçu; (*Ftb.*) faire une passe; (*fig.*) arriver; **to pass away**, disparaître, mourir; **to pass out**, sortir; (*fig.*) s'évanouir.—*n.* passage, défilé, *m.*; gorge, *f.*, col; permis; laissez-passer, *m.*, permission; (*Ftb.*) passe, *f.*; (*fig.*) point, état, *m.*, extrémité, *f.*

passable ['pɑːsəbl], *a.* praticable; navigable (*fleuve etc.*); passable.

passage ['pæsidʒ], *n.* passage, *m.*, traversée, *f.*; (*Arch.*) couloir, corridor, *m.*

pass-book ['pɑːsbuk], *n.* livre de compte, carnet de banque, *m.*

passenger ['pæsindʒə], *n.* voyageur; passager (*par mer ou avion*), *m.*

passer-by ['pɑːsə'bai], *n.* (*pl.* **passers-by** ['pɑːsəz'bai]) passant, *m.*

passing ['pɑːsiŋ], *a.* passager, éphémère, fugitif.—*adv.* extrêmement, éminemment. —*n.* passage; écoulement (*de temps*); (*fig.*) trépas (*mort*), *m.*

passion ['pæʃən], *n.* passion; colère, *f.*, emportement, *m.*

passionate ['pæʃənit], *a.* passionné, ardent; irascible.

passionately ['pæʃənitli], *adv.* à la passion; à la folie, passionnément.

passion-flower ['pæʃənflauə], *n.* passiflore, fleur de la passion, *f.*

passion play ['pæʃənplei], *n.* mystère (de la Passion), *m.*

Passion Week ['pæʃənwiːk]. semaine de la Passion, *f.*

passive ['pæsiv], *a.* and *n.* passif, *m.*

passiveness ['pæsivnis], *n.* passivité, inertie, *f.*

pass-key ['pɑːskiː], *n.* passe-partout, *m.*

Passover ['pɑːsouvə]. la Pâque, *f.*

passport ['pɑːspɔːt], *n.* passeport, *m.*

password ['pɑːswɔːd], *n.* mot de passe; mot d'ordre, *m.*

past [pɑːst], *a.* passé; ancien; dernier (*récent*). —*prep.* au-delà de; près de; sans, hors de; plus de (*âge*); **past three o'clock**, trois heures passées.—*n.* passé, *m.*

paste [peist], *n.* colle (*glu*); pâte (*pour pâtisseries*), *f.*; stras (*faux diamant*), *m.*—*v.t.* coller; **to paste up**, afficher.

pastel ['pæstəl], *n.* pastel, *m.*

pastern ['pæstəːn], *n.* paturon, *m.*

pasteurize ['pɑːstjuəraiz], *v.t.* pasteuriser (*lait*).

pastille [pæs'tiːl], *n.* pastille, *f.*

pastime ['pɑːstaim], *n.* passe-temps, amusement, *m.*, distraction, *f.*

pastor ['pɑːstə], *n.* (*literal and fig.*) pasteur; (*literal*) berger, *m.*

pastoral ['pɑːstərəl], *a.* pastoral.—*n.* pastorale, églogue, *f.*

pastry ['peistri], *n.* pâtisserie, *f.*

pastry cook ['peistrikuk], *n.* pâtissier, *m.*

pasture ['pɑːstʃə], *n.* pâture, *f.*, herbage; pâturage (*champ etc.*), *m.*—*v.t.* faire paître.—*v.i.* paître.

pasty ['peisti], *a.* pâteux.—['pɑːsti], *n.* pâté, *m.*

pat [pæt], *a. and adv.* à propos, tout juste.—*n.* petite tape; caresse, *f.*; rond de beurre, *m.*—*v.t.* taper, tapoter, caresser.

patch [pætʃ], *n.* pièce; mouche (*pour le visage*), *f.*; morceau (*de terre*); pan (*de ciel*), *m.*; tache (*de couleur*), *f.*—*v.t.* rapiécer, raccommoder; arranger.

patching ['pætʃiŋ], *n.* rapiéçage, ravaudage, *m.*

patchwork ['pætʃwəːk], *n.* mélange, *m.*, mosaïque, *f.*

patchy ['pætʃi], *a.* inégal.

pate [peit], *n.* (*colloq.*) caboche, tête, *f.*

patent ['peitənt, 'pætənt], *a.* breveté; (*fig.*) patent, apparent, évident.—*n.* lettres patentes, *f.pl.*, brevet d'invention, *m.*—*v.t.* breveter.

patentee [peitən'tiː], *n.* breveté, *m.*

paternal [pə'təːnl], *a.* paternel.

paternally [pə'təːnəli], *adv.* paternellement.

paternity [pə'təːniti], *n.* paternité, *f.*

paternoster ['pætə'nɔstə], *n.* patenôtre, *f.*, pater, *m.*

path [pɑːθ], *n.* sentier, chemin, *m.*; allée (*dans un jardin*), *f.*

pathless ['pɑːθlis], *a.* sans chemin frayé; (*fig.*) inconnu.

pathetic [pə'θetik], *a. and n.* pathétique, *m.*

pathfinder ['pɑːθfaində], *n.* pionnier, éclaireur, *m.*

pathological [pæθə'lɔdʒikl], *a.* pathologique.

pathologist [pə'θɔlədʒist], *n.* pathologiste, *m.*, *f.*

pathology [pə'θɔlədʒi], *n.* pathologie, *f.*

pathos ['peiθɔs], *n.* pathétique, *m.*

pathway ['pɑːθwei], *n.* sentier; trottoir (*de rue*); accotement (*de route*), *m.*

patience ['peiʃəns], *n.* patience; (*Cards*) réussite, *f.*

patient ['peiʃənt], *a.* patient, endurant.—*n.* malade, *m.*, *f.*; patient; client (*de médecin*), *m.*

patiently ['peiʃəntli], *adv.* patiemment.

patriarch ['peitriɑːk], *n.* patriarche, *m.*

patriarchal [peitri'ɑːkl], *a.* patriarcal.

Patrick ['pætrik]. Pſtrice, *m.*

patrimony ['pætriməni], *n.* patrimoine, *m.*

patriot ['peitriət, 'pætriət], *n.* patriote, *m.*, *f.*

patriotic [peitri'ɔtik], *a.* patriotique (*chose*); patriote (*personne*).

patriotism ['peitriətizm], *n.* patriotisme, *m.*

patrol [pə'troul], *n.* patrouille, ronde, *f.*—*v.t.* faire la ◦patrouille dans.—*v.i.* patrouiller; faire une ronde. [see **prison-van**]

patron ['peitrən], *n.* patron; protecteur; (*Comm.*) client, *m.*; pratique, *f.*

patronage ['pætrənidʒ], *n.* patronage, *m.*, protection, *f.*

patroness ['peitrənes], *n.* patronne, protec-

trice; dame patronnesse (*d'œuvre de bienfaisance*), *f.*

patronize ['pætrənaiz], *v.t.* protéger, patronner; fréquenter (*un magasin*); traiter avec condescendance.

patronizing ['pætrənaiziŋ], *a.* protecteur; **patronizing tone**, ton de condescendance, *m.*

patronymic [pætrə'nimik], *a.* patronymique.—*n.* nom patronymique, *m.*

patten ['pætən], *n.* patin, socque; (*Arch.*) soubassement, *m.*

patter ['pætə], *v.i.* frapper à petits coups, crépiter; trottiner.

pattering ['pætəriŋ], *n.* grésillement; bruit de petits coups, *m.*

pattern ['pætən], *n.* modèle (*pour*); patron (*à couper*); échantillon (*morceau de tissu etc.*); dessin (*de décoration*); exemple, *m.*

patty ['pæti], *n.* petit pâté, *m.*; bouchée (à la reine), *f.*

paucity ['pɔːsiti], *n.* petit nombre, *m.*, disette (*de*), *f.*

Paul [pɔːl]. Paul, *m.*

Paula ['pɔːlə]. Paule, *f.*

paunch [pɔːntʃ], *n.* panse, *f.*, ventre, *m.*

paunchy ['pɔːntʃi], *a.* pansu.

pauper ['pɔːpə], *n.* indigent, *m.*

pauperism ['pɔːpərizm], *n.* paupérisme, *m.*

pauperize ['pɔːpəraiz], *v.t.* réduire à l'indigence.

pause [pɔːz], *n.* pause, *f.*; moment de silence; intervalle, *m.*—*v.i.* faire une pause, s'arrêter.

pave [peiv], *v.t.* paver (*de*); **to pave the way for**, frayer le chemin à *ou* pour.

pavement ['peivmənt], *n.* trottoir (*bord de rue*); dallage; pavé (*de marbre etc.*), *m.*

paver ['peivə], **pavior** ['peivjə], *n.* paveur, *m.*

pavilion [pə'viljən], *n.* pavillon, *m.*, tente, *f.*

paving ['peiviŋ], *n.* pavage, *m.*

paw [pɔː], *n.* patte; (*facet.*) main, *f.*—*v.t.* manier, tripoter (*manier*); **to paw the ground**, piaffer.

pawn (1) [pɔːn], *n.* (*Chess*) pion, *m.*

pawn (2) [pɔːn], *v.t.* engager, mettre en gage. —*n.* gage, *m.*

pawnbroker ['pɔːnbroukə], *n.* prêteur sur gage, *m.*

pawnshop ['pɔːnʃɔp], *n.* mont-de-piété, *m.*

pay [pei], *n.* paie, *f.*; salaire (*ouvrier*), traitement (*fonctionnaire*), *m.*, gages (*domestique*), *m.pl.*; (*Mil.*) solde (*officier*), *f.*, prêt (*soldat*), *m.*—*v.t. irr.* payer, acquitter; s'acquitter de; faire (*compliments etc.*); rendre (*honneur*); **carriage paid**, port payé; **to pay a visit to**, faire une visite à.—*v.i.* payer; rapporter.

payable ['peiəbl], *a.* payable; **payable to bearer**, au porteur; **payable to order**, à l'ordre de.

payee [pei'iː], *n.* porteur, *m.*, bénéficiaire, *m.*, *f.*

payer ['peiə], *n.* payeur, *m.*

pay-load ['peiloud], *n.* (*Av.*) poids utile, *m.*

paymaster ['peimɑːstə], *n.* payeur; trésorier, *m.*

payment ['peimənt], *n.* payement, paiement, versement, *m.*

pea [piː], *n.* pois, *m.*; **green peas**, petits pois, *m.pl.*; **sweet pea**, pois de senteur.

peace [piːs], *n.* paix, *f.*

peaceable ['pi:səbl], *a.* pacifique.
peaceably ['pi:səbli], *adv.* en paix; avec calme.
peaceful ['pi:sful], *a.* paisible; tranquille, calme.
peacefully ['pi:sfuli], *adv.* paisiblement, tranquillement.
peacefulness ['pi:sfulnis], *n.* tranquillité, *f.*, calme, *m.*
peaceless ['pi:slis], *a.* sans paix, agité.
peacemaker ['pi:smeikə], *n.* pacificateur, *m.*
peach [pi:tʃ], *n.* pêche, *f.*
peach tree ['pi:tʃtri:], *n.* pêcher, *m.*
peacock ['pi:kɔk], *n.* paon, *m.*
pea-green ['pi:gri:n], *a.* and *n.* vert pois.
pea-hen ['pi:hen], *n.* paonne, *f.*
peak [pi:k] *n.* cime (*de montagne*), *f.*; pic, sommet, *m.*; visière (*d'une casquette*), *f.*
peaked [pi:kt], *a.* à pic, à pointe; à visière.
peal [pi:l], *n.* carillon (*de cloches*); coup, bruit, grondement (*de tonnerre etc.*); éclat (*de rire*), *m.*—*v.i.* carillonner; retentir, résonner; gronder.
peanut ['pi:nʌt], *n.* arachide, cacahuète, *f.*
pea pod ['pi:pɔd], *n.* cosse de pois, *f.*
pear [peə], *n.* poire, *f.*
pearl [pə:l], *n.* perle, *f.*; **mother-of-pearl**, nacre, *f.*—*v.t.*, *v.i.* perler.
pearl oyster ['pə:l'ɔistə], *n.* huître perlière, *f.*
pearly ['pə:li], *a.* de perle, perlé.
pear tree ['peətri:], *n.* poirier, *m.*
peasant ['pezənt], *n.* paysan, *m.*
peasantry ['pezəntri], *n.* paysans, *m.pl.*
pea soup ['pi:'su:p], *n.* purée de pois, *f.*
peat [pi:t], *n.* tourbe, *f.*
peat bog ['pi:tbɔg], *n.* tourbière, *f.*
pebble [pebl], *n.* caillou, galet (*de plage*), *m.*
pebbly ['pebli], *a.* caillouteux.
peccadillo [peka'dilou], *n.* peccadille, *f.*
peck (1) [pek], *n.* picotin (*d'avoine etc.*), *m.*
peck (2) [pek], *n.* coup de bec (*d'oiseau*), *m.*—*v.t.* becqueter; **a hen-pecked husband**, un mari mené par sa femme.
pectoral ['pektərəl], *a.* and *n.* pectoral, *m.*
peculation [pekju'leiʃən], *n.* péculat, *m.*
peculator ['pekjuleitə], *n.* concussionnaire, *m.*, *f.*
peculiar [pi'kju:liə], *a.* particulier, propre; singulier, bizarre.
peculiarity [pikjuli'æriti], *n.* singularité, particularité, *f.*
peculiarly [pi'kju:liəli], *adv.* particulièrement, singulièrement.
pecuniary [pi'kju:niəri], *a.* pécuniaire.
pedagogic(al) [pedə'gɔdʒik(l)], *a.* pédagogique.
pedagogue ['pedəgɔg], *n.* pédagogue, *m.*, *f.*
pedal [pedl], *n.* pédale, *f.*—*v.i.* pédaler.
pedant ['pedənt], *n.* pédant, *m.*
pedantic [pi'dæntik], *a.* pédant (*personne*), pédantesque (*choses*).
pedantry ['pedəntri], *n.* pédantisme, *m.*, pédanterie, *f.*
peddle [pedl], *v.t.* colporter.—*v.i.* faire le colportage.
peddler [PEDLAR].
pedestal ['pedistl], *n.* piédestal, socle, *m.*
pedestrian [pə'destriən], *a.* à pied, pédestre; (*fig.*) prosaïque.—*n.* piéton, marcheur, *m.*
pedigree ['pedigri:], *n.* généalogie; origine, *f.*; arbre généalogique, *m.*
pediment ['pedimənt], *n.* (*Arch.*) fronton, *m.*

pedlar ['pedlə], *n.* colporteur, *m.*
pedometer [pə'dɔmitə], *n.* podomètre, *m.*
peel [pi:l], *n.* pelure; écorce (*d'orange etc.*), *f.*—*v.t.* peler; éplucher.—*v.i.* se peler; s'écailler.
peep [pi:p], *n.* coup d'œil furtif, *m.*; pointe (*du jour*), *f.*—*v.i.* regarder à la dérobée; paraître, poindre.
peeper ['pi:pə], *n.* curieux, *m.*
peep-hole ['pi:phoul], *n.* judas, *f.*
peeping-Tom ['pi:piŋ'tɔm], *n.* voyeur, *m.*
peer (1) [piə], *v.i.* scruter du regard.
peer (2) [piə], *n.* pair; (*fig.*) égal, pareil, *m.*
peerage ['piəridʒ], *n.* pairie, *f.*; les pairs, *m.pl.*
peeress ['piəris], *n.* pairesse, *f.*
peerless ['piəlis], *a.* incomparable; sans pareil.
peerlessly ['piəlisli], *adv.* incomparablement.
peerlessness ['piəlisnis], *n.* supériorité incomparable, *f.*
peevish ['pi:viʃ], *a.* irritable, maussade.
peevishly ['pi:viʃli], *adv.* maussadement, avec mauvaise humeur.
peevishness ['pi:viʃnis], *n.* maussaderie, humeur acariâtre, *f.*
peewit [PEWIT].
peg [peg], *n.* cheville; patère (*à chapeau etc.*), *f.*; fausset (*de tonneaux*), piquet (*de tente*), *m.*—*v.t.*, *v.i.* cheviller.
pejorative [pə'dʒɔrətiv, 'pi:dʒərətiv], *a.* péjoratif.
Pekinese [pi:ki'ni:z], *a.* pékinois.—*n.* (épagneul) pékinois; Pékinois (*personne*), *m.*
Peking [pi:'kiŋ], Pékin, *m.*
Pekingese [pi:kiŋ'i:z], [PEKINESE].
pelican ['pelikən], *n.* pélican, *m.*
pellet ['pelit], *n.* boulette, *f.*; grain de plomb, *m.*
pellicle ['pelikl], *n.* pellicule, *f.*
pell-mell ['pel'mel], *adv.* pêle-mêle.
pellucid [pə'lju:sid], *a.* transparent, clair, pellucide.
pelmet ['pelmit], *n.* lambrequin, *m.*
pelt (1) [pelt], *v.t.* assaillir, battre.
pelt (2) [pelt], *n.* peau, *f.*—*v.t.* écorcher.
pelting ['peltiŋ], *a.* battant (*pluie*).—*n.* attaque, *f.*, assaut, *m.*; grêle (*de pierres*), *f.*
pelvic ['pelvik], *a.* pelvien.
pelvis ['pelvis], *n.* bassin, *m.*
pemmican ['pemikən], *n.* conserve de viande, *f.*; pemmican, *m.*
pen [pen], *n.* plume, *f.*; parc, enclos (*bestiaux etc.*); poulailler (*pour volaille*), *m.*; **fountain pen**, stylo, *m.*—*v.t.* écrire; rédiger; parquer, enfermer (*bétail*).
penal [pi:nl], *a.* pénal, passible d'une amende; **penal servitude**, travaux forcés, *m.pl.*
penalize ['pi:nəlaiz], *v.t.* infliger une peine à (*quelqu'un*); (*Spt.*) pénaliser.
penalty ['penəlti], *n.* peine; pénalité, amende, *f.*; (*Ftb.*) penalty, *m.*
penance ['penəns], *n.* pénitence, *f.*
pence [PENNY].
pencil [pensl], *n.* crayon, *m.*—*v.t.* dessiner *ou* écrire au crayon.
pencil case ['penslkeis], *n.* porte-crayon, *m.*
pencil sharpener ['pensl'ʃɑ:pnə], *n.* taille-crayon, *m.*
pendant ['pendənt], *n.* pendant, *m.*; pende-loque, *f.*; pendentif, *m.*

pendent ['pendənt], *a.* pendant; suspendu.

pending ['pendiŋ], *a.* pendant, non décidé; en cours.—*prep.* en attendant.

pendulum ['pendjuləm], *n.* pendule, balancier, *m.*

penetrable ['penitrəbl], *a.* pénétrable, sensible.

penetrate ['penitreit], *v.t.*, *v.i.* pénétrer (*dans*).

penetrating ['penitreitiŋ], *a.* pénétrant, perçant; clairvoyant, perspicace.

penetration [peni'treiʃən], *n.* pénétration, *f.*

penguin ['peŋgwin], *n.* manchot, *m.*

pen-holder ['penhouldə], *n.* porte-plume, *m.*

penicillin [peni'silin], *n.* pénicilline, *f.*

peninsula [pi'ninsjulə], *n.* péninsule, presqu'île, *f.*

peninsular [pi'ninsjulə], *a.* péninsulaire.

penitence ['penitəns], *n.* pénitence, *f.*, repentir, *m.*

penitent ['penitənt], *a.* pénitent, repentant.

penitentiary [peni'tenʃəri], *a.* pénitentiaire. —*n.* pénitencier, *m.*; (*Am.*) prison, *f.*

penknife ['pennaif], *n.* canif, *m.*

pennant ['penənt], *n.* (*Naut.*) flamme, *f.*

penniless ['penilis], *a.* sans le sou, sans ressources.

penny ['peni], *n.* (*pl.* **pence** [pens], *of a sum*, or **pennies** ['peniz], *of a number of coins*) penny, *m.*

pension ['penʃən], *n.* pension; pension de retraite, retraite (*d'officiers etc.*), *f.*—*v.t.* **to pension off**, mettre à la retraite.

pensioner ['penʃənə], *n.* pensionnaire, *m.*, *f.*; (*Mil.*) invalide, *m.*

pensive ['pensiv], *a.* pensif, préoccupé, rêveur.

pensively ['pensivli], *adv.* d'un air pensif.

pensiveness ['pensivnis], *n.* air pensif, air préoccupé, *m.*

pent [pent], *a.* **pent up**, enfermé, (*fig.*) étouffé, refoulé.

pentagon ['pentəgən], *n.* pentagone, *m.*

Pentecost ['pentikɔst], Pentecôte, *f.*

penthouse ['penthaus], *n.* appartement sur toit; appentis, *m.*

penultimate [pe'nʌltimit], *a.* pénultième, avant-dernier.

penurious [pi'njuəriəs], *a.* avare; ladre; pauvre (*choses*).

penury ['penjuəri], *n.* pénurie, *f.*

peony ['pi:əni], *n.* pivoine, *f.*

people [pi:pl], *n.* peuple, *m.*, nation, *f.*, gens, *m.pl.*; on, monde, *m.*, personnes (*en général*), *f.pl.*—*v.t.* peupler (*de*).

pepper ['pepə], *n.* poivre, *m.*—*v.t.* poivrer; (*fig.*) cribler de coups.

pepper caster ['pepə'kɑːstə], *n.* poivrière, *f.*

peppercorn ['pepəkɔːn], *n.* grain de poivre, *m.*

peppermint ['pepəmint], *n.* menthe poivrée, *f.*

peppery ['pepəri], *a.* poivré; (*fig.*) irritable.

per [pə:], *prep.* par; le, *m.*, la, *f.*, les, *pl.*; **three francs per pound**, trois francs la livre.

perambulate [pə'ræmbjuleit], *v.t.* parcourir.

perambulation [pəræmbju'leiʃən], *n.* parcours, *m.*; promenade, *f.*

perambulator [pə'ræmbjuleitə], *n.* voiture d'enfant, *f.*

perceive [pə'si:v], *v.t.* apercevoir (*visuellement*), s'apercevoir de (*se rendre compte de*).

percentage [pə'sentidʒ], *n.* pourcentage, *m.*

perceptibility [pəsepti'biliti], *n.* perceptibilité, *f.*

perceptible [pə'septibl], *a.* perceptible, sensible.

perceptibly [pə'septibli], *adv.* perceptiblement, sensiblement.

perception [pə'sepʃən], *n.* perception, sensibilité; découverte, *f.*

perceptive [pə'septiv], *a.* perceptif.

perch (1) [pə:tʃ], *n.* perche (*poisson*), *f.*

perch (2) [pə:tʃ], *n.* perchoir (*à poules etc.*) *m.* —*v.t.*, *v.i.* percher.

percolate ['pə:kəleit], *v.t.*, *v.i.* filtrer, passer.

percolation [pə:kə'leiʃən], *n.* filtration, infiltration, *f.*

percolator ['pə:kəleitə], filtre (à café), *m.*

percussion [pə'kʌʃən], *n.* percussion, *f.*

percussion cap [pə'kʌʃənkæp], *n.* capsule, *f.*

perdition [pə'diʃən], *n.* perdition, ruine, *f.*

peregrinate ['perigrineit], *v.i.* voyager.

peregrination [perigri'neiʃən], *n.* pérégrination, *f.*, voyage à l'étranger, *m.*

peremptorily [pə'remptərili], *adv.* péremptoirement, absolument, formellement.

peremptory [pə'remptəri], *a.* péremptoire, absolu.

perennial [pə'reniəl], *a.* vivace (*plantes*); (*fig.*) éternel.—*n.* plante vivace, *f.*

perfect (1) ['pə:fikt], *a.* parfait; achevé.— [pə'fekt], *v.t.* rendre parfait, perfectionner; achever.

perfect (2) ['pə:fikt], *n.* (*Gram.*) parfait, *m.*

perfection [pə'fekʃən], *n.* perfection, *f.*

perfectly [pə'fiktli], *adv.* parfaitement.

perfidious [pə'fidiəs], *a.* perfide.

perfidiousness [pə'fidiəsnis], **perfidy** ['pə:fidi], *n.* perfidie, *f.*

perforate ['pə:fəreit], *v.t.* perforer, percer.

perforation [pə:fə'reiʃən], *n.* percement, *m.*, perforation; dentelure (*de timbre-poste*), *f.*

perforce [pə'fɔːs], *adv.* forcément, de force.

perform [pə'fɔːm], *v.t.* exécuter, accomplir; (*Theat.*) jouer.—*v.i.* jouer un rôle.

performance [pə'fɔːməns], *n.* accomplissement; ouvrage, *m.*, œuvre (*chose achevée*), *f.*; (*Mach.*) fonctionnement, *m.*; (*Theat.*) représentation; (*Mus.*) exécution; (*Spt.*) performance, *f.*

performer [pə'fɔːmə], *n.* (*Theat.*) acteur, *m.*, actrice, *f.*; (*Mus.*) artiste, *m.*, *f.*

perfume ['pə:fjum], *n.* parfum, *m.*—[pə'fjuːm], *v.t.* parfumer (*de*).

perfumery [pə'fjuːməri], *n.* parfumerie, *f.*

perfunctorily [pə'fʌŋktərili], *adv.* par manière d'acquit; tant bien que mal.

perfunctory [pə'fʌŋktəri], *a.* de pure forme; négligent.

perhaps [pə'hæps], *adv.* peut-être; **perhaps not**, peut-être que non; **perhaps so**, peut-être que oui.

peril ['peril], *n.* péril, danger, *m.*

perilous ['periləs], *a.* périlleux, dangereux.

perilously ['perilasli], *adv.* périlleusement.

perimeter [pə'rimitə], *n.* périmètre, *m.*

period ['piəriəd], *n.* période, *f.*, temps, *m.*, durée; époque; fin, *f.*, terme (*conclusion*); (*Am.*) point (*ponctuation*), *m.*; (*Rhet. etc.*) phrase, *f.*; (*pl.*) (*Physiol.*) règles, *f.pl.*

periodic [piəri'ɔdik], *a.* périodique.

periodical [piəri'ɔdikl], *a.* and *n.* périodique, *m.*

periodically

periodically [piəri'ɔdikli], *adv.* périodiquement.

peripatetic [peripə'tetik], *a.* péripatéticien.

periphery [pə'rifəri], *n.* périphérie, *f.*

periphrasis [pə'rifrəsis], *n.* (*pl.* **periphrases** [pə'rifrəsiːz]) périphrase, *f.*

periscope ['periskoup], *n.* périscope, *m.*

perish ['periʃ], *v.i.* périr (*de*); mourir; dépérir.

perishable ['periʃəbl], *a.* périssable.

peritonitis [peritə'naitis], *n.* péritonite, *f.*

*periwig ['periwig], *n.* perruque, *f.*

periwinkle ['periwiŋkl], *n.* (*Bot.*) pervenche, *f.*; bigorneau (*mollusque*), *m.*

perjure ['pəːdʒə], *v.t.* **to perjure oneself,** se parjurer.

perjurer ['pəːdʒərə], *n.* parjure, *m.,f.*

perjury ['pəːdʒəri], *n.* parjure; (*Law*) faux témoignage, faux serment, *m.*; **wilful perjury,** parjure prémédité.

perk [pəːk], *v.i.* **to perk up,** se ranimer, se raviver.—*n.* (*pl.*) (*fam.*) [PERQUISITE].

perky ['pəːki], *a.* déluré; outrecuidant.

permanency ['pəːmənənsi], **permanence** ['pəːmənəns], *n.* permanence, *f.*

permanent ['pəːmənənt], *a.* permanent; en permanence.

permanently ['pəːmənəntli], *adv.* en permanence.

permeable ['pəːmiəbl], *a.* perméable.

permeate ['pəːmieit], *v.t.* pénétrer.

permissible [pə'misibl], *a.* permis.

permission [pə'miʃən], *n.* permission, *f.*, permis, *m.*

permissive [pə'misiv], *a.* qui permet; toléré.

permit [pə'mit], *v.t.* permettre (*à quelqu'un de . . .*).—['pəːmit], *n.* permis, *m.*

permutation [pəːmju'teiʃən], *n.* permutation, *f.*

pernicious [pə'niʃəs], *a.* pernicieux.

perniciously [pə'niʃəsli], *adv.* pernicieusement.

peroration [perə'reiʃən], *n.* péroraison, *f.*

peroxide [pə'rɔksaid], *n.* peroxyde, *m.*—*v.t.* oxygéner (*cheveux*).

perpendicular [pəːpən'dikjulə], *a.* and *n.* perpendiculaire, *f.*

perpendicularly [pəːpən'dikjuləli], *adv.* perpendiculairement.

perpetrate ['pəːpitreit], *v.t.* commettre; (*Law*) perpétrer.

perpetration [pəːpi'treiʃən], *n.* exécution; (*Law*) perpétration, *f.*

perpetrator ['pəːpitreitə], *n.* auteur (*d'un crime*), *m.*

perpetual [pə'petjuəl], *a.* perpétuel.

perpetually [pə'petjuəli], *adv.* perpétuellement.

perpetuate [pə'petjueit], *v.t.* perpétuer.

perpetuation [pəpetju'eiʃən], *n.* perpétuation, *f.*

perpetuity [pəːpi'tjuːiti], *n.* perpétuité, *f.*

perplex [pə'pleks], *v.t.* embarrasser.

perplexed [pə'plekst], *a.* perplexe, embarrassé.

perplexing [pə'pleksiŋ], *a.* embarrassant.

perplexity [pə'pleksiti], *n.* perplexité, *f.*

perquisite [pə'kwizit], *n.* émolument casuel, *m.*

perry ['peri], *n.* poiré, *m.*

persecute ['pəːsikjuːt], *v.t.* persécuter.

persecuting ['pəːsikjuːtiŋ], *a.* persécuteur.

persecution [pəːsi'kjuːʃən], *n.* persécution, *f.*

persecutor ['pəːsikjutə], *n.* persécuteur, *m.*

perseverance [pəːsi'viərəns], *n.* persévérance, *f.*

persevere [pəːsi'viə], *v.i.* persévérer (*à* ou *dans*).

persevering [pəːsi'viəriŋ], *a.* persévérant.

perseveringly [pəːsi'viəriŋli], *adv.* avec persévérance.

Persia ['pəːʃə], la Perse, *f.*

Persian ['pəːʃən], *a.* de Perse, persan.—*n.* perse (*langue*); Persan (*personne*), *m.*; **the Persian Gulf,** le Golfe Persique.

persist [pə'sist], *v.i.* persister (*dans* ou *à*); continuer.

persistence [pə'sistəns], *n.* persistance, *f.*

persistent [pə'sistənt], *a.* persistant; opiniâtre.

person ['pəːsən], *n.* personne, *f.*; personnage, caractère, *m.*; (*pl.*) personnes, *f.pl.*, gens, *m.pl.,f.pl.*; **young persons,** les jeunes gens.

personage ['pəːsənidʒ], *n.* personnage, *m.*

personal ['pəːsənl], *a.* personnel.

personality [pəːsə'næliti], *n.* personnalité, *f.*

personally ['pəːsənli], *adv.* personnellement.

personate ['pəːsəneit], *v.t.* se faire passer pour; représenter, contrefaire.

personification [pəsɔnifi'keiʃən], *n.* personnification, *f.*

personify [pə'sɔnifai], *v.t.* personnifier.

personnel [pəːsə'nel], *n.* personnel, *m.*

perspective [pə'spektiv], *a.* perspectif.—*n.* perspective, *f.*

perspicacious [pəːspi'keiʃəs], *a.* pénétrant, perspicace; perçant (*la vision*).

perspicacity [pəːspi'kæsiti], *n.* perspicacité, *f.*

perspicuity [pəːspi'kjuːiti], *n.* clarté, *f.*

perspicuous [pə'spikjuəs], *a.* clair, net.

perspiration [pəːspi'reiʃən], *n.* transpiration, sueur, *f.*

perspire [pə'spaiə], *v.i.* transpirer, suer.

persuade [pə'sweid], *v.t.* persuader; **to persuade from,** dissuader de.

persuasion [pə'sweiʒən], *n.* persuasion, *f.*

persuasive [pə'sweisiv], *a.* persuasif.

persuasiveness [pə'sweisivnis], *n.* force persuasive, *f.*

pert [pəːt], *a.* mutin, hardi; impertinent, insolent (*effronté*).

pertain [pə'tein], *v.i.* appartenir.

pertinacious [pəːti'neiʃəs], *a.* obstiné, opiniâtre.

pertinacity [pəːti'næsiti], *n.* obstination, *f.*

pertinence ['pəːtinəns], *n.* convenance, *f.*

pertinent ['pəːtinənt], *a.* pertinent, convenable.

pertly ['pəːtli], *adv.* impertinemment, insolemment.

pertness ['pəːtnis], *n.* impertinence, *f.*

perturb [pə'təːb], *v.t.* agiter, troubler.

perturbation [pəːtə'beiʃən], *n.* agitation, *f.*

perturbed [pə'təːbd], *a.* troublé, inquiet.

Peru [pə'ruː], le Pérou, *m.*

perusal [pə'ruːzl], *n.* lecture, *f.*

peruse [pə'ruːz], *v.t.* lire attentivement.

Peruvian [pə'ruːviən], *a.* péruvien, du Pérou.—*n.* Péruvien (*personne*), *m.*

pervade [pə'veid], *v.t.* pénétrer dans; se répandre dans, remplir.

pervading [pə'veidiŋ], *a.* **all-pervading,** dominant.

perverse [pə'vəːs], *a.* pervers.

510

perversely [pə'vəːsli], *adv.* avec perversité.
perverseness [pə'vəːsnis], **perversity** [pə'vəː siti], *n.* perversité, *f.*
perversion [pə'vəːʃən], *n.* perversion, *f.*
pervert [pə'vəːt], *v.t.* pervertir; fausser, dénaturer.—['pəːvəːt], *n.* perverti, *m.*
perverted [pə'vəːtid], *a.* perverti.
pervious ['pəːviəs], *a.* perméable, pénétrable.
pessimism ['pesimizm], *n.* pessimisme, *m.*
pessimist ['pesimist], *n.* pessimiste, *m., f.*
pessimistic [pesi'mistik], *a.* pessimiste.
pest [pest], *n.* peste, *f.*
pester ['pestə], *v.t.* tourmenter, ennuyer.
pestilence ['pestiləns], *n.* peste, pestilence, *f.*
pestilent ['pestilənt], *a.* pestilentiel, contagieux.
pestilential [pesti'lenʃl], *a.* pestilentiel.
pet (1) [pet], *a.* favori; *pet aversion*, bête noire, *f.*—*n.* chéri, *m.*, chérie, *f.*, favori, *m.*, favorite, *f.*; animal familier; enfant gâté, *m.*—*v.t.* choyer, dorloter; *(Am.)* caresser.
pet (2) [pet], *n.* accès d'humeur, *m.*
petal [petl], *n.* pétale, *m.*
Peter ['piːtə]. Pierre, *m.*
peter out [piːtə'raut], *v.i.* *(colloq.)* s'épuiser; tomber à l'eau *(projet)*, flancher *(machine)*.
petition [pi'tiʃən], *n.* pétition, *f.*—*v.t.* pétitionner.
petitioner [pi'tiʃənə], *n.* *(Law)* requérant, *m.*; pétitionnaire, *m., f.*
petrel ['petrəl], *n.* *(Orn.)* pétrel, *m.*
petrifaction [petri'fækʃən], *n.* pétrification, *f.*
petrify ['petrifai], *v.t.* pétrifier.—*v.i.* se pétrifier.
petrol ['petrəl], *n.* essence, *f.*; *petrol station*, poste d'essence, *m.*
petrol can ['petrəlkæn], *n.* bidon d'essence, *m.*
petroleum [pi'trouliəm], *n.* pétrole, *m.*, huile de pétrole, *f.*
petticoat ['petikout], *n.* jupon, *m.*
pettifogging ['petifɔgiŋ], *a.* avocassier, chicaneur; chicanier *(méthodes etc.)*.
pettiness ['petinis], *n.* petitesse, mesquinerie, *f.*
petty ['peti], *a.* petit; mesquin, chétif; *(Law)* inférieur.
petty officer ['peti'ɔfisə], *n.* *(Navy)* officier marinier, *m.*
petulance ['petjuləns], *n.* irritabilité, *f.*
petulant ['petjulənt], *a.* irritable.
pew [pjuː], *n.* banc d'église, *m.*
pewit ['piːwit], *n.* *(Orn.)* vanneau, *m.*
pewter ['pjuːtə], *n.* étain, potin, *m.*; vaisselle d'étain, *f.*
phalanx ['fælæŋks], *n.* *(pl.* **phalanges** [fə'lændʒiːz]*)* phalange, *f.*
phantom ['fæntəm], *n.* fantôme, *m.*
Pharaoh ['fɛərou], *n.* Pharaon, *m.*
Pharisee ['færisiː], *n.* Pharisien, *m.*
pharmaceutical [fɑːmə'sjuːtikəl], *a.* pharmaceutique.
pharmacy ['fɑːməsi], *n.* pharmacie, *f.*
phase [feiz], *n.* phase, *f.*
pheasant ['fezənt], *n.* faisan, *m.*
phenomenal [fi'nɔmənəl], *a.* phénoménal.
phenomenon [fi'nɔmənən], *n.* *(pl.* **phenomena** [fi'nɔmənə]*)* phénomène, *m.*
phew! [fjuː], *int.* pouf!
phial ['faiəl], *n.* fiole, *f.*
philanthropic [filən'θrɔpik], *a.* philanthropique.

philanthropist [fi'lænθrəpist], *n.* philanthrope, *m., f.*
philanthropy [fi'lænθrəpi], *n.* philanthropie, *f.*
philatelist [fi'lætəlist], *n.* philatéliste, *m., f.*
philharmonic [filhɑː'mɔnik], *a.* philharmonique.
Philip ['filip]. Philippe, *m.*
Philippine ['filipiːn], *a.* philippine.
Philippines ['filipiːnz], **the**, les Philippines, *f.pl.*
Philistine ['filistain], *a.* philistin.—*n.* Philistin *(personne)*, *m.*
philologist [fi'lɔlədʒist], *n.* philologue, *m., f.*
philology [fi'lɔlədʒi], *n.* philologie, *f.*
philosopher [fi'lɔsəfə], *n.* philosophe, *m., f.*
philosophical [filə'sɔfikl], *a.* philosophique; philosophe *(personnes)*.
philosophize [fi'lɔsəfaiz], *v.i.* philosopher.
philosophy [fi'lɔsəfi], *n.* philosophie, *f.*; *natural philosophy*, la physique, *f.*
philter, philtre ['filtə], *n.* philtre, *m.*
phlegm [flem], *n.* flegme, *m.*
phlegmatic [fleg'mætik], *a.* flegmatique.
phobia ['foubiə], *n.* phobie, *f.*
Phoebe ['fiːbi]. Phébé, *f.*
Phoenician [fi'niːʃən], *a.* phénicien.—*n.* Phénicien *(personne)*, *m.*
phoenix ['fiːniks], *n.* phénix, *m.*
phone [foun], *(colloq.)* [TELEPHONE].
phonetic [fə'netik], *a.* phonétique.
phonetics [fə'netiks], *n.pl.* phonétique, *f.*
phoney ['founi], *a.* *(colloq.)* faux, factice.—*n.* charlatan, *m.*
phonograph, see **gramophone**.
phosphate ['fɔsfeit], *n.* phosphate, *m.*
phosphor ['fɔsfə], *n.* phosphore, *m.*
phosphoric [fɔs'fɔrik], *a.* phosphorique.
phosphorus ['fɔsfərəs], *n.* phosphore, *m.*
photo ['foutou], *(colloq.)* [PHOTOGRAPH].
photogenic [foutə'dʒenik], *a.* photogénique.
photograph ['foutəgrɑːf, 'foutəgræf], *n.* photographie, *(colloq.)* photo, *f.*—*v.t.* photographier.
photographer [fə'tɔgrəfə], *n.* photographe, *m., f.*
photographic [foutə'græfik], *a.* photographique.
photography [fə'tɔgrəfi], *n.* photographie, *f.*
photostat ['foutəstæt], *n.* appareil photostat, *m.*
phrase [freiz], *n.* phrase, locution, *f.*; exprimer, nommer; *(Mus.)* phraser.
phraseology [freizi'ɔlədʒi], *n.* phraséologie, *f.*
phrenetic [fre'netik], *a.* fou, frénétique.
phrenologist [fre'nɔlədʒist], *n.* phrénologiste, phrénologue, *m., f.*
phrenology [fre'nɔlədʒi], *n.* phrénologie, *f.*
physic ['fizik], *n.* médecine, *f.*—*v.t.* médicamenter; purger.
physical ['fizikəl], *a.* physique; *physical training*, éducation physique, *f.*
physically ['fizikəli], *adv.* physiquement.
physician [fi'ziʃən], *n.* médecin, *m.*
physicist ['fizisist], *n.* physicien, *m.*
physics ['fiziks], *n.pl.* physique, *f.*
physiognomy [fizi'ɔnəmi, fizi'ɔgnəmi], *n.* physionomie, *f.*
physiological [fiziə'lɔdʒikl], *a.* physiologique.
physiology [fizi'ɔlədʒi], *n.* physiologie, *f.*

511

physiotherapy

physiotherapy [fizio'θerəpi], *n.* physio-thérapie, *f.*

physique [fi'zi:k], *n.* physique, *m.*

pianist ['pianist], *n.* pianiste, *m., f.*

piano ['pjænou, 'pjɑːnou], *n.* piano, *m*; **grand piano**, piano à queue; **to play (on) the piano**, jouer du piano.   [see **music-stool**]

pick [pik], *n.* pic, *m.*, pioche (*outil*), *f.*; choix, *m.*—*v.t.* piquer; cueillir; choisir, trier; ronger (*un os*); chercher (*querelle*); voler à la tire (*dans une poche*); crocheter (*une serrure*); **to pick up**, ramasser, relever.

pickaback ['pikəbæk], *adv.* sur le dos.

pickaxe ['pikæks], *n.* pioche, *f.*

picked [pikt], *a.* d'élite, choisi.

picker ['pikə], *n.* cueilleur, *m.*

picket ['pikit], *n.* piquet, jalon; petit poste, *m.*—*v.t.* former en piquet; guetter (*grévistes* etc.).

pickle [pikl], *n.* saumure, marinade, *f.*; (*pl.*) conserves au vinaigre, *f.pl.*—*v.t.* conserver au vinaigre, mariner; saler.

pickled [pikld], *a.* mariné, conservé au vinaigre; (*pop.*) ivre.

pickpocket ['pikpɔkit], *n.* voleur à la tire, *m.*

pick-up ['pikʌp], *n.* ramassage, *m.*; reprise (*de machine, des affaires*), *f.*; pick-up (*tourne-disque*), *m.*

picnic ['piknik], *n.* pique-nique, *m.*—*v.i.* faire un pique-nique.

pictorial [pik'tɔːriəl], *a.* illustré; de peintre.

pictorially [pik'tɔːriəli], *adv.* avec illustra-tion.

picture ['piktʃə], *n.* tableau, *m.*; peinture; (*fig.*) image, *f.*; **the pictures**, le cinéma.—*v.t.* peindre; (*fig.*) dépeindre, représenter.

picturesque [piktʃə'resk], *a.* pittoresque.

pie [pai], *n.* pâté (*de viande*), *m.*; tourte (*de fruit*), *f.*; (*colloq.*) **as easy as pie**, simple comme bonjour; **to eat humble pie**, avaler des couleuvres.

piebald ['paibɔːld], *a.* pie (*cheval*).

piece [piːs], *n.* pièce (*grand*), *f.*; morceau (*petit*); fragment, bout, *m.*; **a piece of furniture**, un meuble; **a piece of news**, une nouvelle; **to break to pieces**, mettre en pièces; **to take to pieces**, démonter.—*v.t.* rapiécer.

piecemeal ['piːsmiːl], *adv.* par morceaux, peu à peu.

pied [paid], *a.* bariolé, bigarré; pie (*cheval*).

pie dish ['paidiʃ], *n.* tourtière, terrine, *f.*

pier [piə], *n.* jetée, *f.*; ponton (*de rivière*), *m.*; pile (*d'un pont*), *f.*

pierce [piəs], *v.t.* percer, pénétrer.

pierced [piəst], *a.* à jour (*ouvrage*), *m.*

piercing ['piəsiŋ], *a.* perçant; pénétrant.

pier glass ['piəglɔːs], *n.* trumeau, *m.*

piety ['paiəti], *n.* piété, *f.*

pig [pig], *n.* cochon, porc, pourceau, *m.*; **to buy a pig in a poke**, acheter chat en poche.

pigeon ['pidʒin], *n.* timide, craintif.—*n.* pigeon, *m.*; **carrier pigeon**, pigeon voya-geur.

pigeon-hole ['pidʒinhoul], *n.* boulin, *m.*; case (*à papiers* etc.), *f.*; **set of pigeon-holes**, casier, *m.*—*v.t.* classer.

piggery ['pigəri], *n.* étable à cochons, *f.*

piggy ['pigi], *n.* cochon; **piglet** ['piglit], *n.* porcelet, goret, *m.*

---

pigheaded ['pighedid], *a.* têtu, stupide.

pig iron ['pigaiən], *n.* gueuse, *f.*

pigment ['pigmənt], *n.* couleur, *f.*, pigment, *m.*

pigmy [PYGMY].

pigsty ['pigstai], *n.* porcherie, *f.*

pigtail ['pigteil], *n.* queue (*de cheveux*), *f.*

pigtailed ['pigteild], *a.* à queue.

pike [paik], *n.* pique (*arme*), *f.*; brochet (*poisson*), *m.*

pilchard ['piltʃəd], *n.* (*Ichth.*) pilchard, *m.*

pile [pail], *n.* tas, monceau; (*fig.*) (*Build.*) édifice, bâtiment; pieu (*poteau*); poil (*de tissu*), *m.*; **atomic pile**, pile atomique, *f.*; **funeral pile**, bûcher, *m.*—*v.t.* entasser, empiler, amonceler.—*v.i.* **to pile up**, s'empiler, s'entasser.

piles [pailz], *n.pl.* (*Path.*) hémorroïdes, *f.pl.*

pilfer ['pilfə], *v.t.* dérober, chiper.—*v.i.* dérober.

pilferer ['pilfərə], *n.* chapardeur, chipeur, *m.*

pilfering ['pilfəriŋ], *n.* petit vol, larcin, *m.*

pilgrim ['pilgrim], *n.* pèlerin, *m.*

pilgrimage ['pilgrimidʒ], *n.* pèlerinage, *m.*

pill [pil], *n.* pilule, *f.*

pillage ['pilidʒ], *n.* pillage, saccagement, *m.*—*v.t.* saccager, piller.

pillar ['pilə], *n.* pilier, *m.*, colonne, *f.*; (*fig.*) soutien, *m.*

pillar-box ['piləbɔks], *n.* boîte aux lettres, *f.*

pillion ['piljən], *n.* coussinet (*de cheval*), *m.*; siège, *m.* (*ou* selle, *f.*) arrière (*de moto-cyclette*); **to ride pillion**, monter en croupe, monter derrière.

pillory ['piləri], *n.* pilori, *m.*—*v.t.* pilorier, mettre au pilori.

pillow ['pilou], *n.* oreiller, *m.*—*v.t.* reposer, coucher.

pillow-case ['piloukeis], **pillow slip** ['pilou-slip], *n.* taie d'oreiller, *f.*

pilot ['pailət], *n.* pilote, *m.*; **test pilot**, pilote d'essais.—*v.t.* piloter, servir de pilote à.

pilotage ['pailətidʒ], *n.* pilotage, *m.*

pimpernel ['pimpənel], *n.* pimprenelle, *f.*, mouron, *m.*

pimple [pimpl], *n.* bouton, *m.*

pimply ['pimpli], *a.* bourgeonné, pustuleux.

pin [pin], *n.* épingle; cheville (*de bois*), *f.*; (*fig.*) rien, *m.*—*v.t.* épingler, attacher; cheviller.

pinafore ['pinəfɔː], *n.* tablier (*d'enfant*), *m.*

pincers ['pinsəz], *n.pl.* pince, *f.*, tenailles, *f.pl.*

pinch [pintʃ], *n.* pincée (*de sel* etc.); prise (*de tabac*), *f.*; (*fig.*) embarras, *m.*; **at a pinch**, à la rigueur, au besoin.—*v.t.* pincer, serrer, gêner (*habits*); (*pop.*) chiper (*voler*); pincer (*arrêter*).—*v.i.* pincer; se gêner.

pinching ['pintʃiŋ], *a.* pressant, piquant (*froid*).—*n.* pincement, *m.*

pin-cushion ['pinkuʃən], *n.* pelote, *f.*

pine (1) [pain], *n.* pin (*arbre*); bois de pin, *m.*

pine (2) [pain], *v.i.* languir; **to pine after**, soupirer après.

pineapple ['painæpl], *n.* ananas, *m.*

ping [piŋ], *n.* sifflement (*de balle de fusil*), *m.*—*v.i.* siffler.

ping-pong ['piŋpɔŋ], *n.* ping-pong, *m.*

pinion ['pinjən], *n.* aileron, bout d'aile, *m.*—*v.t.* couper le bout de l'aile à; lier.

pink (1) [piŋk], *a.* couleur de rose, rose.—*n.* œillet (*fleur*); rose (*couleur*), *m.*; **in the pink of condition**, en excellente condition;

(colloq.) to be in the pink, se porter à merveille.

pink (2) [piŋk], *v.i.* cliqueter (*moteur*).

pinnace ['pinəs], *n.* pinasse, *f.*

pinnacle ['pinəkl], *n.* pinacle, *m.*

pin-point ['pinpɔint], *v.t.* indiquer exactement.

pin pricks ['pinpriks], *n.pl.* coups d'épingles, *m.pl.*

pint [paint], *n.* pinte (*un demi-litre*), *f.*

pintail ['pinteil], *n.* (*Orn.*) pilet, *m.*

pioneer [paiə'niə], *n.* pionnier, *m.*

pious ['paiəs], *a.* pieux.

piously ['paiəsli], *adv.* pieusement.

pip [pip], *n.* pépin (*de fruit*); (*Rad.*) top, *m.*—*v.i.* piauler (*oiseaux*).

pipe [paip], *n.* tuyau, conduit, *m.*; pipe (*à fumer, à vin etc.*), *f.*; (*Mus.*) pipeau, chalumeau, *m.*—*v.i.* jouer du chalumeau, siffler; (*pop.*) *pipe down!* boucle-la!

pipe-line ['paiplain], *n.* canalisation, *f.*, oléoduc, pipe-line, *m.*

piper ['paipə], *n.* joueur de flûte etc., *m.*

piping ['paipiŋ], *a.* qui joue du chalumeau, sifflant; flûté (*la voix*).—*n.* tubulure, *f.*, tuyautage, *m.*

pipit ['pipit], *n.* (*Orn.*) pipit, *m.*

pippin ['pipin], *n.* reinette, *f.*

piquancy ['pi:kənsi], *n.* goût piquant, *m.*

piquant ['pi:kənt], *a.* piquant.

pique [pi:k], *n.* pique, brouillerie, *f.*

piquet [pi'ket], *n.* (*Cards*) piquet, *m.*

piracy ['paiərəsi], *n.* piraterie, *f.*; (*fig.*) contrefaçon, *f.*, plagiat, *m.*

pirate ['pairit], *n.* pirate; (*fig.*) contrefacteur, *m.*

piratical [pai'rætikl], *a.* de pirate; (*fig.*) de contrefaçon.

pirouette [piru'et], *n.* pirouette, *f.*

pish! [piʃ], *int.* bah!

piss [pis], *v.i.* (*vulg.*) pisser.—*n.* urine, *f.*

pistol [pistl], *n.* pistolet, *m.*

piston ['pistən], *n.* piston, *m.*

piston ring ['pistənriŋ], *n.* segment de piston, *m.*

piston rod ['pistənrɔd], *n.* tige de piston, *f.*

pit [pit], *n.* fosse, (*fig.*) cavité, *f.*; (*Theat.*) parterre; (*Mining*) puits; creux (*de l'estomac*), *m.*; aisselle (*du bras*), *f.*—*v.t.* creuser; marquer de petits creux.

pitch (1) [pitʃ], *n.* jet, lancement (*de caillou, balle*); (*Naut.*) tangage; point, degré, *m.*; pente (*de toit etc.*), *f.*; (*Mus.*) ton, diapason, *m.*; *to play pitch-and-toss*, jouer à pile ou face.—*v.t.* jeter, lancer; établir (*fixer*); dresser (*une tente*).—*v.i.* (*Naut.*) tanguer, plonger; tomber, se jeter.

pitch (2) [pitʃ], *n.* poix, *f.*; *pitch dark*, noir comme dans un four.

pitched [pitʃt], *a.* rangé; *pitched battle*, bataille rangée, *f.*

pitcher ['pitʃə], *n.* cruche, *f.*

pitchfork ['pitʃfɔ:k], *n.* fourche, *f.*

pitching ['pitʃiŋ], *n.* plongement (*de véhicules*) (*Naut.*) tangage, *m.*

pitch pine ['pitʃpain], *n.* pin à trochets, pitchpin, *m.*

piteous ['pitiəs], *a.* piteux, pitoyable (*digne de pitié*).

piteously ['pitiəsli], *adv.* piteusement.

piteousness ['pitiəsnis], *n.* état piteux, *m.*; tristesse, *f.*

pitfall ['pitfɔ:l], *n.* trappe, *f.*, piège, *m.*

pith [piθ], *n.* moelle; vigueur, énergie, *f.*; essentiel, *m.*

pithily ['piθili], *adv.* fortement, vigoureusement.

pithy ['piθi], *a.* plein de moelle; (*fig.*) substantiel, concis.

pitiable ['pitiəbl], *a.* pitoyable, à faire pitié.

pitiful ['pitiful], *a.* pitoyable.

pitifully ['pitifuli], *adv.* pitoyablement.

pitiless ['pitilis], *a.* impitoyable, sans pitié.

pitilessly ['pitilisli], *adv.* impitoyablement, sans pitié.

pitman ['pitmən], *n.* (*pl.* -men [men]) mineur, *m.*

pittance ['pitəns], *n.* pitance, *f.*

pitted ['pitid], *a.* grêlé (*de petite vérole*).

pity ['piti], *n.* pitié, *f.*; dommage (*regret*), *m.*; *what a pity!* quel dommage!—*v.t.* avoir pitié de, plaindre.

pityingly ['pitiiŋli], *adv.* avec pitié.

pivot ['pivət], *n.* pivot, *m.*

placable ['plækəbl], *a.* facile à apaiser.

placard ['plækɑ:d], *n.* placard, *m.*, affiche, pancarte, *f.*—*v.t.* afficher, placarder (*de*).

placate [plə'keit], *v.t.* apaiser.

place [pleis], *n.* lieu, endroit, *m.*, localité; place (*siège etc.*); position, *f.*, rang (*classe*), *m.*; demeure, résidence (*chez soi*), *f.*; emploi (*profession*), *m.*; *come to my place*, venez chez moi; *to take place*, avoir lieu; *out of place*, déplacé, inopportun.—*v.t.* placer, mettre.

placid ['plæsid], *a.* placide, tranquille, calme.

plagiarism ['pleidʒiərizm], *n.* plagiat, *m.*

plagiarist ['pleidʒiərist], *n.* plagiaire, *m.*, *f.*

plagiarize ['pleidʒiəraiz], *v.t.* plagier.

plague [pleig], *n.* peste; (*fig.*) plaie, *f.*, fléau, *m.*—*v.t.* (*fig.*) tourmenter.

plaice [pleis], *n.* carrelet, *m.*; plie franche, *f.*

plaid [plæd], *n.* (*Sc.*) plaid; tartan, *m.*

plain [plein], *a.* uni, plat; simple, sans façon; ordinaire; sans attraits (*mine*); évident (*qui saute aux yeux*); franc (*sincère*); *in plain clothes*, en civil; *plain cooking*, cuisine bourgeoise *ou* au naturel, *f.*—*n.* plaine, *f.*—*adv.* simplement; franchement.

plainly ['pleinli], *adv.* bonnement; distinctement; franchement.

plainness ['pleinnis], *n.* simplicité; clarté; sincérité, *f.*

plain speaking ['plein'spi:kiŋ], *n.* franchise, *f.*

plain-spoken ['plein'spoukn], *a.* franc, clair, explicite.

plaint [pleint], *n.* plainte, *f.*

plaintiff ['pleintif], *n.* plaignant, *m.*

plaintive ['pleintiv], *a.* plaintif.

plaintively ['pleintivli], *adv.* d'une voix plaintive.

plaintiveness ['pleintivnis], *n.* ton plaintif, *m.*

plait [plæt], *n.* natte, tresse (*de cheveux*), *f.*; pli, *m.*—*v.t.* tresser, natter (*cheveux*); plisser.

plaited ['plætid], *a.* tressé (*cheveux*), plissé.

plan [plæn], *n.* plan; dessein, projet; système, *m.*—*v.t.* tracer un plan de; (*fig.*) projeter.

plane (1) [plein], *n.* (*Géom.*) plan; (*Carp.*) rabot; (*colloq.*) avion, *m.*—*v.t.* raboter, aplanir.

plane (2) [plein], **plane tree** ['pleintri:], *n.* platane, *m.*

planet ['plænit], *n.* planète, *f.*

planetarium [plæni'tɛəriəm], *n.* planéta-
rium, *m.*

planetary ['plænitəri], *a.* planétaire.

planing ['pleiniŋ], *n.* rabotage, *m.*

plank [plæŋk], *n.* planche, *f.*, madrier; (*Naut.*)
bordage, *m.*—*v.t.* planchéier; (*Naut.*)
border.

plankton ['plæŋktən], *n.* plancton, *m.*

planner ['plænə], *n.* auteur d'un plan, *m.*;
town planner, urbaniste, *m.*

planning ['plæniŋ], *n.* tracé d'un plan, *m.*;
planification; (*fig.*) invention, *f.*; *town
planning*, urbanisme, *m.*

plant [plɑ:nt], *n.* plante, *f.*; (*Tech.*) matériel,
m.—*v.t.* planter; (*fig.*) poser.

plantain ['plæntin], *n.* plantain, *m.*

plantation [plɑ:n'teiʃən], *n.* plantation, *f.*

planter ['plɑ:ntə], *n.* planteur, colon, *m.*

planting ['plɑ:ntiŋ], *n.* plantage, *m.*, plantation, *f.*

plasma ['plæzmə], *n.* plasma (du sang), *m.*

plaster ['plɑ:stə], *n.* plâtre; (*Pharm.*) emplâtre, *m.*; *sticking plaster*, sparadrap, *m.*
—*v.t.* plâtrer.

plasterer ['plɑ:stərə], *n.* plâtrier, *m.*

plastering ['plɑ:stəriŋ], *n.* plâtrage, *m.*

plastic ['plæstik], *a.* plastique.—*n.* (*pl.*) plas-
tiques, *m.pl.*

plat [PLAIT].

Plate [pleit], **the River**. le Rio de la Plata, *m.*

plate [pleit], *n.* assiette; (*Metal., Phot.*)
plaque, *f.*—*v.t.* plaquer (*de*); laminer;
étamer (*une glace*).

plateau ['plætou, plɑ'tou], *n.* plateau, *m.*

plated ['pleitid], *a.* plaqué.

plateful ['pleitful], *n.* assiettée, *f.*

plate glass ['pleitglɑ:s], *n.* glace sans tain, *f.*

plate-layer ['pleitleiə], *n.* (*Rail.*) poseur de
rails, *m.*

plate rack ['pleitræk], *n.* porte-assiettes, *m.*

platform ['plætfɔ:m], *n.* plateforme; estrade,
f.; (*Rail.*) quai, *m.*

plating ['pleitiŋ], *n.* placage, *m.*; *armor-
plating*, blindage, *m.*

platinum ['plætinəm], *n.* platine, *m.*

platitude ['plætitju:d], *n.* platitude, *f.*

Plato ['pleitou], Platon, *m.*

platoon [plə'tu:n], *n.* (*Mil.*) section, *f.*

platter ['plætə], *n.* écuelle, *f.*; (*Am.*) plat, *m.*

platypus ['plætipəs], *n.* ornithor(h)ynque, *m.*

plaudit ['plɔ:dit], *n.* applaudissement, *m.*

plausible ['plɔ:zibl], *a.* plausible; spécieux.

play [plei], *n.* jeu, *m.*; récréation (*d'enfants*),
f.; essor (*champ libre*); badinage, *m.*; (*Mus.*)
exécution; (*Theat.*) comédie, pièce, *f.*; *fair
play*, franc jeu.—*v.t.* jouer, jouer à; faire
jouer (*une machine etc.*); représenter, faire
(*une pièce, un rôle etc.*); (*Mus.*) jouer de.—
v.i. jouer; folâtrer (*s'amuser*).

play-bill ['pleibil], *n.* affiche de théâtre, *f.*

player ['pleiə], *n.* joueur; (*Theat.*) acteur, *m.*,
actrice, *f.*; artiste, *m.*, *f.*

playfellow ['pleifelou], **playmate** ['plei
meit], *n.* camarade de jeu, *m.*, *f.*

playful ['pleiful], *a.* folâtre, badin.

playfully ['pleifuli], *adv.* en badinant.

playfulness ['pleifulnis], *n.* badinage, enjouement, *m.*

playground ['pleigraund], *n.* cour de récréation, *f.*

playhouse ['pleihaus], *n.* théâtre, *m.*

plaything ['pleiθiŋ], *n.* jouet, joujou, *m.*

playtime ['pleitaim], *n.* récréation, *f.*

playwright ['pleirait], *n.* auteur dramatique,
m., dramaturge, *m.*, *f.*

plea [pli:], *n.* procès, *m.*, cause, *f.*; prétexte,
m., excuse, *f.*

plead [pli:d], *v.t.*, *v.i.* plaider.

pleasant ['plezənt], *a.* agréable, charmant.

pleasantly ['plezəntli], *adv.* agréablement.

pleasantness ['plezəntnis], *n.* agrément,
charme, *m.*

pleasantry ['plezəntri], *n.* plaisanterie, *f.*

please [pli:z], *v.t.* plaire à; *to be pleased*,
être content.—*v.i.* plaire (à); (*impers.*) il
plaît; *as you please*, comme vous voudrez;
if I please, si cela me plaît; (*if you*)
please, s'il vous plaît.

pleased [pli:zd], *a.* charmé, content (*de*);
satisfait (*de choses*).

pleasing ['pli:ziŋ], *a.* agréable, charmant.

pleasurable ['pleʒərəbl], *a.* agréable.

pleasure ['pleʒə], *n.* plaisir; gré (*will*), *m.*

pleasure ground ['pleʒəgraund], *n.* parc,
jardin d'agrément, *m.*

pleat [pli:t], *n.* plissé, *m.*—*v.t.* plisser.

plebeian [plə'bi:ən], *a.* and *n.* plébéien, *m.*

pledge [pledʒ], *n.* gage; nantissement, *m.*;
(*Law*) caution, *f.*—*v.t.* engager; garantir.

plenary ['pli:nəri], *a.* plein, complet, entier.

plenipotentiary [plenipo'tenʃəri], *a.* and *n.*
plénipotentiaire, *m.*, *f.*

plenitude ['plenitju:d], *n.* plénitude, *f.*

plenteous ['plentiəs], *a.* abondant.

plenteously ['plentiəsli], *adv.* abondamment.

plentiful ['plentiful], *a.* abondant.

plenty ['plenti], *n.* abondance, *f.*; *plenty
of*, beaucoup de.

plethora ['pleθərə], *n.* pléthore, *f.*

pleurisy ['pluərəsi], *n.* pleurésie, *f.*

pliable ['plaiəbl], *a.* pliable, flexible.

pliancy ['plaiənsi], *n.* flexibilité, *f.*

pliant ['plaiənt], *a.* pliant, flexible.

pliers ['plaiəz], *n.pl.* pinces, *f.pl.*

plight [plait], *n.* état, *m.*, condition; situation
difficile, *f.*—*v.t.* engager.

plinth [plinθ], *n.* plinthe, *f.*

plod [plɔd], *v.i.* marcher péniblement; (*fig.*)
peiner, travailler assidûment.

plodder ['plɔdə], *n.* piocheur, *m.*

plodding ['plɔdiŋ], *a.* laborieux, piocheur.—
n. travail pénible, *m.*

plop [plɔp], *adv.*, *n.*, *int.* plouf, flac, pouf, *m.*

plot [plɔt], *n.* complot; petit terrain, *m.*;
intrigue (*d'une pièce etc.*), *f.*; *building-
plot*, lotissement, *m.*—*v.t.* comploter;
(*Surv.*) faire le plan de.—*v.i.* comploter.

plotter ['plɔtə], *n.* conspirateur, comploteur,
m.

plotting ['plɔtiŋ], *n.* complots, *m.pl.*; (*Surv.*)
action de rapporter, *f.*

plough [plau], *n.* charrue, *f.*; *the Plough*, le
Chariot, *m.*, la Grande-Ourse, *f.*—*v.t.*
labourer; (*fig.*) sillonner.—*v.i.* labourer.

ploughing ['plauiŋ], *n.* labourage, *m.*

ploughman ['plaumən], *n.* (*pl.* -men [men])
laboureur, *m.*

ploughshare ['plauʃɛə], *n.* soc de charrue, *m.*

plover ['plʌvə], *n.* (*Orn.*) pluvier, vanneau, *m.*

plow, see **plough**.

pluck [plʌk], *v.t.* cueillir (*fleurs, fruits etc.*);
plumer (*volaille*); épiler (*sourcils*).—*n.* cœur,
courage, *m.*

pluckily ['plʌkili], *adv.* courageusement.

plucky ['plʌki], a. courageux.
plug [plʌg], n. tampon, bouchon, m.; bonde (de tonneau); (Elec.) prise de courant; (Teleph.) fiche, f.; **spark plug**, bougie (d'allumage), f.—v.t. tamponner, boucher.
plum [plʌm], n. prune, f.
plumage ['plu:midʒ], n. plumage, m.
plumb [plʌm], a. droit, vertical.—adv. à plomb; (Am., colloq.) complètement.—v.t. plomber; (Naut.) sonder.—n. plomb, m.
plumber ['plʌmə], n. plombier, m.
plumbing ['plʌmiŋ], n. plomberie; tuyauterie, f.
plumb line ['plʌmlain], n. fil à plomb, m.
plume [plu:m], n. plume, f.; plumet, m.—v.t. plumer.
plummet ['plʌmit], n. plomb, m.
plump (1) [plʌmp], a. dodu, potelé, gras.
plump (2) [plʌmp], adv. tout d'un coup; droit.—v.i. **to plump for**, donner tous ses votes pour.
plumpness ['plʌmpnis], n. embonpoint, m., rondeur, f.
plum tree ['plʌmtri:], n. prunier, m.
plunder ['plʌndə], v.t. piller, dépouiller.—n. butin (chose pillée); pillage (acte de piller), m.
plunderer ['plʌndərə], n. pillard, m.
plunge [plʌndʒ], v.t. plonger, précipiter.—v.i. plonger; se précipiter.—n. plongeon, m.
plural ['pluərəl], a. and n. pluriel, m.
plus [plʌs], prep. (Math.) plus.—a. positif.—n. plus, m.—adv. et davantage.
plush [plʌʃ], n. peluche, f.
plutocrat ['plu:tokræt], n. ploutocrate, m., f.
plutocratic [plu:to'krætik], a. ploutocratique.
plutonium [plu'tounjəm], n. plutonium, m.
pluvial ['plu:viəl], a. pluvial.
ply (1) [plai], v.t. manier (fortement); exercer, employer; presser (quelqu'un de prendre quelque chose).—v.i. travailler; faire le service.
ply (2) [plai], n. pli (de tissu); fil (de laine); toron (de corde), m.
plywood ['plaiwud], n. contre-plaqué, m.
pneumatic [nju'mætik], a. pneumatique.
pneumonia [nju'mouniə], n. pneumonie, f.
poach (1) [poutʃ], v.t. braconner, voler.—v.i. braconner.
poach (2) [poutʃ], v.t. pocher (œufs).
poacher ['poutʃə], n. braconnier, m.
poaching ['poutʃiŋ], n. braconnage, m.
pock [pɔk], n. pustule (de petite vérole), f.
pocket ['pɔkit], n. poche, f.; gousset (du gilet), m.; blouse (de billard), f.—v.t. empocher, mettre en poche.
pocket-book ['pɔkitbuk], n. portefeuille (pour l'argent); livre de poche; calepin (carnet), m.
pocketful ['pɔkitful], n. pleine poche, f.
pocket-knife ['pɔkitnaif], n. couteau de poche, canif, m.
pocket money ['pɔkitmʌni], n. argent de poche, m.
pod [pɔd], n. cosse, gousse, f.—v.t. écosser.
podgy ['pɔdʒi], a. gras, potelé.
poem ['pouim], n. poème, m.
***poesy** ['pouizi], n. poésie, f.
poet ['pouit], n. poète, m.
poetaster ['pouitæstə], n. rimailleur, m.
poetess ['pouites], n. poétesse, f.
poetic [pou'etik], **poetical** [pou'etikəl], a. poétique.

poetry ['pouitri], n. poésie, f.
poignancy ['pɔinjənsi], n. piquant, m.; nature poignante, f.
poignant ['pɔinjənt], a. piquant, vif, poignant.
poignantly ['pɔinjəntli], adv. d'une manière piquante.
point [pɔint], n. point (endroit), m.; pointe (bout aiguisé etc.), f.; (Compass) quart de vent; (Spt.) point; (fig.) but; (pl.) (Rail.) aiguillage, m.; **decimal point**, virgule, f.; **in point of fact**, en effet; **not to the point**, hors de propos; **that is not the point**, ce n'est pas là la question; **to make a point of**, se faire un devoir de; **to the point**, à propos.—v.t. aiguiser, tailler (affiler); indiquer; pointer (fusils etc.); (Build.) jointoyer; **to point out**, signaler; faire remarquer.—v.i. se tourner (vers); tomber en arrêt (chiens); **to point at**, montrer du doigt, indiquer.
point-blank ['pɔint'blæŋk], adv. à bout portant; à brûle-pourpoint, carrément.
pointed ['pɔintid], a. pointu; (fig.) mordant.
pointedly ['pɔintidli], adv. d'une manière piquante.
pointer ['pɔintə], n. index; chien d'arrêt, m.
pointing ['pɔintiŋ], n. (Build.) jointoiement, m.
pointless ['pɔintlis], a. sans pointe; (fig.) inutile, fade.
pointsman ['pɔintsmən], n. (pl. -men [men]) (Rail.) aiguilleur, m.
poise [pɔiz], n. poids, équilibre, m.—v.t. balancer, tenir en équilibre.
poison ['pɔizn], n. poison, m.—v.t. empoisonner.
poisoner ['pɔizrnə], n. empoisonneur, m.
poisoning ['pɔizniŋ], n. empoisonnement, m.
poisonous ['pɔiznəs], a. vénéneux (plante); venimeux (serpent etc.); toxique (gaz).
poke (1) [pouk], n. coup de coude ou de poing, m.—v.t. fourrer; pousser (des doigts); remuer, fourgonner (le feu); **to poke fun at**, se moquer de.—v.i. **to poke about**, tâtonner.
poke (2) [pouk], n. *sac, m.; poche, f.
poker ['poukə], n. tisonnier; (Cards) poker, m.
poky ['pouki], a. (colloq.) petit, mesquin.
Poland ['pouland], n. la Pologne, f.
polar ['poulə], a. polaire.
Pole [poul], n. Polonais (personne), m.
pole (1) [poul], n. perche, f.; bâton (de rideau); timon (d'une voiture); échalas (de vignes etc.); mât (de drapeau etc.); poteau (télégraphique), m.
pole (2) [poul], n. (Astron., Geog.) pôle, m.
poleaxe ['poulæks], n. hache d'armes, f.; assommoir, merlin, m.—v.t. assommer.
polecat ['poulkæt], n. putois, m.
polemics [pə'lemiks], n.pl. polémique, f.
pole-star ['poulsta:], n. étoile polaire, f.
pole vault ['poulvɔ:lt], n. saut à la perche, m.
police [pə'li:s], n. police, f.; **county police**, gendarmerie, f.; **police court**, tribunal de simple police, m.; **police station**, commissariat ou poste de police, m.—v.t. policer.
policeman [pə'li:smən], n. (pl. -men [men]) agent de police, gardien de la paix, m.
policewoman [pə'li:swumən], n. (pl. -women [wimin]) femme agent, f.
policy ['pɔlisi], n. politique, f.; plan, m.; **insurance policy**, police d'assurance, f.

poliomyelitis ['pouliomaiə'laitis], (*fam.*) **polio** ['pouliou], *n.* poliomyélite, *f.*
Polish ['pouliʃ], *a.* polonais.—*n.* polonais (*langue*), *m.*
polish ['poliʃ], *v.t.* polir; vernir (*meubles*); cirer (*chaussures*).—*v.i.* se polir.—*n.* poli, *m.*; (*fig.*) élégance, *f.*; **floor polish**, cire à parquet, *f.* **shoe polish**, cirage, *m.*
polished ['poliʃt], *a.* poli.
polisher ['poliʃə], *n.* polisseur; polissoir (*outil*), *m.*; **floor polisher**, cireur de parquet, *m.*
polite [pə'lait], *a.* poli, élégant, complaisant (*pour*).
politely [pə'laitli], *adv.* poliment.
politeness [pə'laitnis], *n.* politesse, *f.*
politic ['politik], *a.* politique.
political [pə'litikl], *a.* politique.
politically [pə'litikli], *adv.* politiquement.
politician [poli'tiʃən], *n.* homme politique; (*pej.*) politicien, *m.*
politics ['politiks], *n.pl.* politique, *f.*
poll [poul], *n.* (*Anat.*) *tête; liste électorale; élection, *f.*, scrutin; sondage (*de l'opinion publique*), *m.*—*v.t.* étêter (*arbres*); voter; obtenir (*un certain nombre de votes*).
pollen ['polən], *n.* pollen, *m.*
pollination [poli'neiʃən], *n.* pollination, *f.*
polling ['poulin], *n.* élection, *f.*; **polling booth**, bureau de scrutin, *m.*
pollute [pə'lju:t], *v.t.* polluer, souiller (*de*).
pollution [pə'lju:ʃən], *n.* pollution, souillure, *f.*
polo ['poulou], *n.* polo, *m.*
polygamist [pə'ligəmist], *n.* polygame, *m.*, *f.*
polygamy [pə'ligəmi], *n.* polygamie, *f.*
polyglot ['poliglət], *a.* and *n.* polyglotte, *m.*, *f.*
polygon ['poligən], *n.* polygone, *m.*
Polynesia [poli'ni:ziə], la Polynésie, *f.*
polypus ['polipəs], *n.* polype, *m.*
polytechnic [poli'teknik], *a.* polytechnique.—*n.* école d'arts et métiers, *f.*
pomade [pə'meid], *n.* pommade, *f.*
pomegranate ['pomgrænit], *n.* grenade, *f.*; **pomegranate tree**, grenadier, *m.*
pommel [pʌml], *v.t.* battre, rosser.—*n.* pommeau (*d'une selle, d'une épée etc.*), *m.*
pomp [pomp], *n.* pompe, *f.*, éclat, faste, *m.*
Pompey ['pompi], Pompée, *m.*
pompon ['pompon], *n.* pompon, *m.*
pomposity [pom'positi], *n.* pompe, *f.*
pompous ['pompəs], *a.* pompeux, fastueux.
pompously ['pompəsli], *adv.* pompeusement.
pond [pond], *n.* étang, vivier, *m.*; mare (*pool*), *f.*
ponder ['pondə], *v.t.* peser, considérer, réfléchir à.—*v.i.* méditer.
ponderous ['pondərəs], *a.* lourd, pesant.
ponderously ['pondərəsli], *adv.* pesamment.
pontiff ['pontif], *n.* pontife, *m.*
pontificate [pon'tifikeit], *n.* pontificat, *m.*—*v.i.* pontifier.
Pontius Pilate ['pontʃəs'pailət]. Ponce Pilate, *m.*
pontoon [pon'tu:n], *n.* ponton; (*Cards*) vingt-et-un, *m.*
pony ['pouni], *n.* poney, petit cheval, *m.*
poodle [pu:dl], *n.* caniche, *m.*
pooh! [pu:], *int.* bah! allons donc!
pooh-pooh ['pu:'pu:], *v.t.* tourner en ridicule.
pool [pu:l], *n.* étang, *m.*, mare; piscine (*pour*

nager); (*Cards, Billiards etc.*) poule; mise en commun, *f.*—*v.t.* mettre en commun.
poop [pu:p], *n.* dunette, poupe, *f.*
poor [puə], *a.* pauvre, indigent; malheureux (*sans joie*); triste (*de pauvre qualité*); mauvais (*pas bon*).
poor-box ['puəboks], *n.* tronc des pauvres, *m.*
poor-house ['puəhaus], *n.* asile des indigents, *m.*
***poor-law** ['puələ:], *n.* loi sur l'assistance publique, *f.*
poorly ['puəli], *a.* indisposé, souffrant.—*adv.* pauvrement, mal, tristement.
poorness ['puənis], *n.* pauvreté; médiocrité, *f.*
pop (1) [pop], *n.* petit bruit vif et sec, *m.*; (*colloq.*) boisson pétillante, *f.*—*v.t.* pousser, fourrer *ou* mettre subitement.—*v.i.* entrer *ou* sortir subitement.—*int.* crac! pan!
pop (2) [pop], *n.* (*Am.colloq.*) papa, *m.*
pop (3) [pop], *a.* and *n.* (*colloq.*) (musique) populaire, *f.*; **the pops**, les chansons en vogue, *f.pl.*
Pope [poup], *n.* Pape, *m.*
popedom ['poupdəm], *n.* papauté, *f.*
popery ['poupəri], *n.* papisme, *m.*
popish ['poupiʃ], *a.* papiste; de papiste (*choses*).
poplar ['poplə], *n.* (*Bot.*) peuplier, *m.*
poplin ['poplin], *n.* popeline, *f.*
poppet ['popit], *n.* poupée, marionnette, *f.*
poppy ['popi], *n.* pavot (*cultivé*); coquelicot (*sauvage*), *m.*
populace ['popjuləs], *n.* populace, *f.*
popular ['popjulə], *a.* populaire; en vogue.
popularity [popju'læriti], *n.* popularité, *f.*
popularize ['popjuləraiz], *v.t.* populariser.
popularly ['popjuləli], *adv.* populairement.
populate ['popjuleit], *v.t.* peupler.
population [popju'leiʃən], *n.* population, *f.*
populous ['popjuləs], *a.* populeux.
porcelain ['pɔ:slin], *n.* porcelaine, *f.*
porch [pɔ:tʃ], *n.* porche, *m.*
porcupine ['pɔ:kjupain], *n.* porc-épic, *m.*
pore (1) [pɔ:], *n.* pore, *m.*
pore (2) [pɔ:], *v.i.* regarder avec grande attention; **to pore over**, dévorer (*un livre*).
pork [pɔ:k], *n.* porc, *m.*
pork-butcher ['pɔ:kbutʃə], *n.* charcutier, *m.*; **pork-butcher's shop**, charcuterie, *f.*
porker ['pɔ:kə], *n.* porc d'engrais, cochon, *m.*
pork pie ['pɔ:k'pai], *n.* pâté de porc, *m.*
pornography [pɔ:'nɔgrəfi], *n.* pornographie, *f.*
porous ['pɔ:rəs], *a.* poreux.
porphyry ['pɔ:firi], *n.* porphyre, *f.*
porpoise ['pɔ:pəs], *n.* marsouin, *m.*
porridge ['pɔridʒ], *n.* bouillie, *f.*
porringer ['pɔrindʒə], *n.* bol à bouillie, *m.*
port (1) [pɔ:t], *n.* port (*ville maritime*), *m.*
port (2) [pɔ:t], *n.* (*Naut.*) bâbord, *m.*
port (3) [pɔ:t], *n.* porto (*vin*), *m.*
portable ['pɔ:təbl], *a.* portatif, transportable.
portal ['pɔ:tl], *n.* portail, *m.*
portcullis [pɔ:t'kʌlis], *n.* herse, *f.*
portend [pɔ:'tend], *v.t.* présager, augurer.
portent ['pɔ:tənt], *n.* mauvais augure, *m.*
portentous [pɔ:'tentəs], *a.* de mauvais augure.
porter ['pɔ:tə], *n.* commissionnaire; concierge (*de maison*); porteur (*de rue*); (*Rail.*) porteur, *m.*
porterage ['pɔ:təridʒ], *n.* port; factage, *m.*

portfolio [pɔːtˈfouliou], n. carton, m.; serviette, f.; (Polit.) portefeuille, m.
port-hole [ˈpɔːthoul], n. sabord, m.
portico [ˈpɔːtikou], n. portique, m.
portion [ˈpɔːʃən], n. partie, part; dot (de mariage), f.—v.t. partager; doter (pour le mariage).
portliness [ˈpɔːtlinis], n. corpulence, f.
portly [ˈpɔːtli], a. d'un port majestueux; corpulent.
portmanteau [pɔːtˈmæntou], n. valise, f.
portrait [ˈpɔːtrit], n. portrait, m.
portray [pɔːˈtrei], v.t. peindre; (fig.) dépeindre, décrire.
Portugal [ˈpɔːtjug(ə)l]. le Portugal, m.
Portuguese [pɔːtjuˈgiːz], a. portugais.—n. portugais (langue); Portugais (personne), m.
pose [pouz], v.t. embarrasser, confondre; poser (une question).—v.i. poser (avec affectation).—n. pose, f.
poser [ˈpouzə], n. question embarrassante, f.
poseur [pouˈzəː], n. poseur, m.
position [pəˈziʃən], n. situation, position, f.
positive [ˈpɔzitiv], a. positif; absolu, sûr; décisif.—n. positif, m.
positively [ˈpɔzitivli], adv. positivement; absolument.
positiveness [ˈpɔzitivnis], n. nature positive, f.
posse [ˈpɔsi], n. détachement (d'agents de police), m.
possess [pəˈzes], v.t. posséder; avoir; jouir de.
possession [pəˈzeʃən], n. possession, f.
possessive [pəˈzesiv], a. possessif.
possessor [pəˈzesə], n. possesseur, m.
posset [ˈpɔsit], n. lait caillé au vin, m.
possibility [pɔsiˈbiliti], n. possibilité, f.; moyen (façon), m.
possible [ˈpɔsibl], a. possible.
possibly [ˈpɔsibli], adv. peut-être.
post (1) [poust], n. emploi; (Mil.) poste; courrier (livraison de lettres), m.; (Post office) poste, f.—v.t. mettre à la poste; (Mil. etc.) poster, affecter.
post (2) [poust], n. poteau (en bois); montant (de porte), m.—v.t. afficher.
postage [ˈpoustidʒ], n. port de lettre, port, affranchissement, m.
postage stamp [ˈpoustidʒstæmp], n. timbre-poste, m.
postal [ˈpoustəl], a. postal; postal order, mandat-poste, m.
postcard [ˈpoustkɑːd], n. carte postale, f.
postdate [poustˈdeit], v.t. postdater.
poster [ˈpoustə], n. affiche, f., placard, m.
posterior [pɔsˈtiəriə], a. postérieur.
posterity [pɔsˈteriti], n. postérité, f.
postern [ˈpoustəːn], a. de derrière.—n. poterne, f.
post-haste [ˈpoustˈheist], adv. en grande hâte.
posthumous [ˈpɔstjuməs], a. posthume.
posthumously [ˈpɔstjuməsli], adv. après décès.
postillion [pɔsˈtiliən], n. postillon, m.
postman [ˈpoustmən], n. (pl. -men [men]) facteur, m.
postmark [ˈpoustmɑːk], n. cachet de la poste, m.
postmaster [ˈpoustmɑːstə], n. receveur des postes, m.
post meridiem [ˈpoustməˈridiəm], (abbr.

p.m. [ˈpiːˈem]) adv. de l'après-midi, du soir.
post-mortem [poustˈmɔːtəm], adv. après décès.—n. autopsie, f.
post office [ˈpoustɔfis], n. bureau de poste, m., poste, f.
postpone [poustˈpoun], v.t. ajourner, différer, remettre.
postponement [poustˈpounmənt], n. ajournement, m., remise, f.
postscript [ˈpoustskript], (abbr. **P.S.** [ˈpiːˈes]) n. post-scriptum, m.
postulate [ˈpɔstjuleit], v.t. postuler.
posture [ˈpɔstʃə], n. posture, pose, f.
post-war [poustˈwɔː], a. d'après guerre.
posy [ˈpouzi], n. petit bouquet, m.
pot [pɔt], n. pot, m.; marmite, f.; pots and pans, batterie de cuisine, f.—v.t. empoter, mettre en pot.
potable [ˈpoutəbl], a. potable.
potash [ˈpɔtæʃ], n. potasse, f.
potassium [pəˈtæsiəm], n. potassium, m.
potato [pəˈteitou], n. (pl. potatoes [pəˈteitouz]) pomme de terre, f.
pot-bellied [ˈpɔtbelid], a. pansu, ventru.
potency [ˈpoutənsi], n. puissance, force, f.
potent [ˈpoutənt], a. puissant, fort; (fig.) efficace.
potentate [ˈpoutənteit], n. potentat, m.
potential [pəˈtenʃəl], a. potentiel, latent.—n. (Elec. etc.) potentiel, m.
potful [ˈpɔtful], n. potée, f.
pother [ˈpɔðə], n. tumulte; bruit, m.
pot-hole [ˈpɔthoul], n. (Geol.) marmite torrentielle; (Motor.) flache, f.
pot-holer [ˈpɔthoulə], n. spéléologue, m., f.
pot-holing [ˈpɔthoulin], n. spéléologie, f.
pothook [ˈpɔthuk], n. crémaillère, f.
potion [ˈpouʃən], n. potion, f.; breuvage, m.
pot-luck [ˈpɔtˈlʌk], n. fortune du pot, f.
pot shot [ˈpɔtʃɔt], n. coup tiré au petit bonheur, m.
pottage [ˈpɔtidʒ], n. potage (épais), m.
potted [ˈpɔtid], a. en pot, en terrine; potted meat, conserve de viande, f.
potter [ˈpɔtə], n. potier, m.—v.i. to potter about, s'amuser à des riens.
pottery [ˈpɔtəri], n. poterie, f.
potting [ˈpɔtin], n. potting shed, serre, resserre, f.—n. (Hort.) mise en pot, f.
pouch [pautʃ], n. poche, f., petit sac, m.; blague (à tabac), f.
poulterer [ˈpoultərə], n. marchand de volailles, m.
poultice [ˈpoultis], n. cataplasme, m.—v.t. mettre un cataplasme à.
poultry [ˈpoultri], n. volaille, f.
pounce [pauns], v.i. fondre (sur).
pound [paund], n. livre; livre sterling; fourrière (clôture), f.—v.t. broyer; (Metal.) bocarder.
poundage [ˈpaundidʒ], n. commission de tant par livre, f.
pounding [ˈpaundin], n. broiement; (Metal.) bocardage, m.
pour [pɔː], v.t. verser.—v.i. couler; pleuvoir à verse (pluie).
pouring [ˈpɔːrin], a. torrentiel (pluie).
pout [paut], v.i. bouder, faire la moue.—n. bouderie, moue, f.
pouting [ˈpautin], a. qui fait la moue; boudeur.

517

poverty [ˈpɔvəti], *n.* pauvreté, misère, indigence, *f.*
poverty-stricken [ˈpɔvətistrikn], *a.* réduit à
la misère, indigent.
powder [ˈpaudə], *n.* poudre, *f.; face powder*,
poudre de riz; *gunpowder*, poudre à
canon; *tooth powder*, poudre dentifrice.—
v.t. réduire en poudre; poudrer (*les cheveux*);
(*Cook.*) saupoudrer; *to powder one's face*,
se poudrer.
powder compact [ˈpaudəkɔmpækt], *n.*
poudrier (*de dame*), *m.*
powdered [ˈpaudəd], *a.* pulvérisé; poudré
(*cheveux*).
powder puff [ˈpaudəpʌf], *n.* houppe, *f.*, pompon, *m.*
powdery [ˈpaudəri], *a.* poudreux; friable.
power [ˈpauə], *n.* pouvoir, *m.*; force
(*physique*); autorité, puissance (*morale*), *f.*;
the Great Powers, les grandes puissances,
f.pl.; *to be in power*, être au pouvoir.
powerful [ˈpauəful], *a.* puissant, fort.
powerfully [ˈpauəfuli], *adv.* puissamment,
fortement.
powerless [ˈpauəlis], *a.* impuissant, faible.
power station [ˈpauəsteiʃən], *n.* usine génératrice, centrale électrique, *f.*
pox [pɔks], *n.* vérole, *f.*; *chicken pox*,
varicelle, *f.*; *small-pox*, petite vérole,
variole, *f.*
practicability [præktikəˈbiliti], *n.* possibilité, praticabilité, *f.*
practicable [ˈpræktikəbl], *a.* praticable.
practical [ˈpræktikl], *a.* pratique; *practical
joke*, mauvaise farce, *f.*
practically [ˈpræktikli], *adv.* en pratique; à
peu près.
practice [ˈpræktis], *n.* pratique, habitude, *f.*,
usage, exercice, *m.*; clientèle (*de médecin,
d'avocat etc.*); intrigue, *f.*
practice [ˈpræktis], *v.t.* pratiquer, mettre en
pratique; exercer, pratiquer (*une profession
etc.*); (*Mus.*) étudier.—*v.i.* (*Mus.*) étudier;
s'exercer (*à*); exercer, faire de la clientèle
(*médecin*).
practised [ˈpræktist], *a.* exercé (*à*); versé
(*dans*); habile.
practising [ˈpræktisiŋ], *a.* praticien, exerçant.
practitioner [prækˈtiʃənə], *n.* praticien, *m.*;
general practitioner, médecin ordinaire,
m.; *medical practitioner*, médecin, *m.*
pragmatic [prægˈmætik], **pragmatical**
[prægˈmætikl], *a.* pragmatique; officieux;
infatué de soi.
pragmatism [ˈprægmətizm], *n.* pragmatisme,
m.
prairie [ˈprɛəri], *n.* prairie, savane, *f.*
praise [preiz], *n.* louange, *f.*, éloge, *m.*—*v.t.*
louer, faire l'éloge de; vanter.
praiseworthy [ˈpreizwəːði], *a.* louable, digne
d'éloges.
pram [præm], *n.* voiture d'enfant, *f.*
prance [prɑːns], *v.i.* fringuer (*cheval*).
prancing [ˈprɑːnsiŋ], *a.* fringant.
prank [præŋk], *n.* escapade, niche, *f.*, tour, *m.*
prate [preit], *v.i.* jaser, babiller, bavarder
(*de*).
prating [ˈpreitiŋ], *a.* bavard, babillard.
pratingly [ˈpreitiŋli], *adv.* en bavard, en
babillard.
prattle [prætl], *v.i.* babiller, jaser, caqueter.—
n. babil, caquetage, bavardage, *m.*

prattler [ˈprætlə], *n.* bavard, babillard, *m.*
prattling [ˈprætliŋ], *n.* bavardage, caquet, *m.*
prawn [prɔːn], *n.* crevette rouge; salicoque, *f.*
pray [prei], *v.t.* prier, supplier.—*v.i.* prier.
prayer [prɛə], *n.* prière, supplication; (*Law*)
demande, *f.*; *the Lord's Prayer*, l'oraison
dominicale, *f.*
prayer book [ˈprɛəbuk], *n.* livre de prières,
m.; liturgie, *f.*
preach [priːtʃ], *v.t., v.i.* prêcher.
preacher [ˈpriːtʃə], *n.* prédicateur, *m.*
preaching [ˈpriːtʃiŋ], *n.* prédication, *f.*
preamble [priːˈæmbl], *n.* préambule, *m.*
prearrange [priːəˈreindʒ], *v.t.* arranger
d'avance.
prebendary [ˈprebandəri], *n.* chanoine,
prébendier, *m.*
precarious [priˈkɛəriəs], *a.* précaire.
precariously [priˈkɛəriəsli], *adv.* précairement.
precariousness [priˈkɛəriəsnis], *n.* nature
précaire; incertitude, *f.*
precaution [priˈkɔːʃən], *n.* précaution, *f.*
precautionary [priˈkɔːʃənri], *a.* de précaution.
precede [priˈsiːd], *v.t.* précéder.
precedence [ˈpresidəns], *n.* préséance, *f.*; *to
have* or *take precedence over*, avoir le
pas sur.
precedent (1) [priˈsiːdənt], **preceding** [priˈ
siːdiŋ], *a.* précédent.
precedent (2) [ˈpresidənt], *n.* précédent, *m.*
precept [ˈpriːsept], *n.* précepte, *m.*
precinct [ˈpriːsiŋkt], *n.* limite, borne, enceinte, *f.*
precious [ˈpreʃəs], *a.* précieux; affecté;
(*fam.*) fameux, fichu.
preciously [ˈpreʃəsli], *adv.* précieusement;
(*fam.*) fameusement, diablement.
preciousness [ˈpreʃəsnis], *n.* haute valeur, *f.*
precipice [ˈpresipis], *n.* précipice, *m.*
precipitate (1) [priˈsipitit], *a.* précipité.—*n.*
(*Chem.*) précipité, *m.*
precipitate (2) [priˈsipiteit], *v.t.* précipiter.—
v.i. se précipiter.
precipitation [prisipiˈteiʃən], *n.* précipitation, *f.*
precipitous [priˈsipitəs], *a.* escarpé, abrupt.
precipitously [priˈsipitəsli], *adv.* à pic, en
précipice; (*fig.*) précipitamment.
precise [priˈsais], *a.* précis, exact; formaliste,
pointilleux, scrupuleux.
precisely [priˈsaisli], *adv.* précisément.
precision [priˈsiʒən], *n.* précision, exactitude,
f.
preclude [priˈkluːd], *v.t.* exclure; empêcher
(*mettre obstacle à*).
preclusion [priˈkluːʒən], *n.* exclusion, *f.*
precocious [priˈkouʃəs], *a.* précoce.
precociousness [priˈkouʃəsnis], *n.* précocité,
f.
preconceived [ˈpriːkənˈsiːvd], *a.* formé
d'avance; *preconceived idea*, idée pré-
conçue, *f.*
precursor [priˈkəːsə], *n.* précurseur, avant-
coureur, *m.*
predatory [ˈpredətəri], *a.* de rapine, de proie,
pillard, rapace.
predecease [priːdiˈsiːs], *v.t.* prédécéder.
predestinate [priːˈdestineit], **predestine**
[priːˈdestin], *v.t.* prédestiner.

predestination [pri:‚desti’neiʃən], *n.* prédestination, *f.*

predetermine [pri:di’tə:min], *v.t.* prédéterminer, arrêter d’avance.

predicament [pri’dikəmənt], *n.* état, *m.*, position difficile, situation fâcheuse; catégorie, *f.*, ordre, *m.*

predicate [’predikit], *n.* prédicat, attribut, *m.*

predict [pri’dikt], *v.t.* prédire.

prediction [pri’dikʃən], *n.* prédiction, prévision, *f.*

predilection [pri:di’lekʃən], *n.* prédilection, *f.*

predispose [pri:dis’pouz], *v.t.* prédisposer.

predisposition [pri:dispə’ziʃən], *n.* prédisposition, *f.*

predominance [pri’dominəns], *n.* prédominance, *f.*, ascendant, *m.*

predominant [pri’dominənt], *a.* prédominant.

predominantly [pri’dominəntli], *adv.* d’une manière prédominante.

predominate [pri’domineit], *v.i.* prédominer, prévaloir.

pre-eminence [pri:’eminəns], *n.* prééminence, supériorité, *f.*

pre-eminent [pri:’eminənt], *a.* prééminent.

pre-eminently [pri:’eminəntli], *adv.* par excellence.

preen [pri:n], *v.t* lisser, nettoyer (ses plumes); *to preen oneself,* se piquer.

pre-engage [pri:in’geidʒ], *v.t.* engager d’avance.

pre-exist [pri:ig’zist], *v.i.* préexister.

pre-existence [pri:ig’zistəns], *n.* préexistence, *f.*

prefabricate [pri:’fæbrikeit], *v.t.* préfabriquer.

preface [’prefis], *n.* préface, *f.*; avant-propos, *m.*—*v.t.* faire une préface à.

prefect [’pri:fekt], *n.* préfet; (*Sch.*) surveillant, *m.*

prefer [pri’fə:], *v.t.* préférer, aimer mieux, avancer, élever (*aux honneurs*); porter (*une accusation*).

preferable [’prefərəbl], *a.* préférable (*à*).

preferably [’prefərəbli], *adv.* préférablement, de préférence.

preference [’prefərəns], *n.* préférence, *f.*

preferential [prefə’renʃl], *a.* préférentiel.

preferment [pri’fə:mənt], *n.* avancement, *m.*, promotion, *f.*

prefix [’pri:fiks], *n.* (*Gram.*) préfixe, *m.*

pregnancy [’pregnənsi], *n.* grossesse, *f.*

pregnant [’pregnənt], *a.* enceinte, grosse; (*fig.*) gros, plein (*de*); fertile, fécond (*en*).

prehensile [pri’hensail], *a.* préhensile.

prehistoric [pri:his’torik], *a.* préhistorique.

prejudge [pri:’dʒʌdʒ], *v.t.* juger d’avance.

prejudice [’predʒudis], *v.t.* prévenir, nuire à (*faire du tort à*).—*n.* prévention, *f.*, préjugé; préjudice, tort (*détriment*), *m.*

prejudiced [’predʒudist], *a.* prévenu.

prejudicial [predʒu’diʃl], *a.* préjudiciable, nuisible (*à*).

prelate [’prelit], *n.* prélat, *m.*

preliminary [pri’liminəri], *a.* and *n.* préliminaire, *m.*

prelude [’prelju:d], *n.* prélude, *m.*

premature [’prematjuə], *a.* prématuré.

prematurely [’premə’tjuəli], *adv.* prématurément.

premeditate [pri’mediteit], *v.t.* préméditer.

premeditated [pri’mediteitid], *a.* prémédité.

premeditation [primedi’teiʃən], *n.* préméditation, *f.*

premier [’pri:miə, ’premiə], *a.* premier (*de rang*).—*n.* premier ministre, *m.*

premise [’premis], *n.* (*Log.*) prémisse, *f.*

premises [’premisiz], *n.pl.* lieux, *m.pl.*; établissement, local, *m.*

premium [’pri:miəm], *n.* prime, *f.*; prix, *m.*

premonition [pri:mə’niʃən], *n.* avertissement; pressentiment, *m.*

prenatal [pri:’neitl], *a.* prénatal.

preoccupied [pri:’okjupaid], *a.* préoccupé.

preordain [pri:o:’dein], *v.t.* ordonner *ou* arranger d’avance.

prep [prep], *a.* (*Sch. fam. abbr.* **preparatory**) préparatoire.

prepaid [pri:’peid], *a.* affranchi, franc de port.—*adv.* franco.

preparation [prepə’reiʃən], *n.* préparation, *f.*; préparatifs, apprêts (*de voyage etc.*), *m.pl.*

preparatory [pri’pærətri], *a.* préparatoire.

prepare [pri’pɛə], *v.t.* préparer.—*v.i.* se préparer, s’apprêter (*à*).

preparedness [pri’pɛə(ri)dnis], *n.* état de préparation, *m.*

prepay [pri:’pei], *v.t. irr* (*conjug. like* PAY) payer d’avance; affranchir (*lettres*).

prepayment [pri:’peimənt], *n.* payement d’avance; affranchissement (*de lettres*), *m.*

preponderance [pri’pondərəns], *n.* prépondérance, *f.*

preponderant [pri’pondərənt], *a.* prépondérant.

preponderate [pri’pondəreit], *v.i.* avoir la prépondérance, l’emporter (*sur*).

preposition [prepə’ziʃən], *n.* préposition, *f.*

prepossessing [pri:pə’zesiŋ], *a.* prévenant, engageant.

preposterous [pri’postərəs], *a.* absurde, déraisonnable.

preposterously [pri’postərəsli], *adv.* absurdement, déraisonnablement.

prerogative [pri’rogətiv], *n.* prérogative, *f.*

Presbyterian [prezbi’tiəriən], *a.* and *n.* presbytérien, *m.*

Presbyterianism [prezbi’tiəriənizm], *n.* presbytérianisme, *m.*

presbytery [’prezbitəri] *n.* presbytère, *m.*

prescience [’preʃəns], *n.* prescience, *f.*

prescribe [pri’skraib], *v.t.* prescrire; (*Med.*) ordonner.—*v.i.* (*Med.*) faire une ordonnance.

prescription [pri’skripʃən], *n.* (*Law*) prescription; (*Med.*) ordonnance, *f.*

presence [’prezəns], *n.* présence, *f.*; air, maintien, *m.*, mine (*aspect*), *f.*; personnage supérieur, *m.*; *presence of mind*, présence d’esprit.

present [’prezənt], *a.* présent; actuel; *at the present moment*, à présent, actuellement; *to be present at*, assister à.—*n.* présent; cadeau, don, *m.*; *for the present*, pour le moment.—[pri’zent], *v.t.* présenter, offrir (*à*).

presentable [pri’zentəbl], *a.* présentable.

presentation [prezən’teiʃən], *n.* présentation, *f.*; don, *m.*

presentiment [pri'zentimənt], n. pressentiment, m.

presently ['prezəntli], adv. tout à l'heure, bientôt; à présent, actuellement.

preservation [prezə'veiʃən], n. salut, m., conservation, préservation (de), f.

preservative [pri'zə:vətiv], a. and n. préservateur, préservatif, m.

preserve [pri'zə:v], n. confiture, f., conserves, f.pl.; réserve, chasse réservée, f.—v.t. conserver (de); conserver; confire (fruits etc.); **preserved fruits**, fruits confits, m.pl.; **preserved meat**, conserves de viande, f.pl.

preserver [pri'zə:və], n. sauveur; conservateur, m.; **life preserver, see life-belt.**

preside [pri'zaid], v.i. présider (à).

presidency ['prezidənsi], n. présidence, f.

president ['prezidənt], n. président, m.; **vice president**, vice-président, m.

presidential [prezi'denʃəl], a. présidentiel; de président.

presiding [pri'zaidiŋ], a. présidant.

press (1) [pres], v.t. presser; serrer, étreindre; satiner (papier); pressurer (fruits); repasser (vêtements); (fig.) insister sur.—v.i. presser, pousser; avancer, se presser.—n. presse, pression, f.; presse (à fruits etc.), m.; armoire à linge, f.; **the press**, la presse.

press (2) [pres], v.t. enrôler (marins) de force.

press agency ['preseidʒənsi], n. agence de presse, f.

press clipping ['presklipiŋ], n. coupure de journal, f.

pressed [prest], a. satiné; **hard pressed**, serré de près; aux abois; **pressed for time**, très pressé.

*****press gang** ['presgæn], n. (Naut.) presse, f.

pressing ['presiŋ], a. urgent, pressant.

pressman ['presmən], n. (pl. -men [men]) journaliste, reporter, m.

pressure ['preʃə], n. pression; tension; urgence, f.; poids (lourdeur), m.; **blood pressure**, tension artérielle.

pressure cooker ['preʃəkukə], n. autoclave; auto-cuiseur, m., cocotte-minute, f.

pressure gauge ['preʃəgeidʒ], n. manomètre, m.

pressurize ['preʃəraiz], v.t. pressuriser.

prestige [pres'ti:ʒ], n. prestige, m.

presumably [pri'zju:məbli], adv. probablement.

presume [pri'zju:m], v.t. présumer; supposer.—v.i. se permettre, avoir l'audace (de), prendre la liberté (de); **to presume upon**, présumer trop de.

presuming [pri'zju:miŋ], a. présomptueux, indiscret.

presumption [pri'zʌmpʃən], n. présomption, f.

presumptive [pri'zʌmptiv], a. présumé; (Law) présomptif.

presumptuous [pri'zʌmptjuəs], a. présomptueux.

presumptuousness [pri'zʌmptjuəsnis], n. présomption, f.

presuppose [pri:sə'pouz], v.t. présupposer.

pretend [pri'tend], v.t. prétexter; feindre.—v.i. prétendre (à); feindre (ae), faire semblant (de).

pretended [pri'tendid], a. prétendu, soidisant.

pretender [pri'tendə], n. prétendant, m.

pretense [pri'tens], n. prétexte, m., simulation; prétention, f.; **to make a pretense of**, faire semblant de; **under false pretenses**, par des moyens frauduleux.

pretension [pri'tenʃən], n. prétention, f.

pretentious [pri'tenʃəs], a. prétentieux, ambitieux.

pretentiousness [pri'tenʃəsnis], n. air prétentieux, m., prétention, f.

preternatural [pri:tə'nætʃərəl], a. surnaturel, contre nature.

pretext ['pri:tekst], n. prétexte, faux semblant, m.; **under the pretext of**, sous prétexte de.

prettily ['pritili], adv. joliment, gentiment.

prettiness ['pritinis], n. gentillesse, f., agrément, m.

pretty ['priti], a. joli, gentil.—adv. assez; passablement; **pretty much**, presque, à peu près.

prevail [pri'veil], v.i. prévaloir, l'emporter (sur); réussir (avoir du succès); dominer.

prevailing [pri'veiliŋ], a. dominant, régnant; général.

prevalence ['prevələns], n. influence, prédominance; fréquence, durée (de temps, maladie etc.), f.

prevalent ['prevələnt], a. régnant, dominant; général.

prevaricate [pri'værikeit], v.i. équivoquer; tergiverser, mentir.

prevarication [priværi'keiʃən], n. tergiversation, f.

prevaricator [pri'værikeitə], n. chicaneur, menteur, m.

prevent [pri'vent], v.t. empêcher, détourner (de); prévenir.

preventable [pri'ventəbl], a. évitable.

prevention [pri'venʃən], n. empêchement, m.

preventive [pri'ventiv], a. préventif.—n. préservatif, m.

preview ['pri:vju:], n. avant-première, f.

previous ['pri:viəs], a. antérieur, préalable.

previously ['pri:viəsli], adv. antérieurement, auparavant.

previousness ['pri:viəsnis], n. antériorité, priorité; (colloq.) anticipation, f.

prey [prei], n. proie, f.; **to be a prey to**, être en proie à.—v.i. **to prey on**, faire sa proie de; tourmenter, obséder (l'esprit).

price [prais], n. prix, m.; **at any price**, à tout prix; **cost price**, prix coûtant; **market price**, prix courant.—v.t. tarifer, mettre un prix à.

priceless ['praislis], a. sans prix, inappréciable; impayable (plaisanterie etc.).

price list ['praislist], n. tarif, m.

prick [prik], n. piqûre; pointe, f.; (fig.) aiguillon (stimulant); remords, m.—v.t. piquer; dresser (les oreilles); aiguillonner (stimuler); (fig.) exciter, tourmenter de remords.

pricker ['prikə], n. poinçon, m., pointe, f.

pricking ['prikiŋ], a. qui pique, piquant.—n. piqûre, f.; picotement (sensation), m.

prickle ['prikl], n. aiguillon, piquant, m.; épine, f.—v.t. piquer.

prickly ['prikli], a. piquant, épineux, hérissé.

pride [praid], n. orgueil, m., fierté; bande (de lions), f.—v.r. **to pride oneself on**, se piquer de, s'enorgueillir de.

prier ['praiə], n. curieux, m.

priest [pri:st], *n.* prêtre, *m.*
priestess ['pri:stes], *n.* prêtresse, *f.*
priesthood ['pri:sthu:d], *n.* prêtrise, *f.*, sacerdoce, clergé, *m.*
priestly ['pri:stli], *a.* de prêtre, sacerdotal.
prig [prig], *n.* faquin, fat; pédant, *m.*
priggish ['prigiʃ], *a.* suffisant, pédant.
priggishly ['prigiʃli], *adv.* avec suffisance.
prim [prim], *a.* affecté, précieux, collet monté.
primacy ['praiməsi], *n.* primauté, *f.*
primal ['praiməl], *a.* primitif; principal.
primarily ['praimərili], *adv.* dans le principe.
primary ['praiməri], *a.* primitif, premier; principal; (*Sch.*) primaire, élémentaire.
primate ['praimit], *n.* primat, *m.*
prime [praim], *a.* premier, principal; de premier rang, de première qualité; *prime minister*, premier ministre, *m.*—*n.* aube, *f.*; commencement; printemps, *m.*; fleur, élite, *f.*, choix (*mieux*), *m.*; première jeunesse, *f.*; *prime of life*, fleur de l'âge, *f.* —*v.t.* amorcer (*fusils*); (*Paint.*) imprimer.
primer [['primə], *n.* premier livre (*de lecture etc.*); (*R.-C. Ch.*) livre d'heures, *m.*
primeval [prai'mi:vəl], *a.* primitif, primordial.
priming ['praimiŋ], *n.* amorçage, *m.*; amorce (*d'un fusil*); (*Paint.*) impression, *f.*
primitive ['primitiv], *a.* and *n.* primitif, *m.*
primitiveness ['primitivnis], *n.* caractère primitif, *m.*
primly ['primli], *adv.* d'un air collet monté.
primness ['primnis], *n.* affèterie, *f.*
primogeniture [praimou'dʒenitjuə], *n.* primogéniture, *f.*
primordial [prai'mɔ:diəl], *a.* primordial.
primrose ['primrouz], *n.* primevère, *f.*
prince [prins], *n.* prince, *m.*
princeliness ['prinslinis], *n.* caractère de prince, *m.*
princely ['prinsli], *a.* de prince, princier; magnifique.—*adv.* en prince, en princesse, magnifiquement.
princess [prin'ses], *n.* princesse, *f.*
principal ['prinsipl], *a.* principal, premier, en chef.—*n.* partie principale, *f.*, chef; directeur, patron; proviseur (*d'un lycée*), *m.*; directrice, *f.*
principality [prinsi'pæliti], *n.* principauté, *f.*
principally ['prinsipli], *adv.* principalement, surtout.
principle ['prinsipl], *n.* principe, *m.*
principled ['prinsipld], *a.* qui a des principes.
print [print], *v.t.* imprimer; faire une empreinte sur; (*Phot. etc.*) tirer; *printed matter*, imprimé(s), *m.* (*pl.*).—*n.* empreinte (*de pas etc.*), impression; estampe, gravure; indienne (*tissu*); (*Phot.*) épreuve, *f.*; (*Print.*) caractère, *m.*
printer ['printə], *n.* imprimeur, typographe, *m.*
printing ['printiŋ], *n.* impression (*tirage*); imprimerie (*art etc.*), *f.*
printing machine ['printiŋmə'ʃi:n], *n.* presse mécanique, *f.*
printing press ['printiŋpres], *n.* presse à imprimer, *f.*
prior ['praiə], *a.* antérieur.—*adv.* antérieurement (*à*), avant.—*n.* prieur, *m.*
prioress ['praiəris], *n.* prieure, *f.*
priority [prai'ɔriti], *n.* priorité, *f.*

priory ['praiəri], *n.* prieuré, *m.*
prise [praiz], *n.* levier, *m.*—*v.t. to prise open*, ouvrir avec un levier.
prism [prizm], *n.* prisme, *m.*
prismatic [priz'mætik], **prismatical** [priz 'mætikəl], *a.* prismatique.
prison [prizn], *n.* prison, *f.*
prisoner ['priznə], *n.* prisonnier, *m.*; (*Law*) *prisoner (at the bar)*, accusé, prévenu, *m.*
prison-van ['priznvæn], *n.* voiture cellulaire, *f.*
pristine ['pristain], *a.* primitif, premier.
privacy ['praivəsi, 'pri.vəsi], *n.* retraite, solitude, intimité, *f.*
private ['praivit], *a.* particulier, personnel, privé; confidentiel, secret; (*Law*) à huis clos.—*n.* (*Mil.*) simple soldat, *m.*
privateer [praivə'tiə], *n.* corsaire, *m.*
privately ['praivitli], *adv.* en particulier; en secret; (*Law*) à huis clos.
privation [prai'veiʃən], *n.* privation, *f.*
privet ['privit], *n.* (*Bot.*) troène, *m.*
privilege ['privilidʒ], *n.* privilège, *m.*, (*Law*) immunité, *f.*—*v.t.* privilégier.
privileged ['privilidʒd], *a.* privilégié.
privily ['privili], *adv.* secrètement, en secret.
privy ['privi], *a.* privé, secret; caché; *Privy Council*, conseil privé, *m.*
prize [praiz], *n.* prise (*ce qu'on prend*), *f.*; prix (*récompense*); lot (*dans une loterie*), *m.*—*v.t.* priser, estimer.
prize-giving ['praizgiviŋ], *n.* distribution des prix, *f.*
prize-winner ['praizwinə], *n.* lauréat, gagnant, *m.*
pro [prou], *prep.* pour; *pros and cons*, le pour et le contre.
probability [prɔbə'biliti], *n.* probabilité, vraisemblance, *f.*
probable ['prɔbəbl], *a.* probable; vraisemblable.
probably ['prɔbəbli], *adv.* probablement.
probate ['proubeit], *n.* vérification (*d'un testament*), *f.*
probation [prə'beiʃən], *n.* probation, épreuve, *f.*; (*Univ. etc.*) examen, stage, *m.*; *on probation*, (*Law*) sous surveillance de la police.
probationary [prə'beiʃənəri], *a.* d'épreuve; de probation.
probationer [prə'beiʃənə], *n.* aspirant, *m.*, stagiaire; novice, *m.*, *f.*
probe [proub], *n.* sonde, *f.*, stylet, *m.*—*v.t.* sonder; (*fig.*) examiner à fond.
probing ['proubiŋ], *a.* pénétrant (*question*).
probity ['proubiti], *n.* probité, *f.*
problem ['prɔbləm], *n.* problème, *m.*
problematic [prɔbli'mætik], **problematical** [prɔbli'mætikəl], *a.* problématique.
proboscis [prə'bɔsis], *n.* (*pl.* **probosces** [prə'bɔsi:z]) trompe, *f.*, (*facet.*) nez, *m.*
procedure [prə'si:dʒə], *n.* procédé, *m.*, procédure, *f.*
proceed [prə'si:d], *v.i.* procéder, avancer, continuer son chemin; provenir (*de*); se mettre (*à*).
proceeding [prə'si:diŋ], *n.* procédé, *m.*; manière d'agir, *f.*; (*pl.*) démarches, *f.pl.*, faits, actes, *m.pl.*
proceeds ['prousi:dz], *n.pl.* produit, montant, *m.*

process ['prouses], *n.* procédé; processus; cours, *m.*, marche, suite (*du temps*), *f.*—*v.t.* (*Ind.*) traiter.

procession [prə'seʃən], *n.* procession, *f.*, cortège, *m.*

processional [prə'seʃənəl], *a.* processionnel. —*n.* hymne processionnel, *m.*

proclaim [prə'kleim], *v.t.* proclamer, déclarer, publier.

proclamation [prɔklə'meiʃən], *n.* proclamation, publication, déclaration; ordonnance, *f.*

proclivity [prə'kliviti], *n.* penchant, *m.*, inclination (à), *f.*

procrastinate [pro'kræstineit], *v.t.* remettre. —*v.i.* retarder.

procrastination [prokræsti'neiʃən], *n.* retardement, délai, *m.*

procrastinator [pro'kræstineitə], *n.* temporiseur, *m.*

procreate ['proukrieit], *v.t.* procréer.

procreation [proukri'eiʃən], *n.* procréation, *f.*

procreative ['proukrieitiv], *a.* procréateur, productif.

proctor ['prɔktə], *n.* (*Univ.*) censeur; (*Law*) procureur, *m.*

procurable [prə'kjuərəbl], *a.* qu'on peut se procurer.

procuration [prɔkju'reiʃən], *n.* gestion des affaires d'autrui; (*Law*) procuration, *f.*

procurator ['prɔkjureitə], *n.* agent d'affaires; (*Law*) procurateur, *m.*

procure [prə'kjuə], *v.t.* procurer, faire avoir, se procurer.

prod [prɔd], *v.t.* pousser du doigt *ou* du bout d'un bâton; piquer; (*fig.*) aiguillonner.—*n.* coup de pointe, *m.*

prodigal ['prɔdigl], *a.* and *n.* prodigue, *m.*, *f.*

prodigality [prɔdi'gæliti], *n.* prodigalité, *f.*

prodigious [prə'didʒəs], *a.* prodigieux.

prodigy ['prɔdidʒi], *n.* prodige, *m.*, *f.*

produce [prə'dju:s], *n.* produit, *m.*—[prə'dju:s], *v.t.* produire; exhiber, montrer; (*Geom.*) prolonger.

producer [prə'dju:sə], *n.* producteur; (*Theat.*) producteur, *m.*

producible [prə'dju:sibl], *a.* productible.

product ['prɔdʌkt], *n.* produit, *m.*; *by-product*, sous-produit, *m.*

production [prə'dʌkʃən], *n.* production, *f.*; (*Chem. etc.*) produit, *m.*; (*Theat.*) mise en scène, *f.*

productive [prə'dʌktiv], *a.* productif; fécond.

productivity [prɔdʌk'tiviti], *n.* productivité, *f.*

profanation [prɔfə'neiʃən], *n.* profanation, *f.*

profane [prə'fein], *a.* profane.—*v.t.* profaner.

profanely [prə'feinli], *adv.* d'une manière profane.

profaner [prə'feinə], *n.* profanateur, *m.*

profanity [prə'fæniti], *n.* conduite profane, impiété, *f.*; langage profane, *m.*

profess [prə'fes], *v.t.* professer, faire profession de, déclarer.

professed [prə'fest], *a.* déclaré, de profession.

professedly [prə'fesidli], *adv.* ouvertement; de profession.

profession [prə'feʃən], *n.* profession, *f.*; état, métier (*emploi*), *m.*

professional [prə'feʃənəl], *a.* de sa profession, professionnel; *professional man*, homme qui exerce une carrière libérale, *m.*—*n.*

homme du métier, homme de l'art; (*Spt.*) professionnel, *m.*

professionalism [prə'feʃənəlizm], *n.* caractère professionnel; (*Spt.*) professionnalisme, *m.*

professionally [prə'feʃənəli], *adv.* par profession; en homme du métier.

professor [prə'fesə], *n.* professeur (d'université), *m.*

professorial [profe'sɔ:riəl], *a.* de professeur, professoral.

professorship [prə'fesəʃip], *n.* professorat, *m.*, chaire, *f.*

proffer ['prɔfə], *n.* offre, *f.*—*v.t.* offrir, proposer.

proficiency [prə'fiʃənsi], *n.* capacité, *f.*; talent, *m.*, compétence, *f.*

proficient [prə'fiʃənt], *a.* versé, fort, compétent.

profile ['proufail], *n.* profil, *m.*; *in profile*, de profil.

profit ['prɔfit], *n.* profit, bénéfice, rapport; (*fig.*) avantage, *m.*—*v.t.* profiter à, faire du bien à; avantager.—*v.i.* profiter (*de*).

profitable ['prɔfitəbl], *a.* profitable, avantageux.

profitably ['prɔfitəbli], *adv.* avantageusement, avec profit.

profiteer [prɔfi'tiə], *n.* profiteur, *m.*—*v.i.* faire des bénéfices excessifs.

profitless ['prɔfitlis], *a.* sans profit, inutile.

profligacy ['prɔfligəsi], *n.* dérèglement, *m.*, dissolution, *f.*, libertinage, *m.*

profligate ['prɔfligit], *a.* débauché, dissolu, libertin.—*n.* libertin, mauvais sujet, *m.*

profound [prə'faund], *a.* profond; approfondi.

profoundly [prə'faundli], *adv.* profondément.

profundity [prə'fʌnditi], *n.* profondeur, *f.*

profuse [prə'fju:s], *a.* prodigue; abondant, excessif (*choses*).

profusely [prə'fju:sli], *adv.* profusément, à profusion.

profuseness [prə'fju:snis], **profusion** [prə'fju:ʒən], *n.* profusion, prodigalité, abondance, *f.*

progenitor [prou'dʒenitə], *n.* aïeul, ancêtre, *m.*

progeny ['prɔdʒəni], *n.* postérité, *f.*, descendants, *m.pl.*

prognostic [prɔg'nɔstik], *a.* pronostique.—*n.* pronostic, *m.*

prognosticate [prɔg'nɔstikeit], *v.t.* pronostiquer.

prognostication [prɔgnɔsti'keiʃən], *n.* pronostic, *m.*

program ['prougræm], *n.* programme, *m.*

progress ['prougres], *n.* progrès, avancement, cours, *m.*; marche, *f.*; voyage (*de cérémonie*), *m.*—[prə'gres], *v.i.* s'avancer, faire des progrès, avancer.

progression [prə'greʃən], *n.* progression, *f.*

progressive [prə'gresiv], *a.* and *n.* progressif, *m.*; (*Polit.*) progressiste, *m.*, *f.*

progressiveness [prə'gresivnis], *n.* marche progressive, *f.*

prohibit [prə'hibit], *v.t.* prohiber, défendre, interdire (à); *smoking prohibited*, défense de fumer.

prohibition [prouhi'biʃən], *n.* prohibition, défense, *f.*

prohibitive [prə'hibitiv], **prohibitory** [prə'hibitri], *a.* prohibitif (*mœurs*); *prohibitive price*, prix exorbitant, *m.*

project ['prɔdʒekt], *n.* projet, dessein, *m.*— [prə'dʒekt], *v.t.* projeter.—*v.i.* avancer, faire saillie.

projectile [prə'dʒektail], *n.* projectile, *m.*

projecting [prə'dʒektiŋ], *a.* saillant, en saillie.

projection [prə'dʒekʃən], *n.* projection, saillie, *f.*; (*Arch.*) ressaut, *m.*

projector [prə'dʒektə], *n.* homme à projets, projeteur; projecteur (*lumière*); (*Cine.*) appareil de projection, *m.*

proletarian [prouli'tɛəriən], *a.* and *n.* prolétaire, *m., f.*

proletariat [prouli'tɛəriət], *n.* prolétariat, *m.*

prolific [prə'lifik], *a.* prolifique; fécond, fertile.

prolix ['prouliks], *a.* prolixe.

prolixity [prə'liksiti], **prolixness** ['prouliks-nis], *n.* prolixité, *f.*

prologue ['proulog], *n.* prologue, *m.*

prolong [prə'lɔŋ], *v.t.* prolonger; retarder, différer (*remettre*); *to be prolonged*, se prolonger.

prolongation [proulɔŋ'geiʃən], *n.* prolongement, *m.*; prolongation (*du temps etc.*), *f.*

promenade [prɔmə'nɑːd], *n.* promenade; esplanade (*au bord de la mer*), *f.*—*v.i.* se promener; se faire voir.

promenader [prɔmə'nɑːdə], *n.* promeneur, *m.*

prominence ['prɔminəns], *n.* proéminence; (*fig.*) distinction, *f.*

prominent ['prɔminənt], *a.* proéminent, saillant; prononcé (*remarquable*); (*fig.*) éminent, distingué.

prominently ['prɔminəntli], *adv.* en saillie; d'une manière frappante.

promiscuity [prɔmis'kjuːiti], **promiscuousness** [prə'miskjuəsnis], *n.* mélange confus, *m.*; promiscuité, *f.*

promiscuous [prə'miskjuəs], *a.* sans distinction de sexe, promiscu; mêlé, confus, sans ordre.

promiscuously [prə'miskjuəsli], *adv.* confusément; en commun, en promiscuité.

promise ['prɔmis], *n.* promesse; (*fig.*) espérance, *f.*—*v.t., v.i.* promettre.

promising ['prɔmisiŋ], *a.* prometteur, qui promet; qui donne des espérances.

promissory ['prɔmisəri], *a.* qui contient une promesse; *promissory note*, billet à ordre, *m.*

promontory ['prɔməntri], *n.* promontoire, *m.*

promote [prə'mout], *v.t.* servir, avancer; promouvoir; encourager; *to promote a company*, lancer une société anonyme.

promoter [prə'moutə], *n.* promoteur, protecteur, instigateur; (*Comm.*) lanceur d'affaires, *m.*

promotion [prə'mouʃən], *n.* promotion, *f.*, avancement, *m.*

prompt [prɔmpt], *v.t.* exciter, porter, pousser; inspirer, suggérer; (*Theat.*) souffler.—*a.* prompt, empressé.

prompter ['prɔmptə], *n.* souffleur, *m.*; *prompter's box*, trou du souffleur, *m.*

promptitude ['prɔmptitjuːd], **promptness** ['prɔmptnis], *n.* promptitude, *f.*, empressement, *m.*

promptly ['prɔmptli], *adv.* promptement, avec empressement.

promptness [PROMPTITUDE].

promulgate ['prɔməlgeit], *v.t.* promulguer.

promulgation [prɔməl'geiʃən], *n.* promulgation, *f.*

promulgator ['prɔməlgeitə], *n.* promulgateur, *m.*

prone [proun], *a.* penché, incliné; couché, étendu; (*fig.*) disposé, porté (à).

proneness ['prounnis], *n.* disposition, inclination, *f.*, penchant, *m.*

prong [prɔŋ], *n.* fourchon, *m.*, dent, *f.*

pronged [prɔŋd], *a.* à fourchons, à dents.

pronoun ['prounaun], *n.* pronom, *m.*

pronounce [prə'nauns], *v.t.* prononcer; déclarer, annoncer, dire.

pronounceable [prə'naunsəbl], *a.* prononçable.

pronouncement [prə'naunsmənt], *n.* prononcement, *m.*, déclaration, *f.*

pronunciation [prənʌnsi'eiʃən], *n.* prononciation, *f.*, accent, *m.*

proof [pruːf], *a.* *proof against*, résistant à, à l'épreuve de; *waterproof*, imperméable. —*n.* preuve; épreuve, *f.*

proofless ['pruːflis], *a.* sans preuve.

proof sheet ['pruːfʃiːt], *n.* (*Print.*) épreuve, *f.*

prop [prɔp], *n.* étai, étançon, (*Hort.*) tuteur, échalas; (*fig.*) appui, soutien; (*Theat.*) (*fam.*) accessoire, *m.*—*v.t.* étayer; appuyer, soutenir; (*Hort.*) échalasser.

propaganda [prɔpə'gændə], *n.* propagande, *f.*

propagandist [prɔpə'gændist], *n.* propagandiste, *m., f.*

propagate ['prɔpəgeit], *v.t.* propager; (*fig.*) répandre; créer, enfanter (*des êtres*).—*v.i.* se propager.

propagation [prɔpə'geiʃən], *n.* propagation, *f.*

propagator ['prɔpəgeitə], *n.* propagateur, *m.*

propel [prə'pel], *v.t.* pousser en avant, faire marcher, propulser.

propeller [prə'pelə], *n.* hélice, *f.*; propulseur, moteur, *m.*

propelling [prə'peliŋ], *a.* propulseur, moteur; *propelling force*, force motrice, *f.*

propensity [prə'pensiti], *n.* penchant, *m.*, tendance, *f.*

proper ['prɔpə], *a.* propre, particulier; convenable, à propos (*comme il faut*); juste, exact (*correct*).

properly ['prɔpəli], *adv.* proprement, comme il faut.

property ['prɔpəti], *n.* propriété, *f.*; bien, *m.*, biens, *m.pl.*; qualité, *f.*; (*Theat., Cine.*) accessoire, *m.*

property tax ['prɔpətitæks], *n.* impôt foncier, *m.*

prophecy ['prɔfəsi], *n.* prophétie, *f.*

prophesy ['prɔfəsai], *v.t.* prophétiser, prédire.

prophet ['prɔfit], *n.* prophète, *m.*

prophetess ['prɔfites], *n.* prophétesse, *f.*

prophetic [prə'fetik], **prophetical** [prə'fetikəl], *a.* prophétique.

propinquity [prə'piŋkwiti], *n.* proximité; parenté (*de personnes*), *f.*

propitiate [prə'piʃieit], *v.t.* rendre propice.

propitiation [prəpiʃi'eiʃən], *n.* propitiation, *f.*

propitiator [prə'piʃieitə], *n.* propitiateur, *m.*

propitiatory [prə'piʃiətri], *a.* and *n.* propitiatoire, *f.*

propitious [prə'piʃəs], *a.* propice, favorable.

propitiousness

propitiousness [prə'piʃəsnis], *n.* nature propice, *f.*

proportion [prə'pɔːʃən], *n.* proportion; partie; portion, *f.*; **in proportion as**, à mesure que.—*v.t.* proportionner.

proportional [prə'pɔːʃənəl], *a.* en proportion; proportionnel.

proportionate [prə'pɔːʃənit], *a.* proportionné.

proposal [prə'pouzl], *n.* proposition; demande en mariage, *f.*

propose [prə'pouz], *v.t.* proposer; offrir; **to propose a toast**, porter un toast.—*v.i.* se proposer; faire une demande en mariage.

proposer [prə'pouzə], *n.* auteur d'une proposition, *m.*

proposition [prɔpə'ziʃən], *n.* proposition; affaire, *f.*

propound [prə'paund], *v.t.* proposer, exposer, mettre en avant.

proprietary [prə'praiətri], *a.* de propriété.— *n.* actionnaires, *m.pl.*

proprietor [prə'praiətə], *n.* propriétaire, *m.*

proprietress [prə'praiətris], *n.* propriétaire, maîtresse, *f.*

propriety [prə'praiəti], *n.* convenance, propriété, *f.*

propulsion [prə'pʌlʃən], *n.* propulsion, *f.*; **jet propulsion**, propulsion à réaction.

prorogation [prourə'geiʃən], *n.* prorogation, *f.*

prorogue [prə'roug], *v.t.* proroger.

prosaic [pro'zeiik], *a.* prosaïque.

proscenium [prə'siːniəm], *n.* proscenium, *m.*, avant-scène, *f.*

proscribe [pro'skraib], *v.t.* proscrire.

proscription [pro'skripʃən], *n.* proscription, *f.*

prose [prouz], *n.* prose, *f.*

prosecute ['prɔsikjuːt], *v.t.* poursuivre; revendiquer (*ses droits etc.*).

prosecution [prɔsi'kjuːʃən], *n.* poursuite, *f.*; procès criminel, *m.*; **witness for the prosecution**, témoin à charge, *m.*

prosecutor ['prɔsikjuːtə], *n.* poursuivant, plaignant, *m.*; **public prosecutor**, procureur de la république, *m.*

prosecutrix ['prɔsikjuːtriks], *n.* poursuivante, plaignante, *f.*

proselyte ['prɔsəlait], *n.* prosélyte, *m.*, *f.*

proselytism ['prɔsəlitizm], *n.* prosélytisme, *m.*

proselytize ['prɔsəlitaiz], *v.t.* convertir.—*v.i.* faire des prosélytes.

prose writer ['prouzraitə], *n.* prosateur, *m.*

prosily ['prouzili], *adv.* prosaïquement, ennuyeusement.

prosiness ['prouzinis], *n.* prosaïsme, *m.*; verbosité, *f.*

prosody ['prɔsədi], *n.* prosodie, *f.*

prospect ['prɔspekt], *n.* vue; perspective, *f.*; (*fig.*) espoir; avenir, *m.*—[prə'spekt], *v.i.* faire des recherches (*minerai, pétrole etc.*), prospecter.

prospective [prə'spektiv], *a.* en perspective; à venir.

prospectively [prə'spektivli], *adv.* pour l'avenir.

prospector [prə'spektə], *n.* explorateur; *orpailleur, *m.*

prospectus [prə'spektəs], *n.* prospectus, *m.*

prosper ['prɔspə], *v.t.* faire prospérer, favoriser.—*v.i.* prospérer, réussir.

prosperity [prɔs'periti], *n.* prospérité, *f.*

prosperous ['prɔspərəs], *a.* prospère; florissant (*affaires*); (*fig.*) heureux; favorable.

prostitute ['prɔstitjuːt], *n.* prostituée, *f.*—*v.t.* prostituer.

prostitution [prɔsti'tjuːʃən], *n.* prostitution, *f.*

prostrate ['prɔstreit]. *v.t.* coucher, prosterner; (*fig.*) renverser; **to prostrate oneself before**, se prosterner devant.— *a.* prosterné; (*fig.*) abattement, *m.*

prostration [prɔs'treiʃən], *n.* prosternation, *f.*; (*fig.*) abattement, *m.*

prosy ['prouzi], *a.* ennuyeux, fastidieux.

protagonist [prou'tægənist], *n.* protagoniste, *m.*

protect [prə'tekt], *v.t.* protéger, défendre; garantir, abriter (*contre le temps etc.*); sauvegarder (*intérêts*).

protection [prə'tekʃən], *n.* protection, défense; garantie, *f.*, abri (*contre le temps etc.*), *m.*; (*Law*) sauvegarde, *f.*

protectionism [prə'tekʃənizm], *n.* protectionnisme, *m.*

protectionist [prə'tekʃənist], *a.* and *n.* protectionniste, *m.*, *f.*

protective [prə'tektiv], *a.* protecteur.

protector [prə'tektə], *n.* protecteur, *m.*

protectorate [prə'tektɔrit], *n.* protectorat, *m.*

protectress [prə'tektris], *n.* protectrice, *f.*

protein ['proutiːn], *n.* protéine, *f.*

protest ['proutest], *n.* protestation, *f.*; (*Comm.*) protêt, *m.*—[prə'test], *v.t.*, *v.i.* protester.

Protestant ['prɔtistənt], *a.* and *n.* protestant, *m.*

Protestantism ['prɔtistəntizm], *n.* protestantisme, *m.*

protestation [prɔtes'teiʃən], *n.* protestation, *f.*

protester [prə'testə], *n.* personne qui fait faire un protêt, *f.*

protocol ['proutəkɔl], *n.* protocole, *m.*

proton ['proutɔn], *n.* proton, *m.*

prototype ['proutətaip], *n.* prototype, *m.*

protract [prə'trækt], *v.t.* prolonger, traîner en longueur.

protraction [prə'trækʃən], *n.* prolongation, *f.*

protractor [prə'træktə], *n.* rapporteur (*instrument*), *m.*

protrude [prə'truːd], *v.t.* pousser en avant, faire sortir.—*v.i.* s'avancer, faire saillie.

protruding [prə'truːdiŋ], *a.* en saillie, saillant.

protrusion [prə'truːʒən], *n.* saillie, *f.*

protuberance [prə'tjuːbərəns], *n.* protubérance, *f.*

protuberant [prə'tjuːbərənt], *a.* protubérant.

proud [praud], *a.* fier (*de*); orgueilleux.

proudly ['praudli], *adv.* fièrement, orgueilleusement.

provable ['pruːvəbl], *a.* prouvable, démontrable.

prove [pruːv], *v.t.* prouver, démontrer; mettre à l'épreuve, éprouver (*la qualité de*); vérifier (*testament etc.*).—*v.i.* se montrer, se révéler.

proved [pruːvd], *a.* prouvé, démontré, reconnu.

provender ['prɔvəndə], *n.* fourrage, *m.*, nourriture (*d'animaux*), *f.*

proverb ['prɔvə:b], *n.* proverbe, *m.*
proverbial [prə'və:biəl], *a.* proverbial.
provide [prə'vaid], *v.t.* pourvoir, fournir; munir; préparer (*à*); stipuler.—*v.i.* pourvoir.
provided [prə'vaidid], *a.* pourvu.—*conj. provided that*, pourvu que (*with subj.*).
providence ['prɔvidəns], *n.* providence (*divine*); prévoyance (*humaine*), *f.*
provident ['prɔvidənt], *a.* prévoyant; économe.
providential [prɔvi'denʃəl], *a.* providentiel, de la providence.
providently ['prɔvidəntli], *adv.* avec prévoyance.
provider [prə'vaidə], *n.* pourvoyeur, fournisseur, *m.*
province ['prɔvins], *n.* province, *f.*; (*fig.*) département, ressort, *m.*
provincial [prə'vinʃəl], *a.* provincial, de province.—*n.* provincial, *m.*
provincialism [prə'vinʃəlizm], *n.* provincialisme, *m.*
proving ['pru:viŋ], *n.* vérification, mise à l'épreuve, *f.*
provision [prə'viʒən], *n.* action de pourvoir; stipulation; (*Law*) disposition (*d'un projet de loi etc.*), *f.*; (*pl.*) vivres, comestibles, *m.pl.*—*v.t.* approvisionner.
provisional [prə'viʒənəl], *a.* provisoire.
provision dealer [prə'viʒəndi:lə], *n.* marchand de comestibles, *m.*
proviso [prə'vaizou], *n.* condition, clause conditionnelle, *f.*
provisory [prə'vaizəri], *a.* provisoire, conditionnel.
provocation [prɔvə'keiʃən], *n.* provocation, *f.*
provocative [prə'vɔkətiv], *a.* provocant, provoquer.
provoke [prə'vouk], *v.t.* provoquer; inciter; fâcher, irriter.
provoker [prə'voukə], *n.* provocateur, *m.*
provoking [prə'voukiŋ], *a.* provocant; ennuyeux, fâcheux, agaçant.
provokingly [prə'voukiŋli], *adv.* d'une manière provocante *ou* contrariante.
provost ['prɔvəst], *n.* prévôt, *m.*; (*Univ.*) principal; (*Sc.*) maire, *m.*
prow [prau], *n.* proue, *f.*
prowess ['prauis], *n.* bravoure, prouesse, *f.*
prowl [praul], *n.* action de rôder, *f.*—*v.i.* rôder.
prowler ['praulə], *n.* rôdeur, *m.*
proximate ['prɔksimit], *a.* proche, immédiat.
proximity [prɔk'simiti], *n.* proximité, *f.*
proximo ['prɔksimou], *adv.* du mois prochain.
proxy ['prɔksi], *n.* mandataire, *m.*, délégué, *m.*; procuration (*chose*), *f.*; *by proxy*, par procuration.
prude [pru:d], *n.* prude, mijaurée, *f.*
prudence ['pru:dəns], *n.* prudence, *f.*
prudent ['pru:dənt], *a.* prudent, sage.
prudential [pru'denʃəl], *a.* de prudence, dicté par la prudence.
prudently ['pru:dəntli], *adv.* prudemment, sagement.
prudery ['pru:dəri], *n.* pruderie, *f.*
prudish ['pru:diʃ], *a.* prude, de prude.
prudishly ['pru:diʃli], *adv.* avec pruderie.
prune [pru:n], *n.* pruneau, *m.*—*v.t.* élaguer, tailler, émonder.
prunella [pru'nelə], *n.* prunelle, *f.*

pruning ['pru:niŋ], *n.* taille, *f.*, élagage, *m.*
pruning shears ['pru:niŋʃiəz], *n.pl.* sécateur, *m.*, cisailles, *f.pl.*
prurience ['pruəriəns], **pruriency** ['pruəriənsi], *n.* démangeaison, *f.*
prurient ['pruəriənt], *a.* qui démange.
Prussia ['prʌʃə], la Prusse, *f.*
Prussian ['prʌʃən], *a.* prussien.—*n.* Prussien (*personne*), *m.*
prussic ['prʌsik], *a.* prussique.
pry [prai], *v.t.* soulever avec un levier.—*v.i.* fureter; fouiller (*dans*); *to pry into*, se mêler de.—*n.* regard scrutateur, regard indiscret, *m.*
prying ['praiiŋ], *a.* scrutateur, curieux.—*n.* curiosité, *f.*
psalm [sɑ:m], *n.* psaume, *m.*
psalmist ['sɑ:mist], *n.* psalmiste, *m.*
psalmody ['sɑ:mədi], *n.* psalmodie, *f.*
psalter ['sɔ:ltə], *n.* psautier, *m.*
pseudonym ['sju:dənim], *n.* pseudonyme, *m.*
pshaw! [pʃɔ:], *int.* bah! fi donc!
psychiatric [saiki'ætrik], *a.* psychiatrique.
psychiatrist [sai'kaiətrist], *n.* psychiatre, *m.*, *f.*
psychiatry [sai'kaiətri], *n.* psychiatrie, *f.*
psychic(al) ['saikik(l)], *a.* psychique.
psycho-analysis [saikouə'næləsis], *n.* psychanalyse, *f.*
psycho-analyst [saikou'ænəlist], *n.* psychanalyste, *m.*, *f.*
psycho-analyze [saikou'ænəlaiz], *v.t.* psychanalyser.
psychological [saikə'lɔdʒikl], *a.* psychologique.
psychologist [sai'kɔlədʒist], *n.* psychologiste, psychologue, *m.*
psychology [sai'kɔlədʒi], *n.* psychologie, *f.*
psychopath ['saikopæθ], *n.* psychopathe, *m.*, *f.*
psychosis [sai'kousis], *n.* psychose, *f.*
ptarmigan ['tɑ:migən], *n.* lagopède, *m.*
ptomaine ['toumein], *n.* ptomaïne, *f.*; *ptomaine poisoning*, intoxication alimentaire, *f.*
puberty ['pju:bəti], *n.* puberté, *f.*
pubescence [pju'besəns], *n.* pubescence, *f.*
pubescent [pju'besənt], *a.* pubescent.
public ['pʌblik], *a.* and *n.* public, *m.*
publican ['pʌblikən], *n.* cafetier, patron de bistro(t); (*Bibl.*) publicain, *m.*
publication [pʌbli'keiʃən], *n.* publication, *f.*
public-house ['pʌblik'haus], *n.* café, *m.*, brasserie, *f.*, bistro(t), *m.*
publicist ['pʌblisist], *n.* publiciste, journaliste; publicitaire, *m.*, *f.*
publicity [pʌb'lisiti], *n.* publicité; réclame, *f.*
publicize ['pʌblisaiz], *v.t.* faire connaître au public.
publicly ['pʌblikli], *adv.* publiquement; en public.
publish ['pʌbliʃ], *v.t.* publier; éditer.
publisher ['pʌbliʃə], *n.* éditeur, *m.*; *bookseller and publisher*, libraire-éditeur, *m.*
puce [pju:s], *a.* puce.
puck (1) [pʌk], *n.* lutin, *m.*
puck (2) [pʌk], (*Spt.*) palet de hockey (sur glace), *m.*
pucker ['pʌkə], *v.t.* rider, plisser; (*Dress.*) faire goder.—*v.i.* goder.—*n.* ride, (*Dress.*) poche, *f.*; mauvais pli, *m.*
puckering ['pʌkəriŋ], *n.* froncement, *m.*
puckish ['pʌkiʃ], *a.* malicieux; de lutin.

525

pudding

pudding ['pudiŋ], *n.* pudding, pouding, *m.*;
puddle [pʌdl], *n.* flaque (d'eau), mare, *f.*—
v.t. troubler, rendre bourbeux.
puerile ['pjuərail], *a.* puéril.
puerility [pjuə'riliti], *n.* puérilité, *f.*
puff [pʌf], *n.* souffle (*d'haleine*), *m.*; bouffée (*de vent, fumée etc.*), *f.*; feuilleté (*pâtisserie*), *m.*; houppe à poudrer (*de dames*), *f.*; bouillon (*de robes*); puff, *m.*, réclame tapageuse, *f.*—*v.t.* souffler, bouffir (*les joues*), gonfler; (*fig.*) faire mousser (*publicité*).—*v.i.* souffler, boursoufler, bouffir, bouffer, se gonfler; haleter.
puffin ['pʌfin], *n.* (*Orn.*) macareux, *m.*
puffiness ['pʌfinis], *n.* boursouflure, enflure, *f.*
puff pastry ['pʌfpeistri], *n.* pâte feuilletée, *f.*
puffy ['pʌfi], *a.* bouffi, gonflé.
pug [pʌg], *n.* carlin (*chien*), *m.*
pugilism ['pju:dʒilizm], *n.* pugilat, *m.*, boxe, *f.*
pugilist ['pju:dʒilist], *n.* boxeur, pugiliste, *m.*
pugilistic [pjudʒi'listik], *a.* de pugilat.
pugnacious [pʌg'neiʃəs], *a.* querelleur; batailleur.
pugnaciously [pʌg'neiʃəsli], *adv.* d'un air batailleur.
pugnacity [pʌg'næsiti], *n.* pugnacité, *f.*
pug nose ['pʌgnouz], *n.* nez épaté, *m.*
puke [pju:k], *v.i.* vomir.
pule [pju:l], *v.i.* piauler.
puling ['pju:liŋ], *n.* cri; piaulement, *m.*
pull [pul], *v.t.* tirer; presser (*la détente*); **to pull a wry face**, faire la grimace; **to pull down**, abattre, démolir; **to pull off**, arracher, enlever; **to pull up**, hisser; se remettre; tirer (*tirer la rame*); **to pull in**, s'arrêter; **to pull round**, se remettre; **to pull through**, guérir, s'en tirer; **to pull up**, s'arrêter.—*n.* action de tirer, traction, *f.*; coup (*d'aviron*), effort, *m.*; secousse, *f.*; (*fig.*) avantage, *m.*; **hard pull**, rude effort.
pullet ['pulit], *n.* poulette, *f.*
pulley ['puli], *n.* poulie, *f.*
pullover ['puləuvə], *n.* pull-over, *m.*
pulmonary ['pʌlmənəri], *a.* pulmonaire.
pulp [pʌlp], *n.* pulpe; pâte (*papier*), *f.*—*v.t.* réduire en pâte.
pulpiness ['pʌlpinis], *n.* nature pulpeuse, *f.*
pulpit ['pulpit], *n.* chaire, *f.*
pulpous ['pʌlpəs], **pulpy** ['pʌlpi], *a.* pulpeux.
pulsate [pʌl'seit], *v.i.* battre; palpiter.
pulsation [pʌl'seiʃən], *n.* pulsation, *f.*
pulsatory ['pʌlsətri], *a.* pulsatoire.
pulse [pʌls], *n.* pouls, *m.*; pulsation, *f.*; plantes légumineuses, *f.pl.*
pulverization [pʌlvərai'zeiʃən], *n.* pulvérisation, *f.*
pulverize ['pʌlvəraiz], *v.t.* pulvériser.
puma ['pju:mə], *n.* puma, couguar, *m.*
pumice ['pʌmis], *n.* pierre ponce, *f.*
pump [pʌmp], *n.* pompe, *f.*; escarpin (*chaussure*), *m.*—*v.t.* pomper; (*fig.*) sonder; **to pump up**, gonfler (*pneu*).—*v.i.* pomper.
pumpkin ['pʌmpkin], *n.* citrouille, courge, *f.*, potiron, *m.*
pump room ['pʌmpru:m], *n.* buvette, *f.*
pun [pʌn], *n.* calembour, jeu de mots, *m.*—*v.i.* faire des calembours.
punch (1) [pʌntʃ], *n.* emporte-pièce; (*Print.*) poinçon, *m.*—*v.t.* percer, poinçonner.

punch (2) [pʌntʃ], *n.* coup de poing, *m.*—*v.t.* donner un coup de poing à.
punch (3) [pʌntʃ], *n.* punch (*boisson*), *m.*
punch bowl ['pʌntʃboul], *n.* bol à punch, *m.*
puncheon ['pʌntʃən], *n.* poinçon, *m.*, pièce (*de vin*), *f.*
punctilio [pʌŋk'tiliou], *n.* exactitude scrupuleuse, *f.*, point d'étiquette, *m.*
punctilious [pʌŋk'tiliəs], *a.* pointilleux.
punctiliousness [pʌŋk'tiliəsnis], *n.* exactitude scrupuleuse, pointillerie, *f.*
punctual ['pʌŋktjuəl], *a.* ponctuel, exact.
punctuality [pʌŋktju'æliti], *n.* ponctualité, exactitude, *f.*
punctually ['pʌŋktjuəli], *adv.* ponctuellement, exactement.
punctuate ['pʌŋktjueit], *v.t.* ponctuer.
punctuation [pʌŋktju'eiʃən], *n.* ponctuation, *f.*
puncture ['pʌŋktʃə], *n.* piqûre; crevaison (*d'un pneu*), *f.*—*v.t.* piquer; crever (*pneu*).
pundit ['pʌndit], *n.* pandit, *m.*
pungency ['pʌndʒənsi], *n.* âcreté; aigreur, *f.*
pungent ['pʌndʒənt], *a.* âcre; piquant, mordant.
pungently ['pʌndʒəntli], *adv.* avec causticité.
puniness ['pju:ninis], *n.* petitesse, nature chétive, *f.*
punish ['pʌniʃ], *v.t.* punir, corriger; malmener.
punishable ['pʌniʃəbl], *a.* punissable.
punishment ['pʌniʃmənt], *n.* punition; peine, *f.*, châtiment, *m.*; **capital punishment**, peine capitale.
punitive ['pju:nitiv], *a.* punitif.
punt [pʌnt], *n.* bachot, *m.*—*v.i.* conduire un bachot (*à la perche*).
puny ['pju:ni], *a.* petit, chétif.
pup [pʌp], *n.* petit chien, petit; (*pej.*) freluquet, fat, *m.*
pupil (1) ['pju:pil], *n.* élève, *m.*, *f.*
pupil (2) ['pju:pil], *n.* pupille (*de l'œil*), *f.*
pupilary ['pju:piləri], *a.* pupillaire.
puppet ['pʌpit], *n.* marionnette, *f.*; **glove puppet**, marionnette à gaine; **puppet government**, gouvernement fantoche, *m.*
puppet show ['pʌpitʃou], *n.* (spectacle de) marionnettes, *f.pl.*
puppy ['pʌpi], *n.* petit chien; (*fig.*) fat, freluquet, *m.*
purblind ['pə:blaind], *a.* myope.
purchase ['pə:tʃis], *n.* achat, *m.*, acquisition, emplette; (*Mech.*) prise, *f.*—*v.t.* acheter, acquérir.
purchase deed ['pə:tʃisdi:d], *n.* contrat d'achat, *m.*
purchaser ['pə:tʃisə], *n.* acquéreur, acheteur, *m.*
purchasing ['pə:tʃisiŋ], *n.* achat, *m.*; **purchasing power**, pouvoir d'achat, *m.*
pure [pjuə], *a.* pur; **pure-bred**, de race.
purely ['pjuəli], *adv.* purement.
pureness ['pjuənis], *n.* pureté, *f.*
purgation [pə'geiʃən], *n.* purgation, *f.*
purgative ['pə:gətiv], *a.* and *n.* purgatif, *m.*
purgatorial [pə:gə'tɔ:riəl], *a.* du purgatoire.
purgatory ['pə:gətəri], *n.* purgatoire, *m.*
purge [pə:dʒ], *v.t.* purger; purifier, épurer.—*n.* purgation, purge, *f.*; (*Polit.*) nettoyage, *m.*

purification [pjuərifiˈkeiʃən], *n.* purification; épuration, *f.*
purifier [ˈpjuərifaiə], *n.* purificateur, *m.*
purify [ˈpjuərifai], *v.t.* purifier.—*v.i.* se purifier.
purist [ˈpjuərist], *n.* puriste, *m., f.*
puritan [ˈpjuəritən], *n.* puritain, *m.*
puritan [ˈpjuəritən], *a.* puritain.
puritanical [pjuəriˈtænikl], *a.* de puritain, puritain.
puritanism [ˈpjuəritənizm], *n.* puritanisme, *m.*
purity [ˈpjuəriti], *n.* pureté, *f.*
purl [pəːl], *v.t.* engrêler (*dentelle*).—*v.i.* murmurer, gazouiller.—*n.* engrêlure (*de dentelle*), *f.*; doux murmure; gazouillement, *m.*
purlieu [ˈpəːljuː], *n.* alentours, environs, *m.pl.*
purloin [pəˈlɔin], *v.t.* dérober, voler.
purple [pəːpl], *a.* violet, mauve; pourpre.—*n.* pourpre, mauve (*couleur*), *m.*; pourpre (*teinture etc.*), *f.*—*v.t.* teindre en pourpre, empourprer, rougir.
purport [ˈpəːpət], *n.* sens, *m.*, teneur, portée, *f.*—[pəˈpəːt], *v.t.* tendre à montrer, signifier, vouloir dire.
purpose [ˈpəːpəs], *n.* but, objet, *m.*, fin, *f.*, dessein, *m.*, intention, *f.*; **on purpose**, exprès, à dessein; **to answer one's purpose**, faire son affaire.—*v.t., v.i.* se proposer, avoir l'intention (*de*).
purposely [ˈpəːpəsli], *adv.* à dessein, exprès.
purr [pəː], *v.i.* ronronner.
purring [ˈpəːriŋ], *a.* qui fait ronron.—*n.* ronron, *m.*
purse [pəːs], *n.* porte-monnaie, *m.*; bourse, *f.*; (*Am.*) sac à main, *m.*—*v.t.* plisser, froncer (*les sourcils etc.*).
purser [ˈpəːsə], *n.* commissaire (*de navire*); (*Mining*) agent comptable, *m.*
pursuance [pəˈsjuːəns], *n.* poursuite, conséquence, *f.*; **in pursuance of**, conformément à.
pursuant [pəˈsjuːənt], *a.* en conséquence (*de*), conforme (*à*).
pursue [pəˈsjuː], *v.t.* poursuivre; suivre, chercher.
pursuer [pəˈsjuːə], *n.* poursuivant, *m.*
pursuit [pəˈsjuːt], *n.* poursuite, recherche; occupation, *f.*; (*pl.*) travaux, *m.pl.*
purulence [ˈpjuəruləns], **purulency** [ˈpjuərulənsi], *n.* purulence, *f.*
purulent [ˈpjuərulənt], *a.* purulent.
purvey [pəˈvei], *v.t.* fournir, approvisionner; procurer.
purveyor [pəˈveiə], *n.* pourvoyeur, fournisseur, *m.*
pus [pʌs], *n.* pus, *m.*
push [puʃ], *v.t.* pousser; (*fig.*) presser, importuner; **to push back**, repousser, faire reculer; **to push down**, faire tomber, renverser.—*v.i.* pousser; faire un effort; **to push off**, pousser au large; **to push on**, pousser en avant.—*n.* impulsion, poussée, *f.*; effort, *m.*; extrémité, *f.*
pushing [ˈpuʃiŋ], *a.* entreprenant.
pusillanimity [pjuːsiləˈnimiti], *n.* pusillanimité, *f.*
pusillanimous [pjuːsiˈlæniməs], *a.* pusillanime.
puss [pus], *n.* (*colloq.*) minet, *m.*, minette, *f.*
pustule [ˈpʌstjuːl], *n.* pustule, *f.*

put [put], *v.t. irr.* mettre, poser, placer; proposer (*solution etc.*); lancer (*poids etc.*); **to put about**, gêner; **to put aside**, mettre de côté; **to put back**, replacer, remettre; **to put by**, mettre de côté; **to put forward**, mettre en avant; **to put off**, ôter; remettre; **to put on**, mettre (*vêtements*); **to put on the light**, allumer; **to put out**, mettre dehors; éteindre (*feu etc.*); **to put up**, installer; loger, caser (*dans un hôtel etc.*).—*v.i.* aller; germer, pousser; (*Naut.*) se mettre; **to put in**, entrer au port; **to put up**, loger (*à* ou *chez*), descendre (*à*); **to put up with**, supporter.
putrefaction [pjuːtriˈfækʃən], *n.* putréfaction, *f.*
putrefy [ˈpjuːtrifai], *v.t.* putréfier.—*v.i.* se putréfier.
putrid [ˈpjuːtrid], *a.* putride.
putridity [pjuːˈtriditi], *n.* putridité, *f.*
putt [pʌt], *v.t.* (*Golf*) poter.
putter [ˈpʌtə], *n.* (*Golf*) poteur, *m.*
putting [ˈputiŋ], *n.* action du mettre, mise, *f.*
putty [ˈpʌti], *n.* mastic, *m.*
puzzle [pʌzl], *n.* (*fig.*) énigme, *f.*; jeu de patience, casse-tête (*jouet*), *m.*; **crossword puzzle**, mots croisés, *m.pl.*—*v.t.* intriguer, embarrasser; **to puzzle one's brains**, se creuser la tête.
pygmean [pigˈmiən], *a.* de pygmée.
pygmy [ˈpigmi], *n.* pygmée, *m., f.*
pyjamas [piˈdʒɑːməz], *n.pl.* pyjama, *m.*
pylon [ˈpailən], *n.* pylône, *m.*
pyramid [ˈpirəmid], *n.* pyramide, *f.*
pyramidal [piˈræmidl], *a.* pyramidal.
pyre [ˈpaiə], *n.* bûcher, *m.*
Pyrenees [pirəˈniːz], **the.** les Pyrénées, *f.pl.*
pyrethrum [paiˈriːθrəm], *n.* (*Bot.*) pyréthre, *m.*
pyrotechnic [paiərouˈteknik], **pyrotechnical** [paiərouˈteknikəl], *a.* pyrotechnique, pyrique.
pyrotechnics [paiərouˈtekniks], *n.pl.* pyrotechnie, *f.*
pyrotechnist [paiərouˈteknist], *n.* artificier, *m.*
python [ˈpaiθən], *n.* python, *m.*
pyx [piks], *n.* ciboire, *m.*

Q

Q, q [kjuː]. dix-septième lettre de l'alphabet, *m.*
quack [kwæk], *a.* de charlatan.—*n.* charlatan; couac, cri du canard, *m.*—*v.i.* crier (comme les canards *etc.*).
quackery [ˈkwækəri], *n.* charlatanisme, *m.*
Quadragesima [kwɔdrəˈdʒesimə]. Quadragésime, *f.*
quadrangle [ˈkwɔdræŋgl], *n.* quadrilatère carré, *m.*; (*Univ.*) cour d'honneur, *f.*
quadrant [ˈkwɔdrənt], *n.* quart de cercle, *m.*
quadratic [kwɔˈdrætik], *a.* du second degré.
quadrennial [kwɔˈdreniəl], *a.* quadriennal.
quadrennially [kwɔˈdreniəli], *adv.* tous les quatre ans.

527

quadrilateral

quadrilateral [kwɔdri'lætərəl], a. quadrilatéral.—n. quadrilatère, m.
quadrille [kwə'dril], n. quadrille, m.; contredanse, f.
quadroon [kwə'druːn], n. quarteron, m.
quadruped ['kwɔdruped], n. quadrupède, m.
quadruple ['kwɔdrupl], a. and n. quadruple, m.—v.t. quadrupler.
quadruplet ['kwɔdruplit], n. quadruplette, f.; (pl.) (colloq.) quads [kwɔdz], quadruplés, m.pl.
quaff [kwæf], v.t. boire à grands traits.
quaffer ['kwæfə], n. buveur, m.
quagmire ['kwægmaiə], n. fondrière, f.
quail (1) [kweil], v.i. perdre courage, fléchir.
quail (2) [kweil], n. (Orn.) caille, f.
quaint [kweint], a. singulier, bizarre; pittoresque.
quaintly ['kweintli], adv. singulièrement, bizarrement.
quaintness ['kweintnis], n. bizarrerie, originalité, f.
quake [kweik], v.i. trembler; branler.—n. tremblement, m.
Quaker ['kweikə], n. Quaker, m.
Quakerism ['kweikərizm], n. Quakerisme, m.
quaking ['kweikiŋ], a. tremblant.—n. tremblement, m.; terreur, f.
qualifiable ['kwɔlifaiəbl], a. qualifiable.
qualification [kwɔlifi'keiʃən], n. qualification, qualité; aptitude, f., talent, m.; réserve, restriction, f.; (pl.) qualités, f.pl., titres, m.pl.
qualified ['kwɔlifaid], a. qui a les qualités requises (pour), propre (à); **qualified teacher**, professeur diplômé, m.
qualify ['kwɔlifai], v.t. rendre capable (de); autoriser (à); modérer.—v.i. se préparer (à).
qualifying ['kwɔlifaiiŋ], a. qualificatif.
quality ['kwɔliti], n. qualité, f.; (colloq.) talent, m.
qualm [kwɑːm], n. nausée, f.; (fig.) scrupule, m.
qualmish ['kwɑːmiʃ], a. qui a mal au cœur.
quandary ['kwɔndəri], n. embarras, m., impasse, f.
quantitative ['kwɔntitətiv], a. quantitatif.
quantity ['kwɔntiti], n. quantité, f.; grand nombre, m.
quantum ['kwɔntəm], n. montant, quantum, m.
quarantine ['kwɔrəntiːn], n. quarantaine, f.—v.t. mettre en quarantaine.
quarrel ['kwɔrəl], n. querelle, dispute, brouille, f.—v.i. se quereller, se brouiller.
quarreller ['kwɔrələ], n. querelleur, m.
quarrelling ['kwɔrəliŋ], n. querelle; dispute, f.
quarrelsome ['kwɔrəlsəm], a. querelleur.
quarrelsomeness ['kwɔrəlsəmnis], n. humeur querelleuse, f.
quarry (1) ['kwɔri], n. carrière, f.—v.t. tirer d'une carrière.
quarry (2) ['kwɔri], n. (Hunt.) curée; proie, f.
quarrying ['kwɔriiŋ], n. extraction d'une carrière, f.
quarryman ['kwɔrimən], n. (pl. -men [men]) carrier, m.
quart [kwɔːt], n. quart de gallon (1,14 litre), m.
quarter ['kwɔːtə], n. quart; quart de quintal

(12,70 kg.); quartier (de ville, de la lune, de mouton etc.), m.; partie, région (d'un pays), f.; côté (direction); trimestre (de l'année), m.; hanche (de navire), f.; (pl.) logement; (Mil.) quartier, m.; **to come to close quarters**, en venir aux mains.—v.t. diviser en quatre; (Mil.) caserner; loger (dans une maison); (Her.) écarteler.
quarter day ['kwɔːtədei], n. jour du terme, m.
quarter-deck ['kwɔːtədek], n. gaillard d'arrière, m.
quartering ['kwɔːtəriŋ], n. division en quatre parties, f.; (Mil.) logement; (Her.) écartèlement, m.
quarterly ['kwɔːtəli], a. trimestriel.—adv. par trimestre, tous les trois mois.
quartermaster ['kwɔːtəmɑːstə], n. (Navy) maître timonier; (Mil.) officier d'approvisionnement, m.
quartet [kwɔː'tet], n. quatuor, m.
quarto ['kwɔːtou], a. and n. in-quarto, m.
quartz [kwɔːts], n. quartz, m.
quash [kwɔʃ], v.t. écraser; (fig.) dompter; (Law) annuler, casser.
quasi ['kweisai], adv. quasi.
quatrain ['kwɔtrein], n. quatrain, m.
quaver ['kweivə], n. tremblement de la voix, trille, m.; (Mus.) croche, f.—v.i. trembler; (Mus.) faire des trilles.
quavering ['kweivəriŋ], a. tremblant, chevrotant.—n. trille, tremolo; tremblement de voix, m.
quay [kiː], n. quai, m.
quayage ['kiːidʒ], n. quayage, m.
queen [kwiːn], n. reine; (Cards etc.) dame, f.
queen bee ['kwiːn'biː], n. reine-abeille, f.
queen like ['kwiːnlaik], **queenly** ['kwiːnli], adv. de reine, digne d'une reine.
queen-mother [kwiːn'mʌðə], n. reine-mère, f.
queer [kwiə], a. bizarre, étrange, drôle.
queerly ['kwiəli], adv. étrangement, bizarrement.
queerness ['kwiənis], n. étrangeté, bizarrerie, f.; malaise, m.
quell [kwel], v.t. réprimer, dompter.
quench [kwentʃ], v.t. éteindre; étancher; étouffer (élan etc.); **to quench one's thirst**, étancher sa soif, se désaltérer.
quenchable ['kwentʃəbl], a. extinguible.
quenchless ['kwentʃlis], a. inextinguible.
querulous ['kweruləs], a. plaintif, maussade.
querulousness ['kweruləsnis], n. humeur chagrine, f.
query ['kwiəri], n. question, f.; point d'interrogation, m.—v.t. mettre en doute.—v.i. questionner.
quest [kwest], n. enquête; recherche, f.; **in quest of**, à la recherche de.
question ['kwestʃən], n. question, interrogation, demande, f.; sujet (problème), m.; (Parl.) interpellation, f.; **out of the question**, absolument impossible; **that is not the question**, il ne s'agit pas de cela; **to ask a question**, poser une question.—v.t. questionner, interroger; mettre en doute.—v.i. se demander (si).
questionable ['kwestʃənəbl], a. contestable, douteux, incertain; suspect, équivoque.
questioner ['kwestʃənə], n. questionneur, m.
questioning ['kwestʃəniŋ], n. questions, f.pl., interrogation, f.

question master [ˈkwestʃənmɑːstə], n. (*Rad.*, *Tel.*) meneur de débats, m.

questionnaire [kwestʃəˈnɛə], n. questionnaire, m.

queue [kjuː], n. queue, f.—v.i. faire la queue.

quibble [kwibl], n. argutie, chicane, f.—v.i. ergoter, chicaner.

quibbler [ˈkwiblə], n. ergoteur, chicaneur, m.

quick [kwik], a. vite, rapide, prompt; agile, leste; vif (*vivant*); (*fig.*) fin.—adv. vite, promptement, lestement.—n. vif, m.; chair vive, f.; **stung to the quick**, piqué au vif; (*collect.*) **the quick**, les vivants, m.pl.

quicken [ˈkwikən], v.t. animer, vivifier; raviver, accélérer, hâter.—v.i. prendre vie, s'animer.

quickening [ˈkwikəniŋ], a. vivifiant, qui ranime.

quicklime [ˈkwiklaim], n. chaux vive, f.

quickly [ˈkwikli], adv. vite; promptement; bientôt.

quickness [ˈkwiknis], n. vitesse; promptitude; activité; pénétration; fréquence (*du pouls*), f.

quicksand [ˈkwiksænd], n. sable mouvant, m.

quickset [ˈkwikset], a. vive; **quickset hedge**, haie vive, f.—n. plante vive, f.

quicksilver [ˈkwiksilvə], n. vif-argent, mercure, m.

quicksilvered [ˈkwiksilvəd], a. étamé.

quicksilvering [ˈkwiksilvəriŋ], n. étamage, m.

quick-tempered [ˈkwikˈtempəd], a. emporté, vif, colérique.

quick-witted [ˈkwikˈwitid], a. à l'esprit vif.

quid [kwid], n. chique; (*slang*) livre sterling, f.

quidnunc [ˈkwidnʌŋk], n. curieux, colporteur de nouvelles, m.

quiescence [kwiˈesəns], n. quiétude, tranquillité, f., repos, m.

quiescent [kwiˈesənt], a. paisible, en repos, tranquille.

quiet [ˈkwaiət], a. tranquille, calme; paisible, silencieux; (*fig.*) modeste; **be quiet!** silence! taisez-vous! **to keep quiet**, se tenir tranquille, rester tranquille.—n. tranquillité, quiétude, f.; repos, calme, m.—v.t. (*also* **quieten** [ˈkwaiətn]) tranquilliser, apaiser, calmer.—v.i. **to quiet(en) down**, s'apaiser, se calmer.

quieten, v.t., v.i. [QUIET].

quieting [ˈkwaiətiŋ], a. calmant, tranquillisant.

quietly [ˈkwaiətli], adv. tranquillement; doucement; en silence, sans bruit, discrètement, sans éclat.

quietness [ˈkwaiətnis], n. tranquillité, f.; calme, repos, m.

quietude [ˈkwaiitjuːd], n. quiétude, tranquillité, f.

quietus [kwaiˈiːtəs], n. repos, m.; mort, f.; (*fig.*) coup de grâce, m.; décharge, quittance, f.

quill [kwil], n. (tuyau de) plume; plume d'oie (*pour écrire*), f.; piquant (*de porc-épic*), m.—v.t. tuyauter, rucher.

quilling [ˈkwiliŋ], n. tuyautage, m., ruche, f.

quilt [kwilt], n. édredon, m., courtepointe, f.—v.t. piquer.

quilting [ˈkwiltiŋ], n. piqué; piquage, m.

quince [kwins], n. coing; cognassier (*arbre*), m.

quinine [ˈkwainain], n. quinine, f.

Quinquagesima [kwiŋkwəˈdʒesimə]. Quinquagésime, f.

quinquennial [kwiŋˈkweniəl], a. quinquennial.

quinquina [kiŋˈkiːnə], n. quinquina, m.

quinsy [ˈkwinzi], n. angine, f.

quint [kwint], n. quinte, f.

quintal [kwintl], n. quintal, m.

quintessence [kwinˈtesəns], n. quintessence, f.

quintet [kwinˈtet], n. quintette, m.

quintuple [ˈkwintjupl], a. quintuple.—v.t. quintupler.

quintuplets [ˈkwintjuplits], (*colloq.*) **quins** [kwinz], n.pl. quintuplés, m.pl.

quip [kwip], n. mot piquant, sarcasme, m.—v.t. railler.

quire [ˈkwaiə], n. main (*de papier*), f.

quirk [kwəːk], n. sarcasme, m., pointe; subtilité (*chicane*), f.

quit [kwit], v.t. irr. quitter, abandonner; **notice to quit**, congé, m.—a. quitte; **to get quit of**, se débarrasser de.

quite [kwait], adv. tout à fait, entièrement, complètement, tout; bien, parfaitement; assez.

quits [kwits], a. quitte.

quiver [ˈkwivə], n. carquois, m.—v.i. trembler, frissonner; palpiter (*la chair*); frémir.

quivering [ˈkwivəriŋ], n. tremblement, frissonnement; battement des paupières, m.

Quixote [ˈkwiksət], **Don**. Don Quichotte, m.

quixotic [kwikˈsɔtik], a. de Don Quichotte; extravagant, exalté.

quiz [kwiz], n. plaisanterie; devinette, f.; examen oral, m., colle, f.; **radio quiz**, jeu radiophonique, m.—v.t. questionner, interroger; [see **question master**]

quizzical [ˈkwizikəl], a. douteur.

quodlibet [ˈkwɔdlibet], n. quolibet, m., subtilité, f.

quoin [kɔin], n. coin, m.

quoit [kɔit], n. palet, m.

quondam [ˈkwɔndəm], a. ci-devant, ancien.

quorum [ˈkwɔːrəm], n. nombre suffisant, quorum, m.

quota [ˈkwoutə], n. quote-part, f.

quotable [ˈkwoutəbl], a. citable.

quotation [kwoˈteiʃən], n. citation; (*Comm.*) cote, f.; (*St. Exch.*) cours, m.[see **comma**]

quote [kwout], v.t. citer; alléguer; (*Comm.*) coter.

quotidian [kwoˈtidiən], a. quotidien, journalier.

quotient [ˈkwouʃənt], n. quotient, m.

R

R, r [ɑː]. dix-huitième lettre de l'alphabet, m.

rabbet [ˈræbət], n. feuillure, rainure, f.—v.t. faire une rainure à.

rabbet-plane [ˈræbətplein], n. guillaume, m.

rabbi ['ræbai], n. rabbin, m.; **chief rabbi**, grand rabbin.

rabbit ['ræbit], n. lapin, m.; **young rabbit**, lapereau, m.

rabble [ræbl], n. foule; populace, canaille, f.

rabid ['ræbid], a. féroce, furieux; enragé (chien).

rabies ['reibi:z], n. rage, hydrophobie, f.

raccoon [rə'ku:n], n. raton laveur, m.

race (1) [reis], n. (Biol.) race, f.

race (2) [reis], n. (Spt.) course, f.; raz, raz de marée (courant), m.—v.i. courir vite, courir, lutter de vitesse; **to go to the races**, aller aux courses.

race-course ['reiskɔːs], n. champ de courses, hippodrome, m.

race-horse ['reishɔːs], n. cheval de course, m.

racer ['reisə], n. coureur; cheval de course, m.

race-track ['reistræk], n. piste, f.

racial ['reiʃəl], a. de (la) race, ethnique.

raciness ['reisinis], n. piquant, m., verve, f.

racing ['reisiŋ], a. de course.—n. les courses, f.pl.

racing car ['reisiŋkɑː], n. automobile de course, f.

racism ['reisizm], n. racisme, m.

rack [ræk], n. râtelier (dans une écurie etc.); chevalet (instrument de tension), m.; roue (instrument de supplice) (Tech.) crémaillère, f.; **luggage rack**, (Rail.) filet, m.—v.t. mettre à la torture; (fig.) tourmenter; **to rack one's brains**, se creuser la cervelle.

racket ['rækit], n. fracas, tapage, tintamarre, caquet, m.; (Ten.) raquette; escroquerie, supercherie, combine, f.

rackety ['rækiti], a. tapageur.

racking ['rækiŋ], a. de torture; atroce (douleur).

racy ['reisi], a. (fig.) vif, piquant, plein de verve (style etc.).

radar ['reidɑː], n. radar, m.

radiance ['reidiəns], **radiancy** ['reidiənsi], n. rayonnement, éclat, m., splendeur, f.

radiant ['reidiənt], a. rayonnant (de); radieux, éclatant.

radiantly ['reidiəntli], adv. en rayonnant, splendidement.

radiate ['reidieit], v.t. émettre comme des rayons.—v.i. rayonner (de).

radiation [reidi'eiʃən], n. rayonnement, m., radiation, f.

radiator ['reidieitə], n. radiateur, m.

radical ['rædikəl], a. radical; fondamental.—n. radical, m.

radicalism ['rædikəlizm], n. radicalisme, m.

radically ['rædikəli], adv. radicalement, essentiellement.

radio ['reidiou], n. radio, la T.S.F., f. [see **wireless**]

radioactive [reidiou'æktiv], a. radio-actif.

radioactivity ['reidiouæk'tiviti], n. radio-activité, f.

radio control ['reidioukən'troul], n. télé-guidage, m.—v.t. téléguider.

radiogram ['reidiougræm], n. radio-gramme, m.

radiography [reidi'ɔgrəfi], n. radiographie, f.

radish ['rædiʃ], n. radis, m.; **horse-radish**, raifort, m.

radium ['reidiəm], n. radium, m.

radius ['reidiəs], n. rayon, m.

radix ['reidiks], n. (pl. **radices** ['reidisi:z]) racine; base, f.

raffle [ræfl], n. loterie, tombola, f.—v.t. mettre en tombola.

raft [rɑːft], n. radeau; train de bois, m.

rafter ['rɑːftə], n. chevron, m.

raftered ['rɑːftəd], a. à chevrons.

rafting ['rɑːftiŋ], n. flottage en train, m.

raftsman ['rɑːftsmən], n. flotteur, m.

rag [ræg], n. chiffon (nettoyage etc.); haillon, m., guenille, loque (de vêtement), f.; (Sch.) chahut, m.; brimade, f.—v.t. (Sch.) chahuter.

ragamuffin ['rægəmʌfin], n. gueux, polisson, va-nu-pieds, m.

rage [reidʒ], n. rage, fureur, f., emportement, m.; furie, manie, f.; **it's all the rage**, cela fait fureur.—v.i. être furieux, être en fureur, s'emporter; (fig.) sévir.

ragged ['rægid], a. en haillons, déguenillé (personnes); en lambeaux, déchiré (choses).

raggedness ['rægidnis], n. délabrement, déguenillement, m.; guenilles, f.pl.

raging ['reidʒiŋ], a. furieux, en fureur; déchaîné, acharné, violent (tempête, guerre etc.).—n. fureur, violence, f.

ragman ['rægmən], n. (pl. **-men** [men]) chiffonnier, m.

rag-time ['rægtaim], n. (Mus.) musique syncopée, f.

raid [reid], n. incursion, f.; raid, coup de main, m.; **air raid**, raid aérien.—v.t. faire une incursion dans; piller; bombarder.

raider ['reidə], n. maraudeur; commando, m.

rail (1) [reil], n. barre, f., barreau (bois, métal etc.), m.; rampe (d'escalier), f.; parapet (de pont etc.); (Rail.) rail, m.—v.t. enclore, griller.

rail (2) [reil], v.i. **to rail at**, criailler, invectiver.

railer ['reilə], n. criailleur, médisant, m.

railing (1) ['reiliŋ], n. grille, f., garde-fou, m.

railing (2) ['reiliŋ], n. injures, invectives, f.pl.

raillery ['reiləri], n. raillerie, f.

railway ['reilwei], n. chemin de fer, m., voie ferrée, f.

railwayman ['reilweimən], n. (pl. **-men** [men]) employé des chemins de fer, cheminot, m.

raiment ['reimənt], n. vêtement, m.

rain [rein], n. pluie, f.—v.t. faire pleuvoir.—v.i. pleuvoir; **it is pouring with rain**, il pleut à verse.

rainbow ['reinbou], n. arc-en-ciel, m.

raincoat ['reinkout], n. imperméable, m.

rainfall ['reinfɔːl], n. pluie annuelle, pluie tombée, f.

rain gauge ['reingeidʒ], n. pluviomètre, m.

rainy ['reini], a. pluvieux.

raise [reiz], v.t. lever; élever; hausser (prix etc.); soulever (élever à une petite hauteur etc.); cultiver (légumes); augmenter, accroître (ajouter à); faire naître (soupçons); pousser (un cri); faire lever (pâte); se procurer (argent); faire (un emprunt etc.).—n. augmentation (de gages), f.

raised [reizd], a. levé; en relief.

raisin [reizn], n. raisin sec, m.

raising ['reiziŋ], n. augmentation, f., accroissement, m.; levée (d'impôts, de troupes, de sièges etc.), f.; élevage (de bestiaux), m.; culture (de plantes etc.), f.

rake (1) [reik], n. (Hort.) râteau.—v.t. (Agric.) râteler; (Hort.) ratisser; ramasser (rassembler); (Mil.) enfiler.

rake (2) [reik], n. roué (libertin), m.

raking ['reikiŋ], a. d'enfilade.—n. (Hort.) ratissage; (Agric.) râtelage, m.

rakish ['reikiʃ], a. dissolu; élancé (navire).

rakishness ['reikiʃnis], n. libertinage; air crâne, m.

rally ['ræli], v.t. rallier, rassembler.—v.i. se rallier, se rassembler; (fig.) se remettre.—n. ralliement, m.

Ralph [reif, rælf]. Raoul, m.

ram [ræm], n. bélier; mouton, m.—v.t. (Law) enfoncer; pilonner, tasser (terre etc.); bourrer (dans un canon).

ramble [ræmbl], n. excursion à pied, grande promenade; (fig.) divagation, f.—v.i. errer, se promener; errer çà et là; (fig.) divaguer.

rambler ['ræmblə], n. excursionniste (à pied), m., f.; (Hort.) rosier grimpant, m.

rambling ['ræmbliŋ], a. errant, vagabond; (fig.) décousu, incohérent.—n. excursions, promenades à l'aventure; (fig.) divagations, f.pl.

ramification [ræmifi'keiʃən], n. ramification, f.

ramify ['ræmifai], v.i. se ramifier.

rammer ['ræmə], n. pilon, m.

ramp [ræmp], n. rampe, montée; (fam.) escroquerie, f.

rampant ['ræmpənt], a. dominant, violent; effréné; (Her.) rampant.

rampart ['ræmpɑːt], n. rempart, m.

ramrod ['ræmrɔd], n. baguette (de fusil), f.; écouvillon (de canon), m.; **stiff as a ramrod**, droit comme un piquet.

ramshackle ['ræmʃækl], a. qui tombe en ruines, délabré.

rancid ['rænsid], a. rance.

rancidity [ræn'siditi], **rancidness** ['rænsidnis], n. rancidité, f.

rancor ['ræŋkə], n. haine, rancune, f.

rancorous ['ræŋkərəs], a. rancunier, haineux.

Randolph ['rændɔlf]. Rodolphe, m.

random ['rændəm], a. fait au hasard.—n. hasard, m.; **at random**, au hasard.

range [reindʒ], n. rangée, f., rang (file), m.; chaîne (de montagnes etc.); étendue, portée, f., fourneau; tir (armes à feu), m.; gamme (de couleurs), f.—v.t. ranger, arranger; aligner (avec); parcourir.—v.i. s'aligner; être rangé.

range finder ['reindʒfaində], n. télémètre, m.

ranger ['reindʒə], n. garde-forestier, m.

rank (1) [ræŋk], n. rang, ordre, m., classe, f.; (Mil.) grade; (fig.) haut rang, m.; station de taxis, f.—v.t. ranger, classer.—v.i. se ranger, être classé; occuper un rang.

rank (2) [ræŋk], a. luxuriant; (fig.) rude; extrême; fétide (odeur).

rankle [ræŋkl], v.i. s'envenimer, s'enflammer.

rankness ['ræŋknis], n. surabondance; grossièreté; rancidité, f.

ransack ['rænsæk], v.t. saccager, piller; fouiller.

ransacking ['rænsækiŋ], n. pillage, m.

ransom ['rænsəm], n. rançon, f.—v.t. rançonner.

rant [rænt], n. déclamation extravagante, f.— v.i. extravaguer; tempêter.

ranter ['ræntə], n. déclamateur, énergumène, m.

ranting ['ræntiŋ], a. d'énergumène, extravagant.

ranunculus [rə'nʌŋkjuləs], n. (Bot.) renoncule, f.

rap [ræp], n. tape, f., petit coup sec, m.—v.t., v.i. frapper.

rapacious [rə'peiʃəs], a. rapace.

rapaciously [rə'peiʃəsli], adv. avec rapacité.

rapaciousness [rə'peiʃəsnis], **rapacity** [rə'pæsiti], n. rapacité, f.

rape (1) [reip], n. (Poet.) rapt, enlèvement, m.—v.t. viol, m.—v.t. enlever de force; violer.

rape (2) [reip], n. (Agric.) colza, m., navette, f.

rapid ['ræpid], a. and n. rapide, m.

rapidity [rə'piditi], **rapidness** ['ræpidnis], n. rapidité, f.

rapidly ['ræpidli], adv. rapidement.

rapier ['reipiə], n. rapière, f.

rapine ['ræpain], n. rapine, f.

rapt [ræpt], a. ravi, extasié; profond (attention).

rapture ['ræptʃə], n. ravissement, transport, m., extase, f.

rapturous ['ræptʃərəs], a. ravissant; joyeux.

rapturously ['ræptʃərəsli], adv. avec transport.

rare [rɛə], a. rare; clairsemé; à moitié cru (viande).

rarefaction [rɛəri'fækʃən], n. raréfaction, f.

rarefy ['rɛərifai], v.t. raréfier.—v.i. se raréfier.

rarely ['rɛəli], adv. rarement.

rareness ['rɛənis], **rarity** ['rɛəriti], n. rareté, f.

rascal [rɑːskl], n. coquin, fripon, gredin, m.

rascality [rɑːs'kæliti], n. friponnerie, gredinerie, coquinerie, f.

rascally ['rɑːskəli], a. coquin, fripon.

rase [RAZE].

rash (1) [ræʃ], a. téméraire; irréfléchi, imprudent.

rash (2) [ræʃ], n. éruption, f.

rasher ['ræʃə], n. tranche, f.

rashly ['ræʃli], adv. témérairement; imprudemment.

rashness ['ræʃnis], n. témérité; précipitation, imprudence, f.

rasp [rɑːsp], n. râpe, f.—v.t. râper; râcler, écorcher (surface, peau).—v.i. grincer, crisser.

raspberry ['rɑːzbəri], n. framboise, f.

raspberry bush ['rɑːzbəribuʃ], n. framboisier, m.

rasping ['rɑːspiŋ], a. grinçant, âpre, rauque (voix).—n. râpage; crissement, m.

rat [ræt], n. rat, m.; **to smell a rat**, se douter de quelque chose.

ratchet ['rætʃit], n. cliquet, m., dent d'engrenage, f.

ratchet-brace ['rætʃitbreis], **ratchet-jack** ['rætʃitdʒæk], n. vilbrequin à cliquet, m.

rate (1) [reit], n. prix, m.; raison, proportion, f.; taux (argent, population); cours (de change); degré, rang, ordre, m.; vitesse; taxe, f., impôt (taxe municipale), m.; **at any rate**, en tout cas; **first-rate**, de première classe.—v.t. évaluer; classer; taxer; faire une estimation; regarder (comme).—v.i. **to rate as**, être classé comme.

rate (2) [reit], v.t. gronder.

531

rateable

rateable ['reitəbl], *a.* imposable; *rateable value,* valeur locative imposable (*d'un immeuble*), *f.*

rate-payer ['reitpeiə], *n.* contribuable, *m.*, *f.*

rather ['rɑːðə], *adv.* plutôt; un peu, quelque peu (*légèrement*); assez, passablement (*suffisamment*).

ratification [rætifi'keiʃən], *n.* ratification, *f.*

ratify ['rætifai], *v.t.* ratifier, approuver.

ratifying ['rætifaiiŋ], *a.* ratificatif.

rating (1) ['reitiŋ], *n.* estimation, évaluation; répartition d'impôt, *f.*; (*Navy*) matelot, *m.*

rating (2) ['reitiŋ], *n.* gronderie, *f.*

ratio ['reiʃiou], *n.* proportion, raison, *f.*, rapport, *m.*

ration ['ræʃən], *n.* ration, *f.*—*v.t.* rationner.

ration book ['ræʃənbuk], *n.* carte d'alimentation, *f.*

rationing ['ræʃəniŋ], *n.* rationnement, *m.*

rational ['ræʃənl], *a.* raisonnable, rationnel.

rationalism ['ræʃnəlizm], *n.* rationalisme, *m.*

rationalist ['ræʃnəlist], *n.* rationaliste, *m.*, *f.*

rationalize ['ræʃnəlaiz], *v.t.* rationaliser.

rationally ['ræʃnəli], *adv.* raisonnablement, rationnellement.

rattan [rə'tæn], *n.* rotin, *m.*

ratten [rætn], *v.t.* intimider; saboter.

rattle [rætl], *v.t.* faire claquer, faire sonner; secouer (*chaines etc.*).—*v.i.* faire un bruit sec; cliqueter, crépiter.—*n.* bruit; cliquetis (*de métaux*); râle (*à la gorge*); hochet (*jouet*), *m.*; crécelle, *f.*

rattlesnake ['rætlsneik], *n.* serpent à sonnettes, crotale, *m.*

rattling ['rætliŋ], *a.* bruyant; (*fig.*) excellent.—*n.* bruit, cliquetis, *m.*

rat-trap ['rættræp], *n.* ratière, *f.*

raucous ['rɔːkəs], *a.* rauque.

ravage ['rævidʒ], *n.* ravage, *m.*—*v.t.* ravager.

ravager ['rævidʒə], *n.* ravageur, dévastateur, *m.*

rave [reiv], *v.i.* être en délire; (*fig.*) extravaguer.

ravel [rævl], *v.t.* embrouiller, entortiller.—*v.i.* s'embrouiller, s'entortiller.

raven (1) [reivn], *n.* (*Orn.*) corbeau, *m.*

raven (2) [rævn], *v.t.* dévorer.

ravenous ['rævənəs], *a.* dévorant, vorace.

ravenously ['rævənəsli], *adv.* avec voracité.

ravenousness ['rævənəsnis], *n.* voracité, rapacité, *f.*

ravine [rə'viːn], *n.* ravin, *m.*

raving ['reiviŋ], *a.* en délire, délirant; furieux, fou.—*n.* délire, *m.*

ravish ['ræviʃ], *v.t.* ravir; enlever; (*fig.*) transporter.

ravisher ['ræviʃə], *n.* ravisseur, *m.*

ravishing ['ræviʃiŋ], *a.* ravissant.

raw [rɔː], *a.* cru; vif, écorché (*égratigné etc.*); (*fig.*) sans expérience, novice; pur (*alcool*); brut (*cuir etc.*); froid et humide (*temps*); *raw materials,* matières premières, *f.pl.*

raw-boned ['rɔːbound], *a.* maigre, décharné.

rawness ['rɔːnis], *n.* crudité, *f.*; froid humide (*du temps*), *m.*; (*fig.*) inexpérience, *f.*

ray (1) [rei], *n.* rayon, *m.*

ray (2) [rei], *n.* (*Ichth.*) raie, *f.*

rayless ['reilis], *a.* sans rayon, sans lumière.

Raymond ['reimənd], *n.* Raymond, *m.*

rayon ['reiən], *n.* rayonne, *f.*

raze [reiz], *v.t.* raser, effleurer; rayer, effacer (*supprimer*); abattre, détruire (*édifice*).

razor ['reizə], *n.* rasoir, *m.*; *safety razor,* rasoir de sûreté.

re [riː, rei], *prep.* au sujet de, à propos de.

reach [riːtʃ], *n.* portée, atteinte; étendue (*capacité*), *f.*; bief (*de canal*), *m.*—*v.t.* atteindre, toucher; passer, donner (*rendre*); arriver à, parvenir à (*accomplir*).—*v.i.* s'étendre de . . . à.

reachable ['riːtʃəbl], *a.* qu'on peut atteindre.

react [riː'ækt], *v.i.* réagir (*sur*).

reaction [riː'ækʃən], *n.* réaction, *f.*

reactionary [riː'ækʃənəri], *a.* and *n.* réactionnaire, *m.*, *f.*

reactor [riː'æktə], *n.* réacteur, *m.*

read [riːd], *v.t. irr.* lire; faire la lecture de; (*fig.*) étudier.—*v.i.* lire; faire la lecture; se lire.

readable ['riːdəbl], *a.* lisible; qui se lit avec plaisir.

readableness ['riːdəblnis], *n.* lisibilité, *f.*

readdress [riːə'dres], *v.t.* faire suivre (*lettre*).

reader ['riːdə], *n.* lecteur; (*Print.*) correcteur; liseur (*amateur de lecture*); (*Sch.*) livre de lecture, *m.*

readily ['redili], *adv.* tout de suite, promptement; volontiers (*de bon gré*), avec plaisir.

readiness ['redinis], *n.* empressement, *m.*; promptitude; facilité; bonne volonté (*complaisance*), *f.*

reading ['riːdiŋ], *n.* lecture; variante (*textuelle*), leçon; hauteur (*de baromètre*), *f.*

reading book ['riːdiŋbuk], *n.* livre de lecture, *m.*

reading desk ['riːdiŋdesk], *n.* pupitre, *m.*

reading lamp ['riːdiŋlæmp], *n.* lampe de travail, *f.*

reading room ['riːdiŋruːm], *n.* salle de lecture, *f.*

readjust [riːə'dʒʌst], *v.t.* rajuster, rectifier.

readjustment [riːə'dʒʌstmənt], *n.* rajustement, *m.*

ready ['redi], *a.* prêt, prompt; facile; vif (*qui comprend vite*); *ready money,* argent comptant, *m.*

ready-made ['redimeid], *a.* tout fait, confectionné.

ready-reckoner ['redi'reknə], *n.* barème, *m.*

ready-witted ['redi'witid], *a.* à l'esprit vif.

reaffirm [riːə'fəːm], *v.t.* réaffirmer.

reafforestation [riːəfɔris'teiʃən], *n.* reboisement, *m.*

real ['riːəl], *a.* réel; vrai, véritable; effectif; (*Law*) immeuble, immobilier. [see **realty**] **estate-agent; house-agent**]

realism ['riːəlizm], *n.* réalisme, *m.*

realist ['riːəlist], *n.* réaliste, *m.*, *f.*

realistic [riːə'listik], *a.* réaliste.

reality [riː'æliti], *n.* réalité, *f.*; réel, *m.*

realizable ['riːəlaizəbl], *a.* réalisable.

realization [riːəlai'zeiʃən], *n.* réalisation; conception nette, *f.*

realize ['riːəlaiz], *v.t.* réaliser; effectuer; se rendre compte de, bien comprendre; se figurer; rapporter (*somme*).

really ['riːəli], *adv.* réellement, en effet, effectivement; vraiment.—*int.* en vérité! à vrai dire!

realm [relm], *n.* royaume, (*fig.*) domaine, *m.*

realty ['riːəlti], *n.* biens immeubles, *m.pl.*

ream [riːm], *n.* rame (*de papier*), *f.*

reap [ri:p], *v.t.*, *v.i.* moissonner; (*fig.*) recueillir.

reaper ['ri:pə], *n.* moissonneur, *m.*

reaping ['ri:piŋ], *n.* moisson, *f.*

reaping machine ['ri:piŋməʃi:n], *n.* moissonneuse, *f.*

reappear [ri:ə'piə], *v.i.* reparaître, réapparaître.

reappearance [ri:ə'piərəns], *n.* réapparition; rentrée (*d'acteur*), *f.*

reappoint [ri:ə'point], *v.t.* réintégrer; renommer.

reappointment [ri:ə'pointmənt], *n.* réintégration, *f.*

rear (1) [riə], *a.* situé à l'arrière; postérieur; *rear wheel*, roue arrière, *f.*—*n.* dernier rang, *m.*; arrière-garde, *f.*; derrière (*d'édifice etc.*), *m.*; *to bring up the rear*, fermer la marche.

rear (2) [riə], *v.t.* élever.—*v.i.* se cabrer.

rear admiral ['riərædmərəl], *n.* contre-amiral, *m.*

re-arm [ri:'ɑ:m], *v.t.*, *v.i.* réarmer.

re-armament [ri:'ɑ:məmənt], *n.* réarmement, *m.*

rearwards ['riəwədz], *adv.* à l'arrière.

reascend [ri:ə'send], *v.t.*, *v.i.* remonter.

reason [ri:zn], *n.* raison, *f.*; raisonnement, *m.*; *the reason why*, la raison pour laquelle; *that stands to reason*, cela va sans dire; *to have reason to believe*, avoir lieu de croire.—*v.t.*, *v.i.* raisonner.

reasonable ['ri:znəbl], *a.* raisonnable; modéré.

reasonableness ['ri:znəblnis], *n.* raison, modération, *f.*

reasonably ['ri:znəbli], *adv.* raisonnablement.

reasoner ['ri:zənə], *n.* raisonneur, logicien, *m.*

reasoning ['ri:zəniŋ], *n.* raisonnement, *m.*

reassemble [ri:ə'sembl], *v.t.* rassembler.—*v.i.* se rassembler.

reassert [ri:ə'sə:t], *v.t.* affirmer de nouveau.

reassess [ri:ə'ses], *v.t.* réévaluer.

reassessment [ri:ə'sesmənt], *n.* réimposition; réévaluation, *f.*

reassign [ri:ə'sain], *v.t.* réassigner.

reassignment [ri:ə'sainmənt], *n.* réassignation, *f.*

reassume [ri:ə'sju:m], *v.t.* réassumer; reprendre (*position*).

reassurance [ri:ə'ʃuərəns], *n.* action de rassurer; (*Comm.*) réassurance, *f.*

reassure [ri:ə'ʃuə], *v.t.* rassurer; (*Comm.*) réassurer.

rebate ['ri:beit], *n.* rabais, *m.*, remise, *f.*—[ri'beit], *v.t.* diminuer, rabattre.

rebel ['rebl], *n.* rebelle, *m.*, *f.*, révolté, *m.*—[ri'bel], *v.i.* se révolter, se soulever (*contre*).

rebellion [ri'beljən], *n.* rébellion, *f.*

rebellious [ri'beljəs], *a.* rebelle.

rebelliously [ri'beljəsli], *adv.* en rebelle.

rebelliousness [ri'beljəsnis], *n.* rébellion, *f.*

rebirth [ri:'bə:θ], *n.* renaissance, *f.*

reborn [ri:'bo:n], *a.* né de nouveau; réincarné.

rebound ['ri:baund], *n.* rebondissement, contre-coup, *m.*—[ri'baund], *v.i.* rebondir.

rebuff [ri'bʌf], *n.* rebuffade, *f.*, échec, *m.*—*v.t.* rebuter, repousser.

rebuild [ri:'bild], *v.t. irr.* (*conjug. like* BUILD) rebâtir, reconstruire.

rebuke [ri'bju:k], *n.* réprimande, *f.*, reproche, *m.*—*v.t.* réprimander, reprendre, censurer.

rebus ['ri:bəs], *n.* rébus, *m.*

rebut [ri'bʌt], *v.t.* rebuter, repousser, réfuter.

recalcitrant [ri'kælsitrənt], *a.* récalcitrant, insoumis, réfractaire.

recall [ri'ko:l], *n.* rappel, *m.*; révocation, *f.*; *beyond recall*, irrévocablement.—*v.t.* rappeler; se rappeler (*se souvenir de*).

recant [ri'kænt], *v.t.* rétracter, désavouer, abjurer.—*v.i.* se rétracter.

recantation [ri:kæn'teiʃən], *n.* rétractation, palinodie, *f.*

recapitulate [ri:kə'pitjuleit], *v.t.* récapituler.

recapitulation [ri:kəpitju'leiʃən], *n.* récapitulation, *f.*

recapture ['ri:'kæptʃə], *n.* reprise, *f.*—*v.t.* reprendre.

recast [ri:'kɑ:st], *v.t. irr.* (*conjug. like* CAST) refondre; (*Theat.*) faire une nouvelle distribu.ion des rôles.

recede [ri'si:d], *v.i.* se retirer (*de*); s'éloigner.

receding [ri'si:diŋ], *a.* fuyant (*le front*), effacé (*menton*).

receipt [ri'si:t], *n.* reçu, *m.*, quittance, *f.*, acquit, *m.*; réception (*le fait de recevoir*); (*pl.*) recette, *f.*, recettes, *f.pl.*; récépissé, *m.*—*v.t.* acquitter.

receive [ri'si:v], *v.t.* recevoir, accepter; accueillir; recéler (*biens volés*).

receiver [ri'si:və], *n.* receveur; receleur (*d'objets volés*); liquidateur (*faillite*); (*Teleph.*) récepteur, *m.*

receiving [ri'si:viŋ], *n.* réception, *f.*; recel (*d'objets volés*), *m.*

recent ['ri:sənt], *a.* récent, frais, nouveau.

recently ['ri:səntli], *adv.* récemment, depuis peu.

receptacle [ri'septəkl], *n.* réceptacle; récipient, *m.*

reception [ri'sepʃən], *n.* réception, *f.*; accueil, *m.*

receptionist [ri'sepʃənist], *n.* réceptionniste, *m.*, *f.*

receptive [ri'septiv], *a.* réceptif (*esprit*).

recess [ri'ses], *n.* enfoncement, *m.*, niche, *f.*; recoin, *m.*; vacances, *f.pl.*

recession [ri'seʃən], *n.* retraite, *f.*; désistement (*d'une revendication*), *m.*; (*St. Exch.*) baisse, *f.*

recidivist [ri'sidivist], *n.* récidiviste, *m.*, *f.*

recipe ['resipi], *n.* (*Cook.*) recette, *f.*

recipient [ri'sipiənt], *n.* personne qui reçoit, *f.*, destinataire (*de lettre*), *m.*, *f.*; (*Chem.*) récipient, *m.*

reciprocal [ri'siprəkl], *a.* réciproque.

reciprocate [ri'siprəkeit], *v.t.* échanger; répondre à.—*v.i.* alterner, se succéder.

reciprocation [risiprə'keiʃən], **reciprocity** [resi'prositi], *n.* réciprocité, *f.*

recital [ri'saitl], *n.* récit, *m.*; narration, énumération, *f.*; (*Mus.*) récital, *m.*

recitation [resi'teiʃən], *n.* récitation, *f.*

recitative [resitə'ti:v], *n.* récitatif, *m.*

recite [ri'sait], *v.t.* réciter, faire le récit de; raconter.

reciter [ri'saitə], *n.* récitateur; diseur, narrateur, *m.*

reck [rek], *v.i.* se soucier de.

reckless ['reklis], *a.* insouciant (*de*); téméraire, insensé.

recklessly ['reklisli], *adv.* témérairement, avec insouciance.

recklessness ['reklisnis], *n.* insouciance, témérité, *f.*

reckon [rekn], *v.t.* compter, calculer; regarder, évaluer (*comme*).—*v.i.* compter; *to reckon on*, compter sur; *to reckon with*, tenir compte de.

reckoner ['rekna], *n.* calculateur, chiffreur, *m.*; *ready-reckoner*, barème, *m.*

reckoning ['rekniŋ], *n.* compte, calcul; écot, *m.*, note (*dans un hôtel*); addition (*dans un restaurant*); (*Naut.*) estime, *f.*

reclaim [ri:'kleim], *v.t.* réformer, corriger; ramener (*de*); réclamer, revendiquer (*ses droits*); défricher (*terre*).

reclaimable [ri:'kleiməbl], *a.* corrigible; cultivable, défrichable (*terre*).

reclaiming [ri:'kleimiŋ], **reclamation** [reklə'meiʃən], *n.* défrichement (*de terre*), *m.*; réforme, correction (*de criminels*), *f.*

recline [ri'klain], *v.i.* s'appuyer, se reposer, se coucher.

reclining [ri'klainiŋ], *a.* incliné, appuyé, couché.

reclothe [ri:'klouð], *v.t.* rhabiller.

recluse [ri'klu:s], *a.* reclus; solitaire, retiré.—*n.* reclus, *m.*

reclusion [ri'klu:ʒən], *n.* réclusion, *f.*

recognition [rekəg'niʃən], *n.* reconnaissance, *f.*

recognizable [rekəg'naizəbl], *a.* reconnaissable.

recognizance [ri'kɔgnizəns], *n.* reconnaissance; (*Law*) obligation contractée, *f.*

recognize ['rekəgnaiz], *v.t.* reconnaître.

recoil [ri'koil], *n.* recul; contre-coup, *m.*; (*fig.*) répugnance, *f.*—*v.i.* reculer; retomber.

recollect [rekə'lekt], *v.t.* se souvenir de, se rappeler.

recollection [rekə'lekʃən], *n.* souvenir, *m.*; mémoire, *f.*

recommence [ri:kə'mens], *v.t.*, *v.i.* recommencer.

recommend [rekə'mend], *v.t.* recommander.

recommendation [rekəmen'deiʃən], *n.* recommandation; apostille (*d'une pétition*), *f.*

recompense ['rekəmpens], *n.* récompense, *f.*; dédommagement, *m.*—*v.t.* récompenser (*de*); dédommager (*de*); compenser, réparer.

reconcilable [rekən'sailəbl], *a.* réconciliable; conciliable (*avec.*)(*choses.*)

reconcile ['rekənsail], *v.t.* réconcilier (*avec*); habituer, accoutumer (*familiariser*); *to reconcile oneself to*, se résigner à.

reconciliation [rekənsili'eiʃən], *n.* réconciliation; conciliation (*de choses*); (*Bibl.*) expiation, *f.*

recondite [ri'kəndait, 'rekəndait], *a.* secret, abstrus, profond, mystérieux.

recondition [ri:kən'diʃən], *v.t.* remettre à neuf, refaire.

reconnaissance [ri'kɔnisəns], *n.* reconnaissance, *f.*

reconnoiter [rekə'nɔitə], *v.t.* reconnaître.—*v.i.* faire une reconnaissance.

reconsider [ri:kən'sidə], *v.t.* considérer de nouveau; revenir sur (*une décision*).

reconsideration [ri:kənsidə'reiʃən], *n.* reconsidération, *f.*

reconstitute [ri:'kɔnstitju:t], *v.t.* reconstituer.

reconstruct [ri:kən'strʌkt], *v.t.* reconstruire.

reconstruction [ri:kən'strʌkʃən], *n.* reconstruction, *f.*

record ['rekɔ:d], *n.* registre, *m.*, archives, *f.pl.*; disque (*de phonographe*); (*Spt.*) record; dossier, *m.*; *keeper of the records*, archiviste, *m.*, *f.*; *long-playing record*, disque longue durée, *m*; *public records*, archives, *f.pl.*; *record library*, discothèque, *f.*; greffe, *m.*—[ri'kɔ:d], *v.t.* enregistrer; graver, imprimer (*dans l'esprit etc.*); mentionner (*fait historique*).

recorder [ri'kɔ:də], *n.* enregistreur, archiviste; greffier; (*Law*) officier judiciaire d'une ville; (*Mus.*) flageolet, *m.*; *tape recorder*, magnétophone, *m.*

recording [ri'kɔ:diŋ], *n.* enregistrement, *m.*

recount (1) [ri'kaunt], *v.t.* raconter.

recount (2) [ri:'kaunt], *v.t.* recompter.—['ri:kaunt], *n.* nouvelle addition des voix (*aux élections*), *f.*

recoup [ri'ku:p], *v.t.* rembourser, dédommager (*de*).

recourse [ri'kɔ:s], *n.* recours, *m.*

recover (1) [ri'kʌvə], *v.t.* recouvrer, retrouver; réparer (*perte*).—*v.i.* se rétablir, guérir; se remettre (*d'une maladie*); se relever (*d'une perte*).

recover (2) [ri:'kʌvə], *v.t.* recouvrir; regarnir.

recovery [ri'kʌvəri], *n.* recouvrement, *m.*; guérison, *f.*; rétablissement, *m.*; (*Écon.*) reprise, *f.*; *past recovery*, incurable, sans remède.

recreant ['rekriənt], *a.* and *n.* lâche, infidèle, *m.*, *f.*, apostat, *m.*

re-create [ri:kri'eit], *v.t.* recréer.

recreation [rekri'eiʃən], *n.* récréation, *f.*, divertissement, *m.*

recriminate [ri'krimineit], *v.i.* récriminer (*contre*).

recrimination [rikrimi'neiʃən], *n.* récrimination, *f.*

recriminatory [ri'kriminətri], *a.* récriminatoire.

recrudescence [ri:kru'desəns], *n.* recrudescence, *f.*

recruit [ri'kru:t], *n.* recrue, *f.*, conscrit, *m.*—*v.t.* rétablir, réparer (*restaurer*); (*Mil.*) recruter.—*v.i.* se recruter, se remettre.

recruiting [ri'kru:tiŋ], **recruitment** [ri'kru:t mənt], *n.* recrutement, *m.*; *recruiting officer*, officier de recrutement, *m.*

rectangle ['rektæŋgl], *n.* rectangle, *m.*

rectangular [rek'tæŋgjulə], *a.* rectangulaire, rectangle, à angle droit.

rectifiable ['rektifaiəbl], *a.* rectifiable.

rectification [rektifi'keiʃən], *n.* rectification, *f.*

rectifier ['rektifaiə], *n.* rectificateur, *f.*; (*Elec.*) redresseur, *m.*

rectify ['rektifai], *v.t.* rectifier; redresser.

rectilineal [rekti'liniəl], *a.* rectiligne.

rectitude ['rektitju:d], *n.* rectitude, droiture, *f.*

rector ['rektə], *n.* (*Ch. of England*) prêtre; (*R.-C.*) curé; (*Univ. etc.*) recteur, principal, *m.*

rectorial [rek'tɔ:riəl], *a.* rectoral.

rectorship ['rektəʃip], *n.* rectorat, *m.*

rectory ['rektəri], *n.* cure, *f.*, presbytère, *m.*

recumbent [ri'kʌmbənt], *a.* couché, étendu; appuyé (*sur*).

recuperate [ri'ku:pəreit], *v.t.* recouvrer, récupérer.—*v.i.* se rétablir, se remettre, reprendre ses forces.

recuperation [riku:pə'reiʃən], *n.* recouvrement; rétablissement (*personne*), *m.*

recur [ri'kə:], *v.i.* revenir; se reproduire.

recurrence [ri'kʌrəns], *n.* retour, *m.*

recurrent [ri'kʌrənt], **recurring** [ri'kə:riŋ], *a.* périodique; (*Anat. etc.*) récurrent.

red [red], *a.* rouge; roux (*cheveux*); vermeil (*lèvres etc.*); **red lead**, minium, *m.*; **red-letter day**, jour de fête, *m.*—*n.* rouge, *m.*

redbreast ['redbrest], *n.* rouge-gorge, *m.*

redden [redn], *v.t., v.i.* rougir.

reddish ['rediʃ], *a.* rougeâtre, roussâtre.

redeem [ri'di:m], *v.t.* racheter; (*Fin.*) rembourser, amortir; retirer (*objets mis en gage*); (*fig.*) réparer.

redeemable [ri'di:məbl], *a.* rachetable.

redeemer [ri'di:mə], *n.* rédempteur, *m.*

redeeming [ri'di:miŋ], *a.* qui rachète.

redemption [ri'dempʃən], *n.* rédemption, *f.*; (*Fin.*) amortissement; rachat (*de billets*), *m.*

red-hot ['redhɔt], *a.* tout rouge, chauffé au rouge, ardent (*charbon*).

redirect [ri:di'rekt], *v.t.* faire suivre (*lettre*).

rediscover [ri:dis'kʌvə], *v.t.* redécouvrir.

redistribution [ri:distri'bju:ʃən], *n.* nouvelle distribution, répartition, *f.*

redness ['rednis], *n.* rougeur; rousseur (*de cheveux*), *f.*

redolence ['redoləns], *n.* parfum, *m.*; senteur, *f.*

redolent ['redolənt], *a.* qui a un parfum de; **redolent of . . .**, qui sent le . . . .

redouble [ri'dʌbl], *v.t., v.i.* redoubler.

redoubt [ri'daut], *n.* redoute, *f.*

redoubtable [ri'dautəbl], *a.* redoutable.

redound [ri'daund], *v.i.* contribuer (*à, en*), résulter (*pour*), rejaillir (*sur*).

redpole, redpoll ['redpoul], *n.* (*pop.*) linotte, *f.*

redraft [ri:'drɑ:ft], *n.* nouveau dessin, *m.*; (*Comm.*) retraite,*f.*—*v.t.* rédiger de nouveau.

redress [ri'dres], *v.t.* redresser, corriger, réparer.—*n.* redressement, *m.*, réparation,*f.*, remède, *m.*

redshank ['redʃæŋk], *n.* (*Orn.*) chevalier, *m.*, gambette, *f.*

redskin ['redskin], *n.* Peau-Rouge, *m., f.*

red tape ['red'teip], *n.* bolduc, *m.*; (*fig.*) routine administrative, *f.*

reduce [ri'dju:s], *v.t.* réduire (*à* ou *en*); maigrir (*chair*); dégrader (*abaisser*); **a person in reduced circumstances**, une personne tombée dans la gêne.—*v.i.* maigrir.

reduction [ri'dʌkʃən], *n.* réduction, *f.*; **a reduction in prices**, une baisse des prix, *f.*; **reduction to the ranks**, cassation, *f.*

redundance [ri'dʌndəns], **redundancy** [ri'dʌndənsi], *n.* redondance, *f.*

redundant [ri'dʌndənt], *a.* redondant, superflu.

re-echo [ri:'ekou], *v.t.* répéter.—*v.i.* retentir. —*n.* écho répété, *m.*

reed [ri:d], *n.* roseau; chalumeau, *m.*; (*Mus.*) anche,*f.*

reed pipe ['ri:dpaip], *n.* chalumeau, pipeau, *m.*

reedy ['ri:di], *a.* couvert de roseaux; flûtée (*voix*).

reef (1) [ri:f], *n.* récif, écueil, *m.*

reef (2) [ri:f], *n.* ris (*de voile*), *m.*—*v.t.* prendre un ris dans.

reef knot ['ri:fnɔt], *n.* nœud plat, *m.*

reek [ri:k], *n.* fumée, *f.*; relent, *m.*—*v.i.* fumer; exhaler; **reeking with**, tout fumant de; *to reek of*, puer, empester.

reel (1) [ri:l], *n.* dévidoir, *m.*; bobine (*de coton*), *f.*; (*Angling*) moulinet, *m.*; (*Cine.*) bobine, bande, *f.*; **newsreel**, les actualités, *f.pl.*—*v.t. to reel off*, dévider, débiter.— *v.i.* tournoyer, chanceler, trébucher.

reel (2) [ri:l], *n.* branle écossais (*danse*), *m.*

re-elect [ri:i'lekt], *v.t.* réélire.

re-election [ri:i'lekʃən], *n.* réélection, *f.*

re-embark [ri:əm'bɑ:k], *v.t.* rembarquer.— *v.i.* se rembarquer.

re-embarkation [ri:embɑ:'keiʃən], *n.* rembarquement, *m.*

re-embody [ri:əm'bɔdi], *v.t.* réincorporer.

re-enact [ri:i'nækt], *v.t.* remettre en vigueur (*une loi*); reconstituer (*un crime*).

re-enactment [ri:i'næktmənt], *n.* remise en vigueur, reconstitution, *f.*

re-engage [ri:in'geidʒ], *v.t.* rengager.

re-enlist [ri:in'list], *v.t., v.i.* (se) rengager.

re-enter [ri:'entə], *v.t., v.i.* rentrer.

re-entrant [ri:'entrənt], *a.* and *n.* rentrant, *m.*

re-establish [[ri:is'tæbliʃ], *v.t.* rétablir.

re-establishment [ri:is'tæbliʃmənt], *n.* rétablissement, *m.*

re-examine [ri:ig'zæmin], *v.t.* examiner de nouveau, revoir.

re-export [ri:iks'pɔ:t], *v.t.* réexporter.

refashion [ri:'fæʃən], *v.t.* refaçonner.

refasten [ri:'fɑ:sn], *v.t.* rattacher; ragrafer.

refection [ri'fekʃən], *n.* repas, *m.*, collation, *f.*

refectory [ri'fektəri], *n.* réfectoire, *m.*

refer [ri'fə:], *v.t.* renvoyer, rapporter; adresser (*à*); remettre à la décision de.—*v.i.* se référer, se rapporter, avoir rapport (*à*); s'en rapporter, se référer (*personnes*); s'adresser (*à*).

referee [refə'ri:], *n.* arbitre, *m., f.*—*v.t., v.i.* (*Spt.*) arbitrer.

reference ['refərəns], *n.* renvoi; rapport (*respect*), *m.*; allusion, *f.*; renseignements, *m.pl.*, références (*de bonne vie et mœurs*), *f.pl.*; (*Comm.*) référence, *f.*; **book of reference**, ouvrage à consulter, *m.*; **with reference to**, au sujet de; **to make reference to**, faire allusion à.

referendum [refə'rendəm], *n.* référendum, *m.*

refill [ri:'fil], *v.t.* remplir.—*v.i.* (*Motor.*) faire le plein (*d'essence*).—[ri:'fil], *n.* objet (*feuilles, pile, ampoule*) de rechange; (*Motor.*) plein (d'essence), *m.*

refine [ri'fain], *v.t.* épurer (*liquides*); (*Metal.*) affiner; raffiner (*sucre etc.*); (*fig.*) purifier.

refined [ri'faind], *a.* raffiné; pur, délicat (*goût*).

refinement [ri'fainmənt], *n.* raffinage (*de sucre*); (*Metal.*) affinage, *m.*; épuration (*de liquides*); (*fig.*) délicatesse, *f.*

refinery [ri'fainəri], *n.* raffinerie (*de sucre*); (*Metal.*) affinerie, *f.*

refit [ri:'fit], *v.t.* réparer; (*Naut.*) radouber.— ['ri:fit], *n.* réparation, *f.* (*Naut.*) refonte, *f.*

reflect [ri'flekt], *v.t.* réfléchir; faire rejaillir sur.—*v.i.* réfléchir; *to reflect upon*, réfléchir à, méditer sur.

reflected [ri'flektid], *a.* réfléchi.

535

reflection

reflection [REFLEXION].
reflective [ri'flektiv], a. réfléchissant; méditatif.
reflector [ri'flektə], n. réflecteur; (Cycl., Motor.) catadioptre, m.
reflex ['ri:fleks], a. réfléchi; (Paint.) reflété; (Physiol. etc.) réflexe.—n. (Paint.) reflet; (Physiol.) réflexe, m.
reflexion [ri'flekʃən], n. réflexion, f.; reflet (lumière etc.), m.; censure, f.; blâme, m.
reflexive [ri'fleksiv], a. réfléchi.
reform [ri'fɔ:m], n. réforme, f.—v.t. réformer; corriger.—v.i. se réformer, se corriger.
re-form [ri:'fɔ:m], v.t. reformer.—v.i. se reformer.
reformation [refɔ:'meiʃən], n. réformation; réforme, f.; the Reformation, (Hist.) la Réforme.
re-formation [ri:fɔ:'meiʃən], n. formation nouvelle, f.
reformer [ri'fɔ:mə], n. réformateur, m.
refract [ri'frækt], v.t. réfracter.
refraction [ri'frækʃən], n. réfraction, f.
refractive [ri'fræktiv], a. réfractif; réfringent.
refractory [ri'fræktri], a. indocile, récalcitrant, intraitable, rebelle; (Chem. etc.) réfractaire; rétif (cheval).
refrain [ri'frein], v.i. se retenir, s'abstenir (de).—n. refrain, m.
refresh [ri'freʃ], v.t. rafraîchir; délasser, restaurer; to refresh oneself, se rafraîchir.
refreshing [ri'freʃiŋ], a. rafraîchissant; réparateur, qui repose.
refreshment [ri'freʃmənt], n. rafraîchissement, m.; refreshment bar, buvette, f.; refreshment car, wagon-restaurant, m.; refreshment room, buffet, m.
refrigerate [ri'fridʒəreit], v.t. réfrigérer, frigorifier.
refrigeration [rifridʒə'reiʃən], n. réfrigération, f.
refrigerator [ri'fridʒəreitə], n. réfrigérateur; (fam.) Frigidaire (marque déposée), m.
refuel [ri:'fjuəl], v.i. (Av.) faire le plein (d'essence).
refuge [refju:dʒ], n. refuge (contre), m.; to take refuge, se réfugier.
refugee [refju'dʒi:], n. réfugié, m.
refulgence [ri'fʌldʒəns], n. éclat, m., splendeur, f.
refulgent [ri'fʌldʒənt], a. éclatant.
refund [ri'fʌnd], v.t. rembourser, rendre.—['ri:fʌnd], n. remboursement, m.
refurnish [ri:'fɔ:niʃ], v.t. remeubler.
refusal [ri'fju:zl], n. refus, m.
refuse ['refju:s], n. rebut, m., ordures (ménagères, de marché), f.pl.; refuse dump, voirie, f.—[ri'fju:z], v.t. refuser; rejeter.—v.i. refuser.
refute [ri'fju:t], v.t. réfuter.
regain [ri'gein], v.t. regagner, reprendre.
regal [ri:gl], a. royal.
regale [ri'geil], v.t. régaler.—v.i. se régaler.
regally [ri:gəli], adv. royalement, en roi.
regard [ri'gɑ:d], n. égard, m.; considération, f.; respect (estime), m.; (pl.) amitiés, f.pl., compliments, m.pl.; out of regard for, par égard pour; with regard to, quant à.—v.t. regarder; considérer; as regards, quant à.

regarding [ri'gɑ:diŋ], prep. quant à, concernant.
regardless [ri'gɑ:dlis], a. peu soigneux (de); sans égard (pour); regardless of, sans se soucier de.
regatta [ri'gætə], n. régate(s), f.(pl.).
regency ['ri:dʒənsi], n. régence, f.
regenerate [ri'dʒenərət], a. régénéré.—[ri:'dʒenəreit], v.t. régénérer.
regenerating [ri'dʒenəreitiŋ], a. régénérateur.
regeneration [ri:dʒenə'reiʃən], n. régénération, f.
regent ['ri:dʒənt], n. régent, m.
regicide ['redʒisaid], n. régicide (crime), m.; régicide (personne), m., f.
régime [rei'ʒi:m], n. (Polit.) régime, m.
regimen ['redʒimən], n. (Gram., Med.) régime, m.
regiment ['redʒimənt], n. régiment, m.
regimental [redʒi'mentl], a. du régiment, de régiment.
regimentation [redʒimen'teiʃən], n. enrégimentation, f.
Reginald ['redʒinəld]. Renaud, m.
region ['ri:dʒən], n. région, f.
regional ['ri:dʒənl], a. régional.
register ['redʒistə], n. registre, m.; liste électorale (de votants), f.—v.t. enregistrer; recommander (lettre, paquet); déclarer (naissance); immatriculer (voiture); déposer (marque de fabrique etc.).
registrar ['redʒistrɑ:], n. (Law) greffier; (Univ.) secrétaire et archiviste; officier de l'état civil (de naissances etc.), m.
registration [redʒis'treiʃən], n. enregistrement; chargement (de lettres); dépôt (d'une marque de fabrique etc.), m.; immatriculation (de véhicule); inscription (des bagages), f.; registration number, (Motor.) numéro minéralogique, m.
registry ['redʒistri], n. enregistrement; (Law) greffe, m.
registry office ['redʒistri'ɔfis], n. bureau de l'état civil, m.
regret [ri'gret], n. regret, m.—v.t. regretter (de), avoir du regret (de).
regretful [ri'gretful], a. plein de regrets; regrettable.
regretfully [ri'gretfuli], adv. avec regret, f. regret.
regrettable [ri'gretəbl], a. fâcheux, regrettable.
regular ['regjulə], a. régulier; réglé; en règle; ordinaire (normal); (fig.) franc, fieffé.
regularity [regju'læriti], n. régularité, f.
regularly ['regjulɑli], adv. régulièrement, m.
regulate ['regjuleit], v.t. régler; diriger.
regulation [regju'leiʃən], a. réglementaire.—n. règlement, m.
regulator ['regjuleitə], n. régulateur, m.
rehabilitate [ri:hə'biliteit], v.t. réhabiliter.
rehabilitation [ri:həbili'teiʃən], n. réhabilitation, f.
rehearsal [ri'hə:sl], n. récit, m.; (Theat.) répétition, f.; dress rehearsal, répétition générale.
rehearse [ri'hə:s], v.t. (Theat.) répéter; (fig.) raconter (narrer).
rehouse [ri:'hauz], v.t. reloger.
reign [rein], n. règne, m.—v.i. régner.

536

reigning ['reiniŋ], *a.* régnant; (*fig.*) dominant (*prevailing*).

reimburse [ri:im'bə:s], *v.t.* rembourser.

reimbursement [ri:im'bə:smənt], *n.* remboursement, *m.*

rein [rein], *n.* rêne, *f.*—*v.t.* conduire à la bride, gouverner, brider; contenir.

reincarnation [ri:inka:'neiʃən], *n.* réincarnation, *f.*

reindeer ['reindiə], *n.* renne, *m.*

reinforce [ri:in'fɔ:s], *v.t.* renforcer; **reinforced concrete**, béton armé, *m.*

reinforcement [ri:in'fɔ:smənt], *n.* renforcement; (*Mil.*) renfort, *m.*

reinstall [ri:in'stɔ:l], *v.t.* réinstaller.

reinstate [ri:in'steit], *v.t.* rétablir.

reinstatement [ri:in'steitmənt], *n.* rétablissement, *m.*

reintroduce [ri:intrə'dju:s], *v.t.* introduire de nouveau, réintroduire.

reinvest [ri:in'vest], *v.t.* replacer.

reinvigorate [ri:in'vigəreit], *v.t.* ranimer.

reissue [ri:'isju:], *v.t.* émettre de nouveau; rééditer (*livre*).—*n.* nouvelle émission; nouvelle édition, *f.*

reiterate [ri:'itəreit], *v.t.* réitérer.

reiteration [ri:itə'reiʃən], *n.* réitération, *f.*

reiterative [ri:'itərətiv], *a.* réitératif.

reject [ri'dʒekt], *v.t.* rejeter.—['ri:dʒekt], *n.* pièce de rebut, *f.*

rejection [ri'dʒekʃən], *n.* rejet, *m.*

rejoice [ri'dʒɔis], *v.t.* réjouir.—*v.i.* se réjouir (*de*).

rejoicing [ri'dʒɔisiŋ], *n.* réjouissance, joie, *f.*

rejoin [ri'dʒɔin], *v.t.* rejoindre.—[ri'dʒɔin], *v.i.* répliquer, répondre.

rejoinder [ri'dʒɔində], *n.* repartie, (*Law*) réplique, *f.*

rejuvenate [ri'dʒu:vəneit], *v.t.* rajeunir.

rejuvenation [ridʒu:və'neiʃən], *n.* rajeunissement, *m.*

rekindle [ri:'kindl], *v.t.* rallumer.

relapse [ri'læps], *n.* rechute, *f.*—*v.i.* retomber (*dans*); récidiver (*criminel*).

relate [ri'leit], *v.t.* raconter; rapporter.—*v.i.* se rapporter, avoir rapport (*à*).

related [ri'leitid], *a.* ayant rapport; parent (*de*); allié (*à*) (*par mariage etc.*).

relating [ri'leitiŋ], *a.* relatif, qui se rapporte (*à*).

relation [ri'leiʃən], *n.* relation, *f.*, rapport; récit (*narration*); parent (*de la famille*); allié (*par mariage*), *m.*; (*pl.*) relations, *f.pl.*, rapports (*contact*), *m.pl.*

relationship [ri'leiʃənʃip], *n.* parenté, *f.*; rapport, *m.*

relative ['relətiv], *a.* relatif (*à*).—*n.* parent (*Gram.*) relatif, *m.*

relatively ['relətivli], *adv.* relativement.

relativity [relə'tivitil], *n.* relativité, *f.*

relax [ri'læks], *v.t.* relâcher, détendre.—*v.i.* se relâcher; se détendre; se délasser.

relaxation [ri:læk'seiʃən], *n.* relâchement, relâche, *m.*, détente, *f.*; (*Med.*) repos, *m.*

relaxing [ri'læksiŋ], *a.* relâchant; énervant, débilitant (*climat*).

relay ['ri:lei], *n.* relais, *m.*—*v.t.* relayer.

re-lay [ri:'lei], *v.t.* poser de nouveau.

release [ri'li:s], *v.t.* relâcher, élargir (*un prisonnier*); décharger (*de*); déclencher.—*n.* élargissement, *m.*; délivrance; décharge

(*d'une obligation*); (*Cine.*) sortie (*d'un film*), *f.*; déclenchement (*de ressort etc.*), *m.*

relegate ['reləgeit], *v.t.* reléguer.

relegation [relə'geiʃən], *n.* relégation, *f.*

relent [ri'lent], *v.i.* s'amollir, s'attendrir; se repentir (*regretter*).

relenting [ri'lentiŋ], *n.* attendrissement, *m.*

relentless [ri'lentlis], *a.* inflexible, impitoyable.

relentlessly [ri'lentlisli], *adv.* impitoyablement.

relentlessness [ri'lentlisnis], *n.* rigueur, dureté, *f.*

relevance ['reləvəns], **relevancy** ['reləvənsi], *n.* relation, *f.*, rapport, *m.*; pertinence, convenance, *f.*, à-propos, *m.*

relevant ['reləvənt], *a.* relatif, applicable (*à*); à propos, pertinent.

reliable [ri'laiəbl], *a.* digne de confiance; sûr, exact, bien fondé (*renseignement*).

reliability [rilaiə'biliti], *n.* crédibilité, véracité; sûreté, *f.*

reliance [ri'laiəns], *n.* confiance, *f.*

relic ['relik], *n.* relique (*de saint* ou *martyr*), *f.*; (*pl.*) restes (*d'un être*), vestiges (*du passé*), *m.pl.*

relief [ri'li:f], *n.* soulagement (*de douleur etc.*); secours (*aide*), *m.*; (*Mil.*) relève, *f.*; (*Sculp. etc.*) relief, *m.*; **relief train**, train supplémentaire, *m.*

relieve [ri'li:v], *v.t.* soulager, adoucir; délivrer (*de*); secourir, aider (*assister*); (*Mil.*) relever (*sentinelle*).

religion [ri'lidʒən], *n.* religion, *f.*

religious [ri'lidʒəs], *a.* religieux; de religion.

religiously [ri'lidʒəsli], *adv.* religieusement.

relinquish [ri'liŋkwiʃ], *v.t.* abandonner; renoncer à.

relinquishment [ri'liŋkwiʃmənt], *n.* abandon, *m.*; renonciation, *f.*

reliquary ['relikwəri], *n.* reliquaire, *m.*

relish ['reliʃ], *n.* goût, *m.*, saveur, *f.*; (*Cook.*) assaisonnement; (*fig.*) charme; appétit, *m.*—*v.t.* goûter, savourer; relever le goût de.

relive [ri:'liv], *v.t.* revivre.

reload [ri:'loud], *v.t.* recharger.

reluctance [ri'lʌktəns], *n.* répugnance, *f.*

reluctant [ri'lʌktənt], *a.* qui a de la répugnance à, qui agit à contre-cœur; peu disposé (*à*).

reluctantly [ri'lʌktəntli], *adv.* à contre-cœur.

rely [ri'lai], *v.i.* compter (*sur*), avoir confiance (*en*).

remain [ri'mein], *v.i.* rester, demeurer.

remainder [ri'meində], *n.* reste, *m.*

remaining [ri'meiniŋ], *a.* de reste, restant.

remains [ri'meinz], *n.pl.* restes; débris, *m.pl.*; **mortal remains**, dépouille mortelle, *f.*

remake [ri:'meik], *v.t. irr.* (*conjug. like* MAKE) refaire.

remand [ri'mɑ:nd], *v.t.* renvoyer à une autre audience.—*n.* renvoi à une autre audience, *m.*

remark [ri'mɑ:k], *n.* remarque, *f.*—*v.t.* remarquer, observer; faire remarquer, faire observer (*à une personne*).

remarkable [ri'mɑ:kəbl], *a.* remarquable.

remarkably [ri'mɑ:kəbli], *adv.* remarquablement.

remarriage [ri:'mæridʒ], *n.* remariage, *m.*

remarry [ri:'mæri], *v.t.* épouser de nouveau. —*v.i.* se remarier.

remedial [ri'mi:djəl], *a.* réparateur; (*Med.*) curatif.
remedy ['remədi], *n.* remède; (*Law*) recours, *m.—v.t.* remédier à, porter remède à.
remember [ri'membə], *v.t.* se souvenir de, se rappeler; reconnaître (*de vue*).
remembrance [ri'membrəns], *n.* souvenir, *m.*, mémoire, *f.*
remind [ri'maind], *v.t.* rappeler à, faire souvenir (*à . . . de*), faire penser à.
reminder [ri'maində], *n.* mémento, *m.*
reminisce [remi'nis], *v.i.* raconter ses souvenirs.
reminiscence [remi'nisəns], *n.* réminiscence, *f.*
reminiscent [remi'nisənt], *a.* qui rappelle.
remiss [ri'mis], *a.* négligent.
remission [ri'miʃən], *n.* rémission, *f.*, pardon; relâchement (*détente*), *m.*; remise (*de dette, peine*), *f.*
remit [ri'mit], *v.t.* relâcher (*détendre*); remettre (*amende* etc.).—*v.i.* se relâcher, se calmer; diminuer.
remittance [ri'mitəns], *n.* remise, *f.*; envoi de fonds, *m.*
remittent [ri'mitənt], *a.* (*Path.*) rémittent.
remnant ['remnənt], *n.* reste; coupon, bout (*de tissu*), *m.*; (*pl.*) restes, débris, *m.pl.*
remodel [ri:'mɔdl], *v.t.* remodeler.
remold [ri:'mould], *v.t.* mouler de nouveau.
remonstrance [ri'mɔnstrəns], *n.* remontrance, *f.*
remonstrate ['remənstreit], *v.i.* remontrer.
remorse [ri'mɔ:s], *n.* remords, *m.*
remorseful [ri'mɔ:sful], *a.* rempli de remords.
remorseless [ri'mɔ:slis], *a.* sans remords, impitoyable.
remorselessness [ri'mɔ:slisnis], *n.* cruauté, inhumanité, *f.*
remote [ri'mout], *a.* éloigné, lointain; reculé (*époque*); distant (*personne*).
remotely [ri'moutli], *adv.* de loin; faiblement.
remoteness [ri'moutnis], *n.* éloignement, *m.*; réserve (*attitude*), *f.*
remount [ri:'maunt], *v.t.*, *v.i.* remonter.—*n.* remonte, *f.*
removable [ri'mu:vəbl], *a.* transportable; (*fig.*) amovible (*fonctionnaire* etc.).
removal [ri'mu:vl], *n.* éloignement, départ; transport; déménagement (*de meubles*); déplacement, *m.*; révocation (*de ses fonctions*), *f.*
remove [ri'mu:v], *n.* degré (*parenté*), *m.*; distance, *f.—v.t.* éloigner; déplacer (*bouger*); transporter; déménager (*meubles*); ôter, enlever (*emporter*); renvoyer (*de ses fonctions*).—*v.i.* s'éloigner, se déplacer; déménager (*changer de domicile*).
removed [ri'mu:vd], *a.* éloigné; *first cousin once removed*, cousin issu de germains, *m.*
remover [ri'mu:və], *n.* déménageur, *m.*; *nail polish remover*, dissolvant (pour ongles), *m.*
remunerate [ri'mju:nəreit], *v.t.* rémunérer.
remuneration [rimju:nə'reiʃən], *n.* rétribution, rémunération, *f.*
remunerative [ri'mju:nərətiv], *a.* rémunérateur; (*Law*) rémunératoire.
rename [ri:'neim], *v.t.* renommer.
rend [rend], *v.t.* irr. déchirer; (*fig.*) fendre.

render ['rendə], *v.t.* rendre; interpréter, traduire; (*Cook.*) fondre (*graisse* etc.).
rendering ['rendəriŋ], *n.* traduction, interprétation, *f.*
renegade ['renigeid]. *n.* renégat, *m.*
renew [ri'nju:], *v.t.* renouveler; renouer (*connaissance*).
renewal [ri'nju:əl], *n.* renouvellement, *m.*; *renewal of subscription*, réabonnement, *m.*
renounce [ri'nauns], *v.t.* renoncer (à); renier.
renouncement [ri'naunsmənt], *n.* renoncement, *m.*, renonciation, *f.*
renovate ['renəveit], *v.t.* renouveler; rajeunir.
renovation [renə'veiʃən], *n.* rénovation, *f.*
renovator ['renəveitə], *n.* rénovateur, *m.*
renown [ri'naun], *n.* renommée, *f.*, renom, *m.*
renowned [ri'naund], *a.* renommé.
rent (1) [rent], *n.* déchirure, fente, *f.*; accroc (*de vêtements*), *m.*
rent (2) [rent], *n.* loyer (*de maison* ou *d'appartement*); fermage (*de ferme*), *m.*; (*pl.*) rentes, *f.pl.*; revenu, *m.*; *ground rent*, rente foncière, *f.—v.t.* louer; prendre à ferme, donner à ferme.—*v.i.* se louer.
rent (3) [rent], *past* and *p.p.* [REND].
rental [rentl], *n.* valeur locative, *f.*
rent-free ['rentfri:], *a.* exempt de loyer.
renunciation [rinʌnsi'eiʃən], *n.* renonciation, *f.*, renoncement, *m.*
reoccupation [ri:ɔkju'peiʃən], *n.* réoccupation, *f.*
reoccupy [ri:'ɔkjupai], *v.t.* réoccuper.
reopen [ri:'oupən], *v.t.* rouvrir.—*v.i.* rentrer (*écoles, tribunaux* etc.).
reopening [ri:'oupniŋ], *n.* réouverture; rentrée (*d'écoles* etc.), *f.*
reorganization [ri:ɔ:gənai'zeiʃən], *n.* réorganisation, *f.*
reorganize [ri:'ɔ:gənaiz], *v.t.* réorganiser.
rep (1) [rep], *a.* de reps.—*n.* reps (*tissu*), *m.*
rep (2) [rep], [REPERTORY].
rep (3) [rep], [REPRESENTATIVE].
repaint [ri:'peint], *v.t.* repeindre.
repair (1) [ri'pɛə], *v.t.* réparer; raccommoder (*vêtements* etc.); (*fig.*) rétablir.—*n.* réparation, *f.*; raccommodage (*de vêtements* etc.); *to keep in repair*, entretenir.
repair (2) [ri'pɛə], *n.* séjour (*retraite*), *m.—v.i.* aller; se rendre (à).
repairer [ri'pɛərə], *n.* réparateur; raccommodeur (*de vêtements*), *m.*
reparable ['repərəbl], *a.* réparable.
reparation [repə'reiʃən], *n.* réparation (*d'une offense*), *f.*
repartee [repɑ:'ti:], *n.* repartie, riposte, *f.*
repast [ri'pɑ:st], *n.* repas, *m.*
repatriate [ri:'pætrieit], *v.t.* rapatrier.
repay [ri'pei], *v.t.* irr. (*conjug. like* PAY) rembourser; (*fig.*) valoir la peine (*de*).
repayment [ri:'peimənt], *n.* remboursement, *m.*
repeal [ri'pi:l], *v.t.* révoquer; abroger (*loi* etc.).—*n.* révocation; abrogation (*de loi*), *f.*
repeat [ri'pi:t], *v.t.* répéter, réitérer; réciter (*par cœur*); bis (*après vers de chanson* etc.).—*n.* répétition; (*Mus.*) reprise, *f.*
repeated [ri'pi:tid], *a.* répété, réitéré.
repeatedly [ri'pi:tidli], *adv.* à plusieurs reprises; souvent, bien des fois.
repeating [ri'pi:tiŋ], *a.* qui répète; à répétition.

repel [ri'pel], *v.t.* repousser; combattre.

repellent [ri'pelənt], *a.* répulsif, répugnant.—*n.* répulsif; (*Med.*) révulsif, *m.*

repent [ri'pent], *v.t.* se repentir de.—*v.i.* se repentir.

repentance [ri'pentəns], *n.* repentir, *m.*

repentant [ri'pentənt], *a.* repentant.

repercussion [ri:pə'kaʃən], *n.* répercussion, *f.*

repertory ['repətri], *n.* répertoire, *m.*; *repertory theatre*, (*fam.*) *rep*, théâtre de province, *m.*

repetition [repi'tiʃən], *n.* répétition; (*Mus.*) reprise, *f.*

repetitive [ri'petitiv], *a.* qui se répète.

repine [ri'pain], *v.i.* murmurer (*contre*); se plaindre (*de*).

repining [ri'painiŋ], *a.* disposé à se plaindre, mécontent.—*n.* plainte, *f.*, regret, *m.*

replace [ri:'pleis], *v.t.* replacer; remplacer (*substituer*).

replacement [ri:'pleismənt], *n.* remplacement, *m.*

replant [ri:'plɑ:nt], *v.t.* replanter.

replay ['ri:plei], *n.* match rejoué, *m.*—[ri:'plei], *v.t.*, *v.i.* rejouer.

replenish [ri'pleniʃ], *v.t.* remplir (*de*).—*v.i.* se remplir.

replenishment [ri'pleniʃmənt], *n.* remplissage, *m.*

replete [ri'pli:t], *a.* plein, rempli (*de*).

repletion [ri'pli:ʃən], *n.* plénitude; (*Med.*) réplétion, *f.*

replica ['replikə], *n.* double, *m.*, copie, *f.*

reply [ri'plai], *n.* réponse; (*Law*) réplique, *f.*—*v.t.*, *v.i.* répondre, répliquer.

repopulate [ri:'pɔpjuleit], *v.t.* repeupler.

report [ri'pɔ:t], *v.t.* rapporter, raconter, dire; rendre compte de: signaler; dénoncer (*à la police*); *to report oneself*, se présenter à.—*n.* rapport; bruit, oui-dire (*rumeur*); compte rendu, procès-verbal (*de réunion etc.*); (*Sch.*) bulletin; coup (*de fusil*), *m.*; réputation (*renom*), *f.*

reporter [ri'pɔ:tə], *n.* rapporteur; reporter (*journaliste*), *m.*

reporting [ri'pɔ:tiŋ], *n.* reportage, *m.*

repose [ri'pouz], *v.t.* reposer.—*v.i.* se reposer.—*n.* repos, *m.*

repository [ri'pɔzitri], *n.* dépôt, *m.*

repossess [ri:pə'zes], *v.t.* rentrer en possession de.

reprehend [repri'hend], *v.t.* réprimander, censurer, blâmer (*de*).

reprehensible [repri'hensibl], *a.* répréhensible, blâmable.

represent [repri'zent], *v.t.* représenter.

representation [reprizen'teiʃən], *n.* représentation, *f.*

representative [repri'zentətiv], *a.* représentatif, qui représente.—*n.* représentant; (*Comm.*) (*fam. abbr. rep*) agent, *m.*

repress [ri'pres], *v.t.* réprimer.

repression [ri'preʃən], *n.* répression, *f.*

repressive [ri'presiv], *a.* répressif.

reprieve [ri'pri:v], *n.* sursis; répit, *m.*—*v.t.* accorder un sursis à; commuer (*une peine*), gracier.

reprimand ['reprimɑ:nd], *n.* réprimande, *f.*— *v.t.* réprimander.

reprint ['ri:print], *n.* réimpression, *f.*—[ri:'print], *v.t.* réimprimer.

reprisal [ri'praizl], *n.* représailles, *f.pl.*

reproach [ri'prouts], *n.* reproche; opprobre (*honte*), *m.*; *above reproach*, irréprochable.—*v.t.* reprocher.

reprobate ['reprəbit], *n.* vaurien, *m.*

reprobation [reprə'beiʃən], *n.* réprobation, *f.*

reproduce [ri:prə'dju:s], *v.t.* reproduire.—*v.i.* se reproduire.

reproduction [ri:prə'dakʃən], *n.* reproduction, *f.*

reproductive [ri:prə'daktiv], *a.* reproducteur.

reproof [ri'pru:f], *n.* reproche, *m.*, réprimande, *f.*

reprove [ri'pru:v], *v.t.* blâmer; censurer.

reproving [ri'pru:viŋ], *a.* réprobateur.

reprovingly [ri'pru:viŋli], *adv.* d'un air *ou* ton réprobateur.

reptile ['reptail], *a.* reptile; (*fig.*) rampant, vil.—*n.* reptile, *m.*

reptilian [rep'tilian], *a.* reptilien.

republic [ri'pablik], *n.* république, *f.*

republican [ri'pablikən], *a.* and *n.* républicain, *m.*

republication [ri:pabli'keiʃən], *n.* nouvelle édition, réimpression (*de livre*), *f.*

republish [ri:'pabliʃ], *v.t.* republier, rééditer.

repudiate [ri'pju:dieit], *v.t.* répudier.

repudiation [ripju:di'eiʃən], *n.* répudiation, *f.*

repugnance [ri'pagnəns], *n.* répugnance, *f.*

repugnant [ri'pagnənt], *a.* répugnant.

repulse [ri'pals], *v.t.* repousser, rebuter.—*n.* échec, refus, *m.*, rebuffade, *f.*; *to meet with a repulse*, essuyer un échec.

repulsion [ri'palʃən], *n.* répulsion, *f.*

repulsive [ri'palsiv], *a.* rebutant; repoussant (*forbidding*).

repulsiveness [ri'palsivnis], *n.* caractère repoussant, *m.*

repurchase [ri:'pə:tʃis], *v.t.* racheter.—*n.* rachat; (*Law*) réméré, *m.*

reputable ['repjutəbl], *a.* honorable, de bonne réputation, considéré.

reputably ['repjutəbli], *adv.* honorablement.

reputation [repju'teiʃən], *n.* réputation, *f.*

repute [ri'pju:t], *v.t.* (*usu. pass.*) réputer, estimer.—*n.* réputation, *f.*, renom, *m.*

reputed [ri'pju:tid], *a.* réputé, censé, qui passe pour.

request [ri'kwest], *n.* demande, prière; (*Law*) requête, *f.*; *request stop*, arrêt facultatif (*autobus*), *m.*—*v.t.* demander; prier.

requiem ['rekwiem], *n.* requiem, *m.*

require [ri'kwaiə], *v.t.* exiger, requérir; avoir besoin de (*manquer de*); (*impers.*) falloir.

requirement [ri'kwaiəmənt], *n.* exigence, nécessité, *f.*, besoin, *m.*; condition requise, *f.*

requisite ['rekwizit], *a.* requis, exigé, nécessaire.—*n.* qualité *ou* condition requise; chose requise, *f.*

requisition [rekwi'ziʃən], *n.* réquisition, *f.*—*v.t.* réquisitionner.

requital [ri'kwaitl], *n.* récompense, *f.*

requite [ri'kwait], *v.t.* récompenser; rendre la pareille à; payer de retour.

reredos ['riədɔs], *n.* retable, *m.*

rescind [ri'sind], *v.t.* rescinder, annuler.

rescue ['reskju:], *n.* délivrance, *f.*; sauvetage, *m.*; *to the rescue*, au secours!—*v.t.* sauver, délivrer (*de*).

rescuer ['reskju:ə], *n.* sauveteur, libérateur, *m.*

research [ri'sə:tʃ], *n.* recherche, *f.*—*v.i.* faire des recherches.

reseat [ri:'si:t], v.t. rasseoir.
resemblance [ri'zemblans], n. ressemblance, f.; (fig.) rapport, m.
resemble [ri'zembl], v.t. ressembler (à); to resemble each other, se ressembler.
resent [ri'zent], v.t. ressentir, se ressentir de; s'offenser de; prendre en mauvaise part.
resentful [ri'zentful], a. rancunier.
resentfully [ri'zentfuli], adv. avec ressentiment.
resentment [ri'zentmant], n. ressentiment, m., rancœur, f.
reservation [rezə'veiʃən], n. réserve, restriction, arrière-pensée, f.; (Am.) terrain réservé, m.; réservation, location (place assise), f.
reserve [ri'zə:v], n. réserve, retenue, prudence; arrière-pensée, f.—v.t. réserver.
reserved [ri'zə:vd], a. réservé.
reservedly [ri'zə:vidli], adv. avec réserve.
reservist [ri'zə:vist], n. réserviste, m., f.
reservoir ['rezəvwa:], n. réservoir, m.
reset [ri:'set], v.t. irr. (conjug. like SET) poser ou fixer de nouveau; (Print.) composer de nouveau; (Surg.) remettre.
resetting [ri:'setin], n. remontage (de pierre précieuse), m.; (Print.) recomposition, f.
resettle [ri:'setl], v.t. rétablir.—v.i. s'établir de nouveau.
resettlement [ri:'setlmant], n. rétablissement, m.
reshape [ri:'ʃeip], v.t. reformer, remanier.
reside [ri'zaid], v.i. résider, demeurer.
residence ['rezidans], n. résidence, demeure, f.; board (and) residence, la table et le logement.
resident ['rezidant], a. résidant; interne (de la maison).—n. habitant; résident, m.
residential [rezi'denʃl], a. résidentiel.
residual [ri'zidjual], a. résiduel.
residuary [ri'zidjuəri], a. de résidu, de reste; universel (légataire).
residue ['rezidju:], n. reste, (Chem.) résidu; reliquat (de dette), m.
resign [ri'zain], v.t. donner sa démission de; renoncer à; to be resigned to or resign oneself to, se résigner à.—v.i. donner sa démission, démissionner (de).
resignation [rezig'neiʃən], n. résignation; cession; démission (de ses fonctions), f.
resigned [ri'zaind], a. résigné; démissionnaire (d'un poste).
resilience [ri'ziliəns], resiliency [ri'ziliənsi], n. rebondissement, m.; élasticité, f.
resilient [ri'ziliənt], a. rebondissant.
resin ['rezin], n. résine; colophane (pour violons), f.
resist [ri'zist], v.t. résister à.—v.i. résister.
resistance [ri'zistəns], n. résistance, f.
resistant [ri'zistənt], a. résistant.
re-sole [ri:'soul], v.t. ressemeler.
resolute ['rezəlju:t], a. déterminé, résolu.
resolutely ['rezəlju:tli], adv. résolument.
resoluteness ['rezəlju:tnis], n. résolution, fermeté, f.
resolution [rezə'lju:ʃən], n. résolution; décision (d'assemblée), f.
resolve [ri'zɔlv], n. résolution, f.—v.t. résoudre; fondre (liquéfier); éclaircir, dissiper (doutes etc.); déterminer, décider (assemblée).—v.i. se résoudre, se décider; se fondre (se dissoudre).

resolved [ri'zɔlvd], a. résolu.
resolvent [ri'zɔlvənt], n. (Med.) résolvant, m.
resonance ['rezənəns], n. résonance, f.
resonant ['rezənənt], a. résonnant, sonore.
resort [ri'zɔ:t], n. ressource, f., recours; séjour, rendezvous (endroit); (Law) ressort, m.; seaside resort, station balnéaire, plage, f.—v.i. recourir, avoir recours (à); se rendre, aller (à).
resound [ri'zaund], v.i. résonner, retentir.
resounding [ri'zaundin], a. retentissant.—n. retentissement, m.
resource [ri'sɔ:s], n. ressource, f.
resourceful [ri'sɔ:sful], a. plein de ressources.
respect [ri'spekt], n. respect, m., estime, f.; égard, m.; (pl.) respects, hommages, m.pl.; in every respect, sous tous les rapports; in respect to, à l'égard de.—v.t. respecter, considérer, avoir égard à.
respectability [rispektə'biliti], n. honorabilité, f; convenances, f.pl.; bienséance, f.
respectable [ri'spektəbl], a. respectable, honorable; comme il faut, convenable.
respectably [ri'spektəbli], adv. comme il faut, très bien.
respectful [ri'spektful], a. respectueux.
respectfully [ri'spektfuli], adv. avec respect; yours respectfully (à un supérieur hiérarchique), veuillez agréer, Monsieur, l'assurance de mes sentiments respectueux.
respecting [ri'spektin], prep. à l'égard de, quant à, touchant.
respective [ri'spektiv], a. respectif, relatif.
respectively [ri'spektivli], adv. respectivement.
respiration [respi'reiʃən], n. respiration, f.
respirator ['respireitə], n. respirateur, m.
respiratory ['respirətri], a. respiratoire.
respire [ri'spaiə], v.t., v.i. respirer.
respite ['respit] n. répit, relâche; (Law) sursis, m.
resplendence [ri'splendəns], n. éclat, m., splendeur, f.
resplendent [ri'splendənt], a. resplendissant (de).
respond [ri'spond], v.i. répondre (à).
respondent [ri'spondənt], n. répondant, (Law) défendeur, m.
response [ri'spons], n. réponse, f.; (fig.) écho; (Eccles.) répons, m.
responsibility [risponsi'biliti], n. responsabilité, f.
responsible [ri'sponsibl], a. chargé (de), responsable (de); digne de confiance.
responsive [ri'sponsiv], a. sensible, facile à émouvoir.
rest (1) [rest], n. repos, m.; (Mus.) pause, f.; appui (soutien), m.; at rest, en repos.—v.t. reposer; faire reposer; (fig.) fonder.—v.i. se reposer; s'appuyer; it rests with me to . . ., c'est à moi de . . .; to rest assured, être assuré.
rest (2) [rest], n. reste, restant, m.; les autres, m.pl.—v.i. demeurer, rester.
restart [ri:'sta:t], v.t., v.i. recommencer.
restaurant ['restərã:], n. restaurant, m.
restful ['restful], a. qui donne du repos, paisible.
resting ['restin], a. couché, se reposant; appuyé, s'appuyant.—n. repos, m.
resting place ['restinpleis], n. lieu de repos, gîte, m.

restitution [resti'tju:ʃən], n. restitution, f.
restive ['restiv], a. rétif; inquiet.
restiveness ['restivnis], n. naturel rétif, m.;
nervosité, f.
restless ['restlis], a. sans repos; inquiet;
agité.
restlessly ['restlisli], adv. sans repos.
restlessness ['restlisnis], n. agitation; insomnie, f.
restock [ri:'stɔk], v.t. repeupler (chasse
réservée); regarnir (boutique), réassortir.
restoration [restə'reiʃən], n. restauration, f.;
rétablissement, m.; restitution (après une
perte injuste), f.
restorative [ri'stɔːrativ], a. and n. fortifiant,
m.
restore [ri'stɔː], v.t. restituer, rendre (redonner); ramener (personne); restaurer (bâtiment etc.); remettre (replacer); rétablir.
restorer [ri'stɔːrə], n. restaurateur, m.
restrain [ri'strein], v.t. retenir, contenir; to
restrain from, empêcher de; to restrain
oneself, se contraindre, se contenir.
restraining [ri'streiniŋ], a. qui restreint,
restrictif.
restraint [ri'streint], n. contrainte; gêne, f.
restrict [ri'strikt], v.t. restreindre.
restriction [ri'strikʃən], n. restriction, f.
restrictive [ri'striktiv], a. restrictif.
result [ri'zʌlt], n. résultat, m.; as a result of,
par suite de.—v.i. résulter; to result in,
aboutir à.
resultant [ri'zʌltənt], a. résultant.—n. résul-
tante, f.
resume [ri'zju:m], v.t. reprendre, renouer,
continuer.
resumption [ri'zʌmpʃən], n. reprise, f.
resurface [ri:'sə:fis], v.t. remettre en état
(route).—v.i. remonter à la surface.
resurgence [ri'sə:dʒəns], n. résurrection, f.
resurrect [rezə'rekt], v.t. ranimer, ressusciter.
resurrection [rezə'rekʃən], n. résurrection, f.
resuscitate [ri'sʌsiteit], v.t. ressusciter.
resuscitation [risʌsi'teiʃən], n. résurrection;
renaissance (des arts etc.); (Med.) ressuscitation, f.
retail ['ri:teil], a. en détail; retail price, prix
de détail m.—n. détail, m., vente au détail, f.
—[ri:'teil], v.t. vendre en détail, détailler;
(fig.) débiter; colporter (nouvelles).
retailer [ri:'teilə], n. détaillant; colporteur (de
nouvelles), m.
retain [ri'tein], v.t. retenir; engager (en payant
des arrhes).
retainer [ri'teinə], n. serviteur, dépendant,
m.; honoraires donnés d'avance (acompte),
m.pl.
retaining [ri'teiniŋ], a. qui retient; retaining wall, mur de soutènement, m.
retake [ri:'teik], v.t. irr. (conjug. like TAKE)
reprendre; (Cine.) retourner (un plan).
retaking [ri:'teikiŋ], n. reprise, f.
retaliate [ri'tælieit], v.i. rendre la pareille à.
retaliation [ritæli'eiʃən], n. représailles, f.pl.
retaliatory [ri'tæliatəri], a. de représailles.
retard [ri'ta:d], v.t. retarder.
retch [ri:tʃ], v.i. avoir des haut-le-cœur.
retching [ri:'tʃiŋ], n. haut-le-cœur, m.
retell [ri:'tel], v.t. irr. (conjug. like TELL)
redire, répéter.
retention [ri'tenʃən], n. conservation; (Med.)
rétention, f.

retentive [ri'tentiv], a. qui retient; tenace,
fidèle (la mémoire).
retentiveness [ri'tentivnis], n. pouvoir de
rétention, m.; fidélité (de la mémoire), f.
reticence ['retisəns], n. réticence, f.
reticent ['retisənt], a. réservé, taciturne.
reticular [re'tikjulə], a. réticulaire.
reticulate [re'tikjulit], a. réticulé.
retina ['retinə], n. rétine, f.
retinue ['retinju:], n. suite, f.; cortège, m.
retire [ri'taiə], v.t. retirer.—v.i. se retirer,
prendre sa retraite.
retired [ri'taiəd], a. retiré, retraité (qui a pris
sa retraite); ancien (qui n'exerce plus cette
profession); on the retired list, en retraite.
retirement [ri'taiəmənt], n. retraite; (fig.)
solitude, f.
retiring [ri'taiəriŋ], a. réservé, timide,
modeste; sortant (d'un emploi).
retort (1) [ri'tɔːt], n. réplique, riposte, f.—
v.i. riposter, répliquer.
retort (2) [ri'tɔːt], n. (Chem.) cornue, f.
retouch [ri:'tʌtʃ], v.t. retoucher.
retrace [ri'treis], v.t. (Paint.) retracer; to
retrace one's steps, revenir sur ses pas,
rebrousser chemin.
retract [ri'trækt], v.t. rétracter.—v.i. se
rétracter, se dédire.
retractable [ri'træktebl], a. (Av.) escamotable.
retransmit [ri:trɑːns'mit], v.t. retransmettre.
retread [ri:'tred], v.t. (Motor.) rechaper
(pneu).—['ri:tred], n. pneu rechapé, m.
retreat [ri'tri:t], n. retraite, f.—v.i. se retirer
(à ou dans); (Mil.) battre en retraite.
retreating [ri'tri:tiŋ], a. qui bat en retraite,
fuyant (le front).
retrench [ri'trentʃ], v.t. retrancher.—v.i. se
retrancher.
retrenchment [ri'trentʃmənt], n. retranchement, m.
retribution [retri'bju:ʃən], n. récompense,
rétribution, f.; (fig.) châtiment, m., vengeance, f.
retrievable [ri'tri:vəbl], a. recouvrable
(argent); réparable (perte).
retrieve [ri'tri:v], v.t. rétablir; réparer (chose
brisée); recouvrer (chose perdue); rapporter
(chien).
retriever [ri'tri:və], n. chien rapporteur, m.
retroaction [ri:trou'ækʃən], n. rétroaction, f.
retroactive [ri:trou'æktiv], a. rétroactif.
retrograde ['retrogreid], a. rétrograde.
retrogression [retro'greʃən], n. rétrogression, rétrogradation, f.
retrogressive [retro'gresiv], a. rétrogressif.
retrospect ['retrospekt], n. regard jeté en
arrière, m.; revue, f.; in retrospect, en
rétrospective.
retrospective [retro'spektiv], a. rétrospectif;
(Law) rétroactif.
retrospectively [retro'spektivli], adv.
rétrospectivement; (Law) rétroactivement.
retroversion [retro'və:ʃən], n. renversement, m.
retrovert [retro'və:t], v.t. renverser.
return [ri'tə:n], v.t. rendre; renvoyer; rembourser (argent etc.); rapporter (intérêt);
(Comm.) rendre compte; élire (candidat); he
was returned, il fut élu.—v.i. revenir;
retourner; rentrer.—n. retour, m.; rentrée, f.;
renvoi, m.; remise en place (chose déplacée),
f.; profit, m.; restitution, f.; remboursement,

541

m.; élection, *f.*; ra port, relevé, état (*impôts etc.*); bilan (*de banque*); (*pl.*) produit, *m.*; **by return mail**, par retour du courrier; **in return for**, en retour de; **nil return**, état néant; **on sale or return**, en dépôt; **return journey**, retour; **return match**, revanche, *f.*; **return ticket**, billet d'aller et retour, *m.*
returnable [ri'tə:nəbl], *a.* restituable.
reunion [ri:'ju:niən], *n.* réunion, *f.*
reunite [ri:ju'nait], *v.t.* réunir.—*v.i.* se réunir.
rev [rev], *n.* (*colloq., Motor.*) tour, *m.*—*v.t.* **to rev the engine**, faire s'emballer le moteur. —*v.i.* s'emballer.
reveal [ri'vi:l], *v.t.* révéler.
reveille [ri'væli], *n.* réveil, *m.*
revel [revl], *n.* (*pl.*) divertissements, *m.pl.*— *v.i.* se réjouir, se divertir; **to revel in**, se délecter à.
revelation [revə'leiʃən], *n.* révélation, *f.*; **Book of Revelation**, Apocalypse, *f.*
reveller ['revələ], *n.* joyeux convive, *m.*
revelry ['revəlri], *n.* réjouissances, *f.pl.*, joyeux ébats, *m.pl.*
revenge [ri'vendʒ], *n.* vengeance; (*Spt.*) revanche, *f.*—*v.t.* venger; se venger de; **to revenge oneself on**, se venger de.
revengeful [ri'vendʒful], *a.* vindicatif.
revengefully [ri'vendʒfuli], *adv.* par vengeance.
revenue ['revənju:], *n.* revenu, *f.*; (*State*) fisc, trésor, *m.*; **revenue officer**, officier de la douane, *m.*
reverberate [ri'və:bəreit], *v.t.* réverbérer; renvoyer (*son, chaleur etc.*).—*v.i.* se répercuter.
reverberation [rivə:bə'reiʃən], *n.* réverbération (*de chaleur*); répercussion, *f.*
revere [ri'viə], *v.t.* révérer, vénérer.
reverence ['revərəns], *n.* révérence, *f.*
reverend ['revərənd], *a.* révérend (*titre ecclésiastique*).
reverent ['revərənt], *a.* révérencieux.
reverently ['revərəntli], *adv.* avec révérence.
reverie ['revəri], *n.* rêverie, *f.*
reversal [ri'və:sl], *n.* annulation; cassation, *f.*
reverse [ri'və:s], *a.* contraire, opposé.—*n.* revers, *m.*; défaite, *f.*; **quite the reverse**, tout le contraire (*de*); **the reverse way**, en sens inverse.—*v.t.* renverser; appliquer en sens inverse; (*Law*) infirmer, casser.—*v.i.* (*Motor.*) faire marche ou machine en arrière.
reversed [ri'və:st], *a.* renversé; inverse.
reversible [ri'və:sibl], *a.* révocable, réversible, à double face (*tissu*).
reversion [ri'və:ʃən], *n.* réversion, *f.*
revert [ri'və:t], *v.i.* revenir (*sur*).
revertible [ri'və:tibl], *a.* réversible.
revetment [ri'vetmənt], *n.* revêtement, *m.*
revictual [ri:'vitl], *v.t.* ravitailler.
revictualling [ri:'vitliŋ], *n.* ravitaillement, *m.*
review [ri'vju:], *n.* revue, revision; critique; revue, *f.*, périodique, *m.*—*v.t.* revoir, reviser; passer en revue; analyser, critiquer (*livre etc.*).
reviewer [ri'vju:ə], *n.* critique, *m., f.*
revile [ri'vail], *v.t.* injurier, insulter, outrager.
revilement [ri'vailmənt], *n.* injure, insulte, *f.*
reviling [ri'vailiŋ], *a.* diffamatoire, outrageant. —*n.* insultes, injures, *f.pl.*
revisal [ri'vaizl], *n.* revision, *f.*
revise [ri'vaiz], *v.t.* revoir, reviser, réviser.

reviser [ri'vaizə], *n.* personne qui revoit, *f.*, reviseur, *m.*
revision [ri'viʒən], *n.* revision, révision, *f.*
revisit [ri:'vizit], *v.t.* revisiter, retourner voir.
revitalize [ri:'vaitəlaiz], *v.t.* revivifier.
revival [ri'vaivl], *n.* rétablissement, *m.*; renaissance (*des arts*); reprise (*d'une pièce*), *f.*; réveil (*religieux*), *m.*
revive [ri'vaiv], *v.t.* ressusciter; raviver.—*v.i.* se ranimer; renaître (*arts etc.*).
revivify (ri'vivifai], *v.t.* revivifier.
revoke ['revəkəbl], *a.* révocable.
revocation [revə'keiʃən], *n.* révocation, *f.*
revoke [ri'vouk], *v.t.* révoquer.—*v.i.* (*Cards*) renoncer.—*n.* (*Cards*) renonce, *f.*
revolt [ri'voult], *n.* révolte, *f.*—*v.i.* se révolter; se soulever.
revolting [ri'voultiŋ], *a.* révoltant.
revolution [revə'lju:ʃən], *n.* révolution, *f.*; tour (*de roue*), *m.*
revolutionary [revə'lju:ʃənəri], *a.* and *n.* révolutionnaire, *m., f.*
revolve [ri'vɔlv], *v.t.* tourner; retourner, repasser, rouler (*dans l'esprit*).—*v.i.* tourner; (*fig.*) retourner, revenir.
revolver [ri'vɔlvə], *n.* revolver, *m.*
revolving [ri'vɔlviŋ], *a.* tournant.
revue [ri'vju:], *n.* (*Theat.*) revue, *f.*
revulsion [ri'vʌlʃən], *n.* révulsion, *f.*
reward [ri'wɔ:d], *n.* récompense, *f.*; prix, *m.* —*v.t.* récompenser.
rewind [ri:'waind], *v.t.* irr. (*conjug. like* WIND) rebobiner (*soie etc.*); remonter (*montre, horloge*); rembobiner (*film*).
rewrite [ri:'rait], *v.t.* irr. (*conjug. like* WRITE) récrire.
rhapsody ['ræpsədi], *n.* rapsodie, *f.*
Rheims [ri:mz]. Reims, *m.*
Rhenish ['reniʃ], *a.* du Rhin.—*n.* vin du Rhin, *m.*
rheostat ['ri:ostæt], *n.* rhéostat, *m.*
rhesus ['ri:səs], *a.* (*Med.*) rhésus.
rhetoric ['retərik], *n.* rhétorique, *f.*
rhetorical [ri'tɔrikl], *a.* de rhétorique; **rhetorical question**, question de pure forme, *f.*
rheum [ru:m], *n.* rhume, catarrhe, *m.*
rheumatic [ru:'mætik], *a.* rhumatismal; **rheumatic fever**, rhumatisme articulaire aigu, *m.*
rheumatism ['ru:mətizm], *n.* rhumatisme, *m.*
rheumatoid ['ru:mətoid], *a.* rhumatoïde; **rheumatoid arthritis**, rhumatisme articulaire, *m.*
Rhine [rain], **the**. le Rhin, *m.*
Rhineland ['rainlænd]. la Rhénanie, *f.*
Rhinelander ['rainlændə], *n.* Rhénan, *m.*
rhinoceros [rai'nɔsərəs], *n.* rhinocéros, *m.*
Rhodesia [rou'di:ziə]. la Rhodésie, *f.*
Rhodesian [rou'di:ziən], *a.* rhodésien.—*n.* Rhodésien (*personne*), *m.*
rhododendron [roudə'dendrən], *n.* rhododendron, *m.*
rhombus ['rɔmbəs], *n.* losange, *m.*
Rhone [roun]. le Rhône, *m.*
rhubarb ['ru:bɑ:b], *n.* rhubarbe, *f.*
rhyme [raim], *n.* rime, *f.*; (*pl.*) vers, *m.pl.*— *v.t., v.i.* rimer; rimailler.
rhythm [riðm], *n.* rythme, *m.*; cadence, *f.*
rhythmical ['riðmikl], *a.* rythmique.
rhythmically ['riðmikli], *adv.* avec rythme.
rib [rib], *n.* côte; baleine (*de parapluie*), *f.*

ringworm

ribald ['ribəld], *a.* grossier, obscène.
ribaldry ['ribəldri], *n.* obscénités, *f.pl.*
ribbed [ribd], *a.* à côtes.
ribbon ['ribən], *n.* ruban; cordon (*de médaille*); lambeau (*morceau de tissu déchiré*), *m.*
rice [rais], *n.* riz, *m.*; *rice field*, rizière, *f.*
rich [ritʃ], *a.* riche; fertile, fécond (*terre*); de haut goût (*fort assaisonné*); voyant (*couleur*); (*fig.*) délicieux, généreux (*vin*); *the rich*, les riches, *m.pl.*; *to grow rich*, s'enrichir.
riches ['ritʃiz], *n.pl.* richesse, *f.*
richly ['ritʃli], *adv.* richement; grandement; (*fam.*) joliment.
richness ['ritʃnis], *n.* richesse; fécondité, *f.*; haut goût, *m.*
rick [rik], *n.* meule, *f.*
rickets ['rikits], *n.pl.* rachitis, rachitisme, *m.*
rickety ['rikiti], *a.* (*fig.*) boiteux (*meuble*).
rickshaw ['rikʃɔː], *n.* pousse-pousse, *m.*
ricochet ['rikəʃei], *n.* ricochet, *m.*—*v.i.* ricocher.
rid [rid], *v.t. irr.* délivrer, débarrasser; *to get rid of*, se débarrasser de.
riddance ['ridəns], *n.* débarras, *m.*
riddle (1) [ridl], *n.* énigme, *f.*
riddle (2) [ridl], *v.t.* cribler.—*n.* crible, *m.*
ride [raid], *v.t. irr.* monter, être monté sur; mener, conduire; faire (*une distance précise*).—*v.i.* monter (*à cheval, à bicyclette etc.*), aller, venir, être ou se promener (*à cheval, à bicyclette, en voiture etc.*); être monté (*sur*); flotter, voguer (*sur*); être (*à l'ancre*); *to ride away*, partir, s'en aller; *to ride back*, revenir, s'en retourner.—*n.* promenade, course (*à cheval, en voiture, à bicyclette etc.*), *f.*; trajet, *m.*; allée cavalière (*sentier dans un bois etc.*), *f.*
rider ['raidə], *n.* cavalier, *m.*, cavalière, *f.*; écuyer, *m.*, écuyère (*de cirque*), *f.*; jockey; codicille (*document*), *m.*
riderless ['raidəlis], *a.* sans cavalier.
ridge [ridʒ], *n.* sommet (*pic*), *m.*, cime; chaîne (*de montagnes*); arête, crête (*d'une montagne*) *f.*; faîte (*de toit*), *m.*; (*Agric.*) sillon, billon, *m.*—*v.t.* sillonner.
ridicule ['ridikjuːl], *n.* ridicule, *m.*—*v.t.* tourner en ridicule, ridiculiser.
ridiculous [ri'dikjuləs], *a.* ridicule.
ridiculously [ri'dikjuləsli], *adv.* ridiculement.
riding (1) ['raidiŋ], *n.* promenade à cheval, *f.*, exercice à cheval, *m.*, équitation, *f.*; (*Naut.*) mouillage, *m.*
riding (2) ['raidiŋ], *n.* (*Yorkshire*) arrondissement, *m.*
riding habit ['raidiŋhæbit], *n.* amazone, *f.*
riding hood ['raidiŋhud], *n.* capuchon, *m.*; *Little Red Riding Hood*, le petit Chaperon rouge.
rife [raif], *a.* abondant, répandu; *to be rife*, régner (*tumulte etc.*), courir (*bruit*).
riff-raff ['rifræf], *n.* racaille, canaille, *f.*
rifle (1) [raifl], *v.t.* piller, dévaliser.
rifle (2) [raifl], *v.t.* rayer (*armes à feu*).—*n.* fusil (*rayé*), *m.*, carabine, *f.*; *rifle gallery* or *range*, tir, *m.*; *rifle practice* or *shooting*, tir au fusil, tir à la carabine, *m.*; *rifle shot*, coup de fusil, *m.*
rifleman ['raiflmən], *n.* (*pl.* -men [men]) carabinier, *m.*
rifling (1) ['raifliŋ], *n.* pillage.

rifling (2) ['raifliŋ], *n.* rayage (*de fusils*), *m.*
rift [rift], *n.* fente; éclaircie (*aux nuages*), *f.*
rig [rig], *n.* gréement; accoutrement (*vêtements*), *m.*—*v.t.* équiper, gréer; (*fig.*) accoutrer, attifer.
rigged [rigd], *a.* gréé.
rigging ['rigiŋ], *n.* gréement, *m.*, agrès, *m.pl.*
right [rait], *a.* droit; direct, en ligne droite; vrai, véritable; bon, propre, convenable; juste, correct; en règle; *all right!* c'est bien! *that is right*, c'est cela; *the right man*, l'homme qu'il faut; *the right road*, le bon chemin; *to be right*, avoir raison; être juste (*compte*); *to put right*, mettre en bon ordre, arranger.—*adv.* droit, tout droit; justement (*avec justice*); comme il faut, bien (*correctement*); tout à fait (*entièrement*); fort (*beaucoup*); très.—*n.* droit, *m.*, justice, raison, *f.*; côté droit, *m.*, droite, *f.*; *on* or *to the right*, à droite; *right of way*, droit de passage; *to put* or *set to rights*, arranger, mettre en ordre.—*v.t.* redresser, corriger (*choses*).—*v.i.* se redresser, se relever.
righteous ['raitʃəs], *a.* juste, droit.
righteously ['raitʃəsli], *adv.* justement.
righteousness ['raitʃəsnis], *n.* droiture, vertu, *f.*
rightful ['raitful], *a.* légitime, véritable.
right-handed ['raithændid], *a.* droitier.
rightly ['raitli], *adv.* bien; à juste titre; comme il faut (*convenablement*); juste (*exactement*).
rightness ['raitnis], *n.* rectitude; droiture; justesse, *f.*
rigid ['ridʒid], *a.* rigide, raide.
rigidity [ri'dʒiditi], *n.* rigidité; raideur, *f.*
rigidly ['ridʒidli], *adv.* rigidement; avec raideur.
rigmarole ['rigməroul], *n.* galimatias, *m.*
rigor ['rigə, 'raigə], *n.* (*Path.*) rigidité, *f.*
rigor ['rigə], *n.* rigueur, *f.*
rigorous ['rigərəs], *a.* rigoureux.
rigorously ['rigərəsli], *adv.* rigoureusement, avec rigueur, à la rigueur.
rile [rail], *v.t.* (*colloq.*) faire enrager, agacer.
rill [ril], *n.* petit ruisseau, *m.*
rim [rim], *n.* bord, rebord, *m.*; jante (*de roue*), *f.*
rime [raim], *n.* givre, *m.*; gelée blanche, *f.*
rimless ['rimlis], *a.* sans monture (*lunettes*).
rind [raind], *n.* écorce, peau, pelure; croûte (*de fromage*); couenne (*de lard*), *f.*
ring (1) [riŋ], *n.* anneau, *m.*, bague (*pour le doigt etc.*), *f.*; cercle, rond, *m.*; arène (*pour se battre*), *f.*; ring (*pour la boxe*), *m.*; (*fig.*) bande, clique, *f.*; (*Comm.*) syndicat, *m.*—*v.t.* mettre un anneau à; entourer.
ring (2) [riŋ], *v.t. irr.* sonner, faire sonner; *to ring someone up*, téléphoner à quelqu'un.—*v.i.* sonner; retentir (*de*), tinter (*aux oreilles*).—*n.* son, tintement, coup de sonnette, *m.*; sonnerie, *f.*; *there's a ring at the door*, on sonne.
ring-dove ['riŋdʌv], *n.* pigeon ramier, *m.*
ringer ['riŋə], *n.* sonneur, *m.*
ringing ['riŋiŋ], *n.* son (*de cloche*), *m.*; sonnerie, *f.*, tintement, retentissement, *m.*
ringleader ['riŋliːdə], *n.* meneur, chef de bande, *m.*
ringlet ['riŋlit], *n.* boucle (*de cheveux*), *f.*
ring-road ['riŋroud], *n.* route de ceinture, *f.*
ringworm ['riŋwəːm], *n.* herpès tonsurant, *m.*

rink [riŋk], *n.* patinoire (*de glace*), *f.*; skating (*pour patinage à roulettes*), *m.*

rinse [rins], *v.t.* rincer.

riot ['raiət], *n.* émeute, *f.*; vacarme, tumulte (*bruit*), *m.*; (*fig.*) festins, *m.pl.*—*v.i.* faire une émeute.

rioter ['raiətə], *n.* émeutier; tapageur, *m.*

riotous ['raiətəs], *a.* séditieux, tumultueux.

rip (1) [rip], *v.t.* fendre, déchirer; **to rip open**, ouvrir.—*n.* déchirure, *f.*

rip (2) [rip], *n.* (*slang*) vaurien, polisson, *m.*

ripe [raip], *a.* mûr.

ripen ['raipən], *v.t.* mûrir, faire mûrir.—*v.i.* mûrir, venir à maturité.

ripeness ['raipnis], *n.* maturité, *f.*

ripening ['raipniŋ], *n.* maturation, *f.*

ripple [ripl], *v.t.* rider.—*v.i.* se rider; onduler. —*n.* ride (*d'eau*), *f.*

rippling ['ripliŋ], *n.* clapotis, murmure, *m.*

rip-roaring ['riprɔːriŋ], *a.* tumultueux; robuste; épatant.

rise [raiz], *v.i. irr.* se lever, se relever (*après une chute, un malheur etc.*); s'élever, monter; se dresser (*montagne etc.*); s'augmenter, hausser (*prix*); aller en montant (*rue*); se soulever (*rébellion*); ressusciter (*les morts*); prendre sa source (*en* ou *dans*).—*n.* lever, *m.*; montée (*de colline etc.*); crue (*des eaux*); hausse (*de prix*), augmentation; source, origine, *f.*

riser ['raizə], *n.* marche (*d'escalier*), *f.*; **early riser**, personne matinale, *f.*

risible ['rizibl], *a.* rieur.

rising ['raiziŋ], *a.* levant; montant (*marée*); (*fig.*) naissant; qui a de l'avenir (*qui promet*). —*n.* lever (*du lit, du soleil*), *m.*; montée (*de colline*); crue (*des eaux*), clôture (*d'assemblée*); résurrection, *f.*; soulèvement, *m.*, insurrection, *f.*

risk [risk], *n.* risque, *m.*—*v.t.* risquer.

risky ['riski], *a.* risqué, hasardeux.

rite [rait], *n.* rite, *m.*, cérémonie, *f.*

ritual ['ritjuəl], *a.* du rite.—*n.* rituel, *m.*

rival [raivl], *a. and n.* rival, *m.*—*v.t.* rivaliser avec.

rivalry ['raivlri], *n.* rivalité, *f.*

rive [raiv], *v.t. irr.* fendre.—*v.i.* se fendre.

river ['rivə], *a.* de rivière, fluvial.—*n.* fleuve (*qui débouche dans la mer*), *m.*; (*autrement*) rivière, *f.*; **down the river**, en aval; **up the river**, en amont.

riverside ['rivəsaid], *a.* au bord de l'eau.—*n.* bord de l'eau, *m.*

rivet ['rivit], *v.t.* river, riveter; attache (*de porcelaine*), *f.*—*v.t.* river, riveter; (*fig.*) fixer.

riveting ['rivitiŋ], *n.* rivetage, *m.*

rivulet ['rivjulit], *n.* ruisseau, *m.*

roach [routʃ], *n.* (*Ichth.*) gardon, *m.*

road [roud], *n.* route, *f.*, chemin, *m.*; chaussée; rue (*en ville*); (*Naut.*) rade, *f.*; **by-road**, chemin détourné; **carriage road**, route carrossable; **cross-roads**, carrefour, *m.*; **high road**, grand-route, *f.*; **roads and bridges**, ponts et chaussées, *m.pl.*

road hog ['roudhɔg], *n.* (*Motor.*) chauffard, *m.*

road-house ['roudhaus], *n.* auberge, hôtellerie, *f.*

road map ['roudmæp], *n.* carte routière, *f.*

road mender ['roudmendə], *n.* cantonnier, *m.*

road metal ['roudmetl], *n.* cailloutis, empierrement, *m.*

roadside ['roudsaid], *n.* bord de la route, *m.*; **by the roadside**, au bord de la route.

roadstead ['roudsted], *n.* rade, *f.*

roadway ['roudwei], *n.* chaussée; voie (*de pont*), *f.*

roadworthy ['roudwəːði], *a.* (*Motor.*) en état de marche.

roam [roum], *v.t.* rôder dans ou parmi.—*v.i.* errer, rôder.

roan [roun], *a.* rouan.

roar [rɔː], *n.* rugissement (*de lion etc.*); mugissement (*de la mer etc.*); éclat (*de rire*); grondement (*de tonnerre etc.*), *m.*—*v.i.* rugir (*lion etc.*); mugir (*mer etc.*); gronder (*tonnerre, canon etc.*); (*colloq.*) vociférer; **to roar with laughter**, rire aux éclats.

roaring ['rɔːriŋ], *a.* rugissant, mugissant; **to do a roaring trade**, faire des affaires d'or.

roast [roust], *v.t.* rôtir; faire rôtir; torréfier (*café*); (*Metal.*) griller.—*v.i.* rôtir; griller. —*a.* rôti; **roast beef**, rosbif, *m.*; **roast pork**, rôti de porc, *m.*

roaster ['roustə], *n.* rôtisseur (*personne*), *m.*; rôtissoire (*chose*), *f.*

roasting ['roustiŋ], *n.* (*Metal.*) brûlant.—*n.* grillage, *m.*; torréfaction (*de café*), *f.*

rob [rob], *v.t.* voler; piller; priver (*de*).

robber ['robə], *n.* voleur, *m.*

robbery ['robəri], *n.* vol, *m.*

robe [roub], *n.* robe, *f.*—*v.t.* vêtir (d'une robe); revêtir (*de*).

robin ['robin], **robin redbreast** [robin'red brest], *n.* (*Orn.*) rouge-gorge, *m.*

robot ['roubət], *n.* automate, robot, *m.*

robust [ro'bʌst], *a.* robuste, vigoureux.

robustness [ro'bʌstnis], *n.* robustesse, vigueur, *f.*

rock (1) [rok], *n.* rocher, roc, *m.*; (*Geol.*) roche, *f.*; sucre d'orge (*bonbon*), *m.*

rock (2) [rok], *v.t.* balancer; bercer, remuer.— *v.i.* se balancer; branler, trembler.

rockery ['rokəri], *n.* jardin de rocaille, *m.*

rocket ['rokit], *n.* fusée, *f.*; **rocket launcher**, lance-fusée.—*v.i.* monter en flèche (*prix*).

rockiness ['rokinis], *n.* nature rocailleuse, *f.*

rocking ['rokiŋ], *n.* balancement; bercement, *m.*

rocking chair ['rokiŋtʃeə], *n.* chaise à bascule, *f.*

rocking horse ['rokiŋhɔːs], *n.* cheval à bascule, *m.*

rock salt ['rɔksɔːlt], *n.* sel gemme, *m.*

rocky ['roki], *a.* rocailleux, rocheux.

rod [rod], *n.* verge, baguette; tringle (*à rideaux etc.*); canne à pêche; perche (= 5,0291 metres); bielle (*de piston*), *f.*

rodent ['roudənt], *n.* (*Zool.*) rongeur, *m.*

rodeo [ro'deiou], *n.* rodéo, *m.*

roe (1) [rou], *n.* œufs (*de poisson*), *m.pl.*

roe (2) [rou], *n.* chevreuil, *m.*, chevrette, *f.*

roebuck ['roubʌk], *n.* chevreuil, *m.*

Roger ['rodʒə], Roger, *m.*

rogue [roug], *n.* coquin, fripon, fourbe, *m.*

roguery ['rougəri], *n.* coquinerie, friponnerie, fourberie, *f.*

roguish ['rougiʃ], *a.* coquin, fripon; (*facet.*) espiègle.

roguishly ['rougiʃli], *adv.* en fripon, en fourbe; (*facet.*) avec espièglerie.

roister [ˈrɔistə], *v.i.* faire du tapage.
roisterer [ˈrɔistərə], *n.* tapageur, *m.*
roistering [ˈrɔistəriŋ], *a.* tapageur, bruyant. —*n.* tapage, *m.*
role [roul], *n.* rôle, *m.*
roll [roul], *n.* rouleau; roulement (*acte de rouler quelque chose*); roulis (*de navire*); petit pain; roulement (*de tambour*); rôle (*liste*), *m.*; (*pl.*) rôles, *m.pl.*; annales, archives, *f.pl.*—*v.t.* rouler; passer au rouleau (*gazon, gravier etc.*); (*Metal.*) laminer.—*v.i.* rouler, se rouler; tourner; (*Naut.*) avoir du roulis.
roll call [ˈroulkɔ:l], *n.* appel, *m.*
roller [ˈroulə], *n.* rouleau; cylindre, *m.*
roller skate [ˈrouləskeit], *n.* patin à roulettes, *m.*
rollicking [ˈrɔlikiŋ], *a.* folâtre, joyeux.
rolling [ˈrouliŋ], *n.* roulement; roulis (*de navire*); (*Metal.*) laminage, *m.*; ***rolling stock***, matériel roulant, *m.*
rolling pin [ˈrouliŋpin], *n.* rouleau, *m.*
Roman [ˈroumən], *a.* romain; aquilin (*nez*).—*n.* Romain (*personne*), *m.*
Romance [roˈmæns], *a.* roman; ***Romance languages***, langues romanes, *f.pl.*
romance [roˈmæns], *n.* roman de chevalerie, *m.*; histoire romanesque; (*Mus.*) romance; (*fam.*) amourette, aventure, *f.*—*v.i.* inventer à plaisir, exagérer, broder.
romanesque [rouməˈnesk], *a.* (*Arch.*) roman.
Romania [roˈmeiniə], [RUMANIA].
romantic [roˈmæntik], *a.* romanesque; romantique (*paysage, style etc.*).
romanticism [roˈmæntisizm], *n.* romantisme, *m.*
romanticist [roˈmæntisist], *n.* romantique, *m.*, *f.*
Rome [roum]. Rome, *f.*
romp [rɔmp], *n.* gamine, garçonnière (*jeune fille*), *f.*; jeu violent, tapage, *m.*—*v.i.* jouer rudement, folâtrer.
rompers [ˈrɔmpəz], *n.pl.* barboteuse, *f.*
romping [ˈrɔmpiŋ], *n.* jeux rudes, *m.pl.*
roof [ru:f], *n.* toit; palais (*de la bouche*), *m.*—*v.t.* couvrir d'un toit; couvrir.
roofing [ˈru:fiŋ], *n.* toiture, *f.*
roof rack [ˈru:fræk], *n.* (*Motor.*) galerie, *f.*
rook (1) [ruk], *n.* freux, *m.*, (*pop.*) corneille, *f.*; (*slang*) tricheur, *m.*—*v.t.*, *v.i.* (*slang*) friponner, filouter.
rook (2) [ruk], *n.* (*Chess*) tour, *f.*
rookery [ˈrukəri], *n.* colonie de freux, *f.*
rookie [ˈruki], *n.* (*slang*) bleu, *m.*
room [ru:m], *n.* place, *f.*, espace, *m.*; chambre, salle, pièce(*d'appartement*),*f.*[see **residence**]
roomful [ˈru:mful], *n.* chambrée, *f.*
roominess [ˈru:minis], *n.* nature spacieuse, grandeur, *f.*
roomy [ˈru:mi], *a.* spacieux, vaste.
roost [ru:st], *n.* juchoir, perchoir, *m.*—*v.i.* se jucher.
rooster [ˈru:stə], *n.* coq, *m.*
root [ru:t], *n.* racine; (*fig.*) source, *f.*—*v.t.* ***to root out***, déraciner, extirper.
rooted [ˈru:tid], *a.* enraciné; (*fig.*) invétéré.
rooting [ˈru:tiŋ], *n.* enracinement, *m.*; ***rooting out***, arrachement, *m.*, extirpation, *f.*
rope [roup], *n.* corde, *f.*; (*Naut.*) cordage, *m.*; (*Mount.*) cordée, *f.*; ***a piece of rope***, un bout de filin.—*v.t.* attacher avec une corde; lier.—*v.i.* filer (*vin etc.*); (*Mount.*) s'encorder.
rope-walker [ˈroupwɔ:kə], *n.* funambule, *m.*, *f.*
ropiness [ˈroupinis], *n.* viscosité, *f.*
ropy [ˈroupi], *a.* qui file, filant, visqueux.
rosary [ˈrouzəri], *n.* chapelet, *m.*
rose (1) [rouz], *n.* rose; (*Tech.*) pomme d'arrosoir; (*Arch.*) rosace, *f.*
rose (2) [rouz], *past* [RISE].
roseate [ˈrouziit], *a.* rosé.
rose bed [ˈrouzbed], *n.* massif de rosiers, *m.*
rosebud [ˈrouzbʌd], *n.* bouton de rose, *m.*
rose-bush [ˈrouzbuʃ], *n.* rosier, *m.*
rose garden [ˈrouzgɑ:dn], *n.* roseraie, *f.*
rosemary [ˈrouzməri], *n.* romarin, *m.*
rosette [roˈzet], *n.* rosette, *f.*
rose window [ˈrouzwindou], *n.* rosace, *f.*
rosin [ˈrɔzin], *n.* colophane, *f.*
rosiness [ˈrouzinis], *n.* couleur rose, *f.*
rostrum [ˈrɔstrəm], *n.* (*Rom. Hist.*) rostres, *m.pl.*; tribune (*estrade*), *f.*
rosy [ˈrouzi], *a.* de rose, rose, rosé, vermeil.
rot [rɔt], *n.* pourriture; (*colloq.*) blague, *f.*—*v.t.* pourrir, faire pourrir; carier (*dent*).—*v.i.* pourrir, se pourrir; se carier (*dent*).
rota [ˈroutə], *n.* ***by rota***, à tour de rôle.
rotary [ˈroutəri], *a.* rotatif, rotatoire.
rotate [roˈteit], *v.t.*, *v.i.* tourner.
rotation [roˈteiʃən], *n.* rotation, succession, *f.*; ***rotation of crops***, assolement, *m.*
rote [rout], *n.* routine, *f.*; ***by rote***, par cœur.
rotten [rɔtn], *a.* pourri; carié (*dent*); gâté (*œuf*).
rottenness [ˈrɔtnnis], *n.* pourriture; carie (*des dents*), *f.*
rotter [ˈrɔtə], *n.* (*fam.*) sale type, *m.*
rotting [ˈrɔtiŋ], *a.* qui pourrit; qui se carie.—*n.* putréfaction, *f.*
rotund [roˈtʌnd], *a.* rond, arrondi.
rotundity [roˈtʌnditi], *n.* rondeur, rotondité, *f.*
rouble [ru:bl], *n.* rouble, *m.*
rouge [ru:ʒ], *n.* rouge, fard, *m.*
rough [rʌf], *a.* rude; hérissé; raboteux (*chemin*); grosse, houleuse (*mer*); orageux (*temps*); âpre (*goût*); dépoli (*verre*); grossier (*manières*); approximatif (*pas exact*); ***rough-and-ready***, fait à la va-vite; ***rough copy*** or ***draft***, brouillon, *m.*; ***rough estimate***, appréciation en gros, *f.*—*adv.* brutalement, rudement.—*n.* voyou, polisson, *m.*; ***rough-and-tumble***, mêlée, bousculade, *f.*
roughcast [ˈrʌfkɑ:st], *v.t.* ébaucher; (*Build.*) crépir.—*n.* ébauche, *f.*; (*Build.*) crépi, *m.*
roughen [rʌfn], *v.t.* rendre rude.
rough-hewn [ˈrʌfhju:n], *a.* ébauché.
rough-house [ˈrʌfhaus], *n.* (*fam.*) chahut, *m.*
roughly [ˈrʌfli], *adv.* rudement; grossièrement; à peu près.
roughness [ˈrʌfnis], *n.* aspérité, rudesse; apreté (*au goût*); agitation (*de la mer*); grossièreté (*de manières*), *f.*; mauvais état (*de rue*), *m.*
round [raund], *a.* rond; circulaire; en rond.—*adv.* en rond; à la ronde; tout autour, à l'entour; ***to go round***, faire le tour de.—*prep.* autour de.—*n.* rond, cercle; tour (*petite promenade*), *m.*; rouelle (*de bœuf etc.*); salve (*d'applaudissements*), *f.*; (*Artill.*) coup de canon, *m.*; ronde (*de veilleurs, police etc.*); (*Golf*) tournée, *f.*; (*Box.*) round, *m.*; ***round***

of ammunition, cartouche, *f.*—*v.t.* arrondir; entourer, faire le tour de (*faire un cercle*); doubler (*cap*); *to round off*, arrondir, finir, compléter; *to round up*, rassembler (*bestiaux etc.*); faire une rafle.—*v.i.* s'arrondir.

roundabout ['raundəbaut], *a.* détourné; indirect.—*n.* manège; (*Motor.*) rondpoint, *m.*

rounded ['raundid], *a.* arrondi.

*roundelay ['raundəlei], *n.* rondeau, *m.*

rounders ['raundəz], *n.pl.* balle au camp, *f.*

roundish ['raundiʃ], *a.* arrondi; rondelet (*personne*).

roundly ['raundli], *adv.* en rond; (*fig.*) rondement.

roundness ['aundnis], *n.* rondeur; (*fig.*) franchise, *f.*

round trip, see **return**.

round-up ['raundʌp], *n.* rassemblement (*de bétail*), *m.*; rafle (*de criminels*), *f.*

roup [ru:p], *n.* pépie (*maladie de volaille*), *f.*

rouse [rauz], *v.t.* éveiller, (*fig.*) réveiller, exciter.

rout [raut], *n.* cohue; déroute (*d'une armée*), *f.*—*v.t.* mettre en déroute.

route [ru:t], *n.* itinéraire, parcours, *m.*—*v.t.* router (*circulation, colis etc.*).

route map ['ru:tmæp], *n.* carte routière, *f.*

routine [ru:'ti:n], *n.* routine, *f.*

rove [rouv], *v.i.* rôder, courir.

rover ['rouvə], *n.* rôdeur, vagabond; pirate; (*Scouting*) éclaireur chevalier, *m.*

roving ['rouviŋ], *a.* errant, vagabond.

row (1) [rau], *n.* tapage, vacarme, *m.*; querelle, scène, *f.*

row (2) [rou], *n.* rang, *m.*, rangée, file; colonne (*de chiffres*), *f.*

row (3) [rou], *n.* promenade en bateau, *f.*—*v.t.* (*Naut.*) faire aller à la rame.—*v.i.* ramer; (*Naut.*) nager.

rowan ['rauən], *n.* (*Sc.*) sorbier des oiseaux, *m.*

rowdy ['raudi], *a.* tapageur.—*n.* voyou, gredin, *m.*

rowdyism ['raudiizm], **rowdiness** ['raudinis], *n.* tapage, *m.*

rower ['rouə], *n.* rameur; (*Naut.*) nageur, *m.*

rowing ['rouiŋ], *n.* canotage, *m.*

rowing-boat ['rouiŋbout], *n.* bateau à rames, *m.*

rowlock ['rʌlək], *n.* tolet, *m.*, dame, *f.*

royal ['rɔiəl], *a.* royal, de roi.

royalist ['rɔiəlist], *a.* and *n.* royaliste, *m.*, *f.*

royally ['rɔiəli], *adv.* royalement, en roi.

royalty ['rɔiəlti], *n.* royauté; (*usu. pl.*) commission, *f.*, droit d'auteur, *m.*

rub [rʌb], *v.t., v.i.* frotter; (*Med.*) frictionner.—*n.* frottement; coup de brosse, *m.*; (*fig.*) difficulté, *f.*, obstacle, *m.*

rubber (1) ['rʌbə], *n.* frotteur; frottoir (*chose*), *m.*; (*pl.*) (*Am.*) caoutchoucs (*chaussures*), *m.pl.*; **India rubber**, caoutchouc, *m.*, gomme (à effacer), *f.*

rubber (2) ['rʌbə], *n.* (*Cards*) rob, *m.*

rubber-stamp ['rʌbəstæmp], *n.* tampon; (*fig.*) béni-oui-oui, *m.*—*v.t.* ratifier.

rubbing ['rʌbiŋ], *n.* frottement; frottage, *m.*; (*Med.*) friction, *f.*

rubbish ['rʌbiʃ], *n.* débris, *m.pl.*; ordures, *f.pl.*; fatras (*sottises*), *m.*

rubbish bin ['rʌbiʃbin], *n.* poubelle, *f.*

rubbish cart ['rʌbiʃkɑːt], *n.* tombereau, *m.*

rubbish dump ['rʌbiʃdʌmp], *n.* dépotoir, *m.*

rubbishy ['rʌbiʃi], *a.* de rebut, sans valeur.

rubble ['rʌbl], *n.* blocaille, *f.*, moellons; décombres, *m.pl.*

rubicund ['ru:bikənd], *a.* rubicond.

rubric ['ru:brik], *n.* rubrique, *f.*

ruby ['ru:bi], *a.* de rubis, vermeil.—*n.* rubis, *m.*; teinte rouge, *f.*, incarnat, *m.*

ruck [rʌk], *n.* peloton (*de coureurs, cyclistes*), *m.*

rucksack ['rʌksæk], *n.* sac à dos, *m.*

ruction ['rʌkʃən], *n.* (*colloq.*) bagarre, dispute, *f.*

rudder ['rʌdə], *n.* gouvernail, *m.*

ruddiness ['rʌdinis], *n.* rougeur, *f.*

ruddy ['rʌdi], *a.* rouge, au teint vermeil.

rude [ru:d], *a.* grossier, impoli; (*fig.*) rude, violent.

rudely ['ru:dli], *adv.* grossièrement; rudement.

rudeness ['ru:dnis], *n.* rudesse; grossièreté; insolence; violence, *f.*

rudiment ['ru:dimənt], *n.* rudiment, *m.*

rudimentary [ru:di'mentri], *a.* rudimentaire.

rue [ru:], *v.t.* se repentir de, regretter.

rueful ['ru:ful], *a.* triste; lamentable.

ruefully ['ru:fuli], *adv.* tristement, déplorablement.

ruff [rʌf], *n.* fraise, collerette, *f.*

ruffian ['rʌfiən], *n.* bandit, *m.*; brute, *f.*

ruffianism ['rʌfiənizm], *n.* brutalité, *f.*

ruffianly ['rʌfiənli], *a.* de brigand, brutal.

ruffle [rʌfl], *n.* manchette, ruche, *f.*—*v.t.* froncer (*le front etc.*); froisser (*sentiments*); ébouriffer (*les cheveux*).

rug [rʌg], *n.* couverture, *f.*; tapis, *m.*

rugby ['rʌgbi], *n.* (*Spt.*) rugby, *m.*

rugged ['rʌgid], *a.* rude; raboteux; âpre; bourru (*personne*).

ruggedness ['rʌgidnis], *n.* rudesse, âpreté, *f.*

ruin ['ru:in], *n.* ruine; perte, *f.*—*v.t.* ruiner.

ruination [ru:i'neiʃən], *n.* perte, *f.*

ruinous ['ru:inəs], *a.* ruineux; en ruine.

ruinously ['ru:inəsli], *adv.* ruineusement.

rule [ru:l], *n.* règle, *f.*; règlement; gouvernement, empire (*domination*), *m.*; (*Law*) ordonnance, *f.*; *as a rule*, en général, d'ordinaire.—*v.t.* régler, diriger; gouverner, régir; (*Law*) décider.—*v.i.* gouverner; (*Law*) décider; *to rule over*, régner sur.

ruler ['ru:lə], *n.* gouvernant, souverain, *m.*; règle (*instrument*), *f.*

ruling ['ru:liŋ], *a.* dominant, régnant, dirigeant.—*n.* (*Law*) ordonnance de juge, décision, *f.*

rum (1) [rʌm], *a.* drôle; (*colloq.*) cocasse.

rum (2) [rʌm], *n.* rhum, *m.*

Rumania [ru:'meinjə], la Roumanie, *f.*

Rumanian [ru:'meinjən], *a.* roumain.—*n.* roumain (*langue*); Roumain (*personne*), *m.*

rumba ['rʌmbə], *n.* rumba, *f.*

rumble ['rʌmbl], *v.i.* gronder, gargouiller.

rumbling ['rʌmbliŋ], *a.* qui gronde; qui gargouille.—*n.* grondement; gargouillement, *m.*

rumbustious [rʌm'bʌstjəs], *a.* (*fam.*) turbulent, tapageur.

ruminant ['ru:minənt], *a.* and *n.* ruminant, *m.*

ruminate ['ru:mineit], *v.i.* ruminer.

rumination [ru:mi'neiʃən], *n.* rumination, *f.*

rummage ['rʌmidʒ], v.t., v.i. fouiller.—n. remue-ménage, m.

rummage sale ['rʌmidʒseil], n. vente d'objets usagés, f.

rumor ['ru:mə], n. rumeur, f.; bruit, m.—v.t. faire courir le bruit de.

rump [rʌmp], n. croupe; culotte (de viande), f.; croupion (de volaille), m.

rumple [rʌmpl], v.t. chiffonner, froisser.—n. pli, m., froissure, f.

rumpus ['rʌmpəs], n. (colloq.) tapage, m.

run [rʌn] (stocking), see **ladder**.

run [rʌn], v.t. irr. courir; encourir; faire courir, faire marcher, conduire (machines); pousser, enfoncer; diriger, exploiter, tenir; **to run down,** dénigrer (décrier); (Hunt.) forcer; **to run for,** courir chercher; **to run in,** enfoncer; arrêter, coffrer; (Motor.) rôder; **to run out,** faire sortir; épuiser; **to run over,** (Motor.) écraser (personne, animal); **to run up,** monter en courant.—v.i. courir; accourir (s'approcher); se sauver (s'échapper); s'étendre; fuir (bateau); couler (liquide); se fondre (couleurs); fondre (se dissoudre); être (exister); courir, circuler; faire le service (autobus etc.); marcher, être en marche (mécanisme); s'écouler (temps); pleurer (les yeux); rouler (avancer en tournant); devenir; filer (navire etc.); suppurer (ulcère etc.); monter (somme); (Am.) se présenter (aux élections); **to run about,** courir çà et là; **to run after,** chercher; **to run against,** courir contre; **to run aground,** échouer; **to run at,** attaquer; **to run away,** se sauver, s'emballer (cheval); s'écouler (liquide etc.); **to run down,** descendre en courant, aller, venir, couler (liquide); s'arrêter (mécanisme); **to run from,** s'enfuir de; **to run for office,** se **stand;** **to run out,** courir dehors; couler, fuir; se terminer, expirer, tirer à sa fin; descendre (marée); **to run over,** déborder (liquide etc.); **to run through,** passer à travers de, parcourir; gaspiller; **to run up,** courir en haut, monter; **to run up to,** s'élever à, monter à.—n. course (action de courir), f.; cours (série); trajet, voyage, m.; durée, f., succès (vogue), m.; irruption (dans une banque etc.), f.; commun (généralité), m.; **in the long run,** à la longue, à la fin.

runaway ['rʌnəwei], a. emballé (cheval).—n. fuyard; fugitif, déserteur, m.

rung (1) [rʌŋ], n. échelon (d'échelle); bâton (de chaise etc.), m.

rung (2) [rʌŋ], p.p. [RING (2)].

runner ['rʌnə], n. coureur; messager, courrier; (Bot.) rejeton, m.; **scarlet runner,** haricot d'Espagne, m.

running ['rʌniŋ], a. courant; de suite (consécutivement).—n. course, f.; écoulement (d'eau), m.

runt [rʌnt], n. bétail petit ou chétif; (fig.) avorton, nain, m.

runway ['rʌnwei], n. (Av.) piste d'envol, f.

rupee [ru:'pi:], n. roupie, f.

rupture ['rʌptʃə], n. rupture; (Med.) hernie, f.—v.t. rompre.—v.i. se rompre.

rural ['ruərəl], a. champêtre, rural, rustique.

ruse [ru:z], n. ruse, f., stratagème, m.

rush (1) [rʌʃ], n. (Bot.) jonc, m.

rush (2) [rʌʃ], n. ruée, f., mouvement précipité, m.; foule, presse (gens), f.—v.t. en-

trainer brusquement; dépêcher; envahir.—v.i. se jeter, se ruer, se précipiter (sur).

rushing ['rʌʃiŋ], a. impétueux.—n. élan, m., précipitation, f.

rusk [rʌsk], n. biscotte, f.

russet ['rʌsit], a. roussâtre.—n. roux, m.; reinette grise (pomme), f.

Russia ['rʌʃə], la Russie, f.

Russian ['rʌʃən], a. russe, de Russie.—n. russe (langue), m.; Russe (personne), m., f.

rust [rʌst], n. rouille, f.—v.i. se rouiller.

rustic ['rʌstik], a. rustique, champêtre.—n. rustre, paysan, m.

rusticate ['rʌstikeit], v.t. reléguer à la campagne; (Univ.) renvoyer temporairement.—v.i. se retirer à ou habiter la campagne.

rustication [rʌsti'keiʃən], n. villégiature, f.; (Univ.) renvoi temporaire, m.

rusticity [rʌs'tisiti], n. simplicité, rusticité, f.

rustiness ['rʌstinis], n. rouille, f.

rustle [rʌsl], v.t. (Am.) voler (du bétail).—v.i. bruire, frémir; faire frou-frou (robe); **to rustle against,** frôler.—n. frôlement; bruissement; frou-frou (de robe), m.

rustler ['rʌslə], n. (Am.) voleur de bétail, m.

rustless ['rʌstlis], a. inoxydable.

rustling ['rʌsliŋ], a. qui fait frou-frou, frémissant.—n. (Am.) vol de bétail, m.

rusty ['rʌsti], a. rouillé; roux (couleur).

rut [rʌt], n. ornière (de route), f.—v.i. sillonner d'ornières.

ruthless ['ru:θlis], a. impitoyable, insensible.

ruthlessly ['ru:θlisli], adv. sans pitié, sans merci.

ruthlessness ['ru:θlisnis], n. cruauté, inhumanité, f.

Rwanda ['rwʌndə]. le Rwanda, le Ruanda, m.

rye [rai], n. seigle, m.

rye grass ['raigro:s], n. ivraie, f., ray-grass, m.

S

S, s [es]. dix-neuvième lettre de l'alphabet, m.

Saar [sɑ:]. la Sarre, f.

Sabbath ['sæbəθ], n. (Jews) sabbat; dimanche; (fig.) repos, m.

sabbatic [sə'bætik], **sabbatical** [sə'bætikəl], a. sabbatique, du sabbat.

saber ['seibə], n. sabre, m.—v.t. sabrer.

sable [seibl], a. de zibeline, de martre; (Her.) de sable.—n. martre, zibeline, f.; (Her.) sable, m.

sabot ['sæbou], n. sabot, m.

sabotage ['sæbətɑ:ʒ], n. sabotage, m.—v.t. saboter.

saboteur [sæbə'tə:], n. saboteur, m.

sac [sæk], n. (Anat.) sac, m.; bourse, f.

saccharine ['sækərin], n. saccharine, f.

sacerdotal [sæsə'doutl], a. sacerdotal.

sack (1) [sæk], n. sac, m.; **to get the sack,** (colloq.) être renvoyé; **to give the sack to,** renvoyer, congédier.—v.t. (colloq.) congédier.

sack (2) [sæk], n. sac, saccagement (d'une ville), m.—v.t. saccager, mettre à sac.

sackcloth ['sækklɔθ], *n.* toile à sac, *f.*
sackful ['sækful], *n.* sac plein, *m.*, sachée, *f.*
sacking (1) ['sækiŋ], *n.* toile à sac, *f.*
sacking (2) ['sækiŋ], *n.* sac, saccagement (*de ville*), *m.*
sacrament ['sækrəmənt], *n.* sacrement, *m.*
sacramental [sækrə'mentl], *a.* sacramentel.
sacred ['seikrid], *a.* sacré; saint (*histoire etc.*); (*fig.*) inviolable.
sacredly ['seikridli], *adv.* saintement; religieusement.
sacredness ['seikridnis], *n.* sainteté, *f.*, caractère sacré, *m.*
sacrifice ['sækrifais], *v.t.*, *v.i.* sacrifier.—*n.* sacrifice, *m.*; victime, *f.*
sacrificer ['sækrifaisə], *n.* sacrificateur, *m.*
sacrificial [sækri'fiʃl], *a.* des sacrifices, sacrificatoire.
sacrilege ['sækrilidʒ], *n.* sacrilège, *m.*
sacrilegious [sækri'lidʒəs], *a.* sacrilège.
sacrilegiously [sækri'lidʒəsli], *adv.* d'une manière sacrilège.
sacrilegiousness [sækri'lidʒəsnis], *n.* caractère sacrilège, *m.*
sacristy ['sækristi], *n.* sacristie, *f.*
sacrosanct ['sækrosæŋkt], *a.* sacro-saint.
sad [sæd], *a.* triste; pitoyable, déplorable; cruel (*perte*)
sadden [sædn], *v.t.* attrister.—*v.i.* s'attrister.
saddle [sædl], *n.* selle, *f.*; **pack-saddle**, bât, *m.*; **side-saddle**, selle d'amazone.—*v.t.* seller; charger, accabler.
saddle-bag ['sædlbæg], *n.* sacoche, *f.*
saddle-bow ['sædlbou], *n.* arçon, *m.*
saddler ['sædlə], *n.* sellier, *m.*
saddle room ['sædlru:m], *n.* sellerie, *f.*
saddlery ['sædləri], *n.* sellerie, *f.*
sadism ['seidizm], *n.* sadisme, *m.*
sadist ['seidist], *n.* sadique, *m.*, *f.*
sadistic [sə'distik], *a.* sadique.
sadly ['sædli], *adv.* tristement; mal, beaucoup, grandement.
sadness ['sædnis], *n.* tristesse, *f.*
safe [seif], *a.* sauf, en sûreté; à l'abri (*de*); sûr; *safe and sound*, sain et sauf.—*n.* coffre-fort (*pour l'argent*); garde-manger (*pour aliments*), *m.*
safe-conduct ['seif'kɔndʌkt], *n.* sauf-conduit, *m.*
safeguard ['seifgɑ:d], *n.* sauvegarde, *f.*—*v.t.* sauvegarder.
safe-keeping ['seif'ki:piŋ], *n.* bonne garde, sûreté, *f.*
safely ['seifli], *adv.* sain et sauf; en sûreté.
safety ['seifti], *a.* de sûreté.—*n.* sûreté, *f.*, salut, *m.*
safety catch ['seiftikætʃ], *n.* cran de sûreté, cran d'arrêt, *m.*
safety lamp ['seiftilæmp], *n.* lampe de sûreté, *f.*
safety match ['seiftimætʃ], *n.* allumette suédoise, *f.*
safety pin ['seiftipin], *n.* épingle de sûreté, *f.*
safety valve ['seiftivælv], *n.* soupape de sûreté, *f.*
saffron ['sæfrən], *a.* couleur safran; de safran. —*n.* safran, *m.*
saffrony ['sæfrəni], *a.* safrané.
sag [sæg], *v.i.* plier, ployer, s'affaisser; se relâcher (*câble*).
saga ['sɑ:gə], *n.* saga, *f.*

sagacious [sə'geiʃəs], *a.* sagace; intelligent (*animal*).
sagaciously [sə'geiʃəsli], *adv.* avec sagacité.
sagaciousness [sə'geiʃəsnis], **sagacity** [sə'gæsiti], *n.* sagacité, *f.*
sage (1) [seidʒ], *a.* sage, prudent.—*n.* sage, *m.*
sage (2) [seidʒ], *n.* sauge (*herbes*), *f.*
sagely ['seidʒli], *adv.* sagement, prudemment.
sagging ['sægiŋ], *a.* affaissé, fléchi, ployé.—*n.* courbure, *f.*, affaissement, *m.*; baisse (*de prix*), *f.*
sago ['seigou], *n.* sagou; sagouier, sagoutier (*arbre*), *m.*
sagy ['seidʒi], *a.* qui a un goût de sauge.
Sahara [sə'hɑ:rə], *the.* le Sahara, *m.*
said [sed], *a.* dit, susdit [SAY].
sail [seil], *n.* voile, *f.*; (*collect.*) voiles, *f.pl.*, voilure; aile (*de moulin à vent*); course ou promenade à la voile (*sur l'eau*), *f.*—*v.t.* naviguer (*sur*), voguer (*sur ou dans*).—*v.i.* faire voile; cingler, naviguer; mettre à la voile, appareiller.
sailable ['seiləbl], *a.* navigable.
sail-cloth ['seilklɔθ], *n.* toile à voiles, *f.*
sailing ['seiliŋ], *a.* à voiles.—*n.* navigation, *f.*; appareillage, *m.*; partance (*départ*), *f.*
sailing boat ['seiliŋbout], *n.* bateau à voiles, *m.*
sailing ship ['seiliŋʃip], *n.* bâtiment à voiles voilier, *m.*
sail-maker ['seilmeikə], *n.* voilier, *m.*
sailor ['seilə], *n.* marin, matelot, *m.*
saint [seint] *strong form,* [sənt] *weak form,* *n.* saint, *m.*, sainte, *f.*; *All Saints' Day,* la Toussaint, *f.*
saintliness ['seintlinis], *n.* sainteté, *f.*
saintly ['seintli], *a.* saint; de saint, vénérable.
sake [seik], *n.* (*used only with* FOR); *art for art's sake,* l'art pour l'art; *for God's sake,* pour l'amour de Dieu; *for the sake of appearances,* pour sauver des apparences; *for the sake of health,* pour cause de santé; *for your sake,* par égard pour vous.
sal [sæl], *n.* sel, *m.*
salaam [sə'lɑ:m], *n.* salamalec, *m.*
salad ['sæləd], *n.* salade, *f.*
salad bowl ['sælədboul], *n.* saladier, *m.*
salad oil ['sælədɔil], *n.* huile de table, *f.*
salamander ['sæləmændə], *n.* salamandre, *f.*
salaried ['sælərid], *a.* qui touche des appointements.
salary ['sæləri], *n.* appointements, *m.pl.*; traitement (*de fonctionnaire*), *m.*
sale [seil], *n.* vente; mise en vente, *f.*; *for sale,* à vendre; *on sale,* en vente; *private sale,* vente à l'amiable; *sale by auction,* vente aux enchères; *to put up for sale,* mettre en vente.
saleable ['seiləbl], *a.* vendable; de bonne vente.
sale-room ['seilru:m], *n.* salle des ventes, *f.*
salesman ['seilzmən], *n.* (*pl.* **-men** [men]) vendeur, marchand; courtier de commerce, *m.*
Salic ['sælik], *a.* salique.
salient ['seiliənt], *a.* and *n.* saillant, *m.*
saliently ['seiliəntli], *adv.* d'une manière saillante.
salify ['sælifai], *v.t.* salifier.
saline ['seilain], *a.* salin.
saliva [sə'laivə], *n.* salive, *f.*

548

salivate ['sæliveit], *v.t.* faire saliver.
sallow ['sælou], *a.* jaunâtre, jaune, blême.
sallowness ['sælounis], *n.* teint blême, *m.*
sally ['sæli], *n.* sortie; (*fig.*) excursion; saillie (*d'esprit*), *f.—v.i.* sortir, faire une sortie.
salmon ['sæmən], *n.* saumon, *m.*
salmon trout ['sæmən'traut], *n.* truite saumonée, *f.*
saloon [sə'lu:n], *n.* (grand) salon, *m.*, salle; (*Am.*) buvette, *f.*, bar, *m.*; conduite-intérieure (*voiture*), *f.*
salsify ['sælsifi], *n.* (*Bot.*) salsifis, *m.*
salt [sɔːlt], *a.* salé; de sel.—*n.* sel, *m.*; *Epsom salts*, sels anglais, *m.pl.—v.t.* saler.
salt-cellar ['sɔːlt'selə], *n.* salière, *f.*
salted ['sɔːltid], *a.* salé; (*fig.*) aguerri.
salter ['sɔːltə], *n.* saunier; saleur, *m.*
salting ['sɔːltiŋ], *n.* salaison, *f.*, salage, *m.*
saltish ['sɔːltiʃ], *a.* un peu salé, saumâtre.
saltless ['sɔːltlis], *a.* sans sel; (*fig.*) insipide.
salt marsh ['sɔːltmɑːʃ], *n.* marais salant, *m.*
salt mine ['sɔːltmain], *n.* mine de sel, *f.*
saltness [sɔːltnis], *n.* salure, *f.*
saltpeter [sɔːlt'pi:tə], *n.* salpêtre, *m.*
saltpeter-works [sɔːlt'pi:təwə:ks], *n.pl.* salpêtrière, *f.*
saltpetrous [sɔːlt'petrəs], *a.* salpêtreux.
salt water ['sɔːltwɔːtə], *n.* eau de mer, *f.*
salty ['sɔːlti], *a.* salé; qui a un goût de sel.
salubrious [sə'lju:briəs], *a.* salubre, sain.
salubriously [sə'lju:briəsli], *adv.* d'une manière salubre.
salubrity [sə'lju:briti], *n.* salubrité, *f.*
salutary ['sæljutəri], *a.* salutaire.
salutation [sælju'teiʃən], *n.* salut, *m.*, salutation, *f.*
salute [sə'lju:t], *n.* salut, *m.*, salutation, salve (*de fusils*), *f.—v.t.* saluer.
Salvador ['sælvədɔ:], **El.** le Salvador, *m.*
Salvadorean [sælvə'dɔ:riən], *a.* salvadorègne.—*n.* Salvadorègne (*personne*), *m.*, *f.*
salvage ['sælvidʒ], *n.* sauvetage, *m.*, objets sauvés, *m.pl.*; (*Ind.*) récupération, *f.—v.t.* récupérer; relever (*navire*).
salvage money ['sælvidʒmʌni], *n.* prix *ou* droit de sauvetage, *m.*
salvage vessel ['sælvidʒvesl], *n.* navire de relevage, *m.*
salvation [sæl'veiʃən], *n.* salut, *m.*; *Salvation Army*, Armée du Salut, *f.*
salve [sælv, sɑːv], *n.* onguent; (*fig.*) remède, baume, *m.—*[sælv], *v.t.* remédier à; (*Naut.*) sauver, sauveter.
salver ['sælvə], *n.* plateau, *m.*
salvo ['sælvou], *n.* réserve, restriction; salve (*d'artillerie*), *f.*
Samaritan [sə'mæritən], *a.* samaritain.—*n.* Samaritain (*personne*), *m.*
same [seim], *a.* même.—*n.* le même.—*n.* la même; même chose, *f.*; ledit, *m.*, ladite, *f.*, lesdits, *m.pl.*; lesdites, *f.pl.*; *all the same*, néanmoins, quand même; *it is all the same*, c'est égal; *just the same*, tout de même; *much about the same*, à peu près de même; *the same to you*, et vous de même.
sameness ['seimnis], *n.* identité, uniformité, *f.*
sample [sɑːmpl], *n.* échantillon, *m.—v.t.* échantillonner; déguster (*vin*).
sampler ['sɑːmplə], *n.* modèle; (*Needlework*) canevas, *m.*

sampling ['sɑːmpliŋ], *n.* échantillonnage, *m.*; gustation (*des mets*), *f.*
sanatorium [sænə'tɔ:riəm], *n.* sanatorium, *m.*
sanctification [sæŋktifi'keiʃən], *n.* sanctification, *f.*
sanctified ['sæŋktifaid], *a.* sanctifié, saint.
sanctify ['sæŋktifai], *v.t.* sanctifier.
sanctimonious [sæŋkti'mouniəs], *a.* papelard, béat, hypocrite.
sanctimoniously [sæŋkti'mouniəsli], *adv.* d'un air béat.
sanctimoniousness [sæŋkti'mouniəsnis], *n.* dévotion affectée; cagoterie, *f.*
sanction ['sæŋkʃən], *n.* sanction, autorité, *f.—v.t.* sanctionner, autoriser.
sanctity ['sæŋktiti], *n.* sainteté, *f.*
sanctuary ['sæŋktjuəri], *n.* sanctuaire, asile, refuge, *m.*
sanctum ['sæŋktəm], *n.* sanctuaire; (*colloq.*) cabinet de travail, *m.*, retraite, *f.*
sand ['sænd], *n.* sable; sablon (*sable fin*), *m.*; (*pl.*) plage, *f.*, bord de la mer, *m.—v.t.* sabler.
sandal [sændl], *n.* sandale, *f.*; santal, *m.*
sandbag ['sændbæg], *n.* sac de terre, *m.*
sand bank ['sændbæŋk], *n.* banc de sable, *m.*
sand drift ['sænddrift], *n.* amas de sable, *m.*
sand eel ['sændi:l], *n.* lançon, *m.*, équille, *f.*
sand glass ['sændglɑːs], *n.* sablier, *m.*
sand martin ['sændmɑːtin], *n.* hirondelle de rivage, *f.*
sand-paper ['sændpeipə], *n.* papier de verre, *m.—v.t.* passer au papier de verre.
sand pit ['sændpit], *n.* sablière, sablonnière, *f.*
sand shoes ['sændʃu:z], *n.pl.* espadrilles, *f.pl.*
sandstone ['sændstoun], *n.* grès, *m.*
sand-storm ['sændstɔ:m], *n.* ouragan de sable, *m.*
sandwich ['sændwitʃ], *n.* sandwich, *m.*
sandwich man ['sændwitʃmən], *n.* (*pl.* **men** [men]) homme-sandwich, homme-affiche, *m.*
sandy ['sændi], *a.* sablonneux, de sable; d'un blond ardent, roux (*couleur*).
sane [sein], *a.* sain, sain d'esprit.
sanguinary ['sæŋgwinəri], *a.* sanguinaire.
sanguine ['sæŋgwin], *a.* sanguin; plein de confiance, confiant.
sanguineness ['sæŋgwinnis], *n.* confiance, assurance, *f.*
sanitary ['sænitəri], *a.* sanitaire, hygiénique; *sanitary napkin*, serviette hygiénique, *f.*
sanitation [sæni'teiʃən], *n.* assainissement, *m.*
sanity ['sæniti], *n.* état sain, jugement sain, *m.*
Sanskrit ['sænskrit], *a.* and *n.* sanscrit, *m.*
Santa Claus ['sæntə'klɔ:z]. Père Noël, *m.*
sap (1) [sæp], *n.* sève, *f.*
sap (2) [sæp], *n.* (*Mil.*) sapé, *f.—v.t.* saper.
sapience ['seipiəns], *n.* sagesse, *f.*
sapient ['seipiənt], *a.* sage.
sapless ['sæplis], *a.* sans sève; sec, desséché.
sapling ['sæpliŋ], *n.* jeune arbre, baliveau, *m.*
saponaceous [sæpə'neiʃəs], *a.* saponacé.
saponify [sə'pɔnifai], *v.t.* saponifier.—*v.i.* se saponifier.
sapper ['sæpə], *n.* sapeur, *m.*
sapphic ['sæfik], *a.* and *n.* (*Pros.*) saphique, *m.*
sapphire ['sæfaiə], *n.* saphir, *m.*
sappiness ['sæpinis], *n.* abondance de sève, *f.*
sappy ['sæpi], *a.* plein de sève.
saraband ['særəbænd], *n.* sarabande, *f.*

Saracen ['særəsn], *a.* sarrasin.—*n.* Sarrasin, *m.*
sarcasm ['sɑːkæzm], *n.* sarcasme, *m.*
sarcastic [sɑːˈkæstik], *a.* sarcastique.
sarcastically [sɑːˈkæstikəli], *adv.* d'une manière *ou* d'un ton sarcastique.
sarcophagus [sɑːˈkɔfəgəs], *n.* sarcophage, *m.*
sardine [sɑːˈdiːn], *n.* sardine, *f.*
Sardinia [sɑːˈdinjə]. la Sardaigne, *f.*
Sardinian [sɑːˈdinjən], *a.* sarde.—*n.* Sarde (*personne*), *m.*, *f.*
sardonic [sɑːˈdɔnik], *a.* sardonique.
sarong [səˈrɔŋ], *n.* pagne, *m.*, jupe (*malaisien*), *f.*
sarsaparilla [sɑːsəpəˈrilə], *n.* salsepareille, *f.*
sash (1) [sæʃ], *n.* ceinture; écharpe (*décoration*), *f.*
sash (2) [sæʃ], *n.* châssis (*de fenêtre*), *m.*
sash window ['sæʃwindou], *n.* fenêtre à guillotine, *f.*
sassafras ['sæsəfræs], *n.* (*Bot.*) sassafras, *m.*
Satan ['seitən]. Satan, *m.*
satanic [səˈtænik], **satanical** [səˈtænikəl], *a.* satanique.
satchel ['sætʃl], *n.* sacoche, *f.*; sac d'écolier, cartable, *m.*
sate [seit], *v.t.* rassasier (*de*), assouvir.
satellite ['sætəlait], *n.* satellite, *m.*
satiate ['seiʃieit], *v.t.* rassasier (*de*).
satiated ['seiʃieitid], *a.* rassasié (*de*); gorgé.
satiety [səˈtaiəti], *n.* satiété, *f.*
satin ['sætin], *a.* de satin.—*n.* satin, *m.*
satin-wood ['sætinwuːd], *n* bois de citronnier, *m.*
satire ['sætaiə], *n.* satire, *f.*
satiric [səˈtirik], **satirical** [səˈtirikəl], *a.* satirique.
satirist ['sætirist], *n.* satirique, *m.*, *f.*
satirize ['sætiraiz], *v.t.* satiriser.
satisfaction [sætisˈfækʃən], *n.* satisfaction; réparation (*récompense*), *f.*
satisfactorily [sætisˈfæktərili], *adv.* d'une manière satisfaisante.
satisfactory [sætisˈfæktri], *a.* satisfaisant.
satisfy ['sætisfai], *v.t.* satisfaire; satisfaire à; acquitter (*dette*); assouvir (*passion*); rassasier (*de*) (*appétit*); *to be satisfied that*, être persuadé, être convaincu que; *to be satisfied with*, être satisfait de, être content de.—*v.i.* satisfaire, donner satisfaction.
satisfying ['sætisfaiiŋ], *a.* satisfaisant; nourrissant (*nourriture*).
saturate ['sætjureit], *v.t.* saturer.
saturation [sætjuˈreiʃən], *n.* saturation, *f.*
Saturday ['sætədei]. samedi, *m.*
Saturn ['sætən]. Saturne, *m.*
Saturnalia [sætəˈneiliə]. saturnales, *f.pl.*
saturnine ['sætənain], *a.* sombre, taciturne.
satyr ['sætə], *n.* satyre, *m.*
sauce [sɔːs], *n.* sauce; (*fig.*) insolence, impertinence, *f.*—*v.t.* assaisonner; flatter (*le goût*); (*fig.*) dire des impertinences à.
sauce boat ['sɔːsbout], *n.* saucière, *f.*
saucer ['sɔːsə], *n.* soucoupe, *f.*; *flying saucer*, soucoupe volante.
saucepan ['sɔːspən], *n.* casserole, *f.*
saucily ['sɔːsili], *adv.* insolemment.
sauciness ['sɔːsinis], *n.* insolence, impertinence, *f.*
saucy ['sɔːsi], *a.* insolent, impertinent.
Saudi Arabia ['saudiəˈreibiə]. l'Arabie Séoudite, *f.*
sauerkraut ['sauəkraut], *n.* choucroute, *f.*

saunter ['sɔːntə], *v.i.* flâner.—*n.* flânerie, *f.*
saunterer ['sɔːntərə], *n.* flâneur, *m.*
sauntering ['sɔːntəriŋ], *a.* de flâneur.—*n.* flânerie, *f.*
sausage ['sɔsidʒ], *n.* saucisse (*à cuire*), *f.*; saucisson (*salami etc.*), *m.*
sausage meat ['sɔsidʒmiːt], *n.* chair à saucisse, *f.*
sausage-roll ['sɔsidʒˈroul], *n.* friand, *m.*
savage ['sævidʒ], *a.* sauvage; féroce.—*n.* sauvage, *m.*, *f.*—*v.t.* attaquer, mordre (*bête*).
savagely ['sævidʒli], *adv.* sauvagement, en sauvage; d'une manière féroce.
savageness ['sævidʒnis], *n.* férocité, brutalité; sauvagerie, *f.*
savagery ['sævidʒəri], *n.* férocité, barbarie, *f.*
savannah [səˈvænə], *n.* savane, prairie, *f.*
save [seiv], *v.t.* sauver (*de*); épargner (*argent etc.*); mettre de côté, économiser.—*v.i.* économiser, faire des économies.—*n.* (*Spt.*) arrêt, *m.*—*prep.* hormis, excepté, sauf.
saver ['seivə], *n.* sauveur, libérateur, *m.*; économe (*ménager*), *m.*, *f.*
saving ['seiviŋ], *a.* économe, ménager.—*n.* épargne; économie, *f.*; salut, *m.*
savings bank ['seiviŋzbæŋk], *n.* caisse d'épargne, *f.*
savior ['seivjə], *n.* sauveur, *m.*
savor ['seivə], *n.* saveur, *f.*; goût, *m.*, odeur, *f.*—*v.t.* goûter, savourer.—*v.i.* avoir du goût; sentir.
savoriness ['seivərinis], *n.* goût agréable, *m.*, saveur, *f.*
savory ['seivəri], *a.* savoureux, appétissant.—*n.* plat épicé, *m.*
saw (1) [sɔː], *past* [SEE].
saw (2) [sɔː], *n.* scie, *f.*—*v.t.*, *v.i.* irr. scier.
saw (3) [sɔː], *n.* adage, dicton (*proverbe*), *m.*
sawdust ['sɔːdʌst], *n.* sciure (de bois), *f.*
saw-mill ['sɔːmil], *n.* scierie, *f.*
sawyer ['sɔːjə], *n.* scieur, scieur de long, *m.*
saxifrage ['sæksifreidʒ], *n.* (*Bot.*) saxifrage, *f.*
Saxon ['sæksən], *a.* saxon, de Saxe.—*n.* saxon (*langue*); Saxon (*personne*), *m.*
saxophone ['sæksəfoun], *n.* saxophone, *m.*
say [sei], *v.t.* irr. dire; parler, répéter, réciter; *I say!* dites donc! *that is to say*, c'est-à-dire; *they say*, on dit.—*n.* dire, mot, ce qu'on a à dire, *m.*
saying ['seiiŋ], *n.* mot, proverbe, dicton, *m.*; sentence, maxime, *f.*
scab [skæb], *n.* croûte (*sur blessure etc.*); gale (*de mouton etc.*), *f.*; [see blackleg]
scabbard ['skæbəd], *n.* fourreau, *m.*
scabbiness ['skæbinis], *n.* état galeux, *m.*
scabby ['skæbi], *a.* couvert de croûtes; galeux.
scabious ['skeibiəs], *a.* scabieux.—*n.* scabieuse (*plante*), *f.*
scaffold ['skæfəld], *n.* échafaud, *m.*—*v.t.* échafauder.
scaffolding ['skæfəldiŋ], *n.* échafaudage, *m.*
scald [skɔːld], *n.* brûlure, *f.*—*v.t.* échauder, ébouillanter.
scalding ['skɔːldiŋ], *n.* échaudage, *m.*
scalding-hot ['skɔːldiŋˈhɔt], *a.* tout bouillant.
scale (1) [skeil], *n.* échelle; (*Mus.*) gamme, *f.*—*v.t.* escalader.
scale (2) [skeil], *n.* écaille (*de poisson*), *f.*
scale (3) [skeil], *n.* bassin, plateau (*balance*), *m.*; *scales* or *pair of scales*, balance, *f.*

scale-maker ['skeilmeikə], *n.* balancier, *m.*

scalene ['skeili:n], *a.* scalène.

scaliness ['skeilinis], *n.* nature écailleuse, *f.*

scaling (1) ['skeiliŋ], *n.* escalade (*montagnes*), *f.*

scaling (2) ['skeiliŋ], *n.* écaillage (*peintures*), *m.*

scallop ['skɔləp], *n.* coquille Saint-Jacques; coquille; dentelure, *f.*, feston, *m.—v.t.* denteler; (*Needlework*) festonner.

scalp [skælp], *n.* cuir chevelu, *m.*, chevelure, *f.*, scalpe; (*fig.*) front, *m.*, tête, *f.—v.t.* scalper.

scalpel ['skælpəl], *n.* (*Surg.*) scalpel, *m.*

scaly ['skeili], *a.* écaillé; (*Bot.*) écailleux.

scamp [skæmp], *n.* chenapan, vaurien, *m.*; *young scamp*, petit polisson, *m.—v.t.* bâcler.

scamper ['skæmpə], *v.i.* courir, s'enfuir.—*n.* course rapide, *f.*

scampi ['skæmpi], *n.pl.* langoustine, *f.*

scan [skæn], *v.t.* scruter; (*Pros.*) scander; (*Rad.*) balayer.

scandal [skændl], *n.* scandale, *m.*; honte; médisance, *f.*

scandalize ['skændəlaiz], *v.t.* scandaliser, choquer; calomnier.

scandal-monger ['skændlmʌŋgə], *n.* médisant, *m.*

scandalous ['skændələs], *a.* scandaleux; honteux.

Scandinavia [skændi'neivjə]. la Scandinavie, *f.*

Scandinavian [skændi'neivjən], *a.* scandinave.—*n.* Scandinave (*personne*), *m.*, *f.*

scanner ['skænə], *n.* scrutateur, *m.*; *radar scanner*, déchiffreur de radar, *m.*

scanning ['skæniŋ], *n.* examen minutieux, *m.*; (*Pros.*) scansion, *f.*; (*Rad.*) balayage, *m.*

scansion ['skænʃən], *n.* scansion, *f.*

scant [skænt], *a.* rare; rétréci; faible; peu de.

scantily ['skæntili], *adv.* faiblement, d'une manière insuffisante.

scantiness ['skæntinis], *n.* insuffisance (*de vivres etc.*); faiblesse (*de poids*), *f.*

scantling ['skæntliŋ], *n.* échantillon, *m.*; (*Carp.*) volige, *f.*, équarrissage, *m.*

scanty ['skænti], *a.* rare; rétréci, faible, peu abondant, insuffisant; clairsemé (*cheveux*).

scapegoat ['skeipgout], *n.* bouc émissaire, *m.*; (*fig.*) souffre-douleur, *m.*

scapegrace ['skeipgreis], *n.* vaurien, mauvais sujet, *m.*

scapement ['skeipmənt], *n.* échappement, *m.*

scapula ['skæpjulə], *n.* (*Anat.*) omoplate, *f.*

scapular ['skæpjulə], *a.* scapulaire.

scapulary ['skæpjulori], *n.* (*R.-C. Ch.*) scapulaire, *m.*

scar [skɑ:], *n.* cicatrice, balafre, *f.—v.t.* cicatriser; balafrer.

scarab ['skærəb], **scarabaeus** [skærə'bi:əs], *n.* scarabée, *m.*

scaramouch ['skærəmu:ʃ], *n.* scaramouche, *m.*

scarce [skɛəs], *a.* rare; *to make oneself scarce*, disparaître, décamper, filer.

scarcely ['skɛəsli], *adv.* à peine, presque pas, guère.

scarcity ['skɛəsiti], *n.* rareté; disette (*famine*), *f.*

scare [skɛə], *n.* panique, frayeur subite, *f.—v.t.* effrayer, épouvanter, effaroucher.

scarecrow ['skɛəkrou], *n.* épouvantail, *m.*

scarf [skɑ:f], *n.* (*pl.* **scarfs** [skɑ:fs], **scarves** [skɑ:vz]) écharpe, *f.*; cache-nez, *m.inv.*; foulard, *m.*

scarifier ['skærifaiə], *n.* scarificateur, *m.*

scarify ['skærifai], *v.t.* scarifier (*peau*), ameublir (*terre*).

scarlatina [skɑ:lə'ti:nə], *n.* (fièvre) scarlatine, *f.*

scarlet ['skɑ:lit], *a.* and *n.* écarlate, *f.*; *scarlet fever*, fièvre scarlatine, *f.*; *scarlet runner*, haricot d'Espagne, *m.*

scarp [skɑ:p], *n.* (*Fort.*) escarpe, *f.—v.t.* escarper.

scarves [SCARF].

scatheless ['skeiðlis], *a.* sans dommage, sain et sauf.

scathing ['skeiðiŋ], *a.* acerbe, cinglant, cassant.

scatter ['skætə], *v.t.* disperser, dissiper; répandre, éparpiller.—*v.i.* se disperser, se répandre.

scattered ['skætəd], *a.* dispersé, éparpillé, épars.

scattering ['skætəriŋ], *n.* éparpillement; petit nombre, *m.*

scavenge ['skævindʒ], *v.t.* ébouer, balayer.

scavenger ['skævindʒə], *n.* boueur; balayeur, *m.*

scavenging ['skævindʒiŋ], *n.* ébouage, balayage, *m.*

scene [si:n], *n.* scène; (*Theat.*) scène, décoration, *f.*; décor; (*fig.*) théâtre, *m.*; *behind the scenes*, dans la coulisse; *scene shifter*, machiniste, *m.*

scenery ['si:nəri], *n.* scène; (*fig.*) vue, perspective, *f.*, paysage, *m.*; (*Theat.*) décors, *m.pl.*

scenic ['si:nik], *a.* scénique.

scent [sent], *n.* odeur, senteur, *f.*, parfum; odorat; flair, nez (*de chien*), *m.*; voie (*de cerf*); (*fig.*) piste (*traces*), *f.—v.t.* parfumer (*de*); sentir, flairer (*animal*).

scent bottle ['sentbɔtl], *n.* flacon de parfum, *m.*

scentless ['sentlis], *a.* sans odeur, inodore.

scent spray ['sentsprei], *n.* vaporisateur, *m.*

sceptic ['skeptik], *n.* sceptique, *m.*, *f.*

sceptical ['skeptikl], *a.* sceptique.

scepticism ['skeptisizm], *n.* scepticisme, *m.*

sceptre ['septə], *n.* sceptre, *m.*

sceptred ['septəd], *a.* portant le sceptre.

schedule ['ʃedju:l, (*Am.*) 'skedju:l], *n.* liste, *f.*, inventaire; (*Comm.*) bilan; (*Law*) bordereau, *m.—v.t.* enregistrer, inventorier.

scheme [ski:m], *n.* arrangement, *m.*, combinaison, *f.*; projet, système, *m.—v.t.* projeter, combiner.—*v.i.* faire des projets; (*fig.*) intriguer.

schemer ['ski:mə], *n.* faiseur de projets; (*fig.*) intrigant, *m.*

scheming ['ski:miŋ], *a.* à projets; intrigant.—*n.* projets *m.pl.*, intrigues, *f.pl.*

schism [sizm], *n.* schisme, *m.*

schismatic [siz'mætik], *n.* schismatique, *m.*, *f.*

schizophrenia [skitso'fri:niə], *n.* (*Med.*) schizophrénie, *f.*

schizophrenic [skitso'fri:nik], *a.* and *n.* schizophrène, *m.*, *f.*

scholar ['skɔlə], *n.* écolier; érudit, savant (*learned person*), *m.*; *day scholar*, externe, *m.*, *f.*

scholarly

scholarly ['skɔləli], *a.* d'érudit, savant.
scholarship ['skɔləʃip], *n.* érudition, *f.*, savoir, *m.*; (*Univ. etc.*) bourse, *f.*
scholastic [skoˈlæstik], *a.* and *n.* scolastique, *m., f.*
scholasticism [skoˈlæstisizm], *n.* scolastique, *f.*
school [sku:l], *n.* école; bande, troupe (*de baleines etc.*), *f.*; **at school**, en classe, à l'école; **boarding school**, pension, *f.*, pensionnat, *m.*; **primary school**, école primaire; **grammar school**, collège, lycée, *m.*; **nursery school**, école maternelle.—*v.t.* instruire, enseigner; réprimander.
schooled [sku:ld], *a.* formé, entraîné, dressé.
schooling ['sku:liŋ], *n.* instruction; réprimande, *f.*
schoolmaster ['sku:lmɑ:stə], *n.* instituteur, professeur, *m.*
schoolmistress ['sku:lmistris], *n.* maîtresse d'école, institutrice, *f.*
schooner ['sku:nə], *n.* (*Naut.*) goélette, *f.*
sciatic [sai'ætik], *a.* sciatique.
sciatica [sai'ætikə], *n.* sciatique, *f.*
science ['saiəns], *n.* science, *f.*
scientific [saiən'tifik], *a.* scientifique.
scientist ['saiəntist], *n.* homme de science, savant, *m.*
Scilly Isles ['siliailz], **the,** les Sorlingues, *f.pl.*
scimitar ['simitə], *n.* cimeterre, *m.*
scintillant ['sintilənt], *a.* scintillant.
scintillate ['sintileit], *v.i.* scintiller.
scintillation [sinti'leiʃən], *n.* scintillation, *f.*, scintillement, *m.*
scion ['saiən], *n.* (*Bot.*) scion; (*fig.*) rejeton, *m.*
scission ['siʃən], *n.* scission, *f.*
scissors ['sizəz], *n.pl.* ciseaux, *m.pl.*
scoff [skɔf], *n.* moquerie, *f.*, sarcasme, *m.*—*v.t.* se moquer de, bafouer.—*v.i.* railler.
scoffer ['skɔfə], *n.* moqueur, railleur, *m.*
scoffing ['skɔfiŋ], *n.* moquerie, dérision, *f.*
scoffingly ['skɔfiŋli], *adv.* par moquerie, en dérision.
scold [skould], *v.t.* gronder, criailler (*après*).—*v.i.* gronder, *f.*
scolding ['skouldiŋ], *a.* bougon.—*n.* semonce, *f.*
sconce [skɔns], *n.* candélabre (*fixé au mur*), *m.*; bobèche (*de bougeoir*), *f.*
scone [skɔn, skoun], *n.* petite galette (ronde), *f.*
scoop [sku:p], *n.* grande cuiller; (*Naut.*) écope; (*Journ. slang*) nouvelle à sensation, *f.*—*v.t.* vider, creuser; (*Naut.*) écoper.
scooter ['sku:tə], *n.* patinette, *f.*; scooter, *m.*
scope [skoup], *n.* portée, étendue; visée; liberté, *f.*
scorch [skɔ:tʃ], *v.t.* brûler, roussir, griller.—*v.i.* se brûler.
scorching ['skɔ:tʃiŋ], *a.* brûlant, très chaud.
score [skɔ:], *n.* entaille, coche, *f.*; compte; vingt, *m.*, vingtaine, *f.*; (*Games*) nombre de points; (*fig.*) motif, *m.*, raison, cause; (*Mus.*) partition, *f.*; **on what score?** à quel titre?—*v.t.* entailler, marquer; rayer; (*Mus.*) orchestrer; **to score out,** rayer, biffer (*texte*).—*v.i.* marquer des points.
scorer ['skɔ:rə], *n.* marqueur, *m.*
scoring ['skɔ:riŋ], *n.* (*Games etc.*) marque; (*Mus.*) orchestration, *f.*
scorn [skɔ:n], *v.t.* mépriser; dédaigner.—*v.i.* mépriser; dédaigner (*de*); **to scorn to fly,**

dédaigner de fuir.—*n.* mépris, dédain, *m.* dérision, *f.*
scornful ['skɔ:nful], *a.* méprisant, dédaigneux.
scornfully ['skɔ:nfuli], *adv.* dédaigneusement, avec dédain.
scornfulness ['skɔ:nfulnis], *n.* caractère dédaigneux, *m.*
scorpion ['skɔ:piən], *n.* scorpion, *m.*
Scot [skɔt], *n.* Écossais, *m.*
Scotch [skɔtʃ], *a.* écossais (*but used* ONLY *in certain fixed expressions, which include the following*) **Scotch terrier,** terrier griffon, *m.*; **Scotch (whisky),** whisky écossais, *m.*; [SCOTS].
scotch [skɔtʃ], *v.t.* entailler; enrayer (*roue*); (*fig.*) annuler.
scot-free [skɔt'fri:], *a.* sans frais; (*fig.*) sain et sauf, indemne.
Scotland ['skɔtlənd]. l'Écosse, *f.*
Scots [skɔts], **Scottish** ['skɔtiʃ], *a.* écossais; *Scots Law,* droit écossais, *m.*
Scotsman ['skɔtsmən], *n.* (*pl.* **-men** [men]) Écossais, *m.*
Scotswoman ['skɔtswumən], *n.* (*pl.* **-women** [wimin]) Écossaise, *f.*
Scottish [SCOTS].
scoundrel ['skaundrəl], *n.* gredin, coquin, scélérat, *m.*
scour (1) ['skauə], *v.t.* nettoyer, récurer, purger, écurer.—*v.i.* écurer; nettoyer.
scour (2) ['skauə], *v.t.* parcourir.—*v.i.* courir.
scourer ['skauərə], *n.* récureur, nettoyeur, *m.*
scourge [skə:dʒ], *n.* fouet; (*fig.*) fléau, *m.*—*v.t.* fouetter, flageller; (*fig.*) châtier.
scourger ['skə:dʒə], *n.* châtieur; (*Eccles. Hist.*) flagellant, *m.*
scourging ['skə:dʒiŋ], *n.* flagellation, *f.*
scouring ['skauəriŋ], *n.* récurage; nettoyage, *m.*
scout [skaut], *n.* éclaireur; scout, *m.*; (*Naut.*) vedette, *f.*; (*Av.*) avion de chasse, *m.*—*v.t.* repousser avec mépris.—*v.i.* aller en éclaireur.
scowl [skaul], *v.i.* se re(n)frogner, froncer le sourcil.—*n.* re(n)frognement, froncement de sourcil, *m.*
scowling ['skauliŋ], *a.* re(n)frogné, menaçant.
scrag [skræg], *n.* corps décharné, squelette, *m.*; **scrag-end,** bout saigneux (*de viande*), *m.*
scragginess ['skræginis], *n.* état raboteux, *m.*; maigreur, *f.*
scraggy ['skrægi], *a.* noueux, rugueux; rabougri.
scramble [skræmbl], *v.t.* (*Teleg.*) brouiller (*message*); *scrambled eggs,* œufs brouillés, *m.pl.*—*v.i.* grimper; se battre, se disputer.—*n.* mêlée, lutte, *f.*
scrap (1) [skræp], *n.* morceau, fragment, bout, *m.*; (*pl.*) bribes, *f.pl.*; restes, *m.pl.*—*v.t.* mettre au rebut.
scrap (2) [skræp], *n.* (*slang*) bagarre, rixe, *f.*
scrap-book ['skræpbuk], *n.* album, *m.*
scrape [skreip], *v.t.* gratter, érafler, râcler; décrotter (*bottes etc.*); (*Cook.*) ratisser; **to scrape together,** amasser petit à petit.—*v.i.* gratter; (*fam.*) râcler (*jouer du violon*); **to scrape through,** passer de justesse; **to bow and scrape,** faire des salamalecs.—*n.* grattage, *m.*; (*fig.*) difficulté, mauvaise affaire, *f.*

552

scraper ['skreipə], n. grattoir; râcloir, m.; (*Agric.*) ratissoire, f.; décrottoir (*pour chaussures*), m.

scrap heap ['skræphi:p], n. tas de ferraille, m.

scraping ['skreipiŋ], n. grattage, m.; ratissure (*de légumes*), f.; **with much bowing and scraping**, avec force révérences.

scrap iron ['skræpaiən], n. ferraille, f.

scratch [skrætʃ], n. égratignure, f.; coup de griffe *ou* d'ongle, m.; raie, rayure (*sur une surface polie*), f.—*v.t.* gratter; rayer (*surface polie*).—*v.i.* gratter; (*Spt.*) renoncer à concourir.

scratcher ['skrætʃə], n. égratigneur; grattoir (*instrument*), m.

scratching ['skrætʃiŋ], n. grattage, m.; égratignure; rayure, f.

scrawl [skrɔ:l], n. griffonnage, m., pattes de mouche, f.pl.—*v.t.*, *v.i.* griffonner.

scrawler ['skrɔ:lə], n. griffonneur, m.

scrawny ['skrɔ:ni], a. décharné, émacié.

scream [skri:m], n. cri perçant, m.—*v.i.* crier, pousser des cris.

screamer ['skri:mə], n. crieur, m.

screaming ['skri:miŋ], a. perçant; qui crie.—n. cris, m.pl.

screech [skri:tʃ], n. cri perçant, m.—*v.i.* crier.

screech owl ['skri:tʃaul], n. effraie, chouette, f.

screen [skri:n], n. écran; paravent (*pliant*); rideau (*d'arbres etc.*), m.; (*fig.*) voile, f., abri, m.; défense, f.—*v.t* mettre à couvert; abriter (*contre*).

screw [skru:], n. à hélice.—n. vis; hélice (*de navire etc.*), f.—*v.t.* visser; (*fig.*) serrer (*presser*); pressurer (*opprimer*).—*v.i.* se visser.

screw bolt ['skru:boult], n. boulon à vis, m.

screw cap ['skru:kæp], n. couvercle à vis, m.

screw-driver ['skru:draivə], n. tournevis, m.

screw nail ['skru:neil], n. vis à bois, f.

screw nut ['skru:nʌt], n. écrou, m.

screw-wrench ['skru:rentʃ], n. clef anglaise, f.

scribble ['skribl], n. griffonnage; barbouillage, m.—*v.t.*, *v.i.* griffonner.

scribbler ['skriblə], n. griffonneur; gratte-papier, m.

scribe [skraib], n. scribe; écrivain, m.—*v.t.* (*Carp.*) tracer.

scrimmage ['skrimidʒ], n. lutte, rixe; (*Ftb.*) mêlée, f.

scrip [skrip], n. petit sac; (*Comm.*) titre *ou* certificat provisoire, m.

script [skript], n. manuscrit; (*Cine.*) scénario, m.

scriptural ['skriptʃuərəl], a. de l'Écriture Sainte, biblique, scriptural.

Scripture ['skriptʃə], n. l'Écriture Sainte, f.

script-writer ['skriptraitə], n. (*Cine.*) scénariste, m., f.

scrofula ['skrɔfjulə], n. scrofule, f.

scrofulous ['skrɔfjuləs], a. scrofuleux.

scroll [skroul], n. rouleau, m.

scrounge [skraundʒ], v.t., v.i. (*slang*) chiper, chaparder, grappiller; **to scrounge on someone**, vivre aux crochets de quelqu'un.

scrounger ['skraundʒə], n. chapardeur, m.

scrub [skrʌb], v.t., v.i. frotter fort; laver, récurer.—n. broussailles, f.pl.; maquis, m.

scrubbing ['skrʌbiŋ], n. frottage, récurage, m.

scrubbing brush ['skrʌbiŋbrʌʃ], n. brosse de cuisine, f.

scrubby ['skrʌbi], a. rabougri, chétif, mal rasé.

scruff [skrʌf], n. nuque, f.

scruple [skru:pl], n. scrupule, m.—*v.i.* se faire scrupule (*de*), hésiter (*à*).

scrupulous ['skru:pjuləs], a. scrupuleux.

scrupulously ['skru:pjuləsli], adv. scrupuleusement.

scrupulousness ['skru:pjuləsnis], n. scrupule, doute, m.

scrutator [skru:'teitə], n. scrutateur, m.

scrutineer [skru:ti'niə], n. pointeur (*de votes*); scrutateur, m.

scrutinize ['skru:tinaiz], v.t. scruter, examiner à fond.

scrutinizing ['skru:tinaiziŋ], a. scrutateur, inquisiteur.

scrutiny ['skru:tini], n. enquête rigoureuse, vérification, f.

scud [skʌd], n. léger nuage, m.; course rapide, f.—*v.i.* s'enfuir; courir (*nuages*).

scuffle [skʌfl], n. bagarre, rixe, mêlée, f.—*v.i.* se battre; traîner les pieds.

scull [skʌl], n. rame; godille, f.—*v.i.* ramer.

scullery ['skʌləri], n. arrière-cuisine, laverie, f.; **scullery maid**, laveuse de vaisselle, f.

sculptor ['skʌlptə], n. sculpteur, m.

sculpture ['skʌlptʃə], n. sculpture, f.—*v.t.* sculpter.

scum [skʌm], n. écume, f.; (*fig.*) rebut (*ordures*), m.; lie, f.—*v.t.* écumer.

scupper ['skʌpə], n. (*Naut.*) dalot, m.—*v.t.* saborder.

scurf [skə:f], n. pellicules (*des cheveux*), f.pl.

scurfy ['skə:fi], a. pelliculeux (*cheveux*).

scurrility [skʌ'riliti], **scurrilousness** ['skʌrilənis], n. grossièreté, f.

scurrilous ['skʌriləs], a. grossier, ordurier.

scurry ['skʌri], n. débandade, f.; tourbillon (*de poussière, de neige etc.*), m.—*v.i.* se hâter.

scurvily ['skə:vili], adv. bassement, vilement.

scurviness ['skə:vinis], n. état scorbutique, m.; (*fig.*) bassesse; mesquinerie (*avarice*), f.

scurvy ['skə:vi], a. scorbutique; (*fig.*) vil, vilain.—n. scorbut, m.

scut [skʌt], n. couette (*de lièvre etc.*), f.

scutcheon ['skʌtʃən], [ESCUTCHEON].

scuttle (1) [skʌtl], n. panier; seau à charbon, m.

scuttle (2) [skʌtl], n. (*Naut.*) hublot, m.; écoutille, f.—*v.t.* saborder.

scuttle (3) [skʌtl] v.i. aller à pas précipités.

scuttling ['skʌtliŋ], a. en fuite, qui détale.—n. sabordage, m.

scythe [saið], n. faux, f.—*v.t.* faucher.

sea [si:], a. de mer, marin, maritime.—n. mer; lame; (*fig.*) multitude, f.; déluge, m.; **at sea**, en mer; **heavy sea**, mer houleuse; **in the open sea**, en pleine mer, au grand large.

seaboard ['si:bɔ:d], n. littoral, rivage, m., côte, f.

sea-borne ['si:bɔ:n], a. transporté par mer.

sea calf ['si:kɑ:f], n. veau marin, m.

sea cow ['si:kau], n. lamantin, m.

sea dog ['si:dɔg], n. loup de mer (*marin*), m.

seafarer ['si:fɛərə], n. homme de mer, marin, m.

seafaring ['si:fɛəriŋ], a. marin; **seafaring man**, marin, m.

sea-front ['si:frʌnt], n. esplanade, f., bord de mer, m.

sea-gauge ['si:geidʒ], *n.* tirant d'eau, *m.*
sea-going ['si:gouiŋ], *a.* de haute mer.
sea gull ['si:gʌl], *n.* mouette, *f.*, goéland, *m.*
sea horse ['si:hɔ:s], *n.* morse, *m.*
sea kale ['si:keil], *n.* chou marin, *m.*
seal (1) [si:l], *n.* cachet; sceau (*officiel*), *m.*; (*Law*) scellés, *m.pl.*; *Privy Seal,* petit sceau.—*v.t.* cacheter; (*Law*) sceller; (*Customs*) plomber.
seal (2) [si:l], *n.* phoque, *m.*
sea legs ['si:legz], *n.pl.* pied marin, *m.*
sea level ['si:levəl], *n.* niveau de la mer, *m.*
sealing ['si:liŋ], *n.* action de sceller, *f.*
sealing wax ['si:liŋwæks], *n.* cire à cacheter, *f.*
sea lion ['si:laiən], *n.* lion de mer, *m.*, otarie, *f.*
seam [si:m], *n.* (*Dress.*) couture; (*Mining*) couche; (*Geol.*) veine, *f.*—*v.t.* coudre; couturer.
seaman ['si:mən], *n.* (*pl.* **-men** [men]) marin, matelot, homme de mer, *m.*
seamanship ['si:mənʃip], *n.* matelotage, *m.*
seamless ['si:mlis], *a.* sans couture.
seamstress ['si:mstris], [SEMPSTRESS].
seamy ['si:mi], *a.* plein de coutures; *the seamy side of life,* les dessous de la vie, *m.pl.*
sea nymph ['si:nimf], *n.* néréide, *f.*
seaplane ['si:plein], *n.* hydravion, *m.*
seaport ['si:pɔ:t], *n.* port de mer, *m.*
sear [siə], *a.* séché, fané, flétri.—*v.t.* brûler; cautériser; faner.
search [sə:tʃ], *n.* recherche; (*Law*) perquisition; (*Customs*) visite, *f.*—*v.t.* chercher, examiner; fouiller; (*Law*) faire une perquisition chez; (*Customs*) visiter.—*v.i.* chercher; fouiller.
searcher ['sə:tʃə], *n.* chercheur, *m.*
searching ['sə:tʃiŋ], *a.* scrutateur, pénétrant; vif, perçant (*vent*).
searchingly ['sə:tʃiŋli], *adv.* minutieusement.
searchlight ['sə:tʃlait], *n.* projecteur, *m.*
search party ['sə:tʃpɑ:ti], *n.* expédition de secours, *f.*
search warrant ['sə:tʃwɔrənt], *n.* mandat de perquisition, *m.*
sea route ['si:ru:t], *n.* voie de mer, *f.*
seascape ['si:skeip], *n.* (*Paint.*) marine, *f.*
Sea Scout ['si:skaut], *n.* (boy-)scout marin, *m.*
sea-shell ['si:ʃel], *n.* coquillage, *m.*
seashore ['si:ʃɔ:], *n.* bord de la mer, rivage, *m.*, côte, *f.*
sea-sick ['si:sik], *a.* qui a le mal de mer.
sea-sickness ['si:siknis], *n.* mal de mer, *m.*
seaside ['si:said], *n.* bord de la mer, *m.*
season ['si:zn], *n.* saison, *f.*; (*fig.*) temps, moment opportun, *m.*—*v.t.* assaisonner (*de*); sécher (*bois*); (*fig.*) accoutumer (*à*).—*v.i.* s'acclimater; se sécher (*bois*).
seasonable ['si:znəbl], *a.* de saison; (*fig.*) à propos, opportun, convenable.
seasonably ['si:znəbli], *adv.* à propos.
seasonal ['si:znəl], *a.* des saisons; saisonnier.
seasoned ['si:znd], *a.* assaisonné (*viande*); (*fig.*) endurci, aguerri, acclimaté.
seasoning ['si:zniŋ], *n.* assaisonnement; séchage (*du bois*), *m.*
season ticket ['si:zn'tikit], *n.* carte d'abonnement, *f.*
seat [si:t], *n.* siège; banc, *m.*; banquette (*dans un véhicule*); (*fig.*) place; demeure (*château*), *f.*; théâtre (*de guerre*); fond (*de pantalon*), *m.*;

take your seats, please! en voiture!—*v.t.* asseoir; faire asseoir; placer.
seated ['si:tid], *a.* assis, placé.
sea wall ['si:wɔ:l], *n.* digue, chaussée, *f.*
seaward ['si:wəd], *a.* tourné vers la mer.—*adv.* vers la mer.
seaweed ['si:wi:d], *n.* algue, *f.*, goémon, varech, *m.*
seaworthiness ['si:wə:ðinis], *n.* navigabilité (*navire*), *f.*
seaworthy ['si:wə:ði], *a.* en bon état (de navigation).
secant ['si:kənt], *a.* sécant.—*n.* sécante, *f.*
secede [si'si:d], *v.i.* se séparer (*de*).
seceder [si'si:də], *n.* scissionnaire, *m.*, *f.*; dissident, *m.*
secession [si'seʃən], *n.* sécession, séparation, *f.*
seclude [si'klu:d], *v.t.* séparer; éloigner.
secluded [si'klu:did], *a.* retiré, isolé, solitaire.
seclusion [si'klu:ʒən], *n.* retraite, solitude, *f.*
second ['sekənd], *a.* second, deuxième; deux (*du mois*); inférieur; *on second thoughts,* à la réflexion.—*n.* témoin, second (*dans un duel*), *m.*; seconde (*temps*), *f.*—*v.t.* seconder, aider; appuyer (*une motion*); [si'kɔnd] détacher (*fonctionnaire*).
secondary ['sekəndri], *a.* secondaire; accessoire.
seconder ['sekəndə], *n.* personne qui appuie, *f.*
second-hand ['sekənd'hænd], *a.* and *adv.* d'occasion.
secondly ['sekəndli], *adv.* secondement; en second lieu.
second-rate ['sekənd'reit], *a.* de second ordre.
secrecy ['si:krəsi], *n.* secret, *m.*; discrétion, *f.*
secret ['si:krit], *a.* secret; retiré (*maison etc.*).—*n.* secret, *m.*
secretarial [sekrə'tɛəriəl], *a.* de secrétaire.
secretariat [sekrə'tɛəriæt], *n.* secrétariat, *m.*
secretary ['sekrətri], *n.* secrétaire, *m.*, *f.*
secretaryship ['sekrətriʃip], *n.* secrétariat, *m.*
secrete [si'kri:t], *v.t.* cacher; (*Physiol.*) sécréter.
secretion [si'kri:ʃən], *n.* sécrétion, *f.*
secretive ['si:krətiv], *a.* réservé; dissimulé.
secretiveness ['si:krətivnis], *n.* caractère cachottier, *m.*
secretly ['si:krətli], *adv.* en secret; intérieurement.
sect [sekt], *n.* secte, *f.*
sectarian [sek'tɛəriən], *a.* de sectaire.—*n.* sectaire, *m.*, *f.*
sectarianism [sek'tɛəriənizm], *n.* esprit de secte, sectarisme, *m.*
section ['sekʃən], *n.* section; coupe, *f.*, profil; (*Mil.*) groupe de combat, *m.*
sectional ['sekʃənəl], *a.* en coupe; en sections.
sector ['sektə], *n.* secteur, *m.*
secular ['sekjulə], *a.* temporel; laïque; séculaire (*année*).
secularity [sekju'læriti], **secularness** ['sekjulənis], *n.* sécularité, mondanité, *f.*
secularization [sekjulərai'zeiʃən], *n.* sécularisation, *f.*
secularize ['sekjuləraiz], *v.t.* séculariser.
secure [si'kjuə], *a.* dans la sécurité, en sûreté; sûr, assuré (*chose*); bien fermé.—*v.t.* mettre en sûreté; assurer (*garantir*); s'assurer de; fermer; barrer (*attacher fortement*); (*fig.*) affermir.
securely [si'kjuəli], *adv.* en sûreté; sûrement; fortement.

secureness [si'kjuənis], *n.* sécurité, *f.*

security [si'kjuəriti], *n.* sécurité, sûreté; garantie, *f.*; (*pl.*) titres, *m.pl.*, valeurs, *f.pl.*; (*Law*) caution, *f.*

sedan [si'dæn] (*Motor.*), *see* **saloon**.

sedate [si'deit], *a.* posé, calme, rassis.

sedately [si'deitli], *adv.* posément, avec calme.

sedateness [si'deitnis], *n.* calme, *m.*

sedative ['sedətiv], *a.* and *n.* sédatif, *m.*

sedentary ['sedntri], *a.* sédentaire; inactif.

sedge [sedʒ], *n.* laiche, *f.*, jonc, *m.*

sediment ['sedimənt], *n.* sédiment, dépôt, *m.*

sedition [si'diʃən], *n.* sédition, *f.*

seditious [si'diʃəs], *a.* séditieux.

seditiousness [si'diʃəsnis], *n.* esprit séditieux, *m.*

seduce [si'dju:s], *v.t.* séduire.

seducer [si'dju:sə], *n.* séducteur, *m.*

seducing [si'dju:siŋ], *a.* séduisant.

seduction [si'dʌkʃən], *n.* séduction, *f.*

seductive [si'dʌktiv], *a.* séducteur, séduisant.

sedulity [si'dju:liti], **sedulousness** ['sed juləsnis], *n.* assiduité, diligence, *f.*

sedulous ['sedjuləs], *a.* assidu, diligent, zélé.

sedulously ['sedjuləsli], *adv.* assidûment, diligemment, avec application.

sedulousness [SEDULITY].

see (1) [si:], *n.* siège épiscopal, évêché; archevêché (*d'un archevêque*), *m.*; **the Holy See**, le Saint-Siège, *m.*

see (2) [si:], *v.t. irr.* voir; comprendre; accompagner, conduire.—*v.i.* voir; s'occuper (*de*); **I will see to it**, j'y veillerai.

seed [si:d], *n.* semence; graine (*de légumes*); (*fig.*) race, *f.*; **to run to seed**, monter en graine.—*v.t.* ensemencer; (*Spt.*) trier.—*v.i.* grener.

seed bed [si:dbed], *n.* semis, *m.*

seed cake ['si:dkeik], *n.* gâteau à l'anis, *m.*

seedling ['si:dliŋ], *n.* semis, sauvageon, *m.*

seedsman ['si:dzmən], *n.* (*pl.* **-men** [men]) grainetier, *m.*

seed-time ['si:dtaim], *n.* semailles, *f.pl.*

seedy ['si:di], *a.* râpé, usé (*vêtement*); souffrant; miteux.

seeing ['si:iŋ], *n.* vue; vision, *f.*—*conj. phr.* **seeing that**, vu que, puisque.

seek [si:k], *v.t. irr.* chercher; poursuivre, en vouloir à (*la vie etc.*).—*v.i.* chercher.

seeker ['si:kə], *n.* chercheur, *m.*

seeking ['si:kiŋ], *n.* recherche, poursuite, *f.*

seem [si:m], *v.i.* sembler, paraître, avoir l'air (*de*).

seeming ['si:miŋ], *a.* apparent, spécieux.—*n.* semblant, *m.*, apparence, *f.*, dehors, *m.*

seemingly ['si:miŋli], *adv.* en apparence, apparemment.

seemliness ['si:mlinis], *n.* bienséance, convenance, *f.*

seemly ['si:mli], *a.* bienséant, convenable; joli.—*adv.* convenablement.

seep [si:p], *v.i.* s'infiltrer, suinter.

seer [si:ə], *n.* prophète, voyant, *m.*

seesaw ['si:sɔ:], *n.* bascule, balançoire, *f.*, va-et-vient, *m.*—*v.i.* faire la bascule.

seethe [si:ð], *v.t.* faire bouillir.—*v.i.* bouillir, bouillonner.

segment ['segmənt], *n.* segment, *m.*

segregate ['segrigeit], *v.t.* séparer.—*v.i.* se diviser.

segregation [segri'geiʃən], *n.* séparation, ségrégation, *f.*

seize [si:z], *v.t.* saisir; se saisir de, s'emparer de; (*Naut.*) amarrer.—*v.i.* (*Mech.*) gripper, caler; se coincer.

seizure ['si:ʒə], *n.* saisie, prise de possession; (*Path.*) attaque, *f.*

seldom ['seldəm], *adv.* rarement.

select [si'lekt], *a.* choisi; d'élite.—*v.t.* choisir.

selection [si'lekʃən], *n.* choix, *m.*

selectness [si'lektnis], *n.* excellence, *f.*

self [self], *pron.* (*pl.* **selves** [selvz]) même, soi-même; (*reflexively*) se.—*n.* le moi, individu, *m.*, personne, *f.*

self-assertion ['selfə'sə:ʃən], *n.* caractère impérieux, *m.*, outrecuidance, *f.*

self-assertive ['selfə'sə:tiv], *a.* autoritaire, outrecuidant.

self-centered ['self'sentəd], *a.* égocentrique.

self-confidence ['self'kɔnfidəns], *n.* confiance en soi-même, assurance, *f.*

self-confident ['self'kɔnfidənt], *a.* sûr de soi-même.

self-conscious ['self'kɔnʃəs], *a.* embarrassé, intimidé; gêné.

self-consciousness ['self'kɔnʃəsnis], *n.* embarras, *m.*, gêne, *f.*

self-contained ['selfkən'teind], *a.* indépendant; avec entrée particulière (*appartement*).

self-control ['selfkən'troul], *n.* sang-froid, *m.*; maîtrise de soi, *f.*

self-defense ['selfdi'fens], *n.* défense personnelle; légitime défense, *f.*

self-denial ['selfdi'naiəl], *n.* abnégation, *f.*; désintéressement, *m.*

self-denying ['selfdi'naiiŋ], *a.* qui fait abnégation de soi.

self-educated ['self'edjukeitid], *a.* autodidacte.

self-esteem ['selfi'sti:m], *n.* amour-propre, *m.*

self-evident ['self'evidənt], *a.* évident en soi, qui saute aux yeux.

self-governed ['self'gʌvənd], *a.* indépendant, autonome.

self-government ['self'gʌvənmənt], *n.* autonomie, *f.*

self-help ['self'help], *n.* efforts personnels, *m.pl.*

self-importance ['selfim'pɔ:təns], *n.* suffisance, vanité, *f.*

self-important ['selfim'pɔ:tənt], *a.* plein de soi, suffisant.

self-inflicted ['selfin'fliktid], *a.* volontaire.

selfish ['selfiʃ], *a.* égoïste.

selfishly ['selfiʃli], *adv.* en égoïste, d'une manière égoïste.

selfishness ['selfiʃnis], *n.* égoïsme, *m.*

selfless ['selflis], *a.* désintéressé.

self-made ['self'meid], *a.* qui s'est fait ce qu'il est; **he is a self-made man**, il est fils de ses œuvres.

self-opinioned ['selfə'pinjənd], **self-opinionated** ['selfə'pinjəneitid], *a.* entêté.

self-possessed ['selfpə'zest], *a.* calme, maître de soi.

self-possession ['selfpə'zeʃən], *n.* sang-froid, aplomb, *m.*

self-praise ['self'preiz], *n.* éloge de soi-même, *m.*

self-preservation ['selfprezə'veiʃən], *n.* conservation de soi-même, *f.*

self-propelled ['selfprə'peld], *a.* autopropulsé.

self-registering ['self'redʒistriŋ], *a.* à registre, enregistreur.

self-reliance ['selfri'laiəns], *n.* confiance en soi, indépendance, *f.*

self-respect ['selfris'pekt], *n.* respect de soi-même, amour-propre, *m.*; dignité, *f.*

self-righteous ['self'raitʃəs], *a.* pharisaïque.

self-sacrifice ['self'sækrifais], *n.* sacrifice de soi-même, *m.*, abnégation, *f.*

self-same ['selfseim], *a.* absolument le même.

self-satisfied ['self'sætisfaid], *a.* content de soi.

self-seeking ['self'si:kiŋ], *a.* égoïste.

self-service ['self'sə:vis], *n.* libre service, self-service, *m.*

self-starter ['self'sto:tə], *n.* démarreur automatique, *m.*

self-styled ['self'staild], *a.* soi-disant, prétendu.

self-sufficiency ['selfsə'fiʃənsi], *n.* suffisance; indépendance, *f.*

self-sufficient ['selfsə'fiʃənt], *a.* suffisant; indépendant.

self-supporting ['selfsə'pɔ:tiŋ], *a.* qui subsiste par ses propres moyens.

self-taught ['self'tɔ:t], *a.* autodidacte.

self-will ['self'wil], *n.* obstination, opiniâtreté, *f.*

self-willed ['self'wild], *a.* obstiné, opiniâtre.

sell [sel], *v.t. irr.* vendre.—*v.i.* se vendre; **to be sold out of an article**, avoir tout vendu, ne plus avoir d'un article.—*n.* attrape, *f.*

seller ['selə], *n.* vendeur, *m.*, vendeuse, *f.*

selling ['seliŋ], *n.* vente, *f.*; **selling off**, liquidation, *f.*

seltzer ['seltsə], **seltzer water** ['seltsə'wɔ:tə], *n.* eau de Seltz, *f.*

selvedge ['selvidʒ], *n.* lisière, *f.*

selves [SELF].

semaphore ['seməfɔ:], *n.* sémaphore, *m.*

semblance ['sembləns], *n.* semblant, *m.*, apparence, *f.*

semi ['semi], *pref.* semi, demi, à demi, à moitié.

semibreve ['semibri:v], *n.* (*Mus.*) ronde, *f.*

semi-circle ['semisə:kl], *n.* demi-cercle, *m.*

semicolon ['semi'koulən], *n.* point-virgule, *m.*

semi-detached ['semidi'tætʃt], *a.* **semi-detached houses**, maisons jumelles, *f.pl.*

semi-final ['semifainl], *n.* demi-finale, *f.*

seminary ['seminəri], *n.* séminaire, *m.*; institution (*école*), *f.*

semi-official ['semiə'fiʃl], *a.* demi-officiel, officieux.

semiquaver ['semikweivə], *n.* (*Mus.*) double croche, *f.*

semitone ['semitoun], *n.* (*Mus.*) demi-ton, semi-ton, *m.*

semolina [semə'li:nə], *n.* semoule, *f.*

sempstress ['sempstris, 'semstris], *n.* couturière, *f.*

senate ['senit], *n.* sénat, *m.*

senator ['senitə], *n.* sénateur, *m.*

senatorial [seni'to:riəl], *a.* sénatorial.

send [send], *v.t. irr.* envoyer, faire parvenir; expédier (*marchandises*); **to send away**, renvoyer, congédier; **to send back**, renvoyer; **to send for**, envoyer chercher, faire venir; **to send forth**, lancer, émettre; **to send in**, faire entrer; **to send on**, faire suivre (*lettres etc.*).—*v.i.* envoyer.

sender ['sendə], *n.* envoyeur; (*Comm.*) expéditeur, *m.*

Senegal ['senigɔ:l]. le Sénégal, *m.*

Senegalese [seniɡə'li:z], *a.* sénégalais.—*n.* Sénégalais (*personne*), *m.*

senile ['si:nail], *a.* de vieillard, sénile.

senility [sə'niliti], *n.* sénilité, *f.*

senior ['si:njə], *a.* aîné; ancien; plus ancien, supérieur.—*n.* aîné; ancien; doyen, *m.*

seniority [si:ni'ɔriti], *n.* priorité d'âge; ancienneté, *f.*

senna ['senə], *n.* séné, *m.*

sensation [sen'seiʃən], *n.* sensation, *f.*

sensational [sen'seiʃənl], *a.* à sensation, à effet.

sensationalism [sen'seiʃənlizm], *n.* recherche du sensationnel, *f.*

sense [sens], *n.* sens; bon sens, sens commun; sentiment, *m.*; signification, *f.*

senseless ['senslis], *a.* sans connaissance, insensible; insensé, absurde (*pas raisonnable*).

senselessly ['senslisli], *adv.* d'une manière insensée; sottement.

senselessness ['senslisnis], *n.* sottise, absurdité, *f.*

sensibility [sensi'biliti], *n.* sensibilité, *f.*; sentiment, *m.*

sensible ['sensibl], *a.* sensé, raisonnable (*intelligent*); sensible (*de*); en pleine connaissance.

sensibly ['sensibli], *adv.* sensiblement; sensément, sagement (*avec intelligence*).

sensitive ['sensitiv], *a.* sensible (*à*); sensitif, impressionnable; susceptible (*ombrageux*).

sensitiveness ['sensitivnis], **sensitivity** [sensi'tiviti], *n.* sensibilité; susceptibilité (*facilité à se vexer etc.*), *f.*

sensitized ['sensitaizd], *a.* (*Phot.*) sensible (*papier*).

sensory ['sensəri], *a.* sensoriel, des sens.

sensual ['sensjuəl], *a.* sensuel; des sens.

sensualist ['sensjuəlist], *n.* sensualiste, *m.*, *f.*, sensuel, *m.*

sensuality [sensju'æliti], *n.* sensualité, *f.*

sentence ['sentəns], *n.* phrase; maxime, *f.*; jugement, arrêt, *m.*, sentence, *f.*—*v.t.* prononcer une sentence *ou* un jugement (*contre*), condamner.

sententious [sen'tenʃəs], *a.* sentencieux.

sententiousness [sen'tenʃəsnis], *n.* caractère sentencieux, *m.*

sentient ['senʃənt], *a.* sensible.

sentiment ['sentimənt], *n.* sentiment; avis, *m.*, pensée, *f.*

sentimental [senti'mentl], *a.* sentimental.

sentimentality [sentimen'tæliti], *n.* sensiblerie, sentimentalité, *f.*

sentinel ['sentinl], **sentry** ['sentri], *n.* sentinelle, *f.*, factionnaire, *m.*

sentry box ['sentriboks], *n.* guérite, *f.*

separable ['separəbl], *a.* séparable, divisible.

separate ['separit], *a.* séparé; disjoint, désuni.—['separeit], *v.t.* séparer; disjoindre, désunir.—*v.i.* se séparer; se disjoindre.

separately ['separitli], *adv.* séparément, à part.

separation [sepə'reiʃən], *n.* séparation; désunion, *f.*

sepia ['si:pjə], *n.* sépia (*couleur*); seiche (*poisson*), *f.*

sepoy ['si:pɔi], n. cipaye, m.
September [sep'tembə]. septembre, m.
septennial [sep'teniəl], a. septennal.
septennially [sep'teniəli], adv. tous les sept ans.
septic ['septik], a. septique; infecté (blessure).
septuagenarian [septjuədʒə'neəriən], a. and n. septuagénaire, m., f.
Septuagesima [septjuə'dʒesimə]. Septuagésime, f.
sepulchral [si'pʌlkrəl], a. sépulcral.
sepulchre ['sepəlkə], n. sépulcre, m.
sepulture ['sepəltʃə], n. sépulture; inhumation, f.
sequel ['si:kwəl], n. suite, conséquence, f.
sequence ['si:kwəns], n. suite, série; succession; (Cine.) séquence, f.
sequester [si'kwestə], v.t. séquestrer.
sequestered [si'kwestəd], a. retiré, écarté; (Law) en séquestre.
sequestrate [si'kwestreit, si'kwestrit], v.t. séquestrer.
sequestration [si:kwəs'treiʃən], n. séquestre, m.; retraite, f., isolement (personne), m.
sequestrator ['si:kwəstreitə], n. (Law) séquestre, m.
sequin [si'kwin], n. sequin, m.
seraglio [se'rɑ:ljou], n. sérail, m.
seraph ['seraf], n. (pl. **seraphim** ['serəfim]) séraphin, m.
seraphic [sə'ræfik], a. séraphique.
Serbia ['sə:biə]. la Serbie, f.
Serbian ['sə:biən], a. serbe.—n. serbe (langue), m.; Serbe (personne), m., f.
sere [SEAR].
serenade [serə'neid], n. sérénade, f.—v.t. donner une sérénade à.
serene [si'ri:n], a. serein, calme; sérénissime (titre).
sereneness [si'ri:nli], adv. avec sérénité.
sereneness [sə'ri:nnis], serenity [si'reniti], n. sérénité, f., calme, m.
serf [sə:f], n. serf, m.
serfdom ['sə:fdəm], n. servage, m.
serge [sə:dʒ], n. serge, f.
sergeant, serjeant ['sɑ:dʒənt], n. sergent (infanterie); maréchal des logis (cavalerie, artillerie); brigadier (police), m.
sergeant major ['sɑ:dʒənt'meidʒə], n. adjudant, m.
serial ['siəriəl], a. paraissant par numéros ou par livraisons; **serial** (story), (roman-) feuilleton, m.
serially ['siəriəli], adv. par numéros.
seriatim [siəri'eitim], adv. par série; successivement.
series ['siəri:z], n. série, suite, succession, f.
serious ['siəriəs], a. sérieux; grave.
seriously ['siəriəsli], adv. sérieusement; gravement.
seriousness ['siəriəsnis], n. sérieux, m.; gravité, f.
serjeant [SERGEANT].
sermon ['sə:mən], n. sermon, m.
sermonize ['sə:mənaiz], v.t. prêcher; sermonner.
sermonizer ['sə:mənaizə], n. sermonneur, m.
serpent ['sə:pənt], n. serpent, m.
serpentine ['sə:pəntain], a. serpentin, sinueux.—n. (Min.) serpentine, f.
serrate ['sereit], a. en scie, dentelé; serraté.

serration [se'reiʃən], n. dentelure, f.
serried ['serid], a. compact, serré.
serum ['siərəm], n. sérum, m.
servant ['sə:vənt], n. serviteur, m., servante, f.; employé (de compagnies etc.), m.; domestique, m.; ordonnance (d'officier), m., f.; **civil servant**, fonctionnaire, m., f.
serve [sə:v], v.t. servir; servir à, être bon à; faire (apprentissage); desservir (localité); signifier (une assignation); **it serves him right**, c'est bien fait.—v.i. servir; être au service; suffire.—n. (fam.) (Ten.) service, m.
server ['sə:və], n. servant; (Ten.) serveur; (Eccles.) acolyte, m.
service ['sə:vis], n. service; (fig.) avantage, m.; utilité; signification (d'assignation); (Mil.) arme, f.—v.t. (Motor.) entretenir, réparer.
serviceable ['sə:visəbl], a. utile (à), avantageux, de bon usage.
serviceableness ['sə:visəblnis], n. utilité, f.
service station ['sə:vissteiʃən], n. station-service, f.
serviette [sə:vi'et], n. serviette de table, f.
servile ['sə:vail], a. servile; asservi.
servility [sə'viliti], n. servilité, bassesse, f.
serving ['sə:viŋ], a. servant, qui sert.
servitude ['sə:vitju:d], n. servitude, f., asservissement, m.; **penal servitude**, travaux forcés, m.pl.
sesame ['sesəmi], n. sésame, m.
session ['seʃən], n. session, séance, f.; (pl.) assises, f.pl.
set [set], v.t. irr. poser, opposer (sceau, signature), mettre, placer, poser; planter (fleurs); fixer; ajuster, arranger (régler); affûter (outil); donner (exemple); (Mus.) mettre en musique; remettre (os); sertir (pierre précieuse); dresser, tendre (piège); déployer (voiles); (Print.) composer; **to set aside**, mettre de côté; **to set at ease**, mettre à l'aise; **to set back**, reculer; **to set forth**, énoncer; **to set forward**, avancer; **to set off**, faire ressortir (faire valoir); **to set up**, ériger, établir (fonder).—v.i. se fixer; diriger, porter (vers ou à); se coucher (soleil); prendre (confitures etc.); **to set about**, commencer, se mettre à; **to set out**, partir, se mettre en route; **to set up** (dans un commerce etc.), s'établir.—a. mis, posé, placé; serti (pierre précieuse); prêt; arrêté, fixe; réglé; d'apparat, préparé (discours); **all set?** ça y est?—n. collection, f., ensemble, assortiment, m., série, f., jeu; service (de porcelaine etc.), m.; parure (de pierres précieuses); mise en plis (cheveux), f.; (Theat.) décor; groupe, m.
set-back ['setbæk], n. recul, échec, m.
set-square ['setskwɛə], n. équerre, f.
settee [se'ti:], n. canapé, m., causeuse, f.
setter ['setə], n. chien d'arrêt, m.; **bone-setter**, rebouteur, rebouteux, m.
setting ['setiŋ], n. mise, pose, f.; coucher (du soleil etc.); décor (naturel ou de théâtre), m. (Mus.) mise en musique, f.; remboîtement (d'os), m.; monture (de pierre précieuse), f.
settle (1) [setl], v.t. fixer; établir; décider, arrêter; assigner (des biens à); coloniser (un pays); accommoder; payer, régler (dettes).—v.i. s'établir, se fixer; se marier; se calmer (devenir tranquille); se poser (oiseau); s'ar-

settle

ranger (*avec*); **to settle down**, se fixer, s'établir; **to settle down to**, s'appliquer à.

settle (2) [setl], *n.* banc (à dossier), *m.*

settled [setld], *a.* établi; calme, tranquille.

settlement ['setlmənt], **settling** ['setliŋ], *n.* établissement, arrangement; dépôt (*au fond des liquides*); accord, contrat, *m.*; colonisation; colonie, *f.*; règlement, solde (*des comptes*) (*Build.*) tassement, *m.*

settler ['setlə], *n.* colon, immigrant, *m.*

set-up ['setʌp], *n.* organisation, *f.*

seven ['sevən], *a.* and *n.* sept, *m.*

sevenfold ['sevənfould], *a.* septuple.—*adv.* sept fois.

seventeen [sevən'ti:n], *a.* and *n.* dix-sept, *m.*

seventeenth ['sevənti:nθ], *a.* dix-septième; dix-sept (*des rois etc.*).—*n.* dix-septième (*fraction*), *m.*

seventh ['sevənθ], *a.* septième; sept (*des rois etc.*).—*n.* septième (*fraction*), *m.*; (*Mus.*) septième, *f.*

seventieth ['sevəntiiθ], *a.* soixante-dixième. —*n.* soixante-dixième (*fraction*), *m.*

seventy ['sevənti], *a.* soixante-dix, *m.*

sever ['sevə], *v.t.* séparer, diviser (*de*); disjoindre; couper.—*v.i.* se séparer (*de*).

several ['sevrəl], *a.* plusieurs, divers; distinct, respectif.

severally ['sevrəli], *adv.* séparément, individuellement.

severance ['sevərəns], *n.* séparation, disjonction; rupture, *f.*

severe [si'viə], *a.* sévère; rigoureux, rude (*temps etc.*); violent, aigu, vif (*douleur etc.*).

severity [si'veriti], *n.* sévérité; rigueur, *f.*

sew [sou], *v.t. irr.* coudre; brocher (*livre*).

sewage ['siu:idʒ], *n.* eaux d'égout, *f.pl.*

sewer (1) ['souə], *n.* couseur, *m.*

sewer (2) ['sju:ə], *n.* égout, *m.*

sewerage ['sju:əridʒ], *n.* système d'égouts, *m.*, égouts, *m.pl.*

sewing ['souiŋ], *n.* couture, *f.*; **sewing machine**, machine à coudre, *f.*

sex [seks], *n.* sexe, *m.*

sexagenarian [seksədʒə'nɛəriən], *a.* and *n.* sexagénaire, *m., f.*

Sexagesima [seksə'dʒesimə], Sexagésime, *f.*

sexennial [sek'seniəl], *a.* sexennal.

sexennially [sek'seniəli], *adv.* tous les six ans.

sextant ['sekstənt], *n.* sextant, *m.*

sextet [seks'tet], *n.* (*Mus.*) sextuor, *m.*

sexton ['sekstən], *n.* sacristain; fossoyeur, *m.*

sextuple ['sekstjupl], *a.* and *n.* sextuple, *m.*

sexual ['seksjuəl], *a.* sexuel.

sexuality [seksju'æliti], *n.* sexualité, *f.*

shabbily ['ʃæbili], *adv.* mal, pauvrement (*mis* ou *vêtu*); (*fig.*) mesquinement.

shabbiness ['ʃæbinis], *n.* état râpé (*de vêtements*), *m.*; (*fig.*) mesquinerie, *f.*

shabby ['ʃæbi], *a.* râpé; mal vêtu, mal mis; (*fig.*) mesquin, ignoble.

shackle [ʃækl], *v.t.* enchaîner; (*fig.*) entraver.

shackles [ʃæklz], *n.pl.* fers, *m.pl.*, chaînes (*fig.*) entraves, *f.pl.*

shad [ʃæd], *n.* alose (*poisson*), *f.*

shade [ʃeid], *n.* ombre, *f.*; ombrage (*d'arbre etc.*); abat-jour (*de lampe etc.*); garde-vue (*pour les yeux*), *m.*; nuance (*couleur*), *f.*; (*pl.*) enfers (*où vivent les immortels*), *m.pl.*; **in the shade**, à l'ombre.—*v.t.* ombrager (*de*); obscurcir; abriter (*protéger*) (*Paint.*) ombrer, nuancer; hachurer (*une carte*).

---

shaded ['ʃeidid], *a.* à l'ombre; ombragé (*de*); (*Paint.*) ombré.

shadiness ['ʃeidinis], *n.* ombrage, *m.*, ombre; (*fig.*) nature suspecte, *f.*

shading ['ʃeidiŋ], *n.* ombres, nuances; hachures, *f.pl.*

shadow ['ʃædou], *n.* ombre, *f.*—*v.t.* ombrager; filer, espionner (*suivre de près*).

shadowing ['ʃædouiŋ], *n.* espionnage, *m.*, filature, *f.*

shadowy ['ʃædoui], *a.* ombragé; sombre (*morne*); vague, chimérique (*irréel*).

shady ['ʃeidi], *a.* ombragé, ombreux; sombre (*noir*); (*colloq.*) louche (*malhonnête*).

shaft [ʃɑ:ft], *n.* flèche, *f.*; dard, trait; brancard (*de charette*); manche (*d'outil, d'arme*); puits (*de mine*); (*Mach.*) arbre, *m.*

shag [ʃæg], *n.* poil rude; caporal (*tabac*); cormoran huppé (*oiseau*), *m.*

shagginess ['ʃæginis], *n.* état poilu, état hérissé, *m.*

shaggy ['ʃægi], *a.* poilu, velu; raboteux (*pays*).

shagreen [ʃə'gri:n], *a.* de peau de chagrin.—*n.* peau de chagrin, *f.*

shah [ʃɑ:], *n.* shah, *m.*

shake [ʃeik], *n.* secousse, *f.*; serrement, *m.*; poignée (de main), *f.*; hochement (de tête), *m.*—*v.t. irr.* secouer, branler, agiter; ébranler, faire trembler; **to shake hands with**, serrer la main à.—*v.i.* trembler (*de*); s'agiter, branler; chanceler (*sur ses jambes*).

shakedown ['ʃeikdaun], *n.* lit improvisé, *m.*

shakily ['ʃeikili], *adv.* en branlant; à pas chancelants.

shaking ['ʃeikiŋ], *n.* secousse, *f.*, ébranlement, tremblement; ballottement (*à cheval*), *m.*

shako ['ʃækou], *n.* shako, *m.*

shaky ['ʃeiki], *a.* branlant; (*fig.*) peu solide; faible, chancelant (*personne*).

shale [ʃeil], *n.* argile schisteuse, *f.*

shall [ʃæl], *v.aux. irr.* (*used as sign of the future*) **I shall go**, j'irai; devoir; vouloir; **shall I go?** dois-je aller ? voulez-vous que j'aille ? **but he shall**, mais je l'y forcerai; **but I shall not**, mais je n'en ferai rien.

shallop ['ʃæləp], *n.* chaloupe, péniche, pinasse, *f.*

shallot [ʃə'lɔt], *n.* échalote, *f.*

shallow ['ʃælou], *a.* peu profond; (*fig.*) superficiel, léger, borné.

shallowness ['ʃælounis], *n.* peu de profondeur; esprit borné, *m.*

sham [ʃæm], *a.* feint, simulé; faux, factice.—*n.* feinte, *f.*, prétexte, *m.*; imposture, frime, *f.*—*v.t.* feindre, simuler; faire le, la ou les.—*v.i.* feindre, faire semblant; jouer la comédie.

shamble [ʃæmbl], *v.i.* marcher en traînant les pieds.

shambles [ʃæmblz], *n.pl.* abattoir, *m.*; (*fig.*) scène de carnage; une belle pagaille, *f.*

shambling ['ʃæmbliŋ], *a.* traînant.

shame [ʃeim], *n.* honte; ignominie (*déshonneur*), *f.*; opprobre, *m.*; **what a shame!** quel dommage!—*v.t.* faire honte à.

shamefaced ['ʃeimfeist], *a.* honteux, confus.

shamefacedly ['ʃeim'feisidli], *adv.* d'un air penaud.

shamefacedness ['ʃeimfeistnis], *n.* mauvaise honte; timidité, *f.*

shameful ['ʃeimful], *a.* honteux; déshonnête.

shamefulness ['ʃeimfulnis], n. honte, igno-minie, f.
shameless ['ʃeimlis], a. éhonté, effronté, impudent.
shamelessly ['ʃeimlisli], adv. sans honte, effrontément.
shamelessness ['ʃeimlisnis], n. effronterie, impudence, f.
shammer ['ʃæmə], n. simulateur, m.
shampoo ['ʃæm'pu:], v.t. frictionner; net-toyer (la tête).—n. shampooing, m.
shamrock ['ʃæmrɔk], n. trèfle (d'Irlande), m.
shank [ʃæŋk], n. jambe, f.
shanty ['ʃænti], n. cabane, bicoque, hutte, f.
shanty-town ['ʃæntitaun], n. bidonville, f.
shape [ʃeip], n. forme, figure; tournure, taille (de personne); façon, coupe (de vêtement), f.—v.t. former, façonner; modeler (sur).
shapeless ['ʃeiplis], a. informe, sans forme.
shapelessness ['ʃeiplisnis], n. absence de forme, difformité, f.
shapeliness ['ʃeiplinis], n. beauté de forme, f., galbe, m.
shapely ['ʃeipli], a. bien fait, beau.
share (1) [ʃɛə], n. soc (de charrue), m.
share (2) [ʃɛə], n. part, portion; (St. Exch.) action, f.; *preferred share*, action privi-légiée.—v.t., v.i. partager; prendre part à; avoir part à.
shareholder ['ʃɛəhouldə], n. actionnaire, m., f.
sharer ['ʃɛərə], n. participant; (Law) parta-geant, m.
sharing ['ʃɛəriŋ], n. partage, m.
shark [ʃɑːk], n. requin; (fig.) escroc, filou (personne), m.
sharp [ʃɑːp], a. tranchant, affilé, qui coupe bien; pointu, aigu; saillant (angle); (fig.) vif, intelligent, pénétrant, perçant; anguleux (traits); piquant, aigre (goût etc.); rusé (astucieux); (Mus.) dièse; *sharp practice*, filouterie, rouerie, f.—adv. précise (l'heure); *at four o'clock sharp*, à quatre heures précises; *look sharp!* faites vite!—n. (Mus.) dièse, m.
sharpen ['ʃɑːpən], v.t. affiler, aiguiser; tailler en pointe, tailler (crayon etc.); (fig.) rendre vif.
sharper ['ʃɑːpə], n. aigrefin, escroc, chevalier d'industrie, m.
sharply ['ʃɑːpli], adv. rudement, vivement; nettement.
sharpness ['ʃɑːpnis], n. tranchant (d'une lame), m.; pointe (acuité); acidité (de fruit); violence (de douleur etc.); âpreté (de langage etc.); netteté (de contour etc.), f.; esprit éveillé (d'enfants etc.), m.
sharp-sighted ['ʃɑːp'saitid], a. à l'esprit délié.
sharp-witted ['ʃɑːp'witid], a. à l'esprit délié.
shatter ['ʃætə], v.t. fracasser, briser en pièces.—v.i. se briser, se fracasser.
shave [ʃeiv], v.t. raser; faire la barbe à; effleurer (friser); (Tech.) planer.—v.i. se raser, se faire la barbe; *to have a close shave*, l'échapper belle; *to have a shave*, se raser, se faire raser.
shaving ['ʃeiviŋ], n. action de raser, f.; copeau (de bois), m.
shaving brush ['ʃeiviŋbrʌʃ], n. blaireau, m.
shaving cream ['ʃeiviŋkri:m], n. crème à raser, f.

shaving soap ['ʃeiviŋsoup], n. savon pour la barbe, m.
shawl [ʃɔːl], n. châle, m.
she [ʃiː], pron. elle; femelle (de certains animaux), f.
sheaf [ʃiːf], n. (pl. sheaves [ʃiːvz]) gerbe, f.; faisceau (de flèches), m.—v.t. engerber, mettre en gerbe.
shear [ʃiə], v.t. irr. tondre.
shearer ['ʃiərə], n. tondeur, m.; tondeuse (machine), f.
shearing ['ʃiəriŋ], n. tonte, tondaison, f.
shears [ʃiəz], n.pl. grands ciseaux, m.pl.; cisailles (pour haie, pour métal), f.pl.
she-ass ['ʃiːæs], n. ânesse, f.
sheath [ʃiːθ], n. (pl. sheaths [ʃiːðz]) gaine, f.; fourreau (à épée); étui (à ciseaux etc.); (Ent.) élytre, m.
sheathe [ʃiːð], v.t. mettre dans le fourreau, rengainer; envelopper; revêtir (de).
sheaves [SHEAF].
she-cat ['ʃiːkæt], n. chatte, f.
shed (1) [ʃed], n. hangar; (Build.) atelier, m.; *cow-shed*, étable (à vaches), f.; *lean-to shed*, appentis, m.
shed (2) [ʃed], v.t. irr. répandre, verser; se dépouiller de, perdre (feuilles etc.); jeter (animal).
shedding ['ʃediŋ], n. effusion (de sang); perte (feuilles etc.), f.
sheen [ʃiːn], n. éclat, lustre, brillant, m.
sheep [ʃiːp], n.inv. mouton, m.; (fig.) brebis, f.; *black sheep*, brebis galeuse; *lost sheep*, brebis égarée.
sheep dip ['ʃiːpdip], n. bain parasiticide, m.
sheep dog ['ʃiːpdɔg], n. chien de berger, m.
sheep-fold ['ʃiːpfould], n. bergerie, f., bercail, m.
sheepish ['ʃiːpiʃ], a. penaud, bête, niais.
sheepishly ['ʃiːpiʃli], adv. d'un air penaud.
sheep pen ['ʃiːppen], n. parc à moutons, m.
sheep-shearing ['ʃiːpʃiəriŋ], n. tonte, f.
sheepskin ['ʃiːpskin], n. peau de mouton; basane (cuir), f.
sheer (1) [ʃiə], a. pur; escarpé, à pic (rocher); *sheer force*, pure force, f.; *sheer non-sense*, pure sottise, f.—adv. tout droit; tout à fait.
sheer (2) [ʃiə], n. (Naut.) tonture; embardée, f.—v.i. faire des embardées; *to sheer off*, pousser au large, s'esquiver.
sheet [ʃiːt], n. drap, m.; feuille (de papier ou métal); nappe (d'eau etc.); (Naut.) écoute (corde), f.; *winding sheet*, linceul, m.
sheet anchor ['ʃiːtæŋkə], n. ancre de miséri-corde; (fig.) ancre de salut, f.
sheet iron ['ʃiːtaiən], n. tôle, f.
sheet lightning ['ʃiːtlaitniŋ], n. éclair en nappe, m.
sheikh [ʃeik], n. cheik, m.
shelf [ʃelf], n. (pl. shelves [ʃelvz] planche, f.; rayon (de bibliothèque), m.; tablette, f.; écueil (dans la mer), m.; *set of shelves*, étagères, f.pl.
shell [ʃel], n. coque (d'œuf, fruits etc.); coquille (œuf vide); cosse (de petits pois etc.); écaille (d'huître, de tortue); carapace (de homard), f.; (Artill.) obus; (fig.) extérieur, m.—v.t. écaler (noisette etc.); écosser (petits pois etc.); égrener (graine); (Mil.) bombarder.
shell-fish ['ʃelfiʃ], n. coquillage, mollusque, m., crustacés, m.pl.

shelling ['ʃeliŋ], n. écossage; égrenage; (Mil.) bombardement, m.

shell-proof ['ʃelpruːf], a. blindé.

shelter ['ʃeltə], n. abri, couvert; (fig.) asile, m.; to take shelter, s'abriter.—v.t. abriter; protéger.—v.i. s'abriter.

sheltered ['ʃeltəd], a. abrité.

shelve [ʃelv], v.t. mettre sur un rayon; (fig.) enterrer.—v.i. aller en pente.

shelves [SHELF].

shelving ['ʃelviŋ], a. en pente, incliné.

shepherd ['ʃepəd], n. berger, pâtre; (fig.) pasteur, m.—v.t. piloter, guider.

shepherdess ['ʃepədes], n. bergère, f.

sherbet ['ʃəːbət], n. sorbet, m.

sheriff ['ʃerif], n. shérif; (Am.) chef de police (d'un comté), m.

sherry ['ʃeri], n. vin de Xérès, m.

shield [ʃiːld], n. bouclier; écran protecteur (Her.) écu, écusson, m.—v.t. défendre de, protéger contre.

shift [ʃift], n. changement; expédient, m., ressource, f.; détour, faux-fuyant (artifice), m.; *chemise de femme; équipe, journée (d'ouvriers), f.—v.t., v.i. changer; changer de place; (fig.) trouver des expédients; to shift for oneself, se débrouiller.

shiftiness ['ʃiftinis], n. manque de franchise, m.

shifting ['ʃiftiŋ], a. changeant; shifting sand, sable mouvant, m.—n. changement; déplacement (de cargaison etc.), m.

shiftless ['ʃiftlis], a. sans initiative; sans énergie; paresseux.

shifty ['ʃifti], a. plein d'expédients; he is a shifty customer, c'est un roublard.

shilling ['ʃiliŋ], n. shilling, m.

shilly-shally ['ʃili'ʃæli], n. irrésolution, f.—v.i. hésiter, être irrésolu.

shimmer ['ʃimə], n. lueur, f.—v.i. miroiter.

shin [ʃin], n. devant de la jambe; jarret (de bœuf), m.

shin-bone ['ʃinboun], n. tibia, m.

shindy ['ʃindi], n. tapage, m.

shine [ʃain], v.i. irr. luire; reluire; briller.—n. brillant, éclat, lustre, m.

shingle (1) [ʃiŋgl], n. bardeau (pour toiture), m.; coiffure à la garçonne, f.

shingle (2) [ʃiŋgl], n. galets, cailloux (au bord de la mer), m.

shingles [ʃiŋglz], n.pl. (Med.) zona, m.

shingly [ʃiŋgli], a. couvert de galets.

shining [ʃainiŋ], a. luisant, brillant.

shiny ['ʃaini], a. luisant, reluisant.

ship [ʃip], n. navire; vaisseau, bâtiment, m.—v.t. embarquer; expédier (marchandises); armer (avirons).—v.i. s'embarquer.

shipboard ['ʃipbɔːd], n. bord de navire, m.

shipbuilder ['ʃipbildə], n. constructeur de navires, m.

shipbuilding ['ʃipbildiŋ], n. construction navale, m.

ship chandler ['ʃip'tʃɑːndlə], n. fournisseur de navires, m.

shipmate ['ʃipmeit], n. camarade de bord, m.

shipment ['ʃipmənt], n. chargement, m.

shipowner ['ʃipounə], n. armateur, m.

shipper ['ʃipə], n. expéditeur, m.

shipping ['ʃipiŋ], a. maritime.—n. vaisseaux, navires, m.pl.; navigation; marine marchande; mise à bord (chargement), f.

ship's boat ['ʃips'bout], n. chaloupe, f.

ship's carpenter ['ʃips'kɑːpintə], n. charpentier du bord, m.

shipshape ['ʃipʃeip], a. en ordre, bien arrangé.

shipwreck ['ʃiprek], n. naufrage, m.—v.t. faire faire naufrage à; to be shipwrecked, faire naufrage.

shipwrecked ['ʃiprekt], a. naufragé.

shipwright ['ʃiprait], n. constructeur de navires, m.

shipyard ['ʃipjɑːd], n. chantier naval, m.

shire ['ʃaiə], n. comté, m.

shirk [ʃəːk], v.t. éviter, éluder.—v.i. finasser; tirer au flanc.

shirker ['ʃəːkə], n. carottier; flanchard, m.

shirt [ʃəːt], n. chemise (d'homme), f.; shirt collar, col de chemise, m.; shirt front, devant de chemise, plastron, m.

shiver (1) ['ʃivə], v.t. briser en morceaux, fracasser.—v.i. se briser en morceaux.—n. fragment, morceau, éclat, m.

shiver (2) ['ʃivə], v.i. grelotter (de froid); frissonner (de peur).—n. frisson, tremblement, m.

shivering ['ʃivəriŋ], a. frissonnant.—n. frissonnement, frisson, m.

shoal [ʃoul], n. banc (de poissons), m.; (fig.) foule, f.; bas-fond, haut-fond (de la mer), m.; in shoals, en foule.

shock (1) [ʃɔk], n. choc, m.; (Elec.) secousse, f.—v.t. choquer, heurter; scandaliser.

shock (2) [ʃɔk], n. moyette (de blé); tignasse (de cheveux), f.

shock absorber ['ʃɔkəbsɔːbə], n. (Motor.) amortisseur, m.

shocking ['ʃɔkiŋ], a. choquant, affreux, dégoûtant.

shockingly ['ʃɔkiŋli], adv. affreusement.

shod [ʃɔd], a. ferré (cheval); chaussé (personne).

shoddy ['ʃɔdi], a. d'effilochage; de pacotille. —n. drap de laine d'effilochage, m.

shoe [ʃuː], n. soulier, m.; chaussure, f.; fer (à cheval); sabot (en bois), m.—v.t. irr. chausser; ferrer (cheval etc.).

shoe-black ['ʃuːblæk], n. cireur, m.

shoe-horn ['ʃuːhɔːn], n. chausse-pied, m.

shoeing ['ʃuːiŋ], n. ferrage, m.

shoeing-smith ['ʃuːiŋsmiθ], n. maréchal ferrant, m.

shoe-lace ['ʃuːleis], n. lacet de chaussure, m.

shoemaker ['ʃuːmeikə], n. cordonnier, m.

shoe-making ['ʃuːmeikiŋ], n. cordonnerie, f.

shoe polish ['ʃuːpɔliʃ], n. cirage, m.

shoot [ʃuːt], v.t. irr. tirer, lancer, darder; décharger, tirer un coup (de fusil etc.); atteindre (une cible); tuer (faire mourir); fusiller; descendre (rapides etc.); to shoot a film, tourner un film; to shoot oneself, se tuer.—v.i. tirer; chasser (gibier); (fig.) s'élancer; filer (étoile etc.); pousser (plante etc.).—n. rejeton, m., pousse (plante), f.; sarment (de vigne); dépôt de décombres (ordures), m.

shooter ['ʃuːtə], n. tireur, m.

shooting ['ʃuːtiŋ], a. lancinant (douleur); shooting star, étoile filante, f.—n. tir (de fusil), m.; chasse au fusil, f.; élancement (de douleur), m.; pousse (de plante); décharge (des ordures), f.; (Cine.) tournage (de film), m.

shooting-brake ['ʃuːtiŋbreik], n. (Motor.) canadienne, f.

shooting gallery ['ʃuːtiŋgæləri], *n.* tir, stand, *m.*

shop [ʃɔp], *n.* boutique (*petit*), *f.*, magasin (*grand*); atelier (*de fabrication*), *m.*—*v.i.* faire des emplettes; *to go shopping*, aller faire des courses.

shop-assistant ['ʃɔpəsistənt], *n.* vendeur, *m.*, vendeuse, commise, *f.*

shopkeeper ['ʃɔpkiːpə], *n.* marchand, *m.*

shoplifter ['ʃɔpliftə], *n.* voleur à l'étalage, *m.*

shoplifting ['ʃɔpliftiŋ], *n.* vol à l'étalage, *m.*

shopper ['ʃɔpə], *n.* acheteur, client, *m.*

shopping center ['ʃɔpiŋsentə], *n.* quartier commerçant, *m.*

shop steward ['ʃɔpstjuəd], *n.* responsable syndical, délégué ouvrier, *m.*

shop-walker ['ʃɔpwɔːkə], *n.* chef de rayon; inspecteur de magasin, *m.*

shop window ['ʃɔp'windou], *n.* devanture, vitrine, *f.*, étalage, *m.*

shopworn ['ʃɔpwɔːn], *a.* défraîchi.

shore [ʃɔː], *n.* rivage, bord, *m.*, plage, côte, *f.*—*v.t.* étayer, étançonner.

short [ʃɔːt], *a.* court; bref; passager (*temps*); petit (*taille*); insuffisant; croquant (*pâte*); brusque (*bourru*); *short circuit*, court-circuit, *m.*; *short story*, conte, *m.*, nouvelle, *f.*; *to cut the matter short*, pour en finir.—*adv.* court, vivement, brusquement; *it falls far short of it*, il s'en faut de beaucoup.

shortbread ['ʃɔːtbred], *n.* (gâteau) sablé, *m.*

short-circuit ['ʃɔːt'səːkit], *v.t.* mettre en court-circuit.

shortcoming ['ʃɔːtkʌmiŋ], *n.* défaut, *m.*, insuffisance, *f.*

shorten [ʃɔːtn], *v.t.* raccourcir; abréger.—*v.i.* (se) raccourcir.

shortening ['ʃɔːtniŋ], *n.* raccourcissement, *m.*

shorthand ['ʃɔːthænd], *n.* sténographie, *f.*

short-handed ['ʃɔːt'hændid], *a.* à court de personnel.

shorthand-typist ['ʃɔːthænd'taipist], *n.* sténodactylographe, (*fam.*) sténodactylo, *f.*

short-lived ['ʃɔːt'livd], *a.* qui vit peu de temps, éphémère.

shortly ['ʃɔːtli], *adv.* bientôt, sous peu; brièvement.

shortness ['ʃɔːtnis], *n.* courte durée, *f.*; peu d'étendue, *m.*; petitesse (*de taille*), *f.*

shorts ['ʃɔːts], *n.pl.* culotte courte, *f.*, caleçon court, slip; short, *m.*

short-sighted ['ʃɔːt'saitid], *a.* myope; (*fig.*) peu prévoyant.

short-sightedness ['ʃɔːt'saitidnis], *n.* myopie, *f.*; (*fig.*) manque de prévoyance, *m.*

short-tempered ['ʃɔːt'tempəd], *a.* vif, pétulant, brusque.

short-winded ['ʃɔːt'windid], *a.* à l'haleine courte; poussif (*cheval*).

shot (1) [ʃɔt], *past* and *p.p.* [SHOOT].

shot (2) [ʃɔt], *a.* chatoyant; *shot silk*, soie gorge-de-pigeon, *f.*—*n.* coup de fusil, coup; trait (*d'arc*), *m.*; balle (*de fusil*), *f.*, boulet (*de canon*); plomb (*de fusil de chasse*), *m.*; (*Artill.*) charge; portée (*étendue*), *f.*; tireur (*personne*) (*Fib.*) coup au but, *m.*; (*Med.*) injection; (*Cine.*) prise, *f.*; *at a shot*, d'un seul coup; *like a shot*, comme un trait; *to be a good shot*, être bon tireur; *to fire a shot*, tirer un coup de feu. [see **shy**]

shot-gun ['ʃɔtgʌn], *n.* fusil de chasse, *m.*

should [ʃud], *v.aux.* (*past of* **shall**, *used as sign of the conditional*) *I should speak*, je parlerais; (= *ought to*, *conditional tense of* devoir) *you should see it*, vous devriez le voir.

shoulder ['ʃouldə], *n.* épaule; (*Tech.*) languette, *f.*; *round shoulders*, dos rond, *m.*—*v.t.* charger sur les épaules; se charger de; porter (*armes*).

shoulder blade ['ʃouldəbleid], *n.* omoplate, *f.*

shout [ʃaut], *v.t.*, *v.i.* crier, huer, pousser des cris; vociférer.—*n.* cri, *m.*; acclamations, *f.pl.*; éclat (*de rire*), *m.*

shouting ['ʃautiŋ], *n.* acclamation, *f.*, cris, *m.pl.*

shove [ʃʌv], *v.t.* pousser; *to shove away*, repousser, éloigner.—*v.i.* pousser.—*n.* coup, *m.*, poussée, *f.*

shovel [ʃʌvl], *n.* pelle, *f.*—*v.t.* ramasser avec la pelle, pelleter.

shovelful ['ʃʌvlful], *n.* pelletée, *f.*

show [ʃou], *v.t.* irr. montrer, faire voir, exposer à la vue; manifester, témoigner, démontrer; indiquer; expliquer; *to show in*, faire entrer; *to show off*, faire valoir.—*v.i.* paraître, se montrer; se faire remarquer; *to show off*, poser, se donner des airs.—*n.* apparence, *f.*; étalage, *m.*, parade, *f.*; spectacle, concours, *m.*; exposition, *f.*

show-case ['ʃoukeis], *n.* montre, vitrine, *f.*

shower ['ʃauə], *n.* ondée (*légère*); averse (*grosse*); pluie, grêle (*de coups*, *pierres etc.*); douche, *f.*—*v.t.* inonder (*de pluie*) (*fig.*) verser.

shower bath ['ʃauəbɑː:θ], *n.* douche, *f.*, bain-douche, *m.*

showery ['ʃauəri], *a.* pluvieux.

show-ring ['ʃouriŋ], *n.* arène de vente, *f.*

show room ['ʃouruːm], *n.* salle d'exposition, *f.*

showy ['ʃoui], *a.* voyant, prétentieux, criard.

shrapnel ['ʃræpnəl], *n.* éclats d'obus, *m.pl.*

shred [ʃred], *n.* lambeau, bout, brin, *m.*; *to tear to shreds*, déchirer en lambeaux.—*v.t.* déchiqueter; râper grossièrement.

shrew [ʃruː], *n.* mégère, femme acariâtre, *f.*

shrewd [ʃruːd], *a.* sagace, fin, perspicace.

shrewdly ['ʃruːdli], *adv.* avec sagacité, avec pénétration, finement.

shrewdness ['ʃruːdnis], *n.* sagacité, pénétration, finesse, *f.*

shrewish ['ʃruːiʃ], *a.* acariâtre.

shrewishly ['ʃruːiʃli], *adv.* en mégère.

shrewishness ['ʃruːiʃnis], *n.* humeur acariâtre, *f.*

shriek [ʃriːk], *n.* cri perçant, *m.*—*v.t.* crier.—*v.i.* jeter un cri aigu.

shrieking ['ʃriːkiŋ], *n.* cris stridents, *m.pl.*

shrift [ʃrift], *n.* confession, *f.*; (*fig.*) *short shrift*, très court délai, *m.*

shrill [ʃril], *a.* aigu, perçant; aigre (*voix*).

shrillness ['ʃrilnis], *n.* son aigu, ton aigu, *m.*

shrilly ['ʃrili], *adv.* d'un ton aigu.

shrimp [ʃrimp], *n.* crevette (*grise*), *f.*

shrine [ʃrain], *n.* châsse, *f.*; tombeau, *m.*; chapelle (*d'un saint*), *f.*

shrink [ʃriŋk], *v.t.* irr. rétrécir, faire rétrécir.—*v.i.* rétrécir, se rétrécir; se retirer; reculer; se ratatiner; se tasser (*en vieillissant*).

shrinkage ['ʃriŋkidʒ], *n.* rétrécissement, *m.*, contraction, *f.*

561

shrinking

shrinking ['ʃriŋkiŋ], *n.* rétrécissement, *m.*; action de reculer, *f.*

*shrive [ʃraiv], *v.t. irr.* confesser.

shrivel [ʃrivl], *v.t.* faire ratatiner, faire recroqueviller, rider, racornir.—*v.i.* se ratatiner, se recroqueviller.

shroud [ʃraud], *n.* linceul, suaire, *m.*; (*Naut.*, *pl.*) haubans, *m.pl.*—*v.t.* (*fig.*) abriter, couvrir.

Shrovetide ['ʃrouvtaid]. les jours gras, *m.pl.*; *Shrove Tuesday*, mardi-gras, *m.*

shrub [ʃrʌb], *n.* arbuste, arbrisseau, *m.*

shrubbery ['ʃrʌbəri], *n.* plantation d'arbrisseaux, *f.*

shrubby ['ʃrʌbi], *a.* plein d'arbrisseaux, touffu.

shrug [ʃrʌg], *n.* haussement d'épaules, *m.*—*v.t.* hausser; *to shrug one's shoulders*, hausser les épaules.

shudder ['ʃʌdə], *v.i.* frissonner, frémir (*de*).—*n.* frissonnement, frémissement, *m.*

shuffle [ʃʌfl], *v.t.* mêler; (*Cards*) battre.—*v.i.* traîner les pieds; battre les cartes; tergiverser (*équivoquer*).

shuffling ['ʃʌfliŋ], *a.* chicaneur, biaiseur; traînant (*allure*).—*n.* marche traînante, *f.*; (*Cards*) battement des cartes, *m.*; (*fig.*) chicane, *f.*

shun [ʃʌn], *v.t.* éviter, fuir.

shunt [ʃʌnt], *v.t.* garer (*train*); détourner.

shunting ['ʃʌntiŋ], *n.* changement de voie, garage, *m.*

shut [ʃʌt], *v.t. irr.* fermer; enfermer; *to shut off*, intercepter, couper (*vapeur etc.*); *to shut out*, exclure; *to shut up*, fermer, enfermer; condamner (*porte etc.*); faire taire.—*v.i.* fermer, se fermer; *shut up!* taisez-vous!

shutter ['ʃʌtə], *n.* volet, contrevent (*à l'extérieur de la fenêtre*), *m.*

shuttle [ʃʌtl], *n.* navette (*tissage*); vanne, *f.*

shuttle-cock ['ʃʌtlkɔk], *n.* volant, *m.*

shuttle service ['ʃʌtləːvis], *n.* navette, *f.*

shy (1) [ʃai], *a.* réservé, timide, honteux.—*v.i.* être ombrageux, faire un écart (*cheval*).

shy (2) [ʃai], *v.t.* jeter, lancer.—*n.* coup de pierre *etc.*); essai, *m.*; *to have a shy at*, s'essayer à (*faire quelque chose*).

shyly ['ʃaili], *adv.* timidement, avec réserve.

shyness ['ʃainis], *n.* timidité, retenue, réserve; fausse honte, *f.*

Siam [sai'æm]. le Siam, *m.*

Siamese [saiə'miːz], *a.* siamois.—*n.* siamois (*langue*); Siamois (*personne*), *m.*

Siberia [sai'biəriə]. la Sibérie, *f.*

Siberian [sai'biəriən], *a.* sibérien.—*n.* Sibérien (*personne*), *m.*

sibilant ['sibilənt], *a.* sifflant.—*n.* lettre sifflante, *f.*

siccative ['sikətiv], *a.* and *n.* siccatif, *m.*

Sicilian [si'siliən], *a.* sicilien.—*n.* Sicilien (*personne*), *m.*

Sicily ['sisili]. la Sicile, *f.*

sick [sik], *a.* malade; qui a des nausées, qui a mal au cœur; (*fig.*) las, dégoûté; *sick headache*, migraine, *f.*; *sick man* or *woman*, malade, *m.*, *f.*; *sick of*, dégoûté de; *to be sea-sick*, avoir le mal de mer; *to be sick*, vomir.

sick-bed ['sikbed], *n.* lit de douleur, *m.*

sicken [sikn], *v.t.* rendre malade; (*fig.*) lasser, dégoûter.—*v.i.* tomber malade.

sickening ['sikniŋ], *a.* écœurant; (*fig.*) dégoûtant.

sickle [sikl], *n.* faucille, *f.*

sick leave ['sikliːv], *n.* congé de convalescence, *m.*

sickliness ['siklinis], *n.* mauvaise santé, *f.*

sick list ['siklist], *n.* rôle des malades, *m.*

sickly ['sikli], *a.* maladif; affadissant, affadi (*goût etc.*).

sickness ['siknis], *n.* maladie, *f.*; nausées, *f.pl.*

sick-nurse ['siknəːs], *n.* garde-malade, *f.*

sick-room ['sikruːm], *n.* chambre de malade, *f.*

side [said], *a.* de côté; latéral; indirect.—*n.* côté; flanc; bord; versant (*de montagne*); parti; (*Spt.*) camp, *m.*; *by his side*, à côté de lui; *side by side*, côte à côte; *this side up* (*caisses*), dessus; *to take sides*, prendre parti; *wrong side out*, à l'envers.—*v.i.* *to side with*, se ranger du côté de.

sideboard ['saidbɔːd], *n.* buffet, *m.*

sided ['saidid], *a.* à côtés, à faces; *two-sided*, à deux faces.

side door ['saiddɔː], *n.* porte latérale, *f.*

side-line ['saidlain], *n.* occupation secondaire, *f.*

sidelong ['saidlɔŋ], *a.* and *adv.* de côté.

side show ['saidʃou], *n.* spectacle forain, *m.*

sidesman ['saidzmən], *n.* (*pl.* -**men** [men]) (*Eccles.*) marguillier, *m.*

side-track ['saidtræk], *v.t.* garer (*train*); (*fig.*) semer (*quelqu'un*).

sidewalk ['saidwɔːk], *n.* (*Am.*) trottoir (*de rue*), *m.*

sideways ['saidweiz], *adv.* de côté; obliquement.

siding ['saidiŋ], *n.* voie d'évitement, voie de garage, *f.*

sidle [saidl], *v.i.* marcher de côté; s'insinuer.

siege [siːdʒ], *n.* siège, *m.*; *to lay siege to*, mettre le siège devant, faire le siège de, assiéger.

Sienna [si'enə]. Sienne, *f.*

sierra [si'eərə], *n.* sierra, *f.*

Sierra Leone [si'eərəli'oun]. le Sierra-Leone, *m.*

siesta [si'estə], *n.* sieste, *f.*

sieve [siv], *n.* tamis (*fin*); crible (*grand*), *m.*

sift [sift], *v.t.* tamiser; cribler; sasser (*farine*); (*fig.*) examiner.

sifting ['siftiŋ], *n.* tamisage; (*fig.*) examen minutieux, *m.*

sigh [sai], *n.* soupir, *m.*—*v.i.* soupirer; *to sigh after*, soupirer après; *to sigh over*, gémir sur.

sighing ['saiiŋ], *n.* soupirs, *m.pl.*

sight [sait], *n.* vue, vision, *f.*; regard, *m.*, yeux, *m.pl.*; guidon, *m.*, hausse (*armes à feu*), *f.*; spectacle, *m.*; *a sight better*, beaucoup mieux; *at first sight*, à première vue; *by sight*, de vue; *in sight*, en vue; *out of sight*, hors de vue; *second sight*, clairvoyance, *f.*; *to catch sight of*, apercevoir; *to come in sight*, apparaître.—*v.t.* apercevoir.

sighted ['saitid], *a.* en vue; qui voit, voyant; *long-sighted*, presbyte; *short-sighted*, myope; (*fig.*) peu clairvoyant.

sightliness ['saitlinis], *n.* beauté, *f.*

sight-reading ['saitriːdiŋ], *n.* (*Mus.*) déchiffrement, *m.*

562

sight-seeing ['saitsi:iŋ], *n.* *to go sight-seeing*, aller voir les curiosités.

sight-seer ['saitsi:ə], *n.* touriste, *m.,f.*, visiteur (*d'une ville*), *m.*

sign [sain], *n.* signe; indice, *m.*; enseigne (*panneau*), *f.*—*v.t., v.i.* signer.

signal ['signəl], *a.* signalé, insigne.—*n.* signal; signe; (*Rail.*) sémaphore, *m.*; (*pl.*) (*Mil.*) les transmissions, *f.pl.*—*v.t.* signaler, faire signe à.—*v.i.* signaler; donner un signal.

signal-box ['signəlbɔks], *n.* poste à signaux, *m.*

signalman ['signəlmən], *n.* (*pl.* **-men** [men]) (*Rail.*) signaleur, *m.*

signaller ['signələ], *n.* signaleur, *m.*

signally ['signəli], *adv.* remarquablement.

signatory ['signətəri], *a.* and *n.* signataire, *m.,f.*

signature ['signətʃə], *n.* signature, *f.*

sign-board ['sainbɔ:d], *n.* enseigne, *f.*

signet ['signit], *n.* sceau; cachet, *m.*

signet ring ['signitriŋ], *n.* chevalière, *f.*

significance [sig'nifikəns], *n.* signification, *f.*, sens, *m.*; importance, *f.*

significant [sig'nifikənt], *a.* significatif.

signification [signifi'keiʃən], *n.* signification, *f.*

signify ['signifai], *v.t.* vouloir dire, signifier; faire connaître; importer.

sign-post ['sainpoust], *n.* poteau indicateur, *m.*

silence ['sailəns], *n.* silence, *m.*; *silence!* (*notice*), défense de parler.—*v.t.* réduire au silence, faire taire.

silent ['sailənt], *a.* silencieux; peu loquace (*qui ne parle pas beaucoup*); muet (*lettre, film*).

silently ['sailəntli], *adv.* silencieusement, en silence; sans bruit.

silent partner ['sailənt'pɑ:tnə], *n.* associé commanditaire, *m.*

Silesia [sai'li:ʃə, sai'li:siə]. la Silésie, *f.*

silex ['saileks], *n.* silex, *m.*

silhouette [silu'et], *n.* silhouette, *f.*

silica ['silikə], *n.* silice, *f.*

silicon ['silikən], *n.* silicium, *m.*

silicosis [sili'kousis], *n.* (*Med.*) silicose, *f.*

silk [silk], *a.* de soie, en soie.—*n.* soie, *f.*; (*pl.*) soieries, *f.pl.*

silken ['silkən], *a.* de soie; soyeux.

silkiness ['silkinis], *n.* nature soyeuse, *f.*

silkworm ['silkwə:m], *n.* ver à soie, *m.*

silky ['silki], *a.* de soie; soyeux.

sill [sil], *n.* seuil (*d'une porte*); rebord (*d'une fenêtre*), *m.*

silliness ['silinis], *n.* sottise, niaiserie, *f.*

silly ['sili], *a.* and *n.* sot, nigaud, niais, *m.*; *silly ass*, imbécile, *m.*; *silly thing*, sottise, *f.*; nigaud (*personne*).

silt [silt], *v.t.* envaser.—*v.i.* s'envaser.—*n.* vase, *f.*, limon, *m.*

silting ['siltiŋ], *n.* envasement, *m.*

silver ['silvə], *a.* d'argent; argenté (*couleur*); argentin (*son*).—*n.* argent, *m.*; monnaie d'argent; argenterie (*vaisselle*), *f.*—*v.t.* argenter; étamer (*miroir*).

silvering ['silvəriŋ], *n.* argenture, *f.*; étamage (*de miroirs*), *m.*

silver-plated ['silvə'pleitid], *a.* argenté, en plaqué.

silversmith ['silvəsmiθ], *n.* orfèvre, *m.*

silvery ['silvəri], *a.* d'argent; argenté (*couleur*); argentin (*son*).

similar ['similə], *a.* semblable, pareil; similaire (*de nature*).

similarity [simi'læriti], *n.* ressemblance, similitude; similarité (*de nature*), *f.*

similarly ['similəli], *adv.* pareillement, d'une manière semblable.

simile ['simili], *n.* comparaison, *f.*

similitude [si'militju:d], *n.* similitude, *f.*

simmer ['simə], *v.i.* bouillir lentement, mijoter.

simmering ['siməriŋ], *n.* mijotement, *m.*

simnel ['simnəl], *n.* gâteau de Pâques *ou* de la mi-carême, *m.*

simper ['simpə], *n.* sourire niais, *m.*—*v.i.* sourire niaisement, minauder.

simpering ['simpəriŋ], *a.* minaudier.—*n.* minauderie, *f.*

simperingly ['simpəriŋli], *adv.* en minaudant.

simple [simpl], *a.* simple; *as simple as ABC*, simple comme bonjour.—*n.* simple, *m.*

simple-hearted ['simpl'hɑ:tid], **simple-minded** ['simplmaindid], *a.* simple, ingénu, naif.

simpleness ['simplnis], *n.* simplicité, *f.*

simpleton ['simpltən], *n.* niais, nigaud, *m.*

simplicity [sim'plisiti], *n.* simplicité, *f.*

simplification ['simplifi'keiʃən], *n.* simplification, *f.*

simplify ['simplifai], *v.t.* simplifier.

simply ['simpli], *adv.* simplement (*sans complexité*); tout bonnement (*et rien de plus*).

simulate ['simjuleit], *v.t.* feindre, simuler.

simulation [simju'leiʃən], *n.* simulation, *f.*

simulator ['simjuleitə], *n.* simulateur, *m.*

simultaneous [siməl'teinjəs], *a.* simultané.

simultaneously [siməl'teinjəsli], *adv.* simultanément.

sin [sin], *n.* péché, *m.*; (*fig.*) offense, *f.*—*v.i.* pécher.

since [sins], *conj.* puisque (*parce que*); depuis que (*temps*).—*prep.* depuis; *since then*, depuis lors.—*adv.* depuis; *ever since*, depuis ce temps-là; *long since*, il y a long-temps.

sincere [sin'siə], *a.* sincère.

sincerely [sin'siəli], *adv.* sincèrement; *yours sincerely* (*lettre amicale mais sans intimité*), veuillez croire, cher Monsieur, à mes sentiments les meilleurs.

sincerity [sin'seriti], *n.* sincérité, bonne foi, *f.*

sine [sain], *n.* (*Trig.*) sinus, *m.*

sinecure ['sainikjuə], *n.* sinécure, *f.*

sinew ['sinju:], *n.* tendon, (*colloq.*) nerf, *m.*

sinewy ['sinju:i], *a.* tendineux; (*fig.*) nerveux, vigoureux.

sinful ['sinful], *a.* pécheur, coupable.

sinfully ['sinfuli], *adv.* d'une manière coupable, en pécheur.

sinfulness ['sinfulnis], *n.* culpabilité, iniquité, *f.*

sing [siŋ], *v.t., v.i.* irr. chanter, célébrer (*louer*); siffler (*vent*); *to make someone sing small*, rabattre le caquet à quelqu'un.

Singapore [siŋə'pɔ:]. Singapour, *m.*

singe [sindʒ], *v.t.* flamber; roussir (*vêtements etc.*); (*Tech.*) griller.—*n.* légère brûlure, *f.*

singeing ['sindʒiŋ], *n.* flambage (*de vêtements etc.*), *m.*; roussissure, *f.*; (*Tech.*) grillage, *m.*

singer ['siŋə], *n.* chanteur, *m.*; cantatrice (*professionnelle*), *f.*

singing ['siŋiŋ], *a.* qui chante; chanteur (*oiseau*).—*n.* chant; bourdonnement (*dans les oreilles*), *m.*

single [siŋgl], *a.* seul, simple, unique; particulier (*individuel*); singulier (*combat*); non marié, célibataire; *single bedroom*, chambre à un lit, *f.*; *single man*, célibataire, garçon, *m.*; *single (ticket)*, billet simple, *m.*; *single woman*, femme non mariée, fille, *f.*—*n.* (*pl.*) (*Ten.*) partie simple, *f.*—*v.t.* choisir; *to single out*, choisir, distinguer de la foule.

single-handed ['siŋgl'hændid], *adv.* tout seul, sans aide.

single-hearted ['siŋgl'hɑ:tid], *a.* sincère, honnête.

singleness ['siŋglnis], *n.* sincérité, simplicité, *f.*

singlet ['siŋglit], *n.* maillot fin, *m.*

single-track ['siŋgltræk], *a.* (*Rail.*) à voie unique; (*Cine.*) à simple piste.

singly ['siŋgli], *adv.* seulement; séparément; individuellement, un à un.

singsong ['siŋsɔŋ], *n.* chant monotone, *m.*

singular ['siŋgjulə], *a.* singulier; étrange (*bizarre*); simple (*pas complexe*), (*Gram.*)—*n.* singulier, *m.*

singularity [siŋgju'læriti], *n.* singularité, *f.*

singularly ['siŋgjulali], *adv.* singulièrement.

sinister ['sinistə], *a.* sinistre; (*Her.*) sénestre.

sink [siŋk], *n.* évier (*de cuisine*); égout (*conduit*), *m.*; *a sink of iniquity*, un cloaque d'iniquité.—*v.t. irr.* faire tomber au fond, enfoncer; couler (*navire*); creuser (*puits etc.*); placer (*argent*) à fonds perdu; amortir (*dette*).—*v.i.* aller au fond, tomber au fond; s'enfoncer, sombrer, couler (*navire*); décliner, s'affaiblir (*santé etc.*); baisser (*prix etc.*); être abattu (*âme, cœur etc.*); descendre, se coucher (*soleil etc.*); dégénérer (*en*).

sinker ['siŋkə], *n.* plomb (*de ligne de pêche*), *m.*

sinking ['siŋkiŋ], *a.* qui coule (*navire*).—*n.* foncement (*de puits etc.*); tassement (*de fondements*); affaissement (*santé*); placement à fonds perdu (*d'argent*); amortissement (*d'une dette*); engloutissement (*de navire*), *m.*

sinking fund ['siŋkiŋfʌnd], *n.* fonds, *m.*, ou caisse d'amortissement (*d'une dette etc.*), *f.*

sinless ['sinlis], *a.* sans péché, innocent; pur.

sinner ['sinə], *n.* pécheur, *m.*, pécheresse, *f.*

sinuous ['sinjuəs], *a.* sinueux.

sinus ['sainəs], *n.* (*Anat.*) sinus, *m.*

sip [sip], *n.* petit coup, *m.*, petite gorgée, *f.*—*v.t., v.i.* boire à petit coups, siroter.

siphon ['saifən], *n.* siphon, *m.*—*v.t.* siphonner.

sir [sə:], *n.* monsieur, *m.*

sire ['saiə], *n.* père; sire (*à un roi*), *m.*; (*pl.*) pères, aïeux, *m.pl.*; *grand-sire*), grandpère, *m.*

siren ['saiərən], *n.* sirène, *f.*

Sirius ['siriəs], (*Astron.*) Sirius, *m.*

sirloin ['sə:lɔin], *n.* aloyau; faux-filet, *m.*

sirocco [si'rɔku], *n.* siroco, *m.*

siskin ['siskin], *n.* (*Orn.*) tarin, *m.*

sissy ['sisi], *n.* (*colloq.*) poule mouillée, *f.*

sister ['sistə], *a.* sœur; du même gabarit (*navire*).—*n.* sœur; (*Med.*) infirmière-major, *f.*

sisterhood ['sistəhud], *n.* communauté de sœurs, *f.*, sœurs, *f.pl.*

sister-in-law ['sistərinlɔ:], *n.* belle-sœur, *f.*

sisterly ['sistəli], *a.* de sœur, en sœur.

sit [sit], *v.t. irr.* asseoir; se tenir sur (*cheval*).—*v.i.* s'asseoir (*acte*); être assis (*attitude*); siéger, tenir séance, se réunir (*assemblée, cour, juge etc.*); couver (*poule etc.*), percher (*oiseau*); poser (*pour un portrait*); *to sit down*, s'asseoir; *to sit up*, se tenir droit; veiller (*s'abstenir du sommeil*).

sit-down strike ['sitdaunstraik], *n.* grève sur le tas, *f.*

site [sait], *n.* situation, *f.*, emplacement (*de bâtiment*); site (*paysage*), *m.*—*v.t.* placer.

sitfast ['sitfɑ:st], *n.* (*Vet.*) cor, durillon, *m.*

sitter ['sitə], *n.* personne assise, *f.*; (*Paint.*) modèle, *m.*

sitting ['sitiŋ], *a.* assis; en séance (*cour etc.*); perché (*oiseau*); qui couve (*poule*).—*n.* séance; audience (*d'une cour*); couvaison (*des œufs*); place (*réservée*); (*Paint.*) séance, *f.*

sitting room ['sitiŋru:m], *n.* petit salon, *m.*

situate (1) ['sitjueit], *v.t.* situer.

situate (2) ['sitjuit], **situated** ['sitjueitid], *a.* situé; (*Law*) sis.

situation [sitju'eiʃən], *n.* situation, position, *f.*, état, *m.*; place, *f.*, emploi, *m.*

six [siks], *a.* and *n.* six, *m.*

sixteen ['siks'ti:n], *a.* and *n.* seize, *m.*

sixteenth [siks'ti:nθ], *a.* seizième; seize (*rois etc.*).—*n.* seizième (*fraction*), *m.*

sixth [siksθ], *a.* sixième; six (*rois etc.*).—*n.* sixième (*fraction*), *m.*; (*Mus.*) sixte, *f.*

sixthly ['siksθli], *adv.* sixièmement.

sixtieth ['sikstiiθ], *a.* soixantième.—*n.* soixantième (*fraction*), *m.*

sixty ['siksti], *a.* and *n.* soixante, *m.*; *about sixty*, une soixantaine (*de*), *f.*

sizable ['saizəbl], *a.* d'une bonne grosseur.

size (1) [saiz], *n.* grandeur, dimension, taille (*physique*); grosseur, *f.*, volume (*espace occupé*); calibre (*de cartouche*); format (*de livre ou de papier*), *m.*; encolure (*de chemise*); pointure (*de gant, de chaussure etc.*), *f.*; effectif (*d'école, de classe etc.*), (*Comm.*) numéro, *m.*—*v.t.* classer, ranger (*par grosseur, par taille*); *to size up*, juger.

size (2) [saiz], *n.* colle, *f.*, encollage, *m.*—*v.t.* coller, encoller.

sized [saizd], *a.* de grosseur; de taille.

sizzle [sizl], *n.* grésillement, *m.*—*v.i.* grésiller.

skate (1) [skeit], *n.* (*Ichth.*) raie, *f.*

skate (2) [skeit], *n.* patin, *m.*; *roller skate*, patin à roulettes.—*v.i.* patiner.

skater ['skeitə], *n.* patineur, *m.*

skating ['skeitiŋ], *n.* patinage, *m.*

skating rink ['skeitiŋriŋk], *n.* patinoire, *f.*

skein [skein], *n.* écheveau, *m.*

skeleton ['skelətən], *n.* squelette, *m.*; (*Tech.*) charpente, carcasse, *f.*

skeleton key ['skelətən'ki:], *n.* passe-partout, *m.inv.*, crochet, *m.*

sketch [sketʃ], *n.* esquisse, *f.*, croquis, *m.*, ébauche; (*Theat.*) saynète, *f.*; (*fig.*) aperçu, *m.*—*v.t.* esquisser, ébaucher.

sketch-book ['sketʃbuk], *n.* cahier de croquis, *m.*

sketchily ['sketʃili], *adv.* incomplètement.

sketchy ['sketʃi], *a.* d'esquisse, ébauché; rudimentaire.

skew [skju:], *a.* oblique, en biais.

skewer ['skju:ə], *n.* brochette, *f.*—*v.t.* embrocher.

ski [ski:], *n.* ski, *m.*—*v.i.* faire du ski.

skid [skid], *n.* (*Motor.*) dérapage (*de*), *m.*, embardée, *f.*; (*Av.*) patin, *m.*—*v.i.* déraper (*bicyclette* ou *véhicule*).

skier ['ski:ə], *n.* skieur, *m.*

skiff [skif], *n.* esquif, *m.*

ski-ing ['ski:iŋ], *n.* le ski, *m.*

ski-lift ['ski:lift], *n.* remonte-pentes, *m.inv.*

skill [skil], *n.* habileté, dextérité, adresse, *f.*

skilled [skild], *a.* habile, adroit; **skilled labor**, main-d'œuvre spécialisée, *f.*; **skilled workman**, ouvrier qualifié, *m.*

skillful ['skilful], *a.* adroit, habile.

skillfully ['skilfuli], *adv.* adroitement, habilement.

skim [skim], *v.t.* écumer; écrémer (*lait*); (*fig.*) raser, effleurer.

skimp [skimp], *v.t.* lésiner; bâcler (*travail*).

skimpy ['skimpi], *a.* mesquin, chiche; étriqué.

skin [skin], *n.* peau, *f.*; **banana skin**, pelure de banane, *f.*; **to escape by the skin of one's teeth**, l'échapper belle; **wet to the skin**, trempé jusqu'aux os.—*v.t.* écorcher (*personne* ou *animal*); peler, éplucher (*fruits* etc.); (*fig.*) écorcher, plumer.

skin-deep ['skindi:p], *a.* superficiel, peu profond.

skinflint ['skinflint], *n.* pince-maille, grigou, ladre, *m.*

skinless ['skinlis], *a.* sans peau.

skinner ['skinə], *n.* écorcheur; pelletier (*marchand*), *m.*

skinny ['skini], *a.* maigre, décharné.

skip [skip], *n.* saut, bond, *m.*—*v.t.* sauter; passer (*en lisant*).—*v.i.* sauter, sautiller, gambader.

skipper ['skipə], *n.* patron (*de navire marchand*); (*Spt.*) chef d'équipe, *m.*

skipping ['skipiŋ], *n.* action de sauter, *f.*; saut à la corde, *m.*

skipping-rope ['skipiŋroup], *n.* corde à sauter, *f.*

skirmish ['skə:miʃ], *n.* escarmouche, *f.*—*v.i.* escarmoucher.

skirmisher ['skə:miʃə], *n.* tirailleur, *m.*

skirmishing ['skə:miʃiŋ], *n.* escarmouches, *f.pl.*

skirt [skə:t], *n.* pan (*d'un habit*), *m.*; jupe (*de robe*); (*pl.*) lisière, extrémité, *f.*, bord (*de forêt* etc.), *m.*; **outskirts**, bords, faubourgs, *m.pl.*—*v.t.* border; longer (*rivière* etc.).

skirting ['skə:tiŋ], **skirting-board** ['skə:tiŋbɔ:d], *n.* bord, *m.*, bordure; (*Arch.*) plinthe, *f.*

skit [skit], *n.* parodie, *f.*

skittish ['skitiʃ], *a.* capricieux, volage.

skittishly ['skitiʃli], *adv.* capricieusement.

skittishness ['skitiʃnis], *n.* légèreté, inconstance, *f.*

skittle [skitl], *n.* quille, *f.*

skittle alley ['skitl'æli], *n.* jeu de quilles, *m.*

skulk [skʌlk], *v.i.* se cacher; rôder (*autour de*).

skull [skʌl], *n.* crâne, *m.*

skull-cap ['skʌlkæp], *n.* calotte, *f.*

skunk [skʌŋk], *n.* putois d'Amérique, *m.*

sky [skai], *n.* ciel, *m.*

sky-blue ['skaiblu:], *a.* bleu ciel, azuré.

sky-high ['skai'hai], *a.* qui touche aux cieux; **to blow up sky-high**, faire sauter jusqu'aux cieux; (*fig.*) tancer vertement.

skylark ['skailɑ:k], *n.* alouette (des champs), *f.*—*v.i.* (*fig.*) faire des farces.

skylarking ['skailɑ:kiŋ], *n.* farces, *f.pl.*

skylight ['skailait], *n.* châssis vitré, *m.*, lucarne faîtière, *f.*

sky-line ['skailain], *n.* horizon, *m.*

sky-scraper ['skaiskreipə], *n.* gratte-ciel, *m.*

slab [slæb], *n.* dalle, plaque, table; tablette (*de chocolat*); dosse, *f.*

slack [slæk], *a.* lâche; faible, mou; détendu (*corde*); négligent; **business is slack**, les affaires ne vont pas; **the slack season**, la morte-saison, *f.*—*n.* menu charbon; mou (*de corde*); (*Eng.*) jeu; (*pl.*) pantalon, *m.*

slacken ['slækən], *v.t.* relâcher, détendre; affaiblir (*la rigueur*); ralentir (*vitesse*).—*v.i.* se relâcher, se détendre; se ralentir; diminuer; tomber.

slackening ['slækniŋ], *n.* relâchement, *m.*

slacker ['slækə], *n.* paresseux, *m.*

slacking ['slækiŋ], *n.* paresse, *f.*

slackly ['slækli], *adv.* mollement, lâchement; négligemment.

slackness ['slæknis], *n.* relâchement, *m.*; négligence, nonchalance (*morale*), *f.*

slag [slæg], *n.* scorie, *f.*; mâchefer, *m.*

slag-heap ['slæghi:p], *n.* crassier, *m.*

slake [sleik], *v.t.* éteindre (*chaux*); **to slake one's thirst**, se désaltérer.

slam [slæm], *v.t.* fermer avec violence, claquer.—*v.i.* se fermer avec bruit.—*n.* (*Cards*) vole, *f.*, chelem, *m.*

slander ['slɑ:ndə], *n.* calomnie; (*Law*) diffamation, *f.*—*v.t.* calomnier; (*Law*) diffamer.

slanderer ['slɑ:ndərə], *n.* calomniateur; (*Law*) diffamateur, *m.*

slanderous ['slɑ:ndərəs], *a.* calomnieux; (*Law*) diffamatoire.

slang [slæŋ], *n.* argot, *m.*, langue verte, *f.*

slangy ['slæŋi], *a.* d'argot, argotique.

slant [slɑ:nt], *v.t.* incliner.—*v.i.* incliner; être de biais, biaiser.—*n.* inclinaison, pente, *f.*; **on the slant**, en écharpe, en biais.

slanting ['slɑ:ntiŋ], *a.* oblique; en écharpe (*coup d'épée* etc.).

slantingly ['slɑ:ntiŋli], **slantwise** ['slɑ:ntwaiz], *adv.* obliquement, en biais.

slap [slæp], *n.* tape, *f.*; soufflet (*sur la figure*), *m.*—*v.i.* souffleter, donner une fessée à (*un enfant*).—*adv.* tout droit, en plein.

slapdash ['slæpdæʃ], *adv.* à la six-quatre-deux, n'importe comment.—*a.* fait à la hâte.

slap-happy ['slæp'hæpi], *a.* toqué.

slapstick ['slæpstik], *n.* (*Theat., Cine.*) **slapstick comedy** (*fam.*), tarte à la crème, *f.*

slash [slæʃ], *n.* taillade; balafre (*sur la figure*), *f.*—*v.t.* taillader; balafrer (*la figure*).—*v.i.* frapper.

slashing ['slæʃiŋ], *a.* mordant, cinglant.

slate [sleit], *n.* ardoise, *f.*—*v.t.* couvrir d'ardoises; (*colloq.*) tancer.

slate-colored ['sleitkʌləd], *a.* ardoisé, gris d'ardoise.

slate pencil ['sleitpensl], *n.* crayon d'ardoise, *m.*

slater ['sleitə], *n.* couvreur en ardoise, *m.*

slating ['sleitiŋ], *n.* toiture en ardoise; (*colloq.*) semonce, *f.*

slattern ['slætən], *n.* femme malpropre, souillon, *f.*

slatternly ['slætənli], *a.* négligent, malpropre, mal soigné.

slaty ['sleiti], *a.* schisteux, d'ardoise; ardoisé (*couleur*).

slaughter ['slɔːtə], *n.* tuerie, boucherie, *f.*, massacre; abattage (*des animaux*), *m.*—*v.t.* massacrer; abattre (*animaux*).

slaughterer ['slɔːtərə], *n.* abatteur, *m.*

slaughter-house ['slɔːtəhaus], *n.* abattoir, *m.*

Slav [slɑːv], *a.* slave.—*n.* Slave (*personne*), *m.*, *f.*

slave [sleiv], *n.* esclave, *m.*, *f.*—*v.i.* travailler comme un esclave, peiner.

slave driver ['sleivdraivə], *n.* (*fig.*) maître sévère et cruel, *m.*

slaver (1) ['sleivə], *n.* négrier, bâtiment négrier, *m.*

slaver (2) ['slævə], *v.i.* baver (*sur*).—*n.* bave, salive, *f.*

slavery ['sleivəri], *n.* esclavage, *m.*

slave trade ['sleivtreid], *n.* traite des noirs, *f.*

slavish ['sleiviʃ], *a.* d'esclave; servile (*imitation etc.*).

slavishly ['sleiviʃli], *adv.* en esclave; servilement.

slavishness ['sleiviʃnis], *n.* servilité, *f.*

Slavonic [slə'vɔnik], *a.* slave.—*n.* slave (*langues*), *m.*

slay [slei], *v.t. irr.* tuer.

slayer ['sleiə], *n.* tueur (*de*), meurtrier, *m.*

slaying ['sleiiŋ], *n.* tuerie, *f.*

sledge [sledʒ], *n.* traîneau, *m.*—*v.i.* (*also to go sledging*) se promener en traîneau.

sledge hammer ['sledʒhæmə], *n.* marteau à deux mains, *m.*

sleek [sliːk], *a.* lisse, luisant, poli; (*fig.*) doucereux, onctueux.

sleekness ['sliːknis], *n.* luisant, *m.*; (*fig.*) douceur, onctuosité, *f.*

sleep [sliːp], *n.* sommeil, *m.*; *beauty sleep*, sommeil avant minuit; *sound sleep*, profond sommeil; *to go to sleep*, s'endormir; *to put a dog to sleep*, tuer un chien.—*v.t. irr.* dormir.—*v.i.* dormir, coucher (*à, chez* ou *dans*).

sleeper ['sliːpə], *n.* dormeur, *m.*; (*Rail.*) traverse, *f.*; (*colloq.*) wagon-lit, *m.*

sleepily ['sliːpili], *adv.* d'un air endormi.

sleepiness ['sliːpinis], *n.* assoupissement, *m.*

sleeping ['sliːpiŋ], *a.* endormi; dormant.—*n.* sommeil, repos, *m.*; *sleeping pills* ou *tablets*, somnifère, *m.*

sleeping bag ['sliːpiŋbæg], *n.* sac de couchage, *m.*

sleeping berth ['sliːpiŋbəːθ], *n.* couchette, *f.*

sleeping car ['sliːpiŋkɑː], *n.* wagon-lit, *m.*

sleeping draft ['sliːpiŋdrɑːft], *n.* somnifère, *m.*

sleeping partner ['sliːpiŋ'pɑːtnə], *n.* associé commanditaire, *m.*

sleepless ['sliːplis], *a.* sans sommeil.

sleeplessness ['sliːplisnis], *n.* insomnie, *f.*

sleep-walker ['sliːpwɔːkə], *n.* somnambule, *m.*, *f.*

sleepy ['sliːpi], *a.* qui a envie de dormir, soporifique (*somnifère*); *to feel sleepy*, avoir sommeil.

sleepy-head ['sliːpihed], *n.* paresseux, *m.*

sleet [sliːt], *n.* neige fondue, *f.*; grésil, *m.*

sleeve [sliːv], *n.* manche, *f.*

sleeveless ['sliːvlis], *a.* sans manches.

sleigh [slei], *n.* traîneau, *m.*

sleight [slait], *n.* habileté, *f.*, escamotage, *m.*; *sleight of hand*, tour de passe-passe, *m.*

slender ['slendə], *a.* mince; élancé; svelte (*taille*); (*fig.*) léger; chétif, maigre.

slenderness ['slendənis], *n.* minceur, légèreté; modicité, *f.*

sleuth(-hound) ['sluːθ(haund)], *n.* (chien) limier, (*fig.*) détective, *m.*

slice [slais], *n.* tranche; écumoire (*ustensile*), *f.*; *fish-slice*, truelle, *f.*; *slice of bread and jam*, tartine de confiture, *f.*—*v.t.* couper en tranches.

slick [slik], *a.* adroit.

slickness ['sliknis], *n.* adresse, habileté, *f.*

slide [slaid], *n.* glissoire, glissade, *f.*; *lantern slide*, diapositive, vue fixe, *f.*—*v.t. irr.* glisser; tirer (*de*).—*v.i.* glisser; couler.

slide rule ['slaidruːl], *n.* règle à calcul, *f.*

sliding ['slaidiŋ], *a.* glissant; à coulisse.—*n.* glissade, *f.*, glissement, *m.*

sliding door ['slaidiŋ'dɔː], *n.* porte à coulisse, *f.*

sliding scale ['slaidiŋ'skeil], *n.* (*Econ.*) échelle mobile, *f.*

slight [slait], *a.* mince, léger; insignifiant; *not in the slightest*, pas le moins du monde.—*n.* manque d'égards; affront, *m.*, insulte, *f.*—*v.t.* traiter sans égards; mépriser.

slightingly ['slaitiŋli], *adv.* avec mépris, avec dédain.

slightly ['slaitli], *adv.* légèrement, un peu.

slightness ['slaitnis], *n.* minceur; légèreté, *f.*

slim [slim], *a.* svelte, mince; (*colloq.*) rusé.—*v.i.* s'amincir.

slime [slaim], *n.* vase, *f.*, limon, *m.*, bave (*de colimaçon*), *f.*

sliminess ['slaiminis], *n.* viscosité, *f.*

slimness ['slimnis], *n.* sveltesse, taille mince, *f.*

slimy ['slaimi], *a.* vaseux, limoneux; visqueux, gluant; (*fam.*) obséquieux.

sling [sliŋ], *n.* fronde; bretelle (*de fusil*), écharpe (*pour un membre cassé*), *f.*—*v.t. irr.* lancer (*avec une fronde*); suspendre (*fusil etc.*).

slinger ['sliŋə], *n.* frondeur, *m.*

slink [sliŋk], *v.i. irr.* s'esquiver, se dérober.

slip [slip], *v.t.* couler; couler; perdre; lâcher; filer (*câble*); pousser (*verrou*); *to slip in*, introduire; *to slip off*, enlever, ôter; *to slip on*, passer, mettre.—*v.i.* glisser; couler (*nœud*); patiner (*roues*); (*fig.*) faire un faux pas; *to slip away*, s'esquiver; *to slip down*, tomber; *to slip in*, se faufiler, entrer furtivement; *to slip up*, (*fam.*) se tromper.—*n.* glissade; combinaison (*sous-vêtement*); laisse (*à chien*), *f.*; engobe (*céramique*); (*Hort.*) scion, *m.*; cale (*de port etc.*); faute d'étourderie, *f.*; lapsus, *m.*; *pillow slip*, taie d'oreiller, *f.*; *slip of paper*, bout de papier, *m.*; *slip of the pen*, erreur de plume, *f.*; *to give someone the slip*, planter quelqu'un là; *to make a slip*, faire un faux pas.

slip-knot ['slipnɔt], *n.* nœud coulant, *m.*

slipper ['slipə], *n.* pantoufle, *f.*

slippered ['slipəd], *a.* en pantoufles.

slipperiness ['slipərinis], *n.* nature glissante; volubilité (*de la langue*), *f.*

slippery ['slipəri], *a.* glissant; incertain, peu sûr; peu stable; matois, rusé; *slippery customer*, rusé compère, *m.*

slipshod ['slipʃɔd], *a.* (*fig.*) négligé; décousu (*style*).

slipstream ['slipstri:m], n. sillage, m.

slipway ['slipwei], n. cale, f.

slit [slit], v.t. irr. fendre.—v.i. se fendre.—n. fente, fissure, f.

slither ['sliðə], v.i. glisser; ramper (reptile).

sliver ['slivə, 'slaivə], n. éclat, m., tranche, f., ruban, m.

slobber ['slɔbə], v.i. baver.

sloe [slou], n. (Bot.) prunelle, f.

sloe tree ['sloutri:], n. prunellier, m.

slogan ['slougən], n. mot d'ordre, m., devise, f., slogan, m.

sloop [slu:p], n. sloop, aviso, m.

slop [slɔp], n. (usu. in pl.) rinçures, f.pl.—v.t. répandre, renverser.

slop basin ['slɔpbeisn], **slop bowl** ['slɔp boul], n. bol à rinçures (de thé), m.

slope [sloup], n. pente, f.; talus, versant, m.—v.i. couper en biais; taluter.—v.i. pencher, aller en pente, incliner.

sloping ['sloupiŋ], a. de biais, en pente.

sloppiness ['slɔpinis], n. état détrempé, m.; mollesse (personne), f.

sloppy ['slɔpi], a. bourbeux, humide; (fig.) mou.

slot [slɔt], n. rainure, mortaise, fente; barre de bois, f.

sloth (1) [slouθ], n. paresse, fainéantise, f.

sloth (2) [slouθ], n. (Zool.) paresseux, aï, m.

slothful ['slouθful], a. paresseux, fainéant.

slot machine ['slɔtməʃi:n], n. distributeur automatique, m.

slouch [slautʃ], n. démarche molle ou lourde, f.; lourdaud (personne), m.—v.i. marcher lourdement; **to slouch along**, marcher d'un pas traînant.

slouching ['slautʃiŋ], a. lourd et gauche.

slough [slau], n. bourbier, m., fondrière; dépouille (de serpent), f.

Slovak ['slouvæk], a. slovaque.—n. Slovaque (personne), m., f.

sloven ['slʌvn], n. sans-soin, mal-soigné, m.

Slovene ['slouvi:n], n. Slovène (personne), m., f.

Slovenian [slo'vi:niən], a. slovène.

slovenliness ['slʌvnlinis], n. malpropreté, saleté, négligence, f.

slovenly ['slʌvnli], a. mal soigné, mal peigné, débraillé.

slow [slou], a. lent, tardif; lourd (pesant); en retard (montre etc.).—adv. lentement.—v.t. ralentir.—v.i. se ralentir.

slowly ['slouli], adv. lentement, tardivement.

slowness ['slounis], n. lenteur; paresse; lourdeur (pesanteur), f.; retard (de montre etc.), m.

slow-worm ['slouwə:m], n. orvet, m.

sludge [slʌdʒ], n. boue, vase, f.; cambouis, m.

slug [slʌg], n. limace, f.; lingot (de fusil), m.

sluggard ['slʌgəd], n. paresseux, m.

sluggish ['slʌgiʃ], a. paresseux, indolent, lourd; lent (ruisseau).

sluggishly ['slʌgiʃli], adv. paresseusement, lourdement.

sluggishness ['slʌgiʃnis], n. paresse; lenteur (de ruisseau), f.

sluice [slu:s], n. écluse; bonde (dans un étang), f.—v.t. lâcher par une écluse; inonder d'eau.

sluice-gate ['slu:sgeit], n. vanne, f.

slum [slʌm], n. taudis, m., (pl.) bas quartiers, m.pl.; **slum clearance**, lutte contre les taudis, f.

slumber ['slʌmbə], n. sommeil, m.—v.i. sommeiller, dormir.

slumberer ['slʌmbərə], n. dormeur, m.

slumbering ['slʌmbəriŋ], a. endormi, assoupi.—n. sommeil, assoupissement, m.

slump [slʌmp], v.i. s'enfoncer soudainement.—n. baisse subite; crise, f.

slur [slə:], n. tache; (Mus.) liaison, f.; **to cast a slur upon**, flétrir, dénigrer.—v.t. tacher, salir; (Mus.) lier; **to slur over**, glisser sur.

slurred [slə:d], a. (Mus.) coulé; brouillé (paroles).

slurring ['slə:riŋ], n. (Mus.) liaison, f.

slush [slʌʃ], n. boue, fange; neige à moitié fondue, f.

slut [slʌt], n. saligaude, souillon, f.

sly [slai], a. sournois, rusé; **on the sly**, en sourdine; **sly dog**, fin matois, m.

slyly ['slaili], adv. avec ruse, sournoisement.

slyness ['slainis], n. ruse, finesse, nature sour-oise, f.

smack (1) [smæk], n. claquement (de fouet), m.; claque (de la main); gifle (sur la figure), f.; gros baiser, m.—adv. **smack in the middle**, en plein milieu.—v.t. faire claquer (fouet, les lèvres); donner une claque à.

smack (2) [smæk], n. (fig.) saveur, f.—v.i. **to smack of**, sentir (le, la etc.).

smack (3) [smæk], n. bateau de pêche, m.

smacking ['smækiŋ], n. claquement, m.; fessée, f.

small [smɔ:l], a. petit; fin, menu; (fig.) chétif, mince, pauvre; modeste, peu considérable; **small arms**, armes portatives, f.pl.; **small fry**, menu fretin, m.; **small letters**, minuscules, f.pl.—n. partie mince, f.; **small of the back**, chute des reins, f.

smallish ['smɔ:liʃ], a. un peu petit, un peu menu.

smallness ['smɔ:lnis], n. petitesse, f.; peu d'importance, m.

smallpox ['smɔ:lpɔks], n. petite vérole, f.

smarmy ['smɑ:mi], a. (pop.) mielleux.

smart [smɑ:t], a. piquant, cuisant, vif; vigoureux, rude; intelligent, éveillé; beau, élégant, pimpant, chic; **look smart!** dépêchez-vous! **smart Aleck**, finaud, m.—n. douleur aiguë, vive douleur, cuisson, f.—v.i. cuire, éprouver une vive douleur.

smarten [smɑ:tn] (**up**), v.t. animer; **to smarten oneself up**, se faire beau, s'attifer.

smarting ['smɑ:tiŋ], a. cuisant, poignant.—n. douleur cuisante, f.

smartly ['smɑ:tli], adv. lestement, vivement; habilement; vigoureusement, rudement; élégamment.

smartness ['smɑ:tnis], n. force, vigueur; élégance, f., éclat (de vêtements), m.; finesse (astuce), f.

smash [smæʃ], v.t. briser, écraser; (fig.) ruiner.—v.i. se briser.—n. fracas, m.; (Fin.) déconfiture, faillite, banqueroute; (Rail.) catastrophe, f.—adv. **to go smash**, faire faillite.

smashing ['smæʃiŋ], a. (pop.) formidable, épatant.

smattering ['smætəriŋ], n. connaissances superficielles, f.pl

smear [smiə], v.t. enduire; (fig.) salir.—n. tache, f.; (fig.) calomnie, atteinte à la réputation, f.

smell

smell [smel], n. odeur, f.; odorat (sens); flair (de chien), m.—v.t., v.i. irr. sentir; flairer (chien).

smelly ['smeli], a. malodorant.

smelt (1) [smelt], n. (Ichth.) éperlan, m.

smelt (2) [smelt], v.t. fondre.

smelting ['smeltiŋ], n. fonte, f.

smile [smail], n. sourire, m.—v.i. sourire.

smiling ['smailiŋ], a. souriant; riant (paysage etc.).

smilingly ['smailiŋli], adv. en souriant.

smirch [smə:tʃ], v.t. souiller, salir.—n. tache, f.

smirk [smə:k], v.i. minauder.—n. sourire affecté, m.

smirking ['smə:kiŋ], a. affecté, minaudier.

smite [smait], v.t. irr. frapper; détruire; châtier; (fig.) charmer.

smith [smiθ], n. forgeron, m.

smithereens [smiðə'ri:nz], n.pl. to smash to smithereens, mettre en miettes.

smithy ['smiði], n. forge, f.

smock [smɔk], n. blouse, f.

smog [smɔg], n. brouillard épais et enfumé, m.

smoke [smouk], n. fumée, f.—v.t., v.i. fumer.

smokeless ['smouklis], a. sans fumée.

smoker ['smoukə], n. fumeur (personne), m.

smoke-stack ['smoukstæk], n. cheminée, f.

smokiness ['smoukinis], n. état enfumé, m.

smoking ['smoukiŋ], a. fumant.—n. habitude de fumer, f.; no smoking, défense de fumer.

smoky ['smouki], a. qui fume, plein de fumée.

smooth [smu:ð], a. uni; égal (régulier); doux (non âpre); poli, lisse (verni); plat (mer); doucereux (personne).—v.t. polir; adoucir; aplanir, unir; dérider (le front); lisser (les cheveux).

smooth-faced ['smu:ðfeist], a. imberbe.

smoothing-iron ['smu:ðiŋaiən], n. fer à repasser, m.

smoothly ['smu:ðli], adv. uniment; sans difficulté; doucement.

smoothness ['smu:ðnis], n. égalité; douceur, f.; calme (de la mer), m.

smooth-tongued ['smu:ð'tʌŋd], a. mielleux, doucereux.

smother ['smʌðə], v.t. suffoquer, étouffer.

smothering ['smʌðəriŋ], a. étouffant, suffocant.—n. étouffement, m.

smoulder ['smouldə], v.i. brûler sans fumée ni flamme; (fig.) couver.

smouldering ['smouldəriŋ], a. qui couve.

smudge [smʌdʒ], v.t. barbouiller, noircir.—n. barbouillage, m., tache, f.

smudgy ['smʌdʒi], a. barbouillé; taché.

smug [smʌg], a. suffisant, content de soi.

smuggle [smʌgl], v.t. passer en contrebande.—v.i. faire la contrebande.

smuggled [smʌgld], a. de contrebande.

smuggler ['smʌglə], n. contrebandier, m.

smuggling ['smʌgliŋ], n. contrebande, fraude, f.

smugness ['smʌgnis], n. suffisance, f.

smut [smʌt], n. tache de suie; (fig.) saleté (grivoiserie), f.—v.t. noircir.

smuttiness ['smʌtinis], n. noirceur (fig.) saleté, f.

smutty ['smʌti], a. noir; (fig.) obscène, grivois.

snack [snæk], n. morceau; casse-croûte, m.

snack-bar ['snækba:], n. snack-bar, m.

snaffle [snæfl], n. mors de bridon, filet, m.—

snag [snæg], n. (fig.) obstacle caché, m.

snail [sneil], n. escargot, limaçon, colimaçon, m.

snail's pace ['sneilzpeis], n. pas de tortue, m.

snake [sneik], n. serpent, m.—v.i. (Naut.) serpenter.

snap [snæp], v.t. saisir, happer; casser, rompre, éclater; faire claquer (fouet etc.); fermer avec un bruit sec; dire d'un ton sec. —v.i. tâcher de mordre ou de happer; se casser, se rompre; craquer; to snap at, (fam.) brusquer.—a. imprévu.—n. coup de dent, m.; cassure, f.; claquement (de fouet etc.); bruit sec; fermoir (de sac à main); biscuit craquant, m.; vivacité, f.

snapdragon ['snæpdrægn], n. muflier, m.

snappy ['snæpi], a. vif; make it snappy! dépêchez-vous!

snapshot ['snæpʃɔt], n. (colloq. snap [snæp]) instantané, m.

snare [snɛə], n. lacet, collet; (fig.) piège, m.— v.t. prendre (au piège).

snarl [sna:l], v.i. grogner; montrer les dents. —n. grognement, m.

snarling ['sna:liŋ], a. hargneux.—n. grognement, m.

snatch [snætʃ], v.t. saisir; to snatch at, chercher à saisir; to snatch from, arracher à; to snatch up, empoigner.—n. by snatches, à bâtons rompus; snatches of conversation, des bribes de conversation, f.pl.

sneak [sni:k], v.t. chiper.—v.i. s'en aller furtivement; (Sch.) cafarder, moucharder.— n. pleutre, pied-plat; cafard, m.

sneaking ['sni:kiŋ], a. rampant, servile; furtif, inavoué.

sneer [sniə], n. rire ou sourire moqueur, sarcasme, ricanement, m.—v.i. ricaner, se moquer (de).

sneering ['sniəriŋ], a. ricaneur, moqueur.—n. ricanement, m.

sneeringly ['sniəriŋli], adv. en ricanant.

sneeze [sni:z], n. éternuement, m.—v.i. éternuer.

sneezing ['sni:ziŋ], n. éternuement, m.

sniff [snif], v.t. flairer.—v.i. renifler.—n. reniflement, m.

snigger ['snigə], v.i. rire du bout des lèvres, ricaner.—n. rire en dessous, m.

snip [snip], n. coup de ciseaux, m.; (pop.) certitude, f.—v.t. couper (d'un coup de ciseaux).

snipe [snaip], n. bécassine, f.—v.i. (Shooting) canarder.

sniper ['snaipə], n. tireur embusqué, franc-tireur, m.

snippet ['snipit], n. petit morceau, m.

snivel [snivl], v.i. être morveux; (fig.) pleurnicher.

sniveller ['snivlə], n. pleurnicheur, m.

snivelling ['snivliŋ], a. morveux; (fig.) pleurnicheur.—n. pleurnicherie, f.

snob [snɔb], n. poseur; fat, snob, m.

snobbery ['snɔbəri], n. snobisme, m.

snobbish ['snɔbiʃ], a. affecté, poseur, prétentieux.

snobbishness ['snɔbiʃnis], n. snobisme, m.

snoop [snu:p], v.i. fureter.

snooper ['snu:pə], n. fureteur, m.

snooze [snu:z], *n.* somme, *m.*—*v.i.* sommeiller.

snore [sno:], *v.i.* ronfler.—*n.* ronflement, *m.*

snorkel ['sno:rkl], *n.* schnorkel, *m.*

snort [sno:t], *v.i.* renâcler, s'ébrouer (*cheval*); ronfler.

snorting ['sno:tiŋ], *n.* ronflement, *m.*

snot [snot], *n.* (*vulg.*) morve, *f.*

snotty ['snoti], *a.* (*vulg.*) morveux.

snout [snaut], *n.* museau; mufle (*de taureau*); groin (*de cochon*), *m.*

snow [snou], *n.* neige, *f.*—*v.i.* neiger, tomber de la neige.

snowball ['snoubo:l], *n.* boule de neige, *f.*

snow-capped ['snoukæpt], *a.* couronné de neige.

snow-drift ['snoudrift], *n.* congère, *f.*, amas de neige, *m.*

snowdrop ['snoudrɔp], *n.* perce-neige, *m.*

snowflake ['snoufleik], *n.* flocon de neige, *m.*

snow-man ['snoumæn], *n.* (*pl.* **-men** [men]) bonhomme de neige, *m.*

snowplow ['snouplau], *n.* chasse-neige, *m.*

snow-shoe ['snoufu:], *n.* raquette, *f.*

snow-storm ['snousto:m], *n.* tempête de neige, *f.*

Snow White ['snou'wait]. Blanche-Neige, *f.*

snow-white ['snouwait], *a.* blanc comme la neige.

snowy ['snoui], *a.* de neige; neigeux.

snub [snʌb], *n.* rebuffade, *f.*; affront, *m.*—*v.t.* rabrouer, rembarrer.

snub-nosed ['snʌbnouzd], *a.* au nez camus.

snuff (1) [snʌf], *n.* tabac (à priser), *m.*; **pinch of snuff**, prise de tabac, *f.*

snuff (2) [snʌf], *n.* lumignon (*de mèche*), *m.*—*v.t.* moucher (*chandelle*).

snuff-box ['snʌfbɔks], *n.* tabatière, *f.*

snuffle [snʌfl], *n.* reniflement, *m.*—*v.i.* nasiller, renifler.

snuffling ['snʌfliŋ], *a.* nasillard.—*n.* nasillement, *m.*

snug [snʌg], *a.* confortable, commode et agréable, où l'on est bien; gentil; serré, compact; **we are very snug here**, nous sommes on ne peut mieux ici.

snuggery ['snʌgəri], *n.* endroit petit et commode (*où l'on se sent chez soi*), *m.*

snuggle [snʌgl], *v.t.* serrer.—*v.i.* se serrer.

snugly ['snʌgli], *adv.* commodément, à son aise.

snugness ['snʌgnis], *n.* confort, bien-être, *m.*

so [sou], *adv.* and *conj.* ainsi, de cette manière, comme cela, comme ça (*de cette façon*); de même, de la même manière, tel (*pareillement*); si, tellement, tant (*à tel point*); aussi, donc (*alors*); **and so on**, et ainsi de suite; **be it so**, soit! **how so?** comment cela? **is that so?** vraiment? **just so!** parfaitement! **Mr. So-and-So**, Monsieur un tel; **or so**, environ, à peu près; **so as to**, de manière à; **so that**, de sorte que.

soak [souk], *v.t.* tremper; (*colloq.*) estamper.—*v.i.* tremper, s'infiltrer.

soaking ['soukiŋ], *a.* qui trempe.—*n.* trempée (*de pluie*), *f.*

soap [soup], *n.* savon, *m.*—*v.t.* savonner.

soap bubble ['soupbʌbl], *n.* bulle de savon, *f.*

soap flakes ['soupfleiks], *n.pl.* savon en paillettes, *m.*

soap-suds ['soupsʌdz], *n.pl.* eau de savon, *f.*

soar [so:], *v.i.* prendre l'essor, s'élever; **to soar over**, planer sur.

soaring ['so:riŋ], *a.* qui s'élève; (*fig.*) élevé.—*n.* essor, élan, *m.*

sob [sɔb], *v.i.* sangloter.—*n.* sanglot, *m.*

sobbing ['sɔbiŋ], *n.* sanglots, *m.pl.*

sober ['soubə], *a.* qui n'a pas bu, qui n'est pas ivre; sobre, tempéré; grave, sérieux; sensé; calme, posé, rassis.—*v.t.* dégriser; (*fig.*) calmer.—*v.i.* **to sober up**, se désenivrer.

soberly ['soubəli], *adv.* sobrement; raisonnablement.

soberness ['soubənis], **sobriety** [sə'braiəti], *n.* sobriété, tempérance; gravité, *f.*

so-called ['sou'kɔ:ld], *a.* soi-disant, prétendu.

soccer ['sɔkə], *n.* (*fam.*) football, *m.*

sociability [souʃə'biliti], *n.* sociabilité, *f.*

sociable ['souʃəbl], *a.* sociable.

social ['souʃəl], *a.* social.

socialism ['souʃəlizm], *n.* socialisme, *m.*

socialist ['souʃəlist], *a.* and *n.* socialiste, *m.*, *f.*

socially ['souʃəli], *adv.* socialement.

society [sə'saiəti], *n.* société; la société, *f.*; le monde, *m.*

sociology [sousi'ɔlədʒi], *n.* sociologie, *f.*

sock [sɔk], *n.* chaussette; semelle (*intérieure*), *f.*

socket ['sɔkit], *n.* emboîture; orbite (*de l'œil*), *f.*; trou, *m.*, cavité; douille (*d'outil etc.*), *f.*

Socrates ['sɔkrəti:z]. Socrate, *m.*

sod [sɔd], *n.* gazon, *m.*; motte de gazon, *f.*

soda ['soudə], *n.* soude, *f.*; **baking soda**, bicarbonate de soude, *m.*

soda water ['soudəwo:tə], *n.* eau de Seltz, *f.*, soda, *m.*

sodden ['sɔdn], *a.* imprégné d'eau, détrempé; pâteux (*pain*); abruti (*d'alcool*).

sodium ['soudiəm], *n.* (*Chem.*) sodium, *m.*

sodomy ['sɔdəmi], *n.* sodomie, *f.*

sofa ['soufə], *n.* canapé, *m.*

soft [sɔft], *a.* mou, mol, mollet; délicat, doux, facile, pas résistant; tendre; efféminé; faible; sot, niais; (*Gram.*) doux; **soft fruits**, fruits rouges, *m.pl.*—*adv.* mollement, doucement.—*int.* doucement! tout doux!

soften [sɔfn], *v.t.* amollir, ramollir; adoucir, apaiser; affaiblir; attendrir (*cœur*).—*v.i.* s'amollir, se ramollir; s'affaiblir; s'attendrir (*cœur*).

softener ['sɔfnə], *n.* chose qui amollit, *f.*

softening ['sɔfniŋ], *n.* amollissement; affaiblissement; attendrissement (*du cœur*), *m.*

soft-headed ['sɔft'hedid], *a.* niais; sot.

soft-hearted ['sɔft'hɑ:tid], *a.* tendre, compatissant.

softly ['sɔftli], *adv.* mollement; doucement; tendrement.

softness ['sɔftnis], *n.* mollesse; faiblesse; niaiserie; douceur, *f.*

soggy ['sɔgi], *a.* détrempé; pâteux (*pain*).

soil (1) [sɔil], *n.* sol, terrain, terroir, *m.*, terre, *f.*

soil (2) [sɔil], *n.* tache, souillure, *f.*—*v.t.* salir, souiller.

sojourn ['sɔdʒən], *n.* séjour, *m.*—*v.i.* séjourner.

sojourning ['sɔdʒəniŋ], *n.* séjour, *m.*

solace ['sɔlis], *n.* consolation, *f.*, soulagement, *m.*—*v.t.* consoler (*de*).

solar ['soulə], *a.* solaire, du soleil.

solder ['sɔ(l)də], *n.* soudure, *f.*—*v.t.* souder.

soldering ['sɔ(l)dəriŋ], *n.* soudure, *f.*; soudage (*action*), *m.*; **soldering iron**, fer à souder, *m.*

soldier

soldier ['souldʒə], *n.* soldat, militaire, *m.*;
foot soldier, fantassin, *m.*; *private soldier*, simple soldat.—*v.i.* servir comme
soldat.
soldierly ['souldʒəli], *a.* de soldat, militaire,
martial.
soldiery ['souldʒəri], *n.* troupes, *f.pl.*, soldats,
m.pl.
sole (1) [soul], *a.* seul, unique.
sole (2) [soul], *n.* plante (*du pied*); semelle (*de
soulier, d'outil etc.*), *f.*—*v.i.* ressemeler.
sole (3) [soul], *n.* (*Ichth.*) sole, *f.*
solecism ['sɔlisizm], *n.* solécisme, *m.*
solely ['soulli], *adv.* seulement, uniquement.
solemn ['sɔləm], *a.* solennel.
solemnity [sə'lemniti], *n.* solennité, *f.*
solemnization [sɔləmnai'zeiʃən], *n.* solen-
nisation; célébration solennelle, *f.*
solemnize ['sɔləmnaiz], *v.t.* solenniser, célébrer.
solemnly ['sɔləmli], *adv.* solennellement.
solenoid ['sɔlinoid], *n.* (*Elec.*) solénoïde, *m.*
solicit [sə'lisit], *v.t.* solliciter.
solicitation [səlisi'teiʃən], *n.* sollicitation, *f.*
solicitous [sə'lisitəs], *a.* désireux; *solicitous
about*, soigneux, attentif à.
solicitude [sə'lisitju:d], *n.* sollicitude, *f.*
solid ['sɔlid], *a.* solide, massif.—*n.* solide, *m.*
solidarity [sɔli'dæriti], *n.* solidarité, *f.*
solidification [səlidifi'keiʃən], *n.* solidification, *f.*
solidify [sə'lidifai], *v.t.* solidifier.—*v.i.* se
solidifier.
solidity [sə'liditi], **solidness** ['sɔlidnis], *n.*
solidité, *f.*
solidly ['sɔlidli], *adv.* solidement.
soliloquize [sə'liləkwaiz], *v.i.* faire un soliloque.
soliloquy [sə'liləkwi], *n.* soliloque, *m.*
soling ['soulin], *n.* ressemelage, *m.*
solitary ['sɔlitəri], *a.* solitaire, retiré, isolé;
seul.
solitude ['sɔlitju:d], *n.* solitude, *f.*
solo ['soulou], *n.* solo, *m.*
soloist ['soulouist], *n.* soliste, *m.*, *f.*
Solomon ['sɔləmən]. Salomon, *m.*
solstice ['sɔlstis], *n.* solstice, *m.*
solubility [sɔlju'biliti], *n.* solubilité, *f.*
soluble ['sɔljubl], *a.* soluble.
solution [sə'lju:ʃən], *n.* solution, *f.*
solvable ['sɔlvəbl], *a.* soluble.
solve [sɔlv], *v.t.* résoudre, expliquer, éclaircir.
solvency ['sɔlvənsi], *n.* (*Fin.*) solvabilité, *f.*
solvent ['sɔlvənt], *a.* dissolvant; (*Comm.*)
solvable.—*n.* dissolvant, *m.*
Somali [so'mɑːli], *a.* somali.—*n.* somali
(*langue*); Somali (*personne*), *m.*
Somalia [so'mɑːliə]. la Somalie, *f.*
Somaliland [so'mɑːlilænd]. la Somalie, *f.*
somber ['sɔmbə], *a.* sombre.
somberly ['sɔmbəli], *adv.* sombrement.
some [sʌm], *a.* quelque, *m.*, *f.*, quelques, *pl.*;
un certain, *m.*, certains, *m.pl.*, plusieurs,
pl.; du, *m.*, de la, *f.*, de l', *m.*, *f.*, des, *pl.*, de;
quelconque; un certain nombre de, un peu
de, une partie de.—*adv.* à peu près, environ,
quelque.—*pron.* quelques-uns, *m.pl.*, quelques-unes, *f.pl.*; les uns, *m.pl.*, les unes,
f.pl., . . . les autres, *pl.*; en.

somebody ['sʌmbədi], **someone** ['sʌmwʌn],
pron. quelqu'un, *m.*, quelqu'une, *f.*, on;
somebody else, quelqu'un d'autre, quelque autre, un autre.
somehow ['sʌmhau], *adv.* d'une manière ou
d'une autre, de façon ou d'autre.
someone [SOMEBODY].
somersault ['sʌməsɔ:lt], *n.* saut périlleux, *m.*,
culbute, *f.*
something ['sʌmθiŋ], *n.* and *pron.* quelque
chose (*de*), *m.*; *something else*, autre
chose, *f.*—*adv.* un peu, quelque peu, tant
soit peu.
sometime ['sʌmtaim], *adv.* autrefois, jadis;
sometime or other, tôt ou tard.—*a.*
ancien.
sometimes ['sʌmtaimz], *adv.* quelquefois,
parfois; tantôt.
somewhat ['sʌmwɔt], *adv.* quelque peu, un
peu; assez.—*n.* un peu, quelque peu, tant
soit peu, *m.*
somewhere ['sʌmwɛə], *adv.* quelque part;
somewhere else, ailleurs.
somnambulist [sɔm'næmbjulist], *n.* somnambule, *m.*, *f.*
somniferous [sɔm'nifərəs], *a.* somnifère.
somnolence ['sɔmnələns], *n.* somnolence, *f.*
somnolent ['sɔmnələnt], *a.* somnolent.
son [sʌn], *n.* fils; (*fig.*) descendant, *m.*
sonata [sə'nɑːtə], *n.* sonate, *f.*
song [sɔŋ], *n.* chanson, *f.*; chant, *m.*; (*fig.*)
ballade, *f.*; *a mere song*, un rien, *m.*, une
bagatelle, *f.*
songster ['sɔŋstə], *n.* chanteur; oiseau chanteur, *m.*
songstress ['sɔŋstris], *n.* chanteuse, *f.*
song thrush ['sɔŋθrʌʃ], *n.* grive chanteuse,
f.
song-writer ['sɔŋraitə], *n.* chansonnier, *m.*
son-in-law ['sʌninlɔ:], *n.* gendre, *m.*
sonnet ['sɔnit], *n.* sonnet, *m.*
sonorous ['sɔnərəs], *a.* sonore.
soon [su:n], *adv.* bientôt; tôt (*de bonne heure*);
as soon as, aussitôt que, dès que; *how
soon?* quand ? *see you soon!* à bientôt; *so
soon*, si tôt; *too soon*, trop tôt.
sooner ['su:nə], *adv.* plus tôt (*de meilleure
heure*); plutôt (*mieux*); *no sooner said
than done*, aussitôt dit, aussitôt fait;
sooner or later, tôt ou tard; *sooner than*,
plutôt que.
soonest ['su:nist], *adv.* le plus tôt.
soot [sut], *n.* suie, *f.*
soothe [su:ð], *v.t.* apaiser, calmer; (*fig.*)
charmer.
soothing ['su:ðiŋ], *a.* calmant, consolant; flatteur.
soothingly ['su:ðiŋli], *adv.* d'un ton doux.
soothsay ['su:θsei], *v.i.* prophétiser, prédire.
soothsayer ['su:θseiə], *n.* devin, *m.*, devineresse, *f.*, prophète, *m.*
sooty ['suti], *a.* de suie, fuligineux; plein *ou*
couvert de suie.
sop [sɔp], *n.* morceau (de pain) trempé; (*fig.*)
pot-de-vin (*pourboire*), *m.*—*v.t.* tremper.
Sophia [sə'faiə]. Sophie, *f.*
sophism ['sɔfizm], *n.* sophisme, *m.*
sophist ['sɔfist], *n.* sophiste, *m.*, *f.*
sophisticate [sə'fistikeit], *v.t.* sophistiquer,
falsifier.

sophisticated [səˈfistikeitid], a. falsifié; blasé (*personne*).

sophistication [səfistiˈkeiʃən], n. sophistication, falsification, f.

sophistry [ˈsɔfistri], n. sophismes, m.pl.

Sophocles [ˈsɔfəkliːz]. Sophocle, m.

soporific [sɔpəˈrifik], a. and n. soporifique, m.

sopping [ˈsɔpiŋ] (**wet**), a. trempé.

soprano [səˈprɑːnou], n. soprano, m., f.

sorcerer [ˈsɔːsərə], n. sorcier, magicien, m.

sorceress [ˈsɔːsəris], n. sorcière, magicienne, f.

sorcery [ˈsɔːsəri], n. sorcellerie, magie, f.

sordid [ˈsɔːdid], a. sordide, sale; bas, vil.

sordidly [ˈsɔːdidli], adv. sordidement.

sordidness [ˈsɔːdidnis], n. sordidité, f.

sore [sɔː], a. douloureux, endolori, sensible; (*fig.*) rude; fâché; **sore throat**, mal à la gorge, m.—n. plaie, f.

sorely [ˈsɔːli], adv. gravement, fortement, cruellement, rudement.

soreness [ˈsɔːnis], n. douleur; sensation pénible, f.

sorrel [ˈsɔrəl], a. saure; alezan.—n. oseille, f.; alezan (*cheval*), m.

sorrily [ˈsɔrili], adv. misérablement, pauvrement.

sorrow [ˈsɔrou], n. chagrin, m., douleur; peine, tristesse, f.—v.i. être affligé.

sorrowful [ˈsɔrəful], a. triste, affligé.

sorrowfully [ˈsɔrəfuli], adv. tristement.

sorrowing [ˈsɔrouiŋ], a. affligé.

sorry [ˈsɔri], a. fâché, désolé (*de*); triste, pauvre, méchant, pitoyable; **I am sorry for you**, je vous plains; **I am sorry to say that** . . ., je regrette d'avoir à dire que . . .; **sorry!** pardon!

sort (1) [sɔːt], n. sorte, f., genre, m., espèce; manière, façon, f.; **nothing of the sort**, pas du tout.

sort (2) [sɔːt], v.t. assortir, classer, distribuer; trier (*lettres etc.*).

sorted [ˈsɔːtid], a. assorti; trié, arrangé, séparé.

sorter [ˈsɔːtə], n. trieur, m.

sortie [ˈsɔːtiː], n. (*Mil.*) sortie, f.; (*Av.*) vol, m.

sorting [ˈsɔːtiŋ], n. triage, tri; assortiment (*classement*), m.

so-so [ˈsouˈsou], a. comme ci comme ça, (*fam.*) couci-couça.

sot [sɔt], n. ivrogne, m., f.

sottish [ˈsɔtiʃ], a. hébété, abruti.

sough [sau, sʌf], v.i. murmurer, soupirer (*vent*).

soughing [ˈsauiŋ], n. bruissement, murmure, m.

soul [soul], n. âme, f.; (*fig.*) être; principe (*essence*), m.; **All Souls' Day**, le jour des morts, m.

soulful [ˈsoulful], a. sentimental.

soulfully [ˈsoulfuli], adv. avec expression; avec sentiment.

soulless [ˈsoullis], a. sans âme; abrutissant.

sound (1) [saund], n. détroit (*goulet*), m.; (*Surg.*) sonde, f.—v.t. sonder (*les profondeurs etc.*); (*Surg.*) ausculter.

sound (2) [saund], a. en bon état, sain; (*fig.*) solide; profond (*sommeil*); valide, bien fondé; **safe and sound**, sain et sauf.

sound (3) [saund], v.t. faire sonner; proclamer.—v.i. sonner; retentir, résonner (*de*); sembler.—n. son, bruit, m.; **to break the**

sound barrier, (*Av.*) franchir le mur du son.

sounding (1) [ˈsaundiŋ], n. sondage, m.; (*Surg.*) auscultation, f.

sounding (2) [ˈsaundiŋ], a. résonnant, retentissant; (*fig.*) pompeux.—n. retentissement, résonnement, m.

sounding balloon [ˈsaundiŋbəˈluːn], n. (*Meteor.*) ballon sonde, m.

sounding-lead [ˈsaundiŋled], n. plomb de sonde, m.

sounding line [ˈsaundiŋlain], n. ligne de sonde, f.

soundless [ˈsaundlis], a. sans bruit, muet.

soundly [ˈsaundli], adv. vigoureusement, rudement, ferme, bien; sainement, solidement; profondément (*sommeil*).

soundness [ˈsaundnis], n. bon état, m.; force, vigueur (*physique*); droiture (*morale*), f.

sound-proof [ˈsaundpruːf], a. insonore.

sound track [ˈsaundtræk], n. (*Cine.*) piste sonore, f.

sound wave [ˈsaundweiv], n. onde sonore, f.

soup [suːp], n. potage, m., soupe, f.; (*colloq.*) **to be in the soup**, être dans le pétrin.

soup ladle [ˈsuːpleidl], n. louche, f.

soup tureen [ˈsuːptjuˈriːn], n. soupière, f.

sour [ˈsauə], a. aigre, acide; tourné (*lait*); (*fig.*) âpre.—v.t. aigrir; (*fig.*) empoisonner.—v.i. s'aigrir.

source [sɔːs], n. source, f.

souring [ˈsauəriŋ], n. aigrissement, m.

sourish [ˈsauəriʃ], a. suret, aigrelet.

sourly [ˈsauli], adv. avec aigreur; (*fig.*) aigrement, âprement.

sourness [ˈsauənis], n. aigreur, acidité; (*fig.*) âpreté, f.

souse [saus], v.t. tremper; faire mariner.—n. marinade, f.

south [sauθ], a. sud, du sud, du midi, méridional.—n. sud, midi, m.—adv. vers le midi, vers le sud, au sud; **South Africa**, l'Afrique du Sud, f.; **South America**, l'Amérique du Sud, f.

south-east [ˈsauθˈiːst], a. sud-est, du sud-est.—n. sud-est, m.—adv. vers le sud-est.

south-easter [ˈsauθˈiːstə], n. vent du sud-est, m.

south-easterly [ˈsauθˈiːstəli], **south-eastern** [ˈsauθˈiːstn], a. du sud-est.

southerly [ˈsʌðəli], **southern** [ˈsʌðən], a. du sud, du midi, méridional.

southerner [ˈsʌðənə], n. méridional, m.; (*Am.*) sudiste, m., f.

southernmost [ˈsʌðənmost], a. à l'extrême sud.

southward [ˈsauθwəd], adv. vers le sud, au sud.

south-west [ˈsauθˈwest], a. sud-ouest, du sud-ouest.—n. sud-ouest, m.—adv. vers le sud-ouest.

southwester [sauˈwestə], [souˈWESTER].

south-westerly [ˈsauθˈwestəli], **south-western** [ˈsauθˈwestən], a. du sud-ouest, sud-ouest.

souvenir [ˈsuːvəniə], n. souvenir, m.

sou'wester, southwester [sauˈwestə], n. vent du sud-ouest; suroît (*coiffure*), m.

sovereign [ˈsɔvrin], a. and n. souverain, m.

sovereignty [ˈsɔvrinti], n. souveraineté, f.

Soviet [ˈsouviet], n. Soviet, m.; **the Soviet Union**, l'Union Soviétique, f.

sow (1) [sau], *n.* truie; gueuse (*de fer*), *f.*
sow (2) [sou], *v.t. irr.* semer.—*v.i.* semer, faire les semailles.
sower ['souə], *n.* semeur, *m.*
sowing ['souiŋ], *n.* semailles, *f.pl.*, ensemencement, *m.*
soya-bean ['sɔiə'biːn], *n.* soya, soja, *m.*
spa [spaː], *n.* source minérale; ville d'eaux, *f.*
space [speis], *n.* espace, *m.*, étendue; place, *f.*; intervalle, *m.*—*v.t.* (*Print.*) espacer.
space ship ['speisʃip], *n.* astronef, *m.*
space suit ['speissjuːt], *n.* combinaison spatiale, *f.*
space travel ['speistrævl], *n.* astronautique, *f.*, voyages interplanétaires, *m.pl.*
space traveller ['speistrævlə], *n.* astronaute, cosmonaute, *m.*, *f.*
spacing ['speisiŋ], *n.* espacement; (*Print.*) interligne, *m.*
spacious ['speiʃəs], *a.* spacieux, vaste.
spaciously ['speiʃəsli], *adv.* spacieusement; amplement.
spaciousness ['speiʃəsnis], *n.* vaste étendue, *f.*
spade [speid], *n.* bêche, pelle (*d'enfant*), *f.*; (*Cards*) pique, *m.*
spadeful ['speidful], *n.* pelletée, *f.*
Spain [spein]. l'Espagne, *f.*
span [spæn], *n.* empan, *m.*; envergure (*d'ailes*), *f.*; moment, instant, *m.*—*v.t.* mesurer; embrasser; traverser.
spangle ['spæŋgl], *n.* paillette, *f.*—*v.t.* pailleter (*de*).
Spaniard ['spænjəd], *n.* Espagnol, *m.*
spaniel ['spænjəl], *n.* épagneul, *m.*
Spanish ['spæniʃ], *a.* espagnol, d'Espagne.— *n.* espagnol (*langue*), *m.*
spank [spæŋk], *v.t.* fesser.—*n.* (*also* spanking (1) ['spæŋkiŋ]) fessée, *f.*
spanking (2) ['spæŋkiŋ], *a.* vigoureux; rapide (*pas*).
spanner ['spænə], *n.* clef à écrous, *f.*; **adjustable spanner**, clef anglaise, *f.*
spar [spaː], *n.* perche, *f.*, poteau; (*Naut.*) espar; (*Box.*) combat d'entraînement, *m.*— *v.i.* faire un assaut amical (*de boxe* ou *de paroles*); se disputer.
spare [spɛə], *v.t.* épargner; ménager, économiser (*dépenser avec précaution*); se passer de (*se priver de*); donner, céder; prêter.—*a.* disponible, de reste (*superflu*); libre (*temps*); (*Motor. etc.*) de rechange; modique, faible, pauvre; maigre, sec (*taille*).
spareness ['spɛənis], *n.* maigreur, *f.*
spare-rib ['spɛə'rib], *n.* côte de porc, *f.*
sparing ['spɛəriŋ], *a.* économe, ménager, frugal, sobre (*de*); parcimonieux.
sparingly ['spɛəriŋli], *adv.* frugalement, avec parcimonie; économiquement.
sparingness ['spɛəriŋnis], *n.* frugalité, épargne, parcimonie, *f.*
spark [spaːk], *n.* étincelle; (*fig.*) lueur, *f.*— *v.i.* produire des étincelles.
spark plug ['spaːkiŋplʌg], *n.* (*Motor.*) bougie (d'allumage), *f.*
sparkle ['spaːkl], *n.* étincellement, éclat, *m.*; vivacité (*d'esprit*), *f.*—*v.i.* étinceler, scintiller; pétiller (*boisson*).
sparkling ['spaːkliŋ], *a.* étincelant; mousseux (*boisson*).
sparling ['spaːliŋ], *n.* (*Ichth.*) éperlan, *m.*
sparrow ['spærou], *n.* moineau, passereau, *m.*
sparrow hawk ['spærouhɔːk], *n.* épervier, *m.*

sparse [spaːs], *a.* épars; éparpillé, clairsemé.
sparsely ['spaːsli], *adv.* d'une manière éparse, de loin en loin.
sparseness ['spaːsnis], *n.* rareté, *f.*; éparpillement, *m.*
Sparta ['spaːtə]. Sparte, *f.*
Spartan ['spaːtən], *a.* spartiate.—*n.* Spartiate (*personne*), *m.*, *f.*
spasm [spæzm], *n.* spasme, accès, *m.*
spasmodic [spæz'mɔdik], spasmodical [spæz'mɔdikəl], *a.* spasmodique.
spasmodically [spæz'mɔdikəli], *adv.* par à-coups.
spastic ['spæstik], *a.* spasmodique.—*n.* paraplégique, *m.*, *f.*
spat (1) [spæt], *past* and *p.p.* [SPIT].
spat (2) [spæt], *n.* guêtre de ville, *f.*
spate [speit], *n.* crue (*de rivière*); (*fig.*) affluence, *f.*
spatter ['spætə], *v.t.* éclabousser (*de*).
spatula ['spætjulə], *n.* spatule, *f.*
spavin ['spævin], *n.* éparvin, *m.*
spawn [spɔːn], *n.* frai, *m.*; (*fig.*) race, engeance, *f.*—*v.t.* (*fig.*) engendrer.—*v.i.* frayer; (*fig.*) naître.
spawning ground ['spɔːniŋgraund], *n.* frayère, *f.*
speak [spiːk], *v.t. irr.* parler; dire; (*Naut.*) héler; **to speak one's mind**, dire sa pensée.—*v.i.* parler; causer (*avec*); faire un discours (*en public*); dire; **so to speak**, pour ainsi dire; **to speak out**, parler à haute voix; **to speak up**, parler plus fort
speaker ['spiːkə], *n.* personne qui parle, *f.*; orateur; (*Parl.*) président; (*Rad.* = **loud-speaker**) haut-parleur, *m.*
speaking ['spiːkiŋ], *a.* parlant, qui parle.—*n.* parole, *f.*, langage, discours, *m.*
speaking-tube ['spiːkiŋtjuːb], *n.* tuyau *ou* tube acoustique, *m.*
spear [spiə], *n.* lance, *f.*—*v.t.* percer d'un coup de lance; harponner (*poisson etc.*).
spear-head ['spiəhed], *n.* fer de lance, *m.*; (*Mil.*) avancée, pointe, *f.*
spearman ['spiəmən], *n.* (*pl.* **-men** [men]) lancier, *m.*
spearmint ['spiəmint], *n.* menthe verte, *f.*
special ['speʃl], *a.* spécial, exprès; extraordinaire. [**special delivery**, see **express**]
specialist ['speʃəlist], *n.* spécialiste, *m.*, *f.*
speciality [speʃi'æliti], specialty ['speʃəlti], *n.* spécialité, *f.*
specialization [speʃəlai'zeiʃən], *n.* spécialisation, *f.*
specialize ['speʃəlaiz], *v.i.* se spécialiser.
specially ['speʃəli], *adv.* particulièrement, surtout.
specie ['spiːʃiː], *n.* espèces, *f.pl.*, numéraire, *m.*
species ['spiːʃiːz], *n.* espèce, *f.*; (*fig.*) genre, *m.*, sorte, *f.*
specific [spi'sifik], *a.* spécifique; précis.
specification [spesifi'keiʃən], *n.* spécification; description précise (*de brevet d'invention*), *f.*
specify ['spesifai], *v.t.* spécifier, déterminer; fixer d'avance (*une heure*).
specimen ['spesimən], *n.* spécimen, modèle, échantillon, *m.*
specious ['spiːʃəs], *a.* spécieux, captieux.
speciousness ['spiːʃəsnis], *n.* spéciosité, apparence plausible, *f.*

speck [spek], *n.* petite tache, marque, *f.*, point; grain (*de poussière*), *m.*—*v.t.* tacher, marquer.

speckle [spekl], *v.t.* tacheter, marqueter, moucheter (*de*).—*n.* moucheture (*peau d'animal*), *f.*

speckled [spekld], *a.* tacheté, marqueté, moucheté.

spectacle ['spektəkl], *n.* spectacle, *m.*; (*pl.*) lunettes, *f.pl.*

spectacle case ['spektəklkeis], *n.* étui à lunettes, *m.*

spectacle maker ['spektəklmeikə], *n.* lunetier, *m.*

spectacular [spek'tækjulə], *a.* théâtral, impressionnant.

spectator [spek'teitə], *n.* spectateur, *m.*; (*pl.*) assistants, *m.pl.*

specter ['spektə], *n.* spectre, fantôme, *m.*

spectral ['spektrəl], *a.* de spectre, spectral.

spectroscope ['spektrəskoup], *n.* spectroscope, *m.*

spectrum ['spektrəm], *n.* (*pl.* **spectra** ['spektrə]) spectre, *m.*

speculate ['spekjuleit], *v.i.* spéculer (*sur*), méditer (*sur*).

speculation [spekju'leiʃən], *n.* spéculation, méditation, *f.*

speculative ['spekjulətiv], *a.* spéculatif, contemplatif; (*Comm.*) spéculateur.

speculatively ['spekjulətivli], *adv.* en théorie.

speculator ['spekjuleitə], *n.* spéculateur, *m.*

speech [spiːtʃ], *n.* parole, *f.*; discours, *m.*, allocution (*public*); langue (*parler*), *f.*; **extempore speech**, improvisation, *f.*; (*Parl.*) **maiden speech**, discours de début.

speech-day ['spiːtʃdei], *n.* (*Sch.*) distribution des prix, *f.*

speechless ['spiːtʃlis], *a.* sans voix; muet, interdit.

speechlessness ['spiːtʃlisnis], *n.* mutisme, *m.*

speed [spiːd], *n.* vitesse, rapidité, célérité; hâte, diligence, promptitude, *f.*; (*fig.*) succès, *m.*; **God-speed !** bon succès! bonne chance!—*v.t. irr.* expédier, hâter; faire réussir (*faciliter*).—*v.i.* se hâter, se dépêcher.

speed-boat ['spiːdbout], *n.* motoglisseur, *m.*; hors-bord, *m.inv.*

speedily ['spiːdili], *adv.* vite, en toute hâte.

speediness ['spiːdinis], *n.* célérité, hâte, *f.*

speed limit ['spiːdlimit], *n.* limitation de vitesse, *f.*

speedometer [spiː'dɔmitə], *n.* indicateur de vitesse, tachymètre, *m.*

speedwell ['spiːdwel], *n.* (*Bot.*) véronique, *f.*

speedy ['spiːdi], *a.* rapide, vite, prompt.

spell (1) [spel], *n.* temps, *m.*, période, *f.*; tour (*de service*), *m.*

spell (2) [spel], *n.* charme, *m.*—*v.t.*, *v.i. irr.* épeler (*nommer les lettres*); orthographier (*écrire correctement*); signifier.

spell-bound ['spelbaund], *a.* charmé, fasciné.

speller ['spelə], *n.* personne qui orthographie *ou* qui épèle, *f.*

spelling ['speliŋ], *n.* orthographe; épellation, *f.*

spelling bee ['speliŋbiː], *n.* concours orthographique, *m.*

spelling book ['speliŋbuk], *n.* abécédaire, syllabaire, *m.*

spelter ['speltə], *n.* zinc, *m.*

spend [spend], *v.t. irr.* dépenser; gaspiller, perdre (*prodiguer*); passer (*temps*).—*v.i.* dépenser; se perdre (*se dissiper*); se consumer.

spending ['spendiŋ], *n.* action de dépenser, dépense, *f.*

spendthrift ['spendθrift], *n.* prodigue, *m.*, *f.*, dissipateur, *m.*

spent [spent], *a.* épuisé; mort (*balle etc.*).

sperm [spəːm], *n.* sperme; frai (*poisson etc.*); blanc de baleine, *m.*

spew [spjuː], *v.t.*, *v.i.* vomir.

spewing ['spjuːiŋ], *n.* vomissement, *m.*

sphere ['sfiə], *n.* sphère, *f.*

spherical ['sferikl], *a.* sphérique.

spherics ['sferiks], *n.pl.* théorie de la sphère, *f.*

spheroid ['sfiərɔid], *n.* sphéroïde, *m.*

sphinx ['sfiŋks], *n.* (*pl.* **sphinxes** ['sfiŋksiz]) sphinx, *m.*

spice [spais], *n.* épice, *f.*—*v.t.* épicer (*de*).

spiciness ['spaisinis], *n.* goût épicé, *m.*

spick-and-span ['spikənd'spæn], *a.* tiré à quatre épingles; bien astiqué.

spicy ['spaisi], *a.* épicé, aromatique, parfumé.

spider ['spaidə], *n.* araignée, *f.*

spigot ['spigət], *n.* fausset; (*Am.*, *Sc.*) robinet, *m.*

spike [spaik], *n.* pointe, *f.*; clou à grosse tête (*de métal*), *m.*; cheville (*de bois*), *f.*; **marline-spike**, épissoir, *m.*—*v.t.* clouer; hérisser. [see **stiletto heels**]

spiked [spaikt], *a.* à pointes, barbelé.

spikenard ['spaiknɑːd], *n.* nard indien, *m.*

spiky ['spaiki], *a.* à pointe aiguë; armé de pointes.

spill (1) [spil], *v.t. irr.* répandre, verser; renverser.—*v.i.* se verser, se répandre.—*n.* culbute (*renversement*), *f.*

spill (2) [spil], *n.* allumette de papier, allumette en copeau, *f.*

spin [spin], *v.t. irr.* filer; faire tourner.—*v.i.* filer (*aller vite*); tourner.—*n.* tournoiement, *m.*; (*Av.*) vrille, *f.*; (*Motor.*) tour, *m.*; promenade, *f.*

spinach ['spinidʒ], *n.* épinards, *m.pl.*

spinal [spainl], *a.* spinal; **spinal column**, colonne vertébrale, *f.*

spindle [spindl], *n.* fuseau; pivot; (*Mach.*) essieu; (*Tech.*) axe, *m.*

spindleful ['spindlful], *n.* fusée, *f.*

spindle-legs ['spindllegz], **spindle-shanks** ['spindlʃæŋks], *n.pl.* jambes de fuseau, *f.pl.*

spindrift ['spindrift], *n.* embrun, *m.*

spine [spain], *n.* épine dorsale; (*Bot.*) épine, *f.*

spineless ['spainlis], *a.* sans épines; (*fig.*) mou, flasque, invertébré.

spinet ['spinit, spi'net], *n.* épinette, *f.*

spinner ['spinə], *n.* fileur, *m.*

spinney ['spini], *n.* petit bois, bosquet, *m.*

spinning ['spiniŋ], *a.* tournoyant, tournant.—*n.* filage (*processus*), *m.*; filature (*art*), *f.*; tournoiement, *m.*

spinning machine ['spiniŋmə'shiːn], *n.* machine à filer, *f.*

spinning mill ['spiniŋmil], *n.* filature, *f.*

spinning top ['spiniŋtɔp], *n.* toupie, *f.*

spinning wheel ['spiniŋwiːl], *n.* rouet, *m.*

spinous ['spainəs], *a.* épineux.

spinster ['spinstə], *n.* fille non mariée, célibataire, *f.*

spinsterhood ['spinstəhud], *n.* célibat, *m.*

spiny ['spaini], *a.* épineux, couvert d'épines; (*fig.*) difficile.

spiraea [spai'ri:ə], *n.* (*Bot.*) spirée, *f.*

spiral ['spaiərəl], *a.* spiral; en colimaçon (*escalier*).—*n.* spirale, *f.*—*v.i.* monter en spirale.

spirally ['spaiərəli], *adv.* en spirale.

spire ['spaiə], *n.* aiguille, flèche, *f.*

spirit (1) ['spirit], *n.* esprit, *m.*, âme, *f.*, fantôme, spectre (*apparition*), *m.*—*v.t.* **to spirit away**, faire disparaître.

spirit (2) ['spirit], **spiritedness** ['spiritidnis], *n.* (*fig.*) ardeur, force, vigueur, *f.*, feu, élan, entrain, *m.*; fougue (*d'un cheval*); verve, bonne humeur, *f.*, entrain, courage, *m.*—*v.t.* animer, encourager.

spirit (3) ['spirit], *n.* (*sing.* or *pl.*) spiritueux, *m. inv.*; liqueur spiritueuse *ou* alcoolique, *f.*; esprit (*de vin etc.*), *m.*; **methylated spirit**, alcool à brûler, *m.*

spirited ['spiritid], *a.* animé, plein de cœur, plein de vivacité; vif, plein de verve; fougueux (*cheval*).

spiritedly ['spiritidli], *adv.* avec ardeur, chaleureusement, avec force, avec entrain.

spiritedness [SPIRIT (2)].

spirit lamp ['spiritlæmp], *n.* lampe à alcool, *f.*

spiritless ['spiritlis], *a.* sans vigueur, mou, énervé; sans courage; abattu (*découragé*).

spirit level ['spiritlevl], *n.* niveau à bulle d'air, *m.*

spiritual ['spiritjuəl], *a.* spirituel.—*n.* chant religieux (*des Noirs*), *m.*

spiritualism ['spiritjuəlizm], *n.* spiritisme (*communication avec les esprits*), *m.*

spiritualist ['spiritjuəlist], *n.* spirite (*adepte du spiritisme*), *m.*, *f.*

spiritualize ['spiritjuəlaiz], *v.t.* spiritualiser.

spirituous ['spiritjuəs], *a.* spiritueux.

spiry ['spaiəri], *a.* en flèche, élancé.

spit (1) [spit], *n.* broche; profondeur de bêche (*plongée dans la terre*), *f.*—*v.t.* embrocher, mettre à la broche.

spit (2) [spit], *n.* crachat, *m.*, salive, *f.*—*v.t. irr.* cracher (*sur* ou *à*).

spite [spait], **spitefulness** ['spaitfulnis], *n.* dépit, *m.*; rancune, malveillance, *f.*; **in spite of**, en dépit de, malgré; **out of spite**, par dépit; **to have a spite against**, en vouloir à.—*v.t.* vexer, blesser, contrarier.

spiteful ['spaitful], *a.* rancunier, malveillant, vindicatif.

spitefully ['spaitfuli], *adv.* par dépit, par rancune.

spitefulness [SPITE].

spitfire ['spitfaiə], *n.* rageur, *m.*

spitter ['spitə], *n.* cracheur, *m.*

spitting ['spitiŋ], *n.* crachement, *m.*

spittle [spitl], *n.* salive, *f.*; (*colloq.*) crachat, *m.*

splash [splæʃ], *v.t.* éclabousser.—*v.i.* éclabousser; clapoter (*vagues*); patauger.—*n.* éclaboussure, *f.*; clapotement, clapotis (*des vagues*); flac (*bruit*), *m.*

splashing ['splæʃiŋ], *n.* éclaboussement (*acte*), *m.*; éclaboussure (*ce qui rejaillit*), *f.*

splashy ['splæʃi], *a.* éclaboussé, bourbeux.

splay [splei], *v.t.* évaser; (*Arch.*) ébraser; épauler (*cheval*).—*n.* écartement; (*Arch.*) ébrasement, *m.*

splay-footed ['spleifutid], *a.* aux pieds plats et tournés en dehors.

spleen [spli:n], *n.* rate, *f.*; (*fig.*) fiel, *m.*, animosité, *f.*; spleen, *m.*, mélancolie, *f.*

splendid ['splendid], *a.* resplendissant, somptueux, magnifique.

splendidly ['splendidli], *adv.* avec éclat, magnifiquement.

splendor ['splendə], *n.* splendeur, *f.*, éclat, *m.*

splenetic [splə'netik], *a.* splénétique, atrabilaire.

splice [splais], *n.* épissure, *f.*, raccordement, *m.*—*v.t.* épisser; (*Carp.*) joindre.

splint [splint], *n.* éclisse, attelle, *f.*—*v.t.* éclisser.

splinter ['splintə], *n.* éclat, éclat de bois, *m.*—*v.t.* briser en éclats.—*v.i.* voler en éclats.

splintery ['splintəri], *a.* plein d'éclats, esquilleux.

split [split], *a.* fendu; **split personality**, dédoublement de la personnalité, *m.*; **split pin**, goupille, *f.*—*n.* fente; (*fig.*) scission, *f.*—*v.t. irr.* fendre; diviser, partager.—*v.i.* se fendre; se quereller.

split-second ['splitsekənd], *a.* ultra-rapide.

splitting ['splitiŋ], *n.* fendage, *m.*; **splitting of the atom**, fission de l'atome, *f.*

splotch [splotʃ], *n.* grosse tache, *f.*, barbouillage, *m.*

splutter ['splʌtə], *v.i.* bredouiller, cracher (*plume* ou *graisse*).—*n.* or **spluttering** ['splʌtəriŋ], bredouillement, crachage, *m.*

spoil [spoil], *v.t. irr.* gâter, abîmer; dépouiller (*de*); ravager (*piller*).—*v.i.* se gâter, s'abîmer.—*n.* butin, *m.*, dépouille, *f.*, pillage, *m.*

spoiled [spoild], *a.* gâté.

spoiler ['spoilə], *n.* personne qui gâte, *f.*; spoliateur (*pilleur*), *m.*

spoiling ['spoiliŋ], *n.* action de gâter; avarie, *f.*

spoil-sport ['spoilspo:t], *n.* trouble-fête, *m.*

spoke [spouk], *n.* rais, rayon, *m.*

spoke-shave ['spoukʃeiv], *n.* (*Carp.*) plane, *f.*

spokesman ['spouksmən] (*pl.* -**men** [men]), **spokeswoman** ['spoukswumən] (*pl.* -**women** [wimin]), *n.* porte-parole, *m.inv.*

spoliate ['spoulieit], *v.t.* spolier, piller.

spoliation ['spouli'eiʃən], *n.* spoliation, *f.*

sponge [spʌndʒ], *n.* éponge, *f.*; (*Artill.*) écouvillon, *m.*—*v.t.* éponger; (*Artill.*) écouvillonner.—*v.i.* **to sponge on**, vivre aux dépens de.

sponge cake ['spʌndʒkeik], *n.* gâteau de Savoie, *m.*

sponger ['spʌndʒə], *n.* pique-assiette, parasite, *m.*

sponginess ['spʌndʒinis], *n.* nature spongieuse, *f.*

sponging ['spʌndʒiŋ], *n.* épongement, *m.*; (*fig.*) écorniflerie, *f.*

spongy ['spʌndʒi], *a.* spongieux.

sponsor ['spɔnsə], *n.* parrain, *m.*, marraine, *f.*; garant (*qui cautionne*), *m.*—*v.t.* répondre pour; parrainer.

sponsorship ['spɔnsəʃip], *n.* parrainage, *m.*

spontaneity [spɔntə'ni:iti], *n.* spontanéité, *f.*

spontaneous [spɔn'teiniəs], *a.* spontané.

spontaneously [spɔn'teiniəsli], *adv.* spontanément.

spool [spu:l], *n.* bobine, *f.*

spoon [spu:n], *n.* cuiller, cuillère, *f.*

spoonbill ['spu:nbil], *n.* (*Orn.*) palette, *f.*

spoonful ['spu:nful], *n.* cuillerée, *f.*

spoor [spuə], *n.* trace, *f.*, empreintes, *f.pl.*

sporadic [spə'rædik], *a.* sporadique.

spore [spɔ:], *n.* spore, *f.*

sport [spɔːt], *n.* jeu, divertissement, amusement, *m.*; moquerie, raillerie, *f.*; jouet; sport, *m.*—*v.t.* faire parade de.—*v.i.* se divertir, s'amuser.

sporting ['spɔːtiŋ], *a.* de sport; sportif.

sportive ['spɔːtiv], *a.* badin, folâtre.

sportively ['spɔːtivli], *adv.* en badinant.

sportiveness ['spɔːtivnis], *n.* folâtrerie, *f.*

sportsman ['spɔːtsmən], *n.* (*pl.* **-men** [men]) sportif, sportsman, *m.*

sportsmanship ['spɔːtsmənʃip], *n.* sportivité, *f.*

spot [spɔt], *n.* tache, *f.*; endroit, lieu, *m.*; **on the spot**, sur place, sur-le-champ.—*v.t.* tacheter, moucheter; tacher; (*fam.*) repérer; (*colloq.*) observer.

spot-check ['spɔt'tʃek], *n.* contrôle-surprise, *m.*

spotless ['spɔtlis], *a.* sans tache; (*fig.*) immaculé, pur, irréprochable.

spotlessness ['spɔtlisnis], *n.* pureté, *f.*

spotted ['spɔtid], *a.* tacheté, moucheté; truité.

spotter ['spɔtə], *n.* (*Mil. Av.*) observateur, *m.*

spotty ['spɔti], *a.* couvert de taches, moucheté, tacheté.

spouse [spauz], *n.* époux, *m.*, épouse, *f.*; mari, *m.*, femme, *f.*

spout [spaut], *n.* tuyau, *m.*; gouttière (*de maison*), *f.*; bec (*de cruche etc.*), *m.*—*v.i.* jaillir; (*fam.*) déclamer.

spouter ['spautə], *n.* (*fam.*) déclamateur, *m.*

spouting ['spautiŋ], *n.* jaillissement, *m.*; déclamation, *f.*

sprain [sprein], *n.* entorse, foulure, *f.*—*v.t.* fouler; se faire une entorse à.

sprat [spræt], *n.* esprot, sprat, *m.*

sprawl [sprɔːl], *v.i.* s'étendre, s'étaler.

spray [sprei], *n.* branche, ramille (*d'arbrisseau etc.*), *f.*; embrun, *m.*; poussière (*d'eau*), *f.*; vaporisateur, *m.*—*v.t.* pulvériser, vaporiser, asperger.

spread [spred], *v.t. irr.* étendre, déployer; répandre; couvrir (*table*); mettre (*nappe*); tendre (*voiles etc.*).—*v.i.* s'étendre, se déployer; se répandre, se propager.—*n.* étendue, *f.*; envergure (*ailes*), *f.*; (*fam.*) festin (*banquet*), *m.*

spreading ['sprediŋ], *a.* étendu, qui se répand.

spree [spriː], *n.* (*colloq.*) bamboche, bombe, *f.*

sprig [sprig], *n.* brin, *m.*, brindille; pointe (*clou*), *f.*

sprightliness ['spraitlinis], *n.* vivacité, *f.*, entrain, *m.*

sprightly ['spraitli], *a.* enjoué, vif, animé, gai.

spring [sprin], *v.t. irr.* (*Naut.*) **to spring a leak**, faire une voie d'eau; **to spring upon**, présenter à l'improviste ... à.—*v.i.* bondir, s'élancer; jaillir (*sourdre*); pousser, naître (*se développer*); paraître, poindre (*jour*); provenir, découler, descendre (*avoir pour ancêtres*).—*n.* saut, bond, élan; ressort (*élasticité*), *m.*; source; cause, origine, *f.*; printemps, *m.*; (*pl.*) suspension (*de voiture*), *f.*

spring-board ['sprinbɔːd], *n.* tremplin, *m.*

springiness ['sprininis], *n.* élasticité, *f.*

springlike ['sprinlaik], *a.* printanier.

spring tide ['sprintaid], *n.* grande marée, *f.*

springy ['sprini], *a.* élastique.

sprinkle ['sprinkl], *v.t.* répandre; arroser (*de*), asperger (*de*) (*eau bénite*); saupoudrer (*de*).

sprinkler ['sprinklə], *n.* (*Eccles.*) aspersoir, *m.*; (*Hort.*) arroseuse à jet tournant, *f.*

sprinkling ['sprinkliŋ], *n.* arrosage, *m.*; (*Eccles.*) aspersion, *f.*; (*fig.*) petit nombre, *m.*

sprint [sprint], *n.* sprint, *m.*—*v.i.* courir à toute vitesse.

sprinter ['sprintə], *n.* coureur de vitesse, sprinter, *m.*

sprite [sprait], *n.* esprit follet, lutin, *m.*

sprout [spraut], *n.* pousse, *f.*, jet, rejeton, *m.*; **Brussels sprouts**, choux de Bruxelles, *m.pl.*—*v.i.* pousser, bourgeonner (*plantes*).

sprouting ['sprautiŋ], *n.* germination, *f.*

spruce (1) [spruːs], *a.* paré, bien mis, pimpant. —*v.t.* attifer.

spruce (2) [spruːs], *n.* sapin (*arbre*), *m.*

spry [sprai], *a.* alerte, plein d'entrain.

spunk [spʌŋk], *n.* amadou; (*colloq.*) cœur, courage, *m.*

spur [spəː], *n.* éperon (*de coq etc.*); (*fig.*) aiguillon, stimulant, *m.*—*v.t.* éperonner; stimuler.

spurious ['spjuəriəs], *a.* faux, falsifié.

spuriousness ['spjuəriəsnis], *n.* fausseté, *f.*

spurn [spəːn], *v.t.* repousser, écarter (*du pied*); mépriser.—*n.* mépris, dédain, *m.*

spurred [spəːd], *a.* éperonné.

spurt [spəːt], *v.t.* faire jaillir.—*v.i.* s'élancer; (*Spt.*) démarrer.—*n.* jaillissement; (*fig.*) effort soudain; (*Spt.*) démarrage, *m.*

sputnik ['spʌtnik, 'sputnik], *n.* spoutnik, *m.*

sputter ['spʌtə], *v.i.* cracher; bredouiller.—*n.* salive, *f.*

sputtering ['spʌtəriŋ], *n.* bredouillement, *m.*

sputum ['spjuːtəm], *n.* crachat, *m.*

spy [spai], *n.* espion, *m.*—*v.t.* scruter; apercevoir.—*v.i.* épier, espionner.

spy-glass ['spaiglɑːs], *n.* longue-vue, *f.*

spying ['spaiiŋ], *n.* espionnage, *m.*

spy ring ['spairiŋ], **spy system** ['spaisistəm], *n.* espionnage, *m.*

squabble [skwɔbl], *n.* dispute, querelle, *f.*—*v.i.* se chamailler.

squabbler ['skwɔblə], *n.* querelleur, *m.*

squad [skwɔd], *n.* (*Mil.*) peloton, *m.*; (*Rail.*) brigade; équipe (*de sauvetage etc.*), *f.*

squadron ['skwɔdrən], *n.* (*Mil.*) escadron, *m.*; (*Av.*) escadrille; (*Naut.*) escadre, *f.*

squadron leader ['skwɔdrənliːdə], *n.* (*Av.*) commandant, *m.*

squalid ['skwɔlid], *a.* malpropre, sale.

squalidness [SQUALOR].

squall [skwɔːl], *n.* cri; coup de vent, *m.*, bourrasque, rafale (*de vent*), *f.*—*v.i.* crier, brailler.

squalling ['skwɔːliŋ], *a.* criard, braillard.— *n.* criaillerie, *f.*

squally ['skwɔːli], *a.* à grains, à rafales.

squalor ['skwɔlə], **squalidness** ['skwɔlidnis], *n.* malpropreté, *f.*

squamous ['skweiməs], *a.* squameux; écailleux.

squander ['skwɔndə], *v.t.* dissiper, gaspiller.

squanderer ['skwɔndərə], *n.* gaspilleur, *m.*, prodigue, *m.*, *f.*

squandering ['skwɔndəriŋ], *n.* gaspillage, *m.*

square [skwɛə], *a.* carré; soldé (*comptes etc.*); (*fig.*) équitable, juste; de superficie (*mesure*). —*n.* carré; carreau (*de verre etc.*), *m.*; case (*d'échiquier*); place (*dans une ville*); place d'armes (*de ville de garnison*), *f.*, parvis (*devant une église*), *m.*—*v.t.* carrer; (*Carp.*)

équarrir; balancer (*comptes*); (*fig.*) régler, ajuster.—*v.i.* cadrer, s'accorder (*avec*).

square-built ['skwɛəbilt], *a.* aux épaules carrées.

squarely ['skwɛəli], *adv.* carrément; (*fig.*) justement.

squareness ['skwɛənis], *n.* forme carrée, *f.*

squaring ['skwɛəriŋ], *n.* équarrissage, *m.*; *squaring of the circle*, quadrature du cercle, *f.*

squarish ['skwɛəriʃ], *a.* à peu près carré.

squash [skwɔʃ], *v.t.* écraser, aplatir; (*fig.*) rembarrer (*personne*).—*n.* écrasement (*aplatissement*), *m.*; foule serrée (*de gens*), *f.*; *lemon squash*, citronnade, *f.*

squashy ['skwɔʃi], *a.* mou et humide.

squat [skwɔt], *a.* accroupi, blotti; trapu, ramassé (*courtaud*).—*v.i.* s'accroupir; se blottir; (*Am.*) s'établir (*sans droit*).

squatter ['skwɔtə], *n.* personne accroupie, *f.*; colon (*sans droit*), *m.*

squatting ['skwɔtiŋ], *n.* accroupissement, *m.*

squaw [skwɔ:], *n.* femme peau-rouge, *f.*

squawk [skwɔ:k], *n.* cri rauque; couac, *m.*—*v.i.* pousser des cris rauques.

squeak [skwi:k], *n.* petit cri aigu, *m.*—*v.i.* pousser des cris aigus; jurer (*instrument de musique*).

squeaking ['skwi:kiŋ], *a.* criard; qui jure (*instrument de musique*).

squeal [skwi:l], *v.i.* pousser des cris perçants. —*n.* cri perçant, *m.*

squeamish ['skwi:miʃ], *a.* qui se soulève (*l'estomac*); trop délicat, difficile (*scrupuleux*).

squeamishly ['skwi:miʃli], *adv.* avec dégoût.

squeamishness ['skwi:miʃnis], *n.* délicatesse exagérée, *f.*, goût difficile, *m.*

squeeze [skwi:z], *n.* compression; cohue, *f.*— *v.t.* serrer, presser; *to squeeze money out of*, extorquer de l'argent à; *to squeeze out*, exprimer; *to squeeze through*, forcer à travers.—*v.i. to squeeze through*, se forcer à travers.

squeezing ['skwi:ziŋ], *n.* étreinte, compression, *f.*; serrement (*de la main*), *m.*

squelch [skweltʃ], *v.t.* écraser, aplatir.

squib [skwib], *n.* pétard, *m.*; (*fig.*) satire, *f.*

squill [skwil], *n.* scille (*plante*), *f.*

squint [skwint], *a.* louche.—*n.* regard louche, *m.*—*v.i.* loucher.

squinting ['skwintiŋ], *a.* louche.—*n.* action de loucher, *f.*, strabisme, *m.*

squire ['skwaiə], *n.* écuyer; châtelain; cavalier servant (*d'une dame*), *m.*—*v.t.* escorter (*une dame*).

squireen [skwaiə'ri:n], *n.* hobereau, *m.*

squirm [skwə:m], *v.i.* se tortiller, se tordre (*de douleur* ou *d'embarras*).

squirrel ['skwirəl], *n.* écureuil, *m.*

squirt [skwə:t], *n.* seringue, *f.*—*v.t.* seringuer, faire jaillir.—*v.i.* jaillir.

stab [stæb], *v.* coup de poignard, de couteau etc., *m.*—*v.t.* poignarder.

stabbing ['stæbiŋ], *a.* lancinant.—*n.* coup de poignard, *m.*

stability [stə'biliti], *n.* stabilité, solidité; (*fig.*) fermeté, *f.*

stabilization [steibilai'zeiʃən], *n.* stabilisation, *f.* [see **tail-plane**]

stabilize ['steibilaiz], *v.t.* stabiliser.

stable (1) [steibl], *a.* stable, fixe, solide; (*fig.*) constant.

stable (2) [steibl], *n.* écurie, *f.*—*v.t.* loger (*chevaux*); établer (*bétail*).

stable-boy ['steiblbɔi], **stableman** ['steibl mən] (*pl.* -**men** [men]), *n.* garçon d'écurie, *m.*

stabling ['steibliŋ], *n.* écuries (*pour chevaux*) étables (*pour bétail*), *f.pl.*

staccato [stə'ka:tou], *a.* saccadé.—*adv.* en staccato.

stack [stæk], *n.* souche (*d'une cheminée*); pile, *f.*, tas (*de charbon, de bois*), *m.*; meule (*de foin etc.*), *f.*—*v.t.* empiler (*bois*); emmeuler (*foin etc.*).

stacking ['stækiŋ], *n.* emmeulage, empilage, entassement, *m.*

stack-yard ['stækjɑ:d], *n.* cour de ferme, *f.*

stadium ['steidiəm], *n.* stade, *m.*

staff [stɑ:f], *n.* (*pl.* **staves** [steivz]) bâton, bourdon (*de pèlerin*), *m.*; hampe (*à drapeau*), *f.*; (*pl.* **staffs**) corps, personnel; (*Mil.*) état-major, *m.*; *to be on the staff*, être attaché à, faire partie du personnel de.—*v.t.* fournir le personnel de.

staff officer [stɑ:f'ɔfisə], *n.* officier d'état-major, *m.*

stag [stæg], *n.* cerf, *m.*

stag beetle ['stægbi:tl], *n.* (*Ent.*) cerf-volant, lucane, *m.*

stage [steidʒ], *n.* estrade (*dans une salle*); (*Theat.*) scène, *f.*; (*fig.*) théâtre, *m.*; étape (*voyage*), *f.*; (*fig.*) degré, *m.*, phase, période, *f.*—*v.t. to stage a play*, monter une pièce.

stage-coach ['steidʒkoutʃ], *n.* diligence, *f.*

stage door ['steidʒ'dɔ:], *n.* entrée des artistes, *f.*

stage effect ['steidʒifekt], *n.* effet scénique, *m.*

stage-hand ['steidʒhænd], *n.* machiniste, *m.*

stage manager ['steidʒ'mænidʒə], *n.* régisseur, *m.*

stage properties ['steidʒ'prɔpətiz], *n.pl.* accessoires de théâtre, *m.pl.*

stage set ['steidʒset], *n.* décor, *m.*

stagger ['stægə], *v.t.* faire chanceler; (*fig.*) étonner; échelonner (*heures, vacances etc.*). —*v.i.* chanceler.

staggering ['stægəriŋ], *a.* chancelant; incertain.—*n.* chancellement; échelonnage, *m.*

stagnancy ['stægnənsi], **stagnation** [stæg neiʃən], *n.* stagnation, *f.*

stagnant ['stægnənt], *a.* stagnant; (*fig.*) inactif, mort.

stagnate [stæg'neit], *v.i.* être stagnant.

stagnation [STAGNANCY].

staid [steid], *a.* posé, sérieux, grave.

staidness ['steidnis], *n.* gravité, *f.*

stain [stein], *n.* tache; (*Paint.*) teinte; (*fig.*) honte, *f.*, opprobre (*disgrâce*), *m.*—*v.t.* tacher (*de*); (*fig.*) souiller; (*Dyeing*) teindre. —*v.i.* se tacher.

stained [steind], *a.* taché; (*fig.*) souillé; (*Dyeing*) teint; *stained glass*, vitrail, *m.*

stainer ['steinə], *n.* teinturier, *m.*

staining ['steiniŋ], *n.* teinture, *f.*

stainless ['steinlis], *a.* sans tache; inoxydable (*acier*).

stair [stɛə], *n.* marche, *f.*; degré; (*pl.*) escalier, *m.*

staircase ['stɛəkeis], *n.* escalier, *m.*; cage d'escalier, *f.*; *back staircase*, escalier de service; *moving staircase*, escalier roulant.

stair-rod ['stɛərɔd], *n.* tringle (de tapis) d'escalier, *f.*
stake [steik], *n.* pieu, poteau, bûcher (de *martyre*); (*Cards etc.*) enjeu, *m.*, mise, *f.* —*v.t.* parier, gager; hasarder (*risquer*); **to stake out,** jalonner.
stalactite ['stæləktait], *n.* stalactite, *f.*
stalagmite ['stæləgmait], *n.* stalagmite, *f.*
stale [steil], *a.* vieux, rassis (*pain*); (*fig.*) suranné, passé, usé.
stalemate ['steilmeit], *v.t.* (*Chess*) faire pat.— *n.* pat, *m.*; (*fig.*) impasse, *f.*
staleness ['steilnis], *n.* vieillesse, *f.*; état rassis (*pain*), *m.*; banalité, *f.*
stalk [stɔːk], *n.* tige; queue (de *fleur*), *f.* trognon (de *chou*), *m.*; démarche fière (*allure*), *f.*—*v.t.* chasser à l'affût.—*v.i.* marcher fièrement.
stalker ['stɔːkə], *n.* chasseur à l'affût, *m.*
stalking ['stɔːkiŋ], *n.* (*Hunt.*) chasse à l'affût, *f.*
stall (1) [stɔːl], *n.* stalle (d'*église ou d'écurie*), étable (à *bétail*); écurie (à *chevaux*); échoppe, boutique, *f.*, étalage; (*Theat.*) fauteuil d'orchestre, *m.*
stall (2) [stɔːl], *v.t.*, *v.i.* caler (*machine*).
stallion ['stæljən], *n.* étalon, *m.*
stalwart ['stɔːlwət], *a.* vigoureux, robuste; vaillant.
stamen ['steimen], *n.* (*Bot.*) étamine, *f.*
stamina ['stæminə], *n.* vigueur, résistance, *f.*
stammer ['stæmə], *v.t.*, *v.i.* bégayer, balbutier.—*n.* bégaiement, *m.*
stammerer ['stæmərə], *n.* bègue, *m.*, *f.*
stammering ['stæməriŋ], *a.* bègue.—*n.* bégaiement, *m.*
stamp [stæmp], *v.t.* frapper du pied; piétiner; empreindre, imprimer; contrôler (*garantir*); estamper (*pièce de monnaie*); timbrer (*documents, lettres etc.*); (*Metal.*) bocarder; estampiller (*marchandises*); affranchir (*payer d'avance*); poinçonner (*billet*).—*v.i.* trépigner, frapper du pied.—*n.* estampe (*outil*), *f.*; coin, poinçon, *m.*; empreinte, marque (*impression*), *f.*; poinçon de contrôle (*sur l'or*); timbre (*sur documents*); (*Metal.*) bocard, *m.*; (*Comm.*) estampille (*sur marchandises*), *f.*; (*fig.*) caractère, *m.*, trempe, *f.*; coup de pied, trépignement; timbre-poste, *m.*; **rubber stamp,** tampon, *m.*
stamp collecting ['stæmpkəlektiŋ], *n.* philatélie, *f.*
stamp collector ['stæmpkə'lektə], *n.* philatéliste, *m.*, *f.*
stamp duty ['stæmp'djuːti], *n.* droit de timbre, *m.*
stampede [stæm'piːd], *n.* débandade, panique, *f.*—*v.i.* fuir en désordre.
stamping ['stæmpiŋ], *n.* contrôlage (*garantie*); timbrage, (*Metal.*) bocardage; piétinement, trépignement (*des pieds*), *m.*
stamp machine ['stæmpmə'ʃiːn], *n.* distributeur automatique de timbres-poste, *m.*
stanch [staːntʃ], **staunch** [stɔːntʃ], *a.* solide, ferme; (*fig.*) sûr, dévoué.—*v.t.* étancher.
stanchion ['staːnʃən], *n.* étançon, étai, *m.*
stanchness ['staːntʃnis], **staunchness** ['stɔːntʃnis], *n.* fermeté; constance, dévotion, *f.*
stand [stænd], *v.t. irr.* mettre debout, placer, poser; endurer, souffrir, supporter, soutenir; subir; résister à; payer (à *boire*).—*v.i.* se tenir; rester debout; se soutenir (*difficilement*); se placer, se mettre (*prendre place*);

être debout; se trouver, être (*bâtiment*); se maintenir (*ne pas lâcher pied*); se présenter (*comme candidat*); **stand by!** attention! *to* **stand aside,** se tenir à l'écart; *to* **stand by,** assister à (*être présent*); défendre, s'en tenir à (*un avis etc.*); se tenir prêt; *to* **stand down,** se retirer; *to* **stand firm,** tenir ferme, tenir bon; *to* **stand for,** soutenir; signifier; *to* **stand in for someone,** remplacer quelqu'un; *to* **stand out,** se dessiner (*être en relief*); résister; *to* **stand still,** s'arrêter, se tenir tranquille; *to* **stand up,** se lever.—*n.* arrêt, *m.*, halte, pause, *f.*; stand, étalage (*exposition etc.*); socle (à *vases etc.*), *m.*; (*fig.*) cessation, résistance, *f.*
standard ['stændəd], *a.* type, standard, normal; étalon; au titre (*argent*); classique (*livre*); (*Hort.*) en plein vent (*arbre*), sur tige (*roses*); régulateur (*prix*).—*n.* étendard, (*Naut.*) pavillon; étalon (de *poids et mesures*); titre (d'*or et d'argent*); (*fig.*) type, modèle; (*Hort.*) arbre en plein vent, *m.*
standard-bearer ['stændədbeərə], *n.* porte-étendard, *m.*
standardization [stændədai'zeiʃən], *n.* étalonnage, *m.*; (*Comm.*) standardisation, *f.*
standardize ['stændədaiz], *v.t.* étalonner, standardiser.
stand-by ['stændbai], *n.* appui, soutien, *m.*, ressource, *f.*
stand-in ['stændin], *n.* remplaçant, *m.*
standing ['stændiŋ], *a.* stagnant; fixe; debout, sur pied (*non abattu*); (*fig.*) invariable.—*n.* position, *f.*; rang, *m.*; durée, date, *f.*, service, *m.*
stand-offish ['stænd'ɔfiʃ], *a.* réservé, distant.
stand-point ['stændpoint], *n.* point de vue, *m.*
standstill ['stændstil], *n.* arrêt, *m.*
stand-to ['stænd'tuː], *n.* (*Mil.*) alerte, *f.*
stanza ['stænzə], *n.* stance, strophe, *f.*
staple (1) [steipl], *a.* établi; principal.—*n.* denrée principale (*marchandises*), *f.*; (*fig.*) fond, *m.*
staple (2) [steipl], *n.* agrafe; gâche (de *serrure*), *f.*—*v.t.* agrafer.
stapler ['steiplə], *n.* agrafeuse (*machine*), *f.*
star [staː], *n.* étoile, *f.*, astre, *m.*; (*Theat., Cine.*) vedette, *f.*—*v.t.* étoiler, parsemer d'étoiles; avoir comme vedettes.—*v.i.* tenir le premier rôle.
starboard ['staːbəd], *n.* tribord, *m.*
starch [staːtʃ], *n.* amidon, *m.*; fécule (*aliment*); (*fig.*) raideur, *f.*—*v.t.* empeser.
starchiness ['staːtʃinis], *n.* raideur, *f.*
starchy ['staːtʃi], *a.* féculent; empesé; (*fig.*) guindé.
stare [stɛə], *v.t.* dévisager.—*v.i.* regarder fixement; ouvrir de grands yeux (*être ébahi*).— *n.* regard fixe; regard ébahi, *m.*
starfish ['staːfiʃ], *n.* étoile de mer, *f.*
star-gazer ['staːgeizə], *n.* astrologue, *m.*, *f.*; rêveur, *m.*
staring ['stɛəriŋ], *a.* voyant, tranchant (*couleur etc.*).
stark [staːk], *adv.* tout, tout à fait.—*a.* raide; stérile (*paysage*).
starless ['staːlis], *a.* sans étoiles.
starling ['staːliŋ], *n.* étourneau, sansonnet, *m.*
starlit ['staːlit], *a.* étoilé.
starry ['staːri], *a.* étoilé; (*fig.*) étincelant; **starry-eyed,** peu pratique.

start [stɑːt], *v.t.* commencer; faire lever (*gibier*); faire partir; mettre en marche (*machine*).—*v.i.* tressaillir (*de* ou *à*); partir (*s'en aller*); commencer, débuter; sursauter (*faire un bond*).—*n.* tressaillement; saut, bond; commencement, début; départ, *m.*; *to wake with a start*, se réveiller en sursaut.

starter ['stɑːtə], *n.* starter (*de course*); (*Motor.*) démarreur, *m.*

starting ['stɑːtiŋ], *n.* tressaillement; départ; commencement, début, *m.*; mise en marche (*de moteur etc.*), *f.*

starting-handle ['stɑːtiŋhændl], *n.* (*Motor.*) manivelle, *f.*

starting point ['stɑːtiŋpɔint], *n.* point de départ, *m.*

starting post ['stɑːtiŋpoust], *n.* poteau de départ, *m.*

startle [stɑːtl], *v.t.* faire tressaillir, effrayer.

startling ['stɑːtliŋ], *a.* étonnant, saisissant.

starvation [stɑːˈveiʃən], *n.* inanition, faim, *f.*

starve [stɑːv], *v.t.* faire mourir de faim; affamer.—*v.i.* mourir de faim.

starveling ['stɑːvliŋ], *n.* affamé, meurt-de-faim, *m.*

starving ['stɑːviŋ], *a.* affamé, mourant de faim.

state [steit], *n.* état, *m.*, condition, *f.*; état (*organisme politique*); rang (*classe*), *m.*; pompe, *f.*, apparat (*pompe*), *m.*; *the United States*, les États-Unis, *m.pl.*—*v.t.* énoncer, déclarer.

state-controlled ['steitkənˈtrould], *a.* étatisé.

statecraft ['steitkrɑːft], *n.* politique, *f.*

stated ['steitid], *a.* réglé, fixe.

stateless ['steitlis], *a.* **stateless person**, apatride, *m.*, *f.*

stateliness ['steitlinis], *n.* majesté, grandeur, *f.*

stately ['steitli], *a.* imposant, majestueux, noble.—*adv.* majestueusement, avec dignité.

statement ['steitmənt], *n.* exposé, énoncé, rapport, *m.*; déclaration, *f.*

statesman ['steitsmən], *n.* (*pl.* **-men** [men]) homme d'État, *m.*

statesmanlike ['steitsmənlaik], *a.* d'homme d'État.

statesmanship ['steitsmənʃip], *n.* science du gouvernement, politique, *f.*

static ['stætik], **statical** ['stætikəl], *a.* statique.

station ['steiʃən], *n.* station, *f.*; rang (*classe*), *m.*; position; (*Rail.*) gare, *f.*; (*Mil.*) poste, *m.*, garnison, *f.*—*v.t.* placer; (*Mil.*) poster.

stationary ['steiʃənəri], *a.* stationnaire; fixe.

stationer ['steiʃənə], *n.* papetier, *m.*

stationery ['steiʃənəri], *n.* papeterie, *f.*

station wagon ['steiʃənwægən], *n.* (*Motor.*) canadienne, *f.*

statistic [stəˈtistik], **statistical** [stəˈtistikəl], *a.* statistique.

statistician [stætisˈtiʃən], *n.* statisticien, *m.*

statistics [stəˈtistiks], *n.pl.* statistique, *f.*

statuary ['stætjuəri], *n.* statuaire, *f.*

statue ['stætjuː], *n.* statue, *f.*

statuesque [stætjuˈesk], *a.* plastique.

stature ['stætʃə], *n.* stature, taille, *f.*

status ['steitəs], *n.* statut légal, *m.*; condition, *f.*, rang, *m.*

statute ['stætjuːt], *n.* statut, *m.*, loi, *f.*

statutory ['stætjutəri], *a.* réglementaire, statutaire.

staunch [STANCH].

stave [steiv], *n.* douve (*de baril*); (*Mus.*) portée, *f.*; verset (*de psaume*), *m.*—*v.t. irr.* crever; défoncer (*baril*); *to stave off*, chasser, repousser, éloigner, écarter, prévenir (*danger*).

staves [STAFF].

stay [stei], *v.t.* arrêter; apaiser (*sa faim*); étayer, accoter (*appuyer*).—*v.i.* rester; demeurer (*séjourner*); descendre; attendre. —*n.* séjour; (*Law*) sursis; soutien, appui (*aide*), *m.*

stay-at-home ['steiəthoum], *a.* and *n.* casanier, *m.*

stead [sted], *n.* lieu, *m.*, place, *m.*

steadfast ['stedfast], *a.* ferme, constant, stable.

steadfastly ['stedfəstli], *adv.* fermement, avec constance.

steadfastness ['stedfəstnis], *n.* fermeté, constance, *f.*

steadily ['stedili], *adv.* fermement, avec persistance.

steadiness ['stedinis], *n.* fermeté; assurance, *f.*

steady ['stedi], *a.* ferme, assuré; posé (*sérieux*); régulier.—*adv.* doucement.—*v.t.* affermir; assujettir (*fixer*); calmer.

steak [steik], *n.* tranche (*de viande*), *f.*; entrecôte, *m.*; *fillet steak*, bifteck dans le filet, *m.*

steal [stiːl], *v.t. irr.* voler, dérober.—*v.i.* se dérober, se glisser furtivement, aller ou venir à la dérobée.

stealer ['stiːlə], *n.* voleur, *m.*

stealing ['stiːliŋ], *n.* vol, *m.*

stealth [stelθ], *n.* *by stealth*, à la dérobée, furtivement.

stealthily ['stelθili], *adv.* à la dérobée, furtivement, à pas de loup.

stealthy ['stelθi], *a.* dérobé, furtif.

steam [stiːm], *n.* vapeur, *f.*—*v.t.* (*Cook.*) cuire à la vapeur.—*v.i.* jeter de la vapeur; fumer.

steamboat ['stiːmbout], *n.* bateau à vapeur, *m.*

steam engine ['stiːmendʒin], *n.* machine à vapeur, *f.*

steamer ['stiːmə], *n.* vapeur, steamer, *m.*

steam gauge ['stiːmgeidʒ], *n.* manomètre, *m.*

steaming ['stiːmiŋ], *a.* fumant.

steam pipe ['stiːmpaip], *n.* tuyau de vapeur, *m.*

steam-roller ['stiːmroulə], *n.* rouleau compresseur, *m.*—*v.t.* (*fig.*) écraser.

steamship ['stiːmʃip], *n.* vapeur, *m.*

steam whistle ['stiːmwisl], *n.* sifflet à vapeur, *m.*

steamy ['stiːmi], *a.* humide.

steed [stiːd], *n.* (*poet*) coursier, *m.*

steel [stiːl], *a.* d'acier, en acier.—*n.* acier; fusil (*pour aiguiser un couteau*); (*fig.*) fer, *m.* —*v.t.* acérer, garnir d'acier; (*fig.*) fortifier, bardé de fer.

steel-clad ['stiːlklæd], *a.* revêtu d'acier, bardé de fer.

steeliness ['stiːlinis], *n.* dureté d'acier; (*fig.*) dureté, *f.*

steel-plated ['stiːlpleitid], *a.* cuirassé.

steel-works ['stiːlwəːks], *n.pl.* aciérie, *f.*

steely ['stiːli], *a.* d'acier; (*fig.*) dur, de fer.

steelyard ['sti:lja:d], *n.* romaine, *f.*

steep (1) [sti:p], *a.* escarpé, à pic; raide (*escalier*).—*n.* pente rapide, *f.*; escarpement, *m.*

steep (2) [sti:p], *v.t.* tremper; (*fig.*) saturer (*de*).

steeping ['sti:piŋ], *n.* trempage, *m.*

steeple [sti:pl], *n.* clocher, *m.*

steeplechase [sti:pltʃeis], *n.* course au clocher, *f.*, steeplechase, *m.*

steepled [sti:pld], *a.* à clocher.

steeple-jack ['sti:pldʒæk], *n.* réparateur de clochers *ou* de cheminées, *m.*

steeply ['sti:pli], *adv.* en pente rapide.

steepness [sti:pnis], *n.* raideur, pente rapide, *f.*

steer [stiə], *n.* bouvillon, jeune bœuf, *m.*—*v.t.* gouverner; diriger; (*Motor. etc.*) conduire. —*v.i.* se diriger.

steerage ['stiəridʒ], *n.* timonerie, *f.*; l'avant; logement des passagers de troisième classe, *m.*

steering ['stiəriŋ], *n.* direction; (*Motor.*) conduite, *f.*

steering wheel ['stiəriŋwi:l], *n.* volant, *m.*

steersman ['stiəzmən], *n.* (*pl.* -men [men]) timonier, *m.*

stellar ['stelə], *a.* stellaire.

stem [stem], *n.* tige; queue (*d'une fleur etc.*); (*fig.*) souche (*d'une famille*), *f.*—*v.t.* refouler (*courant*); (*fig.*) résister à.—*v.i. to stem from*, être issu de.

stench [stentʃ], *n.* puanteur, *f.*

stencil ['stensil], *n.* patron, pochoir, stencil, *m.*—*v.t.* tracer au patron, tirer au stencil.

sten gun ['stengʌn], *n.* fusil mitrailleur, *m., f.*

stenographer [ste'nɔgrəfi], *n.* sténographe, *m., f.*

stenography [ste'nɔgrəfi], *n.* sténographie, *f.*

stentorian [sten'tɔ:riən], *a.* de stentor.

step [step], *n.* mesurer en comptant les pas, arpenter.—*v.i.* faire un pas, marcher pas à pas; marcher, aller; monter (*dans*); descendre (*de*); *to step aside*, s'écarter; *to step back*, reculer; *to step forward*, s'avancer; *to step on*, fouler; *to step over*, enjamber.—*n.* pas; degré, *m.*, marche (*d'escalier*), *f.*; échelon (*d'échelle*); marchepied (*de voiture ou de bicyclette*), *m.*; (*fig.*) démarche; (*pl.*) échelle, *f.*

stepbrother ['stepbrʌðə], *n.* beau-frère, *m.*

stepchild ['steptʃaild], *n.* beau-fils, *m.*, belle-fille, *f.*

stepfather ['stepfɑ:ðə], *n.* beau-père, *m.*

Stephen [sti:vn], Étienne, *m.*

stepmother ['stepmʌðə], *n.* belle-mère, marâtre, *f.*

steppe [step], *n.* steppe (*plaine*), *f.*

stepping ['stepiŋ], *n.* marche, allure, *f.*

stepping-stone ['stepiŋstoun], *n.* (*pl.*) pierres de gué, *f.pl.*; (*fig.*) introduction, *f.*

stepsister ['stepsistə], *n.* belle-sœur, *f.*

stereoscopic [stiəriə'skɔpik], *a.* stéréoscopique.

stereotype ['stiəriətaip], *a.* stéréotypé; cliché. —*n.* stéréotype, *f.*; (*fig.*) cliché, *m.*—*v.t.* clicher; stéréotyper.

stereotyped ['stiəriətaipt], *a.* (*usu. fig.*) stéréotypé.

sterile ['sterail], *a.* stérile.

sterility [stə'riliti], *n.* stérilité, *f.*

sterilization [sterilai'zeiʃən], *n.* stérilisation, *f.*

sterilize ['sterilaiz], *v.t.* stériliser.

sterling ['stə:liŋ], *a.* sterling; (*fig.*) vrai, de bon aloi.

stern (1) [stə:n], *a.* sévère, dur; rigoureux.

stern (2) [stə:n], *n.* (*Naut.*) arrière, *m.*

sternly ['stə:nli], *adv.* sévèrement, durement.

sternmost ['stə:nmoust], *a.* le dernier.

sternness ['stə:nnis], *n.* sévérité, austérité, *f.*

stethoscope ['steθəskoup], *n.* stéthoscope, *m.*

stevedore ['sti:vədo:], *n.* arrimeur; déchargeur, *m.*

stew [stju:], *n.* étuvée, *f.*, ragoût (*de viande*); (*fig.*) embarras, *m.*, confusion, *f.*; *Irish stew*, ragoût de mouton.—*v.t.* étuver; mettre en ragoût, faire un ragoût de.—*v.i.* cuire à l'étuvée; (*fig.*) cuire dans sa peau.

steward ['stju:əd], *n.* intendant; régisseur (*d'une propriété*); économe (*de collège*); commiss..ire (*de bal etc.*); (*Naut.*) steward, *m.*; *steward's room*, cambuse, *f.*

stewardess ['stju:ədis], *n.* femme de chambre (*de bord*), stewardesse, *f.*

stewardship ['stju:ədʃip], *n.* intendance; (*fig.*) administration, *f.*

stewed [stju:d], *a.* étuvé, en ragoût; en compote.

stew-pan ['stju:pæn], *n.* casserole, *f.*

stew-pot ['stju:pɔt], *n.* cocotte, *f.*, faitout, *m.*

stick (1) [stik], *n.* bâton, *m.*; canne (*pour marcher*), *f.*; (*Av.*) manche; chapelet (*de bombes*), *m.*

stick (2) [stik], *v.t. irr.* percer, piquer; enfoncer; coller; *stick no bills*, défense d'afficher.—*v.i.* se coller, s'attacher; rester (*demeurer*); *to stick close*, ne pas quitter; *to stick out*, faire saillie; persister; *to stick to*, s'en tenir à; *to stick up*, se dresser.

stickiness ['stikinis], *n.* viscosité, *f.*

sticking plaster ['stikiŋ'plɔ:stə], *n.* taffetas d'Angleterre, *m.*

stickle [stikl], *v.i.* tenir beaucoup (*à*); se disputer.

stickleback ['stiklbæk], *n.* épinoche, *f.*

stickler ['stiklə], *n.* partisan, *m.*; rigoriste, *m., f.*

sticky ['stiki], *a.* gluant, collant; (*fig.*) difficile (*personne*).

stiff [stif], *a.* raide, rigide, tenace; dur, ferme (*non fluide*); opiniâtre (*entêté*); gêné (*contraint*); courbatu (*muscles*); affecté, guindé (*style*).

stiffen [stifn], *v.t.* raidir; (*fig.*) endurcir.— *v.i.* se raidir; (*fig.*) s'endurcir.

stiffening ['stifniŋ], *n.* raidissement; soutien (*appui*), *m.*

stiffly ['stifli], *adv.* avec raideur; obstinément.

stiff neck ['stifnek], *n.* torticolis, *m.*

stiff-necked ['stifnekt], *a.* opiniâtre, entêté.

stiffness ['stifnis], *n.* raideur; gêne (*contrainte*); opiniâtreté (*entêtement*), *f.*; (*fig.*) air guindé, *m.*

stifle [staifl], *v.t., v.i.* étouffer, suffoquer.—*n.* (*Vet.*) grasset, *m.*

stifling ['staifliŋ], *a.* étouffant, suffocant. —*n.* suffocation, *f.*

stigma ['stigmə], *n.* stigmate, *m.*, flétrissure, *f.*

stigmatize ['stigmətaiz], *v.t.* stigmatiser, flétrir.

stile [stail], *n.* échallier, échalis, *m.*

stiletto [sti'letou], *n.* stylet, *m.*; ***stiletto heels***, talons aiguille, *m.pl.*

still (1) [stil], *a.* silencieux; tranquille, calme, paisible, en repos; immobile; non mousseux (*vin*).—*adv.* encore, toujours; cependant, néanmoins (*malgré tout*).—*v.t.* calmer, apaiser.

still (2) [stil], *n.* alambic, *m.*

still-born ['stilbɔːn], *a.* mort-né.

stillness ['stilnis], *n.* tranquillité, *f.*, calme, *m.*

still room ['stilruːm], *n.* distillerie, *f.*, laboratoire, *m.*

stilt [stilt], *n.* échasse, *f.*; pilotis, pieu (*de pont etc.*), *m.*

stilted ['stiltid], *a.* guindé, pompeux.

stimulant ['stimjulənt], *n.* stimulant, *m.*

stimulate ['stimjuleit], *v.t.* stimuler; (*fig.*) exciter.

stimulating ['stimjuleitiŋ], *a.* stimulant.

stimulation [stimju'leiʃən], *n.* stimulation, *f.*

stimulus ['stimjuləs], *n.* stimulant, aiguillon, stimulus, *m.*

sting [stiŋ], *n.* aiguillon; dard (*d'ortie etc.*), *m.*; piqûre; (*fig.*) pointe, *f.*—*v.t. irr.* piquer; (*fig.*) irriter.

stingily ['stindʒili], *adv.* chichement, mesquinement.

stinginess ['stindʒinis], *n.* mesquinerie, ladrerie, *f.*

stinging ['stiŋiŋ], *a.* piquant; cinglant.—*n.* piqûre, *f.*

stingy ['stindʒi], *a.* avare, mesquin, ladre, chiche.

stink [stiŋk], *n.* puanteur, mauvaise odeur, *f.*—*v.i. irr.* puer; sentir mauvais.

stinking ['stiŋkiŋ], *a.* puant.

stint [stint], *v.t.* limiter, restreindre; ***to stint oneself***, se priver (*de*).—*n.* limite, borne; portion; besogne, *f.*

stipend ['staipend], *n.* traitement (*d'ecclésiastique* OU *de magistrat*), *m.*

stipendiary [sti'pendiəri], *a.* appointé.

stipple [stipl], *v.t.* pointiller.

stippling ['stipliŋ], *n.* pointillage (*processus*); pointillé (*résultat*), *m.*

stipulate ['stipjuleit], *v.i.* stipuler (*de* OU *que*).

stipulation [stipju'leiʃən], *n.* stipulation, condition, *f.*

stipulator ['stipjuleitə], *n.* partie stipulante, *f.*

stir [stəː], *v.t.* remuer; (*fig.*) agiter; ***to stir the fire***, attiser le feu.—*v.i.* remuer, se remuer, bouger.—*n.* remuement, bruit, *m.*; agitation, *f.*

stirring ['stəːriŋ], *a.* remuant; émouvant (*histoire etc.*).—*n.* agitation, *f.*

stirrup ['stirəp], *n.* étrier, *m.*

stirrup cup ['stirəpkʌp], *n.* coup de l'étrier, *m.*

stirrup leather ['stirəp'leðə], *n.* étrivière, *f.*

stitch [stitʃ], *n.* point, *m.*; maille (*en tricot*), *f.*; (*Med.*) point de suture, *m.*; ***a stitch in time saves nine***, un point à temps en épargne cent.—*v.t.* piquer, coudre; brocher (*livres*); (*Med.*) suturer.

stitched [stitʃt], *a.* piqué, broché (*livre*).

stitching ['stitʃiŋ], *n.* couture, *f.*; brochage (*de livre*), *m.*; (*Med.*) suture, *f.*

stoat [stout], *n.* hermine d'été, *f.*

stock (1) [stɔk], *n.* courant, habituel.—*n.* souche (*d'arbre, famille etc.*), *f.*; cep (*de vigne*); bloc (*de bois etc.*), *m.*; monture (*de*

fusil*); (*Hort.*) ente (*pour greffer*), *f.*; (*Cook.*) consommé, *m.*; (*fig.*) race, famille, *f.*; approvisionnement, stock (*réserve*), assortiment (*sélection*), *m.*; (*pl.*) fonds, fonds publics, *m.pl.*, rentes, actions, *f.pl.*; (*Shipbuilding*) chantier, *m.*, cale de construction, *f.*; ceps (*punition*), *m.pl.*; ***rolling stock***, matériel roulant, *m.*; ***to take stock of***, faire l'inventaire de.—*v.t.* pourvoir (*de*); stocker (*magasin*); meubler (*ferme*); empoissonner (*vivier*).

stock (2) [stɔk], *n.*(*St. Exch.*), see **share** (2).

stockade [stɔ'keid], *n.* palissade, *f.*—*v.t.* palissader.

stock book ['stɔkbuk], *n.* livre de magasin, magasinier, *m.*

stock-breeder ['stɔkbriːdə], *n.* éleveur, *m.*

stock-breeding ['stɔkbriːdiŋ], *n.* élevage, *m.*

stockbroker ['stɔkbroukə], *n.* agent de change, *m.*

stock exchange ['stɔkikst'ʃeindʒ], *n.* bourse; compagnie des agents de change, *f.*

stockholder ['stɔkhouldə], *n.* actionnaire, *m.*, *f.*, rentier, *m.*

stocking ['stɔkiŋ], *n.* bas, *m.*

stockpile ['stɔkpail], *n.* stocks de réserve, *m.pl.*—*v.t., v.i.* stocker.

stock-still ['stɔk'stil], *a.* immobile.—*adv.* sans bouger.

stock-taking ['stɔkteikiŋ], *n.* inventaire, *m.*

stocky ['stɔki], *a.* trapu.

stodgy ['stɔdʒi], *a.* pâteux, lourd.

stoic ['stouik], *n.* stoïcien, *m.*

stoic ['stouik], **stoical** ['stouikəl], *a.* stoïcien; (*fig.*) stoïque.

stoicism ['stouisizm], *n.* stoïcisme, *m.*

stoke [stouk], *v.t.* chauffer; tisonner (*le feu*).

stoker ['stoukə], *n.* chauffeur, *m.*

stoking ['stoukiŋ], *n.* chauffage, *m.*, chauffe, *f.*

stole (1) [stoul], *n.* étole; (*Cost.*) écharpe, *f.*

stole (2) [stoul], *past* STEAL.

stolen ['stoulən], *a.* volé, dérobé.

stolid ['stɔlid], *a.* lourd, impassible.

stolidity [stɔ'liditi], **stolidness** ['stɔlidnis], *n.* flegme, *m.*

stomach ['stʌmək], *n.* estomac; (*euph.*) ventre; appétit, *m.*—*v.t.* avaler; endurer.

stomach ache ['stʌməkeik], *n.* mal à l'estomac, *m.*, colique, *f.*

stone [stoun], *a.* de pierre, en pierre; de grès (*céramique*).—*n.* pierre, *f.*; caillou (*galet*); noyau (*de fruits*); pépin (*de raisins*); (*Path.*) calcul; (*Weight*) stone (*kg. 6,348*), *m.*—*v.t.* lapider; ôter les noyaux de (*fruits*).

stone-blind ['stounblaind], *a.* complètement aveugle.

stone-cold ['stounkould], *a.* complètement froid.—*adv.* complètement.

stone-dead ['stoun'ded], *a.* raide mort.

stone-deaf ['stoundef], *a.* complètement sourd.

stone fruit ['stounfruːt], *n.* fruit à noyau, *m.*

stone-mason ['stounmeisən], *n.* maçon, marbrier (*pour tombes*), *m.*

stone's throw ['stounzθrou], *n.* jet de pierre, *m.*

stoneware ['stounwɛə], *n.* grès, *m.*, poterie de grès, *f.*

stonework ['stounwəːk], *n.* maçonnerie, *f.*

stoniness ['stouninis], *n.* nature pierreuse; (*fig.*) dureté, *f.*

stoning ['stouniŋ], *n.* lapidation, *f.*

stony ['stouni], *a.* de pierre; pierreux (*plein de pierres*); (*fig.*) insensible; **stony-hearted**, au cœur de pierre.

stook [stu:k], *n.* tas de gerbes, *m.*—*v.t.* mettre en gerbes.

stool [stu:l], *n.* tabouret; escabeau, *m.*

stoop [stu:p], *v.i.* se pencher, se baisser; se voûter; (*fig.*) s'abaisser.—*n.* inclination, *f.*; (*fig.*) abaissement, *m.*

stooping ['stu:piŋ], *a.* penché, courbé.

stop [stɔp], *n.* halte; pause, *f.*; obstacle; (*Organ*) jeu, registre; arrêt (*de trains etc.*), *m.*; (*Gram.*) **full stop**, point, *m.*—*v.t.* arrêter, empêcher; couper (*le souffle*); suspendre (*paiement etc.*); retenir (*la paye*); (*Mus.*) presser; (*Gram.*) ponctuer; boucher (*trou etc.*); stopper (*machine*); plomber (*dent*).—*v.i.* s'arrêter; stopper.

stopcock ['stɔpkɔk], *n.* robinet d'arrêt, *m.*

stop-gap ['stɔpgæp], *n.* bouche-trou, *m.*

stoppage ['stɔpidʒ], *n.* interruption, halte, *f.*; arrêt (*d'un train etc.*), *m.*; obstruction; retenue (*de salaire*), *f.*; chômage (*arrêt de travail*); plombage (*de dent*), *m.*

stopper ['stɔpə], *n.* bouchon (*en verre*), *m.*—*v.t.* boucher.

stopping ['stɔpiŋ], *n.* arrêt; plombage (*de dent*), *m.*; matière à plomber, *f.*

stop-watch ['stɔpwɔtʃ], *n.* chronomètre, *m.*

storage ['stɔ:ridʒ], *n.* emmagasinage, *m.*, accumulation, *f.*

store [stɔ:], *n.* provision, *f.*; approvisionnement, *m.*, réserve, *f.*; magasin, *m.*, boutique, *f.*; (*fig.*) fonds, trésor, *m.*; **in store**, en réserve; **to lay in a store of**, faire une provision de.—*v.t.* pourvoir, munir, approvisionner (*de*); enrichir (*l'esprit*).

store-house ['stɔ:haus], *n.* magasin, entrepôt, dépôt, *m.*

store-keeper ['stɔ:ki:pə], *n.* garde-magasin; marchand (*boutiquier*), *m.*

store-room ['stɔ:ru:m], *n.* dépôt, office, *m.*; réserve, *f.*

storey, story (1) ['stɔ:ri], *n.* étage, *m.*

storied (1) ['stɔ:rid], *a.* à étage.

storied (2) ['stɔ:rid], *a.* historié.

stork [stɔ:k], *n.* cigogne, *f.*

storm [stɔ:m], *n.* orage, *m.*, tempête, *f.*—*v.t.* donner l'assaut à, prendre d'assaut.—*v.i.* faire de l'orage; (*fig.*) tempêter, s'emporter.

storm bell ['stɔ:mbel], *n.* tocsin, *m.*

storm cloud ['stɔ:mklaud], *n.* nuée, *f.*

storminess ['stɔ:minis], *n.* état orageux, *m.*

storming ['stɔ:miŋ], *n.* assaut, *m.*, prise d'assaut; (*fig.*) rage, *f.*

stormy ['stɔ:mi], *a.* orageux, à l'orage; **stormy petrel**, pétrel, *m.*

story (1) [STOREY].

story (2) ['stɔ:ri], *n.* histoire, *f.*, récit; conte (*littéraire*); mensonge (*tromperie*), *m.*

story-book ['stɔ:ribuk], *n.* livre de contes, *m.*

story-teller ['stɔ:ritelə], *n.* conteur (*narrateur*); menteur (*trompeur*), *m.*

stout [staut], *a.* fort; gros, corpulent; (*fig.*) brave, courageux.—*n.* stout, *m.*, bière brune forte (*boisson*), *f.*

stoutly ['stautli], *adv.* vigoureusement, fort et ferme.

stoutness ['stautnis], *n.* embonpoint, *m.*, corpulence; (*fig.*) fermeté, *f.*

stove (1) [stouv], *past* and *p.p.* [STAVE].

stove (2) [stouv], *n.* poêle; fourneau (*de cuisine*), *m.*

stow [stou], *v.t.* mettre en place; (*Naut.*) arrimer; **to stow away**, emmagasiner.

stowage ['stouidʒ], *n.* mise en place, *f.*, (*Naut.*) arrimage, *m.*

stowaway ['stouəwei], *n.* passager clandestin, *m.*—*v.i.* s'embarquer clandestinement.

straddle [strædl], *v.t.* enfourcher; *v.i.* écarter les jambes, marcher les jambes écartées.

strafe [strɑ:f], *v.t.* mitrailler, bombarder.

straggle [strægl], *v.i.* s'écarter; marcher à la débandade.

straggler ['stræglə], *n.* rôdeur; (*Mil.*) traînard, *m.*

straggling ['strægliŋ], *a.* séparé; éparpillé (*disséminé*).

straight [streit], *a.* droit; (*fig.*) équitable, juste.—*adv.* droit, tout droit, directement; **straight away**, sur-le-champ, tout de suite.

straight-edge ['streitedʒ], *n.* règle à araser, *f.*

straighten [streitn], *v.t.* rendre droit, redresser; (*fig.*) mettre en ordre (*affaires, maison*).

straight-faced ['streit'feisd], *a.* imperturbable.

straightforward [streit'fɔ:wəd], *a.* droit, direct; (*fig.*) franc; simple (*problème*).

straightforwardly [streit'fɔ:wədli], *adv.* avec droiture; (*colloq.*) carrément.

straightforwardness [streit'fɔ:wədnis], *n.* droiture, franchise, *f.*

straightness ['streitnis], *n.* ligne directe; droiture, *f.*

straightway ['streitwei], *adv.* sur-le-champ, à l'instant.

strain (1) [strein], *v.t.* tendre; forcer (*contraindre*); se fouler (*muscles*); filtrer, passer (*liquide*).—*v.i.* s'efforcer; se filtrer (*liquide*).—*n.* grand effort, *m.*, tension; entorse, foulure (*de muscles*), *f.*; ton; chant, *m.*

strain (2) [strein], *n.* race, lignée, *f.*

strained [streind], *a.* forcé, pas naturel (*langage etc.*); tendu.

strainer ['streinə], *n.* passoire, *f.*

straining ['streiniŋ], *n.* tension, *f.*, grand effort, *m.*, exagération, *f.*; filtrage (*d'un liquide*), *m.*

strait [streit], *a.* étroit, serré; strict.—*n.* (*usu. pl.*) (*Geog.*) détroit, *m.*; (*pl.*) gêne, difficulté, *f.*, embarras, *m.*

straiten [streitn], *v.t.* rétrécir (*resserrer*); (*fig.*) gêner.

strait-laced ['streitleist], *a.* lacé étroitement; (*fig.*) sévère, prude.

straitness ['streitnis], *n.* étroitesse, *f.*

strait-waistcoat ['streitweiskout], **strait-jacket** ['streitdʒækit], *n.* camisole de force, *f.*

strand (1) [strænd], *n.* plage, grève, *f.*—*v.t.* jeter à la côte, échouer.—*v.i.* échouer.

strand (2) [strænd], *n.* cordon (*de corde*), *m.*

stranded ['strændid], *a.* échoué; (*fig.*) dans l'embarras.

stranding ['strændiŋ], *n.* échouement, échouage, *m.*

strange [streindʒ], *a.* étrange, singulier, bizarre.

strangely ['streindʒli], *adv.* étrangement, singulièrement.

strangeness ['streindʒnis], *n.* étrangeté, bizarrerie, *f.*

stranger ['streindʒə], *n.* étranger, inconnu, *m.*

strangle ['stræŋgl], *v.t.* étrangler.

strangler ['stræŋglə], *n.* étrangleur, *m.*

strangling ['stræŋgliŋ], *n.* étranglement, *m.*

strangulation [stræŋgju'leiʃən], *n.* strangulation, *f.*

strap [stræp], *n.* courroie, *f.*; lien, *m.*, bande (*de fer*), *f.*—*v.t.* attacher avec une courroie; lier.

strapper ['stræpə], *n.* grand gaillard, *m.*

strapping ['stræpiŋ], *a.* bien découplé, bien bâti.

stratagem ['strætədʒəm], *n.* stratagème, *m.*

strategic [strə'tiːdʒik], **strategical** [strə'tiːdʒikəl], *a.* stratégique.

strategist ['strætədʒist], *n.* stratégiste, *m.*, *f.*

strategy ['strætədʒi], *n.* stratégie, *f.*

stratify ['strætifai], *v.t.* stratifier.

stratocruiser ['stræto'kruːzə], *n.* avion stratosphérique, *m.*

stratosphere ['strætəsfiə], *n.* stratosphère, *f.*

stratum ['straːtəm], *n.* (*pl.* **strata** ['straːtə]) couche, *f.*

straw [strɔː], *a.* de paille.—*n.* paille, *f.*; **it's the last straw**, c'est le comble.—*v.t.* rempailler (*chaise*).

strawberry ['strɔːbəri], *n.* fraise, *f.*; fraisier (*plante*), *m.*

straw-colored ['strɔːkʌləd], *a.* jaune-paille.

straw mat ['strɔː mæt], *n.* paillasson, *m.*

stray [strei], *v.i.* s'égarer, errer, vaguer; s'écarter (*de*).—*a.* égaré; (*fig.*) fortuit.—*n.* épave, *f.*; **waifs and strays**, des épaves, *f.pl.*

straying ['streiiŋ], *n.* égarement, *m.*

streak [striːk], *n.* raie, bande, *f.*; **streak of lightning**, éclair, *m.*—*v.t.* rayer, strier; barioler, bigarrer.—*v.i.* filer.

streaked [striːkt], *a.* rayé (*de*); bariolé, bigarré.

streaky ['striːki], *a.* rayé; veiné (*marbre*); entrelardé (*viande*).

stream [striːm], *n.* courant; cours d'eau, *m.*, rivière, *f.*; ruisseau; (*fig.*) cours; jet (*de lumière etc.*); torrent (*de paroles etc.*), *m.*; **to go down stream**, aller en aval; **to go up stream**, aller en amont.—*v.i.* couler; ruisseler (*sang etc.*); rayonner (*lumière*).

streamer ['striːmə], *n.* banderole; (*Naut.*) flamme, *f.*; (*pl.*) serpentins (*de papier*), *m.pl.*

streamlet ['striːmlit], *n.* petit ruisseau; ru, *m.*

stream-line ['striːmlain], *n.* fil de l'eau, *m.* —*v.t.* caréner; (*fig.*) moderniser.

stream-lined ['striːmlaind], *a.* **stream-lined body**, carrosserie carénée, *f.*; **stream-lined car**, voiture aérodynamique, *f.*

street [striːt], *n.* rue, *f.*

street door ['striːt'dɔː], *n.* porte sur la rue, *f.*

street lamp ['striːt'læmp], *n.* réverbère, *m.*

street sweeper ['striːt'swiːpə], *n.* balayeur de rue (*personne*), *m.*; balayeuse (*machine*), *f.*

strength [streŋθ], *n.* force, *f.*, forces, *f.pl.*; (*Build.*) solidité, *f.*; (*Mil.*) effectif, *m.*

strengthen ['streŋθən], *v.t.* fortifier, affermir, raffermir; (*Mil.*) renforcer.—*v.i.* se fortifier, s'affermir, se raffermir.

strengthener ['streŋθnə], *n.* (*Med.*) fortifiant, *m.*

strengthening ['streŋθniŋ], *a.* fortifiant.

strenuous ['strenjuəs], *a.* énergique, vif, ardent, vigoureux.

strenuously ['strenjuəsli], *adv.* avec zèle, ardemment; vigoureusement.

strenuousness ['strenjuəsnis], *n.* zèle, *m.*, ardeur; vigueur, *f.*

streptococcus [strepto'kɔkəs], *n.* streptocoque, *m.*

streptomycin [strepto'maisin], *n.* streptomycine, *f.*

stress [stres], *n.* force, emphase, *f.*, poids; (*Gram.*) accent, *m.*; violence (*du temps*); (*Mech.*) tension, *f.*—*v.t.* appuyer sur, accentuer.

stretch [stretʃ], *v.t.* tendre (*un élastique*); étendre; déployer (*ailes*); élargir; forcer (*faire violence à*); (*fig.*) exagérer.—*v.i.* s'étendre; s'étirer; se déployer; s'élargir; prêter (*gants, tissu*).—*n.* étendue, tension, extension; section (*de route*), *f.*; (*fig.*) effort, *m.*; **at a stretch**, d'un trait.

stretcher ['stretʃə], *n.* brancard, *m.*, civière; baguette (*à gants*), *f.*, tendeur (*à chaussures*), *m.*

stretcher-bearer ['stretʃʃbɛərə], *n.* brancardier, *m.*

stretching ['stretʃiŋ], *n.* élargissement, *m.*; tension, *f.*

strew [struː], *v.t.* *irr.* répandre, parsemer, semer.

strewing ['struːiŋ], *n.* jonchée, *f.*

striate ['straiit], **striated** [strai'eitid], *a.* strié.

striation [strai'eiʃən], *n.* striure, *f.*

stricken [strikn], *p.p.* [STRIKE].—*a.* affligé; (*Med.*) atteint (*de*).

strict [strikt], *a.* exact, strict, précis; rigide; sévère.

strictly ['striktli], *adv.* strictement, formellement; **strictly speaking**, rigoureusement parlant.

strictness ['striktnis], *n.* exactitude, rigueur; sévérité, *f.*

stricture ['striktʃə], *n.* censure, critique, *f.*; (*Med.*) étranglement, *m.*

stride [straid], *n.* grand pas, *m.*, enjambée, *f.* —*v.i.* *irr.* marcher à grands pas *ou* à grandes enjambées.

strident ['straidənt], *a.* strident.

strife [straif], *n.* lutte, querelle, dispute, *f.*

strike [straik], *v.t.* *irr.* frapper; battre, cogner; asséner, porter (*un coup*); sonner (*l'heure*); rendre (*muet etc.*); établir (*l'équilibre*); allumer (*allumette*); faire (*marché etc.*); amener (*drapeau*); plier (*tente*); **to strike down**, abattre; **to strike off**, retrancher, effacer.—*v.i.* frapper; toucher; échouer (*heurter un écueil etc.*); heurter, donner (*contre*); sonner (*pendule etc.*); (*Hort.*) prendre racine; faire grève, se mettre en grève (*ouvriers*); **to strike out**, se lancer; (*Mus.*) **to strike up**, commencer à jouer.— *n.* grève (*d'ouvriers*), *f.*; **sit-down strike**, débrayage, *m.*; **stay-in-strike**, grève sur le tas.

striker ['straikə], *n.* frappeur, *m.*; gréviste (*ouvrier en grève*), *m.*, *f.*; percuteur (*de fusil*), *m.*

striking ['straikiŋ], *a.* frappant, saisissant; remarquable.—*n.* frappement, *m.*; frappe; sonnerie (*de pendule*), *f.*

strikingly ['straikiŋli], *adv.* d'une manière frappante.

string [striŋ], *n.* ficelle, corde, *f.*; fil; cordon, lacet (*de chaussures etc.*); chapelet (*d'oignons etc.*), *m.*; corde (*de violon*); bride (*de bonnet etc.*); (*fig.*) suite, série, *f.*; **the strings**, les instruments à cordes (*d'un orchestre*), *m.pl.*—*v.t. irr.* garnir de cordes; enfiler (*grains etc.*); (*Mus.*) accorder.

stringed [striŋd], *a.* à cordes (*instrument de musique*).

stringency [ˈstrindʒənsi], *n.* rigueur, *f.*

stringent [ˈstrindʒənt], *a.* rigoureux, strict.

stringy [ˈstriŋi], *a.* fibreux; filandreux (*viande*).

strip [strip], *n.* bande, *f.*, ruban; lambeau, *m.*, langue (*de terre*), *f.*—*v.t.* dépouiller (*de*); dévaliser (*voler*); déshabiller (*dévêtir*); **to strip off**, se dépouiller de.—*v.i.* se déshabiller.

stripe [straip], *n.* raie; barre, bande; marque (*cicatrice*), *f.*; (*Mil.*) chevron, galon, *m.*—*v.t.* rayer, barrer.

striped [straipt], **stripy** [ˈstraipi], *a.* rayé, à raies, zébré.

stripling [ˈstripliŋ], *n.* adolescent, *m.*

strive [straiv], *v.i. irr.* s'efforcer (*de*), faire des efforts (*pour*), se débattre; se disputer (*rivaliser*).

striving [ˈstraiviŋ], *n.* lutte, *f.*, efforts, *m.pl.*

stroke [strouk], *n.* coup; trait; trait de plume; coup d'aviron, *m.*; brassée (*de la nage*), course (*de piston*), *f.*; (*Med.*) coup de sang, *m.*, attaque, *f.*; chef de nage (*de bateau à rames*), *m.*; **at a stroke**, d'un coup, d'un trait.—*v.t.* caresser.

stroking [ˈstroukiŋ], *n.* caresses, *f.pl.*

stroll [stroul], *n.* (courte) promenade, *f.*, tour, *m.*, flânerie, *f.*—*v.i.* errer, flâner.

stroller [ˈstroulə], *n.* flâneur, *m.*

strong [strɔŋ], *a.* fort, solide; (*fig.*) vigoureux, résolu; **strong light**, vive lumière, *f.*

strong-box [ˈstrɔŋbɔks], *n.* coffre-fort, *m.*

stronghold [ˈstrɔŋhould], *n.* forteresse, *f.*, fort, *m.*

strongly [ˈstrɔŋli], *adv.* fortement, fermement.

strong-room [ˈstrɔŋruːm], *n.* cave aux coffres-forts, *f.*

strontium [ˈstrɔnʃiəm], *n.* strontium, *m.*

strop [strɔp], *n.* cuir à rasoir, *m.*—*v.t.* repasser, affiler.

strophe [ˈstroufi, ˈstrɔfi], *n.* stance, strophe, *f.*

structural [ˈstrʌktʃərəl], *a.* de structure, structural.

structure [ˈstrʌktʃə], *n.* construction, structure, *f.*; édifice, *m.*; facture (*de pièce, de poème*), *f.*

struggle [ˈstrʌgl], *n.* lutte, *f.*, effort, *m.*—*v.i.* lutter, se débattre.

struggling [ˈstrʌgliŋ], *n.* lutte, *f.*; effort, *m.*

strum [strʌm], *v.t., v.i.* tapoter, taper (*sur*).

strumming [ˈstrʌmiŋ], *n.* tapotage, *m.*

strut [strʌt], *n.* démarche fière, *f.*; (*Carp. etc*) étai, *m.*—*v.i.* se pavaner, se carrer.

strychnine [ˈstrikniːn], *n.* strychnine, *f.*

stub [stʌb], *n.* souche, *f.*; bout, *m.*

stubble [ˈstʌbl], *n.* chaume, *m.*

stubborn [ˈstʌbən], *a.* obstiné, opiniâtre.

stubbornness [ˈstʌbənnis], *n.* opiniâtreté, *f.*

stubby [ˈstʌbi], *a.* trapu (*taille*).

stucco [ˈstʌkou], *n.* stuc, *m.*

stud (1) [stʌd], *n.* bouton de chemise; clou, *m.* —*v.t.* clouter; parsemer (*de*).

stud (2) [stʌd], *n.* écurie, *f.*; **stud farm**, haras, *m.*

student [ˈstjuːdənt], *n.* étudiant, *m.*, élève, *m., f.*

studied [ˈstʌdid], *a.* étudié (*style etc.*); prémédité (*calculé*).

studio [ˈstjuːdiou], *n.* atelier; (*Cine., Rad.*) studio, *m.*

studious [ˈstjuːdiəs], *a.* studieux; diligent.

studiously [ˈstjuːdiəsli], *adv.* studieusement.

studiousness [ˈstjuːdiəsnis], *n.* application, *f.*

study [ˈstʌdi], *n.* étude, *f.*; soin, *m.*, application (*attention*), *f.*; cabinet d'étude (*pièce*), *m.*; **to be in a brown study**, être dans la lune.—*v.t.* étudier, s'occuper de.—*v.i.* étudier, travailler.

stuff [stʌf], *n.* étoffe, *f.*, tissu, *m.*; (*fig.*) matière, *f.*; fatras (*bêtises*), *m.*—*v.t.* rembourrer; bourrer (*remplir*); boucher (*trou*); (*Taxidermy*) empailler; (*Cook.*) farcir.—*v.t.* se b urrer; se gorger.

stuffing [ˈstʌfiŋ], *n.* bourre (*substances*), *f.*; rembourrage (*opération*), *m.*; (*Cook.*) farce, *f.*; (*Taxidermy*) empaillage, *m.*

stuffy [ˈstʌfi], *a.* privé d'air, renfermé; **to be stuffy**, sentir le renfermé; (*fig.*) avoir des préjugés.

stultify [ˈstʌltifai], *v.t.* rendre nul; contredire (*démentir*); **to stultify oneself**, se rendre ridicule.

stumble [stʌmbl], *v.i.* trébucher, broncher; (*fig.*) faire un faux pas, faillir.—*n.* faux pas, *m.*

stumbling [ˈstʌmbliŋ], *a.* trébuchant.—*n.* trébuchement, *m.*

stumbling block [ˈstʌmbliŋblɔk], *n.* pierre d'achoppement, *f.*

stump [stʌmp], *n.* tronçon, *m.*, souche, *f.*; chicot (*de dent*); trognon (*de chou*); moignon (*de membre*), *m.*; (*Drawing*) estompe, *f.*

stumpy [ˈstʌmpi], *a.* trapu (*personne*).

stun [stʌn], *v.t.* étourdir.

stunning [ˈstʌniŋ], *a.* étourdissant; (*slang*) épatant.

stunt (1) [stʌnt], *v.t.* rabougrir.

stunt (2) [stʌnt], *n.* tour de force, *m.*; réclame, *f.*

stunted [ˈstʌntid], *a.* rabougri.

stupefaction [stjuːpiˈfækʃən], *n.* stupéfaction, *f.*

stupefy [ˈstjuːpifai], *v.t.* hébéter, abrutir; stupéfier.

stupefying [ˈstjuːpifaiiŋ], *a.* stupéfiant.

stupendous [stjuːˈpendəs], *a.* prodigieux, foudroyant.

stupid [ˈstjuːpid], *a.* stupide, sot, bête.

stupidity [stjuːˈpiditi], *n.* stupidité, bêtise, *f.*

stupidly [ˈstjuːpidli], *adv.* stupidement.

stupor [ˈstjuːpə], *n.* stupeur, *f.*

sturdy [ˈstəːdi], *a.* vigoureux, fort, robuste; hardi.

sturgeon [ˈstəːdʒən], *n.* esturgeon, *m.*

stutter [ˈstʌtə], *v.t., v.i.* bégayer.

stutterer [ˈstʌtərə], *n.* bègue, *m., f.*

stuttering [ˈstʌtəriŋ], *n.* bégaiement, *m.*

sty (1) [stai], *n.* étable (*à cochons*), *f.*

sty (2), **stye** [stai], *n.* orgelet (*à l'œil*), *m.*

Stygian [ˈstidʒiən], *a.* stygien.

style [stail], *n.* style; (*fig.*) genre, *m.*, manière, *f.*; titre, *m.*; raison sociale (*d'une compagnie*), *f.*; **to live in style**, avoir un train de maison.—*v.t.* appeler, qualifier de.

stylish ['stailiʃ], a. élégant, de bon ton.
stylus ['stailəs], n. style, m.
styptic ['stiptik], a. and n. (Med.) styptique, m.
suave [swɑːv], a. suave.
suavity ['swɑːviti], n. suavité, f.
subaltern ['sʌbaltən], a. subalterne.—n. (sous-)lieutenant, m.
subconscious [sʌb'kɔnʃəs], a. and n. (Psych.) subconscient, m.
subconsciously [sʌb'kɔnʃəsli], adv. inconsciemment.
subdivide [sʌbdi'vaid], v.t. subdiviser.
subdue [səb'djuː], v.t. subjuguer; dompter, étouffer; subdued light, demi-jour, m.
sub-editor [sʌb'editə], n. secrétaire de la rédaction, m.
subject ['sʌbdʒikt], a. assujetti, soumis; sujet (à), exposé (à).—n. sujet, m.; (Sch.) matière, f.; particulier, m., personne, f.— [səb'dʒekt], v.t. assujettir, soumettre; rendre sujet (à), exposer (à).
subjection [səb'dʒekʃən], n. sujétion, f.
subjective [səb'dʒektiv], a. subjectif.
subjectively [səb'dʒektivli], adv. subjectivement.
subject matter ['sʌbdʒiktmætə], n. sujet, m. matière, f.
subjugate ['sʌbdʒugeit], v.t. subjuguer.
subjunctive [səb'dʒʌŋktiv], a. and n. (Gram.) subjonctif, m.
sublet [sʌb'let], v.t. irr. (conjug. like LET) sous-louer.
sub-lieutenant [sʌblef'tenənt], n. (Navy) enseigne, m.
sublimate ['sʌblimeit], v.t. sublimer.
sublime [sə'blaim], a. and n. sublime, m.
sublimeness [sə'blaimnis], n. sublimité, f.; sublime, m.
sub-machine gun [sʌbmə'ʃiːngʌn], n. mitraillette, f.
submarine ['sʌbməriːn], a. and n. sous-marin, m.
submerge [səb'məːdʒ], v.t. submerger.—v.i. plonger.
submission [səb'miʃən], n. soumission; résignation, déférence, f.
submissive [səb'misiv], a. soumis (à); docile.
submit [səb'mit], v.t. soumettre (à).—v.i. se soumettre (à).
subnormal [sʌb'nɔːml], a. sous-normal.
subordinate [sə'bɔːdinit], a. subordonné (à).—n. subordonné, m.—[sə'bɔːdineit], v.t. subordonner (à).
subordination [səbɔːdi'neiʃən], n. subordination, f.; rang inférieur, m.
suborn [sə'bɔːn], v.t. suborner.
subpoena [sʌb'piːnə], n. (Law) citation, assignation, f.—v.t. citer, assigner.
subscribe [səb'skraib], v.t. souscrire.—v.i. souscrire (à ou pour); s'abonner (à un journal).
subscriber [səb'skraibə], n. abonné (à un journal), m.
subscription [səb'skripʃən], n. souscription, f.; abonnement (à un journal etc.), m.
subsection ['sʌbsekʃən], n. subdivision, f.
subsequent ['sʌbsikwənt], a. subséquent, postérieur.
subsequently ['sʌbsikwəntli], adv. ensuite, après.

subservient [səb'səːvjənt], a. subordonné (à); qui contribue à; obséquieux.
subserviently [səb'səːvjəntli], adv. en sousordre, utilement; servilement.
subside [səb'said], v.i. s'affaisser (être accablé); baisser, s'abaisser, se calmer, s'apaiser (s'adoucir); se taire (personne); to subside into, se changer en.
subsidence ['sʌbsidəns, səb'saidəns], n. affaissement, m.; (fig.) baisse (rivière), f.
subsidiary [səb'sidjəri], a. subsidiaire (à).— n. auxiliaire, m.; filiale (compagnie), f.
subsidize ['sʌbsidaiz], v.t. subventionner.
subsidy ['sʌbsidi], n. subvention, f.
subsist [səb'sist], v.i. subsister, exister.
subsistence [səb'sistəns], n. subsistance, f.; entretien, m.; existence, f.
subsistent [səb'sistənt], a. existant, qui existe.
subsoil ['sʌbsɔil], n. sous-sol, m.
sub-species [sʌbspiːʃiːz], n. sous-espèce, f.
substance ['sʌbstəns], n. substance, f.; fond (l'essentiel), m.; biens (richesses), m.pl.
substantial [səb'stænʃl], a. substantiel, réel, solide; aisé (riche).
substantially [səb'stænʃəli], adv. solidement, fortement, considérablement.
substantiate [səb'stænʃieit], v.t. établir, confirmer.
substantive ['sʌbstəntiv], a. indépendant; (Gram.) substantif.—n. (Gram.) substantif, m.
substitute ['sʌbstitjuːt], v.t. substituer (à).— n. substitut, remplaçant, m.
substitution [sʌbsti'tjuːʃən], n. substitution, f.
substratum [sʌb'strɑːtəm], n. (pl. substrata [sʌb'strɑːtə]) substratum, substrat, m., couche inférieure, f.; (Agric.) sous-sol, m. f.
subtenant ['sʌbtenənt], n. sous-locataire, m., f.
subterfuge ['sʌbtəfjuːdʒ], n. subterfuge, faux-fuyant, m.
subterranean [sʌbtə'reiniən], a. souterrain.
sub-title ['sʌbtaitl], n. sous-titre, m.
subtle [sʌtl], a. subtil, rusé; fin.
subtlety ['sʌtlti], n. subtilité, finesse, f.
subtly ['sʌtli], adv. subtilement.
subtract [səb'trækt], v.t. défalquer; (Arith.) soustraire.
subtraction [səb'trækʃən], n. (Arith.) soustraction, f.
suburb ['sʌbəːb], n. faubourg, m., (pl.) alentours, environs, m.pl., banlieue, f.; garden suburb, cité-jardin, f.
suburban [sə'bəːbən], a. de la banlieue, suburbain.
subvention [səb'venʃən], n. subvention, f.
subversive [səb'vəːsiv], a. subversif.
subway ['sʌbwei], n. passage souterrain; (Am.) métro, m.
succeed [sək'siːd], v.t. succéder à, suivre; to succeed each other, se succéder.—v.i. succéder (à); hériter (une propriété); parvenir (à), réussir (avoir du succès).
succeeding [sək'siːdiŋ], a. suivant (dans le passé); à venir, futur (à l'avenir); successif (consécutif).
success [sək'ses], n. succès, m.; I wish you success! bonne chance!
successful [sək'sesful], a. heureux; couronné de succès, réussi, victorieux; to be successful, réussir.

successfully [sək'sesfuli], *adv.* heureusement, avec succès.

succession [sək'seʃən], *n.* succession, suite, *f.*; avènement (*au trône etc.*), *m.*; postérité (*descendance*), *f.*; **in succession**, successivement, de suite.

successive [sək'sesiv], *a.* successif, consécutif.

successor [sək'sesə], *n.* successeur, *m.*

succinct [sək'siŋkt], *a.* succinct, concis.

succinctly [sək'siŋktli], *adv.* avec concision.

succinctness [sək'siŋktnis], *n.* concision, brièveté, *f.*

succor ['sʌkə], *v.t.* secourir, aider.—*n.* secours, *m.*, aide, *f.*

succulent ['sʌkjulənt], *a.* succulent, plein de jus.

succumb [sə'kʌm], *v.i.* succomber (à).

such [sʌtʃ], *a.* tel, pareil, semblable; **he is such a bore**, il est si ennuyeux; **such a one**, un tel, *m.*, une telle, *f.*; **such a one as**, tel que; **such as it is**, tel quel, *m.*, telle quelle, *f.*; **such as you**, tel que vous.

suchlike ['sʌtʃlaik], *a.* semblable, pareil; de ce genre.

suck [sʌk], *v.t., v.i.* sucer; téter (*à la mamelle*); aspirer.

sucker ['sʌkə], *n.* suceur; (*fig.*) gobeur, *m.*

sucking ['sʌkiŋ], *a.* qui suce, aspirant.—*n.* sucement, *m.*, succion, *f.*

sucking pig ['sʌkiŋpig], *n.* cochon de lait, *m.*

suckle [sʌkl], *v.t.* allaiter, nourrir.

suction ['sʌkʃən], *n.* succion, aspiration, *f.*

Sudan [su'dæn, su'dɑ:n], le Soudan, *m.*

Sudanese [sudə'ni:z], *a.* soudanais.—*n.* Soudanais (*personne*), *m.*

sudden [sʌdn], *a.* subit, soudain; (*fam.*) **all of a sudden**, tout à coup.

suddenly ['sʌdnli], *adv.* subitement, soudain, tout à coup.

suddenness ['sʌdnnis], *n.* soudaineté, *f.*

Sudetenland [su'deitnlænd], les Sudètes, *m.pl.*

suds [sʌdz], **soap-suds** ['soupsʌdz], *n.pl.* eau de savon, lessive, *f.*

sue [sju:], *v.t.* poursuivre (en justice).—*v.i.* implorer.

suède [sweid], *n.* daim (*chaussures*); suède (*gants*), *m.*

suet ['sju:it], *n.* graisse de bœuf, *f.*

suffer ['sʌfə], *v.t.* souffrir; supporter, endurer, subir (*éprouver*); laisser, permettre (*autoriser*).—*v.i.* souffrir (*de*); **to suffer for**, porter la peine de.

sufferable ['sʌfərəbl], *a.* supportable, tolérable.

sufferance ['sʌfərəns], *n.* tolérance, *f.*

sufferer ['sʌfərə], *n.* victime (*de*), *f.*; patient, *m.*

suffering ['sʌfəriŋ], *a.* souffrant.—*n.* souffrance, douleur, *f.*

suffice [sə'fais], *v.t.* suffire à, satisfaire.—*v.i.* suffire.

sufficiency [sə'fiʃənsi], *n.* suffisance; aisance (*financière*), *f.*

sufficient [sə'fiʃənt], *a.* suffisant, assez.

sufficiently [sə'fiʃəntli], *adv.* suffisamment, assez.

suffix ['sʌfiks], *n.* suffixe, *m.*

suffocate ['sʌfəkeit], *v.t., v.i.* suffoquer, étouffer, asphyxier.

suffocating ['sʌfəkeitiŋ], *a.* suffocant, étouffant, asphyxiant.

suffocation [sʌfə'keiʃən], *n.* suffocation, asphyxie, *f.*

suffrage ['sʌfridʒ], *n.* suffrage, *m.*

suffuse [sə'fju:z], *v.t.* répandre, couvrir (*de*); répandre sur; se répandre sur.

suffusion [sə'fju:ʒən], *n.* épanchement, *m.*, suffusion, *f.*

sugar ['ʃugə], *n.* sucre, *m.*; **barley sugar**, sucre d'orge; **brown (unrefined) sugar**, cassonade, *f.*; **powdered sugar**, sucre en poudre; **granulated sugar**, sucre cristallisé; **lump sugar**, sucre cassé.—*v.t.* sucrer; (*fig.*) adoucir.

sugar beet ['ʃugəbi:t], *n.* betterave à sucre, *f.*

sugar bowl ['ʃugəboul], *n.* sucrier, *m.*

sugar cane ['ʃugəkein], *n.* canne à sucre, *f.*

sugared ['ʃugəd], *a.* sucré; (*fig.*) doux.

sugar loaf ['ʃugəlouf], *n.* pain de sucre, *m.*

sugar refinery ['ʃugəri'fainəri], *n.* raffinerie de sucre, *f.*

sugary ['ʃugəri], *a.* sucré; trop sucré.

suggest [sə'dʒest], *v.t.* suggérer; inspirer.

suggestion [sə'dʒestʃən], *n.* suggestion; proposition, idée; nuance, *f.*

suggestive [sə'dʒestiv], *a.* suggestif.

suicidal [sju:i'saidl], *a.* de suicide; fatal.

suicide ['sju:isaid], *n.* suicide (*acte*); suicidé (*personne*), *m.*; **to commit suicide**, se suicider.

suit [sju:t], *n.* suite, collection complète, *f.*, assortiment, *m.*; (*Cards*) couleur; sollicitation, prière; recherche en mariage; (*Law*) instance, *f.*, procès, *m.*; **suit of clothes**, complet (*d'homme*), tailleur (*de femme*), *m.*—*v.t.* adapter; convenir à, aller à; plaire à —*v.i.* s'accorder (à).

suitability [sju:tə'biliti], *n.* convenance, *f.*

suitable ['sju:təbl], *a.* convenable (à); à propos.

suitably ['sju:təbli], *adv.* convenablement.

suite [swi:t], *n.* suite, *f.*, ensemble, *m.*; **suite of rooms**, appartement, *m.*; **suite of furniture**, ameublement complet, *m.*

suitor ['sju:tə], *n.* prétendant (*amoureux*); (*Law*) plaideur, *m.*

sulk [sʌlk], *v.i.* bouder, faire la mine.

sulkily ['sʌlkili], *adv.* en boudant, en faisant la mine.

sulkiness ['sʌlkinis], **sulking** ['sʌlkiŋ], *n.* bouderie, *f.*

sulks [sʌlks], *n.pl.* mauvaise humeur, bouderie, *f.*

sulky ['sʌlki], *a.* boudeur.

sullen ['sʌlən], *a.* maussade, morose. renfrogné.

sullenly ['sʌlənli], *adv.* maussadement, d'un air renfrogné.

sullenness ['sʌlənnis], *n.* air maussade, *m.*

sully ['sʌli], *v.t.* souiller, ternir (*de*).

sulphate ['sʌlfeit], *n.* sulfate, *m.*

sulphide ['sʌlfaid], *n.* sulfure, *m.*

sulphite ['sʌlfait], *n.* sulfite, *m.*

sulphonamide [sʌl'founəmaid], *n.* sulfamide, *m.*

sulphur ['sʌlfə], *n.* soufre, *m.*

sulphuric [sʌl'fjuərik], *a.* sulfurique.

sulphurous ['sʌlfjurəs], *a.* sulfureux.

sultan ['sʌltən], *n.* sultan, *m.*

sultana [sʌl'tɑ:nə], *n.* sultane, *f.*; (*pl.*) raisins de Smyrne, *m.pl.*

sultriness ['sʌltrinis], *n.* chaleur étouffante, *f.*

sultry ['sʌltri], a. d'une chaleur étouffante, étouffant, suffocant; (fam.) épicé, salé (histoire etc.); *it is very sultry*, il fait très lourd.

sum [sʌm], n. somme (d'argent), f.; (Arith.) problème, calcul, m.; *the four sums*, les quatre opérations, f.pl.—v.t. *to sum up*, additionner, faire l'addition de; (fig.) récapituler.

summarily ['sʌmərili], adv. sommairement.

summarize ['sʌməraiz], v.t. résumer sommairement.

summary ['sʌməri], a. sommaire, prompt.— n. sommaire, résumé, m.

summer ['sʌmə], n. été, m.; d'été, estival—n. été, m.; *in summer*, en été.

summer-house ['sʌməhaus], n. pavillon, m.

summing-up ['sʌmiŋʌp], n. résumé, m.

summit ['sʌmit], n. sommet, m., cime, f.; (fig.) comble, m.

summon ['sʌmən], v.t. convoquer (un rassemblement etc.); sommer (ordonner); (Law) citer en justice; assigner (témoins).

summons ['sʌmənz], n. sommation (commandement); convocation, f.; appel (invitation), m.; (Law) citation, f., mandat de comparution, m.—v.t. assigner, citer (en justice), appeler à comparaître.

sump [sʌmp], n. (Mining) puisard, m.; (fond de carter (de voiture), m.

sumptuous ['sʌmptjuəs], a. somptueux.

sumptuously ['sʌmptjuəsli], adv. somptueusement.

sun [sʌn], n. soleil, m.—v.t. exposer au soleil.

sun bath ['sʌnbɑ:θ], n. bain de soleil, m.

sun-bathe ['sʌnbeið], v.i. prendre des bains de soleil.

sunbeam ['sʌnbi:m], n. rayon de soleil, m.

sun-blind ['sʌnblaind], n. store, m.

sunburn ['sʌnbə:n], n. hâle; coup de soleil, m.

sunburnt ['sʌnbə:nt], a. hâlé; basané.

Sunday ['sʌndi], n. dimanche, m.

sunder ['sʌndə], v.t. séparer; couper en deux.

sundial ['sʌndaiəl], n. cadran solaire, m.

sundries ['sʌndriz], n.pl. choses diverses, f.pl.

sundry ['sʌndri], a. divers.

sun-flower ['sʌnflauə], n. tournesol, m.

sunken ['sʌŋkən], a. enfoncé; cave (joues); creux (yeux).

sunless ['sʌnlis], a. sans soleil.

sunlight ['sʌnlait], n. lumière du soleil, f.

sunlit ['sʌnlit], a. ensoleillé.

sunny ['sʌni], a. ensoleillé; (fig.) heureux; *it is sunny*, il fait du soleil.

sunrise ['sʌnraiz], n. lever du soleil, m.

sunset ['sʌnset], n. coucher du soleil, m.

sunshade ['sʌnʃeid], n. parasol, m., ombrelle, f.

sunshine ['sʌnʃain], n. soleil, m., clarté du soleil, f.

sunstroke ['sʌnstrouk], n. coup de soleil, m., insolation, f.

sup [sʌp], n. (Sc.) petit coup, m., gorgée, f.— v.t. boire à petits coups.—v.i. souper.

super ['sju:pə], a. (slang) *it is super*, c'est sensass (sensationnel).

superable ['sju:pərəbl], a. surmontable.

superabundance [sju:pərə'bʌndəns], n. surabondance, f.

superannuate [sju:pər'ænjueit], v.t. mettre à la retraite.

superannuated [sju:pər'ænjueitid], a. mis à la retraite, en retraite (personne); démodé.

superannuation [sju:pərænju'eiʃən], n. mise à la retraite, retraite, f.; *superannuation fund*, caisse de retraites, f.

superb [sju:'pə:b], a. superbe.

superbly [sju:'pə:bli], adv. superbement.

supercilious [sju:pə'siliəs], a. hautain, arrogant.

superciliously [sju:pə'siliəsli], adv. avec hauteur.

superciliousness [sju:pə'siliəsnis], n. hauteur; arrogance, f.

superficial [sju:pə'fiʃl], a. superficiel; de superficie (mesure).

superficiality [sju:pəfiʃi'æliti], n. caractère superficiel, m.

superficially [sju:pə'fiʃəli], adv. superficiellement.

superfine ['sju:pəfain], a. superfin; (Comm.) surfin.

superfluity [sju:pə'flu:iti], n. superfluité, f.; superflu, m.

superfluous [sju:'pə:fluəs], a. superflu, inutile.

superhuman [sju:pə'hju:mən], a. surhumain.

superimpose [sju:pərim'pouz], v.t. superposer, surimposer.

superintend [sju:pərin'tend], v.t. surveiller.

superintendent [sju:pərin'tendənt], n. chef, directeur, inspecteur, surintendant; commissaire de police, m.

superior [sju:'piəriə], a. and n. supérieur, m.

superiority [sjupiəri'oriti], n. supériorité, f.

superlative [sju:pə'lətiv], a. suprême; (Gram.) superlatif.—n. (Gram.) superlatif, m.

superman ['sju:pəmæn], n. (pl. -men [men]) surhomme, m.

supernatural [sju:pə'nætʃərəl], a. and n. surnaturel, m.

supernumerary [sju:pə'nju:mərəri], a. surnuméraire.—n. surnuméraire; (Theat.) figurant, m.

superscribe [sju:pə'skraib], v.t. mettre une adresse, une suscription ou une inscription à.

superscription [sju:pə'skripʃən], n. suscription; inscription; (Coin.) légende, f.; en-tête (de lettre), m.

supersede [sju:pə'si:d], v.t. remplacer.

superseded [sju:pə'si:did], a. démodé, périmé.

supersonic [sju:pə'sonik], a. (onde) ultra-sonore; (Av.) supersonique.

superstition [sju:pə'stiʃən], n. superstition, f.

superstitious [sju:pə'stiʃəs], a. superstitieux.

superstructure [sju:pə'strʌktʃə], n. superstructure, f.

super-tax ['sju:pətæks], n. surtaxe, f.

supervene [sju:pə'vi:n], v.i. survenir.

supervention [sju:pə'venʃən], n. survenance, f.

supervise ['sju:pəvaiz], v.t. surveiller.

supervision [sju:pə'viʒən], n. surveillance; inspection, f.

supervisor ['sju:pəvaizə], n. surveillant, m.

supine [sju:'pain], a. couché sur le dos; (fig.) nonchalant.—['sju:pain], n. (Gram.) supin, m.

supper ['sʌpə], n. souper, m.; *supper time*, heure du souper, f.

supplant [sə'plɑ:nt], v.t. supplanter.

supple [sʌpl], *a.* souple, flexible.
supplement [sʌpli'ment], *v.t.* suppléer à; compléter.—['sʌplimənt], *n.* supplément, *m.*
supplementary [sʌpli'mentəri], *a.* supplémentaire.
suppleness ['sʌplnis], *n.* souplesse, *f.*
suppliant ['sʌpliənt], *a.* and *n.* suppliant, *m.*
supplicate ['sʌplikeit], *v.t.* supplier, implorer.
supplication [sʌpli'keiʃən], *n.* supplication, prière, *f.*
supplier [sə'plaiə], *n.* pourvoyeur; fournisseur, *m.*
supply [sə'plai], *n.* fourniture; provision, *f.*, approvisionnement (*réserve*), *m.*; (*Elec.*) alimentation, *f.*; (*Mil., pl.*) vivres (*ravitaillement*); (*Parl.*) subsides, *m.pl.*—*v.t.* fournir; pourvoir à, subvenir à (*besoins*), ravitailler.
support [sə'pɔ:t], *v.t.* soutenir, supporter; entretenir (*faire vivre*); appuyer (*aider*).—*n.* appui, soutien; support (*physique*); entretien (*des dépendants*), *m.*
supportable [sə'pɔ:təbl], *a.* supportable.
supporter [sə'pɔ:tə], *n.* adhérent, partisan; appui, soutien; (*Spt.*) supporter; (*Her.*) support, *m.*
suppose [sə'pouz], *v.t.* supposer, s'imaginer; *to be supposed to* (*know*), être censé (*savoir*); *suppose we go,* si nous y allions.
supposed [sə'pouzd], *a.* présumé; prétendu, soi-disant; censé.
supposedly [sə'pouzidli], *adv.* censément.
supposing [sə'pouziŋ], *conj.* supposons, supposé (*que*).
supposition [sʌpə'ziʃən], *n.* supposition, *f.*
suppress [sə'pres], *v.t.* supprimer; réprimer (*révolte etc.*); étouffer; *a suppressed laugh,* un rire étouffé.
suppression [sə'preʃən], *n.* suppression; répression; dissimulation (*de la vérité*), *f.*
suppressor [sə'presə], *n.* (*Rad., Tel.*) dispositif anti-parasites, *m.*
suppurate ['sʌpjureit], *v.i.* suppurer.
suppuration [sʌpju'reiʃən], *n.* suppuration, *f.*
supremacy [sju'preməsi], *n.* suprématie, *f.*
supreme [sju'pri:m], *a.* suprême.
supremely [sju'pri:mli], *adv.* suprêmement.
surcharge ['sə:tʃɑ:dʒ], *n.* surcharge, surtaxe, *f.*
sure [ʃuə], *a.* sûr, certain; assuré; *to be sure!* certainement! bien sûr! *to be sure to,* ne pas manquer de.—*adv.* sûrement, à coup sûr.
sure-footed [ʃuə'futid], *a.* au pied sûr.
surely ['ʃuəli], *adv.* sûrement, assurément, à coup sûr.
sureness ['ʃuənis], *n.* certitude, sûreté, *f.*
surety ['ʃuəti], *n.* certitude (*véracité*); sûreté, sécurité (*garantie*), *f.*; (*Law*) garant, *m.*
surf [sə:f], *n.* ressac, *m.*, brisants sur la plage, *m.pl.*
surface ['sə:fis], *n.* surface, *f.*
surfeit ['sə:fit], *n.* rassasiement, *m.*; *to have a surfeit of,* être rassasié de.
surf-riding ['sə:fraidiŋ], *n.* sport de l'aquaplane, planking, surf, *m.*
surge [sə:dʒ], *n.* houle, lame de fond, *f.*—*v.i.* s'enfler, s'élever.
surgeon ['sə:dʒən], *n.* chirurgien, *m.*
surgery ['sə:dʒəri], *n.* chirurgie (*art*), *f.*
surgical ['sə:dʒikl], *a.* chirurgical.
surliness ['sə:linis], *n.* morosité, *f.*

surly ['sə:li], *a.* morose; hargneux (*chien*).
surmise ['sə:maiz], *n.* soupçon, *m.*, conjecture, *f.*—[sə'maiz], *v.t.* soupçonner, conjecturer.
surmount [sə'maunt], *v.t.* surmonter.
surmountable [sə'mauntəbl], *a.* surmontable.
surname ['sə:neim], *n.* nom de famille, *m.*
surpass [sə'pɑ:s], *v.t.* surpasser, l'emporter sur.
surpassable [sə'pɑ:səbl], *a.* qu'on peut surpasser.
surpassing [sə'pɑ:siŋ], *a.* éminent, supérieur, rare.
surplice ['sə:plis], *n.* surplis, *m.*
surplus ['sə:pləs], *a.* de surplus.—*n.* surplus, *m.*; *surplus stock,* solde, *m.*
surprise [sə'praiz], *n.* surprise, *f.*; étonnement, *m.*—*v.t.* surprendre, étonner.
surprising [sə'praiziŋ], *a.* surprenant, étonnant.
surrealism [sə'ri:əlizm], *n.* surréalisme, *m.*
surrender [sə'rendə], *n.* reddition, capitulation, *f.*; abandon (*d'un titre, d'un droit*), *m.*; (*Law*) cession, *f.*—*v.t.* rendre; (*fig.*) abandonner, livrer (*personne etc.*); (*Law*) céder.—*v.i.* se rendre.
surreptitious [sʌrəp'tiʃəs], *a.* subreptice, clandestin; frauduleux.
surreptitiously [sʌrəp'tiʃəsli], *adv.* subrepticement.
surround [sə'raund], *v.t.* entourer, environner (*de*), (*Mil.*) cerner.
surrounding [sə'raundiŋ], *a.* environnant, d'alentour.—*n.* (*pl.*) alentours, environs, *m.pl.*, entourage, milieu, *m.*
surtax ['sə:tæks], *n.* surtaxe, *f.*
survey ['sə:vei], *n.* vue, *f.*, coup d'œil, *m.*; inspection (*examen*); expertise (*évaluation*), *f.*; arpentage (*de terrain etc.*); (*Ordnance*) levé topographique, *m*; *aerial survey,* levé aérophotogrammétrique, *m.*—[sə'vei], *v.t.* arpenter (*terrain*); (*Ordnance*) lever le plan de; (*fig.*) examiner, contempler.
surveying [sə'veiiŋ], *n.* arpentage, levé de plans, *m.*
surveyor [sə'veiə], *n.* inspecteur; arpenteur (*de terrain*); agent voyer (*ponts et chaussées*), *m.*
survival [sə'vaivl], *n.* survivance; survie, *f.*
survive [sə'vaiv], *v.t.* survivre à.—*v.i.* survivre.
surviving [sə'vaiviŋ], *a.* survivant.
survivor [sə'vaivə], *n.* survivant, *m.*
Susan [su:zn]. Suzanne, *f.*
susceptibility [səsepti'biliti], *n.* susceptibilité; sensibilité, *f.*
susceptible [sə'septibl], *a.* susceptible (*de*).
suspect ['sʌspekt], *a.* and *n.* suspect, *m.*—[sə'spekt], *v.t., v.i.* soupçonner.
suspend [sə'spend], *v.t.* suspendre; cesser (*payements*).
suspender [sə'spendə], *n.* (*pl.*) jarretelles (*pour bas*); (*Am.*) bretelles (*pour pantalon*), *f.pl.*
suspense [sə'spens], *n.* suspens, doute, *m.*
suspension [sə'spenʃən], *n.* suspension, *f.*
suspicion [sə'spiʃən], *n.* soupçon, *m.*
suspicious [sə'spiʃəs], *a.* soupçonneux; suspect, louche (*équivoque*).
suspiciously [sə'spiʃəsli], *adv.* avec méfiance; d'une manière suspecte.

suspiciousness [sə'spiʃəsnis], *n.* caractère soupçonneux, *m.*; défiance, méfiance, *f.*

sustain [sə'stein], *v.t.* soutenir, supporter; éprouver, essuyer (*perte*).

sustaining [sə'steiniŋ], *a.* fortifiant, nourrissant.

sustenance ['sʌstinəns], *n.* nourriture, *f.*, aliments, *m.pl.*; entretien, *m.*, subsistance, *f.*

suzerain ['sju:zərein], *a.* and *n.* suzerain, *m.*

suzerainty ['sju:zəreinti], *n.* suzeraineté, *f.*

swab [swɔb], *n.* torchon; (*Naut.*) faubert; tampon (*de coton hydrophile*), *m.*—*v.t.* fauberter; nettoyer.

swaddle [swɔdl], *v.t.* emmailloter.

swaddling ['swɔdliŋ], *n.* emmaillotement, *m.*; **swaddling clothes**, maillot, *m.*

swag [swæg], *n.* (*slang*) butin; (*Australia*) baluchon, *m.*

swagger ['swægə], *v.i.* faire le rodomont; se donner des airs, se vanter.

swaggerer ['swægərə], *n.* fanfaron, *m.*

swaggering ['swægəriŋ], *a.* de fanfaron.—*n.* fanfaronnade, *f.*

swagman ['swægmən], *n.* (*pl.* **-men** [men]) (*Australia*) chemineau, *m.*

swain [swein], *n.* (*poet.*) berger, jeune paysan, *m.*

swallow (1) ['swɔlou], *v.t.* avaler; engloutir (*faire disparaître*); consumer; (*fig.*) gober. —*n.* (*pop.*) avaloir, gosier (*gorge*), *m.*; gorgée (*ce qu'on avale*), *f.*

swallow (2) ['swɔlou], *n.* hirondelle (*oiseau*), *f.*

swallow dive ['swɔloudaiv], *n.* (*Swim.*) saut de l'ange, *m.*

swallower ['swɔlouə], *n.* avaleur, *m.*

swallow-tail ['swɔlouteil], *a.* en queue d'aronde.—*n.* habit à queue de morue, *m.*

swamp [swɔmp], *n.* marais, marécage, *m.*—*v.t.* submerger; faire couler (*bateau*).

swampy ['swɔmpi], *a.* marécageux.

swan [swɔn], *n.* cygne, *m.* [see **swallow dive**]

swank [swæŋk], *n.* pose; (*pop.*) épate, *f.*—*v.i.* (*pop.*) crâner, poser; faire du chiqué.

swanky ['swæŋki], *a.* chic, rupin.

swap [swɔp], *v.t.* (*colloq.*) échanger, troquer. —*n.* troc, échange, *m.*

sward [swɔ:d], *n.* (*poet.*) gazon, *m.*, pelouse, *f.*

swarm [swɔ:m], *n.* essaim (*d'abeilles*), *m.*— *v.i.* essaimer; (*fig.*) accourir en foule.

swarming ['swɔ:miŋ], *n.* essaimage, *m.*

swarthiness ['swɔ:ðinis], *n.* teint basané, *m.*

swarthy ['swɔ:ði], *a.* basané, hâlé.

swashbuckler ['swɔʃbʌklə], *n.* fanfaron, matamore, *m.*

swastika ['swɔstikə], *n.* croix gammée, *f.*

swat [swɔt], *v.t.* écraser, tuer (*mouche*).

swath [swɔ:θ], *n.* andain, *m.*, fauchée, *f.*

swathe [sweið], *v.t.* emmailloter.

sway [swei], *v.t.* manier, porter; balancer (*agiter*); (*fig.*) diriger (*gouverner*); influencer (*l'opinion*).—*v.i.* se balancer.—*n.* empire, *m.*; domination (*règne*), *f.*

swaying ['sweiiŋ], *n.* balancement, *m.*; oscillation, *f.*

swear [swɛə], *v.t. irr.* faire prêter serment à (*témoins etc.*); prêter (*serment*); **to swear at**, injurier.—*v.i.* jurer; prêter serment.

swearer ['swɛərə], *n.* jureur, *m.*

swearing ['swɛəriŋ], *n.* serments; jurons (*gros mots*), *m.pl.*; **swearing in**, prestation de serment, assermentation (*de juges etc.*), *f.*

swear-word ['swɛəwə:d], *n.* juron, gros mot, *m.*

sweat [swet], *n.* sueur, transpiration, *f.*—*v.t.* faire suer.—*v.i.* suer, transpirer.

sweater ['swetə], *n.* chandail, tricot, pullover (*vêtement*), *m.*

sweatiness ['swetinis], *n.* sueur, *f.*, état de sueur, *m.*

sweating ['swetiŋ], *a.* en sueur; tout en sueur. —*n.* moiteur; fatigue, *f.*

sweaty ['sweti], *a.* en sueur.

Swede [swi:d], *n.* Suédois (*personne*), *m.*

swede [swi:d], *n.* (*Bot.*) rutabaga, *m.*

Sweden ['swi:dn], la Suède, *f.*

Swedish ['swi:diʃ], *a.* suédois, de Suède,—*n.* suédois (*langue*), *m.*

sweep [swi:p], *v.t. irr.* balayer; ramoner (*cheminée*); draguer (*rivière*).—*v.i.* passer rapidement.—*n.* coup de balai; ramoneur (*de cheminées*), *m.*; étendue, portée (*distance*), cour'e, *f.*; (*fig.*) sweepstake, *m.*; **to make a clean sweep of**, faire table rase de.

sweeper ['swi:pə], *n.* balayeur; ramoneur (*de cheminées*), *m.*

sweeping ['swi:piŋ], *a.* rapide, irrésistible; (*fig.*) général.—*n.* balayage; ramonage (*de cheminées*), *m.*; (*pl.*) balayures, ordures, *f.pl.*

sweepstake ['swi:psteik], *n.* poule, *f.*; sweepstake, *m.*

sweet [swi:t], *a.* doux, sucré; parfumé (*odeur*); (*Mus.*) suave, mélodieux; frais (*poisson etc.*); (*fig.*) joli, charmant.—*n.* chose douce, *f.*; (*pl.*) entremets, sucreries, *f.pl.*; chéri, *m.*

sweetbread ['swi:tbred], *n.* ris de veau *ou* d'agneau, *m.*

sweeten ['swi:tn], *v.t.* sucrer; purifier (*salle, l'air etc.*); (*fig.*) adoucir.

sweetener ['swi:tnə], *n.* adoucissant, *m.*

sweetening ['swi:tniŋ], *n.* adoucissement, *m.*

sweetheart ['swi:tho:t], *n.* amoureux; amant; bon ami, *m.*

sweetly ['swi:tli], *adv.* doucement, gentiment; mélodieusement.

sweetmeat ['swi:tmi:t], *n.* sucrerie, *f.*, bonbon, *m.*

sweetness ['swi:tnis], *n.* douceur; fraîcheur; mélodie, *f.*; (*fig.*) charme, *m.*

sweet pea ['swi:t'pi:], *n.* pois de senteur, *m.*

sweet shop ['swi:t'ʃɔp], *n.* confiserie, *f.*

sweet william ['swi:t'wiljəm], *n.* œillet de poète, *m.*

swell [swel], *v.t. irr.* enfler, gonfler; aggraver; augmenter (*ajouter à*).—*v.i.* enfler, s'enfler, se gonfler; grossir, croître (*multiplier*); (*fig.*) bouffir (*d'orgueil, de colère etc.*).—*a.* (*colloq.*) à la mode, chic; épatant.—*n.* élévation, montée, *f.*; renflement (*de son*), *m.*; houle (*de mer*), *f.*; (*colloq.*) rupin, élégant, *m.*

swelling ['sweliŋ], *a.* grandissant (*qui augmente*).—*n.* enflure; bouffissure (*pathologique*), *f.*; gonflement (*protubérance*), *m.*, crue (*de rivière*), *f.*; soulèvement (*des vagues*); (*fig.*) mouvement, transport (*de colère etc.*), *m.*

swelter ['sweltə], *v.i.* étouffer de chaleur; **it is sweltering hot**, il fait une chaleur étouffante.

swerve [swə:v], *v.i.* s'écarter, se détourner, faire un écart (*cheval*), faire une embardée (*voiture*).

swerving ['swə:viŋ], *n.* écart, *m.*, déviation, embardée (*de voiture*), *f.*

swift [swift], *a.* vite; rapide, prompt.—*n.* (*Orn.*) martinet, *m.*

swift-footed ['swift'futid], *a.* rapide à la course; au pied léger.

swiftly ['swiftli], *adv.* vite, rapidement.

swiftness ['swiftnis], *n.* rapidité, vitesse, *f.*

swig [swig], *v.t., v.i.* (*pop.*) boire à longs traits. —*n.* long trait (*d'alcool*), *m.*

swill [swil], *v.t.* laver, rincer; boire avidement.—*v.i.* boire; (*colloq.*) s'enivrer.—*n.* lavure de vaisselle, lavure, *f.*; grand coup (*d'alcool*), *m.*

swim [swim], *v.t. irr.* traverser à la nage.— *v.i.* nager; flotter, surnager; (*fam.*) tourner (*la tête*); être inondé (de) (*être submergé*).— *n.* nage, *f.*; **in the swim**, à la page.

swimmer ['swimə], *n.* nageur, *m.*

swimming ['swimiŋ], *n.* natation (*sport*); nage (*action*), *f.*; (*fam.*) étourdissement (*de tête*), *m.*; **by swimming**, à la nage.

swimming baths ['swimiŋbɑːθz], **swimming pool** ['swimiŋpuːl], *n.* piscine, *f.*

swimmingly ['swimiŋli], *adv.* à merveille.

swim-suit ['swimsjuːt], *n.* maillot de bain, *m.*

swindle [swindl], *v.t.* escroquer.—*n.* escroquerie, *f.*

swindler ['swindlə], *n.* escroc, filou, *m.*

swindling ['swindliŋ], *n.* escroquerie, *f.*

swine [swain], *n.inv.* cochon, pourceau, porc; (*pop.*) salaud, *m.*

swing [swiŋ], *v.t. irr.* balancer; brandir (*une arme etc.*).—*v.i.* se balancer; osciller; pendiller, être suspendu.—*n.* oscillation (*mouvement*), *f.*; balancement, *m.*; balançoire (*siège*), *f.*; (*Mus.*) swing, *m.*; **in full swing**, en pleine activité.

swing-door ['swiŋ'dɔː], *n.* porte battante, *f.*

swinging ['swiŋiŋ], *n.* balancement, *m.*, oscillation, *f.*

swipe [swaip], *n.* taloche, *f.*—*v.t.* donner une taloche à; (*fam.*) chiper.

swirl [swəːl], *v.i.* tourbillonner.—*n.* remous, *m.*

swish [swiʃ], *v.t.* cingler, fouetter.—*v.i.* siffler, bruire.

Swiss [swis], *a.* helvétique, suisse.—*n.* Suisse (*personne*), *m.*, Suissesse, *f.*

switch [switʃ], *n.* badine, houssine, gaule; (*Rail.*) aiguille, *f.*; (*Elec.*) commutateur, interrupteur, *m.*—*v.t.* houspiller, cingler; (*Rail.*) aiguiller; changer (*de*); **to switch off**, couper; **to switch on**, ouvrir.—*v.i.* **to switch off**, couper le courant; **to switch on**, mettre le courant.   [see **pointsman**]

switchboard ['switʃbɔːd], *n.* standard (*téléphonique*), *m.*; **switchboard operator**, standardiste, *m.*, *f.*

Switzerland ['switsələnd]. la Suisse, *f.*

swivel [swivl], *n.* émerillon; pivot, *m.*—*v.i.* pivoter.

swoon [swuːn], *v.i.* s'évanouir.—*n.* evanouissement, *m.*

swoop [swuːp], *v.i.* fondre (*sur*).—*n.* **at one (fell) swoop**, d'un seul coup (*fatal*).

sword [sɔːd], *n.* épée, *f.*

sword bearer ['sɔːdbɛərə], *n.* porte-épée, *m.*

sword-fish ['sɔːdfiʃ], *n.* espadon, *m.*

swordsman ['sɔːdzmən], *n.* (*pl.* -**men** [men]) tireur, homme d'épée, *m.*

swordstick ['sɔːdstik], *n.* canne à épée, *f.*

sworn [swɔːn], *a.* juré; (*Law*) assermenté; acharné (*ennemi*).

swot [swɔt], *v.i.* (*Sch. slang*) piocher, bûcher.— *n.* bûcheur, *m.*

sycamore ['sikəmɔː], *n.* sycomore, *m.*

sycophancy ['sikəfənsi], *n.* adulation, *f.*

sycophant ['sikəfənt], *n.* adulateur, *m.*

sycophantic [sikə'fæntik], *a.* adulateur, *m.*

syllabic [si'læbik], *a.* syllabique.

syllable ['siləbl], *n.* syllabe, *f.*

syllabus ['siləbəs], *n.* résumé; sommaire, programme (*surtout d'études scolaires*), *m.*

syllogism ['silədʒizm], *n.* syllogisme, *m.*

sylph [silf], *n.* sylphe, *m.*

sylvan ['silvən], *a.* sylvestre, des bois, champêtre, agreste.

symbol [simbl], *n.* symbole, *m.*

symbolic [sim'bɔlik], **symbolical** [sim'bɔlikl], *a.* symbolique.

symbolism ['simbəlizm], *n.* symbolisme, *m.*

symbolize ['simbəlaiz], *v.t., v.i.* symboliser.

symmetrical [si'metrikl], *a.* symétrique.

symmetry ['simitri], *n.* symétrie, *f.*

sympathetic [simpə'θetik], *a.* sympathique (*nerf*); compatissant.

sympathize ['simpəθaiz], *v.i.* sympathiser (*avec*); compatir (*à*).

sympathizer ['simpəθaizə], *n.* sympathisant, *m.*

sympathy ['simpəθi], *n.* sympathie; compréhension, *f.*; condoléances, *f.pl.*

symphony ['simfəni], *n.* symphonie, *f.*

symposium [sim'pouzjəm], *n.* (*fig.*) recueil d'articles (*sur un seul sujet*), *m.*

symptom ['simptəm], *n.* symptôme, *m.*

symptomatic [simptə'mætik], *a.* symptomatique.

synagogue ['sinəgɔg], *n.* synagogue, *f.*

synchromesh ['siŋkromeʃ], *a.* and *n.* synchromesh, *m.*

synchronize ['siŋkrənaiz], *v.i.* synchroniser (*avec*).

syncopate ['siŋkəpeit], *v.t.* syncoper.

syndic ['sindik], *n.* syndic, *m.*

syndicate ['sindikit], *n.* syndicat, *m.*—['sindikeit], *v.t.* syndiquer.—*v.i.* se syndiquer.

synod ['sinəd], *n.* synode, *m.*

synonym ['sinənim], *n.* synonyme, *m.*

synonymous [si'nɔniməs], *a.* synonyme.

synopsis [si'nɔpsis], *n.* (*pl.* **synopses** [si'nɔpsiːz]) sommaire, *m.*

syntax ['sintæks], *n.* syntaxe, *f.*

synthesis ['sinθisis], *n.* (*pl.* **syntheses** ['sinθisiːz]) synthèse, *f.*

synthesize ['sinθisaiz], *v.t.* synthétiser.

synthetic [sin'θetik], *a.* synthétique.

synthetically [sin'θetikli], *adv.* synthétiquement.

Syria ['siriə]. la Syrie, *f.*

Syriac ['siriæk], *a.* syriaque.—*n.* syriaque (*langue*), *m.*

Syrian ['siriən], *a.* syrien.—*n.* syrien (*langue*); Syrien (*personne*), *m.*

syringe ['sirindʒ], *n.* seringue, *f.*—*v.t.* seringuer.

syrup ['sirəp], *n.* sirop, *m.*

syrupy ['sirəpi], *a.* sirupeux.

system ['sistəm], *n.* système, régime; réseau (*ferroviaire*), *m.*

systematic [sistə'mætik], *a.* systématique.
systematically [sistə'mætikli], *adv.* systématiquement.
systematize ['sistəmətaiz], *v.t.* systématiser.

T

T, t [tiː]. vingtième lettre de l'alphabet, *m.*; *T-square*, té à dessin, *m.*

tab [tæb], *n.* étiquette; patte, *f.*, écusson, *m.*

tabby ['tæbi], *a.* tacheté, moucheté.—*n.* chat moucheté, rayé *ou* tigré, *m.*

tabernacle ['tæbənækl], *n.* tabernacle, *m.*

table [teibl], *n.* table, *f.*; *to be seated at table*, être attablé; *to clear the table*, desservir; *to lay the table*, mettre le couvert; *to sit down to table*, se mettre à table.—*v.t.* déposer (*un projet de loi*).

table-cloth ['teiblklɔθ], *n.* nappe, *f.*

table linen ['teibllinin], *n.* linge de table, *m.*

tablespoon ['teiblspuːn], *n.* cuiller à soupe, *f.*

tablespoonful ['teiblspuːnful], *n.* grande cuillerée, *f.*

tablet ['tæblit], *n.* tablette, *f.*; (*Med.*) comprimé, *m.*

taboo [tə'buː], *a.* and *n.* tabou, *m.*

tabulate ['tæbjuleit], *v.t.* cataloguer.

tacit ['tæsit], *a.* tacite, implicite.

tacitly ['tæsitli], *adv.* tacitement, implicitement.

taciturn ['tæsitə:n], *a.* taciturne.

Tacitus ['tæsitəs]. (*L. Lit.*) Tacite, *m.*

tack [tæk], *n.* petit clou, *m.*, broquette; (*Naut.*) amure, *f.*—*v.t.* clouer; (*Needlework*) bâtir, faufiler.—*v.i.* (*Naut.*) virer vent devant.

tackiness ['tækinis], *n.* viscosité, *f.*

tacking ['tækiŋ], *n.* cloutage, *m.*; (*Needlework*) faufilure, *f.*; (*Naut.*) virement de bord, louvoyage, *m.*

tackle [tækl], *n.* attirail; (*Naut.*) palan; (*Spt.*) plaquage, *m.*; (*fig.*) ustensiles, *m.pl.*; *fishing tackle*, articles de pêche, *m.pl.*—*v.t.* empoigner; (*Ftb.*) plaquer; (*fig.*) attaquer (*travail etc.*).

tacky ['tæki], *a.* collant, visqueux, gluant.

tact [tækt], *n.* toucher; (*fig.*) tact, savoir-faire, *m.*

tactful ['tæktful], *a.* plein de tact.

tactical ['tæktikl], *a.* tactique.

tactician [tæk'tiʃən], *n.* tacticien, *m.*

tactics ['tæktiks], *n.pl.* tactique, *f.*

tactile ['tæktail], *a.* tactile.

tactless ['tæktlis], *a.* sans tact, sans savoir-faire.

tadpole ['tædpoul], *n.* têtard, *m.*

taffeta ['tæfitə], *n.* taffetas, *m.*

taffrail ['tæfreil], *n.* couronnement (*de la poupe*), *m.*

tag [tæg], *n.* ferret, fer, bout ferré, *m.*; étiquette (*fiche*), *f.*; dicton, *m.*—*v.t.* ferrer (*cordon*); (*fig.*) coudre (à).

tail [teil], *n.* queue; (*fig.*) extrémité, *f.*; bout; pan (*d'habit*), *m.*; pile (*de pièce de monnaie*), *f.*; empennage (*d'avion*), *m.*—*v.t.* couper la queue (*d'un animal*); ôter les queues (*de fruits*); (*fam.*) filer (*criminels etc.*).

tail coat ['teilkout], *n.* habit, *m.*

tailed [teild], *a.* à queue.

tailless ['teillis], *a.* sans queue, anoure.

tail-light ['teillait], *n.* feu arrière, *m.*

tailor ['teilə], *n.* tailleur, *m.*

tailor-made ['teilə'meid], *a.* and *n.* tailleur, *m.*

tail-plane ['teilplein], *n.* (*Av.*) stabilisateur, *m.*

taint [teint], *v.t.* corrompre, gâter.—*v.i.* se corrompre; se gâter (*viande*).—*n.* souillure, corruption; tache (*du péché*), *f.*

take [teik], *v.t.* irr. prendre; mener (*quelqu'un*); conduire (*personne en voiture*); porter (*chose*); emmener (*quelqu'un*); enlever (*voler*); soustraire (*retrancher*); saisir; accepter; (*fig.*) supposer; profiter de (*une occasion*); contenir (*avoir de la place pour*); faire (*une promenade etc.*); avoir (*vengeance etc.*); retenir (*chambre etc.*); suivre (*une route etc.*); mettre (*temps*); *to take advantage of*, profiter de; *to take away*, emmener (*personne*), emporter (*choses*), ôter (*retirer*); desservir (*le couvert etc.*); dérober (*voler*); *to take back*, reprendre, remporter; *to take down*, descendre; rabattre (*humilier*); démolir (*maison*); prendre note de (*inscrire*); *to take heed*, prendre garde (à); *to take in*, faire entrer; comprendre (*consister en*); recevoir, recevoir chez soi (*loger*); tromper, duper; faire sa provision de (*vivres etc.*); *to take off*, enlever, ôter, retirer (*vêtement*); caricaturer (*imiter*); *to take out*, faire sortir, sortir (*chose*); promener (*personne*); arracher (*dents*); ôter, enlever (*taches etc.*); *to take over*, se charger de, prendre la succession de (*affaires*); *to take up*, monter, faire monter, soulever (*lever*); ramasser (*relever*); commencer, entamer, aborder (*des études etc.*); occuper (*temps*).—*v.i.* réussir (*avoir du succès*); prendre (*feu etc.*); *to take after*, ressembler à; (*Av.*) *to take off*, décoller; (*fam.*) *to take on*, se lamenter, s'affliger; *to take up with*, s'associer à.—*n.* prise, pêche, quantité (*de poissons*); (*Cine.*) prise de vue, *f.*

take-in ['teikin], *n.* duperie, attrape, *f.*

take-off ['teikɔ:f], *n.* caricature, charge, *f.*; (*Av.*) décollage, *m.*

take-over ['teikouvə], *n.* (*Fin.*) rachat (*d'entreprise*), *m.*; *take-over bid*, offre de rachat, *f.*

taking ['teikiŋ], *a.* attrayant, séduisant; (*colloq.*) contagieux (*maladie*).—*n.* prise; arrestation, *f.*; (*pl.*) recettes (*argent*), *f.pl.*

talc [tælk], *n.* talc, *m.*

talcum powder ['tælkəm'paudə], *n.* talc, *m.*

tale [teil], *n.* conte, récit, *m.*; histoire, *f.*

talent ['tælənt], *n.* talent, *m.*

talented ['tæləntid], *a.* de talent, habile, bien doué.

talisman ['tælizmən], *n.* talisman, *m.*

talk [tɔːk], *v.t.* parler, dire; *to talk over*, cajoler (*quelqu'un*); discuter (*quelque chose*). —*v.i.* parler (*de*); converser, causer; bavarder, jaser (*babiller*); *to talk at*, haranguer.—*n.* entretien, *m.*, propos, *m.pl.*, conversation; causerie (*intime*), *f.*; bavardage, bruit (*racontar*), *m.*; *small talk*, banalités, *f.pl.*

talkative ['tɔːkətiv], *a.* causeur, bavard.

talker ['tɔːkə], *n.* causeur, parleur, *m.*
talking ['tɔːkiŋ], *a.* causeur, bavard.—*n.* conversation, causerie, *f.*
tall [tɔːl], *a.* grand (*personne*); haut (*chose*).
tallboy ['tɔːlbɔi], *n.* chiffonnier, *m.*; (haute) commode-secrétaire, *f.*
tallness ['tɔːlnis], *n.* grande taille, hauteur, *f.*
tallow ['tælou], *n.* suif, *m.*
tallow-candle ['tælou'kændl], *n.* chandelle, *f.*
tally ['tæli], *n.* taille; entaille, marque; étiquette (*à bagages*), *f.*—*v.i.* s'accorder; **to tally with,** s'accorder avec, correspondre à.
tally-ho! ['tæli'hou], *int.* (*Hunt.*) taïaut!
Talmud ['tælmʌd], *n.* talmud, *m.*
talon ['tælən], *n.* serre, griffe, *f.*
tambourine [tæmbə'riːn], *n.* tambour de basque, *m.*
tame [teim], *a.* apprivoisé; domestique; (*fig.*) insipide.—*v.t.* apprivoiser; dompter (*dominer*).
tamely ['teimli], *adv.* avec soumission; sans cœur.
tameness ['teimnis], *n.* apprivoisement, *m.*, domesticité; soumission; (*fig.*) faiblesse (*de style etc.*), *f.*
tamer ['teimə], *n.* dompteur (*de bête sauvage*) *m.*
taming ['teimiŋ], *n.* apprivoisement, *m.*
tamp [tæmp], *v.t.* bourrer, tamponner.
tamper ['tæmpə], *v.i.* **to tamper with,** se mêler (*de*); expérimenter (*avec*); jouer avec; fausser (*serrure etc.*).
tampering ['tæmpəriŋ], *n.* menées secrètes, *f.pl.*
tan [tæn], *n.* tan; tanné (*couleur*); hâle (*de la peau*), *m.*—*v.t.* tanner; bronzer (*la peau*).
tandem ['tændəm], *n.* tandem (*bicyclette*), *m.*
tang [tæŋ], *n.* goût, *m.*, saveur, *f.*
tangent ['tændʒənt], *n.* tangente, *f.*
tangerine [tændʒə'riːn], *n.* mandarine, *f.*
tangible ['tændʒibl], *a.* tangible, palpable.
Tangier(s) [tæn'dʒiə(z)]. Tanger, *m.*
tangle [tæŋgl], *n.* enchevêtrement, *m.*—*v.t.* embrouiller, enchevêtrer.
tangled [tæŋgld], *a.* embrouillé.
tango ['tæŋgou], *n.* tango, *m.*
tank [tæŋk], *n.* réservoir (*bain*), *m.*; (*Mil.*) char (d'assaut), *m.*
tankard ['tæŋkəd], *n.* chope, *f.*
tanker ['tæŋkə], *n.* bateau citerne, *m.*
tanner ['tænə], *n.* tanneur, *m.*
tannery ['tænəri], *n.* tannerie, *f.*
tanning ['tæniŋ], *n.* tannage, *m.*; (*fam.*) rossée, *f.*
tantalize ['tæntəlaiz], *v.t.* tantaliser, tourmenter.
tantalizing ['tæntəlaiziŋ], *a.* tentant, torturant.
tantamount ['tæntəmaunt], *a.* équivalent (*à*).
tantrum ['tæntrəm], *n.* mauvaise humeur, *f.*
Tanzania [tænzə'niːə]. la Tanzanie, *f.*
tap (1) [tæp], *n.* robinet (*bain*); comptoir (*bar*), *m.*; cannelle (*de baril*), *f.*; taraud (*outil*), *m.*; **on tap,** en perce.—*v.t.* tirer (*liquide*); mettre en perce (*baril*); inciser (*arbre*); tarauder (*vis etc.*); (*Surg.*) faire la ponction à.
tap (2) [tæp], *n.* tape, *f.*, petit coup (*à la porte etc.*), *m.*—*v.t.* taper, frapper doucement.—*v.i.* taper, frapper.
tape [teip], *n.* ruban (*de fil*), *m.*; ganse (*sur habit*); bande (*magnétique*), *f.*; **red tape,** (*fig.*) routine administrative, *f.*

tape measure ['teipmeʒə], *n.* mètre ruban, *m.*
taper ['teipə], *n.* bougie effilée, *f.*; (*Eccles.*) cierge, *m.*
tape recorder ['teiprikɔːdə], *n.* magnétophone, *m.*
tape recording ['teiprikɔːdiŋ], *n.* enregistrement magnétique, *m.*
tapering ['teipəriŋ], *a.* effilé.
tapestry ['tæpistri], *n.* tapisserie, *f.*
tape-worm ['teipwəːm], *n.* ver solitaire, *m.*
tapioca [tæpi'oukə], *n.* tapioca, *m.*
tapir ['teipiə], *n.* tapir, *m.*
tappet ['tæpit], *n.* taquet (*de soupape*), *m.*
tapping (1) ['tæpiŋ], *n.* taraudage (*de vis*), *m.*; mise en perce (*de baril*); incision (*d'arbre*); (*Surg.*) ponction, *f.*
tapping (2) ['tæpiŋ], *n.* tapotement, *m.*
tar [tɑː], *n.* goudron; loup de mer (*matelot*), *m.* —*v.t.* goudronner.
tarantella [tærən'telə], *n.* tarentelle (*danse*), *f.*
tarantula [tə'ræntjulə], *n.* tarentule, *f.*
tardily ['tɑːdili], *adv.* tardivement, lentement.
tardiness ['tɑːdinis], *n.* lenteur, *f.*; tardiveté (*de fruit*), *f.*
tardy ['tɑːdi], *a.* lent; en retard, tardif.
tare (1) [tɛə], *n.* tare (*poids*), *f.*
tare (2) [tɛə], *n.* (*Script.*) ivraie; (*pl.*) (*Agric.*) vesce, *f.*
target ['tɑːgit], *n.* cible, *f.*; but, objectif, *m.*
tariff ['tærif], *n.* tarif, *m.*
tarmac ['tɑːmæk], *n.* macadam, *m.*; (*Av.*) piste d'envol, *f.*—*v.t.* goudronner.
tarn [tɑːn], *n.* petit lac (*de montagne*), *m.*
tarnish ['tɑːniʃ], *v.t.* ternir; (*fig.*) souiller, flétrir.—*v.i.* se ternir.
tarpaulin [tɑː'pɔːlin], *n.* (*Naut.*) prélart, *m.*, bâche, toile goudronnée, *f.*
tarry (1) ['tɑːri], *a.* goudronneux, bitumeux.
tarry (2) ['tæri], *v.i.* rester, tarder.
tart (1) [tɑːt], *n.* tarte, tourte, *f.*
tart (2) [tɑːt], *a.* acide, âcre; (*fig.*) aigre.
tartan ['tɑːtən], *n.* tartan, *m.*
tartar ['tɑːtə], *n.* (*Chem.*) tartre, *m.*
tartaric [tɑː'tærik], *a.* tartrique, *f.*
tartish ['tɑːtiʃ], *a.* aigrelet.
tartly ['tɑːtli], *adv.* avec aigreur; (*fig.*) vertement, sévèrement.
tartness ['tɑːtnis], *n.* acidité; (*fig.*) aigreur, *f.*
task [tɑːsk], *n.* tâche, *f.*; devoir (*de*); pensum (*punition*), *m.*; **to take to task,** réprimander, semoncer.
taskmaster ['tɑːskmɑːstə], *n.* chef de corvée, *m.*

Tasmania [tæz'meinjə]. la Tasmanie, *f.*
Tasmanian [tæz'meinjən], *a.* tasmanien.—*n.* Tasmanien (*personne*), *m.*
tassel [tæsl], *n.* gland, *m.*
taste [teist], *v.t.* goûter; (*fig.*) savourer, éprouver.—*v.i.* goûter (*de*); avoir un goût (*de*).—*n.* goût; soupçon (*trace*), *m.*
tasteful ['teistful], *a.* de bon goût.
tastefully ['teistfuli], *adv.* avec goût.
tasteless ['teistlis], *a.* fade, insipide.
tastelessly ['teistlisli], *adv.* insipidement, fadement.
taster ['teistə], *n.* dégustateur, *m.*
tasting ['teistiŋ], *n.* dégustation, *f.*
tasty ['teisti], *a.* (*colloq.*) de bon goût; savoureux.

tatter ['tætə], *n.* haillon, lambeau, *m.*, guenille, *f.*

tattered ['tætəd], *a.* déguenillé, en haillons (*personne*); en lambeaux, tout déchiré (*vêtements etc.*).

tatting ['tætiŋ], *n.* frivolité (*dentelle*), *f.*

tattle [tætl], *n.* babil, caquet, *m.*—*v.i.* bavarder.

tattler ['tætlə], *n.* babillard, bavard, *m.*

tattling ['tætliŋ], *a.* babillard, bavard.

tattoo [tə'tu:], *v.t.* tatouer.—*n.* tatouage, *m.*; (*Mil.*) fête militaire, *f.*

taunt [[tɔ:nt], *n.* injure, *f.*, reproche amer, *m.* —*v.t.* tancer, reprocher à, injurier.

tauntingly ['tɔ:ntiŋli], *adv.* injurieusement.

Taurus ['tɔ:rəs]. (*Astron.*) le Taureau, *m.*

taut [tɔ:t], *a.* raide, tendu; enflé (*voile*).

tautology [tɔ:'tɔlədʒi], *n.* tautologie, *f.*

tavern ['tævən], *n.* taverne, *f.*; cabaret, *m.*

tawdry ['tɔ:dri], *a.* criard, de mauvais goût, prétentieux.

tawny ['tɔ:ni], *a.* fauve.

tawse [tɔ:z], *n.* martinet, *m.*

tax [tæks], *n.* impôt, *m.*, taxe; (*fig.*) contribution, *f.*; *income tax*, impôt sur le revenu; *purchase tax*, taxe de luxe; *tax evasion*, fraude fiscale, *f.*; *surtax*, surtaxe, *f.*—*v.t.* imposer, taxer; (*fig.*) accuser (*de*).

taxable ['tæksəbl], *a.* imposable.

taxation [tæk'seiʃən], *n.* taxation, *f.*

tax-free ['tæks'fri:], *a.* exempt d'impôts.

taxi ['tæksi], *n.* taxi, *m.*

tax-payer ['tækspeiə], *n.* contribuable, *m.*, *f.*

tea [ti:], *n.* thé, *m.*; tisane (*infusion*), *f.*; goûter (*repas*), *m.*

tea caddy ['ti:kædi], *n.* boîte à thé, *f.*

tea cake ['ti:keik], *n.* brioche, *f.*

teach [ti:tʃ], *v.t. irr.* enseigner, instruire; apprendre (*à*).—*v.i.* enseigner, professer.

teachable ['ti:tʃəbl], *a.* disposé à apprendre, docile; enseignable (*chose*).

teacher ['ti:tʃest], *n.* maître, instituteur; professeur (*de lycée*), *m.*

tea chest ['ti:tʃest], *n.* caisse à thé, *f.*

teaching ['ti:tʃiŋ], *n.* enseignement, *m.*

tea-cup ['ti:kʌp], *n.* tasse à thé, *f.*

teak [ti:k], *n.* (*Bot.*) teck, tek, *m.*

teal [ti:l], *n.* (*Orn.*) sarcelle, *f.*

team [ti:m], *n.* attelage, *m.*, (*Spt.*) équipe, *f.*

teapot ['ti:pɔt], *n.* théière, *f.*

tear (1) [tiə], *n.* larme, *f.*, pleur, *m.*

tear (2) [tɛə], *v.t. irr.* déchirer; (*fig.*) arracher; *to tear asunder*, déchirer en deux.—*v.i.* se déchirer.—*n.* déchirure, *f.*; *wear and tear*, usure, *f.*

tear-drop ['tiədrɔp], *n.* larme, *f.*

tearful ['tiəful], *a.* tout en larmes.

tearfully ['tiəfuli], *adv.* les larmes aux yeux.

tearing ['tɛəriŋ], *n.* déchirement, *m.*

tease [ti:z], *v.t.* taquiner, tourmenter; carder (*laine*).—*n.* taquin, *m.*

tea service ['ti:sə:vis], *n.* service à thé, *m.*

teasing ['ti:ziŋ], *a.* taquin.—*n.* taquinerie, *f.*

teaspoon ['ti:spu:n], *n.* cuiller à thé, *f.*

teaspoonful ['ti:spu:nful], *n.* petite cuillerée, *f.*

tea strainer ['ti:streinə], *n.* passe-thé, *m.*

teat [ti:t], *n.* mamelon, tétin, *m.*; tette, *f.*

tea table ['ti:teibl], *n.* table à thé, *f.*

tea time ['ti:taim], *n.* l'heure du thé, *f.*

tea tray ['ti:trei], *n.* plateau à thé, *m.*

tea urn ['ti:ə:n], *n.* fontaine à thé, *f.*

technical ['teknikl], *a.* technique, de l'art; *technical school*, école professionnelle, *f.*

technicality [tekni'kæliti], *n.* caractère technique; terme technique (*mot*), *m.*; (*fig.*) formalité, *f.*

technically ['teknikli], *adv.* techniquement.

technician [tek'niʃən], *n.* technicien, *m.*

technique [tek'ni:k], *n.* technique, *f.*

technologist [tek'nɔlədʒist], *n.* technologue, *m.*, *f.*

technology [tek'nɔlədʒi], *n.* technologie, *f.*

teddy ['tedi], *n.* *teddy bear*, ours en peluche, *m.*

tedious ['ti:diəs], *a.* ennuyeux, fatigant.

tedium ['ti:diəm], *n.* ennui, *m.*

tee [ti:], *n.* dé (*au golf*), *m.*

teem [ti:m], *v.i.* être fécond (*en*); *to teem with*, abonder en.

teeming ['ti:miŋ], *a.* fécond, fertile, surabondant (*de*).

teenager ['ti:neidʒə], *n.* adolescent, *m.*

teens [ti:nz], *n.pl.* l'âge de treize à dix-neuf ans, *m.*; *to be in one's teens*, n'avoir pas vingt ans.

teeth [TOOTH].

teethe [ti:ð], *v.i.* faire ses dents.

teething ['ti:ðiŋ], *n.* dentition, *f.*

teetotal [ti:'toutl], *a.* de tempérance.

teetotal(l)er [ti:'toutlə], *n.* buveur d'eau, *m.*

teetotalism [ti:'toutlizm], *n.* abstinence de boissons alcooliques, *f.*

telegram ['teligræm], *n.* télégramme, *m.*, dépêche, *f.*

telegraph ['teligra:f, -græf], *n.* télégraphe, *m.*; *telegraph office*, bureau télégraphique, *m.*—*v.t.*, *v.i.* télégraphier.

telegraphic [teli'græfik], *a.* télégraphique.

telegraphist [ti'legrəfist], *n.* télégraphiste, *m.*, *f.*

telegraph post ['teligra:fpoust], **telegraph pole** ['teligra:fpoul], *n.* poteau télégraphique, *m.*

telegraph wire ['teligrəfwaiə], *n.* fil télégraphique, *m.*

telegraphy [ti'legrəfi], *n.* télégraphie, *f.*; *wireless telegraphy*, télégraphie sans fil.

telepathy [ti'lepəθi], *n.* télépathie, *f.*

telephone ['telifoun], *n.* téléphone, *m.*; *telephone exchange*, central téléphonique, *m.*; *telephone booth*, cabine téléphonique, *f.*; *telephone operator*, téléphoniste, *m.*, *f.* —*v.t.*, *v.i.* téléphoner.

telephonic [teli'fɔnik], *a.* téléphonique.

teleprinter ['teliprintə], *n.* téléimprimeur, télétype, *m.*

telescope ['teliskoup], *n.* (*Astron.*) télescope, *m.*; longue vue, *f.*

telescopic [teli'skɔpik], *a.* télescopique.

televiewer ['telivju:ə], *n.* téléspectateur, *m.*

televise ['telivaiz], *v.t.* téléviser.

television ['teliviʒən], *n.* télévision, *f.*; *television set*, téléviseur, appareil de télévision, *m.*

tell [tel], *v.t. irr.* dire; faire part de; raconter (*réciter*); montrer, indiquer (*expliquer*); révéler, dévoiler, énumérer (*compter*); avouer (*confesser*); reconnaître (*à*); savoir (*deviner*).—*v.i.* dire; faire son effet, porter (*influer*); juger (*interpréter*).

teller ['telə], *n.* diseur; raconteur; (*Am.*, *Sc.*) caissier (*de banque*); (*Parl.*) scrutateur, *m.*

telling ['teliŋ], *a.* qui porte; expressif.—*n.* récit, *m.*, narration, *f.*

tell-tale ['telteil], *a.* rapporteur; (*fig.*) révélateur.—*n.* rapporteur, *m.* témérité, *f.*

temerity [ti'meriti], *n.* témérité, *f.*

temper ['tempə], *n.* tempérament, *m.*, disposition; humeur; colère (*rage*), *f.*; sangfroid (*équanimité*), *m.*; trempe (*d'acier etc.*), *f.*; *to lose one's temper*, se mettre en colère.—*v.t.* tempérer (*de*); détremper (*couleurs*); tremper (*acier etc.*); (*fig.*) adoucir.

temperament ['tempərəmənt], *n.* tempérament, *m.*

temperamental [tempərə'mentl], *a.* capricieux, instable.

temperance ['tempərəns], *n.* tempérance, *f.*

temperate ['tempərit], *a.* modéré, tempéré (*climat*).

temperature ['tempritʃə], *n.* température, *f.*

tempest ['tempist], *n.* tempête, *f.*

tempestuous [tem'pestjuəs], *a.* orageux, tempétueux.

templar ['templə], *n.* templier, *m.*

temple [templ], *n.* temple, *m.*; (*Anat.*) tempe, *f.*

templet ['templit], *n.* patron, gabarit, *m.*

temporal ['tempərəl], *a.* temporel; (*Anat.*) temporal.

temporarily ['tempərərili], *adv.* temporairement.

temporary ['tempərəri], *a.* temporaire, provisoire.

temporization [tempərai'zeiʃən], *n.* temporisation, *f.*

temporize ['tempəraiz], *v.i.* temporiser.

tempt [tempt], *v.t.* tenter (*de*); pousser (*à*).

temptation [temp'teiʃən], *n.* tentation, *f.*

tempter ['temptə], *n.* tentateur, *m.*

tempting ['temptiŋ], *a.* tentant, séduisant, attrayant; appétissant (*nourriture*).

temptress ['temptris], *n.* tentatrice, *f.*

ten [ten], *a.* dix.—*n.* dix, *m.*; une dizaine (*dix environ*), *f.*

tenable ['tenəbl], *a.* soutenable.

tenacious [ti'neiʃəs], *a.* tenace.

tenaciously [ti'neiʃəsli], *adv.* d'une manière tenace, obstinément.

tenacity [ti'næsiti], *n.* ténacité, *f.*

tenancy ['tenənsi], *n.* location, *f.*

tenant ['tenənt], *n.* locataire, *m.*, *f.*

tench [tentʃ], *n.* (*Ichth.*) tanche, *f.*

tend [tend], *v.t.* garder, soigner.—*v.i.* tendre (*à*); se diriger vers.

tendency ['tendənsi], *n.* tendance, disposition, *f.*

tender (1) ['tendə], *n.* offre (*proposition*); (*Comm.*) soumission, *f.*; *legal tender*, monnaie légale, *f.*—*v.t.* offrir.—*v.i.* *to tender for*, soumissionner pour.

tender (2) ['tendə], *n.* (*Naut.*) allège, *f.*; (*Rail.*) tender, *m.*

tender (3) ['tendə], *a.* tendre; sensible (*vulnérable*).

tender-hearted ['tendə'ha:tid], *a.* sensible, au cœur tendre.

tenderly ['tendəli], *adv.* tendrement.

tenderness ['tendənis], *n.* tendresse; sensibilité (*vulnérabilité*); sollicitude, *f.*

tendon ['tendən], *n.* tendon, *m.*

tendril ['tendril], *n.* (*Bot.*) vrille, *f.*

tenement ['tenimənt], *n.* habitation, maison, *f.*

tenet ['ti:nit, 'tenit], *n.* principe, *m.*

tenfold ['tenfould], *a.* décuple.—*adv.* dix fois.

tennis ['tenis], *n.* tennis; •jeu de paume, *f.*

tennis court ['teniskɔ:t], *n.* court de tennis, tennis; •jeu de paume, *m.*

tennis racket ['tenisrækit], *n.* raquette de tennis, *f.*

tenor ['tenə], *n.* (*Mus.*) ténor, *m.*

tense (1) [tens], *n.* (*Gram.*) temps, *m.*

tense (2) [tens], *a.* tendu, raide.

tensile ['tensail], *a.* ductile (*métal*).

tension ['tenʃən], *n.* tension, *f.*

tent [tent], *n.* tente, *f.*; *bell tent*, tente conique.

tentacle ['tentəkl], *n.* tentacule, *m.*

tentative ['tentətiv], *a.* tentatif, d'essai.

tentatively ['tentətivli], *adv.* en guise d'essai.

tenter-hook ['tentəhuk], *n.* clou à crochet, *m.*; *to be on tenter-hooks*, être sur des épines.

tenth [tenθ], *a.* dixième; dix (*du mois, roi etc.*).—*n.* dixième (*fraction*), *m.*; (*Eccles.*) dîme, *f.*

tenuous ['tenjuəs], *a.* délié, mince, ténu.

tenure ['tenjuə], *n.* tenure, *f.*

tepid ['tepid], *a.* tiède.

tercentenary [tə:'sen'ti:nəri], *a.* de trois siècles.—*n.* tricentenaire, *m.*

term [tə:m], *n.* terme, *m.*; limite; (*Law*) session, *f.*; (*Sch.*) trimestre, *m.*; (*pl.*) conditions, *f.pl.*; prix, *m.*—*v.t.* nommer, appeler.

termagant ['tə:məgənt], *n.* mégère, *f.*

terminable ['tə:minəbl], *a.* terminable.

terminal ['tə:minl], *a.* terminal.—*n.* (*Elec.*) borne, *f.*; *air terminal*, gare aérienne, aérogare, *f.*

terminate ['tə:mineit], *v.t.* terminer, finir.

termination [tə:mi'neiʃən], *n.* fin, terminaison, *f.*

terminology [tə:mi'nɔlədʒi], *n.* terminologie, *f.*

terminus ['tə:minəs], *n.* terminus (*gare*), *m.*; tête de ligne, *f.*

tern [tə:n], *n.* sterne, *m.*, hirondelle de mer, *f.*

ternary ['tə:nəri], *a.* ternaire.

terrace ['teris], *n.* terrasse, *f.*

terraced ['terist], *a.* étagé en terrasse.

terra cotta ['terə'kɔtə], *n.* terre cuite, *f.*

terra firma ['terə'fə:mə], *n.* terre ferme, *f.*

terrestrial [tə'restriəl], *a.* terrestre.

terrible ['teribl], *a.* terrible.

terribly ['teribli], *adv.* terriblement; (*colloq.*) diablement.

terrier ['teriə], *n.* terrier, chien terrier, *m.*

terrific [tə'rifik], *a.* terrible, épouvantable; (*fam.*) formidable.

terrify ['terifai], *v.t.* terrifier.

territorial [teri'tɔ:riəl], *a.* territorial.

territory ['teritəri], *n.* territoire, *m.*

terror ['terə], *n.* terreur, *f.*; effroi, *m.*

terrorism ['terərizm], *n.* terrorisme, *m.*

terrorist ['terərist], *n.* terroriste, *m.*, *f.*

terrorize ['terəraiz], *v.t.* terroriser.

terse [tə:s], *a.* net, concis; bien tourné, élégant.

tersely ['tə:sli], *adv.* nettement; d'une manière concise.

terseness ['tə:snis], *n.* netteté, *f.*

tertian ['tə:ʃən], *a.* tierce.

tertiary ['tə:ʃəri], *a.* tertiaire.

tessellated [tesə'leitid], *a.* tessellé.

593

test [test], *n.* épreuve, *f.*; test; essai, *m.*; pierre de touche, *f.*—*v.t.* éprouver, mettre à l'épreuve, tester; (*Metal.*) coupeller.
testament ['testəmənt], *n.* testament, *m.*
testator [tes'teitə], *n.* testateur, *m.*
testicle ['testikl], *n.* testicule, *m.*
testify ['testifai], *v.t.* témoigner; (*Law*) déposer (*de*).—*v.i.* (*Law*) déposer.
testimonial [testi'mouniəl], *n.* témoignage; certificat, témoignage d'estime, *m.*
testimony ['testiməni], *n.* témoignage, *m.*
testiness ['testinis], *n.* humeur, irritabilité, *f.*
testing ['testiŋ], *n.* épreuve, *f.*, essai, *m.*
test tube ['testtju:b], *n.* éprouvette, *f.*
testy ['testi], *a.* irritable, susceptible.
tetanus ['tetənəs], *n.* tétanos, *m.*
tether ['teðə], *n.* longe, *f.*; *to be at the end of one's tether,* être à bout de forces.—*v.t.* mettre à l'attache, attacher (*à*).
tetrahedron [tetrə'hi:drən], *n.* tétraèdre, *m.*
tetrarch ['tetra:k], *n.* tétrarque, *m.*
Teuton ['tju:tən], *a.* teuton.—*n.* Teuton (*personne*), *m.*
Teutonic [tju:'tonik], *a.* teutonique.
text [tekst], *n.* texte, *m.*
text-book ['tekstbuk], *n.* manuel, livre de classe, *m.*
textile ['tekstail], *a.* textile.—*n.* tissu, textile, *m.*, étoffe, *f.*
textual ['tekstjuəl], *a.* textuel.
texture ['tekstʃə], *n.* tissu, *m.*; contexture (*d'écrits etc.*), *f.*
Thai [tai], *a.* thaïlandais.—*n.* thaïlandais (*langue*); Thaïlandais (*personne*), *m.*
Thailand ['tailænd], *n.* la Thaïlande, *f.*, le Siam, *m.*
Thames [temz], **the.** la Tamise, *f.*
than [ðæn], *conj.* que; de (*between more or less and a number*); que de (*before an infinitive*).
thank [θæŋk], *v.t.* remercier (*de*); rendre grâces à.
thankful ['θæŋkful], *a.* reconnaissant (*de*).
thankfully ['θæŋkfuli], *adv.* avec reconnaissance.
thankfulness ['θæŋkfulnis], *n.* reconnaissance, *f.*
thankless ['θæŋklis], *a.* ingrat; oublié (*non reconnu*).
thanklessness ['θæŋklisnis], *n.* ingratitude, *f.*
thank offering ['θæŋkofəriŋ], *n.* sacrifice d'actions de grâces, *m.*
thanks [θæŋks], *n.pl.* remerciments, remerciments, *m.pl.*, grâces, *f.pl.*—*int.* merci.
thanksgiving ['θæŋksgiviŋ], *n.* actions de grâces, *f.*
that [ðæt], *dem.a.* (*pl.* **those** [ðouz]) ce, cet, *m.*, cette, *f.*; (*emphatically*) ce . . . .-là, cet . . .-là, *m.*, cette . . .-là, *f.*—*dem.pron.* celui-là, *m.*, celle-là (*that one*), *f.*; cela, (*colloq.*) ça, *m.*—*rel.pron.* qui, que, lequel, *m.*, laquelle, *f.*, lesquels, *m.pl.*, lesquelles, *f.pl.*—*conj.* que.
thatch [θætʃ], *n.* chaume, *m.*—*v.t.* couvrir de chaume.
thatcher ['θætʃə], *n.* couvreur en chaume, *m.*
thaw [θɔ:], *n.* dégel, *m.*—*v.t.* dégeler; (*fig.*) fondre, attendrir.—*v.i.* dégeler, se dégeler; (*fig.*) fondre, s'attendrir.
the [ðə], *adv.* (*before vowel* [ði], *def. art.* le, *m.*, la, l', *f.*, les, *pl.*
theater ['θiətə], *n.* théâtre, *m.*
theatrical [θi:'ætrikl], *a.* de théâtre, théâtral.
theatricals [θi:'ætriklz], *n.pl.* spectacle, *m.*

*thee [ði:], *pron.* (*also Poet.*) toi; te.
theft [θeft], *n.* vol, *m.*; *petty theft,* larcin, *m.*
their [ðɛə], *poss.a.* leur, leurs, *pl.*
theirs [ðɛəz], *poss.pron.* le leur, *m.*, la leur, *f.*, les leurs, *pl.*, à eux, *m.pl.*, à elles, *f.pl.*
theism ['θi:izm], *n.* théisme, *m.*
theist ['θi:ist], *n.* théiste, *m.*, *f.*
theistic [θi:'istik], *a.* théiste.
them [ðem], *pron.* eux, *m.pl.*, elles, *f.pl.*; (*obj.*) les; (*dat.*) leur, *pl.*
theme [θi:m], *n.* thème, sujet, *m.*
theme song ['θi:msɔŋ], *n.* chanson leit-motif, *f.*
themselves [ðem'selvz], *pron.* eux-mêmes, *m.pl.*, elles-mêmes, *f.pl.*; (*reflexive*) se, *pl.*
then [ðen], *adv.* alors (*après*); dans ce cas (*puisqu'il en est ainsi*); donc; *but then,* par contre; *by then,* alors, déjà; *now and then,* de temps en temps.—*conj.* donc.
thence [ðens], *adv.* de là, en; dès lors.
thenceforth [ðens'fɔ:θ], **thenceforward** [ðens'fɔ:wəd], *adv.* dès lors, depuis lors, à partir de ce moment-là.
theocracy [θi:'okrəsi], *n.* théocratie, *f.*
theocratic [θi:ə'krætik], *a.* théocratique.
theodolite [θi:'odəlait], *n.* théodolite, *f.*
theologian [θi:ə'loudʒiən], *n.* théologien, *m.*
theological [θi:ə'lodʒikl], *a.* théologique.
theology [θi:'olədʒi], *n.* théologie, *f.*
theorem ['θi:ərəm], *n.* théorème, *m.*
theoretic [θi:ə'retik], **theoretical** [θi:ə'retikəl], *a.* théorique.
theorist ['θi:ərist], **theorizer** ['θi:əraizə], *n.* théoricien, *m.*
theorize ['θi:əraiz], *v.i.* théoriser.
theory ['θi:əri], *n.* théorie, *f.*
therapeutic [θerə'pju:tik], *a.* thérapeutique.
therapeutics [θerə'pju:tiks], *n.pl.* thérapeutique, *f.*
therapist ['θerəpist], *n.* praticien, *m.*
therapy ['θerəpi], *n.* thérapie, *f.*
there [ðɛə], *adv.* là, y; (*impers.*) il; en cela; voilà; *here and there,* çà et là; *over there,* là-bas; *there and then,* séance tenante; *there is* or *there are !* le voilà qui vient! *there is* or *there are,* il y a.
thereabout [ðɛərə'baut], **thereabouts** [ðɛərə'bauts], *adv.* par là, près de là; à peu près, environ (*plus ou moins*).
thereafter [ðɛər'ɑ:ftə], *adv.* après, d'après cela, ensuite.
thereat [ðɛər'æt], *adv.* par là, à cet endroit; (*fig.*) là-dessus, à cela.
thereby [ðɛə'bai], *adv.* par là, par ce moyen.
therefore [ðɛəfɔ:], *adv.* donc, par conséquent.
therefrom [ðɛə'frɔm], *adv.* de là, en.
therein [ðɛər'in], *adv.* là-dedans, en cela; y.
thereof [ðɛər'ɔv], *adv.* en, de cela.
thereon [ðɛər'ɔn], *adv.* là-dessus.
Theresa [tə'ri:zə], Thérèse, *f.*
thereto [ðɛər'tu:], **thereunto** [ðɛər'ʌnti], *adv.* y, à cela; à quoi.
thereupon [ðɛərə'pɔn], *adv.* là-dessus, sur cela, sur ce.
therewith [ðɛə'wið], *adv.* avec cela, de cela, en.
therm [θə:m], *n.* thermie, *f.*
thermal ['θə:məl], *a.* thermal.
thermometer [θə'momitə], *n.* thermomètre, *m.*

thermometrical [θə:mo'metrikl], *a.* thermométrique.

thermonuclear [θə:mo'nju:kliə], *a.* thermonucléaire.

thermos ['θə:mɔs], *a.* (*reg. trade mark*) *thermos flask*, bouteille Thermos *ou* isolante, *f.*

thermostat ['θə:məstæt], *n.* thermostat, *m.*

these [ði:z], *a.* ces, ces . . . -ci, *m.pl.*—*pron.* ceux-ci, *m.pl.*, celles-ci, *f.pl.*

thesis ['θi:sis], *n.* thèse, *f.*

Thespian ['θespiən], *a.* tragique, de la tragédie.

thew [θju:], *n.* tendon, muscle, nerf, *m.*

they [ðei], *pron.* ils, eux, *m.pl.*, elles, *f.pl.*; (*followed by a relative*) ceux, *m.pl.*, celles, *f.pl.*; (*impers.*) on (*les gens*); *they say*, on dit.

thick [θik], *a.* épais; gros (*tuyau*); fort, solide (*porte etc.*); trouble (*boisson*); dru, serré (*touffu*); indistinct (*prononciation*); (*fam.*) intime.—*n.* fort, *m.*; *in the thick of*, au (plus) fort de.—*adv.* (*also thickly* ['θikli]) épais; dru (*vite*); en foule (*l'un après l'autre*).

thicken ['θikn], *v.t.* épaissir; lier (*sauce*).—*v.i.* s'épaissir; augmenter; se lier (*sauce*).

thickening ['θikniŋ], *n.* épaississement, *m.*; liaison (*d'une sauce*), *f.*

thicket ['θikit], *n.* fourré, hallier, taillis, *m.*

thick-headed ['θik'hedid], *a.* sot, bête, stupide.

thickly [THICK].

thickness ['θiknis], *n.* épaisseur; consistance (*composition*), *f.*

thick-set ['θikset], *a.* touffu; trapu (*personne*).

thick-skinned ['θik'skind], *a.* (*fig.*) peu sensible.

thief [θi:f], *n.* (*pl. thieves* [θi:vz]) voleur; larron, *m.*

thieve [θi:v], *v.i.* voler.

thieving ['θi:viŋ], *n.* vol, larcin, *m.*, rapine, *f.*

thievish ['θi:viʃ], *a.* adonné au vol; voleur.

thievishly ['θi:viʃli], *adv.* en voleur; par le vol.

thievishness ['θi:viʃnis], *n.* penchant au vol, *m.*, habitude du vol, *f.*

thigh [θai], *n.* cuisse, *f.*

thigh-bone ['θaiboun], *n.* fémur, *m.*

thimble [θimbl], *n.* dé, *m.*

thimbleful ['θimblful], *n.* un plein dé, *m.*

thin [θin], *a.* mince; maigre (*décharné*); élancé, délié (*svelte*); peu nombreux (*gens*); clair; clairsemé, rare (*arbres etc.*); grêle, faible (*son etc.*).—*adv.* d'une manière éparse, clair.—*v.t.* amincir, allonger (*sauce etc.*); éclaircir; raréfier.

*thine [ðain], *pron.* le tien, *m.*, la tienne, *f.*, les tiens, *m.pl.*, les tiennes, *f.pl.*; à toi.

thing [θiŋ], *n.* chose, *f.*, objet, *m.*, affaire, *f.*; être, *m.*; (*pl.*) affaires, *f.pl.*, effets, *m.pl.*

think [θiŋk], *v.t. irr.* penser; croire (*tenir pour vrai*); imaginer, songer (*avoir l'idée*); trouver, juger (*considérer*).—*v.i.* penser; croire; s'imaginer; songer (*à*); s'aviser (*de*); avoir une idée *ou* opinion (*de*); *to think over*, réfléchir à; *to think up*, inventer.

thinker ['θiŋkə], *n.* penseur, *m.*

thinking ['θiŋkiŋ], *a.* pensant, qui pense, réfléchi.—*n.* pensée, *f.*; jugement, avis, *m.*

thinly ['θinli], *adv.* légèrement (*vêtu*); clairsemé, de loin en loin (*répandu*).

thinness ['θinnis], *n.* ténuité; fluidité; rareté,

f., petit nombre (*quantité*), *m.*; maigreur (*du corps*), *f.*

thin-skinned ['θin'skind], *a.* à la peau mince; (*fig.*) irritable, chatouilleux, susceptible.

third [θə:d], *a.* troisième; trois (*mois, roi etc.*).—*n.* tiers (*fraction*), *m.*; (*Mus.*) tierce, *f.*

thirdly ['θə:dli], *adv.* troisièmement.

thirst [θə:st], *n.* soif, *f.*; *to quench one's thirst*, se désaltérer.—*v.i.* avoir soif (*de*).

thirstily ['θə:stili], *adv.* avidement.

thirstiness ['θə:stinis], *n.* soif, *f.*

thirsty ['θə:sti], *a.* qui a soif; altéré.

thirteen [θə:'ti:n], *a. and n.* treize, *m.*

thirteenth [θə:'ti:nθ], *a.* treizième; treize (*rois etc.*).—*n.* treizième (*fraction*), *m.*

thirtieth ['θə:tiiθ], *a.* trentième; trente (*du mois*).—*n.* trentième (*fraction*), *m.*

thirty ['θə:ti], *a. and n.* trente, *m.*

this [ðis], *a.* (*pl. these* [ði:z]) ce, cet, *m.*, cette, *f.*; ce . . . -ci, cet . . . -ci, *m.*; cette . . . -ci, *f.*—*pron.* celui-ci, *m.*, celle-ci (*this one*), *f.*; ceci, *m.*

thistle [θisl], *n.* (*Bot.*) chardon, *m.*

thistly ['θisli], *a.* plein de chardons.

thither ['ðiðə], *adv.* là, y; *hither and thither*, çà et là.

thong [θɔŋ], *n.* courroie, lanière, sangle, *f.*

thoracic [θɔ'ræsik], *a.* thoracique.

thorax ['θɔ:ræks], *n.* thorax, *m.*

thorn [θɔ:n], *n.* épine, *f.*

thorn bush ['θɔ:nbuʃ], *n.* buisson épineux, *m.*

thorny ['θɔ:ni], *a.* épineux.

thorough ['θʌrə], *a.* entier, complet; achevé, parfait; vrai (*véritable*).

thoroughbred ['θʌrəbred], *a.* pur sang (*cheval*); (*colloq.*) consommé.

thoroughfare ['θʌrəfɛə], *n.* voie de passage, *f.*, passage, *m.*; artère, *f.*; *no thoroughfare*, passage interdit.

thoroughgoing ['θʌrəgouiŋ], *a.* résolu; achevé, consommé.

thoroughly ['θʌrəli], *adv.* tout à fait, entièrement; à fond.

thoroughness ['θʌrənis], *n.* caractère achevé, *m.*, perfection, *f.*

thorough-paced ['θʌrəpeist], *a.* achevé, franc, fieffé.

those [ðouz], *a.* ces; ces . . . -là, *pl.*—*pron.* ceux-là, *m.pl.*, celles-là, *f.pl.*

*thou [ðau], *pron.* tu; *than thou*, que toi.

though [ðou], *conj.* quoique, bien que (*with subj.*); quand même (*même si*).—*adv.* cependant, pourtant.

thought (1) [θɔ:t], *past and p.p.* [THINK].

thought (2) [θɔ:t], *n.* pensée; idée, *f.*; sentiment (*opinion*), *m.*

thoughtful ['θɔ:tful], *a.* pensif, réfléchi; rêveur, méditatif; inquiet (*troublé*); attentif, soucieux (*prévenant*).

thoughtfully ['θɔ:tfuli], *adv.* pensivement, avec attention.

thoughtfulness ['θɔ:tfulnis], *n.* méditation, *f.*, recueillement, *m.*; sollicitude, prévenance (*attentions*), *f.*

thoughtless ['θɔ:tlis], *a.* irréfléchi, insouciant.

thoughtlessly ['θɔ:tlisli], *a.* avec insouciance; sans réflexion.

thoughtlessness ['θɔ:tlisnis], *n.* insouciance, négligence, *f.*

thousand ['θauzənd], *a.* mille; mil (*dates*).—*n.* mille; millier, *m.*, (*pl.*) milliers, *m.pl.*

thousandth ['θauzəndθ], *a.* millième.—*n.* millième (*fraction*), *m.*

thraldom ['θrɔːldəm], *n.* esclavage, asservissement, *m.*

thrall [θrɔːl], *n.* esclave, *m.*, *f.*; esclavage, *m.*

thrash [θræʃ], *v.t.* battre, rosser (*quelqu'un*); [THRESH].

thrasher ['θræʃə], [THRESHER].

thrashing ['θræʃiŋ], *n.* rossée, *f.*; [THRESHING].

thrashing machine [THRESHING MACHINE].

thread [θred], *n.* fil; filet (*de vis*), *m.*—*v.t.* enfiler; traverser (*faire son chemin à travers*).

threadbare ['θredbɛə], *a.* râpé; (*fig.*) rebattu.

threat [θret], *n.* menace, *f.*

threaten [θretn], *v.t.* menacer (*de*).

threatening ['θretniŋ], *a.* menaçant; de menaces.—*n.* menaces, *f.pl.*

threateningly ['θretniŋli], *adv.* avec menaces; d'un air menaçant.

three [θriː], *a.* and *n.* trois, *m.*

three-cornered ['θriːkɔːnəd], *a.* à trois cornes; *three-cornered hat*, tricorne, *m.*

threefold ['θriːfould], *a.* triple.

three-master ['θriːmɑːstə], *n.* trois-mâts, *m.*

three-ply ['θriːplai], *a.* à trois épaisseurs; *three-ply wood*, contreplaqué, *m.*

threescore ['θriːskɔː], *a.* soixante.—*n.* soixantaine, *f.*

thresh [θreʃ], *v.t.* (*Agric.*) battre (*en grange*).

thresher ['θreʃə], *n.* batteur en grange, *m.*

threshing ['θreʃiŋ], *n,* (*Agric.*) battage, *m.*

threshing machine ['θreʃiŋmə'ʃiːn], *n.* batteuse, *f.*

threshold ['θreʃould], *n.* seuil; (*fig.*) début, *m.*

thrift [θrift], **thriftiness** ['θriftinis], *n.* épargne, économie, *f.*

thriftily ['θriftili], *adv.* avec économie.

thriftiness [THRIFT].

thriftless ['θriftlis], *a.* dépensier, prodigue.

thriftlessly ['θriftlisli], *adv.* en prodigue, follement.

thriftlessness ['θriftlisnis], *n.* prodigalité, *f.*, gaspillage, *m.*

thrifty ['θrifti], *a.* ménager, économe, frugal.

thrill [θril], *v.t.* faire frissonner, faire tressaillir (*de*).—*v.i.* frémir, tressaillir (*de*).—*n.* tressaillement, frisson, *m.*

thriller ['θrilə], *n.* (*fam.*) roman *ou* film à sensation, *m.*

thrilling ['θriliŋ], *a.* saisissant, poignant, palpitant.

thrive [θraiv], *v.i. irr.* prospérer; réussir.

thriving ['θraiviŋ], *a.* florissant, vigoureux.

throat [θrout], *n.* gorge, *f.*; gosier, *m.*

throaty ['θrouti], *a.* guttural (*voix*).

throb [θrɔb], *v.i.* battre; palpiter.—*n.* battement, *m.*

throbbing ['θrɔbiŋ], *a.* palpitant, vibrant; lancinant (*douleur*).—*n.* battement; ronflement (*de moteur*), *m.*

throes [θrouz], *n.pl.* douleurs, angoisses, *f.pl.*

thrombosis [θrɔm'bousis], *n.* thrombose, *f.*

throne [θroun], *n.* trône, *m.*

throng [θrɔŋ], *n.* foule, multitude, *f.*—*v.t.* remplir.—*v.i.* accourir en foule, se presser.

thronged [θrɔŋd], *a.* serré (*personnes*); comble (*salle*).

throstle [θrɔsl], *n.* (*Orn.*) grive chanteuse, *f.*

throttle [θrɔtl], *v.t.* étrangler; étouffer.—*n.* gosier; (*Motor. etc.*) papillon, *m.*

through [θruː], *prep.* à travers; au travers de;

par; dans; par suite de (*à cause de*).—*a.* direct (*train, billet etc.*).—*adv.* directement, droit (*sans s'arrêter*); de part en part; d'un bout à l'autre (*dans toute sa longueur*); jusqu'à la fin, jusqu'au bout; complètement; *to be wet through*, être trempé jusqu'aux os; *to fall through*, manquer, échouer (*projet*); *to go through with* (*something*), *to see* (*something*) *through*, mener (quelque chose) à bonne fin.

throughout [θruː'aut], *prep.* dans tout, par tout.—*adv.* d'un bout à l'autre; entièrement.

throw [θrou], *v.t. irr.* jeter; lancer; renverser; tordre (*soie*); démonter, désarçonner (*cavalier*); *to throw aside*, jeter de côté; *to throw away*, jeter, rejeter; gaspiller; *to throw off*, se défaire de, ôter (*vêtements*).—*n.* jet, coup; (*fig.*) élan, *m.*

thrower ['θrouə], *n.* jeteur, lanceur, *m.*

thrush [θrʌʃ], *n.* (*Orn.*) grive, *f.*

thrust [θrʌst], *v.t. irr.* pousser, enfoncer, fourrer; presser.—*v.i.* porter une botte *ou* un coup (*à*); se fourrer.—*n.* coup, *m.*; (*Fenc.*) botte; (*Arch. etc.*) poussée, *f.*

thud [θʌd], *n.* bruit sourd; son mat, *m.*—*v.i.* faire un bruit sourd.

thug [θʌg], *n.* bandit, *m.*

thumb [θʌm], *n.* pouce, *m.*—*v.t.* manier gauchement; feuilleter; salir (avec les pouces).

thumbnail ['θʌmneil], *a.* en raccourci, minuscule.

thumb-screw ['θʌmskruː], *n.* vis à ailettes, *f.*; poucettes (*supplice*), *f.pl.*

thumbstall ['θʌmstɔːl], *n.* poucier, doigtier, *m.*

thump [θʌmp], *v.t.* frapper du poing, cogner.—*n.* coup, *m.*, bourrade, *f.*

thunder ['θʌndə], *n.* tonnerre, *m.*; (*fig.*) foudre, *f.*—*v.i.* tonner; (*fig.*) fulminer.

thunderbolt ['θʌndəboult], *n.* foudre, *f.*

thunder-clap ['θʌndəklæp], *n.* coup de tonnerre, *m.*

thundering ['θʌndəriŋ], *a.* tonnant, foudroyant; (*collog.*) énorme.

thunderous ['θʌndərəs], *a.* orageux; à tout rompre (*applaudissements*).

thunderstorm ['θʌndəstɔːm], *n.* orage (accompagné de tonnerre), *m.*

thunderstruck ['θʌndəstrʌk], *a.* foudroyé; (*fig.*) atterré.

thundery ['θʌndəri], *a.* orageux.

Thursday ['θəːzd(e)i], *n.* jeudi, *m.*

thus [ðʌs], *adv.* ainsi; *thus far*, jusqu'ici.

thwack [θwæk], *n.* coup, *m.*—*v.t.* frapper, rosser, battre.

thwacking ['θwækiŋ], *n.* roulée de coups, raclée, *f.*

thwart [θwɔːt], *v.t.* traverser; (*fig.*) contrarier.—*adv.* en travers.—*n.* banc de rameurs, *m.*

*thy [ðai], *poss.a.* (*also poet.*) ton, *m.*, ta, *f.*, tes, *pl.*

thyme [taim], *n.* thym, *m.*

thyroid ['θairɔid], *a.* thyroïde.

*thyself [ðai'self], *pron.* (*also poet.*) toi-même; toi; (*reflexive*) te.

tiara [ti'ɑːrə], *n.* tiare, *f.*

Tibet [ti'bet]. le Tibet, *m.*

Tibetan [ti'betn], *a.* tibétain.—*n.* tibétain (*langue*); Tibétain (*personne*), *m.*

tibia ['tibiə], n. (Anat.) tibia (os de la jambe), m.

tic [tik], n. tic, m.

tick (1) [tik], n. tic-tac (bruit), m.; marque, f. —v.t. marquer; **to tick off**, pointer.—v.i. faire tic-tac, battre (horloges etc.).

tick (2) [tik], n. coutil (de matelas), m.

ticket ['tikit], n. billet; ticket, m.; étiquette, f.; **return ticket**, billet d'aller et retour; **season ticket**, carte d'abonnement, f.; **single ticket**, billet simple.—v.t. étiqueter, numéroter.

ticket collector ['tikitkəlektə], n. contrôleur, m.

ticket office ['tikitɔfis], n. bureau des billets, guichet, m.

ticking (1) ['tikiŋ], n. tic-tac, battement (de montre etc.), m.

ticking (2) ['tikiŋ], n. coutil, m., toile à matelas, f.

tickle [tikl], v.t., v.i. chatouiller.

tickling ['tikliŋ], n. chatouillement, m.

ticklish ['tikliʃ], a. chatouilleux; critique, délicat.

tidal [taidl], a. de marée; **tidal harbor**, port à marée, m.; **tidal wave**, raz de marée, m.

tide [taid], n. marée, f.; courant (flot), m.; (fig.) époque, f.

tidily ['taidili], adv. proprement, en bon ordre.

tidiness ['taidinis], n. propreté, netteté, f., bon ordre, m.

tidings ['taidiŋz], n.pl. nouvelles, f.pl.

tidy ['taidi], a. rangé, bien arrangé, en ordre, propre, net.—v.t. mettre en ordre; ranger; arranger (papiers etc.).

tie [tai], v.t. lier, attacher; nouer, faire (un nœud).—v.i. se lier, se nouer; être à égalité. —n. lien; nœud (knot); cordon (de chaussure), m.; cravate; (Mus.) liaison; (Games) partie nulle, f.

tier [tiə], n. rang, m.; rangée, f.

tierce [tiəs], n. (Cards) tierce, f.

tiff [tif], n. petite querelle, pique, f.

tiffany ['tifəni], n. gaze de soie (tissu), f.

tiger ['taigə], n. tigre, m.

tiger lily ['taigəlili], n. (Bot.) lis tigré, m.

tiger moth ['taigəmɔθ], n. arctie, f.

tight [tait], a. serré; raide, tendu (corde); trop étroit (vêtements); imperméable; **air-tight** or **water-tight**, imperméable à l'air ou à l'eau.

tighten [taitn], v.t. serrer; tendre (constraindre); (fig.) resserrer.

tight-fisted ['tait'fistid], a. serré, ladre.

tightly ['taitli], adv. ferme, fortement; étroitement serré.

tightness ['taitnis], n. raideur; étroitesse (des vêtements), f.

tight-rope ['taitroup], n. corde raide, f.; **tight-rope walker**, funambule, danseur de corde, m.

tights [taits], n.pl. collant, maillot, m.

tigress ['taigris], n. tigresse, f.

tile [tail], n. tuile, f.; carreau (for flooring), m. —v.t. couvrir de tuiles; carreler (une pièce).

tiler ['tailə], n. couvreur (en tuiles), m.

tile works ['tailwə:ks], n. tuilerie, f.

till (1) [til], prep. jusqu'à.—conj. jusqu'à ce que (with subj.).

till (2) [til], n. caisse, f.

till (3) [til], v.t. labourer, cultiver.

tillable ['tiləbl], a. labourable.

tillage ['tilidʒ], n. labourage, m.

tiller (1) ['tilə], n. laboureur, m.

tiller (2) ['tilə], n. (Naut.) barre du gouvernail, f.

tilt (1) [tilt], n. bâche, banne (toile), f.

tilt (2) [tilt], n. joute; inclinaison, f.—v.t. incliner, faire pencher.—v.i. jouter; incliner, pencher.

tilth [tilθ], n. labourage, m., culture, f.

timber ['timbə], n. bois de construction, m.— v.t. boiser.

timbering ['timbəriŋ], n. boisage, m.

timber-work ['timbəwə:k], n. charpente, f.

timbrel ['timbrəl], n. tambour de basque, tambourin, m.

time [taim], n. temps, m.; saison, époque, f.; terme (période), m.; heure (de la journée), f.; moment, m.; occasion; fois (répétition); époque, f., siècle (d'histoire), m.; mesure, f.; (Dri'ing) pas, m.; **at times**, parfois, à temps d'autre; **in no time**, en un clin d'œil; **in time**, temps; (Mus.) en mesure.—v.t. faire à propos; fixer l'heure de; (Spt.) chronométrer; **ill-timed**, inopportun; **well-timed**, opportun, à propos.

time bomb ['taimbɔm], n. bombe à retardement, f.

time fuse ['taimfju:z], n. fusée à temps, f.

time-honored ['taimɔnəd], a. vénérable; séculaire.

time-keeper ['taimki:pə], n. surveillant, contrôleur, m.

time lag ['taimlæ:g], n. décalage, retard, m.

timeliness ['taimlinis], n. opportunité, f., à-propos, m.

timely ['taimli], a. opportun, à propos.

time-piece ['taimpi:s], n. pendule, f.

time sheet ['taimʃi:t], n. feuille de présence, f.

timetable ['taimteibl], n. indicateur, horaire, m.; (Sch.) emploi du temps, m.

time-worn ['taimwɔ:n], a. usé par le temps.

timid ['timid], a. timide, craintif, peureux.

timidity [ti'miditi], n. timidité, f.

timing ['taimiŋ], n. ajustement, règlement; réglage (de montre etc.), m.

timorous ['timərəs], a. timoré, timide.

timorously ['timərəsli], adv. craintivement.

timorousness ['timərəsnis], n. timidité, f.

tin [tin], n. étain, m.; boîte (de conserve), f.— v.t. étamer.

tincture ['tiŋktʃə], n. teinture, f., extrait, m.; (fig.) nuance, f.—v.t. teindre (de).

tinder ['tində], n. amadou, m.

tinder-box ['tindəbɔks], n. boîte à amadou, f.; briquet à silex, m.

tinfoil ['tinfɔil], n. feuille d'étain, f.

tinge [tindʒ], n. teinte, nuance, f.; soupçon (goût), m.—v.t. teindre.

tingle [tiŋgl], v.i. tinter; picoter, cuire (douleur).

tingling ['tiŋgliŋ], n. tintement (son); picotement, m.

tinker ['tiŋkə], n. rétameur, m.—v.t. rétamer; raccommoder.

tinkle [tiŋkl], v.t. faire tinter.—v.i. tinter.—n. tintement, m.

tinkling ['tiŋkliŋ], n. tintement, m.

tinny ['tini], a. qui abonde en étain; grêle (son).

tin plate ['tinpleit], n. fer-blanc, m.

tinsel ['tinsəl], *a.* de clinquant; (*fig.*) faux.—*n.* clinquant; (*fig.*) faux éclat, *m.*

tinsmith ['tinsmiθ], *n.* ferblantier, *m.*

tint [tint], *n.* teinte, nuance, *f.*—*v.t.* teinter, nuancer (*de*).

tin-tack ['tintæk], *n.* semence étamée, *f.*

tinware ['tinwɛə], *n.* ferblanterie, *f.*

tiny ['taini], *a.* tout petit, minuscule.

tip (1) [tip], *n.* bout, *m.*; extrémité, pointe, *f.*—*v.t.* garnir le bout.

tip (2) [tip], *n.* tape (*coup léger*), *f.*; pourboire (*gratuity*); dépotoir (*débris*); (*Spt.*) tuyau, *m.*—*v.t.* donner un pourboire à; décharger (*véhicule*); (*Spt.*) tuyauter.

tippet ['tipit], *n.* pèlerine, palatine (*fourrure*), *f.*

tipple ['tipl], *v.i.* boire, pinter.—*n.* boisson, *f.*

tippler ['tiplə], *n.* buveur, *m.*

tippling ['tipliŋ], *n.* ivrognerie, *f.*

tipstaff ['tipsta:f], *n.* huissier, *m.*

tipster ['tipstə], *n.* (*Spt.*) tuyauteur, *m.*

tipsy ['tipsi], *a.* gris, ivre.

tiptoe ['tiptou], *n.* pointe du pied, *f.*; **on tip-toe**, sur la pointe des pieds.

tip-top ['tiptəp], *a.* (*colloq.*) excellent.—*n.* comble, sommet, *m.*

tirade [ti'reid, tai'reid], *n.* tirade, diatribe, *f.*

tire (1) [taiə], *n.* pneu (*de roue*), *m.*

tire ['taiə], *v.t.* lasser, fatiguer; ennuyer (*moralement*).—*v.i.* se fatiguer, se lasser.

tired ['taiəd], *a.* las, fatigué; ennuyé.

tiredness ['taiədnis], *n.* fatigue, lassitude, *f.*

tiresome ['taiəsəm], *a.* fatigant; ennuyeux (*assomant*).

tiresomeness ['taiəsəmnis], *n.* nature fatigante, *f.*; ennui, *m.*

tissue ['tiʃju:, 'tisju:], *n.* tissu, *m.*—*v.t.* tisser, broder.

tissue paper ['tiʃju:peipə], *n.* papier de soie, *m.*

tit (1) [tit], *n.* mésange (*oiseau*), *f.*

tit (2) [tit], *n.* **tit for tat**, un prêté pour un rendu.

titanic [tai'tænik], *a.* titanique, titanesque.

titbit ['titbit], *n.* morceau friand, *m.*

tithe [taið], *n.* dîme, *f.*, dixième, *m.*—*v.t.* dîmer.

titillate ['titileit], *v.t.* chatouiller, titiller.

titillation [titi'leiʃən], *n.* titillation, *f.*, chatouillement, *m.*

titlark ['titla:k], *n.* alouette des prés, *f.*

title [taitl], *n.* titre; (*fig.*) droit, document, *m.*—*v.t.* titrer, qualifier (*de*).

titled [taitld], *a.* titré.

title deed ['taitldi:d], *n.* titre (*de propriété*), *m.*

title page ['taitlpeidʒ], *n.* titre, *m.*

titmouse ['titmaus], *n.* (*pl.* **titmice** ['titmais]) mésange, *f.*

titter ['titə], *v.i.* rire tout bas.—*n.* petit rire étouffé, *m.*

tittle [titl], *n.* point, iota, *m.*

tittle-tattle ['titltætl], *n.* caquetage, bavardage, *m.*—*v.i.* jaser, bavarder.

titular ['titjulə], *a.* titulaire.

titulary ['titjuləri], *a.* de titre.—*n.* titulaire, *m.*, *f.*

to [tu], *prep.* à, de (*before infinitive*); pour, afin de (*dans le but de*); à (*un endroit*); en (*before names of countries of the feminine gender and those of the masculine gender beginning with a vowel*); dans (*followed by* le, la, *etc.*); vers (*un endroit*); contre (*pari*); près de (*cour royale etc.*); outre, en addition à (*en plus de*);

pour (*faire quelque chose*); en comparaison de, auprès de (*à côté de*); jusqu'à (*telle ou telle limite*); envers (*à l'égard de*).

toad [toud], *n.* crapaud, *m.*

toadish ['toudiʃ], *a.* de crapaud.

toadstool ['toudstu:l], *n.* champignon vénéneux, *m.*

toady ['toudi], *n.* flagorneur, *m.*—*v.t.* flagorner, aduler.

toadyism ['toudiizm], *n.* flagornerie, servilité, *f.*

toast [toust], *n.* rôtie, tranche de pain grillée, *f.*; toast (*bu à la santé de quelqu'un*), *m.*—*v.t.* rôtir, griller; porter un toast à.

toaster ['toustə], *n.* grille-pain, *m.inv.*

toasting fork ['toustiŋfo:k], *n.* fourchette à rôties, *f.*

toast-master ['toustma:stə], *n.* préposé aux toasts, *m.*

toast rack ['toustræk], *n.* porte-rôties, porte-toasts, *m.inv.*

tobacco [tə'bækou], *n.* tabac, *m.*

tobacco box [tə'bækoubɔks], *n.* boîte à tabac, *f.*

tobacco jar [tə'bækoudʒa:], *n.* pot à tabac, *m.*

tobacconist [tə'bækənist], *n.* marchand de tabac, *m.*; **tobacconist's shop**, bureau de tabac, *m.*

tobacco pouch [tə'bækoupautʃ], *n.* blague à tabac, *f.*

toboggan [tə'bɔgən], *n.* toboggan, *m.*; luge, *f.*—*v.i.* luger.

tocsin ['tɔksin], *n.* tocsin, *m.*

today [tə'dei], *adv.* aujourd'hui.

toddle [tɔdl], *v.i.* trottiner.

toddler ['tɔdlə], *n.* tout petit enfant, *m.*

to-do [tə'du:], *n.* tapage, éclat, *m.*, (*fam.*) histoire, *f.*

toe [tou], *n.* orteil, doigt de pied; devant du sabot, *m.*, pince (*de cheval*), *f.*; bout (*de bas*), *m.*

toe-nail ['touneil], *n.* ongle de pied, *m.*

toffee, toffy ['tɔfi], *n.* caramel au beurre, *m.*

toga ['tougə], *n.* toge, *f.*

together [tə'geðə], *adv.* ensemble, à la fois, en même temps (*simultanément*); de concert (*entre eux*); de suite (*consécutivement*).

Togo ['tougou]. le Togo, *m.*

Togolese [tougo'li:z], *a.* togolais.—*n.* Togolais (*personne*), *m.*

toil [tɔil], *n.* travail dur, labeur, *m.*; peine, *f.*; (*pl.*) piège, *m.*—*v.i.* travailler fort, se fatiguer.

toiler ['tɔilə], *n.* travailleur, *m.*

toilet ['tɔilit], *n.* toilette, *f.*; les toilettes (*dans les hôtels etc.*), *f.pl.*, cabinet d'aisances, *m.*

toiling ['tɔiliŋ], *n.* travail, labeur, *m.*, peine, *f.*

toilsome ['tɔilsəm], *a.* pénible, laborieux, fatigant.

toilsomeness ['tɔilsəmnis], *n.* difficulté, *f.*

token ['toukən], *n.* marque, *f.*; gage (*témoignage*); jeton (*jeux de cartes, téléphone etc.*), *m.*; **book token**, bon de livre, *m.*; **token strike**, grève d'avertissement, *f.*

tolerable ['tɔlərəbl], *a.* tolérable, passable (*assez bon*).

tolerably ['tɔlərəbli], *adv.* passablement, assez.

tolerance ['tɔlərəns], *n.* tolérance, *f.*

tolerant ['tɔlərənt], *a.* tolérant.

tolerate ['tɔlǝreit], v.t. tolérer; supporter.
toleration [tɔlǝ'reiʃǝn], n. tolérance, f.
toll (1) [toul], n. péage; droit; octroi (*impôt municipal*), m.
toll (2) [toul], n. tintement, glas (*de cloche*), m.—v.t., v.i. sonner, tinter (*cloche*).
toll-bar ['toulbɑ:], **toll-gate** ['toulgeit], n. barrière de péage, f.
toll bridge ['toulbridʒ], n. pont à péage, m.
toll call, see **trunk-call**.
toll-house ['toulhaus], n. bureau de péage, m.
tolling ['touliŋ], n. tintement, m.
tomahawk ['tɔmǝhɔ:k], n. tomahawk, m.; hache de guerre, f.
tomato [tǝ'mɑːtou], n. tomate, f.
tomb [tu:m], n. tombeau, m.; tombe, f.
tomboy ['tɔmbɔi], n. garçon manqué, m.
tombstone ['tu:mstoun], n. pierre tombale, f.
tom-cat ['tɔmkæt], n. matou, m.
tome [toum], n. tome, volume, m.
tomfool [tɔm'fuːl], n. sot, bête, niais, m.
tomfoolery [tɔm'fuːlǝri], n. sottise, bêtise, niaiserie, f.
Tommy gun ['tɔmigʌn], n. mitraillette, f.
tomorrow [tǝ'mɔrou], adv. demain.
tomtit ['tɔmtit], n. (*Orn.*) mésange bleue, f.
tom-tom ['tɔmtɔm], n. tam-tam, m.
ton [tʌn], n. tonne (1016,04 *kilogrammes*), f.
tone [toun], n. ton; accent, timbre (*de voix*), m.—v.t. donner le ton à, régler; (*Mus.*) accorder; (*Phot.*) virer; *to tone down*, adoucir, pallier.
toneless ['tounlis], a. sans éclat, sans chaleur (*voix*).
tongs [tɔŋz], n.pl. pincettes; (*Tech.*) tenailles, pinces, f.pl.
tongue [tʌŋ], n. langue, f.; *to hold one's tongue*, se taire.
tongued [tʌŋd], a. à langue.
tongue-tied ['tʌŋtaid], a. qui a la langue liée; (*fig.*) réduit au silence, muet.
tonic ['tɔnik], a. and n. (*Med.*) tonique, fortifiant, m.
tonight [tǝ'nait], n. cette nuit, f., ce soir, m.
tonnage ['tʌnidʒ], n. tonnage, m.
tonsil ['tɔnsl], n. (*Anat.*) amygdale, f.
tonsil(l)itis [tɔnsi'laitis], n. amygdalite, f.
tonsure ['tɔnʃǝ], n. tonsure, f.—v.t. tonsurer.
too [tu:], adv. trop, par trop; aussi, de même, également (*pareillement*); d'ailleurs, de plus; *too much* or *too many*, trop.
tool [tu:l], n. outil, instrument; (*fig.*) agent, m.
tool chest ['tu:lʃest], n. boîte à outils, f.
tooth [tu:θ], n. (*pl.* teeth [ti:θ]) dent, f.; *set of teeth*, râtelier, m.; *wisdom tooth*, dent de sagesse.—v.t. denteler.
toothache ['tu:θeik], n. mal de dents, m.
toothbrush ['tu:θbrʌʃ], n. brosse à dents, f.
toothed [tu:θt], a. à dents; (*Tech.*) denté.
toothless ['tu:θlis], a. sans dents, édenté.
tooth-paste ['tu:θpeist], n. pâte dentifrice, f., dentifrice, m.
tooth-pick ['tu:θpik], n. cure-dents, m.inv.
tooth-powder ['tu:θpaudǝ], n. poudre dentifrice, f.
toothsome ['tu:θsǝm], a. agréable au goût, savoureux, friand.
toothsomeness ['tu:θsǝmnis], n. goût agréable, m.
top (1) [tɔp], a. premier, principal, extrême.—n. haut, sommet, m.; cime (*de montagne etc.*),

f.; faîte (*d'édifice*), m.; (*Naut.*) hune, f.; dessus (*de table*), m.—v.t. couronner, surmonter (*de*).
top (2) [tɔp], n. toupie (*jouet*), f.
topaz ['toupæz], n. topaze, f.
top boots ['tɔpbu:ts], n.pl. bottes à revers, f.pl.
top-coat ['tɔpkout], n. pardessus, m.
tope (1) [toup], v.i. (*colloq.*) pinter, boire.
tope (2) [toup], n. chien de mer, m.
toper ['toupǝ], n. ivrogne, m., f.
top hat ['tɔp'hæt], n. chapeau haut de forme, m.
topic ['tɔpik], n. matière, f., sujet, m.
topical ['tɔpikl], a. d'actualité; (*Med.*) topique.
topmast ['tɔpmɑ:st], n. mât de hune, m.
topmost ['tɔpmoust], a. le plus haut, le plus élevé.
top-sail ['tɔpsl], n. hunier, m.
topographer [tǝ'pɔgrǝfǝ], n. topographe, m.
topog. aphic [tɔpǝ'græfik], **topographical** [tɔpǝ'græfikǝl], a. topographique.
topography [tǝ'pɔgrǝfi], n. topographie, f.
topple ['tɔpl], v.i. tomber, dégringoler.
topsy-turvy ['tɔpsi'tǝ:vi], adv. sens dessus dessous.
torch [tɔ:tʃ], n. torche, f., flambeau, m., lampe de poche, f.
torch-bearer ['tɔ:tʃbɛǝrǝ], n. porte-flambeau, m.
toreador [tɔriǝ'dɔ:], n. toréador, m.
torment (1) ['tɔ:ment], n. tourment, m., torture, f.; supplice, m.
torment (2) [tɔ:'ment], v.t. tourmenter, torturer.
tormentor [tɔ:'mentǝ], n. tourmenteur, bourreau, m.
tornado [tɔ:'neidou], n. tornade, f., ouragan, cyclone, m.
torpedo [tɔ:'pi:dou], n. torpille, f.—v.t. torpiller.
torpedo boat [tɔ:'pi:doubout], n. torpilleur, m.
torpid ['tɔ:pid], a. engourdi, torpide, inerte.
torpor ['tɔ:pǝ], n. torpeur, apathie, f.
torrefaction [tɔri'fækʃǝn], n. torréfaction, f.
torrefy ['tɔrifai], v.t. torréfier.
torrent ['tɔrǝnt], n. torrent, m.
torrential [tɔ'renʃl], a. torrentiel.
torrid ['tɔrid], a. brûlant, torride.
torridness ['tɔridnis], **torridity** [tɔ'riditi], n. chaleur brûlante, f.
torsion ['tɔ:ʃǝn], n. torsion, f.
torso ['tɔ:sou], n. torse, m.
tortoise ['tɔ:tǝs], n. tortue, f.
tortoise-shell ['tɔ:tǝsʃel], a. d'écaille.—n. écaille de tortue, écaille, f.
tortuous ['tɔ:tjuǝs], a. tortueux, sinueux.
tortuousness ['tɔ:tjuǝsnis], n. tortuosité, f.
torture ['tɔ:tʃǝ], n. torture, f.; supplice, m.—v.t. torturer; (*fig.*) faire souffrir.
torturer ['tɔ:tʃǝrǝ], n. bourreau, m.
toss [tɔs], n. jet, lancement, m.; *to win the toss*, gagner (à pile ou face).—v.t. lancer ou jeter (*en l'air*); ballotter; secouer.—v.i. s'agiter.
tossing ['tɔsiŋ], n. secousse, f.; ballottement; hochement, m.
toss-up ['tɔsʌp], n. coup de pile ou face, m.
total [toutl], a. total, complet, entier.—n. total, montant, m., somme, f.—v.t. se monter à.

totalitarian [toutæli'tɛəriən], *a.* (*Polit.*) totalitaire.
totalitarianism [toutæli'tɛəriənizm], *n.* totalitarisme, *m.*
totality [tou'tæliti], *n.* totalité, *f.*, montant, tout, *m.*
totalizator ['toutəlaizeitə], *n.* totalisateur, *m.*
totally ['toutəli], *adv.* totalement, tout à fait, entièrement.
totem ['toutəm], *n.* totem, *m.*
totter ['tɔtə], *v.i.* chanceler; (*fig.*) vaciller, trembler.
tottering ['tɔtəriŋ], *a.* chancelant, tremblant.—*n.* chancellement, *m.*
tottery ['tɔtəri], *a.* chancelant.
touch [tʌtʃ], *v.t.* toucher; toucher à (*s'ingérer dans*); émouvoir (*attendrir*); **to touch up**, retoucher.—*v.i.* toucher; se toucher; **to touch at**, aborder à (*navire*); **to touch upon**, effleurer, (*fig.*) faire allusion à.—*n.* le toucher (*sens tactile*); attouchement (*contact*), *m.*; légère attaque (*d'une maladie*), *f.*; (*fig.*) soupçon (*trace*), *m.*; **it was touch and go**, il s'en est fallu de bien peu; **to get in touch with**, se mettre en rapports, entrer en contact avec; **to keep in touch with**, garder le contact avec.
touchiness ['tʌtʃinis], *n.* irascibilité, *f.*
touching ['tʌtʃiŋ], *a.* touchant, émouvant.—*prep.* concernant, au sujet de.
touch-line ['tʌtʃlain], *n.* (*Ftb.*) ligne de touche, *f.*
touchstone ['tʌtʃstoun], *n.* pierre de touche, *f.*
touch-wood ['tʌtʃwud], *n.* amadou, *m.*
touchy ['tʌtʃi], *a.* irritable, susceptible.
tough [tʌf], *a.* dur, raide, résistant; coriace (*viande*); fort (*solide*); difficile.
toughen ['tʌfn], *v.t.* durcir.—*v.i.* s'endurcir.
toughish ['tʌfiʃ], *a.* un peu dur.
toughly ['tʌfli], *adv.* durement, vigoureusement.
toughness ['tʌfnis], *n.* raideur; dureté, nature coriace (*viande etc.*); (*fig.*) difficulté, *f.*
tour ['tuə], *n.* tour, voyage, *m.*; randonnée, tournée, *f.*—*v.i.* visiter (*un pays*); voyager dans (*un pays*); excursionner.
tourism ['tuərizm], *n.* tourisme, *m.*
tourist ['tuərist], *n.* touriste, *m., f.*, voyageur, *m.*; **tourist agency**, bureau de tourisme, *m.*
tournament ['tuənəmənt], *n.* tournoi; concours, *m.*
tourniquet ['tuənikei], *n.* garrot, *m.*
tousle [tauzl], *v.t.* tirailler, chiffonner; **tousled hair**, cheveux ébouriffés, *m.pl.*
tout [taut], *v.i.* racoler.—*n.* racoleur, *m.*
touting ['tautiŋ], *n.* racolage, *m.*
tow [tou], *n.* filasse, étoupe (*chanvre*); remorque, *f.*; **in tow**, à la remorque.—*v.t.* remorquer, touer, haler.
towage ['touidʒ], *n.* remorquage, touage, halage, *m.*
toward, towards [tu'wɔːd(z)], *prep.* vers, envers; du côté de; à l'égard de (*par respect pour*); sur, environ, vers (*l'heure*).
tow-boat ['toubout], *n.* remorqueur, *m.*
towel ['tauəl], *n.* essuie-mains, *m.inv.*, serviette, *f.*
towelling ['tauəliŋ], *n.* toile pour serviettes, *f.*; tissu-éponge, *m.*

tower ['tauə], *n.* tour, *f.*—*v.i.* **s'élever** (*au-dessus de*), dominer.
towering ['tauəriŋ], *a.* élevé; dominant; violent.
towing ['touiŋ], *n.* remorque, *f.*; halage (*sur canal*), *m.*
towing-boat ['touiŋbout], [TOW-BOAT].
tow(ing)-line ['tou(iŋ)lain], **tow(ing)-rope** ['tou(iŋ)roup], *n.* cable de remorque, *m.*, remorque, *f.*
tow(ing)-path ['tou(iŋ)pɑːθ], *n.* chemin de halage, *m.*
town [taun], *n.* ville, *f.*
town clerk ['taun'klɑːk], *n.* secrétaire de, mairie, *m.*
town council ['taun'kaunsl], *n.* conseil municipal, *m.*
town councilor ['taun'kaunsilə], *n.* conseiller municipal, *m.*
town hall ['taun'hɔːl], *n.* hôtel de ville, *m.*, mairie, *f.*
town planning ['taun plæniŋ], *n.* urbanisme, *m.*
townsfolk [TOWNSPEOPLE].
township ['taunʃip], *n.* commune, *f.*
townsman ['taunzmən], *n.* (*pl.* **-men** [men]) habitant de la ville, bourgeois, *m.*
townspeople ['taunzpiːpl], **townsfolk** ['taunzfouk], *n.* habitants (de la ville), citadins, *m.pl.*
tow-rope [TOW(ING)-LINE].
toxic ['tɔksik], *a.* toxique.
toxicology [tɔksi'kɔlədʒi], *n.* toxicologie, *f.*
toy [tɔi], *n.* jouet, joujou, *m*—*v.i.* jouer; folâtrer; s'amuser (*avec*).
trace (1) [treis], *n.* trace, *f.*; tracé (*calque*), *m.*—*v.t.* tracer; calquer (*dessin*); suivre la trace de (*to track*); (*fig.*) remonter à l'origine de.
trace (2) [treis], *n.* (*usu. pl.*) traits (*harnais*), *m.pl.*
traceable ['treisəbl], *a.* que l'on peut tracer.
tracer ['treisə], *n.* traceur; traçoir (*instrument*), *m.*
tracery ['treisəri], *n.* (*Arch.*) réseau, *m.*
trachea [trə'kiːə], *n.* (*Anat.*) trachée-artère, *f.*
tracing ['treisiŋ], *n.* tracé, tracement; calque, *m.*; **tracing paper**, papier à calquer, *m.*
track [træk], *n.* (*Spt.*) piste, *f.*, chemin (*route*), *m.*; (*Hunt.*) piste; (*Rail.*) voie; (*Astron.*) orbite, *f.*, sillage (*de bateau*), *m.*; **beaten track**, sentier battu, *m.*; (*Cine.*) **sound track**, bande sonore, *f.*—*v.t.* suivre à la piste; haler, remorquer.
tracker ['trækə], *n.* traqueur, *m.*
tracking ['trækiŋ], *n.* action de suivre à la trace, *f.*
trackless ['træklis], *a.* sans trace; sans chemins.
tract [trækt], *n.* étendue; contrée; brochure (*petit livre*), *f.*
tractable ['træktəbl], *a.* traitable, maniable.
tractile ['træktail], *a.* ductile.
traction ['trækʃən], *n.* traction, tension, *f.*
traction engine ['trækʃənendʒin], *n.* locomotive routière, *f.*
tractor ['træktə], *n.* tracteur, *m.*
trade [treid], *n.* commerce, trafic, négoce; métier, *m.*, profession (*vocation*), *f.*; **Board of Trade**, Ministère du Commerce, *m.*; **free trade**, libre-échange, *m.*; (*Comm.*) **trade name**, marque déposée, *f.*—*v.i.* trafiquer, faire le commerce (*de*).

trade-mark ['treidmɑːk], *n.* marque de fabrique, *f.*

trader ['treidə], *n.* négociant, *m.*

tradesman ['treidzmən], *n. (pl. -men* [men]) marchand, boutiquier (*détaillant*); fournisseur, *m.*

trade union ['treid 'juːnjən], *n.* syndicat ouvrier, *m.*

trade unionism ['treid'juːnjənizm], *n.* syndicalisme, *m.*

trade unionist ['treid'juːnjənist], *n.* syndicaliste, *m.*, *f.*

trade winds ['treidwindz], *n.pl.* vents alizés, *m.pl.*

trading ['treidiŋ], *a.* marchand, de commerce.—*n.* négoce, commerce, *m.*

tradition [trə'diʃən], *n.* tradition, *f.*

traditional [trə'diʃənl], *a.* traditionnel.

traduce [trə'djuːs], *v.t.* diffamer, calomnier.

traducer [trə'djuːsə], *n.* calomniateur, *m.*

traffic ['træfik], *n.* trafic; commerce, négoce, *m.*; circulation (*de voitures*), *f.*; (*Rail.*) mouvement, *m.*; **traffic jam**, embouteillage; **traffic light**, feu de signalisation. *m.*—*v.i.* trafiquer, commercer.

trafficker ['træfikə], *n.* trafiquant, *m.*

tragedian [trə'dʒiːdiən], *n.* auteur tragique; tragédien, *m.*

tragedy ['trædʒədi], *n.* tragédie, *f.*

tragic ['trædʒik], **tragical** ['trædʒikəl], *a.* tragique.

tragi-comedy ['trædʒi'kɔmidi], *n.* tragi-comédie, *f.*

tragi-comical ['trædʒi'kɔmikəl], *a.* tragi-comique.

trail [treil], *n.* traînée (*Hunt.*) piste, *f.*—*v.t.* suivre à la piste; traîner (*tirer après soi*).—*v.i.* traîner.

trailer ['treilə], *n.* remorque (*bicyclette, camion etc.*); (*Am.*) roulotte, caravane; (*Cine.*) bande de lancement, *f.*

train [trein], *n.* (*Rail.*) train, *m.*; suite, *f.* cortège (*personnel*), *m.*; série, *f.*, enchaînement (*succession*), *m.*; traînée (*de poudre à canon*); queue, traîne (*de robe*), *f.*; **breakdown train**, train de secours; **freight train**, train de marchandises, *m.*—*v.t.* exercer, instruire; dresser, entraîner (*cheval etc.*); former.—*v.i.* s'entraîner.

train bearer ['treinbɛərə], *n.* porte-queue, *m.*

trainee [trei'niː], *n.* stagiaire, *m.*, *f.*

trainer ['treinə], *n.* dresseur; entraîneur, *m.*

training ['treiniŋ], *n.* éducation, instruction, *f.*; dressage (*de cheval*); entraînement (*de cheval de course*), *m.*

training ship ['treiniŋʃip], *n.* vaisseau-école, *m.*

trait [trei, treit], *n.* trait, *m.*

traitor ['treitə], *n.* traître, *m.*

traitorous ['treitərəs], *a.* traître, perfide.

traitorously ['treitərəsli], *adv.* en traître, perfidement.

traitress ['treitris], *n.* traîtresse, *f.*

trajectory [trə'dʒektəri], *n.* trajectoire, *f.*

tram(-car) ['træm(kɑː)], *n.* tramway, *m.*

trammel ['træml], *n.* tramail (*filet*), *m.*; entrave (*de cheval*), *f.*—*v.t.* entraver, empêtrer (*de*).

tramp [træmp], *v.t.* faire à pied, faire.—*v.i.* aller à pied, marcher lourdement.—*n.* randonnée (*à pied*), *f.*; bruit de pas (*marche pesante*); vagabond, *m.*

trample [træmpl], *v.t.* fouler (*aux pieds*).

trampling ['træmpliŋ], *n.* piétinement, bruit de pas, *m.*

trance [trɑːns], *n.* extase; (*Path.*) catalepsie, *f.*

tranquil ['træŋkwil], *a.* tranquille.

tranquillity [træŋ'kwiliti], *n.* tranquillité, *f.*, calme, *m.*

tranquillize ['træŋkwilaiz], *v.t.* tranquilliser, calmer.

tranquillizer ['træŋkwilaizə], *n.* calmant, *m.*

transact [træn'zækt], *v.t.* traiter, expédier.

transaction [træn'zækʃən], *n.* transaction, affaire, *f.*

transactor [træn'zæktə], *n.* négociateur, *m.*

transalpine [træn'zælpain], *a.* transalpin.

transatlantic [trænzət'læntik], *a.* transatlantique.

transcend [træn'send], *v.t.* dépasser, surpasser.

transcendence [træn'sendəns], **transcendency** [træn'sendənsi], *n.* excellence, transcendance, *f.*

transcendent [træn'sendənt], *a.* transcendant.

transcendental [trænsen'dentl], *a.* transcendantal.

transcribe [træn'skraib], *v.t.* transcrire, copier.

transcriber [træn'skraibə], *n.* copiste, *m.*, *f.*, transcripteur, *m.*

transcript ['trænskript], *n.* copie, *f.*

transcription [træn'skripʃən], *n.* transcription, *f.*

transept ['trænsept], *n.* transept, *m.*

transfer [træns'fəː], *v.t.* transporter; (*Law*) transférer.—['trænsfə], *n.* copie, *f.*; (*Law*) transfert, *m.*

transferable ['trænsfərəbl], *a.* transférable, transmissible.

transference ['trænsfərəns], *n.* transfert, *m.*

transfiguration [trænsfigju'reiʃən], *n.* transfiguration, transformation, *f.*

transfigure [træns'figə], *v.t.* transfigurer.

transfix [træns'fiks], *v.t.* transpercer.

transform [træns'fɔːm], *v.t.* transformer, changer (*en*).—*v.i.* se transformer (*en*).

transformation [trænsfə'meiʃən], *n.* transformation, *f.*, changement, *m.*; **transformation scene**, changement à vue, *m.*

transformer [træns'fɔːmə], *n.* transformateur, *m.*

transfuse [træns'fjuːz], *v.t.* transfuser.

transfusion [træns'fjuːʒən], *n.* transfusion, *f.*

transgress [træns'gres, trænz'gres], *v.t.* transgresser, enfreindre.—*v.i.* transgresser, pécher.

transgression [træns'greʃən], *n.* transgression, infraction, *f.*

transgressor [træns'gresə], *n.* pécheur, *m.*, pécheresse, *f.*

tranship [træn'ʃip], *v.t.* transborder.

transience ['trænziəns], *n.* nature transitoire, courte durée, *f.*

transient ['trænziənt], *a.* passager, transitoire.

transistor [træn'zistə], *n.* transistor, transistron, *m.*

transit ['trænzit], *n.* passage, *m.*; **in transit**, en transit.

transition [træn'ziʃən], *n.* transition, *f.*

transitional [træn'ziʃənl], *a.* de transition.

transitive ['trænzitiv], *a.* qui passe; (*Gram.*) transitif.

601

transitoriness [ˈtrænzitərinis], *n.* nature transitoire, courte durée, *f.*

transitory [ˈtrænzitəri], *a.* transitoire, passager.

translatable [trænsˈleitəbl], *a.* traduisible.

translate [trænsˈleit], *v.t.* traduire; transférer (*évêque*).

translation [trænsˈleiʃən], *n.* traduction; translation (*d'un évêque*), *f.*

translator [trænsˈleitə], *n.* traducteur, *m.*

translucent [trænzˈljuːsənt], *a.* translucide.

transmarine [trænzməˈriːn], *a.* d'outremer.

transmigrate [trænzmaiˈgreit], *v.i.* passer d'un corps dans un autre; émigrer.

transmigration [trænzmaiˈgreiʃən], *n.* transmigration; métempsyc(h)ose (*des âmes*), *f.*

transmissible [trænzˈmisibl], *a.* transmissible.

transmission [trænzˈmiʃən], *n.* transmission, *f.* [(*Motor.*) see **gear-box**]

transmit [trænzˈmit], *v.t.* transmettre, envoyer; (*Rad.*) émettre.

transmitter [trænzˈmitə], *n.* (*Rad.*) émetteur, *m.*

transmutable [trænzˈmjuːtəbl], *a.* transmuable.

transmutation [trænzmjuˈteiʃən], *n.* transmutation, *f.*; changement (*de couleur*, *m.*

transmute [trænzˈmjuːt], *v.t.* transmuer, convertir.

transom [ˈtrænsəm], *n.* traverse (*de fenêtre*), imposte, *f.*

transparency [trænsˈpɛərənsi], *n.* transparence, *f.* (*Phot.*) diapositive, *f.*

transparent [trænsˈpɛərənt], *a.* transparent.

transparently [trænsˈpɛərəntli], *adv.* avec transparence; évidemment.

transpire [trænsˈpaiə, trænzˈpaiə], *v.i.* transpirer; (*fig.*) avoir lieu, arriver.

transplant [trænsˈplɑːnt, trænzˈplɑːnt], *v.t.* transplanter; (*fig.*) déplacer.

transplanting [trænsˈplɑːntiŋ, trænzˈplɑːntiŋ], *n.* transplantation, *f.*

transport [ˈtrænspɔːt], *n.* transport, *m.*— [trænsˈpɔːt], *v.t.* transporter; déporter (*forçat*).

transportation [trænspɔːˈteiʃən], *n.* transport, *m.*; déportation (*des forçats*), *f.*

transporter [trænsˈpɔːtə], *n.* entrepreneur de transports; (pont) transbordeur, *m.*

transporting [trænsˈpɔːtiŋ], *a.* ravissant, transportant.

transposal [trænsˈpouzl], *n.* transposition, *f.*

transpose [trænzˈpouz], *v.t.* transposer.

transubstantiation [trænsəbstænʃiˈeiʃən], *n.* transsubstantiation, *f.*

Transvaal [ˈtrænzvɑːl], **the.** le Transvaal, *m.*

transversal [trænzˈvɑːsl], *a.* transversal.

transversely [trænzˈvɑːsli], *adv.* en travers.

transverse [trænzˈvɑːs], *a.* transverse, transversal.

trap [træp], *n.* trappe, *f.*, piège, *m.*; carriole (*véhicule*), *f.*—*v.t.* prendre au piège, attraper.

trap door [ˈtræpdɔː], *n.* trappe, *f.*

trapeze [trəˈpiːz], *n.* trapèze, *m.*

trapper [ˈtræpə], *n.* trappeur, *m.*

trappings [ˈtræpiŋz], *n.pl.* harnais, *m.*; (*fig.*) parure, *f.*, atours, *m.pl.*

traps [træps], *n.pl.* bagages, *m.pl.*

trash [træʃ], *n.* rebut, *m.*; camelote, *f.*; fatras (*écrits*), *m.*

trashy [ˈtræʃi], *a.* de rebut, sans valeur.

travel [trævl], *v.t.* parcourir; faire (*distance etc.*).—*v.i.* voyager, être en voyage.—*n.* voyage, *m.*

traveller [ˈtrævlə], *n.* voyageur; (*Comm.*) commis voyageur, *m.*; **traveller's check**, chèque de voyage, *m.*

travelling [ˈtrævliŋ], *a.* voyageur, de voyage; ambulant (*itinérant*); **travelling expenses**, frais de déplacement, *m.pl.*; **travelling-case**, nécessaire de voyage, *m.*—*n.* voyage, *m.*, voyages, *m.pl.*

travelogue [ˈtrævələg], *n.* film de tourisme, *m.*

traverse [ˈtrævəs], *a.* oblique.—*n.* traverse, *f.*—*v.t.* traverser; (*Law*) nier.

travesty [ˈtrævəsti], *n.* travestissement, *m.*; parodie, *f.*—*v.t.* travestir, parodier.

trawl [trɔːl], *n.* chalut (*filet*), *m.*—*v.i.* pêcher au chalut.

trawler [ˈtrɔːlə], *n.* chalutier, *m.*

trawling [ˈtrɔːliŋ], *n.* pêche au chalut, *f.*

tray [trei], *n.* plateau, *m.*

treacherous [ˈtretʃərəs], *a.* traître, perfide.

treacherously [ˈtretʃərəsli], *adv.* en traître.

treachery [ˈtretʃəri], *n.* trahison, perfidie, *f.*

treacle [triːkl], *n.* mélasse, *f.*

tread [tred], *v.t. irr.* fouler, écraser.—*v.i.* mettre le pied, marcher (*sur*); se poser (*pieds*).—*n.* pas, *m.*; marche (*d'escalier*); chape (*d'un pneu*), *f.*

treading [ˈtrediŋ], *n.* pas, *m.*; marche, *f.*; foulage (*de raisins etc.*), *m.*

treadle [tredl], *n.* marche; pédale, *f.*

treadmill [ˈtredmil], *n.* trépigneuse, *f.*

treason [triːzn], *n.* trahison, *f.*; **high treason**, lèse-majesté, *f.*

treasonable [ˈtriːznəbl], *a.* de trahison.

treasonably [ˈtriːznəbli], *adv.* par trahison, traîtreusement.

treasure [ˈtreʒə], *n.* trésor, *m.*—*v.t.* garder, priser.

treasurer [ˈtreʒərə], *n.* trésorier, *m.*

treasure-trove [ˈtreʒətrouv], *n.* trésor trouvé, *m.*

treasury [ˈtreʒəri], *n.* trésor, trésor public, *m.*, finances, *f.pl.*, trésorerie, *f.*

treat [triːt], *n.* régal, festin, (*fig.*) plaisir, *m.*—*v.t.* traiter; régaler (*de*).—*v.i.* traiter (*de*); négocier.

treatise [ˈtriːtis], *n.* traité (*de ou sur*), *m.*

treatment [ˈtriːtmənt], *n.* traitement, *m.*

treaty [ˈtriːti], *n.* traité, *m.*

treble [trebl], *a.* triple; (*Mus.*) de dessus, soprano.—*n.* triple; (*Mus.*) dessus, soprano, *m.*—*v.t.*, *v.i.* tripler.

trebling [ˈtrebliŋ], *n.* triplement, *m.*

trebly [ˈtrebli], *adv.* triplement, trois fois.

tree [triː], *n.* arbre; embauchoir (*pour botte*), *m.*; (*fig.*) croix, *f.*

trefoil [ˈtriːfɔil], *n.* trèfle, *m.*

trellis [ˈtɛlis], *n.* treillis, treillage, *m.*

trellised [ˈtrelist], *a.* treillissé.

tremble [trembl], *v.i.* trembler.

trembling [ˈtrembliŋ], *a.* tremblant, tremblotant.—*n.* tremblement, *m.*

tremendous [triˈmendəs], *a.* terrible, épouvantable.

tremendously [triˈmendəsli], *adv.* terriblement.

tremor [ˈtremə], *n.* tremblement, *m.*; secousse, *f.*

tremulous ['tremjuləs], *a.* tremblant, *(fig.)* craintif.

tremulously ['tremjuləsli], *adv.* en tremblant, en tremblotant.

tremulousness ['tremjuləsnis], *n.* tremblotement, *m.*

trench [trentʃ], *n.* fossé, *m.*, tranchée; rigole *(entre sillons etc.)*, *f.*—*v.t.* creuser.

trenchancy ['trentʃənsi], *n.* causticité, *f.*

trenchant ['trentʃənt], *a.* tranchant, caustique.

trencher ['trentʃə], *n.* tranchoir, tailloir, *m.*

trencherman ['trentʃəmən], *n.* (*pl.* **-men** [men]) gros mangeur, *m.*

trend [trend], *n.* direction, tendance, *f.*—*v.i.* se diriger, tendre (*vers*).

trepan [trə'pæn], *n.* (*Surg.*) trépan, *m.*—*v.t.* trépaner.

trepanning [trə'pæniŋ], *n.* trépanation, *f.*

trepidation [trepi'deiʃən], *n.* trépidation, *f.*

trespass ['trespəs], *n.* violation de propriété, *f.*, délit, *m.*; (*Scripture*) offense, *f.*—*v.i.* violer la propriété; empiéter (*sur*); (*Scripture*) pécher; transgresser.

trespasser ['trespəsə], *n.* violateur du droit de propriété; (*Scripture*) pécheur, *m.*, pécheresse, *f.*

tress [tres], *n.* tresse, boucle, *f.*

trestle [tresl], *n.* tréteau, *m.*

trestle bed ['treslbed], *n.* lit de sangle, *m.*

triad ['traiæd], *n.* triade, *f.*

trial ['traiəl], *a.* d'essai.—*n.* expérience, épreuve, *f.*, essai (*Law*) procès, *m.*

triangle ['traiæŋgl], *n.* triangle, *m.*

triangular [trai'æŋjulə], *a.* triangulaire.

tribal [traibl], *a.* tribal.

tribe [traib], *n.* tribu, peuplade; (*fig.*) race, *f.*

tribulation [tribju'leiʃən], *n.* tribulation, *f.*

tribunal [trai'bjuːnl], *n.* tribunal, *m.*

tribune ('tribjuːn], *n.* (*Rom. Hist.*) tribun, *m.*; tribune (*estrade*), *f.*

tributary ['tribjutəri], *a.* tributaire.—*n.* tributaire; affluent (*rivière*), *m.*

tribute ['tribjuːt], *n.* tribut; (*fig.*) hommage, *m.*

trice (1) [trais], *n.* **in a trice**, en un clin d'œil.

trice (2) [trais], *v.t.* (*Naut.*) hisser.

trick [trik], *n.* tour, artifice, *m.*; (*Cards*) levée; ruse, finesse, *f.*; tic (*habitude*), *m.*; **nasty trick**, vilain tour; **to play someone a trick**, faire une niche *ou* jouer un tour à quelqu'un.—*v.t.* duper; tricher (*en jouant*); **to trick out**, parer, orner.

trickery ['trikəri], *n.* tromperie, fourberie, tricherie, *f.*

trickish ['trikiʃ], *a.* trompeur, fourbe, fin.

trickle [trikl], *v.i.* suinter, dégoutter.

trickling ['trikliŋ], *n.* écoulement, *m.*

trickster ['trikstə], *n.* fourbe, escroc, *m.*

tricky ['triki], *a.* fourbe, rusé; (*fig.*) compliqué; délicat (*à manier*).

tricolor ['traikʌlə], *n.* drapeau tricolore, *m.*

tricolored ['traikʌləd], *a.* tricolore.

tricycle ['traisikl], *n.* tricycle, *m.*

trident ['traidənt], *n.* trident, *m.*

tried [traid], *a.* éprouvé.

triennial [trai'eniəl], *a.* triennal.—*n.* (*Bot.*) plante triennale, *f.*

triennially [trai'eniəli], *adv.* tous les trois ans.

trier ['traiə], *n.* (*Law*) juge; arbitre, *m.*; (*fig.*) épreuve, pierre de touche, *f.*

trifle [traifl], *n.* bagatelle; (*Cook.*) sorte de charlotte russe, *f.*—*v.i.* badiner; **to trifle with**, plaisanter avec, se moquer de.

trifler ['traiflə], *n.* personne frivole, *f.*

trifling ['traifliŋ], *a.* de rien, insignifiant, frivole.—*n.* frivolité, *f.*, badinage, *m.*

trigamy ['trigəmi], *n.* trigamie, *f.*

trigger ['trigə], *n.* détente, *f.*

trigonometry [trigə'nɔmətri], *n.* trigonométrie, *f.*

trilateral [trai'lætərəl], *a.* trilatéral.

trill [tril], *n.* trille, *m.*—*v.i.* triller.

trillion ['triljən], *n.* (*since* 1948) trillion; (*before* 1948) quintillion, *m.*

trilogy ['trilədʒi], *n.* trilogie, *f.*

trim [trim], *a.* soigné, coquet, bien mis, bien arrangé.—*n.* bon ordre, *m.*; assiette (*de bateau*), *f.*; orientement (*des voiles*); arrimage (*de cale*), *m.*—*v.t.* arranger, mettre en ordre; garnir, parer (*de*); émonder, tailler (*couper*); (*Naut.*) arrimer (*cargaison*); orienter (*voiles*).—*v.i.* (*Polit. slang*) balancer entre deux partis.

trimly ['trimli], *adv.* bien, gentiment, proprement.

trimmer ['trimə], *n.* (*Polit.*) opportuniste, *m.*, *f.*; (*Naut.*) soutier, *m.*

trimming ['trimiŋ], *n.* garniture; semonce; (*pl.*) parure (*de viande*), *f.*

trimness ['trimnis], *n.* air soigné, bon ordre, *m.*

Trinidad ['trinidæd]. (Île de la) Trinité, *f.*

Trinity ['triniti], *n.* Trinité, *f.*

trinket ['triŋkit], *n.* petit bijou, *m.*, breloque, *f.*

trinomial [trai'noumiəl], *a.* and *n.* trinôme, *m.*

trio ['triːou], *n.* trio, *m.*

trip [trip], *v.t.* renverser, faire tomber.—*v.i.* trébucher, faire un faux pas; fourcher (*la langue*); courir légèrement.—*n.* croc-enjambe, faux pas, *m.*; excursion, *f.*, tour, voyage, *m.*

tripe [traip], *n.* tripes, *f.pl.*

triple [tripl], *a.* triple.—*v.t.* tripler.

triplet ['triplit], *n.* (*Pros.*) tercet; (*Mus.*) triolet, *m.*; (*pl.*) triplés, *m.pl.*

triplicate ['triplikit], *a.* triplé.—*n.* triplicata (*copie*), *m.*

tripod ['traipɔd], *n.* trépied, *m.*

tripper ['tripə], *n.* (*colloq.*) excursionniste, *m.*, *f.*

tripping ['tripiŋ], *a.* agile, léger.—*n.* croc en jambe, faux pas, *m.*; erreur, *f.*; pas léger, *m.*

trireme ['trairiːm], *n.* trirème, *f.*

trisect [trai'sekt], *v.t.* couper en trois.

trisyllabic [traisi'læbik], *a.* trissyllabe.

trisyllable [trai'siləbl], *n.* trissyllabe, *m.*

trite [trait], *a.* usé, banal, rebattu.

triteness ['traitnis], *n.* nature banale, trivialité, *f.*

Triton ['traitən]. Triton, *m.*

triumph ['traiəmf], *n.* triomphe, *m.*—*v.i.* triompher.

triumphal [trai'ʌmfl], *a.* triomphal.

triumphant [trai'ʌmfənt], *a.* triomphant.

triumphantly [trai'ʌmfəntli], *adv.* en triomphe.

triumvir [trai'ʌmvə], *n.* triumvir, *m.*

triumvirate [trai'ʌmvərit], *n.* triumvirat, *m.*

trivet ['trivit], *n.* trépied, *m.*

603

trivial

trivial ['triviəl], *a.* banal, insignifiant, sans importance.
triviality [trivi'æliti], *n.* insignifiance; banalité, *f.*
troat [trout], *n.* bramement, *m.*—*v.t.* bramer, raire (*cerf*).
trochaic [tro'keiik], *a.* trochaïque.
trochee ['trouki], *n.* trochée, *m.*
Trojan ['troudʒən], *a.* troyen.—*n.* Troyen, *m.*
troll [troul], *v.t.* rouler, tourner.
trolley, trolly ['troli], *n.* fardier, chariot; (*Elec.*) trolley, *m.*; *dinner trolley*, table roulante, *f.* [see **tram(-car**)]
trolley bus ['trolibʌs], *n.* trolleybus, *m.*
trollop ['troləp], *n.* souillon, *f.*
trombone [trɔm'boun], *n.* trombone, *m.*
troop [tru:p], *n.* troupe, bande, *f.*—*v.i.* s'attrouper, s'assembler.
trooper ['tru:pə], *n.* (*Mil.*) soldat à cheval, cavalier, *m.*
trophy ['troufi], *n.* trophée, *m.*
tropic ['trɔpik], *n.* tropique, *m.*
tropical ['trɔpikəl], *a.* tropical, des tropiques.
trot [trɔt], *n.* trot, *m.*—*v.i.* trotter, aller au trot; trottiner (*enfant*).
troth [trouθ], *n.* foi, *f.*; *by my troth !* ma foi !
trotter ['trɔtə], *n.* cheval de trot, trotteur, *m.*; (*pl.*) pieds de mouton, pieds de cochon, *m.pl.*
trotting ['trɔtiŋ], *a.* trotteur.—*n.* trot, *m.*
troubadour ['tru:bəduə], *n.* troubadour, *m.*
trouble [trʌbl], *v.t.* agiter; troubler, déranger (*gêner*); tourmenter, affliger (*faire souffrir*); inquiéter (*préoccuper*).—*v.i.* s'inquiéter, se donner la peine (*de*).—*n.* trouble, *m.*; peine (*effort*), affliction, *f.*, souci, chagrin (*tristesse*) ennui (*difficulté*), *m.*; *it is not worth the trouble,* ce n'est pas la peine.
troubled [trʌbld], *a.* inquiet, agité; trouble (*eau etc.*).
troublesome ['trʌblsəm], *a.* ennuyeux, incommode; fatigant, fâcheux.
troublesomeness ['trʌblsəmnis], *n.* ennui, embarras, *m.*, gêne, *f.*
*****troublous** ['trʌbləs], *a.* troublé, agité, orageux.
trough [trɔf], *n.* auge, huche, *f.*; (*Cook.*) pétrin; auget, abreuvoir (*pour boire*), *m.*
trounce [trauns], *v.t.* rosser, étriller.
trouncing ['traunsiŋ], *n.* raclée, *f.*, étrillage, *m.*
trouser-press ['trauzəpres], *n.* presse-pantalon, *m.*
trousers ['trauzəz], *n.pl.* pantalon, *m.*
trousseau ['tru:sou], *n.* trousseau, *m.*
trout [traut], *n.* truite, *f.*
trowel ['trauəl], *n.* truelle, *f.*
Troy [trɔi], Troie, *f.*
troy weight ['trɔiweit], *n.* troy (*poids de douze onces à la livre*), *m.*
truant ['tru:ənt], *n.* fainéant, vagabond, *m.*; *to play truant,* faire l'école buissonnière.
truce [tru:s], *n.* trêve, *f.*
truck [trʌk], *n.* fardier, chariot (*charrette*); (*Am.*) camion; (*Rail.*) wagon, *m.*—*v.i.* troquer.
truckle [trʌkl], *n.* roulette, *f.*—*v.i.* ramper, s'abaisser (*devant*).
truckle bed ['trʌklbed], *n.* grabat, *m.*.
truckling ['trʌkliŋ], *n.* soumission, *f.*, abaissement, *m.*

truculence ['trʌkjuləns], *n.* férocité, truculence, *f.*
truculent ['trʌkjulənt], *a.* brutal, féroce, farouche.
trudge [trʌdʒ], *n.* marche pénible, *f.*—*v.i.* clopiner, marcher péniblement.
true [tru:], *a.* vrai, véritable; fidèle (*véridique*); exact (*juste*); loyal (*honnête*), droit (*vertueux*); *to come true,* se réaliser.—*int.* c'est vrai! c'est juste!—*adv.* juste (*précisément*).—*v.t.* ajuster.
true-bred ['tru:bred], *a.* de bonne race, pur sang; (*fig.*) accompli.
true-hearted ['tru:'hɑ:tid], *a.* au cœur sincère.
trueness ['tru:nis], *n.* fidélité; justesse, *f.*
truffle [trʌfl], *n.* truffe, *f.*; *to stuff with truffles,* truffer.
truism ['tru:izm], *n.* truisme, *m.*
truly ['tru:li], *adv.* vraiment, véritablement.
trump [trʌmp], *n.* trompe, trompette, *f.*; (*Cards*) atout, *m.*—*v.t.* jouer atout, couper.
trumpery ['trʌmpəri], *a.* sans valeur, mesquin.—*n.* rebut, *m.*, blague, *f.*
trumpet ['trʌmpit], *n.* trompette, *f.*—*v.t.* proclamer.—*v.i.* barrir (*éléphant*).
trumpet call ['trʌmpitkɔ:l], *n.* coup de trompette, *m.*
trumpeter ['trʌmpitə], *n.* trompette, *m.*
truncate [trʌŋ'keit], *v.t.* tronquer.
truncheon ['trʌntʃən], *n.* bâton, *m.*; matraque, *f.*
trundle [trʌndl], *v.t.* rouler.
trunk [trʌŋk], *n.* tronc, *m.*; malle (*boîte*); trompe (*d'éléphant*), *f.*; coffre (*d'auto*), *m.*
trunk call ['trʌŋkɔ:l], *n.* (*Teleph.*) appel interurbain, *m.*
trunk road ['trʌŋkroud], *n.* route à grande circulation, *f.*
trunnion ['trʌnjən], *n.* tourillon, *m.*
truss [trʌs], *n.* botte (*de foin etc.*), *f.*; paquet; (*Surg.*) bandage herniaire, *m.*—*v.t.* trousser (*une poule*); lier (*foin*).
trust [trʌst], *n.* confiance (*en*), *f.*; dépôt, *m.*; garde (*charge*), *f.*; crédit; (*Law*) fidéicommis; (*Comm.*) trust, syndicat, *m.*—*v.t.* se fier à, se confier à; faire crédit à (*en matière d'argent*).—*v.i.* avoir confiance (*en* ou *dans*); s'attendre (*à*).
trust deed ['trʌstdi:d], *n.* acte fiduciaire, *m.*
trusted ['trʌstid], *a.* de confiance.
trustee [trʌs'ti:], *n.* gardien, *m.*, dépositaire; (*Law*) fidéicommissaire, *m.*, *f.*
trusteeship [trʌs'ti:ʃip], *n.* administration; tutelle, *f.*, (*Law*) fidéicommis, *m.*
trustiness ['trʌstinis], *n.* fidélité, loyauté, *f.*
trusting ['trʌstiŋ], *a.* plein de confiance.
trustworthiness ['trʌstwə:ðinis], *n.* fidélité (*personne*); exactitude (*des nouvelles etc.*), *f.*
trustworthy ['trʌstwə:ði], *a.* digne de confiance; exact (*nouvelles*).
trusty ['trʌsti], *a.* sûr, fidèle, loyal.
truth [tru:θ], *n.* vérité, *f.*, vrai, *m.*; *to tell the truth . . .,* à vrai dire . . .
truthful ['tru:θful], *a.* véridique, vrai.
truthfully ['tru:θfuli], *adv.* véridiquement, avec vérité.
truthfulness ['tru:θfulnis], *n.* véracité, *f.*
try [trai], *v.t.* essayer; éprouver, mettre à l'épreuve; tenter (*se prêter à*); (*Law*) juger.—*v.i.* essayer, tâcher (*de*).—*n.* essai, *m.*

trying ['traiiŋ], *a.* difficile, pénible.

*tryst [traist], *n.* rendez-vous, *m.*

Tsar [zɑː], *n.* Tsar, *m.*

Tsarina [zɑːˈriːnə], *n.* Tsarine, *f.*

tsetse ['tsetsi], *n.* mouche tsé-tsé, *f.*

tub [tʌb], *n.* cuve, *f.*, baquet; bain (*moderne*), *m.*—*v.t.* encuver; (*Gard.*) encaisser.

tuba ['tjuːbə], *n.* tuba, (*m.*); contrebasse à vent, *f.*

tubby ['tʌbi], *a.* gros, obèse.

tube [tjuːb], *n.* tube; (*Anat.*) conduit, canal; (*Rail.*) métro, *m.*; **inner tube**, chambre à air, *f.*; (*Rad.*) lampe, *f.*

tuber ['tjuːbə], *n.* tubercule, *m.*

tubercular [tjuˈbəːkjulə], *a.* tuberculeux.

tuberculosis [tjubəːkjuˈlousis], *n.* tuberculose, *f.*

tuberose ['tjuːbərous], *a.* tubéreux.—*n.* tubéreuse, *f.*

tuberous ['tjuːbərəs], *a.* tubéreux.

tubular ['tjuːbjulə], *a.* tubulaire.

tuck [tʌk], *n.* pli, *m.*; plisser; serrer; retrousser.

tucker ['tʌkə], *n.* chemisette, collerette, *f.*

Tuesday ['tjuːzd(e)i]. mardi, *m.*; **Shrove Tuesday,** mardi gras.

tuft [tʌft], *n.* touffe (*d'herbe ou de cheveux*); huppe (*d'oiseau*), *f.*

tufted ['tʌftid], *a.* touffu; huppé (*oiseau*).

tug [tʌg], *v.t.* tirer avec effort; remorquer (*to tow*).—*n.* tiraillement; remorqueur (*bateau*), *m.*

tuition [tjuˈiʃən], *n.* instruction, *f.*, enseignement, *m.*; frais d'inscription, *m.*

tulip ['tjuːlip], *n.* tulipe, *f.*

tulle [tjuːl], *n.* tulle, *m.*

tumble [tʌmbl], *n.* culbute, chute, *f.*—*v.t.* culbuter.—*v.i.* tomber; rouler (*descendre en roulant*); dégringoler (*se tourner*).

tumbledown ['tʌmbldaun], *a.* croulant, délabré.

tumbler ['tʌmblə], *n.* verre sans pied; gobelet; culbutant (*pigeon*), *m.*

tumblerful ['tʌmbləful], *n.* plein un grand verre, *m.*

tumbril ['tʌmbril], **tumbrel** ['tʌmbrəl], *n.* tombereau, *m.*

tumefaction [tjuːmiˈfækʃən], *n.* tuméfaction, *f.*

tumefy ['tjuːmifai], *v.t.* tuméfier.—*v.i.* se tuméfier.

tumid ['tjuːmid], *a.* enflé, gonflé; (*fig.*) boursouflé.

tumidity [tjuˈmiditi], **tumidness** ['tjuːmidnis], *n.* enflure; (*fig.*) turgescence, *f.*

tumor ['tjuːmə], *n.* tumeur, *f.*

tumular ['tjuːmjulə], *a.* en monticule.

tumult ['tjuːmʌlt], *n.* tumulte; trouble, *m.*

tumultuous [tjuˈmʌltjuəs], *a.* tumultueux, turbulent, agité.

tumultuousness [tjuˈmʌltjuəsnis], *n.* turbulence, *f.*

tun [tʌn], *n.* tonneau, fût, *m.*; cuve, *f.*

tunable ['tjuːnəbl], *a.* accordable.

tundra ['tʌndrə], *n.* toundra, *f.*

tune [tjuːn], *n.* air; accord, *m.*; (*fig.*) harmonie, humeur, *f.*; **in tune,** d'accord; **out of tune,** faux.—*v.t.* accorder, mettre d'accord.—*v.i.* (*Rad.*) **to tune in,** accrocher (*un poste*).

tuneful ['tjuːnful], *a.* harmonieux, mélodieux.

tuneless ['tjuːnlis], *a.* discordant.

tuner ['tjuːnə], *n.* accordeur, *m.*

tungsten ['tʌŋstən], *n.* tungstène, *m.*

tunic ['tjuːnik], *n.* tunique, *f.*

tuning ['tjuːniŋ], *n.* accord, *m.*, action d'accorder, *f.*

tuning fork ['tjuːniŋfɔːk], *n.* diapason, *m.*

tuning hammer ['tjuːniŋhæmə], *n.* accordoir, *m.*

Tunisia [tjuˈniziə]. la Tunisie, *f.*

Tunisian [tjuˈniziən], *a.* tunisien.—*n.* Tunisien (*personne*).

tunnel [tʌnl], *n.* tunnel, passage souterrain, *m.*—*v.t.* percer un tunnel dans.

tunnelling ['tʌnəliŋ], *n.* construction de tunnels, *f.*

tunny ['tʌni], *n.* (*Ichth.*) thon, *m.*

turban ['təːbən], *n.* turban, *m.*

turbid ['təːbid], *a.* trouble, bourbeux.

turbidity [təːˈbiditi], **turbidness** ['təːbidnis], *n.* état bourbeux, état trouble, *m.*

turbine ['təːbin, 'təːbain], *n.* turbine, *f.*

turbo-prop ['təːbɔprɔp], *a.* (*Av.*) à turbopropulseur.

turbot ['təːbət], *n.* turbot, *m.*

turbulence ['təːbjuləns], **turbulency** ['təːbjulənsi], *n.* turbulence, *f.*, tumulte, *m.*

turbulent ['təːbjulənt], *a.* tumultueux, turbulent.

turbulently ['təːbjuləntli], *adv.* tumultueusement.

tureen [tjuˈriːn], *n.* soupière, *f.*

turf [təːf], *n.* gazon, *m.*; motte de gazon; tourbe (*combustible*), *f.*; (*fig.*) turf, *m.*—*v.t.* gazonner.

turfing ['təːfiŋ], *n.* gazonnement, *m.*

turf-moss ['təːfmɔs], **turf-pit** ['təːfpit], *n.* tourbière, *f.*

turfy ['təːfi], *a.* gazonné; tourbeux.

turgid ['təːdʒid], *a.* gonflé; boursouflé.

turgidity [təːˈdʒiditi], **turgidness** ['təːdʒidnis], *n.* turgescence; (*fig.*) emphase (*de style*), *f.*

Turk [təːk], *n.* Turc (*personne*), *m.*

Turkey ['təːki]. la Turquie, *f.*

turkey ['təːki], *n.* dindon, *m.*; **hen turkey,** dinde, *f.*

Turkish ['təːkiʃ], *a.* de Turquie, turc.—*n.* turc (*langue*), *m.*

turmoil ['təːmɔil], *n.* tumulte, *m.*, agitation, *f.*

turn [təːn], *v.t.* tourner, faire tourner; faire pencher (*la balance*); retourner (*vêtement etc.*); changer, convertir (*transformer*); traduire (*en une autre langue*); soulever (*l'estomac*); émousser (*le tranchant*); (*fig.*) rouler (*dans la tête*); **to turn aside,** détourner, écarter (*de*); **to turn away,** renvoyer, congédier; **to turn back,** faire retourner; **to turn down,** rabattre (*un col*); refuser; **to turn in,** tourner en dedans; **to turn into,** changer en; **to turn off,** couper (*vapeur*), fermer (*robinet*); **to turn on,** donner (*vapeur*), ouvrir (*robinet*); **to turn out,** mettre dehors; éteindre (*lumière*); **to turn over,** retourner, feuilleter (*pages d'un livre*); **to turn tail,** prendre la fuite; **to turn up,** retrousser.—*v.i.* tourner, se tourner; se retourner (*vers*); se détourner (*s'écarter*); se changer (*en*); devenir, se faire; **to turn back,** rebrousser chemin; **to turn from,** s'éloigner de; **to turn in,** se coucher (*aller au lit*); **to turn round,** tourner, se

605

tourner, se retourner; *to turn to*, s'adresser à; *to turn up*, se retrousser; arriver (*se passer*).—*n.* tour; coude, détour (*tournant*); service; changement, *m.*; occasion; tournure (*d'esprit*), *f.*; trait (*de balance*), *m.*; *a bad turn*, un mauvais tour; *a good turn*, un service; *by turns, in turns*, à tour de rôle.

turncoat ['tə:nkout], *n.* renégat, *m.*

turn-cock ['tə:nkɔk], *n.* fontainier, *m.*

turner ['tə:nə], *n.* tourneur, *m.*

turnery ['tə:nəri], *n.* art du tourneur, *m.*

turning ['tə:niŋ], *n.* tournant (*de route etc.*); (*Carp.*) tournage, *m.*

turning-lathe ['tə:niŋleið], *n.* tour, *m.*

turning point ['tə:niŋpɔint], *n.* point décisif, moment critique, *m.*

turnip ['tə:nip], *n.* navet, *m.*

turnkey ['tə:nki:], *n.* guichetier, porte-clefs, *m.*

turn-out ['tə:naut], *n.* équipage, *m.*; tenue, *f.*

turn-over ['tə:nouvə], *n.* chiffre d'affaires; chausson (*pâte*), *m.*

turnpike ['tə:npaik], *n.* barrière de péage, *f.*; autoroute, *f.*

turnspit ['tə:nspit], *n.* tournebroche, *m.*

turnstile ['tə:nstail], *n.* tourniquet, *m.*

turn-table ['tə:nteibl], *n.* plaque tournante; platine, *f.*

turn-up ['tə:nʌp], *n.* revers (*de pantalon*), *m.*

turpentine ['tə:pəntain], *n.* térébenthine, *f.*

turpitude ['tə:pitju:d], *n.* turpitude, *f.*

turquoise ['tə:kwɔiz], *n.* turquoise, *f.*

turret ['tʌrit], *n.* tourelle, *f.*

turreted ['tʌritid], *a.* garni de tourelles.

turtle [tə:tl], *n.* tortue de mer, *f.*; *to turn turtle*, chavirer (*bateau*), capoter (*voiture*).

turtle-dove ['tə:tldʌv], *n.* tourterelle, *f.*

Tuscan ['tʌskən], *a.* toscan.—*n.* Toscan (*personne*), *m.*

Tuscany ['tʌskəni]. la Toscane, *f.*

tush! [tʌʃ], *int.* bah! fi donc!

tusk [tʌsk], *n.* défense (*d'éléphant*), *f.*; croc (*dent*), *m.*

tussle [tʌsl], *n.* lutte, bagarre, *f.*

tut! [tʌt], *int.* bah! allons donc!

tutelage ['tju:tilidʒ], *n.* tutelle, *f.*

tutor ['tju:tə], *n.* précepteur (*dans une famille*); (*Univ.*) maître-assistant, *m.*—*v.t.* instruire, enseigner.

tutorial [tju:'tɔ:riəl], *a.* de précepteur.

tutoring ['tju:təriŋ], *n.* instruction, *f.*

tutorship ['tju:təʃip], *n.* préceptorat, *m.*

twaddle [twɔdl], *n.* bavardage, caquetage, *m.*

*twain [twein], *a.* and *n.* deux, *m.*

twang [twæŋ], *n.* son sec (*d'une corde qui vibre*); accent nasillard (*voix*), *m.*—*v.t.* faire résonner, faire vibrer.—*v.i.* résonner, nasiller.

tweak [twi:k], *v.t.* pincer (*en tordant*).

tweezers ['twi:zəz], *n.pl.* pinces à épiler (*pour poils*), *f.pl.*

twelfth [twelfθ], *a.* douzième; douze (*du mois, des rois etc.*), *m.*; *Twelfth Night*, jour des Rois, *m.*—*n.* douzième (*fraction*), *m.*

twelve [twelv], *a.* and *n.* douze, *m.*; *twelve o'clock*, midi (*noon*), minuit (*midnight*), *m.*

twelvemonth ['twelvmʌnθ], *n.* an, *m.*, année, *f.*

twentieth ['twentiəθ], *a.* vingtième; vingt (*du mois etc.*).—*n.* vingtième (*fraction*), *m.*

twenty ['twenti], *a.* and *n.* vingt, *m.*

twenty-first ['twenti'fə:st], *a.* vingt et unième, vingt et un (*du mois etc.*).

twice [twais], *adv.* deux fois.

twig [twig], *n.* brindille, ramille, *f.*

twilight ['twailait], *a.* crépusculaire.—*n.* crépuscule, *m.*

twill [twil], *n.* étoffe croisée, *f.*

twin [twin], *a.* jumeau; jumelé; (*Bot.*) double, géminé.—*n.* jumeau, *m.*, jumelle, *f.*

twine [twain], *n.* ficelle, *f.*—*v.t.* retordre; enlacer.—*v.i.* s'entrelacer, s'enrouler.

twinge [twindʒ], *n.* élancement; remords (*de conscience*), *m.*—*v.i.* élancer; (*fig.*) torturer.

twinkle [twiŋkl], *v.i.* étinceler.

twinkling ['twiŋkliŋ], *a.* étincelant, scintillant. —*n.* scintillement, clignotement (*des yeux*), *m.*; *in the twinkling of an eye*, en un clin d'œil.

twirl [twə:l], *v.t.* faire tournoyer; friser (*favc¯is*).—*v.i.* tournoyer, tourner rapidement.—*n.* tournoiement, *m.*; pirouette, *f.*

twist [twist], *v.t.* tordre; tortiller, retordre; cercler, entourer; enlacer (*entortiller*); (*fig.*) pervertir (*dénaturer*).—*v.i.* se tordre, s'entrelacer, s'enlacer, s'enrouler.—*n.* cordon, *m.*, corde, *f.*; tortillon (*de papier*), *m.*; carotte (*de tabac*), *f.*

twisted ['twistid], *a.* tordu; (*fig.*) perverti, défiguré, dénaturé.

twisting ['twistiŋ], *a.* tortueux.—*n.* tordage; tortillement, *m.*

twitch [twitʃ], *n.* saccade, *f.*; tic (*contraction spasmodique*); tiraillement (*de douleur*), *m.*—*v.t.* tirer brusquement; crisper.—*v.i.* se contracter nerveusement.

twitching ['twitʃiŋ], *n.* saccade, crispation (*des muscles etc.*), *f.*; tiraillement (*de douleur*), *m.*

twitter ['twitə], *v.t.*, *v.i.* gazouiller.—*n.* gazouillement, *m.*

two [tu:], *a.* and *n.* deux, *m.*

two-edged ['tu:edʒd], *a.* à deux tranchants.

twofold ['tu:fould], *a.* double.—*adv.* doublement, deux fois.

two-stroke ['tu:strouk], *a.* à deux temps.

tycoon [tai'ku:n], *n.* taïcoun; (*fam.*) brasseur d'affaires, manitou, *m.*

type [taip], *n.* type; (*Print.*) caractère; (*pop.*) type, *m.*—*v.t.* [TYPEWRITE].

typewrite ['taiprait], *v.t.* écrire à la machine, dactylographier, taper.

typewriter ['taipraitə], *n.* machine à écrire, *f.*

typewritten ['taipritn], *a.* tapé à la machine.

typhoid ['taifoid], *a.* typhoïde.

typhoon [tai'fu:n], *n.* typhon, *m.*, trombe, *f.*

typhus ['taifəs], *n.* typhus, *m.*

typical ['tipikl], *a.* typique.

typically ['tipikli], *adv.* d'une manière typique.

typify ['tipifai], *v.t.* symboliser.

typing ['taipiŋ], *n.* dactylographie, (*fam.*) dactylo, *f.*

typist ['taipist], *n.* dactylographe, (*fam.*) dactylo, *m.*, *f.*

typography [tai'pɔgrəfi], *n.* typographie, *f.*

tyrannical [ti'rænikl], *a.* tyrannique.

tyrannically [ti'rænikli], *adv.* tyranniquement.

tyrannize ['tirənaiz], *v.i.* faire le tyran; *to tyrannize over*, tyranniser.

tyranny ['tirəni], n. tyrannie, f.
tyrant ['taiərənt], n. tyran, m.
tyre ['taiə], n. pneu (de roue), m.
tyro ['taiərou], n. novice, débutant, m.
Tzar [TSAR].

U

U, u [ju:]. vingt et unième lettre de l'alphabet, m.
ubiquitous [ju'bikwitəs], a. omniprésent.
ubiquity [ju'bikwiti], n. ubiquité, f.
udder ['Adə], n. mamelle, f., pis, m.
ugh! [u:x, u:h, Ax, uf], int. pouah!
ugliness ['Aglinis], n. laideur, f.
ugly ['Agli], a. laid, vilain.
Ukraine [ju'krein], the. l'Ukraine, f.
Ukrainian [ju'kreiniən], a. ukrainien.—n. Ukrainien (personne), m.
ukulele [ju:kə'leili], n. ukulélé, m.
ulcer ['Alsə], n. ulcère, m.
ulcerate ['Alsəreit], v.t. ulcérer.—v.i. s'ulcérer.
ulcerated ['Alsəreitid], a. ulcéré.
ulceration [Alsə'reiʃən], n. ulcération, f.
ulcerous ['Alsərəs], a. ulcéreux.
ullage ['Alidʒ], n. vidange, f.
ulterior [Al'tiəriə], a. ultérieur; without ulterior motive, sans arrière-pensée.
ultimate ['Altimit], a. dernier; extrême.
ultimately ['Altimitli], adv. finalement, à la fin.
ultimatum [Alti'meitəm], n. (pl. ultimata [Alti'meitə]) ultimatum, m.
ultimo ['Altimou], adv. (abbr. ult. [Alt]) du mois dernier.
ultra ['Altrə], n. ultra, m.
ultramarine [Altrəmə'ri:n], a. d'outremer.—n. outremer, m.
ululate ['ju:kə'leili], v.i. ululer.
Ulysses [ju:'lisi:z]. Ulysse, m.
umber ['Ambə], n. (Paint.) terre d'ombre, f.
umbilical [Am'bilikl], a. ombilical.
umbrage ['Ambridʒ], n. ombrage, m.
umbrella [Am'brelə], n. parapluie, m.; umbrella stand, porte-parapluies, m.inv.
umpire ['Ampaiə], n. arbitre, m.—v.t., v.i. arbitrer.
unabashed [Anə'bæʃt], a. sans être confus.
unabated [Anə'beitid], a. sans diminution.
unable [An'eibl], a. incapable (de); to be unable to, ne pas pouvoir.
unabridged [Anə'bridʒd], a. non abrégé; en entier.
unacceptable [Anək'septəbl], a. inacceptable.
unaccommodating [Anə'kɔmədeitiŋ], a. peu accommodant.
unaccompanied [Anə'kAmpənid], a. seul, sans suite.
unaccountable [Anə'kauntəbl], a. inexplicable, inconcevable.
unaccountably [Anə'kauntəbli], adv. inconcevablement.
unaccustomed [Anə'kAstəmd], a. inaccoutumé (à); peu habitué.

unacknowledged [Anək'nɔlidʒd], a. non reconnu; sans réponse (lettre).
unacquainted [Anə'kweintid], a. étranger (à); peu familier (avec).
unadopted [Anə'dɔptid], a. non adopté.
unadorned [Anə'dɔ:nd], a. sans ornement.
unadulterated [Anə'dAltəreitid], a. pur, non frelaté.
unadvisable [Anəd'vaizəbl], a. peu sage, inopportun.
unadvised [Anəd'vaizd], a. malavisé; imprudent (rash).
unadvisedly [Anəd'vaizidli], adv. inconsidérément.
unaffected [Anə'fektid], a. sans affectation; insensible (peu ému).
unaffectedly [Anə'fektidli], adv. sans affectation.
unafraid [Anə'freid], a. sans peur.
unaided [An'eidid], a. seul, sans aide.
unallayed [Anə'leid], a. non apaisé.
unallowable [Anə'lauəbl], a. non permis; inadmissible.
unalloyed [Anə'lɔid], a. pur, sans alliage, sans mélange.
unalterable [An'ɔ:ltərəbl], a. inaltérable, invariable.
unalterably [An'ɔ:ltərəbli], adv. immuablement.
unambitious [Anæm'biʃəs], a. sans ambition.
unanimity [ju:nə'nimiti], n. unanimité, f.
unanimous [ju'næniməs], a. unanime.
unanimously [ju'næniməsli], adv. unanimement, à l'unanimité.
unanswerable [An'a:nsərəbl], a. incontestable.
unanswered [An'a:nsəd], a. sans réponse.
unappeasable [Anə'pi:zəbl], a. implacable.
unappetizing [An'æpitaiziŋ], a. peu appétissant.
unappreciated [Anə'pri:ʃieitid], a. inapprécié.
unapproachable [Anə'proutʃəbl], a. inaccessible, inabordable.
unarmed [An'a:md], a. sans armes.
unascertainable [Anæsə'teinəbl], a. qu'on ne peut constater.
unashamed [Anə'ʃeimd], a. sans honte.
unasked [An'a:skt], a. sans être invité; spontané.—adv. spontanément.
unaspiring [Anə'spaiəriŋ], a. sans ambition.
unassailable [Anə'seiləbl], a. hors d'atteinte; inattaquable, irréfutable.
unassisted [Anə'sistid], a. sans aide.
unassuming [Anə'sju:miŋ], a. sans prétention, modeste.
unattached [Anə'tætʃt], a. sans être attaché (à); en disponibilité.
unattainable [Anə'teinəbl], a. inaccessible.
unattended [Anə'tendid], a. seul, sans suite.
unattested [Anə'testid], a. non attesté.
unattractive [Anə'træktiv], a. peu attrayant, sans attrait.
unauthenticated [Anɔ:'θentikeitid], a. dont l'authenticité n'est pas prouvée.
unauthorized [An'ɔ:θəraizd], a. sans autorisation; illicite, illégal (chose).
unavailable [Anə'veiləbl], a. non valable; inutilisable (billet); indisponible (fonds, personne); qu'on ne peut se procurer (chose).
unavailing [Anə'veiliŋ], a. inutile, inefficace.
unavenged [Anə'vendʒd], a. impuni, non vengé.

607

unavoidable [ʌnə'vɔidebl], *a.* inévitable.
unavoidably [ʌnə'vɔidəbli], *adv.* inévitablement.
unaware [ʌnə'weə], *a.* ignorant; *to be unaware of*, ignorer.
unawares [ʌnə'weəz], *adv.* à l'improviste; à son insu (*sans s'en rendre compte*); *to be taken unawares*, être pris au dépourvu.
unbalanced [ʌn'bælənst], *a.* mal équilibré.
unbearable [ʌn'bɛərəbl], *a.* insupportable, intolérable.
unbearably [ʌn'bɛərəbli], *adv.* insupportablement.
unbeatable [ʌn'biːtəbl], *a.* invincible.
unbeaten [ʌn'biːtn], *a.* invaincu.
unbecoming [ʌnbi'kʌmiŋ], *a.* peu convenable, malséant; qui ne va pas bien (*vêtement*).
unbecomingly [ʌnbi'kʌmiŋli], *adv.* d'une manière peu séante.
unbefitting [ʌnbi'fitiŋ], *a.* qui ne convient pas, peu propre.
unbeknown [ʌnbi'noun], *a.* inconnu; *unbeknown to me*, à mon insu.
unbelief [ʌnbi'liːf], *n.* incrédulité, incroyance, *f.*
unbelievable [ʌnbi'liːvəbl], *a.* incroyable.
unbeliever [ʌnbi'liːvə], *n.* incrédule; sceptique, *m., f.*
unbelieving [ʌnbi'liːviŋ], *a.* incrédule; sceptique.
unbend [ʌn'bend], *v.t. irr.* (*conjug. like* BEND) détendre, relâcher; débander (*l'arc*); (*fig.*) délasser (*l'esprit*).—*v.i.* se détendre.
unbending [ʌn'bendiŋ], *a.* inflexible.
unbiased [ʌn'baiəst], *a.* sans prévention, impartial.
unbidden [ʌn'bidn], *a.* sans être invité.
unbind [ʌn'baind], *v.t. irr.* (*conjug. like* BIND) délier, détacher.
unbleached [ʌn'bliːtʃt], *a.* écru.
unblemished [ʌn'blemiʃt], *a.* sans tache.
unblushing [ʌn'blʌʃiŋ], *a.* qui ne rougit point, éhonté, sans vergogne.
unblushingly [ʌn'blʌʃiŋli], *adv.* sans rougir.
unbolt [ʌn'boult], *v.t.* tirer les verrous de, ouvrir.
unborn [ʌn'bɔːn], *a.* encore à naître; futur, à venir (*chose*).
unbosom [ʌn'buzm], *v.t. to unbosom oneself*, ouvrir son cœur.
unbound [ʌn'baund], *a.* délié; non relié (*livre*).
unbounded [ʌn'baundid], *a.* illimité, infini.
unbreakable [ʌn'breikəbl], *a.* incassable.
unbridled [ʌn'braidld], *a.* débridé; (*fig.*) effréné.
unbroken [ʌn'broukn], *a.* non rompu; continu (*ininterrompu*); indompté (*non vaincu*); intact (*non violé*); non dressé (*animal*).
unbrotherly [ʌn'brʌðəli], *a.* peu fraternel.
unbuckle [ʌn'bʌkl], *v.t.* déboucler.
unburden [ʌn'bɜːdn], *v.t.* décharger; *to unburden oneself*, ouvrir son cœur.
unburied [ʌn'berid], *a.* sans sépulture.
unbusinesslike [ʌn'biznislaik], *a.* peu pratique.
unbutton [ʌn'bʌtn], *v.t.* déboutonner.
uncalled [ʌn'kɔːld], *a.* sans être appelé; *uncalled for*, sans être demandé; gratuit (*superflu*); peu convenable (*mal élevé*); non mérité (*injuste*).

uncanny [ʌn'kæni], *a.* mystérieux, surnaturel.
uncared-for [ʌn'kɛədfɔː], *a.* négligé.
unceasing [ʌn'siːsiŋ], *a.* incessant, sans cesse.
unceasingly [ʌn'siːsiŋli], *adv.* continuellement, sans cesse.
uncensored [ʌn'sensəd], *a.* non expurgé.
unceremonious [ʌnseri'mouniəs], *a.* peu cérémonieux; sans façon.
unceremoniously [ʌnseri'mouniəsli], *adv.* sans cérémonie, sans façon.
uncertain [ʌn'sɜːtin], *a.* incertain, peu sûr.
uncertainty [ʌn'sɜːtinti], *n.* incertitude, *f.*
uncertificated [ʌnsə'tifikeitid], *a.* non diplômé (*instituteur*).
unchain [ʌn'tʃein], *v.t.* déchaîner.
unchallenged [ʌn'tʃælindʒd], *a.* indisputé.
unchangeable [ʌn'tʃeindʒəbl], *a.* inaltérable, immuable.
unchanged [ʌn'tʃeindʒd], *a.* inchangé, toujours le même.
unchanging [ʌn'tʃeindʒiŋ], *a.* invariable, constant.
uncharitable [ʌn'tʃæritəbl], *a.* peu charitable.
uncharitableness [ʌn'tʃæritəblnis], *n.* manque de charité, *m.*
uncharitably [ʌn'tʃæritəbli], *adv.* sans charité.
uncharted [ʌn'tʃɑːtid], *a.* inexploré.
unchaste [ʌn'tʃeist], *a.* incontinent, impudique.
unchecked [ʌn'tʃekt], *a.* non réprimé, sans frein; non vérifié.
unchivalrous [ʌn'ʃivlrəs], *a.* peu chevaleresque.
unchristian [ʌn'kristiən], *a.* peu chrétien.
uncircumcised [ʌn'sɜːkəmsaizd], *a.* incirconcis.
uncivil [ʌn'sivil], *a.* malhonnête, impoli.
uncivilized [ʌn'sivilaizd], *a.* peu civilisé, barbare.
uncivilly [ʌn'sivili], *adv.* malhonnêtement, impoliment.
unclaimed [ʌn'kleimd], *a.* non réclamé.
unclasp [ʌn'klɑːsp], *v.t.* dégrafer, défaire.
unclassified [ʌn'klæsifaid], *a.* non classé.
uncle [ʌŋkl], *n.* oncle, *m.*; (*slang*) *at uncle's*, chez ma tante (*le prêteur sur gage*).
unclean [ʌn'kliːn], *a.* malpropre, sale; impudique (*obscène*); impur.
uncleanliness [ʌn'klenlinis], **uncleanness** [ʌn'kliːnnis], *n.* saleté; (*fig.*) impureté, *f.*
unclench [ʌn'klentʃ], *v.t.* ouvrir, desserrer.
uncloak [ʌn'klouk], *v.t.* dévoiler.
unclose [ʌn'klouz], *v.t.* ouvrir.
unclosed [ʌn'klouzd], *a.* non fermé, ouvert.
unclothe [ʌn'klouð], *v.t.* déshabiller.
unclothed [ʌn'klouðd], *a.* déshabillé, nu.
unclouded [ʌn'klaudid], *a.* sans nuage, serein.
uncock [ʌn'kɔk], *v.t.* désarmer (*fusil etc.*).
uncoil [ʌn'kɔil], *v.t.* dérouler.—*v.i.* se dérouler.
uncombed [ʌn'koumd], *a.* mal peigné, ébourifé.
uncomfortable [ʌn'kʌmftəbl], *a.* peu confortable, incommode; gêné (*personne*).
uncomfortably [ʌn'kʌmftəbli], *adv.* peu confortablement; mal à l'aise.
uncommitted [ʌnkə'mitid], *a.* non commis; non engagé, libre.

uncommon [ʌn'kɔmən], *a.* peu commun; rare.

uncommonly [ʌn'kɔmənli], *adv.* rarement; infiniment (*singulièrement*).

uncommunicative [ʌnkə'mju:nikətiv], *a.* peu communicatif, réservé.

uncomplaining [ʌnkəm'pleiniŋ], *a.* sans plainte, résigné.

uncomplainingly [ʌnkəm'pleiniŋli], *adv.* sans se plaindre, sans plainte.

uncompleted [ʌnkəm'pli:tid], *a.* inachevé, incomplet.

uncomplimentary [ʌnkɔmpli'mentəri], *a.* peu flatteur.

uncompromising [ʌn'kɔmprəmaiziŋ], *a.* peu accommodant, intransigeant.

unconcern [ʌnkən'sə:n], *n.* insouciance, indifférence, *f.*

unconcerned [ʌnkən'sə:nd], *a.* indifférent, insouciant.

unconcernedly [ʌnkən'sə:nidli], *adv.* avec indifférence.

unconditional [ʌnkən'diʃənl], *a.* sans conditions, absolu.

unconditionally [ʌnkən'diʃənəli], *adv.* sans condition.

unconfined [ʌnkən'faind], *a.* libre; illimité.

unconfinedly [ʌnkən'fainidli], *adv.* sans limite.

unconfirmed [ʌnkən'fə:md], *a.* non confirmé.

uncongenial [ʌnkən'dʒi:niəl], *a.* désagréable; peu sympathique.

unconnected [ʌnkə'nektid], *a.* détaché, sans rapport (*avec*); décousu (*style*).

unconquerable [ʌn'kɔŋkərəbl], *a.* invincible.

unconquered [ʌn'kɔŋkəd], *a.* insoumis.

unconscionable [ʌn'kɔnʃənəbl], *a.* déraisonnable.

unconscionably [ʌn'kɔnʃənəbli], *adv.* déraisonnablement.

unconscious [ʌn'kɔnʃəs], *a.* ignorant (*de*); sans connaissance, insensible.—*n.* inconscient, *m.*

unconsciously [ʌn'kɔnʃəsli], *adv.* à son insu.

unconsciousness [ʌn'kɔnʃəsnis], *n.* inconscience, *f.*; évanouissement, *m.*

unconsecrated [ʌn'kɔnsikreitid], *a.* non consacré.

unconsidered [ʌnkən'sidəd], *a.* inconsidéré.

unconstitutional [ʌnkɔnsti'tju:ʃənl], *a.* inconstitutionnel.

unconstrained [ʌnkən'streind], *a.* sans contrainte; aisé (*style*).

unconstraint [ʌnkən'streint], *n.* aisance, *f.*

uncontaminated [ʌnkən'tæmineitid], *a.* sans souillure.

uncontested [ʌnkən'testid], *a.* incontesté.

uncontrollable [ʌnkən'trouləbl], *a.* irrésistible; fou (*rire*).

uncontrollably [ʌnkən'trouləbli], *adv.* irrésistiblement.

uncontrolled [ʌnkən'trould], *a.* irrésistible.

unconventional [ʌnkən'venʃənl], *a.* peu conventionnel.

unconverted [ʌnkən'və:tid], *a.* inconverti.

unconvinced [ʌnkən'vinst], *a.* non convaincu.

unconvincing [ʌnkən'vinsiŋ], *a.* peu convaincant.

uncooked [ʌn'kukt], *a.* non cuit, cru.

uncork [ʌn'kɔ:k], *v.t.* déboucher.

uncorrupted [ʌnkə'rʌptid], *a.* non corrompu (*par*); intègre.

uncouple [ʌn'kʌpl], *v.t.* découpler; débrayer.

uncouth [ʌn'ku:θ], *a.* bizarre; grossier; gauche.

uncouthly [ʌn'ku:θli], *adv.* rudement; gauchement.

uncover [ʌn'kʌvə], *v.t.* découvrir.

uncovered [ʌn'kʌvəd], *a.* découvert.

uncreasable [ʌn'kri:səbl], *a.* infroissable.

uncritical [ʌn'kritikl], *a.* sans discernement.

uncrowned [ʌn'kraund], *a.* non couronné.

unction ['ʌŋkʃən], *n.* onction, *f.*

unctuous ['ʌŋktjuəs], *a.* onctueux.

unctuously ['ʌŋktjuəsli], *adv.* onctueusement.

uncultivated [ʌn'kʌltiveitid], *a.* inculte.

uncultured [ʌn'kʌltʃəd], *a.* sans culture.

uncurl [ʌn'kə:l], *v.t.* dérouler; défriser (*cheveux*).—*v.i.* se dérouler; se défriser (*cheveux*).

uncustomary [ʌn'kʌstəməri], *a.* inaccoutumé.

uncut [ʌn'kʌt], *a.* non coupé; entier; non entamé (*pain etc.*).

undamaged [ʌn'dæmidʒd], *a.* non endommagé; intact (*réputation*).

undated [ʌn'deitid], *a.* sans date.

undaunted [ʌn'dɔ:ntid], *a.* intrépide.

undeceive [ʌndi'si:v], *v.t.* désabuser, détromper.

undecided [ʌndi'saidid], *a.* indécis.

undecipherable [ʌndi'saifərəbl], *a.* indéchiffrable.

undefeated [ʌndi'fi:tid], *a.* invaincu.

undefended [ʌndi'fendid], *a.* sans défense, non défendu; sans défenseur (*accusé*).

undefilable [ʌndi'failəbl], *a.* sans tache, immaculé.

undefinable [ʌndi'fainəbl], *a.* indéfinissable.

undefined [ʌndi'faind], *a.* indéfini.

undelivered [ʌndi'livəd], *a.* non délivré.

undemonstrative [ʌndi'mɔnstrətiv], *a.* peu démonstratif, réservé.

undeniable [ʌndi'naiəbl], *a.* incontestable.

undenominational [ʌndinɔmi'neiʃənl], *a.* laïque (*école*).

under ['ʌndə], *a.* de dessous, inférieur; sous, subalterne, subordonné (*rang*).—*prep.* sous; au-dessous de (*inférieur à etc.*); dans, en (*en état de*); avec, à (*ayant*); *to be under obligations to,* avoir des obligations à; *to be under way* (*ship*), être en marche; *under age,* mineur; *under consideration,* à l'examen; *under cover of,* sous prétexte de; *under discussion,* en discussion; *under the breath,* à demi-voix; *under these circumstances,* dans ces circonstances.—*adv.* dessous, au-dessous; *see under,* voyez ci-dessous.

under-carriage ['ʌndəkæridʒ], *n.* (*Av.*) train d'atterrissage, *m.*

underclothes ['ʌndəklouðz], *n.pl.* sousvêtements, *m.pl.*

undercurrent ['ʌndəkʌrənt], *n.* courant inférieur, *m.*

undercut (1) ['ʌndəkʌt], *n.* filet (de *bœuf*), *m.*

undercut (2) [ʌndə'kʌt], *v.t. irr.* (*conjug. like* CUT) vendre meilleur marché.

under-developed [ʌndədi'veləpt], *a.* sousdéveloppé.

under-dog ['ʌndədɔg], *n.* opprimé, *m.*

underdone [ʌndə'dʌn], *a.* peu cuit, saignant.

609

under-estimate

under-estimate [ˌʌndər'estimeit], *v.t.* sous-estimer.
under-exposed [ˌʌndəriks'pouzd], *a.* (*Phot.*) sous-exposé.
underfelt ['ʌndəfelt], *n.* thibaude, *f.*
underfoot [ˌʌndə'fut], *adv.* sous les pieds.
undergo [ˌʌndə'gou], *v.t. irr.* (*conjug. like* GO) subir; supporter, endurer.
undergraduate [ˌʌndə'grædjuət], *n.* étudiant, *m.*
underground ['ʌndəgraund], *a.* souterrain; clandestin.—*n.* (*Rail.*) métro, *m.*—[ˌʌndə'graund], *adv.* sous terre.
undergrowth ['ʌndəgrouθ], *n.* broussailles, *f.pl.*
underhand [ˌʌndəhænd], *a.* clandestin; sournois (*personne*).—[ˌʌndə'hænd], *adv.* sous main; en cachette.
underline [ˌʌndə'lain], *v.t.* souligner.
underling ['ʌndəliŋ], *n.* subalterne, *m.*, *f.*
underlying [ˌʌndə'laiiŋ], *a.* fondamental.
under-manned [ˌʌndə'mænd], *a.* à court de personnel.
undermentioned [ˌʌndə'menʃənd], *a.* ci-dessous.
undermine [ˌʌndə'main], *v.t.* miner; (*fig.*) détruire.
undermost ['ʌndəmoust], *a.* le plus bas.
underneath [ˌʌndə'ni:θ], *prep.* sous, au-dessous de.—*adv.* dessous, au-dessous, par-dessous, en dessous.
under-nourished [ˌʌndə'nʌriʃt], *a.* sous-alimenté.
underpaid [ˌʌndə'peid], *a.* mal payé.
underpants ['ʌndəpænts], *n.pl.* caleçons, *m.pl.*
under-privileged [ˌʌndə'privilidʒd], *a.* non privilégié.
under-production [ˌʌndəprə'dʌkʃən], *n.* sous-production, *f.*
underrate [ˌʌndə'reit], *v.t.* sous-estimer, déprécier.
under-ripe [ˌʌndə'raip], *a.* pas assez mûr, vert.
under-secretary ['ʌndəsekrətəri], *n.* sous-secrétaire, *m.*, *f.*
under-side ['ʌndəsaid], *n.* dessous, *m.*
undersigned ['ʌndəsaind], *a. and n.* soussigné, *m.*
undersized [ˌʌndə'saizd], *a.* au-dessous de la moyenne.
understand [ˌʌndə'stænd], *v.t. irr.* (*conjug. like* STAND) entendre, comprendre; apprendre, entendre dire (*être informé de*); s'entendre (*à ou en*) (*savoir faire*).—*v.i.* comprendre.
understandable [ˌʌndə'stændəbl], *a.* intelligible; compréhensible.
understanding [ˌʌndə'stændiŋ], *n.* entendement, *m.*; intelligence; compréhension; entente (*accord*), *f.*
understudy ['ʌndəstʌdi], *n.* doublure, *f.*
undertake [ˌʌndə'teik], *v.t. irr.* (*conjug. like* TAKE) entreprendre, se charger (*de*); s'engager (*à*); promettre (*de*).
undertaker ['ʌndəteikə], *n.* entrepreneur des pompes funèbres, *m.*
undertaking [ˌʌndə'teikiŋ], *n.* entreprise, *f.*
undertone ['ʌndətoun], *n.* ton bas, *m.*; *in an undertone*, à voix basse.
underwear ['ʌndəwɛə], *n.* sous-vêtements, *m.pl.*

underworld ['ʌndəwə:ld], *n.* enfer, *m.*; (*fig.*) bas-fonds (*des criminels*), *m.pl.*
underwrite [ˌʌndə'rait], *v.t. irr.* (*conjug. like* WRITE) souscrire; (*Insurance*) assurer.
underwriter ['ʌndəraitə], *n.* assureur, *m.*
undeserved [ˌʌndi'zə:vd], *a.* immérité, non mérité.
undeservedly [ˌʌndi'zə:vidli], *adv.* à tort, injustement.
undesirable [ˌʌndi'zaiərəbl], *a.* peu désirable.
undetected [ˌʌndi'tektid], *a.* non découvert, inaperçu.
undetermined [ˌʌndi'tə:mind], *a.* indéterminé, indéfini.
undeterred [ˌʌndi'tə:d], *a.* sans être découragé.
undeveloped [ˌʌndi'veləpt], *a.* non développé.
undies ['ʌndiz], *n.pl.* (*fam.*) lingerie, *f.*
undigested [ˌʌndi'dʒestid], *a.* non digéré.
undignified [ʌn'dignifaid], *a.* sans dignité.
undiluted [ˌʌndai'lju:tid], *a.* non dilué.
undiminished [ˌʌndi'miniʃt], *a.* non diminué.
undiplomatic [ˌʌndiplo'mætik], *a.* peu diplomatique.
undisciplined [ʌn'disiplind], *a.* indiscipliné.
undisclosed [ˌʌndis'klouzd], *a.* non révélé, caché.
undiscovered [ˌʌndis'kʌvəd], *a.* non découvert.
undisguised [ˌʌndis'gaizd], *a.* sans déguisement.
undismayed [ˌʌndis'meid], *a.* sans peur, sans terreur.
undisputed [ˌʌndis'pju:tid], *a.* incontesté.
undistinguished [ˌʌndis'tiŋgwiʃt], *a.* (*fig.*) sans distinction.
undisturbed [ˌʌndis'tə:bd], *a.* tranquille, calme.
undivided [ˌʌndi'vaidid], *a.* sans partage, tout entier.
undo [ʌn'du:], *v.t. irr.* (*conjug. like* DO) défaire; délier, détacher (*dénouer*); ruiner, perdre (*détruire*).
undoing [ʌn'du:iŋ], *n.* ruine, perte, *f.*
undone [ʌn'dʌn], *a.* ruiné, perdu; défait, délié.
undoubted [ʌn'dautid], *a.* incontestable, certain.
undoubtedly [ʌn'dautidli], *adv.* sans aucun doute.
undress [ʌn'dres], *v.t.* déshabiller.—*v.i.* se déshabiller.—*n.* (*Mil.*) petite tenue, *f.*
undressed [ʌn'drest], *a.* déshabillé.
undrinkable [ʌn'driŋkəbl], *a.* imbuvable, non potable.
undue [ʌn'dju:], *a.* non dû; excessif.
undulate ['ʌndjuleit], *v.i.* onduler, ondoyer.
undulating ['ʌndjuleitiŋ], *a.* accidenté (*terrain*).
undulation [ˌʌndju'leiʃən], *n.* ondulation, *f.*
unduly [ʌn'dju:li], *adv.* indûment; à tort; trop.
undying [ʌn'daiiŋ], *a.* impérissable, immortel.
unearned [ʌn'ə:nd], *a.* qu'on n'a pas gagné; immérité; *unearned income*, rentes, *f.pl.*
unearth [ʌn'ə:θ], *v.t.* déterrer.
unearthly [ʌn'ə:θli], *a.* surnaturel; (*colloq.*) infernal.
uneasily [ʌn'i:zili], *adv.* mal à son aise; difficilement, péniblement, avec gêne.

610

uneasiness [ʌn'i:zinis], *n.* malaise, *m.*, peine; inquiétude (*d'esprit*), *f.*

uneasy [ʌn'i:zi], *a.* inquiet, gêné.

uneatable [ʌn'i:təbl], *a.* immangeable.

uneconomical [ʌni:kə'nɔmikl], *a.* non économique.

uneducated [ʌn'edjukeitid], *a.* sans éducation.

unemotional [ʌni'mouʃənl], *a.* peu impressionnable; peu émotif.

unemployed [ʌnim'plɔid], *a.* sans travail, inoccupé; (*fig.*) inactif, oisif.—*n.pl. the unemployed*, les sans-travail, les chômeurs, *m.pl.*

unemployment [ʌnim'plɔimənt], *n.* manque de travail, chômage, *m.*

unencumbered [ʌnin'kʌmbəd], *a.* non embarrassé (*de*); non hypothéqué (*biens*).

unending [ʌn'endiŋ], *a.* interminable.

unendurable [ʌnin'djuərəbl], *a.* insupportable, intolérable.

un-English [ʌn'iŋgliʃ], *a.* non anglais; indigne d'un Anglais.

unenlightened [ʌnin'laitnd], *a.* peu éclairé.

unenterprising [ʌn'entəpraiziŋ], *a.* peu entreprenant.

unenthusiastic [ʌninθju:zi'æstik], *a.* peu enthousiaste.

unenviable [ʌn'enviəbl], *a.* peu enviable.

unequal [ʌn'i:kwəl], *a.* inégal; au-dessous (*de*); *unequal to the task*, pas à la hauteur de la tâche.

unequalled [ʌn'i:kwəld], *a.* sans égal, sans pareil.

unequivocal [ʌni'kwivəkl], *a.* non équivoque.

unequivocally [ʌni'kwivəkli], *adv.* sans équivoque.

unerring [ʌn'ə:riŋ], *a.* infaillible, sûr.

uneven [ʌn'i:vn], *a.* inégal; raboteux (*terrain*).

unevenly [ʌn'i:vinli], *adv.* inégalement.

unevenness [ʌn'i:vinnis], *n.* inégalité, *f.*

uneventful [ʌni'ventful], *a.* sans incidents, monotone.

unexaggerated [ʌnig'zædʒəreitid], *a.* nullement exagéré.

unexciting [ʌnik'saitiŋ], *a.* peu intéressant.

unexpected [ʌniks'pektid], *a.* inopiné, inattendu; imprévu.

unexpectedly [ʌniks'pektidli], *adv.* à l'improviste.

unexpired [ʌniks'paiəd], *a.* non expiré.

unexplained [ʌniks'pleind], *a.* sans explication, inexpliqué.

unexploded [ʌniks'ploudid], *a.* non éclaté.

unexplored [ʌniks'plɔ:d], *a.* inexploré.

unexposed [ʌniks'pouzd], *a.* non exposé.

unextinguished [ʌniks'tiŋgwiʃt], *a.* non éteint.

unfading [ʌn'feidiŋ], *a.* (*fig.*) impérissable, immortel.

unfailing [ʌn'feiliŋ], *a.* inépuisable, infaillible (*certain*).

unfair [ʌn'fɛə], *a.* injuste; (*Spt.*) pas de jeu.

unfairly [ʌn'fɛəli], *adv.* injustement.

unfairness [ʌn'fɛənis], *n.* injustice, *f.*

unfaithful [ʌn'feiθful], *a.* infidèle.

unfaithfulness [ʌn'feiθfulnis], *n.* infidélité, *f.*

unfaltering [ʌn'fɔ:ltəriŋ], *a.* ferme, assuré; résolu (*actions etc.*).

unfamiliar [ʌnfə'miljə], *a.* peu familier (*avec*); peu connu.

unfashionable [ʌn'fæʃənəbl], *a.* démodé.

unfasten [ʌn'fɑ:sn], *v.t.* ouvrir, détacher, défaire.

unfathomable [ʌn'fæðəməbl], *a.* insondable.

unfavorable [ʌn'feivərəbl], *a.* peu favorable.

unfed [ʌn'fed], *a.* mal nourri.

unfeeling [ʌn'fi:liŋ], *a.* insensible, dur, cruel.

unfeigned [ʌn'feind], *a.* vrai, sincère.

unfeignedly [ʌn'feinidli], *adv.* sincèrement.

unfelt [ʌn'felt], *a.* qu'on ne sent pas.

unfenced [ʌn'fenst], *a.* sans clôture.

unfetter [ʌn'fetə], *v.t.* ôter les fers à; (*fig.*) délivrer.

unfettered [ʌn'fetəd], *a.* libre, sans entraves.

unfilial [ʌn'filiəl], *a.* peu filial.

unfinished [ʌn'finiʃt], *a.* inachevé.

unfit [ʌn'fit], *a.* peu propre; impropre (*à*); incapable (*de*); en mauvaise santé.

unfitting [ʌn'fitiŋ], *a.* inconvenant.

unfix [ʌn'fiks], *v.t.* détacher.

unfixed [ʌn'fikst], *a.* mobile; indécis.

unflagging [ʌn'flægiŋ], *a.* infatigable.

unfledged [ʌn'fledʒd], *a.* sans plumes; (*fig.*) novice.

unflinching [ʌn'flintʃiŋ], *a.* ferme, déterminé.

unfold [ʌn'fould], *v.t.* déplier, déployer; révéler.—*v.i.* se déployer, se dévoiler.

unforeseen [ʌnfɔ:'si:n], *a.* imprévu.

unforgettable [ʌnfə'getəbl], *a.* inoubliable.

unforgiving [ʌnfə'giviŋ], *a.* implacable.

unforgotten [ʌnfə'gɔtn], *a.* pas oublié.

unfortified [ʌn'fɔ:tifaid], *a.* non fortifié, ouvert.

unfortunate [ʌn'fɔ:tʃənit], *a.* infortuné, malheureux.

unfortunately [ʌn'fɔ:tʃənitli], *adv.* malheureusement.

unfounded [ʌn'faundid], *a.* sans fondement.

unframed [ʌn'freimd], *a.* sans cadre.

unfrequented [ʌnfri'kwentid], *a.* peu fréquenté, solitaire.

unfriendliness [ʌn'frendlinis], *n.* disposition peu amicale, *f.*

unfriendly [ʌn'frendli], *a.* peu amical (*personne*); malveillant (*chose*).

unfrock [ʌn'frɔk], *v.t.* défroquer.

unfruitful [ʌn'fru:tful], *a.* infertile, stérile.

unfulfilled [ʌnful'fild], *a.* non accompli.

unfurl [ʌn'fə:l], *v.t.* déferler, déployer.

unfurnished [ʌn'fə:niʃt], *a.* non meublé.

ungainly [ʌn'geinli], *a.* maladroit.

ungenerous [ʌn'dʒenərəs], *a.* peu généreux.

ungentlemanliness [ʌn'dʒentlmənlinis], *n.* impolitesse, *f.*

ungentlemanly [ʌn'dʒentlmənli], *a.* de mauvais ton.

ungodliness [ʌn'gɔdlinis], *n.* impiété, *f.*

ungodly [ʌn'gɔdli], *a.* impie.

ungovernable [ʌn'gʌvənəbl], *a.* ingouvernable; effréné.

ungraceful [ʌn'greisful], *a.* peu gracieux.

ungracious [ʌn'greiʃəs], *a.* peu gracieux, déplaisant.

ungrammatical [ʌngrə'mætikl], *a.* incorrect.

ungrateful [ʌn'greitful], *a.* ingrat (*envers*).

ungratefully [ʌn'greitfuli], *adv.* avec ingratitude.

ungrudging [ʌn'grʌdʒiŋ], *a.* de bon cœur.

ungrudgingly [ʌn'grʌdʒiŋli], *adv.* volontiers, de bon cœur.

unguarded [ʌn'gɑ:did], *a.* sans défense; imprudent, irréfléchi (*inconsidéré*).

unguardedly

unguardedly [ʌnˈgɑːdidli], adv. imprudemment.

unguent [ˈʌŋgwənt], n. onguent, m.

unhallowed [ʌnˈhæloud], a. non sanctifié.

unhampered [ʌnˈhæmpəd], a. non embarrassé (par).

*unhand [ʌnˈhænd], v.t. lâcher.

unhappily [ʌnˈhæpili], adv. malheureusement.

unhappiness [ʌnˈhæpinis], n. malheur, m.

unhappy [ʌnˈhæpi], a. malheureux.

unharmed [ʌnˈhɑːmd], a. sain et sauf.

unharness [ʌnˈhɑːnis], v.t. déharnacher; dételer (d'une charrette).

unhatched [ʌnˈhætʃt], a. non éclos.

unhealthy [ʌnˈhelθi], a. insalubre, malsain; maladif (personne).

unheard [ʌnˈhɜːd], a. sans être entendu; unheard of, inconnu, inouï (extraordinaire).

unheeded [ʌnˈhiːdid], a. inaperçu, négligé.

unheedful [ʌnˈhiːdful], unheeding [ʌn'hiːdiŋ], a. insouciant; inattentif.

unhesitating [ʌnˈheziteitiŋ], a. sans hésitation; résolu.

unhesitatingly [ʌnˈheziteitiŋli], adv. sans hésiter.

unhewn [ʌnˈhjuːn], a. brut; non taillé.

unhinge [ʌnˈhindʒ], v.t. démonter.

unhitch [ʌnˈhitʃ], v.t. décrocher; dételer (cheval).

unholy [ʌnˈhouli], a. profane, impie.

unhook [ʌnˈhuk], v.t. décrocher; dégrafer (vêtements).

unhoped [ʌnˈhoupt], a. inattendu; unhoped for, inespéré.

unhorse [ʌnˈhɔːs], v.t. désarçonner, démonter.

unhurried [ʌnˈhʌrid], a. lent, sans précipitation.

unhurt [ʌnˈhɜːt], a. sain et sauf, sans blessures.

unhygienic [ʌnhaiˈdʒiːnik], a. peu hygiénique.

unicorn [ˈjuːnikɔːn], n. licorne, f.

unidentified [ʌnaiˈdentifaid], a. non identifié.

unification [juːnifiˈkeiʃən], n. unification, f.

uniform [ˈjuːnifɔːm], a. and n. uniforme, m.

uniformity [juːniˈfɔːmiti], n. uniformité, f.

uniformly [ˈjuːnifɔːmli], adv. uniformément.

unify [ˈjuːnifai], v.t. unifier.

unilateral [juːniˈlætərəl], a. unilatéral.

unimaginable [ʌniˈmædʒinəbl], a. inimaginable, inconcevable.

unimaginative [ʌniˈmædʒinətiv], a. peu imaginatif.

unimpaired [ʌnimˈpɛəd], a. inaltéré, intact.

unimpeachable [ʌnimˈpiːtʃəbl], a. irréprochable.

unimpeded [ʌnimˈpiːdid], a. sans empêchement.

unimportance [ʌnimˈpɔːtəns], n. peu d'importance, m., insignifiance, f.

unimportant [ʌnimˈpɔːtənt], a. sans importance, insignifiant.

unimpressed [ʌnimˈprest], a. sans être ému.

unimpressive [ʌnimˈpresiv], a. peu frappant.

uninformed [ʌninˈfɔːmd], a. non informé; ignorant.

uninhabitable [ʌninˈhæbitəbl], a. inhabitable.

uninhabited [ʌninˈhæbitid], a. inhabité.

uninitiated [ʌniˈniʃieitid], a. non initié.

uninjured [ʌnˈindʒəd], a. sain et sauf, sans blessures.

uninspired [ʌninˈspaiəd], a. non inspiré, terne.

uninspiring [ʌninˈspaiəriŋ], a. banal.

unintelligible [ʌninˈtelidʒibl], a. inintelligible.

unintentional [ʌninˈtenʃənl], a. sans intention, involontaire.

unintentionally [ʌninˈtenʃənli], adv. fait sans le vouloir, sans intention.

uninterested [ʌnˈintristid], a. non intéressé, indifférent.

uninteresting [ʌnˈintristiŋ], a. peu intéressant.

uninterrupted [ʌnintəˈrʌptid], a. ininterrompu.

uninvited [ʌninˈvaitid], a. sans invitation.

uninviting [ʌninˈvaitiŋ], a. peu attrayant; peu appétissant (nourriture).

union [ˈjuːniən], n. union, f.; trade union, syndicat ouvrier, syndicat (corporatif), m.

unique [juˈniːk], a. unique.

uniquely [juˈniːki], adv. d'une manière unique.

unison [ˈjuːnizn], n. unisson, m.; in unison, à l'unisson.

unit [ˈjuːnit], n. unité, f.; bloc, élément, m.

unite [juˈnait], v.t. unir (à ou avec); joindre, réunir (efforts etc.).—v.i. s'unir, se réunir; se joindre (à ou avec).

united [juˈnaitid], a. uni; réuni; joint; the United Kingdom, le Royaume-Uni, m.; the United States, les États-Unis, m.pl.

unity [ˈjuːniti], n. unité; union, f.

universal [juːniˈvəːsl], a. universel.

universally [juːniˈvəːsəli], adv. universellement.

universe [ˈjuːnivəːs], n. univers, m.

university [juːniˈvəːsiti], n. université, f.; university degree, grade universitaire, m.

unjust [ʌnˈdʒʌst], a. injuste, inique.

unjustly [ʌnˈdʒʌstli], adv. injustement.

unjustifiable [ʌnˈdʒʌstifaiəbl], a. injustifiable.

unjustified [ʌnˈdʒʌstifaid], a. sans justification.

unkind [ʌnˈkaind], a. désobligeant; peu aimable; cruel.

unkindliness [ʌnˈkaindlinis], n. désobligeance; malveillance, f.

unkindly [ʌnˈkaindli], a. peu propice, défavorable.—adv. sans bienveillance; cruellement, mal.

unkindness [ʌnˈkaindnis], n. manque d'amabilité, m., désobligeance; cruauté, dureté, f.

unknowingly [ʌnˈnouiŋli], adv. sans le savoir, à son insu.

unknown [ʌnˈnoun], a. inconnu; unknown to me (without my knowledge), à mon insu.

unlace [ʌnˈleis], v.t. délacer, détacher.

unladylike [ʌnˈleidilaik], a. peu digne d'une dame, de mauvais ton.

unlatch [ʌnˈlætʃ], v.t. lever le loquet de, ouvrir.

unlawful [ʌnˈlɔːful], a. illégal; illicite.

unlawfully [ʌnˈlɔːfuli], adv. illégalement; illicitement.

unleash [ʌnˈliːʃ], v.t. lâcher (chien).

unleavened [ʌn'levənd], *a.* sans levain; (*Scripture*) azyme.

unless [ʌn'les], *conj.* à moins que . . . ne (*with subjunctive*); à moins de (*followed by infinitive*); si . . . ne . . . pas (*followed by indicative*); si ce n'est, excepté que.

unlicensed [ʌn'laisənst], *a.* non autorisé; (*Comm.*) non patenté.

unlike [ʌn'laik], *a.* différent (*de*); qui ne ressemble pas (*à*).

unlikelihood [ʌn'laiklihud], *n.* invraisemblance, improbabilité, *f.*

unlikely [ʌn'laikli], *a.* improbable, invraisemblable, peu sûr.

unlimited [ʌn'limitid], *a.* illimité.

unlined [ʌn'laind], *a.* non doublé.

unlink [ʌn'liŋk], *v.t.* défaire, détacher.

unload [ʌn'loud], *v.t.* décharger; désarmer (*fusil*).

unlock [ʌn'lɔk], *v.t.* ouvrir.

unlooked-for [ʌn'luktfɔː], *a.* inattendu, imprévu.

unloose [ʌn'luːs], *v.t.* délier, détacher.

unloved [ʌn'lʌvd], *a.* pas aimé.

unluckily [ʌn'lʌkili], *adv.* malheureusement, par malheur.

unlucky [ʌn'lʌki], *a.* malheureux, infortuné; sinistre, de mauvais augure, de mauvais présagé.

unmade [ʌn'meid], *a.* défait; pas fait (*lit*); non empierré (*route*).

unmanageable [ʌn'mænidʒəbl], *a.* ingouvernable; rebelle.

unmanliness [ʌn'mænlinis], *n.* conduite indigne d'un homme, lâcheté, *f.*

unmanly [ʌn'mænli], *a.* indigne d'un homme, lâche; mou, efféminé.

unmannerliness [ʌn'mænəlinis], *n.* grossièreté, impolitesse, *f.*

unmannerly [ʌn'mænəli], *a.* grossier, mal appris, impoli.

unmarked [ʌn'mɑːkt], *a.* non marqué (*de*); inaperçu.

unmarketable [ʌn'mɑːkitəbl], *a.* invendable.

unmarried [ʌn'mærid], *a.* célibataire; **un-married man**, célibataire, *m.*; **un-married woman**, demoiselle; vieille fille, *f.*

unmask [ʌn'mɑːsk], *v.t.* démasquer; (*fig.*) dévoiler.

unmastered [ʌn'mɑːstəd], *a.* indompté.

unmatched [ʌn'mætʃt], *a.* dépareillé; (*fig.*) sans pareil.

unmentionable [ʌn'menʃənəbl], *a.* dont on ne parle pas.

unmerciful [ʌn'məːsiful], *a.* impitoyable, cruel.

unmercifully [ʌn'məːsifuli], *adv.* impitoyablement, sans pitié.

unmerited [ʌn'meritid], *a.* immérité.

unmindful [ʌn'maindful], *a.* peu soucieux (*de*).

unmistakable [ʌnmis'teikəbl], *a.* évident, clair.

unmistakably [ʌnmis'teikəbli], *adv.* évidemment, clairement.

unmitigated [ʌn'mitigeitid], *a.* non adouci; (*colloq.*) fieffé (*gredin etc.*).

unmolested [ʌnmə'lestid], *a.* sans être molesté.

unmotherly [ʌn'mʌðəli], *a.* peu maternel.

unmounted [ʌn'mauntid], *a.* à pied (*sans cheval*); non collé (*photographie etc.*).

unmourned [ʌn'mɔːnd], *a.* sans être pleuré.

unmoved [ʌn'muːvd], *a.* immobile; (*fig.*) non ému.

unmusical [ʌn'mjuːzikl], *a.* peu harmonieux; pas musicien (*personne*).

unmuzzle [ʌn'mʌzl], *v.t.* démuseler.

unnamed [ʌn'neimd], *a.* innommé; anonyme.

unnatural [ʌn'nætʃrəl], *a.* contre nature; dénaturé (*personne*).

unnavigable [ʌn'nævigəbl], *a.* innavigable.

unnecessarily [ʌn'nesəsərili], *adv.* sans nécessité, inutilement; par trop.

unnecessary [ʌn'nesəsəri], *a.* peu nécessaire, inutile.

unneighborly [ʌn'neibəli], *a.* peu obligeant; de mauvais voisin.

unnerve [ʌn'nəːv], *v.t.* énerver; (*fig.*) décourager.

unnoticed [ʌn'noutist], *a.* inaperçu, inobservé.

unnumbered [ʌn'nʌmbəd], *a.* innombrable.

unobjectionable [ʌnəb'dʒekʃənəbl], *a.* irrécusable.

unobliging [ʌnə'blaidʒiŋ], *a.* désobligeant.

unobservant [ʌnəb'zəːvənt], *a.* peu observateur.

unobserved [ʌnəb'zəːvd], *a.* inaperçu.

unobtainable [ʌnəb'teinəbl], *a.* impossible à obtenir.

unobtrusive [ʌnəb'truːsiv], *a.* réservé, discret.

unobtrusively [ʌnəb'truːsivli], *adv.* sans importunité, avec modestie.

unoccupied [ʌn'ɔkjupaid], *a.* inoccupé; libre, disponible (*temps etc.*); inhabité (*maison*).

unofficial [ʌnə'fiʃl], *a.* non officiel.

unofficially [ʌnə'fiʃəli], *adv.* non officiellement.

unopened [ʌn'oupənd], *a.* fermé; non décacheté (*lettre etc.*).

unopposed [ʌnə'pouzd], *a.* sans opposition.

unorganized [ʌn'ɔːgənaizd], *a.* non organisé.

unoriginal [ʌnə'ridʒinəl], *a.* peu original.

unorthodox [ʌn'ɔːθədɔks], *a.* peu orthodoxe.

unostentatious [ʌnɔsten'teiʃəs], *a.* sans faste; modeste.

unostentatiously [ʌnɔsten'teiʃəsli], *adv.* sans ostentation.

unpack [ʌn'pæk], *v.t.* déballer (*marchandises*); dépaqueter (*paquets*).

unpacking [ʌn'pækiŋ], *n.* déballage; dépaquetage (*de petits paquets*), *m.*

unpaid [ʌn'peid], *a.* non payé, sans paye.

unpalatable [ʌn'pælətəbl], *a.* désagréable (au goût).

unparalleled [ʌn'pærəleld], *a.* sans pareil; sans précédent.

unpardonable [ʌn'pɑːdnəbl], *a.* impardonnable.

unparliamentary [ʌnpɑːli'mentəri], *a.* peu parlementaire.

unpatriotic [ʌnpætri'ɔtik], *a.* peu patriotique (*sentiment*); peu patriote (*personne*).

unpaved [ʌn'peivd], *a.* non pavé.[see **unmade**]

unperturbed [ʌnpə'təːbd], *a.* peu ému, impassible.

unphilosophical [ʌnfilə'sɔfikl], *a.* peu philosophique.

unpick [ʌn'pik], *v.t.* découdre.

unpicked [ʌn'pikt], *a.* non cueilli; décousu (*couture*).

unpin

unpin [ʌn'pin], *v.t.* défaire.

unpitied [ʌn'pitid], *a.* qu'on ne plaint pas.

unpitying [ʌn'pitiiŋ], *a.* sans pitié, impitoyable.

unplayable [ʌn'pleiəbl], *a.* injouable.

unpleasant [ʌn'plezənt], *a.* déplaisant, fâcheux.

unpleasantly [ʌn'plezəntli], *adv.* désagréablement.

unpleasantness [ʌn'plezəntnis], *n.* désagrément, *m.*

unplowed [ʌn'plaud], *a.* non labouré.

unpoetical [ʌnpo'etikl], *a.* peu poétique.

unpolished [ʌn'pɔliʃt], *a.* non poli; mat (*or etc.*); non ciré (*chaussures*); dépoli (*verre*), (*fig.*) grossier.

unpolluted [ʌnpə'lju:tid], *a.* non souillé; pur.

unpopular [ʌn'pɔpjulə], *a.* impopulaire.

unpopularity [ʌnpɔpju'læriti], *n.* impopularité, *f.*

unpractical [ʌn'præktikl], *a.* peu pratique.

unpractised [ʌn'præktist], *a.* inexpérimenté.

unprecedented [ʌn'presidəntid], *a.* sans précédent.

unprejudiced [ʌn'predʒudist], *a.* sans préjugés, impartial.

unpremeditated [ʌnpri'mediteitid], *a.* inopiné, improvisé, sans préméditation.

unprepared [ʌnpri'pɛəd], *a.* non préparé; *to be unprepared for*, ne pas s'attendre à.

unpreparedness [ʌnpri'pɛəridnis], *n.* manque de préparation, *m.*

unprepossessing [ʌnpri:pə'zesiŋ], *a.* peu engageant.

unprincipled [ʌn'prinsipld], *a.* sans principes, sans mœurs.

unproductive [ʌnprə'dʌktiv], *a.* improductif; stérile (*terre*).

unproductiveness [ʌnprə'dʌktivnis], *n.* stérilité, *f.*

unprofessional [ʌnprə'feʃənəl], *a.* contraire aux règles d'une profession.

unprofitable [ʌn'prɔfitəbl], *a.* peu lucratif, sans profit; inutile.

unprofitably [ʌn'prɔfitəbli], *adv.* inutilement, sans profit.

unpronounceable [ʌnprə'naunsəbl], *a.* imprononçable.

unpropitious [ʌnprə'piʃəs], *a.* peu propice (*à*).

unprotected [ʌnprə'tektid], *a.* sans protection, sans défense; à découvert.

unprovided [ʌnprə'vaidid], *a.* dépourvu, dénué (*de*); *we were unprovided for that*, nous ne nous attendions pas à cela.

unprovoked [ʌnprə'voukt], *a.* sans provocation; *an unprovoked insult*, une insulte gratuite.

unpublished [ʌn'pʌbliʃt], *a.* inédit.

unpunished [ʌn'pʌniʃt], *a.* impuni.

unqualified [ʌn'kwɔlifaid], *a.* incapable (*de*), incompétent; (*fig.*) sans réserve; (*Law*) inhabile (*à*); non autorisé (*médecins etc.*).

unquenchable [ʌn'kwentʃəbl], *a.* inextinguible.

unquestionable [ʌn'kwestʃənəbl], *a.* incontestable, indubitable.

unquestionably [ʌn'kwestʃənəbli], *adv.* incontestablement; sans contredit.

unravel [ʌn'rævl], *v.t.* démêler, débrouiller.
—*v.i.* se démêler, se débrouiller, s'effiler.

unreadable [ʌn'ri:dəbl], *a.* illisible.

unreadily [ʌn'redili], *adv.* lentement, à contre-cœur.

unreadiness [ʌn'redinis], *n.* manque de préparation *ou* de bonne volonté, *m.*

unready [ʌn'redi], *a.* mal préparé; lent.

unreal [ʌn'ri:əl], *a.* irréel; chimérique, imaginaire.

unrealistic [ʌnri:ə'listik], *a.* peu réaliste.

unreality [ʌnri'æliti], *n.* défaut de réalité, *m.*

unrealizable [ʌn'ri:əlaizəbl], *a.* irréalisable.

unreasonable [ʌn'ri:znəbl], *a.* déraisonnable; exorbitant.

unreasonableness [ʌn'ri:znəblnis], *n.* déraison; absurdité, extravagance (*de demande*), *f.*

unreasonably [ʌn'ri:znəbli], *adv.* sans raison, à l'excès.

unrecognizable [ʌn'rekəgnaizəbl], *a.* méconnaissable.

unrecognized [ʌn'rekəgnaizd], *a.* sans être reconnu; (*fig.*) méconnu (*non apprécié*).

unrecompensed [ʌn'rekəmpenst], *a.* sans récompense.

unreconciled [ʌn'rekənsaild], *a.* irréconcilié.

unrecorded [ʌnri'kɔ:did], *a.* non enregistré.

unredeemable [ʌnri'di:məbl], *a.* irrachetable.

unredeemed [ʌnri'di:md], *a.* non racheté.

unrefined [ʌnri'faind], *a.* non raffiné, brut; (*fig.*) grossier.

unregistered [ʌn'redʒistəd], *a.* non enregistré; non recommandé (*lettre etc.*).

unrelated [ʌnri'leitid], *a.* sans rapport (*avec*); *who is unrelated to*, qui n'est pas parent de.

unrelenting [ʌnri'lentiŋ], *a.* inflexible, implacable.

unreliable [ʌnri'laiəbl], *a.* peu sûr; sur qui *ou* sur quoi l'on ne peut compter.

unrelieved [ʌnri'li:vd], *a.* non soulagé; sans relief.

unremitting [ʌnri'mitiŋ], *a.* incessant, infatigable.

unremunerative [ʌnri'mju:nərətiv], *a.* peu rémunérateur, peu lucratif.

unrepentant [ʌnri'pentənt], *a.* impénitent.

unrepresented [ʌnrepri'zentid], *a.* non représenté.

unrequited [ʌnri'kwaitid], *a.* sans être récompensé; qui n'est pas payé de retour (*amour*).

unreserved [ʌnri'zə:vd], *a.* sans réserve; absolu (*total*).

unreservedly [ʌnri'zə:vidli], *adv.* sans réserve.

unresisting [ʌnri'zistiŋ], *a.* qui ne résiste pas, soumis.

unresolved [ʌnri'zɔlvd], *a.* non résolu; irrésolu, indécis (*personne*).

unresponsive [ʌnris'pɔnsiv], *a.* peu sensible; froid.

unrest [ʌn'rest], *n.* inquiétude, agitation, *f.*

unrestrained [ʌnris'treind], *a.* non restreint; non réprimé; effréné, déréglé.

unrestricted [ʌnri'striktid], *a.* sans restriction.

unretentive [ʌnri'tentiv], *a.* peu tenace; peu fidèle (*la mémoire*).

unrevenged [ʌnri'vendʒd], *a.* non vengé.

unrevised [ʌnri'vaizd], *a.* non revu, non revisé.

unrewarded [ʌnri'wɔ:did], *a.* sans récompense.

unrewarding [ʌnri'wɔ:diŋ], a. peu rémunéra-teur.

unrig [ʌn'rig], v.t. dégréer.

unrighteous [ʌn'raitʃəs], a. injuste, inique.

unrighteousness [ʌn'raitʃəsnis], n. injustice, iniquité, f.

unripe [ʌn'raip], a. pas mûr, vert; (fig.) prématuré.

unrivaled [ʌn'raivəld], a. sans rival, sans égal.

unroll [ʌn'roul], v.t. dérouler, déployer.—v.i. se dérouler se déployer.

unruffled [ʌn'rʌfld], a. tranquille, calme.

unruly [ʌn'ru:li], a. indiscipliné, insoumis, turbulent.

unsaddle [ʌn'sædl], v.t. desseller; débâter (âne); désarçonner (cavalier).

unsafe [ʌn'seif], a. peu sûr, dangereux, hasardeux.

unsaleable [ʌn'seiləbl], a. invendable.

unsalted [ʌn'sɔ:ltid], a. non salé, sans sel.

unsanctified [ʌn'sæŋktifaid], a. non con-sacré, profane.

unsatisfactorily [ʌnsætis'fæktərili], adv. d'une manière peu satisfaisante.

unsatisfactory [ʌn'sætis'fæktəri], a. peu satis-faisant.

unsatisfied [ʌn'sætisfaid], a. peu satisfait.

unsavoriness [ʌn'seivərinis], n. insipidité, fadeur, f.; mauvais goût, m.

unsavory [ʌn'seivəri], a. sans saveur, insipide; repoussant (désagréable).

unscarred [ʌn'skɑ:d], a. sans cicatrices.

unscathed [ʌn'skeiðd], a. sans blessures, sain et sauf.

unscholarly [ʌn'skɔləli], a. illettré, ignorant.

unscientific [ʌnsaiən'tifik], a. peu scienti-fique.

unscientifically [ʌnsaiən'tifikli], adv. peu scientifiquement.

unscrew [ʌn'skru:], v.t. dévisser.

unscrupulous [ʌn'skru:pjuləs], a. peu scrupuleux.

unscrupulously [ʌn'skru:pjuləsli], adv. sans scrupule.

unscrupulousness [ʌn'skru:pjuləsnis], n. manque de scrupule, m.

unseal [ʌn'si:l], v.t. décacheter; desceller.

unsealed [ʌn'si:ld], a. décacheté, ouvert.

unseasonable [ʌn'si:znəbl], a. mal à propos; indu (heure); hors de saison (temps).

unseat [ʌn'si:t], v.t. renverser; désarçonner (d'un cheval); (Polit.) invalider.

unseaworthy [ʌn'si:wə:ði], a. incapable de tenir la mer, innavigable.

unsecured [ʌnsi'kjuəd], a. sans garantie; mal fermé (porte).

unseeing [ʌn'si:iŋ], a. aveugle.

unseemliness [ʌn'si:mlinis], n. inconve-nance, f.

unseemly [ʌn'si:mli], a. inconvenant; indécent.

unseen [ʌn'si:n], a. sans être vu, invisible.

unselfish [ʌn'selfiʃ], a. désintéressé.

unserviceable [ʌn'sə:visəbl], a. inutile, bon à rien.

unsettle [ʌn'setl], v.t. déranger; (fig.) troubler.

unsettled [ʌn'setld], a. mal fixé, mal établi; incertain (temps etc.); irrésolu (personne); dérangé, troublé (esprit); variable, changeant (inconstant).

unshackled [ʌn'ʃækld], a. sans entraves, libre.

unshaken [ʌn'ʃeikn], a. inébranlable, ferme.

unshapely [ʌn'ʃeipli], a. difforme, informe.

unshaved [ʌn'ʃeivd], unshaven [ʌn'ʃeivn], a. non rasé.

unsheathe [ʌn'ʃi:ð], v.t. dégainer.

unship [ʌn'ʃip], v.t. débarquer; démonter (gouvernail etc.); désarmer (avirons).

unshod [ʌn'ʃɔd], a. sans chaussures; déferré (cheval).

unshorn [ʌn'ʃɔ:n], a. non tondu.

unshrinkable [ʌn'ʃriŋkəbl], a. irrétrécissable.

unsightliness [ʌn'saitlinis], n. laideur, f.

unsightly [ʌn'saitli], a. laid, déplaisant.

unsigned [ʌn'saind], a. non signé.

unsisterly [ʌn'sistəli], a. peu digne d'une sœur.

unskilled [ʌn'skild], a. inexpérimenté; non qualifié; unskilled labor, travail de manœuvre, m.; main-d'œuvre non spécia-lisée, f.

unskillful [ʌn'skilful], a. inhabile, maladroit.

unsociable [ʌn'souʃəbl], a. insociable.

unsoiled [ʌn'sɔild], a. sans tache.

unsold [ʌn'sould], a. invendu.

unsoldierly [ʌn'souldʒəli], a. indigne d'un soldat.

unsolicited [ʌnsə'lisitid], a. sans être sollicité.

unsolved [ʌn'sɔlvd], a. non résolu.

unsophisticated [ʌnsə'fistikeitid], a. qui n'est pas frelaté; pur, vrai.

unsought [ʌn'sɔ:t], a. non recherché; spon-tané.

unsound [ʌn'saund], a. défectueux, malsain; faux, erroné; mal établi (crédit); vicieux, pas sain (cheval); of unsound mind, non sain d'esprit.

unsparing [ʌn'spɛəriŋ], a. libéral, prodigue; impitoyable (sans pitié).

unsparingly [ʌn'spɛəriŋli], adv. avec prodi-galité; impitoyablement.

unspeakable [ʌn'spi:kəbl], a. inexprimable; indicible; ignoble, sans nom.

unspecified [ʌn'spesifaid], a. non spécifié.

unspoiled [ʌn'spɔild], a. non corrompu; bien élevé (enfant).

unspoken [ʌn'spoukn], a. non prononcé; tacite.

unsportsmanlike [ʌn'spɔ:tsmənlaik], a. in-digne d'un chasseur ou d'un sportsman.

unspotted [ʌn'spɔtid], a. sans tache.

unstable [ʌn'steibl], a. irrésolu; inconstant; (Mech.) instable.

unstained [ʌn'steind], a. sans tâche.

unstamped [ʌn'stæmpt], a. non timbré, sans timbre.

unsteadily [ʌn'stedili], adv. en chancelant; d'une manière irrégulière.

unsteadiness [ʌn'stedinis], n. instabilité, irrésolution, f.

unsteady [ʌn'stedi], a. chancelant; mal assuré, irrésolu, inconstant, irrégulier (con-duite).

unstinted [ʌn'stintid], a. non restreint, abondant.

unstop [ʌn'stɔp], v.t. déboucher, ouvrir.

unstrengthened [ʌn'streŋθənd], a. non renforcé.

unstressed [ʌn'strest], a. inaccentué, atone.

unsubdued [ʌnsəb'dju:d], a. indompté.

unsubmissive [ʌnsəb'misiv], a. insoumis.

615

unsubmissiveness [ʌnsəb'misivnis], *n.* insoumission, *f.*

unsubstantial [ʌnsəb'stænʃl], *a.* peu substantiel; peu solide; (*fig.*) immatériel; chimérique.

unsuccessful [ʌnsək'sesful], *a.* qui n'a pas réussi, sans succès.

unsuccessfully [ʌnsək'sesfuli] *adv.* sans succès.

unsuitable [ʌn'sju:təbl], *a.* peu convenable, peu propre (*à*).

unsuited [ʌn'sju:tid], *a.* peu fait (*pour*), peu convenable (*à*).

unsullied [ʌn'sʌlid], *a.* sans souillure, sans tache.

unsung [ʌn'sʌŋ], *a.* non célébré.

unsupervised [ʌn'sju:pəvaizd], *a.* non surveillé.

unsupported [ʌnsə'pɔ:tid], *a.* non soutenu; (*fig.*) sans appui.

unsuppressed [ʌnsə'prest], *a.* mal contenu.

unsure [ʌn'ʃuə], *a.* peu sûr.

unsurpassed [ʌnsə'pɑ:st], *a.* non surpassé, sans égal.

unsuspected [ʌnsə'spektid], *a.* insoupçonné; non suspect.

unsuspecting [ʌnsə'spektiŋ], sans soupçon, confiant.

unsuspicious [ʌnsə'spiʃəs], *a.* sans méfiance, confiant.

unsustained [ʌnsə'steind], *a.* non soutenu.

unswayed [ʌn'sweid], *a.* qui ne se laisse pas influencer.

unswerving [ʌn'swə:viŋ], *a.* qui ne s'écarte pas, inébranlable.

unsymmetrical [ʌnsi'metrikl], *a.* asymétrique.

unsympathetic [ʌnsimpə'θetik], *a.* froid, peu compatissant.

unsystematic [ʌnsisti'mætik], *a.* peu systématique.

untainted [ʌn'teintid], *a.* non corrompu; frais (*viande*).

untamable [ʌn'teiməbl], *a.* indomptable.

untamed [ʌn'teimd], *a.* indompté, non apprivoisé.

untapped [ʌn'tæpt], *a.* inexploité (*ressources*).

untarnished [ʌn'tɑ:niʃt], *a.* non terni.

untaught [ʌn'tɔ:t], *a.* ignorant, illettré.

untaxed [ʌn'tækst], *a.* exempt d'impôts.

unteachable [ʌn'ti:tʃəbl], *a.* incapable d'apprendre.

untearable [ʌn'tɛərəbl], *a.* indéchirable.

untempered [ʌn'tempəd], *a.* non trempé (*métal*).

untenable [ʌn'tenəbl], *a.* insoutenable.

untended [ʌn'tendid], *a.* non gardé.

untested [ʌn'testid], *a.* inessayé.

unthanked [ʌn'θæŋkt], *a.* sans être remercié.

unthinking [ʌn'θiŋkiŋ], *a.* inconsidéré, étourdi.

unthinkingly [ʌn'θiŋkiŋli], *adv.* sans y penser.

untidily [ʌn'taidili], *adv.* sans ordre, sans soin.

untidiness [ʌn'taidinis], *n.* désordre, *m.*

untidy [ʌn'taidi], *a.* en désordre; négligé.

untie [ʌn'tai], *v.t.* délier, dénouer; défaire (*nœud*).

until [ən'til], *prep.* jusqu'à; avant.—*conj.* jusqu'à ce que, avant que.

untilled [ʌn'tild], *a.* inculte, en friche.

untimeliness [ʌn'taimlinis], *n.* inopportunité, *f.*

untimely [ʌn'taimli], *a.* prématuré, inopportun.—*adv.* avant terme, prématurément.

untiring [ʌn'taiəriŋ], *a.* infatigable.

untiringly [ʌn'taiəriŋli], *adv.* sans relâche.

***unto** ['ʌntu], *prep.* [TO].

untold [ʌn'tould], *a.* non raconté, non exprimé; sans nombre; inouï.

untouchable [ʌn'tʌtʃəbl], *a.* and *n.* hors caste, paria, intouchable, *m., f.*

untouched [ʌn'tʌtʃt], *a.* non touché; (*fig.*) non ému (*de*).

untoward [ʌn'tɔːd, ʌn'touəd], *a.* insoumis, indocile (*rebelle*); fâcheux.

untraceable [ʌn'treisəbl], *a.* introuvable.

untrained [ʌn'treind], *a.* inexpérimenté (*inexpert*); indiscipliné; non dressé (*animal*).

untrammelled [ʌn'træməld], *a.* sans entraves.

untranslatable [ʌntrɑːns'leitəbl], *a.* intraduisible.

untravelled [ʌn'trævld], *a.* peu connu (*terre*); qui n'a pas voyagé (*personne*).

untried [ʌn'traid], *a.* non essayé; qui n'a pas encore été jugé.

untrimmed [ʌn'trimd], *a.* sans garniture; non émondé (*arbre*).

untrodden [ʌn'trɔdn], *a.* non frayé; non maculé (*neige*).

untroubled [ʌn'trʌbld], *a.* calme, tranquille.

untrue [ʌn'tru:], *a.* faux; inexact (*nouvelle etc.*); déloyal (*à*).

untrustworthiness [ʌn'trʌstwə,ðinis], *n.* inexactitude, fausseté, *f.*

untrustworthy [ʌn'trʌstwə:ði], *a.* indigne de confiance; inexact, mensonger (*nouvelle etc.*).

untruth [ʌn'tru:θ], *n.* contre-vérité, fausseté, *f.*

untruthful [ʌn'tru:θful], *a.* menteur; mensonger (*nouvelle etc.*); perfide, faux, déloyal (*traître*).

untruthfulness [ʌn'tru:θfulnis], *n.* fausseté, *f.*

untutored [ʌn'tju:təd], *a.* peu instruit, ignorant.

untwine [ʌn'twain], *v.t.* détordre; dérouler.

untwist [ʌn'twist], *v.t.* détordre, détortiller, défaire.

unused (1) [ʌn'ju:zd], *a.* non employé, inutilisé; inusité (*mot*).

unused (2) [ʌn'ju:st], *a.* inaccoutumé; *un-used to*, inaccoutumé à.

unusual [ʌn'ju:ʒuəl], *a.* peu commun, rare.

unusually [ʌn'ju:ʒuəli], *adv.* rarement, extraordinairement.

unutterable [ʌn'ʌtərəbl], *a.* inexprimable, indicible.

unuttered [ʌn'ʌtəd], *a.* non prononcé.

unvanquished [ʌn'væŋkwiʃt], *a.* indompté.

unvaried [ʌn'vɛərid], *a.* uniforme.

unvarnished [ʌn'vɑ:niʃt], *a.* non verni; (*fig.*) simple, naturel.

unvarying [ʌn'vɛəriiŋ], *a.* invariable, uniforme.

unveil [ʌn'veil], *v.t.* dévoiler; découvrir.

unventilated [ʌn'ventileitid], *a.* mal aéré.

unversed [ʌn'və:st], *a.* peu versé (*dans*).

unvisited [ʌn'vizitid], *a.* non visité, peu fréquenté.

unwarily [ʌn'wɛərili], *adv.* sans précaution, imprudemment.

unwariness [ʌn'wɛərinis], *n*. imprévoyance, imprudence, *f*.

unwarlike [ʌn'wɔːlaik], *a*. pacifique, peu belliqueux.

unwarrantable [ʌn'wɔrəntəbl], *a*. injustifiable.

unwarrantably [ʌn'wɔrəntəbli], *adv*. inexcusablement.

unwarranted [ʌn'wɔrəntid], *a*. non garanti; *an unwarranted insult*, une insulte gratuite.

unwary [ʌn'wɛəri], *a*. inconsidéré, imprudent.

unwashed [ʌn'wɔʃt], *a*. non lavé, sale, malpropre.

unwavering [ʌn'weivəriŋ], *a*. résolu, inébranlable.

unwearable [ʌn'wɛərəbl], *a*. qu'on ne peut plus porter.

unwearied [ʌn'wiərid], *a*. non lassé, infatigable.

unwelcome [ʌn'welkəm], *a*. importun; fâcheux.

unwell [ʌn'wel], *a*. indisposé, souffrant, mal portant.

unwept [ʌn'wept], *a*. non pleuré, non regretté.

unwholesome [ʌn'houlsəm], *a*. malsain, insalubre.

unwieldy [ʌn'wiːldi], *a*. lourd, pesant, difficile à manier.

unwilling [ʌn'wiliŋ], *a*. peu disposé, mal disposé; *to be unwilling to*, n'être pas disposé à.

unwillingly [ʌn'wiliŋli], *adv*. à contre-cœur, sans le vouloir.

unwillingness [ʌn'wiliŋnis], *n*. mauvaise volonté, *f*.

unwind [ʌn'waind], *v.t. irr. (conjug. like* WIND) dévider; dérouler; *(fig.)* débrouiller. —*v.i.* se dévider.

unwise [ʌn'waiz], *a*. peu sage, malavisé, insensé.

unwisely [ʌn'waizli], *adv*. peu sagement, imprudemment.

unwished (for) [ʌn'wiʃt(fɔː)], *a*. non souhaité.

unwitnessed [ʌn'witnist], *a*. sans témoin, non certifié.

unwitting [ʌn'witiŋ], *a*. inconscient.

unwittingly [ʌn'witiŋli], *adv*. sans le savoir, inconsciemment.

unwomanly [ʌn'wumənli], *a*. indigne d'une femme.

unwonted [ʌn'wountid], *a*. inaccoutumé, rare.

unworkable [ʌn'wəːkəbl], *a*. impraticable.

unworked [ʌn'wəːkt], *a*. inexploité (*mine etc.*).

unworn [ʌn'wɔːn], *a*. non usé, non usagé.

unworthily [ʌn'wəːðili], *adv*. indignement, sans le mériter.

unworthiness [ʌn'wəːðinis], *n*. indignité, *f*.

unworthy [ʌn'wəːði], *a*. indigne (*de*), sans mérite.

unwrap [ʌn'ræp], *v.t.* défaire, désenvelopper.

unwrinkle [ʌn'riŋkl], *v.t.* dérider.

unwrinkled [ʌn'riŋkld], *a*. sans rides, uni.

unwritten [ʌn'ritn], *a*. non écrit; *(fig.)* oral, traditionnel.

unyielding [ʌn'jiːldiŋ], *a*. qui ne cède pas, inflexible.

unyoke [ʌn'jouk], *v.t.* ôter le joug à, dételer.

up [ʌp], *adv*. au haut, en haut, haut; en l'air; levé, sur pied (*pas au lit*); sur l'horizon, debout (*pas assis*); excité; en révolte, en insurrection; fini (*expiré*); élevé (*prix*); en hausse (*valeurs de Bourse*); *it is up to us to do it*, c'est à nous de le faire; *road up*, rue barrée; *to be up to*, être au courant de; *to make up to*, faire des avances à; *up and down*, en haut et en bas, çà et là, de long en large, de haut en bas; *up there*, là-haut; *up to*, jusqu'à la hauteur de; *up to date*, à la dernière mode; à jour; *up to now*, jusqu'ici; *up to then*, jusque-là; *what's up?* (*collog.*) qu'est-ce qu'il y a donc?—*prep*. en haut de, au haut de; en montant; *up hill* or *up stream*, en amont. —*n*. haut, *m.*; *the ups and downs*, les hauts et les bas, *m.pl.*

upbraid [ʌp'breid], *v.t.* reprocher à; réprouver.

upbraiding [ʌp'breidiŋ], *n*. reproche, *m*.

upcast ['ʌpkɑːst], *n*. jet; coup, *m*.

upheaval [ʌp'hiːvl], *n*. soulèvement, *m*.

uphill ['ʌphil], *a*. qui monte; *(fig.)* ardu, pénible.—[ʌp'hil], *adv*. en côte, en montant.

uphold [ʌp'hould], *v.t. irr. (conjug. like* HOLD) soutenir, maintenir.

upholster [ʌp'houlstə], *v.t.* tapisser.

upholsterer [ʌp'houlstərə], *n*. tapissier, *m*.

upholstery [ʌp'houlstəri], *n*. tapisserie, *f*.

upkeep ['ʌpkiːp], *n*. entretien, *m*.

upland ['ʌplənd], *a*. élevé, des hautes terres.

uplands ['ʌpləndz], *n.pl.* terrain élevé, haut pays, *m.*, hautes terres, *f.pl.*

uplift [ʌp'lift], *v.t.* lever, élever, soulever. —['ʌplift], *n*. *(fig.)* inspiration, *f*.

uplifting [ʌp'liftiŋ], *n*. soulèvement, *m*.

upon [ə'pɔn], *prep*. sur; *upon pain of*, sous peine de.

upper ['ʌpə], *a*. supérieur, d'en haut, de dessus, au-dessus; haut; *the Upper House* la Chambre Haute; *upper circle*, troisièmes loges, *f.pl.*; *upper deck*, pont supérieur, *m.*; *upper hand*, dessus, *m.*, supériorité, *f*.

uppermost ['ʌpəmoust], *a*. le plus élevé; *(fig.)* le plus fort.

uppers ['ʌpəz], *n.pl.* empeignes (*de chaussures*), *f.pl.*; *(fam.)* *to be on one's uppers*, être dans la débine.

Upper Volta ['ʌpə'vɔltə]. la Haute Volta, *f*.

uppish ['ʌpiʃ], *a*. fier, arrogant.

uppishness ['ʌpiʃnis], *n*. fierté, arrogance, *f*.

upraise [ʌp'reiz], *v.t.* soulever, élever.

upright ['ʌprait], *a*. droit, debout; d'aplomb, vertical; *(fig.)* honnête (*intègre*).—*adv.* tout droit.—*n*. montant, *m*.

uprightness ['ʌpraitnis], *n*. droiture, intégrité, *f*.

uprising [ʌp'raiziŋ], *n*. lever; soulèvement, *m*.

uproar ['ʌprɔː], *n*. tumulte, désordre; tapage, *m*.

uproarious [ʌp'rɔːriəs], *a*. bruyant; tumultueux.

uproariously [ʌp'rɔːriəsli], *adv*. avec un grand vacarme.

uproot [ʌp'ruːt], *v.t.* déraciner, extirper.

uprooting [ʌp'ruːtiŋ], *n*. déracinement, *m*.

upset [ʌp'set], *v.t. irr. (conjug. like* SET) renverser; *(fig.)* bouleverser.—*v.i.* se renverser;

verser (*véhicules*).—['ʌpset], *n.* bouleversement, *m.*

upshot ['ʌpʃɔt], *n.* résultat, *m.*, fin, *f.*, fin mot, *m.*

upside-down ['ʌpsaid'daun], *adv.* sens dessus dessous.

upstairs ['ʌpsteəz], *a.* d'en haut.—[ʌp'steəz], *adv.* en haut.

upstanding [ʌp'stændiŋ], *a.* droit, debout.

upstart ['ʌpstɑːt], *n.* parvenu, nouveau riche, *m.*

upsurge [ʌp'səːdʒ], *n.* poussée, *f.*

upward ['ʌpwəd], *a.* dirigé en haut; ascendant.—*adv.* or **upwards** ['ʌpwədz], en haut; en montant; *upwards of*, plus de.

Ural ['juərəl] **Mountains**. les Monts Ourals, *m.pl.*

uranium [ju'reiniəm], *n.* uranium, *m.*

urban ['əːbən], *a.* urbain.

urbane [əː'bein], *a.* qui a de l'urbanité, poli.

urbanely [əː'beinli], *adv.* avec urbanité.

urbanity [əː'bæniti], *n.* urbanité, *f.*

urbanize ['əːbənaiz], *v.t.* urbaniser.

urchin ['əːtʃin], *n.* gamin, polisson; (*colloq.*) mioche, gosse, *m.*; *sea urchin*, oursin, *m.*

urge [əːdʒ], *v.t.* presser; pousser, exciter, porter (*à*); alléguer (*insister sur*); *to urge on*, pousser en avant.—*n.* impulsion; poussée, *f.*

urgency ['əːdʒənsi], *n.* urgence, *f.*

urgent ['əːdʒənt], *a.* urgent, instant.

urgently ['əːdʒəntli], *adv.* avec urgence, instamment.

urging ['əːdʒiŋ], *n.* sollicitation, *f.*

uric ['juərik], *a.* urique.

urinal ['juərinl], *n.* urinoir; (*Med.*) urinal, *m.*; vespasienne (*urinoir public*), *f.*

urinate ['juərineit], *v.i.* uriner.

urine ['juərin], *n.* urine, *f.*

urn [əːn], *n.* urne; fontaine (*à thé, à café etc.*), *f.*

Ursula ['əːsjulə] Ursule, *f.*

Uruguay ['juəruɡwai]. l'Uruguay, *m.*

Uruguayan [juəru'gwaiən], *a.* uruguayen.—*n.* Uruguayen (*personne*), *m.*

us [ʌs], *pron.* nous; *for us Frenchmen*, pour nous autres Français.

usable ['juːzəbl], *a.* utilisable, employable.

usage ['juːzidʒ], *n.* usage, *m.*

use [juːs], *n.* usage, emploi, *m.*; utilité, *f.*, avantage, profit, *m.*; habitude, *f.*; (*Law*) usufruit, *m.*; *it is of no use*, cela ne sert à rien; *of use*, utile; *to make use of*, se servir de; *what is the use of that?* à quoi sert cela?—[juːz], *v.t.* user de, faire usage de, employer, se servir de; utiliser; consommer.

used [juːzd], *a.* usité (*mot etc.*), d'occasion (*voiture*); *very little used*, qui a peu servi, presque neuf (*vêtement etc.*).—[juːst] *to be* or *get used to*, s'accoutumer à, s'habituer à.—[juːst], *v. aux. in the expression* used to (*followed by inf.*) *usu. translated by the Imp. Tense in French*; *he used to admire*, il admirait.

useful ['juːsful], *a.* utile.

usefully ['juːsfuli], *adv.* utilement, avec profit.

usefulness ['juːsfulnis], *n.* utilité, *f.*

useless ['juːslis], *a.* inutile; vain.

uselessly ['juːslisli], *adv.* inutilement.

uselessness ['juːslisnis], *n.* inutilité, *f.*

usher ['ʌʃə], *n.* huissier (*de cour de justice*);

sous-maître, *m.*—*v.t.* faire entrer, introduire (*dans*); (*fig.*) annoncer.

usherette [ʌʃə'ret], *n.* (*Cine.*) ouvreuse, *f.*

usual ['juːʒuəl], *a.* usuel, ordinaire, habituel, accoutumé; d'usage; *as usual*, comme d'habitude.

usually ['juːʒuəli], *adv.* ordinairement, d'ordinaire, d'habitude.

usurer ['juːʒərə], *n.* usurier, *m.*

usurious [juː'zjuəriəs], *a.* usuraire.

usurp [juː'zəːp], *v.t.* usurper.

usurpation [juːzə'peiʃən], *n.* usurpation, *f.*

usurper [juː'zəːpə], *n.* usurpateur, *m.*

usury ['juːʒəri], *n.* usure, *f.*

utensil [juː'tensil], *n.* ustensile, *m.*

uterine ['juːtərain], *a.* utérin.

uterus ['juːtərəs], *n.* utérus, *m.*

utilitarian [juːtili'teəriən], *a.* utilitaire.

utilitarianism [juːtili'teəriənizm], *n.* utilitarisme, *m.*

utility [juː'tiliti], *n.* utilité, *f.*

utilizable ['juːtilaizəbl], *a.* utilisable.

utilization [juːtilai'zeiʃən], *n.* utilisation, *f.*

utilize ['juːtilaiz], *v.t.* utiliser.

utmost ['ʌtmoust], *a.* extrême, le dernier, le plus haut, le plus grand; le plus élevé (*prix etc.*).—*n.* extrême, comble, *m.*; *to do one's utmost*, faire tout son possible (*pour*).

Utopia [juː'toupiə]. Utopie, *f.*

Utopian [juː'toupiən], *a.* d'utopie, utopique.

utter (1) ['ʌtə], *a.* entier, complet; absolu; le plus profond (*extrême*); vrai; fieffé (*véritable*).

utter (2) ['ʌtə], *v.t.* pousser; proférer, prononcer; dire; émettre (*fausse monnaie*).

utterable ['ʌtərəbl], *a.* exprimable.

utterance ['ʌtərəns], *n.* énonciation, prononciation, parole, expression, *f.*

utterer ['ʌtərə], *n.* personne qui prononce, *f.*; émetteur (*de fausse monnaie*), *m.*

utterly ['ʌtəli], *adv.* tout à fait, entièrement.

uttermost ['ʌtəmoust], *a.* extrême; le plus reculé.

uvula ['juːvjulə], *n.* (*Anat.*) luette, uvule, *f.*

uvular ['juːvjulə], *a.* uvulaire.

uxorious [ʌk'sɔːriəs], *a.* uxorieux, esclave de sa femme.

uxoriousness [ʌk'sɔːriəsnis], *n.* complaisance excessive pour sa femme, *f.*

V

V, v [viː]. vingt-deuxième lettre de l'alphabet, *m.*

vacancy ['veikənsi], *n.* vacance, place vacante, *f.*; vide, *m.*; lacune (*trou*), *f.*

vacant ['veikənt], *a.* vacant, vide; libre (*inoccupé*); vide d'expression (*regard perdu*).

vacate [və'keit], *v.t.* laisser vacant, quitter.

vacation [və'keiʃən], *n.* vacation, *f.*, vacances, *f.pl.*

vaccinate ['væksineit], *v.t.* vacciner.

vaccination [væksi'neiʃən], *n.* vaccination, vaccine, *f.*

vaccine ['væksiːn], *a.* de vache.—*n.* vaccin, *m.*

vacillate ['væsileit], *v.i.* vaciller; (*fig.*) hésiter.

vacillating ['væsileitiŋ], *a.* vacillant, indécis.

vacillation [væsi'leiʃən], *n.* vacillation, indécision, *f.*

vacuity [və'kju:iti], *n.* vide, *m.*; vacuité, *f.*

vacuous ['vækjuəs], *a.* vide; (*fig.*) bête.

vacuum ['vækjuəm], *n.* vide, *m.*

vacuum cleaner ['vækjuəm'kli:nə], *n.* aspirateur, *m.*

vade-mecum ['veidi'mi:kəm], *n.* vademecum, *f.*

vagabond ['vægəbɔnd], *a.* errant, vagabond. —*n.* vagabond, *m.*

vagary ['veigəri], *n.* caprice, *m.*, lubie, boutade, *f.*

vagina [və'dʒainə], *n.* (*Anat.*) vagin, *m.*

vagrancy ['veigrənsi], *n.* vagabondage, *m.*

vagrant ['veigrənt], *a.* vagabond, errant.—*n.* vagabond, mendiant, *m.*

vague [veig], *a.* vague.

vaguely ['veigli], *adv.* vaguement.

vagueness ['veignis], *n.* vague, *m.*

vain [vein], *a.* vain; faux (*creux*); vaniteux, glorieux (*fier*); *in vain*, en vain.

vainglorious [vein'glɔ:riəs], *a.* vain, vaniteux.

vainglory [vein'glɔ:ri], *n.* vaine gloire, gloriole, *f.*

vainly ['veinli], *adv.* en vain, vainement.

vainness ['veinnis], *n.* vanité, *f.*

valance ['væləns], *n.* frange de lit, *f.*

vale [veil], *n.* (*poet.*) vallon, *m.*, vallée, *f.*

valedictory [væli'diktəri], *a.* d'adieu.—*n.* discours d'adieu, *m.*

valet ['vælit], *n.* valet de chambre, *m.*

valetudinarian [vælitju:di'nɛəriən], *a.* and *n.* valétudinaire, *f.*

valiant ['væliənt], *a.* vaillant, valeureux.

valiantly ['væliəntli], *adv.* vaillamment.

valid ['vælid], *a.* valide, valable.

validate ['vælideit], *v.t.* valider, rendre valable.

validity [və'liditi], **validness** ['vælidnis], *n.* validité, *f.*

validly ['vælidli], *adv.* validement.

validness [VALIDITY].

valise [və'li:z], *n.* valise, *f.*; sac de voyage, *m.*

valley ['væli], *n.* vallée, *f.*, vallon, *m.*

valor ['vælə], *n.* valeur, vaillance, *f.*

valorous ['vælərəs], *a.* valeureux.

valuable ['væljuəbl], *a.* précieux.

valuation [vælju'eiʃən], *n.* évaluation, *f.*

valuator ['væljueitə], *n.* estimateur, *m.*

value ['vælju:], *n.* valeur, *f.*; prix, *m.*—*v.t.* évaluer, estimer.

valued ['vælju:d], *a.* estimé, apprécié.

valueless ['væljulis], *a.* sans valeur.

valuer ['væljuə], *n.* estimateur, commissaire-priseur, *m.*

valve ['vælv], *n.* soupape; valve; (*Rad.*) lampe, *f.*

valved [vælvd], *a.* à soupape; (*Bot.*) valvé, à valves.

valvular ['vælvjulə], *a.* (*Med.*) valvulaire.

vamp [væmp], *n.* empeigne; enjôleuse, femme fatale, *f.*—*v.t.* (*fig.*) raccommoder, rapiécer; (*Mus.*) improviser.

vampire ['væmpaiə], *n.* vampire, *m.*

van [væn], *n.* camionnette, voiture (*de déménagement*), *f.*; (*Rail. etc.*) fourgon, *m.*; avant-garde (*précurseur*), *f.*

vandal [vændl], *n.* vandale, *m.*, *f.*

vandalism ['vændəlizm], *n.* vandalisme, *m.*

vane [vein], *n.* girouette, *f.*

vanguard ['væŋgɑ:d], *n.* avant-garde, *f.*

vanilla [və'nilə], *n.* vanille, *f.*

vanish ['væniʃ], *v.i.* s'évanouir, disparaître.

vanishing point ['væniʃiŋpɔint], *n.* point de fuite, *m.*

vanity ['væniti], *n.* vanité, *f.*

vanquish ['væŋkwiʃ], *v.t.* vaincre.

vanquisher ['væŋkwiʃə], *n.* vainqueur, *m.*

vantage ['vɑ:ntidʒ], *n.* avantage, *m.*, supériorité, *f.*

vapid ['væpid], *a.* fade, insipide; éventé (*boisson alcoolique*).

vapidity [væ'piditi], **vapidness** ['væpidnis], *n.* fadeur, insipidité, *f.*

vapor ['veipə], *n.* vapeur; (*fig.*) fumée, *f.*

vaporish ['veipəriʃ], **vapory** ['veipəri], *a.* vaporeux.

vaporization [veipərai'zeiʃən], *n.* vaporisation, *f.*

vaporize ['veipəraiz], *v.t.* vaporiser.—*v.i.* se vaporiser.

vaporous ['veipərəs], *a.* vaporeux.

variability [vɛəriə'biliti], **variableness** ['vɛəriəblnis], *n.* variabilité; inconstance, *f.*

variable ['vɛəriəbl], *a.* variable; inconstant.

variance ['vɛəriəns], *n.* désaccord, *m.*

variation [vɛəri'eiʃən], *n.* variation, *f.*, changement, *m.*

varicose ['værikous], *a.* variqueux; *varicose vein*, varice, *f.*

varied ['vɛərid], *a.* varié, divers.

variegate ['vɛərigeit], *v.t.* varier; nuancer.

variegated ['vɛərigeitid], *a.* varié, bigarré; (*Bot.*) panaché.

variegation [vɛəri'geiʃən], *n.* bigarrure, *f.*

variety [və'raiəti], *n.* variété, diversité, *f.*

various ['vɛəriəs], *a.* divers, différent.

variously ['vɛəriəsli], *adv.* diversement.

varnish ['vɑ:niʃ], *n.* vernis, *m.*—*v.t.* vernir; vernisser (*poterie etc.*).

varnisher ['vɑ:niʃə], *n.* vernisseur, *m.*

varnishing ['vɑ:niʃiŋ], *n.* vernissure, *f.*; vernissage, *m.*

vary ['vɛəri], *v.t.* varier; diversifier.—*v.i.* varier, changer.

varying ['vɛəriiŋ], *a.* changeant, qui varie, divers.

vascular ['væskjulə], *a.* vasculaire.

vase [vɑ:z], *n.* vase, *m.*

vaseline ['væsəli:n], *n.* (*reg. trade mark*) vaseline, *f.*

vassal [væsl], *n.* vassal, *m.*

vassalage ['væsəlidʒ], *n.* vasselage, *m.*; (*fig.*) servitude, *f.*

vast [vɑ:st], *a.* vaste, immense.—*n.* immensité, *f.*

vastly ['vɑ:stli], *adv.* immensément, excessivement.

vastness ['vɑ:stnis], *n.* vaste étendue, grandeur, *f.*

vat [væt], *n.* cuve, *f.*

vatful ['vætful], *n.* cuvée, *f.*

Vatican ['vætikən], *n.* le Vatican, *m.*

vaudeville ['voudəvil], *n.* vaudeville, *m.*

vault [vɔ:lt], *n.* voûte, cave, *f.*; caveau (*lieu de sépulture*); saut (*bond*), *m.*—*v.t.* voûter.—*v.i.* sauter.

vaulted ['vɔ:ltid], *a.* voûté, en voûte.

vaulter

vaulter ['vɔːltə], *n.* voltigeur, sauteur, *m.*, acrobate, *m.*, *f.*

vaulting ['vɔːltiŋ], *n.* construction de voûtes, *f.*; voûtes, *f.pl.*; voltige (*acrobatie*), *f.*

vaunt [vɔːnt], *n.* vanterie, *f.*—*v.t.* vanter, élever jusqu'aux nues.

vaunter ['vɔːntə], *n.* vantard, *m.*

vaunting ['vɔːntiŋ], *a.* plein de jactance.

vauntingly ['vɔːntiŋli], *adv.* avec jactance.

veal [viːl], *n.* veau, *m.*

vedette [və'det], *n.* vedette, *f.*

veer [viə], *v.t.* virer (*bateau*).—*v.i.* tourner, changer de direction; virer (*bateau*).

vegetable ['vedʒitəbl], *a.* végétal.—*n.* végétal, légume, *m.*

vegetal ['vedʒitl], *a.* végétal.

vegetarian [vedʒi'tɛəriən], *a.* and *n.* végétarien, *m.*

vegetate ['vedʒiteit], *v.i.* végéter.

vegetation [vedʒi'teiʃən], *n.* végétation, *f.*

vegetative ['vedʒitətiv], *a.* végétatif, végétant.

vehemence ['viːiməns], *n.* véhémence; (*fig.*) ardeur, *f.*

vehement ['viːimənt], *a.* véhément, impétueux.

vehemently ['viːiməntli], *adv.* avec véhémence, impétueusement.

vehicle ['viːikl], *n.* véhicule, *m.*, voiture, *f.*

veil [veil], *n.* voile, *m.*; voilette (*de dame*), *f.*—*v.t.* voiler; (*fig.*) déguiser.

vein [vein], *n.* veine; (*fig.*) humeur, *f.*—*v.t.* veiner.

veined [veind], **veiny** ['veini], *a.* veiné.

vellum ['veləm], *n.* vélin, *m.*

velocity [və'lɔsiti], *n.* vélocité, vitesse, rapidité, *f.*

velvet ['velvit], *a.* de velours; (*Bot.*) velouté.—*n.* velours, *m.*

velveteen [velvə'tiːn], *n.* velours de coton, *m.*

velvety ['velviti], *a.* velouté.

venal [viːnl], *a.* vénal.

venality [viː'næliti], *n.* vénalité, *f.*

vend [vend], *v.t.* vendre (*petits articles*).

vending machine, see **slot-machine**.

vendetta [ven'detə], *n.* vendetta, *f.*

vendible ['vendibl], *a.* vendable.

vendor ['vendə], *n.* vendeur, *m.*

veneer [və'niə], *n.* feuille (*de bois etc.*); plaque, *f.*; (*fig.*) vernis, *m.*—*v.t.* plaquer (*de*).

veneering [və'niəriŋ], *n.* placage, *m.*

venerable ['venərəbl], *a.* vénérable.

venerableness ['venərəblnis], *n.* caractère vénérable, *m.*

venerate ['venəreit], *v.t.* vénérer.

veneration [venə'reiʃən], *n.* vénération, *f.*

venerator ['venəreitə], *n.* vénérateur, *m.*

venery ['venəri], *n.* chasse, vénerie, *f.*

Venetian [və'niːʃən], *a.* vénitien, de Venise; **Venetian blind**, jalousie, *f.*; **Venetian shutter**, persienne, *f.*—*n.* Vénitien (*personne*), *m.*

Venezuela [venə'zweilə], le Vénézuéla, *m.*

Venezuelan [venə'zweilən], *a.* vénézuélien.—*n.* Vénézuélien (*personne*), *m.*

vengeance ['vendʒəns], *n.* vengeance, *f.*; **with a vengeance**, furieusement, à outrance.

vengeful ['vendʒful], *a.* vindicatif.

venial ['viːniəl], *a.* véniel, pardonnable.

veniality [viːni'æliti], *n.* vénialité, *f.*

Venice ['venis]. Venise, *f.*

venison ['venizn], *n.* venaison, *f.*

venom ['venəm], *n.* venin, *m.*

venomous ['venəməs], *a.* venimeux (*animal*); vénéneux (*plante*); (*fig.*) méchant.

venous ['viːnəs], *a.* veineux.

vent [vent], *v.t.* donner issue à, exhaler, décharger.—*n.* issue, *f.*, passage, cours; trou de fausse (*de baril*); soupirail (*pour l'air*), *m.*; **to give vent to**, donner libre cours à.

ventilate ['ventileit], *v.t.* ventiler; aérer, (*fig.*) discuter.

ventilation [venti'leiʃən], *n.* ventilation, *f.*; **ventilation shaft**, puits d'aérage, *m.*

ventilator ['ventileitə], *n.* ventilateur, *m.*

ventral ['ventrəl], *a.* ventral.

ventricle ['ventrikl], *n.* ventricule, *m.*

ventriloquism [ven'trilǝkwizm], *n.* ventriloquie, *f.*

ventriloquist [ven'trilǝkwist], *n.* ventriloque, *m.*, *f.*

venture ['ventʃə], *n.* aventure, entreprise, *f.*—*v.t.* aventurer, risquer.—*v.i.* oser, se hasarder, s'aventurer; s'aviser de (*se permettre*).

venturer ['ventʃərə], *n.* personne aventureuse, *f.*

venturesome ['ventʃəsəm], *a.* aventureux, audacieux.

venue ['venjuː], *n.* juridiction, *f.*; lieu de réunion, *m.*

Venus ['viːnəs]. Vénus, *f.*

veracious [və'reiʃəs], *a.* véridique.

veracity [və'ræsiti], *n.* véracité, *f.*

veranda, verandah [və'rændə], *n.* véranda, *f.*

verb [vəːb], *n.* verbe, *m.*

verbal ['vəːbəl], *a.* verbal, littéral.

verbally ['vəːbəli], *adv.* verbalement, mot à mot.

verbatim [vəː'beitim], *adv.* mot pour mot.

verbena [vəː'biːnə], *n.* verveine, *f.*

verbiage ['vəːbiidʒ], *n.* verbiage, *m.*

verbose [vəː'bous], *a.* verbeux, diffus, prolixe.

verbosity [vəː'bositi], *n.* verbosité, *f.*

verdant ['vəːdənt], *a.* verdoyant, vert.

verdict ['vəːdikt], *n.* verdict; (*fig.*) arrêt, *m.*

verdigris ['vəːdigriːs], *n.* vert-de-gris, *m.*

verdure ['vəːdjə], *n.* verdure, *f.*

verge (1) [vəːdʒ], *n.* bord, *m.*; bordure; lisière (*de forêt etc.*); verge (*baguette*), *f.*; **on the verge of setting out**, à la veille de partir.—*v.i.* pencher (*vers*); **to verge on**, toucher à.

verger ['vəːdʒə], *n.* bedeau, huissier à verge, *m.*

verification [verifi'keiʃən], *n.* vérification, *f.*

verifier ['verifaiə], *n.* vérificateur, *m.*

verify ['verifai], *v.t.* vérifier.

verily ['verili], *adv.* en vérité, vraiment.

verisimilar [veri'similə], *a.* vraisemblable.

verisimilitude [verisi'militjuːd], *n.* vraisemblance, *f.*

veritable ['veritəbl], *a.* véritable.

verity ['veriti], *n.* vérité, *f.*

vermicelli [vəːmi'seli], *n.* vermicelle, *m.*

vermicule ['vəːmikjuːl], *n.* vermisseau, *m.*

vermilion [və'miljən], *a.* vermeil.—*n.* vermillon, *m.*

vermin ['vəːmin], *n.* vermine, *f.*

verminous ['vəːminəs], *a.* vermineux.

vernacular [vəˈnækjulə], *a.* du pays, indigène. —*n.* langue vernaculaire, *f.*

vernal [ˈvəːnəl], *a.* printanier.

veronica [vəˈrɔnikə], *n.* véronique, *f.*

versatile [ˈvəːsatail], *a.* qui a des connaissances variées; qui se plie à tout.

versatility [vəːsəˈtiliti], *n.* souplesse, faculté d'adaptation, *f.*

verse [vəːs], *n.* vers, *m.*, poésie; strophe (*stance*), *f.*

versed [vəːst], *a.* versé (*dans*).

versification [vəːsifiˈkeiʃən], *n.* versification, *f.*

versifier [ˈvəːsifaiə], *n.* versificateur, rimailleur, *m.*

versify [ˈvəːsifai], *v.t.* mettre en vers.—*v.i.* versifier.

version [ˈvəːʃən], *n.* version, *f.*

versus [ˈvəːsəs], *prep.* contre.

vertebra [ˈvəːtibrə], *n.* (*pl.* **vertebræ** [ˈvəːtibriː]) vertèbre, *f.*

vertebral [ˈvəːtibrəl], *a.* vertébral.

vertebrate [ˈvəːtibrit], *a.* and *n.* vertébré, *m.*

vertex [ˈvəːteks], *n.* (*pl.* **vertices** [ˈvəːtisiːz]) sommet, zénith, *m.*

vertical [ˈvəːtikl], *a.* vertical.

vertically [ˈvəːtikli], *adv.* verticalement.

vertiginous [vəːˈtidʒinəs], *a.* vertigineux.

vertigo [ˈvəːtigou], *n.* vertige, *m.*

verve [vəːv], *n.* verve, *f.*

very [ˈveri], *a.* vrai, même, véritable.—*adv.* fort, bien, très.

vesper [ˈvespə], *n.* étoile du soir, *f.*; soir *m.*; (*pl.*) vêpres, *f.pl.*

vessel [vesl], *n.* vase; vaisseau, bâtiment, navire, *m.*

vest [vest], *n.* tricot de corps; (*Am.*) gilet, *m.*— *v.t.* vêtir, revêtir; investir (*de*).—*v.i.* échoir (*à*).

vestal [vestl], *a.* vestale, de Vesta; (*fig.*) chaste.—*n.* vestale, *f.*

vestibule [ˈvestibjuːl], *n.* vestibule, *m.*

vestige [ˈvestidʒ], *n.* vestige, *m.*, trace, *f.*

vestment [ˈvestmənt], *n.* vêtement (de cérémonie), *m.*; chasuble, *f.*

vestry [ˈvestri], *n.* sacristie, *f.*

vesture [ˈvestʃə], *n.* vêtements, *m.pl.*

Vesuvius [viˈsuːvjəs]. le Vésuve, *m.*

vetch [vetʃ], *n.* vesce, *f.*

veteran [ˈvetərən], *a.* vieux, ancien, expérimenté.—*n.* vétéran, *m.*

veterinary [ˈvetərinri], *a.* vétérinaire; *veterinary surgeon*, vétérinaire, *m.,f.*

veto [ˈviːtou], *n.* veto, *m.*—*v.t.* mettre son veto à, interdire.

vex [veks], *v.t.* fâcher, vexer, contrarier.

vexation [vekˈseiʃən], *n.* vexation, contrariété, *f.*, chagrin, *m.*

vexatious [vekˈseiʃəs], *a.* vexatoire; irritant, fâcheux, ennuyeux.

vexatiousness [vekˈseiʃəsnis], *n.* caractère vexatoire, *m.*

vexed [vekst], *a.* vexé, fâché; (*fig.*) épineux (*question*).

vexing [ˈveksiŋ], *a.* contrariant, vexant, ennuyeux.

via [ˈvaiə], *prep.* par, par voie de, via.

viability [vaiəˈbiliti], *n.* viabilité, *f.*

viable [ˈvaiəbl], *a.* viable.

viaduct [ˈvaiədʌkt], *n.* viaduc, *f.*

vial [ˈvaiəl], *n.* fiole, *f.*

viands [ˈvaiəndz], *n. pl.* aliments, *m.pl.*; mets, *m.*

viaticum [vaiˈætikəm], *n.* viatique, *m.*

vibrate [vaiˈbreit], *v.t.* faire vibrer.—*v.i.* vibrer, osciller.

vibration [vaiˈbreiʃən], *n.* vibration, oscillation, *f.*

vibrating [vaiˈbreitiŋ], **vibratory** [ˈvaibrə təri], *a.* vibrant, vibratoire.

vicar [ˈvikə], *n.* (*Engl. Ch.*) pasteur; (*R.-C. Ch.*) curé (*de paroisse*), *m.*; *vicar general*, vicaire, *m.*

vicarage [ˈvikəridʒ], *n.* cure, *f.*, presbytère, *m.*

vicarial [viˈkɛəriəl], *a.* de la cure, du curé.

vicarious [viˈkɛəriəs], *a.* vicarial, de vicaire, (*fig.*) de substitution.

vicariously [viˈkɛəriəsli], *adv.* par délégation, par substitution.

vice (1) [vais], *n.* vice, défaut, *m.*; *vice squad*, brigade de mœurs, *f.*

vice (2) [vais], *n.* (*Tech.*) étau, *m.*

vice admiral [ˈvaisædmirəl], *n.* vice-amiral, *m.*

vice chancellor [ˈvaistʃɔːnsələ], *n.* vice-chancelier; (*Univ.*) recteur, *m.*

vice president [ˈvaisprezidənt], *n.* vice-président, *m.*

viceroy [ˈvaisrɔi], *n.* vice-roi, *m.*

vicinity [viˈsiniti], *n.* voisinage, *m.*, proximité, *f.*, alentours, *m.pl.*

vicious [ˈviʃəs], *a.* vicieux; haineux.

viciously [ˈviʃəsli], *adv.* vicieusement; rageusement.

viciousness [ˈviʃəsnis], *n.* nature vicieuse, *f.*, vice, *m.*

vicissitude [viˈsisitjuːd], *n.* vicissitude, *f.*

victim [ˈviktim], *n.* victime, *f.*

victimization [viktimaiˈzeiʃən], *n.* tyrannisation, *f.*

victimize [ˈviktimaiz], *v.t.* exercer des représailles contre, tromper.

victor [ˈviktə], *n.* vainqueur, *m.*

victorious [vikˈtɔːriəs], *a.* victorieux, de victoire.

victoriously [vikˈtɔːriəsli], *adv.* victorieusement, en vainqueur.

victory [ˈviktəri], *n.* victoire, *f.*

victual [vitl], *v.t.* approvisionner, ravitailler.

victualler [ˈvitlə], *n.* pourvoyeur, fournisseur (de vivres), *m.*; *licensed victualler*, débitant de boissons, *m.*

victualling [ˈvitliŋ], *n.* ravitaillement, *m.*

victuals [vitlz], *n.pl.* vivres, *m.pl.*, provisions, *f.pl.*

vie [vai], *v.i.* rivaliser, lutter (*de*); le disputer (*à*).

Vienna [viˈenə]. Vienne, *f.*

Viennese [viːəˈniːz], *a.* viennois.—*n.* Viennois (*personne*), *m.*

Vietnam [vjetˈnæm]. le Vietnam, *m.*

Vietnamese [vjetnəˈmiːz], *a.* vietnamien.—*n.* Vietnamien (*personne*), *m.*

view [vjuː], *n.* vue, perspective, scène, *f.*; regard (*coup d'œil*); aperçu, examen (*exposé*), *m.*; intention, *f.*, dessein, *m.*; opinion, pensée, *f.*; *in view of*, en considération de; *on view*, ouvert au public; *with a view to*, en vue de.—*v.t.* regarder; considérer; examiner, inspecter; explorer.

viewer [ˈvjuːə], *n.* spectateur; téléspectateur, *m.*

viewing [ˈvjuːiŋ], *n.* examen, *m.*, inspection, *f.*

view-point ['vju:pɔint], *n.* point de vue, *m.*

vigil ['vidʒil], *n.* veille, veillée, (*Eccles.*) vigile, *f.*

vigilance ['vidʒiləns], *n.* vigilance, *f.*

vigilant ['vidʒilənt], *a.* vigilant, éveillé.

vigilantly ['vidʒiləntli], *adv.* avec vigilance.

vigorous ['vigərəs], *a.* vigoureux.

vigorously ['vigərəsli], *adv.* vigoureusement.

vigorousness ['vigərəsnis], **vigor** ['vigə], *n.* vigueur, *f.*

vile [vail], *a.* vil, abject, bas; détestable.

vileness ['vailnis], *n.* bassesse, *f.*

vilification [vilifi'keiʃən], *n.* diffamation, *f.*

vilifier ['vilifaiə], *n.* diffamateur, *m.*

vilify ['vilifai], *v.t.* vilipender, dénigrer.

villa ['vilə], *n.* villa; maison de campagne, *f.*

village ['vilidʒ], *n.* village, *m.*

villager ['vilidʒə], *n.* villageois, *m.*

villain ['vilən], *n.* scélérat, gredin; (*Theat.*) traître, *m.*

villainous ['vilənəs], *a.* vil, infâme.

villainy ['viləni], *n.* scélératesse, vilenie, *f.*

vindicate ['vindikeit], *v.t.* soutenir, défendre, justifier; venger.

vindication [vindi'keiʃən], *n.* défense, justification, *f.*

vindicator ['vindikeitə], *n.* défenseur, *m.*

vindictive [vin'diktiv], *a.* vindicatif.

vindictively [vin'diktivli], *adv.* d'une manière vindicative.

vindictiveness [vin'diktivnis], *n.* esprit de vengeance, *m.*

vine [vain], *n.* vigne, *f.*

vine-dresser ['vaindresə], *n.* vigneron, *m.*

vinegar ['vinigə], *n.* vinaigre, *m.*

vine grower ['vaingrouə], *n.* viticulteur, *m.*

vine-growing ['vaingrouiŋ], *n.* viticulture, *f.*

vine harvest ['vainha:vist], *n.* vendange, *f.*

vine prop ['vainprɔp], *n.* échalas, *m.*

vinery ['vainəri], *n.* serre à vignes, *f.*

vineyard ['vinjəd], *n.* vigne, *f.*; vignoble, *m.*

vinicultural [vini'kʌltʃərəl], *a.* vinicole.

viniculture ['vinikʌltʃə], *n.* viniculture, *f.*

vinous ['vainəs], *a.* vineux.

vintage ['vintidʒ], *n.* vendange, *f.*; vinée, récolte de vin (*cueillette*), *f.*; vendanges (*temps de la récolte*), *f.pl.*; **a vintage wine**, un vin de marque, *m.*

vintager ['vintidʒə], *n.* vendangeur, *m.*

vintner ['vintnə], *n.* négociant en vins, *m.*

viny ['vaini], *a.* de vigne, de raisin; de vignoble.

viola (1) [vi'oulə], *n.* (*Mus.*) alto, *m.*; **viola player**, altiste, *m.*, *f.*

viola (2) ['vaiələ], *n.* (*Bot.*) violette, *f.*

violate ['vaiəleit], *v.t.* violer, faire violence à; outrager.

violation [vaiə'leiʃən], *n.* violation, infraction, *f.*; viol (*d'une femme*), *m.*

violator ['vaiəleitə], *n.* violateur, *m.*

violence ['vaiələns], *n.* violence, *f.*; **with violence (of robbery)**, à main armée.

violent ['vaiələnt], *a.* violent; atroce (*douleur*).

violently ['vaiələntli], *adv.* violemment, avec violence.

violet ['vaiəlit], *n.* violette (*plante*), *f.*; violet (*couleur*), *m.*

violin [vaiə'lin], *n.* violon, *m.*

violinist [vaiə'linist], *n.* violoniste, *m.*, *f.*

violist [vi'oulist], *n.* altiste, violiste, *m.*, *f.*

violoncellist [vaiələn'tʃelist], *n.* violoncelliste, *m.*, *f.*

violoncello [vaiələn'tʃelou], *n.* violoncelle, *m.*

viper ['vaipə], *n.* vipère, *f.*

viperish ['vaipəriʃ], **viperous** ['vaipərəs], *a.* de vipère; (*fig.*) venimeux.

virago [vi'ra:gou], *n.* virago, mégère, *f.*

virgin ['və:dʒin], *n.* vierge; virginal, de vierge.—*n.* vierge, *f.*

virginal ['və:dʒinəl], *a.* virginal, de vierge.

Virginia creeper [və'dʒinjə'kri:pə], *n.* vigne vierge, *f.*

virginity [və'dʒiniti], *n.* virginité, *f.*

viridity [vi'riditi], *n.* verdeur, fraîcheur, *f.*

virile ['virail], *a.* viril, mâle.

virility [vi'riliti], *n.* virilité, nature virile, *f.*

virtual ['və:tjuəl], *a.* virtuel; de fait.

virtually ['və:tjuəli], *adv.* virtuellement, de fait.

virtue ['və:tju:], *n.* vertu; (*fig.*) valeur, *f.*, mérite, *m.*

virtuosity [və:tju'ositi], *n.* virtuosité, *f.*

virtuoso [və:tju'ousou], *n.* (*pl.* **virtuosi** [və:tju'ousi]) virtuose, *m.*, *f.*

virtuous ['və:tjuəs], *a.* vertueux.

virtuously ['və:tjuəsli], *adv.* vertueusement.

virtuousness ['və:tjuəsnis], *n.* vertu, *f.*

virulence ['viruləns], *n.* virulence, *f.*

virulent ['virulənt], *a.* virulent.

virus ['vaiərəs], *n.* virus, *m.*

visa ['vi:za], *n.* visa, *m.*—*v.t.* viser.

visage ['vizidʒ], *n.* visage, *m.*, figure, *f.*

viscera ['visərə], *n.pl.* viscères, *m.pl.*

viscid ['visid], *a.* visqueux.

viscosity [vis'kositi], *n.* viscosité, *f.*

viscount ['vaikaunt], *n.* vicomte, *m.*

viscountess ['vaikauntis], *n.* vicomtesse, *f.*

viscountship ['vaikauntʃip], *n.* vicomté, *f.*

viscous ['viskəs], *a.* visqueux, glutineux.

vise [vais], *n.* (*Tech.*) étau, *m.*

visibility [vizi'biliti], *n.* visibilité, *f.*

visible ['vizibl], *a.* visible; clair.

visibly ['vizibli], *adv.* visiblement, à vue d'œil.

vision ['viʒən], *n.* vision, vue, *f.*

visionary ['viʒənəri], *a.* and *n.* visionnaire, *m.*, *f.*

visit ['vizit], *n.* visite, *f.*; séjour (*a stay*), *m.*—*v.t.* visiter, aller, rendre visite à; **I visit the theatre twice a week**, je vais au théâtre deux fois par semaine.—*v.i.* faire des visites.

visitant ['vizitənt], *n.* visiteur, *m.*

visitation [vizi'teiʃən], *n.* inspection; épreuve, *f.*

visiting ['vizitiŋ], *a.* en visite, de visite.—*n.* visites, *f.pl.*

visitor ['vizitə], *n.* visiteur; (*official*) inspecteur, *m.*; **she has visitors**, elle a du monde.

visor ['vaizə], *n.* visière, *f.*

vista ['vistə], *n.* vue, perspective, *f.*

Vistula ['vistjulə], the. la Vistule, *f.*

visual ['viʒuəl], *a.* visuel.

visualize ['viʒuəlaiz], *v.t.* se représenter.

vital [vaitl], *a.* vital, de vie; (*fig.*) essentiel.

vitality [vai'tæliti], *n.* vitalité, *f.*

vitalize ['vaitəlaiz], *v.t.* vivifier; (*fig.*) animer.

vitally ['vaitəli], *adv.* vitalement.

vitals [vaitlz], *n.pl.* parties vitales, *f.pl.*

vitamin ['vitəmin], *n.* vitamine, *f.*

vitiate ['viʃieit], *v.t.* vicier; (*fig.*) corrompre.
vitiation [viʃi'eiʃən], *n.* viciation; (*fig.*) corruption, *f.*
vitreous ['vitriəs], *a.* vitreux; (*Anat.*) vitré.
vitrify ['vitrifai], *v.t.* vitrifier.—*v.i.* se vitrifier.
vitriol ['vitriəl], *n.* vitriol, *m.*
vitriolic [vitri'ɔlik], *a.* vitriolique.
vituperate [vi'tju:pəreit], *v.t.* vilipender, injurier.
vituperation [vitju:pə'reiʃən], *n.* reproches, *m.pl.*, invectives, *f.pl.*
vituperative [vi'tju:pərətiv], *a.* injurieux, hargneux.
vivacious [vi'veiʃəs], *a.* vif, vivace, animé.
vivaciously [vi'veiʃəsli], *adv.* vivement, avec vivacité.
vivaciousness [vi'veiʃəsnis], *n.* vivacité, **vivacity** [vi'væsiti], *n.* vivacité, *f.*
vivary ['vivəri], *n.* vivier, *m.*
vivid ['vivid], *a.* vif, frappant.
vividly ['vividli], *adv.* d'une manière frappante, avec éclat.
vividness ['vividnis], *n.* vivacité, *f.*, éclat, *m.*
vivification [vivifi'keiʃən], *n.* vivification, *f.*
vivify ['vivifai], *v.t.* vivifier.
vivifying ['vivifaiiŋ], *a.* vivifiant.
viviparous [vi'vipərəs], *a.* vivipare.
vivisection [vivi'sekʃən], *n.* vivisection, *f.*
vivisector [vivi'sektə], *n.* vivisecteur, *m.*
vixen ['viksən], *n.* renarde (*bête*); mégère (*femme*), *f.*
vixenish ['viksəniʃ], *a.* de mégère, méchante.
viz. [viz] (*usu.* read namely), *adv.* à savoir.
vizier [vi'ziə], *n.* vizir, *m.*
vocabulary [vo'kæbjulari], *n.* vocabulaire, *f.*
vocal [voukl], *a.* vocal, de la voix.
vocalist ['voukəlist], *n.* chanteur, *m.*, chanteuse, *f.*
vocalize ['voukəlaiz], *v.t., v.i.* vocaliser.
vocally ['voukəli], *adv.* par la voix, vocalement.
vocation [vo'keiʃən], *n.* vocation; profession, *f.*
vocational [vo'keiʃənəl], *a.* professionnel.
vocative ['vɔkətiv], *n.* vocatif, *m.*
vociferate [və'sifəreit], *v.t., v.i.* vociférer.
vociferation [vəsifə'reiʃən], *n.* vocifération, *f.*
vociferous [və'sifərəs], *a.* qui vocifère, bruyant.
vociferously [və'sifərəsli], *adv.* en vociférant.
vodka ['vɔdkə], *n.* vodka, *f.*
vogue [voug], *n.* vogue, *f.*
voice [vɔis], *n.* voix, *f.*; *at the top of one's voice*, à tue-tête.—*v.t.* publier; exprimer.
void [vɔid], *a.* vide, vacant; (*Law*) nul, de nul effet.—*n.* vide, espace vide, *m.*—*v.t.* vider; (*Law*) annuler.
voidable ['vɔidəbl], *a.* annulable.
volatile ['vɔlətail], *a.* volatil; qui vole, volant; inconstant (*volage*).
volatility [vɔlə'tiliti], *n.* volatilité, *f.*
volcanic [vɔl'kænik], *a.* volcanique.
volcano [vɔl'keinou], *n.* volcan, *m.*
vole [voul], *n.* campagnol, *m.*
volition [və'liʃən], *n.* volition, volonté, *f.*
volley ['vɔli], *n.* décharge, salve (*de mousqueterie*); volée (*de canon*), *f.*—*v.t.* (*Ten.*) renvoyer (*la balle*) de volée.
volt [voult], *n.* (*Elec.*) volt, *m.*

voltage ['voultidʒ], *n.* voltage, *m.*
volte-face ['vɔltfa:s], *n.* volte-face, *f.*
volubility [vɔlju'biliti], *n.* volubilité, *f.*
voluble ['vɔljubl], *a.* délié (*langue*); facile (*débit*).
volubly ['vɔljubli], *adv.* avec volubilité.
volume ['vɔljum], *n.* volume; tome (*livre*), *m.*
voluminous [və'lju:minəs], *a.* volumineux.
voluminously [və'lju:minəsli], *adv.* d'une manière volumineuse.
voluminousness [və'lju:minəsnis], *n.* grosseur, *f.*
voluntarily ['vɔləntərili], *adv.* volontairement, spontanément.
voluntariness ['vɔləntərinis], *n.* spontanéité, *f.*
voluntary ['vɔləntəri], *a.* volontaire, spontané; libre; intentionnel.—*n.* (*Mus.*) improvisation, *f.*
volunteer [vɔlən'tiə], *n.* volontaire, *m., f.*—*v.t.* offrir volontairement.—*v.i.* offrir ses services; s'engager comme volontaire.
voluptuary [və'lʌptjuəri], *n.* voluptueux, épicurien, *m.*
voluptuous [və'lʌptjuəs], *a.* voluptueux.
voluptuously [və'lʌptjuəsli], *adv.* voluptueusement.
voluptuousness [və'lʌptjuəsnis], *n.* volupté, *f.*
volute [və'lju:t], *n.* volute, *f.*
voluted [və'lju:tid], *a.* voluté.
volution [və'lju:ʃən], *n.* spirale, *f.*
vomit ['vomit], *v.t., v.i.* vomir.—*n.* vomissement, *m.*
voodoo ['vu:du:], *n.* vaudou, *f.*
voracious [və'reiʃəs], *a.* vorace.
voraciously [və'reiʃəsli], *adv.* avec voracité.
voraciousness [və'reiʃəsnis], **voracity** [və'ræsiti], *n.* voracité, *f.*
vortex ['vɔ:teks], *n.* (*pl.* **vortices** ['vɔ:tisi:z]) tourbillon, *m.*
vortical ['vɔ:tikl], *a.* tourbillonnant, en tourbillon.
votaress ['voutəris], *n.* adoratrice, *f.*
votary ['voutəri], *n.* adorateur, *m.*; (*fig.*) admirateur, *m.*
vote [vout], *n.* vote, *m.*; voix, *f.*—*v.t., v.i.* voter.
voter ['voutə], *n.* votant, *m.*
voting ['voutiŋ], *n.* vote, *m.*; *voting-paper*, bulletin de vote, *m.*
votive ['voutiv], *a.* votif, voué.
vouch [vautʃ], *v.t.* attester; affirmer.—*v.i.* témoigner (*de*), répondre (*de*).
voucher ['vautʃə], *n.* garant, *m.*, garantie; pièce justificative, *f.*; *luncheon voucher*, bon de repas, *m.*
vouchsafe [vautʃ'seif], *v.t.* daigner, accorder.
vow [vau], *n.* vœu, *m.*—*v.t.* vouer.—*v.i.* faire un vœu; jurer.
vowel ['vauəl], *n.* voyelle, *f.*
voyage ['vɔiidʒ], *n.* voyage (*par mer*), *m.*
voyager ['vɔiidʒə], *n.* voyageur, passager, *m.*
vulcanite ['vʌlkənait], *n.* caoutchouc vulcanisé, *m.*, ébonite, *f.*
vulcanize ['vʌlkənaiz], *v.t.* vulcaniser.
vulgar ['vʌlgə], *a.* vulgaire, commun.
vulgarism ['vʌlgərizm], *n.* expression vulgaire, *f.*
vulgarity [vʌl'gæriti], *n.* vulgarité, grossièreté, *f.*; mauvais goût, *m.*
vulgarize ['vʌlgəraiz], *v.t.* vulgariser.

vulnerability [vʌlnərə'biliti], *n.* vulnérabilité, *f.*
vulnerable ['vʌlnərəbl], *a.* vulnérable.
vulpine ['vʌlpain], *a.* de renard; (*fig.*) rusé.
vulture ['vʌltʃə], *n.* vautour, *m.*

W

W, w ['dʌbəljuː]. vingt-troisième lettre de
l'alphabet, *m.*
wad [wɔd], *n.* bourre (*armes à feu etc.*), *f.*;
tampon, paquet (*faisceau*), *m.*—*v.t.* bourrer
(*armes à feu etc.*); ouater (*vêtement etc.*).
wadded ['wɔdid], *a.* ouaté (*de*).
wadding ['wɔdiŋ], *n.* bourre (*armes à feu*);
ouate (*rembourrage*), *f.*
waddle [wɔdl], *v.i.* se dandiner.
waddling ['wɔdliŋ], *n.* dandinement, *m.*
wade [weid], *v.t.* traverser à gué.—*v.i.*
marcher (*dans l'eau ou dans la vase*).
wafer ['weifə], *n.* pain à cacheter, *m.*; gaufrette; (*R.-C. Ch.*) hostie, *f.*
waffle [wɔfl], *n.* gaufre, *f.*
waffle iron ['wɔflaiən], *n.* gaufrier, *m.*
waft [wɔft], *v.t.* porter, transporter; faire
flotter.
wag [wæg], *n.* badin, plaisant, farceur, *m.*—
v.t. remuer, agiter.—*v.i.* s'agiter, remuer, se
mouvoir.
wage [weidʒ], *v.t.* faire.—*n.* [WAGES].
wager ['weidʒə], *n.* gageure, *f.*, pari, *m.*—*v.t.*
gager, parier.
wages ['weidʒiz], *n.pl.* gages (*de serviteur*),
m.pl.; salaire, *m.*, paye (*d'ouvrier*), *f.*
waggery ['wægəri], *n.* espièglerie, plaisanterie, *f.*
waggish ['wægiʃ], *a.* badin, malin, facétieux.
waggishness ['wægiʃnis], *n.* badinage, *m.*,
espièglerie, *f.*
waggle [wægl], *v.t.* remuer.—*v.i.* frétiller.
wagon ['wægən], *n.* charrette, *f.*,
chariot; (*Mil.*) caisson, fourgon; (*Rail.*)
wagon, *m.*
wagtail ['wægteil], *n.* hochequeue, *m.*
waif [weif], *n.* épave, *f.*
wail [weil], *v.t.* pleurer, lamenter.—*v.i.*
pleurer, gémir, se lamenter.—*n.* (*also* **wailing** ['weiliŋ]) cri, *m.*, lamentation, plainte,
f.
wain [wein], *n.* charrette, *f.*
wainscot ['weinzkət], *n.* lambris, *m.*, boiserie,
f.
waist [weist], *n.* ceinture, taille, *f.*
waistband ['weistbænd], *n.* ceinture (*de
pantalon etc.*), *f.*
waistcoat ['weis(t)kout], *n.* gilet, *m.*
wait [weit], *v.t.* attendre.—*v.i.* attendre;
servir (*à table etc.*).—*n.* embuscade, *f.*, guet-
apens, *m.*; attente, *f.*
waiter ['weitə], *n.* garçon, *m.*
waiting ['weitiŋ], *n.* attente, *f.*; service
(*attentions*), *m.*; **no waiting**, stationnement
interdit, *m.*
waiting-maid ['weitiŋmeid], **waiting-
woman** ['weitiŋwumən] (*pl.* **-women**

{wimin}]), *n.* femme de chambre; camériste
(*de princesse etc.*), *f.*
waiting room ['weitiŋruːm], *n.* salle d'attente, *f.*
waitress ['weitris], *n.* servante, fille de service,
f.
waits [weits], *n.pl.* chanteurs de noëls, *m.pl.*
waive [weiv], *v.t.* écarter, mettre de côté;
abandonner, renoncer.
wake (1) [weik], *v.t. irr.* éveiller, réveiller.—
v.i. veiller (*ne pas se coucher*); se réveiller (*de
sommeil*).—*n.* fête de village, *f.*
wake (2) [weik], *n.* sillage (*de navire*), *m.*; (*fig.*)
suite, *f.*
wakeful ['weikful], *a.* éveillé; vigilant.
wakefulness ['weikfulnis], *n.* insomnie, *f.*
waken ['weikən], *v.t.* éveiller, réveiller.—*v.i.*
s'éveiller, se réveiller.
waking ['weikiŋ], **wakening** ['weikniŋ], *a.*
éveillé.—*n.* réveil, *m.*
wale ['weil], *n.* marque (*de fouet*); côte (*de
tissu*); (*pl.*) (*Naut.*) préceinte, *f.*
Wales [weilz]. le Pays de Galles, *m.*
walk [wɔːk], *v.t.* parcourir, traverser à pied;
faire à pied (*distance etc.*); mettre au pas
(*cheval*).—*v.i.* marcher; aller à pied; se
promener (*pour le plaisir*); aller au pas
(*cheval*); **to walk over**, traverser *ou* parcourir à pied.—*n.* marche; promenade, *f.*,
tour, *m.*; allée (*sentier*); démarche, allure, *f.*;
pas (*de cheval*), *m.*; (*fig.*) sphère, *f.*, chemin,
m.; **at a walk**, au pas.
walker ['wɔːkə], *n.* promeneur, marcheur;
piéton, *m.*
walkie-talkie ['wɔːki'tɔːki], *n.* (*fam.*) émetteur-récepteur portatif, *m.*
walking ['wɔːkiŋ], *a.* ambulant; de marche.—
n. la marche; promenade à pied, *f.*
walking stick ['wɔːkiŋstik], *n.* canne, *f.*
walk-over ['wɔːkouvə], *n.* (*Spt.*) **to have a
walk-over**, remporter une victoire facile,
gagner sans concurrent.
wall [wɔːl], *n.* muraille, *f.*, mur, *m.*, paroi, *f.*,
espalier (*à fruits*), *m.*—*v.t.* entourer de
murailles; **to wall up**, murer.
wallet ['wɔlit], *n.* portefeuille, *f.*
wall-eye ['wɔːlai], *n.* œil vairon, *m.*
wallflower ['wɔːlflauə], *n.* giroflée jaune,
ravenelle, *f.*
wall fruit ['wɔːlfruːt], *n.* fruit d'espalier, *m.*
walling ['wɔːliŋ], *n.* muraillement, *m.*; murs,
m.pl.
wallop ['wɔləp], *v.t.* rosser.
walloping ['wɔləpiŋ], *n.* rossée, volée de
coups, raclée, *f.*
wallow ['wɔlou], *v.i.* se vautrer, se rouler.
wall-paper ['wɔːlpeipə], *n.* papier peint, *m.*
walnut ['wɔːlnʌt], *n.* noix, *f.*; noyer (*bois*), *m.*
walnut tree ['wɔːlnʌttriː], *n.* noyer, *m.*
walrus ['wɔːlrəs], *n.* morse, cheval marin, *m.*
Walter ['wɔːltə]. Gauthier, *m.*
waltz [wɔːl(t)s], *n.* valse, *f.*—*v.i.* valser.
waltzer ['wɔːl(t)sə], *n.* valseur, *m.*
waltzing ['wɔːl(t)siŋ], *n.* valse, *f.*
wan [wɔn], *a.* blême, pâle, pâlot.
wand [wɔnd], *n.* baguette, *f.*
wander ['wɔndə], *v.i.* errer; divaguer
(*l'esprit*); délirer.
wanderer ['wɔndərə], *n.* vagabond, *m.*
wandering ['wɔndəriŋ], *a.* errant, vagabond;
nomade (*tribu etc.*); (*fig.*) distrait.—*n.*
course errante, divagation, *f.*; délire, *m.*

wanderlust ['wɔndǝlʌst], *n.* manie des voyages, *f.*

wane [wein], *n.* déclin, *m.*; (*fig.*) décadence, *f.* —*v.i.* décroître (*lune*); (*fig.*) décliner.

wanly ['wɔnli], *adv.* avec pâleur.

wanness ['wɔnnis], *n.* pâleur, *f.*

want [wɔnt], *n.* besoin; manque, défaut (*absence*), *m.*; indigence, misère (*pauvreté*), *f.*; *for want of,* faute de.—*v.t.* avoir besoin de; manquer de; vouloir, désirer (*avoir envie de*); demander (*réclamer*).—*v.i.* manquer (*de*).

wanting ['wɔntiŋ], *a.* qui manque, manquant.

wanton ['wɔntǝn], *a.* folâtre (*capricieux*); licencieux, libertin (*impudique*); gratuit (*sans cause*).—*n.* débauchée, *f.*—*v.i.* folâtrer.

wantonly ['wɔntǝnli], *adv.* en folâtrant; gratuitement.

wantonness ['wɔntǝnnis], *n.* légèreté, *f.*; libertinage, *m.*

war [wɔ:], *n.* guerre, *f.*—*v.i.* faire la guerre (à), lutter (*contre*).

warble [wɔ:bl], *v.t., v.i.* gazouiller; (*fig.*) chanter.

warbler ['wɔ:blǝ], *n.* oiseau chanteur, *m.*; fauvette (*oiseau*), *f.*

warbling ['wɔ:bliŋ], *a.* mélodieux.—*n.* gazouillement, *m.*

ward [wɔ:d], *n.* pupille, *m.*, *f.*; tutelle (*protection*); garde (*de serrure*); salle (*d'hôpital*), *f.*; arrondissement (*de ville*), *m.*—*v.i.* to *ward off,* parer, détourner.

warden [wɔ:dn], *n.* gardien; gouverneur, recteur (*d'université*); directeur (*de collège*), conservateur (*de jardin public*), *m.*

warder ['wɔ:dǝ], *n.* gardien de prison, *m.*

wardress ['wɔ:dris], *n.* gardienne de prison, *f.*

wardrobe ['wɔ:droub], *n.* garde-robe; armoire (*meuble*), *f.*

ward-room ['wɔ:dru:m], *n.* (*Naut.*) carré des officiers, *m.*

ware [wɛǝ], *n.* (*collect.*) articles fabriqués, *m.pl.*; (*pl.*) marchandises, *f.pl.*

warehouse ['wɛǝhaus], *n.* magasin; entrepôt, *m.*—*v.t.* emmagasiner.

warehousing ['wɛǝhauziŋ], *n.* emmagasinage, *m.*

warfare ['wɔ:fɛǝ], *n.* la guerre, *f.*; les opérations, *f.pl.*

warily ['wɛǝrili], *adv.* prudemment, avec circonspection.

wariness ['wɛǝrinis], *n.* prudence, circonspection, *f.*

warlike ['wɔ:laik], *a.* guerrier, martial, belliqueux.

warlock ['wɔ:lɔk], *n.* sorcier, *m.*

warm [wɔ:m], *a.* chaud; (*fig.*) zélé, ardent; chaleureux (*accueil*).—*v.t.* chauffer; réchauffer (*ce qui s'était refroidi*); (*fig.*) échauffer.—*v.i.* chauffer, se chauffer, (*fig.*) s'animer.

warming ['wɔ:miŋ], *n.* chauffage, *m.*

warming pan ['wɔ:miŋpæn], *n.* bassinoire, *f.*

warmly ['wɔ:mli], *adv.* chaudement; (*fig.*) vivement.

war-monger ['wɔ:mʌŋgǝ], *n.* belliciste, *m.*, *f.*

warmth [wɔ:mθ], *n.* chaleur; (*fig.*) ardeur, *f.*

war-office ['wɔ:rɔfis], *n.* ministère de la guerre, *m.*

warn [wɔ:n], *v.t.* avertir, prévenir (*de*); to *warn against,* mettre en garde contre.

warning ['wɔ:niŋ], *n.* avertissement, avis, *m.*

warp [wɔ:p], *n.* chaîne (*tissage*), *f.*—*v.t.* ourdir (*tissage*); faire déjeter (*bois*); (*Naut.*) touer; (*fig.*) fausser, pervertir.—*v.i.* se déjeter, se déformer; gauchir; (*fig.*) dévier (*de*).

warping ['wɔ:piŋ], *n.* ourdissage (*tissage*); déjettement, gauchissement (*de bois*), *m.*

warrant ['wɔrǝnt], *n.* autorisation, garantie, *f.*; ordre, mandat; mandat d'amener, *m.*; (*fig.*) justification, *f.*—*v.t.* garantir, autoriser.

warrant officer ['wɔrǝntɔfisǝ], *n.* (*Mil.*) adjudant; (*Naut.*) premier maître, *m.*

warrantor ['wɔrǝntǝ], *n.* (*Law*) garant, *m.*

warranty ['wɔrǝnti], *n.* garantie, *f.*

warren ['wɔrǝn], *n.* garenne, *f.*

warrior ['wɔriǝ], *n.* guerrier, soldat, *m.*

Warsaw ['wɔ:sɔ:], Varsovie, *f.*

wart [wɔ:t], *n.* verrue, *f.*, poireau, *m.*

warted ['wɔ:tid], **warty** ['wɔ:ti], *a.* couvert de verrues; (*Bot.*) verruqueux.

wary ['wɛǝri], *a.* avisé, prudent; défiant.

wash [wɔʃ], *n.* blanchissage, *m.*, lessive (*de linge*), *f.*; (*Paint.*) lavis; sillage (*de navire*), *m.*—*v.t.* blanchir (*linge*); (*fig.*) mouiller, laver.—*v.i.* se laver; faire la lessive (*blanchisseuse etc.*); to *wash up,* faire la vaisselle.

washable ['wɔʃǝbl], *a.* lavable.

washbasin ['wɔʃbeisn], *n.* lavabo, *m.*, cuvette, *f.*

washer ['wɔʃǝ], *n.* laveur, *m.*; machine à laver; (*Tech.*) rondelle, *f.*

washer-woman ['wɔʃǝwumǝn], *n.* (*pl.* -women [wimin]) blanchisseuse, *f.*

wash-house ['wɔʃhaus], *n.* lavoir, *m.*, buanderie, *f.*

washing ['wɔʃiŋ], *n.* lavage; blanchissage (*du linge*), *m.*

washing machine ['wɔʃiŋmǝʃi:n], *n.* machine à laver, *f.*

wash-leather ['wɔʃleðǝ], *n.* peau de chamois, *f.*

wash-stand ['wɔʃstænd], *n.* toilette, *f.*; lavabo (*petit*), *m.*

wash-tub ['wɔʃtʌb], *n.* baquet, *m.*

washy ['wɔʃi], *a.* humide, mouillé; (*fig.*) fade.

wasp [wɔsp], *n.* guêpe, *f.*; *wasps' nest,* guêpier, *m.*

waspish ['wɔspiʃ], *a.* irascible, irritable.

waspishness ['wɔspiʃnis], *n.* humeur irascible, *f.*

wastage ['weistidʒ], *n.* gaspillage, *m.*

waste [weist], *a.* de rebut; sans valeur; perdu (*inemployé*); inculte (*terre*).—*n.* perte (*mauvais emploi*), *f.*; déchet (*à nettoyer*); gaspillage; rebut, *m.*; terre inculte, *f.*—*v.t.* gaspiller; perdre (*employer mal*); gâcher (*faire sans soin*); ravager, dévaster (*piller*).—*v.i.* s'user, s'épuiser; to *waste away,* dépérir, maigrir.

waste-book ['weistbuk], *n.* brouillard, *m.*

wasteful ['weistful], *a.* dissipateur, prodigue.

wastefulness ['weistfulnis], *n.* prodigalité, perte, *f.*, gaspillage, *m.*

waste paper ['weist'peipǝ], *n.* papier de rebut, *m.*

waste-paper basket ['weistpeipǝ'bɑ:skit], *n.* corbeille à papier, *f.*

waste-pipe ['weistpaip], *n.* tuyau de dégagement; écoulement, *m.*

waster ['weistǝ], **wastrel** ['weistril], *n.* prodigue, *m.*, *f.*, gaspilleur, *m.*

wasting ['weistiŋ], *a.* qui épuise.—*n.* dépérissement, *m.*, consumption (*du corps*), *f.*

watch [wɔtʃ], *n.* montre; veille (*nocturne*); vigilance (*attention*); garde, *f.*; (*Naut.*) quart, *m.*—*v.t.* veiller sur, surveiller, regarder, épier.—*v.i.* veiller (*ne pas dormir*); prendre, garde (*faire attention*); monter la garde; (*Naut.*) faire le quart.

watch-dog ['wɔtʃdɔg], *n.* chien de garde, *m.*

watcher ['wɔtʃə], *n.* surveillant, veilleur, *m.*

watch fire ['wɔtʃfaiə], *n.* feu de bivouac, *m.*

watchful ['wɔtʃful], *a.* vigilant, attentif.

watchfulness ['wɔtʃfulnis], *n.* vigilance, *f.*

watching ['wɔtʃiŋ], *n.* surveillance, *f.*

watch-maker ['wɔtʃmeikə], *n.* horloger, *m.*

watch-making ['wɔtʃmeikiŋ], *n.* horlogerie, *f.*

watchman ['wɔtʃmən], *n.* (*pl.* **-men** [men]) gardien; veilleur de nuit, *m.*

watch-tower ['wɔtʃtauə], *n.* tour de guet, *f.*

watchword ['wɔtʃwə:d], *n.* mot d'ordre, *m.*

water ['wɔ:tə], *a.* d'eau, à eau; aquatique.—*n.* eau; marée (*flux*), *f.*, (*fig.*) ordre, rang, *m.*; **drinking water**, eau potable; **fresh water**, eau douce (*pas salée*).—*v.t.* arroser; donner à boire à, abreuver (*diluer*); moirer (*étoffe*).

water bottle ['wɔ:təbɔtl], *n.* carafe, *f.*; (*Mil. etc.*) bidon, *m.*; bouilloi_e (*pour chauffer le lit*), *f.*

water carrier ['wɔ:təkæriə], *n.* porteur d'eau; broc (*à eau*), *m.*

water cart ['wɔ:təka:t], *n.* voiture d'arrosage, *f.*

water closet ['wɔ:təklɔzit], *n.* toilettes, *f.pl.*, cabinet d'aisances, *m.*

water color ['wɔ:təkʌlə], *n.* aquarelle, *f.*

watercress ['wɔ:təkres], *n.* cresson, cresson de fontaine, *m.*

water cure ['wɔ:təkjuə], *n.* hydrothérapie, *f.*

watered ['wɔ:təd], *a.* arrosé; moiré (*étoffe*).

waterfall ['wɔ:təfɔ:l], *n.* cascade, *f.*; chute d'eau, *f.*

water-fowl ['wɔ:təfaul], *n.* oiseau aquatique, *m.*

waterfront ['wɔ:təfrʌnt], *n.* les quais, *m.pl.*, port, *m.*

water hen ['wɔ:təhen], *n.* poule d'eau, *f.*

wateriness ['wɔ:tərinis], *n.* aquosité, *f.*

watering ['wɔ:təriŋ], *n.* arrosage (*plantes*), *m.*; irrigation (*terre*), *f.*; abreuvage (*animaux*); moirage (*étoffe*), *m.*

watering can ['wɔ:təriŋkæn], *n.* arrosoir, *m.*

watering place ['wɔ:təriŋpleis], *n.* ville d'eaux, station thermale, *f.*; abreuvoir (*pour animaux*), *m.*

water jug ['wɔ:tədʒʌg], *n.* pot à eau, *m.*

water level ['wɔ:təlevl], *n.* niveau d'eau, *m.*

water lily ['wɔ:təlili], *n.* nénuphar, *m.*

water line ['wɔ:təlain], *n.* ligne de flottaison, *f.*

water-logged ['wɔ:təlɔgd], *a.* envahi par les eaux.

watermark ['wɔ:təma:k], *n.* étiage (*de rivière*); filigrane (*sur papier*), *m.*

water-melon ['wɔ:təmelən], *n.* melon d'eau, *m.*, pastèque, *f.*

water mill ['wɔ:təmil], *n.* moulin à eau, *m.*

water pipe ['wɔ:təpaip], *n.* tuyau d'eau, *m.*

water plant ['wɔ:təplɑ:nt], *n.* plante aquatique, *f.*

water polo ['wɔ:təpoulou], *n.* polo nautique, *m.*

water-power ['wɔ:təpauə], *n.* force hydraulique, *f.*

water pressure ['wɔ:təpreʃə], *n.* pression d'eau, *f.*

waterproof ['wɔ:təpru:f], *a.* and *n.* imperméable, *m.*—*v.t.* rendre imperméable, cirer (*un tissu*).

water rat ['wɔ:təræt], *n.* rat d'eau, *m.*

water-rate ['wɔ:təreit], *n.* taux d'abonnement aux eaux de la ville, *m.*

watershed ['wɔ:təʃed], *n.* versant, *m.*

waterspout ['wɔ:təspaut], *n.* trombe, *f.*; tuyau de descente, *m.*

water tank ['wɔ:tətæŋk], *n.* réservoir à eau, *m.*, citerne, *f.*

water-tight ['wɔ:tətait], *a.* étanche.

water-works ['wɔ:təwə:ks], *n.pl.* établissement pour la distribution des eaux, *m.*, mach.ine hydraulique, *f.*

watery ['wɔ:təri], *a.* aqueux; mouillé, plein d'eau; (*poet.*) humide.

watt [wɔt], *n.* (*Elec.*) watt, *m.*

wattage ['wɔtidʒ], *n.* (*Elec.*) wattage, *m.*

wattle [wɔtl], *n.* claie (*d'osier etc.*), *f.*—*v.t.* clayonner.

wave [weiv], *n.* vague, *f.*, flot, *m.*, lame, ondulation; (*poet.*) onde, *f.*; signe (*de la main*), *m.*; **permanent wave**, permanente, indéfrisable, *f.*; **long waves**, (*Rad.*) grandes ondes, *f.*; **short waves**, petites ondes, ondes courtes, *f.pl.*—*v.t.* agiter, faire signe de (*la main*); onduler (*cheveux*).—*v.i.* ondoyer, onduler, s'onder; faire signe (*à*).

waved [weivd], *a.* ondulé.

wave-length ['weivleŋθ], *n.* longueur d'onde, *f.*

waver ['weivə], *v.i.* hésiter, vaciller, balancer.

waverer ['weivərə], *n.* personne indécise, *f.*, esprit vacillant, *m.*

wavering ['weivəriŋ], *a.* indécis, vacillant, irrésolu.—*n.* hésitation, indécision, *f.*

waving ['weiviŋ], *n.* ondoiement, *m.*, ondulation (*blé etc.*), *f.*; geste (*de la main*), *m.*

wavy ['weivi], *a.* ondoyant, onduleux.

wax [wæks], *n.* cire; poix (*de cordonnier*), *f.*; (*colloq.*) colère, *f.*—*v.t.* cirer, enduire de cire.—*v.i.* croître (*lune*), s'accroître; devenir.

wax candle ['wæks'kændl], *n.* bougie, *f.*

waxen ['wæksn], *a.* de cire; cireux.

wax taper ['wæks'teipə], *n.* rat de cave; (*Eccles.*) cierge, *m.*

waxwing ['wækswiŋ], *n.* (*Orn.*) jaseur, *m.*

waxwork ['wækswə:k], *n.* ouvrage de cire, *m.*; (*pl.*) figures de cire, *f.*, *pl.*

waxy ['wæksi], *a.* cireux.

way [wei], *n.* chemin, *m.*, route, voie, *f.*; passage; côté, sens, *m.*, direction; manière, façon, mode, *f.*; moyen, *m.*, méthode, *f.*; état (*condition*), *m.*; **a long way off**, très loin, *f.*; **by a long way** (*by far*), de beaucoup; **by the way**, à propos.

way-bill ['weibil], *n.* feuille de route, *f.*

wayfarer ['weifɛərə], *n.* voyageur, *m.*

wayfaring ['weifɛəriŋ], *a.* qui voyage.

waylay [wei'lei], *v.t.* guetter, guetter au passage.

wayside ['weisaid], *a.* au bord de la route.—*n.* bord de la route, *m.*

wayward ['weiwəd], *a.* capricieux, entêté.

waywardness ['weiwədnis], *n.* humeur capricieuse, *f.*

we [wi:], *pron.* nous; (*indef.*) on; *we Frenchmen*, nous autres Français.

weak [wi:k], *a.* faible, infirme, débile.

weaken [wi:kn], *v.t.* affaiblir; atténuer.—*v.i.* s'affaiblir.

weakening ['wi:kniŋ], *n.* affaiblissement, *m.*

weakling ['wi:kliŋ], *n.* être faible, faiblard, *m.*

weakly ['wi:kli], *a.* faible; infirme, débile.— *adv.* faiblement, sans force.

weak-minded ['wi:k'maindid], *a.* d'esprit faible.

weakness ['wi:knis], *n.* faiblesse; débilité, *f.*; (*fig.*) faible, *m.*

weak-spirited ['wi:k'spiritid], *a.* mou, sans courage.

weal [wi:l], *n.* bien, bien-être, bonheur, *m.*; marque (*sur la peau*), *f.*

wealth [welθ], *n.* richesse, *f.*, richesses, *f.pl.*; profusion, *f.*

wealthy ['welθi], *a.* riche, opulent.

wean [wi:n], *v.t.* sevrer; (*fig.*) détacher.

weaning ['wi:niŋ], *n.* sevrage, *m.*

weanling ['wi:nliŋ], *n.* enfant *ou* animal en sevrage, *m.*

weapon [wepn], *n.* arme, *f.*

wear [weə], *v.t. irr.* porter (*habits*); mettre (*enfiler*); (*to wear out*, user, (*fig.*) épuiser, lasser.—*v.i.* s'user (*s'élimer*); se porter (*habits*); (*fig.*) se conserver.—*n.* usage (*port*), *m.*; usure (*élimage*), *f.*

wearable ['weərəbl], *a.* mettable.

wearied ['wiərid], *a.* fatigué, las; (*fig.*) ennuyé.

wearily ['wiərili], *adv.* péniblement, d'un air las.

weariness ['wiərinis], *n.* fatigue, lassitude, *f.*; (*fig.*) ennui, *m.*

wearisome ['wiərisəm], *a.* ennuyeux; lassant.

wearisomeness ['wiərisəmnis], *n.* nature ennuyeuse, *f.*

weary ['wiəri], *a.* fatigué, las, ennuyé; ennuyeux (*chose*).—*v.t.* lasser, fatiguer; ennuyer.

weasel ['wi:zl], *n.* belette, *f.*

weather ['weðə], *a.* du côté du vent.—*n.* temps, *m.*; (*fig.*) tempête, *f.*—*v.t.* résister à (*tempête etc.*); (*fig.*) tenir tête à.

weather-beaten ['weðəbi:tn], *a.* battu par la tempête; (*fig.*) fatigué; hâlé.

weathercock ['weðəkɔk], *n.* girouette, *f.*

weather-glass ['weðəgla:s], *n.* baromètre, *m.*

weather-proof ['weðəpru:f], *a.* à l'épreuve du (*mauvais*) temps, imperméable.

weather report ['weðəripɔ:t], *n.* bulletin météorologique, *m.*

weather ship ['weðəʃip], *n.* navire météorologique, *m.*

weave [wi:v], *n.* (*Tex.*) tissage, *m.*—*v.t., v.i. irr.* tisser; tresser (*entrelacer*).

weaver ['wi:və], *n.* tisserand, *f.*

weaving ['wi:viŋ], *n.* tissage, *m.*

web [web], *n.* tissu, *m.*; sangle (*pour selle*); toile (*d'araignée*), *f.*

webbed [webd], **webby** ['webi], *a.* palmé.

webbing ['webiŋ], *n.* sangles (*de chaise, lit etc.*), *f.pl.*

web-footed ['webfutid], *a.* palmipède.

wed [wed], *v.t.* épouser, se marier avec.—*v.i.* se marier.

wedded ['wedid], *a.* marié (*à*); conjugal.

wedding ['wediŋ], *a.* de noces, de mariage.— *n.* noce, *f.*, noces, *f.pl.*, mariage, *m.*

wedding ring ['wediŋriŋ], *n.* alliance, *f.*

wedge [wedʒ], *n.* coin, *m.*; cale (*pour tenir immobile*), *f.*—*v.t.* serrer; caler; coincer.

wedge-shaped ['wedʒʃeipt], *a.* en forme de coin, cunéiforme.

wedlock ['wedlɔk], *n.* mariage, *m.*

Wednesday ['wenzd(e)i]. mercredi, *m.*; *Ash Wednesday*, mercredi des Cendres.

weed [wi:d], *n.* mauvaise herbe, *f.*; *widow's weeds*, vêtements de deuil, *m.pl.*—*v.t.* sarcler; (*fig.*) nettoyer; *to weed out*, extirper.

weeder ['wi:də], *n.* sarcleur (*personne*); sarcloir (*outil*), *m.*

weeding ['wi:diŋ], *n.* sarclage, *m.*

weed killer ['wi:dkilə], *n.* herbicide, *m.*

weedy ['wi:di], *a.* plein de mauvaises herbes.

week [wi:k], *n.* semaine, *f.*; *this day week*, d'auj ourd'hui en huit (*avenir*); il y a huit jours (*passé*).

weekday ['wi:kdei], *n.* jour ouvrable, jour de semaine, *m.*

week-end ['wi:k'end], *n.* fin de la semaine, *f.*, week-end, *m.*

weekly ['wi:kli], *a.* de la semaine; hebdomadaire (*revue*).—*n.* hebdomadaire, *m.*—*adv.* par semaine, tous les huit jours.

weep [wi:p], *v.t., v.i. irr.* pleurer; *to weep bitterly*, pleurer à chaudes larmes.

weeping ['wi:piŋ], *a.* qui pleure, éploré; (*Bot.*) pleureur; *weeping willow*, saule pleureur, *m.*—*n.* pleurs, *m.pl.*, larmes, *f.pl.*

weever ['wi:və], *n.* (*Ichth.*) vive, *f.*

weevil ['wi:vl], *n.* charançon, *m.*

weft [weft], *n.* trame, *f.*

weigh [wei], *v.t.* peser; (*fig.*) juger; (*Naut.*) lever (*l'ancre*).—*v.i.* peser.

weigh-bridge ['weibridʒ], *n.* pont à bascule, *m.*

weighing ['weiiŋ], *n.* pesage, *m.*; *weighing machine*, bascule, *f.*

weight [weit], *n.* poids, *m.*; *atomic weight*, masse atomique, *f.*

weighted ['weitid], *a.* chargé (*de*).

weightily ['weitili], *adv.* pesamment.

weightless ['weitlis], *a.* sans poids.

weightlessness ['weitlisnis], *n.* apesanteur, *f.*

weighty ['weiti], *a.* pesant, lourd; (*fig.*) important.

weir [wiə], *n.* barrage, déversoir, *m.*

weird [wiəd], *a.* fantastique, étrange.

weirdness ['wiədnis], *n.* étrangeté, magie, *f.*

welcome ['welkəm], *a.* bienvenu, agréable (*chose*); libre (*à profiter de quelque chose*).— *n.* bienvenue, *f.*, accueil, *m.*; *to bid (someone) welcome*, souhaiter la bienvenue à (*quelqu'un*).—*int.* soyez le bienvenu.—*v.t.* souhaiter la bienvenue à. *bien accueilli! you are welcome*, see **mention**.

weld [weld], *v.t.* souder; (*fig.*) unir.—*n.* soudure, *f.*

welder ['weldə], *n.* soudeur, *m.*

welding ['weldiŋ], *n.* soudure, *f.*

welfare ['welfeə], *n.* bien-être, bien, *m.*; *Welfare State*, état providence, *m.*

well (1) [wel], *n.* puits, *m.*; (*fig.*) source, *f.*; *ink-well*, encrier, *m.*—*v.i.* jaillir (*de*).

well (2) [wel], *a.* bien, en bonne santé; bon; heureux (*fortuné*); utile, profitable; *to get well*, se rétablir; *well off*, aisé (*riche*).—

627

adv. bien; très, fort; comme il faut; *well!* eh bien! *well done!* très bien! bravo! *well, I never!* pas possible!

well-being ['wel'bi:iŋ], *n.* bien-être, *m.*
well-informed ['welin'fɔ:md], *a.* instruit; bien renseigné.
wellingtons ['weliŋtənz], *n.pl.* demi-bottes, *f.pl.*
well-known ['welnoun], *a.* bien connu, célèbre.
well-meaning ['wel'mi:niŋ], *a.* bien intentionné.
well-meant ['wel'ment], *a.* fait à bonne intention.
well-nigh ['welnai], *adv.* presque.
well-timed ['wel'taimd], *a.* à propos, fait à propos.
well-to-do ['weltə'du:], *a.* très aisé, cossu.
well-wisher ['wel'wiʃə], *n.* ami, partisan, *m.*
Welsh [welʃ], *a.* gallois, du pays de Galles.—*n.* gallois (*langue*), *m.*; *the Welsh*, les Gallois, *m.pl.*
Welshman ['welʃmən], *n.* (*pl.* -**men** [men]) Gallois, *m.*
welt [welt], *n.* bordure (*de gant*); trépointe (*de semelle*), *f.*
welter ['weltə], *n.* confusion, *f.*—*v.i.* se vautrer, se rouler.
wen [wen], *n.* loupe, *f.*; goitre, *m.*
wench [wentʃ], *n.* donzelle; (*pej.*) souillon, *f.*
wend [wend], *v.t., v.i.* aller; *to wend one's way*, se diriger (*vers*).
wer(e)wolf ['wə:wulf], *n.* loup-garou, *m.*
west [west], *a.* de l'ouest, occidental.—*n.* ouest, occident, couchant, *m.*—*adv.* à l'ouest.
westerly ['westəli], *a.* d'ouest.—*adv.* vers l'ouest.
western ['westən], *a.* de l'ouest, occidental, ouest, d'occident; à l'ouest (*vue*).—*n.* (*Ciné.*) western, *m.*
westward ['westwəd], *adv.* à l'ouest.
wet [wet], *a.* mouillé, humide; pluvieux (*temps*); *it is wet*, il pleut; *to get wet*, se mouiller; *wet through*, mouillé jusqu'aux os, trempé.—*n.* humidité; pluie, *f.* —*v.t. irr.* mouiller, humecter; arroser.
wetness ['wetnis], *n.* humidité, *f.*; état pluvieux, *m.*
wetting ['wetiŋ], *n.* trempage, *m.*
whack [hwæk], *n.* grand coup, *m.*; (*fam.*) part, *f.*—*v.t.* frapper, battre.
whale [hweil], *n.* baleine, *f.*
whalebone ['hweilboun], *n.* baleine, *f.*
whale oil ['hweilɔil], *n.* huile de baleine, *f.*
whaler ['hweilə], *n.* baleinier, *m.*
wharf [hwɔ:f], *n.* (*pl.* **wharfs** [hwɔ:fs], **wharves** [hwɔ:vz]) quai, embarcadère, débarcadère; entrepôt (*pour marchandises*), *m.*
what [hwɔt], *a.* quel, *m.*, quelle, *f.*, quels, *m.pl.*, quelles, *f.pl.*—*pron.rel.* ce qui, ce que; qui, que; quoi.—*inter. pron.* qu'est-ce qui? que? qu'est-ce que? quoi? *what!* comment!
whatever [hwɔt'evə], **whatsoever** [hwɔtsou'evə], *pron. anal. a.* quoi que ce soit; quelque . . . que; tout ce qui, tout ce que (*all that*).
whatnot ['hwɔtnɔt], *n.* étagère, *f.*
whatsoever [WHATEVER].
wheat [hwi:t], *n.* blé, froment, *m.*
wheaten ['hwi:tn], *a.* de froment.

wheedle ['hwi:dl], *v.t.* cajoler, câliner.
wheedling ['hwi:dliŋ], *a.* cajoleur, câlin.—*n.* cajolerie, câlinerie, *f.*
wheel [hwi:l], *n.* roue, *f.*; volant (*pour conduire*); rouet (*pour filer*), *m.*; révolution, *f.*, tour, cercle (*rotation*); soleil (*feu d'artifice*), *m.*; *driving wheel*, roue motrice, *f.*; *fly-wheel*, volant, *m.*—*v.t.* rouler, faire tourner; brouetter; voiturer.—*v.i.* rouler (*sur des roues*); tourner, se tourner (*en cercle*); tournoyer (*pirouetter*); (*Mil.*) faire une conversion; *to wheel round*, faire volte-face.
wheel-barrow ['hwi:lbærou], *n.* brouette, *f.*
wheel-chair ['hwi:ltʃɛə], *n.* voiture de malade, *f.*, fauteuil roulant, *m.*
wheeled [hwi:ld], *a.* à roues.
wheeling ['hwi:liŋ], *n.* (*Mil.*) conversion, *f.*; tournoiement (*d'oiseau*), *m.*
wheelwright ['hwi:lrait], *n.* charron, *m.*
wheeze [hwi:z], *v.i.* siffler en respirant.
wheezing ['hwi:ziŋ], *n.* sifflement, *m.*
wheezy ['hwi:zi], *a.* poussif, asthmatique.
whelk [hwelk], *n.* buccin, *m.*
whelp [hwelp], *n.* petit (*d'un fauve*), *m.*—*v.i.* mettre bas.
when [hwen], *conj.* quand, lorsque; que, où; *the day when I saw him*, le jour où je l'ai vu.—*inter. adv.* quand est-ce que? quand?
whence [hwens], *adv.* d'où.
whenever [hwen'evə], **whensoever** [hwen sou'evə], *adv.* toutes les fois que, quand, à n'importe quel moment que.
where [hwɛə], *adv.* où; là où.
whereabouts ['hwɛərəbauts], *adv.* où à peu près.—*n. to know someone's whereabouts*, savoir où est quelqu'un.
whereas [hwɛər'æz], *adv.* au lieu que, tandis que; (*Law*) vu que.
whereat [hwɛər'æt], *adv.* à quoi, de quoi; sur quoi.
whereby [hwɛə'bai], *adv.* par lequel, par où.
wherefore ['hwɛəfɔ:], *adv.* pourquoi, c'est pourquoi.
wherein [hwɛər'in], *adv.* en quoi, dans lequel, où.
whereof [hwɛər'ɔv], *adv.* dont, de quoi, duquel.
whereon [hwɛər'ɔn], **whereupon** ['hwɛərə 'pɔn], *adv.* sur quoi, sur lequel; là-dessus.
wheresoever [hwɛəsou'evə], [WHEREVER].
wherever [hwɛər'evə], *adv.* partout où, n'importe où.
wherewith [hwɛə'wið], *adv.* avec quoi; de quoi.
wherewithal [hwɛəwið'ɔ:l], *n. to find the wherewithal to . . .*, trouver les moyens de . . . *ou* l'argent pour . . .
wherry ['hweri], *n.* bachot, *m.*
whet [hwet], *v.t.* aiguiser, affiler; (*fig.*) stimuler.—*n.* aiguisement, repassage; (*fig.*) stimulant, *m.*
whether ['hweðə], *conj.* soit que; si, que; *whether . . . or*, soit . . . soit, si . . . ou, que . . . ou.
whetstone ['hwetstoun], *n.* pierre à aiguiser, *f.*
whey [hwei], *n.* petit lait, *m.*
which [hwitʃ], *a.* quel, *m.*, quelle, *f.*, quels, *m.pl.*, quelles, *f.pl.*; lequel, *m.*, laquelle, *f.*, lesquels, *m.pl.*, lesquelles, *f.pl.*—*rel. pron.*

qui, que, lequel, *m.*, laquelle, *f.*, lesquels, *m.pl.*, lesquelles, *f.pl.*; ce qui, ce que (*that which*), m.

whichever [hwitʃ'evə], *pron.* lequel, *m.*, laquelle, *f.*, lesquels, *m.pl.*, lesquelles, *f.pl.*; quelque . . . que; *whichever you buy*, n'importe lequel que vous achetiez.

whiff [hwif], *n.* bouffée, haleine, *f.*—*v.t.* lancer en bouffées.

while [hwail], *n.* temps, *m.*; *a little while ago*, il y a peu de temps; *it is not worth while*, cela n'en vaut pas la peine.—*v.t.* passer, faire passer; *to while away the time*, tuer le temps.—(*also* **whilst** [hwailst]), *conj.* pendant que (*au cours de*); tandis que (*par contraste*); tant que (*tout le temps que*); en, tout en (*suivi d'un participe présent*).

whilst [WHILE].

whim [hwim], *n.* caprice, *m.*

whimper ['hwimpə], *v.i.* pleurnicher.

whimpering ['hwimpəriŋ], *a.* pleurnicheur, geignard.—*n.* pleurnichement, *m.*

whimsical ['hwimzikl], *a.* fantasque; capricieux.

whimsically ['hwimzikli], *adv.* capricieusement, fantasquement.

whin [hwin], *n.* ajonc, genêt épineux, *m.*

whine [hwain], *v.i.* se plaindre, geindre, pleurnicher.—*n.* pleurnichement, *m.*

whining ['hwainiŋ], *a.* plaintif, dolent.—*n.* gémissement, geignement, *m.*; (*fig.*) plaintes, *f.pl.*

whinny ['hwini], *v.i.* hennir.—*n.* hennissement, *m.*

whip [hwip], *n.* fouet, *m.*; cravache (*de cavalier*), *f.*; (*Parl.*) secrétaire d'un parti, appel fait aux membres d'un parti, *m.*—*v.t.* fouetter; (*fig.*) battre.

whip-cord ['hwipkɔ:d], *n.* fouet; (*Tex.*) fil à fouet, *m.*

whip hand ['hwiphænd], *n.* dessus, avantage, *m.*

whip-lash ['hwiplæʃ], *n.* mèche (*de fouet*), *f.*

whipper-in ['hwipər'in], *n.* piqueur, *m.*

whipper-snapper ['hwipəsnæpə], *n.* petit bout d'homme, *m.*

whippet ['hwipit], *n.* lévrier (*de course*), *m.*

whipping ['hwipiŋ], *n.* coups de fouet, *m.pl.*

whipping-top ['hwipiŋtɔp], *n.* sabot, *m.*

whir [hwə:], *v.i.* tourner avec bruit; vrombir.—(*also* **whirring** ['hwə:riŋ]), *n.* bruissement, ronronnement, *m.*

whirl [hwə:l], *v.t.* faire tourner, faire tournoyer.—*v.i.* tournoyer, tourbillonner; pirouetter.—*n.* tournoiement; tourbillon (*de poussière etc.*), *m.*

whirligig ['hwə:ligig], *n.* tourniquet, *m.*; pirouette, *f.*

whirlpool ['hwə:lpu:l], *n.* tourbillon (*d'eau*), *m.*

whirlwind ['hwə:lwind], *n.* tourbillon, cyclone, *m.*

whirring [WHIR].

whisk [hwisk], *n.* vergette, époussette, verge (*à œufs etc.*), *f.*—*v.t.* épousseter; fouetter (*crème*); battre (*œufs*).—*v.i.* passer rapidement.

whiskered ['hwiskəd], *a.* à favoris; à moustaches (*animal*).

whiskers ['hwiskəz], *n.* favoris, *m.pl.*; moustache (*de chat etc.*), *f.*

whisky, whiskey ['hwiski], *n.* whisky, *m.*

whisper ['hwispə], *n.* chuchotement, *m.*—*v.t.* chuchoter, dire à l'oreille.—*v.i.* chuchoter, parler tout bas.

whispering ['hwispəriŋ], *n.* chuchotement, *m.*

whist [hwist], *n.* whist, *m.*

whistle [hwisl], *n.* sifflet; coup de sifflet; sifflement (*du vent*); (*colloq.*) gosier, bec (*gorge*), *m.*—*v.t.*, *v.i.* siffler.

whistler ['hwislə], *n.* siffleur, *m.*

whistling ['hwisliŋ], *a.* sifflant.—*n.* sifflement, coup de sifflet, *m.*

whit [hwit], *n.* iota, point, atome, brin, *m.*

white [hwait], *a.* blanc; (*fig.*) sans tache, pur. —*n.* blanc; aubier (*de bois*), *m.*

whitebait ['hwaitbeit], *n.* blanchaille, *f.*

whiten [hwaitn], *v.t.* blanchir; (*Build.*) badigeonner.—*v.i.* blanchir.

whiteness ['hwaitnis], *n.* blancheur; pâleur, *f.*

whitening ['hwaitniŋ], *n.* action de blanchir, *f.*; [WHITING (1)].

whitewash ['hwaitwɔʃ], *n.* blanc de chaux, *m.* —*v.t.* blanchir à la chaux; badigeonner.

whither ['hwiðə], *adv.* où, par où.

whithersoever [hwiðəsou'evə], *adv.* n'importe où.

whiting (1) ['hwaitiŋ], **whitening** ['hwaitniŋ], *n.* blanc d'Espagne, *m.*

whiting (2) ['hwaitiŋ], *n.* (*Ichth.*) merlan, *m.*

whitish ['hwaitiʃ], *a.* blanchâtre.

whitlow ['hwitlou], *n.* panaris, *m.*

Whitsun ['hwitsən], *a.* de la Pentecôte; *Whitsunday*, le dimanche de la Pentecôte.

Whitsuntide ['hwitsəntaid]. Pentecôte, *f.*

whiz(z) [hwiz], *v.i.* siffler.

whizzing ['hwiziŋ], *n.* sifflement, *m.*

who [hu:], *pron.* (*rel.*) qui; lequel; (*inter.*) qui? qui est-ce qui?

whodunit [hu:'dʌnit], *n.* (*colloq.*) roman policier, *m.*

whoever [hu:'evə], *pron.* qui, quiconque, qui que ce soit; celui qui.

whole [houl], *a.* tout, entier, tout entier, complet; intégral; bien portant; en grains (*non moulu*).—*n.* tout, ensemble; total, montant, *m.*; somme, totalité, *f.*; *on the whole*, en somme, dans l'ensemble.

whole-hearted [houl'ha:tid], *a.* sincère.

whole-heartedly [houl'ha:tidli], *adv.* sincèrement.

wholesale ['houlseil], *a.* en gros.—*n.* vente en gros, *f.*

wholesome ['houlsəm], *a.* sain, salubre; salutaire; utile.

wholesomeness ['houlsəmnis], *n.* salubrité, nature salutaire, *f.*

wholly ['houlli], *adv.* entièrement, complètement, tout à fait.

whom [hu:m], *pron.* (*rel.*) que, lequel; (*inter.*) qui? qui est-ce que?

whomsoever [hu:msou'evə], *pron.* qui que ce soit que.

whoop [hu:p], *n.* huée, *f.*; cri (*de guerre*), *m.*— *v.t.*, *v.i.* huer, crier.

whooping ['hu:piŋ], *n.* huées, *f.pl.*

whooping cough ['hu:piŋkɔf], *n.* coqueluche, *f.*

whopper ['hwɔpə], *n.* (*slang*) chose énorme, *f.*; mensonge énorme, *m.*; bourde, *f.*

whose [hu:z], *pron.* (*rel.*) dont, de qui; duquel, *m.*, de laquelle, *f.*, desquels, *m.pl.*, desquelles, *f.pl.*; (*inter.*) à qui?

whosoever

whosoever [hu:souʼevə], *pron.* qui que ce soit qui.

why [hwai], *adv.* pourquoi?—*int.* eh bien, mais! tiens!

wick [wik], *n.* mèche, *f.*

wicked [ʼwikid], *a.* méchant, malin.

wickedly [ʼwikidli], *adv.* méchamment.

wickedness [ʼwikidnis], *n.* méchanceté, perversité, *f.*

wicker [ʼwikə], *a.* d'osier, en osier.—*n.* osier, *m.*

wicker-work [ʼwikəwəːk], *n.* clayonnage, *m.*; vannerie, *f.*

wicket [ʼwikit], *n.* guichet, *m.*

wide [waid], *a.* large, grand, ample, vaste, immense (*d'étendue*); **three feet wide**, large de trois pieds; **to open wide**, ouvrir tout grand.—*adv.* loin, au loin, largement; **far and wide**, partout; **wide apart**, écarté, espacé.

wide-awake [ʼwaidəʼweik], *a.* bien éveillé.

widely [ʼwaidli], *adv.* au loin, loin; grandement; largement; **widely known**, bien connu.

widen [waidn], *v.t.* élargir, étendre.—*v.i.* s'élargir, s'étendre.

wideness [ʼwaidnis], *n.* largeur, étendue, *f.*

widening [ʼwaidniŋ], *n.* élargissement, *m.*

wide-spread [ʼwaidspred], *a.* répandu; général, universel.

widow [ʼwidou], *n.* veuve, *f.*

widowed [ʼwidoud], *a.* veuf, veuve; (*fig.*) privé (*de*).

widower [ʼwidouə], *n.* veuf, *m.*

widowhood [ʼwidouhud], *n.* veuvage, *m.*

width [widθ], *n.* largeur, étendue, *f.*

wield [wiːld], *v.t.* manier, tenir.

wife [waif], *n.* (*pl.* **wives** [waivz]) femme, épouse, *f.*

wifely [ʼwaifli], **wife-like** [ʼwaiflaik], *a.* de femme, d'épouse, conjugal.

wig [wig], *n.* perruque, *f.*

wig-maker [ʼwigmeikə], *n.* perruquier, *m.*

wigged [wigd], *a.* à perruque, portant perruque.

wigging [ʼwigiŋ], *n.* (*colloq.*) savon, *m.*, semonce, *f.*

wiggle [wigl], *v.t.* agiter.—*v.i.* se dandiner.

wild [waild], *a.* sauvage; farouche (*non apprivoisé*); effaré, déréglé (*désordonné*); furieux (*de rage*); insensé, extravagant (*fou*); étrange, bizarre (*baroque*); **wild beast**, fauve, *m.*; **wild boar**, sanglier, *m.*; **wildcat**, chat sauvage, *m.*—*n.*(*pl.*) désert, lieu sauvage, *m.*

wilderness [ʼwildənis], *n.* lieu désert, *m.*

wildfire [ʼwaildfaiə], *n.* feu grégeois, *m.*; **like wildfire**, comme l'éclair.

wildly [ʼwaildli], *adv.* d'une manière farouche, d'un air effaré; étourdiment, follement; à tort et à travers.

wildness [ʼwaildnis], *n.* état sauvage; dérèglement, désordre, *m.*; turbulence, licence, *f.*

wile [wail], *n.* (*usu. pl.*) artifice, *m.*, ruse, *f.*

wilful [ʼwilful], *a.* opiniâtre; obstiné, volontaire, prémédité.

wilfully [ʼwilfuli], *adv.* opiniâtrement; à dessein.

wilfulness [ʼwilfulnis], *n.* obstination, opiniâtreté, *f.*

will [wil], *n.* volonté, *f.*; vouloir; bon plaisir, gré (*inclination*); (*Law*) testament, *m.*—

v.t. vouloir, ordonner; léguer (*par testament*).—*v. aux. irr.*, *when used to indicate the future it is not translated*; **he will come**, il viendra; *when used emphatically it is translated by* **vouloir**; **I will not do it**, je ne veux pas le faire.

William [ʼwiljəm]. Guillaume, *m.*

willing [ʼwiliŋ], *a.* bien disposé; de bonne volonté; **to be willing**, vouloir bien, être disposé (*à*).

willingly [ʼwiliŋli], *adv.* volontiers.

willingness [ʼwiliŋnis], *n.* bonne volonté, *f.*, bon vouloir, *m.*; complaisance, *f.*

will-o'-the-wisp [wiləðəʼwisp], *n.* feu follet, *m.*

willow [ʼwilou], *n.* saule, *m.*

willy-nilly [ʼwiliʼnili], *adv.* bon gré mal gré.

wily [ʼwaili], *a.* rusé, fin, astucieux.

win [win], *v.t. irr.* gagner (*bataille, argent etc.*); remporter (*prix, victoire etc.*).—*v.i.* gagner; remporter la victoire, triompher.

wince [wins], *v.i.* sourciller, tressaillir (*de douleur*).—*n.* tressaillement, *m.*

winch [wintʃ], *n.* manivelle, *f.*, treuil (*cabestan*), *m.*

wind (1) [wind], *n.* vent; souffle, *m.*, respiration, haleine (*breath*), *f.*; (*Med.*) vents, *m.pl.* flatuosité, *f.*—*v.t.* faire perdre haleine à essouffler (*cheval*).

wind (2) [waind], *v.t. irr.* enrouler (*en peloton*); dévider (*soie etc.*); **to wind up**, remonter (*pendule etc.*); terminer (*négociations*); (*Comm.*) liquider.—*v.i.* tourner; se rouler, s'enrouler, s'enlacer; faire un détour; serpenter (*route, rivière*).

wind-bag [ʼwindbæg], *n.* (*fig.*) moulin à paroles, *m.*

winded [ʼwindid], *a.* hors d'haleine, essoufflé; **long-winded**, de longue haleine.

winder [ʼwaində], *n.* dévidoir (*appareil*); remontoir (*de montre*), *m.*

windfall [ʼwindfɔːl], *n.* (*fig.*) bonne aubaine, *f.*

wind gauge [ʼwindgeidʒ], *n.* anémomètre, *m.*

winding [ʼwaindiŋ], *a.* sinueux, tortueux; en spirale (*escalier*).—*n.* sinuosité, *f.*; (*Elec.*) enroulement, *m.*

winding sheet [ʼwaindiŋʃiːt], *n.* linceul, *m.*

wind-jammer [ʼwinddʒæmə], *n.* (*Naut.*) voilier, *m.*

windlass [ʼwindləs], *n.* treuil; (*Naut.*) guindeau, cabestan, *m.*

windmill [ʼwindmil], *n.* moulin à vent, *m.*

window [ʼwindou], *n.* fenêtre; glace (*de train, voiture etc.*); montre, vitrine, *f.*, étalage (*de magasin*), *m.*; (*pl.*) vitraux (*d'église*), *m.pl.*

window box [ʼwindouboks], *n.* jardinière, *f.*

window cleaner [ʼwindoukliːnə], *n.* laveur de carreaux, *m.*

window-dresser [ʼwindoudresə], *n.* étalagiste, *m.*, *f.*

window-dressing [ʼwindoudresiŋ], *n.* art de l'étalage; (*fam.*) trompe-l'œil, *m.*

window frame [ʼwindoufreim], *n.* châssis de fenêtre, *m.*

window pane [ʼwindoupein], *n.* carreau, *m.*

window-shopping [ʼwindouʃopiŋ], *n.* lèche-vitrine, *m.*

window shutter [ʼwindouʃʌtə], *n.* volet; contrevent, *m.*

window sill [ʼwindousil], *n.* rebord *ou* appui de fenêtre, *m.*

windpipe [ʼwindpaip], *n.* trachée-artère, *m.*

windshield ['windʃiːld], *n.* (*Motor.*) pare-brise, *m.*
wind-sock ['windsɔk], *n.* (*Av.*) manche à air, *f.*
wind tunnel ['windtʌnl], *n.* (*Av.*) tunnel aérodynamique, *m.*
windward ['windwəd], *adv.* au vent.—*n.* côté du vent, *m.*
windy ['windi], *a.* du vent; venteux; *it is windy*, il fait du vent.
wine [wain], *n.* vin, *m.*—*v.t. to wine and dine*, fêter.
wine-bibber ['wainbibə], *n.* buveur, *m.*, ivrogne, *m.*
wine bin ['wainbin], *n.* porte-bouteilles, *m.*
wine cellar ['wainselə], *n.* cave, *f.*
wineglass ['wainglɑːs], *n.* verre à vin, *m.*
wine-growing ['waingrouiŋ], *a.* viticole.—*n.* viticulture, *f.*
wine merchant ['wainməːtʃənt], *n.* négociant en vins, *m.*
wine-press ['wainpres], *n.* pressoir, *m.*
wine-tasting ['wainteistiŋ], *n.* dégustation de vins, *f.*
wine waiter ['wainweitə], *n.* sommelier, *m.*
wing [wiŋ], *n.* aile; (*Av.*) escadre; (*Theat.*) (*pl.*) coulisse, *f.*; *on the wing*, au vol.—*v.t.* blesser à l'aile.
winged [wiŋd], *a.* ailé; (*fig.*) rapide; blessé à l'aile.
winger ['wiŋə], *n.* (*Ftb.*) ailier, *m.*
wing span ['wiŋspæn], *n.* envergure, *f.*
wink [wiŋk], *n.* clin d'œil, *m.*, œillade, *f.*—*v.i.* cligner de l'œil; clignoter (*lumière*).
winking ['wiŋkiŋ], *a.* clignotant.—*n.* clignotement; clignement d'œil, *m.*
winkle [wiŋkl], *n.* (*Ichth.*) bigorneau, *m.*
winner ['winə], *n.* gagnant; vainqueur (*d'une course etc.*), *m.*
winning ['winiŋ], *a.* gagnant; (*fig.*) attrayant, séduisant.—*n.* (*pl.*) gain, *m.*
winning post ['winiŋpoust], *n.* poteau d'arrivée, but, *m.*
winnow ['winou], *v.t.* vanner.
winter ['wintə], *a.* d'hiver.—*n.* hiver, *m.*; *in winter*, en hiver.—*v.i.* hiverner, passer l'hiver (à).
wintry ['wintri], *a.* d'hiver, hivernal; (*fig.*) glacial.
wipe [waip], *v.t.* essuyer; *to wipe off*, effacer; *to wipe up*, nettoyer.
wiper ['waipə], *n.* **windshield wiper**, essuie-glace, *m.*
wire [waiə], *n.* fil métallique, fil de fer, *m.*; dépêche (*télégramme*), *f.*; *barbed wire*, fil de fer barbelé.—*v.t.* attacher *ou* lier avec du fil de métal; griller; (*fig.*) télégraphier.
wire cutters ['waiəkʌtəz], *n.pl.* cisailles coupe-fil, *f.pl.*
wire-haired ['waiəhɛəd], *a.* à poil dur (*chien*).
wireless ['waiəlis], *a.* sans fil.—*n.* radio, T.S.F., *f.*; *wireless set*, poste de T.S.F., *m.*, radio, *f.*
wire netting ['waiənetiŋ], *n.* grillage, treillis métallique, *m.*
wire rope ['waiəroup], *n.* câble métallique, *m.*
wiring ['waiəriŋ], *n.* (*Elec.*) canalisation, *f.*; câblage, *m.*
wiry ['waiəri], *a.* (*fig.*) nerveux, souple.
wisdom ['wizdəm], *n.* sagesse; prudence, *f.*
wise [waiz], *a.* sage; discret, prudent.—*n.* manière, façon, sorte, guise, *f.*

wise-crack ['waizkræk], *n.* bon mot, *m.*
wisely ['waizli], *adv.* sagement; prudemment.
wish [wiʃ], *n.* souhait, désir, *m.*, envie, *f.*—*v.t., v.i.* souhaiter, désirer, vouloir; *I wish I could*, je voudrais pouvoir; *I wish I were . . .*, je voudrais être . . .; *to wish well to*, vouloir du bien à.
wish-bone ['wiʃboun], *n.* lunette, fourchette, *f.*
wishful ['wiʃful], *a.* désireux (*de*).
wishy-washy ['wiʃiwɔʃi], *a.* faible, pauvre.
wisp [wisp], *n.* bouchon de paille etc., *m.*; mèche (*de cheveux*), *f.*
wisteria [wis'tɛəriə], *n.* glycine, *f.*
wistful ['wistful], *a.* désireux; d'envie, de regret, pensif (*air, regard, sourire*).
wistfully ['wistfuli], *adv.* d'un air de vague regret.
wit [wit], *n.* esprit; entendement, jugement; (*fig.*) bel esprit; (*pl.*) esprit, *m.*, raison, tête, *f.*, sens, bon sens, *m.*; *to be at one's wits' end*, ne savoir que faire.—*v.t.* savoir; *to wit*, c'est-à-dire.
witch [witʃ], *n.* sorcière, magicienne, *f.*
witchcraft ['witʃkrɑːft], *n.* sorcellerie, magie noire, *f.*
witch hazel ['witʃheizl], *n.* (*Bot.*) hamamélis, *m.*
with [wið], *prep.* avec; de, par (*au moyen de*); à, au, à la, aux (*in descriptive phrases*); chez, parmi (*in compagnie de*); auprès de (*de l'envisge de*); malgré (*en dépit de*); *angry with*, fâché contre.
withal [wið'ɔːl], *adv.* avec tout cela, en outre.
withdraw [wið'drɔː], *v.t. irr.* (*conjug. like* DRAW) retirer; rappeler; éloigner (*de*).—*v.i.* se retirer, s'éloigner (*de*).
withdrawal [wið'drɔːəl], *n.* retraite (*des vaincus*), *f.*; retrait (*enlèvement*), *m.*
wither ['wiðə], *v.i.* se flétrir, se faner.
withering ['wiðəriŋ], *a.* écrasant (*sarcastique*).
withers ['wiðəz], *n.pl.* garrot (*de cheval*), *m.*
withhold [wið'hould], *v.t. irr.* (*conjug. like* HOLD) retenir; refuser.
within [wið'in], *prep.* dans, en; à moins de (*pas plus de*); *within a pound or so*, à une livre près; *within reach of*, à portée de.—*adv.* en dedans, à l'intérieur; à la maison, chez soi.
without [wið'aut], *prep.* sans (*manquant de*).—*conj.* à moins que, sans que (*unless*).—*adv.* en dehors, au dehors.
withstand [wið'stænd], *v.t. irr.* (*conjug. like* STAND) résister à, combattre.
withy ['wiði], *a.* d'osier.—*n.* osier, *m.*
witless ['witlis], *a.* sans esprit; sot.
witness ['witnis], *n.* témoin; témoignage (*preuve*), *m.*—*v.t.* témoigner; être témoin de.—*v.i.* témoigner, porter témoignage.
witticism ['witisizm], *n.* bon mot, *m.*
wittily ['witili], *adv.* spirituellement, avec esprit.
wittiness ['witinis], *n.* esprit, caractère spirituel, *m.*
wittingly ['witiŋli], *adv.* sciemment, à dessein.
witty ['witi], *a.* spirituel; plaisant (*facétieux*).
wives [WIFE].
wizard ['wizəd], *n.* sorcier, magicien, *m.*
wizened ['wizənd], *a.* ratatiné, ridé.
wobble [wɔbl], *v.i.* vaciller, ballotter.

wobbling ['wɔbliŋ], *a.* vacillant, branlant.—
n. vacillation, *f.*; dandinement, *m.*

wobbly ['wɔbli], *a.* branlant, vacillant.

woe [wou], *n.* (*fig.*) peine, douleur, *f.*; malheur, *m.*

woebegone ['woubigən], **woeful** ['wouful], *a.* triste, malheureux, abattu.

woefully ['woufuli], *adv.* tristement.

wolf [wulf], *n.* (*pl.* **wolves** [wulvz]) loup, *m.*; *she-wolf*, louve, *f.*

wolf cub ['wulfkʌb], *n.* louveteau, *m.*

wolf dog ['wulfdɔg], *n.* chien-loup, *m.*

wolfish ['wulfiʃ], *a.* de loup; (*fig.*) rapace.

wolves [WOLF].

woman ['wumən], *n.* (*pl.* **women** ['wimin]) femme, *f.*

woman hater ['wumənheitə], *n.* misogyne, *m.*

womanhood ['wumənhud], *n.* état de femme, *m.*

womankind ['wumənkaind], *n.* le sexe féminin, *m.*; les femmes, *f.pl.*

womanly ['wumənli], *a.* de femme.

womanliness ['wumənlinis], *n.* féminité, *f.*

womb [wu:m], *n.* (*Anat.*) matrice, *f.*; (*fig.*) sein, *m.*, flancs, *m.pl.*

women [WOMAN].

wonder ['wʌndə], *n.* étonnement, *m.*, surprise; merveille (*spectacle etc.*), *f.*, miracle, prodige, *m.*—*v.i.* s'étonner, être étonné; se demander; *to wonder whether*, se demander si.

wonderful ['wʌndəful], *a.* étonnant, merveilleux.

wonderfully ['wʌndəfuli], *adv.* étonnamment, merveilleusement.

wonderment ['wʌndəmənt], *n.* étonnement, *m.*

wondrous ['wʌndrəs], *a.* merveilleux.

wondrously ['wʌndrəsli], *adv.* merveilleusement.

wont [wount], *a. to be wont to*, avoir l'habitude de.—*n.* coutume, habitude, *f.*

wonted ['wountid], *a.* accoutumé, habituel.

woo [wu:], *v.t.* faire la cour à; courtiser.

wood [wud], *n.* bois (*matériel ou forêt*), *m.*

woodbine ['wudbain], *n.* chèvrefeuille, *m.*

woodcock ['wudkɔk], *n.* bécasse, *f.*

woodcut ['wudkʌt], *n.* gravure sur bois, *f.*

wood-cutter ['wudkʌtə], *n.* bûcheron, *m.*

wooded ['wudid], *a.* boisé.

wooden ['wudn], *a.* de bois, en bois; (*fig.*) gauche (*mouvement etc.*).

woodland ['wudlənd], *a.* des bois, sylvestre.
—*n.* pays boisé, bois, *m.*

woodman ['wudmən], *n.* (*pl.* -**men** [men]) garde forestier; bûcheron, *m.*

wood nymph ['wudnimf], *n.* nymphe des bois, dryade, *f.*

woodpecker ['wudpekə], *n.* pic, *m.*; *green woodpecker*, pivert, *m.*

wood pigeon ['wudpidʒin], *n.* pigeon ramier, *m.*

wood pulp ['wudpʌlp], *n.* pâte de bois, *f.*

wood-winds ['wudwindz], *n.pl.* (*Mus.*) les bois, *m.pl.*

woodwork ['wudwə:k], *n.* boiserie; menuiserie; charpente, *f.*

wood-worm ['wudwə:m], *n.* artison, *m.*

woody ['wudi], *a.* boisé; ligneux.

wood yard ['wudjɑ:d], *n.* chantier, *m.*

wooer ['wu:ə], *n.* amoureux, prétendant, *m.*

woof [wu:f], *n.* trame, *f.*; tissu (*texture*), *m.*

wooing ['wu:iŋ], *n.* cour, *f.*

wool [wul], *n.* laine, *f.*

woollen ['wulən], *a.* de laine, à laine.—*n.*(*pl.*) tissus de laine, *m.pl.*, laines, *f.pl.*, lainages, *m.pl.*; *woollen cloth*, drap, *m.*; *wool dealer*, marchand de draps, *m.*; *woollen goods*, (*fam.*) *woollies*, lainages, *m.pl.*

woolliness ['wulinis], *n.* nature laineuse; (*fig.*) imprécision, *f.*

woolly ['wuli], *a.* laineux.

Woolsack ['wulsæk], *n.* sac de laine (*siège du Lord Chancellor*), *m.*

word [wə:d], *n.* mot, *m.*; parole (*prononcée*), *f.*; avis, *m.*; nouvelle (*communication*), *f.*; *by word of mouth*, de vive voix; *in a word*, en un mot; *not a word!* bouche close!—*v.t.* exprimer; énoncer; rédiger (*télégramme*).

word-book ['wə:dbuk], *n.* vocabulaire, lexique, *m.*

wordiness ['wə:dinis], *n.* prolixité, verbosité, *f.*

wording ['wə:diŋ], *n.* expression, *f.*; énoncé (*d'un problème*), *m.*

wordy ['wə:di], *a.* verbeux, diffus.

work [wə:k], *v.t.* travailler; façonner (*ouvrager*); se frayer (*un chemin*); payer (*son passage*) en travaillant; broder (*coudre*); faire aller, manœuvrer (*machine etc.*); exploiter (*mine etc.*); *to work off*, user; *to work one-self up*, s'exciter; *to work out*, résoudre (*problème*).—*v.i.* travailler; fonctionner, marcher; aller, jouer; opérer, avoir de l'effet (*agir*); *to work loose*, se desserrer.—*n.* travail; ouvrage, *m.*, besogne (*tâche*); (*fig.*) affaire; (*Lit.*) œuvre, *f.*; (*pl.*) mécanisme (*de moteur*), *m.*; manœuvres (*d'une machine*), *f.pl.*; (*Ind.*) fabrique, usine, *f.*; (*Fort.*) travaux, *m.pl.*; mouvement (*de montre*), *m.*; *road works ahead*, attention, travaux! *to be out of work*, chômer.

workable ['wə:kəbl], *a.* réalisable; exploitable (*mine etc.*).

workaday ['wə:kədei], *a.* de tous les jours.

work-bench ['wə:kbentʃ], *n.* établi, *m.*

work-box ['wə:kbɔks], *n.* boîte à ouvrage, *f.*

worker ['wə:kə], *n.* travailleur; ouvrier; employé, *m.*

workhouse ['wə:khaus], *n.* maison des pauvres, *f.*; hospice, *m.*

working ['wə:kiŋ], *a.* qui travaille, ouvrier; de travail (*vêtements*); *hard-working*, laborieux; *in working order*, en état de fonctionnement; *working capital*, capital d'exploitation, *m.*; *working man*, ouvrier, *m.*—*n.* travail, *m.*; marche, *f.*; fonctionnement, jeu (*de machine*), *m.*; opération; exploitation (*de mine etc.*), *f.*

working class ['wə:kiŋklɑ:s], *n.* classe ouvrière, *f.*

working day ['wə:kiŋ'dei], *n.* jour ouvrable, *m.*

workman ['wə:kmən], *n.* (*pl.* -**men** [men]) ouvrier, artisan, *m.*

workmanlike ['wə:kmənlaik], *a.* bien fait, bien travaillé.

workmanship ['wə:kmənʃip], *n.* ouvrage, travail, *m.*

work-room ['wə:kru:m], **work-shop** ['wə:kʃɔp], *n.* atelier, *m.*

world [wə:ld], *n.* monde; l'univers, (*fig.*) monde, *m.*, vie, *f.*; *all the world over*, dans le monde entier; *a world of good*, un bien infini; *the first world war*, la première guerre mondiale.

worldliness ['wəːldlinis], *n.* mondanité; frivolité, *f.*

worldly ['wəːldli], *a.* mondain, du monde.

worldwide ['wəːldwaid], *a.* universel, répandu partout.

worm [wəːm], *n.* ver, *m.*; chenille, larve, *f.*; filet (*de vis*), *m.—v.t.* miner; *to worm oneself into*, s'insinuer, se faufiler dans.

worm cast ['wəːmkaːst], *n.* déjection de ver (de terre), *f.*

worm-eaten ['wəːmiːtn], *a.* rongé des vers, vermoulu.

worm screw ['wəːmskruː], *n.* tire-bourre, *m.*

wormwood ['wəːmwud], *n.* armoise amère, *f.*; (*fig.*) fiel, *m.*

worried ['wʌrid], *a.* tourmenté, harassé, ennuyé.

worry ['wʌri], *n.* ennui, tracas, souci, *m.—v.t.* tourmenter, tracasser.—*v.i.* tracasser; *don't worry!* soyez tranquille!

worse [wəːs], *a.* pire; plus mauvais; plus malade, plus mal (*santé*).—*n.* pire; plus mauvais, *m.—adv.* plus mal, pis; *far worse*, bien pis, bien pire; *so much the worse*, tant pis.

worsen [wəːsn], *v.i.* empirer.

worsening ['wəːsniŋ], *n.* aggravation, *f.*

worship ['wəːʃip], *n.* culte, *m.*, adoration, *f.*; honneur (*titre*), *m.—v.t.*, *v.i.* adorer.

worshipful ['wəːʃipful], *a.* honorable.

worshipper ['wəːʃipə], *n.* adorateur, *m.*

worst [wəːst], *a.* le plus mauvais, le pire.—*adv.* le pis, le plus mal.—*n.* le plus mauvais, le pire, le pis.—*v.t.* battre, vaincre, défaire.

worsted ['wustid], *a.* de laine peignée.—*n.* laine peignée, *f.*

worth [wəːθ], *a.* qui vaut, valant; qui mérite (*digne*); qui est riche de (*qui possède*); *to be worth doing*, valoir la peine de faire.—*n.* valeur, *f.*; prix, *m.*; *for all one's worth*, de toutes ses forces.

worthily ['wəːðili], *adv.* dignement.

worthiness ['wəːðinis], *n.* mérite, *m.*

worthless ['wəːθlis], *a.* sans valeur, qui ne vaut rien; *worthless fellow*, vaurien, *m.*

worth-while ['wəːθ'hwail], *a.* qui vaut la peine (*de*).

worthy ['wəːði], *a.* digne, honorable; (*colloq.*) brave.—*n.* (*colloq.*) brave homme; homme illustre, *m.*

would [wud], *v.aux. past* and *cond.* [WILL]. *When used emphatically* **would** *is translated by* **vouloir.**

would-be ['wudbi], *a.* prétendu, soi-disant.

wound (1) [waund], *past* and *p.p.* [WIND (2)].

wound (2) [wuːnd], *n.* blessure; plaie, *f.—v.t.* blesser.

wounded ['wuːndid], *a.* blessé.

woven [wouvn], *a.* tissé.

wrack [ræk], *n.* varech, *m.*; ruine, *f.*, débris, *m.*

wraith [reiθ], *n.* revenant, *m.*

wrangle [ræŋgl], *n.* dispute, querelle, *f.—v.i.* se disputer, se quereller.

wrangling ['ræŋgliŋ], *n.* dispute, *f.*, chamailleries, *f.pl.*

wrap [ræp], *v.t.* enrouler, envelopper.—*n.* châle, peignoir, *m.*

wrapper ['ræpə], *n.* enveloppe; toile d'embal-

lage (*pour paquets*); bande (*pour journal*); couverture (*de livre*), *f.*

wrapping ['ræpiŋ], *n.* enveloppe, couverture, *f.*; *wrapping-paper*, papier d'emballage, *m.*

wrath [rɔːθ], *n.* courroux, *m.*, colère, *f.*

wrathful ['rɔːθful], *a.* courroucé.

wreak [riːk], *v.t.* exécuter, satisfaire.

wreath [riːθ], *n.* guirlande, *f.*, feston, *m.*; couronne (*d'épouse etc.*), *f.*

wreathe [riːð], *v.t.* entrelacer, tresser (*de*).—*v.i.* s'entrelacer, s'enrouler.

wreathed [riːðd], *a.* entrelacé.

wreck [rek], *n.* naufrage; navire naufragé, *m.*, épave; (*fig.*) ruine, *f.—v.t.* faire faire naufrage à; (*fig.*) ruiner.

wreckage ['rekidʒ], *n.* débris de naufrage, *m.*, épaves, *f.pl.*

wrecked [rekt], *a.* naufragé; ruiné.

wrecker ['rekə], *n.* pilleur d'épaves, naufrageur, *m.*; (*Motor.*) dépanneuse, *f.* [see **house-breaker**; **train**]

wren [ren], *n.* (*Orn.*) roitelet, *m.*

wrench [rentʃ], *n.* torsion, *f.*, arrachement, *m.*; entorse (*des muscles*); clef (*outil*), *f.—v.t.* arracher (*à ou de*); se fouler (*cheville etc.*).

wrest [rest], *v.t.* arracher (*à*).

wrestle [resl], *v.i.* lutter.

wrestler ['reslə], *n.* lutteur, *m.*

wrestling ['resliŋ], *n.* lutte, *f.*; catch, *m.*; *all-in wrestling*, lutte libre.

wretch [retʃ], *n.* malheureux, *m.*; misérable (*scélérat*), *m.*, *f.*; *poor wretch*, pauvre diable, *m.*

wretched ['retʃid], *a.* malheureux, misérable; vilain, triste; pitoyable, à faire pitié.

wretchedly ['retʃidli], *adv.* malheureusement, misérablement; d'une manière pitoyable.

wretchedness ['retʃidnis], *n.* misère, pauvreté, *f.*

wriggle [rigl], *v.i.* se tortiller, se remuer.

wriggling ['rigliŋ], *n.* tortillement, *m.*

wring [riŋ], *v.t. irr.* tordre; arracher (*à*); presser, serrer (*étreindre*).

wringer ['riŋə], *n.* essoreuse (*à linge*), *f.*

wringing ['riŋiŋ], *a.* *wringing wet*, trempé jusqu'aux os (*personne*); mouillé à tordre (*vêtement*).

wrinkle [riŋkl], *n.* ride (*à la figure etc.*), *f.*; pli, faux pli (*de vêtement*); (*slang*) tuyau (*renseignement*), *m.—v.t.* rider; plisser; *to wrinkle one's brow*, froncer les sourcils.—*v.i.* se rider.

wrinkled [riŋkld], *a.* ridé; (*Bot.*) plissé.

wrist [rist], *n.* poignet, *m.*

wristband ['ristbænd], *n.* poignet, *m.*

wrist watch ['ristwɔtʃ], *n.* montre-bracelet, *f.*

writ [rit], *n.* exploit, mandat, *m.*, ordonnance, (*Parl.*) lettre de convocation, *f.*

write [rait], *v.t.*, *v.i. irr.* écrire; *to write off*, (*Comm.*) passer au compte des profits et pertes.

write-off ['raitɔf], *n.* annulation; non-valeur (*personne*), *f.*

writer ['raitə], *n.* écrivain, *m.*

writhe [raið], *v.i.* se tordre (*de douleur*); se crisper.

writing ['raitiŋ], *n.* écriture (*calligraphie*), *f.*; écrit (*chose écrite*); (*fig.*) ouvrage, document, *m.*; inscription, *f.*; *in writing*, par écrit.

writing case ['raitiŋkeis], *n.* papeterie, *f.*

writing desk ['raitiŋdesk], *n.* pupitre, bureau, secrétaire, *m.*

writing paper ['raitiŋpeipə], *n.* papier à écrire, *m.*
writing table ['raitiŋteibl], *n.* table à écrire, *f.*
written [ritn], *a.* écrit, par écrit.
wrong [rɔŋ], *a.* faux, erroné, inexact (*pas vrai*); mal, mauvais; *to be wrong,* avoir tort (*personne*), n'être pas à l'heure, aller mal (*montre*); *what's wrong with you?* qu'avez-vous? *wrong number,* (*Teleph.*) mauvais numéro, *m.*; *wrong side,* envers, *m.*; *wrong side up,* sens dessus dessous.— *adv.* mal, à tort, à faux.—*n.* mal, *m.*, injustice, *f.*, tort; dommage, *m.*—*v.t.* faire du tort à, nuire à.
wrongdoer ['rɔŋdu:ə], *n.* pervers, méchant, *m.*
wrongdoing ['rɔŋduiŋ], *n.* le mal, *m.*
wrongful ['rɔŋful], *a.* injuste.
wrongfully ['rɔŋfuli], *adv.* à tort, injustement.
wrongly ['rɔŋli], *adv.* mal, à tort; *rightly or wrongly,* à tort ou à raison.
wroth [rouθ], *a.* (*poet.*) en colère, irrité, courroucé.
wrought [rɔːt], *a.* travaillé; façonné; ouvré (*tissu*), *a.* (*poet.*) *wrought iron,* fer forgé, *m.*
wry [rai], *a.* de travers, tordu, tors; *to pull a wry face,* faire la grimace.

X

X, x [eks]. vingt-quatrième lettre de l'alphabet; X, dix, *m.*
Xerxes ['zəːksiːz]. Xerxès, *m.*
Xmas ['krisməs]. (*abbr.* CHRISTMAS) Noël, *m.*
X-ray ['eksrei], *a.* radiographique; *X-ray photograph,* radiographie, *f.*—*n.* (*pl.*) rayons X, *m.pl.*—*v.t.* radiographier.
xylophone ['zailəfoun], *n.* xylophone; (*slang*) claquebois, *m.*

Y

Y, y [wai]. vingt-cinquième lettre de l'alphabet; (l')i grec, *m.*
yacht [jɔt], *n.* yacht, *m.*
yacht club ['jɔtklʌb], *n.* cercle nautique, *m.*
yachting ['jɔtiŋ], *n.* yachting, *m.*
yachtsman ['jɔtsmən], *n.* (*pl.* **-men** [men]) yachtman, *m.*
yak [jæk], *n.* (*Zool.*) ya(c)k, *m.*
yam [jæm], *n.* igname, *f.*
yank [jæŋk], *v.t.* (*fam.*) tirer brusquement.
Yankee ['jæŋki], *n.* Yankee, Américain, *m.*
yap [jæp], *v.i.* japper, aboyer.—*n.* jappement, *m.*
yard (1) [jɑːd], *n.* cour, *f.*, préau, *m.*
yard (2) [jɑːd], *n.* (*Naut.*) vergue, *f.*; (*Measure*) yard (mètre 0,914383), *m.*
yard-arm ['jɑːdɑːm], *n.* bout de vergue, *m.*
yarn [jɑːn], *n.* fil; (*Naut.*) fil de caret, récit, conte (*histoire*), *m.*

yawl [jɔːl], *n.* (*Naut.*) sloop, *m.*; (*Row.*) yole de mer, *f.*
yawn [jɔːn], *n.* bâillement, *m.*—*v.i.* bâiller.
yawning ['jɔːniŋ], *a.* qui bâille; (*fig.*) béant.
*ye [jiː], *pron.pl.* vous.
yea [jei], *adv.* oui; vraiment, en vérité.—*n.* vote affirmatif, *m.*
year [jiə], *n.* an (*unité de temps*), *m.*; année (*particulière*), *f.*; *every year,* tous les ans; *four times a year,* quatre fois par an; *new year,* nouvel an; *next year,* l'an prochain.
year-book ['jiəbuk], *n.* annuaire, *m.*
yearling ['jiəliŋ], *a.* âgé d'un an.—*n.* poulain, *m.*, ou pouliche, *f.*, d'un an.
yearly ['jiəli], *a.* annuel.—*adv.* tous les ans.
yearn [jəːn], *v.i.* *to yearn after,* soupirer après; *to yearn to do something,* brûler de faire quelque chose.
yearning ['jəːniŋ], *n.* désir ardent, *m.*
yeast [jiːst], *n.* levure, *f.*
yell [jel], *n.* hurlement, *m.*—*v.i.* hurler, pousser des hurlements.
yelling ['jeliŋ], *n.* hurlements, *m.pl.*
yellow ['jelou], *a.* jaune; (*slang*) poltron.—*n.* jaune, *m.*—*v.t., v.i.* jaunir.
yellow-hammer ['jelouhæmə], *n.* (*Orn.*) bruant jaune, *m.*
yellowish ['jelouiʃ], *a.* jaunâtre.
yellowness ['jelounis], *n.* couleur jaune, *f.*
yelp [jelp], *v.i.* glapir, japper.
yelping ['jelpiŋ], *n.* glapissement, jappement, *m.*
Yemen ['jemən]. le Yémen, *m.*
Yemeni ['jeməni], *a.* yémenite.—*n.* Yémenite (*personne*), *m.*, *f.*
yeoman ['joumən], *n.* (*pl.* **-men** [men]) fermier-propriétaire, *m.*
yeomanry ['joumənri], *n.* fermiers-propriétaires, *m.pl.*
yes [jes], *adv.* oui; si (*in reply to a negative*).
yes man ['jesmæn], *n.* (*pl.* **men** [men]) (*pop.*) Béni-oui-oui, *m.*
yesterday ['jestəd(e)i], *adv.* and *n.* hier, *m.*; *the day before yesterday,* avant-hier; *yesterday evening,* hier soir.
yet [jet], *conj.* pourtant, cependant, tout de même.—*adv.* encore, déjà; *as yet,* jusqu'ici; *not yet,* pas encore.
yew [juː], *n.* (*Bot.*) if, *m.*
yield [jiːld], *v.t.* produire, rapporter; livrer, céder (*au vainqueur*); *to yield up,* rendre.— *v.i.* se rendre, céder (à); consentir (à).—*n.* rendement, produit, rapport, *m.*
yielding ['jiːldiŋ], *a.* complaisant, facile.—*n.* reddition; soumission, *f.*
yoke [jouk], *n.* joug; attelage, *m.*, paire; palanche (*pour seaux*), *f.*; (*Dress.*) empiècement, *m.*—*v.t.* atteler, accoupler.
yokel ['joukl], *n.* rustre, campagnard, *m.*
yolk [jouk], *n.* jaune (d'œuf), *m.*
yonder ['jɔndə], *adv.* là, là-bas.—*a.* *yonder castle,* ce château-là.
*yore [jɔː], *adv.* autrefois, jadis.
you [juː], *pron.* vous; (*to a child, relative, pet etc.*) tu, te, toi; (*indef.*) on.
young [jʌŋ], *a.* jeune; novice, neuf, inexpérimenté (*non éprouvé*); (*fig.*) naissant; *young folks* or *young people,* jeunes gens, *m.pl.*; *young lady,* demoiselle, *f.*—*n.pl.* les jeunes, les jeunes gens; les petits, *m.pl.*; *with young,* pleine (*animal*).

younger ['jʌŋgə], *a.* plus jeune; cadet (*de deux frères etc.*).

youngest ['jʌŋgist], *a.* le plus jeune.

youngish ['jʌŋiʃ], *a.* assez jeune.

youngster ['jʌŋstə], *n.* jeune homme; gamin, mioche, *m.*, gosse, *m.*, *f.*

your [jɔ:], *a.* votre, (*pl.*) vos; (*to a child, relative, pet etc.*) ton, ta, tes; (*indef.*) son, sa, ses.

yours [jɔ:z], *pron.* le vôtre, *m.*, la vôtre, *f.*, les vôtres, *pl.*; à vous (*your property*); de vous (*by you*); (*to a child, relative, pet etc.*) le tien, la tienne, les tiens, les tiennes; à toi (*your property*); de toi (*by you*).

yourself [jɔ:'self], *pron.* (*pl.* **yourselves** [jɔ:'selvz]) vous-même, toi-même; (*pl.*) vous-mêmes; (*reflexive*) vous, te.

youth [ju:θ], *n.* jeunesse, adolescence, *f.*; jeune homme, adolescent (*personne*), *m.*; (*fig.*) jeunes gens, *m.pl.*

youthful ['ju:θful], *a.* jeune; de jeunesse.

youthfulness ['ju:θfulnis], *n.* jeunesse, *f.*

Yugoslav ['ju:goʊ'slɑ:v], *a.* yougoslave.—*n.* Yougoslave (*personne*), *m.*, *f.*

Yugoslavia [ju:goʊ'slɑ:vjə]. la Yougoslavie, *f.*

****Yule** [ju:l], **Yule-tide** ['ju:ltaid], *n.* Noël, *m.*, fête de Noël, *f.*

Yule log ['ju:llɔg], *n.* bûche de Noël, *f.*

Z

Z, z [zed, (*Am.*) zi:]. vingt-sixième lettre de l'alphabet, *m.*

Zambesi [zæm'bi:zi]. le Zambèze, *m.*

Zambia ['zæmbjə]. la Zambie, *f.*

zany ['zeini], *n.* zani, bouffon, *m.*

zeal [zi:l], *n.* zèle, *m.*

zealot ['zelət], *n.* zélateur, *m.*, fanatique, *m.*, *f.*

zealous ['zeləs], *a.* zélé, zélateur.

zealously ['zeləsli], *adv.* avec zèle.

zebra ['zi:brə], *n.* zèbre, *m.*; **zebra crossing** (*pedestrian crossing*), passage clouté, *m.*

zenith ['zeniθ], *n.* zénith; (*fig.*) apogée, *m.*

zephyr ['zefə], *n.* zéphyr, zéphire, Zéphyre, *m.*

zero ['ziərou], *n.* zéro; (*fig.*) rien, *m.*; **zero hour**, l'heure H, *f.*

zest [zest], *n.* goût, *m.*, saveur, *f.*; zeste (*d'orange, de citron*); (*fig.*) entrain, *m.*, verve, *f.*

Zeus [zju:s]. (*Myth.*) Zeus, *m.*

zigzag ['zigzæg], *a.* en zigzag.—*n.* zigzag, *m.* —*v.i.* aller en zigzag, zigzaguer.

zinc [ziŋk], *n.* zinc, *m.*—*v.t.* zinguer.

zinnia ['zinjə], *n.* (*Bot.*) zinnia, *m.*

Zion ['zaiən]. Sion, *m.*

zip [zip], *n.* sifflement (*de balle*), *m.*; énergie, verve, *f.*—*v.t.* siffler; **zip fastener**, fermeture à glissière, *f.*

zither ['ziðə], *n.* cithare, *f.*

zodiac ['zoudiæk], *n.* zodiaque, *m.*

zone [zoun], *n.* zone, *f.*

zoo [zu:], *n.* jardin zoologique, (*fam.*) zoo, *m.*

zoological [zouə'lɔdʒikl], *a.* zoologique; **zoological gardens**, jardin zoologique, *m.*

zoologist [zou'ɔlədʒist], *n.* zoologiste, zoologue, *m.*, *f.*

zoology [zou'ɔlədʒi] *n.* zoologie, *f.*

zoom [zu:m], *n.* bourdonnement, ronflement, *m.*—*v.i.* vrombir.

Zulu ['zu:lu:], *a.* zoulou.—*n.* Zoulou, *m.*

French Verbs

1. All verbs not marked *irr.* in the French-English section of the Dictionary are either
   (a) regular, and conjugated like AIMER, FINIR or VENDRE according to their ending (see below) or
   (b) anomalous, and conjugated like the verb in that group to which the user is referred.
2. The Imperfect Indicative, Conditional, Imperative, and Imperfect Subjunctive are not given and may be assumed to be formed as follows:
   Imperfect Indicative: by substituting for the final *-ons* of 1st Person Plural, Present Indicative the endings *-ais, -ais, -ait, -ions, -iez, -aient* (except *être: j'étais*).
   Conditional: by substituting for the endings of the Future those of the Imperfect Indicative given above.
   Imperative: (a) 2nd Person Singular, 1st and 2nd Person Plural, by using these forms of

Infinitive	Participles	Present Indicative	Past Historic
REGULAR VERBS First Conjugation Infinitive in *-er*			
aim-*er*	aim-*ant* aim-*é*	aim-*e* aim-*es* aim-*e* aim-*ons* aim-*ez* aim-*ent*	aim-*ai* aim-*as* aim-*a* aim-*âmes* aim-*âtes* aim-*èrent*
Second Conjugation Infinitive in *-ir*			
fin-*ir*	fin-*issant* fin-*i*	fin-*is* fin-*is* fin-*it* fin-*issons* fin-*issez* fin-*issent*	fin-*is* fin-*is* fin-*it* fin-*îmes* fin-*îtes* fin-*irent*
Third Conjugation Infinitive in *-re*			
vend-*re*	vend-*ant* vend-*u*	vend-*s* vend-*s* vend vend-*ons* vend-*ez* vend-*ent*	vend-*is* vend-*is* vend-*it* vend-*îmes* vend-*îtes* vend-*irent*
ANOMALOUS VERBS			
amener	amenant amené	amène amènes amène amenons amenez amènent	amenai . . . amenâmes . . .
appeler	appelant appelé	appelle appelles appelle appelons appelez appellent	appelai . . . appelâmes . . .
assiéger	assiégeant assiégé	assiège assièges assiège assiégeons assiégez assiègent	assiégeai . . . assiégeâmes . . .

French Verbs

the Present Indicative without pronouns (-*er* verbs drop the final *s* of the 2nd Person Singular).

    (*b*) 3rd Person Singular and Plural by using these forms of the Present Subjunctive.

Imperfect Subjunctive: from the 2nd Person Singular of the Past Historic by adding -*se*, -*ses*, -*t*, -*sions*, -*siez*, -*sent*.

3. Exceptions to the above rules are indicated in footnotes.
4. Compound verbs (e.g. DEVENIR, REVENIR, etc.) are given only where they differ from the simple form (e.g. VENIR).
5. Defective verbs are marked † and all existing forms are given.

Future	Present Subjunctive	English
aimer-*ai*	aim-*e*	to like, to love
aimer-*as*	aim-*es*	
aimer-*a*	aim-*e*	
aimer-*ons*	aim-*ions*	
aimer-*ez*	aim-*iez*	
aimer-*ont*	aim-*ent*	
finir-*ai*	fini-*sse*	to finish
finir-*as*	fini-*sses*	
finir-*a*	fini-*sse*	
finir-*ons*	fini-*ssions*	
finir-*ez*	fini-*ssiez*	
finir-*ont*	fini-*ssent*	
vendr-*ai*	vend-*e*	to sell
vendr-*as*	vend-*es*	
vendr-*a*	vend-*e*	
vendr-*ons*	vend-*ions*	
vendr-*ez*	vend-*iez*	
vendr-*ont*	vend-*ent*	
amènerai...	amène	to bring
amènerons...	amènes	
	amène	
	amenions	
	ameniez	
	amènent	
appellerai...	appelle	to call
appellerons . . .	appelles	
	appelle	
	appelions	
	appeliez	
	appellent	
assiégerai . . .	assiège	to besiege
assiégerons . . .	assièges	
	assiège	
	assiégions	
	assiégiez	
	assiègent	

637

French Verbs

Infinitive	*Participles*	*Present Indicative*	*Past Historic*
battre	battant battu	bats bats bat battons battez battent	battis . . . battîmes . . .
céder	cédant cédé	cède cèdes cède cédons cédez cèdent	cédai . . . cédâmes . . .
commencer	commençant commencé	commence commences commence commençons commencez commencent	commençai commenças commença commençâmes commençâtes commencèrent
dépecer	dépeçant dépecé	dépèce dépèces dépèce dépeçons dépecez dépècent	dépeçai dépeças dépeça dépeçâmes dépeçâtes dépecèrent
employer[1]	employant employé	emploie emploies emploie employons employez emploient	employai . . . employâmes . . .
manger	mangeant mangé	mange manges mange mangeons mangez mangent	mangeai mangeas mangea mangeâmes mangeâtes mangèrent
payer[1]	(See footnote)		
rapiécer	rapiéçant rapiécé	rapièce rapièces rapièce rapiéçons rapiécez rapiècent	rapiéçai rapiéças rapiéça rapiéçâmes rapiéçâtes rapiécèrent
rompre	rompant rompu	romps romps rompt rompons rompez rompent	rompis . . . rompîmes . . .

IRREGULAR VERBS

† absoudre	absolvant absous, *m.*, absoute, *f.*	absous absous absout absolvons absolvez absolvent	

[1] All verbs in *-oyer* and *-uyer* change *y* to *i* before a mute *e*.   With verbs in *-ayer*, *y* or *i* may

Future	Present Subjunctive	English
battrai . . . battrons . . .	batte . . . battions . . .	to beat
céderai . . . céderons . . .	cède cèdes cède cédions cédiez cèdent	to yield
commencerai . . . commencerons . . .	commence . . . commencions . . .	to begin
dépècerai . . . dépècerons . . .	dépèce dépèces dépèce dépecions dépeciez dépècent	to cut up
emploierai . . . emploierons . . .	emploie emploies emploie employions employiez emploient	to employ, to use
mangerai . . . mangerons . . .	mange . . . mangions . . .	to eat
		to pay (for)
rapiécerai . . . rapiécerons . . .	rapièce rapièces rapièce rapiécions rapiéciez rapiècent	to patch
romprai . . . romprons . . .	rompe . . . rompions . . .	to break
absoudrai . . . absoudrons . . .	absolve . . . absolvions . . .	to absolve

be used. With *grasseyer*, y is always used.

639

French Verbs

Infinitive	Participles	Present Indicative	Past Historic
† accroire	(used only in the infinitive in the phrase *'faire accroire'*, to make one		
acquérir	acquérant acquis	acquiers acquiers acquiert acquérons acquérez acquièrent	acquis... acquîmes...
† advenir	advenant advenu	il advient	il advint
aller [1]	allant allé	vais vas va allons allez vont	allai... allâmes...
assaillir	assaillant assailli	assaille... assaillons...	assaillis... assaillîmes...
asseoir	asseyant *or* assoyant assis	assieds [2] assieds assied asseyons asseyez asseyent	assis... assîmes...
avoir [3]	ayant eu	ai as a avons avez ont	eus... eûmes...
boire	buvant bu	bois bois boit buvons buvez boivent	bus... bûmes...
bouillir	bouillant bouilli	bous bous bout bouillons bouillez bouillent	bouillis... bouillîmes...
† braire [4]	brayant brait	il brait ils braient	
† bruire [5]	bruissant bruit	il bruit ils bruissent	
† choir	chu	chois chois choit	chus... chûmes...
† clore	clos	clos clos clôt closent	

---

[1] 2nd pers. sing. Imperative: *va*.
[2] The forms in *-oit* (or *-eoit*) (same conjugation as *prévoir*) are accepted by the Académie Française but considered as familiar or even vulgar.

640

Future	Present Subjunctive	English .
believe)		
acquerrai... acquerrons...	acquière acquières acquière acquérions acquériez acquièrent	to acquire
il adviendra	il advienne	to happen
irai... irons...	aille ailles aille allions alliez aillent	to go
assaillirai... assaillirons...	assaille... assaillions...	to assault
assiérai... *or* assoirai... assiérons... *or* assoirons...	asseye[2]... asseyions...	to set to seat
aurai... aurons...	aie aies ait ayons ayez aient	to have
boirai... boirons...	boive boives boive buvions buviez boivent	to drink
bouillirai... bouillirons...	bouille... bouillions...	to boil
il braira ils brairont		to bray
		to rustle
cherrai... *or* choirai... cherrons... *or* choirons...		to fall
clorai... clorons...	close... closions...	to close

[3] Imperative: *aie, ayons, ayez.*
[4] Imperfect Indicative: *il brayait, ils brayaient.*
[5] Imperfect Indicative: *il bruissait, ils bruissaient* or *il bruyait, ils bruyaient.*

French Verbs

Infinitive	Participles	Present Indicative	Past Historic
conclure	concluant conclu	conclus, -s, -t concluons...	conclus... conclûmes...
conduire	conduisant conduit	conduis, -s, -t conduisons...	conduisis... conduisimes...
confire	confisant confit	confis, -s, -t confisons...	confis... confîmes...
connaitre	connaissant connu	connais connais connaît connaissons connaissez connaissent	connus... connûmes...
coudre	cousant cousu	couds... cousons..	cousis... cousimes...
courir	courant couru	cours,-s,-t courons...	courus... courûmes...
craindre	craignant craint	crains,-s,-t craignons...	craignis... craignimes...
croire	croyant cru	crois crois croit croyons croyez croient	crus... crûmes...
croître	croissant [1] crû, *m.*, crue, *f.*	crois crois croit croissons croissez croissent	crûs... crûmes...
cueillir	cueillant cueilli	cueille... cueillons...	cueillis... cueillîmes...
† déchoir [2]	déchu	déchois déchois déchoit déchoyons déchoyez déchoient	déchus... déchûmes...
devoir	devant dû, *m.*, due, *f.*, dus, *m.pl.*	dois dois doit devons devez doivent	dus... dûmes...
dire	disant dit	dis dis dit disons dites disent	dis... dîmes...
† échoir	échéant échu	il échoit ils échoient	il échut ils échurent

[1] The past part. of **accroître** is **accru**, and of **décroître**. **décru** (no circumflex on the *u* of the masculine sing.).　[2] No Imperfect Indicative.

642

Future	Present Subjunctive	English
conclurai... conclurons...	conclue... concluions...	to conclude
conduirai... conduirons...	conduise... conduisions...	to lead to drive
confirai... confirons...	confise... confisions...	to preserve
connaîtrai... connaîtrons...	connaisse... connaissions...	to know
coudrai... coudrons...	couse... cousions...	to sew
courrai... courrons...	coure... courions...	to run
craindrai... craindrons...	craigne... craignions...	to fear
croirai... croirons...	croie croies croie croyions croyiez croient	to believe
croîtrai... croîtrons...	croisse... croissions...	to grow
cueillerai... cueillerons...	cueille... cueillions...	to gather
décherrai... décherrons...	déchoie déchoies déchoie déchoyions déchoyiez déchoient	to fall to lose
devrai... devrons...	doive doives doive devions deviez doivent	to owe to have to
dirai... dirons...	dise... disions...	to say
il échoira or écherra ils échoiront or écherront	il échoie or échée ils échéent	to fall due

French Verbs

Infinitive	Participles	Present Indicative	Past Historic
écrire	écrivant écrit	écris,-s,-t écrivons...	écrivis... écrivîmes...
envoyer	envoyant envoyé	envoie envoies envoie envoyons envoyez envoient	envoyai... envoyâmes...
être[1]	étant été	suis es est sommes êtes sont	fus... fûmes...
† faillir	faillant failli	faut[2]	faillis[3]... faillîmes...
faire	faisant fait	fais fais fait faisons faites font	fis... fîmes...
† falloir[4]	fallu	il faut	il fallut
† férir[5]	féru		
† forfaire (à)	forfait		
† frire	frit	fris fris frit	
fuir	fuyant fui	fuis fuis fuit fuyons fuyez fuient	fuis... fuîmes...
† gésir[6]	gisant	gît gisons gisez gisent	
haïr	haïssant haï	hais,-s,-t haïssons...	haïs... haïmes[7]...
lire	lisant lu	lis,-s,-t lisons...	lus... lûmes...
luire	luisant lui	luis,-s,-t luisons...	luis... luîmes...
maudire	conjugated like the regular verbs in -ir, e.g. finir, except for the past		
médire (de)	médisant médit	médis... médisons...	médis... médîmes...

[1] Imperfect Indic.: *j'étais*; Imperative: *sois, soyons, soyez.*
[2] Only in the phrase *le cœur me faut.*
[3] In current usage followed by an infinitive, *e.g. il faillit tomber*, he nearly fell.
[4] Imperfect Indic.: *il fallait.*

Future	Present Subjunctive	English
écrirai... écrirons...	écrive... écrivions...	to write
enverrai... enverrons...	envoie envoies envoie envoyions envoyiez envoient	to send
serai... serons...	sois sois soit soyons soyez soient	to be
faudrai or faillirai		to fail
ferai... ferons...	fasse... fassions...	to make, to do
il faudra	il faille	to be necessary
		to strike
		to be false (to)
frirai... frirons...		to fry
fuirai... fuirons...	fuie... fuyions...	to flee
		to lie
haïrai... haïrons...	haïsse... haïssions...	to hate
lirai... lirons...	lise... lisions...	to read
luirai... luirons...	luise... luisions...	to gleam
participle (maudit).		to curse
médirai... médirons...	médise... médisions...	to speak ill of

[5] The infinitive is used only in the phrase *sans coup férir*, without striking a blow. *Féru* is adjectival only (*féru d'amour*, lovesick).
[6] The Imperfect Indic., *je gisais*, etc., is used.
[7] The plural is written without a circumflex: *haïmes*, *haïtes*.

French Verbs

Infinitive	Participles	Present Indicative	Past Historic
mettre	mettant mis	mets,-s,-t mettons...	mis... mîmes...
moudre	moulant moulu	mouds mouds moud moulons moulez moulent	moulus... moulûmes...
mourir	mourant mort	meurs meurs meurt mourons mourez meurent	mourus... mourûmes...
mouvoir	mouvant [1]mû, *m.*, mue, *f.*, mus, *m.pl.*	meus meus meut mouvons mouvez meuvent	mus... mûmes...
naître	naissant né	nais nais naît naissons naissez naissent	naquis... naquîmes...
nuire (à)	nuisant nui	nuis,-s,-t nuisons...	nuisis... nuisîmes...
† oindre[2]	oint		
† ouïr[3]	oyant ouï		ouïs... ouïmes...
ouvrir	ouvrant ouvert	ouvre... ouvrons...	ouvris... ouvrîmes...
† paître	paissant	pais pais paît paissons paissez paissent	
plaire	plaisant plu	plais plais plaît plaisons plaisez plaisent	plus... plûmes...
† pleuvoir	pleuvant plu	il pleut	il plut
† poindre	poignant point	il point	
pourvoir	pourvoyant pourvu	pourvois,-s,-t pourvoyons,-yez,-ient	pourvus... pourvûmes...

[1] The past part. of *émouvoir* is *ému*, and of *promouvoir*, *promu* (no circumflex on the *u* of the masculine sing.).

646

Future	Present Subjunctive	English
mettrai... mettrons...	mette... mettions...	to put
moudrai... moudrons...	moule... moulions...	to grind
mourrai... mourrons...	meure meures meure mourions mouriez meurent	to die
mouvrai... mouvrons...	meuve meuves meuve mouvions mouviez meuvent	to move
naîtrai... naîtrons...	naisse... naissions...	to be born
nuirai... nuirons...	nuise... nuisions...	to harm
oindrai...		to anoint
ouïrai... ouïrons...		to hear
ouvrirai... ouvrirons...	ouvre... ouvrions...	to open
paîtrai... paîtrons...	paisse... paissions...	to graze
plairai... plairons...	plaise... plaisions...	to please
il pleuvra	il pleuve	to rain
il poindra ils poindront		to dawn to sting
pourvoirai... pourvoirons...	pourvoie... pourvoyions...	to provide

[2] Imperfect Indic.: *je oignais.*
[3] This verb is seldom used other than in the infinitive and in the compound tenses.

French Verbs

Infinitive	Participles	Present Indicative	Past Historic
pouvoir	pouvant	peux *or* puis	pus...
	pu	peux	pûmes...
		peut	
		pouvons	
		pouvez	
		peuvent	
prendre	prenant	prends	pris...
	pris	prends	primes...
		prend	
		prenons	
		prenez	
		prennent	
prévoir	prévoyant	prévois,-s,-t	prévis...
	prévu	prévoyons, -yez, -ient	prévîmes...
recevoir	recevant	reçois	reçus...
	reçu	reçois	reçûmes...
		reçoit	
		recevons	
		recevez	
		reçoivent	
résoudre	résolvant	résous	résolus...
	résolu *or* résous	résous	résolûmes...
		résout	
		résolvons	
		résolvez	
		résolvent	
rire	riant	ris,-s,-t	ris...
	ri	rions...	rîmes...
savoir[1]	sachant	sais,-s,-t	sus...
	su	savons...	sûmes...
sentir	sentant	sens,-s,-t	sentis...
	senti	sentons...	sentîmes...
† seoir	seyant	il sied	
		ils siéent	
suffire	suffisant	suffis,-s,-t	suffis...
	suffi	suffisons...	suffîmes...
suivre	suivant	suis,-s,-t	suivis...
	suivi	suivons...	suivîmes...
surseoir[2]	sursoyant	sursois,-s,-t	sursis...
	sursis	sursoyons, -yez, -ient	sursîmes...
taire	conjug. like *plaire* except that there is no circumflex on the *i* of the 3rd		
tenir[3]	tenant	tiens	tins
	tenu	tiens	tins
		tient	tint
		tenons	tînmes
		tenez	tîntes
		tiennent	tinrent
† traire	trayant	trais,-s,-t	
	trait	trayons...	

[1] Imperative: *sache, sachons, sachez.*
[2] The Past Historic and the Imperfect Indicative are seldom used.

Future	Present Subjunctive	English
pourrai... pourrons...	puisse... puissions...	to be able
prendrai... prendrons...	prenne... prenions...	to take
prévoirai... prévoirons...	prévoie... prévoyions...	to foresee
recevrai... recevrons...	reçoive reçoives reçoive recevions receviez reçoivent	to receive
résoudrai... résoudrons...	résolve... résolvions...	to resolve
rirai... rirons...	rie... riions...	to laugh
saurai... saurons...	sache... sachions...	to know
sentirai... sentirons...	sente... sentions...	to feel to smell
il siéra ils siéront	il siée ils siéent	to become to suit
suffirai... suffirons...	suffise... suffisions...	to suffice
suivrai... suivrons...	suive... suivions...	to follow
surseoirai... surseoirons...	sursoie... sursoyions...	to delay to suspend
Pers. Sing. Pres. Indic.: *il tait.*		to keep silent about
tiendrai... tiendrons...	tienne tiennes tienne tenions teniez tiennent	to hold
trairai... trairons...	traie... trayions...	to milk

[3] Imperfect Subjunctive: *tinsse, -es, tint, tinssions, -iez, -ent.*

French Verbs

Infinitive	Participles	Present Indicative	Past Historic
vaincre	vainquant vaincu	vaincs vaincs vainc vainquons vainquez vainquent	vainquis... vainquîmes...
valoir	valant valu	vaux, -x, -t valons...	valus... valûmes...
vêtir	vêtant vêtu	vêts, vêts, vêt vêtons...	vêtis... vêtîmes...
vivre	vivant vécu	vis,-s,-t vivons...	vécus... vécûmes...
voir	voyant vu	vois,-s,-t voyons, -yez, -ient	vis... vîmes...
vouloir[1]	voulant voulu	veux veux veut voulons voulez veulent	voulus... voulûmes...

[1] Imperative: *veuille, veuillons, veuillez.*

Future	Present Subjunctive	English
vaincrai... vaincrons...	vainque... vainquions...	to conquer
vaudrai... vaudrons...	[2]vaille... valions...	to be worth
vêtirai... vêtirons...	vête... vêtions...	to clothe
vivrai... vivrons...	vive... vivions...	to live
verrai... verrons...	voie... voyions...	to see
voudrai... voudrons...	veuille... voulions...	to be willing to want, to wish

[2] *prévaloir: prévale, prévalions.*

English Verbs

All verbs not marked *irr.* in the English-French section of the Dictionary come in one of the following categories:

    (*a*) Regular verbs, conjugated like WORK or LIVE.

    (*b*) Verbs ending in -*y* preceded by one or more consonants, e.g. DENY, REPLY, IMPLY, conjugated like CARRY (i.e. the *y* changes to *i* in the Past Tense and Past Participle).

    (*c*) Verbs ending in a single consonant preceded by one or more vowels (but not a diphthong, e.g. WAIT, or a double vowel, e.g. SEEM), which are monosyllabic or in which the stress falls on the last syllable, conjugated like DROP and PREFER (i.e. the final consonant is doubled in the Past Tense and Past Participle).

    N.B.   Apart from those which are irregular, all verbs ending in -*l* preceded by one or more vowels (but not a diphthong, e.g. SAIL, or a double vowel, e.g. PEEL) may double the *l* in the Past and Past Participle even if the stress does not fall on the last syllable, e.g. IMPERIL, DIAL.

    * = obsolete.   *A = obsolete, but still used adjectivally.   † = becoming obsolete.
    †A = becoming obsolete, but still used adjectivally.

Infinitive	Past Tense	Past Participle	French
REGULAR VERBS (*a*)			
work	worked	worked	travailler
live	lived	lived	vivre
REGULAR VERBS (*b*)			
carry	carried	carried	porter
REGULAR VERBS (*c*)			
drop	dropped	dropped	laisser tomber
prefer	preferred	preferred	préférer
imperil	imperilled	imperilled	hasarder
dial	dialled	dialled	composer un numéro
IRREGULAR VERBS			
abide	abode	abode	demeurer
awake	awoke	awoke *or* awaked	éveiller
be *Pres. Indic.* am, art, is, are	was, were	been	être
bear	bore	borne *or* born[1]	porter
beat	beat	beaten	battre
beget	begot *begat	begotten	engendrer
begin	began	begun	commencer
bend	bent	bent	courber
bereave	bereaved *or* bereft	bereaved *or* bereft	priver (de)
beseech	besought	besought	supplier
bid	bade *or* bid	bidden *or* bid	ordonner

[1] *born* = né; *borne* = porté.

Infinitive	Past Tense	Past Participle	French
bind	bound	bound *A bounden[1]	lier
bite	bit	bitten	mordre
bleed	bled	bled	saigner
blow	blew	blown	souffler
break	broke	broken	casser
breed	bred	bred	élever
bring	brought	brought	apporter
build	built	built	construire
burn	burnt *or* burned	burnt *or* burned	brûler
burst	burst	burst	éclater
buy	bought	bought	acheter
Pres. Indic. can	could	——	pouvoir
cast	cast	cast	jeter
catch	caught	caught	attraper
choose	chose	chosen	choisir
cleave (*v.t.*)	cleft *clove	cleft *A cloven[2]	fendre
cling	clung	clung	s'attacher
come	came	come	venir
cost	cost	cost	coûter
creep	crept	crept	ramper
crow	crowed *or* †crew	crowed	chanter (coq)
cut	cut	cut	couper
deal	dealt	dealt	distribuer
dig	dug	dug	creuser
do	did	done	faire
draw	drew	drawn	tirer, dessiner
dream	dreamt *or* dreamed	dreamt *or* dreamed	rêver
drink	drank	drunk *A drunken[3]	boire
drive	drove	driven	conduire

[1] It is his *bounden* duty.　　[2] *Cloven* hoof.　　[3] A *drunken* brawl.

653

English Verbs

Infinitive	Past Tense	Past Participle	French
dwell	dwelt	dwelt	demeurer
eat	ate	eaten	manger
fall	fell	fallen	tomber
feed	fed	fed	nourrir
feel	felt	felt	sentir
fight	fought	fought	combattre
find	found	found	trouver
flee	fled	fled	fuir
fling	flung	flung	lancer
fly	flew	flown	voler
forbear	forbore	forborne	s'abstenir
forbid	forbade *or* forbad	forbidden	interdire
forget	forgot	forgotten	oublier
forsake	forsook	forsaken	abandonner
freeze	froze	frozen	geler
get	got	got *A gotten[1]	obtenir, devenir
gird	girded *or* girt	girded *or* girt	ceindre
give	gave	given	donner
go	went	gone	aller
grind	ground	ground	moudre
grow	grew	grown	croître, devenir
hang[2]	hung	hung	pendre
have *Pres. Indic.* have,*hast, has	had	had	avoir
hear	heard	heard	entendre
heave	heaved *or* hove	heaved *or* hove	soulever
hew	hewed	hewn *or* hewed	tailler
hide	hid	hidden	cacher
hit	hit	hit	frapper

[1] Ill-*gotten* gains; but in America *gotten* is often standard usage as an alternative Past Participle.
[2] To suspend. In the meaning 'to execute by hanging', the verb is regular.

Infinitive	Past Tense	Past Participle	French
hold	held	held	tenir
hurt	hurt	hurt	blesser
keep	kept	kept	garder
kneel	knelt	knelt	s'agenouiller
know	knew	known	savoir
lay	laid	laid	poser
lead	led	led	conduire
lean	leant *or* leaned	leant *or* leaned	pencher
leap	leapt *or* leaped	leapt *or* leaped	sauter
learn	learnt *or* learned	learnt *or* learned	apprendre
leave	left	left	laisser, quitter
lend	lent	lent	prêter
let	let	let	laisser
lie[1]	lay	lain	être couché
light	lit *or* lighted	lit *or* lighted	allumer
lose	lost	lost	perdre
make	made	made	faire
Pres. Indic. may	might	——	pouvoir (permission, probabilité)
mean	meant	meant	signifier
meet	met	met	rencontrer
mow	mowed	mowed *or* mown	faucher
pay	paid	paid	payer
put	put	put	mettre
quit	quitted *or* quit	quitted *or* quit	quitter
read	read	read	lire
rend	rent	rent	déchirer
rid	rid	rid	débarrasser
ride	rode	ridden	aller à cheval *etc.*
ring[2]	rang	rung	sonner

[1] To recline. In the meaning 'to be untruthful', the verb is regular.
[2] (Of a bell). In the meaning 'to put a ring round', the verb is regular.

English Verbs

Infinitive	Past Tense	Past Participle	French
rise	rose	risen	se lever
rive	rived	riven *or* rived	fendre
run	ran	run	courir
saw	sawed	sawn	scier
say	said	said	dire
see	saw	seen	voir
seek	sought	sought	chercher
sell	sold	sold	vendre
send	sent	sent	envoyer
set	set	set	placer
sew	sewed	sewn *or* sewed	coudre
shake	shook	shaken	secouer
Pres. Indic. shall[1]	should[1]	—	—
shear	sheared	shorn *or* sheared	tondre
shed	shed	shed	verser
shine	shone	shone	briller
shoe	shod	shod	chausser
shoot	shot	shot	tirer (au fusil)
show	showed	shown *or* showed	montrer
shrink	shrank	shrunk *A shrunken	rétrécir
shrive	shrove	shriven	se confesser
shut	shut	shut	fermer
sing	sang	sung	chanter
sink	sank	sunk *A sunken[2]	sombrer
sit	sat	sat	être assis
slay	slew	slain	tuer
sleep	slept	slept	dormir
slide	slid	slid	glisser
sling	slung	slung	lancer

[1] Used as auxiliaries only.   [2] *Sunken* cheeks.

Infinitive	Past Tense	Past Participle	French
slink	slunk	slunk	s'esquiver
slit	slit	slit	fendre
smell	smelt *or* smelled	smelt *or* smelled	sentir
smite	smote	smitten	frapper
sow	sowed	sown *or* sowed	semer
speak	spoke *spake	spoken	parler
speed	sped *or* speeded	sped *or* speeded	se hâter
spell	spelt *or* spelled	spelt *or* spelled	épeler
spend	spent	spent	dépenser
spill	spilt *or* spilled	spilt *or* spilled	verser
spin	spun	spun	filer
spit[1]	spat *or* spit	spat *or* spit	cracher
split	split	split	fendre
spoil	spoilt *or* spoiled	spoilt *or* spoiled	gâter
spread	spread	spread	s'étendre
spring	sprang	sprung	s'élancer
stand	stood	stood	être debout
stave	staved *or* stove	staved *or* stove	crever
steal	stole	stolen	voler
stick	stuck	stuck	coller
sting	stung	stung	piquer
stink	stank	stunk	puer
strew	strewed	strewed *or* strewn	répandre
stride	strode	stridden	marcher à grands pas
strike	struck	struck †A stricken[2]	frapper
string	strung	strung	ficeler
strive	strove	striven	s'efforcer
swear	swore	sworn	jurer
sweep	swept	swept	balayer

[1] To expectorate. In the meaning 'to put on a spit', the verb is regular.
[2] *Stricken* in years.

English Verbs

Infinitive	Past Tense	Past Participle	French
swell	swelled	swollen *or* swelled	enfler
swim	swam	swum	nager
swing	swung	swung	se balancer
take	took	taken	prendre
teach	taught	taught	enseigner
tear	tore	torn	déchirer
tell	told	told	dire
think	thought	thought	penser
thrive	thrived *or* throve	thrived *or* thriven	prospérer
throw	threw	thrown	jeter
thrust	thrust	thrust	lancer
tread	trod	trodden	fouler
wake	woke *or* waked	waked	éveiller
wear	wore	worn	porter (vêtements)
weave	wove	woven	tisser
weep	wept	wept	pleurer
wet	wetted *or* wet	wetted *or* wet	mouiller
will	would	——	vouloir
win	won	won	gagner
wind	wound	wound	enrouler
wring	wrung	wrung	tordre
write	wrote	written	écrire